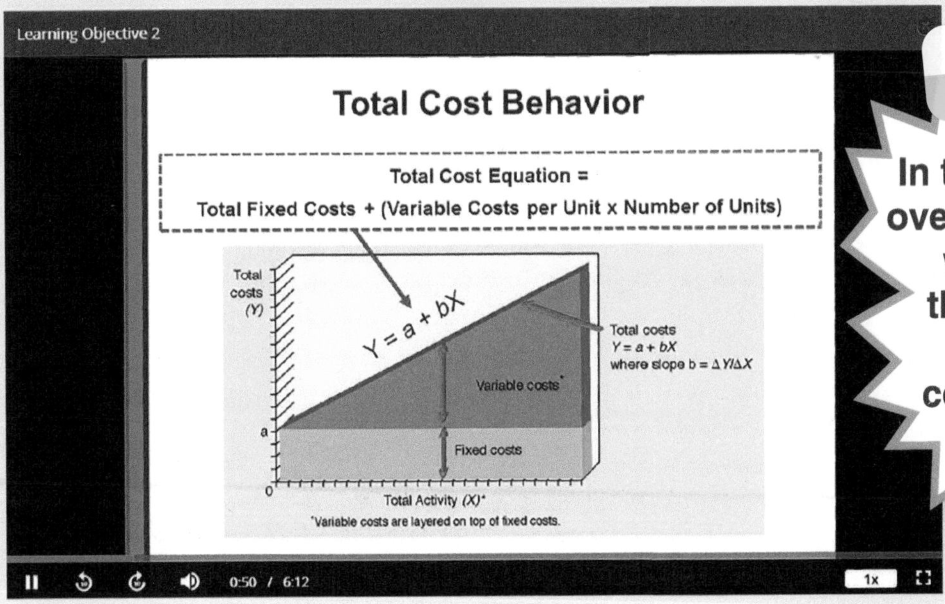

In the same two surveys, over 86% of the students who responded said they would encourage their professor to continue using MBC in future terms.

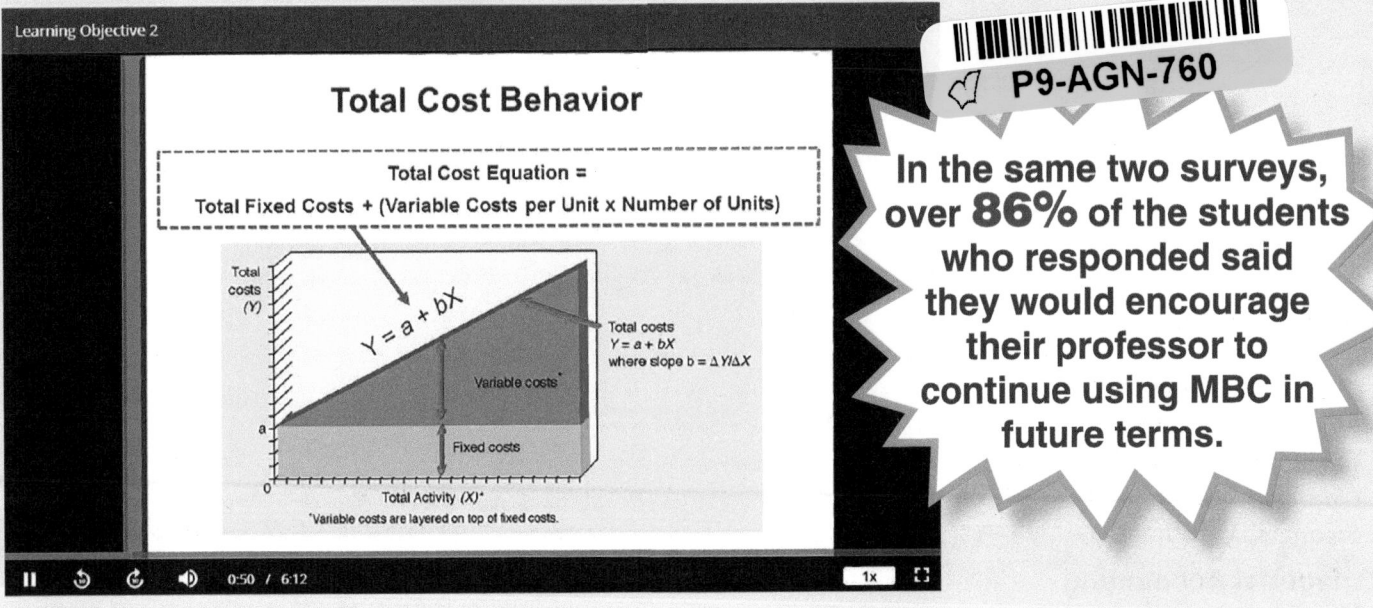

Make Instruction Needs-Based

- Identify where your students are struggling and customize your instruction to address their needs.
- Gauge how your entire class or individual students are performing by viewing the easy-to-use gradebook.
- Ensure your students are getting the additional reinforcement and direction they need between class meetings.

Provide Instruction and Practice 24/7

- Assign homework from your Cambridge Business Publishers' textbook and have myBusinessCourse grade it for you automatically.
- With our eLectures, your students can revisit accounting topics as often as they like or until they master the topic.
- Guided Examples show students how to solve select problems.
- Make homework due before class to ensure students enter your classroom prepared.
- For an additional fee, upgrade MBC to include the eBook and you have all the tools needed for an online course.

LMS Integration

myBusinessCourse integrates with many learning management systems, including **Canvas**, **Blackboard**, **Moodle**, **D2L**, **Schoology**, and **Sakai**. Your gradebooks sync automatically.

Getting Started is as EASY as 1, 2, 3 . . . 4!

1. Sign Up

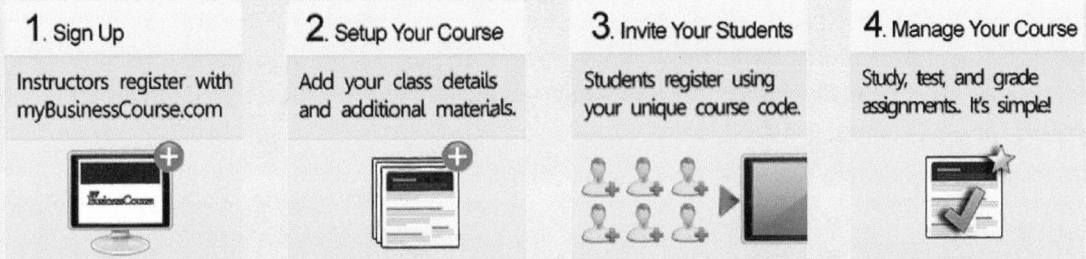

Instructors register with myBusinessCourse.com

2. Setup Your Course

Add your class details and additional materials.

3. Invite Your Students

Students register using your unique course code.

4. Manage Your Course

Study, test, and grade assignments. It's simple!

Want to learn more about myBusinessCourse?

Contact your sales representative or visit www.mybusinesscourse.com.

SECOND EDITION

Intermediate Accounting

Michelle Hanlon
Massachussetts Institute of Technology

Leslie Hodder
Indiana University

Karen Nelson
Texas Christian University

Darren Roulstone
Ohio State University

Amie Dragoo

Cambridge
BUSINESS PUBLISHERS

To my undergraduate accounting professors, Dr. Charles Wootton and Dr. Roann Kopel, who patiently answered my hours of questions about the details of intermediate accounting. Thank you.

—MH

To my extended family, but especially Pat, Brian, Lisa, Maggie, and Will for your support and indulgence as I pursue my dreams. You are my reason.

—LH

To Cindy, Kyle, Sariah, and Rachel for their much appreciated love and support.

—DR

To my husband Mike and our children, Jake, Justin, Julia, and Josie—for your love and steadfast support.

—AD

Cambridge Business Publishers

INTERMEDIATE ACCOUNTING, Second Edition, by Michelle Hanlon, Leslie Hodder, Karen Nelson, Darren Roulstone, and Amie Dragoo.

STUDENT EDITION
Volume 1 ISBN: 978-1-61853-313-5
Volume 2 ISBN: 978-1-61853-335-7

Bookstores & Faculty: To order this book, contact the company via email **customerservice@cambridgepub.com** or call 800-619-6473.

Students: To order this book, please visit the book's website and order directly online.

Printed in the United States of America.
10 9 8 7 6 5 4 3 2 1

About Our Team

Michelle L. Hanlon is the Howard W. Johnson Professor at the MIT Sloan School of Management. She earned her doctorate degree at the University of Washington. Prior to joining MIT, she was a faculty member at the University of Michigan. Professor Hanlon has taught undergraduates, MBA students, Executive MBA students, and Masters of Finance students. She is the winner of the 2013 Jamieson Prize for Excellence in Teaching at MIT Sloan. Professor Hanlon's research focuses primarily on the intersection of financial accounting and taxation. She has published research studies in the *Journal of Accounting and Economics*, the *Journal of Accounting Research*, *The Accounting Review*, the *Review of Accounting Studies*, the *Journal of Finance*, the *Journal of Financial Economics*, the *Journal of Public Economics*, and others. She has won several awards for her research and has presented her work at numerous universities and conferences. Professor Hanlon has served on several editorial boards and currently serves as an editor at the *Journal of Accounting and Economics*. Professor Hanlon is a co-author on two other textbooks—*Financial Accounting* and *Taxes and Business Strategy*. She has testified in front of the U.S. Senate Committee on Finance and the U.S. House of Representatives Committee on Ways and Means about the interaction of financial accounting and tax policy and international tax policy. She served as a U.S. delegate to the American-Swiss Young Leaders Conference in 2010 and worked as an Academic Fellow at the U.S. House Ways and Means Committee in 2015.

Leslie D. Hodder is a full Professor and the Conrad Prebys Endowed Professor of Accounting at Indiana University's Kelley School of Business. She received her B.B.A and M.B.A./M.Acc from the University of New Mexico and her Ph.D. from the University of Texas at Austin. Prior to obtaining her Ph.D., Professor Hodder was Chief Financial Officer of a publicly traded commercial bank holding company in southern California. Professor Hodder was on faculty at Stanford University before joining the Indiana University faculty in 2003. Her research has appeared in top accounting journals, including *The Accounting Review*, *Review of Accounting Studies*, *Contemporary Accounting Research*, and *Accounting Organizations and Society*. She is the past winner of the American Accounting Association's Wildman Award, is a past and present Editor at *The Accounting Review*, and is currently on the Executive Board of the American Accounting Association. Professor Hodder teaches financial-accounting-related topics in the undergraduate, master, and doctoral programs. Over her teaching career, she has developed or co-developed six courses in financial accounting, including Intermediate Financial Accounting I and II, Applied Audit and Accounting Research, and Detecting Earnings Management with a focus on data analytics. Professor Hodder currently teaches intermediate accounting to graduate and undergraduate students.

Karen K. Nelson Karen K. Nelson is the M. J. Neeley Professor of Accounting in the M. J. Neeley School of Business at Texas Christian University. She earned her Ph.D. from the University of Michigan and a bachelor's degree (summa cum laude) from the University of Colorado. Prior to joining TCU, Professor Nelson served on the faculty at Stanford University and Rice University, and as a Visiting Professor at the University of Michigan. A Certified Public Accountant in Colorado, she is a past member of the Standing Advisory Group of the Public Company Accounting Oversight Board. Professor Nelson's research focuses on financial reporting and disclosure issues, including the role of regulators, auditors, and private securities litigation in monitoring financial reporting quality. She has held research seminars at numerous conferences and business schools in the U.S. and abroad. Her research is published in several leading academic journals including *The Accounting Review*, *Journal of Accounting and Economics*, *Journal of Accounting Research*, and the *Review of Accounting Studies*, and has been featured in the popular financial press. She has served on the Editorial Board of *The Accounting Review*. Professor Nelson has taught financial accounting and reporting at the undergraduate, MBA, and Ph.D. levels, and is the recipient of numerous awards for teaching excellence.

Darren T. Roulstone is the John W. Berry Sr., Fund for Faculty Excellence Professor of Accounting at the Ohio State University's Fisher College of Business. He earned his doctorate at the University of Michigan's Ross School of Business and BS and MAcc degrees from Brigham Young University's Marriott School of Business. Professor Roulstone currently directs the Ph.D. program in Accounting and Management Information Systems at Fisher. He teaches a seminar on capital markets research and the core course in financial reporting in Fisher's Master of Accounting program. He has extensive experience teaching intermediate accounting at both the undergraduate and graduate levels. Prior to joining Fisher, he was on the faculty at the University of Chicago's Booth School of Business where he taught financial accounting and financial statement analysis in the full-time, evening, and weekend MBA programs. Professor Roulstone's research focuses on information intermediaries, information acquisition by investors, and textual analysis of corporate disclosure. He serves on the editorial boards of several accounting journals and is currently an associate editor at Management Science. His research has been published in a variety of leading academic journals including *The Accounting Review*, *Journal of Accounting and Economics*, *Journal of Accounting Research*, *Management Science*, and *Review of Accounting Studies*. He is a past president of the American Accounting Association's Financial Accounting and Reporting Section.

Amie L. Dragoo is a Professor of Accounting and Educational Consultant. Former Accounting Department Chair and Associate Professor at Edgewood College, Dr. Dragoo earned her BA and MBA from Michigan State University, and her doctorate from Edgewood College. She holds a CPA license, and for nearly 15 years has been a Becker Professional Education faculty instructor. Prior to her experiences in higher education, she was a senior business assurance associate with PricewaterhouseCoopers LLP (formerly Coopers & Lybrand L.L.P.). Dr. Dragoo has extensive teaching experiences, including courses in Intermediate Accounting I and II, Cost Accounting, Advanced Cost Management, Strategic Financial Management, and other advanced courses in financial and managerial accounting. She has received a number of teaching awards including the School of Business Outstanding Faculty Award and the Estervig-Beaubien Excellence in Teaching and Mentoring Award. She has also worked as an independent consultant, including projects in higher education, and has worked with several corporate clients. Dr. Dragoo's research has been published in the *Journal of Education for Business* and the *Journal of Continuing Higher Education* and she has contributed to numerous articles published by organizations affiliated with the AICPA. She has been involved in many community-oriented programs including the Volunteer Income Tax Assistance (VITA) program.

Preface

Welcome to the Second Edition of *Intermediate Accounting*. This product is the result of extensive market research that included both faculty and students. We created this learning system because, as educators, we didn't feel that the existing textbooks in the intermediate market recognized how the study habits of today's students have evolved, nor did we feel that existing textbooks fully embraced the power of technology in the learning process. This product is not so much a textbook as it is an integrated learning system. Although the print textbook can be used on its own, we created extensive digital resources that integrate with and complement the print book.

"The book is very user friendly. It covers topics efficiently, without distracting students with excess detail."
Maef Woods
Heidelberg University

The emphasis in our approach is to provide students with a demonstration and review problem for each deliberately selected, key learning objective. In this way, students see the application of concepts through a step-by-step illustration and then have the opportunity to immediately practice similar review problems electronically in myBusinessCourse (MBC), our online homework platform. In addition, MBC contains hundreds of instructional videos that were created by one of the authors. There are three general categories of videos; concept overviews, demonstration videos, and worked-out problems. The combination of textbook, videos, and online practice comprise an **active learning** system that recognizes and embraces how today's students prefer to learn and provides students with the tools to master intermediate accounting.

Our approach steers away from dense text (which the average student is not reading) and moves to an active-learning approach where content is delivered in short bursts followed by immediate practice. Because each learning objective for every chapter is self-contained, faculty have the flexibility to pick and choose learning outcomes.

We note the need in the market for a direct incorporation of authoritative guidance. Although other intermediate accounting textbooks include some references to the FASB's standards in a footnote to a chapter, direct citations are rarely included. In our approach, we provide succinct yet thorough, to-the-point explanations in each self-contained learning objective along with direct citations of the most relevant references from the **Codification**. We feel direct citations best prepare the typical intermediate accounting student who will often reference and cite the authoritative standards in practice. This novel approach of combining active-learning with real life authoritative guidance reflects our belief that such an approach best prepares intermediate accounting students for life in practice.

Target Audience

As the title suggests, *Intermediate Accounting* is intended for use following the introductory financial accounting course at either the undergraduate or graduate level. This book supports an intermediate accounting series offered to accounting and some finance majors, typically in a two-course sequence (three-course series in some cases). The topics in intermediate accounting are relevant to approximately 70% of the Financial Accounting Reporting (FAR) section of the Uniform CPA Examination. This rigorous exam ensures that only qualified individuals become licensed as U.S. Certified Public Accountants (CPAs).

"The Action Plan with the Demos, Reviews, and Assignments is my HANDS DOWN favorite. I have specific topics that are important to me, so I use the Action Plan to convey to my students where to focus. The design of the plan allows them to spend more time focused specifically on the topics that I intend to cover in detail."
Stephani Mason
DePaul University

Action Plan

To establish the active-learning approach of the product and highlight its user friendly organization, each chapter opens with an **Action Plan** that identifies each learning objective for the chapter, the related page numbers, the demonstrations, the review applications, and the assignments. This table allows students and faculty to quickly grasp the chapter contents and to efficiently navigate to the desired topic.

Action Plans *summarize each chapter's resources and categorize them by learning objective.*

Demos *are illustrative examples in the textbook that are accompanied by videos (available in MBC) that provide 3-5 minute overviews of each learning objective.*

Assignments *reinforce learning and can be completed by hand or within MBC.*

Action Plan

LO	Topic/Subtopic	Page	Demos	Reviews	Assignments
LO13–1	**Identify and classify intangible items** Intangible Assets :: Goodwill :: Finite Life Intangible Assets :: Indefinite Life Intangible Assets :: Internally Generated Intangible Assets and Goodwill	13-3	D13-1	R13-1	21, 22, 39, 40, 41, 59, 60, 61, 62, 67, 68, 71, 72, 73
LO13–2	**Determine the initial and subsequent measurements of intangible assets** Amortization Expense :: Straight-Line Method :: Finite Useful Life :: Legal Life	13-8	D13-2	R13-2	23, 24, 25, 26, 27, 28, 29, 42, 43, 44, 45, 46, 47, 59, 60, 61, 62, 66, 72
LO13–3	**Record goodwill resulting from an acquisition** Goodwill :: Control of Business :: Residual Value :: No Amortization	13-11	D13-3	R13-3	30, 31, 48, 49, 59, 60, 62, 63, 65, 69, 71
LO13–4	**Account for impairment and derecognition of intangibles** Impairment Testing :: Indicators :: Recoverability Test :: Impairment Test :: Qualitative Assessment :: Quantitative Test :: Derecognition	13-15	D13-4A D13-4B D13-4C D13-4D	R13-4	32, 33, 34, 50, 51, 52, 62, 63, 69, 71, 72
LO13–5	Account for changes in estimates ...				

Learning Objectives *identify the key learning goals of the chapter.*

Reviews *are practice problems that follow Demos and that are accompanied by videos (available in MBC) that demonstrate how to solve each problem.*

Overview, Demo, and Review

We have adopted a straightforward effective layout throughout every chapter of the book. We have included carefully crafted learning objectives that are not extraneous or all-encompassing. Each key learning objective is clearly identified with a distinct red banner and is followed by its own overview, demo, and review problem.

LO 8-3 Account for the impact of sales returns and allowances

In fact, each learning objective represents a **separate learning module**, allowing students and faculty to break down complex topics into manageable subtopics. We believe that students will appreciate this style of learning uniquely adopted in *Intermediate Accounting* because of the current trend in learning preferences. Students prefer to learn by doing with convenient access to explanations and authoritative references for help in the process. For additional support, students have access to short videos for each Demo and Review. The videos can be accessed in MBC.

Overview—Authoritative Foundation

Following each learning objective is a brief explanation of the topic with visual references (diagrams), when helpful. We also include an overview box for each learning objective to provide students with a quick overview of key topics. For topics for which we felt relevant authoritative guidance was important, we included an excerpt from the Codification. **This presentation of the accounting guidance**

minimizes authors' biases and places both students and faculty in a unique authoritative position. Our approach incorporates ASC Glossary definitions whenever possible and terminology that is common in the Codification such as the terms recognition, measurement, derecognition, and disclosure. References to authoritative guidance are distinctly highlighted with black block text as shown below.

> "I'm really impressed with the book and like the integration of the codification. I encourage my colleagues to seriously consider adopting the book."
> Maef Woods
> *Heidelberg University*

Because a sale on account could be considered a 30- or 45-day loan (depending on the specific terms), there is a financing component to a sale on account. Sellers initiating a revenue contract with transfer within one year, do not have to recognize a financing component. This means short-term accounts receivable are typically recorded at the full amount that the seller expects to receive (not adjusted to present value). The authoritative support follows.

606-10-32-15 In determining the transaction price, an entity shall adjust the promised amount of consideration for the effects of the time value of money if the timing of payments agreed to by the parties to the contract (either explicitly or implicitly) provides the customer or the entity with a significant benefit of financing the transfer of goods or services to the customer. In those circumstances, the contract contains a significant financing component.

We cite the Codification a including excerpts where appropriate.

Demonstration

We believe that a presentation focused on demos will inspire the contemporary college learner. Demos are included for each learning objective to illustrate the accounting concept discussed. We include color-coded solutions within the Demo (the **blue text**) because this is the student's first exposure to the relevant topic. We noted that in other intermediate textbooks, it is not uncommon for an accounting concept or a variation to an accounting method to be explained in a paragraph or in a two-page (or more) spread instead of through an illustration. This is how our approach is very different— in our approach, **accounting concepts are predominantly demonstrated**. The active learner can reconstruct the steps independently or attempt the same demo through the online learning system—myBusinessCourse. In the margin adjacent to the journal entries, we also show the impact on the accounting equation and T-accounts to aid in student comprehension. In addition, each demo is accompanied by a short video clip (typically 3 minutes or less) that walks students through the solution to the demo.

Accounting for Sales Returns LO8-3 Demo 8-3

Mass Inc. sells merchandise of $1,000,000 on account, with a cost of $650,000 (65% of sales) during 2020. Mass Inc. grants $16,000 of returns in 2020, the first year of operations. On December 31, 2020, Mass Inc. estimates total returns to be 2% of credit sales. Record the entries for (a) sale of merchandise (b) actual returns granted in 2020 assuming that the company uses a perpetual inventory system and (c) estimated returns at the end of the year.

Demo MBC

Videos, created by the authors that provide step-by-step guidance on solving the problem, are available in MBC.

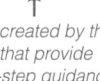

Solution

Mass Inc. recognizes sales and actual returns during the period, and records an adjusting entry at period-end to estimate future returns. **Sales Returns**, a contra revenue account, is debited when an actual return is recorded, resulting in an indirect reduction to sales revenue. Total sales returns are estimated to be $20,000 (0.02 × $1,000,000). Therefore, the refund liability at the end of the year is $4,000 or $20,000 (total estimated returns) less $16,000 (actual returns). Simultaneously, we record an entry to adjust Inventory-Estimated Returns by $2,600 or $13,000 ($20,000 × 0.65) less $10,400 (returned inventory received to date).

To aid in student comprehension, we show the impact on the accounting equation and T-accounts in addition to the journal entries.

2020—To record sale of merchandise

Accounts Receivable	1,000,000	
Sales Revenue		1,000,000
Cost of Goods Sold	650,000	
Inventory		650,000

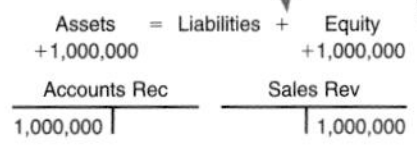

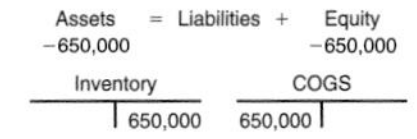

2020—To record actual returns of merchandise

Sales Returns	16,000	
Cash (or Accounts Receivable)		16,000

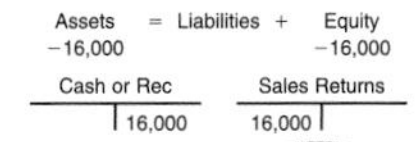

"Students tend not to read textbooks the way they did in the past. My students learn better by seeing an example and then doing a similar problem. The Overview/ Demonstration/Review approach used in the book worked well for my students for that reason. "
Lindsay Meermans
Wittenberg University

Review

At the conclusion of each learning objective, a review problem is provided with answers included at the end of the chapter. These review problems are presented to reinforce concepts presented in the section and to ensure student comprehension. By not providing the review solutions on the same page as the review, we are encouraging students to 'learn by doing.' The demo, along with the overview material, provides the foundation for students to complete the review problems. Again, students have the opportunity to practice the same problem online in myBusinessCourse. We believe that many students will take advantage of the opportunity to work through the problem online because they will gain instant feedback as to whether they completed the solution accurately—and frankly, a digital environment is more in line with how we all function every day. In addition, each review is accompanied by a short video clip (typically 3 minutes or less) that walks students through the solution to the review.

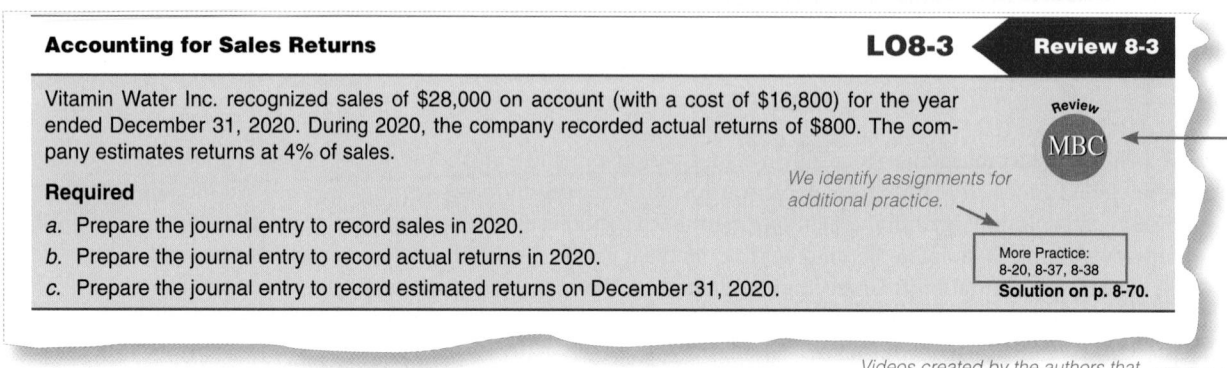

Accounting for Sales Returns **LO8-3** **Review 8-3**

Vitamin Water Inc. recognized sales of $28,000 on account (with a cost of $16,800) for the year ended December 31, 2020. During 2020, the company recorded actual returns of $800. The company estimates returns at 4% of sales.

Review MBC

Required

a. Prepare the journal entry to record sales in 2020.
b. Prepare the journal entry to record actual returns in 2020.
c. Prepare the journal entry to record estimated returns on December 31, 2020.

We identify assignments for additional practice.

More Practice: 8-20, 8-37, 8-38

Solution on p. 8-70.

Videos created by the authors that provide step-by-step guidance on solving the problem are available in MBC.

Integrated Videos in MBC

As noted in the preceding paragraphs, author-created videos are an integral part of the learning system. Time and again, our market research on student preferences and study habits indicates today's students like and rely heavily on video instruction as they learn and apply accounting concepts to homework assignments and projects. Our videos are available through MBC and can be accessed 24/7 by students. To facilitate students' use of the instructional videos while doing their homework, we identify the appropriate video in the margin next to many assignments.

Exercise 11-56
Computing and Recording Interest Capitalization **LO5**
Hint: See Demo 11-5

Weld Corporation is constructing a plant for its own use. Weld capitalizes interest on an annual basis. The following expenditures are made during the current year: January 1, $30,000; July 1, $290,000; September 1, $800,000; and December 31, $2,110,000. The following debts were outstanding throughout the current year.

Construction note, 12%	$100,000
Short-term note payable, 15%	400,000
Accounts payable (noninterest-bearing)	400,000

We identify for student guidance an appropriate video aid in the margin next to assignments.

Required

a. Compute the amount of interest to be capitalized in 2020.
b. Calculate the amount of interest to expense in 2020.
c. Prepare the 2020 summary journal entry to record the construction expenditures and interest, assuming that construction is not complete on December 21, 2020.

Learning in Context

Expanding Your Knowledge

These boxes expand on related topics of the section through examples and discussions going beyond the section's learning objective. These topics can enhance classroom discussions or simply allow the curious student to expand to topics beyond the usual coverage. A representative sample follows.

EXPANDING YOUR KNOWLEDGE **Securitization of Receivables**

Securitization is another way that companies can convert receivables more quickly into cash. In a securitization, assets (such as trade receivables or credit card receivables) are pooled together to form a portfolio. The portfolio is typically transferred to a securitization entity, commonly a trust. Interests in the securitization entity are then sold to investors or the portfolio is used as collateral for debt issuances. Just as in our previous discussions, the seller must determine whether the transfer to the securitization entity represents a *sale* or a *secured borrowing.*

Real World

Students appreciate and become more engaged when they can see the real-world relevance of the content they are learning in class. We included current, real-world examples of financial reporting throughout each chapter in Real World boxes.

KELLOGG

Real World—CONCENTRATION OF CREDIT RISK

KELLOGG [K]

In a recent Form 10-K, Kellogg Company described the credit risk associated with having a narrow base of customers—see below. The risk is that if one customer defaults, the company could be substantially impacted negatively. In an earlier section of the Form 10-K (Management's Discussion and Analysis Section), Kellogg disclosed: "During 2015, our top five customers, collectively, including Wal-Mart, accounted for approximately 34% of our consolidated net sales and approximately 47% of U.S. net sales."

Derivative Instruments And Fair Value Measurements Management believes concentrations of credit risk with respect to accounts receivable is limited due to the generally high credit quality of the Company's major customers, as well as the large number and geographic dispersion of smaller customers. However, the Company conducts a disproportionate amount of business with a small number of large multinational grocery retailers, with the five largest accounts encompassing approximately 29% of consolidated trade receivables at January 2, 2016.

Management Judgment

In each chapter, we emphasize how **management judgment** is required to apply the authoritative guidance. We feel it is important for students to understand that applying accounting rules is often subjective and requires professional judgment.

Management Judgment

There are many financing decisions that management must make related to debt issues. For example, management determines the type and features of new debt and the terms and timing of the issue. Management must also determine whether or not to extinguish debt early, refund debt with alternative debt, or entice debt holders to convert debt to equity in cases of convertible debt. Let's consider a sample of the judgments that management must make in accounting for long-term debt.

- Management determines the method to amortize discounts or premiums and whether a method other than the effective interest method produces results that are not materially different from the effective interest method (p. 16-11).
- In a case where a note is issued at a stated rate that does not equal the market rate, the market rate of a note with similar risks must be determined (p. 16-24).
- In a case where a note is issued for noncash consideration, management must determine whether the fair value of the debt or the fair value of the noncash consideration is more reliable. Further, in cases where the

Chapter Assessment

The challenge in intermediate accounting is applying the concepts to different scenarios. Our assignment material consists of a wide variety of formats, varying levels of complexity, a thorough coverage of learning objectives, and selections with real world data. The materials increase in complexity as you

"There are an ample number of assignments for each learning objective, and I like that the solutions manual is available in Excel."
Lindsay Meermans
Wittenberg University

move through the different categories: questions, brief exercises, exercises, and problems. The questions in each end of chapter section are numbered sequentially from start to finish to avoid confusion for students. All learning objectives are represented in the end of chapter materials.

Each chapter contains approximately 20 questions, 25 brief exercises, 30 exercises, and 15 problems. We prepared a grid plotting each chapter's content across the best competing texts in the marketplace, arranged by learning objective, to ensure that our coverage meets or exceeds the competition. Importantly, our assignments correspond with the listed learning objective ensure that students have the necessary foundational material to complete the corresponding problems.

The last section (Accounting Decisions and Judgments) includes more application-type problems, which are identified as follows:

Real World Analysis: Includes real-world material from actual publicly available financial statements.

Communication Case: Allows students to apply chapter content through a written presentation.

Judgment Case: Pushes students to levels of evaluation and analysis involving relevant content.

Ethics Case: Shows students how decisions have ethical consequences.

Codification Skills: Includes research in the ASC glossary and generally in the Codification on specific topics and through an applied example.

Challenge Problem: Problems either integrate content from multiple chapters or require students to apply the chapter's content in a more complex environment that pushes students beyond the usual content coverage.

Deloitte Trueblood Case: References are provided to cases in the Trueblood case series, prepared by Deloitte professionals, based on recent accounting technical issues that require research and judgment.

Content Highlights

Chapters in this text are organized into two parts.

Part 1: Chapters 1 through 6 offer a review of introductory financial reporting. We begin with the accounting environment and the underlying conceptual framework. We review the accounting double-entry system, including the preparation and presentation of the four financial statements: income statement (including comprehensive income), balance sheet, statement of equity, and statement of cash flows. We also introduce the DuPont framework, which is useful for analysis and interpretation of accounting reports. The first part of the book concludes with a review of time value of money.

Part 2: The second part launches with the chapter on revenue recognition. This chapter is helpful to understanding the remaining chapters, including when revenue (and assets) are recognized, and when expenses (and liabilities) are recognized. Chapters 8 through 22 loosely follow the accounting equation. Specifically, we begin with the chapters covering assets—Chapters 8 through 14, followed by chapters generally covering liabilities or equity (with some asset implications)—Chapters 15 through 21. We conclude part 2 by revisiting the statement of cash flows (from Chapter 5), which addresses the cash flows related to some special topics introduced in part 2. Finally, **Appendix A** reviews the topics of accounting changes and error analysis, which is integrated throughout the text, and **Appendix B** describes key areas of differences between U.S. GAAP and IFRS. New **Appendix C** introduces students to Data Analytics.

Highlights for each chapter are summarized.

CHAPTER 1—**Accounting Environment and the Conceptual Framework**

- Concise presentation with direct citations to the Statements of Financial Accounting Concepts (SFACs) allowing students and faculty the opportunity to interpret the guidance directly.

CHAPTER 2—**Accounting Information System**

- Visual references to the accounting steps provide clarity throughout the chapter.

CHAPTER 3—Income Statement and Comprehensive Income

- Includes an introduction to the topics noncontrolling interest and foreign currency translation
- Upfront overview of accounting changes, errors, and estimates with a reference to specific coverage throughout each content area in the book. This integrated approach eliminates the need for of a separate chapter on accounting changes.

CHAPTER 4—Balance Sheet and Financial Reporting

- Introduction to financial statement disclosures and Form 10-K components provides a base for application of concepts to real world examples.

CHAPTER 5—Statement of Cash Flows and Financial Analysis

- Stronger emphasis on cash flows in first half of the text, emphasizing its importance in reviewing a full set of financial statements.
- Includes an illustration of the interrelations of financial statements, including the comprehensive income statement.
- Ratios introduced within the DuPont framework providing a structure to relate ratios to each other. Also distinguishes investment analysis from creditor analysis.
- Includes an introduction to non-GAAP financial measures.
- Summary grid of ratios with references to coverage throughout the text.

CHAPTER 6—Time Value of Money

- Time value of money calculations (in this chapter and throughout text) are illustrated in Excel, consistent with the new tools provided in the CPA exam and tools most relevant in practice.
- What-if analyses illustrate how a change in a variable affects the output.
- Includes clear applications to leases, pensions, bonds, and debt, as introductions to later chapters.

CHAPTER 7—Revenue Recognition

- Learning objectives centered around the five steps in the revenue recognition process with demos and reviews concentrated on each separate step. Relevant, real-life examples provided in the demos for each step.
- Includes an overview of long-term construction contracts within the chapter. Appendix on long-term construction contracts is only necessary if faculty prefer to incorporate entries specific to the construction industry.

CHAPTER 8—Cash and Receivables

- CECL model incorporated throughout the chapter.

CHAPTER 9—Inventory: Measurement

- Includes *separate* demos on periodic and perpetual inventory systems, giving faculty options for coverage.
- Includes application of initial measurement concepts with inventory.

CHAPTER 10— Inventory: Additional Issues

- Includes a robust, applied discussion of inventory principle changes and errors.

CHAPTER 11—Property, Plant & Equipment: Acquisition & Disposition

- Includes a discussion on judgments used in developing fixed asset capitalization policies.
- Includes a discussion of construction in process, commonly included in PP&E presentations but missing in competing text books.

CHAPTER 12—Depreciation, Impairments, and Depletion

- Includes examples of commonly used accounting conventions for depreciation.
- Illustrates changes in estimate, depreciation methods, and errors in accounting for fixed assets.

CHAPTER 13—Intangible Assets and Goodwill

- Separately presents intangibles as a standalone topic and not intermingled with property, plant, and equipment to decrease confusion for students and also to reflect its prominence on a balance sheet.

CHAPTER 14—**Investments in Debt and Equity Securities**

- Organizes the accounting of investments by method (instead of type) using terminology consistent with the authoritative guidance such as FV-NI and FV-OCI.
- Includes an option to adjust the fair value allowance upon sale of securities or at period-end, and each option is separately labeled in the assignments.
- Visual references to the investment methods provide clarity to aid students in the navigation of the chapter.
- Includes a robust appendix on derivatives.

CHAPTER 15—**Short-Term Liabilities and Contingencies**

- Incorporates subsequent event discussion with contingency overview.
- Includes examples of the accounting for gift card breakage.

CHAPTER 16—**Long-Term Liabilities**

- Demonstrates for students the different variations of bond discounts and premiums for the effective interest method and straight-line method.
- Short demos followed by immediate practice especially conducive to student retention in complex topics.
- Illustrates the accounting for bond issuance costs while the use of Excel facilitates the computation of required interest rates.

CHAPTER 17—**Leases**

- Includes a robust discussion on the key aspects of a lease.
- Logical presentation of lease accounting with an illustration of variations in demos instead of explanations of exceptions in paragraph form.
- Includes a clear presentation of the accounting for lease incentives, including journal entries.
- Applies the lease criteria to multiple lease examples.

CHAPTER 18—**Income Taxes**

- Content adjusted for the recently passed U.S. tax reform act.
- Utilizes a balance sheet approach, consistent with the authoritative guidance.

CHAPTER 19—**Pensions and Postretirement Benefits**

- Coverage of a defined benefit plan is organized by its three main components: PBO, plan assets, and pension expense. This provides a conceptual foundation for the journal entries and worksheets.
- Includes journal entries for defined contribution plans

CHAPTER 20—**Stockholders' Equity**

- Demonstrations include alternative approaches of treasury stock and direct stock retirement.
- Use of graphics help explain the effects of stock dividends, cash dividends, and stock splits.

CHAPTER 21—**Share-Based Compensation and Earnings per Share**

- Tabular format (often seen in financial reports) consistently applied to basic EPS, diluted EPS (many variations), and diluted EPS with multiple securites.
- Short demos followed by immediate practice especially conducive to student retention in complex topics
- Includes a demonstration of restricted stock share awards and restricted stock unit awards.

CHAPTER 22—**Statement of Cash Flows Revisited**

- Focuses on the indirect method given the extraordinarily high usage and the overwhelming feedback that the FASB received to not require the use of the direct method.

APPENDIX A—**Accounting Changes and Error Analysis Revisited**

- Summarizes and references accounting for changes and errors applied to content areas throughout the text.

IFRS Appendix

Appendix B provides a separate section summarizing key differences between U.S. GAAP and IFRS, arranged in the same order as the chapter coverage. The presentation of the IFRS section consistently follows our approach of overview, demo, and review. Including the coverage in a separate section provides faculty with the most flexibility in determining how, when, or whether to introduce specific aspects of IFRS.

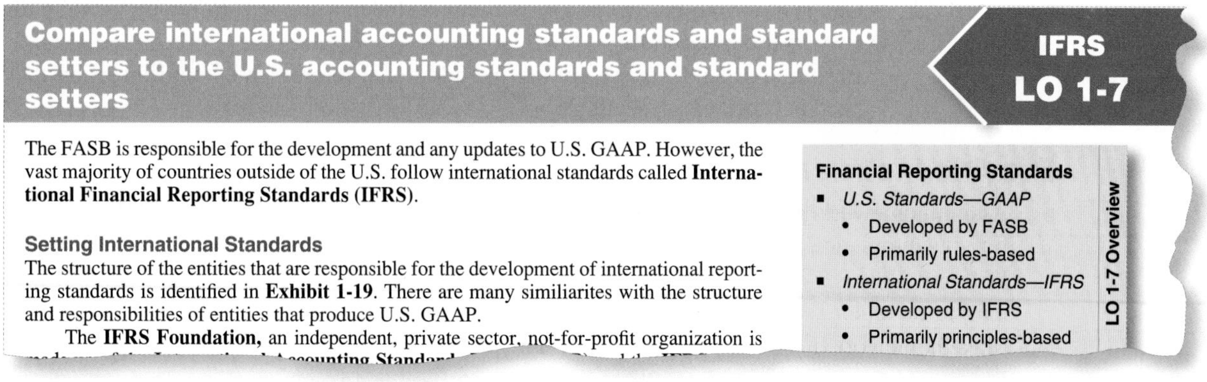

Compare international accounting standards and standard setters to the U.S. accounting standards and standard setters

IFRS
LO 1-7

The FASB is responsible for the development and any updates to U.S. GAAP. However, the vast majority of countries outside of the U.S. follow international standards called **International Financial Reporting Standards (IFRS)**.

Setting International Standards

The structure of the entities that are responsible for the development of international reporting standards is identified in **Exhibit 1-19**. There are many similiarites with the structure and responsibilities of entities that produce U.S. GAAP.

The **IFRS Foundation,** an independent, private sector, not-for-profit organization is

Financial Reporting Standards
- *U.S. Standards—GAAP*
  - Developed by FASB
  - Primarily rules-based
- *International Standards—IFRS*
  - Developed by IFRS
  - Primarily principles-based

LO 1-7 Overview

Data Analytics Appendix

The world in which we live has changed dramatically in recent years. Technology is rapidly altering how accounting is performed and what can be done with the data once they are collected. In this edition, we introduce students to Data Analytics in **Appendix C.** The appendix contains an overview of data analytics, provides examples detailing how data analysis is performed, and requires students to apply some basic techniques.

New To This Edition

- The resources in myBusinessCourse (MBC) have been expanded to include homework assignments.
- Dozens of additional videos have been created by the authors to facilitate student learning.
- Reviews now identify assignments that students can use for additional practice.
- *Hints* now appear in the margin next to many assignments. The *Hints* identify the Demo video that best illustrates the learning objective being applied in the assignment.
- Appendix C on Data Analytics.
- Various topics and assignments have been updated to reflect the most current accounting standards.
- A new Test Bank is available.

Technology that Improves Learning and Complements Faculty Instruction

95% students who used MBC, responded that MBC helped them learn accounting.*

myBusinessCourse is an online learning and assessment program intended to complement your textbook and faculty instruction. Access to **myBusinessCourse** is FREE ONLY with the purchase of a new textbook, but can be purchased separately.

MBC is ideal for faculty seeking opportunities to augment their course with an online component. MBC is also a turnkey solution for online courses. The following are some of the features of MBC.

Increase Student Readiness

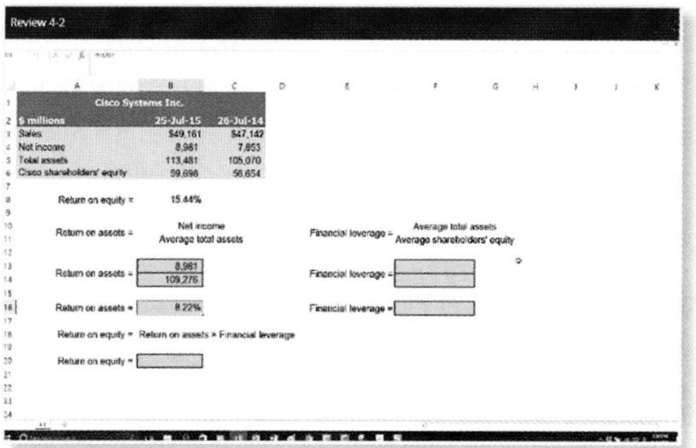

- **Demos** apply each chapter's learning objectives and concepts to a problem. Consistent with the text and created by the authors, these videos are ideal for remediation and online instruction.
- **Reviews** are narrated video demonstrations created by the authors that show students how to solve the Review problems from the textbook.
- Immediate feedback with **auto-graded homework**.
- **Test Bank** questions that can be incorporated into your assignments.
- Instructor **gradebook** with immediate grade results.

86% of students said they would encourage their professor to continue using MBC in future terms.*

Make Instruction Needs-Based

- Identify where your students are struggling and customize your instruction to address their needs.
- Gauge how your entire class or individual students are performing by viewing the easy-to-use gradebook.
- Ensure your students are getting the additional reinforcement and direction they need between class meetings.

Provide Instruction and Practice 24/7

- Assign homework from your Cambridge Business Publishers' textbook and have MBC grade it for you automatically.
- With our Videos, your students can revisit accounting topics as often as they like or until they master the topic.
- Make homework due before class to ensure students enter your classroom prepared.
- For an additional fee, upgrade MBC to include the eBook and you have all the tools needed for an online course.

Integrate with LMS

myBusinessCourse integrates with many learning management systems, including **Canvas**, **Blackboard**, **Moodle**, **D2L**, **Schoology**, and **Sakai**. Your gradebooks sync automatically.

Additional Resources

Financial Accounting Bootcamp

This interactive tutorial is intended for use in programs that either require or would like to offer a tutorial that can be used as a refresher of topics introduced in the first financial accounting course. It is designed as an asynchronous, interactive, self-paced experience for students. Available Learning Modules (You Select) follow.

1. Introducing Financial Accounting (approximate completion time 2 hours)
2. Constructing Financial Statements (approximate completion time 4 hours)
3. Adjusting Entries and Completing the Accounting Cycle (approximate completion time 4 hours)
4. Reporting and Analyzing Cash Flows (approximate completion time 3.5 hours)
5. Analyzing and Interpreting Financial Statements (approximate completion time 3.5 hours)
6. Excel and Time-Value of Money Basics (approximate completion time 2 hours)

This is a separate, saleable item. Contact your sales representative to receive more information or email customerservice@cambridgepub.com.

Guide to Intermediate Accounting Research

The *Guide to Intermediate Accounting Research*, Second Edition, by Shelby Collins, is intended to serve as a supplement to the materials used in an intermediate accounting course. It includes many opportunities to apply Codification guidance to related accounting topics (including, for example, leases, investment accounting, revenue recognition, and consolidation). Students will learn to confidently address and communicate accounting research issues, from start to finish. Students will not only take away the ability to identify the accounting problem (the "researchable question"), but will gain experience locating and applying guidance within the FASB Codification. This is a separate, saleable text (ISBN: 978-1-61853-316-6). Contact your sales representative to receive a desk copy or email customerservice@cambridgepub.com

Companion Casebook

Cases in Financial Reporting, 8th edition by Michael Drake (Brigham Young University), Ellen Engel (University of Illinois—Chicago), D. Eric Hirst (University of Texas – Austin), and Mary Lea McAnally (Texas A&M University). This book comprises 27 cases and is a perfect companion book for

*These statistics are based on the results of two surveys in which 2,330 students participated.

faculty interested in exposing students to a wide range of real financial statements. Each case deals with a specific financial accounting topic within the context of one (or more) company's financial statements. Each case contains financial statement information and a set of directed questions pertaining to one or two specific financial accounting issues. This is a separate, saleable casebook (ISBN 978-1-61853-122-3). Contact your sales representative to receive a desk copy or email customerservice@cambridgepub.com.

Acknowledgments

This product has benefited greatly from the valuable feedback of focus group attendees, survey respondents, reviewers, students, colleagues, and adopters of the first edition. We are extremely grateful to them for their help in making this project a success.

JK Aier, *George Mason University*
Angela Andrews, *Indiana University*
Wendy Bailey, *Northeastern University*
Dereck Barr-Pulliam, *University of Wisconsin*
Mark Bauman, *University of Northern Iowa*
Laura Bearden, *Adrian College*
Rick Berschback, *Walsh College*
Carol Bishop, *Georgia Southwestern*
Shay Blanchette Proulx, *Babson College*
William Brink, *Miami University*
Philip Brown, *Harding University*
Esther Bunn, *Stephen F. Austin State University*
Linda Campbell, *Siena Heights University*
Rodney Carmack, *Arkansas State University*
Thomas Carnes, *Berry College*
Charles Carpenter, *Francis Marion University*
Matthew Carroll, *West Virginia State University*
Mary Ellen Carter, *Boston College*
Jack Cathey, *University of North Carolina—Charlotte*
Richard Cazier, *University of Texas—El Paso*
Sumantra Chakravarty, *California State—Fullerton*
Jeff Chen, *Texas Christian University*
Zhenhua Chen, *University of San Diego*
Xiaoyan Cheng, *University of Nebraska—Omaha*
Lynn Clements, *Florida Southern College*
Robert Collier, *University of Ottawa*
Cheryl Corke, *Genesee Community College*
Patricia Crenny, *Villanova University*
Marc Cussatt, *Washington State University*
Angela Davis, *University of Oregon*
Patricia Davis , *Keystone College*
Scott Dell, *Marian University*
Ming Deng, *Baruch College*
Cynthia Dittmer, *St. Ambrose University*
Tom Downen, *University of North Carolina—Wilmington*
Tim Eaton, *Miami University*
Lisa Eiler, *University of Montana*
David Emerson, *Salisbury University*
James Emig, *Villanova University*
Joseph Faello, *Mississippi State University*
Kevin Feeney, *Southern Connecticut State University*
Mary Fischer, *University of Texas—Tyler*
Linda Flaming, *Monmouth University*
Mitchell Franklin, *Le Moyne College*
Diana Franz, *University of Toledo*
Donna Free, *Oakland University*
Fabio Gaertner, *University of Wisconsin*
Patricia Galletta, *College of Staten Island*
Miriam Gerstein, *Brooklyn College*
John Giles, *North Carolina State University*
Marina Grau, *Houston Community College*
Tony Greig, *University of Wisconsin*
Thomas Guarino, *Plymouth State University*
Kim Guerts, *Crown College*
Hongtao Guo, *Salem State University*
Richard Hale, *Kentucky State University*
Susan Hamlen, *University at Buffalo*
Glen Hansen, *Utica College*
Karen Hennes, *University of Oklahoma*
Julie Huang, *University of Louisville*
Steven Hunt, *Western Illinois University*
Derek Jackson, *Saint Mary's University of Minnesota*
John Jiang, *Michigan State University*
Vicki Jobst, *Benedictine University*
Marsha Keune, *University of Dayton*
Suzanne Kiess, *Jackson College*
Irene Kim, *Catholic University*
Jung Hoon Kim, *Florida International University*
Oksana Kim, *Minnesota State University Mankato*
Robin Knowles, *Texas A&M International University*
Melvin Lamboy-Ruiz, *Iowa State University*
Yvette Lazdowski, *Plymouth State University*
Charles Leflar, *University of Arkansas*
Deborah Leitsch, *Golden Beacom College*
Zining Li, *Loyola Marymount University*
Lihong Liang, *Syracuse University*
Sharon Lightner, *National University*
Lucy Lim, *Howard University*
Ellen Lippman, *University of Portland*
Suzanne Long, *Monroe Community College*
Amanda Sue Marcy, *University of Scranton*
Roger Martin, *University of Virginia*
Sharon Martin, *Case Western Reserve University*
Stephani Mason, *DePaul University*
Katie Maxwell, *University of Arizona*
Brian McAllister, *University of Colorado—Colorado Springs*
Sarah McCoy, *Bentley University*
Terra McGhee, *University of Texas—Arlington*

Lindsay Meermans, *Wittenberg University*
Don Minyard, *University of Alabama*
Toni Molinari, *Clark University*
Al Nagy, *John Carroll University*
Cindy Phipps, *Lakeland College*
Marc Picconi, *College of William & Mary*
James Pierson, *Chatham University*
Byron Pike, *Minnesota State University—Mankato*
Lincoln Pinto, *Concordia University*
Paul Polinski, *University of Washington—Bothell*
Jean Price, *Marshall University*
Richard Price, *University of Oklahoma*
Robert Rankin, *Texas A&M University—Commerce*
Robert Resutek, *University of Georgia*
Cecile Roberti, *Community College of Rhode Island*
Steve Rock, *University of Colorado*
Tom Rosengarth, *Bridgewater College*
Mark Ross, *Western Kentucky University*
John Rossi, *Moravian College*
Brian Routh, *University of Southern Indiana*
Philipp Schaberl, *University of Northern Colorado*
Nadia Schwartz, *Augustana College*
Sarah Shonka McCoy, *Bentley University*
Evan Shough, *Oklahoma City University*
Debra Sinclair, *University of South Florida—St. Petersburg*
Nancy Snow, *University of Toledo*
Greg Sommers, *Southern Methodist University*
Theodore Souigianis, *University of Illinois*
Vicki Stewart, *Texas A & M University—Commerce*
Randall Stone, *East Central University*
Steve Stubben, *University of Utah*
Amy Sun, *University of Houston*
Maya Thevenot, *Florida Atlantic University*
Robin Thomas, *North Carolina State University*
Jake Thornock, *Brigham Young University*
Pamela Trafford, *University of Massachusetts*
Mark Ulrich, *St. John's University*
Huishan Wan, *University of Northern Iowa*
Edie Wasyliszyn, *University of Wisconsin—Superior*
Olena Watanabe, *Iowa State University*
Mary Jeanne Welsh, *La Salle University*
Ben Whipple, *University of Georgia*
Donna Whitten, *Purdue University—Northwest*
Jeff Wilks, *Brigham Young University*
Veronda Willis, *University of Texas—Tyler*
Jennifer Winchel, *University of Virginia*
Maef, *Woods, Heidelberg University*
Suzanne Wright, *Pennsylvania State University*
Hong Xie, *University of Kentucky*
Aleksandra Zimmerman, *Northern Illinois University*

We are particularly thankful for the amazing job our accuracy checkers performed on the 2nd edition. Susan Hamlen, Beth Nodus, and Mark Bauman were extremely thorough and provided many useful suggestions for improving this edition. We are grateful to George Werthman, Debbie McQuade, Terry McQuade, Marnee Fieldman, Katie Jones-Aiello, Lorraine Gleeson, Jocelyn Mousel, Jill Sternard, and the entire team at Cambridge Business Publishers for their encouragement, enthusiasm, and guidance.

Michelle Hanlon *Leslie Hodder* *Karen Nelson* *Darren Roulstone* *Amie Dragoo*

February 2019

Brief Contents

Contents

Chapter 13

Intangible Assets and Goodwill 13-1

Chapter 14

Investments in Debt and Equity Securities 14-1

1 Accounting Environment and the Conceptual Framework

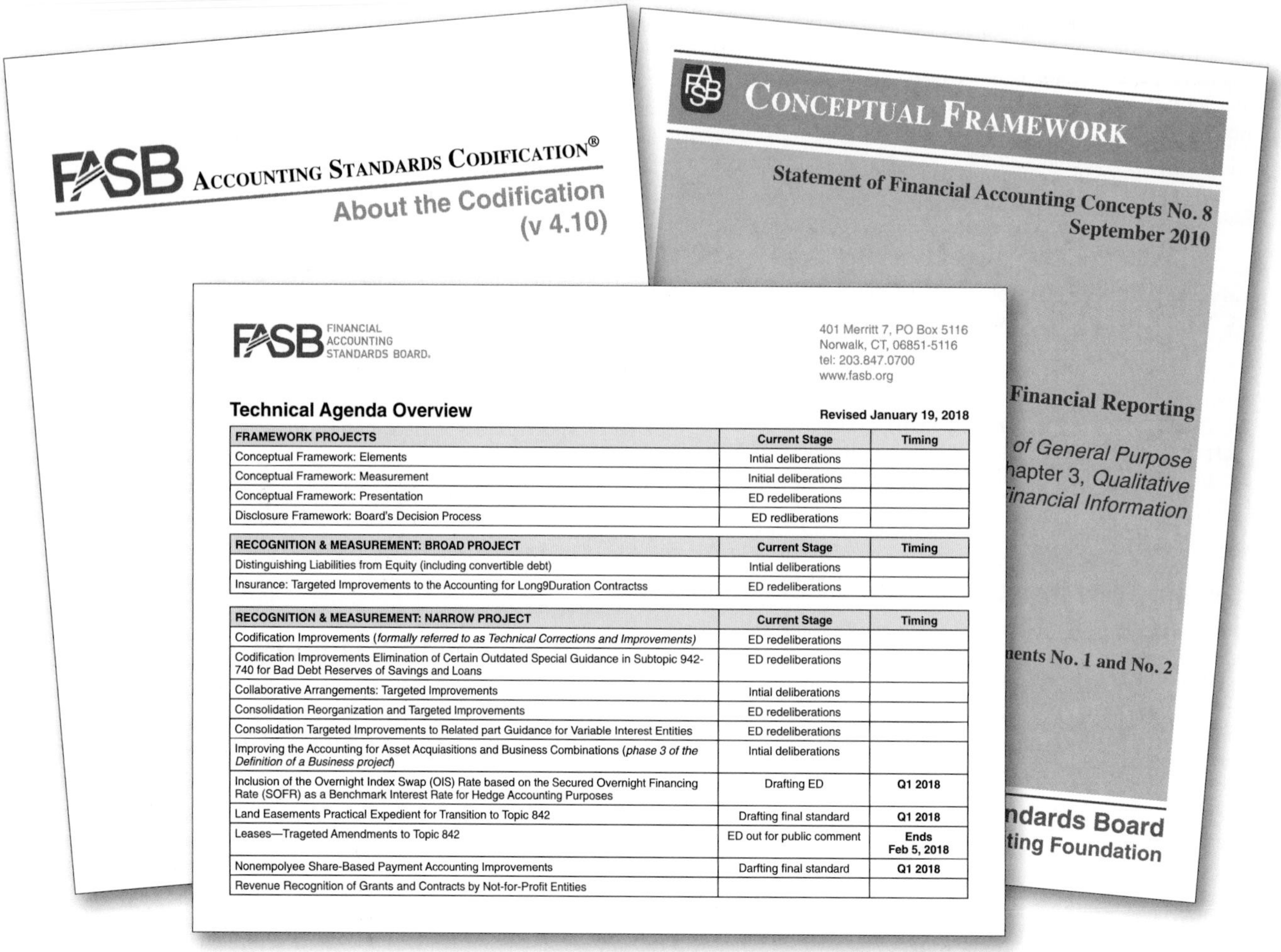

FASB ACCOUNTING STANDARDS CODIFICATION®
About the Codification
(v 4.10)

CONCEPTUAL FRAMEWORK
Statement of Financial Accounting Concepts No. 8
September 2010

Financial Reporting
of General Purpose
hapter 3, Qualitative
inancial Information

nents No. 1 and No. 2

ndards Board
ting Foundation

FASB FINANCIAL ACCOUNTING STANDARDS BOARD.

401 Merritt 7, PO Box 5116
Norwalk, CT, 06851-5116
tel: 203.847.0700
www.fasb.org

Technical Agenda Overview — Revised January 19, 2018

FRAMEWORK PROJECTS	Current Stage	Timing
Conceptual Framework: Elements	Intial deliberations	
Conceptual Framework: Measurement	Initial deliberations	
Conceptual Framework: Presentation	ED redeliberations	
Disclosure Framework: Board's Decision Process	ED redliberations	

RECOGNITION & MEASUREMENT: BROAD PROJECT	Current Stage	Timing
Distinguishing Liabilities from Equity (including convertible debt)	Intial deliberations	
Insurance: Targeted Improvements to the Accounting for Long9Duration Contractss	ED redeliberations	

RECOGNITION & MEASUREMENT: NARROW PROJECT	Current Stage	Timing
Codification Improvements (*formally referred to as Technical Corrections and Improvements)*	ED redeliberations	
Codification Improvements Elimination of Certain Outdated Special Guidance in Subtopic 942-740 for Bad Debt Reserves of Savings and Loans	ED redeliberations	
Collaborative Arrangements: Targeted Improvements	Intial deliberations	
Consolidation Reorganization and Targeted Improvements	ED redeliberations	
Consolidation Targeted Improvements to Related part Guidance for Variable Interest Entities	ED redeliberations	
Improving the Accounting for Asset Acquiasitions and Business Combinations (*phase 3 of the Definition of a Business project*)	Intial deliberations	
Inclusion of the Overnight Index Swap (OIS) Rate based on the Secured Overnight Financing Rate (SOFR) as a Benchmark Interest Rate for Hedge Accounting Purposes	Drafting ED	Q1 2018
Land Easements Practical Expedient for Transition to Topic 842	Drafting final standard	Q1 2018
Leases—Trageted Amendments to Topic 842	ED out for public comment	Ends Feb 5, 2018
Nonempolyee Share-Based Payment Accounting Improvements	Darfting final standard	Q1 2018
Revenue Recognition of Grants and Contracts by Not-for-Profit Entities		

Chapter Preview

We begin with a discussion of the accounting profession's responsibility to provide external decision makers with financial statements that they can use with reasonable levels of reliability and confidence. Preparation of financial statements is guided by the objective of general-purpose financial reporting and conformity with Generally Accepted Accounting Principles (GAAP). We discuss key organizations involved in the development of GAAP and how current GAAP is accessed through the Codification. Accounting rules outlined in GAAP are based on a conceptual framework that consists of: (1) fundamental characteristics, (2) enhancing characteristics, (3) elements, (4) assumptions, (5) principles, and (6) a constraint.

Chapter *Preview provides context for the topics that are presented in the chapter.*

Action Plan *summarizes each chapter's resources and categorizes them by learning objective.*

Assignments *reinforce learning and can be completed by hand or within MBC.*

Action Plan

LO	Topic/Subtopic	Page	Demos	Reviews	Assignments
LO 1–1	**Describe the objective of general-purpose financial reporting** Reporting Objective :: General-Purpose Reporting :: Decision Makers :: Resource Allocation	1-3	D1-1	R1-1	32, 43, 51, 56, 57, 64
LO 1–2	**Identify key organizations that determine GAAP and the factors that drive high-quality reporting** SEC :: AICPA :: FASB :: EITF :: IASB :: Auditors :: Ethics	1-6	D1-2	R1-2	33, 44, 51, 60, 61, 63, 69, 70
LO 1–3	**Describe the qualitative characteristics of, and the constraint on, useful financial information** Fundamental Characteristics :: Enhancing Characteristics :: Cost Constraint	1-16	D1-3A D1-3B D1-3C	R1-3A R1-3B R1-3C	34, 35, 36, 41, 45, 46, 47, 48, 51, 52, 53, 58, 67
LO 1–4	**Explain financial statement elements in the FASB Conceptual Framework** Point in Time Elements :: Period of Time Elements	1-22	D1-4	R1-4	37, 49, 50, 51, 62, 68
LO 1–5	**Describe the four key accounting assumptions** Economic Entity :: Going Concern :: Monetary Unit :: Periodicity	1-24	D1-5	R1-5	38, 41, 42, 51, 52, 53, 54, 55, 62, 68
LO 1–6	**Describe the four key accounting principles** Measurement :: Revenue Recognition :: Expense Recognition :: Full Disclosure	1-26	D1-6	R1-6	39, 40, 41, 42, 51, 52, 53, 54, 55, 56, 57, 58, 59, 62, 65, 66, 68

Learning Objectives *identify the key learning goals of the chapter.*

Demos *are illustrative examples accompanied by videos (available in* **myBusinessCourse**, *MBC) that give 3-5 minute demonstrations for each learning objective.*

Reviews *are practice problems that follow Demos and that are accompanied by videos (available in MBC) that demonstrate how to solve each problem.*

Each learning objective represents a **separate learning module**.

LO 1-1 Describe the objective of general-purpose financial reporting

LO 1-1 Overview

Objective of Financial Reporting
Report financial information:
- About the reporting entity
- Useful to existing and potential investors and creditors
- Useful for making decisions about allocating resources to the company.

Overview box *accompanies each learning objective and provides students with a brief summary of topics to be covered.*

Financial accounting is primarily concerned with the way companies identify, measure, and communicate financial information to external users. **External financial statement users** are those who rely on companies' financial statements and related information to make economic decisions.

Financial reporting is the process of communicating financial information to external financial statement users. Financial information includes financial statements (such as the income statement and balance sheet) and other reports (such as press releases, annual reports, and management forecasts).

Financial statements include the statement of comprehensive income (or a separate income statement along with a comprehensive income report), balance sheet (also called the statement of financial position), statement of stockholders' equity, and the statement of cash flows. Accompanying the financial statements are notes which provide additional information to financial statement users. **This book focuses on the financial reporting of financial statements and the accompanying notes of reporting entities.**

Objective of Financial Reporting

The objective of financial reporting as outlined in the Statement of Financial Accounting Concepts No. 8 follows. (See **LO 1-3** for a discussion on the conceptual framework outlined in the Statements of Financial Accounting Concepts.)

References to **authoritative guidance** *are distinctly highlighted in black blocks with white text.*

SFAC No. 8 OB2 The objective of general-purpose financial reporting is to provide financial information about the reporting entity that is useful to existing and potential investors, lenders, and other creditors in making decisions about providing resources to the entity. Those decisions involve buying, selling, or holding equity and debt instruments and providing or settling loans and other forms of credit.

This flow of financial information to existing and potential investors and creditors is shown in **Exhibit 1-1**. We discuss three important aspects of this objective.

EXHIBIT 1-1
Objective of Financial Reporting

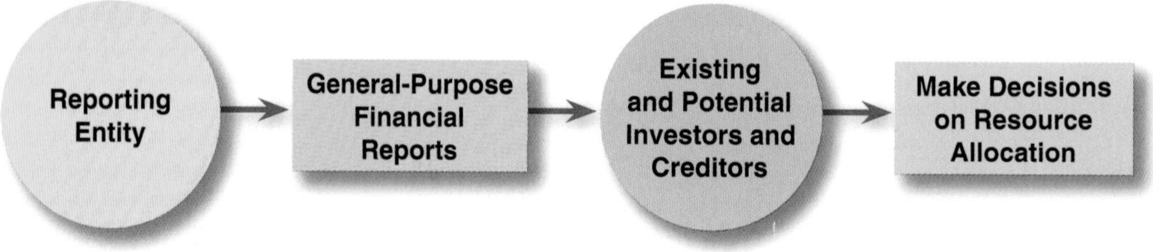

General-Purpose Financial Reports

Key terms *appear in bold font.*

General-purpose financial reports are not designed to show the value of the reporting entity, but provide information to assist existing and potential investors and creditors in assessing performance and estimating the value of an entity. **General-purpose financial reporting** refers to the most efficient and effective way to provide information about a reporting entity to a variety of users external to the company. A **reporting entity** is an identifiable accounting unit with distinct economic activities, separate and apart from its owners or shareholders, creditors, and other entities. The aim of financial reporting is to provide financial information of a reporting entity that meets the needs of external users, namely investors and creditors. We focus our analysis on business entities that issue publicly traded debt or equity securities such that they are required to file financial statements with the Securities and Exchange Commission. Throughout the text we refer to these entities as reporting entities or companies for simplicity.

Investors and Creditors

Financial reporting is focused on the needs of *existing and potential* investors (shareholders) and creditors (lenders). Investors and creditors who are buying, selling, holding, or potentially holding debt and equity securities have the most immediate need for financial information. Importantly, because reporting is general-purpose, the needs of other external users must also be served.

External decision makers often lack direct access to the information generated by the internal operations of a company and thus must rely on general-purpose financial statements. External users, beyond investors and creditors include suppliers, employees, customers, competitors, financial analysts and advisers, brokers, underwriters, attorneys, economists, certain regulatory authorities, legislators, labor unions, researchers, and the general public.

Decisions on Resource Allocation

Resources are limited, and investors and creditors make decisions on how to allocate resources. Reliable information is crucial for investors and creditors to make informed decisions on the most effective way to allocate resources. Decision makers require information about a company's economic resources and claims on those resources, and changes in economic resources and claims. They also require information about financial performance using accrual accounting, current and past cash flows, and other changes not resulting from financial performance such as financing sources and amounts. The result of better investment decisions is an improved allocation of economic resources among competing needs throughout our economy.

Implications of Financial Reporting

Financial reporting has economic consequences for current and potential investors and creditors.

Impact for Investors Reporting accounting information, especially earnings, impacts financial markets. There is a positive relation between a company's reported earnings and the price that its stock sells for on a public exchange. The graph below depicts stock returns trending up during the year for companies that subsequently reported higher earnings (as compared with the prior year) and trending down for companies that subsequently reported lower earnings. This finding highlights the important role that accountants play in the process of reporting earnings, as preparers and auditors. Other findings highlight the impact of earnings components and other balance sheet disclosures for investors.

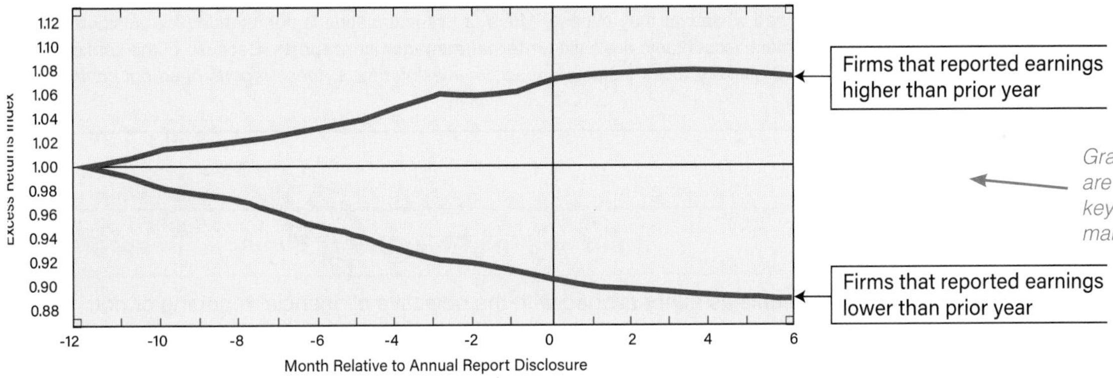

Graphical displays are used to convey key points in a visual manner.

Ball, R., and P. Brown. "An empirical evaluation of accounting income numbers." *Journal of Accounting Research*, Vol. 6, No. 2 (Autumn): 159–178.

Impact for Creditors Creditors supply financing, or capital, to businesses and in return expect repayment plus interest where the repayment terms and interest rate are set by a debt contract. Financial markets use accounting numbers to help price a company's debt and to determine interest rates. Ratings by independent rating agencies indicate the level of risk for a company's ability to pay obligations when they come due. Financial reporting is relevant in this case because it supplies the financial ratios that are key inputs to the pricing of debt in capital markets.

AICPA Pathways Commission

The AICPA Pathways Commission developed a visualization of accounting that is shown in **Exhibit 1-2**. The visualization emphasizes how useful accounting information can lead to better decisions. Useful information is based upon judgment as many areas in accounting are not straight-forward

EXHIBIT 1-2
Pathways Commission: This is Accounting

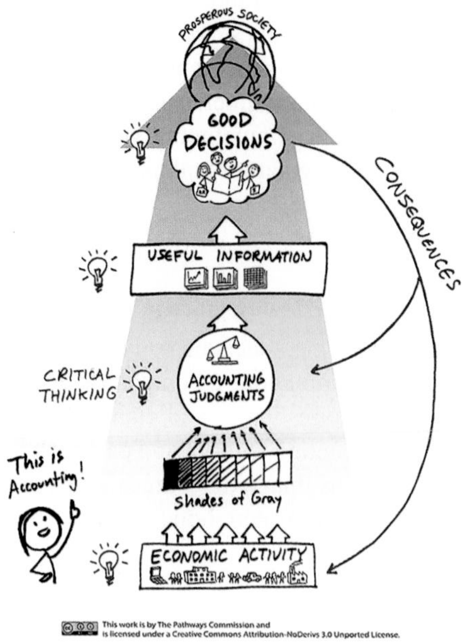

calculations of dollar amounts. This means critical thinking skills are essential in the development of information. Understanding how accounting relates to underlying economic activities and the ultimate decisions of users helps preparers assess the usefulness of information.

General-purpose financial reporting follows accrual accounting. Accrual accounting requires that an event that alters the economic status of a company be recognized in the period in which the event occurs rather than in the period when cash changes hands. Accrual accounting provides a stronger foundation for assessing a company's past and future performance than information solely about cash receipts and cash payments during that period. When companies provide *both* cash and accrual based financial information, investors and creditors are able to gain a better understanding of the financial position and performance of the company.

SFAC No. 6 139 Accrual accounting attempts to record the financial effects on an entity of transactions and other events and circumstances that have cash consequences for the entity in the periods in which those transactions, events, and circumstances occur rather than only in the periods in which cash is received or paid by the entity.

Expanding Your Knowledge *expounds on related topics through examples and discussions.*

EXPANDING YOUR KNOWLEDGE — **Managerial Accounting: What's the Difference?**

Unlike financial accounting, other specialized branches of accounting are designed to handle the *internal information needs* of a company. **Management accounting**, for example, addresses the needs of internal managers, providing them with accounting information so they can maintain control over business operations and product lines, monitor budgets and profit performance, and direct the company's future success. Internal managers in a business can usually obtain whatever financial data they need whenever they choose. Much of this information is not intended for outsiders. The reports generated by management accountants are called **internal management reports**. Because of the confidential nature of these reports and their primary focus on internal decision-making needs, *these reports need not conform to GAAP.*

Demos *illustrate the section's learning objective. Solutions are in blue font, and a brief video walking through the solution is available in* **myBusinessCourse**.

Demo 1-1 LO1-1 Analyzing the Objective of Financial Reporting

Demo MBC

Identify each of the following statements as either aligned with the objective of financial reporting or not.

	Aligned with the objective of financial reporting	Not aligned with the objective of financial reporting
a. Financial reporting consists of general-purpose financial statements, such as an income statement and a cash flow statement, that serve the needs of investors and creditors.	Aligned	
b. Financial reporting consists of a number of specialized financial reports that meet the explicit needs of a variety of user groups within a company.		Not aligned
c. Primary users of financial reporting are a company's managers who make decisions for daily operations.		Not aligned
d. Intended users of financial reporting include individuals who are considering whether to purchase stock in the company. . . .	Aligned	
e. Financial reporting includes both cash-based reporting and accrual-based reporting.	Aligned	

continued

continued from previous page

f. A shareholder or owner of a company is able to obtain financial information (such as monthly sales) by inquiring directly to the company's management. This means financial reporting is beneficial, but not critical, to an investor. . . . . **Not aligned**

g. Financial reporting is necessary because investors and creditors make decisions that require allocation of limited resources. . . . . **Aligned**

Reviews *conclude each LO section and allow students the opportunity to apply their knowledge to ensure comprehension of the topic before advancing.*

Objective of Financial Reporting — LO1-1 — REVIEW 1-1

Indicate whether each of the statements *a* through *f* is true or false.

____ *a.* Management reports are prepared primarily for internal users.

____ *b.* Financial reporting is indirectly concerned with stockholders and creditors.

____ *c.* A company can choose the types of financial statements to report according to the needs of external users.

____ *d.* Providing both cash-basis and accrual-basis information through financial reporting is beneficial to external users.

____ *e.* The addition of notes following financial statements is an optional way for companies to communicate information with investors.

____ *f.* Financial reporting focuses primarily on internal users of financial statements.

Review MBC

More Practice: 1-32, 1-43

Solution on p. 1-41.

MACY'S — Real World—FINANCIAL REPORTING

Financial reporting includes the communication of financial statements *and* other reports. One such report is the Management's Discussion and Analysis of Financial Condition and Results of Operations (MD&A) section of the annual Form 10-K report filed with the SEC. The MD&A focuses on the company's operations and financial results, including the areas of liquidity and capital resources. The MD&A also addresses apparent trends or uncertainties that can materially affect the company's financial results. It often discusses management's views of key business risks and the company's response to these risks along with critical accounting estimates. The following excerpt from the MD&A of a recent Form 10-K of Macy's Inc. provides an example of the type of information included in the MD&A. We see how the reporting has an emphasis on management's *future expectations.*

> **Liquidity and Capital Resources Outlook** Management believes that, with respect to the Company's current operations, cash on hand and funds from operations, together with its credit facility and other capital resources, will be sufficient to cover the Company's reasonably foreseeable working capital, capital expenditure and debt service requirements and other cash requirements in both the near term and over the longer term. The Company's ability to generate funds from operations may be affected by numerous factors, including general economic conditions and levels of consumer confidence and demand . . .

MACY'S [M]

More Practice is a reference to additional assignments that cover similar topics.

Review solutions are provided at the end of the chapter along with a brief video walk through of the solution in **myBusinessCourse**.

Identify key organizations that determine GAAP and the factors that drive high-quality reporting — LO 1-2

Knowing the rules and disclosures required in preparation of financial reports is essential to understanding financial reports. Over time, the accounting profession has developed a body of financial accounting concepts, principles, and procedures intended to ensure that external financial statements are relevant and faithfully representational. This body of concepts, principles, and procedures is known as **Generally Accepted Accounting Principles (GAAP)**. GAAP is intended both to guide and govern the preparation of financial statements in the interest of the public. The description *generally accepted* means that each principle either was established by a

LO 1-2 Overview

Drivers of GAAP Development
- American Institute of Certified Public Accountants (AICPA)
- Securities and Exchange Commission (SEC)
- Financial Accounting Standards Board (FASB)

designated rule-making body, such as the FASB (Financial Accounting Standards Board) or the AICPA (American Institute of Certified Public Accountants), or has achieved general acceptance through practice.

Historical Development of GAAP

The bulk of the development of GAAP has taken place in the *private sector* through the efforts of the AICPA (1939–1973) and the FASB (1973–present). Further, the **Securities and Exchange Commission (SEC)**, a governmental organization established in 1933, has regulatory power over the accounting standards process as shown in **Exhibit 1-3**.

EXHIBIT 1-3
History of Accounting Standard Setting

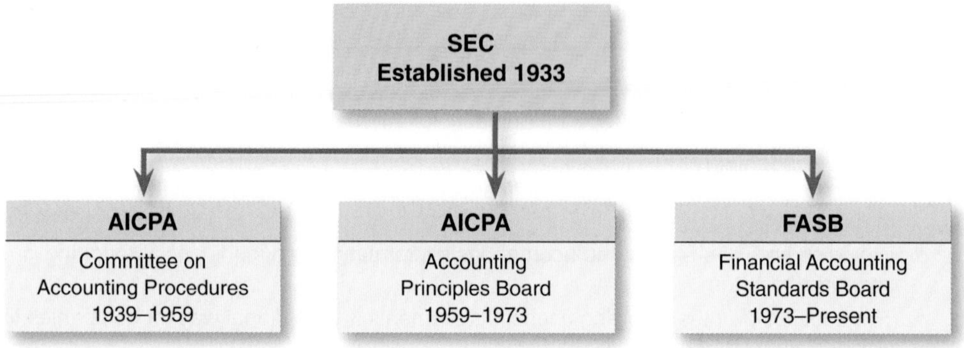

Two outcomes of the 1929 stock market crash and the subsequent Great Depression (blamed in part on inadequate financial disclosure) were the Securities Act of 1933 and the Securities Exchange Act of 1934. After these Acts, and before a company is allowed to issue or sell securities across state lines, it must file a prospectus with the SEC to report information about the company, its officers, and its financial affairs. Under the Securities Act of 1934, the SEC was created as an independent regulatory agency of the government. To that end, a company must file with the SEC its audited financial statements each year (**Form 10-K reports**) and unaudited quarterly statements (**Form 10-Q reports**) after securities have been sold to the public. Aspects of 10-K reports are discussed in Chapter 4. *The objective of the SEC is to ensure that the investor community has adequate information to make investment decisions.*

During the years immediately following the securities acts, the SEC relied primarily on the **American Institute of Certified Public Accountants (AICPA)** to develop accounting standards. The AICPA is a private, professional organization of certified public accountants. In response to the growing need to report reliable financial information, the AICPA created the **Committee on Accounting Procedure (CAP)** in the 1930s to set reporting requirements. The CAP issued 51 Accounting Research Bulletins, which was a substantive start in developing accounting standards. However, CAP was a part-time committee and could not devote sufficient time to formulating accounting standards. In 1959, CAP was replaced by the **Accounting Principles Board (APB)**. The APB designated its pronouncements as Accounting Principles Board Opinions, and 31 were issued over the period 1959 to 1973. However, widespread complaints about the narrow focus on specific issues led to the replacement of the APB by the **Financial Accounting Standards Board (FASB)** in 1973.

Current Development of GAAP

Several aspects of the FASB make it more effective than its predecessors.

- **Small size** The FASB has 7 voting members.
- **Financial independence** The FASB is financed largely through accounting support fees paid by publicly traded companies.
- **Reporting autonomy** FASB members resign from their prior organizations and cannot retain investments in companies.
- **Board representation** Members are not required to be CPAs.
- **Staff and advisory support** The FASB has its own staff, a research group, and an advisory body available to advise on agenda items and proposed releases.
- **Service continuity** FASB members serve full time with renewable 5-year terms.

The FASB's mission is to establish and improve accounting standards that foster financial reporting and provide information to help investors make decisions. Many different entities are involved in the standard setting process as depicted in **Exhibit 1-4**. The FASB is currently at center stage in developing and updating GAAP through the standard setting process.

EXPANDING YOUR KNOWLEDGE **Sarbanes-Oxley Act: Role of the SEC**

The Sarbanes-Oxley Act (SOX) introduced major changes to the regulation of corporate governance and financial practice. The Act was named after the two legislators who sponsored the bill: Senator Paul Sarbanes and Representative Michael Oxley. SOX was passed in response to the financial collapse of Enron and the accounting firm, Arthur Andersen, along with other known cases of fraud. The Act mandated a number of reforms including the following:

- *Oversight board:* **Public Company Accounting Oversight Board** (**PCAOB**) formed to oversee the auditing profession.
- *Personal certification:* Corporate executives must personally certify that the financial statements report fairly, the financial condition and results of operations in all material respects.
- *Nonaudit services:* An auditor is prohibited from providing non-audit services (such as bookkeeping, internal audit services, and consulting services) to an audit client.
- *Internal controls:* Management is required to perform a formal assessment of the effectiveness of its internal controls over financial reporting (often referred to as *Section 404*, the specific section of SOX).
- *Audit committees:* Audit committee members of the Board of Directors of the reporting entity must not be otherwise affiliated with the company.
- *Periodic report review:* The SEC performs some level of review of every public company's periodic reports at least once every three years (or more frequently).

EXHIBIT 1-4
Organizational Structure of Standard Setters

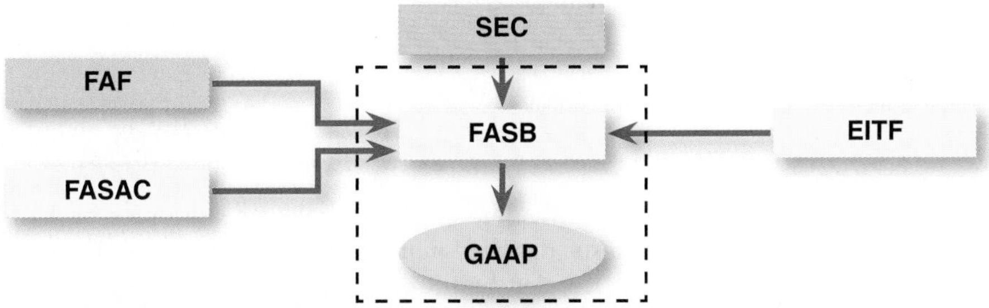

- **FAF**. Members of the FASB are accountable to the **Financial Accounting Foundation (FAF)**, a board of 14–18 trustees. The trustees of the FAF appoint members of the FASB and FASAC, raise funds to support the organization's structure, and periodically review the FASB's basic structure.
- **FASAC**. The **Financial Accounting Standards Advisory Council (FASAC)** is a group of approximately 35 senior-level individuals broadly selected from preparers, users, auditors, and CPA constituencies. Its responsibilities are to work closely with the FASB in an advisory capacity on project issues, priorities or new agenda items, procedural matters, and other matters as requested by the chairman of the FASB.

- **SEC**. The SEC exercises regulatory and enforcement authority over financial accounting as delegated by the Congress. While the SEC relies on the FASB and the accounting profession to establish accounting standards, in certain instances, the SEC has established specific accounting practice rules. Occasionally the SEC prods the accounting profession to move forward in tackling critical problems. When there is disagreement within the accounting profession over major issues, the SEC can exercise its influence to resolve matters.

  The SEC enforces accounting standards. These enforcement powers help to obtain credibility in financial reporting. For example, if the SEC believes that a company's audited financial report contains an irregularity, the SEC may send the company a deficiency letter, which prompts a response by the registrant. If an issue is not quickly resolved (an unusual situation), the SEC can issue a stop-order. Such an order prevents the company from issuing or trading securities on the exchanges. In certain situations, criminal charges may be brought against company executives.

- **EITF**. To overcome the delays caused by the FASB's due process approach, a committee called the **Emerging Issues Task Force (EITF)** was formed in 1984 by the FASB to consider issues of limited importance and scope that require technical guidance and are amenable to quick resolution. Its 10 to 15 members are drawn mainly from senior technical partners of the larger CPA firms and preparer associations. Once approved by the FASB, the conclusions of this group are considered authoritative. For example, the EITF addressed how restricted cash should be presented in the cash flow statement (EITF Issue No. 16-A) resulting in a change to GAAP. This is an example of a narrowly defined question that can be efficiently addressed by the EITF in a timely manner.

Although the AICPA was instrumental in developing GAAP prior to 1973, the AICPA is no longer involved in the development of accounting standards. The AICPA responds primarily to the needs of **CPAs (Certified Public Accountants)** in public practice. A CPA meets education and experience requirements (which vary from state to state), and passes the rigorous Uniform CPA Examination. Hence, its efforts and publications focus on the practice of public accounting. The AICPA establishes standards for audits of private companies, enforces a code of professional ethics for its members, provides educational guidance materials to its members, and develops and grades the Uniform CPA Examination.

EXPANDING YOUR KNOWLEDGE **Institute of Management Accountants**

The Institute of Management Accountants (IMA), is the counterpart of the AICPA for those accountants concerned with the accounting information needs within a company. The IMA sponsors a CMA (Certified Management Certificate) for those who would like to earn a certification for management accountants and financial professionals.

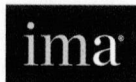

Codification (or ASC)

Prior to 2009, GAAP included approximately 16 different sources, issued by a number of different groups. For example, GAAP included documents issued by the AICPA committees (research bulletin, opinions, and industry guides), and documents issued by the FASB (standards, interpretations, and technical bulletins). To simplify the accessibility of GAAP, the FASB released the **Codification** or **ASC** (Accounting Standards Codification) in 2009, which stores authoritative U.S. GAAP in one place. The Codification can be accessed through the Financial Accounting Research System, which is an online, searchable database that streamlines the research process. The **Accounting Standards Updates (ASUs)** amend the Codification.

The Codification is organized by nine major **areas,** which are listed in **Exhibit 1-5**.

EXHIBIT 1-5
Codification Area List

100 General principles	400 Liabilities	700 Expenses
200 Presentation	500 Equity	800 Broad transactions
300 Assets	600 Revenue	900 Industry

Topics within each of the 9 areas are further organized into relevant **subtopics**, each of which is organized into **sections**. Sections have a standardized number and title formatting. For example, the first section in a subtopic is Section 05, Overview and Background, the second section is Section 10, Objectives, and the third section is Section 15, Scope, and Scope exceptions. Any section preceded by an "S" contains SEC guidance rather than FASB guidance. See **Exhibit 1-6** for a full list of sections with descriptions. Sections are further organized into **paragraphs**.

EXHIBIT 1-6
Codification Section List

Section Number ZZ (XXX-YY-ZZ)	Name of Section	Description of Section
00	Status	References to the Accounting Standards Updates that affect the subtopic.
05	Overview and Background	General overview of the subtopic.
10	Objectives	High-level objectives of the subtopic.
15	Scope and Scope Exceptions	Description of where the guidance applies and where it does not apply. (Unless otherwise indicated, guidance applies to all entities.)
20	Glossary	All glossary terms used in the subtopic.
25	Recognition	Includes the criteria, timing, and financial presentation for recognizing an item.
30	Initial Measurement	Criteria and amounts to measure an item at the initial date of recognition.
35	Subsequent Measurement	Criteria and amounts to measure an item *after* the initial date of recognition. Sources of changes include impairment, credit losses, fair value adjustments, depreciation, and amortization.
40	Derecognition	Criteria, amount and timing to remove an item from the financial records.
45	Other Presentation Matters	Financial statement presentation guidance.
50	Disclosure	Disclosure requirements for a subtopic.

continued

continued from previous page

Section Number ZZ (XXX-YY-ZZ)	Name of Section	Description of Section
55	Implementation Guidance and Illustrations	Implementation guidance and illustrations.
60	Relationships	References to other subtopics that contain related information.
65	Transition and Open Effective Date Information	Guidance for transitioning to the standard.
70	Grandfathered Guidance	Description of content grandfathered after July 1, 2009.
75	XBRL Elements	XBRL elements for the subtopic.
S-ZZ	SEC Section	Relevant SEC content for the subtopic.

Let's look at one specific ASC citation that corresponds to a section in the Codification. In the following case, the authoritative content of identification of a contract is found in the Codification in paragraph 7 as denoted by the ASC citation ASC 606-10-25-7.

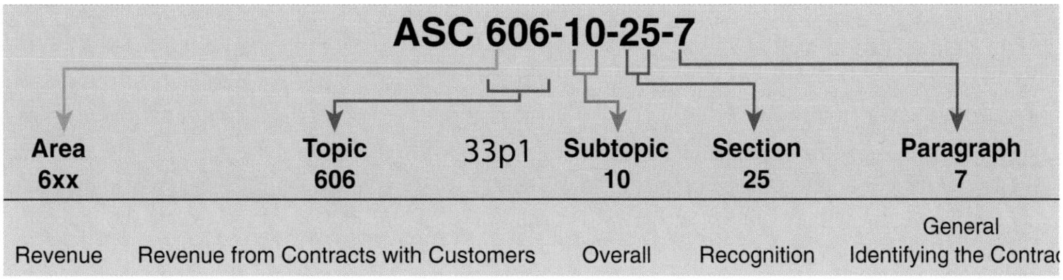

The section names in the Codification incorporate key terms that are used throughout this text to describe the accounting process: recognize, measure, derecognize, and disclose.

- To **recognize** is to record a particular item in financial statements.
- To **measure** is to assign a numerical amount to a financial item.
- To **derecognize** is to remove a financial item from financial statements.
- To **disclose** is to include information about a financial item in the notes accompanying financial statements. In some cases, disclosure relates to disclosure on the face of financial statements. Disclosure, however, is not recognition.

In this chapter we provide direct citations of the Financial Accounting Concepts to provide background for introductory topics. In remaining chapters we directly cite the Codification. We lead a direct citation with an ASC reference, and an ASC definition with ASC Glossary using the following formats:

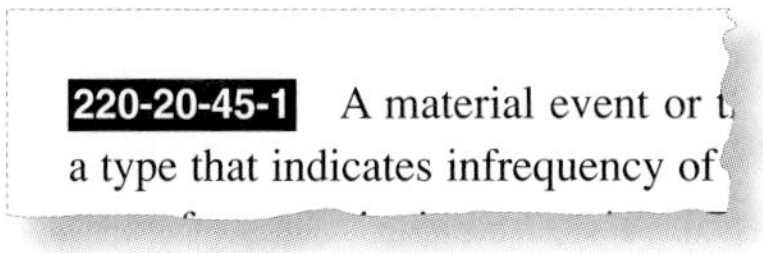

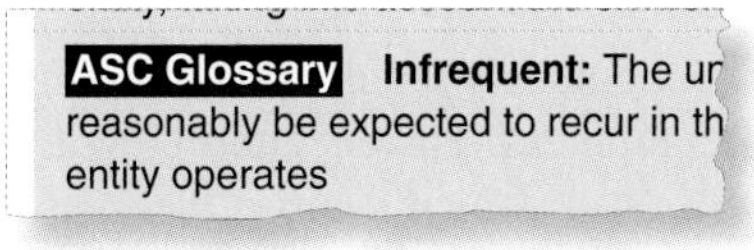

Applying Judgment When Using the Codification

Confronted with a question in practice, accounting professionals consult the Codification to determine whether authoritative support exists to provide the needed guidance. To this end, with Codification citations provided throughout this text, we show **how the financial reporting explanations and demonstrations are grounded in the authoritative guidance.**

Straightforward Analysis At times, guidance obtained through the Codification provides a straightforward "answer" and the next steps are clear. For example, let's assume that a company initiated a transaction with its chief operating officer where the company loaned cash to the officer and received a note. The company wishes to determine whether the note receivable can be combined with other accounts receivable amounts on the balance sheet. Authoritative guidance provides a definitive answer.

850-10-50-2 Notes or accounts receivable from officers, employees, or affiliated entities must be shown separately and not included under a general heading such as notes receivable or accounts receivable.

Analysis with Judgment More commonly, the authoritative guidance provides a framework for recognition or disclosure and the researcher must apply judgment. For example, the researcher makes assumptions, chooses among alternatives, and develops estimates. Sometimes, judgment is required to determine whether an item is recognized at all, as in the case of loss contingencies. Assume that a company exchanges a note receivable in an equipment purchase. Because no cash is exchanged, the company must determine what dollar amount to use to measure the transaction. The following accounting guidance is applicable.

310-10-30-5 [In] circumstances where interest is not stated... the note, the sales price, and the cost of the property, goods, or services exchanged for the note shall be recorded at the fair value of the property, goods, or services or at an amount that reasonably approximates the fair value of the note, whichever is the more clearly determinable.

In this case, the company must determine whether to record the equipment at its fair value, or at the fair value of the note receivable, depending on what management concludes is more clearly determinable.

Let's extend this example—after the equipment is recognized, management must determine how to allocate the expense to future periods. Relevant accounting guidance follows.

360-10-35-4 The cost of a productive facility is one of the costs of the services it renders during its useful economic life. Generally accepted accounting principles (GAAP) require that this cost be spread over the expected useful life of the facility in such a way as to allocate it as equitably as possible to the periods during which services are obtained from the use of the facility. This procedure is known as depreciation accounting, a system of accounting which aims to distribute the cost or other basic value of tangible capital assets, less salvage (if any), over the estimated useful life of the unit (which may be a group of assets) in a systematic and rational manner. It is a process of allocation, not of valuation.

In this case, management has the option to choose a depreciation method that allocates cost in a systematic and rational manner. This opens up the possibility to a variety of depreciation methods such as straight-line or an accelerated method such as declining balance. Management must make *assumptions* about how the equipment will be used.

Let's continue this example—if management subsequently assessed the equipment for impairment, accounting guidance includes the following on the measurement of an impairment loss.

360-10-35-17 An impairment loss shall be recognized only if the carrying amount of a long-lived asset (asset group) is not recoverable and exceeds its fair value.

Management judgment is required in applying the recoverability test and then in determining the fair value of the equipment. The accounting guidance in this case, requires certain disclosures when an impairment loss is recorded such as the method used in determining the fair value. This allows the financial statement user some insight into how certain judgments were made.

While disclosure can be included in any specific note, the accounting policies note is an important source for users to identify methods selected (such as a depreciation method selected for fixed assets) and key assumptions made by management (such as estimates of useful life of fixed assets). We see how the Codification specifically mentions that disclosure should encompass important judgments made.

235-10-50-3 Disclosure of accounting policies shall identify and describe the accounting principles followed by the entity and the methods of applying those principles that materially affect the determination of financial position, cash flows, or results of operations. In general, the disclosure shall encompass important judgments as to appropriateness of principles relating to recognition of revenue and allocation of asset costs to current and future periods; in particular, it shall encompass those accounting principles and methods that involve any of the following:

a. A selection from existing acceptable alternatives
b. Principles and methods peculiar to the industry in which the entity operates, even if such principles and methods are predominantly followed in that industry
c. Unusual or innovative applications of GAAP.

We should mention that recent standard updates in the Codification have required the use of an **asset::liability approach** over a **revenue::expense approach**. In the asset::liability approach, the changes in assets and liabilities determine the changes in revenue and expenses. Although the reverse would typically produce similar results, this is not always the case. In the recently developed revenue recognition standard, for example, revenue is recognized when or as a seller satisfies a performance obligation by transferring an asset to a customer.

606-10-25-23 An entity shall recognize revenue when (or as) the entity satisfies a performance obligation by transferring a promised good or service (that is, an asset) to a customer. An asset is transferred when (or as) the customer obtains control of that asset.

We will continue to see the asset::liability approach as standards are changed and updated in the foreseeable future.

With key authoritative guidance provided throughout this text, we will see firsthand how guidance depends on management's judgment in its application. We will also see the practical application of how guidance is referenced and relied upon in the "real world." The process of researching an issue in practice starts with clearly documenting the facts of the situation and succinctly stating the research question. After identifying the relevant authoritative literature, the researcher develops a conclusion involving application of judgment. This process is often documented in a research report. An example of such a report would usually have the following sections: (1) background information—facts and circumstances, (2) research issue—question(s) to address, (3) applicable authoritative guidance, (4) analysis—financial statement and tax, and (5) conclusions—answer(s) to research questions(s).

Due Process for New Standards

The process to develop standards is transparent, encourages participation and considers stakeholder views. Standard setting follows a due process that provides an opportunity for interested parties to express their views. The standard setting process involves the following steps (see http://www.accountingfoundation.org/jsp/Foundation/Page/FAFSectionPage&cid=1351027541520).

Step 1. Identify topic FASB identifies a financial reporting issue based on requests/recommendations from stakeholders, research by staff, FASB members' concerns, or other means.

Step 2. Make agenda decision After internal research and consultation with stakeholders and others, FASB votes on whether to add a project to the technical agenda.

Step 3. Deliberate at public meeting The issues of the project are discussed at a public meeting.

Step 4. Issue document for public comment The FASB may publish a preliminary document(s) for public comment, which identifies issues and potential solutions. After considering feedback, the FASB may issue an Exposure Draft of the proposed change. A due date is selected for the conclusion of the comment period and all comments are posted on the FASB's website.

Step 5. Host public hearings or round tables For major projects, the FASB may hold public hearings or round table discussions.

Step 6. Re-deliberate based on comments and research The FASB carefully considers the research and comments at additional public meetings.

Step 7. Issue final standard If the final standard is approved by a vote of the FASB, an *Accounting Standards Update* is issued and amends the Codification.

The FASB is influenced in its decisions by various business and special interest groups and by circumstances that are not purely accounting. A political process is involved that must reconcile the general interest, the conceptual and technical characteristics of the issue, and the specific interests of all three groups— preparers, auditors, and users. The success of this process of formulating a consensus on accounting standards depends on the conceptual soundness, absence of bias, and appropriate cost-benefit trade-offs in the application of the FASB's decisions. It also depends on the extent to which interested parties perceive that their interests are served. The various participant groups influencing the FASB in its due diligence process are in **Exhibit 1-7**.

EXHIBIT 1-7
External Users that Influence Standard Setting

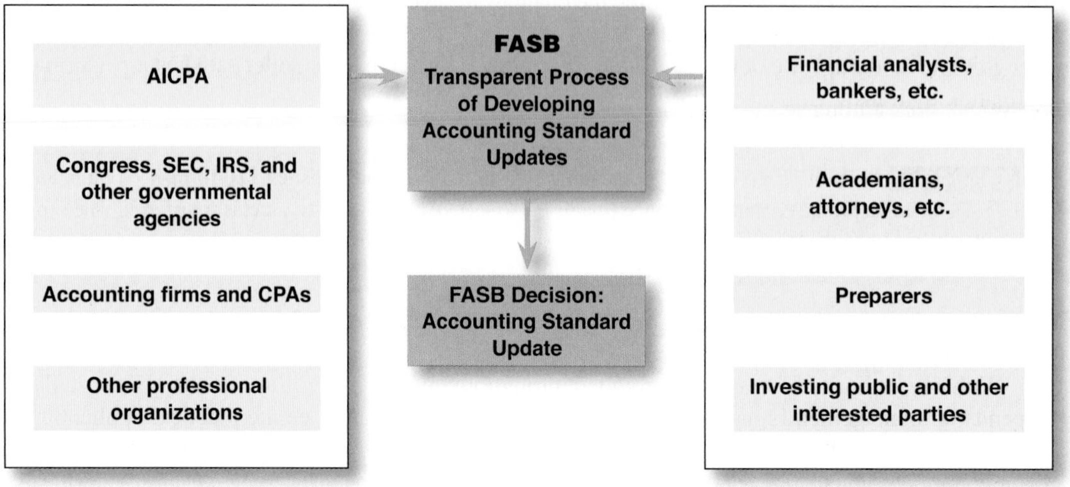

One of the problems in obtaining a consensus is the differing perspectives held by various participants affected by accounting standards. Preparers prefer to not release information that might be of value to their competitors. Companies may also hesitate to release information that reflects badly on their prospects or that is less favorable than expected. Outside users of financial information, on the other hand, prefer to receive as complete a picture of the company as possible. This friction between preparers and users helps to explain why the development of GAAP is a complex and difficult task.

EXPANDING YOUR KNOWLEDGE **Governmental Accounting**

In 1984, the **Government Accounting Standards Board (GASB)** was created to develop financial accounting and reporting standards for U.S. state and local governmental units. The GASB is an independent, private organization of 7 members based in Connecticut. The FAF is responsible for the oversight, administration, financing, and appointment of the GASB. **Governmental Accounting Standards Advisory Council (GASAC)** advises the GASB on issues related to projects, possible new agenda items, project priorities, procedural matters, and other matters as requested by the chair of the GASB.

International Accounting Standards

The International Accounting Standards Board (IASB) is an independent, private-sector organization, established in 2001. The IASB's mission is to develop **International Financial Reporting Standards (IFRS)**, a single set of high quality, understandable, enforceable and globally accepted financial reporting standards based upon clearly articulated principles. One-hundred fifty-seven individual countries and other jurisdictions permit or require IFRS for domestic listed companies. (See http://www.ifrs.org/Use-around-the-world/Pages/Jurisdiction-profiles.aspx for listings—results based on 166 profiles of jurisdictions across the world, making up 99% of the global gross domestic product.)

Differences exist between GAAP and IFRS due in part to the basic approach: GAAP tends to be more **rules-based** (such as defining a materiality threshold of 20%), while IFRS tends to be more **principles-based** (such as stating that the amount must be material without quantifying a specific threshold). In the range from principles-based to rules-based, IFRS is closer to principles-based while U.S. GAAP is closer to rules-based as shown in **Exhibit 1-8**.

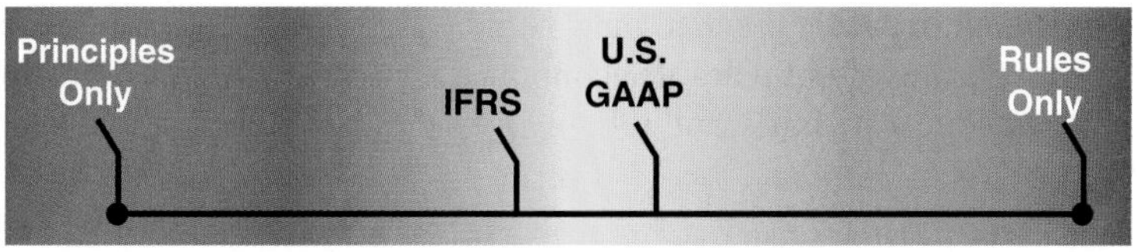

EXHIBIT 1-8
U.S. GAAP and IFRS

While there is some agreement that having one set of global accounting standards is more efficient, it appears that there will continue to be separate U.S. GAAP and IFRS standards for the foreseeable future. As early as 2002, the FASB and the IASB expressed a commitment to **converge** or remove differences between IFRS and GAAP to allow comparability of companies across regions. Subsequently, several initiatives were undertaken to move toward the U.S. adopting IFRS or converging with IFRS. As a result, the IASB has worked with the U.S. on a number of major projects to build commonalities among accounting standards. One such convergence success story was adoption of revenue recognition standards. However, efforts toward convergence of U.S. GAAP with IFRS have lost momentum and the two boards are largely focused on their individual agendas. We recognize that the vast majority of U.S. GAAP and IFRS is similar. However, because differences do exist between IFRS and U.S. GAAP, we highlight those differences in an appendix to this text.

Although convergence is not on the horizon, there is a movement toward a more principles-based approach. In a report issued in July 2003 by the SEC (https://www.sec.gov/news/studies/principlesbased-stand.htm#3) as a result of the Sarbanes-Oxley Act, the SEC recommended that the FASB follow an **objectives-oriented approach**. An objectives-oriented system is more in line with a principles-based system. The characteristics of an objectives-oriented system follow.

- An improved conceptual framework that guides the FASB in developing GAAP (see **LO 1-3**).
- Explain the objective of each standard.
- Provide sufficient detail to allow consistent application.
- Minimize exceptions from the standard.
- Avoid concrete tests that may allow for the evasion of the intent of a standard.

One application of this move toward objectives-oriented standards is the development of a revised revenue recognition standard by the FASB. The new single revenue standard replaced a multitude of industry specific revenue standards disbursed across the Codification.

Factors Driving High-Quality Application of GAAP

In addition to a transparent and participatory process in the development of high quality GAAP standards, along with federal regulations (such as the Sarbanes-Oxley Act), there are further ways to encourage high quality financial reporting. These include the application of auditing standards along with ethical standards of those preparing financial statements.

Independent Auditors

Independent accountants in public practice—most are CPAs—offer services such as auditing. These accountants act as independent and impartial **auditors** of their client's financial statements. Although independent accountants are paid by their clients, legislation makes them responsible to a governmental oversight board in the case of public companies, and to the users of financial statements.

The relationship between preparers of financial statements, auditors, and users is depicted in **Exhibit 1-9**. Preparers (companies) are responsible for developing their financial reports. These reports are audited by the auditor to provide a reliability check to the user.

EXHIBIT 1-9
Relationship of Preparers, Auditors, and Users

A professional accountant in public practice must be independent of the client whose report is to be certified. Even if the reporting of unfavorable economic results poses major problems for the reporting company, the results must be fairly and reliably presumed. Public interest must predominate.

TWITTER [TWTR]

Real World *boxes provide current examples of financial reporting activities of real companies.*

TWITTER Real World — GENERALLY ACCEPTED ACCOUNTING PRINCIPLES

Twitter Inc. includes a statement as part of its Report of Independent Registered Public Accounting Firm in a recent Form 10-K that indicates that its financial statements are presented in conformity with GAAP.

> In our opinion, the accompanying consolidated balance sheets and the related consolidated statements of operations, of comprehensive loss, of redeemable convertible preferred stock, convertible preferred stock and stockholders' equity and of cash flows present fairly, in all material respects, the financial position of Twitter, Inc. and its subsidiaries . . ., and the results of their operations and their cash flows . . . in conformity with accounting principles generally accepted in the United States of America.

Ethics and Financial Reporting

Financial reporting is a service function. To be useful, financial information must be objective and reliable. Thus, it must be free of bias and intentional distortion. Yet because the business environment is complex, financial reporting is also complex. Complexity creates dilemmas, and these dilemmas are made more difficult to resolve by the desires of management to report improved short-term results. Pressures arise to report desired results and to ignore discrepancies—in essence, to bend the rules. Professional organizations such as the AICPA and the IMA maintain a *code of ethics* that offer guidance for members facing ethical dilemmas.

Some of the ethical dilemmas that arise are clear; others are not. The proper action is not always evident. For example, auditors may discover information that is of value to a competitor. Alternatively, the information they learn can raise conflicts between respecting the relationship with the client and their responsibility to disclose information to protect the public. Information can come to the attention of the accountant that could be used for personal gain. Alternatively, the accountant might be asked to use a questionable reporting method. What should be done? *The answer rests on the fact that the accountant's ultimate responsibility is to the public.*

Yet the solution often is neither obvious nor easy. The question ultimately is not always a legal one, but an ethical one. A working rule sometimes suggested for resolving these dilemmas is to ask ourselves if we would be comfortable reading about our actions on today's headline news site.

In facing a difficult ethical dilemma, the first responsibility is to recognize that an ethical issue is present. Recognition assumes a sensitivity that is developed from experience. Second, try to understand the issues and the costs and to identify alternatives. Third, find time to reflect and evaluate. Share your thinking with a person whom you trust and respect and who can keep a confidence. Finally, make the decision and find the best means to communicate it. The decision should meet today's headline news test.

EXPANDING YOUR KNOWLEDGE **Private Company Council**

The FAF established a 9 to 12 member board, the **Private Company Council (PCC)**, to improve the process of setting accounting standards for the *needs of private companies.* In some cases, GAAP has proven to be too burdensome and costly for private companies. The PCC's primary responsibilities are to advise the FASB on private company matters regarding active FASB agenda items and on possible alternatives within existing GAAP. Any proposals by the PCC require endorsement by the FASB. For example, Accounting Standards Update 2014-18 resulted from a PPC project on accounting for identifiable intangible assets in a business combination for private companies.

Demo 1-2 **LO1-2** **Determinants of U.S. GAAP**

Demo MBC

Match each of the following descriptions to one of the following organizations: SEC, AICPA, FASB, or IASB. A description may relate to more than one organization.

	SEC	AICPA	FASB	IASB
a. Developed GAAP from 1939–1973.		✔		
b. Established the CAP and APB which contributed to GAAP . . .		✔		

continued

continued from previous page

	SEC	AICPA	FASB	IASB
c. Develops and updates GAAP currently.			✔	
d. Develops GAAP through a transparent process that involves public meetings, hearings, and deliberations based upon public comments and research			✔	
e. Has regulatory oversight over the FASB.	✔			
f. Has the authority to create GAAP but allows the private sector to be responsible for updates to GAAP	✔			
g. Issues Accounting Standards Updates that amend the Codification			✔	
h. Approves the standards developed by the EITF that become part of GAAP.			✔	
i. Enforces a code of professional ethics and develops the Uniform CPA Examination.		✔		
j. Develops IFRS, a single set of global standards				✔
k. Organized as a private sector board.		✔	✔	✔
l. Organized as a governmental board.	✔			

Determinants of U.S. GAAP **LO1-2** **REVIEW 1-2**

For each statement below, indicate which of the two organizations listed is more accurately described.

a. Acts as an advisory council to the FASB	FASAC	or	FAF
b. Develops international financial reporting standards	SEC	or	IASB
c. Emerged from actions of Congress	FASB	or	SEC
d. Professional organization of CPAs.	AICPA	or	FASB
e. Focused on technical issues, short-term in nature.	EITF	or	FASB
f. Raises funds to support the FASB	FASAC	or	FAF
g. Requires a full-time commitment as a board member	CAP	or	FASB
h. Requires registered companies to file annual financial statements	FASB	or	SEC

Review MBC

More Practice: 1-33, 1-44

Solution on p. 1-41.

Describe the qualitative characteristics of, and the constraint on, useful financial information

LO 1-3

In addition to developing Accounting Standard Updates, the FASB issues updates to the Conceptual Framework. In general, the FASB's **Conceptual Framework** (included in the FASB's Statements of Financial Accounting Concepts or SFAC) provides the *constitution* used by the FASB to guide its deliberations and development of GAAP.

The conceptual framework is the most recent attempt to develop a theoretical underpinning to support resolutions to accounting and reporting problems. The FASB's conceptual framework is reflected in the tone and motives embedded in GAAP. *Yet, the conceptual framework is not considered GAAP and may not be referenced as an authoritative source for financial reporting decisions.*

LO 1-3 Overview

Conceptual Framework
- Qualitative Characteristics
  - Fundamental qualitative characteristics
  - Enhancing qualitative characteristics
- Constraint
  - Cost effectiveness

FASB's conceptual framework is outlined in **Exhibit 1-10**. The overarching theme of the framework is the objective of financial reporting. The remaining aspects of the conceptual framework of qualitative characteristics, elements, assumptions, principles, and constraint are explained in other sections of this chapter.

EXHIBIT 1-10
FASB's Conceptual Framework

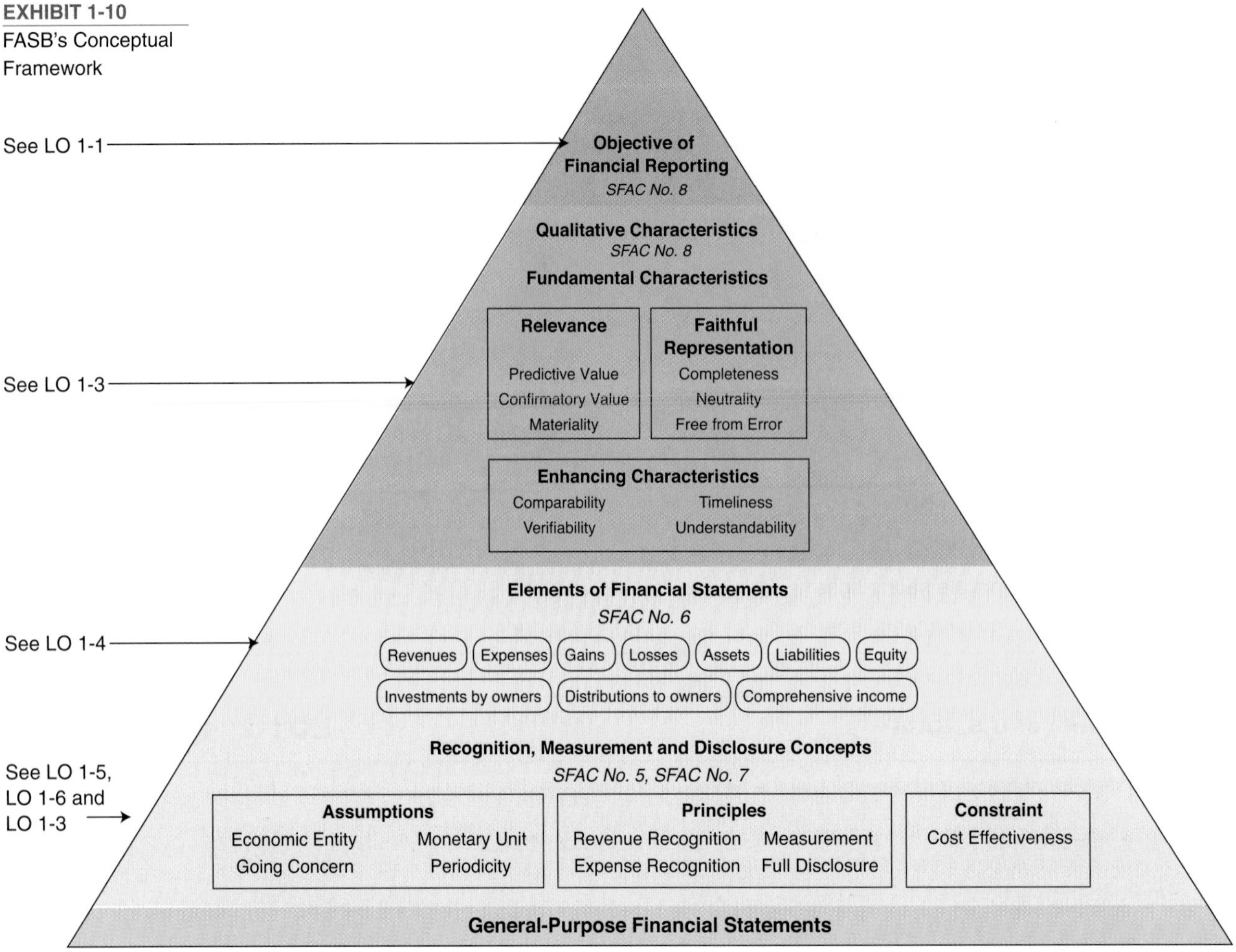

See LO 1-1
Objective of Financial Reporting
SFAC No. 8
Qualitative Characteristics
SFAC No. 8
Fundamental Characteristics
See LO 1-3
Relevance
Predictive Value
Confirmatory Value
Materiality
Faithful Representation
Completeness
Neutrality
Free from Error
Enhancing Characteristics
Comparability
Timeliness
Verifiability
Understandability
Elements of Financial Statements
SFAC No. 6
See LO 1-4
Revenues
Expenses
Gains
Losses
Assets
Liabilities
Equity
Investments by owners
Distributions to owners
Comprehensive income
Recognition, Measurement and Disclosure Concepts
SFAC No. 5, SFAC No. 7
See LO 1-5, LO 1-6 and LO 1-3
Assumptions
Economic Entity
Monetary Unit
Going Concern
Periodicity
Principles
Revenue Recognition
Measurement
Expense Recognition
Full Disclosure
Constraint
Cost Effectiveness
General-Purpose Financial Statements

Fundamental Qualitative Characteristics

The objective of general-purpose financial reporting specifies that *useful financial information* should be provided to financial statement users. What makes information useful? The conceptual framework describes two types of qualitative characteristics to describe useful information: fundamental qualitative characteristics and enhancing qualitative characteristics.

The FASB specified in SFAC No. 8 that two **fundamental qualitative characteristics** of accounting information in terms of usefulness to external decision makers are **relevance** and **faithful representation**. *Relevant information* is capable of making a difference to decision makers—see **Exhibit 1-11** for additional explanation of what makes information relevant.

EXHIBIT 1-11
Fundamental Qualitative Characteristic: Relevance

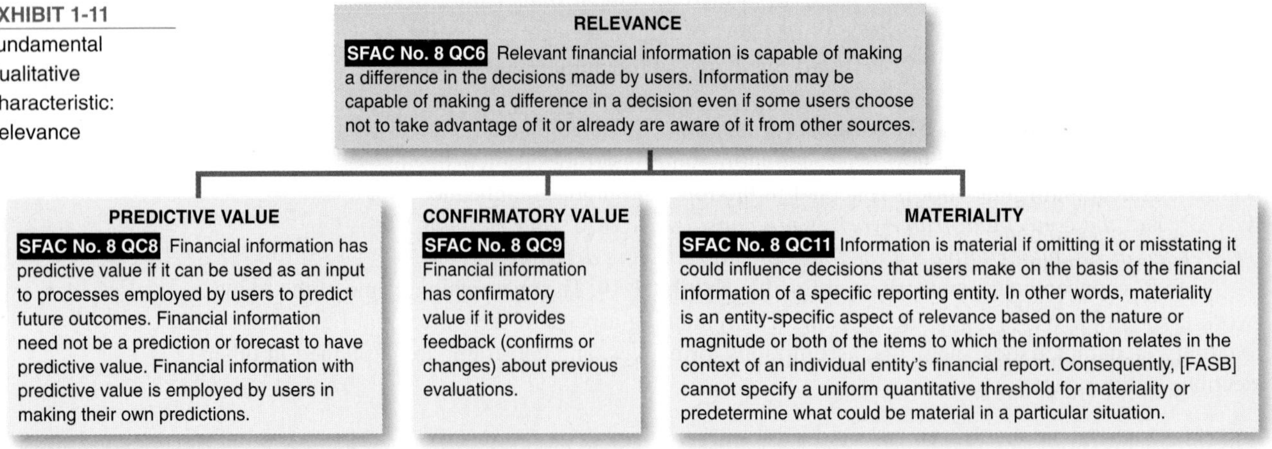

RELEVANCE
SFAC No. 8 QC6 Relevant financial information is capable of making a difference in the decisions made by users. Information may be capable of making a difference in a decision even if some users choose not to take advantage of it or already are aware of it from other sources.
PREDICTIVE VALUE
SFAC No. 8 QC8 Financial information has predictive value if it can be used as an input to processes employed by users to predict future outcomes. Financial information need not be a prediction or forecast to have predictive value. Financial information with predictive value is employed by users in making their own predictions.
CONFIRMATORY VALUE
SFAC No. 8 QC9 Financial information has confirmatory value if it provides feedback (confirms or changes) about previous evaluations.
MATERIALITY
SFAC No. 8 QC11 Information is material if omitting it or misstating it could influence decisions that users make on the basis of the financial information of a specific reporting entity. In other words, materiality is an entity-specific aspect of relevance based on the nature or magnitude or both of the items to which the information relates in the context of an individual entity's financial report. Consequently, [FASB] cannot specify a uniform quantitative threshold for materiality or predetermine what could be material in a particular situation.

Faithfully represented information authentically represents a fact or an occurrence. **Exhibit 1-12** provides additional explanation from the FASB of what makes information a faithful representation.

EXHIBIT 1-12
Fundamental Qualitative Characteristic: Faithful Representation

FAITHFUL REPRESENTATION

SFAC No. 8 QC12 Financial reports represent economic phenomena in words and numbers. To be useful, financial information not only must represent relevant phenomena, but it also must faithfully represent the phenomena that it purports to represent.

COMPLETENESS

SFAC No. 8 QC13 A complete depiction includes all information necessary for a user to understand the phenomenon being depicted, including all necessary descriptions and explanations.

NEUTRALITY

SFAC No. 8 QC14 A neutral depiction is without bias in the selection or presentation of financial information. A neutral depiction is not slanted, weighted, emphasized, deemphasized, or otherwise manipulated to increase the probability that financial information will be received favorably or unfavorably by users. Neutral information does not mean information with no purpose or no influence on behavior. On the contrary, relevant financial information is, by definition, capable of making a difference in users' decisions.*

FREE FROM ERROR

SFAC No. 8 QC15 Faithful representation does not mean accurate in all respects. Free from error means there are no errors or omissions in the description of the phenomenon, and the process used to produce the reported information has been selected and applied with no errors in the process. In this context, free from error does not mean perfectly accurate in all respects. For example, an estimate of an unobservable price or value cannot be determined to be accurate or inaccurate. However, a representation of that estimate can be faithful if the amount is described clearly and accurately as being an estimate, the nature and limitations of the estimating process are explained, and no errors have been made in selecting and applying an appropriate process for developing the estimate.

* The updated conceptual framework *does not* include conservatism as a qualitative characteristic. Understating assets or overstating liabilities in one period often leads to overstating financial performance in later periods which is in conflict with the concept of neutrality. See Statement of Financial Accounting Concepts No. 8 for further discussion.

Fundamental Qualitative Characteristics of Financial Reporting LO1-3 Demo 1-3A

Match examples *a* through *f* with one of the six fundamental qualitative characteristics. Although more than one principle might apply, select the *most relevant* principle for the specific situation.

1. Predictive value
2. Confirmatory value
3. Materiality
4. Completeness
5. Neutrality
6. Free from error

Example	Fundamental Qualitative Characteristic
a. Information reported in a 2020 income statement in a Form 10-K of a public company is used to assess the accuracy of forecasted 2020 sales.	**Confirmatory value**
b. Information reported in the 2020 income statement in a Form 10-K of a public company is used as the basis to prepare a forecast of 2021 sales.	**Predictive value**
c. A company discloses its accounting policy for estimated uncollectible accounts because the policy and the amount recorded could make a difference to users of the financial information.	**Materiality**
d. Actual warranty repairs in 2021 pertaining to 2020 sales of products exceed the warranty reserve on December 31, 2020 by $10,000. Although warranty estimates proved inaccurate, the amounts were reasonable based on information available at the end of 2020.	**Free from error**
e. A company does not deliberately increase its allowance for doubtful accounts in a period of profitability in order to build a cushion for future unprofitable years.	**Neutrality**
f. A company reports the cost of equipment ($500,000) and accumulated depreciation ($100,000) in its financial statements, which provides information on the extent to which assets have been depreciated or used.	**Completeness**

REVIEW 1-3A **LO1-3** **Fundamental Qualitative Characteristics of Financial Reporting**

Review MBC

Match examples *a* through *f* with one of the six fundamental qualitative characteristics. Although more than one principle might apply, choose the *most relevant* characteristic for each situation.

1. Predictive value
2. Confirmatory value
3. Materiality
4. Completeness
5. Neutrality
6. Free from error

____ *a.* Management concludes that a depreciation error discovered will not make a difference to external financial statement users because it represents less than 1% of net income.

____ *b.* The computation for depreciation expense on equipment for 2020 was accurately computed using the original cost of equipment, plus an estimated salvage value and useful life based upon the company's past experiences with similar equipment.

____ *c.* Income derived from discontinued operations is reported separately from income derived from continuing operations in the income statement. This presentation helps financial statements users estimate the amount of income that will continue into future years.

____ *d.* A company supplies extensive information in a note accompanying its financial statements related to its pension plan, including the assumptions used to calculate the pension liability.

____ *e.* The drop in sales reported in 2020 was inconsistent with an investor's projected level of sales based upon a 5-year trend of previously reported sales.

____ *f.* A company discloses a description and a dollar amount of sales to a company in which it has a 25% ownership interest.

More Practice: 1-35, 1-46
Solution on p. 1-41.

Enhancing Qualitative Characteristics

For information to be useful, it must also have enhancing qualitative characteristics. The conceptual framework describes four **enhancing qualitative characteristics** of useful financial information: comparability, verifiability, timeliness, and understandability. Definitions of enhancing qualitative characteristics are included in **Exhibit 1-13**.

EXHIBIT 1-13 Enhancing Qualitative Characteristics

ENHANCING QUALITATIVE CHARACTERISTICS

COMPARABILITY

SFAC No. 8 QC20 Users' decisions involve choosing between alternatives, for example, selling or holding an investment, or investing in one reporting entity or another. Consequently, information about a reporting entity is more useful if it can be compared with similar information about other entities and with similar information about the same entity for another period or another date.

SFAC No. 8 QC23 Comparability is not uniformity. For information to be comparable, like things must look alike and different things must look different. Comparability of financial information is not enhanced by making unlike things look alike any more than it is enhanced by making like things look different.

VERIFIABILITY

SFAC No. 8 QC26 Verifiability helps assure users that information faithfully represents the economic phenomena it purports to represent. Verifiability means that different knowledgeable and independent observers could reach consensus, although not necessarily complete agreement, that a particular depiction is a faithful representation. Quantified information need not be a single point estimate to be verifiable. A range of possible amounts and the related probabilities also can be verified.

TIMELINESS

SFAC No. 8 QC29 Timeliness means having information available to decision makers in time to be capable of influencing their decisions. Generally, the older the information is, the less useful it is. However, some information may continue to be timely long after the end of a reporting period because, for example, some users may need to identify and assess trends.

UNDERSTANDABILITY

SFAC No. 8 QC30 Classifying, characterizing, and presenting information clearly and concisely makes it understandable.

SFAC No. 8 QC31 Some phenomena are inherently complex and cannot be made easy to understand. Excluding information about those phenomena from financial reports might make the information in those financial reports easier to understand. However, those reports would be incomplete and therefore potentially misleading.

SFAC No. 8 QC32 Financial reports are prepared for users who have a reasonable knowledge of business and economic activities and who review and analyze the information diligently. At times, even well-informed and diligent users may need to seek the aid of an adviser to understand information about complex economic phenomena.

- **Comparability** enables financial statement users to identify and understand similarities and differences among financial items. Comparability may be achieved through the consistent use of the same accounting method for the same items either (1) from period to period within a single company or (2) in a single period across different companies.
- **Verifiability** implies a consensus in that different knowledgeable and independent observers would reach a similar conclusion that the financial information is a faithful representation of what it is intended to depict. Financial information can be verified directly (through observation) or indirectly (through checking inputs and recalculating outputs).

- **Timely financial information** is available to financial statement users in time to be capable of influencing decisions. Generally, information becomes less useful over time. On the other hand, releasing information too quickly may increase the likelihood of error.
- **Understandability** means that financial information is classified, characterized, and presented clearly and concisely to financial statement users. However, some financial information is inherently complex. Excluding such information would lead to incomplete reports and may be misleading. It is assumed that financial information is prepared for users who are reasonably informed of business and economic activities. It is also assumed that the financial statement users diligently review and analyze financial information presented. Even so, these users may need to seek assistance on complex financial information.

Enhancing Qualitative Characteristics of Financial Reporting **LO1-3** **Demo 1-3B**

Demo MBC

Match examples *a* through *d* with one of the four enhancing qualitative characteristics. Although more than one characteristic might apply, choose the *most relevant* one for the specific situation.

1. Comparability 2. Verifiability 3. Timeliness 4. Understandability

Example	Enhancing Qualitative Characteristic
a. A company reporting inventory under the LIFO inventory method (last-in, first-out), discloses inventory values under the FIFO inventory method (first-in, first-out). This disclosure allows financial statement users to compare inventory amounts using similar accounting methods across entities.	**Comparability**
b. A company elects to reference accompanying notes to financial statement items. For example, next to long-term debt in the liabilities section of the balance sheet is the reference, "see note 7."	**Understandability**
c. Two independent auditors determine that a company's recorded bond payable value is supported by reviewing bond contracts with creditors.	**Verifiability**
d. For certain filers with the Securities and Exchange Commission, annual financial statements are due 60 days following the end of the fiscal year.	**Timeliness**

Enhancing Qualitative Characteristics of Financial Reporting **LO1-3** **REVIEW 1-3B**

Review MBC

Match examples *a* through *d* with one of the four enhancing qualitative characteristics. Although more than one characteristic might apply, choose the *most relevant* one for the specific situation.

1. Comparability 2. Verifiability 3. Timeliness 4. Understandability

___ *a.* A company with a loan outstanding to a bank provides the bank with monthly, unaudited financial statements.

___ *b.* An independent auditor uses indirect evidence (customer aging, historical collection history, etc.) to evaluate the adequacy of the allowance for doubtful account balance recorded by the client.

___ *c.* A company consistently uses the same method of depreciation (straight-line) year after year, for the same class of assets.

___ *d.* The accounting standards require a tabular reconciliation of warranties, outlining changes in the warranty accrual from the beginning of the period to the end of period. The format of a tabular reconciliation provides a clear picture of how the accrual increased and decreased over the year.

More Practice: 1-36, 1-47
Solution on p. 1-41.

MACY'S

Real World—QUALITATIVE CHARACTERISTICS

MACY'S [M]

Macy's, Inc. reported the following information as part of Note 1 to its financial statements, Organization and Summary of Significant Accounting Policies. The following note excerpt illustrates at least two qualitative characteristics. First, the note explains that the company's financial statements are comparable with other companies using either LIFO or FIFO because the LIFO results approximated FIFO results. Second, the materiality concept is applied because while the LIFO results "approximated" the FIFO results, the difference was not disclosed. This implies that there was a difference, but it was not material because it was not quantified for the financial statement reader.

Merchandise Inventories—Merchandise inventories are valued at lower of cost or market using the last-in, first-out (LIFO) retail inventory method...At January 30, 2016 and January 31, 2015, merchandise inventories valued at LIFO, including adjustments as necessary to record inventory at the lower of cost or market, approximated the cost of such inventories using the first-in, first-out (FIFO) retail inventory method. The application of the LIFO retail inventory method did not result in the recognition of any LIFO charges or credits affecting cost of sales for 2015, 2014 or 2013. The retail inventory method inherently requires management judgments and estimates, such as the amount and timing of permanent markdowns to clear unproductive or slow-moving inventory, which may impact the ending inventory valuation as well as gross margins.

Cost Effectiveness Constraint

Providing financial information comes with a cost. Cost is a constraint on the type and amount of information that is provided through financial reporting.

SFAC No. 8 QC35 Cost is a pervasive constraint on the information that can be provided by financial reporting. Reporting financial information imposes costs, and it is important that those costs are justified by the benefits of reporting that information.

The **cost effectiveness constraint** requires that costs to report financial information are justified by the benefits of reporting that information. Costs include both *provider costs* to collect, process, verify, and disseminate financial information, and *user costs* to analyze and interpret the information provided. If needed information is missing, users incur additional costs to obtain or estimate that information from alternate sources. However, reporting relevant and faithfully representative financial information does not mean that all information that every user finds relevant will be reported.

When the FASB proposes new accounting standards, it applies the cost constraint in determining whether the benefits of reporting information justify the costs incurred to the providers and the users of that information. In part, FASB's process of gathering information from various user groups in developing new standards helps to inform the FASB in making the cost/benefit analysis. Assessing costs and benefits is a subjective process because different entities will estimate costs and benefits differently. However, FASB considers costs and benefits more generally, and not in relation to a specific entity.

Demo 1-3C **LO1-3** **Cost Effectiveness Constraint**

Demo MBC

Identify each statement as an illustration of the cost effectiveness constraint or not.

Example	Illustrates Cost Effectiveness
a. In determining whether to expand disclosure of loss contingencies, the FASB considered the cost to the preparers of disclosing information that may be prejudicial against companies involved in ongoing litigation.	Yes
b. The objective of the newly issued accounting standard to simplify the balance sheet classification of debt is to reduce the cost and complexity of determining the current versus noncurrent balance sheet classification of debt.	Yes
c. A company decides not to review all of its revenue contracts for proper classification under the newly issued revenue recognition standard because of the time and costs involved.	No

Cost Effectiveness Constraint

LO1-3 REVIEW 1-3C

For each situation below, determine whether the proposed action by the company aligns with the cost effectiveness constraint or not.

a. A company's main accountant left the company abruptly one month before the close of the company's fiscal year. In preparing annual statements, the company will incur excessive costs to hire accounting services to compute the ending inventory balance under FIFO (first-in, first-out). The company's president is considering whether to estimate the inventory balance based upon last year's information due to the excessive cost of preparing the information.

b. A reporting error in the computation of an inventory balance in a prior year is estimated to be no more than $10,500. The company estimates that it would cost over $70,000 to perform the detailed research necessary to find the exact amount of the error. The company's accountant is proposing to use the amount of $10,500 to adjust the financial statements to correct the error.

Review MBC

More Practice: 1-21

Solution on p. 1-41.

FASB

Real World—COST EFFECTIVENESS

The FASB issued an exposure draft on the disclosure of certain loss contingencies. After soliciting feedback on the exposure draft, the FASB posted a summary of the feedback on its website in a link called "Comment Letter Summary" on August 8, 2008. As you can see from the summary prepared by the FASB below, the majority of the respondents did not support the amendment and cost was a factor. On July 9, 2012, the FASB voted to remove the topic from its agenda.

> **Comment Letter Summary**—The majority of respondents do not support the proposed Update. These respondents are concerned that the enhanced disclosures in the proposed Update would impose significant costs, force an entity to waive attorney-client privilege and work-product protections, and provide prejudicial information to litigation adversaries that would hinder the entity's defense in litigation. Users generally support the proposed Update and commended the Board's efforts for striking an appropriate balance between providing users with adequate information to assess the potential cash flows from loss contingencies and protecting entities from providing prejudicial information to current and future claimants. See http://www.fasb.org/cs/ContentServer?site=FASB&c=Document_C&pagename=FASB%2FDocument_C%2FDocumentPage&cid=1176157934255 to access the comment letter summary.

Explain financial statement elements in the FASB conceptual framework

LO 1-4

The conceptual framework builds on the objective of financial reporting and the qualitative characteristics of financial information with the definitions of **financial statement elements**. Financial statements consist of financial statement elements. We discuss each of these elements more in-depth in later chapters.

Brief definitions of the ten financial statement elements are included in SFAC No. 6. Three elements describing resources, claims to resources, and residual interest at a point in time (**point in time elements**) are shown in **Exhibit 1-14**.

LO 1-4 Overview

Financial Statement Elements
- Point in time elements
  - Assets, liabilities, equity
- Period of time elements
  - Investment by owners
  - Distributions to owners
  - Comprehensive income
  - Revenues, expenses
  - Gains, losses

EXHIBIT 1-14 Point in Time Elements

Element	Description
Assets	**SFAC No. 6 25** Assets are probable future economic benefits obtained or controlled by a particular entity as a result of past transactions or events.
Liabilities	**SFAC No. 6 35** Liabilities are probable future sacrifices of economic benefits arising from present obligations of a particular entity to transfer assets or provide services to other entities in the future as a result of past transactions or events.
Equity (Net Assets)	**SFAC No. 6 49** Equity or net assets is the residual interest in the assets of an entity that remains after deducting its liabilities.

Seven elements describing the effects of transactions and other events that affect an entity during intervals of time (**period of time elements**) are shown in **Exhibit 1-15**. The two types of elements are related: point in time elements are affected by the period of time elements. The cumulative ending balances of point in time elements appear on the balance sheet. The period of time elements (results of events or circumstances) appear on the income statement, statement of comprehensive income, and/or the stockholders' equity statement. Revenues, expenses, gains, and losses appear on the income statement. Comprehensive income (encompassing revenues, expenses, gains, losses and other comprehensive income) appears on the statement of comprehensive income. Investments by owners and distributions to owners are included on the stockholders' equity statement (along with changes in all equity accounts).

EXHIBIT 1-15
Period of Time Elements

Element	Description
Investments by owners	**SFAC No. 6 66** Investments by owners are increases in equity of a particular business enterprise resulting from transfers to it from other entities of something valuable to obtain or increase ownership interests (or equity) in it. Assets are most commonly received as investments by owners, but that which is received may also include services or satisfaction or conversion of liabilities of the enterprise.
Distributions to owners	**SFAC No. 6 67** Distributions to owners are decreases in equity of a particular business enterprise resulting from transferring assets, rendering services, or incurring liabilities by the enterprise to owners. Distributions to owners decrease ownership interest (or equity) in an enterprise.
Comprehensive income	**SFAC No. 6 70** Comprehensive income is the change in equity of a business enterprise during a period from transactions and other events and circumstances from nonowner sources. It includes all changes in equity during a period except those resulting from investments by owners and distributions to owners.
Revenues	**SFAC No. 6 78** Revenues are inflows or other enhancements of assets of an entity or settlements of its liabilities (or a combination of both) from delivering or producing goods, rendering services, or other activities that constitute the entity's ongoing major or central operations.
Expenses	**SFAC No. 6 80** Expenses are outflows or other using up of assets or incurrences of liabilities (or a combination of both) from delivering or producing goods, rendering services, or carrying out other activities that constitute the entity's ongoing major or central operations.
Gains	**SFAC No. 6 82** Gains are increases in equity (net assets) from peripheral or incidental transactions of an entity and from all other transactions and other events and circumstances affecting the entity except those that result from revenues or investments by owners.
Losses	**SFAC No. 6 83** Losses are decreases in equity (net assets) from peripheral or incidental transactions of an entity and from all other transactions and other events and circumstances affecting the entity except those that result from expenses or distributions to owners.

Demo 1-4 LO1-4 Identification of Financial Statement Elements

For each of the 10 financial statement elements *a* through *j*, provide (1) a brief definition, (2) a relevant example (account or transaction), and (3) the financial statement where the element is reported.

Financial Statement Element	Definition	Example (Accounts or Transaction)	Applicable Financial Statement
a. Asset	Probable future economic benefits obtained by a company.	Cash	Balance sheet
b. Liability	Obligation to transfer cash (or other resources) resulting from past transaction(s).	Accounts payable	Balance sheet

continued

continued from previous page

c. Equity	Owners' residual interest in the assets less liabilities of a company.	Stockholders' equity	Balance sheet
d. Investment by owners	Increase in net assets for an ownership interest.	Common stock issued for cash	Stockholders' equity statement
e. Distribution to owners	Decrease in net assets by transfer of assets to the owners of the company.	Dividend paid in cash	Stockholders' equity statement
f. Comprehensive income	Changes in equity during a period from nonowner sources.	Net unrealized gain or loss—other comprehensive income	Statement of comprehensive income
g. Revenue	Inflow of an asset and/or settlement of a liability from delivery or production of a good or providing a service through ongoing major or central operations.	Sales revenue	Income statement
h. Expense	Outflow of an asset and/or incurrence of a liability from delivery or production of a good or providing a service through ongoing major or central operations.	Selling expense	Income statement
i. Gain	Increase in equity from peripheral or incidental activities and other transactions except those that result from revenues or investment by owners.	Gain on disposal of fixed asset	Income statement
j. Loss	Decrease in equity from peripheral or incidental activities and other transactions except those that result from expenses or distributions to owners.	Loss on disposal of fixed asset	Income statement

Financial Statement Elements **LO1-4** **REVIEW 1-4**

Review MBC

Match each account or transaction *a* through *j* with one of the ten financial statement elements.

Financial Statement Element

1. Asset
2. Liability
3. Equity
4. Investment by owners
5. Distribution to owners
6. Comprehensive income
7. Revenue
8. Expense
9. Gain
10. Loss

Account or Transaction

_____ *a.* Income Tax Payable
_____ *b.* Interest Receivable
_____ *c.* Sales Revenue
_____ *d.* Loss on Impairment of Intangible Asset
_____ *e.* Amortization Expense
_____ *f.* Gain on Litigation Settlement
_____ *g.* Cash Dividend Declared
_____ *h.* Common stock issued for cash
_____ *i.* Shareholders' Equity
_____ *j.* Other Comprehensive Income—Net Unrealized Gain or Loss

More Practice: 1-37, 1-49
Solution on p. 1-41.

Describe the four key accounting assumptions **LO 1-5**

There are four underlying assumptions in the development of accounting standards and in the financial reporting process: economic entity assumption, going concern assumption, monetary unit assumption, and the periodicity assumption. Although these concepts are not specifically referenced in the conceptual framework, they are generally acknowledged concepts that provide a foundation for development of accounting standards. **Exhibit 1-16** defines the four accounting assumptions.

LO 1-5 Overview

Accounting Assumptions
- Economic entity assumption
- Going concern assumption
- Monetary unit assumption
- Periodicity assumption

EXHIBIT 1-16
Assumptions

Assumptions

Economic Entity Assumption
Specific economic activities can be considered an identifiable accounting unit, separate and apart from its owners and from other entities.

Going Concern Assumption
The business entity is not expected to liquidate but to continue operations for the foreseeable future. It is expected to be in business for a period of time sufficient to carry out contemplated operations, contracts, and commitments.*

Monetary Unit Assumption
The results of a company's economic activities are reported in the U.S. dollar, the standard monetary unit in the U.S. It is standard practice in the U.S. to ignore changes in the purchasing power of currency (such as inflation and deflation).

Periodicity Assumption
Changes in a company's financial position are reported over a series of distinct time periods such as months, quarters, and years. A company's economic life is divided up into artificial periods for reporting periods. A **fiscal year** is an annual time period that corresponds to a calendar year or another 12-month period such as a fiscal year ended January 31.

* If a business entity expects to be liquidated in the near future, conventional accounting is not appropriate based on the going concern assumption; such circumstances call instead for the use of liquidation accounting, which values assets and liabilities at estimated net realizable or liquidation values.

Demo 1-5 LO1-5 Identifying Accounting Assumptions

Demo MBC

Each of the four examples below is based on a generally acknowledged accounting assumption. Match each example with one of the four accounting assumptions.

1. Economic entity assumption
2. Going concern assumption
3. Monetary unit assumption
4. Periodicity assumption

Example	Assumption
a. A company that began operations in 2001 reinvests income in retained earnings each year through 2020 without any adjustments for inflation. . .	**Monetary unit assumption**
b. Even though a shareholder holds an ownership interest in a corporation, the corporation owns its assets (equipment, buildings, and so forth). Those assets are not owned directly by its shareholders.	**Economic entity assumption**
c. The segregation of assets and liabilities into the categories of current and noncurrent is supported by the assumption that the company will be in existence beyond one year.	**Going concern assumption**
d. A company with publicly traded securities registered with the Securities and Exchange Commission is required to report financial statement information on a quarterly and annual basis that coincides with its fiscal year.	**Periodicity assumption**

REVIEW 1-5 LO1-5 Accounting Assumptions

Review MBC

Each of the four situations *a* through *d* below is based on a generally acknowledged accounting assumption. Match each situation with one of the four accounting assumptions.

1. Economic entity assumption
2. Going concern assumption
3. Monetary unit assumption
4. Periodicity assumption

____ *a.* The benefit of a widely recognized, favorable reputation of a company is not converted into a dollar amount on its financial statements.

____ *b.* Two legally separate companies (a parent company and a subsidiary company) are consolidated and reported as one company for financial reporting purposes.

____ *c.* A company purchases a patent with a useful life of 10 years. The company amortizes the patent over 10 years rather than reporting the patent at its liquidation value.

____ *d.* A company records an accrual for salaries expense as of the date of its fiscal year-end, December 31, 2020, in order to properly recognize incurred expenses for the fiscal year.

More Practice: 1-38
Solution on p. 1-41.

Describe the four key accounting principles

LO 1-6

Four accounting principles apply when recording and reporting financial information: measurement principle, revenue recognition principle, expense recognition principle, and full disclosure principle. **Exhibit 1-17** defines the four accounting principles.

LO 1-6 Overview

Accounting Principles
- Measurement principle
  - Historical cost
  - Fair value
- Revenue recognition principle
- Expense recognition principle
- Full disclosure principle

EXHIBIT 1-17
Accounting Principles

Principle	Description
Measurement principle	GAAP is a **mixed-attribute** measurement model as described in SFAC No. 5.* The most common ways to measure financial items are at **historical cost** (original exchange price) and at **fair value** (price that would be received to sell an asset or paid to transfer a liability in an orderly transaction between market participants at the measurement date). If an asset is measured at historical cost (*verifiable*), it may be subject to depreciation, depletion, or amortization. If an asset is measured at fair value *(subjective*), the company must disclose the level of reliability of the estimate through the **fair value hierarchy** (introduced below). *The current trend is for accounting standards to allow more valuation of items on the balance sheet at fair value than historical value.*
Revenue recognition principle	Revenue recognition begins with a contract between the seller and the customer where the seller makes a contractual promise to transfer goods or services to a customer in exchange for consideration. Revenue is recognized in the period when the seller satisfies its **performance obligation** (the promise to transfer goods or services to the customer). The five steps in the revenue recognition process are introduced in a section below but are described in detail in Chapter 7.**
Expense recognition principle	There are three approaches to expense recognition described in SFAC No. 6: (1) expense is *directly related to revenue*, meaning expense is recorded at the same time revenue is recognized; (2) expense is *incurred to obtain benefits exhausted within the period*, meaning expense is recorded as incurred; (3) expense is *incurred to obtain benefits over several periods*, meaning expense is allocated systematically and rationally.
Full disclosure principle	Financial statements include the accompanying **notes to financial statements** (adding depth to amounts in the financial statements), **supplementary schedules** (not required for financial reporting but are presented for the purpose of additional analysis), and **modifying comments on the face of financial statements** (clarify or refer to other parts of the financial statements). Financial statements report all relevant information bearing on the economic affairs of the company. The purpose of full disclosure is to provide external users with the accounting information needed to make informed investment and credit decisions. The FASB is currently engaged in a disclosure framework project to improve the effectiveness of disclosures as explained below.

* SFAC No. 5 describes other measurement models including net realizable value, current cost, and present value of future cash flows.

** Revenue recognition standard ASC 606 replaced the revenue recognition principle stated in SFAC No. 5, which explains that revenue is recognized when realized or realizable and earned.

EXPANDING YOUR KNOWLEDGE
FASB Disclosure Framework Project

The intent of the FASB's Disclosure Framework project is to improve disclosure effectiveness through the communication of information that is most important to financial statement users. The project has two components, the board's decision process and the entity's decision process. Also, the proposal updates the definition of materiality and addresses the application of materiality to quantitative and qualitative disclosures. As a result, the FASB hopes to improve disclosure effectiveness by allowing companies to eliminate immaterial disclosures. The FASB is in the process of obtaining input on the proposal.

- The Board's decision process is a review of the disclosure requirements in the accounting standards. To this end, the FASB is initially reviewing the disclosure requirements in five areas: fair value measurement, defined benefit plans, income taxes, inventory, and interim reporting.
- The entity's decision process is concerned with the appropriate exercise of discretion by reporting entities.

Demo 1-6 **LO1-6** **Identifying Accounting Principles**

Demo MBC

Each of the four situations *a* through *d* below is an application of an accounting principle. Match each situation with one of the following four accounting principles.

1. Measurement principle
2. Expense recognition principle
3. Revenue recognition principle
4. Full disclosure principle

Example	Accounting Principle
a. A balance sheet includes a consolidated amount for property, plant, and equipment while a note to the financial statements includes the categories and amounts of property, plant, and equipment, the balance of accumulated depreciation, the depreciation method employed, and average useful lives.	**Full disclosure principle**
b. A purchase of land 15 years ago is recorded in the financial statements at its original acquisition cost, which is verified with the supporting documents from the date of purchase.	**Measurement (historical cost)**
c. When a seller delivers a product in fulfillment of a promise in a revenue contract, the seller recognizes expense (cost of goods sold) for sacrifice of the product sold to the customer. The expense is directly related to the revenue.	**Expense recognition principle**
d. A company receives a cash deposit from a customer for a service to be performed in three months. Even though cash is received now, revenue is not recognized until the performance obligation is satisfied in three months.	**Revenue recognition principle**

REVIEW 1-6 **LO1-6** **Accounting Principles**

Each case *a* through *e* below is an application of an accounting principle. Match each case with one of the following four accounting principles.

1. Measurement principle
2. Expense recognition principle
3. Revenue recognition principle
4. Full disclosure principle

____ *a.* The cost of utilities for the month of June for a company is expensed in that month because the benefits from incurring utilities cost are derived in that same month.

____ *b.* An investment in common stock of another company is adjusted to its quoted price based on the closing stock price on a public exchange. The fair value is considered to be a Level 1 classification in the fair value hierarchy because the market price is observable.

____ *c.* A company elects to present a supplementary schedule on the detail of general and administration expenses, the total of which is shown in the income statement.

____ *d.* A company performs a service in the current month but will not receive payment for 90 days. Because the company satisfied the performance obligation in the current period, the company records revenue in the current period even though payment will be received in the future.

____ *e.* An upfront full payment for a 12-month casualty insurance policy is allocated evenly as expense over the 12-month period that the company receives the benefit from having insurance coverage.

More Practice: 1-39
Solution on p. 1-41.

Fair Value Hierarchy

As described in Exhibit 1-17, fair value is a common GAAP measurement. To increase consistency and comparability in fair value measurements and related disclosures, the FASB developed the fair value hierarchy (ASC 820) to categorize inputs into three levels. The range of subjectivity starts with

Level 1 as the least subjective, moving to Level 3, the most subjective. **Exhibit 1-18** describes fair value hierarchy levels.

- **Level 1 Input** is the quoted price of an identical asset, such as quoted price of shares of common stock traded on a stock exchange.
- **Level 2 Input** includes (1) quoted prices for similar assets or liabilities in active markets, (2) quoted prices for identical or similar assets or liabilities in inactive markets, (3) inputs other than quoted prices that are observable for the asset or liability, and (4) market-corroborated inputs.
- **Level 3 Input** (unobservable input) is developed by the company using the best information available, which can include the company's own data, such as forecasted cash flows.

When a company employs the fair value measurement model when reporting a financial item, the company must include a description in the notes as to whether the fair value input is classified as a Level 1, Level 2, or Level 3 classification. Disclosure of how a Level 3 valuation is determined is more extensive than a Level 1 amount due to the subjectivity of the estimate.

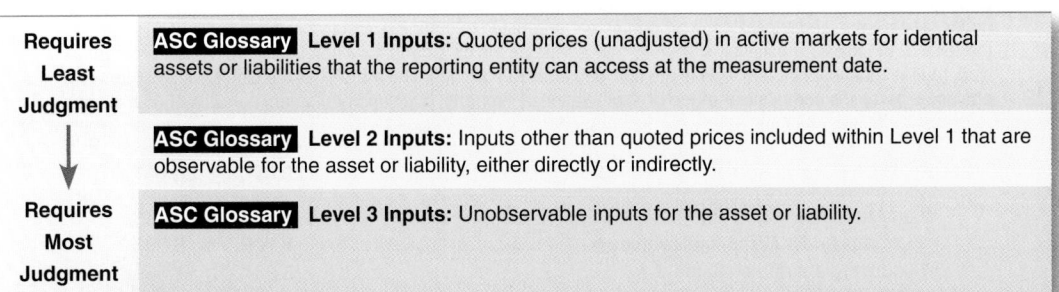

EXHIBIT 1-18
Fair Value Hierarchy Levels

Requires Least Judgment	**ASC Glossary** **Level 1 Inputs:** Quoted prices (unadjusted) in active markets for identical assets or liabilities that the reporting entity can access at the measurement date.
↓	**ASC Glossary** **Level 2 Inputs:** Inputs other than quoted prices included within Level 1 that are observable for the asset or liability, either directly or indirectly.
Requires Most Judgment	**ASC Glossary** **Level 3 Inputs:** Unobservable inputs for the asset or liability.

The FASB standardized a **fair value option** (ASC 825) in measuring financial assets and financial liabilities. This allows companies to *elect* to present financial assets and liabilities at fair value on the face of the financial statements where fair value presentation is not required. Examples of financial assets include investments in other companies and accounts receivable. Examples of financial liabilities include bonds payable and notes payable. Subsequent changes in fair value are reflected in the income statement, or in certain cases other comprehensive income, as unrealized gains or losses.

More on Recognition

General Recognition Criteria SFAC No. 5 describes *four fundamental recognition criteria* that should be met before an item is recognized in financial reporting. When the criteria are met, recognition is subject to a cost-benefit constraint and a materiality threshold. The recognition criteria follow.

- **Definitions** The item meets the definition of an element of financial statements.
- **Measurability** The item has a relevant attribute measurable with sufficient reliability.
- **Relevance** Information about the item is capable of making a difference in user decisions.
- **Reliability** Information about the item is representationally faithful, verifiable, and neutral.

Revenue Recognition The process for revenue recognition begins with the identification of a contract where the performance obligation is outlined. The final step in the revenue recognition process per ASC 606 is satisfaction of a performance obligation. For example, if a customer purchases office products from a retailer, revenue is recognized when the office products are transferred to the customer. This is the point that the performance obligation of the retailer is met, specifically, delivery of the office products. The process becomes more complex when multiple performance obligations exist, there is not a distinctive transaction price, or revenue is recognized over time. These issues are covered in Chapter 7.

Five-Step Revenue Recognition Process

Step 1: Identify the contract(s) with a customer.

Step 2: Identify the performance obligations in the contract.

Step 3: Determine the transaction price.

Step 4: Allocate the transaction price to the performance obligations in the contract.

Step 5: Recognize revenue when (or as) the entity satisfies a performance obligation.

WALGREENS BOOTS ALLIANCE.

Real World—FULL DISCLOSURE

WALGREENS BOOTS ALLIANCE [WBA]

Walgreens Boots Alliance, Inc. reported in its balance sheet the net amount of property, plant, and equipment. Further, it reported more details in a note accompanying the financial statements. To fulfill the principle of full disclosure, the company disclosed the fixed asset categories, accumulated depreciation, depreciation methods, average asset lives, and the accounting policy on repairs.

Property, Plant and Equipment Depreciation is provided on a straight-line basis over the estimated useful lives of owned assets. Estimated useful lives range from 20 years for land improvements, 13 to 50 for buildings and building improvements and 3 to 20 for fixtures, plant and equipment. Leasehold improvements, equipment under capital lease and capital lease properties are amortized over their respective estimate of useful life or over the term of the lease, whichever is shorter. Major repairs, which extend the useful life of an asset, are capitalized; routine maintenance and repairs are charged against earnings. The majority of the Company's fixtures and equipment uses the composite method of depreciation... Property, plant and equipment consists of (in millions):

	2015	2014
Land and land improvements	$ 3,687	$ 3,418
Buildings and building improvements	7,705	6,901
Fixtures, plant and equipment	8,904	7,559
Capitalized system development costs and software	1,491	688
Capital lease properties	821	530
	22,608	19,096
Less: accumulated depreciation and amortization	7,540	6,839
Balance at end of year	$15,068	$12,257

Management Judgment

Management Judgment sections appear in each chapter and identify decisions requiring management judgment that must be made when applying authoritative guidance.

Management judgment is a key part of applying the accounting Codification to financial reporting and financial statements. It is also important in the analysis and interpretation of accounting data.

Reporting Elements of Financial Statements

Judgment is crucial when reporting financial statement elements. As an example, the accounting judgment required for the reporting of equipment was highlighted in the analysis beginning on page 1-10. Management judgment is required for each of the following steps.

- Determination of which measurement is more clearly determinable for initial recognition of equipment.
- Determination of which method to use to allocate the cost of equipment to expense over its useful life based on assumptions of its use.
- Estimations required to apply the selected depreciation method such as the determination of the equipment's estimated useful life.
- Estimations used to test the equipment for impairment.
- Determination of the items to disclose in financial statements including accounting policies.

Applying the Codification to Financial Reporting

Accounting is *not* simply the application of a set of rules known as GAAP. Instead, as illustrated in the above equipment example, we see how applying GAAP through the Codification requires management judgment. Interpreting and applying guidance in specific cases is seldom a straightforward process. Consider the element definitions on page 1-23. The conceptual framework provides definitions of financial statement elements for guidance on how to classify items. However, classification of items into these categories requires management judgment as we see in the following cases.

- Should a payment for an asset improvement that is not a large dollar amount be classified as an *asset* or as an *expense*?
- Should revenue related to a long-term contract be recognized initially as a *liability* or *revenue*, or as some combination?
- Should an unrealized loss on an investment that is recognized as part of *comprehensive income* also be recognized as a *loss*?

The more we are exposed to accounting guidance throughout this text, the more we come to appreciate how critical thinking and judgment are a necessary and crucial part of expertly applying accounting guidance.

Questions *are commonly used to stimulate classroom discussion on key topics.*

Questions

1-1. What is meant by general-purpose financial statements? What is typically reported as part of general-purpose financial statements?
1-2. What is the difference between financial statements and financial reporting?
1-3. What is the basic objective of financial reporting?
1-4. Are a company's financial reports prepared primarily for internal or external users? Is a user expected to have a certain level of sophistication to understand the financial statements?
1-5. Why does financial accounting emphasize communication?
1-6. Do accounting reports include data based on assumptions about the future? If so, provide an example.
1-7. What organization currently formulates generally accepted accounting principles?
1-8. What developments led to the establishment of the FASB?
1-9. What are some key characteristics of the FASB board that contribute to its efficiency in developing accounting standards?
1-10. Briefly explain the SEC's role in establishing accounting standards and enforcing compliance with prescribed accounting standards.
1-11. What constitutes GAAP?
1-12. What is the essence of the FASB's due process procedure?
1-13. What is the Sarbanes Oxley Act? Name two provisions of the Act that influence accounting practices.
1-14. Identify the major events leading to the development of accounting practice standards.
1-15. Briefly explain the due process system used by the FASB to develop an Accounting Standard Update.
1-16. Why is a consensus important with respect to accounting standards? How is a consensus attained at the present time?
1-17. What is the importance of the Codification?
1-18. What is the IASB's primary mission?
1-19. Why do you think the FASB developed a conceptual framework?
1-20. Identify and briefly explain the two qualitative characteristics of accounting information.
1-21. How is the cost effectiveness constraint applied to accounting standard setting?
1-22. Explain the difference between a revenue, a gain, and an investment by owner.
1-23. Explain the difference between an expense, a loss, and a distribution to owner.
1-24. Explain the four basic assumptions that underlie implementation of accounting.
1-25. If a company no longer has a going concern assumption, how are assets and liabilities measured?
1-26. Explain why the periodicity assumption causes accruals and deferrals in accounting.
1-27. Briefly describe four accounting principles.
1-28. Why is GAAP described as a mixed-attribute measurement model?

1-29. Define the revenue recognition principle.

1-30. Describe the different approaches to recognizing expenses.

1-31. What is the fair value hierarchy and what is its relevance to financial statement preparation?

Many of the assignments can be completed online within **myBusinessCourse**.

Brief Exercises

Brief Exercise 1-32
Identifying Objectives of Financial Reporting **LO1**
Hint: See Demo 1-1

Demo videos that relate to an assignment are often identified in the margin.

The objective of financial reporting as outlined in the conceptual framework guides the financial reporting process. Identify whether each of the following phrases aligns with the objective of financial reporting or not.

____ *a.* Provides information on general-purpose financial information.
____ *b.* Provides information on specialized financial information.
____ *c.* Focused on financial reporting needs of internal financial statement users.
____ *d.* Focused on financial reporting needs of external financial statement users.
____ *e.* Provides information for an identifiable accounting unit with distinct economic activities.

Brief Exercise 1-33
Identifying Accounting Entities **LO2**
Hint: See Demo 1-2

Match the following organization *a* through *e* with the appropriate organization description.

a. SEC *b.* AICPA *c.* FASB *d.* EITF *e.* IASB

____ 1. Private sector board with a goal of creating a single set of high quality, globally accepted standards.
____ 2. Committee that identifies, discusses, and resolves accounting issues within the framework of the Codification with an emphasis on timely resolution.
____ 3. U.S. governmental agency with authority granted by Congress, to prescribe and enforce financial reporting standards.
____ 4. Private sector board that is primarily responsible for establishing generally accepted accounting principles.
____ 5. Private sector organization of certified public accountants that establishes audit standards for private companies and develops and grades the Uniform CPA Examination.

Brief Exercise 1-34
Classifying Qualitative Characteristics **LO3**

Match the fundamental qualitative characteristic (*relevance* or *faithful representation*) with the term or phrase *a* through *f* that best supports that characteristic.

a. Free from error ____________ *d.* Neutrality ____________
b. Confirmatory value ____________ *e.* Predictive value ____________
c. Materiality ____________ *f.* Completeness ____________

Brief Exercise 1-35
Applying Qualitative Characteristics **LO3**
Hint: See Demo 1-3A

Identify which qualitative characteristic (predictive value, confirmatory value, materiality, completeness, neutrality, or free from error) applies in each of the following situations *a* through *f*.

____ *a.* An incorrect useful life for equipment entered into the depreciation system was discovered after year-end. An adjustment to correct depreciation expense was recorded before the financial statements were issued.
____ *b.* A company's equity investment is classified as a Level 1, Level 2, or Level 3 fair value measurement. This allows a potential creditor to assess the level of subjectivity of the fair value measurement.
____ *c.* The reported cash flows from investing activities is 25% lower this year than what a shareholder had forecasted for this year.
____ *d.* A shareholder analyzes the future undiscounted lease cash outflows disclosed in a company's financial statements to prepare a 3-year income statement forecast.
____ *e.* To test for impairment of goodwill, a company obtains an appraisal of the business unit associated with the goodwill from a reputable, independent appraiser.
____ *f.* A company presents its financial statements, rounded in thousands (000).

Brief Exercise 1-36
Identifying Violations of Qualitative Characteristics **LO3**
Hint: See Demo 1-3B

Identify which qualitative characteristic (comparability, verifiability, timeliness, or understandability) is potentially violated in each of the situations *a* through *d*.

____ *a.* A company that has utilized straight-line depreciation since its inception, disclosed a change to the average-cost method in 2020, only to change back to straight-line depreciation in 2021.
____ *b.* The newly hired auditors for a company are unable to substantiate the accounts receivable allowance reported in the prior year's financial statement (audited by the prior auditors).

____ *c.* Notes to financial statements do not clearly provide the categories of investments that are consolidated into one line on the balance sheet labeled "investments."

____ *d.* Due to the unexpected resignation of the CFO in January, the company did not issue its annual financial statements (year-end December 31) until June when typically the company would release financial statements in early March.

Brief Exercise 1-37
Identifying Financial Statement Elements **LO4**

Indicate how we would classify each of the following financial statement items.

a. Cost of salaries paid in June for hours worked in June	Expense	or	Liability
b. Cash dividends paid to shareholders	Expense	or	Distribution to owners
c. Common stock issued for land.	Gain	or	Investment by owners
d. Interest income earned on investments owned by a manufacturer	Revenue	or	Gain
e. Cost of goods sold of a manufacturer	Expense	or	Loss

---

Brief Exercise 1-38
Applying Accounting Assumptions **LO5**
Hint: See Demo 1-5

Identify which accounting assumption (economic entity, going concern, monetary unit, or periodicity) applies in each of the following situations *a* through *d*.

____ *a.* American Eagles Corp. reports financial information quarterly and annually.

____ *b.* American Eagles Corp. does not adjust dollar amounts in its financial statements for the effects of inflation.

____ *c.* Debt of American Eagles' individual investors is not consolidated into the financial results of American Eagles Corp.

____ *d.* American Eagles Corp. depreciates its buildings over 40 years.

Brief Exercise 1-39
Applying Accounting Principles **LO6**
Hint: See Demo 1-6

Identify which accounting principle (measurement, revenue recognition, expense recognition, or full disclosure) applies in each of the following situations *a* through *d*.

____ *a.* American Eagles Corp. includes a note accompanying its financial statements describing the expected impact of new accounting standards issued, but not yet adopted.

____ *b.* Investments (classified as trading securities) are reported at fair value on the balance sheet date of American Eagles Corp.

____ *c.* American Eagles Corp. recognizes insurance expense evenly over a 5-year policy term.

____ *d.* Revenue is recorded when American Eagles Corp. meets its performance obligations, even if cash is received prior to or after that point.

Brief Exercise 1-40
Classifying Items Using the Fair Value Hierarchy **LO6**

Classify the reporting to be applied for each of the following securities *a* through *c* according to levels described in the fair value hierarchy (Level 1, Level 2 or Level 3).

____ *a.* Equity securities for which closing prices at the balance sheet date are not available, but where a quoted bid price is available within the last 6 months.

____ *b.* Equity securities delisted from an exchange, and where there is no observable pricing data.

____ *c.* Equity securities for which an official close price is available on an active market exchange.

Brief Exercise 1-41
Applying Qualitative Characteristics, Principles, and Assumptions **LO3, 5, 6**

What qualitative characteristic, accounting principle, or assumption justifies the accounting treatment in each situation *a* through *e*?

____ *a.* Prepayment for an annual license is allocated equally to expense over the next 12 months for Americ Inc.

____ *b.* Williams owns a shoe repair shop, a restaurant, and a service center. Separate financial statements are prepared for each business.

____ *c.* Inventories at Kaylee Inc. are valued at lower of cost or net realizable value.

____ *d.* Although the inflation rate for the most recent fiscal year of Maxim Auto was 6%, no adjustment was made on the year-end statements.

____ *e.* While making a delivery, the driver for A-to-Z Store collided with another vehicle, causing both property damage and personal injury. The party sued A-to-Z for damages that could exceed A-to-Z's insurance coverage. Existence of the suit was disclosed on A-to-Z's most recent financial statements.

Brief Exercise 1-42
Identifying Violations of Accounting Assumptions and Principles **LO5, 6**

Identify the accounting assumption or principle that is violated in each situation *a* through *d*.

____ *a.* Although the economic deterioration is expected to follow straight-line, for efficiency purposes, a company adopts an accelerated tax method of depreciation for financial reporting purposes.

____ *b.* A debt obligation of a fully owned subsidiary is excluded from the consolidated financial statements of the parent company.

____ *c.* Because land has appreciated by over 500% since its original purchase, management thought that it would be more appropriate to report land at fair value.

____ *d.* A company did not report in a note to its financial statements information regarding litigation claims that were probable and estimable because the company did not want any information published that could impact their legal defense.

Exercises

Exercise 1-43
Analyzing the Objective of Financial Reporting **LO1**

Assignments are coded by LO for student reference and instructor organization.

Indicate whether each statement *a* through *h* is true or false.

____ *a.* Financial reporting focuses primarily on external users of financial statements.

____ *b.* General-purpose financial statements are prepared primarily for internal users.

____ *c.* Financial reporting is directly concerned with stockholders and creditors.

____ *d.* Financial reporting requires only a balance sheet, an income statement, and a statement of cash flow, while other statements are optional.

____ *e.* Disclosure notes are considered an integral part of financial statements.

____ *f.* External decision makers include shareholders, bondholders, banks, and competitors.

____ *g.* Because accrual accounting is more predictive of future performance than cash accounting, all financial statements reported follow accrual accounting.

____ *h.* Resource allocation decisions drive the need for financial reporting.

Exercise 1-44
Identifying Influencers of GAAP Development **LO2**
Hint: See Demo 1-2

The following responsibilities relate to the development of GAAP.

____ *a.* Issues Accounting Standard Updates that are included in the Codification.

____ *b.* Arranged the committees that developed GAAP from 1939–1973.

____ *c.* Primarily responsible for the development of GAAP since 1973.

____ *d.* Holds the authority to develop and enforce GAAP but has delegated the development of GAAP to the private sector.

____ *e.* Created the Committee on Accounting Procedure and the Accounting Principles Board.

____ *f.* Includes 7 board members who are devoted to the board on a full-time basis, with renewable 5-year terms.

____ *g.* Primarily responsible for conclusions reached by the Emerging Issues Task Force.

____ *h.* Mission is to ensure that the investor community has the information needed to make decisions on resources allocated to investments.

____ *i.* Responsible for developing the Uniform CPA Examination.

____ *j.* Develops or improves GAAP through a transparent process that often involves public meetings, public comment solicitation, and public hearings.

Required

For each of the responsibilities *a* through *j*, indicate which body 1, 2, or 3 is primarily responsible for that duty.

1. SEC (Securities and Exchange Commission)
2. AICPA (Accounting Institute of Certified Public Accountants)
3. FASB (Financial Accounting Standards Board)

Exercise 1-45
Identifying Qualitative Characteristics **LO3**

Match each of the following qualitative characteristics *a* through *j* with the most closely related qualitative characteristic description 1 through 10.

a. Predictive value
b. Confirmatory value
c. Materiality
d. Completeness
e. Neutrality
f. Free from error
g. Comparability
h. Verifiability
i. Timeliness
j. Understandability

Qualitative Characteristic Descriptions

____ 1. Includes all required information for a financial statement user to understand the economic reality of the company.
____ 2. Has no discrepancies or omissions.
____ 3. Presented in a timely manner so as to influence business decisions.
____ 4. Corrects or confirms past predictions or forecasts.
____ 5. Results from the consistent use of accounting methods across periods and entities.
____ 6. Assists financial statement users in forecasting future trends of a company.
____ 7. Classified and presented clearly and concisely.
____ 8. Results would be similar for independent observers.
____ 9. Data that influences the economic decisions of a financial statement user are reported.
____ 10. Presented without bias.

Exercise 1-46
Applying Fundamental Qualitative Characteristics LO3

The following statements describe the usefulness of accounting information.

____ ____ *a.* A company's Form 10-K statement includes three years of financial statement history, which is a source of information for investors in forecasting future earnings.

____ ____ *b.* An investor reviewed the notes to the financial statements to assess a company's debt structure. The investor was interested in the interest rates on the loans, the terms of the notes, future payments, and related debt covenants.

____ ____ *c.* A company discloses the impact of all recently proposed standards on the company's consolidated financial position, results of operations, and cash flows, regardless if it has a positive, negative, or immaterial impact.

____ ____ *d.* An investor of a company reconciled forecasted sales for 2020 to actual sales for 2020, discovering that the company outperformed its forecast by 20%.

____ ____ *e.* Although not a historically large amount, a company reports the amount of inventory obsolescence due to the subjectivity in estimating the amount.

____ ____ *f.* The observation of a physical inventory count is a way that auditors can obtain assurance that the inventory value recorded in the financial statements is accurate.

Required

For each statement *a* through *f*, indicate which *fundamental qualitative characteristic* best applies (relevance or faithful representation), and then, which subset of the *fundamental characteristic* best applies (predictive value, confirmatory value, materiality, completeness, neutrality, or free from error).

Exercise 1-47
Applying Enhancing Qualitative Characteristics LO3

The following statements describe the usefulness of accounting information.

____ *a.* Management of a company prepares financial statements that are audited by an independent accounting firm. In the opinion of the auditors, the consolidated financial statements present fairly, in all material respects, the financial position, results of operations, and cash flows in conformity with GAAP.

____ *b.* A corporation has a policy to present quarterly financial statements to its shareholders 30 days after quarter-end, and year-end financial statements within 60 days after year-end.

____ *c.* A start up company chose to value inventory using the average cost method after research indicated that the average cost method was the most typical method used by its competitors.

____ *d.* A company's note regarding its income tax accrual is complex, requiring a reasonable understanding of income tax accounting.

____ *e.* A company has continued to use the same inventory costing method since its inception.

Required

For each statement *a* through *e*, indicate which enhancing qualitative characteristic best applies (comparability, verifiability, timeliness, or understandability).

Exercise 1-48
Applying Qualitative Characteristics LO3

During an audit of Gomez Company, the five situations described below were found to exist.

1. The company recorded a $27.50 tool as expense when purchased, although it had a 10-year estimated life and no residual value.
2. For inventory purposes, the company switched from FIFO to LIFO to FIFO for the same items during a five-year period.
3. The company recognizes depreciation using the double-declining balance, but its major competitors recognize depreciation using the straight-line method.

4. The company follows a policy of depreciating plant and equipment on the straight-line basis over a period of time that is 50% longer than the most reliable useful-life estimate.
5. For financial reporting purposes, the company reports fixed assets on a net basis, without providing information on the balance of accumulated depreciation.

Required

a. Identify the qualitative characteristic of accounting information that is directly involved in each situation.
b. For each situation 1 through 5, would we recommend that the company change its accounting policy?

Exercise 1-49
Defining Elements of Financial Statements **LO4**
Hint: See Demo 1-4

The conceptual framework defines the elements of financial statements *a* through *i* below. Important aspects of each element are listed in 1 through 11 below. Match the aspects with the elements by indicating the letter(s) of the element that applies to each aspect. Some aspects can have more than one related element.

Financial Statement Elements

a. Revenues
b. Losses
c. Gains
d. Expenses
e. Liabilities
f. Assets
g. Equity
h. Investments by owners
i. Distributions to owners

Important Aspect of the Element Definition

____ 1. Residual interest in assets after deducting liabilities.
____ 2. Decreases ownership claims.
____ 3. Result from the entity's ongoing major or central operations.
____ 4. Probable future economic benefits obtained by an entity.
____ 5. Using up of assets or incurrence of liabilities.
____ 6. Enhancements of assets or settlements of liabilities.
____ 7. From peripheral or incidental transactions of the entity.
____ 8. Probable future sacrifices arising from present obligations.
____ 9. Increases in equity from peripheral or incidental activities.
____10. Increases in net assets for an ownership interest.
____11. Decreases in net assets by transferring assets to entity owners.

Exercise 1-50
Identifying Financial Statement Elements and Reports **LO4**

The following *a* through *l* is a list of accounts and transactions for Selena Company.

	Account or Transaction	Financial Statement Element	Financial Statement
a.	Sales revenue		
b.	Bonds payable		
c.	Cash dividends issued		
d.	Gain on sale of investment		
e.	Prepaid insurance		
f.	Preferred stock issued for cash		
g.	Other comprehensive income		
h.	Advertising expense		
i.	Loss on sale of building		
j.	Interest payable		
k.	Inventory		
l.	Retained earnings		

Required

For each of the items *a* through *l* listed above, indicate the financial statement element and the applicable financial statement that best applies.

Exercise 1-51
Identifying Conceptual Framework Topics **LO1, 2, 3, 4, 5, 6**

The following topics 1 through 6 are discussed in the context of the FASB's conceptual framework.

1. Objective of general-purpose financial reporting
2. Qualitative characteristics of financial information
3. Accounting principles
4. Accounting assumptions
5. Accounting constraint
6. Financial statement elements

Required

Listed below are subtopics of the above topics. Match the subtopics *a* through *r* with the topics 1 through 6.

____ *a.* Revenue recognition criteria	____ *k.* Fundamental characteristics
____ *b.* Full disclosure	____ *l.* To aid in decision-making on resource allocation
____ *c.* Cost effectiveness	____ *m.* Enhancing characteristics
____ *d.* Assets, liabilities, and equity (defined)	____ *n.* Provide financial information to investors and creditors
____ *e.* Materiality	____ *o.* Expense recognition
____ *f.* Comparability	____ *p.* Going concern
____ *g.* Revenues and expenses (defined)	____ *q.* Predictive value
____ *h.* Monetary unit	____ *r.* Distributions to owners (defined)
____ *i.* Verifiability	
____ *j.* Comprehensive income (defined)	

Exercise 1-52
Identifying and Analyzing Qualitative Characteristics, Principles, Assumptions **LO3, 5, 6**

The FASB's Statements of Financial Accounting Concepts are intended to provide guidance in analyzing and recording transactions and events. Below are several such cases.

a. Sage Company used FIFO in 2019, LIFO in 2020, and FIFO in 2021.
b. Sage acquired land on credit by signing a $66,000, one-year, noninterest-bearing note. The asset account was debited for $66,000. The interest rate for a similar purchase is 10%.
c. Sage issues its annual financial report nine months after the end of the annual reporting period.
d. Sage recognizes all sales revenues on the cash basis.
e. Sage records interest expense only on the payment dates.
f. Sage includes among its financial statement elements an apartment house owned and operated by the owner of the company.
g. Sage never uses notes or supplemental schedules as a part of its financial reports.

Required

Indicate the accounting concept that applies to each case *and* state whether that concept was violated or not. Choose from qualitative characteristics, accounting assumptions, and accounting principles.

Exercise 1-53
Identifying Principles, Assumptions, Constraint **LO3, 5, 6**

Following are accounting assumptions, accounting principles, and constraints, lettered *a* through *i.*

Assumptions, Principles, and Constraints

a. Economic entity assumption	*f.* Measurement principle
b. Going concern assumption	*g.* Expense recognition principle
c. Periodicity assumption	*h.* Full-disclosure principle
d. Monetary unit assumption	*i.* Cost effectiveness constraint
e. Revenue recognition principle	

Match the following phrases 1 through 9 with their best assumption, principle or constraint.

Key Phrase

____ 1. Recognition of revenue when performance obligation is met.
____ 2. Common denominator—U.S. dollar.
____ 3. Expenses recorded as revenue is incurred, as expense is incurred, or systematically over time.
____ 4. Preparation cost versus value of benefit to the user.
____ 5. Separate and apart from its owners and other entities.
____ 6. Report all relevant information.
____ 7. Reporting periods—such as monthly, quarterly, or yearly.
____ 8. Historical cost and fair value measurements.
____ 9. Business continuity for the foreseeable future.

Exercise 1-54
Applying Principles and Assumptions **LO5, 6**

Identify the accounting assumption or principle that best supports the accounting decision in 1 through 8.

____ 1. Land is reported on the balance sheet, as a total of two purchase amounts (for land purchased in 1980 and land purchased in 2020).
____ 2. The rationale for a company's change in depreciation methods, as well as the financial statement impact, is explained in a note accompanying the financial statements.

____ 3. The company is assumed to exist over at least the period of time the building is being depreciated, which is 40 years.
____ 4. A parent company is consolidated with a wholly owned subsidiary to produce consolidated financial statements.
____ 5. Cost of goods sold is recorded at the same time as the related product is sold.
____ 6. The depreciable cost of equipment is allocated to expense over the useful life of the equipment.
____ 7. A public company reports financial results for each quarter and year-end.
____ 8. A company records a liability for receipt of a payment related to a service to be performed next month.

Exercise 1-55
Identifying Violations of Principles and Assumptions **LO5, 6**

Identify the accounting assumption or principle that is most violated in each of the cases 1 through 8.

____ 1. Thrive Inc. adjusted amounts in its financial statements for the effect of inflation over the past five years.
____ 2. Soni Corp. recorded a sale at the time of the customer order, even though the item was shipped several days later.
____ 3. Harper Inc. adopted the new revenue recognition accounting standard in the current year but failed to disclose the impact on financial statements, which is material.
____ 4. The expense for a one-year maintenance contract for Lazer Inc. was recorded in January of the year of the contract.
____ 5. A personal loan of the president of Lee Corp. was included in the liabilities on the balance sheet of Lee Corp.
____ 6. Equipment recorded in the accounting records of Atlanta Inc. appreciated $100,000 from 2019 to 2020. Atlanta Inc. recorded this unrealized gain in the income statement as it increased the asset value.
____ 7. Bell Tech Inc., a private corporation, provides financial statements to its shareholders every two years.
____ 8. Wilderness Inc. depreciated fixed assets (over 5 years) in its current financial statements even though liquidation of the company was imminent.

Accounting Decisions and Judgments *assignments include more application-type problems and require critical thinking.*

Accounting Decisions and Judgments

AD&J 1-56
Evaluating a Change in Accounting Principle **LO 1, 6**

Real World Analysis **Ford Motor Company** disclosed the following note accompanying its December 31, 2015, annual financial statements.

> **Change in Accounting—Pension and Other Postretirement Employee Benefits ("OPEB").** On December 31, 2015, we adopted a change in accounting method for certain components of expense related to our defined benefit pension and OPEB plans. Under the new method, we recognize remeasurement gains and losses immediately in net income and use fair value to calculate the expected return on plan assets. Historically, we recognized remeasurement gains and losses as a component of Accumulated other comprehensive income/(loss) and amortized them as a component of net periodic benefit cost, subject to a corridor, over the remaining service period of our active employees. In addition, we previously used a market-related value of plan assets that recognized changes in fair value over time to calculate the expected return on plan assets.
>
> We believe this change in accounting method is preferable as it better recognizes the current performance of our pension and OPEB plans in our net income in the year incurred. Additionally, our segment reporting shown in Note 24 now provides better transparency into the underlying operating results of Ford's Automotive business units. We have retrospectively applied this change in accounting method to all prior periods. As of January 1, 2013, the cumulative effect of the change resulted in a decrease of $18 billion in Retained earnings and an increase of $18 billion in Accumulated other comprehensive income/(loss), both components of total equity in our consolidated and sector balance sheets.

Required
Does this change in reporting aid the decisions of those using Ford's financial statements? Explain.

AD&J 1-57
Evaluating an Annual Report **LO1, 6**

Real World Analysis Obtain an electronic copy of the Form 10-K for the **Coca-Cola Company** for the year ended December 31, 2015, which is on the SEC Edgar website (https://www.sec.gov/edgar/searchedgar/companysearch.html). Search for "Coca Cola Co."

Required
Answer the following questions based on its 2015 financial statements.

a. On what date does the annual reporting period end? Is the company a calendar-year reporting firm?
b. What were the net operating revenues for 2015?
c. What was the net increase (decrease) in cash and cash equivalents for 2015?

d. What were the total assets at the end of the 2015 reporting period?

e. What is the title of the first note to the consolidated financial statements? How many notes were provided?

f. What is the name of the auditing firm?

g. What references to recently issued accounting guidance are included in the notes? What does the reporting say, if anything, about their expected future impact on Coca-Cola Company's financial statements?

h. Do the financial statements refer to GAAP at any point?

i. How does the company apply the expense recognition principle to the following?

  i. Intangible assets with definitive lives.
  ii. Property, plant, and equipment.
  iii. Inventories.

Red blocks highlight the type of assignment in the Accounting Decisions and Judgments section.

AD&J 1-58 Communicating Conceptual Framework Violations LO3, 6

Communication Case The following two independent cases arguably violate part(s) of the FASB's conceptual framework.

Case A. Financial statements of Gold Corporation include the following note: "During the current year, plant assets were written down by $8,000,000. This write-down will reduce future expenses. Depreciation and other expenses in future years will be lower, and as a result this will benefit profits of future years."

Case B. During an audit of the Silver Company, certain liabilities, such as taxes, appear to be overstated. Also, some semi-obsolete inventory items appear undervalued, and the tendency is to expense rather than to capitalize as many items as possible. Management states that "the company has always taken a very conservative view of the business and its future prospects." Management suggests that it does not wish to weaken the company by reporting any more earnings or paying any more dividends than are absolutely necessary because it does not expect business to continue to be good. It points out that the lower valuations for assets do not hurt anything for the company but do create reserves for "hard times."

Required

For each case, write a one-half page memo explaining to the CFO the nature of any violations of accepted accounting and reporting practices *and*, in those instances, what part(s) of the conceptual framework is directly violated.

AD&J 1-59 Evaluating Intangible Assets LO6

Judgment Case The value of Coca-Cola Company's internally generated brand name has been estimated at about $80 billion. Even though Coca-Cola Company reports on its financial statements over $12 billion of goodwill and other intangible assets, almost none of this reported value is due to Coca-Cola Company's brand.

Required

a. What are arguments in favor of *including* a value for Coca-Cola Company's brand on its financial statements?

b. In contrast, what are arguments in favor of *excluding* a value for Coca-Cola Company's brand on its financial statements?

AD&J 1-60 Assessing Alternative Approaches to Setting Accounting Standards LO2

Real World Analysis Consider the following approaches to setting accounting standards.

a. Private sector exclusively.

b. Public sector exclusively.

c. Private and public sectors jointly.

Required

Explain and assess the three approaches to setting accounting standards. Include a consideration of the politics of a standard-setting approach.

AD&J 1-61 Analyzing a Convergence with International Financial Reporting Standards LO2

Judgment Case What advantages do we see the United States gaining from achieving a greater harmonization with (less diversity from) international accounting standards? What are the disadvantages of converging with IFRS?

AD&J 1-62 Assessing the Treatment of Research and Development Costs LO4, 5, 6

Ethics Case You are hired as the assistant in the finance department of a medium-sized publicly traded company. Realizing the importance of accounting for your job, you complete a two-semester introductory course in financial accounting at night at a local college. In this course you learned that basic research and development costs are expensed during the period they are incurred. You recall, however, that accountants believe in allocating the costs of a given activity with the revenues resulting from that activity.

Your company has developed an important breakthrough in laser equipment. The cost of development has been considerable. If this cost were capitalized this year and written off against expected future revenues from the new machine, this year's earnings per share would increase by 10% rather than show a modest decline.

Your manager favors capitalization because the company's CEO wants to continue a 20-quarter record of increasing earnings per share figures. She asks your opinion based on your recent exposure to accounting standards.

You research your company's past practice in this area and you reread the accounting standards on research and development costs. Although your company has not previously experienced the level of R&D expenses associated with the present project, past practice in your company is to expense these costs. Your reading of the accounting standards confirms what you recall from class, namely, that these expenses should be expensed.

Your manager is adamant to adopt the alternative position and is known to be intolerant of views differing from her own.

Required

Explain and outline how you would approach your forthcoming meeting with the manager.

AD&J 1-63
Analyzing Neutrality in Standard Setting **LO2**

Communication Case Write a one-half page discussion on whether the FASB should follow a policy of neutrality in standard setting. Should the Board devote attention to economic consequences?

AD&J 1-64
Distinguishing Accrual-Basis and Cash-Basis Accounting **LO1**

Real World Analysis The conceptual framework states that the objective of financial reporting is to provide information that is helpful to current and potential investors and creditors in assessing the amounts, timing, and uncertainty of future net cash inflows to the entity. Yet the revenue and expense recognition concepts described in the conceptual framework are predicated on the accrual basis of accounting.

Required

Distinguish between the cash basis and the accrual basis of accounting. Address any seeming conflict between the two positions. Use examples of how expenses and revenues are treated in both systems.

AD&J 1-65
Analyzing Violations of Full Disclosure **LO6**

Judgment Case Explain how each of the following items, as reported on Siesta Corporation's balance sheet, violated (if it did) the full-disclosure principle.

a. There was no comment or explanation that the company changed its inventory method from FIFO to LIFO at the beginning of the current reporting period. A large changeover difference was involved.
b. Equity reported only two amounts: capital stock, $150,000; and retained earnings, $130,000. Capital stock has a total par value of $100,000 and originally sold for $150,000 cash.
c. Sales revenue was $960,000 and cost of goods sold, $600,000; but the first line reported on the income statement was revenues, $360,000.
d. No earnings per share (EPS) amounts were reported.
e. Currents assets amounted to $314,000 and current liabilities, $205,000; the balance sheet reported as a single amount, working capital, $109,000.
f. The income statement showed only the following three classifications.

i. Gross revenues. ii. Costs. iii. Net profit.

AD&J 1-66
Analyzing Comparability, Consistency, and Allocation in Inventory Methods **LO6**

Real World Analysis An automobile manufacturer switched its inventory method for financial reporting from LIFO to FIFO. In its letter to shareholders, the manufacturer explained that other automobile manufacturers (competitors) have consistently used the FIFO method. Therefore, by changing over to FIFO, the reported net income was restated on a comparable basis to the other companies. Effective 15 years later, the automobile manufacturer switched back to LIFO. In an accompanying note, the auto manufacturer explained that the change was made to more accurately match current costs with current revenues. The results from prior years were restated so all years were reported on the same basis.

Required

a. Are the reasons for the original change from LIFO to FIFO, taken alone, reasonable arguments for not continuing to use the same inventory cost-flow assumption? Explain.
b. How does the later change to LIFO produce a more accurate allocation of current costs with current revenues?

AD&J 1-67
Analyzing Qualitative Characteristics **LO3**

Real World Analysis A company's management determined that fraud-related losses due to certain leasing transactions were immaterial, thus were not disclosed in the financial statements. The fraud-related losses were less than 10% of the company's $2.2 billion in shareholder equity.

Required

a. Explain the qualitative characteristics of accounting information that are arguably at issue and assess the situation.

b. Suppose the controller is informed by the president that the amount should be considered immaterial. The controller believes the amount is likely material. What should the controller do?

AD&J 1-68
Identifying Violations of Elements, Principles, Assumptions **LO4, 5, 6**

Challenge Problem An inspection of the annual financial statements and the accounting records revealed that Massey Hardware had violated accounting assumptions, accounting principles, and constraints. The following transactions were involved.

1. Merchandise purchased for resale was delivered on June 5. The invoice price was $50,000 with terms n/30. The following month on July 1, the account was paid (cash was credited for $50,000) and an entry was recorded to increase inventory for $50,000 and to decrease cash for $50,000.
2. Accounts receivable of $95,000 was reported on the balance sheet on June 30 for a sale shipped the following month.
3. In June, usual and ordinary repairs on operational assets were recorded as an increase to operational assets.
4. Treasury stock (stock of the company that was sold and subsequently bought back from stockholders) was debited to treasury stock (asset account) and was reported on the balance sheet as an asset at the purchase cost, $76,000.
5. Depreciation expense of $227,000 was recorded as a deduction directly from retained earnings on the balance sheet.
6. Income tax expense of $18,000 was recorded as a deduction directly from retained earnings on the balance sheet.
7. The company issued stock for land on June 30. The stock had a par value of $1,000, but the fair value was not easily determinable. The fair value of the land was estimated to be $3,000. The company recorded the entry as an increase to land for $1,000 and an increase to common stock for $1,000.

Required

For each transaction, identify the inappropriate treatment *and* what element, assumption, and/or principle was violated.

AD&J 1-69
Codification Skills
Defining Terms in ASC Glossary **LO2**

Codification Skills The Codification has a Master Glossary that provides definitions of important accounting terms. Define the following accounting terms.

a. Fair value (used in the topic of Receivables).

b. Public business entity.

c. Securities and Exchange Commission registrant.

AD&J 1-70
Codification Skills
Researching using the Codification **LO2**

Codification Skills Refer to the Codification to answer the following questions.

a. What is the topic number of debt?

b. What are the titles of sections 5, 25, and 50 in topic 505, subtopic 10?

c. What are the titles of sections 5, 25, and 50 in topic 505, subtopic 20?

d. What is the ASC reference for the content of the presentation of receivables from officers, employees, or affiliates? FASB ASC ____-____-____-____

e. What is the ASC reference for the five steps in the revenue recognition process? FASB ASC ____-____-____-____

Answers to Review Exercises

Solutions to the Review problems are at the end of each chapter. Video walkthroughs of Review solutions are available in **myBusinessCourse**.

Review 1-1

a. True, *b.* False, *c.* False, *d.* True, *e.* False, *f.* False

Review 1-2

a. FASAC, *b.* IASB, *c.* SEC, *d.* AICPA, *e.* EITF, *f.* FAF, *g.* FASB, *h.* SEC

Review 1-3A

a. materiality, *b.* free from error, *c.* predictive value, *d.* completeness, *e.* confirmatory value, *f.* neutrality

Review 1-3B

a. timeliness, *b.* verifiability, *c.* comparability, *d.* understandability

Review 1-3C

a. No, the company will need to incur the costs to provide the information that is routinely required by companies to prepare.

b. Yes, the estimate may be used due to the excessive cost of determining an exact amount, as long as the company is confident that the amount is not materially understated.

Review 1-4

a. 2. Liability, *b.* 1. Asset, *c.* 7. Revenue, *d.* 10. Loss, *e.* 8. Expense, *f.* 9. Gain, *g.* 5. Distribution to owners, *h.* 4. Investment by owners, *i.* 3. Equity, *j.* 6. Comprehensive income.

Review 1-5

a. 3. Monetary unit assumption, *b.* 1. Economic entity assumption, *c.* 2. Going concern assumption, *d.* 4. Periodicity assumption.

Review 1-6

a. 2. Expense recognition principle, *b.* 1. Measurement principle (fair value), *c.* 4. Full disclosure principle, *d.* 3. Revenue recognition principle, *e.* 2. Expense recognition principle

2 Accounting Information System

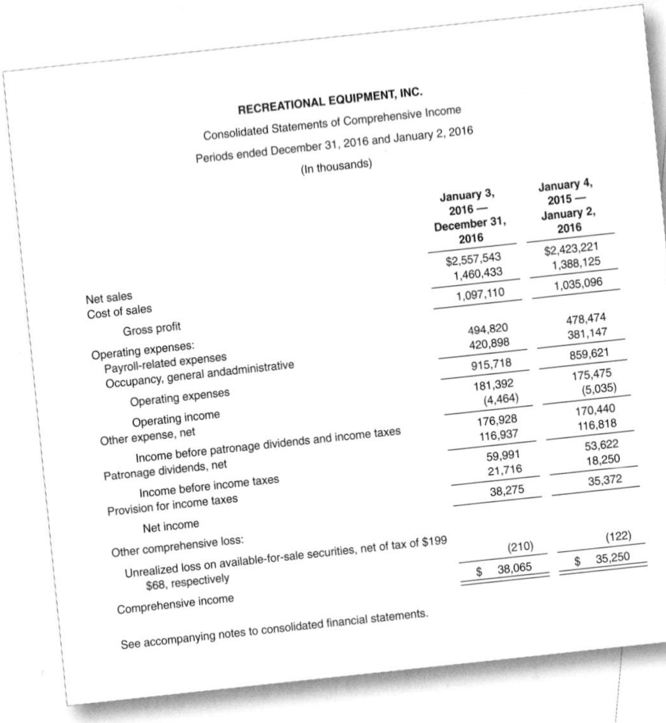

RECREATIONAL EQUIPMENT, INC.

Consolidated Statements of Comprehensive Income

Periods ended December 31, 2016 and January 2, 2016

(In thousands)

	January 3, 2016 — December 31, 2016	January 4, 2015 — January 2, 2016
Net sales	$2,557,543	$2,423,221
Cost of sales	1,460,433	1,388,125
Gross profit	1,097,110	1,035,096
Operating expenses:		
Payroll-related expenses	494,820	478,474
Occupancy, general andadministrative	420,898	381,147
Operating expenses	915,718	859,621
Operating income	181,392	175,475
Other expense, net	(4,464)	(5,035)
Income before patronage dividends and income taxes	176,928	170,440
Patronage dividends, net	116,937	116,818
Income before income taxes	59,991	53,622
Provision for income taxes	21,716	18,250
Net income	38,275	35,372
Other comprehensive loss:		
Unrealized loss on available-for-sale securities, net of tax of $199 $68, respectively	(210)	(122)
Comprehensive income	$ 38,065	$ 35,250

See accompanying notes to consolidated financial statements.

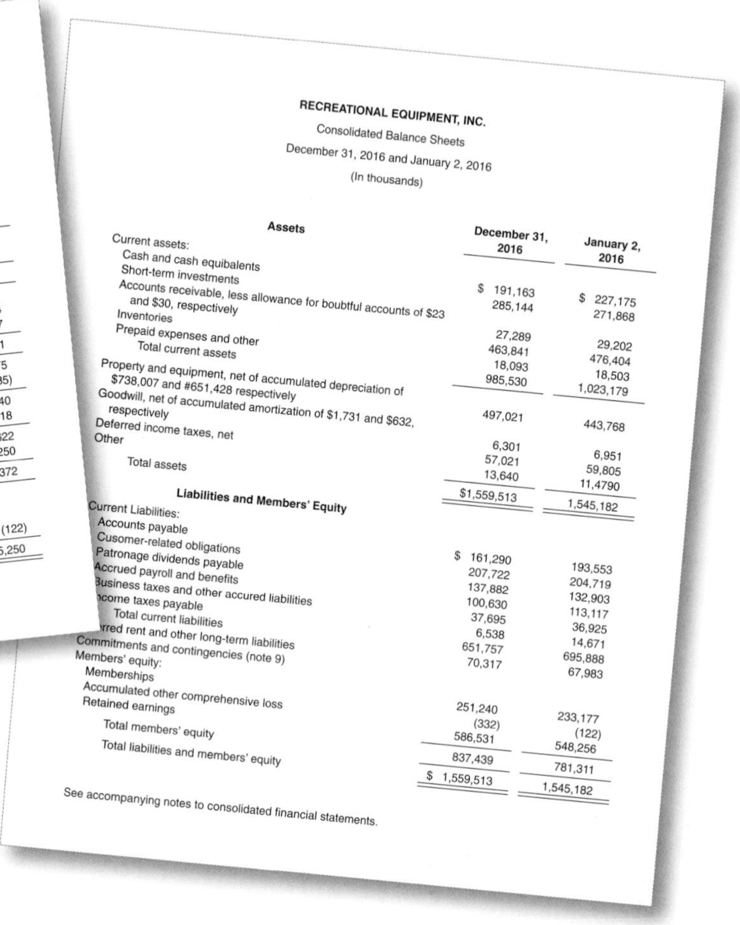

RECREATIONAL EQUIPMENT, INC.

Consolidated Balance Sheets

December 31, 2016 and January 2, 2016

(In thousands)

Assets	December 31, 2016	January 2, 2016
Current assets:		
Cash and cash equibalents	$ 191,163	$ 227,175
Short-term investments	285,144	271,868
Accounts receivable, less allowance for boubtful accounts of $23 and $30, respectively	27,289	29,202
Inventories	463,841	476,404
Prepaid expenses and other	18,093	18,503
Total current assets	985,530	1,023,179
Property and equipment, net of accumulated depreciation of $738,007 and #651,428 respectively	497,021	443,768
Goodwill, net of accumulated amortization of $1,731 and $632, respectively	6,301	6,951
Deferred income taxes, net	57,021	59,805
Other	13,640	11,4790
Total assets	$1,559,513	1,545,182
Liabilities and Members' Equity		
Current Liabilities:		
Accounts payable	$ 161,290	193,553
Cusomer-related obligations	207,722	204,719
Patronage dividends payable	137,882	132,903
Accrued payroll and benefits	100,630	113,117
Business taxes and other accured liabilities	37,695	36,925
ncome taxes payable	6,538	14,671
Total current liabilities	651,757	695,888
rred rent and other long-term liabilities	70,317	67,983
Commitments and contingencies (note 9)		
Members' equity:		
Memberships	251,240	233,177
Accumulated other comprehensive loss	(332)	(122)
Retained earnings	586,531	548,256
Total members' equity	837,439	781,311
Total liabilities and members' equity	$ 1,559,513	1,545,182

See accompanying notes to consolidated financial statements.

Chapter Preview

Computerized programs are important to modern processing of accounting information. It is important to understand the information inputs to this automated process. The adage Garbage-In, Garbage-Out is very true. The modern professional manager must understand the information inputted, the processing of this information within the accounting system, and the output of financial reports. This chapter explains the accounting processes that occur from the initiation of a transaction to the preparation of financial statements. Financial statements are an important output of the accounting information system, providing information for assessing a company's profitability, its ability to generate cash flows, and its financial position. Working through the process allows us to understand the automated processing and to make proper inferences from the reports generated.

Action Plan

LO	Topic/Subtopic	Page	Demos	Reviews	Assignments
LO 2–1	**Analyze the effects of economic transactions using the accounting equation** Economic Transactions :: Accounts :: Assets :: Liabilities :: Stockholders' Equity :: Double-Entry System	2-3	D2-1	R2-1	14, 31, 52, 61, 62
LO 2–2	**Identify, record, and post transactions** Chart of Accounts :: Normal Balances :: Accounting Cycle :: Identify :: Record :: Post	2-5	D2-2A D2-2B	R2-2	15, 16, 17, 19, 20, 21, 22, 23, 25, 32, 33, 34, 35, 36, 39, 51, 53, 54, 64, 65, 66
LO 2–3	**Prepare an unadjusted trial balance** Account Balances :: Debit Balances :: Credit Balances :: Debit Credit Equality	2-13	D2-3	R2-3	18, 34, 36, 37, 38, 51, 53, 54, 64, 67
LO 2–4	**Identify, record, and post adjusting journal entries** Deferral of Expense :: Deferral of Revenue :: Accrual of Expense :: Accrual of Revenue	2-14	D2-4A D2-4B D2-4C D2-4D	R2-4	19, 20, 21, 22, 23, 24, 25, 26, 27, 34, 39, 40, 41, 42, 43, 44, 46, 51, 54, 55, 56, 57, 58, 59, 60, 63, 64
LO 2–5	**Prepare an adjusted trial balance** Adjusting entries :: Account Balances :: Debit Balances :: Credit Balances :: Debit Credit Equality	2-22	D2-5	R2-5	28, 34, 45, 46, 51, 54, 55, 56, 57, 64
LO 2–6	**Prepare financial statements from an adjusted trial balance** Income Statement :: Statement of Stockholders' Equity :: Balance Sheet	2-23	D2-6	R2-6	29, 34, 47, 50, 51, 54, 55, 56, 57, 62, 64
LO 2–7	**Prepare and post closing entries and prepare a post-closing trial balance** Closing Entries :: Income Summary :: Dividends :: Retained Earnings :: Post-Closing Balance Sheet	2-25	D2-7A D2-7B	R2-7	30, 34, 48, 49, 50, 51, 54, 55, 56, 57
LO 2–8	**APPENDIX 2A—Convert from cash-basis net income to accrual-basis net income** Cash Receipts :: Accrual-Basis Revenue :: Cash Payments :: Accrual-Basis Expense	2-29	D2-8	R2-8	71, 74, 75, 80
LO 2–9	**APPENDIX 2B—Prepare reversing entries** Reversing Journal Entries :: Optional Step	2-31	D2-9	R2-9	72, 76, 77, 81
LO 2–10	**APPENDIX 2C—Utilize an accounting worksheet** Unadjusted Trial Balance :: Adjusting Entries :: Adjusted Trial Balance :: Financial Statements	2-32	D2-10	R2-10	73, 78, 79, 82

LO 2-1 Analyze the effects of economic transactions using the accounting equation

LO 2-1 Overview

Accounting Equation

Assets = Liabilities + Stockholders' Equity

- Reflects basic identity of a company
- Remains in balance after recording each economic transaction and event

The accounting process begins with an **economic transaction or event** that has a direct impact on the financial position of a company. The effects of a transaction or event are recorded in **accounts**, which describe specific resources, obligations, and their changes. **Accounts are organized into one of three categories of assets, liabilities, and stockholders' equity**. The relation of these categories of accounts is expressed in the following equation, which reflects assets (resources) on the left and the financing of those resources on the right.

Assets = Liabilities + Stockholders' Equity

The accounting equation reflects *the basic identity of a corporation*. Assets of a corporation are claimed by creditors (liabilities) and by owners (stockholders' equity). **Stockholders' equity**, also called *shareholders' equity*, is the residual interest in assets of a corporation after deducting liabilities. **Exhibit 2-1** expands the accounting equation to show examples of accounts within each of the three categories.

EXHIBIT 2-1
Accounting Identity of a Corporation

Assets		Liabilities		Stockholders' Equity
Probable future economic benefits	=	*Probable future sacrifices of economic benefits*	+	*Residual interest in assets*
Examples cash, accounts receivable, prepaid expense, supplies, inventory, equipment, building, intangible assets		*Examples* accounts payable, salaries payable, accrued expenses, notes payable, bonds payable, deferred revenue		*Examples* paid-in capital: common stock; retained earnings: revenue, expense, dividends

Economic transactions or events are recorded in an accounting system in such a way as to affect at least two accounts. For the accounting equation to stay in balance, a change in one amount in the equation requires an offsetting change in another amount in the equation. This duality is called the **double-entry system**. The double-entry system ensures that the accounting equation remains in balance.

As an example, let's consider an increase in equipment, an asset account. In a double-entry system, and based upon the underlying economics of the transaction, this increase in assets is offset with another account (or accounts) that maintains the equality of the accounting equation. It could be offset by an increase to liabilities (note payable) for a note issuance, an increase in stockholders' equity (common stock) for a stock issuance, or a decrease in assets (cash) for a cash payment. In the double-entry system, we need to analyze how each economic transaction affects the accounting equation.

The category of stockholders' equity is further divided into two main components: paid-in capital and retained capital, usually called retained earnings in practice. **Paid-in capital** is the amount invested by shareholders into the corporation, while **retained earnings** is the amount of income (revenue less expenses) recognized by the corporation (net of dividends) since the inception of the company. Paid-in capital includes a number of additional accounts beyond common stock such as preferred stock, paid-in capital in excess of par, accumulated other comprehensive income, and treasury stock (a deduction)—all discussed in later chapters. **Exhibit 2-2** shows how specific accounts within the components of paid-in capital and retained earnings impact stockholders' equity. Issuances of common stock and revenue increase stockholders' equity while expenses and dividends decrease stockholders' equity. Any change in a stockholders' equity account must be offset by another account to assure that the accounting equation remains in balance.

EXHIBIT 2-2
Components of Stockholders' Equity

Stockholders' Equity

Paid-in capital	Retained earnings
+ Common stock	+ Revenue
	− Expense
	− Dividends

Analysis of Transactions Using Accounting Equation

LO2-1 Demo 2-1

Demo MBC

For each of the seven transactions shown below for Consult Inc., show the impact on the components of the accounting equation. The accounting equation should remain in balance (such that *assets equal liabilities plus stockholders' equity*) after considering the effects of each transaction.

Transactions and solutions

1. Owners invested $25,000 in Consult Inc. in exchange for shares of common stock.

Assets	=	Liabilities	+	Stockholders' Equity
Cash				*Common Stock*
$25,000	=	$0	+	**$25,000**

Analysis: From the company perspective, assets (cash) increase as stockholders' equity increases (common stock) with the latter reflecting the increase in owners' claims on assets contributed.

2. Consult Inc. paid $1,000 in attorney fees to help launch the business.

Assets	=	Liabilities	+	Stockholders' Equity
Cash				Legal Expense
$(1,000)	=	$0	+	**$(1,000)**

Analysis: The decrease in assets (cash) causes stockholders' equity to decrease through the recognition of legal expense.

3. Consult Inc. borrowed $10,000 from a bank by signing a note payable.

Assets	=	Liabilities	+	Stockholders' Equity
Cash		Note Payable		
$10,000	=	**$10,000**	+	$0

Analysis: Assets (cash) increase and liabilities (note payable) increase when Consult Inc. incurs an obligation to repay in the future the cash received now.

4. Consult Inc. purchased $4,000 of supplies on account from Office Gear Inc.

Assets	=	Liabilities	+	Stockholders' Equity
Supplies		Accounts Payable		
$4,000	=	**$4,000**	+	$0

Analysis: Assets (supplies) increase when Consult Inc. purchases supplies with an obligation to pay an amount at a later date, which is a liability.

5. Consult Inc. performed consulting services for $2,000 cash.

Assets	=	Liabilities	+	Stockholders' Equity
Cash				Service Revenue
$2,000	=	$0	+	**$2,000**

Analysis: Consult Inc. performs services for cash, resulting in an increase in assets (cash) and an increase in stockholders' equity through the recognition of revenue.

6. Consult Inc. declared a cash dividend of $500 payable to shareholders.

Assets	=	Liabilities	+	Stockholders' Equity
		Dividends Payable		Retained Earnings
$0	=	**$500**	+	**$(500)**

Analysis: Consult Inc. declares a dividend (but has not yet paid the dividend), which causes liabilities to increase (dividends payable) and stockholders' equity to decrease through a reduction in retained earnings. Dividends are not an expense but rather a direct reduction to retained earnings.

7. Consult Inc. paid $3,000 on account to Office Gear Inc.

Assets	=	Liabilities	+	Stockholders' Equity
Cash		Accounts Payable		
$(3,000)	=	**$(3,000)**	+	$0

Analysis: Consult Inc. decreases assets (cash) when it makes a payment on account, which causes its obligations (liabilities) to decrease.

REVIEW 2-1 **LO2-1** **Analysis of Transactions Using Accounting Equation**

Review MBC

For each of the seven separate transactions below, show the impact on the components of the accounting equation.

1. Tax Services Inc. provided $1,000 of tax services on account this month.
2. Eagle Brand Inc. incurred utility costs for this month of $850, payable next month.
3. Texako Inc. paid $50,000 in dividends this month that were declared last month.
4. Post Corp. purchased equipment at a cost of $25,000 this month by issuing a note payable.
5. Atlanta Inc. paid $2,200 cash for one year of insurance coverage.
6. Quality Products Inc. paid $8,000 cash for supplies to be used later this month.
7. Fast Food Inc. paid $3,000 cash for salaries this month.

More Practice: 2-14, 2-31
Solution on p. 2-58.

LO 2-2 Identify, record, and post transactions

LO 2-2 Overview

Identify, Record, and Post Transactions

- *Identify* the accounts affected by a transaction
- *Record* the impact on the accounts in a journal
- *Post* the impact to individual account balances in a ledger

An **accounting information system** is designed to record accurate financial data in a timely and chronological manner, facilitate retrieval of financial data in a form useful to management, and simplify periodic preparation of financial statements for external use. An accounting information system uses debits and credits to record transactions and events.

All accounts, such as cash, payables, and common stock, are organized in an accounting system using a **ledger**, also called a *general ledger*. The beginning balance, increases, decreases, and an ending balance are maintained and continually updated in the ledger for each account.

Each account in the ledger is assigned a unique account number in a **chart of accounts**. Accounts are typically numbered by the order of the balance sheet: asset accounts, liability accounts, stockholders' equity accounts. Having a master set of account names with identification numbers allows for consistent recording by all departments and segments of the company. **Exhibit 2-3** shows an excerpt from a chart of accounts. The number of accounts in a chart of accounts varies by the size and complexity of the transactions of a company. The chart of accounts is tailored for a company's industry and specific needs.

EXHIBIT 2-3
Example Chart of Accounts (excerpt)

Assets		Liabilities		Stockholders' Equity	
Acct. No.	**Account Name**	**Acct. No.**	**Account Name**	**Acct. No.**	**Account Name**
100	Cash	202	Accounts payable	302	Common stock
104	Accounts receivable	204	Salaries payable	304	Retained earnings
106	Inventory	206	Accrued expenses	310	Dividends
160	Equipment	240	Notes payable	400	Sales revenue
162	Accumulated depreciation	242	Bonds payable	515	Salaries expense

Normal Account Balances

Debit and credit rules complement the double-entry system. The debit and credit system is used as a recording and balancing procedure. This system divides accounts into two sides. The **debit (Dr.)** side is always the left side, and the **credit (Cr.)** side is always the right side. These terms carry no further meaning. The **T-account** is a form of *a ledger* used for summarizing transactions; it takes the form of the letter T.

Account Title (Acct #)	
Left side Debit	*Right side* Credit

In the accounting equation (Assets = Liabilities + Stockholders' Equity), the accounts on the left side of the equation (assets) usually have a net normal debit balance and the accounts on the right side of the equation (liabilities and stockholders' equity) usually have a net normal credit balance. To ensure that the accounting equation is always in balance, the left side (debit accounts) must always equal the right side (credit accounts). This means that each transaction in a double-entry accounting system consists of at least one debit amount and one credit amount.

Exhibit 2-4 shows the debit and credit side of each in the accounting equation. It is important to see that although stockholders' equity has a net normal credit balance, two of the four accounts that make up stockholders' equity have normal debit balances—see dividends and expenses.

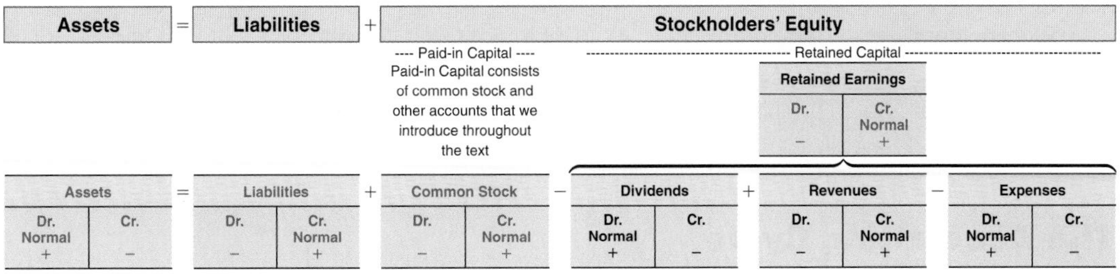

EXHIBIT 2-4
Debit and Credit Impact on the Accounting Equation

A debit or a credit can mean an increase or decrease depending on the account type and its normal balance. For example, to increase an asset (that has a normal debit balance) we require a debit. To increase a liability (that has a normal credit balance) we require a credit. **Exhibit 2-5** illustrates the debit or credit impact depending on the normal balance of the account.

EXHIBIT 2-5
Impact of Debits and Credits on Account Types

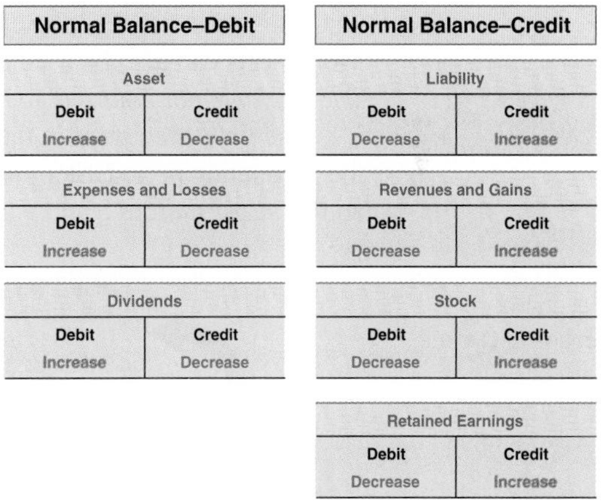

Accounts can be further classified as permanent or temporary. **Permanent accounts** are those appearing in the balance sheet: assets, liabilities, and stockholders' equity. The term permanent means that balances in these accounts are carried over from one period to the next. **Temporary accounts** report changes in retained earnings (a permanent account) from dividends and income-generating activities that appear in the income statement: revenues, expenses, gains, and losses. For example, when a bill for utilities is paid, the utilities expense account describes the reason for the decrease in cash. **Temporary accounts are closed (meaning set to zero) and their balances transferred to the permanent account (retained earnings) at the end of each accounting period**.

Identify Normal Account Balances

LO2-2 **Demo 2-2A**

Demo MBC

For each account listed below, indicate the account type (asset, liability, or stockholders' equity), balance type (permanent or temporary), normal balance (debit or credit), and how to increase and decrease the account (using a debit or credit).

Account Name	Account Type	Permanent or Temporary	Normal Balance	To Increase Account	To Decrease Account
1. Cash	Asset	Permanent	Debit	Debit	Credit
2. Accounts receivable	Asset	Permanent	Debit	Debit	Credit
3. Accounts payable	Liability	Permanent	Credit	Credit	Debit
4. Notes payable	Liability	Permanent	Credit	Credit	Debit
5. Common stock	Stockholders' Equity	Permanent	Credit	Credit	Debit
6. Dividends	Stockholders' Equity	Temporary	Debit	Debit	Credit

continued

continued from previous page

	Account Name	Account Type	Permanent or Temporary	Normal Balance	To Increase Account	To Decrease Account
7.	Sales revenue	Stockholders' Equity	Temporary	Credit	Credit	Debit
8.	Interest revenue	Stockholders' Equity	Temporary	Credit	Credit	Debit
9.	Cost of goods sold	Stockholders' Equity	Temporary	Debit	Debit	Credit
10.	Interest expense	Stockholders' Equity	Temporary	Debit	Debit	Credit

The Accounting Cycle

The **accounting cycle**, shown in **Exhibit 2-6**, is a series of sequential steps leading to the preparation of financial statements. This cycle is repeated each accounting period. Accounting application software is commonly used to perform the majority of the accounting cycle steps. Accounting software functions as an accounting system by recording and processing accounting transactions. Examples of accounting application software include QuickBooks and Sage software packages (for small to mid-size companies) and SAP and Oracle PeopleSoft Enterprise Resource Planning Systems (for mid-size to large companies). Worksheets can also be used to facilitate financial statement preparation as discussed in Appendix 2C. *The fundamental nature of the process, however, is the same regardless of the technology used.*

The first three steps in the accounting cycle require the most time and effort and take place during the accounting period. Steps 4 through 7 occur at the end of each accounting period (monthly, quarterly, and/or yearly). Steps 8 and 9 take place at the end of the accounting period with the fiscal year-end.

EXHIBIT 2-6
Steps in the Accounting Cycle

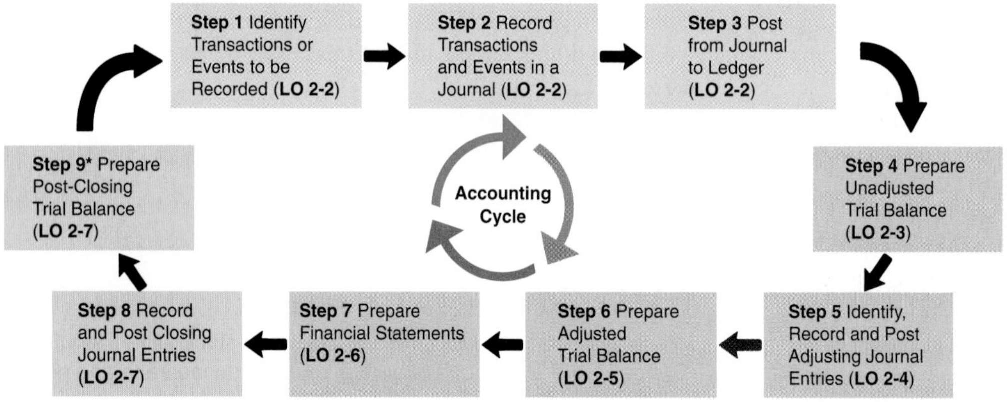

* As an optional step, a company can record and post reversing entries at the beginning of the next accounting period. Reversing entries are discussed in Appendix 2B.

Steps in Accounting Cycle
Step 1: Identify transactions
Step 2: Record transactions
Step 3: Post transactions
Step 4: Prepare unadjusted trial balance
Step 5: Identify, record, post adjusting entries
Step 6: Prepare adjusted trial balance
Step 7: Prepare financial statements
Step 8: Record and post closing journal entries
Step 9: Prepare post-closing trial balance

Identify Transactions and Events to be Recorded—Step 1

The purposes of the first step in the accounting cycle are to identify the **transactions and events** that cause a change in the company's resources, obligations, and equity, and to collect relevant economic data about those transactions. Events that change a company's resources, obligations, and equity are categorized as external, internal, or some combination of both. Transactions are types of external events.

External events include the exchange of resources and obligations between the reporting company and outside parties. These exchanges are either reciprocal transfers or nonreciprocal transfers. In a **reciprocal transfer**, the company both transfers and receives resources (such as a sale of goods). In a **non-reciprocal transfer**, the company either transfers or receives resources (such as a payment of cash dividends). External events also include economic and environmental events beyond the control of the company, including casualty losses and changes in the market value of assets and liabilities. External events generally require a journal entry.

Internal events occur within the company, affecting its resources or obligations, and do not involve outside parties. Examples are recognition of depreciation of long-lived assets and the use of inventory for production. These events generally require a journal entry. However, a number of events, such as increases in the value of a brand name, are not recorded. GAAP provides guidelines on which transactions should be recorded in the accounting information system.

Transactions are often accompanied by a **source document**, generally a record (electronic or paper) that describes the exchange, the parties involved, the date, and the amount. Examples are sales invoices, freight bills, and cash register receipts. Certain events (such as the accrual of interest) are not signaled by a separate transaction or source document. Recording these transactions requires reference to the underlying contract supporting the original exchange of resources. Source documents are essential for the initial recording of transactions in a journal and are also used for subsequent tracing and verification, for evidence in legal proceedings, and for audits of financial statements.

Record Transactions and Events in a Journal—Step 2

Step 2 measures and records the economic effect of transactions in a journal. A **general journal** is a chronological record of transactions, organized in a debit-credit format. A general journal includes the (1) date, (2) debited accounts listed first (positioned at the far left) and credited accounts listed next (slightly indented to the right), (3) account numbers, (4) dollar amounts (debits in the first column and credits in the next column), and (5) a brief, optional explanation. Companies may also use special journals to record multiple transactions of a similar type, such as for sales, cash receipts, purchases, and cash payments.

For example, a journal entry is recorded on January 1, 2020, when owners invest $25,000 in Consult Inc. in exchange for shares of common stock. Assuming that Cash and Common Stock had account numbers of 100 and 302, respectively, we record the following.

Steps in Accounting Cycle
Step 1: Identify transactions
Step 2: Record transactions
Step 3: Post transactions
Step 4: Prepare unadjusted trial balance
Step 5: Identify, record, post adjusting entries
Step 6: Prepare adjusted trial balance
Step 7: Prepare financial statements
Step 8: Record and post closing journal entries
Step 9: Prepare post-closing trial balance

Jan. 1, 2020—To record issuance of common stock for cash

Date	Account Name	Acct. No.	Dr.	Cr.
Jan. 1	Cash	100	25,000	
	Common Stock.	302		25,000

Post from Journal to Ledger—Step 3

Transferring transaction data from the journal to the ledger is called **posting**. Posting reclassifies the data from the journal's chronological format to an account classification format in the ledger. Recall that a ledger holds individual accounts, grouped according to account type. A T-account was introduced previously as a form of a ledger.

We commonly use the T-account for ledger presentation; however, **Exhibit 2-7** shows one example of a formalized general ledger used in practice. This general ledger depicts the following columns for each account identified with a unique account number: (1) date, (2) explanation of the transaction, (3) journal identification reference column, (4) debit column for an amount, (5) credit column for an amount, and (6) the account balance column. In a computerized accounting system, a journal entry automatically generates a posting to the corresponding ledger accounts.

Steps in Accounting Cycle
Step 1: Identify transactions
Step 2: Record transactions
Step 3: Post transactions
Step 4: Prepare unadjusted trial balance
Step 5: Identify, record, post adjusting entries
Step 6: Prepare adjusted trial balance
Step 7: Prepare financial statements
Step 8: Record and post closing journal entries
Step 9: Prepare post-closing trial balance

EXHIBIT 2-7
Formal General Ledger (excerpt)

Cash					**No. 100**
Date	**Explanation**	**Ref.**	**Debit**	**Credit**	**Balance**
2020 Jan. 1	Issued common stock for cash.	J1	25,000		25,000

Common Stock					**No. 302**
Date	**Explanation**	**Ref.**	**Debit**	**Credit**	**Balance**
2020 Jan. 1	Issued common stock for cash.	J1		25,000	25,000

When the $25,000 cash debit from the general journal entry is posted to the Cash ledger account and to the Common Stock ledger account, J1 is entered in the reference column indicating the journal page number from which this amount is posted. Cross-referencing is important when posting large numbers of transactions, detecting and correcting errors, and maintaining an audit trail.

Accounting systems usually have two types of ledgers: the general ledger and subsidiary ledgers. The **general ledger** holds the control accounts. **Subsidiary ledgers** support general ledger accounts that consist of many separate individual accounts. For example, a company with a substantial number of customer accounts receivable maintains one ledger account per customer, stored in an accounts receivable subsidiary ledger. The individual customer account is called the subsidiary account. The general ledger holds only the control account, the balance of which reflects the sum of all the individual customer account balances. Only control accounts are used in preparing financial statements.

Demo 2-2B **LO2-2** **Identify, Record, and Post Transactions**

Demo MBC

Resilient Recreation Equipment Inc. (RREI), a retail store selling gear and apparel for outdoor activities, began operations in 2020. For each of the ten transactions listed below for RREI, *record* the necessary journal entry and *post* the journal entry to the ledger. Each account has been assigned an account number.

1. June 1: Issued 20,000 shares of its own common stock in exchange for $10 cash per share.

Assets = Liabilities + Equity
+200,000 +200,000

RECORD IN JOURNAL

June 1, 2020—To record issuance of common stock

June 1	Cash.	100	200,000	
	Common Stock (20,000 × $10). . . .	302		200,000

POST TO LEDGER

Cash		100
June 1	200,000	

Common Stock		302
	200,000	June 1

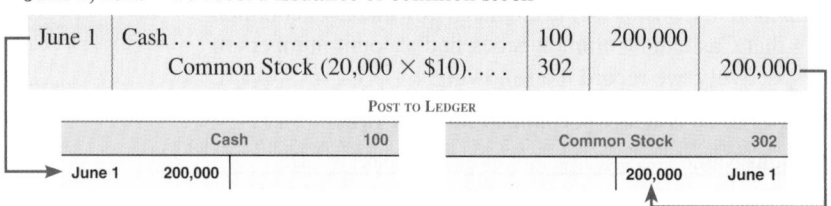

2. June 2: Purchased equipment for use in operating the business at a cost of $60,000 by signing a 6-month, 10% note payable. The equipment has an estimated 5-year useful life and no salvage value (the estimated value from the disposal or trade-in of the asset).

Assets = Liabilities + Equity
+60,000 +60,000

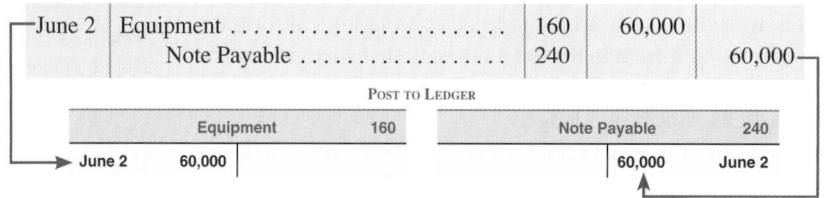

RECORD IN JOURNAL

June 2, 2020—To record issuance of a note for equipment

June 2	Equipment	160	60,000	
	Note Payable	240		60,000

POST TO LEDGER

Equipment		160
June 2	60,000	

Note Payable		240
	60,000	June 2

continued

continued from previous page

3. June 3: Paid $3,000 cash for a six-month insurance coverage. Coverage is effective immediately.

RECORD IN JOURNAL

June 3, 2020—To record prepaid insurance

June 3	Prepaid Insurance	108	3,000	
	Cash	100		3,000

Assets	= Liabilities +	Equity
+3,000		
−3,000		

POST TO LEDGER

Prepaid Insurance			108
June 3	3,000		

Cash			100
June 1	200,000	3,000	June 3

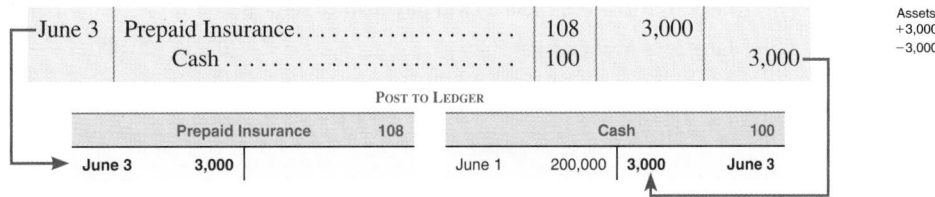

4. June 5: Purchased $100,000 of inventory on account.*

*This inventory purchase is accounted for using the perpetual inventory system, which requires an increase in the inventory account at acquisition—later chapters discuss inventory methods in detail.

RECORD IN JOURNAL

June 5, 2020—To record purchase of inventory on account

June 5	Inventory	106	100,000	
	Accounts Payable	202		100,000

Assets	= Liabilities +	Equity
+100,000	+100,000	

POST TO LEDGER

Inventory			106
June 5	100,000		

Accounts Payable			202
		100,000	June 5

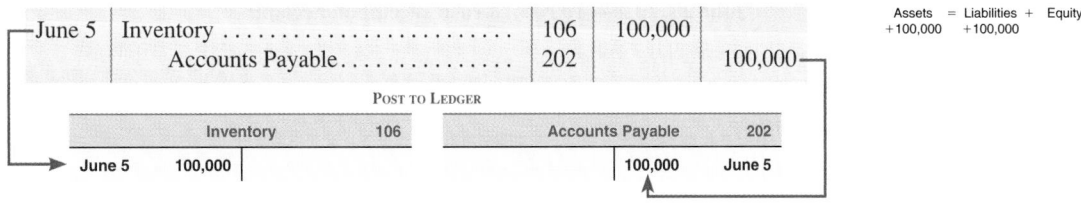

5. June 10: Received a $1,000 cash advance from customer for training sessions scheduled for later this month. Because cash is received in advance of completing a performance obligation, Deferred Revenue (a liability account) is credited.

RECORD IN JOURNAL

June 10, 2020—To record cash received prior to completion of performance obligation

June 10	Cash	100	1,000	
	Deferred Revenue	208		1,000

Assets	= Liabilities +	Equity
+1,000	+1,000	

POST TO LEDGER

Cash			100
June 1	200,000	3,000	June 3
June 10	1,000		

Deferred Revenue			208
		1,000	June 10

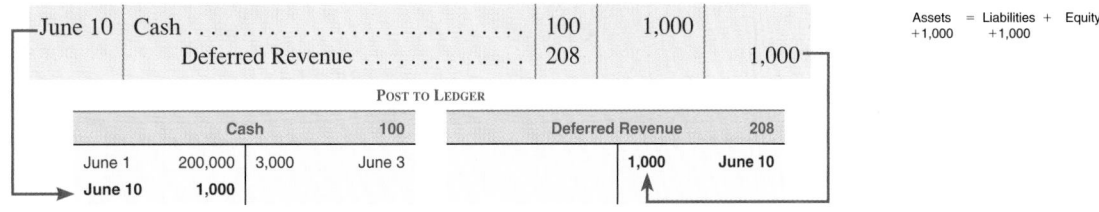

6. June 25: Sold products at a selling price of $46,000 (cost of $25,000) on account.*

*Sales revenue and cost of goods sold are recorded simultaneously according to the expense recognition principle because cost of good sold (expense) is directly related to the sale (revenue).

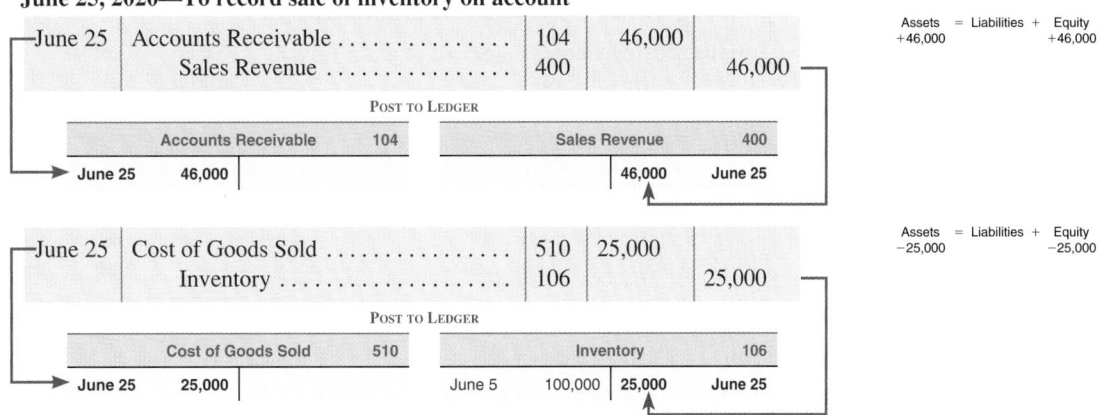

RECORD IN JOURNAL

June 25, 2020—To record sale of inventory on account

June 25	Accounts Receivable	104	46,000	
	Sales Revenue	400		46,000

Assets	= Liabilities +	Equity
+46,000		+46,000

POST TO LEDGER

Accounts Receivable			104
June 25	46,000		

Sales Revenue			400
		46,000	June 25

June 25	Cost of Goods Sold	510	25,000	
	Inventory	106		25,000

Assets	= Liabilities +	Equity
−25,000		−25,000

POST TO LEDGER

Cost of Goods Sold			510
June 25	25,000		

Inventory			106
June 5	100,000	25,000	June 25

continued

continued from previous page

7. June 26: Paid $20,000 cash to reduce the company's accounts payable from inventory previously purchased on account.

Assets = Liabilities + Equity
−20,000 −20,000

RECORD IN JOURNAL

June 26, 2020—To record cash payment to settle account

June 26	Accounts Payable	202	20,000	
	Cash	100		20,000

POST TO LEDGER

Accounts Payable			202
June 26	**20,000**	100,000	June 5

Cash			100
June 1	200,000	3,000	June 3
June 10	1,000	**20,000**	**June 26**

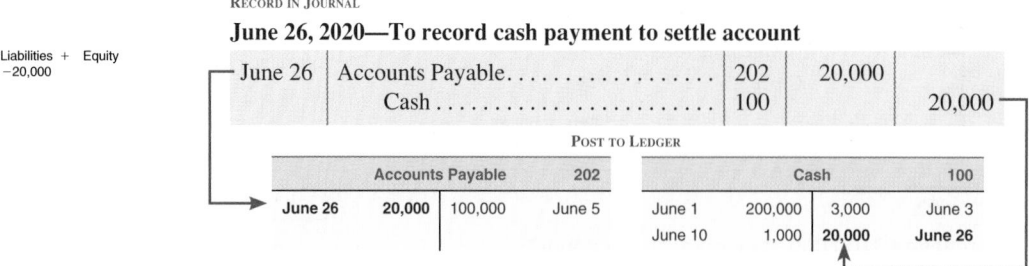

8. June 28: Received $10,000 cash as payment towards the company's accounts receivable from sales previously made on account.

Assets = Liabilities + Equity
+10,000
−10,000

RECORD IN JOURNAL

June 28, 2020—To record cash receipt on account

June 28	Cash	100	10,000	
	Accounts Receivable	104		10,000

POST TO LEDGER

Cash			100
June 1	200,000	3,000	June 3
June 10	1,000	20,000	June 26
June 28	**10,000**		

Accounts Receivable			104
June 25	46,000	**10,000**	**June 28**

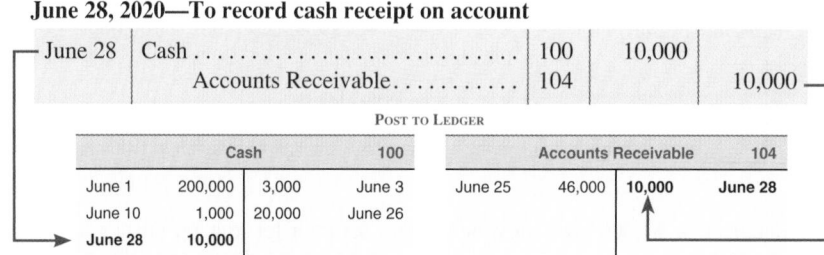

9. June 29: Paid $2,000 cash for rent of retail space for June.

Assets = Liabilities + Equity
−2,000 −2,000

RECORD IN JOURNAL

June 29, 2020—To record cash lease payment

June 29	Lease Expense	520	2,000	
	Cash	100		2,000

POST TO LEDGER

Lease Expense			520
June 29	**2,000**		

Cash			100
June 1	200,000	3,000	June 3
June 10	1,000	20,000	June 26
June 28	10,000	**2,000**	**June 29**

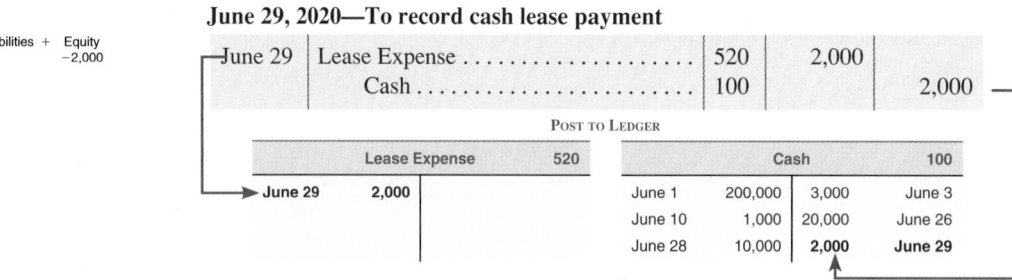

10. June 30: Paid $2,500 cash dividends to company stockholders.*

*We use the dividend account (a temporary account) to record the impact on stockholders' equity. Alternatively, a company can debit retained earnings directly.

Assets = Liabilities + Equity
−2,500 −2,500

RECORD IN JOURNAL

June 30, 2020—To record cash dividends paid

June 30	Dividends	310	2,500	
	Cash	100		2,500

POST TO LEDGER

Dividends			310
June 30	**2,500**		

Cash			100
June 1	200,000	3,000	June 3
June 10	1,000	20,000	June 26
June 28	10,000	2,000	June 29
		2,500	**June 30**

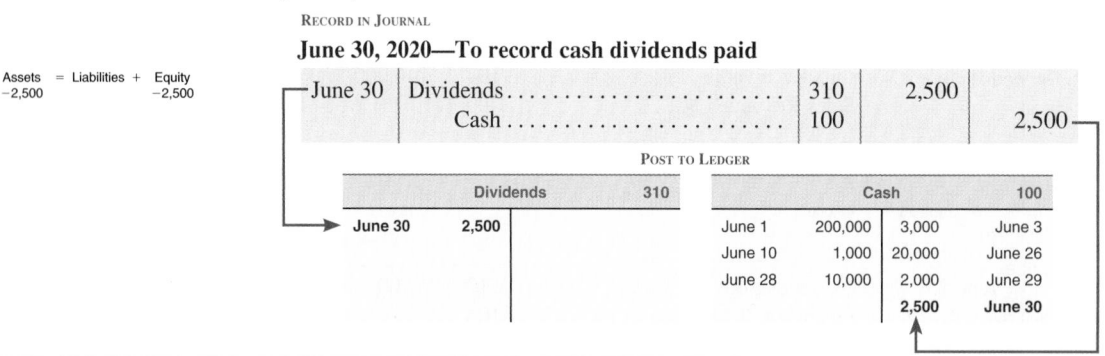

Post Journal Entries to General Ledger

Exhibit 2-8 shows RREI's general ledger in T-account form after the 10 journal entries above are posted to ledger accounts. The ending balance in each T-account is determined by calculating the *net* *balance* of the debit side and credit side of the T-account. A net debit balance is shown on the left side of the T-account while a net credit balance is shown on the right side.

EXHIBIT 2-8
General Ledger Accounts

Assets = Liabilities + Stockholders' Equity

Assets

Cash 100

June 1	200,000	3,000	June 3
June 10	1,000	20,000	June 26
June 28	10,000	2,000	June 29
		2,500	June 30
June 30 Bal.	**183,500**		

Accounts Receivable 104

June 25	46,000	10,000	June 28
June 30 Bal.	**36,000**		

Inventory 106

June 5	100,000	25,000	June 25
June 30 Bal.	**75,000**		

Prepaid Insurance 108

June 3	3,000		
June 30 Bal.	**3,000**		

Equipment 160

June 2	60,000		
June 30 Bal.	**60,000**		

Liabilities

Accounts Payable 202

June 26	20,000	100,000	June 5
		80,000	**June 30 Bal.**

Deferred Revenue 208

		1,000	June 10
		1,000	**June 30 Bal.**

Note Payable 240

		60,000	June 2
		60,000	**June 30 Bal.**

Stockholders' Equity

Common Stock 302

		200,000	June 1
		200,000	**June 30 Bal.**

Dividends 310

June 30	2,500		
June 30 Bal.	**2,500**		

Revenue

Sales Revenue 400

		46,000	June 25
		46,000	**June 30 Bal.**

Expense

Cost of Goods Sold 510

June 25	25,000		
June 30 Bal.	**25,000**		

Lease Expense 520

June 29	2,000		
June 30 Bal.	**2,000**		

Identify, Record, and Post Transactions

LO2-2 **REVIEW 2-2**

Review MBC

Part One—Identification of Account Types and Normal Balances

For each account listed below for KPMB Consulting Inc. (a newly formed consulting firm), indicate the account type (asset, liability, or stockholders' equity) and normal balance (debit or credit).

Account	Account No.	Account Type			Normal Balance	
		Asset	Liability	Equity	Debit	Credit
1. Cash	100					
2. Accounts Receivable	104					
3. Supplies	107					
4. Prepaid Insurance	108					
5. Equipment	160					
6. Accounts Payable	202					
7. Deferred Service Revenue	208					
8. Note Payable	240					
9. Common Stock	302					
10. Consulting Revenue	402					
11. Salaries Expense	515					
12. Lease Expense	520					

Part Two—Recording and Posting Transactions

Enter each of the following transactions in a general journal for KPMB Consulting Inc. Use the chart of accounts from Part One. Next, post the journal entries to ledger accounts set up in the form of T-accounts.

1. June 1 Sold 1,000 shares of common stock for $40,000 cash.
2. June 2 Purchased office equipment that cost $30,000 by signing a two-year, 7% interest-bearing note payable. The equipment has a useful life of 5 years.
3. June 3 Purchased $5,000 of supplies on account. *Hint*: Debit Supplies.

continued

continued from previous page

4. June 4 Performed $2,000 of consulting services on account.
5. June 5 New client agreed to consulting proposal with $1,000 of work to begin next month.
6. June 6 Paid $6,000 cash for a 6-month insurance policy (June through November).
7. June 13 Paid $2,500 cash toward payable for June 3 purchase of supplies.
8. June 15 Received $1,200 cash in advance for consulting services to be performed in two weeks.
9. June 20 Performed consulting services for $5,000 cash.
10. June 30 Paid $3,500 cash for salaries for the month of June.
11. June 30 Paid $4,500 cash for June rent for a short-term lease.

More Practice:
2-15, 2-16, 2-17, 2-32, 2-33, 2-35
Solution on p. 2-59.

LO 2-3 Prepare an unadjusted trial balance

LO 2-3 Overview

Unadjusted Trial Balance
- Prepare at the end of the accounting period
- Compile the ending balances of the individual ledger accounts
- List debits and credits in separate columns
- Ensure that total debits equal total credits

The **unadjusted trial balance** is a list of general ledger accounts and their account balances in the following order: assets, liabilities, stockholders' equity, revenues, expenses, gains, and losses. The unadjusted trial balance is prepared before the adjusting entries are recorded.

Prepare an Unadjusted Trial Balance—Step 4

Steps in Accounting Cycle
Step 1: Identify transactions
Step 2: Record transactions
Step 3: Post transactions
Step 4: Prepare unadjusted trial balance
Step 5: Identify, record, post adjusting entries
Step 6: Prepare adjusted trial balance
Step 7: Prepare financial statements
Step 8: Record and post closing journal entries
Step 9: Prepare post-closing trial balance

In step 4, an unadjusted trial balance is typically prepared at the end of the reporting period, after all transaction entries are recorded in the journals and posted to the ledger. The debit balances are listed in the left column and the credit balances in the right column, with the totals of the two columns in agreement.

The unadjusted trial balance is a means for checking that the sum of debit account balances equals the sum of credit account balances. If the sums of debit and credit balances are not equal, the error must be found and corrected. A reexamination of source documents and postings is one way to discover the source of an error. Equality of debits and credits does not, however, imply that the accounts are error-free. An unposted journal entry, an incorrectly classified account, and an erroneous journal entry amount are errors that are not revealed through an inequality of debits and credits.

Demo 2-3 **LO2-3** **Unadjusted Trial Balance**

Demo MBC

Prepare an unadjusted trial balance for RREI by compiling the ending balances in each of the individual ledger accounts using ending balances included in **Exhibit 2-8**.

Solution

To prepare the unadjusted trial balance, list the accounts (in account number order) along with the ending debit or credit balances. The total debits of $387,000 equal the total credits of $387,000.

continued

continued from previous page

Unadjusted Trial Balance
June 30, 2020

Acct. No.	Account	Debit	Credit
100	Cash	$183,500	
104	Accounts receivable	36,000	
106	Inventory	75,000	
108	Prepaid insurance	3,000	
160	Equipment	60,000	
202	Accounts payable		$ 80,000
208	Deferred revenue		1,000
240	Note payable		60,000
302	Common stock		200,000
310	Dividends	2,500	
400	Sales revenue		46,000
510	Cost of goods sold	25,000	
520	Lease expense	2,000	
	Totals	$387,000	$387,000

Unadjusted Trial Balance LO2-3 **REVIEW 2-3**

Using the information from Review 2-2, prepare an unadjusted trial balance for KPMB Consulting Inc. as of June 30, 2020.

Review MBC

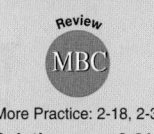

More Practice: 2-18, 2-36

Solution on p. 2-61.

Identify, record, and post adjusting journal entries LO 2-4

Many changes in a company's economic resources and obligations occur continuously in time. For example, interest accrues daily on debts, as does lease expense on office buildings. Other resources and obligations, such as employee salaries, originate as service is rendered, with payment to follow at specified dates. The end of the accounting period generally does not coincide with the receipt or payment of cash associated with these types of resource changes. **Accrual-basis accounting (required under GAAP) demands the recording of deferrals and accruals at the end of each accounting period using revenue and expense recognition principles**. (*Cash-basis accounting*, which is used by some small companies and for tax accounting purposes, requires the recording of entries generally when cash is exchanged—See Appendix 2A.)

Adjusting journal entries
- **Deferrals of revenue and expense**
  - Cash flows occur in current period
  - Revenue and expense recorded in a later period
- **Accruals of revenue and expense**
  - Revenue and expense recorded in current period
  - Cash flows occur in a later period

LO 2-4 Overview

SFAC No. 6 145 Accrual accounting uses accrual, deferral, and allocation procedures whose goal is to relate revenues, expenses, gains, and losses to periods to reflect an entity's performance during a period instead of merely listing its cash receipts and outlays.

Identify, Record, and Post Adjusting Journal Entries—Step 5

Adjusting journal entries are used to record resource changes that span more than one time period to ensure the accuracy of financial statements. Adjusting journal entries generally record a resource or obligation change and usually involve both a permanent and a temporary account. *Adjusting journal entries are recorded and dated as of the last day of the accounting period.* They are recorded in the

Steps in Accounting Cycle
Step 1: Identify transactions
Step 2: Record transactions
Step 3: Post transactions
Step 4: Prepare unadjusted trial balance
Step 5: Identify, record, post adjusting entries
Step 6: Prepare adjusted trial balance
Step 7: Prepare financial statements
Step 8: Record and post closing journal entries
Step 9: Prepare post-closing trial balance

general journal and posted to ledger accounts. Source documents from earlier transactions are the primary information sources for adjusting journal entries.

Cash is not typically involved in adjusting journal entries. However, corrections of errors involving the cash account discovered at the end of the accounting period are sometimes recorded as adjusting journal entries. Also, an entry to adjust the cash balance to a bank balance is recorded as an adjusting journal entry.

Adjusting journal entries are classified into two categories.

- Deferrals of expense and revenue (See **Demo 2-4A** and **Demo 2-4B**.)
- Accruals of expense and revenue (See **Demo 2-4C** and **Demo 2-4D**.)

For deferrals, recognition of revenues and expenses is delayed to future periods, even though the cash flows occur now. A deferral of revenue is recorded as a liability while a deferral of expense is recorded as an asset. Revenue and expense recognition take place in a future period.

SFAC No. 6 141 Deferral is concerned with past cash receipts and payments—with prepayments received (often described as collected in advance) or paid: it is the accounting process of recognizing a liability resulting from a current cash receipt (or the equivalent) or an asset resulting from a current cash payment (or the equivalent) with deferred recognition of revenues, expenses, gains, or losses. Their recognition is deferred until the obligation underlying the liability is partly or wholly satisfied or until the future economic benefit underlying the asset is partly or wholly used or lost.

For accruals, recognition of revenues and expenses occurs in the current accounting period while the cash flows occur in the future. An accrual of revenue is recorded as an asset while an accrual of expenses is recorded as a liability. The recording of cash flows takes place in a future period.

SFAC No. 6 141 Accrual is concerned with expected future cash receipts and payments: it is the accounting process of recognizing assets or liabilities and the related liabilities, assets, revenues, expenses, gains, or losses for amounts expected to be received or paid, usually in cash, in the future.

DEFERRED EXPENSE

Deferrals of Expense

A cash outflow for the purchase of an asset that occurs prior to a company using the asset is a **deferral of expense** (including allocation such as depreciation and amortization). An asset is debited and cash is credited at the time of purchase. Deferrals of expense result in the recording of current assets such as supplies, prepaid insurance, prepaid internet services, prepaid lease expense, and advertising, as well as noncurrent assets such as buildings and equipment. An asset is recognized as an expense when the asset is used or consumed. The original cash outflow and subsequent recognition of expense through an adjusting journal entry is shown in **Exhibit 2-9**. (The phrase *current assets* is used to classify assets reasonably expected to be realized in cash or sold or consumed generally in one year or less—see Chapter 4 for details.)

In the case of property, plant, and equipment, its usage or consumption each year is estimated. Property, plant, and equipment is the balance sheet category used to account for many productive assets with a useful life exceeding one year. Over time, capital expenditures for these assets are allocated over the period that revenue (that the assets help produce) is recognized. **Depreciation** is a systematic and rational allocation of plant asset cost over its estimated useful life. Depreciation is an estimate of the expiration of costs due to equipment usage, deterioration, and obsolescence. The most common way to estimate depreciation is to allocate the cost of an asset evenly over its expected useful life, called **straight-line depreciation**. Annual straight-line depreciation is calculated by taking the original cost of an asset less the salvage value, divided by the useful life of the asset (in years). Depreciation is covered in more detail in a later chapter. Amortization, a systematic and rational allocation of the cost of an intangible asset over its useful life, is covered in a later chapter.

Straight-Line Depreciation:
$$\frac{\text{Cost} - \text{Salvage value}}{\text{Useful Life}}$$

In the case of leases, we assume in this chapter that all leases are short-term leases (duration of 12 months or less) where lease payments are recognized as expense on a straight-line basis. For example, if a company makes a 6-month lease payment in advance, the amount is recognized as expense evenly over the 6-month period. Any deferred amount is called **prepaid lease expense** and recognized as a current asset. More complex lease arrangements are discussed in a later chapter.

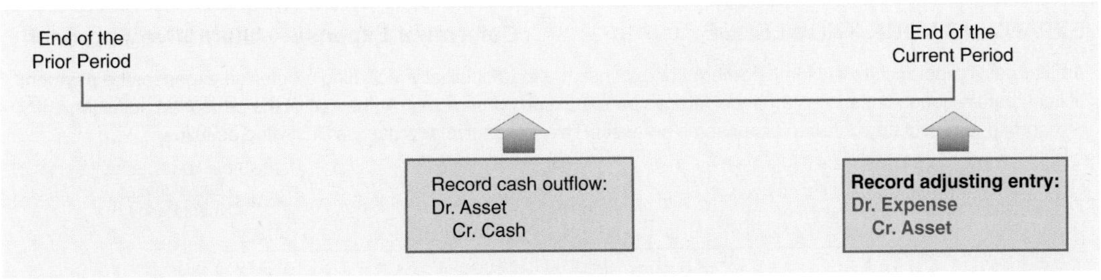

EXHIBIT 2-9
Adjusting Journal Entry for a Deferral of Expense

Adjusting Journal Entries—Deferrals of Expense

LO2-4 **Demo 2-4A**

Demo MBC

Refer to information from **Demo 2-2B**. During the month of June, RREI (*a*) used a month of insurance coverage, and (*b*) incurred one month of depreciation on its equipment. Record the related adjusting journal entries on June 30, 2020, and post these entries to the ledger.

Solution

Prepaid Insurance Recall that the company prepaid for a 6-month insurance policy on June 3, 2020. On the unadjusted trial balance, the full $3,000 payment is reflected in Prepaid Insurance (a deferral of an expense). However, $500 of this payment ($3,000/6) is for coverage of June 2020. The expense recognition principle requires recognition of a $500 expense for the partial expiration of the asset. RREI adjusts Prepaid Insurance and recognizes the expense as follows.

RECORD IN JOURNAL

June 30, 2020—To adjust prepaid insurance for expiration

June 30	Insurance Expense	526	500	
	Prepaid Insurance.	108		500

Assets = Liabilities + Equity
−500 −500

POST TO LEDGER

Insurance Expense	526	
June 30	500	
June 30 Bal.	500	

Prepaid Insurance			108
June 3	3,000	500	June 30
June 30 Bal.	2,500		

The credit to Prepaid Insurance records the reduction in the asset that occurs for June as insurance benefits were received. The remaining $2,500 balance in Prepaid Insurance reflects insurance coverage for the following five months.

Depreciation Recall that RREI paid $60,000 for equipment (useful life of 5 years or 60 months) on June 2, 2020. At June 30, an adjusting entry is required to reflect one month of usage for $1,000 ($60,000/60 months). The adjusting entry requires a debit to Depreciation Expense and a credit to Accumulated Depreciation, a contra asset account.

RECORD IN JOURNAL

June 30, 2020—To record depreciation expense

June 30	Depreciation Expense	528	1,000	
	Accumulated Depreciation.	162		1,000

Assets = Liabilities + Equity
−1,000 −1,000

POST TO LEDGER

Depreciation Expense	528	
June 30	1,000	
June 30 Bal.	1,000	

Accumulated Depreciation			162
		1,000	June 30
		1,000	June 30 Bal.

The adjusting entry reduces the net book value of equipment. A **contra account** has a balance opposite that of the account to which it relates. Accumulated Depreciation in this example is associated with the Equipment account. The net of the Equipment account less the Accumulated Depreciation account is the net undepreciated account balance (or net book value). The use of a contra account provides financial statement users both the original cost and net book value of the asset. The usual balance sheet presentation of net equipment follows.

Assets—Noncurrent Assets	
Equipment.	$60,000
Less: Accumulated depreciation	1,000
Equipment, net book value	$59,000

EXPANDING YOUR KNOWLEDGE **Deferral of Expense—Alternative Approach**

An alternative approach exists for the deferral of expense. Instead of initially recording a deferred expense, the payment of cash before goods or services are received can be *expensed immediately*. At the end of the period, an adjusting entry is recorded to reflect any deferred expense as an asset. This alternative approach is illustrated as follows.

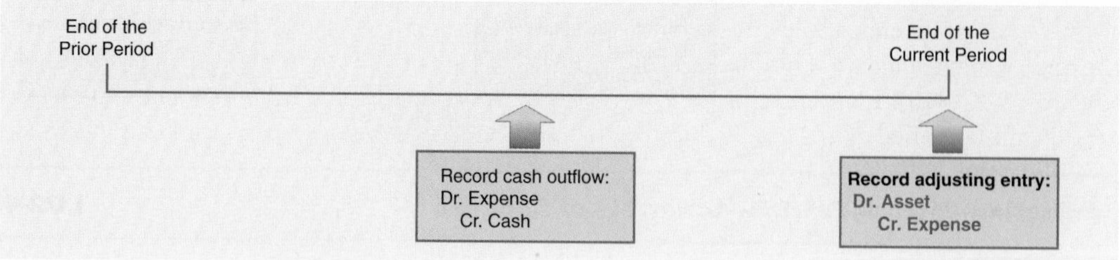

Consider this alternative approach applied to RREI above; this means that the $3,000 paid for insurance is expensed on June 2.

Assets = Liabilities + Equity
−3,000 −3,000

Ins Exp: 3,000 |
Cash: | 3,000

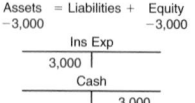

June 2, 2020—To record insurance payment (6-month policy)

June 2	Insurance Expense	526	3,000	
	Cash	100		3,000

At the June 30 period-end, the $2,500 unexpired insurance expense ($3,000 less the $500 insurance expired for June) is recorded as an asset.

Assets = Liabilities + Equity
+2,500 +2,500

Prep Ins: 2,500 | ; balance 2,500
Ins Exp: 3,000 | 2,500 ; balance 500

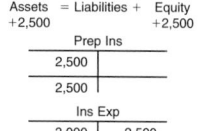

June 30, 2020—To adjust prepaid insurance account

June 30	Prepaid Insurance.	108	2,500	
	Insurance Expense	526		2,500

We see that in both the original approach and the alternative, the ending balance in Prepaid Insurance ($2,500) and the ending balance of Insurance Expense ($500) are identical.

Deferrals of Revenue

DEFERRED REVENUE

The basis for revenue recognition under the revenue recognition accounting standard is the existence of a **contract** (a legally enforceable agreement) between two entities. This means that when cash is received in exchange for a company's obligation to transfer goods or services in the future under a revenue contract, a liability is created called a **contract liability**. A **deferral of revenue** is the accounting process of recognizing a contract liability at the time of the cash inflow. We use a number of deferred revenue accounts that are specific types of contract liabilities; examples are in **Exhibit 2-10**. (Revenue recognition is discussed in more depth in Chapter 7.)

606-10-45-2 If a customer pays consideration, or an entity has a right to an amount of consideration that is unconditional (that is, a receivable), before the entity transfers a good or service to the customer, the entity shall present the contract as a contract liability when the payment is made or the payment is due (whichever is earlier). A contract liability is an entity's obligation to transfer goods or services to a customer for which the entity has received consideration (or an amount of consideration is due) from the customer.

606-10-45-5 This guidance uses the terms contract asset and contract liability but does not prohibit an entity from using alternative descriptions in the statement of financial position.

EXHIBIT 2-10
Examples of Contract Liabilities

Account Titles	Alternative Account Titles*
Deferred revenue	Unearned sales revenue
Deferred service revenue	Unearned service revenue
Deferred subscription revenue	Unearned subscription revenue
Deferred service contract revenue	Unearned service contract revenue
Deferred coupon revenue	Unearned coupon revenue
Deferred franchise rights revenue	Unearned franchise rights revenue
Deferred royalty revenue	Unearned royalty revenue

*Under the prior revenue recognition standard, revenue was recognized when realized or realizable and *earned*. As a company provided goods or services, the related revenue was earned and thus recognized. End of period adjustments transferred amounts from unearned revenue accounts to recognized (earned) revenue accounts.

A company (seller) will recognize deferred revenue (contract liability) in the amount of a prepayment for its performance obligation to transfer control of a good or service to a customer. Revenue is subsequently recognized when (or as) the company satisfies a performance obligation through a transfer of control of the promised good or service to a customer. **A company recognizes revenue at the point when the performance obligation is satisfied.**

Deferrals of revenue can also result from contracts with customers outside of the revenue recognition accounting standard. For example, the guidance for leases is included in a separate accounting standard (ASC 840). For certain lease types, rent received in advance from a tenant under a lease agreement is classified as a current liability called deferred lease revenue. Lease accounting is covered in a later chapter.

The original cash inflow and subsequent recognition of revenue through an adjusting journal entry is shown in **Exhibit 2-11**.

EXHIBIT 2-11
Adjusting Journal Entry for a Deferral of Revenue

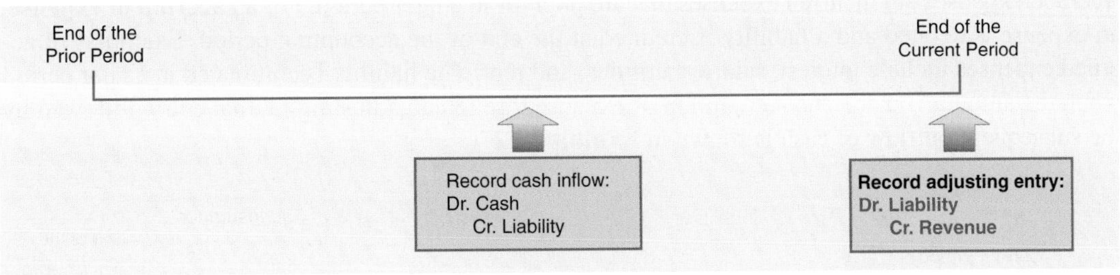

Adjusting Journal Entries—Deferral of Revenue **LO2-4** **Demo 2-4B**

Demo MBC

As of June 30, RREI fulfilled its performance obligation under its revenue contract related to the $1,000 advance cash receipt on June 10. Record the adjusting journal entry on June 30, 2020, and post the entry to the ledger.

Solution

On the unadjusted trial balance of RREI, the full $1,000 payment is reflected as deferred revenue. RREI eliminates deferred revenue and recognizes revenue as follows.

RECORD IN JOURNAL

June 30, 2020—To record cash advance

June 30	Deferred Revenue	208	1,000	
	Training Revenue.	402		1,000

Assets	= Liabilities	+ Equity
	−1,000	+1,000

POST TO LEDGER

Deferred Revenue			208
June 30	1,000	1,000	June 10
		0	June 30 Bal.

Training Revenue			402
		1,000	June 30
		1,000	June 30 Bal.

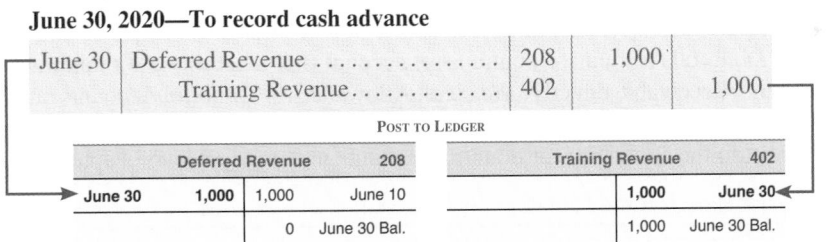

EXPANDING YOUR KNOWLEDGE **Deferral of Revenue—Alternative Approach**

An alternative approach is available in accounting for a deferral of revenue. Instead of initially deferring revenue, a receipt of cash before goods or services are received is *recognized fully as revenue.* At the end of the period, an adjusting entry is recorded to reflect any deferral of revenue as a liability. This alternative approach is illustrated below.

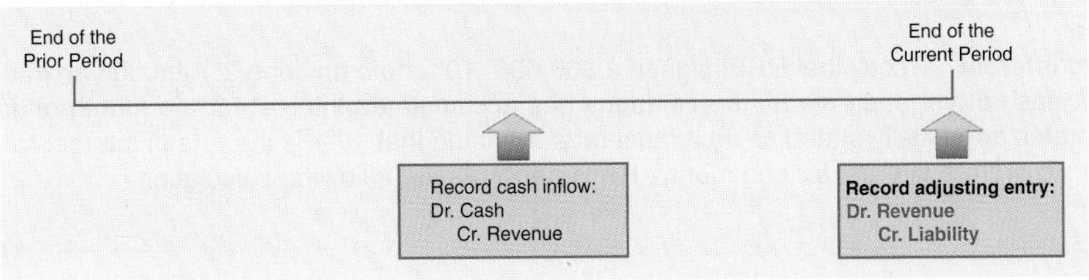

continued

continued from previous page

Applying this alternative approach to RREI, the full $1,000 received in advance of services to be performed is recorded as training revenue on June 10.

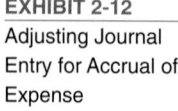

Assets = Liabilities + Equity
+1,000 +1,000

Cash
1,000 |

Training Rev
| 1,000

June 10, 2020—To record cash advance

June 10	Cash	100	1,000	
	Training Revenue.	402		1,000

On June 30, the Deferred Revenue account balance is zero because training revenue is fully recognized on June 30; therefore no adjusting entry is required. Under either approach, training revenue recorded is $1,000 for June, and Deferred Revenue is $0 as of June 30, 2020.

Accruals of Expense

ACCRUED EXPENSE

Accrued expenses are incurred expenses that are paid for in a later period. For an **accrual of expense**, an expense is debited and a liability is credited at the end of the accounting period. Examples of accrued expenses include interest, salaries, utilities, and rent. The liability is eliminated in a later period when the amount is paid. The recognition of expense through an adjusting journal entry, followed by the subsequent outflow of cash is shown in **Exhibit 2-12.**

EXHIBIT 2-12
Adjusting Journal Entry for Accrual of Expense

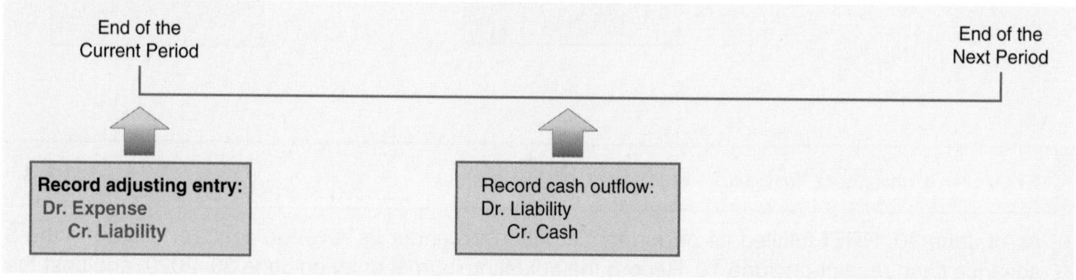

There are some adjusting journal entries for accrued expenses that operate differently. For example, the accrual for bad debt expense is an adjusting entry that does not exactly follow the flow of entries outlined in **Exhibit 2-12**. The bad debt accrual results as part of the process in adjusting accounts receivable to **net realizable value**, or the amount that the company estimates it will ultimately collect on the receivables. The adjusting entry includes a debit to Bad Debt Expense and a credit to the Allowance for Doubtful Accounts, a contra-asset account (not a liability). We might wonder—Why not credit Accounts Receivable directly? We credit Allowance for Doubtful Accounts rather than Accounts Receivable because the identities of the specific uncollectible accounts are not yet known. We discuss the adjustment to the allowance for doubtful accounts in detail in a later chapter.

Demo 2-4C **LO2-4** **Adjusting Journal Entries—Accrual of Expense**

Demo MBC

Consider the following information for RREI: (a) incurred interest expense on the 6-month, $60,000, 10% note payable, (b) incurred $3,000 of salaries that relate to hours worked in June that will be paid in July, and (c) determined that an increase to the Allowance for Doubtful Accounts of $1,950 is necessary to recognize accounts receivable at net realizable value. Record the related adjusting journal entries on June 30, 2020, and post the entries to the ledger.

Solution

Accrued interest Recall that RREI signed a $60,000, 10% note on June 2. Although an interest payment has not yet been made, the company has accumulated interest for the month of June. Interest rates are usually stated as an annual rate; meaning that 10% is the rate of interest for the full year. To prorate interest for one month, RREI performs the following calculation.

continued

continued from previous page

Interest	=	Face Value of Note	×	Annual Interest Rate	×	Fraction of Year
$500	=	$60,000	×	10%	×	1/12

Record in Journal

June 30, 2020—To record accrued interest expense

June 30	Interest Expense	542	500	
	Interest Payable	210		500

Assets = Liabilities + Equity
+500 −500

Post to Ledger

Interest Expense		542	
June 30	500		
June 30 Bal.	500		

Interest Payable			210
		500	June 30
		500	June 30 Bal.

Accrued salaries The unpaid salaries for employee services provided in June is accrued in an adjusting journal entry.

Record in Journal

June 30, 2020—To record accrued salaries expense

June 30	Salaries Expense	515	3,000	
	Salaries Payable	204		3,000

Assets = Liabilities + Equity
+3,000 −3,000

Post to Ledger

Salaries Expense		515	
June 30	3,000		
June 30 Bal.	3,000		

Salaries Payable			204
		3,000	June 30
		3,000	June 30 Bal.

Bad debt Expense RREI records the following entry to adjust accounts receivable to net realizable value.

Record in Journal

June 30, 2020—To record estimated bad debt expense

June 30	Bad Debt Expense	540	1,950	
	Allowance For Doubtful Accounts	105		1,950

Assets = Liabilities + Equity
−1,950 −1,950

Post to Ledger

Bad Debt Expense		540	
June 30	1,950		
June 30 Bal.	1,950		

Allowance for Doubtful Accounts			105
		1,950	June 30
		1,950	June 30 Bal.

Accruals of Revenue

ACCRUED REVENUE

To accrue revenue as of the reporting date, an asset is debited and revenue is credited. Examples of **accruals of revenue** include unbilled services, commissions, and interest. Revenue can be unbilled because it is partially complete, or the timing of the invoice process does not coincide with the end of the accounting period. The invoice process is the recurring accounting process that results in the recording of accounts receivable and revenues; in the case where an invoice is not yet sent at the end of a reporting period, revenue must be accrued.

The asset is eliminated in a later period when payment is received from the customer. The recognition of revenue through an adjusting journal entry, followed by the subsequent inflow of cash is shown in **Exhibit 2-13**.

EXHIBIT 2-13
Adjusting Journal Entry for Accrual of Revenue

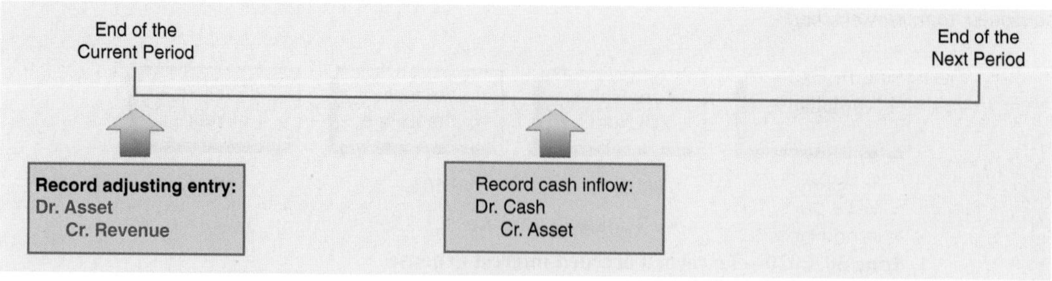

Demo 2-4D **LO2-4** **Adjusting Journal Entries—Accrual of Revenue**

Demo MBC

RREI has satisfied its performance obligations for $3,000 of unrecorded training revenue that has not been billed. Record the adjusting journal entry on June 30, 2020, and post it to the ledger.

Solution

Accounts receivable is recorded when a company has an unconditional right to consideration. Accounts Receivable is increased by $3,000 for unbilled services.

RECORD IN JOURNAL

June 30, 2020—To record accounts receivable

Assets	= Liabilities +	Equity
+3,000		+3,000

June 30	Accounts Receivable	104	3,000	
	Training Revenue	402		3,000

POST TO LEDGER

Accounts Receivable			104
June 25	46,000	10,000	June 28
June 30	**3,000**		
June 30 Bal.	39,000		

Training Revenue			402
		1,000	June 30
		3,000	**June 30**
		4,000	June 30 Bal.

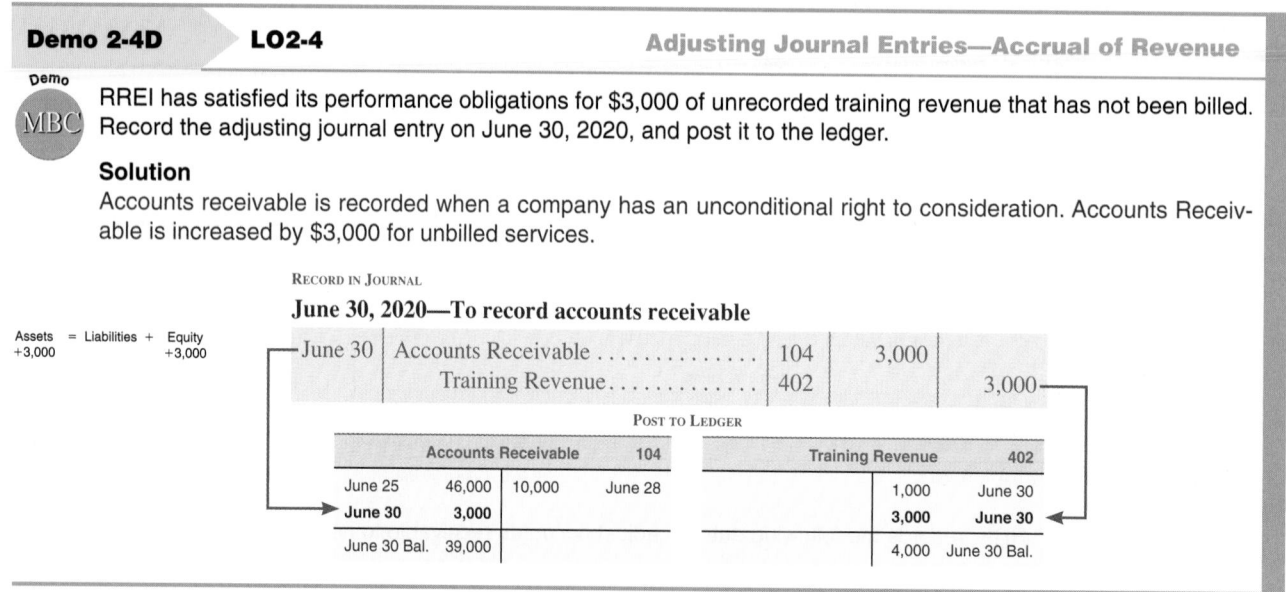

Summary of Deferral and Accrual Adjusting Entries

Exhibit 2-14 summarizes the deferral and accrual adjusting journal entries.

EXHIBIT 2-14
Adjusting Journal Summary

Type of Adjusting Journal Entry	Before Adjusting Journal Entry	Adjusting Journal Entry
Deferral of expense	Asset overstated Expense understated	Dr. Expense Cr. Asset
Deferral of revenue	Liability overstated Revenue understated	Dr. Liability Cr. Revenue
Accrual of expense	Liability understated Expense understated	Dr. Expense Cr. Liability
Accrual of revenue	Asset understated Revenue understated	Dr. Asset Cr. Revenue

REVIEW 2-4 **LO2-4** **Adjusting Journal Entries**

Review MBC

Refer to information from KPMB Consulting Inc. in Review 2-2 and Review 2-3. Prepare the June 30, 2020, adjusting entry for each of the following items and post those entries to the ledger accounts. The following accounts are added to KPMB Consulting Inc.'s chart of accounts: Insurance Expense

continued

continued from previous page

(526), Depreciation Expense (528), Accumulated Depreciation (162), Interest Expense (542), Interest Payable (210), Utilities Expense (540), Utilities Payable (215), Supplies Expense (541).

1. One month of insurance expense expired.
2. Equipment is depreciated for the month of June.
3. $500 of KPMB's performance obligations have been satisfied as of June 30, 2020, related to the June 15 advance payment.
4. Interest expense is incurred for the month of June.
5. Utility expense incurred for June of $1,100 will be paid in July.
6. Revenue of $750 has not been billed related to performance obligations completed as of June 30, 2020.
7. Supplies inventory on June 30, 2020, based on a physical count is $3,300. Recall that the Supplies account has a $5,000 balance, recorded when supplies were purchased.

More Practice: 2-26, 2-40, 2-43
Solution on p. 2-61.

Prepare an adjusted trial balance

LO 2-5

At this point in the cycle, the transaction journal entries and the adjusting journal entries have been recorded and posted and an adjusted trial balance is prepared. This **adjusted trial balance** lists all the account balances that appear in financial statements (with the exception of retained earnings, which does not yet reflect the current year's net income or dividends).

LO 2-5 Overview

Adjusted Trial Balance
- Prepare at the end of the accounting period after adjusting journal entries are posted
- Add new accounts when applicable
- Ensure that total debits equal total credits
- Use to prepare financial statements

Prepare the Adjusted Trial Balance—Step 6

The purpose of the adjusted trial balance is to prove debit-credit equality, taking all adjusting journal entries into consideration.

The account balances in the adjusted trial balance reflect the effects of adjusting journal entries. New accounts not appearing in the unadjusted trial balance usually emerge from the adjustment process. The financial statements can now be prepared from the adjusted trial balance.

Steps in Accounting Cycle
Step 1: Identify transactions
Step 2: Record transactions
Step 3: Post transactions
Step 4: Prepare unadjusted trial balance
Step 5: Identify, record, post adjusting entries
Step 6: Prepare adjusted trial balance
Step 7: Prepare financial statements
Step 8: Record and post closing journal entries
Step 9: Prepare post-closing trial balance

Adjusted Trial Balance **LO2-5** **Demo 2-5**

Demo MBC

Refer to information from **Demo 2-3** and **Demo 2-4A** through **Demo 2-4D**. Prepare an adjusted trial balance for RREI by compiling the ending balance from each of the individual ledger accounts (including adjustments from the recording of adjusting entries).

Solution

To prepare the adjusted trial balance, list the accounts (in account number order) along with the ending debit or credit balances from the unadjusted trial balance in **Demo 2-3**, updated for new ledger accounts and new balances of some existing accounts included in **LO 2-4**. The total debits of $396,450 equal the total credits of $396,450.

continued

continued from previous page

Adjusted Trial Balance
June 30, 2020

Acct. No.	Account	Debit	Credit
100	Cash	$183,500	
104	Accounts receivable	39,000	
105	Allowance for doubtful accounts		$ 1,950
106	Inventory	75,000	
108	Prepaid insurance	2,500	
160	Equipment	60,000	
162	Accumulated depreciation		1,000
202	Accounts payable		80,000
204	Salaries payable		3,000
208	Deferred revenue		
210	Interest payable		500
240	Note payable		60,000
302	Common stock		200,000
310	Dividends	2,500	
400	Sales revenue		46,000
402	Training revenue		4,000
510	Cost of goods sold	25,000	
515	Salaries expense	3,000	
520	Lease expense	2,000	
526	Insurance expense	500	
528	Depreciation expense	1,000	
540	Bad debt expense	1,950	
542	Interest expense	500	
	Totals	$396,450	$396,450

REVIEW 2-5 **LO2-5** **Adjusted Trial Balance**

Review MBC

Using the information from Review 2-3 and Review 2-4, prepare an adjusted trial balance for KPMB Consulting Inc. as of June 30, 2020.

More Practice: 2-28, 2-46

Solution on p. 2-63.

LO 2-6 Prepare financial statements from an adjusted trial balance

LO 2-6 Overview

Financial Statements

- *Income statement*: statement of profitability for a given period of time
- *Statement of stockholders' equity:* statement of changes in stockholders' equity components for a given period of time
- *Balance sheet:* Balances at a point in time of assets, liabilities, and stockholders' equity

Financial statements are the culmination of the accounting cycle. Financial statements are produced for a period of time (or at a point in time), typically at month-end, quarter-end, or year-end. Financial statements communicate financial information about a company to its external users.

Prepare Financial Statements—Step 7

We explain the preparation of the income statement, stockholders' equity statement, and balance sheet—each prepared directly from the adjusted trial balance. In later chapters we expand explanations of financial statements and include the statement of cash flows and the statement of comprehensive income.

Income Statement

The income statement is prepared first because net income must be known before the stockholders' equity statement is completed. The account balances of revenues and expenses are reported on the income statement. The income statement summarizes the profits (losses) of a company over a specific period of time.

Statement of Stockholders' Equity

The statement of stockholders' equity summarizes the changes in each major component of stockholders' equity from the beginning of the period to the end of the period. One major component of stockholders' equity is retained earnings, which is increased by net income (or decreased by net loss) from the income statement and is decreased by declared dividends. **Changes in retained earnings that are reported in a statement of retained earnings are captured within the statement of stockholders' equity.**

Another major component of stockholders' equity is common stock, which is increased by the issuance of any common stock for the period. Other adjustments to a statement of stockholders' equity are discussed in later chapters.

Steps in Accounting Cycle
Step 1: Identify transactions
Step 2: Record transactions
Step 3: Post transactions
Step 4: Prepare unadjusted trial balance
Step 5: Identify, record, post adjusting entries
Step 6: Prepare adjusted trial balance
Step 7: Prepare financial statements
Step 8: Record and post closing journal entries
Step 9: Prepare post-closing trial balance

Balance Sheet

The balance sheet is a summary of the ending balances of assets, liabilities, and stockholders' equity at a point in time. Those account balances are reported on the balance sheet. The ending balance of retained earnings is transferred from the statement of stockholders' equity; thus, the balance sheet is prepared after the statement of stockholders' equity is completed.

Preparation of Financial Statements — LO2-6 — Demo 2-6

Demo MBC

Refer to the information in **Demo 2-5**. Prepare the June income statement, the June statement of stockholders' equity, and the June 30 balance sheet from the adjusted trial balance of RREI.

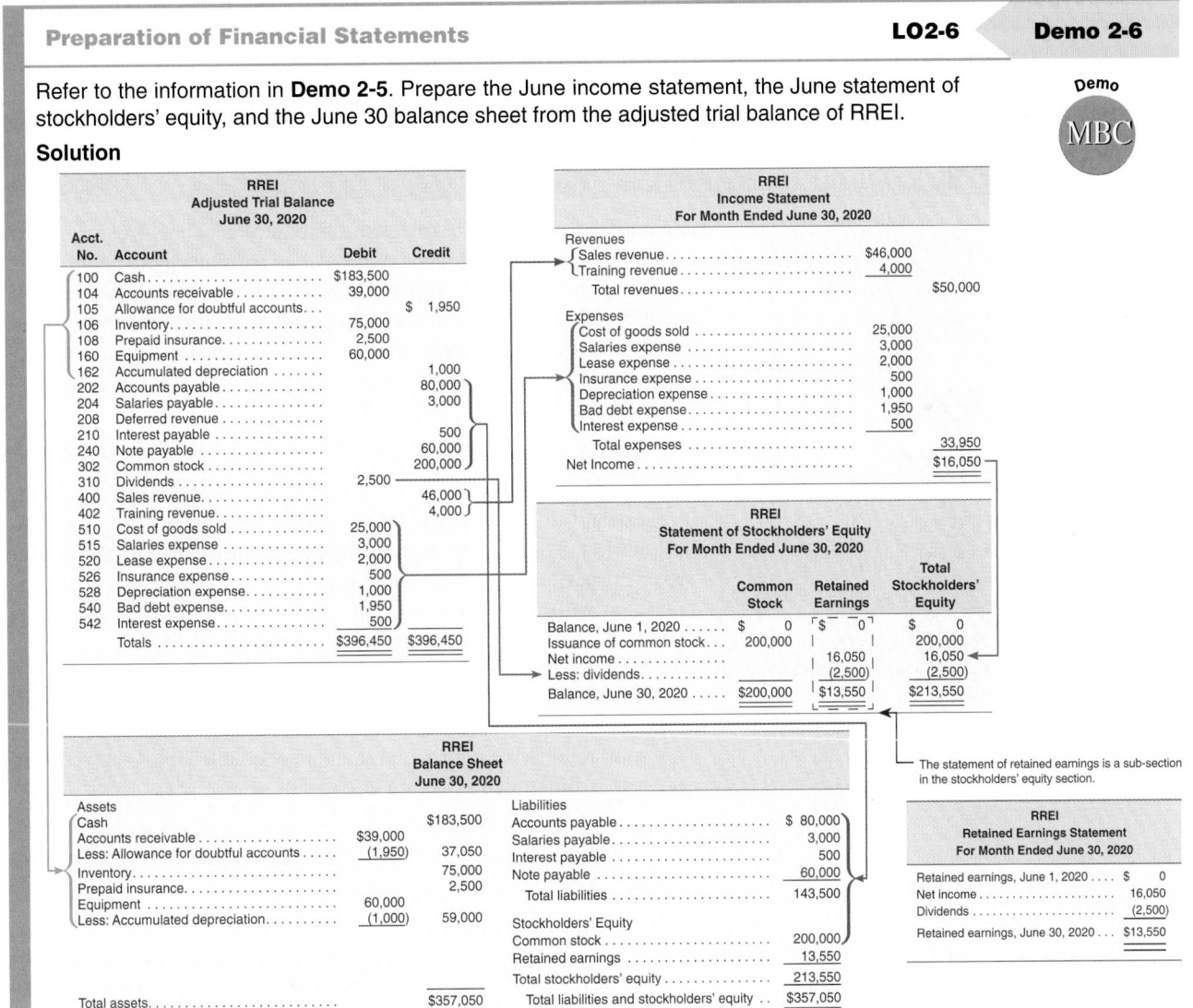

Solution

RREI
Adjusted Trial Balance
June 30, 2020

Acct. No.	Account	Debit	Credit
100	Cash	$183,500	
104	Accounts receivable	39,000	
105	Allowance for doubtful accounts		$ 1,950
106	Inventory	75,000	
108	Prepaid insurance	2,500	
160	Equipment	60,000	
162	Accumulated depreciation		1,000
202	Accounts payable		80,000
204	Salaries payable		3,000
208	Deferred revenue		
210	Interest payable		500
240	Note payable		60,000
302	Common stock		200,000
310	Dividends	2,500	
400	Sales revenue		46,000
402	Training revenue		4,000
510	Cost of goods sold	25,000	
515	Salaries expense	3,000	
520	Lease expense	2,000	
526	Insurance expense	500	
528	Depreciation expense	1,000	
540	Bad debt expense	1,950	
542	Interest expense	500	
	Totals	$396,450	$396,450

RREI
Income Statement
For Month Ended June 30, 2020

Revenues		
Sales revenue	$46,000	
Training revenue	4,000	
Total revenues		$50,000
Expenses		
Cost of goods sold	25,000	
Salaries expense	3,000	
Lease expense	2,000	
Insurance expense	500	
Depreciation expense	1,000	
Bad debt expense	1,950	
Interest expense	500	
Total expenses		33,950
Net Income		$16,050

RREI
Statement of Stockholders' Equity
For Month Ended June 30, 2020

	Common Stock	Retained Earnings	Total Stockholders' Equity
Balance, June 1, 2020	$ 0	$ 0	$ 0
Issuance of common stock	200,000		200,000
Net income		16,050	16,050
Less: dividends		(2,500)	(2,500)
Balance, June 30, 2020	$200,000	$13,550	$213,550

The statement of retained earnings is a sub-section in the stockholders' equity section.

RREI
Retained Earnings Statement
For Month Ended June 30, 2020

Retained earnings, June 1, 2020	$ 0
Net income	16,050
Dividends	(2,500)
Retained earnings, June 30, 2020	$13,550

RREI
Balance Sheet
June 30, 2020

Assets		
Cash		$183,500
Accounts receivable	$39,000	
Less: Allowance for doubtful accounts	(1,950)	37,050
Inventory		75,000
Prepaid insurance		2,500
Equipment	60,000	
Less: Accumulated depreciation	(1,000)	59,000
Total assets		$357,050

Liabilities	
Accounts payable	$ 80,000
Salaries payable	3,000
Interest payable	500
Note payable	60,000
Total liabilities	143,500
Stockholders' Equity	
Common stock	200,000
Retained earnings	13,550
Total stockholders' equity	213,550
Total liabilities and stockholders' equity	$357,050

EXPANDING YOUR KNOWLEDGE **Financial Statements: The Full Reporting Package**

The following statements are included within a full set of financial statements. Each of these statements is explained in more depth in the chapter(s) indicated.

- **Income statement** Reports the net profits (net losses) of a company for a period of time (Chapter 3).
- **Statement of comprehensive income** Reports the changes in stockholders' equity not resulting from transactions with owners for a period of time (Chapter 3).
- **Statement of stockholders' equity** Reports the changes in stockholders' equity accounts over a period of time (Chapters 3 and 20).
- **Balance sheet** Reports the financial position of a company at a point in time (Chapter 4).
- **Statement of cash flows** Reports and classifies changes in cash over a period of time as operating activities, investing activities, or financing activities (Chapters 5 and 22).

REVIEW 2-6 **LO2-6** **Financial Statement Preparation**

Review MBC

More Practice: 2-29, 2-47

Solution on p. 2-63.

Refer to the solution of Review 2-5. Using the adjusted trial balance of KPMB Consulting Inc. as of June 30, 2020, prepare the June income statement, the June statement of stockholders' equity, and the June 30 balance sheet.

LO 2-7 Prepare and post closing entries and prepare a post-closing trial balance

LO 2-7 Overview

Closing Entries

- Close expenses and revenues to income summary
- Close income summary to retained earnings
- Close dividends to retained earnings
- Prepare post-closing balance sheet with all permanent accounts

Steps in Accounting Cycle

Step 1: Identify transactions
Step 2: Record transactions
Step 3: Post transactions
Step 4: Prepare unadjusted trial balance
Step 5: Identify, record, post adjusting entries
Step 6: Prepare adjusted trial balance
Step 7: Prepare financial statements
Step 8: Record and post closing journal entries
Step 9: Prepare post-closing trial balance

Closing entries transfer the balances of temporary accounts (revenues, expenses, gains, losses, and dividends) to retained earnings by reducing these accounts to a zero balance. The permanent accounts (assets, liabilities, and stockholders' equity) are not closed as their ending balances are carried over to the next period. The retained earnings account is the only permanent account involved in the closing process.

Prepare and Post Closing Entries—Step 8

The balances of all temporary accounts (revenues, expenses, gains, losses, and dividends) are set to zero at the end of each accounting period. This is done so that these accounts can start at zero for the next period. Otherwise the performance of one period would be jumbled with the performance of one or more other periods. Some companies use the **income summary account**, a temporary *clearing account*, to accumulate the balances of revenues, expenses, gains, and losses for closing purposes. The balances in the income summary account (the net income or net loss) and dividends are transferred to retained earnings, a permanent account. This 4-step closing process is illustrated in **Demo 2-7A**.

Record and Post Closing Journal Entries

LO2-7 **Demo 2-7A**

Demo MBC

Refer to the information in **Demo 2-5** and **Demo 2-6**. Record and post the closing entries for RREI as of June 30, 2020. Assume that the company uses the income summary account as a temporary clearing account for revenues, expenses, gains, and losses.

Solution

Step 1: Revenues and gains are closed to income summary. To close out an account, the balance is reduced to zero and the amount is transferred to income summary.

June 30, 2020—To close revenue accounts to income summary

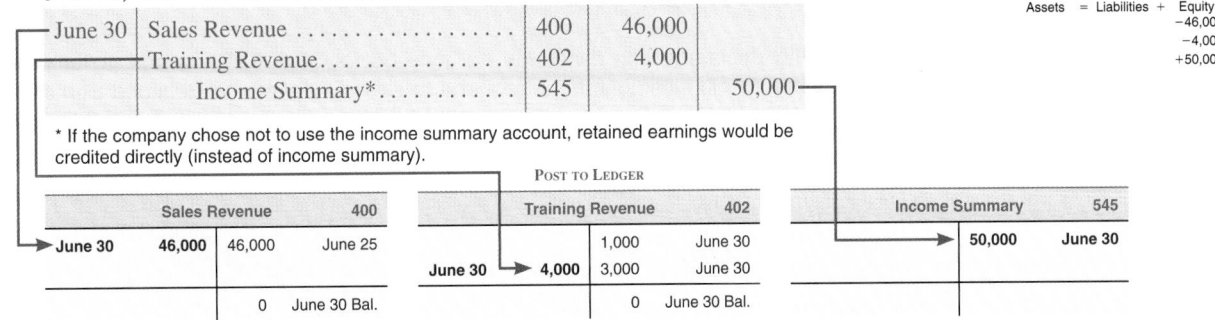

June 30	Sales Revenue	400	46,000	
	Training Revenue	402	4,000	
	Income Summary*	545		50,000

Assets	= Liabilities	+ Equity
		−46,000
		−4,000
		+50,000

* If the company chose not to use the income summary account, retained earnings would be credited directly (instead of income summary).

Post to Ledger

Sales Revenue 400

June 30	**46,000**	46,000	June 25
		0	June 30 Bal.

Training Revenue 402

		1,000	June 30
June 30	**4,000**	3,000	June 30
		0	June 30 Bal.

Income Summary 545

		50,000	**June 30**

Step 2: Expenses and losses are closed to income summary.

June 30, 2020—To close expense accounts to income summary

June 30	Income Summary*	545	33,950	
	Cost of Goods Sold	510		25,000
	Salaries Expense	515		3,000
	Lease Expense	520		2,000
	Insurance Expense	526		500
	Depreciation Expense	528		1,000
	Bad Debt Expense	540		1,950
	Interest Expense	542		500

Assets	= Liabilities	+ Equity
		−33,950
		+33,950

*If the company chose not to use the income summary account, retained earnings would be debited directly (instead of income summary).

Post to Ledger

Income Summary 545

June 30	**33,950**	50,000	June 30
		16,050	June 30 Bal.

Lease Expense 520

June 29	2,000	**2,000**	**June 30**
June 30 Bal.	0		

Bad Debt Expense 540

June 30	1,950	**1,950**	**June 30**
June 30 Bal.	0		

Cost of Goods Sold 510

June 25	25,000	**25,000**	**June 30**
June 30 Bal.	0		

Insurance Expense 526

June 30	500	**500**	**June 30**
June 30 Bal.	0		

Interest Expense 542

June 30	500	**500**	**June 30**
June 30 Bal.	0		

Salaries Expense 515

June 30	3,000	**3,000**	**June 30**
June 30 Bal.	0		

Depreciation Expense 528

June 30	1,000	**1,000**	**June 30**
June 30 Bal.	0		

Step 3: Steps 1 and 2 leave a net balance in the Income Summary account equal to net income (credit balance) or net loss (debit balance) for the period. The Income Summary account is closed by transferring its amount to Retained Earnings. RREI makes the following entry to close Income Summary to Retained Earnings.

continued

continued from previous page

June 30, 2020—To close income summary to retained earnings

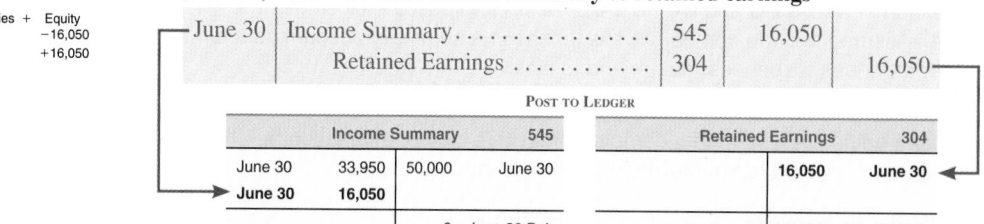

Assets = Liabilities + Equity −16,050 +16,050

June 30	Income Summary	545	16,050	
	Retained Earnings	304		16,050

POST TO LEDGER

Income Summary			545
June 30	33,950	50,000	June 30
June 30	**16,050**		
		0	June 30 Bal.

Retained Earnings			304
		16,050	**June 30**
		16,050	June 30 Bal.

Step 4: When RREI declared cash dividends on June 30 for $2,500, Dividends, a temporary account, is debited. A fourth closing entry is required to close Dividends to Retained Earnings. *If RREI had opted instead to debit Retained Earnings directly when declaring dividends, this closing entry is unnecessary.*

June 30, 2020—To close dividends to retained earnings

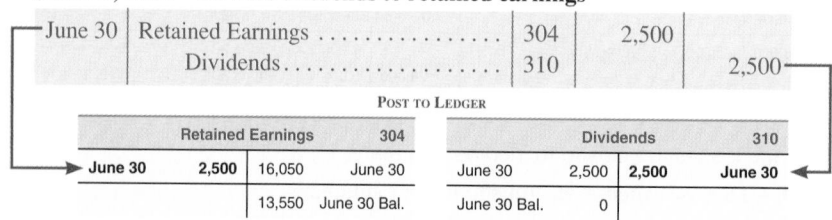

Assets = Liabilities + Equity −2,500 +2,500

June 30	Retained Earnings	304	2,500	
	Dividends	310		2,500

POST TO LEDGER

Retained Earnings			304
June 30	**2,500**	16,050	June 30
		13,550	June 30 Bal.

Dividends			310
June 30	2,500	**2,500**	**June 30**
June 30 Bal.	0		

Temporary accounts now have zero balances and are ready for the next period's accounting cycle. The net result of closing entries is to transfer, in the accounting system, to Retained Earnings an amount equal to earnings less dividends declared for a period. The entries are then posted to ledger accounts to prepare a post-closing trial balance.

EXPANDING YOUR KNOWLEDGE — **Computerized Closing Process**

In most computerized accounting systems, year-end closing is performed by software. The accounting database is automatically updated with the closing entries when the menu item to close the accounting period is selected. However, an income summary account might not be visible even though the net income amount (and not the individual revenue and expense amounts) is posted to the retained earnings account.

Prepare a Post-Closing Trial Balance—Step 9

Steps in Accounting Cycle
Step 1: Identify transactions
Step 2: Record transactions
Step 3: Post transactions
Step 4: Prepare unadjusted trial balance
Step 5: Identify, record, post adjusting entries
Step 6: Prepare adjusted trial balance
Step 7: Prepare financial statements
Step 8: Record and post closing journal entries
Step 9: Prepare post-closing trial balance

A post-closing trial balance lists the balances of permanent accounts only after the closing process is complete (the temporary accounts have balances of zero). This step is taken to check for debit-credit equality after the closing entries are posted. The retained earnings account is at the correct ending balance and is the only permanent account with a balance different from the one shown in the adjusted trial balance.

Demo 2-7B **LO2-7** **Prepare a Post-Closing Trial Balance**

Demo MBC

Refer to the information in **Demo 2-5** and **Demo 2-7A**. Prepare a post-closing trial balance from the trial balance adjusted for the closing entries.

continued

continued from previous page

Solution

To prepare the post-closing trial balance, list the accounts (in account number order) along with the ending debit or credit balances. A number of the ending balances from the adjusted trial balance in **Demo 2-5** have been adjusted through the closing process in **Demo 2-7A**. All of the final ending balances in the ledgers are included here. The total debits of $360,000 equal the total credits of $360,000.

Post-Closing Trial Balance
June 30, 2020

Acct. No.	Account	Debit	Credit
100	Cash	$183,500	
104	Accounts receivable	39,000	
105	Allowance for doubtful accounts		$ 1,950
106	Inventory	75,000	
108	Prepaid insurance	2,500	
160	Equipment	60,000	
162	Accumulated depreciation		1,000
202	Accounts payable		80,000
204	Salaries payable		3,000
208	Deferred revenue		
210	Interest payable		500
240	Note payable		60,000
302	Common stock		200,000
304	Retained earnings		13,550
	Totals	$360,000	$360,000

Closing Entries and Post-Closing Trial Balance **LO2-7** **REVIEW 2-7**

Refer to the solution for Review 2-5.

1. Record and post the Closing Entries for KPMB Consulting Inc. as of June 30, 2020. Assume that the company uses the Income Summary account as a temporary clearing account for revenues, expenses, gains, and losses. Use the following additional accounts: Income Summary (545), and Retained Earnings (304).
2. Prepare a post-closing trial balance.

Review MBC

More Practice: 2-30, 2-48, 2-49

Solution on p. 2-64.

Management Judgment

Management judgment is an important part of applying the accounting information system and in the interpretation of accounting analytics.

Management Judgment Required in the Accounting Cycle

Application of the accounting cycle requires a number of judgments for management. Let's consider a few of the judgments demanded.

- Determining the accounting method used: accrual or cash basis. See Appendix 2A for cash basis accounting.
- Determining the accounting software package used to record transactions.
- Establishing a chart of accounts; see an excerpt of a chart of accounts in Exhibit 2-3.
- Determining the fiscal year-end and reporting periods (monthly, quarterly, annually reporting).
- Determining accounting policies to follow such as the revenue recognition policy and depreciation policy.
- Determining whether or not to use reversing entries; see Appendix 2B for reversing entries.

- Determining financial reports to produce for internal and external use including the use of integrated reporting.

Management Judgment Required in Setup of Accounts

Establishing a chart of accounts is a crucial step as it determines how detailed or summarized information will be organized in financial reports. A chart of accounts also can be tailored to specific industries to make reports more relevant for decision-makers.

Management Judgment for Data Analytics

The use of data analytics, where large data sets often called *big data* can be analyzed, is a way for companies to gain a competitive edge through skilled analysis of information. Data analytics tools are used by accountants to link nonfinancial information with financial information for purposes of integrated reporting. This can lead to more reliable forecasts, more comprehensive and robust reporting, and generally more useful information for management decision-making. Understanding how to link nonfinancial data to financial data summarized through the accounting cycle requires critical thinking and management judgment.

APPENDIX 2A LO 2-8 Convert from cash-basis net income to accrual-basis net income

LO 2-8 Overview

Convert from Cash Basis to Accrual Basis
- **Cash receipts (cash to accrual)**
  - Adjust for changes in accounts receivable and deferred revenue
- **Cash payments (cash to accrual)**
  - Adjust for changes in prepaid expenses and accrued liabilities

This text applies the accrual basis of accounting, which is required under GAAP. The accrual basis records expenses when incurred and revenues when performance obligations are met. Recognition in the accounting records often occurs before or after the payment or receipt of cash. Several of the adjusting entries in this section record resource changes of this type. For example, one adjusting entry records interest expense before cash is paid, while another adjusting entry records training revenue after cash is received.

Cash-basis accounting, which generally records an entry only upon exchange of cash, typically does not require many adjusting entries. Cash-basis accounting is used by some small companies and, in some instances, for income tax accounting. Earnings under the accrual basis more fully reflect the resource changes affecting a company's net assets for a period.

Conversion of Receipts (Cash Basis) to Revenue (Accrual Basis)

To convert cash received from customers from a cash basis to an accrual basis, the company must take into account changes in accounts receivable and deferrals of revenue.

Hint: This solution can also be set up using T-accounts.

Deferred Rent Revenue	
	Beg Bal
Rent revenue	Cash receipts
	End Bal

Rent Receivable	
Beg Bal	
Rent revenue	Cash receipts
End Bal	

Cash receipts from customers (cash-basis)	
Subtract beginning accounts receivable (asset)	← Cash receipt this year, but revenue in prior year
Add ending accounts receivable (asset)	← No cash receipt yet, but revenue in current year
Add beginning deferred revenue (liability)	← No cash receipt yet, but revenue in current year
Subtract ending deferred revenue (liability)	← Cash receipt this year, but revenue next year
Revenue (accrual-basis)	

Conversion of Disbursements (Cash Basis) to Operating Expenses (Accrual Basis)

To convert cash paid for operating expenses from a cash basis to an accrual basis, the company must take into account changes in prepaid expenses and accrued liabilities.

	Cash paid for operating expenses (cash-basis)
Cash paid last year, but expense this year →	Add beginning prepaid expense (asset)
Cash paid this year, but expense next year →	Subtract ending prepaid expense (asset)
Cash paid this year, but expense last year →	Subtract beginning accrued liabilities (liability)
No cash payment yet, but expense this year →	Add ending accrued liabilities (liability)
	Operating expenses (accrual-basis)

Prepaid Expense	
Beg Bal	
Cash Payments	Oper Expense
End Bal	

Accrued Expense	
	Beg Bal
Cash Payments	Oper Expense
	End Bal

Conversion from Cash Basis to Accrual Basis

LO2-8 Demo 2-8

Cruise Inc. maintains cash records during the year, but is required to report financial statements on an accrual basis. Cruise Inc. compiles the following information.

As of December 31	2019	2020
Accounts receivable	$5,000	$18,000
Deferred revenue	4,000	2,500
Prepaid operating expenses	7,200	8,800
Accrued liabilities	2,000	12,000

For Year Ended	2020
Cash receipts from customers	$200,000
Cash paid for operating expenses	100,000

Convert Cruise Inc.'s cash receipt and cash disbursement records to an accrual basis.

Solutions

Conversion of Receipts (Cash-Basis) to Revenue (Accrual-Basis):

Cash receipts from customers (cash-basis)	$200,000
Subtract beginning accounts receivable (asset)	(5,000)
Add ending accounts receivable (asset)	18,000
Add beginning deferred revenue (liability)	4,000
Subtract ending deferred revenue (liability)	(2,500)
Revenue (accrual-basis)	$214,500

Conversion of Disbursements (Cash-Basis) to Operating Expenses (Accrual-Basis):

Cash paid for operating expenses (cash-basis)	$100,000
Add beginning prepaid expense (asset)	7,200
Subtract ending prepaid expense (asset)	(8,800)
Subtract beginning payable (liability)	(2,000)
Add ending payable (liability)	12,000
Operating expenses (accrual-basis)	$108,400

Conversion from Cash Basis to Accrual Basis

LO2-8 REVIEW 2-8

Armour Athletics maintains its accounting records on a cash basis during the year. It must convert its information to an accrual basis at year-end. The following information is available for Armour Athletics for 2020.

As of December 31	2019	2020
Accounts receivable	$6,600	$8,800
Deferred revenue	2,500	2,400
Accrued liabilities	3,900	4,400
Prepaid lease expense	1,200	1,000

For Year Ended December 31	2020
Cash receipts from customers	$60,000
Cash paid for operating expenses	38,000
Depreciation expense	5,000

Required

Calculate net income on an accrual basis for Armour Athletics for 2020

More Practice: 2-75

Solution on p. 2-65.

APPENDIX 2B LO 2-9 Prepare reversing journal entries

LO 2-9 Overview

Reversing Journal Entries
- Reverse deferral or accrual on the first day of the following accounting period
- Utilize to simplify journal entries in period following adjustment

Depending on a company's accounting system and its accounting policy, **reversing journal entries** can be used to simplify certain journal entries for the next accounting period.

Reversing journal entries are **optional** entries that are (1) dated the first day of the next accounting period, and (2) use the same accounts and amounts as an adjusting journal entry but with the debits and credits reversed.

Reversing journal entries are *appropriate* only for adjusting journal entries that (1) defer the recognition of revenue or expense items recorded originally as revenue or an expense in full or (2) accrue revenue or expense items during the current period (for example, salaries expense). Thus, if a deferral or accrual adjusting journal entry increases an asset or liability, a reversing journal entry is appropriate.

Reversing journal entries are *inappropriate* for adjusting journal entries that adjust assets and liabilities recorded for cash flows preceding the recognition of revenues and expenses (for example, depreciation) and for some other adjusting journal entries, such as reclassifications and estimations.

Demo 2-9 **LO2-9** **Reversing Journal Entries**

Demo MBC

Recall that RREI paid $3,000 for a six-month insurance premium on June 3. One month of coverage expired on June 30. RREI also incurred $3,000 of salaries that relate to hours worked in June that will be paid in July.

a. Record June and July journal entries for insurance (deferral of expense) with and without reversing entries.

b. Record June and July journal entries for salaries (accrual of expense) with and without reversing entries. Assume that salaries of $3,000 were paid on July 8, 2020.

Solution

Deferral of Insurance Expense–With Reversing Entry:

Prep Ins	
2,500	2,500
2,000	
2,000	

Ins Exp	
3,000	2,500
2,500	2,000
1,000	

Initial Purchase June 3, 2020	Adjusting Entry June 30, 2020	Reversing Entry July 1, 2020	Adjusting Entry July 31, 2020
Insurance Expense . . . 3,000 Cash 3,000	Prepaid Insurance . . .2,500 Insurance Expense 2,500	Insurance Expense . . . 2,500 Prepaid Insurance 2,500	Prepaid Insurance . . . . 2,000 Insurance Expense 2,000

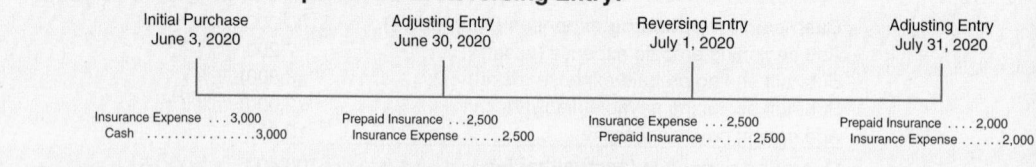

Deferral of Insurance Expense–Without Reversing Entry:

Prep Ins	
3,000	500
	500
2,000	

Ins Exp	
500	
500	
1,000	

Initial Purchase June 3, 2020	Adjusting Entry June 30, 2020	July 1, 2020	Adjusting Entry July 31, 2020
Prepaid Insurance . . . . 3,000 Cash 3,000	Insurance Expense . . . . .500 Prepaid Insurance 500		Insurance Expense . . . . .500 Prepaid Insurance 500

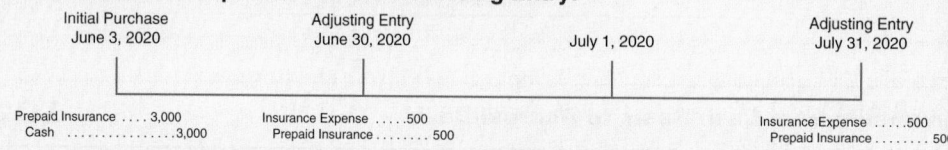

With or without reversing journal entry, insurance expense recorded in June and July of 2020 is $1,000 and the balance in prepaid insurance is $2,000 on July 31, 2020. Use of the reversing journal entry, however, saves the cost and effort of reviewing the relevant accounts and source documents to determine the subsequent year's entry. The reversing journal entry makes the necessary adjustments to the accounts while the information used in making the adjusting journal entries is available.

Accrual of Salaries Expense–With Reversing Entry:

Salaries Pay	
3,000	3,000
	0

Salaries Exp	
3,000	3,000
3,000	
3,000	

Adjusting Entry June 30, 2020	Reversing Entry July 1, 2020	Payment of Salaries July 8, 2020
Salaries Expense . . . . . 3,000 Salaries Payable 3,000	Salaries Payable . . . .3,000 Salaries Expense 3,000	Salaries Expense . . . . . 3,000 Cash 3,000

continued

continued from previous page

Accrual of Salaries Expense–Without Reversing Entry:

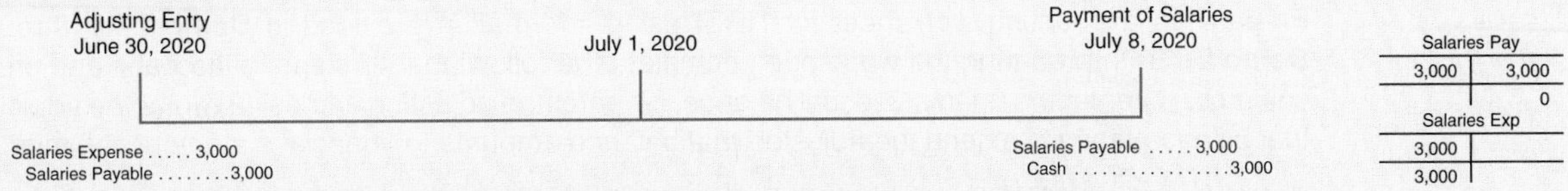

In this example, the reversing journal entry simplifies the subsequent payroll entry, which can now be recorded in a manner identical to all other payrolls (recorded when salaries are paid). With or without reversing entries, salaries expense recognized through July 8, 2020, is $3,000.

Reversing Journal Entries

LO2-9 **REVIEW 2-9**

At the end of the December 31, 2020, annual accounting period, Madison Corp. made the following adjusting entries.

1.	Dec. 31	Salaries Expense	4,500	
		Salaries Payable		4,500
2.	Dec. 31	Prepaid Insurance	5,000	
		Insurance Expense		5,000
3.	Dec. 31	Depreciation Expense	2,500	
		Accumulated Depreciation		2,500
4.	Dec. 31	Amortization Expense	3,800	
		Patent		3,800
5.	Dec. 31	Payroll Tax Expense	2,800	
		Payroll Taxes Payable		2,800

Required

Assuming that Madison Corp. uses reversing entries, prepare the reversing entries that would be made on January 1, 2021, for the adjusting entries above, where applicable.

More Practice: 2-72, 2-76, 2-77
Solution on p. 2-66.

Utilize an accounting worksheet

APPENDIX 2C
LO 2-10

Accounting Worksheets

- Enter the unadjusted trial balance
- Enter the adjusting journal entries
- Enter the adjusted trial balance
- Extend the adjusted trial balance to the financial statement columns

LO 2-10 Overview

To expedite the accounting cycle, some companies use a worksheet as an aid. The worksheet is a tool for organizing accounting information for the purpose of recording adjusting and closing entries and preparing financial statements. An **accounting worksheet** is a multicolumn workspace that provides an organized format for performing several end-of-period accounting cycle steps and for preparing financial statements before posting adjusting journal entries. It also provides evidence, for audit trail purposes, of an organized and structured accounting process that can be more easily reviewed than other methods of analysis.

In manual accounting systems, worksheet input is developed by transferring account name and balance information manually from the general ledger to the worksheet. With most computerized systems, this task is accomplished automatically. Computer spreadsheet and accounting software programs can be used to generate worksheets quickly and with relative ease. These programs offer important labor and time savings in the planning and mechanical plotting of adjusting journal entries on the worksheet. This type of software is a powerful tool for accomplishing several steps in the accounting cycle.

Worksheets are optional and assist with only a portion of the accounting cycle. Formal adjusting journal entries are recorded in the accounting information system in addition to those entered on the worksheet.

Demo 2-10 **LO2-10** **Preparation of an Accounting Worksheet**

Demo MBC

Prepare an accounting worksheet for RREI using information provided in **Demo 2-2B** through **Demo 2-7B**. In preparing the worksheet, complete the following four steps in the debit and credit columns: (1) enter the unadjusted trial balance, (2) enter the adjusting entries, (3) enter the adjusted trial balance, and (4) extend the adjusted trial balance amounts to financial statement columns.

Solution

Explanations for each of the four steps in preparing the accounting worksheet follow.

Worksheet for Month Ended June 30, 2020

		Step One		Step Two		Step Three		Step Four			
		Unadjusted Trial Balance		Adjusting Entries		Adjusted Trial Balance		Income Statement		Balance Sheet	
Acct. No.	Description	Debit	Credit	Debit	Credit	Debit	Credit	Debit	Credit	Debit	Credit
100	Cash	$183,500				$183,500				$183,500	
104	Accounts receivable	36,000		(7)$ 3,000		39,000				39,000	
105	Allowance for doubtful accounts				(6) $1,950		$ 1,950				$ 1,950
106	Inventory	75,000				75,000				75,000	
108	Prepaid insurance	3,000			(1) 500	2,500				2,500	
160	Equipment	60,000				60,000				60,000	
162	Accumulated depreciation				(2) 1,000		1,000				1,000
202	Accounts payable		$80,000				80,000				80,000
204	Salaries payable				(5) 3,000		3,000				3,000
208	Deferred revenue		1,000	(3) 1,000							
210	Interest payable				(4) 500		500				500
240	Note payable		60,000				60,000				60,000
302	Common stock		200,000				200,000				200,000
304	Retained earnings, June 1, 2020		0								
310	Dividends	2,500				2,500				2,500	
400	Sales revenue		46,000				46,000		$46,000		
402	Training revenue				(3) 1,000 (7) 3,000		4,000		4,000		
510	Cost of goods sold	25,000				25,000		$25,000			
515	Salaries expense			(5) 3,000		3,000		3,000			
520	Lease expense	2,000				2,000		2,000			
526	Insurance expense			(1) 500		500		500			
528	Depreciation expense			(2) 1,000		1,000		1,000			
540	Bad debt expense			(6) 1,950		1,950		1,950			
542	Interest expense			(4) 500		500		500			
	Totals	$387,000	$387,000	$10,950	$10,950	$396,450	$396,450	33,950	50,000	362,500	346,450
	Net income							16,050			16,050
	Totals							$50,000	$50,000	$362,500	$362,500

Step One: Enter Unadjusted Trial Balance

Enter the unadjusted trial balance in the first two columns of the worksheet by inserting the year-end balances of all ledger accounts. The retained earnings balance is the beginning-of-year balance (zero in this case) because no transactions have affected this account. Confirm the debit-credit equality of the totals.

Step Two: Enter Adjusting Journal Entries

Enter the following adjusting journal entries from RREI Inc.

(1)	June 30	Insurance Expense	526	500	
		Prepaid Insurance	108		500
(2)	June 30	Depreciation Expense	528	1,000	
		Accumulated Depreciation	162		1,000
(3)	June 30	Deferred Revenue	208	1,000	
		Training Revenue	402		1,000

continued

continued from previous page

(4)	June 30	Interest Expense	542	500	
		Interest Payable	210		500
(5)	June 30	Salaries Expense	515	3,000	
		Salaries Payable	204		3,000
(6)	June 30	Bad Debt Expense	540	1,950	
		Allowance for Doubtful Accounts . . .	105		1,950
(7)	June 30	Accounts Receivable	104	3,000	
		Training Revenue	402		3,000

The worksheet adjusting journal entries are facilitating entries only and are not formally recorded in the general journal at this point. If a new account is created by an adjusting journal entry, it is inserted in its normal position.

Step Three: Enter Adjusted Trial Balance
Enter the adjusted trial balance by adding or subtracting across the unadjusted trial balance sheet columns and adjusting journal entries columns for each account. For example, the adjusted balance of the prepaid insurance account of $2,500 is the sum of its unadjusted balance $3,000 and the $500 decrease from the adjusting journal entry.

Step Four: Extend the Adjusted Trial Balance Amounts to Financial Statements
Each account in the adjusted trial balance is extended to one of the three sets of remaining debit-credit columns. Temporary accounts are sorted to the income statement columns (revenues to the credit column, expenses to the debit column). Permanent accounts are sorted to the balance sheet columns.

Total the income statement columns. Income (ignoring taxes) is the difference between the debit and credit column totals. A net credit represents income; a net debit represents a loss. For RREI, pretax income is $16,050 ($50,000 − $33,950). The net income amount is also added to the balance sheet credit column to balance the balance sheet as an increase to retained earnings.

Financial statements are prepared directly from the last three sets of worksheet columns. The formal adjusting journal entries are then recorded and posted.

Accounting Worksheet **LO2-10** **REVIEW 2-10**

Refer to information in Reviews 2-2 through 2-7. Prepare an accounting worksheet for KPMB Consulting Inc. for the month of June 2020.

Review MBC

More Practice: 2-78, 2-79
Solution on p. 2-66.

Questions

2-1. How are the income statement and balance sheet related?

2-2. Explain the benefits of the double-entry system. What additional benefits does the debit-credit convention provide?

2-3. For each transaction, enter the names of the relevant accounts affected in the appropriate columns.

	Debit	Credit
a. Credit sale	________	________
b. Cash collection on account	________	________
c. Pay rent in advance	________	________
d. Purchase equipment for cash	________	________

continued

continued from previous page

	Debit	Credit
e. Declare cash dividends	________	________
f. Issue common stock at par	________	________
g. Accrue interest expense	________	________

2-4. Indicate with a ✔ in the column whether each listed account is a temporary or permanent account.

	Temporary	Permanent
a. Sales	___	___
b. Cash	___	___
c. Cost of goods sold	___	___
d. Prepaid lease expense	___	___
e. Accumulated depreciation	___	___
f. Dividends	___	___
g. Retained earnings	___	___
h. Income summary	___	___
i. Advertising expense	___	___
j. Deferred revenue	___	___
k. Accounts payable	___	___
l. Lease expense	___	___
m. Loss on sale of fixed asset	___	___

2-5. Number the following steps in the accounting cycle to indicate their normal sequence of completion.

____ *a.* Post.
____ *b.* Identify transaction to be recorded.
____ *c.* Identify, record, and post adjusting entries.
____ *d.* Record and post closing entries.
____ *e.* Prepare financial statements.
____ *f.* Record current transactions.
____ *g.* Prepare post-closing trial balance.
____ *h.* Prepare adjusted trial balance.
____ *i.* Prepare unadjusted trial balance.

2-6. Why do some companies record an expense or revenue upon routine payment or receipt of cash, and prior to the expiration of cost or the recognition of revenue?

2-7. Provide two examples each for (*a*) a recording error that would not cause the trial balance to be out of balance and (*b*) an error that would create an imbalance.

2-8. Some adjusting entries give rise to accounts not previously represented in the ledger, and others do not. Give two examples of each type of adjusting entry.

2-9. A company's Deferred Revenue account (contract liability) increased from $19,000 to $27,000 during the current year. The company collected $55,000 cash for revenue contracts. Determine the amount of revenue recognized in the current year.

2-10. Which account in an unadjusted trial balance might reflect its beginning balance? Which account in an adjusted trial balance also might reflect such a balance?

2-11. Provide three examples of internal cost allocations that require adjusting entries.

2-12. Explain the nature and purpose of closing entries.

2-13. A company first closes revenue accounts (total $25,000) and then closes expense accounts (total $15,000). What is the balance in the Income Summary account after the second closing entry (give amount, and state whether it is a debit or a credit)? What does the balance represent?

Brief Exercises

Brief Exercise 2-14
Applying the Accounting Equation **LO1**
Hint: See Demo 2-1

Show the effect on the accounting equation for each of the following transactions for Savers Inc. for the month of January.

a. Purchased inventory on account from supplier.
b. Sold inventory on account to customer.
c. Collected cash from customer account.
d. Paid cash to supplier on account.
e. Paid a dividend to shareholders.

Brief Exercise 2-15
Preparing Journal Entries **LO2**
Hint: See Demo 2-2B

Prepare journal entries for the following transactions for Kaboom Inc.

a. Paid $1,200 cash for a 6-month insurance policy.
b. Declared dividends of $2,000 cash.

c. Paid $3,000 cash in salaries for the month.
d. Provided $8,000 in services for customers on account.
e. Collected one-half of the amount due from customers in part *d.*

Brief Exercise 2-16 Recording Journal Entries **LO2** *Hint:* See Demo 2-2B

Prepare journal entries for each of the following transactions of Alma Inc.

a. Issues stock to shareholders in exchange for $10,000 cash.
b. Purchases $3,000 of equipment by signing a note payable.
c. Performs $2,500 of services for customers on account.
d. Pays $1,000 cash for legal services.

Brief Exercise 2-17 Posting Journal Entries **LO2** *Hint:* See Demo 2-2B

Trek Inc. recorded the following journal entries *a* through *h* in January 2020, its first period of operations.

	Account	No.	Debit	Credit
a.	Cash	100	2,000	
	Common Stock.	302		2,000
b.	Operating Expense.	525	1,300	
	Cash	100		1,300
c.	Accounts Receivable	104	450	
	Service Revenue.	400		450
d.	Cash	100	250	
	Accounts Receivable	104		250
e.	Equipment	160	750	
	Cash	100		750
f.	Accounts Receivable	104	500	
	Service Revenue.	400		500
g.	Cash	100	1,200	
	Common Stock.	302		1,200
h.	Operating Expense.	525	400	
	Accounts Payable.	202		400

Post the journal entries *a* through *h* to T-accounts (as ledgers), and determine the ending balance in each T-account.

Brief Exercise 2-18 Preparing an Unadjusted Trial Balance **LO3** *Hint:* See Demo 2-3

Using the following T-Accounts, prepare an unadjusted trial balance for Perry Inc. Assume that the trial balance is dated January 31, 2020. Ignore account numbers.

Cash		Accounts Receivable		Equipment		Accounts Payable	
4,000	2,000	1,000	800	1,100		2,000	3,000
800		600					450

Note Payable		Common Stock		Service Revenue		Legal Expense	
	1,100		2,000		600	450	

Brief Exercise 2-19 Recording Asset Purchase and Depreciation **LO2, 4**

AtoZ Co. purchased equipment on June 1, 2020, for $50,000. The company plans to depreciate the asset evenly over its useful life of 10 years.

a. Record the entry for the purchase on June 1, 2020.
b. Record the required adjusting entry on December 31, 2020.

Brief Exercise 2-20 Recording Prepaid Asset and Year-End Adjustment **LO2, 4**

AtoZ Co. purchased a 3-year insurance policy on August 1, 2020, for $10,800.

a. Record the entry for the purchase of the insurance coverage on August 1, 2020, recording the full amount as prepaid insurance.
b. Record the required adjusting entry on December 31, 2020.

Brief Exercise 2-21 Recording Deferred Revenue and Year-End Adjustment **LO2, 4**

On January 1, 2020, Colo Inc. contracts with a customer to provide services in March 2020 for $1,000. The customer paid the full contract price on January 1, 2020.

a. Record the entry for the receipt of cash on January 1, 2020, recording the full amount as a deferred revenue.
b. Record the required adjusting entry on March 31, 2020.

Brief Exercise 2-22 Recording Accrued Expenses **LO2, 4**

AtoZ Co. incurred $1,000 of utility costs for the month of December 2020 (payment due in January), which are unrecorded at year-end.

a. Record the entry for the adjustment on December 31, 2020.
b. Record the payment for the utility costs in January 2021.

Brief Exercise 2-23
Recording Accrued Revenues **LO2, 4**

AtoZ Co. provided delivery services for $5,000 to a customer on December 31, 2020, that has not yet been billed to the customer.

a. Record the year-end adjustment required on December 31, 2020.
b. Record the receipt of cash from the customer in January 2021.

Brief Exercise 2-24
Recording Accrued Interest Expense **LO4**

Alaska Inc. borrowed $40,000 by signing a one-year note payable on November 1, 2020. The note bears interest at 10% and interest is payable upon maturity of the note.

a. Record this financing transaction on November 1, 2020.
b. Record the year-end adjusting entry required on December 31, 2020. *Hint:* Prorate the annual interest of 10% for two months.
c. Record the entry to repay the note on November 1, 2021.

Brief Exercise 2-25
Recording Asset Purchase and Depreciation **LO2, 4**

Juan Inc. purchased equipment for $200,000 cash on June 30, 2020. The equipment has an estimated useful life of 10 years with no salvage value. The company will depreciate the asset evenly over its useful life.

a. Record the purchase of equipment on June 30, 2020.
b. Record the adjusting entry required on December 31, 2020.
c. Provide the balance sheet presentation of equipment on December 31, 2020.

Brief Exercise 2-26
Recording Adjusting Entries **LO4**

Prepare the adjusting journal entries required on December 31, 2020, for Walker Corp. using the following information. Assume that no adjusting journal entries were recorded in 2020 prior to year-end.

a. Interest expense of $150 for the month of December 2020 will be paid in January 2021.
b. Unbilled revenue for services performed in December 2020 is $500. The company will prepare and forward invoices for this amount in January 2021 to customers with a 30-day collection term.
c. $1,500 cash was received in advance on November 30, 2020, for future services to be performed by Walker Corp. and was recorded as deferred service revenue. The services were performed in December 20, 2020.
d. Walker Corp. acquired a two-year insurance policy on January 1, 2020, for $4,800 cash that was recorded initially as prepaid insurance.
e. Depreciation on equipment is $6,000 for 2020.

Brief Exercise 2-27
Analyzing Financial Statement Impacts
LO4

Referring to the information in Brief Exercise 2-26, indicate the income statement and balance sheet impacts in each case *a* through *e* if Walker Corp. failed to record the necessary adjusting entry(ies).

Brief Exercise 2-28
Preparing an Adjusted Trial Balance **LO5**
Hint: See Demo 2-5

The following is the unadjusted trial balance for Walker Corp. as of December 31, 2020. Prepare an adjusted trial balance after posting the adjusting entries required in Brief Exercise 2-26.

Unadjusted Trial Balance
December 31, 2020

Accounts	Debit	Credit
Cash	$ 8,000	
Accounts receivable	3,500	
Supplies	1,800	
Prepaid insurance	4,800	
Equipment	25,000	
Accumulated depreciation		
Accounts payable		$ 1,200
Interest payable		
Deferred revenue		1,500
Note payable		10,000
Common stock		25,000
Service revenue		9,000
Salaries expense	3,600	
Depreciation expense		
Interest expense		
Insurance expense		
Totals	$46,700	$46,700

Brief Exercise 2-29
Preparing Financial Statements **LO6**
Hint: See Demo 2-6

Brown Inc. prepared the following adjusted trial balance on December 31, 2020, based on its first year of operations. Using this adjusted trial balance, prepare an income statement for the year ended December 31, 2020, and a balance sheet as of December 31, 2020.

Adjusted Trial Balance
December 31, 2020

Accounts	Debit	Credit
Cash	$ 6,600	
Accounts receivable	3,000	
Prepaid insurance	1,200	
Other assets	5,200	
Equipment, net	20,000	
Accounts payable		$ 4,000
Note payable		8,000
Common stock		8,000
Service revenue		40,000
Selling expenses	8,000	
General and administrative expenses	15,000	
Interest expense	1,000	
Totals	$60,000	$60,000

Brief Exercise 2-30
Recording Closing Entries **LO7**
Hint: See Demo 2-7

Lakeside Inc. reports balances in the following temporary accounts on December 31, 2020. Prepare closing entries as of December 31, 2020. Assume that the company uses the Income Summary account as a temporary clearing account for revenues, expenses, gains, and losses.

Service revenue	$100,000	Interest expense	$ 3,000
Operating expenses	60,000	Income tax expense	11,850
Interest revenue	2,500	Dividends	5,000

Exercises

Exercise 2-31
Analyzing Transactions Using the Accounting Equation **LO1**
Hint: See Demo 2-1

Dynamic Corporation completed the following transactions during the month of March 2020.

1. Issued 20,000 shares of its own common stock for $200,000 cash.
2. Borrowed $100,000 cash in return for a 9%, one-year note payable.
3. Purchased equipment at a net cash cost of $100,000 with cash.
4. Purchased inventory on account for $80,000. Assume that the company uses the perpetual inventory system.
5. Sold merchandise for $100,000 (and a cost of $60,000); collected $70,000 cash, and the balance is due in one month. *Hint:* Consider two parts to the transaction—one for sales and one for cost of goods sold.
6. Paid $25,000 cash for operating expenses.
7. Paid for half of the merchandise previously purchased on account in transaction 4.
8. Collected 40% of the balance due on the sales in transaction 5.
9. Paid cash for an insurance premium, $1,200 for one year of coverage (debit prepaid insurance).
10. Paid legal fees for the month of March, $10,000 cash.

Required
Indicate the effects on the accounting equation for each of the 10 transactions. Provide your answer in the format illustrated in **Demo 2-1**.

Exercise 2-32
Recording Journal Entries **LO2**
Hint: See Demo 2-2B

Refer to the information in Exercise 2-31 to complete the following requirement.

Required
Prepare journal entries to record the ten transactions from Exercise 2-31.

Exercise 2-33
Classifying Financial Items
LO2

The following accounts were used in recording the 2020 adjusting entries of Jackson Corp, a nutritions lab.

1. Prepaid insurance
2. Interest expense
3. Property taxes payable
4. Note receivable
5. Interest payable
6. Common stock
7. Accumulated depreciation
8. Allowance for doubtful accounts
9. Interest revenue
10. Depreciation expense
11. Sales
12. Accounts receivable
13. Accrued expense
14. Cost of goods sold
15. Deferred subscription revenue

Required

a. Classify each account as asset, liability, revenue, expense, or paid-in capital. Indicate if the account is a contra account.

b. Indicate the account's normal balance (debit or credit).

c. Indicate whether a debit or credit is needed to increase the account.

Exercise 2-34
Accounting Cycle Ordering and Objective **LO2, 3, 4, 5, 6, 7**

The following nine steps that constitute the accounting cycle are in column 3 in scrambled order. In the right most column is a brief statement of the objective of each step, also in scrambled order.

Sequence (ordering)	Matching (step with objective)	Step	Objective
______	______	Record.	*a.* Verification after closing entries.
______	______	Prepare adjusted trial balance.	*b.* Communication to outside (and potential) stakeholders.
______	______	Identify transactions.	*c.* Verification before adjusting entries.
______	______	Prepare financial statements.	*d.* Transfer from journal to ledger.
______	______	Record and post closing entries.	*e.* Recording of resource changes not accompanied by new source documents.
______	______	Post.	*f.* An activity based on source documents.
______	______	Identify, record, and post adjusting entries.	*g.* An original input into the accounting system.
______	______	Prepare unadjusted trial balance.	*h.* Obtaining a zero balance in the revenue, expense, and dividend accounts.
______	______	Prepare post-closing trial balance.	*i.* Verification after adjusting entries.

Required

a. In the first column, indicate the sequential order, *1* through *9*, for each of the accounting steps in column 3.

b. In the second column, indicate the corresponding letter, *a* through *i*, of the description that best matches each accounting step in column 3.

Exercise 2-35
Preparing Journal Entries **LO2**
Hint: See Demo 2-2B

Dyna Corp., a legal firm, completed the following transactions during the month of January, its first month of operations.

Jan. 1	Issued 10,000 shares of common stock for $50,000 cash.
Jan. 3	Purchased $60,000 of office equipment by paying $5,000 cash and by signing a one-year, 10% interest-bearing note payable for the remaining balance.
Jan. 3	Purchased $3,000 supplies on account. *Hint*: Debit Supplies.
Jan. 4	Performed $4,000 of legal services on account.
Jan. 6	Received a $1,500 cash deposit from a new client for legal work to commence next month.
Jan. 10	Paid $5,000 cash for a 12-month insurance policy.
Jan. 13	Paid cash to settle the account for supplies purchased on January 3.
Jan. 20	Performed legal services for $5,000 cash.
Jan. 30	Collected $2,000 cash from customer on account for legal services performed on January 4.
Jan. 31	Paid $3,000 cash in salaries for the month of January.
Jan. 31	Paid $1,000 cash dividends to shareholders.
Jan. 31	Paid $5,000 cash for January rent.

Required

Analyze each of the above transactions and record the general journal entry for each, omitting explanations. Ignore any month-end adjusting entries.

Exercise 2-36
Posting Journal Entries and preparing Trial Balance **LO2, 3**

Use the information in Exercise 2-35 and complete the following requirements.

Required

a. Post each journal entry to T-accounts (serving as a ledger).

b. Prepare an unadjusted trial balance from the ledger in part *a*.

Exercise 2-37
Resolving Errors and Correcting a Trial Balance **LO3**

Century Inc., a consulting firm, prepared the following unadjusted trial balance.

Account	Debit	Credit
Cash	$ 71,126	
Accounts receivable	62,000	
Allowance for doubtful accounts	(4,000)	
Inventory		$ 36,000
Equipment	363,000	
Accumulated depreciation		24,000
Accounts payable	36,000	
Notes payable		50,000
Common stock, par $10		360,000
Retained earnings (correct)		28,000
Revenues		150,000
Expenses	120,000	
Totals	$648,126	$648,000

Assume we examine the accounts and identify the following four errors.

1. Equipment purchased for $15,000 at year-end was debited to Expenses.
2. Sales on credit of $1,658 were debited to Accounts Receivable for $1,784 and credited to Revenues for $1,658.
3. A $12,000 cash collection on accounts receivable was debited to Cash and credited to Revenues.
4. The inventory amount is understated by $4,000 because the entry to record the purchase of inventory was incorrectly recorded in COGS (cost of goods sold is included in expenses).

Required

Prepare a corrected unadjusted trial balance.

Exercise 2-38
Resolving Errors and Correct a Trial Balance **LO3**

The following trial balance provided by Specialty Stores Inc. is not in balance.

Account	Debits	Credits
Cash	$ 81,800	
Accounts receivable	64,100	
Allowance for doubtful accounts		$ 2,300
Inventory	88,800	
Prepaid insurance	800	
Land	10,000	
Equipment	200,000	
Accumulated depreciation		60,000
Accounts payable		36,500
Interest payable		500
Deferred revenue	1,800	
Notes payable		100,000
Common stock		140,000
Retained earnings		28,000
Sales		272,100
Salaries expense	80,000	
Operating expense	110,500	
Interest expense	2,400	
Totals	$640,200	$639,400

Upon a detailed examination of the accounting records, the following items were discovered.

1. A $1,200 posting (debit) to Inventory was omitted.
2. A $500 payment on account was debited to Operating Expense and credited to Cash.
3. A sale of $3,200 on account (supported by an invoice) was recorded as a debit to Accounts Receivable for $2,300 and a credit to Sales for $2,300.
4. The total amount of interest expense in the ledger is $4,000, instead of $2,400 incorrectly included in the trial balance.

5. Depreciation expense for the period of $20,000 was debited to Accumulated Depreciation and credited to Operating Expense.

Required

Prepare a corrected unadjusted trial balance.

Exercise 2-39
Preparing Adjusting Journal Entries
LO2, 4

Baker Corp., which produces fine confections, had the following transactions during 2020.

Jan. 1	Purchased insurance policy for $4,800 cash that expires on December 31, 2021.
Mar. 31	Borrowed $30,000 cash from a bank and signed a one-year note payable, with interest of 8% due at maturity.
June 30	Purchased equipment for $20,000 cash. The equipment will be depreciated evenly over five years.
Dec. 1	A key customer borrows $6,000 cash and signs a 1-year note that requires the customer to pay the loan of $6,000 plus interest of 10% upon maturity.
Dec. 15	$1,800 cash collected for a performance obligation to be completed in January 2021. *Hint:* Credit Deferred Service Revenue when collected.

Required

a. Prepare the original journal entry for each transaction on the date provided.
b. Provide the 2020 adjusting journal entry (if applicable) for each situation.

Exercise 2-40
Preparing Adjusting Journal Entries **LO4**

Rivers Corp., which sponsors river tours, adjusts and closes its accounts each December 31. The following situations require adjusting entries at the current year-end.

1. Equipment is to be depreciated for the full year: cost is $45,000, and the estimated useful life is five years.
2. The accounts receivable balance at December 31 is $8,000. The company estimates that 5% of receivables will not be collected. (Assume a zero beginning balance in the allowance for doubtful accounts.)
3. Property taxes for the current year have not yet been recorded or paid. A statement for the current year was received near the end of December for $4,000; if paid after February 1 in the next year, a 10% penalty is assessed.
4. Office supplies that cost $400 were purchased during the year and debited to Supplies. A physical count of inventory showed $100 of supplies at the prior year-end and $150 at the current year-end.
5. Rivers received $10,000 cash for 12 monthly tours to take place from September of the current year to August of the following year. The total amount collected on September 1 of this year was credited to Service Revenue.
6. Rivers received a note receivable from a customer dated November 1 of the current year. It is a $6,000, 10% note, due in one year. At the maturity date, Rivers will collect the amount of the note plus interest for one year.
7. Salaries earned from December 29 through 31 of this year, but not yet recorded or paid, are $4,800.
8. Interest expense of $400 incurred, but not yet recorded, for November and December of this year will not be paid until April 30 of next year.

Required

Prepare the necessary adjusting journal entries on December 31 for each situation.

Exercise 2-41
Analyzing Adjusting Journal Entries—Prepaid Asset and Deferred Revenue **LO4**

Voss Inc., an accounting firm, adjusts and closes its accounts each December 31. Below are two situations requiring adjusting entries.

1. During the current year, supplies were purchased for $750 cash. The inventory of supplies at the prior year-end was $150. At the current year-end, inventory remaining was $240. Prepare the adjusting entry required for each of the following separate cases.
   a. Case A—the $750 was debited to Supplies Expense. What is the balance of supplies at year-end?
   b. Case B—the $750 was debited to Supplies. What is the balance of supplies at year-end?
2. On June 1, the company collected $8,400 cash, which is for services to be performed over the next 12 months. Prepare the adjusting entry required for each of the following separate cases.
   a. Case A— the $8,400 was credited to Service Revenue. What is the balance of deferred service revenue at year-end?
   b. Case B—the $8,400 was credited to Deferred Service Revenue. What is the balance of deferred service revenue at year-end?

Exercise 2-42
Analyzing Adjusting Journal Entries—Prepaid Assets **LO4**

1. On December 31, 2020, the supplies account showed a current balance of $1,400. During 2021, purchases of supplies amount to $4,000. An inventory of supplies on December 31, 2021, showed a current balance of $2,000. Prepare the adjusting entry required on December 31, 2021, under each of the following separate cases.

a. Case A—purchases of supplies were debited to Supplies. What is the balance of the supplies account on December 31, 2021?

b. Case B—purchases of supplies were debited to Supplies Expense. What is the balance of the supplies account on December 31, 2021?

2. On December 31, 2020, the prepaid insurance account showed a debit balance of $3,600, which was for coverage for the three months, January through March of 2021. On April 1, 2021, the company purchased another policy covering a two-year period starting from that date. The two-year premium of $38,400 was paid and debited to prepaid insurance.

   a. Prepare the adjusting entry required on December 31, 2021, to account for insurance expense for the entire year.

   b. What is the balance in the prepaid insurance account on December 31, 2021?

Exercise 2-43
Preparing Adjusting Journal Entries **LO4**

Pacific Company adjusts and closes its books each December 31. It is now December 31, 2020, and the following information is available for preparing accounting adjustments.

1. The Accounts Receivable balance at December 31 is $16,000. The company estimates that 5% of receivables will not be collected. (Assume a zero beginning balance in the Allowance For Doubtful Accounts.)
2. Unpaid and unrecorded salaries incurred at December 31 are $2,400.
3. The company paid a two-year insurance premium in advance on April 1, 2020, for $4,800 cash, which was debited to Prepaid Insurance.
4. Equipment which cost $40,000, is to be depreciated for the full year. The estimated useful life is 10 years, and the equipment will be depreciated evenly over its useful life.
5. Pacific Company leased a warehouse on June 1, 2020, for one year only. The company was required to pay the full amount of rent one year in advance on June 1, for $4,800 cash, which was debited to Lease Expense.
6. The company received from a customer a 9% note with a face amount of $6,000. The note was dated September 1, 2020; the principal plus the interest is payable one year later. Note Receivable was debited, and Sales was credited on September 1, 2020.
7. On December 30, 2020, the property tax bill was received in the amount of $2,500. This amount applied only to 2020 and had not been previously recorded or paid. Taxes are due, and will be paid, on January 15, 2021.
8. On April 1, 2020, the company signed a $30,000, 10% note payable. On that date, Cash was debited and Note Payable credited for $30,000. The note is payable on March 31, 2021, for the face amount plus interest for one year.
9. The company purchased a patent on January 1, 2020, at a cost of $5,950. On that date, the Patent was debited and Cash credited for $5,950. The patent has an estimated useful life of 17 years and no residual value. *Hint:* Record the estimated consumption of the patent as amortization expense.

Required

Prepare the adjusting entry required on December 31, 2020, for each situation 1 through 9.

Exercise 2-44
Analyzing Accrual Accounting Adjustments **LO4**

The following balances for Experts Inc. were obtained from its accounting information system.

As of (or For Year Ended) December 31	2019	2020
Supplies	$ 3,400	$4,800
Accounts receivable	12,000	9,800
Salaries payable	3,000	1,400
Prepaid lease expense	0	4,400

Required

1. If supplies expense in the income statement is $18,000, what was the cost of supplies purchased in 2020?
2. Assuming no write-offs of accounts receivable, what was the cash collected on accounts receivable in 2020 if revenue recognized in the income statement for 2020 is $537,800?
3. If salaries paid during the year were $200,000, what was salaries expense for 2020?
4. If a 6-month lease payment made in advance was $6,600, what was lease expense for 2020? On approximately what date was the payment made?

Exercise 2-45
Analyzing an Adjusted Trial Balance **LO5**

Below is an adjusted trial balance (partial) for Lazer Tag Inc. as of December 31, 2020.

Adjusted Trial Balance (Partial)
December 31, 2020

Acct. No.	Account	Debit	Credit
104	Accounts receivable	$ 40,000	
106	Supplies	9,000	
108	Prepaid insurance	7,600	
160	Deferred revenue		$ 6,600
202	Salaries payable		8,000
208	Interest payable		2,000
400	Sales revenue		800,000
405	Event revenue		19,800
502	Salaries expense	200,000	
510	Supplies expense	7,000	
515	Insurance expense	4,320	
520	Interest expense	2,000	

Additional information

a. Last year, a corporate client paid a 12-month event fee of $26,400 cash for one planned event per month at Lazer Tag to be applied over 12 months.

b. Supplies available on December 31, 2019, were $6,000.

c. A two-year insurance policy was purchased on September 1, 2020. The policy was paid in full on September 1, 2020. Premiums had increased from the prior policy.

Required

1. If interest expense relates to six months of interest expense on a 10% note payable, what is the amount of the note payable?
2. What was the adjusting journal entry to accrue unpaid, but incurred salaries, on December 31, 2020?
3. How many months remain in the 12-month corporate client contract?
4. What amount of supplies was purchased during 2020?
5. What was the price of the two-year policy signed on September 1, 2020? By how much did the current policy's monthly premium increase over the prior policy's monthly premium?

Exercise 2-46
Preparing Adjusting Journal Entries and Trial Balance **LO4, 5**

Discovery Inc., an electronics retailer, commenced operations on January 1, 2020. The unadjusted trial balance for Discovery as of March 31, 2020, follows.

Unadjusted Trial Balance
March 31, 2020

Acct. No.	Account	Debit	Credit
100	Cash	$ 52,000	
104	Accounts receivable	49,000	
105	Supplies	4,500	
106	Inventory	75,000	
108	Prepaid insurance	3,000	
155	Building	150,000	
160	Equipment	80,000	
202	Accounts payable		$ 45,000
208	Deferred service revenue		1,800
240	Note payable		125,000
302	Common stock		110,000
300	Retained earnings		88,200
310	Dividends	1,500	
400	Sales		350,000
510	Cost of goods sold	200,000	
515	Operating expenses	15,000	
520	Salaries expenses	90,000	
	Totals	$720,000	$720,000

Additional information

1. Examination of supplies indicates that $3,000 of supplies are still available on March 31, 2020.
2. One year of insurance coverage was purchased on January 1, 2020, for $3,000 cash.
3. Building and equipment (purchased on January 1, 2020) will be depreciated evenly over the useful lives of 30 years and 8 years, respectively.
4. $800 of the $1,800 in deferred service revenue relates to service obligations to be performed after March 31, 2020.
5. Annual interest on the note payable is 8%. Interest is due in one year upon the maturity of the note. The note was issued on January 1, 2020.
6. Utilities for March 2020 of $800 have been incurred but not yet paid.
7. At the end of March, the company provided a new service to customers for in-home assessments. The company will bill customers $600 in April for services performed in March.
8. Additional general ledger accounts, currently with a zero balance, are:

170 Accumulated Depreciation—Building	516 Supplies Expense
171 Accumulated Depreciation—Equipment	517 Insurance Expense
203 Utilities Payable	518 Depreciation Expense
209 Interest Payable	519 Utilities Expense
403 Service Revenue	530 Interest Expense

Required

a. Prepare all necessary adjusting entries as of March 31 for the three-month period ended March 31, 2020.
b. Prepare an adjusted trial balance on March 31, 2020.
c. Compute net income for the three months ended March 31, 2020.

Exercise 2-47
Preparing Financial Statements **LO6**

The adjusted trial balance of Monona Inc. as of December 31, 2020, follows.

Adjusted Trial Balance
December 31, 2020

Acct. No.	Account	Debit	Credit
100	Cash	$ 36,000	
104	Accounts receivable	70,000	
105	Allowance for doubtful accounts		$ 3,550
106	Inventory	80,000	
108	Prepaid insurance	4,800	
150	Land	11,450	
155	Building	200,000	
156	Equipment	60,000	
162	Accumulated depreciation		12,500
202	Accounts payable		75,000
204	Salaries payable		4,500
208	Deferred service revenue		2,000
210	Interest payable		500
240	Note payable		150,000
302	Common stock		185,000
304	Retained earnings		12,000
310	Dividends	5,000	
400	Sales revenue		500,000
402	Service revenue		25,000
510	Cost of goods sold	240,000	
512	Salaries expense	230,000	
520	Repair expense	2,000	
526	Insurance expense	3,600	
528	Depreciation expense	13,200	
540	Interest expense	12,000	
542	Bad debt expense	2,000	
	Totals	$970,050	$970,050

Required

a. Prepare the income statement for the year ended December 31, 2020.

b. Prepare the statement of stockholders' equity for the year ended December 31, 2020. Assume that the common stock was issued prior to 2020.

c. Prepare the balance sheet on December 31, 2020.

Exercise 2-48
Preparing Closing Entries **LO7**
Hint: See Demo 2-7A

The following selected accounts and amounts are from the adjusted trial balance for Seattle Inc.

Sales	$55,000	Cost of goods sold	$26,500
Service revenue	1,000	Interest expense	2,000
Operating expenses	12,000	Dividends	5,500
Income tax expense	2,500		

Required

Prepare the closing entries for revenues, expenses, and dividends. Use the Income Summary account to close income statement amounts.

Exercise 2-49
Preparing Closing Entries **LO7**

Following is a partial adjusted trial balance for Accel Inc. for its year ended December 31, 2020.

Acct. No.	Description	Debit	Credit
310	Retained earnings		$1,200,000
315	Dividends	$ 13,000	
400	Sales		800,000
405	Consulting revenue		50,000
500	Costs of goods sold	500,000	
502	Salaries expense	80,000	
510	Supplies expense	7,000	
515	Insurance expense	12,000	
520	Interest expense	2,000	

Required

Prepare the closing entries for revenues, expenses, and dividends. Use the Income Summary account to close income statement amounts.

Exercise 2-50
Preparing Financial Statements and Closing Entries **LO6, 7**

Hayley Inc. prepared the following adjusted trial balance as of December 31, 2020.

Adjusted Trial Balance
December 31, 2020

Account	Debit	Credit
Cash	$ 30,000	
Accounts receivable	32,000	
Inventory	40,000	
Prepaid insurance	1,200	
Equipment	225,000	
Accumulated depreciation—equipment		$ 45,000
Accounts payable		35,000
Salaries payable		4,000
Interest payable		400
Note payable		50,000
Common stock		110,000
Retained earnings		80,000
Dividends	3,000	
Sales		350,000
Cost of goods sold	200,000	
Salaries expense	119,200	
Repair expense	2,100	
Insurance expense	1,500	
Selling expense	2,200	
Depreciation expense	13,200	
Interest expense	5,000	

Totals	$674,400	$674,400

Required

a. Prepare the income statement for Hayley Inc. for the year ended December 31, 2020.
b. Prepare closing entries as of December 31, 2020.

Exercise 2-51 Matching Accounting Concepts and Terminology **LO2, 3, 4, 5, 6, 7**

Terms relating to concepts discussed in this chapter along with descriptions of the terms follow.

Descriptions

____ *a.* Allows for revenues and expenses to be recorded in the appropriate accounting period
____ *b.* Record of similar transactions such as sales or cash receipts
____ *c.* Equates assets to liabilities plus stockholders' equity
____ *d.* To transfer from the journal to the ledger
____ *e.* Transfer of temporary account balance to a permanent account balance
____ *f.* Form of a ledger
____ *g.* All-purpose record of transactions in a chronological sequence
____ *h.* List of ending balances of accounts before adjusting entries are recorded
____ *i.* Provides evidence of a transaction
____ *j.* Master list of accounts and unique identifiers
____ *k.* List of ending balances of accounts after adjusting entries are recorded
____ *l.* Process repeated each accounting period leading to financial reporting

Required

Match each of the terms or phrases 1 through 12 with the most closely aligned description *a* through *l*.

Problems

Problem 2-52 Analyzing Transactions Using the Accounting Equation **LO1**

The following selected transactions were completed during 2020 by Rotan Corp., a furniture retailer.

1. Issued 20,000 shares of its own common stock, par $1, for $12 cash per share. *Hint*: Credit Paid-In Capital in Excess of Par—Common Stock for any excess above par.
2. Borrowed $100,000 cash on a 9%, one-year note, interest payable at maturity on April 30, 2021.
3. Purchased equipment for use in operating the business at a net cash cost of $164,000; paid in full.
4. Purchased merchandise for resale at a cost of $140,000 cash. Assume a perpetual inventory system. (*Hint*: Debit Inventory.)
5. Purchased merchandise for resale on credit terms 2/10, n/60. The merchandise will cost $9,800 if paid within 10 days; after 10 days, the payment will be $10,000. The company always takes the discount; therefore, such purchases are recorded net of discount.
6. Sold merchandise for $180,000, with a cost of $100,000; collected $165,000 cash, and the $15,000 balance is due in one month. *Hint:* Consider two parts to the transaction—one for sales and one for cost of goods sold.
7. Paid $40,000 cash for operating expenses.
8. Paid 75% of the balance for the merchandise purchased in part 5 within 10 days; the remaining 25% balance was unpaid at year-end.
9. Collected 50% of the balance due on the sale in part 6; the remaining 50% balance is uncollected at year-end.
10. Paid $600 cash for an insurance premium; the premium was for two years of coverage. (*Hint*: Debit Prepaid Insurance.)
11. Purchased for $63,000 cash a tract of land for company operations.
12. Paid $10,000 cash damages to a customer who was injured on the company premises.

Required

Show the effects using the accounting equation for each of the 12 transactions above. Provide answers in the format of **Demo 2-1**.

Problem 2-53
Journaling, Posting, and Preparing an Unadjusted Trial Balance **LO2, 3**

Refer to the information in Problem 2-52 to complete the following requirements.

Required

a. Enter each of the transactions 1 through 12 in a general journal entry. Use the number of the transaction in place of the date.

b. Set up T-accounts as a ledger and then post the journal entries. Use the following chart of accounts: Cash (100), Accounts Receivable (104), Inventory (106), Prepaid Insurance (108), Equipment (160), Land (161), Accounts Payable (202), Note Payable (240), Common Stock (302), Paid-in Capital in Excess of Par—Common Stock (303), Sales (400), Cost of Goods Sold (510), Operating Expenses (522), Loss on Damages (530).

c. Prepare an unadjusted trial balance.

Problem 2-54
Applying the Entire Accounting Cycle **LO2, 3, 4, 5, 6, 7**

The post-closing trial balance for Wilson Corp., a retailer, at December 31, 2019, follows.

Acct. No.	Account	Debit	Credit
101	Cash	$ 27,000	
102	Accounts receivable	21,000	
103	Allowance for doubtful accounts		$ 1,000
104	Inventory (perpetual inventory system)	35,000	
105	Prepaid insurance (20 months remaining)	900	
200	Equipment (20-year estimated life, no residual value)	50,000	
201	Accumulated depreciation—equipment		22,500
300	Accounts payable		7,500
301	Salaries payable		
302	Income taxes payable (for 2019)		4,000
400	Common stock, par $1		80,000
401	Retained earnings		18,900
500	Sales		
600	Cost of goods sold		
601	Operating expenses		
602	Income tax expense		
700	Income summary		
	Totals	$133,900	$133,900

The following transactions occurred during 2020 in the order shown (use the number at the left in place of a date).

1. Sales revenue was $30,000, of which $10,000 was on credit; the cost, provided using perpetual inventory, was $19,500.
2. Collected $17,000 cash on accounts receivable.
3. Paid $4,000 cash toward income taxes payable (2019).
4. Purchased $40,000 of merchandise, of which $8,000 was on credit.
5. Paid $6,000 cash toward accounts payable.
6. Sales revenue was $72,000 (in cash); cost was $46,800.
7. Paid $19,000 cash in operating expenses.
8. On July 1, 2020, issued 1,000 shares of common stock, par $1, for $1,000 cash.
9. Purchased $100,000 of merchandise, of which $27,000 was on credit.
10. Sales revenue was $98,000, of which $30,000 was on credit; cost, $63,700.
11. Collected $26,000 cash toward accounts receivable.
12. Paid $28,000 cash toward accounts payable.
13. Paid $18,000 cash for various operating expenses.

Required

a. Prepare general journal entries for each of the transactions above for 2020.

b. Set up T-accounts as the general ledger for each of the accounts listed in the above trial balance and enter the December 31, 2019, balances. Post the journal entries from *a*.

c. Prepare an unadjusted trial balance.

d. Prepare December 31, 2020, adjusting entries for the following additional information.

1. Increase the allowance for doubtful accounts by $200. *Hint:* Debit Operating Expenses.
2. Accrued income tax expense is $11,784. *Hint:* Credit Income Taxes Payable.
3. Accrued salaries were $300.
4. Use straight-line depreciation for equipment.
5. Adjust prepaid insurance account for current year expense.

e. Post adjusting journal entries from *d* to the ledger.
f. Prepare an adjusted trial balance.
g. Prepare the income statement and balance sheet.
h. Prepare the closing entries.
i. Post the closing entries to the ledger.
j. Prepare a post-closing trial balance.

Problem 2-55
Preparing Adjusting Entries, Trial Balances, Financial Statements, Closing, and Post-Closing Trial Balance **LO4, 5, 6, 7**

Milwaukee Corp. prepared its unadjusted trial balance dated December 31, 2020, as follows.

Unadjusted Trial Balance
December 31, 2020

Account	Debit	Credit
Cash	$ 40,000	
Accounts receivable	60,000	
Allowance for doubtful accounts		$ 6,000
Inventory	70,000	
Land	150,000	
Equipment	780,000	
Accumulated depreciation—equipment		100,000
Accounts payable		22,000
Note payable		200,000
Common stock		400,000
Retained earnings		50,000
Sales revenue		900,000
Subscription revenue		24,000
Cost of goods sold	270,000	
Lease expense	45,000	
Interest expense	12,000	
Selling expense	40,000	
Insurance expense	30,000	
Internet expense	15,000	
Salaries expense	110,000	
General and administrative expense	80,000	
Totals	$1,702,000	$1,702,000

Additional information for accounting adjustments

1. Equipment has a total estimated useful life of 14 years and an estimated residual value of $80,000. Milwaukee Corp. uses straight-line depreciation and accounts for depreciation expense as a general and administrative expense.
2. The company estimates an increase in the allowance for doubtful accounts of $9,000 is required in order to recognize accounts receivable of $60,000 at net realizable value.
3. The note payable requires 8% interest to be paid semiannually, every October 1 and April 1.
4. $5,000 of salaries were earned in December but not recorded or paid.
5. Internet expense represents a payment made on January 2, 2020, for two years of internet services (2020 and 2021).
6. Insurance expense represents payment made for a one-year policy, paid June 30, 2020. Coverage begins on that date.
7. Subscription revenue represents cash received for a one-and-one-half-year subscription to a journal published by Milwaukee Corp. The subscription period begins July 1, 2020.

Required

a. Record the required adjusting journal entries. The company adjusts its accounts at year-end only.
b. Prepare the adjusted trial balance.
c. Prepare the income statement for 2020 and the balance sheet at year-end 2020.
d. Prepare closing entries.

Problem 2-56
Preparing Adjusting Entries, Trial Balances, Financial Statements, and Closing Entries **LO4, 5, 6, 7**

Spectrum Inc., a calendar-year firm, began operations as a retailer in January 2020. The following information pertains to transactions in 2020.

Unadjusted Trial Balance
December 31, 2020

Account	Debit	Credit
Cash	$ 180,000	
Accounts receivable	197,000	
Allowance for doubtful accounts	3,000	
Inventory	200,000	
Equipment	110,000	
Accounts payable		$ 40,000
Long-term note payable, 10%		100,000
Common stock		200,000
Sales		2,500,000
Cost of goods sold	1,800,000	
Salaries expense	60,000	
Lease expense	70,000	
Utility expense	40,000	
Selling expense	80,000	
General and administrative expense	100,000	
Totals	$2,840,000	$2,840,000

Additional information for accounting adjustments

1. The note payable calls for interest payments every February 1. The note is due in full on January 31, 2024.
2. A month-to-month lease agreement required a $15,000 cash advance lease payment for January 2021 rent. The company's policy is to charge lease payments initially to lease expense.
3. Equipment costing $110,000 cash was purchased in early February. It has an estimated residual value of $10,000 and a five-year useful life. Spectrum uses the straight-line method of depreciation.
4. The company estimates an increase in the allowance for doubtful accounts of $12,500 is required to recognize accounts receivable of $197,000 at net realizable value.
5. Income tax payable, not previously recorded, totals $130,000.
6. Dividends of $117,000 are declared.

Required

a. Record the required adjusting journal entries.
b. Prepare the adjusted trial balance.
c. Prepare the income statement for 2020 and the balance sheet at year-end 2020.
d. Prepare closing entries.
e. Prepare a post-closing trial balance.

Problem 2-57
Preparing Adjusting Entries, Trial Balances, Financial Statements, and Closing Entries **LO4, 5, 6, 7**

The unadjusted trial balance for Brown Inc. follows.

Unadjusted Trial Balance
December 31, 2020

Account	Debit	Credit
Cash	$ 6,320	
Accounts receivable	6,000	
Prepaid lease expense	19,200	
Supplies	11,000	
Equipment	20,000	
Accumulated depreciation—equipment		$ 3,000
Accounts payable		2,000
Note payable		8,000
Common stock		20,000
Retained earnings		8,000
Dividends	10,000	
Service revenue		50,000
Interest expense	480	
Salaries expense	13,000	
Utility expense	2,000	
Miscellaneous expense	3,000	
Totals	$91,000	$91,000

Additional information for accounting adjustments

1. Brown was required to pay the entire rental for a one-year lease beginning July 1 for $13,200 cash. Brown recorded the payment as a debit to Prepaid Lease Expense.
2. A year-end count revealed $2,000 of supplies still available.
3. Annual depreciation expense on the equipment is $1,000.
4. Unpaid and unrecorded salaries is $2,000 at year-end.
5. The note payable calls for annual interest of 8%, payable each September 30. The principal amount of the note is not due for several years.

Required

a. Record the required adjusting journal entries.
b. Prepare the adjusted trial balance.
c. Prepare the income statement for 2020 and the balance sheet at year-end 2020.
d. Prepare closing entries.

Problem 2-58
Preparing Adjusting Journal Entries **LO4**

The following transactions and events for Stellar Corp. are being reviewed for possible adjusting entries at December 31, 2020 (the end of its accounting period).

1. Equipment used in operations cost $420,000; it was purchased on July 1, 2017. It has an estimated useful life of 12 years. Straight-line depreciation is used.
2. The company estimates an increase in the allowance for doubtful accounts of $3,000 is required to recognize accounts receivable of $300,000 at net realizable value.
3. At the beginning of 2020, supplies amounted to $600. During 2020, supplies of $8,800 were purchased; this amount was debited to Supplies Expense. An inventory of supplies at the end of 2020 showed $400 still available. However, the January 1 balance of $600 is still recorded in the supplies account.
4. On July 1, 2020, the company paid a three-year insurance premium of $2,160; this amount was debited to Prepaid Insurance.
5. On August 1, 2020, the company borrowed $120,000 cash from Shar Bank. The loan was for 12 months at 9% interest payable at maturity date.
6. On December 31, 2020, salaries earned by employees but not yet paid (or recorded) was $18,000.
7. On September 1, 2020, the company loaned $60,000 cash to another company. The loan was at 10% per year and was due in six months; interest is payable at maturity. Cash was credited for $60,000, and Note Receivable was debited on September 1 for the same amount.

8. On January 1, 2020, Supplies amounted to $200. During 2020, supplies that cost $4,000 were purchased and debited to Supplies. At the end of 2020, a physical inventory count revealed that supplies still available were $800.
9. At the end of 2020, property taxes for 2020 of $59,000 were assessed on property owned by the company. The taxes are due no later than February 1, 2021. The taxes have not been recorded on the books because payment has not yet been made.
10. The company borrowed $120,000 cash from the bank on December 1, 2020. A 60-day note payable was signed at 9% interest payable on maturity date. On December 1, 2020, Cash was debited and Note Payable credited for $120,000.
11. On July 1, 2020, the company paid the city a $1,000 license fee for the next 12 months. On that date, Cash was credited and License Expense debited for $1,000.
12. The company owns three SUVs used by its executives. A six-month maintenance contract on them was signed on October 1, 2020, whereby a local garage agreed to do "all the required maintenance." Payment was made for the following six months in advance; specifically, on October 1, 2020, Cash was credited and Repair Expense was debited for $9,600.

Required

Prepare the adjusting entry (or entries) that are necessary, if any, on December 31, 2020, for each item 1 through 12.

Problem 2-59
Preparing Adjusting Journal Entries **LO4**

Rona Company is a calendar-year manufacturer. Rona is reviewing the following transactions for possible adjusting entries at December 31, 2020.

1. One of Rona Company's liabilities is a 12%, $40,000 long-term note payable, which requires interest to be paid each March 1 and September 1.
2. Rona Company owns a $20,000, 10% bond, which it purchased at face value and which pays interest each August 1 and February 1.
3. Rona Company performed and completed services for a customer in December for a $12,000 total fee. The customer was not billed and did not remit payment in the current year. The customer has a strong credit rating.
4. Depreciation of $30,000 is to be recorded.
5. Salaries totaling $15,000 were earned but not paid or recorded at year-end. The first payroll in 2021 is expected to total $45,000.
6. Rona paid $4,800 cash for a one-year insurance policy on September 1, 2020. Rona records the full amount on September 1 as insurance expense.

Required

Prepare the adjusting entry (or entries) that are necessary, if any, on December 31, 2020, for each item 1 through 6.

Problem 2-60
Analyzing Financial Statements and Preparing Accounting Adjustments **LO4**

Fannie Corp. started operations on January 1, 2020. It is now December 31, 2020, the end of its annual accounting period and the company has just prepared the following financial statements.

Fannie Corp.
Income Statement
For Year Ended December 31, 2020

Service revenue		$100,000
Expenses		
Salaries	$30,000	
Repairs	5,000	
Service	25,000	
Other miscellaneous	10,000	70,000
Net income		$ 30,000

Fannie Corp.
Balance Sheet
December 31, 2020

Assets		**Liabilities**	
Cash	$ 7,500	Accounts payable	$ 8,000
Note receivable, 8%	1,200	Note payable, 6%	24,000
Supplies	6,000	Total liabilities	32,000
Equipment	90,000	**Stockholders' Equity**	
Other assets	7,300	Common stock	50,000
		Retained earnings	30,000
		Total stockholders' equity	80,000
Total assets	$112,000	Total liabilities and stockholders' equity	$112,000

The above statements (unaudited) were presented to a local bank, at the bank's request, to support a loan request. The bank requested that the statements be examined by an independent CPA. Among other accounting issues, we find that the following items were not considered by the company in preparing the income statement and balance sheet.

1. Service revenue amounting to $2,000 had been collected but the related obligations had not been performed as of December 31, 2020.
2. At December 31, 2020, salaries earned by employees but not yet paid or recorded amount to $9,000.
3. A count of supplies at December 31, 2020, showed $4,000 of supplies still available. (Supplies are used in repairs.)
4. Depreciation on the equipment acquired on January 3, 2020, was not recorded. The estimated useful life is 10 years.
5. The note receivable received was from a customer and was dated November 1, 2020; the principal plus interest is payable April 30, 2021.
6. The note payable to the local bank was dated June 1, 2020; the principal plus interest is payable May 31, 2021.
7. Income tax expense is $1,386. Assume that no income tax has been recorded. Record all as income taxes payable.

Required

a. Prepare the adjusting entries that are necessary, if any, on December 31, 2020, for each item 1 through 7.

b. Determine the effect of each item 1 through 7 on the following categories by indicating the amount reported, the adjustments, and the adjusted amount.

1. Net income
2. Assets
3. Liabilities
4. Stockholders' equity

Accounting Decisions and Judgments

AD&J 2-61
Evaluating an Annual Report LO1

Real World Analysis Obtain a digital copy of Form 10-K for **Coca-Cola Company** for the year ended December 31, 2015, which can be found on the SEC Edgar website (https://www.sec.gov/edgar/searchedgar/companysearch.html).

Required

a. Did the average gross margin ratio change from 2014 to 2015? What might have caused the change? (*Hint:* Review the Management's Discussion and Analysis section of the Form 10-K.)

b. Locate the note about accounting for advertising costs. How are prepaid advertising costs treated for accounting purposes?

c. What are the company's policies regarding amortization of intangibles?

d. Can you determine the amount of cash paid to suppliers in 2015? If not, what other information would you need?

e. Although interest payable is not separately listed in either the balance sheet or the notes, can you determine the change in that account during 2015?

AD&J 2-62
Analyzing MD&A
LO1, 6

Real World Analysis Use Form10-K for **Coca-Cola Company** for the year ended December 31, 2015 which can be found on the SEC Edgar website (https://www.sec.gov/edgar/searchedgar/companysearch.html) to answer the following questions pertaining to Coca-Cola's MD&A (Management's Discussion and Analysis of Financial Condition and Results of Operations) section.

Required

a. Describe the types of information contained in the MD&A section most likely to be found elsewhere in the financial statements and notes. Why is this information repeated?

b. Describe the types of information in the MD&A section, other than that of a prospective nature, that probably would not be found elsewhere in the financial statements and notes.

c. Describe the types of information in the MD&A section of a prospective nature, that probably would not be found elsewhere in the financial statements and notes.

AD&J 2-63
Recording Adjusting Entries **LO4**

Ethics Case Adjusting journal entries are not necessarily supported by source documents or exchanges of resources between parties and might therefore be more easily omitted, altered, or forgotten.

Required

Considering the adjusting entries discussed in this chapter, prepare a one-half page written description of intentional alterations of adjusting journal entries that would constitute unethical behavior on the part of accountants.

AD&J 2-64
Discussing Ethical Responsibilities of Accountants
LO2, 3, 4, 5, 6

Ethics Case Refer to the Statement of Ethical Professional Practice produced by the Institute of Management Accountants Inc. at https://www.imanet.org/.

Required

Discuss in writing (one-half page) the responsibilities that the accounting staff has toward the shareholders of a corporation, relative to transaction recording and financial reporting.

AD&J 2-65
Distinguishing Events and Transactions
LO2

Communication Case As a staff accountant in a large retailing firm, you have had significant experience developing information for financial reporting purposes. During lunch with a colleague in the marketing department, you explain how the accounting information system is designed to record all events affecting the firm. Your colleague has always wondered why some events warrant formal recording in the accounts whereas others do not.

For example, your colleague wonders why an upturn in demand for expensive sports shoes marketed by the firm does not warrant the recording of increased income before sale. She asked:

> We cannot fill all the orders we receive for these shoes. Why can't we recognize our profit as soon as we receive these items from the manufacturer? I know the firm does not wait until receipt of cash to accrue interest on its financial investments. Yet I also know that increases in the value of our company's stock are not recognized in our accounts as increases in the value of our assets. However, outside parties have made that assessment. I am confused.

Required

Write a short one-half page memo to your colleague distinguishing three types of events that may or may not be recorded in the accounts, as a way of explaining the items she has raised.

AD&J 2-66
Communicating the Need for Journals in an AIS System **LO2**

Communication Case Systems Inc. produces and markets a wide variety of information and communication technology products. Although current demand for its products has increased enough to justify continued growth in production systems, the VP of finance is concerned that continuing recessionary factors may reverse the good fortune of the company. Yet, if the firm is to grow, it must overhaul its AIS. The VP has discussed the AIS project with you, the controller of this company, and cannot understand your insistence that the system have a strong journalizing capability. The VP argues:

> The whole purpose of AIS is to culminate in accurate financial statements each year. Why not simply record each transaction directly into the accounts? I just do not understand the need to record transactions into a temporary record first.

The VP is removed from the day-to-day operational traffic within the firm but has some responsibility for the outcome of the AIS project. The volume of transactions of the medium-sized firm is substantial.

Required

Prepare a one-half page memo to the VP explaining the need for the journal entry step in AIS of Systems Inc.

AD&J 2-67
Differentiating between Adjusted and Unadjusted Trial Balances **LO3**

Communication Case In your post as director of accounting information systems, you periodically must communicate with your staff about technical aspects of accounting to help them set up the information system in the most effective manner. George, one of the analysts who has some knowledge of accounting, asked you to clarify the differences between the unadjusted and adjusted trial balances. For example, George is confused about what inventory balance will appear in each.

Required

Write a short one-half page memo to George explaining the differences between the two trial balances. Assume that this company is considering more than one way of recognizing cost of goods sold in the accounts.

Appendix—Questions

2-68. Explain the purpose and nature of reversing entries. Why are they recorded and posted?

2-69. Xanthon Company owes a $4,000, three-year, 9% note payable. Interest is paid each November 30. At the end of the accounting period, December 31, the following adjusting entry was made:

Interest Expense.	30	
Interest Payable		30

Would you recommend using a reversing entry in this situation? Explain.

2-70. Explain which accounting cycle steps are affected by the use of a worksheet.

Appendix—Brief Exercises

App—Brief Exercise 2-71 Calculating Accrual Amounts LO8 *Hint:* See Demo 2-8

Skechers Inc. calculated its cash receipts from customers as $28,000 and its cash payments for operating expenses as $20,000 for the year ended December 31, 2020. The beginning and ending balances of accounts receivable were $3,500 and $2,800, respectively. The beginning and ending balances of accrued expenses were $1,800 and $3,200, respectively.

Required

a. Calculate revenues on an accrual basis for 2020.
b. Calculate operating expenses on an accrual basis for 2020.

App—Brief Exercise 2-72 Recording Reversing Entries LO9 *Hint:* See Demo 2-9

Hancock Inc. utilizes reversing journal entries in accounting for accrual adjustments. Salaries earned for the three-day period ending December 31, 2020, are $3,800, which will be paid in 2021. When Hancock salaries are paid, they are recorded as salaries expense.

Required

a. Record the adjusting journal entry at year-end.
b. Record the reversing entry to be recorded on January 1, 2021.
c. Record the payment of salaries in January 2021.

App—Brief Exercise 2-73 Preparing an Accounting Worksheet LO10

Ripley Corp. prepared an accounting worksheet as of June 30, 2020. An excerpt follows.

Accounting Worksheet excerpt
June 30, 2020

Sales revenue.	$150,000
Cost of goods sold	80,000
Operating expenses	30,000
Interest revenue	2,000
Interest expense.	5,000
Income tax expense	11,000

Required

Prepare a summarized income statement based upon the following excerpt from Ripley's accounting worksheet.

Appendix—Exercises

App—Exercise 2-74
Converting from Cash-Basis to Accrual-Basis Accounting **LO8**
Hint: See Demo 2-8

Leigh Inc. maintains its accounting records on a cash basis. Leigh collected $86,000 in cash from customers during 2020 and paid $28,000 cash for operating expenses in 2020. Leigh determined the 2020 beginning and ending balances for the following accounts.

As of December 31	2019	2020
Accounts receivable	$4,900	$6,500
Deferred revenue	2,200	1,800
Prepaid operating expenses	4,900	7,500
Accrued liabilities	5,000	6,000

Required

a. Convert cash collected from customers to revenue on an accrual basis.
b. Convert cash paid for operating expense to operating expenses on an accrual basis.

App—Exercise 2-75
Converting from Cash-Basis to Accrual-Basis Accounting **LO8**

Brooks Corp. maintains its accounting records on a cash basis during the year. Brooks converts its information to an accrual basis at year-end. The following information is available for Brooks for 2020.

As of December 31	2019	2020
Accounts receivable	$68,000	$72,000
Deferred revenue	8,800	7,000
Accrued liabilities	16,000	16,500
Prepaid lease expense	6,200	4,500

For Year Ended December 31	2020
Cash receipts from customers	$612,000
Cash paid for operating expenses	480,000
Depreciation expense	50,000

Required

Calculate net income on an accrual basis for Brooks Corp. for 2020.

App—Exercise 2-76
Preparing Reversing Entries **LO9**

On December 31, 2020, Nutra Corp made the following adjusting entries.

	Account	Debit	Credit
1.	Salaries Expense	32,000	
	Salaries Payable		32,000
2.	Bad Debt Expense	2,000	
	Allowance for Doubtful Accounts		2,000
3.	Income Tax Expense	48,000	
	Income Tax Payable		48,000
4.	Depreciation Expense	100,000	
	Accumulated Depreciation		100,000

Required

a. Prepare reversing entries as of January 1, 2021, for items 1 through 4 that are appropriate.
b. For each adjusting entry, explain how we decide whether to reverse it or not.

App—Exercise 2-77
Preparing Reversing Entries **LO9**

At the end of its annual accounting period on December 31, 2020, Ran Corp. made the following adjusting entries.

	Account	Debit	Credit
1.	Property Tax Expense	400	
	Property Taxes Payable		400
	(These are paid once each year.)		
2.	Supplies	2,000	
	Supplies Expense		2,000
	(Supplies are debited to supplies expense when purchased.)		
3.	Patent Amortization Expense	1,000	
	Patents		1,000
4.	Warranty Expense	300	
	Warranty Liability		300
5.	Salaries Expense	4,500	
	Salaries Payable		4,500

Required

a. Prepare the applicable reversing entries that could be made on January 1, 2021.
b. Explain, for each adjusting entry, how you decided whether to reverse it or not.

App—Exercise 2-78
Completing an Accounting Worksheet **LO10**
Hint: See Demo 2-10

Olivia Inc.'s adjusted trial balance on June 30, 2020, is included on the following accounting worksheet.

Worksheet for Month Ended June 30, 2020

Account	Adjusted Trial Balance		Income Statement		Balance Sheet	
	Debit	Credit	Debit	Credit	Debit	Credit
Cash	$ 3,000					
Accounts receivable	3,100					
Prepaid insurance	1,000					
Equipment	20,000					
Accumulated depreciation		$ 5,000				
Accounts payable		3,500				
Salaries payable		1,000				
Common stock		15,000				
Service revenue		9,000				
Salaries expense	2,500					
Lease expense	800					
Insurance expense	600					
Depreciation expense	2,500					
Totals	$33,500	$33,500				
Net income						
Totals						

Required

Complete the right-most 4 columns of the accounting worksheet.

App—Exercise 2-79
Completing an Accounting Worksheet **LO10**
Hint: See Demo 2-10

The unadjusted trial balance is included on the following worksheet for Mastery Financial Inc.

Worksheet for the Year Ended December 31, 2020

Account	Unadjusted Trial Balance		Adjusting Entries		Adjusted Trial Balance		Income Statement		Balance Sheet	
	Debit	Credit	Debit	Credit	Debit	Credit	Debit	Credit	Debit	Credit
Cash	$ 8,000									
Accounts receivable	12,000									
Supplies	6,500									
Equipment	34,100									
Accumulated depreciation		$ 3,400								
Accounts payable		4,200								
Salaries payable										
Common stock		40,000								
Retained earnings		5,000								
Service revenue		40,000								
Salaries expense	20,000									
Lease expense	9,600									
Insurance expense	2,400									
Supplies expense										
Depreciation expense										
Totals	$92,600	$92,600								
Net income										
Totals										

Additional information for accounting adjustments

1. Supplies still available at December 31, 2020, total $5,000.
2. Depreciation expense for the year for equipment was $3,400.
3. Unbilled revenue for services performed was $2,000 as of December 31, 2020.
4. Salaries incurred but unpaid were $2,400 on December 31, 2020.

Required

Complete the right-most 8 columns of the accounting worksheet.

Appendix—Problems

App—Problem 2-80
Cash-Basis and Accrual-Basis Statements **LO8**

Anchor Corp. compiled the following information related to its operations for the year 2020.

As of December 31	2019	2020
Accounts receivable	$12,000	$12,500
Deferred revenue	5,000	4,800
Salaries payable.	1,200	1,800
Prepaid insurance.	2,900	1,300
Accrued liabilities	12,000	11,000

For Year Ended December 31	2020
Cash receipts from services performed	$100,000
Cash paid to employees for salaries	65,000
Cash paid for insurance	3,000
Cash paid for other operating expenses.	30,000
Cash paid for equipment, 10-year useful life . . .	60,000

Required

a. Prepare a cash-based statement of income.

b. Prepare an accrual-based statement of income.

App—Problem 2-81
Preparing Reversing Entries **LO9**

Rona Company is a calendar-year manufacturer. Rona is reviewing the following transactions for possible adjusting entries at December 31, 2020.

1. One of Rona Company's liabilities is a 12%, $40,000 long-term note payable, which requires interest to be paid each March 1 and September 1.
2. Rona Company owns a $20,000, 10% bond, which it purchased at face value and which pays interest each August 1 and February 1.
3. Rona Company performed and completed services for a customer in December for a $12,000 total fee. The customer was not billed and did not remit payment in the current year. The customer has a strong credit rating.
4. Depreciation of $30,000 is to be recorded.
5. Salaries totaling $15,000 were earned but not paid or recorded at year-end. The first payroll in 2021 is expected to total $45,000.
6. Rona paid $4,800 cash for a one-year insurance policy on September 1, 2020. Rona records the full amount on September 1 as insurance expense.

Required

For each of the 6 items described above, provide the following:

a. December 31, 2020, adjusting entry.

b. January 1, 2021, reversing entry (if a reversing entry is not appropriate, explain why).

c. Entry for the associated transaction to occur in 2021 if one is expected.

App—Problem 2-82
Preparing an Accounting Worksheet and Financial Statements **LO10**

Data Corp. is currently completing the end-of-the-period accounting process. At December 31, 2020, the following unadjusted trial balance was developed from its general ledger.

Account	Debit	Credit
Cash.	$ 60,260	
Accounts receivable	38,000	
Allowance for doubtful accounts.		$ 2,000
Inventory (perpetual inventory system)	105,000	
Supplies	900	
Long-term note receivable, 14%.	12,000	
Equipment	180,000	
Accumulated depreciation, equipment		64,000
Patent.	8,400	
Interest receivable		
Accounts payable.		23,000
Interest payable		
Income taxes payable.		
Property taxes payable.		
Deferred revenue		
Mortgage payable, 12%		60,000
Common stock, par $10		115,000
Retained earnings		32,440
Sales.		700,000

continued

continued from previous page

Account	Debit	Credit
Investment revenue		1,120
Training revenue		3,000
Cost of goods sold	380,000	
Selling expenses	164,400	
General and administrative expenses	55,000	
Interest expense	6,600	
Income tax expense		
Gain on sale		10,000

Additional data for adjustments and other purposes

1. The company estimates an increase in the allowance for doubtful accounts of $500 is required to recognize accounts receivable of $38,000 at net realizable value. Classify bad debt expense as a selling expense.
2. Interest on the long-term note receivable was last collected on August 31, 2020.
3. Estimated useful life of the equipment is 10 years; residual value is $20,000. Allocate 10% of depreciation expense to general and administrative expense and the balance to selling expenses to reflect proportionate use. Use straight-line depreciation.
4. Estimated remaining economic life of the patent is 14 years (from January 1, 2020) with no residual value. Use straight-line amortization and classify as selling expense (as it is used in sales promotion).
5. Interest on the mortgage payable was last paid on November 30, 2020.
6. On June 1, 2020, the company entered into a contract with a customer to provide training for its product for one year and collected $3,000 cash payment in advance for the year; the entire amount was credited to training revenue on this date.
7. On December 31, 2020, the company received a bill for its calendar year 2020 property taxes of $1,300. The payment is due February 15, 2021. Assume that it will be paid on that date and classify it as a general and administrative expense.
8. Supplies remaining at December 31, 2020, amount to $300; classify supplies used as a selling expense.
9. Accrued income tax expense is $35,132, which has not been recorded.

Required

a. Enter the above unadjusted trial balance on a worksheet.
b. Enter the adjusting entries and complete the worksheet.
c. Prepare the income statement for 2020 and the balance sheet at December 31, 2020.

Answers to Review Exercises

Review 2-1

1.

Assets	=	Liabilities	+	Stockholders' Equity
Accounts receivable				Tax Service Revenue
$1,000	=	$0	+	$1,000

2.

Assets	=	Liabilities	+	Stockholders' Equity
		Accounts Payable		Utilities Expense
$0	=	$850	+	$(850)

3.

Assets	=	Liabilities	+	Stockholders' Equity
Cash		Dividends Payable		
$(50,000)	=	$(50,000)	+	$0

4.

Assets	=	Liabilities	+	Stockholders' Equity
Equipment		Note Payable		
$25,000	=	$25,000	+	$0

5.

Assets	=	Liabilities	+	Stockholders' Equity
Prepaid insurance				
$2,200		$0		$0
Cash	=		+	
$(2,200)				

6.

Assets	=	Liabilities	+	Stockholders' Equity
Supplies				
$8,000				
Cash				
$(8,000)	=	$0	+	$0

7.

Assets	=	Liabilities	+	Stockholders' Equity
Cash				Salaries Expense
$(3,000)	=	$0	+	$(3,000)

Review 2-2

Part One

Account	Account No.	Account Type: Asset	Liability	Stockholders' Equity	Normal Balance: Debit	Credit
Cash	100	✔			✔	
Accounts receivable	104	✔			✔	
Supplies	107	✔			✔	
Prepaid insurance	108	✔			✔	
Equipment	160	✔			✔	
Accounts payable	202		✔			✔
Deferred service revenue	208		✔			✔
Note payable	240		✔			✔
Common stock	302			✔		✔
Consulting revenue	402			✔		✔
Salaries expense	515			✔	✔	
Lease expense	520			✔	✔	

Review 2-2

Part Two

June 1—To record sale of common stock

Assets +40,000 = Liabilities + Equity +40,000

1.	June 1	Cash	100	40,000	
		Common Stock	302		40,000

June 2—To record purchase of equipment with a note

Assets +30,000 = Liabilities +30,000 + Equity

2.	June 2	Equipment	160	30,000	
		Note Payable	240		30,000

June 3—To record purchase of supplies on account

Assets +5,000 = Liabilities +5,000 + Equity

3.	June 3	Supplies	107	5,000	
		Accounts Payable	202		5,000

June 4—To record service revenue on account

Assets +2,000 = Liabilities + Equity +2,000

4.	June 4	Accounts Receivable	104	2,000	
		Consulting Revenue	402		2,000

5. No Entry Required

June 6—To record prepaid insurance

6.	June 6	Prepaid Insurance	108	6,000	
		Cash	100		6,000

Assets = Liabilities + Equity
+6,000
−6,000

June 13—To record payment on account

7.	June 13	Accounts Payable	202	2,500	
		Cash	100		2,500

Assets = Liabilities + Equity
−2,500 −2,500

June 15—To record payment in advance of performance obligation

8.	June 15	Cash	100	1,200	
		Deferred Service Revenue	208		1,200

Assets = Liabilities + Equity
+1,200 +1,200

June 20—To record cash receipt for performance obligation

9.	June 20	Cash	100	5,000	
		Consulting Revenue	402		5,000

Assets = Liabilities + Equity
+5,000 +5,000

June 30—To record salaries paid

10.	June 30	Salaries Expense	515	3,500	
		Cash	100		3,500

Assets = Liabilities + Equity
−3,500 −3,500

June 30—To record rent paid

11.	June 30	Lease Expense	520	4,500	
		Cash	100		4,500

Assets = Liabilities + Equity
−4,500 −4,500

Assets = Liabilities + Stockholders' Equity

Assets

Cash			100
June 1	40,000	6,000	June 6
June 15	1,200	2,500	June 13
June 20	5,000	3,500	June 30
		4,500	June 30
June 30 Bal.	29,700		

Accounts Receivable			104
June 4	2,000		
June 30 Bal.	2,000		

Supplies			107
June 3	5,000		
June 30 Bal.	5,000		

Prepaid Insurance			108
June 6	6,000		
June 30 Bal.	6,000		

Equipment			160
June 2	30,000		
June 30 Bal.	30,000		

Liabilities

Accounts Payable			202
June 13	2,500	5,000	June 3
		2,500	June 30 Bal.

Deferred Service Revenue			208
		1,200	June 15
		1,200	June 30 Bal.

Note Payable			240
		30,000	June 2
		30,000	June 30 Bal.

Stockholders' Equity

Common Stock			302
		40,000	June 1
		40,000	June 30 Bal.

Revenue

Consulting Revenue			402
		2,000	June 4
		5,000	June 20
		7,000	June 30 Bal.

Expense

Salaries Expense			515
June 30	3,500		
June 30 Bal.	3,500		

Lease Expense			520
June 30	4,500		
June 30 Bal.	4,500		

Review 2-3

Unadjusted Trial Balance
June 30, 2020

Acct. No.	Description	Debit	Credit
100	Cash	$29,700	
104	Accounts receivable	2,000	
107	Supplies	5,000	
108	Prepaid insurance	6,000	
160	Equipment	30,000	
202	Accounts payable		$ 2,500
208	Deferred service revenue		1,200
240	Note payable		30,000
302	Common stock		40,000
402	Consulting revenue		7,000
515	Salaries expense	3,500	
520	Lease expense	4,500	
	Totals	$80,700	$80,700

Review 2-4

Assets = Liabilities + Equity
−1,000 −1,000

RECORD IN JOURNAL

June 30, 2020—To adjust prepaid insurance

	Date	Account	Ref.	Debit	Credit
1.	June 30	Insurance Expense ($6,000/6)	526	$1,000	
		Prepaid Insurance	108		$1,000

POST TO LEDGER

Insurance Expense	526		
June 30	1,000		
June 30 Bal.	1,000		

Prepaid Insurance	108		
June 6	6,000	1,000	June 30
June 30 Bal.	5,000		

Assets = Liabilities + Equity
−500 −500

RECORD IN JOURNAL

June 30, 2020—To record depreciation expense

	Date	Account	Ref.	Debit	Credit
2.	June 30	Depreciation Expense [($30,000/5)/12]	528	500	
		Accumulated Depreciation	162		500

POST TO LEDGER

Depreciation Expense	528		
June 30	500		
June 30 Bal.	500		

Accumulated Depreciation	162		
		500	June 30
		500	June 30 Bal.

Assets = Liabilities + Equity
−500 +500

RECORD IN JOURNAL

June 30, 2020—To record partial satisfaction of performance obligation

	Date	Account	Ref.	Debit	Credit
3.	June 30	Deferred Service Revenue	208	500	
		Consulting Revenue	402		500

POST TO LEDGER

Deferred Service Revenue	208		
June 30	500	1,200	June 15
		700	June 30 Bal.

Consulting Revenue	402		
		2,000	June 4
		5,000	June 20
		500	June 30
		7,500	June 30 Bal.

RECORD IN JOURNAL

June 30, 2020—To record interest expense

4.	June 30	Interest Expense ($30,000 × 0.07/12)	542	175	
		Interest Payable	210		175

Assets	= Liabilities	+ Equity
	+175	−175

POST TO LEDGER

Interest Expense		542	
June 30	175		
June 30 Bal.	175		

Interest Payable		210	
		175	June 30
		175	June 30 Bal.

RECORD IN JOURNAL

June 30, 2020—To record utilities expense

5.	June 30	Utilities Expense	540	1,100	
		Utilities Payable	215		1,100

Assets	= Liabilities	+ Equity
	+1,100	−1,100

POST TO LEDGER

Utilities Expense		540	
June 30	1,100		
June 30 Bal.	1,100		

Utilities Payable		215	
		1,100	June 30
		1,100	June 30 Bal.

RECORD IN JOURNAL

June 30, 2020—To record accounts receivable

6.	June 30	Accounts Receivable	104	750	
		Consulting Revenue	402		750

Assets	= Liabilities	+ Equity
+750		+750

POST TO LEDGER

Accounts Receivable		104	
June 4	2,000		
June 30	750		
June 30 Bal.	2,750		

Consulting Revenue		402	
		2,000	June 4
		5,000	June 20
		500	June 30
		750	June 30
		8,250	June 30 Bal.

RECORD IN JOURNAL

June 30, 2020—To record supplies expense

7.	June 30	Supplies Expense	541	1,700	
		Supplies ($5,000 − $3,300)	107		1,700

Assets	= Liabilities	+ Equity
−1,700		−1,700

POST TO LEDGER

Supplies Expense		541	
June 30	1,700		
June 30 Bal.	1,700		

Supplies		107	
June 3	5,000	1,700	June 30
June 30 Bal.	3,300		

Review 2-5

Adjusted Trial Balance
June 30, 2020

Acct. No.	Description	Debit	Credit
100	Cash	$29,700	
104	Accounts receivable	2,750	
107	Supplies	3,300	
108	Prepaid insurance	5,000	
160	Equipment	30,000	
162	Accumulated depreciation		$ 500
202	Accounts payable		2,500
208	Deferred service revenue		700
210	Interest payable		175
215	Utilities payable		1,100
240	Note payable		30,000
302	Common stock		40,000
402	Consulting revenue		8,250
515	Salaries expense	3,500	
520	Lease expense	4,500	
526	Insurance expense	1,000	
528	Depreciation expense	500	
540	Utilities expense	1,100	
541	Supplies expense	1,700	
542	Interest expense	175	
	Totals	$83,225	$83,225

Review 2-6

KPMB Consulting Inc.
Income Statement
For Month Ended June 30, 2020

Revenues		
Consulting revenue		$ 8,250
Expenses		
Salaries expense	$3,500	
Lease expense	4,500	
Insurance expense	1,000	
Depreciation expense	500	
Utilities expense	1,100	
Supplies expense	1,700	
Interest expense	175	
Total operating expenses		12,475
Net Loss		$ (4,225)

KPMB Consulting Inc.
Statement of Stockholders' Equity
For Month Ended June 30, 2020

	Common Stock	Retained Earnings	Total Stockholders' Equity
Balance, June 1, 2020	$ 0	$ 0	$ 0
Issuance of common stock	40,000		40,000
Net loss		(4,225)	(4,225)
Less: dividends			0
Balance, June 30, 2020	$40,000	$(4,225)	$35,775

KPMB Consulting Inc.
Balance Sheet
June 30, 2020

Assets			Liabilities	
Cash		$29,700	Accounts payable	$ 2,500
Accounts receivable		2,750	Deferred service revenue	700
Supplies		3,300	Interest payable	175
Prepaid insurance		5,000	Utilities payable	1,100
Equipment	$30,000		Note payable	30,000
Less: Accumulated depreciation	(500)	29,500	Total liabilities	34,475
			Stockholders' Equity	
			Common stock	40,000
			Retained earnings	(4,225)
			Total stockholders' equity	35,775
Total assets		$70,250	Total Liabilities and Stockholders' Equity	$70,250

Review 2-7

June 30, 2020—To close revenue accounts to income summary

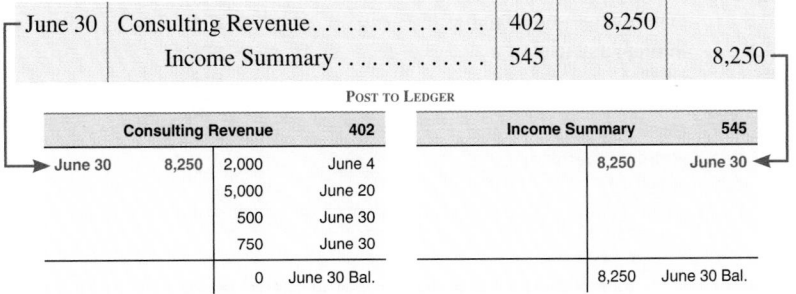

June 30	Consulting Revenue	402	8,250	
	Income Summary	545		8,250

Assets = Liabilities + Equity
−8,250
−8,250

POST TO LEDGER

Consulting Revenue			402
June 30	8,250	2,000	June 4
		5,000	June 20
		500	June 30
		750	June 30
		0	June 30 Bal.

Income Summary			545
		8,250	June 30
		8,250	June 30 Bal.

June 30, 2020—To close expense accounts to income summary

June 30	Income Summary	545	12,475	
	Salaries Expense	515		3,500
	Lease Expense	520		4,500
	Insurance Expense	526		1,000
	Depreciation Expense	528		500
	Utilities Expense	540		1,100
	Supplies Expense	541		1,700
	Interest Expense	542		175

Assets = Liabilities + Equity
−12,475
+12,475

POST TO LEDGER

Income Summary			545
June 30	12,475	8,250	June 30
June 30 Bal.	4,225		

Insurance Expense			526
June 30	1,000	1,000	June 30
June 30 Bal.	0		

Supplies Expense			541
June 30	1,700	1,700	June 30
June 30 Bal.	0		

Salaries Expense			515
June 30	3,500	3,500	June 30
June 30 Bal.	0		

Depreciation Expense			528
June 30	500	500	June 30
June 30 Bal.	0		

Interest Expense			542
June 30	175	175	June 30
June 30 Bal.	0		

Lease Expense			520
June 30	4,500	4,500	June 30
June 30 Bal.	0		

Utilities Expense			540
June 30	1,100	1,100	June 30
June 30 Bal.	0		

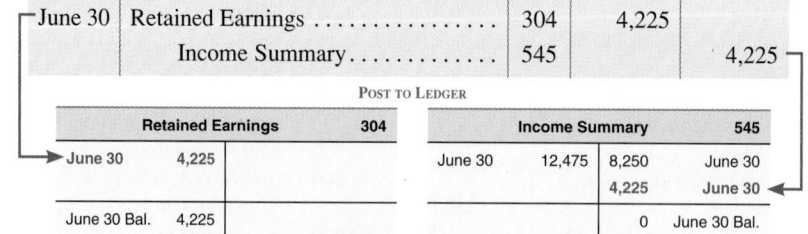

Assets	= Liabilities +	Equity
		−4,225
		+4,225

June 30, 2020—To close income summary to retained earnings

June 30	Retained Earnings	304	4,225	
	Income Summary.	545		4,225

POST TO LEDGER

Retained Earnings			304
June 30	4,225		
June 30 Bal.	4,225		

Income Summary			545
June 30	12,475	8,250	June 30
		4,225	June 30
		0	June 30 Bal.

Post-Closing Trial Balance
June 30, 2020

Acct. No.	Description	Debit	Credit
100	Cash.	$29,700	
104	Accounts receivable	2,750	
107	Supplies	3,300	
108	Prepaid insurance.	5,000	
160	Equipment	30,000	
162	Accumulated depreciation . . .		$ 500
202	Accounts payable.		2,500
208	Deferred service revenue		700
210	Interest payable		175
215	Utilities payable		1,100
240	Note payable		30,000
302	Common stock		40,000
304	Retained earnings	4,225	
	Totals	$74,975	$74,975

Review 2-8

Cash receipts from customers (cash-basis)	$60,000
Subtract beginning accounts receivable (asset). . . .	(6,600)
Add ending accounts receivable (asset).	8,800
Add beginning deferred revenue (liability)	2,500
Subtract ending deferred revenue (liability)	(2,400)
Revenue (accrual-basis)	$62,300

Cash paid for operating expenses (cash-basis) . . .	$38,000
Add beginning prepaid expense (asset).	1,200
Subtract ending prepaid expense (asset).	(1,000)
Subtract beginning accrued liabilities (liability)	(3,900)
Add ending accrued liabilities (liability).	4,400
Operating expenses (accrual-basis).	$38,700

Net income	
Revenue.	$62,300
Operating expenses	(38,700)
Depreciation expense.	(5,000)
Net income (accrual-basis).	$18,600

Review 2-9

1.

Salaries Payable	4,500	
Salaries Expense		4,500

Salaries Payable: 4,500 (debit) | Bal. 4,500 (credit)

Salaries Expense: | 4,500 (credit)

Assets = Liabilities + Equity
−4,500 +4,500

2.

Insurance Expense	5,000	
Prepaid Insurance.		5,000

Insur Expense: 5,000 (debit) |

Prepaid Insur: Bal. 5,000 (debit) | 5,000 (credit)

Assets = Liabilities + Equity
−5,000 −5,000

3. No reversing entry made.
4. No reversing entry made.
5.

Payroll Taxes Payable	2,800	
Payroll Tax Expense.		2,800

Payroll Tax Pay: 2,800 (debit) | Bal. 2,800 (credit)

Payroll Tax Exp: | 2,800 (credit)

Assets = Liabilities + Equity
−2,800 +2,800

Review 2-10

KPMB Consulting Inc.
Worksheet for Month Ended June 30, 2020

Acct. No.	Description	Unadjusted Trial Balance		Adjusting Entries		Adjusted Trial Balance		Income Statement		Balance Sheet	
		Debit	Credit	Debit	Credit	Debit	Credit	Debit	Credit	Debit	Credit
100	Cash.	$29,700				$29,700				$29,700	
104	Accounts receivable	2,000		$ 750		2,750				2,750	
107	Supplies	5,000			$1,700	3,300				3,300	
108	Prepaid insurance.	6,000			1,000	5,000				5,000	
160	Equipment	30,000				30,000				30,000	
162	Accumulated depreciation . . .				500		$ 500				$ 500
202	Accounts payable		$ 2,500				2,500				2,500
208	Deferred service revenue		1,200	500			700				700
210	Interest payable				175		175				175
215	Utilities payable				1,100		1,100				1,100
240	Note payable		30,000				30,000				30,000
302	Common stock		40,000				40,000				40,000
304	Retained earnings										
402	Consulting revenue.		7,000		1,250		8,250		$8,250		
515	Salaries expense	3,500				3,500		$ 3,500			
520	Lease expense	4,500				4,500		4,500			
526	Insurance expense			1,000		1,000		1,000			
528	Depreciation expense.			500		500		500			
540	Utilities expense			1,100		1,100		1,100			
541	Supplies expense			1,700		1,700		1,700			
542	Interest expense			175		175		175			
	Totals	$80,700	$80,700	$5,725	$5,725	$83,225	$83,225	12,475	8,250	70,750	74,975
	Net income							(4,225)			(4,225)
	Totals							$ 8,250	$8,250	$70,750	$70,750

3 Income Statement and Comprehensive Income

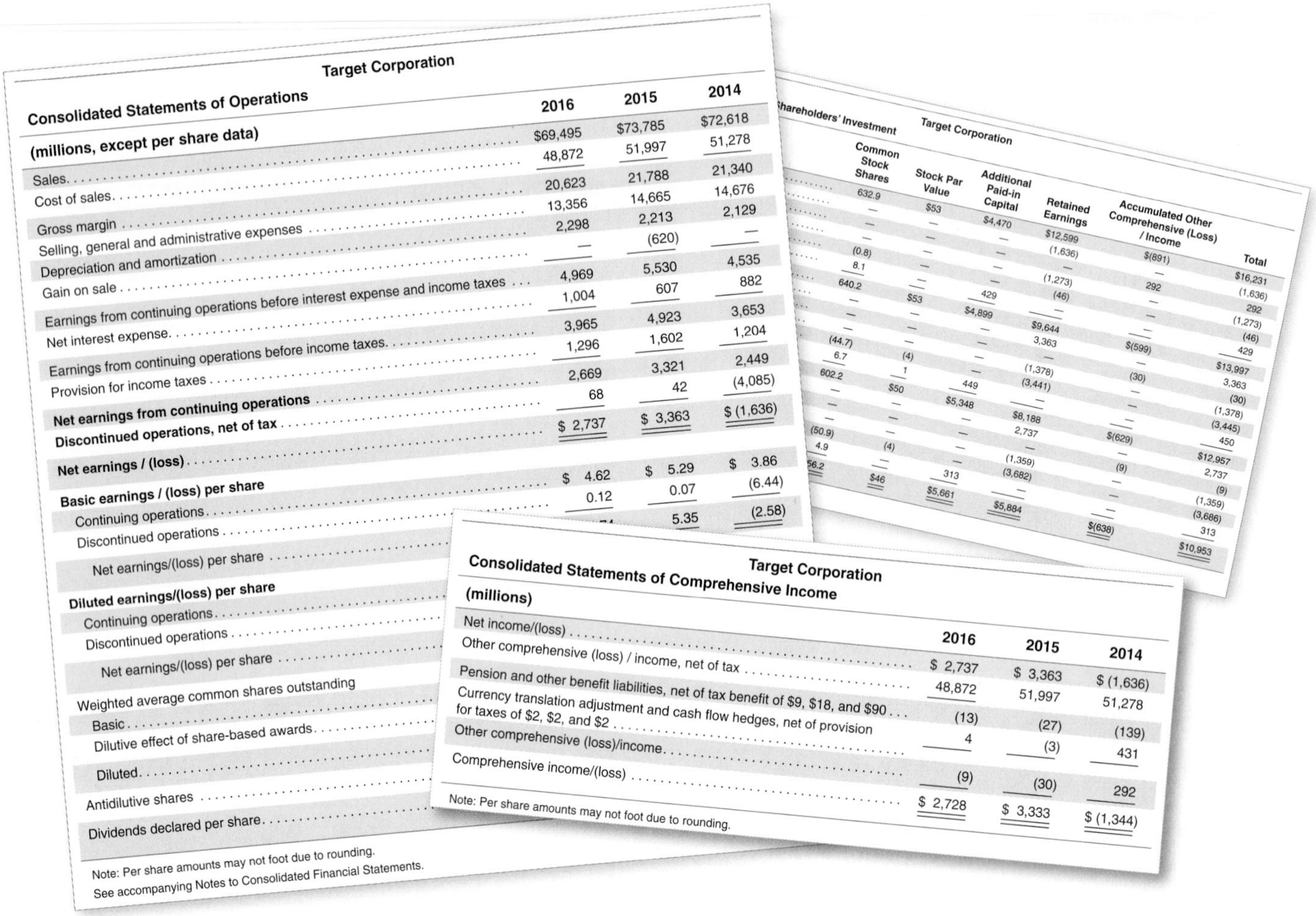

Target Corporation

Consolidated Statements of Operations

(millions, except per share data)	2016	2015	2014
Sales	$69,495	$73,785	$72,618
Cost of sales	48,872	51,997	51,278
Gross margin	20,623	21,788	21,340
Selling, general and administrative expenses	13,356	14,665	14,676
Depreciation and amortization	2,298	2,213	2,129
Gain on sale	—	(620)	—
Earnings from continuing operations before interest expense and income taxes	4,969	5,530	4,535
Net interest expense	1,004	607	882
Earnings from continuing operations before income taxes	3,965	4,923	3,653
Provision for income taxes	1,296	1,602	1,204
Net earnings from continuing operations	2,669	3,321	2,449
Discontinued operations, net of tax	68	42	(4,085)
Net earnings / (loss)	$ 2,737	$ 3,363	$ (1,636)
Basic earnings / (loss) per share			
Continuing operations	$ 4.62	$ 5.29	$ 3.86
Discontinued operations	0.12	0.07	(6.44)
Net earnings/(loss) per share		5.35	(2.58)
Diluted earnings/(loss) per share			
Continuing operations			
Discontinued operations			
Net earnings/(loss) per share			
Weighted average common shares outstanding			
Basic			
Dilutive effect of share-based awards			
Diluted			
Antidilutive shares			
Dividends declared per share			

Note: Per share amounts may not foot due to rounding.
See accompanying Notes to Consolidated Financial Statements.

Target Corporation

Consolidated Statements of Comprehensive Income

(millions)	2016	2015	2014
Net income/(loss)	$ 2,737	$ 3,363	$ (1,636)
Other comprehensive (loss) / income, net of tax	48,872	51,997	51,278
Pension and other benefit liabilities, net of tax benefit of $9, $18, and $90	(13)	(27)	(139)
Currency translation adjustment and cash flow hedges, net of provision for taxes of $2, $2, and $2	4	(3)	431
Other comprehensive (loss)/income	(9)	(30)	292
Comprehensive income/(loss)	$ 2,728	$ 3,333	$ (1,344)

Note: Per share amounts may not foot due to rounding.

Chapter Preview

This chapter explains *what* information is in the income statement and *how* this information is classified. Management often makes determinations that affect income presentation such as whether to classify a business component as a discontinued operation. Income statement classifications affect both the *quality of earnings* and a financial statement user's ability to predict the amounts, timing, and uncertainty of future cash flows using reported income. We begin by reviewing the format of the income statement, including the presentation of unusual items, discontinued business components, and earnings per share. We then review the format and composition of comprehensive income and stockholders' equity statements. We conclude by discussing the reporting of changes in accounting principles and accounting estimates, as well as the correction of errors.

Action Plan

LO	Topic/Subtopic	Page	Demos	Reviews	Assignments
LO 3–1	**Prepare an income statement using single-step and multiple-step formats, focusing on income from continuing operations** Operating :: Nonoperating :: Income Tax :: Net Income	3-3	D3-1	R3-1	18, 19, 20, 31, 32, 33, 34, 35, 36, 37, 38, 39, 40, 50, 51, 52, 60, 61, 62, 63, 64, 65, 66, 68
LO 3–2	**Report the impact of unusual and infrequent items** Unusual :: Infrequent :: Income from Continuing Operations :: Disclosure	3-7	D3-2	R3-2	21, 39, 50, 53, 54, 55, 60, 61, 62, 64
LO 3–3	**Prepare an income statement to include discontinued operations** Business Component :: Sold or Held for Sale :: Strategic Shift :: Intraperiod Tax Allocation	3-9	D3-3A D3-3B	R3-3	22, 23, 24, 41, 42, 43, 44, 45, 50, 52, 56, 60, 61, 64, 67
LO 3–4	**Disclose earnings per share on the income statement** Net Income :: Preferred Dividends :: Weighted Average Common Shares :: Earnings Per Share	3-15	D3-4A D3-4B	R3-4	24, 25, 33, 34, 35, 36, 38, 42, 44, 45, 50, 51, 52, 54, 55, 60, 61, 62, 63, 69
LO 3–5	**Report other comprehensive income** Net Income :: Other Comprehensive Income :: Comprehensive Income :: Single or Separate Statements	3-18	D3-5	R3-5	26, 38, 40, 46, 50, 57, 61, 62, 68, 69, 70
LO 3–6	**Describe the statement of stockholders' equity** Common Stock :: Retained Earnings :: Accumulated Other Comprehensive Income :: Separate Retained Earnings Statement	3-21	D3-6	R3-6	27, 37, 40, 47, 50, 54, 57, 62, 66
LO 3–7	**Report changes in accounting estimate, changes in accounting principle, and error corrections** Prospective Treatment :: Retrospective Treatment :: Modified Retrospective Treatment :: Restatement	3-22	D3-7A D3-7B D3-7C	R3-7	28, 29, 30, 47, 48, 49, 50, 58, 59, 60, 64, 68
LO 3-8	**APPENDIX 3A—Describe interim financial reporting** Discrete View :: Integral-Part View :: Quarterly Reporting	3-30	D3-8	R3-8	71, 72, 73, 74, 75, 76, 77

LO 3-1 Prepare an income statement using single-step and multiple-step formats, focusing on income from continuing operations

LO 3-1 Overview

Income Statement Formats

Single-step format
- Revenues and gains less expenses and losses
- No distinction between operating and nonoperating items

Multiple-step format
- Typically includes subtotals: gross profit and operating income
- Operating and nonoperating items reported separately

The **income statement** reports revenues, gains, expenses, and losses of a company *for a specified period of time.* (See Exhibit 1-15 in Chapter 1 to review definitions of these financial statement elements.) The income statement is the primary source of information on a company's current operating performance. Investors, lenders, analysts, and others utilize this and other information for predicting the amount, timing, and uncertainty of the company's future income and cash flows. (The income statement is also called a statement of income, statement of earnings, statement of operations, and profit and loss statement.)

Income from continuing operations specifies the revenues, gains, expenses, and losses associated with the parts of a company that are expected to continue into the future. In contrast, **income (loss) from discontinued operations** (operations that have been disposed of or are held for sale) are reported in a separate section and are addressed later in the chapter.

While the accounting standards include a definition of income from continuing operations, the standards do not specify its format.

ASC Glossary: **Income from Continuing Operations:** Income after applicable income taxes but excluding the results of discontinued operations, the cumulative effect of accounting changes, translation adjustments, purchasing power gains and losses on monetary items, and increases and decreases in the current cost or lower recoverable amount of nonmonetary assets and liabilities.

Income from continuing operations is made up of operating items, nonoperating items, and income tax (See **Exhibit 3-1**). The majority of companies separate operating activities from nonoperating activities when presenting financial information in an income statement.

EXPANDING YOUR KNOWLEDGE — Usefulness and Limitations of an Income Statement

Investors and creditors use reported earnings in different ways to assess cash flow prospects.

- **Performance evaluation** Income components are used to assess a company's performance relative to prior results, expectations, industry and competitor results.
- **Future earning prediction** The income statement provides a basis for predicting future results, with special emphasis on differentiating recurring and nonrecurring amounts.
- **Risk assessment** Income results provide a basis for a financial statement user to assess risk about predicting future financial results.

Financial statement users are limited by a number of factors inherent in the reporting process.

- **Estimates and judgment** Measurements in financial statements commonly involve estimates, classifications, summarizations, judgments, and allocations.
- **Selection of accounting methods** Income components are impacted by accounting methods used. Explanations of underlying assumptions or methods better enable one to compare results across companies.
- **Other sources of information** Financial statement users must rely on additional information in analyzing financial statements such as economic indicators and analyst expectations. Also, some items are omitted from the income statement because they cannot be reliably measured, such as internally generated goodwill and investments in human capital.

RALPH LAUREN; U.S. BANCORP

Real World—OPERATING INCOME VS. NONOPERATING INCOME

RALPH LAUREN [RL]
U.S. BANCORP [USB]

What is considered *operating income* for one company may be considered *nonoperating income* for another. Consider interest revenue and interest expense. For **Ralph Lauren Corporation**, Interest expense and Interest and other income, net are classified in its income statement as nonoperating. For **U.S. Bancorp**, Total interest income and Total interest expense are the first two items on its income statement as they relate to its primary operations.

EXHIBIT 3-1 Items Included in Income from Continuing Operations

Component	Description
Operating Items	Revenues and expenses of a company's primary or major operations.*
Revenues	▪ Sales: Main source of revenue, reported net of discounts, returns, and allowances.
Expenses	▪ Cost of goods sold: Direct cost of goods sold in generating revenues. ▪ Selling expenses: Expenses incurred by the company in its efforts to generate revenues. Examples include: • Marketing expense • Delivery expense • Promotional materials expense • Vehicle expense • Advertising expense • Sales salaries expense ▪ General and administrative expenses: Expenses incurred by the company to maintain its operations that are not directly related to production of goods and services. Examples include: • Administrative salaries and benefit expense • Bonus expense • Insurance expense • Legal expense • Utilities expense • Depreciation on corporate office ▪ Other operating expenses: Items management feels are important to identify separately such as the following examples: restructuring costs, research and development costs, and amortization of intangible assets.
Nonoperating Items	▪ Revenue and expense items that are not components of the company's primary operations but are related to secondary or auxiliary activities. ▪ Gains and losses or changes in equity resulting from peripheral transactions of an entity.
Other revenues and gains	Examples are interest revenue, royalty revenue, dividend revenue, and gains from the sale of investments.
Other expenses and losses	Examples are interest expense, litigation losses, and losses from the sale of investments.
Income Tax	Portion of state and federal income tax expenses applicable to income from continuing operations. This chapter uses a 25% tax rate; which is the 21% federal tax rate plus an estimated 4% allowance for state and local taxes.

*Operating items also include gains or losses on the sale of fixed assets not classified as discontinued operations.

360-10-45-5 A gain or loss recognized . . . on the sale of a long-lived asset (disposal group) that is not a discontinued operation shall be included in income from continuing operations before income taxes in the income statement of a business entity. If a subtotal such as income from operations is presented, it shall include the amounts of those gains or losses.

Income Statement Formats

Although the accounting standards do not require a specific format for the income statement, the income statement items are typically organized in one of two general ways: a multiple-step format or a single-step format. Within these two general formats, companies alter the order of listings or groupings of items in a wide variety of ways.

Multiple-Step Income Statement Format

The **multiple-step format** distinguishes among various operations and activities that affect income. Importantly, operating and nonoperating items are *separated* in the multiple-step format. The multiple-step statement typically presents two subtotals not found on the single-step statement.

- **Gross profit** (or *gross margin*)—Sales revenue less cost of goods sold.
- **Operating income** (or *income from operations*)—Operating revenues less operating expenses.

Single-Step Income Statement Format

The **single-step format** uses only two broad classifications: (1) revenues and gains, and (2) expenses and losses. It is called a single-step statement because only one step is involved in computing and displaying income. Many companies use a single-step format but add a separate section showing the effects of income taxes.

Numerous variations of the single-step format exist. For example, revenue items such as interest income or investment income are sometimes netted against related expenses. The key characteristic of a single-step statement is that only two broad classifications are used in determining income from continuing operations. As a result, there is no priority implied in reporting one revenue or expense item over another revenue or expense item. In **Demo 3-1**, we show both the multiple-step and the single-step income statement presentations.

NIKE Real World—INCOME STATEMENT PRESENTATION

NIKE [NKE]

NIKE Inc. reported the following consolidated statement of income in the multiple-step format in its recent Form 10-K. This is a condensed version of the income statement because it does not provide all of the details for revenues and expenses on the face of its income statement. We see that Nike provides references to where more detailed information is available.

NIKE, INC.
Consolidated Statement of Income (excerpt)
For Year Ended May 31, 2015

$ millions	**2015**
Income from continuing operations	
Revenues	$30,601
Cost of sales	16,534
Gross profit	14,067
Demand creation expense	3,213
Operating overhead expense	6,679
Total selling and administrative expense	9,892
Interest expense (income), net (Notes 6, 7 and 8)	28
Other (income) expenses, net (Note 17)	(58)
Income before income taxes	4,205
Income tax expense (Note 9)	932
Net income	$ 3,273

Demo 3-1 **LO3-1** **Multiple-Step and Single-Step Income Statement Formats**

Demo MBC

The following items are taken from the adjusted trial balance of Kabella Corp., a merchandiser, on December 31, 2020. Prepare an income statement using the multiple-step and the single-step formats for the year ended December 31, 2020. Assume a tax rate of 25%.

Sales revenue	$1,000,000	Loss on sale of bond	$ 1,000
Gain on sale of investment	5,000	Interest revenue	3,000
Cost of goods sold	645,000	Interest expense	5,000
Selling expenses	90,000	Research and development expense	25,000
General and administrative expenses	60,000		

continued

continued from previous page

Solution Multiple-Step Format

KABELLA CORPORATION Income Statement For Year Ended December 31, 2020		
Sales revenue		$1,000,000
Cost of goods sold		645,000
Gross profit		355,000
Operating expenses		
Selling	$90,000	
General and administrative	60,000	
Research and development	25,000	
Total operating expenses		175,000
Operating income		180,000
Other revenues and gains		
Interest revenue	3,000	
Gain on sale of investment	5,000	8,000
Other expenses and losses		
Interest expense	5,000	
Loss on sale of bond	1,000	6,000
Income before income taxes		182,000
Income tax expense ($182,000 × 25%)		45,500
Net income		$ 136,500

Solution Single-Step Format

KABELLA CORPORATION Income Statement For Year Ended December 31, 2020	
Revenues and gains	
Sales revenue	$1,000,000
Interest revenue	3,000
Gain on sale of investment	5,000
Total revenues and gains	1,008,000
Expenses and losses	
Cost of goods sold	645,000
Selling	90,000
General and administrative	60,000
Research and development	25,000
Interest expense	5,000
Loss on sale of bond	1,000
Total expenses and losses	826,000
Income before income taxes	182,000
Income tax expense ($182,000 × 25%)	45,500
Net income	$ 136,500

We see how the multiple-step statement provides a distinction between operating and nonoperating activities while the single-step statement does not. Net income of $136,500 is the same in each statement. The single-step format has the advantage of simplicity and avoids the need to develop labels for subtotals. The multiple-step format is potentially more informative to decision makers because it highlights key items. Retailers, for example, often use a multiple-step format to report gross profit, emphasizing the relation between sales and cost of sales.

Multiple-Step and Single-Step Income Statement Formats LO3-1 REVIEW 3-1

Review MBC

Golden Corp.'s records show the following information at December 31, 2020, which is its accounting year-end.

Sales revenue	$450,000	Interest expense	$ 10,000
Gain on sale of investment	20,000	Loss on sale of patent	3,000
Selling expenses	35,000	Cost of goods sold	300,000
General and administrative expense	65,000		

Part One—Multiple-Step Income Statement

Using the information from Golden Corp., compute the following subtotals that are shown in a *multiple-step income statement.* Assume an income tax rate of 25%.

a. Gross profit
b. Operating income
c. Income before income taxes
d. Income tax expense
e. Net income

continued

continued from previous page

Part Two—Single-Step Income Statement

Compute the following subtotals that are shown in a *single-step income statement* for Golden Corp. Assume an income tax rate of 25%.

a. Total revenues and gains
b. Total expenses and losses
c. Income before income taxes
d. Income tax expense
e. Net income

More Practice: 3-20, 3-32
Solution on p. 3-51.

LO 3-2 Report the impact of unusual and infrequent items

LO 3-2 Overview

Unusual and/or Infrequent Items
- Highly abnormal and/or not expected to recur
- Report separately in income from continuing operations or disclose in notes to financial statements

The quality of earnings impacts the ability of a financial statement user to predict future earnings. Assessing earnings quality requires *judgment* by the financial statement user in determining which income statement items are **permanent** in nature (will likely continue into the future) and which items are **transitory** in nature (will likely *not* continue into the future). GAAP requires companies to highlight material **unusual and/or infrequent items** to assist financial statement users in projecting future earnings. The terms unusual and infrequent are defined in **Exhibit 3-2**.

EXHIBIT 3-2
Unusual and Infrequent Items Defined

Concept	Definition
ASC Glossary **Unusual:**	The underlying event or transaction should possess a high degree of abnormality and be of a type clearly unrelated to, or only incidentally related to, the ordinary and typical activities of the entity, taking into account the environment in which the entity operates
ASC Glossary **Infrequent:**	The underlying event or transaction should be of a type that would not reasonably be expected to recur in the foreseeable future, taking into account the environment in which the entity operates

A material event or transaction that a company considers to be unusual or infrequent (or both) is reported as a separate item in income from continuing operations (illustrated in **Demo 3-2**), or disclosed in the notes to the financial statements. (Earlier standards required items that were both unusual and infrequent to be reported as "extraordinary" items; this classification was eliminated as part of FASB's initiative to reduce the complexity in the standards.) Authoritative guidance on the reporting requirements follow.

> **220-20-45-1** A material event or transaction that an entity considers to be of an unusual nature or of a type that indicates infrequency of occurrence or both shall be reported as a separate component of income from continuing operations. The nature and financial effects of each event or transaction shall be presented as a separate component of income from continuing operations or, alternatively, disclosed in notes to financial statements. Gains or losses of a similar nature that are not individually material shall be aggregated. Such items shall not be reported on the face of the income statement net of income taxes. Similarly, the EPS effects of those items shall not be presented on the face of the income statement.

In determining whether an item is unusual, the company must consider the environment in which it operates. The environment includes factors such as geographical location and industry type. What is unusual for one company may not be unusual for another company because of differences in environments. In a similar way, the environment that a company operates in can affect whether an event or transaction will recur in the foreseeable future. The past occurrence for a particular company of an event provides evidence in assessing whether the event will recur in the foreseeable future.

Examples of items that may be unusual and/or infrequent to a company follow.

- Casualty loss such as property damage from natural forces such as hail or earthquake.
- Impairment of assets that might occur with receivables, inventories, fixed assets, or intangibles.
- Sale of the only investment held in a company's history.
- Restructuring charges due to a company downsize.

A restructuring is defined in the Codification.

ASC Glossary **Restructuring:** A program that is planned and controlled by management, and materially changes either the scope of a business undertaken by an entity, or the manner in which that business is conducted.

A liability for restructuring or exit costs and the associated expense are recorded in the period that the restructuring event occurs, not simply when a plan is in place as described in the standards.

420-10-25-2 A liability for a cost associated with an exit or disposal activity is incurred when the definition of a liability included in FASB Concepts Statement No. 6, Elements of Financial Statements, is met. Only present obligations to others are liabilities under the definition. An obligation becomes a present obligation when a transaction or event occurs that leaves an entity little or no discretion to avoid the future transfer or use of assets to settle the liability. An exit or disposal plan, by itself, does not create a present obligation to others for costs expected to be incurred under the plan; thus, an entity's commitment to an exit or disposal plan, by itself, is not the requisite past transaction or event for recognition of a liability.

CATERPILLAR

Real World—RESTRUCTURING COSTS: UNUSUAL OR INFREQUENT?

CATERPILLAR [CAT]

The following excerpt from a recent 10-K of Caterpillar Inc. describes its restructuring costs as reported in 2015, 2014, and 2013.

> **Restructuring Costs** Restructuring costs for 2015, 2014 and 2013 were $908 million, $441 million and $200 million, respectively. The 2015 restructuring costs . . . were recognized in Other operating (income) expense . . . [and] in Cost of goods sold. Restructuring costs for 2014 and 2013 were recognized in Other operating (income) expense.
>
> The restructuring costs in 2015 were primarily related to several restructuring programs across the company. The restructuring costs in 2014 were primarily related to a reduction in workforce at our Gosselies, Belgium, facility. The most significant charges in 2013 were for the restructuring of management and support functions and the closure or downsizing of several facilities related to our mining business.

Reporting an Unusual and/or Infrequent Item LO3-2 Demo 3-2

Demo MBC

Refer to the information for the multiple-step income statement in **Demo 3-1** with one addition: The company incurred a $20,000 loss due to damages sustained from a hailstorm. Kabella concludes that the amount is material and resulted from an infrequently recurring event. Prepare an income statement in the multiple-step format, separately reporting the $20,000 loss.

continued

continued from previous page

Solution

KABELLA CORPORATION Income Statement For Year Ended December 31, 2020		
Sales revenue		$1,000,000
Cost of goods sold		645,000
Gross profit		355,000
Operating expenses		
Selling	90,000	
General and administrative	60,000	
Research and development	25,000	
Total operating expenses		175,000
Operating income		180,000
Other revenues and gains		
Interest revenue	3,000	
Gain on sale of investment	5,000	8,000
Other expenses and losses		
Interest expense	5,000	
Loss on sale of bond	1,000	
Loss from hailstorm damage	**20,000**	26,000
Income before income taxes		162,000
Income tax expense ($162,000 × 25%)		40,500
Net income		$ 121,500

REVIEW 3-2 **LO3-2** **Reporting an Unusual and/or Infrequent Item**

Review MBC

More Practice: 3-21, 3-39
Solution on p. 3-51.

Refer to the information from Golden Corp. from Review 3-1. Assume that the company also incurred an unusual and infrequent loss of $25,000 for restructuring of its operations. Compute the following subtotals that are shown in a *multiple-step income statement* for Golden Corp. Assume an income tax rate of 25%.

a. Gross profit
b. Operating income
c. Income before income taxes
d. Income tax expense
e. Net income

LO 3-3 Prepare an income statement to include discontinued operations

LO 3-3 Overview

Discontinued Business Component

- Sale of component before balance sheet date
  - Income/loss from discontinued component, net of tax
  - Gain/loss on disposal, net of tax
- Sale of component after balance sheet date
  - Income/loss from discontinued component, net of tax
  - Impairment loss on discontinued component, net of tax

The sale or disposal of a major component of a company's business impacts predictions of future income and cash flow. The income (loss) pertaining to a discontinued business component and the gain (loss) on disposal of this business component are not indicative of future income. To make this distinction, income (loss) from discontinued operations are *separately identified in the income statement (net of tax) and presented after income from continuing operations for all years presented.*

For a disposal to be classified as discontinued operations, (1) a business component is held for sale, sold, or disposed of other than by sale (such as abandoned) *and* (2) the disposal represents a strategic shift. These criteria are further explained in **Exhibit 3-3**.

EXHIBIT 3-3 Criteria for Identifying Discontinued Operations

Criteria	Description
Elimination of a business component	**A business component is held for sale*, sold, or disposed of other than by sale (such as abandoned).** **ASC Glossary** **Component of an Entity:** A component of an entity comprises operations and cash flows that can be clearly distinguished, operationally and for financial reporting purposes, from the rest of the entity. A component of an entity may be a reportable segment or an operating segment, a reporting unit, a subsidiary, or an asset group.
Existence of a strategic shift	**The disposal represents a strategic shift.** **205-20-45-1C** Examples of a strategic shift that has (or will have) a major effect on an entity's operations and financial results could include a disposal of a major geographical area, a major line of business, a major equity method investment, or other major parts of an entity.

* The accounting standards provide criteria on whether an asset is held for sale including the requirement that generally the sale is probable (likely to occur) within the following year. See ASC 360-10-45-9 for the full set of criteria.

To report the results of discontinued operations separately in the income statement, the results are removed from income from continuing operations for all years presented. This helps financial statement users in evaluating separately income from operations that will continue into the future. For example, Spectrum Brands Holdings declared its intent to sell its Global Batteries and Appliances components in 2018. At the date of its fiscal year-end of September 30, 2018, the income (loss) pertaining to its Global Batteries and Appliances components is reported separately in all years presented in the comparative income statements. Even in the previous fiscal years of 2016 and 2017, the income results from the Global Batteries and Appliances components are reclassified into the separate discontinued operations section. As a result, income from continuing operations for 2016, 2017, and 2018 provides information for financial statement users in predicting future performance of Spectrum Brands Holdings without taking into account the Global Batteries and Appliances components.

After a business component is classified as held for sale, the sale may or may not be complete at the time of the next reporting date. In **Demo 3-3A**, we consider a sale completed by the next reporting date. In **Demo 3-3B**, we consider a sale completed after the reporting date.

Discontinued Business Component Sold *During* Reporting Period

Two categories of income from discontinued operations result when a business component is sold as of the financial statement date.

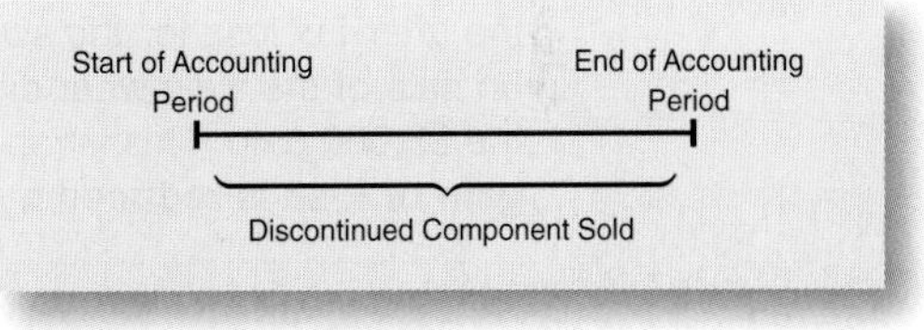

1. Results of operations for the discontinued business component, net of tax
2. Gain or loss from disposal of the business component, net of tax

These two items are reported separately on the income statement, or combined as one item. If combined, the amount of the gain or loss must be disclosed.

205-20-45-3 The statement in which net income of a business entity is reported . . . for current and prior periods shall report the results of operations of the discontinued operation, including any gain or loss recognized . . . in the period in which a discontinued operation either has been disposed of or is classified as held for sale.

205-20-45-3B A gain or loss recognized on the disposal (or loss recognized on classification as held for sale) shall be presented separately on the face of the statement where net income is reported or disclosed in the notes to financial statements.

The reported amounts are shown in the income statement after adjusting for tax effects. Determining the tax effects is an **intraperiod tax allocation** process. *Intra* means that the item, income taxes in this case, is allocated among various items within a given accounting period. Thus, a portion of the total income taxes is allocated to discontinued operations in a given accounting period.

205-20-45-3A The results of all discontinued operations, less applicable income taxes (benefit), shall be reported as a separate component of income.

EXPANDING YOUR KNOWLEDGE — **Predicting Future Performance**

A financial statement user's ability to predict the uncertainty of future cash flows requires one to differentiate between a recurring item (permanent in nature) and a nonrecurring item (transitory in nature) on the income statement.

- *Operating Income* While operating income is likely to recur in the future, unusual and/or infrequent items can be included that would not be expected to recur. Also, discretionary spending amounts (such as spending on advertising campaigns and research and development projects) may not recur to the same extent.
- *Nonoperating Items* Certain items in nonoperating income are unlikely to recur. For example, interest expense can be expected to recur, but an unusual and/or infrequent item such as a loss from a flood or restructuring costs may not be expected to recur.
- *Discontinued Operations* By their nature, the financial effects of discontinued operations are not expected to recur.

Financial statement users utilize the information disclosed on the face of income statements and in accompanying notes to predict what costs will recur to better estimate future cash flows. *Earnings quality* affects the ability of the financial statement user to predict future financial performance from the information reported.

Demo 3-3A LO3-3 Discontinued Operations—Component Sold as of Financial Statement Date

Demo MBC

Kabella Corp.'s swimwear division is a business component and a major line of business. Assume that Kabella sold its swimwear division during the year. The loss reported by the division was $25,000 before taxes and the company's tax rate is 25%. In addition, the sale of the business component resulted in a net gain of $5,000 before taxes. The following December 31, 2020, account balances exclude amounts from the swimwear business component. Prepare an income statement for 2020, including the presentation for discontinued operations.

Sales revenue	$850,000	Loss on sale of bond	$ 1,000
Gain on sale of investment	5,000	Interest revenue	3,000
Cost of goods sold	500,000	Interest expense	5,000
Selling expenses	80,000	Research and development expense	25,000
General and administrative expenses	40,000	Loss from hailstorm damage	20,000

Solution

First, the loss on the swimwear division results in tax savings of $6,250 ($25,000 × 25%). This means the after-tax loss for the swimwear division is $18,750 ($25,000 − $6,250). Second, the after tax gain on sale of the swimwear division is $3,750 after subtracting the taxes of $1,250 ($5,000 × 25%) from the $5,000 gain. This intraperiod tax allocation follows. **Whether a loss or a gain, the amount of that gain or loss is reduced by its tax effect.**

Loss from discontinued component	$(25,000)	
Gain on disposal of discontinued component		$5,000
Tax savings	6,250	
Additional taxes		(1,250)
Gain or (loss) net of tax	$(18,750)	$3,750

continued

continued from previous page

The following income statement for Kabella Corp. illustrates the presentation of discontinued operations of a business component sold as of the financial statement date.

KABELLA CORPORATION
Income Statement
For Year Ended December 31, 2020

Sales revenue		$850,000	
Cost of goods sold		500,000	
Gross profit		350,000	
Operating expenses			
Selling	$80,000		
General and administrative	40,000		
Research and development	25,000		
Total operating expenses		145,000	
Operating income		205,000	Continuing Operations
Other revenues and gains			
Interest revenue	3,000		
Gain on sale of investment	5,000	8,000	
Other expenses and losses			
Interest expense	5,000		
Loss on sale of bond	1,000		
Loss from hailstorm damage	20,000	26,000	
Income from continuing operations before income taxes		187,000	
Income tax expense		46,750	
Income from continuing operations		140,250	
Discontinued operations			
Loss from discontinued component, net of tax savings of $6,250		**(18,750)**	Discontinued Operations
Gain on disposal of discontinued component, net of tax of $1,250		**3,750**	
Net income		$125,250	

Discontinued Business Component Sold *After* Reporting Period

In the prior example, the discontinued component was sold **before** year-end. Let's now assume that a component was identified as discontinued but was *not sold during the reporting period.* Two categories of income from discontinued operations result when a business component is sold after the reporting period.

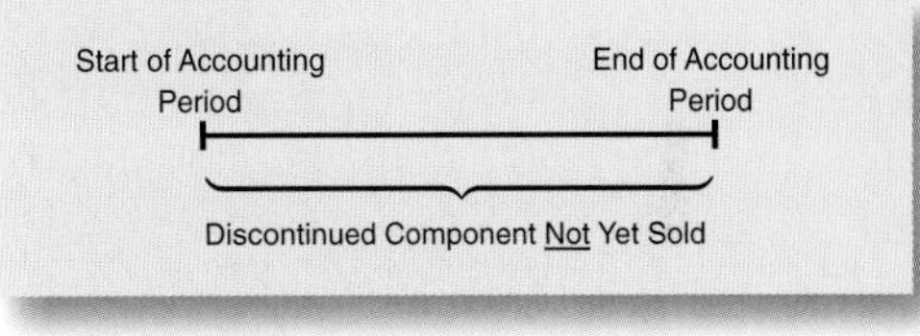

1. Results of operations for the discontinued business component during the reporting period, net of tax.
2. When applicable, impairment loss for the net of the component's carrying value over its fair value less costs to sell, net of tax.

360-10-35-40 A loss [expected disposal loss on assets classified as held for sale] shall be recognized for any initial or subsequent write-down to fair value less cost to sell.

These two items can be reported separately on the income statement, or combined as one item. If combined, the amount of the impairment loss must be disclosed. The reported amounts are shown in the income statement after adjusting for tax effects. (In subsequent periods, recoverability of losses is allowed, but this is limited to the cumulative amount of recorded unrealized losses as explained in Chapter 12.)

The balance sheet is also affected when a business component is held for sale: the assets and liabilities of the discontinued operation must be separately presented at the reporting date. For example, applicable amounts in property, plant, and equipment accounts are reclassified to assets held for sale.

205-20-45-10 In the period(s) that a discontinued operation is classified as held for sale and for all prior periods presented, the assets and liabilities of the discontinued operation shall be presented separately in the asset and liability sections, respectively, of the statement of financial position. Those assets and liabilities shall not be offset and presented as a single amount.

TARGET

Real World—REPORTING DISCONTINUED OPERATIONS

TARGET [TGT]

Target Corporation reported a loss from discontinued operations in 2014 due to the deconsolidation of its Canadian segment. The $4.1 billion loss drove an overall loss of $1.6 billion in 2014. The discontinued operations classification helps investors and creditors make sense of a $(1.636) billion net loss for 2014 followed by $3.363 billion net income for 2015.

Consolidated Statements of Operations (millions)	2015	2014	2013
Sales	$73,785	$72,618	$71,279
Cost of sales	51,997	51,278	50,039
Gross margin	21,788	21,340	21,240
Selling, general and administrative expenses	14,665	14,676	14,465
Depreciation and amortization	2,213	2,129	1,996
Gain on sale	(620)	—	(391)
Earnings from continuing operations before interest expense and income taxes	5,530	4,535	5,170
Net interest expense	607	882	1,049
Earnings from continuing operations before income taxes	4,923	3,653	4,121
Provision for income taxes	1,602	1,204	1,427
Net earnings from continuing operations	3,321	2,449	2,694
Discontinued operations, net of taxes	42	(4,085)	(723)
Net earnings/(loss)	$ 3,363	$ (1,636)	$ 1,971

Demo 3-3B **LO3-3** **Discontinued Operations—Component Not Sold as of Financial Statement Date**

Demo

MBC

Refer to the information in **Demo 3-3A**. Assume now that the division was held for sale on December 31, 2020. The business component experienced a loss of $40,000 before taxes ($30,000 after the tax savings of $10,000 or $40,000 × 25%). Also, the fair value of the business component was estimated to be $8,000 below its carrying value before the tax savings of $2,000, or $8,000 × 25%. The following income statement for Kabella shows the presentation of discontinued operations of a business component still held as of the financial statement date.

continued

continued from previous page

KABELLA CORPORATION
Income Statement
For Year Ended December 31, 2020

Sales revenue		$850,000	Continuing Operations
Cost of goods sold		500,000	
Gross profit		350,000	
Operating expenses			
Selling	$80,000		
General and administrative	40,000		
Research and development	25,000		
Total operating expenses		145,000	
Operating income		205,000	
Other revenues and gains			
Interest revenue	3,000		
Gain on sale of investment	5,000	8,000	
Other expenses and losses			
Interest expense	5,000		
Loss on sale of bond	1,000		
Loss from hailstorm damage	20,000	26,000	
Income from continuing operations before income taxes		187,000	
Income tax expense ($187,000 × 25%)		46,750	
Income from continuing operations		140,250	
Discontinued operations			Discontinued Operations
Loss from discontinued component, net of tax savings of $10,000		**(30,000)**	
Impairment loss on discontinued component, net of tax savings of $2,000		**(6,000)**	
Net income		$104,250	

Disclosure of Discontinued Operations

A company must disclose in its notes to the financial statements, additional information regarding the business component sold or held for sale. This information includes a description of the events leading to the disposal or expected disposal, the expected manner and timing of that disposal, and if not reported separately on the face of the income statement, any gains or losses recognized. If applicable, the company must disclose a description of the circumstances leading to a change in plans to dispose and any significant continuing involvement with a discontinued operation after disposal. Full disclosure requirements are included in ASC 205-20-50.

Discontinued Operations — LO3-3 — REVIEW 3-3

Review MBC

Golden Corp. disposed of a business component prior to its year-end at a loss of $4,500 before tax. The company incurred a loss from the discontinued component of $18,000 during the year. The following records for Golden Corp. for the year ended December 31, 2020, *exclude* amounts related to the discontinued business component.

Sales revenue	$450,000	Interest expense	$ 10,000
Gain on sale of investment	20,000	Loss on sale of patent	3,000
Selling expense	35,000	Cost of goods sold	300,000
General and administrative expense	65,000	Restructuring costs	25,000

continued

continued from previous page

Part One—Discontinued Business Component Sold During Reporting Period

Compute the following subtotals that are shown in a *multiple-step income statement* for Golden Corp. Assume an income tax rate of 25%.

a. Gross profit
b. Operating income
c. Income from continuing operations before income taxes
d. Income tax expense
e. Income from continuing operations
f. Loss from discontinued component, net of tax
g. Net income

Part Two—Discontinued Business Component Sold After Reporting Period

Assume the same information from Golden Corp. in Part One except that the sale of the discontinued component was not complete as of December 31, 2020. On December 31, 2020, the fair value of the business component was $50,000, estimated costs to sell were $7,000, and the carrying value was $60,000. Compute the following subtotals that are shown in a *multiple-step income statement* for Golden Corp. for the year ended December 31, 2020. Assume an income tax rate of 25%.

a. Gross profit
b. Operating income
c. Income from continuing operations before income taxes
d. Income tax expense
e. Income from continuing operations
f. Loss from discontinued component, net of tax
g. Net income

More Practice:
3-22, 3-23, 3-41, 3-43
Solution on p. 3-51.

LO 3-4 Disclose earnings per share on the income statement

LO 3-4 Overview

Earnings per Share

$$\frac{\text{Net income} - \text{Preferred dividends}}{\text{Weighted average common shares outstanding}}$$

- Report (or disclose) separately per share information for discontinued operations

Companies must report earnings per share information on the face of the income statement. **Earnings per share (EPS)** relates the income of a company to a single share of stock.

260-10-45-2 Entities with simple capital structures, that is, those with only common stock outstanding, shall present basic per-share amounts for income from continuing operations and for net income on the face of the income statement.

Earnings per share is computed by dividing reported net income available to the holders of common stock by the weighted average number of common shares outstanding during the period. For the computation of EPS on common stock, net income must be reduced by any preferred stock dividend claims because such dividends are not available to common stock owners and have not been subtracted in computing income. **Demo 3-4A** illustrates the computation of earnings per share with no discontinued business component.

If the income statement includes discontinued operations, per-share amounts are reported for (1) income from continuing operations, (2) income from discontinued operations, (3) gain or loss recognized on the business component, and (4) net income. The per-share amounts for the discontinued items can be reported on the face of the income statement or in the notes accompanying the financial statements. **Demo 3-4B** illustrates the computation of earnings per share with a discontinued business component.

260-10-45-3 An entity that reports a discontinued operation in a period shall present basic and diluted per-share amounts for that line item either on the face of the income statement or in the notes to the financial statements.

The accounting standards require the disclosure of both basic and diluted earnings per share. However, in Chapter 3, we only consider companies with a simple capital structure where no common stock exists that upon a potential conversion or exercise would dilute (decrease) earnings per common share. These complex scenarios resulting in the disclosure of diluted earnings per share are discussed in Chapter 21.

Earnings Per Share—With Continuing Operations Only

LO3-4 **Demo 3-4A**

Demo MBC

Kabella Corp. reports net income of $140,250 for 2020 with no discontinued operating business components. In other words, all of Kabella's net income is attributed to income from continuing operations. Weighted average common shares outstanding for 2020 for Kabella were 100,000 and Kabella had no preferred stock outstanding. Calculate earnings per share and prepare the earnings per share section of the income statement for the year ended December 31, 2020.

Solution

Earnings per Share Calculation

$$\text{Earnings per share: } \frac{\text{Net income} - \text{Preferred dividends}}{\text{Weighted average common shares outstanding}} = \frac{\$140{,}250 - \$0}{100{,}000} = \$1.40$$

Income Statement Presentation of Earnings per Share

KABELLA CORPORATION
Income Statement (Excerpt)
For Year Ended December 31, 2020

Net income	$140,250
Earnings per share	**$1.40**

UPS

Real World—EPS PRESENTATION

UNITED PARCEL SERVICE [UPS]

United Parcel Service Inc. reported the following earnings per share information in a recent Form 10-K.

Years Ended December 31 (in millions, except per share amounts)	2015	2014	2013
Net income	$4,844	$3,032	$4,372
Basic earnings per share	$ 5.38	$ 3.31	$ 4.65
Diluted earnings per share	$ 5.35	$ 3.28	$ 4.61

Earnings Per Share—With Discontinued Operations

LO3-4 **Demo 3-4B**

Demo MBC

Next assume that Kabella Corp. reported income from continuing operations of $140,250, a loss from discontinued component (net of tax savings) of $18,750, a gain on disposal of discontinued component of $3,750 (net of tax), and net income of $125,250 as shown in **Demo 3-3A**. For 2020, Kabella had 100,000 weighted average common share outstanding and no preferred stock outstanding. Calculate earnings per share and prepare a multiple-step income statement, including the earnings per share presentation, for the year ended December 31, 2020.

continued

continued from previous page

Solution

Earnings per Share Calculation To calculate earnings per share, divide each relevant income statement amount by the weighted average common shares outstanding.

	Income Statement Amount	Weighted Average Common Shares	Earnings Per Share
Income from continuing operations	$140,250	100,000	$1.40
Loss from discontinued component, net of tax savings	(18,750)	100,000	(0.19)
Gain on disposal of discontinued component, net of tax	3,750	100,000	0.04
Net income	$125,250	100,000	$1.25

Income Statement Presentation The earnings per share amounts calculated above are included in the income statement following the reporting of net income.

KABELLA CORPORATION
Income Statement
For Year Ended December 31, 2020

Sales revenue		$850,000	Continuing Operations
Cost of goods sold		500,000	
Gross profit		350,000	
Operating expenses			
Selling	$80,000		
General and administrative	40,000		
Research and development	25,000		
Total operating expenses		145,000	
Operating income		205,000	
Other revenues and gains			
Interest revenue	3,000		
Gain on sale of investment	5,000	8,000	
Other expenses and losses			
Interest expense	5,000		
Loss on sale of bond	1,000		
Loss from hailstorm damage	20,000	26,000	
Income from continuing operations before income taxes		187,000	
Income tax expense		46,750	
Income from continuing operations		140,250	
Discontinued operations			Discontinued Operations
Loss from discontinued component, net of tax savings of $5,000		(18,750)	
Gain on disposal of discontinued component, net of tax of $1,000		3,750	
Net income		$125,250	
Per share			
Income from continuing operations		**$1.40**	Earnings per Share
Loss from discontinued component, net of tax savings		**(0.19)**	
Gain on disposal of discontinued component, net of tax		**0.04**	
Net income		**$1.25**	

REVIEW 3-4 LO3-4 Earnings per Share

Review MBC

Part One—Earnings Per Share with Continuing Operations Only

Assume that Golden Corp. reported net income of $24,000 for the year ended December 31, 2020, with no discontinued operating business components. Weighted average common shares outstanding for 2020 for Golden Corp. were 10,000. Golden Corp. declared and paid $1,000 in preferred stock dividends. Calculate earnings per share.

continued

continued from previous page

Part Two—Earnings per Share with Discontinued Operations

Assume that Golden Corp. reported income from continuing operations of $24,000, incurred a loss from a discontinued component of $13,500 (after tax), and reported a loss on disposal of the business component of $3,375 (after tax) for the year ended December 31, 2020. Weighted average common shares outstanding for 2020 for Golden Corp. were 10,000. Golden Corp. declared and paid $1,000 in preferred stock dividends. Prepare the earnings per share section of the income statement for the year ended December 31, 2020.

More Practice:
3-24, 3-25, 3-44, 3-45
Solution on p. 3-51.

EXPANDING YOUR KNOWLEDGE — Noncontrolling Interest

A company (parent) prepares financial statements where it combines its own activities with those of one or more additional companies (subsidiaries) in which it has a more than 50% but less than 100% ownership interest. The combined income statement is labeled a **consolidated income statement**. When a company prepares a consolidated income statement, the company allocates consolidated net income to itself (parent) and to other investors (noncontrolling interest). **Noncontrolling interest** is the interest (less than a 50% ownership) in the subsidiaries *not* owned by the parent company. Earnings per share calculations for the parent company are based on income attributable to the parent. Authoritative guidance follows.

ASC Glossary Noncontrolling interest: The portion of equity (net assets) in a subsidiary not attributable, directly or indirectly, to a parent. A noncontrolling interest is sometimes called a minority interest.

810-10-50-1A A parent with one or more less-than-wholly-owned subsidiaries shall disclose . . . Separately, on the face of the consolidated financial statements, both of the following: (1) The amounts of consolidated net income and consolidated comprehensive income (2) The related amounts of each attributable to the parent and the noncontrolling interest.

260-10-45-11A For purposes of computing EPS in consolidated financial statements (both basic and diluted), if one or more less-than-wholly-owned subsidiaries are included in the consolidated group, income from continuing operations and net income shall exclude the income attributable to the noncontrolling interest in subsidiaries.

This allocation is illustrated in a recent 3M Company Form 10-K report for the year ended December 31, 2017.

Net income including noncontrolling interest	$4,869
Less: Net income attributable to noncontrolling interest	11
Net income attributable to 3M	$4,858
Weighted average 3M common shares outstanding—basic	597.5
Earnings per share attributable to 3M common shareholders—basic	$8.13

Report other comprehensive income — LO 3-5

Comprehensive income includes all changes in equity during a period from transactions and events from nonowner sources. **Comprehensive income equals net income or net loss plus (minus) other comprehensive income (loss), net of tax.**

Other comprehensive income (OCI) includes revenues, expenses, gains, and losses that are included in comprehensive income but not in net income in accordance with GAAP. Examples include unrealized holding gains (or losses) on certain types of debt investments and foreign currency translation adjustments. We will discuss additional examples of other comprehensive income items in later chapters. (A list of of other comprehensive income items is included at ASC 220-10-45-10A.)

LO 3-5 Overview

Financial Statement Presentation Options
- Single continuous statement of comprehensive income
- Two separate, but consecutive statements of income and comprehensive income

Two presentation formats are acceptable for the statement of comprehensive income.

- **Single continuous statement of comprehensive income.** This is a statement that extends a traditional income statement to include elements of other comprehensive income to arrive at comprehensive income.
- **Two separate but consecutive statements of income and comprehensive income.** The first statement is the income statement that ends with net income. The second statement begins with net income and includes elements of other comprehensive income to arrive at comprehensive income.

Single Statement	Two Statements
Revenues	Revenues
(Expenses)	(Expenses)
Net income	Net income
OCI (net of tax)	
Comp Inc	Net income
	OCI (net of tax)
	Comp Inc

Demo 3-5 illustrates the two presentation formats for comprehensive income. Authoritative support for the presentation of comprehensive income follows.

220-10-45-1A An entity reporting comprehensive income in a single continuous financial statement shall present its components in two sections, net income and other comprehensive income.

220-10-45-1B An entity reporting comprehensive income in two separate but consecutive statements shall present the following: (a) Components of and the total for net income in the statement of net income; (b) Components of and the total for other comprehensive income as well as a total for comprehensive income in the statement of comprehensive income, which shall be presented immediately after the statement of net income. A reporting entity shall begin the second statement with net income.

Demo 3-5 LO3-5 Statement of Comprehensive Income Presentations

The following items are from the adjusted trial balance of Kabella Corp. for the year ended December 31, 2020. Assume a tax rate of 25% and prepare (1) a single continuous statement of comprehensive income and (2) two separate statements of income and comprehensive income.

Sales revenue	$850,000	Interest revenue	$ 3,000
Gain on sale of investment	5,000	Interest expense	5,000
Cost of goods sold	500,000	Research and development expense	25,000
Selling expenses	80,000	Loss from hail damage	20,000
General and administrative expenses	40,000	Foreign currency translation adjustment, loss	6,500
Loss on sale of bond	1,000		

Solution

Single Continuous Statement of Comprehensive Income

KABELLA CORPORATION
Statement of Comprehensive Income
For Year Ended December 31, 2020

Sales revenue	$850,000
Cost of goods sold	500,000
Gross profit	350,000
Operating expenses	145,000
Operating income	205,000
Other revenue and gains	8,000
Other expenses and losses	26,000
Income before income taxes	187,000
Income tax expense ($187,000 × 25%)	46,750
Net income	140,250
Other comprehensive income:	
Foreign currency translation adjustment, less tax savings of $1,625*	**(4,875)**
Comprehensive income	$135,375

* Loss after tax is $4,875, computed as $6,500 less $1,625 ($6,500 × 25%).

Separate Statements of Income and Comprehensive Income

KABELLA CORPORATION
Income Statement
For Year Ended December 31, 2020

Sales revenue	$850,000
Cost of goods sold	500,000
Gross profit	350,000
Operating expenses	145,000
Operating income	205,000
Other revenue and gains	8,000
Other expenses and losses	26,000
Income before income taxes	187,000
Income tax expense	46,750
Net income	$140,250

KABELLA CORPORATION
Statement of Comprehensive Income
For Year Ended December 31, 2020

Net income	$140,250
Other comprehensive income:	
Foreign currency translation adjustment, less tax savings of $1,625	**(4,875)**
Comprehensive income	$135,375

UPS

Real World—STATEMENT OF COMPREHENSIVE INCOME

United Parcel Service Inc. elected to present *two separate financial statements*: a statement of consolidated income and a statement of consolidated comprehensive income (loss) for its reporting year. The separate statement of consolidated comprehensive income (loss) presented in its recent Form 10-K follows.

UNITED PARCEL SERVICE [UPS]

Statements of Consolidated Comprehensive Income (Loss)

For Year Ended December 31 (in millions)	2015	2014	2013
Net income	$4,844	$3,032	$4,372
Change in foreign currency translation adjustment, net of tax	(440)	(331)	(260)
Change in unrealized gain (loss) on marketable securities, net of tax	(1)	1	(7)
Change in unrealized gain (loss) on cash flow hedges, net of tax	6	280	67
Change in unrecognized pension and postretirement benefit costs, net of tax	489	(3,084)	3,094
Comprehensive income (loss)	$4,898	$ (102)	$7,266

Statement of Comprehensive Income Presentations

LO3-5 **REVIEW 3-5**

Silver Corp. has service revenue of $250,000, operating expenses of $230,000, and an unrealized holding gain of $5,000 on debt security investments for the year ended December 31, 2020. The income tax rate is 25%.

Prepare (1) a single continuous statement of comprehensive income and (2) two separate but consecutive statements of income and comprehensive income. Ignore earnings per share disclosure.

Review MBC

More Practice: 3-26, 3-46

Solution on p. 3-51.

EXPANDING YOUR KNOWLEDGE — OCI: Foreign Currency Translation Adjustment

It is often necessary to consolidate entities for financial reporting purposes under the economic entity assumption. However, what if one entity is in a foreign country and its financial amounts are measured in a foreign currency, which is different from the currency of the reporting entity? *To consolidate the two financial statements, all financial amounts must be expressed in the currency of the reporting entity.* The process of expressing amounts measured in a **functional currency** to amounts measured in the **domestic entity's reporting currency** is called **foreign currency translation**. The translation adjustment is reported in *other comprehensive income*. Consider these two measures.

- **Functional currency** Currency of the primary economic environment in which the entity generates and expends cash.
- **Domestic entity's reporting currency** Currency in which a reporting entity prepares its financial statements.

Prior to translation, a foreign entity must first determine whether its financial statements are stated in its functional currency. If not, the foreign entity must first measure its financial statements in its functional currency. The effects of remeasurement to a foreign entity's functional currency are generally recognized in the income statement of the foreign entity. Guidance on the appropriate exchange rates to use for remeasurement and translation is included in ASC 830. VF Corporation provides the following explanation of the measurement and translation policies in a note to its 2015 annual financial statements.

> **Summary of Significant Accounting Policies** The financial statements of most foreign subsidiaries are measured using the foreign currency as the functional currency. Assets and liabilities denominated in a foreign currency are translated into U.S. dollars using exchange rates in effect at the balance sheet date, and revenues and expenses are translated at average exchange rates during the period. Resulting translation gains and losses, and transaction gains and losses on long-term advances to foreign subsidiaries, are reported in other comprehensive income (loss) ("OCI").

LO 3-6 Describe the statement of stockholders' equity

LO 3-6 Overview

Statement of Stockholders' Equity
- Includes beginning balances, changes, and ending balances of equity accounts
- Accounts include common stock, retained earnings, and accumulated other comprehensive income
- Ending balances appear in stockholders' equity section of the balance sheet

The sources and changes in stockholders' equity accounts from the beginning of the reporting period to the end of the reporting period are presented in the **statement of stockholders' equity** (also called statement of shareholders' equity). Companies commonly present changes in each stockholders' equity account in a separate column in the statement of stockholders' equity as illustrated in **Demo 3-6**. The components of stockholders' equity often include paid-in capital (such as common stock), retained earnings, and accumulated other comprehensive income. **Accumulated other comprehensive income (AOCI)** is a permanent balance sheet account that holds the balance of other comprehensive income, accumulated over time. The components of stockholders' equity are discussed in more depth in Chapter 20.

The statement of stockholders' equity is typically presented for three years in its own separate financial statement (although disclosure is an option).

205-10-45-2 In any one year it is ordinarily desirable that the statement of financial position, the income statement, and the statement of changes in equity be presented for one or more preceding years, as well as for the current year.

505-10-50-2 If both financial position and results of operations are presented, disclosure of changes in the separate accounts comprising shareholders' equity (in addition to retained earnings) and of the changes in the number of shares of equity securities during at least the most recent annual fiscal period and any subsequent interim period presented is required to make the financial statements sufficiently informative. Disclosure of such changes may take the form of separate statements or may be made in the basic financial statements or notes thereto.

Demo 3-6 **LO3-6** **Statement of Stockholders' Equity Presentation**

Demo MBC Kabella Corp. reports December 31, 2019, normal balances in common stock, retained earnings, and accumulated other comprehensive income of $500,000, $250,000, and $18,000, respectively. Assume (a) no changes in common stock in 2020, (b) net income of $130,900, which increased retained earnings, and dividends of $10,000, which decreased retained earnings in 2020, and (c) an unrealized holding loss on debt securities of $4,550 (net of tax), which reduced accumulated other comprehensive income in 2020. Prepare (1) a statement of stockholders' equity, (2) the stockholders' equity section of the balance sheet, and (3) a retained earnings statement for 2020.

Solution

Statement of Stockholders' Equity

KABELLA CORPORATION
Statement of Stockholders' Equity

	Common Stock	Retained Earnings	Accumulated Other Comprehensive Income	Total
Beginning balance, December 31, 2019	$500,000	$250,000	$18,000	$768,000
Net income		130,900		130,900
Dividends		(10,000)		(10,000)
Other comprehensive Income:				
Unrealized holding loss on debt securities, net of tax savings			(4,550)	(4,550)
Ending balance, December 31, 2020	**$500,000**	**$370,900**	**$13,450**	**$884,350**

continued

continued from previous page

Stockholders' Equity Section of the Balance Sheet The ending balances in the stockholders' equity statement are reported in the stockholders' equity section of the balance sheet.

KABELLA CORPORATION
Balance Sheet (Excerpt)
December 31, 2020

Stockholders' equity	
Common stock	$500,000
Retained earnings	370,900
Accumulated other comprehensive income	13,450
Total stockholders' equity	$884,350

Retained Earnings Statement Some companies present separately the items affecting retained earnings in a statement of retained earnings, although this is not common. The retained earnings statement follows. We see that the statement of retained earnings is fully captured within the statement of stockholders' equity—see the Retained Earnings column in the statement of stockholders' equity and match it with the retained earnings statement here.

KABELLA CORPORATION
Retained Earnings Statement

Retained earnings, December 31, 2019	$250,000
Net income	130,900
Dividends	(10,000)
Retained earnings, December 31, 2020	$370,900

Statement of Stockholders' Equity **LO3-6** **REVIEW 3-6**

On December 31, 2019, Bronze Inc. had the following balances in stockholders' equity accounts: common stock, $300,000 credit balance; accumulated other comprehensive income, $35,000 credit balance; and retained earnings, $280,000 credit balance. During 2020, the company reported net income of $180,000, declared and paid dividends of $100,000, issued common stock of $50,000, and reported a foreign currency translation loss adjustment of $10,000 (after tax). Prepare a statement of stockholders' equity for Bronze Inc. for the year ended December 31, 2020.

Review MBC

More Practice: 3-27

Solution on p. 3-52.

Report changes in accounting estimate, changes in accounting principle, and error corrections

LO 3-7

This section explains the reporting for changes in accounting estimates and changes in accounting principles. It also describes the accounting treatment when a material error is discovered after the financial statements are issued.

Other Reporting Items
- Changes in accounting estimates—prospective approach
- Changes in accounting principles—retrospective, prospective, or modified retrospective approach
- Error correction—restatement

LO 3-7 Overview

Change in Accounting Estimate

Estimates (such as are made in determining depreciation expense or bad debt expense) are frequently required in accounting. However, subsequent experience and additional information often make it possible to improve these estimates. Revisions of accounting estimates such as the useful lives or residual values of depreciable assets, net realizable value of receivables, and warranty costs are considered changes in accounting estimates. As a company gains experience in such areas as depreciable assets, receivables, and warranties, it develops a basis for revising one or more of its prior accounting estimates. For example, the estimated useful life of equipment in use (and depreciated) for six years might be changed from an original 10-year to a 15-year estimated life because the equipment has remained in good repair and will be useful for longer than originally expected.

GAAP does not require a change to prior accounting results for a change in estimate. Instead, the new estimate is to be used during the current and remaining periods. Thus, a change in estimate is made on a **prospective basis** (future-oriented basis) as illustrated in **Demo 3-7A**.

250-10-45-17 A change in accounting estimate shall be accounted for in the period of change if the change affects that period only or in the period of change and future periods if the change affects both. A change in accounting estimate shall not be accounted for by restating or retrospectively adjusting amounts reported in financial statements of prior periods or by reporting pro forma amounts for prior periods.

The accounting standards require disclosure of the impact on income and per-share amounts for a change in estimate when the change affects several periods and is material. This disclosure is required because the change in estimate could impact the comparability of financial information from year to year.

250-10-50-4 The effect on income from continuing operations, net income (or other appropriate captions of changes in the applicable net assets or performance indicator), and any related per-share amounts of the current period shall be disclosed for a change in estimate that affects several future periods, such as a change in service lives of depreciable assets. Disclosure of those effects is not necessary for estimates made each period in the ordinary course of accounting for items such as uncollectible accounts or inventory obsolescence; however, disclosure is required if the effect of a change in the estimate is material.

UPS

Real World—ESTIMATION IN ACCRUAL ACCOUNTING

UNITED PARCEL SERVICE [UPS]

Estimation is inherent in preparing financial statements under accrual accounting. United Parcel Service included the following description of its use of estimation in its recent Form 10-K.

> **Use of Estimates** The preparation of our consolidated financial statements requires the use of estimates and assumptions that affect the reported amounts of assets and liabilities, the reported amounts of revenues and expenses, and the disclosure of contingencies. Estimates have been prepared on the basis of the most current and best information, and actual results could differ materially from those estimates.

Demo 3-7A LO3-7 Change in Accounting Estimate

Demo MBC

Equipment that cost $24,000 is being depreciated on a straight-line basis over a 10-year estimated useful life with no residual value. At the start of the seventh year, management determines that the total estimated useful life of the equipment is 14 years (with zero residual value). What is depreciation expense in year seven?

Solution

No changes are made to previously issued financial statements. Instead, the company takes a prospective approach by adjusting the current year's income statement with the newly obtained information. After determining the net book value of equipment, the company will depreciate this entire amount (because of zero residual value) over the remaining useful life of 8 years (14 years – 6 years). For year seven, depreciation is computed as follows.

Computation of Annual Depreciation in Year Seven

Original cost	$24,000
Accumulated depreciation to date of change ($24,000 × 6/10)	(14,400)
Net book value	$ 9,600
Annual depreciation over remaining useful life ($9,600/8 years)	$ 1,200

Assets = Liabilities + Equity
−1,200 −1,200

Deprec Exp: 1,200 |
Accum Deprec: | Bal 14,400; 1,200

Year 7—To record depreciation expense

Depreciation Expense	1,200	
Accumulated Depreciation		1,200

Change in Accounting Principle

There are two general circumstances driving a change in accounting principle.

- **Voluntary change in accounting principle** A change in circumstances can result in a *voluntary change* from one acceptable accounting principle to another acceptable accounting principle as illustrated in **Demo 3-7B**. When this happens, a **retrospective adjustment** is made to apply the change to prior periods and this new accounting principle is used for the current period. (The prospective treatment is applied if it is impractical to use retrospective treatment.)
- **Required change in accounting principle based on a Codification update** An update to the Codification can result in a change in the accounting for a particular transaction or event. When this happens, we look to the standards to see whether we make a retrospective adjustment, or follow a prospective approach, or a **modified retrospective approach.** The modified approach is where the new standard is applied to the current period only (prior financial statements are not restated) and a cumulative effect adjustment is added to or subtracted from beginning retained earnings of the current period. The required approach depends on the circumstances of the standard update.

The following authoritative guidance explains how the retrospective approach requires that all financial statements presented reflect the change, and how adjustments to the beginning carrying values of assets, liabilities, and retained earnings may be required.

250-10-45-5 An entity shall report a change in accounting principle through retrospective application of the new accounting principle to all prior periods, unless it is impracticable to do so. Retrospective application requires all of the following:(a) The cumulative effect of the change to the new accounting principle on periods prior to those presented shall be reflected in the carrying amounts of assets and liabilities as of the beginning of the first period presented. (b) An offsetting adjustment, if any, shall be made to the opening balance of retained earnings (or other appropriate components of equity or net assets in the statement of financial position) for that period. (c) Financial statements for each individual prior period presented shall be adjusted to reflect the period-specific effects of applying the new accounting principle.

An exception to the accounting treatment of a change in accounting principle is one where an accounting estimate is effected by a change in accounting principle. Such a change includes a change in depreciation or amortization methods. The accounting standards provide that a change in depreciation or amortization methods is treated prospectively, not retrospectively as illustrated in a later chapter.

250-10-45-18 Distinguishing between a change in an accounting principle and a change in an accounting estimate is sometimes difficult. In some cases, a change in accounting estimate is effected by a change in accounting principle. One example of this type of change is a change in method of depreciation, amortization, or depletion for long-lived, nonfinancial assets (hereinafter referred to as depreciation method). The new depreciation method is adopted in partial or complete recognition of a change in the estimated future benefits inherent in the asset, the pattern of consumption of those benefits, or the information available to the entity about those benefits. The effect of the change in accounting principle, or the method of applying it, may be inseparable from the effect of the change in accounting estimate. Changes of that type often are related to the continuing process of obtaining additional information and revising estimates and, therefore, shall be considered changes in estimates for purposes of applying this Subtopic.

For a change in accounting principle, a company must disclose (1) the nature and reason for the change including an explanation of why the new method is preferable, (2) the method of applying the change, and (3) the indirect effects such as a change in profit sharing due to the change in principle (ASC 250-10-50-1).

Demo 3-7B **LO3-7** **Change in Accounting Principle**

Alexa Inc. reported the following comparative income statement amounts for 2019.

Previously Issued Comparative Income Statements—2019	2018	2019
Sales	$100,000	$120,000
Cost of goods sold	60,000	65,000
Gross margin	$ 40,000	$ 55,000

In 2020, Alexa Inc.'s management decides to change its inventory method. If the new inventory method had been used in all previous periods, cost of goods sold would have been $5,000 less in 2018 and $4,000 less in 2019, than was recorded using the old inventory method. In 2020, sales were $130,000 and cost of goods sold were $68,000 using the new inventory method. (1) Prepare a three-year, partial income statement presentation for 2018, 2019, and 2020. (2) Indicate how the December 31, 2019, opening balance of retained earnings in the company's stockholders' equity statement would be affected by this change in accounting principle. Ignore income taxes.

Solution

Income Statement Presentation Alexa Inc. reports the following comparative income statements for 2018–2020, with all years reflecting the application of the new inventory method. Cost of goods sold is adjusted from $60,000 to $55,000 in 2018; it is adjusted from $65,000 to $61,000 in 2019; and it is reported as is under the new method in 2020. With a change in accounting principle, currently issued financial statements recast the prior years as if the new method had been used all along.

Currently Issued Comparative Income Statements—2020	2018	2019	2020
Sales	$100,000	$120,000	$130,000
Cost of goods sold	55,000	61,000	68,000
Gross margin	$ 45,000	$ 59,000	$ 62,000

Statement of Stockholders' Equity Presentation In applying a retrospective adjustment, a company reports the cumulative effect of the change in prior periods (net of tax) as an adjustment to beginning retained earnings of the earliest reporting year presented. The following schedule is an excerpt from the stockholders' equity statement illustrating the adjustment to beginning retained earnings for the cumulative effect of the change in prior periods. Ignore income taxes for this presentation. (An entry also is made to decrease inventory and decrease retained earnings, net of tax, for the prior period adjustment.)

ALEXA INC. Statement of Stockholders' Equity (excerpt)	Retained Earnings
Balance, December 31, 2019	$ #
Cumulative effect of change in accounting principle	9,000
Adjusted balance, December 31, 2019	$ #

EXPANDING YOUR KNOWLEDGE **Change in Reporting Entity**

A change in a reporting entity results when reporting consolidated statements in place of individual company statements or when reporting the effects of changing the composition of a consolidated or combined group. To allow meaningful comparisons across reporting periods, the retrospective approach is applied to these changes. For example, if a company began to consolidate its financial statement because ownership in its investment exceeded 50% in that year, the prior year is restated as if they had been consolidated all along. This allows for comparability across periods.

EXPANDING YOUR KNOWLEDGE **Earnings Management**

A financial statement user's ability to assess the amount, timing, and uncertainty of future cash flows can be affected by a company's efforts to manage earnings. **Earnings management** is the shifting of income into different reporting periods; that is, shifted from periods where the revenues or expenses were actually incurred. The following are examples of earnings management.

- Smoothing income (spreading out expenses or revenues over several reporting periods) to avoid income fluctuations and to meet income targets or investor expectations.
- Changing the timing of purchases or sales to change a particular period's earnings results.
- Increasing reserves or allowances (such as an inventory obsolescence reserve or allowance for doubtful accounts) to defer income to future periods. For example, a company intentionally inflates expenses by increasing an inventory reserve in a year with unexpected profits. In a later year, the company decreases the reserve, incurring less expense to offset an unexpected income shortfall.
- Decreasing reserves or allowances to meet current income targets.
- Changing accounting methods or assumptions without appropriate justification to adjust revenues or expenses reported.

These types of adjustments affect the quality of earnings because they artificially adjust income to align to a predetermined goal or expectation. As a result, the information provided in the income statement becomes less useful to financial statement users in predicting future cash flows. Ultimately, financial statement users lose a degree of confidence in financial reporting, which is the basis of investor decision-making in capital markets. Why would management intentionally use earnings to misrepresent financial performance? Research suggests at least four reasons. Source: WSJ Oct 1, 2012.

- To influence its stock price.
- To hit earnings benchmarks due to outside pressure.
- To hit earnings benchmarks due to inside pressure.
- Due to senior managers fear for their career.

Error Correction

An accounting error occurs when a transaction or event is recorded incorrectly or is not recorded at all. Examples of errors include inaccurate depreciation calculations, inaccurate entering of service lives, or an incorrect capitalization of a repair expense. A *material error* not discovered until after the release of the financial statements must be corrected through a **prior period adjustment**, illustrated in **Demo 3-7C**. A prior period adjustment is an entry to correct an error through an adjustment of a balance sheet account and typically the retained earnings account and is recorded in the period that the error is discovered. The adjustments are excluded from the determination of net income for the current period. (On the other hand, an error considered immaterial would be corrected in the current period.)

Previously issued financial statements of all prior periods must be restated to reflect the correction. The cumulative effect on periods prior to those presented is made to the opening balance of retained earnings, similar to retrospective treatment. Authoritative guidance follows.

ASC Glossary **Restatement:** The process of revising previously issued financial statements to reflect the correction of an error in those financial statements.

250-10-45-23 Any error in the financial statements of a prior period discovered after the financial statements are issued or are available to be issued...shall be reported as an error correction, by restating the prior-period financial statements. Restatement requires all of the following:

a. The cumulative effect of the error on periods prior to those presented shall be reflected in the carrying amounts of assets and liabilities as of the beginning of the first period presented.

b. An offsetting adjustment, if any, shall be made to the opening balance of retained earnings (or other appropriate components of equity or net assets in the statement of financial position) for that period.

c. Financial statements for each individual prior period presented shall be adjusted to reflect correction of the period-specific effects of the error.

250-10-50-7 When financial statements are restated to correct an error, the entity shall disclose that its previously issued financial statements have been restated, along with a description of the nature of the error. The entity also shall disclose both of the following: (a) The effect of the correction on each financial statement line item and any per-share amounts affected for each prior period presented (b) The cumulative effect of the change on retained earnings or other appropriate components of equity or net assets in the statement of financial position, as of the beginning of the earliest period presented.

Demo 3-7C **LO3-7** **Error Correction**

Demo MBC

Equipment that cost the Bailey Retail Company $10,000 (with a 10-year estimated useful life and no residual value) was purchased on January 1, 2017. The total cost was erroneously debited to an expense account in 2017 and no depreciation was recorded subsequent to 2017. The error is discovered on December 29, 2020. Record the correcting entry required in 2020, ignoring the income tax effect.

Solution

December 29, 2020—To record a correction of an error

Assets	=	Liabilities	+	Equity
+10,000				−1,000
−4,000				+7,000

Equipment		Deprec Exp	
10,000		1,000	

Accum Deprec		Ret Earnings	
	4,000		7,000

Equipment	10,000	
Depreciation Expense ($10,000 / 10)	1,000	
Accumulated Depreciation ($1,000 × 4)		4,000
Retained Earnings—Prior Period Adjustment ($10,000 − $3,000)		7,000

Equipment is debited for the original cost of the equipment of $10,000. Depreciation Expense is debited for current year's depreciation expense of $1,000 (cost of $10,000 divided by the useful life of 10 years). Accumulated Depreciation is credited for $4,000 (depreciation accumulated from 2017 to 2020). Lastly, Retained Earnings is credited for $7,000, to correct years 2017 to 2020 ($10,000 erroneously expensed less $3,000 for the correct expense).

The correction would be reflected throughout all financial statements presented. Similar to the presentation in **Demo 3-7B**, the opening balance of retained earnings would be adjusted for corrections prior to the financial statements presented. In our example, if 2019 and 2020 comparative financial statements were presented, both years would reflect the corrections. In addition, the impact of the errors on 2017 and 2018 would be reflected as an adjustment to opening retained earnings (January 1, 2019).

Summary of Accounting Changes and Error Correction

Exhibit 3-4 includes a summary of the accounting treatments for error corrections and accounting changes. While **LO 3-7** provides an overview of the accounting treatment for each type, we expand on these explanations with more examples throughout this text. **Exhibit 3-4** is a road map for the application of these concepts in later chapters.

EXHIBIT 3-4 Summary of the Accounting Changes and Treatment of Error Correction

Accounting Change	Description	Accounting Treatment	Additional Coverage
Change in estimate	Change an accounting estimate due to changes in circumstance or new facts.	Prospective treatment	**LO 8-4.** Change in allowance for doubtful account estimates **LO 12-4.** Change in depreciation estimates **LO 13-5.** Change in intangible estimates **Appendix A.** Recap
Change in accounting principle effected by a change in estimate	Effects of a change in accounting principle are inseparable from the effects of a change in accounting estimate.	Prospective treatment	**LO 12-5.** Change in depreciation method **Appendix A.** Recap

continued

continued from previous page

Accounting Change	Description	Accounting Treatment	Additional Coverage
Change in accounting principle	Substitution of one generally accepted accounting principle for another.	▪ Retrospective treatment typically applied. ▪ Prospective treatment applied only if it is impractical to use retrospective treatment. ▪ Retrospective, prospective, or modified retrospective treatment applied in implementing a new standard, as required.	**LO 10-6.** Change in inventory method **LO 18-10.** Tax effects of change in accounting principle **Appendix A.** Recap
Error correction	Correction of a transaction that is recorded incorrectly or not at all.	▪ Retrospective treatment ▪ Restatement of previously issued financial statements if error is discovered in a subsequent accounting period.	**LO 10-7.** Inventory errors **LO 12-6.** Property, plant and equipment errors **LO 18-10.** Tax effects of error corrections **Appendix A.** Recap
Change in reporting entity	Presentation of financial statements that are effectively those of a *different* reporting entity.	Retrospective treatment	**Appendix A.** Recap

Principle Change, Estimate Change, and Error Correction

LO3-7 **REVIEW 3-7**

For each of the six scenarios *a* through *f* occurring in 2020, indicate (1) type of adjustment (principle change, estimate change, or error), (2) accounting treatment (retrospective, restatement, or prospective), and (3) whether an adjustment to retained earnings is required.

Review MBC

Accounting Change or Error	Type (Principle Change, Estimate Change, or Error)	Accounting Treatment (Retrospective, Restatement, or Prospective)	Adjustment to Retained Earnings Required
a. Projected salvage value used in determining depreciation for a building purchased in 2015 (useful life of 30 years) is adjusted in 2020.			
b. In 2020, the company discovered that the accrual for vacation was incorrectly calculated resulting in an understatement of expense for 2019 by a material amount.			
c. In 2020, the company adopted a new accounting standard that resulted in an increase in expense for 2020 and would have increased expense in previous years if adopted earlier. The new standard requires retrospective treatment.			
d. The company changed from the LIFO inventory method to the FIFO inventory method in 2020. Cost of goods sold would have been lower in previous years had FIFO been used.			
e. New equipment was purchased in 2019 and added to the automated depreciation system. However, instead of selecting "straight-line" depreciation method, "MACRS" depreciation (a tax depreciation method) was erroneously selected resulting in a material overstatement of depreciation expense for 2019.			
f. Actual returns of inventory in 2020 were less than the amount estimated as a refund liability at the 2019 year-end.			

More Practice:
3-28, 3-29, 3-30, 3-49

Solution on p. 3-52.

Management Judgment

Presentation of the income statement, the reporting of comprehensive income, and the reporting of accounting changes and errors are dependent on decisions made by management.

Income Statement Presentation and Reporting of Comprehensive Income

Management must choose the type of format to use for the income statement and for reporting comprehensive income. Management must also determine which categories to present on financial statements. Items will be reported separately depending on judgments of materiality and usefulness to financial statement users. For example, ASC 360-10-50-1 requires the reporting of depreciation expense *either* on the face of the income statement or in notes to financial statements. In another example, restructuring charges can be presented *separately* as a component of income from continuing operations if material. As shown earlier in ASC 220-20-45-1, a material event or transaction that is unusual or infrequent is reported as a *separate* component of income from continuing operations. Determining whether an item meets this threshold for separate reporting requires judgment. A quick summary follows.

- Choice of income statement presentation: single-step vs. multiple-step, or some combination.
- Choice in reporting OCI: separate or continuous statement of comprehensive income.
- Classification of items as either operating or nonoperating in a multiple-step statement.
- Identifying material, unusual, and/or infrequent transactions requiring separate reporting.

Classification of a Disposal as Discontinued Operations

Classifying a disposal as discontinued operations requires management judgment.

- Does the disposal of assets meet the definition of a *component*?
- If the component has not been sold as of the balance sheet date, does it meet the criteria for an asset *held-for-sale*?
- Does the disposal represent a *strategic shift*, resulting in a major effect on the company's operations and financial results?

In determining whether a disposal represents a strategic shift, management analyzes relevant qualitative and quantitative factors. For example, management considers that a qualitative factor in support of a strategic shift is that the component represents a separate reporting segment. Management considers a quantitative factor in support of a strategic shift when that component represents more than 15% of total revenues.

Accounting for Changes in Principles and for Errors

Voluntary change in accounting principle As we explained in reference to ASC 250-10-50-1, a company must disclose why a voluntary change in accounting principle is *preferable*. In such a case, management determines that the new method is preferable based on analysis of the circumstances. Authoritative guidance (for SEC registrants) follows which emphasizes the role of business judgment.

> **250-10-S99-4** In the case of changes for which objective criteria for determining preferability have not been established by authoritative bodies, business judgment and business planning often are major considerations in determining that the change is to a preferable method because the change results in improved financial reporting.

Change in accounting estimate The process of developing and updating accounting estimates requires management judgment. Events, facts, or circumstances can change *after* an estimate is made requiring an adjustment to that estimate.

Correction of an Error When an accounting error is discovered, management must determine whether the error is *material* to previously issued financial statements. A qualitative characteristic of useful information is materiality (introduced in Chapter 1). Deciding whether an item is material to a company requires judgment as there are no pre-established thresholds to determine whether an item is or is not material. In fact, a uniform numerical threshold of let's say 5% cannot be used as the sole way of determining materiality—it needs to be combined with other analysis pertaining to that situation. Ultimately, an item is considered material if there is a substantial likelihood that a reasonable person would consider it material or important.

250-10-S99-1 The use of a percentage as a numerical threshold, such as 5%, may provide the basis for a preliminary assumption that—without considering all relevant circumstances—a deviation of less than the specified percentage with respect to a particular item on the registrant's financial statements is unlikely to be material. The staff has no objection to such a "rule of thumb" as an initial step in assessing materiality. But quantifying, in percentage terms, the magnitude of a misstatement is only the beginning of an analysis of materiality; it cannot appropriately be used as a substitute for a full analysis of all relevant considerations. Materiality concerns the significance of an item to users of a registrant's financial statements. A matter is "material" if there is a substantial likelihood that a reasonable person would consider it important.

Describe interim financial reporting

APPENDIX 3A
LO 3-8

Interim Financial Reporting
- Report on a more timely basis (quarterly)
- Report some items as incurred (*discrete view*)
- Allocate some items to multiple periods (*integral-part view*)

LO 3-8 Overview

Annual financial statements are not the most timely source of information for investors. Companies often issue **interim reports**, usually quarterly, to provide timely information. The SEC requires a quarterly Form 10-Q for publicly traded companies.

Reporting more frequently than once each year presents financial reporting challenges. For example, many retailers conduct a large percentage of their business in the fourth quarter of the calendar year, the holiday season. Results of the fourth quarter often determine whether the company will be profitable. In preparing quarterly reports, management must decide which costs to expense in the first three quarters and which costs are more appropriately capitalized and expensed in the fourth quarter.

More generally, the reasons for difficulties in presenting interim reports include:

- Seasonality of revenues, costs, and expenses.
- Major costs that occur in one interim period but benefit other interim periods within the same reporting year.
- Seasonality of production activities.
- Unusual and/or infrequent items that occur in one interim period.
- Selection of the appropriate income tax rate for each interim period.

There are two opposing conceptual views on the treatment of the interim period.

- **Discrete view** Each interim period is viewed as a basic reporting period—it stands alone and is not simply part of the annual period. Under this view, revenue and expense recognition, accruals, and deferrals for the interim period follow the same principles and procedures used for an annual period. For example, expense in one interim period is not allocated to another period.
- **Integral-part view** Each interim period is viewed as an integral part of the annual period. Revenue, expense, deferrals, and accruals are affected by judgments made at the end of each interim period about the results of operations for the remainder of the annual period. For example, an expense incurred in one interim period can be allocated among other interim periods within the reporting year.

The accounting standards primarily consider the interim period as an integral part of the annual period, with the discrete approach used for specific items as illustrated in Demo 3-8.

270-10-45-1 Interim financial information is essential to provide investors and others with timely information as to the progress of the entity. The usefulness of such information rests on the relationship that it has to the annual results of operations. Accordingly, each interim period should be viewed primarily as an integral part of an annual period.

The following guidance is provided by GAAP regarding interim reporting.

270-10-45-3 Revenue from products sold or services rendered shall be recognized as the entity satisfies a performance obligation by transferring a promised good or service to a customer. Those revenues shall be recognized during an interim period on the same basis as followed for the full year in accordance with Topic 606 on revenue from contracts with customers.

270-10-45-4 Costs associated with revenue - those costs that are associated directly with or allocated to the products sold or to the services rendered and that are charged against income in those interim periods in which the related revenue is recognized.

All other costs and expenses—those costs and expenses that are not allocated to the products sold or to the services rendered and that are charged against income in interim fiscal periods as incurred, or are allocated among interim periods based on an estimate of time expired, benefit received, or other activity associated with the periods.

270-10-45-8 Gains and losses that arise in any interim period similar to those that would not be deferred at year end shall not be deferred to later interim periods within the same fiscal year.

740-270-25-2 The tax (or benefit) related to ordinary income (or loss) shall be computed at an estimated annual effective tax rate and the tax (or benefit) related to all other items shall be individually computed and recognized when the items occur.

270-10-45-11A Effects of disposals of a component of an entity and unusual or infrequently occurring transactions and events that are material with respect to the operating results of the interim period shall be reported separately. Gains or losses from disposal of a component of an entity and unusual or infrequently occurring items shall not be prorated over the balance of the fiscal year.

The minimum data to be reported include (ASC 270-10-50-1):

- Sales, income taxes, net income, and comprehensive income.
- Income effects of a discontinued component.
- Disposal of a component of a business.
- Unusual and/or infrequent items.
- Contingent items.
- Earnings per share.
- Seasonal revenue, costs, or expenses.
- Significant changes in estimates or provisions for income taxes.
- Changes in accounting principles or estimates.
- Fair value assumptions and methods used to estimate the fair value of financial instruments.
- Significant changes in financial position.

TARGET

Real World—QUARTERLY REPORTING

TARGET [TGT]

Target Corporation reported its third quarter results as of October 29, 2016, in its Form 10-Q filed with the SEC. Its consolidated statements of operations included results for the following periods.

- Three months ended October 29, 2016
- Three months ended October 31, 2015
- Nine months ended October 29, 2016
- Nine months ended October 31, 2015

The following excerpt from its 10-Q is the consolidated statement of operations for the three months ended October 29, 2016 (excluding per share information).

continued

continued from previous page

Statement of Operations—unaudited (millions)	2016
Sales	$16,441
Cost of sales	11,471
Gross margin	4,970
Selling, general and administrative expenses	3,339
Depreciation and amortization	570
Earnings from continuing operations before interest expense and income taxes	1,061
Net interest expense	142
Earnings from continuing operations before income taxes	919
Provision for income taxes	311
Net earnings from continuing operations	608
Discontinued operations, net of tax	—
Net earnings	$ 608

Interim Financial Reporting

LO3-8 **Demo 3-8**

Demo MBC

Following are first quarter data, ended March 31, 2020, for Gilmore Corp. Determine the expense that is reported in the interim financial statements for the three-month period ended March 31, 2020.

Unusual loss	$ 15,000	Shipping expense	$ 7,000
Operating asset cost (10-year useful life)	480,000	Cost of goods sold	241,000
Salaries expense	89,000	Annual property tax expense for 2020 (estimated)	12,000
Advertising expense (benefits first and second quarterly equally)	18,000		

Solution

Unusual loss	$ 15,000
Depreciation expense ($480,000 / 10 × 3/12)	12,000
Salaries expense	89,000
Advertising expense ($18,000 / 2)	9,000
Property tax expense ($12,000 / 4)	3,000
Shipping expense	7,000
Cost of goods sold	241,000
Total expense reported in quarter	$376,000

The unusual loss is recognized in the period incurred. Depreciation expense is allocated based upon the time expired (3 months). Salaries expense, cost of goods sold, and selling expense are charged against income in the quarter that the related revenues are recognized. Advertising expense is charged over the time benefits are received (two quarters). Property tax is accrued for a partial period (3 months) to reach a full year for the annual period.

Interim Financial Reporting

LO3-8 **REVIEW 3-8**

Review MBC

Match each of the transactions or events, 1 through 7, with the most appropriate interim accounting treatment, *a*, *b*, or *c*.

Accounting Treatment

a. Fully recognize in the financial statements of the current interim period.

b. Fully defer item until a later reporting period.

continued

continued from previous page

c. Amortize or accrue (recognize partly in the current interim period and partly in subsequent interim periods).

Transaction or Event

_____ 1. Utilities expense allocable to consumption during the current interim period.
_____ 2. Estimated accrual for a legal contingency.
_____ 3. Annual insurance premium paid in the current interim period.
_____ 4. Loss due to fire experienced in the current interim period.
_____ 5. Estimate for bonuses to executives paid at the end of the year if the company reaches certain profitability measures. Management estimates that the company will likely reach the profitability targets.
_____ 6. Annual estimated pension expense.
_____ 7. Temporary declines in the market value of finished goods inventory.

More Practice: 3-74, 3-75

Solution on p. 3-52.

Questions

3-1. Explain the usefulness and the limitations of the income statement.

3-2. Explain the concept of quality of earnings.

3-3. Explain the basic difference between revenues and gains, and provide examples of each.

3-4. Explain the basic difference between expenses and losses, and provide examples of each.

3-5. Describe the two formats used for income statements. Explain why actual income statements are often a combination of these two formats.

3-6. Explain how gross profit is computed for a retail business.

3-7. Explain how cost of goods sold is reported on a single-step income statement and on a multiple-step income statement.

3-8. List the four major income subtotals, or captions, in their order of appearance, on a typical multiple-step income statement.

3-9. What factors might companies take into consideration when one chooses between the two alternative formats for the income statement?

3-10. How are items that are unusual and/or infrequent reported on the income statement?

3-11. Define a prior period adjustment. How is a prior period adjustment reported?

3-12. Define intraperiod tax allocation.

3-13. Define earnings per share (EPS). Why is it required as an integral part of the income statement?

3-14. A company reports the following amounts for 2020.

Loss from continuing operations	$(40,000)
Gain from the sale of discontinued operations.	$ 90,000
Net income	$ 50,000
Average number of common shares outstanding . . .	25,000 shares

Prepare the EPS presentation. Which EPS amount is likely to be the most relevant? Explain.

3-15. Explain what is meant by a change in estimate. Explain the basic approach used to account for and report a change in estimate.

3-16. A company has a machine that cost $20,000 when acquired at the beginning of year 1. It has been depreciated using the straight-line method on the basis of a 10-year useful life and no residual value. At the start of year 5, the total useful life was changed to 8 years. Compute the amount of depreciation expense per year that should be recorded for the remaining useful life of the machine.

3-17. What items are reported on a statement of retained earnings (as incorporated into the statement of stockholders' equity)? Explain how it provides a link between the current income statement and the balance sheet.

Brief Exercises

Brief Exercise 3-18 Preparing a Single-Step Income Statement **LO1** *Hint:* See Demo 3-1

The following information is from Atlanta Corp. for the 12 months ended December 31, 2020. Prepare a single-step income statement (excluding the earnings per share disclosures) assuming a tax rate of 25%. Report income tax expense in its own separate section.

Sales revenue	$800,000	Interest expense	$5,000
Costs of goods sold	500,000	Gain on sale of short-term investments	8,800
Selling and administrative expenses	150,000		

Brief Exercise 3-19 Preparing Multiple-Step Income Statement **LO1** *Hint:* See Demo 3-1

Refer to the information in Brief Exercise 3-18 Prepare a multiple-step income statement (excluding the earnings per share disclosures).

Brief Exercise 3-20 Computing Income Statement Subtotals **LO1**

The following selected items are taken from the adjusted trial balance of Dion Inc. at December 31, 2020. Assuming an income tax rate of 25%, determine the following amounts:

a. Gross profit.
b. Operating income (loss).
c. Nonoperating income (loss).
d. Income tax expense.
e. Net income (loss).

Adjusted Trial Balance (Selected Accounts)	Debit	Credit
Sales revenue		$3,000,000
Costs of goods sold	$1,600,000	
Selling and administrative expenses	900,000	
Loss on sale of investments	50,000	
Interest revenue		15,000

Brief Exercise 3-21 Preparing the Nonoperating Items Section of an Income Statement **LO2** *Hint:* See Demo 3-2

Gomez Inc. reported the following *pretax* amounts for 2020. Assuming an income tax rate of 25%, prepare the income statement beginning with *Operating income*. Ignore the earnings per share disclosures.

Loss from discontinued operations	$48,000	Operating income	$400,000
Gain on sale of investments	5,000	Loss on sale of patent	48,000
Interest expense	18,000		

Brief Exercise 3-22 Reporting Discontinued Operations **LO3** *Hint:* See Demo 3-3A

Leigh Corp. disposed of its Knit Products Division in June of 2020 at a loss of $38,000 before tax. Prior to the sale, the Knit Products Division (considered a separate business component) reported a net loss from operations of $405,000 before tax. Leigh Corp. reported income from continuing operations of $900,000 before tax for 2020.

a. Assuming an income tax rate of 25%, prepare an income statement beginning with *Income from Continuing Operations*. Ignore earnings per share disclosures.
b. Repeat the requirements of part *a* but now assume that the Knit Products Division reported income from operations of $80,000 in 2020.

Brief Exercise 3-23 Reporting Discontinued Operations **LO3** *Hint:* See Demo 3-3B

On October 31, 2020, Leigh Corp. approved a formal plan to dispose of its Knit Products Division. On December 31, 2020, the Knit Products Division was held for sale but had not been sold. The Knit Products Division (considered a separate business component) reported a net loss from operations of $505,000 before tax for the year ended December 31, 2020. The Knit Products Division has a book value and fair value (after selling expenses) of $3,600,000 and $3,300,000, respectively. Leigh Corp. reported income from continuing operations of $900,000 before tax for 2020.

a. Assuming an income tax rate of 25%, prepare an income statement beginning with *Income from Continuing Operations*. Ignore earnings per share disclosures.
b. Repeat the requirements of part *a* but now assume that the book value of the Knit Products Division is $3,200,000 on December 31, 2020.

Brief Exercise 3-24
Reporting Earnings per Share **LO3, 4**

Refer to the information in Brief Exercise 3-23. Prepare the earnings per share section of the income statement for Leigh Corp. assuming weighted average common shares outstanding for 2020 were 150,000.

Brief Exercise 3-25
Computing Earnings per Share **LO4**
Hint: See Demo 3-4A

Lee Corp. had 200,000 weighted average common shares outstanding in 2020 and 5,000 weighted average preferred shares outstanding in 2020. Lee Corp. reported net income of $450,000 in 2020, and declared and paid $50,000 and $10,000 of common stock and preferred stock dividends, respectively. Compute earnings per share for Lee Corp. for 2020.

Brief Exercise 3-26
Preparing a Statement of Comprehensive Income **LO5**
Hint: See Demo 3-5

Sanders Inc. reported net income of $550,000 for the year ended December 31, 2020. The company had a pretax unrealized holding gain on debt securities of 14,000 and a pretax loss on foreign currency translation adjustment of $40,000. The company's tax rate is 25%. Prepare a separate statement of comprehensive income beginning with *net income*.

Brief Exercise 3-27
Preparing a Retained Earnings Statement **LO6**

In 2020, Lucky Inc. reported net income of $48,000 and declared and paid a common stock cash dividend of $20,000. Assuming that the company had a beginning balance of $344,000 in retained earnings, prepare a retained earnings statement for 2020.

Brief Exercise 3-28
Reporting a Change in Estimate **LO7**

In 2020, Nordsom Corp. increased its warranty accrual by $30,000 based upon recent experiences with product returns resulting from manufacturing defects originating in 2019, but not discovered until 2020.

a. Classify the accounting change.
b. Determine the proper accounting approach.

Brief Exercise 3-29
Reporting a Change in Accounting Principle **LO7**

CostKo Corp. reported net income of $1,000,000 and $1,100,000 in 2018 and 2019, respectively. In 2020, the company changed its method of accounting for inventory from weighted average to FIFO (first-in, first-out). As a result of using the new method (FIFO), net income would have been $1,100,000 and $1,302,000 in 2018 and 2019, respectively.

a. Classify the accounting change.
b. Determine the proper accounting approach.
c. In reporting comparative income statements in 2020, what net income amounts are included for 2018 and 2019?

Brief Exercise 3-30
Reporting an Accounting Error **LO7**

An error considered material of $125,000 (net of tax) to Netbic Corp. was discovered in 2020 that originated in 2019. The error represents an overstatement of the company's previously reported revenues. Assuming an unadjusted beginning balance in retained earnings of $2,000,000, a 2020 net loss of $50,000, and that no dividends were declared or paid in 2020, prepare its statement of retained earnings for 2020. *Hint:* Adjust the beginning balance of retained earnings for the error.

Exercises

Exercise 3-31
Computing Retained Earnings and Net Income **LO1**

The following selected balance sheet amounts are from Aerial Inc. as of December 31, 2020.

Selected Balance Sheet Amounts

Assets		Liabilities	
Cash	$14,000	Accounts payable	$ 4,800
Accounts receivable	5,000	Note payable	10,000
Supplies	3,800	Stockholders' equity	
Equipment	25,000	Common stock	10,000
		Paid-in capital in excess of par	5,000

Required

a. Compute retained earnings as of December 31, 2020 assuming retained earnings is the only missing category in the selected balance sheet amounts above.
b. Determine net income assuming that the balance in retained earnings on January 1, 2020, was $2,500; dividends declared during 2020 were $4,500; and no other items affected retained earnings during 2020.

Exercise 3-32
Computing Gross Profit and Operating Income **LO1**

Following is an excerpt from the Packer Inc. year-end trial balance dated December 31, 2020.

Selected Adjusted Trial Balance Amounts

Acct. No.	Description	Debit	Credit
400	Sales revenue		$70,000
402	Consulting revenue		1,000
404	Gain on sale of investments		2,800
510	Cost of goods sold	$25,000	
511	Selling expense	11,000	
512	Salaries expense	3,000	
520	Rent expense	2,000	
526	Insurance expense	500	
528	Depreciation expense	1,000	
530	Research and development expense	5,000	
535	Loss on sale of investments	1,800	
540	Interest expense	500	
542	Income tax expense	1,950	

Required

a. Compute gross profit for 2020.
b. Compute operating income for 2020.

Exercise 3-33
Preparing a Single-Step Income Statement **LO1, 4**

The following items are from the adjusted trial balance of Bailey Corp. on December 31, 2020, the end of its annual accounting period. Assume an average 25% income tax on all items. Weighted average shares of common stock outstanding for 2020 were 10,000.

Sales revenue	$645,200	Selling expenses	$136,000
Depreciation for the period	6,000	General and administrative expenses	110,000
Rent revenue	2,400	Interest revenue	900
Gain on sale of investment	2,000	Interest expense	1,500
Cost of goods sold	330,000	Loss on sale of investment	22,000

Required

Prepare a single-step income statement for the 12 months ended December 31, 2020, including the earnings per share disclosures. Report income taxes in its own section.

Exercise 3-34
Preparing a Multiple-Step Income Statement **LO1, 4**

Refer to the information in Exercise 3-33 to complete the following requirement.

Required

Prepare a multiple-step income statement for the 12 months ended December 31, 2020, including the earnings per share disclosure. Assume that rent revenue is a nonoperating revenue.

Exercise 3-35
Preparing a Single-Step and a Multiple-Step Income Statement **LO1, 4**

The following selected items are taken from the adjusted trial balance of Amick Corp. at December 31, 2020.

Sales revenue	$950,000
Cost of goods sold	575,000
Dividends received on investment in stocks	6,500
Interest expense	4,200
Loss on sale of investments	48,000
Promotion expense	15,000
Shipping expense	25,000
Depreciation (50% selling, 50% general and administrative)	20,000
Salaries (general and administrative)	80,000
Other general and administrative expenses	23,000
Salaries (selling)	85,300
Interest revenue	2,500
Income tax rate	25%
Common stock	20,000 shares

Required

a. Prepare a single-step income statement (including earnings per share). Include income taxes in its own section.
b. Prepare a multiple-step income statement (including earnings per share).

Exercise 3-36
Preparing a Single-Step and a Multiple-Step Income Statement **LO1, 4**

Lewis Company's records show the following information at December 31, 2020, its annual year-end.

Sales revenue	$95,000	Interest expense	$ 4,000
Service revenue	35,000	Earthquake loss on building	15,000
Gain on sale of short-term investments	11,000	Loss on sale of warehouse*	3,000
Selling expense	18,000	Cost of goods sold	45,000
General and administrative expense	12,000	Common stock shares outstanding	10,000 shares
Depreciation expense (administrative)	6,000	Income tax rate	25%

* Loss on sale of warehouse is considered nonoperating.

Required

a. Prepare a single-step income statement (including earnings per share).
b. Prepare a multiple-step income statement (including earnings per share).

Exercise 3-37
Preparing a Multiple-Step Income Statement and a Retained Earnings Statement **LO1, 6**

The following pretax amounts are taken from the accounts of J&J Inc. at December 31, 2020, its annual year-end ($ thousands). Assume an average 25% tax rate on all items.

Sales revenue	$ 340
Cost of goods sold	170
Selling and administrative expenses	90
Gain on sale of land held for speculation	30
Prior period adjustment, correction of error from 2019, pretax (a debit)	16
Interest expense	2
Cash dividends declared and paid	5
Retained earnings, December 31, 2019	103
Common stock, outstanding	10,000 shares

Required

a. Prepare a multiple-step income statement, including intraperiod income tax allocation and EPS disclosure.
b. Determine the December 31, 2020, balance in retained earnings.

Exercise 3-38
Computing Financial Statement Measures **LO1, 4, 5**

The following pretax amounts are taken from the adjusted trial balance of Mastery Inc. on December 31, 2020, its annual year-end. Assume that the income tax rate for all items is 25%. The average number of common shares outstanding during the year was 20,000.

Balance, retained earnings, December 31, 2019	$ 90,000
Sales revenue	600,000
Cost of goods sold	210,000
Selling expenses	72,000
Administrative expenses	68,000
Gain on sale of investments	20,000
Unrealized holding gain on debt investments, net of tax	8,500
Prior period adjustment, understatement of depreciation from prior period (2019)	40,000
Dividends declared and paid	32,000

Required

Compute the following amounts for the year-end financial statements of 2020.

a. Gross profit (2020).
b. Operating income (2020).
c. Net income (2020).
d. Earnings per share (2020).
e. Comprehensive income (2020).
f. Retained earnings balance (December 31, 2020).

Exercise 3-39
Computing Net Sales and Net Income Attributable to Controlling Interest **LO1, 2**

The following pretax amounts are taken from the adjusted trial balance of Gilmore Corp. at December 31, 2020, its annual year-end.

Dividends declared and paid	$ 35,000	Casualty loss	$ 22,000
Sales revenue, net	300,000	Common stock (par $5)	200,000
Cost of goods sold	100,000	Beginning retained earnings, December 31, 2019	60,000
Operating expenses	60,000	Net income attributable to noncontrolling interest	5,000

Required

Compute the following for 2020, assuming an income tax rate of 25%.

a. Net income
b. Net income attributable to controlling interest (2020).

Exercise 3-40 Preparing an Income Statement and a Statement of Comprehensive Income **LO1, 5, 6**

The following pretax amounts are taken from the adjusted trial balance of Avoca Auto Corp. at December 31, 2020, its annual year-end.

Sales revenue	$260,000
Cost of goods sold	110,000
Operating expenses	80,000
Gain on debt retirement	20,000
Interest expense	8,000
Loss from discontinued operations	50,000
Retained earnings balance, December 31, 2019	30,000
Dividends declared and paid	25,000
Unrealized holding gain on debt investment securities, net of tax	4,000
Common stock, weighted average shares outstanding	10,000 shares

Required

a. Prepare a single-step income statement. Assume an average 25% tax rate on all items. Include earnings per share disclosures.
b. Prepare a statement of comprehensive income by showing a separate but consecutive statement of comprehensive income. Ignore earnings per share disclosures.
c. Compute the ending retained earnings balance at December 31, 2020.

Exercise 3-41 Reporting Discontinued Operations—Disposal in Subsequent Year **LO3**

On October 1, 2020, Blain Company approved a formal plan to sell the McKay Division, considered a component of the business. The sale will occur on March 31, 2021. The division had operating income of $500,000 (pretax) for the year ended December 31, 2020, but expects to incur an operating loss of $100,000 for the first quarter of 2021. Blain determines the carrying value and fair value (net of selling costs) of the McKay Division to be $5,000,000 and $4,800,000, respectively, on December 31, 2020. Blain's tax rate for 2020 is 25%. Weighted average number of common shares outstanding in 2020 is 300,000.

Required

a. Assume Blain Company's income from continuing operations is $2,300,000. Prepare a partial income statement beginning with *income from continuing operations*. Include earnings per share disclosures.
b. How does the answer to part *a* change if the fair value of the McKay Division's net assets were $5,200,000 instead of $4,800,000 on December 31, 2020?

Exercise 3-42 Reporting on Discontinued Operations —Disposal in Current Year **LO3, 4**

On August 1, 2020, Fischer Inc. decided to discontinue the operations of its Services Division, which qualifies as a business component. An agreement was formalized to sell this component for $156,000 cash. The book value of the assets of the Services Division was $180,000. The disposal date was August 1, 2020. The income tax rate is 25%, and the accounting year-end is December 31. On December 31, 2020, the pretax income from all operations, including an operating loss of $20,000 incurred by the Services Division prior to August 1, 2020, was $400,000. There were 50,000 weighted average common shares outstanding during 2020.

Required

Prepare a partial income statement beginning with income from continuing operations. Include the earnings per share disclosures.

Exercise 3-43 Computing and Reporting Discontinued Operations **LO3**

Jules Inc. reported net income of $1,681,500, income from continuing operations of $1,800,000 (after tax), and a loss from a discontinued component of $480,000 (pretax) for the year ended December 31, 2020. The company's tax rate is 25%. The decision to dispose of the component was made on June 1, 2020, and the component was sold on November 30, 2020.

Required

Compute net proceeds from the sale of the discontinued component if the carrying value of the business component was $475,000 on November 30, 2020 (the date of sale).

Exercise 3-44
Reporting an Income Statement with Irregular Items **LO3, 4**

The following pretax amounts are taken from the adjusted trial balance of Goal Corp. at December 31, 2020, its annual year-end. Assume an average 25% tax rate on all items.

Sales revenue	$220,000	Gain on sale of fixed asset (pretax)	$25,000
Service revenue	50,000	Restructuring costs (pretax)	20,000
Cost of goods sold	130,000	Loss on discontinued operations (pretax)	5,000
Operating expenses	88,000	Common stock outstanding	10,000 shares

Required

Prepare a single-step income statement, including the section on earnings per share.

Exercise 3-45
Reporting Earnings per Share Disclosures **LO3, 4**

Siera Inc. had 350,000 shares of common stock outstanding throughout 2020 that declared and paid dividends of $50,000 in 2020. The company also had 30,000 shares of preferred stock that paid dividends of $5,000 in 2020 (declared in 2020). The company reported the following amounts in its income statement for the year ended December 31, 2020 (pretax).

Income from continuing operations	$1,250,000
Loss from discontinued operations	35,000

Required

a. Prepare the earnings per share section of the income statement for the year ended December 31, 2020 assuming a tax rate of 25%.

b. Repeat requirement of part *a* except now assume that the company reported income from discontinued operations of $35,000.

Exercise 3-46
Reporting a Statement of Comprehensive Income **LO5**
Hint: See Demo 3-5

Wagner Inc. has service revenue of $2,000,000, operating expenses of $1,200,000, and an unrealized holding loss of $100,000 on debt security investments for the year ended December 31, 2020. Its income tax rate is 25%.

Required

a. Prepare a single continuous statement of comprehensive income. Ignore earnings per share disclosures.

b. Prepare two separate statements of income and comprehensive income. Ignore earnings per share disclosures.

Exercise 3-47
Preparing a Statement of Stockholders' Equity with a Prior Period Error **LO6, 7**

In 2019, the first year of operations for Sprint Co., the company reported net income of $45,000 and declared and paid dividends of $14,000. No other items affected retained earnings in 2019. On December 31, 2019, the company had the following balances in stockholders' equity accounts (other than retained earnings): common stock, $100,000 credit balance; accumulated other comprehensive income, $5,000 debit balance. During 2020, the company reported net income of $88,000, declared and paid dividends of $20,000, and reported a foreign currency translation gain of $8,500 (after tax). Also in 2020, the company discovered that its 2019 depreciation expense was understated by $10,000 before taxes and the amount is material to the company. Assume a tax rate of 25%.

Required

a. Prepare a statement of stockholders' equity for Sprint Co. for the year ended December 31, 2020.

b. Prepare a separate statement of retained earnings for the year ended December 31, 2020.

Exercise 3-48
Recording a Change in Accounting Estimate **LO7**
Hint: See Demo 3-7A

Epsom Company purchased a machine that cost $40,000 on January 1, 2012. The estimated useful life was 12 years, and the estimated residual value was $0. Straight-line depreciation is used. At the start of 2020, before making any adjusting entry to record depreciation expense for that year, the company decided that the machine should be depreciated over a 15-year total useful life.

Required

a. Prepare the adjusting entry at December 31, 2020, for annual depreciation expense.

b. Prepare the correcting entry required, if any, at December 31, 2020. If none is required, provide the reason.

Exercise 3-49 Recording a Change in Estimate, an Error Correction, and a Change in Principle **LO7**

On December 31, 2020, Alexa Company is preparing adjusting entries for its annual year-end. The following situations confront the company.

1. Equipment #101 with a cost of $7,700 was purchased on January 1, 2018. It is being depreciated on a straight-line basis over an estimated useful life of 10 years with no residual value. At December 31, 2020, it has been determined that the estimated total useful life is 6 years instead of 10.
2. Equipment #502 with a cost of $4,550 was purchased on January 1, 2017. It is being depreciated on a straight-line basis over an estimated useful life of seven years with no residual value. At December 31, 2020, it was discovered that no depreciation had been recorded on this equipment for 2017 or 2018, but it was recorded for 2019.
3. In 2020, Alexa decided to change inventory methods from the weighted-average method to the FIFO method. Net income reported in 2019 applying the weighted-average method was $95,000. If FIFO had been applied in 2019, net income would have been $101,000.

Required

a. For equipment #101, provide the required adjusting entry for depreciation expense at December 31, 2020.
b. For equipment #502, provide the required adjusting entry for depreciation expense at December 31, 2020.
c. For equipment #502, provide any necessary correcting entry. Ignore income taxes.
d. In reporting comparative income statements in 2020, what net income amount is presented for 2019?

Exercise 3-50 Distinguishing Concept Terminology **LO1, 2, 3, 4, 5, 6, 7**

Terms relating to concepts discussed in this chapter along with descriptions of those terms follow.

____ 1. Operating income	*a.* Event not related to the typical activities of a company
____ 2. Nonoperating income	*b.* Relating income available to common shareholders to one share of stock
____ 3. Gross profit	*c.* Allocating the tax effect to an item within a period of time
____ 4. Unusual event	*d.* Result from a change in accounting principle or an error correction
____ 5. Infrequent event	*e.* Revenues and expenses from a company's central operations
____ 6. Discontinued operations	*f.* Result specified when adopting an accounting standard update
____ 7. Intraperiod tax allocation	*g.* Nonowner changes in equity
____ 8. Earnings per share	*h.* An eliminated business component representing a strategic shift
____ 9. Comprehensive income	*i.* Results from a change in accounting estimate
____ 10. Prospective treatment	*j.* Event not expected to recur in the foreseeable future
____ 11. Retrospective treatment	*k.* Sales revenue less cost of goods sold
____ 12. Modified retrospective treatment	*l.* Revenues, expenses, gains, and losses from a company's peripheral operations

Required

Match each term, *1* through *12* with the most appropriate description *a* through *l*.

Problems

Problem 3-51 Preparing a Single-Step and a Multiple-Step Income Statement **LO1, 4**

The following pretax information is taken from the adjusted trial balance of Trader J's Corp. at December 31, 2020, its annual year-end.

Sales revenue, net	$950,000	Interest expense	$ 9,000
Gain on sale of investment	8,000	Recovery from prior expropriation loss	80,000
Depreciation expense	25,000	Loss on sale of long-term investments	10,000
Selling expense	140,000	Cost of goods sold	550,000
General and administrative expenses	92,300	Casualty loss	30,000
Rent revenue	18,000	Average income tax rate on all items	25%
Investment revenue	7,000	Common stock outstanding	40,000 shares

Required

a. Prepare a single-step income statement including the earnings per share disclosures.
b. Prepare a multiple-step income statement including the earnings per share disclosures. Assume that rent revenue is nonoperating.

Problem 3-52
Preparing a Multiple-Step Income Statement **LO1, 3, 4**

The following data are taken from the adjusted trial balance of Retail Corp. at December 31, 2020, its annual year-end.

Sales revenue	$400,000
Cost of goods sold	102,000
Depreciation expense (70% administrative expense, 30% selling expense)	50,000
Rent revenue	4,000
Interest expense	6,000
Investment revenue	2,500
Selling expenses (excluding depreciation)	105,500
General and administrative expenses (excluding depreciation)	46,000
Gain on sale of noncurrent asset	6,000
Loss on sale of long-term investments	3,600
Loss due to discontinued operations	10,000
Average income tax rate on all items	25%
Weighted average common stock outstanding	20,000 shares

Required

Prepare a multiple-step income statement, including the earnings per share disclosure. Assume that rent revenue and the gain on sale of noncurrent asset are nonoperating.

Problem 3-53
Reorganizing an Income Statement in Proper Layout and Titles **LO2**

Graphics Inc. prepared the following income statement at its year-end, December 31, 2020.

Profit and Loss
December 31, 2020

Sales income		$196,000
Cost of sales		64,000
Gross profit		132,000
Costs		
Salaries	$30,000	
Depreciation	12,000	
Selling	42,000	
General and administrative	16,000	
Interest	6,000	
Sale of long-term investments, loss	10,000	
Loss on discontinued operations	8,600	122,800
Other income		
Service	7,400	
Interest	2,800	10,200
Taxable profit		19,400
Tax (25%)		4,900
Net profit		$ 14,500

Required

The statement above has some poor titles, lacks proper organization, and reports some incorrect subtotals. Recast the above statement in an accurate, multiple-step statement in proper form.

Problem 3-54
Preparing a Multiple-Step Income Statement with Earnings Per Share Disclosure **LO2, 4, 6**

The following amounts are taken from the accounting records of Trans Corp. at December 31, 2020, its annual year-end.

Sales revenue	$340,000
Service revenue	64,000
Cost of goods sold	170,000
Selling and administrative expenses	86,000
Investment revenue	6,000
Interest expense	4,000
Infrequent item: loss on sale of long-term investment	10,000
Loss due to fire damage	14,000
Cash dividends declared and paid	8,000
Prior period adjustment, correction of error from prior period, pretax (a debit)	12,000
Balance, retained earnings, December 31, 2019	80,300
Common stock (par $5) outstanding	30,000 shares
Average income tax rate on all items	25%

Required

a. Prepare a multiple-step income statement, including tax allocation and earnings per share disclosure. Assume that service revenue is nonoperating.

b. Compute the ending balance at December 31, 2020, for retained earnings.

Problem 3-55
Preparing a Multiple-Step Income Statement with Earnings Per Share Disclosure **LO2, 4**

The following pretax amounts are taken from the accounts of Stone Corp. at December 31, 2020, its annual year-end.

Sales revenue	$550,000
Cost of goods sold	280,000
Selling expenses	70,000
Administrative expenses (includes $20,000 of restructuring costs)	100,000
Interest revenue	1,000
Interest expense	3,000
Unusual item: Gain from sale of noncurrent asset (nonoperating)	20,000
Loss from discontinued operations	40,000
Balance, retained earnings, December 31, 2019	95,000
Cash dividends declared and paid	15,000
Prior period adjustment, correction of error (omitted a loss from prior period)	8,000
Common stock (par $1) outstanding	40,000 shares
Average income tax rate on all items	25%

Required

a. Prepare a multiple-step income statement, including tax allocation and earnings per share disclosure.

b. Compute the ending balance at December 31, 2020, for retained earnings.

Problem 3-56
Preparing the Discontinued Operations Section of the Income Statement **LO3**

At its September 1, 2020, meeting, the board of directors of Jolie Inc. approved a plan for disposing of its candy vending division. The vending machine operation is a separate business component and had incurred a loss before tax of $150,000 for the eight-month period ending September 1, 2020. A tentative agreement has been reached with Macur Corporation to buy the vending division for $2 million, with delivery of all the assets and operations to Macur as of April 1, 2021. Jolie will continue operating the division until it is delivered to Macur. The book value of the vending machine operation is $2,100,000 on December 31, 2020. An operating loss of $30,000 before tax effects is experienced during the last four months of 2020. Assume an income tax rate of 25%.

Required

a. Present the discontinued operations section of the 2020 income statement for Jolie Company. Assume that the after-tax income from continuing operations in 2020 is $500,000. Ignore the earnings per share disclosure.

b. Actual operations of the vending machine division for the first three months of 2021 result in an operating loss before taxes of $40,000, and the sale of the net assets of the division results in an actual pretax loss of $180,000. Present the discontinued operations section of comparative income statements for 2020 and 2021 for Jolie Company. Assume that after-tax income from continuing operations is $600,000 in 2021.

c. How would the answer change to part *a* if the book value of the vending machine operation were $1,900,000 on December 31, 2020, instead of $2,100,000?

Problem 3-57
Preparing a Statement of Comprehensive Income and a Stockholders' Equity Statement **LO5, 6**

The following pretax amounts are taken from the adjusted trial balance of Gomez Corp. at December 31, 2020, its annual year-end.

Sales revenue	$1,000,000	Unrealized holding loss on debt securities	$ 12,000
Cost of goods sold	560,000	Foreign currency translation adjustment, loss	18,000
Operating expenses	280,000	Common stock, 50,000 shares outstanding	150,000
Interest expense	50,000		

Other information:

- Assume an average 25% corporate tax rate on all items.
- Assume no changes in common stock in 2020.
- Accumulated other comprehensive income had a $40,000 credit balance on December 31, 2019.
- Retained earnings had a $387,000 credit balance on December 31, 2019.
- Dividends declared and paid in 2020 were $50,000.

Required

a. Prepare two separate but consecutive statements of income and comprehensive income. Ignore earnings per share disclosures.

b. Prepare a statement of stockholders' equity.

Problem 3-58
Restating in Proper Form an Income Statement and a Statement of Retained Earnings with Error Correction **LO7**

The records of Glacier Corporation for 2020 provided the following pretax data.

Income Statement Data—2020	
Income before discontinued operation	$80,000*
Loss from discontinued operation	20,000*
Pretax income	$60,000

Statement of Retained Earnings—2020	
Beginning balance, December 31, 2019	$170,000
Less: Correction of accounting error	(30,000)*
Corrected balance, December 31, 2019	140,000
Add: Net income, 2020	60,000
Less: Dividends declared and paid during 2020	(40,000)
Ending balance, December 31, 2020	$160,000

Required

Properly format the income statement (beginning with income from continuing operations before tax) and the statement of retained earnings. Both statements should be prepared on an after-tax basis as applicable (apply intraperiod tax allocation). Assume that the three items indicated with an asterisk are subject to a 25% income tax effect.

Problem 3-59
Reporting a Change in Principle, Change in Estimate, and Correction of an Error **LO7**

Express Corp. was audited by an independent CPA at December 31, 2020, its annual year-end. During the audit, the following situations were found that needed attention.

1. On December 29, 2018, a $12,000 asset purchase was debited in full to 2018 operating expenses. The asset has a six-year estimated life and no residual value. The company uses straight-line depreciation for such assets.
2. Prior to recording 2020 depreciation expense, the company decided, based on new information, that a large machine that originally cost $128,000 should be depreciated over a total useful life of 14 years instead of 20 years. (This is not an error correction.) The machine was acquired January 2, 2015. Assume that the residual value of $8,000 was not changed. Provide the 2020 adjusting entry and any other entries due to the change in useful life. Annual straight-line depreciation is calculated as cost less residual value, divided by useful life.
3. In late December 2020, the company disposed of old equipment for $6,000 cash. Annual depreciation was $2,000. At the beginning of 2020, the accounts appeared as follows.

Equipment (cost)	$18,000
Accumulated depreciation	13,000

At the date of disposal, the following entry was made. No depreciation was recorded for 2020.

Cash	6,000	
Equipment		6,000

4. A patent that originally cost $3,400 is being amortized over its useful life of 17 years at $200 per year. After the 2019 adjusting entry it was amortized down to a book value of $800. At the end of 2020, it was determined in view of a competitor's patent that the patent will have no economic value to the company by the end of 2021. Straight-line amortization is used.
5. The company decided to change inventory methods in 2020. If the new inventory method had been used in all previous periods, 2019 cost of goods sold would have been $8,000 more than was recorded using the old inventory method. The company used the new inventory method in the current year.

Required

a. For each situation above, identify whether it represents an accounting error, change in estimate, or change in accounting principle.

b. Prepare any necessary journal entries. Ignore income tax considerations.

Problem 3-60
Preparing a Multiple-Step Income Statement with Irregular Items and Tax Allocations
LO1, 2, 3, 4, 7

The following trial balance of the Petro Corp. at December 31, 2020, has been adjusted, *except* that income tax expense has not yet been allocated.

PETRO CORPORATION
Selected Trial Balance Amounts
December 31, 2020

Accounts	Debit	Credit
Net sales, excluding Plastics Division		$10,750,000
Net sales, Plastics Division		2,200,000
Cost of sales, excluding Plastics Division	$5,920,000	
Cost of sales, Plastics Division	1,650,000	
Selling and administrative expenses, excluding Plastics Division	2,600,000	
Selling and administrative expenses, Plastics Division	660,000	
Interest revenue		65,000
Gain on litigation settlement		200,000
Gain on disposal of Plastics Division		150,000

Other financial data for the year ended December 31, 2020.

1. Income taxes: Tax rate on all types of income, 25%.
2. The gain from litigation settlement is a taxable gain and is considered unusual and infrequent.
3. Discontinued operations: On October 31, 2020, Petro sold its Plastics Division for $2,950,000, when the carrying amount was $2,800,000. For financial statement reporting, this sale was considered a disposal of a component of a business.
4. Capital structure: Common stock, $10 par, 215,000 weighted average shares outstanding.

Required

Prepare an income statement for Petro using the multiple-step format for the year ended December 31, 2020, including the earnings per share disclosure.

Problem 3-61
Classifying Effects of Transactions among Financial Statements **LO1, 2, 3, 4, 5**

The following amounts (considered material) required analysis to indicate on which financial statement and section the amounts are reported.

1. Total amount of cash and credit sales for the period.
2. A client suffered a casualty loss (a fire) amounting to $500,000.
3. Gain on sale of a business component resulting in a strategic shift.
4. A client company paid $175,000 damages assessed by the courts as a result of an injury to a customer on the company premises three years earlier.
5. A client sold a fixed asset and reported a gain of $70,000.
6. Cost of goods sold for the period.
7. The major supplier of raw materials to a client company experienced a prolonged strike. As a result, the client company reported a loss of $150,000. This is the first such loss; however, the client has three major suppliers, and strikes are not unusual in those industries.
8. A client owns several large blocks of common stock of other corporations. The shares have been held for a number of years and are viewed as a long-term investment. During the past year, 20% of the stock was sold to meet an unusual cash demand. Additional sales of the stock are not anticipated.
9. Selling expenses.
10. Cash dividends declared and paid.
11. Restructuring charges.
12. Gain due to a foreign currency translation adjustment.
13. Rent collected on office space temporarily leased.
14. Interest expense of the year paid in cash plus interest accrued on liabilities.
15. Dividends received on stocks held as an investment.

16. Damages paid as a result of a lawsuit by an individual injured while shopping in the store; the litigation lasted three years.
17. Loss due to expropriation of a plant in a foreign country.
18. Adjustment due to correction during current year of an error; the error was made two years earlier.
19. Interest collected on November 30 of the current year from a customer on a 90-day note.
20. Year-end bonus of $50,000 paid to employees for performance during the year.

Required

Classify each item as (a) operating income, (b) nonoperating income (other revenues, gains, expenses, and losses), (c) adjustment to retained earnings, (d) other comprehensive income, or (e) discontinued operation.

Accounting Decisions and Judgments

AD&J 3-62
Evaluating an Annual Report **LO1, 2, 4, 5, 6**

Real World Analysis Obtain an electronic copy of the Form 10-K for the **Coca-Cola Company** for the year ended December 31, 2015, which can be found on the SEC Edgar website (https://www.sec.gov/edgar/searchedgar/companysearch.html). Search for Coca Cola Co. To become familiar with the 2015 financial statements, complete the following requirements.

a. Are the statements comparative? Why are comparative statements usually presented?
b. Are the statements consolidated? What do we understand this to mean?
c. Is this a retail, a financial, or a manufacturing company? Explain.
d. How many different kinds of revenue were reported? How many different kinds of expenses were reported?
e. How were interest expense and interest revenue reported on the income statement?
f. Was the total amount of depreciation expense separately reported on the income statement?
g. Were any unusual or infrequently occurring (but not both) items reported on the income statement in 2014 or 2015?
h. Was there any indication of an accounting change? If so, explain how it was reported and what type of change it was.
i. How many EPS amounts were reported?
j. What subtotals were reported on the income statement? Please list them.
k. What was the profit margin (net income divided by revenue) for 2015?
l. What basis was used for valuing inventories?
m. What was the primary depreciation method used for accounting purposes?
n. What was the amount of income tax expense for 2015?
o. In 2015, what was the total amount of cash dividends declared on (a) common stock and (b) preferred stock?
p. Did the auditor's report express any reservations about the financial statements? Explain.
q. Did the company present a single statement of comprehensive income or two separate statements of income and comprehensive income?

AD&J 3-63
Preparing Single-Step and Multiple-Step Income Statements **LO1, 4**

Real World Analysis In its Year 8 annual report, **Georgia-Pacific Corporation**, a large manufacturer of building and paper products, identifies the following revenue, expense, gain, and loss accounts and amounts ($ millions). Assume that Georgia-Pacific has issued no preferred shares and has 90.6 million shares of common stock outstanding. The company's fiscal year ends on December 31.

Account	Amount	Account	Amount
Cost of sales	$10,326	Depreciation and cost of timber harvested	$ 935
Interest expense	443	Loss from early retirement of debt	21
Net sales	13,336	Selling, general, and administrative expense	1,141
Provision for income taxes	202		

Required

a. Assume that Georgia-Pacific desired to report the above accounts in a single-step format except for a second step for income taxes. Prepare a single-step statement, including EPS computations for Year 8.

b. Assume that Georgia-Pacific desired to report the above accounts in a multiple-step format. Prepare a multiple-step statement, including EPS computations for Year 8.

AD&J 3-64 Preparing Comparative Income Statements with Discontinued Operations, Preferred Dividends, and EPS **LO1, 2, 3, 7**

Real World Analysis In its 2015 annual report, **General Electric Co. (GE)** reported that

> Discontinued operations primarily included our Consumer business, most of our CLL business, our Real Estate business, and our U.S. mortgage business (WMC). Results of operations, financial position and cash flows for these businesses are separately reported as discontinued operations for all periods presented. Income (loss) from discontinued operations, net of tax were $(7,795) million in 2015 and $5,691 million in 2014.

GE's earnings from continuing operations after income taxes attributable to GE common shareholders were $1,679 million in 2015 and $9,523 million in 2014. The average common shares outstanding were 9,944 million shares in 2015 and 10,045 million shares in 2014. GE declared $18 million in preferred stock dividends in 2015 and $0 in 2014.

Required

Prepare the comparative income statements for GE covering 2015 and 2014, beginning with income from continuing operations. Include earnings per share disclosures.

3-65 **AD&J** Analyzing a Multiple-Step Income Statement **LO1**

Real World Analysis **Quality Food Centers (QFC)** is the largest independent supermarket chain and is the second largest chain in food market share in the Seattle/Puget Sound region. It operates over 50 stores in the Pacific Northwest. QFC has a reputation for premium quality perishables and superior service. Following are the comparative income statements for QFC as they appear in its Year 4 annual report.

QUALITY FOOD CENTERS, INC.
Income Statements

For Years Ending (in thousands)	Year 2	Year 3	Year 4
Sales	$460,106	$518,260	$575,879
Cost of sales and related occupancy expenses	343,118	386,895	430,711
Marketing, general, and administrative expenses	80,143	92,468	105,956
Operating income	36,845	38,897	39,212
Interest expense	0	0	0
Interest income	864	880	933
Earnings before income taxes	37,709	39,777	40,145
Taxes on income			
Current	10,628	11,207	11,593
Deferred	2,005	2,576	2,175
Total income taxes	12,633	13,783	13,768
Net earnings	$ 25,076	$ 25,994	$ 26,377

Required

a. Does QFC report a single-step or multi-step format? Does it disclose any unusual or infrequent items? Does it carry significant debt?

b. Does QFC report gross profit? Should it?

c. What other financial statement labels would be comparable to "earnings before income taxes"?

AD&J 3-66
Correcting Financial Statement Deficiencies **LO1, 6**

Challenge Problem The following annual income statement and statement of retained earnings are prepared for Airco Corporation.

AIRCO CORPORATION
Profit Statement
December 31, 2020

Sales income		$123,000
Service income		20,000
Total		143,000
Cost of sales		65,000
Gross profit		78,000
Costs		
Salaries, wages, etc.	$35,000	
Depreciation and write-offs	7,000	
Rent	3,000	
Taxes, property	500	
Utilities	2,100	
Promotion	900	
Sales return	2,000	
Sundry	6,700	(57,200)
Special items		
Profit on asset sold		6,000
Inventory shortage		(2,800)
Pretax profit		24,000
Income tax		3,200
Net profit		$ 20,800

AIRCO CORPORATION
Earned Surplus
December 31, 2020

Balance, earned surplus		$27,000
Add		
Profit		20,800
Correction of inventory error of 2019 (pretax)		5,000
Total		52,800
Deduct		
Earthquake loss (pretax)	$13,000	
Dividends	15,000	27,000
Balance		$25,800

Required

Evaluate Airco's financial statement presentation and format. There are at least 20 failures by the company regarding proper reporting, terminology, and format.

a. Identify 8 corrections for the income statement.
b. Identify 6 corrections for the statement of retained earnings.

AD&J 3-67
Analyzing Income Disclosures with Discontinued Operations **LO3**

Judgment Case Excerpts from Stanley Inc.'s comparative income statements for years 2017 through 2019 follow.

$ millions	2019	2018	2017
Income from continuing operations, after tax	$30	$(15)	$20
Discontinued operations			
Income from operations of discontinued component, net of tax	0	10	15
Gain on disposal of discontinued component, net of tax	50	0	0
Net income (loss)	$80	$ (5)	$35

Additional information

In 2018, income from continuing operations after tax included a $40 loss from an earthquake, net of tax. The earthquake loss is considered to be infrequent and unusual.

Required

a. Stanley has experienced volatile earnings over the three-year period shown. Do you expect this volatility to continue based on the information provided? Explain.

b. Net income increased from a loss of $5 million in 2018 to a profit of $80 million in 2019. The company's common stock price increased only 20% during that same period. Why might this be the case? Relate the 20% increase in stock price to components of net income.

c. Would we expect net income in 2020 to be more or less than the amount reported in 2019? More specifically, assuming no new, unusual, nonrecurring items, what would we estimate net income to be in 2020?

AD&J 3-68 Searching the Codification to Define Key Terms **LO1, 5, 7**

Codification Skills Refer to the Codification and identify and report the definition for each of the following terms.

1. Net income
2. Comprehensive income
3. Other comprehensive income
4. Change in accounting principle
5. Accounting change
6. Retrospective application
7. Error in previously issued financial statements

AD&J 3-69 Researching the Codification for Proper Citation **LO4, 5**

Codification Skills Research the Codification and report the proper citation that provides guidance on each of the following topics.

a. Comprehensive income presentation options — FASB ASC ___-___-___-___

b. Other comprehensive income item examples — FASB ASC ___-___-___-___

c. Objectives of basic and diluted earnings per share — FASB ASC ___-___-___-___

d. Income statement presentation earnings per share — FASB ASC ___-___-___-___

AD&J 3-70 Researching the Codification for Authoritative Guidance **LO5**

Codification Skills A company is preparing its annual financial statements for the year ended December 31, 2020. The company would like to review examples of a single continuous statement of comprehensive income. Identify the source of authoritative guidance that provides such examples.

FASB ASC ___-___-___-___

Appendix—Brief Exercises

App—Brief Exercise 3-71 Estimating Bonuses for Interim Financial Statements **LO8**

In January 2020, management of Clip Inc. estimates that its year-end bonus to executives will be $500,000 for 2020. The amount paid in 2019 was $440,000. Final determination of the amount to be paid is made at year-end.

Required

Determine the amount, if any, of bonus expense that should be reflected in Clip's quarterly income statement for the three months ended March 31, 2020. Justify and explain your answer.

App—Brief Exercise 3-72 Allocating Expenses to Interim Financial Statements **LO8**

In September 2020, Crystal Resorts spent $300,000 in advertising for the coming ski season. The ski season lasts from October through the following March, with business expected to be spread evenly over this period. The fiscal year for Crystal Resorts ends March 31, 2021.

Required

Determine the amount of expense that should be included in Crystal Resorts' interim financial statements for the quarter ending September 30 and for December 31, 2020. Justify and explain your answer.

App—Brief Exercise 3-73 Estimating Income Taxes for Interim Financial Statements **LO8**

Proctor Inc. reported income before income taxes of $100,000 and $150,000 in the first two quarters of 2020. Management's estimate of the annual effective tax rate is 35% at the end of the first quarter and is 30% at the end of the second quarter.

Required

Determine the income tax expense for the first two quarters of 2020.

Appendix—Exercises

App—Exercise 3-74
Reporting Items on Interim Financial Statements **LO8**

For interim reporting, items can be treated in one of four ways.

a. Recognized in interim statements of the current interim period.
b. Recognized in the current interim period but require special disclosure.
c. Deferred in their entirety (that is, not recognized until some later interim period or not recognized at all).
d. Amortized or accrued (recognized partly in the current interim period and partly in subsequent interim periods).

The following items 1 through 10 require a decision on how they are reported on interim statements. Match the letters *a, b, c,* or *d* from above with the numbered items on how best to report it on the interim statements.

____ 1. Salaries allocable to services rendered during the current period.
____ 2. Inventories estimated by use of the gross margin method.
____ 3. Temporary declines in the market value of inventories.
____ 4. Short-term stock investment gains from recoveries of market value (not in excess of previously recognized market declines).
____ 5. Materials and salaries allocable to products sold this period.
____ 6. Costs benefiting two or more interim periods.
____ 7. Increase in gross margin due to liquidation of a layer of LIFO-based inventory expected to be replenished by year-end.
____ 8. Quantity discounts allowed to customers based on the annual volume of their purchases.
____ 9. Contingencies and other uncertainties that can affect fairness of presentation.
____10. Income tax on income of first quarter where total income for the first quarter puts the company in a low tax bracket; subsequent operations are expected to be sufficiently profitable that by the end of the second quarter and thereafter taxable income of the company will be in a higher bracket.

App—Exercise 3-75
Reporting Transactions and Events in Interim Financial Statements **LO8**

Following are six independent cases on how accounting transactions and events might be reported on a company's interim financial reports. State whether the proposed decision is acceptable, not acceptable, or either depending on specific factors according to generally accepted accounting principles as applicable to interim financial data. Support your answer with a brief explanation.

____ 1. Company management was reasonably certain it would have an employee strike in the third quarter. As a result, it shipped heavily during the second quarter but plans to defer the recognition of the sales in excess of its normal sales. The deferred sales will be recognized as sales in the third quarter, when the strike is in progress. Management thinks this is more representative of normal second- and third-quarter operations.
____ 2. The company takes a physical inventory at year-end for annual financial statement purposes. Inventory and cost of sales reported in interim quarterly statements are based on estimated gross profit rates because a physical inventory would result in a temporary shutdown of operations. The company has reliable perpetual inventory records.
____ 3. The company is planning to report one-fourth of its annual pension expense each quarter.
____ 4. The company wrote down inventory to reflect lower of cost or market in the first quarter of this year. At year-end, the market exceeds the original acquisition cost of this inventory. Consequently, management plans to write the inventory back up to its original cost as a year-end adjustment.
____ 5. The company realized a large gain on the sale of investments at the beginning of the second quarter. The company wants to report one-third of the gain in each of the remaining quarters.
____ 6. The company has estimated its annual audit fee. Management plans to prorate this expense equally over the four quarters.

CMA adapted

Appendix—Problems

App—Problem 3-76
Reporting Interim Income under Different Situations **LO8**

Dunn Manufacturing Company's budgeted activities for 2020 follow.

Net sales (1,000,000 units).	$6,000,000
Cost of goods sold	3,600,000
Gross margin	2,400,000
Selling, general, and administrative expenses	1,400,000
Operating earnings	1,000,000
Nonoperating income	100,000
Earnings before income taxes	1,100,000
Estimated income taxes (current and deferred)	385,000
Net earnings	$ 715,000
Earnings per share of common stock	$ 7.15

Dunn has operated profitably for many years and has experienced a seasonal pattern of sales volume and production. Sales volume of Dunn for 2020 is expected to follow a quarterly pattern of 10%, 20%, 35%, and 35% because of the seasonality of the industry. Due to production and storage capacity limitations, it is expected that Dunn's production will follow a pattern of 20%, 25%, 30%, and 25% during the four quarters of 2020.

At the end of the first quarter of 2020, Dunn prepared and issued the following interim report for public release.

Net sales (100,000 units)	$ 600,000
Cost of goods sold	360,000
Gross margin	240,000
Selling, general, and administrative expenses	290,000
Operating loss	(50,000)
Loss from warehouse fire	(175,000)
Loss before income taxes	(225,000)
Estimated income taxes	0
Net loss	$(225,000)
Loss per share of common stock	$ (2.25)

The following additional information is available for the first quarter just completed, but was not included in the public information released.

1. The company uses a standard cost system in which standards are set at currently attainable levels on an annual basis. Production during the quarter was 200,000 units, of which 100,000 were sold.
2. The selling, general, and administrative expenses were budgeted on a basis of $1,000,000 fixed expenses for the year plus 40 cents of variable expenses per unit of sales.
3. The warehouse fire loss met the conditions of an unusual and infrequent loss. The warehouse had an undepreciated cost of $475,000, and $300,000 was recovered from insurance on the warehouse. No other gains or losses are anticipated this year from similar events or transactions, nor has Dunn had any similar losses in preceding years. The full loss will be deductible as an ordinary loss for income tax purposes.
4. The effective income tax rate, for federal and state taxes combined, is expected to average 35% of earnings before income taxes during 2020. There are no permanent differences between pretax accounting income and taxable income.
5. Earnings per share were computed on the basis of 100,000 shares of capital stock outstanding. Dunn has only one class of stock issued, no long-term debt outstanding, and no stock option plan.

Required

a. For the additional information items 1 through 5 above, state whether Dunn has prepared its interim income statement in an acceptable or not acceptable manner per U.S. GAAP. Explain.

b. Identify one weakness in the form and content of Dunn's interim report without reference to the additional information.

c. Without reference to the specific situation of Dunn, what are the minimum standards of disclosure for interim financial data (published interim financial reports) for publicly traded companies?

App—Problem 3-77
Challenges in Reporting Interim Financial Statements LO8

The unaudited quarterly financial statements issued by many corporations are prepared on the same basis as annual statements, with minor exceptions.

Required

a. Under what circumstances would there be a difference between the basis used to prepare interim statements and that for annual statements?

b. Why are there problems in using interim statements to predict annual income?

c. How might quarterly income be affected by the behavior of costs incurred in the repairs and maintenance of manufacturing equipment account?

Answers to Review Exercise

Review 3-1

Part One a. $150,000 b. $50,000 c. $57,000 d. $14,250 e. $42,750

Part Two a. $470,000 b. $413,000 c. $57,000 d. $14,250 e. $42,750

Review 3-2

a. $150,000 b. $25,000 c. $32,000 d. $8,000 e. $24,000

Review 3-3

Part One a. $150,000 b. $25,000 c. $32,000 d. $8,000 e. $24,000 f. $(16,875) g. $7,125

Part Two a. $150,000 b. $25,000 c. $32,000 d. $8,000 e. $24,000 f. $(26,250) g. $(2,250)

Review 3-4

Part One $2.30

Part Two

Per share	
Income from continuing operations	$ 2.30
Loss from discontinued component, net of tax	(1.35)
Loss on disposal of discontinued component, net of tax	(0.34)
Net income	$ 0.61

Review 3-5

1.

SILVER CORPORATION
Statement of Comprehensive Income
For Year Ended December 31, 2020

Service revenue	$250,000
Operating expenses	230,000
Income before income taxes	20,000
Income tax expense ($20,000 × 25%)	5,000
Net income	15,000
Unrealized holding gain on debt security investments, net of tax	3,750
Comprehensive income	$ 18,750

2.

SILVER CORPORATION
Income Statement
For Year Ended December 31, 2020

Service revenue	$250,000
Operating expenses	230,000
Income before income taxes	20,000
Income tax expense ($20,000 × 25%)	5,000
Net income	$ 15,000

SILVER CORPORATION
Statement of Comprehensive Income
For Year Ended December 31, 2020

Net income	$15,000
Unrealized holding gain on debt security investments, net of tax	3,750
Comprehensive income	$18,750

Review 3-6

BRONZE INC.
Statement of Stockholders' Equity

	Common Stock	Retained Earnings	Accumulated Other Comprehensive Income	Total
Beginning balance, December 31, 2019	$300,000	$280,000	$35,000	$615,000
Net income		180,000		180,000
Dividends		(100,000)		(100,000)
Issue common stock	50,000			50,000
Other comprehensive income				
Foreign currency translation adjustment, net of tax			(10,000)	(10,000)
Ending balance, December 31, 2020	$350,000	$360,000	$25,000	$735,000

Review 3-7

a. Change in accounting estimate, prospective, no adjustment.

b. Error, restatement, adjust retained earnings to correct for understatement of expense in prior year.

c. Change in accounting principle, retrospective, adjust retained earnings to correct for understatement of expense in prior year.

d. Change in accounting principle, retrospective, adjust retained earnings to correct for overstatement of expense in prior years.

e. Error, restatement, adjust retained earnings to correct for overstatement of expense in prior year.

f. Change in accounting estimate, prospective, no adjustment.

Review 3-8

1. a 2. a 3. c 4. a 5. c 6. c 7. b

4 Balance Sheet and Financial Reporting

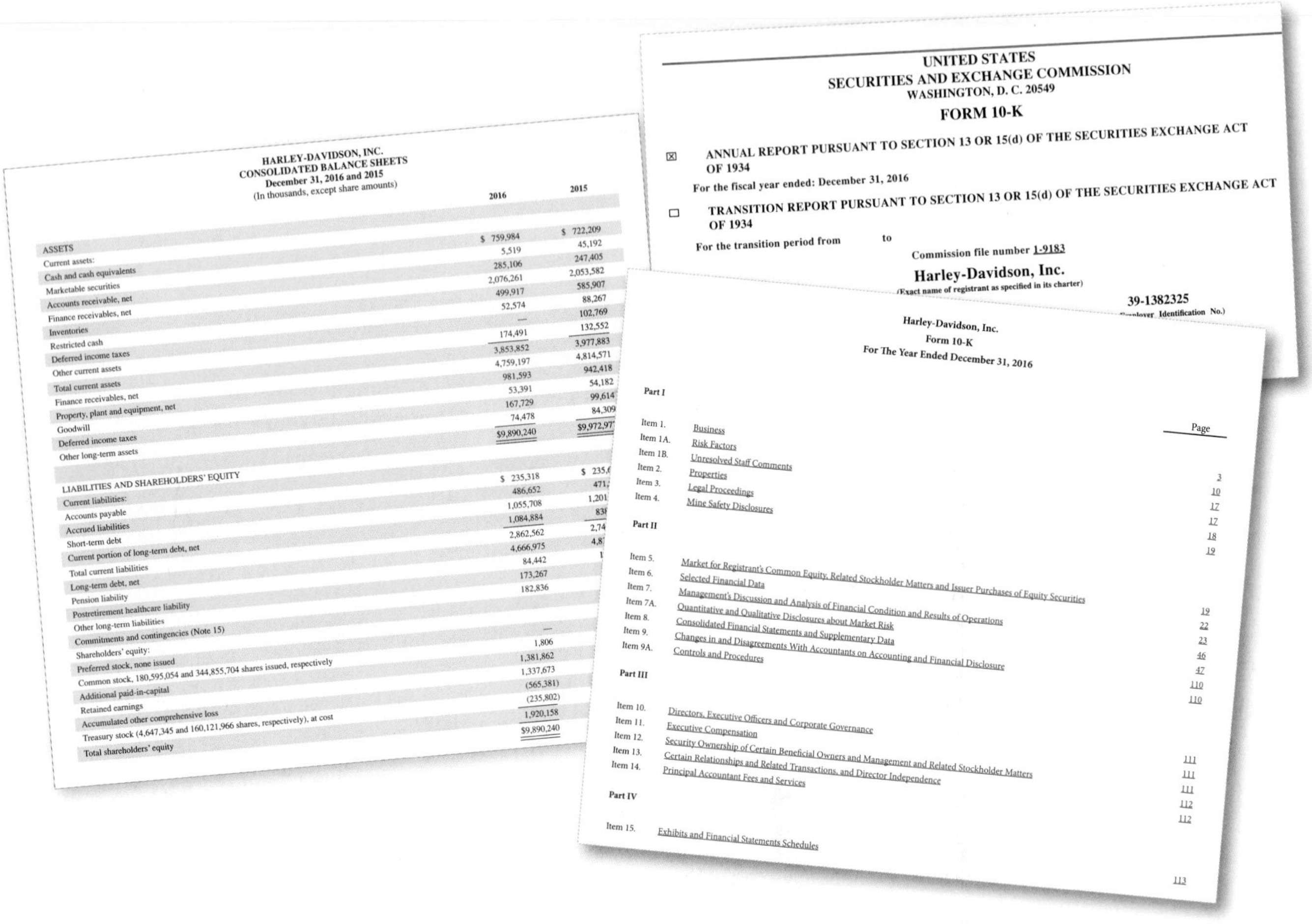

HARLEY-DAVIDSON, INC.
CONSOLIDATED BALANCE SHEETS
December 31, 2016 and 2015
(In thousands, except share amounts)
ASSETS
LIABILITIES AND SHAREHOLDERS' EQUITY
UNITED STATES
SECURITIES AND EXCHANGE COMMISSION
WASHINGTON, D. C. 20549
FORM 10-K
ANNUAL REPORT PURSUANT TO SECTION 13 OR 15(d) OF THE SECURITIES EXCHANGE ACT OF 1934
For the fiscal year ended: December 31, 2016
TRANSITION REPORT PURSUANT TO SECTION 13 OR 15(d) OF THE SECURITIES EXCHANGE ACT OF 1934
Commission file number 1-9183
Harley-Davidson, Inc.
39-1382325
Harley-Davidson, Inc.
Form 10-K
For The Year Ended December 31, 2016
Part I
Part II
Part III
Part IV

Chapter Preview

The balance sheet provides economic information at a point in time about an entity's resources (*assets*), claims against those resources (*liabilities*), and the remaining claim accruing to the owners (*stockholders' equity*). We begin this chapter with a discussion on how to classify items for balance sheet presentation and how to prepare a classified balance sheet. We then examine additional aspects of financial reporting including the accompanying notes to financial statements, the components of a Form 10-K, and segment reporting (Appendix 4A).

Action Plan

LO	Topic/Subtopic	Page	Demos	Reviews	Assignments
LO 4–1	**Identify classifications of asset, liability, and equity accounts on the balance sheet** Current Assets :: Noncurrent Assets :: Current Liabilities :: Noncurrent Liabilities :: Paid-in Capital :: Retained Earnings :: Accumulated Other Comprehensive Income :: Treasury Stock :: Noncontrolling Interests	4-3	D4-1A D4-1B D4-1C	R4-1	22, 23, 40, 41, 42, 43, 58, 69, 70, 73, 74
LO 4–2	**Prepare a classified balance sheet** Current and Noncurrent Classifications :: Working Capital	4-12	D4-2	R4-2	24, 25, 26, 27, 28, 29, 30, 31, 32, 33, 44, 45, 46, 47, 48, 49, 59, 60, 61, 62, 63, 64, 65, 66, 71, 72, 74
LO 4–3	**Explain notes accompanying financial statements** Significant Accounting Policies :: Fair Value Measurement :: Related Party Transactions :: Subsequent Events :: Errors, Fraud, and Illegal Acts :: Other Separate Notes	4-15	D4-3	R4-3	34, 35, 36, 49, 50, 51, 52, 53, 62, 66, 74, 75
LO 4–4	**Identify and describe sections of Form 10-K** Selected Financial Data :: MD&A :: Financial Statements and Supplementary Data :: Directors and Executive Officers :: Executive Compensation	4-23	D4-4	R4-4	37, 38, 39, 54, 55, 56, 57, 67, 68, 74
LO 4–5	**APPENDIX 4A—Describe requirements of segment reporting** Revenue Test :: Operating Profit Test :: Identifiable Asset Test :: Combined Sales Test	4-32	D4-5	R4-5	74, 81, 82, 83, 84, 85, 86, 87, 88, 89

LO 4-1 Identify classifications of asset, liability, and equity accounts on the balance sheet

LO 4-1 Overview

Balance Sheet Classifications
- Assets
  - Current and noncurrent
- Liabilities
  - Current and noncurrent
- Stockholders' equity
  - Paid-in capital
  - Retained earnings
  - Accumulated other comprehensive income
  - Treasury stock
  - Noncontrolling interests

The **balance sheet**, also referred to as the **statement of financial position**, is the financial statement that shows the balances of individual accounts making up assets, liabilities, and stockholders' equity at a specific point in time. Totals presented on the balance sheet illustrate that the balance sheet equation is in balance.

Assets = Liabilities + Stockholders' Equity

The balance sheet equation highlights that funds are raised from creditors (liabilities) or from owners (stockholders' equity) to acquire the entity's assets. The balance sheet is regularly reported at the close of business on the last day of each reporting period. However, a balance sheet can be constructed at any point in time.

Assets, liabilities, and equity (stockholders' equity) are finanical statement elements defined in Chapter 1 and repeated in **Exhibit 4-1**.

EXHIBIT 4-1
Defining Assets, Liabilities, and Equity

Element	Description
Assets	**SFAC No. 6 25** Assets are probable future economic benefits obtained or controlled by a particular entity as a result of past transactions or events.
Liabilities	**SFAC No. 6 35** Liabilities are probable future sacrifices of economic benefits arising from present obligations of a particular entity to transfer assets or provide services to other entities in the future as a result of past transactions or events.
Equity (also called Net Assets)	**SFAC No. 6 49** Equity or net assets is the residual interest in the assets of an entity that remains after deducting its liabilities.

The balance sheet classification categories included in **Exhibit 4-2** are representative of current reporting practices. A **classified balance sheet** is organized into these or similar categories that combine permanent accounts of comparable nature and function.

EXHIBIT 4-2
Classification of Balance Sheet Accounts

Assets	=	Liabilities	+	Stockholders' Equity
Current assets		Current liabilities		Paid-in capital
Noncurrent assets				Retained earnings
Long-term investments		Noncurrent liabilities		Accumulated other comprehensive income (AOCI)
Property, plant, and equipment				Treasury stock
Intangible assets				Noncontrolling interests
Other assets				

Balance Sheet

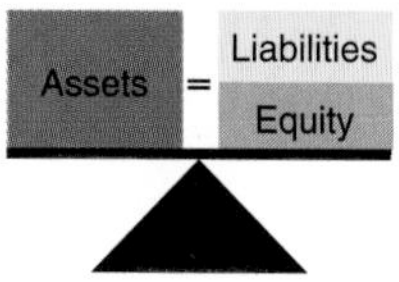

Generally, assets are grouped into two categories: **current assets** and **noncurrent assets**. Within these categories, it is common practice for assets to be classified and presented in decreasing order of **liquidity** (meaning convertibility into cash). Those items nearest to cash (that is, readily convertible at any time without restriction) are listed first. Assets with least liquidity (or least likely to be converted to cash) are listed last. In **Demo 4-1A**, we distinguish between current and noncurrent assets on the balance sheet. A similar classification exists for liabilities.

As discussed in Chapter 1, GAAP is a mixed-attribute measurement model because some items are recognized at historical cost and some items are recognized at fair value. This is illustrated in a typical balance sheet. For example, in the noncurrent asset section, certain types of long-term debt investments are recognized at historical cost while certain types of long-term debt investments are recognized at fair value. Besides following the relevant accounting standards, companies can choose to recognize even more items at fair value by electing the *fair value option*. Companies can elect to apply the **fair value option method** to eligible financial assets and financial liabilities. The fair value option is applied to receivables in Chapter 8, to investments in Chapter 14, and to financial liabilities in Chapter 16. Authoritative guidance follows.

825-10-25-1 This Subtopic permits all entities to choose, at specified election dates, to measure eligible items at fair value (the fair value option).

The fair value option is applied to each individual asset or liability generally at the date of purchase or origination and this election is generally not revocable. Unrealized gains or losses determined when adjusting assets or liabilities to fair value at reporting dates are recognized in net income.

825-10-35-4 A business entity shall report unrealized gains and losses on items for which the fair value option has been elected in earnings (or another performance indicator if the business entity does not report earnings) at each subsequent reporting date.

VF CORP.

Real World—ACCOUNTING EQUATION

VF CORP [VFC]

The following illustration organizes the balance sheet amounts from a recent annual report of VF Corporation using the balance sheet categories shown in **Exhibit 4-2**. This illustration demonstrates that the accounting equation is in balance ($ millions).

Assets		=	Liabilities		+	Stockholders' Equity	
Current assets	$4,163		Current liabilities	$1,942		Paid-in capital	$3,299
Noncurrent assets			Noncurrent liabilities	2,313		Retained earnings	3,129
Investments	0			$4,255		AOCI	(1,043)
PP&E	988					Treasury stock	0
Intangible assets	3,901					Noncontrolling interests	0
Other assets	588						$5,385
	$9,640			$9,640			

Current Asset Classification

The terms **current assets** and **operating cycle** are defined in the authoritative guidance as follows.

ASC Glossary **Current Assets:** Current assets is used to designate cash and other assets or resources commonly identified as those that are reasonably expected to be realized in cash or sold or consumed during the normal operating cycle of the business.

210-10-45-3 A one-year time period shall be used as a basis for the segregation of current assets in cases where there are several operating cycles occurring within a year. However, if the period of the operating cycle is more than 12 months, as in, for instance, the tobacco, distillery, and lumber businesses, the longer period shall be used. If a particular entity has no clearly defined operating cycle, the one-year rule shall govern.

ASC Glossary **Operating Cycle:** The average time intervening between the acquisition of materials or services and the final cash realization constitutes an operating cycle.

The normal operating cycle of a business is the average length of time from the expenditure of cash for inventory to the collection of cash from the sale of that inventory. The normal operating cycle of a typical manufacturer is shown in **Exhibit 4-3**.

EXHIBIT 4-3
Operating Cycle of a Manufacturing Company

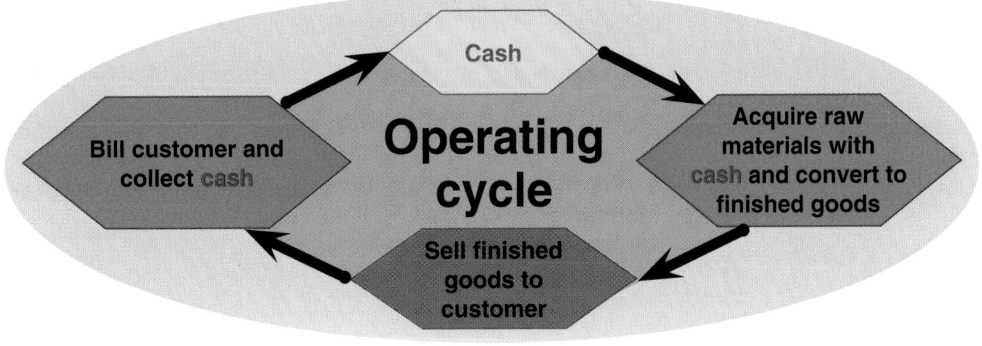

Most companies use one year as the time period for classifying items as current or long-term because either the operating cycle is less than one year or the length of the operating cycle is difficult to measure reliably. Typical accounts classified as a current asset are identified in **Exhibit 4-4**.

EXHIBIT 4-4
Examples of Current Asset Accounts

Current Asset	Description
Cash [Chapter 8]	Items immediately available to pay obligations such as cash on hand, cash in the bank, money orders, cashier's checks, and certified checks.
Cash equivalents [Chapter 8]	Short-term (maturity of 3 months or less), highly liquid investments in securities readily convertible into known amounts of cash with low risk of loss. Examples of cash equivalents include commercial paper, money market funds, and U.S. Treasury bills. Cash and cash equivalents are often combined into one line item on the balance sheet.
Restricted cash [Chapter 8]	Cash restricted for a particular purpose that is not available for general use. Depending on the length of the restriction and the ultimate intended use of cash, restricted cash can be reported as current or noncurrent.
Short-term investments [Chapter 14]	Debt or equity investments where the company has the intent and ability to sell within the next year (or operating cycle, if longer).
Accounts receivable (Trade receivables) [Chapters 2, 7, 8]	Results from the satisfaction of performance obligations incurred during a company's normal course of business through an informal credit agreement. Receivables are recognized at net realizable value or net of any expected credit losses (accounts receivable less allowance for doubtful accounts).
Nontrade receivables [Chapter 8]	Amounts owed to a company from sources such as tax refunds, contracts, investees, finance receivables, installment notes, sale of assets, and advances to employees.
Notes receivable [Chapter 8]	Receivables, with a maturity date within the following year, supported by formal contractual agreements.
Inventories [Chapters 9, 10]	Inventories consist of goods owned by a business and held either for use in the manufacture of products or as products awaiting sale. Merchandisers have one category of inventory (merchandise inventory) while manufacturers have three categories of inventory: raw materials (goods purchased for use in the manufacture of inventory), work-in-process (inventory items requiring further processing) and finished goods (manufactured goods held for sale).
Prepaid expenses [Chapter 2]	Cash outlays made in advance of receipt of service such as rent and advertising.

Noncurrent Asset Classification

Two important distinctions between current and noncurrent assets are that long-term assets are not completely used up in a single operating cycle *and* management plans to retain long-term assets beyond one year from the balance sheet date or beyond the operating cycle if it is longer. Typical accounts included in noncurrent assets are identified in **Exhibit 4-5**. If a company determines that a reported asset has no future economic benefit, it is written off and recognized in the income statement as a loss.

EXHIBIT 4-5
Examples of Noncurrent Asset Accounts

Noncurrent Asset	Description
Long-term investments [Chapter 14]	Long-term assets not used directly in the operations of a company including the following: ▪ Investments in equity or debt of another company; investor has the intent and ability to hold at least one year. ▪ Investments in nonconsolidated subsidiaries, including long-term receivables from nonconsolidated subsidiaries. ▪ Funds set aside for long-term future use, such as bond sinking funds (to retire bonds payable), expansion funds, stock retirement funds, and long-term savings deposits. ▪ Cash surrender value of life insurance policies carried by a company. ▪ Long-term investments in tangible assets, such as land and buildings, held for speculation.

continued

continued from previous page

Noncurrent Asset	Description
Property, plant, and equipment (Fixed assets) [Chapter 11]	Long-term tangible assets and other noncurrent assets used in continuing operations that are not held for resale including the following: ▪ Items that are depreciable, such as buildings, machinery, fixtures, and leasehold improvements, presented net of accumulated depreciation. ▪ Items that are subject to depletion, including mineral deposits, timberland, and agricultural land, presented net of depletion. ▪ Items that are not subject to depreciation, such as land or construction in process, recorded at cost.
Intangible assets and goodwill [Chapter 13]	Assets that lack physical substance (other than financial assets, such as accounts receivable or investments). Examples include patents, franchises, and goodwill. Intangible assets that are subject to amortization are reported net of accumulated amortization. Goodwill (not subject to amortization) arises when a company acquires another and the purchase price exceeds the fair value of the net assets acquired in the purchase. Although goodwill can be developed internally, it is not recognized unless a company is purchased.
Other assets [Chapters 12, 18]	Assets not easily included under alternative asset classifications. Examples include long-term prepaid expenses (deferred charges), idle fixed assets, deferred tax assets (net), long-term receivables, and noncurrent assets held for resale.

MACY'S Real World—REPORTING ASSETS ON THE BALANCE SHEET

MACY'S [M]

Macy's Inc. reported the following current assets and noncurrent assets in its classified balance sheet in a recent annual report.

Macy's, Inc.
Consolidated Balance Sheets (excerpt)

January 30, $ millions	2016	2015
Assets		
Current assets		
Cash and cash equivalents	$ 1,109	$ 2,246
Receivables	558	424
Merchandise inventories	5,506	5,417
Prepaid expenses and other current assets	479	493
Total current assets	7,652	8,580
Property and equipment—net	7,616	7,800
Goodwill	3,897	3,743
Other intangible assets—net	514	496
Other assets	897	711
Total assets	$20,576	$21,330

EXPANDING YOUR KNOWLEDGE — Balance Sheet: Usefulness and Limitations

The classifications on the balance sheet provide useful information to financial statement users.

Liquidity The balance sheet provides information that helps users assess a company's ability to pay current liabilities from its current assets, which is evidence of a company's liquidity.

Financial Flexibility The balance sheet provides insight into the risk profile of a company and its flexibility to alter amounts and timing of cash flows in response to unexpected needs and opportunities. Is the company in a position to finance new activities with relative ease without incurring excessive debt?

Solvency The ability of a company to pay debts as they come due is an indicator of a company's solvency. A balance sheet provides information on the level of debt and its relation to assets.

continued

continued from previous page

There are, however, limitations with information from a balance sheet.

Historical Cost A number of balance sheet values are not updated to fair value such as property, plant and equipment, causing comparisons between companies to be misleading.

Estimations The typical balance sheet includes many estimated amounts, such as expected credit losses from uncollectible receivables and the estimated liability arising from warranties. Other estimates are accumulated depreciation, amortization, income taxes, contingencies, and pension liabilities. The usefulness of such numbers depends on the quality of the estimates.

Omissions Certain assets and liabilities do not appear in financial statements. For example, the values of research and development activity and of human resources are difficult to quantify, which helps explain their exclusion from the balance sheet.

Demo 4-1A **LO4-1** **Classifying Assets on the Balance Sheet**

Demo MBC

Beree Inc. has the following asset accounts, 1 through 15, included in its adjusted trial balance on December 31, 2020. Indicate whether each balance sheet account should be classified as *current* or *noncurrent*.

Account	Current	Noncurrent
1. Cash	✔	
2. Supplies	✔	
3. Land, held for speculation		✔
4. Land, used in operations		✔
5. Equipment, retired and held for sale	✔	
6. Accounts receivable	✔	
7. Patent		✔
8. Cash equivalents	✔	
9. Prepaid insurance	✔	
10. Building		✔
11. Equity investments (intend to sell within a year)	✔	
12. Equity investments (intend to hold beyond a year)		✔
13. Bond sinking fund		✔
14. Finished goods inventory	✔	
15. Accumulated depreciation—Equipment		✔

Current Liability Classification

Liabilities are classified and generally reported based on time to maturity. The current liability section is listed first, followed by the noncurrent liability section. In **Demo 4-1B**, we distinguish between current and noncurrent liabilities on the balance sheet. Current liabilities include those obligations expected to be liquidated using current assets or refinanced by other short-term liabilities. Typically, accounts payable or notes payable (short-term) are listed first, although there is no prescribed ordering of current liabilities. Typical accounts included in current liabilities are described in **Exhibit 4-6**. In each case, if the normal operating cycle of a company is longer than a year, the amount is due within the normal operating cycle (instead of one year).

EXHIBIT 4-6
Examples of Current Liability Accounts

Current Liability	Description
Accounts payable (trade payables) [Chapter 15]	Obligations relate to the acquisition of inventories, supplies, and services used in the production and sale of goods or services.
Short-term notes payable [Chapter 15]	Formal written promises to pay a principal amount and are typically associated with interest charges.

continued

continued from previous page

Current Liability	Description
Current maturities of long-term debt [Chapter 15]	Portion of long-term debt that is due within the next year, and is expected to be paid with current assets or will result in the creation of other current liabilities.
Callable obligations [Chapter 15]	Obligations due on demand under the contract provisions in effect at the balance sheet date.
Deferred revenue [Chapters 2, 7, 15]	Cash is received in exchange for a company's obligation to transfer goods or services in the future under a revenue contract.
Accrued liabilities [Chapters 2, 15]	Incurred but unpaid expenses for items such as salaries, payroll taxes, interest, taxes, and utilities.

Noncurrent Liability Classification

A long-term (noncurrent) liability is an obligation that does not require the use of current assets for payment (or the incurrence of another current liability) during the next reporting year (or operating cycle if longer). Typical accounts included in noncurrent liabilities are identified in **Exhibit 4-7**. In each case, the amount is due after one year, or the normal operating cycle if longer than one year.

EXHIBIT 4-7
Examples of Noncurrent Liability Accounts

Noncurrent Liability	Description
Bonds payable [Chapter 16]	Debt security issued to secure large amounts of capital on a long-term basis. Reported net of bond discounts (contra account) and bond premiums (adjunct account).
Long-term notes payable [Chapter 16]	Formal written promises to pay an amount due after the following year, and are typically associated with interest charges.
Pension liabilities [Chapter 19]	Long-term net obligation to provide future benefits attributed to employee services rendered to date.
Other long-term liabilities [Chapters 15, 17, 18]	Obligations such as long-term lease liabilities and deferred tax liabilities (net). Also includes certain contingencies or obligations dependent upon a future event such as the settlement of a legal matter or future warranty claim.

MACY'S

Real World—REPORTING LIABILITIES ON THE BALANCE SHEET

MACY'S [M]

Macy's Inc. reported the following current liabilities and noncurrent liabilities in its classified balance sheet in a recent annual report.

January 30, $ millions	2016	2015
Current liabilities		
Short-term debt	$ 642	$ 76
Merchandise accounts payable	1,526	1,594
Accounts payable and accrued liabilities	3,333	3,109
Income taxes	227	296
Total current liabilities	5,728	5,075
Long-term debt	6,995	7,233
Deferred income taxes	1,477	1,443
Other liabilities	2,123	2,201
Total liabilities	$16,323	$15,952

Classifications on the Balance Sheet

We illustrated a typical presentation of a classified balance sheet. Companies, however, can instead present a balance sheet with groups of similar accounts, such as those with a similar nature, function, or measurement bases. For example, a company can group together accounts that relate to certain functions of the company such as investing or financing, or group together assets valued similarly (fair value or amortized cost). The objective of providing more homogeneous groupings is to provide more useful information to financial statement users.

Exposure Draft of SFAC No. 8 PR 36 Subtotals represent broad classes of often heterogeneous items. In contrast, line items can reflect more homogeneous classes of items and usually are more useful to resource providers in faithfully representing the differences in effects of transactions, events, or circumstances. Therefore, creating line items that include classes of items that are as nearly homogeneous as possible is a critical aspect of presentation. Homogeneity enhances the ability to faithfully represent a line item.

EXPANDING YOUR KNOWLEDGE **Management Intent**

Management intent can play a role in the classification of balance sheet items. For example, investments can be classified as current or noncurrent depending on management's intent. How long does management expect to hold an investment? As another example, consider land. If land is used in continuing operations, it is classified as *property, plant, and equipment.* If land is being held for speculative purposes, where management intends to sell the land at a future date when circumstances are favorable, land is classified as an *investment.* If land is not used in operations and is held for sale, it is included in *current assets* or *other assets*, depending on how long management estimates that it will be held for sale.

Demo 4-1B **LO4-1** **Classifying Liabilities on the Balance Sheet**

Demo MBC

Beree Inc. has the following liability accounts, 1 through 12, included in its adjusted trial balance on December 31, 2020. Indicate whether each balance sheet account should be classified as *current* or *noncurrent.*

Account	Current	Noncurrent
1. Accounts payable	✔	
2. Note payable, due in three months	✔	
3. Current maturities of long-term debt	✔	
4. Bonds payable, due in 5 years		✔
5. Mortgage payable, due in 10 years		✔
6. Accrued salaries	✔	
7. Accrued interest	✔	
8. Deferred revenue (short-term)	✔	
9. Dividends payable	✔	
10. Income taxes payable	✔	
11. Obligations under pension plans		✔
12. Note payable, due in 24 months		✔

Stockholders' Equity

Stockholders' equity items are classified and presented in order of permanence. This means that paid-in capital accounts, which typically change the least, are usually listed first. Equity accounts that are used to report accumulated earnings and are updated on an ongoing basis are listed last. For common stock, the number of authorized shares is reported either on the face of the balance sheet or in the notes, while the number of shares issued and outstanding are reported on the face of the balance sheet. For preferred stock, the number of authorized shares issued and outstanding are recognized on the face of the balance sheet or in a note. Typical stockholders' equity accounts are identified in **Exhibit 4-8**. In **Demo 4-1C**, we prepare the stockholders' equity section of the balance sheet.

210-10-S99-1-29 For each class of common shares state, on the face of the balance sheet, the number of shares issued or outstanding, as appropriate . . ., and the dollar amount thereof.

210-10-S99-1-28 Preferred stocks which are not redeemable or are redeemable solely at the option of the issuer. . . . State on the face of the balance sheet or in a note, for each issue, the number of shares authorized and the number of shares issued or outstanding, as appropriate.

MACY'S

Real World—REPORTING STOCKHOLDERS' EQUITY

MACY'S [M]

Macy's Inc. reported the following shareholders' equity (stockholders' equity) accounts in its classified balance sheet in a recent annual report.

January 30, $ millions	2016	2015
Shareholders' equity		
Common stock (310.3 and 340.6 shares outstanding) . . .	$ 3	$ 4
Additional paid-in capital . . .	621	1,048
Accumulated equity . . .	6,334	7,340
Treasury stock . . .	(1,665)	(1,942)
Accumulated other comprehensive loss . . .	(1,043)	(1,072)
Total Macy's Inc. shareholders' equity . . .	4,250	5,378
Noncontrolling interest . . .	3	0
Total shareholders' equity . . .	$4,253	$5,378

EXHIBIT 4-8
Stockholders' Equity Accounts

Equity Account	Description
Paid-in capital (Contributed capital) [Chapters 3, 20]	Paid-in capital includes the following: ▪ Common stock: par value (or stated value) of the issued or outstanding common stock of the company. ▪ Preferred stock: par value (or stated value) of the issued or outstanding preferred stock of the company. ▪ Paid-in capital in excess of par: reports the value of assets received by the company above the par (or stated value) of the capital stock given in exchange.
Retained earnings [Chapters 3, 20]	Retained earnings is a company's accumulated net earnings, less dividends paid out, since the company's inception. A portion of retained earnings can be restricted for specific purposes, such as for contractual reasons or management's intent to restrict dividend availability due to, for example, an upcoming plant expansion. A restriction is typically indicated in notes to financial statements. However, a company can elect to formally transfer (through a journal entry) restricted retained earnings into a separate account—Appropriated Retained Earnings. Appropriated retained earnings is identified separately in the stockholders' equity section of the balance sheet.
Accumulated other comprehensive income [Chapters 3, 20]	Accumulated other comprehensive income is the accumulation of revenues, expenses, gains, and losses included in comprehensive income but not in net income.
Treasury stock [Chapter 20]	Capital stock that has been issued and then reacquired by the company, but not retired. Amount is shown as a deduction in stockholders' equity.
Noncontrolling interests [Chapter 3]	Noncontrolling interest is the amount of a company's net assets owned by outside investors in one of a company's subsidiaries that is not part of its controlling interest. A company (parent) prepares financial statements where it combines its own activities with those of one or more additional companies (subsidiaries) in which it has a more than 50% but less than 100% ownership interest. The combined balance sheet is labeled a consolidated balance sheet. When a company prepares a consolidated balance sheet, the company allocates consolidated net assets to itself (parent) and to other investors (noncontrolling interest). Noncontrolling interest is the interest (less than a 50% ownership) in the net assets of the subsidiaries not owned by the parent company.

EXPANDING YOUR KNOWLEDGE — Industry Unique Balance Sheets

Balance sheet classification can vary by industry. For example, the balance sheet of a financial institution such as U.S. Bancorp does not distinguish current assets from noncurrent assets as you would see in a typical balance sheet of a manufacturing company. Financial institutions *do not use a current asset designation because nearly all their assets are readily marketable.*

U.S. Bancorp
Consolidated Balance Sheet (Assets only, $ millions)
December 31, 2015

Assets	
Cash and due from banks	$ 11,147
Investment securities	105,587
Loans held for sale	3,184
Loans, net	256,986
Premises and equipment	2,513
Goodwill	9,361
Other intangible assets	3,350
Other assets	29,725
Total assets	$421,853

Demo 4-1C LO4-1 Stockholders' Equity Balance Sheet Presentation

Demo MBC

Randall Inc. had the following balances on December 31, 2020, for its stockholders' equity accounts. Prepare the stockholders' equity section of its balance sheet as of December 31, 2020.

Retained earnings	$100,000
Common stock ($1 par value, 100,000 shares authorized, 25,000 shares issued and outstanding)	25,000
Paid-in capital in excess of par	80,000
Accumulated other comprehensive income	35,000
Noncontrolling interests	14,000
Treasury stock (100 shares)	3,000

Solution

Randall Inc.
Balance Sheet (Stockholders' Equity Section only)
December 31, 2020

Common stock ($1 par value, 100,000 shares authorized, 25,000 share issued and outstanding)	$ 25,000
Paid-in capital in excess of par	80,000
Retained earnings	100,000
Accumulated other comprehensive income	35,000
Less: Treasury stock, 100 shares	(3,000)
Total equity attributable to Randall Inc. stockholders	237,000
Equity attributable to noncontrolling interests	14,000
Total stockholders' equity	$251,000

Balance Sheet Classification

LO4-1 **REVIEW 4-1**

Review MBC

Match each account *a* through *n* with one of the 12 balance sheet classifications.

Balance Sheet Classification	Account
1. Current assets	____ *a.* Machinery
2. Investments	____ *b.* Income tax receivable
3. Property, plant, and equipment	____ *c.* Franchise
4. Intangible assets	____ *d.* Raw materials inventory
5. Other assets	____ *e.* Dividends payable
6. Current liabilities	____ *f.* Common stock
7. Long-term liabilities	____ *g.* Shares held by noncontrolling stockholders
8. Paid-in capital	
9. Retained earnings	____ *h.* Bonds payable
10. Accumulated other comprehensive income	____ *i.* Cash surrender value of life insurance
11. Treasury stock	____ *j.* Deferred revenue (current)
12. Noncontrolling interests	____ *k.* Investment in IBM common stock (with intent to hold at least 1 year)
	____ *l.* Noncurrent receivable (due from supplier)
	____ *m.* Paid-in capital in excess of par—common stock
	____ *n.* Foreign currency translation adjustment

More Practice: 4-40, 4-41, 4-43
Solution on p. 4-62

Prepare a classified balance sheet

LO 4-2

The **classified balance sheet** (illustrated in **Demo 4-2**) organizes accounts according to the categories listed in **Exhibit 4-2**. The primary characteristic of a classified balance sheet is the distinction made between current and noncurrent assets and liabilities.

Classified Balance Sheet
- Presents balances in asset, liability, and equity accounts
- Classifies assets and liabilities as current and noncurrent
- Allows for determination of a company's working capital

LO 4-2 Overview

210-10-05-4 The balance sheets of most entities show separate classifications of current assets and current liabilities (commonly referred to as classified balance sheets) permitting ready determination of working capital.

With current assets and current liabilities identified on a classified balance sheet, **working capital** (current assets less current liabilities) is readily determinable. Without a distinction between current and noncurrent amounts, financial statement users can only estimate working capital. The amount of working capital provides useful information to financial statement users on the company's ability to pay short term obligations when they become due as explained in the ASC definition of working capital. Ratios are discussed in more detail in Chapter 5.

ASC Glossary **Working Capital** Working capital (also called net working capital) is represented by the excess of current assets over current liabilities and identifies the relatively liquid portion of total entity capital that constitutes a margin or buffer for meeting obligations within the ordinary operating cycle of the entity.

Demo 4-2 **LO4-2** **Preparing a Classified Balance Sheet**

Demo MBC

The following balances are from the adjusted trial balance of Burr Inc. on December 31, 2020, its annual year-end. Prepare a classified balance sheet for Burr Inc. as of December 31, 2020. Assume that the company has 5,000 authorized shares of common stock ($1 par value), with 2,000 shares issued and outstanding. Also assume that the company has 1,000 authorized shares of preferred stock ($40 par value), with 200 shares issued and outstanding.

Account	Debit	Credit
Cash	$ 20,000	
Accounts receivable	37,000	
Allowance for doubtful accounts		$ 2,000
Short-term investments	40,000	
Inventory	95,000	
Prepaid expenses (short-term)	1,000	
Bond sinking fund	35,000	
Advances to suppliers (short-term)	4,000	
Dividends	10,000	
Rent receivable (short-term)	2,000	
Investment in subsidiary	22,000	
Deposits, long-term	25,000	
Land	30,000	
Building	450,000	
Accumulated depreciation, building		210,000
Equipment	60,000	
Accumulated depreciation, equipment		20,000
Franchise	12,000	
Accumulated other comprehensive income or loss	4,000	
Mortgage payable, long term		54,000
Accounts payable, trade		6,000
Dividends payable		10,000
Deferred revenue (current)		3,000
Interest payable		4,000
Bonds payable, due in 2025		98,000
Common stock		2,000
Paid-in capital in excess of par—common stock		198,000
Preferred stock		8,000
Paid-in capital in excess of par—preferred stock		88,000
Retained earnings, January 1*		56,000

*Assuming that Burr Inc.'s net income for 2020 was $88,000, ending retained earnings is $134,000 (beginning retained earnings of $56,000 plus net income of $88,000 minus dividends of $10,000).

continued

continued from previous page

Solution

Burr Inc.
Balance Sheet
December 31, 2020

Assets		
Current assets		
Cash		$ 20,000
Accounts receivable	$ 37,000	
Less: Allowance for doubtful accounts	(2,000)	35,000
Short-term investments		40,000
Inventory		95,000
Prepaid expenses		1,000
Rent receivable		2,000
Advances to suppliers		4,000
Total current assets		197,000
Investments		
Investment in subsidiary		22,000
Bond sinking fund		35,000
Total investments		57,000
Property, plant, and equipment		
Land	30,000	
Building	450,000	
Equipment	60,000	
Less: Accumulated depreciation	(230,000)	
Net property, plant, and equipment		310,000
Intangible assets		
Franchise		12,000
Other assets		
Deposits		25,000
Total assets		**$601,000**

Liabilities and Stockholders' Equity	
Current liabilities	
Accounts payable	$ 6,000
Dividends payable	10,000
Deferred revenue	3,000
Interest payable	4,000
Total current liabilities	23,000
Long-term liabilities	
Bonds payable	98,000
Mortgage payable	54,000
Total long-term liabilities	152,000
Stockholders' equity	
Preferred stock ($40 par value, 1,000 shares authorized, 200 shares issued and outstanding)	8,000
Common stock ($1 par value, 5,000 shares authorized, 2,000 shares issued and outstanding)	2,000
Paid-in capital in excess of par	286,000
Retained earnings	134,000
Accumulated other comprehensive loss	(4,000)
Total stockholders' equity	426,000
Total liabilities and stockholders' equity	**$601,000**

The *report format* of the classified balance sheet lists assets followed by liabilities and stockholders' equity. Alternatively, a company can use the *account format* of the classified balance sheet where assets are displayed on the left side of the page and liabilities and stockholders' equity are displayed on the right side of the page as shown in **Demo 4-2**. While the presentation style differs, the content is exactly the same.

EXPANDING YOUR KNOWLEDGE **Potential for a New Balance Sheet Presentation**

In 2004, the FASB and the IFRS initiated a joint financial statement presentation project to enhance the usefulness of information provided in financial statements. A draft of the proposed standard requires that an entity classify its assets and liabilities on the balance sheet according to how those items relate to its major activities or functions. Thus, unlike current practice, assets, liabilities, and equity would be *classified into the categories of operating, investing, and financing.* Within each category, a distinction would be made between current and noncurrent items. The categories of operating, investing, and financing arguably would better align across the statement of cash flows, the statement of comprehensive income, and the balance sheet. The project was suspended in 2011 as efforts focused on other projects. Although the project is not on the current FASB agenda, the potential for a major change to the balance sheet presentation is possible if the project is revisited.

Operating
Investing
Financing

REVIEW 4-2 **LO4-2** **Preparing a Classified Balance Sheet**

Review MBC

The following balances are from the post-closing trial balance of Koll's Store. Prepare a classified balance sheet for Koll's Store as of December 31, 2020.

Account	Debit	Credit
Cash	$ 88,000	
Accounts receivable	310,000	
Allowance for doubtful accounts		$ 13,000
Inventory	500,000	
Supplies	9,000	
Short-term investments	224,000	
Equipment	440,000	
Building	800,000	
Accumulated depreciation—equipment		160,000
Accumulated depreciation—building		220,000
Patent	6,000	
Accounts payable		325,000
Salaries payable		45,000
Deferred revenue		12,000
Income tax payable		72,000
Note payable, 5%, 3-year		900,000
Common stock, $1 par, 10,000 authorized shares		5,000
Paid-in capital in excess of par—common stock		295,000
Retained earnings		330,000
Totals	$2,377,000	$2,377,000

More Practice: 4-32, 4-46, 4-47

Solution on p. 4-62.

LO 4-3 Explain notes accompanying financial statements

LO 4-3 Overview

Notes to Financial Statements
- Summary of significant accounting policies
- Expanded information on items such as intangible assets, investments, debts, taxes, and leases
- Fair value measurement
- Related party transactions
- Subsequent events
- Errors, fraud, and illegal acts

Notes to financial statements are a way to provide additional information to financial statement users in accordance with the full disclosure principle introduced in Chapter 1. As an example, **Harley-Davidson Inc.**, a motorcycle manufacturer, reported its annual 2015 financial statements along with additional information that included *22 notes extending over 49 pages*. We refer to the Harley-Davidson notes as we describe in this section the types of notes typically included in annual reports.

Notes Accompanying Financial Statements

Disclosure notes are narrative explanations of items such as the company's accounting policies, pension plans, maturity dates on payables and receivables, restrictions relating to long-term debt, subsequent events, and contingencies (including pending lawsuits). **Notes are intended to complement and supplement the financial statements.** A note can refer to a single amount in financial statements, to several amounts, or to a situation that is not directly reflected in any statement.

Supporting schedules can be presented separately or incorporated into notes. Supporting schedules are presented by companies when a particular financial statement item involves a number of changes or important components. **Parenthetical notes** are used on the face of the financial statements to disclose information. For example, we see Harley-Davidson's balance sheet on the first page of this chapter includes a parenthetical note referencing Note 15 next to the line item *Commitments and Contingencies*.

A list of the 22 notes included in the **Harley-Davidson** 2015 annual report is inclued below. *Summary of Significant Accounting Policies* is the first note accompanying the financial statements. Although there is no required order of the remaining notes, in general, disclosures move through the balance sheet from assets, to liabilities, to stockholders' equity, followed by miscellaneous items.

1. Summary of Significant Accounting Policies	12. Income Taxes
2. Additional Balance Sheet and Cash Flow Information	13. Employee Benefit Plans & Other Postretirement Benefits
3. Acquisition	14. Leases
4. Goodwill and Intangible Assets	15. Commitments and Contingencies
5. Finance Receivables	16. Capital Stock
6. Asset-Backed Financing	17. Share-Based Awards
7. Fair Value Measurements	18. Earnings Per Share
8. Fair Value of Financial Instruments	19. Reportable Segments and Geographic Information
9. Derivative Instruments and Hedging Activities	20. Related Party Transactions
10. Accumulated Other Comprehensive Loss	21. Supplemental Consolidating Data
11. Debt	22. Subsequent Events

Throughout this text, we present a number of required disclosures for typical notes to financial statements. In practice, companies rely on a **financial statement disclosure checklist** to prepare note disclosures. The checklist is a comprehensive document that outlines disclosures required for financial statement items and includes a reference to the Codification guidance for each requirement.

We examine five examples of note disclosures. Beyond these five, as we see in the Harley-Davidson list, a company has other notes supporting financial statement items such as investments, intangible assets, debt, income taxes, leases, and so forth. In **Demo 4-3**, we distinguish between a disclosure of a significant accounting policy from a separate disclosure in a note or recognition on the face of the financial statements. Other than errors, fraud, and illegal acts, the list of notes in the Harley-Davidson report includes all of the following examples.

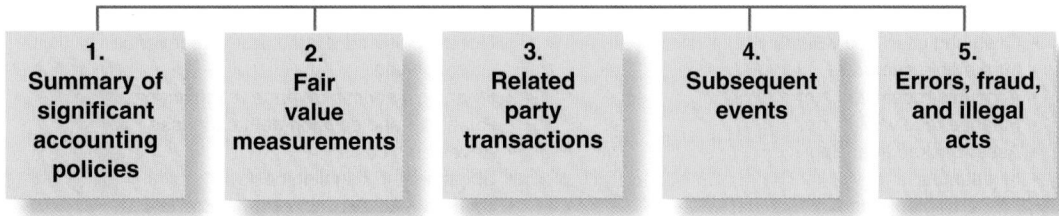

1. **Summary of significant accounting policies**
2. **Fair value measurements**
3. **Related party transactions**
4. **Subsequent events**
5. **Errors, fraud, and illegal acts**

Summary of Significant Accounting Policies

The disclosure of accounting policies describes the signficant accounting principles followed by the company and the methods of applying those principles that materially affect the financial statements. For example, a company discloses its accounting policy on revenue recognition. The accounting standards indicate that the preferred location of the significant accounting policies note is the first disclosure note.

235-10-50-6 Disclosure [of significant accounting policies] is preferred in a separate summary of significant accounting policies preceding the notes to financial statements (notes), or as the initial note, under the same or a similar title.

The accounting standards provide guidance on the type of information to include in the accounting policies note and provide examples of disclosures.

235-10-50-3 Disclosure of accounting policies shall identify and describe the accounting principles followed by the entity and the methods of applying those principles that materially affect the determination of financial position, cash flows, or results of operations. In general, the disclosure shall encompass important judgments as to appropriateness of principles relating to recognition of revenue and allocation of asset costs to current and future periods; in particular, it shall encompass those accounting principles and methods that involve any of the following:

- A selection from existing acceptable alternatives.
- Principles and methods peculiar to the industry in which the entity operates, even if such principles and methods are predominantly followed in that industry.
- Unusual or innovative applications of GAAP.

235-10-50-4 Examples of disclosures by an entity commonly required with respect to accounting policies would include, among others, those relating to the following:

- Basis of consolidation.
- Depreciation methods.
- Amortization of intangibles.
- Inventory pricing.

- Recognition of revenue from contracts with customer.
- Recognition of revenues from leasing operations.

A company must also disclose the nature of its operations and its use of estimates to assist financial statement users in their assessment of the risks and uncertainties of the company's operations.

275-10-05-5 Information about the nature of operations is helpful because the various kinds of businesses in which reporting entities operate have diverse degrees and kinds of risks. Certain of these risks are inherent to the business in which an entity is engaged. By knowing the nature of an entity's business and the principal markets for its products or services, a financial statement user is alerted, indirectly, about the risks common to that business.

275-10-05-6 There is a need to communicate explicitly to users of financial reports that the inescapable use of estimates in the preparation of financial information, including the estimation of fair values for assets carried at such a basis, results in the reporting of values that are approximations rather than exact amounts. If users understand better the inherent limitations on precision in financial statements, they will be better able to make decisions.

Disclosures of accounting policies should not duplicate details included in other parts of financial statements. A listing of topics included in Harley-Davidson's note on significant accounting policies is provided next.

The following sections are included in Note 1: Summary of Significant Accounting Policies accompanying the Harley-Davidson Inc. 2015 annual report.

- Principles of consolidation and basis of presentation
- Use of estimates
- Cash and cash equivalents
- Marketable securities
- Accounts receivable, net
- Finance receivables, net
- Asset-backed financing
- Inventories
- Property, plant and equipment
- Goodwill
- Long-lived assets
- Product warranty and recall campaigns
- Derivative financial instruments
- Motorcycles and related products revenue recognition
- Financial services revenue recognition
- Research and development expenses
- Advertising costs
- Shipping and handling costs
- Share-based award compensation costs
- Income tax expense
- Accounting standards not yet adopted

Fair Value Measurements

To increase consistency and comparability in fair value disclosures, the FASB requires disclosure on a company's fair value measurements using the fair value hierarchy. FASB developed categories for companies to classify fair value measurements: Level 1, Level 2, and Level 3. The fair value hierarchy consists of **Level 1** (quotes prices in active markets for identical assets), **Level 2** (significant other observable inputs), and **Level 3** (significant unobservable inputs) measurements. Using a consistent framework improves consistency from period to period within a company and comparability of information across companies. Classifying fair value measurements also provides more information to financial statement users regarding the source and reliability of the financial measurements.

The distinction between recurring items and nonrecurring items is important when identifying disclosure requirements. A **recurring item** is an item that the company evaluates period after period because it is continually maintained such as a balance in cash equivalents or investments. A **nonrecurring item** is a one-time or sporadic event such as an impairment of property, plant, and equipment, goodwill, intangible assets, or investments. Another example of a nonrecurring item is the valuation at fair value of a business component held for sale.

820-10-50-1 A reporting entity shall disclose information that helps users of its financial statements assess both of the following:

a. For assets and liabilities that are measured at fair value on a recurring or nonrecurring basis in the statement of financial position after initial recognition, the valuation techniques and inputs used to develop those measurements

b. For recurring fair value measurements using significant unobservable inputs (Level 3), the effect of the measurements on earnings (or changes in net assets) or other comprehensive income for the period.

To meet these requirements, the following disclosure items are required (ASC 820-10-50-2):

- Fair value at the end of the reporting period for recurring measurements.
- Fair value at the relevant measurement date for nonrecurring items.
- Level of the fair value hierarchy (Level 1, 2, or 3).
- Amount, reasons, and policies of transfers between Level 1 and Level 2 categories for recurring basis measurements.
- Description of the valuation techniques and inputs used in Level 2 and Level 3 measurements.
- For recurring Level 3 measurements, reconciliation of activity during the period, gains and losses in the period, and a sensitivity analysis to changes in unobservable inputs.
- For recurring and nonrecurring Level 3 measurements, a description of the valuation processes.

As we see from this disclosure list, the depth of disclosure is much greater for a Level 3 measurement which requires management estimation and judgment. The following disclosure for **Harley-Davidson** is included below as an example of a fair value measurement disclosure.

Note 7— Fair Value Measurements Certain assets and liabilities are recorded at fair value in the financial statements; some of these are measured on a recurring basis while others are measured on a non-recurring basis. Assets and liabilities measured on a recurring basis are those that are adjusted to fair value each time a financial statement is prepared. Assets and liabilities measured on a nonrecurring basis are those that are adjusted to fair value when required by particular events or circumstances. In determining the fair value of assets and liabilities, the Company uses various valuation techniques. The availability of inputs observable in the market varies from instrument to instrument and depends on a variety of factors including the type of instrument, whether the instrument is actively traded, and other characteristics particular to the transaction. For many financial instruments, pricing inputs are readily observable in the market, the valuation methodology used is widely accepted by market participants, and the valuation does not require significant management discretion. For other financial instruments, pricing inputs are less observable in the market and may require management judgment.

The Company assesses the inputs used to measure fair value using a three-tier hierarchy. The hierarchy indicates the extent to which inputs used in measuring fair value are observable in the market. Level 1 inputs include quoted prices for identical instruments and are the most observable.

Level 2 inputs include quoted prices for similar assets and observable inputs such as interest rates, foreign currency exchange rates, commodity prices. The Company uses the market approach to derive the fair value for its level 2 fair value measurements. Forward contracts for foreign currency, commodities and interest rates are valued using current quoted forward rates and prices; and investments in marketable securities and cash equivalents are valued using publicly quoted prices.

Level 3 inputs are not observable in the market and include management's judgments about the assumptions market participants would use in pricing the asset or liability.

Recurring Fair Value Measurements The following tables present information about the Company's assets and liabilities measured at fair value on a recurring basis as of December 31 (in thousands):

	2015	Quoted Prices in Active Markets for Identical Assets (Level 1)	Significant Other Observable Inputs (Level 2)	Significant Unobservable Inputs (Level 3)
Assets:				
Cash equivalents	$555,910	$390,706	$165,204	$—
Marketable securities	81,448	36,256	45,192	—
Derivatives	16,235	—	16,235	—
Total	$653,593	$426,962	$226,631	$—
Liabilities:				
Derivatives	$ 1,300	$ —	$ 1,300	$—

continued

continued from previous page

Nonrecurring Fair Value Measurements Repossessed inventory is recorded at the lower of cost or net realizable value through a nonrecurring fair value measurement. Repossessed inventory was $17.7 million and $13.4 million at December 31, 2015 and 2014, for which the fair value adjustment was $8.6 million and $5.0 million at December 31, 2015 and 2014, respectively. Fair value is estimated using Level 2 inputs based on the recent market values of repossessed inventory.

Related Party Transactions

When a company engages in a transaction where one of the parties has the ability to influence the actions and policies of another or when a nontransacting third party has the ability to influence the policies of the transacting parties, the transaction is labeled a **related party transaction**. Such transactions cannot be assumed to be at arm's length because the conditions necessary for a competitive, free-market interaction are not likely to exist.

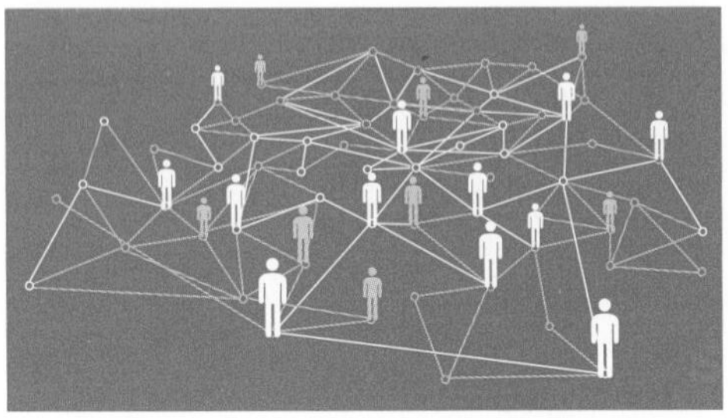

850-10-05-3 Examples of related party transactions include transactions between:

- A parent entity and its subsidiaries.
- Subsidiaries of a common parent.
- An entity and trusts for the benefit of employees, such as pension and profit-sharing trusts that are managed by or under the trusteeship of the entity's management
- An entity and its principal owners, management, or members of their immediate families
- Affiliates. [A party that, directly or indirectly through one or more intermediaries, controls, is controlled by, or is under common control with an entity.]

850-10-05-4 Transactions between related parties commonly occur in the normal course of business. Examples of common transactions with related parties are:

- Sales, purchases, and transfers of real and personal property
- Services received or furnished, such as accounting, management, engineering, and legal services
- Use of property and equipment by lease or otherwise
- Borrowings, lendings, and guarantees
- Maintenance of compensating bank balances for the benefit of a related party
- Intra-entity billings based on allocations of common costs
- Filings of consolidated tax returns.

For related party transactions, the accounting standards require the following disclosures.

- The nature of the relationship(s) involved.
- A description of the transaction, even when no amounts or nominal amounts were involved, for each period for which income statements are presented.
- Dollar amounts of transactions for each period for which income statements are presented.
- Any amounts due to or from related parties as of the balance sheet date, and the terms and manner of settlement planned.

ASC 850-10-50 provides additional information on related party disclosures.

Harley-Davidson Inc. reported related party transactions in a note accompanying its 2015 annual consolidated financial statements as follows.

Note 20—Related Party Transactions A director of the Company is Chairman and Chief Executive Officer and an equity owner of Fred Deeley Imports Ltd. (Deeley Imports), the exclusive distributor of the Company's motorcycles in Canada until August 2015. On August 4, 2015, the Company completed its purchase of certain assets and liabilities from Deeley Imports including, among other things, the acquisition of the exclusive right to distribute the Company's motorcycles and other products in Canada. As a result of the acquisition, the Company no longer does business with Deeley Imports. Refer to Note 3 for further details.

In 2015, the Company recorded $111.3 million Motorcycles and Related Products revenue and Financial Services revenue from Deeley Imports which represents sales to Deeley Imports through August 4, 2015. The Company had no finance receivables balances due from Deeley Imports at December 31, 2015.

Subsequent Events

Subsequent events take place between the balance sheet date and the release of financial statements. A material subsequent event is disclosed in notes to financial statements. Such items can include the sale of a business component, the issuance of stock or bonds, or significant damage incurred due to a natural disaster. Subsequent events are discussed in depth in Chapter 15.

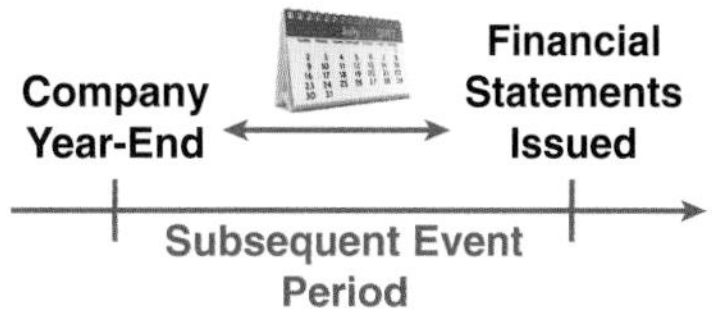

ASC Glossary **Subsequent Events:** Events or transactions that occur after the balance sheet date but before financial statements are issued or are available to be issued.

A subsequent events note for **Harley-Davidson Inc.** included in its 2015 annual report follows.

> **Note 22—Subsequent Events** In January 2016, HDFS issued \$600.0 million of medium-term notes that mature in January 2019 and have an annual interest rate of 2.25% and \$600.0 million of medium-term notes that mature in January 2021 and have an annual interest rate of 2.85%.

Errors, Fraud, and Illegal Acts

Errors

Fraud

Illegal Acts

While not common to financial statement disclosure, material errors (unintentional mistakes) and fraud or illegal acts (intentional misstatements) must be disclosed in financial statements. As explained in an earlier chapter, past financial statements must be corrected for a material error. Bribes, kickbacks, illegal political contributions, and other violations of statutes and regulations constitute illegal acts. A company's management is responsible for the completeness of financial statement disclosures, which includes relevant information pertaining to illegal acts. If the company's auditor discovers an illegal act such as bribery, the auditor ensures that the amount is disclosed, along with all known facts about the illegal act.

Fraudulent financial reporting generally can be traced to poor internal control or to poor industry or overall business conditions. Extreme pressures on management, such as a major decline in revenue, unrealistic profit or other performance goals, or bonus plans that depend on short-term performance, can fuel fraudulent financial reporting. The opportunity to engage in fraudulent financial reporting is present when conditions such as the following exist.

- The board of directors or an audit committee of the board does not carefully review the reporting process.
- The company has engaged in unusual or complicated transactions.
- The system of internal control is weak.
- Internal audit staff is small or poorly trained and underfunded.
- There is extensive need for judgment in making accounting estimates.

MEAD JOHNSON NUTRITION

Real World—DISCLOSURE OF AN ILLEGAL ACT

MEAD JOHNSON NUTRITION COMPANY [MJN]

Mead Johnson Nutrition Company disclosed the following information in its 2014 Form 10-K regarding an investigation of bribery involving a subsidiary in China which resulted in a \$12 million settlement with the SEC in a release dated July 28, 2015 (www.sec.gov).

> **Note 20 Contingencies** The Company has substantially progressed in its internal investigation of certain business activities of the Company's local subsidiary in China. The Company's investigation focused on certain expenditures that were made in connection with the promotion of the Company's products and certain expenditures otherwise made in its China business. Certain of such expenditures were made in violation of Company policies and may have been made in violation of applicable U.S. and/or local laws, including the U.S. Foreign Corrupt Practices Act (the "FCPA"). The investigation has been conducted by outside legal counsel and was overseen by a committee of independent members of the Company's board of directors. The results of the investigation are being discussed with the SEC and the Department of Justice (the "DOJ"), both of which are responsible for FCPA enforcement and frequently examine these issues in tandem, and the Company is responding to their requests for additional information which are common in FCPA investigations. At this time, the Company is unable to predict the scope, timing or outcome of this ongoing matter or any regulatory or legal actions that may be commenced related to this matter. If a violation of the FCPA or other laws is determined to have occurred, the Company could become subject to monetary penalties as well as civil and criminal sanctions.

The ethical climate of an organization can contribute to or inhibit fraudulent financial reporting. The attitude that top management conveys about issues of honesty in general and truthful reporting in particular influences the actions of other managers in positions of responsibility. The accounting profession must try to prevent fraudulent financial reporting, and it must determine responsibility when it occurs. The Sarbanes-Oxley Act in particular has instituted penalties (including criminal penalties) for executives involved in the reporting of fraudulent financial information.

COCA-COLA Real World—ADDITIONAL INFORMATION ON SUSTAINABILITY

Sustainability reporting has emerged as a common practice adopted by many companies across the world even though reporting is optional. Sustainability reporting is a way for companies to communicate their social and environmental initiatives. The most widely adopted framework for sustainability reporting is the Global Reporting Initiative (GRI) Sustainability Reporting Framework, which emphasizes the environmental and social impacts important to stakeholders. External assurance of sustainability reports is offered by independent auditing firms. **Coca-Cola Company** issues an annual sustainability report. Its 2014/2015 report discusses its 2020 goals.

> Our dashboard below provides an overview of our 2020 sustainability commitments. These commitments extend across the entire Coca-Cola system, which includes all of our nearly 250 independent bottling partners. We have set ambitious targets to drive system wide change beyond small operational improvements. We do not own most of the companies that comprise our bottling system, but we feel it is important to strive for large-scale success and to provide leadership that will raise the bar for our system and our industry.

The dashboard for Coca-Cola Company included the following.

- Me: Well-being
- We: Women's economic empowerment
  Human & workplace rights
  Sustainable communities
- World: Water stewardship
  Sustainable packaging
  Climate protection
  Sustainable agriculture

Demo 4-3 LO4-3 Financial Statement Disclosure

Demo MBC

The following financial reporting items are from Verdes Inc. for the year ended December 31, 2020. Match each financial reporting item, *a* through *h*, with one of the three disclosure options. Provide a brief description of the disclosure recommended.

Disclosure options

1. Disclose in the summary of significant accounting policies note.
2. Disclose as a separate note.
3. Recognize on the face of the balance sheet.

	Financial Reporting Item	Suggested Financial Statement Disclosure
a.	Verdes provided funds to its subsidiary through a two-year loan agreement.	[2] In a *separate related party note*, describe the nature of the relationship with the subsidiary, including a description of the financing transaction and amount due.
b.	Verdes uses the FIFO (first-in, first-out) inventory method to account for its inventory costs.	[1] In the *summary of significant accounting policies note*, indicate the method used to account for inventory.
c.	Verdes holds a number of investments at year-end that are accounted for differently because of the classification of the investment type.	[2] In a *separate investments note*, provide the dollar amount of investments comprising the various investment category types.
d.	Verdes holds both current and noncurrent assets and liabilities.	[3] On the *face of the balance sheet*, classify assets and liabilities as current or noncurrent.
e.	Verdes estimated damages (considered material) on its production facilities due to a fire that occurred in January 2021.	[2] In a *separate subsequent event note*, describe the nature of the subsequent event and an estimate of the damages if available.

continued

continued from previous page

	Financial Reporting Item	Suggested Financial Statement Disclosure
f.	Verdes depreciates its equipment on a straight-line basis over different periods (of years) depending on the asset category.	[1] In the *summary of significant accounting policies note*, indicate the method used to depreciate assets and include the average useful lives for major asset categories over which the assets are depreciated.
g.	Verdes Co. holds a number of notes payable outstanding with financial institutions, in various amounts with various due dates, and various fair value amounts.	[2] In a *separate debt note,* indicate the composition of debt and include terms, amounts, due dates, fair value, and other information that would be important to the financial statement user.
h.	Verdes Co. follows a revenue recognition policy where revenue is recognized when a contractual obligation is satisfied at the point that control of the product is transferred to the customer.	[1] In the *summary of significant accounting policies note*, describe the revenue recognition policy.

Financial Statement Disclosure

LO4-3 **REVIEW 4-3**

Review MBC

Match each of the following financial statement disclosure excerpts, *a* through *i*, with one of the six disclosure options where we would likely see the excerpt. Assume financial statements are issued as of December 31, 2020.

Disclosure options

1. Disclose as a separate note on the summary of significant accounting policies.
2. Disclose as a separate note on fair value.
3. Disclose as a separate note on related parties.
4. Disclose as a separate note on subsequent events.
5. Disclose as a separate note on errors, fraud, or illegal acts.
6. Disclose as a separate note on a subject not indicated in the list above.

Financial Statement Disclosure Excerpts for Dillon Corp.

____ *a.* On January 5, 2021, the company declared cash dividends of $1.00 per share payable on January 31, 2021, for shareholders of record on January 10, 2021.

____ *b.* The company recognizes trade accounts receivable at net realizable value by recording an allowance for doubtful accounts to reflect expected credit on collection.

____ *c.* The company is subject to a variety of legal actions arising in the ordinary course of business, which are subject to uncertainties.

____ *d.* The company entered into a lease agreement with Unite Inc. (a company owned by the company's president) to lease administrative office space.

____ *e.* The company has two defined benefit plans that allow for employees to contribute up to the maximum allowed under the IFRS rules.

____ *f.* After year-end, but before statements are released, the company entered into a new credit agreement that provides for a $100,000 unsecured credit line.

____ *g.* The company expenses production costs of magazine, television, and other advertisements as of the initial date of the advertisement event.

____ *h.* The company identified a prior period adjustment for in-transit inventory that was incorrectly recorded as a sale in the prior year.

____ *i.* The company determined that cash equivalents at December 31, 2020, are classified as Level 1 in the fair value hierarchy.

More Practice: 4-35, 4-36, 4-50, 4-51, 4-53

Solution on p. 4-62.

LO 4-4 Identify and describe sections of Form 10-K

LO 4-4 Overview

Annual Report on Form 10-K
- Selected financial data
- MD&A
- Financial statements and supplementary data
- Directors and executive officers and corporate governance
- Executive compensation

Most U.S. public companies are required to produce a report on **Form 10-K** each year and file it with the Securities and Exchange Commission (SEC). The Form 10-K provides a comprehensive overview of a company's business and financial condition and includes audited financial statements. Large accelerated registrants (as defined by the SEC based upon the number of shares held by public investors) must file the Form 10-K within 60 days after year-end and accelerated filers must file within 75 days after year-end.

Selected Content of the Form 10-K

Financial reporting in the Form 10-K extends beyond the financial statements and accompanying notes to include other required items such as selected financial data and management's discussion and analysis of financial condition and results of operations. An overview of financial reporting in the Form 10-K is illustrated in **Exhibit 4-9**.

EXHIBIT 4-9
Financial Reporting in the Form 10-K

Financial reporting			
Area directly affected by the Codification			
Basic financial statements			
Financial statements and reports	Notes to financial statements	Supplementary information	Other means of providing financial information
	Examples:	Examples:	Examples:
■ Balance sheet ■ Statement of comprehensive income ■ Statement of cash flows ■ Statement of stockholders' equity ■ Auditors' report ■ Management reports	■ Accounting policies ■ Contingencies ■ Inventory methods ■ Fair value measurements ■ Alternative measures	■ Segment information ■ Oil and gas reserves information ■ Quarterly financial data	■ Selected financial data ■ Management's discussion and analysis ■ Board and executive officers and corporate governance ■ Executive compensation

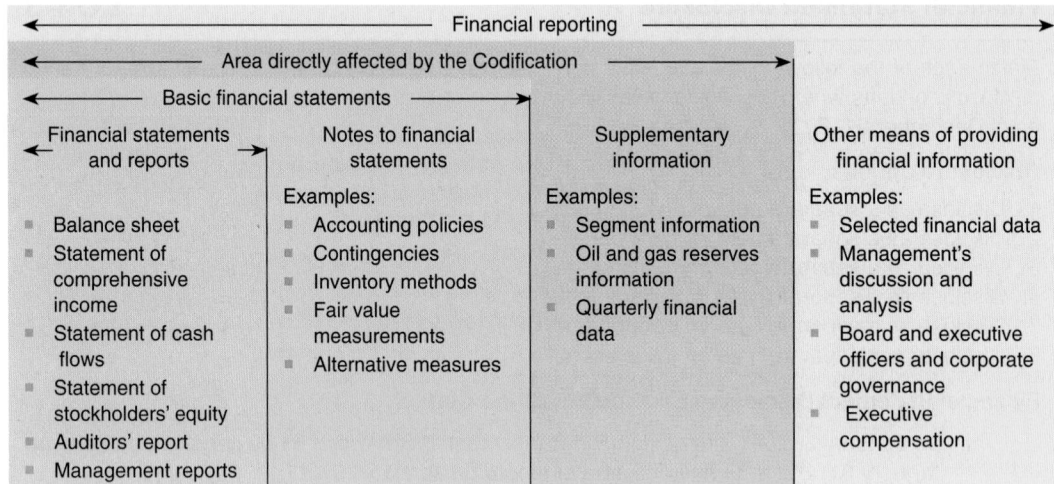

The required sections of the Form 10-K are organized into Items 1 through 15 as shown below. The requirements for these items are outlined at https://www.sec.gov/files/form10-k.pdf. In this section, we provide a brief overview of certain items relevant to the topics in this text: Items 6, 7, 8, 10, and 11. In **Demo 4-4**, we classify items from a Form 10-K by item number.

SEC Form 10-K Items

Item 1:	Business
Item 1A:	Risk factors
Item 1B:	Unresolved staff comments
Item 2:	Properties
Item 3:	Legal proceedings
Item 4:	Mine safety disclosures
Item 5:	Market for registrant's common equity & related stockholder matters & issuer purchases of equity securities
Item 6:	Selected financial data
Item 7:	Management's discussion and analysis of financial condition and results of operations
Item 7A:	Quantitative and qualitative disclosures about market risk
Item 8:	Financial statements and supplementary data
Item 9:	Changes in and disagreements with accountants on accounting and financial disclosure
Item 9A:	Controls and procedures
Item 9B:	Other information

continued

continued from previous page

Item 10:	Directors and executive officers and corporate governance
Item 11:	Executive compensation
Item 12:	Security ownership of certain beneficial owners and management and related stockholder matters
Item 13:	Certain relationships and related transactions, and director independence
Item 14:	Principal accountant fees and services
Item 15:	Exhibits, financial statement schedules

Selected Financial Data—Item 6

The **Selected financial data** section includes specific financial information about the company for the last five years including the following.

- Net sales or operating revenues.
- Income (loss) from continuing operations.
- Income (loss) from continuing operations per common share.
- Total assets.
- Long-term obligations and redeemable preferred stock.
- Cash dividends declared per common share.

EXPANDING YOUR KNOWLEDGE **XBRL and Big Data**

The SEC has a rule requiring companies to provide financial statement information in a universal format that is intended to improve the usefulness of information. Companies provide their financial statements to the SEC in interactive data format using the **eXtensible Business Reporting Language** (**XBRL**), a type of computer language. In XBRL, there is a **taxonomy** or standard list of tags. Each item in the financial statements is associated with a tag from the taxonomy that corresponds to a specific financial reporting item. In the XBRL format, financial statement information is downloaded into spreadsheets, analyzed through commercial software, and used within investment models. Interactive data has the potential to increase the speed, accuracy, and usefulness of financial disclosure, and to reduce reporting costs over time.

Big data is a phrase used to describe the voluminous amount of data and information being generated, stored, processed, and analyzed by companies. As a result of the formating of financial information into XBRL, such information is well positioned for big data analysis. For example, a company could identify research and development costs across companies and across industries.

Selected financial data disclosure for **Harley-Davidson Inc.** for the last five years follows.

Item 6. Selected Financial Data (In thousands, except per share amounts)	**2015**	**2014**	**2013**	**2012**	**2011**
Statement of income data:					
Revenue:					
Motorcycles & Related Products	$5,308,744	$5,567,681	$5,258,290	$4,942,582	$4,662,264
Financial Services	686,658	660,827	641,582	637,924	649,449
Total revenue	5,995,402	6,228,508	5,899,872	5,580,506	5,311,713
Income from continuing operations	752,207	844,611	733,993	623,925	548,078
Income from discontinued operations, net of tax	—	—	—	—	51,036
Net income	$ 752,207	$ 844,611	$ 733,993	$ 623,925	$ 599,114
Weighted-average common shares:					
Basic	202,681	216,305	222,475	227,119	232,889
Diluted	203,686	217,706	224,071	229,229	234,918
Earnings per common share from continuing operations:					
Basic	$ 3.71	$ 3.90	$ 3.30	$ 2.75	$ 2.35
Diluted	3.69	3.88	3.28	2.72	2.33
Earnings per common share from discontinued operations:					
Basic	$ —	$ —	$ —	$ —	$ 0.22
Diluted	—	—	—	—	0.22

continued

continued from previous page

Earnings per common share:					
Basic	$ 3.71	$ 3.90	$ 3.30	$ 2.75	$ 2.57
Diluted	3.69	3.88	3.28	2.72	2.55
Dividends paid per common share	1.240	1.100	0.840	0.620	0.475
Balance sheet data:					
Total assets	$9,991,167	$9,528,097	$9,405,040	$9,170,773	$9,674,164
Total debt	6,890,388	5,504,629	5,259,170	5,102,649	5,722,619
Total equity	1,839,654	2,909,286	3,009,486	2,557,624	2,420,256

Management's Discussion and Analysis—Item 7

A section entitled **Management's Discussion and Analysis of Financial Condition and Results of Operations (MD&A)** is required of all SEC registrants. The MD&A section precedes the financial statements in the Form 10-K. The MD&A section provides a narrative of the financial highlights for the reporting period, supplementing the technical information found in financial statements and notes. This section is written by management covering such topics as the mission of the company, major investments, marketing activities, financial strategies, the company's product and service lines, results of operations, effects of newly adopted accounting standards, and risk conditions. Companies also must disclose prospective information relating to future trends, commitments, and events that can materially affect a company's operations or liquidity.

The Securities and Exchange Commission (in Regulation S-K) requires the following components in the MD&A.

1. Liquidity
2. Capital resources
3. Results of operations
4. Off-balance sheet arrangements
5. Tabular disclosure of contractual obligations

The MD&A requirements are intended to satisfy three principal objectives.

- To provide a narrative explanation of a company's financial statements from the perspective of the company's management.
- To enhance full disclosure by providing a more thorough background of the financial statements presented.
- To provide information on the quality and variability of a company's net income and cash flows to aid an investor in predicting future financial performance.

(The MD&A requirements are defined by the SEC. See Interpretation: Commission Guidance Regarding Management's Discussion and Analysis of Financial Condition and Results of Operations Securities and Exchange Commission, 17 CFR Parts 211, 231 and 241.)

The MD&A section of Form 10-K is a helpful resource to potential investors and creditors in providing more context to the financial statements. For example, explanation on past trends and on management's expectations for future trends provides additional background for investment decisions. Excerpts from **Harley-Davidson**'s MD&A section of its 2015 Form 10-K follow. (The full MD&A is available in the Form 10-K from http://investor.harley-davidson.com.)

Outlook (excerpt)

In 2016, the Company expects to increase its spending on customer-facing marketing by approximately 65% from 2015 levels and it expects to increase its spending on new product development by approximately 35% from 2015 levels. This spending reallocation would represent an approximate $70 million increase in the Company's spending to drive demand compared to 2015.

Results of Operations 2015 Compared to 2014 (excerpt)

Consolidated operating income was down 9.8% in 2015 driven by a decrease in operating income from the Motorcycles segment which decreased by $127.7 million compared to 2014. Operating income for the Financial Services segment increased by $2.4 million during 2015 as compared to 2014.

continued

continued from previous page

New Accounting Standards Not Yet Adopted (excerpt)

In February 2015, the FASB issued ASU No. 2015-02 Amendments to the Consolidation Analysis (ASU 2015-02). ASU No. 2015-02 amends the guidance within Accounting Standards Codification (ASC) Topic 810, "Consolidation," to change the analysis that a reporting entity must perform to determine whether it should consolidate certain legal entities.

Critical Accounting Estimates (excerpt)

Product Warranty—Estimated warranty costs are reserved for motorcycles, motorcycle parts and motorcycle accessories at the time of sale. The warranty reserve is based upon historical Company claim data used in combination with other known factors that may affect future warranty claims. The Company updates its warranty estimates quarterly to ensure that the warranty reserves are based on the most current information available.

Liquidity and Capital Resources as of December 31, 2015 (excerpt)

Operating Activities—The decrease in operating cash flow in 2015 compared to 2014 was due primarily to lower net income and increased wholesale lending. At the end of 2015, inventory was higher, as the Company increased its year-over-year fourth quarter production to maximize manufacturing efficiencies and prepare for the 2016 first quarter shipments.

EXPANDING YOUR KNOWLEDGE **Forward-Looking Statements and Safe Harbor**

The MD&A includes managers' views about future financial performance. The AICPA issued a statement on the services to be provided by practitioners related to prospective financial statements. The statement defines a financial forecast and a financial projection (Financial Forecasts and Projections, New York: AICPA 2015). Key aspects of the definitions follow.

- A **financial forecast** is a prospective financial statement that presents an entity's *expected* financial position, results of operations, and cash flows. A financial forecast is based on the responsible party's assumptions reflecting the conditions it expects to exist and the course of action it expects to take, based upon the responsible party's knowledge and beliefs. A financial forecast may be expressed as a single monetary point or a range of points based upon assumptions.
- A **financial projection** is a prospective financial statement that presents, given one or more hypothetical assumptions, an entity's expected financial position, results of operations, and cash flows. A financial projection is sometimes prepared to present one or more hypothetical courses of action for evaluation, as in response to a question such as, "What would happen if . . . ?" A financial projection is based on the responsible party's knowledge and belief of the assumptions reflecting conditions it expects would exist and the course of action it expects would be taken, given one or more hypothetical assumptions. A projection, like a forecast, may contain a range of points.

An annual report contains a variety of forecasts in different forms. For example, the allowance for doubtful accounts is a forecast of future uncollectible accounts. Depreciation expense is a forecast of how an asset cost is allocated to an asset's forecasted useful life. Management statements in the MD&A often forecast future dividend payments or capital cash outflows. The requirement that managers disclose in their MD&A prospective information could lead to fears that managers will face consequences if future results do not match projections. For this reason, a *safe harbor rule* is established to protect companies that have an error in a forecast as long as the forecast was prepared on a reasonable basis and disclosed in good faith—see the following from the 10-K of Harley-Davidson.

> The Company intends that certain matters discussed by the Company are "forward-looking statements" intended to qualify for the safe harbor from liability established by the Private Securities Litigation Reform Act of 1995. These forward looking statements can generally be identified as such because the context statement will include words such as the Company "believes," "anticipates," "expects," "plans," "estimates," or words of similar meaning. Similarly, statements that describe future plans, objectives, outlooks, targets, guidance or goals are also forward-looking statements. Such forward-looking statements are subject to certain risks and uncertainties that could cause actual results to differ materially from those anticipated as of the date of this report... The Company disclaims any obligation to publicly update such forward looking statements to reflect subsequent events or circumstances.

Financial Statements and Supplementary Data—Item 8

The Form 10-K includes comparative financial statements with accompanying note disclosures plus any *required* supplementary information. Comparative financial statements highlight the nature and trends of current changes affecting the company. Two annual balance sheets, three annual statements of comprehensive income, three annual statements of cash flows, and three annual stockholders' equity reconciliations are presented. This presentation emphasizes that statements for a series of periods are more useful than a statement for a single period.

Required supplementary information is information that the FASB views as an essential part of financial reporting. Supplementary data follows the notes to financial statements. An example of supplementary data includes quarterly financial statements. Authoritative guidelines for the measurement and presentation of the supplementary information have been established. Although not audited, auditors apply certain limited procedures such as reviewing for deficiencies in, or the omission of, certain information. In its annual report on 2015 Form 10-K, **Harley-Davidson Inc.** provides (1) Supplemental Consolidating Data, and (2) Quarterly Financial Data as supplementary data.

Auditors' Report

The auditors' report accompanies the audited financial statements of Item 8 of the Form 10-K. The **auditors' report** expresses the auditors' professional opinion on financial statements. Although the auditors have sole responsibility for all opinions expressed in the auditors' report, company management has the primary responsibility for the financial statements themselves, including the notes. Compilation and presentation of accounting information and all supporting text contained in a company's financial statements are management's concern and responsibility. The auditors, in rendering their opinion, affirm or disaffirm what management has compiled and presented.

When an audit (independent examination of a company's financial records) is complete, the auditors are required to draft an opinion paragraph that best communicates their professional opinion about the company's financial statements. The auditors can render one of four opinions.

1. **Unqualified opinion** An unqualified opinion (clean opinion) is provided when the auditor concludes that the statements fairly present the results of operations, financial position, and cash flows in conformance with GAAP and provide reasonable assurance that the financial statements are free of material misstatement.
2. **Qualified opinion** A qualified opinion is provided when the auditor takes limited exception to the client's financial statements in a way that does not invalidate the statements as a whole. A qualified opinion must explain the reasons for the exception and its effect on the financial statements.
3. **Adverse opinion** An adverse opinion is provided when the financial statements do not fairly present the results of operations, financial position, and cash flows. Material exceptions require an adverse opinion. An adverse opinion means that the statements, taken as a whole, are not presented in accordance with GAAP. Adverse opinions are rare.
4. **Disclaimer of opinion** When the auditors have not been able to obtain sufficient evidence, they must state that they are unable to express an opinion (that is, they issue a disclaimer). The disclaimer must provide the reasons the auditor did not give an opinion.

Most opinions are unqualified. The audit report for **Harley-Davidson Inc.** is provided next. A major purpose of the auditors' opinion is to assure the reader that financial statements conform with GAAP. Without such assurance, an investor or creditor is ill-advised to rely on a company's statements when making investment or lending decisions. We see that the report also includes a paragraph in which the auditors provide an opinion on internal controls from financial reporting.

> Report of Independent Registered Public Accounting Firm
> To the Board of Directors and Shareholders of Harley-Davidson, Inc.:
>
> We have audited the accompanying consolidated balance sheets of Harley-Davidson, Inc. as of December 31, 2015 and 2014, and the related consolidated statements of income, comprehensive income, shareholders' equity and cash flows for each of the three years in the period ended December 31, 2015. Our audits also included the financial statement schedule listed in the index at item 15(a). These financial statements and schedule are the responsibility of the Company's management. Our responsibility is to express an opinion on these financial statements and schedule based on our audits.
>
> We conducted our audits in accordance with the standards of the Public Company Accounting Oversight Board (United States). Those standards require that we plan and perform the audit to obtain reasonable assurance about whether the financial statements are free of material misstatement. An audit includes

continued

continued from previous page

examining, on a test basis, evidence supporting the amounts and disclosures in the financial statements. An audit also includes assessing the accounting principles used and significant estimates made by management, as well as evaluating the overall financial statement presentation. We believe that our audits provide a reasonable basis for our opinion.

In our opinion, the financial statements referred to above present fairly, in all material respects, the consolidated financial position of Harley-Davidson, Inc. at December 31, 2015 and 2014, and the consolidated results of its operations and its cash flows for each of the three years in the period ended December 31, 2015, in conformity with U.S. generally accepted accounting principles. Also in our opinion, the related financial statement schedule, when considered in relation to the basic financial statements taken as a whole, presents fairly in all material respects the information set forth therein.

We also have audited, in accordance with the standards of the Public Company Accounting Oversight Board (United States), Harley-Davidson, Inc.'s internal control over financial reporting as of December 31, 2015, based on criteria established in Internal Control—Integrated Framework issued by the Committee of Sponsoring Organizations of the Treadway Commission (2013 framework) and our report dated February 18, 2016 expressed an unqualified opinion thereon.

/s/ Ernst & Young LLP
Milwaukee, Wisconsin

Management Reports

Management reports reference the audited financial statements of Item 8 of the Form 10-K. The Sarbanes-Oxley Act (introduced in Chapter One) requires disclosures by management asserting their responsibility for financial information presented in the Form 10-K and for assessment of the company's internal control procedures. Two management reports for Harley-Davidson are provided: Management's Report on Internal Control Over Financial Reporting and the Chief Executive Officer Certification. The first report indicates that management takes responsibility for evaluating the effectiveness of its internal controls over financial reporting. In the second report, the president and CEO of the company certifies the financial statements. Required by the Sarbanes-Oxley Act, a CEO (chief executive officer) and CFO (chief financial officer) certify the annual report by signing an executive officer certification report. In signing the report, among other things, the executive officer certifies that he or she has reviewed the report and is not aware of untrue statements of material fact or omissions that would make the reports misleading. Certifications are typically included as exhibits to the Form 10-K.

Management's Annual Report on Internal Control over Financial Reporting

Our management is responsible for establishing and maintaining adequate internal control over financial reporting, as such term is defined in Rule 13a-15(f) of the Exchange Act. Under the supervision and with the participation of our management, including our Chief Executive Officer and Chief Financial Officer, we conducted an evaluation of the effectiveness of our internal control over financial reporting based upon criteria established in Internal Control—Integrated Framework (2013) by the Committee of Sponsoring Organizations of the Treadway Commission. Based on that evaluation, our management concluded that our internal control over financial reporting was effective as of December 26, 2015.

The Company's management is responsible for establishing and maintaining adequate internal control over financial reporting, as such term is defined in Exchange Act Rules 13a-15(f). Under the supervision and with the participation of management, including the principal executive officer and principal financial officer, management conducted an evaluation of the effectiveness of the Company's internal control over financial reporting based on the criteria established in Internal Control – Integrated Framework (2013 Framework) issued by the Committee of Sponsoring Organizations of the Treadway Commission. Based on management's evaluation under the framework in Internal Control – Integrated Framework, management has concluded that the Company's internal control over financial reporting was effective as of December 31, 2015. Ernst & Young LLP, an independent registered public accounting firm, has audited the Consolidated Financial Statements included in this Annual Report on Form 10-K and, as part of its audit, has issued an attestation report, included herein, on the effectiveness of the Company's internal control over financial reporting.

PepsiCo has a strong history of doing what's right. We realize that great companies are built on trust, strong ethical standards and principles. Our financial results are delivered from that culture of accountability, and we take responsibility for the quality and accuracy of our financial reporting.

Matthew S. Levatich	John A. Olin
President and Chief Financial Officer	Senior Vice President and Chief Financial Officer

Chief Executive Officer Certification (Excerpt)
Pursuant to Rule 13a-14(a) under the Securities Exchange Act of 1934
I, Matthew S. Levatich, certify that:

1. I have reviewed this annual report on Form 10-K of Harley-Davidson, Inc.;
2. Based on my knowledge, this report does not contain any untrue statement of a material fact or omit to state a material fact necessary to make the statements made, in light of the circumstances under which such statements were made, not misleading with respect to the period covered by this report;
3. Based on my knowledge, the financial statements, and other financial information included in this report, fairly present in all material respects the financial condition, results of operations and cash flows of the registrant as of, and for, the periods presented in this report;
4. The registrant's other certifying officer and I are responsible for establishing and maintaining disclosure controls and procedures...
5. The registrant's other certifying officer and I have disclosed, based on our most recent evaluation of internal control over financial reporting, to the registrant's auditors and the audit committee of registrant's board of directors:
   a. All significant deficiencies and material weaknesses in the design or operation of internal control over financial reporting which are reasonably likely to adversely affect the registrant's ability to record, process, summarize and report financial information; and
   b. Any fraud, whether or not material, that involves management or other employees who have a significant role in the registrant's internal control over financial reporting.

Date: February 18, 2016

/S/ Matthew S. Levatich
Matthew S. Levatich
President and Chief Executive Officer

Directors and Executive Officers and Corporate Governance—Item 10

The Form 10-K discloses the names and experiences of the board of directors and executive officers, the company's code of ethics, and certain qualifications for directors and committees of the board of directors. The **board of directors** consists of elected members from the shareholder group who oversee the executive management of the company and represent the shareholders. The board of directors assist management in establishing the broad goals of a company. Examples of items that would be overseen by the board of directors include hiring and firing of company executives, dividend policies, executive compensation, and acquisitions and divestitures. The decisions of the board of directors directly impact the operations of the corporation and thus the reporting. For example, decisions by the board of directors to declare a dividend result in the recognition of a dividend payable and a decision by the board to sell off a component leads to the classification of a business component as a discontinued operation.

EXPANDING YOUR KNOWLEDGE — Corporate Governance

In compliance with requirements of Item 10 of the Form 10-K, Harley-Davidson Inc. provides a link to its Financial Code of Ethics. The code is signed by the company's CEO, CFO, controller, and employees in the accounting and finance areas (or support areas). The full Financial Code of Ethics is at http://investor.harley-davidson.com/. Following is an excerpt (first 5 of 11 points) from that code of ethics.

1. I will act honestly and ethically in all my professional relationships.
2. I will endeavor to avoid all conflicts of interests with the Company and in any case will immediately and fully disclose any transaction or relationship that reasonably could be expected to give rise to an actual or perceived conflict of interest between the Company and me in accordance with the Conflict of Interest process.
3. I will ensure, to the best of my knowledge, the timely and understandable disclosure of information that is accurate, complete, objective, and relevant in all reports and documents filed with or submitted to the Securities and Exchange Commission or any other governmental, private or public regulatory agency or in other public communications that the Company makes.
4. I will endeavor to comply with all laws, rules and regulations of federal, state, provincial and local governments, and other appropriate private and public regulatory agencies.
5. I will act in good faith, responsibly, with due care, competence and diligence, without misrepresenting material facts or allowing my independent judgment to be subordinated, in all of my professional relationships.

Executive Compensation—Item 11

The SEC regulates disclosure of top executive salary information for its registrants. (Although required as Item 11 on Form 10-K, many companies fulfill this requirement by incorporating the information by reference to the Proxy statement, an SEC required report to shareholders.) An SEC registrant is required to disclose information concerning the amount and type of compensation paid to its CEO, CFO, and the three other most highly compensated executive officers. The registrant must disclose the criteria used in arriving at executive compensation decisions and the relation between the company's executive compensation practices and corporate performance. An excerpt from the 2015 Proxy statement of **Harley-Davidson Inc.** follows.

Summary Compensation Table ($ thousands)

Name and Principal Position	Year	Salary	Bonus	Stock Awards	Option Awards	Non-Equity Incentive Plan Compensation	Change in Pension Value	All Other Compensation	Total
Matthew S. Levatich	2015	$902	$307	$1,500	$968	$1,455	$1,285	$ 52	$6,470
President and COO	2014	669	221	641	474	1,481	1,508	439	5,434
	2013	635	191	559	419	1,153	675	105	3,736

EXPANDING YOUR KNOWLEDGE — Marketing through an Annual Report

A company can produce an annual report, separate from the Form 10-K. Although it typically includes many of the same items of a Form 10-K such as financial statements and notes, it does not include all requirements of the SEC. However, an annual report is in large part a marketing item for current and potential shareholders and creditors. Accordingly, an annual report is more visually appealing with pictures, charts, and graphs. An annual report usually begins with a letter to shareholders where top executives offer an overview of the company's operations, its financial position, and its future plans. For example, Coca Cola Company produced a 2016 Form 10-K and a 2016 Annual Review. The 2016 Annual Review includes a letter to shareowners, selected financial data, company highlights, descriptions of new products, and more.

Items of the Annual Report on Form 10-K — LO4-4 — Demo 4-4

Demo MBC

Match the information items *a* through *g* with the item of the Form 10-K filing in which that information is disclosed.

Form 10-K Items

1. Selected financial data—Item 6
2. Management's discussion and analysis—Item 7
3. Financial statements and supplementary data—Item 8
4. Directors and executive officers and corporate governance—Item 10
5. Executive compensation—Item 11

Solution

	Description	Form 10-K Item
a.	An opinion of the results of an examination of the financial statements of a company by an independent examiner.	**[3] Financial statements and supplementary data**
b.	Evidence provided by management of a company to investors and creditors regarding the company's financial condition, changes in financial condition, and the results of operations.	**[2] Management's discussion and analysis**
c.	Summary of salaries, bonuses, and stock compensation for highly compensated executive officers	**[5] Executive compensation**
d.	Includes the income statement, statement of comprehensive income (combined with the income statement or consecutive to the income statement), the balance sheet, the statement of stockholders' equity, the statement of cash flows, and the accompanying notes to the financial statements.	**[3] Financial statements and supplementary data**
e.	Selected financial information provided for a five-year period of time.	**[1] Selected financial data**
f.	Unaudited information providing additional supporting information to the financial statements.	**[3] Financial statements and supplementary data**
g.	Presentation of the names and backgrounds of the board of directors of the corporation.	**[4] Directors and executive officers and corporate governance**

REVIEW 4-4 **LO4-4** **Annual Report on Form 10-K**

Review MBC

Match each of the following Form 10-K excerpts, *a* through *f*, with one of the five parts of the annual report on Form 10-K where we are likely to find the excerpt.

Parts of an Annual Report on Form 10-K

1. Management's discussion and analysis of financial condition and results of operations
2. Selected financial data
3. Supplementary data to the financial statements
4. Auditors' report
5. Management report

Financial Statement Disclosure

_____ *a.* Based on the assessment, management concluded that, as of December 31, 2015, the Company's internal control over financial reporting is effective. (Source: 3M Company 10-K)

_____ *b.* The following selected financial data were reported ($ millions):

	2015	2014	2013	2012	2011
Total assets.	$90,093	$92,023	$90,055	$86,174	$79,974

(Source: Coca Cola Company 10-K)

_____ *c.* Unaudited quarterly data included the following net income numbers ($ thousands):

March 31	June 30	September 30	December 31	Year Ended, December 31
$19,180	$6,344	$128,225	$103,230	$256,979

(Source: Under Armour Inc. 10-K)

_____ *d.* Earnings before interest and income taxes ("EBIT") increased 10% for fiscal 2016, driven by revenue growth and gross margin expansion, while selling and administrative expense was flat as a percent of revenues. (Source: NIKE Inc. 10-K)

_____ *e.* In our opinion, such consolidated financial statements present fairly, in all material respects, the financial position of The Boeing Company and subsidiaries as of December 31, 2015 and 2014, and the results of their operations and their cash flows for each of the three years in the period ended December 31, 2015, in conformity with accounting principles generally accepted in the United States of America. (Source: The Boeing Company 10-K)

_____ *f.* Our net sales for fiscal 2016 decreased $281 million, or 2 percent, compared with fiscal 2015 primarily due to a decrease in net sales at Gap and Banana Republic, partially offset by an increase in net sales at Old Navy and Athleta. (Source: Gap Inc. 10-K)

More Practice: 4-55, 4-56, 4-57
Solution on p. 4-62.

Management Judgment

Many decisions by management contribute to the amounts reported in the balance sheet and items reported in the notes accompanying financial statements.

Elements Reported in the Balance Sheet

Management judgment is important in determining amounts reported in the balance sheet. Following are examples of items that are impacted by management judgment, including whether those items are classified as current or noncurrent.

- Accounts receivable is recorded net of expected credit losses, estimated based upon historical trends, adjusted to reflect current information and reasonable and supportable forecasts prepared by management.
- Inventory measured under certain assumptions is reported at the lower of cost or net realizable value, where cost is based on cost flow assumptions (determined by management) and net realizable value is estimated by management based on selling price less reasonably predictable costs of completion, disposal, and transportation.
- An investment is classified as noncurrent if management determines that they have the intent and ability to hold the investment beyond one year.

- Recognition of contingencies as liabilities is based on whether management determines that the resolution of a future event resulting in a loss is probable and the amount of the loss is estimable.

These examples show that the seemingly straightforward presentation of account balances in a simple accounting equation is the result of numerous decisions made by management requiring judgment and estimations, guided by authoritative support in the Codification.

Items Reported in Note Disclosures

Although authoritative guidance is provided for note disclosures, there are many aspects of disclosures that are dependent on management judgment, some examples of which follow.

- Disclosures of significant accounting policies and judgments related to the appropriateness of accounting principles chosen (see p. 4-16).
- Explicit disclosures of the inescapable use of accounting estimates in the preparation of financial statements (see p. 4-17).
- Disclosures of fair value measurements, with more disclosures surrounding level 3 measurements that are the most subjective in nature (see p. 4-18).
- Disclosure of subsequent events, if material (see p. 4-20).
- Explanations in the MD&A of past performance, including expectations for future results (see p. 4-25).

An important point is that management must decide which accounting items are significant or material. For example, to determine whether an accounting policy is significant, management may consider the usefulness of the related account on the financial statements. Disclosure effectiveness is improved if immaterial or redundant amounts are removed from financial reporting.

Describe requirements of segment reporting

APPENDIX 4A
LO 4-5

Accounting standards use a *modified management approach* to identify potentially reportable segments. The idea is that the way a company is organized for management of its various business activities and the financial information that is used for managing those operations should determine the segment information to be reported. The focus is on financial information that management uses to make decisions about its operations. This management approach is modified to require reporting on a reasonable number of segments. If too many segments are identified, aggregation criteria are used to develop a smaller number of reportable segments. Quantitative thresholds are used to determine the minimum size of operating segments that must be reported.

LO 4-5 Overview

Determination of a reportable segment
- Revenue test
- Operating profit (loss) test
- Identifiable asset test
- Combined revenue test

280-10-05-3 The guidance in this Subtopic requires that general-purpose financial statements include selected information reported on a single basis of segmentation. The method for determining what information to report is referred to as the management approach. The management approach is based on the way that management organizes the segments within the public entity for making operating decisions and assessing performance. Consequently, the segments are evident from the structure of the public entity's internal organization, and financial statement preparers should be able to provide the required information in a cost-effective and timely manner.

An **operating segment** is defined as a component of a company:

- That engages in business activities from which it may earn revenues and incur expenses (including transactions with other company components).
- Whose operating results are regularly reviewed by the company's "chief operating decision maker" to make segment resource allocation decisions and to assess segment performance.
- For which discrete financial information is available.

The accounting standards provide for aggregating the information from operating segments if the segments have similar economic characteristics and are similar in each of the following areas:

- Nature of the products and services.
- Nature of the production processes.
- Type or class of customer for the products and services.
- Methods used to distribute products and services.
- Nature of the regulatory environment, if applicable.

Quantitative Thresholds for Reporting Segments

In addition to meeting the definition of an operating segment, there also are several quantitative thresholds which determine the operating segments that must be separately reported (illustrated in **Demo 4-5**). A company must report information about an operating segment if the segment meets three thresholds based on: revenue, profit or loss, and assets.

Revenue Test

Report as a segment if the reported revenue, including sales to both external and internal customers, is 10% or more of the combined revenue, internal and external, of all reported operating segments.

Operating Profit Test

Report as a segment if the absolute amount of reported profit or loss is 10% or more of the greater, in absolute amount, of:

- Combined reported profit of all operating segments that did not report a loss, or
- Combined reported loss of all operating segments that did report a loss.

Identifiable Assets Test

Report as a segment if assets are 10% or more of the combined assets of all operating segments.

Combined Revenue Test

If combined external operating segment revenues are less than 75% of total external company revenue, then additional segments must be identified. If the 75% test is not met, management must identify additional individual segments, even though they do not meet any of the three quantitative thresholds, until the 75% test is met. The segments and other business activities that are not separately reported are combined into an "all other" category for reporting purposes.

Segment Disclosures

The required quantitative information that must be disclosed for each reportable segment includes measures of: *profit or loss* and *total assets*. Along with quantitative information, a company should disclose general information about the segment including factors in determining the segment and a description of its product and service offerings. Any of the following items that are included in the measure of segment profit or loss that is reviewed by the chief operating decision maker must also be reported.

- Revenues from external customers.
- Revenues from transactions with other operating segments.
- Interest revenue.
- Interest expense.
- Depreciation, depletion, and amortization expenses.
- Any unusual items.
- Equity in the net income of investees accounted for by the equity method.

- Income tax expense or benefit.
- Significant noncash items other than depreciation, depletion, and amortization expense.

The company also should disclose a reconciliation of segment revenues to total revenues, of segment profit or loss to total income before taxes, of segment assets to total assets.

Reliance on major customers is required to be disclosed. If revenues from transactions with a single external customer amount to 10% or more of a company's revenues, the company must disclose the amount of revenues from that customer, along with the identity of the segment or segments reporting the revenues. The company does not need to disclose the identity of a major customer or the amount of revenues that each segment reports from that customer.

Information on geographic areas is required to be disclosed as indicated in the following authoritative guidance.

280-10-50-42 A public entity shall report the following geographic information unless it is impracticable to do so.

a. Revenues from external customers attributed to the public entity's country of domicile and attributed to all foreign countries in total from which the public entity derives revenues. If revenues from external customers attributed to an individual foreign country are material, those revenues shall be disclosed separately. A public entity shall disclose the basis for attributing revenues from external customers to individual countries.

b. Long-lived assets other than financial instruments, long-term customer relationships of a financial institution, mortgage and other servicing rights, deferred policy acquisition costs, and deferred tax assets located in the public entity's country of domicile and located in all foreign countries in total in which the public entity holds assets. If assets in an individual foreign country are material, those assets shall be disclosed separately.

VF CORP.

Real World—REPORTABLE SEGMENTS

VF CORP [VFC]

The following illustrates revenues by segment reported by VF Corporation on its identified segments.

$ thousands	2015	2014	2013
Coalition revenues:			
Outdoor & Action Sports	$ 7,400,446	$ 7,198,994	$ 6,379,167
Jeanswear	2,792,244	2,801,754	2,810,994
Imagewear	1,082,565	1,104,038	1,065,952
Sportswear	635,056	650,203	624,693
Contemporary Brands	344,089	400,431	415,053
Other	122,344	126,741	123,789
Total coalition revenues	$12,376,744	$12,282,161	$11,419,648

Segment Reporting | **LO4-5** | **Demo 4-5**

Demo MBC

In 2020, Diverse Inc. reports total revenue of $31,000, profit before income taxes of $4,070, and total assets of $81,000. The company identifies eight operating segments as candidates for reporting, based on the definition of an operating segment, with the following segment-specific financial information. Determine which segments are reportable. For simplification, assume no intercompany transactions.

continued

continued from previous page

Operating Segment	Segment Revenue	Pretax Operating Profit (Loss)	Identifiable Assets
Auto parts	$ 8,000	$ 270	$ 7,000
Software production and sales	6,500	900	3,000
Software consulting	200	100	100
Electronics production and sales	10,500	2,300	12,000
Electronics equipment rental	300	100	1,000
Real estate	400	(150)	600
Warehouse leasing	100	50	300
Finance	5,000	500	57,000
Totals	$31,000	$4,070	$81,000

Solution

Revenue Test Any operating segment with revenue equal to or greater than $3,100 (10% × $31,000) meets the test. Four meet the threshold (Auto parts, Software Production and Sales, Electronics Production and Sales, and Finance) and are required to be separately reported.

Operating Profit Test The criterion for this test is 10% of the greater of (1) the absolute value of combined profit for segments reporting a profit: 10% × ($4,070 + $150), or $422, and (2) the absolute value of the combined loss for segments reporting a loss: 10% × $150, or $15. Therefore, the criterion amount is $422. Segments with operating profit (loss) greater than $422 must be reported separately. Three meet the threshold (Software Production and Sales, Electronics Production and Sales, and Finance) and are required to be separately reported. The only segment to report a loss is real estate. The absolute value of the loss, $150, does not exceed $422. Therefore, the real estate segment does not meet the operating profit test.

Identifiable Assets Test Any operating segment with identifiable assets greater than $8,100 (10% × $81,000) must be separately reported. This means Electronic Production and Sales, and Finance must be reported separately.

Thus, the four reporting segments are: Auto parts, Software Production and Sales, Electronics Production and Sales, and Finance.

Combined Revenue Test Four operating segments do not meet the threshold amounts and do not need to be reported separately. However, if combined operating segment revenues are less than 75% of total company revenue, or $23,250 (75% × $31,000) for the company, then additional segments must be identified. The sum of the revenues for the reportable segments is $30,000 ($8,000 + $6,500 + $10,500 + $5,000); thus, 96.8% ($30,000/$31,000) of the total reported revenue is included in the reportable segments. The 75% requirement is met without considering additional aggregation of operating segments in this case. If the 75% test is not met, management must identify additional individual segments, even though they do not meet any of the three quantitative thresholds, until the 75% test is met. Finally, the segments and other business activities that are not separately reported are combined into an "all other" category for reporting purposes.

Segment Reporting

LO4-5 **REVIEW 4-5**

Review MBC

Tebow Inc. operates as a single operating segment, with sales throughout the world. In 2020, sales, pretax operating profit, and identifiable assets reported by customer location consist of the following.

	Sales	Pretax Operating Profit	Identifiable Assets
United States	$40,000	$4,300	$45,000
Asia, other than China	13,000	1,400	12,500
Europe	12,000	1,250	13,000
China	11,000	(1,100)	10,750
Canada	9,200	930	9,000
Oceania	3,000	325	2,900
Middle East	2,000	180	1,400
Africa	1,400	(170)	1,400
Latin America	1,250	90	1,100
Totals	$92,850	$7,205	$97,050

a. Compute the revenue test threshold and determine the identifiable segments.
b. Compute the operating profit threshold and determine the identifiable segments.
c. Compute the total asset threshold and determine the identifiable segments.
d. Conduct the combined revenue test.

More Practice: 4-84, 4-85

Solution on p. 4-62.

Questions

4-1. What is the purpose of a balance sheet?

4-2. What does a balance sheet report? Why is it dated differently from the income statement and the statement of cash flows?

4-3. Explain the relation between the balance sheet and full disclosure.

4-4. Define current assets and current liabilities and emphasize their interrelation.

4-5. Why are market (fair) values not used exclusively in balance sheets? What option is available to financial statement preparers to recognize at fair value, items that would typically be recognized at historical cost?

4-6. What would the investment category include in a balance sheet?

4-7. Distinguish between tangible and intangible assets.

4-8. Why is the caption "other assets" sometimes necessary? Name two items that might be reported under this classification.

4-9. Distinguish between current and noncurrent liabilities.

4-10. What is stockholders' equity? What are the main components of stockholders' equity?

4-11. What are comparative financial statements? Why are they important?

4-12. What is meant by subsequent events? Why are they reported?

4-13. Why are notes to financial statements important? How does a company determine when a note should be included?

4-14. What is the auditors' report? Why is it important to the statement user?

4-15. Are financial statements the representation of company management, the independent auditor, or both? Explain.

4-16. What is the full-disclosure principle? What is the purpose of notes to financial statements?

4-17. What is the Form 10-K? What items must be included in the Form 10-K?

4-18. Briefly describe three reports associated with financial statements reported in a Form 10-K.

4-19. Describe what is included in the Management's Discussion and Analysis section of the Form 10-K.

4-20. What are the accounting policies of a company? What, if any, are the requirements for disclosing information about accounting policies?

4-21. What must a company disclose about related party transactions?

Brief Exercises

Brief Exercise 4-22
Classifying Current and Noncurrent Assets and Liabilities **LO1**

Classify the following assets and liabilities as current or noncurrent for the typical company.

a. Bond payable, 10-year maturity
b. Cash equivalents
c. Building (in use)
d. Note receivable, 2-year maturity
e. Accounts payable
f. Income taxes payable

Brief Exercise 4-23
Classifying Current and Noncurrent Assets **LO1**
Hint: See Demo 4-1A

Review the following separate items and determine the proper classification as of December 31, 2020, as a current or noncurrent asset, or some combination.

a. $50,000, long-term note receivable, with an installment payment of $5,000 due June 30, 2021.
b. $5,000 investment in equity securities where the company (owner of the investment) intends to sell the securities sometime in 2021.
c. $40,000 investment in land that is held for speculative purposes.
d. $14,000 in accounts receivable, with an associated allowance for doubtful accounts of $1,000.

Brief Exercise 4-24
Preparing the Current Asset Section **LO2**

Prepare the current asset section of a classified balance sheet given the following account balances on December 31, 2020.

Accounts receivable	$45,000	Cash equivalents	$ 1,000
Allowance for doubtful accounts	2,000	Equipment	100,000
Accounts payable	50,000	Inventory	50,000
Cash	14,000	Prepaid insurance	1,000

Brief Exercise 4-25
Preparing the Investments Section **LO2**

Prepare the investment section of a classified balance sheet given the following account balances on December 31, 2020.

Bond sinking fund	$100,000
Debt investments (expected to be held to maturity in 2025)	40,000
Land (in use)	45,000
Land held for speculation	25,000
Prepaid insurance (for January 2021 coverage paid in advance)	5,000

Brief Exercise 4-26
Preparing the Property, Plant, and Equipment Section **LO2**

Prepare the property, plant, and equipment section of a classified balance sheet given the following account balances on December 31, 2020.

Land	$28,000	Accumulated depreciation—building	$ 25,000
Accumulated depreciation—equipment	5,000	Building	200,000
Equipment	40,000	Land held for speculation	20,000

Brief Exercise 4-27
Preparing the Intangible Assets Section **LO2**

Prepare the intangible asset section of a classified balance sheet given the following account balances on December 31, 2020.

Patents	$12,000	Franchise	$80,000
Cash	75,000	Goodwill	19,000
Investment in equity securities—long-term	35,000		

Brief Exercise 4-28
Preparing the Current Liabilities Section **LO2**

Prepare the current liabilities section of a classified balance sheet given the following account balances on December 31, 2020.

Dividends payable	$ 4,000	Accounts payable	$60,000
Bonds payable (matures December 2028)	50,000	Income taxes payable	14,000
Interest payable	1,000	Deferred revenue (long-term)	5,000
Note payable (due June 30, 2021)	20,000		

Brief Exercise 4-29 Preparing the Long-term Liabilities Section **LO2**

Prepare the long-term liabilities section of a classified balance sheet given the following account balances on December 31, 2020.

Bonds payable (due in 2026)	$100,000	Net pension liability (long-term)	$30,000
Note payable (due November 1, 2021)	5,000	Income taxes payable	21,000
Note payable (due December 31, 2025)	45,000		

Brief Exercise 4-30 Preparing the Stockholders' Equity Section **LO2**

Prepare the stockholders' equity section of a classified balance sheet given the following account balances on December 31, 2020.

Preferred stock, par $15, authorized 20,000 shares	$255,000
Cash received above par of preferred stock	25,000
Common stock, no-par, 60,000 shares issued (100,000 shares authorized)	200,000
Retained earnings	150,000

Brief Exercise 4-31 Preparing a Classified Balance Sheet **LO2** *Hint:* See Demo 4-2

Prepare a classified balance sheet given the following account balances on December 31, 2020. Next, compute working capital on that same date.

Cash	$ 2,000	Accounts payable	$ 62,000
Accounts receivable	60,000	Notes payable (long-term)	70,000
Inventory	2,500	Income taxes payable	2,200
Franchise	35,000	Retained earnings, unadjusted	45,800
Prepaid insurance	1,200	Interest payable	700
Common stock (no-par, 10,000 shares issued and outstanding)	50,000	Equipment, net	130,000

Brief Exercise 4-32 Preparing a Classified Balance Sheet **LO2** *Hint:* See Demo 4-2

Prepare a classified balance sheet given the following account balances from a post-closing trial balance dated December 31, 2020.

Account	Debit	Credit
Cash	$180,000	
Accounts receivable	215,000	
Allowance for doubtful accounts		$15,000
Inventory	103,200	
Building	220,000	
Accumulated depreciation—building		45,000
Franchise	45,000	
Accounts payable		168,000
Salaries payable		25,000
Bonds payable		210,000
Common stock		100,000
Retained earnings		199,000
Accumulated other comprehensive income		1,200
Totals	$763,200	$763,200

Brief Exercise 4-33 Determining Current Assets and Current Liabilities from Other Accounts **LO2**

Determine the missing amounts from a balance sheet dated December 31, 2020.

Missing amounts: Total current assets and Total current liabilities. There are no other missing amounts.

Given amounts: Equipment, net $27,000, Patent $6,000, Notes payable $8,000, Common stock $18,000, Retained earnings $5,000, Total liabilities $20,000

Brief Exercise 4-34
Determining Where to Disclose Financial Reporting Items **LO3**
Hint: See Demo 4-3

Match the following financial reporting items *a* through *f* with the most proper means of disclosure, 1 through 3. Assume a December 31, 2020, annual year-end for financial statements.

Means of Disclosure

1. Disclose as part of the summary of significant accounting policies note.
2. Disclose as a separate note.
3. Report on the face of the balance sheet.

Financial Reporting Item

____ *a.* Inventory costing method
____ *b.* Components of long-term debt
____ *c.* Subsequent event details
____ *d.* Depreciation method
____ *e.* Related party transactions
____ *f.* Current assets

Brief Exercise 4-35
Identifying Disclosure Types **LO3**

The following items were identified in preparing year-end, December 31, 2020, financial statements for Lakeside Inc.

____ *a.* Guaranteed the loan of its shareholder with a 25% ownership interest.
____ *b.* Determined that long-term debt investments at December 31, 2020, are classified as Level 2 in the fair value hierarchy.
____ *c.* Incurred a loss due to a flood on December 31, 2020.
____ *d.* Currently investigating indications of bribes paid by employees of one of its subsidiaries in China for marketing opportunities for its products.
____ *e.* Guaranteed the loan of one of its suppliers.
____ *f.* Secured a new bank loan on January 15, 2021.
____ *g.* Inventories are valued at the lower of cost (first-in, first-out) or market.

In each situation, indicate the type of disclosure that should be considered: (1) summary of significant accounting policies, (2) fair value measurement, (3) related party transactions, (4) subsequent events, (5) errors, fraud, and illegal acts, or (6) none of the above.

Brief Exercise 4-36
Defining Disclosure Categories **LO3**

Match the disclosure categories 1 through 6, with the descriptions, *a* through *f*.

Disclosure Categories

1. Summary of significant accounting policies
2. Fair value measurement
3. Related party transactions
4. Subsequent events
5. Error
6. Fraud or illegal act

Descriptions

____ *a.* Description of events taking place after year-end but before the issuance of financial statements.
____ *b.* Measurement disclosure classified as Level 1, Level 2, or Level 3
____ *c.* Intentional misstatement of amounts in the financial statements.
____ *d.* Conducting business with another entity where one has the ability to influence the other.
____ *e.* Unintentional misstatement of amounts in the financial statements.
____ *f.* Descriptions of accounting methods and policies.

Brief Exercise 4-37
Defining Elements of the Form 10-K **LO4**
Hint: See Demo 4-4

Match the Form 10-K components 1 through 7, with the descriptions, *a* through *g*.

Form 10-K Components

1. Selected financial data
2. MD&A
3. Auditor's report
4. Executive compensation summary
5. Chief executive officer certification
6. Directors and executive officers
7. Financial statements and supplementary information

Descriptions

____ *a.* Disclosure of salary measurements of key officers of the company.
____ *b.* Personally signed statement of key officer of the company indicating no knowledge of misstatements in the financial statements.
____ *c.* Listing of specific measurements of financial items for the most recent 5 years.
____ *d.* Balance sheet, statement of comprehensive income, statement of stockholders' equity, cash flows, notes.
____ *e.* Names and experiences of the boards of directors, CEO, and CFO.
____ *f.* Explanation of financial results of recent years along with prospective information.
____ *g.* Opinion on the fair representation of financial statements by an independent party.

Brief Exercise 4-38
Classifying Statements as Items in the Form 10-K **LO4**
Hint: See Demo 4-4

The following items are included in the fiscal year 2017 Form 10-K of **United Natural Foods Inc.**

____ 1. Steven L. Spinner [President and CEO]: fiscal 2017 base salary, $922,500.
____ 2. As we continue to aggressively pursue new customers, expand relationships with existing customers and pursue opportunistic acquisitions, we expect net sales for fiscal 2018 to grow over fiscal 2017.
____ 3. Basic earnings per share is calculated by dividing net income by the weighted average number of common shares outstanding during the period.
____ 4. Eric F. Artz , age 49, has served as a member of the Board since October 2015.
____ 5. Net sales of $9,274, $8,470, $8,185, $6,794, $6,064, for the fiscal years of 2017, 2016, 2015, 2014, and 2013, respectively. ($ millions)

For each statement 1 through 5, indicate the Item number of the Form 10-K where the statement would be included or incorporated by reference.

Brief Exercise 4-39
Identifying Which Items are Disclosed in the Annual Report on Form 10-K **LO4**

In each situation, indicate whether the item is included in the annual report on Form 10-K or not.

____ *a.* Press release on a company's earning per share
____ *b.* Management's discussion and analysis
____ *c.* Executive compensation
____ *d.* Analyst report on earnings expectations
____ *e.* Corporate tax return
____ *f.* Financial statements and accompanying notes
____ *g.* Auditors' report

Exercises

Exercise 4-40
Classifying Balance Sheet Accounts **LO1**

The following are classifications included on a typical classified balance sheet.

Balance Sheet Classifications

a. Current assets.
b. Investments.
c. Property, plant, and equipment.
d. Intangible assets.
e. Other assets.
f. Current liabilities.
g. Long-term liabilities.
h. Paid-in capital.
i. Retained earnings.
j. Accumulated other comprehensive income.
k. Noncontrolling interests.

Required

Use the letters *a* to *k* from the balance sheet classifications above to indicate the usual classification for each of the 22 balance sheet items listed below. Also indicate whether an account is a *contra* account.

____ 1. Accumulated depreciation.
____ 2. Bonds payable (due in 10 years).
____ 3. Accounts payable (trade).
____ 4. Investment in stock of another company (long-term holding).
____ 5. Land (in use).
____ 6. Unrealized gain on foreign currency translation adjustment.
____ 7. Office supplies inventory.
____ 8. Restricted cash (release not expected for two years).
____ 9. Accumulated income less accumulated dividends.
____ 10. Deferred revenue (short-term).
____ 11. Bond sinking fund (to retire long-term bonds).
____ 12. Prepaid insurance.
____ 13. Accounts receivable (trade).
____ 14. Short-term investment.
____ 15. Allowance for doubtful accounts.
____ 16. Building (in use).
____ 17. Common stock (par $10).
____ 18. Interest revenue earned but not collected.
____ 19. Shares held by noncontrolling stockholders.
____ 20. Patent.
____ 21. Land, held for investment.
____ 22. Paid-in capital in excess of par—common stock.

Exercise 4-41
Classifying Balance Sheet Accounts **LO1**

Classify the following amounts as (*a*) current assets, (*b*) investments, (*c*) property, plant, and equipment, (*d*) other assets, (*e*) current liabilities, (*f*) long-term liabilities, (*g*) paid-in capital, or (*h*) retained earnings.

____ 1. Note payable (due in two years).
____ 2. Bond sinking fund.
____ 3. Investment in common stock of subsidiary.
____ 4. Deferred lease revenue (for the first quarter of the following year).
____ 5. Deferred tax liability, net.
____ 6. Accumulated net income since inception, less dividends.
____ 7. No-par common stock.
____ 8. Accrued pension liability (long-term).
____ 9. Customer advances.
____ 10. Accumulated depreciation.
____ 11. Prepaid insurance.
____ 12. Investment in U.S. Treasury bills.
____ 13. Leasehold improvements.
____ 14. Raw materials inventory.
____ 15. Furniture and fixtures.
____ 16. Construction in process (company's building under construction).

Exercise 4-42
Reporting Financial Items in the Balance Sheet **LO1**

Alexa Corp. is preparing its balance sheet at December 31, 2020. The following items are under consideration.

1. Note payable, long term, $80,000 originating on December 31, 2020. This note will be paid in installments. The first installment of $10,000 is to be paid August 1, 2021.
2. Bonds payable, 5%, $200,000 at December 31, 2020. Annual interest on the bond is paid on January 1, 2021.
3. Bond sinking fund, $40,000; this fund is being accumulated to retire the bonds at maturity.
4. Rent paid in advance for the first quarter of 2021 on a short-term lease, $6,000.
5. Accounts payable, $14,000, due to suppliers in terms ranging from 30 to 60 days.
6. A 3-year, 8%, $40,000 note payable to bank originating on November 1, 2020, requires quarterly interest payments.
7. Year-end bonuses, based upon 2020 reported net income, are estimated to be $30,000 and are payable March 15, 2021.

Required

For each of the items described above, determine the amount(s) to be recognized on the balance sheet and classify each amount as one of the following: (a) current assets, (b) investments, (c) property, plant, and equipment, (d) other assets, (e) current liabilities, or (f) long-term liabilities. More than one amount may apply to an item.

Exercise 4-43
Classifying Accounts on the Balance Sheet **LO1**

Typical balance sheet classifications follow.

Balance Sheet Classifications

a. Current assets.
b. Investments.
c. Property, plant, and equipment.
d. Intangible assets.
e. Other assets.
f. Current liabilities.
g. Long-term liabilities.
h. Paid-in capital.
i. Retained earnings.
j. Accumulated other comprehensive income.
k. Noncontrolling interests.

Required

Use the letters *a* to *k* from the balance sheet classifications above to indicate the usual classification for each of the 22 balance sheet items listed below.

____ 1. Preferred stock.
____ 2. Accrued salaries.
____ 3. Long-term receivable.
____ 4. Cash surrender value of life insurance.
____ 5. Income tax payable.
____ 6. Current maturities of 10-year bond payable.
____ 7. Interest payable.
____ 8. Work in process inventory.
____ 9. Long-term debt callable due to a covenant violation.
____ 10. Copyrights.
____ 11. Accounts receivable—trade.
____ 12. Accumulated depreciation—equipment.
____ 13. Land (in use).
____ 14. Dividends payable.
____ 15. Note receivable (due in 2 years).
____ 16. Last month rent of a one-year lease received in advance.
____ 17. Goodwill.
____ 18. Land held for speculation.
____ 19. Prepaid insurance (6 month prepayment).
____ 20. Accrued utilities expense.
____ 21. Paid-in capital in excess of par—common stock.
____ 22. Note payable (due in 6 months).

Exercise 4-44
Computing Missing Amounts on a Classified Balance Sheet **LO2**

The consolidated balance sheet of Mutron Lock Inc. follows.

Consolidated Balance Sheet
As of December 31, 2020

Assets		
Current assets		
Cash and cash equivalents.		$ 10,195
Marketable securities		*a*
Accounts receivable	$153,682	
Allowance for doubtful accounts. . .	*b*	147,421
Inventories		201,753
Prepaid expenses.		8,902
Total current assets		*c*
Property, plant, and equipment		
Land	12,482	
Building.	*d*	
Equipment and machinery	195,467	
Accumulated depreciation	(103,675)	
Total property, plant, and equipment		261,056
Investments		14,873
Other assets.		7,926
Total assets.		$661,774

Liabilities and Stockholders' Equity		
Current liabilities		
Accounts payable	$85,476	
Notes payable.	*e*	
Income taxes payable.	6,421	
Current portion of long-term debt	4,893	
Accrued expenses	5,654	
Total current liabilities		$110,763
Long-term debt.		122,004
Deferred income taxes		*f*
Pension liability.		35,136
Total liabilities		*g*
Stockholders' equity		
Preferred stock, no-par value (authorized 10,000 shares, issued 2,400 shares).	*h*	
Common stock, $5 par value (authorized 400,000 shares, issued 20,000 shares)	*i*	
Additional paid-in capital.	73,725	
Total contributed capital		*j*
Retained earnings		
Appropriated	25,000	
Unappropriated.	*k*	181,471
Total retained earnings and contributed capital.		*l*
Less treasury stock (3,421 shares).		21,809
Total stockholders' equity		347,668
Total liabilities and stockholders' equity . . .		$ *m*

Required

For each of the items *a* through *m*, determine the balances that appear on the complete balance sheet.

Exercise 4-45
Computing Retained Earnings and Preparing a Classified Balance Sheet **LO2**

The following data, in no particular order, are from the accounts of Brown Corp. as of December 31, 2020, its annual year-end. All amounts are accurate, all accounts have normal balances, total debits equal total credits, and all amounts are in $ thousands.

Accounts payable (trade)	$ 8	Deferred revenue	$ 2
Debt retirement fund (long-term)	4	Cash dividends payable	5
Accounts receivable	17	Inventory.	30
Income taxes payable.	4	Land held for future business site.	18
Short-term investments, marketable securities (cost which approximates fair value).	10	Equipment and furniture	70
Bonds payable (long-term)	51	Net income for 2020	35
Accumulated depreciation, equipment and furniture.	6	Dividends (cash) declared (a debit)	3
Common stock, par $1 (100,000 shares authorized)	70	Prepaid expenses (short-term).	1
Cash.	20	Patent.	4
Retained earnings, December 31, 2019.	17	Prepaid rent (long-term)	2
Allowance for doubtful accounts.	2	Investment in capital stock of Zinc Products Corporation (long-term).	26
		Premium on common stock	5

Required

a. Compute the year-end balance of retained earnings.

b. Prepare a classified balance sheet as of December 31, 2020.

c. Compute working capital on December 31, 2020.

Exercise 4-46
Preparing a Classified Balance Sheet **LO2**
Hint: See Demo 4-2

The ledger of Bama Inc. had the following account balances on December 31, 2020.

Accounts payable	$33,200	Office equipment	$ 9,500
Accounts receivable	9,500	Raw materials inventory	9,600
Accrued expenses (credit)	800	Allowance for bad debts	500
Bonds payable, 8%	25,000	Accumulated depreciation	9,000
Common stock ($100 par)	70,000	Rent expense paid in advance on a short-term lease	3,000
Cash	10,000	Sinking fund to retire long-term debt	7,000
Retained earnings (to be computed)	?	Land held for future plant site	14,000
Plant equipment	31,200	Note receivable, 9%, due 2022	6,749
Finished goods inventory	13,100	Work in process inventory	23,300
Investments*	13,000		

*Of the balance in the investments account, $4,000 will be converted to cash in the coming year; the remainder is a long-term investment.

Required

Prepare a classified balance sheet for Bama Inc. on December 31, 2020.

Exercise 4-47
Preparing a Classified Balance Sheet **LO2**

The following balances are from the post-closing trial balance of Armour Inc.

Account Title	Debit	Credit
Cash	$ 16,000	
Accounts receivable	65,000	
Allowance for doubtful accounts		$ 7,500
Inventory	90,000	
Prepaid insurance	1,200	
Short-term investments	28,000	
Equipment	100,000	
Building	300,000	
Accumulated depreciation—equipment		20,000
Accumulated depreciation—building		7,500
Goodwill	30,300	
Accounts payable		45,000
Salaries payable		5,000
Interest payable		1,500
Income tax payable		9,000
Notes payable, 8%, 5-year		250,000
Bonds payable, 7%, 10-year		15,000
Common stock		200,000
Retained earnings		70,000
Totals	$630,500	$630,500

Required

a. Prepare a classified balance sheet for Armour Inc. as of December 31, 2020.
b. Compute working capital on December 31, 2020.

Exercise 4-48 Correcting the Presentation of a Classified Balance Sheet **LO2**

The following draft of a balance sheet was prepared for Roslyn Corp., but includes a number of errors in classification, presentation, and computation.

Roslyn Corp.
Balance Sheet
December 31, 2020

Assets		Liabilities and Stockholders' Equity	
Cash	$ 120,000	Liabilities	
Building	565,000	Accounts payable	$ 200,000
		Note payable	177,000
Equipment	110,000	Dividends payable	10,000
Accounts receivable	241,000	Deferred revenue	3,000
		Accumulated depreciation	80,000
Investments, short-term	140,000	Bonds payable	200,000
Inventory	325,000	Total	670,000
Prepaid rent	5,000	Stockholders' equity	
		Common stock	475,000
Investments, long-term	140,000	Retained earnings	555,000
Franchise	40,000	Accumulated other comprehensive income	(14,000)
		Total stockholders' equity	1,016,000
Total assets	$1,686,000	Total liabilities and stockholders' equity	$1,686,000

Additional information

- Note payable includes interest due of $2,000. The note plus interest is due in 6 months.
- Net accounts receivable of $241,000 consists of accounts receivable of $257,000 minus an allowance for doubtful accounts of $16,000.
- Common stock includes $175,000 attributed to additional paid-in capital.
- Included in the cash balance is $20,000 of cash restricted for 9 months due to a debt covenant.

Required

Prepare a corrected classified balance sheet for Roslyn Corp. on December 31, 2020.

Exercise 4-49 Preparing a Current Asset Section along with Note Disclosures **LO2, 3**

The following selected balances are from the post-closing trial balance of WKO Inc. as of December 31, 2020.

Cash	$ 75,000	Equipment	$80,000
Investments	98,000	Accumulated depreciation	15,000
Accounts receivable	75,000	Franchise, net	15,000
Inventory	80,000	Customer deposits received in advance	4,000
Note receivable	100,000	Accounts payable	65,000

Additional information

1. Included in the cash balance is $25,000 of cash restricted for 18 months due to a debt agreement.
2. Included in investments is $28,000 of short-term investments at fair value and the remaining is long-term, also recognized at fair value.
3. 5% of the accounts receivable balance of $75,000 is estimated to be uncollectible.
4. Inventory is valued at the lower of cost or market. The cost value is determined using the average cost method.
5. The note receivable of $100,000 is due in 21 months. The interest rate is 6% and the note originated on September 30, 2020. Interest is paid quarterly with the first payment due January 1, 2021.

Required

a. Prepare the current asset section of the classified balance sheet for WKO Inc. on December 31, 2020.

b. Prepare a list of four notes, regarding all assets, to be included in the significant accounting policy note accompanying the financial statements of WKO Inc. on December 31, 2020.

Exercise 4-50
Preparing Note Disclosures for Financial Statements **LO3**

Match each of the following excerpts *a* through *i* from actual financial statements with one of the five disclosure options where we are likely to find the excerpt.

Disclosure Options

1. Disclose as a separate note on the summary of significant accounting policies.
2. Disclose as a separate note on fair value.
3. Disclose as a separate note on related parties.
4. Disclose as a separate note on subsequent events.
5. Disclose as a separate note on errors, fraud, or illegal acts.
6. Disclose as a separate note on a subject not indicated in the list above.

Financial Reporting Items

____ *a.* On February 16, 2016, VF's Board of Directors declared a quarterly cash dividend of $0.37 per share, payable on March 18, 2016 to shareholders of record on March 8, 2016. (Source: VF Corporation 10-K (December 31, 2015))

____ *b.* We classify time deposits and other investments that are highly liquid and have maturities of three months or less at the date of purchase as cash equivalents. (Source: Coca-Cola Company 10-K)

____ *c.* As of March 1, 2014, the Company retired all existing treasury stock. Upon retirement, the treasury stock balance as of March 1, 2014 was reduced for the amount originally recorded for the shares repurchased. (Source: The Gap Inc. 10-K)

____ *d.* The Company has an operating lease agreement with an entity controlled by the Company's CEO to lease an aircraft for business purposes. (Source: Under Armour Inc. 10-K)

____ *e.* The Company identified a prior period error in the classification of available-for-sale securities ("AFS") for the first and second quarters of 2015. The Company concluded that the error was not material to any of its previously issued financial statements. (Source: Under Armour Inc. 10-K)

____ *f.* Subsequent to fiscal year-end, the Company repurchased approximately 7.8 million shares of the Company's common stock at an average price per share of $30.15 for a total of approximately $234 million. (Source: Whole Foods Market Inc. 10-K)

____ *g.* During the three months ended January 31, 2015, the Company recorded a cumulative adjustment to net sales for $7.7 million related to amounts owed to a customer resulting from an incorrect calculation of contractual obligations to that customer from fiscal year 2009 through fiscal year 2014. (Source: United Natural Foods Inc. 10-K)

____ *h.* We review the carrying amount of long-lived assets for impairment whenever events or changes in circumstances indicate that the carrying amount of an asset may not be recoverable. (Source: The Gap Inc. 10-K)

____ *i.* Level 3 inputs are not observable in the market and include management's judgments about the assumptions market participants would use in pricing the asset or liability. (Source: Harley-Davidson Inc. 10-K)

Exercise 4-51
Identifying Where Items are Disclosed in Financial Statements and Notes **LO3**
Hint: See Demo 4-3

Match each of the following financial reporting items *a* through *j* from a company with a December 31, 2020, year-end with one of the following four reporting options:

1. Disclosed as part of the summary of significant accounting policies note.
2. Disclosed as a separate note.
3. Reported on the face of the balance sheet.
4. Not reported as part of the financial statements and accompanying notes.

Financial Reporting Items

____ *a.* Separate reporting of current and noncurrent liabilities.

____ *b.* Bond issuance that took place on January 10, 2021.

____ *c.* Use of straight-line method to amortize a patent (intangible asset with a finite life).

____ *d.* Sale of property to a sibling of the CEO (Chief Executive Officer).

____ *e.* Use of the average cost method to account for inventory.

____ *f.* Management's discussion and analysis of financial condition and results of operations.

____ *g.* The balance of inventory on December 31, 2021, and 2020.

____ *h.* Explanation of how the allowance for doubtful accounts was estimated.

____ *i.* Components of pension costs and a description of assumptions used to estimate pension liability.

____ *j.* Number of shares of common stock issued and outstanding.

Exercise 4-52
Identifying Where Items are Disclosed in Financial Statements and Notes **LO3**
Hint: See Demo 4-3

The following excerpts *a* through *e* are reported items from financial statements and accompanying notes. Indicate where the excerpt is likely reported, 1, 2 or 3.

1. Disclosed as part of the summary of significant accounting policies note.
2. Disclosed as a separate note.
3. Reported on the face of the balance sheet.

Financial Statement Excerpts

____ *a.* Nonvested shares of restricted stock had a market value of $37.0 million at the end of 2015. The market value of the shares that vested during 2015, 2014, and 2013 was $14.1 million, $20.1 million and $9.7 million, respectively.

____ *b.* Inventories are stated at the lower of cost or net realizable value. Cost is determined on the first-in, first-out ("FIFO") method and is net of discounts or rebates received from vendors.

____ *c.* Preferred Stock, par value $1; shares authorized, 25,000,000; no shares outstanding in 2015 and 2014.

____ *d.* Depreciation of property, plant and equipment is computed using the straight-line method over the estimated useful lives of the assets, ranging from 3 to 10 years for machinery and equipment and up to 40 years for buildings.

____ *e.* The company has $110.1 million of international lines of credit with various banks, which are uncommitted and can be terminated at any time by either the company or the banks.

Exercise 4-53
Classifying Disclosures and Analyzing Financial Statement Impact **LO3**

The following items are considered in the preparation of financial statements for Forde Inc. for the year ended December 31, 2020.

1. The company is currently investigating whether a foreign division paid bribes to governmental officials in the Bahamas in order to obtain a sales contract with the government. The company is working with the SEC to resolve the matter.
2. A loan to a 5% shareholder was made on June 30, 2020, for $10,000. Interest is due annually beginning one year from the origination of the loan.
3. On January 15, 2021, a business component met the criteria to be classified as held for sale. At that time, impairment is estimated to be $30,000.
4. Short-term investments are valued at Level 1 in the fair value hierarchy for $40,550. Total net unrealized gain (affecting net income) related to the investments is $1,500.
5. Depreciation is determined on a straight-line basis for buildings and leasehold improvements over 2 to 40 years.
6. On February 1, 2021, the company declared a quarterly cash dividend of $0.40 per share, payable on March 15, 2021, for shareholders of record on March 10, 2021.
7. Goodwill and other acquired intangible assets with indefinite lives are not amortized but are tested for impairment annually.
8. Equipment is measured at fair value of $27,000 on a nonrecurring basis using significant unobservable inputs (Level 3). The total related impairment loss is $3,000.
9. Land was sold to the company president at a price significantly under its appraised value.
10. All highly liquid investments with an original maturity of 90 days or less are considered to be cash equivalents.

Required

For each of the items listed above, complete the following table:

Item Number	Note Disclosure Category	Balance Sheet	Income Statement
#	List Category	Yes or no	Yes or no

For the note disclosure category, choose from the following items: (1) summary of significant accounting policies, (2) fair value measurement, (3) related party transactions, (4) subsequent events, (5) errors, fraud, and illegal acts. For each item, indicate whether we would expect to potentially see an item affected on the face of the balance sheet and/or on the face of the income statement.

Exercise 4-54
Researching a Form 10-K **LO4**

Obtain an electronic copy of the annual report on Form 10-K for **Under Armour Inc.** for the year ended December 31, 2016, which can be found on the SEC Edgar website (https://www.sec.gov/edgar/searchedgar/companysearch.html).

Required

Use Form 10-K to answer the following questions.

1. Selected financial data
   a. In what item number is selected financial data included?
   b. What is gross profit for the year ended December 31, 2016 (in thousands)?
2. MD&A
   a. In what item number is MD&A included?
   b. What was the percentage increase in net revenues of the Apparel division from 2015 to 2016?
   c. At December 31, 2016 what percentage of cash and cash equivalents were held by foreign subsidiaries?
3. Financial statements and supplementary data
   a. In what item number are financial statements and supplementary data included?
   b. What is the balance of accounts payable on December 31, 2015 (in thousands)?
   c. What is the total commitment of the company to pay future minimum sponsorship and other marketing payments (in thousands)?
4. Directors and Executive Officers*
   a. In what item number are directors and executive officers included?
   b. In what year did Kevin A. Plank become chairman of the board?
   c. What is the average age of the 10 directors elected at the 2017 annual meeting?
5. Executive Compensation*
   a. In what item number is executive compensation included?
   b. What is the total adjusted 2016 compensation for Kevin A. Plank (founder)?
   c. What is the total 2017 retention equity award granted to Kevin A. Plank (founder)?
   d. What is the total 2017 retention equity award granted to Michael Lee (Chief Digital Officer)?

   **Hint:* The proxy statement (incorporated by reference) is labeled *DEF 14A* and can be found using the SEC Edgar website.

Exercise 4-55
Identifying Where Items are Disclosed in Form 10-K **LO4**

The following excerpts *1* through *7* are from financial statements and accompanying notes on Form 10-K. Indicate which section *a* through *g* that the excerpt is reported.

1. Statement from the CEO (chief executive officer) and CFO (chief financial officer) that they have evaluated controls over financial reporting.
2. Additional financial reporting information communicated to financial statement users as required by FASB. This information is not audited but is subject to limited procedures by auditors.
3. Statement from executive officers that they are responsible for the integrity of financial statements.
4. Statement from independent evaluators on whether the financial statements are presented fairly and in compliance with GAAP.
5. Financial reports plus the accompanying disclosure notes.
6. Statements about a company's products and results of operations including explanation of trends.
7. Certain financial information (such as net sales and net income) reported over the past five years.

Section of the Annual Report on Form 10-K

____ *a.* Management's discussion and analysis of financial condition and results of operations
____ *b.* Selected financial data
____ *c.* Financial statements
____ *d.* Supplementary data
____ *e.* Auditors' report
____ *f.* Management's report on internal controls over financial reporting
____ *g.* Management's responsibility for financial reporting

Exercise 4-56
Identifying Where Items are Disclosed in Form 10-K **LO4**

The following excerpts *a* through *e* are from financial statements and accompanying notes of companies' Form 10-K. Indicate from which section, *1* through *5*, that the excerpt is reported.

1. Management's discussion and analysis of financial condition and results of operations
2. Selected financial data

3. Required supplementary data
4. Auditors' report
5. Management report

Financial Reporting Excerpts

____ *a.* Dividends per share are $1.3300, $1.1075, $0.9150, $0.7575, and $0.6525, for years 2015, 2014, 2013, 2012, and 2011, respectively.

____ *b.* 2015 revenue growth was negatively impacted by unseasonably warm weather in the fourth quarter, a softer retail environment and the 53rd week in 2014.

____ *c.* Our responsibility is to express opinions on these financial statements, on the financial statement schedule and on the Company's internal control over financial reporting based on our integrated audits.

____ *d.* Based on this assessment [of the company's internal control over financial reporting], the company's management has determined that VF's internal control over financial reporting was effective as of January 2, 2016.

____ *e.* Net income was $288,709, $170,811, $459,864, and $312,209 for the first, second, third, and fourth quarter, respectively.

Exercise 4-57
Identifying What Information is in Form 10-K Disclosures and Reports **LO4**

Match the Form 10-K disclosure, report, or item, 1 through 14, with the list of disclosures, *a* through *n*.

Form 10-K Disclosure, Report, or Item

1. Auditors' report
2. Noncontrolling interest
3. Unqualified opinion
4. Required supplementary information
5. Statement of financial position
6. Classified balance sheet
7. Current assets
8. Management's Discussion and Analysis
9. Subsequent event
10. Current liabilities
11. Related party
12. Selected financial information
13. Annual report on Form 10-K
14. Normal operating cycle

Description of Disclosure

____ *a.* Balances of assets, liabilities, and equity at a point in time.

____ *b.* Items expected to be realized in cash within a year or the normal operating cycle if longer.

____ *c.* Length of time from the expenditure of cash for inventory, to accounts receivable, and back to cash.

____ *d.* Obligations expected to be liquidated using current assets or refinanced by short-term debt.

____ *e.* Net assets owned by shareholders outside of the controlling shareholders.

____ *f.* Presents assets and liabilities as current and noncurrent.

____ *g.* One entity has the ability to influence the actions of another entity.

____ *h.* Material event taking place after the balance sheet date but before financial statement issuance.

____ *i.* Annual financial report filed with the SEC.

____ *j.* Statement expressing an opinion on financial statements by an independent assessor.

____ *k.* Auditor concludes that financial statements are presented in conformance with GAAP.

____ *l.* Certain financial statement information presented over the latest 5 years.

____ *m.* Includes financial highlights and description of trends for the periods presented in the financial statements.

____ *n.* Supportive details to the financial statements that are unaudited.

Problems

Problem 4-58
Classifying Accounts and Disclosures on the Balance Sheet **LO1**

Following are the usual balance sheet classifications *a* through *k*.

Balance sheet classifications

a. Current assets.
b. Investments.
c. Property, plant, and equipment.
d. Intangible assets.
e. Other assets.
f. Current liabilities.
g. Long-term liabilities.
h. Paid-in capital.
i. Retained earnings.
j. Accumulated other comprehensive income.
k. Noncontrolling interests.

Following are common accounts and disclosures on the balance sheet.

Balance sheet items

____ 1. Cash.
____ 2. Cash set aside to meet long-term purchase commitment.
____ 3. Land (used as plant site).
____ 4. Accrued salaries.
____ 5. Investment in the capital stock of another company (long term; not a controlling interest).
____ 6. Inventory of damaged goods.
____ 7. Idle plant, held for disposal.
____ 8. Investment in bonds of another company (long-term).
____ 9. Cash surrender value of life insurance policy.
____ 10. Goodwill.
____ 11. Natural resource (timber tract).
____ 12. Allowance for doubtful accounts.
____ 13. Finance receivables, long term.
____ 14. Service revenue collected in advance.
____ 15. Accrued interest payable.
____ 16. Accumulated amortization on patent.
____ 17. Prepaid rent expense.
____ 18. Short-term investment (common stock).
____ 19. Deferred revenue.
____ 20. Net of accumulated revenues, gains, expenses, losses, and dividends.
____ 21. Trade accounts payable.
____ 22. Current maturity of long-term debt.
____ 23. Land (held for speculation).
____ 24. Notes payable (short-term).
____ 25. Special cash fund accumulated to build plant five years from the balance sheet date.
____ 26. Bonds issued—to be paid within six months.
____ 27. Long-term investment in rental building.
____ 28. Copyright.
____ 29. Land purchased for future use.
____ 30. Accumulated depreciation.
____ 31. Franchise.
____ 32. Accounts receivable.
____ 33. Deferred tax liability, net.
____ 34. Common stock (at par value).
____ 35. Pension liability.
____ 36. Foreign currency exchange adjustment.
____ 37. Contributed capital in excess of par.
____ 38. Equipment.
____ 39. Unamortized bond discount (on bonds payable long-term).
____ 40. Cash equivalent.

Required

Enter the classification *a* through *k* for each balance sheet item to indicate its usual balance sheet classification. Indicate whether an account is a contra account.

Problem 4-59
Preparing and Interpreting a Classified Balance Sheet **LO2**

The following data are taken from the accounts of Spice Corp. on December 31, 2020, its annual year-end.

Cash	$ 20,000	Mortgage payable (long term)	$ 54,000
Accounts receivable	37,000	Accounts payable	56,000
Short-term investment (cost which approximates market)	40,000	Dividends (cash) payable (payable March 1, 2021)	10,000
Inventory	35,000	Deferred revenue	3,000
Prepaid expense (current)	1,000	Interest payable	4,000
Bond sinking fund (to pay bonds at maturity)	35,000	Accumulated depreciation, building	210,000
Advances to suppliers (current)	4,000	Accumulated depreciation, equipment	20,000
Cash dividends declared during 2020	10,000	Allowance for doubtful accounts	2,000
Supplies	2,000	Bonds payable (maturity 2025)	102,000
Investment in stock (at fair value)	22,000	Common stock, $4 par (50,000 shares issued and outstanding)	200,000
Unamortized discount on bonds payable	4,000	Preferred stock, $10 par (8,000 shares, issued and outstanding)	80,000
Note receivable (long-term)	25,000		
Land (building site in use)	30,000	Additional paid-in capital—preferred stock	16,000
Building	450,000		
Equipment	120,000	Retained earnings, December 31, 2019	6,000
Franchise (used in operations)	16,000	Net income for 2020	88,000
Total debits	$851,000	Total credits	$851,000

Required

a. Prepare a classified balance sheet in good form.

b. Answer the following questions related to the information above.

1. By what percentage was the building depreciated?
2. Provide the entry that was made to record the 2020 dividend declaration.
3. Provide the entry that was made for the advances to suppliers. Assume cash transactions.
4. Compute working capital on December 31, 2020.

Problem 4-60
Preparing a Classified Balance Sheet **LO2**

Following is the chart of accounts for Pavin Corp. for 2020.

Accounts payable.
Accounts receivable.
Accrued expenses.
Accumulated amortization.
Accumulated depreciation
Allowance for doubtful accounts.
Amortization expense.
Bad debt expense.
Bonds payable.
Bond sinking fund.
Buildings.
Cash.
Cash surrender value of life insurance policies.
Common stock.
Cost of goods sold.
Deferred tax liabilities, net.
Depreciation expense.
Discount on bonds payable.
Dividends payable.
Equipment.
Finished goods.
Gain on sale of marketable securities.
General and administrative expense.
Goodwill.
Income tax expense.
Income tax payable.
Interest payable.
Investment in common stock, not intended for resale.
Investment in subsidiaries.
Land.
Licenses.
Loss on sale of land.
Marketable securities (short-term).
Miscellaneous expense.
Overhead.
Paid-in capital in excess of par—common stock.
Patents.
Prepaid expense.
Purchases.
Raw materials.
Restricted cash (long-term).
Retained earnings.
Salaries expense.
Salaries payable.
Sales revenue.
Travel and entertainment expense.
Work in process.

Required

Prepare a classified balance sheet in proper form as of December 31, 2020. Use "x" instead of amounts.

Problem 4-61
Preparing an Income Statement, a Statement of Retained Earnings, and a Classified Balance Sheet **LO2**

The adjusted trial balance and other related data for Nentenda Inc. at December 31, 2020, follow.

Adjusted Trial Balance, December 31, 2020

Debit Balance Accounts		Credit Balance Accounts	
Cash	$ 38,600	Reserve for bad debts	$ 1,100
Land (used for building site)	29,000	Accounts payable (trade)	15,000
Cost of goods sold	125,500	Revenues	245,000
Short-term investments	42,000	Income tax payable	7,500
Goodwill	12,000	Note payable (short-term)	12,000
Merchandise inventory	29,000	Common stock, $10 par, authorized 50,000 shares	100,000
Office supplies inventory	2,000	Reserve for depreciation, building	90,000
Patent	7,000	Retained earnings, December 31, 2019	47,000
Operating expenses	55,000	Accrued salaries	2,100
Income tax expense	17,500	Premium on common stock	15,000
Bond discount (unamortized)	7,500	Reserve for patent amortization	4,000
Prepaid insurance	900	Cash advance from customer (short-term)	3,000
Building (at cost)	150,000	Accrued property taxes	800
Land (held for speculation)	31,000	Note payable (long-term)	16,000
Interest receivable	300	Deferred revenue	1,500
Accounts receivable (trade)	22,700	Bonds payable, 11% ($25,000 due June 1, 2021)	75,000
Note receivable, 5% (long-term investment)	26,000		
Cash surrender value of life insurance policy	9,000		
Dividends, paid cash during 2020	15,000		
Prior period adjustment (correction of error from prior year—no income tax effect)	15,000		
Total debits	$635,000	Total credits	$635,000

Required

a. Prepare a single-step income statement including the earnings per share disclosure.

b. Prepare a separate statement of retained earnings.

c. Prepare a classified balance sheet in good form. Update accounts names as appropriate.

Problem 4-62
Preparing an Income Statement, Balance Sheet, and a Subsequent Event Note Disclosure **LO2, 3**

Following are accounts and balances, in random order, from the adjusted trial balance of Deck Corp. at December 31, 2020. Debits equal credits, all amounts are correct, *all accounts have normal balances*, and a perpetual FIFO inventory system is used.

Work in process inventory	$ 29,000	Cash on hand for change	$ 400
Interest receivable	2,200	Preferred stock, $100 par, authorized 5,000 shares	60,000
Common stock, no-par, authorized 100,000 shares, issued 40,000	150,000	Deferred revenue	900
Cash in bank	30,000	Finished goods inventory	43,000
Trademarks, net	1,400	Note receivable (short term)	4,000
Land held for speculation	27,000	Bonds payable, 6% (due in 6 years)	50,000
Supplies inventory	600	Accounts payable (trade)	17,000
Goodwill	18,000	Reserve for bad debts	1,400
Raw materials inventory	13,000	Notes payable (short term)	7,200
Bond sinking fund	10,000	Office equipment	25,000
Accrued property taxes	1,400	Land (used as building site)	8,000
Accounts receivable (trade)	29,000	Short-term investments (at market)	15,500
Salaries payable	2,100	Retained earnings, December 31, 2019	23,200
Mortgage payable (due in three years)	10,000	Cash dividends on common stock declared and paid during 2020	20,000
Building	130,000	Revenues during 2020	500,000
Prepaid expense	1,900	Cost of goods sold for 2020	300,000
Equipment held for sale	7,800	Expenses for 2020 (including income taxes)	100,000
Deposits (cash collected from customers on sales orders to be delivered next quarter; no revenue yet recognized)	1,000	Income taxes payable	40,000
Long-term investment in bonds of Kaline Corp. (at cost, to be held to maturity)	50,000	Interest payable	1,000
Patents, net	14,000	Accumulated depreciation, office equipment	1,600
Premium on preferred stock	8,000	Accumulated depreciation, building	5,000

Required

a. Prepare a single-step income statement including the earnings per share disclosure.

b. Prepare a classified balance sheet in good form. Update account names as necessary.

c. Assume that between December 31, 2020, and issuance of the financial statements, a flood damaged the finished goods inventory in an amount estimated to be $20,000. This event has not been (and should not have been) recognized in 2020. However, disclosure in the 2020 statements is required. Prepare the necessary disclosure.

Problem 4-63 Correcting Terminology and Classification of Items for a Balance Sheet **LO2**

The following balance sheet was submitted for review prior to publication in the annual report of Hi-Tech Company for the year ended December 31, 2020.

Hi-Tech Company
Balance Sheet
December 31, 2020

Assets		
Cash		$2,000
Accounts receivable	$4,050	
Less: Allowance for doubtful accounts	(50)	4,000
Inventories		3,250
Investment in subsidiary		300
Fixed		
Land at cost	400	
Building, machinery and fixtures, at cost	4,000	
Less: reserve for depreciation	(1,490)	2,910
Deferred charges and other assets		
Cash surrender value of life insurance		20
Receivables, long-term		15
Plant assets held for early resale		30
Total assets		$12,525
Liabilities		
Notes payable to bank		$ 550
Current maturities of bonds payable		600
Accounts payable—trade		2,100
Income tax payable		500
Accrued expenses		750
9% Bonds payable in annual installments of $600	$4,200	
Less: current maturity	600	3,600
Capital		
Common stock—authorized, issued, and outstanding 100,000 shares of $10 par		1,000
Capital surplus		300
Earned surplus		3,125
Total liabilities		$12,525

Additional information

- Capital surplus consists of the difference between the par value of $10 per share of capital stock and the price at which the stock was actually issued.

Required

Revise the above classified balance sheet in good form. Pay special attention to correcting poor terminology and identifying the proper classification of items.

Problem 4-64
Correcting Format, Terminology and Classification of Items in a Balance Sheet **LO2**

The president of Artar Company suspects that its financial statements are not well prepared. The president provides the following statement for review.

Artar Company
Balance Sheet
For Year Ended December 31, 2020

Resources	
Liquid assets	
Cash in banks	$ 8,700
Receivables from various sources net of reserve for bad debts ($200)	4,500
Inventories	10,000
Cash for daily use	800
Total	24,000
Permanent assets	
Treasury stock, 100 shares	4,000
Fixed assets (net of depreciation)	26,000
Grand total	$54,000
Obligations and Net Worth	
Short-term	
Trade payables	$ 4,500
Salaries accrued	600
Total	5,100
Fixed:	
Mortgage	8,000
Net worth	
Capital stock, no-par, 5,000 shares authorized, 800 shares issued	27,000
Retained earnings	13,900
Total	40,900
Grand total	$54,000

Required

Revise the above balance sheet in good form. Pay special attention to correcting format and poor terminology, and identifying the proper classification of items. Assume equipment has a cost of $30,000.

Problem 4-65
Recording Adjusting and Correcting Entries, and Preparing a Classified Balance Sheet from Accounts **LO2**

Electro Corp. prepared the following trial balance as of December 31, 2020. The adjusting entries for 2020 have been made, except for the items specifically noted below.

Cash	$15,000	
Accounts receivable	16,000	
Inventories	16,000	
Equipment	22,400	
Land	6,400	
Building	7,600	
Miscellaneous assets (long-term)	1,100	
Accounts payable		$ 5,500
Note payable, 10%		8,000
Common stock (par $10)		38,500
Retained earnings		32,500
Totals	$84,500	$84,500

There are errors and omissions reflected in the above trial balance, including the following. No correction has yet been recorded.

1. The $16,000 balance in accounts receivable represents the entire amount owed to the company; of this amount, $12,400 is from trade customers, and 5% of that amount is estimated to be uncollectible. The remaining amount owed to the company represents a long-term advance to a customer.
2. Inventories include $2,000 of goods incorrectly valued at twice their cost (meaning they are reported at $4,000).
3. Office supplies still available at year-end total $500 and are included in the balance of inventories.

4. When the equipment and building were purchased new on January 1, 2015, they had estimated lives of 10 and 25 years, respectively. They have been depreciated using the straight-line method on the assumption of zero residual value, and depreciation has been credited directly to the asset accounts. Depreciation has been recorded for 2020.
5. The balance in the land account includes a $1,000 payment made as a deposit of earnest money on the purchase of an adjoining tract. The option to buy it has not yet been exercised and probably will not be exercised during the coming year.
6. The interest-bearing note dated April 1, 2020, matures March 31, 2021. Interest on it has not been recorded.
7. There are 2,500 common stock shares outstanding.

Required

a. Prepare correcting and adjusting entries for the 7 items above.

b. Prepare a classified balance sheet based upon the information provided after making all necessary adjusting and correcting entries.

Problem 4-66 Preparing an Income Statement, a Classified Balance Sheet, and Financial Statement Note Disclosures **LO2, 3**

The following adjusted accounts are organized by Denver Corp. as of December 31, 2020.

Denver Corporation
Adjusted Trial Balance
December 31, 2020

Debit Balance Accounts	
Cost of goods sold	$230,000
Operating expenses	130,000
Income tax expense	51,500
Cash	44,000
Short-term investments (at fair value)	12,000
Accounts receivable	70,000
Merchandise inventory	72.000
Office supplies inventory	2,000
Investment in bonds of Sigma Corp. (long-term)	33,000
Land	10,000
Plant and equipment	135,000
Franchise (less amortization)	8,000
Idle equipment held for disposal	7,500
Dividends declared and paid during 2020	40,000
	$845,000
Credit Balance Accounts	
Sales revenue	$490,000
Accumulated depreciation, plant and equipment	40,000
Accounts payable	50,000
Income taxes payable	11,000
Bonds payable	50,000
Allowance for doubtful accounts	3,000
Premium on bonds payable (unamortized)	1,000
Common stock, par $10 (authorized 50,000 shares)	150,000
Excess of issue price over par of common stock	18,000
Retained earnings, January 1, 2020	32,000
	$845,000

Additional information

1. Inventory cost is recorded at the lower of cost or market, where market is computed using the average cost method.
2. Plant and equipment consists of a building ($120,000) and equipment ($15,000). The building and equipment are depreciated using the straight-line method over estimated useful life. The estimated useful life of the building is 20 years and the equipment is 5 years.
3. Franchise is amortized using the straight-line method over a period of 10 years.
4. The 9% bonds were issued on January 1, 2018, and have a 10-year maturity date.

Required

a. Prepare an income statement for Denver Corp. (including earnings per share disclosure) for the year ended December 31, 2020.

b. Prepare a classified balance sheet for Denver Corp. as of December 31, 2020.
c. Identify the accounts from the classified balance sheet where disclosure is likely is in the (1) summary of significant accounting policies disclosure note or (2) as a separate disclosure note.

Problem 4-67
Identifying Items of Disclosure in the Annual Report on Form 10-K **LO4**

Obtain an electronic copy of the annual report on Form 10-K for the **Coca-Cola Company** for the year ended December 31, 2015, which can be found on the SEC Edgar website (https://www.sec.gov/edgar/searchedgar/companysearch.html). Use the annual report to answer the following questions.

Required

a. What items are included in the annual report on Form 10-K? Provide a list with Item number and title.
b. Who is the Executive Vice President and President of Coca-Cola North America?
c. What selected financial data is highlighted? Over what periods?
d. What categories of "challenges and risks" are discussed in the Management's Discussion and Analysis section?
e. What is the explanation provided by management for the decrease in gross profit margin from 2014 to 2015?
f. What accounting firm signed the audit opinion for Coca-Cola Company?
g. How many executive officers signed the Report of Management?
h. How many notes accompany the financial statements of Coca-Cola Company?
i. Does the company have a related party note? Subsequent events note?

Problem 4-68
Researching a Form 10-K **LO4**

Obtain an electronic copy of the annual report on Form 10-K for Apple Inc. for the year ended September 30, 2017, which can be found on the SEC Edgar website (https://www.sec.gov/edgar/searchedgar/companysearch.html).

Required

Use Form 10-K to answer the following questions.

1. Selected financial data
   a. In what item number is selected financial data included?
   b. What years are presented in the schedule?
   c. How many lines of information in the schedule pertain to the balance sheet?
   d. What is the balance of commercial paper on September 30, 2016 (in millions)?
2. MD&A
   a. In what item number is MD&A included?
   b. What was the percentage change in the sale of iPhones from 2016 to 2017?
   c. What was the percentage change in the sale of Macs from 2016 to 2017?
   d. How does Apple organize its operating segments?
   e. What is the gross margin percentage for 2017? What range does the company estimate gross margin percentages to be during the first quarter of 2018?
3. Financial statements and supplementary data
   a. In what item number are financial statements and supplementary data included?
   b. How many topics are included in the summary of significant accounting policies note?
   c. What is the measurement of Level 2 commercial paper on September 30, 2017?
   d. How many related party transactions are disclosed in the notes?
   e. How many incidents of errors and illegal acts are disclosed in the notes?
   f. How many subsequent events are disclosed in the notes?
   g. How many reportable segments are disclosed in the notes?
4. Directors and Executive Officers*
   a. In what item number are directors and executive officers included?
   b. How many members are on the board of directors?
   c. In what year did Andrea Jung join the board of directors?
5. Executive Compensation*
   a. In what item number is executive compensation included?
   b. What is the total 2017 compensation for Tim Cook (CEO)?
   c. What percentage of total compensation for Angela Ahrendts (Senior Vice President, Retail) is made up of stock awards in 2017?

**Hint:* The proxy statement (incorporated by reference) is labeled DEF 14A and is on the SEC Edgar website.

Accounting Decisions and Judgments

AD&J 4-69 Understanding and Interpreting Current Asset Disclosures **LO1**

Real World Analysis The current asset section of Callaway Golf, a manufacturer of golf equipment, is shown below.

Current assets ($ thousands)	Current Year	Prior Year
Cash and cash equivalents	$ 45,618	$ 26,204
Accounts receivable, net	73,466	124,470
Inventories, net	149,142	97,094
Deferred taxes	51,029	23,810
Other current assets	4,301	10,208
Total current assets	$323,606	$281,786

Required

a. What types of assets are likely included in cash equivalents?

b. Notes reveal that its allowance for doubtful accounts rose by $2,893 ($9,939 − $7,046). Why might this have happened even though receivables (net) declined?

c. What items are we likely to find in the account "other current assets"?

AD&J 4-70 Classifying Balance Sheet Items **LO1**

Real World Analysis The left-hand column provides balance sheet classifications. The items in the right-hand column are taken from the actual balance sheets of the identified companies.

Balance Sheet Classifications	Balance Sheet Accounts
a. Current asset	____ 1. Net property (Ford Motor Company)
b. Noncurrent asset	____ 2. Goodwill (Marriott International Inc.)
c. Current liability	____ 3. Accrued liabilities (short-term) (The Boeing Company)
d. Noncurrent liability	____ 4. Cash and cash equivalents (Harley-Davidson Inc.)
e. Stockholders' equity	____ 5. Equity attributable to noncontrolling interests (Coca-Cola Co.)
	____ 6. Pension and postretirement benefits (Sears Holdings Corporation)
	____ 7. Current portion of long-term debt (Nike Inc.)
	____ 8. Equity investment in Alliance Boots (Walgreens Boots Alliance Inc.)
	____ 9. Accrued wages and withholdings (United Parcel Service Inc.)
	____ 10. Additional paid-in capital (Target Corporation)

Required

Identify each account, 1 through 10, with the most appropriate classification *a* through *e*. A classification can be used more than once.

AD&J 4-71 Reporting and Ordering Current Assets in a Balance Sheet **LO2**

Real World Analysis The balance sheet of Ford Motor Company, a major U.S. automobile and truck producer, lists five items in its current assets. These five items are listed alphabetically below. Present these items in the order which Ford reported them in its annual report. *Hint*: As with nearly all companies, Ford lists current assets by liquidity from most to least liquid.

$ millions	December 31, 2015
a. Cash and cash equivalents	$ 5,386
b. Inventories	8,319
c. Marketable securities	18,181
d. Other current assets	1,851
e. Receivables, net	5,173
Total current assets	$38,910

AD&J 4-72
Reporting and Ordering Stockholders' Equity Accounts **LO2**

Real World Analysis The **ON Semiconductor Corporation** lists the following six accounts within stockholders' equity.

$ millions	**December 31, 2015**
a. Accumulated deficit	$ (709.4)
b. Accumulated other comprehensive loss	(42.3)
c. Additional paid-in capital	3,420.3
d. Common stock, $.01 par value (Shares issued outstanding, 412 million)	$ 5.3
e. Non-controlling interest in consolidated subsidiary	23.7
f. Treasury stock	(1,065.7)
Total	$1,631.9

Required

Present these items in the format and order which we expect to see them in the company's balance sheet. The company is a manufacturer of energy efficient electronics. *Hint:* The Accumulated Deficit account is a common title for the Retained Earnings account when it has a debit balance.

AD&J 4-73
Defining Key Accounting Terms **LO1**

Codification Skills Refer to the Codification and identify definitions for the following: (1) cash equivalents, (2) current assets, (3) current liabilities, (4) operating cycle, and (5) operating segment.

AD&J 4-74
Identifying Codification Citations for Professional Guidance with Various Disclosures **LO1, 2, 3, 4, 5**

Codification Skills Refer to the Codification and identify the proper citation that provides guidance on each of the following topics.

a. Reporting of current liabilities on a classified balance sheet FASB ASC ___-___-___-___

b. Presentation of comparative financial statements FASB ASC ___-___-___-___

c. Tests for determining reportable operating segments FASB ASC ___-___-___-___

d. Requiring disclosure about accounting policies FASB ASC ___-___-___-___

AD&J 4-75
Identifying Codification Sources for Guidance with Quarterly Statements **LO3**

Codification Skills A company is preparing its first quarter financial statements after having reported annual statements as of December 31, 2020. The company is drafting notes to its quarterly financial statements and is unsure whether to include the policy on significant accounting policies as reported at year-end in its first quarter financial statements (unaudited). Identify what guidance is available in the Codification to help determine the proper disclosure.

FASB ASC ___-___-___-___

Appendix—Questions

4-76. The accounting standards require disclosures in three areas: operating segments, geographical areas, and major customers. Are these three areas independent of each other? When might they be? When might they not be?

4-77. What is the difference, if any, between the terms *operating segment* and *reportable segment*? Explain how each is determined.

4-78. What are the criteria used to determine whether operating segments can be combined into a single segment?

4-79. When the reportable segments do not account for at least 75% of the company's reported revenue, how are these aggregation criteria used to increase the amount of revenue included in reportable operation segments?

4-80. Briefly describe the tests for determining a reportable segment.

Appendix—Brief Exercises

App—Brief Exercise 4-81
Determining of Reportable Segments using the Revenue Test **LO5**
Hint: See Demo 4-5

Jets Inc. had six operating segments reporting the following amount of revenue per segment. Considering the criteria for determining a reportable segment based only upon the revenue test, what segments are reportable?

Segment	A	B	C	D	E	F	Total
Operating revenue	$9,100	$4,000	$8,000	$10,800	$3,500	$9,000	$44,400

App—Brief Exercise 4-82
Determining of Reportable Segments using the Profit (Loss) Test **LO5**
Hint: See Demo 4-5

Jets Inc. had six operating segments reporting the following amount of profit (loss) per segment. Considering the criteria for determining a reportable segment based only upon the operating profit (loss), what segments are reportable?

Segment	A	B	C	D	E	F	Total
Operating profit (loss).	$1,000	$500	$588	$2,900	$2,100	$(700)	$6,388

App—Brief Exercise 4-83
Determining of Reportable Segments using the Identifiable Assets Test **LO5**
Hint: See Demo 4-5

Jets Inc. had six operating segments reporting the following amount of identifiable assets per segment. Considering the criteria for determining a reportable segment based only upon identifiable assets, what segments are reportable?

Segment	A	B	C	D	E	F	Total
Identifiable assets.	$50,000	$23,000	$45,000	$60,000	$21,500	$32,000	$231,500

Appendix—Exercises

App—Exercise 4-84
Determining Major Customer Disclosures **LO5**

Mango Company operates as a single operating segment, but it has large sales to a small number of customers. In 2020, Mango had the following sales to customers.

California Company	$16,000,000	Texas Inc.	$ 3,000,000
Oregon Inc..	8,000,000	Domestic governments.	19,000,000
Montana Corp.	5,000,000	Foreign governments	14,500,000
Arizona Company.	4,000,000	Other sales.	40,000,000

Additional information

a. Other sales include sales to many customers, none of which exceeds $1,000,000.

b. Oregon Inc. and Arizona Company are both subsidiaries of Utah Inc. Direct sales to Utah total $1,000,000 and are included in other sales.

c. Sales to domestic governments include $14,000,000 to federal governmental agencies, with the remainder being to local governmental agencies.

d. Sales to foreign governments include $8,500,000 in sales to the Canadian government, with the remainder being to various other foreign governments, none more than $1,000,000.

Required

Determine the major customer disclosures that must be made in accordance with accounting standards. Write a one-half-page memo to the chief financial officer explaining the answer and providing a sample disclosure to be included in Mango Company financial statements.

App—Exercise 4-85
Reporting Segments and Major Customers **LO5**

Keefe Corp. has expanded rapidly, and segment reporting has become an accounting issue. The company has no intersegment sales. The following annual data are available for 2020, which has a year-end of December 31 ($ millions).

Operating Segments	Total Segment Revenues	Operating Profit (Loss)	Identifiable Assets
A.	$620	$200	$400
B.	100	20	80
C.	340	70	300
D.	190	(30)	140
E.	180	(25)	180
F.	70	10	120
G.	120	(20)	140
All others.	380	(25)	140

Additional Information

- The "all others" includes five operating segments, none with revenues or assets greater than $80 million and none with an operating profit.
- Operating segments A and B have very similar products and production processes but serve different customer types and use quite different product distribution systems. This is partly because operating segment B is in a regulated environment but operating segment A is not.
- Operating segments F and G have very similar products, production processes, and product distribution systems but are organized as separate divisions because they serve substantially different types of customers. Neither F nor G is in a regulated environment.

Required

a. Determine what are reportable segments without regard to aggregation criteria.

b. If the requirements for reportable segments are not yet met, apply appropriate aggregation criteria to identify additional reportable segments.

c. Assume Keefe has sales totaling $220 million to the U.S. federal government, primarily from operating segments A and C. Other significant customers include annual revenues of $190 million from Ikon Tech (primarily sales of segment D) and $100 million in sales by segment E to the French government. What, if any, disclosures must Keefe make regarding major customers?

Appendix—Problems

App—Problem 4-86
Reporting Segments and Applying Segment Tests **LO5**

Anntem Corp. has three product divisions: Health-care, Agricultural, and Food. Health-care has three separate groups: pharmaceuticals, consumer health care, and medical devices. The Health-care manager receives separate financial information for each group. The CEO of Anntem makes major decisions for all three divisions. In 2020, Anntem reports the following.

- Revenues of $12,300,000, which includes interest revenue of $100,000 that is not allocated to any division.
- Income before taxes of $1,500,000 after deducting all expenses, including some that are not allocated to divisions.
- Total assets of $22,000,000, some of which are headquarters and not included in any division.
- Intercompany sales are priced at market prices, and profits on intersegment sales total $50,000.
- The same accounting methods used for corporate reporting are used in measuring sales, profits, and assets at the division and group level.

Division and group level information for 2020 follows ($ thousands).

	Health-Care Division					
	Pharmaceuticals	Consumer Health Care	Medical Devices	Total Health-Care Division	Agricultural Products Division	Food Products Division
Sales to external customers	$ 6,000	$3,000	$1,200	$10,200	$1,000	$1,000
Intersegment sales	500	0	0	500	0	700
Income (loss) before taxes	1,800	200	(400)	1,600	200	100
Segment assets as of Dec. 31	10,000	3,500	1,500	15,000	4,000	2,000
Depreciation and amortization*	300	100	100	500	150	100
Capital expenditures†	400	200	100	700	200	200

*An additional depreciation of $50 on headquarters facilities is not included in segment amounts.

†An additional $200 of capital expenditures was incurred for facilities for headquarters.

Required

a. Assume all the groups within the Health-care products qualify as operating segments, as do the Agricultural products and Food products divisions. Determine which of these five are reportable operating segments.

b. Show the quantitative information that is required to be reported by Anntem for 2020. All revenues, expenses, or assets not included above as part of an operating segment are unallocated corporate items.

Appendix—Accounting Decisions and Judgments

App—AD&J 4-87 Applying Segment Tests to an Operating Segment **LO5**

Real World Analysis In a recent Form 10-K, the **Coca-Cola Company** reported consolidated net operating revenues, operating income, and identifiable operating assets were $44,294, $8,728, and $74,305, respectively for 2015. The following additional information is reported for its "Eurasia and Africa" operating segment ($ millions).

Eurasia and Africa	2015
Net operating revenues:	
Third party	$2,423
Intersegment	36
Total net revenues	2,459
Operating income (loss)	987
Interest income	—
Interest expense	—
Depreciation and amortization	44
Equity income (loss)—net	14
Income (loss) before income taxes	1,004
Identifiable operating assets	1,148
Investments	1,061
Capital expenditures	19

Required

Does Coca-Cola's Eurasia and Africa segment meet the criteria for requiring a segment to be reported? Show computations.

App—AD&J 4-88 **Real World Analysis** Reporting Segment Information by Geographical Region **LO5**

Real World Analysis **Cisco Systems** is the worldwide leader in networking. Its fiscal year-end is the last Saturday in July, which was July 31 for the fiscal Year 9 annual report. The Cisco Year 9 annual report provides segment information in Note 11.

> **Segment Information and Major Customers**
> The Company's operations involve the design, development, manufacture, marketing, and technical support of networking products and services . . . The Company conducts business globally and is managed geographically. The Company's management relies on an internal management accounting system. This system includes sales and standard cost information by geographic theater. Sales are attributed to a theater based on the ordering location of the customer.
>
> The Company's management makes financial decisions and allocates resources based on the information it receives from this internal system. Information from this internal management system differs from the amounts reported under generally accepted accounting principles due to certain corporate level adjustments. These corporate level adjustments are primarily sales related reserves, credit memos, and returns. Based on

the criteria set forth in the accounting standards, the Company has four reportable segments: the Americas, Europe, Middle East and Africa, hereafter EMEA, Asia/Pacific, and Japan.

Summarized financial information by segment for Year 9, Year 8, Year 7:

$ millions	Year 9	Year 8	Year 7
Net sales			
Americas	$ 8,069	$5,731	$3,968
EMEA	3,216	2,114	1,551
Asia/Pacific	825	535	453
Japan	566	459	587
Corporate adjustments	(522)	(351)	(107)
Total	$12,154	$8,488	$6,452
Standard margin*			
Americas	$ 5,836	$4,260	
EMEA	2,380	1,565	
Asia/Pacific	586	395	
Japan	436	340	
Corporate adjustments	(1,324)	(996)	
Total	$ 7,914	$5,564	

*Standard margin by segment not tracked by the Company prior to fiscal year 8.

The standard margins above differ from the amounts recognized under generally accepted accounting principles because the Company does not allocate certain production overhead, manufacturing variances, and other production related costs to the theaters. Enterprise-wide information is provided in accordance with the accounting standards. Geographic sales information is based on the ordering location of the customer. Property and equipment information is based on the physical location of the assets.

The following is net sales and property and equipment information for geographic areas. In Year 9, Year 8, and Year 7, no single customer accounted for 10% or more of the Company's net sales.

$ millions	Year 9	Year 8	Year 7
Net sales:			
U.S.	$ 7,435	$5,231	$3,615
All other countries	5,241	3,608	2,944
Corporate adjustments	(522)	(351)	(107)
Total	$12,154	$8,488	$6,452
Property and equipment, net:			
U.S.	$ 687	$ 527	$ 412
All other countries	114	72	56
Total	$ 801	$ 599	$ 468

Required

a. What information does Cisco provide about its investment in and the profitability of its various products, such as routers, LAN and ATM switches, access servers, and network management software? Why does it provide (or not provide) this information?

b. In managing its various geographical segments, what measure of profitability does the company use? How might it differ from operating profit as determined under generally accepted accounting principles?

c. Comment on whether any geographical regions are substantially more profitable than others in fiscal Year 9. Explain why we get the result we do in this analysis. *Hint:* Profit margin is equal to (Net sales − Standard margin)/Net sales.

d. In what geographical region have Cisco's sales grown the most rapidly over the past two years? In general, what does the segment information in Note 11 provide that might not be known without the disclosure of this information?

Communication Case Many financial analysts and professional accountants argue that companies should continue to report segment data. On the other hand, many managers argue strongly against segment disclosures.

App—AD&J 4-89 Examining the Reasons For and Against Segment Reporting **LO5**

Required

In a one-page report, outline the following three points.

a. The reasons for requiring financial reporting by segments.
b. The reasons against requiring financial reporting by segments.
c. The accounting difficulties in implementing segment reporting.

Answers to Review Exercises

Review 4-1

a. 3 *b.* 1 *c.* 4 *d.* 1 *e.* 6 *f.* 8 *g.* 12 *h.* 7 *i.* 2 *j.* 6 *k.* 2 *l.* 5 *m.* 8 *n.* 10

Review 4-2

KOLL'S STORE
Balance Sheet
December 31, 2020

Assets			Liabilities and Stockholders' Equity	
Current assets			**Current liabilities**	
Cash		$ 88,000	Accounts payable	$ 325,000
Accounts receivable	$310,000		Salaries payable	45,000
Less: Allowance for doubtful accounts	(13,000)	297,000	Deferred revenue	12,000
Investments		224,000	Income tax payable	72,000
Inventory		500,000	Total current liabilities	454,000
Supplies		9,000	**Long-term liabilities**	
Total current assets		1,118,000	Note payable, 5%, 3-year	900,000
Property, plant, and equipment			Total long-term liabilities	900,000
Building	800,000		**Stockholders' equity**	
Equipment	440,000		Common stock ($1 par, 10,000 shares authorized, 5,000 shares issued and outstanding)	5,000
Accumulated depreciation	(380,000)			
Net property, plant, and equipment		860,000	Paid-in capital in excess of par	295,000
Intangible assets			Retained earnings	330,000
Patent		6,000	Total stockholders' equity	630,000
Total assets		**$1,984,000**	**Total liabilities and stockholders' equity**	**$1,984,000**

Review 4-3

a. 4 *b.* 1 *c.* 6 *d.* 3 *e.* 6 *f.* 4 *g.* 1 *h.* 5 *i.* 2.

Review 4-4

a. 5 *b.* 2 *c.* 3 *d.* 1 *e.* 4 *f.* 1

Review 4-5

a. $9,285; Identifiable segments: United States, Asia (other than China), Europe, China.
b. $848; Identifiable segments: United States, Asia (other than China), Europe, China, Canada.
c. $9,705; Identifiable segments: United States, Asia (other than China), Europe, China.
d. Revenues of identifiable segments are 92% of total revenue; therefore the 75% threshold is met.

5 Statement of Cash Flows and Financial Analysis

MACY'S, INC.
CONSOLIDATED STATEMENTS OF CASH FLOWS
(millions)

	2015	2014	2013
Cash flows from operating activities:			
Net income	$1,070	$1,526	$1,486
Adjustments to reconcile net income to net cash provided by operating activities:			
Impairments, store closing and other costs	288	87	88
Depreciation and amortization	1,061	1,036	1,020
Stock-based compensation expense	65	73	62
Amortization of financing costs and premium on acquired debt	(14)	(5)	(8)
Changes in assets and liabilities:			
(Increase) decrease in receivables	(45)	22	(58)
(Increase) decrease in merchandise inventories	(60)	44	(249)
(Increase) decrease in prepaid expenses and other current assets	0	(3)	(2)
Increase in other assets not separately identified	(1)	(61)	(1)
Increase (decrease) in merchandise accounts payable	(78)	(21)	101
Increase (decrease) in accounts payable, accrued liabilities and other items not separately identified	(144)	37	48
Increase (decrease) in current income taxes	(69)	(65)	7
Increase (decrease) in deferred income taxes	(1)	29	(142)
Increase (decrease) in other liabilities not separately identified	(88)	10	197
Net cash provided by operating activities	1,984	2,709	2,549
Cash flows from investing activities:			
Purchase of property and equipment	(777)	(770)	(607)
Capitalized software	(336)	(298)	(256)
Acquisition of Bluemercury, Inc., net of cash acquired	212	0	0
Disposition of property and equipment	204	172	132
Other, net	29	(74)	(57)
Net cash used by investing activities	(1,092)	(970)	(788)
Cash flows from financing activities:			
Debt issued	499	1,044	400
Financing costs	(4)	(9)	(9)
Debt repaid	(152)	(870)	(124)
Dividends paid	(456)	(421)	(359)
Increase (decrease) in outstanding checks	(83)	133	24
Acquisition of treasury stock	(2,001)	(1,901)	(1,571)
Issuance of common stock	163	258	315
Proceeds from noncontrolling interest	5	0	0
Net cash used by financing activities	(2,029)	(1,766)	(1,324)
Net increase (decrease) in cash and cash equivalents	(1,137)	(27)	437
Cash and cash equivalents beginning of period	2,246	2,273	1,836
Cash and cash equivalents end of period	$1,109	$2,246	$2,273
Supplemental cash flow information:			
Interest paid	$ 383	$ 413	$ 388
Interest received	2	2	2
Income taxes paid (net of refunds received)	635	834	835

Important Information Regarding Non-GAAP Financial Measures

The Company reports its financial results in accordance with generally accepted accounting principles ("GAAP"). However, management believes that certain non-GAAP financial measures provide users of the Company's financial information with additional useful information in evaluating operating performance. Management believes that providing changes in comparable sales on an owned plus licensed basis, which includes the impact of growth in comparable sales of departments licensed to third parties supplementally to its results of operations calculated in accordance with GAAP assists in evaluating the Company's ability to generate sales growth, whether through owned businesses or departments licensed to third parties, on a comparable basis, and in evaluating the impact of changes in the manner in which certain departments are operated. Management believes that excluding certain items that may vary substantially in frequency and magnitude from diluted earnings per share attributable to Macy's, Inc. shareholders and from operating income and EBITDA as percentages to sales are useful supplemental measures that assist in evaluating the Company's ability to generate earnings and leverage sales, respectively, and to more readily compare these metrics between past and future periods. Management also believes that EBITDA and Adjusted EBITDA are frequently used by investors and securities analysts in their evaluations of companies, and that such supplemental measures facilitate comparisons between companies that have different capital and financing structures and/or tax rates. In addition, management believes that ROIC is a useful supplemental measure in evaluating how efficiently the Company employs its capital. The Company uses some of these non-GAAP financial measures as performance measures for components of executive compensation.

Non-GAAP financial measures should be viewed as supplementing, and not as an alternative or substitute for, the Company's financial results prepared in accordance with GAAP. Certain of the items that may be excluded or included in non-GAAP financial measures may be significant items that could impact the Company's financial position, results of operations and cash flows and should therefore be considered in assessing the Company's actual financial condition and performance. Additionally, the amounts received by the Company on account of sales of departments licensed to third parties are limited to commissions received on such sales. The methods used by the Company to calculate its non-GAAP financial measures may differ significantly from methods used by other companies to compute similar measures. As a result, any non-GAAP financial measures presented herein may not be comparable to similar measures provided by other companies.

Change in Comparable Sales

The following is a tabular reconciliation of the non-GAAP financial measure of changes in comparable sales on an owned plus licensed basis, to GAAP comparable sales (i.e., on an owned basis), which the Company believes to be the most directly comparable GAAP financial measure.

	2015	2014	2013	2012	2011
Increase (decrease) in comparable sales on an owned basis (note 1)	(3.0)%	0.7%	1.9%	3.7%	5.3%
Impact of growth in comparable sales of departments licensed to third parties (note 2)	0.5%	0.7%	0.9%	0.3%	0.4%
Increase (decrease) in comparable sales on an owned plus licensed basis	(2.5)%	1.4%	2.8%	4.0%	5.7%

Notes:

(1) Represents the period-to-period percentage change in net sales from stores in operation throughout the year presented and the immediately preceding year and all online sales, adjusting for the 53rd week in 2012, excluding commissions from departments licensed to third parties. Stores undergoing remodeling, expansion or relocation remain in the comparable sales calculation unless the store is closed for a significant period of time. Definitions and calculations of comparable sales differ among companies in the retail industry.

(2) Represents the impact of including the sales of departments licensed to third parties occurring in stores in operation throughout the year presented and the immediately preceding year and all online sales, adjusting for the 53rd week in 2012, in the calculation. The Company licenses third parties to operate certain departments in its stores and online and receives commissions from these third parties based on a percentage of their net sales. In its financial statements prepared in conformity with GAAP, the Company includes these commissions (rather than sales of the departments licensed to third parties) in its net sales. The Company does not, however, include any amounts in respect of licensed department sales (or any commissions earned on such sales) in its comparable sales in accordance with GAAP (i.e., on an owned basis). The Company believes that the amounts of commissions earned on sales of departments licensed to third parties are not material to its results of operations for the periods presented.

Chapter Preview

The purpose of the statement of cash flows is to provide relevant information about a company's cash inflows and outflows for a period that assists investors and creditors in projecting the company's future net cash flows. We review the presentation of the statement of cash flows using the indirect method. Next, we examine the interrelations of financial statements, and compute ratios frequently used by investors and creditors to evaluate and compare companies. We also describe horizontal and vertical analyses, and conclude by examining non-GAAP measures, which are increasingly reported in annual reports.

Action Plan

LO	Topic/Subtopic	Page	Demos	Reviews	Assignments
LO 5-1	**Identify operating, investing, and financing activities** Classifying Cash Inflows :: Classifying Cash Outflows :: Operating Activities :: Investing Activities :: Financing Activities	5-3	D5-1	R5-1	20, 21, 37, 38, 61, 72, 75, 76, 78, 79
LO 5-2	**Prepare an indirect statement of cash flows** Cash from Operating Activities :: Cash from Investing Activities :: Cash from Financing Activities :: Noncash Investing and Financing Activities	5-6	D5-2	R5-2	21, 22, 23, 24, 25, 38, 39, 40, 41, 42, 43, 44, 61, 62, 63, 64, 72, 75, 79, 80, 85
LO 5-3	**Describe the interrelations of financial statements** Income Statement :: Statement of Comprehensive Income :: Statement of Stockholders' Equity :: Balance Sheet :: Statement of Cash Flows	5-11	D5-3A D5-3B	R5-3	26, 27, 45, 46, 65
LO 5-4	**Perform an investment analysis using the DuPont Framework** Return on Equity :: Return on Assets :: Financial Leverage :: Profit Margin :: Asset Turnover	5-17	D5-4A D5-4B D5-4C	R5-4	28, 29, 31, 32, 47, 48, 49, 50, 54, 55, 56, 67, 68, 69, 70, 73, 74, 77
LO 5-5	**Perform a credit analysis using key ratios** Current Ratio :: Quick Ratio :: Current Cash Debt Coverage :: Total Liabilities-to-Equity :: Times Interest Earned :: Cash Debt Coverage :: Free Cash Flow	5-24	D5-5A D5-5B	R5-5	30, 33, 51, 52, 53, 55, 56, 67, 69, 70, 74
LO 5-6	**Perform horizontal and vertical analyses** Horizontal Analysis :: Vertical Analysis	5-29	D5-6A D5-6B	R5-6	34, 57, 66, 67, 71
LO 5-7	**Recognize non-GAAP financial measures** Non-GAAP Disclosure :: MD&A :: Reconciliation to GAAP Measure	5-31	D5-7	R5-7	35, 36, 58, 59, 60
LO 5-8	**APPENDIX 5A—Prepare the operating activities section of the statement of cash flows using the direct method** Operating Activities :: Receipts from Customers :: Payments to Suppliers :: Payments for Operating Expenses	5-36	D5-8	R5-8	75, 79, 81, 82, 83, 84, 85, 86

LO 5-1 Identify operating, investing, and financing activities

LO 5-1 Overview

Cash Flows

- *Operating*: Cash flows not from investing or financing activities
- *Investing*: Cash flows related to purchases and sales of noncurrent fixed assets and investments
- *Financing*: Cash flows related to external financing

The statement of cash flows explains the change in cash over the period and provides relevant, disaggregated information about cash inflows and outflows. Unlike the income statement that is prepared on an accrual basis, the statement of cash flows reflects *only* cash flows. The statement of cash flows is prepared as one of the required reports in a company's presentation of annual results.

230-10-15-3 A business entity . . . that provides a set of financial statements that reports both financial position and results of operations shall also provide a statement of cash flows for each period for which results of operations are provided.

Information about the cash available for debt payments, dividends, investments, and capital expenditures is important to both investors and creditors. Of particular interest is the amount of cash a company generates from its operating activities, which must eventually pay for the company's debts and dividends and provide for growth. The statement of cash flows also provides useful information about a company's borrowing patterns, subsequent repayments, new investments by owners, and dividend distributions.

230-10-10-2 Information provided in a statement of cash flows, if used with related disclosures and information in the other financial statements, should help investors, creditors, and others (including donors) to do all of the following:

a. Assess the entity's ability to generate positive future net cash flows
b. Assess the entity's ability to meet its obligations, its ability to pay dividends, and its needs for external financing
c. Assess the reasons for differences between net income and associated cash receipts and payments
d. Assess the effects on an entity's financial position of both its cash and noncash investing and financing transactions during the period.

The sources of cash flows provide valuable information to investors and creditors in assessing a business. For example, did cash inflows result from continuing operations or from a specific event such as a sale of stock? Were *cash outflows* used for continuing operations or for paying off debt? To provide a meaningful framework for investors and creditors, cash flows are classified into three types: operating, investing, and financing.

Cash Flows from Operating Activities

Cash flows from operating activities include all cash flows not defined as investing or financing activities. Classified as operating are both the cash inflows and the cash outflows related to activities that generate net income. Common operating cash flows are listed in **Exhibit 5-1**. The difference between operating cash inflows and outflows is called the *net cash provided (used) by operating activities*. Typically, the net amount is an inflow because, over the long term, cash collections from operations must exceed cash outflows for a going concern. Many analysts consider this the most important subtotal in the statement of cash flows because it provides a measure similar to net income on a cash basis.

EXHIBIT 5-1
Cash Flows from **Operating** Activities

Cash Inflows—Cash Received from:	Cash Outflows—Cash Paid for:
Customers for goods or services	Purchase of goods for resale
Refunds from suppliers	Salaries and other operating expenses
Dividends from investments	Income taxes, duties, and fines
Interest on receivables	Interest on liabilities

Cash Flows from Investing Activities

Cash flows from investing activities include cash inflows and outflows related to disposing of or acquiring property, plant, and, equipment; the sale or purchase of investments and other long-term assets; and the extension and collection of loans. Cash flows from investing activities exclude payments for inventories, which are included in operating activities. Typical investing cash flows are listed in **Exhibit 5-2**. The difference between investing cash inflows and outflows is called *net cash provided (used) by investing activities.*

EXHIBIT 5-2
Cash Flows from **Investing** Activities

Cash Inflows—Cash Received from:	Cash Outflows—Cash Paid for:
Sale of property, plant, and equipment	Purchase of property, plant, and equipment
Sale of debt and equity investments in other companies*	Investments in debt and equity investments in other companies*
Collection of a loan (excluding interest, which is an operating activity)	Loans to other entities
Sale of patents or other intangible assets	Purchase of patents or other intangible assets

*Cash flows from investments are classified as operating cash flows if those assets are acquired specifically for resale and are carried at fair value in a trading account—we cover this in a later chapter.

Cash Flows from Financing Activities

Cash flows from financing activities include both cash inflows and outflows related to issuance of debt and equity. Cash inflows occur by borrowing from creditors or by issuing stock to owners to obtain cash for financing the business. Cash outflows occur when principal is repaid to creditors and when distributions are made to owners. Typical financing cash flows are listed in **Exhibit 5-3**. The difference between these cash inflows and outflows is called *net cash provided (used) by financing activities.*

EXHIBIT 5-3
Cash Flows from **Financing** Activities

Cash Inflows—Cash Received from:	Cash Outflows—Cash Paid for:
Issuance of a company's own stock	Dividends and other cash distributions to owners
Issuance of bonds or other debt (short-term and long-term)	Reacquiring previously issued capital stock
Sale of treasury stock (covered in later chapter)	Principal payments on loans or payments to retire bonds or other debt

In sum, the change from one balance sheet date to another is a result of operating, investing, and financing activities. In **Demo 5-1**, we classify cash flows as operating, investing, or financing depending on their source.

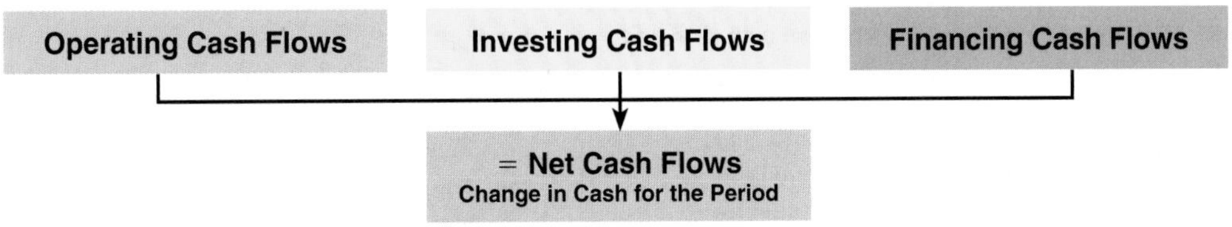

NIKE [NKE]

NIKE Real World—CASH FLOW ACTIVITIES

The following excerpt from the Management's Discussion and Analysis Section of Nike Inc.'s annual report on Form 10-K explains key changes in the three sections of the statement of cash flows.

> ***Cash provided by operations*** was $4,680 million for fiscal 2015 compared to $3,013 million for fiscal 2014. Our primary source of operating cash flow for fiscal 2015 was Net income of $3,273 million. Our fiscal 2015 change in working capital was a net cash inflow of $256 million as compared to a net cash outflow of $488 million for fiscal 2014. Our investments in working capital decreased due to increases in accrued liabilities. . . These amounts were partially offset by higher inventory levels resulting from business growth and West Coast port delays in North America, as well as lower Income taxes payable as a result of tax payments made in fiscal 2015.
>
> ***Cash used by investing activities*** was $175 million for fiscal 2015, compared to a $1,207 million use of cash for fiscal 2014. The primary driver of the decrease in Cash used by investing activities was the net change in short-term investments (including sales, maturities and purchases) from net purchases to net sales/maturities. In fiscal 2015, there were $935 million of net sales/maturities compared to $328 million of net purchases of short-term investments in the same period of fiscal 2014.
>
> ***Cash used by financing activities*** was $2,790 million for fiscal 2015 compared to $2,914 million for fiscal 2014, a decrease of $124 million, as increased dividends were more than offset by an increase in proceeds from the exercise of stock options and the excess tax benefits from share-based payment arrangements.

Demo 5-1 **LO5-1** **Classification of Cash Flows**

Demo MBC

A company has the following cash flows, 1 through 12, in the current year. For each item, indicate the type of cash flow (inflow or outflow), along with the classification of the cash flow (operating, investing, or financing).

	Cash Inflow or Cash Outflow	Operating, Investing, or Financing Activity
1. Proceeds from stock issuance	Inflow	Financing
2. Payment to retire bonds	Outflow	Financing
3. Proceeds from the sale of plant assets	Inflow	Investing
4. Loans made to others	Outflow	Investing
5. Receipts from customers	Inflow	Operating
6. Interest payments	Outflow	Operating
7. Proceeds from borrowing	Inflow	Financing
8. Payments to purchase own capital stock	Outflow	Financing
9. Sale of land	Inflow	Investing
10. Purchase of equity security for investment	Outflow	Investing
11. Dividends received	Inflow	Operating
12. Payment for salaries to employees	Outflow	Operating

REVIEW 5-1 **LO5-1** **Classification of Cash Flows**

Review MBC

Match each transaction *a* through *i* with one of the 3 classifications on the statement of cash flows.

Classification on Statement of Cash Flows

1. Cash Flows from Operating Activities
2. Cash Flows from Investing Activities
3. Cash Flows from Financing Activities

Transaction

____ *a.* Purchase of equipment for cash
____ *b.* Payment of state income tax
____ *c.* Purchase of a patent for cash
____ *d.* Payment of dividends
____ *e.* Payment for utilities for the month
____ *f.* Payment on short-term debt
____ *g.* Principal payment on long-term loan
____ *h.* Purchase of inventory for cash
____ *i.* Sale of equity investment for cash

More Practice:
5-20, 5-21, 5-37, 5-38
Solution on p. 5-63.

Prepare an indirect statement of cash flows

LO 5-2

LO 5-2 Overview

Indirect Statement of Cash Flows

- Classify cash flows as operating, investing, and financing
- Reconcile cash balance from beginning to end of period
- Reconcile net income to net cash flows from operating activities in the operating activities section

The three types of cash flows—operating, investing, and financing—are included in three separate sections in the statement of cash flows.

In the statement of cash flows, the operating, investing, and financing totals are added together to account for the total change in cash from the beginning of the period to the end of the period. "Cash" includes cash, cash equivalents, and restricted cash. Cash equivalents (highly liquid investment with little credit risk) and restricted cash (cash not available for general use) were introduced in Chapter 4. In other words, cash at the beginning of the period is reconciled to cash at the end of the period through operating, investing, and financing activities as follows.

+/− Net cash flows from operating activities for the period
+/− Net cash flows from investing activities for the period
+/− Net cash flows from financing activities for the period
+/− Net change in cash during the period
\+ Cash at the beginning of the period
= Cash at the end of the period

230-10-45-24 A statement of cash flows for a period shall report net cash provided or used by operating, investing, and financing activities and the net effect of those flows on the total of cash, cash equivalents, and amounts generally described as restricted cash or restricted cash equivalents during the period. The statement of cash flows shall report that information in a manner that reconciles beginning and ending totals of cash, cash equivalents, and amounts generally described as restricted cash or restricted cash equivalents.

Two formats are available for displaying cash flow information. *They differ in the approach used to calculate net cash flows from operating activities only.* The two formats are the **indirect method** and the **direct method**. The direct method is described in an appendix to this chapter.

The vast majority of companies elect to report their statement of cash flows using the indirect method. Under this method, net income (reported on an accrual basis) is adjusted to arrive at net cash flows from operating activities (reported on a cash basis). In other words, *operating cash flows are determined indirectly through adjustments to net income.* Computation and presentation of information pertaining to investing and financing activities are identical under both methods. In **Demo 5-2**, we see a simple example of a statement of cash flows using the indirect approach. A later chapter revisits the statement of cash flows, incorporating more complex accounts and transactions that we cover in the remaining chapters.

Cash Flows from Operating Activities

The operating activities section starts with net income. Adjustments are made to net income to arrive at net cash from operating activities, a cash-based amount. These adjustments include noncash revenue and expense adjustments, and changes in operating assets and operating liabilities (there are some exceptions to using current items as outlined in a later chapter).

INDIRECT METHOD

Net Income
\+ Noncash expenses and losses
− Noncash revenues and gains
− Increase in operating (non-cash) assets
\+ Decrease in operating (non-cash) assets
− Decrease in operating liabilities
\+ Increase in operating liabilities
+/− Cash flows classified as operating, but not included in net income
= Net cash flows from operating activities

Noncash Revenue and Expense Adjustments

Expenses not involving cash payments are added back to net income to arrive at cash from operating activities. The more common adjustments include depreciation and amortization changes. Losses on the sale of investments, including investments in property, plant, and equipment, or the settlement of nonoperating liabilities are added back to net income because the cash effects of these transactions are classified as investing or financing activities.

Noncash revenues are subtracted from net income. One example of a noncash revenue is income accrued on a bond purchased at a discount. Gains on the sale of investments, including investments in property, plant, and equipment, or the settlement of nonoperating liabilities are reversed from net income because the cash effects of these transactions are classified as investing or financing activities.

Changes in Current Assets and Current Liabilities

To reconcile net income to cash provided by operating activities, increases in operating assets (other than cash) are subtracted from net income and decreases in operating assets (other than cash) are added to net income. For example, an increase in accounts receivable is subtracted from net income because the corresponding sales increased net income, but did not result in the collection of cash. A decrease in accounts receivable is added to net income because it reflects cash received from customers that was not included in income this period.

Decreases in operating liabilities are subtracted from net income, and increases in operating liabilities are added to net income. For example, an increase in accounts payable is added to net income because the corresponding expense decreased net income without affecting cash. A decrease in accounts payable is subtracted from net income because it reflects a cash payment on account but not an expense of the current period.

Cash Flows from Investing and Financing Activities

Certain activities are classified as investing and financing activities. Unlike operating activities, investing and financing cash flows are always *directly reported* in the statement of cash flows. For example, the sale of equipment is reported as a positive amount (cash inflow) while a purchase of equipment is reported as a negative amount (cash outflow) in the investing activities section. Similarly, the sale of common stock is reported as a positive amount (cash inflow) while a purchase of stock for the treasury is reported as a negative amount (cash outflow) in the financing activities section.

Financial Statement Disclosures

Noncash investing and financing activities involve an exchange of value other than cash that must be disclosed in financial statements. A transaction may involve no cash (such as settling a debt in full by issuing the company's capital stock to the creditor) or be partly in cash (such as settling a debt with 30% cash and 70% capital stock). **These noncash and part-cash activities are either reported in a separate schedule at the bottom of the statement of cash flows or disclosed in the notes.**

Additional examples of noncash transactions follow.

- Purchase of property, plant, and equipment through debt financing.
- Conversion of debt securities (bonds payable) to equity securities (common stock).
- Issuance of stock to purchase assets such as land or equipment.
- Exchange of a noncurrent asset for another noncurrent asset.

230-10-50-3 Information about all investing and financing activities of an entity during a period that affect recognized assets or liabilities but that do not result in cash receipts or cash payments in the period shall be disclosed.
230-10-50-6 If there are only a few such noncash transactions, it may be convenient to include them on the same page as the statement of cash flows. Otherwise, the transactions may be reported elsewhere in the financial statements, clearly referenced to the statement of cash flows.

In addition, a company must disclose cash paid for interest and taxes and information about restricted cash and cash equivalents. Authoritative guidance follows.

230-10-50-2 If the indirect method is used, amounts of interest paid (net of amounts capitalized)...and income taxes paid during the period shall be disclosed.

230-10-50-7 An entity shall disclose information about the nature of restrictions on its cash, cash equivalents, and amounts generally described as restricted cash or restricted cash equivalents.

Indirect Method of Cash Flows

LO5-2 **Demo 5-2**

Demo MBC

The income statement and balance sheet along with additional information are provided for Lakers Inc. for the year ended December 31, 2020. Prepare a statement of cash flows for the year ended December 31, 2020, using the indirect method.

Lakers Inc.
Statement of Comprehensive Income
For Year Ended December 31, 2020

Sales	$66,000
Salaries expense	24,500
Depreciation expense	4,000
Selling and administrative expenses	12,000
Interest expenses	3,500
Net income	22,000
Other comprehensive income	
Unrealized gain on investment	2,000
Comprehensive income	$24,000

Lakers Inc.
Balance Sheet

December 31	2019	2020	Difference
Cash and cash equivalents	$ 42,000	$ 71,000	$29,000
Accounts receivable	31,000	40,000	9,000
Plant assets	82,000	81,000	(1,000)
Accumulated depreciation	(20,000)	(14,000)	6,000
Investment	0	14,000	14,000
Total assets	$135,000	$192,000	$57,000
Salaries payable	$ 3,000	$ 5,000	$ 2,000
Notes payable, long-term	46,000	40,000	(6,000)
Common stock, par $10	61,000	101,000	40,000
Paid-in capital in excess of par	9,000	17,000	8,000
Retained earnings	16,000	27,000	11,000
Accumulated other comprehensive income	0	2,000	2,000
Total liabilities and stockholders' equity	$135,000	$192,000	$57,000

Additional information

1. Details for the plant assets account.
   (a) Purchased plant assets for cash, $30,000.
   (b) Sold plant assets for $21,000; recorded as:

Cash	21,000	
Accumulated Depreciation	10,000	
Plant Assets		31,000

2. Depreciation expense for 2020 is $4,000.
3. Recorded a $2,000 unrealized gain in OCI at year-end for a debt investment purchased during the year for $12,000.
4. Details for the long-term notes payable account.*

Borrowed cash	$40,000
Principal payments on note	46,000

5. Retained earnings statement.

Balance, December 31, 2019	$16,000
Net income	22,000
Cash dividend paid	(11,000)
Balance, December 31, 2020	$27,000

6. Issued common stock for cash ... $48,000
7. No significant noncash activities exist.
8. All sales are on account.

* Note payable of $46,000 was paid off and a new note was issued for $40,000.

Solution
Cash Flows from Operating Activities

Noncash adjustment Depreciation of $4,000 is added back to net income because it is a noncash expense item. The unrealized gain affecting OCI did not impact net income; thus it is not an adjusting entry on the cash flow statement.

Increase in operating asset Credit sales ($66,000) increased accounts receivable, yet accounts receivable increased a net of $9,000, implying $57,000 of collections on account. Because the $66,000 included in net income exceeds the $57,000 cash received, a $9,000 reconciling adjustment is required to remove the excess of accrued revenue over cash received.

Increase in operating liability Salaries expense of $24,500 increased salaries payable, yet salaries payable increased a net of $2,000, implying $22,500 of salary payments. Because the $24,500 reducing net income is greater than the $22,500 cash paid, a $2,000 adjustment is required to remove the excess of accrual expense over salary payments made.

continued

continued from previous page

The complete cash flows from operating activities section for Lakers Inc. follows.

Cash flows from operating activities	
Net income	$22,000
Adjustments:	
Depreciation expense	4,000
Increase in accounts receivable	(9,000)
Increase in salaries payable	2,000
Net cash provided by operating activities	$19,000

Cash Flows from Investing Activities

Lakers Inc. purchased plant assets for $30,000 cash. This is an investing cash outflow. Lakers Inc. also sold plant assets as noted in the additional information provided for Lakers Inc. The $21,000 proceeds are an investing cash inflow. The two transactions listed in the additional information help explain the changes in accumulated depreciation and plant assets accounts during 2020.

Plant Assets			
Beg. bal.	82,000	31,000	Original cost of equip. sold
Purchases	30,000		
End. bal.	81,000		

Accumulated Depreciation			
Acc. dep. of equip. sold	10,000	20,000	Beg. bal.
		4,000	Dep. exp.
		14,000	End. bal.

Lakers Inc. also purchased a debt investment for $12,000 during the year resulting in a cash outflow of $12,000.

Cash flows from investing activities	
Cash paid for acquisition of plant assets	$(30,000)
Cash received from sale of plant assets	21,000
Cash paid for purchase of investment	(12,000)
Net cash used by investing activities	$(21,000)

Cash Flows from Financing Activities

Lakers Inc. borrowed $40,000 cash (financing cash inflow) and paid $46,000 principal (financing cash outflow) on its long-term notes payable. These changes account for the $6,000 net decrease in long-term debt on the balance sheet ($46,000 − $40,000). The retained earnings statement reveals $11,000 of dividends declared and paid in 2020, a financing cash outflow. There is no dividends payable account, meaning all dividends declared were paid. The last item is common stock issuance for $48,000, a financing cash inflow.

Cash flows from financing activities	
Cash received from long-term debt issuance	$40,000
Cash paid on long-term debt	(46,000)
Cash paid for dividends	(11,000)
Cash received from sale of common stock	48,000
Net cash provided by financing activities	$31,000

All balance sheet account changes are explained by the transaction analysis above, and so there are no further items to disclose in the statement of cash flows. For example, the change in equipment and accumulated depreciation balances are reconciled above. The $11,000 retained earnings increase is explained by the $22,000 of net income less $11,000 of dividends.

Statement of Cash Flows

We combine the three sections of the statement of cash flows to complete the statement of cash flows that follows. Net operating cash inflows of $19,000, less net investing cash outflows of $21,000, plus net financing cash inflows of $31,000, equals *the net change in cash of $29,000.* This change in cash plus the beginning cash balance of $42,000 equals the ending cash balance of $71,000.

continued

continued from previous page

Lakers Inc.
Statement of Cash Flows, Indirect Method
For Year Ended December 31, 2020

Cash flows from operating activities	
Net income	$22,000
Adjustments:	
Depreciation expense	4,000
Increase in accounts receivable	(9,000)
Increase in salaries payable	2,000
Net cash provided by operating activities	19,000
Cash flows from investing activities	
Cash paid for acquisition of plant assets	(30,000)
Cash received from sale of plant assets	21,000
Cash paid for purchase of investment	(12,000)
Net cash used by investing activities	(21,000)
Cash flows from financing activities	
Cash received from long-term debt issuance	40,000
Cash paid on long-term debt	(46,000)
Cash paid for dividends	(11,000)
Cash received from sale of common stock	48,000
Net cash provided by financing activities	31,000
Net increase in cash and cash equivalents during 2020	29,000
Cash and cash equivalents, December 31, 2019	42,000
Cash and cash equivalents, December 31, 2020	$71,000

NIKE

Real World—CONSOLIDATED STATEMENT OF CASH FLOWS

The following consolidated statement of cash flows was reported in the annual report on Form 10-K for **Nike Inc.** Notice how noncash investing and financing items are disclosed at the bottom of the statement of cash flows. In addition, the required disclosure of cash paid for interest and taxes is included at the end of the presentation.

NIKE [NKE]

For Year Ended (in millions)	2015
Cash provided by operations	
Net income	$3,273
Income charges (credits) not affecting cash:	
Depreciation	606
Deferred income taxes	(113)
Stock-based compensation	191
Amortization and other	43
Net foreign currency adjustments	424
Net gain on divestitures	—
Increase (decrease) in accounts receivable	(216)
(Increase) in inventories	(621)
(Increase) in prepaid expenses and other current assets	(144)
(Decrease) increase in accounts payable, accrued liabilities, and income taxes payable	1,237
Cash provided by operations	4,680
Cash used by investing activities	
Purchases of short-term investments	(4,936)
Maturities of short-term investments	3,655
Sales of short-term investments	2,216
Investments in reverse repurchase agreements	(150)
Additions to property, plant and equipment	(963)
Disposals of property, plant and equipment	3
Proceeds from divestitures	—
Cash used by investing activities	(175)

continued

continued from previous page

Cash used by financing activities	
Net proceeds from long-term debt issuance	—
Long-term debt payments, including current portion	(7)
(Decrease) increase in notes payable	(63)
Payments on capital lease obligations	(19)
Proceeds from exercise of stock options and other stock issuances	514
Excess tax benefits from share-based payment arrangements	218
Repurchase of common stock	(2,534)
Dividends—common and preferred	(899)
Cash used by financing activities	(2,790)
Effect of exchange rate changes on cash and equivalents	(83)
Net increase (decrease) in cash and equivalents	1,632
Cash and equivalents, beginning of year	2,220
Cash and equivalents, end of year	$3,852
Supplemental disclosure of cash flow information:	
Cash paid during the year for:	
Interest, net of capitalized interest	$ 53
Income taxes	1,262
Noncash additions to property, plant, and equipment	206
Dividends declared and not paid	240

REVIEW 5-2 LO5-2 Statement of Cash Flows

Review MBC

Bell Corp. compiled the following annual information for year-end 2020. Prepare a statement of cash flows for the year ended December 31, 2020, for Bell Corp. Assume that cash at the beginning of the year is $44,000.

Increase in cash	$26,000	Increase in common stock	$ 40,000
Increase in accounts receivable	14,000	Increase in retained earnings	25,300
Decrease in merchandise inventory	22,700	Net income	113,610
Decrease in supplies	1,000	Depreciation expense	45,000
Decrease in accounts payable	5,000	Gain on sale of equipment	2,500
Decrease in salaries payable	9,000	Equipment purchases (cash)	57,600
Decrease in utilities payable	400	Book value of equipment sold	8,000
Decrease in notes payable	30,000	Dividends paid	88,310

More Practice: 5-39, 5-40, 5-41, 5-42, 5-43, 5-44

Solution on p. 5-63.

LO 5-3 Describe the interrelations of financial statements

LO 5-3 Overview

Interrelations of Financial Statements

- *Net income*; income statement to statement of comprehensive income
- *Net income and other comprehensive income*; comprehensive income statement to stockholders' equity statement
- *Ending equity balances*; stockholders' equity statement to balance sheet
- *Cash balances*; balance sheet to statement of cash flows

Analysis of financial reports requires an understanding of the interrelations among financial statements, often called **articulation**. The financial statements present financial statement elements. Descriptions of the ten financial statement elements are reviewed below.

Element	Description
Assets	**SFAC No. 6 25** Assets are probable future economic benefits obtained or controlled by a particular entity as a result of past transactions or events.
Liabilities	**SFAC No. 6 35** Liabilities are probable future sacrifices of economic benefits arising from present obligations of a particular entity to transfer assets or provide services to other entities in the future as a result of past transactions or events.

continued

continued from previous page

Element	Description
Equity (Net Assets)	**SFAC No. 6 49** Equity or net assets is the residual interest in the assets of an entity that remains after deducting its liabilities.
Investments by owners	**SFAC No. 6 66** Investments by owners are increases in equity of a particular business enterprise resulting from transfers to it from other entities of something valuable to obtain or increase ownership interests (or equity) in it. Assets are most commonly received as investments by owners, but that which is received may also include services or satisfaction or conversion of liabilities of the enterprise.
Distributions to owners	**SFAC No. 6 67** Distributions to owners are decreases in equity of a particular business enterprise resulting from transferring assets, rendering services, or incurring liabilities by the enterprise to owners. Distributions to owners decrease ownership interest (or equity) in an enterprise.
Comprehensive Income	**SFAC No. 6 70** Comprehensive income is the change in equity of a business enterprise during a period from transactions and other events and circumstances from nonowner sources. It includes all changes in equity during a period except those resulting from investments by owners and distributions to owners.
Revenues	**SFAC No. 6 78** Revenues are inflows or other enhancements of assets of an entity or settlements of its liabilities (or a combination of both) from delivering or producing goods, rendering services, or other activities that constitute the entity's ongoing major or central operations.
Expenses	**SFAC No. 6 80** Expenses are outflows or other using up of assets or incurrences of liabilities (or a combination of both) from delivering or producing goods, rendering services, or carrying out other activities that constitute the entity's ongoing major or central operations.
Gains	**SFAC No. 6 82** Gains are increases in equity (net assets) from peripheral or incidental transactions of an entity and from all other transactions and other events and circumstances affecting the entity except those that result from revenues or investments by owners.
Losses	**SFAC No. 6 83** Losses are decreases in equity (net assets) from peripheral or incidental transactions of an entity and from all other transactions and other events and circumstances affecting the entity except those that result from expenses or distributions to owners.

Given an event or transaction, we need answers to the following questions to determine which financial statement elements were affected.

1. Was an asset acquired, created, or enhanced; *or* was it disposed or impaired?
2. Was a liability incurred or settled?
3. Was there a transaction with an owner?

We apply the definitions of financial statement elements in **Demo 5-3A**.

Applying Definitions of Financial Statement Elements — LO5-3 — Demo 5-3A

Demo MBC

Using the definitions of financial statement elements determine whether the following transactions give rise to comprehensive income. For all examples, assume no changes in assets and liabilities, other than the changes indicated.

Transaction	Impact on Comprehensive Income
1. Cash increased $5,000. Loans payable increased $5,000.	An asset was acquired or enhanced by $5,000, and a liability of $5,000 was incurred. Because this resulted in no change in net assets, there can be no recognition of comprehensive income.
2. Cash increased $5,000 and the transaction was not with an owner.	An asset was acquired or enhanced by $5,000. Because liabilities did not change, there was a change in net assets of $5,000. This change was not attributable to a transaction with an owner, so comprehensive income is recognized.
3. Cash increased $5,000 and the transaction was with an owner.	An asset was acquired or enhanced by $5,000. Because liabilities did not change, there was a change in net assets of $5,000. Because the change was attributable to a transaction with an owner, there can be no recognition of comprehensive income.

Financial Statements A complete set of financial statements includes the following:

- A **balance sheet** displays assets, liabilities and net assets (equity) at a point in time.
- A **statement of stockholders' equity** displays sources of changes in equity accounts between two balance sheet dates. These sources include transactions with owners and other transactions, not with owners.
- A **statement of comprehensive income** displays sources of changes in net assets not attributable to transactions with owners between two balance sheet dates.
- The **income statement** is a sub-part of the **statement of comprehensive income** that displays revenues, expenses, and certain gains and losses not included in other comprehensive income.
- The **statement of cash flows** displays changes in cash between two balance sheet dates.

The interrelations among financial statements derive from the balance sheet equation. The balance sheet equation states that for any amount of resources (assets) there is an equal amount of claims on those resources (by creditors and owners):

Assets = Liabilities + Equity (Net Assets)

The **balance sheet** presents individual accounts making up assets, liabilities, and equity. Totals are presented so that financial statement users can see that the balance sheet equation is in balance as shown in the Lakers Inc. balance sheet from the prior section.

Lakers Inc.
Balance Sheet

At December 31	2019	2020
Cash and cash equivalents	$ 42,000	$ 71,000
Accounts receivable	31,000	40,000
Plant assets	82,000	81,000
Accumulated depreciation	(20,000)	(14,000)
Investment	0	14,000
Total assets	$135,000	$192,000
Salaries payable	$ 3,000	$ 5,000
Notes payable, long-term	46,000	40,000
Common stock, par $10	61,000	101,000
Paid-in capital in excess of par	9,000	17,000
Retained earnings	16,000	27,000
Accumulated other comprehensive income	0	2,000
Total liabilities and stockholders' equity	$135,000	$192,000

The balance sheet equation is true by construction, not by any law of nature. Because the balance sheet equation is true at all points in time, it must be true that over any reporting period, the change in assets equals the change in liabilities plus the change in equity. In the equation below the symbol Δ represents "change."

$$\Delta\text{Assets} = \Delta\text{Liabilities} + \Delta\text{Equity}$$

Given comparative balance sheets, the remaining financial statements explain the sources of changes in financial statement elements on the balance sheet over the reporting period.

The **statement of stockholders' equity** shows changes in equity resulting from transactions with owners and changes not resulting from transactions with owners. Transactions with owners include stock issuances, stock repurchases, and dividends. Changes in equity not attributable to transactions with owners include net income and other comprehensive income.

The Lakers Inc. statement of stockholders' equity is below. The columns correspond to line items shown in the equity section of the balance sheets.

Lakers Inc.
Statement of Stockholders' Equity

	Common Stock	Paid-in Capital in Excess of Par	Retained Earnings	Accumulated OCI	Total Stockholders' Equity
Balance, December 31, 2019....	$ 61,000	$ 9,000	$16,000	$ 0	$ 86,000
Issuance of common stock......	40,000	8,000			48,000
Net income..................			22,000		22,000
Dividends..................			(11,000)		(11,000)
Unrealized gain on investments..				2,000	2,000
Balance, December 31, 2020....	$101,000	$17,000	$27,000	$2,000	$147,000

From the statement of stockholders' equity we can see that net assets increased because Lakers issued $48,000 of stock, earned $22,000 of net income, declared dividends of $11,000, and recorded an unrealized gain on investments of $2,000 during the period (all totaling $61,000). Because financial statement users benefit from understanding the components of comprehensive income and net income, companies prepare a statement of comprehensive income, shown for Lakers Inc. below.

Lakers Inc.
Statement of Comprehensive Income
For Year Ended December 31, 2020

Sales............................	$66,000
Salaries expense..................	24,500
Depreciation expense...............	4,000
Selling and administrative expenses ...	12,000
Interest expense...................	3,500
Net income.......................	$22,000
Other comprehensive income	
Unrealized gain on investments	2,000
Comprehensive income.............	$24,000

The statement of comprehensive income shows major sources of revenues, expenses, gains, losses, and other comprehensive income. Lakers reported net income of $22,000 and other comprehensive income of $2,000 during the period.

We know from the balance sheet that the balance of Cash was $42,000 at the beginning of the period and $71,000 at the end. Because financial statement users benefit from understanding components of changes in cash over the period, companies prepare a statement of cash flows.

Just like the other financial statements that explain changes over the period, the indirect method statement of cash flows derives from the balance sheet equation:

$$\Delta\textbf{Assets} = \Delta\textbf{Liabilities} + \Delta\textbf{Equity}$$

The change in assets is simply the change in cash plus the change in assets other than cash:

$$\Delta\textbf{Cash} + \Delta\textbf{Noncash Assets} = \Delta\textbf{Liabilities} + \Delta\textbf{Equity}$$

Subtracting the change in noncash assets from both sides shows that the total change in cash is equal to the net change in liabilities and equity minus the change in noncash assets:

$$\Delta\textbf{Cash} = -\Delta\textbf{Noncash Assets} + \Delta\textbf{Liabilities} + \Delta\textbf{Equity}$$

Breaking out the change in equity into net income and other changes in equity not included in net income shows that net income is an important source of the total change in cash. This equation illustrates that the change in cash is made up of the items on the right of the equation, which are shown in the three sections of operating, investing, and financing.

$$\Delta\text{Cash} = \text{Net Income} - \Delta\text{Noncash Assets} + \Delta\text{Liabilities} + \Delta\text{Equity (excluding net income)}$$

Lakers' statement of cash flows explaining the details of its $29,000 change in cash ($71,000 − $42,000) is shown below.

Lakers Inc.
Statement of Cash Flows, Indirect Method
For Year Ended December 31, 2020

Cash flows from operating activities	
Net income	$22,000
Adjustments:	
Depreciation expense	4,000
Increase in accounts receivable	(9,000)
Increase in salaries payable	2,000
Net cash inflow from operating activities	19,000
Cash flows from investing activities	
Cash paid for acquisition of plant assets	(30,000)
Cash received from sale of plant assets	21,000
Cash paid for purchase of investment	(12,000)
Net cash outflow from investing activities	(21,000)
Cash flows from financing activities	
Cash received from long-term debt issuance	40,000
Cash paid on long-term debt	(46,000)
Cash paid for dividends	(11,000)
Cash received from sale of common stock	48,000
Net cash inflow from financing activities	31,000
Net increase in cash and cash equivalents during 2020	29,000
Cash and cash equivalents, December 31, 2019	42,000
Cash and cash equivalents, December 31, 2020	$71,000

The interrelations among the financial statements of Lakers Inc. are shown in **Demo 5-3B**.

Interrelations of Financial Statements

LO5-3 Demo 5-3B

Demo MBC

Lakers Inc. reported the following financial statements for the year ended December 31, 2020. Answer the questions following the financial statements (ignore taxes).

Lakers Inc.
Statement of Comprehensive Income
For Year Ended December 31, 2020

Sales	$66,000
Salaries expense	24,500
Depreciation expense	4,000
Selling and administrative expenses	12,000
Interest expense	3,500
Net income	$22,000
Other comprehensive income	
Unrealized gain on investments	2,000
Comprehensive income	$24,000

Lakers Inc.
Statement of Stockholders' Equity

	Common Stock	Paid-in Capital in Excess of Par	Retained Earnings	Accumulated OCI	Total Stockholders' Equity
Balance, December 31, 2019	$ 61,000	$ 9,000	$16,000	$ 0	$ 86,000
Issuance of common stock	40,000	8,000			48,000
Net income			22,000		22,000
Dividends			(11,000)		(11,000)
Unrealized gain on investments				2,000	2,000
Balance, December 31, 2020	$101,000	$17,000	$27,000	$2,000	$147,000

Lakers Inc.
Balance Sheet

At December 31	2019	2020
Cash and cash equivalents	$ 42,000	$ 71,000
Accounts receivable	31,000	40,000
Plant assets	82,000	81,000
Accumulated depreciation	(20,000)	(14,000)
Investment	0	14,000
Total assets	$135,000	$192,000
Salaries payable	$ 3,000	$ 5,000
Notes payable, long-term	46,000	40,000
Common stock, par $10	61,000	101,000
Paid-in capital in excess of par	9,000	17,000
Retained earnings	16,000	27,000
Accumulated other comprehensive income	0	2,000
Total liabilities and stockholders' equity	$135,000	$192,000

Lakers Inc.
Statement of Cash Flows, Indirect Method
For Year Ended December 31, 2020

Cash flows from operating activities	
Net income	$22,000
Adjustments:	
Depreciation expense	4,000
Increase in accounts receivable	(9,000)
Increase in salaries payable	2,000
Net cash inflow from operating activities	19,000
Cash flows from investing activities	
Cash paid for acquisition of plant assets	(30,000)
Cash received from sale of plant assets	21,000
Cash paid for purchase of investment	(12,000)
Net cash outflow from investing activities	(21,000)
Cash flows from financing activities	
Cash received from long-term debt issuance	40,000
Cash paid on long-term debt	(46,000)
Cash paid for dividends	(11,000)
Cash received from sale of common stock	48,000
Net cash inflow from financing activities	31,000
Net increase in cash and cash equivalents during 2020	29,000
Cash and cash equivalents, December 31, 2019	42,000
Cash and cash equivalents, December 31, 2020	$71,000

Solution

Interrelation Questions	Title	Amount
1. What amounts appear on both the statement of comprehensive income and on the stockholders' equity statement?	Net Income	$ 22,000
	Other comprehensive income	2,000
2. What ending balances appear on both the stockholders' equity statement and the balance sheet?	Common stock	101,000
	Paid-in capital in excess of par	17,000
	Retained earnings	27,000
	Accumulated other comprehensive income	2,000
3. What amount appears on both the statement of comprehensive income and on the statement of cash flows?	Net Income	22,000
4. What amounts appear on both the balance sheet and on the statement of cash flows?	Cash and cash equivalents, beginning	42,000
	Cash and cash equivalents, ending	71,000

REVIEW 5-3 **LO5-3** **Interrelations of Financial Statements**

Review MBC

Find the missing amounts *a* through *g* for Crystal Corp. using knowledge of the interrelations of financial statements. *Hint:* Calculate *d* before calculating *c*.

Net income, 2020	$ (a)
Retained earnings, December 31, 2020	(b)
Retained earnings, December 31, 2019	8,800
Dividends, 2020	5,000
Common stock, December 31, 2020	75,000
Total stockholders' equity, December 31, 2020	(c)
Other comprehensive income, 2020	2,500
Accumulated other comprehensive income, December 31, 2019	16,000
Accumulated other comprehensive income, December 31, 2020	(d)
Comprehensive income, 2020	16,900
Total assets, December 31, 2020	(e)
Total assets, excluding cash, December 31, 2020	(f)
Total liabilities, December 31, 2020	41,800
Cash, December 31, 2019	5,000
Cash, December 31, 2020	3,500
Change in cash, 2020	(g)

More Practice:
5-27, 5-45, 5-46
Solution on p. 5-64.

LO 5-4 Perform an investment analysis using the DuPont Framework

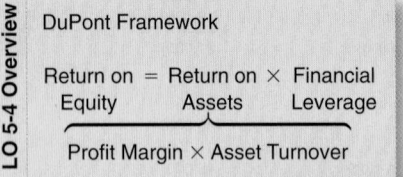

LO 5-4 Overview

DuPont Framework

Return on Equity = Return on Assets × Financial Leverage

Return on Assets = Profit Margin × Asset Turnover

Investors and creditors use several tools to analyze financial statements including ratio, vertical, and horizontal analyses. We begin this section by examining ratios primarily from an owner's perspective. The next section reviews ratios primarily from a creditor's perspective, followed by a section on horizontal and vertical analyses of financial statements.

Investor decisions on buying, selling, or holding investments are influenced by the returns expected on those investments. Investor expectations depend on an assessment of the amount, timing, and uncertainty of future net cash inflows to the company.

SFAC No. 8 OB3 Decisions by existing and potential investors about buying, selling, or holding equity and debt instruments depend on the returns that they expect from an investment in those instruments, for example, dividends, principal and interest payments, or market price increases. . . . Investors', lenders', and other creditors' expectations about returns depend on their assessment of the amount, timing, and uncertainty of (the prospects for) future net cash inflows to the entity. Consequently, existing and potential investors, lenders, and other creditors need information to help them assess the prospects for future net cash inflows to an entity.

This means owners need information to help them assess the potential for future net cash inflows to an entity. Ratio analysis is a tool for assessing the financial information made available to owners through the financial reporting process. In general, **ratios** measure key relations between financial statement items. The first ratio that we review is a ratio important to *owners* in assessing the profitability of investments (or potential investments): the return on equity ratio.

Return on Equity and its Interpretation Using DuPont Model

Return on equity (**ROE**) is a common profitability measure used by management and investors. ROE relates net income (from the income statement) to stockholders' equity (from the balance sheet). This measure answers a question critical to investors: *How effectively has the company managed capital invested by stockholders?*

The ROE measure is calculated at the aggregate level of a company by dividing net income by average stockholders' equity. To improve company performance as reflected in this ratio, we need to understand what drives this ratio. Further, we can break down ROE into components that better inform management about ways that can make a meaningful impact on ROE.

One method to disaggregate ROE is the **DuPont model** introduced by E.I. Dupont de Nemurs as a tool for managers to evaluate company performance. Instead of viewing ROE as simply a measure of profitability, the DuPont model breaks down ROE into three drivers: **profitability**, **activity**, and **leverage**. See **Exhibit 5-4** for a summary of these DuPont Model components.

EXHIBIT 5-4
Components of DuPont Model

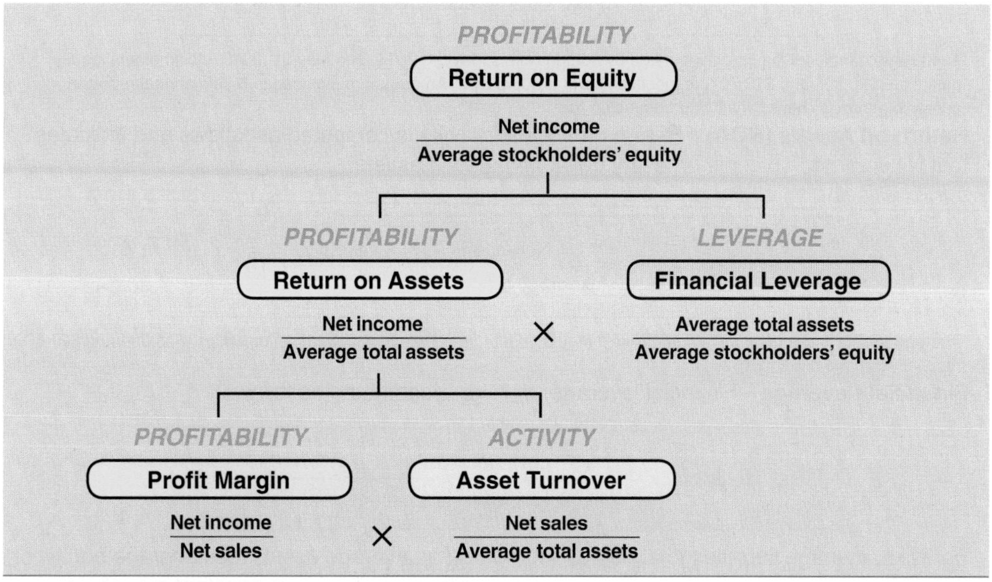

- **Return on Equity** (**ROE**) is the top-level profitability measure in the DuPont model. ROE measures the return the company has earned on the reported value (book value) of the stockholders' investment. This key indicator analyzes the return on investment from the perspective of stockholders. Investment includes capital contributions plus undistributed retained earnings.
- **Return on assets** is equal to net income divided by average assets. Return on assets is a measure of profitability that assesses a company's utilization of assets to generate profits. To increase a company's return on assets, managers focus both on the balance sheet and income statement. The return on assets will increase if existing assets generate higher profits, or if profit remains constant but total assets decline.
- **Financial leverage** is an indicator of how a company's assets are financed (debt vs. equity). In the DuPont analysis, the leverage ratio is measured by dividing average total assets by average total stockholders' equity. The financial leverage ratio increases when a company's debt level increases relative to its equity level.
- **Profit margin**, a profitability ratio, measures the percent of profit recognized on each dollar of net sales. Management can increase profit margin by increasing its gross profit margin (gross profit/net sales) and/or by reducing its operating expenses relative to sales dollars.
- **Asset turnover** measures the amount of net sales generated for each asset dollar invested. Management can increase asset turnover by increasing sales volume without increasing assets, or by reducing the level of assets without reducing the level of sales. This is an activity measure because its focus is on how to more efficiently utilize assets to produce sales.

We use **Demo 5-4A** to examine each of the components of the DuPont model. We then examine how these measures interact to affect ROE in **Demo 5-4B**. We conclude with additional ratios that support categories within the DuPont model in **Demo 5-4C**.

Component Analysis of DuPont Model **LO5-4** **Demo 5-4A**

Demo MBC

Selected information from **Nike Inc.**'s annual report on Form 10-K follows. Compute the following ratios in the DuPont model as applied to Nike: (a) return on equity, (b) return on assets, (c) financial leverage, (d) profit margin, and (e) asset turnover.

$ millions	**2015**
Average total assets	$20,097
Average stockholders' equity	11,766
Net sales	30,601
Net income	3,273

continued

continued from previous page

Solution

a. **Return on Equity (ROE)** ROE for Nike follows and indicates that shareholders earned a 28% return on investment.

$$\text{Return on Equity} = \frac{\text{Net income}}{\text{Average stockholders' equity*}} = \frac{\$3{,}273}{\$11{,}766} = 28\%$$

*Average stockholders' equity is calculated by adding Nike's May 31, 2014, and May 31, 2015, stockholders' equity balances ($10,824 and $12,707, respectively) and dividing by 2. Amounts are included in Nike's annual reported accessible through https://www.nike.com/us/en_us/.

b. **Return on Assets (ROA)** Return on assets for Nike is computed as follows and indicates that Nike earned 16 cents on every dollar invested in assets.

$$\text{Return on Assets} = \frac{\text{Net income}}{\text{Average total assets*}} = \frac{\$3{,}273}{\$20{,}097} = 16\%$$

*Average assets is calculated by adding Nike's May 31, 2014, and May 31, 2015, asset balances ($18,594 and $21,600, respectively) and dividing by 2.

c. **Financial Leverage** Financial leverage for Nike is computed as follows.

$$\text{Financial Leverage} = \frac{\text{Average total assets}}{\text{Average stockholders' equity}} = \frac{\$20{,}097}{\$11{,}766} = 1.71$$

For Nike, average liabilities total $8,331 (computed as average assets less average equity, or $20,097 − $11,766, using the balance sheet equation). If Nike holds constant average assets, but increases equity to $13,000 then liabilities would decline to $7,097, and the financial leverage ratio would decline to 1.55. Conversely, if Nike decreases equity to $11,000, the financial leverage ratio would increase to 1.83. When liabilities equal total stockholders' equity, the financial leverage ratio is 2.0. The higher the financial leverage, the more the company relies on debt over equity financing. Risk increases with higher leverage because failure to service debt can result in bankruptcy. These ratios for Nike are summarized below:

Analysis of Financial Leverage for Nike Inc.

Case	Assets	Stockholders' Equity	Liabilities	Financial Leverage
Less debt	$20,097	$13,000	$ 7,097	1.55
Current debt and equity . . .	**20,097**	**11,766**	**8,331**	**1.71**
More debt	20,097	11,000	9,097	1.83
Equal debt and equity.	20,097	10,048	10,049	2.00

d. **Profit Margin** Nike's profit margin calculation is shown below and indicates that it earned 11 cents of income for each sales dollar.

$$\text{Profit Margin} = \frac{\text{Net income}}{\text{Net sales}} = \frac{\$3{,}273}{\$30{,}601} = 11\%$$

e. **Asset Turnover** Nike's asset turnover ratio is shown below and indicates that $1.52 in sales was generated for each asset dollar invested.

$$\text{Asset Turnover} = \frac{\text{Net sales}}{\text{Average total assets}} = \frac{\$30{,}601}{\$20{,}097} = 1.52$$

Integration of DuPont Model Components

Return on equity increases with profitability, leverage, and asset turnover, as long as the company is profitable and reports a positive balance in stockholders' equity. **Exhibit 5-5** combines the ratios for Nike within the DuPont model to show a **first level analysis**. The return on equity of 28% is *disaggregated* into the equation Profitability times Leverage: 16% × 1.7 = 28% (rounded). It can be further disaggregated into the equation Profitability times Activity times Leverage: 11% × 1.52 × 1.7 = 28% (rounded).

An interesting implication of this model is that management can work toward increasing ROE through initiatives that improve profit margin and asset turnover, while also taking steps to manage leverage. Focusing on each of the drivers of ROE provides opportunities for management to improve financial results.

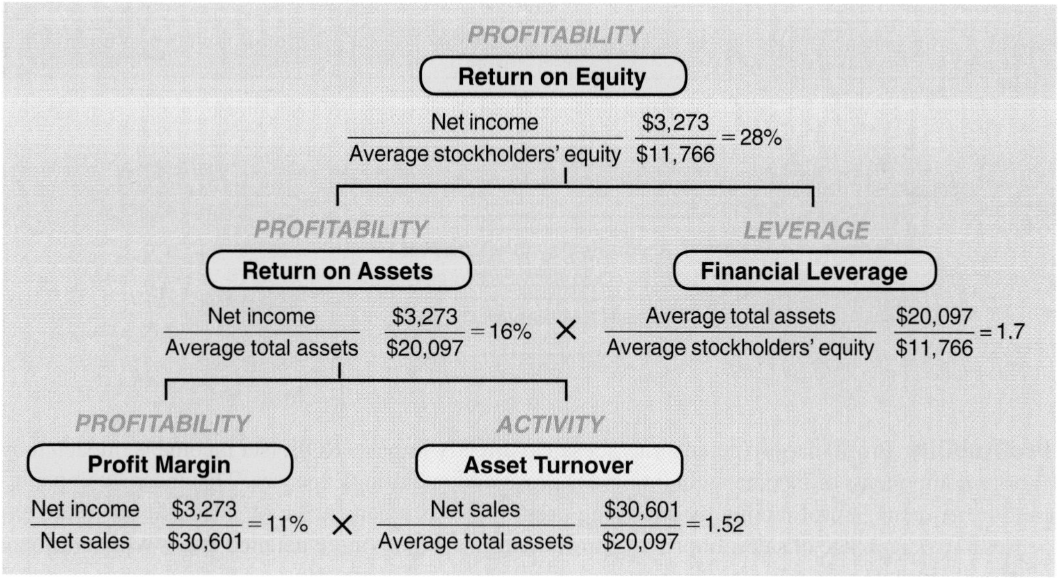

EXHIBIT 5-5
First Level Analysis of the Disaggregation of Return on Equity

Integration Analysis of DuPont Model Components

LO5-4 **Demo 5-4B**

Demo MBC

Return on equity can be disaggregated into its components of profitability (profit margin), activity (asset turnover), and leverage (financial leverage). Demonstrate how the product of the components is equal to return on equity for Nike.

Solution

Components of Return on Equity								
A		**B**		**A × B**		**C**		**A × B × C**
Profit Margin		**Asset Turnover**		**Return on Assets**		**Financial Leverage**		**Return on Equity**
11%	×	1.5	=	16.5%	×	1.7	=	28%

We see how changes in the components of the return on equity (due to changes in assets, stockholders' equity, sales, or net income) can impact ROE. For example, changes in financial results can cause an increase in asset turnover, which could improve return on equity. Alternatively, an increase in financial leverage or profit margin can cause return on equity to increase. In some cases, adjustments to financial results impact more than one ratio. The challenge for management is to find the right balance of profitability, activity, and leverage that produces the largest return for shareholders.

Additional Layers of the DuPont Model

We have reviewed how profitability, activity, and leverage all impact return on equity. **Exhibit 5-6** shows how we can further dissect these three components by assessing factors that influence them. Many other ratios can be examined when we move to detailed analysis of financial statement components. For now, we focus on commonly used ratios.

EXHIBIT 5-6
Supporting Ratios—DuPont Model

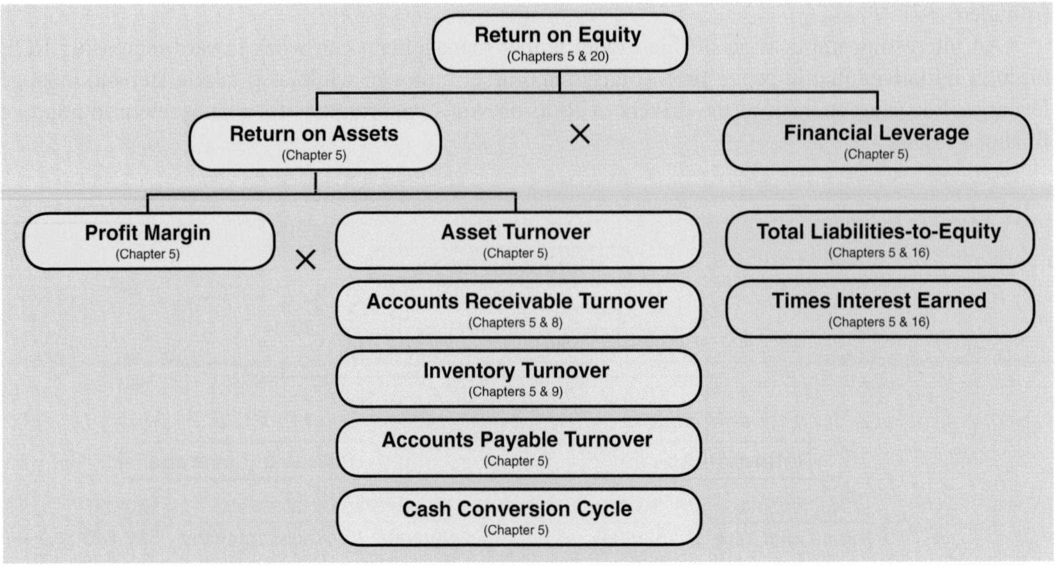

Profitability Profit margin (net income/net sales) directly impacts ROE. Net income is impacted by various components of income including gross profit and operating expenses. This means companies can further manage profitability by analyzing gross profit as a percentage of sales and operating expenses as a percentage of sales. Improving profit margins at these more detailed levels will contribute to improvements in overall profit margin.

Leverage While a high return on equity is desirable, a company will not increase debt to the maximum levels possible to maximize its return on equity through leverage. Although debt can be a cost effective means of funding, which is beneficial to stockholders, an increase in debt increases required debt payments thus increasing the risk of default. A company must balance the maintenance of a satisfactory return to shareholders with the risk of default due to added debt. We examine two ratios, total liabilities-to-equity and times interest earned, from a creditor perspective in the next section to help us here.

Activity We explained how asset turnover (net sales/total assets) directly impacts ROE. However, a more detailed analysis would examine the activity of major asset categories. Improvements in activity of major asset categories will contribute to improvements in the overall asset turnover ratio. In **Demo 5-4C**, we examine the categories of receivables, inventory, and payables. There are other categories that we examine later such as equipment (analyzed through the fixed asset turnover ratio discussed in Chapter 12).

$$\frac{\text{Net credit sales}}{\text{Average accounts receivable}}$$

- **Accounts receivable turnover** measures, on average, how effectively companies use customer credit. Extending credit can increase sales, but can also lead to credit losses. Accounts receivable turnover is affected by a number of factors including changes in credit policies. For example, if sales are not affected, changing payment terms from 60 days to 45 days would increase the accounts receivable turnover due to the more rapid collection of accounts receivable balances. Other things equal, increasing accounts receivable turnover increases overall asset turnover.

$$\frac{365}{\text{Acounts receivable turnover}}$$

- **Average days to collect receivables** is the accounts receivable turnover expressed in days. In other words, it estimates the average collection period.
- **Inventory turnover** measures the number of times, on average, that inventory is sold and replaced during the period. A low inventory turnover ratio may mean the company has excess

amounts invested in inventory, risking damage, obsolescence, and exposure to fluctuating market prices. If inventory turnover is too high, the company risks not having enough stock to meet customer demand. Other things equal, increasing the inventory turnover results in an increase in overall asset turnover.

$\frac{\text{Cost of good sold}}{\text{Average inventory}}$

- **Average days in inventory** is the inventory turnover expressed in days. In other words, it estimates the average holding period of inventory.

$\frac{365}{\text{Inventory turnover}}$

- **Accounts payable turnover** measures the rate at which a company pays off its suppliers during the period. An increase in the accounts payable turnover ratio indicates that a company is paying amounts due to suppliers at a faster rate. However, delaying payment to suppliers resulting in a decrease in accounts payable turnover reduces required cash levels at any given time (given no other changes).

$\frac{\text{Cost of goods sold}}{\text{Average acounts payable}}$

- **Average days payable outstanding** is the accounts payable turnover expressed in days. In other words, it estimates the average payment terms.

$\frac{365}{\text{Acounts payable turnover}}$

- **Cash conversion cycle** measures the average time (in days) to sell inventories, collect the receivables from the sale, pay the payables incurred for the inventory purchase, and return to cash. It is calculated by adding average days to collect receivables and average days in inventory and then subtracting average days payable outstanding. Management strives to decrease the cash conversion cycle because each time a cash conversion cycle is completed, a company generates both profit and cash flow. Reducing a cash conversion cycle can be achieved by collecting receivables more quickly, selling inventory more quickly, and/or delaying payment on payables. The median cash conversion cycle for all publicly traded companies was 62 days in 2015.

Average days to collect receivables
+ Average days in inventory
− Average days payables outstanding
= Cash conversion cycle

Additional Layer Analysis of DuPont Model

LO5-4 **Demo 5-4C**

Demo MBC

Additional financial statement information for Nike follows. Compute the following *activity ratios*: (a) accounts receivable turnover and average days to collect receivables, (b) inventory turnover and average days in inventory, (c) accounts payable turnover and average days payable outstanding, and (d) cash conversion cycle.

$ millions	**2015**
Average accounts receivable	$ 3,396
Average inventory	4,142
Average accounts payable	2,031
Net sales	30,601
Cost of goods sold	16,534

Solution

a. **Accounts Receivable Turnover and Average Days to Collect Receivables** For Nike, **accounts receivable turnover** indicates that on average, receivables are collected 9.0 times during the year.The **average days to collect receivables** indicates that accounts receivable were outstanding, on average, for 41 days before collection.

$$\text{Accounts Receivable Turnover} = \frac{\text{Net credit sales}}{\text{Average accounts receivable (gross)}} = \frac{\$30{,}601}{\$3{,}396} = 9.0$$

$$\text{Average Days to Collect Receivables} = \frac{\text{365 days}}{\text{Accounts receivable turnover}} = \frac{365}{9.0} = 41\,\text{days}$$

b. **Inventory Turnover and Average Days in Inventory** The **inventory turnover** for Nike is 4.0 indicating that on average, inventory was sold 4.0 times during the year. The **average days in inventory** of 91 days means that inventory sat for 91 days, on average, before being sold.

continued

continued from previous page

$$\text{Inventory Turnover} = \frac{\text{Cost of goods sold}}{\text{Average inventory}} = \frac{\$16{,}534}{\$4{,}142} = 4.0$$

$$\text{Average Days in Inventory} = \frac{365 \text{ days}}{\text{Inventory turnover}} = \frac{365}{4.0} = 91 \text{ days}$$

c. **Accounts Payable Turnover and Average Days Payable Outstanding** The **accounts payable turnover** for Nike is 8.1 indicating that on average, NIKE paid off its suppliers 8.1 times during the year. The **average days payable outstanding** of 45 means that accounts payable was outstanding for 45 days, on average, before being paid.

$$\text{Accounts Payable Turnover} = \frac{\text{Cost of goods sold}}{\text{Average accounts payable}} = \frac{\$16{,}534}{\$2{,}031} = 8.1$$

$$\text{Average Days Payable Outstanding} = \frac{365 \text{ days}}{\text{Accounts payable turnover}} = \frac{365}{8.1} = 45 \text{ days}$$

d. **Cash Conversion Cycle** The **cash conversion cycle** for Nike is 87 days, indicating a cycle of 87 days from the time cash is used to purchase inventory until cash is collected on the sale of the inventory.

$$\textbf{Cash Conversion Cycle} = \text{Average days to collect receivables} + \text{Average days in inventory} - \text{Average days payable outstanding}$$

$$= 41 \text{ days} + 91 \text{ days} - 45 \text{ days} = 87 \text{ days}$$

REVIEW 5-4 LO5-4 Investment Analysis Using DuPont Framework

Fastenal Inc. is a wholesale distributor of industrial and construction supplies with stores located primarily in North America. The following information is in a recent annual report on Form 10-K.

$ millions	December 31, 2015	December 31, 2016
Net sales	$3,869	$3,962
Cost of sales	1,920	1,997
Net income	516	499
Accounts receivable	468	500
Inventories	913	993
Total assets	2,532	2,669
Accounts payable	126	109
Total liabilities	731	736
Stockholders' equity	1,801	1,933

a. Calculate the return on equity for 2016.

b. Disaggregate the 2016 return on equity into its DuPont components of profitability (profit margin), activity (asset turnover) and leverage (financial leverage). Demonstrate how the product of the components is equal to return on equity.

c. Compute the following activity ratios for 2016: (1) accounts receivable turnover, (2) inventory turnover, and (3) accounts payable turnover.

More Practice: 5-47, 5-48
Solution on p. 5-64.

Perform a credit analysis using key ratios

LO 5-5

Credit Analysis
- Liquidity ratios
  - Current ratio
  - Quick ratio
  - Current cash debt coverage
- Solvency ratios
  - Total liabilities-to-equity
  - Times interest earned
  - Cash debt coverage
  - Free cash flow

LO 5-5 Overview

While the prior section focused mainly on investment analysis, this section focuses mainly on credit analysis. Creditors such as banks, public debt investors, and private lenders, focus on the return of principal plus interest. **Creditors supply capital to businesses and in return expect repayment plus interest where the repayment terms and interest rate are set by a debt contract.** For creditors, there are fewer opportunities for gains beyond amounts specified by the debt contract. So, although ratios described under investment equity analysis are relevant to creditors, more attention is focused on liquidity and solvency measures.

Liquidity is a measure of the availability of cash for *short-term needs.* Creditors are at risk for nonpayment, so measures that focus on a company's ability to pay required interest are critical. Ratios help creditors to quickly respond to threats of nonpayment. Common liquidity ratios include the current ratio, working capital, quick ratio, and current cash debt coverage. We apply these ratios in **Demo 5-5A**.

- **Current Ratio** is a measure of short-term liquidity. It indicates a company's ability to meet short-term obligations from current assets. Investors and creditors use this ratio to assess whether a company has the ability to pay debts coming due within the year.

  $\frac{\text{Current assets}}{\text{Current liabilities}}$

- **Working Capital** is a variation to the current ratio. As with the current ratio, comparing current obligations with current resources allows investors and creditors a means to assess a company's ability to satisfy short-term obligations when due.

  Current assets − Current liabilities

- **Quick Ratio** is a liquidity ratio that only includes the most liquid assets of cash, short-term investments (marketable securities), and accounts receivable. The purpose of the quick ratio is to analyze a company's ability to pay its current debts with only its most liquid assets. This ratio is a more rigorous test of liquidity than the current ratio.

  $\frac{\text{Cash + Market securities + Receivables}}{\text{Current liabilities}}$

- **Current Cash Debt Coverage** measures whether a company can pay its current debts with cash provided from operating activities. An entity's liquidity is dependent on its ability to generate additional cash to cover debt payments. A higher ratio means a company is generating more cash flow relative to current obligations.

  $\frac{\text{Cash provided by operating activities}}{\text{Average current liabilities}}$

Solvency refers to a company's ability to satisfy its obligations to creditors. Solvency is essential to the economic survival of a company over time. Solvency ratios include static, or balance sheet based ratios. Solvency ratios also include flow measures, referred to as coverage ratios. These ratios measure a company's risk of being unable to make required principal and interest payments. As equity approaches zero, the liabilities to equity of the company is considered insolvent and the liabilities to equity ratio is undefined, which can eventually lead to bankruptcy. We apply certain of these solvency ratios in **Demo 5-5B**.

- **Total liabilities-to-equity** measures the proportion of liabilities to equity in a company's capital structure. It indicates how much a company relies on debt financing compared to equity financing. As the liabilities-to-equity ratio increases, risk increases and solvency decreases. A ratio greater than 1.0 indicates that total liabilities exceed total stockholders' equity.

  $\frac{\text{Total liabilities}}{\text{Total stockholders' equity}}$

- **Times interest earned** measures the profit before tax that is available to make required interest payments. Income before taxes and interest expense is divided by gross interest expense (without an offset by interest revenue). This measure assumes that interest is the only required payment because the principal would be refinanced when due. As the times interest earned ratio increases, risk decreases and solvency increases.

  $\frac{\text{Income before interest and taxes}}{\text{Interest expense}}$

- **Cash debt coverage** measures a company's ability to pay debts with cash provided from operating activities. Increases to this ratio indicate more flexibility in that a company is better able to pay off obligations without liquidating assets or incurring additional liabilities.

  $\frac{\text{Cash provided by operating activities}}{\text{Average total liabilities}}$

- **Free cash flow** measures the discretionary cash that a company has to invest in long term assets, to retire debt, or to make distributions to shareholders. In calculating free cash flow, capital expenditures are deducted as these are typically necessary costs to continue operations and to

  Cash provided by operating activities − Capital expenditures − Cash dividends

remain competitive. Likewise, companies usually maintain a steady dividend payment if a dividend policy has been established or followed. The remaining cash flow from operations (if any) is considered to be the amount of cash that is available for discretionary purposes such as debt reduction or new investment purchases. The higher the free cash flow, the more flexibility a company has in making cash flow decisions and the higher the tolerance for unexpected events such as an economic downturn or a new investment opportunity.

Accounting information is important in assessing a company's liquidity and solvency and this relation is reinforced in the FASB Concept Statement.

SFAC No. 8 OB13 Information about the nature and amounts of a reporting entity's economic resources and claims can help users to identify the reporting entity's financial strengths and weaknesses. That information can help users to assess the reporting entity's liquidity and solvency, its needs for additional financing, and how successful it is likely to be in obtaining that financing. Information about priorities and payment requirements of existing claims helps users to predict how future cash flows will be distributed among those with a claim against the reporting entity.

Financial statement users can identify the financial strengths and weaknesses of a company through information reported on the company's economic resources and claims to those resources. Accounting information is also useful in predicting a company's need for and ability to obtain additional financing. To this end, liquidity and solvency ratios help creditors assess the risk of receiving interest and principal payments.

Demo 5-5A LO5-5 Liquidity Ratios

Demo MBC

The following additional information is from the 2015 Form 10-K of **Nike Inc.** ($ millions). Compute the following liquidity ratios: (a) current ratio, (b) quick ratio, and (c) current cash debt coverage.

Current assets	$15,976	Short term investments	$2,072
Current liabilities	6,334	Cash provided by operations	4,680
Cash and cash equivalents	3,852	Average current liabilities	5,681
Accounts receivable	3,358		

Solution

Current Ratio Nike's **current ratio** of 2.5 indicates that the company had $2.50 of current assets for every $1.00 of current liabilities.

$$\text{Current Ratio} = \frac{\text{Current assets}}{\text{Current liabilities}} = \frac{\$15,976}{\$6,334} = 2.5$$

Quick Ratio Cash and cash equivalents ($3,852) plus short-term investments ($2,072), plus accounts receivable ($3,358) divided by current liabilities ($6,334) equals 1.5. Nike's **quick ratio** of 1.5 means that it had $1.50 of very liquid assets for every $1.00 of current liabilities.

$$\textbf{Quick Ratio} = \frac{\text{Cash} + \text{Marketable securities} + \text{Accounts receivable}}{\text{Current liabilities}} = \frac{\$9,282}{\$6,334} = 1.5$$

Current Cash Debt Coverage Nike's **current cash debt coverage ratio** is 0.82, meaning it was able to pay off $0.82 for every $1.00 of current liabilities with cash provided by operating activities.

$$\text{Current Cash Debt Coverage} = \frac{\text{Cash provided by operating activities}}{\text{Average current liabilities}} = \frac{\$4,680}{\$5,681} = 0.82$$

Solvency Ratios

LO5-5 **Demo 5-5B**

Demo MBC

The following additional information is from the 2015 Form 10-K of Nike Inc. ($ millions). Compute the following solvency ratios: (a) total liabilities-to-equity, (b) times interest earned, (c) cash debt coverage, and (d) free cash flow.

Total liabilities	$ 8,893	Interest expense	$ 60
Average total liabilities	8,332	Cash provided by operations	4,680
Total stockholders' equity	12,707	Cash paid for capital expenditures	963
Income before taxes and interest expense	4,233	Cash paid for dividends	899

Solution

Total Liabilities-to-Equity The **total liabilities-to-equity** ratio indicates that Nike was financed with approximately $0.70 of liabilities for each $1.00 of stockholders'equity.

$$\text{Total Liabilities-to-Equity} = \frac{\text{Total liabilities}}{\text{Total stockholders' equity}} = \frac{\$8,893}{\$12,707} = 0.70$$

Times Interest Earned Nike has a high **times interest earned** ratio of 70.6, indicating it had ample profit available to pay its required interest payments.

$$\text{Times Interest Earned} = \frac{\text{Income before taxes and interest expense}}{\text{Interest expense, gross}} = \frac{\$4,233}{\$60} = 70.6$$

Cash Debt Coverage Nike's **cash debt coverage** ratio is 0.56 indicating that it had $.56 in cash generated from operating activities for every dollar of debt.

$$\text{Cash Debt Coverage} = \frac{\text{Cash provided by operating activities}}{\text{Average total liabilities}} = \frac{\$4,680}{\$8,332} = 0.56$$

Free Cash Flow Nike's **free cash flow** is $2,818 ($4,680 − $963 − $899) indicating a surplus in cash generated from operating activities after paying for capital expenditures and dividends for the period.

$$\text{Free Cash Flow} = \text{Cash provided by operating activities} - \text{Capital expenditures} - \text{Cash dividends} = \$2,818$$

EXPANDING YOUR KNOWLEDGE

Credit Ratings

Independent agencies provide opinions regarding the ability of companies to repay obligations when they become due. This opinion of a company's creditworthiness is a *credit rating*, which is based on company, industry, and economic factors. Company ratios are some of the most important factors. Moody's Investor Services is one of the more influential credit rating agencies. Moody's highest credit rating is Aaa for an investment grade security. Moody's lowest rating for a speculative grade investment is a C, which typically means the company is in default. Ratings are crucial to a company because they affect the cost of the company's debt and the interest rate that the company must pay. Ratios used by Moody's are published along with definitions. The following table has a selection of Moody's ratios that are similar to those in this chapter. We see that analysts such as Moody's adjust ratios to fit their needs. Ratios are flexible in this regard. We also see the median value for top-rated companies (Moody's reports this for all grades). For example, for every $1 invested in assets of an Aaa rated company, it generates 20.9 cents of EBITA.

continued

continued from previous page

Moody's Ratio	**Formula**	**Aaa Rated Median**	**Similar Ratio: Chapter 5 Ratio**	**Similar Ratio: Formula**
EBITA**/Average Assets	EBITA (Earnings before interest, taxes, depreciation, amortization) / Average of Current and Previous Year Assets	20.9%	Return on assets	Net income / Average total assets
EBITA Margin	EBITA / Net Revenue	25.1%	Profit margin	Net income / Sales
EBITA/Interest Expense	EBITA / Interest Expense	28.90	Times interest earned	Income before interest and taxes / Interest expense, gross
Funds from Operations/Debt	Funds From Operations / (Short-Term Debt + Long-Term Debt)	133.5%	Cash debt coverage	Operating cash flows / Average total liabilities
Debt/Book Capitalization	(Short-Term Debt + Long-Term Debt) / (Short-Term Debt + Long-Term Debt + Deferred Taxes + Minority Interest + Book Equity)	19.3%	Total liabilities-to-assets	Total liabilities / Total assets

* Moody's data retrieved from 2013 median values using Moody's Financial Metrics™ Key Ratios By Rating And Industry For North American Nonfinancial Corporations: December 2013 (Excel Data Supplement).

** EBITA is defined as earnings from continuing operations before interest, taxes, and amortization.

REVIEW 5-5 **LO5-5** **Credit Analysis Using Key Ratios**

Review MBC

Calculate the following measures for **Fastenal Inc.** for 2016 using the information provided in Review 5-4 and the additional information provided below from a recent annual report on Form 10-K.

Liquidity: (a) current ratio, (b) quick ratio, and (c) current cash debt coverage.

Solvency: (d) total liabilities-to-equity, (e) times interest earned, (f) cash debt coverage, and (g) free cash flow.

$ millions	**December 31, 2015**	**December 31, 2016**
Net cash provided by operating activities....	$ 547	$ 514
Capital expenditures....................	155	190
Cash dividends.........................	327	347
Cash and cash equivalents	129	113
Marketable securities...................	0	0
Current assets	1,665	1,721
Current liabilities......................	373	276
Interest expense.......................	3	7
Income before taxes and interest expense...	829	796

More Practice: 5-51, 5-52, 5-53

Solution on p. 5-64.

Summary of Financial Statement Ratios

Financial ratios can be organized into four categories: profitability, activity, solvency, and liquidity. **Exhibit 5-7** provides a summary of ratios from this chapter along with references to later discussions. We also cover additional ratios in later chapters such as the profitability ratios of **earnings per share** (Chapter 21), **price-to-earnings ratio** (Chapter 20), and **payout ratio** (Chapter 20); and solvency ratios of **book value per share** (Chapter 20) and **total liabilities-to-total assets** (Chapter 16).

NIKE

Real World—PUBLISHED FINANCIAL STATEMENT RATIOS

NIKE [NKE]

Nike Inc. reported the following ratios in the Selected Financial Data section of its 2015 annual report on Form 10-K. The ratios are a mix of profitability, activity, and liquidity ratios.

Profitability ratios:	Return on equity, return on assets
Activity ratios:	Inventory turns
Liquidity ratio:	Current ratio

Financial History	2015	2014	2013	2012	2011
Return on equity	27.8%	24.6%	23.1%	22.0%	21.8%
Return on assets	16.3%	14.9%	15.3%	15.1%	15.0%
Inventory turns	4.0	4.1	4.2	4.5	4.8
Current ratio at May 31	2.5	2.7	3.5	3.0	2.9

EXHIBIT 5-7
Summary of Financial Statement Ratios

Ratio	Formula	Focus	Chapter
Profitability: Focus on profit generation			
1. Return on equity	Net income / Average stockholders' equity	Return on investments made by owners	Chapters 5, 20
2. Return on assets	Net income / Average total assets	Return on all assets, regardless of how financed	Chapter 5
3. Profit margin	Net income / Net sales	Profitability of each dollar of sales revenue	Chapter 5
Activity: Focus on productivity (activity) of assets			
4. Asset turnover	Net sales / Average total assets	Efficiency of asset utilization	Chapter 5
5. Accounts receivable turnover	Net credit sales / Average accounts receivable	Efficiency of credit policies and collection of trade accounts	Chapters 5, 8
6. Average days to collect receivables	365 / Accounts receivable turnover	Average number of days to collect receivables	Chapters 5, 8
7. Inventory turnover	Cost of goods sold / Average inventory	Number of times inventory was sold during the period	Chapters 5, 9
8. Average days in inventory	365 / Inventory turnover	Average number of days inventory is held	Chapters 5, 9
9. Fixed asset turnover ratio	Net sales / Average fixed assets	Efficiency of fixed asset utilization	Chapters 5, 12
10. Accounts payable turnover	Cost of goods sold / Average accounts payable	Number of times a company pays off its supplier during the period	Chapter 5
11. Average days payable outstanding	365 / Accounts payable turnover	Average number of days it takes for a company to pay off its invoices from suppliers	Chapter 5
12. Cash conversion cycle	Average days to collect receivables + Average days in inventory − Average days payable outstanding	Measures the days to convert cash to inventories, receivables to cash, cash to payables	Chapter 5
Solvency: Focus on long-term financial viability			
13. Financial leverage	Average total assets / Average stockholders' equity	Proportion of assets provided by creditors relative to owners	Chapter 5
14. Total liabilities-to-equity	Total liabilities / Total stockholders' equity	Proportion of resources provided by creditors relative to owners	Chapters 5, 16
15. Times interest earned	Income before interest and taxes / Interest expense, gross	Number of times income could pay for interest	Chapters 5, 16
16. Cash debt coverage	Cash provided by operating activities / Average total liabilities	Measures ability to pay debt with yearly cash flow	Chapter 5
17. Free cash flow	Cash Provided by operating activities − Capital expenditures − Cash dividends	Measures cash generated after capital investments and dividend payments	Chapter 5

continued

continued from previous page

Ratio	Formula	Focus	Chapter
Liquidity: Focus on short-term debt paying ability			
18. Current ratio	Current assets / Current liabilities	Test of short-term liquidity	Chapters 5, 15
19. Quick ratio	(Cash + Marketable securities + Receivables) / Current liabilities	Rigorous test of short-term liquidity	Chapters 5, 15
20. Working capital	Current assets − Current liabilities	Test of short-term liquidity	Chapters 4, 5
21. Current cash debt coverage	Cash provided by operating activities / Average current liabilities	Measures ability to pay current debt with yearly cash flow	Chapter 5

LO 5-6 Perform horizontal and vertical analyses

LO 5-6 Overview

Financial Statement Analyses
- **Horizontal Analysis**
  - Percentage change/Base period amount
- **Vertical Analysis**
  - ***Balance sheet***
    Balance sheet amount/Total assets
  - ***Income statement***
    Income statement amount/Total revenue

Horizontal analysis, or **trend analysis**, is a tool to examine financial statement information across time by examining changes, often presented as percentages. The percentage change is calculated by dividing the dollar change by the base period amount. **Demo 5-6A** illustrates this.

Vertical analysis, or **common size analysis**, is a tool used to examine individual financial statement items (or a group of items) relative to a base amount. In the income statement, a typical base is *total revenue* while in the balance sheet, a typical base is *total assets*. **Demo 5-6B** illustrates this.

Demo 5-6A LO5-6 Horizontal Analysis

Demo MBC

Following are the balance sheets for Lakers Inc. as of December 31, 2019, and 2020, along with the income statements for the years ended December 31, 2019, and 2020. Prepare a horizontal analysis of the balance sheet and the income statement of Lakers Inc.

Solution

Lakers Inc.
Balance Sheets

At December 31	2019	2020	Dollar Change	Percentage Change
Current assets	$ 73,000	$111,000	**$38,000**	**52%**
Noncurrent assets	62,000	81,000	**19,000**	**31**
Total assets	$135,000	$192,000	**$57,000**	**42**
Current liabilities	$ 3,000	$ 5,000	**$ 2,000**	**67%**
Noncurrent liabilities	46,000	40,000	**(6,000)**	**(13)**
Stockholders' equity	86,000	147,000	**61,000**	**71**
Total liabilities and stockholders' equity	$135,000	$192,000	**$57,000**	**42**

Horizontal analysis includes a dollar change over the year, computed by subracting the December 31, 2019, balance from the December 31, 2020, balance. The percentage change is calculated by dividing the dollar change by the base period (December 31, 2019, amount). For example, the dollar change in current assets of $38,000 is equal to $111,000 less $73,000. The percentage change in current assets of 52% is computed by dividing $38,000 by $73,000. The same steps are applied to the income statement below.

continued

continued from previous page

Lakers Inc.
Income Statement

For Years Ended December 31	2019	2020	Dollar Change	Percentage Change
Sales	$62,000	$66,000	$ 4,000	6%
Expenses	39,000	44,000	5,000	13
Net income	$23,000	$22,000	$(1,000)	–4

Vertical Analysis

LO5-6 **Demo 5-6B**

Demo MBC

The balance sheets as of December 31, 2019, and December 31, 2020, follow for Lakers Inc. along with the income statements for the years ended December 31, 2019, and 2020. Prepare a vertical analysis of the balance sheet and the income statement of Lakers Inc.

Solution

Balance sheet: For 2019, the percentages are calculated by dividing each balance sheet amount by total assets ($135,000). For 2020, the percentages are calculated by dividing each balance sheet amount by total assets ($192,000).

Income statement: For 2019, the percentages are calculated by dividing each income statement amount by total revenue ($62,000). For 2020, the percentages are calculated by dividing each income statement amount by total revenue ($66,000).

LAKERS INC.
Balance Sheets

At December 31	2019	2020	Percentage of 2019 Assets	Percentage of 2020 Assets
Current assets	$ 73,000	$111,000	54%	58%
Noncurrent assets	62,000	81,000	46%	42%
Total assets	$135,000	$192,000	100%	100%
Current liabilities	$ 3,000	$ 5,000	2%	3%
Noncurrent liabilities	46,000	40,000	34%	21%
Stockholders' equity	86,000	147,000	64%	76%
Total liabilities and stockholders' equity	$135,000	$192,000	100%	100%

LAKERS INC.
Income Statements

For Years Ended December 31	2019	2020	Dollar Change	Percentage of 2019 Revenue	Percentage of 2020 Revenue
Sales	$62,000	$66,000	$ 4,000	100%	100%
Expenses	39,000	44,000	5,000	−63%	−67%
Net income	$23,000	$22,000	$(1,000)	37%	33%

REVIEW 5-6 **LO5-6** **Horizontal and Vertical Analyses**

Review MBC

Prepare a horizontal analysis and a vertical analysis of the balance sheets and income statements for Fastenal Company below ($ millions).

Income Statement	2016	2015
Revenues	$3,962	$3,869
Costs of goods sold	1,997	1,920
Gross margin	1,965	1,949
Operating expenses	1,169	1,120
Operating income	$ 796	$ 829

Balance Sheet	2016	2015
Current assets	$1,721	$1,665
Noncurrent assets	948	867
Total assets	$2,669	$2,532
Current liabilities	$ 276	$ 373
Noncurrent liabilities	460	358
Total liabilities	736	731
Stockholders' equity	1,933	1,801
Total liabilities and stockholders' equity	$2,669	$2,532

More Practice:
5-34, 5-57
Solution on p. 5-64.

LO 5-7 Recognize non-GAAP financial measures

LO 5-7 Overview

Non-GAAP Financial Measures

- Information **not** presented in accordance with GAAP
- Information *voluntarily* presented as management interpretation
    - Included in the MD&A section, press release, and so forth
    - Not included in the financial statements and accompanying notes
    - Requires a reconciliation between the non-GAAP measure and the closest GAAP measure

Non-GAAP financial measures provide information to financial statement users that management would like to convey. A non-GAAP measure is based upon assumptions that deviate from GAAP. For example a pro forma income disclosure may present earnings of the company excluding nonrecurring gains and losses the company considers unusual and infrequent. Another example of a non-GAAP measure is the reporting of an industry specific ratio. **These disclosures are not calculated or presented in accordance with GAAP and have no defined meaning or uniform characteristics.** The Securities and Exchange Commission defines a non-GAAP financial measure in its Regulation G: Conditions for Use of Non-GAAP Financial Measures.

SEC Regulation G For purposes of Regulation G, a non-GAAP financial measure is a numerical measure of a registrant's historical or future financial performance, financial position or cash flows that: excludes amounts, or is subject to adjustments that have the effect of excluding amounts, that are included in the most directly comparable measure calculated and presented in accordance with GAAP in the statement of income, balance sheet or statement of cash flows (or equivalent statements) of the issuer; or includes amounts, or is subject to adjustments that have the effect of including amounts, that are excluded from the most directly comparable measure so calculated and presented.

Why would management wish to report non-GAAP measures? Where would this information appear in the annual report on Form 10-K? We will address these and other aspects of non-GAAP disclosures in this section. Having the ability to identify non-GAAP disclosures is critical due to their lack of standardization. Although non-GAAP disclosures were once infrequent, in recent years, they have become common in quarterly and annual financial reporting.

Let's begin by looking at a non-GAAP disclosure recently reported by Macy's in its Form 10-K. We will use this example to help explain non-GAAP disclosures.

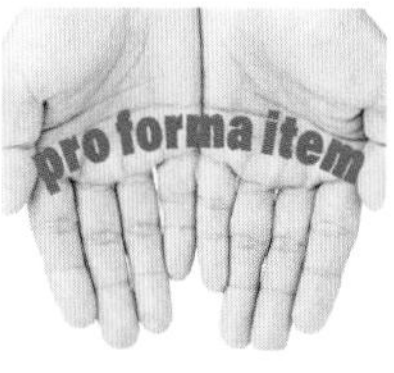

Examples of Non-GAAP Disclosures

In the Management's Discussion and Analysis of Financial Condition and Results of Operations section (MD&A) of the Form 10-K report, Macy's Inc. provides an overview of the company's operation for 2015. **Exhibit 5-8** has an excerpt from that overview.

> Adjusted EBITDA (earnings before interest, taxes, depreciation and amortization, impairments, store closing and other costs) as a percent to net sales was 12.5% in 2015, as compared to 14.0% in 2014.

EXHIBIT 5-8
MD&A Section of Macy's Inc. (from its 2015 Overview)

This excerpt does not use terms defined in GAAP such as income from continuing operations or gross profit. Instead, Macy's Inc. chose to describe a change based upon EBITDA, which is a non-GAAP measure. Because a non-GAAP disclosure is essentially any voluntary disclosure that falls outside of a GAAP standard, the types of disclosures are endless.

Following are examples of non-GAAP disclosures included in other annual reports of retailers.

- Gap Inc. reported *free cash flow* as a non-GAAP measure. Management asserts that this internal metric is an important driver of business.
- American Eagle Outfitters Inc. reported *non-GAAP earnings* per share, explained as GAAP earnings per share adjusted to remove asset impairments and restructuring charges. Management believes this metric is useful as another means to evaluate company performance.
- Walgreens Boots Alliance Inc. reported *adjusted operating income*, resulting from non-GAAP adjustments to operating income. The adjustments included adding back LIFO provision and a loss on sale of a business. Management asserts that the non-GAAP measure provides additional insights and perspectives about the operating performance of the company from period to period.

As we see from these examples, the types of non-GAAP disclosures vary. What is common, however, is for companies to exclude certain expense and revenues to highlight what they assert are non-recurring revenues and expenses. Each example is consistently and properly identified in the text of the MD&A as a non-GAAP measure. Non-GAAP disclosures must not be reported in audited financial statements or notes accompanying financial statements. They are increasingly seen in the MD&A section, in press releases, and in other reports.

Disclosure Requirements of Non-GAAP Measures

In a later section of its MD&A, Macy's Inc. provides more information on its non-GAAP measure—see **Exhibit 5-9**. In this excerpt, the management of Macy's explains that the company's key motivation for disclosing EBITDA is that it provides additional useful information and facilitates comparisons from period to period. The company explains that the measures are supplemental in nature and are not substitutes for GAAP measures. The company emphasized that the methods used to calculate non-GAAP measures can vary significantly from company to company.

An important point to remember about non-GAAP information is that management is presenting information it believes is useful and should be viewed, beyond the information required under GAAP. This provides management a tremendous amount of latitude in the presentation of information. In response to the reporting of non-GAAP measures, and to protect the interests of financial statement users, the **SEC requires companies to provide a reconciliation between all non-GAAP measures reported and the most directly comparable GAAP measure for each non-GAAP measure**. The required reconciliation (See **Demo 5-7**) allows financial statement users to assess which items were excluded or included to arrive at the non-GAAP measure.

SEC Regulation G Regulation G requires the registrant to provide the following information as part of the disclosure or release of the non-GAAP financial measure: presentation of the most directly comparable financial measure calculated and presented in accordance with GAAP; and a reconciliation (by schedule or other clearly understandable method), which shall be quantitative for historic measures and quantitative, to the extent available without unreasonable efforts, for prospective measures, of the differences between the non-GAAP financial measure presented and the most directly comparable financial measure or measures calculated and presented in accordance with GAAP.

EXHIBIT 5-9
MD&A Section of Macy's Inc.

Important Information Regarding Non-GAAP Financial Measures

The Company reports its financial results in accordance with generally accepted accounting principles ("GAAP"). However, management believes that certain non-GAAP financial measures provide users of the Company's financial information with additional useful information in evaluating operating performance. . . Management believes that excluding certain items that may vary substantially in frequency and magnitude from diluted earnings per share attributable to Macy's Inc. shareholders and from operating income and EBITDA as percentages to sales are useful supplemental measures that assist in evaluating the Company's ability to generate earnings and leverage sales, respectively, and to more readily compare these metrics between past and future periods. Management also believes that EBITDA and Adjusted EBITDA are frequently used by investors and securities analysts in their evaluations of companies, and that such supplemental measures facilitate comparisons between companies that have different capital and financing structures and/or tax rates... Non-GAAP financial measures should be viewed as supplementing, and not as an alternative or substitute for, the Company's financial results prepared in accordance with GAAP. Certain of the items that may be excluded or included in non-GAAP financial measures may be significant items that could impact the Company's financial position, results of operations and cash flows, and should therefore be considered in assessing the Company's actual financial condition and performance. . . The methods used by the Company to calculate its non-GAAP financial measures may differ significantly from methods used by other companies to compute similar measures. As a result, any non-GAAP financial measures presented herein may not be comparable to similar measures provided by other companies.

Demo 5-7 LO5-7 Non-GAAP Disclosures

Demo MBC

An excerpt from the reconciliation for Macy's Inc. located in its MD&A section follows. Based upon the reconciliation of the GAAP measure to the non-GAAP measure provided by Macy's Inc., answer the questions that follow.

Macy's Inc. Reconciliation of GAAP Measure to Non-GAAP Measure	2015
Net Income	**$1,070**
Net Income	$1,070
Add back interest expense—net	361
Add back federal, state and local income tax expense	608
Add back (deduct) impairments, store closing and other costs and gain on sale of leases	288
Add back depreciation and amortization	1,061
Adjusted EBITDA	**$3,388**

Solution

Question	Answer
1. What is the reported non-GAAP measure?	Adjusted EBITDA
2. What is the closest GAAP measure to the reported non-GAAP measure?	Net income
3. How many adjustments are described between the GAAP measure and the reported non-GAAP measure?	Four adjustments are identified: (1) interest expense, (2) taxes, (3) impairments, store closings, and other costs, gain on sale of leases, and (4) depreciation and amortization.
4. Why did Macy's choose to disclose the non-GAAP measure (Refer to **Exhibit 5-9**)?	Management explains that the additional information was included to provide useful information for evaluation of the company and to enhance comparability from period to period.
5. Where is the non-GAAP measure reported?	MD&A Section of the annual report on Form 10-K.

GAP

Real World—FREE CASH FLOW

GAP INC. [GPS]

Gap Inc. reported the following free cash flow in its MD&A section of its recent Form 10-K. Notice that free cash flow is clearly identified as a *non-GAAP financial measure*.

Free Cash Flow Free cash flow is a non-GAAP financial measure. We believe free cash flow is an important metric because it represents a measure of how much cash a company has available for discretionary and non-discretionary items after the deduction of capital expenditures, as we require regular capital expenditures to build and maintain stores and purchase new equipment to improve our business. We use this metric internally, as we believe our sustained ability to generate free cash flow is an important driver of value creation. However, this non-GAAP financial measure is not intended to supersede or replace our GAAP result. The following table reconciles free cash flow, a non-GAAP financial measure, from a GAAP financial measure.

For Fiscal Year Ended ($ millions)	2015	2014	2013
Net cash provided by operating activities	$1,594	$2,129	$1,705
Less: Purchases of property and equipment	(726)	(714)	(670)
Free cash flow	$ 868	$1,415	$1,035

Non-GAAP Disclosures

LO5-7 **REVIEW 5-7**

Review MBC

General Electric reported the following information in its MD&A section of a recent annual report on Form 10-K.

Industrial Segment Organic Operating Profit ($ millions)	2017
Industrial segment profit (GAAP)	$14,740
Adjustments:	
Acquisitions	388
Business dispositions (other than dispositions of businesses acquired for investment)	(84)
Currency exchange rates	4
Industrial segment organic operating profit (Non-GAAP)	$15,048

Industrial segment organic operating profit growth measures industrial segment profit excluding the effects of acquisitions, business dispositions and currency exchange rates. We believe that this measure provides management and investors with a more complete understanding of underlying operating results and trends of established, ongoing operations by excluding the effect of acquisitions, dispositions and currency exchange, which activities are subject to volatility and can obscure underlying trends. We also believe that presenting industrial segment organic operating profit growth separately for our industrial businesses provides management and investors with useful information about the trends of our industrial businesses and enables a more direct comparison to other nonfinancial businesses and companies. Management recognizes that the term "industrial segment organic operating profit growth" may be interpreted differently by other companies and under different circumstances. Although this may have an effect on comparability of absolute percentage growth from company to company, we believe that these measures are useful in assessing trends of the respective businesses or companies and may therefore be a useful tool in assessing period-to-period performance trends.

Required

a. What is the non-GAAP measure that is reported?

b. What GAAP measure is used in the reconciliation to compare to the non-GAAP measure?

c. Why is this disclosure included in the MD&A section of the Form 10-K and not in the notes accompanying the financial statements?

d. Why is this non-GAAP measure reported?

More Practice: 5-36, 5-58, 5-59, 5-60

Solution on p. 5-65.

Management Judgment

Although the format of the statement of cash flows is prescribed by GAAP, management judgment is an important part of the preparation of this statement including the process of categorizing cash flows.

Transactions That Directly Impact Net Cash Flows for a Period

Management can directly impact the timing of certain cash flows. This timing of cash flows can shift income to or from specific periods. As examples, the following activities by management, which are *not* prohibited by accounting standards, increase net cash flows provided by operating activities for a given reporting period.

- Accelerate collections from credit customers by offering discounts.
- Accelerate cash receipts by selling receivables (or other assets).
- Delay cash payments to suppliers for credit purchases.
- Delay or decrease discretionary cash expenditures.

In many of these cases, the positive impact on reported cash flows affects the current period only; there is a corresponding negative impact on cash flows in some other period for several of these cases.

Classification of Cash Flows as Operating, Investing, or Financing

Management must decide into which section cash flows are to be reported.

- *Payments are not classified solely based on the type of purchase.* As an example, a purchase of land is typically reported as an investing activity. However, if the purchase of land is done by a developer with the intent to divide it into lots for sale, the purchase of land is recorded as an operating activity.
- *Payments can have aspects of more than one class of cash flows.* As an example, a company purchases many types of equipment that will either be resold directly to customers or rented to customers. Also, customers have an option to rent the equipment for 6 months prior to deciding whether to continue to rent the equipment or purchase it. Should the company classify the purchase of the various equipment as operating activities (in the case of a sale to a customer) or as investing activities (in the case of a lease to a customer)? GAAP requires the cash flows to be classified into separately identifiable sources if possible, but this requires judgment. If separation is not possible, such as when a single piece of equipment is rented for a short time and then sold, then GAAP requires that the predominant source of cash flows be determined for proper classification.

Reporting of Non-GAAP Measures in Financial Reporting

Management judgment is necessary when determining the presentation of non-GAAP measures in the MD&A section. Application of management judgment extends to the following issues.

- Whether or not to present a non-GAAP measure(s).
- What non-GAAP measure is to be disclosed.
- How to calculate the non-GAAP measure.
- How to relate the non-GAAP measure to a GAAP measure.

Prepare the operating activities section of the statement of cash flows using the direct method

APPENDIX 5A
LO 5-8

The direct method for reporting a company's net cash flow from operating activities reports the same total cash provided or used as is shown in the indirect method. The difference is that the direct method reports gross operating cash inflows and outflows, while the indirect method reports a reconciliation of net income to cash provided or used by operating activities. The direct method statement begins with the individual cash inflows (such as from customers, interest and dividends on investments, and refunds from suppliers) and then deducts individual cash outflows (purchases of goods for resale, interest on debt obligations, income taxes, and salaries and wages). These totals are not available on the indirect method statement. To prepare the statement of cash flows using the direct method, each major category of the income statement is converted from an accrual basis to a cash basis and reported separately, as illustrated in **Demo 5-8**. If a company elects to use the direct method, the reconciliation of net income to cash provided or used by operating activities that would have been reported under the indirect method must appear in a supplementary schedule.

Cash Flows from Operating Activities—Direct Method

+	Cash received from customers
−	Cash payments to suppliers
−	Cash payments to employees
−	Cash payments for operating expenses
	Net cash flows from operating activities

LO 5-8 Overview

Operating Activities Section—Direct Method

LO5-8 Demo 5-8

Following is the income statement for Lakers Inc. from earlier Demos along with selected balance sheet data. Convert each of the four line items in the income statement to a cash basis. Prepare a full statement of cash flows under the direct method.

Demo MBC

Lakers Inc.
Income Statement
For Year Ended December 31, 2020

Sales (all on credit)	$66,000
Salaries expense	24,500
Depreciation expense	4,000
Selling and administrative expenses	12,000
Interest expense	3,500
Net income	$22,000

Lakers Inc.
Balance Sheet Data

At December 31	2019	2020
Accounts receivable	$31,000	$40,000
Salaries payable	3,000	5,000

Solution

Sales Credit sales ($66,000) from the income statement increase accounts receivable. The related cash flow is collections on accounts receivable. This amount can be derived from the cash receipts journal or through an analysis of accounts receivable as follows. Cash collections are reported as cash collected from customers in the operation section of the direct method statement of cash flows.

Accounts receivable, December 31, 2019	$31,000
Sales in 2020	66,000
Accounts receivable, December 31, 2020	(40,000)
Cash collections in 2020	**$57,000**

Accounts Rec

31,000	
66,000	57,000
40,000	

Salaries Salaries expense ($24,500) from the income statement is related to salaries payable, which increased $2,000 during 2020. The related cash flow is salary payments, determined through an analysis of salaries payable as follows. Salary payments are reported as payment to employees in the operating section of the direct method statement of cash flows.

Salary payable, December 31, 2019	$ 3,000
Salaries expense in 2020	24,500
Salary payable, December 31, 2020	(5,000)
Salary payments in 2020	**$22,500**

Salaries Payable

	3,000
22,500	24,500
	5,000

continued

continued from previous page

Depreciation Depreciation expense ($4,000) from the income statement is not a cash flow and therefore is not disclosed in the operating section of the direct method statement of cash flows. This amount, however, appears in the reconciliation of net income and net operating cash flow.

Selling and Administrative and Interest Selling and administrative expenses of $12,000 and interest expense of $3,500 are reported on the income statement. However, the balance sheet shows no associated payable accounts. Therefore, we assume the recognized expense amounts represent cash expenditures.

Statement of Cash Flows—Direct Method

Following is the statement of cash flows using the direct method. In comparing this statement to the indirect statement in **Demo 5-2**, we see that the net cash inflow from operating activities of $19,000 is the same. However, the composition of the operating activities section is different. The investing and financing activities sections are identical.

LAKERS INC.
Statement of Cash Flows, Direct Method
For Year Ended December 31, 2020

Cash flows from operating activities	
Cash received from customers	$57,000
Cash payments to employees	(22,500)
Cash payments for selling and administrative activities	(12,000)
Cash payments for interest	(3,500)
Net cash provided by operating activities	19,000
Cash flows from investing activities	
Cash paid for acquisition of plant assets	(30,000)
Cash received from sale of plant assets	21,000
Cash paid for purchase of investment	(12,000)
Net cash used by investing activities	(21,000)
Cash flows from financing activities	
Cash received from long-term debt issuance	40,000
Cash paid on long-term debt	(46,000)
Cash paid for dividends	(11,000)
Cash received from sale of common stock	48,000
Net cash provided by financing activities	31,000
Net increase in cash and cash equivalents during 2020	29,000
Cash and cash equivalents, December 31, 2019	42,000
Cash and cash equivalents, December 31, 2020	$71,000

Identical to Indirect Cash Flow Method

EMC CORP. [EMC]

EMC CORP. **Real World—DIRECT METHOD OF CASH FLOWS**

EMC Corporation, a technology based company, is involved in the growing trends of cloud computing, Big Data, mobile, social networking, and security. EMC reports cash flows using the direct method of cash flows.

Consolidated Statements of Cash Flows For Year Ended December 31 ($ millions)	2015
Cash flows from operating activities:	
Cash received form customers	$25,737
Cash paid to suppliers and employees	(19,312)
Dividends and interest received	100
Interest paid	(138)
Income taxes paid	(1,001)
Net cash provided by operating activities	$ 5,386

Operating Activities Section—Direct Method

LO5-8 **REVIEW 5-8**

The following financial information for Toma Inc. is from its 2020 annual report. Convert each of the six items in the income statement to a cash basis. Prepare the operating activities section of the statement of cash flows under the direct method.

Review MBC

Income Statement For Year Ended December 31, 2020	
Sales	$18,000
Salaries expense	9,000
Rent expense	800
Depreciation expense	350
Utilities expense	1,000
Miscellaneous expenses	3,500
Net income	$ 3,350

Changes in Current Assets and Liabilities in 2020	
Increase in accounts receivable	$300
Decrease in salaries payable	500
Decrease in utilities payable	150

More Practice: 5-82, 5-83

Solution on p. 5-65.

Questions

5-1. What is the purpose of the statement of cash flows?

5-2. Compare the purposes of the balance sheet, income statement, and statement of cash flows.

5-3. Explain the three major sections in the statement of cash flows.

5-4. What items are included in the change in cash on a statement of cash flows?

5-5. List three major cash inflows and three major cash outflows under (a) operating activities, (b) investing activities, and (c) financing activities.

5-6. Explain why cash paid during the period for purchases and for salaries is not specifically reported as cash outflows on the statement of cash flows using the indirect method.

5-7. Explain why an adjustment must be made to compute cash flow from operating activities for depreciation expense.

5-8. What is meant by "noncash investing and financing activities" in the statement of cash flows?

5-9. Explain the relation between the balance in the cash account and the statement of cash flows.

5-10. Why are ratios of financial statement values useful? Under what conditions are they most revealing?

5-11. How can the return on equity be disaggregated using the DuPont Model?

5-12. What factors can make improvements to the cash conversion cycle?

5-13. Identify some ratios that support: (a) profitability, (b) activity, and (c) financial leverage.

5-14. In assessing a company, are creditors interested in all categories of ratios: profitability, activity, liquidity, and long-term solvency?

5-15. Define and describe two liquidity ratios.

5-16. How are the following categories of ratios different: profitability, activity, solvency, and liquidity?

5-17. How is a vertical analysis different from a horizontal analysis?

5-18. What are some challenges in analyzing non-GAAP disclosures that a company makes in an annual report on Form 10-K?

5-19. Why does the Securities and Exchange Commission require a reconciliation of a reported non-GAAP measure to a GAAP measure?

Brief Exercises

Brief Exercise 5-20 Classifying Cash Flows **LO1** *Hint:* See Demo 5-1

Classify each of the following cash flows as an (1) operating activity, (2) investing activity, or (3) financing activity.

_____ *a.* Cash paid for dividends.

_____ *b.* Cash received from the sale of land.

_____ *c.* Cash received on sale of merchandise.

_____ *d.* Cash received on the issuance of a note payable.

_____ *e.* Cash paid for interest on a note payable.

_____ *f.* Cash paid to reduce the principal balance of a note payable.

Brief Exercise 5-21
Classifying Cash Flows **LO1, 2**

Classify each of the following items as a (1) cash from operating activity, (2) cash from investing activity, (3) cash from financing activity, or (4) noncash financing and/or investing activity.

____ *a.* Cash received from sale of common stock.
____ *b.* Common stock issued in exchange for equipment to be used in operations.
____ *c.* Cash paid for the acquisition of plant assets.
____ *d.* Cash paid to employees for salaries.
____ *e.* Refinancing a short-term note with a long-term note.
____ *f.* Cash received from dividends on investments held.
____ *g.* Sale of long-term investment in equity securities.

Brief Exercise 5-22
Preparing the Cash Flow from Operating Activities Section **LO2**

Sarasota Corp. reported net income of $50,000, which included depreciation expense of $6,500. It also reported a decrease in accounts receivable and salaries payable of $3,500 and $2,000, respectively. Further, it reported an increase in inventory of $7,000 and an increase in accounts payable of $4,800. Calculate its net cash provided by operating activities.

Brief Exercise 5-23
Preparing the Cash Flow from Operating Activities Section **LO2**

Atlas Corp. reported the following amounts for the year ended December 31, 2020. Calculate the company's net cash provided by operating activities for the year ended December 31, 2020.

Net income	$230,000	Depreciation expense	$28,000
Decrease in accounts payable	8,800	Increase in accounts receivable	13,000
Increase in prepaid rent	3,000	Increase in interest payable	1,200

Brief Exercise 5-24
Preparing the Cash Flow from Investing Activities Section **LO2**

Gomez Corp. reported the following items for the year ended December 31, 2020. Calculate cash flows from investing activities for the year ended December 31, 2020.

Purchased an investment in debt securities (long-term) for cash	$ 30,000
Sold equipment for cash, previously used in operations	25,000
Paid cash for dividends	10,000
Issued common stock for cash	100,000
Retired a 10-year bond payable by repaying the face value at maturity	80,000
Sold investment in equity securities (held for one-year)	11,000
Borrowed cash by signing a nine-month note payable	15,000
Extended a loan to a customer for a building expansion	8,000

Brief Exercise 5-25
Preparing the Cash Flow from Financing Activities Section **LO2**

Refer to the information in Brief Exercise 5-24. Calculate cash flows from financing activities for the year ended December 31, 2020.

Brief Exercise 5-26
Computing Ending Stockholders' Equity **LO3**

Streep Corp. is in its first year of operations and it reported the following amounts. Compute the total amount of stockholders' equity as of December 31, 2020.

Common stock, December 31, 2020	$45,000	Dividends declared and paid, 2020	$ 4,500
Other comprehensive income, 2020	5,000	Net income, 2020	18,000

Brief Exercise 5-27
Identifying Interrelations of Financial Statements **LO3**
Hint: See Demo 5-3B

When considering the interrelations of financial statements, name at least two specific financial statements where:

____ *a.* Net income is reported.
____ *b.* Retained earnings is reported.
____ *c.* Ending cash balance for the period is reported.
____ *d.* Accumulated other comprehensive is reported.

Brief Exercise 5-28
Computing Return on Equity **LO4**
Hint: See Demo 5-4A

Compute return on equity from the selected 2016 balance sheet and annual income statement information of **VF Corporation** ($ millions).

Sales	$12,251	Total assets	$9,640
Net income	1,232	Average stockholders' equity	5,508

Brief Exercise 5-29
Computing Margin, Turnover, and Leverage **LO4**
Hint: See Demo 5-4B

Using DuPont analysis, compute return on equity from the following information provided for **United Parcel Service Inc.** for the year ended December 31, 2015.

Profit margin (Net income/ Sales)	8.30%
Asset turnover (Sales/ Average total assets)	1.58
Financial leverage (Average total assets/Average stockholders' equity)	15.86

Brief Exercise 5-30
Computing Liquidity and Solvency Ratios **LO5**
Hint: See Demo 5-5A

The following selected financial information is provided for **United Parcel Services Inc.** for the year ended December 31, 2015 ($ millions).

Total liabilities	$35,820	Cash	$2,730
Current liabilities	10,696	Marketable securities	1,996
Total assets	38,311	Accounts receivable	7,252
Current assets	13,208		

Compute the following ratios.

a. Current ratio *b.* Quick ratio *c.* Total liabilities-to-equity

Brief Exercise 5-31
Computing Activity Ratios **LO4**
Hint: See Demo 5-4C

The following amounts are summarized from information included in the **Whole Foods Market Inc.**'s 2015 annual report on Form 10-K ($ millions).

Sales	$15,389	Inventory, average balance	$471
Cost of goods sold	9,973	Accounts payable, average balance	286
Accounts receivable, average balance	208		

Compute the following ratios.

a. Accounts receivable turnover
b. Average days to collect receivables
c. Inventory turnover
d. Average days in inventory
e. Accounts payable turnover
f. Average days payable outstanding
g. Cash conversion cycle

Brief Exercise 5-32
Solving for Unknown Financial Statement Amounts **LO4**

Financial information for **Target Corporation** for the fiscal year ended January 30, 2016, follows ($ millions).

Sales	$73,785	Asset turnover	1.812
Profit margin	4.558%	Financial leverage	3.021

Compute the following amounts.

a. Net income
b. Average total assets
c. Average stockholders' equity
d. Return on equity

Brief Exercise 5-33
Computing Cash Flow Based Measures **LO5**
Hint: See Demo 5-5B

The following amounts are from information in the 2015 annual report of **Target Corporation** ($ millions).

Cash provided by operating activities	$ 5,140	Cash paid for capital expenditures	$1,438
Average current liabilities	12,179	Cash paid for dividends	1,362
Average total liabilities	27,240		

Compute the following ratios for 2015.

a. Current cash debt coverage *b.* Cash debt coverage *c.* Free cash flow

Brief Exercise 5-34
Performing a Horizontal and Vertical Analysis **LO6**
Hint: See Demo 5-6A, Demo 5-6B

Complete a vertical and horizontal analysis of the following income statement from Gomez Corporation.

Income Statement	**2020**	**2019**
Revenues	$50,000	$55,000
Costs of goods sold	32,000	36,000
Gross margin	18,000	19,000
Operating expenses	11,000	12,500
Net income	$ 7,000	$ 6,500

Brief Exercise 5-35
Identifying Non-GAAP and GAAP Measures **LO7**
Hint: See Demo 5-7

Whole Foods Market Inc. reported the following reconciliation in the MD&A section of its 2015 annual report on Form 10-K ($ millions).

Net cash provided by operating activities	$1,129
Development cost of new locations	(516)
Other property and equipment expenditures	(335)
Free cash flow	$ 278

a. What is the GAAP measure included in this reconciliation?
b. What is the non-GAAP measure included in this reconciliation?

Brief Exercise 5-36
Identifying GAAP and Non-GAAP Measures **LO7**

Identify each of the following items *a* through *h* as a (1) GAAP measure or (2) a non-GAAP measure.

____ *a.* EBITA
____ *b.* Gross profit
____ *c.* Income from continuing operations
____ *d.* Pro forma income statement
____ *e.* Current assets
____ *f.* Working capital
____ *g.* Free cash flow
____ *h.* Adjusted operating income

Exercises

Exercise 5-37
Classifying Items in the Statement of Cash Flows **LO1**

The following items are commonly reported in a statement of cash flows (indirect method presentation). For each item 1 through 20, determine (a) in which section the item is presented (operating [O], investing [I], or financing [F]) and (b) whether the associated dollar amount is added [A] or subtracted [S] in the statement.

____ ____ 1. Payments of short-term debt.
____ ____ 2. Repurchases of common stock.
____ ____ 3. Purchases of property and equipment.
____ ____ 4. Sale of investments classified as long-term.
____ ____ 5. Proceeds from the issuance of common stock.
____ ____ 6. Increase in prepaid expenses and other current assets.
____ ____ 7. Acquisition for cash of a competitor.
____ ____ 8. Increase in current income tax payable.
____ ____ 9. Decrease in accounts payable.
____ ____ 10. Dividends paid to stockholders.
____ ____ 11. Depreciation and amortization.
____ ____ 12. Payment of current maturities of long-term debt.
____ ____ 13. Increase in income tax receivable.
____ ____ 14. Decrease in inventories.
____ ____ 15. Decrease in accounts receivable.
____ ____ 16. Decrease in deferred revenue.
____ ____ 17. Loss on disposal of fixed assets.
____ ____ 18. Increase in accrued salaries and payroll taxes.
____ ____ 19. Loss on impairment of assets.
____ ____ 20. Acquisition of intangibles assets.

Exercise 5-38
Classifying Transactions in the Statement of Cash Flows **LO1, 2**

The following transactions are from Diaz Corp. for the year ended December 31, 2020.

____ 1. Paid cash to acquire assets for operations.
____ 2. Cash dividends declared but not paid.
____ 3. Cash proceeds from note payable.
____ 4. Sale of assets used in operations for cash.
____ 5. Loaned cash in exchange for long-term note receivable.*
____ 6. Purchased long-term stock investment for cash.
____ 7. Collected cash to settle notes receivable (principal only).*
____ 8. Purchased a patent for cash.
____ 9. Paid salaries in cash.
____ 10. Paid off debt by giving 60% cash and 40% treasury stock.
____ 11. Issued common stock for cash.
____ 12. Paid cash dividend.
____ 13. Purchased company's own common stock for cash.
____ 14. Paid cash to settle notes payable.
____ 15. Sales revenue collected in cash.

* Note receivable does not relate to the financing of goods or services.

Required

Classify each of the transactions, 1 through 15, into one of the following categories, *a*, *b*, *c*, *d*, or *e*.

a. Cash inflow (outflow) from operating activities.
b. Cash inflow (outflow) from investing activities.
c. Cash inflow (outflow) from financing activities.
d. Non-cash investing or financing activity.
e. Not a cash inflow or outflow.

Exercise 5-39 Indirect Method—Preparing the Operating Activities Section **LO2**

The following data are from the accounting records of Clooney Company.

Net income (accrual basis)	$40,000	Amortization of patent	$ 100
Depreciation expense	7,800	Increase in long-term liabilities	10,000
Decrease in salaries payable	1,200	Sale of capital stock for cash	25,000
Decrease in trade accounts receivable	1,800	Accounts payable increase	4,000
Increase in merchandise inventory	2,500		

Required

Prepare the operating activities section of the statement of cash flows for Clooney Company using the indirect method.

Exercise 5-40 Indirect Method—Preparing the Operating Activities Section **LO2**

Pitt Corp. reported net income of $450,000 for the year ended December 31, 2020. Depreciation expense was $48,000 and was reported as part of operating expenses in the income statement. Following are changes in account balances from December 31, 2019, to December 31, 2020.

Increase in accounts receivable	$21,000	Increase in accounts payable	$ 8,000
Increase in inventories	75,000	Decrease in salaries payable	44,000
Decrease in prepaid insurance	12,000		

Required

Prepare the operating activities section of the statement of cash flows for Pitt Company using the indirect method.

Exercise 5-41 Indirect Method—Preparing a Statement of Cash Flows **LO2**
Hint: See Demo 5-2

Range Company has the following selected data from its annual period ended December 31, 2020.

Paid cash dividend	$10,000
Purchase of equipment	60,000
Increase in merchandise inventory	14,000
Borrowed on a long-term note	25,000
Acquired land as a future company site; paid in full by issuing 3,000 shares of Range capital stock, $10 par, when the market price per share was $15	?
Increase in prepaid expenses	3,000
Decrease in accounts receivable	7,000
Payment of bonds payable in full	97,000
Increase in accounts payable	5,000
Cash from disposal of fixed assets (sold at book value)	12,000
Decrease in rent receivable	2,000

Income statement	2020
Sales revenue	$400,000
Rent revenue	10,000
Cost of goods sold	(190,000)
Depreciation expense	(20,000)
Remaining expenses	(97,000)
Net income	$103,000

Required

Prepare a statement of cash flows for the Range Company for the year ended December 31, 2020, using the indirect method. The beginning-year cash balance was $62,000.

Exercise 5-42
Indirect Method—Preparing a Statement of Cash Flows **LO2**
Hint: See Demo 5-2

Calex Inc. reported the following comparative balance sheets.

Balance Sheets	Dec. 31, 2019	Dec. 31, 2020
Cash and cash equivalents	$ 4,000	$10,750
Accounts receivable	3,000	2,000
Equipment	10,000	15,000
Accumulated depreciation	(1,000)	(2,000)
Total assets	$16,000	$25,750
Salaries payable	$ 1,000	$ 2,000
Long-term notes payable	5,000	5,000
Capital stock	8,000	8,000
Retained earnings	2,000	10,750
Total liabilities and stockholders' equity	$16,000	$25,750

Additional information

1. Net income for the current year was $9,750.
2. No disposals of equipment took place during the year.

Required

Prepare the statement of cash flows for Calex for the year ended December 31, 2020, using the indirect method.

Exercise 5-43
Indirect Method—Preparing a Statement of Cash Flows **LO2**
Hint: See Demo 5-2

Kidman Corp. reported the following financial statements for the year ended December 31, 2020.

Balance Sheet, December 31	2019	2020	Difference
Cash and cash equivalents	$ 24,000	$ 62,000	$38,000
Accounts receivable	19,000	15,000	(4,000)
Merchandise inventory	31,000	59,000	28,000
Land	20,000	4,000	(16,000)
Equipment	48,000	72,000	24,000
Accumulated depreciation	(12,000)	(24,000)	(12,000)
Total assets	$130,000	$188,000	$58,000
Accounts payable	$ 16,000	$ 18,000	$ 2,000
Notes payable, long-term	7,000	2,000	(5,000)
Bonds payable	—	30,000	30,000
Common stock (no-par)	80,000	92,000	12,000
Retained earnings	27,000	46,000	19,000
Total liabilities and stockholders' equity	$130,000	$188,000	$58,000

Income Statement For Year Ended December 31, 2020	
Revenues	$152,000
Costs of goods sold	82,000
Depreciation	12,000
Other expenses	14,000
Loss on sale of land	10,000
Net income	$ 34,000

Required

Prepare the statement of cash flows for Kidman Corp. for the year ended December 31, 2020, using the indirect method.

Exercise 5-44
Indirect Method—Preparing a Statement of Cash Flows **LO2**

The accounting records of Guci Corp. show the following data for the current year.

Balance Sheet

December 31	2019	2020	Difference
Cash	$ 100	$ 65	$ (35)
Accounts receivable	300	200	(100)
Merchandise inventory	100	300	200
Equipment, net	1,800	2,200	400
Total assets	$2,300	$2,765	$465
Accounts payable	$ 275	$ 240	$ (35)
Salaries payable	50	25	(25)
Bonds payable	600	700	100
Common stock (no-par)	1,100	1,200	100
Retained earnings	275	600	325
Total liabilities and stockholders' equity	$2,300	$2,765	$465

Income Statement
For Year Ended December 31, 2020

Revenues	$3,000
Costs of goods sold	1,700
Depreciation	400
Other expenses	385
Net income	$ 515

Additional information

1. Equipment was sold for its book value of $400.
2. Equipment purchased during the year was $1,200.
3. Cash dividends declared and paid were $190.

Required

Prepare the statement of cash flows for Guci Corp for the year ended December 31, 2020, using the indirect method.

Exercise 5-45
Applying Interrelations of Financial Statements **LO3**

The following information is from three separate companies.

	Case 1	Case 2	Case 3
Net income, 2020	$ 28,000	$ (h)	$ 90,000
Retained earnings, December 31, 2020	(a)	870,000	(n)
Retained earnings, December 31, 2019	10,000	780,000	254,500
Dividends, 2020	8,000	35,000	(o)
Common stock, December 31, 2020	(b)	(i)	150,000
Total stockholders' equity, December 31, 2020	112,000	(j)	480,000
Other comprehensive income, 2020	(c)	0	(p)
Accumulated other comprehensive income, December 31, 2019	3,000	0	2,500
Accumulated other comprehensive income, December 31, 2020	2,000	0	(q)
Comprehensive income, 2020	(d)	(k)	103,000
Total assets, December 31, 2020	(e)	2,200,000	880,000
Total assets, excluding cash, December 31, 2020	(f)	(l)	825,000
Total liabilities, December 31, 2020	92,000	900,000	(r)
Cash, December 31, 2019	5,000	75,000	(s)
Cash, December 31, 2020	10,000	(m)	(t)
Change in cash, 2020	(g)	(10,000)	10,000

Required

Fill in the missing amounts, *a* through *t*, for each of the three separate companies.

Exercise 5-46 Using Interrelations of Financial Statements **LO3**

Answer each of the following separate questions. If the missing amount cannot be determined with the information given, explain what is needed to answer the questions.

a. Given comprehensive income of $43,000, and other comprehensive income of $4,000, determine net income for the same period.
b. Given accumulated other comprehensive income on January 1 of $560,000, and other comprehensive income for the year of $65,000 (gain), what is accumulated other comprehensive income at year-end?
c. Assuming no dividend payments, determine net income if retained earnings increased by $20,000.
d. Given an ending balance of stockholders' equity of $76,000, an ending balance in no-par common stock of $50,000, and an ending balance in retained earnings of $34,000, determine the ending balance in accumulated other comprehensive income.
e. Given the information in part *d*, can other comprehensive income for the year be determined? Why or why not?
f. If cash decreased during the year by $9,000, and ending cash totaled $5,000, determine beginning cash for the period.

Exercise 5-47 Computing and Disaggregating Return on Equity **LO4**

Following are selected balance sheet and income statement information from **Ralph Lauren Corporation**'s 2015 annual report on Form 10-K.

$ millions	April 2, 2016	March 28, 2015
Sales.	$7,230	$7,451
Net income	396	702
Total assets.	6,213	6,106
Total stockholders' equity	3,744	3,891

Required

a. Calculate Ralph Lauren's return on equity for the fiscal year ended April 2, 2016.
b. Disaggregate return on equity to its DuPont components of activity (profit margin), activity (asset turnover), and leverage (financial leverage). Demonstrate how the product of the components is equal to return on equity.

Exercise 5-48 Computing, Disaggregating, and Analyzing Return on Equity **LO4**

Selected balance sheet and income statement information follows for **American Eagle Outfitters Inc.** and **Abercrombie & Fitch Co.**

American Eagle Outfitters Inc.		
$ millions	January 30, 2016	January 31, 2015
Sales.	$3,522	$3,283
Net income	218	80
Total assets.	1,612	1,697
Total stockholders' equity . . .	1,051	1,140

Abercrombie & Fitch Co.		
$ millions	January 30, 2016	January 31, 2015
Sales.	$3,519	$3,744
Net income	39	52
Total assets.	2,433	2,505
Total stockholders' equity . . .	1,291	1,390

Required

a. Calculate return on equity for the fiscal year ended January 30, 2016, for each company.
b. Disaggregate return on equity to its DuPont components of profitability (profit margin), activity (asset turnover), and leverage (financial leverage) for each company. Demonstrate how the product of the components is equal to return on equity.
c. Analyze the results. What are the drivers for the differences (if any) between the ratios of the two companies?

Exercise 5-49 Computing Activity Ratios **LO4**
Hint: See Demo 5-4C

Selected balance sheet and income statement information follows for **Ralph Lauren Corporation**.

Ralph Lauren Corporation		
$ millions	April 2, 2016	March 28, 2015
Sales.	$7,230	$7,451
Cost of goods sold	3,218	3,242
Accounts receivable, gross.	771	906
Inventory.	1,125	1,042
Accounts payable	151	210

Required

Compute the following ratios for its fiscal year ended April 2, 2016.

a. Accounts receivable turnover
b. Average days to collect receivables
c. Inventory turnover
d. Average days in inventory
e. Accounts payable turnover
f. Average days payable outstanding
g. Cash conversion cycle

Exercise 5-50
Computing Activity Ratios **LO4**
Hint: See Demo 5-4C

Selected balance sheet and income statement information follows for the **3M Company**.

3M Company			
$ millions	**Dec. 31, 2015**	**Dec. 31, 2014**	**Dec. 31, 2013**
Sales	$30,274	$31,821	$30,871
Cost of goods sold	15,383	16,447	16,106
Accounts receivable, gross	4,245	4,332	4,357
Inventory	3,518	3,706	3,864

Required

Compute the following ratios for the fiscal years ended December 31, 2015, and December 31, 2014.

a. Accounts receivable turnover
b. Average days to collect receivables
c. Inventory turnover
d. Average days in inventory

Exercise 5-51
Computing and Analyzing Liquidity and Solvency Ratios **LO5**

Selected balance sheet and income statement information follows for the **3M Company**.

3M Company		
$ millions	**Dec. 31, 2015**	**Dec. 31, 2014**
Interest expense	$ 149	$ 142
Income before interest and taxes	6,946	7,135
Cash	1,798	1,897
Marketable securities	118	1,439
Accounts receivable	4,245	4,332
Current assets	10,986	12,303
Current liabilities	7,118	5,964
Total assets	32,718	31,209
Total liabilities	20,971	18,067
Total stockholders' equity	11,747	13,142

Required

a. Compute the following ratios for the fiscal years ended December 31, 2015, and December 31, 2014.
   1. Current ratio
   2. Quick ratio
   3. Total liabilities-to-equity
   4. Times interest earned

b. Comment on the trends from 2014 to 2015 for 3M company regarding liquidity and solvency.

Exercise 5-52
Computing and Analyzing Liquidity and Solvency Ratios **LO5**

Selected balance sheet and income statement information follows for **Gap Inc.** and **American Eagle Outfitters Inc.** for the fiscal year ended January 30, 2016.

For Year Ended Jan. 30, 2016 ($ millions)	Gap Inc.	American Eagle Outfitters Inc.
Interest expense	$ 59	$ 1
Income before interest and taxes	1,524	322
Cash and cash equivalents	1,370	260
Marketable securities	—	—
Accounts receivable	282	81
Current assets	3,985	723
Current liabilities	2,535	464
Total assets	7,473	1,612
Total liabilities	4,928	561
Total stockholders' equity	2,545	1,051

Required

a. Compute the following ratios for the fiscal year ended January 30, 2016.
1. Current ratio
2. Quick ratio
3. Total liabilities-to-equity
4. Times interest earned

b. Comment on liquidity and solvency comparing the ratio results from the two companies.

Exercise 5-53 Computing and Analyzing Cash Flow Ratios **LO5**

Selected financial information for **Gap Inc.** and **American Eagle Outfitters Inc.** follows.

$ millions	Gap Inc.	American Eagle Outfitters Inc.
Current liabilities, January 30, 2016	$2,535	$464
Current liabilities, January 31, 2015	2,234	459
Total liabilities, January 30, 2016	4,928	561
Total liabilities, January 31, 2015	4,707	557
Cash provided by operating activities, 2016	1,594	342
Cash paid for capital expenditures, 2016	726	164
Cash paid for dividends, 2016	377	97

Required

a. For each company, compute the following ratios for the fiscal year ended January 30, 2016: current cash debt coverage, cash debt coverage, and free cash flow.

b. Briefly comment on the results.

Exercise 5-54 Solving for Financial Amounts and Ratios **LO4**

Selected financial information for Laurel Corporation follows.

$ millions	Dec. 31, 2019	Dec. 31, 2020
Sales	$5,100	(a)
Net income	425	(b)
Total assets	3,500	3,800
Total stockholders' equity	1,600	1,800
Return on equity		25.88%
Profit margin		0.08
Asset turnover		(c)
Financial leverage		(d)

Required

Determine the missing amounts, *a* through *d*, using accounting knowledge.

Exercise 5-55 Solving for Financial Amounts **LO4, 5**

Selected financial information for Crombie Corporation follows.

$ millions	Dec. 31, 2020	$ millions	Dec. 31, 2020
Interest expense	$149,000	Total assets	5,000,000
Income before interest and taxes	(a)	Total liabilities	(d)
Cash	(b)	Total stockholders' equity	2,300,000
Marketable securities	205,000	Total liabilities-to-equity	(e)
Accounts receivable	480,000	Current ratio	0.91
Current assets	(c)	Times interest earned	6.00
Current liabilities	1,100,000	Quick ratio	0.75

Required

Determine the missing amounts, *a* through *e*, using accounting knowledge.

Exercise 5-56 Analyzing Effects of Transactions for Liquidity and Solvency **LO4, 5**

A creditor is concerned with both the liquidity and solvency trends of Dyckman Company. The following information is available for Dyckman Company at the current year-end ($ thousands).

Current Assets	Total Assets	Current Liabilities	Total Liabilities	Total Stockholders' Equity
$5,000	$19,000	$4,800	$9,000	$10,000

Dyckman informs this creditor that the company is considering the following transactions.

a. Issuance of common stock for cash for $1 million.

b. Issuance of bonds payable for cash for $1 million.

c. Early retirement of $1 million long-term notes payable with cash.

d. Pay off short term note payable of $500,000.

Required

The creditor wishes to assess the immediate impact that each transaction would have on liquidity and solvency. This creditor measures liquidity using the current ratio, and measures solvency using the total liabilities-to-equity ratio. For each transaction, identify whether it has a positive, negative, or no effect on (1) liquidity and (2) solvency.

Exercise 5-57
Performing a Horizontal and Vertical Analysis **LO6**

Financial statements for Eagle Corp. follow.

Income Statement	2019	2020
Revenues	$375,000	$400,000
Costs of goods sold	232,500	250,000
Gross margin	142,500	150,000
Operating expenses	92,000	90,000
Net income	$ 50,500	$ 60,000

Balance Sheet	2019	2020
Current assets	$ 28,000	$ 35,000
Noncurrent assets	200,000	195,000
Total assets	$228,000	$230,000
Current liabilities	$ 27,000	$ 30,000
Noncurrent liabilities	95,000	90,000
Total liabilities	122,000	120,000
Stockholders' equity	106,000	110,000
Total liabilities and stockholders' equity	$228,000	$230,000

Required

a. Prepare a horizontal analysis for the period from 2019 to 2020.

b. Prepare a vertical analysis for the years ended 2019 and 2020.

Exercise 5-58
Interpreting Non-GAAP Disclosures **LO7**
Hint: See Demo 5-7

The **Boeing Company** reported the following information in its MD&A section of a recent annual report on Form 10-K.

Earnings From Operations—The following table summarizes Earnings from operations.

Years Ended December 31 ($ millions)	2015	2014	2013
Commercial Airplanes	$5,157	$6,411	$5,795
Defense, Space & Security	3,274	3,133	3,235
Boeing Capital	50	92	107
Unallocated pension and other postretirement benefit expense	(298)	(1,387)	(1,314)
Other unallocated items and eliminations	(740)	(776)	(1,261)
Earnings from operations (GAAP)	$7,443	$7,473	$6,562
Unallocated pension and other postretirement benefit expense	298	1,387	1,314
Core operating earnings (Non-GAAP)	$7,741	$8,860	$7,876

Earnings from operations in 2015 decreased by $30 million compared with 2014 primarily reflecting a fourth quarter charge of $885 million related to the 747 program at Commercial Airplanes and higher charges of $410 million related to the USAF KC-46A Tanker recorded by Commercial Airplanes and our Boeing Military Aircraft (BMA) segment, partially offset by lower unallocated pension and other postretirement benefit expense of $1,089 million.

Non-GAAP Measures: Core Operating Earnings, Core Operating Margin, and Core Earnings Per Share
Our Consolidated Financial Statements are prepared in accordance with Generally Accepted Accounting Principles in the United States of America (GAAP), which we supplement with certain non-GAAP financial information. These non-GAAP measures should not be considered in isolation or as a substitute for the related GAAP measures, and other companies may define such measures differently . . . Core operating earnings, core operating margin and core earnings per share exclude the impact of certain pension and other postretirement benefit expenses that are not allocated to business segments . . . Management uses core operating earnings, core operating margin and core earnings per share for purposes of evaluating and forecasting underlying business performance. Management believes these core earnings measures provide investors additional insights into operational performance as unallocated pension and other postretirement benefit cost primarily represent costs driven by market factors and costs not allocable to U.S. government contracts.

Required

a. What is the non-GAAP measure reported?

b. What GAAP measure is used in the reconciliation to compare to the non-GAAP measure?

c. Why is this disclosure included in the MD&A section of the Form 10-K and not in the notes accompanying the financial statements?

d. Why is this non-GAAP measure reported?

Exercise 5-59
Analyzing Non-GAAP Disclosures **LO7**

The following excerpts are from the annual report on Form 10-K for **Walgreens Boots Alliance Inc.**

Excerpt 1: For Year Ended ($ millions)	2017
Operating income (GAAP)	$5,557
Cost transformation	835
Acquisition-related costs	474
Acquisition-related amortization	332
Adjustments to equity earnings in AmerisourceBergen	187
LIFO provision	166
Asset recovery	(11)
Adjusted operating income (Non-GAAP measure)	$7,540

Excerpt 2: For Year Ended ($ millions)	2017
Sales	$118,214
Cost of sales	89,052
Gross profit	29,162
Selling, general and administrative	23,740
Equity earnings in AmerisourceBergen	135
Equity earnings in Alliance Boots	—
Operating income	$ 5,557

Required

a. Where do we expect to find (1) *Excerpt One* and (2) *Excerpt Two* within the annual report on Form 10-K?

b. What is the non-GAAP measure reported?

c. What GAAP measure is used in the reconciliation in comparison with the non-GAAP measure?

d. What is the percentage difference in comparing the non-GAAP measure to the GAAP measure?

e. The largest reconciling item is cost transformation. What other term can be used for such costs?

Exercise 5-60
Analyzing Non-GAAP Disclosures **LO7**

The following excerpt is from the MD&A section of annual report on Form 10-K for **3M Company**.

Net Debt (non-GAAP measure) The Company defines net debt as total debt less the total of cash, cash equivalents and marketable securities. 3M considers net debt and its components to be an important indicator of liquidity and a guiding measure of capital structure strategy. Net debt is not defined under U.S. generally accepted accounting principles and may not be computed the same as similarly titled measures used by other companies. The following table provides net debt as of December 31, 2016 and 2015.

At December 31 ($ millions)	2016	2015
Total debt	$11,650	$10,797
Less: Cash and cash equivalents and marketable securities	2,695	1,925
Net debt (non-GAAP measure)	8,955	8,872

In 2016, net debt rose by $83 million to a net debt balance of $9.0 billion (as of December 31, 2016), as 3M progressed on its capital structure strategy. Debt levels were higher due to 2016 issuances, with this increase partially offset by the September 2016 repayment of $1 billion aggregate principal amount of medium-term notes. Cash and cash equivalents and marketable securities were higher in both the U.S. and internationally.

In addition, on the balance sheet, 3M Company reports the following balances

At December 31 ($ millions)	2016	2015
Cash and cash equivalents	$ 2,398	$ 1,798
Marketable securities—current	280	118
Marketable securities—noncurrent	17	9
Short-term borrowings and current portion of long-term debt	972	2,044
Long-term debt	10,678	8,753

Required

a. What is the non-GAAP measure reported?

b. What initial GAAP measure is used in the reconciliation to compare to the non-GAAP measure?

c. Reconcile the GAAP measure components to the amounts presented on the balance sheet for each year.

d. Compute the percentage change from 2015 to 2016 for (1) the initial GAAP measure presented and (2) the non-GAAP measure.

e. The company indicates that the non-GAAP measure is an indicator of liquidity. Are the components of the non-GAAP measure primarily current or noncurrent?

Problems

Problem 5-61 Classifying Transactions on the Statement of Cash Flows **LO1, 2**

The following transactions are from Zomez Corp. for the year ended December 31, 2020.

____ 1. Purchase of equity securities for cash (with intent to hold for one year).
____ 2. Increase in prepaid expenses during the year.
____ 3. Increase in deferred revenue for the year.
____ 4. Payment of cash dividends by the company.
____ 5. Cash proceeds from sale of land.
____ 6. Depreciation expense.
____ 7. Purchase of an asset in exchange for stock.
____ 8. Retirement of bonds with cash.
____ 9. Retirement of bonds with issuance of common stock.
____ 10. Cash proceeds from issuance of preferred stock.
____ 11. Increase in interest payable for the year.
____ 12. Increase in salaries payable for the year.
____ 13. Issuance of bonds for cash.
____ 14. Cash acquisition of patents.
____ 15. Cash principal payment on mortgage.
____ 16. Increase in accounts receivable for the year.
____ 17. Amortization of patents.
____ 18. Loss on sale of equipment.
____ 19. Cash proceeds from sale of used equipment.
____ 20. Increase in bonus payable for the year.

Required

Classify each of the transactions into one of the following categories.

a. Operating—addition to net income (indirect method).

b. Operating—subtraction from net income (indirect method).

c. Cash flows from investing activities.

d. Cash flows from financing activities.

e. Reported as a noncash investing and/or financing transaction.

Problem 5-62
Indirect Method—Preparing a Statement of Cash Flows **LO2**

A comparative balance sheet for Anthro Corp. follows. Net income for 2020 was $25,000, and cash dividends of $10,000 were paid in 2020. No buildings and equipment were sold in 2020. Land was sold at cost.

Comparative Balance Sheet

December 31	2019	2020
Assets		
Cash	$ 20,000	$ 38,000
Accounts receivable	150,000	170,000
Inventory	200,000	230,000
Land	85,000	70,000
Building and equipment	175,000	200,000
Accumulated depreciation	(65,000)	(80,000)
Total assets	$565,000	$628,000
Liabilities and Stockholders' Equity		
Accounts payable	$ 75,000	$ 90,000
Income taxes payable	42,000	30,000
Notes payable (long term)	80,000	100,000
Preferred stock	75,000	75,000
Common stock (no-par)	175,000	200,000
Retained earnings	118,000	133,000
Total liabilities and stockholders' equity	$565,000	$628,000

Required

Prepare a statement of cash flows for the year ended December 31, 2020, using the indirect method.

Problem 5-63
Correcting a Poorly Prepared Statement of Cash Flows **LO2**

The following statement of cash flows was incorrectly prepared by Blum Corporation. The correctly reported income statement also follows.

Statement of Cash Flows
For Year Ended December 31, 2020

Cash received from operations	
Net income	$102,000
Depreciation expense	40,000
Amortization of patent	9,000
Decrease in accounts receivable balance	5,000
Increase in inventory balance	(10,000)
Increase in wages payable balance	4,000
Machinery, old (sold at book value on credit)	7,000
Long-term note given for land purchased	29,000
Total funds received	$186,000
Cash spent	
Retirement of mortgage	$ 60,000
Cash dividends	20,000
Machinery (new)	50,000
Acquired land; issued capital stock in full payment (6,000 shares, par $5)*	36,000
Invested in capital stock of Costner Corporation (classified as noncurrent)	10,000
Increase in cash balance	10,000
Total funds spent	$186,000

*Market price is $6 per share.

Income Statement
For Year Ended December 31, 2020

Sales revenue	$320,000
Cost of goods sold	120,000
Depreciation expense	40,000
Amortization of patent	9,000
Salaries and wages	11,000
Remaining expenses (all cash)	38,000
Net income	$102,000

Required

Restate the statement of cash flow in correct form using proper titles and subtotals. Use the indirect method, and assume that cash at the beginning of the period was $28,000.

Problem 5-64
Indirect Method—Preparing a Statement of Cash Flows and Comparative Balance Sheets from Financial Data **LO2**

Linda Ray, the president of GEI Corporation, requires a statement of cash flows for its annual report ending December 31, 2020. The following balance sheet data are from GEI.

1. Cash account balances: December 31, 2019, $43,000; December 31, 2020, $18,000.
2. The net balance in Accounts Receivable decreased by $10,000 during the year from $60,000 to $50,000. The company had no short-term investments.
3. Inventory increased $9,000 from $71,000 to $80,000.
4. Accounts Payable increased $3,000 during the year from $29,000 to $32,000. Income Tax Payable increased $4,000 during the year from $4,000 to $8,000. Salaries Payable decreased by $5,000 during the year from $9,000 to $4,000. There were no other current liabilities.
5. During December 2020, the company settled a $10,000 note payable (fully liquidating the outstanding balance) by issuing shares of its own common stock with equal value.
6. Cash expenditures during 2020 were (*a*) payment of long-term debts, $64,000; (*b*) purchase of fixed assets, $74,000 (ending balance of $159,000); (*c*) payment of a cash dividend, $16,000; and (*d*) purchase of land as an investment, $25,000.
7. Sale and issuance of GEI common stock for $20,000 cash. The December 31, 2019, balance of Common Stock was $50,000.
8. Issuance of a long-term mortgage note, $30,000 cash.
9. Balance of Accumulated Depreciation is $52,000 on December 31, 2020.
10. Retained Earnings on December 31, 2019, is $67,000.
11. Sold fixed assets; the following entry was made:

Cash	5,000	
Accumulated Depreciation	12,000	
Fixed Assets		15,000
Gain on Sale of Fixed Assets		2,000

Following is summary income statement data for GEI.

Sales revenue (net credit sales)	$ 295,000
Cost of goods sold	(140,000)
Depreciation expense	(14,000)
Patent amortization*	(1,000)
Income tax expense	(17,000)
Selling and administrative expenses	(42,000)
Gain on sale of fixed assets	2,000
Net income	$ 83,000

*Net patent balance on December 31, 2020, is $8,000.

Required

a. Prepare comparative balance sheets as of December 31, 2019, and December 31, 2020.
b. Prepare a statement of cash flows using the indirect method.

Problem 5-65
Determining Missing Amounts Using Interrelations of Financial Statements **LO3**

The following abbreviated financial statements of Polo Corp. contain missing values.

Statement of Comprehensive Income

Net income, 2020	$ (a)
Other comprehensive income, 2020 (debit bal.)	(5,000)
Comprehensive income, 2020	$ 275,000

Changes in Accumulated Other Comprehensive Income from the Statement of Stockholders' Equity

Accumulated other comprehensive income, December 31, 2019	$ 70,000
Other comprehensive income, 2020	(b)
Accumulated other comprehensive income, December 31, 2020	$ (c)

Retained Earnings Statement

Retained earnings, December 31, 2019	$ 400,000
Net income, 2020	(d)
Dividends, 2020	(80,000)
Retained earnings, December 31, 2020	$ (e)

Balance Sheet

Assets	
Cash, December 31, 2020	$ (f)
Total assets, excluding cash, December 31, 2020	1,300,000
Total assets, December 31, 2020	$1,600,000
Liabilities	
Total liabilities, December 31, 2020	$ 810,000
Stockholders' Equity	
Common stock (no-par), December 31, 2020	(g)
Retained earnings, December 31, 2020	(h)
Accumulated other comprehensive income, December 31, 2020	(i)
Total stockholders' equity, December 31, 2020	$ (j)

Statement of Cash Flows

Net cash flows from operating activities	$ 290,000
Net cash flows from investing activities	(400,000)
Net cash flows from financing activities	(k)
Change in cash, 2020	50,000
Cash, December 31, 2019	(l)
Cash, December 31, 2020	$ (m)

Required

Determine the missing amounts, *a* through *m*, from the financial statements.

Problem 5-66
Preparing Financial Statements **LO6**

Media Inc., a graphics provider, reported the following information for 2020.

Selected Accounts from the Balance Sheet December 31, 2019

Accounts receivable	$ 5,000
Prepaid insurance	10,000
Supplies	2,500
Equipment, net	40,000
Accounts payable (suppliers)	20,000*
Deferred lease revenue	6,500
Salaries payable	3,500
Common stock (no-par)	13,500
Retained earnings	25,000

* The December 31, 2020, balance is $25,000.

Income Statement For Year Ended December 31, 2020

Sales	$100,000
Insurance expense	(7,500)
Depreciation expense	(5,000)
Supplies expense	(15,000)
Salaries expense	(30,000)
Lease revenue	6,000
Net income	$ 48,500

Statement of Cash Flows For Year Ended December 31, 2020

Cash flows from operating activities		
Collections from customers	$45,000	
Insurance payments	(12,500)	
Payments to suppliers	(22,500)	
Payments to employees	(26,000)	
Rental receipts	9,500	
Net cash used by operating activities		$(6,500)
Cash flows from investing activities		—
Cash flows from financing activities		—
Cash balance, December 31, 2019		11,000
Cash balance, December 31, 2020		$ 4,500

Required

Prepare the December 31, 2020, balance sheet.

Problem 5-67
Computing Liquidity Ratios and Activity Ratios; Performing Horizontal Analysis **LO4, 5, 6**

The following data are taken from **VF Corporation** in its 2015 annual report on Form 10-K.

VF Corporation

At December ($ millions)	2015	2014
Assets		
Current assets		
Cash	$ 946	$ 972
Accounts receivable	1,320	1,276
Inventory	1,612	1,483
Other current assets	286	301
Total current assets	4,164	4,032
Property, plant and equipment	988	942
Intangible assets	2,113	2,433
Goodwill	1,788	1,825
Other assets	587	613
Total assets	$ 9,640	$9,845

continued

continued from previous page

VF Corporation At December ($ millions)	2015	2014
Liabilities and Stockholders' Equity		
Current liabilities		
Short-term borrowings	$ 450	$ 22
Current portion of long-term debt	13	4
Accounts payable	690	691
Accrued liabilities	789	897
Total current liabilities	1,942	1,614
Long-term debt	1,402	1,414
Other liabilities	911	1,186
Total liabilities	4,255	4,214
Stockholders' equity		
Preferred stock	—	—
Common stock	106	108
Additional paid-in capital	3,193	2,993
Accumulated other comprehensive income	(1,043)	(702)
Retained earnings	3,129	3,232
Total stockholders' equity	5,385	5,631
Total liabilities and stockholders' equity	$ 9,640	$9,845

Additional Information ($ millions)	2015
Net sales	$12,251
Cost of goods sold	6,394
Net income	1,232
Income before interest and taxes	1,669
Interest expense	89
Cash provided from operating activities	1,147
Cash paid for dividends	565
Cash paid for capital expenditures	255

Required

a. Calculate the following liquidity ratios for 2015: current ratio and quick ratio.

b. Calculate the following activity ratios for 2015: accounts receivable turnover, average days to collect receivables, inventory turnover, and average days in inventory.

c. Calculate the following cash flow ratios for 2015: current cash debt coverage, cash debt coverage, and free cash flow.

d. Prepare a horizontal analysis for the change in balance sheet accounts from 2014 to 2015.

Problem 5-68
Computing Profitability and Solvency Ratios **LO4**

Refer to the information in Problem 5-67 for VF Corporation to answer the following requirements.

Required

a. Calculate the following profitability ratio: return on equity.

b. Disaggregate return on equity into its DuPont components of profitability (profit margin), activity (asset turnover), and leverage (financial leverage). Demonstrate how the product of the components is equal to return on equity.

c. Calculate the following solvency ratios: total liabilities-to-equity, and times interest earned.

Problem 5-69
Analyzing Competitors on Liquidity, Solvency, and Profitability Measures **LO4, 5**

The following financial statement information is for two competitors: **VF Corporation** and **Columbia Sportswear Company**.

$ millions	VF Corp. 2015	Columbia Sportswear Co. 2015
Assets		
Current assets		
Cash	$ 946	$ 370
Accounts receivable	1,320	372
Inventory	1,612	474
Other current assets	286	33
Total current assets	4,164	1,249
Property, plant and equipment	988	292
Intangible assets	2,113	139
Goodwill	1,788	69
Other assets	587	97
Total assets	$ 9,640	$1,846
Liabilities and Stockholders' Equity		
Current liabilities		
Short-term borrowings	$ 450	$ 2
Current portion of long-term debt	13	
Accounts payable	690	217
Accrued liabilities	789	147
Total current liabilities	1,942	366
Long-term debt	1,402	55
Other liabilities	911	9
Total liabilities	4,255	430
Stockholders' equity		
Common stock	106	35
Additional paid-in capital	3,193	
Accumulated other comprehensive income	(1,043)	(21)
Retained earnings	3,129	1,386
Non-controlling interest		16
Total stockholders' equity	5,385	1,416
Total liabilities and stockholders' equity	$ 9,640	$1,846

Additional Information ($ millions)		
Net sales	$12,251	$2,326
Cost of goods sold	6,394	1,253
Net income	1,232	180
Income before interest and taxes	1,669	248
Interest expense	89	1

Required

Compute the ratios below and briefly analyze the two competitors in the following three areas.

a. Liquidity—current ratio and quick ratio.

b. Solvency—total liabilities-to-equity and times interest earned.

c. Profitability—return on equity and profit margin.

Problem 5-70
Analyzing Competitors on Liquidity, Solvency, and Profitability Measures **LO4, 5**

The following financial statement information is from two competitors, **Walgreens Boots Alliance Inc.** and **CVS Health Corporation**, for their respective 2015 fiscal year-end.

$ millions	Walgreens Boots Alliance Inc. 2015	CVS Health Corp. 2015
Assets		
Current assets		
Cash	$ 3,000	$ 2,459
Short-term investments		88
Accounts receivable	6,849	11,888
Inventories	8,678	14,001
Other current assets	1,130	1,942
Total current assets	19,657	30,378
Property, plant and equipment	15,068	9,855
Intangible assets	12,351	13,878
Goodwill	16,372	38,106
Other assets	5,334	1,440
Total assets	$ 68,782	$ 93,657
Liabilities and Stockholders' Equity		
Current liabilities		
Short-term borrowings	$ 1,068	
Current portion of long-term debt		$ 1,197
Accounts payable	10,088	7,490
Claims and discounts payable		7,653
Accrued liabilities	5,401	6,829
Total current liabilities	16,557	23,169
Long-term debt	13,315	26,267
Other liabilities	7,610	6,979
Total liabilities	37,482	56,415
Redeemable noncontrolling interest		39
Stockholders' equity		
Common stock	12	17
Additional paid-in capital	9,953	30,948
Accumulated other comprehensive income	(214)	(358)
Retained earnings	25,087	35,506
Treasury stock	(3,977)	(28,917)
Non-controlling interest	439	7
Total stockholders' equity	31,300	37,203
Total liabilities and stockholders' equity	$ 68,782	$ 93,657

Additional Information ($ millions)		
Net sales	$103,444	$153,290
Cost of goods sold	76,520	126,762
Net income	4,279	5,237
Income before interest and taxes	5,916	9,454
Interest expense	605	838
Cash provided by operating expenses	5,664	8,412

Required

Analyze the financial statements of the two competitors by answering the following questions. Include support for your answers.

a. Which competitor has the stronger liquidity position?
b. Which competitor has the stronger return on equity?
c. Use the DuPont model to identify which component(s) of return on equity drives the difference (if any) between the two competitors' return on equity.

d. Which company has a stronger long-term solvency position?
e. Which company has a stronger cash to debt coverage?
f. Which competitor has a higher rate of productivity on its assets?

Problem 5-71
Performing Horizontal and Vertical Analysis of the Balance Sheet and Income Statement **LO6**

The following financial statement information is from **Walgreens Boots Alliance Inc.** its 2015 and 2014 fiscal year-ends ($ millions).

Walgreens Boots Alliance Inc.
Balance Sheet

December 31	2015	2014
Assets		
Current assets		
Cash	$ 3,000	$ 2,646
Accounts receivable	6,849	3,218
Inventories	8,678	6,076
Other current assets	1,130	302
Total current assets	19,657	12,242
Property, plant and equipment	15,068	12,257
Equity investment	—	7,336
Intangible assets	12,351	1,180
Goodwill	16,372	2,359
Other assets	5,334	1,876
Total assets	$68,782	$37,250
Liabilities and Stockholders' Equity		
Current liabilities		
Short-term borrowings	$ 1,068	$ 774
Accounts payable	10,088	4,315
Accrued liabilities	5,401	3,806
Total current liabilities	16,557	8,895
Long-term debt	13,315	3,716
Other liabilities	7,610	4,022
Total liabilities	37,482	16,633
Redeemable noncontrolling interest		
Stockholders' equity		
Common stock	12	80
Additional paid-in capital	9,953	1,172
Accumulated other comprehensive income	(214)	136
Retained earnings	25,087	22,322
Treasury stock	(3,977)	(3,197)
Non-controlling interest	439	104
Total stockholders' equity	31,300	20,617
Total liabilities and stockholders' equity	$68,782	$37,250

Walgreens Boots Alliance Inc.
Income Statement

For Year Ended December 31	2015	2014
Net sales	$103,444	$76,392
Cost of goods sold	76,520	54,823
Gross margin	26,924	21,569
Operating expenses	22,886	18,609
Other expenses, gains, losses	(182)	1,028
Net income	$ 4,220	$ 1,932

Required

a. Prepare a horizontal analysis of the change in balances from 2014 to 2015.
b. Prepare a vertical analysis of the income statement and balance sheet for 2014 and 2015.

Accounting Decisions and Judgments

AD&J 5-72
Evaluating an Annual Report **LO1, 2**

Real World Analysis Obtain an electronic copy of the Form 10-K for **Coca-Cola Company** for the year ended December 31, 2015, which can be found on the SEC Edgar website (https://www.sec.gov/edgar/searchedgar/companysearch.html).

Required

a. Did Coca-Cola increase its total common dividend payment in 2015?
b. Does Coca-Cola use the direct or indirect method of presenting its statement of cash flows?
c. What was Coca-Cola's total liabilities-to-equity ratio as of December 31, 2015? What is a key limitation of this ratio?
d. Why are depreciation and amortization added to net income to obtain cash flow from operations?
e. Depreciation and amortization for 2015 amounted to $1,970 million in the statement of cash flows. However, the allowance for depreciation included in Note 7 decreased by $842 ($10,625 to $9,783) million. Why are the two amounts not the same?
f. Does Coca-Cola present its balance sheet in the form that stresses the financing form of the accounting identity?

AD&J 5-73
Analyzing Return on Equity and its Components **LO4**

Real World Analysis Obtain electronic copies of the annual reports on Form 10-K for **Gap Inc.** and **Abercrombie & Fitch Co.** for the fiscal years ended February 1, 2014, January 31, 2015, and January 30, 2016, from the SEC Edgar website (https://www.sec.gov/edgar/searchedgar/companysearch.html).

Required

a. Calculate return on equity for fiscal years ended February 1, 2014, January 31, 2015, and January 30, 2016, for each company.
b. Disaggregate return on equity into its DuPont components of profitability (profit margin), activity (asset turnover), and leverage (financial leverage) for each company. Demonstrate how the product of the components is equal to return on equity.
c. Analyze your results. What are the drivers for the differences (if any) between the ratios of the two companies?

AD&J 5-74
Computing Key Ratios **LO4, 5**

Real World Analysis Obtain electronic copies of the annual reports on Form 10-K for **Walgreens Boots Alliance Inc.** for fiscal year ended August 31, 2015, from the SEC Edgar website (https://www.sec.gov/edgar/searchedgar/companysearch.html). *Hint:* See how the company reports noncontrolling interest on financial statements. In this case, use earnings attributable to the controlling interest in the numerator and equity of the controlling interest (CI) in the denominator.

Required

Compute the following ratios for 2015.

a. Return on equity
b. Current ratio
c. Quick ratio
d. Total liabilities-to-equity
e. Times interest earned

AD&J 5-75
Interpreting Statements of Cash Flows for Several Competitors **LO1, 2, 8**

Real World Analysis Obtain electronic copies of the annual reports on Form 10-K for the companies listed below from the SEC Edgar website (https://www.sec.gov/edgar/searchedgar/companysearch.html).

1. **Abercrombie & Fitch Co.** (January 30, 2016)
2. **Gap Inc.** (January 30, 2016)
3. **American Eagle Outfitters** (January 30, 2016)
4. **The TJX Companies Inc.** (January 30, 2016)
5. **J. Crew Group Inc.** (January 20, 2016)
6. **Ralph Lauren Corporation** (April 2, 2016)
7. **Lululemon Athletica Inc.** (January 31, 2016)
8. **Urban Outfitters Inc.** (January 31, 2016)
9. **Guess? Inc.** (January 30, 2016)

Required

Answer the following questions for each of the 9 companies listed above.

a. Determine whether report the statement of cash flows is presented using the indirect method of cash flows or the direct method of cash flows.
b. Which sections of the statement of cash flows are outflows and which sections are inflows?
c. By how much did cash increase or decrease during the period?

d. What (if any) noncash items are disclosed?

e. What observations can you make based on the data collected for this group of retail competitors?

Real World Analysis The following items are taken from actual statements of cash flows of the indicated companies.

AD&J 5-76 Identifying Where Items are Reported within a Statement of Cash Flows **LO1**

Item (Company)

____ 1. Capital expenditures for property and equipment (**American Eagle Outfitters**)
____ 2. Proceeds from issuance of short-term debt (**Ralph Lauren Corporation**)
____ 3. Dividends paid (**Target Corporation**)
____ 4. Depreciation and amortization (**Whole Foods Market Inc.**)
____ 5. Purchases of marketable securities and investments (assume non-trading) (**3M Company**)
____ 6. Changes in accrued expenses and other current liabilities (**Gap Inc.**)
____ 7. Cash paid for business acquisitions (**United Parcel Service Inc.**)
____ 8. Software purchases (**VF Corporation**)
____ 9. Increase in current income taxes (**Macy's Inc.**)

Required

Identify each item, 1 through 9, with its reported location in the statement of cash flows. Use the following symbols *O*, *I*, or *F*.

O Cash flows from operations.
I Cash flows from investing activities.
F Cash flows from financing activities.

Judgment Case Increasing accounts receivable turnover contributes to an increase in return on equity. To increase the accounts receivable turnover, a company must consider different ways to reduce investment in accounts receivable with similar sales results.

AD&J 5-77 Consulting Management when Analyzing Accounts Receivable Turnover **LO4**

Required

a. As a manager responsible for increasing return on equity, what actions might we suggest to increase return on receivables?

b. What unintended consequences can these suggestions have that could negatively affect operational performance? What can a company do to reduce receivables without negatively impacting performance?

Codification Skills Identify and list the definitions from the Codification for the following:

AD&J 5-78 Using the Codification in Defining Cash Flow Activities **LO1**

1. operating activities.
2. financing activities.
3. investing activities.

Codification Skills Research the Codification and identify the proper citation that provides guidance on each of the following topics.

AD&J 5-79 Using the Codification to Cite Guidance on Cash Flow Disclosures **LO1, 2, 8**

a. Disclosure of noncash investing and financing activities. FASB ASC ____-____-____-____

b. Disclosure of interest and income taxes paid (indirect method). FASB ASC ____-____-____-____

c. Examples of cash inflows from financing activities. FASB ASC ____-____-____-____

d. Purpose of the statement of cash flows. FASB ASC ____-____-____-____

Codification Skills A company has reported amounts in its balance sheet for cash, cash equivalents, and restricted cash. In preparing its statement of cash flows, management is uncertain as to which balance(s) to include in the beginning and ending cash balance. Identify the relevant authoritative guidance on this issue.

AD&J 5-80 Using the Codification to Research Guidance on What is Included in Cash **LO2**

FASB ASC ____-____-____-____

Appendix—Brief Exercises

App Brief Exercise 5-81
Direct and Indirect Methods—Demonstrating the Difference Between Direct and Indirect Cash Flow Methods **LO8**

a. Explain the basic difference between the direct and indirect methods of reporting on the statement of cash flows.

b. Use net income of $5,000, sales revenue of $100,000, and an increase in accounts receivable of $10,000, to illustrate the basic difference between the direct and indirect methods of reporting on the statement of cash flows. Assume that the increase in accounts receivable reflects the amount by which credit sales exceed cash collections on account.

c. Which method provides the most relevant information to investors and creditors?

App Brief Exercise 5-82
Direct Method—Preparing the Operating Activities Section of the Statement of Cash Flows **LO8**
Hint: See Demo 5-8

TJ Company reported the following cash flows. Prepare the operating activities section of the statement of cash flows using the direct method.

Cash paid to suppliers	$40,000	Cash received from customers.	$60,000
Cash paid to employees.	5,000	Cash paid for taxes.	3,000

Appendix—Exercises

App Exercise 5-83
Direct Method—Preparing a Statement of Cash Flows **LO8**

Lauder Corp. reported the following financial statements.

Balance Sheet

December 31	2019	2020	Difference
Cash.	$ 24,000	$ 62,000	$38,000
Accounts receivable	19,000	15,000	(4,000)
Merchandise inventory	31,000	59,000	28,000
Land	20,000	4,000	(16,000)
Equipment	48,000	72,000	24,000
Accumulated depreciation	(12,000)	(24,000)	(12,000)
Total assets.	$130,000	$188,000	$58,000
Accounts payable.	$ 16,000	$ 18,000	$ 2,000
Notes payable, long-term	7,000	2,000	(5,000)
Bonds payable	—	30,000	30,000
Common stock (no-par)	80,000	92,000	12,000
Retained earnings	27,000	46,000	19,000
Total liabilities and stockholders' equity . . .	$130,000	$188,000	$58,000

Income Statement

For Year Ended December 31	2020
Revenues.	$152,000
Costs of goods sold	82,000
Depreciation.	12,000
Other expenses	14,000
Loss on sale of land	10,000
Net income.	$ 34,000

Required

Prepare the statement of cash flows using the direct method for Lauder Corp. for the year ended December 31, 2020.

Appendix—Problems

App Problem 5-84
Direct Method—Preparing a Statement of Cash Flows **LO8**

Refer to the information in Problem 5-64 to complete the following requirement.

Required

Prepare a complete statement of cash flows using the direct method.

Appendix—Accounting Decisions and Judgments

App AD&J 5-85
Comparing the Direct and Indirect Methods for Reporting Cash Flows **LO2, 8**

Judgment Case The FASB initiated a joint project with the AICPA entitled Financial Statement Presentation. A copy of the FASB exposure draft dated July 1, 2010, and initial feedback is accessible on the FASB's website. Access the exposure draft at https://www.fasb.org/jsp/FASB/Page/SectionPage&cid=1176157086783 to answer the following questions.

Required

a. Which method does the FASB prefer, the direct method or the indirect method?

b. What advantages does the FASB propose as support for the preferred method?

c. What disadvantages does the FASB propose are prevalent if companies select the alternative method?

d. Given these advantages and disadvantages, which method would you propose and why? Are there other factors to consider in choosing one method over another?

App AD&J 5-86
Determining Financial Amounts from the Statement of Cash Flows Under the Direct Method **LO8**

Challenge Problem The statement of cash flows using the direct method for Collins Industries follows.

Consolidated Statement of Cash Flows
For Year Ended October 31, 2020

Cash flows from operating activities	
Cash received from customers	$157,845,373
Cash paid to suppliers and employees	(150,697,953)
Income taxes paid	(1,456,095)
Interest paid, net	(1,628,444)
Net cash provided by operating activities	4,062,881
Cash flows from investing activities	
Capital expenditures	(5,958,283)
Sale of property and equipment	478,150
Expenditures for other assets	(284,849)
Other, net	—
Net cash used by investing activities	(5,764,982)
Cash flows from financing activities	
Principal payments of long-term debt and capitalized leases	(2,598,936)
Addition to long-term debt and capitalized leases	6,854,316
Purchase of common stock	(862,525)
Payment of dividends	(1,735,911)
Net cash provided by financing activities	1,656,944
Net increase (decrease) in cash	45,157
Cash at beginning of year	189,152
Cash at end of year	$ 143,995
Reconciliation of net loss to net cash provided by operations:	
Net income	$ 3,027,100
Depreciation and amortization	1,795,336
Common stock issued for benefit of employees	—
Decrease in receivables	1,399,922
Decrease in inventories	414,780
Decrease in prepaid expenses	395,578
Decrease in accounts payable	(2,183,531)
Decrease in accrued expenses	(717,215)
Gain on sale of property and equipment	(69,089)
Net cash provided by operating activities	$ 4,062,881

Required

Determine the following amounts using Collin's statement of cash flows.

a. Total sales. (Assume all receivables relate to sales.)

b. Book value of property and equipment sold.

c. Cost of goods sold. (Assume that $70,000,000 of $150,697,953 line item "cash paid to suppliers and employees" was paid to suppliers.)

d. Total of operating expenses other than cost of goods sold, noncash expenses, and interest. (Assume the line item "interest paid, net" equals interest expense less interest revenue.)

e. Net income. (This amount is given, but we must calculate it from the information provided along with the results calculated for part *a*, *b*, *c*, and *d*.)

Answers to Review Exercises

Review 5-1

a. Cash flows from investing activities

b. Cash flows from operating activities

c. Cash flows from investing activities

d. Cash flows from financing activities

e. Cash flows from operating activities

f. Cash flows from financing activities

g. Cash flows from financing activities

h. Cash flows from operating activities

i. Cash flows from investing activities

Review 5-2

Bell Corp.
Statement of Cash Flows
For Years Ended December 31, 2020

Cash flows from operating activities	
Net income	$113,610
Adjustments:	
Depreciation expense	45,000
Gain on sale of equipment	(2,500)
Increase in accounts receivable	(14,000)
Decrease in supplies	1,000
Decrease in merchandise inventory	22,700
Decrease in accounts payable	(5,000)
Decrease in salaries payable	(9,000)
Decrease in utilities payable	(400)
Net cash inflow from operating activities	151,410
Cash flows from investing activities	
Purchase of equipment	(57,600)
Sale of equipment*	10,500
Net cash outflow from investing activities	(47,100)
Cash flows from financing activities	
Decrease in notes payable	(30,000)
Issuance of common stock	40,000
Cash paid for dividends	(88,310)
Net cash outflow from financing activities	(78,310)
Net increase in cash during 2020	26,000
Cash, January 1, 2020	44,000
Cash, December 31, 2020	$ 70,000

*$8,000 + $2,500 = $10,500.

Review 5-3

a. $14,400 ($16,900 – $2,500)
b. $18,200 ($8,800 + $14,400 – $5,000)
c. $111,700 ($75,000 + $18,200 + 18,500)
d. $18,500 ($16,000 + $2,500)
e. $153,500 ($3,500 + $150,000)
f. $150,000 ($153,500 – $3,500)
g. ($1,500) ($3,500 – $5,000)

Review 5-4

a. 0.27
b. 0.13 × 1.52 × 1.39 = 0.27
c. 8.19, 2.10, 17.00

Review 5-5

a. 6.24
b. 2.22
c. 1.58
d. 0.38
e. 113.71
f. 0.70
g. ($23)

Review 5-6

Horizontal analysis Income Statement	2016	2015	Dollar Change	Percentage Change
Revenues	$3,962	$3,869	$ 93	2%
Costs of goods sold	1,997	1,920	77	4%
Gross margin	1,965	1,949	16	1%
Operating expenses	1,169	1,120	49	4%
Operating income	$ 796	$ 829	$(33)	−4%

Horizontal analysis Balance Sheet	2016	2015	Dollar Change	Percentage Change
Current assets	$1,721	$1,665	$ 56	3%
Noncurrent assets	948	867	81	9%
Total assets	$2,669	$2,532	137	5%
Current liabilities	$ 276	$ 373	$ (97)	−26%
Noncurrent liabilities	460	358	102	28%
Total liabilities	736	731	5	1%
Stockholders' equity	1,933	1,801	132	7%
Total liabilities and stockholders' equity	$2,669	$2,532	$137	5%

Vertical analysis Income Statement	2016	2015	Percentage of 2016 Revenues	Percentage of 2015 Revenues
Revenues	$3,962	$3,869	100%	100%
Costs of goods sold	1,997	1,920	50%	50%
Gross margin	1,965	1,949	50%	50%
Operating expenses	1,169	1,120	30%	29%
Net income	$ 796	$ 829	20%	21%

Vertical analysis Balance Sheet	2016	2015	Percentage of 2016 Assets	Percentage of 2015 Assets
Current assets	$1,721	$1,665	64%	66%
Noncurrent assets	948	867	36%	34%
Total assets	$2,669	$2,532	100%	100%
Current liabilities	$ 276	$ 373	10%	15%
Noncurrent liabilities	460	358	17%	14%
Total liabilities	736	731	28%	29%
Stockholders' equity	1,933	1,801	72%	71%
Total liabilities and stockholders' equity	$2,669	$2,532	100%	100%

Review 5-7

a. Industrial segment organic operating profit.

b. Industrial segment profit.

c. The financial statements are prepared according to GAAP standards. Industrial segment organic operating profit is not a GAAP standard. Because the company reports industrial segment organic operating profit in the MD&A, a reconciliation between GAAP and the non-GAAP measure is required.

d. General Electric's management believes that the industrial segment organic profit measure provides a more complete summary of operating results, allows more information useful for trend analysis, and allows a more direct comparison to other nonfinancial businesses and companies.

Review 5-8

Cash flows from operating activities	
Cash received from customers	$17,700
Cash payments to employees	(9,500)
Cash payments for selling and administrative activities	(5,450)
Net cash inflow from operating activities	$ 2,750

6 Time Value of Money

International Business Machines Corporation

2016 Annual Report on Form 10-K
Footnote D. Financial Instruments

Loans and Long-Term Receivables

Fair values are based on discounted future cash flows using current interest rates offered for similar loans to clients with similar credit ratings for the same remaining maturities. At December 31, 2016 and 2015, the difference between the carrying amount and estimated fair value for loans and long- term receivables was immaterial. If measured at fair value in the financial statements, these financial instruments would be classified as Level 3 in the fair value hierarchy.

The Gap, Inc.

2016 Annual Report on Form 10-K
Note 1. Organization and Summary of Significant Accounting Policies (excerpt)

Impairment of Long-Lived Assets

We review the carrying amount of long-lived assets for impairment whenever events or changes in circumstances indicate that the carrying amount of an asset may not be recoverable. Events that result in an impairment review include a significant decrease in the operating performance of the long-lived asset, or the decision to close a store, corporate facility, or distribution center. Long-lived assets are considered impaired if the carrying amount exceeds the estimated undiscounted future cash flows of the asset or asset group. For impaired assets, we recognize a loss equal to the difference between the carrying amount of the asset or asset group and its estimated fair value, which is recorded in operating expenses in the Consolidated Statements of Income. The estimated fair value of the asset or asset group is based on discounted future cash flows of the asset or asset group using a discount rate commensurate with the related risk. The asset group is defined as the lowest level for which identifiable cash flows are available and largely independent of the cash flows of other groups of assets, which for our retail stores is primarily at the store level.

Target Corporation

2016 Annual Report on Form 10-K
Note 10. Fair Value Measurements (excerpt)

Significant Financial Instruments not Measured at Fair Value[(a)]	2016		2015	
(millions)	Carrying Amount	Fair Value	Carrying Amount	Fair Value
Debt[(b)]	$11,715	$12,545	$11,859	$13,385

(a) The carrying amounts of certain other current assets, accounts payable, and certain accrued and other current liabilities approximate fair value due to their short-term nature.

(b) The fair value of debt is generally measured using a discounted cash flow analysis based on current market interest rates for the same or similar types of financial instruments and would be classified as Level 2. These amounts exclude unamortized swap valuation adjustments and capital lease obligations.

Ford Motor Company

2017 Annual Report on Form 10-K
Note 17. Retirement Benefits (excerpt)

Defined benefit pension and OPEB plan obligations are remeasured at least annually as of December 31 based on the present value of projected future benefit payments for all participants for services rendered to date. The measurement of projected future benefits is dependent on the provisions of each specific plan, demographics of the group covered by the plan, and other key measurement assumptions. For plans that provide benefits dependent on salary assumptions, we include a projection of salary growth in our measurements. No assumption is made regarding any potential future changes to benefit provisions beyond those to which we are presently committed (e.g., in existing labor contracts).

Chapter Preview

We begin by describing the compounding of *interest* (the cost of using money over time) as it applies to different compounding periods. We apply the time value of money concept in computations of the future value and the present value of *lump-sum amounts* (single amounts) and *annuities* (streams of equal payments). We show the formulas underlying time value of money calculations, but we emphasize the use of *Excel tools* for calculations as they are widespread in use by accountants. We conclude by applying the time value of money concept to common accounting and business situations such as the recording of bonds, pension obligations, and lease liabilities.

Action Plan

LO	Topic/Subtopic	Page	Demos	Reviews	Assignments
LO 6–1	**Explain the calculation of compound interest** Annual Compounding :: Semiannual Compounding :: Quarterly Compounding :: Monthly Compounding	6-3	D6-1	R6-1	18, 37, 38, 52, 64, 89
LO 6–2	**Apply future value concepts to a single amount** Accumulation :: Lump-Sum Amount :: Future Value :: Excel Formula	6-5	D6-2	R6-2	19, 20, 37, 38, 41, 42, 51, 52, 53, 64, 71, 72, 73
LO 6–3	**Apply present value concepts to a single amount** Discounting :: Lump-Sum Amount :: Present Value :: Excel Formula :: Traditional Approach :: Expected Cash Flow Approach	6-8	D6-3A D6-3B D6-3C	R6-3	21, 22, 23, 24, 39, 40, 41, 42, 43, 51, 52, 53, 64, 65, 67, 71, 72, 73, 85, 91
LO 6–4	**Apply future value concepts to an ordinary annuity and an annuity due** Ordinary Annuity :: Annuity Due :: Deferred Annuity :: Excel Formula	6-13	D6-4A D6-4B D6-4C	R6-4	25, 26, 44, 45, 48, 49, 50, 51, 52, 53, 63, 64, 66, 70, 71, 72, 73
LO 6–5	**Apply present value concepts to an ordinary annuity and an annuity due** Ordinary Annuity :: Annuity Due :: Deferred Annuity :: Excel Formula	6-16	D6-5A D6-5B D6-5C	R6-5	27, 28, 29, 30, 31, 32, 36, 46, 47, 48, 49, 50, 51, 52, 53, 54, 63, 64, 65, 66, 68, 69, 70, 71, 72, 73
LO 6–6	**Apply time value of money concept to common accounting scenarios** Bonds :: Lease Payments :: Pension Obligations :: Capital Investment Decisions :: Debt Retirement	6-19	D6-6	R6-6	33, 34, 35, 53, 55, 56, 57, 58, 59, 60, 61, 62, 64, 74, 75, 76, 77, 78, 79, 80, 81, 82, 83, 84, 86, 87, 88, 91, 92, 93
LO 6–7	**APPENDIX 6A—Apply time value of money concept to bond interest amortization** Bond Interest :: Discount on Bond Payable :: Premium on Bond Payable :: Effective Interest Method of Amortization	6-22	D6-7	R6-7	94, 97, 99
LO 6–8	**APPENDIX 6B—Apply time value of money concept using a financial calculator and compound interest tables** Financial Calculator :: Compound Interest Tables :: Factors :: Interpolation	6-25	D6-8A D6-8B	R6-8	90, 95, 96, 98, 100

LO 6-1 Explain the calculation of compound interest

LO 6-1 Overview

Compound Interest
Interest earned on principal plus accumulated interest compounded
- Annually
- Semiannually
- Quarterly
- Monthly

In business terms, **interest** is the cost of using money over time. More specifically, **interest expense** is the recognition during a reporting period of a borrower's cost for using resources. **Interest revenue** is the recognition during a reporting period of a lender's return for loaning resources. This definition of interest is in close agreement with the definition used by economists, who prefer to say that interest represents the **time value of money**.

We know that a thousand dollars today is worth more in one year's time than a thousand dollars received one year from now. The assumption is that today's dollars can be put to work earning interest. Today's money has a future value equal to its **principal** (face amount) plus whatever interest can be earned over the period of time it could be invested. Let's say that $1,000 earns 3% interest over a one-year period. In that case, the $1,000 is increased by $30 interest ($1,000 × 3%) for a total of $1,030 in one year. The time value of money ignores changes in inflation or in what a dollar can purchase due to changing prices—instead, it is focused on growth in dollars due to investing.

Compound interest results from earning interest on an initial investment (principal) plus earning interest on interest. In compound interest problems, it is assumed that interest is allowed to accumulate. **This means that compound interest includes interest on previously computed and recorded interest.**

Annual Compounding

The following table illustrates **annual compounding** over three years on an initial bank deposit.

Year	Principal Balance: Beginning of Year	5% Annual Interest	Principal Balance: End of Year
2020	$10,000	$ 500	$10,500
2021	10,500	525	11,025
2022	11,025	551	11,576
Total Interest		**$1,576**	

In the first year, the principal balance of $10,000 earns $500 of interest. That ending balance of $10,500 ($10,000 + $500) earns interest the following year at 5%: $10,500 × 5% = $525. We see that interest is earned not only on the initial investment of $10,000 but also on its earnings. In 2022, interest earned is even higher at $551 because interest is earned on the balance of $11,025.

Quarterly Compounding

In the prior example, interest was compounded annually. Compound interest periods of less than one year yield even more interest. When interest periods of less than one year are used, the annual interest rate given must be converted to an equivalent rate for the time period specified for compounding purposes. **Quoted interest rates are annual interest rates unless otherwise stated.**

To convert an annual rate to a compounding period of less than a year, simply divide the annual rate by the number of compounding periods within the year. To demonstrate, we add quarterly compounding to the interest illustration above.

Quarter 2020	Principal Balance: Beginning of Period	1.25% Quarterly Interest	Principal Balance: End of Period
First quarter	$10,000	$125	$10,125
Second quarter	10,125	127	10,252
Third quarter	10,252	128	10,380
Fourth quarter	10,380	130	10,510
Total Interest		$510	

The number of compounding periods in one year is now 4. Interest for one quarter is ¼ of 5%, or 1.25%. The first-year's interest with quarterly compounding would total $510 compared to $500 under annual compounding.

The quarterly compounding for the first year produces $10 more interest than annual compounding ($510 vs. $500). **The shorter the compounding time period, the greater the accumulated interest**. Quarterly compounding at 1.25% is equivalent to an annual interest rate of 5.1% ($510 ÷ $10,000). This equivalent rate is called the **effective rate** or the **annual yield**. As shown in this example, whenever interest is compounded more often than annually, the effective interest rate (5.1%) is greater than the stated interest rate (5.0%).

Compounding Options

Semiannual, quarterly, monthly, weekly, and daily compounding are all in common use. When interest periods of less than one year are used, the annual interest rate stated must be converted to an equivalent rate for the time period specified for compounding purposes. Also, the number of corresponding **compounding periods** over the life of the investment must be determined as illustrated in **Demo 6-1**. For example, when there is semiannual compounding over a 5 year period at an annual interest rate of 5%, the number of compounding periods is equal to 2 semiannual periods × 5 years, or 10 compounding periods, and the stated interest rate is 2.5%, or 5% ÷ 2, per semiannual period.

Accounting uses many applications of present and future value concepts. Some of the more common applications of time value of money are for the valuation of accounts such as bonds, lease liabilities, and pension obligations, discussed later. More generally, ASC 820 describes present value techniques used to estimate the fair value of assets and liabilities necessary for financial reporting and disclosure purposes. **The purpose of this chapter is to provide the foundation necessary for application of several accounting procedures in practice today**.

Compound Interest — LO6-1 — Demo 6-1

Demo MBC

Determine the number of compounding periods per year *and* compute the interest rate per compounding period for the following four compound interest scenarios.

Compounding	Annual Interest Rate	Number of Compounding Periods per Year	Interest Rate per Compounding Period
1. Annual.	5%	1	5% ÷ 1 = 5.00%
2. Semiannual.	5%	2	5% ÷ 2 = 2.50%
3. Quarterly	5%	4	5% ÷ 4 = 1.25%
4. Monthly	5%	12	5% ÷ 12 = 0.42%

Compound Interest — LO6-1 — REVIEW 6-1

Review MBC

For the following separate cases, *a* through *h*, for an investment of $10,000, complete the table by indicating (1) the interest rate per compounding period, and (2) the *total* number of compounding periods over the full term of the investment.

Compounding	Annual Interest Rate	Term	Interest Rate per Compounding Period	Total Number of Compounding Periods
a. Annual.	7%	5 years		
b. Quarterly	8%	8 years		
c. Monthly	6%	5 years		
d. Semiannual. . . .	8%	10 years		
e. Annual.	6%	3 years		
f. Quarterly	6%	5 years		
g. Monthly	6%	4 years		
h. Semiannual. . . .	6%	8 years		

More Practice: 6-18

Solution on p. 6-48.

EXPAND YOUR KNOWLEDGE **Simple Interest**

With **simple interest**, interest is earned on the principal balance only. Simple interest is the product of the principal amount at the beginning of each year multiplied by the period's interest rate. Interest is paid periodically (typically yearly or at the end of the contract) only on the initial principal and not on interest accumulated but not yet paid. This means a three-year $10,000 loan at a rate of 5% simple interest produces interest of $500 each year ($10,000 × 5%). *Investments specifying simple interest are rare.* The following table illustrates **simple compounding** over three years on a bank deposit, assuming that the $500 interest is withdrawn each year. Total interest over the three-year period is $1,500. This compares to the interest under annual compounding of $1,576 in the prior compounding interest example.

Year	Principal Balance: Beginning of Year	5% Annual Interest	Principal Balance: End of Year
2020	$10,000	$ 500	$10,000
2021	10,000	500	10,000
2022	10,000	500	10,000
Total Interest		$1,500	

LO 6-2 Apply future value concepts to a single amount

LO 6-2 Overview

Future Value of Single Amounts
- Compute end-point value of a single amount invested over time
- Solve using FV function in Excel

A **lump-sum amount** is a single amount. It often refers to a one-time-only investment amount, which involves an amount that earns compound interest from the start to the end of an investment time frame resulting in an ending amount.

Present value refers to an amount earlier than the end-point of an investment. **Future value** refers to an amount later than the starting point of an investment. If the amount invested at the start is known, the future value of that lump-sum amount at the end can be projected, provided the *interest rate* and *number of compounding periods* are specified. The time value of money amounts can be determined in a number of ways as described in **Exhibit 6-1**.

EXHIBIT 6-1
Options for Computing Time Value of Money

Computing Options	Coverage	Description
Formula	Chapter 6	An unknown amount is determined by solving formulas, which mathematically depict the process of interest accumulation over time.
Excel	Chapter 6	An unknown amount is determined using functions in Excel. The arguments (or inputs to functions) are present value, future value, number of periods, interest rate, and payment. We enter the known arguments and solve for the remaining unknown argument.
Compound interest tables	Appendix 6B	An unknown amount is determined by applying factors from present value and future value tables. Factors are selected from tables based upon a desired interest rate and a desired number of compounding periods.
Financial calculator	Appendix 6B	An unknown amount is determined using functions on a financial calculator. The functionality of calculators vary, but similar to Excel, we enter the known variables and solve for the remaining unknown variable.

FYI: Visit https://office.live.com/start/Excel.aspx for free access to Microsoft Excel Online by creating a Microsoft account.

Accountants mainly use Excel in practice. The AICPA recently addded Microsoft Excel as a tool for the CPA exam. Thus, after a brief introduction to formulas behind the computations, we focus on using Excel, including assignments. Appendix 6B to this chapter relies on interest tables and a calculator, and includes assignments for both methods.

We begin with an explanation of the steps to compute the future value of a single amount through a formula. By understanding the logic in computing future value, we gain a better understanding of the steps automatically done in Excel.

TARGET

Real World—PRESENT VALUE DISCLOSURE

In notes accompanying a recent Form 10-K for **Target Corporation**, a number of references were made to time value of money calculations including the following.

- Capital leases: disclosed the present value of future minimum lease payments.
- Defined benefit pension plan: disclosed the present value of benefit obligations.
- Financial instruments: disclosed fair value of debt measured using a discounted cash flow analysis.
- General liability and workers' compensation: recorded liabilities at estimated net present value.

TARGET [TGT]

Future Value of a Single Amount—Computation through Formula

Assume that we have a lump-sum amount of $10,000 to invest today for 3 years, earning 5% interest, compounded annually. What is the future value of this lump-sum amount at the end of 3 years? Today's (present value) amount increases to a future value amount from **compounding** of interest and is illustrated as follows.

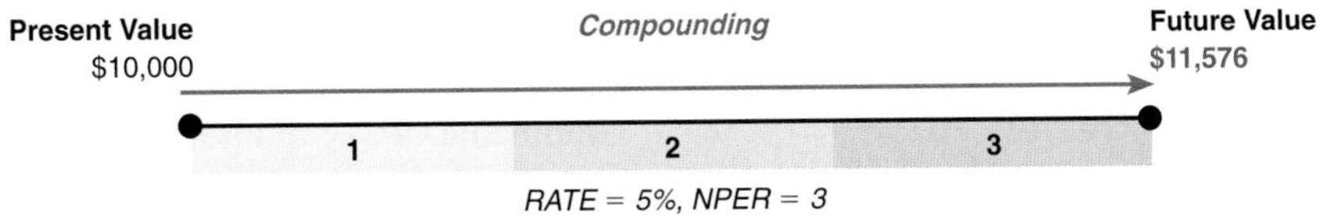

FYI: We use variables names similar to that used in Excel.

The future value of $10,000 after one year is $10,500, computed as $10,000 × 1.05. After the full three years, the future value is $11,576, computed as $10,000 × 1.05 × 1.05 × 1.05.

The formula that drives this **accumulation** of interest is in **Exhibit 6-2**. This formula for the future value of a single amount is where *FV* (future value) is defined in terms of *PV* (present value), *RATE* (interest), and *NPER* (number of compounding periods).

EXHIBIT 6-2
Future Value of a Single Amount Formula

$$FV = PV \times (1 + RATE)^{NPER}$$

We use the following formula to solve for the future value of $10,000 on deposit for 3 periods at an interest rate of 5%; this yields a future value of $11,576.

$$FV = PV \times (1 + RATE)^{NPER} = \$10{,}000 \times (1 + 0.05)^3 = \$10{,}000 \times (1.15763^*) = \$11{,}576$$

*To simplify this calculation, prepared tables (at the end of this chapter) can be used that include these factors. For example, the factor from the *Future Value of $1 Table* for 5% and 3 years is 1.15763. This factor of 1.15763 is multiplied by $10,000 to arrive at a future value of $11,576.30. Use of tables is explained further in Appendix 6B.

Future Value of a Single Amount—Computation through Excel

The same result is obtained using Excel. The formula to solve for future value is preset in the **future value function** in Excel. The inputs to the function are called **arguments** (commonly referred to as **variables**). After entering values in Excel for each argument, the function will return the fair value. The arguments in Excel are defined as follows.

Excel Argument	Description
RATE	Market or effective rate of interest for each compounding period.
NPER	Number of compounding periods.
FV	Future value or the value at a future date that assumes an investment increased by interest accumulation.
PV	Present value or the value today of a future amount that is discounted to the present with interest discounting.

After selecting the future value (FV) function in Excel, enter the known arguments: interest rate (5%), number of periods (3), and present value (−$10,000). The **syntax** (or the layout of the function and its related arguments) of the future value function in Excel is =FV(RATE,NPER,PMT,PV).

The FV function in Excel solves for the future value of $11,576 based upon the values of the arguments entered. When we enter a present value amount as a negative number (representing a *cash outflow*), Excel reports a future value amount as a positive number (representing a *cash inflow*). The opposite is also true—when entering a positive number for the present value (representing a *cash inflow*), Excel reports a negative number as the future value (representing a *cash outflow*). In **Demo 6-2**, we compute the future value of different amounts under different compounding scenarios.

	Excel Arguments				Excel Function
	RATE	NPER	PV	FV	=FV(RATE,NPER,PMT,PV)*
Given	5%	3	(10,000)	?	= FV(0.05,3,0,− 10000)
Solution				$11,576.25	

*In the future value function, we enter zero for PMT because there are no periodic payments in this example—we discuss periodic payments in **LO 6-4**.

Future Value of a Single Amount—Change in Values of Arguments

The following table demonstrates how changing the values of the arguments affects the future value of $11,576.25 (from the previous example). In the first case, the interest rate is increased from 5% to 7%. Because interest is compounded at a higher rate of return, the future value increases to $12,250.43. In the second case, the number of periods that the investment earns interest increases from 3 periods to 5 periods. Additional compounding periods cause an increase in the future value to $12,762.82. In the last case, the initial investment increases to $15,000, resulting in an increase in the future value to $17,364.38.

	Excel Arguments				Excel Function
	RATE	NPER	PV	FV	=FV(RATE,NPER,PMT,PV)
Original	5%	3	$(10,000)	$11,576.25	= FV(0.05,3,0,− 10000)
Increase interest rate	7%	3	(10,000)	12,250.43	= FV(0.07,3,0,− 10000)
Increase number of periods	5%	5	(10,000)	12,762.82	= FV(0.05,5,0,− 10000)
Increase present value	5%	3	(15,000)	17,364.38	= FV(0.05,3,0,− 15000)

EXPANDING YOUR KNOWLEDGE — Graphical Display of Interest Compounding

The following graphical display of interest compounding illustrates the relations among future values, interest rates, and periods of time. A $10,000 initial investment grows differently at a 10% interest rate versus a 5% interest rate or a 0% interest rate. After 10 years at a 10% interest rate, the $10,000 increases to $25,937, while at a 5% interest rate, the initial investment increases to $16,289. As you can see by looking at the trend lines, the future value grows at an increasing rate as the interest rate increases.

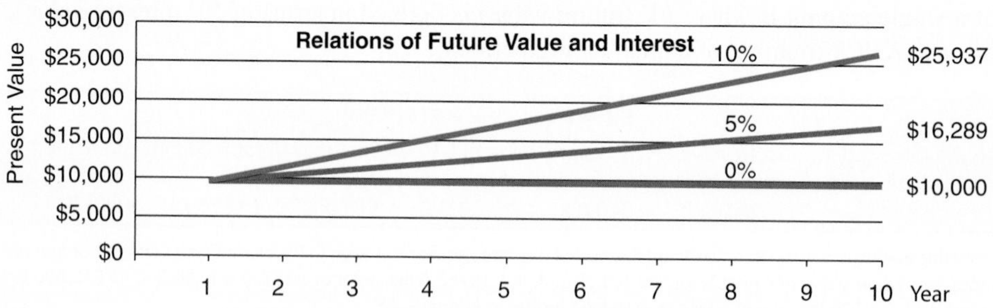

Demo MBC

Demo 6-2 **LO6-2** **Future Value of a Single Amount**

For the separate investments *A* through *F*, complete the following table by indicating (1) the Excel formula required to calculate the future value of the investment, and (2) the future value amount of the investment.

Investment	Compounding	Annual Interest Rate	Initial Cost	Investment Period	Excel Formula	Future Value Amount
Investment A	Annually	6%	$ (5,000)	3 years	**FV(0.06, 3,0,− 5000)**	**$ 5,955.08**
Investment B	Annually	8%	(6,000)	5 years	**FV(0.08, 5,0,− 6000)**	**8,815.97**
Investment C	Semiannually	6%	(5,000)	4 years	**FV(0.03, 8,0,− 5000)**	**6,333.85**
Investment D	Semiannually	8%	(4,000)	6 years	**FV(0.04,12,0,− 4000)**	**6,404.13**
Investment E	Quarterly	6%	(10,000)	5 years	**FV(0.015,20,0,−10000)**	**13,468.55**
Investment F	Quarterly	8%	(8,000)	4 years	**FV(0.02,16,0,− 8000)**	**10,982.29**

Future Value of a Single Amount

LO6-2 **REVIEW 6-2**

Review MBC

Laurel Inc. is considering a $5,000 investment with an expected annual return of 6%, compounded semiannually over 5 years. Compute the estimated future value of the investment with these terms. Next, compute the estimated future value of the investment assuming that the following arguments change while other arguments remain the same: (1) interest rate increases to 8%, (2) number of years increases to 10, (3) initial cost of the investment increases to $6,000, and (4) compounding is adjusted to quarterly. Consider each change separately.

Terms	Original Investment	Increase Interest Rate	Increase Periods	Increase Present Value	Increase Compounding
Annual interest rate . . .	6%	8%	6%	6%	6%
Compounding	Semiannual	Semiannual	Semiannual	Semiannual	Quarterly
Number of years	5	5	10	5	5
Initial Cost	$(5,000)	$(5,000)	$(5,000)	$(6,000)	$(5,000)
Future value	$ a	$ b	$ c	$ d	$ e

More Practice:
6-19, 6-37, 6-38
Solution on p. 6-48.

Apply present value concepts to a single amount

LO 6-3

Present Value of Single Amounts
- Compute *current value* of a future, single amount (discounting)
- Compute *current value* of a future *estimated amount(s)*
  - Traditional approach
  - Expected cash flow approach

LO 6-3 Overview

To determine the present value of a future amount, the future amount must be discounted to the present. **Discounting** is a mathematical process for reducing a future value to a present value. If the dollar amount at the end of an investment period (future value) is known, the amount of money needed at the start of the investment period (present value) can be determined, as long as the *interest rate* and *number of interest compounding periods* are known.

Present Value of a Single Amount—Computation through Formula

Assume that we desire a future value of $11,576 in 3 years. If we assume an interest rate of 5% (compounded annually), *what lump-sum amount must we invest today to have an accumulated future value of $11,576 in 3 years?* The present value of this single amount is illustrated as follows.

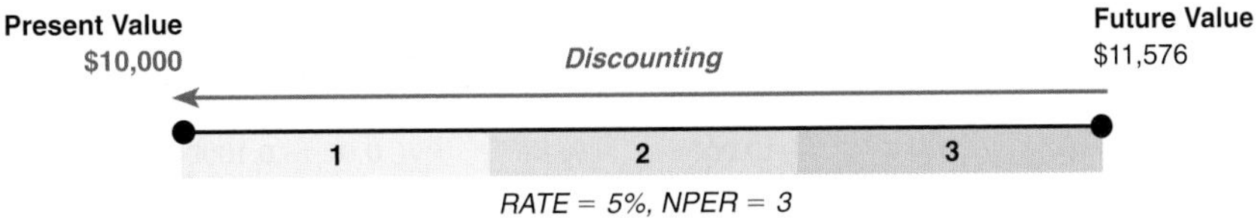

We again illustrate this computation in two ways: through a formula and through Excel. The formula for the present value of a single amount is in **Exhibit 6-3**, where *PV* (present value) is defined in terms of *FV* (future value), *RATE* (interest), and *NPER* (number of compounding periods). This formula is derived by taking the future value of a single amount equation from **Exhibit 6-2** and dividing each side of that equation by $(1 + RATE)^{NPER}$.

EXHIBIT 6-3
Present Value of a Single Amount Equation

$$V = \frac{FV}{(1+RATE)^{NPER}}$$

We use the following formula to solve for the present value of $11,576 on deposit for 3 periods at an interest rate of 5%; this yields a present value of $10,000 as follows.

$$PV = \frac{FV}{(1+RATE)^{NPER}} = \frac{\$11,576}{(1+0.05)^3} = \$10,00$$

Present Value of a Single Amount—Computation through Excel

We obtain the same result by using Excel. After choosing the present value (PV) function in Excel, we enter values for the arguments: interest rate (5%), number of periods (3), and future value ($11,576). The **syntax** of the present value function in Excel is =PV(RATE,NPER,PMT,FV). The function solves for the present value of $10,000 (rounded) based upon the values of the arguments entered.

	Excel Arguments				Excel Function
	RATE	NPER	PV	FV	=PV(RATE,NPER,PMT,FV)
Given	5%	3	?	$11,576	= PV(0.05,3,0,11576)
Solution			$(9,999.78)		

Present Value of a Single Amount—Change in Values of Arguments

The following table demonstrates how changing the values of the arguments affects the present value of the investment from the previous example. In the first case, the interest rate is increased from 5% to 7%. Because interest is compounded at a higher rate of return, the present value required to return $11,576 decreases to $9,449.46. In the second case, the number of periods that the investment earns interest increases from 3 periods to 5 periods, which also results in a decrease in the investment required to return $11,576. In the third case, the desired future value increases to $12,000, which requires a higher upfront investment of $10,366.05.

	Excel Arguments				Excel Function
	RATE	NPER	FV	PV	=PV(RATE,NPER,PMT,FV)
Original	5%	3	$11,576	$ (9,999.78)	= PV(0.05,3,0,11576)
Increase interest rate	7%	3	11,576	(9,449.46)	= PV(0.07,3,0,11576)
Increase number of periods	5%	5	11,576	(9,070.10)	= PV(0.05,5,0,11576)
Increase present value	5%	3	12,000	(10,366.05)	= PV(0.05,3,0,12000)

In **Demo 6-3A**, we compute the present value of different amounts under different compounding scenarios. In **Demo 6-3B**, we examine situations where a present value amount and a future value amount are known, and instead solve for the interest rate or the number of periods. In Excel, the syntax of the RATE function is =RATE(NPER,PMT,PV,FV) and the syntax of the NPER function is =NPER(RATE,PMT,PV,FV).

Demo 6-3A **LO6-3** **Present Value of a Single Amount**

Demo MBC

For the following separate investments *A* through *F*, complete the table by indicating (1) the Excel formula required to calculate the present value of the investment, and (2) the present value amount of the investment.

Investment	Compounding	Annual Interest Rate	Future Value	Investment Period	Excel Formula	Present Value Amount
Investment A	Annually	6%	$ 8,000	3 years	PV(0.06, 3,0, 8000)	$ (6,716.95)
Investment B	Annually	8%	4,000	5 years	PV(0.08, 5,0, 4000)	(2,722.33)
Investment C	Semiannually	6%	15,000	4 years	PV(0.03, 8,0,15000)	(11,841.14)
Investment D	Semiannually	8%	6,000	6 years	PV(0.04,12,0, 6000)	(3,747.58)
Investment E	Quarterly	6%	5,000	5 years	PV(0.015,20,0, 5000)	(3,712.35)
Investment F	Quarterly	8%	10,000	4 years	PV(0.02,16,0,10000)	(7,284.46)

Demo 6-3B **LO6-3** **Solving for Unknown Arguments**

Demo MBC

Solve the following two separate questions.

a. Jacob invests $10,000 today and leaves it on deposit for three years to accumulate to a future amount of $11,576. What is the interest rate earned on this investment of $10,000?

b. Josie invests $10,000 today earning 5% and wants to achieve a future amount of $11,576. How many periods must Josie invest $10,000 to accumulate to $11,576?

continued

continued from previous page

Solutions

a. **Solving for Interest Rate** The RATE function is illustrated as follows.

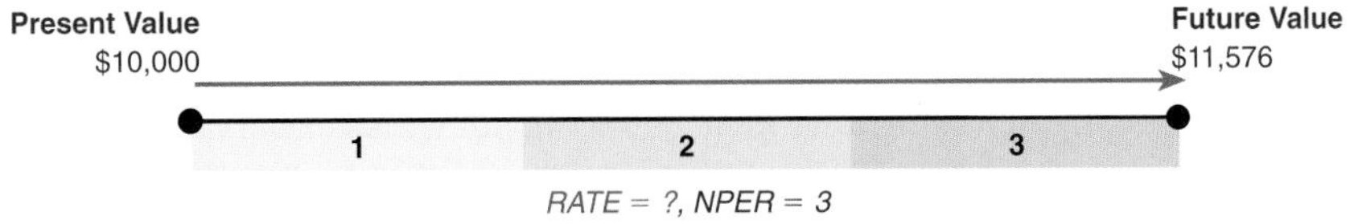

We choose the RATE function in Excel, and then enter the known variables of present value (−$10,000), future value ($11,576), and number of periods (3). The result of 5% is the interest rate that Jacob must earn on a $10,000 investment over 3 years to accumulate to $11,576. Because we are entering both an inflow and an outflow, we enter the cash outflow of $10,000 as a negative amount and the cash inflow of $11,576 as a positive amount. *Entering both values as either negative or positive will result in an error in Excel.*

	Excel Arguments				Excel Function
	RATE	NPER	PV	FV	=RATE(NPER,PMT,PV,FV)
Given	?	3	(10,000)	11,576	= *RATE(3,0,−10000,11576)*
Solution	5%				

b. **Solving for Number of Periods** The NPER function is illustrated as follows.

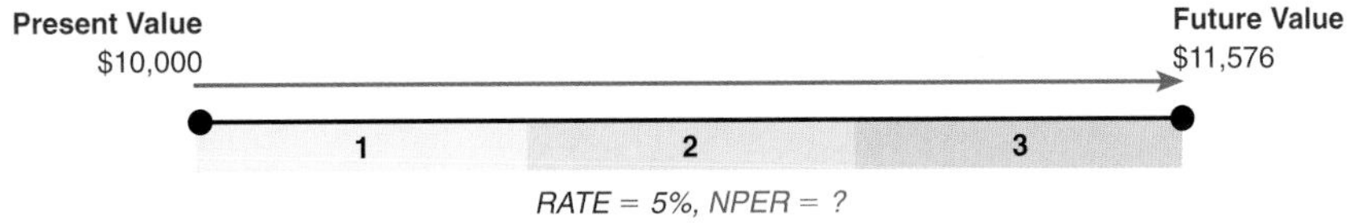

We choose the NPER function in Excel, and then enter the known variables of present value (−$10,000), future value ($11,576), and interest rate (0.05). The result of 3 is the number of periods that Josie must invest $10,000 to return $11,576, assuming an interest rate of 5%. We again enter the cash outflow of $10,000 as a negative and the cash inflow of $11,576 as a positive amount.

	Excel Arguments				Excel Function
	RATE	NPER	PV	FV	=NPER(RATE,PMT,PV,FV)
Given	5%	?	(10,000)	11,576	= *NPER(0.05,0,−10000,11576)*
Solution		3			

Expected Cash Flow Approach—Warranty

There are two approaches in computing present value in order to estimate the fair value of an asset or liability: the traditional approach and the expected cash flow approach. In the **traditional approach**, risk in future cash flows is reflected in the *interest rate* used to discount the cash flows. The rate can be set without a formal assessment of the uncertainty of individual cash flows. The higher the risk, the higher the interest rate.

For example, in computing the present value of a bond contract for the payment of interest over time and a principal value at the end of the bond term, a company uses a single interest rate to measure the present value of the bond. The single interest rate is set according to the level of associated risk.

SFAC No. 7 43 In effect, although not always by conscious design, the traditional approach assumes that a single interest rate convention can reflect all the expectations about the future cash flows and the appropriate risk premium . . . For assets and liabilities with contractual cash flows, it is consistent with the manner in which marketplace participants describe assets and liabilities, as in "a 12 percent bond."

However, SFAC No. 7 outlines an alternative method to measure the risk of cash flows in a present value calculation. The **expected cash flow** approach, illustrated in **Demo 6-3C**, incorporates a range of potential cash flows and assigns probabilities to cash flow amounts within the range. In this way, the risk is applied directly to the cash flows allowing accountants to recognize uncertainties in groups of cash flows. The expected cash flow approach is appropriate for situations where payments are estimated and not contractual.

SFAC NO. 7 45 The Board found the expected cash flow approach to be a more effective measurement tool than the traditional approach in many situations. In developing a measurement, the expected cash flow approach uses all expectations about possible cash flows instead of the single most-likely cash flow.

For example, a cash flow might be $100 (30% probability) or $400 (70%) probability. The expected cash flow is $310.

$100 × 30%	$ 30
$400 × 70%	280
Expected cash flow.	$310

These cash flows are discounted using the **risk-free rate of return**, which is the rate of return on an investment with zero risk, such as the return on a three-month U.S. Treasury instrument.

SFAC No. 7 40 In the expected cash flow approach discussed in this Statement, only the third factor listed in paragraph 39 (the time value of money, represented by the risk-free rate of interest) is included in the discount rate.

Demo 6-3C LO6-3 Present Value of Warranty—Expected Cash Flow Approach

Demo MBC

Briggs Inc. offers a two-year warranty on defects for all engines sold. Briggs uses the expected cash flow approach to measure the fair value of its warranty obligation. In using this method, Briggs assigns the following probabilities to estimated cash flows over the two-year warranty period.

Year	Estimate of Cash Outflow	Probability	Expected Cash Flow
2021	$ 80,000	30%	$ 24,000
	95,000	40%	38,000
	105,000	30%	31,500
		100%	**$ 93,500**
2022	$ 95,000	20%	$ 19,000
	110,000	60%	66,000
	120,000	20%	24,000
		100%	**$109,000**

Assuming that cash flows occur at year-end, and the risk-free rate of return is 5%, calculate the present value of the two years of estimated warranty outflows.

Solutions

The present value of the warranty cash flows using the expected cash flow approach is $187,913.83 ($89,047.62 + $98,866.21).

	Excel Arguments				Excel Function
	RATE	NPER	PV	FV	=PV(RATE,NPER,PMT,FV)
Given	5%	1	?	(93,500)	= PV(0.05,1,0,−93500)
Solution			$89,047.62		

	Excel Arguments				Excel Function
	RATE	NPER	PV	FV	=PV(RATE,NPER,PMT,FV)
Given	5%	2	?	(109,000)	= PV(0.05,2,0,−109000)
Solution			$98,866.21		

REVIEW 6-3 LO6-3 Present Value

Review MBC

Part One—Present Value of Single Amount Laurel Inc. is considering an investment that will grow to $8,000 with an expected annual return of 6%, compounded semiannually over 5 years. Compute the amount that must be invested today (present value) under those assumptions. Next, compute the estimated present value assuming that the following variables change while other variables remain the same: (1) interest rate increases to 8%, (2) the number of years increases to 10, (3) the future value increases to $10,000, and (4) compounding is adjusted to quarterly. Consider each change separately.

Terms	Original Investment	Increase Interest Rate	Increase Periods	Increase Present Value	Increase Compounding
Annual interest rate . . .	6%	8%	6%	6%	6%
Compounding.	Semiannual	Semiannual	Semiannual	Semiannual	Quarterly
Number of years.	5	5	10	5	5
Future value	$8,000	$8,000	$8,000	$10,000	$8,000
Present value	$(a)	$(b)	$(c)	$(d)	$(e)

continued

continued from previous page

Part Two—Solving for Unknown Argument The following four investment cases are missing the value of one key argument. Solve for the unknown argument in each separate case. Assume interest is compounded annually.

	Investment 1	Investment 2	Investment 3	Investment 4
RATE . . .	**(a)**%	6%	6%	5%
NPER . . .	8	**(b)**	4	3
PV.	$(8,000)	$(7,734)	$ **(c)**	$(10,000)
FV.	$12,000	$10,350	$3,900	$ **(d)**

Part Three—Expected Cash Flow Approach Laurel Inc. is estimating legal costs related to an environmental remediation anticipated in 10 years. Due to uncertainties related to legal services required at that time, the company prepared the following estimates.

Legal Cash Outflow	Probability
$250,000	40%
200,000	30%
100,000	20%
50,000	10%

a. Compute the expected cash outflow for legal costs using the expected cash approach.

b. Assuming a 4% risk-free rate, determine the present value of the expected cash outflow.

More Practice: 6-39, 6-41, 6-43
Solution on p. 6-48.

EXPANDING YOUR KNOWLEDGE — Applications of Time Value of Money

Where does time value of money apply to topics in this text? In Chapter 1, we introduced the *fair value hierarchy*, which requires fair value estimates to be classified as a Level 1, 2, or 3. A Level 3 estimate is based on unobservable inputs that reflect a company's assumptions. An example of a Level 3 estimate is where a company estimates the fair value of an asset or liability based on the *present value* of expected future cash flows. A preview of upcoming topics follows.

Topic	Chapter	Application
Notes receivable	Chapter 8	Noncurrent note receivables are recorded at *present value* of cash flows discounted at the market rate of interest. Interest is amortized using the effective interest rate method.
Asset retirement obligations	Chapter 11	Obligations for asset retirements (such as dismantling, closure, and removal costs) are capitalized at the *present value* of those future costs.
Noncurrent fixed asset impairment	Chapter 12	When an asset's carrying amount is adjusted to fair value and when quoted market prices are unavailable, fair value is estimated by taking the *present value* of future net cash inflows using a rate reflecting the risk involved.
Intangible assets impairment	Chapter 13	Similar to noncurrent assets, in certain cases, fair value is estimated by taking the *present value* of future net cash inflows using a rate reflecting the risk involved.
Held-to-maturity debt securities	Chapter 14	Discounts (or premiums) on held-to-maturity debt securities are amortized over the debt term using the effective interest rate method and the *present value* function.
Noncurrent payables	Chapter 16	Noncurrent payables (notes, bonds) are recorded at *present value* of cash flows discounted at the market rate of interest. Interest is amortized using the effective interest rate method.
Leases	Chapter 17	Lease liabilities and lease assets are capitalized at the *present value* of lease payments.
Pensions	Chapter 19	Projected benefit obligation is the actuarial *present value* of benefits attributed to employee service rendered to date, as measured by the benefit formula using estimated future salary levels.

LO 6-4 Apply future value concepts to an ordinary annuity and an annuity due

LO 6-4 Overview

Future Value of Annuities
- Compute end-point value of a series of uniform payments
  - Ordinary annuity: end of period payments
  - Annuity due: beginning of period payments
  - Deferred annuity: Delayed annuity payments

An **annuity** is a series of *uniform payments* (sometimes called rents) occurring at *uniform intervals over a specified investment time frame*. We determine the future value of an annuity using a *single interest rate*. The term *payments* is used because it includes annuity amounts that take the form of either cash payments into an annuity type of investment or cash withdrawals from an annuity type of investment. In cases where payments or withdrawals are uneven or unequal, each cash amount is considered a lump-sum amount and not an annuity.

There are two distinct types of annuities: an ordinary annuity and an annuity due. The distinction is in the timing of the payments. With an **ordinary annuity** (or an annuity in arrears), the payments (or receipts) occur at the **end** of each interest compounding period. With an **annuity due** (or an annuity in advance), payments (or receipts) occur at the **beginning** of each interest compounding period. Unless otherwise stated, all annuities are assumed to be ordinary annuities, meaning that every payment occurs at the end of the interest period.

Future Value of an Ordinary Annuity—Computation through Formula

Assume that we make 3 payments of $5,000 on deposit at a financial institution at the **end** of each of the next 3 years, earning interest of 6%. *What is the future value of this ordinary annuity stream of three $5,000 payments?* The future value of this ordinary annuity stream is illustrated as follows.

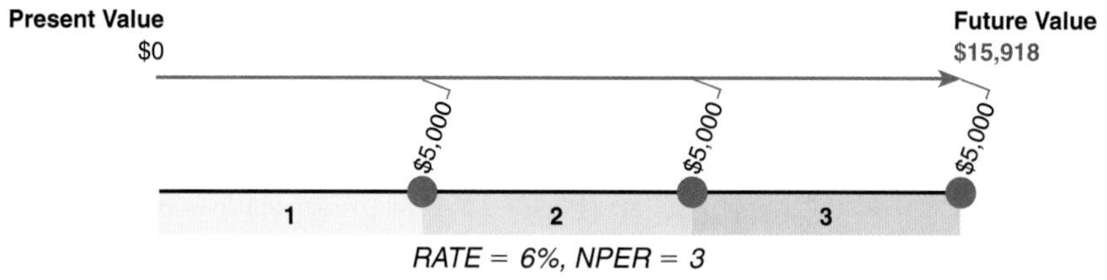

To compute the **future value of an ordinary annuity**, we use the formula to find the future value of each payment and total them.

$$FV = PV \times (1 + RATE)^{(NPER - 1)} + PV \times (1 + RATE)^{(NPER - 2)} + PV \times (1 + RATE)^{(NPER - 3)}$$

Assuming an interest rate of 6% and that the $5,000 payments are made at the **end** of each period, the calculation follows.

$$FV = \$5{,}000 \times (1 + 0.06)^2 + \$5{,}000 \times (1 + 0.06)^1 + \$5{,}000 \times (1 + 0.06)^0 = \$15{,}918$$

Future Value of an Ordinary Annuity—Computation through Excel

The same result is obtained using Excel. The following additional arguments in Excel are relevant.

Excel Argument	Description
PMT	Fixed payment per period.
TYPE	Enter *0* or leave blank: signifies that payments are made at the end of the period (ordinary annuity). Enter *1*: signifies that payments are made at the beginning of the period (annuity due).

After choosing the future value function (FV) in Excel, we enter measurements for the arguments: interest rate (6%), number of periods (3), and annuity payment (−$5,000). The **syntax** of the future value function in Excel is =FV(RATE,NPER,PMT,PV,TYPE). We use the same future value function that we used for the lump sum calculation earlier, except now we include PMT (the annuity payment) and exclude PV (the lump sum). The default in Excel is an ordinary annuity,

	Excel Arguments						Excel Function
	RATE	NPER	PMT	PV	FV	TYPE	=FV(RATE,NPER,PMT,PV,TYPE)
Given	6%	3	(5,000)	—	?	—	*= FV(0.06,3,−5000,0,0)*
Solution					$15,918.00		

so no entry is required for *TYPE*, although a zero may be entered. The result is $15,918, the future value of the ordinary annuity stream based on the values of the arguments entered. See also **Demo 6-4A**.

Future Value of an Ordinary Annuity—Change in Values of Arguments

The following table demonstrates how a change in a variable affects the future value of the annuity stream from the previous example. In the first case, the interest rate is increased to 8% from 6%. Because interest is compounded at a higher rate of return, the future value of the $5,000 annuity payments increases to $16,232. In the second case, the number of periods that the investment earns interest increases from 3 periods to 5 periods resulting in a future value of $28,185.46. In the third case, payments increase to $6,000, resulting in a higher future value of $19,101.60.

	RATE	NPER	PMT	FV	Excel Formula
Original	6%	3	$(5,000)	$15,918.00	= FV(0.06,3,−5000)
Increase interest rate	8%	3	(5,000)	16,232.00	= FV(0.08,3,−5000)
Increase periods	6%	5	(5,000)	28,185.46	= FV(0.06,5,−5000)
Increase payment	6%	3	(6,000)	19,101.60	= FV(0.06,3,−6000)

Future Value of an Ordinary Annuity **LO6-4** **Demo 6-4A**

Demo MBC

For the following *end of period* annuity streams *A* through *F*, complete the table by indicating the (a) Excel formula required to calculate the future value of the ordinary annuity stream, and (b) future value amount of the ordinary annuity stream.

Investment	Compounding	Annual Interest Rate	Payment	Investment Period	Excel Formula	Future Value Amount
Annuity A	Annually	5%	$(15,000)	3 years	**FV(0.05, 3,−15000)**	**$47,287.50**
Annuity B	Annually	7%	(10,000)	5 years	**FV(0.07, 5,−10000)**	**57,507.39**
Annuity C	Semiannually	5%	(6,000)	4 years	**FV(0.025, 8,− 6000)**	**52,416.70**
Annuity D	Semiannually	7%	(2,500)	6 years	**FV(0.035,12,− 2500)**	**36,504.90**
Annuity E	Quarterly	4%	(500)	5 years	**FV(0.01,20,− 500)**	**11,009.50**
Annuity F	Quarterly	8%	(1,000)	4 years	**FV(0.02,16,− 1000)**	**18,639.29**

Future Value of an Annuity Due—Computation through Formula

Assume now that we make 3 payments of $5,000 on deposit at the beginning of each of the next 3 years, earning interest of 6%. *What is the future value of this annuity stream of three $5,000 payments due at the beginning of the period (annuity due)?* The future value of this annuity due stream is illustrated as follows.

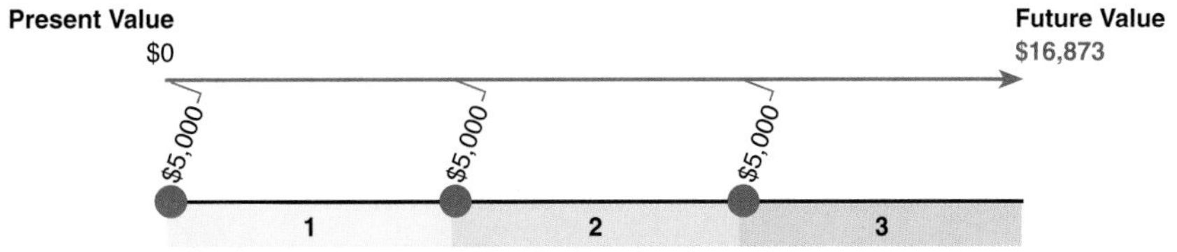

RATE = 6%, *NPER* = 3

To compute the **future value of an annuity due**, we use the formula to find the future value of each payment and total them.

$$FV = PV \times (1 + RATE)^{NPER} + PV \times (1 + RATE)^{(NPER-1)} + PV \times (1 + RATE)^{(NPER-2)}$$

Assuming an interest rate of 6% and that the payments are made at the **beginning** of each period, the calculation follows.

$$FV = \$5{,}000 \times (1 + 0.06)^3 + \$5{,}000 \times (1 + 0.06)^2 + \$5{,}000 \times (1 + 0.06)^1 = \$16{,}873$$

Future Value of an Annuity Due—Computation through Excel

After choosing the future value function (FV) function in Excel, we enter measurements for the known arguments: interest rate (6%), number of periods (3), annuity payment

	Excel Arguments						Excel Function
	RATE	NPER	PMT	PV	FV	TYPE	=FV(RATE,NPER,PMT,PV,TYPE)
Given	6%	3	(5,000)	—	?	1	= FV(0.06,3,−5000,0,1)
Solution					$16,873.08		

(−$5,000), and type (1). By entering a value of *1* for type, the future value is calculated assuming beginning of period payments. The result is $16,873.08, the future value of the annuity due stream based on the variables entered. See also **Demo 6-4B**.

Demo 6-4B **LO6-4** **Future Value of an Annuity Due**

For the following *beginning of period* annuity streams *A* through *F*, complete the table by indicating (1) the Excel formula required to calculate the future value of the annuity stream, and (2) the future value amount of the annuity stream.

Investment	Compounding	Annual Interest Rate	Payment	Investment Period	Excel Formula	Future Value Amount
Annuity A	Annually	5%	$(15,000)	3 years	**FV(0.05, 3,−15000,0,1)**	**$49,651.88**
Annuity B	Annually	7%	(10,000)	5 years	**FV(0.07, 5,−10000,0,1)**	**61,532.91**
Annuity C	Semiannually	5%	(6,000)	4 years	**FV(0.025, 8,− 6000,0,1)**	**53,727.11**
Annuity D	Semiannually	7%	(2,500)	6 years	**FV(0.035,12,− 2500,0,1)**	**37,782.58**
Annuity E	Quarterly	4%	(500)	5 years	**FV(0.01,20,− 500,0,1)**	**11,119.60**
Annuity F	Quarterly	8%	(1,000)	4 years	**FV(0.02,16,− 1000,0,1)**	**19,012.07**

Future Value of a Deferred Annuity

A **deferred annuity** occurs when an annuity stream is delayed (see **Demo 6-4C**). This means that the payments begin after a certain number of periods after the date of the initial agreement.

For example, after two years, LA Bakery deposits $5,000 into an account at the end of each of the next 5 years at an interest rate of 7%. *What is the future value of the annuity stream?* The future value of this ordinary annuity stream is illustrated as follows.

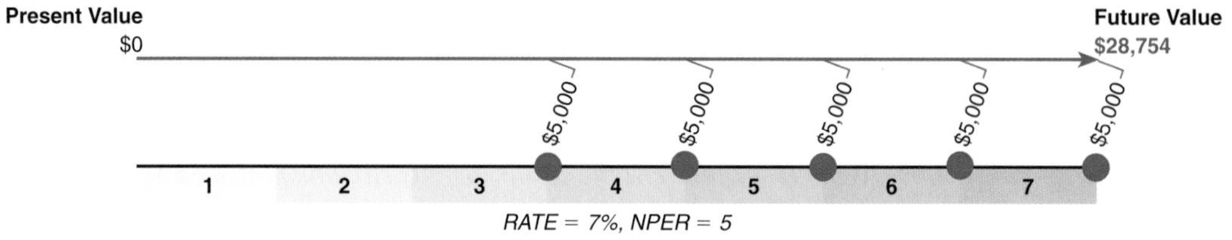

The initial period is ignored for this future value calculation because no investment took place during the deferral period. This means the calculation for the annuity is the same as it is for a 5-year ordinary annuity. The future value of the ordinary stream is $28,754, calculated using the future value function in Excel.

	Excel Arguments						Excel Function
	RATE	NPER	PMT	PV	FV	TYPE	=FV(RATE,NPER,PMT,PV,TYPE)
Given	7%	5	(5,000)	—	?	—	= FV(0.07,5,−5000)
Solution					$28,753.70		

Demo 6-4C **LO6-4** **Future Value of a Deferred Annuity**

After a 3-year deferral, Laurel Inc. deposits $8,000 at the *end* of each year for 10 years (which is years 4 through 13). The annuity stream is expected to earn interest of 6% annually.

a. What is the future value of the ordinary annuity stream?

b. What is the future value of the ordinary annuity stream if the first payment is deferred for three years?

Solution

a. The future value of the annuity stream at the end of the 13 years is calculated as follows.

FV(0.06,10,−8000) = $105,446.36

b. If the first payment is deferred for three years, the future value of the annuity is still $105,446.36. Because no investment took place during the deferral period, the future value is equivalent to an investment that has no deferral.

Future Value of Annuities **LO6-4** **REVIEW 6-4**

For the following separate annuity streams *A* through *F*, complete the table by indicating the future value amount of the annuity stream.

Review MBC

Investment	Frequency of Payments	Annual Interest Rate	Payment	Number of Payments	Beg. or End of Period Payment	Deferral of Annuity Payment	Future Value Amount
Annuity A	Annually	6%	$(1,250)	2	End	n/a	$______
Annuity B	Semiannually	8%	(4,000)	6	End	n/a	______
Annuity C	Semiannually	6%	(8,000)	8	End	n/a	______
Annuity D	Annually	8%	(4,100)	6	Beginning	n/a	______
Annuity E	Semiannually	6%	(800)	10	Beginning	2 years	______
Annuity F	Semiannually	8%	(3,000)	8	Beginning	1 year	______

More Practice: 6-44, 6-45
Solution on p. 6-48.

Apply present value concepts to an ordinary annuity and an annuity due

LO 6-5

A common business question is, "What's the current value (in today's dollars) of a stream of future cash flows?" We measure this value using the present value of an annuity function, considering whether the uniform payments occur at the end of the period (ordinary annuity) or at the beginning of the period (annuity due).

Present Value of Annuities

- Compute *current value* of a series of uniform payments
  - Ordinary annuity: end of period payments
  - Annuity due: beginning of period payments
  - Deferred annuity: Delayed annuity payments

LO 6-5 Overview

Present Value of an Ordinary Annuity—Computation through Formula

Assume that we make 3 payments of $5,000 on deposit at the **end** of each of the next 3 years, earning interest of 6%. *What is the present value of this ordinary annuity stream of three $5,000 payments made at the end of each period?* The present value of this ordinary annuity stream is illustrated as follows.

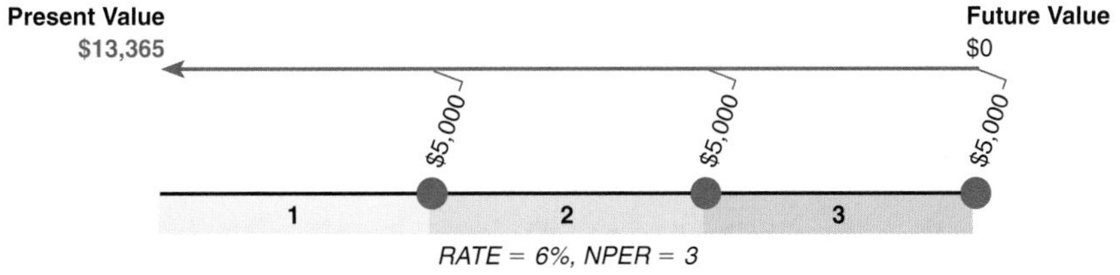

To compute the **present value of an ordinary annuity**, we use the formula to find the present value of each payment and then total them.

$$PV = \frac{FV}{(1 + RATE)^{(NPER-2)}} + \frac{FV}{(1 + RATE)^{(NPER-1)}} + \frac{FV}{(1 + RATE)^{(NPER-0)}}$$

Assuming an interest rate of 6% and that the $5,000 payments are made at the **end** of each period, the calculation follows.

$$PV = \frac{\$5,000}{(1+0.06)^1} + \frac{\$5,000}{(1+0.06)^2} + \frac{\$5,000}{(1+0.06)^3} = \$13,365$$

Present Value of an Ordinary Annuity—Computation through Excel

After choosing the present value (PV) function in Excel, we enter measurements for the arguments: interest rate (6%), number of periods (3), and annuity payment (−$5,000). The **syntax** of the present value function is =PV(RATE,NPER,PMT,FV,TYPE). No entry is required for TYPE because the default in Excel is for an *ordinary* annuity. The result is $13,365.06, the present value of the annuity stream based on the variables entered. This result means that if $13,365.06 were invested today at 6%, it would produce 3 payments of $5,000 at the end of each annual period. After the 3 payments, the investment would have a $0 value. See also **Demo 6-5A**.

	Excel Arguments						Excel Functions
	RATE	NPER	PMT	PV	FV	TYPE	=PV(RATE,NPER,PMT,FV,TYPE)
Given	6%	3	(5,000)	?	—	—	= PV(0.06,3,−5000)
Solution				$13,365.06			

Present Value of an Ordinary Annuity—Change in Variables

The following table demonstrates how a change in a variable affects the present value of the annuity stream from the previous example. In the first case, the interest rate is increased to 8% from 6%. Because interest is compounded at a higher rate of return, the present value of the annuity stream decreases to $12,885.48. In the second case, the number of periods that the investment earns interest increases from 3 periods to 5 periods resulting in an increase in the present value to $21,061.82. In the last case, the payment increases to $6,000, which increases the present value of this annuity stream to $16,038.07.

	Excel Arguments				Excel Functions
	RATE	NPER	PMT	PV	=PV(RATE,NPER,PMT,FV,TYPE)
Original	6%	3	$(5,000)	$13,365.06	= PV(0.06,3,−5000)
Increase interest rate	8%	3	(5,000)	12,885.48	= PV(0.08,3,−5000)
Increase periods	6%	5	(5,000)	21,061.82	= PV(0.06,5,−5000)
Increase payment	6%	3	(6,000)	16,038.07	= PV(0.06,3,−6000)

Demo 6-5A **LO6-5** **Present Value of an Ordinary Annuity**

Demo MBC

For the following *end of period* annuity streams *A* through *D*, complete the table by indicating (1) the Excel formula required to calculate the present value of the ordinary annuity stream, and (2) the present value amount of the ordinary annuity stream.

Investment	Frequency of Payments	Annual Interest Rate	Payment	Number of Payments	Excel Formula	Present Value Amount
Annuity A	Annually	5%	$15,000	3	**PV(0.05, 3,15000)**	**$(40,848.72)**
Annuity B	Annually	7%	10,000	6	**PV(0.07, 6,10000)**	**(47,665.40)**
Annuity C	Semiannually	5%	6,000	8	**PV(0.025, 8, 6000)**	**(43,020.82)**
Annuity D	Semiannually	7%	2,500	12	**PV(0.035,12, 2500)**	**(24,158.34)**

Present Value of an Annuity Due—Computation through Formula

Assume that we make 3 payments of $5,000 on deposit at the beginning of each of the next 3 years, earning interest of 6%. *What is the present value of this annuity stream of three $5,000 payments made at the beginning of each period (annuity due)?* The present value of this annuity due stream is illustrated as follows.

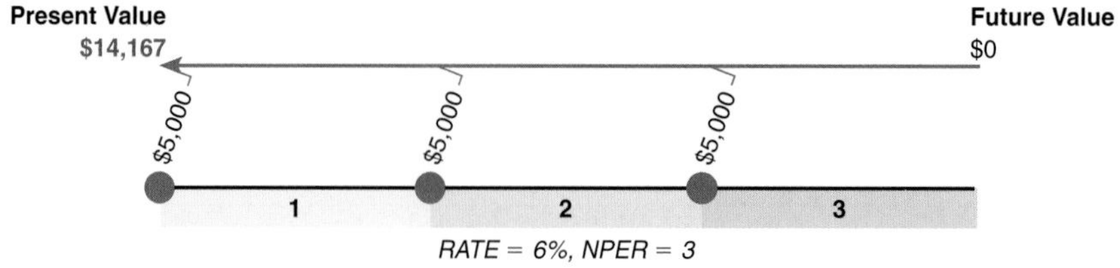

To compute the **present value of an annuity due**, use the formula to find the present value of each payment and total them.

$$PV = \frac{FV}{(1+RATE)^{(NPER-3)}} + \frac{FV}{(1+RATE)^{(NPER-2)}} + \frac{FV}{(1+RATE)^{(NPER-1)}}$$

Assuming an interest rate of 6% and that the payments are made at the **beginning** of each period, the calculation follows.

$$PV = \frac{\$5{,}000}{(1+0.06)^0} + \frac{\$5{,}000}{(1+0.06)^1} + \frac{\$5{,}000}{(1+0.06)^2} = \$14{,}167$$

Present Value of an Annuity Due—Computation through Excel

After choosing the present value (PV) function in Excel, we enter measurements for the arguments: interest rate (6%), number of periods (3), annuity payment (−$5,000), and type (1). The result is $14,166.96, the present value of the annuity stream based on the variables entered. See also **Demo 6-5B**.

	Excel Arguments						Excel Functions
	RATE	NPER	PMT	PV	FV	TYPE	=PV(RATE,NPER,PMT,FV,TYPE)
Given	6%	3	(5,000)	?	—	1	= PV(0.06,3,−5000,0,1)
Solution				$14,166.96			

Present Value of an Annuity Due

LO6-5 **Demo 6-5B**

For the following *beginning of period* annuity streams *A* through *D*, complete the table by indicating (1) the Excel formula required to calculate the present value of the annuity due stream, and (2) the present value amount of the annuity due stream.

Investment	Frequency of Payments	Annual Interest Rate	Payment	Number of Payments	Excel Formula	Present Value Amount
Annuity A	Annually	5%	$(15,000)	3	PV(0.05, 3,−15000,0,1)	$42,891.16
Annuity B	Annually	7%	(10,000)	6	PV(0.07, 6,−10000,0,1)	51,001.97
Annuity C	Semiannually	5%	(6,000)	8	PV(0.025, 8,− 6000,0,1)	44,096.34
Annuity D	Semiannually	7%	(2,500)	12	PV(0.035,12,− 2500,0,1)	25,003.88

Present Value of a Deferred Annuity

A deferred annuity occurs when an annuity stream is delayed—see **Demo 6-5C**. When computing the present value of a deferred annuity, interest is recognized during the deferral period.

For example, after two years of deferred rent, Leasing Inc. receives rental income of $20,000 a year for 8 years, beginning at the end of year 3. Given an interest rate of 6%, *what is the present value of the payment stream?* The present value of this annuity stream is illustrated as follows.

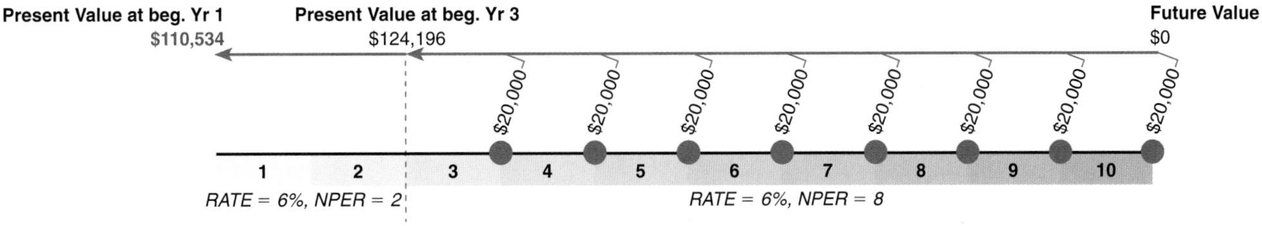

The first step is to measure the present value of the ordinary annuity stream of $20,000 for 8 years. This present value measurement is $124,196. The next step is to measure the present value of the lump-sum amount of $124,196 discounted at 6% for two years. This final present value measurement is $110,534. This means that the present value of a stream of 8 rental payments of $20,000, beginning at the end of year 3 is $110,534.

	Excel Arguments						Excel Functions
	RATE	NPER	PMT	PV	FV	TYPE	=PV(RATE,NPER,PMT,FV,TYPE)
Given	6%	8	(20,000)	?	—	—	= PV(0.06,8,−20000)
Solution				$124,196			

	Excel Arguments						Excel Functions
	RATE	NPER	PMT	PV	FV	TYPE	=PV(RATE,NPER,PMT,FV,TYPE)
Given	6%	2	—	?	(124,196)	—	= PV(0.06,2,0,−124,196)
Solution				$110,534			

Demo 6-5C **LO6-5** **Present Value of a Deferred Annuity**

Demo MBC

Johnson received a defined retirement benefit, which will commence in 10 years. At that time, Johnson receives monthly cash payments of $2,000 for 15 years with the first payment scheduled for the end of the initial month of benefit. Assuming an interest rate of 6%, what is the value of the annuity today? Assume annual compounding during the deferral period.

Solutions

The present value of the ordinary annuity stream of $2,000 per month for 15 years, discounted at 6% (or 0.005 per month), is calculated as follows.

PV(0.005,180,−2000) = $237,007.03

The final step is to calculate the present value of the lump sum $237,007.03 to be received in 10 years.

PV(0.06,10,0,−237007.03) = $132,343.49

REVIEW 6-5 **LO6-5** **Present Value of Annuities**

Review MBC

For the following separate annuity streams *A* through *F*, complete the table by indicating the present value amount of the annuity stream.

Investment	Frequency of Payments	Annual Interest Rate	Payment	Number of Payments	Beg. or End of Period Payment	Deferral of Annuity Payment	Present Value Amount
Annuity A	Annually	6%	$(1,250)	2	End	n/a	$_______
Annuity B	Semiannually	8%	(4,000)	6	End	n/a	_______
Annuity C	Semiannually	6%	(8,000)	8	End	2 years*	_______
Annuity D	Annually	8%	(4,100)	6	Beginning	n/a	_______
Annuity E	Semiannually	6%	(800)	10	Beginning	n/a	_______
Annuity F	Semiannually	8%	(3,000)	8	Beginning	1 year*	_______

*Assume semiannual compounding during the deferral period.

More Practice: 6-46, 6-47, 6-54
Solution on p. 6-48.

LO 6-6 Apply time value of money concept to common accounting scenarios

LO 6-6 Overview

Application of Time Value of Money
- Issuance of bonds
- Lease payments
- Pension obligations
- Capital Investment Decisions
- Debt retirement

The time value of money concept has many applications in accounting for monetary assets and liabilities, both in recording entries and in disclosures accompanying financial statements. Monetary assets and liabilities are defined in the accounting guidance as follows:

ASC Glossary Monetary Assets: Money or a claim to receive a sum of money the amount of which is fixed or determinable without reference to future prices of specific goods or services.

ASC Glossary Monetary Liability: An obligation to pay a sum of money the amount of which is fixed or determinable without reference to future prices of specific goods and services.

In this section, we review monetary items related to bonds, notes, leases, and pensions. See also **Demo 6-6**.

Bond Issuance Price

A **bond** is a debt security issued by companies and governmental units to secure large amounts of capital on a long-term basis. In return for capital, the issuing company formally agrees to pay periodic cash interest based upon a stated interest rate during the bond term and to return the principal (face value) at the end of the bond term.

While cash interest payments are based on the stated interest rate, the **market or effective rate** for the bond changes. A bond's market or effective interest rate is the rate that discounts the bond's cash interest payments and principal (maturity value) to the bond's current selling price (present value). The market rate changes with changes in the bond's risk, driven by economic, industry, and company conditions. The bond's selling price is equal to the present value of the periodic cash interest payments (annuity) plus the present value of the return of principal (lump-sum amount).

Issuance of Bonds—Annual Interest

	Excel Arguments						Excel Functions
	RATE	NPER	PMT	PV	FV	TYPE	=PV(RATE,NPER,PMT,FV,TYPE)
Given	9%	10	(8,000)	?	(100,000)	—	= PV(0.09,10,−8000, −100000)
Solution				$93,582.34			

Assume that Wings Inc. issued 100, 10-year, 8%, $1,000 bonds on January 1 with cash interest payable annually on December 31. The interest rate for bonds of similar risk is 9%. *What is the selling price of the bonds?* To answer this, we calculate the present value of the cash interest payments of $8,000 per year (8% × $100,000) and of the maturity value ($100,000) using a 9% discount rate, which results in a selling price for the bonds of $93,582.34. We see how the present value of the principal lump sum amount and the present value of the cash interest payments are computed in one function in Excel.

We see that the bonds sell at a **discount**—meaning the selling price ($93,582.34) is less than the stated value ($100,000). A discount exists when the market price (which is used to discount the cash outflows) is greater than the stated interest rate. If the market rate was anything less than the stated rate, the bonds would sell at a **premium**—meaning a value above the stated value.

Issuance of Bonds—Semiannual Interest

Assume instead that 100, 10-year, 8%, $1,000 bonds are issued on January 1 with cash interest payable semiannually on July 1 and January 1. The market price for bonds of similar risk is 9%. *What is the selling price of the bonds?* Because the bonds pay cash interest semiannually, the interest rates and periods must be adjusted to reflect semiannual compounding periods as follows.

- Semiannual market rate: 9% ÷ 2 = 4.5%
- Semiannual periods: 10 years × 2 = 20 periods
- Semiannual cash interest payment: 8% × $100,000 ÷ 2 = $4,000

	Excel Arguments						Excel Functions
	RATE	NPER	PMT	PV	FV	TYPE	=PV(RATE,NPER,PMT,FV,TYPE)
Given	4.5%	20	(4,000)	?	(100,000)	—	= PV(0.045,20,− 4000, − 100000)
Solution				$93,496.03			

The selling price of $93,496.03 for these bonds is computed by discounting the semiannual cash interest payments and principal to the present. Again, see how the present value of the principal lump sum amount and the present value of the cash interest payments are computed in one function in Excel. For further discussion on bonds, see Appendix 6A.

Lease Payment

In accounting for most leases, future lease payments are discounted to present value when measuring the lease liability. Time value of money concepts are also used in determining the lease payment that the **lessor** (owner of the asset) charges to the **lessee** (entity who is leasing the asset).

Assume that Leasing Inc. leases equipment to Wings Inc. over a 5-year period with payments due annually starting immediately on January 1, 2020. The equipment has a fair value of $50,000, a useful life of 5 years, and no salvage value. Leasing Inc. requires a rate of return on this lease of 12%. *What is the annual lease payment determined by Leasing Inc.?* The lease payment of $12,384.36 is measured using the PMT function in Excel.

	Excel Arguments						Excel Functions
	RATE	NPER	PMT	PV	FV	TYPE	=PMT(RATE,NPER,PV,FV,TYPE)
Given	12%	5	?	(50,000)	—	1	= PMT(0.12,5,−50000,0,1)
Solution			$12,384.36				

Pension Obligations

In the case of **defined benefit plans**, employers pay an amount to eligible employees during their retirement period as specified by the pension agreement. The benefit is earned through an employee's service to the company. In estimating the pension obligation, employers must estimate the eventual retirement payments to employees and discount the payments to the present.

Assume that Wings Inc. pays retirement benefits to one employee (Justin) who is estimated to retire in 10 years. Justin's annual benefit is equal to 50% of his annual salary at the date of retirement, estimated to be $70,000. The benefit

	Excel Arguments						Excel Functions
	RATE	NPER	PMT	PV	FV	TYPE	=PV(RATE,NPER,PMT,FV,TYPE)
Given	6%	15	(35,000)	?	—	—	= PV(0.06,15,−35000)
Solution				$339,928.71			

	Excel Arguments				Excel Functions
	RATE	NPER	PV	FV	=PV(RATE,NPER,PMT,FV)
Given	6%	10	?	(339,929)	= PV(0.06,10,0,339928.71)
Solution			$189,814.42		

is to be paid at the end of each annual period of retirement, which is estimated to be 15 years. *What is the present value of the pension benefit obligation?* Assuming an interest rate of 6% and annual compounding, the present value of the deferred annuity of $35,000 (50% × $70,000) *at the start of the retirement benefit period* is equal to $339,929, using the present value function in Excel. Next, the present value of the deferred annuity of $339,929 is calculated to equal $189,814.42.

Lease or Buy

Companies often face situations where they must choose between the purchase or lease of a noncurrent asset. Assume that Northern Airlines is negotiating to acquire four new planes. Three alternatives are available.

1. Purchase the aircraft for $35 million each, payment due immediately.
2. Purchase the aircraft by paying $20 million immediately and $20 million each year for 11 more years.
3. Lease the aircraft for $21.5 million payable at the end of each year for 12 years.

The relevant market rate of interest (the discount rate) for ventures of this type is 10%. *Assuming that Northern has sufficient resources, which alternative is least expensive?* Ignore tax considerations. To compare the three options, the present value of each is determined.

	Excel Arguments						Excel Functions
	RATE	NPER	PMT	PV	FV	TYPE	=PV(RATE,NPER,PMT,FV,TYPE)
Given	10%	12	(20,000,000)	?	—	1	= PV(0.1,12,−20000000,0,1)
Solution				$149,901,220			

	Excel Arguments						Excel Functions
	RATE	NPER	PMT	PV	FV	TYPE	=PV(RATE,NPER,PMT,FV,TYPE)
Given	10%	12	(21,500,000)	?	—	—	= PV(0.1,12,−21500000)
Solution				$146,494,374			

Option One The present value is $35 million × 4 planes = $140 million.

Option Two The present value of an annuity stream with the first payment due immediately is $149.9 million.

Option Three The present value of the lease payments with the first payment due in one year is $146.5 million. Based on an interest rate of 12%, the least expensive option is option one.

Debt Retirement

Loan payments are calculated using the time value of money concept. Assume that on January 1, 2020, Wings Inc. signed a note payable for $75,000. The debt is to be paid off in 10 years with annual payments due on December 31. The note accrues interest at a rate of 10%, compounded annually. *What is the annual payment on the note?* The annual payment is $12,205.90 measured using the PMT Excel function.

	Excel Arguments						Excel Functions
	RATE	NPER	PMT	PV	FV	TYPE	=PMT(RATE,NPER,PV,FV,TYPE)
Given	10%	10	?	75,000	—	—	= PMT(0.1,10,75000)
Solution			$(12,205.90)				

Demo 6-6 LO6-6 Application of Time Value of Money

Answer the questions for each of the following applications of the time value of money. Use Excel for calculations.

Topic	Application	Solution
Bonds	New Co. issued $50,000, 6%, 10-year bonds payable on January 1, 2020. Calculate the selling price of the bonds if the bonds pay cash interest semiannually ($50,000 × 3% = $1,500) and the market rate of interest on similar bonds is 7%.	**$46,446.90** **PV(0.035,20,−1500,−50000)**
Leases	Lessor Inc. leased equipment to Williams Inc. for a 10-year term, which is the estimated life of the equipment. The fair value of the equipment is $30,000 and the first annual payment is due at the inception of the lease. Calculate the annual lease payment assuming that Lessor Inc. is interested in a 10% return on its investment and the equipment has no salvage value.	**$4,438.51** **PMT(0.1,10,−30000,0,1)**

continued

continued from previous page

Topic	Application	Solution
Debt	Debtor Co. borrowed $35,000 and agreed to pay off the loan over 5 years by making equal semiannual payments. What is the payment amount if the first payment is due at the end of the first 6 months and the interest rate is 8%?	**$(4,315.18)** **PMT(0.04,10,35000)**
Capital Decisions	Retail Inc. is considering two options for leasing equipment: pay $40,000 upfront or pay 5 annual installments of $10,000, with the first installment due immediately. If Retail Inc.'s borrowing rate is 8%, what option is better?	**PV of annual installments: $43,121.27** **PV(0.08,5,−10000,0,1)** **Select the $40,000 upfront payment as it is less than the present value of installment payments.**

Application of Time Value of Money

LO6-6 **REVIEW 6-6**

Review MBC

Answer the questions for each of the following applications of the time value of money. Use Excel for calculations.

Topic	Application	Solution
Leases	Lessee Co. leased a building beginning on December 31, 2020, for 15 years requiring annual lease payments of $80,000 with the first annual lease payment due immediately. Calculate the present value of the lease liability at the inception of the lease assuming an interest rate of 6%.	
Pension	A CEO will retire on December 31, 2020. Retirement benefits are fixed payments of $10,000 at each month-end for 15 years. What is the present value of the pension liability on December 31, 2020, assuming an interest rate of 6%?	
Bonds	Neww Co. issues $50,000, 6%, 10-year bonds payable on January 1, 2020. Calculate the selling price of the bonds if the bonds pay cash interest semiannually and the market rate of interest on similar bonds is 5%.	
Debt	Debtor Inc. would like to establish a debt retirement fund to pay off a $250,000 debt due 5 years from today. If the fund is estimated to earn interest at 4% per year, what amount must be deposited semiannually (beginning in six months) to reach $250,000?	

More Practice:
6-33, 6-34, 6-35, 6-55, 6-57, 6-61

Solution on p. 6-48.

Management Judgment

Management judgment does *not* apply to the mechanical process of calculating a present value or a future value amount in Excel. However, management judgment is involved in determining the variables that are entered into these calculations. For calculations in this chapter, these variables were provided. However, in practice, some variables are easily determinable like a fixed payment, but many variables are estimated such as an interest rate.

Estimated Rate Requires Judgment

Management judgment is required in estimating interest rates such as in the following cases.

- A bond selling price is determined by taking the present value of contractual payments, discounted at the market rate. The market rate is determined based on bonds of similar risk.
- A lease payment is determined by solving for that payment given the terms of the lease, the present value (and residual value) of the leased asset, and the rate. The rate is estimated based upon the lessor's desired rate of return.
- The future value of a bond sinking fund is calculated by using planned funding payments, number of periods, and the estimated rate of return on those funds.

Estimated Payment Requires Judgment

Management judgment is required in estimating future payments such as in the following cases.

- In the case of certain pension funds, the payment to employees expected to retire in the future must be estimated. The payment is determined by a pension formula, but may be based upon the employee's salary at the time of retirement.
- The fair value of an asset in some cases is estimated by the present value of its net cash flows. For example, the gross profit obtained from selling goods produced on a piece of equipment over its useful life could be estimated as payments in calculating the present value of the equipment.

Estimated Number of Periods Requires Judgment

Management judgment is required in estimating the number of periods such as in the following cases.

- In our above pension example, the number of periods must be estimated when determining the present value of the payments if the pension benefits will be paid until the retiree is deceased.
- In our above equipment example, the estimated useful life of the equipment (number of periods) must be estimated in determining the present value.

Traditional vs. Expected Cash Flow Approach

Management must determine whether to use the traditional approach or the expected cash flow approach (described earlier on page 6-10) when determining present value when there are risks in the cash flows. In other words, when the payments are not fixed or easily determinable, management must factor in risk by choosing an *appropriate interest rate* (traditional method) or factor in risk by using *expected cash flows* by assigning probabilities to cash flows. This was illustrated in Demo 6-3C where the present value of warranties was determined using the expected cash flow method. While the probabilities related to potential cash flows were provided in this demo , these values must be estimated by management in practice.

APPENDIX 6A LO 6-7 Apply time value of money concept to bond interest amortization

LO 6-7 Overview

Bond Interest Amortization
- Amortize bond discount (premium) using effective interest method over bond term

A bond payable is a long-term debt instrument that typically requires cash interest payments over the bond term and payment of principal at the end of the bond term. A bond can be issued at an amount below the principal amount (discount) or at an amount above the principal amount (premium). The difference between the principal value and the issuance price is amortized over the life of the bond. Present value concepts are applied in calculating both the issuance price and the amortization of the discount or premium over the bond term.

Effective Interest Method of Amortization

The price of a bond is determined based on the present value of both the principal paid at maturity (lump-sum amount) and the periodic cash interest payments made over the bond term (payments). The present value of the lump-sum payment and the interest payments are computed in one formula in Excel.

Starr Inc. sold a $200,000, 5% bond due in 5 years, with cash interest payments due at the end of each year. The market rate of debt of similar risk is 6%. The cash flows with this bond are illustrated here.

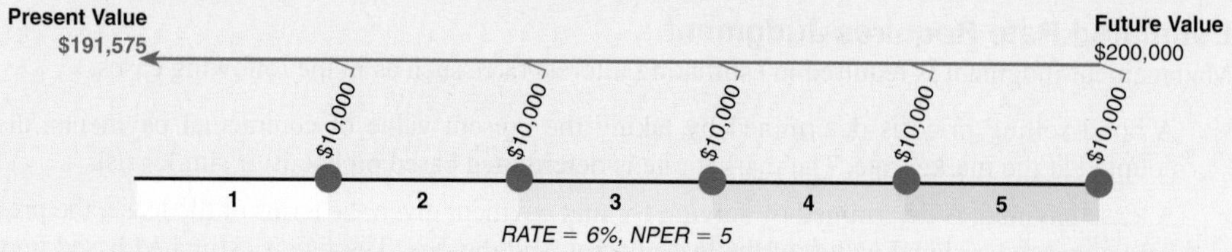

The $191,575 present value of the bond is computed using Excel. The bond discount of $8,425 is the difference between the bond's principal ($200,000) and the bond's selling price ($191,575). The **effective interest method**, illustrated in **Demo 6-7,** is used to amortize the bond discount to interest expense over the life of the bond. With the effective interest method, interest expense is determined by multiplying the effective (market) rate of interest by the carrying value of the bond at the *beginning* of the interest period. Interest expense increases each period because interest expense fluctuates with the increasing bond carrying value. This means that the base for calculating interest expense each period is increasing as the bond moves toward the face value.

	Excel Arguments						Excel Functions
	RATE	NPER	PMT	PV	FV	TYPE	=PV(RATE,NPER,PMT,FV,TYPE)
Given	6%	5	(10,000)	?	(200,000)	—	=PV(0.06,5,−10000,−200000)
Solution				$191,575			

The cash interest paid each period is calculated by multiplying the face amount of the bond by the stated interest rate for the period. The difference between the market interest amount and the cash interest amount is used to adjust the bond book value each period until the bond reaches its face amount. The following amortization table illustrates how interest expense is recognized over the life of the bond. Amortization of interest on notes receivable is illustrated in Chapter 8 and amortization for bonds and notes payable is illustrated in Chapter 16.

Effective Interest Amortization—Discount

Annual Period	Cash (Stated Interest)[a]	Interest Expense (Market Interest)[b]	Discount on B.P. Amortization[c]	Bond Payable, Net (Carrying Value)[d]
				$191,575
1	$10,000	$11,495	$1,495	193,070
2	10,000	11,584	1,584	194,654
3	10,000	11,679	1,679	196,333
4	10,000	11,780	1,780	198,113
5	10,000	11,887	1,887	200,000
	$50,000	$58,425	$8,425	

[a] Stated rate × Bond face value
[b] Market rate × Bond payable, net, beginning of year
[c] Interest expense − Cash
[d] Bond payable, net, beginning of year + Discount amortization

Bond Interest Amortization LO6-7 **Demo 6-7**

Demo MBC

Prepare an effective interest table for $75,000 of 6%, 5-year bonds payable, issued on January 1, 2020. The bonds pay interest annually on December 31. The market rate of interest is 8%.

Solutions

Effective Interest Amortization—Discount

Date	Cash (Stated Interest)	Interest Expense (Market Interest)	Discount on B.P. Amortization	Bonds Payable, Net (Carrying Value)
				$69,011
Dec. 31, 2020 . . .	$ 4,500	$ 5,521	$1,021	70,032
Dec. 31, 2021 . . .	4,500	5,603	1,103	71,135
Dec. 31, 2022 . . .	4,500	5,691	1,191	72,326
Dec. 31, 2023 . . .	4,500	5,786	1,286	73,612
Dec. 31, 2024 . . .	4,500	5,889	1,388	75,000
	$22,500	$28,490	$5,989	

Note Interest Amortization Table **LO6-7** **REVIEW 6-7**

Sicily Inc. purchases equipment on January 1, 2020, by issuing a 3-year, $20,000 note, requiring no periodic cash interest payments. The market rate of interest is 7%. Prepare an effective interest rate table for this note issued for equipment. *Hint:* The amounts in the cash column will be zero.

Review MBC

More Practice: 6-97, 6-99

Solution on p. 6-48.

APPENDIX 6B
LO 6-8

Apply time value of money concept using a financial calculator and compound interest tables

LO 6-8 Overview

Alternative Ways to Solve Time Value of Money Problems
- Financial calculator
- Compound interest tables

Financial calculators and compound interest tables are additional tools available to help solve time value of money situations. Financial calculators operate similarly to Excel in that known variables are entered and the calculator computes the unknown variable as shown in **Demo 6-8A**. Compound interest tables provide factors that can be used to simplify the process of determining present and future values through formulas as shown in **Demo 6-8B**.

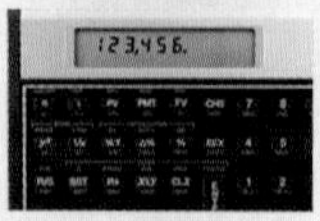

Time Value of Money—Financial Calculator

While financial calculators can operate differently, most financial calculators have keys for present value (PV), future value (FV), number of time periods (N), interest key (*%i*), and a compute key (CPT). Hewlett Packard and Texas Instruments manufacture popular types of financial calculators; however, the time value of money operations differ. When using a financial calculator, it is important to understand the functionality of the type and model of financial calculator used. After clearing data stored in memory, enter each variable followed by the appropriate calculator key.

Demo 6-8A **LO6-8** **Time Value of Money—Financial Calculator**

Demo
MBC

Demonstrate time value of money functions through a financial calculator in the following two cases.

a. **Future value of a single amount** Lowe Inc. has a lump-sum amount of $10,000 to invest today for 3 years, earning 5% interest, compounded annually. What is the future value of this lump-sum amount at the end of 3 years using a *financial calculator*?

b. **Present value of an ordinary annuity** Lowe Inc. is to receive $1,000 per year, beginning one year from today, for a period of 5 years, earning 6% interest compounded annually. What is the present value of this ordinary annuity stream using a *financial calculator*?

Solutions

a. **Future value of a single amount** Each of the following inputs are entered followed by the appropriate variable. Financial calculators are typically programed to enter percentages as whole numbers (such as 5 instead of 0.05). Also, the number of rounded digits can be adjusted, which is usually up to 12 digits.

Inputs

10000		PV
5		%i
3		N
CPT	FV	

Output
11576.25

b. **Present Value of an Ordinary Annuity** Each of the following inputs are entered followed by the appropriate variable.

Inputs

1000		PMT
6		%i
5		N
CPT	PV	

Output
4212.36

Time Value of Money—Compound Interest Tables

Published **compound interest tables** can be used to solve time value of money situations as shown in **Demo 6-8B**. These tables contain **factors** based on a $1 amount, with different combinations of interest rates and number of periods which are derived from present and future value formulas. These factors can then be multiplied by the actual amount for the situation to obtain the present or future value. Six tables are included at the end of this chapter.

Table 6A-1: Future value of $1
Table 6A-2: Present value of $1
Table 6A-3: Future value of ordinary annuity of $1
Table 6A-4: Present value of ordinary annuity of $1
Table 6A-5: Future value of annuity due of $1
Table 6A-6: Present value of annuity due of $1

One advantage of using tables is it eliminates many tedious calculations required in formula calculations. The disadvantages of using the tables are that it is more time consuming than using a financial calculator or Excel, and the situations are limited to the interest rates and number of periods published in tables.

Future Value of a Single Amount—Computation through Table

Assume that we have a lump-sum amount of $5,000 to invest today for 5 years, earning 8% interest, compounded annually. What is the future value of this lump-sum amount at the end of 3 years?

If using the tables to solve for this problem, first locate the appropriate table. In this case it is the *Future Value of $1 table* (**Table 6A-1**). Then find the interest rate column and read down the column to the intersecting line representing the number of interest periods involved, found at the left-hand side of the table. For our example, the intersection of 5 years and 8% rate results in a factor of 1.46933. We take this future value factor and multiply it by today's $5,000 amount.

Future value = Present value × Factor
= $5,000 × 1.46933 = $7,347

Present Value of a Single Amount—Computation through Table

Assume that we will receive $8,000, 10 years from today. Also assume an interest rate of 5% compounded annually. What is the present value of this $8,000 future lump sum?

If using the tables to solve for this problem, first locate the appropriate table, which is the *Present Value of $1 table* (**Table 6A-2**). Then find the interest rate column and read down the column to the intersecting line representing the number of interest periods involved, found at the left-hand side of the table. For our example, the intersection of 10 years and 5% interest results in a factor of 0.61391. Multiply this future value factor by the $8,000 future amount.

Present value = Future value × Factor
= $8,000 × 0.61391 = $4,911

Determination of Interest Rate—Computation through Table with Interpolation

Determination of an unknown interest rate or unknown number of periods sometimes requires interpolation because the table values are limited. Assume that $5,000 is deposited in a savings account at compound interest and that a $15,000 balance is expected at the end of year 10. What is the implicit interest rate, assuming annual compounding?

Future value = Present value × Factor
$15,000 = $5,000 × Factor
Thus: Factor = $15,000/$5,000 = 3.000000

From the *Future Value of $1 table*, the 3.00000 value for 10 periods falls somewhere between 2.83942 (which is compounded at 11%) and 3.10585 (which is compounded at 12%). The interest rate that corresponds to the 3.00000 value being sought is closer to 3.10585 (12%) than it is to 2.83942 (11%)—approximately 6/10 of the way from 11% to 12%. As an approximation, 11.6% might be used.

Future Value of an Ordinary Annuity—Computation through Table

Assume that an annuity payment stream of $5,000 is deposited annually at the end of each period at 8% interest for 6 years. What is the future value of this annuity stream?

To use tables to solve for this problem, first locate the appropriate table, which is the *Future value of Ordinary Annuity of $1* (**Table 6A-3**). Then find the interest rate column and read down the column to the intersecting line representing the number of interest periods involved. For our example, the intersection of 6 years and 8% interest results in a factor of 7.33593. Multiply this future value factor by the $5,000 annuity amount.

Future value = Present value × Factor
= $5,000 × 7.33593 = $36,680

Future Value of Annuity Due—Computation through Table

Assume that an annuity payment stream of $5,000 is deposited annually at the *beginning of each period* at 8% interest for 6 years. What is the future value of this annuity stream?

To use tables to solve for this problem, first locate the appropriate table, which is the *Future Value of an Annuity Due of $1* (**Table 6A-5**). Then find the interest rate column and read down the column to the intersecting line representing the number of interest periods involved. For our example, the intersection of 6 years and 8% interest results in a factor of 7.92280. Multiply this future value factor by the $5,000 annuity amount.

Future value = Present value × Factor
= $5,000 × 7.92280 = $39,614

Present Value of an Ordinary Annuity—Computation through Table

If an annuity payment stream of $10,000 is deposited annually at the end of each period at 6% interest for 5 years, what is the present value of this annuity stream? To use tables to solve for this problem, first locate the appropriate table, which is the *Present Value of an Ordinary Annuity of $1* (**Table 6A-4**). Then find the interest rate column and read down the column to the intersecting line representing the number of interest periods involved. For our example, the intersection of 5 years and 6% interest results in a factor of 4.21236. Multiply this present value factor by the $5,000 annuity amount.

Present value = Future value × Factor
= $5,000 × 4.21236 = $21,062

Present Value of Annuity Due—Computation through Table

If an annuity payment stream of $10,000 is deposited annually at the beginning of each period at 6% interest for 5 years, what is the present value of this annuity stream? With an annuity due, each payment is made one period sooner than in the case of the ordinary annuity. This means that one way to find the annuity due factor is to multiply the equivalent ordinary annuity factor by $(1 + i)$.

To use tables to solve for this problem, first locate the appropriate table, which is the *Present Value of an Annuity Due of $1* (**Table 6A-6**). Then find the interest rate column and read down the column to the intersecting line representing the number of interest periods involved. For our example, the intersection of 5 years and 6% interest results in a factor of 4.46511. Multiply this present value factor by the $5,000 annuity amount.

Present value = Future value × Factor
= $5,000 × 4.46511 = $22,326

Time Value of Money—Compound Interest Tables

LO6-8 Demo 6-8B

Demo MBC

Complete the following table by indicating (1) the relevant factor from the present value or future value table, and (2) the amount of the present or future value for each separate case *a* through *f*. Assume that the number of periods is 10 and the interest rate is 6% with annual compounding for each case. Round each answer to the nearest $1.

	Time Value of Money Case	Table (source)	Factor	Answer
a.	Current value of $5,000 to be received in 5 years.	Present value of $1	**0.55839**	**$2,792**
b.	Current value of a stream of $100 payments made at the end of each period.	Present value of ordinary annuity of $1	**7.36009**	**$ 736**
c.	Future value of a stream of $100 payments made at the end of each period.	Future value of ordinary annuity of $1	**13.18079**	**$1,318**
d.	Future value of a stream of $100 payments made at the beginning of each period.	Future value of annuity due of $1	**13.97164**	**$1,397**
e.	Current value of a stream of $100 payments made at the beginning of each period.	Present value of annuity due of $1	**7.80169**	**$ 780**
f.	Future value of $2,000 in 10 years from now.	Future value of $1	**1.79085**	**$3,582**

Future Value and Present Value Interest Tables

Table 6A-1 Future value of 1: FV1 = $(1 + i)^n$

This table shows the compund amount (future value) of $1 at various interest rates and for various time periods. It is used to compute the future value of single payments, where i = interest; and n = number of periods.

n	2%	3%	4%	5%	6%	7%	8%	9%	10%	11%	12%	15%
1 . . .	1.02000	1.03000	1.04000	1.05000	1.06000	1.07000	1.08000	1.09000	1.10000	1.11000	1.12000	1.15000
2 . . .	1.04040	1.06090	1.08160	1.10250	1.12360	1.14490	1.16640	1.18810	1.21000	1.23210	1.25440	1.32250
3 . . .	1.06121	1.09273	1.12486	1.15763	1.19102	1.22504	1.25971	1.29503	1.33100	1.36763	1.40493	1.52088
4 . . .	1.08243	1.12551	1.16986	1.21551	1.26248	1.31080	1.36049	1.41158	1.46410	1.51807	1.57352	1.74901
5 . . .	1.10408	1.15927	1.21665	1.27628	1.33823	1.40255	1.46933	1.53862	1.61051	1.68506	1.76234	2.01136
6 . . .	1.12616	1.19405	1.26532	1.34010	1.41852	1.50073	1.58687	1.67710	1.77156	1.87041	1.97382	2.31306
7 . . .	1.14869	1.22987	1.31593	1.40710	1.50363	1.60578	1.71382	1.82804	1.94872	2.07616	2.21068	2.66002
8 . . .	1.17166	1.26677	1.36857	1.47746	1.59385	1.71819	1.85093	1.99256	2.14359	2.30454	2.47596	3.05902
9 . . .	1.19509	1.30477	1.42331	1.55133	1.68948	1.83846	1.99900	2.17189	2.35795	2.55804	2.77308	3.51788
10 . . .	1.21899	1.34392	1.48024	1.62889	1.79085	1.96715	2.15892	2.36736	2.59374	2.83942	3.10585	4.04556
11 . . .	1.24337	1.38423	1.53945	1.71034	1.89830	2.10485	2.33164	2.58043	2.85312	3.15176	3.47855	4.65239
12 . . .	1.26824	1.42576	1.60103	1.79586	2.01220	2.25219	2.51817	2.81266	3.13843	3.49845	3.89598	5.35025
13 . . .	1.29361	1.46853	1.66507	1.88565	2.13293	2.40985	2.71962	3.06580	3.45227	3.88328	4.36349	6.15279
14 . . .	1.31948	1.51259	1.73168	1.97993	2.26090	2.57853	2.93719	3.34173	3.79750	4.31044	4.88711	7.07571
15 . . .	1.34587	1.55797	1.80094	2.07893	2.39656	2.75903	3.17217	3.64248	4.17725	4.78459	5.47357	8.13706
16 . . .	1.37279	1.60471	1.87298	2.18287	2.54035	2.95216	3.42594	3.97031	4.59497	5.31089	6.13039	9.35762
17 . . .	1.40024	1.65285	1.94790	2.29202	2.69277	3.15882	3.70002	4.32763	5.05447	5.89509	6.86604	10.76126
18 . . .	1.42825	1.70243	2.02582	2.40662	2.85434	3.37993	3.99602	4.71712	5.55992	6.54355	7.68997	12.37545
19 . . .	1.45681	1.75351	2.10685	2.52695	3.02560	3.61653	4.31570	5.14166	6.11591	7.26334	8.61276	14.23177
20 . . .	1.48595	1.80611	2.19112	2.65330	3.20714	3.86968	4.66096	5.60441	6.72750	8.06231	9.64629	16.36654
21 . . .	1.51567	1.86029	2.27877	2.78596	3.39956	4.14056	5.03383	6.10881	7.40025	8.94917	10.80385	18.82152
22 . . .	1.54598	1.91610	2.36992	2.92526	3.60354	4.43040	5.43654	6.65860	8.14027	9.93357	12.10031	21.64475
23 . . .	1.57690	1.97359	2.48472	3.07152	3.81975	4.74053	5.87146	7.25787	8.95430	11.02627	13.55235	24.89146
24 . . .	1.60844	2.03279	2.56330	3.22510	4.04893	5.07237	6.34118	7.91108	9.84973	12.23916	15.17863	28.62518
25 . . .	1.64061	2.09378	2.66584	3.38635	4.29187	5.42743	6.84848	8.62308	10.83471	13.58546	17.00006	32.91895

Table 6A-2 Present value 1: $PV1 = 1/(1 + i)^n$

This table shows the present value of $1 discounted at various rates of interest and for various time periods. It is used to compute the present value of single payments.

n	2%	3%	4%	5%	6%	7%	8%	9%	10%	11%	12%	15%
1 . . .	0.98039	0.97087	0.96154	0.95238	0.94340	0.93458	0.92593	0.91743	0.90909	0.90090	0.89286	0.86957
2 . . .	0.96117	0.94260	0.92456	0.90703	0.89000	0.87344	0.85734	0.84168	0.82645	0.81162	0.79719	0.75614
3 . . .	0.94232	0.91514	0.88900	0.86384	0.83962	0.81630	0.79383	0.77218	0.75131	0.73119	0.71178	0.65752
4 . . .	0.92385	0.88849	0.85480	0.82270	0.79209	0.76290	0.73503	0.70843	0.68301	0.65873	0.63552	0.57175
5 . . .	0.90573	0.86261	0.82193	0.78353	0.74726	0.71299	0.68058	0.64993	0.62092	0.59345	0.56743	0.49718
6 . . .	0.88797	0.83748	0.79031	0.74622	0.70496	0.66634	0.63017	0.59627	0.56447	0.53464	0.50663	0.43233
7 . . .	0.87056	0.81309	0.75992	0.71068	0.66506	0.62275	0.58349	0.54703	0.51316	0.48166	0.45235	0.37594
8 . . .	0.85349	0.78941	0.73069	0.67684	0.62741	0.58201	0.54027	0.50187	0.46651	0.43393	0.40388	0.32690
9 . . .	0.83676	0.76642	0.70259	0.64461	0.59190	0.54393	0.50025	0.46043	0.42410	0.39092	0.36061	0.28426
10 . . .	0.82035	0.74409	0.67556	0.61391	0.55839	0.50835	0.46319	0.42241	0.38554	0.35218	0.32197	0.24718
11 . . .	0.80426	0.72242	0.64958	0.58468	0.52679	0.47509	0.42888	0.38753	0.35049	0.31728	0.28748	0.21494
12 . . .	0.78849	0.70138	0.62460	0.55684	0.49697	0.44401	0.39711	0.35553	0.31863	0.28584	0.25668	0.18691
13 . . .	0.77303	0.68095	0.60057	0.53032	0.46884	0.41496	0.36770	0.32618	0.28966	0.25751	0.22917	0.16253
14 . . .	0.75788	0.66112	0.57748	0.50507	0.44230	0.38782	0.34046	0.29925	0.26333	0.23199	0.20462	0.14133
15 . . .	0.74301	0.64186	0.55526	0.48102	0.41727	0.36245	0.31524	0.27454	0.23939	0.20900	0.18270	0.12289
16 . . .	0.72845	0.62317	0.53391	0.45811	0.39365	0.33873	0.29189	0.25187	0.21763	0.18829	0.16312	0.10686
17 . . .	0.71416	0.60502	0.51337	0.43630	0.37136	0.31657	0.27027	0.23107	0.19784	0.16963	0.14564	0.09293
18 . . .	0.70016	0.58739	0.49363	0.41552	0.35034	0.29586	0.25025	0.21199	0.17986	0.15282	0.13004	0.08081
19 . . .	0.68643	0.57029	0.47464	0.39573	0.33051	0.27651	0.23171	0.19449	0.16351	0.13768	0.11611	0.07027
20 . . .	0.67297	0.55368	0.45639	0.37689	0.31180	0.25842	0.21455	0.17843	0.14864	0.12403	0.10367	0.06110
21 . . .	0.65978	0.53755	0.43883	0.35894	0.29416	0.24151	0.19866	0.16370	0.13513	0.11174	0.09256	0.05313
22 . . .	0.64684	0.52189	0.42196	0.34185	0.27751	0.22571	0.18394	0.15018	0.12285	0.10067	0.08264	0.04620
23 . . .	0.63416	0.50669	0.40573	0.32557	0.26180	0.21095	0.17032	0.13778	0.11168	0.09069	0.07379	0.04017
24 . . .	0.62172	0.49193	0.39012	0.31007	0.24698	0.19715	0.15770	0.12640	0.10153	0.08170	0.06588	0.03493
25 . . .	0.60953	0.47761	0.37512	0.29530	0.23300	0.18425	0.14602	0.11597	0.09230	0.07361	0.05882	0.03038

Table 6A-3 Future Value of an Ordinary Annuity of *n* Payments of 1 Each: $FVA = \left[\frac{(1+i)^n - 1}{i}\right]$

This table shows the future value of an ordinary annuity of $1 at various rates of interest and for various time periods. It is used to compute the future value of a series of payments made at the end of each interest compounding period.

n	2%	3%	4%	5%	6%	7%	8%	9%	10%	11%	12%	15%
1 . . .	1.00000	1.00000	1.00000	1.00000	1.00000	1.00000	1.00000	1.00000	1.00000	1.00000	1.00000	1.00000
2 . . .	2.02000	2.03000	2.04000	2.05000	2.06000	2.07000	2.08000	2.09000	2.10000	2.11000	2.12000	2.15000
3 . . .	3.06040	3.09090	3.12160	3.15250	3.18360	3.21490	3.24640	3.27810	3.31000	3.34210	3.37440	3.47250
4 . . .	4.12161	4.18363	4.24646	4.31013	4.37462	4.43994	4.50611	4.57313	4.64100	4.70973	4.77933	4.99338
5 . . .	5.20404	5.30914	5.41632	5.52563	5.63709	5.75074	5.86660	5.98471	6.10510	6.22780	6.35285	6.74238
6 . . .	6.30812	6.46841	6.63298	6.80191	6.97532	7.15329	7.33593	7.52333	7.71561	7.91286	8.11519	8.75374
7 . . .	7.43428	7.66246	7.89829	8.14201	8.39384	8.65402	8.92280	9.20043	9.48717	9.78327	10.08901	11.06680
8 . . .	8.58297	8.89234	9.21423	9.54911	9.89747	10.25980	10.63663	11.02847	11.43589	11.85943	12.29969	13.72682
9 . . .	9.75463	10.15911	10.58280	11.02656	11.49132	11.97799	12.48756	13.02104	13.57948	14.16397	14.77566	16.78584
10 . . .	10.94972	11.46388	12.00611	12.57789	13.18079	13.81645	14.48656	15.19293	15.93742	16.72201	17.54874	20.30372
11 . . .	12.16872	12.80780	13.48635	14.20679	14.97164	15.78360	16.64549	17.56029	18.53117	19.56143	20.65458	24.34928
12 . . .	13.41209	14.19203	15.02581	15.91713	16.86994	17.88845	18.97713	20.14072	21.38428	22.71319	24.13313	29.00167
13 . . .	14.68033	15.61779	16.62684	17.71298	18.88214	20.14064	21.49530	22.95338	24.52271	26.21164	28.02911	34.35192
14 . . .	15.97394	17.08632	18.29191	19.59863	21.01507	22.55049	24.21492	26.01919	27.97498	30.09492	32.39260	40.50471
15 . . .	17.29342	18.59891	20.02359	21.57856	23.27597	25.12902	27.15211	29.36092	31.77248	34.40536	37.27971	47.58041
16 . . .	18.63929	20.15688	21.82453	23.65749	25.67253	27.88805	30.32428	33.00340	35.94973	39.18995	42.75328	55.71747
17 . . .	20.01207	21.76159	23.69751	25.84037	28.21288	30.84022	33.75023	36.97370	40.54470	44.50084	48.88367	65.07509
18 . . .	21.41231	23.41444	25.64541	28.13238	30.90565	33.99903	37.45024	41.30134	45.59917	50.39594	55.74971	75.83636
19 . . .	22.84056	25.11687	27.67123	30.53900	33.75999	37.37896	41.44626	46.01846	51.15909	56.93949	63.43968	88.21181
20 . . .	24.29737	26.87037	29.77808	33.06595	36.78559	40.99549	45.76196	51.16012	57.27500	64.20283	72.05244	102.44358
21 . . .	25.78332	28.67649	31.96920	35.71925	39.99273	44.86518	50.42292	56.76453	64.00250	72.26514	81.69874	118.81012
22 . . .	27.29898	30.53678	34.24797	38.50521	43.39229	49.00574	55.45676	62.87334	71.40275	81.21431	92.50258	137.63164
23 . . .	28.84496	32.45288	36.61789	41.43048	46.99583	53.43614	60.89330	69.53194	79.54302	91.14788	104.60289	159.27638
24 . . .	30.42186	34.42647	39.08260	44.50200	50.81558	58.17667	66.76476	76.78981	88.49733	102.17415	118.15524	184.16784
25 . . .	32.03030	36.45926	41.64591	47.72710	54.86451	63.24904	73.10594	84.70090	98.34706	114.41331	133.33387	212.79302

Table 6A-4 Present Value of an Ordinary Annuity of n Payments of 1 Each: $PVA = \left[\frac{1-1/(1+i)^n}{i}\right]$

n	2%	3%	4%	5%	6%	7%	8%	9%	10%	11%	12%	15%
1 . . .	0.98039	0.97087	0.96154	0.95238	0.94340	0.93458	0.92593	0.91743	0.90909	0.90090	0.89286	0.86957
2 . . .	1.94156	1.91347	1.88609	1.85941	1.83339	1.80802	1.78326	1.75911	1.73554	1.71252	1.69005	1.62571
3 . . .	2.88388	2.82861	2.77509	2.72325	2.67301	2.62432	2.57710	2.53129	2.48685	2.44371	2.40183	2.28323
4 . . .	3.80773	3.71710	3.62990	3.54595	3.46511	3.38721	3.31213	3.23972	3.16987	3.10245	3.03735	2.85498
5 . . .	4.71346	4.57971	4.45182	4.32948	4.21236	4.10020	3.99271	3.88965	3.79079	3.69590	3.60478	3.35216
6 . . .	5.60143	5.41719	5.24214	5.07569	4.91732	4.76654	4.62288	4.48592	4.35526	4.23054	4.11141	3.78448
7 . . .	6.47199	6.23028	6.00205	5.78637	5.58238	5.38929	5.20637	5.03295	4.86842	4.71220	4.56736	4.16042
8 . . .	7.32548	7.01969	6.73274	6.46321	6.20979	5.97130	5.74664	5.53482	5.33493	5.14612	4.96764	4.48732
9 . . .	8.16224	7.78611	7.43533	7.10782	6.80169	6.51523	6.24689	5.99525	5.75902	5.53705	5.32825	4.77158
10 . . .	8.98259	8.53020	8.11090	7.72173	7.36009	7.02358	6.71008	6.41766	6.14457	5.88923	5.65022	5.01877
11 . . .	9.78685	9.25262	8.76048	8.30641	7.88687	7.49867	7.13896	6.80519	6.49506	6.20652	5.93770	5.23371
12 . . .	10.57534	9.95400	9.38507	8.86325	8.38384	7.94269	7.53608	7.16073	6.81369	6.49236	6.19437	5.42062
13 . . .	11.34837	10.63496	9.98565	9.39357	8.85268	8.35765	7.90378	7.48690	7.10336	6.74987	6.42355	5.58315
14 . . .	12.10625	11.29607	10.56312	9.89864	9.29498	8.74547	8.24424	7.78615	7.36669	6.98187	6.62817	5.72448
15 . . .	12.84926	11.93794	11.11839	10.37966	9.71225	9.10791	8.55948	8.06069	7.60608	7.19087	6.81086	5.84737
16 . . .	13.57771	12.56110	11.65230	10.83777	10.10590	9.44665	8.85137	8.31256	7.82371	7.37916	6.97399	5.95423
17 . . .	14.29187	13.16612	12.16567	11.27407	10.47726	9.76322	9.12164	8.54363	8.02155	7.54879	7.11963	6.04716
18 . . .	14.99203	13.75351	12.65930	11.68959	10.82760	10.05909	9.37189	8.75563	8.20141	7.70162	7.24967	6.12797
19 . . .	15.67846	14.32380	13.13394	12.08532	11.15812	10.33560	9.60360	8.95011	8.36492	7.83929	7.36578	6.19823
20 . . .	16.35143	14.87747	13.59033	12.46221	11.46992	10.59401	9.81815	9.12855	8.51356	7.96333	7.46944	6.25933
21 . . .	17.01121	15.41502	14.02916	12.82115	11.76408	11.83553	10.01680	9.29224	8.64869	8.07507	7.56200	6.31246
22 . . .	17.65805	15.93692	14.45112	13.16300	12.04158	11.06124	10.20074	9.44243	8.77154	8.17574	7.64465	6.35866
23 . . .	18.29220	16.44361	14.85684	13.48857	12.30338	11.27219	10.37106	9.58021	8.88322	8.26643	7.71843	6.39884
24 . . .	18.91393	16.93554	15.24696	13.79864	12.55036	11.46933	10.52876	9.70661	8.98474	8.34814	7.78432	6.43377
25 . . .	19.52346	17.41315	15.62208	14.09394	12.78336	11.65358	10.67478	9.82258	9.07704	8.42174	7.84314	6.46415

Table 6A-5 Future Value of an Annuity Due of n Payments of 1 Each: $FVAD = \left[\frac{(1+i)^n-1}{i}\right] \times (1+i)$

This table shows the future value of an annuity due of $1 at various rates of interest and for various time periods. It is used to compute the future value of a series of payments made at the beginning of each interest compounding period.

n	2%	3%	4%	5%	6%	7%	8%	9%	10%	11%	12%	15%
1 . . .	1.02000	1.03000	1.04000	1.05000	1.06000	1.07000	1.08000	1.09000	1.10000	1.11000	1.12000	1.15000
2 . . .	2.06040	2.09090	2.12160	2.15250	2.18360	2.21490	2.24640	2.27810	2.31000	2.34210	2.37440	2.47250
3 . . .	3.12161	3.18363	3.24646	3.31013	3.37462	3.43994	3.50611	3.57313	3.64100	3.70973	3.77933	3.99338
4 . . .	4.20404	4.30914	4.41632	4.52563	4.63709	4.75074	4.86660	4.98471	5.10510	5.22780	5.35285	5.74238
5 . . .	5.30812	5.46841	5.63298	5.80191	5.97532	6.15329	6.33593	6.52333	6.71561	6.91286	7.11519	7.75374
6 . . .	6.43428	6.66246	6.89829	7.14201	7.39384	7.65402	7.92280	8.20043	8.48717	8.78327	9.08901	10.06680
7 . . .	7.58297	7.89234	8.21423	8.54911	8.89747	9.25980	9.63663	10.02847	10.43589	10.85943	11.29969	12.72682
8 . . .	8.75463	9.15911	9.58280	10.02656	10.49132	10.97799	11.48756	12.02104	12.57948	13.16397	13.77566	15.78584
9 . . .	9.94972	10.46388	11.00611	11.57789	12.18079	12.81645	13.48656	14.19293	14.93742	15.72201	16.54874	19.30372
10 . . .	11.16872	11.80780	12.48635	13.20679	13.97164	14.78360	15.64549	16.56029	17.53117	18.56143	19.65458	23.34928
11 . . .	12.41209	13.19203	14.02581	14.91713	15.86994	16.88845	17.97713	19.14072	20.38428	21.71319	23.13313	28.00167
12 . . .	13.68033	14.61779	15.62684	16.71298	17.88214	19.14064	20.49530	21.95338	23.52271	25.21164	27.02911	33.35192
13 . . .	14.97394	16.08632	17.29191	18.59863	20.01507	21.55049	23.21492	25.01919	26.97498	29.09492	31.39260	39.50471
14 . . .	16.29342	17.59891	19.02359	20.57856	22.27597	24.12902	26.15211	28.36092	30.77248	33.40536	36.27971	46.58041
15 . . .	17.63929	19.15688	20.82453	22.65749	24.67253	26.88805	29.32428	32.00340	34.94973	38.18995	41.75328	54.71747
16 . . .	19.01207	20.76159	22.69751	24.84037	27.21288	29.84022	32.75023	35.97370	39.54470	43.50084	47.88367	64.07509
17 . . .	20.41231	22.41444	24.64541	27.13238	29.90565	32.99903	36.45024	40.30134	44.59917	49.39594	54.74971	74.83636
18 . . .	21.84056	24.11687	26.67123	29.53900	32.75999	36.37896	40.44626	45.01846	50.15909	55.93949	62.43968	87.21181
19 . . .	23.29737	25.87037	28.77808	32.06595	35.78559	39.99549	44.76196	50.16012	56.27500	63.20283	71.05244	101.44358
20 . . .	24.78332	27.67649	30.96920	34.71925	38.99273	43.86518	49.42292	55.76453	63.00250	71.26514	80.69874	117.81012
21 . . .	26.29898	29.53678	33.24797	37.50521	42.39229	48.00574	54.45676	61.87334	70.40275	80.21431	91.50258	136.63164
22 . . .	27.84496	31.45288	35.61789	40.43048	45.99583	52.43614	59.89330	68.53194	78.54302	90.14788	103.60289	158.27638
23 . . .	29.42186	33.42647	38.08260	43.50200	49.81558	57.17667	65.76476	75.78981	87.49733	101.17415	117.15524	183.16784
24 . . .	31.03030	35.45926	40.64591	46.72710	53.86451	62.24904	72.10594	83.70090	97.34706	113.41331	132.33387	211.79302
25 . . .	32.67091	37.55304	43.31174	50.11345	58.15638	67.67647	78.95442	92.32398	108.18177	126.99877	149.33393	244.71197

Table 6A-6 Present Value of an Annuity Due of *n* Payments of 1 Each: $PVAD = \left[\frac{1-1(1+i)^n}{i}\right] \times (1+i)$

This table shows the present value of an annuity due of $1 at various rates of interest and for various time periods. It is used to compute the present value of a series of payments made at the beginning of each interest compounding period.

n	2%	3%	4%	5%	6%	7%	8%	9%	10%	11%	12%	15%
1 . . .	1.00000	1.00000	1.00000	1.00000	1.00000	1.00000	1.00000	1.00000	1.00000	1.00000	1.00000	1.00000
2 . . .	1.98039	1.97087	1.96154	1.95238	1.94340	1.93458	1.92593	1.91743	1.90909	1.90090	1.89286	1.86957
3 . . .	2.94156	2.91347	2.88609	2.85941	2.83339	2.80802	2.78326	2.75911	2.73554	2.71252	2.69005	2.62571
4 . . .	3.88388	3.82861	3.77509	3.72325	3.67301	3.62432	3.57710	3.53130	3.48685	3.44371	3.40183	3.28323
5 . . .	4.80773	4.71710	4.62990	4.54595	4.46511	4.38721	4.31213	4.23972	4.16987	4.10245	4.03735	3.85498
6 . . .	5.71346	5.57971	5.45182	5.32948	5.21236	5.10020	4.99271	4.88965	4.79079	4.69590	4.60478	4.35216
7 . . .	6.60143	6.41719	6.24214	6.07569	5.91732	5.76654	5.62288	5.48592	5.35526	5.23054	5.11141	4.78448
8 . . .	7.47199	7.23028	7.00205	6.78637	6.58238	6.38929	6.20637	6.03295	5.86842	5.71220	5.56376	5.16042
9 . . .	8.32548	8.01969	7.73274	7.46321	7.20979	6.97130	6.74664	6.53482	6.33493	6.14612	5.96764	5.48732
10 . . .	9.16224	8.78611	8.43533	8.10782	7.80169	7.51523	7.24689	6.99525	6.75902	6.53705	6.32825	5.77158
11 . . .	9.98259	9.53020	9.11090	8.72173	8.36009	8.02358	7.71008	7.41766	7.14457	6.88923	6.65022	6.01877
12 . . .	10.78685	10.25262	9.76048	9.30641	8.88687	8.49867	8.13896	7.80519	7.49506	7.20652	6.93770	6.23371
13 . . .	11.57534	10.95400	10.38507	9.86325	9.38384	8.94269	8.53608	8.16073	7.81369	7.49236	7.19437	6.42062
14 . . .	12.34837	11.63496	10.98565	10.39357	9.85268	9.35765	8.90378	8.48690	8.10336	7.74987	7.42355	6.58315
15 . . .	13.10625	12.29607	11.56312	10.89864	10.29498	9.74547	9.24424	8.78615	8.36669	7.98187	7.62817	6.72448
16 . . .	13.84926	12.93794	12.11839	11.37966	10.71225	10.10791	9.55948	9.06069	8.60608	8.19087	7.81086	6.84737
17 . . .	14.57771	13.56110	12.65230	11.83777	11.10590	10.44665	9.85137	9.31256	8.82371	8.37916	7.97399	6.95423
18 . . .	15.29187	14.16612	13.16567	12.27407	11.47726	10.76322	10.12164	9.54363	9.02155	8.54879	8.11963	7.04716
19 . . .	15.99203	14.75351	13.65930	12.68959	11.82760	11.05909	10.37189	9.75563	9.20141	8.70162	8.24967	7.12797
20 . . .	16.67846	15.32380	14.13394	13.08532	12.15812	11.33560	10.60360	9.95012	9.36492	8.83929	8.36578	7.19823
21 . . .	17.35143	15.87747	14.59033	13.46221	12.46992	11.59401	10.81815	10.12855	9.51356	8.96333	8.46944	7.25933
22 . . .	18.01121	16.41502	15.02916	13.82115	12.76408	11.83553	11.01680	10.29224	9.64869	9.07507	8.56200	7.31246
23 . . .	18.65805	16.93692	15.45112	14.16300	13.04158	12.06124	11.20074	10.44243	9.77154	9.17574	8.64465	7.35866
24 . . .	19.29220	17.44361	15.85684	14.48857	13.30338	12.27219	11.37106	10.58021	9.88322	9.26643	8.71843	7.39884
25 . . .	19.91393	17.93554	16.24696	14.79864	13.55036	12.46933	11.52876	10.70661	9.98474	9.34814	8.78432	7.43377

REVIEW 6-8 **LO6-8** **Compound Interest Table**

Review MBC

Complete the following table for investments *a* through *f* by indicating the relevant factor from the present value or future value table and the final present or future value amount.

Investment	Compounding	Annual Interest Rate	Amount	Investment Period	Payment at Beg. or End of Period	Future Value or Present Value	Factor	Answer
a. Annuity	Annually	5%	$1,000	2 years	End	Future	______	$______
b. Annuity	Semiannually	4%	500	3 years	Beginning	Present	______	______
c. Annuity	Semiannually	6%	7,000	4 years	Beginning	Future	______	______
d. Single Payment	Annually	5%	4,500	6 years	n/a	Present	______	______
e. Single Payment	Semiannually	6%	8,000	5 years	n/a	Future	______	______
f. Single Payment	Semiannually	4%	4,800	4 years	n/a	Present	______	______

More Practice: 6-98

Solution on p. 6-48.

Questions

6-1. Explain what is meant by the time value of money.

6-2. Assuming that the annual rate of interest is stated as 12%, what is the interest rate for the following compounding periods: (a) semiannual, (b) quarterly, (c) monthly?

6-3. What is the fundamental difference between simple interest and compound interest?

6-4. Briefly explain each of the following:

a. Future value of $1.

b. Present value of $1.

c. Future value of annuity of *n* payments of $1 each.

d. Present value of annuity of *n* payments of $1 each.

6-5. What is the future value of $10,000 earning 10% per year for two years?

6-6. Contrast a future value of $1 with the present value of $1.

6-7. If $15,000 were deposited in an account at 8% interest, compounded annually, what would be the balance in the account at the end of (a) 10 years? (b) 15 years? (c) 25 years?

6-8. Assume that we have a legal contract that specifies that we will receive $200,000 cash in the future. Assuming a 9% interest rate, what would be the present value of that contract if the amount will be received in (a) 10 years, (b) 15 years, or (c) 25 years from today?

6-9. Assume that we deposit $20,000 in an account for a three-year period. How much cash would we receive at period end if 12% simple interest per annum is accumulated in the fund at the end of each quarter?

6-10. Assume that we will receive $100,000 cash from a trust fund six years from now. What is the present value of the $100,000, assuming 12% interest on a quarterly basis?

6-11. What are the three characteristics of an annuity? Explain what would happen if any of these characteristics were changed.

6-12. If $20,000 is deposited in an account at the end of each of *n* annual periods and will earn 9%, what will be the balance in the account at the date of the last deposit (an ordinary annuity), assuming that *n* equals (a) 10 years, (b) 15 years, and (c) 25 years?

6-13. Explain the difference between (a) future value of an ordinary annuity, and (b) future value of an annuity due.

6-14. Explain the difference between (a) present value of an ordinary annuity, and (b) present value of an annuity due.

6-15. Compute the present value of an annuity of five payments of $9,000 each using a 12% interest rate, assuming (a) an ordinary annuity, and (b) an annuity due. Explain why the two amounts are different.

6-16. Compute the future value of an annuity of six payments of $5,000 each using a 10% interest rate, assuming (a) an ordinary annuity, and (b) an annuity due. Explain why the two amounts are different.

6-17. A company creates a building fund by contributing $100,000 per year to it for 10 years. Explain how we identify whether this situation is an ordinary annuity or an annuity due.

Brief Exercises

Brief Exercise 6-18 Identifying Number of Compounding Periods and Rate per Period **LO1** *Hint:* See Demo 6-1

Complete the following table.

Investment	Cost	Annual Interest Rate	Term	Compounding	Interest Rate per Compounding Period	Total Number of Compounding Periods
Investment A	$ 50,000	5%	5 years	Quarterly	______	______
Investment B	50,000	6%	5 years	Monthly	______	______
Investment C	100,000	8%	10 years	Quarterly	______	______
Investment D	100,000	10%	10 years	Monthly	______	______

Brief Exercise 6-19 Computing the Future Value of a Single Amount **LO2** *Hint:* See Demo 6-2

Evans invested $50,000 today in a mutual fund earning 5% interest, compounded annually.

a. What is the value of the mutual fund in 5 years?

b. What is the value of the mutual fund in 20 years?

Brief Exercise 6-20 Solving for Number of Compounding Periods **LO2**

Lawren plans to invest $10,000 today. Assuming that the investment earns 8% compounded quarterly, how many quarters must Lawren invest the amount to achieve a goal of $15,000?

Brief Exercise 6-21 Computing the Present Value of a Single Amount **LO3**

Depp is reviewing an investment that will provide a payout of $30,000 in five years. If Depp considers a 7% interest rate (compounded annually) acceptable, what amount is Depp willing to pay for the investment today?

Brief Exercise 6-22
Computing the Present Value of a Single Amount **LO3**
Hint: See Demo 6-3A

Reynolds must accumulate $40,000 in eight years to purchase replacement equipment. Reynolds plans to invest funds today to have the $40,000 accessible at that time.

a. Assuming a 6% return compounded annually on its investment, how much must Reynolds invest now to reach the goal?

b. Assuming an 8% return compounded annually on its investment, how much must Reynolds invest now to reach the goal?

Brief Exercise 6-23
Solving for Interest Rate per Period **LO3**
Hint: See Demo 6-3B

Scarlett has $25,000 available today to invest for 20 years. Scarlett desires an investment fund balance of $100,000 at that time. What interest rate (compounded annually) must Scarlett earn to reach the desired balance in 20 years?

Brief Exercise 6-24
Solving for Number of Compounding Periods **LO3**
Hint: See Demo 6-3B

Foxx has $25,000 available today to invest at a rate of return of 8%, compound annually. How many years would it take for the initial balance to reach $75,000?

Brief Exercise 6-25
Computing the Future Value of an Annuity **LO4**
Hint: See Demo 6-4A

Stone will deposit $7,500 at the end of each year for 10 years in a fund that earns 7%, compounded annually. What is the total amount of the fund at the end of 10 years?

Brief Exercise 6-26
Computing the Future Value of an Annuity **LO4**
Hint: See Demo 6-4B

Refer to information in Brief Exercise 6-25, what amount would be accumulated in the fund if the annual deposits were instead made at the *beginning* of each year?

Brief Exercise 6-27
Computing the Present Value of an Annuity **LO5**

In repayment of a loan today, Nicholas agreed to pay a financial institution $1,000 at the end of each month over a 3 year period, beginning one month from today. Assuming the interest rate on the loan is 8.5%, what is today's amount of the loan?

Brief Exercise 6-28
Computing the Present Value of an Annuity **LO5**

Refer to information in Brief Exercise 6-27, what is the loan amount if the first payment is made immediately?

Brief Exercise 6-29
Computing the Value of Deferred Annuity **LO5**
Hint: See Demo 6-5C

What is the present value of 4 years of annual cash receipts of $8,000 at the end of each year that begins two years from today, assuming a 6% interest rate?

Brief Exercise 6-30
Solving for Annuity Amount per Period **LO5**

Samuel borrowed $25,000 to purchase a vehicle on January 1, 2020, by signing a five-year note with a 6% interest rate. Assuming end of month payments and monthly compounding, what is the monthly payment on the loan?

Brief Exercise 6-31
Solving for Number of Compounding Periods **LO5**

Leonardo Inc. invests $20,944 at the end of each year in an investment fund that earns 5% interest. How many years will it take for the company to reach $200,000?

Brief Exercise 6-32
Solving for the Interest Rate per Period **LO5**

Wick borrowed $8,000 and agreed to make 10 annual payments of $1,036 at the end of each year. What is the interest rate of this loan?

Brief Exercise 6-33
Determining Bond Price **LO6**
Hint: See Demo 6-6

On January 1, 2020, Arrow Inc. issued $100,000, 5% bonds due in 10 years. The bonds pay annual interest at the end of each year equal to 5% of face value. The current market interest rate for bonds with similar risk is 6%. Determine the selling price of the bonds.

Brief Exercise 6-34
Determining Lease Liability **LO6**
Hint: See Demo 6-6

Applied Inc. signed a 10-year lease for its corporate office space on January 2, 2020. The first annual payment of $40,000 is due immediately. Assuming an interest rate of 7%, what is the present value of the lease liability?

Brief Exercise 6-35
Determining Annual Loan Payment **LO6**

Americ Inc. borrowed $80,000 on January 1, 2020, with repayment scheduled over a 10-year period, with payments due at the end of each year at an interest rate of 7%. What is Americ's annual payment on this loan?

Brief Exercise 6-36
Solving for Annuity Amount per Period **LO5**

Aflack Inc. borrowed $10,000 and agreed to pay off the loan over 5 years by making equal year-end payments, compounded annually at 10%.

a. What is the annual payment amount?

b. What is the annual payment amount if the interest rate increased to 12%?

Exercises

Exercise 6-37
Computing Future Value of Single Amount with Changes in Compounding Periods **LO1, 2**
Hint: See Demo 6-2

Vision Inc. is considering the following investment opportunities.

Investment	Compounding	Annual Interest Rate	Cost	Term
Investment A. . . .	Annually	6%	$100,000	5 years
Investment B. . . .	Semiannually	6%	100,000	5 years
Investment C . . .	Quarterly	6%	100,000	5 years
Investment D . . .	Monthly	6%	100,000	5 years

Required

a. Compute the future value under each of the investment options.

b. Which option is preferable?

Exercise 6-38
Computing Future Value of Single Amount Under Different Assumptions **LO1, 2**
Hint: See Demo 6-2

Abbot Inc. is considering the following investment opportunities.

Investment	Compounding	Annual Interest Rate	Cost	Investment Period
Investment A. . . .	Semiannually	6%	$50,000	5 years
Investment B. . . .	Quarterly	8%	60,000	10 years
Investment C . . .	Monthly	10%	40,000	8 years
Investment D . . .	Monthly	5%	80,000	10 years

Required

Compute the future value under each of the investment options. Round interest rate percentages to two decimal places.

Exercise 6-39
Computing Present Value of Single Amount Under Different Assumptions **LO3**
Hint: See Demo 6-3A

Consider the following four separate investment scenarios.

Future Amount	Compounding	Annual Interest Rate	Investment Period
$10,000	Annually	5%	5 years
50,000	Semiannually	6%	10 years
60,000	Quarterly	8%	5 years
80,000	Monthly	10%	10 years

Required

Compute the present value under each of the four separate investment options.

Exercise 6-40
Computing Present Value of Several Single Amounts **LO3**

The following cash inflows are predicted over the next five years: $10,000, $15,000, $20,000, $25,000 and $30,000 at the end of years one, two, three, four, and five, respectively.

Required

Compute the total present value of the five cash flows at the beginning of year one, assuming annual compounding at a 6% interest rate.

Exercise 6-41
Solving for Unknown Variables for Different Investments **LO2, 3**

Consider the following four *separate* investment scenarios.

	Investment 1	Investment 2	Investment 3	Investment 4
RATE	?%	6%	5%	8%
NPER	5	?	10	12
PV............	$(5,000)	$(22,000)	$?	$(82,000)
FV............	$ 8,000	$ 35,000	$18,000	$?

Required
Solve for the unknown variables in each of the four separate investment scenarios. Assume interest is compounded annually in each case.

Exercise 6-42
Solving for Unknown Variables for Different Investment Needs **LO2, 3**

Answer the requirements in each of the following two separate cases.

1. At today's date, Etna Inc. has $40,000 that is deposited in an investment account until needed. It is anticipated that $111,000 will be needed at the end of 10 years to expand manufacturing. What approximate rate of interest is required to accumulate $111,000, assuming compounding on an annual basis?
2. Visi Inc. plans an addition to its building as soon as adequate funds are accumulated. The company has estimated that the addition will cost $200,000. At today's date, $90,600 cash is available for investment, and such a fund pays 6% interest (compounded annually). How many periods would be required to accumulate the $200,000?

Exercise 6-43
Computing Expected Cash Outflows and Their Present Value **LO3**
Hint: See Demo 6-3C

Minerals Inc. anticipates environmental costs at the end of a 10-year production cycle. Due to the uncertainties of the remedies available in 10 years, the company has developed the following estimates.

Cash Outflow	Probability
$500,000	30%
550,000	25%
600,000	25%
700,000	20%

Required

a. Compute the expected cash outflow for the environmental costs.

b. Determine the present value of the expected cash outflow assuming an interest rate of 5%.

Exercise 6-44
Computing Future Value of Annuities, Deferrals **LO4**

For the following separate annuity streams *A* through *F*, complete the table by indicating the future value amount of the annuity stream.

Investment	Frequency of Payments	Annual Interest Rate	Payment	Number of Payments	Beginning or End of Period Payment	Deferral of Annuity Payment	Future Value Amount
Annuity A	Annually	5%	$(5,500)	6	End	n/a	$_____
Annuity B	Annually	6%	(6,500)	4	Beginning	n/a	_____
Annuity C	Annually	7%	(20,000)	8	End	3 years	_____
Annuity D	Semiannually	5%	(3,400)	6	End	n/a	_____
Annuity E	Semiannually	6%	(2,500)	4	Beginning	n/a	_____
Annuity F	Semiannually	7%	(22,000)	8	End	2 years	_____

Exercise 6-45
Computing Future Value of Annuity Deposits—With and Without Deferred Payment **LO4**

Fargo Inc. decides to accumulate a debt retirement fund by making ten equal annual deposits of $15,000 at the end of the next ten years. Assume the fund accumulates annual compound interest at 7% per year, which is added to the fund balance.

Required

a. What is the balance in the fund immediately after the last deposit?

b. What is the balance in the fund after the last deposit assuming that the first payment is deferred for 3 years?

Exercise 6-46
Computing Present Value of Annuity Payments Under Different Assumptions **LO5**

Consider the following four separate investment scenarios.

	Investment 1	Investment 2	Investment 3	Investment 4
Annual interest rate	7%	6%	5%	8%
Investment period................	5 years	6 years	5 years	10 years
Compounding periods	Quarterly	Annually	Semiannually	Monthly
Payment per compounding period ...	$5,000	$18,000	$10,000	$1,000
First payment	Beg. of period	End of period	End of period	Beg. of period

Required

Compute the present value of the annuity stream for each of the four investment scenarios.

Exercise 6-47
Computing Present Value of a Deferred Annuity **LO5**
Hint: See Demo 6-5C

J. Johnson receives a defined retirement benefit, which commences in 15 years. At that time, Johnson is to receive monthly cash payments of $1,500 for 10 years with the first payment scheduled for the end of the initial month of benefit. Assume an interest rate of 6%.

Required

What is the value of the deferred annuity as of today? Assume annual compounding during the deferral period.

Exercise 6-48
Computing Annuity Amounts Under Different Situations **LO4, 5**

1. Julie has $25,000 in a fund that earns 10% annual compound interest. If she desires to withdraw it in five equal annual amounts, starting today (at beginning of period), how much would she receive each year?
2. Jules deposits $250 each semiannual period starting today (at beginning of period); this account earns 3% (annual rate). What is the balance in the account at the end of year 10?
3. Jill purchases a new automobile that cost $14,000. She receives a $4,000 trade-in allowance for her old auto and signs an 8% note for $10,000. The note requires eight equal quarterly payments starting at the end of the first quarter from date of purchase. What is the amount of each payment?
4. June deposits $2,000 at the end of each year in an investment account for five years at compound interest. The fund has a balance of $12,456 at the date of the last deposit. What rate of interest did she earn?
5. On January 1, Jin owed a debt of $15,130. An agreement was reached that she would pay the debt plus compound interest in 24 monthly installments of $700, the first payment to be made at the end of January. What rate of annual interest is she paying?

Exercise 6-49
Computing Annuity Amounts Under Different Situations **LO4, 5**

1. Oliver Inc. plans to establish a debt retirement fund, beginning December 31, 2020. Contributions of $20,000 are made to a trustee annually, beginning December 31, 2020, so that the desired amount of $90,120 is available in four years, the date of the last payment. Compute the required interest rate that must be earned by the fund on an annual basis to satisfy these requirements.
2. Polus Inc. decides to create a plant expansion fund by making equal annual deposits of $30,000 on each January 1. Interest at 10% compounded annually is added to the fund balance each year-end. How many deposits are required to accumulate a fund of $313,077?

Exercise 6-50
Computing Present and Future Values Under Different Assumptions **LO4, 5**

Consider the following four *separate* investment scenarios.

	Investment 1	Investment 2	Investment 3	Investment 4
RATE	?%	7%	6%	1%
NPER	10	?	4	24
PV..............	$240,000	$10,000	$?	$(24,000)
PMT	$ (35,000)	$ (2,300)	$(18,000)	$?
TYPE	End of period	Beginning of period	End of period	Beginning of period

Required

Determine the unknown variables in each of the four separate investment scenarios.

Exercise 6-51
Computing Future and Present Values **LO2, 3, 4, 5**

1. What is the present value of $5,000 to be received after 5 years, discounted at 5%?
2. What is the future value of $10,000 at the end of 4 years, compounded at 6%?
3. What is the present value of equal payments of $18,000 due at the end of each of 8 periods, discounted at 5%?
4. What is the future value of equal payments of $25,000 made at the beginning of each of 5 periods, compounded at 7%?
5. What is the present value of equal payments of $20,000 made at the end of 8 periods, compounded at 6%? The payments are deferred for 3 years.

Exercise 6-52
Computing Future and Present Value Under Different Investment Assumptions LO1, 2, 3, 4, 5

1. If we invest $10,000 in an account at 4% interest compounded annually, what is the account balance at the end of five years?
2. We wish to accumulate an investment fund of $40,000 at the end of six years by making a single deposit now. What amount must we deposit now assuming annual compounding of 6%?
3. If we deposit $250,000 in an investment fund on January 1, which earns interest of 8% compounded annually, what annual payment can we withdraw each year over the next 20 years? Assume that our first withdrawal is at the end of the first year.
4. If we make a payment of $575 each month starting today into a fund that earns 6%, how many months does it take to accumulate $100,000? Assume monthly compounding of interest.

Exercise 6-53
Computing Future and Present Value Under Different Investment Assumptions LO2, 3, 4, 5, 6

1. Stone Inc. deposits $40,000 today into a special fund that is needed at the end of six years. A financial institution serves as the fund trustee and pays 10% interest on the fund balance. Compute the fund balance at the end of year 6 assuming annual compounding.
2. On January 15, 2020, Southwest Inc. adopts a plan to accumulate funds for environmental improvements on July 2, 2024, at an estimated cost of $2,000,000. Southwest plans to make four equal annual deposits in a fund that earns interest at 10% compounded annually. The first deposit is made on July 1, 2020. Compute the amount of the annual deposit.
3. Hanks Inc. establishes a debt retirement fund to retire debt of $72,820. Hanks makes three equal annual contributions of $20,000, starting on January 1, 2020. The fund earns interest at 10%, compounded annually. The $72,820 debt must be paid on December 31, 2022. What is the balance of the fund at the end of 2022?
4. Gold Inc. invests $10,000 today in a mutual fund. Gold anticipates leaving this fund alone for 12 years. The fund is increased each year-end by specified compound interest rates as follows: years 1 to 4 inclusive, 8%; 5 to 8 inclusive, 9%; and 9 to 12 inclusive, 10%. Compute the fund balance at the end of year 12.

Exercise 6-54
Determining Present Value of Annuities, Deferrals LO5

For the following separate annuity streams *A* through *F*, complete the table by indicating the future present amount of the annuity stream.

Investment	Frequency of Payments	Annual Interest Rate	Payment	Number of Payments	Beginning or End of Period Payment	Deferral of Annuity Payment	Present Value Amount
Annuity A.	Annually	5%	$(5,000)	4	End	n/a	$______
Annuity B	Annually	6%	(3,500)	8	Beginning	n/a	______
Annuity C	Annually	7%	(10,000)	6	End	2 years*	______
Annuity D	Semiannually	5%	(1,400)	10	End	n/a	______
Annuity E	Semiannually	6%	(7,500)	8	Beginning	n/a	______
Annuity F	Semiannually	7%	(12,000)	4	End	2 years**	______

*Assume annual compounding during the deferral period.
**Assume semiannual compounding during the deferral period.

Exercise 6-55
Determining Selling Prices of Bonds Under Different Interest Assumptions LO6

Olay Inc. issues $100,000, 8%, 10-year bonds payable on January 1, 2020. Calculate the selling price of the bonds under the following separate assumptions.

a. The bonds pay cash interest annually ($8,000) and the market rate of interest on similar bonds is 10%.
b. The bonds pay cash interest annually ($8,000) and the market rate of interest on similar bonds is 8%.
c. The bonds pay cash interest annually ($8,000) and the market rate of interest on similar bonds is 6%.
d. The bonds pay cash interest semiannually ($4,000) and the market rate of interest on similar bonds is 10%.
e. The bonds pay cash interest semiannually ($4,000) and the market rate of interest on similar bonds is 8%.
f. The bonds pay cash interest semiannually ($4,000) and the market rate of interest on similar bonds is 6%.

Exercise 6-56
Determining Asset Cost When Paying with Cash and Notes Payable LO6

Ked Inc. purchases equipment, which has a cash price of $6,726. Terms are arranged for a $2,000 cash down payment plus payment of the remaining $4,726, plus 15% compound interest per annum, through three equal payments. The purchase occurs on January 1, 2020, and the three payments occur on each December 31 thereafter.

Required

a. Compute the amount of each annual payment.
b. What does Ked record for the cost of equipment?
c. What total amount of interest was paid?

Exercise 6-57
Computing Annuity Amounts to a Debt Retirement Fund **LO6**

On January 1, 2020, Chang Inc. establishes a bond sinking fund (a bond retirement fund) amounting to $100,000. A trustee has agreed to handle the fund and to increase it each year on a 10% annual compound interest basis. Chang is to make equal annual contributions to the fund during the next four years, starting in 2020.

Required

a. Compute the amount of the required annual deposits assuming payments begin on December 31, 2020.

b. Compute the amount of the required annual deposits assuming payments begin on January 1, 2021.

Exercise 6-58
Computing the Annual Debt Payments **LO6**

On September 1, 2020, Sault Inc. incurs a $60,000 debt. Arrangements are made to pay this debt in three equal annual installments starting immediately at compound interest of 10%.

Required

a. Is this an ordinary annuity or an annuity due?

b. Compute the amount of the equal annual payments.

c. Compute the annual payment assuming the payments are made annually at the end of each annual period beginning on September 1, 2021.

Exercise 6-59
Computing the Annual Lease Payments **LO6**

On January 1, 2020, Alpha Inc. leased equipment to Omega Company. Selected information for Alpha relating to the lease follows.

Lease term	10 years (expected life of the equipment)
Lease payments ...	Due annually on January 1, beginning immediately on January 1, 2020
Lease liability.....	$85,000 (at lease inception)
Interest rate.......	10%

Required

Determine the annual lease payment charged by Alpha Inc.

Exercise 6-60
Computing the Exchange Price for an Asset Sale **LO6**

On April 1, 2020, Linden sold a patent to Bell Company in exchange for a $100,000 noninterest-bearing note due on April 1, 2021. There was no established exchange price for the patent, and the note had no ready market. The prevailing rate of interest for a note of this type at April 1, 2020, was 9%. The collection of the note receivable from Bell is reasonably assured.

Required

Calculate the amount that Linden should record as note receivable and sales revenue on April 1, 2020.

Exercise 6-61
Computing the Value of a Pension Agreement and Interest **LO6**

On January 1, the Wiek Company contracted with its president, J. May, to make a single deposit immediately to establish a fund with a trustee that pays May $40,000 per year for each of the three years following retirement. May will retire in 10 years on December 31, and the three equal annual payments are to be made by the trustee each December 31 starting in the 11th year. The trustee will add to the fund 8% annual compound interest each year-end. The fund is to have a zero balance on December 31, immediately after the last payment in May.

Required

a. Compute the present value of the pension obligation.

b. How much of the total amount paid to May during the payout period is provided by interest earned during that time?

Exercise 6-62
Applying Present Value in Deciding to Lease or Buy **LO6**

Express Inc. is considering whether to lease or buy equipment with a useful life of 10 years. If the company were to purchase the equipment, it would cost $25,000 upfront. However, if the company were to lease the equipment, the lease payment would be $4,500 annually, with the first payment due immediately. Considering a 10% interest rate, which alternative, lease or buy, is recommended?

Exercise 6-63
Computing Present and Future Values Under Different Assumptions **LO4, 5**

Complete the following table by solving for the present value in each of the separate cases. In each case, one variable changes from the original scenario.

	Original	Increase Interest Rate	Increase Periods	Increase Payment	Beginning of Period
RATE ...	8%	10%	8%	8%	8%
NPER ...	10	10	8	10	10
PMT	$(50,000)	$(50,000)	$(50,000)	$(75,000)	$(50,000)
PV......	$?	$?	$?	$?	$?
FV......	$ 0	$ 0	$ 0	$ 0	$ 0
TYPE ...	0	0	0	0	1

Exercise 6-64 Distinguishing Among Time Value of Money Concepts **LO1, 2, 3, 4, 5, 6**

Following is a list of key terms or phrases, 1 through 14, along with their descriptions in *a* through *n*.

Terms

____ 1. Interest expense
____ 2. Interest revenue
____ 3. Present value of a single amount
____ 4. Present value of an ordinary annuity
____ 5. Present value of an annuity due
____ 6. Future value of a single amount
____ 7. Future value of an ordinary annuity
____ 8. Future value of an annuity due
____ 9. Deferred annuity
____ 10. Compounding
____ 11. Discounting
____ 12. Principal
____ 13. Effective interest rate
____ 14. Time value of money

Descriptions

a. Current value of an equal stream of payments, starting at the end of the first period.
b. Process of earning interest on previously recorded interest.
c. Amount that an equal stream of payments, starting at the beginning of the period, will grow to.
d. Recognition of a borrower's cost for using resources.
e. Process of reducing a future amount to the present value by compound interest.
f. Current value of an equal stream of payments, starting at the beginning of the first period.
g. Money in the future is worth less than the same amount today.
h. Recognition by the lender of the amount earned for loaning resources.
i. True compounded rate that equates the price of an instrument to the present value of the interest payments and face value.
j. Amount that an equal stream of payments, starting at the end of the period, will grow to.
k. Equivalent amount today of a future single amount.
l. Equal stream of payments that begins after a specific period of time.
m. Future value of a single amount in current dollars.
n. Face amount of a bond.

Required

Match each term, 1 through 14, with the most appropriate description *a* through *n*.

Problems

Problem 6-65 Computing Interest Rates and Fund Balances for Different Investments **LO3, 5**

Answer the requirements for each of the following separate cases.

Case 1. On September 1, 2020, Parker deposits $30,000 in an investment account that is expected to accumulate to $32,700 by August 31, 2021. Interest is compounded annually.

Required

Compute the expected compound annual interest rate.

Case 2. On May 1, 2021, Parker deposits $200,000 in an investment account that is expected to accumulate to $251,942 on April 30, 2024. Interest is compounded annually.

Required

Compute the expected compound annual interest rate.

Case 3. On October 1, 2021, Parker deposits $10,000 in an investment account that is expected to have a fund balance of $25,000 at the end of 10 years. Interest is compounded annually.

Required

a. Compute the expected compound annual interest rate.
b. If the funds are not withdrawn, what would be the fund balance at the end of 20 years?

Problem 6-66
Computing the Value of Assets and Liabilities Using Annuities **LO4, 5**

For each of the separate cases below, assume that the annual interest rate is 6% and that compounding is semiannual.

a. How much accumulates by the end of eight years if $6,000 is deposited each semiannual interest period in an investment account at the (1) end of each period, and (2) start of each period?

b. What are the periodic payments each period on a $67,000 debt that is to be paid in semiannual installments over a six-year period assuming compound interest and payments are made at the (1) beginning of each period, and (2) end of each period?

c. A machine is purchased that has a list price of $45,000. Full payment occurs with $9,000 cash and five equal semiannual payments of $6,000 each. The first payment is made at the end of the first semiannual period after purchase date. How much should be recorded in the accounts as the cost of the machine?

d. An investment is being contemplated. This investment produces an estimated end-of-period cash income of $26,000 semiannually for five years. At the end of its productive life, the investment has an estimated recovery value of $4,500. Determine a reasonable estimate of the present value of the investment.

Problem 6-67
Computing Present Value Using Cash Flows that are Expected vs. Most Likely **LO3**

A noncurrent asset is expected to provide up to $10,000 in end-of-period cash flows annually over the next 6 years. The probabilities of cash flows from the asset follows. The risk free interest rate is 6%. A 10% interest rate reflects the uncertainty of collecting the cash flows.

	Cash Inflow	Probability
Year 1	$ 8,000	20%
	10,000	80%
Year 2	7,000	15%
	10,000	85%
Year 3	7,000	25%
	10,000	75%
Year 4	6,500	25%
	10,000	75%
Year 5	6,000	20%
	10,000	80%
Year 6	5,000	30%
	10,000	70%

Required

a. Calculate the present value of the future cash inflows using the expected cash flow approach. Round the present value of the cash flows for each year to the nearest dollar.

b. Calculate the present value of the future cash inflows using the traditional approach of using the most likely amount as an estimate of future cash flows. Round the present value of the cash flows for each year to the nearest dollar.

Problem 6-68
Computing Future Value of Deferred Annuity **LO5**

E. Lane has a daughter, Lois, who is 15 years old today. For her birthday, E. Lane invests $20,000 toward her college education. E. Lane stipulates that Lois can withdraw four equal annual amounts from the fund, the first withdrawal to be made on her 18th birthday. Assume an 8% compound interest rate.

Required

Compute the amount of each of the four withdrawals by Lois that will fully deplete the fund on the date of the final withdrawal.

Problem 6-69
Computing Present Value of Deferred Annuity **LO5**

Phillips Inc. plans to expand sales activities into the western part of the country. To execute its strategy, the company is budgeting four year-end cash outflows of $100,000 beginning in two years.

Required

Assuming a 6% interest compounded annually, what is the present value of the annuity stream?

Problem 6-70
Computing the Present Value of Debt Annuities **LO4, 5**

Answer the requirements for each of the following separate cases.

a. On June 1, Felicity Inc. owed a $45,000 overdue debt. The bank agreed to allow payment of it over the next three years at 12% compound interest, with payments to be made each quarter. Compute the periodic payments assuming that the first payment is made (1) August 31 and (2) June 1.

b. Steff Inc. rents a warehouse from Derr Inc. for $20,000 annual rent, payable in advance on each January 1. Steff proposes to sign a three-year lease and to pay an amount for all three years' rent in advance. Derr agrees to the proposal with the stipulation that the $60,000 is paid immediately (on January 1). Steff had expected some discount on the $60,000 because returns on excess funds are earning above 8% per annum. What amount should Steff offer to pay Derr upfront for the lease?

Problem 6-71
Computing the Interest Rate in Debt Annuities **LO2, 3, 4, 5**

Answer the requirements for each of the following separate cases.

a. On September 1, Cooper Inc. decides to deposit $500,000 in a debt retirement fund. The company needs $947,000 to pay a debt 10 years later. What rate of compound interest must the fund earn to meet the cash requirement to pay the debt?

b. BW Inc. owes a $200,000 debt that is payable eight years from now. BW wants to pay the debt in full immediately. The creditor has agreed to settle the debt in full for $108,100 cash. What rate of compound discount is the creditor applying to the note?

c. On May 1, 2021, Fed Inc. owes a $100,000 debt that is to be paid in three equal annual payments. The first payment is to be made on April 30, 2022. The interest rate is 7%. Compute the amount of the equal annual payments.

Problem 6-72
Computing Present and Future Values for Different Business Situations **LO 2, 3, 4, 5**

Answer the requirements for each of the following separate cases. Assume annual compounding unless otherwise indicated.

a. On January 1, year 1, $30,000 is deposited in a fund at 6% compound interest. At the end of year 5, what will the fund balance be, assuming that compounding is (1) annually, (2) semiannually, and (3) quarterly?

b. On January 1, year 1, a machine is purchased at an invoice price of $20,000. The full purchase price is to be paid at the end of year 5. Assuming 12% compound interest, what did the machine cost if compounding is (1) annually, (2) semiannually, and (3) quarterly?

c. If $6,000 is deposited in a fund today and will increase to $12,798 in 13 years, what is the implicit compound interest rate?

d. If the present value of $15,000 is $5,864 at 11% compound annual discount, what is the number of periods?

e. On January 1, year 1, a company decided to establish a fund by making 10 equal annual deposits of $6,000, starting on December 31. The fund will be increased by 9% compounded interest. What will be the fund balance at the end of year 10 (immediately after the last deposit)?

f. On January 1, year 1, a company decided to establish a fund by making 10 equal annual deposits of $9,000, starting on January 1. The fund will be increased by 7% compound interest. What will be the balance in the fund at the end of year 10?

g. J. Dee is at retirement and has a large amount of ready cash on January 1. She wants to deposit enough cash in a fund to receive back $40,000 each December 31 for the next five years, starting this year. Assuming 10% compound interest, how much cash must Dee deposit on January 1?

h. Ace Inc. is considering the purchase of license rights on January 1, year 1. The rights will generate $8,000 net cash inflow each January 1 for five years, starting January 1, year 1. At the end of year 5, the rights will have no value. Assuming a 14% compound interest rate, what should Ace be willing to pay for the rights on January 1, year 1?

i. At the start of January in year 1, Bigbay Inc. creates a fund expected to equal $552,026 in seven years by making seven equal annual deposits of $60,000, starting on December 31 of year 1. What is the implicit compound interest rate for this fund?

j. The present value of several future equal year-end cash payments of $30,000 each is $141,366 assuming 11% compound discount. What is the expected number of cash payments?

k. Mia will retire 10 years from now and wants to establish a fund today that will pay $30,000 cash at the end of each of the first five years after retirement. Specific dates are these: date of a single deposit by Mia, January 1, year 1; date of first cash payment from the fund to Mia, December 31, year 11. The fund will pay 10% compound interest. How much cash must Mia deposit on January 1, year 1, to provide the five equal annual year-end cash payments from the fund?

Problem 6-73
Computing Future Values Under Different Investment Scenarios **LO 2, 3, 4, 5**

Answer the requirements for each of the following separate cases.

Case 1. On January 1, 2020, Joy Brown deposited $20,000 in an investment account that would accumulate at 11% annual compound interest for four years.

Required
Compute the investment account balance at the end of the fourth year.

Case 2. On March 1, 2020, Phil Gray deposited $15,000 in an investment account that would accumulate to $16,873 at the end of three years, assuming annual compound interest.

Required
Compute the expected interest rate in this case.

Case 3. On September 1, 2020, Dan Jones deposited $7,000 in an investment account that would accumulate to $11,108, assuming 8% annual compound interest.

Required
Compute the expected number of periods in this case.

Case 4. Wolf Company established a construction fund on July 1, 2021, by making a single deposit of $360,000. Also, at the end of each fiscal year, on June 30, the company will make a $60,000 deposit in the fund. The fund and its deposits will earn 5% compound interest each year.

Required
Compute the fund balance at June 30, 2025.

Problem 6-74
Computing Present Values for Bonds, Notes, and Leases **LO6**

Broderick Company entered into the following transactions in 2020.

a. On December 31, 2020, the company issued 6%, 15-year, $10,000 bonds that pay cash interest semiannually on June 30 and December 31. The market rate of interest for bonds with similar risk is 7%.
b. The company purchased equipment on December 30, 2020. The seller agreed to accept a down payment of $10,000 and a two-year, noninterest-bearing note of $45,000 (this amount includes the principal and all interest) due in two years. Assume that the market rate of interest for this debt is 13%.
c. The company leased a building beginning on December 31, 2020, for 10 years that requires annual lease payments of $60,000 with the first lease payment due on December 31, 2020. The market rate of interest for this lease is 6%.

Required
Compute the present value as of December 31, 2020, for the (a) bond, (b) noninterest-bearing note, and (c) lease liability.

Problem 6-75
Applying Present Value Concepts to Equipment Purchase **LO6**

Rye Inc. is considering purchasing a used machine. The company plans to keep the machine for 10 years, at which time the residual value is expected to be zero. An analysis of the capacity of the machine and the costs of operating it (including materials used in production) indicates that the machine would increase after-tax net cash inflow by approximately $200,000 per year.

Required
a. Compute the approximate amount that Rye should be willing to pay today for the machine assuming a target earnings rate of 12% per year. Assume that the earnings are realized at each year-end.
b. What price should be paid assuming a $50,000 residual value at the end of the 10 years?

Problem 6-76
Applying Future and Present Values to Liquidate Assets to Settle Debt **LO6**

Wilson Inc. is planning to pay off some of its debts. On January 1, 2020, the company has the following investment accounts.

Date Established	Amount Deposited (single deposit for each)	Annual Compound Interest Rate
January 1, 2009	$20,000	8%
January 1, 2015	30,000	10%

The company's outstanding debts on January 1, 2020, that it wishes to pay off follow.

Due Date	Type of Note	Note*
December 31, 2023	Noninterest-bearing	$ 60,000
December 31, 2030	Noninterest-bearing	200,000

*Amount for each note is the single sum to be paid at maturity (includes both principal and interest).

Required

a. Compute the total value of the company's two investment accounts on January 1, 2020.

b. Compute the total amount for which the two debts can be settled on January 1, 2020. Assume a 12% market rate of interest.

c. Assume the company uses the total from the investment accounts to pay off its two debts on January 1, 2020. Does Wilson have a cash shortage or cash excess? By how much?

Problem 6-77
Applying Present Values to Determine Pension Funding **LO6**

Marke Inc. provides retirement benefits to its employees. The following information pertains to three employees eligible for retirement benefits that are equal to annual (end of year) payments of 50% of salary before retirement. A. Smith is eligible for 10 years of benefits, and B. Jones and C. Wills are eligible for 15 years of benefits. Invested funds earn 10% interest compounded annually.

Employee	Estimated Salary Before Retirement	Estimated Date of Retirement
A. Smith	$ 70,000	December 31, 2025
B. Jones	100,000	December 31, 2025
C. Will	50,000	December 31, 2025

Required

a. Determine the present value of the retirement benefits on December 31, 2025.

b. Determine the present value of the retirement benefits on January 1, 2020.

c. Assume the company previously set aside funds for retirement that are worth $100,000 on January 1, 2020. As of January 1, 2020, what annual payment to an investment fund must the company make to have fully funded pension obligation on December 31, 2025, assuming a 10% interest rate?

Problem 6-78
Determining a Fair Value Estimate of Future Remediation Costs **LO6**

Inteli Inc. is required to record the present value of estimated cash flows for environment remediation, which is expected to take place in 15 years. The cost of the remediation is estimated as follows, along with the probabilities of incurring the expenses.

Costs	Probability
$1,000,000	0.40
900,000	0.40
800,000	0.20

Required

a. Assuming an interest rate of 8%, what is the present value of the remediation costs?

b. The present value of the remediation costs represents the fair value of the obligation. How would this amount be classified according to the fair value hierarchy? *Hint:* See fair value hierarchy in Exhibit 1-18.

Problem 6-79
Computing Loan Payments to Fund Expansion **LO6**

The owner of I-Haul is considering expanding into the Northwest region. Expansion is estimated to cost $10 million, including the development of facilities and the purchase of additional trucks. The owner elects to borrow the money from a local bank at an annual 10% interest rate. The owner also agrees to pay back the loan in 20 semiannual payments over a 10-year period with equal payments to begin in six months.

Required

a. What is the periodic loan payment?

b. If the loan were paid off in equal annual payments beginning in one year, what would the loan payments equal?

Problem 6-80
Applying Time Value of Money Concept to a Mortgage **LO6**

Laura Ray buys a house for $150,000. She makes a down payment of $30,000 cash and takes out a 12% mortgage for the remaining balance. The bank requires that she pay off the mortgage in 25 equal annual installments, beginning one year from today.

Required

a. Determine the annual amount of the 25 installments.
b. What is the total amount paid by Ray (over the 25 years) for the $150,000 house?
c. How much of the total in part *b* is interest charges?

Problem 6-81
Applying Time Value of Money Concept to the Sale of a Business **LO6**

G. Smith wishes to sell her business and receives the following three offers.

a. $568,000 cash (to be received immediately).
b. $200,000 cash today plus an annual installment of $60,000 at each year-end for 10 years.
c. $96,000 cash at each year-end for 10 years minus a required owner investment of $20,000 today to correct certain conditions.

Required

Which offer should the owner accept if each alternative is equally risky and the required return is 10% per year?

Problem 6-82
Applying Time Value of Money Concept to Bonus Options **LO6**

Linda Reed is an executive of VIP Inc. and has earned a bonus. She has the option of taking the $60,000 bonus today or $114,000 cash five years from today.

Required

a. Determine the interest rate that equates the two bonus options. *Hint*: This is the interest rate at which Linda is indifferent between the two options.
b. If Linda has investment opportunities that yield 14% or higher returns, which option should she elect?

Accounting Decisions and Judgments

AD&J 6-83
Interpreting a Credit Agreement **LO6**

Real World Analysis Anheuser-Busch, the global brewer, reported the following credit agreement in note 4 of its Year 8 consolidated financial statements.

> The company has in place a single committed revolving credit agreement totaling $1 billion, which expires in January of Year 11. The agreements provide that under certain circumstances the company may select among various loan arrangements with differing maturities and among a variety of interest rates, including a negotiated rate. At December 31, Year 8 and Year 7, the company had no outstanding borrowings under the agreement. Fees under the agreement were $0.6 million, $0.6 million, and $0.7 million, in Year 8, Year 7, and Year 6, respectively.

Required

a. What amount (denote by an interest rate) did the company pay to maintain its line of credit in Year 8?
b. Is the rate in part *a* an unusual rate? Explain.

AD&J 6-84
Considering the Discounting of Deferred Taxes **LO6**

Real World Analysis Tax law specifies different timing for certain expense deductions than is required under GAAP. Deferred tax liabilities are commonly found in company balance sheets. For example, if a $1 million machine is depreciated over 10 years for book purposes using the straight-line method, but more rapidly for establishing the liability for taxes payable to the government, the book tax expense exceeds the tax liability. The difference is a deferred tax liability, which is extinguished in future periods when depreciation for book purposes exceeds that taken for tax. Coca-Cola Company, for example, shows a deferred tax liability of $424 million as of December 31, Year 8.

Required

Would it be logical to show the deferred tax liability at its discounted value on the balance sheet? If we agree with that logic, why do we believe it is not done in practice?

AD&J 6-85
Analyzing Debt Maturity Disclosure **LO3**

Real World Analysis 3M Company reported the following debt maturities over the next five years in a disclosure note in its Year 5 annual report:

Maturities of long-term debt for the five years subsequent of December 31, Year 5 are as follows (in millions):

Year 6	Year 7	Year 8	Year 9	Year 10	After Year 10	Total
$1,125	$744	$993	$622	$1,203	$5,191	$9,878

Required

a. Assuming end of year payments discounted at 5%, what is the present value of the debt commitments? Round the present value of each year's payment to the nearest dollar. (Also assume debt payments were made in Year 11 for payments after Year 10.)

b. How does the amount you calculated in part *a* differ from the total provided in the note?

AD&J 6-86
Setting Up a Fund to Retire Debt—Single Payments and Annuities **LO6**

Real World Analysis The Year 8 balance sheet of Merck (in note 8), dated December 31, shows $499 million of 6.8% Euronotes due December 31, Year 15. Merck is a pharmaceutical manufacturer. Assume that the principal amount of these notes must be retired in equal amounts on December 31 of each year. It is now December 31, Year 8. Assume that a sinking fund, earning interest at 10% compounded annually, is used to retire the debt.

Required

a. If Merck sets up a fund by investing a single amount on January 1, Year 9, to refund only the principal amount of the debentures due on December 31, Year 15 (a single principal payment), what amount is required?

b. Repeat part *a* assuming that the single amount is deposited at December 31, Year 9.

c. Repeat part *a* assuming that a sinking fund is used with equal payments each December 31, beginning December 31, Year 9 and ending December 31, Year 15.

d. Repeat part *c* assuming that the payments begin December 31, Year 8, and end December 31, Year 14.

AD&J 6-87
Setting Up a Fund to Retire Debt—Single Payments and Annuities **LO6**

Real World Analysis Reported as part of Coca-Cola's long-term debt as of December 31, Year 8, was $150 million of notes, which carry interest at 6%. Interest is paid semiannually. The notes are due December 31, Year 13 (in note 6).

Required

a. Suppose Coca-Cola were to establish a bond sinking fund by making a single lump-sum payment on January 1, Year 9. If the fund would earn 10% interest compounded annually, what single amount is necessary on January 1, Year 9, to retire the notes on December 31, Year 13? (The sinking fund would not be used to pay interest.)

b. Assume the facts in part *a*, but suppose, instead, that equal payments into the fund are to begin January 1, Year 9, and end January 1, Year 12. What is the amount of each annual payment required to retire the notes on December 31, Year 13? Interest on the fund will be 10% compounded annually.

c. How many consecutive payments of $41.21 million on December 31 of each year would have to be made into the fund beginning on December 31, Year 9, to retire the $150 million debt at December 31, Year 13, if interest at 10% compounded annually is earned on the fund?

AD&J 6-88
Applying Present Values to Compare the Cost of Two Alternative Assets **LO6**

Communication Case Viable Corp. purchases machines for use in its plant. Machine Type A is typical of these machines. Currently, Viable is considering the purchase of a new Type A machine. Two different brand names are being considered. Viable expects a 12% return on its plant investments.

	Brand A	Brand B
Cost (cash basis)	$100,000	$90,000
Operating expense to operate the machine (per year)	$7,000	$8,000
Estimated useful life (years)	8	8
Estimated residual value (% of cost)	20%	10%

Required

a. Compute the present value of the costs of the two alternative brands of machines. (Assume that all variables, other than the four listed above, are identical for both brands.)

b. Which machine should Viable purchase? Are any other factors besides our computations relevant? Prepare the response in memo form to senior management.

Judgment Case An investment firm advertised a 20% return on its investments and provided this example in its promotion brochure: A $10,000 investment is expected to increase to $30,000 after 10 years.

AD&J 6-89
Computing an Implicit Interest Rate and Assessing Promotional Material **LO1**

Required

a. Compute the actual interest rate implicit in the promotional investment return.

b. Is the advertised 20% rate of return correct, or is it misleading? Explain. *Hint*: What would simple interest yield?

Challenging Problem A component product is presently being manufactured using equipment that is fully depreciated. With suitable annual overhauls and an upfront cost of $20,000, it can be used by the company for another three years. The cost of these overhauls is expected to be $40,000 per year (payable at the beginning of each year), and at the end of the third year the overhauled machine is expected to have a salvage value of $10,000.

AD&J 6-90
Applying Present Values to Decide Whether to Overhaul or Replace Assets **LO8**

A new machine can be purchased for $134,350 cash with an expected life of three years and no expected salvage value at the end of three years. The projected sales and cost of operations for both the old and new machines for each of the next three years follow. Assume that the time value of money for this company is 10% per year, and ignore income taxes.

Product Data	Old Machine	New Machine
Unit sales per year (via transfers to other production departments).	20,000	20,000
Out-of-pocket operating costs per unit*	$8.00/unit	$7.50/unit

*Assume these cash outflows occur at the end of each year.

Required

a. Should the old machine be overhauled *or* should the new equipment be acquired? Explain.

b. If the component product can be purchased at a cost of $10.30 per unit from outside suppliers, should it then be purchased or be manufactured internally? Explain. Assume that payments to external suppliers are made at the end of each year.

c. At what level of output (unit sales per year) would management be indifferent to (1) buying the component from outside suppliers at $10.30 per unit, and (2) manufacturing it internally on the new equipment?

Codification Skills Refer to the Codification and identify the definition for each of the following.

AD&J 6-91
Searching the Codification to Define Key Terms **LO3, 6**

1. Present value
2. Discount rate
3. Asset retirement obligation
4. Interest method defined in the codification

Codification Skills Research the Codification and report the proper citation that provides guidance on each of the following topics.

AD&J 6-92
Researching the Codification for Proper Citation **LO6**

a. Using present value to estimate the fair value of uncertainties in long-lived assets

FASB ASC ____-____-____-____

b. Using present value to account for notes exchanged for property, goods, or services

FASB ASC ____-____-____-____

c. Accounting for discounts and premiums in notes as the difference between the present and face value

FASB ASC ____-____-____-____

d. Interest rate used when computing the present value of a lease liability

FASB ASC ____-____-____-____

Codification Skills A company is preparing annual financial statements, which includes the valuation of impairment on a building. The company is unsure as to how to use the expected cash flow technique to estimate the fair value of the asset for impairment. What guidance is available in the Codification to help determine the proper disclosure?

FASB ASC ____-____-____-____

AD&J 6-93
Researching the Codification for Authoritative Guidance **LO6**

Appendix—Brief Exercises

App—Brief Exercise 6-94
Identifying the Stated and Market Rates **LO7**

UPPS Inc. issued a $5,000, 5% bond on January 1, 2020, for $4,738. The market rate of interest for bonds of this type is 7%. What is the (a) stated interest for 2020, and (b) market interest for 2020?

App—Brief Exercise 6-95
Applying Present and Future Value Tables **LO8**

What table value should be used to compute the balance in a fund at the end of year 11 if $100,000 is deposited at the date the fund is established and we assume 6% annual interest rate with interest compounding semiannually?

Brief Exercise 6-96
Applying Present and Future Value Tables **LO8**

What table value should be used to compute the present value of $50,000, assuming 8% compound interest, quarterly compounding, and six years of discounting?

Appendix—Exercises

App—Exercise 6-97
Preparing an Effective Interest Table for Bonds **LO7**
Hint: See Demo 6-7

Prepare an effective interest table for $100,000, 5%, 5-year bonds payable, issued on January 1, 2020. The bonds pay cash interest semiannually on June 30 and December 31. The market rate of interest is 6%.

App—Exercise 6-98
Applying Present and Future Value Tables **LO8**
Hint: See Demo 6-8B

Complete the following table assuming that the number of periods is 10 and the interest rate is 6% annual compounding:

Time Value of Money Example	Table (Source)	Factor	Answer
Current value of $10,000 received in 10 years.	______	______	$______
Current value of a stream of $1,000 payments made at each period end.	______	______	______
Future value of a stream of $1,000 payments made at each period end.	______	______	______
Future value of a stream of $1,000 payments made at each beginning of the period.	______	______	______
Current value of a stream of $1,000 payments made at each beginning of the period.	______	______	______
Future value of $10,000 (as of today) in 10 years.	______	______	______

Appendix—Problems

App—Problem 6-99
Preparing an Effective Interest Table for Notes **LO7**

Fox Inc. purchases land on January 1, 2020, and issues a 5-year, $50,000, zero-interest-bearing note. The market rate of interest is 8% and Fox uses the effective interest rate method to amortize discounts and premiums.

Required

Prepare an effective interest table for this land purchase using a note.

App—Problem 6-100
Applying Present and Future Value Tables **LO8**

Refer to Problem 6-65 and apply interest compounding tables to answer requirement for cases 1, 2, and 3, with the following modifications: For case 3 only, (1) for requirement *a*, estimate the implicit interest rate through interpolation, and (2) for requirement *b*, use the closest full percentage point available on the table to estimate the present value of the fund in 20 years.

Answers to Review Exercises

Review 6-1

a. 7%, 5
b. 2%, 32
c. 0.5%, 60
d. 4%, 20
e. 6%, 3
f. 1.5%, 20
g. 0.5%, 48
h. 3%, 16

Review 6-2

a. $6,719.58, FV(0.03,10,0,–5000)
b. $7,401.22, FV(0.04,10,0,–5000)
c. $9,030.56, FV(0.03,20,0,–5000)
d. $8,063.50, FV(0.03,10,0,–6000)
e. $6,734.28, FV(0.015,20,0,–5000)

Review 6-3

Part One

a. $5,952.75, PV(0.03,10,0,8000)
b. $5,404.51, PV(0.04,10,0,8000)
c. $4,429.41, PV(0.03,20,0,8000)
d. $7,440.94, PV(0.03,10,0,10000)
e. $5,939.76, PV(0.015,20,0,8000)

Part Two

a. 5%, RATE(8,0,–8000,12000)
b. 5, NPER(0.06,0,–7734,10350)
c. $(3,089.17), PV(0.06,4,0,3900)
d. $11,576.25, FV(0.05,3,0,–10000)

Part Three

a. $185,000, ($250,000 × 40%) + ($200,000 × 30%) + ($100,000 × 20%) + ($50,000 × 10%) = $185,000
b. $124,979.37, (PV(0.04,10,0,–185000))

Review 6-4

a. $ 2,575.00, FV(0.06,2,-1250)
b. $26,531.90, FV(0.04,6,–4000)
c. $71,138.69, FV(0.03,8,–8000)
d. $32,483.49, FV(0.08,6,–4100,0,1)
e. $ 9,446.24, FV(0.03,10,–800,0,1)
f. $28,748.39, FV(0.04,8,–3000,0,1)

Review 6-5

a. $ 2,291.74, PV(0.06,2,–1250)
b. $20,968.55, PV(0.04,6,–4000)
c. $49,895.25, PV(0.03,8,–8000), PV(0.03,4,0,–56157.54)
d. $20,470.11, PV(0.08,6,–4100,0,1)
e. $ 7,028.89, PV(0.03,10,–800,0,1)
f. $19,421.38, PV(0.04,8,–3000,0,1), PV(0.04,2,0,–21006.16)

Review 6-6

Leases: $823,598.71, PV(0.06,15,–80000,0,1)
Pension: $1,185,035.15, PV(0.005,180,–10000)
Bonds: $53,897.29, PV(0.025,20,–1500,–50000)
Debt: $(22,831.63), PMT(0.02,10,0,250000)

Review 6-7

Effective Interest Amortization—Discount

Date	Cash (Stated Interest)	Interest Expense (Market Interest)	Discount on N.P. Amortization	Note Payable, Net (Carrying Value)
				$16,326*
Dec. 31, 2020	$0	$1,143**	$1,143	17,469***
Dec. 31, 2021	0	1,223	1,223	18,692
Dec. 31, 2022	0	1,308	1,308	20,000
	$0	$3,674	$3,674	

* PV(0.07,3,0,–20000) **$16,326 × 0.07 = $1,143 ***$16,326 + $1,143 = $17,469

Review 6-8

a. 2.0500 $2,050
b. 5.7135 $2,857
c. 9.1591 $64,114
d. 0.7462 $3,358
e. 1.3439 $10,751
f. 0.8535 $4,097

7 Revenue Recognition

Ford Motor Company

NOTE 4. REVENUE The following table disaggregates our revenue by major source for the period ended December 31, 2017 (in millions):

	Automotive	Financial Services	All Other	Consolidated
Vehicles, parts, and accessories	$140,171	$ —	$—	$140,171
Used vehicles	2,956	—	—	2,956
Extended service contracts	1,236	—	—	1,236
Other revenue (a)	815	219	10	1,044
Revenues from sales and services	145,178	219	10	145,407
Leasing income	475	5,552	—	6,027
Financing income	—	5,184	—	5,184
Insurance income	—	158	—	158
Total revenues	$145,653	$11,113	$10	$156,776

(a) Primarily includes commissions and vehicle-related design and testing services.

Revenue is recognized when obligations under the terms of a contract with our customer are satisfied; generally this occurs with the transfer of control of our vehicles, parts, accessories, or services. Revenue is measured as the amount of consideration we expect to receive in exchange for transferring goods or providing services. Sales, value add, and other taxes we collect concurrent with revenue-producing activities are excluded from revenue. Incidental items that are immaterial in the context of the contract are recognized as expense. The expected costs associated with our base warranties and field service actions continue to be recognized as expense when the products are sold (see Note 23). We recognize revenue for vehicle service contracts that extend mechanical and maintenance coverages beyond our base warranties over the life of the contract. We do not have any material significant payment terms as payment is received at or shortly after the point of sale.

ASU 2014-09, Revenue - Revenue from Contracts with Customers. On January 1, 2017, we adopted the new accounting standard ASC 606, Revenue from Contracts with Customers and all the related amendments ("new revenue standard") to all contracts using the modified retrospective method. We recognized the cumulative effect of initially applying the new revenue standard as an adjustment to the opening balance of retained earnings. The comparative information has not been restated and continues to be reported under the accounting standards in effect for those periods. We do not expect the adoption of the new revenue standard to have a material impact to our net income on an ongoing basis.

A majority of our sales revenue continues to be recognized when products are shipped from our manufacturing facilities. For certain vehicle sales where revenue was previously deferred, such as vehicles subject to a guaranteed resale value recognized as a lease and transactions in which a Ford-owned entity delivered vehicles, we now recognize revenue when vehicles are shipped in accordance with the new revenue standard.

The new revenue standard also provided additional clarity that resulted in reclassifications to or from Revenue, Cost of sales, and Financial Services other income/(loss), net.

Chapter Preview

The FASB provides a framework for revenue recognition **(ASC 606)**. Its purpose is to improve comparability across industries, reduce complexities in application, and improve disclosures for investors and creditors. This framework not only dictates reporting requirements, but also impacts business processes and internal controls underlying revenue recognition reporting. We begin with a review of the *five steps of the revenue recognition process* as identified in the standard. We then apply the five steps, followed by more in-depth applications for each step. More complex revenue recognition arrangements are also explored followed by accounting for contracts, costs, and an overview of disclosure requirements. While accounting guidance outlines steps of revenue recognition, each step requires management judgment. How revenue is recognized is often under scrutiny by the Securities and Exchange Commission in its oversight of filings from its registrants.

Action Plan

LO	Topic/Subtopic	Page	Demos	Reviews	Assignments
LO 7–1	**Apply the five-step revenue recognition process** Contract :: Performance Obligation :: Transaction Price :: Transaction Price Allocation :: Revenue Recognition	7-3	D7-1	R7-1	18, 19, 48, 49, 67, 94
LO 7–2	**Identify the contract with the customer—Step 1** Contract Validity :: Commercial Substance :: Approval :: Rights and Obligations :: Payment Terms :: Collectibility	7-5	D7-2	R7-2	20, 21, 50, 51, 80, 94, 95
LO 7–3	**Identify performance obligations in the contract—Step 2** Distinct Performance Obligation :: Materiality :: License :: Franchise :: Customer Options	7-8	D7-3	R7-3	22, 23, 24, 25, 26, 52, 53, 54, 55, 71, 81, 82, 94, 95
LO 7–4	**Determine the transaction price—Step 3** Fixed Consideration :: Variable Consideration :: Consideration Payable :: Refund Liability	7-13	D7-4A D7-4B	R7-4	27, 28, 29, 30, 31, 56, 57, 58, 59, 60, 61, 62, 81, 82, 83, 84, 85, 86, 89, 94
LO 7–5	**Allocate the transaction price to performance obligations in the contract—Step 4** Observable Standalone Selling Price :: Estimated Standalone Selling Price :: Allocation Approaches	7-18	D7-5A D7-5B	R7-5	32, 33, 48, 63, 64, 65, 66, 68, 81, 82, 85, 87, 92, 94
LO 7–6	**Recognize revenue when (or as) the seller satisfies a performance obligation—Step 5** Recognition at a Point in Time :: Recognition Over Time :: Contract Liability :: Contract Asset	7-22	D7-6A D7-6B D7-6C	R7-6	31, 34, 35, 36, 37, 38, 39, 54, 55, 62, 63, 64, 65, 67, 68, 69, 70, 71, 72, 81, 82, 83, 84, 85, 87, 93, 94, 95
LO 7–7	**Recognize revenue after a contract modification** Contract Modification :: Distinct Goods or Services :: Standalone Prices	7-30	D7-7	R7-7	40, 41, 73, 74, 88, 95
LO 7-8	**Recognize revenue in more complex revenue arrangements** Bill-and-Hold :: Consignment :: Repurchase :: Principal :: Agent	7-33	D7-8A D7-8B D7-8C D7-8D	R7-8	42, 43, 44, 45, 75, 76, 77, 78, 90
LO 7-9	**Describe accounting for contract costs and disclosure requirements for revenue recognition.** Costs to Obtain Contract :: Costs to Fulfill Contract :: Practical Expedient :: Disclosure Requirements	7-39	D7-9	R7-9	46, 47, 53, 79, 83, 91, 96
LO 7-10	**APPENDIX 7A—Apply the revenue recognition process to long-term contracts expected to be profitable** Revenue Over Time :: Revenue at Point in Time :: Cost-to-Cost Method	7-43	D7-10A D7-10B	R7-10	101, 102, 103, 105, 106, 107, 108, 110, 111, 112
LO 7-11	**APPENDIX 7B—Apply the revenue recognition process to long-term contracts expected to be unprofitable** Overall Contract Loss :: Current Period Loss	7-48	D7-11A D7-11B	R7-11	104, 109, 113, 114

LO 7-1 Apply the five-step revenue recognition process

LO 7-1 Overview

Revenue Recognition Basics
Step 1: Identify the contract
Step 2: Identify the performance obligations
Step 3: Determine the transaction price
Step 4: Allocate the transaction price to performance obligations
Step 5: Recognize revenue when (or as) each performance obligation is satisfied through a transfer of control of goods or services to a customer

Accounting guidance indicates that the objective of the revenue recognition standard is to guide entities in reporting useful information to users of financial statements about the nature, amount, timing, and uncertainty of revenue and cash flows arising from a contract with a customer. This guidance applies to all customer contracts except for those topics addressed in other standards such as leases, insurance, and financial instruments.

To meet this objective, the **core principle of the revenue recognition standard** is as follows.

606-10-10-2 The core principle of the guidance in this Topic is that an entity shall recognize revenue to depict the transfer of promised goods or services to customers in an amount that reflects the consideration to which the entity expects to be entitled in exchange for those goods or services.

Revenue is recognized according to this core principle by applying a five-step process (ASC 606-10-05-4).

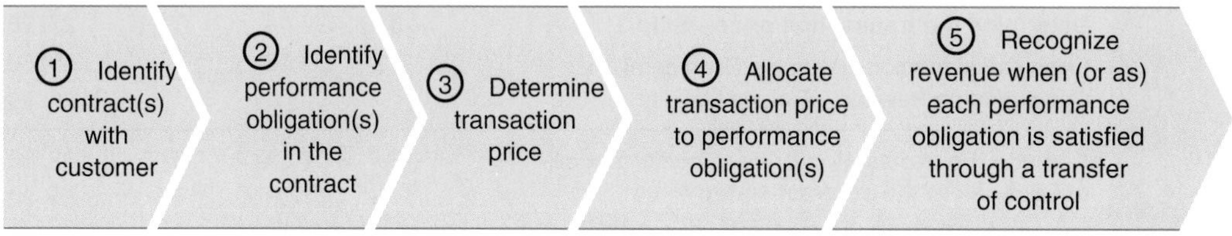
① Identify contract(s) with customer
② Identify performance obligation(s) in the contract
③ Determine transaction price
④ Allocate transaction price to performance obligation(s)
⑤ Recognize revenue when (or as) each performance obligation is satisfied through a transfer of control

A company must fulfill all five steps in the revenue recognition process before revenue is recognized. All five steps can occur simultaneously, also known as a point in time (as in **Demo 7-1** below) or they can occur over time (illustrated in later sections). **Revenue is recognized in the final step of the process when (or as) a company satisfies a performance obligation by transferring control of promised goods or services to a customer.** The transfer of goods or services arises from the company's ordinary activities or those activities that are ongoing, major, or central.

Key terms used in the revenue recognition process follow.

Term or Phrase	Definition
Revenue	**ASC Glossary** Inflows or other enhancements of assets of an entity [a seller] or settlements of its liabilities (or a combination of both) from delivering or producing goods, rendering services, or other activities that constitute the entity's [seller's] ongoing major or central operations.
Contract	**ASC Glossary** An agreement between two or more parties that creates legally enforceable rights and obligations.
Customer	**ASC Glossary** A party that has contracted with an entity [a seller] to obtain goods or services that are an output of the entity's [seller's] ordinary activities in exchange for consideration.
Performance obligation	**ASC Glossary** A promise in a contract with a customer to transfer to the customer either: (a) A good or service (or a bundle of goods or services) that is distinct or (b) A series of distinct goods or services that are substantially the same and that have the same pattern of transfer to the customer.
Standalone selling price	**ASC Glossary** The price at which an entity [a seller] would sell a promised good or service separately to a customer.
Transaction price	**ASC Glossary** The amount of consideration to which an entity [a seller] expects to be entitled in exchange for transferring promised goods or services to a customer, excluding amounts collected on behalf of third parties.

As we see from the steps in the revenue recognition process outlined above, the process begins with a contract (which may be written, oral, or implied by a seller's customary business practices) and ends when control of a good or service transfers to a customer. When a customer receives goods or services, the customer receives an asset. In the case of services, the asset may exist only for a moment before being consumed. When a seller accepts a performance obligation and receives advance payment, it incurs a liability. The FASB decided that focusing on the recognition and measurement of the assets and liabilities arising from a contract would bring discipline to the earning process and ultimately result in a more consistent application of the revenue standard.

Transfer of control is determined primarily from the perspective of the customer. **Exhibit 7-1** describes **five indicators that control has transferred from the seller to the customer** at a point in time, allowing the seller to recognize revenue. Identifying the point of transfer of control can be straightforward or can require substantial management judgment. The indicators listed in **Exhibit 7-1** are factors for a seller to consider when determining the point of transfer (ASC 606-10-25-30). Not all indicators must be met for a customer to gain control of an asset. However, the factors are typically present when control has passed to the customer.

EXHIBIT 7-1
Five Indicators that Control Transferred from Seller to Customer

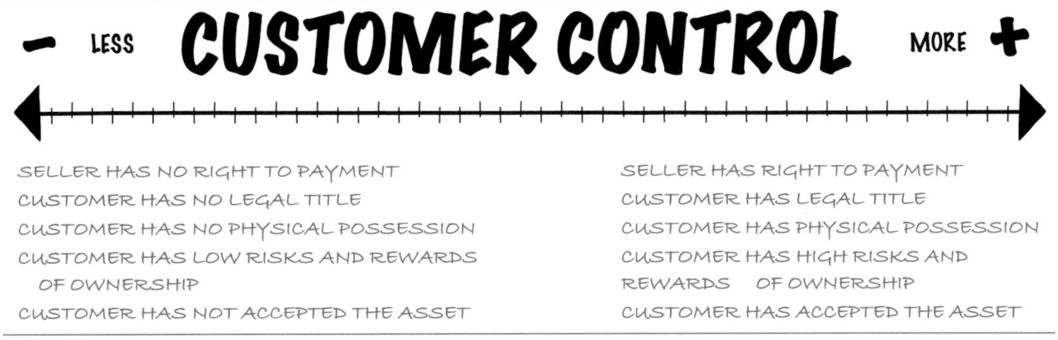
- LESS
CUSTOMER CONTROL
MORE +
SELLER HAS NO RIGHT TO PAYMENT
CUSTOMER HAS NO LEGAL TITLE
CUSTOMER HAS NO PHYSICAL POSSESSION
CUSTOMER HAS LOW RISKS AND REWARDS OF OWNERSHIP
CUSTOMER HAS NOT ACCEPTED THE ASSET
SELLER HAS RIGHT TO PAYMENT
CUSTOMER HAS LEGAL TITLE
CUSTOMER HAS PHYSICAL POSSESSION
CUSTOMER HAS HIGH RISKS AND REWARDS OF OWNERSHIP
CUSTOMER HAS ACCEPTED THE ASSET

ALPHABET

Real World—REVENUE RECOGNITION POLICY

Alphabet Inc. reported the following revenue recognition policy in a recent Form 10-K Report, which aligns with Step 5 in the revenue recognition process.

> Revenues are recognized when control of the promised goods or services is transferred to our customers in an amount that reflects the consideration we expect to be entitled to in exchange for those goods or services.

ALPHABET [GOOGL]

Application of the Five-Step Revenue Recognition Process — LO7-1 — Demo 7-1

Demo MBC

A seller, REII Inc. initiates a contract with a customer to provide one product (a ski sweater) for $100 on June 1, 2020. The cost of the sweater to REII is $60. On June 1, 2020, the ski sweater is transferred to the customer and the customer remits $100 to REII.

Required

a. Using REII's sale, demonstrate the five steps of the revenue recognition process.

b. Record the journal entry for REII on June 1, 2020.

Solution

a. Five Steps in the Revenue Recognition Process

① Identify contract — The contract requires REII to provide a ski sweater in exchange for $100. As explained above, a contract can be implied by common business practice.

② Identify performance obligation — There is one performance obligation or promise: REII provides one ski sweater to the customer.

③ Determine transaction price — The transaction price of the ski sweater is $100.

④ Allocate transaction price — $100 is allocated to one performance obligation, the seller's obligation to provide one sweater to the customer.

⑤ Recognize revenue — The contract is satisfied immediately when REII provides the sweater to the customer and collects $100 cash. Revenue is recognized when the asset (inventory) is physically exchanged for $100 cash. The risks, rewards, and legal ownership of the sweater pass to the customer who has accepted the sweater and receives its benefits.

continued

continued from previous page

b. REII records the following journal entry on June 1, 2020.

June 1, 2020—To recognize revenue and record cost of sales

Cash	100	
Sales Revenue		100
Cost of Goods Sold	60	
Inventory		60

Assets	=	Liabilities	+	Equity
+100				+100
−60				−60

Cash		Sales Rev	
100			100
Inventory		**COGS**	
	60	60	

In **Demo 7-1**, revenue is recognized at *a single point in time* for a contract containing a *single performance obligation.* Many variations to this simple scenario can make the application of the five steps of revenue recognition more complex. For example, what if the customer also received loyalty points for the purchase, which granted the customer discounts on future purchases? What if the customer paid a deposit for the sweater because it was out of stock and available to ship the following week? What if the customer returned the sweater the following week? These are just a few of the complicating factors we explore in later sections when we take a deeper dive into each of the five steps of revenue recognition.

EXPANDING YOUR KNOWLEDGE — **Portfolio Approach**

A company generally applies the revenue recognition model to *a single contract with a customer.* However, as a practical expedient, a **portfolio approach** is acceptable under certain conditions. The portfolio approach allows companies to combine contracts for purposes of revenue recognition when it is more practical than accounting for each contract separately. To elect the portfolio approach, the company must reasonably expect that the effect of applying a portfolio approach to a group of contracts (or performance obligations) would not differ materially from considering each contract (or performance obligation) separately. For example, a telecommunications company that sells cellular phones and service plans to many customers might combine similar contracts executed on the same day in applying steps 2 through 5 of the revenue recognition model.

REVIEW 7-1 — **LO7-1** — **Application of the Five-Step Revenue Recognition Process**

Review MBC

More Practice: 7-18, 7-19, 7-48, 7-49
Solution on p. 7-74.

On June 1, 2020, REII Inc. initiates a written contract with a customer to repair a snowboard for $75 with payment due upon completion of the repair. REII Inc. completes the repair on June 5, 2020, at which time the customer picks up the snowboard and pays $75 to REII Inc. using a credit card.

Required

Use this example to demonstrate the five steps of the revenue recognition process.

LO 7-2 Identify the contract with the customer—Step 1

LO 7-2 Overview

Step 1: Identify the Contract with Customer

Conditions of a Valid Contract
- Commercial substance
- Approval by both parties
- Identifiable rights and obligations
- Identifiable payment terms
- Probable collection of consideration

Step 1 in the revenue recognition process is to identify the contract with a customer or an agreement with enforceable rights and obligations.

606-10-25-2 A contract is an agreement between two or more parties that creates enforceable rights and obligations. Enforceability of the rights and obligations in a contract is a matter of law. Contracts can be written, oral, or implied by an entity's customary business practices. The practices and processes for establishing contracts with customers vary across legal jurisdictions, industries, and entities. In addition, they may vary within an entity (for example, they may depend on the class of customer or the nature of the promised goods or services). An entity shall consider those practices and processes in determining whether and when an agreement with a customer creates enforceable rights and obligations.

The contract between the seller and the customer must be a **valid contract**. After a valid contract is established, it is not uncommon for a contract to be modified at a later point. In this section, we review the indicators of a valid contract. In a later section, we review the steps to take when a contract is modified.

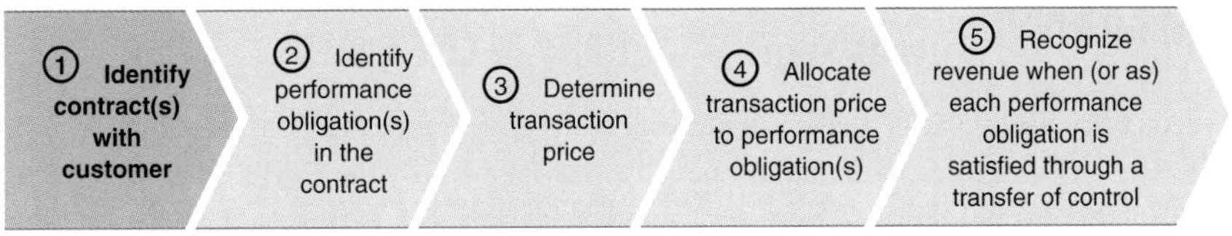
① Identify contract(s) with customer
② Identify performance obligation(s) in the contract
③ Determine transaction price
④ Allocate transaction price to performance obligation(s)
⑤ Recognize revenue when (or as) each performance obligation is satisfied through a transfer of control

Conditions of a Valid Contract

In the prior section, we identified a contract between a retailer and a customer where the retailer promised a ski sweater to a customer for consideration. In Step 1 of the revenue recognition process, we must determine whether the contract is *valid*. The revenue recognition standard identifies the conditions of a valid contract, outlined in **Exhibit 7-2**. A contract that creates enforceable rights and obligations is established when all five conditions are met (ASC 606-10-25-1).

EXHIBIT 7-2
Five Conditions of a Valid Contract

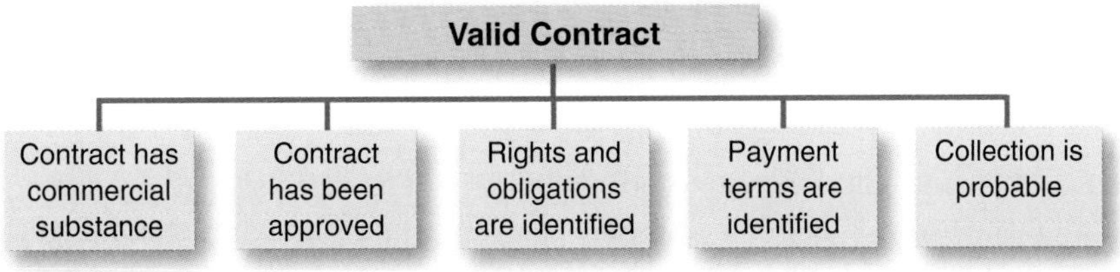
Valid Contract
Contract has commercial substance
Contract has been approved
Rights and obligations are identified
Payment terms are identified
Collection is probable

LO7: Contract for a ski sweater
Condition met:
☑ Seller's cash increases as a result of the contract.

Contract has Commercial Substance This means the risk, timing, or amount of the seller's future cash flows is expected to change due to the contract. There also must be a valid business reason for the transaction to occur. If there is no change in the risk, timing, or amount of the seller's future cash flows, there likely is no contract. For example, a contract may *not* have commercial substance if a customer can use a good for free during a 3-month trial period. The risks of owning the product have not passed to the customer if the customer can return the good before the end of the trial period at no cost.

☑ Transaction is part of normal business practices.

Contract has Approval This means that the parties to the contract have approved the contract and have committed to perform their obligations. Commitments may be stipulated through a written agreement, oral agreement, or through other relevant normal business practices. This means a contract can be formally or informally approved by both parties, depending on the situation. All relevant facts and circumstances should be considered in determining whether both parties substantially intend to be bound by the terms of the contract.

☑ Seller provides sweater and customer provides payment.

Rights are Identified This condition requires an identification of the rights of each party regarding the goods or services to be transferred. This is necessary because without a clear indication of the rights of each party, assessing at which point control is transferred to the customer is difficult. If either party has the unilateral right to terminate a contract without compensating the other party, then the rights and obligations are not clear, making the contract invalid.

☑ Price of the sweater is clearly identified.

Payment Terms are Identified This condition requires identifiable payment terms for the goods or services to be transferred and is necessary for determination of the transaction price. While this does not require a fixed or explicitly stated price in the contract, there must be sufficient information to allow an estimate of the transaction price.

☑ Collection in full is expected immediately.

Collection is Probable This means that collection of substantially all of the consideration is probable. This means the customer must have the intent and ability to pay substantially all of the consideration to the seller at the time the amount is due. **Consideration** is the benefit (such as money, goods, or services) that is bargained for between the parties of a contract. Sometimes contracts are written in a way to lower the seller's exposure to credit risk. For example, a seller might require an advance payment on the contract (such as a prepayment or deposit). Or, the seller might have the right to discontinue providing goods and/or services to a customer in the event of nonpayment. In either of these cases, the seller has reduced exposure to the risk of noncollection, which in turn can fulfill the fifth condition of a contract. (The revenue recognition standard *does not allow* the seller to consider its ability to repossess an asset transferred to a customer as a way to mitigate credit risk to meet the fifth condition of a valid contract.)

WELLS FARGO BANK

Real World—VALIDITY OF CONTRACTS

WELLS FARGO BANK N.A. [WFC]

In 2016, **Wells Fargo Bank N.A.** was the subject of an investigation by the Consumer Financial Protection Bureau (CFPB), which resulted in the largest penalty ever imposed by the CFPB. In a press release issued by the CFPB on September 8, 2016, (https://www.consumerfinance.gov/) the CFPB indicated that Wells Fargo must pay a $100 million fine for the widespread practice of opening accounts without knowledge of its customers. To boost sales to reach targets, Wells Fargo employees would secretly open new accounts on behalf of its customers and transfer money from existing accounts. The estimate of the number of unauthorized new accounts was two million! Wells Fargo's violations included (1) opening deposit accounts and transferring funds without authorization, (2) applying for credit card accounts without authorization, (3) issuing and activating debit cards without authorization, and (4) creating phony email addresses for the purposes of online services. In reviewing the criteria included in this section for a valid contract, it is clear that Wells Fargo did not have a valid contract with its customers. Both parties did not approve the arrangements (a condition of a valid contract). Even though this occurred while the previous revenue standard (ASC 605) was in place, recognition of revenue is not supported under either standard in this case.

In some cases, the validity of contracts can require in-depth analysis, judgment, and a review of legal enforceability. However, in other cases, the analysis is more straightforward. See **Demo 7-2** for an exercise on this topic.

When a contract with a customer *does not meet* the conditions of a valid contract and the seller receives consideration from the customer, the seller shall recognize revenue for consideration received only when *one or more* of the following events have occurred.

606-10-25-7

a. The entity has no remaining obligations to transfer goods or services to the customer, and all, or substantially all, of the consideration promised by the customer has been received by the entity and is nonrefundable.
b. The contract has been terminated, and the consideration received from the customer is nonrefundable.
c. The entity has transferred control of the goods or services to which the consideration that has been received relates, the entity has stopped transferring goods or services to the customer (if applicable) and has no obligation under the contract to transfer additional goods or services, and the consideration received from the customer is nonrefundable.

Until one of these events has occurred, the seller records a liability (not revenue) for the consideration received in advance of the contract being considered a valid contract.

Demo 7-2 LO7-2 Validity of a Contract

Demo MBC

In each of the following *separate* contract scenarios, indicate (1) which specific condition of a valid contract listed in **Exhibit 7-2** is addressed, and (2) how the validity of a contract is affected by facts in each scenario.

a. A contract between a seller and a customer is approved verbally although the seller's agreements are typically in writing.
b. A seller enters a contract fully confident that it will not collect 100% of the amount due from the customer.
c. A seller is still negotiating a sales agreement with a new customer even though the customer took control of the product sold under the open contract.
d. A seller and customer agree to a contract that includes sufficient information to allow the parties to estimate the transaction price, but the price was not included in the contract.
e. A seller and a customer transfer the same good back and forth multiple times.

continued

continued from previous page

Solution

a. **Whether the contract has been approved**
For a contract to be legally enforceable, both parties must approve the contract. If the typical practice for the company is to execute written contracts, a verbal contract might not be customary with business practices, which can call into question the validity of the contract. Additional facts of the situation must be analyzed to understand why the parties deviated from typical business practices and to determine whether both parties granted approval.

b. **Whether collection is probable**
The issue is not whether the seller expects to collect in full but whether the seller expects to collect substantially all of the amount due. To enhance the probability of collection, the seller might offset the credit risk by requiring advance payments or by requiring contractual rights to cease to provide services in the case of nonpayment. Additional facts of the situation must be analyzed to understand more fully, the collectibility of the contract.

c. **Whether the entities' rights and obligations are identified**
A valid contract requires that each party's rights be identified. Even though the goods were transferred, if there is not a clear understanding of the rights and obligations transferred, there may not be a valid contract in place.

d. **Whether payment terms are identified**
A valid contract does not require a specific price as long as there is sufficient information to estimate the prices and there is a legally enforceable right to payment to the seller. For example, the contract might specify goods will be provided at the prevailing price in a specified market.

e. **Whether the contract has commercial substance**
If the economic positions of the parties changed based on the contract, the contract likely has commercial substance, which is required for a valid contract. In this case, the economic positions of the parties have not changed. The parties are transferring goods back and forth multiple times to increase volume and sales with no other substance. If the economic position of the parties has not changed, it is likely that the contract does not have commercial substance.

One can see that the revenue recognition standard requires much judgment on the part of management and the auditors—the decision of whether a contract exists and whether revenue is recognized depends on the facts and circumstances of the situation.

Validity of a Contract — LO7-2 — REVIEW 7-2

In each of the following *separate* contract scenarios, indicate (1) which specific condition of a valid contract listed in **Exhibit 7-2** is addressed, and (2) how the validity of a contract is affected by facts in each scenario.

a. A five-year contract entered into and approved by two parties includes a termination clause that allows either party to cancel at any time during the five-year period for no additional compensation.
b. A customer purchased clothing online without signing a written contract.
c. A contract between two parties includes a promise for payment to include cash plus stock.
d. Because a seller is concerned about the viability of a particular customer, the seller stipulates shipment of goods will stop if the customer fails to make timely payments.
e. A seller enters into a contract with a customer to sell an asset at a specific price. The customer agrees to sell the asset back to the seller at the same price.

More Practice:
7-20, 7-21, 7-50, 7-51
Solution on p. 7-74.

Identify the performance obligations in the contract—Step 2 — LO 7-3

A performance obligation is a contractual promise to transfer a good or service to a customer. Companies must identify the performance obligations in each contract and determine which promises will be accounted for as separate performance obligations as illustrated in **Demo 7-3**.

LO 7-3 Overview

Step 2: Identify Performance Obligations
Separate performance obligations in a contract are:
- Capable of being distinct
- Identifiable from other contract promises
- Material in the context of a contract

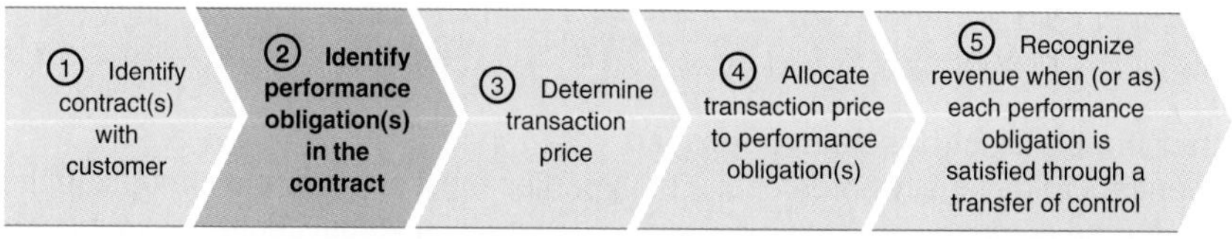
① Identify contract(s) with customer
② Identify performance obligation(s) in the contract
③ Determine transaction price
④ Allocate transaction price to performance obligation(s)
⑤ Recognize revenue when (or as) each performance obligation is satisfied through a transfer of control

Identification of Separate Performance Obligation(s)

A contract can incorporate multiple performance obligations. For example, consider a company such as TDS Telecom, which can offer a customer a bundle of goods such as a phone, phone service, data service, renewal options, or even free gifts such as speakers or a TV. Identifying separate performance obligations in an industry with constantly evolving products and services such as the telecommunications industry can be challenging.

Examples of performance obligations include (but are not limited to) the following:

- Sale of goods, for example, by a manufacturer or a merchandiser
- Performing an agreed-upon task or service
- Constructing, manufacturing, or developing an asset
- Granting a license of technology, franchises, patents, trademarks, and similar items
- Service-type warranties
- Granting of customer options for additional goods or services:
  - Sales incentive plans
  - Customer loyalty programs
  - Contract renewal options
  - Discounts on future purchases
  - Prospective volume discount plans

Separate Performance Obligations		
Capable of being distinct	Distinct within context of a contract	Material

A **separate performance obligation** is a performance obligation that is distinct. A performance obligation (or a series of goods or services with the same pattern of transfer to a customer) is distinct if (1) a promised good or service is capable of being distinct and (2) the promised good or service is distinct within the context of the contract. In determining the number of separate performance obligations, immaterial performance obligations (in the context of the contract) can be ignored.

Capable of Being Distinct

A good or service is capable of being distinct if the good or service is beneficial to the customer. A customer can benefit from a promised good or service if the good or service can be used, consumed, sold for an amount that is greater than scrap value, or held for an economic benefit. For some goods or services, a customer might be able to benefit from a good or service on its own. For other goods or services, a customer might be able to benefit from the good or service only in combination with other readily available resources. A **readily available resource** is a good or service that is sold separately or has already been obtained. Evidence that a customer can benefit from a good or service can be derived in a number of ways.

For example, the fact that a seller regularly sells a good or service separately would indicate that a customer can benefit from the good or service. Or, as another example, a promise to produce an architectural plan and a promise to construct a building based on the architectural plan are two separate performance obligations. Providing a plan is separately identifiable from providing a finished building. The customer can benefit separately from both the plan and from the finished building.

606-10-25-19a The customer can benefit from the good or service either on its own or together with other resources that are readily available to the customer (that is, the good or service is capable of being distinct).

Distinct within the Context of a Contract

A performance obligation is distinct within the context of a contract if that promise can be identified separately from other promises within the contract. This means that the promises in the contract are (1) not integrated or bundled into a combined product or service, (2) not the result of goods or services modifying other goods or services, or (3) not interrelated.

For example, the software on a phone (such as camera, clock, and navigation guide) is not distinct from the phone itself because the phone is necessary for the operation of the software. In another case, providing a sweetener in an iced tea at a coffee shop is not a separate obligation from providing the iced tea. Another example is that a nonrefundable registration (joining) fee for a fitness facility and a monthly facility usage fee are considered to be one performance obligation, even though the fitness facility can charge separately for these items. Overall, the objective is to determine whether the promise, in the context of the contract, is to transfer goods and services individually or to transfer them combined (or as an integrated bundle).

606-10-25-19b The entity's promise to transfer the good or service to the customer is separately identifiable from other promises in the contract (that is, the promise to transfer the good or service is distinct within the context of the contract).

606-10-25-21

a. The entity provides a significant service of integrating goods or services with other goods or services promised in the contract into a bundle of goods or services that represent the combined output or outputs for which the customer has contracted.

b. One or more of the goods or services significantly modifies or customizes, or are significantly modified or customized by, one or more of the other goods or services promised in the contract.

c. The goods or services are highly interdependent or highly interrelated. In other words, each of the goods or services is significantly affected by one or more of the other goods or services in the contract. For example, in some cases, two or more goods or services are significantly affected by each other because the entity would not be able to fulfill its promise by transferring each of the goods or services independently.

Materiality Threshold

The revenue standard does not require companies to *separately* account for promised goods or services if they are immaterial to the context of the contract. For example, if as part of a service contract, a seller provides an email with a monthly account statement, the seller might consider the providing of a monthly email to be immaterial within the context of the contract. This means the service would not be considered a separate performance obligation. (However, immaterial items that are material in the aggregate within the context of a contract, require further analysis.)

606-10-25-16A An entity is not required to assess whether promised goods or services are performance obligations if they are immaterial in the context of the contract with the customer.

Licenses, Warranties, and Customer Options

Further explanations of licenses, warranties, and customer options are provided in the paragraphs below.

License A contract can include a license combined with other promises. Each promise must be evaluated to determine whether it is distinct. A license establishes rights to intellectual property and the obligations of a seller to provide those rights. As an example, a franchise establishes rights for a franchisee. The franchisor grants rights to individuals or business entities to use a particular name and offer specified services or products for a period of time. In this chapter, we consider the recognition of revenue from the perspective of the franchisor. In a later chapter, we consider the accounting for franchise costs from the perspective of the franchisee.

Service-Type Warranties Companies can offer a warranty as part of a contract. Certain warranties (service-type warranties) that provide assurances in addition to agreed upon specifications of the related product are considered separate performance obligations. The accounting for warranties is addressed in Chapter 15.

Customer Options Sometimes sellers grant customers options or the right to acquire additional goods and services as part of a contract. The right to additional goods and services is not an enforceable obligation of the customer but an option. A customer option may or may not represent an additional performance obligation of the seller. A customer option is considered a separate performance obligation when it is *material in the context of a contract*. In these cases, the customer would not have the option or right to free or discounted services or goods, unless they entered into the original contract.

This means the customer is paying for two things in the context of the contract: a good or service now and the right to a good or service in the future.

> **606-10-55-42** If, in a contract, an entity grants a customer the option to acquire additional goods or services, that option gives rise to a performance obligation in the contract only if the option provides a material right to the customer that it would not receive without entering into that contract . . . If the option provides a material right to the customer, the customer in effect pays the entity in advance for future goods or services, and the entity recognizes revenue when those future goods or services are transferred or when the option expires.

Volume discounts that are prospective (rights to discounts that apply only to optional purchases in the future) should be evaluated to determine whether the customer is provided a material right that could only be obtained through the revenue contract. Volume discounts that are retroactive (adjustments to prior purchases because a certain volume was reached) are evaluated as variable consideration and affect the transaction price (see **LO 7-4**).

Determining whether a customer option is material requires judgment. To make this determination, consider this question: Would the same class of customer receive the same option to acquire additional goods and services if they had not entered into the revenue contract? For example, a customer enters into a contract to purchase a good and receives a 50% discount coupon on a subsequent purchase. If 15% discount coupons are widely available to the public, the net benefit to the customer is a 35% discount coupon (50% − 15%). The contract would have two performance obligations—one for the purchase of the good and one for a 35% coupon on a future purchase. This means that the customer is actually paying the seller for two items: for the good received now and for future goods.

Evaluation of materiality should also consider *qualitative factors* such as what a new customer would pay for the same option, the pricing of similar items by competitors, availability of options during a renewal period, and whether benefits accumulate (such as points in a loyalty rewards program accumulating with each dollar of customer purchases). If the option or right granted to a customer is determined to be material within the context of the contract, it is considered to be a separate performance obligation. **Determining the number of separate performance obligations in a contract is important because the remaining steps of the revenue recognition process are applied separately to each performance obligation.**

Demo 7-3 LO7-3 Identification of Separate Performance Obligation(s)

Determine how many separate performance obligations are included in the following *separate* contract examples.

a. A builder enters into an agreement with a customer to build an addition to the customer's home for $80,000, payable when completed. The builder (also acting as contractor) is responsible for all aspects of the project including construction services, plumbing, electrical, carpentry, painting, design, preparation, and cleanup.

Solution

Construction services can be sold separately to a customer and the customer could benefit from the individual services. However, the promise is for a finished addition to the house. These individual services cannot be separated from the overall promise in the contract to provide a finished addition because the services are highly interrelated and one or more services modifies another. Therefore, the building of the addition is considered **one performance obligation**.

b. Amazing Inc. enters into a contract with a customer to sell an electronic tablet and two years of data services. The customer receives an electronic tablet at a discounted value of $75 (retail value is $200) and agrees to pay a monthly fee of $20 for data service. Amazing also sells the tablet without data service and sells data services without the purchase of a tablet.

Solution

There are **two performance obligations** in the arrangement: the tablet and monthly data service. The tablet and monthly data service can be purchased separately, thus the tablet and monthly data service each provides a benefit and represents a separate promise. Further, because the tablet can be used without the data service, and the data service can be used with a different device, the two elements are not highly interdependent. (Allocation of a transaction price to various performance obligations is discussed in a later step.)

continued

continued from previous page

c. Bitware Inc. enters into a contract with a customer to provide a software license. The customer accesses the software by entering a unique 10-digit code. The software is functional on the customer's own computer. Within this contract, the customer has access to Bitware's customer service by phone or online for 12 months after the software download. Customer service contracts for this software are available from other service providers.

Solution

The seller has **two performance obligations**: to provide the software license and to provide customer support. The first promise, the license, grants the customer the right to use the intellectual property. The second promise, the right to customer service, benefits the customer and is separately identifiable from the right to use the software.

d. Epik, a healthcare software provider, enters into an arrangement to provide software and 1,000 hours of consulting services for $750,000. The software and the consulting services are distinct. Epik also provides an option to its customer to purchase 100 additional hours of consulting services over the next month at a rate of $225 per hour, which represents a 10% discount off the price of consulting services. During the same period, Epik launches a general advertising campaign to offer a 10% discount for consulting services.

Solution

There are **two performance obligations**: the transfer of the software and the transfer of the 1,000 hours of consulting services. The option to purchase 100 additional hours of consulting services at a discount does not provide a material customer option because similar customers can receive the discount without entering into a contract.

e. Gapp Inc. sponsors a customer loyalty point program where customers earn one loyalty point for every $5 spent on clothing and accessories at any Gapp Inc. store. Loyalty program members often exchange accumulated loyalty points for free products at Gapp. An individual customer makes a purchase of denim jeans at Gapp on June 1, 2020, for $60 and earns 12 loyalty points.

Solution

There are **two performance obligations**: the purchase of denim jeans and the loyalty points distributed. The loyalty points are a material customer option for additional goods because they can accumulate and equate to free products.

RAYTHEON Real World—PERFORMANCE OBLIGATION(S)

RAYTHEON COMPANY [RTN]

Raytheon Company is a technology and innovation leader specializing in defense and other government markets. The vast majority of revenue is from long-term contracts associated with the design, development, manufacture, or modification of complex aerospace or defense equipment or services. Raytheon reported the following revenue recognition policy in a recent Form 10-Q Report, which indicates that the bulk of the contracts are made up of a single performance obligation due to the integrative nature of the contracts.

> For most of our contracts, the customer contracts with us to provide a significant service of integrating a complex set of tasks and components into a single project or capability (even if that single project results in the delivery of multiple units). Hence, the entire contract is accounted for as one performance obligation. Less commonly, however, we may promise to provide distinct goods or services within a contract in which case we separate the contract into more than one performance obligation.

EXPANDING YOUR KNOWLEDGE — "Material" Customer Option?

The revenue recognition standard requires a customer option to be defined as a separate performance obligation only if the option is material in *the context of an individual contract.* FASB's intent is to allow companies to disregard immaterial items at the contract level. If a company establishes thousands of contracts in a year, a sophisticated system is required to review materiality at a contract level. Consider, for example, a cell phone provider.

Case One A customer has signed a one-year agreement for cellular service for a total price of $1,200. The customer also receives an option to renew service at a discounted price. The renewal option has a standalone selling price of $20. The cell phone provider considers the $20 option *to be immaterial* to the contract price of $1,200.

continued

continued from previous page

Case Two A customer has entered into a month-to-month cellular contract for $100 per month. The customer also receives an option to renew cell phone service at a discounted price. The standalone selling price of the renewal option is $10. In this case, the cell phone provider considers the $10 option to be *material* to the contract price of $100.

As outlined in these cases, a $10 option can be material, whereas a $20 option might not be material considering the context of the individual contracts. Because the standard does not require a review of options in total in determining materiality, the total value of options considered immaterial at a contract level, can be material at a company level. Still, these options will not be considered separate performance obligations.

REVIEW 7-3 LO7-3 Identification of Separate Performance Obligation(s)

Review MBC

In each of the following *separate* contract scenarios, determine and describe the number of performance obligations.

a. An optometrist enters into a contract with a customer to sell a pair of contacts along with two free boxes of contact solution. The optometrist sells contacts and solution separately, but the contacts require solution to work properly. Alternative brands of solution are compatible with the contacts.

b. A manufacturer purchased specialized industrial equipment for $350,000 plus installation services with a cost of $35,000. Due to the nature of the equipment, the installation is highly specialized and involves additional modifications of the equipment at the site of the installation.

c. A retail customer enters into a contract for a three-year license for anti-virus software. The purchase includes an initial software download and subsequent software updates over the three-year license period. Because new viruses emerge quickly, the software is expected to change and adapt extensively over the three-year license period.

d. A service provider enters into a contract with a customer for one year of home security monitoring for $360. Under the sales contract, the service provider guarantees a rate of $295 per year for years two and three as long as there is no lapse in service. The rates for security monitoring are expected to increase by 10% per year without the renewal options.

e. A franchisee enters into a contract with a franchisor for the right to operate a fast food location, using the company's (1) logo, design, and advertising materials, (2) menu items, recipes, and supplier contacts, (3) store designs, and (4) daily operating instructions for a five-year period beginning on January 1, 2020. The upfront fee of $250,000 also includes the purchase of equipment for $50,000, to be delivered 3 weeks after the date of the contract.

f. A retailer sells barbecue sauce with a coupon attached for 50 cents off the next purchase of barbecue sauce. The barbecue sauce typically sells for $2.00 a bottle.

g. A customer purchased a refrigerator from a home improvement retail store. Because the customer had no means to transport the refrigerator to her home to benefit from its use, she also rented a truck through the store for two hours. At the same time, the customer purchased vehicle insurance from the store because she was not sure if she would be covered through her own insurance plan.

h. An owner of a rental property enters into a contract with a service provider to manage its property over a one-year period. Management services vary each day but include items such as managing occupancy, maintenance, and accounting services.

More Practice: 7-52, 7-53
Solution on p. 7-74.

LO 7-4 Determine the transaction price—Step 3

LO 7-4 Overview

Step 3: Determine Transaction Price

- Fixed consideration (*determines transaction price*)
- Variable consideration (*estimates transaction price*)
  - Expected value method
  - Most likely amount method
- Consideration payable to the customer (*reduces transaction price*)
- Refund liability (*reduces transaction price*)

The next step in the revenue recognition process is to determine the **transaction price**, which is the amount of consideration that the company expects to be entitled to in exchange for the transfer of promised goods or services to a customer. The transaction price *excludes* amounts collected on behalf of third parties such as certain sales taxes.

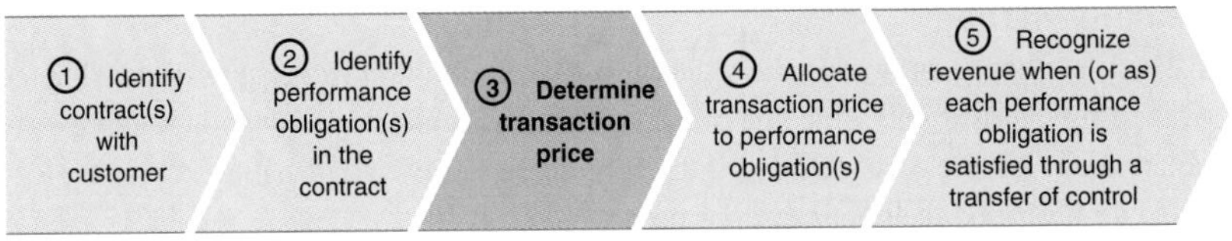
① Identify contract(s) with customer
② Identify performance obligation(s) in the contract
③ Determine transaction price
④ Allocate transaction price to performance obligation(s)
⑤ Recognize revenue when (or as) each performance obligation is satisfied through a transfer of control

In this section, we explore how the transaction price is determined. Consideration is fixed, variable, or includes some elements of both. The transaction price is also affected by other factors such as consideration payable to customers, refund liabilities, time value of money, and noncash consideration. In addition, as shown in LO7-8, when a company simply arranges for services to be provided, the transaction price includes only the fee or commission that the company is entitled to for the transfer of the goods or services.

Determine Transaction Price					
Fixed Consideration	Variable Consideration	Consideration Payable to Customer	Refund Liability	Time Value of Money	Noncash Consideration

Fixed Consideration

With **fixed consideration**, determination of the transaction price is simple. For example, a builder enters into a contract with a customer to construct an addition to a customer's home for $80,000. The transaction price is stated in the contract and is not contingent on other events. In another example, REII Inc. sold one ski sweater for fixed consideration of $100. The transaction price is *fixed* and easily determinable.

Variable Consideration

Variable consideration results when the price of goods or services a seller is entitled to depends on future events, or when a price varies due to discounts, incentives, credits, or other similar items. If the consideration promised in a contract includes a variable amount, the company must estimate the amount of consideration the company is entitled to upon the exchange. Examples of variable consideration include the following:

- Price concessions
- Retroactive volume discounts
- Rebates and refunds
- Bonuses, incentives, and royalties
- Revenue contingent on future event occurring
- Cash discounts (see Chapter 8)

The revenue recognition standard provides two choices to estimate variable consideration: the expected value method and the most likely amount method. See **Demo 7-4A**. Companies should choose the method that is the better predictor of revenue and that method should be applied consistently with the following constraint outlined in the accounting standards:

606-10-32-11 An entity shall include in the transaction price some or all of an amount of variable consideration . . . only to the extent that it is probable that a significant reversal in the amount of cumulative revenue recognized will not occur when the uncertainty associated with the variable consideration is subsequently resolved.

Expected Value Method

606-10-32-8a The expected value is the sum of probability-weighted amounts in a range of possible consideration amounts. An expected value may be an appropriate estimate of the amount of variable consideration if an entity has a large number of contracts with similar characteristics.

To use the expected value method, a company needs data necessary to consider and quantify the possibilities of all possible outcomes.

For example, assume consideration is variable due to the potential for a retroactive volume discount such that the unit price declines for all contracted units when the customer reaches specified sales volumes for additional units. Consideration to be received might be $100 (35% probability), $200 (35% probability), or $300 (30% probability). Under the expected value method, variable consideration is estimated at $195.

$100 × 35%	$ 35
$200 × 35%	70
$300 × 30%	90
Variable consideration	$195

Most Likely Amount Method

606-10-32-8b The most likely amount is the single most likely amount in a range of possible consideration amounts (that is, the single most likely outcome of the contract). The most likely amount may be an appropriate estimate of the amount of variable consideration if the contract has only two possible outcomes (for example, an entity either achieves a performance bonus or does not).

For example, if the consideration to be received might be $400 or $0 but the most likely amount is $400, variable consideration is estimated at $400.

The seller is required to use the method that best predicts the amount of revenue to be collected. The availability of alternative methods does not imply companies have a free choice to use either if one is significantly more predictive than the other.

Demo 7-4A **LO7-4** **Estimating Transaction Price when it Includes Variable Consideration**

Demo MBC

Example One—Expected Value Method Diaz Inc. develops website ads for customers. Contract terms and conditions are similar across its various contracts. Contracts typically include a fixed fee plus variable consideration for a performance bonus earned when website ads are delivered ahead of schedule. Based on Diaz's historical experience, the bonus amounts and associated probabilities for achieving each bonus on a new customer's contract follow.

Bonus Amount	Probability of Outcome
$ 0	15%
5,000	40%
10,000	45%

Diaz has a large number of contracts that have characteristics that are similar to the new contract. As a result, Diaz determines that using the expected value method would better predict the amount of consideration to which it will be entitled than using the most likely amount method. What is Diaz Inc.'s transaction price for the performance bonus based upon the *expected value method*?

Solution

Diaz estimates $6,500 of variable consideration to include in the transaction price using the expected value method, calculated as follows.

Bonus Amount		Probability of Outcome		Revenue Recognized
$ 0	×	15%	=	$ 0
5,000	×	40%	=	2,000
10,000	×	45%	=	4,500
		Expected consideration		$6,500

Example Two—Most Likely Amount Method Diaz Inc. develops website ads for customers. Contract terms and conditions are similar across its various contracts. Contracts typically include a fixed fee plus variable consideration for a performance bonus related to the timing to complete the website ad. If the website ad is finished by the deadline stated in the contract, Diaz Inc. will receive a bonus of $5,000. If the website ad is not finished by the deadline, Diaz Inc. receives no bonus. Based upon its historical experience, Diaz believes that the most likely amount of the bonus consideration is $5,000. What is Diaz Inc.'s transaction price for the performance bonus based upon the *most likely amount method*?

Solution

Diaz estimates $5,000 of variable consideration to include in the transaction price using the most likely amount method, calculated as follows.

Bonus Amount	Most Likely Outcome
$ 0	n/a
$5,000	$5,000

EXPANDING YOUR KNOWLEDGE **Constraint on Variable Consideration**

A seller recognizes variable consideration only to the extent a probable significant reversal of revenue will not occur in the future. The revenue recognition standard outlines factors that could increase the likelihood of a revenue reversal (not all inclusive).

606-10-32-12 Factors that could increase the likelihood or the magnitude of a revenue reversal include, but are not limited to, any of the following:

a. The amount of consideration is highly susceptible to factors outside the entity's [seller's] influence. Those factors may include volatility in a market, the judgment or actions of third parties, weather conditions, and a high risk of obsolescence of the promised good or service.
b. The uncertainty about the amount of consideration is not expected to be resolved for a long period of time.
c. The entity's [seller's] experience (or other evidence) with similar types of contracts is limited, or that experience (or other evidence) has limited predictive value.
d. The entity [seller] has a practice of either offering a broad range of price concessions or changing the payment terms and conditions of similar contracts in similar circumstances.
e. The contract has a large number and broad range of possible consideration amounts.

Consideration Payable to a Customer

As part of a contract, a seller can pay consideration to a customer. Examples of consideration paid or payable to a customer include credits (coupons), volume discounts, rebates, cooperative advertising arrangements, and slotting fees (shown in **Demo 7-4B**). The payment of consideration need not take place at the same time as the revenue contract. Expected **consideration payable** is generally treated as a reduction of the transaction price.

Selling price
Less: Consideration payable
Transaction price recorded as sales revenue

Unpaid consideration at a reporting period is recorded as a current liability. If however, the payment to the customer is in exchange for a distinct good or service received from the customer, the transaction is recorded separately as a typical purchase from a supplier. Further, if consideration payable is greater than the fair value of the distinct good or service received from the customer, the excess is treated as a reduction to the transaction price.

606-10-32-25 An entity shall account for consideration payable to a customer as a reduction of the transaction price and, therefore, of revenue unless the payment to the customer is in exchange for a distinct good or service . . . that the customer transfers to the entity.

606-10-32-26 If consideration payable to a customer is a payment for a distinct good or service from the customer, then an entity shall account for the purchase of the good or service in the same way that it accounts for other purchases from suppliers. If the amount of consideration payable to the customer exceeds the fair value of the distinct good or service that the entity receives from the customer, then the entity shall account for such an excess as a reduction of the transaction price. If the entity cannot reasonably estimate the fair value of the good or service received from the customer, it shall account for all of the consideration payable to the customer as a reduction of the transaction price.

Reducing the Transaction Price for Consideration Payable — LO7-4 — Demo 7-4B

Demo MBC

Kallog Inc., a cereal manufacturer, sells its cereal line to a large grocery store chain. Kallog also pays the grocery chain a **slotting fee**, which is a payment for desired shelf position in the store. The slotting fee is negotiated as part of the sales contract. For the month of June 2020, cash sales to a grocery store were $10,000, cost of inventory was $4,000, and the slotting fee was $500. Kallog did not receive a distinct good or service in exchange for the $500. What is Kallog's transaction price?

Solution

The slotting fee is consideration payable because it is paid by the seller in connection with the contract and is not paid for a distinct good or service. The transaction price (recorded as sales revenue) is measured as follows.

Selling price	$10,000
Less: Consideration payable	500
Transaction price recorded as sales revenue	$ 9,500

continued

continued from previous page

Instead of recording the consideration payable (slotting fees) as an advertising expense, it is reported as a reduction to the transaction price because it was negotiated as part of the contract.†

† Recognition of revenue is in a later section (LO 6). Looking ahead, the following summary entries for the month of June are required by Step 5 for revenue recognition assuming Kallog pays the slotting fee in a future month.

To record sales

Cash	10,000	
Sales Revenue		9,500
Consideration Payable		500

To record cost of goods sold

Cost of Goods Sold	4,000	
Inventory		4,000

Refund Liability—Sales with Right of Return

A company recognizes a refund liability (usually a *current liability*) if the company receives consideration from a customer and expects to refund some or all of the consideration in the future. The **refund liability** is the amount of consideration received (or receivable) that the company does not expect to be entitled to. The amount of refund liability should be adjusted at the end of each reporting period. The most common refund liability is a sale with the right of return. Other refund liabilities include retroactive price adjustments and refunds due to poor customer satisfaction with a service provided.

The right of return affects the transaction price but is *not* considered to be a performance obligation. The expected value of sales returns is estimated in the same way as other variable consideration: using either the expected value method or the most likely amount method. The transaction price recorded as sales revenue in the income statement is reduced by the refund liability. In other words, sales revenue is recorded only for goods not expected to be returned. The recording of returns is discussed further in Chapter 8.

Time Value of Money

The revenue recognition standard provides guidance on accounting for arrangements with significant financing components. The determination of whether a financing component is significant is assessed at the contract level and involves judgment, with an evaluation of both qualitative and quantitative factors. In determining the transaction price in contracts with significant financing components, companies adjust consideration amounts for the effect of the time value of money when the timing of payments provides the customer with financing benefits. A contract with a customer does not have a significant financing component if any of the following factors exist:

606-10-32-17

a. The customer paid for the goods or services in advance, and the timing of the transfer of those goods or services is at the discretion of the customer.

b. A substantial amount of the consideration promised by the customer is variable, and the amount or timing of that consideration varies on the basis of the occurrence or nonoccurrence of a future event that is not substantially within the control of the customer.

c. The difference between the promised consideration and the cash selling price of the good or service . . . arises for reasons other than the provision of finance to either the customer or the entity, and the difference between those amounts is proportional to the reason for the difference.

In addition, the following practical expedient is applicable to contracts with short-term payment receipts.

606-10-32-18 As a practical expedient, an entity need not adjust the promised amount of consideration for the effects of a significant financing component if the entity expects, at contract inception, that the period between when the entity transfers a promised good or service to a customer and when the customer pays for that good or service will be one year or less.

See Chapter 8 for recording significant financing components in the recording of notes receivable.

Noncash Consideration

The fair value (at a contract's inception) of noncash consideration received from a customer must be included in determining the transaction price. If the fair value of the consideration is not reasonably estimable, the value of the consideration is estimated indirectly by reference to the standalone selling price of the goods or services promised to the customer. Noncash consideration can be in the form of property, plant, and equipment, or a financial instrument. A customer might contribute goods or services to facilitate a seller's fulfillment of a performance obligation. An entity should include the customer's contribution of goods or services in the transaction price as noncash consideration only if the entity obtains control of those goods or services.

As an example, assume that on January 1, 2020, Atlanta Inc. enters into a contract with Green Mfg. to build equipment. Atlanta Inc. pays Green Mfg. $2 million and agrees to provide necessary materials with a fair value of $250,000 to be used in the manufacturing of the equipment. Atlanta Inc. will deliver the materials to Green Mfg. approximately three months after development of the equipment commences. Green Mfg. obtains control of the materials upon delivery by Atlanta Inc. and could elect to use the materials for other projects. In this case, Green Mfg. determines the transaction price to be $2,250,000 or $2 million plus the noncash consideration of $250,000.

Transaction Price **LO7-4** **REVIEW 7-4**

In each of the following separate revenue contract scenarios, determine the transaction price *and* determine whether the transaction price is fixed, variable, or some combination of both.

a. Merc Inc. sells $100,000 of inventory during 2020 to customers for $130,000. Merc Inc. accepts returns up to 6 months after the date of purchase. Based on historical trends, 5% of inventory that Merc Inc. sells is returned.

b. Krowgar Co. sells a brand new cereal product to Mart Inc. for $3,000. Krowgar agrees to reimburse Mart Inc. $500 for anticipated shortfalls in the selling price collected by Mart Inc. for the launch of the product.

c. IT Inc. enters into a contract with Smit Co. to install a new technology system. IT Inc. will receive a bonus of $5,000 (in addition to a fixed fee of $50,000) if the installation is completed before year-end. The bonus decreases by $1,000 per week after year-end. IT Inc. estimates that there is a 70% probability that the contract will be completed by the agreed-upon completion date, a 20% probability that it will be completed one week after year-end, and a 10% probability that it will be completed two weeks after year-end.

d. Sisko Inc. enters into a contract with Davi Co. to install a new technology system. Sisko Inc. will receive a bonus of $5,000 (in addition to a fixed fee of $50,000) if the installation is completed before year-end. The bonus decreases by $1,000 per week after year-end. Based on Sisko's history of meeting deadlines, Sisko estimates that the most likely amount of the bonus to be received is $5,000.

More Practice:
7-56, 7-57, 7-58, 7-59
Solution on p. 7-74.

Allocate the transaction price to performance obligations in the contract—Step 4

LO 7-5

After the performance obligations are identified and the transaction price is established, the next step is to allocate the transaction price to the separate performance obligations.

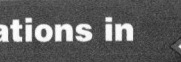

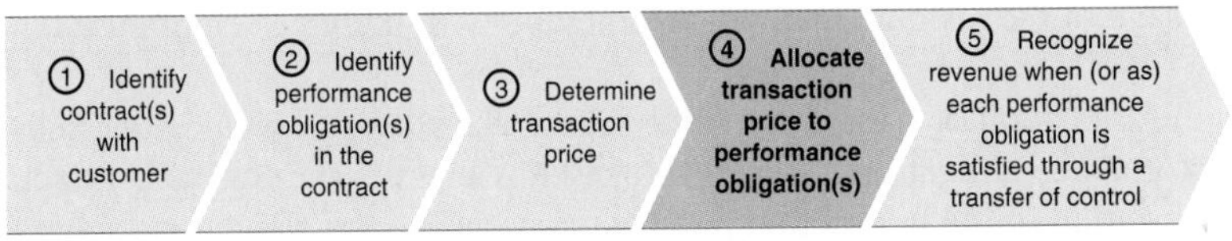
① Identify contract(s) with customer
② Identify performance obligation(s) in the contract
③ Determine transaction price
④ Allocate transaction price to performance obligation(s)
⑤ Recognize revenue when (or as) each performance obligation is satisfied through a transfer of control

LO 7-5 Overview

Step 4: Allocate Transaction Price Based on Relative Standalone Selling Prices

- Observable standalone selling prices
- Estimated standalone selling prices
  - Adjusted market assessment approach
  - Expected cost plus a margin approach
  - Residual approach

The transaction price is allocated to each performance obligation based on the **standalone selling price** or the price at which a company would sell a promised good or service separately to a customer. The company must determine the standalone selling prices for each material distinct performance obligation and then allocate the transaction price based on each item's relative standalone selling price compared to the total standalone selling price of all performance obligations in the contract.

606-10-05-4 Step 4: Allocate the transaction price to the performance obligations in the contract—An entity typically allocates the transaction price to each performance obligation on the basis of the relative standalone selling prices of each distinct good or service promised in the contract. If a standalone selling price is not observable, an entity estimates it.

Determine standalone selling price of each performance obligation			
Observable	Estimated: Adjusted Market Assessment Approach	Estimated: Expected Cost Plus a Margin Approach	Estimated: Residual Approach
Allocate transaction price to performance obligations based upon relative standalone selling prices			

The strongest evidence of a standalone selling price is when goods or services are sold separately. In such a case, standalone prices are **observable.**

606-10-32-32 The best evidence of a standalone selling price is the observable price of a good or service when the entity sells that good or service separately in similar circumstances and to similar customers. A contractually stated price or a list price for a good or service may be (but shall not be presumed to be) the standalone selling price of that good or service.

Other times, however, the standalone selling price must be **estimated**. Three methods for estimating a standalone selling price are the (1) **adjusted market assessment approach**, (2) **expected cost plus a margin approach**, and (3) **residual approach**.

606-10-32-33 When estimating a standalone selling price, an entity shall consider all information (including market conditions, entity-specific factors, and information about the customer or class of customer) that is reasonably available to the entity. In doing so, an entity shall maximize the use of observable inputs and apply estimation methods consistently in similar circumstances.

Adjusted Market Assessment Approach

In the adjusted market assessment approach, a company estimates the price that a customer in a market (in which it is actively selling goods or services) would be willing to pay for these goods or services. Information can be obtained from competitors' prices. This method is easier to apply if a seller has been active in a market for a period of time or a competitor offers a similar product and it can be used as a basis for this analysis.

Expected Cost Plus a Margin Approach

In the expected cost plus a margin approach, a company forecasts its expected costs of satisfying a performance obligation and then adds an appropriate margin for that good or service to compute the standalone selling price of that good or service.

Residual Approach

In the residual approach, the standalone selling price of one (or more) of the goods or services is known. The remaining good or service is valued at the sales price left to be allocated. This method can *only* be used to estimate the standalone selling price of a good or service if one of the following criteria is met.

- The seller sells the same good or service to different customers for different amounts.
- The good or service does not have an established price because it has not been sold before.

Due to restrictions placed on usage of the residual method, this method will likely be seldom used in practice.

In **Demo 7-5A** we show the allocation of transaction price in the case where the standalone selling price for each separate performance obligation is observable or known at the start of the contract. In **Demo 7-5B** we show the allocation of the transaction price when not all of the standalone selling prices are observable, which means that some must be estimated.

In the examples and assignments in this chapter, we state the price that the goods or services are sold for including the price that is stated to the customer for each component. The objective, however, is to determine how to *allocate revenue to the performance obligations according to the revenue recognition standards for financial accounting purposes*. For example, a customer might be told that after buying ten products, the eleventh is free. However, for financial accounting purposes, the revenue recognition standard requires that revenue be allocated to all eleven products.

Transaction Price Allocation—Standalone Selling Prices Are Observable LO7-5 Demo 7-5A

Demo MBC

Example One—Total Standalone Selling Price Equals Total Transaction Price

A customer enters into a contract with B-Buys Inc. to purchase a computer and computer services for a combined price of $1,200 (stated to the customer as $1,000 for the computer and $200 for the computer services).The sale of the computer and the services are considered separate performance obligations. B-Buys Inc. sells the same computers to other customers for $1,000 each and provides computer services (technical assistance) to other customers for $200 per year. This means that the standalone selling price for the computer is $1,000 and the standalone selling price for computer services is $200. *In this case, the total transaction price of $1,200 equals the total standalone selling price of $1,200.* Allocate the total $1,200 transaction price to each separate performance obligation.

Solution

Performance Obligations	Transaction Price as Stated	Standalone Selling Price	Allocated Transaction Price
Computer	$1,000	$1,000	$1,000
Services	200	200	200
	$1,200	$1,200	$1,200

The transaction price of $1,200 is the amount recognized as revenue in Step 5, with $1,000 allocated to the computer and $200 to the computer services.

Example Two—Total Standalone Selling Price Does Not Equal Total Transaction Price

Assume the same circumstances as in Example One except that the customer pays a *combined discounted selling price of $900 (stated to the customer as $800 for the computer and $100 for the service). In this case, the total transaction price of $900 does not equal the total standalone selling price of $1,200.* Allocate the total $900 transaction price to each separate performance obligation.

Solution

Performance Obligations	Transaction Price as Stated	Standalone Selling Price	Selling Price Ratio	Allocated Transaction Price
Computer	$800	$1,000	1,000/1,200 or 5/6	$750 (5/6 × $900)
Services	100	200	200/1,200 or 1/6	150 (1/6 × $900)
	$900	$1,200	1,200/1,200 or 6/6	$900

The transaction price of $900 is the amount recognized as revenue in Step 5, with $750 allocated to the computer and $150 to the computer services. The total allocated revenue recognized can never exceed the total transaction price.

ALPHABET

Real World—MULTIPLE PERFORMANCE OBLIGATIONS

ALPHABET [GOOGL]

Alphabet Inc. reported the following revenue recognition policy in a recent Form 10-K Report, indicating the use of two approaches described above: (1) allocation of transaction price with observable standalone selling prices and (2) allocation of transaction price using the expected cost plus a margin approach.

> **Arrangements with Multiple Performance Obligations** Our contracts with customers may include multiple performance obligations. For such arrangements, we allocate revenue to each performance obligation based on its relative standalone selling price. We generally determine standalone selling prices based on the prices charged to customers or using expected cost plus margin.

Demo 7-5B LO7-5 Transaction Price Allocation—Standalone Selling Prices Are Estimated

Demo MBC

Example One—Adjusted Market Assessment Approach and Expected Cost Plus a Margin Approach

5M Inc. enters into a contract with a customer to sell three products in exchange for $200, the total transaction price (stated to the customer as $75 for Product A, $100 for Product B, and $25 for Product C). 5M regularly sells Product A, so the market price is directly observable at $75 per product. The standalone selling price of Products B and C are not observable. 5M Inc. gathers additional information regarding Products B and C. Two competitors sell an item similar to product B for an average selling price of $100. The estimated cost of Product C is $36 and the company has a typical profit margin of 40%. Allocate the total $200 transaction price to each separate performance obligation.

Solution

The standalone selling prices of Products A, B, and C are estimated as follows.

Product A	$ 75	*Directly observable*—known standalone selling price
Product B	100	*Adjusted market assessment approach*—estimated based upon competitors' prices
Product C	50	*Expected cost plus a margin*—estimated based on cost plus margin ($36 × 1.40)
	$225	

The customer received a discount because the combined price of the bundled goods was $200, which was less than the estimated standalone selling prices of the individual products, which total $225. Because there is no observable evidence of where to allocate the $25 ($225 − $200) discount, the discount is allocated proportionately as follows.

Performance Obligations	Transaction Price as Stated	Standalone Selling Price	Selling Price Ratio	Allocated Transaction Price*	
Product A	$ 75	$ 75	75/225 or 3/9	$ 67	(3/9 × $200)
Product B	100	100	100/225 or 4/9	89	(4/9 × $200)
Product C	25	50	50/225 or 2/9	44	(2/9 × $200)
	$200	$225	225/225 or 9/9	$200	

*Amounts rounded.

The $200 transaction price is the amount recognized as revenue in Step 5, with $67 allocated to Product A, $89 to Product B, and $44 to Product C.

Example Two—Residual Approach

5M Inc. enters into a contract with a customer to sell three products in exchange for $200, the total transaction price. 5M regularly sells Product A for $75 and Product B for $95 on a standalone basis. The standalone selling price of Product C is not observable because it is a new product and is currently not sold by competitors. Because Product C has not been sold before and does not have an established price, the residual approach can be used to estimate the selling price of Product C. Allocate the total $200 transaction price to each separate performance obligation.

Solution

The standalone selling prices of Products A, B, and C are summarized as follows.

Performance Obligations	Standalone Selling Price	Allocated Transaction Price
Product A	$75 (*Observable*)	$ 75
Product B	95 (*Observable*)	95
Product C		30*
		$200

*$200 − $75 − $95 = $30

The $200 transaction price is the amount recognized as revenue in Step 5, with $75 allocated to Product A, $95 to Product B, and $30 to Product C.

EXPAND YOUR KNOWLEDGE **Estimating Standalone Price**

Estimating standalone price *requires judgment.* The revenue recognition standard indicates that we cannot presume that a list price or a contractually stated price is a standalone selling price. The revenue recognition standard provides examples of items to consider in estimating a standalone selling price.

Market Conditions to Consider

- Potential limits on the selling price of the product.
- Competitor pricing for a similar product.
- Current market trends that will likely affect the pricing.
- The entity's market share and position.
- Effects of the geographic area on pricing.

Entity-Specific Factors to Consider

- Profit objectives and internal cost structure.
- Pricing practices and pricing objectives.
- Effects of customization on pricing.
- Pricing practices used to establish pricing of bundled products.

Allocation of Transaction Price

LO7-5 **REVIEW 7-5**

Cellular Inc. is offering a promotion for new customers signing a contract: purchase a new handset, a one-year service agreement, and set of headphones for $710. The transaction price as stated to the customer is $150 for the handset, $480 for the one-year service agreement, and $80 for the set of headphones. Allocate the $710 transaction price under the following separate cases.

a. The three items (service, handset, and headphones) are sold separately by Cellular. The standalone selling prices of the handset, one-year service agreement, and headphones are $150, $480, and $80, respectively.

b. The three items (service, handset, and headphones) are sold separately by Cellular. The standalone selling prices of the handset, one-year service agreement, and headphones are $200, $480, and $80, respectively.

c. Two of the three items (service and handset) are sold separately by Cellular. The standalone selling prices of the handset and one-year service agreement are $200 and $480, respectively. Because Cellular has never sold headphones prior to this promotion, Cellular determined the average selling price of similar headphones in the market place to be $100.

d. Two of the three items (service and handset) are sold separately by Cellular. The standalone selling prices of the handset and one-year service agreement are $200 and $480, respectively. Cellular purchased the headphones for $64 a pair and expects a gross profit margin of 40%.

e. Two of the three items (service and handset) are sold separately by Cellular. The standalone selling prices of the handset and one-year service agreement are $200 and $480, respectively. Cellular has never sold headphones prior to this promotion, and is not able to obtain a reliable comparable market price because the headphones are unique and nothing comparable is available on the market.

More Practice: 7-32, 7-33, 7-66
Solution on p. 7-75.

Recognize revenue when (or as) the seller satisfies a performance obligation—Step 5

LO 7-6

The final step of revenue recognition is to recognize revenue as distinct performance obligations are satisfied. According to the accounting guidance:

> **606-10-25-23** An entity shall recognize revenue when (or as) the entity satisfies a performance obligation by transferring a promised good or service (that is, an asset) to a customer. An asset is transferred when (or as) the customer obtains control of that asset.

LO 7-6 Overview

Step 5: Recognize Revenue When Seller Satisfies a Performance Obligation

- Revenue recognized at a point in time
- Revenue recognized over time

① Identify contract(s) with customer → ② Identify performance obligation(s) in the contract → ③ Determine transaction price → ④ Allocate transaction price to performance obligation(s) → **⑤ Recognize revenue when (or as) each performance obligation is satisfied through a transfer of control**

Recognition of Revenue	
At Point in Time	Over Time

Control can transfer to a customer **at a point in time** or **over time**. Control implies the customer can direct the use and obtain the benefits of that good or service. In evaluating the transfer of control, management should consider guidance mainly from the perspective of the customer to determine if revenue is recognized at a point in time or over time. **When a company has multiple performance obligations, each performance obligation is analyzed to determine when control has transferred to the customer for each respective performance obligation.**

Recognition of Revenue Over Time

Revenue is recognized *over time* if *any one* of the following three criteria in **Exhibit 7-3** is met.

EXHIBIT 7-3 Revenue Recognition Over Time Criteria

Revenue Recognition Over Time Criteria	Contract Example
606-10-25-27a The customer simultaneously receives and consumes the benefits provided by the [seller's] performance as the [seller] performs.	Six-month security monitoring at a retail store.
606-10-25-27b The [seller's] performance creates or enhances an asset (for example, work in process) that the customer controls as the asset is created or enhanced.	Contract to build customized equipment for a customer where the customer owns the work in process.
606-10-25-27c The [seller's] performance does not create an asset with an alternative use to the [seller] . . . and the [seller] has an enforceable right to payment for performance completed to date.	Contract to build customized equipment for a customer where the customer does not take physical possession of the equipment until fully built. The customer is obligated to pay costs incurred plus the agreed upon profit if a cancellation occurs.

If one criterion is met, the seller must recognize revenue over time, proportionately with the rate of satisfaction of the performance obligation. If a seller **does not** satisfy a performance obligation over time, the performance obligation is satisfied **at a point in time.**

How is revenue recognized over time? With some service revenue contracts, revenue is earned evenly over the contract period, thus revenue is recognized on a **straight-line basis**. Other times, as in many long-term contracts, revenue is earned based on the **extent of progress toward satisfaction of performance obligations**. Progress toward the satisfaction of performance obligations may be measured through input measures or output measures.

606-10-25-31 For each performance obligation satisfied over time . . . an entity shall recognize revenue over time by measuring the progress toward complete satisfaction of that performance obligation. The objective when measuring progress is to depict an entity's performance in transferring control of goods or services promised to a customer (that is, the satisfaction of an entity's performance obligation).

606-10-55-17 Output methods recognize revenue on the basis of direct measurements of the value to the customer of the goods or services transferred to date relative to the remaining goods or services promised under the contract. Output methods include methods such as surveys of performance completed to date, appraisals of results achieved, milestones reached, time elapsed, and units produced or units delivered.

606-10-55-20 Input methods recognize revenue on the basis of the entity's efforts or inputs to the satisfaction of a performance obligation (for example, resources consumed, labor hours expended, costs incurred, time elapsed, or machine hours used) relative to the total expected inputs to the satisfaction of that performance obligation.

Judgment is needed to determine what is the measure that best captures progress that has been made. One common input method to estimate the amount of revenue to record over time is the **cost-to-cost method**, which measures the input of costs incurred relative to total expected costs to be incurred. In computing the percentage completion, costs due to inefficiencies (such as unexpected amounts of wasted materials, labor, or other resources) that were not reflected in the price of the contract are *excluded* from the calculation. The percentage completion is applied to total contract revenue (transaction price) to measure the amount of revenue to recognize to date.

$$\text{Percent complete} = \frac{\text{Total costs incurred to date (excluding inefficiencies)}}{\text{Most recent estimate of total project costs}}$$

$$\text{Recognized revenue} = \text{Percent complete} \times \text{Total contract revenue}$$

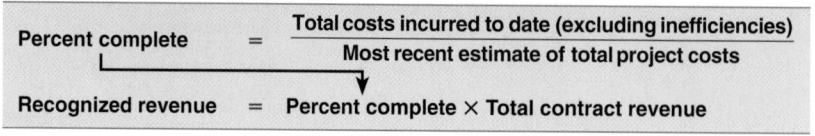

However, if the company estimates a net contract loss, the net contract loss is recognized immediately. See Appendix 7A and Appendix 7B for a presentation of journal entries for long-term construction contracts.

Recognition of Revenue at a Point in Time

If none of the criteria included in **Exhibit 7-3** are met, revenue is recognized at a point in time—when control of the asset passes to the customer. The factors included earlier in **Exhibit 7-1** are key in determining whether control has passed to the customer. For example, does the customer have physical possession of the asset or does the seller have the right to payment?

Contract Liabilities and Contract Assets

Definitions of terms contract liability and contract asset are as follows.

Balance Sheet Accounts	Point of Revenue Recognition
Contract Liability	**ASC Glossary** An entity's [seller's] obligation to transfer goods or services to a customer for which the [seller] has received consideration (or the amount is due) from the customer.
Contract Asset	**ASC Glossary** An entity's [seller's] right to consideration in exchange for goods or services that the [the seller] has transferred to a customer when that right is conditioned on something other than the passage of time (for example, [the seller's] future performance).

When a customer performs first (a prepayment), the seller recognizes a contract liability. This means a seller records a liability if a customer's payment occurs before transfer of control of the good or service to the customer. The seller recognizes revenue at the point when the performance obligation is satisfied. As shown in Exhibit 2-10, we use a variety of account names to refer to a contract liability such as deferred revenue, deferred service revenue, and deferred royalty revenue.

On the other hand, when a seller first satisfies a performance obligation by transferring control of a promised good or service, the seller has earned a right to consideration from the customer and, therefore, recognizes either a receivable or a contract asset. **Contract assets** represent *conditional rights* to consideration. The right would be conditional, for example, when a seller must satisfy another performance obligation in the contract before it is entitled to payment from the customer. If an entity has an *unconditional right* to receive consideration from the customer, a **receivable** is recognized and presented separately from other contract assets. A right is unconditional if nothing other than the passage of time is required before payment of that consideration is due.

606-10-45-1 When either party to a contract has performed, an entity [seller] shall present the contract in the statement of financial position as a contract asset or a contract liability, depending on the relationship between the entity's [seller's] performance and the customer's payment. An entity [seller] shall present any unconditional rights to consideration separately as a receivable.

For example, a seller enters into a contract to deliver two products to a customer which will be delivered at two different times. The delivery of each product is considered a separate performance obligation. The customer is not required to pay for both products until 30 days after *both* products are delivered. After the first product is delivered, the seller debits Contract Asset (not a receivable) and credits Sales Revenue. This is because the seller does not have an unconditional right to consideration until the second product is delivered. After the second product is delivered, the contract asset is reclassified to a receivable. If however, the customer is required to pay for each individual product 30 days after delivery of the product, the company debits Accounts Receivable and credits Sales Revenue after delivery of the first (and second) product.

606-10-45-2 If a customer pays consideration, or an entity has a right to an amount of consideration that is unconditional (that is, a receivable), before the entity transfers a good or service to the customer, the entity shall present the contract as a contract liability when the payment is made or the payment is due (whichever is earlier). A contract liability is an entity's obligation to transfer goods or services to a customer for which the entity has received consideration (or an amount of consideration is due) from the customer.

606-10-45-3 If an entity performs by transferring goods or services to a customer before the customer pays consideration or before payment is due, the entity shall present the contract as a contract asset, excluding any amounts presented as a receivable. A contract asset is an entity's right to consideration in exchange for goods or services that the entity has transferred to a customer.

In **Demo 7-6A**, we review three examples where revenue is recognized at a point in time. In **Demo 7-6B**, we review three examples where the satisfaction of at least one performance obligation is recognized as revenue over time.

Demo 7-6A LO7-6 Recognition of Revenue at a Point in Time

Demo MBC

Example One—Revenue Recognized at a Point in Time

A seller, REII Inc., enters into a contract to deliver customized ski equipment to a customer for $500 (cost is $250). The customer pays a $100 deposit upfront on October 15, 2020, while the remaining $400 ($500 − $100) is due on delivery, expected in three weeks. Prepare the journal entries required on October 15 and on November 7, 2020 (the date that the customized ski equipment is picked up by the customer and balance is paid in full).

Solution

Revenue is recognized on delivery of the ski equipment because that is the point at which control of the product is transferred to the customer. This means that only at this point is the fifth step of the revenue recognition process complete. Because the $100 was received in advance of the delivery of the product, REII Inc. will recognize deferred revenue (a contract liability). Deferred revenue will be reversed and recognized as revenue when delivery of the customized product takes place.

October 15, 2020—To record customer prepayment

Assets = Liabilities + Equity
+100 +100
Cash: 100 (debit) | Deferred Rev: 100 (credit)

Cash	100	
Deferred Revenue		100

November 7, 2020—To recognize revenue and reduce inventory

Assets = Liabilities + Equity
+100 +100
Cash: 100, 400 (debit) | Deferred Rev: 100 (debit), 100 (credit) | Sales Rev: 500 (credit)

Deferred Revenue	100	
Cash	400	
Sales Revenue		500

Assets = Liabilities + Equity
−250 −250
Inventory: 250 (credit) | COGS: 250 (debit)

Cost of Goods Sold	250	
Inventory		250

Example Two—Revenue Recognized at a Point in Time

Gapp Inc. sponsors a customer loyalty point program where customers earn one loyalty point for every $5 spent on clothing and accessories at any Gapp Inc. store or through online purchases. Loyalty program members can exchange accumulated loyalty points for free products at Gapp Inc. (such as one loyalty point equals $1 of free products). It is common for loyalty program members to accumulate and redeem loyalty points for free products. During June of 2020, customers purchased products with a sales value of $20,000, earning $4,000 in loyalty points. Based on past history of promotional programs, Gapp Inc. estimates a standalone selling price of $0.75 per loyalty point or $3,000 in total. The standalone selling price of the products purchased is $20,000.

Required

a. Assuming that there are two performance obligations (product sales and loyalty points), allocate the transaction price to the products and loyalty points.

b. Record the entry for sales for the month of June. (Ignore the cost entries.)

c. Assuming that 1,600 loyalty points were redeemed in June, and Gapp Inc. still expects 3,000 points to be redeemed in total, record the entry to recognize revenue on the redeemed loyalty points. (Ignore the cost entries.)

Solution

a. The transaction price would be allocated as follows (Step 4).

Performance Obligations	Transaction Price as Stated	Standalone Selling Price	Selling Price Ratio	Allocated Transaction Price*
Sale of product	$20,000	$20,000	20/23	$17,391 (20/23 × $20,000)
Loyalty points	—	3,000	3/23	2,609 (3/23 × $20,000)
	$20,000	$23,000	23/23	$20,000

*Amounts rounded.

continued

continued from previous page

b. Gapp Inc. records the following journal entry for the month of June for the transfer of control of product to the customer (point in time sale). Revenue allocated to the customer option (loyalty points) is deferred until the rewards are redeemed for additional product.

June 30, 2020—To record sales transaction

Cash	20,000	
Deferred Revenue		2,609
Sales Revenue		17,391

Assets	=	Liabilities	+	Equity
+20,000		+2,609		+17,391

Cash: 20,000 (debit)
Sales Rev: 17,391 (credit)
Deferred Rev: 2,609 (credit)

c. Gapp Inc. would recognize revenue related to the customer options for June for $1,391 or [(1,600 pts/3,000 pts) × $2,609]. Gapp Inc. records the following entry:

June 30, 2020—To record customer redemption of loyalty points

Deferred Revenue	1,391	
Sales Revenue		1,391

Assets	=	Liabilities	+	Equity
		−1,391		+1,391

Deferred Rev: 1,391 (debit) | 2,800 (credit)
Sales Rev: 17,200 (credit), 1,391 (credit)

Example Three—Revenue Recognized at a Point in Time

A contractor enters into a three-year construction contract with Dental Inc. to build an office building. The contract has the following conditions.

- The office building plan is based upon a standard model frequently built by the contractor.
- Non-refundable payments are required including a payment equal to 10% of the contract up front, interim billing totaling 50% of the contract at the end of 18 months, and 40% at the end of the contract if the project meets the prescribed requirements.
- Dental Inc. can cancel the contract at any time (with a termination penalty); any work in process is the property of the contractor. Any payments made to the contractor before the cancellation date remain with the contractor.
- Physical possession and title do not pass until completion of the contract.
- Total estimated contract revenue is $300 million and total estimated contract cost is $200 million.
- Year one cost is $120 million (including $20 million related to contractor-caused inefficiencies).

Determine the amount of revenue that the contractor should recognize during the first year of the contract.

Solution

First, the contractor must evaluate whether revenue should be recognized at a point in time or over time. In reviewing the revenue recognition criteria in **Exhibit 7-3**, this situation does not warrant revenue recognition over time.

- Dental Inc. does not enjoy use of the building or have control of the building over its life, as it does not own the work in process.
- The building has alternative uses (is not customized).
- The contractor does not have an enforceable right of payment for work to date. Payments are not based upon performance but on a preset schedule, thus, at any point in time, the contractor may not have been compensated for the work completed.

Therefore, no revenue (or expense) is recorded in 2020. Instead, revenue (and expense) would be recognized in income at the completion of the project when control of the building is transferred to Dental Inc.

Recognition of Revenue Over Time

LO7-6 **Demo 7-6B**

Demo MBC

Example One—Revenue Recognized Over Time

On June 1, 2020, Forde Auto Manufacturer sells for cash, 500, three-year maintenance contracts to its customers for $1,000,000. The customers will benefit from the maintenance contracts over the three-year protection period. The standalone selling price of each maintenance contract is $2,000. Prepare Forde's journal entry (1) to record the sale of maintenance contracts, and (2) to record any adjusting entry on June 30, 2020. Ignore cost entries.

continued

continued from previous page

Solution

Revenue on the maintenance contract is recognized over time because the customer will benefit from the service over the three-year period. The entries to record the deferral of revenue on June 1 and the entry to record the recognition of revenue on a straight-line basis follow.

Assets = Liabilities + Equity
+1,000,000 +1,000,000
Cash: 1,000,000 (debit)
Def Serv Rev: 1,000,000 (credit)

June 1, 2020—To defer service revenue

Cash	1,000,000	
Deferred Service Revenue		1,000,000

Assets = Liabilities + Equity
−27,778 +27,778
Def Serv Rev: 27,778 (debit) | 1,000,000 (credit)
Service Rev: 27,778 (credit)

June 30, 2020—To recognize revenue for one month

Deferred Service Revenue	27,778	
Service Revenue ($1,000,000 / 36 months)		27,778

Example Two—Includes Revenue Recognized Over Time

On January 1, 2020, Top Buys Inc. enters into a contract with a customer for a combined discounted selling price of $940 (stated to the customer as $700 for a computer, payable at the date of sale, and $240 for one year of computer service, payable at $20 per month). Standalone selling price of the computer is $960 and the standalone selling price of the computer service is $240. The allocation of the transaction price of $940 is calculated as follows (Step 4).

Performance Obligations	Transaction Price as Stated	Standalone Selling Price	Selling Price Ratio	Allocated Transaction Price
Computer	$700	$ 960	960/1,200 or 4/5	$752 (4/5 × $940)
Services	240	240	240/1,200 or 1/5	188 (1/5 × $940)
	$940	$1,200	1,200/1,200 or 5/5	$940

Record the journal entries for Top Buys Inc. on (a) January 1 at the point of sale, and (b) January 31, 2020, the date of the first monthly payment. Assume that service revenue is recognized on a straight-line basis.

Solution

The allocated transaction price for the computer ($752) is recognized as revenue when the customer takes control of the computer at the time of sale. The $188 service revenue is recognized over the one-year contract term at $16.00 per month ($188/12, rounded). A contract asset of $52 ($752 − $700) is established at the time that the revenue for the computer is recorded. The contract asset represents the difference between the revenue recognized (allocated transaction price of $752) and the consideration received (amount billed to the customer for the computer of $700). This asset is reduced each month by the portion of the monthly computer service fee that was allocated to the computer of $4.00 per month ($52/12, rounded). On January 1, 2020, the following entry would be reported upon the sale of the computer.

Assets = Liabilities + Equity
+700 +752
+52
Cash: 700 (debit)
Sales Rev: 752 (credit)
Contract Asset: 52 (debit)

January 1, 2020—To record sale of computer

Cash	700	
Contract Asset	52	
Sales Revenue		752

On the first date of the monthly service payment (and for each of the 11 months remaining in the contract), Top Buys Inc. would record the following entry.

Assets = Liabilities + Equity
+20 +16
−4
Cash: 700, 20 (debit)
Sales Rev: 752, 16 (credit)
Contract Asset: 52 (debit) | 4 (credit)

January 31, 2020—To record service revenue

Cash ($240/12)	20	
Contract Asset ($52/12)*		4
Service Revenue ($188/12)*		16

*Amounts rounded.

Example Three—Includes Revenue Recognized Over Time

A contractor enters into a three-year construction contract with a customer to build an office building. The contract has the following characteristics.

continued

continued from previous page

- The office building is highly customized to the customer's specifications.
- Non-refundable, interim progress payments are required.
- The customer can cancel the contract at any time (with a termination penalty); any work in process is the property of the customer.
- Total estimated contract revenue is $300,000 and total estimated contract cost is $200,000.
- Year one cost is $140,000 (including $20,000 related to contractor-caused inefficiencies).

Determine the amount of revenue that the contractor should recognize during the first year of the contract, assuming that the company uses the cost-to-cost method to estimate progress toward satisfaction of its performance obligation.

Solution

First, the contractor must evaluate whether revenue should be recognized at a point in time or over time. In reviewing the revenue recognition criteria, this situation does warrant revenue recognition over time because:

- Customer has control of the building over its life, as it owns land and the work in process.
- The building is highly customized, thus built for a specific use.
- The contractor does have an enforceable right of payment for work to date because progress billings are required.

Therefore, revenue will be recorded during the project, over time.

Progress toward satisfaction of the performance obligation is estimated as follows. Contract inefficiencies are not included in the cost-to-cost measurement.

$$\textbf{Percent complete} = \frac{\$120{,}000 \text{ (Costs incurred to date excluding inefficiencies)}}{\$200{,}000 \text{ (Total estimated costs)}} = 60\%$$

Computation of recognized revenue

Revenue ($300,000 × 60%)	$180,000
Costs (excluding inefficiencies)	120,000
Gross profit	60,000
Contract inefficiencies	20,000
Adjusted contract margin	$ 40,000

Under the cost-to-cost method, 60% of revenue is recognized (or $180,000) which results in a gross profit of $60,000 and an adjusted contract margin of $40,000.

Licenses

A license establishes the rights of a customer to intellectual property of an entity (such as software, motion pictures, music, franchises, and patents). The revenue recognition standard provides guidance on whether to recognize revenue over time or at a point in time for a license depending on whether the customer has the right to access or use the intellectual property.

606-10-55-58a An entity should account for a promise to provide a customer with a right to access the entity's intellectual property as a performance obligation satisfied over time because the customer will simultaneously receive and consume the benefit from the entity's performance of providing access to its intellectual property as the performance occurs.

606-10-55-58b An entity's promise to provide a customer with the right to use its intellectual property is satisfied at a point in time.

To determine whether a customer has the right to access or the right to use the intellectual property, the seller considers the classification of intellectual property.

- **Functional intellectual property** Functional intellectual property has significant standalone functionality. For example, if a license transfers a right to use intellectual property, the intellectual property has significant standalone functionality. Thus, the customer's use of the intellectual property is not affected by the seller's continuing activity. A functional intellectual property has the ability to perform a task or be played, such as game software or film content. In this case, revenue would generally be recognized at a single point in time. (If, however, the functionality of the intellectual property is expected to substantively change during the license term and the customer is required to use the updated property, the license grants a right to access.)

- **Symbolic intellectual property** Symbolic intellectual property does not have significant standalone functionality: substantially all of the utility is derived from association with the seller or the seller's ongoing activities. If a license provides the right of access to the seller's intellectual property, the customer's use of the intellectual property is affected by the seller's continuing activity. In this case, revenue would generally be recognized over time. Symbolic intellectual property includes items such as brands, trade names, and logos.

In **Demo 7-6C**, we review the process of revenue recognition of a license.

Demo 7-6C LO7-6 Recognition of License Revenue

On January 1, 2020, franchisor grants a license to a franchisee to use the franchisor's trade name of Tasty Taco and to sell the Tasty Taco menu for 10 years. The license is a contract between the franchisee and the franchisor. The franchisor receives a fixed fee of $500,000 on January 1, 2020, plus a royalty equal to 5% of customer's sales over the term of the license of 10 years. In addition to the license, the franchisor provides restaurant equipment for $150,000 (cost of $130,000), due upon delivery of the equipment on February 1, 2020. The price of the equipment and the license fee represent standalone selling prices. The franchisor expects to provide services related to the license evenly over the license term. These activities are customary business practices of the franchisor and include product improvements, pricing strategies, advertising campaigns, and operational suggestions to support the franchise name and menu. None of these activities directly transfers goods or services to the franchisee.

Record the journal entry on (a) January 1, 2020, the date of contract, (b) February 1, 2020, the date of the delivery of the equipment, and (c) December 31, 2020, assuming that the franchisee reported sales of $350,000 for 2020.

Solution

The contract has two distinct performance obligations, a promise to grant a license and a promise to transfer equipment. Each promise is distinct because the license and the equipment are not interdependent. The franchisee benefits from the license separately from the equipment (i.e. the equipment could be used for other purposes or even be sold for cash.)

The transaction price consists of fixed consideration ($500,000 plus $150,000) and variable consideration (fee based upon sales). Because the license and equipment were sold at standalone selling prices, the price allocated to the license will be $500,000 plus the fee based upon sales, and the price allocated to the equipment will be $150,000. The fee based upon sales is allocated entirely to the franchise license because it relates entirely to the franchisor's promise to grant the franchise license.

Because the franchisor's continuing activities affect the value of the franchise over the 10-year period, revenue will be recognized over time. Therefore, the franchisor would defer the initial license fee on January 1, 2020, and recognize revenue over the license term.

Assets	=	Liabilities	+	Equity
+500,000		+500,000		

Cash: 500,000 (debit) | Def License Rev: 500,000 (credit)

January 1, 2020—To record receipt and deferral of license fee

Cash	500,000	
Deferred License Revenue		500,000

On February 1, 2020, the revenue (and cost) related to the equipment will be recognized when control of the equipment is transferred to the franchisee.

Assets	=	Liabilities	+	Equity
+150,000				+150,000

Cash: 500,000; 150,000 (debit) | Sales Rev: 150,000 (credit)

Assets	=	Liabilities	+	Equity
−130,000				−130,000

Inventory: 130,000 (credit) | COGS: 130,000 (debit)

February 1, 2020—To record transfer of control of equipment

Cash	150,000	
Sales Revenue		150,000
Cost of Goods Sold	130,000	
Inventory		130,000

Because the service related to the license is provided evenly over the lease term, the fixed license revenue will be recognized on a straight-line basis. The franchisor would record the following entry on December 31, 2020.

continued

continued from previous page

December 31, 2020—To record franchise revenue

Deferred License Revenue ($500,000/10)	50,000	
Accounts Receivable ($350,000 × 0.05)	17,500	
Franchise Revenue		67,500

Assets	=	Liabilities	+	Equity
+17,500		−50,000		+67,500

Accounts Rec: 17,500 (debit)
Def License Rev: 50,000 (debit) | 500,000 (credit)
Franchise Rev: 67,500 (credit)

The royalty fee based on franchisee revenue is recognized as revenue as sales of the franchisee are recognized.

Revenue Recognition LO7-6 REVIEW 7-6

Answer the requirements for each of the following separate cases.

a. Face North Co. required an advance payment of $200 on January 15, 2020, from a customer for a customized order of sweatshirts. The customer picked up the sweatshirts on January 31, 2020, and paid the remaining balance of $100. Determine the amount of revenue that Face North Co. would record on January 15, 2020, and January 31, 2020.

b. Roote Co. sold backpacks to customers in September of 2020 at full price for $10,000. At the point of sale, Roote Co. provided customers 100 coupons for $40 off on the purchase of a backpack in October 2020. The coupon is considered a separate performance obligation. Roote Co. estimates the standalone selling price of the backpacks to be $10,000 and the standalone selling price of the coupons to be $2,000 ($40 × 50 coupons expected to be redeemed). Determine the revenue that Roote Co. records in September for the sale of full price backpacks, and the amount of revenue deferred for the coupons.

c. On January 15, 2020, Construction Inc. entered into a contract with a customer to build an addition to its corporate headquarters for $4,000,000. The customer owns the construction in process during the construction process and the customer is under obligation to pay for any work completed, even if the contract is cancelled. The addition is expected to be completed in two years for a total cost of $2,400,000. Actual costs incurred through December 31, 2020, are $1,400,000. Determine the amount of revenue to record in 2020.

d. On January 15, 2020, Quality Inc. entered into a contract with a retailer to build a parking ramp for $2,000,000. Quality Inc. owns the construction in process and the parking lot is located in a commercial district with access to a number of businesses. The parking ramp is expected to be completed in two years for a total cost of $1,600,000. Actual costs incurred through December 31, 2020, are $900,000. Determine the amount of revenue to record in 2020.

e. On January 1, 2020, Franchisee Inc. enters into a contract with Franchisor Inc. for the right (beginning immediately) to operate a fast food location, using the company's (a) logo, design, and advertising materials, (b) menu items, recipes, and supplier contacts, (c) store designs, and (d) daily operating instructions for a five-year period. The upfront fee of $250,000 also includes accounting services for the franchise for one year only, beginning on January 1, 2020. The standalone selling price of the franchise services and accounting services are $245,000 and $5,000, respectively. Determine the amount of revenue to recognize for Franchisor Inc. on January 1, 2020, and December 31, 2020.

More Practice: 7-35, 7-37, 7-69, 7-70, 7-72

Solution on p. 7-75.

Recognize revenue after a contract modification LO 7-7

It is not uncommon for modifications to contracts to take place at some point during the contract term. **Contract modifications** create or alter the rights and obligations of parties to the contract.

Contract Modification (LO 7-7 Overview)

- Adds distinct goods or services at standalone selling price(s)
  - Account for as a new separate contract
- Adds distinct goods or services not at standalone selling price(s)
  - Terminate original contract and account for under new combined contract
- Adds nondistinct goods or services
  - Cumulative catch-up adjustment

606-10-25-10 A contract modification is a change in the scope or price (or both) of a contract that is approved by the parties to the contract . . . A contract modification exists when the parties to a contract approve a modification that either creates new or changes existing enforceable rights and obligations of the parties to the contract. A contract modification could be approved in writing, by oral agreement, or implied by customary business practices.

Accounting standards guide the treatment of contract modifications depending on whether the modification provides for additional distinct goods or services at standalone selling prices. The three options are outlined below and illustrated in **Demo 7-7**.

Contract Modification			
	New Separate Contract; No Change to Original Contract	**New Combined Contract after Terminating Original Contract**	**Cumulative Catch-up with No New Contract**
Adds distinct goods/services	Yes	Yes	No—Additional goods or services are not distinct
Increase in contract price is reflective of standalone prices	Yes	No—Contract price increases are not reflective of standalone prices of additional goods and services	Not applicable

For a modification to be accounted for as a new separate contract, both conditions must be met: the modification provides distinct goods or services and the change in contract price reflects standalone prices. For example, a manufacturer modifies a contract to sell additional distinct goods at an observable standalone selling price. In this case, revenue is recognized under the new and old contract separately.

A contract modification is treated prospectively if the additional goods and services are distinct, but the contract price is not adjusted for standalone prices. This means that the remaining consideration will be allocated to the remaining performance obligations, including those added in the modification. For example, a service contract is modified to extend service for an additional year at a reduced rate (below the standalone selling price.) In this case, the original contract is terminated and a new combined contract is created for all remaining goods and services. The revenue for all remaining goods or services to be provided is recorded at a **blended price** of the new and old contract.

However, if the additional goods or services are not distinct, the modification is accounted for as a cumulative catch-up adjustment. For example, a contractor and customer modify a long-term construction contract to build an office building which causes an increase in costs and the transaction price. In this case, the contract modification is considered part of the original contract and is therefore part of a single performance obligation. The effect of the modification on the transaction price and on percentage of completion are recorded as an adjustment (increase or decrease) to revenue on the date of the contract modification.

Demo 7-7 LO7-7 Revenue Recognition with a Contract Modification

Demo MBC

Example One—Contract Modification Resulting in a New Separate Contract

Over a 9-month period, Diaz Co. promises to sell 220 units of product to one of its customers for $2,200 ($10 per unit). After Diaz Co. has transferred control of 100 units of product to the customer, the contract is modified to require the delivery of an additional 50 units (a total of 270 units) to the customer. When the contract is modified, the price of the contract increases by $400 ($8 × 50 units). The standalone selling price of the 50 additional units at the time of the contract modification is $8 per unit, and the additional units are distinct from the original units. Determine the amount of revenue that will be recognized for (1) the 120 units remaining in the original contract, and (2) the 50 additional units resulting from the contract modification.

Solution

Because the 50 new units are distinct and have a standalone price, the agreement to sell the 50 units is considered a *new separate contract* and is accounted for as follows.

Remaining Contract Revenue to Recognize		
Remaining sales in the original contract:	120 units (220 − 100) × $10 (original contract price)	= $1,200
Sales under the contract modification:	50 units × $8 (modified contract price)	= 400
Total remaining revenue to recognize.		$1,600

continued

continued from previous page

Example Two—Contract Modification Resulting in a New Combined Contract (adapted from ASC 606-10-55-114)

Assume the circumstances with Diaz Co. in Example One are the same except that the customer identifies a quality issue unique to the first 100 units purchased. As a result, Diaz Co. agrees to a price concession on the additional 50 units to compensate for the quality issue. The price of the additional 50 units is determined to be $5 per unit. (Standalone selling price of the new units is still considered to be $8 per unit.) Determine the amount of revenue that will be recognized for the (1) 120 units remaining in the original contract, and (2) 50 additional units resulting from the contract modification.

Solution

While the additional 50 units are distinct, the units are not sold at their standalone selling price because the price concession is related to quality deficiencies of the previous units of product sold. Therefore, the modification results in the termination of the original contract and the creation of a new combined contract. Revenue per unit for the remaining units will be recorded at a blended price of the new and old contract.

Remaining Contract Revenue to Recognize

Remaining sales in the original contract:	120 units (220 − 100) × $10	$1,200
Sales under the contract modification:	50 units × $5	250
		$1,450
Blended revenue per unit:	$1,450/170 units (120 + 50).	$ 8.53
Total remaining revenue to recognize	$8.53 × 170 units.	$1,450

Example Three—Contract Modification Resulting in a Cumulative Catch-Up Adjustment

A builder enters into a two-year contract with a customer for $350,000 to manufacture customized equipment (a single performance obligation). After 6 months, the builder and customer agree to modify the floor plans which results in an increase in both the transaction price and total expected costs by $75,000 and $50,000, respectively. Is the contract modification treated as (1) a new contract or (2) as part of the original contract? What type of adjustment is required?

Solution

Contact modification is treated as part of the original contract and accounted for with cumulative catch-up adjustment. If the company uses the cost-to-cost method to measure its progress toward satisfying the performance obligation, the percentage of completion takes into account the adjusted transaction price and estimated total contract costs. The updated percentage of completion is applied to total contract revenue to measure revenue recognized to date.

Contract Modification LO7-7 REVIEW 7-7

Answer the requirements for each of the following separate cases.

a. On January 1, 2020, Manufac Co. enters into a contract with a retailer to sell 250 distinct items of merchandise for $50,000 ($200 per item) over a 12-month period. On March 31, 2020, the parties to the contract agree to a contract modification to add an additional 80 items for $220 each within the original contract period. The $220 per unit price for the additional items represents the standalone selling price of these items on the date of the modification. If 200 items had already been sold under the original contract, how would revenue be allocated to the remaining 50 items under the original contract and the 80 items per the contract modification?

b. Assume the same information as in part *a* except that the new items under the contract modification are not sold at the standalone selling price (the standalone selling price is not $220 per unit). If 200 items had already been sold under the original contract, how would revenue be allocated to the remaining 50 items under the original contract and the 80 items per the contract modification?

Review MBC

More Practice: 7-40, 7-41, 7-73

Solution on p. 7-75.

LO 7-8 Recognize revenue in more complex revenue arrangements

LO 7-8 Overview

Complex Revenue Arrangements
- Bill-and-hold arrangement
- Consignment arrangement
- Repurchase arrangement
- Principal/agent arrangement

In this section we explore four situations that add complexity to Step 5 of revenue recognition in determining whether control of the asset has transferred to the customer: (1) bill-and-hold arrangements (**Demo 7-8A**), (2) consignment arrangements (**Demo 7-8B**), (3) repurchase arrangements—**Demo 7-8C**, and (4) principal/agent arrangements—**Demo 7-8D**.

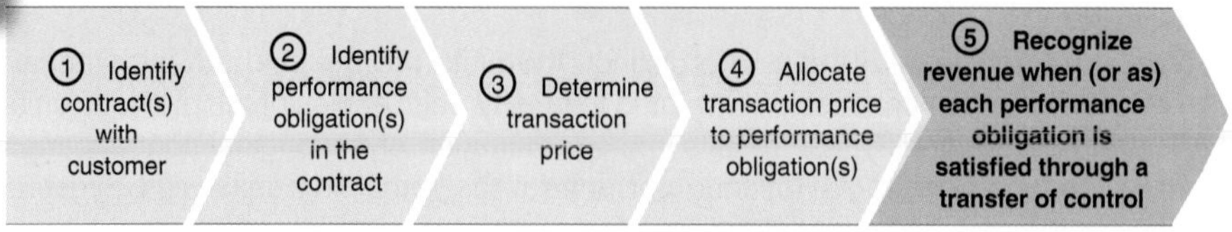
① Identify contract(s) with customer
② Identify performance obligation(s) in the contract
③ Determine transaction price
④ Allocate transaction price to performance obligation(s)
⑤ Recognize revenue when (or as) each performance obligation is satisfied through a transfer of control

Bill-and-Hold Arrangement

A **bill-and-hold arrangement** takes place when a customer is billed for goods that are completed and ready to deliver, but the seller does not actually ship the goods until a later time period. Even though the physical asset has not passed to the customer, the seller must still evaluate whether control has passed to the customer. The revenue recognition standard identifies the following additional criteria (beyond the criteria previously outlined for a transfer of control in **Exhibit 7-1**) that *all* must be met to determine whether control has passed to the customer. This criteria prevents companies from shifting sales into the current period (overstating revenue) when the risks and rewards of ownership have *not* passed to the customer in the current period.

606-10-55-83

a. The reason for the bill-and-hold arrangement must be substantive (for example, the customer has requested the arrangement).
b. The product must be identified separately as belonging to the customer.
c. The product currently must be ready for physical transfer to the customer.
d. The entity [seller] cannot have the ability to use the product or to direct it to another customer.

Demo 7-8A **LO7-8** **Transfer of Control under a Bill-and-Hold Arrangement**

Demo MBC

Brow Inc. enters into a contract during August of 2020 to supply 1,000 units of product to a retailer. Brow Inc. must deliver the units in 2020 at a date to be specified by the retailer. The retailer expects to have sufficient shelf space at the time of delivery but does not currently have the shelf space to hold the order. Brow Inc. has inventory of 200,000 units of product, excluding the 1,000 units relating to the contract with the retailer. Even though the 1,000 units of product are interchangeable with other units, the 1,000 units are ready for immediate shipment at the request of the customer, segregated from inventory (beginning on September 1, 2020) and will not be used to fulfill other orders. Payment for the 1,000 units is due September 30, 2020. The units are sold at $50 per unit while the cost to Brow Inc. is $30 per unit. Record the entry for Brow Inc. on September 1, 2020.

Solution

Brow Inc. should recognize revenue on September 1, 2020, when the 1,000 units are segregated from the rest of the inventory because the inventory cannot be used to fulfill other orders and is ready for transfer to the customer. The reason for the bill-and-hold transaction is substantive (lack of shelf space). Brow Inc. records the following entry on September 1, 2020.

September 1, 2020—To record sale of units in bill-and-hold arrangement

Accounts Receivable	50,000	
Sales Revenue (1,000 × $50)		50,000
Cost of Goods Sold	30,000	
Inventory (1,000 × $30)		30,000

Assets = Liabilities + Equity
+50,000 +50,000
Accounts Rec: 50,000 (debit) | Sales Rev: 50,000 (credit)

Assets = Liabilities + Equity
−30,000 −30,000
Inventory: 30,000 (credit) | COGS: 30,000 (debit)

Consignment Arrangement

A **consignment arrangement** occurs when a company (**consignor**) ships goods to a distributor (**consignee**), but retains control of the goods until a predetermined event occurs, such as the sale of the product to a customer. This means that even though the consignee can have physical possession of the asset, the consignee might not have control of the asset. The following indicators from the revenue recognition standard can be used to evaluate whether an agreement is a consignment arrangement.

606-10-55-80

- The product is controlled by the entity [consignor] until a specified event occurs, such as the sale of the product to a customer of the dealer [consignee], or until a specified period expires.
- The entity [consignor] is able to require the return of the product or transfer the product to a third party (such as another dealer).
- The dealer [consignee] does not have an unconditional obligation to pay for the product (although it might be required to pay a deposit).

The consignee exercises due diligence in holding the product and selling the product for the consignor. The consignee forwards the selling price to the consignor after the product is sold while the consignor pays the consignee a commission related to the sale. The consignor carries the inventory on its balance sheet; the consignee does not carry the inventory on its balance sheet. The consigner records sales at the selling price of the product while the consignee records commission revenue.

Transfer of Control under a Consignment Arrangement LO7-8 Demo 7-8B

Demo MBC

On June 1, Consignor Inc. ships 50 items of inventory to Consignee Inc. who has agreed to sell the products to the end customers in exchange for a 10% commission on the sale. The products sell to the end customer for $250 while the cost to Consignor Inc. for each product is $140. On June 30, 2020, 25 items are sold by Consignee Inc. for cash, and Consignor Inc. is automatically notified at month-end. On July 2, 2020, Consignee Inc. remits cash less commission to Consignor Inc. electronically. Record the entries on June 1, June 30, and July 2, 2020, for Consignor Inc. and for Consignee Inc.

Solution

June 1, 2020—Consignor Inc. ships products to Consignee Inc.
No entries required (Consignor may or may not record a journal entry to reclassify inventory from finished goods inventory to consigned inventory).

Consignee Inc.
June 30, 2020—To record cash collection on sale of products

Cash (25 × $250)	6,250	
Commission Revenue (0.10 × $6,250)		625
Payable to Consignor ($6,250 − $625)		5,625

Assets = Liabilities + Equity
+6,250 = +5,625 + +625
Cash: 6,250 (Dr) | Pay to Consignor: 5,625 (Cr) | Commission Rev: 625 (Cr)

Consignor Inc.
June 30, 2020—To record sale of inventory held by Consignee Inc.

Due from Consignee ($6,250 − $625)	5,625	
Commission Expense (0.10 × $6,250)	625	
Sales Revenue (25 × $250)		6,250

Assets = Liabilities + Equity
+5,625 = + −625, +6,250
Due from Consignee: 5,625 (Dr) | Sales Rev: 6,250 (Cr) | Commission Exp: 625 (Dr)

Cost of Goods Sold	3,500	
Inventory (25 × $140)		3,500

Assets = Liabilities + Equity
−3,500 = + −3,500
Inventory: 3,500 (Cr) | COGS: 3,500 (Dr)

Consignee Inc.
July 2, 2020—To record remittance of cash (net) to Consignor Inc.

Payable to Consignor	5,625	
Cash		5,625

Assets = Liabilities + Equity
−5,625 = −5,625 +
Cash: 6,250 | 5,625 | Pay to Consignor: 5,625 | 5,625

Consignor Inc.
July 2, 2020—To record receipt of cash (net) from Consignee Inc.

Cash	5,625	
Due from Consignee		5,625

Assets = Liabilities + Equity
+5,625
−5,625
Due from Consignee: 5,625 | 5,625 | Cash: 5,625 (Dr)

Repurchase Arrangement

A repurchase right is an obligation to repurchase a good after it is sold to a customer. This right might be specified in a sales contract or in a separate arrangement with the customer. Repurchase rights can be a:

- Seller's obligation to repurchase the good (**forward arrangement**).
- Seller's right to repurchase the good (**call option**).
- Customer's right to require the seller to repurchase the good (**put option**).

Forward Arrangement and Call Option

Revenue is not recognized in the forward arrangement or call option because the seller's obligation or repurchase rights *limit the customer's ability to control the good.* If the repurchase price is less than the original selling price of the asset, the transaction is accounted for as a lease (see chapter on lease accounting). If the repurchase price is equal to or greater than the original selling price of the asset, the transaction is accounted for as a financing agreement. In this case, a liability is recorded and any corresponding interest is recognized.

Forward Arrangement or Call Option (ASC 606-10-55-68)

Repurchase price < Original selling price → Lease
Repurchase price ≥ Original selling price → Financing Agreement

Put Option

In a put option, *the customer has control over the good* and has the choice of retaining the good, selling it to a third party, or selling it back to the seller. Thus, the accounting treatment depends on whether the repurchase price is less than or greater than the expected market value of the asset. If the repurchase price is less than or equal to the expected market value, the customer is expected to retain the good, so this is treated as a sale with the right or return. However, if the repurchase price is greater than the expected market value, the customer has a significant economic incentive to sell back to the seller (exercise the put option). In this case, and similar to the forward arrangement and call option described above, the seller accounts for the transaction as a lease if the repurchase price is less than the original selling price. If the repurchase price is equal to or greater than the original selling price, the transaction is accounted for as a financing agreement.

Put Option (ASC 606-10-55-72 to 76)

If Repurchase price ≤ Expected market value → Sale with Right of Return
If Repurchase price > Expected market value
  Repurchase price < Original selling price → Lease
  Repurchase price ≥ Original selling price → Financing Agreement

Demo 7-8C **LO7-8** **Transfer of Control under Repurchase Arrangements**

Demo MBC

Example One—Forward Arrangement in which Repurchase Price Exceeds Original Sales Price
Manufacturing Inc. enters into a contract to sell equipment on January 1, 2020, to a customer, Bell Corp., for $51,440. As part of the contract, Manufacturing Inc. agrees to repurchase this equipment two years later for $60,000. The interest rate for a financing arrangement with commensurate risk is 8%. The equipment is repurchased from Bell Corp. on December 31, 2021, for the agreed upon repurchase price. Record the entries for Manufacturing Inc. on January 1, 2020, December 31, 2020, and December 31, 2021, ignoring the cost entries.

Solution
Because the seller is obligated to repurchase the equipment, the transaction is a *forward arrangement.* The transaction is accounted for as a financing agreement (not a sale) because the repurchase price is greater than the original sales price. The equipment is not derecognized by Manufacturing Inc. because it is considered collateral for the loan rather than a sale of equipment to Bell.

Assets = Liabilities + Equity
+51,440 +51,440
Cash: 51,440 (Dr) | Liab to Bell: 51,440 (Cr)

January 1, 2020—To record initiation of financing transaction

Cash	51,440	
Liability to Bell Corp.		51,440

continued

continued from previous page

December 31, 2020—To record interest on financing transaction

Interest Expense	4,115	
Liability to Bell Corp. ($51,440 × 0.08)		4,115

Assets = Liabilities + Equity
+51,440 +51,440
Liab to Bell: 51,440; 4,115 | Interest Exp: 4,115

December 31, 2021—To record interest on financing transaction

Interest Expense	4,445	
Liability to Bell Corp. [($51,440 + $4,115) × 0.08]		4,445

Assets = Liabilities + Equity
+4,445 −4,445
Liab to Bell: 51,440; 4,115; 4,445 | Interest Exp: 4,115; 4,445

December 31, 2021—To record settlement of liability

Liability to Bell Corp. ($51,440 + $4,115 + $4,445)	60,000	
Cash		60,000

Assets = Liabilities + Equity
−60,000 −60,000
Cash: 51,440 | 60,000 — Liab to Bell: 60,000 | 51,440; 4,115; 4,445; —

Example Two—Put Option in which Repurchase Price Exceeds Expected Market Value
Refer to Example One but assume instead that the contract gave the option to the customer to require the seller to repurchase the asset for $65,000 when the fair value of the asset at the end of two years is expected to be $61,000. The repurchase price of $65,000 is greater than the original selling price of the equipment of $51,440.

Solution
Because the customer can require the seller to repurchase the asset, it is considered a *put option.* In this case, the customer would have an economic incentive to sell back the equipment because the expected fair value is less than the repurchase price. ***Therefore, the transactions are recorded as a financing arrangement as shown above in Example One for the forward option.***

Example Three—Put Option in which Expected Market Value Exceeds Repurchase Price
Refer to Example Two but assume instead that the repurchase price is $61,000 and the fair value is expected to be $65,000. Again, the repurchase price (of $61,000) is greater than the original selling price of the equipment of $51,440.

Solution
In this case, the repurchase is unlikely so the transaction is treated as a sale with a right of return. The seller estimates the refund liability to be zero because it does not expect the customer to return the equipment.

January 1, 2020—To record sale of equipment

Cash	51,440	
Sales Revenue		51,440

Assets = Liabilities + Equity
+51,440 +51,440
Cash: 51,440 | Sales Rev: 51,440

Principal/Agent Arrangement

A **principal** promises to provide goods or services to its customers. An **agent** arranges for goods or services to be provided by the principal to an end customer, usually for a fee. A principal (not an agent) has substantive control of the goods or services before they are transferred to a customer. Indicators to consider in deciding who has control of the goods or services before transfer include:

- Who is primarily responsible for fulfilling the promise to provide a good or service?
- Who bears inventory risk before transfer to the customer?
- Who has discretion in establishing prices for the goods or services?

Accounting implications of being an agent or principal follow.

- **Principal** Recognize revenue at *the gross amount* paid by the customer and recognize the full cost of the product or service. Revenue is recognized when control of the good or service is transferred from the principal to the customer.
- **Agent** Recognize revenue in the *amount of the fee or commission it expects to be entitled to* for facilitating the transfer of goods or services. Revenue is recognized when the agent fulfills its performance obligation to facilitate a transaction between a principal and a customer.

606-10-55-37B When (or as) an entity that is a principal satisfies a performance obligation, the entity recognizes revenue in the gross amount of consideration to which it expects to be entitled in exchange for the specified good or service transferred.

606-10-55-38 An entity is an agent if the entity's performance obligation is to arrange for the provision of the specified good or service by another party. An entity that is an agent does not control the specified good or service provided by another party before that good or service is transferred to the customer. When (or as) an entity that is an agent satisfies a performance obligation, the entity recognizes revenue in the amount of any fee or commission to which it expects to be entitled in exchange for arranging for the specified goods or services to be provided by the other party.

Demo 7-8D LO7-8 Estimating Revenue for Principals and Agents

Demo MBC

Example One—Recognizing Revenue as a Principal

Find-a-Hotel Inc. negotiates with major hotel chains to obtain access to rooms at reduced rates and sells the overnight stays to its customers through its website. Find-a-Hotel Inc. contracts with hotel chains to buy a specific number of overnight stays at agreed-upon rates and must pay for these overnight stays regardless of whether it is able to resell them. Customers search for available overnight stays on Find-a-Hotel Inc.'s website where overnight stays are priced according to the discretion of Find-a-Hotel Inc. After purchase, Find-a-Hotel Inc. emails the confirmation number to the customer and resolves any booking service complaints. The hotel chains fulfill the obligation of providing the hotel stay and remedies for service dissatisfaction with the hotel stay.

On June 1, 2020, Find-a-Hotel Inc. purchases a room from a hotel chain in Miami for $75 for an overnight stay. A customer purchases the overnight stay through Find-a-Hotel Inc. on its website for $90 on June 7, 2020, to be used on June 10, 2020.

a. Determine whether Find-a-Hotel Inc. is a principal or an agent.
b. Record Find-a-Hotel Inc.'s entries on June 1, 2020, on June 7, 2020, and on June 10, 2020.

Solution

a. Find-a-Hotel Inc. is the **principal** and should recognize revenue at the gross amount charged to customers. Find-a-Hotel Inc. controls the overnight stays prior to transfer of the hotel stay to the customer. Find-a-Hotel has the ability to direct the use of the overnight stays, has the inventory risk in holding the overnight stays and has discretion in pricing the overnight stays. The indicators support Find-a-Hotel Inc. as the principal.

b. Find-a-Hotel Inc. would record the following journal entry to record sales at the gross amount of $90, and the cost of purchase for a service performed that day.

June 1, 2020—To record purchase of overnight stay

Inventory	75	
Cash		75

Assets = Liabilities + Equity
+75
−75
Inventory: 75 | ; Cash: | 75

Find-a-Hotel Inc. would record revenue at the time that control of the overnight stay is transferred to the end customer from Find-a-Hotel Inc. on June 10, 2020. Therefore, revenue would be deferred as a contract liability by Find-a-Hotel Inc. when cash is collected on June 7, 2020.

June 7, 2020—To record sale of overnight stay to end customer

Cash	90	
Deferred Revenue		90

Assets = Liabilities + Equity
+90 +90
Cash: 90 | 75 ; Deferred Rev: | 90

June 10, 2020—To record revenue for sale of overnight stay

Deferred Revenue	90	
Sales Revenue		90

Assets = Liabilities + Equity
−90 +90
Deferred Rev: 90 | 90 ; Sales Rev: | 90

Cost of Goods Sold	75	
Inventory		75

Assets = Liabilities + Equity
−75 −75
Inventory: 75 | 75 ; COGS: 75 |

continued

continued from previous page

Example Two—Recognizing Revenue as an Agent

Refer to Example One but assume instead that Find-a-Hotel Inc. enters into a contract with a major hotel chain to sell its rooms online. Find-a-Hotel Inc. facilitates payments between the customer and the hotel chain. The price of the overnight stays are set by the hotel chain and Find-a-Hotel Inc. receives a 10% commission on each overnight stay sold through its website. Find-a-Hotel Inc. is not responsible for any hotel cancellations. The hotel chain fulfills the obligation of providing the overnight stay and remedies for service dissatisfaction.

Find-a-Hotel Inc. advertises available hotel rooms from various hotel chains on its website. A customer purchases an overnight stay through Find-a-Hotel Inc. on its website for $90 on June 7, 2020, to be used on June 10, 2020. Find-a-Hotel collects the full amount from the customer and electronically forwards this amount, less its commission, to the hotel chain on June 8, 2020.

a. Determine whether Find-a-Hotel Inc. is a principal or an agent.
b. Record Find-a-Hotel Inc.'s entries on June 7, 2020, on June 8, 2020, and on June 10, 2020.

Solution

a. Find-a-Hotel Inc. is the **agent**, facilitating a transaction between the principal (hotel chain) and the customer. Find-a-Hotel Inc. does not control the overnight stays before they are transferred to the customer. Find-a-Hotel Inc. does not control the price of the overnight stays, nor is it responsible for any cancellations by the customer.
b. Find-a-Hotel Inc. should record revenue when the overnight stays are purchased by the customers. Find-a-Hotel Inc. would record the following journal entry to record the collection of cash from the customer.

June 7, 2020—To record sale of collection of cash from customer

Cash	90	
Accounts Payable (hotel chain) ($90 × 0.90)		81
Commission Revenue ($90 × 0.10)		9

Assets = Liabilities + Equity
+90 +81 +9
Cash: 90 |
Accounts Payable: | 81
Commission Rev: | 9

June 8, 2020—To record payment to hotel chain

Accounts Payable	81	
Cash		81

Assets = Liabilities + Equity
−81 −81
Cash: 90 | 81
Accounts Payable: 81 | 81

June 10, 2020—Customer stays the night
Find-a-Hotel records no entry on June 10, 2020, because revenue was recorded at the date that Find-a-Hotel facilitated the transaction between the hotel chain and the customer.

Complex Revenue Arrangements LO7-8 REVIEW 7-8

Review MBC

Answer the requirements for each of the following separate complex revenue cases.

a. On December 31, 2020, Batteries Inc. sold 5,000 batteries to a retail customer with payment terms net 30, with shipment scheduled for February 15, 2021. On December 31, 2020, the units are clearly segregated in Batteries Inc.'s warehouse for shipment to the customer, but the units may be used to fulfill other customer orders as long as the units are replaced before the scheduled shipment date. Determine the type of complex revenue arrangement and the date that Batteries Inc. should record revenue for the sale of the 5,000 batteries to its customer.
b. On February 1, 2020, Supplier Inc. shipped product to Chocolate Inc. with a sales value of $5,000. Chocolate Inc. entered into a contract with Supplier Inc. in which it only is responsible for purchasing the product that it sells to the end customer. Any unused product can be returned to Supplier Inc. at no cost to Chocolate Inc. Also, Supplier Inc. can recall any unsold product held by Chocolate Inc. at any time for sale at other locations. For the month of February, Chocolate Inc. sold $4,000 of product and paid Supplier Inc. for the purchase electronically on February 28, 2020. Chocolate Inc. will hold the excess product into March, as it is likely that $500 of the amount will be sold. Determine the type of complex revenue arrangement and the amount of revenue that Supplier Inc. should record in February 2020.

continued

continued from previous page

c. TicketMajor Inc. purchases tickets in large blocks for various live concerts. TicketMajor Inc. then sells the tickets online to the customers. TicketMajor Inc. is responsible for pricing the tickets and is responsible for any unsold tickets. Ticket purchases are nonrefundable after the customer purchases the tickets online. In February of 2020, TicketMajor Inc. purchased tickets worth $50,000 and sold tickets worth $35,000, for which concerts had taken place. Determine the type of complex revenue arrangement and how much revenue TicketMajor Inc. reports in February of 2020.

d. On January 1, 2020, Zappit Inc. sells equipment to Solo Inc. for $15,000. As stipulated in the revenue contract, Zappit Inc. will buy back the equipment on December 31, 2020, for $15,000. The relevant interest rate is 5%. Determine the type of complex revenue arrangement and the amount of revenue that Zappit Inc. should record on January 1, 2020.

More Practice:
7-42, 7-43, 7-44, 7-45, 7-78

Solution on p. 7-76.

LO 7-9 Describe accounting for contract costs and disclosure requirements for revenue recognition

LO 7-9 Overview

Disclosure Requirements
- Disaggregated revenue
- Contracts with customers
- Performance obligations
- Significant judgments
- Practical expedients
- Contract cost assets
  - Costs to obtain a contract
  - Costs to fulfill a contract

Revenue and the associated bad debt expense are presented on the income statement, and assets and liabilities associated with revenue contracts are presented on the balance sheet. These include contract assets, contract liabilities, and accounts receivable (net of the allowance for doubtful accounts). In addition, ASC 340 requires a number of disclosures in notes to financial statements and provides guidance on the reporting of contract costs.

Contract Costs

Sellers may incur costs to obtain a contract or fulfill a contract, both of which are illustrated in Demo 7-9. **Costs to obtain a contract**, include items such as marketing costs, bid and proposal costs, sales commissions, and legal costs. These are amounts due to third parties (including company employees), not to customers. Costs incurred to obtain a contract are recognized as assets if they meet both of the following criteria.

1. Costs are incremental (costs that would not have been incurred if the contract had not been obtained).
2. Costs are recoverable (directly charged to customer or expected to be recovered through the margin in the contract).

340-40-25-1 An entity shall recognize as an asset the incremental costs of obtaining a contract with a customer if the entity expects to recover those costs.

Generally, all *other* costs incurred to obtain a contract are expensed as incurred. However, the accounting guidance offers the following **practical expedient**:

340-40-25-4 As a practical expedient, an entity may recognize the incremental costs of obtaining a contract as an expense when incurred if the amortization period of the asset that the entity otherwise would have recognized is one year or less.

The asset recognized from capitalizing costs to obtain a contract is amortized on a systematic basis consistent with the pattern of the transfer of the goods or services to which the asset relates. For example, if a sales commission were paid on the origination of a contract (and not on contract renewals), the contract asset would likely be amortized over the expected length of the customer relationship. Assets recognized from the costs to obtain a contract are subject to impairment testing.

Sellers can incur **costs to fulfill a contract** before transferring goods or services. Costs to fulfill a contract are recognized as an asset if the costs meet all of the following criteria (ASC 340-40-25-5).

1. Costs relate directly to a contract or an anticipated contract that the seller can specifically identify.
2. Costs generate or enhance resources used to satisfy performance obligations in the future.
3. Costs are recoverable.

Fulfillment costs include direct labor, direct materials, and allocation of costs that relate directly to the unsatisfied performance obligations in a contract. Fulfillment costs do not include general and administrative costs, costs of wasted resources, costs that relate to satisfied performance obligations, or where it's unclear whether they relate to unsatisfied performance obligations. Shipping and handling activities performed *before* the customer obtains control of the good are activities to fulfill the entity's promise to transfer the good.

The revenue recognition standard allows an **election for shipping and handling fees** incurred *after* the title has passed to the customer. Shipping costs that occur *after* title has passed to the customer can be recognized as fulfillment costs (in which case, the associated revenue is recognized when control of the asset passes to the customer) or as an additional performance obligation (in which case, the associated revenue is recognized as the performance [shipping] takes place).

606-10-25-18B If shipping and handling activities are performed after a customer obtains control of the good, then the entity may elect to account for shipping and handling as activities to fulfill the promise to transfer the good.

The asset recognized from capitalizing the costs to fulfill a contract is amortized on a systematic basis consistent with the pattern of the transfer of the goods or services to which the asset relates. Assets recognized from the costs to fulfill a contract are subject to impairment testing.

Accounting for and Reporting of Contract Costs

LO7-9 **Demo 7-9**

Demo MBC

Example One—Costs to Obtain a Contract

On January 1, 2020, Arrens Co. enters into a contract with a customer where a sales staff member receives a 10% commission on the contract, totaling $5,000, to be paid during the year. The contract calls for Arrens to deliver product throughout the calendar year and Arrens expects to recover the commission on the contract. The contract does not have a renewal option. How would Arrens account for the contract cost on January 1, 2020?

Solution

Arrens can recognize the commission cost as an asset and amortize it over the life of the contract.

January 1, 2020—To record contract cost

Contract Cost	5,000	
Salaries Payable		5,000

Assets = Liabilities + Equity
+5,000 +5,000
Contract Cost: 5,000 (debit) | Salaries Payable: 5,000 (credit)

However, because the contract is not longer than a year, Arrens could instead expense the commission cost as incurred under the practical expedient.

January 1, 2020—To record contract cost

Contract Cost Expense	5,000	
Salaries Payable		5,000

Assets = Liabilities + Equity
+5,000 −5,000
Salaries Payable: 5,000 (credit) | Contract Cost Exp: 5,000 (debit)

Example Two—Costs to Fulfill a Contract

Hampshire Inc. enters into a service contract with a customer for a three-year period. Hampshire incurs costs of $5,000 at the outset of the contract that relate directly to the contract and are critical to Hampshire's obligation to fulfill the contract. There are no refund rights in the contract, and automatic billing takes place monthly. Costs are expected to be recovered. How would Hampshire Inc. account for the contract costs on January 1, 2020?

Solution

Hampshire should recognize the costs incurred at the outset of the contract as an asset since they (1) relate directly to the contract, (2) enhance the resources of the company to perform under the contract, and (3) are expected to be recovered. An asset is recognized and amortized on a systematic basis consistent with the pattern of transfer of the services to the customer.

January 1, 2020—To record contract cost

Contract Cost	5,000	
Cash		5,000

Assets = Liabilities + Equity
+5,000
−5,000
Contract Cost: 5,000 (debit) | Cash: 5,000 (credit)

Financial Reporting

Revenue is presented in the income statement when the five steps of the revenue recognition process have been satisfied. The balance sheet displays contract assets and contract liabilities. As discussed earlier in the chapter, a contract asset is recorded when a company transfers goods or services to a customer before payment is due, excluding any amounts reported as receivables. Similar to accounts receivable, a contract asset is a company's right to consideration in exchange for goods or services that the entity has transferred to a customer. However, accounts receivable is recorded when the company has an unconditional right to consideration. This means only the passage of time is required for the company to receive the consideration. A contract asset is conditional in that the company may have to perform additional services or deliver additional goods to the customer prior to being entitled to the consideration. A contract liability is recognized when a customer pays in advance for a seller's performance obligation to transfer goods or services in the future.

Because they are interdependent, contract assets and liabilities (excluding accounts receivable) should be presented on a **net basis**, as either a contract asset or a contract liability. The netting of contract assets and contract liabilities is performed at the contract level.

31 October 2014 TRG Meeting; agenda paper no. 7 The boards decided that the remaining rights and performance obligations in a contract should be accounted for and presented on a net basis, as either a contract asset or a contract liability. The boards noted that the rights and obligations in a contract with a customer are interdependent—the right to receive consideration from a customer depends on the entity's performance and, similarly, the entity performs only as long as the customer continues to pay. The boards decided that those interdependencies are best reflected by accounting and presenting on a net basis the remaining rights and obligations in the statement of financial position.

The net contract asset or liability is presented separately from the refund liability. Management should evaluate any resulting contract asset or receivable for impairment in accordance with the accounting guidance in evaluating the impairment of receivables (ASC 310).

Financial Statement Disclosures

The **objective** of the disclosure requirements is to provide sufficient information to enable users of financial statements to understand the nature, amount, timing, and uncertainty of revenue and cash flows arising from contracts with customers. To achieve that objective, a seller shall disclose qualitative and quantitative information about all of the following:

- **Disaggregated revenue** Sellers shall disclose revenue disaggregated into categories that illustrate how economic factors affect the nature, amount, timing, and uncertainty of revenue and cash flows.
- **Contracts with customers** The opening and closing balances of contract assets and liabilities should be provided. Significant components of changes in balances should be provided, including the amount of revenue recognized in the current period that was deferred in prior years. The company should disclose information about significant payment terms, the nature of goods and services promised, obligations for returns, and warranties provided. The revenue recognition standard includes examples of required disclosures, and addresses more complex topics such as cumulative catch-up adjustments and impairments.
- **Performance obligations** The company should provide information about performance obligations, including when they are typically satisfied, the nature of goods and services provided, the allocation of transaction prices to distinct obligations, and the timing of revenue recognition.
- **Significant judgments and changes in judgments** Sellers shall disclose information about the timing of satisfaction of performance obligations, determination of the transaction price and the amounts allocated to performance obligations, methods used to recognize revenue over time and justification for those methods.

AMAZON

Real World—SHIPPING COSTS: A PERFORMANCE OBLIGATION?

The FASB in ASU 2016-10 provides guidance to allow an entity to elect to account for shipping and handling activities performed after control of a good has been transferred to the customer as a fulfillment cost. Prior to this amendment, companies interpreting the new revenue recognition standards were wondering if shipping obligations were a separate performance obligation. Consider Amazon Inc., who serves retail customers through the web. Without ASU 2016-10 amendment, it is quite possible that Amazon would have three performance obligations: to provide the good, to ship the good, and to insure the good through the shipment process. If that were the case, Amazon would have had to allocate the transaction price to the three performance obligations, including shipping, whether the customer paid for shipping or not. Even further, the timing of the recognition of the three performance obligations would be different: revenue for shipping and insurance would be recognized over the shipping period, while revenue on the product purchase would be recognized when control of the good was transferred to the customer. The amendment simplified the accounting for such transactions, allowing companies that ship free on board to elect to avoid treating shipping as a separate performance obligation.

AMAZON [AMZN]

Contract Costs and Revenue Disclosures — LO7-9 — REVIEW 7-9

Match each term or phrase, 1 through 9, with its best description, *a* through *i*.

Review MBC

Term or Phrase

____ 1. Net basis of presentation
____ 2. Capitalized costs to fulfill a contract
____ 3. Objective of financial disclosure for revenue
____ 4. Performance obligation or cost to fulfill a contract
____ 5. Accounts receivable
____ 6. Capitalized costs to obtain a contract
____ 7. Short-term costs to obtain a contract
____ 8. Contract asset
____ 9. Contract liability

Description

a. Practical expedient to allow immediate expense treatment.
b. Direct and recoverable contract costs, incurred to satisfy future performance obligations.
c. Incremental and recoverable costs incurred prior to contract.
d. Offsetting contract assets against contract liabilities on a contract basis.
e. Shipping costs incurred after title has passed to a customer.
f. Unconditional right to consideration.
g. Results from a transfer of goods or services to customer before payment is due.
h. Increase the understanding of the nature, amount, timing, and uncertainty of revenue arising from contracts.
i. Prepayment for a good or service.

More Practice: 7-46, 7-47
Solution on p. 7-76.

Management Judgment

The aim of ASC 606 is to establish the principles for companies to use when recognizing revenue. A *principles-based approach* requires management judgment.

606-10-10-1 The objective of the guidance in this Topic is to establish the principles that an entity shall apply to report useful information to users of financial statements about the nature, amount, timing, and uncertainty of revenue and cash flows arising from a contract with a customer.

Management considers all relevant information in applying the standard and consistently applies the standard across all of its revenue contracts.

606-10-10-3 An entity shall consider the terms of the contract and all relevant facts and circumstances when applying this guidance. An entity shall apply this guidance, including the use of any practical expedients, consistently to contracts with similar characteristics and in similar circumstances.

Each step of the revenue recognition process requires judgment. We highlight some of the judgments described in this chapter.

Step 1: Identify contract(s) with customer

- Determining whether a contract meets the five conditions of validity (p. 7-6).
- Determining when and how to account for contract modifications (p. 7-31).

Step 2: Identify performance obligation(s) in the contract

- Determining whether a promise meets the criteria to be treated as a separate performance obligation (p. 7-9).
- Determining whether a separate performance obligation (such as a customer option) is material (p. 7-11).

Step 3: Determine the transaction price

- Estimating variable consideration through the expected value method or the most likely amount method (p. 7-14).
- Determining whether consideration payable is made for a distinct good or service (p. 7-16).
- Estimating a refund liability (p. 7-17).
- Determining whether a financing component is significant (p. 7-17).

Step 4: Allocate transaction price to performance obligation(s)

- Determining standalone selling prices when the amount is not observable using the adjusted market assessment approach, the expected cost plus a margin approach or the residual approach (p. 7-18).
- Considering all relevant information when estimating standalone selling prices (p. 7-22).

Step 5: Recognize revenue when (or as) each performance obligation is satisfied through a transfer of control

- Identifying the point of transfer of a promised good or service using indicators (p. 7-4).
- Evaluating the criteria to determine whether revenue should be recognized over time (p. 7-23).
- Estimating the amount of revenue to recognize over time, as progress is made toward satisfying the promise(s) of the contract (p. 7-23).
- Determining whether a customer has the right to access or use intellectual property (p. 7-28).
- Determining when to recognize revenue under a bill-and-hold arrangement, consignment arrangement, repurchase arrangement, and a principal/agent arrangement (p. 7-33).
- Determining whether a contract cost meets the criteria for capitalization (p. 7-39).

In general, management must determine the proper disclosures, including the disclosure of significant judgments made and changes in judgments (p. 7-41).

APPENDIX 7A LO 7-10 Apply the revenue recognition process to long-term contracts expected to be profitable

LO 7-10 Overview

Long-term Contracts—Profitable

- Single performance obligation satisfied over time
  - Gross profit recognized over time
- Single performance obligation satisfied at a point in time
  - Gross profit recognized at end of the project

This section reviews the accounting for profitable long-term contracts where the performance obligation is satisfied over time (formerly called *percentage-of-completion method*) and where the performance obligation is satisfied at a point in time (formerly called *completed contract method*).

In analyzing long-term contracts, first determine whether revenue is recognized over time or at a point in time (see the criteria included in **LO 7-6**). In **Demo 7-10A**, we demonstrate the journal entries for a long-term contract where revenue is recognized over time. As construction costs are incurred, they are accumulated in **Construction in Process**, an inventory account. Progress billings are not directly recorded as revenues but are debited to **Accounts Receivable** and credited to **Billings on Contracts**, a contra inventory account. On a periodic basis, revenue (and expense) is recorded using a method to measure the company's progress toward satisfaction of the performance obligation. Earlier, in **Demo 7-6B**, we demonstrated the cost-to-cost input measure as a way to measure progress. This is a common input method to estimate the amount of revenue to recognize over time in long-term contracts. In recording periodic revenues (**Revenue from Long-Term Contracts**) and expenses (**Cost of Construction**), the difference (gross profit), is debited to Construction in Process. Finally, a journal entry is recorded to close the Construction in Process account and Billings on Contracts at the completion of the project.

When revenue is recognized over time on a long-term construction contract, inventory is carried at cost plus recognized gross profit. If Construction in Process exceeds Billings on Contracts, the net difference is reported as a *current asset*. The net debit balance represents the contractor's net ownership interest in the construction project. If Construction in Process is less than Billings on Contracts, the net difference represents the customer's net ownership interest in the project. The net credit balance is reported as a *current liability* in the contractor's financial statements. As mentioned earlier, the remaining reported rights and obligations in a contract (Construction in Process and Billings on Contracts) should be presented in the financial statements on a *net basis*.

In **Demo 7-10B**, we demonstrate the journal entries for a long-term contract where revenue is recognized at a point in time. In this case, all revenue and expense recognition is deferred until the end of the contract. As construction costs are incurred, they are accumulated in Construction in Process. Progress billings are not directly recorded as revenues but are debited to Accounts Receivable and credited to Billings on Contracts.

At the completion of the contract, all the accounts are closed, and the entire gross profit on the construction project is recognized. Income is recognized as the difference between the accumulated credit balance in Billings on Contracts and the debit balance in Construction in Process, assuming that the total price of the contract has been billed. The accumulated amount of billings on contracts is recognized as revenue from long-term contracts, and the accumulated amount of construction in process inventory on completion of the contract is recognized as cost of construction (an expense). In the financial statements, Construction in Process inventory is carried at cost on the balance sheet and the income statement reflects no impact from the contract until the time of completion of the contract.

Long-Term Contract: Revenue Recognized Over Time—Cost-to-Cost Basis LO7-10

Demo 7-10A

Demo

MBC

Ace Construction Co. has contracted to erect a building for $1.5 million, starting construction on February 1, 2019, with a planned completion date of August 1, 2021. Total costs to complete the contract are estimated at $1.35 million, so the estimated gross profit is projected to be $150,000 ($1.5 million − $1.35 million). Progress billings payable within 10 days after billing will be made on a predetermined schedule. Assume the following data pertain to the construction period spanning three calendar years.

Construction Project—Three-Year Summary (Contract Price: $1,500,000)

As of December 31	2019	2020	2021
1. Costs incurred during current year	$ 350,000	$ 550,000	$ 465,000
2. Cumulative costs incurred to date	350,000	900,000	1,365,000
3. Estimated costs to complete at year-end	1,000,000	460,000	0
4. Estimated total costs for project	$1,350,000	$1,360,000	$1,365,000
5. Progress billings during year	$ 300,000	$ 575,000	$ 625,000
6. Cumulative billings to date	300,000	875,000	1,500,000
7. Collections on billings during year	270,000	555,000	675,000
8. Cumulative collections to date	270,000	825,000	1,500,000

Estimated completion costs increased by $10,000 in 2020, and by another $5,000 in 2021. The total cost to complete the project is $1,365,000 at the end of 2021. Estimated contract profit as of December 31, 2021, is therefore revised from the original estimate of $150,000 to $135,000 ($1.5 million − $1.365 million). Assume the contract meets the 3 criteria to recognize revenue over time. Thus, for each year of the construction project (a) record construction in process inventory, progress billings, and collections, (b) record revenue and expenses using the cost-to-cost method, and (c) prepare the financial statement presentation.

continued

continued from previous page

Solution

a. **Record Construction in Process Inventory, Progress Billings, and Collections of Progress Billings**

The three journal entries to record the construction in process inventory, progress billings, and collections of progress billings each year for Ace Construction follow.

CIP	
350,000	
550,000	
465,000	

Cash, Payables, Etc.	
270,000	350,000
555,000	550,000
675,000	465,000

Accounts Rec	
300,000	270,000
575,000	555,000
625,000	675,000

Billings	
	300,000
	575,000
	625,000

	2019		2020		2021	
Construction in Process	350,000		550,000		465,000	
Cash, Payables, etc.		350,000		550,000		465,000
Accounts Receivable	300,000		575,000		625,000	
Billings on Contracts		300,000		575,000		625,000
Cash	270,000		555,000		675,000	
Accounts Receivable		270,000		555,000		675,000

b. **Record Revenues and Expenses**

The cost-to-cost method is used to determine percent complete as follows.

Calculation of Percent Complete	2019	2020	2021
Cost incurred to date	$ 350,000	$ 900,000	$1,365,000
Estimated total costs	1,350,000	1,360,000	1,365,000
Percent complete	25.926%	66.176%	100.000%

The percent completed is computed as costs incurred to date divided by the estimate of total costs to complete. For example, estimated total costs at the end of 2019 ($1,350,000) equals costs incurred to date ($350,000) plus estimated costs to complete at the end of 2019 ($1,000,000). For 2019, the percent complete of 25.926% is equal to $350,000 (costs incurred to date) divided by $1,350,000 (estimate of total costs). Revenue recognized to date is equal to the percent complete multiplied by the total contract price of $1.5 million.

Calculation of Revenue to Date	2019	2020	2021
2019: $1.5 million × 0.25926	$388,890	$ —	$ —
2020: $1.5 million × 0.66176	—	992,640	—
2021: $1.5 million × 1.00000	—		1,500,000

To determine revenue for each year, revenue recorded in prior years is subtracted from the total revenue recognizable.

Current period revenue = (Percent complete × Total contract revenue) − Revenue recognized in prior periods

In 2020, for instance, the revenue to be recognized is the total revenue recognizable of $992,640 less the revenue recognized in 2019 of $388,890, or $603,750. The gross profit to be recognized is the difference between revenue and costs incurred in the period.

Calculation of Gross Profit per Period	2019	2020	2021	Total
Revenue for the current period	$388,890	$603,750	$507,360	$1,500,000
Costs incurred in current period	350,000	550,000	465,000	1,365,000
Gross profit for the period	$ 38,890	$ 53,750	$ 42,360	$ 135,000

The entry to record the recognition of revenue and expense in each period is as follows.

CIP	
350,000	
38,890	
550,000	
53,750	
465,000	
42,360	1,500,000
0	

Billings	
1,500,000	300,000
	575,000
	625,000
	0

Cost of Construct	
350,000	
550,000	
465,000	

Rev from Contracts	
	388,890
	603,750
	507,360

	2019		2020		2021	
Construction in Process	38,890		53,750		42,360	
Cost of Construction	350,000		550,000		465,000	
Revenue from Long-Term Contracts		388,890		603,750		507,360

continued

continued from previous page

The following journal entry closes out Billings on Contracts and Construction in Process at the completion of the project.

Billings on Contracts	1,500,000	
Construction in Process		1,500,000

c. **Financial Statement Presentation**
Construction in process exceeds billings on contracts in 2019 and 2020; thus, on the balance sheet the net amount is presented as an asset in 2019 and 2020. On the income statement, revenue, costs, and gross profit are presented.

Long-Term Contract Revenue Recognized Over Time

		2019		2020	2021
Balance Sheet:					
Current assets					
Accounts receivable		$ 30,000		$ 50,000	
Inventory					
Construction in process.	$388,890		$992,640		
Less: Billings on contracts	300,000		875,000		
Construction in process in excess of billings. . .		$ 88,890		$117,640	
Income Statement:					
Revenue from long-term contracts.		$388,890		$603,750	$507,360
Cost of construction		350,000		550,000	465,000
Gross profit.		$ 38,890		$ 53,750	$ 42,360

Long-Term Contract: Revenue Recognized at a Point in Time

LO7-10 **Demo 7-10B**

Demo MBC

Refer to **Demo 7-10A** but assume instead that the Ace Construction contract did not meet the criteria to recognize revenue over time. For the three years of the construction project (a) record construction in process inventory, progress billings, and collections; (b) record revenue and expenses at the project completion; (c) prepare the financial statement presentation; and (d) compare the gross profit recorded in **Demo 7-10A** and **Demo 7-10B**.

Solution

a. **Record Construction in Process Inventory, Progress Billings, and Collections of Progress Billings**
The journal entries to record the construction in process inventory, progress billings, and collections of progress billings each year for Ace Construction follow. This step is the same as we illustrated above when revenue was recognized over time.

	2019		2020		2021	
Construction in Process	350,000		550,000		465,000	
Cash, Payables, etc.		350,000		550,000		465,000
Accounts Receivable	300,000		575,000		625,000	
Billings on Contracts		300,000		575,000		625,000
Cash	270,000		555,000		675,000	
Accounts Receivable		270,000		555,000		675,000

CIP	
350,000	
550,000	
465,000	

Cash, Payables, Etc.	
270,000	350,000
555,000	550,000
675,000	465,000

Accounts Receiv	
300,000	270,000
575,000	555,000
625,000	675,000
0	

Billings	
	300,000
	575,000
	625,000

b. **Record Revenue and Expense Recognition at Project Completion**
The journal entries to recognize revenue and expense upon completion of Ace's contract in August 2021 follow.

continued

continued from previous page

Cost of Construct	
1,365,000	

Rev from Contracts	
	1,500,000

CIP	
350,000	1,365,000
550,000	
465,000	
0	

Billings	
	300,000
	575,000
	625,000
	0

Billings on Contracts	1,500,000	
Revenue from Long-Term Contracts		1,500,000
Cost of Construction	1,365,000	
Construction in Process		1,365,000

c. **Financial Statement Presentation**
The balance sheet and income statement presentations of the contract follow.

Long-Term Contract Revenue: Recognized at a Point in Time

	2019		2020		2021
Balance Sheet					
Current assets					
Accounts receivable		$30,000		$50,000	
Inventory					
Construction in process	$350,000		$900,000		
Less: Billings on contracts	300,000		875,000		
Construction in process in excess of billings		$50,000		$25,000	
Income Statement					
Revenue from long-term contracts		—		—	$1,500,000
Cost of construction		—		—	1,365,000
Gross profit		—		—	$ 135,000

d. **Compare Gross Profit Recognized**
The following table shows the differences in gross profit between the two methods on a year-to-year basis. We see that total gross profit totaled over the three years is the same for each method.

Gross Profit When:	Revenue Recognized at Point in Time	Revenue Recognized Over Time
2019	$ —	$ 38,890
2020	—	53,750
2021	135,000	42,360
Total	$135,000	$135,000

REVIEW 7-10 **LO7-10** **Long-Term Profitable Construction Project**

Review MBC

BuildMore Construction Co. contracted to construct an addition for $400,000. Construction started in January 2020 and was completed in November 2021. Data relating to the contract follow.

	2020	2021
Costs incurred during year	$150,000	$170,000
Estimated additional costs to complete	190,000	
Billings during year	200,000	200,000
Cash collections during year	140,000	260,000

Required

a. Record the journal entries for 2020 and 2021 under the assumption that revenue is recognized at a point in time.

b. Record the journal entries for 2020 and 2021 under the assumption that revenue is recognized over time.

More Practice:
7-105, 7-107, 7-108
Solution on p. 7-76.

Apply the revenue recognition process to long-term contracts expected to be unprofitable

APPENDIX 7B
LO 7-11

When the costs necessary to complete a contract result in contract losses, two situations are possible.

1. Loss results in an unprofitable contract.
2. Contract remains profitable, but there is a current-year loss.

In **Demo 7-11A**, we demonstrate the accounting for a contract with an overall loss. Whether revenue is recognized at a point in time or over time, the projected loss is recognized in full in the period in which the loss is estimated. In **Demo 7-11B**, we demonstrate the accounting for a contract with a current-year loss, but overall, the contract remains profitable. When revenue is recognized at a point in time, no additional entry is necessary because all gross profit is deferred, and an overall loss is not expected. However, with a contract for which revenue is recognized over time, a loss period results from the usual computation of the percent complete applied to total revenue, which ends up being less than costs incurred.

Long-term Contracts
- Overall loss on unprofitable contract:
  - Recognize loss in full in period when loss is known
- Current period loss, but overall profitable contract
  - Revenue at a Point in Time: no periodic loss recognized
  - Revenue Over Time: Partially reverse previously reported profits

LO 7-11 Overview

Overall Loss on an Unprofitable Contract

LO7-11 **Demo 7-11A**

Demo MBC

Refer to information in **Demo 7-10A**. Suppose that Ace's costs incurred are $350,000 in 2019 and $550,000 in 2020, and at the end of 2020, Ace's estimate of costs to complete the contract increases from $460,000 to $625,000. This means costs incurred through 2020 total $900,000, and the total estimated cost of the contract becomes $1,525,000. Thus, at the end of 2020 there is now an expected loss on the contract of $25,000 ($1,500,000 − $1,525,000). Assume that actual costs incurred in 2021 are $625,000.

Required

a. Record the loss in 2020 assuming revenue is recognized at a point in time.

b. Assume the contract meets the three criteria to recognize revenue over time. For each year of the construction project, (1) record construction in process inventory, progress billings, and collections; (2) record revenue and expenses using the cost-to-cost method; and (3) prepare the financial statement presentation.

Solution

a. **Reporting Loss—Revenue Recognized at a Point in Time**

The journal entry to record the loss at the end of 2020 follows.

December 31, 2020—To record contract loss

Loss on Long-Term Contracts	25,000	
Construction in Process		25,000

Assets = Liabilities + Equity
−25,000 −25,000

CIP	
	25,000

Loss on Contracts	
25,000	

b. **Reporting Loss—Revenue Recognized over Time**

1. **Record Construction in Process Inventory, Progress Billings, and Collections of Progress Billings**

The three journal entries to record the construction in process inventory, progress billings, and collections of progress billings each year for Ace Construction follow.

	2019		2020		2021	
Construction in Process	350,000		550,000		625,000	
Cash, Payables, etc.		350,000		550,000		625,000
Accounts Receivable	300,000		575,000		625,000	
Billings on Contracts		300,000		575,000		625,000
Cash	270,000		555,000		675,000	
Accounts Receivable		270,000		555,000		675,000

CIP	
350,000	
550,000	
625,000	

Cash, Payables, Etc.	
270,000	350,000
555,000	550,000
675,000	625,000

Accounts Rec	
300,000	270,000
575,000	555,000
625,000	675,000

Billings	
	300,000
	575,000
	625,000

continued

continued from previous page

2. Recording Revenues and Expenses

The amount of revenue recognized to date each year is computed in the usual way. Each year, the percent complete is calculated based on the cost-to-cost method and applied to the total contract revenue of $1,500,000 to determine revenue recognized to date.

Calculation of Percent Complete	2019	2020	2021
Cost incurred to date	$ 350,000	$ 900,000	$1,525,000
Estimated total costs	1,350,000	1,525,000	1,525,000
Percent complete	25.926%	59.016%	100.000%

Calculation of Revenue to Date	2019	2020	2021
2019: $1.5 million × 0.25926	$388,890	$ —	$ —
2020: $1.5 million × 0.59016	—	885,240	—
2021: $1.5 million × 1.00000	—		1,500,000

The company records the following entries to recognize revenue and expense each year.

Assets = Liabilities + Equity: Assets 38,890; Equity +388,890, −350,000
CIP: 350,000; 38,890; balance 388,890
Rev from Contracts: 388,890
Cost of Construct: 350,000

December 31, 2019—To record contract revenue and expense

Construction in Process ($388,890 – $350,000)	38,890	
Cost of Construction	350,000	
Revenue from Long-Term Contracts		388,890

In 2020, the company estimates an overall contract loss of $25,000, calculated as $1,500,000 minus $1,525,000. Therefore, Construction in Process is credited for the $25,000 loss and the profit of $38,890 recognized in the prior year (which now must be reversed). The Cost of Construction ($496,350 + $63,890) reflects an acceleration of costs to recognize the overall loss immediately in the period in which the company first knows there will be a loss on the project.

Assets = Liabilities + Equity: Assets −63,890; Equity +496,350, −560,240
CIP: 350,000; 38,890; 550,000 | 63,890; balance 875,000
Rev from Contracts: 388,890; 496,350
Cost of Construct: 350,000; 560,240

December 31, 2020—To record contract revenue and expense

Cost of Construction ($496,350 + $63,890)	560,240	
Construction in Process ($38,890 + $25,000)		496,350
Revenue from Long-Term Contracts ($885,240 – $388,890)		63,890

Because actual costs in 2021 were as expected, no additional profit or loss is reported in 2021.

Assets = Liabilities + Equity: Equity +614,760, −614,760
Cost of Construct: 350,000; 560,240; 614,760
Rev from Contracts: 388,890; 496,350; 614,760

December 31, 2021—To record contract revenue and expense

Cost of Construction ($1,525,000 – $350,000 – $560,240)	614,760	
Revenue from Long-Term Contracts ($1,500,000 – $885,240)		614,760

The balance in the Construction in Process account equals the balance in Billings on Contracts. When the contract is completed, a journal entry is made to close the Construction in Process and the Billings on Contracts accounts.

Assets = Liabilities + Equity: Assets −1,500,000; Liabilities −1,500,000
CIP: 350,000; 38,890; 550,000; 625,000 | 63,890; 1,500,000; balance 0
Billings: 1,500,000 | 300,000; 575,000; 625,000; balance 0

Billings on Contracts	1,500,000	
Construction in Process		1,500,000

3. Financial Statement Presentation

Long-Term Contract Revenue Recognized Over Time

	2019		2020		2021
Balance Sheet					
Current assets					
Accounts receivable		$ 30,000		$ 50,000	
Inventory					
Construction in process	$388,890		$875,000		
Less: Billings on contracts	300,000		875,000		
Construction in process in excess of billings		$ 88,890		$ 0	

continued

continued from previous page

	2019	2020	2021
Income Statement			
Revenue from long-term contracts	$388,890	$496,350	$614,760
Cost of construction	350,000	560,240	614,760
Gross profit (loss)	$ 38,890	$ (63,890)*	$

*Equals the overall loss of $25,000 plus the elimination of the previously recognized profit of $38,890.

Current Period Loss on Overall Profitable Contract

LO7-11 **Demo 7-11B**

Demo MBC

Refer to information in **Demo 7-10A**. Suppose Ace's costs incurred through the end of 2020 are as reported, but the estimate of costs to complete the contract has increased from the original estimate of $460,000 to $550,000. This means costs totaling $900,000 have already been incurred, and the total estimated cost of completing the construction contract is $1,450,000. The contract still generates a gross profit of $50,000 ($1,500,000 − $1,450,000).

Required

a. Record the loss in 2020 assuming revenue is recognized at a point in time.
b. Record the entries over the remaining contract life assuming revenue is recognized over time.

Solution

a. **Reporting at a Point in Time—Loss Incurred**
No entry is needed in 2020 to record the current year loss. At completion of the contract, the usual revenue, cost of construction, and gross profit entries are made, but the gross profit is reduced to $50,000.

b. **Reporting Over Time—Loss Incurred**
The computation of the loss for 2020 follows.

Construction costs to December 31, 2020	$ 900,000
Estimated costs to complete	550,000
Estimated total costs of contract	$1,450,000
Percent complete ($900,000/$1,450,000)	62.069%
Revenue recognizable as of December 31, 2020 ($1,500,000 × 0.62069)	$ 931,035
Revenue recognized in prior periods	388,890
Revenue to be recognized in 2020	542,145
Cost of construction in 2020	550,000
Loss on construction contract in 2020	$ (7,855)

The journal entry to record revenue, cost of construction, and loss for 2020 follows.

December 31, 2020—To record contract loss

Cost of Construction	550,000	
Construction in Process		7,855
Revenue from Long-Term Contracts		542,145

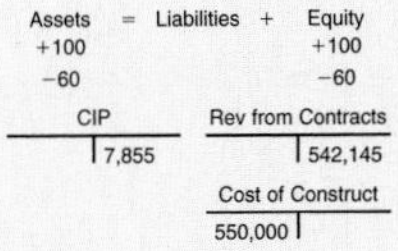

Assets = Liabilities + Equity
+100
−60
+100
−60
CIP
7,855
Rev from Contracts
542,145
Cost of Construct
550,000

The $7,885 reduction in Construction In Process represents a partial reversal of profit recognized in 2019.

Profit recognized through December 31, 2019	$38,890
Revised profit through December 31, 2020 ($50,000 × 0.62069)	31,035
Reduction in profit (construction in process)	$ 7,855

continued

continued from previous page

In 2021, Ace Construction recognizes the remaining revenue of $568,965 ($1,500,000 less the $931,035 recognized in prior years) and costs of $550,000, yielding a gross profit of $18,965.

	Revenues	Expenses	Gross Profit
Total over life of contract.	$1,500,000	$1,450,000	$50,000
Recognized in prior periods	931,035	900,000	31,035
Recognized in 2021	$ 568,965	$ 550,000	$18,965

REVIEW 7-11 **LO7-11** **Unprofitable Construction Project**

Review MBC

BuildMore Construction Co. contracted to construct an addition to a building for $300,000. Construction started in January 2020 and was completed in November 2022. Data relating to the contract follow.

	2020	2021	2022
Costs incurred to date	$ 80,000	$190,000	$330,000
Estimated costs for completion.	170,000	135,000	0
Customer billings to date	100,000	200,000	300,000
Customer collections to date	80,000	160,000	300,000

Required

a. Record the journal entries for 2020, 2021, and 2022 under the assumption that revenue is recognized at a point in time.

b. Record the journal entries for 2020, 2021, and 2022 under the assumption that revenue is recognized over time.

More Practice: 7-109, 7-113
Solution on p. 7-76.

Questions

7-1. What are the five steps in the revenue recognition process?

7-2. From a seller's perspective, why does a customer prepayment result in a contract liability such as deferred revenue?

7-3. What are indicators that a customer has taken control of an asset? Why is this concept important in the revenue recognition process?

7-4. Explain the components of a valid contract.

7-5. How does a seller determine whether the modification of a contract represents a new separate contract or the termination of an existing contract and replacement with a new combined contract?

7-6. What criteria are used to determine whether a contract has single or multiple performance obligations?

7-7. Are nonrefundable membership fees to an art museum considered to be a separate performance obligation? Why or why not?

7-8. Does a right of return represent a separate performance obligation?

7-9. What is variable consideration? What is the constraint when including variable consideration in the transaction price? Identify specific examples of variable consideration.

7-10. In determining variable consideration, when is it appropriate to use the expected value method? When is it appropriate to use the most likely amount method?

7-11. How is a transaction price determined when noncash consideration is received?

7-12. What is the difference between a principal and an agent? How is revenue recognized differently for a principal in contrast to an agent?

7-13. Describe three approaches to estimate the standalone selling price of a good or service when the selling price is not directly observable.

7-14. When is revenue recognized over time instead of at one point in time?

7-15. If a seller of goods to a customer has an obligation to later repurchase goods from that customer, the transaction is treated as a financing agreement. Explain.

7-16. What is a consignment arrangement? How is revenue recognized on a consignment transaction?

7-17. For a long-term construction project, when is revenue recognized if revenue is recognized (a) at a point in time? (b) over time?

Brief Exercises

Brief Exercise 7-18 Identifying the Five Steps of Revenue Recognition **LO1** *Hint:* See Demo 7-1

A customer purchases a pair of shoes from a retailer at a local mall on June 1, 2020, for $60, which is the stand-alone selling price of the shoes. The customer paid for the shoes with a credit card and immediately takes possession of the shoes. Use this example to demonstrate the five steps of the revenue recognition process.

Brief Exercise 7-19 Identifying the Five Steps of Revenue Recognition **LO1**

Match each of the following items *a* through *e* to each of the steps 1 through 5 in the revenue recognition process.

____ *a.* The price for performing a federal tax return is $200 and a state tax return is $100 if contracted separately.
____ *b.* Tax Prep Inc. will prepare the year-end federal tax return and state tax return for Customer J.
____ *c.* The total price for the year-end tax preparation is $300.
____ *d.* Customer J enters into an agreement with Tax Prep Inc. for Tax Prep Inc. to prepare Customer J's federal and state tax returns.
____ *e.* The federal and state tax returns are completed and approved by Customer J.

Brief Exercise 7-20 Identifying Contract Validity **LO2**

For each item *a* through *h*, indicate whether the item is (1) required for a valid contract, or (2) not required for a valid contract.

____ *a.* Valid business purpose
____ *b.* Written agreement
____ *c.* Identifiable payment terms
____ *d.* Cash consideration only
____ *e.* 99% probability of collection
____ *f.* Identifiable rights and obligations
____ *g.* Fixed contract price
____ *h.* Contract length exceeding one year

Brief Exercise 7-21 Assessing Contract Validity **LO2** *Hint:* See Demo 7-2

Match each of the following contract parts, *a* through *c*, with the most relevant of the following five contract conditions: (1) commercial substance, (2) approval, (3) identifiable rights and obligations, (4) identifiable payment terms, and (5) probable collection.

a. How a contract is approved: verbally, in writing, customary business practice.
b. Identification of a specific transaction price or a range of transaction prices.
c. Estimate of collectibility of consideration due.

Brief Exercise 7-22 Identifying Performance Obligations **LO3**

A customer hired a contractor to construct a storage facility next to the customer's home. The contract includes promises to provide the materials for the facility, to lay the foundation, construct the facility, and install fixtures within the facility. The contractor is able to identify the standalone prices for each of these aspects of the job based upon other contracts for these individual services. How many performance obligations are in the contract?

Brief Exercise 7-23 Identifying Performance Obligations **LO3** *Hint:* See Demo 7-3

Brewer Co. produces and sells coffee brewing machines that operate by loading individual, prefilled cups of flavored ground coffee. Brewer sells to retailers the brewing machines for $75 and the prefilled cups (pack of 24 for $12). The customer cannot operate the machine without the prefilled cups and these prefilled cups cannot be purchased from other vendors. Brewer expects that the retail customer will buy 12 refill packs throughout each year of the machine's useful life. How many performance obligations are in the contract?

Brief Exercise 7-24 Identifying Performance Obligations **LO3**

Marina Co. sells motor boats and provides off-season storage for boats. The boats sell for $35,000 per boat and off-season storage sells for a total of $400 for the months of September through April. Marina Co. enters into a contract to sell a boat and storage (for the period of September 2020 to April 2021) for a bundled price of $34,000. How many performance obligations are in the contract?

Brief Exercise 7-25 Identifying Performance Obligations **LO3**

Supreme Fitness, a health club, enters into contracts with customers for one year of membership to any of its health clubs for $50 per month for a minimum 12-month period. Supreme Fitness also charges a $50 nonrefundable joining fee to partially compensate for the initial activities of customer initiation and registration. How many performance obligations are in the contract?

Brief Exercise 7-26
Identifying Performance Obligations **LO3**
Hint: See Demo 7-3

SpeedyTax sells a yearly subscription, which provides support to customers in preparing tax returns electronically. The annual subscription includes explanations of new tax laws and access to online tax assistance. If a customer purchases a one-year subscription, the customer is entitled to a renewal of the subscription for the following year at a 25% discount. The 25% discount is not available unless the subscription is purchased in the current year. How many performance obligations are in the contract?

Brief Exercise 7-27
Computing a Transaction Price
LO4
Hint: See Demo 7-4A

On June 1, 2020, Consulting Inc. enters into a contract with a customer to build a website for its start-up business for $25,000, plus a possible performance bonus. The contract includes the creation of the website as a vehicle to communicate information about the customer's products, to sell products, and to collect payment for the products. The pricing of the customized website project includes a performance bonus of $5,000 to be paid to Consulting Inc. if the website is completed by July 31, 2020. The performance bonus will be reduced for each week beyond the due date (up to three weeks). Based on Consulting Inc.'s historical experience and the assessment of its current capabilities, the following outcomes are estimated. Indicate which method is appropriate in estimating the variable consideration. Estimate the transaction price for Consulting Inc.'s revenue contract.

Completion Date	Probability of Outcome	Performance Bonus
July 31, 2020	60%	$5,000
Aug. 7, 2020	20%	4,000
Aug. 14, 2020	15%	3,000
Aug. 21, 2020	5%	2,000

Brief Exercise 7-28
Computing a Transaction Price
LO4
Hint: See Demo 7-4A

Refer to the information in Brief Exercise 7-27. Assume the same facts except that Consulting Inc. is unable to estimate the probabilities of all possible outcomes. Based on past experience, Consulting Inc. believes that there is a 70% chance that it will complete the customized website by July 31, 2020, and a 30% chance that it will not. Indicate which method is appropriate in estimating the variable consideration. Compute the transaction price for Consulting Inc.'s revenue contract.

Brief Exercise 7-29
Estimating Sales Returns **LO4**

Guccii Inc. sells $350,000 of inventory during March 2020 to customers for $500,000. Guccii Inc. accepts returns up to 3 months after the date of purchase. Based on historical trends, 10% of inventory that Guccii Inc. sells is returned. Determine revenue to be recognized during March 2020.

Brief Exercise 7-30
Estimating Sales Returns **LO4**

Lacey Inc. manufactures hair products that it sells to multiple distributors. Lacey developed a new line of shampoo that it sold to distributors in the month of July 2020 for $30,000 (cost of $15,000). If the distributors fail to sell the new product (shampoo), the product can be returned to Lacey Inc. for a full refund. Because this is a new product line, Lacey is unable to estimate the amount of returns. No actual returns took place in July of 2020.

a. Determine revenue to be recognized during July 2020.
b. Determine the balance in refund liability on July 31, 2020.

Brief Exercise 7-31
Accounting for Consideration Payable **LO4, 6**
Hint: See Demo 7-4B

Furniture Manufacturer Inc. sells 1,000 chairs to a retailer for $500,000 (with a cost of $300,000) in June 2020. Additionally, Furniture Manufacturer Inc. agrees to pay $5,000 toward an advertising promotion campaign that the retailer will provide. The retailer will provide the advertising electronically and through local print media. The cost for the advertising campaign was negotiated as part of the revenue contract.

a. Prepare the entry for June 2020 to record Furniture Manufacturer Inc.'s sales revenue and cost of sales, assuming cash collected is net of the advertising fee.
b. Prepare the entry in June 2020 to record Furniture Manufacturer Inc.'s sales revenue and cost of sales now assuming that $500,000 cash is collected this month. The advertising fee will be paid next month to the customer.

Brief Exercise 7-32
Allocating a Transaction Price **LO5**
Hint: See Demo 7-5A

Seven Flags Park offers a promotion for free parking to customers who purchase a one day pass to enjoy thrill rides at its park plus two meal vouchers for a total of $75. Seven Flags sells each of the contract promises separately during the same timeframe for the following standalone prices: Day pass = $45, Parking = $20, and Two meal vouchers = $30. Compute the allocated transaction price of the day pass, two meals, and parking for Seven Flags assuming the sale of 500 promotional packages on July 15, 2020.

Brief Exercise 7-33
Allocating a Transaction Price Using Adjusted Market Assessment *and* Using Expected Cost plus a Margin **LO5**
Hint: See Demo 7-5B

Clothing Warehouse Inc. sells men's formal business suits. Clothing Warehouse offers complimentary custom fitting for a purchase made in the store for a business suit with a minimum price of $300. Providing the business suit and providing the fitting service are considered separate performance obligations. Compute the allocated transaction price of a business suit and a custom fitting for the following two separate cases.

a. Use the *adjusted market assessment approach* and assume that Clothing Warehouse Inc.'s direct competitor prices its fitting services for $60 per business suit. The business suit has a standalone selling price of $300.

b. Use the *expected cost plus a margin approach* and assume that the labor and material charges for a fitting are $40 while the typical margin above cost is 35%. The business suit has a standalone selling price of $300.

Brief Exercise 7-34
Classifying License Revenue and Describing Revenue Recognition **LO6**

Software Inc. sells access to a license for accounting software packages for small to mid-sized companies. Customers can choose two different options. For the first option, customers can choose to purchase the software to be downloaded on the customer's personal computer for $375. Although Software Inc. provides occasional software updates, the updates are not critical to the continued utility of the software. For the second option, the customer can choose to purchase cloud-based access to the software package for $20 per month, with the price guaranteed for two years.

a. How would Software Inc. classify its intellectual property for each option—functional intellectual property or symbolic intellectual property?

b. How would Software Inc. recognize revenue under each option—immediately or deferred and recognized over the term of the agreement?

Brief Exercise 7-35
Recognizing Franchise Revenue **LO6**

Pizza Extravaganza grants franchisees the right to operate a pizzeria using the company's name, menu items, décor, and general operational program. A franchisee pays a $250,000 initial fee for management training, and extensive planning documents. After the franchise opens, the franchisee can choose to sign an annual agreement and pay a fee of $75,000 per year for additional training, accounting services, and real-time consulting services. A new franchise agreement is signed on June 1, 2020, and the new pizzeria opened up for business on December 31, 2020. A franchisee signed up for a year of consulting services on December 31, 2020.

When is revenue recognized for (a) the $250,000 initial fee, and (b) $75,000 consulting fee?

Brief Exercise 7-36
Recording Advance Payment on Revenue **LO6**

On January 1, 2020, Colorado Inc. contracts with a customer to provide services in March 2020 for $800. The customer paid the contract price in advance of the service on March 1, 2020, while the service took place on March 8, 2020. Prepare the journal entries required for Colorado Inc. related to this revenue contract.

Brief Exercise 7-37
Determining Timing of Revenue Recognition **LO6**

For each of the following *separate* scenarios, determine at what date, or over what period of time, revenue will be recognized.

a. Ace Company is under contract to build an athletic facility for a local college for $15,000,000. The structure, while in process, is owned by the college. The college owns the work in process and is under obligation to pay for any work completed, even if the contract is canceled. The facility is expected to be completed after two years.

b. On December 31, 2020, Zulu Sales Company sold a special machine (serial no. 1713) for $200,000 and collected $80,000 cash. The remainder plus 10% interest is payable December 31, 2021. Zulu will deliver the machine on January 5, 2021. The customer has an excellent credit rating.

c. On January 2, 2020, the Daily Journal collected $400 cash from a customer for a two-year subscription to an electronic newspaper with daily postings.

Brief Exercise 7-38
Computing Income Statement Effect of Revenue Recognition on Long-Term Construction Contract **LO6**

On January 1, 2020, BuilderOne Inc. enters into a contract with a customer to redesign and update an office building for a price of $2,400,000. The construction is estimated to take three years at a total estimated cost of $2,000,000. Costs incurred in 2020 total $400,000. Determine the revenue and expense amounts to be recognized in the income statement in 2020 assuming that the company appropriately recognizes revenue over time using the cost-to-cost method.

Brief Exercise 7-39
Computing Income Statement Effect of Revenue Recognition on Long-Term Construction Contract **LO6**

Refer to the information in Brief Exercise 7-38. Assume the same facts except that the company appropriately recognizes revenue at a point in time. Determine the revenue and expense amounts to be recognized in the income statement in 2020.

Brief Exercise 7-40
Identifying a Contract Modification **LO7**

A wholesaler enters into a contract with a retailer to sell 5,000 distinct items of merchandise for $25,000 ($50 per item) over a 12-month period. The parties to the contract modify the agreement after 6 months to sell an additional 200 items for $60 each. The $60 per unit price of the additional items represents the standalone selling price of these items on the date of the modification.

a. Would the change to the agreement be accounted for as (1) a new separate contract with no change to the original contract or (2) a new contract after terminating the original contract?

b. Would the answer to part *a* change if the $60 per unit price for the additional distinct items did not represent the standalone selling price?

Brief Exercise 7-41
Identifying Accounting Treatment for Contract Modifications **LO7**

Match each of the contract modifications *a* to *c* with the proper accounting treatment, 1 through 3.

Accounting treatment

1. New separate contract with no change to original contract
2. Termination of original contract and creation of a new combined contract
3. Cumulative catch-up adjustment with no new contract

Contract modifications

____ *a.* Contract modification of distinct goods not reflective of standalone selling prices.
____ *b.* Contract modification of non-distinct goods.
____ *c.* Contract modification of distinct goods at standalone selling prices.

Brief Exercise 7-42
Timing of Revenue Recognition on Bill-and-Hold Arrangement **LO8**
Hint: See Demo 7-8A

On June 5, 2020, Quantum Corp. sold 500 units to a manufacturer. Payment is due in 30 days according to the normal credit arrangements with this customer. However, the units will not be shipped to the manufacturer for 2 to 6 weeks due to an unexpected change in the manufacturer's production schedule. Quantum Corp. has isolated the units in its storage facility and will ship the items when the manufacturer can accommodate the items. If the units were shipped to the manufacturer on July 6, 2016, when would Quantum Corp. recognize revenue?

Brief Exercise 7-43
Recognizing Revenue on Consignment Arrangement **LO8**

A magazine distributor ships a supply of weekly issues to a chain of grocery stores on March 1, 2020. The grocery chain will receive a 20% commission on any magazines sold. Any magazines not sold at the end of the week are returned to the distributor at the same time that the inventory of the next weekly issue is dropped off at the grocery store. At what point in the process does the distributor recognize revenue?

Brief Exercise 7-44
Classifying Repurchase Arrangements **LO8**

Indicate how each of the following contractual arrangements would be treated for accounting purposes: (1) leasing agreement, (2) financing agreement, or (3) sale with the right of return.

____ *a.* Contract obligates the seller to repurchase merchandise sold to a customer where the repurchase price is greater than the original selling price.
____ *b.* Contract obligates the seller to repurchase merchandise sold to a customer where the repurchase price is less than the original selling price.
____ *c.* Contract gives the right to the seller to repurchase merchandise sold to a customer where the repurchase price is less than the original selling price.
____ *d.* Contract gives the right to the seller to repurchase merchandise sold to a customer where the repurchase price is equal to the original selling price.
____ *e.* Contract gives the right to the customer to obligate the seller to repurchase merchandise sold to the customer where the repurchase price is less than the expected market value.
____ *f.* Contract gives the right to the customer to obligate the seller to repurchase merchandise sold to the customer where the repurchase price is greater than the expected market value and greater than the original selling price.

Brief Exercise 7-45
Recording Principal and Agent Revenue Entries **LO8**
Hint: See Demo 7-8D

Travel-by-Air Inc. sells discounted airline tickets to travelers on three major airlines. The discounted airfares are established by the airline companies that fulfill the promised flights. After purchase, customers must contact the airline companies directly for changes to or questions about their airline tickets. The customer pays for the airline ticket through the website of Travel-by-Air. Travel-by-Air forwards the payment for the airline tickets to the airlines less a 10% commission fee. In August of 2020, Travel-by-Air collected cash from customers totaling $40,000, and forwarded $36,000 (fees collected less commission) to the airlines. Prepare the entry recorded by Travel-by-Air Inc. to (a) recognize revenue, and (b) remit payment to the airlines.

Brief Exercise 7-46
Identifying the Reporting of Contract Revenues and Costs in Financial Statements **LO9**

Indicate how each of the following items would be included in the financial statements of a seller: (1) expense on the income statement, (2) asset on the balance sheet, or (3) liability on the balance sheet.

____ *a.* Costs to obtain a three-year contract that are expected to be recovered over the contract term.
____ *b.* Direct costs to fulfill a three-year contract's performance obligations that are expected to be recovered over the contract term.
____ *c.* Receipt of a down payment on a contract expected to be satisfied in two months.
____ *d.* Unconditional right to consideration.
____ *e.* Conditional right to consideration.
____ *f.* Costs to obtain a two-year contract that are *not* expected to be recovered over the contract term.

Brief Exercise 7-47
Identifying the Reporting of Contract Revenues and Costs in Financial Statements **LO9**

For the following items 1 to 6, indicate whether the item would be (a) expensed as incurred, (b) capitalized as an asset, or (c) may be either expensed as incurred or capitalized as an asset.

____ 1. Sales commission costs to obtain a two-year revenue contract that are recoverable.
____ 2. Sales commission costs to obtain a two-year revenue contract that are not expected to be recovered.
____ 3. Sales commission costs to obtain a revenue contract that are recoverable with an amortization period of 9 months.
____ 4. Direct labor costs incurred to fulfill a two-year revenue contract that are identifiable, generate resources used to satisfy performance obligations in the future, and are recoverable.
____ 5. General and administrative costs incurred to fulfill a two-year revenue contract.
____ 6. Shipping and handling costs incurred after title has passed to a customer for a point in time sale.

Exercises

Exercise 7-48
Identifying the Five Steps in the Revenue Recognition Process **LO1, 5**

A customer is interested in buying a pair of tennis shoes from Zap's, an online retailer, on June 1, 2020, for $80. The customer took advantage of a special offer, allowing for a purchase of a second pair of shoes at half price. The customer purchased and paid for both pairs of shoes with a credit card for a total of $120. Shipping was paid by Zap's (FOB destination) and the shoes were expected to arrive at the customer's home on June 4, 2020. The standalone selling price of each pair of shoes was $80. Use this example to identify and demonstrate the five steps of the revenue recognition process.

Exercise 7-49
Identifying the Five Steps in the Revenue Recognition Process **LO1**
Hint: See Demo 7-1

Match each step 1 through 5 with the sales process described in *a* through *e*.

Revenue Recognition Steps
Step 1: Identify the contract with customer.
Step 2: Identify the performance obligation(s).
Step 3: Determine the transaction price.
Step 4: Allocate the transaction price to performance obligation(s).
Step 5: Recognize revenue when (or as) each performance obligation is satisfied through a transfer of control.

Description of the Steps in a Sale of an Electronic Tablet
____ *a.* The total price for the tablet and two years of services is $600.
____ *b.* Customer takes possession of the electronic tablet and benefits from the data service over two years.
____ *c.* Customer will receive the electronic tablet immediately and will benefit from two years of data services for the tablet.
____ *d.* The standalone selling price of the tablet is $400 and of the two-year service contract is $200.
____ *e.* Customer agrees to purchase an electronic tablet plus two years of data services for an agreed upon price.

Exercise 7-50
Identifying the Requirements of a Valid Contract **LO2**
Hint: See Demo 7-2

Match each condition 1 through 5 with the descriptions in *a* through *e*.

Conditions of a Valid Contract
1. Contract has commercial substance.
2. Contract has approval.
3. Rights and obligations are identified.
4. Payment terms are identified.
5. Collection is probable.

Description of Contract Conditions

____ *a.* Intention by each party of a contract to abide by the terms of the contract.
____ *b.* Intention and ability of a customer to pay substantially all of the consideration due per contract.
____ *c.* Information stated in contract about payment terms.
____ *d.* Business purpose for the transfer of goods to a customer in exchange for consideration is identified in the contract.
____ *e.* Information regarding the rights and obligations of each party in a contract.

Exercise 7-51
Identifying the Validity of a Contract's Features **LO2**

The following are items from separate contractual agreements.

a. A contract for the sale of packaging to a manufacturer over a three-year period allows for the price of the packaging to increase with changes in the Consumer Price Index (to be determined at the end of each year).
b. The amount of a seller's future cash inflows are expected to change by $100 as result of a contract.
c. A customer is negotiating a contract with its supplier for specialized equipment. The specifications of the equipment have been determined as well as the price. The date and means of delivery are still under negotiation.
d. A wholesaler sells electronics to a retailer in January. Due to the slow payment for a previous order, the wholesaler requested a 50% deposit upfront for the purchase. The wholesaler expects the remaining 50% payment to be collected.
e. A customer purchases dog food at a retailer for cash of $20 through a self-service, automated checkout register. The customer did not sign a written agreement to purchase the item or verbally agree to purchase the item.
f. A hospital treats an uninsured patient for emergency services. The amount billed to the patient for services was $1,500, but the average collection amount from an uninsured patient is approximately 10% of billed services.

Required

Indicate which of the following requirements of a valid contract is primarily addressed in each of the separate cases above: (1) commercial substance, (2) approval, (3) identifiable rights and obligations, (4) identifiable payment terms, and (5) probable collection. Describe in 1 or 2 sentences how management judgment is required in determining whether the indicated requirement of a valid contract is met.

Exercise 7-52
Identifying the Number of Performance Obligations **LO3**
Hint: See Demo 7-3

Answer the following requirements for each *separate* case that involves contracts with performance obligations.

a. A retailer enters into a contract with a customer to sell an electric toothbrush, bundled with the replacement parts for the toothbrush. The retailer also sells the replacement parts and toothbrushes separately. The customer can use the toothbrush without the replacement parts, but the replacement parts have no use without the toothbrush. How many performance obligations exist in the bundling of the toothbrush and the replacement parts?
b. A contractor enters into a revenue contract to build a house for a customer. The contractor is responsible for the overall management of the project and identifies various goods and services that are provided, including architectural design, site preparation, construction of the home, plumbing and electrical services, painting, and carpentry. The contractor regularly sells these goods and services individually to customers. For example, the contractor can be contracted to paint a home. How many performance obligations are included in the contract to build the home assuming that the goods and services provided are limited to the descriptive list provided above?
c. Gateway Inc. enters into a contract with a customer to provide a license for use of new accounting software, installation services, and three years of subsequent customer support. The customer purchased the accounting software, scheduled installation services one week later, and is guaranteed customer support for three years beyond the software purchase date. The installation services require some configuration but no serious modifications. External consultants would have the knowledge to perform similar services (installation and customer support). The subsequent customer support does not significantly affect the software's benefit or value to the customer. How many performance obligations are included in this revenue contract?
d. Assume the same circumstances in part *c* above except that Gateway Inc. is supplying highly customized software, where the customer has a number of requests for changes to the standard software to accommodate industry specific reporting requirements. The customization affects both the software product and the installation process. How many performance obligations are included in this revenue contract?

Exercise 7-53
Identifying the Number of Performance Obligations **LO3, 9**

The following *separate* scenarios describe contracts with performance obligations.

a. Nikey Inc. shipped a pair of tennis shoes to a customer with the terms FOB shipping point. The shipping charges are material to the cost of the shoes. However, Nikey Inc. has elected to classify the shipping and handling costs as contract fulfillment costs.

b. Home Concepts Inc. contracts with a customer to sell and install an underground pool. The pool is operational without any customization or modification. The pool installation could be performed by other service providers.

c. Lance Inc. regularly purchases supplies from Vendor Inc. in the amount of $10,000 per month. If Lance Inc. reaches $80,000 of purchases during the calendar year, Vendor Inc. will provide Lance Inc. a rebate check of 3% on the $80,000 purchases (or $2,400) payable on January 15th of the following year. *Hint:* Consideration for the current revenue contract depends on a future event—whether or not the purchase threshold is met.

d. Builders Inc., a contractor, enters into a contract to build an exercise facility for a customer. Builder's Inc. is responsible for the overall management of the project and identifies a number of promised goods and services: engineering, site clearance, foundation, procurement, construction, piping and wiring, installation, and finishing.

e. Discovery Inc., a technology company, licenses to a customer its patent rights to an electronic process for five years and also promises to manufacture the electronic component for the customer for two years, while the customer develops its own manufacturing capability. The customer expects no significant updates to the electronic process.

f. Home Concepts Inc. enters into a contract with a customer to provide one of its popular models of outdoor hot tubs. The hot tub is widely available and is not customized in any way. However, the customer has contracted with Home Concepts to order replacement filters every 6 months over the next three years for the maintenance of the hot tub. The filters are not available from other vendors but are sold separately by Home Concepts Inc.

g. Appliances Inc. sells a refrigerator (selling price of $1,200) to a customer, who also receives a free trial size packet of a cleaning solution (standalone selling price of $1.50).

h. Sun Show Inc. sells sunglasses (selling price of $20) to a customer, who also receives a free trial size packet of a cleaning solution (standalone selling price of $1.50).

i. Lance Inc. regularly purchases supplies from Vendor Inc. in the amount of $10,000 per month. If Lance Inc. reaches $80,000 of purchases during the calendar year, Vendor Inc. will lower its selling price by 10% for Lance's purchases in the following year. The 10% volume discount is not available to customers outside of this promotion. *Hint:* Consideration for the current revenue contract is not contingent upon or affected by future purchases.

Required

Indicate the number of performance obligations in each of the scenarios *a* through *i*.

Exercise 7-54
Identifying and Recording Customer Option for Additional Merchandise **LO3, 6**

A large clothing retailer chain, Koll's, offers a sales incentive program where customers receive direct credit toward future purchases based upon the dollar amount of purchases today. For every $50 spent today, the customer will earn a $5 credit to be used at Koll's in two weeks. The credit expires 5 days after it becomes active. Not all customers will redeem the credit in the 5-day window of time. Based upon historical trends, Koll's estimates that 35% of the credits will be redeemed.

Required

a. Determine how many performance obligations are included in a sales transaction during the sales incentive program.

b. Assuming that Koll's sold $500,000 of merchandise (cost of $200,000) during the first day of the sales incentive period, record the journal entry(ies) to record sales revenue. Assume all sales were cash sales.

c. Record a summary entry to recognize revenue (if any) during the 5-day merchandise credit redemption period, assuming that 35% of the credits are redeemed.

d. Record a summary entry to recognize revenue (if any) at the conclusion of the 5-day merchandise credit redemption period, assuming that no credits are redeemed.

Exercise 7-55
Identifying and Recording Customer Option for Additional Merchandise **LO3, 6**

Pets Inc. launches a new advertising promotion where, for each purchase over $30, it offers a coupon for a 35% discount on a future purchase of $30 or more. There is a limit of one coupon per customer. Pets Inc. estimates that 28% of customers receiving the coupon will redeem the coupon on an average purchase of $40. Sales on the first day of the one-week promotional period totaled $200,000 resulting in 2,000 coupons distributed. Assume all sales were cash sales. Cost of sales is 45% of the selling price.

Required

a. Determine how many performance obligations are included in a sales transaction during the advertising promotion program. Assume that coupons readily available to the public online or in company fliers have a maximum value of 20% off a purchase of $30 or more.

b. Record the journal entry to record revenue in the first day of the promotion period using the relative percentages to allocate standalone selling prices.

c. Only 25% of the coupons were redeemed during the redemption period on qualifying purchases of $18,500. Record the entry for the redemption of the coupons, ignoring the cost entries.

d. If the coupon offered were instead 20% on purchases of $30 or more (otherwise, same facts as before), how would the answers change to parts *a* and *b*, if at all?

Exercise 7-56
Determining the Transaction Price for a Revenue Contract **LO4**

A contractor enters into a revenue contract with a customer to build customized equipment for $100,000 with a performance bonus of $55,000 that will be paid based on how quickly the equipment is completed. The amount of the performance bonus decreases by 15% of the original bonus per week for every week beyond the agreed-upon completion date. The contractor has had experiences with similar contracts and thus has the data to predict the timing of completion of the contract. Therefore, the contractor concludes that the expected value method is the best predictor of revenue. The contractor estimates that there is a 65% probability that the contract will be completed by the agreed-upon completion date, a 25% probability that it will be completed one week late, and a 10% probability that it will be completed two weeks late.

Required

Determine the transaction price for revenue recognition for the contractor.

Exercise 7-57
Determining the Transaction Price for a Revenue Contract **LO4**
Hint: See Demo 7-4A

A contractor enters into a revenue contract to construct customized equipment for a customer. The contract price is $100,000 plus a $50,000 bonus if the customized equipment is completed by a specified date. The contract is expected to take three years to complete. The contractor has extensive experience in building customized equipment. The award fee is paid only if the customized equipment is completed by the agreed upon date. Otherwise, the contractor receives no bonus. The contractor estimates that it is 80% likely that the contract will be completed successfully and in advance of the target date.

Required

Determine the transaction price for revenue recognition for the contractor.

Exercise 7-58
Determining the Transaction Price for a Revenue Contract **LO4**

Equipment Inc. sells machinery to a customer for $1 million payable in 6 months. At the inception of the contract, Equipment Inc. believes that it is likely that the customer will not pay the full contract price due to a possible price concession. Equipment Inc. has been offered up to a $250,000 price concession if it provides demonstrations of the equipment to potential customers of Equipment Inc. Equipment Inc. estimates that the customer will pay at least $750,000, which is sufficient to cover Equipment Inc.'s cost of sales. Equipment Inc. is interested in the contract and thus willing to accept the lower contract price because it wants to grow its presence in this market. Equipment Inc. concludes it is probable it will collect $750,000.

Required

Determine the transaction price for revenue recognition for the seller.

Exercise 7-59
Measuring the Transaction Price **LO4**

The following are separate revenue contract scenarios.

1. Loyola Inc. sells $50,000 of inventory during the year to customers for $100,000. Loyola Inc. accepts returns up to 3 months after the date of purchase. Loyola estimates returns to be 6% of sales.
2. Nakoma Corp. sells product offering a retroactive volume discount on certain cumulative sales volumes as follows: 0 to 500 cost $10 each; 501 to 1,000 units cost $9 each; 1,001 units and beyond cost $8 each. For Nakoma's largest customer, Nakoma estimates the likelihood of cumulative purchases for the year as follows: 15% for 400 units, 50% for 800 units, and 35% for 1,200 units. The revenue contract stipulates that the price per unit of product will be adjusted retroactively once specified sales volumes are met. Cumulative sales to Nakoma's largest customer were 200 units in the first quarter.
3. Spectrum Inc. is entering into a revenue contract with a new customer for $20,000. Spectrum agrees to pay an up-front fee of $2,500 to the new customer in order to obtain the new contract as a way to compensate the customer for additional up-front processing costs. This payment is not associated with any distinct goods or services.
4. Lakeside Inc. enters into a revenue contract with a customer to provide services. Under the contract, Lakeside will receive a $10,000 bonus (beyond the established fees of $72,000) if the services are completed by the established date and within the required specifications. Based on Lakeside's history of completing past contracts, Lakeside estimates that the most likely amount of the bonus is $10,000.
5. Atlanta Inc. enters into a revenue contract with a customer to provide services. Under the contract, Atlanta Inc. will receive 100 shares of the customer's common stock ($1 par value per share). At the contract's inception, the stock is trading on an exchange at $25 per share.

Required

For each of the separate revenue contracts *1* through *5* (a) measure the transaction price and (b) determine whether the transaction price is fixed, variable, or some combination of both.

Exercise 7-60 Determining Transaction Price and Refund Liability **LO4**

A distributor sells jewelry to a retail chain with the stipulation that 30% of the jewelry can be returned within six months. Actual returns have averaged 25% in each of the last 10 years. The distributor sells 10,000 items to retailers on account in January of 2020. Jewelry was sold to the distributor for $10 per item.

Required

a. Determine the transaction price for the sale of jewelry by the distributor for January of 2020.

b. Determine the balance in Refund Liability on January 31, 2020, if the company had actual returns of $4,500 in January 2020.

Exercise 7-61 Determining Transaction Price and Refund Liability **LO4**

In January 2020, a retailer sells 100 paper shredders to customers for $100 each. The terms of the sales include a right for the customer to return a shredder within 180 days of the sale date. Based on historical trends, the retailer uses the expected value method and estimates a 40% probability that 8 paper shredders will be returned, a 45% probability that 9 paper shredders will be returned, and a 15% probability that 12 paper shredders will be returned. The retailer also concludes it is highly probable that there will not be a significant reversal of revenue recognized based on this return estimate. Thus, the agreement is a valid contract. Assume no actual returns in January 2020.

Required

Determine (1) the transaction price for the sale of shredders for January 2020, and (2) the refund liability balance on January 31, 2020. Round expected returns to the nearest whole unit.

Exercise 7-62 Recording a Payment by Seller to Customer **LO4, 6**

On March 18, 2020, Kudos Corporation sells snack products to a retail warehouse club chain in the amount of $50,000 (cost of $30,000). The contract includes an obligation for the warehouse club to run certain advertising campaigns for the snack products in exchange for $4,000 cash from Kudos Corporation on the contract date. The comparable price for this type of advertising campaign to be conducted by a third party is $4,000.

Required

a. Prepare Kudos' journal entry on March 18, 2020, for the sale of merchandise and the purchase of advertising services.

b. Assume instead that Kudos sold $50,000 of product to a customer (cost of $30,000) and has agreed to pay the customer $1,000 in slotting fees for preferential product placement in displays. Kudos will pay the $1,000 fee on April 30, 2020. Prepare Kudos' journal entry on March 18, 2020, for the sale of the product and on April 30, 2020, for the payment of the slotting fee.

Exercise 7-63 Allocating Transaction Price to Performance Obligations and Recording Sales **LO5, 6**

On June 1, 2020, Forde Auto Manufacturer sells a 4-door sedan to a dealer for $30,000, which includes three years of maintenance. The standalone selling price of the vehicle is $30,000 and the standalone selling price of the maintenance contract is $2,000. In addition, Forde offered a $500 cash incentive (per vehicle purchased) to the dealer if the vehicle was purchased in the first week of June 2020.

Required

a. How should the transaction price be allocated among the performance obligation(s) for sales made in the first week of June? Round each price to the nearest dollar.

b. Prepare Forde's journal entry to record the sale of vehicles for cash, assuming that dealers purchased 20 vehicles during the first week of June 2020. (Ignore the cost of sales entries.)

Exercise 7-64 Allocating Transaction Price to Performance Obligations and Recording Sales **LO5, 6**

Maximum Inc. (retailer) has a loyalty program that rewards its customers one point per $1 spent. Points are redeemable for $0.20 off future purchases. A customer purchases products (cost of $140) for cash at the usual selling price of $200 and earns 200 points redeemable for $40 off future purchases of goods or services. The retailer expects redemption of 180 points or 90% of points earned.

Required

a. How should the transaction price be allocated among the performance obligation(s)? Round each price to the nearest dollar.

b. Prepare Maximum's journal entry to record the $200 sale to the customer where the customer earned 200 loyalty points.

Exercise 7-65
Allocating Transaction Price to Performance Obligations and Recording Sales **LO5, 6**

Value Dealership Inc. markets and sells vehicles to retail customers. Along with a new vehicle purchase, a customer will receive a free annual maintenance contract for one year from the date of purchase. The standalone selling price of a vehicle is $30,000 and the standalone selling price for the annual maintenance contract is $500. During October 2020, Value Dealership Inc. sold 30 vehicles for $30,250 per vehicle, each with a free annual maintenance contract.

Required

a. Ignoring the cost entries, record the journal entry in October 2020 for Value Dealership's sale of vehicles with the associated maintenance contracts to customers. Round prices to the nearest dollar.

b. Assume the same information above except that the standalone selling price of the annual maintenance contract is not known because this was the first time Value Dealership offered the service. Value Dealership is uncertain as to what services, on average, a customer will take advantage of during the year of the contract. The Dealership researched competitor prices and determined that the average selling price for a maintenance service contract is $650. Ignoring the cost entries, record the journal entry in October 2020 for Value Dealership's sale of vehicles to its customers.

c. Assume the same information (original scenario) above except that the standalone selling price of the annual maintenance contract is not known because this was the first time Value Dealership offered the service. Value Dealership determined that the cost of the annual contract is $400 for the year and the expected profit margin on the service contract is 35%. Ignoring the cost entries, record the journal entry in October 2020 for Value Dealership's sale of vehicles to its customers.

Exercise 7-66
Allocating Transaction Price to Performance Obligations **LO5**

Pet Lodge Inc., which offers day and overnight kennel services for pets, is offering a promotion for new customers signing a contract: purchase 3 overnight stays, a 10-visit day pass punch card, and a new leash for $260. The total transaction price of $260 is stated to the customer as $90 for the overnight stay, $150 for the punch card, and $20 for the leash. Allocate the $260 transaction price under the following *separate* scenarios. Round allocated prices to the nearest dollar.

a. The three items (overnight stays, day pass punch card, and leash) are sold separately by Pet Lodge Inc. The standalone selling prices of the overnight stays, day pass punch card, and a new leash are $90, $150, and $20, respectively.

b. The three items (overnight stays, day pass punch card, and leash) are sold separately by Pet Lodge Inc. The standalone selling prices of the overnight stays, day pass punch card, and leash are $105, $180, and $25, respectively.

c. Two of the three items (overnight stay and day pass punch card) are sold separately by Pet Lodge Inc. The standalone selling prices of the overnight stays and day pass punch card are $90, $150, respectively. Because Pet Lodge Inc. has never sold leashes prior to this promotion, Pet Lodge Inc. determined the average selling price of similar leashes in the market place to be $25.

d. Two of the three items (overnight stays and day pass punch card) are sold separately by Pet Lodge Inc. The standalone selling prices of the overnight stays and day pass punch card are $90, $150, respectively. Pet Lodge Inc. purchased the leashes for $15 each and expects a gross profit margin of 50%.

e. Two of the three items (overnight stays and day pass punch card) are sold separately by Pet Lodge Inc. The standalone selling prices of the overnight stays and day pass punch card are $90, $150, respectively. Pet Lodge Inc. has never sold leashes prior to this promotion, and is not able to obtain a reliable comparable market price because the leashes are unique and there is nothing comparable on the market.

Exercise 7-67
Identifying Customer Control and Recording Advance Payment **LO1, 6**

Allstar Inc. sells uniforms and spirit clothing to local school teams. Allen High School placed an order for 50 items for a total selling price of $2,200 on September 14, 2020. The cost of the merchandise to Allstar Inc. is $1,115. To place the order, Allstar Inc. required a $500 down payment on September 14, 2020. Delivery of the order to Allen is completed on October 7, 2020, at which time the remaining balance was collected from Allen.

Required

a. Demonstrate the five steps of the revenue recognition process for this scenario.

b. Record Allstar's entry on September 14, 2020.

c. Record Allstar's entries on October 7, 2020.

Exercise 7-68
Allocating Transaction Price to Performance Obligations and Recording Sales **LO5, 6**

Software Supplier Inc. sells to a customer a perpetual software license and post-contract customer support for a 12-month period, commencing at the time that the software is activated. Software Supplier Inc. charges $300 upfront when the software is purchased and $20 a month for 12 months, due at the end of the month. Software Supplier Inc. sells the software separately for $400 while the standalone selling price of the post-contract customer support is $200.

Required

a. How should the transaction price be allocated among the performance obligation(s)? Round to the nearest dollar.

b. Prepare Software Supplier's journal entry to record sale of software to the customer and the entry for the first monthly payment.

Exercise 7-69
Computing Revenue and Gross Profit on Long-Term Construction Contract **LO6**
Hint: See Demo 7-6B

Supplier Corp. enters into a government contract in 2020 to provide computer equipment for $2 million. The contract consists of a single performance obligation to provide specified equipment in three years. Total costs estimated by Supplier Corp. for the contract are $1.4 million. The equipment is highly specialized and has no alternative uses. As negotiated in the contract, any costs incurred by Supplier Corp. plus a specified profit margin will be paid to Supplier Corp. in the event of a contract cancellation. Actual costs incurred in 2020 were $650,000 including unexpected cost overruns of $80,000 due to labor inefficiencies.

Required

a. Would revenue be recognized over time or at a point in time for this contract?

b. Calculate (1) recognized revenue, (2) the gross profit, and (3) adjusted contract margin to be recorded in 2020. Round answers to the nearest dollar.

Exercise 7-70
Computing Revenue and Gross Profit on Long-term Construction Contract **LO6**

Refer to the information in Exercise 7-69. Assume that at the end of 2021, the estimate of total costs has increased to $1.50 million due to an increase in cost of materials. Actual costs incurred to date are $1,150,000, excluding year one inefficiencies. Round answers to the nearest dollar.

Required

a. Calculate (1) recognized revenue, (2) the gross profit, and (3) adjusted contract margin to be recorded in 2021.

b. Calculate (1) cumulative recognized revenue, (2) cumulative gross profit, and (3) cumulative adjusted contract margin at the end of 2021.

Exercise 7-71
Identifying Performance Obligations and Recording Revenue from Franchise Rights **LO3, 6**

The Krispy Donuts franchise has agreements with 100 franchisees across the United States to operate bakeries. On January 1, 2020, Krispy Donuts grants a franchisee the right to operate a bakery in Minneapolis, Minnesota, using Krispy Donuts brand name, recipe, and other business concepts for a price of $500,000. On January 1, 2020, the franchisee made a down payment to the franchisor of $50,000 and paid the remaining $450,000 upfront fee on March 31, 2020. In exchange for the $500,000 payment, the franchisee received franchise rights, which include benefits of a national advertising campaign over the ten-year period (starting on the contract date) to promote the brand name of Krispy Donuts. The payment also includes the purchase of kitchen equipment from the franchisor (fair value of $60,000), and upfront training and assistance in setting up the franchise (fair value of $20,000). The training and assistance will be performed before the opening of the bakery. Equipment was delivered on April 1, 2020, and had a cost of $40,000. Krispy Donuts uses the residual method to measure the standalone value of the franchise rights.

Required

a. How many performance obligations are included in the franchise arrangement?

b. When does the franchisor recognize revenue for each performance obligation?

c. Prepare the journal entries for the Krispy Donuts franchisor through the opening of the bakery on June 1, 2020.

d. Assuming the franchisor has a December 31 year-end, prepare any journal entries required on December 31, 2020.

Exercise 7-72
Computing Revenue to be Recognized Under Different Scenarios **LO6**

Answer the requirements for each of the following separate cases.

a. Organic Foods Inc. required an advance payment of $50 on March 1, 2020, from a customer for a customized fruit basket. The customer picked up the basket on March 5, 2020, and paid the remaining balance of $75. Determine the amount of revenue that Organic Foods Inc. would record on March 1, 2020, and March 5, 2020.

b. Eagle Inc. sold apparel to customers in May of 2020 for $100,000. At the point of sale, Eagle Inc. provided customers 1,000 coupons for 30% off purchases in June and July of 2020. The coupon is considered a separate performance obligation. Eagle Inc. estimates the standalone selling price of the apparel to be $100,000 and the standalone selling price of the coupons to be $15,000 ($30 estimated coupon value x 500 coupons expected to be redeemed). Determine the amount of revenue that Eagle would record in May for the sale of apparel, and the amount of revenue deferred for the customer options (coupon promotion).

c. JJ Construction Inc. entered into a contract with a customer to build a corporate office on January 1, 2020, for $15,000,000. The customer owns the construction in process during the construction process and the customer is under obligation to pay for any work completed, even if the contract is canceled. The office is expected to be completed in three years for a total cost of $9,500,000. Actual costs incurred through December 31, 2020, are $3,990,000. Determine the amount of revenue to record in 2020 assuming that the cost-to-cost method is used.

d. JJ Construction Inc. entered into a contract with a customer to build a movable storage facility on January 1, 2020, for $1,500,000. JJ Construction Inc. owns the work in process and constructs this type of storage unit for a number of customers. The customer made a down payment of 10% of the project, with an additional 10% due at the end of year one and the remaining due when it takes control of the facility. The facility is expected to be completed in two years for a total cost of $1,200,000. Actual costs incurred through December 31, 2020, are $500,000. Determine the amount of revenue to record in 2020.

e. On January 1, 2020, Franchisee Inc. enters into a contract with Italian Fine Dining Inc. for the right (beginning immediately) to operate an Italian Fine Dining restaurant and receive on-going consulting services for a five-year period. The upfront fee of $150,000 also includes specialized equipment for $20,000. The standalone selling price of the franchise services and specialized equipment are $130,000 and $20,000, respectively. The equipment (with a cost of $15,000) was transferred to the franchisee on March 1, 2020. Determine the amount of revenue to recognize for Italian Fine Dining Inc. on January 1, 2020, March 1, 2020, and December 31, 2020.

Exercise 7-73
Recording Revenue Under a Contract Modification **LO7**

Traders Inc. enters into a three-year office maintenance contract with its customer for $420,000 ($140,000 per year). $140,000 per year is the standalone selling price for one year of maintenance service. At the end of the second year, both parties agree to modify the maintenance contract as follows: (1) the fee for the third year is reduced to $110,000, and (2) the contract is extended for an additional two years for $200,000 ($100,000 per year). The standalone selling price for one year of service at the time of modification is $120,000. Maintenance fees are billed annually by Traders Inc.

Required

a. Record Traders Inc.'s journal entry to recognize revenue for each of the first two years of the contract. Assume that the contract price was paid in cash.

b. Record Traders Inc.'s journal entry to recognize revenue for each of the years three through five of the contract, taking into account the contract modification.

Exercise 7-74
Recognizing Revenue Under a Contract Modification **LO7**

On August 1, 2020, a retailer enters into an arrangement with a customer to sell 10 items for $2,000 ($200 per item) over a four-month period. During August and September of 2020, the retailer sold 5 of the 10 items to the customer. On October 1, 2020, the contract is modified to include 8 additional items, with a transaction price of $250 per item. Because the additional items have added features, the standalone selling price of the additional items is $250 per item at the date of the contract modification.

Required

a. Describe how the retailer should account for the contract modification.

b. Determine the amount of revenue to be recognized for the remaining units (the 5 under the original contract and the 8 under the contract modification) to be sold under the revenue contract(s).

Exercise 7-75
Determining Revenue Contract Classification and Recognition Timing **LO8**
Hint: See Demo 7-8A

Smith Manufacturing Inc. sells $250,000 of equipment to a customer on August 15, 2020, and the equipment is prepared to ship on that date. However, Smith Manufacturing Inc. receives a last minute request from the customer to hold the shipment for 15-45 days due to delay in construction of a facility where the new equipment will be installed. The equipment is customized for the customer, and it cannot be used for any other purposes. Smith bills the customer on August 15, 2020, with payment due in 30 days. The equipment was shipped to the customer on September 8, 2020.

Required

a. How would this type of revenue contract be classified? Explain.

b. At what date is revenue recognized by Smith Manufacturing for the sale of equipment?

Exercise 7-76
Recording Revenue Under Different Repurchase Agreements **LO8**

On January 1, 2020, Miller Inc. sells equipment to Smith Inc. for $55,000. As stipulated in the revenue contract, Miller Inc. will buy back the equipment on December 31, 2020, for $58,850. The relevant interest rate is 7%.

Required

a. Prepare the seller's journal entry on January 1, 2020.

b. Prepare the seller's journal entry on December 31, 2020.

c. Assume instead that Miller has the *option* to buy back the equipment and the fair value of the equipment is expected to decline through 2020. How would the answers to parts *a* and *b* change (if at all)?

d. Assume instead that Smith has the option to require Miller to buy back the equipment after one year for $58,850 (an amount greater than the expected market value of the equipment at that time). How would the answers to parts *a* and *b* change (if at all)?

Exercise 7-77 Recording Revenue and Receivables Under a Consignment Arrangement **LO8**
Hint: See Demo 7-8B

On March 15, 2020, Drexel Corp. provides goods to a retailer through consignment where Drexel Corp. retains ownership of the goods until the goods are sold to the retailer's customer. Sale to the final customer is documented when the goods are scanned at the cash register of the retailer. Drexel Corp. receives a daily report on the number of units sold by the retailer to the end customer. Any unsold product can be returned to Drexel Corp. at anytime. Drexel Corp. has the right through the contract to recall any goods shipped and to transfer the goods to another retailer as a way to increase the rate of sales to the final customer. After the sale of the products to the final customer, the retailer cannot return the items to Drexel Corp. During March of 2020, Drexel Corp. transferred 1,200 units to the retailer, and the retailer sold 1,000 units. The product cost Drexel Corp. $80 per unit and the product was sold for $115 per unit to the end customer. The retailer sent a payment to Drexel Corp. for the cash collected on the sale of product less a 10% commission on April 7, 2020.

Required

a. At what date should Drexel Corp. recognize revenue? Explain.

b. Record Drexel's entries on March 15, 2020, March 31, 2020, and April 7, 2020.

Exercise 7-78 Determining Type of Revenue Arrangement and the Timing or Amount of Revenue Recognized **LO8**

Answer the requirements for each of the following separate revenue arrangements.

a. On December 31, 2020, Quality Wholesalers Inc. sold merchandise to a retailer with payment terms net 30. The merchandise is clearly segregated in Wholesalers Inc.'s distribution center, ready for shipment to the customer, but the units are not scheduled to ship until March 1, 2021 (or earlier if requested by retailer). Due to structural damage from a fire at one of the retailer's locations, the retailer does not currently have the capacity to hold the merchandise, but would like to have the merchandise available if needed. Determine (1) the type of complex revenue arrangement, and (2) the date that Quality Wholesalers Inc. should record the sale of the merchandise to its customer.

b. On February 1, 2020, Atlanta Inc. sells equipment to Raleigh Inc. for $200,000. As stipulated in the revenue contract, Raleigh Inc. can sell back the equipment on December 31, 2020, for $15,000. (The expected value of the equipment at that time is $20,000.) The relevant interest rate is 7%. Determine (1) the type of complex revenue arrangement, and (2) the amount of revenue that Atlanta Inc. should record on February 1, 2020.

c. On April 1, 2020, Container Store Inc. shipped merchandise to Office Plus Inc. with a sales value of $15,000. Container Store Inc. entered into a contract with Office Plus Inc. in which it only is responsible for purchasing the merchandise that it ultimately sells to its customers. Any unsold merchandise can be returned to Container Store Inc. at no cost to Office Plus Inc. and Container Store Inc. can request return of merchandise held by Office Plus Inc. at any time. For the month of April, Office Plus Inc. sold $10,000 of the shipped merchandise and paid Packaging Plus Inc. for the purchase electronically on April 30, 2020. Determine (1) the type of complex revenue arrangement, and (2) the amount of revenue that Container Store Inc. should record in April 2020.

d. MyTickets Inc. facilitates the purchase of concert tickets to customers through its vast social media network. MyTickets Inc. has access to blocks of tickets from a large number of vendors that are advertised through its network. When a customer purchases a ticket, MyTickets Inc. electronically forwards the payment to the vendor, less a commission of 15%. Any issues with the performances associated with the tickets are managed by the vendors. In March of 2020, MyTickets Inc. sold tickets worth $45,000, of which $8,000 of the concerts have not yet taken place. Determine (1) the type of complex revenue arrangement, and (2) how much revenue MyTickets Inc. reports in March of 2020.

Exercise 7-79 Accounting for Contract (Commission) Costs **LO9**

Alexis Inc. pays commissions to sales agents for initial sales of 18-month contracts for product purchases. The cost of commissions will be recovered over the contract period. Alexis Inc. concludes that the commission payment is an incremental cost of obtaining the contract and recognizes an asset for the commissions paid.

Required

a. What period of time should Alexis Inc. use to amortize the commission costs? Explain.

b. If instead the contract was a 12-month contract, would the accounting treatment for commission costs change assuming that the cost of commissions will be recovered over the contract period? Explain.

c. How would our answer to *a* change if Alexis instead concluded that the cost of commissions would not be recovered over the contract period?

Problems

Problem 7-80
Evaluating the Validity of a Contract (Rights and Collectibility) **LO2**

Answer the requirements for each of the following cases involving four distinct industries: real estate, telecommunication, pharmaceutical, and healthcare.

a. *Real Estate Industry.* A stated contract price on a real estate contract is $1,000,000. A price concession is expected of $100,000 on the contract price. In evaluating the validity of a contract, is the $1,000,000 contract price or the price net of the price concession ($900,000) considered in evaluating the probability of collectibility on the contract?

b. *Telecommunication Industry.* In determining the validity of a contract, it will be important to determine the length of the contract. A telecommunication company arranges for a prepaid, month-to-month, cellular contract with a customer. The customer pays for a month of cellular service on the first day of the service period. A typical customer will remain on the month-to-month contract for a two-year period. In evaluating the validity of a contract, what is the length of contract?

c. *Pharmaceutical Industry.* A pharmaceutical company leases a medical device to a customer over a five-year period. In addition, the pharmaceutical company provides training services over the initial two-year period. How is this contract evaluated under the revenue recognition standard?

d. *Healthcare Industry.* A hospital treats a patient in an emergency situation for services with a retail price of $10,000. Due to the seriousness of the injury, the hospital was unable to evaluate the patient's intent and ability to pay for the services at the time the services were provided. Is a valid contract in place given that the provider fulfilled its obligations to provide services to the patient?

Problem 7-81
Accounting for Upfront Fees and Recording and Allocating Revenue
LO3, 4, 5, 6

CharterX Inc. establishes a contract with a customer to deliver both a cable television receiver (equipment) and cable television service for 15 months. In exchange, the customer pays a $75 upfront fee for installation of the cable television receiver (which must be returned to CharterX Inc. at the end of the contract term) and $80 a month for the premium package of 200+ channels. The $75 upfront fee has no standalone selling price as it is not sold separately. The $80 charge per month for cable services is at its standalone selling price. The company has determined that the contract for the receiver is not a lease.

Required

a. (1) How many performance obligations are established in the revenue contract? (2) Record the entry by the seller at the initiation of the contract assuming 100 contracts are initiated. (3) Record the entry by the seller one month after initiation of the contract.

b. CharterX Inc. also offers a bundled package where a customer receives the 15-month cable subscription (and cable television receiver) along with an internet connection for an upfront fee of $75 plus $100 a month (stated to the customer as $80 per month for cable service, and an additional $20 per month for internet service). The standalone selling price of the internet connection is $40 per month. (1) How many performance obligations are established in the revenue contract? (2) Record the entry by the seller at the initiation of the contract assuming 100 new customers sign up for the bundled option. (3) Record the entry by the seller one month after initiation of the contract. Round amounts to the nearest dollar.

Problem 7-82
Determining Transaction Price and Recording Entries for a Customer Loyalty Program
LO3, 4, 5, 6

Best Burritos Inc., a restaurant chain, sponsors a new customer loyalty program. For every purchase, the customer swipes their reward card that tracks their spending at the restaurant. Every cumulative $50 spent earns the customer a free menu item. It is common for customers to track spending using the loyalty card and to accumulate the right to free menu items.

For the month of June 2020, Best Burritos Inc. records sales of $150,000 with 70% of the sales registered on loyalty cards. The average value of a food item expected to be redeemed by a customer, as a free menu item, is $6.50. The average redemption rate is estimated at 60%. Round amounts to the nearest dollar.

Required

a. Determine the transaction price for the product and for the customer loyalty program.

b. Record the journal entry for the June 2020 sales. Ignore the cost of sales entry.

c. At the end of June 2020, 300 items are redeemed for $1,800. Record the redemption entry in June 2020.

Problem 7-83
Determining Transaction Price and Recording Revenue and Commission Entries
LO4, 6, 9

On January 1, 2020, Packaging Inc. enters into a one-year contract with 5M Inc. to deliver packaging materials. The contract stipulates that the price per case of packaging materials will be adjusted retroactively once 5M Inc. reaches certain sales volumes, defined as follows.

Cumulative Sales Volume	Price Per Case
0–100,000 cases	$80
100,001–300,000 cases	70
300,001 cases and above	60

Volume is determined based on sales during the calendar year and price adjustments are computed retroactively on the cumulative sales volume. Any refunds earned by 5M Inc. are paid at the end of the calendar year. There are no minimum purchase requirements. Packaging Inc.'s cost per case is $40. Packaging Inc. estimates that the total sales volume for the year will be 200,000 cases based on past experiences with 5M Inc. During the first quarter ended March 31, 2020, Packaging Inc. sells 80,000 cases to 5M Inc. at a contract price of $80 per case.

Required

a. Determine Packaging Inc.'s transaction price for the sale of 80,000 cases.

b. Record Packaging Inc.'s journal entries for the first quarter sales and cost of sales.

c. Assume that the sales representative assigned to 5M Inc. received a commission of $5,000 on the origination of the contract on January 1, 2020. (Commissions are not paid on contract renewals.) While the contract is in effect for one year, 5M Inc. has indicated its intent to renew the contract for the following year. Packaging Inc. expects the contract to continue to be renewed for an additional three years (beyond December 31, 2021). Record the entries related to the commission on January 1, 2020, and on December 31, 2020.

Problem 7-84
Determining Transaction Price and Recording Revenue and Refund Entries **LO4, 6**

Refer to the original facts in Problem 7-83. This contract continues into the next quarter with the following results.

- Packaging Inc. sells 90,000 cases of packaging material during the second quarter period ended June 30, 2020.
- Due to expansion of product lines by 5M Inc., Packaging Inc. increases its estimate of total sales volume to 350,000 cases for the calendar year.

Required

a. Explain how Packaging Inc. should account for this change.

b. Record the journal entries related to sales and cost of sales that are required for the second quarter.

Problem 7-85
Determining Transaction Price and Recording Revenue and Refund Entries **LO4, 5, 6**

Home Warehouse Inc. sells lighting fixtures to customers for $50 per unit (cost of $30 per unit). A rebate coupon is issued with each sale that can be redeemed by the customer for $10 per unit in the future. Home Warehouse Inc. estimates that 25% of eligible rebates will be redeemed based on its experience with similar programs, and rebate redemption rates available in the marketplace for similar programs.

Required

a. Assuming that Home Warehouse Inc. sells 215 lighting fixtures to customers on January 1, 2020, record the journal entry to reflect sales and cost of goods sold.

b. If Home Warehouse Inc. estimates that the *most likely amount* of sales returns is 30 units, how would the entries in part *a* change? Assume that the estimated rebate percentage is applied to sales before an estimate of returns. *Hint:* In the cost of goods sold entry, record a debit to Estimated Inventory Returns for the cost of 30 units.

Problem 7-86
Determining Transaction Price Using Probability-Weighted Estimates **LO4**

Star Supplier Inc. enters into a contract to sell component parts to a manufacturer. The price for the first 1,000 units is $90 each and the price for all units in excess of 1,000 is $50 each. The price for the first 1,000 is not retroactively adjusted once volumes exceed 1,000 units (only units after 1,000 will be discounted). Star Supplier Inc. believes the manufacturer will purchase a minimum of 1,000 components. After the initial 1,000 components, Star Supplier Inc. believes there is a 55% probability that the manufacturer will purchase an additional 200 components, a 25% probability the manufacturer will purchase an additional 500 units, and a 20% probability that the manufacturer will purchase an additional 700 units. Star Supplier Inc.'s assumptions are based on historical experience with similar contracts, and information determined through the relationship with the manufacturer and its planned production levels. Star Supplier Inc. has determined that a probability-weighted estimate is more predictive of the amount of revenue to be collected instead of determining the most likely amount of the average transaction price.

Required

a. Compute the probability weighted consideration.

b. Compute the probability weighted number of parts.

c. Compute the probability weighted component price per unit.

d. How is the probability weighted component price per unit used in accounting for the contract?

Problem 7-87
Allocating a Transaction Price and Recording Revenue and Cost of Revenue **LO5, 6**

A retailer initiates an advertising campaign, which allows a customer to receive a coupon for a free gaming system DVD with the purchase of three gaming system DVDs in a single purchase for $75 (3 × $25). To receive the free gaming system DVD coupon, the customer fills out a request form and mails it to the retailer prior to the expiration date. The retailer estimates, based on recent experience with similar promotions, that 80% of the customers will complete the mail-in rebate required to receive the free gaming system DVD. The cost of the DVD to the retailer is $18, and its standalone selling price is $25.

Required

a. How is the consideration allocated to the performance obligations in the revenue contract?

b. Prepare the journal entry for sales and cost of sales for 40 sales transactions in which 3 gaming system DVDs were sold as part of each transaction. Round to the nearest dollar.

c. Assume the retailer has no past experience to estimate the amount of redemption. (1) Show how the consideration is allocated to the performance obligations in the revenue contract. (2) Prepare the journal entry for sales and cost of sales for 40 sales transactions in which 3 gaming system DVDs were sold as part of each transaction.

Problem 7-88
Accounting for a Product and Service Contract Sale with a Contract Modification **LO7**

Stapler Inc. offers a color laser printer for $350 (the standalone selling price). The cost of the printer for Stapler Inc. is $210 per printer. Available separately is a two-year product replacement plan (to replace or repair the printer) for $80. The product replacement plan has a standalone selling price of $80 for the two-year period. In the first week of June 2020, the company sold 1,000 printers with the two-year product replacement plan. One year after the sale of the printers, Stapler Inc. offers an incentive for its customers to extend the service plan one additional year. The offer allows customers to modify their contract and extends the replacement plan for one additional year for $35. In June 2021, 300 customers agreed to the terms of contract modification and paid the $35 fee. Stapler Inc. incurred warranty costs of $0, $8,000, and $20,000 in years ending May 31, 2020, 2021, and 2022, respectively.

Required

a. Record the seller's journal entries required from the original purchase of the printer and service agreements through the end of the extended contracts in 2022 for the following.
   1. Sale of printer and service agreements.
   2. Revenue related to the service agreements for the period June 1, 2020, to May 31, 2021.
   3. Payment received for contract extension.
   4. Revenue earned June 1, 2020, to May 31, 2021, for original contracts (no extensions).
   5. Revenue earned June 1, 2020, to May 31, 2021, for original contracts (with extensions).
   6. Warranty costs for the period June 1, 2020, to May 31, 2021.
   7. Revenue earned June 1, 2021, to May 31, 2022, for original contracts (with extensions).
   8. Warranty costs for the period June 1, 2021, to May 31, 2022.

b. Reconcile the contract liability account from 2020–2022. *Hint:* Begin with the contract liability from the original service contract and add or subtract, as appropriate, reversals and extensions to the contract liability.

c. Compute the gross profit percentage on the printer sales and the profitability margin on the service contract sales in total (for all contracts and years combined).

Accounting Decisions and Judgments

AD&J 7-89
Researching and Analyzing the Accounting Treatment for Upfront Customer Payments **LO4**

Judgment Case A Transition Resource Group for Revenue Recognition (TRG) was established by the FASB to comment on questions from companies transitioning to ASC 606. The topic of TRG Memo No. 59 is the accounting for payment to customers in the revenue recognition process. The following is a summary of an example presented by the TRG.

> Service Provider makes a $1 million payment to a customer as part of the negotiations in a contract to provide IT outsourcing services. The payment to the customer was negotiated because the customer will incur costs to terminate employees and dispose of equipment that is currently utilized in the operations to be outsourced. The entity estimates that the customer will pay a fee of $6 million for five years of services. The contract is cancellable at the end of any month for no penalty, although Service Provider expects the customer to continue to purchase services for five years because the customer has limited ability to perform the services internally given the customer terminated employees and disposed of equipment. Additionally, the customer has incurred significant setup costs and will incur the significant setup costs to change vendors. Finally, Service Provider knows from past experience with entering into similar contracts with other customers that most customers do not cancel contracts. Service Provider has no previous revenue from contracts with this customer.

Required

a. Locate TRG Memo No. 59 from the FASB website (fasb.org) and indicate (1) the date of the memo, (2) the main question addressed by the TRG, and (3) the Codification standard that is referenced for the question.

b. The TRG Memo No. 59 references ASC 606-10-32-27 in the discussion regarding the timing of recognition of consideration payable as a reduction of revenue when consideration payable was accounted for as a reduction of a transaction price. Why is this Codification reference relevant? Briefly summarize how two different views evolved from this particular Codification reference.

c. In the example provided above, how would the consideration payable be recognized under the two different views described in part *b*?

d. What view do you support in reference to this example? Explain.

AD&J 7-90 Analyzing Principal and Agent Arrangements **LO8**

Real World Analysis **Alphabet Inc.** (Google) reported the following disclosure in a recent Form 10-Q.

> For ads placed on Google Network Members' properties, we evaluate whether we are the principal (i.e., report revenues on a gross basis) or agent (i.e., report revenues on a net basis). Generally, we report advertising revenues for ads placed on Google Network Members' properties on a gross basis, that is, the amounts billed to our customers are recorded as revenues, and amounts paid to publishers are recorded as cost of revenues. We are the principal because we control the advertising inventory before it is transferred to our customers. Our control is evidenced by our sole ability to monetize the advertising inventory, being primarily responsible to our customers, having discretion in establishing pricing, or a combination of these.
>
> As it relates to Google's other revenues, the most significant judgment is determining whether we are the principal or agent for app sales and in-app purchases through the Google Play store. We report revenues from these transactions on a net basis because our performance obligation is to facilitate a transaction between app developers and end users, for which we earn a commission. Consequently, the portion of the gross amount billed to end users that is remitted to app developers is not reflected as revenues.

Required

a. Does Google report the following transactions at gross or net (revenue)?
1. Sales revenue: App sales
2. Sales revenue: In-app customer purchases through Google Play store
3. Advertising revenue: ads placed on Google Network Members' properties

b. What accounting guidance did Google use to determine whether to record revenue at net or at gross?

c. If App sales (net) were $3 million, and Google receives a 10% commission on each transaction, what is the gross amount billed to the end users? Make a case for why the gross amount is not recorded on Google's financial statements.

AD&J 7-91 Analyzing the Accounting for Contract Costs **LO9**

Real World Analysis **Raytheon Company** is a technology and innovation leader specializing in defense and other government markets. The vast majority of revenue is from long-term contracts associated with the design, development, manufacture, or modification of complex aerospace or defense equipment or related services. Raytheon disclosed the following information in a recent Form 10-Q.

> Deferred Commissions—Our incremental direct costs of obtaining a contract, which consist of sales commissions primarily for our security software sales at Forcepoint, are deferred and amortized over the period of contract performance or a longer period, generally the estimated life of the customer relationship if renewals are expected and the renewal commission is not commensurate with the initial commission. We classify deferred commissions as current or noncurrent based on the timing of when we expect to recognize the expense. The current and noncurrent portions of deferred commissions are included in prepaid expenses and other current assets and other assets, net, respectively, in our consolidated balance sheets. At April 2, 2017 and December 31, 2016, we had $32 million of deferred commissions. In the first quarters of 2017 and 2016, we had $5 million and $2 million, respectively, of amortization expense related to deferred commissions.

Other information (in millions)	First Quarter ended April 2, 2017
Prepaid expenses and other current assets.	$ 457
Other assets, net	2,383

Required

a. How do deferred commissions meet the criteria to capitalize costs to obtain a contract?

b. Is it possible for Raytheon to have a standard period of time to amortize contract costs (such as five years)? Why or why not?

c. Why do you believe contract costs are not shown separately on its balance sheet?

AD&J 7-92
Analyzing the Allocation of Transaction Price **LO5**

Real World Analysis Workday Inc. is a leading provider of enterprise cloud applications for finance and human resources. Workday Inc. disclosed the following information in a recent Form 10-Q.

> Some of our contracts with customers contain multiple performance obligations. For these contracts, we account for individual performance obligations separately if they are distinct. The transaction price is allocated to the separate performance obligations on a relative standalone selling price basis. We determine the standalone selling prices based on our overall pricing objectives, taking into consideration market conditions and other factors, including the value of our contracts, the cloud applications sold, customer demographics, geographic locations, and the number and types of users within our contracts.

General Dynamics Corporation is a global aerospace and defense company that offers a broad portfolio of products and services. It disclosed the following information in a recent Form 10-Q.

> For contracts with multiple performance obligations, we allocate the contract's transaction price to each performance obligation using our best estimate of the standalone selling price of each distinct good or service in the contract. The primary method used to estimate standalone selling price is the expected cost plus a margin approach, under which we forecast our expected costs of satisfying a performance obligation and then add an appropriate margin for that distinct good or service.

Required

a. What guidance does GAAP provide on allocating a transaction price to multiple performance obligations?

b. How do Workday Inc. and General Dynamics Corporation differ in how they allocate a transaction price to multiple performance obligations?

c. What do you believe is a reason that these two companies approach allocation differently?

AD&J 7-93
Recording Entries for Long-Term Deferred Franchise Revenue **LO6**

Challenge On June 30, 2020, City Fresh Market enters into a franchise agreement with Baker, which grants Baker franchise rights to open a City Fresh Market in a defined geographical area. City Fresh Market will provide advertising of the franchise over the three-year franchise agreement. After an initial fee of $35,000 (paid on June 30, 2020), Baker has agreed to pay $20,000 at the end of each of the following three years. Baker's borrowing rate is 8%.

Required

a. Record the entry for City Fresh Market on June 30, 2020, upon inception of the franchise agreement. *Hint:* Record a discount on note receivable for the difference between the present value of the note and the carrying amount of $60,000.

b. Record the entries for City Fresh Market on December 31, 2020, to record interest revenue and franchise revenue.

c. Repeat parts *a* and *b* but instead assume that City Fresh Market will not provide any continuing services over the term of the franchise (nor any advertising promotions).

AD&J 7-94
Defining Key Terms in the Codification **LO1, 2, 3, 4, 5, 6**

Codification Skills Refer to the Codification and identify the definition for each of the following: (1) contract asset, (2) contract liability, (3) contract, (4) customer, (5) performance obligation, (6) revenue, (7) standalone selling price, and (8) transaction price.

AD&J 7-95
Researching the Codification **LO2, 3, 6, 7**

Codification Skills Research the Codification and report the proper citation that provides guidance on each of the following topics.

a. Validity of a contract FASB ASC ____-____-____-____

b. Accounting for contract modifications FASB ASC ____-____-____-____

c. Distinct good or service FASB ASC ____-____-____-____

d. Recognition of revenue over time FASB ASC ____-____-____-____

AD&J 7-96
Researching the Codification **LO9**

Codification Skills A seller is accounting for shipping and handling costs that take place after the customer receives control of the product. More specifically, goods were placed with a carrier and the terms of the shipping were FOB shipping. The seller would like to understand the accounting treatment of such costs and whether an election applies. Also, the seller would like to know if shipping costs should be accrued if the related revenue is recognized before the goods are shipped. Identify the relevant authoritative guidance. FASB ASC ____-____-____-____

Appendix—Questions

7-97. Explain the difference between the two acceptable methods of accounting for long-term construction contracts.

7-98. What are two different approaches to determining the extent of progress toward completion of a construction project? Identify some specific types of measurements for each.

7-99. Why is the ending inventory of construction in process different in amount when revenue is recognized over time as compared to revenue recognized at a point in time? Explain by how much the amounts will differ.

7-100. When a loss is projected on a long-term construction contract, in what period(s) is the loss recognized (a) when revenue is recognized over time, and (b) when revenue is recognized at a point in time?

Appendix—Brief Exercises

App—Brief Exercise 7-101 Reporting Contracts in a Balance Sheet **LO10**

Indicate how the following item is reported in the financial statements of a company: The balance of $250,000 in a billings account, which is less than $300,000 in a construction in process account.

App—Brief Exercise 7-102 Accounting for Contracts Over Time **LO10**

On January 1, 2020, Miller Construction Company contracted to build a parking lot for the city of St. Louis for $750,000. Prepare the 2020 journal entries for the following transactions and estimates relating to the contract assuming that revenue is recognized over time.

a. Construction costs incurred during 2020 . . . $200,000
b. Progress billings $190,000
c. Cash collections $175,000
d. Estimated costs to complete $400,000

App—Brief Exercise 7-103 Accounting for Contracts at a Point in Time **LO10**

Refer to the facts in Appendix Brief Exercise 7-102 *except* that Miller Construction accounts for the contract assuming revenue is recognized at a point in time. Prepare the 2020 journal entries.

App—Brief Exercise 7-104 Recording Entries for an Unprofitable Contract **LO11**

Refer to the facts in Appendix Brief Exercise 7-102 *except* that 2020 construction costs incurred during the year were $400,000 instead of $200,000. Prepare the 2020 journal entries to record profit or loss assuming (1) revenue is recognized over time, and (2) revenue is recognized at a point in time.

Appendix—Exercises

App—Exercise 7-105 Recording Long-Term Construction: Recognize Revenue at a Point in Time and Over Time **LO10**

Watson Construction Company contracted to build a plant for $500,000. Construction started in January 2020 and was completed in November 2021. Watson uses the cost-to-cost method to measure the completion of its performance obligations. Data relating to the contract follow.

	2020	2021
Costs incurred during year	$290,000	$120,000
Estimated additional costs to complete	125,000	
Billings during year	270,000	230,000
Cash collections during year	250,000	250,000

Required

a. Provide the 2020 and 2021 journal entries for Watson assuming revenue is recognized at a point in time. Provide entries for (1) construction costs incurred, (2) progress billings, (3) cash collections, and (4) revenues and expenses.

b. Provide the 2020 and 2021 journal entries for Watson assuming revenue is recognized over time. Provide entries for (1) construction costs incurred, (2) progress billings, (3) cash collections, (4) revenues and expenses, and (5) to close out accounts upon completion of the contract.

App—Exercise 7-106
Preparing Financial Statement Presentation for Long-Term Contracts **LO10**

Refer to the information in Appendix Exercise 7-105 to complete the following requirements.

Required

a. What is the income statement impact of the contract assuming (1) revenue is recognized at a point in time, and (2) that revenue is recognized over time for 2020 and 2021?

b. What is the balance sheet impact of the contract assuming (1) revenue is recognized at a point in time, and (2) that revenue is recognized over time for 2020 and 2021?

App—Exercise 7-107
Recording Long-Term Construction: Recognize Revenue Over Time **LO10**
Hint: See Demo 7-10A

Mullen Construction contracted to build a municipal warehouse for the city of Dallas for $750,000. The contract specified that the city would pay Mullen each month the progress billings, less 10%, which was to be held as a retention reserve. At the end of the construction, the final payment would include the reserve. Each billing, less the 10% reserve, must be paid within 10 days after submission of a billing to the city. Transactions relating to the contract follow.

2020—Construction costs incurred during the year, $200,000; estimated costs to complete, $400,000; progress billing, $190,000; and collections per the contract.

2021—Construction costs incurred during the year, $350,000; estimated costs to complete, $115,000; progress billings, $280,000; and collections per the contract, assuming revenue from the contract is appropriately recognized over time.

2022—Construction costs incurred during the year, $100,000. The remaining billings were submitted by October 1, and final collections were completed on November 30.

Required

a. Provide the 2020, 2021, and 2022 entries for (1) construction costs incurred, (2) progress billings, (3) cash collections, (4) revenues and expenses, and (5) to close out accounts upon completion of the contract, assuming revenue from the contract is appropriately recognized over time.

b. Complete the following table.

Year	Revenue Recognized	Expense Recognized	Receivable, Ending Balance	Construction in Process, Ending Balance	CIP in Excess of Billings, Ending Balance
2020					
2021					
2022					

App—Exercise 7-108
Recording Long-term Construction: Recognize Revenue at a Point in Time **LO10**
Hint: See Demo 7-10B

Refer to the information in Appendix Exercise 7-107 *except* assume that revenue is recognized at a point in time.

Required

a. Provide the 2020, 2021, and 2022 entries for (1) construction costs incurred, (2) progress billings, (3) cash collections, and (4) revenues and expenses.

b. Complete the following table.

Year	Revenue Recognized	Expense Recognized	Receivable, Ending Balance	Construction in Process, Ending Balance	CIP in Excess of Billings, Ending Balance
2020					
2021					
2022					

App—Exercise 7-109
Recording Long-term Construction: Recognize Revenue at a Point in Time and Over Time **LO11**

Smith Construction contracted with a developer to build an apartment building with retail space for $3,000,000. Information relating to this contract follows.

	2020	2021	2022
Costs incurred to date	$1,180,000	$2,330,000	$3,150,000
Estimated costs for completion.	1,320,000	720,000	0
Customer billings to date	1,000,000	2,000,000	3,000,000
Customer collections to date	750,000	1,750,000	3,000,000

Required

a. Provide the 2020, 2021, and 2022 journal entries assuming revenue is recognized at a point in time. Provide entries for (1) construction costs incurred, (2) progress billings, (3) cash collections, and (4) losses, revenues and expenses.

b. Provide the 2020, 2021, and 2022 journal entries assuming revenue is recognized over time. Provide entries for (1) construction costs incurred, (2) progress billings, (3) cash collections, (4) revenues and expenses, and (5) to close out accounts upon completion of the contract.

Appendix—Problems

App—Problem 7-110
Recording and Reporting Long-Term Construction: Recognize Revenue at a Point in Time and Over Time LO10

Thrasher Construction contracted to construct a building for $975,000. The contract provided for progress payments. Thrasher's accounting year ends December 31. Work began under the contract on July 1, 2020, and was completed on September 30, 2022. Construction activities follow.

2020—Construction costs incurred during the year, $180,000; estimated costs to complete, $630,000; progress billings during the year, $153,000; and collections, $140,000.

2021—Construction costs incurred during the year, $450,000; estimated costs to complete, $190,000; progress billings during the year, $382,500; and collections, $380,000.

2022—Construction costs incurred during the year, $195,000. Because the contract was completed, the remaining balance was billed and later collected in full per the contract.

Required

a. Provide the 2020, 2021, and 2022 journal entries assuming revenue is recognized over time. Provide entries for (1) construction costs incurred, (2) progress billings, (3) cash collections, (4) revenues and expenses, and (5) to close out accounts upon completion of the contract. Assume cost-to-cost ratio is used to estimate efforts toward satisfying a performance obligation.

b. Prepare income statement and balance sheet presentations for this contract for each year; assume that revenue is recognized over time.

c. Prepare income statement and balance sheet presentations for this contract for each year; assume that revenue is recognized at a point in time.

App—Problem 7-111
Recording Long-Term Construction: Comparing Entries and Financial Statement Presentations LO10

Wallen Corporation contracted to construct an office building for Ragee Company for $1 million. Construction began on January 15, 2020, and was completed on December 1, 2021. Wallen's year-end is December 31. Transactions by Wallen relating to the contract follow.

	2020	2021
Costs incurred to date	$400,000	$ 850,000
Estimated costs to complete	420,000	
Progress billings to date	410,000	1,000,000
Progress collections to date	375,000	1,000,000

Required

a. Provide the 2020 and 2021 journal entries assuming revenue is recognized at a point in time. Provide entries for (1) construction costs incurred, (2) progress billings, (3) cash collections, and (4) revenues and expenses.

b. Provide the 2020 and 2021 journal entries assuming revenue is recognized over time. Provide entries for (1) construction costs incurred, (2) progress billings, (3) cash collections, (4) revenues and expenses, and (5) to close out accounts upon completion of the contract. Assume cost-to-cost method to estimate efforts toward satisfying a performance obligation.

c. For part *a*, prepare the income statement and balance sheet presentations for this contract for each of the years 2020 and 2021.

d. For part *b*, prepare the income statement and balance sheet presentations for this contract for each of the years 2020 and 2021.

e. What is the nature of the item "costs in excess of billings" that would appear on the balance sheet?

App—Problem 7-112
Recording Long-Term Construction: Comparing Entries and Financial Statement Presentations **LO10**

Precision Construction has agreed to build a 5-story office building for the Mountain States Bank Corporation. The contract calls for a contract price of $15,000,000 for the building, with progress payments being made by Mountain States as the construction proceeds. The period of construction is estimated to be 30 months. The contract is signed on February 1, 2020, and construction begins immediately. Precision Construction uses the cost-to-cost method to measure the completion of its performance obligations. The building is completed and turned over to Mountain States Bank on December 1, 2022. Data on costs incurred, estimated costs to complete, progress billings, and progress payments over the period of construction follow.

$ thousands	2020	2021	2022
Costs incurred this period	$ 1,500	$ 7,875	$ 3,825
Costs incurred to date	1,500	9,375	13,200
Estimated costs to complete at year-end	10,500	3,125	0
Estimated total costs of project	12,000	12,500	13,200
Progress billings this period	1,200	6,000	7,800
Progress payments received this period	825	6,300	7,875

Required

a. Provide the 2020, 2021, and 2022 journal entries assuming revenue is recognized at a point in time. Provide entries for (1) construction costs incurred, (2) progress billings, (3) cash collections, and (4) revenues and expenses.

b. Provide the 2020 and 2021 journal entries assuming revenue is recognized over time. Provide entries for (1) construction costs incurred, (2) progress billings, (3) cash collections, (4) revenues and expenses, and (5) to close out accounts upon completion of the contract.

c. For part *a*, prepare the income statement and balance sheet presentations for this contract for each of the years 2020, 2021, and 2022.

d. For part *b*, prepare the income statement and balance sheet presentations for this contract for each of the years 2020, 2021, and 2022.

App—Problem 7-113
Determining Profit or Loss Reported for Long-Term Construction: Overall Contract Loss—Revenue Recognized Over Time versus Point in Time **LO11**

Leggo Construction has agreed to build an addition for an office building for a contract price of $2,000,000. The period of construction is estimated to be three years. The contract is signed on January 1, 2020, and construction begins immediately. The building is completed on December 31, 2022. Data on costs incurred, and estimated costs to complete over the period of construction follow.

$ thousands	2020	2021	2022
Costs incurred this period	$ 500	$ 625	$975
Estimated costs to complete at year-end	1,000	1,025	0

Required

a. Determine the profit or loss to be reported in each of the years 2020, 2021, and 2022 assuming the company recognizes revenue *over time*.

b. Determine the profit or loss to be reported in each of the years 2020, 2021, and 2022 assuming the company recognizes revenue *at a point in time*.

App—Problem 7-114
Determining Profit or Loss Reported for Long-Term Construction: Current Period Loss—Revenue Recognized Over Time versus Point in Time **LO11**

Dueplo Construction has agreed to build an addition for an office building for a contract price of $2,000,000. The period of construction is estimated to be three years. The contract is signed on January 1, 2020, and construction begins immediately. The building is completed on December 31, 2022. Data on costs incurred, and estimated costs to complete over the period of construction follow.

$ thousands	2020	2021	2022
Costs incurred this period	$ 500	$525	$575
Estimated costs to complete at year-end	1,000	600	0

Required

a. Determine the profit or loss to be reported in each of the years 2020, 2021, and 2022 assuming the company recognizes revenue *over time*.

b. Determine the profit or loss to be reported in each of the years 2020, 2021, and 2022 assuming the company recognizes revenue *at a point in time*.

Answers to Review Exercise

Review 7-1

Step 1 A written contract requires REII Inc. to provide repair on a snowboard for $75.
Step 2 There is one performance obligation or promise: REII Inc. will provide repair to a customer's snowboard.
Step 3 Transaction price of the service is $75.
Step 4 $75 is allocated to one performance obligation, the seller's obligation to repair a snowboard.
Step 5 The contract is satisfied at the time REII Inc. returns the repaired snowboard to the customer and collects cash of $75. Revenue is recognized at the point when control of the repaired snowboard is transferred to the customer and exchanged for $75 cash.

Review 7-2

a. **Whether the parties' rights are identified** The termination clause, if substantive, does not allow for enforceable rights by either party, thus making the contract invalid.

b. **Whether the contract has been approved** An approval does not need to be in writing for a valid contract if the customary business practice is to require approval through an online acceptance process.

c. **Whether the payment terms are identified** Payment terms in a valid contract may include noncash consideration (stock) as part of the transaction price and is measured at fair value.

d. **Whether collection is probable** With an ability to stop the transfer of goods, the seller may have limited its exposure to material uncollectible amounts. Assuming that management considers collection to be probable, and considering that shipment will stop if the customer fails to make timely payments, the contract is valid.

e. **Whether the contract has commercial substance** Because the economic conditions of the seller and customer have not changed, the contract lacks commercial substance. Therefore, the contract is not valid.

Review 7-3

a. Two performance obligations: contacts and solution. Contacts and solution are sold separately (distinct) and are distinct within the context of the contract.

b. One performance obligation: installed customized equipment. Equipment and installation are modified by each other because the installation includes equipment customizations.

c. One performance obligation: license for anti-virus for three years. Initial software download and updates are interrelated. Overall promise in the contract is to provide anti-virus protection for three years.

d. Two performance obligations: home security monitoring and renewal option. Renewal option is considered material in the context of the contract and is not available without the initial purchase of the monitoring service.

e. Two performance obligations: franchise rights and equipment. Equipment and franchise are distinct. The items included in the upfront franchise fee are interrelated.

f. Two performance obligations: barbecue sauce and discount coupon. The discount coupon is a customer option that is material to the contract for the sale of the product and is only available through purchase of the product.

g. Three performance obligations: refrigerator, truck rental, vehicle insurance. The customer benefits from each of the three items on their own and the items are not significantly combined, customized, or interrelated.

h. One performance obligation: management services. Items included within management services are interrelated. Overall promise is to provide management services.

Review 7-4

a. $123,500; variable consideration: Sales price of $130,000 less sales returns of $6,500.

b. $2,500; fixed consideration: Sales of $3,000 less consideration payable of $500.

c. $54,600; $50,000 (fixed consideration) plus $4,600 (variable consideration): [($5,000 × 0.70) + ($4,000 × 0.20) + ($3,000 × 0.10)].

d. $55,000; $50,000 (fixed consideration) plus $5,000 (variable consideration).

Review 7-5

a. Performance Obligations	Transaction Price as Stated	Standalone Selling Price	Selling Price Ratio	Allocated Transaction Price*
Handset	$150	$150	150/710	$150
Service	480	480	480/710	480
Headphone	80	80	80/710	80
	$710	$710	710/710	$710

*Amounts rounded.

b. Performance Obligations	Transaction Price as Stated	Standalone Selling Price	Selling Price Ratio	Allocated Transaction Price*
Handset	$150	$200	200/760	$187
Service	480	480	480/760	448
Headphone	80	80	80/760	75
	$710	$760	760/760	$710

c. Performance Obligations	Transaction Price as Stated	Standalone Selling Price	Selling Price Ratio	Allocated Transaction Price*
Handset	$150	$200	200/780	$182
Service	480	480	480/780	437
Headphone	80	100	100/780	91
	$710	$780	780/780	$710

d. Performance Obligations	Transaction Price as Stated	Standalone Selling Price	Selling Price Ratio	Allocated Transaction Price*
Handset	$150	$200	200/770	$184
Service	480	480	480/770	443
Headphone	80	90 (estimated)	90/770	83
	$710	$770	770/770	$710

e. Performance Obligations	Transaction Price as Stated	Standalone Selling Price	Selling Price Ratio	Allocated Transaction Price*
Handset	$150	$200	200/710	$200
Service	480	480	480/710	480
Headphone	80	30 (estimated)	30/710	30
	$710	$710	710/710	$710

*Amounts rounded.

Review 7-6

a. January 15, 2020, $0; January 31, 2020, $300

b. $8,333, $1,667

c. $2,333,333

d. $0

e. January 1, 2020, $0, December 31, 2020, $54,000 ($245,000/5 + $5,000)

Review 7-7

a. 50 items under original contract: $10,000; 80 items under the contract modification: $17,600

b. 50 items under original contract: $10,615; 80 items under the contract modification: $16,985*

*Blended price = ($10,000 + $17,600)/(50 + 80) = $212.31/unit

50 × $212.31 = $10,615

80 × $212.31 = $16,985

Review 7-8

a. Bill-and-hold, February 15, 2021
b. Consignment, $4,000
c. Principal and agent (TicketMajor is a principal), $35,000
d. Forward arrangement (financing agreement), $0

Review 7-9

a. 7 b. 2 c. 6 d. 1 e. 4 f. 5 g. 8 h. 3 i. 9

Review 7-10

a.

	2020		2021	
Construction in Process	150,000		170,000	
Cash, Payables, etc.		150,000		170,000
Accounts Receivable	200,000		200,000	
Billings on Contracts		200,000		200,000
Cash	140,000		260,000	
Accounts Receivable		140,000		260,000

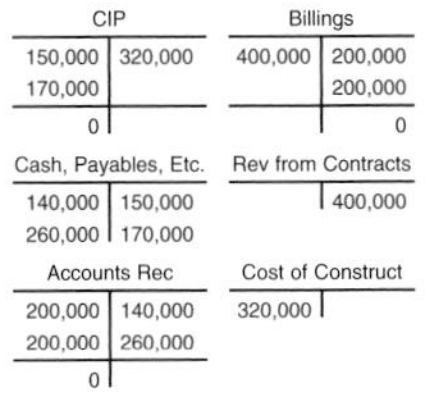

CIP
150,000 | 320,000
170,000
0
Billings
400,000 | 200,000
200,000
0
Cash, Payables, Etc.
140,000 | 150,000
260,000 | 170,000
Rev from Contracts
400,000
Accounts Rec
200,000 | 140,000
200,000 | 260,000
0
Cost of Construct
320,000

November 2021

Billings on Contracts	400,000	
Revenue from Long-Term Contracts		400,000

Cost of Construction	320,000	
Construction in Process		320,000

b. The solution for the first three entries in part *a* apply in part *b* along with the following additional entries.

	2020		2021	
Construction in Process	26,000		53,529	
Cost of Construction	150,000		170,000	
Revenue from Long-Term Contracts		176,471[1]		223,529[2]

[1]$400,000 × $150,000/$340,000 [2]$400,000 − $176,471

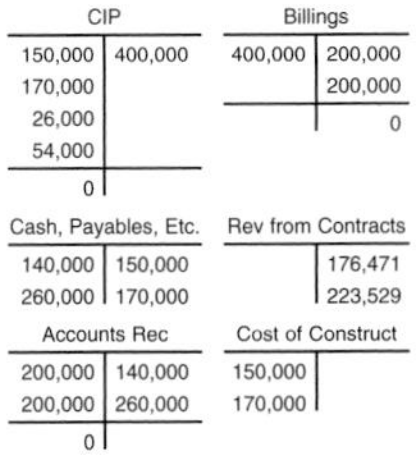

Billings on Contracts	400,000	
Construction in Process		400,000

Review 7-11

a.

	2020		2021		2022	
Construction in Process	80,000		110,000		140,000	
Cash, Payables, etc.		80,000		110,000		140,000
Accounts Receivable	100,000		100,000		100,000	
Billings on Contracts		100,000		100,000		100,000
Cash	80,000		80,000		140,000	
Accounts Receivable		80,000		80,000		140,000

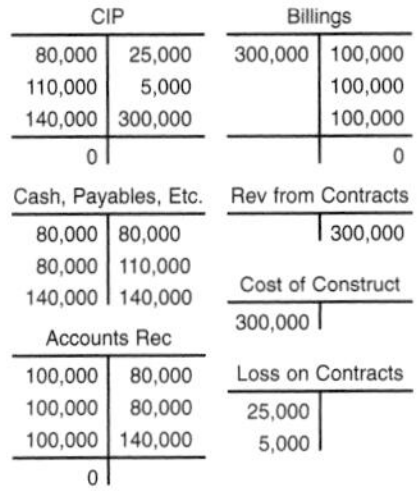

December 31, 2021—To record contract loss

Loss on Long-Term Contracts	25,000	
Construction in Process		25,000

December 31, 2022—To record contract loss

Loss on Long-Term Contracts	5,000	
Construction in Process		5,000

December 31, 2022—To close out progress billings and construction in process

Cost of Construction	300,000	
Construction in Process		300,000

Billings on Contracts	300,000	
Revenue from Long-Term Contracts		300,000

b. The solutions for the first three entries in part *a* apply in part *b* along with the following additional entries.

December 31, 2020—To record contract revenue and expense

Construction in Process ($96,000 – $80,000)	16,000	
Cost of Construction	80,000	
Revenue from Long-Term Contracts ($80,000/$250,000 × $300,000)		96,000

CIP	
80,000	41,000
16,000	5,000
110,000	300,000
140,000	
0	

Billings	
300,000	100,000
	100,000
	100,000
	0

Cash, Payables, Etc.	
80,000	80,000
80,000	110,000
140,000	140,000

Rev from Contracts	
	96,000
	79,385
	124,615

Accounts Rec	
100,000	80,000
100,000	80,000
100,000	140,000
0	

Cost of Construct	
80,000	
120,385	
129,615	

December 31, 2021—To record contract revenue and expense

Cost of Construction ($79,385 + $41,000)	120,385	
Construction in Process ($16,000* + $25,000**)		41,000
Revenue from Long-Term Contracts ([$190,000/$325,000 × $300,000] – $96,000)		79,385

*Reversal of prior year profit recognized.

**Total contract loss computed as $300,000 – ($190,000 + $135,000).

December 31, 2022—To record contract revenue and expense

Cost of Construction ($124,615 + $5,000)	129,615	
Construction in Process ($330,000 – $190,000 – $135,000)		5,000
Revenue from Long-Term Contracts ($300,000 – $96,000 – $79,385)		124,615

December 31, 2022—To close out progress billings and construction in process

Billings on Contracts	300,000	
Construction in Process		300,000

8 Cash and Receivables

Wal-Mart Stores, Inc.
Consolidated Balance Sheet

(Amounts in millions)	As of Ja 2017
ASSETS	
Current assets:	
Cash and cash equivalents	$ 6,867
Receivables, net	5,835

AMAZON.COM, INC.
CONSOLIDATED BALANCE SHEET
(in millions, except per share data)

	December 31,	
ASSETS	**2015**	**2016**
Current assets:		
Cash and cash equivalents	$ 15,890	$ 19,334
Marketable securities	3,918	6,647
Inventories	10,243	11,461
Accounts receivable, net and other	5,654	8,339
Total current assets	35,705	45,781

Lowe's Companies, Inc.
Consolidated Balance Sheet
(In millions, except par value and percentage data)

	February 3, 2017
Assets	
Current assets:	
Cash and cash equivalents	$ 558
Short-term investments	100
Merchandise inventory - net	10,458
Other current assets	884
Total current assest	**12,000**

THE HOME DEPOT, INC. AND SUBSIDIARIES
CONSOLIDATED BALANCE SHEET

amounts in millions, except share and per share data	January 29, 2017
ASSETS	
Current assets:	
Cash and Cash Eequivalents	$ 2,538
Receivables, net	2,029
Merchandise Inventories	6,867
Other current assets	608
Total current assets	17,724

Chapter Preview

We begin by exploring the types and classifications of cash and cash related accounts. We then review the reporting of accounts receivable including its measurement at net realizable value. Next we examine the topic of notes receivable, or formalized promises to receive amounts under specific terms. We explain how companies account for the sale of receivables and the use of receivables as collateral to secure cash loans. We also review the disclosures related to cash and receivables, and analyze receivables through ratios.

Action Plan

LO	Topic/Subtopic	Page	Demos	Reviews	Assignments
LO 8–1	**Classify cash, cash equivalents, restricted cash, and compensating balances** Cash :: Cash Equivalents :: Restricted Cash :: Compensating Balances :: Balance Sheet Classification	8-3	D8-1	R8-1	17, 33, 34, 59, 60, 85, 86
LO 8–2	**Account for sales and collections on account including the impact of cash discounts** Gross Method :: Net Method :: Cash Discount :: Discount Period	8-6	D8-2A D8-2B	R8-2	18, 19, 35, 36, 59, 61, 62, 78, 84
LO 8–3	**Account for the impact of sales returns and allowances** Sales Returns :: Variable Consideration :: Refund Liability :: Estimated Returns Inventory	8-11	D8-3	R8-3	20, 37, 38, 46, 59, 61, 86
LO 8–4	**Measure and record accounts receivable at net realizable value using the allowance method** Net Realizable Value :: Allowance Method :: CECL Model :: Aging Schedule :: Expected Credit Losses	8-13	D8-4A D8-4B	R8-4	21, 22, 23, 24, 39, 40, 41, 42, 43, 44, 45, 46, 59, 62, 63, 64, 65, 66, 75, 76, 77, 80, 81, 85, 86
LO 8–5	**Measure and record notes receivable** Note Receivable :: Face Value:: Effective Interest Method :: Discount on Note Receivable	8-20	D8-5A D8-5B D8-5C D8-5D	R8-5	25, 26, 46, 47, 48, 49, 50, 51, 59, 67, 68, 69, 79, 82, 86, 87
LO 8–6	**Account for the sale of receivables and use as collateral for borrowing** Secured Borrowing :: Collateral :: Sale With Recourse :: Sale Without Recourse :: Recourse Liability	8-27	D8-6A D8-6B D8-6C D8-6D	R8-6	27, 28, 29, 30, 31, 46, 52, 53, 54, 55, 56, 57, 59, 70, 71, 72, 73, 85
LO 8–7	**Describe receivable disclosures and ratio analyses** Accounts Receivable Turnover :: Average Days to Collect Receivables	8-32	D8-7	R8-7	32, 58, 59, 60, 74, 77, 79, 80
LO 8–8	**APPENDIX 8A—Apply cash controls** Cash Reconciliations :: Bank Reconciliation :: Accounting Controls	8-36	D8-8A D8-8B	R8-8	83, 92, 93, 94, 95, 96, 99, 100, 101, 102, 103, 106, 107, 108, 109
LO 8–9	**APPENDIX 8B—Account for impairment of noncurrent receivables** Bad Debt Expense :: Allowance for Doubtful Accounts :: Effective Interest Method :: Expected Credit Losses	8-42	D8-9	R8-9	97, 98, 104, 105, 110

LO 8-1 Classify cash, cash equivalents, restricted cash, and compensating balances

LO 8-1 Overview

Reporting of Cash and Cash Items
- **Cash:** Current Asset
- **Cash equivalent:** With Cash or as a separate current asset
- **Restricted cash:** Separate asset
- **Compensating balances:**
  - Cash (not legally restricted)
  - Separate asset (legally restricted)

The accounting standards provide guidance on how to classify cash and cash related items. Cash available for current operations and cash equivalents (short-term, highly liquid investments) are classified as current assets on the balance sheet. For an item to qualify as a cash equivalent, there needs to be an insignificant risk of a change in the asset's value due to changes in interest rates. Companies must establish a policy on which particular short-term, highly liquid investments are reported as cash equivalents on the balance sheet. Restricted cash items, including compensating balances, however, are typically reported separately from cash and cash equivalents. One exception is that compensating balances that are not legally restricted can be combined with cash.

The definitions of cash, cash equivalents, restricted cash, and compensating balances along with a summary of reporting requirements follow. Appendix 8A provides a discussion of cash controls including bank reconciliations.

Term	Definition
Cash	**ASC Glossary** Consistent with common usage, cash includes not only currency on hand but demand deposits with banks or other financial institutions. Cash also includes other kinds of accounts that have the general characteristics of demand deposits in that the customer may deposit additional funds at any time and also effectively may withdraw funds at any time without prior notice or penalty. **Report as** Cash.
Cash equivalents	**ASC Glossary** Cash equivalents are short-term, highly liquid investments that have both of the following characteristics: (a) Readily convertible to known amounts of cash and (b) So near their maturity that they present insignificant risk of changes in value because of changes in interest rates. Generally, only investments with original maturities of three months or less qualify under that definition. Original maturity means original maturity to the entity holding the investment. **230-10-45-6** Not all investments that qualify are required to be treated as cash equivalents. An entity shall establish a policy concerning which short-term, highly liquid investments that satisfy the definition of cash equivalents are treated as cash equivalents. **Report as** Cash or as a separate current asset.
Restricted cash	Cash restricted for a particular purpose and not available for general use including legal restrictions and voluntary management restrictions. **Report as** Separate asset from Cash if material.
Compensating balances	Minimum cash balance required by a lender to be maintained at the financial institution of the lender, which may be legally restricted for use. **210-10-S99-1** In cases where compensating balance arrangements exist but are not agreements which legally restrict the use of cash amounts shown on the balance sheet, describe in the notes to the financial statements these arrangements and the amount involved, if determinable. **Report as** Separate asset from Cash if legally restricted; otherwise report with Cash.

EXPANDING YOUR KNOWLEDGE **Defining Restricted Cash**

While restricted cash is reported separately from cash and cash equivalents on the balance sheet, recall from Chapter 5 that they are combined for cash flow purposes. In the statement of cash flows, the reconciliation of cash includes the change during a period in the total of (1) cash, (2) cash equivalents, and (3) amounts generally described as restricted cash or restricted cash equivalents. When these three amounts are presented in more than one line item on the balance sheet, disclosure is required to reconcile amounts between the two financial statements. The FASB has not specifically defined restricted cash in the Codification. However, disclosures on the nature of the restrictions on cash and cash equivalents provide insight into the availability of amounts on the balance sheet and about the sources and uses of restricted cash and restricted cash equivalents during a reporting period.

Exhibit 8-1 shows examples of cash, cash equivalents, restricted cash, and compensating balances.

EXHIBIT 8-1
Types of Cash, Cash Equivalents, Restricted Cash, and Compensating Balances

Types of Cash, Cash Equivalents, Restricted Cash, and Compensating Balances

Cash	Cash Equivalents	Restricted Cash and Compensating Balances
Coins, currency. Petty cash funds. Deposits with financial institutions.* Cashier's checks, certified checks, and money orders.	U.S. Treasury obligations, Short-term T-bills. Commercial paper: Short-term unsecured notes issued by large corporations. Money market funds: Certain mutual funds with investments in cash equivalents. Certificates of deposits.	Cash held as collateral, cash held by a third party, and escrow accounts. Dividend funds and payroll funds. Bond sinking fund: Cash accumulated in a fund to pay toward bond retirement. Legally restricted deposits at a lender's institution (compensating balance).

* If a depositor overdraws an account (such as writing checks that exceed the bank balance) but has positive balances in other accounts with that same bank, it is proper to offset the negative and positive balances. However, if the company does not have another offsetting positive balance at the *same bank*, the negative balance will be recognized as *accounts payable on the balance sheet*.

BEST BUY

Real World—DISCLOSING RESTRICTED CASH

BEST BUY [BBY]

Best Buy Co. Inc. included the following accounting policies for cash, cash equivalents, and restricted cash in its first note in a recent Form 10-K.

> **Cash and Cash Equivalents** Cash primarily consists of cash on hand and bank deposits. Cash equivalents consist of money market funds, treasury bills, commercial paper, corporate bonds and deposits with an original maturity of 3 months or less when purchased. The amounts of cash equivalents at January 31, 2015, and February 1, 2014, were $1,660 million and $1,705 million, respectively, and the weighted-average interest rates were 0.4% and 0.5%, respectively. Outstanding checks in excess of funds on deposit (book overdrafts) totaled $0 million and $62 million at January 31, 2015, and February 1, 2014, respectively, and are reflected within accounts payable in our Consolidated Balance Sheets.
>
> **Restricted Assets** Restricted cash totaled $292 million at January 31, 2015, of which $184 million is related to continuing operations and included in other current assets and $108 million is included in current assets held for sale in our Consolidated Balance Sheet. Restricted cash totaled $310 million at February 1, 2014 and is included in other current assets or other assets in our Consolidated Balance Sheet. Such balances are pledged as collateral or restricted to use for vendor payables, general liability insurance and workers' compensation insurance.

Demo 8-1 **LO8-1** **Reporting Cash, Cash Equivalents, and Other Current Assets**

Demo MBC

Loft Inc. is preparing its December 31, 2020, financial statements and gathers the following information. Determine Loft's balances for the following balance sheet classifications on December 31, 2020: Cash; Cash Equivalents; and Other Current Assets.

1. Loft Inc. borrowed $50,000 from First Bank through a one-year note on June 30, 2020, that legally requires the company to maintain a 10% or a $5,000 (0.10 × $50,000) compensating balance. This amount must remain on deposit at the bank during the loan period (legally restricted for use). On December 31, 2020, the company has a balance of $8,500 with First Bank. (Ignore the classification of the remaining loan proceeds.)
2. A cashier's check in the amount of $1,000 made payable to Loft Inc. dated December 29, 2020, is in Loft's possession on December 31, 2020.
3. Loft Inc. has a balance of $10,000 in its savings account on December 31, 2020.
4. Loft Inc. has invested $4,000 in a six-month U.S. Treasury bill on December 1, 2020, when the investment was two months from maturity.
5. On December 15, 2020, Loft Inc. purchased $40,000 of commercial paper of General Electricity Inc. with a 30-day term. Loft Inc. believes that there is a low risk of loss on the investment due to Generally Electricity's strong credit rating from an independent rating agency.

Solution

Cash	$14,500 ($8,500 − $5,000) + $1,000 + $10,000
Cash Equivalents	44,000 ($4,000 + $40,000)
Other Current Assets	5,000

Explanation:

- **Cash** consists of the amount of cash on deposit at First Bank that is not restricted or $8,500 less $5,000. It also includes the cashier's check that has not been deposited ($1,000) and the deposit in savings ($10,000).
- **Cash Equivalents** consist of the investment in the U.S. Treasury bill of $4,000 and the investment of commercial paper of $40,000. Both investments mature in less than three months from Loft's purchase date and have a low risk of loss.
- **Other Current Assets** consist of the compensating balance that Loft Inc. is legally required to maintain at First Bank during the term of the $50,000 loan. Since this requirement reduces liquidity by restricting a portion of cash, the amount is classified separately on the balance sheet.

EXPANDING YOUR KNOWLEDGE **Cost of Borrowing with Compensating Balances**

A requirement from a lender that a compensating balance be maintained increases the effective cost of borrowing. For example, a company borrows $500,000 through a 6% note payable and is required to maintain $20,000 on deposit as security for the note. The effective rate of borrowing is annual interest of $30,000 ($500,000 × 0.06) divided by available cash proceeds of $480,000 ($500,000 − $20,000), or 6.25%.

Some transactions of a company result in items that are not classified as cash or cash equivalents, although they are related to cash. For example, a company may advance cash to employees for travel or other business expenses. Such an amount would not be considered cash for classification purposes but would be considered a current asset (typically a prepaid expense). Or, a company may receive checks from customers that are postdated for a later time (such as next month). Such checks would not be available for immediate deposit so should be classified as accounts receivable. Also, short-term, liquid investments (marketable securities such as money market funds or treasury bills) that do not qualify as cash equivalents would be classified on the balance sheet as short-term investments.

Classification of Cash Related Items **LO8-1** **Review 8-1**

Match each item *a* through *h* with one of the financial statement classifications, 1 through 5.

Review MBC

Financial Statement Classifications

1. Cash
2. Cash equivalent
3. Other current asset (not cash)
4. Noncurrent asset (not cash)
5. Current liability

Items

____ *a.* Certified checks held in treasury.
____ *b.* Cash held in an escrow fund, the fund is expected to accrue interest for two years.
____ *c.* One-year T-bill purchased two months before its maturity date.
____ *d.* Compensating balance held against long-term debt, where the funds are legally restricted from withdrawal.
____ *e.* Negative cash balance due to outstanding checks exceeding cash on deposit.
____ *f.* Travel advance of cash to an employee for business travel.
____ *g.* Deposit in a money market fund with a 2-month maturity date. The fund is considered highly liquid with a low risk of loss.
____ *h.* Cash deposited in a 5-year bond sinking fund.

More Practice: 8-17, 8-33, 8-34
Solution on p. 8-70.

Account for sales and collections on account including the impact of cash discounts — LO 8-2

Accounting for Cash Discounts
- **Gross Method**
  - Accounts receivable recorded at gross value
  - *Sales discounts* recorded only if customer pays *within* discount period
- **Net Method**
  - Accounts receivable recorded net of discount
  - *Sales discounts forfeited* recorded only if customer pays *after* discount period

LO 8-2 Overview

We previously explained that revenue is recognized in the final step of the revenue recognition process: recognize revenue when (or as) a company satisfies a performance obligation by transferring control of a promised good or service to a customer. Typically, control is transferred at the point of delivery of the product or service. At the point of revenue recognition, if credit is extended in the place of cash, a receivable is recorded. Accounting standards describe a receivable as follows.

606-10-45-1 An entity shall present any unconditional rights to consideration separately as a receivable.

Accounts receivable, also called **trade receivables**, result from the satisfaction of obligations incurred during a company's normal course of business through an informal credit agreement. Receivables are supported by sales invoices or other documents rather than by formal written promises, and they include amounts expected to be collected either during the year following the balance sheet date or within the company's operating cycle, whichever is longer.

Because a sale on account could be considered a 30- or 45-day loan (depending on the specific terms), there is a financing component to a sale on account. Sellers initiating a revenue contract with transfer within one year, do not have to recognize a financing component. This means short-term accounts receivable are typically recorded at the full amount that the seller expects to receive (not adjusted to present value). The authoritative support follows.

606-10-32-15 In determining the transaction price, an entity shall adjust the promised amount of consideration for the effects of the time value of money if the timing of payments agreed to by the parties to the contract (either explicitly or implicitly) provides the customer or the entity with a significant benefit of financing the transfer of goods or services to the customer. In those circumstances, the contract contains a significant financing component.

606-10-32-18 As a practical expedient, an entity need not adjust the promised amount of consideration for the effects of a significant financing component if the entity expects, at contract inception, that the period between when the entity transfers a promised good or service to a customer and when the customer pays for that good or service will be one year or less.

Nontrade receivables arise from many other sources, such as from tax refunds, loans made to officers, contracts, investees, finance receivables, installment notes, sale of assets, and advances to employees. Nontrade receivables are generally reported separately from trade receivables. Accounting standards describe certain receivables requiring separate disclosure as follows.

850-10-50-2 Notes or accounts receivable from officers, employees, or affiliated entities must be shown separately and not included under a general heading such as notes receivable or accounts receivable.

EXPANDING YOUR KNOWLEDGE **Trade Discounts**

Typically, a single invoice price for a product is published. Then, several different **trade discounts** often apply depending on the type and quantity of product ordered, or the particular customer placing the order. *These trade discounts reduce the final sales price.* Assume an item priced at $50 is offered at a trade discount of 40% for orders over 1,000 units. This means the unit price for an order of 1,100 units is $30 ($50 × 0.60). The percentage discount can be changed for different order quantities without changing the basic $50 price. For accounting, the listed invoice price less the trade discount is treated as the gross price to which cash discounts apply. Trade discounts are not accounted for separately, but they do define the invoice price.

Companies frequently offer a **cash discount**, also called **sales discounts**, for payment received within a designated period. Cash discounts are used to increase sales, to encourage early payment by a customer, and to increase the likelihood of collection. Typical sales terms are 2/10, n/30. That is, the customer is given a 2% cash discount if payment is made within 10 days of the invoice date; otherwise, the full amount net of any returns or allowances is due in 30 days. *Cash discounts are considered variable consideration because the company is uncertain as to whether the customer will provide payment within the discount period.* Companies can record cash discounts using the gross method or net method. Both methods report revenue net of discounts actually taken, but the composition of the revenue accounts, and period-end adjusting entries, vary.

- Under the **gross method**, when cash discounts are offered, the receivable and sale are recorded at the gross amount. A company records sales discounts only if the customer pays within the discount period. For example, in the first line of **Exhibit 8-2**, revenue originally measured at $100 under the gross method, is reduced to $98 if the customer pays within the discount period. Otherwise, revenue remains at $100 if the customer pays after the discount period.
- Under the **net method**, when cash discounts are offered, the receivable and sale are recorded at the net amount (gross invoice price less available cash discount). A company records sales discount forfeitures only if the customer fails to pay within the discount period. For example, in the second line of **Exhibit 8-2**, revenue originally measured at $98 under the net method, remains at $98 if the customer pays within the discount period. Otherwise, revenue is increased to $100 if the customer pays after the discount period.

In **Exhibit 8-2**, both methods reveal *identical revenues* when the customer pays within the discount period ($98) or when the customer pays after the discount period ($100). The two methods are further illustrated in **Demo 8-2A** and **Demo 8-2B**.

EXHIBIT 8-2
Gross Method versus Net Method

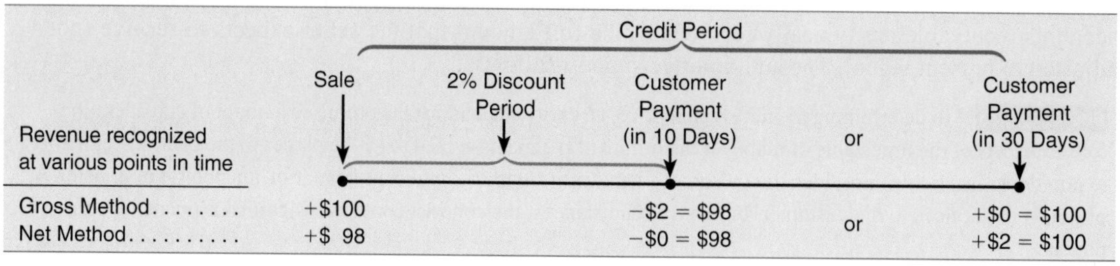

Accounting for Sales and Collections under the Gross Method   LO8-2   Demo 8-2A

On June 1, 2020, Home Store transfers control of merchandise to Gomez at a gross sales price of $1,000 and a cost of $550. Credit terms are 2/10, n/30. Home Store accounts for sales transactions under the gross method.

a. Record the entries for Home Store on June 1, 2020, the date of the sale of merchandise.

b. On June 8, 2020, Gomez paid half of the balance due. Record the entry for Home Store on June 8, 2020.

c. On June 30, 2020, Gomez paid the remaining amount due. Record the entry for Home Store on June 30, 2020.

d. Show the income statement presentation of revenue for the month of June 2020.

Solutions

a. Home Store records the following entry upon sale of the merchandise to Gomez under the gross method. Sales and accounts receivable are recorded at 100% of the sales amount.

June 1, 2020—To record sale of merchandise (both sales and cost entries)

Accounts Receivable	1,000	
Sales Revenue		1,000

Assets = Liabilities + Equity: +1,000 (Assets); +1,000 (Equity). Accounts Rec: 1,000 | . Sales Rev: | 1,000.

Cost of Goods Sold	550	
Inventory		550

Assets = Liabilities + Equity: −550 (Assets); −550 (Equity). Inventory: | 550. COGS: 550 | .

b. Gomez's partial payment on June 8, 2020, is within the 10-day discount period. The discount is recorded in the account, **Sales Discount**, which is a contra account to sales. Home Store records the following entry upon receipt of payment.

June 8, 2020—To record partial payment within discount period

Cash ($500 − $10)	490	
Sales Discount ($500 × 0.02)	10	
Accounts Receivable		500

Assets = Liabilities + Equity: +490, −500 (Assets); −10 (Equity). Cash: 490 | . Sales Discount: 10 | . Accounts Rec: 1,000 | 500.

c. Home Store records the following entry on receipt of the remaining balance on June 30, 2020.

June 30, 2020—To record final payment after discount period

Cash	500	
Accounts Receivable		500

Assets = Liabilities + Equity: +500, −500 (Assets). Cash: 490, 500 | . Accounts Rec: 1,000 | 500, 500.

d. Home Store recognizes the following amounts in its income statement for the month ended June 30, 2020.

Financial Statement Presentation of Revenue—Gross Method

Income Statement—Excerpt
For Month Ended June 30, 2020

Sales revenue	$1,000
Less: Sales discounts	10
Net sales revenue	990
Interest revenue	0
Total revenue	$ 990

KELLOGG

Real World—CASH DISCOUNTS

KELLOGG [K]

Kellogg Company offers cash discounts that they refer to as "prompt payment discounts." Accounts receivable is recorded in the balance sheet net of these discounts as noted below in its recent Form 10-K.

> **Accounts receivable** Accounts receivable consists principally of trade receivables, which are recorded at the invoiced amount, net of allowances for doubtful accounts and prompt payment discounts. Trade receivables do not bear interest. The allowance for doubtful accounts represents management's estimate of the amount of probable credit losses in existing accounts receivable, as determined from a review of past due balances and other specific account data. Account balances are written off against the allowance when management determines the receivable is uncollectible. The Company does not have off-balance sheet credit exposure related to its customers.

Demo 8-2B LO8-2 Accounting for Sales and Collections under the Net Method

Demo MBC

On June 1, 2020, Home Store transfers control of merchandise to Gomez at a gross sales price of $1,000 and a cost of $550. Credit terms are 2/10, n/30. Home Store accounts for sales transactions under the net method.

a. Record the entries for Home Store on June 1, 2020, the date of the sale of merchandise.
b. On June 8, 2020, Gomez paid half of the balance due. Record the entry for Home Store on June 8, 2020.
c. On June 30, 2020, Gomez paid the remaining amount due. Record the entry for Home Store on June 30, 2020.
d. Show the income statement presentation of revenue for the month of June 2020.

Solution

a. Home Store records the following entry upon sale of the merchandise to Gomez under the net method. Sales and accounts receivable are recorded at 98% of the sales amount (100% less the 2% discount).

June 1, 2020—To record sale of merchandise (both sales and cost entries)

Assets = Liabilities + Equity: Assets +980; Equity +980. Accounts Rec: 980 (debit). Sales Rev: 980 (credit).

Accounts Receivable ($1,000 × 0.98)	980	
Sales Revenue		980

Assets = Liabilities + Equity: Assets −550; Equity −550. Inventory: 550 (credit). COGS: 550 (debit).

Cost of Goods Sold	550	
Inventory		550

b. Gomez pays half of the balance on June 8, 2020, which is within the 10-day discount period. Home Store records the following entry on receipt of payment (equal to one-half of $980).

June 8, 2020—To record partial payment within discount period

Assets = Liabilities + Equity: Assets +490, −490. Cash: 490 (debit). Accounts Rec: 980 (debit), 490 (credit).

Cash	490	
Accounts Receivable		490

c. Gomez pays the remaining balance on June 30, 2020, after the discount period. Under the net method, a new account must be created to record the lost discount. This new account is **Sales Discount Forfeited**, a revenue account, similar to interest revenue. Sales discounts forfeited is reported in the *other revenue and gains* section of the income statement. The net method specifically identifies discounts forfeited by customers. Home Store records the following entry on receipt of final payment.

June 30, 2020—To record final one-half payment after discount period

Assets = Liabilities + Equity: Assets +500, −490; Equity +10. Cash: 490, 500 (debit). Sales Disc Forfeit: 10 (credit). Accounts Rec: 980 (debit), 490, 490 (credit).

Cash	500	
Sales Discount Forfeited		10
Accounts Receivable		490

continued

continued from previous page

d. Home Store recognizes the following amounts in its income statement for the month ended June 30, 2020.

Financial Statement Presentation of Revenue—Net Method

Income Statement—Excerpt For Month Ended June 30, 2020	
Sales revenue	$980
Less: Sales discounts	0
Net sales revenue	980
Sales discounts forfeited	10
Total revenue	$990

Under both the gross and net methods, the total amount of revenue recognized for the month is identical ($990). However, the composition of revenue differs. Net sales revenue is higher under the gross method at $990 compared to $980 under the net method. Sales discounts forfeited of $10 is only recorded under the net method. As a result, gross margin (sales revenue less cost of goods sold) will be higher under the gross method by $10.

Both methods are currently used in practice. However, theoretically, the net method is desirable because it results in the recognition of receivables at the amount of expected consideration to be received (assuming customers typically take a discount). With typically short collection periods on receivables, the occurrence of significant differences between the net and gross method at any point in time is likely to be considered immaterial.

EXPANDING YOUR KNOWLEDGE **Incentive to take Cash Discounts?**

A cash discount can be an incentive to pay early even when a percentage of, say, 2% does not seem large. Assume a company purchases merchandise with a $1,000 gross sales price on 2/10, n/30 terms. The company decides to pay on the 30th day following the sale, meaning it pays $1,000 without advantage of the $20 cash discount. This decision to delay payment cost $20, which is an annualized interest rate of 37.2%. The $20 "interest," or amount of discount lost, is slightly over 2% of $980, the amount that would have satisfied the seller if paid within the discount period. *This rate was paid for a borrowing period of 20 days.* The factor 365/20 represents the number of 20-day periods in a year, which yields the annualized rate.

$$\frac{0.02 \times \$1,000}{\$980} \times \frac{365 \text{ days}}{20 \text{ days}} = 37.2\%$$

Gross Method versus Net Method in Recording Cash Discounts — LO8-2 — Review 8-2

On January 1, 2020, Vitamin Water Inc. sold merchandise for $2,800 on credit terms 2/10, n/45.

Required

Ignore cost of sales entries for all of the following requirements.

a. Under the *gross method,* record (1) the sales transaction on January 1, 2020, and (2) the collection of the account, assuming collection took place on January 5, 2020.

b. Under the *gross method,* record (1) the sales transaction on January 1, 2020, and (2) the collection of the account, assuming collection took place on January 25, 2020.

c. Under the *net method,* record (1) the sales transaction on January 1, 2020, and (2) the collection of the account, assuming collection took place on January 5, 2020.

d. Under the *net method,* record (1) the sales transaction on January 1, 2020, and (2) the collection of the account, assuming collection took place on January 25, 2020.

Review MBC

More Practice: 8-18, 8-19, 8-35, 8-36

Solution on p. 8-70.

LO 8-3 Account for the impact of sales returns and allowances

LO 8-3 Overview

Sales Returns and Allowances
- Actual returns: Reduce receivables (or cash) and net sales
- Estimated returns at reporting date:
  - Reduce net sales and increase current liabilities (or decrease net receivables)

Return privileges are frequently part of a comprehensive marketing program aimed to maintain competitiveness. **Sales returns** are unacceptable merchandise taken back. **Sales allowances** are price reductions made to encourage customers to keep merchandise not meeting their preferences or having minor damage. Sales returns and allowances can be substantial.

Sales returns and allowances are forms of *variable consideration*. The seller is uncertain as to the amount of returns or allowances that will be extended to the customer, thus making the eventual transaction price uncertain at the time revenue is recognized. Accounting standards describe the transaction price as the amount of consideration that the company is expected to be entitled to.

606-10-32-2 The transaction price is the amount of consideration to which an entity expects to be entitled in exchange for transferring promised goods or services to a customer . . . The consideration promised in a contract with a customer may include fixed amounts, variable amounts, or both.

A company estimates sales returns based upon prior experiences and changes expected in the future such as a favorable change in economic conditions. The amount of estimated returns is recorded as a **Refund Liability** at the sales value. An asset is also recorded, titled **Inventory—Estimated Returns**, for the cost of inventory expected to be returned to the stock of the company. A material discrepancy between estimated and actual returns and allowances is treated as a change in accounting estimate and can affect future estimates. For example, if a company estimates returns at 1% of sales, but actual experience shows that returns are 1.5% of sales, the company would increase its future estimates of returns (provided trend are expected to continue). Authoritative guidance in this area follows.

606-10-32-10 An entity shall recognize a refund liability if the entity receives consideration from a customer and expects to refund some or all of that consideration to the customer. A refund liability is measured at the amount of consideration received (or receivable) for which the entity does not expect to be entitled (that is, amounts not included in the transaction price). The refund liability (and corresponding change in the transaction price and, therefore, the contract liability) shall be updated at the end of each reporting period for changes in circumstances.

While a company should record an estimate for sales returns with each sale and adjust the transaction price accordingly, companies would typically estimate sales returns at a report date for practical reasons and record an adjusting entry for estimated returns. In **Demo 8-3** we account for sales returns by estimating returns at the end of the period. A sales allowance is accounted for similarly but without the entries showing an inventory impact because the inventory remains with the buyer.

Demo 8-3 **LO8-3** **Accounting for Sales Returns**

Demo MBC

Mass Inc. sells merchandise of $1,000,000 on account, with a cost of $650,000 (65% of sales) during 2020. Mass Inc. grants $16,000 of returns in 2020, the first year of operations. On December 31, 2020, Mass Inc. estimates total returns to be 2% of credit sales. Record the entries for (a) sale of merchandise (b) actual returns granted in 2020 assuming that the company uses a perpetual inventory system and (c) estimated returns at the end of the year.

Solution

Mass Inc. recognizes sales and actual returns during the period, and records an adjusting entry at period-end to estimate future returns. **Sales Returns**, a contra revenue account, is debited when an actual return is recorded, resulting in an indirect reduction to sales revenue. Total sales returns are estimated to be $20,000 (0.02 × $1,000,000). Therefore, the refund liability at the end of the year is $4,000 or $20,000 (total estimated returns) less $16,000 (actual returns). Simultaneously, we record an entry to adjust Inventory-Estimated Returns by $2,600 or $13,000 ($20,000 × 0.65) less $10,400 (returned inventory received to date).

continued

continued from previous page

2020—To record sale of merchandise

Accounts Receivable	1,000,000	
Sales Revenue		1,000,000

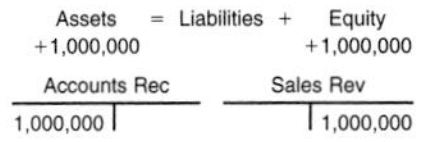

Cost of Goods Sold	650,000	
Inventory		650,000

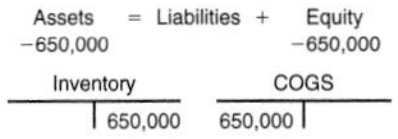

2020—To record actual returns of merchandise

Sales Returns	16,000	
Cash (or Accounts Receivable)		16,000

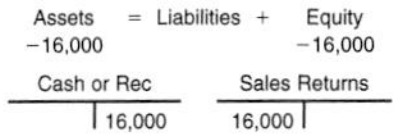

Inventory ($16,000 × 0.65)	10,400	
Cost of Goods Sold		10,400

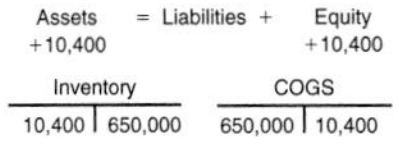

December 31, 2020—To record an estimate of future returns

Sales Returns ($20,000 − $16,000)	4,000	
Refund Liability		4,000

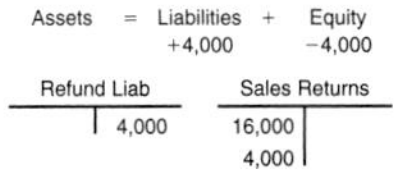

Inventory—Estimated Returns	2,600	
Cost of Goods Sold ([$20,000 × 0.65] − $10,400)		2,600

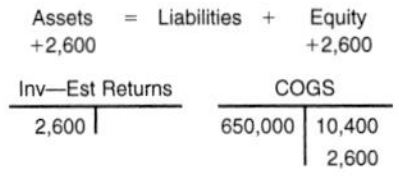

In practice at the end of a period, a company may use an account such as **Allowance for Sales Returns** (a contra Accounts Receivable account) instead of **Refund Liability** if the sales amount for the return is associated with outstanding accounts receivable. In other words, if receivables related to the returns have not been collected, a company may credit the Allowance for Sales Returns instead of Refund Liability.

TARGET

Real World—ESTIMATING SALES RETURNS

TARGET [TGT]

Target Corporation recognizes revenues net of estimated returns as indicated by the following accounting policy note accompanying its financial statements in its recent Form 10-K.

> Our retail stores generally record revenue at the point of sale . . . Guests may return national brand merchandise within 90 days of purchase and owned and exclusive brands within one year of purchase. Revenues are recognized net of expected returns, which we estimate using historical return patterns as a percentage of sales and our expectation of future returns.

Accounting for Sales Returns LO8-3 Review 8-3

Vitamin Water Inc. recognized sales of $28,000 on account (with a cost of $16,800) for the year ended December 31, 2020. During 2020, the company recorded actual returns of $800. The company estimates returns at 4% of sales.

Review MBC

Required

a. Prepare the journal entry to record sales in 2020.
b. Prepare the journal entry to record actual returns in 2020.
c. Prepare the journal entry to record estimated returns on December 31, 2020.

More Practice:
8-20, 8-37, 8-38
Solution on p. 8-70.

LO 8-4 Measure and record accounts receivable at net realizable value using the allowance method

LO 8-4 Overview

Allowance Method
- Follow the CECL model
- Apply expected loss rates to age categories
- Adjust allowance to desired ending balance
- Report receivables at net realizable value

When credit is extended, some amount of uncollectible receivables is inevitable. Companies attempt to develop a credit policy neither too conservative (leading to excessive lost sales) nor too liberal (leading to excessive uncollectible accounts). Past records of payment and the financial condition and income of customers are key inputs to the credit-granting decision.

Allowance Method

The **Current Expected Credit Loss Model** (CECL model) is required for the accounting of expected losses on financial instruments measured at amortized cost beginning in 2020 (with optional adoption in 2019) based on a recently passed accounting standard. Financial instruments under this standard include accounts receivable. Under the CECL model, companies use the **allowance method** to estimate and recognize expected losses on receivables. We describe the accounting processes under the allowance method. Then, we describe how the allowance is estimated.

Under the allowance method, an adjustment to the allowance for doubtful accounts is recorded as an adjusting entry at period-end as a debit to Bad Debt Expense and a credit to the Allowance for Doubtful Accounts. The **allowance for doubtful accounts** (also referred to as a **provision for doubtful accounts**) is a contra account to accounts receivable and is used because the identity of specific uncollectible accounts is unknown at the time of the adjusting entry. Net accounts receivable, which is gross accounts receivable less the allowance for doubtful accounts, is an estimate of the **net realizable value** of the receivables or the amount expected to be collected. Authoritative guidance follows.

326-20-30-1 The allowance for credit losses* is a valuation account that is deducted from the amortized cost basis of the financial asset(s) to present the net amount expected to be collected on the financial asset… An entity shall report in net income (as a credit loss expense*) the amount necessary to adjust the allowance for credit losses for management's current estimate of expected credit losses on financial asset(s).

* Bad debt expense and the allowance for doubtful accounts are referred to in the authoritative literature as **credit loss expense** and the **allowance for credit losses**, respectively. We use the terms *bad debt expense* and the *allowance for doubtful accounts* as we believe that companies will continue to use these long-standing account titles.

The following illustrates the allowance method. At the end of its first year of operations, Gomez Company determines that the allowance for doubtful accounts should be $9,000 based on expected losses on its $300,000 receivable balance. Gomez records the following entry on December 31, 2020.

Assets	=	Liabilities	+	Equity
−9,000				−9,000

AFDA: credit 9,000 | Bad Debt Exp: debit 9,000

December 31, 2020—To establish allowance for doubtful accounts

Bad Debt Expense	9,000	
Allowance for Doubtful Accounts		9,000

Of the $300,000 of accounts receivable that customers owe (or gross accounts receivable), Gomez does not expect to collect $9,000 (or the balance in the allowance for doubtful accounts). This means that Gomez expects to collect $291,000 (net accounts receivable). The balance sheet of Gomez Company shows the following.

Trade accounts receivable, less allowance of $9,000	**$291,000**

After an allowance is established, specific accounts are later written-off. When Gomez established the allowance, it was unclear which specific accounts would ultimately be determined to be uncollectible. A **write-off** of a specific account would not typically occur unless the company has exhausted all methods of collections. When specific accounts are determined to be uncollectible, they are removed from accounts receivable (or derecognized) and that part of the allowance is no longer needed. (Namely, Allowance for Doubtful Accounts is debited and Accounts Receivable is credited.) The adjusting entry to establish the allowance recognized the estimated economic effect of future uncollectible accounts. This means that write-offs of specific accounts do not further reduce total assets unless they exceed the estimate.

After a customer's account is written off, the customer might decide to pay all or part of the balance owed (perhaps to improve their credit standing). This unexpected collection of an account previously written off is called a **recovery** and requires two journal entries. First, the company reverses the write-off and reinstates the customer's account. Next, the collection of the newly reinstated account is recorded. Both write-offs and recoveries are recognized as they occur. Authoritative guidance follows.

326-10-35-8 Writeoffs of financial assets, which may be full or partial writeoffs, shall be deducted from the allowance. The writeoffs shall be recorded in the period in which the financial asset(s) are deemed uncollectible. Recoveries of financial assets and trade receivables previously written off shall be recorded when received.

Demo 8-4A describes the accounting for establishing an allowance, and recording an account write-off and recovery.

Entries Under the Allowance Method — LO8-4 — Demo 8-4A

Demo MBC

Part One: Establishing an Allowance and Recording an Account Write-Off

Rally Company establishes an allowance for doubtful accounts of $5,960 on December 31, 2020 related to its accounts receivable balance of $177,500. Rally Company decides on February 1, 2021, not to pursue collection of Baker's $500 account. The likelihood of collection does not support further collection efforts.

a. Record Rally's entry to establish the allowance for doubtful accounts on December 31, 2020, assuming a zero beginning balance.

b. Record Rally's entry on February 1, 2021, to write-off the Baker account.

c. Measure net accounts receivable before *and* after the Baker account write-off.

Solution

a. Rally would record the following entry to establish its allowance for doubtful accounts.

December 31, 2020—To establish allowance for doubtful accounts

Bad Debt Expense	5,960	
Allowance for Doubtful Accounts		5,960

Assets	=	Liabilities	+	Equity
−5,960				−5,960

b. Rally would record the following entry to write-off the Baker account.

February 1, 2021—To write-off Baker account

Allowance for Doubtful Accounts	500	
Accounts Receivable, Baker		500

Assets	=	Liabilities	+	Equity
+500 −500				

Accounts Receivable

	Debit	Credit	
Beg. bal.	177,500		
		500	Write-off
End. bal.	177,000		

Allowance for Doubtful Accounts

	Debit	Credit	
		5,960	Beg. bal.
Write-off	500		
		5,460	End. bal.

c. The write-off entry in part *b* affects neither income nor the net amount of accounts receivable outstanding. Instead, it is the culmination of the process that began with the adjusting entry to estimate bad debt expense. The write-off entry changes only the components of net accounts receivable (namely, gross accounts receivable and the allowance for doubtful accounts), not the net amount of $171,540.

	Before Baker Write-Off	After Baker Write-Off
Accounts receivable	$177,500	$177,000
Less: Allowance for doubtful accounts	(5,960)	(5,460)
Net accounts receivable	$171,540	$171,540

continued

continued from previous page

Part Two: Recovery of an Account Previously Written-Off

Assume that Baker pays $250 on account on March 1, 2021, after the above write-off entry was recorded. No further payments are expected from Baker on account.

a. Record Rally's entry on March 1, 2021, for the partial recovery of the Baker account.

b. Measure net accounts receivable before and after the partial Baker account recovery.

Solution

a. When amounts are received on account after a write-off, the write-off entry is reversed to reinstate the receivable and then cash collection is recorded. The debit and credit adjustments to Baker's account receivable provide a record of the partial reinstatement and collection of the account.

March 1, 2021—To record partial collection on the Baker account, previously written-off

Assets	= Liabilities	+ Equity
+250		
−250		

Accounts Receivable, Baker	250	
Allowance for Doubtful Accounts		250

Assets	= Liabilities	+ Equity
+250		
−250		

Cash	250	
Accounts Receivable, Baker		250

Accounts Receivable

Prior bal.	177,000	250	Cash collection
Recovery	250		
End. bal.	177,000		

Allowance for Doubtful Accounts

		5,460	Prior bal.
		250	Recovery
		5,710	End. bal.

b. The accounts receivable balance remains unchanged while the allowance is reinstated for the $250 Baker partial account collection. The allowance must be reinstated to properly reflect managements' overall estimate of the uncollectible amount.

	After Baker Write-Off	After Baker Recovery
Accounts receivable	$177,000	$177,000
Less: Allowance for doubtful accounts	(5,460)	(5,710)
Net accounts receivable	$171,540	$171,290

During the year, Rally would record sales and collections on account and any write-offs or recoveries. These transactions impact the balances in accounts receivable and the allowance for doubtful accounts. What if write-offs (net of recoveries) for the period were $6,000 (or any amount above the established allowance)? The Allowance for Doubtful Accounts would have an unadjusted ending debit balance. This will impact the journal entry required at the next reporting date to adjust the allowance to the desired ending balance which we will discuss in **Demo 8-4B**.

Estimating Accounts Receivable at Net Realizable Value

The allowance for doubtful accounts is analyzed and adjusted at reporting dates through an adjusting journal entry to report net accounts receivable at the amount that the company expects to collect. However, how do we determine the appropriate balance in the allowance for doubtful accounts? First thing to consider is that the balance is an *estimate determined by management guided by the requirements of the CECL model. The measurement of the allowance requires a high degree of judgment.* Adjustments to the allowance for doubtful accounts are considered changes in estimate and are accounted for prospectively. The allowance can be measured using a variety of methods—the standards do not designate a specific method but suggests options. The accounting standards provide the following considerations in measuring the allowance.

Reflect Loss Expected Over the Receivable's Life

The loss on receivables should reflect **expected credit losses** expected to be incurred over the entire time that the receivable is expected to be outstanding. In other words, any risk of loss should be considered, even if the company is exposed to losses on the receivable in the latter part of the receivable's life, such as the last 5 days of an expected life of 60 days.

326-20-30-6 An entity shall estimate expected credit losses over the contractual term of the financial asset(s).

Consider Relevant Available Information

The CECL model requires companies to analyze available information that is relevant in estimating the collections on receivables as long as the information is reasonably available with undue cost and effort. Information can include internal and external information to the company, qualitative and quantitative information, information related to a specific customer, or to the broader environment. Companies should consider past events such as incurred losses on collections but should also consider current conditions and forecasted information, such as changes in economic conditions that affect collections. For example, is there a future event that could affect a major customer's ability to make payments on account that would indicate collectibility issues, even if the customer has always paid on time in the past? A good place to start is to look at historical trends, but the standards require companies to adjust the historical information to reflect **current information** and **reasonable and supportable forecasts** of the future. Authoritative support follows.

326-20-30-7 When developing an estimate of expected credit losses on financial asset(s), an entity shall consider available information relevant to assessing the collectibility of cash flows. This information may include internal information, external information, or a combination of both relating to past events, current conditions, and reasonable and supportable forecasts. An entity shall consider relevant qualitative and quantitative factors that relate to the environment in which the entity operates and are specific to the borrower(s). When financial assets are evaluated on a collective or individual basis, an entity is not required to search all possible information that is not reasonably available without undue cost and effort...An entity may find that using its internal information is sufficient in determining collectibility.

326-20-30-9 An entity shall not rely solely on past events to estimate expected credit losses. When an entity uses historical loss information, it shall consider the need to adjust historical information to reflect the extent to which management expects current conditions and reasonable and supportable forecasts to differ from the conditions that existed for the period over which historical information was evaluated. The adjustments to historical loss information may be qualitative in nature and should reflect changes related to relevant data (such as changes in unemployment rates, property values, commodity values, delinquency, or other factors that are associated with credit losses on the financial asset or in the group of financial assets).

EXPANDING YOUR KNOWLEDGE **Adjusting Historical Information for Future Expectations**

Historical information might not reflect management's expectations about the future. Accounting standards (ASC 326-20-55-4) suggest items to consider in updating historical information for current conditions and to prepare reasonable and supportable forecasts.

- Customer's financial condition, credit rating, credit score.
- Customer's ability to make payments.
- Nature and volume of receivables.
- Volume and severity of past due amounts.
- Entity's credit policies and procedures.
- Quality of the company's credit review system.
- Experience, ability, and depth of management.
- Environmental factors including market condition.

Consider Receivables as a Pool When Risks are Similar

Receivables with similar risk are pooled together when estimating collectibility of accounts. If a receivable does not share the risk of a pool, it should be evaluated separately. One way to pool receivables is based upon past due status. An **aging of accounts receivable schedule** categorizes the individual receivables by age or the extent to which the accounts are past due. For example, an aging schedule could divide a receivable balance into 3 categories: current, 1-45 days due, and over 45 days due. The allowance for doubtful accounts is estimated by taking each age category and multiplying by an **expected credit loss rate** for that category. The reasoning behind this method is that older accounts are less likely to be collected, thus a higher loss rate is applied to older accounts. Key questions to ask when adjusting the historical loss rate to an expected credit loss rate follow.

- Do the historical loss rates reflect current and reasonable and supportable forecasts?

- Does the historical loss rate for the current category reflect the risk of loss in the future, even though amounts are not overdue at this time?

Other ways that receivables could be pooled are by credit ratings or industry.

326-20-30-2 An entity shall measure expected credit losses of financial assets on a collective (pool) basis when similar risk characteristic(s) exist… If an entity determines that a financial asset does not share risk characteristics with its other financial assets, the entity shall evaluate the financial asset for expected credit losses on an individual basis.

Reflect Loss Even if Remote

The accounting standards require the estimate of a credit loss to reflect a risk of loss, even if **remote**. For example, if there is a 98% chance that a loss will be zero and a 2% chance of a total loss, the estimated loss should reflect the 2% likelihood of a loss. There would *not* be an accrual recorded for an allowance for doubtful accounts when historical experience adjusted for current conditions and reasonable and supportable forecasts provides an expectation that nonpayment of the receivable balance is zero. If nonpayment is even remote (1% for example), an allowance is required. It would be challenging for a company to establish a zero-loss expectation for a receivable; thus, a situation where no allowance is recorded would be rare.

326-20-30-10 An entity's estimate of expected credit losses shall include a measure of the expected risk of credit loss even if that risk is remote, regardless of the method applied to estimate credit losses.

Demo 8-4B **LO8-4** **Adjusting Accounts Receivable to Net Realizable Value**

Demo MBC

Part One: Estimating the Allowance for Doubtful Accounts Using a Single Rate

Rally Company uses a single 3% historical loss rate on its accounts receivable balance based on past experiences. This example assumes that the receivables are pooled into a single category because the individual account balances have similar characteristics and thus similar risks of losses. The 3% historical loss rate is based upon historical trends. However, analysis of available information and a preparation of a forecast of expected cash collections support the use of 3% as the *expected credit loss rate.* Rally's accounts receivable balance on December 31, 2020, is $177,500. The allowance account reflects an unadjusted, $500 *credit* balance.

a. Prepare the journal entry to adjust accounts receivable to net realizable value on December 31, 2020.

b. Determine how accounts receivable is recognized on the balance sheet at December 31, 2020.

Solution

a. Given an accounts receivable balance of $177,500 on December 31, 2020, the required ending allowance credit balance is $5,325 (0.03 × $177,500). With a $500 beginning *credit* balance, the adjusting entry increases the allowance account by $4,825 ($5,325 − $500), yielding the $5,325 desired ending credit balance.

December 31, 2020—To adjust the allowance

Assets	=	Liabilities	+	Equity
−4,825				−4,825

Bad Debt Expense	4,825	
Allowance for Doubtful Accounts		4,825

Allowance for Doubtful Accounts		
	500	Beg. bal.
	4,825	**Adjustment required**
	5,325	Estim. ending bal. on Dec. 31, 2020

b. Rally's December 31, 2020, balance sheet would report the following.

Trade accounts receivable, less allowance of $5,325	**$172,175**

continued

continued from previous page

Part Two: Estimating the Allowance for Doubtful Accounts Using an Aging of Accounts
The following aging schedule for Rally Inc. categorizes the balance of receivables of $177,500 on December 31, 2020, according to age. An account is considered past due if it is not collected by the end of the period specified in the credit terms. For example, an account arising from a November 1 sale with terms 2/10, n/30, is due December 1. If the account remains unpaid at December 31, the aging analysis classifies the account as 1 to 30 days past due.

Aging Schedule

Customer	Receivable Balance Dec. 31, 2020	Current	Past Due 1–30 Days	Past Due 31–60 Days	Past Due Over 60 Days
Denk.	$ 500	$ 400	$ 100		
Dragoo	53,960	8,400	9,490	29,130	6,940
Evans	54,000	54,000			
Field	1,650		1,350	$ 300	
Harris	90			30	$ 60
King	20,800	700	20,060	40	
Zabot	46,500	46,500			
Total	$177,500	$110,000	$31,000	$29,500	$7,000

Application of Loss Rates to Age Categories

Age Category	Total Balances	Loss Rate	Amount Estimated to be Uncollectible
Not past due (current).	$110,000	0.2%	$ 220
1–30 days past due	31,000	1.0	310
31–60 days past due	29,500	8.0	2,360
Over 60 days past due	7,000	40.0	2,800
	$177,500		$5,690

Rally's aging schedule illustrates the application of the historical loss rates to age categories. The $177,500 accounts receivable balance on December 31, 2020, is divided into four age classifications, with a historical loss rate applied to each age category. *Rally's historical loss rates increase with the age of the accounts from 0.2% to 40%.* As accounts are collected and removed from a category, the proportion represented by uncollectible accounts increases. Rally uses the aging schedule and historical loss rates to estimate bad debt on its accounts receivable balance. The company believes that historical loss rates are a reasonable basis for estimating expected credit losses because (1) the composition of the current receivables is of similar risk and characteristics of the historical receivables, and (2) a reasonable forecast supports the continued use of the loss rates.

a. Prepare the journal entry to record bad debt expense on December 31, 2020, assuming the allowance account reflects an unadjusted $500 *credit* balance.

b. Prepare the journal entry to record bad debt expense on December 31, 2020, assuming the allowance account reflects an unadjusted $500 *debit* balance.

Solution

a. With a $500 *credit* balance in the allowance for doubtful accounts before adjustment, the entry to adjust the allowance would be recorded as follows.

December 31, 2020—To adjust allowance for doubtful accounts

	Debit	Credit
Bad Debt Expense	5,190	
Allowance for Doubtful Accounts		**5,190**

Assets = Liabilities + Equity
−5,190 −5,190

Allowance for Doubtful Accounts		
	500	Beg. bal.
	5,190	**Adjustment required**
	5,690	Estim. ending bal. on Dec. 31, 2020

continued

continued from previous page

b. The computation in Rally's aging schedule yields a required ending balance of $5,690 (credit) in the allowance account at December 31, 2020. Because the allowance balance is $500 (debit balance) before adjustment, the allowance account is increased $6,190, yielding an ending $5,690 balance.

December 31, 2020—To adjust allowance for doubtful accounts

Assets	= Liabilities	+ Equity
−6,190		−6,190

Bad Debt Expense	6,190	
Allowance for Doubtful Accounts		**6,190**

Allowance for Doubtful Accounts

Debit		Credit	
Beg. bal.	500		
		6,190	**Adjustment required**
		5,690	Estim. ending bal. on Dec. 31, 2020

EXPANDING YOUR KNOWLEDGE — Alternative to Estimating Net Realizable Value

As an alternative approach to estimating net realizable value of accounts receivable, a company may adjust the allowance for doubtful accounts based upon a bad debt loss rate applied to credit sales. First, a bad debt loss rate is estimated based upon the relation between actual bad debt losses and net credit sales. Next, the rate is multiplied by the current period's credit sales to arrive at the adjustment to bad debt expense and the allowance for doubtful accounts. This method however, may only be used to estimate net realizable value if the result in the *net value of the receivables* does not differ materially from the *net realizable value of receivables* calculated under the allowance method.

For example, assume that experience shows that 1.2% of Rally's credit sales are not collected. Barring changes in Rally's credit policies or major changes in the economy, Rally expects this rate to continue. Record bad debt expense on December 31, 2020, by applying the bad debt loss rate of 1.2% to credit sales when credit sales are $500,000 for the year and the allowance account has an unadjusted $500 *debit* balance. The required 2020 year-end adjusting entry follows.

December 31, 2020—To adjust allowance for doubtful accounts

Assets	= Liabilities	+ Equity
−6,000		−6,000

AFDA		Bad Debt Exp	
	6,000	6,000	

Bad Debt Expense ($500,000 × 0.012)	6,000	
Allowance for Doubtful Accounts		6,000

After this entry is posted, the balance in the allowance account is $5,500 ($6,000 credit from the adjusting entry less the prior $500 debit balance). This approach is only appropriate under GAAP if the net realizable value does not differ materially from net receivables of $5,500.

EXPANDING YOUR KNOWLEDGE — Direct Write-Off Method For Tax Purposes

Under the direct write-off method, when uncollectible accounts are not probable or estimable or are immaterial, no adjustment to income or receivables is made until specific accounts are considered uncollectible. In other words, no allowance for doubtful accounts is established. If a specific account is considered uncollectible, Bad Debt Expense is debited and Accounts Receivable is credited. The recognition of an allowance under the CECL model is required even if the chance of a write-off is remote. Therefore, unless there is a *zero-loss expectation*, the allowance method (not the direct write-off method) would be used under GAAP. *However, for tax purposes, the direct write-off method is the primary method used.*

REVIEW 8-4 — LO8-4 Measuring and Recording Receivables at Net Realizable Value

At its annual year-end of December 31, 2020, the accounts of Rolo Inc. show the following.

1. Credit sales for 2020 of $3,200,000.
2. Allowance for doubtful account balance, December 31, 2020, $10,000 *credit* (unadjusted).
3. Accounts receivable balance, December 31, 2020, $400,000.
4. Aging schedule at December 31, 2020, for accounts receivable.

continued

continued from previous page

Status of Individual Accounts Receivable	Amount
Not past due	$300,000
Past due 1–60 days	90,000
Past due over 60 days	10,000

Required

a. Prepare the December 31, 2020, adjusting entry to adjust accounts receivable to net realizable value for each of the following independent assumptions concerning expected loss rates.
1. Expected loss rate on total receivables at year-end, 3.0%.
2. Expected loss rates on aging schedule: not past due, 2%; past due 1–60 days, 6%; and past due over 60 days, 15%.

b. Determine accounts receivable at net realizable value recognized on the December 31, 2020, balance sheet for *each* assumption in part *a*.

c. On January 15, 2021, record the entry for the write-off of a specific account (Johnson Inc.) for $1,400. (Assume that the allowance was determined under assumption 2 of part *a*.)

d. On January 31, 2021, record the unanticipated recovery of the $1,400 for Johnson Inc. account previously written off on January 15, 2021.

More Practice:
8-41, 8-42, 8-43, 8-44
Solution on p. 8-71.

Measure and record notes receivable

LO 8-5

A **note receivable** is a written promise to receive specified amounts on specific payment date(s). When the note term is one year or less, the note is classified as short-term. Otherwise, the note is classified as long-term. Notes receivable often arise from revenue contracts with extended payment terms but can also arise from other transactions such as the sale of equipment or a loan to another entity. Notes receivable provide (1) extended payment terms, (2) more security than sales invoices and other commercial trade documents, (3) a formal basis for charging interest, and (4) negotiability (ability to transfer ownership). **Exhibit 8-3** defines common terms used in accounting for notes receivable.

Notes Receivable
- Stated rate = Market rate
  - Note is measured at face value
- Stated rate < Market rate
  - Note is measured at a discount
- Stated rate > Market rate
  - Note is measured at a premium

LO 8-5 Overview

EXHIBIT 8-3
Note Receivable Terminology

Note Terminology	Definition
Face value	Amount due at a note's maturity date.
Stated rate	Interest rate used to determine the cash interest receipts which can be 0% if no cash interest receipts are required. Stated as an annual rate.
Market rate (Effective rate)	Interest rate on a similar investment in the market involving similar risk and where the issuer has a similar crediting rating. Stated as an annual rate.
Interest-bearing note	Note requiring periodic cash interest receipts based on terms of the note.
Noninterest-bearing note	Note requiring no periodic cash interest receipts (the stated rate is equal to zero). Instead, all amounts are received at maturity.
Discount on note receivable	Contra account equal to the excess of the face value of a note over its present value. A discount decreases the carrying value of a note receivable. Discount represents deferred interest revenue that will be recognized over the term of the note.
Premium on note receivable	Adjunct account equal to the excess of the present value of a note over its face value. A premium increases the carrying value of a note receivable. Premiums represent a reduction of interest revenue that will be recognized over the term of the note.

The measurement basis for a note receivable is the present value of the cash expected to be collected on the note, discounted at the market rate in effect at the inception of the note. If present value and face value do not differ materially, the note is recognized at face value. If the face value of the note is greater than the present value of the note, a **discount on note receivable** is recorded. If the face value of the note is less than the present value of the note, a **premium on note receivable** is recorded. A discount (premium) is amortized over the life of the note as an increase (decrease) to interest revenue.

Present Value of Payments Equals the Fair Value of Note

The present value of payments equals the note's face value when the stated rate is equal to the market rate. In this case, the company records the note receivable at its face value and accrues interest over the term of the note as illustrated in **Demo 8-5A**.

Demo 8-5A LO8-5 Noncurrent Note Receivable [Stated Rate = 10%; Market Rate = 10%]

Demo MBC

On April 1, 2020, Lionel Company loaned $12,000 cash to Baylor Company and received a three-year, 10% note. Cash interest is due each March 31, and the principal is due at the end of the third year. The stated rate and market rate are equal. Record the journal entries over the term of the note for Lionel Company assuming a December 31 year-end.

Solution

Receipt of Note The present value of the principal and cash interest receipts on April 1, 2020, is $12,000 because the stated and market rates are equal. The entry to record the note follows.

	RATE	NPER	PMT	PV	FV	Excel Formula
Given	10%	3	−1,200	?	−12,000	=PV(0.10,3,−1,200,−12000)
Solution				$12,000		

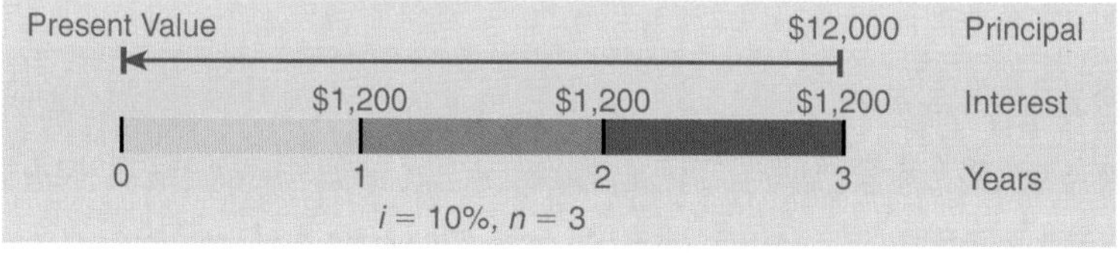

April 1, 2020—To record receipt of note

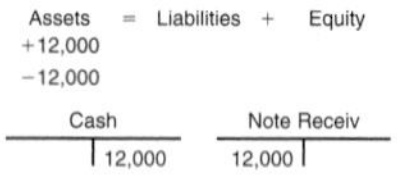

Note Receivable	12,000	
Cash		12,000

Interest Revenue Accrual and Interest Receipt Cash interest received equals interest revenue recognized over the term of the note, as indicated in the following interest receivable accrual and cash receipt entries. Accrued interest revenue is equal to the face value of the note of $12,000 multiplied by the stated rate of 10%, multiplied by the fraction of the year or 9 months divided by 12 months. An accrual of interest revenue is required at December 31 in order to recognize interest revenue in the correct period even though the cash will not be received until the next accounting period. The computation for interest assumes months of equal length.

December 31, 2020, 2021, 2022—To accrue interest revenue

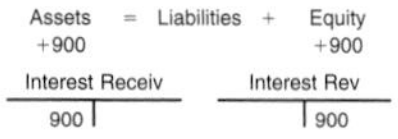

Interest Receivable	900	
Interest Revenue ($12,000 × 0.10 × 9/12)		900

March 31, 2021, 2022, 2023—To record receipt of interest

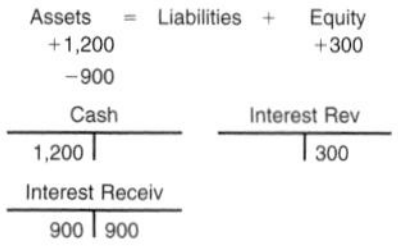

Cash	1,200	
Interest Receivable		900
Interest Revenue ($12,000 × 0.10 × 3/12)		300

Note Collection In addition to cash interest collected on March 31, 2023, Lionel received the principal of the note, reflected in the following entry.

March 31, 2023—To record cash received on note maturity

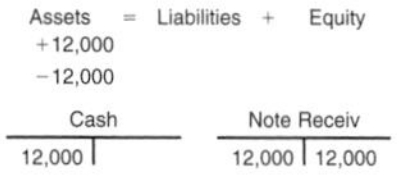

Cash	12,000	
Note Receivable		12,000

Present Value of Payments Does Not Equal the Fair Value of Note

The present value of payments (discounted at the market rate) does not equal the note's face value when the stated rate is not equal to the market rate. For example, the stated rate can be zero or an unrealistic interest rate. In these cases, the company records the note receivable at its face value and records either a discount on note receivable or a premium on note receivable for the difference between the face value and the present value of the note.

A company can receive a note in exchange for property, goods, or services. The present value of the note receivable is measured using either (a) the fair value of the goods or services provided or the fair value of the note, whichever is more clearly determinable, or (b) the present value of the note discounted at the market rate also called the **imputed interest rate** (if the fair value of the goods or services or the note cannot be determined). Authoritative guidance follows.

835-30-25-10 In circumstances where interest is not stated, the stated amount is unreasonable, or the stated face amount of the note is materially different from the current cash sales price for the same or similar items or from the fair value of the note at the date of the transaction, the note, the sales price, and the cost of the property, goods, or service exchanged for the note **shall be recorded at the fair value of the property, goods, or service or at an amount that reasonably approximates the fair value of the note, whichever is the more clearly determinable.** That amount may or may not be the same as its face amount, and any resulting discount or premium shall be accounted for as an element of interest over the life of the note.

835-30-25-11 In the absence of established exchange prices for the related property, goods, or service or evidence of the fair value of the note,...the present value of a note that stipulates either no interest or a rate of interest that is clearly unreasonable **shall be determined by discounting all future payments on the notes using an imputed rate of interest.** This determination shall be made at the time the note is issued, assumed, or acquired; any subsequent changes in prevailing interest rates shall be ignored.

If a note were exchanged solely for cash and no other services, promises or merchandise, the cash value is considered the present value of the note, even if the interest rate is unreasonable or unrealistic. In other words, the amount of cash exchanged is equal to the carrying value of the note at the inception of the note.

835-30-25-4 When a note is received or issued solely for cash and no other right or privilege is exchanged, it is presumed to have a present value at issuance measured by the cash proceeds exchanged.

Next, we review three scenarios: (1) interest-bearing note where the market rate exceeds the stated rate (**Demo 8-5B**), (2) zero-interest bearing note (**Demo 8-5C**), and (3) interest-bearing note where the stated rate exceeds the market rate (**Demo 8-5D**).

Noncurrent Note Receivable [Stated Rate = 3%; Market Rate = 10%] LO8-5 Demo 8-5B

Demo MBC

Fox Company sold equipment on January 1, 2020, to Laker Company and received a two-year, $10,000 note with a 3% stated rate. Cash interest is due each December 31, and the entire principal is due December 31, 2021. The market rate is 10%. The equipment has an original cost of $35,000 and accumulated depreciation of $24,000 on January 1, 2020. Record the journal entries over the term of the note for Fox Company.

Solution

Receipt of Note The present value of the note is measured by taking the present value of cash interest receipts and the present value of the note at maturity, discounted at the market rate of 10%. The present value calculation for the note follows.

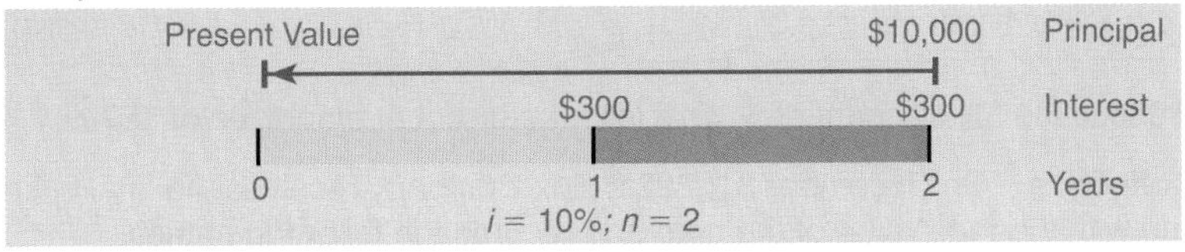

	RATE	NPER	PMT	PV	FV	Excel Formula
Given	10%	2	−300	?	−10,000	=PV(0.10,2,−300,−10000)
Solution				$8,785		

continued

continued from previous page

The measurement of the present value of this note is $8,785. When the stated and market rates are different, the face value and the present value of the note differ. The note is recorded at the face value of $10,000, less the discount of $1,215 for a net amount of $8,785. The loss of $2,215 on the sale is equal to the present value of the note of $8,785 less the carrying value of the equipment of $11,000.

January 1, 2020—To record sale in exchange for note receivable

Assets = Liabilities + Equity
+24,000 −2,215
+10,000
−1,215
−35,000
Accum Deprec: 24,000 (Dr)
Loss on Sale of Equip: 2,215 (Dr)
Discount on NR: 1,215 (Cr)
Note Receiv: 10,000 (Dr)
Eqiupment: 35,000 (Cr)

Loss on Sale of Equipment	2,215	
Accumulated Depreciation	24,000	
Note Receivable	10,000	
Discount on Note Receivable		1,215
Equipment		35,000

Interest Receipt and Discount Amortization On December 31, 2020, interest revenue is recorded, cash interest is received, and a portion of the discount is recognized as interest revenue through the effective interest method. Under the **effective interest method**, the market interest each period is determined by multiplying the market rate by the carrying value of the note at the *beginning* of the interest period. The cash interest received each period is calculated by multiplying the face amount of the note by the stated rate applicable to the interest period. The difference between the market interest amount and the cash interest amount is used to adjust the note's carrying value each period until the note reaches its face amount.

The following amortization schedule illustrates how interest revenue is recognized over the life of the note. The components of the journal entry for each period to record the receipt of interest and amortization of discount are included in this schedule.

Effective Interest Amortization—Discount

Date	Cash (Stated Interest)[a]	Interest Revenue (Market Interest)[b]	Discount on N.R. Amortization[c]	Note Receivable, Net (Carrying Value)[d]
Jan. 1, 2020				$ 8,785
Dec. 31, 2020	$300	$ 879	$ 579	9,364
Dec. 31, 2021	300	936	636	10,000
Totals	$600	$1,815	$1,215	

[a] Note face value × Stated rate.
[b] Note carrying value, beginning of year × Market rate.
[c] Market interest − Stated interest.
[d] Note carrying value, beginning of year + Discount amortization.

Under the effective interest method, the carrying value of the note is always equal to the present value of the remaining cash flows discounted at the market rate in effect at the inception of the note.

The Fox Company records the following journal entry for the receipt of interest and the amortization of the discount.

December 31, 2020—To record receipt of interest and amortization of discount

Assets = Liabilities + Equity
+300 +879
+579
Cash: 300 (Dr)
Interest Rev: 879 (Cr)
Discount on NR: 579 (Dr) | 1,215 (Cr)

Cash	300	
Discount on Note Receivable	579	
Interest Revenue		879

Financial Statement Presentation The balance sheet on December 31, 2020, reports the following.

Note receivable, less discount of $636	9,364

The net discount of $636 is the full discount of $1,215 less the discount amortized of $579.

Note and Interest Collection On December 31, 2021, Fox Company receives the final cash interest payment along with the face value of the note and records the following entries.

continued

continued from previous page

December 31, 2021—To record receipt of cash interest and amortization of discount

Cash	300	
Discount on Note Receivable	636	
Interest Revenue		936

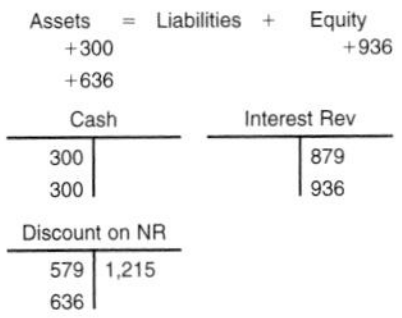

Assets = Liabilities + Equity
+300 +936
+636
Cash
300
300
Interest Rev
879
936
Discount on NR
579 1,215
636

December 31, 2021—To record principal payment received for the note

Cash	10,000	
Note Receivable		10,000

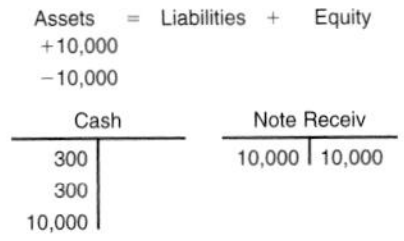

Noncurrent Note Receivable [Stated Rate = 0%; Market Rate = 10%] LO8-5 Demo 8-5C

Demo MBC

On June 30, 2020, Atlas Company sells inventory and receives in exchange a three-year, noninterest-bearing note for $8,000 with an implicit rate of interest of 10%. Record the journal entries over the term of the note for Atlas Company, assuming that Atlas has a June 30 fiscal year-end.

Solution

Receipt of Note The sales revenue of $6,011 is measured as the present value of the note, discounted using the implicit interest rate.

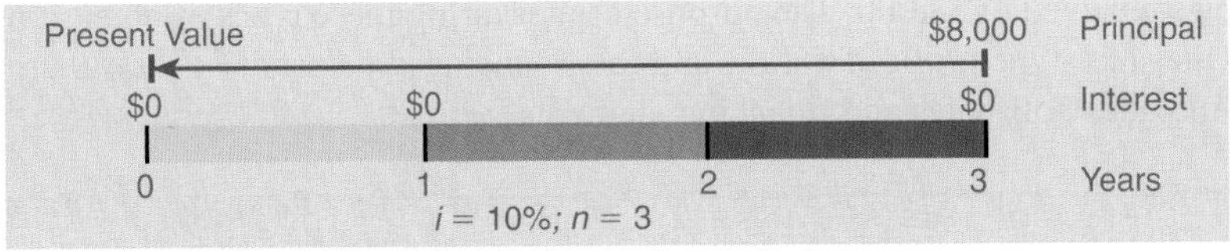

	RATE	NPER	PMT	PV	FV	Excel Formula
Given	10%	3	0	?	−8,000	=PV(0.10,3,0,−8000)
Solution				$6,011		

Upon receipt of the note for the sale of inventory, Atlas records the following entry.

June 30, 2020—To record receipt of note in exchange for inventory

Note Receivable	8,000	
Discount on Note Receivable ($8,000 − $6,011)		1,989
Sales Revenue		6,011

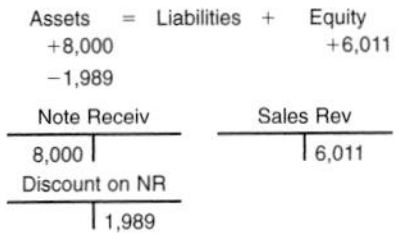

Discount Amortization The following amortization schedule illustrates how interest revenue is recognized over the life of the note.

Effective Interest Amortization—Discount

Date	Cash (Stated Interest)	Interest Revenue (Market Interest)	Discount on N.R. Amortization	Note Receivable, Net (Carrying Value)
June 30, 2020				$6,011
June 30, 2021	$0	$ 601	$ 601	6,612
June 30, 2022	0	661	661	7,273
June 30, 2023	0	727	727	8,000
Totals	$0	$1,989	$1,989	

In the case of a note with a 0% stated rate, the amount of interest revenue recognized each period is equal to the discount amortization. Even though the note does not pay cash interest on a periodic basis, the note does pay interest indirectly. The fair value of the inventory sold is $6,011 but the proceeds from the note are $8,000. The difference of $1,989 or the discount is recognized as interest revenue over the term of the note. Assuming adjusting entries are only made on June 30, the following entries to accrue interest revenue are recorded.

continued

continued from previous page

Assets = Liabilities + Equity
+601 +601

Discount on NR		Interest Rev	
601	1,989		601

June 30, 2021—To record amortization of discount

Discount on Note Receivable	601	
Interest Revenue		601

Assets = Liabilities + Equity
+661 +661

Discount on NR		Interest Rev	
601	1,989		601
661			661

June 30, 2022—To record amortization of discount

Discount on Note Receivable	661	
Interest Revenue		661

Assets = Liabilities + Equity
+727 +727

Discount on NR		Interest Rev	
601	1,989		601
661			661
727			727

June 30, 2023—To record amortization of discount

Discount on Note Receivable	727	
Interest Revenue		727

Note Receivable Collection

Assets = Liabilities + Equity
+8,000
−8,000

Cash		Note Receiv	
8,000		8,000	8,000

June 30, 2023—To record principal payment received on note

Cash	8,000	
Note Receivable		8,000

The sum of the sales revenue of $6,011 and the interest revenue over the term of the note of $1,989 equals the total cash flows received of $8,000. The purpose of measuring these types of notes at present value is to separate the sales-type profit of $6,011 and the financing-type profit of $1,989 arising from a transaction that includes both sales and financing elements.

Demo 8-5D LO8-5 Noncurrent Note Receivable [Stated Rate = 10%; Market Rate = 6%]

Demo MBC

On January 1, 2020, Broadway Company sells specialized equipment with a fair value of $13,283 to King Company and received a three-year, 10%, $12,000 note. Cash interest is due each December 31, and the principal is due at the end of the third year. The prevailing market rate is 6%. Record the journal entries over the term of the note for Broadway Company.

Solution

Receipt of Note The note is recorded at the fair value of the equipment determined to be $13,283 on January 1, 2020. The premium on the note is equal to the excess of the fair value of the equipment of $13,283 over the face value of the note of $12,000, or $1,283. Broadway records the following entry at the inception of the note.

Assets = Liabilities + Equity
+12,000 +13,283
+1,283

Note Receiv		Sales Rev	
12,000			13,283

Premium on NR	
1,283	

January 1, 2020—To record sale of equipment in exchange for note receivable

Note Receivable	12,000	
Premium on Note Receivable	1,283	
Sales Revenue		13,283

The net book value of the note at the time of issuance is $13,283 ($12,000 + $1,283) which is the note receivable plus the premium on the note receivable.

Interest Receipt and Premium Amortization The following amortization schedule illustrates how interest revenue is recognized over the note term.

continued

continued from previous page

Effective Interest Amortization—Premium

Date	Cash (Stated Interest)[a]	Interest Revenue (Market Interest)[b]	Premium on N.R. Amortization[c]	Note Receivable, Net (Carrying Value)[d]
Jan. 1, 2020......				$13,283
Dec. 31, 2020......	$1,200	$ 797	$ 403	12,880
Dec. 31, 2021......	1,200	773	427	12,453
Dec. 31, 2022......	1,200	747	453	12,000
Totals	$3,600	$2,317	$1,283	

[a] Note face value × Stated rate.
[b] Note carrying value, beginning of year × Market rate.
[c] Stated interest − Market interest.
[d] Note carrying value, beginning of year − Premium amortization.

On December 31, 2020 and 2021, Broadway Company records the following journal entries for the receipt of cash interest and the amortization of the premium on the note receivable.

December 31, 2020—To record receipt of cash interest and amortization of premium

Cash	1,200	
Premium on Note Receivable		403
Interest Revenue..............		797

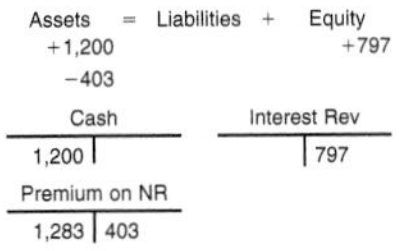

December 31, 2021—To record receipt of cash interest and amortization of premium

Cash	1,200	
Premium on Note Receivable		427
Interest Revenue..............		773

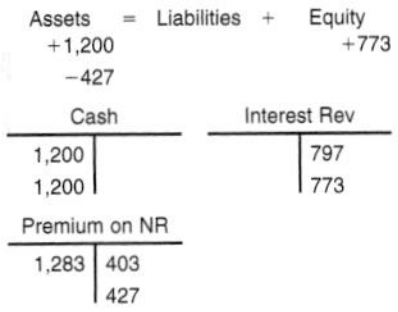

Assets = Liabilities + Equity
+1,200 +773
−427
Cash
1,200
1,200
Interest Rev
797
773
Premium on NR
1,283 403
427

Note and Interest Collection

On December 31, 2022, Broadway receives the final cash interest payment along with the face value of the note and records the following entries.

December 31, 2022—To record receipt of cash interest and amortization of premium

Cash	1,200	
Premium on Note Receivable		453
Interest Revenue..............		747

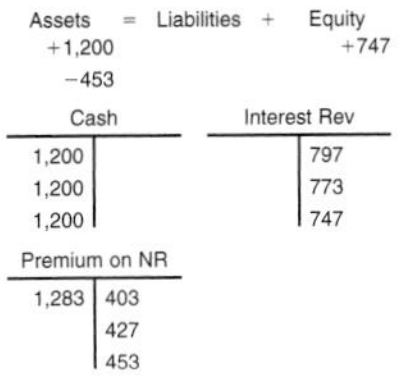

December 31, 2022—To record principal payment received on note

Cash	12,000	
Note Receivable..............		12,000

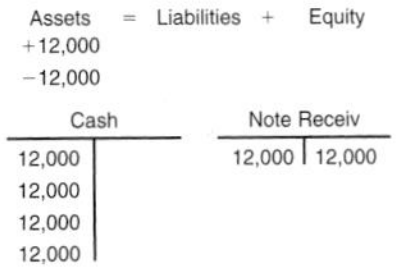

Total interest revenue recognized over the course of the note totals $2,317 ($797 + $773 + $747). Interest revenue recognized is equal to the cash interest receipts over the note term of $3,600 (3 years × $1,200) less the premium on the note receivable of $1,283.

Measuring of Note Receivable and Interest

LO8-5 **Review 8-5**

On January 1, 2020, Capital Inc. sells equipment financed through a $25,000 note, issued by Cola Company. Cola Company agrees to repay the $25,000 proceeds on December 31, 2021. The prevailing market rate on similar notes is 8%. Assume that the cost of the equipment is equal to the selling price. Calculate the net note receivable amount recognized on January 1, 2020, and the interest revenue and cash interest to be recognized in 2020 for each of the following four separate scenarios.

Review MBC

continued

continued from previous page

Case	Stated Rate	Market Rate	Note Receivable, Net January 1, 2020	Interest Revenue 2020	Cash Interest 2020
1 . . .	8%	8%	*a.* _____	*b.* _____	*c.* _____
2 . . .	5%	8%	*d.* _____	*e.* _____	*f.* _____
3 . . .	0%	8%	*g.* _____	*h.* _____	*i.* _____
4 . . .	8%	6%	*j.* _____	*k.* _____	*l.* _____

More Practice:
8-47, 8-48, 8-49, 8-50, 8-51
Solution on p. 8-71.

LO 8-6 Account for the sale of receivables and use as collateral for borrowing

LO 8-6 Overview

Classify arrangement as a sale or secured borrowing
Secured borrowing:
- Receivables remain on books
- Record liability for borrowing

Sale:
- Derecognize receivables
- Record gain or loss on sale
- Record recourse liability if applicable

To obtain cash, companies frequently sell accounts receivable or use them as collateral for loans (also referred to as **secured borrowings**). The company providing the cash is usually a finance company or bank.

Selling receivables or using receivables to obtain cash loans effectively shortens the operating cycle, hastens the return of cash to productive purposes, and alleviates short-run cash-flow problems. The costs of these arrangements include initial fees and interest on loans collateralized by the receivables. Certain risks might be retained by the company, including bearing the cost of bad debts, cash discounts, and sales returns and allowances.

The key financial reporting issue is whether an arrangement involving receivables is a sale or a borrowing transaction.

- In a borrowing, the receivables remain on the owner's books because they are still owned, and a liability is recorded to reflect the owner's obligation to repay the amount borrowed.
- In a sale, the owner derecognizes the receivables and records a gain or loss because the receivables are no longer an asset.

The remaining discussion explains the various ways to dispose of receivables as summarized here.

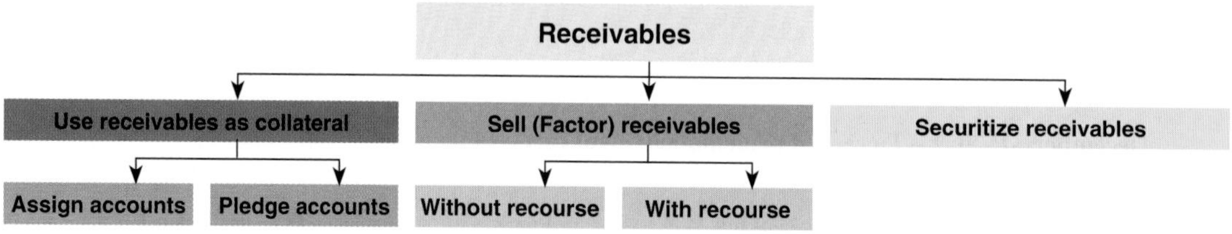

Using Accounts Receivable as Collateral for Borrowing

An entity wishing to borrow money may use accounts receivable as collateral. In this case the entity may either **pledge** the receivables or **assign** specific accounts receivable to a lender (assignee). In both cases, the entity usually retains title to the receivables, continues to receive payments from customers, bears collection costs and the risk of bad debts, and agrees to use any cash collected from customers to pay for the loan. When receivables are assigned, a formal promissory note often allows the assignee to seek payment directly from the receivable proceeds if the loan is not paid when due.

The loan proceeds are typically less than the face value of the receivables assigned to compensate for sales adjustments and to give the assignee a margin of protection. The assignee charges a service fee and interest on the unpaid balance each month. The loan balance is reported among the borrower's other liabilities.

EXPANDING YOUR KNOWLEDGE — **Conditions for a Sale of Receivables**

An arrangement involving receivables is accounted for as a sale only if the seller surrenders control over the receivables. If the seller of receivables retains a *beneficial interest* (right to receive cash flows from the receivables), the buyer might be unable to sell the assets, implying that control has not been completely relinquished by the seller. The seller has surrendered control if *each of the following three conditions are met* (ASC 860-10-40-5).

1. Receivables have been isolated from the seller.
2. Buyer has the right to pledge or exchange the receivables.
3. Seller is not obligated to repurchase receivables from the buyer of receivables.

The recourse obligation, by itself, does not prevent the recording as a sale. Nor does an option held by the seller to repurchase the receivables necessarily require recording the arrangement as a loan. If the arrangement does not qualify as a sale, it would be recorded as a secured borrowing.

Using Receivables as Collateral for Borrowing

LO8-6 **Demo 8-6A**

Demo MBC

Prepare journal entries for the following four chronological steps in a secured borrowing.

1. On November 30, 2020, Franklin Corporation secures a loan with a finance company using its accounts receivable of $80,000 as collateral for the loan. Franklin agrees to remit customer collections as payment on the loan. Loan proceeds are 85% of the receivables less a $1,500 flat-fee finance charge. In addition, the finance company charges 12% interest on the unpaid loan balance, payable at the end of each month.

Solution

November 30, 2020—To record receipt of loan proceeds

Cash ([0.85 × $80,000] − $1,500)	66,500	
Finance Expense	1,500	
Note Payable (0.85 × $80,000)		68,000

Assets = Liabilities + Equity
+66,500 = +68,000 + −1,500
Cash: 66,500 |
Finance Exp: 1,500 |
Note Payable: | 68,000

2. By the end of December, Franklin has collected $46,000 cash on $50,000 of the assigned accounts less $3,000 sales returns (previously recorded as a refund liability) and $1,000 sales discounts.

Solution

December 31, 2020—To record collection on account

Cash ($50,000 − $1,000 − $3,000)	46,000	
Sales Discount	1,000	
Refund Liability	3,000	
Accounts Receivable		50,000

Assets = Liabilities + Equity
+46,000 −50,000 = −3,000 + −1,000
Cash: 66,500, 46,000 |
Sales Discount: 1,000 |
Accounts Rec: Bal. 80,000 | 50,000
Refund Liab: 3,000 |

December 31, 2020—To record payment to finance company

Note Payable ($46,000 − $680)	45,320	
Interest Expense ($68,000 × 0.12 × 1/12)	680	
Cash		46,000

Assets = Liabilities + Equity
−46,000 = −45,320 + −680
Cash: 66,500, 46,000 | 46,000
Note Payable: 45,320 | 68,000
Interest Exp: 680 |

3. In January 2021, $2,000 of the accounts are written off as uncollectible (the original $80,000 of receivables is included in the normal bad debt estimation process). Also, another $25,000 is collected on account.

Solution

January 31, 2021—To record collection and write-off

Cash	25,000	
Allowance for Doubtful Accounts	2,000	
Accounts Receivable		27,000

Assets = Liabilities + Equity
+25,000 +2,000 −27,000
Accounts Receiv: Bal. 80,000 | 50,000, 27,000
Cash: 66,500, 46,000, 25,000 | 46,000
AFDA: 2,000 |

4. The loan is paid in full on January 31, 2021.

continued

continued from previous page

Solution

January 31, 2021—To record payment of remaining loan balance

Assets	=	Liabilities	+	Equity
−22,907		−22,680		−227

Cash: 66,500 | 46,000; 46,000 | 22,907; 25,000 |

Note Payable: 45,320 | 68,000; 22,680 |

Interest Exp: 680 |; 227 |

Note Payable ($68,000 − $45,320)	22,680	
Interest Expense ($22,680 × 0.12 × 1/12)	227	
Cash		22,907

Total cash paid from the borrower to the lender of $68,907 ($46,000 + $22,907) is made up of the principal of $68,000 plus interest expense of $680 plus $227.

Sale of Accounts Receivable without Recourse

Selling (or factoring) receivables transfers ownership of the receivables to the **factor** (buyer of the receivables). Agreements to transfer accounts receivable are made on a nonrecourse or recourse basis.

- In **sales without recourse**, the factor assumes the risk of collection losses. The fee is higher under nonrecourse arrangements because more risk is transferred.
- In **sales with recourse**, the factor can collect amounts from the seller if the customer (original debtor) fails to pay.

A nonrecourse arrangement generally constitutes an ordinary sale of receivables because the factor has no recourse against the seller of the receivables for uncollectible accounts. Control over the receivables generally passes to the factor. The factor typically assumes legal title to the receivables, the cost of uncollectible accounts, and collection responsibilities. However, any adjustments or defects in the receivables (sales discounts, returns, and allowances) are typically the responsibility of the seller because these represent preexisting conditions.

Upon sale, the receivables are removed from the seller's books, cash is debited, and a finance fee is recognized immediately as a loss on sale. The factor might hold back an amount to cover probable sales adjustments. This amount is recorded as a receivable on the seller's books.

Demo 8-6B **LO8-6** **Sale of Receivables Without Recourse**

Demo MBC

On December 1, 2020, Largo Inc. factors without recourse $200,000 of accounts receivable with a finance company. The factor charges a 12% finance fee and retains an amount equal to 10% of the accounts receivable for sales adjustments. The factor estimates bad debt expense of $1,500 related to the $200,000 receivables purchased.

a. Record Largo's entry for the transfer of receivables on December 1, 2020, assuming that the arrangement qualifies as a sale.

b. Record the factor's entry for the transfer of receivables on December 1, 2020.

Solutions

a. Largo records the following entry for the sale of accounts receivable to the factor.

December 1, 2020—To record sale of receivables by Largo Inc.

Assets	=	Liabilities	+	Equity
+25,000				
+2,000				
−27,000				

Cash: 156,000 |

Loss on Sale of Rec: 24,000 |

Rec from Factor: 20,000 |

Accounts Rec: Bal. 200,000 | 200,000

Cash ($200,000 − $20,000 − $24,000)	156,000	
Receivable from Factor (0.10 × $200,000)	20,000	
Loss on Sale of Receivables (0.12 × $200,000)	24,000	
Accounts Receivable		200,000

b. The factor records the following entries upon receipt of the accounts receivable from Largo. Because the accounts receivable are purchased without recourse, the factor also records an estimate of bad debt expense related to the receivables.

continued

continued from previous page

December 1, 2020—To record purchase of receivables by factor

Accounts Receivable	200,000	
Payable to Largo (0.10 × $200,000)		20,000
Financing Revenue (0.12 × $200,000)		24,000
Cash ($200,000 − $20,000 − $24,000)		156,000

Assets = Liabilities + Equity
+200,000 +20,000 +24,000
−156,000

Accounts Rec: 200,000 (Dr) | Payable to Largo: 20,000 (Cr)
Cash: 156,000 (Cr) | Financing Rev: 24,000 (Cr)

December 1, 2020—To record allowance related to purchased receivables

Bad Debt Expense	1,500	
Allowance for Doubtful Accounts		1,500

Assets = Liabilities + Equity
−1,500 −1,500

AFDA: 1,500 (Cr) | Bad Debt Exp: 1,500 (Dr)

Sale of Accounts Receivable with Recourse

When receivables are factored with recourse, the seller bears the risk and cost of bad debts. The finance company has recourse against the seller in the event of default by the original customer. The value of the recourse is estimated as a **recourse liability**.

Sale of Receivables With Recourse

LO8-6 **Demo 8-6C**

Demo MBC

On December 1, 2020, Largo Inc. factors with recourse $200,000 of accounts receivable with a finance company. The factor charges a 6% finance fee and retains an amount equal to $10,000 of the accounts receivable for sales adjustments. Because the sale is with recourse, the fees and charges are lower. Largo estimates its recourse liability for bad debts to be $3,000 (bad debts have not yet been recorded).

a. Record Largo's entry for the transfer of receivables on December 1, 2020, assuming that the arrangement qualifies as a sale.

b. Record the factor's entry for the transfer of receivables on December 1, 2020.

Solutions

a. The entry to record the transfer by Largo follows.

December 1, 2020—To record sale of receivables by Largo Inc.

Cash ($200,000 − $10,000 − $12,000)	178,000	
Receivable from Factor	10,000	
Loss on Sale of Receivables ([0.06 × $200,000] + $3,000)	15,000	
Recourse Liability		3,000
Accounts Receivable		200,000

Assets = Liabilities + Equity
+178,000 +3,000 −15,000
+10,000
−200,000

Cash: 178,000 (Dr) | Recourse Liab: 3,000 (Cr)
Rec from Factor: 10,000 (Dr) | Loss on Sale of Rec: 15,000 (Dr)
Accounts Rec: Bal. 200,000 (Dr) | 200,000 (Cr)

b. The entry to record the transfer by the factor follows.

December 1, 2020—To record purchase of receivables by factor

Accounts Receivable	200,000	
Payable to Largo		10,000
Financing Revenue (0.06 × $200,000)		12,000
Cash ($200,000 − $10,000 − $12,000)		178,000

Assets = Liabilities + Equity
+200,000 +10,000 +12,000
−178,000

Cash: 178,000 (Cr) | Payable to Largo: 10,000 (Cr)
Accounts Rec: 200,000 (Dr) | Financing Rev: 12,000 (Cr)

T-MOBILE

Real World—SALE OF RECEIVABLES

T-MOBILE [TMUS]

T-Mobile US Inc. is a wireless company in the U.S., currently providing wireless communications services, including voice, messaging and data, to over 55 million customers in the postpaid, prepaid, and wholesale markets. In a recent Form 10-K, T-Mobile described its treatment of receivables sold along with a two-year factoring arrangement "to sell certain service accounts receivable on a revolving basis with a current maximum funding limit of $640 million, subject to change upon notification to certain third parties. Sales of receivables occur daily and are settled on a monthly basis."

Factoring Arrangement—Sales of Receivables The sales of receivables through the factoring arrangement are treated as sales of financial assets. Upon sale, T-Mobile derecognizes the receivables, as well as the related allowances, and recognizes the net proceeds in cash provided by operating activities. As of December 31, 2014, T-Mobile derecognized net receivables of $768 million through the factoring arrangement. For the year ended December 31, 2014, T-Mobile received net cash proceeds of $610 million. The proceeds were net of a receivable for the remainder of the purchase price ("deferred purchase price"), which is received from collections on the service receivables. T-Mobile recognizes the deferred purchase price in cash provided by operating activities due to the short duration of the receivables sold and the nature of the related activity. The deferred purchase price represents a financial asset that can be settled in such a way that T-Mobile may not recover substantially all of its recorded investment due to the creditworthiness of customers. As a result, T-Mobile elected at inception to classify the deferred purchase price as a trading security carried at fair value with unrealized gains and losses from changes in fair value included in selling, general and administrative expense.

Discounting a Note Receivable

Just as we saw with accounts receivable, a company may sell a note receivable to a factor such as a financial institution, or otherwise use a note receivable as collateral for a loan, in order to obtain immediate access to cash. A sale of a note to a factor is called **discounting**. The factor charges a finance fee for the transaction.

Demo 8-6D LO8-6 Discounting a Note Receivable

Demo MBC

On April 1, 2020, Wyoming Inc. received a $3,000, 6%, one-year note from a sale of equipment to Neilson Company. Interest on the note is due at maturity. Wyoming discounted the note on August 1, 2020, with recourse to a bank. Assume that the discounting qualifies as a sale and that the bank charges 8%. Prepare Wyoming's 2020 entries related to the note.

Solutions

The bank charges a 8% fee on the full maturity value of the note, prorated for 8 months or the period of time from August 1, 2020 (date of the discounting) to April 1, 2021 (the maturity of the note). The full maturity value equals the principal plus interest on the note receivable. The net proceeds to Wyoming of $3,010 equal the total maturity value ($3,180) less the fee ($170). The calculation of the proceeds to Wyoming follow.

Principal value	$3,000
Add: Interest to maturity ($3,000 × 0.06)	180
Total maturity value subject to discount	3,180
Subtract: Interest charged by bank ($3,180 × 0.08 × 8/12)	170
Proceeds to Wyoming	$3,010

The bank charges interest on the maturity value a full eight months before that value is reached, effectively raising the interest cost to Wyoming. Wyoming records the following entries to discount the note. First, Wyoming accrues interest revenue through the date of the discounting. Next, Wyoming records the discounting of the note.

August 1, 2020—To accrue interest revenue

Assets	= Liabilities	+ Equity
+60		+60

Interest Receiv		Interest Rev	
60			60

Interest Receivable	60	
Interest Revenue ($3,000 × 0.06 × 4/12)		60

continued

continued from previous page

August 1, 2020—To record discounting of note

Cash (see proceeds calculation above)	3,010	
Loss on Sale of Note Receivable ($3,010 − $3,000 − $60)	50	
Note Receivable		3,000
Interest Receivable		60

Assets	= Liabilities	+ Equity
+3,010		−50
−3,000		
−60		

Cash		Loss on Sale of NR	
3,010		50	

Note Receiv	
3,000	3,000

Interest Receiv	
60	60

After August 1, the note is no longer an asset of Wyoming and is removed from its books. The loss of $50 equals the book value of the note plus accrued interest ($3,060) less the proceeds ($3,010). Two factors contribute to the loss: the note was transferred relatively early in its term, and the bank charged a higher interest rate. If the note had been held longer before it was discounted, the total interest charged by the bank would have been reduced, thus increasing the proceeds.

EXPANDING YOUR KNOWLEDGE — **Securitization of Receivables**

Securitization is another way that companies can convert receivables more quickly into cash. In a securitization, assets (such as trade receivables or credit card receivables) are pooled together to form a portfolio. The portfolio is typically transferred to a securitization entity, commonly a trust. Interests in the securitization entity are then sold to investors or the portfolio is used as collateral for debt issuances. Just as in our previous discussions, the seller must determine whether the transfer to the securitization entity represents a *sale* or a *secured borrowing.*

Secured Borrowings and Sales of Receivables **LO8-6** **Review 8-6**

On April 1, 2020, Time Co. is considering *three* scenarios that accelerate the collection of outstanding accounts receivable totaling $300,000: a secured borrowing, selling the receivables with recourse; and selling the receivables without recourse. Prepare all entries required for Time Co. on April 1, 2020, for these three separate scenarios.

1. *Secured borrowing.* The finance company will extend a loan equal to 75% of the accounts receivable assigned. The finance company charges a finance fee of 1.5% of the accounts receivable balance and 9% interest on the loan.
2. *Sell accounts receivable without recourse.* The finance company charges 8% as a finance fee and withholds 15% of the receivables for sales returns, allowances, and discounts. Time Co. expects 1% of the accounts receivable balance to be uncollectible.
3. *Sell accounts receivable with recourse.* The finance company charges 5% as a finance fee and withholds 10% of the receivables for sales returns, allowances, and discounts. Time Co. expects 1% of the accounts receivable balance to be uncollectible.

Review MBC

More Practice: 8-53, 8-54, 8-55, 8-56, 8-57

Solution on p. 8-72.

Describe receivable disclosures and ratio analyses — LO 8-7

Companies disclose important information related to receivables in the notes to financial statements. Along with the review of these notes, investors and creditors perform ratio analyses to provide additional information on the valuation and collectibility of accounts receivable.

LO 8-7 Overview

Ratio Analyses
- **Accounts receivable turnover**
  - Net sales/Average net accounts receivable
- **Average days to collect receivables**
  - 365/Accounts receivable turnover

Receivable Disclosures

Disclosure on receivables should take into account the following requirements (ASC 310-10-50).

- Accounting policies for trade receivables.
- Major categories of receivables not presented separately in the balance sheet.
- Balance in the allowance for doubtful accounts.

- Policy for charging off uncollectible trade accounts receivable, the policy on determining past due accounts, and amounts of certain past due amounts or those on nonaccrual status.
- Receivables that serve as collateral for borrowings.
- Activity in the allowance for doubtful accounts for each period, including all of the following:
  - Balance in the allowance at the beginning and end of each period.
  - Current period provisions.
  - Direct write-downs charged against the allowance.
  - Recoveries of amounts previously charged off.
- Description of the entity's accounting policies and methodology used to estimate the allowance for doubtful accounts, including factors affecting management's judgment, risk characteristics, and any changes in policies.
- Significant purchases or sales of receivables.
- The fair value (excluding trade receivables due within one year or less (ASC 825-10-50-8)).

Concentration of Credit Risk

Companies are required to disclose all significant concentrations of credit risk from receivables and other financial instruments. A **concentration of credit risk** occurs when a company has receivables from different entities whose ability to pay is subject to common economic risks or receivables are concentrated with a major customer. For example, if a substantial portion of a company's accounts receivable arises from sales to agribusiness companies, macroeconomic changes affecting agribusiness could have a significant effect on the collectibility of those receivables.

KELLOGG [K]

KELLOGG Real World—CONCENTRATION OF CREDIT RISK

In a recent Form 10-K, Kellogg Company described the credit risk associated with having a narrow base of customers—see below. The risk is that if one customer defaults, the company could be substantially impacted negatively. In an earlier section of the Form 10-K (Management's Discussion and Analysis Section), Kellogg disclosed: "During 2015, our top five customers, collectively, including Wal-Mart, accounted for approximately 34% of our consolidated net sales and approximately 47% of U.S. net sales."

> **Derivative Instruments And Fair Value Measurements** Management believes concentrations of credit risk with respect to accounts receivable is limited due to the generally high credit quality of the Company's major customers, as well as the large number and geographic dispersion of smaller customers. However, the Company conducts a disproportionate amount of business with a small number of large multinational grocery retailers, with the five largest accounts encompassing approximately 29% of consolidated trade receivables at January 2, 2016.

EXPANDING YOUR KNOWLEDGE — Fair Value Option

Companies have the option to record certain financial assets and liabilities, including receivables, at fair value in the balance sheet. This **fair value option election** is irrevocable and generally must be made at the time of purchase. Under the fair value option, companies measure the receivables at fair value at every reporting date with changes in fair value included in net income. Assume that Lynx Co. elects the fair value option for a note receivable. The fair value at the beginning of the period is $300,000 and the fair value at the end of the period is $325,000. Lynx Co. prepares the following journal entry to record the change in fair value during the period.

Assets	=	Liabilities	+	Equity
+25,000				+25,000

Note Receiv		Unreal Gain or Loss—Inc	
25,000			25,000

Note Receivable	25,000	
Net Unrealized Gain or Loss—Income		25,000

The note receivable is reported on the balance sheet at the adjusted amount of $325,000 and the unrealized gain of $25,000 is reported in the income statement.

Accounts Receivable Ratios

The **accounts receivable turnover ratio** measures, on average, how often receivables are collected during the year. The results help determine the efficiency of credit policies and the trends in collection of trade accounts. This ratio is computed by dividing net sales by average accounts receivable.

The **average days to collect receivables** measures the average number of days that an accounts receivable is outstanding before receipt of payment. This ratio is computed by dividing 365 (days) by the accounts receivable turnover ratio.

Accounts Receivable Ratios

LO8-7 **Demo 8-7**

Demo MBC

The following financial information is provided for competitors: **Amazon** (Amazon.com Inc.) and **Best Buy** (Best Buy Co. Inc.). For both Amazon and Best Buy, compute the accounts receivable turnover and the average days to collect receivables. Briefly analyze your results.

$ millions	Accounts Receivable 2015	Accounts Receivable 2014	Accounts Receivable 2013	Sales 2015	Sales 2014
Best Buy	$1,162	$1,280	$1,308	$ 39,528	$40,339
Amazon	6,423	5,612	4,767	107,006	88,988

Best Buy fiscal year-ends: January 30, 2016, January 31, 2015, and February 1, 2014.
Amazon fiscal year-ends: December 31, 2015, December 31, 2014, and December 31, 2013.

Solution

Accounts Receivable Turnover

Amazon			**2015**	**2014**
Accounts Receivable Turnover	=	$\frac{\text{Net sales}}{\text{Average net accounts receivable}}$	$\frac{\$107,006}{\$6,018} = 17.78$	$\frac{\$88,988}{\$5,190} = 17.15$

Average receivables for 2015: ($6,423 + $5,612)/2
Average receivables for 2014: ($5,612 + $4,767)/2

Best Buy			**2015**	**2014**
Accounts Receivable Turnover	=	$\frac{\text{Net sales}}{\text{Average net accounts receivable}}$	$\frac{\$39,528}{\$1,221} = 32.37$	$\frac{\$40,339}{\$1,294} = 31.17$

Average receivables for 2015: ($1,162 + $1,280)/2
Average receivables for 2014: ($1,280 + $1,308)/2

Average Days to Collect Receivables

Amazon			**2015**	**2014**
Average Days To Collect Receivables	=	$\frac{\text{365 days}}{\text{Accounts receivable turnover}}$	$\frac{365}{17.78} = 20.53$ days	$\frac{365}{17.15} = 21.28$ days

Best Buy			**2015**	**2014**
Average Days To Collect Receivables	=	$\frac{\text{365 days}}{\text{Accounts receivable turnover}}$	$\frac{365}{32.37} = 11.28$ days	$\frac{365}{31.17} = 11.71$ days

continued

continued from previous page

Although Best Buy's receivable turnover and average collection days are stronger than Amazon's, the two companies experienced a slight improvement from 2014 to 2015. This means that the companies are collecting receivables more quickly than the prior year.

The ratios between the two companies are different due to the composition of receivables. In its Form 10-K, Best Buy indicates that receivables "consist principally of amounts due from mobile phone network operators for commissions earned; banks for customer credit card, debit card and electronic benefits transfer (EBT) transactions; and vendors for various vendor funding programs." In its Form 10-K, Amazon indicates that receivables include "amounts primarily related to vendor and customer receivables." It would follow that the terms and conditions of the receivables would be different for at least a portion of the receivables between the two companies.

REVIEW 8-7 **LO8-7** **Accounts Receivable Ratios**

Review MBC

The following financial information is provided for competitors: Ford Motor Company and General Motors Company. For both Year 2 and Year 3, and for both companies, compute the (a) accounts receivable turnover ratio and (b) average days to collect receivables.

$ millions	Accounts Receivable, Net Year 3	Accounts Receivable, Net Year 2	Accounts Receivable, Net Year 1	Sales Year 3	Sales Year 2
Ford Motor Co.	$11,102	$11,042	$11,708	$141,546	$140,566
General Motors Co. . .	9,638	8,337	9,078	156,849	145,922

More Practice: 8-32, 8-58

Solution on p. 8-72.

Management Judgment

Accounting for Receivables

Accounting for receivables, particularly the determination of the net realizable value of receivables, requires management judgment. The following examples show how the process of recording and reporting receivables depends on estimations and judgments.

- Estimation of sales returns to adjust the refund liability account at the end of the period (p. 8-11).
- Application of the CECL model to adjust accounts receivable to net realizable value.
  - Requires an estimation of *expected* credit losses over the lifetime of the receivable (p. 8-15).
  - Requires an analysis of current information and reasonable and supportable forecasts of the future (p. 8-16).
  - Requires a pooling of receivables when receivables share risk characteristics (p. 8-16).
- Estimation of a recourse liability when receivables are sold with recourse (p. 8-30).
- Determination of concentrations of credit risk for disclosure purposes (p. 8-33).

All receivables are at risk for credit losses over the life of the receivable. And because there is no threshold for recognizing credit losses (recognized even if remote), management must make a judgment on expected credit losses for all holdings. Estimates must be continually reassessed and estimates must be adjusted as more information becomes available.

Guidance for Management Judgment

The accounting guidance that follows highlights the critical role of management in estimating expected credit losses (emphasis added).

326-20-30-1 An entity shall report in net income (as a credit loss expense) the amount necessary to adjust the allowance for credit losses for **management's current estimate** of expected credit losses on financial asset(s).

326-20-55-6 Estimating expected credit losses is **highly judgmental** and generally will require an entity to make **specific judgments**.

For example, judgments are critical in the approach used to determine the appropriate historical period to use for the analysis and the methods used to analyze historical periods. Judgments are also critical in determining the approach used to develop forecasts while the accounting guidance does not indicate how the forecast should be developed or the length of the forecast. The guidance does not even specify what approach to use but does require consistent application of techniques that are practical and relevant to the situation.

326-20-55-7 Because of the subjective nature of the estimate, this Subtopic does not require specific approaches when developing the estimate of expected credit losses. Rather, an entity should use judgment to develop estimation techniques that are applied consistently over time and should faithfully estimate the collectibility of the financial assets by applying the principles in this Subtopic. An entity should utilize estimation techniques that are practical and relevant to the circumstance. The method(s) used to estimate expected credit losses may vary on the basis of the type of financial asset, the entity's ability to predict the timing of cash flows, and the information available to the entity.

Apply cash controls

APPENDIX 8A
LO 8-8

The need to safeguard cash is crucial in businesses. The risk of theft is directly related to the ability of individuals to access the accounting system and obtain custody of cash. Companies address this problem through the **internal control system**. An internal control system is a set of policies and procedures designed to protect assets, ensure compliance with laws and company policy, and provide accurate accounting records.

The following discussion highlights two of the most common elements of cash control and management: cash reconciliations and bank account reconciliations.

Internal Controls Over Cash (LO 8-8 Overview)
- Cash drawers: reconcile sales reports to cash inflows
- Petty cash funds: reconcile vouchers to cash outflows
- Cash in bank: reconcile bank balance to cash in books

Cash Reconciliations

Internal control environments for the control of daily cash flows include a cash reconciliation process. Companies commonly use **cash drawers** to collect and maintain cash needed for sales transactions in retail environments. A minimum balance is maintained in the cash drawers to process customer cash transactions (to return the appropriate change to customers). A company will include the minimum amount of cash maintained in cash drawers as part of its cash balance. We can imagine that for large corporations that maintain many retail locations, this amount could be significant. Periodically, and typically at the end of an employee's shift, the amount of cash in a cash drawer is reconciled to the amount of cash reported in the point of sale system (system that scans and records sales transaction) that is used to recognize the sales entries. **Cash Short and Over** is an expense (debit balance) or revenue account (credit balance) used to recognize any differences between the sales recorded and actual cash available.

Less commonly, a **petty cash fund** might be used to provide ready currency for routine disbursements in an office environment for such things as supplies and delivery charges. (In most cases, miscellaneous expenses would be processed through cashless transactions through company credit cards, which are independently reconciled back to supporting documentation.) Petty cash systems foster internal control through the requirement that someone other than the recipient of cash must authorize the disbursement. A record of each disbursement is made, the fund is created and replenished by check and is reconciled, and the replenishment check is written by someone other than the custodian of the fund.

Demo 8-8A LO8-8 Cash Reconciliations

Demo MBC

Part One: Cash Drawer Reconciliation At the close of the day on June 1, 2020, Krogar Inc. accumulated the following information for its 10 cash drawer totals (1) cash drawer count of funds at the end of the day and (2) the amount of sales recorded through the POS system.

	Cash Drawer Count	Sales Recorded
Cash collected	$22,340.20	$22,440.80
Checks collected	5,300.80	5,340.80
Credit cards collected	38,960.40	38,960.40
Total collections	$66,601.40	$66,742.00

Required
Prepare the adjusting entry for the reconciliation between the cash drawer and recorded sales. Assume that the sales amounts have been automatically recorded in the accounting system as a debit to Cash and a credit to Sales Revenue.

Solution
The company will prepare a reconciliation to highlight the differences between the amount of sales recorded in the accounting system of $66,742.00, and the cash collected of $66,601.40.

	Cash Drawer Count	Sales Recorded	Difference Over (Short)
Cash collected	$22,340.20	$22,440.80	$(100.60)
Checks collected	5,300.80	5,340.80	(40.00)
Credit cards collected	38,960.40	38,960.40	0
Total collections	$66,601.40	$66,742.00	$(140.60)

Krogar would record the following journal entry to adjust the accounting records.

June 1, 2020—To record cash over and short

Assets = Liabilities + Equity
−140.60 −140.60
Cash: 140.60 (credit) | Cash Over/Short: 140.60 (debit)

Cash Over and Short	140.60	
Cash		140.60

Part Two: Petty Cash Fund Reconciliation Prepare journal entries for the following steps illustrating a typical petty cash fund operation.

1. A $3,000 petty cash fund is established at a specific location on January 1, 2020, to be maintained by a cash custodian.

Solution

January 1, 2020—To establish a petty cash fund

Assets = Liabilities + Equity
+3,000
−3,000
Petty Cash: 3,000 (debit) | Cash: 3,000 (credit)

Petty Cash	3,000	
Cash		3,000

2. At the end of the first month, $560 remains in the fund. The following individual vouchers accompany the fund: postage, $900; office supplies, $700; and taxi fares, $800 ($2,400 in total). There is a $40 cash shortage ($2,440 − $2,400). Presumably, a voucher was lost, or a voucher understates the amount disbursed. The fund is replenished on January 31, 2020 for $2,440.

Solution

January 31, 2020—To replenish petty cash fund and record related expenses

Assets = Liabilities + Equity
−2,440 −900 −700 −800 −40
Cash: 2,440 (credit) | Postage Exp: 900 (debit) | Off Supp Exp: 700 (debit) | Transport Exp: 800 (debit) | Cash Over/Short: 40 (debit)

Postage Expense	900	
Office Supplies Expense	700	
Transportation Expense	800	
Cash Over and Short	40	
Cash		2,440

continued

continued from previous page

This entry is recorded by the accounting department, not the custodian. Replenishment of the petty cash fund occurs whenever the fund runs low and at the end of each fiscal period for proper reporting of expenses and cash balance. Cash Short and Over is debited for the short fall of $40.

3. The fund is increased to $5,000 on February 1, 2020, because of increased office cash needs.

Solution

February 1, 2020—To increase petty cash fund

Petty Cash	2,000	
Cash		2,000

Assets = Liabilities + Equity
+2,000
−2,000

Petty Cash		Cash	
2,000			2,000

When a petty cash fund is increased, decreased, or closed, an entry is made affecting both the Petty Cash and the Cash accounts.

Bank Reconciliation

Banks prepare monthly statements showing beginning and ending balances and transactions occurring during the month. Because differences are likely to exist between the bank balance and the company's cash balance per the accounting records, a monthly reconciliation is essential. Bank reconciliations are used (1) to determine whether the bank account and the company's cash balance are in agreement after taking into account unrecorded items, (2) to isolate recording errors and other problems in the bank's records or the company's recording system, (3) to establish the correct ending cash balance, and (4) to supply information for adjusting entries. The reconciliation process begins with the two cash balances (bank and book) and lists the differences between those balances and the true ending cash balance.

Bank Reconciliation **LO8-8** **Demo 8-8B**

Demo MBC

On August 31, 2020, the bank statement for West Company reported an ending $38,660 balance, and the Cash account shows an ending $34,880 cash balance.

Bank Statement	
August 1 balance	$32,000
Deposits recorded in August	77,300
Checks cleared in August	(71,240)
Note collected (including $100 interest)	1,100
NSF check, J. Fox	(300)
August service charges	(200)
August 31 balance	$38,660

Company's Cash Account	
August 1 balance	$30,000
August deposits	75,300
August disbursements*	(70,420)
August 31 balance	$34,880

*Per cash payments journal.

Additional data, end of July: Deposits in transit, $5,000, and checks outstanding, $8,000 (these two amounts were taken from the July bank reconciliation). End of August: Cash (undeposited), $990. This amount will be deposited September 1. A check written by West in the amount of $240 for a repair bill in August is included in the cleared checks. West recorded the check for $420, the correct amount, debiting repair expense. The payee will bill West for the remaining $180 due.

Reconcile the bank statement's ending $38,660 balance, and the cash per book's ending $34,880 Cash balance. Prepare any necessary adjusting journal entries.

continued

continued from previous page

Solution

Bank Reconciliation
August 31, 2020

Bank balance, August 31	$38,660	Book balance, August 31	$34,880
Additions:		Additions:	
Cash (undeposited)	990	Note collected by bank:	
Deposits in transit, August 31		Principal	1,000
($5,000 + $75,300 − $77,300)	3,000	Interest	100
		Error in recording repair payment	180
Deductions:		Deductions:	
Outstanding checks August 31		NSF check, J. Fox	(300)
($8,000 + $70,240† − $71,240)	(7,000)	Bank service charges	(200)
		Total	35,660
		Cash shortage*	(10)
Correct cash balance	$35,650	Correct cash balance	$35,650

† Per cash journal as corrected: $70,420 − $180 payment overstatement. * Discovered in preparing the reconciliation.

Step 1: Reconciling Items to the Bank Balance Unless the bank made an error, the majority of the reconciling items to the bank balance are due to timing. This means that, given more time, the items would not be different between book and bank. Thus, no adjusting entries are required for the following reconciling items.

- **Cash (undeposited)** This is the cash held by the company but not deposited at August 31. This amount, usually representing undeposited checks, is *added* to the bank balance.
- **Deposits in transit** These are deposits made too late to the close of the bank's monthly closing date to be reflected in the bank statement. This amount is determined by comparing the company's record of deposits with the deposits listed in the bank statement. Deposits late in the period reflected on the book but not on the bank balance are *added* to the bank balance.
- **Outstanding checks** This amount is determined by comparing checks written with checks cleared. Checks recorded by the company but not reflected in the bank balance are *subtracted* from the bank balance.

Step 2: Reconciling Items to the Book Balance Items are entered to reconcile the company's cash ledger account to the correct cash balance. These are amounts the company did not know at August 31. *Each of these items requires an adjusting journal entry to correct the cash balance.*

- **Collections by bank** A note receivable with a face value of $1,000 plus $100 accrued interest was collected by the bank but was not recorded by West. The required adjusting entry follows.

August 31, 2020—To record collection of note receivable and interest

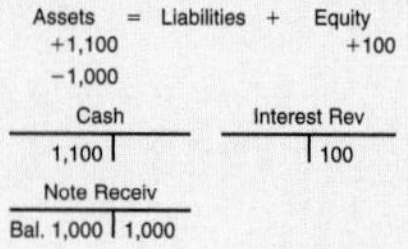

Cash	1,100	
Note Receivable		1,000
Interest Revenue		100

- **Recording Errors** West recorded a $240 check in the cash payments journal in the amount of $420, causing the book balance to be understated by $180 ($420 − $240). West corrects the recording error with the following entry.

August 31, 2020—To correct error in recording

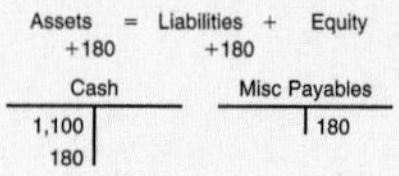

Cash	180	
Miscellaneous Payables		180

Repair expense is correctly stated at $420. This entry corrects the cash disbursement amount and establishes a payable for the amount due.

continued

continued from previous page

- **Nonsufficient funds (NSF) check** A $300 check from customer J. Fox, which was not supported by sufficient funds in Fox's checking account, was returned to West by the bank. West had deposited the check, increased cash, and decreased accounts receivable, but the bank was unable to credit West's account. The $300 amount is included in the $75,300 deposits recorded in August.

August 31, 2020—To record nonsufficient funds

Accounts Receivable, J. Fox	300	
Cash		300

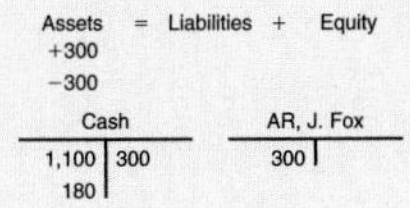

- **Bank service charges** The bank debited West's account for $200 of bank charges in August. West deducts this amount from the cash account.

August 31, 2020—To record bank service charge

Miscellaneous Expenses	200	
Cash		200

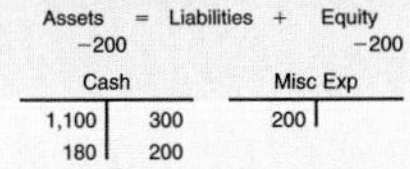

- **Cash shortage** This is the amount by which the cash balance to this point in the reconciliation ($35,660) exceeds the correct cash balance, previously determined to be $35,650. Such a small amount is written off. If a shortage occurs regularly, if the difference is larger, or if West suspects theft, further investigation is warranted. The write-off is accomplished with the following entry.

August 31, 2020—To record cash shortage

Miscellaneous Expenses	10	
Cash		10

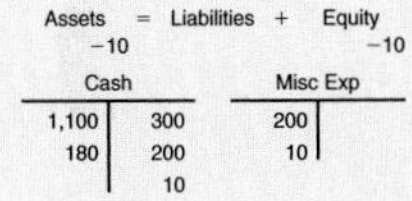

Assets = Liabilities + Equity
−10
−10
Cash
1,100 300
180 200
10
Misc Exp
200
10

Summary Book and bank balances are now reconciled to the same value of $35,650. The cash ledger balance is increased $770 ($1,000 + $100 + $180 − $300 − $200 − $10) as a result. When more than one bank account exists, each is reconciled separately with an individual subsidiary cash ledger account. The sum of the correct ending subsidiary cash ledger balances then equals the cash balance for reporting purposes.

Separation of duties is an important internal control attribute and applies to personnel involved in reconciling bank accounts. For example, a person having responsibility for the bank reconciliation, cash disbursements, and accounting for cash could write and deliberately fail to record an unauthorized check. When the canceled check is returned, outstanding checks could be understated by the amount of the check, in turn overstating the correct cash balance by the amount of the check. The cash account would appear reconciled. Someone other than the cashier should prepare the bank reconciliation.

EXPANDING YOUR KNOWLEDGE — Internal Controls for Cash

Internal controls for cash should:

- Separate custody of and accounting for cash.
- Account for all cash transactions.
- Maintain only the minimum cash balance needed.
- Provide for periodic test counts of cash balances.
- Permit reconciliation of ledger and bank cash-account balances.
- Achieve an adequate return on idle cash balances.
- Result in the physical control of cash.

The following minimum procedures apply in most **cash receipt** situations.

1. Separate the responsibilities for handling cash, for recording cash transactions, and for reconciling cash balances. This separation reduces the possibility of theft and of concealment through false recording.
2. Assign cash-handling and cash-recording responsibilities to different persons to ensure an uninterrupted flow of cash from receipt to deposit. This control requires immediate counting, immediate recording, and timely deposit of all cash received.

3. Maintain close supervision of all cash-handling and cash-recording functions. This control includes both routine and surprise cash counts, internal audits, and daily reports of cash receipts, payments, and balances.

Although **cash disbursement** controls are tailored to each company's needs, certain common procedures apply.

1. Separate the responsibilities for cash disbursement documentation, check writing, check signing, check mailing, and record keeping.
2. Except for internal cash funds (petty cash), make all cash disbursements by check.
3. Develop tight controls and authorization procedures over the check authorization and signing procedures.
4. Require adequate documentation and verification for checks or electronic payments.
5. Supervise all cash disbursements and record-keeping functions.

REVIEW 8-8 LO8-8 Cash Controls

Review MBC

Part One—Cash Drawer Reconciliation

At the end of the business day of May 1, 2020, Pet Supplies Inc. compiled the following amounts from cash drawer reconciliations of cash receipts: Cash collected: $8,549.20; checks collected: $2,341.90; cash refunds made: $143.80. From the retail point of sales system through the input of the electronic register, amounts compiled were as follows: Cash collected: $8,650.80; checks collected: $2,341.90, and cash refunds made: $163.80. Record the necessary adjusting entry, assuming that sales had been automatically recorded from information in the point of sales system.

Part Two—Petty Cash Fund Reconciliation

The Koller Company utilizes a petty cash system for making small payments. Record the journal entries required for the following petty cash transactions completed during June 2020.

1. On June 1, 2020, the company treasurer prepared a $750 check payable to petty cash; the cash was given to the custodian. The petty cash fund has a beginning balance of $0.
2. Expenditures by the custodian through June 30 were postage $50, office supplies $210, office equipment repairs $50, coffee room supplies $100, office birthday party $25, and miscellaneous items $50. The ending fund balance is $265. The fund was replenished on June 30, 2020, back to a level of $750.

Part Three—Bank Reconciliation

Reconciling items on Smith's Inc. prior period *March 31* bank reconciliation follow.

Deposits in transit	$500
Checks outstanding	(100)

April transactions for Smith follow.

Transactions	Bank	Book
Checks recorded	$5,750	$5,900
Deposits recorded	3,800	4,500
Service charges recorded	15	—
Direct deposits to bank	800	—
Electronic payments from bank	80	—
Balance, April 30, 2020	4,540	4,785

More Practice: 8-99, 8-100, 8-101, 8-102, 8-103

Solution on p. 8-72.

Prepare a bank reconciliation for April 2020.

Account for impairment of noncurrent receivables

APPENDIX 8B
LO 8-9

Impairment of Noncurrent Receivables
- Reduce net carrying value to present value of expected future cash flows
- Discount cash flows using *original* effective interest rate of note

LO 8-9 Overview

Use of the Current Expected Credit Loss Model (CECL model) was introduced in **LO 8-4** but it is also applicable to impairment of noncurrent receivables such as a note receivable. Expected losses over the expected life of a note receivable, using historical, current, and reasonable and supportable forecasts should be considered. Even if the likelihood of a loss is remote, the risk of loss should be recognized. This situation arises if principal or interest payments are unlikely to be collected, or if payments will not be received as scheduled. (A payment delay reduces the present value of the note receivable, causing it to be impaired.)

Creditors determine whether a note receivable is impaired during normal note receivable review procedures. Impairments can also result from a formal restructuring agreement between the creditor and the debtor. (This is a type of troubled debt restructuring—see Chapter 16 for a discussion.)

A creditor is required to recognize the value of an impaired note receivable at the present value of expected future cash flows discounted at the note's effective rate (the rate implicit in the original agreement). The FASB concluded that impaired note receivable values should reflect changes in expected future cash flows, but not other changes that might affect fair value. Therefore, rather than change the interest rate to reflect general changes in interest rates, or changes in risk premiums, the creditor applies the original effective rate. Any adjustment to the carrying value is accomplished with a debit to Bad Debt Expense and a credit to Allowance for Doubtful Accounts.

FORD

Real World—IMPAIRMENT OF 'AUTO' RECEIVABLES

FORD [F]

Ford Motor Company's non-consumer receivables mainly reflect credit extended to dealers in the form of lines of credit to purchase new Ford and Lincoln vehicles as well as used vehicles. These receivables are evaluated quarterly by management for potential losses. As a result, the company records both an allowance and impairments on receivables. The section on impairment below describes the process as explained here in the text.

> **Specific Allowance for Impaired Receivables.** Dealer financing is evaluated by segmenting individual loans by the risk characteristics of the loan (such as the amount of the loan, the nature of the collateral, and the financial status of the debtor). The loans are analyzed to determine whether individual loans are impaired, and a specific allowance is estimated based on the present value of the expected future cash flows of the receivable discounted at the loan's original effective interest rate or the fair value of the collateral adjusted for estimated costs to sell.
>
> After establishing the collective and the specific allowance for credit losses, if management believes the allowance does not reflect all losses inherent in the portfolio due to changes in recent economic trends and conditions, or other relevant factors, an adjustment is made based on management judgment.

Recording Impairment of a Note Receivable

LO8-9 **Demo 8-9**

Demo MBC

Crane Company, a calendar-year firm, sold merchandise (selling price of $10,000) to Delo Inc. on January 1, 2020, and received a two-year, 6%, $10,000 note issued at stated value. The note calls for annual interest to be paid each December 31. Crane collected the 2020 interest on schedule. However, interest and principal was not paid on December 31, 2021, according to the note agreement.

At December 31, 2021, with knowledge of financial difficulties for Delo, Crane expects that the 2021 (last) interest payment will not be collected and that only $6,000 of the principal due December 31, 2021, will be collected. The $6,000 principal amount is expected to be collected on December 31, 2023. The current interest rate for notes of similar risk is 14%.

Record the following journal entries for Crane.

a. Record the receipt of the note in exchange for merchandise on January 1, 2020.
b. Record the receipt of interest on December 31, 2020.
c. Record the accrual of interest on December 31, 2021.

continued

continued from previous page

d. Record the impairment of the note receivable on December 31, 2021.
e. Record the accrual of interest on December 31, 2022, assuming no change in loss estimates and the use of the effective interest method.
f. Record the receipt of payment from Delo on December 31, 2023, assuming that payment was received for $6,000.

Solution

a. Receipt of the Note

January 1, 2020—To record receipt of note

Assets = Liabilities + Equity: +10,000 Assets; +10,000 Equity
Note Receiv: 10,000 (Dr) | Sales Rev: 10,000 (Cr)

Note Receivable	10,000	
Sales Revenue		10,000

b. Receipt of Interest

December 31, 2020—To record receipt of interest

Assets = Liabilities + Equity: +600 Assets; +600 Equity
Cash: 600 (Dr) | Interest Rev: 600 (Cr)

Cash	600	
Interest Revenue		600

c. Interest Accrual

December 31, 2021—To record interest accrual

Assets = Liabilities + Equity: +600 Assets; +600 Equity
Interest Receiv: 600 (Dr) | Interest Rev: 600, 600 (Cr)

Interest Receivable	600	
Interest Revenue		600

d. Impairment Loss

December 31, 2021—To record impairment loss on note receivable

Assets = Liabilities + Equity: −4,660, −600 Assets; −5,260 Equity
Interest Receiv: 600 (Dr), 600 (Cr) | Bad Debt Exp: 5,260 (Dr) | AFDA: 4,660 (Cr)

Bad Debt Expense ($4,660 + $600)	5,260	
Interest Receivable ($10,000 × 0.06)		600
Allowance for Doubtful Accounts ($10,000 − $5,340)		4,660

	RATE	NPER	PMT	PV	FV	Excel Formula
Given	6%	2	0	?	−6,000	=PV(0.06,2,0,−6000)
Solution				$5,340		

The adjusted note receivable value of $5,340 is measured as the present value of the expected cash flows discounted at 6%. The 14% rate is not used to discount the cash flows because the accounting standards require the original interest rate effective at the issuance of the note of 6%.

e. Interest Accrual

December 31, 2022—To record interest accrual

Assets = Liabilities + Equity: +320 Assets; +320 Equity
Interest Receiv: 600, 320 (Dr), 600 (Cr) | Interest Rev: 600, 320 (Cr)

Interest Receivable ($5,340 × 0.06)	320	
Interest Revenue		320

f. Derecognition of the Note Receivable

December 31, 2023—To record derecognition of note receivable

Assets = Liabilities + Equity: +6,000, +4,660, −320, −10,000 Assets; +340 Equity
Cash: 600, 6,000 (Dr) | Interest Rev: 600, 320, 340 (Cr) | AFDA: 4,660 (Dr), 4,660 (Cr) | Interest Receiv: 600, 320 (Dr), 600, 320 (Cr) | Note Receiv: 10,000 (Dr), 10,000 (Cr)

Cash	6,000	
Allowance for Doubtful Accounts	4,660	
Interest Receivable		320
Note Receivable		10,000
Interest Revenue [($5,340 + $320) × 0.06]		340

Impairment of a Note Receivable

LO8-9 **Review 8-9**

Prince Inc., a calendar-year firm, has a 6%, $20,000 note receivable from the sale of merchandise. The note was issued when the market rate was 6%. The note is due December 31, 2024. Annual interest is due each December 31. On December 31, 2020, Prince reviews the collectibility of its note and determines that only $15,000 is likely to be received on the due date from this note. Although Prince received the 2020 interest payment, the company does not expect to receive further interest payments. On December 31, 2024, Prince received $14,200 and expects no further payments.

Required

a. Prepare the entry to record the note receivable impairment on December 31, 2020.

b. Prepare the December 31 entry to accrue interest at year-ends for 2021, 2022, and 2023. Prince chooses to recognize interest revenue using the effective interest method.

c. Prepare the entry to record the final receipt of principal.

More Practice:
8-97, 8-98, 8-104, 8-105
Solution on p. 8-73.

Questions

8-1. Define cash as it is used for accounting purposes.

8-2. What are cash equivalents and how are they reported on the balance sheet?

8-3. In what circumstances, if any, is it permissible to offset a bank overdraft against a positive balance in another bank account?

8-4. Define a compensating balance and explain the related reporting requirements.

8-5. Which of the following items should not be recorded in the cash account?

a. Money orders.
b. Postdated checks.
c. Ordinary checks.
d. Postage stamps
e. Currency.
f. Cash deposited in savings accounts.
g. Certificates of deposit.
h. Deposits in checking accounts.

8-6. Crown Co. sold merchandise for $500, terms 2/10, n/30. Explain these terms and prepare the journal entry for the sale under the gross method and under the net method. Which approach is preferable? Why?

8-7. What is the difference between a cash discount and a trade discount?

8-8. In addition to recognizing the sale of a product, describe why an asset and liability are recorded when we estimate returns.

8-9. Briefly describe the allowance method for estimating bad debt expense and the allowance for doubtful accounts for trade receivables. What guidance is available in the accounting standards for estimating the allowance for doubtful accounts?

8-10. Under the allowance method, is the income statement affected when a specific account is determined to be uncollectible?

8-11. It sometimes happens that a receivable that has been written off as uncollectible is recovered. Describe the accounting procedures in such an event.

8-12. What is an accounts receivable aging schedule and how is it used to estimate the allowance for doubtful accounts?

8-13. What accounting guidance is available in determining whether a financing arrangement involving receivables is considered either a sale or a secured borrowing?

8-14. Which party is responsible for uncollectible accounts if an owner sells its receivables to a factor (1) with recourse or (2) without recourse? How is this reported in the financial statements?

8-15. Why are long-term notes recorded at the present value of all future cash flows specified in the note, using the market interest rate?

8-16. When are short-term notes exempt from valuation at present value?

Brief Exercises

Brief Exercise 8-17
Classifying Items as Cash and Cash Equivalents **LO1**
Hint: See Demo 8-1

Which of the following items would be included in *cash and cash equivalents* on the balance sheet?

a. Checking account balance
b. Certificate of deposit (six-month term)
c. Savings account balance
d. Postdated checks received
e. Treasury bills purchased when two months remain in term
f. Compensating balance on deposit for a short-term loan
g. Sinking fund to retire a bond in five years

Brief Exercise 8-18
Recording Cash Discount Entries—Gross Method **LO2**
Hint: See Demo 8-2A

Lynx Inc. sells apparel merchandise to Dyson Inc. at a gross sales price of $350, credit terms 2/10, n/30 on July 10, 2020. Dyson pays for the merchandise in full on July 19, 2020. Record the entries required on July 10, 2020, and July 19, 2020, for Lynx Inc. assuming use of the *gross* method in accounting for credit sales. Omit the cost of goods sold entry.

Brief Exercise 8-19
Recording Cash Discount Entries—Net Method **LO2**
Hint: See Demo 8-2B

Lynx Inc. sells apparel merchandise to Dyson Inc. at a gross sales price of $350, credit terms 2/10, n/30 on July 10, 2020. Dyson pays for the merchandise in full on July 19, 2020. Record the entries required on July 10, 2020, and July 19, 2020, for Lynx Inc. assuming use of the *net* method in accounting for credit sales. Omit the cost of goods sold entry.

Brief Exercise 8-20
Recording Estimated Returns **LO3**
Hint: See Demo 8-3

Fizer recognized sales of $500,000 in 2020 on merchandise with a cost of $260,000. Actual sales returns in 2020 were $2,800. Based on historical trends, the company estimates returns to be 1.5% of sales. Assuming all sales are on account, record the adjusting entry for estimated sales returns on December 31, 2020.

Brief Exercise 8-21
Computing Bad Debts Under the Allowance Method Based on Receivables **LO4**

A company has a credit balance of $600 in its allowance for doubtful accounts. The amount of credit sales for the period is $80,000, and the balance in accounts receivable is $15,000. Assume that the expected credit losses are estimated to be 9% of accounts receivable.

a. What is (1) bad debt expense for the year and (2) the ending balance in the allowance for doubtful accounts?
b. How would the answer to part *a* change (if at all) if the company had a debit balance of $600 in its allowance for doubtful accounts before any adjustment?

Brief Exercise 8-22
Computing Bad Debts Under the Allowance Method Based on Sales **LO4**

Solstice Inc. has a credit balance of $600 in its allowance for doubtful accounts. The amount of credit sales for the period is $80,000, and the balance in accounts receivable is $15,000. Assume that the bad debt estimates are 0.5% of credit sales. What is (1) bad debt expense for the year and (2) the ending balance in the allowance for doubtful accounts?

Brief Exercise 8-23
Determining Cash Collections through Account Analysis **LO4**

Lewis Company had a beginning balance and ending balance in accounts receivable of $650,000, and $760,000, respectively. Sales on credit were $4,500,000 for the year and the company wrote off accounts totaling $3,300 during the year. What were cash collections from sales during the year?

Brief Exercise 8-24
Determining Bad Debt Expense through Account Analysis **LO4**

Phelps Company had a beginning balance of $10,000 in the allowance for doubtful accounts, wrote off accounts totaling $3,300 during the year, and estimated the ending balance in the allowance to be $15,200 based on an analysis of the accounts receivable aging schedule. What is bad debt expense for the year?

Brief Exercise 8-25
Determining Sales and Interest Revenue using Short-Term Note Receivable **LO5**

A one-year, $5,000, 12% note was received by Nadia Company for a credit sale. Assuming a market rate of 12%, determine (1) the value of sales revenue recognized upon issuance of the note and (2) interest revenue recognized over the term of the note.

Brief Exercise 8-26
Determining Sales and Interest Revenue using Long-term Note Receivable **LO5**

A four-year, $5,000, noninterest-bearing note was received by Willis Company for a credit sale. Assuming a market rate of 12%, determine (1) sales revenue recognized upon issuance of the note and (2) interest revenue recognized over the term of the note.

Brief Exercise 8-27
Recording a secured borrowing **LO6**
Hint: See Demo 8-6A

On April 1, 2020, NYC Corporation secures a loan with a finance company, using its accounts receivable of $50,000 as collateral for the loan. NYC Corporation agrees to remit customer collections as payments on the loan. Loan proceeds are 80% of the receivables less a 2% finance charge on the balance of the assigned receivables. In addition, the finance company charges 10% interest on the unpaid loan balance, payable at the end of each month. Record the April 1, 2020, entry for NYC Corporation.

Brief Exercise 8-28 Recording a Sale of Accounts Receivable With Recourse **LO6** *Hint:* See Demo 8-6C

Exon Company sold accounts receivable of $10,000 (with an allowance for doubtful accounts of $300) for $9,000 cash, with recourse. Estimated obligations due to the with-recourse provision amounted to $700. Record the sale of receivables entry for Exon Company.

Brief Exercise 8-29 Recording a Sale of Accounts Receivable Without Recourse **LO6** *Hint:* See Demo 8-6B

Bappa Apparel manufactures fine sportswear for many national retailers and frequently sells its receivables to factors as a means of accelerating cash collections. Bappa sold $100,000 of receivables to a factor. The receivables were sold without recourse. The factor charged 6% and held back 5% for sales adjustments. Record Bappa's required entry.

Brief Exercise 8-30 Recording Purchase of Accounts Receivable Without Recourse **LO6**

Refer to Brief Exercise 8-29 above. Assume that the factor estimates that expected credit losses are 2% of the accounts receivable balance. Record the journal entry for the factor at the time the receivables are purchased.

Brief Exercise 8-31 Discounting a Note Receivable **LO6** *Hint:* See Demo 8-6D

Sonic Inc. received from a customer a $1,000, 9% interest-bearing note that will mature in three months. Two months later, Sonic Inc. discounted the note to the bank to yield 12%. Provide the required journal entry made by the company at the time the note was discounted.

Brief Exercise 8-32 Computing Receivable Ratios **LO7** *Hint:* See Demo 8-7

Broadway Inc. recognized credit sales of $200,000 for the year ended December 31, 2020. The accounts receivable balances at December 31, 2019, and at December 31, 2020, were $18,880 and $22,000, respectively. Compute Broadway's receivable turnover ratio and its average days to collect receivables for 2020.

Exercises

Exercise 8-33 Classifying Cash and Non-Cash Items on a Balance Sheet **LO1**

Tropical Inc. is preparing its December 31 financial statements, and it must determine the proper balance sheet classification of the items listed below.

	Balance Sheet	
Financial Statement Item	**Include in Cash Amount**	**Classification (If Not Cash)**
1. Coins and currency, $1,000.		
2. Checks received from customers, $12,000.		
3. Certificates of deposit (CDs), $16,000.		
4. Petty cash fund, $800.		
5. Postage stamps, $120.		
6. First Star checking account balance, $42,000.		
7. Postdated check from customer, $200.		
8. Money order from customer, $300.		
9. Cash in savings account, $20,000.		
10. Bank draft from customer, $800.		
11. Investment in commercial paper, 30-day term , $160.		
12. Utility deposit to a utilities company (refundable), $100.		
13. Certified check from customer, $2,000.		
14. NSF (non-sufficient fund) check from R. Roe, $400.		
15. Cash advance to company executive, collectible upon demand, $40,000.		
16. Hometown Credit Union, checking account, overdraft, $4,000.		
17. Travel advances to employees, $240.		
18. Cashier's check, $500.		

Required

Complete the table above. (a) Indicate whether each amount would be classified as cash. (b) Indicate an alternative classification if the amount is excluded from cash.

Exercise 8-34
Classifying Cash-Related Items on a Balance Sheet **LO1**

Olympian Inc. is preparing its 2020 financial statements; its annual accounting period ends December 31. The following items, related to cash, are under consideration.

a. A $900 check received from a customer, dated February 1, 2021, is held by Olympian.
b. A customer's check was included in the December 20 deposit. It was returned by the bank stamped NSF (non-sufficient funds). No entry has yet been made by Olympian Inc. to reflect the return.
c. A 6-month, $20,000 CD (certificate of deposit) on which $1,000 of interest accrued to December 31 has just been recorded by debiting interest receivable and crediting interest revenue.
d. Postage stamps that cost $30 are in the cash drawer.
e. A cashier's check of $200 payable to Olympian Inc. is in the cash drawer; it is dated December 29.
f. Three checks, dated December 31, 2020, totaling $465, payable to vendors who have sold merchandise to Olympian Inc. on account, were not mailed by December 31, 2020. They have not been entered as payments in the check register and ledger.
g. Olympian Inc. has a note receivable that matures December 31, 2020. The note is for $20,000 and bears interest at 9%, having been outstanding for three months. The company plans to include the full amount due of $20,000 plus interest in its cash balance even though payment was not received until January 1, 2021.
h. The company has invested in a U.S. Treasury bill, originating December 15, 2020, and maturing February 1, 2021, for $2,500.
i. The company is legally required to maintain $25,000 at its bank as a compensating balance.

Required

Indicate how each item *a* through *i* should be reported on a balance sheet as of December 31, 2020.

Exercise 8-35
Accounting for Sales on Credit: Gross Method **LO2**

On December 29, 2020, Sabre Company sold merchandise for $2,000 on credit terms, 3/10, n/60. The accounting period ends December 31.

Required

Provide the following entries under the gross method.

a. To record the 2020 sale. Omit the cost of good sold entry.
b. To record collection of the account, assuming collection took place on January 5, 2021.
c. To record collection of the account, assuming collection took place on April 1, 2021.
d. Indicate what should be reported on the balance sheet and income statement for both 2020 and 2021 assuming
   1. Parts *a* and *b* occur. 2. Parts *a* and *c* occur.

Exercise 8-36
Accounting for Sales on Credit: Net Method **LO2**

On December 29, 2020, Sabre Company sold merchandise for $2,000 on credit terms, 3/10, n/60. The accounting period ends December 31.

Required

Provide the following entries under the net method.

a. To record the 2020 sale. Omit the cost of good sold entry.
b. To record collection of the account, assuming collection took place on January 5, 2021.
c. To record collection of the account, assuming collection took place on April 1, 2021.
d. Indicate what should be reported on the balance sheet and income statement for both 2020 and 2021 assuming
   1. Parts *a* and *b* occur. 2. Parts *a* and *c* occur.

Exercise 8-37
Recording Entries for Sales and Estimated Returns **LO3**
Hint: See Demo 8-3

Lacey Company recorded sales of $2,000,000 for the year ended December 31, 2020. During 2020, the company recorded actual returns and allowances of $25,000. As of December 31, 2020, Lacey estimates sales returns at 3% of sales. It is the company's policy to provide refunds on account.

Required

a. Prepare the journal entry to record sales in 2020 assuming all sales are on account. Cost of goods sold is 40% of the selling price.

b. Prepare the journal entry to record actual returns in 2020.
c. Prepare the adjusting entry, if any, related to estimated returns on December 31, 2020.
d. Assuming that actual returns were $30,000 in 2021, prepare the journal entry for actual returns.

Exercise 8-38 Recording Sales with Expected Returns **LO3**

Novelty Inc. developed a new product in 2020 and its financial results follow. To increase acceptance by retailers, Novelty sold the product to retailers with an unconditional right of return, which expires on February 1, 2021. Novelty estimates returns to be 30%. All sales are on credit. Cash collections related to that year's sales were $40,000 in 2020 and $113,000 in 2021. Novelty uses the perpetual inventory system.

Sales in 2020	$180,000
Cost of goods sold for 2020	120,000
Returns of 2020 sales in 2020	12,000 (cost $8,000)
Returns of 2020 sales in January 2021	15,000 (cost $10,000)

Required

a. Prepare the 2020 sales journal entry for Novelty Inc.
b. Record actual returns in 2020.
c. Record actual returns in 2021 (for January) and any required adjusting entries.

Exercise 8-39 Classifying Items Related to Receivables and Payables in a Balance Sheet **LO4**

When examining the accounts of WholeFoods Company, we ascertain that balances relating to both receivables and payables are included in a single controlling account (called receivables), which has an $18,000 debit balance. An analysis of the details of this account reveals the following.

Items	Debit	Credit
Accounts receivable—customers	$40,000	
Accounts receivable—officers (current collection expected)	2,500	
Travel advances to sales staff	1,000	
Accounts payable for merchandise		$19,250
Unpaid salaries		3,300
Credit balances in customer accounts (accounts receivable)		2,000
Cash received in advance from customers for goods not yet shipped		450
Allowance for doubtful accounts, adjusted		500

Required

Indicate how each of the items should be reported on WholeFoods Company's balance sheet.

Exercise 8-40 Analyzing Transactions Data to Estimate Accounts Receivable **LO4**

The following information relates to Kulver's Company for 2020.

- Accounts receivable beginning balance: $100,000
- Collections on customers' accounts: $502,000
- Purchases of inventory held for sale (at cost): $480,000
- Ending inventory on December 31, 2020 (at cost): $116,667
- Mark-up on inventory is 50% of cost

Required

a. Estimate the value of ending accounts receivable given the information above.
b. If the balance in the ledger for accounts receivable is $75,000 on December 31, 2020, what are some possible reasons that this amount is different from the amount estimated in part *a*?

Exercise 8-41 Estimating and Recording Bad Debt Estimates and Write-offs; Reporting of Accounts Receivable **LO4**

Master Company's December 31, 2019, balances related to accounts receivable follow.

Accounts receivable	$400,000 Dr.
Allowance for doubtful accounts	20,000 Cr.

During 2020, $45,000 of accounts receivable is considered uncollectible, and no more effort to collect these accounts will be made. Total sales for 2020 are $1,200,000, of which $200,000 are cash sales. A total of $900,000 was collected on account during 2020.

Required

a. Assuming that Master uses the allowance method to estimate net accounts receivable and uses 9% of accounts receivable as its estimate of expected credit losses, prepare the (1) journal entries to record write-offs and bad debt expense for 2020, and (2) disclosure on gross and net accounts receivable on the balance sheet at December 31, 2020.

b. How would the answers to part *a* change (if at all) assuming instead that the unadjusted balance in the allowance for doubtful accounts was a debit balance of $5,000?

Exercise 8-42
Estimating and Recording Bad Debt Estimates and Write-offs; Reporting of Accounts Receivable **LO4**

At December 31, 2020, its annual year-end, the accounts of Sun Systems Inc. show the following.

1. Sales revenue for 2020, $180,000, of which one-sixth was on account.
2. Allowance for doubtful accounts, balance December 31, 2019, $900 credit.
3. Accounts receivable, balance December 31, 2020 (prior to any write-offs of uncollectible accounts during 2020), $18,050.
4. Uncollectible accounts to be written off, December 31, 2020, $1,050.
5. Aging schedule at December 31, 2020, showing the following breakdown of total accounts receivable.

Status	Amount
Not past due	$10,000
Past due 1–60 days	4,000
Past due over 60 days	3,000

Required

a. Prepare the 2020 entry to write off the uncollectible accounts.

b. Prepare the 2020 adjusting entry to record bad debt expense for each of the following independent assumptions concerning expected bad debt loss rates.
   1. Based on credit sales, 1.5%.
   2. Based on total receivables at year-end, 2.5%.
   3. Based on aging schedule: not past due, 0.5%; past due 1–60 days, 1%; and past due over 60 days, 8%.
   4. Based on direct write-off method

c. Prepare the 2020 balance sheet disclosure relating to accounts receivable for each assumption 1 through 4 of part *b*. Describe the positives and negatives of the four methods in part *b*.

Exercise 8-43
Recording Write-Offs and Computing Net Realizable Value of Receivables **LO4**

Andler Inc. estimates that an allowance of $8,000 is required on its accounts receivable balance of $160,000 on December 31, 2020.

Required

a. What is the net realizable value of its accounts receivable on December 31, 2020?

b. On February 1, 2021, the company determined that $2,000 of specific accounts receivable would be written off. Prepare the journal entry required to write-off these accounts. What is the net realizable value of accounts receivable after the write-off?

c. On February 15, 2021, the company unexpectedly collected $500 of the accounts written off on February 1, 2021. Prepare the journal entry required upon collection of these accounts. What is the net realizable value of accounts receivable after the collection?

Exercise 8-44 Preparing an Aging Schedule to Estimate Allowance for Doubtful Accounts **LO4**

A review of open invoices of Sketchers Inc. results in the following report.

Invoice	Amount	Date (each from this year)
#496	$ 509.42	5-Dec
#495	761.97	2-Dec
#427	304.62	5-Nov
#100	121.18	28-Jun
#300	823.81	3-Oct
#410	744.73	31-Oct
#204	69.66	25-Aug
#498	845.38	28-Dec
#499	306.83	28-Dec
#487	830.31	28-Nov
#310	230.72	8-Oct
#178	714.68	7-Aug
#497	372.26	5-Dec
#488	158.78	29-Nov
#105	20.81	5-Jul
	$6,815.15	

Required

a. Organize the list of open invoices as of December 31 into a table with the following aging categories across the top: (1) less than 30 days, (2) 31–60 days, (3) 60–90 days, and (4) greater than 90 days.

b. Assume that the company estimates the allowance for doubtful accounts based upon the following percentages applied to the appropriate aging categories: (1) 1% for less than 30 days, (2) 5% for 31–60 days, (3) 30% for 60–90 days, and (4) 60% for greater than 90 days. What is the ending allowance for doubtful accounts as estimated by the company?

Exercise 8-45 Computing Bad Debt Expense from Transactions Data **LO4**

Modern Oil estimates uncollectible accounts using the allowance method. The following pertains to its year 2020.

- Allowance for Doubtful Accounts, December 31, 2019, balance: $508,000
- Allowance for Doubtful Accounts, December 31, 2020, balance: $491,000
- Accounts formally authorized to be written off in 2020: $88,000
- Unexpected collection of accounts receivable on accounts written off in 2020: $5,000

Required

Compute bad debt expense in 2020 for this company.

Exercise 8-46 Analyzing Accounts and Notes Receivable; Computing Interest, Estimating Value, and Recording Bad Debts **LO3, 4, 5, 6**

Following are four *separate* scenarios.

1. On December 31, 2020, Helena Company, a California real estate firm, received two $20,000 notes from customers in exchange for services rendered. The 8% note from El Dorado Company is due in nine months, and the 3% note from Newcastle Company is due in five years. The market interest rate for similar notes on December 31, 2020, was 8%. At what amounts should the two notes be reported in Helena's December 31, 2020, balance sheet?
2. EPPA, an environmental management firm, issued to Dara, a $10,000, 8%, five-year installment note that required five equal annual year-end payments. This note was discounted to yield a 9% rate to Dara. What is the total amount of interest revenue to be recognized by Dara on this note?
3. On July 1, 2020, Lezix Company, a maker of denim clothing, sold goods in exchange for a $100,000, one-year, noninterest-bearing note. At the time of the sale, the market rate of interest was 12% on similar notes. At what amount should Lezix record the note receivable on July 1, 2020?
4. The records of Quest Company included the following accounts (with normal balances).

Cash sales	$1,200,000
Credit sales	900,000
Balance in accounts receivable, December 31, 2019	180,000
Balance in accounts receivable, December 31, 2020	200,000
Balance in allowance for doubtful accounts, December 31, 2019	3,000 (Cr.)
Accounts written off as uncollectible during 2020	5,000

The company estimates bad debts as 2% of receivables at year-end to be uncollectible. Prepare the adjusting entry at December 31, 2020, to adjust the allowance for doubtful accounts.

Required

Analyze each of the four separate scenarios and answer the requirements.

Exercise 8-47
Recording and Reporting Transactions with Short-Term, Interest-Bearing Note Receivable **LO5**
Hint: See Demo 8-5A

On April 1, 2020, Welsch Company sold merchandise to Customer Rodriguez for $18,000, terms 2/10, n/30. Because of nonpayment by Rodriguez, Welsch received an $18,000, 10%, 12-month note dated May 1, 2020. The stated rate and the market rate are equal. The company's annual reporting period ends December 31. Customer Rodriguez paid the note in full, plus cash interest, on its maturity date.

Required

a. Prepare all entries for Welsch related to the above transactions, including any year-end adjustments.
b. Show what should be presented on the 2020 income statement and balance sheet.

Exercise 8-48
Recording and Reporting Transactions with Short-Term, Interest-Bearing Note Receivable **LO5**

On May 1, 2020, Swimm Company sold merchandise to Customer Lochte and received a $26,400 (face amount), one-year, noninterest-bearing note. The market rate of interest is 10%. The annual reporting period for Swimm Company ends on December 31. Customer Lochte paid the note in full on its maturity date.

Required

a. Prepare all entries for Swimm Company related to the above transactions, including any year-end adjustments. Amortize the discount on the note receivable using the straight-line method. *Hint:* Under the straight-line method, we amortize the discount equally over the 12-months.
b. Show what should be presented on the 2020 income statement and balance sheet.

Exercise 8-49
Recording Entries for Long-Term Note Receivable; Effective Interest Amortization **LO5**
Hint: See Demo 8-5B

On January 1, 2020, Jacobs Company sells land financed through a $40,000 note, issued by Andress Company. The note is a $40,000, 8%, annual interest bearing note. Andress agrees to repay the $40,000 proceeds on December 31, 2021. The prevailing interest rate on similar notes is 11%. Assume that the cost of the land is equal to the selling price.

Required

Prepare all entries for Jacobs over the note term, including any year-end adjustments. Use the effective interest method to amortize the discount.

Exercise 8-50
Preparing Entries and Interest Schedule for Long-Term Note Receivable; Effective Interest Amortization **LO5**

On July 1, 2020, Stealth Company sold a machine that had a list price of $36,000. The customer paid $6,000 cash and signed a three-year, $30,000 note that specified a stated interest rate of 3%. Annual interest on the full amount of the principal is payable each June 30. The principal is payable on June 30, 2023. The market rate of interest for a note of this risk is 10%.

Required

a. Compute the present value of this note.
b. Prepare an effective interest schedule for this note.
c. Prepare all entries required by Stealth for this note through its maturity date, including year-end adjustments.

Exercise 8-51
Preparing Entries and Interest Schedule for Long-Term Note Receivable; Effective Interest Amortization **LO5**
Hint: See Demo 8-5C

On April 1, 2020, Mountain Company sold merchandise and received a $12,000, three-year, noninterest-bearing note. The market rate is 10%. The company uses the effective interest method to amortize any discount.

Required

Prepare all entries for Mountain Company over the note's term, including year-end adjustments.

Exercise 8-52
Preparing Entries for a Secured Borrowing and Subsequent Collections and Payments **LO6**

A note payable was executed by Sterling Inc. to Miami Finance Company. Sterling Inc. used $240,000 of its accounts receivable as collateral for the loan. The contract provided that Miami would advance 85% of the gross amount of the receivables. Sterling Inc. continues to collect payments for the receivables and the cash from customers is then remitted to the finance company. The cash remitted is first applied to the finance charges, with the remainder applied to principal.

During the first month, customers owing $164,000 paid cash, less sales returns and allowances of $6,400, originally recorded as a refund liability. The finance charge at the end of the first month was $1,400.

During the second month, the remaining receivables were collected in full, except for $1,600 written off as uncollectible. Final settlement was effected with the finance company, including payment of an additional finance charge of $600.

Required

a. Record the entries for Sterling to record the secured borrowing.
b. Record the entries for Sterling to record (1) the collections and (2) the payment to Miami for the first month.
c. Record the entries for Sterling to record (1) the collections for the second month and (2) the final payment to Miami.

Exercise 8-53 Recording the Sale of Accounts Receivable Without Recourse **LO6**

On April 1, 2020, DOS Company sold $20,000 accounts receivable to PS2 Finance Company to obtain immediate cash. The related allowance for doubtful accounts was $800. The financial agreement specified a price of $16,000 on a without-recourse basis.

Required

Prepare the journal entry for DOS Company to sell the accounts receivable.

Exercise 8-54 Recording the Sale of Accounts Receivable With Recourse **LO6**

On April 1, 2020, DOS Company sold $20,000 accounts receivable to PS2 Finance Company to obtain immediate cash. The related allowance for doubtful accounts was $800. The financial agreement specified a price of $17,000 on a with-recourse basis. DOS estimated a $400 recourse liability.

Required

Prepare the journal entry for DOS Company to sell the accounts receivable.

Exercise 8-55 Recording the Sale of Accounts Receivable Without Recourse **LO6** *Hint:* See Demo 8-6B

Apparel Inc. manufactures sportswear for retailers and frequently sells its receivables to factors as a means of accelerating cash collections. On December 1, 2020, Apparel Inc. sold $100,000 of its receivables to Factor Bank. The receivables were sold without recourse. The factor charged 8% and held back 5% for sales adjustments. Bad debts estimated on the receivables is $500.

Required

Record all journal entries related to the sale of accounts receivable for (a) Apparel Inc., and (b) Factor Bank.

Exercise 8-56 Recording the Sale of Accounts Receivable With Recourse **LO6** *Hint:* See Demo 8-6C

Cappa Apparel manufactures sportswear for retailers and frequently sells its receivables to factors as a means of accelerating cash collections. On December 1, 2020, Cappa sold $100,000 of its receivables to Factor Bank. The receivables were the sale with recourse. The factor charged 6% and held back 10% for sales adjustments. Cappa records a $4,000 recourse obligation.

Required

Record all journal entries related to the sale of accounts receivable for (a) Cappa Apparel, and (b) Factor Bank.

Exercise 8-57 Recording Entries for the Discounting of a Note Receivable **LO6** *Hint:* See Demo 8-6D

Aerobic Sports Company completed the following 2020 transactions related to a note receivable.

a. February 1, 2020—Received a $200,000, 9%, interest-bearing, six-month note from Temple Company for land that had a carrying value of $60,000.
b. March 1, 2020—Discounted (sold with recourse) the note to Local Bank at a 12% interest rate. Assume the discounting qualifies as a sale.

Required

Prepare the journal entries, including any interest earned, that Aerobic Sports Company should make on February 1, 2020, and March 1, 2020.

Exercise 8-58 Performing Ratio Analysis of Receivables and Interpreting the Results **LO7** *Hint:* See Demo 8-7

NIKE Inc. designs, develops, markets, and sells athletic footwear, apparel, equipment, and accessories worldwide. **Under Armour Inc.** develops, markets, and distributes branded performance apparel, footwear, and accessories for men, women, and youth. The following financial information is reported by both companies.

$ millions	Accounts Receivable Year 3	Accounts Receivable Year 2	Accounts Receivable Year 1	Sales Year 3	Sales Year 2
Nike	$3,241.0	$3,358.0	$3,789.0	$32,376.0	$30,601.0
Under Armour	433.6	332.3	248.3	3,963.3	3,084.4

Required

a. Compute the accounts receivable turnover ratio and the average days to collect receivables for year three and for year two for both Nike and Under Armour.

b. Analyze the year-to-year results for both companies.

Exercise 8-59
Matching Key Terms and Descripitons
LO1, 2, 3, 4, 5, 6, 7

Terms relating to concepts discussed in this chapter along with descriptions of the terms are included in the following two lists.

Terms

____ 1. Petty cash
____ 2. Compensating balance
____ 3. Cash equivalents
____ 4. Bank reconciliation
____ 5. Trade discount
____ 6. Cash discount
____ 7. Allowance method
____ 8. Accounts receivable aging
____ 9. Direct write-off
____10. Factoring
____11. Assignment
____12. Recourse liability
____13. Accounts receivable turnover
____14. Average days to collect receivables
____15. Note receivable

Description of Terms

a. Measure of how often receivables are collected during the year.
b. A schedule that shows the correct cash balance for both the bank and the company.
c. Reduces accounts receivable to net realizable value.
d. A special cash fund used to make small payments.
e. Contractual obligation to receive specific amounts on specific dates.
f. Sale of accounts receivable to a third party at a discount to obtain cash immediately.
g. Negotiable instruments that are accepted by a bank for immediate deposit and withdrawal.
h. A loan constraint that requires a minimum balance at all times in a bank account.
i. Estimated value of liability due to potential payments to factor for defaulted accounts receivable.
j. Schedule that organizes accounts receivable balances by due date.
k. Number of days on average, before payment is made to satisfy a receivable balance.
l. Reduces accounts receivable only when specific accounts are known to be uncollectible.
m. Reduction in selling price depending on customer type and/or quantity ordered.
n. Reduction in payment required due to timing of payment.
o. Using accounts receivable as collateral for a loan from a third party.

Required

Match each term, 1 through 15, with the most appropriate description *a* through *o*.

Problems

Problem 8-60
Analyzing Options to Use Receivables to Improve Liquidity **LO1, 7**

Pier Imports Inc. is a merchandiser with a December 31 year-end. Management is reviewing its financial statements in December, anticipating its year-end. The company is concerned about its liquidity situation as evidenced by its declining current asset ratio over the past year. The projected ratio at year-end is 0.83 (current assets of $500,000 over current liabilities of $600,000). The following suggestions are offered as ways to improve its liquidity position for financial statement reporting.

1. Pledge current accounts receivable to obtain a $75,000 short-term loan, discounted at $8,000. Half of the proceeds would be used to pay down accounts payable.
2. Pledge current accounts receivable to obtain a $75,000 long-term loan. Half of the proceeds would be used to pay down accounts payable.
3. Sell receivables of $100,000 to a factor with a 20% fee. Half of the proceeds would be used to pay down accounts payable.
4. Hold open the year-end for one extra week to collect on its receivables ($20,000) and record additional sales ($20,000) while paying down accounts payable ($20,000).

Required

a. Estimate the impact on the current asset ratio for each of these suggestions.

b. Are there any ethical issues with each of these options? Explain.

Problem 8-61
Analyzing Financial Results of Merchandising Transactions under the Gross and Net Methods **LO2, 3**

On August 12, 2020, Espresso Inc. sells merchandise worth $20,000 (gross sales price) to Crescendo Inc., terms 4/10, n/30. Espresso grants cash discounts on amounts paid within the discount period. Espresso estimates unrecorded returns at the end of the reporting period.

Required

a. Prepare Espresso's journal entries (ignoring cost of goods sold) for the following transactions under the gross method.

Aug.	12	Sales of $20,000 of merchandise to Crescendo.
	17	Returns and allowances of $3,000 (gross) are granted Crescendo.
	19	Espresso collects $11,520 cash from Crescendo on its account.
	24	Returns and allowances of $2,400 (gross) are granted Crescendo on items not yet paid for.
	27	Remainder of the Crescendo account is collected in full.
Sept.	12	Returns and allowances of $1,000 cash (gross) are granted Crescendo on merchandise paid for on August 19.
	14	Returns and allowances of $1,000 cash (gross) are granted Crescendo on merchandise paid for on August 27.

b. Prepare Espresso's journal entries (ignoring cost of goods sold) for the following transactions under the net method.

c. Prepare a table showing the effect on Espresso's net income from sales, sales returns and allowances, and sales discounts under both the gross method and net method (ignoring cost of goods sold). Compute the net cash flow of these events and compare it to the net income effect.

Problem 8-62
Recording and Reporting Accounts Receivable Transactions and Write-Offs **LO2, 4**

Provided below is a chronological log of a sale on credit by Lumber Inc. to Anton.

Dec. 24, 2016—Sold merchandise to Anton, $2,000, terms 2/10, n/30.
Jan. 2, 2017—Anton paid half of the receivable and took the discount.
Dec. 31, 2019—Anton has failed to pay the receivable and Lumber Inc. wrote Anton's account off as uncollectible.
Dec. 31, 2021—Anton unexpectedly paid its debt to Lumber Inc. in full, including 6% annual interest (not compounded, compute to the nearest month).

Required

a. Prepare the entry(ies) that Lumber Inc. should make at each of the above dates (ignore any cost of goods sold entries). Record sales using the net method.

b. Indicate how Anton's account receivable should be reported by Lumber Inc. at each December 31, its annual year-end.

Problem 8-63
Recording Entries to Estimate Bad Debt Expense Including the Write-Off and Subsequent Collection of an Account **LO4**

The accounts of Long Company provided the following information at December 31, 2020, its annual year-end.

Accounts receivable balance, December 31, 2019	$ 25,500
Allowance for doubtful accounts balance, December 31, 2019	1,500
Total sales revenue during 2020 (1/6 are on credit)	480,000
Uncollectible account to be written off during 2020 (A. Smith)	500
Cash collected on accounts receivable during 2020	85,000

Required

a. Prepare the entry to write off customer A. Smith's overdue account.

b. Prepare all entries related to accounts receivable and the allowance account for the following three cases:

1. Bad debt losses assume 1% of credit sales.
2. Bad debt losses assume 8% of the ending balance of accounts receivable.
3. Bad debt losses assuming the following aging schedule.

Age	Accounts Receivable	Probability of Noncollection
Less than 30 days . . .	$14,000	2%
31–90 days.	3,500	10
91–120 days.	1,500	30
More than 120 days . .	1,000	60

c. Indicate how the results are reported on the 2020 income statement and balance sheet for each case in part *b.*
d. Explain and evaluate each of the three methods in part *b.*
e. On August 1, 2021, customer A. Smith paid her overdue account in full. Provide the required entry(ies).

Problem 8-64
Correcting for Errors in Recording Estimates of Bad Debts Expense LO4

Right Aid Inc. has been in business for five years but has never had an audit of its financial statements. We are assigned to audit Right Aid as of December 31, 2020. Its books have been adjusted but not closed as of December 31, 2020. We find that its balance sheet incorrectly carries no allowance for doubtful accounts. Instead, uncollectible accounts have been expensed as written off, and recoveries have been credited to income as collected. The company's policy has been to write off, at December 31 of each year, those accounts on which no collections have been received after three months. The credit terms provide for equal monthly collections over two years after the date of sale.

We recommend, and the company agrees, to revise its accounts for 2020 to account for bad debts on the allowance basis. The allowance is to be based on a percentage of credit sales that is derived from the experience of prior years. Statistics for the past five years follow.

		Year of Sale					Year of Sale			
		2016	2017	2018	2019	2020	2016	2017	2018	2019
Year	Credit Sales	Accounts Receivable Written Off					Recoveries			
2016 . . .	$100,000	$ 550								
2017 . . .	250,000	1,500	$1,000				$300			
2018 . . .	300,000	500	4,000	$1,300				$850		
2019 . . .	325,000	—	1,200	4,500	$1,500				$500	
2020 . . .	275,000	—	—	2,700	5,000	$1,400				$600

Accounts receivable at December 31, 2020, are as follows.

From 2020 sales.	$ 15,000
From 2021 sales.	135,000
	$150,000

Required

a. Compute the uncollectible percentage on accounts for the combined years of 2016 through 2018.
b. Using the percent from part *a*, compute the uncollectible estimate. Also compute the write-offs, the recoveries, and the net write-offs for each year 2019 and 2020.
c. Prepare the journal entry to establish the allowance for doubtful accounts at December 31, 2020. Debit Prior Period Adjustment as this is a correction of an accounting error. Support each debit and credit with computations; ignore income taxes.

AICPA adapted

Problem 8-65
Analyzing Accounts Receivable, Bad Debts Expense, and Write-Offs LO4

The following *separate* scenarios require an analysis of bad debt expense.

1. Roundtree Inc., a manufacturer of natural foods, reported credit sales of $1,150,000 in 2021. Roundtree also reported the following balances.

	December 31, 2020	December 31, 2021
Accounts receivable	$250,000	$325,000
Allowance for doubtful accounts. . . .	15,000	27,500

Roundtree wrote off $5,000 of accounts during 2021. Under the cash basis of accounting, what would Roundtree have recognized as 2021 sales?

2. Brynn Inc., an electronics servicing company, reported $40,000 of gross cash sales (on which there were $2,000 of actual returns and allowances) and $60,000 of gross credit sales (on which $3,000 of cash discounts were taken) in 2020. The beginning and ending balances of accounts receivable in 2020 were $20,000

and $15,000, respectively. Brynn uses the direct write-off method for bad debts and recorded no bad debts in 2020. Under the cash basis of accounting, what amount of revenue would Brynn record in 2020?

3. Vantage Company had a beginning balance of $250,000 in the allowance for doubtful accounts, wrote off accounts totaling $10,000 during the year, and estimated the ending balance in the allowance to be 10% of accounts receivable based on an analysis of the December 31, 2020, accounts receivable balance of $3,000,000. What is bad debt expense for the year?
4. Seven Flags Inc. had a beginning balance and ending balance in accounts receivable of $140,000, and $260,000, respectively. Sales on credit were $2,000,000 for the year and the company wrote off accounts totaling $28,000 during the year. What were cash collections on sales during the year? If the company estimates expected bad debt expense as 0.5% of sales, what is the net realizable value of accounts receivable at year-end?

Required

Analyze each case separately and answer the requirements.

Problem 8-66
Estimating Uncollectible Accounts, Recording Write-Offs, and Applying an Aging Schedule **LO4**

At the beginning of 2020, the credit balance in the Allowance for Doubtful Accounts for Master Healthcare Inc. was $200,000. On an interim basis (during the year), the provision (expense) for doubtful accounts is estimated based on a percentage of net credit sales. Total sales revenue for 2020 amounted to $75 million, of which one-third was on credit. Based on the latest available information, the 2020 provision needed for doubtful accounts is estimated to be 0.75% of net credit sales. During 2020, uncollectible receivables amounting to $220,000 were written off.

Required

a. Compute the ending balance in Master Healthcares's Allowance for Doubtful Accounts at December 31, 2020.

b. Prepare its 2020 entries to write-off in uncollectible accounts and to estimate its allowance for doubtful accounts.

c. At the end of the year, the allowance is estimated based upon the following aging of accounts receivable. What is the estimated Allowance for Doubtful Accounts balance at December 31, 2020?

	Accounts Receivable	Probability of Collection	Number of Items
Less than 30 days	$ 650,000	95%	2,600
31–90 days............	200,000	90%	1,000
91–120 days...........	110,000	70%	733
Greater than 120 days	40,000	40%	1,600
	$1,000,000		

d. What information is available from the aging analysis in part *c* that is not apparent when using the percentage of credit sales approach?

Problem 8-67
Recording Entries and Reporting Short-Term Notes With and Without Stated Interest Rates **LO5**

On November 1, 2020, Rouse Inc. sold merchandise on credit to Customer A for $14,000 and received a six-month, 12%, interest-bearing note. On this same date, Customer B purchased identical merchandise for the same price and credit terms except that the note received by Rouse was noninterest-bearing (the interest was included in the face of the note). The annual accounting period for Rouse ends December 31.

Required

a. For the Customer A note:
   1. Prepare the journal entries required on November 1 and December 31 of 2020, and on May 1 of 2021.
   2. Indicate how this note impacts individual line items on the 2020 income statement and balance sheet.

b. For the Customer B note:
   1. Prepare the journal entries required on November 1 and December 31 of 2020, and on May 1 of 2021.
   2. Indicate how this note impacts individual line items on the 2020 income statement and December 31, 2020, balance sheet.

Problem 8-68
Recording Entries for Long-Term Note Receivable including Interest Revenue **LO5**

Savoy Inc. sold a building and the land on which it is located on January 1, 2020, and received a $150,000 noninterest-bearing note receivable that matures December 31, 2022. The $150,000 is to be paid in full on the maturity date. The sale was recorded as follows by Savoy. It has been determined that 12% is a realistic interest rate for this note. The annual reporting period ends December 31. The accounts have not been adjusted or closed for 2020.

Note Receivable	150,000	
Accumulated Depreciation, Building	100,000	
Building		150,000
Land		60,000
Gain on Sale of Assets		40,000

Required

a. Compute the present value of this note at January 1, 2020.

b. Prepare journal entries required as of the following dates.

1. January 1, 2020
2. December 31, 2020
3. December 31, 2021
4. December 31, 2022

Problem 8-69
Recording Entries and Preparing Effective Interest Table for Long-Term Note Receivable LO5

Watt Service Inc. completed a major renovation contract and billed the customer $56,000 on January 1, 2020. Cash of $16,000 was collected, and a 5% note was received for the remaining $40,000, payable in three equal annual installments (including principal plus interest) each December 31 of 2020, 2021, and 2022. The market rate of interest for notes with comparable risk is 12%.

Required

a. Compute the amount of each of the three annual payments on the note.

b. Compute the present value of the note at January 1, 2020.

c. Prepare an effective interest schedule for the note.

d. Prepare the journal entries required as of the following dates.

1. January 1, 2020
2. December 31, 2020
3. December 31, 2021
4. December 31, 2022

Problem 8-70
Recording Entries for the Assignment of Accounts Receivable LO6

Verona Company finances some of its current operations by using its accounts receivable as collateral for short-term cash loans. On July 1, 2020, Verona used its accounts receivable amounting to $50,000 as collateral for a loan from Adams Finance Company. The finance company advanced 80% of the accounts assigned, less a commission charge of 2% of the total accounts assigned. Also, the finance company charges 10% interest on the unpaid loan balance, payable at each month-end.

In July 2020, Verona Company collected $26,000 of these accounts, and in conformity with the contract, submitted the amount to the finance company for interest and principal.

In August 2020, Verona Company collected an additional $16,000 and paid the remaining amount due to the finance company.

Required

a. Record Verona's entry for the secured borrowing on July 1.

b. Record Verona's entry to collect accounts receivable and submit payment to the finance company in July 2020.

c. Record Verona's entry to collect accounts receivable and submit payment to the finance company in August 2020.

Problem 8-71
Recording Entries for the Sale of Accounts Receivable for the Company and the Factor LO6

Michael Company sells merchandise for $100,000 on credit and then sells those receivables to a finance company. All events occur within the current reporting year.

Required

Prepare journal entries to account for all events for the following two *separate* situations.

a. The receivables are sold on a *nonrecourse* basis. The factor charges 8% as a finance fee and withholds 10% of the receivables for sales returns, allowances, and discounts. The factor absorbs sales adjustments beyond 10%. The factor estimates that 0.5% of the receivables are uncollectible. Accounts receivable are collected less actual adjustments as follows: uncollectible accounts, $500; sales returns and allowances, $6,000; and sales discounts, $6,000. Prepare journal entries to account for these events for the:

1. Michael Company
2. Factor (finance company)

b. The receivables are sold on a *recourse* basis. The fee is 4%, and 15% is withheld. Michael expects $500 of uncollectible. Michael bears the cost of all sales adjustments and uncollectible accounts. Accounts receivable are collected less actual adjustments as follows: uncollectible accounts, $500; sales returns and allowances, $5,000; and sales discounts, $5,000. Prepare journal entries to account for these events for Michael Company only.

Problem 8-72
Recording Entries for the Discounting of a Note Receivable **LO6**

On May 1, 2020, Mark Company sold merchandise to Customer Kim for $40,000, credit terms 2/10, n/30. At the end of May, Customer Kim could not make payment. Instead, a six-month, 12% note receivable of $40,000 was received by Mark (dated June 1, 2020). Mark Company's accounting period ends December 31. On August 1, 2020, Mark discounted (sold) this note, with recourse, to City Bank at 14% interest. On the maturity date, Customer Kim paid the bank in full for the note.

Required

a. Prepare the required entry(ies) for Mark Company on May 1, 2020 (ignoring cost of goods sold).

b. Prepare the required entries for Mark Company on June 1, 2020, and August 1, 2020.

c. Assume instead that Mark sold the accounts receivable (without recourse) to a factor on May 2, 2020. The factor charges 8% as a finance fee and withholds 10% of the receivables for sales returns, allowances, and discounts. Prepare Mark's entry on May 2, 2020.

Problem 8-73
Preparing Entries for Sale of a Note with Subsequent Default and Non-Default **LO6**

On October 15, 2021, Farb Company sold identical merchandise for $12,000 on credit terms 2/10, n/30, to two different customers, designated as Customer X and Customer Y. Farb's annual reporting period ends December 31. These sales were recorded as follows.

	Customer X	Customer Y
Accounts receivable	$11,760	$11,760
Sales revenue.	11,760	11,760

The following events occurred for each customer. (Both transactions were recorded as sales.)

Customer X

Nov. 1, 2021	Could not pay the account; signed a $12,000, 10% note payable, due in 6 months on April 30, 2022.
Dec. 1, 2021	Sold (discounted) the X note to State Bank, with recourse, at 12% interest.
Apr. 30, 2022	Customer X defaulted.
July 31, 2022	Collected in full on the defaulted note plus an additional interest charge of 10% after due date.

Customer Y

Nov. 1, 2021	Could not pay the account; signed a $12,600 noninterest-bearing note, due in 6 months on April 30, 2022.
Dec. 1, 2021	Sold (discounted) the Y note to State bank, with recourse, at 12% interest.
Apr. 30, 2022	Customer Y paid the note in full on the maturity date.

Required

a. For the Customer X note, prepare the journal entries required as of the following dates.

1. November 1, 2021
2. December 1, 2021
3. December 31, 2021
4. April 30, 2022
5. July 31, 2022

b. For the Customer Y note, prepare the journal entries required as of the following dates.

1. November 1, 2021
2. December 1, 2021
3. December 31, 2021
4. April 30, 2022

Problem 8-74
Analyzing and Interpreting Ratios on Receivables **LO7**

A manufacturer-dealer of heavy equipment disclosed the following information related to its selling activities and receivables balances.

$ thousands	2021	2020	2019
Ending accounts receivable, gross	?	?	$3,000
Total net sales	$14,000	$12,000	9,000
Net credit sales	11,000	9,500	7,000
Collections on accounts receivable	7,900	7,700	6,000
Ending allowance for doubtful accounts	300	200	400
Accounts written off	400	500	600

Required

a. Determine the ending gross accounts receivable balance for (1) 2020 and (2) 2021.

b. Did the accounts receivable turnover rise or fall from 2020 to 2021, and by how much?

c. Compute the average days to collect receivables for (1) 2020 and (2) 2021. Comment on the factors that might have caused these two ratios to change in 2021.

d. What effect does a significant increase in bad debt expense have on (1) accounts receivable turnover and (2) average days to collect receivables?

e. What effect does factoring of accounts receivable, accounted for as a sale, have on (1) accounts receivable turnover and (2) average days to collect receivables? Explain the effect in both real and economic terms.

Accounting Decisions and Judgments

AD&J 8-75
Analyzing Bad Debt Expense and Analyzing Receivables Ratios **LO4**

Real World Analysis Information from a sciences and publishing company follows ($ millions).

For Year Ended December 31	Year 8	Year 7	Year 6
From statement of cash flows			
Net income	$333	$291	$496
Provision for losses on accounts receivable	105	81	65
From income statements			
Operating revenue	$3,719	$3,534	$3,074

December 31	Year 8	Year 7
From balance sheets		
Accounts receivable, net of allowance for doubtful accounts (Year 8, $212; Year 7, $183)	$951	$972

Bad debt expense on accounts receivable is substantial in relation to earnings. Assume a corporate tax rate of 40%. Information on accounts receivable written off and recoveries of accounts receivable previously written off was not available from the annual reports.

Required

a. What effect would each of the following have on Year 8 net income and Year 8 ending balance sheet accounts? Ignore differences between tax and financial reporting systems.
   1. Failure to provide for any bad debt expense.
   2. Failure to write off a worthless account of $0.6 million.

b. Assuming insignificant recoveries of bad debts previously written off, estimate write-offs of accounts receivable in Year 8.

c. For both Year 8 and Year 7, compute and comment on
   1. The relation between bad debt expense and operating revenue.
   2. The composite rate of uncollectible accounts as a percentage of gross accounts receivable.
   3. The relation between bad debt expense and write-offs.

AD&J 8-76 Drawing Inferences from Annual Reports Regarding Uncollectible Accounts, Write-Offs, and Cash Collections **LO4**

Real World Analysis Excerpts from **Ameritech**'s Year 8 annual report follow ($ millions).

Income Statement	Year 8	Year 7
Revenues	$17,154	$15,998
Net income	3,606	2,296

Balance Sheet		
Current assets		
Receivables, less allowance for uncollectibles of $338 and $308, respectively	$ 3,052	$ 3,078

Notes		
Provision for uncollectibles	$ 385	$ 355

Required

Answer the following questions assuming that Ameritech uses the allowance method to estimate bad debts (provision for uncollectibles) and that all revenues are credit sales.

a. Are estimated uncollectible accounts increasing or decreasing as a percentage of revenues?

b. What amount of write-offs of accounts receivable were recorded during Year 8?

c. What amount of cash was collected on receivables during Year 8?

d. If the provision for uncollectibles appeared in the statement of cash flows, where would it be shown? Explain.

AD&J 8-77 Comparing Alternative Methods of Recording and Reporting Bad Debts **LO4, 7**

Real World Analysis Notes to the Year 4 annual report of **Tyrex Oil Company**, located in Casper, Wyoming, follow.

> **Bad Debts**—The direct write-off method of accounting for uncollectible accounts receivable is utilized whereby an account is written off only when determined to be uncollectible. The results of this method do not vary materially from the preferred method.

Notes to the Year 4 annual report of **Wyoming Oil and Minerals Inc.**, which engages principally in the exploration, development, and production of oil and gas, included the following.

> The Company uses the direct write-off method for bad debts which expenses uncollectible accounts in the year they become uncollectible. Any difference between this method and the allowance method is not material.

The Year 4 balance sheet of **Sci Systems Inc.**, a government contracting firm, included the following.

June 30	Year 4	Year 3
Accounts receivable, net of $4,267,000 allowance in Year 4 and $4,600,000 in Year 3	$247,004,000	$201,919,000

Neither its income statement nor its statement of cash flows listed bad debt expense. Its notes included the following.

> Income tax expense differs from amounts currently payable, as certain revenues and expenses are reported in periods which differ from those in which they are taxed. The principal differences are that for income tax purposes: (a) income from certain long-term contracts is reported in accordance with income tax regulations; (b) accelerated depreciation of certain fixed assets is used; (c) the direct write-off method for doubtful accounts is used.

A later note described the differences between financial and tax reporting.

Expenses not currently deductible:	
Bad debt provision	$4,267,000

Required

a. Which of the three companies is using a method of recognizing bad debts for financial statement purposes different from the other two? Explain.

b. Why do you think the direct write-off method was used by some of these companies for financial statement purposes?

c. For Sci Systems, comment on the amounts reported for:
1. Year 4 ending allowance for doubtful accounts.
2. Year 4 bad debt expense.

AD&J 8-78
Inferring the Method Used to Record Cash Discounts **LO2**

Real World Analysis A recent annual report of **Knape & Vogt Manufacturing**, a manufacturer of home furnishings and storage systems, disclosed the following.

Current assets	
Accounts receivable, less allowance of $841,886 for doubtful accounts and cash discounts	$27,045,057

Required

Explain which method you believe was used to account for its cash discounts.

AD&J 8-79
Drawing Inferences from Disclosures for Receivables **LO5, 7**

Real World Analysis **Continental Medical Systems Inc.**, located in Mechanicsburg, Pennsylvania, is a provider of comprehensive medical rehabilitation programs and services. The company's Year 4 annual report disclosed the following information relating to notes receivable.

Balance Sheet	June 30, Year 4
Other receivables (in current assets)	$10,778,000
Notes receivable (in noncurrent assets)........	31,454,000

Disclosure The fair value of notes receivable was estimated by discounting the future cash flows using current rates available to similar borrowers under similar circumstances. All notes receivable bear interest at 5% to 12% and require future principal payments of approximately $547,000 in Year 5, $3,742,000 in Year 6, $1,015,000 in Year 7, $683,000 in Year 8, $661,000 in Year 9, and $25,353,000 thereafter. The current portion of these long-term notes is included in other receivables in the consolidated balance sheets.

Required

a. What can we say about the average term of the notes?

b. What can we say about the interest rates at which these notes were issued by customers of Continental Medical? Why would interest rates vary so much?

c. Do you believe the stated interest rate and the prevailing market rate at date of issue are similar or quite different? Explain.

AD&J 8-80
Analyzing Balance Sheet Amounts and Notes Related to Doubtful Accounts **LO4, 7**

Real World Analysis **Coca-Cola Company** financial statements provide partial information about uncollectible accounts ($ millions).

Balance Sheet (December 31)	2015	2014
Trade accounts receivable, less allowances of $352 and $331, respectively	$3,941	$4,466

Trade Accounts Receivable We record trade accounts receivable at net realizable value. This value includes an appropriate allowance for estimated uncollectible accounts to reflect any loss anticipated on the trade accounts receivable balances and charged to the provision for doubtful accounts. We calculate this allowance based on our history of write-offs, the level of past-due accounts based on the contractual terms of the receivables, and our relationships with, and the economic status of, our bottling partners and customers. We believe our exposure to concentrations of credit risk is limited due to the diverse geographic areas covered by our operations. Activity in the allowance for doubtful accounts was as follows:

continued

continued from previous page

Year Ended December 31 ($ millions)	2015	2014	2013
Balance at beginning of year	$331	$ 61	$53
Net charges to costs and expenses[1]	45	308	30
Write-offs	(10)	(13)	(14)
Other[2]	(14)	(25)	(8)
Balance at end of year	$352	$331	$61

[1]The increase in 2014 was primarily related to concentrate sales receivables from our bottling partner in Venezuela. See Hyperinflationary Economies discussion below for additional information.

[2]Other includes foreign currency translation and the impact of transferring certain assets to assets held for sale.

Required

a. Is Coca-Cola using the allowance method or the direct write-off method?

b. Can we determine bad debt expense for 2015?

c. Can we determine whether Coca-Cola uses the income statement method or the balance sheet method to estimate bad debt expense?

d. Assume that Coca-Cola uses a single composite rate of gross accounts receivable to estimate bad debts. Has the percentage of uncollectible accounts increased or decreased in 2015 relative to 2014? What might have caused the change?

e. Using the results from part *d* for 2015, estimate the maximum amount for Coca Cola's 2015 bad debt expense. (Sales for 2015 were $44,294 million.)

AD&J 8-81 Analyzing the Gross and Net Methods of Recording Sales and Communicating the Results **LO4**

Communication Case Assume you are the controller of a large wholesaler that sells most of its product to retailers on credit terms. The distribution and accounting functions for this company are relatively decentralized. For example, branches decide how to record routine operating transactions.

The accountant for the Washington branch, Toni Altair, is charged with implementing the accounting system at that branch. Toni joined the firm recently and has yet to make a decision on whether to use the gross method or the net method to record credit sales. The firm has an established discount program providing an incentive for quick payment by retailers. Toni has asked you to clarify when adjusting entries are necessary for material cash discounts at the end of the period under both methods. A considerable proportion of the firm's customers do not remit payment within the cash discount period.

Required

As the controller, send Toni a memo explaining when an adjusting entry is required at the end of a fiscal period under the gross and net methods for material cash discounts. Include in your message the general journal entries that would be required.

AD&J 8-82 Determining Whether Receivable Financing is a Sale or Loan **LO5**

Judgment Case The following situations involve transactions that should be classified as either a sale or a loan.

a. Sherman Company assigns $400,000 of accounts receivable as collateral for a loan (notification basis). Interest is charged on the monthly outstanding loan balance, and a 2% finance fee is charged immediately on the accounts assigned.

b. Hopper Company factors $50,000 of accounts receivable on a nonrecourse basis. The finance company charges an 8% fee and withholds 10% to cover sales adjustments. The finance company obtains title to the receivables and assumes collection responsibilities.

c. Pine Company factors $40,000 of accounts receivable on a recourse basis. Pine assumes the cost of all sales adjustments. The receivables are part of a much larger group of receivables. Pine's business is stable, and sales adjustments are readily estimable. Pine is compelled under the financing agreement to reimburse the finance company for any losses due to default by original customers.

d. Helms Company factors $80,000 of accounts receivable on a recourse basis. Helms assumes the cost of all sales adjustments and retains the option to repurchase the receivables. The option is easily satisfied in this market.

e. Gilbert Company discounts on a nonrecourse basis a $20,000 note received in a sale.

f. Franklin Company discounts on a recourse basis a $10,000 note received in a sale. The only provision of the financing agreement is that Franklin must reimburse the bank in the event of default by the original maker of the note.

g. Puget Company discounts on a recourse basis a $30,000 note received in a sale. The bank allows Puget to revoke the arrangement within four months.

h. Bellingham Company discounts on a recourse basis a $35,000 note received in a sale. Under the agreement, the bank may not sell or otherwise dispose of the note.

i. Pobedy Company pledges all of its accounts receivable as collateral for a loan. Pobedy must use the proceeds from the accounts receivable to service the loan. Pobedy retains title to the receivables. In the event of default by Pobedy on the loan, the finance company has a claim against any of these receivables for payment of the loan.

Required

For each of the situations, refer to the three conditions of ASC 860 and explain whether the financing of the receivables should be recorded as a sale or a loan.

AD&J 8-83
Analyzing Ethical Considerations in a Bank Reconciliation Process **LO8**

Ethics Case Assume Blueridge recently hired you as a junior accountant. Blueridge is a closely held, medium-sized retailing firm. One of your first assignments is to prepare the June bank reconciliation. The following information is available from its June bank statement and company records.

Deposits in transit.	$ 7,200	Outstanding checks	$9,750
Balance per bank statement. . .	16,500	NSF check returned	3,000
Bank service charges.	30	Deposit of $3,300 incorrectly recorded by the company as . . .	3,030

Your manager, the chief accountant for the company, who has limited cash disbursement responsibilities, tells you that the unadjusted balance of cash per the ledger at the end of June is unavailable. She also tells you that the reconciliation is needed immediately for a report to the vice president of finance. She instructs you to reduce the above outstanding check total by $2,600 "to adjust for earlier discrepancies." Accompanying the bank statement are canceled checks. Among them is a $2,600 check written to an individual not employed with the company, signed by your manager.

Required

a. Assuming that the information above is correct and complete, prepare the June bank reconciliation.

b. Comment on why the supervisor might have withheld information and made the unusual request for adjusting the bank reconciliation.

c. Describe your options and responsibilities in this situation, including ethical considerations and possible implications.

AD&J 8-84
Analyze the Interest Rate on Cash Discounts **LO2**

Judgment Case Maxfield Company sells $2,000 worth of merchandise on credit terms, 4/10, n/30. The buyer paid on the 15th day following the sale.

Required

Assuming a 365-day year, prepare a report addressing the following questions.

a. What is the effective annual interest rate paid by the buyer in this case?

b. How sensitive is this annual interest rate to:
   1. The number of days between the last day of the discount period and the payment date?
   2. The gross purchase price?
   3. The cash discount percentage?

AD&J 8-85
Searching the Codification to Define Key Terms **LO1, 4, 6**

Codification Skills Refer to the Codification and identify the definition for each of the following: (1) cash equivalents, (2) cash, (3) recourse, and (4) uncollectibility.

AD&J 8-86
Researching the Codification for Proper Citation **LO1, 3, 4, 5**

Codification Skills Research the Codification and report the proper citation that provides guidance on each of the following topics.

a. Reporting of restricted cash	FASB ASC	___-___-___-___
b. Basis for recording estimated sales returns	FASB ASC	___-___-___-___
c. Methods for calculating the allowance for doubtful accounts	FASB ASC	___-___-___-___
d. Basis for recording a note receivable (for cash) at present value	FASB ASC	___-___-___-___

Codification Skills A company is preparing annual financial statements, which includes the valuation of a note receivable. This note has no stated interest rate but must be discounted to its present value for accounting purposes. The company is unsure as to what interest rate to use to discount the note. Identify the relevant authoritative guidance.

FASB ASC [ ]-[ ]-[ ]-[ ]

AD&J 8-87 Researching the Codification for Authoritative Guidance **LO5**

Appendix—Questions

8-88. Why is a petty cash fund replenished at the end of a reporting period?

8-89. Where (if at all) do items in (a) through (g) belong in the following bank reconciliation?

Balance from bank statement, June 30	$ x,xxx.xx	Balance from company cash account, June 30	$ x,xxx.xx
Additions.	+	Additions.	+
Deductions	–	Deductions	–
June 30 correct cash balance.	$9,600.00	June 30 correct cash balance.	$9,600.00

a. Note collected by bank for the depositor on June 29; notification was received July 2 when the June 30 bank statement was received.

b. Checks drawn in June that had not cleared the bank by June 30.

c. Check of a depositor with a similar name that was returned with checks accompanying June 30 bank statement and was subtracted from the company's bank account.

d. Bank service charge for which notification was received on receipt of bank statement.

e. Deposit mailed June 30 that reached bank July 1 (not yet included in the bank statement).

f. Notification of charge for imprinting the company's name on blank checks was received with the June 30 bank statement.

g. Upon examination of the cash receipts journal, the company discovered that one receipt was omitted in arriving at the total that was posted to the cash account in the ledger.

8-90. Explain the basic purposes of a bank reconciliation.

8-91. Define the following terms related to accounting for cash.

a. Deposits in transit.

b. Checks outstanding.

c. NSF check.

d. Correct cash balance.

e. Cash short and cash over.

Appendix—Brief Exercises

Amounts from cash drawer of Retail Plus's deposits totaled $38,452.74 from its two retail locations at the end of the day, March 18, 2020. Revenue recorded for cash sales totaled $38,606.92, reported from the electronic register which produces a sales report at the end of each day. Prepare the journal entry to record sales on March 18, 2020. (Ignore cost of goods sold entries.)

App—Brief Exercise 8-92 Recording Entries for a Cash Drawer Reconciliation **LO8**

A petty cash fund was established on March 1, 2020, for $250. On March 15, 2020, the custodian requested a replenishment of the fund through the submission of the following receipts: office supplies, $45.68; miscellaneous expense, $8.48; and delivery charges $125. Record the following entries:

a. To establish the fund

b. To replenish the fund.

App—Brief Exercise 8-93 Recording Entries for a Petty Cash Fund **LO8**

The following information pertains to Zapp's Co., an apparel retailer, at December 31, 2020. In Zapp's December 31, 2020, balance sheet, at what amount should cash be reported?

App—Brief Exercise 8-94 Computing Cash Using Bank Reconciliation Information **LO8**

Bank statement balance	$10,000
Balance per books	15,000
Deposits in transit	5,000
Outstanding checks	1,000
Unrecorded electronic payment on bank statement	1,000

App—Brief Exercise 8-95
Preparing a Bank Reconciliation **LO8**

Foster Company, as a matter of policy, deposits all cash receipts and makes all payments by check. The following were taken from the cash records of the company. Reconcile the bank account as of June 30.

Deposits in transit	$1,950
Checks outstanding	400
June note collected (including 10% interest)	1,100
June bank charges	5
Bank balance, June 30	1,645
Book balance, June 30	2,100

App—Brief Exercise 8-96
Analyzing an Internal Control Environment **LO8**

A small manufacturer receives some payments through the mail through checks and others are electronically deposited in the company's bank account. For the payments that are received through the mail, the office administrator prepares a list of checks (including date, payee, amount, account number) and forwards the list to the controller. The office administrator deposits the checks and forwards the deposit slip to the controller. At the end of each month, the controller reconciles the bank statement to the accounting records. What suggestions would we have to improve the internal control environment?

App—Brief Exercise 8-97
Recording a Note Receivable Impairment **LO9**

At December 31, 2020, Kendall Co. held a $20,000, 6% note receivable from a customer. Kendall Co. is concerned with the general economic outlook and thinks that there is a possibility of default on the note receivable, but that default is not probable. Kendall Co. estimates that there is a 10% chance of a $5,000 default and a 90% chance of no default over the life of the note receivable. Record any necessary journal entry to recognize a loss on impairment.

App—Brief Exercise 8-98
Recording a Note Receivable Impairment **LO9**

Refer to the information in Appendix Brief Exercise 8-96. Assume, instead, that the company has adopted the Current Expected Credit Loss (CECL) Model to estimate impairment loss. Record any necessary journal entry to recognize a loss on impairment.

Appendix—Exercises

App—Exercise 8-99
Preparing Petty Cash Entries and Reporting of Petty Cash **LO8**

Main Company decided to use a petty cash system for making small payments. All petty cash expenditures were for administrative expenses. The company's annual year-end is December 31. The following transactions were completed during December 2020.

1. On December 1, 2020, the company treasurer prepared a $400 check payable to petty cash; the cash was given to the custodian.
2. Expenditures by the custodian (and signed receipts received) through December 20 were: postage, $80; office supplies, $70; subscriptions, $36; office equipment repairs, $120; coffee room supplies, $30; and miscellaneous items, $24. On December 20 the treasurer fully replenished the fund.
3. Expenditures by the custodian through December 31 were: postage, $26; office supplies, $36; subscriptions, $14; office equipment repairs, $42; coffee room supplies, $20; and miscellaneous items, $12. The fund was replenished on December 31.

Required

a. Prepare the necessary journal entries that should be made relating to the petty cash fund on:
   1. December 1, 2020
   2. December 20, 2020
   3. December 31, 2020

b. Indicate how the petty cash fund should be reported on the balance sheet. The regular cash account showed an ending cash balance of $193,000.

c. How are the petty cash transactions reported in the 2020 income statement?

App—Exercise 8-100
Recording Cash Reconciliation Adjustment **LO8**

Fashionable Inc. compiled the following amounts from cash drawer reconciliations of cash receipts: Cash collected: $38,932.20; checks collected: $2,310.77; cash refunds made: $328.12. Per the retail point of sales system through the input of the electronic register, amounts compiled were as follows: Cash collected: $39,002.10; checks collected: $2,342.77, and cash refunds made: $302.12. Record the necessary adjusting entry at the end of the day assuming that sales had been automatically recorded from information in the point of sales system.

App—Exercise 8-101
Preparing Entries to Establish, Reimburse, and Increase Petty Cash **LO8**

As a part of its newly designed internal control system, Waters Inc. established a petty cash fund. Transactions for the first month follow.

1. Wrote a check for $500 on August 1 and gave the cash to the fund custodian.
2. Count of petty cash on August 15 totaled $60. The fund is replenished on August 15.
3. Count of petty cash on August 31 totaled $34. The fund is replenished on August 31.
4. A summary of the petty cash expenditures made by the custodian follows.

	August 1–15	August 16–31
Postage used	$ 40	$ 58
Supplies purchased and used	265	190
Delivery expense	98	178
Miscellaneous expenses	35	40
Total	$438	$466

5. Increased the petty cash fund by $300 on August 31.

Required

Prepare the journal entries required on:

a. August 1, 2020
b. August 15, 2020
c. August 31, 2020

App—Exercise 8-102
Preparing a Bank Reconciliation and Recording Adjusting Entries **LO8**

a. Jones Company received its June 30 bank statement. A summary of this statement follows.

Bank balance, June 1	$23,000
Deposits and other credits	11,600
Checks and other debits	(12,120)
Interest earned on this statement	100
Bank balance, June 30	$22,580

Account transactions reflected in the bank statement follow.

Deposits	
June 1	$ 2,000
June 8	3,000
June 17	4,500
June 22	2,100
Total	$11,600

Checks					
June 2	#61	$1,000	June 17	#65	$ 400
June 7	#63	2,000	June 23	#60	1,100
June 9	#66	3,000	June 27	#67	2,100
June 14	#64	1,420	June 28	#59	1,100
		June total for checks	$12,120		

b. Transaction details involving the Jones Company's Cash account per its book follow.

Cash Account

Balance June 1		$23,900					
Deposits		12,300	Checks			$13,220	
June 8	$3,000		#60	$1,100	#65	$ 400	
June 17	4,500		#61	1,000	#66	3,000	
June 22	2,100		#62	900	#67	2,100	
June 30	2,700		#63	2,000	#68	1,300	
			#64	1,420			

c. A summary bank reconciliation at May 31 follows.

Bank balance	$23,000
Add deposits outstanding	2,000
Deduct check #59 outstanding	1,100
Book balance	$23,900

Required

a. Prepare the June bank reconciliation from this information.

b. Prepare any period-end adjusting entries required.

App—Exercise 8-103
Preparing a Bank Reconciliation and Adjusting Entries **LO8**

Reconciliation of Markus Theater's bank account at May 31 follows.

Balance from bank statement	$5,250	Balance from books	$5,932
Deposits in transit	750	Bank service charge	(7)
Checks outstanding	(75)		
Correct bank cash balance, May 31	$5,925	Correct book cash balance, May 31	$5,925

June transactions	Bank	Books
Checks recorded	$5,750	$5,900
Deposits recorded	4,050	4,500
Service charges recorded	6	—
Collection by bank ($1,000 note plus interest)	1,050	—
NSF check returned with June 30 statement (to be redeposited; assumed to be collectible)	25	—
Balances, June 30	4,569	4,525

Required

a. Prepare a bank reconciliation for June 2020.

b. Prepare all journal entries that should be made based on the June bank reconciliation.

App—Exercise 8-104
Preparing Entries for Note Receivable Impairment, Interest Accrual, and Receipt of Principal **LO9**

Gumco Inc., a calendar-year firm, carries a $12,000, 8% note received from the sale of merchandise worth $12,000 at January 1, 2020. The note is due December 31, 2023. Annual interest is due each December 31.

On December 31, 2020, Gumco reviews the collectibility of its notes and determines that only $9,000 is likely to be received on the due date.

Although Gumco received the 2020 interest payment, the company does not expect to receive further interest payments. On December 31, 2023, Gumco received $8,800 and expects no further payments.

Required

a. Prepare the entry to record the note receivable impairment. Illustrate the portion of the balance sheet showing the note.

b. Prepare the December 31, 2021, and 2022, entries to accrue interest. Gumco recognizes interest revenue using the effective interest method.

c. Prepare the entry to record the final receipt from the note.

App—Exercise 8-105
Computing Bad Debt Expense for Note Receivable Impairment **LO9**

On January 1, 2021, Wyoming Company received a $30,000, three-year note from a sale of equipment to Neil Company. This note has a market rate of 8%. On December 31, 2021, Wyoming estimated that Neil would only pay 50% of the note at maturity because of financial issues. What is the amount of bad debt expense that Wyoming would record on December 31, 2021?

Appendix—Problems

App—Problem 8-106
Adjusting for Cash Drawer Reconciliation **LO8**

Sunglasses Inc. accumulated the following information for its 5 cash drawers from its 5 retail kiosks with totals (1) from cash drawer counts of receipts at the end of the day and (2) the amount of sales recorded through the cash registers.

	Cash Drawer Count	Sales Recorded
Cash collected	$ 4,899.02	$ 4,756.62
Checks collected	234.12	234.12
Credit cards collected	41,032.21	41,032.21
Total collections	$46,165.35	$46,022.95

Required

Prepare the adjusting entry for the reconciliation between the cash drawer and recorded sales. Assume that the sales amounts have been automatically recorded in the accounting system as a debit to Cash and a credit to Sales Revenue.

App—Problem 8-107 Preparing Petty Cash Entries and a Bank Reconciliation **LO8**

Heiden Company instituted a petty cash fund on December 1, 2020 for $500. On December 31, 2020, the custodian presented the following receipts.

Supplies purchased and used	$98.45
Delivery charges	80.20
Online advertising fees	75.00
Miscellaneous expense	60.87

The fund was replenished on December 31, 2020, and was increased by $100. The following additional information was available regarding the company's bank account.

Cash balance per books, December 31, 2020	$1,090.81
Cash balance per bank statement, December 31, 2020	546.15
Deposits in transit, December	474.46
Outstanding checks, December	160.25
Bank service charge, December	25.00
Unrecorded electronic deposit per bank statement	1,000.00
Unrecorded electronic payment per bank statement	325.45
Cash not deposited (outside of petty cash fund)	880.00

Required

a. Record the journal entries to (1) establish the fund, (2) replenish the fund, and (3) increase the balance of the fund.

b. Prepare a bank reconciliation for the month of December.

c. Prepare a partial balance sheet to illustrate the presentation of the cash balance.

App—Problem 8-108 Preparing a Bank Reconciliation and Recording Adjusting Entries **LO8**

The following information is available to United Inc. in preparation of its March bank reconciliation.

a.

Company Cash Account			
March 1 balance	28,350		
Deposits	51,468	53,000	Checks

b. Bank statement for month, dated March 31.

Balance, March 1	$30,800
Deposits	51,198
Checks cleared	(54,118)
NSF check (Customer Zinny)	(100)
Note collected for depositor (including interest, $80)	1,680
Interest on bank balance	36
Bank service charge	(14)
Balance, March 31	$29,482

c. Additional information

1. The company overstated one of its deposits by $20; the bank recorded it correctly.
2. The bank cleared a $178 check as $187; the error has not yet been corrected by the bank.
3. End of February: deposits in transit, $1,550; checks outstanding, $4,000.

Required

a. Using this information, compute the March 31 (1) deposits in transit and (2) checks outstanding.
b. Prepare a bank reconciliation for March.
c. Prepare all journal entries that should be made based on the bank reconciliation in part *b.*

App—Problem 8-109
Preparing a Bank Reconciliation and Recording Adjusting Entries **LO8**

Ample Inc. carries its checking account with Commerce Bank. The company is ready to prepare its December 31 bank reconciliation. The following data are available.

1. The November 30 bank reconciliation showed the following: (1) cash (held back each day by Ample), $400 (included in Ample's Cash account); (2) deposit in transit, #51, $2,000; and (3) checks outstanding, #121, $1,000; #130, $2,000; and #142, $3,000.
2. A summary of Ample's Cash account for December follows.

Balance, December 1	$ 64,000
Deposits: #52–#55, $186,500; #56, $3,500	190,000
Checks: #143–#176, $191,000; #177, $2,500; #178, $3,000; and #179, $1,500	(198,000)
Balance, December 31 (includes $400 cash held each day for change)	$ 56,000

3. A summary of Ample's monthly bank statement at December 31 follows.

Balance, December 1	$ 67,600
Deposits: #51–#55	188,500
Checks: #130, $2,000; #142, $3,000; #143–#176, $191,000	(196,000)
Note collected for Ample Co. (including $720 in interest)	6,720
Fund transfer received for foreign revenue (not yet recorded by Ample)	10,000
NSF check, Customer Belinda	(200)
United Fund (per transfer authorization signed by Ample)	(50)
Bank service charges	(20)
Balance, December 31	$ 76,550

Required

a. Using this information, compute the December 31 (1) deposits in transit and (2) checks outstanding.
b. Prepare the December 31 bank reconciliation.
c. Prepare all journal entries that should be made based on the bank reconciliation in part *b.*

App—Problem 8-110
Record Note Receivable Impairment Entries **LO9**

Thames Inc. loaned Windsor Company $40,000 on January 1, 2016. The 8%, seven-year, simple-interest note called for annual interest payments each December 31. The note is due December 31, 2022. Windsor made the required interest payments through December 31, 2019.

In early January 2020, Windsor began to default on some of its other debts and asked Thames to renegotiate the original note agreement, asking for an extension of the maturity date. Thames refused but could see that the remaining scheduled payments on the note were in jeopardy.

Thames reevaluated the Windsor note and estimated that the remaining interest payments would be only 75% of the original amounts (based on the original principal amount) and that only 50% of the principal amount would be collected. Thames uses the interest method to account for interest after recording note impairment.

Required

a. Record the note impairment as of January 1, 2020.
b. Prepare the December 31, 2020, journal entries, assuming the reestimated interest payment is received.
c. The note is revalued on January 1, 2021. Thames now expects to collect only one more payment on the note receivable: $10,000 on December 31, 2022 (no further interest is expected to be collected). Prepare the January 1, 2021, entry to record the additional impairment.
d. Prepare the journal entries to be recorded on December 31, 2021, and December 31, 2022, assuming the new cash flow estimate is realized.

Answers to Review Exercises

Review 8-1

a. 1 *c.* 2 *e.* 5 *g.* 2

b. 4 *d.* 4 *f.* 3 *h.* 4

Review 8-2

a. **January 1, 2020—To record sale on account under the gross method**

Accounts Receivable	2,800	
Sales Revenue		2,800

Assets = Liabilities + Equity: +2,800 = +2,800
Accounts Rec: 2,800 | ; Sales Rev: | 2,800

January 5, 2020—To record collection on account under the gross method

Cash ($2,800 − $56)	2,744	
Sales Discount ($2,800 × 0.02)	56	
Accounts Receivable		2,800

Assets = Liabilities + Equity: +2,744, −2,800 = −56
Cash: 2,744 | ; Sales Discount: 56 | ; Accounts Rec: 2,800 | 2,800

b. **January 1, 2020—To record sale on account under the gross method**

Accounts Receivable	2,800	
Sales Revenue		2,800

Assets = Liabilities + Equity: +2,800 = +2,800
Accounts Rec: 2,800 | ; Sales Rev: | 2,800

January 25, 2020—To record collection on account under the gross method

Cash	2,800	
Accounts Receivable		2,800

Assets = Liabilities + Equity: +2,800, −2,800
Cash: 2,800 | ; Accounts Rec: 2,800 | 2,800

c. **January 1, 2020—To record sale on account under the net method**

Accounts Receivable ($2,800 × 0.98)	2,744	
Sales Revenue		2,744

Assets = Liabilities + Equity: +2,744 = +2,744
Accounts Rec: 2,744 | ; Sales Rev: | 2,744

January 5, 2020—To record collection on account under the net method

Cash	2,744	
Accounts Receivable		2,744

Assets = Liabilities + Equity: +2,744, −2,744
Cash: 2,744 | ; Accounts Rec: 2,744 | 2,744

d. **January 1, 2020—To record sale on account under the net method**

Accounts Receivable ($2,800 × 0.98)	2,744	
Sales Revenue		2,744

Assets = Liabilities + Equity: +2,744 = +2,744
Accounts Rec: 2,744 | ; Sales Rev: | 2,744

January 25, 2020—To record collection on account under the net method

Cash	2,800	
Sales Discount Forfeited		56
Accounts Receivable		2,744

Assets = Liabilities + Equity: +2,800, −2,744 = +56
Cash: 2,800 | ; Sales Discount Forfeit: | 56 ; Accounts Rec: 2,744 | 2,744

Review 8-3

2020—To record the sale of merchandise

Accounts Receivable	28,000	
Sales Revenue		28,000

Assets = Liabilities + Equity: +28,000 = +28,000
Accounts Rec: 28,000 | ; Sales Rev: | 28,000

Cost of Goods Sold	16,800	
Inventory		16,800

Assets = Liabilities + Equity: −16,800 = −16,800
COGS: 16,800 | ; Inventory: | 16,800

2020—To record the return of merchandise

Assets = Liabilities + Equity: Assets −800; Equity −800
Cash or Receiv: Cr. 800 | Sales Returns: Dr. 800

Sales Returns	800	
Cash or Accounts Receivable		800

Assets = Liabilities + Equity: Assets +480; Equity +480
Inventory: Dr. 480 | COGS: Cr. 480

Inventory	480	
Cost of Goods Sold		480

December 31—To record estimated returns

Assets = Liabilities + Equity: Liabilities +320; Equity −320
Refund Liab: Cr. 320 | Sales Returns: Dr. 320

Sales Returns [(0.04 × $28,000) − $800]	320	
Refund Liability		320

Assets = Liabilities + Equity: Assets +192; Equity +192
Inv—Est Returns: Dr. 192 | COGS: Cr. 192

Inventory—Estimated Returns ($320 × ($16,800/$28,000))	192	
Cost of Goods Sold		192

Review 8-4

a. **(1) December 31, 2020—To record bad debt expense**

Assets = Liabilities + Equity: Assets −2,000; Equity −2,000
AFDA: Cr. 10,000 Bal., 2,000 | Bad Debt Exp: Dr. 2,000

Bad Debt Expense	2,000	
Allowance for Doubtful Accounts ([$400,000 × 0.03] − $10,000)		2,000

(2) December 31, 2020—To record bad debt expense

Assets = Liabilities + Equity: Assets −2,900; Equity −2,900
AFDA: Cr. 10,000 Bal., 2,900 | Bad Debt Exp: Dr. 2,900

Bad Debt Expense	2,900	
Allowance for Doubtful Accounts*		2,900

*([$300,000 × 0.02] + [$90,000 × 0.06] + [$10,000 × 0.15]) − $10,000 = $2,900

b. (1) $388,000 ($400,000 − $12,000) (2) $387,100 ($400,000 − $12,900)

c. **January 15, 2020—To record account write-off**

Assets = Liabilities + Equity: Assets +1,400, −1,400
Accounts Rec: Dr. Bal. 400,000; Cr. 1,400 | AFDA: Dr. 1,400; Cr. 10,000 Bal., 2,900

Allowance for Doubtful Accounts	1,400	
Accounts Receivable		1,400

d. **January 31, 2021—To record unexpected collection on account**

Assets = Liabilities + Equity: Assets +1,400, −1,400
Accounts Rec: Dr. Bal. 400,000, 1,400; Cr. 1,400 | AFDA: Dr. 1,400; Cr. 10,000 Bal., 2,900, 1,400

Accounts Receivable	1,400	
Allowance for Doubtful Accounts		1,400

Assets = Liabilities + Equity: Assets +1,400, −1,400
Cash: Dr. 1,400 | Accounts Rec: Dr. Bal. 400,000, 1,400; Cr. 1,400, 1,400

Cash	1,400	
Accounts Receivable		1,400

Review 8-5

a. $25,000
b. $2,000 ($25,000 × 0.08)
c. $2,000 ($25,000 × 0.08)
d. $23,663 PV(0.08,2,−1250,−25000)
e. $1,893 ($23,663 × 0.08)
f. $1,250 ($25,000 × 0.05)
g. $21,433 PV(0.08,2,0,−25000)
h. $1,715 ($21,433 × 0.08)
i. $0
j. $25,917 PV(0.06,2,−2000,−25000)
k. $1,555 ($25,917 × 0.06)
l. $2,000 ($25,000 × 0.08)

Review 8-6

April 1, 2020—To record assignment of receivables

Cash ([0.75 × $300,000] − $4,500)	220,500	
Finance Expense (0.015 × $300,000)	4,500	
Note Payable (0.75 × $300,000)		225,000

Assets = Liabilities + Equity
+220,500 +225,000 −4,500
Cash: 220,500 (Dr.)
Note Payable: 225,000 (Cr.)
Finance Exp: 4,500 (Dr.)

April 1, 2020—To record sale of receivables without recourse

Cash ($300,000 − $45,000 − $24,000)	231,000	
Receivable from Factor (0.15 × $300,000)	45,000	
Loss on Sale of Receivables (0.08 × $300,000)	24,000	
Accounts Receivable		300,000

Assets = Liabilities + Equity
+231,000 −24,000
+45,000
−300,000
Cash: 231,000 (Dr.)
Loss on Sale of Rec: 24,000 (Dr.)
Rec from Factor: 45,000 (Dr.)
Accounts Rec: Bal. 300,000 (Dr.) | 300,000 (Cr.)

April 1, 2020—To record sale of receivables with recourse

Cash ($300,000 − $15,000 − $30,000)	255,000	
Receivable from Factor (0.10 × $300,000)	30,000	
Loss on Sale of Receivables [(0.05 × $300,000) + $3,000]	18,000	
Recourse Liability (0.01 × $300,000)		3,000
Accounts Receivable		300,000

Assets = Liabilities + Equity
+255,000 +3,000 −18,000
+30,000
−300,000
Cash: 255,000 (Dr.)
Loss on Sale of Rec: 18,000 (Dr.)
Rec from Factor: 30,000 (Dr.)
Recourse Liab: 3,000 (Cr.)
Accounts Rec: Bal. 300,000 (Dr.) | 300,000 (Cr.)

Review 8-7

Accounts receivable turnover ratio:

Ford Motor: Year 3: 12.78 ($141,546 ÷ [{$11,102 + $11,042}/2]) Year 2: 12.36 ($140,566 ÷ [{$11,042 + $11,708}/2])

General Motors: Year 3: 17.45 ($156,849 ÷ [{$9,638 + $8,337}/2]) Year 2: 16.76 ($145,922 ÷ [{$8,337 + $9,078}/2])

Average days to collect receivables:

Ford Motor: Year 3: 28.6 days (365 ÷ 12.78) Year 2: 29.5 days (365 ÷ 12.36)

General Motors: Year 3: 20.9 days (365 ÷ 17.45) Year 2: 21.8 days (365 ÷ 16.76)

Review 8-8

Part One May 1, 2020—To record cash over and short

Cash Over and Short	81.60	
Cash		81.60

Assets = Liabilities + Equity
−81.60 −81.60
Cash: 81.60 (Cr.)
Cash Over/Short: 81.60 (Dr.)

Part Two June 1, 2020—To establish petty cash fund

Petty Cash	750	
Cash		750

Assets = Liabilities + Equity
+750
−750
Petty Cash: 750 (Dr.)
Cash: 750 (Cr.)

June 30, 2020—To record replenishment of the petty cash fund

Postage Expense	50	
Office Supplies Expense	210	
Office Repair Expense	50	
Coffee Room Supplies Expense	100	
Office Social Expense	25	
Miscellaneous Expense	50	
Cash		485

Assets = Liabilities + Equity
−485 −485
Cash: 485 (Cr.)
Misc Expenses: 485 (Dr.)

Part Three

Bank balance, unadjusted	$4,540	Book balance, unadjusted	$4,785
Deposits in transit	1,200	Service charge	(15)
Outstanding checks	(250)	Bank direct deposits	800
		Bank electronic payment	(80)
Adjusted bank balance	$5,490	Adjusted book balance	$5,490

Review 8-9

a. **December 31, 2020—To record loan impairment**

Assets = Liabilities + Equity
−8,119 −8,119
AFDA: | 8,119
Bad Debt Exp: 8,119 |

Bad Debt Expense	8,119	
Allowance for Doubtful Accounts		8,119

b. **December 31, 2021—To record interest revenue**

Assets = Liabilities + Equity
+713 +713
AFDA: 713 | 8,119
Interest Rev: | 713

Allowance for Doubtful Accounts	713	
Interest Revenue		713

December 31, 2022—To record interest revenue

Assets = Liabilities + Equity
+756 +756
AFDA: 713, 756 | 8,119
Interest Rev: | 713, 756

Allowance for Doubtful Accounts	756	
Interest Revenue		756

December 31, 2023—To record interest revenue

Assets = Liabilities + Equity
+801 +801
AFDA: 713, 756, 801 | 8,119
Interest Rev: | 713, 756, 801

Allowance for Doubtful Accounts	801	
Interest Revenue		801

c. **December 31, 2024—To record receipt of principal on note receivable**

Assets = Liabilities + Equity
+14,200 +49
+5,849
−20,000
Cash: 14,200 |
AFDA: 713, 756, 801, 5,849 | 8,119
Interest Rev: | 713, 756, 801, 49
Note Receiv: Bal. 20,000 | 20,000

Cash	14,200	
Allowance for Doubtful Accounts ($8,119 − $713 − $756 − $801)	5,849	
Note Receivable		20,000
Interest Revenue (to balance)		49

9 Inventory: Measurement

Target Corporation Consolidated Statements of Financial Position	January 28, 2017	January 30, 2016
(millions, except footnotes)		
Assets		
Cash and cash equivalents, including short-term investments of $1,110 and $3,008	$ 2,512	$ 4,046
Inventory	8,309	8,601
Assets of discontinued operations	69	322
Other current assets	1,100	1,161
Total current assets	$11,990	$14,130

12. Inventory

The vast majority of our inventory is accounted for under the retail inventory accounting method (RIM) using the last-in, first-out (LIFO) method. Inventory is stated at the lower of LIFO cost or market. The cost of our inventory includes the amount we pay to our suppliers to acquire inventory, freight costs incurred in connection with the delivery of product to our distribution centers and stores, and import costs, reduced by vendor income and cash discounts. The majority of our distribution center operating costs, including compensation and benefits, are expensed in the period incurred. Inventory is also reduced for estimated losses related to shrink and markdowns. The LIFO provision is calculated based on inventory levels, markup rates, and internally measured retail price indices.

Under RIM, inventory cost and the resulting gross margins are calculated by applying a cost-to-retail ratio to the inventory retail value. RIM is an averaging method that has been widely used in the retail industry due to its practicality. The use of RIM will result in inventory being valued at the lower of cost or market because permanent markdowns are taken as a reduction of the retail value of inventory.

We routinely enter into arrangements with vendors whereby we do not purchase or pay for merchandise until the merchandise is ultimately sold to a guest. Activity under this program is included in sales and cost of sales in the Consolidated Statements of Operations, but the merchandise received under the program is not included in inventory in our Consolidated Statements of Financial Position because of the virtually simultaneous purchase and sale of this inventory. Sales made under these arrangements totaled $2,202 million, $2,261 million, and $2,040 million in 2016, 2015, and 2014, respectively.

STARBUCKS CORPORATION
CONSOLIDATED BALANCE SHEETS
(in millions, except per share data)

ASSETS	Oct 2, 2016	Sep 17, 2015
Current assest:		
Cash and cash equivalents	$ 2,128.8	$ 1,530.1
Short-term investments	134.4	81.3
Accounts receivable, net	768.8	719.0
Inventories	1,378.5	1,306.4
Prepaid expenses and other current assets	350.0	334.2
Total current assets	$4,760.5	$3,971.0

	Oct 2, 2016	Sep 17, 2015
Coffee:		
Unroasted	$ 561.6	$ 529.4
Roasted	300.4	279.7
Other merchandise held for sale	308.6	318.3
Packaging and other supplies	207.9	179.0
Total	$1,378.5	$1,306.4

Other merchandise held for sale includes, among other items, serveware and tea. Inventory levels vary due to seasonality, commodity market supply and price fluctuations.

As of October 2, 2016, we had committed to purchasing green coffee totaling $466 million under fixed-price contracts and an estimated $641 million under price-to-be-fixed contracts. As of October 2, 2016, approximately $7 million of our price-to-be-fixed contracts were effectively fixed through the use of futures contracts. Price-to-be-fixed contracts are purchase commitments whereby the quality, quantity, delivery period and other negotiated terms are agreed upon, but the date, and therefore the price, at which the base "C" coffee commodity price component will be fixed has not yet been established. For most contracts, either Starbucks or the seller has the option to "fix" the base "C" coffee commodity price prior to the delivery date. For other contracts, Starbucks and the seller may agree upon pricing parameters determined by the base "C" coffee commodity price. Until prices are fixed, we estimate the total cost of these purchase commitments. We believe, based on relationships established with our suppliers in the past, the risk of non-delivery on these purchase commitments is remote.

Inventories

Inventories are stated at the lower of cost (primarily moving average cost) or market. We record inventory reserves for obsolete and slow-moving inventory and for estimated shrinkage between physical inventory counts. Inventory reserves are based on inventory obsolescence trends, historical experience and application of the specific identification method. As of October 2, 2016 and September 27, 2015, inventory reserves were $39.6 million and $33.8 million, respectively.

Chapter Preview

We begin this chapter by determining what items to include and exclude in inventory. The allocation of costs between ending inventory and cost of goods sold is demonstrated under the periodic system using the cost-flow assumptions of the specific identification, average cost, FIFO (first-in, first-out), and LIFO (last-in, last-out) methods. Next, the allocation of costs is demonstrated under the perpetual inventory system using the cost-flow assumptions of the moving average, FIFO, and LIFO inventory methods. Additional topics related to LIFO are described, including the LIFO reserve, LIFO liquidation, and the dollar-value LIFO method. We conclude with inventory ratio analyses.

Action Plan

LO	Topic/Subtopic	Page	Demos	Reviews	Assignments
LO 9–1	**Determine the initial recognition and measurement of inventory** In Transit Inventory :: Goods on Consignment :: Repurchase Agreement :: Estimated Sales Returns	9-3	D9-1	R9-1	27, 28, 42, 43, 44, 67, 68, 83, 92, 93, 94
LO 9–2	**Demonstrate accounting in a periodic inventory system** Periodic Inventory System :: Gross Method :: Net Method	9-5	D9-2A D9-2B	R9-2	27, 29, 42, 45, 46, 47, 49, 50, 51, 67, 68, 70, 71, 72, 83, 89
LO 9–3	**Demonstrate specific identification, average cost, FIFO, and LIFO in a periodic inventory system** Periodic Inventory System :: Specific Identification :: Average Cost :: FIFO :: LIFO	9-9	D9-3A D9-3B D9-3C D9-3D	R9-3	30, 31, 32, 52, 54, 55, 56, 57, 65, 67, 73, 75, 76, 83, 84, 89, 90, 93
LO 9–4	**Demonstrate accounting in a perpetual inventory system** Perpetual Inventory System :: Gross Method :: Net Method	9-15	D9-4A D9-4B	R9-4	33, 34, 35, 48, 49, 50, 51, 67, 70, 72
LO 9–5	**Demonstrate moving average, FIFO, and LIFO in a perpetual inventory system** Perpetual Inventory System :: Moving Average :: FIFO :: LIFO	9-17	D9-5A D9-5B D9-5C	R9-5	36, 37, 53, 54, 55, 57, 65, 67, 69, 74, 75, 83, 93
LO 9–6	**Explain and compute a LIFO reserve** LIFO Inventory Reserve :: Allowance to Reduce FIFO to LIFO	9-21	D9-6	R9-6	38, 58, 67, 76, 85, 86, 87, 88
LO 9–7	**Describe and compute the effect of LIFO liquidation** LIFO Liquidation :: Voluntary :: Involuntary :: Disclosure	9-22	D9-7	R9-7	39, 59, 60, 67, 77, 78, 93
LO 9–8	**Apply the dollar-value LIFO method** Dollar-Value LIFO :: Base Year :: Price Indices :: Inventory Layers	9-24	D9-8	R9-8	40, 61, 62, 63, 64, 65, 67, 79, 80, 81, 82
LO 9–9	**Perform inventory ratio analysis and interpretation** Inventory Turnover :: Average Days in Inventory	9-27	D9-9	R9-9	41, 66, 67, 84, 91

LO 9-1 Determine the initial recognition and measurement of inventory

LO 9-1 Overview

Inventory Considerations
- Recognition
  - In-transit inventory
  - Consigned inventory
  - Repurchase agreements
- Measurement
  - Acquisition cost
  - Cost to prepare item for sale

Recall from Chapter 7 that *control* of a good, such as inventory, implies that a company can direct its use and derive its benefits. **Inventories** are goods controlled by a company and held either for use in the manufacture of products or as products awaiting sale.

ASC Glossary **Inventory**—The aggregate of those items of tangible personal property that have any of the following characteristics: (a) Held for sale in the ordinary course of business (b) In process of production for such sale (c) To be currently consumed in the production of goods or services to be available for sale.

Depending on the nature of a company's business, inventory can consist of virtually any tangible good or material. **We focus on inventory of a merchandiser (retailer or wholesaler) that purchases goods in a form ready for sale.**

Recognition of Inventory

All inventoriable goods controlled by a company on an inventory date should be recognized on a company's balance sheet as inventory, regardless of their location. At any time, a company can hold goods that it does not control or control goods that it does not hold. *This means that care must be taken to identify goods properly includable in inventory.* Exhibit 9-1 summarizes the treatment of inventory that is in transit during a physical inventory count or included as part of a consignment or a repurchase agreement. These concepts are applied in **Demo 9-1**.

EXHIBIT 9-1 Adjustments to the Physical Inventory Count

Inventory Scenario	Treatment of Inventory
Goods in transit shipped f.o.b. *destination* from supplier to merchandiser.	Include in inventory of supplier.
Goods in transit shipped f.o.b. *shipping* from supplier to merchandiser.	Include in inventory of merchandiser.
Goods in transit shipped f.o.b. *destination* from a merchandiser to a customer.	Include in inventory of merchandiser.
Goods in transit shipped f.o.b. *shipping* from a merchandiser to a customer.	Include in inventory of customer.
Consigned inventory, owned by a consignor but held by a consignee.	Include in inventory of consignor.
Inventory sold to customer with seller repurchase requirements.	Include in inventory of seller.

Goods in Transit Goods purchased and in transit should be included in the purchaser's inventory provided that control has passed to the purchaser. Control for goods in transit is typically determined by legal title.

- If goods are shipped **f.o.b. (free on board) destination**, legal title passes when buyer receives goods from carrier.
- If goods are shipped **f.o.b. (free on board) shipping**, legal title passes when goods are released to carrier.

Goods on Consignment A **consignment** relationship is one where a company (consignor) ships goods to a distributor (consignee) but retains legal title of the goods until a predetermined event occurs, such as the sale of the product to a customer. Goods on consignment should be *included* in inventory of the consignor (owner of the inventory) when the consignee (holder of the inventory) does not take control of the inventory. Accordingly, inventory held on consignment by the consignee should be *excluded* from the consignee's inventory.

Goods Under Repurchase Agreements Some companies enter into repurchase agreements to sell and later buy back inventory items at prearranged prices. One motivation for such a transaction is that it provides a way for a company to finance its inventory purchases. In other words, the seller gains immediate access to cash by selling the inventory and later repurchases the same inventory at a predetermined price. In a case where the seller is *obligated* to buy back the inventory, the seller retains control of the inventory and the inventory would remain on the seller's balance sheet. See Chapter 7 for additional discussion on the accounting for repurchase agreements.

Estimated Sales Returns At times, sales agreements permit goods to be returned to the seller. For any amounts received (or receivable) for which a seller does not expect to be entitled, the company records a refund liability. The company would also record an asset (inventory—estimated returns) for the right to recover the inventory estimated to be returned. See Chapter 8 for an expanded discussion on accounting for sales returns.

606-10-55-27 An asset recognized for an entity's right to recover products from a customer on settling a refund liability initially should be measured by reference to the former carrying amount of the product (for example, inventory) less any expected costs to recover those products (including potential decreases in the value to the entity of returned products). At the end of each reporting period, an entity should update the measurement of the asset arising from changes in expectations about products to be returned. An entity should present the asset separately from the refund liability.

EXPANDING YOUR KNOWLEDGE — **Manufacturing Inventory**

A manufacturing entity acquires raw materials and component parts to manufacture finished products, and then sells them. Through the various stages of the manufacturing process, at least four categories of inventories arise.

- **Raw materials inventory** Tangible goods purchased for direct use in the manufacture of goods for resale such as zinc used in the production of batteries.
- **Work-in-process inventory** Goods requiring further processing before completion and sale, such as unfinished batteries in the production process. Work-in-process inventory includes the cost of direct material, direct labor, and allocated manufacturing overhead costs incurred to date.
- **Finished goods inventory** Manufactured items completed and held for sale, such as packaged batteries ready for sale. Finished goods inventory cost includes the cost of direct material, direct labor, and allocated manufacturing overhead related to its manufacture.
- **Manufacturing supplies inventory** Grease and lubrication oils for machinery, cleaning materials, and other items that make up an insignificant part of finished products.

The flow of inventory costs in a manufacturing setting follows. The inventory valuation methods discussed in this chapter are used in recording cost flows through the manufacturing process.

Initial Measurement of Inventory

Inventory cost is measured by the total cash equivalent outlay made *to acquire goods and to prepare them for sale to customers*. Such cost includes the purchase cost, transportation costs (also called freight-in), transportation insurance, storage fees, sales tax, tariffs, and other costs to prepare inventory for sale. The initial measurement of inventory is reduced by **purchase (cash) discounts** offered by sellers to encourage timely payment from buyers (which speeds up cash flow and reduces borrowing costs for the seller). The accounting for purchase discounts is shown in LO 9-2 (periodic system) and LO 9-4 (perpetual system). Inventory costs do *not* include abnormal costs such as excessive spoilage costs or abnormal shipping costs for a rush delivery. Instead, abnormal costs are expensed as incurred.

Merchandise inventory represents goods purchased for resale by a retailer or a wholesaler. For most merchandisers, goods acquired are not physically altered by the purchaser because the goods are in finished form.

330-10-30-1 The primary basis of accounting for inventories is cost, which has been defined generally as the price paid or consideration given to acquire an asset. As applied to inventories, cost means in principle the sum of the applicable expenditures and charges directly or indirectly incurred in bringing an article to its existing condition and location. It is understood to mean acquisition and production cost, and its determination involves many considerations.

330-10-30-7 Unallocated overheads shall be recognized as an expense in the period in which they are incurred. Other items such as abnormal freight, handling costs, and amounts of wasted materials (spoilage) require treatment as current period charges rather than as a portion of the inventory cost.

EXPANDING YOUR KNOWLEDGE **Period Costs**

Period costs are generally expensed in the period incurred (meaning they are excluded from inventory) because they are indirectly related to the purchase or manufacturing of goods. Examples are:

- **General, selling, and administrative expenses** Ordinarily treated as period expenses because they relate more directly to accounting periods than to inventory. Chapter 7 explains accounting for shipping and handling costs.
- **330-10-30-8** "Under most circumstances, general and administrative expenses shall be included as period charges, except for the portion of such expenses that may be clearly related to production and thus constitute a part of inventory costs (product charges). Selling expenses constitute no part of inventory costs . . . General and administrative expenses ordinarily shall be charged to expense as incurred."
- **Interest costs** Normally expensed as incurred. However, in certain cases where a company constructs assets (for internal use or as discrete projects for sale) over a considerable period of time, some interest can be capitalized—see Chapter 11 for more information on capitalization of interest.

Demo 9-1 **LO9-1** **Recognition and Measurement of Inventory**

Demo MBC

Part One: Recognition of Inventory

Indicate whether each item, 1 through 7, should be *included* or *excluded* from ending inventory of Nadia Inc. on December 31, 2020.

Inventory Description	Include in Dec. 31, 2020 Inventory	Exclude from Dec. 31, 2020 Inventory
1. Merchandise inventory out at a dealer, on consignment.	✔	
2. Inventory held on consignment for another company.		✔
3. Merchandise inventory purchased, in transit, shipped f.o.b. shipping point.	✔	
4. Merchandise inventory purchased, in transit, shipped f.o.b. destination.		✔
5. Merchandise inventory sold, in transit, shipped f.o.b. shipping point.		✔
6. Merchandise inventory sold, in transit, shipped f.o.b. destination.	✔	
7. Inventory sold where Nadia Inc. has an obligation to later repurchase the inventory at a specified price.	✔	

Solution

In the four instances where Nadia Inc. is in control of the inventory, the inventory is included on the company's balance sheet on December 31, 2020. In the three other cases, Nadia Inc. is not in control of the inventory; therefore, inventory is excluded from its balance sheet.

Part Two: Initial Measurement of Inventory

Indicate which costs would be included in the initial measurement of merchandise inventory.

a. _✔_ Sales tax on merchandise purchased

b. ___ Cost of freight to ship merchandise to customer (freight-out)

c. _✔_ Insurance on merchandise stored before sale

d. _✔_ Labor costs for placing merchandise on shelves for sale

e. ___ Water damage to merchandise held for sale due to flood

f. _✔_ Labor costs for unloading truck of merchandise received from vendor

TARGET [TGT]

TARGET **Real World—INVENTORY ON CONSIGNMENT**

Target Corporation described a consignment arrangement in a recent Form 10-K where merchandise is not owned by Target until the merchandise is sold. Because the inventory is simultaneously purchased and sold, Target does not include inventory on its balance sheet for the consigned inventory that was purchased because the sale takes place immediately. All merchandise held on consignment (and not yet sold) is also excluded from Target's balance sheet.

continued

continued from previous page

Inventory We routinely enter into arrangements with vendors whereby we do not purchase or pay for merchandise until the merchandise is ultimately sold to a guest. Activity under this program is included in sales and cost of sales in the Consolidated Statements of Operations, but the merchandise received under the program is not included in inventory in our Consolidated Statements of Financial Position because of the virtually simultaneous purchase and sale of this inventory. Sales made under these arrangements totaled $2,261 million, $2,040 million, and $1,833 million in 2015, 2014, and 2013, respectively.

Measurement of Ending Inventory **LO9-1** **REVIEW 9-1**

The unadjusted inventory balance of Conway Corp. is $800,000 on December 31, 2020, based upon a physical inventory count. A number of items must be considered before the inventory valuation is finalized.

1. On December 31, the physical inventory excluded $10,000 of merchandise inventory shipped f.o.b. destination to Conway Corp. from a vendor. The inventory arrived on January 5, 2021.
2. On December 31, the physical inventory included $1,500 of merchandise held on consignment. The consignor is PackagingPlus Inc.
3. $75,000 of in-transit merchandise was shipped f.o.b. shipping point to a customer and was excluded from the physical inventory count. The merchandise was shipped on December 28, 2020, and is expected to arrive at the customer's site on December 31, 2020.
4. On December 31, the physical inventory excluded $25,000 of merchandise inventory held on consignment by a customer. Conway Corp. is the consignor.
5. Goods are in-transit from a vendor to Conway Corp. on December 31, 2020. The invoice cost was $40,000 and the goods were shipped f.o.b. shipping point on December 26, 2020. The merchandise was excluded from the physical inventory count because the merchandise had not been received.
6. Merchandise with a cost of $30,000 is held in the receiving department for return, but Conway still controls this inventory. The merchandise was excluded from the physical inventory count.

Required

Calculate the adjusted inventory balance on December 31, 2020.

More Practice: 9-28, 9-43, 9-44

Solution on p. 9-53.

Demonstrate accounting in a PERIODIC inventory system LO 9-2

The majority of inventory accounting issues stem from the need to determine the cost of goods sold as reported on the income statement and, simultaneously, the inventory values to be reported on the balance sheet. This means that the dollar amount of cost of goods available for sale for the accounting period must be allocated between expense (cost of goods sold) and assets (ending inventory) by the end of the accounting period as illustrated in **Exhibit 9-2**.

Accounting under a Periodic Inventory System (LO 9-2 Overview)

- Determine ending inventory through a physical inventory count
- Determine COGS after physical inventory count
- Use temporary accounts until inventory is determined
- Account for purchase discounts under the gross or net method

EXHIBIT 9-2
Allocation of Inventory Costs

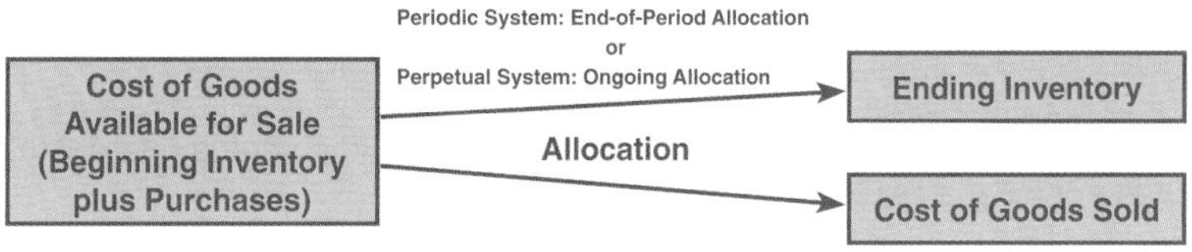

This allocation is measured using either a *periodic inventory system* or a *perpetual inventory system.*

- Periodic system, the inventory value for financial reporting purposes is determined only at particular times, such as at the end of a reporting period.

- Perpetual system, the inventory value is determined by measuring the ongoing physical flow of inventory, and cost is maintained on a continual basis within the accounting information system.

Cost Flow in a Periodic System Under a **periodic inventory system**, an actual physical count of the goods is taken at the end of each accounting period for which financial statements are prepared. The goods are counted, weighed, or otherwise measured, and the quantities are then multiplied by unit costs to value the inventory. *The values for ending inventory and cost of goods sold are only determined on a periodic basis, after a physical inventory count.* Within the periodic inventory system, *temporary accounts* (purchases, freight-in, purchase discounts, and purchase returns and allowances) are used until the inventory adjusting entry is made *after* the physical inventory count occurs as shown in **Exhibit 9-3**. These temporary accounts are income statement accounts and, thus, are reflected in equity in the balance sheet equation illustrations below.

EXHIBIT 9-3
Periodic Inventory System: Calculation of Cost of Goods Sold

Cost of Goods Sold Calculation	Source of Amounts
Beginning Inventory	Carried over from prior period
+ Purchases, net*	Recorded in temporary purchase accounts
= Cost of goods available for sale	Subtotal
− Ending inventory	Obtained from physical inventory count
= Cost of goods sold	Residual value

*Purchases + Freight-in − Purchase discounts − Purchase returns = Purchases, net

Accounting for Purchase Discounts in a Periodic System Purchase discounts can be recorded using either the gross method or the net method.

- Under the **gross method**, purchases are recorded at the full value and **purchase discounts** are recorded at a subsequent date, only if taken. See **Demo 9-2A**.
- Under the **net method**, purchases are initially recorded net of the discount; if a discount is not taken, the lost discount is recorded as **interest expense**, representing a finance charge. See **Demo 9-2B**.

EXPANDING YOUR KNOWLEDGE **Annualized Cost of a Lost Discount**

Many buyers make timely payments and take advantage of cash discounts because of the savings. For example, purchase discount terms of 1/10, n/30 are equivalent to an annualized interest rate of about 18% ([1%/ 20 days] × 365 days) if payment is delayed to the 30th day after purchase. Lost discounts are are actually a financing cost, although only the net method reports them as such.

Demo 9-2A LO9-2 Periodic Inventory System—Gross Method

Demo MBC

Gross Method

CostKo Inc. uses a periodic inventory system and begins the month of June 2020, with $300 in inventory.

Part One: Record journal entries for the following seven transactions, listed in chronological order, using the *gross method* for recording purchase discounts.

1. **Purchase of Inventory** CostKo purchased inventory on June 2, 2020, for $800, with terms 2/10, n/30, using the gross method.

Assets = Liabilities + Equity
+800 −800
Purchases 800 | Accounts Payable | 800

June 2, 2020—To record inventory purchases using gross method

Purchases	800	
Accounts Payable		800

2. **Incur Transportation Costs** On June 2, 2020, CostKo paid shipping charges of $75 related to the purchase of inventory (f.o.b. shipping point).

Assets = Liabilities + Equity
−75 −75
Cash | 75 Freight-in 75 |

June 2, 2020—To record transportation costs on purchases

Freight-In	75	
Cash		75

continued

continued from previous page

3. **Payment on Account within Discount Period** CostKo paid half its account payable balance on June 11, 2020, which falls within the discount period.

June 11, 2020—To record payment on account within discount period

Accounts Payable	400	
Purchase Discount ($400 × 0.02)		8
Cash ($400 × 0.98)		392

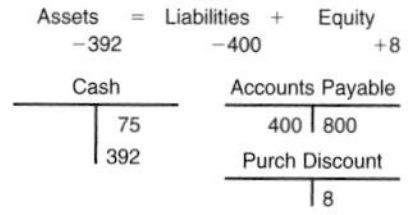

4. **Payment on Account after the Discount Period** CostKo paid $300 on account on June 13, after the discount period.

June 13, 2020—To record payment on account after discount period

Accounts Payable	300	
Cash		300

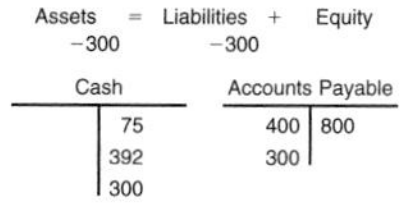

5. **Granted Purchase Allowance** On June 15, 2020, CostKo received a $100 credit from a supplier due to CostKo's return of defective inventory.

June 15, 2020—To record purchase allowance

Accounts Payable	100	
Purchase Returns and Allowances		100

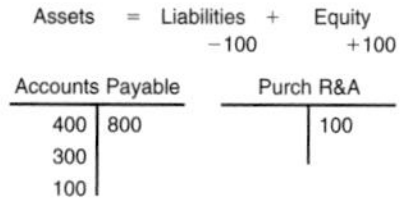

6. **Sale of inventory** CostKo sold inventory on June 20, 2020, with a retail price of $600.

June 20, 2020—To record sale of inventory

Accounts Receivable	600	
Sales		600

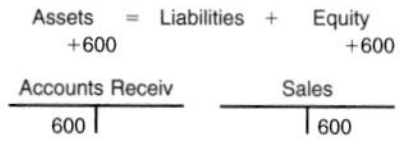

Under the periodic system, only revenue is recorded at the time of sale; cost of goods sold is not recorded until the end of the period *after* a physical inventory count.

7. **Physical Inventory Count to Adjust Ending Inventory** At month end, CostKo completed a physical inventory count and determined the cost of ending inventory on June 30, 2020, to be $617.

June 30, 2020—To adjust ending inventory based on a physical inventory count

Inventory, Ending (based on physical inventory)	617	
Purchase Discount	8	
Purchase Returns and Allowances	100	
Cost of Goods Sold (to balance)	450	
Purchases		800
Freight-In		75
Inventory, Beginning		300

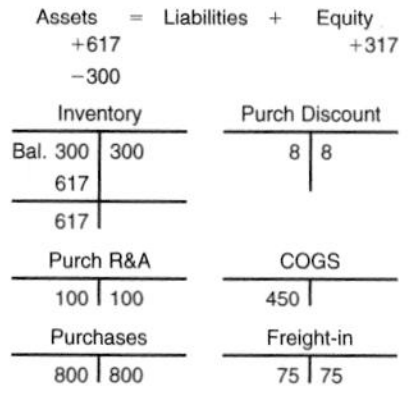

Cost of goods sold (also called cost of sales) is computed as a residual amount (beginning inventory plus net purchases less ending inventory). End-of-period entries are made to close the purchases accounts, to close out beginning inventory, record cost of goods sold, and to record the balance of ending inventory (ending inventory replaces beginning inventory).

Part Two: Show the cost of goods sold calculation for the month of June.

Cost of Goods Sold Calculation	
Beginning Inventory	$ 300
+ Purchases, net*	767
= Cost of goods available for sale	$1,067
− Ending inventory	(617)
= Cost of goods sold	$ 450

*$800 + 75 − 8 − 100 = $767

Demo 9-2B **LO9-2** **Periodic Inventory System—Net Method**

Demo MBC

Net Method

CostKo Inc. uses a periodic inventory system and begins the month of June 2020, with $300 in inventory. Record journal entries for the following three transactions, listed in chronological order, using the *net method* for recording purchase discounts.

1. **Purchase of Inventory** CostKo purchased inventory for $800 on June 2, 2020, with terms 2/10, n/30, net of the 2% purchase discount.

June 2, 2020—To record inventory purchases using net method

Purchases	784	
Accounts Payable ($800 × 0.98)		784

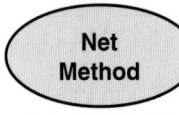

Assets = Liabilities + Equity: +784 (Liabilities), −784 (Equity)

Purchases		Accounts Payable	
784			784

2. **Payment on Account within Discount Period** CostKo paid half of its accounts payable balance on June 11, 2020; payment falls within the discount period thereby reducing inventory at the net purchase price.

June 11, 2020—To record payment on account within discount period

Accounts Payable	392	
Cash ($784/2)		392

Assets = Liabilities + Equity: −392 (Assets), −392 (Liabilities)

Cash		Accounts Payable	
	392	392	784

3. **Payment on Account after the Discount Period** CostKo paid the remaining accounts payable balance on June 13, 2020, after the discount period, recording interest expense for the unused discounts.

June 13, 2020—To record payment on account after discount period

Accounts Payable ($400 − $8)	392	
Interest Expense* ($400 × 0.02)	8	
Cash		400

Assets = Liabilities + Equity: −400 (Assets), −392 (Liabilities), −8 (Equity)

Cash		Accounts Payable	
	392	392	784
	400	392	
			0

Interest Exp	
8	

*Alternatively, a company may use a separate expense account, Purchase Discount Lost, to track amounts separately from other interest expense. If CostKo had not paid the remaining account balance as of June 30, the company would record an entry to accrue interest (Dr. Interest Expense and Cr. Interest Payable) for the lost discount.

REVIEW 9-2 **LO9-2** **Periodic Inventory System**

Review MBC

The following March 2020 transactions relate to PetPlus Inc.

March	5	Purchase of inventory with a list price of $14,000, a trade discount of 20% (which buyers get with certainty), and with terms 2/10, n/30.
	8	Returned $1,000 of inventory (damaged in shipment) to the supplier (the $1,000 is the value after the trade discount).
	14	Paid $4,900 ($5,000 of inventory less a purchase discount of 2%, or $100) on account.
	31	Paid the remaining account balance.

Required

a. Prepare journal entries prior to a physical inventory for these transactions assuming the company uses the periodic inventory system and the *gross method* for recording purchase discounts.

b. Prepare journal entries prior to a physical inventory for these transactions assuming the company uses the periodic inventory system and the *net method* for recording purchase discounts.

More Practice: 9-29, 9-45, 9-46, 9-71

Solution on p. 9-53.

LO 9-3 Demonstrate specific identification, average cost, FIFO, and LIFO in a PERIODIC inventory system

LO 9-3 Overview

Periodic Inventory Cost-Flow Assumptions
- Specific Identification
- Average Cost
- FIFO
- LIFO

Exhibit 9-2 showed that total cost of goods available for sale during each period must be allocated between cost of goods sold and cost of ending inventory. *If inventory unit acquisition costs are constant over time, the choice of an allocation process will not affect the result.* However, inventory item costs—both acquisition and manufacturing costs—typically vary, trending up or down in response to economic conditions. For inventory accounting purposes, this price variability creates a need for management to select an inventory **cost-flow method** (an assumption) for use in allocating total cost of goods available for sale between expenses (cost of goods sold) and assets (ending inventory).

Inventory Cost-Flow Assumptions in a Periodic Inventory System

In a *periodic inventory system*, the quantity of ending inventory is computed at the end of each period. We consider four methods available to companies for use in a periodic inventory system to allocate these costs: (1) specific identification, (2) average cost, (3) first-in, first-out (FIFO), and (4) last-in, first-out (LIFIO). The frequency in use of these methods is shown in **Exhibit 9-4**. See the reasoning for using various methods later in the chapter.

A summary of the methods is provided in **Exhibit 9-5**. We see that each method results in a unique flow of costs through the accounting system.

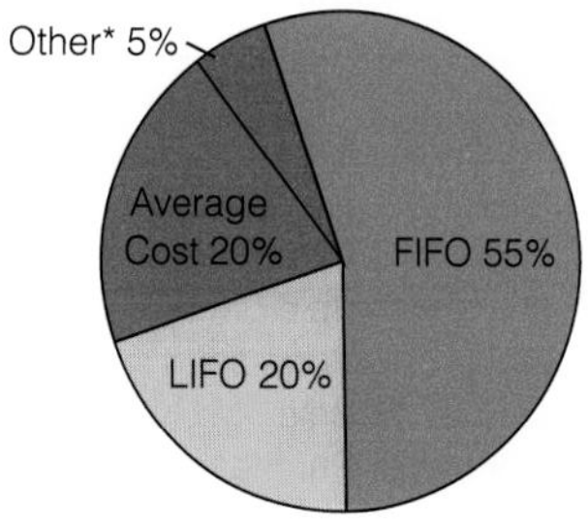

*Includes specific identification.

EXHIBIT 9-4
Frequency of Inventory Method Usage

EXHIBIT 9-5
Summary of Inventory Methods (Periodic Inventory System)

Inventory Method	Description	Inventory Flow	Valuation of Ending Inventory (EI) and Costs of Goods Sold (COGS)
Specific Identification Demo 9-3A	Each inventory item is uniquely identified so that each item sold and in ending inventory is identifiable.	Matches physical inventory flow.	**EI:** Identify and value specific units of inventory at actual cost. **COGS:** Identify and value specific units sold at actual cost.
Average Cost Demo 9-3B	Applies an average cost to units in ending inventory and units sold.	Applies an assumed inventory flow.	Calculate average unit cost and apply average unit cost to: **EI** units, and **COGS** units.
FIFO (First-In, First-Out) Demo 9-3C	Treats first goods purchased or manufactured as the first units sold.	Applies an assumed inventory flow.	**EI:** Start with *the most recent purchases* first until we reach total units remaining; add up the associated costs. **COGS:** Start with *the earliest purchases* first until we reach total units sold; add up the associated costs.
LIFO (Last-In, First-Out) Demo 9-3D	Treats last goods purchased or manufactured as the first units sold.	Applies an assumed inventory flow.	**EI:** Start with *the earliest purchases* first until we reach total units remaining. **COGS:** Start with *the most recent purchases* first until we reach total units sold; add up the associated costs.

The physical movement of goods is typically on a first-in, first-out basis, especially if the product is perishable or subject to obsolescence. However, the cost-flow method used to account for the value of both the inventory used up during the period and the inventory remaining at the end of the period is based on an *assumed flow* of products. For example, the assumed flow of goods for LIFO and FIFO are the exact opposite—LIFO assumes that the latest purchases are sold whereas FIFO assumes that the earliest purchases are sold as depicted in **Exhibit 9-6**. *Except for the specific identification method, inventory accounting concerns the flow of costs through the accounting system, not the flow of goods physically in and out of a company.* This means the physical flow of goods will not always match the accounting and valuation of the physical flow of goods.

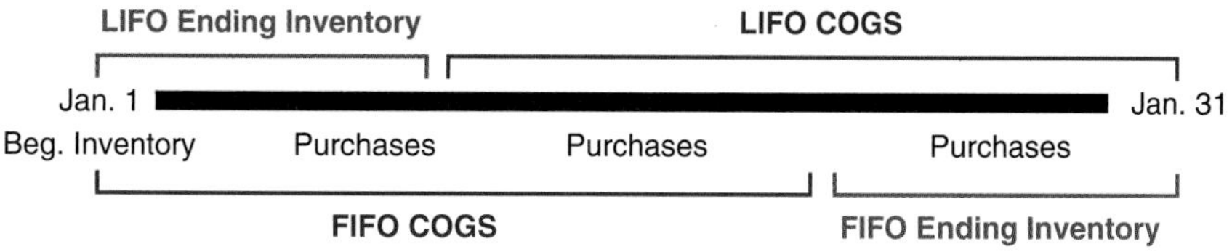

EXHIBIT 9-6
Visually Showing the LIFO and FIFO Inventory Methods

Demo 9-3A **LO9-3** **Specific Identification—Periodic Inventory System**

Demo MBC

Specific Identification —Periodic—

We use the Chase Corporation to demonstrate the four inventory methods. Beginning inventory and related transactions in January follow. Chase began the month with 200 units of inventory, purchased 800 units, and sold 700 units, to end the month with 300 units (200 + 800 − 700 = 300). For simplicity, we assume that beginning inventory is the same under all methods for this demo and for all other examples in this chapter where ending inventory under multiple methods is calculated.

Date	Unit Price	Units Purchased	Units Sold	Balance of Units
January 1 Beginning Balance. . .	$1.00			200
January 9 Purchase	1.10	300		500
January 10 Sale			400	100
January 15 Purchase	1.16	400		500
January 18 Sale			300	200
January 24 Purchase	1.26	100		300

Cost of goods available for sale (beginning inventory plus purchases) for the period follows.

Date	Units	Cost per Unit	Total Cost
January 1	200	$1.00	$ 200
January 9	300	1.10	330
January 15	400	1.16	464
January 24	100	1.26	126
Total cost of goods available for sale (COGAS)	1,000		$1,120

Chase had 1,000 units available for sale in the month of January with a total cost of $1,120. Of the units available for sale, 700 units were sold (400 + 300), while 300 (1,000 − 700) remained in ending inventory.

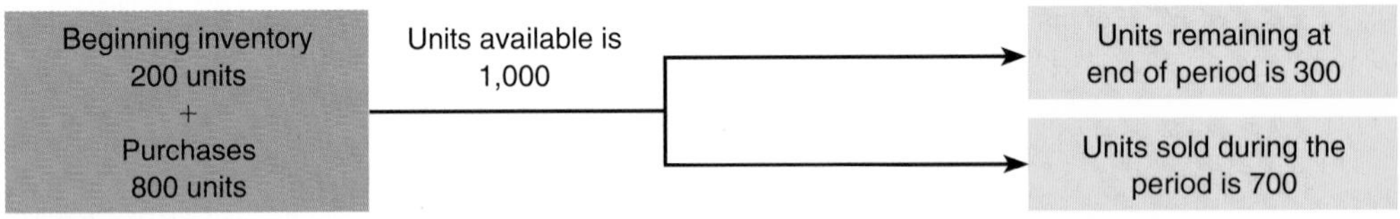

Chase must allocate the total cost of $1,120 between the ending units and the sold units. *Recall that under the periodic inventory system, the allocation occurs at the end of the period, after a physical inventory count. Assume Chase performs this count monthly.*

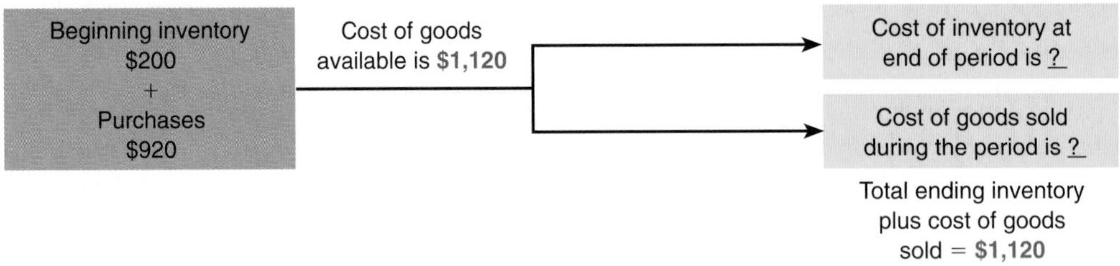

At the end of the period, Chase determines that 300 units in ending inventory are specifically identified as follows: (1) 50 units from the January 1 beginning inventory, (2) 175 units from the January 15 purchase, and (3) 75 units from the January 24 purchase.

Compute the value of ending inventory (January 31) and cost of goods sold (for January) using the *specific identification method* for Chase.

continued

continued from previous page

Solution

Specific Identification: Ending Inventory

Date	Units	Cost per Unit	Total Cost
January 1	50	$1.00	$ 50
January 15	175	1.16	203
January 24	75	1.26	95
Ending inventory	300		$348

Cost of goods sold is calculated as follows.*

Specific Identification: Cost of Goods Sold

COGAS	$1,120
Less ending inventory	348
COGS	$ 772

*Alternatively, cost of goods sold is calculated based on the valuation of the specific items sold:

Date	Units	Cost per Unit	Total Cost
January 1 (200 − 50 units)	150	$1.00	$150
January 9 (300 units)	300	1.10	330
January 15 (400 − 175 units)	225	1.16	261
January 24 (100 − 75 units)	25	1.26	31
Total cost of goods sold	700		$772

Average Cost—Periodic Inventory System

LO9-3 **Demo 9-3B**

Demo MBC

Average Cost —Periodic—

Refer to the transaction data in **Demo 9-3A**. Compute the value of ending inventory (January 31) and cost of goods sold (for January) using the *average-cost method* for Chase.

Solution

A **weighted-average unit cost** is computed by dividing cost of goods available for sale of $1,120 by the number of units in the beginning inventory plus units purchased during the period (200 + 300 + 400 + 100).

$$\frac{\text{Cost of goods available for sale}}{\text{Total units available for sale}} = \frac{\$1,120}{1,000 \text{ units}} = \$1.12 \text{ per ur}$$

The weighted-average unit cost is then applied to the units in the ending inventory to compute the ending inventory balance.

Average Cost: Ending Inventory

Weighted average cost per unit	$1.12
× Ending inventory units	× 300
Ending inventory	$ 336

Costs of goods sold is calculated as follows.*

Average Cost: Cost of Goods Sold

COGAS	$1,120
Less ending inventory	336
COGS	$ 784

* Alternatively, cost of goods sold is calculated as $1.12 multiplied by units sold of 700 to arrive at $784.

Demo 9-3C LO9-3 FIFO—Periodic Inventory System

Demo MBC

FIFO —Periodic—

Refer to the transaction data in **Demo 9-3A**. Compute the value of ending inventory (January 31) and cost of goods sold (for January) under the *FIFO inventory method* for Chase.

Solution

To calculate the cost of the 300 items remaining in inventory, start with *the most recent purchases* first and move to earlier purchases until we reach the total ending units.

FIFO: Ending Inventory

Date	Units	Cost per Unit	Total Cost
January 24	100	$1.26	$126
January 15	200	1.16	232
Ending inventory. . .	300		$358

Costs of goods sold is calculated as follows.*

FIFO: Cost of Goods Sold

COGAS.	$1,120
Less ending inventory. . . .	358
COGS.	$ 762

* Alternatively, cost of goods sold is calculated based on the unit cost of the 700 units sold, starting with the *earliest inventory purchases* as follows:

Date	Units	Cost per Unit	Total Cost
January 1	200	$1.00	$200
January 9	300	1.10	330
January 15 . . .	200	1.16	232
Total	700		$762

Demo 9-3D LO9-3 LIFO—Periodic Inventory System

Demo MBC

LIFO —Periodic—

Refer to the transaction data in **Demo 9-3A**. Compute the value of ending inventory (January 31) and cost of goods sold (for January) under the *LIFO inventory method* for Chase.

Solution

To calculate the cost of the 300 items remaining in inventory, start with *the earliest purchases* first and move to later purchases until we reach the total ending units.

LIFO: Ending Inventory

Date	Units	Cost per Unit	Total Cost
January 1 . . .	200	$1.00	$200
January 9 . . .	100	1.10	110
Total	300		$310

Costs of goods sold is calculated as follows.*

LIFO: Cost of Goods Sold

COGAS.	$1,120
Less ending inventory. . . .	310
COGS.	$ 810

*Alternatively, cost of goods sold is calculated based on the unit cost of the 700 units sold, starting with the *most recent inventory units*, as follows:

Date	Units	Cost per Unit	Total Cost
January 24 . . .	100	$1.26	$126
January 15 . . .	400	1.16	464
January 9	200	1.10	220
Total	700		$810

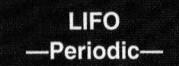

Comparing Inventory Methods

Inventory and COGS amounts are calculated differently under the four different inventory methods as shown in **Exhibit 9-7**. In periods of rising prices (as seen in the Chase example), FIFO inventory (COGS) is the highest (lowest), LIFO inventory (COGS) is the lowest (highest), and the average-cost inventory is in between the two. It is not possible to predict where inventory (COGS) will fall under the specific identification method because it is based on which items are chosen to be sold.

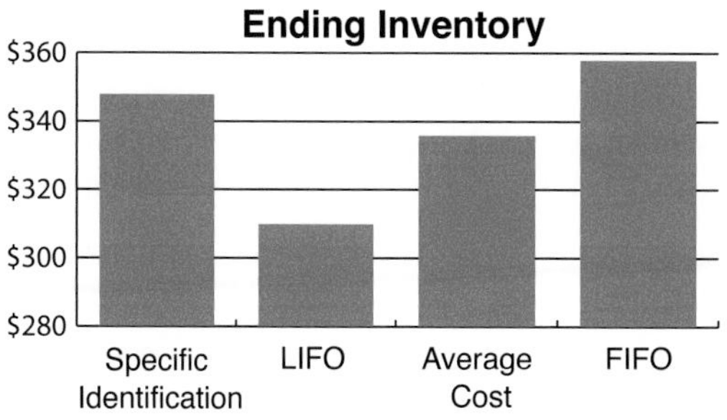

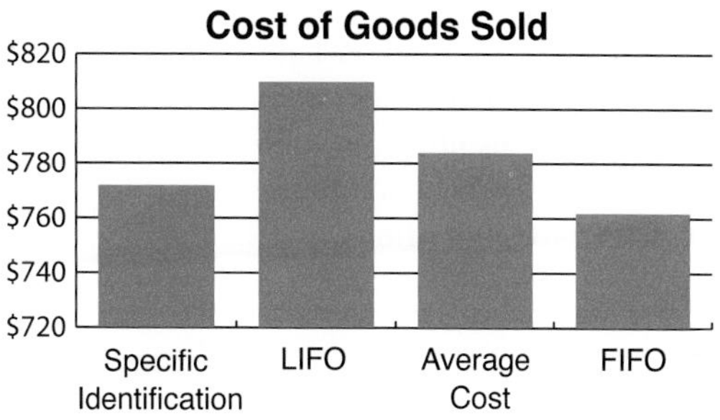

EXHIBIT 9-7 Comparison of Inventory and COGS Values under Periodic Inventory Systems

Exhibit 9-8 summarizes the advantages and disadvantages of each method, **assuming rising prices.** Although in many industries, such as manufacturing, costs have risen over time, in some industries, such as high tech, costs have often fallen. The analysis here assumes costs are rising.

EXHIBIT 9-8 Advantages and Disadvantages of Periodic Inventory Valuation Methods

Inventory Method	Advantages	Disadvantages
Specific Identification	▪ Only method to directly relate costs to actual physical flow.	▪ Income manipulation possible because items can be arbitrarily selected for sale (*purposely* sell a higher or lower priced item). ▪ Only feasible in certain situations (such as small quantities of expensive items).
Average Cost	▪ Systematic and objective. ▪ Consistent application of *same unit costs* on both the balance sheet (EI) and income statement (COGS).	▪ Average price can be quite different from the current cost of inventory (especially if there are upgrades or rising prices). ▪ Batches of inventory lose identity.
FIFO* (First-In, First-Out)	▪ Systematic and objective. ▪ Assumed flow tends to be consistent with physical flow of inventory. ▪ EI on balance sheet approximates current costs.	▪ Lower (older) costs are matched with current (higher) sales revenue on income statement. ▪ Results in higher income (due to older costs), thus higher taxes than under LIFO.
LIFO* (Last-In, First-Out)	▪ Systematic and objective. ▪ Current (higher) costs are matched with current (higher) sales revenue on income statement. ▪ Results in lower income (due to higher costs), thus lower taxes than under FIFO. Taxes are deferred until inventory quantities decline causing older layers to liquidate. ▪ Inventory values are not likely to require write-downs to market, see next chapter.	▪ Assumed flow tends to be inconsistent with physical flow of inventory. ▪ Lower (older) EI costs on the balance sheet do not approximate current costs. ▪ Reports lower profits than under FIFO. ▪ Can encourage inventory purchases at year-end to avoid liquidation of LIFO layers.

*If instead, costs are falling, opposite trends occur. This means that under LIFO (as compared to FIFO), ending inventory would be higher, COGS would be lower, and net income would be higher. LIFO would no longer be tax advantageous and would therefore not be used. If on the other hand, costs rise and fall over time, it is not possible to make assumptions on cost trends.

Phantom Profit in FIFO When costs are rising, reported income under FIFO is higher than under LIFO or average cost. The higher profits result because lower (older) costs are matched with current (higher) sales revenue on the income statement. This effect on income is called a **phantom profit** (or inventory profit) because a portion of the reported gross profit must be used to replace inventory the next period (at higher prices). Phantom profit is the difference between the cost of goods sold at FIFO (old) cost and the cost of goods sold measured at current cost.

Due to the common inflationary behavior in prices, companies did not think that the phantom profits in FIFO should be subject to taxation. Specifically, companies have to incur higher, current costs to replace inventory but can only deduct the lower, older costs on their tax returns when using FIFO. This led to the LIFO method, which was approved by the IRS. However, the IRS also requires that companies that use LIFO for tax purposes also use LIFO for financial reporting. This is known as the **LIFO Conformity Rule**. While LIFO must be reported on the face of financial statements under this rule, the company can disclose non-LIFO valuation amounts in the notes accompanying financial statements.

The use of LIFO has declined over time largely due to changes in the types of companies in the economy. For example, in high technology industries, costs are generally falling (one can get more powerful but cheaper computers now relative to ten years ago). In industries where prices are not rising, LIFO does not offer any benefits.

REVIEW 9-3 **LO9-3** **Inventory Methods under the Periodic Inventory System**

Review MBC

Robin Inc.'s inventory records show the following data relative to an item sold.

Date		Units	Unit Cost
May 1	Inventory.	1,100	$20.50
May 3	Purchases.	10,000	20.80
May 7	Sales.	5,000	
May 20	Purchases.	8,000	21.00
May 22	Sales.	8,500	
May 30	Purchases.	3,000	21.50

Assuming that Robin maintains a periodic inventory system with a monthly physical count, compute ending inventory on May 31 under (1) specific identification, (2) average cost, (3) FIFO, and (4) LIFO. The actual ending units remaining at May 31 are from the following dates: May 1, 500 units; May 3, 1,800 units; May 20, 4,000 units, and May 30, 2,300 units.

More Practice: 9-52, 9-73

Solution on p. 9-54.

LO 9-4 Demonstrate accounting in a PERPETUAL inventory system

LO 9-4 Overview

Accounting Under a Perpetual Inventory System

- Adjust Inventory and COGS accounts directly in the accounting system
- Inventory and COGS balances available continually
- Verify Inventory balance through a physical inventory count
- Account for purchase discounts under the gross or net method

Unlike the periodic system where the inventory balance is determined only at particular points in time, the inventory balance under a perpetual system is determined on a continual basis.

Cost Flow in a Perpetual System When a perpetual inventory system is used, detailed perpetual inventory records are maintained for each inventory item as they are purchased and sold. This means that inventory and cost of goods sold accounts are adjusted directly for transactions affecting inventory as shown in **Exhibit 9-9**. The physical quantity and the valuation of inventory at any time are available from accounting records.

All companies using a perpetual inventory system still perform periodic physical inventory counts to *verify* inventory amounts. A physical count is usually made annually for auditing purposes to compare the inventory available with the perpetual record and to provide data for any adjusting entries needed (errors and losses due to theft or spoilage, for example). When a difference is found between the perpetual inventory records and a physical count, the perpetual inventory records are adjusted to the physical count. In such cases, the inventory account is debited or credited as necessary for the correction, and an inventory correction account, such as Loss on Inventory Shortage or Gain on Inventory Overage, is debited or credited. The balance in the inventory correction account is included as part of cost of goods sold in the income statement.

Ending Inventory Calculation	Source of Amounts
Beginning inventory	Carried over from prior period
+ **Purchases, net**	Recorded in inventory account
Cost of goods available for sale	Subtotal
− Cost of goods sold	Recorded in cost of goods sold account continually
Ending inventory	Balance maintained continually

EXHIBIT 9-9
Perpetual Inventory System: Calculation of Ending Inventory

Accounting for Purchase Discounts in a Perpetual System As with the periodic system, purchase discounts in a perpetual system can be recorded either using the gross method or the net method.

- Under the **gross method**, purchases are recorded at the full value (increase to inventory and accounts payable). If payment is made within the discount period, inventory is credited (reduced to net value). See **Demo 9-4A**.
- Under the **net method**, purchases are initially recorded net of the discount. If a discount is *not* taken, interest expense is debited representing the finance charge. See **Demo 9-4B**.

Perpetual Inventory System—Gross Method LO9-4 Demo 9-4A

Demo MBC

Gross Method

CostKo Inc. uses a *perpetual inventory system*, follows the gross method, and begins the month of June 2020, with $300 of inventory. Record journal entries for the following seven transactions, listed in chronological order.

1. **Purchase of Inventory** CostKo purchased inventory for $800 on June 2, 2020, with terms 2/10, n/30, using the gross method.

June 2, 2020—To record inventory purchases using gross method

Inventory	800	
Accounts Payable		800

Assets = Liabilities + Equity
+800 = +800
Inventory: Bal. 300; 800 | Accounts Payable: 800

2. **Payment for Transportation** On June 2, 2020, CostKo paid shipping charges (f.o.b. shipping point) of $75 related to the purchase of inventory.

June 2, 2020—To record transportation costs on purchases

Inventory	75	
Cash		75

Assets = Liabilities + Equity
+75
−75
Inventory: Bal. 300; 800; 75 | Cash: 75

3. **Payment on Account within Discount Period** CostKo paid half its accounts payable balance on June 11, 2020, which falls within the discount period.

June 11, 2020—To record payment on account within discount period

Accounts Payable	400	
Inventory		8
Cash		392

The cash discount reduces the value of inventory, previously recorded at full or gross value.

Assets = Liabilities + Equity
−8 = −400
−392
Cash: 75; 392 | Accounts Payable: 400 | 800
Inventory: Bal. 300; 800; 75 | 8

4. **Payment on Account after the Discount Period** CostKo paid $300 on account on June 13, after the discount period.

June 13, 2020—To record payment on account after discount period

Accounts Payable	300	
Cash		300

Assets = Liabilities + Equity
−300 = −300
Cash: 75; 392; 300 | Accounts Payable: 400; 300 | 800

5. **Return of Inventory** On June 15, 2020, CostKo returned $100 of inventory.

June 15, 2020—To record return of inventory

Accounts Payable	100	
Inventory		100

The $100 credit is recorded as a reduction in inventory.

Assets = Liabilities + Equity
−100 = −100
Inventory: Bal. 300; 800; 75 | 8; 100
Accounts Payable: 400; 300; 100 | 800

continued

continued from previous page

6. **Sale of inventory** CostKo sold inventory on June 20, 2020, with a retail price of $600 and a cost of $400.

June 20, 2020—To record sale of inventory

Assets = Liabilities + Equity
+600 | +600
−400 | −400
Accounts Receiv: 600 |
Sales: | 600
Inventory: Bal. 300 | 8; 800 | 100; 75 | 400
COGS: 400 |

Accounts Receivable	600	
Sales		600
Cost of Goods Sold	400	
Inventory		400

Under the perpetual system, revenue and cost of goods sold are both recorded at the time of sale.

7. **Adjust Ending Inventory Balance** CostKo preformed a physical inventory count on June 30, 2020, and discovered that the inventory recorded exceeds the physical inventory count by a number of units with a total cost of $50.

June 30, 2020—To record inventory shortage

Assets = Liabilities + Equity
−50 | −50
Inventory: Bal. 300 | 8; 800 | 100; 75 | 400; | 50; 617 |
Loss on Inv Short: 50 |

Loss on Inventory Shortage	50	
Inventory		50

Under the perpetual system, the balance sheet on June 30, 2020, will include adjusted inventory of $617. The income statement for June will include as expense, cost of goods sold of $450, made up of the balances in COGS of $400 and Inventory Shortage of $50. Compare this to the periodic system in **Demo 9-2A**. Ending inventory is $617, and the inventory shortage is absorbed in the cost of goods sold amount of $450. While the COGS amount reported is the same in both systems, only the perpetual system isolates the expense due to inventory shortage within the account details.

Demo 9-4B LO9-4 Perpetual Inventory System—Net Method

Demo MBC

Net Method

CostKo Inc. uses a perpetual inventory system. Record journal entries for the following three transactions, listed in chronological order, using the *net method* for recording purchase discounts.

1. **Purchase of Inventory** CostKo records inventory purchases of $800 on June 2, 2020, with terms 2/10, n/30, net of the 2% purchase discount.

June 2, 2020—To record inventory purchases using net method

Assets = Liabilities + Equity
+784 | +784
Inventory: 784 |
Accounts Payable: | 784

Inventory	784	
Accounts Payable		784

2. **Payment on Account within Discount Period** CostKo paid half of its accounts payable balance on June 11, 2020; payment falls within the discount period.

June 11, 2020—To record payment on account within discount period

Assets = Liabilities + Equity
−392 | −392
Cash: | 392
Accounts Payable: 392 | 784

Accounts Payable	392	
Cash ($784/2)		392

3. **Payment on Account after the Discount Period** CostKo paid the remaining accounts payable balance on June 13, 2020, after the discount period.

June 13, 2020—To record payment on account after discount period

Assets = Liabilities + Equity
−400 | −392 | −8
Cash: | 392; | 400
Accounts Payable: 392 | 784; 392 |; | 0
Interest Exp: 8 |

Accounts Payable ($400 − $8)	392	
Interest Expense ($400 × 0.02)	8	
Cash		400

Perpetual Inventory System **LO9-4** **REVIEW 9-4**

The following March 2020 transactions relate to PetPlus Inc.

March	5	Purchase of inventory for $11,200, with terms 2/10, n/30.
	8	Returned $1,000 of inventory (damaged in shipment) to the supplier.
	14	Paid $4,900 ($5,000 of inventory less discount of $100) on account.
	31	Paid the remaining accounts payable balance.

Review MBC

Required

a. Prepare journal entries for these transactions assuming the company uses the perpetual inventory system and the *gross method* for recording purchase discounts.

b. Prepare journal entries for these transactions assuming the company uses the perpetual inventory system and the *net method* for recording purchase discounts.

More Practice: 9-34, 9-35, 9-48
Solution on p. 9-54.

Demonstrate moving average, FIFO, and LIFO in a PERPETUAL inventory system

LO 9-5

In a *perpetual inventory system*, each receipt and each sale of an inventory item is recorded in the inventory records to maintain an up-to-date perpetual inventory balance. This means the perpetual inventory records provide the units and costs applied to each purchase and sale. We will consider three methods for companies to use in a perpetual inventory system to allocate these costs: (1) moving average, (2) first-in, first-out (FIFO), and (3) last-in, first-out (LIFO). A summary of these methods is in **Exhibit 9-10**. (While specific identification can be used under a perpetual inventory system, it is not shown here as its results are identical to results using the periodic system.)

LO 9-5 Overview

Perpetual Inventory System
- Moving average
- FIFO
- LIFO

EXHIBIT 9-10 Summary of Inventory Methods (Perpetual Inventory System)

Inventory Method	Description	Inventory Flow	Valuation of Ending Inventory (EI) and Costs of Goods Sold (COGS)
Moving Average **Demo 9-5A**	Provides a current average cost on a continual basis.	Applies an assumed inventory flow.	Calculate a new moving-average unit cost after each purchase; apply moving-average unit cost to: **EI** units, and **COGS** units.
FIFO* **(First-In, First-Out)** **Demo 9-5B**	Requires maintaining inventory layers by unit costs throughout the period to assign the proper cost to each sale using earliest purchases first.	Applies an assumed inventory flow.	**EI** consists of the latest purchases. **COGS** is determined for each sale based on the earliest purchases.
LIFO **(Last-In, First-Out)** **Demo 9-5C**	Requires maintaining inventory layers by unit costs throughout the period to assign the proper cost to each sale using latest purchases first.	Applies an assumed inventory flow.	**EI** consists of the earliest purchases. **COGS** is determined for each sale based on the most recent purchases.

FIFO produces the same results whether a periodic system or a perpetual system is used. This means that cost of goods sold as determined by the earliest goods purchased is the same if determined on a continual basis or if calculated at period-end. In contrast, using LIFO, cost of goods sold is determined by the latest goods purchased, which is different if determined on a continual basis or if calculated at period end because the "latest goods" are different goods depending on the point in time.

Moving Average—Perpetual Inventory System **LO9-5** **Demo 9-5A**

Refer to the transaction data in **Demo 9-3A**. Compute the value of ending inventory (January 31) and cost of goods sold (for January) under *the moving-average inventory method* for Chase.

Demo MBC

Solution

Application of the moving-average inventory method in a perpetual inventory system is shown in the following table.

continued

Moving Average —Perpetual—

continued from previous page

	Purchases			Sales			Inventory Balance		
Date	Units	Unit Cost	Total Cost	Units	Unit Cost	Total Cost	Units	Unit Cost	Total Cost
January 1							200	$1.00	$200
January 9	300	$1.10	$330				500	1.06*	530
January 10				400	$1.06	$424	100	1.06	106
January 15	400	1.16	464				500	1.14**	570
January 18				300	1.14	342	200	1.14	228
January 24	100	1.26	126				300	1.18***	$354
Totals			$920			$766			

*On January 9, the $1.06 moving-average cost is derived by dividing total cost of $530 (or $200 + $330) by total units (500 units). Then, on January 10, the 400 units sold are valued at the latest moving-average unit cost of $1.06.

**On January 15, the $1.14 moving-average cost is derived by dividing total cost of $570 (or $106 + $464) by total units (500). Then, on January 18, the 300 units sold are valued at the latest moving-average unit cost of $1.14.

***The January 24 ending inventory of 300 units is valued at the latest moving-average unit cost of $1.18, derived by dividing total cost of $354 (or $228 + $126) by total units (300).

Ending inventory balance	**$354**
Cost of goods sold† ($424 + $342)	**766**

†Alternatively, cost of goods sold of $766 is calculated as follows:

Moving Average: Cost of Goods Sold	
COGAS.	$1,120 (= $200 + $920)
Less ending inventory.	354
COGS.	$ 766

Demo 9-5B **LO9-5** **FIFO—Perpetual Inventory System**

Demo MBC

FIFO —Perpetual—

Refer to the transaction data in **Demo 9-3A**. Compute the value of ending inventory (January 31) and cost of goods sold (for January) under the *FIFO inventory method* for Chase.

Solution

Application of the FIFO inventory method in a perpetual inventory system is demonstrated in the following table.

	Purchases			Sales			Inventory Balance		
Date	Units	Unit Cost	Total Cost	Units	Unit Cost	Total Cost	Units	Unit Cost	Total Cost
January 1							200	$1.00	$200
							200	1.00	200
January 9	300	$1.10	$330				300	1.10	330
				200	$1.00	$200			
January 10				200	1.10	220	100	1.10	110
							100	1.10	110
January 15	400	1.16	464				400	1.16	464
				100	1.10	110			
January 18				200	1.16	232	200	1.16	232
							200	1.16	232
January 24	100	1.26	126				100	1.26	126
Totals			$920			$762			$358

continued

continued from previous page

Under the FIFO inventory method in a perpetual inventory system, a cost is assigned to each sale of inventory, based on the earliest units purchased. For example, the 400 units sold on January 10 are made up of *all* of the 200 units of beginning inventory (at a unit cost of $1.00) and the remaining 200 units from the January 9 purchase (at a cost of $1.10 per unit).

Ending inventory balance on January 24 ($232 + $126)	**$358**
Cost of goods sold for January† ($200 + $220 + $110 + $232).	**762**

†Alternatively, cost of goods sold of $762 is calculated as follows:

FIFO: Cost of Goods Sold	
COGAS.	$1,120
Less ending inventory.	358
COGS.	$ 762

LIFO—Perpetual Inventory System

LO9-5 **Demo 9-5C**

Demo MBC

LIFO —Perpetual—

Refer to the transaction data in **Demo 9-3A**. Compute the value of ending inventory (January 31) and cost of goods sold (for January) under the *LIFO inventory method* for Chase.

Solution

	Purchases			Sales			Inventory Balance		
Date	**Units**	**Unit Cost**	**Total Cost**	**Units**	**Unit Cost**	**Total Cost**	**Units**	**Unit Cost**	**Total Cost**
January 1							200	$1.00	$200
January 9	300	$1.10	$330				200 300	1.00 1.10	200 330
January 10				300 100	$1.10 1.00	$330 100	100	1.00	100
January 15	400	1.16	464				100 400	1.00 1.16	100 464
January 18				300	1.16	348	100 100	1.00 1.16	100 116
January 24	100	1.26	126				100 100 100	1.00 1.16 1.26	100 116 126
Totals			$920			$778			$342

Under the LIFO inventory method in a perpetual inventory system, a cost is assigned to each sale of inventory, based on the latest units purchased. For example, the 400 units sold on January 10 consist of *all* of the 300 units purchased on January 9 (at a unit cost of $1.10) and the remaining 100 units from beginning inventory (at a cost of $1.00 per unit).

Ending inventory balance on January 24 ($100 + $116 + $126).	**$342**
Cost of goods sold for January† ($330 + $100 + $348)	**778**

†Alternatively, cost of goods sold of $778 is calculated as follows:

LIFO: Cost of Goods Sold	
COGAS.	$1,120
Less ending inventory.	342
COGS.	$ 778

COCA-COLA Real World—INVENTORY METHODS

COCA-COLA CO.
[KO]

Coca-Cola Company chose two inventory methods to value its inventory: average cost and FIFO.

Inventories Inventories consist primarily of raw materials and packaging (which includes ingredients and supplies) and finished goods (which include concentrates and syrups in our concentrate operations and finished beverages in our finished product operations). Inventories are valued at the lower of cost or market. We determine cost on the basis of the average cost or first-in, first-out methods. Inventories consisted of the following (in millions):

December 31	2015	2014
Raw materials and packaging	$1,564	$1,615
Finished goods	1,032	1,134
Other	306	351
Total inventories	$2,902	$3,100

REVIEW 9-5 LO9-5 Inventory Methods under a Perpetual Inventory System

Review MBC

Robin Inc.'s inventory records show the following data relative to an item sold regularly.

Date		Units	Unit Cost
May 1	Inventory	1,100	$20.50
May 3	Purchases	10,000	20.80
May 7	Sales	5,000	
May 20	Purchases	8,000	21.00
May 22	Sales	8,500	
May 30	Purchases	3,000	21.50

Assuming that Robin maintains a perpetual inventory system, compute ending inventory on May 31 under (1) moving average, (2) FIFO, and (3) LIFO.

More Practice:
9-36, 9-37, 9-53
Solution on p. 9-55.

LO 9-6 Explain and compute a LIFO reserve

LO 9-6 Overview

LIFO Reserve
Inventory at FIFO, average cost, or standard cost
Less Inventory at LIFO
LIFO Inventory Reserve

Many companies that report inventory at LIFO cost do not use LIFO for internal accounting and control purposes, in part because the method is costly to operate. For *internal and control purposes*, most companies use FIFO, average, or standard cost. (While, not the focus of this chapter, manufacturers often record inventory at standard costs where unit costs for material, labor, and manufacturing overhead are predetermined. At the end of the period, they convert these results to LIFO for *external financial reporting*. For example, if a FIFO inventory system is maintained in a company's accounting records, the difference between the inventory value at FIFO and the inventory value at LIFO is the LIFO reserve as illustrated in **Exhibit 9-11**.

EXHIBIT 9-11
LIFO Reserve

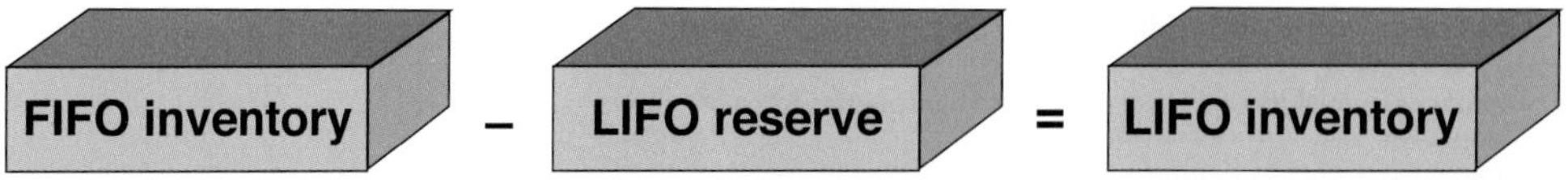

The difference between LIFO and FIFO (or other method used) is the **LIFO reserve**, which is recorded using an **inventory allowance account** (Allowance to Reduce Inventory to LIFO Basis) as shown in **Demo 9-6**. This inventory allowance account is a contra account to the inventory account. The allowance balance is adjusted at the end of each reporting period to reflect the current year-end balance. The entry to adjust the allowance for the *change* in the difference between LIFO and the inventory method used internally also affects cost of goods sold. In some cases, the conversion to LIFO can be outside of the accounts. In this case, the difference between FIFO (or other method) and LIFO is computed and used for external reporting in financial statements. No formal entry is made in the accounting records for this treatment of the allowance.

LIFO Reserve LO9-6 Demo 9-6

Demo MBC

At the end of 2020, its first year of operations, Erie Company's value of inventory using LIFO is $12,000 and if that same inventory is valued using FIFO the value is $18,000 resulting in a difference, or LIFO Reserve, of $6,000. At the end of 2021, the value of inventory using FIFO exceeds the value of inventory if LIFO were used by $4,000. Erie Company has a December 31 year-end. Prepare the journal entries on December 31, 2020, and December 31, 2021, to adjust the LIFO reserve.

Solution

December 31, 2020—To create year-end LIFO allowance

Cost of Goods Sold ($18,000 − $12,000)	6,000	
Allowance to Reduce FIFO Inventory to LIFO Basis		6,000

Assets = Liabilities + Equity
−6,000 −6,000
COGS: 6,000 |
Inventory Allow: | 6,000

December 31, 2021—To adjust year-end LIFO allowance

Allowance to Reduce FIFO Inventory to LIFO	2,000	
Cost of Goods Sold ($6,000 − $4,000)		2,000

Assets = Liabilities + Equity
−2,000 −2,000
COGS: 6,000 | 2,000
Inventory Allow: 2,000 | 6,000
| 4,000

FORD MOTOR CO. Real World—LIFO RESERVE

FORD MOTOR CO. [F]

Ford Motor Company accounts for inventory using the LIFO method. On its balance sheet, inventory is reported at $8,319 million and $7,870 million for years ended 2015 and 2014, respectively. In the note below, Ford reconciles inventory recorded at LIFO to inventory recorded at FIFO. Its FIFO inventory would have been 11.3% and 12.9% higher in 2015 and 2014, respectively.

Inventories All inventories are stated at the lower of cost and net realizable value. Cost for a substantial portion of U.S. inventories is determined by a last-in, first-out (LIFO) basis. LIFO was used for 27% and 28% of total inventories at December 31, 2015 and 2014, respectively. Cost of other inventories is determined by costing methods that approximate a first-in, first-out (FIFO) basis.

Inventories at December 31 ($ millions)	2015	2014
Raw materials, work-in-process, and supplies	$4,005	$3,859
Finished products	5,254	5,026
Total inventories under FIFO	9,259	8,885
LIFO adjustment	(940)	(1,015)
Total inventories	$8,319	$7,870

LIFO Reserve LO9-6 REVIEW 9-6

Review MBC

At the end of the annual accounting period, the inventory records of Boynton Company reveal the following. Boynton's first year of operations was 2020; also, it uses FIFO for internal purposes and LIFO for income tax and external reporting purposes.

Inventories at December 31	2020	2021
Ending inventory at FIFO	$280,000	$325,000
Ending inventory at LIFO	100,000	140,000

Required

a. Assume that the inventory difference is recognized in the accounts. Prepare the necessary journal entry at each year-end to record any LIFO reserve.
b. Illustrate how inventory is shown on Boynton's comparative balance sheets for 2020 and 2021.

More Practice: 9-38, 9-58
Solution on p. 9-55.

LO 9-7 Describe and compute the effect of LIFO liquidation

LO 9-7 Overview

LIFO Liquidation
- Elimination of prior years' inventory layers
- Voluntary or involuntary liquidation
- Disclosed in financial statements

Over time, when a company uses LIFO, it develops **inventory layers** for each year that inventory increases. An issue arises under LIFO when a company ends the year with an inventory quantity lower than that at the beginning of the year under a periodic inventory system. This is called **LIFO liquidation**, where prior years' inventory layer(s) are eliminated.

In periods of rising prices, the liquidated inventory layers consist of lower priced inventory items. The impact on the financial statements is that lower cost inventory (reflected in the older LIFO layers) are expensed in the current period. This means that lower priced inventory is matched against current revenue prices.

We show an example in **Exhibit 9-12** where the company *liquidated* much of its prior (base) year inventory. This company began the period with a single layer under LIFO inventory of 40,000 units and added a second layer of 10,000 units (purchases) during the year. It ended the period with 6,000 units. As a result of the liquidation of much of the base inventory, the cost of goods sold of 44,000 units includes 34,000 units with an old cost ($1 per unit) matched against current revenue. This liquidation of part of the LIFO base layer distorts reported income relative to income under the normal LIFO relation between cost and revenue.

EXHIBIT 9-12
LIFO Liquidation

Current Year Purchases Layer	$15,000 (10,000 × $1.50)
Base Layer	$40,000 (40,000 × $1.00)

	Units	Unit Cost	Total Cost
Beginning inventory (single layer of LIFO inventory)	40,000	$1.00	$40,000
Add purchases	10,000	1.50	15,000
Cost of goods available for sale	50,000		55,000
Ending inventory	6,000	1.00	6,000
Cost of goods sold	44,000		$49,000
Sales (44,000 units) from:			
Purchases	10,000	1.50	15,000
Beginning inventory layer	34,000	1.00	34,000
Cost of goods sold	44,000		$49,000

There are two possible reasons for a liquidation of an earlier layer(s).

- **Voluntary Liquidation** Management decides to reduce normal inventory quantity for some reason, such as a decline in demand, anticipation of reduced inventory replenishment costs, or anticipated changes in the product.
- **Involuntary Liquidation** An inventory reduction can be forced on the company by uncontrollable causes, such as shortages, strikes, delayed delivery dates, and unexpected demand.

Inventory liquidation often occurs sporadically during a year. Under the periodic LIFO method, a company will typically replace inventory liquidations, especially involuntary ones, before year-end. This replacement avoids a lower cost of goods sold and thereby avoids higher taxable income. When replacement is anticipated, entries can be made quarterly to avoid misleading readers of interim financial statements. If the impact of LIFO liquidation is material to a company, the income effect of LIFO liquidation will be disclosed in notes accompanying financial statements.

330-10-S99-3 Such disclosure [income realized as a result of LIFO inventory liquidation] would be required in order to make the financial statements not misleading. Disclosure may be made either in a footnote or parenthetically on the face of the income statement.

Computation of LIFO Liquidation — LO9-7 — Demo 9-7

Demo MBC

Refer to the information in **Exhibit 9-12**. Determine the LIFO liquidation profit or loss (assume a 25% tax rate).

Solution

Cost of goods sold assuming liquidation had not occurred (44,000 × $1.50)	$66,000
Cost of goods sold with liquidation (see Exhibit 9-12)	49,000
Increase in pretax income	$17,000
After-tax increase in income ($17,000 × 0.75)	$12,750

Before taxes, income increased by $17,000, which because of the LIFO conformity rule, caused taxes to increase by $4,250 ($17,000 × 0.25). The after-tax income effect of the LIFO liquidation is $12,750 or $17,000 multiplied by (1 − Tax rate).

SEARS

Real World—LIFO LIQUIDATION

SEARS HOLDING CORP. [SHLD]

Sears Holdings Corporation operates a national network of stores with 1,725 full-line and specialty retail stores in the U.S. operating through Kmart and Sears. Sears values half of its inventory using LIFO. Sears provides information on the LIFO reserve, which is necessary to convert inventory in its financial statements to FIFO to allow for comparability with other companies using FIFO. Sears disclosed that liquidation of older LIFO layers (valued at lower amounts than current inventory replacement costs) resulted in a decrease to cost of sales.

> **Merchandise Inventories** Approximately 50% of consolidated merchandise inventories are valued using LIFO. To estimate the effects of inflation on inventories, we utilize external price indices determined by an outside source, the Bureau of Labor Statistics. If the FIFO method of inventory valuation had been used instead of the LIFO method, merchandise inventories would have been $43 million higher at January 31, 2015 and $70 million higher at February 1, 2014. During 2014 and 2013, a reduction in inventory quantities resulted in a liquidation of applicable LIFO inventory quantities carried at lower costs in prior years. This LIFO liquidation resulted in a decrease in cost of sales of approximately $32 million and $7 million in 2014 and 2013, respectively.

LIFO Liquidation — LO9-7 — REVIEW 9-7

Review MBC

Southeast Inc. has maintained a periodic inventory system and the LIFO inventory method for over 20 years. The earliest layers of LIFO inventory date back 15 years. The company had beginning inventory at January 1, 2020, consisting of three layers, starting with the oldest layer of 150,000 units.

Units	Unit Cost	Total Cost
150,000	$10.00	$1,500,000
80,000	12.00	960,000
15,000	20.00	300,000
245,000		$2,760,000

During the year, an involuntary liquidation of inventory occurred. Ending inventory dropped to 120,000 units. The current replacement value of inventory is $35 per unit.

Required

What is the LIFO liquidation profit or loss assuming a 25% tax rate?

More Practice: 9-39, 9-59, 9-60

Solution on p. 9-55.

LO 9-8 Apply the dollar-value LIFO method

LO 9-8 Overview

Dollar-Value LIFO Method

- Restate ending inventory at base-year dollars
- Arrange restated inventory balance into layers
- Match layers to the appropriate price indices
- Restate layers into current year dollars

Pooling inventory items is a way to reduce the risk of a LIFO liquidation as described in the previous section. With pooling, the average cost for the entire pool of items, not the individual item's cost, is used in computing cost of goods sold and ending inventory values. Thus, even if one or two items in the pool experience a surge in usage for some reason to the point where low-cost inventory base layers are encroached upon, if the pool is large enough, the average cost of the pool will not be materially affected. This advantage is lost if a pool is too small to get the protection of the average cost or if the particular item experiencing liquidation constitutes a major portion of the pool.

Dollar-Value LIFO is a type of inventory costing method that pools inventory (see **Demo 9-8**), decreasing the chance of liquidation of LIFO layers. The dollar-value LIFO method uses price indices related to the inventory, instead of units and unit costs, and is applied to inventory pools, rather than to each individual product. These features of dollar-value LIFO simplify inventory measurement because most detailed computations of the unit cost LIFO method are avoided. The phrase *dollar-value* emphasizes that LIFO inventory each period is determined for *pools of inventory dollars*, rather than for separate units, and that the unit costs of individual products in the inventory pool lose their identities.

The conversion to dollar-value LIFO is not recorded internally in a company's accounts. The dollar-value LIFO approach determines the LIFO amounts of the ending inventory and therefore of cost of goods sold for income tax and external reporting purposes. The company continues to implement and use either the FIFO or average cost results for internal purposes. This means that when applying dollar-value LIFO, the beginning FIFO inventory amount for the company, meaning the first year of operations or the first year where a LIFO layer exists, is used as the base year LIFO inventory amount. The company continues to use FIFO for internal records. Only at year-end is dollar-value LIFO computed. The LIFO reserve adjustment to convert FIFO valuations to dollar-value LIFO is recorded as demonstrated earlier in LO 9-6.

Computation of dollar-value LIFO is described in the following four steps, assuming that the reporting period is a fiscal year, and a periodic inventory system is used.

Step One: Restate Ending Inventory at Base Year Dollars

FIFO inventory is restated to base year prices. While the initial year is at then-current prices, the following years are not. Using dollar-value LIFO allows us to isolate what changes are made due to changes in quantity, not simply changes in the price of goods by dividing ending inventory by the related year's price index. The price index used in dollar-value LIFO is determined in one of two ways:

- An external price index
- An internally generated price index

Many companies prefer to use a general price-level index published monthly by the federal government (for example, Ford's description earlier in the chapter). One such index is the **Consumer Price Index for Urban Consumers** (CPI). Because this general index does not closely measure changes in the prices of specific goods, some companies prefer to use a more specific price index. Such indices are available for many basic commodities, such as farm products and basic minerals, as well as for many manufactured items. A company desiring to use an index that closely captures changes in value of the items in its own inventory can elect to use a specific index based on the current cost of goods the company actually purchases.

Step Two: Arrange Restated Inventory Balance into Layers

After restating inventory into base year dollars, the balance is then arranged into layers. The restated inventory balance is allocated to the oldest layers first. A new layer is added if the restated balance is higher than the prior year's restated inventory balance. Layers built up in prior years are liquidated however, if the restated inventory balance is lower than the restated prior year balance.

Step Three: Match Layers to the Appropriate Price Indices

Each layer is matched to the price index from the year where the layer originated. If no new layer is created in a particular year, that year's index will not be used in the dollar-value LIFO calculations.

Step Four: Restate Layers of Inventory into Current Year Dollars

The last step is to restate the inventory layers into current dollars. Each layer is multiplied by its matching price index determined in step three. Layers are added up to arrive at ending dollar-value LIFO inventory for that year.

Dollar-Value LIFO Method **LO9-8** **Demo 9-8**

Demo MBC

On December 31, 2020, Electronics Inc. had a base year inventory value of $6,100 calculated using FIFO, which will be used as the base year LIFO inventory amount (2020 is Electronics Inc.'s first year of operations). The corporation continues to use FIFO for internal reporting, but will report inventory under dollar-value LIFO method for taxes and external reporting. FIFO ending inventory balances for 2021 and 2022 were $8,930 and $9,490, respectively. Price indices were 1.000, 1.220, and 1.279, for years 2020, 2021, and 2022, respectively. Compute dollar-value LIFO ending inventory at the end of years 2020, 2021, and 2022, and record the adjusting entries on December 31, 2021, and December 31, 2022, to adjust the LIFO reserve.

Solution

Date	Ending Inventory at FIFO (Year-end prices)	÷	Price Index	=	Ending Inventory (Base year prices) [1]		Inventory Layers [2]	Price Index [3]	Ending Inventory (Dollar-Value LIFO) [4]
2020 . . .	$6,100		1.000		$6,100	→	$6,100	1.000	$6,100
2021 . . .	8,930		1.220		7,320	→	6,100	1.000	$6,100
							1,220	1.220	1,488
									$7,588
2022 . . .	9,490		1.279		7,420	→	6,100	1.000	$6,100
							1,220	1.220	1,488
							100	1.279	128
									$7,716

Explanation of the dollar-value solution.

[1] Restate Ending Inventory at Base Year Prices The first step is to divide the ending inventory by the year's **price index** to arrive at inventory in base year dollars as follows.

Year	Ending Inventory/Price Index	Ending Inventory at Base Year Prices
2020	$6,100/1.000	$6,100
2021	$8,930/1.220	7,320
2022	$9,490/1.279	7,420

[2] Arrange Restated Inventory Balance into Layers In 2021, the inventory of $7,320 consists of the older layer of $6,100 while the residual makes up a new layer of inventory of $1,220 ($7,320 − $6,100). In 2022, the inventory value of $7,420 is made up of the two preexisting layers ($6,100 and $1,220), plus a new layer of $100 ($7,420 − $6,100 − $1,220). Because inventory increased (even after taking out the effect of increasing prices), no liquidation of older layers took place.

[3] Match Layers to the Appropriate Price Index Each layer is matched to its originating price index. For example, in 2021, the $6,100 layer originated from year 2020, thus the index of 1.000 used. The new layer of $1,220 originated in 2021, thus the index of 1.222 is used.

[4] Restate Layers of Inventory into Current Year Dollars Layers are now restated into current dollars. For example, in year 2022, the three layers are restated to current year dollars.

continued

continued from previous page

Inventory Layer		Price Index		Dollar-Value LIFO Inventory
$6,100	×	1.000	=	$6,100
1,220	×	1.220	=	1,488
100	×	1.279	=	128
				$7,716

Inventory under dollar-value LIFO is $6,100, $7,588, and $7,716, for the year-ends of 2020, 2021, and 2022, respectively. Information for the adjusting entries follows along with the year-end adjusting entries.

	A	B	C	D
	Ending Inventory at FIFO	Ending Inventory at LIFO	LIFO Reserve [B − A]	Adjustment to LIFO Reserve [C − Prior Year C]
Dec. 31, 2020 . . .	$6,100	$6,100	$ —	$ —
Dec. 31, 2021 . . .	8,930	7,588	(1,342)	(1,342)
Dec. 31, 2022 . . .	9,490	7,716	(1,774)	(432)

December 31, 2021—To adjust the year-end LIFO allowance

Assets = Liabilities + Equity
−1,342 −1,342
Inventory Allow: 1,342 (credit) | COGS: 1,342 (debit)

	Debit	Credit
Cost of Goods Sold	1,342	
Allowance to Reduce FIFO Inventory to LIFO		1,342

December 31, 2022—To adjust the year-end LIFO allowance

Assets = Liabilities + Equity
−432 −432
Inventory Allow: 1,342, 432 (credit) | COGS: 1,342, 432 (debit)

	Debit	Credit
Cost of Goods Sold	432	
Allowance to Reduce FIFO Inventory to LIFO		432

EXPANDING YOUR KNOWLEDGE **Double-Extension Method**

The first step in dollar-value LIFO is to restate inventory layers into base year dollars using a relevant price index such as the CPI. The **double-extension method** can be used if relevant price indices are not available. In this method, the company determines the current price of representative items to the base year items and develops an index to apply to the current year. For example, assume there are 1,000 base year units costing $10 per unit, which totals $10,000. At the end of year one, a representative product costs $12 per unit and the company holds 1,050 units of that product, which totals $12,600. This means the index at the end of year one is 1.26, computed as $12,600/$10,000.

REVIEW 9-8 LO9-8 Dollar-Value LIFO Method

Review MBC

On January 1, 2021, L. Bryan Company changed from FIFO to LIFO for income tax and external reporting purposes. At that date, the beginning FIFO inventory (the base inventory for LIFO purposes) was $75,000. The following information is available from L. Bryan's records for the year-ends 2020 through 2023.

Year	Ending Inventory at FIFO	Index
2020	$ 75,000	1.00
2021	88,000	1.10
2022	100,000	1.15
2023	75,000	1.20

Required

Calculate ending inventory for each year using the dollar-value LIFO method and record the adjusting entries on December 31, 2021, 2022, and 2023 to adjust the LIFO reserve.

More Practice: 9-40, 9-61, 9-62, 9-63

Solution on p. 9-56.

Perform inventory ratio analysis and interpretation — LO 9-9

Inventory Ratios

Inventory Ratios (LO 9-9 Overview)
- Inventory turnover (COGS/Average inventory)
- Average days in inventory (365/Inventory turnover)

Using different inventory cost-flow assumptions can produce significant differences in accounting ratios that involve either cost of sales figures or inventory values as well as others that are affected by these calculations. Analysts should consider making the necessary adjustments to the amounts reported in financial statements before drawing conclusions when comparing the results of operations across companies using different cost-flow assumptions.

Two key ratios used to measure inventory activity are the inventory turnover ratio and the days in inventory (illustrated in **Demo 9-9**).

- **Inventory turnover** (COGS / Average inventory) measures the number of times, on average, that inventory is sold during the period; generally, a higher value is preferred.
- **Average days in inventory** (365 / Inventory turnover) measure helps investors and creditors understand how many days of resources are required to be devoted to inventory before the time of sale; generally, a lower value is preferable.

$$\frac{\text{COGS}}{\text{Average inventory}}$$

$$\frac{365}{\text{Inventory turnover}}$$

Inventories often constitute a large portion of current assets. They are also less liquid than cash and short-term securities. Companies whose current assets are mainly in inventories have less flexibility to meet their obligations out of current assets. This means it is important for investors and creditors to assess whether the company is managing its inventory. If inventory turnover is lower than the industry average or its competitors' ratio, the company might be holding excess inventory. If inventory turnover is higher than the industry average or its competitors' ratio, the company might not have sufficient inventory to support operations and the needs of its customers.

Inventory Ratio Analysis and Interpretation — **LO9-9** — **Demo 9-9**

Demo MBC

Refer to the results of **Demos 9-3A, 9-3B, 9-3C, 9-3D, 9-5A, 9-5B, and 9-5C**. Prepare a table summarizing (a) cost of goods sold, (b) gross profit, (c) inventory turnover, and (d) average days in inventory for Chase Corporation for each of the inventory methods illustrated in this chapter: specific identification (periodic), average cost (periodic), FIFO (periodic), LIFO (periodic), moving average (perpetual), FIFO (perpetual), and LIFO (perpetual). Assume that inventory sells for $2 per unit. Provide a brief interpretation of results.

Solution

Inventory Method	Specific Identification	Average Cost (periodic)	FIFO (periodic)	LIFO (periodic)	Moving Average (perpetual)	FIFO (perpetual)	LIFO (perpetual)
COGAS	$1,120	$1,120	$1,120	$1,120	$1,120	$1,120	$1,120
Less ending Inventory	348	336	358	310	354	358	342
COGS	**$ 772**	**$ 784**	**$ 762**	**$ 810**	**$ 766**	**$ 762**	**$ 778**
Sales ($2 per unit)	$1,400	$1,400	$1,400	$1,400	$1,400	$1,400	$1,400
Less COGS	772	784	762	810	766	762	778
Gross profit	**$ 628**	**$ 616**	**$ 638**	**$ 590**	**$ 634**	**$ 638**	**$ 622**
Average inventory	$ 274	$ 268	$ 279	$ 255	$ 277	$ 279	$ 271
Inventory turnover	***2.82**	**2.93**	**2.73**	**3.18**	**2.77**	**2.73**	**2.87**
Average days in inventory	****129**	**125**	**134**	**115**	**132**	**134**	**127**

$$^{*}\text{ Inventory turnover} = \frac{\text{Cost of goods sold}}{\text{Average inventory}} = \frac{\$772}{\$274 \text{ or } [(\$200 \text{ Beginning inventory} + \$348 \text{ Ending inventory})/2]} = 2.82$$

$$^{**}\text{Average days in inventory} = \frac{365}{\text{Inventory turnover}} = \frac{365}{2.82} = 129 \text{ days}$$

continued

continued from previous page

The following observations are made based on this summary of Chase where *inventory prices rose over time.*

- Cost of goods sold is higher under LIFO than under FIFO, while the average method falls between them.
- Gross profit is lower under LIFO than under FIFO, while the average method falls between them.
- Inventory turnover is higher (days in inventory is lower) under LIFO than under FIFO, while the average method falls between them.
- Although the ratios differ across methods, the actual physical flow of inventory is the same across all methods. Thus, it is important for inventory to be measured using a consistent method over time so that an analysis of ratios over time provides useful information to investors and creditors.
- Differences in the numbers above illustrate why results under different accounting methods are not comparable. If a user wants to compare Chase, which uses LIFO, to a competitor that uses FIFO, that user should adjust Chase's numbers to be as if the company used FIFO (by using the disclosed LIFO Reserve) before computing the ratios above. The ratios are then comparable for the two companies after the adjustment is made.

NIKE

Real World—INVENTORY RATIO ANALYSIS

NIKE INC. [NKE]

Nike Inc. highlights the trend of its inventory turnover ("turns") in a recent report on Form 10-K under Item 6—Selected Financial Data. Inventory turns are reported for the most recent 5 years.

	2015	2014	2013	2012	2011
Return on equity	27.8%	24.6%	23.1%	22.0%	21.8%
Return on assets	16.3%	14.9%	15.3%	15.1%	15.0%
Inventory turns*	4.0	4.1	4.2	4.5	4.8
Current ratio at May 31	2.5	2.7	3.5	3.0	2.9
Price/earnings ratio at May 31	27.5	25.9	22.8	23.0	19.3

*Inventory "turn" in 2015 is calculated as: (1) Average inventory for 2015 ($4,337) and 2014 ($3,947) is $4,142; (2) Cost of sales is $16,534; (3) Inventory turn is 4.0, computed as $16,534/$4,142.

REVIEW 9-9 **LO9-9** **Inventory Ratio Analysis**

Review MBC

Gap Inc. reported the following information in a recent Form 10-K ($ millions).

End of Year 1, Merchandise inventory	$ 1,889
End of Year 2, Merchandise inventory	1,873
End of Year 3, Merchandise inventory	1,830
Year 2, COGS and occupancy expenses	10,077
Year 3, COGS and occupancy expenses	9,876

Required

Compute the (a) inventory turnover and (b) average days in inventory for Year 2 and for Year 3 for Gap Inc.

More Practice: 9-41, 9-66
Solution on p. 9-56.

Management Judgment

We discussed the recognition of inventory using the cost of a specific item or basing the cost on cost-flow assumptions. For many companies, specific identification is prohibitively costly or not feasible.

330-10-30-10 The cost to be matched against revenue from a sale may not be the identified cost of the specific item which is sold, especially in cases in which similar goods are purchased at different times and at different prices. While in some lines of business specific lots are clearly identified from the time of purchase through the time of sale and are costed on this basis, ordinarily the identity of goods is lost between the time of acquisition and the time of sale.

So instead, management most often chooses an inventory method based upon assumptions of how inventory costs flow in the accounting system.

Management Choice of Inventory Method

We discussed several methods employing assumptions including average cost, FIFO, and LIFO.

330-10-30-11 Accordingly, if the materials purchased in various lots are identical and interchangeable, the use of identified cost of the various lots may not produce the most useful financial statements. This fact has resulted in the general acceptance of several assumptions with respect to the flow of cost factors such as FIFO, average, and LIFO to provide practical bases for the measurement of periodic income.

The average cost method is appealing when a mix of inventories of different purchase values occurs. The FIFO approach is a convenient and logical cost-flow assumption for many items. This is because the physical flow of goods most commonly follows FIFO. While LIFO does not generally follow physical flow, it does result in lower payments, which may impact management's choice of inventory method. However, accounting may be more complex under LIFO because companies commonly keep their internal records on FIFO and convert to LIFO at reporting dates.

In general, the decision by management to select an inventory method affects reported inventory and net income. For example, in a recent 10-K, Caterpillar Inc. disclosed that had the FIFO method been in use, inventories would have been $1,934 million higher than the inventory balance reported at December 31, 2017, of $10,018 million. **GAAP requires that the major objective in selecting a method should be to choose the one that most clearly reflects periodic income.** Thus, choosing an inventory method that best matches physical flow of inventory or a method that most clearly reflects the balance sheet presentation is not specifically required.

330-10-30-9 Cost for inventory purposes may be determined under any one of several assumptions as to the flow of cost factors, such as first-in first-out (FIFO), average, and last-in first-out (LIFO). The major objective in selecting a method should be to choose the one which, under the circumstances, most clearly reflects periodic income.

The authoritative guidance also indicates that uniform methods in a specific industry are useful to financial statement users.

330-10-30-14 Although selection of the method should be made on the basis of the individual circumstances, financial statements will be more useful if uniform methods of inventory pricing are adopted by all entities within a given industry.

Disclosure of Inventory Method

Information on which inventory valuation method(s) a company ultimately selects to value its inventories is disclosed in notes to financial statements. This information often appears in its first note, which describes the company's accounting policies. More detailed disclosures are often provided in additional notes. For example, Coca-Cola Company values some inventory using the average cost method and some inventory using FIFO. A company may determine that for certain segments of inventory, a different method is a better reflection of periodic income.

330-10-30-15 While the basis of stating inventories does not affect the overall gain or loss on the ultimate disposition of inventory items, any inconsistency in the selection or employment of a basis may improperly affect the periodic amounts of income or loss. Because of the common use and importance of periodic statements, a procedure adopted for the treatment of inventory items shall be consistently applied in order that the results reported may be fairly allocated between years.

Management Decisions in Measuring Inventory

While management judgment is directly involved in the choice of an inventory method, other inventory decisions also require management judgment. For example, the determination of costs to include in inventory can be subjective. As indicated in the accounting guidance in an earlier section, abnormal freight, handling costs, and amounts of wasted materials should be charged to expense in the current period. This means, for example, that management must determine when freight is abnormal. Does a more costly rush order to stock merchandise inventory or shipping slow-moving inventory to an alternate location result in additional inventory costs or immediate expense?

Under LIFO, determining how to group inventory items into pools is subjective. As a result, it is possible for management to strategically group items to either cause or avoid liquidation, which impacts reported net income. This type of earning management reduces the quality of earnings for the period.

Questions

9-1. Why should managers be concerned with the level and flow of merchandising inventories?

9-2. List and briefly explain the typical inventory classifications for a merchandiser and for a manufacturer.

9-3. What general rule is applied in determining what items should be included in inventory? How does the location of inventory affect this rule?

9-4. Indicate for each of the following whether it is included in the valuation of Mart Inc.'s inventory.

a. Goods held by agents for Mart Inc.
b. Goods held by Mart Inc. for sale on commission.
c. Goods held by Mart Inc. but awaiting return to vendor.
d. Goods returned to Mart Inc. from buyers.

9-5. Assume that we are in the process of adjusting and closing the books at period-end (for the *purchaser* of inventory). For inventory purposes, how would the purchaser treat the following goods in transit?

a. Invoice received for $10,000, shipped f.o.b. shipping point.
b. Invoice received for $18,000, shipped f.o.b. destination.
c. Invoice received for $6,000, shipped f.o.b. shipping point and delivery refused on the last day of the period because of damaged condition.

9-6. Explain the two main journal entries of a periodic inventory system, including for purchases and the period-end adjusting entry. Describe how cost of goods sold is computed.

9-7. Why is cost of goods sold sometimes characterized as a residual amount? In which inventory system is this characterization appropriate?

9-8. Which of the following items should be included in determining the unit cost for inventory purposes in a periodic inventory system?

a. Purchase returns.
b. Cash discounts on credit purchases.
c. Freight on goods purchased.

9-9. What does it mean to have an assumed inventory cost-flow? Which inventory methods apply assumed inventory cost-flows?

9-10. What are some considerations when choosing between a periodic and perpetual inventory system?

9-11. Assuming the LIFO method, what is meant by inventory liquidation? Why is liquidation a serious problem for LIFO but not FIFO?

9-12. What are the primary objectives to be considered in selecting a particular inventory cost-flow method? Why is the selection important?

9-13. Briefly explain the differences between periodic and perpetual inventory systems. Under what circumstances is each generally used?

9-14. Does the adoption of a perpetual inventory system eliminate the need for a physical count or measurement of inventories? Explain.

9-15. Explain the specific identification cost inventory method and explain when the method is appropriate.

9-16. Distinguish between average cost and moving average in determining inventory unit cost. When is each typically used? Explain.

9-17. Explain the essential features of first-in, first-out (FIFO). What are the primary advantages and disadvantages of FIFO? Explain the difference in the application of FIFO under a periodic inventory system and a perpetual inventory system. In contrast with LIFO, how does FIFO affect cash flow?

9-18. Explain the essential features of last-in, first-out (LIFO). What are the primary advantages and disadvantages of LIFO? Explain the differences in application of LIFO under the periodic and perpetual inventory systems.

9-19. What is meant by inventory layers? Why are they important with respect to the FIFO and LIFO methods?

9-20. Compare the balance sheet and income statement effects of FIFO with those of LIFO (a) when prices are rising, and (b) when prices are falling.

9-21. Explain why a company's management might be reluctant to use LIFO in a period of rising inventory costs even though such use would reduce the company's current income tax liability.

9-22. How does dollar-value LIFO result in less liquidation of LIFO layers compared to unit cost LIFO?

9-23. In describing a company's inventory position, the phrase LIFO reserve is sometimes used. What is meant by LIFO reserve? What alternative phrase is used?

9-24. What is the difference between a voluntary and involuntary LIFO liquidation?

9-25. If the Bureau of Labor Statistics computes a price index of 1.15 for a merchandise pool with a base year value of $200,000, why might a company report a dollar-value LIFO amount of $250,000 for this merchandise pool?

9-26. Identify two financial statement ratios used to analyze inventory accounts. Explain how they are calculated.

Brief Exercises

Brief Exercise 9-27 Classifying Goods and Costs as Inventory or Not **LO1** *Hint:* See Demo 9-1

For each of the following items, indicate whether it would be reported as inventory in the financial statements of the seller.

a. Goods sold where the company (seller) has the right to repurchase the inventory at a specified time and price.
b. Goods sold when returns are estimable.
c. Freight-in charges for the receipt of merchandise inventory.
d. Freight-out charges for delivery of merchandise to customer.
e. Goods out on consignment at another location.
f. Goods from another company, held on consignment at its facilities.

Brief Exercise 9-28 Identifying Goods in Transit as Inventory or Not **LO1**

On December 31, 2020, Diamond Co. is determining whether goods in-transit should be included or excluded from the physical inventory count. One shipment in-transit *to* Diamond Co. for $20,000 was shipped f.o.b. destination from a vendor. The goods are expected to arrive on January 2, 2021. One shipment in-transit *from* Diamond Co. for $8,000 was shipped f.o.b. destination to a customer. The merchandise is expected to arrive on January 3, 2021. What shipment amount(s) (if any) should be included in the physical inventory count on December 31, 2020?

Brief Exercise 9-29 Periodic System—Calculating Cost of Goods Sold from Component Accounts **LO2**

Symmetrical Inc. maintains a periodic inventory system. On January 1, 2020, the inventory balance was $25,000. The physical inventory count on December 31, 2020, resulted in an ending inventory balance of $30,000. The company reported purchases of $150,000, freight charges on purchases of $8,000, and purchase returns of $1,000. What should the company report as cost of goods sold for 2020?

Brief Exercise 9-30 Periodic System—Calculating Ending Inventory and Cost of Sales using Average Cost **LO3** *Hint:* See Demo 9-3B

The following information is available for Water's Inc.

Date	Units	Unit Cost
January 1, 2020 (beginning inventory)	100	$50.00
Purchases: January 10, 2020.	75	52.00
January 15, 2020.	150	52.50
January 30, 2020.	100	55.00

The company maintains a periodic inventory system. A physical inventory count shows 125 units in stock on January 31. What is (a) ending inventory on January 31, and (b) cost of goods sold for January, using the average-cost method? Round unit costs to two decimal places.

Brief Exercise 9-31
Periodic System—Calculating Ending Inventory and Cost of Sales using FIFO **LO3**
Hint: See Demo 9-3C

Refer to the information in Brief Exercise 9-30 except that the company uses the FIFO inventory method. What is (a) ending inventory on January 31, and (b) cost of goods sold for January, using the FIFO inventory method?

Brief Exercise 9-32
Periodic System—Calculating Ending Inventory and Cost of Sales using LIFO **LO3**
Hint: See Demo 9-3D

Refer to the information in Brief Exercise 9-30 except that the company uses the LIFO inventory method. What is (a) ending inventory on January 31, and (b) cost of goods sold for January, using the LIFO inventory method?

Brief Exercise 9-33
Perpetual System—Recording Purchases, Returns, and Sales **LO4**

Track Bicycles Inc. maintains a perpetual inventory system and began 2020 with $40,000 of merchandise inventory. During January 2020, the company purchased inventory of $100,000 on account, returned $2,500 of defective goods, and sold inventory with a cost of $110,000 for $180,000 on account. Prepare the journal entries for the month of January for Track Bicycles Inc. for the following inventory transactions: (a) Inventory purchases, (b) Inventory returns, and (c) Inventory sales.

Brief Exercise 9-34
Perpetual System—Recording Purchases and Payments with Discounts using Gross Method **LO4**
Hint: See Demo 9-4A

Track Bicycles Inc. purchased merchandise inventory on February 1, 2020, for $85,000 on account, terms 2/10, n/30. The company maintains a perpetual inventory system and accounts for purchases using the gross method. The full balance of $85,000 was paid on February 9, 2020. Record the purchases entry on February 1, 2020, and the payment entry on February 9, 2020.

Brief Exercise 9-35
Perpetual System—Recording Purchases and Payments with Discounts using Net Method **LO4**
Hint: See Demo 9-4B

Refer to the information in Brief Exercise 9-34 except that the company accounts for purchases using the net method. Record the purchases entry on February 1, 2020, and the payment entry on February 9, 2020.

Brief Exercise 9-36
Perpetual System—Calculating Ending Inventory and Cost of Sales using Moving Average **LO5**
Hint: See Demo 9-5A

Upland Co.'s inventory records showed the following data accounted for in a perpetual inventory system.

Date		Units	Unit Cost
June 1	Inventory.	500	$8.00
June 3	Purchases.	1,000	8.40
June 7	Sales (at $16 per unit)	700	
June 20	Purchases.	680	9.00
June 22	Sales (at $16 per unit)	1,100	

What is (a) ending inventory on January 31, and (b) cost of goods sold for January, using the moving-average method? Round unit costs to two decimal places.

Brief Exercise 9-37
Perpetual System—Calculating Ending Inventory and Cost of Sales using FIFO **LO5**
Hint: See Demo 9-5B

Refer to the information in Brief Exercise 9-36 except that the company accounts for inventory using the FIFO inventory method. What is (a) ending inventory on January 31, and (b) cost of goods sold for January, using the FIFO inventory method?

Brief Exercise 9-38
Recording Entry to Adjust LIFO Reserve **LO6**
Hint: See Demo 9-6

Savers Inc. reports inventory under the LIFO method but maintains inventory records internally using the FIFO method. The difference between FIFO and LIFO at the end of 2019 was $10,000 (FIFO inventory is higher). At the end of 2020, FIFO inventory exceeds LIFO inventory by $13,000. Record the journal entry to adjust the LIFO reserve at December 31, 2020.

Brief Exercise 9-39
Computing LIFO Liquidation **LO7**
Hint: See Demo 9-7

Heiden Inc. accounts for inventory using the LIFO inventory method. Beginning inventory on January 1 consists of 10,000 units at a cost of $5 per unit. During the year, the company sold more items than purchased, causing the ending inventory balance on December 31, 2020, to drop to 7,500 units. Assuming a tax rate of 40%, and a current replacement cost of inventory of $8 per unit, what is the LIFO liquidation effect on pretax and after-tax income?

Will Inc. accounts for inventory using the dollar-value LIFO method. The following information is available for the years 2020 through 2022.

Brief Exercise 9-40
Computing Ending Inventory under Dollar-Value LIFO **LO8**
Hint: See Demo 9-8

Year	Ending Inventory at FIFO	Price Index
2020	$ 5,000	1.00
2021	8,000	1.10
2022	10,000	1.13

What is its ending inventory under the dollar-value LIFO method for the years 2020, 2021, and 2022?

Target Corporation reported the following information in a recent Form 10-K.

Brief Exercise 9-41
Computing Inventory Ratios **LO9**
Hint: See Demo 9-9

Consolidated Statements of Operations ($ millions)	Fiscal Year Ended January 30, 2016
Cost of sales	$51,997

Consolidated Statements of Financial Position ($ millions)	January 30, 2016	January 31, 2015
Inventory	$8,601	$8,282

What is the (a) inventory turnover ratio, and (b) average days in inventory, for the fiscal year ended January 30, 2016?

Exercises

Below is a list of items related to merchandising transactions.

Exercise 9-42
Determining Merchandise and Costs to be Included or Excluded from Inventory **LO1**
Hint: See Demo 9-1

a. Merchandise out on consignment.
b. Merchandise purchased, in transit (shipped f.o.b. shipping point).
c. Merchandise purchased, in transit (shipped f.o.b. destination).
d. Merchandise held on consignment.
e. Merchandise sold, in transit (shipped f.o.b. destination).
f. Merchandise sold, in transit (shipped f.o.b. shipping point).
g. Freight charges on goods purchased.
h. Freight charges on goods sold.
i. Merchandise sold by the merchandiser but where the merchandiser agreed to repurchase the merchandise at a certain price.
j. Merchandise sold where a 5% return is estimated.

Required
For each item *a* through *j*, indicate whether the item should be included in a year-end balance sheet as inventory or whether the item should be excluded from inventory. If the item should be excluded from inventory, indicate the proper accounting treatment.

The unadjusted inventory balance of Ultim Corp. is $100,000 on December 31, 2020, based on a physical inventory count. The following items must be considered before the inventory valuation is finalized.

Exercise 9-43
Determining Merchandise to be Included or Excluded from Ending Inventory **LO1**

a. On December 31, the physical inventory excluded $250 of merchandise inventory set aside for shipment to a customer, which has not yet shipped.
b. On December 31, the physical inventory excluded $1,000 of merchandise inventory out on consignment in the customers' showrooms.
c. On December 31, the physical inventory excluded $800 of merchandise held on consignment.

d. $750 of in-transit merchandise was shipped f.o.b. destination to a customer and was excluded from the physical inventory count. The merchandise was turned over to a common carrier on December 28, 2020, and is expected to arrive at the customer on January 2, 2021.

e. Ultim Corp. ordered merchandise on December 26, 2020. The merchandise ($800) was shipped to Ultim Corp. f.o.b. shipping point, and was expected to arrive January 2, 2021. The merchandise was not included in the physical inventory count.

f. A return to a vendor of merchandise for $1,000 was in-transit on December 31, 2020, and was excluded from the physical inventory count. The merchandise was shipped f.o.b. shipping point on December 30, 2020.

Required

For each item *a* through *f*, determine and explain any adjustments required to the physical inventory balance of $100,000 for Ultim Corp.

Exercise 9-44
Determining Merchandise to be Included or Excluded from Ending Inventory **LO1**

The unadjusted inventory balance of Sara Ann Corp. is $500,000 on December 31, 2020, based on a physical inventory count. The following items must be considered before the inventory valuation is finalized.

a. On December 31, the physical inventory excluded $500 of merchandise inventory shipped to Sara Ann Corp. from a vendor f.o.b. destination that arrived on January 1, 2021.

b. On December 31, the physical inventory included $18,000 of merchandise inventory held on consignment by a customer. Sara Ann Corp. is the consignor.

c. On December 31, the physical inventory included $800 of merchandise held on consignment. The consignor is Sara Ann's largest vendor.

d. $18,000 of in-transit merchandise was shipped f.o.b. shipping point to a customer and was excluded from the physical inventory count. The merchandise was shipped on December 28, 2020, and is expected to arrive at the customer on December 31, 2021.

e. Goods are in-transit from a vendor to Sara Ann on December 31, 2020. The invoice cost was $12,000 and the goods were shipped f.o.b. shipping point on December 28, 2020. The merchandise was excluded from the physical inventory count because they had not been delivered.

f. Merchandise with a cost of $300 is held in the receiving department for return. The merchandise was excluded from the physical inventory count.

Required

Determine whether any adjustments are needed to Sara Ann's physical inventory balance of $500,000 due to the transactions *a* through *f* outlined above.

Exercise 9-45
Periodic System—Recording Inventory-Related Entries using the Gross Method **LO2**
Hint: See Demo 9-2A

Unite Inc. maintains a periodic inventory system and uses the gross method to record purchases. The following transactions occurred during the month of March 2020 for its major inventory line.

a. Purchase of merchandise inventory on March 1, 2020, for $24,000 on account, terms 1/10, n/30.

b. Paid $240 cash for freight charges on March 1, 2020, related to the purchase.

c. Returned $180 of merchandise on March 5, 2020, and received a credit from the vendor.

d. Paid the balance due to the vendor on March 8, 2020.

e. Sold merchandise inventory on March 15, 2020, for $15,000.

Required

Prepare journal entries for transactions *a* through *e*.

Exercise 9-46
Computing Income and Recording Period-End Adjusting Entry—Periodic System **LO2**

The records of Whirlpools Inc. show the following data for 2020.

Sales revenue.	$400,000	Beginning inventory	$50,000
Purchases.	$280,000	Expenses including income taxes . . .	$90,000
Net income as a percent of sales revenue	15%	Tax rate for 2020.	25%

Required

a. Reconstruct the income statement for this company. Assume a periodic inventory system.

b. Prepare the required journal entry at period end to record ending inventory. Assume a periodic inventory system.

Exercise 9-47
Periodic System—Using Knowledge of Financial Statement Relations to Compute Missing Amounts **LO2**

The following information relates to Payleast Shoes Company.

	2020	2021	2022
Net sales	$90,000	$110,000	$130,000
Beginning inventory	12,000	e	j
Purchases (gross)	70,000	82,500	99,000
Purchase returns and allowances	(6,000)	(5,000)	(8,800)
Purchase discounts	(4,000)	(2,500)	(1,900)
Freight-in	3,000	f	10,000
Cost of goods available for sale	a	93,500	k
Ending inventory	15,000	g	26,000
Cost of sales	b	75,500	l
Gross profit	c	h	39,700
Gross profit as a percentage of sales	d	i	m

Required
Assuming the company uses the periodic inventory system, solve for the missing amounts *a* through *m* for years 2020 through 2022.

Exercise 9-48
Perpetual System—Recording Inventory-Related Entries using the Gross Method **LO4**
Hint: See Demo 9-4A

Columbus Music Inc. maintains a perpetual inventory system and uses the gross method to record purchases. The following transactions occurred during the month of March 2020, for its major inventory line.

a. Purchase of merchandise inventory on March 1, 2020, for $24,000 on account, terms 1/10, n/30.
b. Paid cash of $240 for freight charges on March 1, 2020, related to the purchase.
c. Returned $180 of merchandise on March 5, 2020, and received a credit from the vendor.
d. Paid the balance due to the vendor on March 8, 2020.
e. Sold merchandise inventory on March 15, 2020, for $15,000 with a cost of $10,000.

Required
Prepare journal entries for transactions *a* through *e*.

Exercise 9-49
Perpetual and Periodic Systems—Recording Inventory-Related Entries using the Gross Method **LO2, 4**

The following transactions are from Sharper Vision Corporation.

1. Purchased inventory on December 10, 2020, with a list price of $3,750, a trade discount of 20%, and with terms 2/10, n/30.
2. Returned $500 of inventory to the supplier on December 15, 2020.
3. Paid $2,000 cash on account on December 19, 2020.
4. Paid the remaining balance on January 5, 2021.

Required
a. Prepare journal entries for the transactions 1 through 4, assuming that the company uses the perpetual inventory system and the gross method for recording purchase discounts.
b. Prepare journal entries for the transactions 1 through 4, assuming that the company uses the periodic inventory system and the gross method for recording purchase discounts.

Exercise 9-50
Perpetual and Periodic Systems—Recording Inventory-Related Entries using the Net Method **LO2, 4**

Refer to the information from Exercise 9-49. Assume that the company uses the net method for recording purchases.

Required
a. Prepare journal entries for the transactions 1 through 4, assuming that the company uses the perpetual inventory system, including any adjusting entry required on December 31, 2020.
b. Prepare journal entries for the transactions 1 through 4, assuming that the company uses the periodic inventory system, including any adjusting entry required on December 31, 2020.

Exercise 9-51
Recording Entries under the Periodic and Perpetual Inventory Systems **LO2, 4**

The records for Upland Inc. at December 31, 2020, show the following.

	Units	Unit Price
Sales during period (for cash)	10,000	$20 (sales price)
Inventory at beginning of period	2,000	12 (cost)
Merchandise purchased during period (for cash)	16,000	12 (cost)
Purchase returns during period (cash refund)	100	12 (cost)
Inventory at end of period (physically counted)	7,900	12 (cost)

Total expenses (excluding cost of goods sold), $60,000

Required

a. Prepare entries for the transactions reflected above assuming a periodic inventory system for:
1. Merchandise sales.
2. Merchandise purchases.
3. Merchandise returns.
4. Total expenses.
5. To record cost of sales and ending inventory balance.

b. Prepare entries for the transactions reflected above assuming a perpetual inventory system for:
1. Merchandise sales.
2. Merchandise purchases.
3. Merchandise returns.
4. Total expenses.
5. To record cost of sales and ending inventory balance.

Exercise 9-52
Periodic System—Calculating Ending Inventory and Cost of Sales using Average Cost, FIFO, and LIFO
LO3

Leven Company began operations on December 1, 2019. The following information is available for the company's merchandise inventory. A physical inventory taken on March 31, 2020, showed 1,500 units available. Leven uses a periodic inventory system.

Date	Units	Unit Cost
January 1, 2020 (beginning inventory)	800	$ 9.00
Purchases: January 5, 2020	1,500	10.00
January 25, 2020	1,200	10.50
February 16, 2020	600	12.00
March 26, 2020	900	13.00

Required

a. Compute ending inventory and cost of goods sold for the quarter ended March 31, 2020, using:
1. Average Cost method.
2. FIFO method.
3. LIFO method.

b. Which method results in the:
1. Highest gross profit?
2. Lowest gross profit?
3. Highest ending inventory balance?
4. Lowest ending inventory balance?

Exercise 9-53
Perpetual System—Calculating Ending Inventory and Cost of Sales using Moving Average, FIFO, and LIFO **LO5**

April Inc. maintains a perpetual inventory system and recorded the following information for the month of January.

Date	Units	Unit Cost
Inventory, January 1	475	$10.50
Purchase, January 10	200	12.00
Purchase, January 20	100	13.25
Purchase, January 28	300	14.00
Sale, January 5	250	
Sale, January 13	100	
Sale, January 31	160	
Inventory, January 31	565	

Required

Compute ending inventory and cost of goods sold for the month ending January 31 using:
1. Average Cost method.
2. FIFO method.
3. LIFO method.

Exercise 9-54
Periodic and Perpetual Systems—Calculating Ending Inventory and Cost of Sales using Average Cost (Moving Average), FIFO, and LIFO **LO3, 5**

Undew Inc.'s inventory records showed the following data for an item it sells regularly.

Date		Units	Unit Cost
Jan. 1	Inventory.	2,000	$10.00
Jan. 3	Purchases.	18,000	10.40
Jan. 7	Sales (at $26 per unit)	7,000	
Jan. 20	Purchases.	6,000	11.00
Jan. 22	Sales (at $27 per unit)	16,000	
Jan. 30	Purchases.	3,000	12.00

Required

a. Assuming that Undew maintains a periodic inventory system, compute ending inventory and cost of goods sold for the month ending January 31 using (1) average cost, (2) FIFO, and (3) LIFO. Round per unit cost to two decimal places.

b. Assuming that Undew maintains a perpetual inventory system, compute ending inventory and cost of goods sold for the month ending January 31 using (1) moving average, (2) FIFO, and (3) LIFO.

Exercise 9-55
Periodic and Perpetual Systems—Calculating Ending Inventory and Cost of Sales using FIFO and LIFO **LO3, 5**

The inventory records of Cyrus Inc. showed the following data for its merchandise inventory.

Date		Units	Unit Cost
Jan. 1	Inventory.	30	$38.00
Jan. 3	Purchase	45	40.00
Jan. 7	Sale	50	
Jan. 10	Purchase	50	41.60
Jan. 20	Sale	50	
Jan. 30	Purchase	50	43.20

Required

Compute cost of goods sold and ending inventory for the month ending June 30 using:

a. FIFO (periodic inventory system).
b. LIFO (periodic inventory system).
c. FIFO (perpetual inventory system).
d. LIFO (perpetual inventory system).

Exercise 9-56
Periodic System—Computing Cost of Sales and Gross Profit under FIFO and LIFO **LO3, 5**

The owner of Valley Cycle wants to maximize after-tax cash flows and is considering switching from FIFO. The following data are available for its first quarter of 2020. In addition, sales for the first quarter totaled 110 units, and a physical inventory taken on March 31, 2020, showed 50 units available in inventory. Valley uses the periodic inventory system.

Date	Units	Unit Cost
January 1, 2020 (beginning inventory).	30	$180
Purchases: January 15, 2020.	40	205
February 12, 2020.	50	215
March 19, 2020	40	230

Required

a. Which of the following inventory flow methods would we recommend that Valley use to produce the greatest after-tax cash flows: FIFO or LIFO?

b. Prepare a table showing the gross profit and gross profit percentage for each method in part *a* assuming all units for the quarter were sold for $300 each.

Exercise 9-57
Periodic and Perpetual Systems—Calculating Ending Inventory and Cost of Sales using Average Cost and Moving Average **LO3, 5**

The inventory records of Urban Inc. show the following data for its merchandise inventory.

Date		Units	Unit Cost
Jan 1	Inventory.	30	$38.00
Jan 3	Purchase	45	40.00
Jan 7	Sale	50	
Jan 10	Purchase	50	41.60
Jan 20	Sale	50	
Jan 30	Purchase	50	43.20

Required

Compute cost of goods sold and ending inventory for the month ending June 30 (round unit costs to two decimals) using:

a. Average Cost (periodic inventory system).

b. Moving average (perpetual inventory system).

Exercise 9-58
Recording and Reporting a LIFO Reserve **LO6**

At the end of the annual accounting period, the inventory records of Boton Company show the following. The company uses FIFO for internal purposes and LIFO for income tax and external reporting purposes.

	2020	2021
Ending inventory at FIFO	$100,000	$180,000
Ending inventory at LIFO	40,000	70,000

Required

a. Assume that the inventory difference is recognized in the accounts, and the balance in the allowance account was zero at the beginning of 2020. Provide the necessary journal entry at year-end 2020 and 2021.

b. Show how inventory should be shown on its 2020–2021 comparative balance sheets.

c. If the company reported cost of goods sold of $480,000 in 2021 using LIFO, what would cost of goods sold be using FIFO?

Exercise 9-59
Computing and Analyzing a LIFO Liquidation **LO7**
Hint: See Demo 9-7

Chide's storage facility was shut down due to a strike in December 2020, resulting in a drastic reduction in inventory. The company had switched to LIFO effective January 1, 2020. The following data are available. Chide is on a calendar-year reporting basis.

	Units	Unit Cost
Beginning inventory (Base layer of LIFO—January 1)	20,000	$1.00
Inventory purchases during 2020	450,000	1.25
Total available for sale	470,000	
Sales (valued on a LIFO basis) from:		
Purchases	450,000	1.25
Base inventory layer	10,000	1.00
Total	460,000	
Ending inventory (December 31, 2020)	10,000	

Required

a. What is the LIFO liquidation after-tax profit or loss assuming a 25% tax rate?

b. What is the accounting explanation for LIFO liquidation?

Exercise 9-60
Computing and Disclosing a LIFO Liquidation **LO7**

Southeast Inc. has maintained a periodic inventory system and the LIFO inventory method for over 20 years. The earliest layer of LIFO inventory of 30,000 units dates back 15 years. The company had beginning inventory (January 1, 2020) made up of the following three layers.

Units	Unit Cost	Total Cost
30,000	$20.00	$ 600,000
25,000	25.00	625,000
5,000	50.00	250,000
		$1,475,000

At its December 31 year-end, an involuntary liquidation of beginning inventory occurred. Beginning inventory dropped to 40,000 units. The current replacement value of inventory is $50.

Required

a. What is the effect of the LIFO liquidation on after-tax profit or loss assuming a 25% tax rate?

b. What disclosure is required based on the answer to part *a*?

Exercise 9-61
Computing Ending Inventory using Dollar-Value LIFO **LO8**
Hint: See Demo 9-8

On January 1, 2020, Benn Company changed from FIFO to LIFO for income tax and external reporting purposes. At that date, the beginning FIFO inventory (the base inventory for LIFO purposes) was $140,000. The following information is available from Benn's records for the years 2020 through 2023.

Year	Ending Inventory on a FIFO Basis	Price Index
2020	$165,000	1.1
2021	174,000	1.2
2022	201,500	1.3
2023	200,000	1.2

Required

Compute the ending inventory on a dollar-value LIFO basis for each year, 2020 through 2023.

Exercise 9-62
Computing Ending Inventory using Dollar-Value LIFO **LO8**
Hint: See Demo 9-8

On January 1, 2020, Bay Inc. adopted dollar-value LIFO, and its inventory priced at current costs was $30,000. The following information is available on its inventories for 2020 through 2022.

Year	Ending Inventory at December 31	Year-End Conversion Factor*
2020	$34,000	1.10
2021	40,000	1.22
2022	36,000	1.15

*Computed as: Current (year-end) price index ÷ Base-year price index

Required

Compute the ending inventory on a dollar-value LIFO basis for each year, 2020 through 2022.

Exercise 9-63
Computing and Recording Ending Inventory using Dollar-Value LIFO **LO8**

On January 1, 2020, Crow Company changed from FIFO to LIFO for income tax and external reporting purposes. On that same date, the beginning FIFO inventory (the base inventory for LIFO purposes) was $95,000. The following information is available from Crow's records for years 2020 through 2023.

Year	Ending Inventory on a FIFO Basis	Ending Inventory at Base Year Costs
2020	$125,000	113,600
2021	110,000	84,600
2022	115,000	85,200
2023	130,000	92,900

Required

a. Compute the price indices used to calculate ending inventory at base year costs. Round to two decimals. *Hint:* Divide ending inventory on a FIFO basis by ending inventory at base year for each year.

b. Compute the ending inventory on a dollar-value LIFO basis for each year, 2020 through 2023.

c. Prepare the journal entry at each year-end, 2020 through 2023, to adjust inventory to LIFO.

Exercise 9-64
Computing Ending Inventory using Dollar-Value LIFO **LO8**

Brennan Bottlers uses LIFO for income tax and external reporting purposes. The LIFO base inventory at the end of 2020 for the inventory pool amounted to $170,000. The physical inventory of the inventory pool taken at the end of 2021, priced at 2021 costs on a FIFO basis, amounted to $220,000. The price level for 2020 was 100 and for 2021 was 110.

Required

Using the price indices provided, compute the 2021 ending dollar-value LIFO inventory.

Exercise 9-65
Periodic and Perpetual Systems—Calculating Ending Inventory and Cost of Sales using Average Cost, Moving Average, FIFO, LIFO, and Dollar-Value LIFO **LO3, 5, 8**

The inventory records of Mod Oil Company for January 2020 showed the following data for an item of its merchandise for sale (assume that the six transactions occurred in the order shown).

	Units	Unit Cost	Total
Beginning inventory (Jan. 1)	500	$6.00	$ 3,000
Jan. 3 Purchases	600	6.10	3,660
Jan. 5 Sales (900 units)			
Jan. 10 Purchases	600	6.20	3,720
Jan. 20 Sales (500 units)			
Jan. 25 Purchases	400	6.30	2,520
Jan. 28 Sales (300 units)			
Total available for sale	2,100		$12,900

Its ending inventory of 400 units can be specifically identified as follows: 100 units from the January 3 purchase, 50 units from the January 10 purchase, and 250 units from the January 25 purchase.

Required

Compute cost of goods sold and ending inventory for the month ended January 31 using:

a. Specific Identification (periodic inventory system).
b. Average Cost (periodic inventory system).
c. FIFO (periodic inventory system).
d. LIFO (periodic inventory system).
e. Moving average (perpetual inventory system).
f. FIFO (perpetual inventory system).
g. LIFO (perpetual inventory system).
h. Dollar-value LIFO (periodic inventory system). Assume that the beginning inventory is the base layer at a cost of $6.00 per unit. The price index for January 2020 is 1.05.

Exercise 9-66
Analyzing the Impact on Ratios from Changing Inventory Prices **LO9**

Consider two companies that are identical except for the way they value inventory. One company uses FIFO (Company F), while the other uses LIFO (Company L). Assume prices are rising in the markets in which these companies buy materials. Indicate for each ratio below which company (Company F, Company L, or neither) will have the larger ratio value.

Ratio	Company with the Larger Ratio Value
a. Current	________
b. Working capital to total assets	________
c. Inventory turnover	________
d. Debt to equity	________
e. Debt to total assets	________
f. Book value per share	________
g. Return on total assets	________
h. Earnings per share	________

Exercise 9-67
Matching Terms Relating to Inventory Concepts and Procedures with their Descriptions **LO1, 2, 3, 4, 5, 6, 7, 8, 9**

Following are terms relating to inventory concepts and procedures along with descriptions of those terms.

Terms

___ 1. Free on board shipping
___ 2. Free on board destination
___ 3. Gross method—purchase discounts
___ 4. Net method—purchase discounts
___ 5. Consignee
___ 6. Consignor
___ 7. Perpetual inventory system
___ 8. Periodic inventory system
___ 9. Specific Identification
___ 10. Average Cost method
___ 11. Moving Average method
___ 12. Repurchase agreement
___ 13. LIFO reserve
___ 14. LIFO liquidation

Description of Terms

a. Requires each inventory item to be distinguishable from another
b. Occurs when the seller of inventory agrees to buy back the inventory at set terms
c. Purchase discounts lost are treated as a finance charge
d. Ownership passes when the seller transfers goods to carrier
e. An average inventory cost is computed based upon an entire period
f. Purchase discounts are only recorded if taken
g. Elimination of prior period's inventory layer
h. Owner of inventory held at a separate location
i. Requires a physical count of inventory in order to determine COGS
j. Requires average inventory calculations throughout the period
k. Measures the difference between inventory valued at FIFO vs. LIFO
l. Ownership passes when the buyer receives goods from carrier
m. Requires a physical inventory to verify inventory balances
n. Acts as a sales agent to sell merchandise

Required

Match each term, *1* through *14*, with the best description *a* through *n*.

Problems

Problem 9-68
Determining the Ending Inventory Balance After Correcting for Errors
LO1

On December 31, 2020, Patco computed an ending inventory valuation of $250,000. The accounts for 2020 have been adjusted and closed. Subsequently, the independent auditor located several discrepancies in the 2020 ending inventory. These were discussed with the accounting manager, who then prepared the following table.

1. Merchandise in store (at 50% above cost)	$250,000
2. Merchandise out on consignment at sales price (cost of inventory is $4,000)	10,000
3. Goods held on consignment from Davis Electronics at sales price (sales commission, 20% of sales price, included)	4,000
4. Goods purchased, in transit (shipped FOB shipping point, estimated freight, not included, $800), invoice price	5,000
5. Goods out on approval, sales price, $2,500, cost, $1,000	2,500
Total inventory as corrected	$271,500

Required

The auditor did not agree with the "corrected" inventory amount of $271,500. Compute the correct ending inventory amount by modifying the "corrected" balance of $271,500.

Problem 9-69
Perpetual System—Determining FIFO Inventory and Costs; Recording Purchases and Sales; Computing Gross Margin **LO5**

Walsh Company maintains perpetual inventory records on a FIFO basis for the three main products distributed by the company. A physical inventory is taken at each year-end to check the perpetual inventory records. The following information relates to one of its products for the month ended June 2020.

Date		Units	Unit Cost
June 1	Beginning inventory	9,000	$8.10
	Purchases and sales (in order)		
June 3	Purchase #1	5,000	8.15
June 4	Sale #1	10,000	
June 8	Purchase #2	16,000	8.20
June 9	Sale #2	11,000	
June 15	Purchase #3	4,000	8.40
June 18	Purchase #4	7,000	8.25
June 20	Sale #3	14,000	
June 29	Purchase #5	5,000	8.10
June 30	Ending inventory (per count)	10,500	

Required

a. Reconstruct the perpetual inventory record for this product.

b. Prepare eight journal entries (in chronological order) for the above five purchases and three sales. Assume that the selling price is $22 per unit. Also prepare a journal entry for any inventory shortage.

c. Prepare the income statement ending with gross margin. Compute the gross profit as a percentage of sales from this income statement.

Problem 9-70
Periodic and Perpetual Systems—Recording Purchases and Sales and Year-End Adjustments; Preparing an Income Statement
LO2, 4

Carlisle Company reports the following summary results from its transactions during 2020 for its main product. Total expenses (excluding damaged goods, cost of goods sold, and income taxes) were $47,800.

	Units	Unit Price
Beginning inventory	6,000	$18 (cost)
Purchases	20,000	18 (cost)
Purchase returns	1,000	18 (cost)
Sales (gross)	18,000	25 (selling price)
Sales returns	100	25 (selling price)
Damaged merchandise (unsalable)	100	18 (cost)
Ending inventory or physical count (salable)	6,900	
Inventory shortage	?	

Required

a. Prepare the following journal entries for the transactions summarized above assuming that the company uses the perpetual inventory system.

1. Purchase of inventory
2. Return of inventory to suppliers
3. Sale of inventory
4. Return of sales from customers
5. Write-off of inventory
6. Recording of expenses
7. Year-end adjustment for any inventory shortage

b. Prepare the following journal entries for the transactions summarized above assuming that the company uses the periodic inventory system.

1. Purchase of inventory
2. Return of inventory to suppliers
3. Sale of inventory
4. Return of sales from customers
5. Recording of expenses
6. Year-end adjustment to record inventory and cost of sales

c. Prepare a multiple-step income statement under both the periodic and the perpetual inventory systems. Assume 10,000 shares of common stock are outstanding, and the tax rate is 40%.

Problem 9-71
Recording Inventory and Sales Transactions; Preparing an Income Statement **LO2**

Gamit Company completed the following selected (and summarized) transactions during 2020.

1. Merchandise inventory at January 1, 2020, $105,000 (at cost).
2. During the year, purchased merchandise for resale at a quoted price of $200,000 on credit, terms 2/10, n/30. Immediately paid 85% of the cash cost.
3. Paid freight on merchandise purchased, $10,000 cash.
4. Paid 40% of the accounts payable within the discount period. The remaining payables were unpaid at the end of 2020 and were still within the discount period.
5. Merchandise that had a quoted price of $3,000 (terms 2/10, n/30) was returned to a supplier. A cash refund of $2,940 was received because the items were unsatisfactory.
6. During the year, sold merchandise for $370,000, of which 10% was on credit, terms 2/10, n/30.
7. Some merchandise was returned by the customer. Merchandise was originally sold for $600, of which $400 cash was refunded. *Hint:* Debit Sales Returns and Allowances for cash refund.
8. Operating expenses (administrative and distribution) paid in cash, $120,000.
9. Excluded from the purchase given in transaction *2* and from the physical count of ending inventory was a shipment for $7,000 (net of discount). This shipment was in transit, FOB shipping point, at December 31, 2020. The invoice is received.
10. Sold the returned merchandise for $195.

A physical count of ending inventory was $110,000 at cost. The company's average income tax rate is 25%. Accounting policies followed by the company are (1) its annual accounting period ends December 31, (2) a periodic inventory system is used, (3) purchases and accounts payable are recorded net of cash discounts, (4) all cash discounts are taken.

Required

a. Prepare the journal entries for transactions 2 through 11 along with the year-end entry to record ending inventory and cost of goods sold.

b. Prepare a multiple-step income statement for the year ended December 31, 2020. Assume that 20,000 shares of common stock are outstanding.

c. Show how ending inventory and accounts payable should be reported on the balance sheet at December 31, 2020.

Problem 9-72
Periodic and Perpetual Systems—Recording Purchases and Sales, and Year-End Adjustments; Computing Gross Profit under both Systems **LO2, 4**

Diaz Inc. uses the gross method to record purchases. Its inventory balance on August 1, 2020, is $4,000. The following transactions occurred during the month of August 2020 for its major inventory item.

Aug. 1	Purchase of merchandise inventory for $18,000 on account, terms 2/10, n/30.
Aug. 2	Shipping charges of $500 cash paid on delivery of merchandise (shipped f.o.b. shipping point).
Aug. 3	After inspection of the merchandise, $800 of inventory was returned to the vendor for account credit.
Aug. 8	Paid balance on account to vendor.
Aug. 15	Sold merchandise inventory on account for $10,000 with a cost of $6,000.
Aug. 20	Sold merchandise inventory on account for $8,000 with a cost of $4,800.
Aug. 31	Physical inventory count indicated that the ending inventory balance at cost was $9,500.

Required

a. Prepare journal entries for the August transactions assuming that the company uses the perpetual inventory system.

b. Prepare journal entries for the August transactions assuming that the company uses the periodic inventory system.

c. Compute the gross profit and gross profit as a percentage of sales under both the perpetual and the periodic inventory systems for August.

Problem 9-73
Periodic System—Computing Inventory, Cost of Sales, and Gross Profit under Specific Identification, Average Cost, FIFO, and LIFO **LO3**

Beats Inc. has the following data for one of its major inventory items being sold. Assume that the transactions occurred as dated. A physical inventory count on June 30 showed 9,000 units available, which are specifically identified as: 2,000 units from June 1 inventory; 1,000 units from June 7 purchase; and 6,000 units from June 20 purchase.

Date	Units	Unit Cost
June 1, Beginning inventory	8,000	$8.00
Purchases		
June 7	6,000	8.40
June 20	8,000	9.00
Sales		
June 15 (at $24)	9,000	
June 30 (at $26)	4,000	

Required

a. Compute ending inventory, cost of goods sold, and gross margin for this item using:

1. Specific Identification (periodic inventory system).
2. Average Cost (periodic inventory system).
3. FIFO (periodic inventory system).
4. LIFO (periodic inventory system).

b. Which method(s) in part *a* is based on actual physical flow of inventory? Which method(s) in part *a* is based on an assumed physical flow of inventory?

Problem 9-74
Perpetual System—Computing Inventory and Costs of Goods Transferred Out using Moving Average, FIFO, and LIFO **LO5**

Jonson Inc. shows the following data for its raw material inventory used in the manufacturing process.

Date		Units	Unit Cost
Oct. 1	Inventory	4,000	$14.00
Oct. 4	Purchase #1	3,000	15.40
Oct. 5	Transfer out #1	5,000	
Oct. 20	Purchase #2	8,000	16.00
Oct. 24	Transfer out #2	7,000	
Oct. 31	Purchase #3	3,000	16.80

Required

Compute cost of materials transferred out (to work in process) and the valuation of its raw materials ending inventory assuming use of (round unit costs to two decimals):

a. Average Cost—Perpetual system.

b. FIFO—Perpetual system.

c. LFO—Perpetual system.

Problem 9-75
Periodic and Perpetual Systems—Compute Inventory, Cost of Sales, and Gross Margin using Average Cost, Moving Average, FIFO, and LIFO
LO3, 5

Clayton Company shows the following transactions, in the order given, for its major inventory item.

Date		Units	Unit Cost
Nov. 1	Inventory	3,000	$6.90
Nov. 3	Purchase	6,000	7.20
Nov. 5	Sales (at $15)	4,000	
Nov. 13	Purchase	5,000	7.50
Nov. 20	Sales (at $15)	9,000	
Nov. 22	Purchase	11,000	7.66
Nov. 28	Sales (at $18)	9,000	
Nov. 30	Purchase	6,000	7.80

Required

Compute ending inventory, cost of goods sold, and gross margin using the following:

a. Average Cost (periodic inventory system).
b. FIFO (periodic inventory system).
c. LIFO (periodic inventory system).
d. Moving Average (perpetual inventory system).
e. FIFO (perpetual inventory system).
f. LIFO (perpetual inventory system).

Problem 9-76
Periodic System—Preparing an Income Statement using LIFO and FIFO; Disclosure of Inventory Method Change
LO3, 6

Adele Inc., at the beginning of 2020, changed from FIFO to LIFO. The following data for 2020 are for its main inventory item. Total expenses for 2020 (excluding cost of goods sold and income taxes) is $40,000, and its average income tax rate is 40%. Assume 10,000 shares of its common stock are outstanding.

	Units	Unit Cost
Beginning inventory (LIFO base inventory), Jan. 1, 2020	10,000	$3.10
Purchases and sales (in order):		
1. Purchase	8,000	$3.20
2. Sales (at $8.00)	9,000	
3. Sales (at $8.25)	5,000	
4. Purchase	7,000	3.20
5. Purchase	6,000	3.40
6. Sales (at $8.75)	8,000	
7. Purchase	3,000	3.60

Required

a. Prepare an income statement for 2020 using LIFO and the periodic inventory system.
b. Prepare an income statement for 2020 using FIFO and the periodic inventory system.
c. Prepare a disclosure note for the change in 2020 from FIFO to LIFO, explaining the net effect if FIFO had been used (instead of LIFO) in 2020 on ending inventory and net income (in total and per share).

Problem 9-77
Preparing an Income Statement from Purchases and Sales Transactions and with a LIFO Liquidation; Analyzing Year-End Options for Income Effects **LO7**

Case Equipment Co. switched from FIFO to LIFO for tax *and* financial reporting purposes 12 years ago to gain cash savings. This strategy was successful, saving the company several million dollars in tax payments as inventory prices rose over that period. However, market prices began to level off in the recent two years. Case's records show the following information as of December 25, 2020. Its total expenses (excluding cost of goods sold and income taxes) for 2020 are $1,668,000, and its average income tax rate is 25%.

	Units	Unit Cost	Unit Sales Price
Beginning inventory			
LIFO base inventory	10	$ 88,000	
Additional LIFO layers	24	216,000	
Purchases and sales			
Jan. 15 Purchased	8	240,000	
Feb. 20 Sold	16		$320,000
Aug. 1 Sold	18		300,000
Nov. 10 Purchased	12	225,000	
Dec. 1 Sold	11		298,000

Required

a. Assume that no other transactions take place during 2020. Prepare an income statement for 2020 using LIFO and a periodic inventory system. Compute earnings per share assuming 10,000 shares of stock are outstanding.
b. Assume that Case Co. is presented with two opportunities in the final week of December 2020.
   1. Option #1 is to sell five units for $300,000 each.
   2. Option #2 is to purchase five units for $320,000 each.

   An independent appraiser claims that units in both options are priced fairly. What do we recommend for Case assuming we use the impact on net income as the basis to choose between the two opportunities?

Problem 9-78
Periodic System—Calculating Inventory and Cost of Sales using LIFO and FIFO, and with a LIFO Liquidation; Calculating Gross Margin **LO7**

Lucas Inc. maintains a LIFO, periodic inventory system. The following data were available for its January 1, 2020, beginning inventory, consisting of two layers.

	Units	Unit Cost	Total Cost
Layer one	12,000	$25	$300,000
Layer two	8,000	$30	240,000
			$540,000

Required

a. The purchase price of inventory was steady at $50 per unit during 2020. Calculate ending inventory and cost of goods sold if 20,000 units were purchased and 20,000 units were sold (at $75 per unit) during 2020.

b. If replacement cost remains at $50 per unit, calculate ending inventory and cost of goods sold if 20,000 units were purchased and 30,000 units were sold (at $75 per unit) during 2020.

c. Calculate the gross margin and gross margin percentage for both part *a* and part *b*. What is the source of the difference (if any) between the results of parts *a* and *b*?

d. Complete requirements of parts *a* through *c* assuming that the company uses FIFO instead of LIFO.

Problem 9-79 Converting FIFO Inventory to Dollar-Value LIFO and Preparing Year-End Adjustments to the LIFO Reserve **LO8**

Stetson Industries has been using FIFO for all internal and external reporting purposes. At the start of 2020, the company adopted dollar-value LIFO for external financial statement and income tax purposes. Its derived internal price indices for 2019–2022 are: 2019 is 1.00; 2020 is 1.10; 2021 is 1.15; and 2022 is 1.20. The FIFO inventory records reported the following for its single inventory pool.

Year		FIFO Basis
2019	Ending inventory.	$500,000
2020	Ending inventory.	583,000
2021	Ending inventory.	713,000
2022	Ending inventory.	720,000

Required

a. Convert the ending FIFO inventory amounts to a LIFO basis for 2020, 2021, and 2022, assuming the dollar-value LIFO method and using the internal price indices provided.

b. Prepare the December 31 year-end journal entry for 2020, 2021, and 2022 to convert inventory from FIFO to LIFO.

Problem 9-80 Computing Ending Inventory using Dollar-Value LIFO; Converting Dollar-Value LIFO to Current Cost **LO8**

Ohio Inc. maintains its internal inventory records on a FIFO basis. On January 1, 2020, Ohio changed to dollar-value LIFO for external reporting and income tax purposes. The following data are available for Ohio Inc.'s inventory. Its base inventory is $200,000.

	2020	2021	2022
Ending inventory at current-year cost.	$280,000	$320,000	$350,000
LIFO conversion index	1.20	1.30	1.45

Required

a. Compute its ending inventory on a dollar-value LIFO basis for 2020, 2021, and 2022.

b. Assume that its 2023 ending inventory on a dollar-value LIFO basis is $288,390 and its 2023 LIFO conversion index is 1.50. What is its ending inventory on a current cost basis?

Problem 9-81 Converting FIFO to Dollar-Value LIFO and Preparing Income Statements under Both Methods **LO8**

Yun Inc. has been using FIFO since its inception for internal management reports, external reporting to shareholders, and income tax purposes. On January 1, 2020, it decided to change from FIFO to dollar-value LIFO for external reporting and income tax purposes. FIFO will continue in use for internal purposes. Yun has a single LIFO inventory pool. It will apply the dollar-value approach for converting from FIFO to LIFO and will use an internal conversion index computed each year. Price indices are 1.10 for 2020 and 1.15 for 2021. FIFO results for the recent three-year period follow.

	Year 2019			Year 2020			Year 2021		
	Units	Unit Cost	Total	Units	Unit Cost	Total	Units	Unit Cost	Total
Sales revenue.			$18,200			$24,280			$23,300
Cost of goods sold (FIFO)									
Beginning inventory	800	$2.50	2,000	600	$3.00	1,800	700	$3.30	2,310
Purchases.	2,000	3.00	6,000	2,500	3.30	8,250	2,400	3.45	8,280
Ending inventory.	(600)	3.00	(1,800)	(700)	3.30	(2,310)	(900)	3.45	(3,105)
Cost of goods sold	2,200		$ 6,200	2,400		$ 7,740	2,200		$ 7,485

Required

a. Convert the FIFO results to LIFO for 2020 and 2021 using the dollar-value method.

b. Assume $8,000 in operating expenses, a 30% average tax rate, and 4,000 shares of common stock outstanding for both 2020 and 2021. Prepare income statements for 2020 and 2021 with two headings for each year as follows (FIFO is for internal reports and LIFO is for external reports and tax returns).

2020		2021	
FIFO	LIFO	FIFO	LIFO

Problem 9-82
Converting FIFO to Dollar-Value LIFO; Preparing Income Effects under Both Methods; and Note Disclosure for Dollar-Value LIFO Adoption
LO8

Eastshore Inc. sells three main products on a regular basis. The products form one inventory pool. The company used FIFO through 2019 for all purposes. Beginning in 2020, FIFO was continued for internal management and accounting purposes; however, dollar-value LIFO was adopted for income tax and external reporting purposes. Eastshore uses its own price index using actual unit costs of the product pool. The following data (for the three products combined) are for the three years following adoption of LIFO.

FIFO Basis per Accounts	Units	Cost	Total
2019			
Ending inventory	2,000	$3.00	$ 6,000
2020			
Purchases	7,000	3.30	23,100
Sales	6,000		
Ending inventory	3,000	3.30	9,900
2021			
Purchases	10,000	3.60	36,000
Sales	7,000		
Ending inventory	6,000	3.60	21,600
2022			
Purchases	5,000	3.75	18,750
Sales	7,000		
Ending inventory	4,000	3.75	15,000

Required

a. Convert the ending inventory at FIFO to a dollar-value LIFO basis for 2020, 2021, and 2022.

b. Assume an average tax rate of 25% and a FIFO pretax income of $5,000 for 2020, 2021, and 2022. Prepare a table (that includes the annual inventory difference, pretax income, tax expense, and net income) that compares the results of FIFO versus dollar-value LIFO for 2020, 2021, and 2022. Which method should be used if we wish to have greater tax savings?

c. Prepare a proper note to the 2020 financial statements assuming that LIFO is used for external reporting and tax purposes.

Problem 9-83
Computing Inventory Values, Identifying Inventory Costs, and Applying Moving Average, FIFO and LIFO **LO1, 2, 3, 5**

Answer the following requirements for each separate case.

1. The following information was available for Mason Corporation for 2020.

Sales	$100,000
Beginning inventory	36,000
Freight out	9,000
Purchases	43,000
Sales commissions	5,000
Cost of goods sold	60,000

   a. What is Mason's ending inventory?
   b. What is Mason's gross margin?

2. Which of the following, if any, is included in inventory cost? Assume costs are material.
   - Warehouse Costs
   - Insurance on Raw Materials in Transit

3. Kemp Company had the following consignment transactions during December 2020.

Inventory on consignment to Ace Company	$9,000
Freight paid by Kemp	450
Inventory received on consignment from Fenn Inc.	6,000
Freight paid by Fenn	250

No sales of consigned goods were made through December 31, 2020. Kemp's December 31, 2020, balance sheet should include consigned inventory at what value?

4. Ward Inc. had an inventory of 1,600 units valued at $4.00 each to begin the month. Ward sold 800 units on the 15th of the month, and purchased 2,400 units at $4.80 each on the next to the last day of the month.
   a. What is the month-end inventory cost using moving average and the perpetual system?
   b. What is the month-end inventory cost using FIFO and the periodic system?
   c. What is the month-end inventory cost using LIFO and the periodic system?
   d. What is the month-end inventory cost using LIFO and the perpetual system?

Problem 9-84
Compute Average Cost, FIFO, and LIFO Financial Statement Amounts and Ratios
LO3, 9

Patter Inc. maintains a periodic inventory system. The following transactions occurred during 2020 for its major inventory item (in order of occurrence). The total of its other expenses (excluding cost of goods sold and income taxes) during 2020 was $40,000, and its tax rate is 40%.

	Units	Unit Cost
1. Beginning inventory	1,000	$100
2. Purchase	900	80
3. Sale (at $200)	800	
4. Purchase	800	102
5. Sale (at $200)	200	

Required

a. Compute ending inventory, cost of goods sold, and gross margin using:
   1. Average Cost (periodic inventory system).
   2. FIFO (periodic inventory system).
   3. LIFO (periodic inventory system).

b. Which method results in the highest tax liability? Explain why this occurred.

c. Compute the gross profit ratio, inventory turnover ratio, and average days in inventory under each of the three inventory methods in part *a.*

Accounting Decisions and Judgments

AD&J 9-85
Analyzing LIFO versus FIFO Inventory Effects
LO6

Judgment A retailer of apparel and home furnishings reported inventories of $4,646 million and $4,033 million in its December 28, Year 6, and December 30, Year 5 balance sheets, respectively. Also, it reported net income of $1,271 million and $1,801 million for Year 6 and Year 5, respectively. Assume that the company's inventories have been valued on a LIFO basis for the last several years. The company disclosed that if the first-in, first-out (FIFO) method of inventory valuation had been used instead of the LIFO method, merchandise inventories would have been $730 and $711 million higher at December 28, Year 6, and December 30, Year 5, respectively.

Required

a. What would have been the effect on the company's pretax income for Year 6 if inventories had always been valued on a FIFO rather than a LIFO basis?

b. Why is the company required to disclose the adjustment required to restate LIFO inventory amount to a FIFO inventory amount?

c. For what reasons might this company use FIFO for internal reporting even though it is using LIFO for external reporting?

AD&J 9-86
Analyzing LIFO Adoption and Inventory Effects of LIFO versus Average Costs **LO6**

Real World Analysis The following two notes are taken from the **Owens-Illinois** Year 8 annual report. Owens-Illinois is a manufacturer of glass containers and packaging products.

> **INVENTORY VALUATION** The Company values most domestic inventory lower of last-in, first-out (LIFO) cost or market. Other inventories are valued at the lower of standard costs (which approximate average costs), average costs, or market.

Major classes of inventory ($ millions)	Year 8	Year 7
Finished goods	$608.9	$447.3
Work in process	35.0	9.4
Raw materials	123.6	92.5
Operating supplies	70.6	43.2
	$838.1	$592.4

If inventories valued on the LIFO method had been valued at standard or average costs, which approximate current costs, consolidated inventories would be higher than reported by $6.1 million and $21.6 million at December 31, Year 8 and Year 7, respectively. Also, inventories that are valued at the lower of standard costs (which approximate average costs), average costs, or market at December 31, Year 8 and Year 7, were approximately $506.4 million and $313.0 million, respectively.

Required

a. What effect would there have been on the Owens-Illinois Year 8 net income if the company had consistently used standard or average costs to value its inventories over time? Use a 25% tax rate.

b. What effect would there have been on retained earnings as of December 31, Year 8, if Owens-Illinois had consistently used standard or average costs to value its inventories over time?

AD&J 9-87
Evaluating Inventory Reporting Under LIFO versus FIFO **LO6**

Real World Analysis Merck, a major pharmaceutical and health-care firm, disclosed the following note for inventories in its Year 8 annual financial statements.

Inventories at December 31 (in millions)	Year 8	Year 7
Finished goods	$1,701.2	$1,230.6
Raw materials and work in process	851.6	849.7
Supplies	71.1	64.8
Total (approximates current cost)	2,623.9	2,145.1
Reduction to LIFO cost	—	—
Total	$2,623.9	$2,145.1

Inventories valued at LIFO comprised approximately 37% and 42% of inventories at December 31, Year 8 and Year 7, respectively.

Required

a. What basis do you believe Merck uses to account for its inventories internally?

b. Why do you believe Merck reduces its inventories to LIFO cost?

c. If Merck were to adjust its inventories to LIFO cost at the end of Year 7 by a reduction of, say, $10 million, what is the impact on:

1. Income before tax for Year 7? Assume that Merck's reduction to LIFO cost in Year 6 was $8 million.
2. Retained earnings as of January 1, Year 8? (Assume a 25% tax rate.)

AD&J 9-88
Computing the LIFO Reserve, Difference in Income for FIFO versus LIFO, Shares Outstanding, and Average Tax Rate **LO6**

Challenge Problem Pedro's Inc. is an electronics company that manufactures and markets a wide range of products. The company switched to the LIFO method for substantially all domestic inventories at the beginning of 2020. Pedro's income statement ("Consolidated Statements of Earnings") for 2020 and 2021, and the asset section of its 2020 and 2021 balance sheet ("Consolidated Statements of Financial Position") follow. Notes to its financial statements stated that it would have reported basic earnings per share of $4.63 if it had used the FIFO method in 2021.

Required

a. Compute its average income tax rate for 2021.

b. Compute the number of weighted average shares outstanding used for EPS.

c. Compute the difference in 2020 net income and pretax income between FIFO and LIFO.

d. Compute its LIFO reserve at December 31, 2021.

PEDRO'S INC. AND CONSOLIDATED SUBSIDIARIES
Consolidated Statements of Earnings
For Year Ended December 31, 2020 and 2021

In thousands, except per share data	2021	2020
Revenues		
Net sales	$2,023,885	$1,869,944
Equity earnings	5,333	8,605
Royalty income	5,123	2,958
Interest income	10,871	2,406
Gain on involuntary conversion	9,038	—
Total revenues	2,054,250	1,883,913
Cost and expenses		
Cost of products sold	1,445,638	1,304,596
Selling, administrative and general expenses (includes internal research and development expenditures: 2021—$68,184; 2020—$72,593)	396,026	367,804
Interest expense	50,081	33,895
Other (income)	(2,943)	2,430
Total costs and expenses	1,888,802	1,708,725
Pretax earnings	165,448	175,188
Federal, state, and foreign income taxes	59,561	74,155
Net earnings	$ 105,887	$ 101,033
Earnings per share		
Earnings per share	$ 3.78	$ 3.77
Earnings per share assuming full dilution	$ 3.71	$ 3.56

PEDRO'S INC. AND CONSOLIDATED SUBSIDIARIES
Consolidated Statements of Financial Position—Asset Section Only
At December 31, 2020 and 2021

In thousands	2021	2020
Current assets		
Cash	$ 18,105	$ 32,440
Marketable securities—at cost, which approximates market	906	1,908
Accounts receivable, less allowances (2021, $7,732; 2020, $6,148)	324,593	284,355
Inventories, less LIFO reserve (2021, $______; 2020, 21,178)	429,203	388,810
Other current assets	73,558	50,870
Total current assets	846,365	758,383
Investments and other assets		
Unconsolidated financial subsidiary	24,722	19,559
Unconsolidated real estate subsidiary	18,296	5,659
Unconsolidated joint venture	37,498	—
Affiliated companies and other investments	48,914	45,327
Other assets	45,992	58,595
Total investments and other assets	175,422	129,140
Property, plant, and equipment		
Land	26,669	23,215
Buildings	226,546	209,013
Machinery and equipment	448,137	389,503
Construction in process	68,932	66,225
	770,284	687,956
Less allowances for depreciation and amortization	255,701	231,684
Total property, plant, and equipment	514,583	456,272
Cost of acquired businesses in excess of net assets at acquisition dates—net of amortization	76,693	77,168
Total assets	$1,613,063	$1,420,963

AD&J 9-89
Analyzing Year-End Inventory Purchases when using LIFO and any Ethical Issues and Profit Shifting Concerns
LO2, 3

Ethics Case Best Inc. uses a periodic inventory system and LIFO to value its ending inventory for income tax and external reporting purposes. Near the end of 2020, the following records and estimates are available for its single inventory item.

	Units	Unit Cost
Beginning inventory (LIFO basis)		
Base inventory (normal minimum level)	8,000	$40
Incremental inventory layer	5,000	50
Purchases (actual)	60,000	70
Sales* (at $100 per unit)	65,000	
Expenses* (excluding income taxes)	$1,400,000	

*Including estimates for remainder of 2020.

On December 27, 2020, the company has an opportunity to purchase no fewer than 30,000 units of its usual inventory item at $60 (a special price) with 10-day credit terms. Delivery is immediate, and the offer will expire January 3, 2021. The question has been posed whether the purchase (and delivery) should be consummated in 2020 or 2021; management has tentatively decided to make the purchase in 2020.

Required

a. What purchase year do we recommend? Support the recommendation with reasons and pro forma (as if) income statement and balance sheet data. Assume that 50,000 shares of common stock are outstanding and that the tax rate is 30%.

b. Explain and illustrate why EPS would be changed if the purchase is made in 2020.

c. Would we suspect the shifting of profit among periods in this situation if Best Inc. elected to make the purchase in 2020? Does this create an ethical issue? Explain.

AD&J 9-90
Analyzing Bonus Agreements, Ethical Issues involving LIFO and Business Decisions, and Profit Shifting Across Periods
LO3

Ethics Case R. Baker, S. Cook, and T. Dayton formed a partnership to import furniture. Their initial partnership agreement provided for equal investments, equal sharing of responsibilities, equal work, equal salaries, and equal shares of the partnership income. After a few years of operation, sales took off and the business prospered. On January 1, 2020, they incorporated as BCD Inc., with each of the former partners owning 1/3 of the stock of the corporation. The board of directors of BCD comprised Baker, Cook, and Dayton. The board elected Cook as chairman of the board of directors, Baker as president of the corporation in charge of operations, and Dayton as vice president and controller (Dayton was a CPA). Annual compensation of the three officers was set as follows.

Cook	$130,000	plus bonus equal to 2% of annual net income
Baker	135,000	plus bonus equal to 1% of annual net income
Dayton	140,000	plus 5% of annual decrease in income tax payments

The compensation plan was intended as an incentive device as well as to reflect the relative contributions of the three officers to corporate success. In particular, the bonus plan was intended to motivate Cook and Baker (who represented the corporation in the business community) to increase sales and to encourage Dayton (the accountant) to decrease income tax payments. During 2021, 2022, and 2023, sales and income increased steadily. In the year ended December 31, 2023, net income of the corporation was $500,000, which put the annual earnings of all three officers at $140,000 (this amount cannot be verified). Income tax payments for 2023 were $150,000. During 2024, net income, computed on the basis of the FIFO inventory method, which BCD used, increased to $750,000. This increase in corporate income was destined to put Cook's annual earnings at $145,000 and Baker's at $142,500 but to leave Dayton's at $140,000 (neither Baker nor Cook was aware of this). A major reason for the increase in corporation income was Dayton's skill at controlling costs; however, the compensation plan did not adequately reflect this factor. Dayton tried to persuade Cook and Baker to renegotiate his salary, but they refused because they knew little about finance and accounting and were unable to appreciate Dayton's effectiveness at controlling expenses. They were convinced that the reason for the success of BCD was their superlative sales and management skills.

The cost to BCD of its imported furniture was rising rapidly near the end of 2024 and, due to increased competition, the outlook for the company's sales was not bright for 2025. Without notifying Cook or Baker, Dayton changed inventory methods from FIFO to LIFO, effective January 1, 2024. Also, near year-end 2024, Dayton, who controlled all purchases of inventory, stocked up on inventory in response to a pending 20% cost increase announced by BCD's suppliers; the price increase was to become effective in January 2025. Because of the change to LIFO, income tax payments for 2024 decreased to $70,000.

Required

a. What was the likely effect of the change in inventory method on reported income of BCD for 2024? On the annual bonuses of Baker and Cook?

b. What was the likely effect of stocking up of inventory on reported income of 2024? On the annual earnings of Baker and Cook?

c. What was the effect of Dayton's actions on his annual bonus? Does this raise any ethical issues? Explain.

d. What conclusions about accounting income can we draw from this situation?

AD&J 9-91 Computing and Analyzing Accounts Receivable and Inventory Ratios **LO9**

Challenge Problem **Fastenal Company** supplies parts for manufacturing including fastener and other industrial and construction supplies and safety supplies. Fastenal Company reported the following information in a recent Form 10-K.

$ thousands	2016	2015
Trade accounts receivable, net of allowance for doubtful accounts of $11,249 and $11,729, respectively	$ 499,716	$ 468,375
Inventories	992,989	913,263
Sales	3,962,036	3,869,187
Cost of sales	1,997,259	1,920,253

For 2014, trade accounts receivable (net of allowance of $12,619) was $462,077 and inventories was $869,224. Also, bad debt expense was $8,550 in 2016, and $8,769 in 2015.

Required

a. Compute inventory turnover, days in inventory, gross profit, and gross margin percentage for 2016 and 2015.

b. Compute accounts receivable turnover ratio and average days to collect receivables for 2016 and 2015.

c. Determine the amount of accounts receivable write-offs in 2016.

d. Evaluate the ratio trends from the calculations in parts *a* through *c*.

AD&J 9-92 Searching the Codification to Define Key Terms **LO1**

Codification Skills Refer to the Codification and identify the definition for each of the following: (1) inventory, (2) vendor, (3) repurchase agreement, and (4) customer.

AD&J 9-93 Researching the Codification for Proper Citation **LO1, 3, 5, 7**

Codification Skills Research the Codification and report the proper citation that provides guidance on each of the following topics.

a. How to choose an inventory method FASB ASC ____-____-____-____

b. Consistent use of an inventory method FASB ASC ____-____-____-____

c. Consigned inventory FASB ASC ____-____-____-____

d. Disclosure of LIFO liquidation FASB ASC ____-____-____-____

e. Disclosure of inventory method used FASB ASC ____-____-____-____

f. If LIFO is used, disclosure of the difference between current cost and LIFO cost of inventory FASB ASC ____-____-____-____

AD&J 9-94 Researching the Codification for Authoritative Guidance **LO1**

Codification Skills A company is preparing annual financial statements, which includes the valuation of inventory with repurchase agreements. One repurchase agreement with a vendor *requires the company* to buy back inventory while another *grants the company the option* to buy back the inventory. Identify the relevant authoritative guidance to differentiate between these two types of inventory arrangements.

FASB ASC ____-____-____-____

Answers to Review Exercises

Review 9-1

$800,000 − $1,500 + $25,000 + $40,000 + $30,000 = $893,500

Review 9-2

a. **Gross Method**

Assets = Liabilities +11,200 + Equity −11,200
Accounts Payable: Cr 11,200 | Purchases: Dr 11,200

March 5, 2020—Purchase of inventory

Purchases ($14,000 × 0.80)	11,200	
Accounts Payable		11,200

Assets = Liabilities −1,000 + Equity +1,000
Accounts Payable: Dr 1,000, Cr 11,200 | Purchase R&A: Cr 1,000

March 8, 2020—Inventory return

Accounts Payable	1,000	
Purchase Returns and Allowances		1,000

Assets −4,900 = Liabilities −5,000 + Equity +100
Cash: Cr 4,900 | Accounts Payable: Dr 1,000, 5,000, Cr 11,200 | Purch Discount: Cr 100

March 14, 2020—Payment within discount period

Accounts Payable	5,000	
Purchase Discount		100
Cash		4,900

Assets −5,200 = Liabilities −5,200 + Equity
Cash: Cr 4,900, 5,200 | Accounts Payable: Dr 1,000, 5,000, 5,200, Cr 11,200

March 31, 2020—Payment after discount period

Accounts Payable ($11,200 − $1,000 − $5,000)	5,200	
Cash		5,200

b. **Net Method**

Assets = Liabilities +10,976 + Equity −10,976
Accounts Payable: Cr 10,976 | Purchases: Dr 10,976

March 5, 2020—Purchase of inventory

Purchases ($14,000 × 0.80 × 0.98)	10,976	
Accounts Payable		10,976

Assets = Liabilities −980 + Equity +980
Accounts Payable: Dr 980, Cr 10,976 | Purchases: Dr 10,976, Cr 980

March 8, 2020—Inventory return

Accounts Payable ($1,000 × 0.98)	980	
Purchases		980

Assets −4,900 = Liabilities −4,900 + Equity
Cash: Cr 4,900 | Accounts Payable: Dr 980, 4,900, Cr 10,976

March 14, 2020—Payment within discount period

Accounts Payable	4,900	
Cash		4,900

Assets −5,200 = Liabilities −5,096 + Equity −104
Cash: Cr 4,900, 5,200 | Accounts Payable: Dr 980, 4,900, 5,096, Cr 10,976 | Interest Exp: Dr 104

March 31, 2020—Payment after discount period

Accounts Payable ($10,976 − $980 − $4,900)	5,096	
Interest Expense ($5,200 − $5,096)	104	
Cash ($5,096/0.98)		5,200

Review 9-3

1. $181,140 (computed as $10,250 + $37,440 + $84,000 + $49,450)
2. $180,191 (computed as $20.95 or ($463,050/22,100) × 8,600)
3. $182,100 (computed as (3,000 × $21.50) + (5,600 × $21.00))
4. $178,550 (computed as (1,100 × $20.50) + (7,500 × $20.80))

Review 9-4

a. **Gross Method**

March 5, 2020—Purchase of inventory

Inventory	11,200	
Accounts Payable		11,200

Assets = Liabilities + Equity: +11,200 = +11,200
Inventory: 11,200 (Dr) | Accounts Payable: 11,200 (Cr)

March 8, 2020—Inventory return

Accounts Payable	1,000	
Inventory		1,000

Assets = Liabilities + Equity: −1,000 = −1,000
Inventory: 11,200 (Dr) 1,000 (Cr) | Accounts Payable: 1,000 (Dr) 11,200 (Cr)

March 14, 2020—Payment within discount period

Accounts Payable	5,000	
Inventory ($5,000 × 0.02)		100
Cash		4,900

Assets = Liabilities + Equity: −100, −4,900 = −5,000
Inventory: 11,200 (Dr) 1,000, 100 (Cr) | Accounts Payable: 1,000, 5,000 (Dr) 11,200 (Cr) | Cash: 4,900 (Cr)

March 31, 2020—Payment after discount period

Accounts Payable ($11,200 − $1,000 − $5,000)	5,200	
Cash		5,200

Assets = Liabilities + Equity: −5,200 = −5,200
Cash: 4,900, 5,200 (Cr) | Accounts Payable: 1,000, 5,000, 5,200 (Dr) 11,200 (Cr)

b. **Net Method**

March 5, 2020—Purchase of inventory

Inventory ($11,200 × 0.98)	10,976	
Accounts Payable		10,976

Assets = Liabilities + Equity: +10,976 = +10,976
Inventory: 10,976 (Dr) | Accounts Payable: 10,976 (Cr)

March 8, 2020—Inventory return

Accounts Payable ($1,000 × 0.98)	980	
Inventory		980

Assets = Liabilities + Equity: −980 = −980
Inventory: 10,976 (Dr) 980 (Cr) | Accounts Payable: 980 (Dr) 10,976 (Cr)

March 14, 2020—Payment within discount period

Accounts Payable	4,900	
Cash		4,900

Assets = Liabilities + Equity: −4,900 = −4,900
Cash: 4,900 (Cr) | Accounts Payable: 980, 4,900 (Dr) 10,976 (Cr)

March 31, 2020—Payment after discount period

Accounts Payable ($10,976 − $980 − $4,900)	5,096	
Interest Expense ($5,200 − $5,096)	104	
Cash ($5,096 / 0.98)		5,200

Assets = Liabilities + Equity: −5,200 = −5,096 −104
Cash: 4,900, 5,200 (Cr) | Accounts Payable: 980, 4,900, 5,096 (Dr) 10,976 (Cr); balance 0 | Interest Exp: 104 (Dr)

Review 9-5

1. $181,546 (computed as 8,600 × $21.11)
2. $182,100 (computed as (5,600 × $21) + (3,000 × $21.50))
3. $180,650 (computed as (1,100 × $20.50) + (4,500 × $20.80) + (3,000 × $21.50))

Review 9-6

a. **December 31, 2020—Adjust LIFO reserve**

Cost of Goods Sold	180,000	
Allowance to Reduce FIFO Inventory to LIFO Basis		180,000

Assets = Liabilities + Equity: −180,000 = −180,000
Inventory Allow: 180,000 (Cr) | COGS: 180,000 (Dr)

December 31, 2021—Adjust LIFO reserve

Cost of Goods Sold	5,000	
Allowance to Reduce FIFO Inventory to LIFO Basis		5,000

Assets = Liabilities + Equity: −5,000 = −5,000
Inventory Allow: 180,000, 5,000 (Cr); balance 185,000 | COGS: 180,000, 5,000 (Dr)

b.

Balance Sheet (excerpt) For Year Ended December 31	2021	2020
Inventory.	$140,000	$100,000

Review 9-7

Cost of goods sold for the liquidated layers assuming liquidation had not occurred ((245,000 − 120,000) × $35)	$4,375,000
Cost of goods sold for the liquidated layers ($300,000 + $960,000 + $300,000).	1,560,000
Increase in pretax income	$2,815,000
After-tax increase in income ($2,815,000 × 0.75).	$2,111,250

Review 9-8

Date	Ending Inventory (Year-end prices)	÷	Price Index	=	Ending Inventory (Base year prices)	Inventory Layers	Price Index	Ending Inventory (Dollar-Value LIFO)
2020 . . .	$ 75,000		1.00		$75,000	$75,000	1.00	$75,000
2021 . . .	88,000		1.10		80,000	75,000	1.00	75,000
						5,000	1.10	5,500
								$80,500
2022 . . .	100,000		1.15		86,957	75,000	1.00	$75,000
						5,000	1.10	5,500
						6,957	1.15	8,000
								$88,500
2023 . . .	75,000		1.20		62,500	62,500	1.00	$62,500

Assets = Liabilities + Equity
−7,500 −7,500
Inventory Allow: 7,500 | COGS: 7,500

December 31, 2021—To adjust inventory to LIFO

Cost of Goods Sold	7,500	
Allowance to Reduce FIFO Inventory to LIFO Basis		7,500

$7,500 = $88,000 – $80,500.

Assets = Liabilities + Equity
−4,000 −4,000
Inventory Allow: 7,500, 4,000 | COGS: 7,500, 4,000

December 31, 2022—To adjust inventory to LIFO

Cost of Goods Sold	4,000	
Allowance to Reduce FIFO Inventory to LIFO Basis		4,000

$4,000 = $11,500 – $7,500; $11,500 = $100,000 – $88,500.

Assets = Liabilities + Equity
−1,000 −1,000
Inventory Allow: 7,500, 4,000, 1,000 | COGS: 7,500, 4,000, 1,000

December 31, 2023—To adjust inventory to LIFO

Cost of Goods Sold	1,000	
Allowance to Reduce FIFO Inventory to LIFO Basis		1,000

$1,000 = $12,500 – $11,500; $12,500 = $75,000 – $62,500.

Review 9-9

a. Inventory turnover: Year 2: 5.36 ($10,077/$1,881) Year 3: 5.33 ($9,876/$1,852)

b. Average days in inventory: Year 2: 68.1 (365/5.36) Year 3: 68.5 (365/5.33)

10 Inventory: Additional Issues

Whole Foods Market, Inc.
Consolidated Balance Sheets
(In millions)

	September 25, 2016	September 27, 2015
Assets		
Current assests:		
Cash and cash equivalents	$ 351	$ 237
Short-term investments - available-for-sale securities	379	155
Restricted cash	122	127
Accounts receivable	242	218
Merchandise inventories	517	500
Prepaid expenses and other current assets	167	108
Deferred income taxes	197	199
Total current assets	1,975	1,544

Inventories

The Company values inver... ...e lower of cost or market. Cost was determined using the dollar value retail last-in, first-out ("LIFO") method for approximately 91.8% and 92.2% of inventories in fiscal years 2016 and 2015, respectively. Under the LIFO method, the cost assigned to items sold is based on the cost of the most recent items purchased. As a result, the costs of the first items purchased remain in inventory and are used to value ending inventory. The excess of estimated current costs over LIFO carrying value, or LIFO reserve, was approximately $42 million and $49 million at September 25, 2016 and September 27, 2015, respectively. Costs for remaining inventories are determined by the first-in, first-out method. Cost before the LIFO adjustment is principally determined using the item cost method, which is calculated by counting each item in inventory, assigning costs to each of these items based on the actual purchase cost (net of vendor allowances) of each item and recordin... cost of items sold.

Gross Profit

Gross profit totaled approximately $5.4 billion, $5.4 billion and $5.0 billion in fiscal years 2016, 2015 and 2014, respectively. Gross profit as a percentage of sales decreased 78 basis points in fiscal year 2016 compared to the prior fiscal year. Net LIFO inventory reserves decreased approximately $7 million during fiscal year 2016 compared to an increase of ...ximately $1 million and $16 million in fiscal years 2015 and 2014, respectively. The decrease in fiscal years 2016 and ... increase in cost of goods sold as a percentage of sales, primarily reflecting our ongoing value strategy.

Cost of Goods Sold

Cost of goods sold includes cost of inventory sold during the period (net of discounts and allowances), distribution and food preparation costs, and shipping and handling costs. The Company receives various rebates from third-party vendors in the form of purchase or sales volume discounts and payments under cooperative advertising agreements. Purchase volume discounts are calculated based on actual purchase volumes. Volume discounts and cooperative advertising discounts in excess of identifiable advertising costs are recognized as a reduction of cost of goods sold when the related merchandise is sold. The Company utilizes forward purchases to limit its exposures to changes in commodity prices. All forward purchase commitments are established at current prices and recorded through cost of goods sold at settlement.

Chapter Preview

We begin by comparing the cost of inventory to its net realizable value (or to market in certain cases). We do this because accounting standards require inventory adjustments to reflect any decrease in the revenue-generating power of inventory. Next, we describe methods for estimating inventory values in lump sum purchases, and through the use of the gross profit method. We review the reporting requirements of purchase commitments and analyze the impacts of inventory method changes and inventory errors. We conclude with two inventory estimation methods that are common to retail environments: the average cost and conventional retail methods.

Action Plan

LO	Topic/Subtopic	Page	Demos	Reviews	Assignments
LO 10–1	**Apply lower-of-cost-or-net realizable value rule to inventory** Cost :: Net Realizable Value (NRV) :: Allowance to Reduce Inventory to NRV	10-3	D10-1	R10-1	21, 22, 23, 40, 41, 42, 43, 44, 45, 70, 71, 72, 87, 91, 93
LO 10–2	**Apply lower-of-cost-or-market rule to inventory** Cost :: Market Value :: Ceiling :: Floor :: Allowance to Reduce Inventory to Market Value	10-7	D10-2	R10-2	24, 25, 46, 47, 70, 73, 74, 92
LO 10–3	**Demonstrate the relative sales value method to allocate costs to inventory** Lump Sum Purchase :: Relative Sales Value :: Allocation of Purchase Price	10-10	D10-3	R10-3	26, 48, 49, 70, 91
LO 10–4	**Demonstrate the gross profit method to estimate inventory** Markup on Sales :: Markup on Costs :: Estimated COGS :: Estimated Ending Inventory	10-11	D10-4	R10-4	27, 28, 29, 50, 51, 52, 53, 54, 55, 70, 75, 76, 90
LO 10–5	**Demonstrate the accounting for purchase commitments** Noncancelable :: Estimated Liability on Purchase Commitment :: Estimated Loss on Purchase Commitment :: Disclosure	10-13	D10-5	R10-5	30, 31, 56, 57, 70, 77, 91, 92
LO 10–6	**Describe the accounting treatment for changes in inventory methods** Retrospective Adjustment :: Prospective Adjustment :: Direct Effect ::Indirect Effect	10-15	D10-6A D10-6B	R10-6	32, 33, 34, 58, 59, 60, 61, 70, 78, 79, 80, 81, 91, 92
LO 10–7	**Explain the accounting treatment of inventory errors** Material Inventory Errors :: Retained Earnings—Prior Period Adjustment :: Counterbalancing :: Noncounterbalancing	10-20	D10-7	R10-7	35, 36, 62, 63, 64, 70, 82, 83, 85, 91
LO 10–8	**Estimate inventory using the average cost and conventional retail methods** Average Cost Method :: Conventional Method:: Lower-of-Average-Cost-or-Market ::Markups:: Markdowns :: Cost Ratio	10-23	D10-8A D10-8B D10-8C	R10-8	37, 38, 39, 65, 66, 67, 68, 69, 70, 84, 86, 88, 89
LO 10–9	**APPENDIX 10A—Estimate inventory using LIFO retail and dollar-value LIFO retail methods** LIFO Retail :: Dollar-Value LIFO Retail :: Inventory Layers :: Cost Ratio :: Change to LIFO Retail :: Conversion Price Index	10-29	D10-9A D10-9B	R10-9	88, 96, 97, 98, 99, 100, 101, 102, 103, 104, 105

LO 10-1 Apply lower-of-cost-or-net realizable value rule to inventory

LO 10-1 Overview

Lower-of-Cost-or-Net Realizable Value Rule
- Applies to inventory methods other than LIFO and the retail inventory method
- Defines net realizable value as selling price less completion, disposal, and transportation costs

Ordinarily, the basis of recording inventory (measured using the methods described in the prior chapter) is cost of the inventory. However, when there is a loss in utility of inventory as explained in the following accounting guidance, the company must recognize a loss in the income statement and carry inventory on the balance sheet at a value less than cost.

330-10-35-2 Under certain circumstances cost may not be the amount properly chargeable against the revenues of future periods. A departure from cost is required in these circumstances because cost is satisfactory only if the utility of the goods has not diminished since their acquisition; a loss of utility shall be reflected as a charge against the revenues of the period in which it occurs. Thus, in accounting for inventories, a loss shall be recognized whenever the utility of goods is impaired by damage, deterioration, obsolescence, changes in price levels, or other causes.

In other words, a departure from the cost basis of pricing inventory is required when the utility of the inventory is no longer as great as the cost of the inventory.

As shown in **Exhibit 10-1**, in cases where a company measures the cost of inventory either through the LIFO inventory method or the retail inventory method, it follows the **lower-of-cost-or-market rule**. Under this rule, a company records inventory at the lower of cost or market where market is defined as replacement cost (within specified limits). The lower-of-cost-or-market rule is discussed in LO 10-2. For all other inventory methods, a company follows the lower-of-cost-or-net realizable value rule which is discussed in this section.

EXHIBIT 10-1 Inventory Measurement Practices

Inventory Method	Inventory Measurement Approach
• LIFO • Retail Inventory	**Lower-of-Cost-or-Market** LO 10-2
All other inventory methods including FIFO, average cost	**Lower-of-Cost-or-Net Realizable Value** LO 10-1

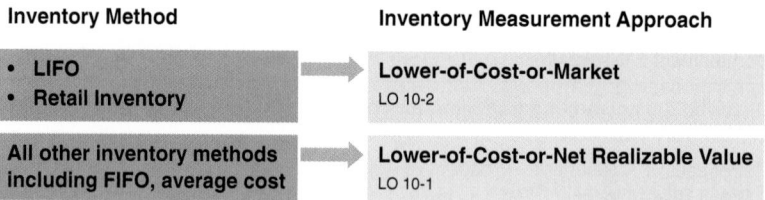

330-10-35-1B Inventory measured using any method other than LIFO or the retail inventory method (for example, inventory measured using first-in, first-out (FIFO) or average cost) shall be measured at the lower of cost and net realizable value. When evidence exists that the net realizable value of inventory is lower than its cost, the difference shall be recognized as a loss in earnings in the period in which it occurs. That loss may be required, for example, due to damage, physical deterioration, obsolescence, changes in price levels, or other causes.

Lower-of-Cost-or-Net Realizable Value Rule

The write-down in inventory is measured through the **lower-of-cost-or-net realizable rule**, where inventory is to be recorded at the lower of:

- **Cost**—any method other than LIFO or the retail inventory method such as average cost, FIFO, or specific identification, OR
- **Net realizable value**—estimated selling price less reasonably predictable costs of completion, disposal, and transportation.

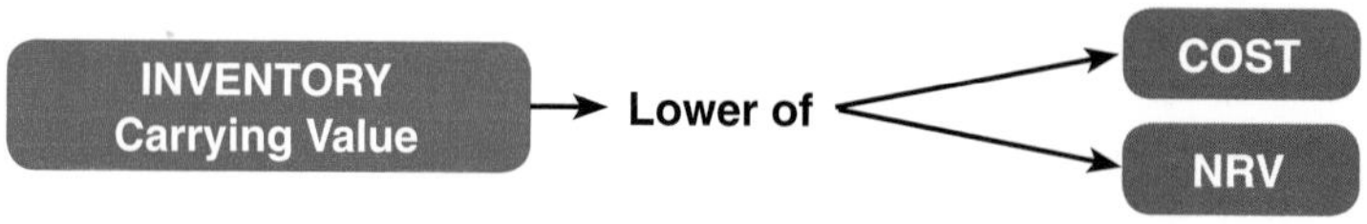

The lower-of-cost-or-net realizable value rule identifies and reduces the value of inventory when a low selling price might not cover the costs to acquire or produce the merchandise. A low selling price can be due to several factors including damage, obsolescence, and competitive pressure. **This reduction is identified and recorded while the inventory is held, instead of in a subsequent period when the inventory is sold.**

For example, a retailer holds inventory consisting of a single line of office products, all purchased during 2020 at a cost of $165 per unit. Late in the year, competition in the office products market causes the net realizable value to drop substantially from $200 a unit to $150 a unit. The retailer's ending inventory for 2020 is valued and reported at $150 per unit, which represents a $15 loss per unit based on the $165 original purchase cost. This $15 per unit loss is reported in the retailer's 2020 financial statements, the period during which the decline in net realizable value took place.

Application of the Lower-of-Cost-or-Net Realizable Rule

Three approaches are available to determine the overall inventory valuation in applying the lower-of-cost-or-net realizable value rule.

- Comparison of cost and net realizable value separately for each item of inventory.
- Comparison of cost and net realizable value separately for each classification of inventory.
- Comparison of total cost with total net realizable value for the inventory.

Demo 10-1 illustrates application of these three approaches. The individual unit basis produces the most conservative inventory value because units with a net realizable value greater than cost are not allowed to offset items with a net realizable value less than cost. This offsetting occurs to some extent in the other approaches. Recall that the overall purpose of applying the lower-of-cost-or-net-realizable-value (or market) is to reflect clearly and fairly the income of the period. The most common practice is to apply the lower-of-cost-or-net-realizable-value (or market) rule separately to each item of inventory. However, applying it to the entire stock of inventory may convey the most information for accounting purposes if, for example, there is only one end-product category. In this case, if the value of total inventory is not below its cost, a remeasurement of individual items may not lead to a more useful result. Management judgment is required on which approach to apply. Consistency in application over time is essential.

330-10-35-8 Depending on the character and composition of the inventory, the [inventory] guidance . . . may properly be applied either directly to each item or to the total of the inventory (or, in some cases, to the total of the components of each major category). The method shall be that which most clearly reflects periodic income.

If cost is lower than net realizable value, no entry is necessary. However, if net realizable value is lower than cost, an adjustment is required to recognize the inventory holding loss. The adjustment reduces the carrying value of inventory and net income. A company does not reverse the loss in later periods even in the event that the net realizable value increases. (The following refers to the write-down of LIFO inventories to lower-of-cost-or-market, which is applied by reference to the valuation of non-LIFO and non-retail method inventories by paragraph 330-10-S35-1.)

330-10-S99-2 Based on FASB ASC paragraph 330-10-35-14, the staff believes that a write-down of inventory to the lower of cost or market at the close of a fiscal period creates a new cost basis that subsequently cannot be marked up based on changes in underlying facts and circumstances.

Recognition of Inventory Losses

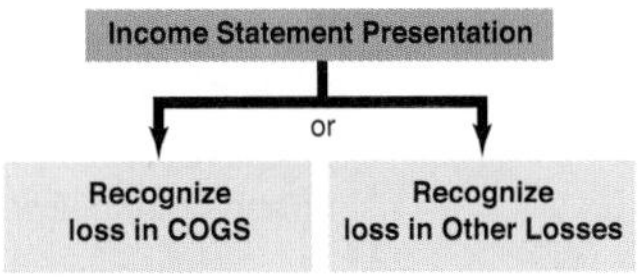

The adjustment of inventory to net realizable value results in a reduction to equity and a reduction to assets. While the accounting guidance provided above indicates that losses are recognized in earnings, more specific guidance is not provided. As a result, companies **report the adjustment of inventory to net realizable value in the income statement either in cost of goods sold *or* separately in the other expenses and losses section**. However, any significant losses that are considered unusual or infrequent should be reported in the other expenses and losses section. See the discussion in Chapter 3 on reporting unusual and/or infrequent items.

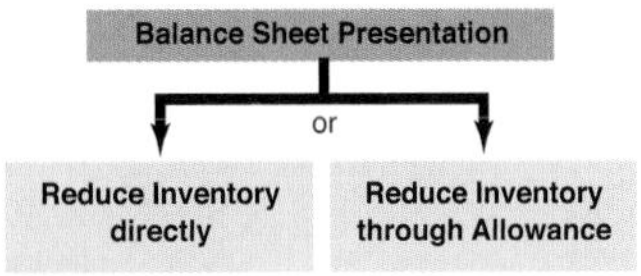

For the asset reduction, either inventory is credited or a contra inventory account, Allowance to Reduce Inventory to Net Realizable Value, is credited. If an allowance account is used for the adjustment, the original inventory value is maintained in the accounting system (similar to using an allowance for doubtful accounts to adjust receivables to net realizable value). While inventory is held, the allowance account is maintained. An allowance account is not reversed later if the net realizable value increases. If the inventory is sold, the balance in the allowance account is closed out to cost of goods sold and a new allowance is reestablished as needed. The Allowance to Reduce Inventory to Net Realizable Value would typically be adjusted at a reporting period date and not at each sale.

EXPANDING YOUR KNOWLEDGE **Inventory at Net Realizable Value: An Exception**

Under unusual circumstances, inventory may be properly stated at a value above cost basis. For example, inventory items may, in some rare cases, be valued at sales price (less disposal costs), even if this value is above the cost value. Inventory may be shown at selling prices that are above cost in the following cases.

330-10-35-16

a. Inventories of gold and silver, when there is an effective government-controlled market at a fixed monetary value
b. Inventories representing agricultural, mineral, and other products, with all of the following criteria:
1. Units of which are interchangeable
2. Units of which have an immediate marketability at quoted prices
3. Units for which appropriate costs may be difficult to obtain.

Where such inventories are stated at sales prices, they shall be reduced by expenditures to be incurred in disposal.

Stating inventories above cost is not uncommon in these cases. When inventory is stated at a value above cost, this fact should be fully disclosed in financial statements.

Demo 10-1 LO10-1 Application of Lower-of-Cost-or-Net Realizable Value Rule

Demo MBC

Star Inc. is a merchandiser, selling women's and men's shoes. The cost and net realizable values for merchandise inventory (accounted for using FIFO or average cost) are provided below as of December 31, 2020.

a. Compute lower-of-cost-or-net realizable value by individual item, classification, and in total.
b. Record the entry to adjust inventory using the individual item approach. (1) Prepare the journal entry to record the holding loss on inventory using an allowance account to adjust inventory and cost of goods sold to adjust equity. (2) Prepare the journal entry to record the holding loss on inventory using an allowance account to adjust inventory and a separate loss account to adjust equity.
c. Show the financial statement impact for each approach described in part *b* assuming cost of goods sold is $100,000 before adjustment.
d. Record the adjustment to reduce inventory to net realizable value on December 31, 2021, assuming that cost and net realizable values are determined to be $90,500 and $83,000, respectively. Assume that the January 1, 2021, inventory was sold during 2021. Adjust cost of goods sold for any adjusting entry.

Solution

a. **Lower-of-cost-or-net realizable value**

			Lower-of-Cost-or-Net Realizable Value Applied to:		
Inventory	**Cost**	**Net Realizable Value**	**Individual Items**	**Classification**	**Total**
Women's Shoes					
Athletic	$10,000	$ 9,500	$ 9,500		
Fashion sneakers . . .	8,000	9,000	8,000		
	18,000	18,500		$18,000	
Men's Shoes					
Athletic	21,000	22,000	21,000		
Fashion sneakers . . .	32,000	29,000	29,000		
	53,000	51,000		51,000	
Total	$71,000	$69,500			$69,500
Inventory at lower-of-cost-or-net realizable value. . . .			**$67,500**	**$69,000**	**$69,500**

Inventory recorded at the lower-of-cost-or-net realizable value is $67,500 if the rule is applied to each item, $69,000 if the rule is applied to each category, and $69,500 if the rule is applied to total inventory. The application of the lower-of-cost-or-net realizable rule resulted in the lowest value when applied to each individual inventory item.

continued

b. **Inventory Adjustment—2020**

(1) The adjustment required is $3,500, which is the cost of $71,000 less the net realizable value of $67,500.

December 31, 2020—To reduce cost of inventory to net realizable value

Cost of Goods Sold	3,500	
Allowance to Reduce Inventory to Net Realizable Value		3,500

Assets = Liabilities + Equity
−3,500 −3,500
Allow to Reduce Inv: 3,500 (credit)
COGS: 3,500 (debit)

(2) The entry to record a loss of $3,500 follows.

December 31, 2020—To reduce cost of inventory to net realizable value

Holding Loss on Inventory	3,500	
Allowance to Reduce Inventory to Net Realizable Value		3,500

Assets = Liabilities + Equity
−3,500 −3,500
Allow to Reduce Inv: 3,500 (credit)
Hold Loss on Inv: 3,500 (debit)

c. **Financial Statement Impact of the Inventory Adjustment—2020**

	(1)	(2)
Balance Sheet Assets, at December 31, 2020		
Inventory	$ 71,000	$ 71,000
Allowance to reduce inventory to net realizable value	(3,500)	(3,500)
Inventory, net	$ 67,500	$ 67,500
Income Statement, for year ended December 31, 2020		
Cost of goods sold	$103,500	$100,000
Other expenses and losses		
Holding loss on inventory	0	3,500

d. **Inventory Adjustment—2021**

On December 31, 2021, the balance of the Allowance to Reduce Inventory to Net Realizable Value is a credit of $3,500 before adjustment. The allowance account is adjusted as follows.

Amount required in the allowance ($90,500 − $83,000)	$7,500
Unadjusted balance in the allowance	3,500
Adjustment to allowance required	$4,000

The entry to adjust the allowance account follows.

December 31, 2021—To reduce cost of inventory to net realizable value

Cost of Goods Sold	4,000	
Allowance to Reduce Inventory to Net Realizable Value		4,000

Assets = Liabilities + Equity
−4,000 −4,000
Allow to Reduce Inv: 3,500, 4,000 (credit); balance 7,500
COGS: 3,500, 4,000 (debit)

NIKE

Real World—LOWER-OF-COST-OR-NET REALIZABLE VALUE

In the Critical Accounting Policies section of the MD&A of a recent Form 10-K, Nike Inc. reported the following information related to its inventory reserves. The excess of cost over net realizable value is recorded in cost of sales.

NIKE INC. [NKE]

> **Inventory Reserves** We also make ongoing estimates relating to the net realizable value of inventories based upon our assumptions about future demand and market conditions. If we estimate that the net realizable value of our inventory is less than the cost of the inventory recorded on our books, we record a reserve equal to the difference between the cost of the inventory and the estimated net realizable value. This reserve is recorded as a charge to Cost of sales. If changes in market conditions result in reductions in the estimated net realizable value of our inventory below our previous estimate, we would increase our reserve in the period in which we made such a determination and record a charge to Cost of sales.

REVIEW 10-1 LO10-1 Application of Lower-of-Cost-or-Net Realizable Value Rule

Review MBC

Anne Taylor Inc. has the following information for six inventory items on June 30, 2020.

Item No.	Quantity	Selling Price	Cost to Sell	Cost per Unit
#110	50	$55	$5	$50
#115	80	78	5	75
#125	20	60	3	45
#210	60	25	2	20
#220	40	46	3	50
#225	90	35	2	30

Required

a. Determine the inventory cost to report on the company's balance sheet as of June 30, 2020, assuming that the company applies the lower-of-cost-or-net realizable value rule to each individual inventory item.

b. Record the entry to adjust inventory to the lower-of-cost-or-net realizable value by adjusting inventory through an allowance account and expense through cost of goods sold.

More Practice:
10-23, 10-42, 10-43
Solution on p. 10-56.

LO 10-2 Apply lower-of-cost-or-market rule to inventory

LO 10-2 Overview

Lower-of-Cost-or-Market Rule
- Applies only to LIFO and retail inventory cost methods
- Defines market as replacement cost limited to a ceiling and a floor

We discussed the lower-of-cost-or-net realizable value rule in the previous section. This rule applies to inventory when the cost flow assumption is *not* the LIFO or retail inventory methods. When companies use the LIFO inventory method or the retail inventory method, the rule that applies is that inventory is recorded at the **lower-of-cost-or-market** as illustrated in **Demo 10-2**. Market is limited to a ceiling and a floor as explained in the accounting guidance that follows.

ASC Glossary Market: As used in the phrase lower of cost or market, the term market means current replacement cost (by purchase or by reproduction, as the case may be) provided that it meets both of the following conditions:

a. Market shall not exceed the net realizable value

b. Market shall not be less than net realizable value reduced by an allowance for an approximately normal profit margin.

330-10-35-1C A departure from the cost basis of pricing inventory measured using LIFO or the retail inventory method is required when the utility of the goods is no longer as great as their cost. Where there is evidence that the utility of goods in their disposal in the ordinary course of business will be less than cost, whether due to damage, physical deterioration, obsolescence, changes in price levels, or other causes, the difference shall be recognized as a loss of the current period. This is generally accomplished by stating such goods at a lower level commonly designated as market.

In other words, market is defined as replacement cost unless **replacement cost** exceeds the **ceiling** or replacement cost is less than the **floor**. Any required adjustments to lower inventory to market value are recorded in the same way as illustrated in LO 10-1 when following the lower-of-cost-or-net realizable value rule.

Floor	Market	Ceiling
Net realizable value less an amount equal to the approximate normal profit margin. A normal profit margin is that achieved on sale of the inventory item or on similar items under normal circumstances.	Replacement cost or the current purchase or reproduction cost.	Net realizable value of inventory or the estimated selling price of the goods in the ordinary course of business less reasonably predictable costs of completion and disposal.

Inconsistency in Applying the Inventory Adjustment Rules

The net impact of the two rules (lower-of-cost-or-market and lower-of-cost-or-net realizable value) is to recognize inventory holding losses earlier in the period when the loss occurs (as estimated). While potential losses are recognized in the period when estimated, gains are not realized until the period in which the inventory is sold. In the period of sale, the company benefits from a higher selling price as the market or net realizable value increases. (Recall that holding gains are not recognized, nor can holding losses be reversed with a favorable increase in market price or net realizable value.) This results in inconsistent reporting and a lack of representational faithfulness of the economic transactions. This means bad news is recognized but good news is delayed. While inconsistent, the recognition of a gain on inventory before control of a good or service has transferred to a customer is not allowed under the revenue recognition standard. Thus, early recognition of a gain does not meet the requirements for recognizing revenue on a sales contract.

EXPANDING YOUR KNOWLEDGE **Why Establish a Ceiling and a Floor for Market?**

The ceiling and floor constraints prevent inventory from being stated at an amount in excess of net selling price or below net selling price less a normal margin of profit. The *ceiling* (maximum value) applies to obsolete, damaged, or out-of-style items—so these losses are recognized in the period of occurrence instead of being carried forward in inventory. The *floor* (minimum value) deters the establishment of unreasonably low inventory values—causing losses on these items to be recognized before sale while increasing profits in future periods when the items are sold.

Application of Lower-of-Cost-or-Market Rule **LO10-2** **Demo 10-2**

The following per unit data are for five products of Diamond Inc. as of December 31, 2020. Calculate the per unit value for each item *A* through *E* when applying the lower-of-cost-or-market rule to ending inventory.

	Item A	Item B	Item C	Item D	Item E
Estimated selling price	$ 85	$ 90	$ 80	$ 75	$ 70
Estimated cost to complete and sell	25	30	20	15	12
Estimated normal profit margin	9	9	8	8	7
Original cost	100	100	100	45	40
Replacement cost	55	65	45	40	45

Solution

We first need to determine the market value. The ceiling is computed as estimated selling price net of selling and completion costs (net realizable value). The floor is computed as net realizable value less estimated normal profit margin.

continued

continued from previous page

	Item A	Item B	Item C	Item D	Item E
Estimated selling price	$85	$90	$80	$75	$70
Less estimated cost to complete and sell	25	30	20	15	12
Net realizable value (ceiling)	**$60**	**$60**	**$60**	**$60**	**$58**
Subtract: Estimated normal profit margin	9	9	8	8	7
Net realizable value less profit (floor)	**$51**	**$51**	**$52**	**$52**	**$51**

From the above, we can determine the market value to use to compare to cost to determine the lower of cost or market. We summarize the decision below.

	Item A	Item B	Item C	Item D	Item E
Replacement cost	$55	$65	$45	$40	$45
Ceiling	60	60	60	60	58
Floor	51	51	52	52	51
Market	55	60	52	52	51
Cost	100	100	100	45	40
Lower-of-cost-or-market	**$55**	**$60**	**$52**	**$45**	**$40**

The market value is the replacement cost unless the amount is limited by the ceiling or floor. One way to think about this is that **out of the three values (replacement cost, ceiling, and floor), always use the middle amount as market value.**

- For item A, the replacement cost of $55 falls between the ceiling and floor so it is considered the market price. Because the market value of $55 is lower than the cost of $100, the inventory value is reduced to $55.
- For item B, the replacement cost exceeds the ceiling, so the market is capped at the ceiling of $60. Because market of $60 is less than the cost of $100, the inventory is written down to the market value of $60.
- For item C, the replacement cost of $45 is too low because it is lower than the floor. Therefore, market is limited to $52, or the floor. The last step is to compare the value of cost to market. The inventory is reduced to the market value of $52 because this value is lower than the cost of $100.

The last two items follow similar analyses but in each of these cases the original cost is less than the determined market value.

WHOLE FOODS MARKET

Real World—LOWER-OF-COST-OR-MARKET

WHOLE FOODS MARKET INC. [WFM]

Whole Foods Market Inc. records inventory at the lower of cost (dollar value retail) or market as reported in a recent Form 10-K.

> **Inventories** The Company values inventories at the lower of cost or market. Cost was determined using the dollar value retail last-in, first-out ("LIFO") method for approximately 92.2% and 93.5% of inventories in fiscal years 2015 and 2014, respectively. Under the LIFO method, the cost assigned to items sold is based on the cost of the most recent items purchased. As a result, the costs of the first items purchased remain in inventory and are used to value ending inventory. The excess of estimated current costs over LIFO carrying value, or LIFO reserve, was approximately $49 million and $48 million at September 27, 2015 and September 28, 2014, respectively. Costs for remaining inventories are determined by the first-in, first-out method. Cost before the LIFO adjustment is principally determined using the item cost method, which is calculated by counting each item in inventory, assigning costs to each of these items based on the actual purchase cost (net of vendor allowances) of each item and recording the actual cost of items sold.

Application of Lower-of-Cost-or-Market Rule

LO10-2 REVIEW 10-2

Review MBC

Anne Taylor Inc. has the following information for six inventory items on June 30, 2020. The normal profit margin is 30% of selling price.

Item No.	Quantity	Selling Price per Unit	Cost to Sell per Unit	Cost per Unit	Replacement Cost per Unit
#110	50	$24	$5	$16	$18
#115	80	22	4	14	15
#125	20	35	6	31	28
#210	60	40	6	29	35
#220	40	18	4	10	13
#225	90	30	8	26	18

Required

a. Determine the inventory cost to report on the balance sheet on June 30, 2020, assuming that the company applies the lower-of-cost-or-market value rule to each individual inventory item.

b. Record the entry to adjust inventory to the lower-of-cost-or-market value by adjusting inventory through an allowance account and expense through cost of goods sold.

More Practice: 10-24, 10-46, 10-47

Solution on p. 10-57.

Demonstrate the relative sales value method to allocate costs to inventory

LO 10-3

Two or more different types of inventory items may be purchased for a **lump sum** (also called a basket purchase). A separate cost for each type is required for accounting purposes. Allocation of the total cost should be related to the economic utility or revenue-producing ability of each kind or group of items. If the sales value of a particular item is a reasonable indication of its relative utility, the cost allocation can be made on the basis of the **relative sales value** of the individual inventory items as illustrated in **Demo 10-3**.

Relative Sales Value Method
- Use when purchasing multiple items at one lump sum price
- Allocate lump sum cost to individual items based upon the relative value of individual sales amounts

LO 10-3 Overview

Relative Sales Value Method

LO10-3 Demo 10-3

Demo MBC

Lee Inc., a packing plant, purchases 1,000 bushels of apples (ungraded) for $2,000 on June 1, 2020. After purchase, the apples are sorted into three grades at a cost of $70 for a total price of $2,070 ($2,000 + $70). Sorting produces the following results: grade A, 200 bushels; grade B, 300 bushels; and grade C, 500 bushels. Lee sells the sorted apples at different retail prices per bushel: grade A, $5; grade B, $4; and grade C, $2.50.

a. Allocate the lump sum cost of $2,070 to the three grades of apples: A, B, and C.

b. Record the June 1, 2020, lump sum purchase allocated to each grade of apples.

c. Calculate the total gross profit and gross profit percentage for each grade of apples assuming all apples are sold at the prices listed.

Solution

a. **Allocation of Lump Sum Cost**

Grade	Quantity (Bushels)	Unit Selling Price	Total Selling Value	Fraction of Total Sales Value	Allocated Cost[1]
A	200	$5.00	$1,000	$1,000/$3,450	$ 600
B	300	4.00	1,200	$1,200/$3,450	720
C	500	2.50	1,250	$1,250/$3,450	750
	1,000		$3,450		$2,070

[1]Fraction of total sales value x Total cost of $2,070.

continued

continued from previous page

The lump sum purchase price is allocated to each grade of apples based upon the relative selling price of the apple grades. Allocation based upon relative selling price is preferred over a uniform allocation of costs because the different grades of apples provide different levels of benefit to Lee. Lee's projected sales value for all of the apples is $3,450. The percentage of each individual grade is computed as a percentage of the total sales value, $3,450. Finally, each percentage is multiplied by the lump sum cost of $2,070 to arrive at the cost for each grade.

b. **Recording Lump Sum Purchase** The following entry is recorded on the date of purchase. The lump sum cost of $2,070 is allocated to the three types of apples based upon the relative sales price of each type of apple.

Assets = Liabilities + Equity
+2,070
−2,070

Inventory		Cash	
2,070			2,070

June 1, 2020—To allocate lump sum purchase price to inventory items

Inventory—Grade A Apples (200 units)	600	
Inventory—Grade B Apples (300 units)	720	
Inventory—Grade C Apples (500 units)	750	
Cash		2,070

c. **Calculation of Gross Profit and Gross Profit Percentage** Sales less allocated cost equals gross profit. For grade A apples, the gross profit of $400 is equal to $1,000 less $600. The gross profit percentage is equal to the gross profit of $400 divided by sales of $1,000. Because the cost is allocated on the same relative basis as sales, the gross profit percentage remains consistent across all inventory items.

Grade	Sales Value	Allocated Cost	Gross Profit[1]	Gross Profit Percentage[2]
A	$1,000	$600	$400	40%
B	1,200	720	480	40%
C	1,250	750	500	40%
	$3,450	$2,070	$1,380	

[1]Sales value less allocated cost. [2]Gross profit / Sales value.

REVIEW 10-3 LO10-3 Relative Sales Value Method

Review MBC

On June 1, 2020, Resort Inc. purchased and subdivided land at a cost of $600,000 cash. The land was divided as follows.

- 10% used for public spaces.
- 40% divided into 10 premier lots to sell for $50,000 each.
- 40% divided into 15 premium lots to sell for $35,000 each.
- 10% divided into 5 standard lots to sell for $20,000 each.

Required

a. Prepare the entry for the purchase of the lots. Use the relative sales value method to allocate the total cost of $600,000 to the three categories of lots. Assume a perpetual inventory system.

b. As of June 30, 2020, Resort Inc. had sold 6 premier lots, 10 premium lots, and 4 standard lots. Compute the valuation of inventory by category as of June 30, 2020.

More Practice: 10-26, 10-48, 10-49

Solution on p. 10-57.

LO 10-4 Demonstrate the gross profit method to estimate inventory

LO 10-4 Overview

Gross Profit Method
- Determine markup on sales
  - If markup on cost is provided, convert to markup on sales
- Estimate cost of goods sold and ending inventory

Although generally unacceptable for use in external financial statements, the gross profit method is used by many companies to estimate the cost of inventory for many other purposes such as estimating a month end's ending inventory when no physical count is taken or estimating the amount of inventory lost to theft. The **gross profit method**, or **gross margin method**, assumes that a constant gross margin estimated on recent sales can be used to estimate cost of goods sold for current sales, which is then used to compute an estimate of ending inventory. See **Demo 10-4**.

Applying the Gross Profit Method

The gross profit method is illustrated in the following two steps.

Step One: Determine Gross Profit as a Percentage of Sales

In applying the gross profit method, a company first estimates **gross profit as a percentage of sales**, also called **markup on sales**, based on prior sales history. This percentage is derived by simply taking gross profit and dividing by sales. For retailers however, **gross profit as a percentage of cost**, also called **markup on cost**, is a commonly used measure. In this case, we must convert gross profit as a percentage of cost to gross profit as a percentage of sales as follows.

$$\textbf{Gross profit as a percentage of sales} = \frac{\textbf{Gross profit as a percentage of cost}}{\textbf{(1 + Gross profit as a percentage of cost)}}$$

Step Two: Estimate Ending Inventory

An estimate of ending inventory is determined as follows. Cost of goods sold is estimated by multiplying sales for the period by (1 − Gross profit as a percentage of sales). Through this calculation, cost of goods sold is estimated based on the *past* relation of cost of goods sold to sales, then applied to *current* sales. Ending inventory is then computed (estimated) by subtracting the estimated cost of goods sold from the cost of goods available for sale.

Beginning inventory
Add: Purchases
Cost of goods available for sale
Subtract: Cost of goods sold (estimated)
Ending inventory (estimated)

Gross Profit Method—Uses and Limitations

The gross profit method has several potential applications.

- To test the reasonableness of an inventory valuation determined by some other means, such as a physical inventory count or from perpetual inventory records.
- To estimate the ending inventory for interim financial reports prepared during the year when it is impractical to count the inventory physically and a perpetual inventory system is not used.
- To estimate the cost of inventory destroyed by an accident, such as fire or a storm. Valuation of inventory lost is necessary to account for the accident and to establish a basis for insurance claims and income taxes.
- To develop estimates of inventory, gross profit, and cost of goods sold for budgeting purposes.

The gross profit method has limitations.

- The past gross margin rate may not appropriately reflect markup changes relating to the current or future periods. This affects reliability of results.
- Gross margin rates (markup rates) may vary widely on different types of inventory. Most companies carry a number of different lines of merchandise, each having a different markup rate. A change during the period in the markup rate on one or more lines or a shift in the relative quantities of each line sold (shifts in sales mix) changes the average gross margin rate. This change affects the reliability of the results.

When the gross profit method is applied in a situation that involves broad aggregations of inventory items with largely different markup rates, the computations should be developed for each separate class. The estimate of the total inventory is then determined by adding the estimates for the separate classes.

Demo 10-4 **LO10-4** **Estimate Inventory Using Gross Profit Method**

Demo MBC

In 2020, Diaz Inc. reports net sales revenues of $20,000, beginning inventory of $5,000, and net purchases of $13,000. Past experience shows a consistent mark up on cost of 25%. The following data for 2019 reflects this. Without a physical inventory count, estimate Diaz's inventory balance on December 31, 2020, using the gross profit method.

2019	Amount	Percentage of Cost	
Sales	$15,000	125%	($15,000/$12,000)
Cost of goods sold	12,000	100%	($12,000/$12,000)
Gross profit	$ 3,000	25%	($3,000/$12,000)

Solution

Step One: Determine Gross Profit as a Percentage of Sales Gross profit as a percentage of cost must first be converted to gross profit as a percentage of sales as follows.

$$\text{Gross profit as a percentage of sales} = \text{Gross profit as a percentage of cost}/(1 + \text{Gross profit as a percentage of cost})$$
$$= 0.25/(1 + 0.25)$$
$$= 0.20 \text{ or } \mathbf{20\%}$$

Alternatively, gross profit as a percentage of sales is calculated as $3,000 in gross profit divided by $15,000 in sales, or 20%.

Step Two: Estimate Ending Inventory Without performing a physical inventory, Diaz estimates ending inventory of $2,000, calculated as follows.

Estimation of December 31, 2020, Ending Inventory

Beginning inventory	$ 5,000
Add: Purchases, net	13,000
Cost of goods available for sale	18,000
Subtract: Cost of goods sold, estimated ($20,000 × (1 − 0.20))	(16,000)
Ending inventory, estimated	$ 2,000

REVIEW 10-4 **LO10-4** **Gross Profit Method**

Review MBC

On May 20, 2020, a flood destroyed Atlas Inc.'s inventory storage facility. It is estimated that $20,000 can be realized from the sale of undamaged inventory. Based on recent history, markup is 30% of cost. The accounting records for inventory reveal the following.

Inventory at May 1, 2020	$1,100,000
Purchases from May 1, 2020, to May 20, 2020	650,000
Net sales from May 1, 2020, to May 20, 2020	2,000,000

Calculate the estimated loss of inventory based on the gross profit method.

More Practice: 10-27, 10-50, 10-52, 10-53, 10-55

Solution on p. 10-57.

LO 10-5 Demonstrate accounting for purchase commitments

LO 10-5 Overview

Purchase Commitments—Material and Noncancelable
- Record unrealized losses if the contract price exceeds market price or net realizable value (as applicable)
- Disclose the commitment

To lock in prices and assure sufficient quantities, companies often contract with suppliers to purchase a specified quantity of materials during a future period at an agreed upon unit cost. **Purchase commitments** (contracts) that are noncancelable and are material, require disclosure in the financial statements and at times, a financial statement adjustment as shown in **Demo 10-5**.

A commitment to purchase goods that have not been shipped to the buyer does not result in a journal entry at a reporting date unless the contract price is greater than the market price (LIFO or retail inventory method) or net realizable value (other inventory methods). In other words, if the buyer expects to incur a loss upon purchase, the loss is recognized in the period of the market price (or net realizable value) decline. Subsequent recoveries of estimated losses are not recognized.

> **330-10-35-17** A net loss on firm purchase commitments for goods for inventory, measured in the same way as are inventory losses, shall be recognized in the accounts. The recognition in a current period of losses arising from the decline in the utility of cost expenditures is equally applicable to similar losses which are expected to arise from firm, uncancelable, and unhedged commitments for the future purchase of inventory items.

Losses on purchase commitments are *not recognized when sale of future inventory items is assured without a price concession* as indicated in accounting guidance.

> **330-10-35-18** The utility of such commitments is not impaired, and hence there is no loss, when the amounts to be realized from the disposition of the future inventory items are adequately protected by firm sales contracts or when there are other circumstances that reasonably assure continuing sales without price decline.

Purchase Commitment — LO10-5 — Demo 10-5

Demo MBC

Baey Company enters into a purchase contract during October 2020 that requires Baey to purchase inventory for $250,000 (50,000 units x $5 per unit) in 2021. The contract price is estimated to be the current market price of the inventory and the company uses the FIFO inventory method.

a. Record an entry (if required) on December 31, 2020, if the net realizable value of the inventory under contract is estimated to be $240,000.

b. Record the entry on June 1, 2021, when Baey purchased the 50,000 units of inventory for $250,000, assuming that the net realizable value of the inventory is $235,000.

Solution

a. **Estimate Loss on Purchase Commitment** The estimated loss of $10,000 ($250,000 – $240,000) is recognized on the 2020 income statement in the other expenses and losses section, and the liability is recognized on the balance sheet. This treatment recognizes the loss in the period when it became probable.

December 31, 2020—To record estimated loss on purchase commitment

Estimated Loss on Purchase Commitment ($250,000 - $240,000)	10,000	
Estimated Liability on Purchase Commitment		10,000

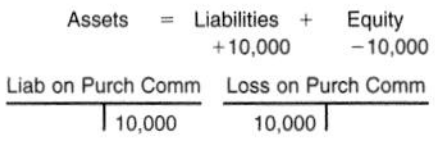

b. **Record Purchase of Inventory Under Commitment** When the goods are acquired on June 1, 2021, Cash is credited for the purchase price. Inventory is debited at net realizable value, Estimated Liability on Purchase Commitment is reversed or debited for $10,000, and Loss on Purchase Contract is debited for $5,000. The purchase entry follows.

June 1, 2021—To record purchase of materials

Inventory	235,000	
Estimated Liability on Purchase Commitment	10,000	
Loss on Purchase Contract ($240,000 – $235,000)	5,000	
Cash		250,000

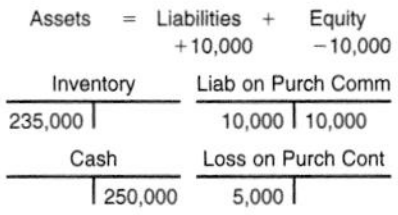

EXPANDING YOUR KNOWLEDGE — **Hedging Against Purchase Commitment Risks**

A purchase commitment protects a buyer from future price increases, but what about price decreases? If prices decline, a buyer is contracted to purchase the goods at the higher, set price. To offset the risk of declining prices, a company can purchase a hedge. With a hedge, the company that is committed to *purchase* goods at a set price enters into a second contract (hedge) to *sell* the goods at this same price to a third party (seller of the hedge). The company would only take advantage of the hedge if market prices *dropped*—otherwise there is no advantage in selling the goods at the contract price. The company must separately evaluate the accounting for the hedge. Fair value hedges are discussed in the chapter on investments.

Inventory Disclosures

ASC 330-10-50 requires the following disclosures related to inventory.

- Basis for stating inventories and the nature and effect on income of any change in basis.
- Substantial and unusual losses resulting from subsequent measurement of inventory.
- Inventory stated above cost.
- Inventory stated at sales price.
- Net losses recognized on firm purchase commitments.
- Disclosures of significant estimates.

Other inventory disclosures include the composition of inventory (such as raw materials or finished goods for a manufacturer), inventory financing arrangements, and the effects of any LIFO liquidations.

TARGET

Real World—PURCHASE COMMITMENTS

TARGET CORP [TGT]

Target Corporation discloses the value of purchase commitments in a recent Form 10-K. Target does not consider purchase orders as part of purchase commitments because they are cancelable.

> **Commitments** Purchase obligations, which include all legally binding contracts such as firm commitments for inventory purchases, merchandise royalties, equipment purchases, marketing-related contracts, software acquisition/license commitments, and service contracts, were $1,950 million and $2,411 million at January 30, 2016 and January 31, 2015, respectively. These purchase obligations are primarily due within three years and recorded as liabilities when inventory is received. We issue inventory purchase orders, which represent authorizations to purchase that are cancelable by their terms. We do not consider purchase orders to be firm inventory commitments. If we choose to cancel a purchase order, we may be obligated to reimburse the vendor for unrecoverable outlays incurred prior to cancellation. Real estate obligations, which include commitments for the purchase, construction or remodeling of real estate and facilities, were $279 million and $243 million at January 30, 2016 and January 31, 2015, respectively. These real estate obligations are primarily due within one year, a portion of which is recorded as liabilities.

REVIEW 10-5 **LO10-5** **Purchase Commitment**

Review MBC

On May 1, 2020, Sonic Inc. entered into a noncancelable contract to purchase 80,000 units of raw materials inventory at $20 per unit, which is the fair market value of the inventory at that date. The contract period extends through May 2021. Sonic's accounting period ends December 31. On December 31, 2020, inventory was being sold for $18 per unit. On March 25, 2021, Sonic purchased the 80,000 units; the selling price per unit of inventory on this date was $17. The company maintains a perpetual inventory system and the FIFO inventory method.

Prepare journal entries required, if any, on (a) May 1, 2020, (b) December 31, 2020, and (c) March 25, 2021. Assume no selling costs.

More Practice: 10-30, 10-31, 10-56, 10-57
Solution on p. 10-57.

LO 10-6 Describe accounting treatment for changes in inventory methods

LO 10-6 Overview

Change in Accounting Method
- Retrospective adjustment
  - Voluntary change in accounting principle
- Prospective adjustment
  - Retrospective approach is impractical
- Expense indirect effect of accounting change

Once a company chooses an inventory method, there is a presumption that the chosen method is consistently applied. Financial statement users rely on consistent application of principles from one period to the next to allow for comparative financial analysis. However, under certain circumstances, a company may voluntarily change from one generally accepted accounting method to another or may be required to change an accounting method due to a Codification update as described in Chapter 3.

Generally, when a company *voluntarily* changes an accounting principle, a **retrospective adjustment** for reporting purposes is made to apply the new accounting principle to prior periods and to the current period (unless is is impracticable to do so). This adjustment is reflected after tax—we cover the tax effect in Chapter 18.

250-10-45-5 An entity shall report a change in accounting principle through retrospective application of the new accounting principle to all prior periods, unless it is impracticable to do so. Retrospective application requires all of the following:

a. The cumulative effect of the change to the new accounting principle on periods prior to those presented shall be reflected in the carrying amounts of assets and liabilities as of the beginning of the first period presented.
b. An offsetting adjustment, if any, shall be made to the opening balance of retained earnings (or other appropriate components of equity or net assets in the statement of financial position) for that period.
c. Financial statements for each individual prior period presented shall be adjusted to reflect the period-specific effects of applying the new accounting principle.

250-10-45-6 If the cumulative effect of applying a change in accounting principle to all prior periods can be determined, but it is impracticable to determine the period-specific effects of that change on all prior periods presented, the cumulative effect of the change to the new accounting principle shall be applied to the carrying amounts of assets and liabilities as of the beginning of the earliest period to which the new accounting principle can be applied. An offsetting adjustment, if any, shall be made to the opening balance of retained earnings (or other appropriate components of equity or net assets in the statement of financial position) for that period.

For example, let's assume that a company changes from average cost to the FIFO inventory method at the beginning of 2020. The company would adjust its accounting records and adjust its external reporting to reflect the change. For reporting purposes for the year ended December 31, 2020, the company will:

- Retroactively adjust all affected financial statements for each individual year presented to reflect the FIFO method, as if it had been used in all prior years. (The statement of cash flows would not be affected for a change in accounting principle.)
- Adjust the opening retained earnings balance of the earliest year presented for any cumulative effect of the change prior to the years presented.

To adjust its accounting records, the company records an adjustment to retained earnings on January 1, 2020, for the cumulative net effect of using FIFO prior to the year 2020. (Recall that all years prior to 2020 are closed, which prohibits a company from recording entries into prior years.) This process is demonstrated in **Demo 10-6A**.

Generally, companies that change *to the LIFO method* report the change **prospectively** (as shown in **Demo 10-6B**) because reconstructing LIFO inventory layers is prohibitively expensive or impossible. (With a prospective adjustment, no entry is required to adjust the accounting records at the time of the change.) Past costs and purchase prices necessary for reconstructing inventory layers are typically unavailable for any prior period. Instead, the beginning inventory balance in the current year serves as the base layer or beginning balance for LIFO. If retrospective application is impracticable, the company should disclose the reasons that it is impractical along with a description of the alternative accounting presentation.

250-10-45-7 If it is impracticable to determine the cumulative effect of applying a change in accounting principle to any prior period, the new accounting principle shall be applied as if the change was made prospectively as of the earliest date practicable.

Many companies that change accounting principles report both direct and indirect effects.

- Direct effects—The **direct effects** of the change are those adjustments made to account balances and earnings amounts to reflect the new principle.
- Indirect effects—Had the new accounting principle been in effect in prior years, certain nondiscretionary items based on earnings, including bonus arrangements and royalties, would have been different. These are **indirect effects** of the accounting principle change. Indirect costs are

not retrospectively applied to financial statements. Instead, any indirect costs are recorded in the current period as incurred.

250-10-45-8 Retrospective application shall include only the direct effects of a change in accounting principle, including any related income tax effects. Indirect effects that would have been recognized if the newly adopted accounting principle had been followed in prior periods shall not be included in the retrospective application. If indirect effects are actually incurred and recognized, they shall be reported in the period in which the accounting change is made.

When indirect effects of a change in accounting principle are recognized in the current year's financial statements, a description and the amount of the indirect effects (including applicable per-share amounts) should be disclosed. If practical to do so, the amount of the total recognized indirect effects (and applicable per-share amounts) that are attributable to each prior period presented should also be disclosed.

Demo 10-6A **LO10-6** **Change in Inventory Method—Retrospective Approach**

Demo MBC

Gomez Inc. began operations on January 1, 2018, electing to use the LIFO inventory method for financial reporting and tax purposes. In 2020, Gomez Inc. decided to change its inventory costing method from LIFO to FIFO for financial reporting and tax purposes. Its reporting year ends on December 31. The following data for Gomez is available for 2018-2020.

	2018—LIFO Method Used		2019—LIFO Method Used		2020—Year of Change to FIFO	
	FIFO	LIFO	FIFO	LIFO	FIFO	LIFO
Beginning inventory		$ 0		$ 45,000		$ 50,000
Purchases		200,000		225,000		250,000
Ending inventory	$47,000	45,000	$60,000	50,000	$80,000	68,000
Cost of goods sold		155,000		220,000		232,000
Operating expenses		40,000		40,000		40,000
Sales		210,000		300,000		310,000

The financial statements as reported under the LIFO inventory method in 2018 and 2019 included the following disclosures (ignoring taxes).

Income Statement—Two-year presentation under LIFO

Income Statement	2018	2019
Sales	$210,000	$300,000
Cost of goods sold	155,000	220,000
Operating expenses	40,000	40,000
Net income	$ 15,000	$ 40,000

Balance Sheet—Two-year presentation under LIFO

Balance Sheet at Dec. 31	2018	2019
Assets		
Inventory	$45,000	$50,000

Retained Earnings Statement—Two-year presentation under LIFO

Retained Earnings	2018	2019
Retained earnings, beginning	$ 0	$15,000
Net income	15,000	40,000
Retained earnings, ending	$15,000	$55,000

continued

a. Prepare three years of comparative income statements (2018-2020) that would be reported *after* the change from LIFO to FIFO.
b. Prepare two years of comparative balance sheets (2019-2020) that would be reported *after* the change from LIFO to FIFO.
c. Prepare two years of comparative retained earnings statements (2019-2020) that would be reported *after* the change from LIFO to FIFO.
d. Record the change in accounting principle for internal accounting records on January 1, 2020, ignoring taxes.
e. Assume that Gomez's executive compensation arrangement includes a bonus based on income, and that the 2019 bonus to be paid in 2020 would have been $1,000 higher under the new inventory method. Record the required entry in 2020 assuming that the original bonus was already recorded, and the 2019 bonus payment will be retroactively adjusted based upon the revised financial statements for the change in accounting principle (based on a decision by the board of directors).

Solution

a. **Comparative Income Statement Presentation**

The change to FIFO in 2020 would require retrospective application to all years reported.

First, cost of goods sold under the FIFO inventory method for the three years is calculated by adding beginning FIFO inventory and purchases, and then subtracting ending FIFO inventory.

COGS—Assuming FIFO Inventory Method	2018	2019	2020
Beginning inventory	$ 0	$ 47,000	$ 60,000
Purchases	200,000	225,000	250,000
Less ending inventory	47,000	60,000	80,000
Cost of goods sold	$153,000	$212,000	$230,000

The three comparative years of income statements reflect cost of goods sold under the FIFO inventory method as follows.

Income Statement—Three-year presentation under FIFO

Income Statement	2018	2019	2020
Sales	$210,000	$300,000	$310,000
Cost of goods sold	153,000	212,000	230,000
Operating expenses	40,000	40,000	40,000
Net income	$ 17,000	$ 48,000	$ 40,000

b. **Comparative Balance Sheet Presentation**

Inventory is presented under the FIFO inventory method for both years.

Balance sheet—Two-year presentation under FIFO Balance at Dec. 31	2019	2020
Assets		
Inventory	$60,000	$80,000

c. **Comparative Retained Earnings Statement Presentation**

The cumulative adjustment of $2,000 is the difference between the January 1, 2019, retained earning balance under LIFO ($15,000) and the January 1, 2019, retained earnings balance under FIFO ($17,000). The comparative retained earnings statements are presented as follows.

Retained earnings—Two Year Presentation

Retained Earnings	2019	2020
Beginning balance, as reported	$15,000	$ 65,000
Add: Adjustment for cumulative effect on prior years of changing to FIFO	2,000	—
Beginning balance, as adjusted	17,000	65,000
Net income	48,000	40,000
Ending balance	$65,000	$105,000

continued

continued from previous page

The retrospective approach applies the same method consistently to each year shown in the comparative statements. The 2019 financial statements, shown comparatively with those of 2020, are retrospectively restated to reflect the new method. Net income for 2019 as reported in the 2020 comparative income statements ($48,000) is restated and thus does not equal the amount reported in the previously issued 2019 annual report ($40,000).

d. **Record Change in Accounting Principle—Retrospective Approach**
The entry to record an accounting principle change affecting prior years is made as of the beginning of the current year (2020). The difference in inventory between FIFO and LIFO on January 1, 2020, is $10,000 ($60,000 − $50,000) and the difference between retained earnings under FIFO and LIFO is $10,000 ($65,000 − $55,000).

The journal entry at the beginning of 2020 is recorded as follows.

Assets = Liabilities + Equity
+10,000 +10,000
Inventory: 10,000 (debit) | Ret Earnings: 10,000 (credit)

January 1, 2020—To retrospectively adjust retained earnings for change to FIFO

Inventory	10,000	
Retained Earnings		10,000

e. **Record Indirect Cost**
The indirect costs recognized in 2020 are expensed as incurred.

Assets = Liabilities + Equity
+1,000 −1,000
Bonus Payable: 1,000 (credit) | Comp Exp: 1,000 (debit)

2020—To record indirect cost based on retrospective adjustment in net income

Compensation Expense	1,000	
Bonus Payable		1,000

Demo 10-6B **LO10-6** **Change in Inventory Method—Prospective Approach**

Using the data from **Demo 10-6A**, let's instead assume that the company reported inventory on the FIFO basis in 2018 and 2019 and then changed to LIFO in 2020. Due to the company's inability to apply LIFO in prior periods, a prospective approach is adopted. Prepare a schedule to calculate cost of goods sold for the years of 2018, 2019, and 2020.

Solution
Cost of goods sold under a prospective approach matches the cost of goods sold previously calculated under FIIFO in 2018 and 2019 of $153,000 and $212,000, respectively. In 2020, cost of goods sold is computed by taking beginning inventory under FIFO, adding purchases, and subtracting ending inventory under LIFO. With the prospective approach, two years are reported using one inventory method and one year using another inventory method, *which makes comparability difficult.*

Cost of Goods Sold—Prospective Treatment	2018	2019	2020
Beginning inventory	$ 0	$ 47,000	$ 60,000
Purchases.	200,000	225,000	250,000
Less ending inventory.	47,000	60,000	68,000
Cost of goods sold	$153,000	$212,000	$242,000

REVIEW 10-6 **LO10-6** **Change in Inventory Method**

Sonic Corporation changed from average cost to FIFO on January 1, 2021, for reporting inventory. Inventory balances under both methods follow. Sonic Corporation has a December 31 year-end.

Inventory balances at December 31	2020	2019
Ending inventory, average cost	$150,000	$110,000
Ending inventory, FIFO.	90,000	75,000

continued

continued from previous page

a. Prepare the January 1, 2021, entry to record the accounting change. Ignore taxes.

b. Show how the December 31, 2020, inventory balance is presented on the comparative December 31, 2021, balance sheet assuming the amount is material enough for the company to restate prior years reported in financial statements. Ignore taxes.

Review MBC

More Practice: 10-34, 10-58, 10-59, 10-60

Solution on p. 10-57.

Describe accounting treatment of inventory errors

LO 10-7

Inventory Errors
- Error discovered in current period
- Error discovered in subsequent period
  - Affects balance sheet only
  - Affects balance sheet and income statement
    - Counterbalancing
    - Noncounterbalancing

LO 10-7 Overview

Errors in inventory discovered *before* the release of financial statements can be corrected and adjustments made to the accounting records and financial statements. However, if a *material error* is not discovered until after the release of the financial statements, the materiality of the impact on financial statements must be determined. Also, some inventory errors affect more than one reporting period.

Restatement of financial statements for a *material error* is required as well as related adjustments to the accounting records. A summary of the accounting treatment for material errors is illustrated in **Exhibit 10-2**. The accounting treatment of three examples of inventory errors is illustrated in **Demo 10-7**.

EXHIBIT 10-2
Accounting for an Error

Type of Error	Financial Statement Presentation	Entries	Example
Error discovered in *same* accounting period.	No impact on prior periods.	Reverse incorrect entry and record correct entry.	Inadvertently include consigned inventory in the merchandise inventory account. (Discovered in the current accounting period.)
Error discovered in subsequent accounting period: *affects balance sheet only.*	Restatement of *all* financial statements presented.	Record reclassification entry (if amount currently on the balance sheet).	Misclassify work-in-process as finished goods inventory. (Discovered in a subsequent accounting period).
Error discovered in subsequent accounting period: *affects balance sheet and income statement* and is **counterbalancing** (or an error that self-corrects within two consecutive accounting periods).	Restatement of *all* financial statements presented.	Record correcting entry *only* if discovered before self-correction of the error.	Overstate ending inventory due to a mathematical error. (Discovered in a subsequent accounting period.)
Error discovered in subsequent accounting period: *affects balance sheet and income statement* and is **noncounterbalancing** (or an error that does not self-correct within two consecutive accounting periods).	Restatement of *all* financial statements presented.	Record an entry to correct the error.	Inadvertently record an inventory purchase as equipment to be depreciated over 10 years. (Discovered in a subsequent accounting period.)

Demo 10-7 **LO10-7** **Inventory Errors**

Demo MBC

The following **correct** information for Halle Inc. is used as the starting point for the following example.

Correct Financial Data, $ thousands	2020	2021
Beginning inventory	$ 3	$ 8
Add: Net purchases	12	12
Subtract: Ending inventory	8	8
Cost of goods sold	$ 7	$12
Nes sales	$10	$16
Subtract: Cost of goods sold	7	12
Gross margin	3	4
Operating expenses	1	1
Pretax income	$ 2	$ 3

Ending Inventory Overstated, Purchases Amount Correct

Assume that 2020 ending inventory is overstated by $1,000 such that ending inventory is recorded in 2020 as $9,000. The 2021 ending inventory of $8,000 is correct and the 2020 net purchases amount of $12,000 is correct. Ignore income taxes.

a. Present how the error is reflected in the original pretax income schedule provided above.
b. Assuming that the error is discovered in 2022, record any necessary journal entries in 2022 and describe financial statement reporting.
c. Assuming that the error is discovered in 2021, record any necessary journal entries in 2021 and describe financial statement reporting.
d. Assuming that the error is discovered in 2020, record any necessary journal entries in 2020 and describe financial statement reporting.

Solution

a. **Pretax Income Schedule**

The error in ending inventory causes an understatement of cost of goods sold and an overstatement of both gross margin and pretax income by the same amount in 2020. In 2021, beginning inventory is overstated by $1,000 causing cost of goods sold to be overstated and both gross margin and pretax income to be understated by the same amount. *The net impact is that the error in 2020 reverses in 2021, thus, is a counterbalancing error.*

$ thousands	2020	2021
Beginning inventory	$ 3	$ 9
Add: Net purchases	12	12
Subtract: Ending inventory	9	8
Cost of goods sold	$ 6	$13
Net sales	$10	$16
Subtract: Cost of goods sold	6	13
Gross margin	4	3
Other expenses	1	1
Pretax income	$ 3	$ 2

b. **Entry after Self Correction**

No entry is required in 2022 after self-correction, although all financial statements are restated to show the correct amounts (assuming the amount is material).

c. **Entry before Self Correction**

Because the entry did not self-correct, the following entry is recorded in 2021, and all financial statements are restated to show the correct amounts.

continued

continued from previous page

January 1, 2021—To correct error made in 2020

Retained Earnings—Prior Period Adjustment	1,000	
Inventory		1,000

Assets = Liabilities + Equity
−1,000 −1,000

Inventory		Ret Earnings—PPA	
Bal. 9,000	1,000	1,000	

d. **Entry in Year of Error**
Because the entry was discovered in the year of the error, inventory can be corrected in 2020, which results in correct financial statements in 2020.

December 31, 2020—To correct error made in 2020

Cost of Goods Sold	1,000	
Inventory		1,000

Assets = Liabilities + Equity
−1,000 −1,000

Inventory		COGS	
Bal. 9,000	1,000	1,000	

STEIN MART

Real World—INVENTORY ERROR

Stein Mart Inc. disclosed the impact on net income and retained earnings of several adjustments in 2012 that included the following errors in accounting for inventory.

STEIN MART INC. [SMRT]

> **Restatement of Previously Issued Financial Statements** Inventory markdowns—We identified and corrected errors related to the incorrect treatment of certain inventory markdowns as promotional (temporary). Based on analysis of various factors, these inventory markdowns should have been accounted for as permanent markdowns. Under the retail inventory method of accounting used by us, promotional markdowns do not impact the value of unsold inventory and thus do not impact cost of sales until the merchandise is sold. Conversely, permanent markdowns reduce the value of unsold inventory and impact cost of sales at the time the markdowns are taken.

Inventory Errors LO10-7 REVIEW 10-7

The following table includes five separate descriptions of errors related to inventory accounted for under the periodic inventory method in year 2020. Indicate whether costs of goods sold on the income statement and ending inventory on the balance sheet, for both years 2020 and 2021, are overstated, understated, or unaffected by the error.

Review MBC

Inventory Error	2020 Cost of Goods Sold	2020 Ending Inventory	2021 Cost of Goods Sold	2021 Ending Inventory
a. Merchandise purchased on December 31, 2020, on credit was included in ending inventory. However, the purchase was *not* recorded until 2021 when the invoice was received from vendor.				
b. Ending inventory was understated because of an error in the physical inventory records.				
c. Goods held on consignment were inadvertently counted in the physical inventory.				
d. A purchase was shipped f.o.b. shipping point on December 31, 2020. The purchase was recorded but the item was *not* included in the physical inventory records.				
e. A purchase was shipped f.o.b. shipping point on December 31, 2020. The purchase was *not* recorded and the item was *not* included in the physical inventory records.				

More Practice: 10-35, 10-64
Solution on p. 10-57.

LO 10-8 Estimate ending inventory using the average cost and conventional retail methods

LO 10-8 Overview

Retail Inventory Methods
- Average cost method
  - Net markups and net markdowns included in cost ratio
- Conventional retail method
  - Only net markups are included in cost ratio
  - Value of ending inventory approximates LCM

The **retail inventory method** is used by retailers that sell a wide variety of items. In such situations, perpetual inventory procedures can be impractical, and a complete physical inventory count is usually taken only annually. Two major advantages of the retail inventory method are its ease of use and reduced recordkeeping requirements. The retail method is acceptable under GAAP for financial reporting even though it is an estimation method.

330-10-30-13 In some situations a reversed markup procedure of inventory pricing, such as the retail inventory method, may be both practical and appropriate. The business operations in some cases may be such as to make it desirable to apply one of the acceptable methods of determining cost to one portion of the inventory or components thereof and another of the acceptable methods to other portions of the inventory.

The retail inventory method requires both retail and actual cost data to complete the following steps.

- Compute ending inventory at retail.
- Compute a cost-to-retail ratio (referred to as the **cost ratio**) or the ratio of goods available for sale *at cost* to goods available for sale *at retail.*
- Convert ending inventory at retail to cost by applying the cost ratio.

The retail inventory method requires that a careful record be kept of all changes to the original sales price because these changes affect the inventory cost computation. To apply the retail inventory method, it is important to distinguish among the following terms.

Net Markups: Markups + Additional markups − Additional markup cancellations	
Markup (Initial markup)	The original or initial amount that the merchandise is marked up above cost. It is the difference between the purchase cost and the original sales price.
Additional markup	Any increase in the sales price above the original sales price. The original sales price is the base from which additional markup is measured.
Additional markup cancellation	Cancellation of all, or some, of an additional markup.

Net Markdowns: Markdowns − Markdown cancellations	
Markdown	A reduction in the original sales price.
Markdown cancellation	Cancellation of a markdown. The increase in the sales price (that does not exceed the original sales price) after a reduction in the original sales price or markdown.

To illustrate the computations for net markups and net markdowns, let's assume that an item that cost $8 is originally marked to sell at $10. This item is subsequently marked up $1 to sell at $11, then marked back down (markup cancellation) to $10. The item was then marked down to $7, but $2 of the markdown was canceled, yielding a final sales price of $9. Net markups and net markdowns are calculated as follows.

Calculation of Net Markups and Net Markdowns	
Net Markups	$0 computed as ($1 − $1)
Net Markdowns.	$1 computed as (−$3 + $2)

Average Cost and Conventional Retail Inventory Methods

The retail inventory method can be applied in different ways to estimate the cost of ending inventory such as the **average cost method** (**Demo 10-8A**) and the **conventional method**, also referred to as the **lower of average-cost-or-market method** (**Demo 10-8B**). Under the average cost method, both net markups and net markdowns are *included* in the calculation of goods available for sale at retail.

However, under the conventional retail method, net markdowns are *excluded* from the calculation of goods available for sale at retail but are still part of the estimated ending inventory at retail. Because the denominator of the cost ratio under the conventional method excludes net markdowns, the denominator is higher than under the average cost method. **This reduces the cost ratio and thus produces a lower (more conservative) estimate of the value of ending inventory under the conventional method.**

The cost ratio under both methods is computed on total goods available for sale (the sum of beginning inventory plus purchases). Thus, this cost ratio reflects the relation of cost-to-retail values for all inventory items available for sale, including beginning inventory.

Application of the retail inventory method requires that internal records be kept to provide data on:

- Sales revenue.
- Beginning inventory valued at both cost and retail.
- Purchases during the period valued at both cost and retail.
- Adjustments to the original retail price, such as additional markups, markup cancellations, markdowns, markdown cancellations, and employee discounts.
- Other adjustments, such as interdepartmental transfers, returns, breakage, and damaged goods.

Retail Inventory Method—Average Cost Method

LO10-8 Demo 10-8A

Demo MBC

The following data is used to illustrate the average cost method for Harbor Inc.

	At Cost	At Retail
Inventory at the beginning of period	$ 550	$ 900
Purchases during period	6,290	8,900
Additional markups during period		225
Additional markup cancellations during period		25
Markdowns during period		600
Markdown cancellations during period		100
Sales revenue for the period		8,500

Compute ending inventory at cost under the average cost method for Harbor Inc.

Solution

Step One: Calculate Ending Inventory at Retail

Goods available for sale at cost and retail are calculated along with ending inventory at retail. Ending inventory at retail is estimated at $1,000.

Retail Inventory Method—Average Cost Method	Cost	Retail
Goods available for sale		
Beginning inventory	$ 550	$ 900
Add (Subtract):		
Net purchases	6,290	8,900
Net markups*		200
Net markdowns**		(500)
Total goods available for sale	$6,840	9,500
Subtract:		
Net sales		(8,500)
Estimated ending inventory at retail		$1,000

*Net Markups	
Additional markups	$225
Additional markup cancellations	(25)
Net markups	$200

**Net Markdowns	
Markdowns	$(600)
Markdown cancellations	100
Net markdowns	$(500)

continued

continued from previous page

Step Two: Calculate Cost Ratio
The cost ratio is calculated as follows.

$$\frac{\text{Goods available for sale at cost}}{\text{Goods available for sale at retail}} = \frac{\$6,840}{\$9,500} = 0.720$$

Step Three: Estimate Retail Inventory at Cost
The ending inventory at retail is multiplied by the cost ratio to estimate ending inventory at cost of $720.

Estimated ending inventory at cost	
Estimated ending inventory at retail	$1,000
× Cost ratio	0.720
Estimated ending inventory at cost	$ 720

Demo 10-8B **LO10-8** **Retail Inventory Method—Conventional Method**

Demo MBC

Using the data for Harbor Inc. included in **Demo 10-8A**, let's now assume that the company is using the conventional retail method to estimate ending inventory at cost.

Solution
Step One: Calculate Ending Inventory at Retail
Net markdowns are excluded from the calculation of goods available for sale.

Retail Inventory Method—Conventional Method	Cost	Retail
Goods available for sale		
Beginning inventory	$ 550	$ 900
Add:		
Net purchases	6,290	8,900
Net markups		200
Total goods available for sale	$6,840	10,000
Subtract:		
Net sales		(8,500)
Net markdowns		(500)
Estimated ending inventory at retail		$ 1,000

Step Two: Calculate Cost Ratio
The cost ratio is calculated as follows. See how the cost ratio of 0.684 (below) is lower than the cost ratio under the average cost method of 0.720 calculated in **Demo 10-8A**.

$$\frac{\text{Goods available for sale at cost}}{\text{Goods available for sale at retail}} = \frac{\$6,840}{\$10,000} = 0.684$$

Step Three: Estimate Retail Inventory at Cost
The ending inventory at retail is multiplied by the cost ratio in order to estimate ending inventory at cost of $684.

Estimated ending inventory at cost	
Estimated ending inventory at retail	$1,000
× Cost ratio	0.684
Estimated ending inventory at cost	$ 684

Complicating Factors for Retail Inventory Method

Several items can complicate the computation of ending inventory using the retail inventory method. In overcoming such complications, it is essential to protect the integrity of the computed cost ratio and the estimated ending inventory at retail. Accounting treatment for six complicating factors are outlined in **Exhibit 10-3** and applied in **Demo 10-8C**.

EXHIBIT 10-3 Complicating Factors in the Retail Inventory Method

Factor	Accounting Treatment
(1) Freight-in	Add to goods available for sale at cost (but not at retail) because freight adds to the cost of merchandise. (Markups will automatically provide for freight-in expenditures.)
(2) Purchase returns and allowances	Purchase returns: deduct from goods available for sale at both cost and retail. Purchase allowances: deduct only in the cost column. (Any associated sales price reduction would be reflected in markdowns.)
(3) Abnormal casualty losses	Subtract from goods available for sale at both cost and retail (before the calculation of the cost ratio) because they will not be sold (such as missing inventory due to fire or theft). Removal from both cost and retail eliminates their effect on the cost ratio as if they had not been purchased in the first place. Damaged merchandise is set up in a special inventory account at its net realizable value.
(4) Sales returns and allowances	Subtract from gross sales because this is a contra account to the sales revenue account. If the returned merchandise is placed back into inventory for resale, no change in the cost column is needed because the cost has already been included in the purchases amount. Merchandise not returned to inventory (because of damage, for example) is deducted at retail, from gross sales. The original cost of the merchandise is deducted from ending inventory at cost, after applying the cost ratio to ending inventory at retail. The merchandise is set up in a special inventory account at its net realizable value.
(5) Discounts to employees	Subtract in the retail column after the calculation of the cost ratio. Discounts to employees that result from selling merchandise below the normal sales price and that are not caused by market value decreases are different from markdowns. (General sales discounts are *not* subtracted from sales to avoid the overstatement of inventory. Sales discounts are a financial incentive to customer to prompt early payment rather than an adjustment to selling price.)
(6) Normal spoilage	Normal spoilage is the retail value of the units lost under normal conditions, including expected shrinkage and breakage. Deduct below the cost ratio at retail because the expected cost of normal spoilage is included implicitly in determining the selling price and does not reflect market value changes.

Retail Inventory Method—Conventional Method with Complicating Items LO10-8 Demo 10-8C

Demo MBC

Shoreline Inc. compiled the following cost and retail data.

	At Cost	At Retail
Inventory at the beginning of period	$ 6,050	$ 11,000
Purchases during period	57,120	102,000
Net markups		600
Net markdowns		4,500
Sales revenue for the period		71,200

The company has the following six additional factors corresponding to the six items in **Exhibit 10-3**. These items are not reflected in the amounts above. Using the conventional retail method, compute ending inventory at cost for Shoreline Inc. Round the cost ratio to three decimals.

	At Cost	At Retail
(a) Freight-in	$1,020	
(b) Purchase returns	560	$1,000
(c) Abnormal casualty loss	3,630	6,600
(d) Sales returns (merchandise placed back into inventory)		1,200
(e) Discounts to employees		200
(f) Normal spoilage		1,300

continued

continued from previous page

Solution

Step One: Calculate Ending Inventory at Retail

The six additional items are added to our previous computation to estimate inventory at retail.

Retail Inventory Method—Conventional Method	Cost	Retail
Goods available for sale		
Beginning inventory	$ 6,050	$ 11,000
Add/(Subtract):		
Purchases	57,120	102,000
Freight-in (a)	1,020	
Purchase returns (b)	(560)	(1,000)
Net markups		600
Casualty loss (c)	(3,630)	(6,600)
Total goods available for sale	$60,000	106,000
Subtract:		
Sales less sales returns ($71,200 − $1,200 (d))		(70,000)
Discounts to employees (e)		(200)
Normal spoilage (f)		(1,300)
Net markdowns		(4,500)
Estimated ending inventory at retail		$ 30,000

Step Two: Calculate Cost Ratio

$$\frac{\text{Goods available for sale at cost}}{\text{Goods available for sale at retail}} = \frac{\$60,000}{\$106,000} = 0.566$$

Step Three: Estimate Retail Inventory at Cost

Estimated ending inventory at cost	
Estimated ending inventory at retail	$30,000
× Cost ratio	0.566
Estimated ending inventory at cost	$16,980

REVIEW 10-8 **LO10-8** **Retail Inventory Method—Conventional Method**

Review MBC

Information relating to the computation of inventory for 2020 for Starz Store Inc. follows. Estimated normal spoilage is 1% of sales.

	At Cost	At Retail
Beginning inventory	$120,000	$ 250,000
Sales		1,000,000
Purchases	450,000	900,000
Freight-in	50,000	
Markups		110,000
Markup cancellations		50,000
Markdowns		90,000
Markdown cancellations		5,000

Required

Calculate the estimated ending inventory for 2020 using the conventional retail method. Round the cost ratio to three decimal places.

More Practice: 10-65, 10-66, 10-67, 10-68

Solution on p. 10-57.

Management Judgment

Lower-of-Cost-or-Net Realizable Rule and the Lower-of-Cost-or-Market Rule

Management judgment is important for adjustments to inventory. Examples follow.

- Selecting whether to apply the rules to individual items, categories, or inventory totals is a decision based on management judgment (see p. 10-4).
- Estimating the selling price, costs of completion and disposal, normal profit margin, and replacement cost used to measure market or net realizable value requires management judgment (see LO 10-1 and LO 10-2).

The following example describes items considered in estimating net realizable value.

Ralph Lauren Corp.—MD&A Section of MD&A Substantially all of our inventories are comprised of finished goods, which are stated at the lower of cost or estimated realizable value, with cost primarily determined on a weighted-average cost basis. The estimated net realizable value of inventory is determined based on an analysis of historical sales trends of our individual product lines, the impact of market trends and economic conditions, and a forecast of future demand, giving consideration to the value of current orders in-house for future sales of inventory, as well as plans to sell inventory through our factory stores, among other liquidation channels. Estimates may differ from actual results due to the quantity, quality, and mix of products in inventory, consumer and retailer preferences and market conditions. Reserves for inventory shrinkage, representing the risk of physical loss of inventory, are estimated based on historical experience and are adjusted based upon physical inventory counts. Our historical estimates of these costs and the related provisions have not differed materially from actual results.

Retail Inventory Method

A cost-to-cost ratio is applied to estimated retail inventory that requires the identification and estimation of markdowns, normal spoilage (including expected shrinkage and breakage), and abnormal casualty losses (see LO 10-8). For example, a decision to mark down inventory at retail may include considerations such as current and expected demand, economic trends, customer preferences, and age of merchandise. The following example describes estimates used in applying the retail inventory method.

Macy's Inc.—MD&A Section of Form 10-K Merchandise inventories are valued at the lower of cost or market using the last-in, first-out (LIFO) retail inventory method. Under the retail inventory method, inventory is segregated into departments of merchandise having similar characteristics and is stated at its current retail selling value. The retail inventory method inherently requires management judgments and estimates, such as the amount and timing of permanent markdowns to clear unproductive or slow-moving inventory, which may impact the ending inventory valuation as well as gross margins.

Purchase Commitments

Estimating an expected loss due to a purchase commitment requires management to estimate the net realizable value of inventory under commitment (or market value depending on the inventory method used) (see LO 10-5).

Gross Profit Method

Although not a GAAP method, management may find it necessary to estimate inventory balances, such as for interim reporting or for estimating inventory losses. Estimating the gross profit rate used to estimate an ending inventory balance requires management judgment (see LO 10-4).

APPENDIX 10A
LO 10-9

Estimate ending inventory using LIFO retail and dollar-value LIFO retail methods

LO 10-9 Overview

Retail Inventory Methods
- LIFO Retail
  - Allocate inventory to layers, applying relevant cost ratio
  - Account for a change to LIFO Retail
- Dollar-Value LIFO
  - First convert inventory to base year dollars
  - Allocate inventory to layers, applying relevant cost ratio and cost indices

Other options under the retail inventory method are the LIFO retail method (**Demo 10-9A**) and the dollar-value LIFO retail method (**Demo 10-9B**). As we discussed in the previous chapter, the advantages of LIFO are better matching of current (higher) expenses with current (higher) sales and lower tax payments (assuming rising prices).

LIFO Retail Method

A number of retailers account for inventory using the **LIFO retail inventory method.** In applying the LIFO retail method, for simplification, we assume that prices remain stable within each period. Because of this price stability assumption, any increase or decrease from the beginning to the end of the year is due to quantity changes. Net markups and net markdowns are assumed to relate entirely to purchases, rather than to beginning inventory and are accounted for in the ratio calculation.

Demo 10-9A **LO10-9** **LIFO Retail Method**

Demo MBC

Zeva Inc. decided to adopt LIFO on January 1, 2019. Assume the following information for Zeva.

2019 Amounts	At Cost	At Retail
Beginning inventory	$17,400	$ 30,000
Purchases	90,480	147,000
Net additional markups		8,800
Net markdowns		5,000
Sales		140,000

Using the LIFO retail method, compute ending inventory at cost assuming Zeva Inc. has a December 31, calendar year-end.

Solution

Step One: Calculate Ending Inventory at Retail

The 2019 ending inventory at retail is $40,800, calculated as follows.

Retail Inventory Method—Average Cost Method	Cost	Retail
Goods available for sale		
Beginning inventory	$ 17,400	$ 30,000
Add (Subtract):		
Net purchases	90,480	147,000
Net markups		8,800
Net markdowns		(5,000)
Subtotal (excluding beginning inventory)	90,480	150,800
Total goods available for sale	$107,880	180,800
Subtract:		
Net sales		(140,000)
Estimated ending inventory at retail		$ 40,800

Step Two: Calculate Cost Ratios for Current Year and Prior Year

The 2018 and 2019 cost ratios are computed as follows.

2018 Cost Ratio

$$\frac{\text{Beginning inventory at cost}}{\text{Beginning inventory at retail}} = \frac{\$17,400}{\$30,000} = 0.58$$

continued

continued from previous page

2019 Cost Ratio				
Subtotal (excluding beginning inventory) at cost / Subtotal (excluding beginning inventory) at retail	=	$90,480 / $150,800	=	0.60

Step Three: Estimate LIFO Retail Inventory at Cost
The beginning inventory layer is made up of $30,000 (beginning inventory at retail) at a cost ratio of 0.58. Because inventory increased to $40,800, the addition of $10,800 ($40,800 − $30,000) is attributed to an increase in inventory quantity. The appropriate cost ratio to apply to the current year is 0.60. Each layer is multiplied by the appropriate cost ratio to arrive at ending inventory at dollar-value LIFO of $23,880 (total).

2019 Ending Inventory At Year-End Retail Prices (STEP ONE)		Inventory Layers at Retail Prices		Cost Ratio (STEP TWO)	2019 Ending Inventory at LIFO Cost (STEP THREE)
$40,800 →	2018	$30,000	×	0.58	$17,400
→	2019	10,800	×	0.60	6,480
		$40,800			$23,880

Dollar-Value LIFO Retail Inventory Method

The **dollar-value LIFO method** requires that a distinction be maintained between base year inventory and subsequent incremental layers. Inventory layers at base-year retail prices are valued by applying two different ratios related to the year that the inventory layer is added: (1) a conversion price index, and (2) a cost ratio.

Dollar-Value LIFO Method **LO10-9** **Demo 10-9B**

Demo MBC

Zeva Inc. decided to adopt the dollar-value LIFO method on January 1, 2019. Assume the following information for Zeva for the three years of 2019, 2020, and 2021. Calculate the dollar-value LIFO ending inventory for (a) 2019, (b) 2020, and (c) 2021.

	2019		2020		2021	
Amount	**At Cost**	**At Retail**	**At Cost**	**At Retail**	**At Cost**	**At Retail**
Beginning inventory	$17,400	$ 30,000	$?	$?	$?	$?
Purchases	90,480	147,000	101,500	169,000	115,800	186,800
Net additional markups		8,800		9,000		7,000
Net markdowns		5,000		6,000		4,000
Sales		140,000		162,800		197,800
External Price Index	102		106		110	

Solution

a. **Dollar-Value LIFO Ending Inventory Calculation—2019**
For 2019, as calculated in the previous example in steps one and two, ending LIFO inventory at retail is $40,800 and the cost ratios are 0.58 and 0.60 for the years 2018, and 2019, respectively. Under dollar-value LIFO however, ending LIFO inventory at retail of $40,800 is first converted to base year dollars as illustrated below.

continued

continued from previous page

In step three, first, the 2019 ending inventory at retail is divided by the current year index to derive ending inventory at base year prices of $40,000 ($40,800/1.02). Next, the $40,000 is divided into two layers: the beginning inventory layer of $30,000 and the residual, which represents the current year layer of $10,000. Each layer is then multiplied by the appropriate conversion price index and the cost ratio to arrive at ending inventory at dollar-value LIFO of $23,520 (total).

2019 Ending Inventory at Base-Year Retail Prices		Inventory Layers at Base-Year Retail Prices		Conversion Price Index		Cost Ratio	2019 Ending Inventory at Dollar-Value LIFO
$40,000	2018	$30,000	×	1.00	×	0.58	$17,400
	2019	10,000	×	1.02	×	0.60	6,120
		$40,000					$23,520

b. **Dollar-Value LIFO Ending Inventory Calculation—2020**

Step One: Calculate Ending Inventory at Retail

The 2020 ending inventory at retail is $50,000, calculated as follows.

Retail Inventory Method—Average Cost Method	Cost	Retail
Goods available for sale		
Beginning inventory*	$ 24,480	$ 40,800
Add (Subtract):		
Net purchases	101,500	169,000
Net markups		9,000
Net markdowns		(6,000)
Subtotal (excluding beginning inventory)	101,500	172,000
Total goods available for sale	$125,980	212,800
Subtract:		
Net sales		(162,800)
Estimated ending inventory at retail		$ 50,000

* $24,480 = Beginning inventory at retail of $40,800 × 2019 cost ratio of 0.60.

Step Two: Calculate Cost Ratio

The 2020 cost ratio is computed as follows.

2020 Cost Ratio

$$\frac{\text{Subtotal (excluding beginning inventory) at cost}}{\text{Subtotal (excluding beginning inventory) at retail}} = \frac{\$101,500}{\$172,000} = 0.59$$

Step Three: Estimate Dollar-Value LIFO Retail Inventory

First, the 2020 ending inventory at retail is divided by the current year index to derive ending inventory at base year prices of $47,170 ($50,000/1.06). Next, the $47,170 is divided into three layers: the 2018 layer of $30,000, the 2019 layer of $10,000, and the residual, which represents the current year layer of $7,170. Each layer is then multiplied by the appropriate conversion price index and cost ratio to arrive at ending inventory at dollar-value LIFO of $28,004 (total).

2020 Ending Inventory at Base-Year Retail Prices		Inventory Layers at Base-Year Retail Prices		Conversion Price Index		Cost Ratio	2020 Ending Inventory at Dollar-Value LIFO
$47,170	2018	$30,000	×	1.00	×	0.58	$17,400
	2019	10,000	×	1.02	×	0.60	6,120
	2020	7,170	×	1.06	×	0.59	4,484
		$47,170					$28,004

continued

continued from previous page

In 2020, ending inventory in base year dollars increased from $40,000 to $47,170. The increase results in a new LIFO layer for 2020 of $7,170.

c. Dollar-Value LIFO Ending Inventory Calculation—2021

Step One: Calculate Ending Inventory at Retail

The 2021 ending inventory at retail is $42,000, calculated as follows

Retail Inventory Method—Average Cost Method	Cost	Retail
Goods available for sale		
Beginning inventory*	$ 29,500	$ 50,000
Add/(Subtract):		
Net purchases	115,800	186,800
Net markups		7,000
Net markdowns		(4,000)
Subtotal (excluding beginning inventory)	115,800	189,800
Total goods available for sale	$145,300	239,800
Subtract:		
Net sales		(197,800)
Estimated ending inventory at retail		$ 42,000

* $29,500 = Beginning inventory at retail of $50,000 × 2020 cost ratio of 0.59.

Step Two: Calculate Cost Ratio

The 2021 cost ratio is computed as follows.

2021 Cost Ratio

$$\frac{\text{Subtotal (excluding beginning inventory) at cost}}{\text{Subtotal (excluding beginning inventory) at retail}} = \frac{\$115{,}800}{\$189{,}800} = 0.61$$

Step Three: Estimate Dollar-Value LIFO Retail Inventory

First, the 2021 ending inventory at retail is divided by the current year index to derive ending inventory at base year prices of $38,182 ($42,000/1.10). Next, the $38,182 is divided into two layers: the 2018 inventory layer of $30,000, and the residual, which represents the 2019 layer of $8,182. Each layer is then multiplied by the appropriate conversion price index and the cost ratio to arrive at ending inventory at dollar-value LIFO of $22,407 (total).

2021 Ending Inventory at Base-Year Retail Prices		Inventory Layers at Base-Year Retail Prices		Conversion Price Index		Cost Ratio	2021 Ending Inventory at Dollar-Value LIFO
$38,182 →	2018	$30,000	×	1.00	×	0.58	$17,400
↘	2019	$ 8,182	×	1.02	×	0.60	5,007
							$22,407

In 2021, ending inventory in base year dollars decreased from $47,170 to $38,182. The decrease results in a liquidation of the entire 2020 layer of $7,170 (base year dollars) and part of the 2019 layer (a reduction of $1,818 in base year dollars or $10,000 less $8,182).

WHOLE FOODS MARKET

Real World—DOLLAR-VALUE LIFO METHOD

Whole Foods Market Inc. included the following note in its 2015 Form 10-K that described the inventory method used, retail dollar-value LIFO. As discussed in Chapter 9, the LIFO reserve is disclosed which allows financial statement users to convert inventory to a FIFO basis for comparability purposes.

WHOLE FOODS MARKET INC. [WFM]

continued

continued from previous page

Summary of Significant Accounting Policies The Company values inventories at the lower of cost or market. Cost was determined using the dollar value retail last-in, first-out ("LIFO") method for approximately 92.2% and 93.5% of inventories in fiscal years 2015 and 2014, respectively. Under the LIFO method, the cost assigned to items sold is based on the cost of the most recent items purchased. As a result, the costs of the first items purchased remain in inventory and are used to value ending inventory. The excess of estimated current costs over LIFO carrying value, or LIFO reserve, was approximately $49 million and $48 million at September 27, 2015 and September 28, 2014, respectively. Costs for remaining inventories are determined by the first-in, first-out method. Cost before the LIFO adjustment is principally determined using the item cost method, which is calculated by counting each item in inventory, assigning costs to each of these items based on the actual purchase cost (net of vendor allowances) of each item and recording the actual cost of items sold.

REVIEW 10-9 LO10-9 LIFO Retail and Dollar Value LIFO Retail Methods

Review MBC

Part One—LIFO Retail Method

Data for Solar Stores follow for the year 2020. On January 1, 2020, when the LIFO retail method was adopted, beginning inventory was $250 at cost and $380 at retail.

Year	Purchases at Cost	Purchases at Retail	Net Additional Markups	Net Additional Markdowns	Sales	Index
2020	$900	$1,700	$115	$80	$1,600	104

Required

Compute the inventory value under LIFO Retail method for the year 2020. Round cost ratio to 3 decimal places.

Part Two—Dollar Value LIFO Retail Method

Data for Solar Stores for the years 2020 and 2021 follow. On January 1, 2020, when the dollar-value LIFO retail method was adopted, beginning inventory was $200 at cost and $333 at retail.

Year	Purchases at Cost	Purchases at Retail	Net Additional Markups	Net Additional Markdowns	Sales	Index
2020	$ 800	$1,350	$ 50	$ 30	$1,300	104
2021	1,000	1,650	100	140	1,450	106

Required

Compute the inventory values under dollar-value LIFO Retail method on December 31, 2020, and December 31, 2021.

More Practice: 10-96, 10-97, 10-98, 10-99
Solution on p. 10-57.

Questions

10-1. How is the lower-of-cost-or-net realizable rule applied to inventory valuation?

10-2. Why are the ceiling and floor values used in determining market in the application of the lower-of-cost-or-market rule?

10-3. How should damaged or obsolete merchandise at the end of the period be valued for inventory purposes?

10-4. What types of inventory does GAAP allow to be measured at selling price in excess of cost?

10-5. What are the basic assumptions underlying the relative sales value method when used in allocating costs for inventory purposes?

10-6. What basic assumption is implicit in the gross profit method?

10-7. Approximate the value of ending inventory using the following data.

Cost of goods available for sale	$170,000
Sales	150,000
Gross margin rate (on sales)	25%

10-8. Refer to the information in Question 10-7 but assume now that the 25% provided is the markup on cost of goods sold. Approximate the value of ending inventory.

10-9. Distinguish between gross profit rate on sales and gross profit percentage on cost of goods sold.

10-10. List four uses of the gross profit method.

10-11. Why is it generally desirable to apply the gross profit method by classes of merchandise?

10-12. Briefly outline the accounting and reporting of losses on purchase commitments when (a) the purchase contract is subject to revision or cancellation, and (b) it is noncancelable and a loss is probable.

10-13. When is a change in inventory methods justifiable? How is the change applied to a company's financial statements?

10-14. Explain the effect of each of the following errors in the ending inventory of a retail business (ignore income taxes).

a. Incorrectly excluded 300 units of commodity C, valued at $3 per unit, from the ending inventory; the purchase on credit was recorded.

b. Incorrectly excluded 400 units of commodity D, valued at $4 per unit, from the ending inventory; the purchase on credit was not recorded.

c. Incorrectly included 100 units of commodity A, valued at $5 per unit, in the ending inventory; the purchase on credit was recorded.

d. Incorrectly included 200 units of commodity B, valued at $3 per unit, in the ending inventory; the purchase on credit was not recorded.

10-15. Assume that inventory, cost $1,000, was sold on credit for $1,200 and held pending pickup by the customer. The goods were incorrectly included in the ending inventory. What is the pretax effect of this error if (a) the sale was not recorded, and (b) the sale was correctly recorded? Assume that a periodic inventory system is used.

10-16. Explain the basics of the retail method of estimating inventories (average). What data must be accumulated to apply the retail method?

10-17. The ending inventory estimated by the retail inventory method is $90,000. A physical inventory of the merchandise extended at retail shows $75,000. Suggest possible reasons for the discrepancy.

10-18. What are the primary uses of the retail method of estimating inventories?

10-19. When are markdowns and markdown cancellations excluded in computing the cost ratio in the retail inventory method?

10-20. Explain the similarity in computing the cost ratio under the average cost method and the conventional method of estimating inventories.

Brief Exercises

Brief Exercise 10-21
Identifying a Loss in Applying Lower-of-Cost-or-Net Realizable Value
LO1

Ward Company has determined its December 31, 2020, inventory on a FIFO basis as $400,000. Information pertaining to that inventory follows.

Estimated selling price	$408,000
Estimated cost of disposal	20,000

Ward records losses that result from applying the lower-of-cost-or-net realizable value rule. At December 31, 2020, what does Ward recognize as a holding loss, if any, on inventory?

Brief Exercise 10-22
Recording a Loss in Applying Lower-of-Cost-or-Net Realizable Value
LO1
Hint: See Demo 10-1

On December 31, 2020, Vale Inc. estimated the cost of inventory under the average cost method to be $88,000 and the net realizable value of inventory to be $85,000. The company maintains a perpetual inventory system and the company has not previously recorded a holding loss on inventory.

a. Prepare the journal entry to record the holding loss on inventory using an allowance account to reduce inventory and cost of goods sold to adjust expense.

b. Prepare the journal entry to record the holding loss on inventory using an allowance account to reduce inventory and a separate loss account to adjust equity.

Brief Exercise 10-23
Identifying a Loss in Applying Lower-of-Cost-or-Net Realizable Value
LO1
Hint: See Demo 10-1

Information related to three products of Adelle Corporation follows.

	Product A	Product B	Product C
Estimated selling price	$20	$25	$28
Original cost (FIFO)	15	20	18
Cost of disposal	2	4	3
Cost of completion	5	0	2

a. What inventory value is reported in the balance sheet for total inventory under the lower-of-cost-or-net realizable value rule assuming each individual item is evaluated?

b. What inventory value is reported in the balance sheet for total inventory under the lower-of-cost-or-net realizable value rule assuming that the inventory in total is evaluated?

Brief Exercise 10-24
Determining Inventory Values in Applying Lower-of-Cost-or-Market **LO2**
Hint: See Demo 10-2

Information related to two products of AMC Corporation follows. Compute the inventory values reported in the balance sheet for Products A and B under the lower-of-cost-or-market rule.

	Product A	Product B
Estimated selling price	$30	$80
Original cost (LIFO)	15	75
Replacement cost	35	70
Cost of disposal	2	4
Gross margin	8	24

Brief Exercise 10-25
Determining Inventory Values in Applying Lower-of-Cost-or-Market **LO2**

On December 31, 2020, Hale Inc. estimated the cost of inventory under the FIFO inventory method to be $100,000 and the market value of inventory to be $95,000. The company maintains a perpetual inventory system and the company has not previously recorded a holding loss on inventory.

a. Prepare the journal entry to record the holding loss on inventory using an allowance account to reduce inventory and cost of goods sold to adjust equity.

b. Prepare the journal entry to record the holding loss on inventory using an allowance account to reduce inventory and a separate loss account to adjust equity.

Brief Exercise 10-26
Recording Purchase Entry Using Relative Sales Value Method
LO3
Hint: See Demo 10-3

Bick Company purchased 2,600 bushels of ungraded apricots for $5,400. The apricots were sorted as follows: grade 1, 1,000 bushels; grade 2, 700 bushels; and grade 3, 900 bushels. The current market prices for graded apricots follow: grade 1, $5 per bushel; grade 2, $3 per bushel; and grade 3, $1 per bushel. The company uses a perpetual inventory system. Prepare the entry to record the purchase.

Brief Exercise 10-27
Estimating Inventory Using Gross Profit Method **LO4**
Hint: See Demo 10-4

Lin Co. sells its merchandise at a gross margin of 30%. The following amounts are among those pertaining to Lin's operations for the six months ended June 30, 2020. On June 30, 2020, Lin's inventory is destroyed by fire. Compute the estimated cost of this destroyed inventory.

Sales	$200,000
Beginning inventory	50,000
Purchases	130,000

Brief Exercise 10-28
Calculating Gross Profit Percentage Given Percentage of Cost
LO4

The following are calculations of gross profit as a percentage of cost: 25%, 30%, and 35%. Compute gross profit as a percentage of sales for each of the three percentage of cost figures. Round to two decimal places.

Brief Exercise 10-29
Calculating Gross Profit Percentage Given Estimated Inventory
LO4

The following information is available for Fox Inc. for its first quarter of 2020.

Cost of goods available for sale	$220,000
Net sales	280,000
Ending inventory estimated using the gross profit method	38,000

a. Determine cost of goods sold for the first quarter of 2020.

b. Determine gross profit percentage used to estimate ending inventory.

Brief Exercise 10-30 Recording Inventory Entries with Purchase Commitments on Reporting Dates **LO5**

On November 1, 2020, 5M Corporation entered into a purchase contract (not subject to revision or cancellation) to purchase 500 units of inventory for $50 per unit before January 1, 2021. The company uses LIFO inventory method.

a. If the inventory has a market price of $45 per unit on November 30, 2020, what entry (if any) does 5M Corporation record?
b. If instead the inventory has a market price of $55 per unit on November 30, 2020, what entry (if any) does 5M Corporation record?

Brief Exercise 10-31 Recording Inventory Entries with Purchase Commitments on Reporting and Purchase Dates **LO5** *Hint:* See Demo 10-5

November 1, 2020, 5M Corporation entered into a purchase contract (not subject to revision or cancellation) to purchase 500 units of inventory for $50 per unit before January 1, 2021. The company uses LIFO inventory method.

a. If the inventory has a market price of $40 per unit on November 30, 2020, what entry (if any) does 5M Corporation record?
b. Record the purchase of 500 units on December 15, 2020, if the market price remained at $40 per unit. Assume that the company applies the perpetual inventory method.

Brief Exercise 10-32 Reporting a Retrospective Change in Inventory Method **LO6**

Blues Corp. changed its method of accounting for inventory from LIFO to FIFO in 2020 for financial accounting purposes. The 2020 ending inventory was $40,000 under LIFO and $55,000 under FIFO. Blues Corp. reports 2020 and 2019 comparative results. (a) What inventory method is used to report results for 2019 and 2020? (b) Where in financial statements is it reported, if anywhere, the cumulative effect of prior years not presented?

Brief Exercise 10-33 Recording Indirect Effect of an Accounting Change **LO6**

Annually, Frontier Company pays a bonus on pretax income of 2% that is paid out to employees. In 2020, a change in method to account for inventory results in a retrospective increase of $280,000 in pretax income of the prior year (2019).

a. Prepare the journal entry for the current year to record the bonus payable, assuming no change in the bonus is possible.
b. When and where is this bonus reported in financial statements? Ignore income taxes.

Brief Exercise 10-34 Reporting a Prospective Change in Inventory Method **LO6**

Blues Corp. changed its method of accounting for inventory from FIFO to LIFO in 2020 for financial accounting purposes. The 2020 ending inventory was $40,000 under LIFO and $55,000 under FIFO. Blues Corp. reports 2020 and 2019 comparative results. What inventory method is used for the beginning inventory valuation in the year of change for reporting comparative financial statements?

Brief Exercise 10-35 Identifying Financial Statement Impacts of Inventory Errors **LO7**

For each of the following *separate* errors, determine the effect on (1) cost of goods sold, and (2) pretax income in the year of the error.

a. Overstatement of ending inventory.
b. Understatement of ending inventory.
c. Overstatement of beginning inventory.
d. Understatement of beginning inventory.
e. Overstatement of purchases.
f. Understatement of purchases.

Brief Exercise 10-36 Reporting an Inventory Error **LO7** *Hint:* See Demo 10-7

In 2021, AJ Inc. discovered errors in previously reported financial statements that overstated ending inventory on December 31, 2020, by $10,000 and on December 31, 2019, by $15,000. Prepare the correcting entry required on January 1, 2021, ignoring income taxes.

Brief Exercise 10-37 Valuing Inventory Using Conventional Retail Method **LO8** *Hint:* See Demo 10-8B

At December 31, 2020, the following information is available from Palo Company's accounting records. If sales are $553,000 and markdowns total $7,000, compute estimated inventory at the end of 2020 using the conventional retail method.

	Cost	Retail
Inventory January 1, 2020	$ 73,500	$101,500
Purchases	416,500	577,500
Additional markups	—	21,000
Available for sale	$490,000	$700,000

Brief Exercise 10-38
Valuing Inventory Using Average Cost Retail Method **LO8**
Hint: See Demo 10-8A

Dean Company uses the retail inventory method to estimate its inventory for interim statement disclosures. Data relating to the computation of the inventory at July 31, 2020, follow. Compute estimated inventory on July 31, 2020, using the average cost retail method.

	Cost	Retail
Beginning inventory, February 1, 2020	$ 180,000	$ 250,000
Purchases	1,020,000	1,575,000
Markups, net		175,000
Sales		1,725,000
Markdowns, net		125,000

Brief Exercise 10-39
Valuing Inventory Using Conventional Retail Method **LO8**
Hint: See Demo 10-8B

Using the information from Brief Exercise 10-38, determine estimated inventory at the end of 2020 using the conventional retail method.

Exercises

Exercise 10-40
Valuing Inventory Using Lower-of-Cost-or-Net Realizable Value **LO1**

Ubber Company had 1,000 units of inventory at the end of the accounting period. The unit cost was $60, and estimated distribution cost was $3 per unit.

Required

Compute the unit valuation of inventory based on lower-of-cost-or-net realizable value under each separate case *a* through *h*.

Case	Unit Selling Price	Case	Unit Selling Price
a.	$61	e.	$59
b.	66	f.	53
c.	68	g.	73
d.	50	h.	65

Exercise 10-41
Calculating Lower-of-Cost-or-Net Realizable Value **LO1**
Hint: See Demo 10-1

The following information is from Guccii Company's individual inventory items as of December 31, 2020.

Inventory	Quantity	Cost per Unit	Net Realizable Value per Unit
Classification: Premium			
Item 1	80	$180	$185
Item 2	150	100	98
Item 3	200	165	175
Item 4	140	158	120
Classification: Classic			
Item 5	100	100	98
Item 6	50	90	95
Item 7	500	105	115
Item 8	280	80	75

Required

a. Calculate lower-of-cost-or-net realizable value applying the rule to each individual item.
b. Calculate lower-of-cost-or-net realizable value applying the rule by inventory category.
c. Calculate lower-of-cost-or-net realizable value applying the rule to total inventory.
d. Explain how the amounts differ across the calculations from *a* through *c*. Is this always the case?

Exercise 10-42
Calculating Lower-of-Cost-or-Net Realizable Value **LO1**

Anne Traylor Inc. has the following information for its six inventory items on June 30, 2020.

Inventory Item	Quantity	Selling Price	Cost to Sell	Inventory Cost
#100	70	$24	$5	$16
#101	100	22	4	17
#115	50	35	6	31
#118	120	40	6	29
#120	25	18	4	10
#128	45	30	8	26

Required

Determine the inventory cost to report on the balance sheet on June 30, 2020, assuming that the company applies the lower-of-cost-or-net realizable value rule to each individual inventory item.

Exercise 10-43
Reporting Lower-of-Cost-or-Net Realizable Value **LO1**

Anne Traylor Inc. has the following information for its six inventory items on June 30, 2020. Additional selling costs include a 5% commission on the sales price of each product.

Inventory Item	Selling Price	Inventory Cost	Transportation Cost
#100	$24	$16	2
#101	22	17	2
#115	35	31	3
#118	32	29	3
#120	18	10	2
#128	30	26	2

Required

Determine the value per unit reported on its balance sheet on June 30, 2020, for the six inventory items from application of the lower-of-cost-or-net realizable value rule.

Exercise 10-44
Recording Inventory at Lower-of-Cost-or-Net Realizable Value **LO1**

The records of Loren Company show the following inventory data.

	Cost	Net Realizable Value
2018 Beginning inventory	$ 8,000	$ 8,000
2018 Ending inventory	10,000	12,000
2019 Ending inventory	16,000	15,000
2020 Ending inventory	8,000	6,000
2021 Ending inventory	24,000	20,000
2022 Ending inventory	16,000	14,000
2023 Ending inventory	20,000	22,000

Required

Record the journal entry required for each year, 2018 through 2023, to adjust the allowance to reduce inventory to net realizable value. Assume that the allowance is only adjusted at the end of the year and that for each year, all of the beginning inventory is sold by the end of the year. Adjust cost of goods sold for any necessary adjustments.

Exercise 10-45
Recording Inventory at Lower-of-Cost-or-Net Realizable Value **LO1**

Inventory balances in 2020 are shown below for Colbert Corporation.

Inventory Date	Original Cost	Net Realizable Value	Purchases
Jan. 1, 2020	$6,000	$6,000	$ 0
Dec. 31, 2020	7,000	6,800	50,000

Required

a. Prepare year-end journal entries to apply lower-of-cost-or-net realizable value rule to inventory on December 31, 2020, assuming that the company adjusts inventory through the allowance account, and adjusts equity through cost of goods sold.

b. Prepare year-end journal entries to apply lower-of-cost-or-net realizable value rule to inventory on December 31, 2020, assuming that the company adjusts the inventory account directly, and adjusts equity through a separate loss account.

c. Identify the primary advantage and disadvantage of the procedures followed in part *a* and part *b*.

Exercise 10-46
Valuing Inventory at Lower-of-Cost-or-Market **LO2**
Hint: See Demo 10-2

Gard Inc. has compiled the following information related to its five products. Also, costs of disposal are estimated to be 10% of selling price, and gross profit is estimated to be 25% of the selling price.

	#1	#2	#3	#4	#5
Estimated selling price	$330	$380	$410	$500	$650
Original cost	225	240	300	315	450
Replacement cost	250	350	245	330	415

Required
Determine the value of inventory applying the lower-of-cost-or-market rule.

Exercise 10-47
Valuing Inventory at Lower-of-Cost-or-Market **LO2**

Management of Tarry Company takes the position that under the lower-of-cost-or-market rule, the two items below are reported in ending inventory at $33,200 (total).

- Edgers: 600 in inventory; cost is $22 each; replacement cost is $16 each; estimated sale price is $30 each; estimated distribution cost is $3 each; and normal profit is 10% of sale price.
- Hedge clippers: 400 in inventory; cost is $50 each; replacement cost is $36 each; estimated sale price is $90 each; estimated distribution cost is $28 each; and normal profit is 20% of sale price.

Required
a. Compute your inventory valuation by item for the Tarry Company inventory reported above. Identify the source of the error if Tarry's estimate differs from your own.
b. Prepare the entry, if any, to report inventory at the lower-of-cost-or-market. Assume a perpetual inventory system and that all adjustments directly impact cost of goods sold and inventory.

Exercise 10-48
Valuing Inventory and Recording Entries Using Relative Sales Value Method **LO3**
Hint: See Demo 10-3

AVC Inc. purchased 1,200 bags of pecans that cost $4,200. The company also incurred $300 for transportation and grading. The pecans graded out as follows.

Grade	Quantity (bags)	Current Market Price per Bag
A	400	$6.75
B	600	6.00
C	100	4.50
Waste	100	—

Required
Assume the relative sales value method is used to allocate lump sum costs.
a. Prepare the purchase entry assuming a perpetual inventory system.
b. Determine the value of ending inventory assuming the following quantities are in inventory: grade A, 100 bags; grade B, 80 bags; and grade C, 40 bags.
c. Prepare the entry for sale of 20 bags of grade A pecans at a market price of $6.75 cash per bag.

Exercise 10-49
Valuing Inventory and Recording Entries Using Relative Sales Value Method **LO3**

Arizona Developers purchased and subdivided a tract of land that cost $900,000. The subdivisions were divided on the following basis.

- 10% used for streets, alleys, and parks
- 50% divided into 100 lots selling at $4,000 each
- 30% divided into 200 lots selling at $3,000 each
- 10% divided into 100 lots selling at $2,000 each

Required
a. Prepare the entry for the purchase of the lots. Use the relative sales value method to allocate the total cost of $900,000 to the three categories of lots. Assume a perpetual inventory system.
b. During the final month of the year, the paving was completed (included in the $900,000 cost) and several sales occurred. Inventory remaining at the first year-end was: 20 of the $4,000 lots; 50 of the $3,000 lots; and 10 of the $2,000 lots. (i) Compute the valuation of inventory at the first year-end. (ii) Prepare the entry for sales and cost of goods sold for each category of lots 1, 2 and 3 separately. Assume cash sales.

Exercise 10-50 Estimating Inventory Using Gross Profit Method **LO4**

The following data is from Netflicks Company for 2020.

Sales revenue	$120,000
Beginning inventory	16,000
Purchases	80,000

Required

For each separate case *a* through *e*, estimate ending inventory. Round ratios to three decimals.

a. Markup is 50% on cost.
b. Markup is 60% on sales.
c. Markup is 25% on cost.
d. Markup is 40% on sales.
e. Markup is 60% on cost.

Exercise 10-51 Estimating Inventory Using Gross Profit Method **LO4**

Assume that we are auditing the records of Forde Corporation. A physical inventory has been taken by the company under our observation. However, the valuation extensions have not been completed. The records of the company show the following account data. The gross margin last period was 35% of net sales; we anticipate that it will be 25% for the year under audit.

Sales, gross	$630,000	Beginning inventory	$200,000
Sales returns (returned to inventory)	10,000	Freight-in	14,000
Purchases, gross	310,000	Purchase returns and allowances	4,000

Required

Estimate the cost of ending inventory using the gross profit method.

Exercise 10-52 Estimating Inventory Loss Using Gross Profit Method **LO4**
Hint: See Demo 10-4

On November 15, 2020, a fire destroyed Youngstown Inc.'s warehouse where inventory is stored. It is estimated that $20,000 can be realized from sale of usable but damaged inventory. The accounting records concerning inventory reveal the following. Based on recent records, gross margin has averaged 35% of net sales.

Inventory at Nov. 1, 2020	$240,000
Purchases from Nov. 1, 2020, to Nov. 15, 2020	280,000
Net sales from Nov. 1, 2020, to Nov. 15, 2020	400,000

Required

a. Calculate the estimated loss of inventory using the gross profit method.
b. Assume instead that the markup is 35% of cost. Estimate the cost of ending inventory using the gross profit method.

AICPA adapted

Exercise 10-53 Estimating Inventory Loss Using Gross Profit Method **LO4**
Hint: See Demo 10-4

The accounting records of Butler Company reveal the following information.

Inventory, January 1	$ 20,000
Purchases to July 19	200,000
Net sales to July 19	170,000

Before the company opened for business on July 20, its assets were totally destroyed by flood. The insurance company adjuster found that the average rate of gross margin for the past few years had been 40%.

Required

a. Estimate the value of inventory destroyed assuming that the gross margin percentage given was based on sales. Round ratios to two decimals.
b. Estimate the value of inventory destroyed assuming that the gross margin percentage given was based on cost of sales. Round ratios to two decimals.

Exercise 10-54 Computing Gross Profit and Cost Percentages Given Ending Inventory Balances **LO4**

Harris Inc. with a December 31 year-end, applies a periodic inventory method in reporting inventory. Because its physical inventory counts take place at year end, Harris estimates ending inventory for its quarterly reports using the gross profit method. The following information is available for Harris.

Inventory, December 31, 2019 (based on physical count)	$ 45,000	Purchases, 2021	$175,000
Inventory, March 31, 2020 (estimated)	20,000	Net sales, 2020	200,000
Inventory, June 30, 2020 (estimated)	59,000	Net sales, 2021	180,000
Purchases, 2020	125,000		

Required

a. Estimate gross profit percentage for first quarter 2020.

b. Estimate cost percentage for first quarter 2020.

c. Estimate gross profit percentage for second quarter 2020.

d. Estimate cost percentage for second quarter 2020.

Exercise 10-55
Estimating Inventory Loss Using Gross Profit Method **LO4**

Dart Company's accounting records reveal the following.

Inventory, January 1, 2020	$ 500,000
Purchases during 2020	2,500,000
Sales during 2020	3,200,000

A physical inventory taken on December 31, 2020, shows an ending inventory of $575,000. Dart's gross margin on sales has remained constant at 25% in recent years. Dart suspects some inventory theft by a new employee.

Required

At December 31, 2020, compute an estimate of the cost of missing inventory.

Exercise 10-56
Accounting for Inventory Transactions with Purchase Commitments **LO5**

During 2020, Moss Company signed a contract with a supplier to purchase 30,000 subassemblies at $30 each during 2021. The company uses the FIFO method to account for inventory.

Required

a. The cost of subassemblies had declined and the estimated net realizable value is $850,000 on December 31, 2020. Prepare any year-end entry required for this cost decline.

b. The subassemblies are received in 2021 when the net realizable value is estimated at $850,000. The contract was paid in full. Prepare the required purchase entry in 2021.

Exercise 10-57
Accounting for Inventory Transactions with Purchase Commitments **LO5**
Hint: See Demo 10-5

Nov. 1, 2020 Sonic Inc. entered into a purchase contract (not subject to revision or cancellation) to purchase 20,000 units of inventory at $7 per unit (to be used in manufacturing). The contract period extends through February 2021, and Sonic applies a perpetual inventory system and the FIFO inventory method.

Dec. 31, 2020 At Sonic's December 31 year-end, inventory was being sold at a price of $5 per unit.

Jan. 25, 2021 Sonic purchased the 20,000 units contracted; however, the selling price per unit of inventory on this date was $4.75.

Required

Prepare any necessary journal entries or disclosures on the following dates. *Note:* The selling prices above are net of selling costs.

a. November 1, 2020 (initiation of contract).

b. December 31, 2020 (reporting period).

c. January 25, 2021 (purchase date).

Exercise 10-58
Recording Entry and Determining Effect on Net Income for Change in Accounting Principle **LO6**

Sterling Co. changed from FIFO to average cost on January 1, 2021. Inventory balances on December 31, 2021, under both methods follow. Sterling Co. has a December 31 year-end.

Inventory balances	2020	2019
Ending inventory, average cost	$15,000	$10,000
Ending inventory, FIFO	9,000	7,000

Required

a. Prepare the entry on January 1, 2021, to record the accounting change. Ignore taxes.

b. Show how its 2020 income statement is impacted when retroactively adjusted for the change in accounting principle. Ignore taxes.

Exercise 10-59
Recording Entry and Determining Effect on Reporting for Change in Accounting Principle
LO6
Hint: See Demo 10-6

Refer to the information in Exercise 10-58. Assume that instead the company is changing from average cost to FIFO in 2021 for reporting inventory.

Required

a. Prepare the entry in the company's accounting system on January 1, 2021, to record the accounting change. Ignore taxes.

b. For external reporting purposes on December 31, 2021, the company reports comparative balance sheets for 2021 and 2020. What amount of inventory is reported on the December 31, 2020, balance sheet?

c. What cumulative effect of change in accounting principle is reported in retained earnings at year-end 2021? At year-end 2020? Assume comparative financial statement presentation of years ended December 31, 2021, and 2020. Ignore taxes.

Exercise 10-60
Change from Average Cost to FIFO: Reporting
LO6

Park Company began operations on January 1, 2018. The following information includes the financial statement impacts of both the average cost and FIFO inventory methods.

	Inventory Balance		Cost of Goods Sold			
	Average Cost	FIFO	Average Cost	FIFO	Sales	Operating Expenses
December 31, 2018 . . .	$30,000	$35,000	$150,000	$145,000	$250,000	$40,000
December 31, 2019 . . .	34,000	48,000	160,000	151,000	255,000	40,400
December 31, 2020 . . .	37,500	61,500	170,000	160,000	230,000	40,800

Required

a. Prepare three-year comparative income statements assuming the company uses the average cost inventory method.

b. Prepare three-year comparative income statements assuming the company uses the FIFO inventory method.

c. Prepare three-year comparative income statements assuming the company changes from the average cost method to the FIFO method in 2020.

Exercise 10-61
Change in Inventory Methods: Entries and Reporting **LO6**

Pier2 Company computed net income under the following two inventory methods for the recent four years. Ignore income taxes.

Year	Average Cost Inventory	FIFO Inventory
2017	$180,000	$195,000
2018	185,000	190,000
2019	190,000	200,000
2020	200,000	205,000

Required

a. Prepare the January 1, 2020, journal entry assuming the company changed from average cost to FIFO in 2020.

b. Assuming the change in part *a*, compute net income reported in 2020, 2019, and 2018, assuming a comparative income statement with two prior years reported.

c. Prepare the January 1, 2020, journal entry assuming the company changed from FIFO to average cost in 2020.

d. Assuming the change in part *c*, compute net income reported in 2020, 2019, and 2018, assuming a comparative income statement with two prior years reported.

e. Instead, assume that the company changes to LIFO beginning in 2020. The company is unable to estimate the LIFO amounts for earlier years. What entry does the company record for the change in accounting method?

Exercise 10-62
Recording Entries to Correct Inventory Errors
LO7

A company purchased merchandise on credit at December 31, 2020, for $6,000. That merchandise was in its warehouse that same day. This purchase was *not* recorded in 2020 because the accounting department did not receive the invoice from the vendor. In 2021, the invoice was received, reported, and paid.

Required

a. Assuming that financial statements are not yet issued for 2020 when this error is discovered, what journal entry, if any, is recorded? The company applies periodic inventory.

b. Assuming that financial statements are already issued for 2020 when this error is discovered, what journal entry, if any, is recorded? Ignore income taxes.

Exercise 10-63
Analyzing Impact of Inventory Errors on Reporting **LO7**

The records of Largo Company reveal the following.

Sales revenue.		$205,000
Cost of goods sold		
Beginning inventory	$ 10,000	
Purchases.	105,000	
Goods available for sale	115,000	
Ending inventory.	25,000	90,000
Gross margin		115,000
Accrued expenses		60,000
Income (pretax)		$ 55,000

The following errors were found and they have *not* been corrected.

1. Revenues collected in advance of $5,000 are included in Sales Revenue.
2. Accrued expenses not recognized of $7,000.
3. Goods costing $10,000 are incorrectly included in ending inventory (they are being held on consignment from Carter Inc.). No purchase was recorded.
4. Goods costing $5,000 are correctly included in ending inventory; however, no purchase was recorded (assume a credit purchase).

Required

a. Prepare a revised income statement on a correct basis.
b. Identify incorrect amounts on the balance sheet *if the errors were not corrected.*

Exercise 10-64
Analyzing Impact of Inventory Errors on Accounts **LO7**

The following table has six *separate* descriptions of inventory errors using the periodic inventory method.

Inventory Error	Cost of Goods Sold	Pretax Income	Ending Inventory
a. Overstated ending inventory.	______	______	______
b. Ending inventory and purchases overstated	______	______	______
c. Ending inventory understated.	______	______	______
d. Ending inventory and purchases understated . . .	______	______	______
e. Beginning inventory overstated	______	______	______
f. Beginning inventory understated	______	______	______

Required

For each of the six *separate* scenarios, indicate what effect—overstated, understated, or no effect—the error has on cost of goods sold, pretax income, and ending inventory. Ignore income taxes.

Exercise 10-65
Estimating Inventory Using Retail Inventory Method—Conventional **LO8**
Hint: See Demo 10-8C

Retail-Mart values its inventory using the conventional retail inventory method. It discloses the following data for the month of June 2020.

	Cost	Selling Price
Inventory, June 1	$ 53,800	$ 80,000
Markdowns.		21,000
Markups		29,000
Markdown cancellations.		10,000
Markup cancellations		9,000
Purchases.	173,200	223,600
Sales.		250,000
Purchase returns and allowances	3,000	3,600
Sales returns and allowances.		10,000

Required

Compute estimated inventory at June 30, 2020, using the conventional retail inventory method. Round the cost ratio to three decimals.

AICPA adapted

Exercise 10-66
Estimating Inventory Using Retail Inventory Method—Conventional
LO8

Wally-Mart values its inventory using the conventional retail inventory method. It discloses the following data for a recent period.

	At Cost	At Retail
Beginning inventory	$101,000	$150,000
Purchases	323,000	563,000
Purchases returns	6,000	10,000
Freight-in	8,000	
Additional markups		12,000
Additional markup cancellations		5,000
Markdowns		9,000
Markdown cancellations		2,000
Sales		540,000
Sales returns (and restored to inventory)		6,000

Required

Compute estimated ending inventory for the period end using the conventional retail inventory method. Round the cost ratio to three decimals.

Exercise 10-67
Estimating Inventory Using Retail Inventory Method—Conventional
LO8

Outlet Store applies the conventional retail inventory method. Information relating to the computation of inventory for 2020 follows. Estimated normal shrinkage is 2% of sales.

	At Cost	At Retail
Beginning inventory	$ 40,000	$ 80,000
Sales		600,000
Purchases	300,000	590,000
Freight-in	8,000	
Markups		60,000
Markup cancellations		20,000
Markdowns		25,000
Markdown cancellations		5,000

Required

Calculate estimated ending inventory for 2020 using the conventional retail method. Round all cost ratios to three decimals.

Exercise 10-68
Estimating Inventory Using Retail Inventory Method—Average Cost
LO8

Rainey Retailers disclosed the following data for January.

	At Cost	At Retail
Beginning inventory	$ 20,000	$ 26,000
Sales		310,000
Sales returns (items restored to inventory)	5,000	
Purchases	150,000	300,000
Purchases returns	3,000	6,000
Freight-in	9,000	

Required

Calculate estimated ending inventory using the retail inventory method at average cost. Round all cost ratios to two decimals.

Exercise 10-69
Calculating Cost to Retail Percentage and Markdowns Using Retail Inventory Method—Conventional
LO8

Baldor Company reports inventory at cost of $30,000 and retail of $65,000 on January 1, 2020. Purchases in 2020 are $20,000 at cost and $30,000 at retail. Sales for 2020 are $79,000. It made additional markups of $8,000 (with cancellations of $3,000). Baldor uses the conventional retail inventory method and estimates ending inventory at $10,000. Markdowns were taken during the year but the dollar amount is unavailable.

Required

a. Compute the cost ratio.
b. Compute net markdowns.

Exercise 10-70
Recording a Loss in Applying Lower-of-Cost-or-Net Realizable Value
LO1, 2, 3, 4, 5, 6, 7, 8

Terms and phrases relating to concepts discussed in this chapter along with descriptions of those terms and phrases follow.

Key Inventory Terms and Phrases	Description of Terms and Phrases
___ 1. Net realizable value	*a.* Requires retroactive restatement of financial statements
___ 2. Lower-of-cost-or-market	*b.* Method for valuing inventory applying to LIFO and retail methods
___ 3. Allowance to reduce inventory to net realizable value	*c.* Cancellation of additional markup
___ 4. Gross profit method	*d.* Inventory estimation that is not acceptable under GAAP
___ 5. Estimated loss on purchase commitment	*e.* Method that approximates lower-of-cost-or-market
___ 6. Change in inventory method	*f.* Not usually practical to retroactively restate or adjust financial statements
___ 7. Change from FIFO to LIFO	*g.* Reduction in original sales price
___ 8. Markdown	*h.* Selling price net of completion and disposal costs
___ 9. Additional markup cancellation	*i.* Theft of inventory that exceeds expectations
___ 10. Retail inventory method—Conventional Method	*j.* Dollar amount required to purchase an inventory item
___ 11. Abnormal casualty loss	*k.* Unrealized when contract price is greater than market price
___ 12. Replacement cost	*l.* Requires net markups and markdowns in cost-to-retail percentage
___ 13. Retail inventory method—Average Method	*m.* Adjusted in accounting records in the period discovered
___ 14. Immaterial error	*n.* Allows for estimation of inventory values when multiple items are purchased at one price
___ 15. Relative sales value method	*o.* Contra inventory account

Required

Match each term, 1 through 15, with the best description *a* through *o*.

Problems

Problem 10-71
Valuing Inventory Using Lower-of-Cost-or-Net Realizable Value **LO1**

Printer Inc. discloses the following ending inventory data.

Classification	Quantity	Cost per Unit	NRV per unit
Paper			
Stock X	400	$300	$330
Stock Y	120	250	230
Ink			
Stock D	40	70	65
Stock E	20	55	62
Toner			
Stock A	16	75	70
Stock B	8	95	80
Stock C	14	100	110

Required

a. Determine the valuation of inventory at cost and at the lower-of-cost-or-net realizable value assuming application by (a) individual items, (b) classifications, and (c) total inventory. The unit costs of the three categories are significantly different; however, within each category the unit costs are similar.

b. Prepare the entry to record the ending inventory for *each* approach in part *a* assuming perpetual inventory and any inventory holding loss is recognized as a separate loss and reduces inventory through an allowance account.

c. Of the three applications in part *a*, which one appears preferable in this situation? Explain.

Problem 10-72
Preparing Income Statement Using Lower-of-Cost-or-Net Realizable Value Method **LO1**

York Inc.'s income statements for 2020 and 2021 follow. The inventory amounts are valued at cost.

	2020	2021
Sales	$107,000	$97,000
Cost of goods sold		
Beginning inventory	25,000	20,000
Purchases	75,000	73,000
Total goods available	100,000	93,000
Ending inventory	20,000	15,000
Cost of goods sold	80,000	78,000
Gross margin	27,000	19,000
Operating expenses	14,000	12,000
Pretax income	$ 13,000	$ 7,000

Inventory valued at lower-of-cost-or-net realizable value would have been:

- $25,000 at the beginning of 2020 (the same as cost)
- $18,000 at the end of 2020, and $12,000 at the end of 2021

Required

Restate the 2020 and 2021 comparative income statements and balance sheets applying the lower-of-cost-or-net realizable value rule for each of the following procedures. Disregard income taxes. Assume that all December 31, 2020, inventory was sold before December 31, 2021.

a. Adjust an allowance account to reduce inventory and adjust cost of goods sold to decrease equity.
b. Adjust an allowance account to reduce inventory and adjust a separate loss account to decrease equity.

Problem 10-73
Recording and Reporting Using Lower-of-Cost-or-Market Method **LO2**

Cool Aire Inc. discloses the following data relating to inventories for 2021.

Inventory Date	Original Cost	Lower of Cost or Market
January 1, 2021	$40,000	$40,000
December 31, 2021	50,000	46,000

It also reports the following annual data.

For Year Ended December 31	2021
Sales	$240,000
Purchases	135,000
Administrative and selling expenses	49,000

The company values inventories on the basis of lower-of-cost-or-market and uses the periodic inventory system. Ignore income taxes.

Required

a. Prepare the entry to apply the lower-of-cost-or-market rule at December 31, 2021. Adjust an allowance account to reduce inventory and adjust a separate loss account to decrease equity.
b. Prepare an income statement for 2021. Report the inventory amount for the balance sheet at cost and at lower-of-cost-or-market at December 31 for 2021.

Problem 10-74
Recording Entries Using Lower-of-Cost-or-Market Rule **LO2**

Neutra Fresh uses a perpetual inventory system. It discloses the following annual data.

For Year Ended December 31	2020	2021
Sales revenue	$160,000	$240,000
Cost of goods sold	80,000	120,000
Remaining expenses	40,000	70,000

Its cost of goods sold is based on inventories valued at cost. Assume for each year that all of the beginning inventory is sold by year end. Additional information regarding its inventories follows.

Inventory	Cost	Market
January 1, 2020	$12,000	$16,000
December 31, 2020	20,000	18,000
December 31, 2021	26,000	20,000

Required

a. Prepare the entries to apply the lower-of-cost-or-market rule at December 31, 2020, and 2021. Adjust an allowance account to reduce inventory and adjust a loss account to decrease equity.

b. Prepare comparative income statements for 2020 and 2021 following part *a*. Ignore income taxes.

c. Prepare the entries to apply the lower-of-cost-or-market rule at December 31, for 2020, and 2021. Adjust an allowance account to reduce inventory and adjust cost of goods sold to decrease equity.

d. Prepare comparative income statements for 2020 and 2021 following part *c*. Ignore income taxes.

Problem 10-75
Estimating Inventory Using Gross Profit Method **LO4**

Georgia Company discloses the following information on September 1, 2020.

Inventory, January 1, 2020	$100,000
Purchases, January 1 to September 1	600,000
Sales, January 1 to September 1	800,000
Purchase returns and allowances	6,000
Sales returns (goods returned to stock)	10,000
Freight-in	8,000

A fire destroys its entire inventory on September 1, 2020, except (i) for goods marked to sell at $12,000, which had an estimated residual value of $8,000, and (ii) for goods in transit to which Georgia had ownership (and this purchase had been recorded). Invoices recorded on the latter show merchandise cost of $4,000 and freight-in of $200. The average rate of gross margin on sales in recent years has been 30%.

Required

a. Estimate the inventory fire loss.

b. Under what conditions would our estimate in part *a* be questionable?

Problem 10-76
Estimating Inventory Using Gross Profit Method **LO4**

Wood Wholesale's warehouse burned down on April 1, 2021. The following information (up to the date of the fire) was taken from the records of the company: inventory, January 1, $30,000; gross sales, $160,000; purchases, $90,000; sales returns (restored to stock), $5,000; purchase returns and allowances, $2,000; and freight-in, $8,000. The cost of goods sold and gross margin for the past three years follow.

Year	Cost of Goods Sold	Gross Margin
2018	$500,000	$125,000
2019	460,000	120,000
2020	500,000	120,000

Required

a. Estimate the cost of the inventory destroyed in the fire.

b. Under what conditions would our estimate in part *a* be questionable?

Problem 10-77
Accounting for Inventory Transactions with Purchase Commitments **LO5**

On December 1, 2020, Aude Corp. entered into a purchase commitment (not subject to revision or cancellation) to purchase 10,000 items of inventory at $20 per unit before January 31, 2021. The market price of inventory on December 1, 2020, is $20. Aude Corp. applies a perpetual inventory system and the LIFO inventory method.

Required

a. On December 5, 2020, 1,000 items of inventory are purchased when the market price is $21 per item. Record the purchase entry.

b. Assume the market price is $19 on December 5, 2020, when 1,000 items of inventory are purchased. Record the purchase entry.

c. On its December 31, 2020, year-end, the market price of inventory is $19. Record the entry, if any, that is necessary at year-end.

d. The remaining units of inventory per contract were purchased on January 15, 2021, when the market price was $18.50. Record the purchase entry.

Problem 10-78 Reporting Effects and Recording Entries with Change in Inventory Costing Method **LO6**

Management of Pepsee Corp. is considering switching inventory methods from average cost to FIFO to follow industry standards. Assume the following data is available for the year ended December 31, 2020.

	Units	Unit Cost
January 1, 2020 (beginning inventory)	60	$200
Purchases		
January 15, 2020	40	215
June 12, 2020	50	218
November 19, 2020	40	220

Sales for the year totaled 110 units at $230 per unit. A physical inventory taken on December 31, 2020, showed 50 units available. Valley uses the periodic inventory method. If the company had been using the FIFO inventory method in prior years, the beginning inventory unit cost would have been $212.

Required

a. Compute the effect on pretax income for 2020 if the company changes from average cost to FIFO, assuming that the company uses a periodic inventory system. Round unit costs to two decimals.

b. Explain the accounting treatment when a company moves to FIFO.

c. Prepare the journal entry, if any, required at January 1, 2020, for the change to FIFO.

Problem 10-79 Change in Inventory Accounting Method **LO6**

Bennz Inc. began operations in 2019. After initially selecting the LIFO inventory method, Bennz Inc. changed from LIFO to FIFO in 2020. Net income for the two most recent years and inventory balances under both methods follow.

Year	Net Income
2020	$30,000 (computed under FIFO)
2019	20,000 (computed under LIFO)

Inventory Balances	2020	2019	2018
Ending inventory, FIFO	$15,000	$10,000	$8,000
Ending inventory, LIFO	9,000	7,000	4,000

Required

a. Prepare the journal entry necessary in 2020 to record the accounting change.

b. Compute the net income that is reported in the 2019 retained earnings statement.

Problem 10-80 Change in Accounting Principle **LO6**

Appel Inc. reported the following information under the average cost method.

Average Cost	2017	2018	2019	2020
Beginning inventory	$ 45,000	$ 50,000	$ 35,000	$ 40,000
Purchases	450,000	380,000	400,000	440,000
Ending inventory	(50,000)	(35,000)	(40,000)	(58,000)
Cost of goods sold	$445,000	$395,000	$395,000	$422,000

During 2021, Appel Inc. decided to change its method in accounting for inventory to the FIFO method. It compiled the following information for ending inventory under the FIFO method.

2016	$50,000	2019	$48,000
2017	60,000	2020	65,000
2018	42,000		

Required

a. Compute cost of goods sold for each year 2017 through 2020 using the FIFO inventory method.
b. Explain how the company presents its comparative financial information in 2021 for the inventory method change.

Problem 10-81
Change in Inventory Costing Method **LO6**

Armstrong Inc. began operations in 2018. Armstrong Inc. computed net income under the following two inventory methods for the prior three years. Ignore taxes for the requirements below.

Year	Average Cost Inventory	LIFO Inventory
2018	$35,000	Unavailable
2019	38,000	Unavailable
2020	50,000	Unavailable

Required

a. Prepare the 2021 journal entry required assuming that the company changed from the average cost method to the LIFO method in 2021. Describe the financial statement reporting implications of this change.
b. Prepare the 2021 journal entry required assuming that the company changed from the average cost method to the LIFO method in 2021. Assume that the company is able to reconstruct LIFO records for 2020 *only* and determined that ending inventory based on 2020 LIFO activity is $45,000. Describe the financial statement reporting implications of this change in method.

Problem 10-82
Analyzing Impacts on Accounts Due to Inventory Errors **LO7**

Dexter Company has completed the income statement and balance sheet at December 31, 2020. Dexter maintains a periodic inventory system. Subsequently, during an audit, the following items were discovered.

a. Selling expenses amounting to $7,000 were not accrued.
b. A conditional sale on credit for $12,000 was recorded on December 31, 2020. The goods, which cost $8,000, were included in ending inventory; they had not been shipped because the customer's address was not known and the credit had not been approved. Ownership had not passed.
c. Merchandise purchased on December 31, 2020, on credit for $6,000 was included in ending inventory because the goods were received. A purchase was not recorded because the accounting department had not received the invoice from the vendor.
d. Ending inventory was overstated by $15,000 because of an addition error on the inventory sheet.
e. A sale return (on account) on December 31, 2020, was not recorded: sales amount was $15,000, and cost was $8,000. Ending inventory did not include the goods returned.

Required

For each item *a* through *e* indicate whether the following four accounts are overstated, understated, or not affected. If accounts other than the ones listed are affected by the error, indicate the account(s) and the impact on the account in the "Other" column.

	Net Sales	Cost of Goods Sold	Gross Margin	Ending Inventory	Other
a.	______	______	______	______	______
b.	______	______	______	______	______
c.	______	______	______	______	______
d.	______	______	______	______	______
e.	______	______	______	______	______

Problem 10-83
Analyzing Impacts on Accounts Due to Inventory Errors (P10-21) **LO7**

On January 3, 2021, Jonah Inc. engaged an independent CPA to perform an audit for the year ended December 31, 2020. Jonah uses a perpetual inventory system. The CPA did not observe the inventory count on December 31, 2020; as a result, a special examination was made of the inventory records. The financial statements prepared by the company (uncorrected) showed the following: ending inventory, $72,000; accounts receivable, $60,000; accounts payable, $30,000; sales, $400,000; and pretax income, $51,000.

The following items *a* through *m* were uncovered during the audit.

a. Merchandise that cost $18,000 was excluded from the physical inventory count, and the related sale for $23,000 was recorded. The goods had been segregated in the warehouse for shipment; however, control of the inventory had not passed to the customer.

b. Merchandise that cost $10,000 was out on consignment to Barr Company and was excluded from the ending inventory. The merchandise was recorded as a sale of $25,000 when shipped to Barr on December 2, 2020.

c. Merchandise costing $1,500 was received on December 28, 2020. but was excluded from the physical inventory count. The auditor located the source documents with the purchasing agent; they indicated, "On consignment from Baker Company."

d. Merchandise costing $2,000 was received on January 8, 2021, and the related purchase invoice recorded January 9. The invoice showed the shipment was made on December 29, 2020, F.O.B. destination. The merchandise was excluded from inventory.

e. Merchandise that cost $11,000, was sold on December 31, 2020, for $16,000, shipped F.O.B. shipping point. The sale was recorded; however, the cost of the in-transit inventory was added to the inventory.

f. Merchandise that cost $6,000 was excluded from ending inventory and not recorded as a sale for $7,500 on December 31, 2020. The goods had been specifically segregated. Control of the inventory will not pass to the customer until delivery.

g. Merchandise that cost $15,000 was included in ending inventory. The related purchase has not been recorded. The goods had been shipped by the vendor F.O.B. destination, and the invoice, but not the goods, was received on December 30, 2020.

h. Merchandise in transit that cost $7,000 was excluded from inventory because it was not yet received. The shipment from the vendor was F.O.B. shipping point. The purchase was recorded on December 29, 2020, when the invoice was received.

i. Merchandise that cost $8,000 was included in ending inventory because it was received. The merchandise had been rejected because of incorrect specifications and was being held for return to the vendor. The merchandise was recorded as a purchase on December 26, 2020.

Required

Complete a row in the following table for each item *a* through *m*. Each item has one column for each of six financial statement amounts (unadjusted balances). Show the specific correction to each balance and the final corrected balance for each financial statement amount.

Data	Ending Inventory	Accounts Receivable	Accounts Payable	Sales	Net Purchases	Pretax Income
Prelim. bal. . . .	$72,000	$60,000	$30,000	$400,000	$160,000	$51,000

AICPA adapted

Problem 10-84
Estimating Ending Inventory Using Retail Inventory Method—Conventional and Average Cost **LO8**

Discount Mart reports the following for 2020.

Sales (gross)	$800,000
Sales returns (restored to inventory)	2,000
Additional markups	9,000
Additional markup cancellations	5,000
Markdowns	7,000
Markdown cancellations	3,000
Purchases	
At retail	850,000
At cost	459,500
Purchase returns	
At retail	4,000
At cost	2,200
Freight on purchases	7,000
Beginning inventory	
At cost	45,000
At retail	80,000

Required

a. Estimate ending inventory for 2020 using the average cost method. Round all cost ratios to three decimals.

b. Estimate ending inventory for 2020 using the conventional retail method. Round all cost ratios to three decimals.

Problem 10-85
Estimating Ending Inventory Using Retail Inventory Method—Conventional **LO7**

Auditors are examining the accounts of Detroit Retail. Auditors were present when Detroit's personnel physically counted its inventory; however, the auditors performed their own tests. Detroit's records provided the following data for the current year.

	At Retail	At Cost
Inventory, beginning-year	$ 300,000	$180,500
Net purchases	1,453,000	955,000
Freight-in		15,000
Additional markups	31,000	
Additional markup cancellations	14,000	
Markdowns	8,000	
Employee discounts	2,000	
Sales	1,300,000	
Inventory, year-end (per physical count valued at retail)	475,000	

Required

a. Compute ending inventory using the conventional method as an audit test of the overall reasonableness of the physical inventory count. Round the cost ratio to three decimals.

b. Compute the difference between estimated inventory in part *a* and the physical inventory value. Identify at least four factors that the auditors should consider in reconciling any difference in these values.

Problem 10-86
Analyzing Use of Retail Inventory Method—Conventional **LO8**

Hudson Company, which is both a wholesaler and a retailer, purchases its inventories from various suppliers. Additional facts for Hudson's wholesale operations follow.

- Hudson incurs substantial warehousing costs.
- Hudson uses the lower-of-cost-or-market rule.
- Replacement cost of inventories is below net realizable value and above net realizable value less the normal profit margin. Original cost of inventories is above replacement cost and below net realizable value.
- Hudson determines the estimated cost of its ending inventories held for sale at retail using the retail inventory method, which approximates lower of average cost or market.
- Hudson incurs markups and markdowns

Required

a. Explain how Hudson should account for warehousing costs related to its wholesale inventories.

b. Explain why the lower-of-cost-or-market method is used to report inventory.

c. Compute the amount Hudson's wholesale inventories are reported at on the balance sheet. Explain the application of the lower-of-cost-or-market method in this situation.

d. Identify how Hudson should treat the following items in its calculation of the cost ratio used to determine the estimated cost of its ending retail inventories in.

1. Freight-in costs.
2. Net markups.
3. Net markdowns.

e. Explain how Hudson's retail inventory method approximates lower of average cost or market.

AICPA adapted

Accounting Decisions and Judgments

AD&J 10-87
Analyzing Inventory Values: Replacement Cost, International Firm **LO1**

Real World Analysis **British Petroleum Company** (BP) is the parent company of one of the world's largest international petroleum and petrochemical groups. It engages in exploration and production, refining and marketing, and chemicals. BP also has interests in nutrition. BP provides the following statement in note 1 to its Year 8 annual report, prepared in accordance with IFRS.

> The accounts are prepared under the historic cost convention . . . Profit and loss determined under the historic cost convention includes stock holding gains and losses and, as a consequence, does not necessarily reflect underlying trading credits.

Stock holding gains or losses represent the difference between the replacement cost of sales and the historical cost of sales calculated using the first-in, first-out method. BP's income statement reports the following pretax figures.

$ millions	Year 8	Year 7
Replacement cost operating profit	$7,371	$10,811
Stock holding gains (losses)	(1,391)	(939)
Total	$5,980	$ 9,872

Required

a. Identify a more descriptive title for the amount reported as "Total."

b. Estimate BP's income for Year 8 if BP used a LIFO cost-flow assumption to value its inventories.

AD&J 10-88 Recording a Loss in Applying Lower-of-Cost-or-Net Realizable Value **LO8, 9**

Real World Analysis Kmart Corporation is a major operator of specialty stores. Kmart's January 31, Year 8, annual report includes the following information in its note 1.

> Inventories are stated at the *lower of cost or market* using primarily the retail method. The last-in, first-out (LIFO) method, using internal inflation indices, was used to determine cost for $6,148, $5,990, and $5,883 million of inventory as of year-end Year 8, Year 7, and Year 6, respectively. Inventories valued on LIFO were $407, $457, and $440 million lower than the amounts that would have been reported using the first-in, first-out (FIFO) method at year-end Year 8, Year 7, and Year 6, respectively.

Required

a. Identify the method used by Kmart to value its inventories.

b. Identify the value Kmart reports in its balance sheet for inventories as of January 31, Year 8.

c. Compute the effect on Kmart's reported operating income before tax for the year ended January 31, Year 8, if it had only used FIFO for its entire existence.

AD&J 10-89 Analyzing the Reporting of Inventory **LO8**

Real World Analysis An excerpt from the annual report of the Coca-Cola Company follows.

> Inventories consist primarily of raw materials and packaging (which includes ingredients and supplies) and finished goods (which includes concentrates and syrups in our concentrate operations and finished beverages in our finished products operations). Inventories are valued at the lower of cost or market. We determine cost on the basis of the average cost of first-in, first-out methods. Inventories consisted of the following (in millions):

December 31	2015	2014
Raw materials and packaging	$1,564	$1,615
Finished goods	1,032	1,134
Other	306	351
Total inventories	$2,902	$3,100

Required

a. Identify the method Coca-Cola uses here to report its inventories. Identify the method used for its cost basis.

b. Is its method for the cost basis permitted under GAAP? Is it allowed for IRS income tax reporting?

AD&J 10-90 Estimating Inventory Using Gross Profit Method **LO4**

Challenge Problem The manager of Seton Books, a book retailer, requires an estimate of inventory cost for a quarterly financial report to the owner on March 31, 2020. In the past, the gross margin method was used because of the difficulty and expense of taking a physical inventory at interim dates. The company sells both fiction and nonfiction books. Due to their lower turnover rate, nonfiction books are typically marked up at 60% on cost. Fiction, on the other hand, has a 40% markup rate on cost. The manager has used an average markup of 50% to estimate interim inventories. You are asked by the manager to estimate inventory cost as of March 31, 2020. The following data are available.

	Fiction	Nonfiction	Total
Inventory, January 1, 2020	$ 200,000	$ 80,000	$ 280,000
Purchases	1,200,000	400,000	1,600,000
Freight	10,000	4,000	14,000
Sales	1,180,000	320,000	1,500,000

Required

a. Using an estimated markup on cost of 50%, estimate inventory as of March 31, 2020, based on the gross margin method applied to combined fiction and nonfiction books. Round gross margin ratios to three decimals.

b. Estimate ending inventory as of March 31, 2020, based on the gross profit method applied separately to fiction and nonfiction books. Round gross margin ratios to three decimals.

c. Explain which method is preferable in this situation.

AD&J 10-91 Recording a Loss in Applying Lower-of-Cost-or-Net Realizable Value **LO1, 3, 5, 6, 7**

Codification Skills Refer to the Codification and identify the definition for each of the following: (1) market, (2) net realizable value, (3) firm purchase commitment, (4) change in accounting principle, and (5) error.

AD&J 10-92 Researching the Codification for Proper Citation **LO2, 5, 6**

Codification Skills Research the Codification and report the proper citation that provides guidance on each of the following topics.

a. Application of the lower-of-cost-or-market rule. FASB ASC ___-___-___-___

b. Application of lower-of-cost-or-market to total inventory or to inventory categories. FASB ASC ___-___-___-___

c. Recording purchase commitment losses. FASB ASC ___-___-___-___

d. Conditions making retrospective treatment for a change in accounting principle impracticable. FASB ASC ___-___-___-___

AD&J 10-93 Researching the Codification for Authoritative Guidance **LO1**

Codification Skills A company is preparing annual financial statements, which includes the valuation of inventory previously marked down to net realizable value. Currently, the net realizable value of the inventory is greatly improved due to changing market conditions. The company would like to reverse the write-down to net realizable value to reflect the current value of the inventory. Identify the relevant authoritative guidance.

FASB ASC ___-___-___-___

Appendix—Questions

10-94. What are the primary differences between the dollar-value LIFO retail method and the retail inventory method under average cost?

10-95. When dollar-value LIFO retail is adopted, why must the ending inventory of the period prior to the base year often be recomputed?

Appendix—Brief Exercises

APP—Brief Exercise 10-96 Estimating Inventory Using LIFO Retail Method **LO9**

Dean Company uses the retail inventory method to estimate its inventory for interim statement purposes. Data relating to the inventory at July 31, 2020, follow. Estimate inventory at July 31, 2020, using the LIFO retail method.

	Cost	Retail
Beginning inventory, January 31, 2020	$ 180,000	$ 250,000
Purchases	1,020,000	1,575,000
Markups, net		175,000
Sales		1,725,000
Markdowns, net		125,000

APP—Brief Exercise 10-97 Estimating Inventory Using Dollar-Value LIFO Retail Method **LO9**

On December 31, 2019, Jason Company adopted the dollar-value LIFO retail inventory method. Inventory data for 2020 follow. Estimate inventory at December 31, 2020, using the dollar-value LIFO retail method.

	LIFO Cost	Retail
Inventory, December 31, 2019	$360,000	$500,000
Inventory, December 31, 2020	?	660,000
Increase in price level for 2020	10%	
Cost to retail ratio for 2020	70%	

Appendix—Exercises

APP—Exercise 10-98 Estimating Inventory Using Retail Inventory Method—LIFO **LO9** *Hint:* See Demo 10-9A

The following data from 2020 are for Rand Stores. On January 1, 2020, it adopted the LIFO retail method when its beginning inventory was $200 at cost and $333 at retail.

Year	Purchases at Cost	Purchases at Retail	Net Additional Markups	Net Additional Markdowns	Sales	Index
2020	$800	$1,400	$0	$30	$1,300	104

Required

Compute inventory value under the LIFO retail method for the year 2020.

APP—Exercise 10-99 Estimating Inventory Using Retail Inventory Method—Dollar-Value LIFO **LO9** *Hint:* See Demo 10-9B

The following data for Randolf Stores is for years 2020 through 2022. On January 1, 2020, it adopted the dollar-value LIFO retail method when its beginning inventory was $200 at cost and $333 at retail.

Year	Purchases at Cost	Purchases at Retail	Net Additional Markups	Net Additional Markdowns	Sales	Index
2020	$ 800	$1,400	$ 50	$ 30	$1,300	104
2021	1,000	1,600	100	140	1,450	108
2022	1,300	2,340	200	270	2,400	110

Required

Compute inventory value under dollar-value LIFO retail method for each year 2020 through 2022.

APP—Exercise 10-100 Estimating Inventory Using Retail Inventory Method—Dollar-Value LIFO **LO9**

Ripley Retail used the retail inventory method, determined on a retail conventional basis, for a number of years for both external and internal reporting and for tax purposes. On January 1, 2021, it changed to dollar-value LIFO retail for both external reporting and income tax purposes, but retained average cost with the conventional method for internal purposes. At year-end 2020 and 2021, the retail inventory computations (conventional method) for internal purposes follow.

	Year 2020		Year 2021	
	At Cost	At Retail	At Cost	At Retail
Beginning inventory, January 1	$ 17,000	$ 30,000	$ 28,000	$ 50,000
Purchases	151,000	268,000	175,450	325,000
Net additional markups		2,000		3,000
Total	$168,000	300,000	$203,450	
Cost ratio	0.56		0.54	
Sales		(245,000)		(305,000)
Net markdowns		(5,000)		(9,000)
Inventory, December 31				
At retail		$ 50,000		$ 64,000
At cost (conventional method)	$ 28,000		$ 34,560	

Required

a. Compute inventory values (at cost and at retail) that are used as the base inventory and the ending inventory for 2021 for conversion purposes. Explain why conventional retail inventory values are not appropriate for this purpose. Round cost ratios to two decimals.

b. Convert the FIFO retail inventory results computed in part *a* to the dollar-value LIFO retail basis for external reports and income tax use at the end of 2021. The price index for 2021 is 1.12. Round cost ratios to two decimals.

APP—Exercise 10-101
Estimating and Recording Inventory Using Retail Inventory Method—Dollar-Value LIFO and Conventional **LO9**

Anderson Company used the retail inventory method for a number of years. On January 1, 2021, the company changed to dollar-value LIFO retail for external reporting and income tax purposes. The following data are available from its inventory records for the year ended December 31, 2020.

For Year Ended December 31	At Cost	At Retail
January 1, 2020, inventory	$48,000	$ 95,000
Purchases	80,000	170,000
Net additional markups		4,000
Net markdowns		8,000
Sales revenue		190,000

Required

a. Compute the December 31, 2020, retail inventory balance using (round cost ratios to three decimals)
1. Conventional retail method
2. FIFO method

b. Prepare the adjusting entry to restate inventory to FIFO, and to be used as the base inventory for the dollar-value LIFO retail method, assuming it had been using the conventional retail method. Round cost ratios to three decimals.

Appendix—Problems

APP—Problem 10-102
Estimating Ending Inventory Using Dollar-Value LIFO Retail Inventory Method **LO9**

Tonbon Retailers maintains its internal inventory records on a FIFO (not lower-of-cost-or-market) basis. At interim reporting dates, Tonbon converts its book balances to a LIFO basis for reporting purposes by using the dollar-value LIFO retail method. The following data for the quarter ended March 31, 2021, are available.

For Quarter Ended March 31, 2021	At Cost	At Retail
Base layer from 2019 (when LIFO was adopted); index = 100	$ 19,750	$ 38,500
Additional LIFO layer added in 2020; index = 104; cost ratio = 0.60	30,900	51,500
Beginning inventory, 2021; index = 110	49,500	90,000
Purchases (net)	231,000	400,000
Net additional markups		30,000
Net markdowns		10,000
Sales returns		6,000
Sales (gross)		396,000
Price index at end of March 2021 = 125		

Required

Compute ending inventory at March 31, 2021, assuming the dollar-value LIFO retail inventory method. Round all cost ratios and price index ratios to three decimals.

APP—Problem 10-103 Estimating Ending Inventory Using Retail Inventory Methods **LO9**

Burrbery's Department Store reports the following data for 2021. Burrbery's external price index is 100 for 2020, and 105 for 2021. (Round cost ratios to 3 decimals.)

For Year Ended December 31, 2021	At Cost	At Retail
Beginning inventory (FIFO cost)	$ 750	$ 1,500
Purchases	30,000	52,500
Markups		4,500
Markup cancellations		1,500
Markdowns		3,750
Markdown cancellations		3,000
Sales		37,500

Required

a. Estimate ending inventory using the conventional retail method.
b. Estimate ending inventory using the average cost method.
c. Estimate ending inventory using the dollar-value LIFO retail method.

APP—Problem 10-104 Estimating Ending Inventory Using Retail Inventory Method—Dollar-Value LIFO **LO9**

Black Company changed to the dollar-value LIFO retail method for external reporting and income tax purposes on January 1, 2019. The following data are available from Black's records for the year ended December 31, 2020.

For Year Ended December 31, 2020	At Cost	At Retail
Purchases	$140,000	$200,000
Net additional markups		8,000
Net markdowns		8,000
Sales		160,000

The December 31, 2019, ending inventory was $176,000 at retail and $102,900 at dollar-value LIFO cost. Relevant external price indexes are: 2018 (base year) = 110; 2019 = 121; and 2020 = 126.5.

Required

Compute the December 31, 2020, ending inventory using the dollar-value LIFO retail method. Round all cost ratios to three decimals. *Hint*: New price ratios using 2018 as the base year (index = 100) must be computed.

APP—Problem 10-105 Estimating Ending Inventory Using Retail Inventory Method—LIFO **LO9**

Babel Inc. incorporated and started its operations in 2019. At that time, the company elected the LIFO retail inventory method to estimate ending inventory. The following data are available for Babel.

For Year Ended December 31, 2020	At Cost	At Retail
Beginning inventory	$ 25,000	$ 36,000
Purchases	120,000	156,000
Net additional markups		16,000
Net markdowns		10,000
Sales		160,000

Required

With no price level changes in 2020, estimate ending inventory on December 31, 2020, using the LIFO retail inventory method.

Answers to Review Exercises

Review 10-1

a. $14,860; computed as ($2,500 + $5,840 + $900 + $1,200 + $1,720 + $2,700).

b. **June 30, 2020—To adjust inventory to lower-of-cost-or-net realizable value**

Cost of Goods Sold ($15,300 − $14,860)	440	
Allowance to Reduce Inventory to Net Realizable Value		440

Assets = Liabilities + Equity
−3,500 −3,500
Allow to Reduce Inv: 440 (credit)
COGS: 440 (debit)

Review 10-2

a. #110: $800, #115: $1,120, #125: $560, #210: $1,740, #220: $400, #225: $1,620.

b. **June 30, 2020—To adjust inventory to lower-of-cost-or-market**

Assets = Liabilities + Equity
−780 −780
Inventory Allow: 780 (credit) | COGS: 780 (debit)

Cost of Goods Sold	780	
Allowance to Reduce Inventory to Market Value		780

Review 10-3

a. **June 1, 2020—To record purchase of lots**

Assets = Liabilities + Equity
+600,000
−600,000
Inventory: 600,000 (debit) | Cash: 600,000 (credit)

Inventory—Executive Lots	266,667	
Inventory—Premium Lots	280,000	
Inventory—Standard Lots	53,333	
Cash		600,000

b. **June 1, 2020—Computation of remaining inventory**

Inventory—Executive Lots ($266,667 x 4/10)	$106,667
Inventory—Premium Lots ($280,000 x 5/15)	93,333
Inventory—Standard Lots ($53,333 x 1/5)	10,667
Total	$210,667

Review 10-4

$190,000; computed as ($1,750,000 − [$2,000,000 × 0.77] − $20,000)

Review 10-5

a. **May 1, 2020—No entry required.**

b. **December 31, 2020—To record loss on purchase commitment**

Assets = Liabilities + Equity
+160,000 −160,000
Liab on Purch Comm: 160,000 (credit) | Loss on Purch Comm: 160,000 (debit)

Estimated Loss on Purchase Commitment	160,000	
Estimated Liability on Purchase Commitment		160,000

c. **March 25, 2021—To record purchase of inventory**

Assets = Liabilities + Equity
+1,360,000 −160,000 −80,000
−1,600,000
Inventory: 1,360,000 (debit) | Liab on Purch Comm: 160,000 (debit) 160,000 (credit)
Cash: 1,600,000 (credit) | Loss on Purch Cont: 80,000 (debit)

Inventory	1,360,000	
Estimated Liability on Purchase Commitment	160,000	
Loss on Purchase Contract	80,000	
Cash		1,600,000

Review 10-6

a. **January 1, 2021—To record retrospective adjustment**

Assets = Liabilities + Equity
−60,000 −60,000
Inventory: Bal. 150,000 (debit) 60,000 (credit) | Ret Earnings: 60,000 (debit)

Retained Earnings	60,000	
Inventory ($150,000 - $90,000)		60,000

b. December 31, 2020, balance sheet: Inventory $90,000

Review 10-7

a. understated, unaffected, overstated, unaffected.

b. overstated, understated, understated, unaffected.

c. understated, overstated, overstated, unaffected.

d. overstated, understated, understated, unaffected.

e. unaffected, understated, unaffected, unaffected.

Review 10-8

$58,880; computed as ($115,000[a] × 0.512[b])

[a] $250,000 + $960,000 − $1,000,000 − $85,000 − $10,000 = $115,000

[b] ($120,000 + $500,000)/($250,000 + $960,000) = 0.512

Review 10-9

Part One: $320 (($380 × 0.658[c]) + ($135 × 0.519[d]))

[c] $250/$380 = 0.658

[d] $900/($1,700 + $115 − $80) = 0.519

Part Two: December 31, 2020: $233; from (($333 × 1.00 × 0.60) + ($55 × 1.04 × 0.58))
December 31, 2021: $328; from ($233 + ($144 × 1.06 × 0.62))

11 Property, Plant, and Equipment: Acquisition and Disposition

NIKE, Inc. Consolidated Balance Sheets

(In millions)	May 31, 2017	May 31, 2016
ASSETS		
Current assets:		
Cash and equivalents	$ 3,808	$ 3,138
Short-term investments	2,371	2,319
Accounts receivable, net	3,677	3,241
Inventories	5,055	4,838
Prepaid expenses and other current assets	1,150	1,489
Total current assets	16,061	15,025
Property, plant and equipment, net	3,989	3,520
Identifiable intangible assets, net	283	281
Goodwill	139	131
Deferred income taxes and other assets	2,787	2,422
TOTAL ASSETS	$23,259	$21,379

Property, Plant and Equipment and Depreciation

Property, plant and equipment are recorded at cost. Depreciation is determined on a straight-line basis for land improvements, buildings and leasehold improvements over 2 to 40 years and for machinery and equipment over 2 to 15 years.

Depreciation and amortization of assets used in manufacturing, warehousing and product distribution are recorded in *Cost of sales*. Depreciation and amortization of all other assets are recorded in *Operating overhead expense*.

NOTE 3 — Property, Plant and Equipment

...nd equipment, net included the following:

	As of May 31, 2017	As of May 31, 2016
	$ 285	$ 286
...ements	1,564	1,467
...pment and internal-use software	3,867	3,510
...rovements	1,484	1,338
...process	758	437
..., plant and equipment, gross	7,958	7,038
...lated depreciation	3,969	3,518
TOTAL PROPERTY, PLANT AND EQUIPMENT, NET	**$ 3,989**	**$ 3,520**

Capitalized interest was not material for the years ended May 31, 2017 , 2016 and 2015 .

Chapter Preview

Accounting principles governing the reporting of property, plant, and equipment are important given the enormous investment in such assets. These assets provide the infrastructure by which companies conduct their business and generate revenue. This chapter describes categories of property, plant, and equipment and the proper classification of acquisition costs. Acquisitions can take place in many ways, and we explain the accounting treatment for lump-sum acquisitions, acquisitions through debt and equity issuances, and acquisitions through donations. We explore two additional categories of costs that increase the asset base of fixed assets: interest capitalization and asset retirement obligations. We also examine accounting implications of activities subsequent to asset acquisition including expenditures on improvements and repairs, disposals, and asset exchanges.

Action Plan

LO	Topic/Subtopic	Page	Demos	Reviews	Assignments
LO 11–1	**Determine costs to capitalize for land, land improvements, equipment, buildings, and construction in process** Land :: Land Improvements :: Equipment :: Buildings :: Construction in Process :: Self-Constructed Assets	11-3	D11-1A D11-1B	R11-1	23, 24, 33, 43, 44, 45, 46, 47, 48, 64, 71, 72, 73, 74, 75, 78, 88, 90, 91, 92, 93, 95
LO 11–2	**Determine costs to capitalize for lump-sum purchases of property, plant, and equipment** Lump-Sum Purchase :: Relative Fair Value :: Proportional Method :: Incremental Method	11-7	D11-2	R11-2	25, 49, 50, 71, 75
LO 11–3	**Account for acquisition of property, plant, and equipment through debt and equity issuances** Acquisition with Debt :: Note Payable :: Discount on Note Payable :: Acquisition with Equity :: Common Stock	11-9	D11-3A D11-3B	R11-3	26, 27, 43, 51, 52, 53, 71, 73, 74, 87, 95
LO 11–4	**Account for acquisition of property, plant, and equipment through donation** Acquisition through Donation :: Fair Value :: Contribution Revenue	11-12	D11-4	R11-4	28, 54, 71, 74
LO 11–5	**Calculate capitalized interest** Interest Capitalization :: Qualifying Assets :: Actual Interest :: Avoidable Interest :: Weighted Average Accumulated Expenditures	11-13	D11-5	R11-5	29, 30, 31, 44, 55, 56, 57, 58, 71, 75, 76, 77, 78, 86, 96
LO 11–6	**Account for asset retirement obligations** Asset Retirement Obligation :: Present Value :: Depreciation :: Accretion	11-18	D11-6	R11-6	32, 59, 71, 79, 94, 95, 96, 97
LO 11–7	**Account for property, plant, and equipment related costs after acquisition** Maintenance and Ordinary Repairs :: Improvements and Replacements :: Additions :: Rearrangements	11-20	D11-7	R11-7	33, 50, 60, 61, 62, 71, 72, 74, 80, 89
LO 11–8	**Account for disposal of property, plant, and equipment** Voluntary Disposal :: Involuntary Disposal :: Update Depreciation Expense :: Gain or Loss on Disposal	11-23	D11-8	R11-8	34, 35, 36, 37, 63, 64, 71, 72, 80, 81, 85
LO 11–9	**Account for exchange of property, plant, and equipment** Asset Exchange :: Commercial Substance :: Lack of Commercial Substance :: Gain or Loss on Exchange	11-25	D11-9A D11-9B	R11-9	38, 39, 40, 41, 42, 65, 66, 67, 68, 69, 70, 71, 73, 82, 83, 84, 95, 96

LO 11-1 Determine costs to capitalize for land, land improvements, equipment, buildings, and construction in process

LO 11-1 Overview

Accounting for Acquisition Costs
- Record at historical cost
- Include costs necessary to prepare asset for intended use
- Include land, improvements, equipment, buildings, and CIP

Tangible assets used in a company's operations have the following characteristics.

- Actively used in operations rather than held as investments or for resale.
- Expected to provide benefits beyond the current accounting period.
- Have physical substance.

Tangible assets used in a company's operations are generally reported in the noncurrent asset section of the balance sheet at historical cost under headings such as **property, plant, and equipment**; **plant assets**; or **fixed assets**. Historical cost is described in the authoritative guidance.

> **360-10-30-1** [The] historical cost of acquiring an asset includes the costs necessarily incurred to bring it to the condition and location necessary for its intended use.

Historical cost, arising from arm's-length transactions between unrelated parties, is considered objective and reliable. It represents the fair value of the asset at the time of acquisition. Historical cost is often criticized as irrelevant when prices of specific assets change subsequent to acquisition. Price changes can render the recorded book value of assets less meaningful. However, the difficulty of measuring the fair value of plant assets reliably is an obstacle to fair value measurement.

The expense recognition principle requires that costs be deferred or held in asset accounts until revenues are generated beyond the current accounting period. This means costs to obtain and to make a fixed asset ready for its intended use are capitalized because they are required to obtain the benefits expected of the asset. To **capitalize** a cost means to debit the acquisition cost to an appropriate asset account. It is important to classify expenditures correctly because an incorrect classification affects reported income for the entire life of the asset. For example, if costs are misclassified as capital expenditures and carried as asset accounts, then current income is overstated, and future income is understated by depreciation of those costs.

Straight-Line Depreciation $\frac{\text{Cost-Salvage Value}}{\text{Useful Life}}$

After plant assets are placed into service, the historical acquisition cost is allocated to expense through the process of depreciation. Depreciation expense is not recognized until the asset begins to produce benefits. Recall that we have been using the straight-line method to depreciate assets up to this point. Other depreciation methods are introduced in Chapter 12. While fixed assets are recorded at historical cost and depreciated, there are instances where the fair value of a fixed asset drops below its book value requiring recognition of a loss. Impairment of fixed assets is discussed in Chapter 12.

Categories of Fixed Assets

Exhibit 11-1 describes the categories of fixed assets, provides examples of acquisition costs, and describes the proper accounting treatment for each. **Demo 11-1A** applies these concepts.

Following are examples of items *excluded* from fixed assets. These items are expensed in the current period.

- Interest on debt incurred to purchase plant assets because the asset is already in its intended condition for use.
- Costs of training employees to use plant assets because training costs enhance the value of employees, not assets.
- Annual property taxes and insurance costs because these costs only maintain or protect the asset over the period.
- Ordinary repairs because they are expected to yield benefits only in the current period. However, major expenditures made subsequent to acquisition that produce a future benefit are capitalized (see LO 11-7).

EXHIBIT 11-1
Property, Plant, and Equipment Categories

Property, Plant, and Equipment	Examples of Acquisition Costs	Accounting Treatment
Land: Property currently in service as a building site or in other productive use.	▪ Purchase price, assumed property taxes, commissions, closing costs, legal fees, title search costs. ▪ Clearing, grading, filling, draining, and surveying, which are required for general land use and add permanent value to the land. ▪ Removing structures (razing costs) if land is acquired for redevelopment or use as a building site. (Proceeds from salvaged materials reduce the costs capitalized.) ▪ Assessments for local government-maintained improvements including streets, sidewalks, sewers, and streetlights.	Record at historical cost with *no* depreciation because the land value will not diminish over time or be exhausted by production activities.
Land Improvements: Site enhancements that are not permanent.	Driveways, parking lots, fencing, sprinkler systems, and landscaping.	Record at historical cost and depreciate over useful life because improvements are subject to damage, require maintenance, and must eventually be replaced.
Equipment: Tangible property used in the company's operations.	Purchase price (net of purchase discounts[1]) or manufactured cost, installation, sales tax, freight, ownership registration, legal costs, trial runs, testing costs.	Record at historical cost and depreciate over useful life.
Buildings: Permanent or temporary structures used in a company's operations (excluding the cost of land).	Purchase price or manufactured cost, commissions, inspection costs.	Record at historical cost and depreciate over useful life.
Construction in process (also called **construction in progress):**[2] Plant assets (such as equipment or building) in the process of being manufactured for a company's own use.	Self-constructed asset: ▪ Incremental direct material and direct labor costs incurred to produce the asset. ▪ Allocated variable and fixed overhead costs (indirect manufacturing costs such as utility costs, insurance, supervision, and equipment maintenance)[3] incurred to produce the asset. ▪ Architectural fees, cost of permits, excavation costs, professional fees, and interest costs[4] paid to construct a building. Fixed assets constructed by other companies: ▪ Progress billings and other construction costs.	▪ Costs accumulate *in construction in process* while the asset is under construction and are reported as a long-term asset. ▪ Costs shift from construction in process to *equipment* or *building* upon completion. **Depreciate the asset only upon completion and placement into service.** ▪ Any costs incurred for a self-constructed asset above the fair value of a similar asset should be expensed as incurred.

[1] Discounts not taken may be recorded by companies as a financing expense, rather than as an increase to the asset balance.

[2] Because construction in process is not actively used in production, it is not an operational asset. However, construction in process is often shown as part of property, plant, and equipment on the balance sheet.

[3] Under full-costing, a company prorates indirect costs to construction in process. However, a company can choose to apply no *indirect* costs to construction in process, but instead expense such costs as incurred.

[4] Interest costs related to borrowings for construction projects are discussed under LO 11-5.

Demo 11-1A LO11-1 Acquisition Costs Classified as Property, Plant, & Equipment

Demo MBC

Vista Company recently acquired several plant assets and began construction on a building. (a) Classify the costs incurred by Vista into the account categories of land, land improvement, equipment, building, construction in process, and period expense. (b) Record the summary journal entry required assuming all purchases were in cash, and construction of the building is still underway at period-end.

(a) Cost Incurred	**Amount**	**Land**	**Land Improvement**	**Equipment**	**Building**	**Construction in Process**	**Period Expense**
Invoice price of equipment	$ 50,000			$50,000			
2% cash discount taken on equipment purchase	(1,000)			(1,000)			
4% sales tax on equipment . . .	2,000			2,000			
Insurance and freight on equipment purchase	600			600			
Cost of land parcel	100,000	$100,000					
Commission and title insurance on land purchase	7,000	7,000					
Setup, testing, and practice runs on equipment	2,000			2,000			
Cost to train employees on equipment.	500						$ 500
Interest on debt incurred to purchase equipment	1,200						1,200
Cost to remove structures from land.	30,000	30,000					
Proceeds on materials salvaged from structures removed	(2,000)	(2,000)					
Excavation of foundation	3,500					$ 3,500	
Surveying and grading	12,000	12,000					
Concrete and labor for foundation.	26,000					26,000	
Property tax paid for the four months after the land acquisition.	550						550
Asphalt for parking lot.	11,000		11,000				
Fencing for property	6,000		6,000				
Total		**$147,000**	**$17,000**	**$53,600**	**$0**	**$29,500**	**$2,250**

(b) Vista Company would record the following summary journal entry.

Assets = Liabilities + Equity
+247,100 −2,250
−249,350

PP&E		CIP	
217,600		29,500	

Cash		Expense	
	249,350	2,250	

To record expenditures during the year

Land	147,000	
Land Improvement.	17,000	
Equipment	53,600	
Construction in Process	29,500	
Training Expense	500	
Interest Expense.	1,200	
Property Tax Expense	550	
Cash		249,350

Accumulated costs in Construction in Process are reclassified to Building after completion of the building.

Self-Constructed Assets

The actual cost of a self-constructed asset does not necessarily equal fair value. If total construction costs exceed the fair value of a similar asset of equal capacity and quality, the excess is recognized as a *loss* in the period incurred—see **Demo 11-1B**. Consistent with the valuation of other assets, the maximum valuation allowed for self-constructed assets is fair value. Failure to do so carries forward cost elements that have no future benefit, causing overstated depreciation in future years.

Self-Constructed Assets — LO11-1 — Demo 11-1B

Demo MBC

Kalvin Inc. completes a project to manufacture equipment with total construction in process costs as follows.

Materials	$200,000
Labor	500,000
Incremental overhead	60,000
Applied general overhead	40,000
Total	$800,000

a. Prepare the summary journal entry on June 1, 2020, to transfer costs from construction in process to equipment if the equipment's fair value at completion is $820,000.

b. Prepare the summary journal entry on June 1, 2020, to transfer costs from construction in process to equipment if the equipment's fair value at completion is $780,000.

Solution

a. **Fair Value Exceeds Construction Costs**

Cost of construction is less than the fair value of equipment. Thus, the equipment is recorded at the cost of construction.

June 1, 2020—To transfer costs from construction in process to equipment

Equipment	800,000	
Construction in Process		800,000

Assets = Liabilities + Equity
+800,000
−800,000

Equipment		CIP	
800,000		Bal. 800,000	800,000

b. **Construction Costs Exceed Fair Value**

Fair value of equipment exceeds construction costs. The excess of fair value over construction costs is expensed in the current period as a loss.

June 1, 2020—To transfer costs from construction in process to equipment

Equipment	780,000	
Loss on Construction of Equipment	20,000	
Construction in Process		800,000

Assets = Liabilities + Equity
+780,000 −20,000
−800,000

Equipment		Loss on Construct	
780,000		20,000	

CIP	
Bal. 800,000	800,000

Real World—PROPERTY AND EQUIPMENT

TARGET CORP. [TGT]

Target Corporation reports five categories of property and equipment including construction-in-progress in its recent report on Form 10-K. Net property and equipment made up 63% of total assets for its two fiscal years reported.

Property and equipment ($ millions)	January 30, 2016	January 31, 2015
Land	$ 6,125	$ 6,127
Buildings and improvements	27,059	26,613
Fixtures and equipment	5,347	5,329
Computer hardware and software	2,617	2,552
Construction-in-progress	315	424
Accumulated depreciation	(16,246)	(15,093)
Property and equipment, net	$25,217	$25,952

REVIEW 11-1 **LO11-1** **Property, Plant, and Equipment Cost Classification**

Review MBC

Sterling Company holds fixed assets at a number of locations and incurred the following costs for the year ended December 31, 2020. Classify the costs incurred by Sterling into the account categories of (1) land, (2) land improvement, (3) equipment, (4) building, (5) construction in process, and (6) period expense. Assume that the construction of the building is still underway while the self-constructed equipment is complete as of December 31, 2020. Cost of the self-constructed equipment is less than the fair value of the equipment.

a. Invoice price of new equipment purchased.
b. Installation costs of equipment purchased.
c. Cost of insurance purchased for coverage during shipment of equipment to its facility.
d. Cost of equipment modifications necessary during the installment process.
e. Purchase price of land intended for use for a new facility.
f. Legal fees associated with the review of the contract to purchase the land.
g. Property taxes for the first year after purchase.
h. Costs to demolish existing building on the new property.
i. Costs of clearing and filling land.
j. Costs of paving the parking lot.
k. Costs of adding lighting to the parking area.
l. Architecture fees for plans for the new building.
m. First billing for construction on building by outside contractor.
n. Materials costs of self-constructed equipment.
o. Labor costs of self-constructed equipment.
p. Manufacturing overhead costs applied to self-constructed equipment.

More Practice: 11-45, 11-46

Solution on p. 11-47.

LO 11-2 Determine costs to capitalize for lump-sum purchases of property, plant, and equipment

LO 11-2 Overview

Lump-Sum Purchase

- **Proportional Method:** Allocate lump-sum cost to individual items based upon relative fair value of individual items
- **Incremental Method:** Allocate part of lump-sum cost to the asset(s) with a determinable fair value, and the remainder to the other asset

Sometimes several fixed assets are acquired for a single lump-sum price that might be lower than the sum of the individual asset prices to induce a larger purchase. In other cases, the assets are attached, as in the case of land and a building. This type of acquisition, called a **lump-sum purchase**, or **basket purchase**, requires allocation of a portion of the single lump-sum price to each asset acquired.

If the goods purchased are identical in nature, the purchase price is allocated evenly to the goods. If however, the goods are not identical, the allocation of the purchase price is based on the best available indicator of the **relative fair values** of the assets. Possible indicators include market prices of similar assets, current appraised value, assessed value for property tax purposes, expected manufacturing cost savings, and the present value of estimated future net cash flows.

Two methods are common in allocation of costs to assets under a lump-sum purchase—see **Demo 11-2**.

- **Proportional method** Each fixed asset is valued according to the ratio of its fair value to the total fair value of the group of fixed assets.
- **Incremental method** If the value of only the first of two assets in a group is determinable, the second asset is valued at the cost remaining to be allocated.

Under either method, the portions of the lump-sum price *directly attributable* to particular assets in the group are assigned in full to those assets. For example, land appraisal costs are assigned only to the land account. Allocation of the remaining lump-sum purchase price is then made to each asset.

Lump-Sum Purchase

LO11-2 **Demo 11-2**

Demo MBC

Example One—Proportional Method of Allocating Lump-Sum Purchase

The negotiated acquisition price paid for land, storage facility, and equipment for a purchase on December 1, 2020, is $90,000. These assets are individually appraised (as the best available indication of value in this case) as follows: land, $30,000; storage facility, $50,000; and equipment, $20,000. Allocate the single lump-sum price using the proportional method and record the entry for the purchase.

Solution

Proportional allocation

Land	$ 30,000	($30,000/$100,000) or 30%
Storage facility	50,000	($50,000/$100,000) or 50%
Equipment	20,000	($20,000/$100,000) or 20%
	$100,000	

Allocation of lump-sum sale price of $90,000

Land (30% × $90,000)	$27,000
Storage facility (50% × $90,000)	45,000
Equipment (20% × $90,000)	18,000
	$90,000

December 1, 2020—To record lump-sum purchase

Land	27,000	
Storage facility	45,000	
Equipment	18,000	
Cash		90,000

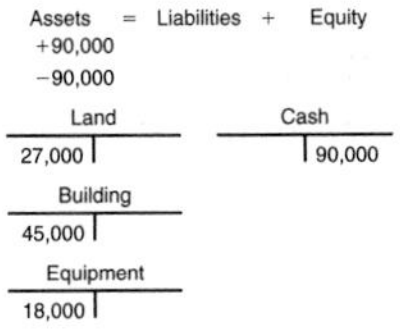

Example Two—Incremental Method of Allocating Lump-Sum Purchase

The negotiated acquisition price paid for land, storage facility, and equipment for a purchase on December 1, 2020, is $90,000. While the land and the storage facility are appraised at $30,000 and $50,000, respectively, the fair value of the equipment is indeterminable because it is highly specialized. Allocate the single lump-sum price using the incremental method and record the entry for the purchase transaction.

Solution

Incremental allocation

Land	$30,000	
Storage facility	50,000	
Equipment	10,000	($90,000 − $30,000 − $50,000)
	$90,000	

December 1, 2020—To record lump-sum purchase

Land	30,000	
Storage facility	50,000	
Equipment	10,000	
Cash		90,000

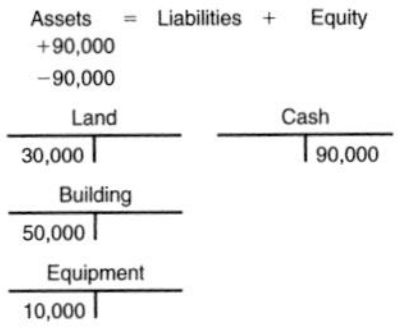

REVIEW 11-2 **LO11-2** **Lump-Sum Purchase**

Review MBC

Allied Construction purchased a total of five printer-and-desk sets from Office Supplies for a combined purchase price of $600 for each set. Office Supplies sells the items on an individual basis as follows: printer, $300; desk, $350.

Required

Allocate the single lump-sum purchase price using the proportional method. Prepare the journal entry for the purchase transaction.

More Practice: 11-25, 11-49
Solution on p. 11-48.

LO 11-3 Account for acquisition of property, plant, and equipment through debt and equity issuances

LO 11-3 Overview

Acquisition of Property, Plant, and Equipment
- ***Debt*** Record either at the fair value of the fixed asset or at the present value of debt payments, whichever is more objective and reliable
- ***Equity*** Record either at the fair value of the fixed asset or at the fair value of securities issued, whichever is more objective and reliable

Property, plant, and equipment is not only purchased through asset disbursements, but can also be purchased through the issuance of debt (See **Demo 11-3A**) or equity (See **Demo 11-3B**).

Acquisition of Property, Plant, and Equipment Using Debt

In accordance with the cost principle, the recorded cost of an asset purchased on credit (a deferred payment) is based on one of the following, whichever is more objective and reliable.

- Fair value of the fixed asset.
- Present value of the future cash payments required by the debt agreement discounted at the prevailing (market) interest rate for that type of debt.

Equipment can be purchased with a formalized debt arrangement with a creditor such as a **note payable.** A note payable typically requires the debtor to pay interest (recognized as interest expense) over the term of the note. If a fixed asset is purchased through the issuance of a note payable requiring interest payments at the market rate of interest, the acquisition is recorded at the face value of the note payable.

If the note payable does *not* bear interest (or the interest rate is *below* the market rate of interest) and the current cash price of the asset is determinable, the excess to be paid over the cash price is treated as interest expense and is allocated over the term of the debt. If the cash price is *not* determinable, the prevailing interest rate is used to determine total interest cost and to compute the asset's present value for recording purposes. The valuation of assets acquired in exchange for debt securities is similar to the valuation of long-term notes receivable, discussed in Chapter 8.

Demo 11-3A **LO11-3** **Acquisition of Equipment Using a Note Payable**

Demo MBC

Example One—Acquisition of Equipment through a Noninterest-Bearing Note, Prevailing Interest Rate Known

Feller Company acquires a machine on January 1, 2020, with a noninterest-bearing, two-year note. The note has no stated rate, but the prevailing interest rate is 10% on liabilities of similar risk and duration. The face amount of the note is $25,000. Record the required journal entries on January 1, 2020, December 31, 2020, and December 31, 2021. Ignore depreciation entries for the asset.

Solution

	RATE	NPER	PV	FV	Excel Formula
Given	10%	2	?	(25,000)	PV(0.10,2,0,-25000)
Solution			$20,661		

The cash equivalent cost of the machine is unknown; so, the asset is recorded at the present value of the note discounted at 10%, which is $20,661.

continued

continued from previous page

The difference between the present value (fair value) of the equipment of $20,661 and the note payable amount of $25,000 is included in the account, **Discount on Note Payable** (a contra liability account) for $4,339. On January 1, 2020, the net liability balance is $20,661, which is the note payable of $25,000 less the discount of $4,339. The discount is recognized as interest expense over the life of the note under the effective interest method. Feller's entries over the life of the note to record the asset, recognize interest expense on the note, and record payment on the note follow.

January 1, 2020—To acquire equipment by issuing a note

Equipment	20,661	
Discount on Note Payable ($25,000 − $20,661)	4,339	
Note Payable		25,000

Assets = Liabilities + Equity
+20,661 = −4,339, +25,000
Equipment: 20,661 (Dr)
Note Payable: 25,000 (Cr)
Discount on NP: 4,339 (Dr)

December 31, 2020—To accrue interest on note payable

Interest Expense	2,066	
Discount on Note Payable ($20,661 × 0.10)		2,066

Assets = Liabilities + Equity
+2,066, −2,066
Interest Exp: 2,066 (Dr)
Note Payable: 4,339 (Dr) | 2,066 (Cr)

December 31, 2021—To record interest and payment on note payable

Note Payable	25,000	
Interest Expense	2,273	
Discount on Note Payable ([$20,661 + $2,066] × 0.10)		2,273
Cash		25,000

Assets = Liabilities + Equity
−25,000 = −25,000, +2,273, −2,273
Cash: 25,000 (Cr)
Note Payable: 25,000 (Dr) | 25,000 (Cr)
Interest Exp: 2,066, 2,273 (Dr)
Discount on NP: 4,339 (Dr) | 2,066, 2,273 (Cr)

Example Two—Acquisition of Equipment through a Noninterest-Bearing Note, Imputed Interest Rate

Feller Company acquires a machine on January 1, 2020, with a noninterest-bearing, two-year note. The note has no stated rate, and the prevailing interest rate of liabilities of similar risk and duration is unknown. The face amount of the note is $25,000. The purchase price of the equipment is $21,000. Record the required journal entries on January 1, 2020, December 31, 2020, and December 31, 2021. Ignore depreciation entries for the asset.

Solution

Because the note is noninterest-bearing and the market rate of interest on the note payable is unknown, the present value of the note is inferred from the fair value of the equipment. The interest rate is imputed from the fair value of the equipment and the terms of the note payable.

	RATE	NPER	PV	FV	Excel Formula
Given	?	2	21,000	(25,000)	*RATE(2,0,21000,−25000)*
Solution	9.109%				

The difference between the present value (fair value) of the equipment of $21,000 and the face value of the note payable of $25,000 is a discount of $4,000. On January 1, 2020, the net liability balance is $21,000 or the note payable of $25,000 less the discount of $4,000. The discount is recognized as interest expense over the life of the note under the effective interest method, applying an effective interest rate of 9.109%. Feller's entries over the life of the note to record the asset, recognize interest expense on the note, and record payment on the note follow.

January 1, 2020—To acquire equipment by issuing a note

Equipment	21,000	
Discount on Note Payable ($25,000 − $21,000)	4,000	
Note Payable		25,000

Assets = Liabilities + Equity
+21,000 = −4,000, +25,000
Equipment: 21,000 (Dr)
Note Payable: 25,000 (Cr)
Discount on NP: 4,000 (Dr)

December 31, 2020—To accrue interest on note payable

Interest Expense	1,913	
Discount on Note Payable ($21,000 × 0.09109)		1,913

Assets = Liabilities + Equity
+1,913, −1,913
Interest Exp: 1,913 (Dr)
Discount on NP: 4,000 (Dr) | 1,913 (Cr)

December 31, 2021—To record interest and payment on note payable

Note Payable	25,000	
Interest Expense	2,087	
Discount on Note Payable ([$21,000 + $1,913] × 0.09109)		2,087
Cash		25,000

Assets = Liabilities + Equity
−25,000 = −25,000, +2,087, −2,087
Cash: 25,000 (Cr)
Note Payable: 25,000 (Dr) | 25,000 (Cr)
Interest Exp: 1,913, 2,087 (Dr)
Discount on NP: 4,000 (Dr) | 1,913, 2,087 (Cr)

Acquisition of Property, Plant, and Equipment Using Equity

When equity securities are issued to acquire plant assets, the assets are recorded either at the fair value of the asset or at the fair value of the securities issued, whichever is more objective and reliable. The fair value of the securities issued is typically reliable for publicly traded securities. If the shares are not publicly traded, a determination of the fair value of the fixed asset can be a more reliable measure of fair value.

Demo 11-3B **LO11-3** **Acquisition of Equipment Using Common Stock**

Demo MBC

On January 1, 2020, Medford Inc. purchases used equipment. The equipment is in reasonable condition but is not normally sold before the end of its useful life. Thus, the equipment has no reliable fair value. In payment for this equipment, Medford issues 2,000 shares of its common stock. Medford's common stock, with a $1 par, is publicly traded and currently trades at $10 per share. Medford has 10 million common shares outstanding. Record the purchase of the equipment on January 1, 2020.

Solution

The proper valuation for the equipment is 2,000 shares multiplied by $10, or $20,000. The purchase is recorded as follows.

Assets = Liabilities + Equity
+20,000 +2,000
+18,000

Equipment: 20,000 |
Common Stock: | 2,000
Paid-in Cap—CS: | 18,000

January 1, 2020—Purchase of equipment with common stock

Equipment ($10 × 2,000 shares)	20,000	
Common Stock ($1 × 2,000 shares)		2,000
Paid-in Capital in Excess of Par—Common Stock ($20,000 − $2,000). . .		18,000

CAMPBELL SOUP

Real World—FINANCING ACQUISITIONS

CAMPBELL SOUP CO. [CPB]

Campbell Soup Company reported in a recent Form 10-K that it financed the acquisition of the assets of Garden Fresh Gourmet through the issuance of commercial paper (debt).

> On June 29, 2015, we completed the acquisition of the assets of Garden Fresh Gourmet for approximately $230 million. Garden Fresh Gourmet is a provider of refrigerated salsa in North America, and it also produces hummus, dips and tortilla chips. We funded the Garden Fresh Gourmet acquisition through the issuance of commercial paper.

REVIEW 11-3 **LO11-3** **Acquisition of Property, Plant, and Equipment Using Debt and Equity**

Review MBC

On January 1, 2020, Silver Co. purchased equipment by making a $50,000 down payment and issuing a noninterest-bearing note for $200,000 due in two years. The fair value of the equipment is unknown. An 8% interest rate per year is typical of this transaction. The company amortizes interest expense using the effective interest method. Ignore any journal entries for depreciation expense.

Required

a. Prepare the entry to record the purchase on January 1, 2020.

b. Prepare the entry on December 31, 2020, to record interest expense.

c. Prepare the entry on December 31, 2021, to record interest expense and the full payment of the note.

d. Assume instead that Silver Co. issued 2,000 shares of its own $1 par value common stock in exchange for the equipment, along with the $50,000 down payment. At the date of exchange, the stock was trading on the market at $75 per share. Prepare the entry to record the equipment purchase.

More Practice: 11-52, 11-53
Solution on p. 11-48.

Account for acquisition of property, plant, and equipment through donation

LO 11-4

Shareholders and other parties occasionally donate assets and services to companies. For example, municipalities donate land and buildings to induce a company to locate in a particular area, thereby improving the local tax base and increasing employment. Fixed assets received as a contribution are recognized at fair value in the period received as illustrated in **Demo 11-4**. The fair value of the donated asset can be estimated through available fair values on similar assets or through appraisals. Along with the asset, the recipient records the receipt as contribution revenue, net of any amounts paid.

LO 11-4 Overview

Recipient of Donation
- Record asset(s) received at fair value
- Record contribution revenue at fair value

958-605-25-2 Contributions received shall be recognized as revenues or gains in the period received and as assets, decreases of liabilities, or expenses depending on the form of the benefits received.

Acquisition of a Building through Donation

LO11-4 **Demo 11-4**

On December 31, 2020, Melbourne Inc. donated a building (fair value $400,000) and the land on which it is located (fair value $100,000) to Standford Corporation. Standford incurred $5,000 of legal transfer costs. Record the donation received by Standford on December 31, 2020.

Solution

The following entry records Standford's receipt of the donated building and land.

December 31, 2020—To record donation received

Building	400,000	
Land	100,000	
Cash		5,000
Contribution Revenue ($500,000 − $5,000)		495,000

Assets = Liabilities + Equity
+400,000 +495,000
+100,000
−5,000

Building: 400,000 (debit)
Land: 100,000 (debit)
Cash: 5,000 (credit)
Contrib Rev: 495,000 (credit)

EXPANDING YOUR KNOWLEDGE — Accounting by the Donor

The donor of an asset records expense at fair value. Before recording the donation, the donor will record a gain or loss, if necessary, to adjust the asset to its fair value. If a donor pledges or promises to donate an asset in the future and the promise is unconditional, the donor records the expense and a liability at the time of the pledge. Referring to **Demo 11-4**, record the donation made by Melbourne Inc. on December 31, 2020, assuming that the carrying value of the building and land on Melbourne's books are $400,000 and $75,000, respectively, prior to donation.

Entries for the Donor (Melbourne)

December 31, 2020—To record increase in land value by donor

Land	25,000	
Gain on Disposal ($100,000 − $75,000)		25,000

Assets = Liabilities + Equity
+25,000 +25,000

Land: Bal. 75,000; 25,000 (debit)
Gain on Disposal: 25,000 (credit)

December 31, 2020—To record donation of land and building by donor

Contribution Expense	500,000	
Land		100,000
Building		400,000

Assets = Liabilities + Equity
−100,000 −500,000
−400,000

Land: Bal. 75,000; 25,000 (debit) | 100,000 (credit)
Contrib Exp: 500,000 (debit)
Building: Bal. 400,000 (debit) | 400,000 (credit)

Fixed Assets Acquired through Donation

LO11-4 **REVIEW 11-4**

Hanlon donated a building and the land on which it is located to Sustainable Solutions on December 31, 2020. The property was reliably appraised at a value of $500,000 (25% related to the land). Sustainable Solutions paid transfer costs of $5,000. The building has an estimated remaining life of 30 years (no residual value).

continued

continued from previous page

More Practice: 11-28, 11-54
Solution on p. 11-48.

Required

Prepare the entries for Sustainable Solutions to record the (a) transfer on December 31, 2020, and (b) depreciation for 2021. Assume a full year of depreciation and use of the straight-line method.

LO 11-5 Calculate capitalized interest

LO 11-5 Overview

Capitalized Interest
- Capitalize the lesser of actual interest or avoidable interest
- Include as part of fixed asset cost
- Depreciate over life of fixed asset
- Disclosures required

Interest cost incurred during the construction of a fixed asset is considered to be a cost necessary for placing the asset into its intended condition for use in the business. That is, the asset cannot generate revenue until it is completed, and the interest incurred until completion is capitalized (added to the asset balance) through a process called **interest capitalization**. When interest is capitalized, interest expense is reduced and the fixed asset account is increased. Capitalized interest is subsequently expensed as part of periodic depreciation expense. This process is illustrated in **Demo 11-5**.

835-20-10-1 The objectives of capitalizing interest are to obtain a measure of acquisition cost that more closely reflects an entity's total investment in the asset and to charge a cost that relates to the acquisition of a resource that will benefit future periods against the revenues of the periods benefited.

Calculation of Capitalized Interest

Interest is capitalized on **qualifying assets** or assets constructed for a company's own use or constructed as discrete projects for sale or lease, such as ships or real estate developments. Qualifying assets are *not* routinely produced. The capitalization period begins when three conditions are met as described in the accounting guidance.

835-20-25-3 The capitalization period shall begin when the following three conditions are present:
a. Expenditures for the asset have been made.
b. Activities that are necessary to get the asset ready for its intended use are in progress.
c. Interest cost is being incurred.
Interest capitalization shall continue as long as those three conditions are present.

If the first condition is not met, the conceptual basis for interest capitalization is absent. If the second condition is not met, construction activities are not the cause of the opportunity cost. If the third condition is not met, there is no interest to capitalize.

The amount of interest capitalized is the lesser of the following two measures.

- **Actual interest**—actual interest cost incurred on all debt outstanding.
- **Avoidable interest**—interest that the company could have avoided if it had not borrowed funds for the project.

835-20-30-2 The amount of interest cost to be capitalized for qualifying assets is intended to be that portion of the interest cost incurred during the assets' acquisition periods that theoretically could have been avoided (for example, by avoiding additional borrowings or by using the funds expended for the assets to repay existing borrowings) if expenditures for the assets had not been made.

835-20-30-6 The total amount of interest cost capitalized in an accounting period shall not exceed the total amount of interest cost incurred by the entity in that period.

Actual Interest

Total actual interest cost incurred during the capitalization period is calculated by multiplying the debt amount by the annual interest rate for the period the debt is outstanding. Actual interest is divided into two portions: **specific debt** (project related debt) and **general debt** (not directly related to the project). This allows us to determine separately the weighted average interest rate on specific debt and general debt. To compute the weighted average interest rate on general debt, divide the total interest on general debt by the total general debt amount. Interest revenue earned on borrowed funds not yet used for a construction project cannot offset the interest expense on that debt.

Avoidable Interest

The first step in the computation of avoidable interest is to compute the **weighted average accumulated expenditures**. We need to determine what interest could have been avoided if expenditures on constructed assets were applied instead to retire debt or for other needs. To compute weighted average accumulated expenditures, each capital expenditure is weighted for the period outstanding during the capitalization period. For example, if a capital expenditure took place on March 1, 2020, the expenditure receives a weight of 10/12 of a capitalization period of 12 months. In other words, cash was sacrificed from March 1 to December 31, which is 10 months out of the year. The individually weighted expenditures are added up to arrive at weighted average accumulated expenditures.

Avoidable interest is calculated by taking weighted average accumulated expenditures multiplied by an appropriate interest rate.

In determining which interest rate to use, first determine how much of the weighted average accumulated expenditures match up to specific debt. For example, if weighted average expenditures are $100,000 and specific debt is $75,000, avoidable interest includes $75,000 multiplied by the specific debt interest rate. The remaining weighted average expenditures of $25,000 ($100,000 less $75,000) is multiplied by the weighted average general debt interest rate.

835-20-30-3 If an entity's financing plans associate a specific new borrowing with a qualifying asset, the entity may use the rate on that borrowing as the capitalization rate to be applied to that portion of the average accumulated expenditures for the asset that does not exceed the amount of that borrowing. If average accumulated expenditures for the asset exceed the amounts of specific new borrowings associated with the asset, the capitalization rate to be applied to such excess shall be a weighted average of the rates applicable to other borrowings of the entity.

Land deserves special mention in the process of interest capitalization. When land is developed for sale, interest is capitalized and added to land cost based on expenditures made for its development. If land is to be used as a building site, the amount of interest capitalized on the land expenditures becomes part of the building cost (not land) and is depreciated over the life of the building. Idle land is not a qualifying asset; however, once construction commences, the historical cost of the land and expenditures to make the land ready for use are included in weighted average accumulated expenditures.

835-20-15-8 Land that is not undergoing activities necessary to get it ready for its intended use is not a qualifying asset. If activities are undertaken for the purpose of developing land for a particular use, the expenditures to acquire the land qualify for interest capitalization while those activities are in progress. The interest cost capitalized on those expenditures is a cost of acquiring the asset that results from those activities. If the resulting asset is a structure, such as a plant or a shopping center, interest capitalized on the land expenditures is part of the acquisition cost of the structure. If the resulting asset is developed land, such as land that is to be sold as developed lots, interest capitalized on the land expenditures is part of the acquisition cost of the developed land.

Capitalized interest (included as part of the fixed asset cost) is expensed through the normal depreciation process for fixed assets.

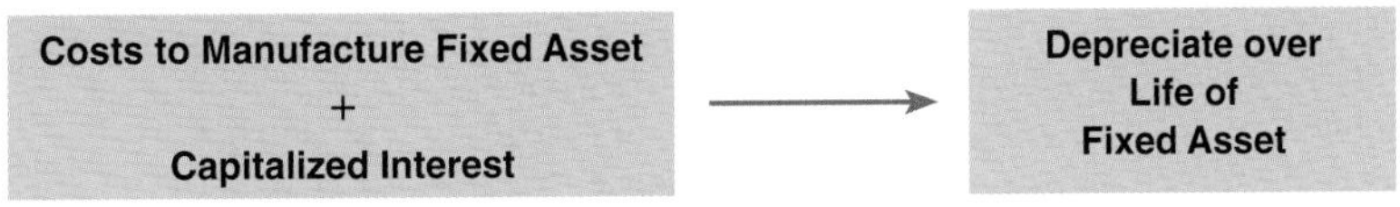

Companies must disclose total interest cost for the accounting period, including the capitalized and the amount expensed in its financial statements.

835-20-50-1 An entity shall disclose the following information with respect to interest cost in the financial statements or related notes:

a. For an accounting period in which no interest cost is capitalized, the amount of interest cost incurred and charged to expense during the period.

b. For an accounting period in which some interest cost is capitalized, the total amount of interest cost incurred during the period and the amount thereof that has been capitalized.

WAL-MART

Real World—INTEREST CAPITALIZATION

WAL-MART STORES INC. [WTM]

Wal-Mart Stores Inc. reports the following information in a recent Form 10-K. Property and equipment include construction in progress, which has no estimated useful life listed because it is not depreciated until placed in service. Related to the construction is information about interest capitalized, amounting to $39 million in 2016.

Property and equipment are stated at cost. Gains or losses on disposition are recognized as earned or incurred. Costs of major improvements are capitalized, while costs of normal repairs and maintenance are charged to expense as incurred. The following table summarizes the Company's property and equipment balances and includes the estimated useful lives that are generally used to depreciate the assets on a straight-line basis:

Fiscal Years Ended January 31 ($ millions)	Estimated Useful Lives	2016	2015
Land	N/A	$ 25,624	$ 26,261
Buildings and improvements	3–40 years	96,845	97,496
Fixtures and equipment	1–30 years	47,033	45,044
Transportation equipment	3–15 years	2,917	2,807
Construction in progress	N/A	4,539	5,787
Property and equipment		$176,958	$177,395
Accumulated depreciation		(66,787)	(63,115)
Property and equipment, net		$110,171	$114,280

Leasehold improvements are depreciated or amortized over the shorter of the estimated useful life of the asset or the remaining expected lease term. Total depreciation and amortization expense for property and equipment, property under financing obligations and property under capital leases for fiscal 2016, 2015 and 2014 was $9.4 billion, $9.1 billion and $8.8 billion, respectively. Interest costs capitalized on construction projects were $39 million, $59 million and $78 million in fiscal 2016, 2015 and 2014, respectively.

Demo 11-5 LO11-5 Interest Capitalization

Demo MBC

The following information is provided for Rodgers Inc. for a long-term construction project that is expected to be completed in the second quarter of 2021. The project is an addition to an existing stadium, which is a qualifying asset.

Capital Expenditures for 2020

Date	Actual Expenditures
January 1, 2020	$2,220,720
March 1, 2020	300,000
June 30, 2020	500,000
December 31, 2020	500,000

Outstanding Debt in 2020

Debt	Issuance Date	Debt Amount	Interest Rate
Construction loan	January 1, 2020	$ 800,000	12%
Note payable	January 1, 2020	1,000,000	13%
Note payable	March 1, 2019	600,000	8%
Bond payable	January 1, 2015	150,000	10%
Note payable	June 30, 2019	600,000	12%

a. Calculate actual interest for 2020 and the weighted average interest rate on general debt in 2020.

b. Calculate avoidable interest for 2020.

c. Record the journal entries in 2020 to record capital expenditures and interest. Show how Rodgers will disclose interest costs in its December 31, 2020, financial statements.

continued

continued from previous page

Solution

a. **Actual Interest Costs and Weighted Average Interest Rate on General Debt**

Actual interest costs and the weighted average interest rate on general date are computed as follows.

Debt	Issuance Date	Debt Amount	Interest Rate	Interest Amount
Specific Debt				
Construction loan	January 1, 2020	$ 800,000	12%	$ 96,000
		$ 800,000		$ 96,000
General Debt				
Note payable	January 1, 2020	$1,000,000	13%	$130,000
Note payable	March 1, 2019	600,000	8%	48,000
Bond payable	January 1, 2015	150,000	10%	15,000
Note payable	June 30, 2019	600,000	12%	72,000
		$2,350,000		$265,000
Total Interest ($96,000 + $265,000).				$361,000
Weighted average interest rate on general debt ($265,000/$2,350,000)				11%

Total actual interest cost incurred during the capitalization period is $361,000. Of this total, $96,000 relates to specific debt and $265,000 relates to general debt. With only one construction loan, the interest rate on specific debt is straightforward at 12%. However, with four general debt amounts, the weighted average interest rate must be computed. To compute the weighted average interest rate on general debt, divide the total interest on general debt of $265,000 by the total general debt amount of $2,350,000 to arrive at 11%.

b. **Avoidable Interest**

The following schedule calculates the weighted average accumulated expenditures for the capitalization period. The first expenditure took place on January 1, thus the expenditure was outstanding for 100% of the year. The second expenditure took place on March 1, 2020, so the expenditure receives a weight of 10/12 of the capitalization period (12 months). The third expenditure was outstanding for half of the year while the final expenditure took place on the last day of the year, so it is not included in the weighted average expenditures for the year.

Date	A Actual Expenditures	B Months Outstanding	C* Percentage of Capitalization Period	A × C Weighted Average Accumulated Expenditures
January 1, 2020	$2,220,720	12	100%	$2,220,720
March 1, 2020.	300,000	10	83%	250,000
June 30, 2020.	500,000	6	50%	250,000
December 31, 2020 . . .	500,000	0	0%	0
				$2,720,720

* Percentage of capitalization period outstanding (or Column B divided by 12 months).

Next, the weighted average accumulated expenditures are allocated to the specific debt amount of $800,000. The remaining amount allocated to general debt is $1,920,720, which is the total of $2,720,720 less the specific debt of $800,000. *Remember that specific debt to the project is always considered first when calculating avoidable interest.* The 12% (specific debt interest rate) is applied to specific debt and 11% (weighted average interest rate on general debt) is applied to the general debt. Total avoidable interest for 2020 is $307,279 calculated based on weighted average accumulated expenditures.

Debt Category	A Weighted Average Accumulated Expenditures	B Interest Rate	A × B Avoidable Interest
Specific Debt	$ 800,000	12%	$ 96,000
General Debt	1,920,720	11%	211,279
	$2,720,720		$307,279

continued

continued from previous page

Lastly, we capitalize the lesser of actual interest or avoidable interest, which in this case is the avoidable interest of $307,279. Avoidable interest is capitalized to Construction in Process during the construction period (and eventually to Building—Stadium).

Actual interest.	$361,000	
Avoidable interest.	307,279	Lesser amount

c. **Journal Entries to Record Expenditures and Interest Capitalization**
The company records the following entries in 2020.

Assets = Liabilities + Equity
+2,220,720
−2,220,720
CIP: 2,220,720 | Cash: 2,220,720

January 1, 2020—To record payment for stadium expansion

Construction in Process	2,220,720	
Cash		2,220,720

Assets = Liabilities + Equity
+300,000
−300,000
CIP: 2,220,720; 300,000 | Cash: 2,220,720; 300,000

March 1, 2020—To record payment for stadium expansion

Construction in Process	300,000	
Cash		300,000

Assets = Liabilities + Equity
+500,000
−500,000
CIP: 2,220,720; 300,000; 500,000 | Cash: 2,220,720; 300,000; 500,000

June 30, 2020—To record payment for stadium expansion

Construction in Process	500,000	
Cash		500,000

Assets = Liabilities + Equity
+500,000
−500,000
CIP: 2,220,720; 300,000; 500,000; 500,000 | Cash: 2,220,720; 300,000; 500,000; 500,000

December 31, 2020—To record payment for stadium expansion

Construction in Process	500,000	
Cash		500,000

Assets = Liabilities + Equity
+307,279 −53,721
−361,000
CIP: 2,220,720; 300,000; 500,000; 500,000; 307,279 | Cash: 2,220,720; 300,000; 500,000; 500,000; 361,000
Interest Exp: 53,721

December 31, 2020—To record interest expense and interest capitalized

Construction in Process	307,279	
Interest Expense ($361,000 − $307,279)	53,721	
Cash		361,000

The amount capitalized as construction in process is transferred to the building account when complete. Rodgers will disclose total interest cost, including the amount capitalized and the amount expensed in its financial statements:

Total Interest Cost $361,000 → **$307,279 Interest Cost Capitalized**
→ **$ 53,721 Interest Cost Expensed**

REVIEW 11-5 LO11-5 Interest Capitalization

Review MBC

The following information is provided for Hodge Inc. for a long-term construction project that is expected to be completed in January 2021. The construction project is for a building intended for the company's own use. The capital expenditure on January 31, 2020, is for the purchase of land for the building site. All debt was outstanding for the full year. All debt is considered general debt with the exception of the $900,000 note payable, which is related directly to the construction project.

Date of Capital Expenditures for 2020	Actual Expenditures
Jan. 31, 2020	$ 300,000
May 1, 2020	800,000
July 31, 2020	1,000,000
Dec. 1, 2020	600,000

continued

continued from previous page

Outstanding Debt in 2020	Debt Amount	Interest Rate
Note payable	$ 900,000	7%
Note payable	350,000	6%
Bond payable	1,000,000	8%
Note payable	600,000	7%

a. Compute weighted average accumulated expenditures.

b. Compute interest to be capitalized and interest to be expensed for the first year. Round the weighted average interest rate to 3 decimals.

c. Prepare the journal entry to record interest for 2020.

More Practice: 11-55, 11-56, 11-57, 11-58

Solution on p. 11-48.

Account for asset retirement obligations

LO 11-6

Some companies employ plant assets that require substantial costs of dismantling, closure, removal, and site reclamation at the end of their useful lives. These costs are called **asset retirement obligations (AROs).**

ASC Glossary Asset Retirement Obligation: An obligation associated with the retirement of a tangible long-lived asset.

The following items are examples of requirements or obligations by law, regulation, or contract that lead to AROs.

- Dismantle offshore oil and gas facilities.
- Close and reclaim mining facilities.
- Decommission nuclear facilities.
- Close and reclaim landfill sites and hazardous waste storage facilities.

LO 11-6 Overview

Asset Retirement Obligation
- Recognize present value of ARO in carrying value of related asset
- Recognize a corresponding liability
- Derecognize the asset through depreciation
- Accrete liability over life of related asset and derecognize when activities are complete

The present value of an ARO is added to the carrying value of the related long-term asset, and a corresponding liability is established. (See **Demo 11-6.**) The liability and increase in asset carrying value are recognized when the company has a legal obligation to perform upon retirement of the asset and the amount is reasonably estimable. For example, the present value of the projected cost to dismantle an offshore oil facility is added to the cost of the oil facility at the same time as a liability for the ARO is recognized. The AROs are capitalized at the present value of estimated future costs using an interest rate that reflects the risk of the cash flows. Alternatively, a company may apply the expected cash flow approach discussed in Chapter 6, where the risk is applied to the cash flows. The cash flows adjusted for the probability of payment are then discounted using a risk-free rate of return. The rationale for capitalizing these costs to the asset (rather than expensing the amount immediately) is that the incurrence of the obligation for future closure and removal is integral to operating the asset.

Fixed Asset	#
Asset Retirement Obligation	#

410-10-25-4 An entity shall recognize the fair value of a liability for an asset retirement obligation in the period in which it is incurred if a reasonable estimate of fair value can be made. If a reasonable estimate of fair value cannot be made in the period the asset retirement obligation is incurred, the liability shall be recognized when a reasonable estimate of fair value can be made.

410-20-25-5 Upon initial recognition of a liability for an asset retirement obligation, an entity shall capitalize an asset retirement cost by increasing the carrying amount of the related long-lived asset by the same amount as the liability.

As the asset is used in operations, depreciation on the carrying value, which includes the present value of the closure and removal costs, is recognized. Changes in the liability due to the passage of time are measured by applying the effective interest method allocation to the amount of the liability at the beginning of the period. The amount increases the liability and the expense is classified as **accretion expense** (an operating expense). The liability (and the fixed asset) is derecognized when

Depreciation Expense	#
Accumulated Depreciation	#

Accretion Expense	#
Asset Retirement Obligation	#

Asset Retirement Obligation . . . #
Cash . . . #

the closure and removal activities are completed and the expenditures are made. If the expenditures are greater (less) than the amount of the ARO, the company will record a loss (gain) on settlement of the ARO.

Demo 11-6 LO11-6 Asset Retirement Obligation

Demo MBC

Lakeside Company, a calendar-year firm, completed the construction of a hazardous waste disposal plant in December 2020, and it is placed into service in January 2021. Lakeside treats contaminated soils, rendering them fit for use in agriculture. Data for capitalization and subsequent depreciation follow.

- Total construction cost of the plant excluding closure and removal costs are $200 million. The plant has a useful life of 20 years (straight-line depreciation).
- Federal regulations require the plant to be dismantled and land reclaimed at the end of the plant's life.
- Estimated cost to dismantle and reclaim the property is $37,205,800.
- Dismantling and reclamation activities will be completed one year following the end of the plant's useful life (assume end-of-year cash flows).
- Discount rate is 6%.

a. Record the capitalization of the asset retirement obligation on December 31, 2020. (Assume that the construction cost of the plant has been recorded.)
b. Record depreciation and accretion expense on December 31, 2021.
c. Record settlement of the asset retirement obligation for $38 million on December 31, 2041.

Solution

a. **Recognition of an Asset Retirement Obligation**

	RATE	NPER	PV	FV	Excel Formula
Given	6%	21	?	(37,205,800)	*PV(0.06,21,0,−37205800)*
Solution			$10,944,287		

The present value of the asset retirement obligation is $10,944,287. Twenty-one years is used in the present value calculation because the cash flows occur one year after the end of the asset's useful life.

The following entry is recorded to recognize the asset retirement obligation.

Assets = Liabilities + Equity
+10,944,287 +10,944,287
Building: Bal. 200,000,000; 10,944,287
ARO: 10,944,287

December 31, 2020—To record asset retirement obligation

Building—Waste Disposal Facility . . .	10,944,287	
Asset Retirement Obligation . . .		10,944,287

b. **Recognition of Depreciation Expense and Accretion Expense**

On December 31, 2021, depreciation expense is recognized on the full value of the plant (construction costs plus the asset retirement obligation) divided by the 20-year useful life.

Assets = Liabilities + Equity
−10,547,214 −10,547,214
Accum Deprec: 10,547,214
Deprec Exp: 10,547,214

December 31, 2021—To record depreciation expense

Depreciation Expense ($200,000,000 + $10,944,287)/20 . . .	10,547,214	
Accumulated Depreciation—Waste Disposal Facility. . .		10,547,214

The liability continues to grow by 6% each year. The liability is debited (extinguished) when cash and other resources are applied to the dismantling effort.

Assets = Liabilities + Equity
+656,657 −656,657
Accretion Exp: 656,657
ARO: 10,944,287; 656,657

December 31, 2021—To record accretion expense

Accretion Expense . . .	656,657	
Asset Retirement Obligation ($10,944,287 × 6%) . . .		656,657

c. **Settlement of Asset Retirement Obligation**

Lakeside would record the following entry upon settlement of the asset retirement obligation.

Assets = Liabilities + Equity
−38,000,000 −37,205,800 −794,200
Cash: 38,000,000
ARO: 37,205,800 | 37,205,800 Bal.
Loss on ARO: 794,200

December 31, 2041—To record settlement of asset retirement obligation

Asset Retirement Obligation . . .	37,205,800	
Loss on Settlement of Asset Retirement Obligation . . .	794,200	
Cash . . .		38,000,000

BOEING

Real World—ASSET RETIREMENT OBLIGATION

The Boeing Company disclosed the following information related to asset retirement obligations in a recent report on Form 10-K. While the company has recorded liabilities related to certain asset retirement obligations that can be reasonably estimated, other retirement obligations are not recorded because they are not estimable.

THE BOEING CO. [BA]

Asset Retirement Obligations We record all known asset retirement obligations for which the liability's fair value can be reasonably estimated, including certain asbestos removal, asset decommissioning and contractual lease restoration obligations. Recorded amounts are not material. We also have known conditional asset retirement obligations, such as certain asbestos remediation and asset decommissioning activities to be performed in the future, that are not reasonably estimable due to insufficient information about the timing and method of settlement of the obligation. Accordingly, these obligations have not been recorded in the Consolidated Financial Statements. A liability for these obligations will be recorded in the period when sufficient information regarding timing and method of settlement becomes available to make a reasonable estimate of the liability's fair value. In addition, there may be conditional asset retirement obligations that we have not yet discovered (e.g., asbestos may exist in certain buildings but we have not become aware of it through the normal course of business), and therefore, these obligations also have not been included in the Consolidated Financial Statements.

Asset Retirement Obligation LO11-6 REVIEW 11-6

BPP Company maintains underground storage tanks for its operations. A new storage tank is installed and made ready for use at a cost of $1,300,000 on January 1, 2020. The useful life of the storage tank is estimated at 20 years. At the end of its useful life, the company is legally required to remove the tank and restore the area at an estimated cost of $225,000. The appropriate discount rate for the company is 7%.

Review MBC

Required

a. Record the storage tank asset purchase and associated asset retirement obligation on January 1, 2020.

b. Record any required adjusting entries on December 31, 2020.

c. Assume that on December 31, 2039, the tank is safely removed at a cost of $300,000. Record the required journal entry.

More Practice: 11-32, 11-59

Solution on p. 11-49.

Account for property, plant, and equipment related costs after acquisition

LO 11-7

Capital expenditures that increase the (1) original useful life or (2) productivity of an asset (the quantity or quality of service) above the original level estimated at acquisition are capitalized. A capitalized post-acquisition expenditure is depreciated over the number of periods benefited, which can be less than the remaining useful life of the original asset.

The service potential of assets and their estimated useful life at acquisition assume a certain minimum level of maintenance and repair. Costs for maintenance and ordinary repairs are **revenue expenditures** expensed in the period incurred. Some companies expense all post-acquisition expenditures less than a certain dollar amount (for example, $500). This policy is supported by the accounting characteristic of materiality (which also applies to the capitalization of interest in LO 11-5).

Subsequent Acquisition Costs
- Capitalize expenditures that increase the original useful life or productivity of an asset
- Depreciate capital expenditures over periods benefited
- Expense ordinary maintenance and repairs in period incurred

LO 11-7 Overview

835-20-15-4 Minimum threshold levels are common in inventory and property, plant, and equipment accounting. Many entities do not include the costs of minor items in inventory, and many entities do not capitalize individual items of property, plant, and equipment, the costs of which are less than a specified threshold. Such thresholds are designed to minimize the burden of capitalizing large numbers of assets and accounting for those costs as the assets are used. Those thresholds are justified on the grounds that the assets whose costs are charged to expense as purchased are immaterial both individually and in the aggregate.

A company does not accrue for a planned major maintenance activity. Before the maintenance activity is initiated, the company does not have an obligation.

360-10-25-5 The use of the accrue-in-advance (accrual) method of accounting for planned major maintenance activities is prohibited in annual and interim financial reporting periods.

Expenditures that result from accident, neglect, intentional abuse, or theft are recognized as losses in the current period. For example, if equipment is damaged during installation, the repair cost is recognized as a loss. After repair, the equipment is no more valuable than it was before the mishap.

It is important to classify expenditures correctly. An incorrect classification affects reported income for the entire life of the asset. If costs are misclassified as capital expenditures and carried as asset accounts, for example, then current income is overstated, and future income is understated by depreciation of those costs. Classification and accounting treatment of subsequent costs are described in **Exhibit 11-2** and applied in **Demo 11-7**.

EXHIBIT 11-2
Treatment of Subsequent Acquisition Costs

Subsequent Cost	Definition	Examples	Accounting Treatment
Maintenance and Ordinary Repairs	Costs necessary to keep assets in operating condition, without prolonging the original estimate of the asset's useful life.	■ Lubrication, cleaning, adjustment, and painting. ■ Relatively small costs for parts, labor, and related supplies for asset maintenance.	■ Expense in the period incurred.
Improvements or Replacements	Replacement of a major component of a plant asset with a significantly improved component or with one of comparable quality, which increases the useful life or productivity of the asset.	■ Replacement of an old shingle roof with a fireproof tile roof. ■ Update to an electrical system in a building. ■ Replacement of an engine with a similar engine. ■ Major repair benefiting several future periods.	■ *Substitution:* Remove old component and add new component. (Use if carrying value of old asset is available.) ■ *Capitalization:* Add new component to asset value. (Use if old asset is significantly depreciated.) ■ *Reduction of accumulated depreciation:* Reduce accumulated depreciation to lengthen life of the related asset. (Use if life of asset is extended but improved quality is not a result.)
Additions	Extensions, enlargements, or expansions of an *existing* asset.	■ Extra wing or room added to a building. ■ Cutting an entrance through existing wall. ■ Add air conditioning system. ■ Add a fire sprinkling system.	■ Record in plant assets at cost: Depreciate over the shorter of its own service life or the remaining life of the original asset.
Rearrangements	Costs of reinstallation, rerouting, or rearrangements to extend benefits beyond the current accounting period.	■ Rearrangement of factory equipment to increase efficiency. ■ Relocation of a company plant.	■ Capitalize and depreciate if material and adds benefit to future periods. ■ Expense if does not clearly add benefit to future period.

Management Judgment

Capitalizing Fixed Assets

A company's fixed asset capitalization policy provides guidance on how to account for fixed asset transactions relevant to the company's operations. A policy (with adequate controls to ensure compliance) facilitates consistent and accurate accounting of fixed asset transactions. Management judgment is required both in establishing the policy and in applying the policy. Items that may be included in a fixed asset capitalization policy follow.

- **Threshold for capitalization** Defines a materiality threshold (such as $1,000) that automatically allows for all items under this amount to be expensed.
- **Categories of fixed assets** Identifies fixed asset categories such as land, building, and equipment by type.
- **Types of costs to capitalize** Identifies specific examples of costs incurred to get an asset ready for its intended use. For example, it identifies shipping costs as part of the costs to get an asset ready for its intended use.
- **Grouping of assets** Identifies whether fixed asset costs are recorded individually or as a group. For example, it indicates whether equipment items on an assembly line will be grouped together or each item would be recorded separately.
- **Distinctions between repairs and improvements** Defines and gives examples of what should be recorded as a repair (expense) and what should be recorded as an improvement (asset).
- **Useful life and depreciation method** Identifies standard useful lives and depreciation methods by fixed asset type. This is relevant in the next chapter where we discuss depreciation methods.
- **Asset retirement obligations** Provides guidance on how to identify and measure a retirement obligation.

Subsequent Acquisition Costs

LO11-7 **Demo 11-7**

Arthur Inc. incurred the following costs subsequent to the acquisition of its current fixed asset pool during 2020. Record the entry for each example, assuming cash purchases.

Example One—Ordinary Repair Arthur incurred $18,000 of costs for employees to repair equipment that malfunctioned.

Solution

Because the expenditure is incurred to keep the asset in present working condition, the amount is classified as an **ordinary repair** and is expensed in 2020.

2020—To record repair expense

Repair Expense	18,000	
Cash		18,000

Assets = Liabilities + Equity
−18,000 −18,000
Repair Exp: 18,000 (debit)
Cash: 18,000 (credit)

Example Two—Replacement A shingle roof that has an original cost of $60,000 and is 80% depreciated is replaced by a tile roof costing $100,000.

Solution

The replacement of the roof (a major component) is treated as a **replacement**. The new asset is capitalized, replacing the old asset.

2020—To remove cost of original roof

Accumulated Depreciation ($60,000 × 80%)	48,000	
Loss on Asset Improvement ($60,000 − $48,000)	12,000	
Building		60,000

Assets = Liabilities + Equity
+48,000 −12,000
−60,000
Building: 60,000 (credit)
Loss on Improv: 12,000 (debit)
Accum Deprec: 48,000 (debit)

2020—To capitalize asset replacement

Building	100,000	
Cash		100,000

Assets = Liabilities + Equity
+100,000
−100,000
Building: 100,000 (debit) | 60,000 (credit)
Cash: 100,000 (credit)

Example Three—Addition Arthur completed the manufacture of a new storage facility with an estimated useful life of 15 years for $90,000. The new facility is attached to an existing building with a remaining useful life of 20 years.

Solution

The new storage facility is considered an **addition** to an existing asset and is capitalized and depreciated over 15 years (shorter of 15 and 20 years).

2020—To capitalize asset addition

Building	90,000	
Cash		90,000

Assets = Liabilities + Equity
+90,000
−90,000
Building: 90,000 (debit)
Cash: 90,000 (credit)

Example Four—Rearrangement The purchasing department was relocated from the corporate office to the plant at a cost of $40,000 to improve the timeliness and effectiveness of the ordering process in conjunction with a move to streamline inventory management. The future years of benefit are estimated to be 5 years.

Solution

The relocation of the facilities of the company is considered a **rearrangement** because it benefits future periods. The amount is capitalized and depreciated over 5 years.

2020—To capitalize asset rearrangement

Building	40,000	
Cash		40,000

Assets = Liabilities + Equity
+40,000
−40,000
Building: 40,000 (debit)
Cash: 40,000 (credit)

SEARS

Real World—PROPERTY AND EQUIPMENT

SEARS HOLDINGS CORP. [SHLD]

Sears Holdings Corporation disclosed its policy on capitalizing costs subsequent to acquisition in a recent Form 10-K.

> Property and equipment are recorded at cost, less accumulated depreciation. Additions and substantial improvements are capitalized and include expenditures that materially extend the useful lives of existing facilities and equipment. Maintenance and repairs that do not materially improve or extend the lives of the respective assets are expensed as incurred.

REVIEW 11-7 **LO11-7** **Subsequent Acquisition Costs**

Review MBC

The corporate office building of Lorge Inc. has an original cost of $2,000,000 and accumulated depreciation of $1,000,000 at the beginning of the current year. During the current year, the following expenditures relating to the building are made.

a. Incurred ordinary repairs	$ 38,000
b. Completed an extension to the building adding 20 additional office spaces	750,000
c. Removed original roof (cost of $200,000 and 50% depreciated) and replaced it with a new roof (solar enhanced)	400,000
d. Completed an update to the electrical system (old costs not known)	120,000

Required

Prepare journal entries to record each event *a* through *d* assuming all items are paid in cash.

More Practice: 11-60, 11-61, 11-62

Solution on p. 11-49.

LO 11-8 Account for disposal of property, plant, and equipment

LO 11-8 Overview

Disposal of Property, Plant, and Equipment
- May be voluntary or involuntary
- Update depreciation expense to time of disposal
- Record gain or loss for the difference between proceeds and net book value

The disposal of plant assets can be *voluntary* (a result of a sale, exchange, or abandonment) or *involuntary* (a result of a casualty such as a fire, a storm, or a government's exercise of its right of eminent domain). In either case, a gain or loss is recorded upon disposal (even if the company must replace the item in an involuntary disposal).

> **605-40-25-3** Involuntary conversions of nonmonetary assets to monetary assets are monetary transactions for which gain or loss shall be recognized even though an entity reinvests or is obligated to reinvest the monetary assets in replacement nonmonetary assets.

If the asset to be disposed of is subject to depreciation, it is depreciated through the date of disposal to update the recorded book value. Applicable property taxes, insurance premiums, and similar costs also are accrued through the date of disposal. Then, the original cost of the asset and its related accumulated depreciation are derecognized. The difference between the book value of a plant asset and the amount received on disposal is recorded as a gain or loss as illustrated in **Demo 11-8**. The **gain or loss on disposal** is reported in the income statement as part of income from continuing operations.

Demo 11-8 **LO11-8** **Disposal of Property, Plant, and Equipment**

Demo MBC

Example One—Gain on Disposal On February 1, 2016, Brown Company paid $32,000 for office equipment with an estimated service life of five years and an estimated residual value of $2,000. Brown uses straight-line depreciation and decides to sell the asset on July 1, 2020, for $8,000. Record the entry on July 1, 2020, for the sale of the office equipment. Depreciation was last updated on December 31, 2019.

continued

continued from previous page

Solution

The entries for Brown, a calendar-year company, at the date of disposal follow.

July 1, 2020—To update depreciation expense through date of disposal

Depreciation Expense ([($32,000 − $2,000)/5 years] × 1/2)............	3,000	
Accumulated Depreciation..................................		3,000

Assets = Liabilities + Equity
−3,000 −3,000

Accum Deprec: 23,500 Bal.; 3,000 | Deprec Exp: 3,000

July 1, 2020—To record sale of equipment

Cash	8,000	
Accumulated Depreciation ([$32,000 − $2,000]/60 months) × 53 months ...	26,500	
Gain on Sale of Equipment ($8,000 − $5,500)...................		2,500
Equipment		32,000

Assets = Liabilities + Equity
+8,000 +2,500
+26,500
−32,000

Cash: 8,000 | Equipment: Bal. 32,000; 32,000
Accum Deprec: 26,500; 23,500 Bal.; 3,000 | Gain on Sale of Equip: 2,500

Example Two—Loss on Disposal Assume the same facts in Example One except that the equipment had a fair value of zero at the date of disposal of July 1, 2020. Record the entry on July 1, 2020, for the disposal of the office equipment.

Solution

Brown records the following entries at the date of disposal.

July 1, 2020—To update depreciation expense through date of disposal

Depreciation Expense ([($32,000 − $2,000)/5 years] × 1/2)............	3,000	
Accumulated Depreciation..................................		3,000

Assets = Liabilities + Equity
−3,000 −3,000

Accum Deprec: 23,500 Bal.; 3,000 | Deprec Exp: 3,000

July 1, 2020—To record disposal of equipment

Accumulated Depreciation ([$32,000 − $2,000]/60 months) × 53 months..	26,500	
Loss on Disposal of Equipment ($32,000 − $26,500)	5,500	
Equipment		32,000

Assets = Liabilities + Equity
+26,500 −5,500
−32,000

Equipment: Bal. 32,000; 32,000 | Loss on Disposal: 5,500
Accum Deprec: 26,500; 23,500 Bal.; 3,000

STARBUCKS

Real World—ASSET DISPOSALS

In its accounting policy disclosure for property, plant, and equipment in a recent Form 10-K, Starbucks Corporation described its policy on disposals as follows (emphasis added).

> **Property, Plant and Equipment** The portion of depreciation expense related to production and distribution facilities is included in cost of sales including occupancy costs on our consolidated statements of earnings. The costs of repairs and maintenance are expensed when incurred, while expenditures for refurbishments and improvements that significantly add to the productive capacity or extend the useful life of an asset are capitalized. ***When assets are disposed of, whether through retirement or sale, the net gain or loss is recognized in net earnings.*** Long-lived assets to be disposed of are reported at the lower of their carrying amount or fair value less estimated costs to sell.

STARBUCKS CORP. [SBUX]

Disposal of Property, Plant, and Equipment **LO11-8** **REVIEW 11-8**

Equipment with an estimated residual value of $5,000 and an estimated useful life of 10 years is purchased for $80,000 on January 1, 2016. Record the entries required on disposal of the equipment under the following three *separate* scenarios assuming that the disposal took place on July 1, 2020. Depreciation was last updated on December 31, 2019.

a. Equipment is sold for $34,000 cash.

b. Equipment is sold for $54,000 cash.

c. Equipment is disposed of due to damage as a result of a flood. The company expects to receive no insurance recovery on the loss.

Review MBC

More Practice: 11-34, 11-35, 11-36, 11-37, 11-63

Solution on p. 11-50.

LO 11-9 Account for exchange of property, plant, and equipment

LO 11-9 Overview

Exchange of Property, Plant, and Equipment
- ***Full* gain (loss) recognition**
  - All exchanges with losses
  - Exchanges with gains and commercial substance
- ***Partial or no gain* recognition**
  - Exchanges with gains and lack of commercial substance

A company can acquire a fixed asset by exchanging another asset, rather than giving up cash (monetary asset). Nonmonetary asset exchanges are described as either having or lacking commercial substance. **Commercial substance** occurs when the company's future cash flows are expected to significantly change as a result of the exchange. An exchange has commercial substance if the risk, timing, or amount of future cash flows associated with the new asset are different from the old asset. For example, if a newer vehicle is exchanged for an older vehicle, the anticipated future cash flows on maintenance should be lower with the new vehicle. On the other hand, if a vehicle is exchanged for another vehicle (same model, mileage, etc.), cash flows would not be expected to change. Thus, the exchange *lacks* commercial substance.

If a loss is determined upon an exchange, the full loss is recognized regardless of whether the exchange has or lacks commercial substance. This avoids the capitalization of an asset at a value greater than its fair value. If a gain is determined upon an exchange with commercial substance, the full gain is recorded. However, **a gain determined upon an exchange that lacks commercial substance is either deferred or only partially recognized as described below.** This exclusion of gain recognition prevents companies from trading similar properties simply to record a gain in its financial statements.

The following is required in recording an asset exchange.

- Asset given up is removed from books (credit original cost and debit accumulated depreciation).
- Cash is recorded (debit cash received and credit cash given).
- New asset value is recorded (fair value of asset given up, plus cash paid or less cash received ***or*** fair value of asset received, whichever is more clearly determinable).
- Gain or loss is recorded to balance the entry, *unless there is an exception* as described below.

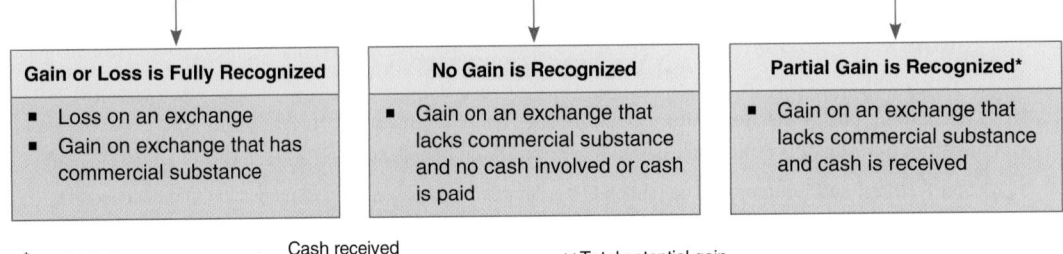

Gain or Loss is Fully Recognized
- Loss on an exchange
- Gain on exchange that has commercial substance

No Gain is Recognized
- Gain on an exchange that lacks commercial substance and no cash involved or cash is paid

Partial Gain is Recognized*
- Gain on an exchange that lacks commercial substance and cash is received

$$^{*}\text{Partial Gain: } \frac{\text{Cash received}}{\text{Cash received plus fair value of other assets received}} \times \text{Total potential gain}$$

If cash exchanged is 25% or more of the fair value of the exchange, the entire gain is recognized (ASC 845-10-25-6).

Demo 11-9A shows examples where a gain or loss is fully recognized. **Demo 11-9B** shows cases with exceptions, where gains are either fully or partially deferred because the transactions lack commercial substance.

Demo 11-9A LO11-9 Exchange of Equipment—Full Gain and Loss Recognized

Demo MBC

The following information for Tacoma Inc. is used in each of the cases that follow. The accumulated depreciation on the asset transferred is updated before the entry for exchange is recorded.

Asset transferred	Crane
Original cost	$50,000
Accumulated depreciation at date of exchange, after depreciation update entry	40,000

continued

continued from previous page

Example One—Exchange with Gain and Commercial Substance

Tacoma exchanges its crane with a fair value of $12,000 for a used truck with no determinable fair value. Assuming that the transaction has commercial substance, record the journal entry for the exchange of assets.

Solution

Any gain or loss is *fully recognized* because the transaction has commercial substance. The truck (new asset) is valued at $12,000, the fair value of the crane transferred, in the following entry.

Equipment—Vehicle (fair value of asset given up)	12,000	
Accumulated Depreciation—Crane	40,000	
Gain on Asset Exchange (to balance)		2,000
Equipment—Crane		50,000

Assets	= Liabilities	+ Equity
+12,000		+2,000
+40,000		
−50,000		

Equipment: Bal. 50,000 | 50,000; 12,000 |
Gain on Exchange: | 2,000
Accum Deprec: 40,000 | 40,000 Bal.

Example Two—Exchange with Gain, Cash Paid, and Commercial Substance

Tacoma exchanges its crane, with a fair value of $12,000, and $15,000 cash for a new truck with a $30,000 list price. The exchange has commercial substance. Record the journal entry for the exchange of assets.

Solution

Any gain or loss is *fully recognized* because the transaction has commercial substance. The truck is recorded at $27,000 ($12,000 fair value of asset given up plus $15,000 cash paid). The fair value of the crane (plus cash paid) is a more reliable value to use for fair value than a list price (dealers often sell at a price different from the list price). The following entry is recorded upon the exchange of assets.

Equipment—Vehicle ($12,000 + $15,000)	27,000	
Accumulated Depreciation—Crane	40,000	
Cash		15,000
Gain on Asset Exchange (to balance)		2,000
Equipment—Crane		50,000

Assets	= Liabilities	+ Equity
+27,000		+2,000
+40,000		
−15,000		
−50,000		

Cash: | 15,000
Equipment: Bal. 50,000 | 50,000; 27,000 |
Accum Deprec: 40,000 | 40,000 Bal.
Gain on Exchange: | 2,000

Example Three—Exchange with Loss, Cash Received, and Commercial Substance

Tacoma exchanges its crane (fair value $8,000) for other equipment and receives $5,000 on the exchange. The exchange has commercial substance.

a. Record the journal entry for the exchange of assets.
b. Explain how the answer to part *a* changes if the transaction lacked commercial substance.

Solution

a. **Exchange with Loss and Commercial Substance**

Any gain or loss is *fully recognized* because the transaction has commercial substance. The implied fair value and valuation of the acquired equipment is $3,000 ($8,000 fair value of asset given up less $5,000 cash received). The entry for the asset exchange follows.

Equipment ($8,000 − $5,000)	3,000	
Accumulated Depreciation—Crane	40,000	
Cash	5,000	
Loss on Asset Exchange (to balance)	2,000	
Equipment—Crane		50,000

Assets	= Liabilities	+ Equity
+3,000		−2,000
+40,000		
+5,000		
−50,000		

Cash: 5,000 |
Equipment: Bal. 50,000 | 50,000; 3,000 |
Accum Deprec: 40,000 | 40,000 Bal.
Loss on Exchange: 2,000 |

b. **Exchange with Loss and Lack of Commercial Substance**

The entry is exactly the same as in part *a* if the transaction were to lack commercial substance because Tacoma incurred a loss. *Losses are fully recognized whether or not the transaction has commercial substance.*

Demo 11-9B LO11-9 Exchange of Equipment—Partial or No Gain Recognized

Demo MBC

The following information for Tacoma Inc. is used in each of the cases that follow. The accumulated depreciation on the asset transferred is updated before the entry for exchange is recorded.

Asset transferred	Crane
Original cost	$50,000
Accumulated depreciation at date of exchange, after depreciation update entry	40,000

Example One—Exchange with Gain, No Cash, and Lacks Commercial Substance
Tacoma exchanges its crane worth $12,000 for another crane. The exchange lacks commercial substance. Record the journal entry for the exchange of assets.

Solution
The potential gain is $2,000, which is equal to the fair value of the asset given up ($12,000) less its book value ($10,000 or $50,000 − $40,000). However, *gains on exchanges lacking commercial substance are fully deferred if no cash is exchanged.* In this case, the valuation of the acquired crane is reduced to the book value of the crane transferred ($10,000). The following entry is recorded upon the exchange of assets.

Assets = Liabilities + Equity
+10,000
+40,000
−50,000

Equipment: Bal. 50,000 | 50,000; 10,000
Accum Deprec: 40,000 | 40,000 Bal.

Equipment—New Crane ($50,000 − $40,000)	10,000	
Accumulated Depreciation—Old Crane	40,000	
Equipment—Old Crane		50,000

Example Two—Exchange with Gain, Cash Paid, and Lacks Commercial Substance
Tacoma exchanges its crane and $15,000 cash for similar equipment with a $30,000 list price. The fair value of the crane to be exchanged is not determinable. The dealer quoted a cash price of $27,000 without the exchange. The exchange lacks commercial substance. Record the journal entry for the exchange of assets.

Solution
The potential gain of $2,000 is equal to the fair value of the assets received ($27,000), less cash paid ($15,000), less book value of assets given up ($10,000). However, *gains on exchanges lacking commercial substance are fully deferred if cash is paid (not received).* Therefore, the new crane is valued at $25,000, the sum of the book values of assets transferred, crane ($10,000) and cash paid ($15,000).

Assets = Liabilities + Equity
+25,000
+40,000
−15,000
−50,000

Cash: | 15,000
Equipment: Bal. 50,000 | 50,000; 25,000
Accum Deprec: 40,000 | 40,000 Bal.

Equipment—New Crane ($10,000 + $15,000)	25,000	
Accumulated Depreciation—Old Crane	40,000	
Cash		15,000
Equipment—Old Crane		50,000

Example Three—Exchange with Gain, Cash Received, and Lacks Commercial Substance
Assume that the fair value of the crane to be exchanged is $12,000. Tacoma trades its crane for a used crane with a fair value of $10,000 and receives $2,000 on the exchange. The exchange lacks commercial substance. Record the journal entry for the exchange of assets.

Solution
The potential gain is $2,000, which is equal to the fair value of the asset given up ($12,000) less book value ($10,000). *Because cash is received and the transaction lacks commercial substance, a partial gain is recognized in the asset exchange.* The partial gain is calculated as follows.

($2,000/[$2,000 + $10,000]) × $2,000 total potential gain = $333 (partial gain to recognize)

Equipment (new crane) is recorded at $12,000 fair value of asset given up, less $5,000 cash received, less the deferred gain ($2,000 − $333) in the following entry.

continued

continued from previous page

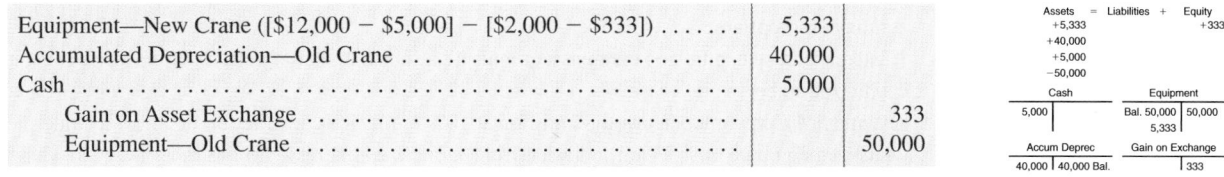

Equipment—New Crane ([$12,000 − $5,000] − [$2,000 − $333])	5,333	
Accumulated Depreciation—Old Crane	40,000	
Cash	5,000	
Gain on Asset Exchange		333
Equipment—Old Crane		50,000

Assets = Liabilities + Equity
+5,333 +333
+40,000
+5,000
−50,000

Cash	
5,000	

Equipment	
Bal. 50,000	50,000
5,333	

Accum Deprec	
40,000	40,000 Bal.

Gain on Exchange	
	333

EXPANDING YOUR KNOWLEDGE — Fair Value Is Unknown

In the unusual case where the fair value of the asset received or given cannot be determined, the company would record the new asset at the book value of the asset given up, adjusted for any cash exchanged. No gain or loss would be recorded on the exchange.

Exchange of Assets — LO11-9 — REVIEW 11-9

Lambou Corporation exchanged old equipment that cost $250,000 (accumulated depreciation of $140,000) for new equipment. The fair value of the new equipment is $125,000. The fair value of the old equipment could not be reliably estimated.

Required

Prepare the entry to record acquisition of new equipment under each of the following separate cases.

a. Transaction has commercial substance. No cash is involved.
b. Transaction has commercial substance. Cash of $25,000 is paid by Lambou.
c. Transaction lacks commercial substance. No cash is involved.
d. Transaction lacks commercial substance. Cash of $12,000 is paid by Lambou.
e. Transaction lacks commercial substance. Cash of $5,000 is received by Lambou.

Review MBC

More Practice: 11-65, 11-66, 11-67, 11-68, 11-69

Solution on p. 11-50.

Questions

11-1. Identify categories of long-term assets used in operations that have physical substance. Under what balance sheet caption are these assets reported?

11-2. How does the measurement principle apply to the acquisition of fixed assets? What implications does the expense recognition principle have for fixed asset accounting?

11-3. Distinguish between expenditures for improvements and expenditures for repairs and maintenance. What accounting implications are involved?

11-4. To determine the cost of equipment, how are the following items treated: (a) invoice price, (b) freight-in, (c) title verification costs, (d) installation costs, (e) testing costs, and (f) cost of a major overhaul before operational use?

11-5. A machine was purchased on the following terms: cash, $100,000, plus five annual payments of $5,000 each. How is the acquisition cost of the machine determined? Explain.

11-6. How is an asset's acquisition cost determined when the consideration given consists of equity securities?

11-7. How are assets recorded when they are acquired by exchanging another asset?

11-8. When several fixed assets are purchased for a single lump-sum consideration, cost allocation is usually employed. Explain the procedure. Why is cost allocation necessary?

11-9. Should donated assets be recorded in the accounts? If so, how are they recorded and at what value?

11-10. Under what conditions is general overhead allocated to a self-constructed asset?

11-11. Some businesses construct plant assets for their own use. What costs are capitalized for these assets? Explain what to do about (a) general company overhead and any incremental costs incurred and (b) costs of construction in excess of the purchase price from an outsider.

11-12. In general, what amount of interest is capitalized as a part of the cost of an asset?

11-13. For what types of assets is requiring a substantial completion or processing time for interest capitalization inappropriate?

11-14. If interest can be capitalized on an asset requiring a substantial completion period, when must interest capitalization begin and cease?

11-15. Assume 5M Company borrowed $2 million at 10% to finance construction of a new loading pier, which turned out to cost $3 million aside from capitalized interest. 5M has other debt. To what extent, if any, can interest in excess of $2,000,000 be capitalized in any full year the pier is under construction? As to the other debt, how is the interest rate determined for capitalization purposes?

11-16. Miller Inc. added a new wing to a plant building at a cost of $300,000 plus $10,000 spent in making passageways through the walls of the old structure. The plant is 10 years old and is being depreciated by an equal amount each year over a 30-year life. Over what period should the new wing be depreciated?

11-17. When are post-acquisition costs capitalized rather than expensed?

11-18. What is the nature of a gain or loss on disposal of a fixed asset when cash is received?

11-19. Outline the accounting steps related to the disposition of a fixed asset, assuming it is not traded in on another asset.

11-20. If interest is capitalized, what is the effect on income in the current year? What is the effect on income in future years?

11-21. Explain how to compute the amount of gain to be recognized in an exchange lacking commercial substance and where cash is received.

11-22. What value is assigned to a fixed asset received in exchange when the transaction has commercial substance, cash is also received, and the fair value of the asset transferred is known?

Brief Exercises

Brief Exercise 11-23
Determining Amount of PP&E to Capitalize
LO1

Williams Corporation purchased an old building and the land on which it is located for $500,000. The old building will be demolished at a net cost of $15,000. A new building will be built on the site. Williams also incurred the following costs: closing fees including commissions of $30,000, and title insurance costing $2,500. Williams assumed property taxes for the 6 months prior to the purchase totaling $10,000. Determine the amount Williams should capitalize for land and building related to the purchase.

Brief Exercise 11-24
Determining Amount of PP&E to Capitalize
LO1

AMP Corporation purchased new manufacturing equipment with an invoice cost of $50,000, plus sales tax of 6% on the selling price. AMP also incurred a freight charge of 10% of the selling price to obtain the equipment and paid an outside consultant $500 for installation of the equipment. AMP retained the services of the consultant for an additional few days for $1,000 to help employees train on the equipment's operations. Insurance premiums increased by $300 for the year related to the equipment usage. The company also received $1,000 for the residual value of the machine that was replaced. Determine the amount AMP should capitalize for equipment related to this purchase.

Brief Exercise 11-25
Determining Costs in a Lump-Sum Acquisition
LO2
Hint: See Demo 11-2

Serena Inc. purchases land and a building for $500,000. An independent appraisal indicates that the land has a value of $80,000 and the building has a value of $450,000. Determine the amount Serena should capitalize for land and building related to the purchase.

Brief Exercise 11-26
Recording Asset Acquisition through Equity **LO3**
Hint: See Demo 11-3B

Venus Company issued 50 shares of its own $1 par common stock in exchange for equipment. The stock was actively traded for $50 a share, and the company's management estimates that the equipment has a fair value at the date of acquisition of approximately $2,600. Prepare the journal entry to record the purchase.

Brief Exercise 11-27
Recording Asset Acquisition through Debt **LO3**

Teslla Corporation purchased land by signing a note with the seller requiring $10,000 immediately and $28,000 three years from purchase. The note is noninterest-bearing, but the interest rate for similar land purchases with notes is 10%.

a. Compute the value recorded in the Land account.
b. Compute the interest Teslla records for the first year of the note.

Brief Exercise 11-28 Recording Donated Assets **LO4** *Hint:* See Demo 11-4

Pitt Company received a vacant building as a donation. The building has an original cost of $200,000 on the donor's books and was 25% depreciated. The building is appraised at $160,000. Record Pitt Company's journal entry related to the donated building.

Brief Exercise 11-29 Calculating Weighted Average Accumulated Expenditures **LO5**

Jolie Company made the following cash expenditures this year on a self-constructed building with work starting January 2, 2020.

Jan. 2	$ 40,000
Sep. 1	60,000
Dec. 1	120,000

The building is still under construction at year-end. Compute the weighted average accumulated expenditures for the purpose of capitalizing interest.

Brief Exercise 11-30 Calculating Actual Interest and Weighted Average Interest Rate **LO5**

Weighted average accumulated expenditures are $400,000 on a project for which work steadily progressed during the current year. The following debt was outstanding during the current year.

Construction loan	$100,000 at 10%
Note payable	500,000 at 8%
Mortgage payable.	150,000 at 12%

a. Compute the total actual interest expense for the current year.
b. Compute the weighted average interest rate on the general debt. Round to four decimals.

Brief Exercise 11-31 Calculating Avoidable Interest **LO5**

Refer to the information in Brief Exercise 11-30. Calculate avoidable interest for the purpose of interest capitalization.

Brief Exercise 11-32 Recording Asset Retirement Obligation **LO6** *Hint:* See Demo 11-6

Martina Company is in the first year of building a storage facility that will contain hazardous building materials. The company is required to remove the storage facility and dispose of its contents at the end of 10 years, which is the useful life of the facility. Martina estimates the dismantling and removal costs to be $120,000 in 10 years. Prepare the journal entry, if any, that is recorded in this first year relating to the restoration costs. The appropriate discount rate is 9%.

Brief Exercise 11-33 Classifying Costs after Acquisition **LO1, 7**

Vertex Company incurred the following costs *a* through *d.* Determine whether each amount is capitalized or expensed in its financial statements.

a. Cost to train employees to run new technology in equipment used in manufacturing.
b. Film applied to windows, which reduces radiant energy entering the building, thus expecting to reduce air-conditioning costs over the next 5 years. The useful life of the windows is not affected.
c. Sound system (wiring, speakers, etc.) added to office buildings to improve the working environment.
d. Cost of replacing gravel parking lot with new asphalt.

Brief Exercise 11-34 Computing Gain or Loss on Disposal **LO8**

On July 1, one of Renee Company's delivery vans was destroyed in an accident. On that date, the van's carrying value was $5,000. On July 15, Renee received and recorded a $1,400 invoice for a new engine installed in the van earlier in May and another $1,000 invoice for various repairs done at the same time. In August, Renee received $7,000 from its insurance policy on the van; Renee plans to use those funds to replace the van. Compute the amount Renee reports as a gain or loss on disposal of the van in its income statement.

Brief Exercise 11-35 Computing Gain or Loss on Disposal **LO8**

On September 1, 2020, Boundary Inc. sold equipment for $24,000, which originally had cost $50,000 on December 31, 2015. The equipment is estimated to have no salvage value at the end of its estimated useful life of 10 years. The company uses straight-line depreciation. Compute the gain or loss on disposal of this equipment on September 1, 2020.

Brief Exercise 11-36 Recording Gain or Loss on Disposal **LO8**

Edgewater Inc. purchased equipment on January 1, 2018, for $36,000. The equipment has an estimated salvage value of $3,000 and an estimated useful life of 8 years. The company depreciates the asset using the straight-line method. On May 30, 2020, Edgewater Inc. sold the equipment for $22,000.

a. Record the May 30, 2020, entry to update depreciation assuming that depreciation was last updated on December 31, 2019.
b. Record the May 30, 2020, entry for the sale of this equipment.

Brief Exercise 11-37
Determining Gain or Loss on Disposal **LO8**

For each of the following three assets, determine the gain or loss on disposal.

Asset	Original Cost of Fixed Asset	Accumulated Depreciation, Balance	Cash Received upon Disposal of Asset	Gain or Loss
#1	$8,000	$6,000	$ 0	a
#2	8,000	5,000	1,500	b
#3	8,000	6,000	2,500	c

Brief Exercise 11-38
Assigning Value to Assets in Nonmonetary Exchange Lacking Commercial Substance **LO9**

Silo Inc. owns an asset originally costing $75,000, with accumulated depreciation of $38,000. The asset's fair value is $38,000. Silo trades in this old asset and pays $4,500 for a new asset. If the transaction lacks commercial substance, record Silo's journal entry for the exchange.

Brief Exercise 11-39
Assigning Value to Assets in Nonmonetary Exchange with Commercial Substance **LO9**

DD Inc. traded in its old building (costing $350,000 with accumulated depreciation of $100,000) for a new building with a fair value of $160,000 along with $80,000 cash from the trade. If the transaction has commercial substance, what amount does DD assign to the new building?

Brief Exercise 11-40
Assigning Value to Assets in Nonmonetary Exchange with Commercial Substance **LO9**

Mariot Inc. trades its old equipment for new equipment with a $12,000 fair market value. Mariot paid $7,000 cash on the exchange. If the transaction has commercial substance, what amount does Mariot assign to the new equipment?

Original cost of old equipment	$10,000
Accumulated depreciation on old equipment	6,000

Brief Exercise 11-41
Assigning Value to Assets in Nonmonetary Exchange Lacking Commercial Substance **LO9**

Mariot trades in its old equipment for new equipment with a $12,000 fair value. Mariot paid $7,000 cash on the exchange. If the transaction lacks commercial substance, what amount does Mariot assign to the new equipment?

Original cost of old equipment	$10,000
Accumulated depreciation on old equipment	6,000

Brief Exercise 11-42
Assigning Value to Assets in Nonmonetary Exchange Lacking Commercial Substance **LO9**

Mariot trades in its old equipment for new equipment. Mariot received $4,000 cash on the exchange. The fair value of the new equipment is $14,000. If the transaction lacks commercial substance, what amount does Mariot assign to the new equipment?

Original cost of old equipment	$10,000
Accumulated depreciation on old equipment	6,000

Exercises

Exercise 11-43
Recording Land Acquisition Costs **LO1, 3**

Following are descriptions of land purchases in four *separate cases*.

1. At the midpoint of the current year, a $40,000 check is given for land, and the buyer assumes the liability for unpaid taxes in arrears of $1,000 at the end of last year and those assessed for the current year of $900.
2. A company issues 14,000 shares of $1 par common stock with a fair value of $6 per share (based upon a recent sale of 10 shares) for land. The land is recently appraised at $80,000 by independent and competent appraisers.
3. A company's offer to purchase land for $8,000 cash two years ago was rejected. Instead, the company acquires the land by issuing 1,000 shares of $1 par common stock (fair value of the stock is $7.80 per share based on several recent large transactions under normal weekly stock trading volume).
4. A company issues 1,000 shares of $40 par common stock for land. The fair value was $60 per share at the time of the land purchase (stock sells regularly with an average daily volume of 5,000 shares). The seller had earlier offered to sell the land for $59,000 cash. Competent appraisers value the land at $61,000.

Required

a. Determine the cost used for recording the land acquired in each of the cases.

b. Record the journal entry for each case on the date of the land's acquisition.

Exercise 11-44
Analyzing Acquisition Costs **LO1, 5**

During the current year, Castle Corp. completed construction of its new corporate headquarters. Castle purchased land with an old building for $375,000. The land was valued at $350,000 and the building at $25,000. Castle demolished the building. Additional expenditures on the project follow.

1. Interest of $73,500 on construction financing incurred after completion of construction of the headquarters building.
2. Cost of $1,800,000 for construction of the new building.
3. Interest of $93,000 (lesser of actual and avoidable interest) on construction financing paid during construction of the headquarters building.
4. Payment of $9,250 for delinquent real estate taxes assumed by Castle upon purchase of the land and building.
5. Liability insurance premium of $6,000 covering the construction period.
6. Cost of $32,500 for razing the existing building.
7. Costs of $68,000 to move into the new headquarters.
8. Purchase of office equipment for $50,000, terms 2/10, n/30. Payment was made within 10 days and the company records purchases net of discount.

Required

Assuming no previous acquisitions of plant assets, determine Castle's ending balance for each of the plant asset accounts of (a) Land, (b) Building, and (c) Equipment, given the above information. Compute (d) total expense, if any, to be recognized from the above expenditures.

AICPA adapted

Exercise 11-45
Classifying Acquisition Costs **LO1**
Hint: See Demo 11-1A

Evonne Company incurred the following expenditures during 2020.

a. Land purchase on January 1, 2020.
b. Legal fees associated with the purchase of land.
c. Title and recording fees.
d. Costs to demolish existing building on new property.
e. Costs of clearing and draining of land.
f. Excavation fees for the foundation of the new building.
g. Installation of watering system for lawn.
h. Property taxes paid on June 30, 2020, for the 12 months ended June 30, 2020.
i. Paving parking lot and driveway.
j. Survey costs for new building.
k. Architecture fees for plans on the new building.
l. Landscaping costs—indefinite life.
m. Net invoice cost of equipment.
n. Maintenance on the first month of using a new machine.
o. Sales and federal excise taxes on equipment.
p. Installation costs of equipment.

Required

Indicate how each cost is classified in the financial statements (land, land improvement, equipment, building, construction in process, expense, or some combination). Assume construction was not completed on the new building at the end of 2020.

Exercise 11-46
Determining Ending Balances in Land and Building Accounts **LO1**

Maldive Company completes the construction of a building. The following *separate items* are the costs relevant to the purchase of the lot and construction of the building.

Cash payments to contractor	$100,000
Sales tax on construction materials used in addition to contractor payments	3,000
Cost of land (building site)	50,000
Gross cost to raze old building on land	20,000
Proceeds from old building salvage	5,000
Utility charges for electricity used in construction	2,000
Capitalized interest on construction	3,000

Required

Determine the ending balance for the Land account and for the Building account.

Exercise 11-47
Recording Costs for Self-Constructed Asset **LO1**

Amethyst Company constructed a building and incurred the following costs directly associated with construction. The building is valued at $77,500 (fair value) upon completion.

Materials	$25,000
Labor	40,000
Incremental overhead	15,000
Interest on construction loan incurred before completion	2,500
Interest on construction loan incurred after completion	1,000
Total	$83,500

Required

Prepare summary journal entries to record costs of (1) construction and (2) completion of the building. Assume that all qualifying interest during the current year is capitalized to the building.

Exercise 11-48
Recording Acquisition Costs **LO1**

Following are three *separate* cases.

1. Equipment with a list price of $30,000 is purchased; terms are 2/10, n/30. Payment is made within the discount period.
2. Equipment with a list price of $20,000 is purchased; terms are 2/10, n/30. Payment is made after the discount period. Any purchase discounts lost are recorded as interest expense.
3. Equipment listed at $9,000 is purchased and invoiced at 2/10, n/30. To take advantage of the discount, the company borrows $8,000 by issuing a 60-day, 15% note, which is paid with interest at its maturity date.

Required

Prepare journal entries for each *separate* case for (a) equipment acquisition, and (b) cash payment.

Exercise 11-49
Recording a Lump-Sum Acquisition **LO2**

Freeman Company purchased a tract of land on which were located a warehouse and an office building. The cash purchase price was $140,000 plus $10,000 in fees connected with the purchase. The following information relates to the property.

	Tax Assessment	Seller's Book Value	Original Cost
Land	$20,000	$10,000	$10,000
Warehouse	40,000	20,000	60,000
Building	60,000	50,000	80,000

Required

Prepare the journal entry to record this purchase.

Exercise 11-50
Recording a Lump-Sum Acquisition **LO2, 7**

Tires Outlet purchases the following used items at an auction for $40,000 cash: a drill press, a lathe, and a heavy-duty air compressor. The equipment is in excellent condition except for the electric motor on the lathe, which will cost $900 to replace with a new motor. Tires Outlet determines that selling prices for the used items are as follows: drill press, $8,400; lathe with an operational motor, $24,000; and air compressor, $10,500.

Required

Prepare the entry to record (a) acquisition of the equipment and (b) replacement of the motor.

Exercise 11-51
Recording Purchase of Equipment through Debt **LO3**
Hint: See Demo 11-3A

O'Reilly Company purchases equipment by making a down payment of $10,000 cash. In addition, O'Reilly signs a note requiring monthly payments of $2,000, starting one month after purchase and continuing for a total of 20 months. The contract calls for no interest, yet the prevailing interest rate is 12% on similar transactions.

Required

a. Record the entry required for the purchase of this equipment.
b. Record the entry to recognize interest expense, one month after this purchase.

Exercise 11-52
Recording Purchase of Equipment through Debt and Equity **LO3**

On January 1, 2020, Vale Inc. acquires equipment with a 10-year useful life by issuing a two-year, zero-interest bearing installment note payable when the market rate is 14% for this transaction. Terms are $7,000 cash payment immediately plus payments of $5,000 cash at the end of each of the next two years. The company uses the effective interest method to amortize interest expense and the straight-line method to estimate depreciation expense.

Required

a. Prepare the entry to record the purchase of this equipment.
b. Prepare the entry at the end of year one for (1) payment and interest and (2) depreciation expense.
c. Prepare the entry at the end of year two for (1) payment and interest and (2) depreciation expense.
d. Assume instead that Vale exchanged 100 shares of its own $1 par common stock along with $7,000 cash for the equipment. The stock was not actively traded but the equipment was estimated to have a fair value at the date of acquisition of $16,000. Prepare the entry to record the purchase.

Exercise 11-53 Recording Purchase of Equipment through Debt and Equity **LO3**

On January 1, 2020, Sidelines Company purchases equipment with an estimated 6-year useful life by making a $7,000 cash payment and issuing a noninterest-bearing note for $24,000 due in two years. The fair value of the equipment is unknown. An 11% annual interest rate is typical of this transaction. The company uses the effective interest method to amortize interest expense and the straight-line method to estimate depreciation expense.

Required

a. Prepare the entry to record the purchase on January 1, 2020.
b. Prepare the entry on December 31, 2020, to record (1) interest expense and (2) depreciation expense.
c. Indicate the balance sheet presentation related to this transaction as of December 31, 2020.
d. Prepare the entry on December 31, 2021, to record (1) interest expense and payment of the note and (2) depreciation expense.
e. Assume instead that Sidelines exchanged 500 shares of its own $10 par value common stock along with $7,000 cash for the equipment. At the date of the exchange, the stock was trading on the market at $40 per share. Prepare the entry to record the purchase of equipment.

Exercise 11-54 Recording Acquisition of Equipment through Donation **LO4**

A shareholder donated a building and the land on which it is located to Clemson Inc. The property was reliably appraised at a value of $160,000 (25% related to the land). Clemson Inc. paid transfer costs of $4,000 cash. The building has an estimated remaining life of 25 years (no residual value).

Required

Prepare Clemson's entries to record the (a) transfer of the building and land, and (b) depreciation expense at the end of the first year. Assume a full year of depreciation and use of the straight-line method.

Exercise 11-55 Computing Interest Capitalization Amounts **LO5**
Hint: See Demo 11-5

Whit Company spent a total of $300,000 cash on a construction project during 2018 and 2019. During 2020, Whit spends an additional $600,000 evenly during the year on the project and completes construction at the end of 2020. Debt outstanding during 2020 follows.

Accounts payable average balance	$ 50,000
10% bond payable	700,000
12% construction loan	200,000

Required

a. Compute the amount of interest to be capitalized in 2020.
b. Calculate the amount of interest to expense in 2020.

Exercise 11-56 Computing and Recording Interest Capitalization **LO5**
Hint: See Demo 11-5

Weld Corporation is constructing a plant for its own use. Weld capitalizes interest on an annual basis. The following expenditures are made during the current year: January 1, $30,000; July 1, $290,000; September 1, $800,000; and December 31, $2,110,000. The following debts were outstanding throughout the current year.

Construction note, 12%	$100,000
Short-term note payable, 15%	400,000
Accounts payable (noninterest-bearing)	400,000

Required

a. Compute the amount of interest to be capitalized in 2020.
b. Calculate the amount of interest to expense in 2020.
c. Prepare the 2020 summary journal entry to record the construction expenditures and interest, assuming that construction is not complete on December 21, 2020.

Exercise 11-57
Computing and Recording Interest Capitalization **LO5**

Bullock Company is constructing a building for its own use and has been capitalizing interest based on average expenditures on a quarterly basis since the project began last year. The following expenditures are made during the first quarter: January 1, $2,800,000; February 1, $2,550,000; and March 31, $3,650,000. Bullock had the following debts outstanding during this quarter.

Note payable, 10%, incurred specifically to finance construction.	$1,600,000
Short-term note payable, 15%	2,500,000
Mortgage note payable, 8%	1,200,000

Required

a. Compute interest to be capitalized and interest to be expensed for this first quarter.
b. Prepare the entry to record the construction expenditures and the interest.
c. Explain what effect, if any, the cost of land on which the building is being erected has on the amount of interest capitalized.

Exercise 11-58
Computing and Recording Interest Capitalization **LO5**

The following information is from Bowin Inc. for a long-term construction project that is expected to be completed in January 2021. The construction project is for a building intended for the company's own use. The capital expenditure on January 1, 2020, is for the purchase of land for the building site. No new construction loans were opened for the project in 2020. All debt was outstanding for the full year.

Capital Expenditures for 2020

Date	Actual Expenditures
Jan. 1, 2020.	$ 30,000
Mar. 31, 2020.	900,000
June 30, 2020.	1,800,000
Nov. 30, 2020.	900,000

Outstanding Debt in 2020

Debt	Debt Amount	Interest Rate
Note payable	$1,000,000	8%
Note payable	800,000	8%
Bond payable	2,000,000	10%
Note payable	500,000	9%

Required

a. Compute interest to be capitalized and the interest to be expensed in 2020.
b. Prepare the entry to record the construction expenditures and interest for 2020.
c. Prepare the entry for depreciation in 2021 assuming that the project is completed on January 1, 2021. Assume that the building has a useful life of 30 years, and that the company uses the straight-line depreciation method.

Exercise 11-59
Recording Asset Retirement Obligation **LO6**
Hint: See Demo 11-6

BPP Company maintains underground storage tanks for its operations. A new storage tank was installed and made ready for use at a cost of $1,000,000 on January 1, 2020. The useful life is estimated at 15 years, at which time the company is legally required to remove the tank and restore the area at an estimated cost of $100,000. The appropriate discount rate for the company is 12%.

Required

a. Record the storage tank asset and the related asset retirement obligation on January 1, 2020.
b. Record any required adjusting entries on December 31 2020.
c. Assume that on December 31, 2035, the tank is safely removed at a cost of $115,000. Record the required journal entry.

Exercise 11-60
Recording Subsequent Expenditures **LO7**
Hint: See Demo 11-7

After 25% of the useful life had expired on equipment with an original cost of $100,000 and no salvage value, a major component of the equipment is unexpectedly replaced. The old component was expected to last as long as the equipment itself, and the company's accounting records on the component indicate it originally cost $20,000 and had no expected salvage value. The replacement component cost $30,000 and has no usefulness beyond that of the equipment.

Required

Prepare the entries to record the component replacement, assuming a cash purchase.

Exercise 11-61
Recording Subsequent Expenditures **LO7**

The plant building of Xon Corporation is old (estimated remaining useful life is 12 years) and needs continuous maintenance and repairs. The company's accounts show that the building originally cost $300,000; and accumulated depreciation was $200,000 at the beginning of the current year. During the current year, the following expenditures relating to the plant building are made.

1.	Continuing, frequent, and low-cost repairs	$17,000
2.	Added a new storage shed attached to the building; estimated useful life of eight years	36,000
3.	Removed roof with original cost, $40,000; replaced it with guaranteed, modern roof	50,000
4.	Unusual and infrequent repairs due to damage from flood; repairs did not increase the use, value, or the economic life of the asset	6,000
5.	Complete overhaul of the plumbing system (old costs unknown)	12,500

Required

Prepare the journal entry to record each item 1 through 5, assuming all items are paid in cash.

Exercise 11-62
Classifying Subsequent Expenditures **LO7**

The following items relate to company expenditures after the original acquisition of property, plant, and equipment.

____ 1. An improvement made to equipment to increase its fair value and its production capacity by 25% without extending the equipment's useful life.
____ 2. An improvement made to equipment to extend the equipment's useful life by 25%.
____ 3. Minor repair of a roof due to hail damage.
____ 4. Replacement of a roof due to hail damage where the book value of the original roof is known.
____ 5. Replacement of a roof due to hail damage where the book value of the original roof is unknown.
____ 6. Rearrangement of a manufacturing assembly line expected to materially impact the current year.
____ 7. Rearrangement of a manufacturing assembly line expected to materially impact the next three years.
____ 8. Major repair to an equipment engine that will increase the useful life of the asset.

Required

Identify the proper accounting treatment for each item *1* through *8* from the following: (a) capitalize and depreciate, (b) expense in current year, (c) decrease accumulated depreciation, or (d) record as new asset after removing old asset.

Exercise 11-63
Recording Fixed Asset Disposal **LO8**
Hint: See Demo 11-8

Manchester Company sells equipment on June 1, 2021, for $139,000 cash. Manchester incurred $800 of removal and selling costs on disposal. The equipment cost $250,000 when it was purchased on January 2, 2018. Its estimated residual value and useful life were $40,000 and 10 years, respectively. Manchester uses straight-line depreciation and records annual depreciation on each December 31.

Required

a. Prepare the journal entries needed to record the asset disposal on June 1, 2021.
b. Record the journal entries if the equipment were abandoned (zero fair value) on June 1, 2021.

Exercise 11-64
Recording Fixed Asset Disposal **LO1, 8**

On April 1, 2020, one of the two large production machines used by Evert Company stripped a gear, causing major internal damage. On April 5, 2020, the company decided to purchase a new machine (cost of $182,500) so that production could continue. On January 1, the accounts showed the following for the old machine: original cost, $90,000; accumulated depreciation, $63,000 (20-year life; no residual value). The company did not accept a trade-in offer of $13,500. Instead, the old machine was sold on April 5 to another company for $24,000. Evert spent $3,000 cleaning and $1,000 moving the machine prior to shipping. Insurance premiums (prepaid) on the old machine were $450; the unused portion of the premium is applied to the new machine. That insurance was paid on January 1 and covered the period January 1 through December 31.

Required

a. Record the entry for Evert Company to purchase equipment on April 5, 2020.
b. Record the entries for Evert Company on April 5, 2020, to dispose of the old machine, including any required updates for depreciation and for insurance expense.

Exercise 11-65
Recording Asset Exchanges **LO9**

Minneapolis Inc. has equipment with an original cost of $35,000 and accumulated depreciation of $20,000. This equipment was traded in for new equipment with a list price of $40,000. The new machine can be purchased without a trade-in for $37,500 cash. The difference between the fair value of the new asset and the fair value of the old asset will be paid in cash.

Required

Prepare the entry to record acquisition of the new machine under each of the following *separate cases.*

a. The new machine is purchased for cash with no trade-in.
b. The transaction has commercial substance. The old equipment is traded in, and $25,000 cash is paid.
c. The same as in part *b* except that the transaction lacks commercial substance.

Exercise 11-66
Recording Asset Exchanges **LO9**

Miley Corp. exchanges old equipment that cost $10,000 (accumulated depreciation of $4,500) for new equipment. The fair value of the new equipment is $8,000. The fair value of the old equipment cannot be reliably estimated.

Required
Prepare the entry to record acquisition of the new equipment under each of the following separate cases.

a. Transaction has commercial substance. No cash is involved.
b. Transaction has commercial substance. Cash of $3,000 is paid by Miley.
c. Transaction lacks commercial substance. No cash is involved.
d. Transaction lacks commercial substance. Cash of $1,000 is paid by Miley.
e. Transaction lacks commercial substance. Cash of $2,000 is received by Miley.

Exercise 11-67
Reporting an Asset Exchange **LO9**

Clarkson Co. and Keyes Inc. exchange equipment. Information related to this exchange for both companies follows.

	Clarkson Co.	Keys Inc.
Equipment given up:		
Equipment (original cost)	$30,000	$35,000
Accumulated depreciation.	10,000	12,000
Fair value	18,000	24,000
Cash exchanged.	(5,500)	5,500

Required
a. Record the exchange for *Clarkson Co.* assuming the transaction has commercial substance.
b. Record the exchange for *Keyes Inc.* assuming the transaction has commercial substance.
c. Record the exchange for *Clarkson Co.* assuming the transaction lacks commercial substance.
d. Record the exchange for *Keyes Inc.* assuming the transaction lacks commercial substance.

Exercise 11-68
Reporting an Asset Exchange **LO9**

Two independent companies, Levine and Shelton, are in the home-building business. Each owns a tract of land for development, but each company prefers to build on the other's land. Accordingly, they agree to exchange their land. An appraiser is hired, and from the appraiser report and the companies' records, the following information is drawn.

Land	Levine Co.	Shelton Co.
Cost (same as book value).	$ 80,000	$50,000
Fair value based on appraisal	100,000	90,000

The exchange of land is made. Based on the difference in appraised values, Shelton also pays $10,000 cash to Levine. The transaction lacks commercial substance.

Required
a. For financial reporting purposes, what does *Levine* recognize as a pretax gain on this exchange?
b. For financial reporting purposes, what does *Shelton* recognize as a pretax gain on this exchange?
c. After the exchange, at what value does *Levine* record its newly acquired land?
d. After the exchange, at what value does *Shelton* record its newly acquired land?

Exercise 11-69
Recording an Asset Exchange **LO9**

Science Center trades an electron microscope with an original cost of $200,000 and accumulated depreciation of $80,000 for new optical equipment. The old equipment has a fair value of $160,000 at trade-in time, and Science Center receives $30,000 cash on the trade-in. The transaction lacks commercial substance.

Required
Prepare the entry for Science Center to record the exchange.

Exercise 11-70
Recording an Asset Exchange **LO9**

a. Huson Company traded in equipment along with $10,000 cash for a newer type of equipment. The transaction has no commercial substance. The following information relates to equipment values on the exchange date. Record Huson's entry for this exchange of equipment.

	Carrying Value	Fair Value
Old equipment	$60,000	$ 90,000
New equipment.	80,000	100,000

b. VM Company traded equipment with an original cost of $50,000 and accumulated depreciation of $20,000 for similar productive equipment with a fair value of $30,000. VM also received $15,000 cash with this exchange. The transaction lacks commercial substance. Record VM's entry for this exchange of equipment.

Exercise 11-71
Defining Concept Terminology **LO1, 2, 3, 4, 5, 6, 7, 8, 9**

Following are terms relating to concepts in this chapter along with descriptions of those terms.

Terms	Description of Terms
____ 1. Historical cost	*a.* Issued as one way to finance fixed asset acquisitions.
____ 2. Capitalization	*b.* Expansion of an existing asset requiring capitalization and depreciation.
____ 3. Self-constructed asset	*c.* Expensed over the life of the related fixed asset.
____ 4. Lump-sum purchase	*d.* Requires an update to depreciation expense.
____ 5. Capitalized interest	*e.* Requires a credit to revenue at the fair value of the asset.
____ 6. Asset retirement obligation	*f.* Type of transaction, which changes future cash flows.
____ 7. Accretion expense	*g.* Value must not exceed fair value.
____ 8. Addition	*h.* Requires cost allocation based upon relative fair value of individual assets.
____ 9. Repairs	*i.* Guiding accounting principle for recording fixed assets.
____10. Disposal of fixed asset	*j.* Discrete construction projects for sale, lease, or for internal usage.
____11. Commercial substance	*k.* Increase in an asset retirement obligation for a period.
____12. Equipment	*l.* Expenditures not capitalized as an asset on the balance sheet.
____13. Noninterest-bearing note	*m.* To record costs on the balance sheet as an asset.
____14. Donated fixed assets	*n.* Present value of obligations at the end of an asset's life.
____15. Qualifying assets	*o.* Tangible property used in a company's operations.

Required

Match each term 1 through 15 with the best description *a* through *o*.

Problems

Problem 11-72
Recording Asset Acquisition Costs
LO1, 7, 8

The following transactions 1 through 6 relate to fixed assets.

1. Purchased land and buildings for $157,800 cash. The purchaser agrees to pay $1,800 for taxes already assessed. The purchaser borrows $100,000 at 15% interest (principal and interest due in one year) from the bank to help make the cash payment. The property is appraised for taxes as follows: land, $50,000; and building, $100,000.
2. Prior to use of the property purchased in part 1, the following expenditures were made.

Repair and renovation of building.	$16,000
Installation of electrical wiring.	4,000
Removal of separate facility	600
Sold scrap lumber from facility removal	100
Construction of new driveway.	3,000
Repair of existing driveways.	1,200
Deposits with utilities for connections.	100
Painting company name on two sides of building.	1,800
Installation of wire fence around property.	5,000

3. Purchased a tract of land for $64,000; assumed taxes already assessed totaling $360. Paid title fees of $100 cash, and attorney fees of $600 cash, in connection with the purchase.
4. The land purchased in part 3 is leveled, and two retaining walls are built to stop erosion. Cost of this work is $6,000 cash. The property is being held as a future plant site.
5. Purchased a used machine for $17,000 cash. Subsequent to purchase, the following expenditures are made.

General overhaul prior to use	$2,400
Installation of machine	600
Cost of moving machine	300
Cost of removing two small machines to make way for larger machine purchased	200
Cost of reinforcing floor prior to installation	800
Testing costs prior to operation	120
Cost of (new) tool kit essential to adjustment of machine for various types of work	440

6. Immediately sold the machine described in part 5 for $16,000 cash after discovering that the machine was not compatible with its operations.

Required

Prepare journal entries to record each of the transactions 1 through 6.

Problem 11-73
Recording Acquisition Scenarios **LO1, 3, 9**

Equipment with a fair value of $30,000 is acquired in a non-cash exchange. Below are five *separate assumptions* as to the consideration given in this non-cash exchange.

a. Gave up bonds held as a long-term investment in held-to-maturity securities; the bonds originally cost $56,000 and had been written down by 50% because of a perceived permanent loss of value.
b. Gave up inventory carried at $19,000 on the most recent balance sheet as part of its perpetual inventory carried at lower of cost or net realizable value. When originally acquired, the inventory had a cost of $19,800.
c. Gave up used equipment with a book value of $12,000 and a fair value of $13,400 *plus* $16,600 cash. When new, the used equipment cost $17,600. The transaction lacks commercial substance.
d. Gave up land with a book value of $15,000 and a fair value of $30,000.
e. Gave up a noninterest-bearing note for $34,500 and maturing in one year. Notes of similar risk required 15% interest at the date of exchange.

Required

Prepare the journal entry required for acquisition under each of the separate cases *a* through *e*.

Problem 11-74
Recording Acquisition Scenarios **LO1, 3, 4, 7**

Review of the property, plant, and equipment accounts of James Company reveals the following transactions.

1. On January 1, 2020, new equipment is purchased with a list price of $30,000. The company did not take advantage of a 1% cash discount available upon full payment of the invoice within 10 days. Shipping costs paid by the seller were $100. Installation costs are $400, representing 10% of the monthly salary of the manager (installation took two days). A wall is moved two feet at a cost of $800 to make room for the equipment. Cash discounts not taken are considered interest expense.
2. During January 2020, the first month of operations, the newly purchased equipment became inoperative due to a product defect. The seller repaired the equipment at no cost; however, the specially trained operator was idle during the two weeks the machine was inoperative. The operator was paid regular wages ($650) during the period, although the only work performed was to observe the repair by the factory representative.
3. On January 1, 2020, the company bought fixtures with a list price of $4,500; the company paid $1,500 cash and issued a one-year, noninterest-bearing note payable for the balance. The current interest rate for this type of note was 15%.
4. On January 1, 2020, the company purchased an automatic counter to be attached to a machine in use, cost $700. The estimated useful life of the counter was 7 years, and the estimated life of the machine was 10 years.
5. On July 1, 2020, a contractor completed construction of a building for the company. The company paid the contractor with a $400,000 face value, 20-year, 8% bonds payable, at which time financial consultants advised that the bonds would sell at 96 ($384,000).
6. On December 31, the company received a property donation from the city for future expansion of its manufacturing facilities. The fair value of this property is estimated at $40,000, although the cost of the property on the city's records is $10,000.

Required

a. Prepare the journal entries to record each of the transactions *1* through *6* as of the date of occurrence. The company uses straight-line depreciation.

b. Record depreciation at the end of 2020 for (1) equipment, (2) fixtures, and (3) building. None of these assets is expected to have a residual value except fixtures (residual value is $500). Estimated useful lives are: fixtures, 5 years; equipment, 10 years; and building, 40 years. Provide a separate entry for each asset.

Problem 11-75
Analyzing Multiple Acquisition Scenarios
LO1, 2, 5

At December 31, 2020, accounts in the property, plant, and equipment section of Hine Inc.'s balance sheet had the following balances.

Land	$ 600,000	Leasehold improvements	$ 800,000
Buildings	1,300,000	Equipment	1,600,000

During 2021, the following transactions occurred.

1. Land site #101 is acquired for $3 million. To acquire the land, Hine pays a $180,000 commission to a real estate agent. Costs of $30,000 are incurred to clear the land. During the course of clearing the land, timber and gravel are recovered and sold for $16,000.
2. A second tract of land (site #102) with a building is acquired for $600,000. The closing statement indicates that the land value is $400,000 and the building value is $200,000. Shortly after acquisition, the building is demolished at a cost of $40,000. A new building is constructed for $300,000 plus the following costs.

Excavation fees	$12,000
Architectural design fees	6,000
Building permit fee	4,000

   Actual interest was $12,500 and avoidable interest was $10,000 during the construction period. The building was completed and occupied on September 30, 2021.
3. A third tract of land (site #103) is acquired for $1,500,000 and is put on the market for resale.
4. Extensive work is done to a building occupied by Hine under a lease agreement that expires on December 31, 2030. The total cost of the work was $250,000 and consisted of the following (the lessor paid half the costs incurred for the extension to the current working area).

Item	Estimated Cost	Useful Life (years)
Painting of ceilings	$ 10,000	1
Electrical work	90,000	10
Construction of extension to current working area	150,000	25
	$250,000	

5. During December 2021, $120,000 is spent to improve leased office space. The related lease will terminate on December 31, 2024, and is not expected to be renewed.
6. A group of new machines is purchased under a royalty agreement, which provides for payment of royalties based on units of production for the machines. The invoice price of the machines was $270,000, freight costs were $2,000, unloading costs were $3,000, and royalty payments for 2021 were $44,000.

Required

a. Prepare a detailed analysis of the changes in each of the following balance sheet accounts for 2021: land, buildings, leasehold improvements, and equipment. Ignore the related accumulated depreciation accounts.

b. List items from transactions 1 through 6, which were not used to determine the balances in part *a*, and indicate where, or whether, these items are included in Hine's financial statements.

AICPA adapted

Problem 11-76
Calculating and Recording Capitalized Interest **LO5**

Rose Company began construction of a small building on January 1, 2021. The company's only debt during the first quarter was an unrelated long-term $300,000 note bearing interest at 11% with a maturity date of December 31, 2023. On May 1, 2021, the company borrowed $100,000 on a 9% construction note (interest-bearing); the note matures on April 30, 2022. The company capitalizes interest on the building on the basis of average quarterly cumulative expenditures. As of the end of each quarter of the six-month construction period, construction expenditures (not including interest) are shown below. Rose's reporting-year ends on December 31. Interest is paid quarterly. The construction expenditures follow.

2021	Expenditure		2021	Expenditure	
Jan. 1	Land	$ 20,000	April 30	Construction	$200,000
Jan. 31	Construction	70,000	May 31	Construction	170,000
Feb. 28	Construction	100,000	June 30	Construction	80,000
Mar. 31	Construction	180,000			

Required

a. Compute the interest cost to be capitalized and expensed each quarter.

b. Record journal entries related to construction *and* interest cost for quarter one and for quarter two. Record costs directly to the Land and the Building accounts.

Problem 11-77
Calculating and Recording Capitalized Interest **LO5**

Dobie Industries began construction of a new plant for its own use on January 1, 2021. During the entirety of 2021, Dobie had the following debt outstanding.

Accounts payable (noninterest-bearing).	$ 80,000
Short-term note payable (14%)	500,000
Bonds payable (12%, issued at par).	1,300,000

On April 1, 2021, Dobie borrowed an additional $500,000 on a 14%, one-year construction note to help finance the plant construction. Interest on all debt is paid at the end of each quarter. The average accumulated expenditures on construction for each quarter of 2021 have already been computed. Assume that these amounts include the correct amounts of previously capitalized interest. The payments and average accumulated expenditures follow.

Quarter	Payments to Contractors	Weighted Average Accumulated Expenditures
1	$150,000	$150,000
2	450,000	300,000
3	750,000	675,000
4	950,000	850,000

Required

a. Compute the interest cost to be capitalized and expensed each quarter.

b. Record journal entries related to construction and interest cost for quarters one, two, three, and four. Record costs directly to the Building account.

Problem 11-78
Recording Capitalized Interest and Costs for Self-Constructed Assets **LO1, 5**

Mannheim Company begins construction of a manufacturing facility on January 4 of the current year. Mannheim uses its own employees and subcontractors to complete the facility. The following list provides information relevant to the construction. The facility is completed December 27 of that year.

1. At the beginning of January, Mannheim obtains construction financing: a 10%, $12,000,000 loan with principal payable at the end of construction provides significant financing for the project. Interest on the loan is payable semiannually. Mannheim pays the interest and principal when due.
2. Mannheim also has (1) $40,000,000 of 12% bonds payable issued at face value seven years before, which pay interest every June 30 and December 31, and (2) an 11% $20,000,000 note paying interest every December 31, outstanding the entire year.
3. Mannheim owns the land site (cost, $4,000,000). In January, a subcontractor is employed to raze the old building (cost, $800,000; accumulated depreciation, $600,000) on the site for $80,000. Mannheim received $10,000 from salvaged materials.
4. Also in January, subcontractors survey, grade, and prepare the land for construction at a cost of $200,000 and excavate the foundation of the new facility for $1,000,000.
5. In January, a subcontractor poured and finished the foundation for $1,500,000. This work is financed separately through a one-year, 9% loan. Mannheim secured the financing at the beginning of January
6. The total material cost for construction excluding other items in this list is $8,000,000.
7. Payments to subcontractors excluding others in this list amount to $2,000,000.

8. Payments to Mannheim employees for work on construction are $16,000,000.
9. In October, a subcontractor remodeled space for a research lab within the facility for $300,000.
10. Incidental fees and other costs associated with facility construction were $150,000.
11. For purposes of interest capitalization, Mannheim assumes an even distribution of cash payments for all construction costs throughout the year (use a simple average) and capitalizes interest once per year as an adjusting entry. Construction costs are accumulated in Mannheim's facility under the construction in progress account.
12. The fair value of the building upon completion is $25,000,000.

Required

Prepare journal entries to account for all aspects of construction and related events for the twelve items above. For simplicity, include the cost of any land improvements in the average accumulated expenditures for the building.

Problem 11-79
Recording Asset Retirement Obligation
LO6

Alaska Industries has just completed construction of an oil drilling facility at a cost of $10 million. The facility has a useful life of 10 years, is expected to have a $1 million residual value, and is depreciated on the straight-line basis. The facility is completed at the end of the current year. Under environmental regulations, Alaska Industries is required to dismantle and remove the facility at the end of its useful life and bear any cleanup costs, which are inevitable in such operations. The cost to comply with the law is estimated to be $666,108. The appropriate discount rate is 7%. Assume that dismantling and cleanup can be accomplished within the first month after closing the facility.

Required

a. Record the capitalization of dismantling and cleanup costs.
b. Compute the increase in annual depreciation as a result of capitalizing the dismantling and cleanup costs.
c. Prepare the entry at the end of 10 years to extinguish the liability, assuming that there is no change in estimates and that the entire liability is paid in cash at the end of 10 years.

Problem 11-80
Recording Subsequent Costs of Asset Acquisitions **LO7, 8**

The plant asset accounting records of Reston Company reflected the following at the beginning of the current year.

Plant building (residual value, $30,000; estimated useful life, 20 years)	$150,000
Accumulated depreciation, plant building	90,000
Equipment (residual value, $35,000; estimated useful life, 10 years)	180,000
Accumulated depreciation, equipment	90,000

During the current year ending December 31, the following transactions (summarized) relating to the above accounts were completed.

1. Expenditures for nonrecurring, relatively large repairs that tend to increase economic utility but not the economic lives of assets follow.

Plant building	$45,000
Equipment	15,000
Replacement of original electrical wiring system of plant building (original cost, $18,000, 75% depreciated)	29,000

2. Additions follow.

Plant building—added small wing to plant building to accommodate new equipment acquired; wing has useful life of 18 years and no residual value	$54,000
Equipment—added special protection devices to 10 machines; devices are attached to the machines and have to be replaced every five years (no residual value)	10,000

3. Outlays for maintenance, parts, and labor to keep assets in normal working condition follow.

Quarter	Plant Building	Equipment
1	$1,600	$ 1,900
2	1,800	6,100
3	1,600	1,000
4	2,000	10,000

Required

Prepare the necessary journal entries to record transactions 1, 2 and 3.

Problem 11-81
Recording Asset Disposal **LO8**

Equipment that cost $36,000 on January 1, 2015, is sold for $20,000 on June 30, 2020. It had been depreciated over a 10-year life by the straight-line method, assuming its residual value would be $3,000. A warehouse that cost $300,000, residual value $30,000, was being depreciated over 20 years by the straight-line method. When the structure was 15 years old, an additional wing was constructed at a cost of $180,000. The estimated life of the wing considered separately was 15 years, and its residual value is $20,000. The accounting period ends December 31.

Required

a. Prepare journal entries required to record the following.
   1. Sale of the equipment.
   2. Cost of additional wing to the warehouse; costs paid in cash.
   3. Depreciation on the warehouse and its additional wing after the latter has been in use for one year.

b. Show how the warehouse and additional wing is reported on the balance sheet (under the Building account) prepared immediately after the depreciation recorded in part *a*.

Problem 11-82
Recording Asset Exchanges **LO9**

Trader Jo Inc. has a policy of trading in equipment after one year's use. The following information is available from Trader Jo's records. Assume a five-year estimated useful life and no residual value for all assets. Trader Joe uses straight-line depreciation.

Jan. 1, 2018	Acquired asset A for $24,000 cash.
Jan. 1, 2019	Exchanged asset A for asset B. Asset B had a fair value of $28,000. Paid $6,000 cash in the exchange.
Jan. 1, 2020	Exchanged asset B for asset C. Asset C had a fair value of $32,000. Paid $8,000 cash in the exchange.
Jan. 1, 2021	Exchanged asset C for asset D. Asset D had a fair value of $22,000. Received $4,000 cash in the exchange.

Required

a. Assume that the transactions lack commercial substance. Prepare the journal entry required for each exchange.

b. Assume that the transactions have commercial substance. Prepare the journal entry required for each exchange.

Problem 11-83
Recording Asset Exchange **LO9**

Part 1 Two equipment items were exchanged (transaction *lacked commercial substance*) when the accounts of the two companies involved reflected the following. The fair value of asset M was reliably determined to be $2,800; no reliable estimate can be made of asset N.

Account	Company M (denoted as asset M)	Company N (denoted as asset N)
Equipment	$8,000	$8,200
Accumulated depreciation . . .	5,500	4,800

Required

a. Prepare the exchange entry for each company assuming that no cash difference is involved.

b. Prepare the exchange entry for each company assuming that a cash difference of $800 is paid by Company M to Company N.

Part 2 Two fixed assets were exchanged (transaction *had commercial substance*) when the accounts of the two companies reflected the following. The fair value of asset A was reliably determined to be $4,500; no reliable estimate can be made for asset B.

Account	Company A (denoted as asset A)	Company B (denoted as asset B)
Equipment	$10,000	$14,000
Accumulated depreciation . . .	7,000	10,500

Required

a. Prepare the exchange entry for each company assuming that no cash difference was involved.

b. Prepare the exchange entry for each company assuming that a cash difference of $1,200 is paid by Company A to Company B.

Problem 11-84
Recording Asset Exchanges **LO9**

For the following five transactions, all items of property refer to fixed assets, *not* inventory, unless specified to the contrary. List prices are not necessarily equal to the fair value.

1. Land carried on the books of Company A at $18,000 is exchanged for equipment carried on the books of Company B at $25,000 (cost, $35,000; accumulated depreciation, $10,000). Fair value of both assets is $30,000. Prepare the journal entry for both Company A and Company B assuming that the transaction has commercial substance.
2. Equipment, which cost Company A $6,000 ($3,000 accumulated depreciation), has a fair value of $3,400. It is traded to a dealer, plus a $5,600 cash payment, for new equipment that has a $12,400 list price. Prepare the journal entry for Company A, assuming that the transaction lacks commercial substance.
3. Equipment that cost Company A $6,000, on which $5,000 depreciation has been accumulated, is traded to a dealer along with $6,300 cash. The new equipment would have cost $7,000 if only cash had been paid; its list price is $7,500. Prepare the journal entry for Company A assuming that the transaction lacks commercial substance.
4. Land carried on the books of Company A at $90,000 is exchanged for land carried on the books of Company B at $78,000. Fair value of each tract is $100,000. Prepare the journal entry for Company B assuming that the transaction lacks commercial substance.
5. Fixtures that cost Company A $15,000 ($9,000 accumulated depreciation) and are worth $8,000 are traded to Company B along with $500 cash. In exchange, Company A receives fixtures from Company B carried by Company B at a cost of $13,000 less $6,000 accumulated depreciation. Prepare the journal entries for both Company A and Company B if necessary assuming that the transaction lacks commercial substance.

Required

Prepare journal entries where necessary to record transactions 1 through 5.

Accounting Decisions and Judgments

AD&J 11-85
Analyzing Asset Disposals **LO8**

Real World Analysis **Ameritech Corporation** is the parent corporation of five Bell companies serving the Great Lakes region. The company's Year 8 annual report included the following information ($ millions).

From notes:	Depreciation based on straight-line method and group methods of depreciation.	
	Gross capital expenditures	$2,982
	Depreciation expense	2,475
From statement of cash flows:	Investing activities section: net capital expenditures	2,954
From balance sheet:	Increase in accumulated depreciation	1,521

The group method of depreciation treats all assets within a group as having a uniform useful life and applies a depreciation rate based on the total cost of the group. No gain or loss is recognized on disposal under this method. Accumulated depreciation is reduced by the difference between the cost of the assets disposed of and cash proceeds.

Required

a. Assuming that all plant assets are depreciated on the group basis, estimate the original cost of plant assets retired in Year 8.

b. Assuming that the straight-line method is applied individually to all plant assets and that gains and losses on plant asset disposals were approximately equal in amount during Year 8, estimate the average proportion of useful life remaining at disposal on the plant assets retired in Year 8. What additional information would be helpful in answering this question?

AD&J 11-86
Estimating Capitalized Interest **LO5**

Real World Analysis **Geneva Steel Corporation** has the only integrated steel mill west of the Mississippi River. The corporation's Year 5 annual report disclosed the following information related to its construction projects, debt and interest cost ($ thousands).

- Construction in progress, a component of total property, plant, and equipment, increased from $63,889 to $80,876 in Year 5.
- Interest capitalized in Year 5 was $5,674. This amount is disclosed in the notes.
- Interest-bearing debt outstanding at the end of Year 4: $190,000 of 9.5% notes; $135,000 of 11.125% notes; and $32,350 of 9% credit line.

Required

a. Using the above information from its annual report, estimate the interest potentially capitalizable in Year 5.

b. Provide at least three reasons why the estimate in part *a* differs from the amount reported by Geneva Steel. Assume that construction payments are made uniformly during the year.

AD&J 11-87
Estimating the Fair Value of Plant Assets Acquired on Credit
LO3

Real World Analysis **Super Valu Stores Inc.** is a large food-marketing company. Information from the company's Year 5 annual report follows. Independent retailers use funds loaned by Super Valu to finance acquisitions of property used in retail food operations. Super Valu records these loans in its long-term notes receivable account.

Year 5 ($ thousands)	Ending Balance
Long-term notes receivable (net)	$36,731

Additional information from its annual report:

> Notes range in length from 1 to 10 years, with the average being 6 years, and may be noninterest-bearing or bear interest at rates ranging primarily from 5 to 12%.

Assume the following for Super Valu Stores.

1. Its notes receivable account consists of one 8-year, 10% note with seven years remaining in its term as of the end of Year 5.
2. Super Valu finances 100% of the asset acquisitions for the retailers.
3. Annual payments on the note are received at each year-end, include principal and interest, and are a constant amount each year.

Required

Determine the fair value of the assets financed by Super Valu at the date of acquisition by the retailers (debtors).

AD&J 11-88
Analyzing Property, Plant, and Equipment Activity **LO1**

Real World Analysis The following information is reported in the Year 8 financial statements of the **Coca-Cola Company** ($ millions).

Balance sheet	
Net property, plant, and equipment, January 1, Year 8.	$3,743
Net property, plant, and equipment, December 31, Year 8.	3,669
Cash flows	
Property, plant, and equipment purchases, Year 8	863
Property, plant, and equipment, disposals, Year 8	54
Selected financial data	
Depreciation expense, Year 8.	381

Required

a. Determine the net book value of property, plant, and equipment disposed of during Year 8.

b. Estimate the net gain or loss from disposals and exchanges of property, plant, and equipment for Year 8.

AD&J 11-89
Analyzing Acquisition Costs: Expenditures Subsequent to Acquisition **LO7**

Judgment Case Assume that the fair value of equipment acquired in a noncash transaction is not determinable by reference to a cash purchase.

Required

a. Explain how the acquiring company determines the capitalizable cost of equipment obtained through each of the following exchanges.
   1. Bonds that have a determinable fair value.
   2. Common stock that does not have a determinable fair value.
   3. Equipment in exchange (commercial substance is lacking) that has a determinable fair value.

b. Assume that the equipment was acquired and has been used by the acquiring company for three years. Expenditures related to the equipment must be made. Identify six types of expenditures that might be involved and explain the proper accounting for each.

AICPA adapted

AD&J 11-90
Analyzing a Court Settlement: Capitalize versus Expense **LO1**

Judgment Case A large automobile manufacturer, which operates in Michigan, agreed in a court settlement to the following.

1. Install pollution control equipment on its manufacturing facility at an estimated cost of $18 million.
2. Pay specified medical expenses for children living near its facilities who were suffering from lead poisoning through polluted water; tentatively estimated cost of $20 million is to be paid as families incur expenses.
3. Pay the city and state a civil penalty of $200,000 over a four-year term in equal $50,000 installments.

Required

a. For each item 1, 2, and 3, discuss the propriety of capitalizing versus expensing the cost.

b. Identify the amount attributed to each item 1, 2, and 3 immediately after the settlement (before any payments are made) and how each be accounted for or disclosed.

AD&J 11-91
Analyzing Related Incidental Costs **LO1**

Communication Case The invoice price of a machine is $20,000. Various other costs relating to the acquisition and installation of the machine amount to $5,000 and include transportation, wiring, special base, and so forth. The machine has an estimated life of 10 years and no residual value.

Anne Wade, the owner of the business, suggests that the incidental costs of $5,000 be debited to expense immediately for three reasons: (1) if the machine should be sold, these costs could not be recovered, (2) the inclusion of the $5,000 in the Equipment account will not necessarily result in a closer approximation of the fair value of this asset over the years because of the possibility of changing price levels, and (3) debiting the $5,000 to expense immediately will reduce federal income taxes.

Required

Write a one-page memo as its company accountant to Anne Wade addressing each of the points she raises.

AICPA adapted

AD&J 11-92
Analyzing Costs after Acquisition **LO1**

Judgment Case One of our clients, a savings bank with several local branches, recently acquired ownership of a lot and building located in a historical part of the city. The building is dilapidated and unsuitable for human habitation. The bank thought at the time that it was acquiring a site for a new branch. Although a firm of architects recommended demolition, the city council, in whose discretion such activity rests, refused consent to demolish the building in view of its historical and architectural value.

To comply with safety requirements and to make the building suitable for use as a branch location, the bank spent $250,000 restoring and altering the old building. It had paid $90,000 for the building and lot and had contemplated spending $200,000 on a new building after demolishing the old structure. Somewhat similar old buildings in less run-down condition could have been bought in the same area for about the same $90,000 price. It is possible, even likely, that some of these that were not so old could have been demolished without governmental intervention, and the bank could have carried out its original plan.

Now that the restoration is finished and the bank is making final plans to open its newest branch in the restored building, the bank has been informed by the State Historical Commission that the building qualifies for and will receive a plaque designating it as a historical site. The designation will be of some value in attracting traffic to the site, the building will probably be pointed out during tours of the city, and so on. Under present laws, receipt of the designation may well mean that the bank can never demolish the structure and is obligated to preserve it, even if the property is later vacated.

Required

a. Discuss the pros and cons of capitalizing the entire $250,000 spent on restoration of the building.

b. How should the $90,000 original expenditure be treated? What would have been the cost of the land if the bank had been able to carry out its original plans?

c. Our client is likely to seek advice as to proper accounting for subsequent costs—repairs, depreciation, possible improvements, etc. What advice do we provide for these costs?

AD&J 11-93
Accounting for Land Costs **LO1**

Communication Case Write a 1-page memo comparing and contrasting the accounting for the following expenditures related to land for your client, Jim Smith, who works for Caspar Golfing, a golfing supply retailer. Jim is concerned about the variety of treatments afforded expenditures on land. Jim does not have an accounting background. In your memo, refer to the general principle for inclusion of expenditures in property, plant, and equipment and why you believe the expenditure should or should not be included in the land account.

a. The cost of constructing a paved parking lot on land already owned by Caspar. Currently, customers must park on a gravel lot next to Caspar's retail outlet.

b. The net cost, after salvage proceeds, to raze an old building on a tract of land just purchased by Caspar. A practice putting green will be constructed in its place.

c. The net cost, after salvage proceeds, to raze the original building constructed several years ago by Caspar to house the retail operations. Caspar intends to build a larger building to be used for the same purpose.

d. The allocated cost of a building on a second tract of land just purchased by Caspar. The land and building were valued separately by a reliable appraiser, but Caspar was able to purchase the package at a lump-sum price considerably lower than the sum of the land and building fair values. Caspar plans to demolish the building and construct a second retail outlet on the property.

AD&J 11-94
Accounting for Closure and Removal Costs
LO6

Communication Case Simba Clark, the director of Shareholder Services of a large multinational corporation headquartered in the U.S., has asked you for help. Simba will address the shareholders meeting tomorrow. One of the questions sent to her from a large shareholder concerns the issue of accounting for closure and removal costs. As the controller of this firm, you are in the best position to help Simba. Her email to you included the following.

> I am aware that there is accounting guidance on recording asset retirement obligations related to the closure and removal costs. I understand that a major shareholder has questions to fully understand the financials as they relate to asset retirement obligations. Although I have some knowledge of accounting, I am only vaguely familiar with this accounting guidance. Can you help me out with guidance in addressing our shareholders?

Required

Draft a one-page email message to Simba explaining the financial statement impact from accounting for closure and removal costs.

AD&J 11-95
Searching the Codification to Define Key Terms **LO1, 3, 6, 9**

Codification Skills Refer to the Codification and identify the definition for each of the following: (1) historical cost, (2) asset retirement obligation, (3) accretion expense, (4) nonmonetary assets and liabilities, and (5) expenditures defined in the Codification.

AD&J 11-96
Researching the Codification for Proper Citation **LO5, 6, 9**

Codification Skills Research the Codification and report the proper citation that provides guidance on each of the following topics.

a. Assets qualifying for interest capitalization. FASB ASC ___-___-___-___

b. Interest capitalization as the lesser of avoidable and actual interest. FASB ASC ___-___-___-___

c. Determination of whether a transaction has commercial substance. FASB ASC ___-___-___-___

d. Period when an asset retirement obligation is recorded. FASB ASC ___-___-___-___

AD&J 11-97
Researching the Codification for Authoritative Guidance
LO6

Codification Skills A company is preparing annual financial statements that includes the valuation of an asset retirement obligation. The asset retirement obligation relates to a legal liability for an environmental remediation expected to take place in 10 years. The obligation was initially recorded 5 years ago. Due to new information on the process required for the remediation, the company expects the cost previously recorded to increase by 25%. The company is unsure as to whether this change is considered to be a change in estimate or an error. Also, the company is not sure what interest rate to use to quantify the liability for the financial statements. Identify the relevant authoritative guidance.

FASB ASC ___-___-___-___

Answers to Review Exercises

Review 11-1

a. Equipment
b. Equipment
c. Equipment
d. Equipment
e. Land
f. Land
g. Period expense
h. Land
i. Land
j. Land improvement
k. Land improvement
l. Construction in process
m. Construction in process
n. Equipment
o. Equipment
p. Equipment (Alternatively, indirect costs may be expensed as incurred.)

Review 11-2

Printer.	$300	($300/$650)
Desk.	350	($350/$650)
	$650	

To record lump sum purchase

Equipment—Printer ($3,000 × 300/650)	1,385	
Equipment—Desk ($3,000 × 350/650)	1,615	
Cash		3,000

Assets = Liabilities + Equity
+1,385
+1,615
−3,000

Equipment: 1,385 | ; 1,615 |
Cash: | 3,000

Review 11-3

a. **January 1, 2020—To record purchase of equipment through debt**

Equipment	221,468	
Discount on Note Payable ($200,000 − (PV(0.08,2,0,−200000))	28,532	
Cash		50,000
Note Payable		200,000

Assets = Liabilities + Equity
+221,468 −28,532
−50,000 +200,000

Cash: | 50,000
Note Payable: | 200,000
Equipment: 221,468 |
Discount on NP: 28,532 |

b. **December 31, 2020—To record interest expense**

Interest Expense ($171,468 × .08)	13,717	
Discount on Note Payable		13,717

Assets = Liabilities + Equity
+13,717 −13,717

Discount on NP: 28,532 | 13,717
Interest Exp: 13,717 |

c. **December 31, 2021—To record interest expense and payment of note**

Note Payable	200,000	
Interest Expense	14,815	
Discount on Note Payable (($171,468 + $13,717) × 0.08)		14,815
Cash		200,000

Assets = Liabilities + Equity
−200,000 −200,000 −14,815
+14,815

Cash: | 50,000; | 200,000
Note Payable: 200,000 | 200,000
Interest Exp: 13,717 | ; 14,815 |
Discount on NP: 28,532 | 13,717; | 14,815

d. **January 1, 2020—To record purchase of equipment through equity**

Equipment ([$75 × 2,000] + $50,000)	200,000	
Cash		50,000
Common Stock ($1 × 2,000)		2,000
Paid-in Capital in Excess of Par—Common Stock ($200,000 − $50,000 − $2,000)		148,000

Assets = Liabilities + Equity
+200,000 +2,000
−50,000 +148,000

Cash: | 50,000
Common Stock: | 2,000
Equipment: 200,000 |
Paid-in Capital—CS: | 148,000

Review 11-4

a. **December 31, 2020—To record acquisition of equipment through donation**

Building ($500,000 × 0.75)	375,000	
Land ($500,000 × 0.25)	125,000	
Cash		5,000
Contribution Revenue ($500,000 − $5,000)		495,000

Assets = Liabilities + Equity
+375,000 +495,000
+125,000
−5,000

Cash: | 5,000
Building: 375,000 |
Land: 125,000 |
Contrib Rev: | 495,000

b. **December 31, 2021—To record depreciation expense**

Depreciation Expense ($375,000/30)	12,500	
Accumulated Depreciation		12,500

Assets = Liabilities + Equity
−12,500 −12,500

Accum Deprec: | 12,500
Deprec Exp: 12,500 |

Review 11-5

a. Weighted average accumulated expenditures: $1,275,000 ($275,000 + $533,333 + $416,667 + $50,000)

b. Capitalized interest: $90,375 (($900,000 × 0.07) + ($375,000 × 0.073))

Interest expense: $115,625 ($206,000 ($63,000 + $21,000 + $80,000 + $42,000) − $90,375) *c.* **December 31, 2020—To record interest expense and capitalized interest**

Assets = Liabilities + Equity
+90,375 −115,625
−206,000
Cash: Cr 206,000 | Interest Exp: Dr 115,625 | CIP: Dr 90,375

Construction in Process	90,375	
Interest Expense	115,625	
Cash		206,000

Review 11-6

a. **January 1, 2020—To record asset retirement obligation**

Assets = Liabilities + Equity
+1,358,144 +58,144
−1,300,000
Cash: Cr 1,300,000 | ARO: Cr 58,144 | Equipment: Dr 1,358,144

Equipment—Storage Tank	1,358,144	
Asset Retirement Obligation (PV(0.07,20,0,−225000))		58,144
Cash		1,300,000

b. **December 31, 2020—To record depreciation expense**

Assets = Liabilities + Equity
−67,907 −67,907
Accum Deprec: Cr 67,907 | Deprec Exp: Dr 67,907

Depreciation Expense ($1,358,144/20)	67,907	
Accumulated Depreciation—Storage Tank		67,907

December 31, 2020—To record accretion expense

Assets = Liabilities + Equity
+4,070 −4,070
ARO: Cr 58,144, 4,070 | Accretion Exp: Dr 4,070

Accretion Expense ($58,144 × 0.07)	4,070	
Asset Retirement Obligation		4,070

c. **December 31, 2039—To record settlement of ARO**

Assets = Liabilities + Equity
−300,000 −225,000 −75,000
Cash: Cr 1,300,000, 300,000 | ARO: Dr 225,000; Cr 225,000 Bal. | Loss on ARO: Dr 75,000

Asset Retirement Obligation	225,000	
Loss on Settlement of Asset Retirement Obligation	75,000	
Cash		300,000

Review 11-7

a. **To record repair expense**

Assets = Liabilities + Equity
−38,000 −38,000
Cash: Cr 38,000 | Repair Exp: Dr 38,000

Repair Expense	38,000	
Cash		38,000

b. **To record addition**

Assets = Liabilities + Equity
+750,000
−750,000
Building: Dr Bal. 2,000,000, 750,000 | Cash: Cr 38,000, 750,000

Building	750,000	
Cash		750,000

c. **To record removal of old roof**

Assets = Liabilities + Equity
+100,000 −100,000
−200,000
Building: Dr Bal. 2,000,000, 750,000; Cr 200,000 | Loss on Improv: Dr 100,000
Accum Deprec: Dr 100,000; Cr 1,000,000 Bal.

Accumulated Depreciation ($200,000 × 1/2)	100,000	
Loss on Asset Improvement	100,000	
Building		200,000

To capitalize replacement

Assets = Liabilities + Equity
+400,000
−400,000
Building: Dr Bal. 2,000,000, 750,000, 400,000; Cr 200,000 | Cash: Cr 38,000, 750,000, 400,000

Building	400,000	
Cash		400,000

d. **To record improvement**

Assets = Liabilities + Equity
+120,000
−120,000
Accum Deprec: Dr 100,000, 120,000; Cr 1,000,000 Bal. | Cash: Cr 38,000, 750,000, 400,000, 120,000

Accumulated Depreciation	120,000	
Cash		120,000

Review 11-8

a. **July 1, 2020—To update depreciation expense**

Depreciation Expense	3,750	
Accumulated Depreciation—Equipment		3,750

Assets = Liabilities + Equity: Assets −3,750; Equity −3,750
Accum Deprec: 30,000 Bal.; 3,750 (credit) | Deprec Exp: 3,750 (debit)

July 1, 2020—To record disposal of equipment

Cash	34,000	
Accumulated Depreciation	33,750	
Loss on Sale of Equipment	12,250	
Equipment		80,000

Assets = Liabilities + Equity: Assets +34,000, +33,750, −80,000; Equity −12,250
Cash: 34,000 (debit) | Equipment: Bal. 80,000 (debit); 80,000 (credit)
Accum Deprec: 33,750 (debit); 30,000, 3,750 Bal. (credit) | Loss on Sale of Equip: 12,250 (debit)

b. **July 1, 2020—To update depreciation expense**

Depreciation Expense	3,750	
Accumulated Depreciation—Equipment		3,750

Assets = Liabilities + Equity: Assets −3,750; Equity −3,750
Accum Deprec: 30,000 Bal.; 3,750 (credit) | Deprec Exp: 3,750 (debit)

July 1, 2020—To record disposal of equipment

Cash	54,000	
Accumulated Depreciation	33,750	
Gain on Sale of Equipment		7,750
Equipment		80,000

Assets = Liabilities + Equity: Assets +54,000, +33,750, −80,000; Equity +7,750
Cash: 54,000 (debit) | Equipment: Bal. 80,000 (debit); 80,000 (credit)
Accum Deprec: 33,750 (debit); 30,000 Bal., 3,750 (credit) | Gain on Sale of Equip: 7,750 (credit)

c. **July 1, 2020—To update depreciation expense**

Depreciation Expense	3,750	
Accumulated Depreciation—Equipment		3,750

Assets = Liabilities + Equity: Assets −3,750; Equity −3,750
Accum Deprec: 3,750 (credit) | Deprec Exp: 3,750 (debit)

July 1, 2020—To record disposal of equipment

Accumulated Depreciation	33,750	
Loss on Sale of Equipment	46,250	
Equipment		80,000

Assets = Liabilities + Equity: Assets +33,750, −80,000; Equity −46,250
Equipment: Bal. 80,000 (debit); 80,000 (credit) | Loss on Sale of Equip: 46,250 (debit)
Accum Deprec: 33,750 (debit); 30,000 Bal., 3,750 (credit)

Review 11-9

a. **To record exchange with commercial substance; no cash involved**

Equipment (fair value of asset received)	125,000	
Accumulated Depreciation	140,000	
Gain on Asset Exchange		15,000
Equipment		250,000

Assets = Liabilities + Equity: Assets +125,000, +140,000, −250,000; Equity +15,000
Equipment: Bal. 250,000, 125,000 (debit); 250,000 (credit) | Accum Deprec: 140,000 (debit); 140,000 Bal. (credit)
Gain on Exchange: 15,000 (credit)

b. **To record exchange with commercial substance; cash is paid**

Equipment (fair value of asset received)	125,000	
Accumulated Depreciation	140,000	
Loss on Asset Exchange	10,000	
Cash		25,000
Equipment		250,000

Assets = Liabilities + Equity: Assets +125,000, +140,000, −25,000, −250,000; Equity −10,000
Cash: 25,000 (credit) | Equipment: Bal. 250,000, 125,000 (debit); 250,000 (credit)
Accum Deprec: 140,000 (debit); 140,000 Bal. (credit) | Loss on Exchange: 10,000 (debit)

c. **To record exchange without commercial substance; no cash involved**

Equipment ($250,000 − $140,000)	110,000	
Accumulated Depreciation	140,000	
Equipment		250,000

Assets = Liabilities + Equity: Assets +110,000, +140,000, −250,000
Equipment: Bal. 250,000, 110,000 (debit); 250,000 (credit) | Accum Deprec: 140,000 (debit); 140,000 Bal. (credit)

d. **To record exchange without commercial substance; cash is paid**

Assets	=	Liabilities	+	Equity
+122,000				
+140,000				
−12,000				
−250,000				

Cash	
	12,000

Equipment	
Bal. 250,000	250,000
122,000	

Accum Deprec	
140,000	140,000 Bal.

Equipment ($250,000 − $140,000 + $12,000)	122,000	
Accumulated Depreciation	140,000	
Cash		12,000
Equipment		250,000

e. **To record exchange without commercial substance; cash is received**

Assets	=	Liabilities	+	Equity
+105,769				+769
+140,000				
+5,000				
−250,000				

Cash	
5,000	

Equipment	
Bal. 250,000	250,000
105,769	

Accum Deprec	
140,000	140,000 Bal.

Gain on Exchange	
	769

Equipment ($125,000 − [$20,000 − $769])	105,769	
Accumulated Depreciation	140,000	
Cash	5,000	
Gain on Asset Exchange ([$5,000/$130,000] × $20,000)		769
Equipment		250,000

12 Depreciation, Impairments, and Depletion

The Boeing Company

Note 1—Summary of Significant Accounting Policies

Property, Plant and Equipment—Property, plant and equipment are recorded at cost, including applicable construction-period interest, less accumulated depreciation and are depreciated principally over the following estimated useful lives: new buildings and land improvements, from 10 to 40 years; and new machinery and equipment, from 4 to 20 years. The principal methods of depreciation are as follows: buildings and land improvements, 150% declining b
and machinery and equipment, sum-of-the-years' digits. Capitalized internal use software is included in Other as
amortized using the straight-line method over 5 years. We periodically evaluate the appropriateness of remai
preciable lives assigned to long-lived assets, including assets that may be subject to a management plan for dis

Ford Motor Company

Net Property Net property is reported at cost, net of accumulated depreciation and impairments. We capitalize new assets when we expect to use the asset for more than one year. Routine maintenance and repair costs are expensed when incurred. Property and equipment are depreciated primarily using the straight-line method over the estimated useful life of the asset. Useful lives range from 3 years to 36 years. The estimated useful lives generally are 14.5 years for machinery and equipment, 8 years for software, 30 years for land improvements, and 36 years for buildings. Tooling generally is amortized over the expected life of a product program using a straight-line method.

Net property at December 31 follows (in millions):

	2016	2017
Land	$ 391	$ 411
Buildings and land improvements	10,308	11,096
Machinery, equipment, and other	34,149	37,533
Software	2,803	3,118
Construction in progress	2,170	2,608
Total land, plant and equipment, and other	49,821	54,766
Accumulated depreciation	(27,804)	(29,862)
Net land, plant and equipment, and other	22,017	24,904
Tooling, net of amortization	10,055	10,423
Total	$32,072	$35,327

Ford Motor Company

Note 2. Summary of Significant Accounting Policies

Long-Lived Asset Impairment—We test long-lived asset groups for recoverability at the operating seg
when changes in circumstances indicate the carrying value may not be recoverable. Events that trigger a test for recoverability include material adverse changes in projected revenues and expenses, significant underperformance relative to historical and projected future operating results, significant negative industry or economic trends, and a significant adverse change in the manner in which an asset group is used or in its physical condition. When a triggering event occurs, a test for recoverability is performed, comparing projected undiscounted future cash flows to the carrying value of the asset group. If the test for recoverability identifies a possible impairment, the asset group's fair value is measured relying primarily on a discounted cash flow method. An impairment charge is recognized for the amount b which the carrying value of the asset group exceeds its estimated fair value. When an impairment loss is recognize
to be held and used, the adjusted carrying amount of those assets is depreciated over their remaining us
impairment of long-lived assets was recorded in 2015.

EOG Resources, Inc.

Note 1: Summary of Significant Accounting Policies

Depreciation, depletion and amortization of the cost of proved oil and gas properties is calculated using the unit-of-production method. The reserve base used to calculate depreciation, depletion and amortization for leasehold acquisition costs and the cost to acquire proved properties is the sum of proved developed reserves and proved undeveloped reserves. With respect to lease and well equipment costs, which include development costs and successful exploration drilling costs, the reserve base includes only proved developed reserves. Estimated future dismantlement, restoration and abandonment costs, net of salvage values, are taken into account.

Chapter Preview

For financial reporting purposes, the cost of property, plant, and equipment can be thought of as a long-term prepayment of an expense. A portion of the cost is assumed to benefit each period of use, and depreciation expense is a systematically determined amount recognized for this purpose. How such costs should be allocated to an asset's life is determined through the depreciation process. In the first part of this chapter, we explore a variety of estimation methods including straight-line, sum-of-the-years'-digits, declining-balance, units-of-production, and group and composite methods. We estimate depreciation for a full year but we also allocate depreciation to partial periods. Other aspects of depreciation we consider include subsequent changes in depreciation estimates, changes in depreciation methods, and errors in depreciation calculations. We explain the steps to determine asset impairment and calculate key ratios. Last, we describe accounting for natural resources such as oil, gas, and minerals.

Action Plan

LO	Topic/Subtopic	Page	Demos	Reviews	Assignments
LO 12–1	**Calculate depreciation using straight-line, sum-of-the-years'-digits, declining-balance, and units-of-production methods** Depreciation Expense :: Allocation of Costs :: Uniform Rate :: Accelerated Rate :: Output/Input Measure	12-3	D12-1A D12-1B D12-1C D12-1D	R12-1	24, 25, 26, 46, 47, 48, 49, 50, 85, 86, 87, 107, 111, 112, 114, 118, 119
LO 12–2	**Account for depreciation in partial periods** Prorate Partial Period :: Policy Convention :: Full-year :: Half-year :: Full-month	12-11	D12-2A D12-2B	R12-2	27, 28, 29, 30, 51, 52, 53, 54, 55, 56, 57, 62, 85, 88, 89, 90, 92, 93, 97, 98
LO 12–3	**Calculate depreciation using group and composite depreciation methods** Group Method :: Homogeneous Assets :: Composite Method :: Heterogeneous Assets	12-15	D12-3	R12-3	31, 58, 59, 60, 85, 91, 108, 113, 115, 118
LO 12–4	**Account for changes in estimate as they relate to depreciation** Change in Estimate :: Change in Residual Value :: Change in Useful Life :: Prospective Treatment :: Disclosure	12-17	D12-4	R12-4	32, 34, 61, 66, 67, 69,73, 85, 92, 93, 95, 96, 97, 117
LO 12–5	**Account for changes in depreciation methods** Treat as Change in Estimate :: Prospective Treatment :: Disclosure	12-19	D12-5	R12-5	33, 35, 63, 64, 65, 68, 69, 85, 94, 95, 98, 117
LO 12–6	**Account for errors in reporting property, plant, and equipment** Accounting Error :: Retrospective Treatment :: Prior Period Adjustment :: Retained Earnings :: Disclosure	12-20	D12-6	R12-6	36, 37, 38, 70, 71, 72, 73, 85, 96, 97, 98, 117
LO 12–7	**Account for impairments of property, plant, and equipment** Impairment Indicator :: Asset Recoverability Test :: Measurement of Impairment Loss	12-21	D12-7	R12-7	39, 40, 74, 75, 85, 92, 93, 99, 117, 118
LO 12–8	**Account for assets held for sale** Discontinue Depreciation :: Fair Value Less Selling Costs :: Recoverability of Losses :: Other Assets	12-24	D12-8	R12-8	41, 42, 76, 77, 85, 100
LO 12–9	**Describe property, plant, and equipment disclosures and ratio analyses** Required Disclosures :: Asset Turnover :: Return on Assets :: Fixed Asset Turnover	12-28	D12-9	R12-9	43, 78, 79, 85, 101, 102, 109
LO 12–10	**Record acquisition and depletion of natural resources** Depletion Cost Base :: Acquisition Costs :: Exploration Costs :: Development Costs :: Restoration Costs	12-30	D12-10A D12-10B	R12-10	44, 45, 80, 81, 82, 83, 84, 103, 104, 105, 106, 110, 116
LO 12–11	**APPENDIX 12A—Calculate MACRS (tax) depreciation** MACRS :: Tax Depreciation :: Asset Classes :: Statutory Percentages :: Depreciation Acceleration	12-34	D12-11	R12-11	122, 123, 124, 125, 126

LO 12-1 Calculate depreciation using straight-line, sum-of-the-years'-digits, declining-balance, and units-of-production methods

LO 12-1 Overview

Depreciation (Allocation) of Cost Based on:
- Uniform rate: Straight-line method
- Accelerated rate: Sum-of-the-years'-digits and declining-balance methods
- Output/Input measures: Units-of-production method

Depreciation recognition transfers a portion of both acquisition costs and capitalized post-acquisition costs of plant assets through a debit to an expense account called **Depreciation Expense**. The allocation to expense takes place over the estimated life of a fixed asset in a systematic and rational manner. The phrase **systematic and rational** implies that depreciation methods should be both precisely specified, rather than arbitrary, and defensible on the grounds that the result follows logically from the asset's use. The corresponding credit is to **Accumulated Depreciation**, a contra asset account. Depreciation expense is an **allocation of costs** for a particular period while accumulated depreciation is the cumulative balance of depreciation at a particular point in time. Companies have a number of depreciation methods available when choosing a systematic method including methods that allocate costs by time (even or accelerated rates) and by output or input measures.

360-10-35-4 The cost of a productive facility is one of the costs of the services it renders during its useful economic life. Generally accepted accounting principles (GAAP) require that this cost be spread over the expected useful life of the facility in such a way as to allocate it as equitably as possible to the periods during which services are obtained from the use of the facility. This procedure is known as depreciation accounting, a system of accounting which aims to distribute the cost or other basic value of tangible capital assets, less salvage (if any), over the estimated useful life of the unit (which may be a group of assets) in a systematic and rational manner. It is a process of allocation, not of valuation.

Depreciation expense for a nonmanufacturing company is classified as a selling or administrative expense, depending on the asset's function. Manufacturing companies include depreciation on plant assets used in manufacturing inventory in the inventory account. When goods are sold, depreciation becomes part of the cost of goods sold expense. Accumulated depreciation appears in the noncurrent asset section of the balance sheet either parenthetically or as a line item deduction from gross property, plant, and equipment. Separate asset and related accumulated depreciation accounts are maintained to preserve records on the historical cost of the asset. Terms that provide the background for depreciation calculations are defined as follows.

Terminology	Description
Book value or **Net carrying value**	Capitalized asset cost less accumulated depreciation, reported on the balance sheet.
Residual value, Salvage value, or **Scrap value**	▪ Estimated net recoverable amount (after any estimated disposal costs) from disposal or trade-in of an asset. ▪ Portion of an asset's acquisition cost not consumed through use, and not allocated to expense through depreciation. ▪ Often assigned no value due to materiality (insignificant amounts) or practicality (uncertainties in measuring).
Useful life or **Service life**	▪ Economic life of an asset or the period that the company plans to benefit from the use of the asset.* ▪ Requires assumptions about potential obsolescence, patterns of usage, and maintenance. ▪ Developed by management through prior experiences in estimating useful life and through consideration of typical industry practices. ▪ Characterized in time (such as years) or in units of input or output (such as hours of usage).
Depreciable cost or **Allocation base**	▪ Total amount of depreciation to be recognized over the useful life of the asset. ▪ Equal to the total capitalized asset cost less salvage value.
Allocation method or **Depreciation method**	Method to systematically allocate a fixed asset's cost by time or by input/output.

* Economic life can be less than the physical life of the asset. For example, a company's policy might be to replace equipment after 3 years with new equipment to maintain high efficiencies.

EXPANDING YOUR KNOWLEDGE **Fair Value vs. Book Value of Fixed Assets**

Depreciation is *not* a valuation process. Gradual fair value changes are *not* recorded in the plant asset accounts, and the book value of a plant asset typically does not equal its fair value. Periodic fair value changes are *not* a sufficiently reliable or objective basis for depreciation accounting, and they are not the result of arm's-length transactions. The cost principle supports the objective of original cost as the depreciation base and the expense recognition principle supports the allocation of expense to the periods revenue is generated by using the fixed asset. For example, equipment is expensed over its useful life of 5 years during which time the company generates revenue from selling products produced by the equipment.

Calculation of Depreciation Expense

In this section, we review four methods of depreciation: (1) straight-line depreciation—**Demo 12-1A** (uniform rate method), (2) sum-of-the-years' digits—**Demo 12-1B** (accelerated rate method), (3) declining-balance—**Demo 12-1C** (accelerated rate method), and (4) units-of-production—**Demo 12-1D** (output/input method). The straight-line method is the most popular method in use as illustrated in **Exhibit 12-1**. Ease of use partially explains the method's popularity. The straight-line method also results in higher current earnings levels for growth companies, an effect that is attractive to managers whose compensation is tied to earnings performance.

EXHIBIT 12-1
Depreciation Methods in Use

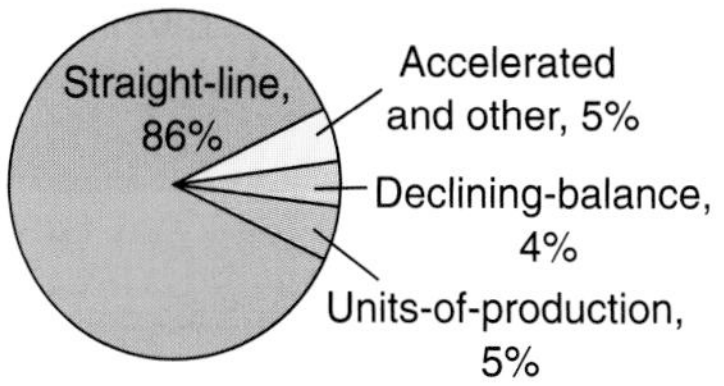

Straight-Line Depreciation Method

The **straight-line method** is based on the assumption that a fixed asset declines in usefulness at a constant rate. The straight-line method relates depreciation directly to the passage of time rather than to the asset's use, resulting in a constant amount of depreciation recognized per rate. The formula for computing periodic straight-line depreciation follows.

$$\textbf{Annual straight-line depreciation expense} = \frac{\textbf{Acquisition cost} - \textbf{Residual value}}{\textbf{Estimated useful life in years}}$$

The straight-line depreciation method is logically appealing as well as systematic and rational. It is especially appropriate when the decline in service potential is approximately the same each period, the use of the asset is roughly the same each period, and repairs and maintenance expenditures are constant over the asset's useful life. This method is not appropriate for assets whose decline in service potential or benefits produced relates not to the passage of time, but rather to other variables, such as units produced or hours in service. The straight-line method also is inappropriate when obsolescence is the primary factor in depreciation.

Straight-Line Depreciation Method **LO12-1** **Demo 12-1A**

Demo MBC

The following information is used to illustrate straight-line depreciation.

Equipment acquisition cost, January 1, 2020	$6,600
Residual value	$600
Estimated useful life, in years	5
Estimated productive output, in units	10,000

a. Record the adjusting entry for 2020 depreciation expense applying the straight-line method.
b. Prepare a depreciation schedule showing depreciation expense, accumulated depreciation, and book value of the equipment over its useful life.
c. Show the balance sheet presentation of equipment on December 31, 2020.

Solution

a. **Straight-Line Depreciation Expense**
Annual straight-line depreciation expense of $1,200 is calculated as follows.

$$\frac{\text{Acquisition cost} - \text{Residual value}}{\text{Estimated useful life in years}} = \frac{(\$6{,}600 - \$600)}{5} = \$1{,}200 \text{ per year}$$

continued

continued from previous page

The entry to record depreciation expense as an adjusting entry at the end of 2020 follows.

December 31, 2020—To record depreciation expense

Depreciation Expense	1,200	
Accumulated Depreciation.		1,200

Assets = Liabilities + Equity
−1,200 −1,200
Accum Deprec: 1,200 (credit)
Deprec Exp: 1,200 (debit)

Straight-line depreciation frequently is expressed in terms of a percentage rate: the ratio of annual depreciation expense to depreciable cost. This asset has a 20% straight-line rate ($1,200/$6,000). In other words, in each year, 20% of depreciable cost is recognized as depreciation. This rate also equals the reciprocal of useful life, or 1/5 (20%).

b. **Straight-line Depreciation Schedule**

The following schedule shows the book value of equipment each year using the straight-line method over the useful life of equipment.

	Depreciation for the Period			End of Period	
Reporting Period	Depreciable Cost*	Depreciation Rate	Depreciation Expense	Accumulated Depreciation	Book Value**
Jan. 1, 2020.					$6,600
Dec. 31, 2020.	$6,000	0.20	$1,200	$1,200	5,400
Dec. 31, 2021.	6,000	0.20	1,200	2,400	4,200
Dec. 31, 2022.	6,000	0.20	1,200	3,600	3,000
Dec. 31, 2023.	6,000	0.20	1,200	4,800	1,800
Dec. 31, 2024.	6,000	0.20	1,200	6,000	600 ← Residual value

* Depreciable cost equals acquisition cost less residual value or $6,600 − $600.

** Book value equals original cost less accumulated depreciation.

In the schedule above, we can see that the depreciation expense is equal each year given a January 1 purchase date. Also, total depreciation expense over five years equals $6,000 or the depreciable cost of the asset. The book value at the end of each period is equal to the original cost of equipment of $6,600 less the balance in accumulated depreciation. For example, on December 31, 2020, the book value of $5,400 is equal to $6,600 (cost) less $1,200 (accumulated depreciation).

c. **Balance Sheet Presentation**

Net equipment appears on the balance sheet at December 31, 2020, as illustrated in the following excerpt.

Assets	
Equipment	$6,600
Less: Accumulated depreciation.	1,200
Equipment, net	$5,400

Sum-of-the-Years'-Digits Depreciation Method

Accelerated depreciation methods recognize greater amounts of depreciation early in the useful life of plant assets and lesser amounts later. Thus, the recognition of depreciation is accelerated. *Accelerated methods are based on the assumption that newer assets produce more benefits per period because they are more productive and require less maintenance and repairs.* Accelerated methods allocate more of the acquisition cost to expense in earlier periods when greater benefits are obtained. In later periods, less depreciation is allocated to expense when an asset is projected to provide less benefit or when repair and maintenance expenses are projected to increase. The principal accelerated methods in use today are the sum-of-the-years'-digits method and the declining-balance method.

360-10-35-7 The declining-balance method is an example of one of the methods that meet the requirements of being systematic and rational. If the expected productivity of the asset or ability of the asset to generate revenue is relatively greater during the earlier years of its life, or maintenance charges tend to increase during later years, the declining-balance method may provide the most satisfactory allocation of cost. That conclusion also applies to other methods, including the sum-of-the-years'-digits method, that produce substantially similar results.

The formula for computing periodic **sum-of-the-years' digits** depreciation expense follows.

Annual sum-of-the-years'-digits depreciation expense = Depreciable cost × Fraction

The fraction for the first year of an asset purchased on January 1, 2020, with a five-year useful life is **5/15** computed from the following components.

Numerator: number of years remaining in the useful life at the beginning of the period. The numerator declines with each year of asset use. For 2020, the numerator is 5 because there are 5 years remaining at the beginning of 2020.

Denominator: sum of the integers from 1 up to the number of years of useful life (sum of the years' digits). For an asset with a useful life of five years, the denominator is $1 + 2 + 3 + 4 + 5$, or 15. This sum also equals $n(n + 1)/2$ where n is the useful life in years, or in this case: $5(5 + 1)/2 = 15$.

The sum-of-the-years' digits method is systematic and rational and is especially appropriate for assets supplying proportionately greater benefits early in their useful life. For example, high-technology equipment often provides more benefits early in its life and then becomes obsolete as technology changes. Accelerated methods are applicable when obsolescence is an important factor in the estimate of useful life. An asset with a three-year useful life is 50% depreciated at the end of its first year under the sum-of-the-years' digits method: $3/(3 + 2 + 1) = 3/6$, or 50%. If the asset becomes obsolete in its second year, most of the asset is already depreciated.

Sum-of-the-Years'-Digits Depreciation Method — LO12-1 — Demo 12-1B

Demo MBC

Using the information for equipment in **Demo 12-1A**, answer the following.

a. Record the adjusting entry for 2020 depreciation expense applying the sum-of-the-years'-digits depreciation method.

b. Prepare a depreciation schedule showing depreciation expense, accumulated depreciation, and book value of the equipment over its useful life.

Solution

a. **Sum-of-the-Years'-Digits Depreciation Expense**

Under sum-of-the-years' digits method, depreciation expense in 2020 is calculated as follows: an asset with a 5-year useful life, the fraction for year one is equal to the numerator of 5 (number of remaining years) divided by the denominator of 15, or $5(5 + 1)/2$.

Depreciable base × Fraction = Sum-of-the-years'-digits annual depreciation
($6,600 − $600) × (5/15) = $2,000

The entry to record depreciation expense as an adjusting entry at the end of 2020 follows.

December 31, 2020—To record depreciation expense

Depreciation Expense	2,000	
Accumulated Depreciation.		2,000

Assets = Liabilities + Equity
−2,000 −2,000
Accum Deprec | 2,000
Deprec Exp 2,000 |

b. **Sum-of-the-Years'-Digits Depreciation Schedule**

The following schedule shows the book value of equipment each year using the sum-of-the-years'-digits depreciation method over the useful life of equipment.

	Depreciation for the Period			End of Period	
Reporting Period	**Depreciable Cost**	**Depreciation Rate**	**Depreciation Expense**	**Accumulated Depreciation**	**Book Value**
Jan. 1, 2020.					$6,600
Dec. 31, 2020.	$6,000	5/15	$2,000	$2,000	4,600
Dec. 31, 2021.	6,000	4/15	1,600	3,600	3,000
Dec. 31, 2022.	6,000	3/15	1,200	4,800	1,800
Dec. 31, 2023.	6,000	2/15	800	5,600	1,000
Dec. 31, 2024.	6,000	1/15	400	6,000	600 ← Residual value

continued

continued from previous page

In the schedule on the previous page, we can see that depreciation expense is the greatest in the first year and decreases each year after that. Also, total depreciation expense over five years equals $6,000 because, in total, 15/15 of the $6,000 depreciable cost is allocated to expense.

Declining-Balance Depreciation Method

The formula for computing periodic **declining balance** depreciation expense is

Annual declining-balance depreciation = Book value at beginning of year × Depreciation rate

The declining-balance method (an accelerated method) is different from other methods in two ways:

- Residual value is not subtracted from cost when computing depreciation.
- A constant depreciation rate is applied to a declining-balance (book value) rather than to a constant depreciable cost. The depreciation rate is a multiple of the straight-line rate. For example, the **double-declining-balance depreciation method** is used when a company depreciates an asset at 2 times the straight-line rate. An asset with a useful life of 5 years has a double-declining rate of 40% (2 × 1/*n*, or 2 × 1/5), where *n* equals the number of estimated years of service. Companies may use other multiples in applying the declining-balance method of depreciation such as 1.5 for the 150% declining balance method disclosed by the Boeing Company in the Chapter Preview.

It is important that assets are not depreciated below their residual value. Because residual value is not subtracted in the declining balance method, depreciation expense in the final year is computed as the amount necessary to reach the required accumulated depreciation amount at the end of the asset's useful life.

Demo 12-1C **LO12-1** **Double-Declining-Balance Depreciation Method**

Demo MBC

Using the information for equipment in **Demo 12-1A**, answer the following.

a. Record the adjusting entry for 2020 depreciation expense applying the double-declining-balance depreciation method.

b. Prepare a depreciation schedule showing depreciation expense, accumulated depreciation, and book value of the equipment over its useful life.

Solution

a. **Double-Declining-Balance Depreciation Expense**

Under the double-declining-balance method, depreciation expense in 2020 is calculated as follows. For an asset with a useful life of 5 years, the double-declining depreciation rate is 40%, which is equal to the straight-line rate of 20% (or 1/5 years) multiplied by 2.

Book value at beginning of year × Depreciation rate = Double-declining-balance annual depreciation
$6,600 × 40% = $2,640

The entry to record depreciation expense as an adjusting entry at the end of 2020 follows.

December 31, 2020—To record depreciation expense

Depreciation Expense	2,640	
Accumulated Depreciation.		2,640

Assets = Liabilities + Equity
−2,640 −2,640
Accum Deprec: 2,640 (credit)
Deprec Exp: 2,640 (debit)

b. **Double-Declining-Balance Depreciation Schedule**

The following schedule shows the book value of equipment each year using the double-declining-balance depreciation method over the useful life of the equipment.

continued

continued from previous page

	Depreciation for the Period			End of Period	
Reporting Period	**Beginning of Period Book Value**	**Depreciation Rate**	**Depreciation Expense**	**Accumulated Depreciation**	**Book Value**
Jan. 1, 2020					$6,600
Dec. 31, 2020	$6,600	0.40	$2,640	$2,640	3,960
Dec. 31, 2021	3,960	0.40	1,584	4,224	2,376
Dec. 31, 2022	2,376	0.40	950	5,174	1,426
Dec. 31, 2023	1,426	0.40	570	5,744	856
Dec. 31, 2024	856	0.40	256*	6,000	600 ← Residual value

*Depreciation expense stops when accumulated depreciation equals the $6,000 depreciable cost, leaving the $600 residual value intact. Thus, the maximum depreciation for 2024 is $256 ($856 less $600) rather than 40% of $856.

Annual depreciation expense declines along with the declining book value under this method. The book value at the beginning of any year is reduced by depreciation in all previous years. For example, 2021 depreciation is computed by taking the book value on January 1, 2021, of $3,960 multiplied by 40% to arrive at $1,584. Residual value is not subtracted in computing double-declining depreciation. The double-declining-balance method requires a forced amount or a plug in the final year of depreciation to reach the final desired accumulated depreciation amount (in this case, $6,000). Under this accelerated method, an asset may be fully depreciated before the end of its useful life.

Real World—DEPRECIATION METHODS

BOEING COMPANY [BA]

The Boeing Company offers products and services in the segments of commercial airplanes, defense, space and security, and capital. In a recent Form 10-K, Boeing disclosed that it uses different depreciation methods for different classes of property, plant, and equipment.

> **Property, Plant and Equipment**—Property, plant and equipment are recorded at cost, including applicable construction-period interest, less accumulated depreciation and are depreciated principally over the following estimated useful lives: new buildings and land improvements, from 10 to 40 years; and new machinery and equipment, from 4 to 20 years. The principal methods of depreciation are as follows: buildings and land improvements, 150% declining balance; and machinery and equipment, sum-of-the-years' digits. Capitalized internal use software is included in Other assets and amortized using the straight-line method over 5 years. We periodically evaluate the appropriateness of remaining depreciable lives assigned to long-lived assets, including assets that may be subject to a management plan for disposition.

Units-of-Production Method

In the **units-of-production method**, or **activity method**, the number of units of output (such as units of production) or input (such as hours of service) are used to measure asset use. A constant amount of depreciable cost is allocated to each unit as a cost of production, and so annual depreciation amounts fluctuate with changes in the volume of input or output. In other words, depreciation is aligned with the level of a company's productivity.

The formula for computing periodic units-of-production depreciation expense follows.

$$\textbf{Depreciation rate per unit of output (input)} = \frac{\textbf{Depreciable cost}}{\textbf{Estimated productive output (input) in units}}$$

$$\textbf{Annual depreciation expense} = \textbf{Depreciation rate per unit of output (input)} \times \textbf{Actual units of output (input)}$$

The input-output methods allocate costs in a systematic and rational manner. However, a problem arises when an input measure varies without a corresponding effect on the output of service. For example, the increasingly heavy traffic in urban areas causes vehicles to run many more hours per week with no increase in their productive service. Also, for many assets, such as buildings, furniture, and office equipment, application of these methods is impracticable because no measure of service or output is available. In other cases, tracking of input or output measures may prove to be too costly. Mining, oil-drilling, and steelmaking equipment are often depreciated using this method.

Demo 12-1D **LO12-1** **Units-of-Production Depreciation Method**

Demo MBC

Using the information for equipment in **Demo 12-1A**, answer the following.

a. Record the adjusting entry for 2020 depreciation expense applying the units-of-production depreciation method assuming that there are 1,800 actual units of production in 2020.

b. Prepare a depreciation schedule showing depreciation expense, accumulated depreciation, and book value of the equipment over its useful life, assuming the following estimated units of production: 2021: 2,000 units; 2022: 2,400 units; 2023: 1,800 units; and 2024: 2,000 units.

Solution

a. **Units-of-Production Depreciation Expense**

Under the units-of-production method, depreciation expense for 2020 is

$$\frac{\text{Depreciable cost}}{\text{Estimated output}} = \frac{\$6,600 - \$600}{10,000 \text{ units}} = \$0.60 \text{ per unit of output}$$

Given 1,800 units produced in 2020, depreciation expense is $1,080 ($0.60 per unit of output × 1,800 units).

The entry to record depreciation expense as an adjusting entry at the end of 2020 follows.

Assets = Liabilities + Equity
−1,080 −1,080
Accum Deprec 1,080
Deprec Exp 1,080

December 31, 2020—To record depreciation expense

Depreciation Expense	1,080	
Accumulated Depreciation.		1,080

b. **Units-of-Production Depreciation Schedule**

The following schedule shows the book value of equipment each year using the units-of-production method.

	Depreciation for the Period			End of Period	
Reporting Period	Units of Output	Depreciation per Unit	Depreciation Expense	Accumulated Depreciation	Book Value
Jan. 1, 2020.					$6,600
Dec. 31, 2020.	1,800	0.60	$1,080	$1,080	5,520
Dec. 31, 2021.	2,000	0.60	1,200	2,280	4,320
Dec. 31, 2022.	2,400	0.60	1,440	3,720	2,880
Dec. 31, 2023.	1,800	0.60	1,080	4,800	1,800
Dec. 31, 2024.	2,000	0.60	1,200	6,000	600 ← Residual value

If the actual output does not equal the planned output, depreciation expense in the last year of the asset's life would be recorded at an amount that results in accumulated depreciation of $6,000 (cost of $6,600 less the residual value of $600). In other words, depreciation expense must not accumulate to more than $6,000.

Comparison of Depreciation Methods

The following table highlights how the pattern of depreciation expense by year varies depending on the method selected.

Depreciation Expense by Year	Straight-Line Demo 12-1A	Sum-of-the Years'-Digits Demo 12-1B	Double-Declining-Balance Demo 12-1C	Units-of-Production Demo 12-1D
2020	$1,200	$2,000	$2,640	$1,080
2021	1,200	1,600	1,584	1,200
2022	1,200	1,200	950	1,440
2023	1,200	800	570	1,080
2024	1,200	400	256	1,200
	$6,000	$6,000	$6,000	$6,000

Straight-line depreciation is constant each year, whereas accelerated depreciation decreases each year. In the early years of the equipment's life, depreciation is higher under the accelerated methods, while in the later years of the equipment's life, depreciation expense is higher under the straight-line method. Under the units-of-production approach, depreciation expense varies according to usage. No matter which method is selected however, accumulated depreciation equals $6,000 at the end of the asset's useful life. The trends of the various depreciation methods over time are illustrated in **Exhibit 12-2**.

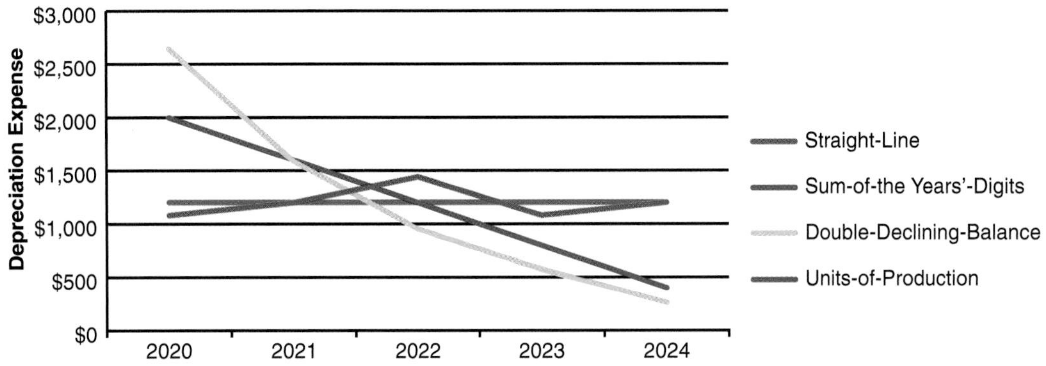

EXHIBIT 12-2
Depreciation Expense Over Time by Method

The choice of depreciation method depends on a variety of factors. Accounting information system costs are an important factor such as the amount of detailed information that must be tracked and the capabilities of the system to retrieve information for depreciation calculations. For example, the units-of-production method requires tracking of input or output measures that may not be otherwise tracked in the accounting system. On the other hand, the straight-line method is simple to apply, projects consistent results over time, and requires no extra tracking of input or output measures. The straight-line method is appropriate when deterioration of a fixed asset is a function of time. Expected obsolescence can also affect the choice of method. Accelerated methods might be appropriate, for example, when a fixed asset is subject to rapid obsolescence.

Many companies employ straight-line depreciation for *financial accounting* and accelerated depreciation for *tax reporting*, typically resulting in higher earnings reported to shareholders and lower tax liabilities. Unlike in inventory accounting, there is no requirement for an alignment of tax and financial accounting depreciation methods. The accounting guidance concludes that an accelerated tax method is unacceptable for financial reporting in certain cases.

360-10-35-9 If the number of years specified by the Accelerated Cost Recovery System of the Internal Revenue Service (IRS) for recovery deductions for an asset does not fall within a reasonable range of the asset's useful life, the recovery deductions shall not be used as depreciation expense for financial reporting.

Other factors affecting depreciation policy are a belief that depreciation methods that maximize net income have a positive effect on share price and management's desire to maximize its own financial well-being through compensation contracts based on earnings. Although both factors may contribute to the dominance of the straight-line method, research suggests that stock prices are not directly affected by the choice of depreciation method.

The latitude in adoption of depreciation methods and the variety of estimates of useful life and residual value are at odds with the uniformity and consistency objectives of financial reporting. In fact, companies may develop their own depreciation method as long as costs are allocated in a systematic and rational manner. The large dollar amount of depreciation expense reported, combined with the inherently approximate nature of depreciation, results in a potentially difficult comparison problem for financial statement users. To further complicate matters, many companies use more than one depreciation method, making it difficult to compare income across companies.

Real World—PROPERTY, PLANT, AND EQUIPMENT

3M COMPANY [MMM]

3M is a diversified technology company. In a recent Form 10-K, 3M disclosed that it records depreciation using the straight-line method. 3M also disclosed the range of useful lives over which depreciation is allocated on its major classes of assets.

> **Property, plant and equipment**—Property, plant and equipment, including capitalized interest and internal engineering costs, are recorded at cost. Depreciation of property, plant and equipment generally is computed using the straight-line method based on the estimated useful lives of the assets. The estimated useful lives of buildings and improvements primarily range from ten to forty years, with the majority in the range of twenty to forty years. The estimated useful lives of machinery and equipment primarily range from three to fifteen years, with the majority in the range of five to ten years. Fully depreciated assets are retained in property and accumulated depreciation accounts until disposal. Upon disposal, assets and related accumulated depreciation are removed from the accounts and the net amount, less proceeds from disposal, is charged or credited to operations. Property, plant and equipment amounts are reviewed for impairment whenever events or changes in circumstances indicate that the carrying amount of an asset (asset group) may not be recoverable. An impairment loss would be recognized when the carrying amount of an asset exceeds the estimated undiscounted future cash flows expected to result from the use of the asset and its eventual disposition. The amount of the impairment loss recorded is calculated by the excess of the asset's carrying value over its fair value. Fair value is generally determined using a discounted cash flow analysis.

REVIEW 12-1 LO12-1 Depreciation Methods

Review MBC

Alpine Inc. purchased equipment on January 1, 2020, with a cost of $225,000. The estimated residual value at the end of its estimated useful life of 6 years is $10,000. Data relating to the equipment follow.

Estimated service life, in years	6
Estimated service hours	100,000
Actual service hours in 2020	20,000
Actual service hours in 2021	18,000

Required

Compute depreciation expense for 2020 and 2021 assuming (1) straight-line, (2) sum-of-the-years'-digits, (3) double-declining-balance, and (4) units-of-production depreciation methods.

More Practice: 12-26, 12-46, 12-47, 12-48

Solution on p. 12-58.

LO 12-2 Account for depreciation in partial periods

LO 12-2 Overview

Depreciation in Partial Periods
- Prorate for partial period
- Adopt policy convention
  - Full-year convention
  - Half-year convention
  - Full-month convention

Most plant assets are not placed in service at the beginning of a reporting period, nor are disposals typically made on an asset's service-entry anniversary date. Companies adjust for fractional periods in two different ways. Some companies compute the exact amount of depreciation for each fractional period—see **Demo 12-2A**. To avoid the complexities of fractional-year depreciation, other companies adopt a **policy convention**, examples of which are included in **Exhibit 12-3**—see **Demo 12-2B**. These conventions satisfy GAAP if the results are not materially different from the exact calculation. **The same policy must be used consistently to achieve similar results from period to period.**

Accounting Convention	Description
Full-year convention—Beginning of period	Annual depreciation is based solely on the basis of the balance in the fixed asset account at the beginning of the year. Assets disposed of during the year are depreciated a full year, and assets purchased during the year are not depreciated that year.
Full-year convention—End of period	Compute annual depreciation solely on the basis of the balance in the fixed asset account at the end of the year. Assets purchased during the year are depreciated a full year, and assets disposed of during the year are not depreciated that year.
Half-year convention	Compute one-half of a year's depreciation in both the year of purchase and the year of retirement, regardless of the date of purchase or retirement.
Full-month convention	Compute a full month of depreciation during the month of purchase and no depreciation in the month of disposal.

EXHIBIT 12-3
Accounting Conventions

Depreciation Prorated for Partial Period

LO12-2 **Demo 12-2A**

Demo MBC

The following information is used to illustrate partial period depreciation computed as the exact amount of depreciation for each fractional period.

Equipment acquisition cost, at April 1, 2020	$6,600
Residual value	$600
Estimated useful life, in years	5
Estimated productive output, in units	10,000
Actual productive unit output, 2020	1,000

Using the information above, compute depreciation expense each year over the life of the equipment using (a) the straight-line method, (b) the sum-of-the-years'-digits method, and (c) the double-declining-balance method. In addition, calculate depreciation expense for 2020 only under (d) the units-of-production method.

Solution

a. **Straight-Line Method**

Recall from the last section that annual depreciation under the straight-line method is $1,200 or ($6,600 − $600)/5. When an asset is purchased during the year, the asset's fractional service period is applied to the annual depreciation amount as illustrated.

	Depreciation for the Period				End of Period	
Reporting Period	Depreciable Cost*	Depreciation Rate	Partial Period	Depreciation Expense	Accumulated Depreciation	Book Value
Jan. 1, 2020 . . .						$6,600
Dec. 31, 2020 . . .	$6,000	0.20	9/12	$ 900	$ 900	5,700
Dec. 31, 2021 . . .	6,000	0.20		1,200	2,100	4,500
Dec. 31, 2022 . . .	6,000	0.20		1,200	3,300	3,300
Dec. 31, 2023 . . .	6,000	0.20		1,200	4,500	2,100
Dec. 31, 2024 . . .	6,000	0.20		1,200	5,700	900
Dec. 31, 2025 . . .	6,000	0.20	3/12	300	6,000	600 ← Residual value

* Depreciable cost equals acquisition cost less residual value, or $6,600 − $600.

In 2020, 9 out of 12 months of depreciation are recorded while in 2025, 3 out of 12 months of depreciation are recorded. In total, exactly 5 full years of depreciation are recorded from 2020 to 2025.

b. **Sum-of-the-Years' Digits-Method**

To prorate depreciation using the sum-of-the-years'-digits method, each layer of depreciation is prorated and allocated to the appropriate year. In other words, the first layer of depreciation of $2,000 (5/15 × $6,000) is allocated 9/12 to 2020 (for the months of April to December) and 3/12 to 2021 (for the months January to March). The pattern continues through the life of the asset and is demonstrated in the following schedule.

continued

continued from previous page

	Depreciation for the Period				End of Period	
Reporting Period	**Depreciable Cost**	**Depreciation Rate**	**Partial Period**	**Depreciation Expense**	**Accumulated Depreciation**	**Book Value**
April 1, 2020 . . .						$6,600
Dec. 31, 2020 . . .	$6,000	5/15	9/12	$1,500	$1,500	5,100
Dec. 31, 2021 . . .	6,000	5/15	3/12	500 ⎤ 1,700	2,000	
	6,000	4/15	9/12	1,200 ⎦	3,200	3,400
Dec. 31, 2022 . . .	6,000	4/15	3/12	400 ⎤ 1,100	3,600	
	6,000	3/15	9/12	900 ⎦	4,500	2,100
Dec. 31, 2023 . . .	6,000	3/15	3/12	300 ⎤ 900	4,800	
	6,000	2/15	9/12	600 ⎦	5,400	1,200
Dec. 31, 2024 . . .	6,000	2/15	3/12	200 ⎤ 500	5,600	
	6,000	1/15	9/12	300 ⎦	5,900	700
Dec. 31, 2025 . . .	6,000	1/15	3/12	100	6,000	600 ← Residual value

c. **Double-Declining-Balance Method**

To prorate depreciation using the double-declining-balance method, the first year is prorated for a partial year (9/12 of the year in this case). Just as with full-year depreciation per year, depreciation will end when the asset has been depreciated up to its residual value.

	Depreciation for the Period				End of Period	
Reporting Period	**Beginning of Period Book Value**	**Depreciation Rate**	**Partial Period**	**Depreciation Expense**	**Accumulated Depreciation**	**Book Value**
April 1, 2020 . . .						$6,600
Dec. 31, 2020 . . .	$6,600	0.40	9/12	$1,980	$1,980	4,620
Dec. 31, 2021 . . .	4,620	0.40		1,848	3,828	2,772
Dec. 31, 2022 . . .	2,772	0.40		1,109	4,937	1,663
Dec. 31, 2023 . . .	1,663	0.40		665	5,602	998
Dec. 31, 2024 . . .	998	0.40		398†	6,000	600 ← Residual value

†Depreciation expense stops when accumulated depreciation equals the $6,000 depreciable cost, leaving the $600 residual value intact. Thus, the maximum depreciation for 2024 is $398 ($6,000 less $5,602) rather than $399 (40% of $998).

d. **Units-of-Production Method**

The units-of-production method automatically adjusts for partial year depreciation. The output (in this case, number of units produced) in the partial-year period is applied to the depreciation rate in the normal manner.

In 2020, the number of units produced by the equipment is 1,000 units, which is a portion of the units that could be produced over a full year. With a $0.60 rate of depreciation per unit of production ($6,000/10,000 units), depreciation would automatically be calculated at a prorated value of $600 (1,000 units × $0.60).

Demo 12-2B LO12-2 Policy Convention Applied to Partial Period

Demo MBC

The following information is used to illustrate partial period depreciation computed using accounting policy conventions.

Equipment acquisition cost, at April 1, 2020 . . .	$ 6,600
Residual value . . .	$ 600
Estimated useful life, in years . . .	5
Estimated productive output, in units . . .	10,000

continued

continued from previous page

Using the information above, compute depreciation expense each year over the life of the equipment using the straight-line method and (a) full-year convention—beginning of period, (b) full-year convention—end of period, (c) half-year convention, and (d) full-month convention. In addition, provide a table comparing annual depreciation expense across the various methods over the equipment's useful life.

Solution

a. **Full-Year Convention—Beginning of Period**
No depreciation is recognized in 2020 on the equipment, while $1,200 is recognized in each year 2021 through 2025.

b. **Full-Year Convention—End of Period**
Straight-line depreciation of $1,200 on the equipment is recognized each year 2020 through 2024, with no depreciation expense recognized in 2025.

c. **Half-Year Convention**
In 2020 and 2025, a half-year of depreciation or $600 (1/2 × $1,200) of straight-line depreciation is recognized, while $1,200 is recognized in years 2021 through 2024.

d. **Full-Month Convention**
Because the asset was purchased on April 1, the full-month convention results in the same depreciation amount as when computing actual depreciation in **Demo 12-2A**. The company would recognize $900 of depreciation expense in 2020, $1,200 of depreciation expense in the years 2021 through 2024, and $300 of depreciation expense in 2025.

Depreciation is summarized in the table below for the various straight-line methods illustrated above. For comparison, prorated depreciation from **Demo 12-2A** is shown in the first row. In all cases, accumulated depreciation at the end of the asset's useful life is equal to $6,000, the depreciable cost of the equipment.

Straight-Line Depreciation Method	**Depreciation Expense**						
	2020	**2021**	**2022**	**2023**	**2024**	**2025**	**Total**
Prorated depreciation (Demo 12-2A) . . .	$ 900	$1,200	$1,200	$1,200	$1,200	$ 300	$6,000
a. Full-year—Beg. of period	0	1,200	1,200	1,200	1,200	1,200	6,000
b. Full-year—End of period.	1,200	1,200	1,200	1,200	1,200	0	6,000
c. Half-year.	600	1,200	1,200	1,200	1,200	600	6,000
d. Full-month.	900	1,200	1,200	1,200	1,200	300	6,000

Partial Period Depreciation

LO12-2 **REVIEW 12-2**

Part One—Depreciation Prorated for Partial Period
Alpine Inc. purchased equipment on September 1, 2020, at a cost of $225,000. The estimated residual value at the end of its estimated life of 6 years is $10,000. Data relating to the equipment follow.

Estimated service life, in years.	6
Estimated service hours	100,000
Actual service hours in 2020	5,000
Actual service hours in 2021	18,000

Compute depreciation expense for 2020 and 2021 under the (1) straight-line, (2) sum-of-the-years'-digits, (3) double-declining-balance, and (4) units-of-production depreciation methods. Prorate partial depreciation expense for each partial period.

Part Two—Policy Convention Applied to Partial Period
Assume the same information as in Part One, except now assume that the equipment was purchased on September 8, 2020. Compute depreciation expense each year over the life of the equipment using the straight-line method and (1) full-year convention—beginning of period, (2) half-year convention, and (3) full-month convention.

Review MBC

More Practice:
12-27, 12-51, 12-52, 12-53
Solution on p. 12-58.

LO 12-3 Calculate depreciation using group and composite depreciation methods

LO 12-3 Overview

Depreciation Methods
- Group Depreciation
  - Similar assets grouped together for depreciation calculations
- Composite Depreciation
  - Dissimilar assets grouped together for depreciation calculations

Rather than track all information for each individual fixed asset, companies can instead group items together for the purpose of depreciation computations. Plant assets are sometimes grouped together for application of an average depreciation rate that reflects the characteristics of the group. There are two approaches in grouping items for depreciation purposes.

- **Group depreciation**—used for homogeneous or similar assets, such as delivery trucks having similar costs, useful lives, and residual values.
- **Composite depreciation—**used for heterogeneous or dissimilar assets, such as industrial equipment with different costs, useful lives, and residual values.

The group and composite depreciation systems are identical with respect to calculations and journal entries. For demonstration purposes, the composite method is outlined in **Demo 12-3**.

The **composite annual depreciation rate** equals the rate of total cost depreciated each year.

$$\textbf{Composite annual depreciation rate} = \frac{\textbf{Annual group straight-line depreciation}}{\textbf{Total group acquisition cost}}$$

The **composite group useful life** is the ratio of total group depreciable cost to annual group straight-line depreciation. The ratio yields the number of years over which depreciation is taken.

$$\textbf{Composite group useful life} = \frac{\textbf{Group depreciable cost}}{\textbf{Annual group straight-line depreciation}}$$

Composite annual depreciation expense for the group of assets is the composite annual depreciation rate multiplied by the balance in the group asset acquisition account. Composite annual depreciation is expensed over the composite group useful life, provided there are no material changes in the assets of the group.

Composite annual depreciation = Composite annual depreciation rate × Total group acquisition cost

Although the original cost for each asset acquired is maintained, only a control account for accumulated depreciation is used. Gains and losses are not recognized on disposal. Instead, the asset control account is credited for the original cost of the item, and the accumulated depreciation account is debited for the difference between cash received and the original cost of the item. In other words, the gain or loss is collapsed within the accumulated depreciation account. *Over time, unrecorded gains often offset unrecorded losses within the accumulated depreciation account.*

360-10-S99-1 Gains and losses resulting from the disposition of revenue producing equipment should not be treated as adjustments to the provision for depreciation in the year of disposition, but should be shown as a separate item in the statement of income. If such equipment is depreciated on the basis of group of composite accounts for fleets of like vehicles, gains (or losses) may be charged (or credited) to accumulated depreciation with the result that depreciation is adjusted over a period of years on an average basis. It should be noted that the latter treatment would not be appropriate for (1) an enterprise (such as an airline) which replaces its fleet on an episodic rather than a continuing basis or (2) an enterprise (such as a car leasing company) where equipment is sold after limited use so that the equipment on hand is both fairly new and carried at amounts closely related to current acquisition cost.

If no changes occur in the makeup of the group during the entire composite life, annual depreciation does not change. When assets are added or disposed of before the end of their useful lives, the original depreciation rate is maintained if the changes are not material to the overall depreciable cost and useful life composition of the group. Depreciation is computed with the old rate and the new balance in the group asset control account, which reflects the addition or deletion of assets. Material changes in the makeup of composite groups may require changes in depreciation rates.

Composite Depreciation Method

LO12-3 **Demo 12-3**

Demo MBC

Columns *A* through *D* in the composite depreciation table provide information for heterogeneous assets purchased in early 2020.

a. Complete the composite depreciation table by calculating total acquisition cost, total residual value, and total annual straight-line depreciation.

b. Calculate the composite annual depreciation rate, the composite group useful life, and the composite annual depreciation expense for 2020. Round annual depreciation rate to three decimals.

c. Record the entry for the disposal of one unit of Asset #2 on February 15, 2021, for $18,000.

d. Determine the composite depreciation expense for 2021.

Solution

a. **Composite Depreciation Table**

	A	B	C	D	E	F	G
					(*A* × *B*)	(*A* × *C*)	(*E* − *F*)/*D*
Asset	**Quantity**	**Unit Acquisition Cost**	**Unit Residual Value**	**Unit Useful Life**	**Total Acquisition Cost**	**Total Residual Value**	**Total Annual Straight-Line Depreciation**
1	10	$50,000	$5,000	15	**$500,000**	**$50,000**	**$30,000**
2	4	20,000	4,000	10	**80,000**	**16,000**	**6,400**
3	5	8,000	600	8	**40,000**	**3,000**	**4,625**
4	25	3,000	0	3	**75,000**	**0**	**25,000**
					$695,000	**$69,000**	**$66,025**

b. **Composite Annual Depreciation Rate, Useful Life, and Annual Depreciation**

The composite annual depreciation rate, the composite group useful life, and the 2020 composite annual depreciation expense are computed as follows.

$$\text{Composite annual depreciation rate} = \frac{\text{Annual group straight-line depreciation}}{\text{Total group acquisition cost}} = \frac{\$66{,}025}{\$695{,}000} = 0.095$$

$$\text{Composite group useful life} = \frac{\text{Group depreciable cost}}{\text{Annual group straight-line depreciation}} = \frac{\$626{,}000 \text{ or } (\$695{,}000 - \$69{,}000)}{\$66{,}025} = 9.48 \text{ years}$$

$$\begin{aligned}\text{2020 Composite Annual Depreciation Expense} &= \text{Composite annual depreciation rate} \times \text{Total group acquisition cost}\\ &= 0.095 \times \$695{,}000\\ &= \$66{,}025\end{aligned}$$

Ignoring any disposals or additions, in 9.48 years, the group is fully depreciated and has a net book value equal to total group depreciable cost of $626,000 (or $66,025 × 9.48 years + rounding difference of $83 due to using 9.48 instead of 9.48126). The composite life is not the simple average useful life of the group, but rather depends on the relative contribution each type of asset makes to the total depreciable cost of the group. For example, Asset #1 contributes $450,000 of depreciable cost to the group, and each unit of Asset #1 has a useful life of 15 years, whereas Asset #4 contributes only $75,000 to depreciable cost, and each unit has a useful life of 3 years. The composite life is therefore closer to the useful life of Asset #1.

c. **Disposal of Asset #2**

The following entry is made to dispose of one unit of Asset #2 for $18,000 on February 15, 2021.

February 15, 2021—To record disposal of one unit of Asset #2

Cash	18,000	
Accumulated Depreciation (to balance).	2,000	
Equipment—Asset #2		20,000

Assets = Liabilities + Equity
+18,000
+2,000
−20,000

Cash: 18,000 (debit)
Accum Deprec: 2,000 (debit)
Equipment: 20,000 (credit)

continued

continued from previous page

d. **Calculation of Composite Depreciation Expense**
The disposal affects 2021 depreciation, computed as follows.

2021 Composite Annual Depreciation = Composite annual depreciation rate × Total group acquisition cost
= 0.095 × ($695,000 − $20,000)
= $64,125

The original rate continues to be applied because no *significant* change in the group has occurred in this case.

Grouping items may be more efficient and cost effective in cases where a company has many individual fixed assets. However, differences in the useful life and depreciable cost among group assets raise concerns about group and composite systems. The group of assets in this example is depreciated for 10 years. Before the end of the first 10 years, Assets #3 and #4 have probably been retired. After the group is fully depreciated, Asset #1 remains in service. Critics charge that composite and group systems compromise the allocation of acquisition costs against periods of use. However, group and composite systems are widely used in companies reporting the use of the straight-line method.

REVIEW 12-3 **LO12-3** **Composite Depreciation Method**

Review MBC

6M Company owns a production plant that consists of the following, all acquired on January 1, 2020.

	Cost	Estimated Residual Value	Estimated Life (years)
Building	$2,000,000	$250,000	30
Equipment	600,000	10,000	15
Other equipment	50,000	0	5

Required

a. Compute total straight-line depreciation for 2020 on all items combined. Round straight-line depreciation for each item to the nearest dollar.
b. Compute the composite depreciation rate (based on original cost) and the composite life (to the nearest full year) of the assets. Round depreciation rates to 3 decimals.
c. Prepare the journal entry to record 2020 composite depreciation.
d. Assume that all of the Other Equipment was sold in 2021 for cash of $6,000. Prepare the entry for the sale of the equipment.

More Practice: 12-31, 12-58, 12-59
Solution on p. 12-59.

LO 12-4 Account for changes in estimate as they relate to depreciation

LO 12-4 Overview

Change in Estimate Affecting Depreciation
- Change of residual value, useful life
- Prospective treatment
- No change to prior reporting
- Disclosure

Revisions of useful lives or residual values of depreciable assets are considered changes in accounting estimates for reporting purposes. For example, unexpected competitive pressures can increase the risk of obsolescence causing a decrease in the estimated useful life of an asset. As a company gains experience in such areas as depreciable assets, it develops a basis for revising one or more of its prior accounting estimates. In cases of estimate changes, prior results are not adjusted. Instead, the new estimate is used during the current and remaining periods—see **Demo 12-4**. Thus, a change in estimate is made on a prospective (future-oriented) basis and the financial statement effects (when material) should be disclosed in the notes accompanying the financial statements.

250-10-50-4 The effect on income from continuing operations, net income (or other appropriate captions of changes in the applicable net assets or performance indicator), and any related per-share amounts of the current period shall be disclosed for a change in estimate that affects several future periods, such as a change in service lives of depreciable assets. Disclosure of those effects is not necessary for estimates made each period in the ordinary course of accounting for items such as uncollectible accounts or inventory obsolescence; however, disclosure is required if the effect of a change in the estimate is material.

Change in Accounting Estimate

LO12-4 **Demo 12-4**

Demo MBC

Equipment that cost $24,000 is being depreciated on a straight-line basis over a 10-year estimated useful life with no residual value. Early in the seventh year, management, having had experience with the equipment, determines that the total useful life will be 14 years (with no residual value). Compute depreciation expense in the seventh year and record the associated journal entry.

Solution

First the book value is determined at the time of the change in estimate. Then, depreciation is calculated using the current estimate of salvage value and the remaining useful life.

Computation of Updated Annual Depreciation

Original cost	$24,000
Less accumulated depreciation to date of change ($24,000 × 6/10)	14,400
Book value (at date of change in estimate)	$ 9,600
Annual depreciation over remaining life: ($9,600/8 years)	$ 1,200

The following journal entry is required to record depreciation in year 7.

Year 7—To record depreciation expense

Depreciation Expense	1,200	
Accumulated Depreciation		1,200

Assets = Liabilities + Equity
−1,200 −1,200
Accum Deprec | 1,200
Deprec Exp 1,200 |

COCA-COLA

Real World—DEPRECIATION ESTIMATES

Coca-Cola Company provided the following disclosure on prospective changes to useful lives and residual values of depreciable assets in its annual report.

COCA-COLA COMPANY [KO]

Property, Plant, and Equipment: Property, plant, and equipment are stated at cost. Depreciation expense is computed using the straight-line method over the estimated useful lives of 20 to 40 years for buildings and improvements and three to 20 years for machinery and equipment. Leasehold improvements are amortized over the shorter of the asset's life or the remaining contractual lease term.

The Company prospectively revised the estimated useful lives and residual values of certain fixed assets based on the results of a comprehensive analysis of the Company's historical fixed asset experience. This historical experience was positively impacted by various programs implemented by the Company in recent years designed to improve asset management and enhance functionality. Specifically, the Company implemented operational systems to track and monitor assets, structured maintenance and refurbishment programs, and enhanced purchase specification requirements. The study confirmed that these programs have extended the useful lives of certain fixed assets, principally vehicles and cold drink equipment, and increased the value of certain assets upon disposition. These changes in accounting estimates generally result in certain of the Company's operating assets being depreciated over longer useful lives, although the Company's asset life ranges generally did not change. The changes in estimates decreased depreciation expense by approximately $161 million, or $0.23 per diluted common share after tax.

Change in Accounting Estimate

LO12-4 **REVIEW 12-4**

Review MBC

Assume the following information for Monona Company.

Fixed asset: Equipment purchased January 1, 2018
Useful life: 10 years — Residual value: $6,500
Original cost: $350,000 — Depreciation method: Straight-line

On January 1, 2020, the company determined that the equipment's life will only extend to a total of 8 years and the residual value is expected to be $1,500. Compute depreciation expense to be recorded in 2020.

More Practice: 12-32, 12-34, 12-61
Solution on p. 12-59.

LO 12-5 Account for changes in depreciation methods

LO 12-5 Overview

Change in Depreciation Method
- Prospective treatment
  - Treat as a change in estimate
  - Make no change to prior reporting
  - Utilize new method in current and future periods
  - Disclosure

Under certain circumstances, a company can change from one depreciation method to another depreciation method such as from sum-of-the-years'-digits depreciation method to straight-line depreciation method. Generally when this happens, **a company treats this as a change in accounting estimate, accounted for prospectively**. The accounting standards refer to a change in depreciation method more specifically as a **change in accounting estimate effected by a change in accounting principle**. While other changes in accounting methods are accounted for retrospectively, the standards distinguish a change in depreciation method from other changes. In this case, management may be unable to separately determine the effects of changing the accounting principle from the effects of changing its estimates. In other words, the change in estimate is accomplished by changing the method. A change in depreciation relates to the continuing process of obtaining additional information and revising estimates and, therefore, is treated as other changes in estimates with prospective treatment—see **Demo 12-5**.

250-10-45-18 Distinguishing between a change in an accounting principle and a change in an accounting estimate is sometimes difficult. In some cases, a change in accounting estimate is effected by a change in accounting principle. One example of this type of change is a change in method of depreciation, amortization, or depletion for long-lived, nonfinancial assets (hereinafter referred to as depreciation method). The new depreciation method is adopted in partial or complete recognition of a change in the estimated future benefits inherent in the asset, the pattern of consumption of those benefits, or the information available to the entity about those benefits. The effect of the change in accounting principle, or the method of applying it, may be inseparable from the effect of the change in accounting estimate. Changes of that type often are related to the continuing process of obtaining additional information and revising estimates and, therefore, shall be considered changes in estimates.

Companies disclose the impact of the change in estimate on financial statements, including the nature and reason for the change and the method of applying the change, in a note to financial statements.

Demo 12-5 **LO12-5** **Change in Depreciation Method**

Demo MBC

Kellog Company purchased equipment on January 1, 2020, and depreciated the equipment using sum-of-the-years'-digits depreciation method. Information related to the equipment follows.

Acquisition cost.	$8,000
Residual value	$500
Estimated useful life, in years.	4

On January 1, 2022, the company's management changes from sum-of-the-years'-digits to straight-line depreciation for its depreciable assets. Compute depreciation expense for 2022 and record the related journal entry.

Solution

The company treats the change from an accelerated method of depreciation to the straight-line method as a change in estimate. No change is made to prior reported information. First, we compute the book value of the equipment on January 1, 2022. The company would have recorded two years of depreciation under sum-of-the-years'-digits. The sum of the years digits is 10 or (1 + 2 + 3 + 4) and is used in the following depreciation calculation.

	Depreciation for the Period			End of Period	
Reporting Period	Depreciable Cost	Depreciation Rate	Depreciation Expense	Accumulated Depreciation	Book Value
Jan. 1, 2020. . . .					$8,000
Dec. 31, 2020. . . .	$7,500	4/10	$3,000	$3,000	5,000
Dec. 31, 2021. . . .	7,500	3/10	2,250	5,250	2,750

continued

continued from previous page

On January 1, 2022, the asset has a book value of $2,750. Depreciation expense using the straight-line method is $1,125 per year for the asset's remaining useful life or ($2,750 − $500)/2.

	Depreciation for the Period			End of Period	
Reporting Period	Depreciable Cost	Depreciation Rate	Depreciation Expense	Accumulated Depreciation	Book Value
Dec. 31, 2022.	$2,250	0.50	$1,125	$6,375	1,625
Dec. 31, 2023.	2,250	0.50	1,125	7,500	500 ← Residual value

The following journal entry is required to record depreciation for 2022.

December 31, 2022—To record depreciation expense

Depreciation Expense	1,125	
Accumulated Depreciation.		1,125

Assets = Liabilities + Equity
−1,125 −1,125

Accum Deprec		Deprec Exp	
	1,125	1,125	

EXPANDING YOUR KNOWLEDGE **Systematic Change in Depreciation Method**

Companies can systematically choose to use *accelerated depreciation* for the first half of a fixed asset's useful life and use *straight-line depreciation* for the second half of a fixed asset's useful life. In this way, the company is able to allocate higher expenses to earlier periods where greater benefits were derived from the asset's use. The company may also avoid having to force a depreciation amount in the final year under the declining-balance method, or having a fully depreciated asset before the end of its service life.

Change in Depreciation Method **LO12-5** **REVIEW 12-5**

Hondae Inc. purchased equipment on June 30, 2017, at a cost of $380,000. The company estimated a $3,000 salvage value and that the equipment would have a useful life of 15 years. The company elected to use the double-declining-balance method until January 1, 2020, at which time the company changes to the straight-line method of depreciation for the equipment.

Compute depreciation expense for 2020.

Review MBC

More Practice: 12-33, 12-35, 12-63, 12-64, 12-65, 12-68
Solution on p. 12-59.

Account for errors in reporting property, plant, and equipment — LO 12-6

LO 12-6 Overview

Accounting Errors
- Retrospective treatment
  - Restate past financial statements
  - Record an entry to correct retained earnings and balance sheet account(s)
  - Disclose nature and amount of error

An accounting error occurs when a transaction or event is recorded incorrectly or is not recorded at all.

For example, an error may be discovered in a depreciation calculation, an incorrect service life may have been entered, or an expense may have been incorrectly capitalized as a fixed asset. If an error is identified within the same accounting period, the error is reversed and the correct entry recorded. However, if a *material error* is not discovered until after the release of financial statements, the error must be corrected through a **prior period adjustment.** A prior period adjustment is an entry to correct an error through an adjustment of a balance sheet account and typically a retained earnings account. The adjustment is **retrospectively** applied with the presentation of all prior periods restated reflecting the adjustment—see **Demo 12-6**. The adjustments are excluded from the determination of net income for the current period.

250-10-45-23 Any error in the financial statements of a prior period discovered after the financial statements are issued or are available to be issued . . . shall be reported as an error correction, by restating the prior-period financial statements.

Demo 12-6 **LO12-6** **Correction of Error**

Demo MBC

On January 1, 2020, Coe pays $5,000 for ordinary repairs and debits the equipment account. Depreciation is 10% per year. Coe discovers the error in 2021. Ignoring income taxes, record the journal entry to correct the error on January 1, 2021. (The income tax effect of error adjustments is addressed in Chapter 18.)

Solution

Assuming that the error is material, the company calculates the financial statement adjustment as follows.

Correct repair expense for 2020.	$5,000
Less: Depreciation expense recorded in 2020 ($5,000 × 0.10).	500
Understated expense in 2020.	$4,500

For 2020, repair expense is understated by $5,000 and depreciation expense is overstated by $500. Income before taxes is overstated by the difference of $4,500. Assets and retained earnings are overstated by $4,500 as well. To correct the error, the company records the following entry, ignoring income taxes.

Assets	= Liabilities	+ Equity
+500		−4,500
−5,000		

Accum Deprec: 500 | ; Ret Earnings—PPA: 4,500 | ; Equipment: | 5,000

January 1, 2021—To correct for repair expense improperly capitalized

Accumulated Depreciation ($5,000 × 0.10)	500	
Retained Earnings—Prior Period Adjustment	4,500	
Equipment		5,000

REVIEW 12-6 **LO12-6** **Correction of Depreciation Error**

Review MBC

Hondae Inc. purchased equipment on January 1, 2019, at a cost of $380,000. The company estimated a $3,000 salvage value and that the equipment will have a useful life of 15 years. The company elects to use the straight-line depreciation method. In entering the information for the asset into the depreciation system, the service life was inadvertently entered as 5 years instead of 15 years.

Ignoring income taxes, record the journal entry to correct the error discovered in 2021.

More Practice: 12-70, 12-71, 12-72

Solution on p. 12-59.

LO 12-7 Account for impairments of property, plant, and equipment

LO 12-7 Overview

Asset Impairment

- Impairment indicator is present
- Recoverability test
- Impairment test

Plant assets that lose a significant portion of utility suffer an impairment of value. **Asset impairments** are caused by casualty, obsolescence, lack of demand for a company's products, negligence, or mismanagement. Other reasons for recognizing an impairment include decisions to close a plant or sell a product line, orders to take a product off the market, and expropriation of assets by a foreign government. Land, although not depreciated, also is subject to impairment loss for reasons such as permanent erosion or changing demographics and competition.

Identification of Asset Impairment

Asset impairments lead to a write-down of assets to fair value. The write-down is recorded as expense in the income statement, reported in the other expenses and losses section. Restoration of a loss is *prohibited* for assets held for use in the company's business. The steps to identify whether an impairment loss is recorded are illustrated in **Exhibit 12-4**, which is demonstrated in **Demo 12-7**.

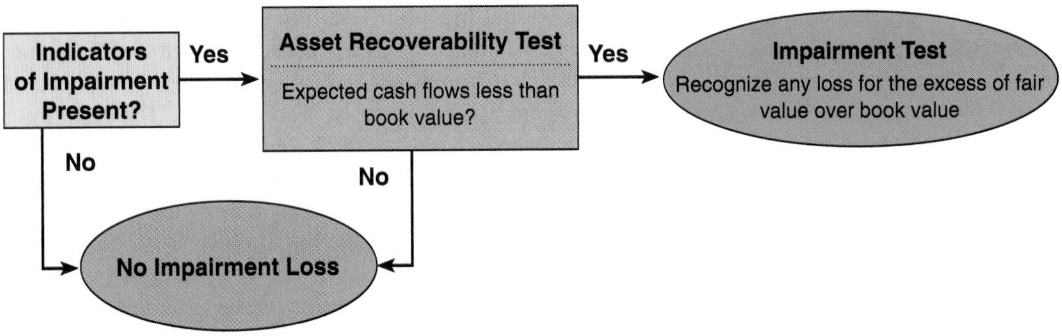

EXHIBIT 12-4
Accounting for Impairment of Property, Plant, and Equipment

Indicators of Impairment

There is no requirement to periodically review assets for impairment. Instead, companies should review for impairment whenever events or changes in circumstances imply that the carrying value might not be recoverable. The following are examples of factors suggesting that an asset currently in use is impaired.

- A decline in fair value of the asset.
- A change in manner in which the asset is used; for example, current underutilization of capacity.
- A change in legal or business climate or an adverse action by a regulator; for example, a plant closing due to noncompliance with environmental regulations.
- A cost overrun on assets being acquired or constructed.
- A current-period cash-flow loss combined with a history of losses associated with the asset.

If one of the above (or a similar event or circumstance) is present, the asset must be reviewed for impairment.

360-10-35-21 A long-lived asset (asset group) shall be tested for recoverability whenever events or changes in circumstances indicate that its carrying amount may not be recoverable.

Step 1—Asset Recoverability Test

If a condition indicates possible impairment, the company performs the **asset recoverability test.**

Asset impaired if: Recoverable cost < Carrying value

One of the assumptions inherent in reporting assets at cost less accumulated depreciation is that carrying value will be recovered. Otherwise, an impairment loss is *implied.* The **recoverable cost** of an asset in use equals the total estimated future net cash inflows (*undiscounted*) expected to be generated by the asset through use and disposal. Net cash inflows are the cash flows expected to be generated by the asset less the cash flows needed to obtain the inflows. If recoverable cost is less than carrying value, the company moves to step 2.

360-10-35-17 An impairment loss shall be recognized only if the carrying amount of a long-lived asset (asset group) is not recoverable and exceeds its fair value. The carrying amount of a long-lived asset (asset group) is not recoverable if it exceeds the sum of the undiscounted cash flows expected to result from the use and eventual disposition of the asset (asset group) . . . An impairment loss shall be measured as the amount by which the carrying amount of a long-lived asset (asset group) exceeds its fair value.

Step 2—Impairment Test

An impairment loss is *recognized* for an asset in use if its fair value is less than its carrying value (net of depreciation to date). The loss is measured as follows.

Impairment loss = Asset carrying value − Asset fair value

The loss is reported as a component of income from continuing operations.

Fair value is the amount at which the asset could be purchased or sold in an active market. If quoted market prices are unavailable, fair value is estimated by taking the present value of future net cash inflows using a rate reflecting the risk involved. Alternatively, a company can apply the expected cash flow approach discussed in Chapter 6, where the risk is applied to the cash flows. The cash flows adjusted for the probability of payment are then discounted using a risk-free rate of return.

The recoverability test compares recoverable cost to carrying value, while the impairment test compares fair value to carrying value. The use of recoverable cost rather than fair value in the recoverability test yields fewer impairment losses and is consistent with the need to investigate for impairment losses on an exception basis only. The recoverability test recognizes the inherent uncertainty in asset valuation. Only clearly impaired assets are written down. If an impairment loss is recognized, fair value is treated as the asset's new cost basis and is the basis for depreciation calculations over the remaining useful life of the asset.

360-10-35-20 If an impairment loss is recognized, the adjusted carrying amount of a long-lived asset shall be its new cost basis. For a depreciable long-lived asset, the new cost basis shall be depreciated (amortized) over the remaining useful life of that asset. Restoration of a previously recognized impairment loss is prohibited.

Notes to financial statements should describe any impairment losses including a description, the amount, and the method used to determine the fair value of the asset.

360-10-50-2 All of the following information shall be disclosed in the notes to financial statements that include the period in which an impairment loss is recognized:

a. A description of the impaired long-lived asset (asset group) and the facts and circumstances leading to the impairment.
b. If not separately presented on the face of the statement, the amount of the impairment loss and the caption in the income statement or the statement of activities that includes that loss.
c. The method or methods for determining fair value.
d. If applicable, the segment in which the impaired long-lived asset (asset group) is reported.

Demo 12-7 LO12-7 Impairment of Fixed Assets

Demo MBC

Ithaca Inc. owns $2,000,000 (original cost) of specialized equipment used in the production of one of its products. The equipment was purchased and installed in January 2010 when the company estimated an expected useful life of 20 years and a residual value of $200,000. Ithaca uses straight-line depreciation. In January 2020, one of Ithaca's competitors completed the development of a competing product with expanded features. The demand for Ithaca's product immediately declined by 40%. In January of 2020, Ithaca estimates the total remaining future net cash inflows from operating the equipment to be $550,000 and the fair value of the equipment to be $400,000. The equipment is expected to have no residual value and is expected to be used for the next five years only.

a. Assess the equipment for impairment and record any losses on impairment that are necessary.
b. Determine carrying value of the equipment after making any required adjustments in part *a*.

Solution

a. **Evaluation for Impairment**

A change in market conditions is an indication that the equipment should be reviewed for potential impairment. The recoverable cost of equipment of $550,000 is less than the carrying value of $1,100,000 (calculated below), which indicates that the company must perform the impairment test.

Original cost of equipment	$2,000,000
Less accumulated depreciation (10 years × [$2,000,000 − $200,000]/20 years).	900,000
Carrying value on December 31, 2019.	$1,100,000

The fair value of the equipment is $400,000, while carrying value of the equipment is $1,100,000, resulting in a loss on impairment of $700,000. The entry to record loss on impairment follows.

continued

continued from previous page

January 2020—To record loss on impairment

Loss on Impairment ($1,100,000 − $400,000)	700,000	
Accumulated Depreciation		700,000

Assets = Liabilities + Equity
−700,000 −700,000

Accum Deprec	
	900,000 Bal.
	700,000
	1,600,000

Loss on Impair	
700,000	

b. **Carrying Value of Equipment**
Carrying value of equipment after recording the loss for impairment is $400,000, which is $2,000,000 less the balance in accumulated depreciation of $1,600,000.

FORD

Real World—IMPAIRMENT OF ASSETS

Ford Motor Company, a global automotive and mobility company based in Dearborn, Michigan, disclosed its policy on asset impairment in a recent Form 10-K.

FORD MOTOR COMPANY [F]

Long-Lived Asset Impairment—We test long-lived asset groups for recoverability at the operating segment level when changes in circumstances indicate the carrying value may not be recoverable. Events that trigger a test for recoverability include material adverse changes in projected revenues and expenses, significant underperformance relative to historical and projected future operating results, significant negative industry or economic trends, and a significant adverse change in the manner in which an asset group is used or in its physical condition. When a triggering event occurs, a test for recoverability is performed, comparing projected undiscounted future cash flows to the carrying value of the asset group. If the test for recoverability identifies a possible impairment, the asset group's fair value is measured relying primarily on a discounted cash flow method. An impairment charge is recognized for the amount by which the carrying value of the asset group exceeds its estimated fair value. When an impairment loss is recognized for assets to be held and used, the adjusted carrying amount of those assets is depreciated over their remaining useful life. No impairment of long-lived assets was recorded in 2015.

Impairment of Fixed Assets — LO12-7 — REVIEW 12-7

Information on three plant assets currently used in operations follows.

Plant Asset	Carrying Value	Recoverable Cost	Fair Value
#201	$400,000	$450,000	$390,000
#202	465,000	420,000	400,000
#203	600,000	400,000	250,000

Review MBC

Required

a. Which plant asset(s), if any, requires an impairment loss to be recognized, and for what amount? Assume that indicators of impairment are present in all cases.

b. Record the entry for the impairment loss (if any).

More Practice:
12-39, 12-40, 12-74, 12-75
Solution on p. 12-59.

Account for assets held for sale — LO 12-8

An **asset held for sale** meets *all* of the following criteria (360-10-45-9).

1. Management commits to a plan to sell the asset.
2. Asset is available for immediate sale in its present condition.
3. An active program to locate a buyer and other actions required to sell the asset have commenced.
4. Sale of the asset is probable, and is generally expected to be completed within one year.

Assets Held for Sale (LO 12-8 Overview)
- Discontinue depreciation
- Report at lower of carrying value or fair value less selling costs
- Report in "Other Assets" on the balance sheet

5. Asset is being actively marketed for sale at a price that is reasonable in relation to its current fair value.
6. Actions required to complete the plan indicate that it is unlikely that significant changes to the plan will be made or that the plan will be withdrawn.

If an asset qualifies as an asset held for sale, the carrying value reported is the lower of:
- **Carrying value**, or
- **Fair value less estimated direct costs to sell the asset**

When the fair value of the asset less costs to sell is the lower of the two amounts, a loss is recognized and the asset is written down to that amount—see **Demo 12-8**. This results in recognition of losses for many assets before disposal. (Recall from Chapter 3 that assets held for sale that meet specified criteria are classified as discontinued operations. Any related impairment loss is properly classified in the discontinued operations section of the income statement, net of tax.)

Recoverability of carrying value is not an issue for assets held for disposal because the value of such assets will be realized at sale, not through use. The focus is on *valuation* rather than allocation of cost for these assets. **Thus, recoverability of losses are allowed limited to the cumulative amount of prior recorded losses.** In other words, the asset's value may not exceed the carrying value at the time the decision to dispose of the asset was made.

360-10-35-40 A loss shall be recognized for any initial or subsequent write-down to fair value less cost to sell. A gain shall be recognized for any subsequent increase in fair value less cost to sell, but not in excess of the cumulative loss previously recognized (for a write-down to fair value less cost to sell).

Assets subject to environmental liabilities, real estate in various parts of the country, and other assets can be held many years before disposal. Assets held for disposal are not subject to further depreciation and should be reported as *other assets* rather than as *property, plant, and equipment* in the balance sheet because the assets are no longer in use.

360-10-35-43 A long-lived asset (disposal group) classified as held for sale shall be measured at the lower of its carrying amount or fair value less cost to sell . . . A long-lived asset shall not be depreciated (amortized) while it is classified as held for sale. Interest and other expenses attributable to the liabilities of a disposal group classified as held for sale shall continue to be accrued.

Management Judgment

Grouping Assets for Impairment Testing

A company must determine whether to group assets for impairment testing or to test assets individually. The authoritative literature indicates that impairment testing should represent the lowest level for which identifiable cash flows are largely independent of cash flows from other assets and liabilities.

360-10-35-23 For purposes of recognition and measurement of an impairment loss, a long-lived asset or assets shall be grouped with other assets and liabilities at the lowest level for which identifiable cash flows are largely independent of the cash flows of other assets and liabilities.

Management's determination of whether and how to group assets for impairment testing can impact the results of the impairment test (and whether or not a loss is recognized). For example, net cash flows from one asset within a group will offset a shortfall of another asset within a group when applying impairment tests. As an example, assume that Transport Inc. is under contract with a municipality to operate ten bus routes. Assets and cash flows designated to provide the service are discrete and measurable. One route operates at a loss and the company is unable to recover the carrying amount of the assets dedicated to that route. If the municipality requires all ten routes for the contract, it would be appropriate to group assets for the ten routes together to test for impairment. This means revenues from the other nine routes are dependent upon operating the unprofitable route.

Applying Impairment Testing

Beyond the judgment required for asset grouping, the remaining steps in impairment testing require judgment. For assets not held for sale, the existence of an impairment indicator, the measurement of expected cash flows, and the rate used to discount future cash flows to fair value are all subjective items. For an asset held for sale, determination of the fair value of the asset is also subjective. For example, a *subjective* appraisal may be used to measure fair value, or *subjective* expected cash flows are discounted to present value using a *subjective* discount rate. Although we provide these amounts in demos for purposes of calculations, in reality, these items are difficult to estimate.

Management Judgment Highlighted in Financial Reporting

As discussed in Chapter 3, a financial statement user's ability to predict future cash flows depends on the user's ability to distinguish between *recurring* and *nonrecurring* income statement items. Information disclosed in the notes about impairment losses (or on the face of the income statement in the case of losses related to discontinued operations) is used by investors and creditors to assess the quality of earnings. For example, large write-offs in one year can cause seemingly large increases in net income in one or more subsequent years. This is because of the reduction in depreciation expense that follows the write-down of a depreciable asset. Because of the importance of impairment information to financial statement users, companies highlight the judgments involved in impairment testing. The following is a just a sample of disclosures from recent Form 10-Ks (from note disclosures and MD&A sections) highlighting the judgment involved in impairment tests.

- The fair value [determined for measuring impairment], based on hierarchy input Level 3, is determined using management's best estimate based on a discounted cash flow model based on future store operating results using internal projections or based on a review of the future benefit the Company anticipates receiving from the related assets.—**Whole Foods Market Inc.**
- Management's judgments regarding the existence of impairment indicators are based on market conditions and operational performance, such as operating income and cash flows.—**Wal-Mart Stores Inc.**
- Our impairment loss calculations require management to make assumptions and to apply judgment to estimate future cash flows and asset fair values, including forecasting useful lives of the assets and selecting the discount rate that reflects the risk inherent in future cash flows.—**American Eagle Outfitters Inc.**
- For asset groups classified as held for sale, the carrying value is compared to the fair value less cost to sell. We estimate fair value by obtaining market appraisals, valuations from third party brokers, or other valuation techniques.—**Target Corporation.**

Asset Held for Sale — LO12-8 — Demo 12-8

Demo MBC

In 2020, Pier Company decides to remove a fixed asset from daily operations and expects to dispose of the asset early in 2021. On December 31, 2020, the asset has a cost of $60,000 and accumulated depreciation of $20,000. The fair value of the asset is $32,000, and estimated costs to sell are $2,000.

a. Record the entry for the impairment loss (if any) on December 31, 2020.
b. Determine the adjusted carrying value of the assets held for sale on December 31, 2020.
c. Record any required adjusting entries on December 31, 2021, assuming that the asset is still held for sale and has a fair value of $36,000 with no change in selling costs.
d. Determine the adjusted carrying value of the assets held for sale on December 31, 2021.

Solution

a. **Impairment Loss on December 31, 2020**

The new carrying value equals $30,000—which is the lower of:

- $40,000 carrying value before adjustment ($60,000 − $20,000).
- $30,000 fair value less cost to sell ($32,000 − $2,000).

A loss of $10,000 (reduction in carrying value) is immediately recognized; and going forward, the asset will no longer be depreciated.

continued

continued from previous page

Assets = Liabilities + Equity
−10,000 −10,000

Accum Deprec: 20,000 Bal.; 10,000; 30,000
Loss on Impair: 10,000

December 31, 2020—To record impairment of asset held for sale

Loss on Impairment ($40,000 – $30,000).	10,000	
Accumulated Depreciation.		10,000

b. **Carrying Value of Asset Held for Sale on December 31, 2020**
On December 31, 2020, the carrying value of the fixed asset held for sale is $30,000, which is the $60,000 cost less accumulated depreciation of $30,000.

c. **Impairment Loss on December 31, 2021**
No depreciation adjustment is recorded. However, on December 31, 2021, the asset is adjusted to $34,000, which is the current fair value of $36,000 less the costs of disposal of $2,000. The new carrying value at December 31, 2021, is $34,000, an increase of $4,000 over the previous carrying value of $30,000, resulting in a gain of $4,000. Carrying value may not exceed $40,000 for this asset.

Assets = Liabilities + Equity
+4,000 +4,000

Accum Deprec: 4,000 | 20,000 Bal.; 10,000; 26,000
Gain on Recovery: 4,000

December 31, 2021—To record recovery of impairment on asset held for sale

Accumulated Depreciation.	4,000	
Gain on Recovery of Impaired Asset ($34,000 – $30,000)		4,000

d. **Carrying Value of Asset Held for Sale on December 31, 2021**
On December 31, 2021, the carrying value of the fixed asset held for sale is $34,000, which is the $60,000 cost less accumulated depreciation of $26,000.

BOEING

Real World—ASSETS HELD FOR SALE

THE BOEING COMPANY [BA]

The Boeing Company disclosed its accounting policy on impairment of assets held for sale in a recent report on Form 10-K.

> **Impairment review for assets under operating leases and held for sale or release**—We evaluate for impairment assets under operating lease or assets held for sale or re-lease when events or changes in circumstances indicate that the expected undiscounted cash flow from the asset may be less than the carrying value. We use various assumptions when determining the expected undiscounted cash flow, including our intentions for how long we will hold an asset subject to operating lease before it is sold, the expected future lease rates, lease terms, residual value of the asset, periods in which the asset may be held in preparation for a follow-on lease, maintenance costs, remarketing costs and the remaining economic life of the asset. We record assets held for sale at the lower of carrying value or fair value less costs to sell . . . When we determine that impairment is indicated for an asset, the amount of impairment expense recorded is the excess of the carrying value over the fair value of the asset.

REVIEW 12-8 LO12-8 Assets Held for Sale

Review MBC

Information on three plant assets currently held for sale follows.

Plant Asset	Original Cost	Accumulated Depreciation	Fair Value	Selling Costs
#101	$25,000	$20,000	$ 5,500	$ 250
#102	44,000	8,800	30,000	1,500
#103	88,000	44,000	40,000	4,000

Required

a. Which plant asset(s), if any, requires an impairment loss to be recognized, and for what amount?
b. Record the journal entry for the impairment loss (if any).

More Practice:
12-41, 12-42, 12-76, 12-77
Solution on p. 12-59.

Describe property, plant, and equipment disclosures and ratio analyses

LO 12-9

LO 12-9 Overview

Asset Turnover Ratio
- Activity ratio
- Net sales/Average total assets

Return on Assets
- Profitability ratio
- Net income/Average total assets

Fixed Asset Turnover Ratio
- Activity ratio
- Net sales/Average fixed assets

Disclosures

Disclosures about depreciation methods used help financial statement users interpret the meaning and impact of depreciation on income and financial position. The following disclosures are required related to depreciation and depreciable assets for each reporting period (360-10-50-1):

- Depreciation expense.
- Balances of major classes of depreciable assets, by nature or function.
- Accumulated depreciation by asset or in total.
- General description of depreciation methods used with respect to major classes of assets.

Companies should also disclose information on depreciation methods and information on post-acquisition costs and idle plant assets. Many users arguably find it useful to disclose the amounts of any fully depreciated assets still in service at a financial reporting date. Significant liens on assets should be disclosed in the liability section rather than as an offset against assets.

Ratio Analysis

Efficiency and profitability of assets are measured in several ways, including through the following three ratios—see also **Demo 12-9**.

Asset turnover (Net sales/Average total assets)—measures efficiency of asset utilization or the amount of sales generated for each dollar invested in company assets. Management can increase asset turnover by increasing sales volume without increasing assets or by reducing the level of assets without reducing the level of sales as explained in Chapter 5.

Return on assets (Net income/Average total assets)—measures profitability of assets or the net income earned on average assets. Return on assets assesses a company's utilization of assets to generate net income. As explained in Chapter 5, to increase return on assets, management seeks to increase profits with the same level of assets and/or to decrease assets with the same level of profitability.

Fixed asset turnover ratio (Net sales/Average fixed assets)—measures effectiveness of fixed assets. Managing the profitability of long-term assets contributes to overall company profitability.

Relation between Depreciation Method and Return on Assets

Return on assets gradually increases as plant assets age, regardless of depreciation method. The numerator of the ratio is reduced by only one year's depreciation, whereas the denominator is reduced by the cumulative depreciation recognized to date, causing the ratio to increase over time.

However, when assets are relatively new, straight-line depreciation yields higher rates of return relative to accelerated methods. Straight-line depreciation maintains higher earnings during early years of an asset's life. As assets age, the relation reverses, and accelerated methods yield higher rates of return. The graph displayed in **Exhibit 12-5** illustrates these points.

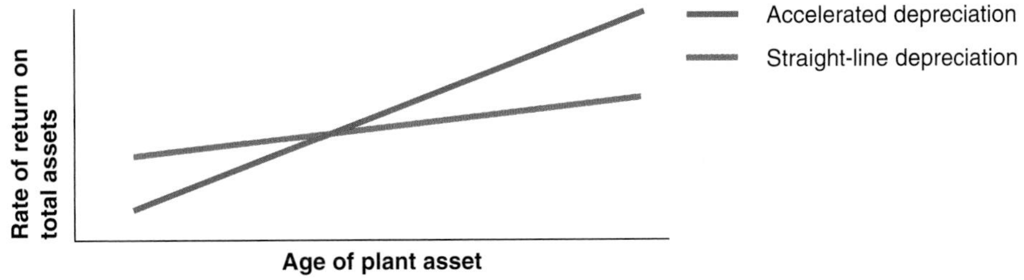

EXHIBIT 12-5
Rate of Return on Assets over Plant Asset's Life

Financial statement users should be aware of depreciation's gradually increasing effect on rates of return, as well as the differential impact of method choice, when comparing different companies and when evaluating the same company across different periods. The ratio of accumulated depreciation to total plant asset cost provides an indication of the percentage of total useful life that has expired.

Demo 12-9 **LO12-9** **Ratio Analysis**

Demo MBC

The following financial information is provided for **Target Corporation**. Compute the company's (a) asset turnover ratio, (b) return on assets, and (c) fixed asset turnover ratio for fiscal years 2014 and 2015. Analyze the results.

	Property, Plant, and Equipment	Total Assets	Net Sales	Net Income (Loss)
Fiscal Year 2013...	$26,412	$44,325		
Fiscal Year 2014...	25,952	41,172	$72,618	$(1,636)
Fiscal Year 2015...	25,217	40,262	73,785	3,363

Target's fiscal years 2013, 2014, and 2015 end on February 1, 2014, January 31, 2015, and January 30, 2016, respectively.

Solution

	FY 2015	FY 2014
Asset Turnover $= \dfrac{\text{Net Sales}}{\text{Average Total Assets}^{1}} =$	$\dfrac{\$73{,}785}{\$40{,}717} = 1.81$	$\dfrac{\$72{,}618}{\$42{,}749} = 1.70$

[1]Average total assets for 2015 is $40,717, which is ($40,262 + $41,172)/2.
Average total assets for 2014 is $42,749, or ($41,172 + $44,325)/2.

The efficiency of asset utilization improved from 2014 to 2015. While assets overall decreased due primarily to a decrease in assets from discontinued operations, net sales rose in 2015. Generally speaking, the combination of assets owned by the company in 2015 generated sales at a higher rate than the combination of assets owned in 2014.

	FY 2015	FY 2014
Return on Assets $= \dfrac{\text{Net Income}}{\text{Average Total Assets}} =$	$\dfrac{\$3{,}363}{\$40{,}717} = 0.08$	$\dfrac{\$(1{,}636)}{\$42{,}749} = (0.04)$

The profitability of assets improved from 2014 to 2015. While assets overall decreased due primarily to a decrease in assets from discontinued operations, net income rose in 2015 without the offsetting loss from discontinued operations in 2014.

	FY 2015	FY 2014
Fixed Asset Turnover $= \dfrac{\text{Net Sales}}{\text{Average Fixed Assets}^{1}} =$	$\dfrac{\$73{,}785}{\$25{,}585} = 2.88$	$\dfrac{\$72{,}618}{\$26{,}182} = 2.77$

[1]Average fixed assets for 2015 is $25,585, or ($25,217 + $25,952)/2.
Average fixed assets for 2014 is $26,182, or ($25,952 + $26,412)/2.

The efficiency of fixed assets improved from 2014 to 2015. The company generated $2.88 in sales dollars for each dollar invested in fixed assets compared to $2.77 in the prior year.

BOEING Real World—DISCLOSURE OF PROPERTY, PLANT AND EQUIPMENT

BOEING COMPANY [BA]

The **Boeing Company** provided the following disclosure in a recent Form 10-K for property, plant and equipment.

> **Note 1: Summary of Significant Accounting Policies—Property, Plant and Equipment**
> Property, plant and equipment are recorded at cost, including applicable construction-period interest, less accumulated depreciation and are depreciated principally over the following estimated useful lives: new buildings and land improvements, from 10 to 40 years; and new machinery and equipment, from 4 to 20 years. The principal methods of depreciation are as follows: buildings and land improvements, 150% declining balance; and machinery and equipment, sum-of-the-years' digits. Capitalized internal use software is included in Other assets and amortized using the straight line method over 5 years. We periodically evaluate the appropriateness of remaining depreciable lives assigned to long-lived assets, including assets that may be subject to a management plan for disposition.

continued

Long-lived assets held for sale are stated at the lower of cost or fair value less cost to sell. Long-lived assets held for use are subject to an impairment assessment whenever events or changes in circumstances indicate that the carrying amount may not be recoverable. If the carrying value is no longer recoverable based upon the undiscounted future cash flows of the asset, the amount of the impairment is the difference between the carrying amount and the fair value of the asset.

Note 8—Property, Plant and Equipment

Property, Plant and Equipment at December 31 consisted of the following:	2017	2016
Land	$ 530	$ 535
Buildings and land improvements	14,125	13,796
Machinery and equipment	14,577	13,569
Construction in progress	1,081	1,790
Gross property, plant and equipment	30,313	29,690
Less accumulated depreciation	(17,641)	(16,883)
Total	$12,672	$12,807

Depreciation expense was $1,548, $1,418 and $1,357 for the years ended December 31, 2017, 2016 and 2015, respectively. Interest capitalized during the years ended December 31, 2017, 2016 and 2015 totaled $110, $170 and $158, respectively.

Ratio Analysis

LO12-9 **REVIEW 12-9**

The following information relates to Harley-Davidson Inc., which has a December 31 year-end. Compute its (a) asset turnover ratio, (b) return on assets ratio, and (c) fixed asset turnover ratio for 2015 and 2016.

$ thousands	Fixed Assets	Total Assets	Revenue	Net Income
2014	$883,077	$9,528,097		
2015	942,418	9,972,977	$5,995,402	$752,207
2016	981,593	9,890,240	5,996,458	692,164

More Practice:
12-43, 12-78, 12-79
Solution on p. 12-59.

Record acquisition and depletion of natural resources

LO 12-10

Natural resources, or **wasting assets**, refer to assets that are consumed physically in production. Natural resources must be discovered and developed before they can be extracted, processed, and sold. Natural resources include timberland, oil and gas, and various types of mineral deposits, such as gold, silver, copper, and coal. Natural resources are classified either as property, plant, and equipment, or as a separate category, and represent rights to exploit a natural resource.

Acquisition costs, exploration costs, development costs, and restoration costs are capitalized as the base for depletion. A description of these categories along with examples are provided in **Exhibit 12-6**.

LO 12-10 Overview

Natural Resources
- Determine depletion base
  - Acquisition costs
  - Exploration costs
  - Development costs
  - Restoration costs
- *Deplete* natural resources when removed using units-of-production method
- *Expense* as cost of goods sold when inventory is sold

EXHIBIT 12-6
Depletion Cost Base

Depletion Cost Base	Costs Incurred	Example
Acquisition costs	Costs incurred to purchase, lease, or otherwise acquire the rights to property for purposes of exploring for and producing a natural resource. (Acquisition costs will be expensed if acquisition efforts fail to identify natural resources.)	Costs to lease property where expected mineral resources will be found.
Exploration costs	Costs incurred to identify areas that may warrant testing or to test specific areas for the presence of a natural resource.	Costs to drill or dig to identify specific sites of natural resources.
Development costs[1]	Costs incurred to provide facilities for extracting, treating, gathering, and storing the natural resource.	Cost of a mineshaft.
Restoration costs	Costs incurred to restore property to its original condition after the natural resource extraction is completed. Capitalized at the fair value of costs (sometimes calculated as the present value of future cash flows). See further discussion of asset retirement obligations in Chapter 11.	Cost to replant trees where timberland was extracted.

[1]Development costs that are tangible assets—such as equipment that can be moved to other sites and has alternative uses—can be depreciated separately. An alternative method for depreciation may be appropriate (such as straight-line) when the equipment has alternate uses.

Transfer of the cost of a natural resource from the **Natural Resource** asset account to the **Inventory** account each period is called **depletion.** The **depletion base** equals total capitalized cost less residual value. The depletion base, similar to depreciable cost for a plant asset, is the total amount of depletion to be recognized over the life of the natural resource. The residual value reduces the depletion base.

Natural resources are depleted using a **units-of-production method**. The depletion rate is calculated by taking the depletion cost base (described above) and dividing by the total activity base (such as tons of ore) as shown in **Demo 12-10A**. The rate is then applied to the actual amount of natural resource extracted to arrive at the amount of natural resources depleted. The depletion rate is based on estimated amounts. Any changes in estimates of these amounts are accounted for *prospectively*. The amount of depletion is typically credited to a natural resource account (such as Mine Property) directly. However, companies sometimes elect to credit a contra asset account instead.

$$\textbf{Depletion rate per unit of output} = \frac{\textbf{Depletion base}}{\textbf{Estimated activity base in units}}$$

$$\textbf{Annual depletion} = \textbf{Depletion rate} \times \textbf{Actual activity base in units}$$

Demo 12-10A **LO12-10** **Natural Resource Acquisition, Depletion, Sale**

Demo MBC

On January 1, 2020, Burlington Inc. acquires and begins operating a large copper mine. The company incurs costs of $4 million to lease, explore, and develop the mine. The company estimates the property will yield 2 million tons of copper ore.

a. Record the entry on January 1, 2020, to acquire the mine.
b. Record the entry for depletion of 300,000 tons of copper ore in 2020.
c. Record the cost of sale entry for the sale of 250,000 of the 300,000 tons of copper ore produced in 2020. (Ignore the entry to recognize sales revenue.)

Solution

a. **Acquisition of Mine Property**
Burlington records the following entry for acquisition of the property.

January 1, 2020—To acquire mine property

Mine Property	4,000,000	
Cash		4,000,000

Assets = Liabilities + Equity
+4,000,000
−4,000,000
Mine Property: 4,000,000 (debit)
Cash: 4,000,000 (credit)

b. **Depletion of Copper Ore**
In 2020, the company extracts 300,000 tons of copper ore. The unit depletion rate per ton of production using the units-of-production method follows.

continued

$$\text{Unit depletion rate per ton} = \frac{\text{Depletion base}}{\text{Estimated recoverable tons of ore}} = \frac{\$4{,}000{,}000}{2{,}000{,}000} = \$2.00 \text{ per ton}$$

$$\text{Depletion amount} = \$2.00 \text{ per ton} \times 300{,}000 \text{ tons extracted} = \$600{,}000$$

The following entry is required to account for the depletion of ore from the mine.

2020—To record depletion of ore

Inventory—Copper Ore	600,000	
Mine Property		600,000

Assets = Liabilities + Equity
+600,000
−600,000

Inventory: 600,000 |
Mine Property: 4,000,000 | 600,000

c. **Sale of Copper Ore**

Depletion becomes a portion of cost of goods sold when the copper ore is sold. The journal entry to record cost of goods sold follows.

December 31, 2020—To record sale of copper ore

Cost of Goods Sold ($2 per ton × 250,000 tons)	500,000	
Inventory—Copper Ore		500,000

Assets = Liabilities + Equity
−500,000 −500,000

Inventory: 600,000 | 500,000; 100,000 |
COGS: 500,000 |

Ending balance for the Inventory–Copper Ore account is $100,000, which is $2 per ton multiplied by 50,000 tons (300,000 tons − 250,000 tons). This means 300,000 tons were depleted. Of the depleted tons, 250,000 tons were sold, and 50,000 tons remain in ending inventory.

Exploration Costs in Oil and Gas

Oil and gas companies incur large costs exploring for oil and gas deposits. Extensive exploration activities are undertaken when management expects the overall results from such activities not only to repay the costs of the exploration *but also* to earn a fair return. When a company pursues exploration by drilling wells in the search for oil and gas reserves, there is considerable risk that some wells will be dry, or unsuccessful. With a large, well-developed exploration program of drilling in areas where there are indications that mineral resources are present, companies expect to have some successful wells that locate recoverable oil and gas, and they expect that these successful efforts will be sufficiently productive to earn the company a fair return on its overall investment. Because oil and gas are regularly traded commodities, market prices are readily available, and an estimate of the fair value of the discovery can be made. An important accounting issue is how to record the **exploration cost** of discovered mineral resources. Accounting for other components of the depletion base does not change.

There are two methods allowed in U.S. GAAP for determining the amount of exploration costs to capitalize and include in the depletion base—both methods are illustrated in **Demo 12-10B**.

- **Successful-efforts method**—only exploration costs of successful wells are capitalized in the cost of the natural resource; exploration costs of unsuccessful wells are expensed as incurred.

932-360-25-3 Under the successful efforts method, certain types of costs may be capitalized as construction-in-progress pending further information about the existence of future benefits, but as soon as the additional information becomes available, and it is known whether future benefits exist, those costs are either reclassified as an amortizable asset or charged to expense.

- **Full-cost method**—all exploration costs are capitalized in the cost of the natural resource as long as the estimated value of reserves discovered from the successful wells is equal to or greater than the amount to be capitalized.

936-360-25-1 Full cost accounting is addressed in the Securities and Exchange Commission (SEC) literature.

Because exploration costs are often very large in the oil and gas industry, the two methods can result in very different financial statements. Companies must disclose which method is followed (successful-efforts or full-cost), how extraction costs are treated (expense, or deplete and depreciate), and information about capitalization of exploratory well costs (**932-235-50-1 to 1B**).

Demo 12-10B **LO12-10** **Depletion of Exploration Costs in Oil**

Demo MBC

Wildcat Exploration incurs costs in 2020 of $2 million each in drilling 20 different oil wells exploring for oil and gas, for a total exploration cost of $40 million (assume cash payments). Nineteen of the wells are unsuccessful, but one well does result in the discovery of recoverable oil reserves. Assume only exploration costs in the depletion base for simplicity.

Wildcat's one successful well has estimated reserves of 10 million barrels and the type of crude oil discovered has a current market price of $8 per barrel. Thus, the estimated fair value of the reserves in the successful well is $80 million ($8 × 10 million barrels).

Required

a. Record the entry for exploration costs using the successful-effort method.
b. Record the entry for exploration costs using the full-cost method.

Solutions

a. **Successful-efforts method**

If the successful-efforts method is used, the exploration costs of the 19 unsuccessful wells are expensed, and the exploration costs of the one successful well of $2 million are recorded as an asset. The following entry records the exploration activities using the successful-efforts method.

Assets = Liabilities + Equity
+2,000,000 −38,000,000
−40,000,000

Oil Reserve: 2,000,000 |
Explor Exp: 38,000,000 |
Cash: | 40,000,000

2020—To record exploration costs using successful-efforts method

Cost of Oil Reserve	2,000,000	
Exploration Expense	38,000,000	
Cash		40,000,000

b. **Full-cost method**

If the full-cost method is used, all of the exploration costs, or $40 million, are capitalized as the cost of the oil reserve since this amount is less than the estimated value of oil discovered from this exploration effort ($80 million).

Assets = Liabilities + Equity
+40,000,000
−40,000,000

Oil Reserve: 40,000,000 |
Cash: | 40,000,000

2020—To record exploration costs using full-cost method

Cost of Oil Reserve	40,000,000	
Cash		40,000,000

EOG RESOURCES

Real World—NATURAL RESOURCES

EOG RESOURCES INC. [EOG]

EOG Resources Inc. reported the following information regarding natural resources in a recent Form 10-K. EOG Resources Inc. operates in most of the productive basins in the United States with a current focus on crude oil and, to a lesser extent, liquids-rich natural gas plays. Natural resources were included within the category of property, plant, and equipment as shown in its financial statements.

CONSOLIDATED BALANCE SHEETS

At December 31 (In Thousands)	2015	2014
Property, Plant and Equipment		
Oil and Gas Properties (Successful Efforts Method)	$50,613,241	$46,503,532
Other Property, Plant and Equipment	3,986,610	3,750,958
Total Property, Plant and Equipment	54,599,851	50,254,490
Less: Accumulated Depreciation, Depletion and Amortization	(30,389,130)	(21,081,846)
Total Property, Plant and Equipment, Net	$24,210,721	$29,172,644

Accounting for Natural Resources **LO12-10** **REVIEW 12-10**

Maine Company purchased the rights to a mine for $4,000,000 on January 1, 2020. The mine is expected to provide 1,200,000 tons of minerals. In 2020, the company extracted 230,000 tons of minerals and sold 200,000 tons.

Required

a. Calculate 2020 depletion for Maine Company. Round the depletion rate to two decimals.

b. Determine the ending inventory balance of minerals on December 31, 2020.

Review MBC

More Practice: 12-44, 12-45, 12-80, 12-81, 12-82

Solution on p. 12-59.

Calculate MACRS (tax) depreciation

APPENDIX 12A

LO 12-11

MACRS Depreciation

- Utilize for tax purposes, not for book purposes
- Classifies assets into specific classes
- Uses statutory depreciation rates
- Accelerates depreciation

LO 12-11 Overview

Depreciation under GAAP and under the Internal Revenue Code are different matters. Under both authorities, depreciation acts to reduce income before tax, and total depreciation over the life of an asset is limited to the original cost. However, under U.S. GAAP, depreciation guidelines are intended to allocate an asset's historical cost to the accounting periods in which the asset is used, in accordance with the expense recognition principle.

In contrast, tax depreciation is geared to the revenue needs and economic policies of the government, which change in response to economic conditions and the fiscal policies of elected administrations. Currently, tax depreciation provides an incentive for replacement, modernization, and expansion of industrial facilities through accelerated depreciation schedules, which allow tax deductions early on. The amount of depreciation recognized for financial reporting purposes is generally different from the amount claimed as a tax deduction. In fact, in some cases, immediate or 100% expensing is allowed for tax purposes.

The **modified accelerated cost recovery system (MACRS)** was enacted by the Tax Reform Act of 1986. MACRS modifies the use of estimated useful life and ignores residual value in determining the depreciation deduction. Assets are assigned to a class with a specified life over which depreciation deductions are taken. For example, two of the classes of personal property under MACRS are three-year property, which includes small tools, horses, assets used in research and development activities, and five-year property which includes automobiles, light trucks, computers, and machinery and equipment not included in other categories.

The annual MACRS deduction is determined by multiplying the asset's cost by the statutory recovery percentage pertinent to the asset's class as shown in **Demo 12-11**. A **half-year convention** is built into the first and last year's percentage for each property class. Under the half-year convention, an asset is assumed to begin service in the middle of the year of purchase, reflecting, on average, a mid-year acquisition date. Under MACRS, the estimated residual value and estimated useful life of an asset are ignored.

The recovery percentages for three- and five-year property follow.

Recovery Percentages

Year	Three-Year	Five-Year
1	33.33%	20.00%
2	44.45	32.00
3	14.81[1]	19.20
4	7.41	11.52[1]
5		11.52
6		5.76
	100.00%	100.00%

[1]Denotes year in which MACRS depreciation is less than or equal to straight-line depreciation; the schedule switches to straight-line depreciation in that year.

There is also what is known as 'bonus depreciation' that is put into the tax code at various times to provide further incentives for investment. Bonus depreciation was expanded under the recent Tax Cuts and Jobs Act (TCJA) in the U.S. to allow full expensing (100% of cost deduction in the first year) for certain assets. The TCJA provides for a phase down of bonus depreciation such that starting in 2023 the bonus depreciation amount is 80% of the cost of the asset and by 2027 bonus depreciation will no longer be allowed. Taxpayers can elect out of bonus depreciation for any class of property for any year.

Demo 12-11 **LO12-11** **MACRS Depreciation Calculation**

Demo MBC

Assume that equipment in the three-year class is purchased for $10,000. The company reports on a calendar-year basis and uses straight-line depreciation for financial reporting purposes. The equipment has a four-year useful life (useful life and class life are not necessarily the same) and residual value of $2,000. Compute annual depreciation over the life of the equipment for tax purposes and financial reporting purposes. Assume the taxpayer does not use bonus depreciation.

Solution

Year	Tax Basis of Asset	MACRS Rate	MACRS Depreciation	Straight-Line Depreciation
1	$10,000	0.3333	$ 3,333[1]	$2,000[2]
2	10,000	0.4445	4,445	2,000
3	10,000	0.1481	1,481	2,000
4	10,000	0.0741	741	2,000
			$10,000	$8,000

[1] $10,000 × 0.3333 [2] ($10,000 − $2,000)/4

Total depreciation for tax purposes under MACRS is $10,000 and total depreciation for financial reporting purposes under the straight-line method is $8,000.

EXPANDING YOUR KNOWLEDGE **Disposal of an Asset: Tax vs. Book Impact**

On a tax basis under MACRS, an asset is fully depreciated. However, under GAAP, an asset is depreciated to salvage value. What is the impact of this difference at the time of sale? Let's assume that the asset in **Demo 12-11** was sold for $3,000 at the end of year four. For tax purposes, the sale would result in a $3,000 gain because the tax basis is $0. For book purposes, the sale would result in a $1,000 gain ($3,000 − $2,000). Over the asset's life for tax purposes, the net effect on taxable income is $(7,000) or $10,000 of depreciation expense less a $3,000 gain. Over the asset's life for book purposes, the net effect on taxable income is $(7,000) or $8,000 of depreciation expense less a $1,000 gain. While there is no net difference, companies view the decrease in taxes in earlier years desirable, supported by the concepts of time value of money. Additional discussion on the accounting for deferred tax differences between book and tax are discussed in Chapter 18.

REVIEW 12-11 **LO12-11** **MACRS Depreciation**

Review MBC

Delta Company purchased machinery in 2020 for $50,000 that qualifies as a five-year class asset for tax depreciation purposes. The equipment has a useful life of ten years and a residual value of $8,000. Delta chooses to use the MACRS tax depreciation tables to compute its depreciation deduction for tax purposes. Compute Delta's depreciation tax deduction for each applicable tax year using the MACRS five-year table (see table earlier in this section).

More Practice: 12-124, 12-125

Solution on p. 12-59.

Questions

12-1. Explain the concept of depreciation.

12-2. A company reported $2 million of depreciation expense in its income statement. Explain what this means to a friend who has little or no background in accounting. Also explain what it does not imply.

12-3. List several factors a company should consider in choosing a depreciation method.

12-4. Explain the meaning of the balance in accumulated depreciation.

12-5. What are the primary causes of depreciation? What effect do changes in the fair value of an asset being depreciated have on the depreciation estimates?

12-6. Explain the three factors (other than depreciation method) that must be considered in allocating the cost of a fixed asset.

12-7. Explain the effects of depreciation on (a) the income statement and (b) the balance sheet.

12-8. In estimating the service life of a fixed asset, obsolescence should be considered. Explain this factor.

12-9. Explain the relation of depreciation to (a) cash flow and (b) fixed assets.

12-10. Explain the relation between depreciation and replacement of the assets being depreciated.

12-11. Compare the effect of the straight-line and units-of-production methods of depreciation on the per unit cost of output for a manufacturing company.

12-12. What is meant by accelerated methods of depreciation? Under what circumstances would these methods generally be appropriate?

12-13. Which method, sum-of-the-years'-digits or double-declining-balance, will always produce the larger amount of depreciation in the first year of an asset's useful life? Support your response.

12-14. Explain the basic accounting policy problems that arise with respect to depreciation when a company's reporting year and the asset year do not coincide. Consider the case of a company that closes its books on June 30 and has purchased a depreciable asset on January 1.

12-15. Explain when and in what amount an impairment loss is recognized on a plant asset in use.

12-16. Explain when and in what amount an impairment loss is recognized on a plant asset held for disposal.

12-17. How are the composite and group depreciation systems similar?

12-18. Explain the difficulties that may arise when group or composite depreciation is used.

12-19. What are some of the advantages of using group or composite depreciation systems?

12-20. What are the differences between natural resources and depreciable assets?

12-21. Describe the types of costs incurred by companies in connection with natural resources. Generally, how is each treated for accounting purposes when incurred?

12-22. How do companies determine the amount of depletion to be charged as an expense each accounting period?

12-23. Describe the successful-efforts method and the full-cost method of accounting for exploration costs. Which method is required for financial reporting?

Brief Exercises

Brief Exercise 12-24 Computing Straight-Line Depreciation **LO1**

On January 1, 2020, equipment is purchased for $240,000. The company incurred installation costs of $600 and freight charges on delivery of $1,000. The equipment has a $20,000 residual value and an expected useful life of five years.

a. Determine depreciation expense for 2020 using the straight-line depreciation method.

b. How does the answer to part *a* change if the appraised value of equipment were $45,000 on December 31, 2020?

Brief Exercise 12-25 Computing Units-of-Production Depreciation **LO1**

On January 1, 2020, equipment is purchased for $150,000 that has an estimated residual value of $1,000 and an estimated useful life of 10 years. The equipment is expected to produce 50,000 units of output over its useful life. The equipment produced 5,500 units in its first year. Determine depreciation expense for 2020, using units-of-production depreciation method.

Brief Exercise 12-26 Computing Depreciation Using Multiple Depreciation Methods **LO1**

On January 1, 2020, Walker Inc. acquired equipment for $40,000. The expected useful life is 10 years and the residual value is $800. Total service hours for the equipment are estimated to be 10,000 while actual hours for 2020 were 900. Compute depreciation expense in 2020, under the following methods.

a. Straight-line

b. Sum-of-the-years'-digits

c. Double-declining-balance

d. Units-of-production

Brief Exercise 12-27 Computing Partial Period Depreciation Using Multiple Depreciation Methods **LO2** *Hint:* See Demo 12-2A

On August 31, 2020, DHS Company acquired equipment for $40,000. The expected useful life is 5 years and the residual value is $800. Compute depreciation expense in 2020 under the following methods.

a. Straight-line

b. Sum-of-the-years'-digits

c. Double-declining-balance

Brief Exercise 12-28 Computing Partial Period, Straight-Line Depreciation **LO2**

Garcia Company purchased a building for $625,000 on March 1, 2020, with an estimated residual value of $50,000. Assuming a useful life of 40 years and that the company uses the straight-line depreciation method, compute depreciation expense for 2020.

Brief Exercise 12-29
Computing Partial Period, Double-Declining-Balance Depreciation **LO2**

Silhouette Company purchased a machine that was installed and placed in service on July 1, 2020, at a cost of $60,000, including installation cost. Salvage value was estimated at $10,000. The machine is being depreciated over 10 years by the double-declining-balance method. For the year ended December 31, 2021, what amount should Silhouette report as depreciation expense?

Brief Exercise 12-30
Computing Partial Period, Sum-of-the-Years'-Digits Depreciation **LO2**

A machine with a five-year estimated useful life and an estimated 10% salvage value was acquired on April 30, 2019, for $56,000. On December 31, 2020, what is the balance of accumulated depreciation on this asset, using sum-of-the-years'-digits method?

Brief Exercise 12-31
Computing Composite Depreciation **LO3**

Taser Company owns the following assets acquired on January 1, 2020.

Asset	Cost	Residual Value	Estimated Useful Life
A.	$60,000	$1,000	10 years
B.	15,000	0	5 years
C.	70,000	2,000	8 years

a. Compute the composite annual depreciation rate. Round to two decimals.
b. Compute the composite group useful life.
c. Compute composite depreciation expense for 2020.

Brief Exercise 12-32
Computing Depreciation with an Estimate Change **LO4**
Hint: See Demo 12-4

Whitney Company purchases equipment on July 1, 2020, for $34,000. This equipment has a useful life of five years and a residual value of $4,000. The company uses the straight-line depreciation method. On January 1, 2022, the company extended the estimate of the total useful life to six years and adjusted the salvage value to $2,000. Compute depreciation expense for 2022.

Brief Exercise 12-33
Computing Depreciation with a Change in Depreciation Method **LO5**

Whitney Company purchased equipment on January 1, 2020, for $90,000. This equipment has a useful life of 6 years and a residual value of $5,000. The company uses the double-declining depreciation method. On January 1, 2023, the company changes its depreciation method to the straight-line method. Compute depreciation expense for 2023.

Brief Exercise 12-34
Computing Depreciation Expense for Change in Useful Life **LO4**

Phelps Company purchases equipment on January 1, 2019, for $36,000 which will be depreciated using the sum-of-years'-digits method. The equipment has a residual value of $6,000 and a useful life of three years. In 2020, Phelps decides that the machine has an original total useful life of four years and $3,000 salvage value. What is depreciation expense for 2020?

Brief Exercise 12-35
Computing Depreciation Expense for Change in Depreciation Method **LO5**
Hint: See Demo 12-5

Phelps Company purchases equipment on January 1, 2019, for $36,000 which will be depreciated using the sum-of-years'-digits method. The equipment has a residual value of $6,000 and a useful life of three years. In 2020, Phelps changes its depreciation method for equipment to the straight-line method. What is depreciation expense for 2020?

Brief Exercise 12-36
Recording Depreciation Error Correction **LO6**

Whitney Company purchased equipment on January 1, 2020, for $90,000. This equipment has a useful life of ten years and a residual value of $5,000. The company uses the straight-line depreciation method. In 2021, the company discovered that it had incorrectly recorded depreciation for 2020 as $5,800. Ignoring income taxes, record the correcting entry on January 1, 2021.

Brief Exercise 12-37
Recording Depreciation Error Correction **LO6**

Ordinary repairs of $10,000 in January of 2018 were inadvertently debited to an equipment account. The equipment was originally purchased in January of 2018 and had a useful life of 6 years. Record the entry to correct the error assuming that the error was discovered in 2020. Ignore income taxes for simplification.

Brief Exercise 12-38
Recording Depreciation Error Correction **LO6**

Assume the same information in Brief Exercise 12-37 *except* that the error was discovered in January of 2019, before the accounts were closed for 2018. Record the entry to correct the error.

Brief Exercise 12-39
Identifying and Recording Impairment Loss on Fixed Asset **LO7**
Hint: See Demo 12-7

Supreme Inc. has equipment with an original cost of $800,000, and accumulated depreciation of $300,000. Supreme is aware of a general market decline in the value of this equipment due to upgrades that are now available. Supreme estimates the total remaining future net cash inflows from operating the equipment to be $400,000. The fair value of the plant is estimated to be $300,000 based on conditions in the local market. Prepare the entry, if any, that Supreme should make to record the decline in value.

Brief Exercise 12-40 Identifying and Recording Impairment Loss on Fixed Asset **LO7**

Assume the same information in Brief Exercise 12-39, except that the original cost of the equipment is $650,000. Prepare the entry, if any, that Supreme should make to record the decline in value.

Brief Exercise 12-41 Recording Impairment Loss on Asset Held for Sale **LO8** *Hint:* See Demo 12-8

WellCon Corporation, a calendar-year corporation, plans to dispose of a plant asset with a carrying value of $50,000 (cost is $75,000 and accumulated depreciation is $25,000) on December 31, 2020, after recording depreciation on the asset. The fair value of the asset is $40,000 at the time, and estimated costs to sell are $5,000. The asset remains in WellCon's possession one year later. The fair value and estimated costs to sell are revised to $32,000 and $4,000, respectively, on that date. Provide the entries on December 31, 2020, and 2021, to record the impairment loss and revaluation.

Brief Exercise 12-42 Recording Impairment Loss on Asset Held for Sale **LO8** *Hint:* See Demo 12-8

Assume the same information in Brief Exercise 12-41, *except* that the fair value and estimated costs to sell are revised to $42,000 and $2,000 on December 31, 2021. Provide the entries on December 31, 2020, and 2021, to record the impairment loss and revaluation.

Brief Exercise 12-43 Computing Asset Ratios **LO9** *Hint:* See Demo 12-9

The following information relates to **Macy's Inc.**

$ millions	Total Assets	Revenue	Net Income
Fiscal Year 2015	$20,576	$27,079	$1,070
Fiscal Year 2014	21,330		

Macy's fiscal years for 2015 and 2014 end on January 30, 2016, and January 31, 2015, respectively.

a. Compute the asset turnover ratio for fiscal year 2015.
b. Compute the return on assets ratio for fiscal year 2015.

Brief Exercise 12-44 Computing Depletion **LO10** *Hint:* See Demo 12-10A

Mining Corporation bought land for $150,000 (residual value $10,000) that is estimated to yield 300,000 pounds of a removable natural resource. The amounts of natural resources extracted in 2020 and 2021 were 35,000 and 45,000 pounds, respectively. Determine depletion for 2020 and for 2021. Round the depletion rate to two decimals.

Brief Exercise 12-45 Recording Depletion Entries **LO10**

Western Mining Inc. acquires a zinc mine in January of 2020, at a cost of $1,200,000 with an estimated 360,000 tons of zinc. Western Mining Inc. also incurs costs of $118,000 to develop the area around the site necessary to access the mine. The land is estimated to have a value of $75,000 after the zinc is mined. At the end of 2020, 60,000 tons of zinc were mined and 50,000 tons were sold by December 31, 2020.

a. Record the entry for acquisition of the zinc mine.
b. Record the entries for depletion and for the cost of the sale of zinc in 2020.

Exercises

Exercise 12-46 Preparing Depreciation Schedules Using Various Depreciation Methods **LO1**

Frito Inc. acquired equipment on January 1, 2020, at a cost of $20,000 that is estimated to have a useful life of five years and a residual value of $5,000.

Required

Prepare a depreciation schedule showing depreciation expense, accumulated depreciation, and book value for the entire life of the asset using the following methods.

a. Straight-line method.
b. Sum-of-the-years'-digits method.
c. Double-declining-balance method.

Exercise 12-47 Computing Depreciation Using Various Depreciation Methods **LO1**

To demonstrate the computations involved in several methods of depreciating a fixed asset, the following data are used for equipment purchased on January 1, 2020.

Cost and residual value		Estimated service life	
Acquisition cost	$12,500	Years	5
Residual value	500	Service hours	10,000
		Productive output (units)	24,000

Required

Compute annual depreciation using each of the following methods.

a. Straight-line depreciation: Compute the depreciation rate and amount for *each year.*

b. Units-of-production method using service hours as a measure of input: Compute the depreciation rate and amount of depreciation expense for the *first year* assuming 2,200 service hours of actual operation.

c. Units-of-production method using units produced as a measure of output: Compute the depreciation rate and amount of depreciation expense for the *first year* assuming 4,000 units of output.

d. Sum-of-the-years'-digits method: Compute the depreciation amount for *each year.*

e. Double-declining-balance method: Compute the depreciation amount for *each year.*

Exercise 12-48
Preparing Depreciation Schedules Using Various Depreciation Methods **LO1**

ISPN Company acquired equipment that cost $36,000 on January 1, 2020, which will be depreciated on the assumption that it will last six years and have a $2,400 residual value. Several possible methods of depreciation are under consideration.

Required

Prepare a schedule that shows annual depreciation expense, accumulated depreciation, and book value over the asset's useful life assuming the following.

a. Sum-of-the-years'-digits method.

b. Units-of-production method. Estimated output is a total of 105,000 units, of which 12,000 will be produced in the first year, 18,000 in the second and third years, 15,000 in the fourth year, and 21,000 in the fifth and sixth years.

Exercise 12-49
Identifying Depreciation Methods and Preparing Schedules **LO1**

Veto Company bought equipment on January 1, 2020, for $45,000. The expected life is 10 years, and the residual value is $5,000. Based on three acceptable depreciation methods, the annual depreciation expense and balance of accumulated depreciation at the end of 2020 and 2021 are shown below.

	Case A		Case B		Case C	
Year	Annual Expense	Accumulated Amount	Annual Expense	Accumulated Amount	Annual Expense	Accumulated Amount
2020 . . .	$9,000	$ 9,000	$4,000	$4,000	$7,273	$ 7,273
2021 . . .	7,200	16,200	4,000	8,000	6,545	13,818

Required

a. Identify the depreciation method used in each case A, B, and C.

b. Based on the answer to part *a*, prepare a depreciation schedule that shows annual depreciation expense, accumulated depreciation, and book value over the life of the asset for each case A, B, and C.

c. Which method results in the highest net income in year 1?

d. Which method results in the highest net income in year 10?

Exercise 12-50
Identifying Depreciation Methods **LO1**

On January 1, 2020, Urban Company acquired a machine for $15,000. The estimated residual value of the machine is $1,000, and the estimated useful life is five years. Urban's year-end is December 31.

Required

Identify the method of depreciation used by Urban if 2021 depreciation expense is (a) $3,600, (b) $2,800, and (c) $3,733.

Exercise 12-51
Recording and Preparing Schedule Using Sum-of-the-Years'-Digits Method Depreciation, Partial Year **LO2**

An asset was purchased October 1, 2020, costing $20,000, with a residual value of $4,000 and an estimated three-year useful life.

Required

a. Prepare a schedule of depreciation that shows annual depreciation expense, accumulated depreciation, and book value over the useful life of the asset assuming that the company depreciated the asset using the sum-of-the-years'-digits method.

b. Record the entry to recognize depreciation in 2020.

c. Record the entry to recognize depreciation in 2021.

Exercise 12-52
Computing Partial Period Depreciation under Multiple Depreciation Methods LO2

To demonstrate the computations involved in several methods of depreciating a fixed asset, the following information is provided.

Cost and residual value		Estimated service life	
Acquisition cost.	$12,500	Years.	5
Residual value	500	Service hours	10,000
		Productive output (units).	24,000

Required

Compute the annual depreciation using each of the following methods assuming that the asset was purchased on August 1, 2020.

a. Straight-line depreciation: Compute the depreciation rate and amount for each year.

b. Units-of-production method using service hours as a measure of input: Compute the depreciation rate and amount for the *first partial year* assuming 900 service hours of actual operation.

c. Units-of-production method using units produced as a measure of output: Compute the depreciation rate and amount for the *first partial year* assuming 1,800 units of output.

d. Sum-of-the-years'-digits method: Compute the depreciation amount for *each year*.

e. Double-declining-balance method: Compute the depreciation amount for *each year*.

Exercise 12-53
Computing Partial Period Depreciation under Multiple Depreciation Methods LO2

Cruz Company purchased a computer on June 30, 2020, for $42,000. The computer had a salvage value of $12,000 and useful life of six years.

Required

a. Using the declining-balance depreciation method (200%), determine depreciation expense for 2021.

b. Using the declining-balance depreciation method (150%), determine depreciation expense for 2021.

c. Using the straight-line depreciation method, determine depreciation expense for 2021.

Exercise 12-54
Computing and Recording Depreciation Entries under Multiple Depreciation Methods LO2

Jackson Company's records show the following property acquisitions and disposals during the first two years of operations.

Year	Acquisition Cost of Property	Estimated Useful Life (Years)	Disposal Amount
2020	$50,000	10	—
2021	20,000	10	$7,000*

*Disposal relates to property acquired in 2020.

Property is depreciated for one-half year in the year of acquisition. Property disposed of is depreciated for one-half year in its year of disposal. Assume no residual values. There are no sale proceeds upon retirement.

Required

a. Compute depreciation expense for 2020 and for 2021, and the balances of the property and related accumulated depreciation accounts, at the end of each year under the straight-line method.

b. Prepare entries for the acquisition, periodic depreciation, and retirement of the property assuming the straight-line method.

Exercise 12-55
Computing Partial Period Depreciation under Multiple Depreciation Methods LO2
Hint: See Demo 12-2A

Asset	Acquisition Date	Depreciation Method	Acquisition Cost	Useful Life	Salvage Value
#1	Jan. 1, 2020	Straight-line	$10,000	4 years	$ 500
#2	Aug. 30, 2020	Double-declining-balance	14,500	8 years	1,000
#3	Feb. 1, 2021	Sum-of-the-years'-digits	18,000	4 years	800
#4	Jul. 31, 2021	Straight-line	33,800	8 years	0

Required

Compute depreciation expense for 2021 for each asset #1, #2, #3, and #4.

Exercise 12-56
Computing Depreciation and Recording Disposal Using Multiple Depreciation Conventions **LO2**
Hint: See Demo 12-2B

Whitney Company purchases equipment on July 12, 2020, for $34,000. This equipment has a useful life of five years and a residual value of $4,000. The company depreciates this asset using the straight-line depreciation method.

Required

a. Compute depreciation using the following variations to the straight-line depreciation method.
1. Compute depreciation for 2020 using the exact date outstanding, commencing depreciation on July 13, 2020, and using 360 days as the allocation base.
2. Compute full year, annual depreciation for 2020 based on the balance in the equipment account at the beginning of the period.
3. Compute full year, annual depreciation for 2020 based on the balance in the equipment account at the end of the period.
4. Compute depreciation for 2020 assuming one-half of a year's depreciation in both the year of purchase and the year of retirement, regardless of the date of purchase or retirement.
5. Compute depreciation for 2020 assuming a full month of depreciation during the month of purchase and no depreciation in the month of disposal.

b. Assume that the asset was retired on January 1, 2023. Prepare the entry for disposal of the asset assuming that the company uses the exact rate outstanding to calculate depreciation. How does the answer differ if the company used the full year (beginning of the period) depreciation method?

Exercise 12-57
Recording Depreciation of Post Acquisition Costs **LO2**

Foster Company purchased a new computer system on January 2, 2020, for $1,200,000. The system has a useful life of six years, considering obsolescence. Its residual value is $20,000. Foster uses the straight-line method. The following events took place in 2021.

- **March 1**: Peripheral equipment costing $30,000 was added to the system. This equipment has a useful life of seven years and a residual value of $2,000. This equipment can be used with several different computers. Foster can replace the computers before the disposal of this equipment.
- **September 1**: An additional memory device was added to the computers, costing $250,000. This device has no utility apart from the computer system but will increase the total residual value of the computers to $40,000.

Required

Provide the general journal entry to record depreciation expense for 2021 on the computers and related equipment.

Exercise 12-58
Recording Composite Depreciation **LO3**

Wilson Company owns the following machines, all acquired on January 1, 2020.

Machine	Original Cost	Estimated Residual Value	Estimated Life (Years)
A.	$14,000	$ 0	4
B.	20,000	2,400	8
C.	36,000	4,000	10
D.	38,000	2,000	12

Required

a. Prepare a schedule based on straight-line depreciation that shows for each machine the following: cost, residual value, depreciable cost, life in years, and annual depreciation.

b. Compute the composite depreciation rate rounded to four decimals (based on cost) and the composite life.

c. Prepare the entry to record 2020 composite depreciation.

Exercise 12-59
Recording Entries Using Composite Depreciation Method **LO3**

California Utilities owns a power plant that consists of the following assets, all acquired on January 1, 2020.

	Cost	Estimated Residual Value	Estimated Life (Years)
Building	$300,000	$10,000	30
Machinery	95,000	0	10
Other equipment	50,000	5,000	6

Required

a. Compute the total straight-line depreciation for 2020 on all items combined.

b. Compute the composite depreciation rate rounded to two decimals (based on cost) and the composite life of the plant.

c. Provide the entry to record 2020 composite depreciation.

d. Assume that all of the Other equipment was sold in 2023 for $6,000 cash. Prepare the entry for the sale of that equipment.

Exercise 12-60 Recording Entries Using Group Depreciation Method **LO3**

Ohio Company owns 10 warehouses of similar type except for varying size. The group system of depreciation is applied to the 10 warehouses, and the rate is 6% each year on cost. At the end of 2020, the asset account, Warehouses, showed a balance of $5,300,000 (residual value $300,000), and the Accumulated Depreciation account showed a balance of $2,400,000. At the start of 2021, Warehouse #8, costing $400,000, was torn down. Materials salvaged from the demolition were sold for $53,000, and $15,000 was spent on demolition.

Required

Provide entries to record (a) depreciation for 2020, (b) disposal of the warehouse in 2021, and (c) depreciation for 2021.

Exercise 12-61 Recording Entry for a Change in Estimate **LO4**

Exon Company purchased equipment for $100,000 on January 1, 2018. The equipment has an estimated residual value of $3,000 and an estimated useful life of 8 years. The company depreciates the equipment using the straight-line method. On January 1, 2021, the company determines that the total useful life is 6 years and the estimated residual value is $1,000.

Required

Prepare the entry to record depreciation expense for 2021.

Exercise 12-62 Computing Depreciation with Subsequent Costs, Change in Depreciation Estimates **LO2**

Assume the following information for Macro Company.

Original asset: Office building purchased Jan. 1, 2014.	Original cost: $800,000.
Useful life: 20 years.	Straight-line depreciation is used.
Salvage value: $0	

On July 1, 2020, at a cost of $150,000, wall partitions were added to the third-floor executive office suite to increase the number of private offices (an addition). The partitions do not extend the life of the building and have no separate utility apart from the building.

Required

a. Compute annual depreciation expense for each year 2014 through 2019.

b. Compute annual depreciation expense for 2020.

Exercise 12-63 Recording Depreciation with a Change in Depreciation Method **LO5**

Pier Exports purchases equipment on January 1, 2018, at a cost of $75,000. The company estimates that there will be no salvage value and that the equipment will have a useful life of 10 years. The company elects to use the double-declining-balance method until 2021, at which time the company changes to the straight-line method of depreciation for the equipment.

Required

Prepare the depreciation entry for 2021.

Exercise 12-64 Describing Financial Statement Impact of a Change in Depreciation Method **LO5**

Vale Company's policy is to depreciate equipment using the double-declining-balance method. However, in 2020, the company decided to change its policy to depreciate equipment using the straight-line depreciation method. The net book value of equipment on January 1, 2020, is $85,000. If straight-line depreciation had been used prior to January 1, 2020, the net book value of equipment on January 1, 2020, would have been $90,000. Depreciation for 2020 under the straight-line method is $11,000 and under the double-declining balance method is $13,000.

Required

Describe the financial statement implications of the change to the straight-line method for (a) financial statements prior to 2020, (b) 2020 financial statements, and (c) post 2020 financial statements.

Exercise 12-65 Recording a Change in Depreciation Method **LO5**

Quest Company has equipment that it acquired on January 1, 2015, for $300,000. The life of the asset was estimated to be 10 years total with a $5,000 residual value. At the beginning of 2020, the company changes its depreciation method to the straight-line method from the double-declining balance method.

Required

Prepare the 2020 entry for depreciation expense.

Exercise 12-66
Recording and Reporting a Change in Depreciation Estimate **LO4**

Bellico Company, which has a calendar fiscal year, purchased its only depreciable plant asset on January 1, 2019, and depreciates it as follows.

Original cost	$10,000	Estimated useful life	Three years
Estimated residual value	1,000	Depreciation method	Sum-of-years'-digits

In 2020, Bellico increased the estimated residual value to $2,000 and increased the total estimated useful life to five years for financial accounting purposes. Additional information follows.

	2019	2020
Revenue	$40,000	$50,000
Expenses other than depreciation and tax	25,000	30,000
Tax rate	30%	30%

Required

a. Provide the 2019 entry for depreciation and the ending 2019 accumulated depreciation balance.
b. Provide the 2020 entry for depreciation and the ending 2020 accumulated depreciation balance.
c. Provide the comparative 2019 and 2020 income statements, including disclosures related to the change in accounting estimate.

Exercise 12-67
Recording and Reporting a Change in Estimated Useful Life **LO4**

Petty Corporation has been depreciating equipment over a 10-year life on a straight-line basis. The equipment, which costs $24,000, was purchased on January 1, 2016. The equipment has an estimated residual value of $6,000. On the basis of experience since acquisition, management has decided to depreciate the equipment over a total life of 14 years instead of 10, with no change in the estimated residual value. The change is to be effective on January 1, 2020. The annual financial statements are prepared on a comparative basis (2019 and 2020 are presented). Income before depreciation for 2019 and 2020 was $49,800 and $52,800, respectively. Disregard income tax considerations.

Required

a. Prepare the journal entries to be recorded in 2016–2019 for annual depreciation. Determine the ending balance in accumulated depreciation on December 31, 2019.
b. Prepare the entry to record depreciation expense in 2020, the year of the change.
c. Illustrate how the change should be reported on the 2020 balance sheet *and* income statement, which are accompanied by the 2019 results for comparative purposes (shares of common stock outstanding are 100,000).

Exercise 12-68
Recording a Change in Depreciation Method **LO5**
Hint: See Demo 12-5

Southern Corporation has been depreciating equipment over a 10-year life using the sum-of-the-years'-digits method. The equipment was acquired January 1, 2016, and cost $68,000 (estimated residual value, $13,000). The company decided to change to straight-line depreciation, effective at the beginning of 2020, with no change in the estimated useful life or the residual value. The annual accounting period ends December 31.

Required

a. Compute accumulated depreciation on December 31, 2019, before the change in depreciation method.
b. Prepare the journal entry for depreciation expense in 2020.

Exercise 12-69
Recording a Change in Depreciation Method and Change in Useful Life **LO4, 5**

Texas Inc. has made several accounting changes to improve its expense allocation method. Assume that it is the end of 2020 and that the accounting period ends on December 31. The books have not been adjusted or closed at the end of 2020. Among the changes are the following.

1. **Equipment A** that costs $50,000 (estimated useful life 10 years, residual value $6,000) has been depreciated using the sum-of-the-years'-digits method. Early in the eighth year (2020), it was decided to change to straight-line depreciation (with no change in residual value or estimated life).
2. **Equipment B** that cost $17,000 (with no residual value) is being depreciated over its estimated useful life of 20 years using the straight-line method. Early in the sixth year (2020), it was decided that the useful life would not last longer than 13 years from the date of acquisition.

Required

Prepare the entry to record the 2020 depreciation for Equipment A and for Equipment B. Disregard income tax considerations.

Exercise 12-70
Recording Depreciation Error Correction **LO6**

Hondae Inc. purchased equipment on January 1, 2018, at a cost of $200,000. The company estimated a $5,000 salvage value and that the equipment will have a useful life of 10 years. The company elected to use the straight-line depreciation method. In entering the information for the asset into the depreciation system, the salvage value was inadvertently entered as $50,000 instead of $5,000. Ignoring income taxes, record the journal entry to correct the error discovered in 2021.

Exercise 12-71
Recording Error Corrections Related to Equipment **LO6**

On April 1, 2021, the following 2020 errors were discovered after the 2020 financial statements were issued.

a. Equipment purchased on January 1, 2020, with a cost of $20,000, salvage value of $1,200, and useful life of 8 years was incorrectly expensed as maintenance cost. The company uses the straight-line method to depreciate all equipment.

b. In 2020, fully depreciated equipment with an original cost of $25,000 and no salvage value was sold for $2,000. The company's entry for the sale was a debit to cash for $2,000 and a credit to equipment for $2,000.

c. Equipment purchased on June 30, 2020, with a cost of $65,000, salvage value of $4,500 and a useful life of 8 years was incorrectly entered into the depreciation system as having a useful life of 18 years.

Required

Prepare entries to correct each of the errors *a*, *b*, and *c*, discovered in 2021. Ignore income taxes.

Exercise 12-72
Recording and Reporting an Error, Comparative Statements **LO6**

Beckham Corporation had never been audited before December 31, 2020, the current year. Before the arrival of the auditor, the controller prepared comparative financial statements showing the results of 2019 and 2020. The accounts for 2020 have not been closed. The auditors discovered that an invoice dated January 2017 for $9,000 (paid in cash at the time) was debited to 2017 operating expenses, although it was for the purchase of equipment. The equipment has an estimated useful life of 10 years and no estimated residual value.

Reported income reflected on the financial statements prepared by the company (before discovery of the error) were 2017, $11,000; 2018, $22,000; 2019, $30,000; and 2020, $33,000. Disregard income tax considerations and assume that Beckham uses straight-line depreciation.

Required

a. Determine the correct net income for the years 2017, 2018, 2019, and 2020.

b. Provide the entries to record the (1) correction of the 2020 error and (2) depreciation expense for 2020.

c. Show how the correction is reported on the 2020 comparative balance sheet, retained earnings statement, and income statement. Include a proper note disclosure.

Exercise 12-73
Recording Errors and Changes in Estimates **LO4, 6**

On January 1, 2018, Zale Company purchased a building for $400,000. The building was estimated to have a useful life of 30 years and no residual value and was depreciated using the straight-line method. In 2020, the company revised the estimated total useful life to 25 years and adjusted the residual to $5,000. In addition, in 2020, the company discovered that building improvements of $6,000 made in early 2019 were incorrectly expensed as repair expense.

Required

a. Provide the journal entry to record the adjustment for the error discovered in 2020. Assume that the error is material to the company.

b. Provide the journal entry in 2020 to record depreciation expense.

Exercise 12-74
Identifying and Recording Impairment Loss on Plant Asset **LO7**

Three cases are provided below concerning a plant asset currently used in operations.

Case	Carrying Value	Recoverable Cost	Fair Value
A.	$40,000	$60,000	$45,000
B.	45,000	65,000	40,000
C.	60,000	40,000	30,000

Required

a. Which cases(s), if any, require an impairment loss to be recognized, and for what amount? Assume that indicators of impairment are present in all cases.

b. Record the entry for the impairment loss on the case(s) identified in part a (if any).

Exercise 12-75
Identifying and Recording Impairment Loss on Equipment **LO7**

Bolt Company purchased equipment on January 1, 2018, for $34,000. This equipment has an estimated useful life of five years, a residual value of $4,000, and is depreciated using the sum-of-the-years'-digits method. At the beginning of 2020, Bolt suspects that the original investment in the asset will not be realized; the total remaining future cash inflow expected to be produced through use of the equipment, including the original residual value, is $10,000. The equipment's fair value at January 1, 2020, is $7,000.

Required

a. Determine whether the asset is impaired and, if so, the amount of the impairment loss on January 1, 2020.
b. Compute depreciation for 2020.

Exercise 12-76
Recording Impairment Loss on Asset Held for Sale **LO8**
Hint: See Demo 12-8

Down Manufacturing Company has a small facility called Plant XT that has not been used for several years because of low product demand. The company does not expect to use the facility in the foreseeable future. Efforts are being made to sell the plant for $350,000, but a realistic recovery amount is $200,000 (net of disposal costs). The accounting records show cost, $1,450,000; accumulated depreciation, $800,000.

Required

a. Provide the entry that Down should make to record the impairment of value.
b. What is the net book value after the entry is recorded for impairment?

Exercise 12-77
Recording Impairment Loss on Asset Held for Sale **LO8**

Three cases are provided below concerning a plant asset currently held for sale.

Case	Original Cost	Accumulated Depreciation	Fair Value	Selling Costs
1	$ 96,000	$ 50,000	$ 45,000	$1,500
2	45,000	1,000	30,000	1,000
3	280,000	150,000	140,000	7,000

a. Which cases(s), if any, require an impairment loss to be recognized, and for what amount?
b. Record the entry for the impairment loss on the case(s) identified in part *a* (if any).

Exercise 12-78
Computing Asset Ratios **LO9**
Hint: See Demo 12-9

The following information relates to **Nike Inc.**

$ millions	Total Fixed Assets	Total Assets	Revenue	Net Income
Fiscal Year 2016	$3,520	$21,396	$32,376	$3,760
Fiscal Year 2015	3,011	21,597	30,601	3,273
Fiscal Year 2014	2,834	18,594		

Nike's fiscal years 2016, 2015, and 2014, end on May 31, 2016, 2015, and 2014, respectively.

Required

a. Compute the asset turnover ratio for fiscal years 2016 and 2015.
b. Compute the return on assets ratio for fiscal years 2016 and 2015.
c. Compute the fixed asset turnover ratio for fiscal years 2016 and 2015.

Exercise 12-79
Solving for Unknown Amounts Through Ratio Analysis **LO9**

Financial information for **Under Armour Inc.** for the fiscal year ended January 30, 2016, follows ($ thousands except for ratios).

Average fixed assets	$ 671,371	Asset turnover	1.48237
Revenues	$4,825,335	Return on assets	0.07895

Required

a. Compute average total assets.
b. Compute net income.
c. Compute fixed asset turnover.

Exercise 12-80
Recording Entries Related to the Purchase and Depletion of Natural Resources **LO10**

On May 1, 2020, Star Mines Inc. purchased an ore mine for $3,000,000 to access an estimated 1,555,000 tons of ore. The company incurred development costs of $225,000 related to the mine and purchased equipment for the mine for $450,000 with a useful life of 8 years. The equipment has no use outside of this mine project. The company is expected to restore the land for alternative uses after mining is complete. The present value of the restoration cost is estimated to be $100,000. The company extracted 180,000 tons of ore in 2020 and sold 150,000 tons.

Required

a. Record the entry for purchase of the mine and equipment. Assume all purchases were for cash.

b. Record the entry for (i) depletion of the ore and (ii) sale of ore in 2020. Round the depletion rate to two decimals.

c. Record the entry for depreciation of the equipment assuming that the equipment is depreciated in proportion to the depletion of the mine.

Exercise 12-81 Calculating Depletion of Natural Resources and Related Cost of Goods Sold **LO10**

Arizona Mining Company acquired property with copper ore reserves estimated at 2 million pounds for $1,800,000. The property will have an estimated value of $100,000 after the ore has been extracted. Before any ore could be removed, it was necessary to incur $500,000 of developmental costs. In the first year, 200,000 pounds were removed and 160,000 pounds of ore were sold; in the second year, 400,000 pounds were removed and 410,000 pounds were sold. In the course of the second year's production, discoveries were made that indicated that if an added $1,460,000 is spent on developmental costs during the third year, future removable ore will total 2.5 million pounds. After these added costs were incurred, production for the third year amounted to 510,000 pounds with sales of 450,000 pounds.

Required

Calculate depletion *and* cost of goods sold that the company reports on its income statement for *each* of the three years. Assume FIFO (first-in, first-out) inventory flow.

Exercise 12-82 Calculating Depletion, Depreciation, and Ending Inventory **LO10**

Atlas Company purchased the rights to a copper mine for $3,000,000 on January 1, 2020. The mine is expected to provide 700,000 tons of copper. Atlas also purchased equipment on June 30, 2020, for $60,000 (residual value $5,000) that will be used for other projects. The estimated useful life is 6 years. In 2020, the company extracted 50,000 tons of copper and sold 30,000 tons.

Required

a. Calculate depletion for Atlas Company for 2020. Round depletion rates to two decimals.

b. Calculate depreciation expense for Atlas Company for 2020 assuming the company uses straight-line depreciation.

c. Determine ending inventory of copper on December 31, 2020.

Exercise 12-83 Calculating Depletion, Depreciation, and Ending Inventory **LO10**

Aerial Company acquired land containing natural resources that it planned to extract for $5 million on January 1, 2020. The amount allocated to the land is $200,000. Surveys estimate that the recoverable reserves will total 4 million tons. The company paid an additional $400,000 for development to prepare for the extraction of the resources. The company also incurred $200,000 to build roads with a useful life of 8 years. The roads will not be used for other projects. The company is obligated to restore the site after the extraction of resources. The present value of this obligation is $50,000. 480,000 tons of natural resources were extracted in 2020 and 450,000 tons were sold in 2020.

Required

a. Determine depletion for the natural resource in 2020.

b. Assuming that the company depreciates the cost of roads using units-of-production, determine depreciation expense for 2020.

c. Compute cost of goods sold for 2020, and ending inventory on December 31, 2020.

Exercise 12-84 Recording Entries Using the Full-Cost and Successful-Efforts Methods **LO10**
Hint: See Demo 12-10B

In 2020, Star Oil Co. incurred exploration costs related to exploring and drilling for oil. Costs were allocated to 5 drilling areas: Area 1: $50,000, Area 2: $25,000, Area 3: $15,000, Area 4: $70,000, Area 5: $45,000.

Of the 5 areas explored, Areas 2, 4, and 5 have successfully resulted in discovery of recoverable oil reserves while Areas 1 and 3 have been abandoned. The estimated value of the oil discovered in the successful drilling areas is $1,500,000.

Required

a. Record the entry for exploration costs using the successful-efforts method.

b. Record the entry for exploration costs using the full-cost method.

Exercise 12-85
Defining Chapter Terms **LO1, 2, 3, 4, 5, 6, 7, 8, 9**

Terms relating to concepts discussed in this chapter along with descriptions of the terms are included in the following two lists:

Chapter 12 Terms	Description of Terms
____ 1. Depreciation expense	*a.* Cost of fixed asset plus subsequent acquisition costs less accumulated depreciation
____ 2. Depreciable cost	*b.* Ratio that divides net sales by average total assets
____ 3. Book value	*c.* Expense fluctuates with changes in input or output units
____ 4. Straight-line depreciation	*d.* Ratio that divides net income by average total assets
____ 5. Units-of-production depreciation method	*e.* Allocation of expense over the life of a fixed asset
____ 6. Composite depreciation	*f.* Does not require a recoverability test before an impairment loss is recorded
____ 7. Depreciation policy conventions	*g.* Depreciation is determined by grouping dissimilar assets
____ 8. Change in depreciation method	*h.* Treated prospectively with no change to prior financial statements
____ 9. Error in depreciation calculation	*i.* Treated retroactively, which requires updates to previously reported information
____ 10. Recoverability test	*j.* Acquisition costs of fixed assets less residual value divided by estimated useful life
____ 11. Impairment loss measurement	*k.* Requires the comparison of fixed asset book value to expected cash flows
____ 12. Return on assets	*l.* Cost of fixed asset plus subsequent acquisition costs less salvage value
____ 13. Asset turnover	*m.* Consistent use of a variation of the application of a depreciation method
____ 14. Assets held for sale	*n.* Requires the comparison of fixed asset book value to fair value

Required

Match each term, *1* through *14*, with the most appropriate description *a* through *n*.

Problems

Problem 12-86
Computing Depreciation Using Various Depreciation Methods **LO1**

Quick Producers acquired factory equipment on January 1, 2020, costing $39,000. In view of pending technological developments, it is estimated that the machine will have a resale value upon disposal in four years of $8,000 and that disposal costs will be $500. Data relating to the equipment follow.

Estimated Service Life	
Years	4
Service hours	20,000

Calendar Year	Actual Service Hours
2020	5,700
2021	5,000
2022	4,800
2023	4,400

Required

a. Prepare a depreciation schedule (for 2020 through 2023) that shows annual depreciation expense, accumulated depreciation, and book value, using the units-of-production method with service hours as a measure of input assuming accounts are closed each December 31.

b. Compute depreciation expense for the *first and second years* assuming (1) straight-line, (2) sum-of-the-years'-digits, and (3) double-declining-balance depreciation.

Problem 12-87
Identifying Depreciation Methods **LO1**

Equipment was acquired for $80,000 on January 1, 2020, that has a six-year estimated life and a residual value of $8,000. Third-year depreciation expense under the four methods listed below (but not in the same order) amounted to (1) $12,000, (2) $11,852, (3) $13,714, and (4) $19,800. The depreciation methods used were (a) double-declining-balance, (b) units-of-production, (c) straight-line, and (d) sum-of-the-years'-digits.

The units-of-production method assumed that 800,000 units could be produced; the actual output in the first three years was 200,000 units, 180,000 units, and 220,000 units.

Required
Match the third-year depreciation amounts, *1* through *4*, to the depreciation methods, *a* through *d*.

Problem 12-88 Computing Partial Period Depreciation Using Various Depreciation Methods **LO2**

Refer to the information from Problem 12-86, but instead assume that the company purchased the equipment on March 1, 2020, instead of January 1, 2020, and that service hours were as follows.

Calendar Year	Actual Service Hours
2020	4,700
2021	5,000
2022	4,800
2023	4,400
2024	1,000

Required
Compute depreciation expense *each year* for the life of the asset assuming (1) units-of-production, (2) straight-line, (3) sum-of-the-years'-digits, and (4) double-declining-balance depreciation.

Problem 12-89 Preparing Depreciation Schedules Using Various Depreciation Methods, Partial Period **LO2**

Constar Company purchased a machine that cost $145,000 on October 31, 2020. The company estimated that the machine would have a net resale value of $8,000 at the end of its useful life. Data related to the machine follows.

Estimated Service Life		Calendar Year	Actual Output (Units)
Years	5	2020	1,600
Output (units)	8,000	2021	1,900
		2022	1,000
		2023	1,800
		2024	1,700

Required
Prepare a depreciation schedule that shows annual depreciation expense, accumulated depreciation, and book value, for the asset over its useful life for each of the following methods.

a. Straight-line.
b. Unit-of-production using actual output. Round depreciation rate to two decimals.
c. Sum-of-the-years'-digits.
d. Double-declining-balance.

Problem 12-90 Determining Ending Balances in Property, Plant, and Equipment; Determining Gain/Loss on Asset Disposition **LO2**

Selected accounts included under property, plant, and equipment on McLory Company's balance sheet at December 31, 2019, had the following balances (at original cost).

Land	$220,000	Buildings	$600,000
Land improvements	75,000	Machinery and equipment	650,000

During 2020, the following transactions occurred.

1. A plant facility consisting of land and building was acquired from Club Company in exchange for 10,000 shares of McLory's common stock. On the acquisition date, McLory's stock had a closing market price of $39 per share on a national stock exchange. The plant facility was carried on Club's accounts at $95,000 for land and $130,000 for the building at the exchange date. Current appraised values for the land and building, respectively, are $120,000 and $240,000.
2. A tract of land was acquired for $85,000 as a potential future building site.
3. Machinery was purchased at a total cost of $250,000. Additional costs were incurred as follows.

Freight and unloading	$ 5,000
Sales and use taxes	10,000
Installation	25,000

4. Expenditures totaling $90,000 were made for new parking lots, streets, and sidewalks at the corporation's various plant locations. These improvements had an estimated useful life of 15 years.

5. A machine that cost $50,000 on January 1, 2012, was scrapped on June 30, 2020. Double-declining depreciation has been recorded on the basis of a 10-year life.
6. A machine was sold for $25,000 on July 1, 2020. Original cost of the machine was $37,000 at January 1, 2017, and it was depreciated on the straight-line basis over an estimated useful life of eight years and a residual value of $ 1,000.

Required

a. Determine the ending balances at December 31, 2020, in each of the following accounts: (1) land, (2) land improvements, (3) buildings, and (4) machinery and equipment.
b. Compute the gain or loss on scrapping equipment on June 30, 2020.
c. Compute the gain or loss on sale of equipment on July 1, 2020.

Problem 12-91
Recording Depreciation and Disposal Using Composite Depreciation
LO3

Fixed assets acquired on January 1, 2020, by Sculley Company are to be depreciated under the composite system. Details regarding each asset are provided in the schedule below.

Asset	Cost	Estimated Residual Value	Estimated Life (years)
A.	$180,000	$20,000	10
B.	60,000	0	6
C.	152,000	32,000	15
D.	24,800	800	8

Required

a. Calculate the composite life and annual composite depreciation rate (based on cost) for assets A, B, C, and D. Provide the entry to record depreciation after one full year of use. Round the depreciation rate to four decimals.
b. During 2021, it was necessary to replace Asset B, which was sold for $32,000. The replacement asset will cost $72,000 and will have an estimated residual value of $6,000 at the end of its estimated six-year useful life. Record the disposal and substitution, which was a cash acquisition.
c. Record depreciation at the end of 2021.

Problem 12-92
Computing Depreciation and Impairment with an Asset Addition and Change in Estimate LO2, 4, 7

On October 1, 2019, I-Toys Inc. purchased plastic molding equipment for $200,000. The equipment has an eight-year useful life and no residual value. The company uses the 150% declining-balance method of depreciation, has a calendar fiscal year, and computes fractional year depreciation to the nearest month.

On October 1, 2020, the company added a component to the molding equipment that increases the production rate. The component costs $20,000 and does alter the useful life of the molding equipment by extending it to a total of 10 years.

On April 1, 2021, the company decided to write down the recorded value of the molding equipment to $30,000, its fair value, because of a protracted downturn in demand for plastic toys. The total estimated future cash flows from the use and disposal of the equipment are estimated to be $45,000.

Required

a. Compute 2019 depreciation expense on the molding equipment.
b. Compute 2020 depreciation expense on the molding equipment, assuming the company includes the new component in the Equipment account.
c. Compute 2021 depreciation through April 1. Prepare the journal entry to record the impairment loss.

Problem 12-93
Recording Depreciation and Preparing Schedule Given Change in Estimate, Change in Method, Impairment LO2, 4, 7

In 2020, Spencer Company purchased equipment that experienced the following four events requiring modification to its accounts. Spencer has a calendar year-end.

1. On June 30, 2020, equipment is purchased for $240,000. The equipment has a $40,000 residual value and an expected useful life of five years.
2. A new component is added to the equipment on June 30, 2021, costing $150,000. As a result, the residual value of the original equipment is raised to $60,000. The useful life of the equipment is unchanged, and the component has no useful life separate from the equipment.
3. The remaining useful life of the equipment is changed to two years as of January 1, 2022. Residual value is unaffected.

4. The equipment becomes totally impaired as a result of a casualty on September 1, 2023. Recoverable cost and fair value are zero. The equipment functions normally through that date. Because the equipment is uninsured, Spencer charges the remaining book value to a loss account.

Required

a. For the following depreciation methods 1 through 3, provide journal entries to record (1) purchase of equipment on June 30, 2020; (2) depreciation expense for 2020, (3) purchase of component in 2021, (4) depreciation expense in 2021, (5) depreciation expense in 2022, and (6) loss on disposal in 2023 including an update to depreciation expense.
   1. Straight-line.
   2. Sum-of-the-years'-digits.
   3. Double-declining-balance *and* assume that the company changes accounting methods to the straight-line method on January 1, 2022.

b. Prepare a schedule proving that total charges reconcile to the total cost of the equipment.

Problem 12-94 Recording and Reporting a Change in Accounting Depreciation Method **LO5**

On January 1, 2016, Jordon Corporation purchased equipment that cost $23,000 with an estimated useful life of 10 years and no estimated residual value. The company uses double-declining-balance depreciation. At the start of 2021, the company decided to switch to straight-line depreciation (no change in useful life or residual value).

Net income before depreciation and before the effects of the accounting change was $40,000 in 2020, and $47,000 in 2021. Disregard income tax considerations.

Required

a. Prepare the 2021 (the year of change) entry to properly record depreciation expense.

b. Show how depreciation expense is reported in the 2020 and 2021 comparative income statements.

Problem 12-95 Determining Depreciation Expense with Changes in Depreciation Assumptions and Methods **LO4, 5**

An asset purchased January 1, 2017, costing $10,000 with a 10-year useful life and no salvage value was depreciated under the straight-line method during its first three years.

Required

Answer the following questions. Consider each question separately, using the original information for the asset.

a. During 2020, the estimate of the total useful life was adjusted to 17 years. Determine depreciation expense in 2020.

b. If management changed its depreciation method to double-declining-balance in 2020, determine depreciation expense in 2020.

c. During 2020, management determined that the asset would have an estimated residual value of $1,000. What is depreciation expense in 2020?

Problem 12-96 Reporting Errors and Changes in Estimates **LO4, 6**

Universal Corporation reported the following information for the current year (2020) and the prior year (2019).

Income Statement	2020	2019
Total revenues	$45,000	$30,000
Total expenses	40,000	28,000
Net income	$ 5,000	$ 2,000

Retained Earnings Statement	2020	2019
Retained earnings, beginning balance...	$2,000	$ 0
Net income	5,000	2,000
Retained earnings, ending balance	$7,000	$2,000

In 2020, before the financial statements have been reported, the following items were discovered.

1. The company understated expenses by $1,000 in 2019 due to a payroll tax accrual that was not recorded. The payroll tax was paid in 2020.
2. In 2020, the company changed the useful life of equipment purchased on January 1, 2019, from 8 years to 10 years. The equipment had a cost of $5,000 with a $500 estimated salvage value. Expenses currently recorded in 2020 do not reflect the change in useful life.

Required

Adjust the comparative financial statements reported above based on the errors identified. Ignore income taxes.

Problem 12-97
Recording Depreciation Expense, Correct for Error, Account for Change in Estimate **LO2, 4, 6**

The following information relates to the property, plant, and equipment of BWW Company.

	Original Cost	Salvage Value	Estimated Useful Life	Acquisition Date
Land	$ 400,000	—	—	Jan. 2, 2018
Land improvements	100,000	$ 0	15 years	Jun. 30, 2018
Buildings	1,200,000	100,000	30 years	Jan. 2, 2018
Equipment:				
Equipment A	250,000	25,000	8 years	Sep. 30, 2018
Equipment B	500,000	40,000	10 years	Jan. 1, 2019
Equipment C	150,000	0	8 years	Jun. 30, 2020

During 2020, the records of BWW Company indicated the following.

1. Use of straight-line depreciation for all depreciable assets.
2. Fair value of land (based on a recent appraisal) was $1,000,000.
3. Land improvements relate to various costs that took place in June of 2018, related to upgrades to parking lots, sidewalks, and lighting systems. The company adjusted the estimated total useful life to 12 years.
4. Discovered that the estimated useful life for Equipment B was erroneously entered into the depreciation system at 15 years instead of 10. Thus, the depreciation entries through December 31, 2019, were calculated incorrectly using 15 years.

Required

a. Prepare the entry for 2020 depreciation expense. Ignore taxes.
b. Prepare the entry to correct the depreciation error discovered in 2020. Ignore taxes.

Problem 12-98
Computing Depreciation Expense and Carrying Value Given Error, Change in Method **LO2, 5, 6**

The following information relates to the property, plant, and equipment of Holly Company.

	Acquisition Cost	Acquisition Date	Residual Value	Estimated Life	Depreciation Method
Land	$ 60,000	Jun. 30, 2018			
Land Improvement	10,000	Aug. 31, 2018	$ 0	15 yrs	Straight-line
Building	560,000	Jun. 30, 2018	50,000	40 yrs	Straight-line
Equipment #10	45,000	Aug. 1, 2018	1,000	10 yrs	Double-declining
Equipment #15	120,000	Jun. 30, 2019	18,000	10 yrs	Double-declining
Equipment #20	110,000	Jul. 31, 2019	2,500	10 yrs	Double-declining

During 2020, the company revealed the following items.

1. Expensed a total of $100,000 in 2018 related to costs of the building that should have been capitalized as building costs.
2. Made decision to change its policy to depreciate equipment starting in 2021 using the straight-line method.
3. Residual value of $18,000 for Equipment #15 was inadvertently entered into the depreciation system as $1,800.
4. Land value appreciated to $90,000 as of December 31, 2020.

Required

For 2018, 2019, and 2020, compute depreciation expense, accumulated depreciation, and the balance in each property, plant, and equipment account listed above. Prepare these values based on both the (a) original numbers and (b) corrected numbers.

Problem 12-99
Recording Asset Impairment and Subsequent Depreciation **LO7**

Gates Inc., a calendar-year firm, currently uses a plant asset in operations that originally cost $110,000 and has a useful life of eight years and a $10,000 residual value at the end of its useful life. Gates uses the straight-line method. As a result of a recent law restricting the use of the product produced by the asset, Gates reviews the asset for impairment. As of January 1, 2020, the beginning of the asset's third year of useful life, total remaining cash inflows attributable to the asset are estimated to be $120,000, while total cash outflows in running and maintaining the machine are estimated to be $65,000. Based on quoted prices and the condition of the asset, Gates estimates the fair value of the asset to be $40,000. The cost to sell the asset is approximately $5,000. Gates plans to continue to use the asset in production, although at a much lower rate of utilization.

Required

a. Record the impairment loss on January 1, 2020.

b. Record depreciation of the asset on December 31, 2020. Assume no change in estimated residual value at the end of the asset's useful life.

Problem 12-100 Recording Impairment and Revaluation of Assets Held for Sale **LO8**

Refer to the information in Problem 12-99, *except* that Gates decides to remove the asset from operations and hold it for disposal.

Required

a. Record the impairment loss on January 1, 2020.

b. Assume the asset remains in Gate's possession on December 31, 2020, at which time the asset's fair value is $30,000 (no change in selling costs). Record the entry to revalue the asset.

c. Instead of the facts in part *b*, assume that on December 31, 2020, the fair value is assessed at $45,000 (no change in selling costs). Record the entry to revalue the asset.

Problem 12-101 Analyzing Asset Ratios **LO9**

The following data and assumptions apply to a calendar-year company holding a depreciable asset.

Date of asset purchase	January 1, 2020
Cost	$ 20,000
Residual value	$ 0
Useful life	4 years
Annual income before taxes, depreciation, and interest	$ 35,000
Tax rate	40%
Interest expense per year	$ 5,000
Total assets on January 1, 2020, including plant asset	$100,000

Required

a. Demonstrate that the rate of return on total assets increases each year of the asset's useful life (assume straight-line depreciation).

b. Show that straight-line depreciation yields a higher rate of return on total assets early in this asset's life relative to sum-of-the-years'-digits. In later years, show this relation reverses.

Problem 12-102 Analyzing the Effect of Depreciation Method on Financial Statement Results **LO9**

On January 1, 2020, Velio Company, a tool manufacturer, acquired new industrial equipment for $4 million. The new equipment had a useful life of four years, and the residual value was estimated to be $400,000. Velio estimates that the new equipment can produce 14,000 tools in its first year. Production is then estimated to decline by 1,000 units per year over the remaining useful life of the equipment.

The following depreciation methods are under consideration: (1) double-declining, (2) straight-line, (3) sum-of-the-years'-digits, and (4) units-of-production.

Required

a. Which depreciation method would result in maximum income for financial statement reporting for the three-year period ending December 31, 2022? Prepare a schedule showing the amount of accumulated depreciation at December 31, 2022, under the method selected. Ignore present value, income tax, and deferred income tax considerations in the answer.

b. Which depreciation method would result in minimum income for tax reporting for the three-year period ending December 31, 2022? (Assume that all four methods are allowable for tax purposes.)

AICPA adapted

Problem 12-103 Recording Depreciation and Depletion Entries **LO10**

Colorado Mining Corporation bought mineral-bearing land for $150,000 that engineers estimate will yield 200,000 pounds of economically removable ore. The land will have a value of $30,000 after the ore is removed.

To work the property, Colorado built structures and sheds on the site that cost $30,000; these will last 10 years, and because their use is confined to mining and it would be expensive to dismantle and move them, they will have no residual value. Machinery that cost $39,000 was installed at the mine, and the added cost for installation was $7,000. This machinery should last 15 years. Like that of the structures, the usefulness of the machinery is confined to these mining operations. Dismantling and removal costs when the property has been fully worked will approximately equal the value of the machinery at that time; therefore, Colorado does not plan to use the structures or the machinery after the minerals have been removed.

In the first year, Colorado removed only 10,000 pounds of ore. However, production increased to 30,000 pounds in the second year. It is expected that all of the removable ore will be extracted within eight years from the start of operations.

Required

a. Prepare a schedule showing the carrying value of (1) natural resources, (2) facilities, and (3) machinery at the end of year one and year two. Use the units-of-production method of depreciation for all three classifications.

b. In the first year, 80% of production was sold and in the second year the inventory carried over from the first year plus 80% of the second year's production was sold. Prepare entries to record (1) accumulated depreciation and accumulated depletion and (2) cost of goods sold, for both year one and year two. Use accounts labeled Accumulated Depreciation and Accumulated Depletion.

Problem 12-104
Recording Depreciation and Depletion Entries **LO10**

On July 1, 2020, Miller Mining, a calendar-year corporation purchased the rights to a copper mine. Of the total purchase price, $2.8 million was allocable to the copper. Estimated reserves were 1.0 million tons of copper. Miller expects to extract and immediately sell 10,000 tons of copper each month. Production began immediately. The selling price is $25 per ton. To aid production, Miller also purchased some new equipment on July 1, 2020. The equipment cost $76,000 and had an estimated useful life of 8.333 years. After all the copper is removed from this mine, the equipment will be of no use to Miller and will be sold for an estimated $4,000. Assume straight-line depreciation on the equipment.

Required

a. If sales and production conform to expectations, what is Miller's depletion expense on this mine for financial accounting purposes for calendar year 2020?

b. If sales and production conform to expectations, what is Miller's depreciation expense on the new equipment for financial accounting purposes for calendar year 2020?

c. Repeat part *b*, but assume units-of-production depreciation.

Problem 12-105
Computing Depletion and Preparing Financial Reporting of Natural Resources **LO10**

Miller Company's investment in a gravel quarry was $6,000,000, of which $400,000 represented land value after removal of the gravel. Geologists engaged to estimate the removable gravel reported originally that 5 million cubic yards (units) could be extracted. In the first year, 880,000 units were extracted and 820,000 units were sold. In the second year, 830,000 units were extracted and sales were 850,000 units.

At the start of the third year, management of Miller had the quarry examined again, at which time it was determined that the remaining removable gravel was 2 million units. Production and sales for the third year amounted to 400,000 units. In the fourth year, production was 750,000 units and sales amounted to 600,000 units.

Required

a. Calculate the depletion rate for Year One and Year Two. Round depletion rates to two decimals.

b. Calculate the depletion rate for Year Three and Year Four. Round depletion rates to two decimals.

c. Calculate the total amount of depletion and the total amount of cost of goods sold for *each* of the four years. Assume a FIFO (first-in, first-out) basis.

d. Show how the gravel inventory and the gravel quarry are reported on Miller's balance sheet at the end of the fourth year. Assume that an accumulated depletion account is used.

Problem 12-106
Accounting for Oil Exploration Costs **LO10**

GeoTech, a company involved in developing and marketing natural resources, began a new development project by purchasing land for the purpose of exploiting its natural resources. During the first year, $300,000 was spent on exploring for the location of the ore (1/3 of the efforts were successful).

Required

Record entries for the current year involving the natural resource exploration efforts begun this year under the (a) successful-efforts method and (b) full-cost method.

Accounting Decisions and Judgments

AD&J 12-107 Analyzing Depreciation and Capital Maintenance LO1

Real World Analysis Ameritech Corporation is the parent corporation of five Bell companies serving the Great Lakes region. Selected amounts from the company's Year 9 financial statements appear below (in $ millions).

Statement of cash flows	
Net income	$3,606
Depreciation and amortization	2,717
Net cash flow from operations	4,810

Statement of shareholders' equity	
Dividends declared	$1,341

Additional assumptions:

1. Average consumer price index for all urban consumers (CPI-U) was 391 in Year 1 and 488 in Year 9.
2. Ameritech purchased all its existing property, plant, and equipment and tangibles in Year 1.
3. The CPI-U provides a reasonable approximation to the increase in replacement cost of Ameritech's plant assets and intangibles since acquisition.

Required

a. Ignoring inflation, or the change in replacement cost of plant assets, has Ameritech generated sufficient resources from operations in Year 9 to replace the portion of the historical cost of its depreciable and amortizable assets allocated to expense in Year 9?

b. Redo part *a*, incorporating the effect of inflation and dividends in the answer. Interpret the results.

AD&J 12-108 Analyzing Composite Depreciation LO3

Real World Analysis Juno Lighting is a manufacturer of track and recessed lighting fixtures. Excerpts from its Year 8 balance sheet and notes to the annual report of Juno Lighting include the following (in $ thousands).

Balance Sheet—Property and Equipment	
Land	$ 7,279
Building and improvements	31,580
Tools and dies	7,884
Machinery and equipment	7,135
Computer equipment	5,043
Office furniture and equipment	2,606
Total property and equipment	$61,527

Summary of Accounting Policies—Property and equipment are stated at cost. Depreciation is computed over estimated useful lives using the straight-line method for financial reporting purposes and accelerated methods for income tax reporting. Useful lives for property and equipment are as follows.

Building and improvements	20–40 years
Tools and dies	3 years
Machinery and equipment	7 years
Computer equipment	5 years
Office furniture and equipment	5 years

For simplicity, assume that all depreciable plant assets were acquired in Year 8 and have no residual value. Use 40 years for the useful life of building and improvements.

Required

a. If Juno Lighting adopts the composite depreciation system for financial reporting purposes in Year 8 and plans to use as few asset groups as possible, how would we group the assets?

b. Determine the composite rate of depreciation and the composite life for each group established under part *a*.

c. Assume that in Year 9, new computer equipment costing $400,000, with no residual value and a useful life of five years, is acquired. Also assume that in Year 9 the company retired computer equipment with an original cost of $150,000. Compute depreciation in Year 9 under the composite method of depreciation.

AD&J 12-109 Analyzing Financial Statements and Perform Ratio Analysis LO9

Real World Analysis Following are excerpts from the financial statements of Coca-Cola Company.

Financial Statements (excerpts)

$ millions	Total Assets	Revenue	Net Income	Depreciation and Amortization
December 31, 2015	$90,093	$44,294	$7,366	$1,735
December 31, 2014	92,023	45,998	7,124	1,716
December 31, 2103	90,055			

Property, Plant, and Equipment, $ millions	2015
Land	$ 717
Buildings and improvements	4,914
Machinery, equipment and vehicle fleet	16,723
	22,354
Less accumulated depreciation	9,783
Property, plant and equipment—net	$12,571

Notes to Financial Statements—Property, Plant and Equipment
Property, plant and equipment are stated at cost. Repair and maintenance costs that do not improve service potential or extend economic life are expensed as incurred. Depreciation is recorded principally by the straight-line method over the estimated useful lives of our assets, which are reviewed periodically and generally have the following ranges: buildings and improvements: 40 years or less; and machinery, equipment and vehicle fleet: 20 years or less. Land is not depreciated, and construction in progress is not depreciated until ready for service. Leasehold improvements are amortized using the straight-line method over the shorter of the remaining lease term, including renewals that are deemed to be reasonably assured, or the estimated useful life of the improvement. Depreciation is not recorded during the period in which a long-lived asset or disposal group is classified as held for sale, even if the asset or disposal group continues to generate revenue during the period. Depreciation expense, including the depreciation expense of assets under capital lease, totaled $1,735 million, $1,716 million and $1,727 million in 2015, 2014 and 2013, respectively. Amortization expense for leasehold improvements totaled $18 million, $20 million and $16 million in 2015, 2014 and 2013, respectively.

Required

a. What method of depreciation is reflected in Coca-Cola's financial statements?

b. Compute Coca-Cola's 2015 and 2014 rate of return on total assets.

c. What was the effect of depreciation in 2015 on its rate of return, assuming a tax rate of 24%?

d. If Coca-Cola had been using an accelerated depreciation method, would the rate of return would be higher or lower than the result from part *b*?

AD&J 12-110
Analyzing the Reporting of Oil and Gas Exploration Costs **LO10**

Real World Analysis In a supplemental section of its Year 5 annual report, Texaco Inc., a major oil company, provides the following disclosures pertaining to its oil and gas operations.

Costs incurred in fiscal Year 5 ($ millions)	
Proved property acquisition	$ 38
Unproved property acquisition	51
Exploration	403
Development	1,322
Total	$1,814

Another part of the supplemental section shows for the same period exploration expenses totaling $306 million, and depreciation, depletion, and amortization totaling $1,198 million. Texaco also reports capitalized costs for fiscal years ending December 31, Year 5 and Year 4, as follows.

$ millions	Year 5	Year 4
Proved properties	$22,208	$24,137
Unproven properties	955	1,015
Support equipment and facilities	1,083	1,081
Gross capitalized costs	24,246	26,233
Accumulated depreciation, depletion, and amortization	16,396	16,872
Net capitalized costs	$ 7,850	$ 9,361

Texaco Inc. uses the successful-efforts method to account for exploration costs.

Required

a. What amount of exploration costs that Texaco incurred in Year 5 was capitalized?

b. If Texaco were using the full-cost method of accounting for exploration costs, what amount of exploration costs would be capitalized in Year 5? List any assumptions needed to answer this question.

c. Determine the amount of capitalized costs removed (retired or otherwise disposed of) from the capitalized costs account and the amount of related accumulated depreciation, depletion, and amortization.

AD&J 12-111 Analyzing Depreciable Tangible Assets Fully Depreciated but Still in Use **LO1**

Communication Case Case 1. Baker Corporation has some fully depreciated fixed assets that are still used in its business.

a. Discuss the possible reasons why this can happen.

b. Comment on the significance of the continued use of these fully depreciated assets.

Communication Case Case 2. In the past, fully depreciated assets and related accumulated depreciation balances have been merged with other assets still used in operations and related depreciation on the balance sheet. Describe the propriety of this accounting treatment, including a consideration of other possible treatments and the circumstances in which they would be appropriate.

AICPA adapted

AD&J 12-112 Analyzing Depreciation and Gain or Loss on Disposal **LO1**

Communication Case Some major car rental companies account for the gain or loss on disposal of their used cars as an adjustment to depreciation expense in the period of disposal rather than reporting gains or losses on disposal.

Required

Explain on what grounds, if any, such a procedure could be justified. Would the answer be different if the procedure were used by relatively few (instead of most) companies in the industry?

AD&J 12-113 Analyzing Depreciation as Single Asset Unit or Separate Subunits **LO3**

Communication Case In situations where depreciable properties are treated as units rather than as part of a group of assets depreciated on a composite or group basis, the question sometimes arises as to what constitutes an appropriate property unit for accounting purposes. For example, a building as a single entity may be designated as the basic property unit. Alternatively, the elevators, escalators, heating and air-conditioning system, other mechanical equipment, plumbing, electrical system, and basic building structure could be accounted for as separate property units.

Required

a. What accounting problems arise if an item that could be accounted for as a single property unit is instead accounted for as a number of separate asset units?

b. Identify and explain some advantages of accounting separately for smaller property units as opposed to aggregation as a single property unit.

AD&J 12-114 Analyzing the Financial Statement Impact of Capitalization Policies **LO1**

Ethics Case **Example One:** Bill Gates, the manager of a large division of a major corporation has significant input to accounting policy for the division and has authority over all line decisions, including purchasing, maintenance, and capital expenditures. The manager has occupied the position for three years; the average time for promotion to the corporate staff level is five years.

The manager has successfully endorsed capitalizing all post-acquisition costs, including improvements and general maintenance and repair. His justification is that all maintenance increases the useful life or productivity of assets relative to lower levels of such costs. In addition, he has recommended postponing many routine repairs on equipment used in manufacturing the division's product. Furthermore, he has resisted requests from lower managers to upgrade and expand facilities in several important areas. Divisions are evaluated on rate of return on investment (ROI), the ratio of divisional income to divisional investment.

Ethics Case **Example Two:** The executive management team for a waste management firm was charged by the Securities and Exchange Commission for financial fraud. Among other things, management was found to have avoided recognition of depreciation expense on equipment by assigning inflated salvage values to the equipment and extending their useful lives. The updated salvage values and useful lives are unrepresentative of estimates chosen by most firms in the industry.

Required

Write a one-page report addressing the ethical factors relevant to the example above of financial reporting and disclosure. Comment on the propriety of the accounting chosen, GAAP flexibility, and the degree to which underlying economic effects are disclosed.

AD&J 12-115 Analyzing the Use of Composite Depreciation **LO3**

Judgment Case MotoCross Bicycles Inc. uses straight-line depreciation for all its depreciable plant assets. All assets are depreciated individually except manufacturing machinery, which is depreciated using the composite method. During the year, MotoCross exchanged a delivery truck with Trike Company for a larger delivery truck. MotoCross paid cash equal to 10% of the larger truck's value.

Required

a. What factors should have influenced MotoCross's selection of the straight-line method?

b. How should MotoCross account for and report the truck exchange transaction?

c. 1. What benefits should MotoCross derive from using the composite method rather than the individual basis for manufacturing machinery?

2. How should MotoCross have calculated the manufacturing machinery's annual depreciation expense in its first year of operations?

AICPA adapted

AD&J 12-116 Analyzing the Accounting Process of Depletion **LO10**

Communication Case A friend of yours recently inherited capital stock in Megamining Corporation. The friend has just received the first annual financial report from the company since the inheritance. One aspect of the report in particular troubles your friend, and you have been asked for an explanation of what the company seems to be saying. The excerpt reads:

> Depletion of mines is computed on the basis of an overall unit rate applied to the pounds of principal products sold from mine production. The corporation makes no representation that the annual amount represents the depletion actually sustained or the decline, if any, in mine values attributable to the year's operations, or that it represents anything other than a general provision for the amortization of the remaining book value of mines.

Specifically, your friend, asks the following: (1) Is the depletion amount reported on the income statement meaningless? (2) Are the company's mines becoming more or less valuable? (3) What is the significance of the book value of the company's mines?

Required

Write a one-page response to your friend's questions. Identify each element of your response with the three questions your friend has asked.

AD&J 12-117 Defining Terms **LO4, 5, 6, 7**

Codification Skills Refer to the Codification and identify the definition for each of the following: (1) change in accounting estimate effected by a change in accounting principle, (2) change in accounting estimate, (3) error in previously issued financial statements, and (4) impairment.

AD&J 12-118 Performing Accounting Research **LO1, 3, 7**

Codification Skills Research the Codification and report the proper citation that provides guidance on each of the following topics.

a. Process of depreciation FASB ASC ___-___-___-___

b. Support for accelerated depreciation methods FASB ASC ___-___-___-___

c. Indications of fixed asset impairment FASB ASC ___-___-___-___

d. Measuring impairment for fixed assets held for sale FASB ASC ___-___-___-___

e. Treatment of gains/losses on sales of assets accounted for using the composite method FASB ASC ___-___-___-___

AD&J 12-119 Performing Accounting Research **LO1**

Codification Skills A company is preparing annual financial statements, which includes the valuation of property, plant, and equipment. The company uses accelerated depreciation for tax purposes. The company wishes to simplify its record keeping by using the same method for depreciation for tax purposes as it does for financial statement reporting. Identify the relevant authoritative guidance. FASB ASC ___-___-___-___

Appendix—Questions

12-120. Explain what is meant by MACRS depreciation. Explain why MACRS may not conform to GAAP.

12-121. In computing a corporation's total tax computed on its tax return, is tax or GAAP depreciation used?

Appendix—Brief Exercises

App—Brief Exercise 12-122 Computing MACRS Depreciation **LO11**

Bryan Company acquired equipment on January 1, 2020, for $20,000. It is estimated that the equipment has a four-year life and a residual value of $5,000. For purposes of this exercise, ignore bonus depreciation and apply MACRS (three-year asset) for tax purposes. Determine tax depreciation under MACRS for the life of the asset. What percentage of the asset is depreciated after two years?

App—Brief Exercise 12-123
Comparing MACRS Depreciation to Straight-Line Depreciation **LO11**

Refer to the information in Brief Exercise 12-122 and compute depreciation using the straight-line method over the life of the asset. What percentage of the asset is depreciated after two years? How does the percentage compare to the equivalent percentage in the MACRS example?

Appendix—Exercises

App—Exercise 12-124
Compute MACRS Depreciation **LO11**

Delton Company purchased machinery in 2020 for $200,000, which qualifies as a five-year class asset for tax depreciation purposes. The equipment has a useful life of ten years and a residual value of $2,000. Delton does not use bonus depreciation.

Required
Compute Delton's depreciation tax deduction for each applicable tax year using the MACRS tables.

App—Exercise 12-125
Computing MACRS Depreciation **LO11**
Hint: See Demo 12-11

Refer to the information in Exercise 12-124 except assume the asset qualifies as a three-year class asset.

Required
Compute Delton's depreciation tax deduction for each applicable tax year using the MACRS tables.

Appendix—Problem

App—Problem 12-126
Computing MACRS Depreciation **LO11**

Delton Company purchased equipment on January 1, 2020, for $200,000, which qualifies as a three-year class asset for tax depreciation purposes. The equipment has a useful life of six years and no residual value.

Required

a. Compute Delton's depreciation tax deduction for each year using the MACRS tables.
b. Compute Delton's depreciation tax deduction for each year using bonus depreciation where 100% of the cost of the asset is taken as a deduction in 2020.
c. Compute the present value of tax benefits from depreciating this asset for tax purposes as in part *b.* Assume that (a) Delton has an applicable 10% after-tax minimum rate of return, (b) it has sufficient income to obtain the tax benefits of depreciation in each year, (c) tax payments for a tax year are made at year-end, and (d) the applicable tax rate is 25%. What is the effect of this amount on the present value of the net cash flows of purchasing this asset?
d. Repeat the requirements of part *c*, but now consider the tax benefits from depreciating this asset for tax purposes using bonus depreciation from part *b.*

Answers to Review Exercises

Review 12-1

1.	2.	3.	4.
2020: $35,833	2020: $61,429	2020: $75,000	2020: $43,000
2021: $35,833	2021: $51,190	2021: $50,000	2021: $38,700

Review 12-2
Part One

1.	2.	3.	4.
2020: $11,944	2020: $20,476	2020: $25,000	2020: $10,750
2021: $35,833	2021: $58,016	2021: $66,667	2021: $38,700

Part Two

	2020	2021	2022	2023	2024	2025	2026*	Total
Full-Year—Beg. of Period. . .	$ 0	$35,833	$35,833	$35,833	$35,833	$35,833	$35,835	**$215,000**
Half-Year.	17,917	35,833	35,833	35,833	35,833	35,833	17,918	**215,000**
Full-Month.	11,944	35,833	35,833	35,833	35,833	35,833	23,891	**215,000**

*Amounts adjusted in final year due to rounding.

Review 12-3

a. Total straight-line depreciation: $107,666 ($58,333 + $39,333 + $10,000)

b. Composite depreciation rate: 0.041 ($107,666/$2,650,000)
Composite life: 22 years [($2,650,000 − $260,000)/$107,666]

c. **December 31, 2020—To record composite depreciation expense**

Assets = Liabilities + Equity
−107,666 −107,666
Accum Deprec | 107,666 ; Deprec Exp 107,666 |

Depreciation Expense	107,666	
Accumulated Depreciation		107,666

d. **2021—To record sale of equipment**

Assets = Liabilities + Equity
+6,000
+44,000
−50,000
Cash 6,000 | ; Accum Deprec 44,000 | 107,666
Equipment | 50,000

Cash	6,000	
Accumulated Depreciation (to balance)	44,000	
Other Equipment		50,000

Review 12-4

$46,633 [($350,000 − $68,700 − $1,500)/6 years]

Review 12-5

$21,072 [($266,394* − $3,000)/150 months × 12 months]

*$380,000 − ($25,333 + $47,289 + $40,984)

Review 12-6

January 1, 2021—To correct depreciation error

Assets = Liabilities + Equity
+100,534 +100,534
Accum Deprec 100,534 | ; Ret Earnings—PPA | 100,534

Accumulated Depreciation ([$75,400 − $25,133] × 2)	100,534	
Retained Earnings—Prior Period Adjustment		100,534

Review 12-7

a. Plant Asset #202: $65,000 loss; Plant Asset #203: $350,000 loss.

b. **To record impairment loss on plant assets**

Assets = Liabilities + Equity
−415,000 −415,000
Accum Deprec | 415,000 ; Loss on Impair 415,000 |

Loss on Impairment ($65,000 + $350,000)	415,000	
Accumulated Depreciation		415,000

Review 12-8

a. Plant Asset #102: $6,700 loss; Plant Asset #103: $8,000 loss.

b. **To record impairment loss on assets held for sale**

Assets = Liabilities + Equity
−14,700 −14,700
Accum Deprec | 14,700 ; Loss on Impair 14,700 |

Loss on Impairment ($6,700 + $8,000)	14,700	
Accumulated Depreciation		14,700

Review 12-9

a. Asset turnover:	2016: 0.60	2015: 0.61
b. Return on assets:	2016: 0.07	2015: 0.08
c. Fixed asset turnover:	2016: 6.23	2015: 6.57

Review 12-10

a. $765,900 ($3.33 × 230,000)

b. $99,900 ($3.33 × 30,000)

Review 12-11

2020	2021	2022	2023	2024	2025	Total
$10,000	$16,000	$9,600	$5,760	$5,760	$2,880	$50,000

13 Intangible Assets and Goodwill

3M Company
Acquired Intangible Assets

The carrying amount and accumulated amortization of acquired finite-lived intangible assets, in addition to the balance of non-amortizable intangible assets, as of December 31, follow:

(Millions)	2016	2015
Customer related intangible assets	**$ 1,939**	$ 1,973
Patents	**602**	616
…echnology-based intangible assets	**524**	525
…e-lived tradenames	**420**	421
…mortizable intangible assets	**211**	216
…oss carrying amount	**$ 3,696**	$ 3,751
…ated amortization — customer related	**(797)**	(668)
…ed amortization — patents	**(497)**	(481)
…ed amortization — other technology based	**(302)**	(252)
…ed amortization — definite-lived tradenames	**(236)**	(215)
Accumulated amortization — other	**(173)**	(169)
Total accumulated amortization	**$(2,005)**	$(1,785)
…inite-lived intangible assets — net	**$ 1,691**	$ 1,966
…tizable intangible assets (primarily tradenames)	**629**	635
…angible assets — net	**$ 2,320**	$ 2,601

…enames acquired by 3M are not amortized because they have been in existence …ears, have a history of leading-market share positions, have been and are …e continuously renewed, and the associated products of which are expected to … flows for 3M for an indefinite period of time.

…xpense for the years ended December 31 follows:

…pense	2016	2015	2014
	$ 262	$ 229	$ 228

…ation expense for acquired amortizable intangible assets recorded as of …6 follows:

(Millions)	2017	2018	2019	2020	2021	After 2021
Amortization expense	$ 223	$ 202	$ 190	$ 180	$ 164	$ 732

The preceding expected amortization expense is an estimate. Actual amounts of amortization expense may differ from estimated amounts due to additional intangible asset acquisitions, changes in foreign currency exchange rates, impairment of intangible assets, accelerated amortization of intangible assets and other events. 3M expenses the costs incurred to renew or extend the term of intangible assets.

3M Company
Research, development and related expenses: These costs are charged to operations in the period incurred and are shown on a separate line of the Consolidated Statement of Income. Research, development and related expenses totaled $1.735 billion in 2016, $1.763 billion in 2015 and $1.770 billion in 2014. Research and development expenses, covering basic scientific research and the application of scientific advances in the development of new and improved products and their uses, totaled $1.225 billion in 2016, $1.223 billion in 2015 and $1.193 billion in 2014. Related expenses primarily include technical support; internally developed patent costs, which include costs and fees incurred to prepare, file, secure and maintain patents; amortization of externally acquired patents and externally acquired in-process research and development; and gains/losses associated with certain corporate approved investments in R&D-related ventures, such as equity method effects and impairments.

3M Company
Intangible assets: Intangible asset types include customer related, patents, other technology-based, tradenames and other intangible assets acquired from an independent party. Intangible assets with a definite life are amortized over a period ranging from one to twenty years on a systematic and rational basis (generally straight line) that is representative of the asset's use. The estimated useful lives vary by category, with customer related largely between seven to seventeen years, patents largely between five to thirteen years, other technology-based largely between two to fifteen years, definite lived tradenames largely between three and twenty years, and other intangibles largely between two to ten years. Costs related to internally developed intangible assets, such as patents, are expensed as incurred, primarily in "Research, development and related expenses."

Intangible assets with a definite life are tested for impairment whenever events or circumstances indicate that the carrying amount of an asset (asset group) may not be recoverable. An impairment loss is recognized when the carrying amount of an asset exceeds the estimated undiscounted cash flows used in determining the fair value of the asset. The amount of the impairment loss recorded is calculated by the excess of the asset's carrying value over its fair value. Fair value is generally determined using a discounted cash flow analysis.

Intangible assets with an indefinite life, namely certain tradenames, are not amortized. Indefinite-lived intangible assets are tested for impairment annually, and are tested for impairment between annual tests if an event occurs or circumstances change that would indicate that the carrying amount may be impaired. An impairment loss generally would be recognized when the fair value is less than the carrying value of the indefinite-lived intangible asset.

Chapter Preview

In this chapter we study the broad topic of intangibles. We begin with a description of intangible assets and goodwill and explore the proper accounting treatment. Some intangibles have a finite life while others have an indefinite life. We review subsequent measurement of recognized intangible assets and goodwill, including amortization (where applicable) and impairment recognition. We explain how changes in estimates are treated prospectively. We also review procedures for derecognizing intangible assets upon disposition and for recording research and development costs.

Action Plan

LO	Topic/Subtopic	Page	Demos	Reviews	Assignments
LO13–1	**Identify and classify intangible items** Intangible Assets :: Goodwill :: Finite Life Intangible Assets :: Indefinite Life Intangible Assets :: Internally Generated Intangible Assets and Goodwill	13-3	D13-1	R13-1	21, 22, 39, 40, 41, 59, 60, 61, 62, 67, 68, 71, 72, 73
LO13–2	**Determine the initial and subsequent measurements of intangible assets** Amortization Expense :: Straight-Line Method :: Finite Useful Life :: Legal Life	13-8	D13-2	R13-2	23, 24, 25, 26, 27, 28, 29, 42, 43, 44, 45, 46, 47, 59, 60, 61, 62, 66, 72
LO13–3	**Record goodwill resulting from an acquisition** Goodwill :: Control of Business :: Residual Value :: No Amortization	13-11	D13-3	R13-3	30, 31, 48, 49, 59, 60, 62, 63, 65, 69, 71
LO13–4	**Account for impairment and derecognition of intangibles** Impairment Testing :: Indicators :: Recoverability Test :: Impairment Test :: Qualitative Assessment :: Quantitative Test :: Derecognition	13-15	D13-4A D13-4B D13-4C D13-4D	R13-4	32, 33, 34, 50, 51, 52, 62, 63, 69, 71, 72
LO13-5	**Account for changes in estimates with intangible assets** Change in Residual Value :: Change in Useful Life :: Prospective Treatment	13-21	D13-5	R13-5	35, 36, 53, 54, 61
LO13–6	**Account for research and development costs** Research and Development Expense :: Alternative Future Use :: Software Development Costs :: Technological Feasibility :: Disclosure	13-22	D13-6A D13-6B	R13-6	37, 38, 55, 56, 57, 58, 59, 61, 64, 66, 70, 71, 72

LO 13-1 Identify and classify intangible items

LO 13-1 Overview

Intangibles
- Recognize acquired intangible assets
  - Finite life intangible assets
  - Indefinite life intangible assets
  - Goodwill
- Expense internally generated intangible costs

Recall from Chapter 1 that an asset is a probable future economic benefit controlled by the company. **Intangible assets** are one type of asset. This category includes assets (other than financial assets) that lack physical substance. **Goodwill** is classified as an intangible but separately from intangible assets. Goodwill originates from a business combination and represents the economic benefits obtained from that purchase that are not individually identified and separately recognized.

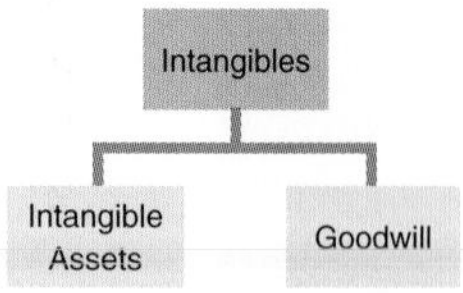

ASC Glossary Intangible Assets: Assets (not including financial assets) that lack physical substance. (The term intangible assets is used to refer to intangible assets other than goodwill.)

ASC Glossary Goodwill: An asset representing the future economic benefits arising from other assets acquired in a business combination . . . that are not individually identified and separately recognized.

Identification of Assets: Intangible Assets and Goodwill

Seven common assets, classified as goodwill or other intangible assets, are described in **Exhibit 13-1**. Included with each description is a discussion of the asset's useful life. The **useful life** of an asset is the period over which the asset is expected to contribute (directly or indirectly) to future cash flows.

350-30-35-2 The useful life of an intangible asset to an entity is the period over which the asset is expected to contribute directly or indirectly to the future cash flows of that entity.

Useful life can be **finite** (such as 20 years) or **indefinite** (such as having options for continual renewals). As described in the accounting guidance, an asset is considered to have an indefinite life when there are no factors that limit how long the asset will contribute to cash flows in the foreseeable future.

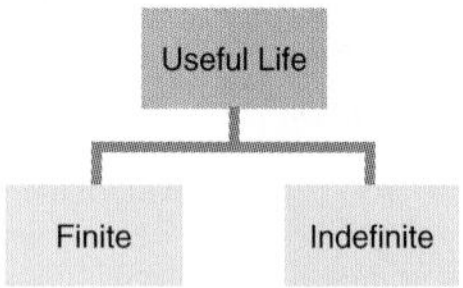

350-35-35-4 If no legal, regulatory, contractual, competitive, economic, or other factors limit the useful life of an intangible asset to the reporting entity, the useful life of the asset shall be considered to be indefinite. The term indefinite does not mean the same as infinite or indeterminate. The useful life of an intangible asset is indefinite if that life extends beyond the foreseeable horizon—that is, there is no foreseeable limit on the period of time over which it is expected to contribute to the cash flows of the reporting entity.

In estimating the useful life of an asset with a finite life, several factors included in the authoritative guidance must be considered.

350-30-35-3 The estimate of the useful life of an intangible asset to an entity shall be based on an analysis of all pertinent factors, in particular, all of the following factors with no one factor being more presumptive than the other:

a. The expected use of the asset by the entity.
b. The expected useful life of another asset or a group of assets to which the useful life of the intangible asset may relate.
c. Any legal, regulatory, or contractual provisions that may limit the useful life . . .
d. The entity's own historical experience in renewing or extending similar arrangements, consistent with the intended use of the asset by the entity, regardless of whether those arrangements have explicit renewal or extension provisions . . .
e. The effects of obsolescence, demand, competition, and other economic factors . . .
f. The level of maintenance expenditures required to obtain the expected future cash flows from the asset . . .

This means that while the life of an intangible asset may be legally defined (such as a patent's legal life), an asset's useful life (period of benefit) may differ. For example, the usefulness of a patent may be less than the legal life because new discoveries make the original patent less beneficial. **In this chapter we see that the classification of an intangible as having a finite or indefinite life impacts its subsequent measurement.**

EXHIBIT 13-1
Goodwill and Intangible Assets

Asset	Description	Useful Life
Patent	▪ Exclusive right recognized by law and registered with the U.S. Patent Office. ▪ Enables the holder to use, manufacture, sell, and control the item, process, or activity covered by the patent without interference by others.	Patents have a finite life, limited to a legal life of 20 years, although, the useful life of many patents is often shorter because technological improvements may cause the products or processes to lose their competitive advantage sooner.*
Copyright	▪ Form of protection given by law to the authors of literary, musical, artistic, and similar works. ▪ Includes the right to print, reprint, sell, or distribute copies, and to perform and record the work.	Copyright law protects a copyright for the life of the author plus 70 years. Copyrights are not renewable thus have a finite life. The useful life may be shorter than the legal life depending on the benefit period.
Trademark (Trade name)	▪ Name, symbol, or other distinctive identity given to a company, product, or service.	Registered trademarks and trade names can be renewed for successive 10-year periods, extending their legal lives indefinitely. However, the useful life may be shorter than the legal life depending on the benefit period so the useful life may be finite or indefinite.
Customer list	▪ Compilation of customer information including names and contact information.	A customer list may have a finite or indefinite useful life depending upon the length of time of the customer relationships that develop from the list.
Franchise	▪ Granted by a franchisor for the right to use a particular name and offer specified services/products. ▪ Also granted by government entities for the right to use public properties or to furnish public services.	Franchise contracts legally specify the rights and obligations of the franchisor and franchisee, and the finite period of time for which the franchise is valid. However, the contract may be renewable on a continual basis, which may indicate an indefinite useful life.
Licenses	▪ Contractual operating rights often granted by a governmental body.	Licenses specify a finite license period. However, a license may be renewable on a continual basis, which could indicate an indefinite useful life.
Goodwill	▪ Arises when a company acquires another company and the purchase price exceeds the fair value of the identifiable net assets acquired in the purchase. ▪ Although goodwill may be developed internally, it is not recognized unless a company is purchased.	Goodwill is associated with a purchased business unit and is considered to have an indefinite useful life as long as the operations of the business unit continue.

*A company may extend the life of a current patent by making a small change and applying for a new patent. If the new patent and old patent essentially provide the same benefits, the old patent costs may be added to the new patent costs and amortized over the new useful life.

For intangible assets to be recognized, they must have probable future economic benefits. Three classifications of intangible assets are outlined in **Exhibit 13-2**. In all three classifications, the intangible asset has been acquired from a third party, either directly through a purchase of an intangible asset

EXHIBIT 13-2
Asset Classification of Intangibles

Asset Classification	Financial Statement Classification	Examples
1. Finite Life Intangible Asset—Acquired	Intangible asset	▪ Purchase price of a patent (20-year useful life) from a third party. ▪ Legal and filing fees paid to a legal firm to register a patent.[1]
2. Indefinite Life Intangible Asset—Acquired	Intangible asset	▪ Purchase of a trademark (indefinite life) as part of a business acquisition. ▪ Legal and filing fees paid to a legal firm to register a trademark.[1]
3. Goodwill (Indefinite Life)—Acquired (See LO 13-3)	Goodwill	▪ Excess of the purchase price of a company over the fair value of the identifiable net assets due to items such as: • Strong reputation • Desirable physical location • Management talent pool • Trade secrets

[1] Fees paid for services outside of the company (such as legal fees) are capitalized as intangible assets even if the intangible asset itself is internally developed.

or payment of registration fees establishing ownership (such as a registering of a patent) or indirectly through a purchase of a company (resulting in goodwill). Asset recognition of *acquired* intangible assets and goodwill is outlined in the accounting guidance.

350-30-05-3 Intangible assets acquired individually or with a group of other assets should be recognized as assets in accordance with Section 350-30-25.

805-30-25-1 The acquirer shall recognize goodwill as of the acquisition date . . .

While intangible assets may be acquired individually or with a group of other assets, intangible assets may also be acquired in a **business combination** or when one company purchases another company. For example, the purchase of another company might include the purchase of the company's license agreements, franchise agreements, patents, acquired in-process research and development, or its customer lists. **Acquired in-process research and development** relates to intellectual property purchased that is part of incomplete research and development projects and is initially recorded as an indefinite life intangible asset until the project is complete. All intangible assets that are identifiable should be recorded at fair value upon purchase of the company. **Identifiable assets** are assets that arise from contractual or legal rights or are separable (capable of being separated from the company and sold, transferred, or exchanged). The excess of the cash paid for the acquired business over the fair value of all identifiable net assets is recorded as goodwill. The recording of goodwill is discussed in more detail in LO 13-3.

805-20-25-10 The acquirer shall recognize separately from goodwill the identifiable intangible assets acquired in a business combination. An intangible asset is identifiable if it meets either the separability criterion or the contractual-legal criterion described in the definition of identifiable.

ASC Glossary Identifiable: An asset is identifiable if it meets either of the following criteria:

a. It is separable, that is, capable of being separated or divided from the entity and sold, transferred, licensed, rented, or exchanged, either individually or together with a related contract, identifiable asset, or liability, regardless of whether the entity intends to do so.

b. It arises from contractual or other legal rights, regardless of whether those rights are transferable or separable from the entity or from other rights and obligations.

A company can incur subsequent costs related to intangibles. Specifically, a patent often does not become established until it has been successfully defended in court; thus, the costs of a successful court defense should be recognized as part of the cost of the patent. If the suit is lost, the legal costs are expensed and the patent is evaluated for impairment. Impairments are discussed in LO 13-4.

Recognition of Expenses: Internally Generated Intangible Assets and Goodwill

Assigning costs to the internal development or maintenance of intangible assets that are not specifically identifiable or that are related to an entity as a whole is difficult. Therefore, **costs to develop intangible assets internally are generally expensed as incurred.**

350-30-25-3 Costs of internally developing, maintaining, or restoring intangible assets that are not specifically identifiable, that have indeterminate lives, or that are inherent in a continuing business or nonprofit activity and related to an entity as a whole, shall be recognized as an expense when incurred.

This means a patent acquired from *a third party* is recognized as an intangible asset, while costs incurred *within a company* to develop a patent are expensed. Thus, for internally developed intangibles, and patents in particular, the allowable capitalized cost oftentimes *understates* the true value compared to a purchased intangible at the date of acquisition. The following examples of internal company costs would result in expense recognition, and not asset recognition.

- Salaries paid to engineers within a company that result in a patent (20-year useful life).
- Supplies used by engineers to develop a patent.
- Salaries paid to designers within a company that result in a trademark (indefinite life).
- Salaries paid to a company's in-house attorney to register a patent.

EXPANDING YOUR KNOWLEDGE — **Revenue Contract Costs**

Revenue contract costs (introduced in Chapter 7) are another form of intangible assets. Recall that costs to obtain a contract (due to a third party) are recognized as an asset if incremental and recoverable. Such costs include sales commissions due to employees. Costs to fulfill a contract are capitalized as an asset if directly related to a contract, generate resources used to satisfy the performance obligation, and are recoverable. Such costs include direct labor, direct materials, and allocated indirect costs. The asset recognized from capitalizing the costs to obtain a contract is amortized on a systematic basis consistent with the pattern of the transfer of the goods or services to which the asset relates. Such assets are subject to impairment testing.

Advertising Expense

In general, advertising costs are either expensed as incurred or expensed the first time advertising takes place with the exception of advertising costs incurred after related revenues are recognized. In this case, advertising costs are accrued when the related revenues are recognized. A company must disclose the accounting policy selected and the total amount charged to advertising expense for each income statement presented.

720-35-25-1 The costs of advertising within the scope of this Subtopic shall be expensed either as incurred or the first time the advertising takes place, except for those costs described in paragraph 720-35-25-1A. The accounting policy selected from these two alternatives shall be applied consistently to similar kinds of advertising activities. Deferring the costs of advertising until the advertising takes place assumes that the costs have been incurred for advertising that will occur. Such costs shall be expensed immediately if such advertising is not expected to occur. Examples of the first time advertising takes place include the first public showing of a television commercial for its intended purpose and the first appearance of a magazine advertisement for its intended purpose.

720-35-25-1A Expenditures for some advertising costs are made after recognizing revenues related to those costs. For example, some entities assume an obligation to reimburse their customers for some or all of the customers' advertising costs (cooperative advertising). When revenues related to the transactions creating those obligations are recognized before the expenditures are made, those obligations shall be accrued and the advertising costs expensed when the related revenues are recognized.

Classification of Intangible Items — LO13-1 — Demo 13-1

Demo MBC

For each of the following ten intangible items, (a) determine whether the item should be recognized as an asset (intangible asset or goodwill) or as expense, and (b) if the item should be recognized as an asset, indicate whether the asset has a finite useful life or an indefinite useful life.

	Intangible Item	Initial Recording: Intangible Asset, Goodwill or Expense	For Assets Only: Finite Useful Life or Indefinite Useful Life
1.	Research costs to internally develop a customer list over a three-year period.	**Expense**	**n.a.**
2.	Purchase of a patent with an expected useful life of 10 years.	**Intangible asset**	**Finite useful life**
3.	Purchase of a copyright, allowing certain printing rights for 50 years.	**Intangible asset**	**Finite useful life**
4.	Purchase of a company for $50,000 over the fair value of its identifiable net assets.	**Goodwill**	**Indefinite useful life**
5.	Customer list purchased from a research institution with a benefit period estimated to be 5 years.	**Intangible asset**	**Finite useful life**
6.	Purchase of a trademark, expected to be renewed indefinitely.	**Intangible asset**	**Indefinite useful life**
7.	Legal costs incurred for an outside counsel to register a patent, which was internally developed.	**Intangible asset**	**Finite useful life**
8.	Legal costs incurred for an outside counsel to successfully defend a patent internally developed.	**Intangible asset**	**Finite useful life**
9.	Legal costs incurred for an outside counsel that failed to defend a patent internally developed.	**Expense**	**n.a.**
10.	Research and development costs incurred by the company's technology division to develop a patent.	**Expense**	**n.a.**

MACY'S

Real World—INTANGIBLE ASSETS

MACY'S [M]

Macy's Inc. reported the following information in a recent Form 10-K regarding its intangible assets. Macy's Inc. holds the following types of intangible assets: finite life intangible assets (labeled *amortizing intangible assets*) and indefinite life intangible assets (labeled *non-amortizing intangible assets*). Accumulated amortization is reported separately from the asset account.

Goodwill and Other Intangible Assets The following summarizes the Company's goodwill and other intangible assets:

(millions)	Jan. 30, 2016	Jan. 31, 2015
Non-amortizing intangible assets		
Goodwill	$9,279	$9,125
Accumulated impairment losses	(5,382)	(5,382)
	3,897	3,743
Tradenames	414	414
	$4,311	$4,157
Amortizing intangible assets		
Favorable leases	$ 149	$ 177
Tradenames	43	—
Customer relationships	—	188
	192	365
Accumulated amortization		
Favorable leases	(90)	(106)
Tradenames	(2)	—
Customer relationships	—	(177)
	(92)	(283)
	$ 100	$ 82

In March 2015, the Company completed its acquisition of Bluemercury, Inc., a luxury beauty products and spa retailer. Goodwill during 2015 increased as a result of this acquisition. Also as a result of the acquisition of Bluemercury, the Company established intangible assets relating to definite lived tradenames and favorable leases. Definite lived tradenames are being amortized over their respective useful lives of 20 years. Favorable lease intangible assets are being amortized over their respective lease terms (weighted average remaining life of approximately six years). Customer relationship intangible assets relating to the acquisition of The May Department Stores Company are fully amortized as of January 30, 2016.

REVIEW 13-1 LO13-1 Classification of Intangible Items

Review MBC

Classify each of the following nine intangible items as one of the following: (a) finite life intangible asset, (b) indefinite life intangible asset other than goodwill, (c) goodwill, or (d) expense.

____ 1. Cost to purchase a franchise (10-year term).
____ 2. Incurred operational costs, which generated internal goodwill due to improved brand recognition.
____ 3. As part of the purchase of another company, a noncompete agreement was purchased that expires in 5 years.
____ 4. Allocated salaries of top management for time spent negotiating a three-year employment contract with the union.
____ 5. Incurred legal fees to register the company's trademark (renewable indefinitely).
____ 6. Incurred design costs (developed jointly by marketing and research staff) for a major overhaul of a product.
____ 7. License fee paid to a state government to operate in the state for two years.
____ 8. Excess of purchase price over the fair value of identifiable net assets acquired through a business combination.
____ 9. Research project purchased through a company acquisition that has the potential to produce one to two new patents over the next year.

More Practice: 13-21, 13-39
Solution on p. 13-42.

Determine the initial and subsequent measurements of intangible assets

LO 13-2

Intangible assets are initially measured at the cost of purchase. In subsequent periods, the costs of intangible assets with a *finite useful life* are **amortized** or allocated over the asset's estimated useful life (limited to the asset's legal life). Intangible assets with an *indefinite useful life* are **not amortized** on a periodic basis. However, both finite life intangible assets and indefinite life intangible assets are evaluated periodically for impairment (as discussed later in LO 13-4).

LO 13-2 Overview

Measurement of Intangible Assets
- Initial measurement
  - Recognize intangible asset at cost
- Subsequent measurement
  - Amortize finite life intangible asset
  - Do not amortize indefinite life intangible asset

350-30-35-1 The accounting for a recognized intangible asset is based on its useful life to the reporting entity. An intangible asset with a finite useful life shall be amortized; an intangible asset with an indefinite useful life shall not be amortized.

Initial Measurement of Intangible Assets

Intangible assets are recorded at acquisition at current cash-equivalent cost. Cost includes purchase price, transfer and legal fees, and other expenditures related to acquisition to bring the asset to its condition and location for intended use.

When an intangible asset is acquired in whole or in part for *noncash consideration*, its cost is any cash paid plus the fair value of the noncash consideration given or the fair value of the assets acquired, whichever is more reliably measurable. For example, if a company acquires a patent by issuing capital stock, the cost of the patent should be measured as the fair value of that stock. If the shares issued do not have an established fair value, evidence of the fair value of the patent itself should be used as the measure of cost of the transaction.

805-50-30-2 Asset acquisitions in which the consideration given is cash are measured by the amount of cash paid, which generally includes the transaction costs of the asset acquisition. However, if the consideration given is not in the form of cash (that is, in the form of noncash assets, liabilities incurred, or equity interests issued) and no other generally accepted accounting principles (GAAP) apply...measurement is based on either the cost which shall be measured based on the fair value of the consideration given or the fair value of the assets (or net assets) acquired, whichever is more clearly evident and, thus, more reliably measurable.

Sometimes an intangible asset may be grouped with other intangibles in a basket purchase. Similar to the fixed asset discussion in Chapter 11, each intangible asset is valued according to its fair value relative to the total fair value of the group of intangibles.

805-50-30-3 Acquiring assets in groups requires not only ascertaining the cost of the asset (or net asset) group but also allocating that cost to the individual assets (or individual assets and liabilities) that make up the group... The cost of a group of assets acquired in an asset acquisition shall be allocated to the individual assets acquired or liabilities assumed based on their relative fair values and shall not give rise to goodwill.

Subsequent Measurement of Finite Life Intangible Assets

The cost (less residual value) of a finite life intangible asset must be allocated to expense in a rational and systematic manner over the legal life or the estimated useful life of the asset, whichever is shorter. See LO 13-1 for a list of factors relevant for estimating useful life. The **straight-line method** should be applied unless a company determines that another systematic method is more appropriate. For example, a patent of a high-technology company might be expected to generate most of its benefits in the early periods of its existence, suggesting an accelerated form of amortization. (Just as with fixed assets, a change in amortization method is considered a *change in accounting estimate effected by a change in accounting principle* that requires prospective treatment.)

350-30-35-6 A recognized intangible asset shall be amortized over its useful life to the reporting entity unless that life is determined to be indefinite. If an intangible asset has a finite useful life, but the precise length of that life is not known, that intangible asset shall be amortized over the best estimate of its useful life. The method of amortization shall reflect the pattern in which the economic benefits of the intangible asset are consumed or otherwise used up. If that pattern cannot be reliably determined, a straight-line amortization method shall be used.

Amortization of an intangible asset usually involves a period-end adjusting entry. The amount to be amortized is recorded as a debit to amortization expense and as a credit directly to the intangible asset account (most common) as shown in **Demo 13-2,** or to the account, Accumulated Amortization (contra account to the asset account). Amortization expense and accumulated amortization must be disclosed in the financial statements or in the accompanying notes.

EXPANDING YOUR KNOWLEDGE — **Disclosure of Intangible Assets**

A number of the disclosure requirements for intangible assets follow.

Finite intangible assets

1. The gross carrying amount and accumulated amortization, in total and by major intangible asset class.
2. The aggregate amortization expense for the period.
3. The estimated aggregate amortization expense for each of the five succeeding fiscal years.

Indefinite life intangible assets

1. The total carrying amount for each major intangible asset class.
2. The entity's accounting policy on the treatment of costs incurred to renew or extend the term of a recognized intangible asset.

Goodwill

1. The gross amount and accumulated impairment losses at the beginning of the period.
2. Additional goodwill recognized and derecognized during the period.

Demo 13-2 LO13-2 Initial and Subsequent Measurement of Intangible Asset

Demo MBC

On January 1, 2020, Alto Company purchased for cash a patent that cost $27,200. The patent has a 20-year legal life that began on January 1, 2019. Applying the straight-line method, Alto uses the remaining legal life as the patent's useful life for amortization purposes. In January of 2021, Alto Company wins a patent infringement suit. Legal costs are $4,750.

Required

a. Record Alto Company's journal entries for (1) purchase of the patent in 2020, (2) amortization of the patent in 2020, (3) defense of the patent in 2021, and (4) amortization of the patent in 2021.

b. Determine the carrying value of the patent on December 31, 2021.

c. Record Alto Company's journal entry on January 1, 2020, for the purchase of the patent if, *instead of cash,* Alto issued a zero-interest note payable for $32,000 due in 2 years. The current interest rate for this type of financing is 8%. Assume that the fair value of the patent is uncertain.

Solution

a. **Journal Entries for the Patent**

January 1, 2020—To record purchase of patent

Patent	27,200	
Cash		27,200

Assets = Liabilities + Equity
+27,000
−27,000

December 31, 2020—To record amortization of patent

Amortization Expense	1,432	
Patent ($27,200/19)		1,432

Assets = Liabilities + Equity
−1,432 −1,432

January 31, 2021—To record costs to successfully defend patent

Patent	4,750	
Cash		4,750

Assets = Liabilities + Equity
+4,750
−4,750

December 31, 2021—To record amortization of patent

Amortization Expense	1,695	
Patent ([$27,200 − $1,432 + $4,750]/18)		1,695

Assets = Liabilities + Equity
−1,695 −1,695

Cash

Debit	Credit
	27,200
	4,750

Patent

Debit	Credit
27,200	1,432
4,750	1,695
28,823	

Amort Exp

Debit	Credit
1,432	
1,695	

continued

continued from previous page

b. **Carrying Value of the Patent on December 31, 2021**
Patent $28,823 ($27,200 − $1,432 + $4,750 − $1,695)

c. **Purchase of a Patent with a Note Payable**
The discount on the note payable is $4,565, which is $32,000 (note payable) less the present value of the note of $27,435. The patent is recorded at the present value of the note payable.

	RATE	NPER	PMT	PV	FV	Excel Formula
Given	8%	2	0	?	(32,000)	=PV(0.08,2,0,−32000)
Solution				$27,435		

January 1, 2020—To record purchase of patent with a note payable

Patent	27,435	
Discount on Note Payable	4,565	
Note Payable		32,000

Assets = Liabilities + Equity
+27,435 −4,565
+32,000

Patent
27,435 |

Discount on NP
4,565 |

Note Payable
| 32,000

Real World—FINITE LIFE INTANGIBLE ASSETS, AMORTIZATION

BOEING [BA]

The Boeing Company reported the following information in a recent report on Form 10-K regarding finite life intangible assets (labeled *finite-lived acquired intangible assets*) and related amortization.

Note 1—Summary of Significant Accounting Policies—Our finite-lived acquired intangible assets are amortized on a straight-line basis over their estimated useful lives as follows: developed technology, from 5 to 14 years; product know-how, from 6 to 30 years; customer base, from 3 to 19 years; distribution rights, from 3 to 27 years; and other, from 3 to 32 years.

Note 2—Goodwill and Acquired Intangibles—The gross carrying amounts and accumulated amortization of our acquired finite-lived intangible assets were as follows at December 31:

	2015		2014	
	Gross Carrying Amount	Accumulated Amortization	Gross Carrying Amount	Accumulated Amortization
Distribution rights	$2,245	$ 673	$2,245	$ 550
Product know-how	503	244	494	216
Customer base	600	403	619	381
Developed technology	455	357	500	386
Other	198	157	202	148
Total	$4,001	$1,834	$4,060	$1,681

Amortization expense for acquired finite-lived intangible assets for the years ended December 31, 2015 and 2014 was $224 and $227. Estimated amortization expense for the five succeeding years is as follows:

	2016	2017	2018	2019	2020
Estimated amortization expense	$211	$204	$185	$154	$145

During 2015 and 2014 we acquired $15 and $87 of finite-lived intangible assets, of which $0 and $24 related to non-cash investing and financing transactions.

Subsequent Measurement of Intangible Assets LO13-2 REVIEW 13-2

Review MBC

CosKo Inc. purchased the following three intangible assets in 2020.

1. A patent was purchased on March 31, 2020, for $50,000 when the remaining legal life (also its useful life) was 15 years.
2. On November 1, 2020, the company purchased a second patent for $85,000 cash. Upon acquisition, 5 years of the patent's legal life of 20 years had already expired. However, the company estimates that the useful life is expected to be only 10 years.

continued

continued from previous page

3. On November 30, 2020, the company purchased a trademark for $15,000. The company considers the life of the trademark to be indefinite.

Record the entry on December 31, 2020, to recognize amortization expense, if any, related to the three intangible assets.

More Practice:
13-26, 13-45
Solution on p. 13-42.

LO 13-3 Record goodwill resulting from an acquisition

LO 13-3 Overview

Goodwill
- Record when control of a business is purchased
- Equals residual of purchase price over fair value of identifiable net assets purchased
- Evaluate for impairment but do not amortize

Goodwill arises when a company acquires control of another company and the purchase price exceeds the fair value of identifiable net assets acquired in the purchase. Thus, the company must separately identify acquired assets and liabilities, including any intangible assets, before the residual (goodwill) is determined. Identifiable assets (including intangible assets) are either capable of being separated from the entity or arise from contractual or other legal rights. In fact, some of the intangibles that an acquiring company identifies would *not* have been previously recognized as assets by the acquired company as described in the authoritative guidance. (Recall that *internally generated intangibles* such as a patent or customer list would not be recognized on the financial statements of the acquired company.)

> **805-20-25-4** The acquirer's application of the recognition principle and conditions may result in recognizing some assets and liabilities that the acquiree had not previously recognized as assets and liabilities in its financial statements. For example, the acquirer recognizes the acquired identifiable intangible assets, such as a brand name, a patent, or a customer relationship, that the acquiree did not recognize as assets in its financial statements because it developed them internally and charged the related costs to expense.

To illustrate, goodwill is $200,000 for the purchase of a company for $1 million when the fair value of identifiable net assets purchased is $800,000—see **Exhibit 13-3**. Goodwill is a *residual value and is an unidentifiable intangible asset.* **Goodwill results when a company acquires control of a business or business unit of another company.**

EXHIBIT 13-3
Goodwill Resulting from a Purchase of a Company

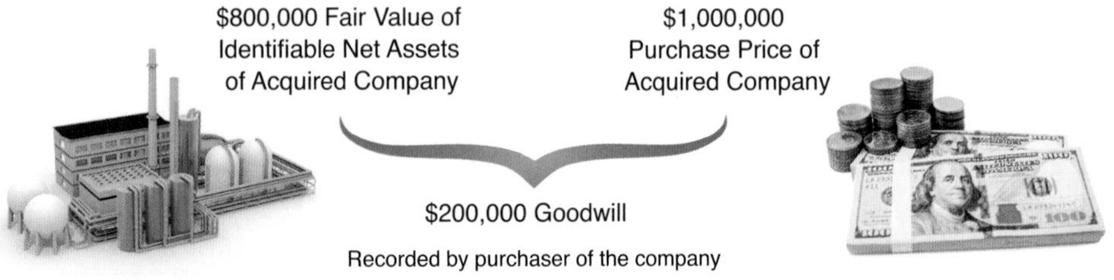

Goodwill represents expected economic benefits that are not separable or identifiable. Goodwill typically arises from favorable characteristics or factors that benefit the company's operations and future revenue streams. Examples of such favorable factors follow.

- Superior management team.
- Outstanding sales organization.
- Favorable position due to weakness in management of one or more competitors.
- Effective advertising.
- Secret manufacturing process.
- Exceptionally strong labor relations.
- Outstanding credit rating.
- Exceptional reputation for total quality.
- Unfavorable developments with a competitor.
- Favorable association with a supplier.
- A highly advantageous strategic location.

Any of these factors can give rise to increased growth and earnings power, leading to an increase in value of the company beyond the value of its individual, identifiable assets. However, they do not meet the definition of intangible assets because they are not separable or contractual. That is, they derive value from their association with the other assets of the company and cannot be sold separately. Thus, goodwill can be measured only when a business unit is sold in its entirety. In the absence of a sale, there is no market or arm's-length transaction with which to measure the goodwill a company creates as it engages in business activities. Accordingly, goodwill is recorded only at the time of purchase of control of another company or a business unit of another company as illustrated in **Demo 13-3**. Because goodwill differs from other separable intangible assets, it must be presented as a separate line item on the balance sheet.

350-20-45-1 The aggregate amount of goodwill shall be presented as a separate line item in the statement of financial position.

Goodwill is not amortized but is subject to impairment testing as indicated in the accounting guidance.

350-20-35-1 Goodwill shall not be amortized. Instead, goodwill shall be tested at least annually for impairment at a level of reporting referred to as a reporting unit.

Recording of Goodwill **LO13-3** **Demo 13-3**

Demo MBC

Hotel Company obtains financial statements and other financial data on Café Inc. and estimates the fair value of Café Inc.'s identifiable assets at $600,000 and the fair value of its identifiable liabilities at $400,000 as shown below.

Balance Sheet, December 31, 2020	As Reported	Fair Value	Difference
Assets			
Cash	$ 30,000	$ 30,000	$ —
Accounts receivable	90,000	85,000	(5,000)
Inventory	60,000	60,000	—
Other current assets	33,000	30,000	(3,000)
Property, plant, and equipment (net)	220,000	235,000	15,000
Patent	—	20,000	20,000
Acquired in-process research and development	—	50,000	50,000
Other assets	85,000	90,000	5,000
Total assets	$518,000	$600,000	$82,000
Liabilities			
Short-term notes payable	$ 85,000	$ 85,000	$ —
Accounts payable	45,000	45,000	—
Other current liabilities	30,000	30,000	—
Long-term debt	250,000	240,000	(10,000)
Total liabilities	410,000	400,000	(10,000)
Stockholders' equity	108,000	200,000	92,000
Total liabilities and stockholders' equity	$518,000	$600,000	$82,000

Record the journal entry for acquisition of Café Inc. by Hotel Company for $230,000 cash on December 31, 2020.

Solution

Several assets have an estimated fair value different from the carrying value reported in Café Inc.'s published financial statements. (Indeed, two intangible assets were not recorded at all—patent and in-process research and development.) The total fair value of Café Inc.'s net assets is determined to be $200,000 ($600,000 total assets less liabilities of $400,000). This is shown as stockholders' equity in the fair value column. This value is established not by estimating the value of Café Inc. as a company, but by netting the fair values of individual assets and liabilities. This value is similar to the liquidation value. If the company were broken up and sold as individual assets, and the liabilities were paid off at current fair values, the resulting net cash to be distributed to the owners would be approximately $200,000.

Although the fair value of the net assets is determined to be $200,000, Hotel negotiated a purchase price with the owners to acquire Café Inc. for $230,000. This purchase price exceeds the current fair value of identifiable net assets of $200,000; thus, goodwill is the difference, or $30,000. When Hotel acquires Café Inc., it records the assets and liabilities of Café Inc. at fair value and records goodwill of $30,000.

continued

continued from previous page

Assets	= Liabilities	+ Equity
+630,000	+400,000	
−230,000		

Cash		Assets (Other than Cash and Goodwill)	
30,000	230,000	570,000	

Goodwill		Liabilities	
30,000			400,000

December 31, 2020—To record purchase of Café Inc.

Cash	30,000	
Accounts Receivable	85,000	
Inventory	60,000	
Other Current Assets	30,000	
Property, Plant, and Equipment	235,000	
Patent	20,000	
Acquired In-Process Research and Development	50,000	
Other Assets	90,000	
Goodwill ($230,000 − $200,000)	**30,000**	
Short-Term Notes Payable		85,000
Accounts Payable		45,000
Other Current Liabilities		30,000
Long-Term Debt		240,000
Cash		230,000

The assets and liabilities of Café Inc. are recorded at current fair values in Hotel's financial records because this reflects the cost Hotel incurred for these items. Goodwill is not amortized but instead is evaluated for impairment as discussed in the next section.

EXPANDING YOUR KNOWLEDGE — Bargain Purchase

When the fair value of identifiable net assets acquired is *greater* than the purchase price, the acquiring company has made what is sometimes called a **bargain purchase**. Even though it would seem that the seller could benefit from selling the assets individually rather than selling the company as a whole, such situations do occasionally occur. For example, the seller may not have the time or resources to take on the efforts or risks of selling the assets separately. The difference between the purchase price and the fair value of assets is recorded as a gain. Assume that on December 31, 2020, Hotel Co. purchases Café Inc. for $180,500, which is $19,500 less than the fair value of net assets acquired. The difference of $19,500 ($200,000 − $180,500) is recorded as a gain.

805-30-25-2 Occasionally, an acquirer will make a bargain purchase, which is a business combination in which the amount [of the identifiable assets acquired and liabilities assumed] exceeds the aggregate of the [consideration transferred]. If that excess remains after applying the requirements [to reassess the identification of assets acquired and liabilities assumed], the acquirer shall recognize the resulting gain in earnings on the acquisition date.

Disclosure in the case of a bargain purchase includes the following from the accounting guidance.

805-30-50-1f [The] acquirer shall disclose all of the following information for each business combination that occurs during the reporting period: In a bargain purchase...both of the following:

1. The amount of any gain recognized . . . and the line item in the income statement in which the gain is recognized
2. A description of the reasons why the transaction resulted in a gain.

Assets	= Liabilities	+ Equity
+600,000	+400,000	+19,500
−180,500		

December 31, 2020—To record bargain purchase of Café Inc.

Cash	30,000	
Accounts Receivable	85,000	
Inventory	60,000	
Other Current Assets	30,000	
Property, Plant, and Equipment	235,000	
Patent	20,000	
Acquired In-Process Research and Development	50,000	
Other Assets	90,000	
Gain on Bargain Purchase ($200,000 − $180,500)		**19,500**
Short-Term Notes Payable		85,000
Accounts Payable		45,000
Other Current Liabilities		30,000
Long-Term Debt		240,000
Cash		180,500

Real World — GOODWILL

BOEING [BA]

The Boeing Company reported the following information in a recent Form 10-K. While total goodwill is $5.1 million on December 31, 2015, its balance is made up of purchases that comprise four reportable segments.

Note 2 – Goodwill and Acquired Intangibles Changes in the carrying amount of goodwill by reportable segment for the years ended December 31, 2015 and 2014 were as follows:

	Commercial Airplanes	Boeing Military Aircraft	Network & Space Systems	Global Services & Support	Total
Balance at January 1, 2014	$2,108	$964	$1,513	$458	$5,043
Acquisitions	45		57		102
Goodwill adjustments	(22)		(4)		(26)
Balance at December 31, 2014	$2,131	$964	$1,566	$458	$5,119
Acquisitions	**6**	**15**			**21**
Goodwill adjustments	**(14)**				**(14)**
Balance at December 31, 2015	**$2,123**	**$979**	**$1,566**	**$458**	**$5,126**

Recording of Goodwill

LO13-3 **REVIEW 13-3**

On January 1, 2020, the balance sheet of Naperville Company (a sole proprietorship) follows.

Assets		Liabilities	
Cash	$ 15,000	Accounts payable	$ 25,000
Accounts receivable, net of allowance	40,000	Noncurrent note payable	65,000
Inventory	60,000	Total liabilities	90,000
Plant and equipment, net of depreciation	200,000	Owners' equity	255,000
Land	30,000		
Total assets	$345,000	Total liabilities and equity	$345,000

On January 1, 2020, Chicago Inc. purchased all of the assets and assumed all of the liabilities listed on the above balance sheet for $365,000 cash. The assets, on date of purchase, were valued by Chicago Inc. as follows: cash, $15,000; accounts receivable, net, $35,000; inventory, $70,000; plant and equipment, net, $230,000; land, $60,000; and license, $10,000. The liabilities were valued at their carrying amounts.

Required

a. Compute the amount of goodwill included in the purchase price paid by Chicago Inc.

b. Prepare the entry that Chicago Inc. makes to record the purchase of Naperville Company.

c. Determine the minimum amount of goodwill that Chicago Inc. can amortize at the end of 2020.

More Practice: 13-31, 13-49

Solution on p. 13-43.

LO 13-4 Account for impairment and derecognition of intangibles

LO 13-4 Overview

Impairment and Derecognition of Intangibles
- Impairment
  - Finite life intangible assets
    - Recoverability test
    - Impairment test
  - Indefinite life intangible assets and goodwill
    - Qualitative assessment
    - Quantitative test
- Derecognition
  - Amortize asset to date of disposal
  - Record gain or loss if applicable

An intangible asset can be overstated if its carrying amount is not recoverable. If an asset is determined to be impaired, the company must reduce the asset account and record an impairment loss. Impairment testing varies by intangible asset type—namely, finite life intangible asset vs. indefinite life intangible asset vs. goodwill as shown below.

Asset Type	Impairment Analysis and Testing
Finite life intangible asset Demo 13-4A	1. Perform recoverability test if indicator(s) is present. 2. Perform impairment test if recoverability test indicates impairment.
Indefinite life intangible asset Demo 13-4B	1. Perform qualitative assessment at least annually (*bypass if moving directly to Step 2*). 2. Perform the quantitative test if indicator(s) is present from the qualitative assessment. Quantitative test is also used to measure any resulting impairment loss.
Goodwill Demo 13-4C	1. Perform qualitative assessment at least annually (*bypass if moving directly to Step 2*). 2. Perform the quantitative goodwill impairment test if indicator(s) is present from the qualitative assessment. Quantitative test is also used to measure any resulting impairment loss.

Impairment of Finite Life Intangible Assets

A finite life intangible asset is evaluated for impairment when events or circumstances indicate that the carrying value of the asset may not be recoverable. Examples of indicators would be an adverse change in the legal or business environment that could impact value, or a significant adverse change in how an intangible asset is being utilized.

If an indicator is present signaling possible impairment, the company performs a **recoverability test**. If the undiscounted sum of future net cash inflows expected to be received from use of the identifiable intangible asset is less than its carrying value and its carrying value is greater than its fair value, the asset is considered to be impaired. An impairment loss is recognized immediately for the difference between book value and fair value. The newly revised book value of the asset is amortized over the expected remaining useful life of the asset. A subsequent reversal of a previously recognized loss is prohibited. (This guidance is the same as discussed in Chapter 12 when evaluating potential impairment of fixed assets.)

350-30-35-14 An intangible asset that is subject to amortization shall be reviewed for impairment . . . by applying the recognition and measurement provisions . . . [An] impairment loss shall be recognized if the carrying amount of an intangible asset is not recoverable and its carrying amount exceeds its fair value. After an impairment loss is recognized, the adjusted carrying amount of the intangible asset shall be its new accounting basis. Subsequent reversal of a previously recognized impairment loss is prohibited.

Impairment of Finite Life Intangible Asset—Patent

LO13-4 **Demo 13-4A**

Edge Inc. purchased a patent for $40,000 on January 1, 2020, with a 10-year estimated life. While preparing financial statements on December 31, 2020, Edge Inc. had an indication that the carrying value of the patent might not be recoverable due to a newly issued, superior product produced by a competitor. Edge Inc. learns that the estimated future net undiscounted cash flows for the patent totals $25,000 while the present value of future estimated net cash flows is $18,400. Record the entry, if any, for an impairment loss on the patent at December 31, 2020.

Solution

First, Edge Inc. performs the recoverability test because an indicator (competitive pressure) is present signaling potential impairment. The carrying value of the patent is measured as follows.

December 31, 2020—Calculation of carrying value of patent

Original cost of patent.	$40,000
Less accumulated amortization ($40,000/10).	4,000
Carrying value on December 31, 2020.	$36,000

In this example, Edge Inc.'s recoverable cost of $25,000 is *less than* the carrying value of $36,000 indicating that the company should proceed to Step 2. Because the carrying value is greater than the fair value of the patent, an impairment loss is recognized for $17,600, computed as follows.

December 31, 2020—Measurement of impairment loss

Fair value (present value of future cash flows).	$18,400
Less carrying value of the patent	36,000
Impairment loss	$17,600

Edge Inc. records the following entry.

December 31, 2020—To record impairment loss on patent

Impairment Loss	17,600	
Patent		17,600

Assets = Liabilities + Equity
−17,600 −17,600

Patent: 17,600 (credit)
Impair Loss: 17,600 (debit)

Real World—IMPAIRMENT OF FINITE LIFE INTANGIBLE ASSETS

BOEING [BA]

Boeing Company reported the following information in a recent Form 10-K regarding finite life intangible asset impairment testing.

> **Note 1—Summary of Significant Accounting Policies**—We evaluate the potential impairment of finite-lived acquired intangible assets whenever events or changes in circumstances indicate that the carrying amount may not be recoverable. If the carrying value is no longer recoverable based upon the undiscounted future cash flows of the asset, the amount of the impairment is the difference between the carrying amount and the fair value of the asset.

Impairment of Indefinite Life Intangible Assets

Indefinitely-lived intangible assets must be reviewed for possible impairment at least annually. This review involves a **qualitative assessment** of factors indicating impairment. If the qualitative assessment indicates that it is *more likely than not* that the asset is impaired, the company must estimate the fair value of the asset and compare it to the carrying value—a **quantitative test**. If the fair value is greater than the carrying value, the asset is considered impaired and a loss is recognized. The qualitative assessment can save the company the effort and expense of estimating fair value in those cases where impairment is not likely. However, management can opt to bypass the qualitative assessment and move directly to the quantitative test if it wishes to do so.

350-30-35-18 An intangible asset that is not subject to amortization shall be tested for impairment annually and more frequently if events or changes in circumstances indicate that it is more likely than not that the asset is impaired.

350-30-35-18A An entity may first perform a qualitative assessment . . . to determine whether it is necessary to perform the quantitative impairment test . . . An entity has an unconditional option to bypass the qualitative assessment for any indefinite-lived intangible asset in any period and proceed directly to performing the quantitative impairment test . . . An entity may resume performing the qualitative assessment in any subsequent period. If an entity elects to perform a qualitative assessment, it first shall assess qualitative factors to determine whether it is more likely than not (that is, a likelihood of more than 50 percent) that an indefinite-lived intangible asset is impaired.

Demo 13-4B LO13-4 Impairment of Indefinite Life Intangible Asset—Trade Name

Demo MBC

Edge Inc. has an intangible asset recorded for a trade name with a carrying value of $275,000 on December 31, 2020. Edge Inc. determines that it is *more likely than not* that the intangible asset is impaired based on qualitative indicators. The fair value of the trade name on December 31, 2020, is $90,434. Prepare the entry, if any, to record impairment of the trade name on December 31, 2020. Assume an interest rate of 6% and that the company expects to continually renew the trade name.

Solution

Because indicators of impairment are present, Edge Inc. must compare the fair value to the carrying value of the trade name to determine possible impairment.

The impairment loss is measured as follows.

December 31, 2020—Calculation of impairment loss

Fair value	$ 90,434
Less carrying value of the trade name	275,000
Impairment loss	$184,566

Edge Inc. records the following entry.

December 31, 2020—To record impairment loss on trade name

Impairment Loss	184,566	
Trade Name		184,566

Assets = Liabilities + Equity
−184,566 −184,566
Trade Name: 184,566 (credit)
Impair Loss: 184,566 (debit)

BOEING Real World — IMPAIRMENT OF INDEFINITE LIFE INTANGIBLE ASSETS

BOEING [BA]

Boeing Company reported the following information in a recent report on Form 10-K regarding indefinite life intangible asset impairment testing. On December 31, 2015, the company had indefinite-life intangible assets with carrying amounts of $490 million relating to trade names.

> **Note 1 – Summary of Significant Accounting Policies**—Indefinite-lived intangibles consist of brand and trade names acquired in business combinations. We test these intangibles for impairment by comparing their carrying value to current projections of discounted cash flows attributable to the brand and trade names. Any excess carrying value over the amount of discounted cash flows represents the amount of the impairment.

Impairment of Goodwill

Goodwill is not amortized on a periodic basis. Instead, similar to other indefinitiely-lived intangible assets, goodwill must be tested for impairment at least annually. The annual goodwill impairment test can be performed any time during the fiscal year provided the test is performed at the same time every year. Impairment of goodwill exists when the carrying amount of a reporting unit that includes goodwill exceeds its fair value. A goodwill impairment loss is recognized for the amount that the carrying amount of a reporting unit, including goodwill, exceeds its fair value, limited to the total amount of goodwill allocated to that reporting unit. (Private businesses can elect to amortize goodwill; however, we assume in the assignments that companies do *not* have this option.)

A company can first consider **qualitative factors** to determine whether it is necessary to perform the quantitative goodwill impairment test. In the qualitative assessment, the company determines whether it is *more likely than not* that the fair value of the reporting unit is less than the carrying amount. ASC 350-20-35 includes a number of factors to consider in the qualitative assessment process. Factors include (not all-inclusive): macroeconomic conditions beyond general economic conditions, industry and market considerations, cost factors, overall financial performance, relevant entity-specific events, reporting unit specific events, and a sustained decrease in share price.

If after assessing these factors, the company determines that it is *more likely than not* that the fair value of the reporting unit is less than its carrying value, the company performs the quantitative goodwill impairment test. Otherwise, no further testing is necessary.

350-20-35-3 An entity may first assess qualitative factors . . . to determine whether it is necessary to perform the quantitative goodwill impairment test . . . If determined to be necessary, the quantitative impairment test shall be used to identify goodwill impairment and measure the amount of a goodwill impairment loss to be recognized (if any).

The **quantitative goodwill impairment test** is used to both identify the existence of impairment and to measure the amount of the impairment loss. If the carrying amount of the reporting unit exceeds its fair value, the excess is recorded as an impairment loss (not to exceed the amount of goodwill allocated to the reporting unit). If the fair value of the reporting unit exceeds its carrying value, goodwill is not considered impaired. A company can choose to bypass the qualitative assessment and move directly to the quantitative test.

350-20-35-2 Impairment of goodwill is the condition that exists when the carrying amount of a reporting unit that includes goodwill exceeds its fair value. A goodwill impairment loss is recognized for the amount that the carrying amount of a reporting unit, including goodwill, exceeds its fair value, limited to the total amount of goodwill allocated to that reporting unit.

350-20-35-3B An entity has an unconditional option to bypass the qualitative assessment described in the preceding paragraph for any reporting unit in any period and proceed directly to performing the quantitative goodwill impairment test. An entity may resume performing the qualitative assessment in any subsequent period.

In this section, we focus on the impairment testing of goodwill of a reporting unit. However, the identifiable fixed assets of the reporting unit may also meet the requirements for impairment testing as discussed in Chapter 12. In this case, the fixed assets would be tested first and any losses recognized before testing for goodwill impairment as indicated in the accounting guidance.

350-20-35-31 If goodwill and another asset (or asset group) of a reporting unit are tested for impairment at the same time, the other asset (or asset group) shall be tested for impairment before goodwill. For example, if a significant asset group is to be tested for impairment under the Impairment or Disposal of Long-Lived Assets Subsections of Subtopic 360-10 (thus potentially requiring a goodwill impairment test), the impairment test for the significant asset group would be performed before the goodwill impairment test. If the asset group was impaired, the impairment loss would be recognized prior to goodwill being tested for impairment.

Demo 13-4C **LO13-4** **Impairment of Goodwill**

Demo MBC

Rayovak Inc. purchased several distinct companies over the past few years. One company Rayovak purchased for $28 million in 2018 resulted in goodwill of $1 million. This purchase became Rayovak's new Home and Garden Division. Unexpectedly, the division reported losses in the current year of 2020. Due to the magnitude of the losses reported, management determines through a qualitative assessment that it is *more likely than not* that goodwill recorded upon the purchase of the company is impaired. On December 31, 2020, the balance of net assets of the Home and Garden Division is $31.2 million including Goodwill. The fair value of the division estimated through an appraisal is $30.8 million. Record the entry, if any, for goodwill impairment related to the Home and Garden Division on December 31, 2020. Assume that the company recorded no impairment losses in 2018 and 2019.

Solution

Because the fair value of $30.8 million is less than the carrying value of $31.2 million, the division is considered impaired. Rayovak determines the impairment on the division as follows.

December 31, 2020—Determine impairment loss of goodwill ($ millions)

Fair value of Home and Garden Division (based on appraisal)	$30.8
Less carrying value of the Home and Garden Division including goodwill	31.2
Impairment of Goodwill	$ 0.4

As a result, Rayovak records the following entry.

December 31, 2020—To record impairment loss of goodwill

Impairment Loss	400,000	
Goodwill		400,000

Assets = Liabilities + Equity
−400,000 −400,000
Goodwill: 400,000 (credit)
Impair Loss: 400,000 (debit)

The *full loss* of $400,000 is reported as a reduction to Goodwill because the measured loss is less than the original value of Goodwill of $1,000,000.

COCA COLA

Real World — GOODWILL IMPAIRMENT

COCA COLA [KO]

Coca Cola Company reported the following information regarding goodwill impairment testing in a recent report on Form 10-K. Coca Cola indicates that it uses discounted cash flow models to determine fair value for purposes of this testing.

Note 1—Business and Summary of Significant Accounting Policies (excerpt)—In order to test for goodwill impairment, the Company compares the fair value of the reporting unit to its carrying value, including goodwill. If the fair value of the reporting unit is lower than its carrying amount, goodwill is written down for the amount by which the carrying amount exceeds the fair value. However, the loss recognized cannot exceed the carrying amount of goodwill. We typically use discounted cash flow models to determine the fair value of a reporting unit. The assumptions used in these models are consistent with those we believe a hypothetical marketplace participant would use. The Company has the option to perform a qualitative assessment of goodwill in order to determine whether it is more likely than not that the fair value of a reporting unit is less than its carrying amount, including goodwill and other intangible assets. If the Company concludes that this is the case, it must perform the testing discussed above. Otherwise, the Company does not need to perform any further testing.

Derecognition of Intangible Assets

When an intangible asset is sold, exchanged, or otherwise disposed of, its carrying value is derecognized and a gain or loss on disposal must be recognized. If the intangible asset to be disposed of is subject to amortization, it is first amortized up to the date of disposal to update the recorded book value. Then the carrying value of the asset is removed from the accounts. The gain or loss equals the difference between the net proceeds from the disposal and the adjusted book value, and is reported as a component of income from continuing operations as shown in the following demonstration.

Derecognition of Intangible Asset—Patent

LO13-4 **Demo 13-4D**

Demo MBC

On January 1 of the current year, Millennial Inc. sold a patent. Millennial originally paid $25,000 for the patent, which now has a book value of $15,000. The terms of sale include cash payments of $5,000 payable on December 31 of each of the next four years. The sale agreement did not specify any interest; however, 6% would be a reasonable rate for this type of transaction.

Record the sale of the patent for Millennial Corporation.

Solution

Note Receivable	20,000	
Patent		15,000
Gain on Sale of Patent ($20,000 − $15,000 − $2,674)		2,326
Discount on Note Receivable ($20,000 − $17,326)		2,674

Assets	= Liabilities	+ Equity
+17,326		+2,326
−15,000		

Patent: credit 15,000
Note Receivable: debit 20,000
Discount on NR: credit 2,674
Gain on Sale—Patent: credit 2,326

The discount on note receivable is the difference between the face value of the note receivable of $20,000 (4 × $5,000) and the present value of the note receivable ($17,326). The resulting gain of $2,326 is the difference between the carrying value of the patent ($15,000) and the fair value of the note receivable ($17,326).

	RATE	NPER	PMT	PV	Excel Formula
Given	6%	4	(5,000)	?	=PV(0.06,4,−5000)
Solution				$17,326	

Impairment and Derecognition of Intangibles

LO13-4 **REVIEW 13-4**

Review MBC

Celestial Co. has the following information for its three intangible assets.

1. **Patent:** A patent was purchased for $220,000 on September 1, 2019. Celestial Co. estimated the useful life of the patent to be 10 years. On December 31, 2020, the estimated future cash flows attributed to the patent were $200,000. On December 31, 2020, the fair value of the patent was estimated to be $180,000. Assume that there is an indication that the asset may not be recoverable.
2. **Trademark:** Celestial Co. paid $15,000 for a trademark on March 1, 2018. The trademark is considered to have an indefinite life. The fair value of the trademark on December 31, 2020, is $12,500.
3. **Goodwill:** Celestial Co. recorded goodwill of $30,000 in January 2019, related to a purchase of another company. The carrying value of goodwill is $30,000 on December 31, 2020. On December 31, 2020, the reporting unit for which the goodwill relates had a fair value of $295,000. The book value of the net assets of the reporting unit (including goodwill) is $300,000. Assume no impairment losses were recognized on goodwill in 2018 or 2019.

Required

a. Determine the carrying value of each intangible asset on December 31, 2020, before impairment testing.

b. Determine the impairment loss, if any, recorded in 2020 related to the three intangible assets.

c. Assume that the patent is sold for cash on June 1, 2021, for $200,000. Compute the gain or loss on disposal.

More Practice: 13-34, 13-52

Solution on p. 13-43.

LO 13-5 Account for changes in estimates with intangible assets

LO 13-5 Overview

Change in Estimate Affecting Amortization
- Change in residual value, useful life
- Prospective treatment
- No change to prior reporting

Revisions of accounting estimates used for amortization such as the useful lives or residual values of intangible assets are considered changes in accounting estimates for reporting purposes. Circumstances may change that constitute a basis for revising one or more accounting estimates. In such cases, prior results and carrying values are not adjusted. Instead, the new estimate is used during the current and remaining periods. Thus, a change in estimate is made on a prospective (future-oriented) basis.

250-10-45-17 A change in accounting estimate shall be accounted for in the period of change if the change affects that period only or in the period of change and future periods if the change affects both. A change in accounting estimate shall not be accounted for by restating or retrospectively adjusting amounts reported in financial statements of prior periods or by reporting pro forma amounts for prior periods.

Demo 13-5 LO13-5 Change in Estimate—Intangible Asset

Demo MBC

Inger Company bought a patent in January 2016, for $6,800. For the first four years, it was amortized on the assumption that the total useful life would be eight years. At the start of the fifth year, management determined that six years would be the probable total useful life. Record annual amortization expense for 2020 and determine the carrying value of the patent on December 31, 2020.

Solution

Measurement of amortization

Original cost	$6,800
Less accumulated amortization to date of change ($6,800 × 4/8)	3,400
Difference (amortized over 2 years of remaining life)	$3,400
Annual amortization over remaining life ($3,400/2 years)	$1,700

The following journal entry is required for the 2020 amortization expense.

December 31, 2020—To record amortization expense

Amortization Expense	1,700	
Patent		1,700

Assets	= Liabilities +	Equity
−1,700		−1,700

Patent		Amort Exp
Bal 3,400	1,700	1,700
1,700		

The carrying value of the patent on December 31, 2020, is $1,700 ($6,800 − $3,400 − $1,700).

REVIEW 13-5 LO13-5 Change in Estimate—Patent

Review MBC

Advance Inc. purchased a patent on June 1, 2018, for $50,000 with an estimated useful life of 10 years. In January 2019, Advance Inc. incurred $5,000 in legal fees to successfully defend the patent. In 2020, Advance Inc. revised the estimated life of the patent to a total of 12 years.

a. Record the entry for amortization expense in 2020.

b. Determine the carrying value of the patent on December 31, 2020.

More Practice: 13-35, 13-36, 13-53

Solution on p. 13-43.

Account for research and development costs

LO 13-6

> **Research and Development Costs (R&D)**
> - Generally expense R&D as incurred
> - Recognize as assets:
>   - Materials, equipment, facilities, and intangibles with alternative future uses
>   - Computer software development costs when technological feasibility is reached
> - Disclose annual costs in the notes to the financial statements
>
> LO 13-6 Overview

Broadly defined, **research and development (R&D)** includes the activities undertaken by companies to create new products and processes, or to improve existing ones, and to discover new knowledge that may be of value in the future. Because of uncertainty whether specific research and development activities provide clear future benefits, and whether costs can be measured reasonably, accounting standards require that *R&D costs should generally be recorded as expense as incurred.* Thus, accounting for R&D is primarily a matter of classifying expenditures as R&D expenses for purposes of disclosure. Note however, that if assets such as buildings or equipment purchased for R&D activities have alternative uses, their costs may be recognized as assets and depreciated over their useful lives. Depreciation expense, in this case, is classified as R&D expense. One exception to the rule that R&D must be expensed is made for certain software development costs, explained in the next section.

730-10-25-1 Research and development costs encompassed by this Subtopic shall be charged to expense when incurred . . .

For many companies, R&D is a very important part of ongoing activities and can be a large and significant expenditure. Thus, the total amount of research and development costs is disclosed in the financial statements.

Company	2017 R&D	R&D/Sales
Bristol-Myers Squibb	$ 6.4 billion	33%
Pfizer Inc.	$ 7.7 billion	15%
PepsiCo, Inc.	$737 million	1.2%
Anheuser-Busch inBev. . . .	$276 million	0.5%

730-10-50-1 Disclosure shall be made in the financial statements of the total research and development costs charged to expense in each period for which an income statement is presented.

The Codification defines the terms "Research" and "Development" as follows.

ASC Glossary **Research** is planned search or critical investigation aimed at discovery of new knowledge with the hope that such knowledge will be useful in developing a new product or service (referred to as product) or a new process or technique (referred to as process) or in bringing about a significant improvement to an existing product or process.

ASC Glossary **Development** is the translation of research findings or other knowledge into a plan or design for a new product or process or for a significant improvement to an existing product or process whether intended for sale or use. It includes the conceptual formulation, design, and testing of product alternatives, construction of prototypes, and operation of pilot plants.

Research and development costs do not include *routine or periodic alterations* to existing products, production lines, manufacturing processes, and other ongoing operations even though those alterations may represent improvements. However, research and development costs do include activities that are intended to bring about *significant improvements* to an existing product or service. General and administrative costs that are not clearly related to research and development activities are *not* included as R&D expense.

730-10-25-2e Indirect costs. Research and development costs shall include a reasonable allocation of indirect costs. However, general and administrative costs that are not clearly related to research and development activities shall not be included as research and development costs.

In **Demo 13-6A**, we will differentiate between R&D expenses and non-R&D expenses. In **Demo 13-6B**, we will apply accounting guidance specifically related to software development costs.

Identifying Research and Development Expense

The accounting treatment for costs identified with research and development activities is described in **Exhibit 13-4**.

EXHIBIT 13-4
Accounting Treatment of Research and Development Costs

R&D Expenditures	Accounting Treatment of R&D Costs: R&D Expense as Incurred	Accounting Treatment of R&D Costs: Alternative Accounting Treatment
1. Materials, equipment, and facilities acquired for particular research and development projects, with no alternative future uses.	✔	
2. Materials, equipment, and facilities acquired for research and development activities with alternative future uses.		Recognize as assets and subsequently expense (as R&D) when used or depreciated.
3. Salaries and wages of those engaged in research and development activities.	✔	
4. Intangible asset acquired for a specific research project with no alternative future use.	✔	
5. Intangible asset acquired for a number of research projects.		Recognize as a finite or indefinite life intangible asset. Amortization is classified as R&D expense.
6. Cost of research and development services performed by another company.	✔	
7. Reasonable allocation of indirect costs of a facility dedicated to R&D activities (rent, utilities, etc.).	✔	

Demo 13-6A **LO13-6** **Identification of Research and Development Expense**

Classify each of the following eight expenditures as to the type of cost (R&D expense or non-R&D expense) and the appropriate treatment in the financial statements.

Expenditure	Type of Cost	Financial Statement Presentation
1. Research in a technology lab aimed at discovery of a new product.	**R&D Expense**	**Expense in income statement**
2. Engineering updates in the early phase of commercial production.	**Non-R&D Expense**	**Expense in income statement**
3. Design costs incurred in the development of a product alternative.	**R&D Expense**	**Expense in income statement**
4. Testing costs of samples of new product alternatives.	**R&D Expense**	**Expense in income statement**
5. Quality control during commercial production.	**Non-R&D Expense**	**Expense in income statement**
6. Modification of a product design.	**R&D Expense**	**Expense in income statement**
7. Design of preproduction prototypes.	**R&D Expense**	**Expense in income statement**
8. Equipment purchased to create the prototypes, which will be used for a number of projects over a projected 10-year period.	**R&D Expense (as depreciated)**	**Recognize on the balance sheet as equipment.** **Depreciation over the 10-year period is recorded as R&D expense in the income statement.**

Research and development costs take place *before* the start of commercial production. **Commercial production** begins when a business component is developed to the point that it meets the basic functional and economic requirements for the sale or use of the component. Activities that take place after commercial production include activities such as running trial productions, and troubleshooting flaws in production equipment or processes. Commercial production activities are recorded as operating expenses.

Product Development over Time →

Research and Development Activity	Commercial Production and Product Sales
R&D expense	Non-R&D expense

Accounting for Software Research and Development Costs

The accounting standards related to a specific type of research and development activity, internally developed computer software, allow for some exceptions to the general accounting treatment described above. Initial recognition of software development costs is described as follows (ASC 985-20-25).

1. All costs incurred to establish the **technological feasibility** of a computer software product are to be treated as research and development and expensed as incurred.
2. Once the **technological feasibility** of the software product is established, subsequent costs incurred to obtain product masters are to be capitalized as an intangible asset.

Establishment of technological feasibility occurs when the company has completed all planning, designing, coding, and testing activities that are necessary to establish that the computer software can be manufactured to meet its design specifications including functions, features, and technical performance requirements. Evidence of reaching technological feasibility can be shown through either (1) the completion of a detailed program design or (2) the completion of a working model of the product.

A **detailed program design** includes:

- A product design by a company with the necessary skills, hardware, and software technology to produce the product.
- Confirmation of the completeness of the design by documentation and tracing of design to product specifications.
- Resolution of any identified high-risk development issues by coding and testing.

Alternatively, a company can establish the technological feasibility of a software product by completing a **working model** of the product that is consistent with the product design and that has been confirmed by testing. A working model consists of the same software language as the final product, performs all the major functions planned for the product, and is ready for initial customer testing.

Software development costs are to be expensed as incurred until technological feasibility is met. Subsequent costs for further coding, testing, debugging, and producing masters of the software product to be duplicated in producing salable products until the product release date are capitalized and amortized over the economic life of the software. After the release date, costs are expensed as operating, but not as research and development.

Software Development over Time →

Research and Development Activity until Technological Feasibility	Research and Development Activity after Technological Feasibility	Product Release and Sale of Product
R&D expense	Intangible asset	Amortization of intangible asset
		Non-R&D expense

The capitalized software costs are amortized to expense on a product-by-product basis. Amortization commences when the product begins to be marketed. The annual amortization is the *greater* of the amount measured through the **revenue method** or the **straight-line method**.

Revenue method

$$\textbf{Amortization expense} = \frac{\textbf{Current product revenue}}{\textbf{Total anticipated product revenue}} \times \textbf{Capitalized software costs}$$

Straight-line method

$$\textbf{Amortization expense} = \frac{\textbf{Capitalized software costs}}{\textbf{Useful life}}$$

While the preceding example relates to the development of computer software to be sold or leased, costs incurred to develop software internally are accounted for in a similar way. After development is complete, costs are capitalized while the coding, training, and installation take place.

EXPANDING YOUR KNOWLEDGE — **What about Start-up Costs?**

Newly formed organizations may incur a number of start-up costs during the first few years of inception. Such costs include legal, accounting, regulatory fees, travel, training, recruiting, etc. Also, a company will likely incur losses during its first few years of operations. Are there any exceptions in GAAP that would allow a company to defer these costs? The short answer is no. Start-up costs and initial losses are required to be expensed as incurred. With start-up companies, it is too difficult to predict the timing of future cash flows related to the upfront costs so deferral is not supported under GAAP.

720-15-25-1 Costs of start-up activities, including organization costs, shall be expensed as incurred.

Demo 13-6B LO13-6 Accounting for Software Research and Development Costs

During 2018 and 2019, Software Inc. incurred $3 million developing a working model of a new software program. During calendar year 2020, an additional $1 million of costs is incurred on the final coding and testing of the product masters. The product is available for sale as of the beginning of 2021 and is expected to have a four-year economic life.

Sales revenues and anticipated future revenues in 2021 are as follows.

$ millions	2021
Current-year revenue	$1.2
Anticipated revenue in future years	4.8
Total	$6.0

Record the entries for (1) initial research and development costs in 2018 and 2019, (2) additional research and development costs in 2020, and (3) amortization expense in 2021. Assume all amounts were paid for in cash.

Solution

The costs of development incurred in 2018 and 2019 are expensed as R&D because they take place prior to the establishment of the technological feasibility of the product.

2018 and 2019—To record research and development expense

Assets	= Liabilities +	Equity
−3,000,000		−3,000,000

Cash		R&D Exp	
	3,000,000	3,000,000	

	Debit	Credit
Research and Development Expense	3,000,000	
Cash		3,000,000

Costs incurred in 2020 are subsequent to the production of a working model (after technological feasibility) and are therefore capitalized as the cost of the intangible software asset.

continued

continued from previous page

December 31, 2020—To recognize intangible asset

Software Intangible Asset	1,000,000	
Cash		1,000,000

Assets = Liabilities + Equity
+1,000,000
−1,000,000
Cash: 1,000,000 (credit) | Software Intang: 1,000,000 (debit)

To determine the amount of amortization in 2021, compute the amount of amortization under both the revenue and the straight-line methods and record the larger amount.

Revenue Method

$$\text{Amortization expense} = \frac{\text{Current period revenue}}{\text{Total anticipated revenue}} \times \text{Capitalized software costs}$$

$$\$200{,}000 = \frac{\$1{,}200{,}000}{(\$1{,}200{,}000 + \$4{,}800{,}000)} \times \$1{,}000{,}000$$

Straight-line Method

$$\text{Amortization expense} = \text{Capitalized software costs} \div \text{Useful life}$$

$$\$250{,}000 = \$1{,}000{,}000 \div 4$$

The greater amortization amount is given by the straight-line method; therefore, $250,000 is the amount amortized in 2021.

December 31, 2021—To amortize software development costs

Software Amortization Expense	250,000	
Software Intangible Asset		250,000

Assets = Liabilities + Equity
−250,000   −250,000
Software Intang: 1,000,000 | 250,000   Software Amort Exp: 250,000 |

At each balance sheet date, the Software Intangible Asset is written down to net realizable value if that value is less than the remaining unamortized cost. If it is written down to net realizable value, the Software Intangible Asset cannot be written back up later.

3M Real World — RESEARCH AND DEVELOPMENT

3M [MMM]

The 3M Company reported the following information regarding research and development in its recent report on Form 10-K. It is interesting to note that the company spent a total of $1.763 billion in research and development costs in 2015.

> **Note 1 – Significant Accounting Policies**—Research, development and related expenses: These costs are charged to operations in the period incurred and are shown on a separate line of the Consolidated Statement of Income. Research, development and related expenses totaled $1.763 billion in 2015, $1.770 billion in 2014 and $1.715 billion in 2013. Research and development expenses, covering basic scientific research and the application of scientific advances in the development of new and improved products and their uses, totaled $1.223 billion in 2015, $1.193 billion in 2014 and $1.150 billion in 2013. Related expenses primarily include technical support; internally developed patent costs, which include costs and fees incurred to prepare, file, secure and maintain patents; amortization of externally acquired patents and externally acquired in-process research and development; and gains/losses associated with certain corporate approved investments in R&D-related ventures, such as equity method effects and impairments.

Research and Development Costs   LO13-6   REVIEW 13-6

Part One—Identification of Research and Development Expense

Review MBC

For each of the following expenditures *a* through *g*, indicate the appropriate *initial* accounting classification: (1) R&D expense, (2) non-R&D expense, or (3) asset.

__ *a.* Routine quality reviews to improve upon the qualities of an existing product.

__ *b.* Engineering activity required to advance the design of a product to the point that it meets specific functional requirements necessary to be ready to manufacture.

continued

continued from previous page

__ *c.* Costs to adapt a product requirement to meet a current customer's specific need.

__ *d.* Testing of a product prototype.

__ *e.* Seasonal design change to an existing product.

__ *f.* Purchase of a facility with alternative possible uses to be used to perform ongoing research activities.

__ *g.* Salaries and related expenses of employees developing a design that represents a significant improvement to a current product.

Part Two—Accounting for Computer Software Development Costs

During 2020, Streamline Inc. developed a new personal computer database sports management software package. Total expenditures (all cash) on the project were $1,800,000, of which 30% occurred after the technological feasibility of the product had been established. The product was completed and offered for sale on January 1, 2021. During 2021, revenues from sales of the product totaled $800,000. The package is expected to be successfully marketable for five years, and the total revenues over the life of the product are estimated to be $12,000,000.

a. Prepare the journal entries to account for the development of this product in 2020.

b. Prepare the journal entry to record the amortization of capitalized computer software development costs for 2021.

More Practice:
13-38, 13-57, 13-64
Solution on p. 13-43.

Management Judgment

In accounting for intangibles, management judgment is required from initial recognition to disposal of the intangibles. We explain some of the items requiring management judgment.

Identification of Intangibles in a Business Combination

Management must determine the identifiable net assets of an acquisition to determine the residual amount of goodwill. Intangibles such as acquired in-process research and development and customer lists must first be identified before goodwill is recognized (p. 13-5).

Useful Life

The determination of amortization expense of finite life intangible assets requires management to estimate the useful life (and residual value) of the assets. Some factors to consider in estimating the useful life of an intangible asset are included on page 13-3. Changes in estimates are treated prospectively.

Impairment Testing

Management may choose to perform qualitative assessments for indefinite life intangible assets before moving to a quantitative test. Management would need to apply judgment to conclude that an indefinite life intangible asset or goodwill is not impaired based on a qualitative assessment.

350-30-35-18D An entity shall evaluate, on the basis of the weight of the evidence, the significance of all identified events and circumstances that could affect the significant inputs used to determine the fair value of the indefinite-lived intangible asset for determining whether it is more likely than not that the indefinite-lived intangible asset is impaired.

These amounts are subjective and require management to make assumptions. If the company performs a quantitative test, judgment is required because the fair value of the asset must be estimated. In similar ways, impairment testing of finite life intangible assets and goodwill also require management judgment (see LO 13-4).

Identification of Research and Development Costs

For disclosure purposes, management must identify research and development costs. This requires judgment in determining what costs meet the definition of research and development costs provided in the Codification. For example, management must differentiate between costs that are routine to an existing product and costs that bring about significant improvements to an existing product. Also, management must determine a reasonable allocation of indirect costs.

Software Development

Intangible costs related to software development may be capitalized after the point of technological feasibility until the release date (p. 13-24). However, management must determine these dates by examining the facts and circumstances of the particular project.

Questions

13-1. What distinguishes intangible assets from tangible assets? How are intangible assets reported on the balance sheet?

13-2. What outlays are properly considered part of the cost of an intangible asset?

13-3. What factors should determine whether an intangible asset is amortized and, if so, over what period of time?

13-4. Describe two classifications of intangible assets.

13-5. What is a franchise right? A trademark?

13-6. Define goodwill and the basis on which goodwill is amortized.

13-7. What is a bargain purchase? How does it arise? How is it treated for accounting purposes?

13-8. What is the maximum number of years over which a patent can be amortized? What determines this maximum? Under what circumstances, if any, should a shorter amortization period be used?

13-9. How are organization costs (start-up costs) treated for accounting purposes?

13-10. What are the guidelines for accounting for research and development (R&D) costs?

13-11. Distinguish between trademarks and copyrights.

13-12. Provide examples of situations in which the accounting carrying value of an intangible asset can increase. Does the accounting value of an intangible necessarily bear close relation to its economic value?

13-13. What are the primary characteristics of goodwill?

13-14. What are examples of items that may contribute to goodwill?

13-15. Under what circumstances is goodwill recognized?

13-16. Under what circumstances might goodwill be amortized?

13-17. Explain impairment of the value of a finite life intangible asset. Assume that a patent originally costing $50,000 (accumulated patent amortization, $35,000) is being evaluated for a possible impairment. The estimated cash flows from the patent are $5,000. Its estimated current fair value is $1,000. Provide any indicated entry; if none, explain why.

13-18. Explain impairment evaluation of an indefinite life intangible asset, other than goodwill.

13-19. Explain impairment evaluation of goodwill.

13-20. Carter Company owns a trademark that it purchased originally for $40,000; accumulated amortization to the current date is $26,000. The trademark has just been sold for $10,000 cash. Provide any required entry.

Brief Exercises

Brief Exercise 13-21 Classifying Intangible Costs **LO1**

In 2020, Downey Co. purchased a patent from a research institution for $25,000 (20-year estimated useful life), paid $3,000 to a company for a trademark (indefinite life), and paid $50,000 in salaries to employees working on a product modification. Determine how the three amounts would initially be recorded by Downey Co. in 2020:

(1) intangible asset—finite life, (2) intangible asset—indefinite life, (3) research and development expense, or (4) non-research and development expense.

Brief Exercise 13-22
Classifying Intangible Costs **LO1**
Hint: See Demo 13-1

The following costs were incurred by Athletica Co. For each item, indicate the proper accounting treatment: (1) expense as incurred, (2) capitalize and assess for impairment, or (3) capitalize, amortize, and assess for impairment.

____ *a.* Start-up costs including legal fees and registration fees.
____ *b.* Research and development cost.
____ *c.* Goodwill recorded based upon a purchase of another company.
____ *d.* Purchase of a patent.
____ *e.* Costs to internally develop a patent.
____ *f.* Purchased trademark with indefinite life.

Brief Exercise 13-23
Recording the Purchase of a Patent **LO2**

On July 1, 2020, Beckham Inc. purchased a patent from a research firm by issuing 4,000 shares of its $1 par value common stock. On the date of purchase, the stock was trading on a public exchange for $10 per share. Record the purchase of the patent by Beckham Inc.

Brief Exercise 13-24
Computing Subsequent Carrying Amount of Patents **LO2**
Hint: See Demo 13-2

In January 2020, Ford Co. purchased a patent from a research institution for $250,000. The patent was estimated to have a useful life of 15 years. In December 2021, Ford Co. defended the patent in legal proceedings and successfully retained rights of ownership of the patent. The estimated life of the patent did not change from its original estimate. Legal expenses were $20,000. Determine the carrying value of the patent on December 31, 2021.

Brief Exercise 13-25
Computing Subsequent Carrying Amount of Patents **LO2**

Assume the same information in Brief Exercise 13-24 except that the legal defense was unsuccessful in defending the patent. The fair value of the patent on December 31, 2021, is now estimated to be $50,000 with a 2-year useful life.

a. Record the entry for the legal fees of $20,000.
b. Determine the carrying value of the patent on December 31, 2021.

Brief Exercise 13-26
Recording the Purchase and Amortization of Patents **LO2**
Hint: See Demo 13-2

Harrison Co. purchased a patent on August 31, 2020, for $80,000 from a researcher. The patent has a legal life of 20 years, but the estimated useful life of the patent is 10 years with no expected residual value.

a. Record the entry for the purchase of the patent on August 31, 2020.
b. Record the entry to record the amortization of the patent on December 31, 2020.

Brief Exercise 13-27
Reporting Intangible Costs **LO2**

Hanks Co. recorded the following amounts for 2020.

- Research and development costs, $50,000.
- Patent, acquired on January 1, 2020, with 10-year useful life, $35,000.
- Goodwill from purchase of a company, $100,000.
- Acquired customer list with an indefinite useful life, $20,000.
- Legal fees paid on December 31, 2020, to register a patent (internally developed, 15-year useful life), $5,000.

a. Determine the amounts to be included on the balance sheet on December 31, 2020. Assume no asset is impaired.
b. Determine amounts to be included on the income statement for the year 2020. Assume no impairment losses were recorded.

Brief Exercise 13-28
Computing the Carrying Value of Intangibles **LO2**

On January 3, 2020, Munn and Cody entered into a noncompetition agreement in connection with Munn's purchase of a trademark from Cody. Munn paid Cody $800,000, of which 75% related to the trademark and 25% reflected Cody's agreement not to compete for a period of five years in the line of business covered by the trademark. Munn considers the life of the trademark to be indefinite. Determine Munn's carrying value of the trademark and noncompete agreement on December 31, 2020. Assume no impairment loss was recognized on the intangibles in prior periods.

Brief Exercise 13-29
Recording Franchise Entries **LO2**

Cleaners Inc. signed a contract with Super-Cleaners, Incorporated. The agreement provided for the payment of a franchise fee by Cleaners Inc. and subsequent periodic franchise royalties based on sales. In return for these royalties, Super-Cleaners will provide specified services in the future (such as promotional suggestions) for 10 years. The franchise fee was $100,000, payable on January 1, 2020. Provide the entries that Cleaners Inc. should make on January 1, 2020, and on December 31, 2020. Disregard any franchise royalties based on sales.

On January 3, 2020, Munn acquired all noncash assets and assumed all liabilities of Saturn Company at a cash purchase price of $1,200,000. Munn determined that the fair value of the assets acquired in the transaction is $1,400,000 and the fair value of liabilities is $600,000. The book value of the net assets at the purchase date was $750,000. Determine the amount of goodwill recorded by Munn upon purchase of Saturn Company.

Brief Exercise 13-30 Computing Goodwill **LO3** *Hint:* See Demo 13-3

GoldStar Inc. acquired all assets and assumed all liabilities of Silver Company at a cash purchase price of $980,000. The carrying value of the assets acquired was $1,300,000 and the carrying value of the liabilities acquired was $500,000. GoldStar Inc. estimated that assets were undervalued by $100,000 due to unrecorded intangibles of $75,000 (fair value) and undervalued land and equipment of $25,000 (as compared to fair value). Determine the amount of goodwill recorded by Silver Company upon purchase of GoldStar Inc.

Brief Exercise 13-31 Computing Goodwill **LO3**

Freeman Co. acquired another business and paid (among other amounts) $36,000 for its goodwill in 2018. On December 31, 2020, the net book value of the business is $440,000 and the fair value of the business is $425,000. Determine the amount of goodwill impairment (if any) on December 31, 2020. Assume no impairment losses were recognized on goodwill in prior periods.

Brief Exercise 13-32 Computing Goodwill Impairment **LO4** *Hint:* See Demo 13-4C

Assume the same information in Brief Exercise 13-32 except that the fair value of the business is estimated at $445,000. Determine the amount of goodwill impairment (if any) on December 31, 2020.

Brief Exercise 13-33 Computing Goodwill Impairment **LO4** *Hint:* See Demo 13-4C

Eastwood Co. is evaluating the following two intangible assets for impairment at year-end. Record any journal entries required to recognize impairment of the intangible assets.

Brief Exercise 13-34 Recording Entry for Impairment of Intangible Assets **LO4** *Hint:* See Demo 13-4A, 13-4B

Intangible Asset	Carrying Value	Future Estimated Net Cash Flows	Fair Value
Patent	$65,000	$50,000	$35,000
Trademark	10,000	No foreseeable limit	12,000

Munn Inc., reported a patent as a noncurrent asset on December 31, 2020, as follows.

Brief Exercise 13-35 Computing Intangible Asset Carrying Value with a Change in Estimate **LO5** *Hint:* See Demo 13-5

Patent	$192,000
Less accumulated amortization	(24,000)
Net patent	$168,000

Transactions related to the patent included the following: The patent was purchased from Grey Company on January 2, 2019, when the remaining legal life was 16 years. On January 2, 2021, Munn determined that the remaining useful life of the patent was only eight years from the date of its acquisition. Determine the carrying value of the patent on December 31, 2022.

Mills Inc. purchased a patent in January of 2015 for $40,000 and chose to amortize the patent over its useful life of 20 years. However, in 2020, the company decided that the total useful life of the patent would only be 10 years based upon new technology advancing in the company's internal research and development department.

a. What entry would the company record for amortization of the patent in 2020?
b. What impact would this change have on prior periods?

Brief Exercise 13-36 Accounting for a Change in Estimate—Patent **LO5** *Hint:* See Demo 13-5

Determine whether the following items would be classified in the financial statements of Jackson Co. as research and development expense or operating expense.

Brief Exercise 13-37 Identifying Research and Development Costs **LO6** *Hint:* See Demo 13-6A

Salaries of employees working on the modification of a product design	$45,000
Cost of materials used during work on the modification of a product design	5,000
Salaries of employees working on the improvement of an existing product	60,000

During 2019, Accounting Software Inc. incurred $200,000 developing a working model of a new software program. During calendar 2020, an additional $50,000 of costs is incurred on the final coding and testing of the product masters. The product is available for sale as of the beginning of 2021 and is expected to have a four-year economic life. Costs incurred in 2021 pertaining to the production of the software and training materials totaled $210,000. Determine how the costs would initially be recorded: (1) research and development expense, (2) non-research and development expense, or (3) intangible asset.

Brief Exercise 13-38 Determining Classification of Software Costs **LO6**

Exercises

Exercise 13-39
Classifying Intangible Assets, Research and Development Expense, and Non-Research and Development Expense
LO1

The following items, 1 through 22, represent various types of company expenditures.

____ 1. Acquired a patent from a technology firm.
____ 2. Paid a consulting firm to assist with the graphic artwork for a new trademark.
____ 3. Increase in the value of a company over the past year due to significant technological advances in product design driving a larger loyal customer base.
____ 4. Payroll and related expenses of employees involved in researching a potential product's market opportunity, cost, and production processes.
____ 5. Internal costs incurred to prepare, file, and secure patents.
____ 6. Costs incurred to develop a copyright internally over a two-year period.
____ 7. Purchased a company for an amount in excess of the fair value of the identifiable net assets.
____ 8. Customer relationships purchased through a business combination.
____ 9. Acquired a franchise license to increase product distribution.
____10. Paid legal fees to organize and incorporate a new business.
____11. Legal costs paid to a law firm in applying for a patent (a patent that was internally generated).
____12. Allocated salaries of an in-house attorney who registered a newly developed patent.
____13. Purchased a customer list to be used for new sales opportunities.
____14. In-process research and development acquired through an acquisition of a company.
____15. Salaries incurred to discover ways to make minor improvements to the current features of an existing product.
____16. Acquired rights to exclusive distribution of a specific product in a certain geographical area.
____17. Patent costs incurred where the future economic benefit derived from the transactions cannot be determined.
____18. Trade names purchased through a business combination.
____19. Scientific research and the application of scientific advances in the development of new products and processes.
____20. Purchased a copyright from a competitor that ceased operations.
____21. Incurred salaries and related costs of employees developing significant improvements to the functionality of an existing product.
____22. Allocated utilities and overhead for a research lab in a corporate office building.

Required

For each item, indicate the proper classification: (a) intangible asset, (b) research and development expense, (c) non-research and development expense, or (d) not recorded.

Exercise 13-40
Classifying Intangible Costs on the Balance Sheet **LO1**

The adjusted trial balance of Lawrence Corporation showed the following selected account balances (all debits) at December 31, 2020, the end of the annual reporting period.

Cash	$ 44,000	Trademark	$ 19,000
Patent, net	14,000	Prepaid insurance (two-thirds is long-term)	6,000
Accounts receivable (net of allowance)	90,000	Copyright, net	12,000
Prepaid rent expense (current)	1,000	Equipment (net of accumulated depreciation)	300,000
Marketable equity securities (current)	50,000	Notes receivable, trade (short-term)	10,000
Franchise, net	18,000	R&D expense	39,000
Rent revenue receivable (current)	3,000	Noncompete agreement	12,000
Goodwill	60,000		

Required

Prepare the asset section of Lawrence's balance sheet at December 31, 2020. Include the proper balance sheet classifications with separate captions for current assets; property, plant, and equipment; intangible assets; and other assets. Assume that all required amortization entries have been made.

Exercise 13-41
Classifying Intangible Assets **LO1**
Hint: See Demo 13-1

The following examples of intangible costs are included in recent Form 10-Ks of the following public companies.

1. **Starbucks Corporation:** Acquired customer base, the acquired workforce including store partners in the region that have strong relationships with these customers, the existing geographic retail and online presence, and the expected geographic presence in new channels for a total cost of $815.6 million.

2. Coca-Cola Company: Sells products under certain trademarks. For example, Glacéau Vitaminwater is a brand owned by Coca-Cola. Trademarks totaled $6.0 billion in 2015.
3. Boeing: Expenditures involve experimentation, design, development and related test activities for defense systems included in the total of $3.3 billion.
4. Under Armour: Through the acquisition of MyFitnessPal in 2015, Under Armour acquired the following intangible items: a nutrition database valued at $4.5 million (10-year estimated useful life), a user-base valued at $38.3 million (10-year estimated useful life), technology valued at $3.2 million (5-year estimated useful life), a trade name valued at $2.3 million (5-year estimated useful life), and goodwill valued at $402.7 million. Goodwill reflects unidentified intangible assets acquired, including operational synergies across the Company, assembled workforces, the value of integrating acquired technologies, and engaging and growing the connected fitness community.
5. Walgreens Boots Alliance Inc.: Upon acquisition of the remaining interest in Alliance Boots, the company's acquisition included a number of intangible assets including loyalty card holders valued at $742 million (12-year estimated useful life), and pharmacy licenses valued at $2.5 billion (indefinite useful life).

Required

For each of the intangible costs described in items 1 through 5, indicate the following:

a. Classification: (1) finite life intangible asset, (2) indefinite life intangible asset other than goodwill, (3) goodwill, or (4) research and development expense.

b. Presentation in the financial statements: (1) asset on the balance sheet, (2) expense on the income statement.

Exercise 13-42
Recording Purchase of Patent through Debt and Equity Issuances
LO2
Hint: See Demo 13-2

On January 1, 2020, Century Inc. purchased from an inventor a patent with a list price of $110,000. Century paid for the patent as follows: cash, $40,000; issuance of 1,000 shares of its own common stock, par $10 (fair value, $20 per share); and a note payable due at the end of three years, face amount, $50,000, noninterest-bearing. The current interest rate for this type of financing is 12%.

Required

Record Century Inc.'s entry for the purchase of the patent.

Exercise 13-43
Accounting for Organization Costs
LO2

Perry Inc. was organized during 2019 and started operations in 2020. Cash expenditures during 2019 and early 2020 were the following.

Professional fees (attorney fees) for articles of incorporation	$20,000
Professional fees (accounting fees) to research tax status of organization	15,000
Meetings and promotional activities incidental to organization	15,000
Filing and related fees	5,000
Purchase of office equipment	50,000

Required

Prepare a summary journal entry to record the cash expenditures related to the startup of a new company.

Exercise 13-44
Recording Correcting Entries for Intangible Asset Account **LO2**

In examination of the following intangible asset account that we have been asked to review, we receive the following information supporting the ending account balance on December 31, 2020.

Intangible Asset			
Jan. 1	Goodwill	15,000	
Jan. 15	Research and development	12,000	
April 1	Prepaid advertising	6,000	
June 30	Patent	8,000	
July 10	Research and development	14,000	
Oct. 5	Bond discount	4,800	
Dec. 31	Legal expense to successfully defend patent	1,500	
End. bal.		61,300	

Required

Prepare the correcting entries to adjust the intangible asset account on December 31, 2020. Assume that the patent has a useful life of 8 years and that there are no indicators of impairment on intangible assets. Also, instead of using a general intangible asset account, use more specific intangible asset accounts.

Exercise 13-45
Recording Entries Related to Patent **LO2**

During 2020, Starnes Corporation developed a patent. Starnes incurred the following costs related to the development of the patent: tests to perfect the use of the patent for production processes, $6,000; research costs in the research laboratory, $21,000; and depreciation on equipment (that has alternative future uses) used in developing the patent, $4,000. In addition, in late December 2020, the company incurred legal fees for the patent registration, $7,000. The expected life of the patent is 20 years. On September 30, 2021, Starnes Corporation defended its patent in court after incurring legal fees of $3,000. The total estimated life of the patent at that time was adjusted to 15 years remaining from September 30, 2021.

Required

Record journal entries for the following items.

a. Patent development and registration costs incurred in 2020.
b. Legal fees paid in 2021.
c. Amortization expense in 2021.
d. Amortization expense in 2022.

Exercise 13-46
Determining Carrying Value and Amortization of Intangible Assets
LO2

Review the following information pertaining to Denzel Company.

1. A patent was purchased on January 2, 2018, for $65,000 when the remaining legal life was 16 years. On January 2, 2020, Denzel determined that the remaining useful life of the patent was only eight years from the date of its acquisition.
2. On January 1, 2020, Denzel Company purchased a second patent for $80,000 cash. At January 1, 2020, 6 years of the patent's legal life of 20 years had already expired.
3. On June 30, 2020, Denzel Company paid a firm $8,000 for a new trademark. Denzel considers the life of the trademark to be indefinite.
4. On November 1, 2020, Denzel Company acquired all noncash assets and assumed all liabilities of Lee Company at a cash purchase price of $120,000. Denzel determined that the fair value of the identifiable net assets acquired in the transaction is $117,000.

Required

a. What is the carrying value of intangible assets on December 31, 2020? Assume no impairment losses were recognized in prior periods.
b. What is amortization expense for 2020?

Exercise 13-47
Recording Sale of a Patent **LO4**
Hint: See Demo 13-4D

On January 1 of the current year, Macey Corporation sold a patent. Macey Corporation originally paid $50,000 for the patent, which now has a book value of $9,000. The terms of sale included cash payments as follows.

1. $5,000 down payment.
2. $5,000 per year, payable on December 31 of each of the next two years.

The sale agreement did not specify any interest; however, 10% would be a reasonable rate for this type of transaction.

Required

Record the sale of the patent for Macey Corporation.

Exercise 13-48
Determining the Initial Value of Goodwill **LO3**
Hint: See Demo 13-3

On April 1, 2020, Penn Corporation purchased all the assets and assumed all the liabilities of Suber Company for $140,000 cash. Suber's total identifiable asset values were as follows: Suber's book value, $200,000; estimated fair value, $230,000. Suber's total liabilities were $105,000 (fair value and book value).

Required

Calculate the amount of goodwill purchased by Penn Corporation on April 1, 2020.

Exercise 13-49
Recording Goodwill upon Acquisition **LO3**

On January 1, 2020, the balance sheet of Naperville Company (a sole proprietorship) was as follows.

Assets		**Liabilities**		
Accounts receivable (net of allowance)	$ 60,000	Current	$38,000	
Inventory	90,000	Noncurrent	80,000	$118,000
Plant and equipment (net of depreciation)	200,000	**Equity**		
Land	30,000	Owners' equity		262,000
Total assets	$380,000	Total liabilities and owners' equity		$380,000

On January 1, 2020, Chicago Corporation purchased all of the assets and assumed all of the liabilities listed on the above balance sheet for $290,000 cash. The assets, on date of purchase, were valued by Chicago Corporation as follows: accounts receivable (net), $50,000; inventory, $85,000; plant and equipment (net), $200,000; and land, $45,000. In addition, Chicago Corporation estimated purchased intangible assets of $2,000 for customer list and $8,000 for trade names (both previously unrecorded). The liabilities were valued at their carrying amounts.

Required

a. Compute the amount of goodwill included in the purchase price paid by Chicago Corporation.
b. Provide the entry that Chicago Corporation should make to record the purchase of Naperville Company.
c. What is the minimum amount of goodwill that Chicago Corporation can amortize at the end of 2020?

Exercise 13-50
Computing Impairment of Goodwill LO4
Hint: See Demo 13-4C

Dow Corporation has assembled the following information for one of its divisions on December 31, 2020.

	Fair Value	Book Value
Total identifiable assets (exclusive of goodwill)		$2,400,000
Goodwill		200,000
Liabilities		1,000,000
Fair value of the division	$1,550,000	

Required

a. Determine the impairment loss (if any) for the Dow Corporation division.
b. How would your answer change if the fair value of total identifiable assets (exclusive of goodwill) were $1,650,000 instead?

Exercise 13-51
Computing Impairment of Patent LO4
Hint: See Demo 13-4A

In January 2017, Idea Company purchased a patent for a new consumer product for $170,000. At the time of purchase, the remaining legal life of the patent was 17 years. However, because of the competitive nature of the market, the patent was estimated to have a useful life of 10 years. During 2021, it was determined that there was a potential health hazard present in the product. As a result, the estimated future cash flows from the patent on December 31, 2021, are estimated to be $80,000 while the fair value of the patent is estimated to be $69,300. Total estimated useful life remains unchanged.

Required

a. Determine annual amortization expense for 2017–2021.
b. Determine the carrying value of the patent on December 31, 2021, before assessing for impairment.
c. What amount should Idea record as an impairment loss (if any) in 2021? What is the adjusted carrying value of the patent on December 31, 2021?
d. Assume that the potential health hazard was resolved in 2022. As a result, the future cash flows from the patent on December 31, 2022, are estimated to be $65,000 while the fair value of the patent is estimated to be $54,000. What amount should Idea record as a loss (or recovery) on impairment (if any) in 2022? What is the adjusted carrying value of the patent on December 31, 2022?

Exercise 13-52
Computing Impairment of Intangible Assets LO4

Stiller Company had the following information for its three intangible assets.

1. Patent: A patent was purchased for $100,000 on June 30, 2018. Stiller estimated the useful life of the patent to be 15 years. On December 31, 2020, the estimated future cash flows attributed to the patent were $85,000. The fair value of the patent was $75,000.
2. Trademark: A trademark was purchased for $5,000 on August 31, 2019. The trademark is considered to have an indefinite life. The fair value of the trademark on December 31, 2020, is $2,500.
3. Goodwill: Stiller recorded goodwill in January 2019, related to a purchase of another company. The carrying value of goodwill is $30,000 on December 31, 2020. On December 31, 2020, the segment for which the goodwill relates had a fair value of $580,000. The book value of the net assets of the segment (including goodwill) is $600,000.

Required

a. Classify each of the intangible assets above as a finite life intangible or an indefinite life intangible.
b. Determine the carrying value of each asset on December 31, 2020, prior to testing for impairment, assuming that the company uses the straight-line method to amortize intangible assets, and no impairment was reported prior to 2020.

c. Test each asset for impairment assuming that the qualitative assessment indicated that further impairment testing was warranted.

d. Determine the carrying value of each asset on December 31, 2020, after impairment testing.

Exercise 13-53
Recording Amortization with a Change in Estimate **LO5**
Hint: See Demo 13-5

On January 1, 2018, Kelley Company purchased a new patent for $10,200 and started amortizing it over its legal life of 20 years. At the start of 2021, Kelley estimated that the total useful life of the patent (from acquisition date) was 12 years.

Required

a. What should Kelley record as amortization expense on the patent for 2021?

b. What is the carrying value of the patent on December 31, 2021?

c. Record the entry for amortization in 2021.

Exercise 13-54
Accounting for Various Intangible Costs: Amortization, Change in Estimate **LO5**

Munn Inc. reported other noncurrent asset account balances on December 31, 2020, as follows.

Patent	$192,000
Accumulated amortization	(24,000)
Net patent	$168,000

Transactions during 2021 and other information relating to Munn's other noncurrent assets include the following.

a. The patent was purchased from Grey Company on January 2, 2019, when the remaining legal life was 16 years. On January 1, 2021, Munn determined that the remaining useful life of the patent was only eight years from the date of its acquisition.

b. On January 1, 2021, in connection with the purchase of a trademark from Cody Corp., the parties entered into a noncompetition agreement. Munn paid Cody $800,000, of which 75% related to the trademark and 25% reflected Cody's agreement not to compete for a period of five years in the line of business covered by the trademark. Munn considers the life of the trademark to be indefinite.

c. On January 1, 2021, Munn acquired all the noncash assets and assumed all liabilities of Amboy Company at a cash purchase price of $1,200,000. Munn determined that the fair value of the identifiable net assets acquired in the transaction is $800,000.

d. Munn incurred the following research and development costs in 2021.

Salaries and related expenses related to the development of patents	$125,000
Supplies	15,000
Allocated facility costs	20,000

Required

a. Prepare a schedule of amortization for 2021 relating to Munn's intangible assets assuming straight-line amortization.

b. Prepare the balance sheet presentation of intangible assets for Munn on December 31, 2021, and the income statement presentation for the year ended December 31, 2021.

Exercise 13-55
Identifying Research and Development Costs **LO6**
Hint: See Demo 13-6A

Hyland Company's research and development (R&D) records contained the following information for 2020.

Materials used in R&D projects	$ 400,000
Equipment acquired that will have significant alternative future uses including future R&D projects	2,000,000
Depreciation expense for 2020 on above equipment	500,000
Personnel costs involved in R&D projects	1,000,000
Consulting fees paid to outsiders for R&D projects	100,000
Indirect costs reasonably allocable to R&D projects	200,000
	$4,200,000

Required

Determine the amount of research and development costs debited to expense and reported on Hyland's 2020 income statement.

Exercise 13-56
Identifying Research and Development Costs
LO6
Hint: See Demo 13-6A

Diaz Company incurred the following costs during the year 2020.

1. Salaries expense related to design for a trademark with an indefinite estimated life	$ 6,000
2. Materials used for research and development projects for the current year	10,000
3. Fees paid to external consultants related to research and development projects	30,000
4. Trouble-shooting in connection with breakdowns during production	18,000
5. Design of tooling involving new technology	9,000
6. Cost of equipment (purchased January 2019) that will have alternative uses over 6 years	80,000
7. Salaries expense related to updates to an existing product	40,000
8. Allocation of rent expense for a facility partially used for research and development activities	15,000
9. Routine testing of product during commercial production	28,000

Required
Determine the amount of research and development costs that would be disclosed in the financial statements of Diaz company for the year 2020.

Exercise 13-57
Amortizing Software Development Costs
LO6

During 2020, the E-Software Company capitalized computer software costs in the amount of $4,000,000. During 2020, the first year the product is released to sell, sales total $2,000,000. Estimated future sales for the remaining three-year life (through 2023) of the product are $14,000,000.

Required
Record the amount of amortization of capitalized computer development software costs for 2020.

Exercise 13-58
Accounting for Software Development Costs
LO6
Hint: See Demo 13-6B

During 2020, PC Software Inc. developed a new personal computer database management software package. Total expenditures on the project were $3,000,000, of which 40% occurred after the technological feasibility of the product had been established. The product was completed and offered for sale on January 1, 2021. During 2021, revenues from sales of the product totaled $4,800,000. The package is expected to be successfully marketable for five years, and the total revenues over the life of the product are estimated to be $20,000,000.

Required
a. Prepare the journal entries to account for the development of this product in 2020.
b. Prepare the journal entries to record the amortization of capitalized computer software development costs in 2021.
c. What disclosures are required in the December 31, 2021, financial statements regarding computer software costs?
d. Suppose this product were developed for internal use. How would your answers to (*a*), (*b*), and (*c*) change?

Problems

Problem 13-59
Recording Entries for Intangibles **LO1, 2, 3, 6**

Our new client, Laser Company, is being audited for the first time on December 31, 2021, the end of the accounting period. In the course of our examination, we encounter in the ledger an asset account titled "Intangibles" (balance, $85,224) presented below.

Intangibles					
June 30, 2019	Goodwill	9,000	2,890	Amortization, 5%	Dec. 31, 2020
Dec. 31, 2019	R&D	10,700	4,486	Amortization, 5%	Dec. 31, 2021
Apr. 1, 2020	Goodwill	14,600			
June 30, 2020	Patent	9,600			
Dec. 31, 2020	R&D	13,900			
June 1, 2021	Goodwill	12,900			
July 1, 2021	Bond discount	4,800			
Dec. 31, 2021	R&D	17,100			
End. bal.		85,224			

By tracing entries to the journal and other supporting documents, we ascertain the following facts.

1. The June 30, 2019, entry was made when the first six months' operations were profitable, although a small loss had been anticipated. At the direction of the company president, and with the approval of the board of directors, an entry was made debiting Intangibles and crediting Retained Earnings for $9,000.

2. All debit entries dated December 31 pertaining to research and development (R&D) arise from the fact that the company has continuously engaged in an extensive R&D program to keep its products competitive and to develop new products. The debits represent half of the costs of the R&D program for each year and were transferred at year-end from the R&D expense account.
3. The April 1, 2020, entry was made after an extensive advertising campaign had seemingly proved successful. Sales rose 8% after the campaign and never dropped again to less than a 4% increase over their former level. The debit represents the expenditures for the campaign.
4. The $9,600 debit on June 30, 2020, represents the purchase price of a patent bought because the company feared that if it fell into other hands, it would damage the company's products competitively. See (7) for amortization information.
5. The debit for June 1, 2021, was made after Laser acquired another company, which will continue to operate as a 100%-owned subsidiary. The price represented an excess payment of $12,900 over the fair values of identifiable net assets acquired (which were properly recorded) and was based on an expectation of continued high profitability.
6. The July 1, 2021, debit for $4,800 represents a discount on a 10-year, $100,000 bond issue marketed by the company on that date. The amount is not material; therefore, straight-line amortization is appropriate.
7. The two credits to the intangibles account represent 5% of the ending balance in the intangibles account at the end of 2020 and 2021, respectively; the offsetting debit was to amortization expense. The patent will be amortized over 10 years, computed to the nearest month.

Required

a. Provide journal entries to reclassify balances in the "Intangibles" account to appropriate accounts. The balance in the "Intangibles" account should be zero when you are finished. We must report intangible assets in appropriately titled accounts (such as "Patents" and "Goodwill"). *Hint:* To review the entry for error correction, see Chapter 3.

b. Provide correct amortization entries for all years and make any other necessary adjustments. Determine the final account balances immediately prior to the 2021 closing entries. Assume that the unadjusted retained earnings balance on January 1, 2021, was $20,000 (credit).

Problem 13-60
Recording Entries and Reporting Intangibles
LO1, 2, 3

Transactions during 2021, the first year of the newly organized J's Discount Foods Corporation, included the following.

Jan. 2 Paid $8,000 attorney's fees and other related costs for assistance in securing the corporate charter, drafting bylaws, and advising on operating in other states (which the company intends to do).

Jan. 31 Paid $2,000 for advertising the grand opening. In addition, during the grand opening the company gave away samples of its products, which were taken from inventory; cost $8,000 (perpetual system).

Feb. 1 Paid an invoice received from the financial institution that underwrote the company's $400,000 par value stock at a 10% premium. Under the contract, the underwriter charged 1% of the gross proceeds from the stock sale. The stock issuance has already been recorded.

Mar. 1 Paid $30,000 to a franchisor for the right to open a Tastee Food lunch counter on the company's premises. The initial franchise runs 10 years from March 1 and can be renewed upon payment of a second amount to be computed later on the basis of sales under the initial franchise.

May 1 Acquired a newly issued patent for $10,200 with a 20-year life.

July 1 Paid $6,400 for registration to secure a trademark enabling the company to market under the now protected name J's Recipe. The trademark has an indefinite life.

Oct. 1 Obtained a license from the city to conduct operations in a newly opened department. The license, which cost $600, runs for one year and is renewable.

Nov. 1 Acquired another business and paid (among other amounts) $36,000 for its goodwill.

Required

a. Provide the journal entry that J's should make for each of the above transactions. December 31 is the end of the annual accounting period; three adjusting entries are required on this date. Assume that qualitative assessment does not indicate impairment on any intangible assets held.

b. Classify each of the intangible assets (and their amounts) for balance sheet reporting at the end of 2021.

Problem 13-61
Reporting Intangible Assets **LO1, 2, 5, 6**

Able Company provided information on its intangible assets as follows.

1. A patent was purchased from East Development Company for $1,500,000 on January 1, 2020. Able estimated the remaining useful life of the patent to be 10 years.
2. On January 1, 2021, a franchise was purchased from the West Company for $500,000. In addition, 5% of revenue from the franchise must be paid to West. Revenue from the franchise for 2021 was $1,200,000. Able Company estimates the useful life of the franchise to be 10 years and records a full year's amortization (straight-line) in the year of purchase.
3. Able incurred R&D costs in 2021 as follows.

Materials (all used during 2021)	$120,000
Personnel	140,000
Indirect costs	60,000
	$320,000

Able estimates that these costs will be recouped by December 31, 2025.

4. On January 1, 2021, Able, based on new events that have occurred in the field, estimates that the remaining life of the patent purchased on January 1, 2020, is only five years from January 1, 2021.

Required

a. Prepare a schedule showing the intangible assets that should be reported on Able Company's balance sheet at December 31, 2021.

b. Prepare an income statement for the year ended December 31, 2021, as a result of the above transactions. Assume a 35% average income tax rate.

AICPA adapted

Problem 13-62
Recording Entries for Intangible Assets **LO1, 2, 3, 4**

Brannen Manufacturing Corporation was incorporated on January 3, 2020. The corporation's financial statements for its first year's operations were not examined by a CPA. We have been engaged to examine the financial statements for the year ended December 31, 2021, and our examination is substantially completed. The corporation's adjusted trial balance appears as follows.

Adjusted Trial Balance

December 31, 2021	Debit	Credit
Cash	$ 11,000	
Accounts receivable	68,500	
Allowance for doubtful accounts		$ 500
Inventories	38,500	
Machinery	80,000	
Equipment	29,000	
Accumulated depreciation		10,000
Patents	102,000	
Prepaid expenses	10,500	
Franchise, net	24,000	
Goodwill	24,000	
Licensing agreement 1	50,000	
Licensing agreement 2	59,000	
Accounts payable		147,500
Deferred revenue		12,500
Capital stock		317,000
Retained earnings, January 1, 2021	17,000	
Sales revenue		668,500
Cost of goods sold	454,000	
Selling and general expenses	173,000	
Interest expense	3,500	
Other expenses	12,000	
Totals	$1,156,000	$1,156,000

The following information relates to accounts that may still require adjustment.

1. Patents for Brannen's manufacturing process were acquired January 2, 2021, for $68,000. An additional $34,000 was spent in December 2021, to defend the patent and was included in the cost of patents. The company was not successful in defending the patent.
2. The balance in the Franchise account properly reflects the carrying value of a franchise payment made on January 1, 2020, for a 5-year term. No amortization has yet been recorded in 2021.
3. On January 3, 2020, Brannen purchased Licensing Agreement 1, which was believed to have an indefinite useful life. The balance in the Licensing Agreement 1 account includes its purchase price of $48,000 and costs of $2,000 related to the acquisition. On January 1, 2021, Brannen bought Licensing Agreement 2, which has a life expectancy of 10 years. The balance in the Licensing Agreement 2 account includes the $58,000 purchase price and $2,000 in acquisition costs, but it has been reduced by a credit of $1,000 for the advance collection of 2022 revenue from the agreement. No amortization on License Agreement 2 has been recorded.
4. In early 2021, an explosion caused a permanent reduction in the expected revenue producing value of Licensing Agreement 1. The fair value of the agreement is estimated at 60% of its carrying value. No entry has been made for the explosion in 2021.
5. The balance in the Goodwill account includes (1) $8,000 paid December 30, 2020, for an advertising program that management believes will assist in increasing Brannen's sales over a period of three to five years following the disbursement and (2) legal expenses of $16,000 incurred for Brannen's incorporation on January 3, 2020.

Required

Prepare journal entries as of December 31, 2021, as required by the information provided above. Ignore income taxes.

AICPA adapted

Problem 13-63
Accounting for the Impairment of Goodwill
LO3, 4

During 2020, Evergreen Corporation had been negotiating to purchase all of Pine Company's noncash assets and to assume all of its liabilities for a single cash price. The target closing date is January 1, 2021. Evergreen requested, and was provided, considerable data, including the following midyear balance sheet (summarized). Evergreen also independently estimated fair values of the assets and liabilities for each category provided on the balance sheet of Pine Co.

Balance Sheet, June 30, 2020	Book Value of Pine Co.	Fair Value Developed by Evergreen Corp.
Assets		
Cash	$ 19,000	$ 0**
Accounts receivable*	60,000	58,000
Inventory	140,000	90,000
Property, plant, and equipment*	300,000	285,000
Land	11,000	40,000
Franchise (unamortized balance)	20,000	21,000
Total	$550,000	$494,000
Liabilities		
Current liabilities	$ 40,000	$ 37,000
Bonds payable	200,000	200,000
Equity		
Stockholders' equity	310,000	—
Total	$550,000	

* Net of the allowance for doubtful accounts and accumulated depreciation, respectively.
**Cash will not be purchased by Evergreen Corporation.

Required

a. Compute the amount of goodwill recorded by Evergreen Corporation for this purchase assuming that Pine Company is created as a new segment of Evergeen, all goodwill is assigned to that segment, and the purchase price is $267,000.

b. Provide the entry for Evergreen Corporation to record the purchase of Pine Company.

c. Provide the entry (if any) at the end of 2021 to adjust goodwill for impairment assuming the following information.

Carrying value of the segment	$250,000
Fair value of the segment	230,000

Problem 13-64
Identifying Research and Development Costs
LO6

Murray Company builds a research facility at a cost of $40 million with an expected useful life of 20 years and zero salvage value in January of 2020. Murray incurs the following additional expenditures in 2020.

Salaries and wages for researchers	$500,000
Materials utilized for research project (no alternative usage)	100,000
Purchase of equipment with alternative uses (to be used over project life of 4 years)	200,000
Fees for consultants on research projects	80,000
Salaries attributed to the development of a patent	100,000
Legal fees paid to file for patent registration	3,000

Required

Determine the total amount of research and development expense for 2020.

Accounting Decisions and Judgments

AD&J 13-65
Analyzing Goodwill
LO3

Real World Analysis In a recent annual report on Form 10-K, **United Parcel Service Inc.** (UPS) provides a note describing its acquisitions of another company during the year, an extract of which follows.

> In August 2015, we acquired Coyote, a U.S.-based truckload freight brokerage company for $1.829 billion. This acquisition will allow us to expand our existing portfolio by adding large scale truckload freight brokerage and transportation management services to our Supply Chain & Freight reporting segment. In addition, we expect to benefit from synergies in purchased transportation, backhaul utilization, cross-selling to customers, as well as technology systems and industry best practices. The acquisition was funded using cash from operations and issuances of commercial paper.
>
> The estimates of deferred income taxes and goodwill are subject to change based on the final determination of fair values of acquired assets and assumed liabilities. The purchase price allocation for acquired companies can be modified for up to one year from the date of acquisition.
>
> The following table summarizes the estimated fair values of the Coyote assets acquired and liabilities assumed at the acquisition date (in millions):

Coyote Assets Acquired and (Liabilities) Assumed	
Cash and cash equivalents	$ 18
Accounts receivable	249
Other current assets	1
Property, plant, and equipment	17
Goodwill	1,233
Intangible assets	664
Other non-current assets	2
Accounts payable and other current liabilities	(132)
Other non-current liabilities	(11)
Deferred tax liability	(212)
Total purchase price	$1,829

> The goodwill recognized of approximately $1.233 billion is attributable to synergies anticipated from more efficient usage of our existing transportation networks and the assembled workforce of Coyote. We have allocated $709 and $524 million of the recognized goodwill to the U.S. Domestic Package and Supply Chain & Freight segments, respectively. None of the goodwill is expected to be deductible for income tax purposes.
>
> The intangible assets acquired of approximately $664 million primarily consist of $426 million of customer relationships (amortized over 10 years), $27 million of non-compete agreements (amortized over 4 years),

and $200 million of trade name, which has an indefinite useful life. The carrying value of acquired accounts receivable approximates fair value.

Required

a. Provide a summary entry UPS would make to record the acquisition. Assume that UPS paid cash for the acquisition.

b. What effect, if any will the excess of cost over identifiable net assets acquired in these acquisitions have on UPS's earnings in future years?

AD&J 13-66
Analyzing Software Development Costs
LO2, 6

Real World Analysis In the notes to its Year 8 financial statements, **Unisys Corporation**, a computer software company, discloses the following regarding its treatment of the cost of software development.

> The cost of development of computer software to be sold or leased is capitalized and amortized to cost of net sales over the estimated revenue-producing lives of the products, but not in excess of three years following product release. Unamortized marketable software costs, reported in the balance sheet, at December 31, Year 8 and Year 7 were $246.6 and $259.0 million, respectively.

In the statement of cash flows, Unisys shows amortization expense for marketable software for Year 8 of $111.8 million.

Required

a. What amount did Unisys capitalize in Year 8 for the development of marketable software?

b. Suppose the capitalized marketable software cost shown at December 31, Year 7, relates to one software product that was released for sale at that date. The product is expected to produce revenues totaling $1,000 million over a three-year useful life.

1. What would be the minimum amortization amount that would be recorded in Year 8?
2. Suppose revenues from the software product totaled $400 million in Year 8. What would be the amount of amortization that Unisys would report in Year 8?
3. Given that $111.8 million of amortization was recorded and assuming the facts in (2) above, estimate the amount of revenue generated by this product in Year 8.

AD&J 13-67
Analyzing Goodwill and Other Intangibles **LO1**

Real World Analysis The following information is a summary of items included in a recent Form 10-K of **Coca Cola Company**.

Intangible Asset ($ millions)	Classification	Dec. 31, 2015
Trademarks	Indefinite life	$ 5,989
Bottlers' franchise rights	Indefinite life	6,000
Goodwill	Indefinite life	11,289
Other	Indefinite life	164
Customer relationships	Definite life	294
Bottlers' franchise rights	Definite life	192
Trademarks	Definite life	167
Other	Definite life	37
		$24,132

Required

a. What is the primary difference in the accounting for intangibles with finite lives versus indefinite lives?

b. Why are some intangible assets (such as trademarks) listed in both classifications?

c. What is the largest intangible asset? What percentage of total intangible assets does this specific asset represent?

AD&J 13-68
Analyzing the Accounting for Intangibles **LO1**

Judgment Case The National Broadcasting Company (NBC), one of the major television network companies, incurred costs of $750,000 in the development of its N logo shown at intervals in its TV broadcasts. Shortly after the N logo was announced and first used by NBC, it was discovered that an educational TV network in Nebraska had already been using a similar logo. To obtain exclusive rights to its already costly logo, NBC agreed, in an out-of-court settlement, to pay $55,000 cash to Nebraska Network and to furnish it with various new and used color TV equipment without cost (NBC book value, $350,000). The equipment to be transferred was conservatively valued at $500,000 by independent appraisers. A spokesman for the Nebraska Network said the equipment to be provided by NBC would have cost $750,000 if bought new and that for the two years preceding the settlement, efforts to get a $750,000 appropriation from the Nebraska legislature to buy such equipment had been unsuccessful. Terms of the settlement provided that $2,500 of the cash settlement was to be paid to William Korbus, who had designed the Nebraska Network's N logo at a cost of $100. Delivery of the equipment to the Nebraska Network was to begin approximately three months after the announced settlement and was to occur over a four-month interval.

Required

a. Briefly explain how you believe NBC should account for its original costs of $750,000 related to the logo. How should it account for the settlement with the Nebraska Network and Korbus?

b. Assuming that accounting principles for not-for-profit organizations such as the Nebraska Network were similar to those for a commercial entity, briefly explain how Nebraska Network should account for the settlement.

AD&J 13-69 Assessing Goodwill Appreciation **LO3, 4**

Ethics Case Blass Equipment Corporation, a retail farm implements dealer, has increased its annual sales volume to a level 10 times greater than the annual sales of the dealership when purchased over 10 years ago. At that time, a material amount of goodwill was recorded. The goodwill is still carried at its original value at purchase.

The board of directors of Blass recently received an offer to negotiate the sale of the company to a larger competitor. As a result, the majority of the board members want to increase the current amount of goodwill on the balance sheet because of the larger sales volume developed through intensive promotion and the current market prices of the company's products. However, a few of the company's board members would prefer to eliminate goodwill altogether from the balance sheet in order to prevent "possible misinterpretations." Goodwill was properly recorded when the business was acquired.

Required

a. Discuss the meaning of the term goodwill. Do not discuss goodwill arising from consolidated statements or the conditions under which goodwill is recorded.

b. Discuss the propriety of
1. Increasing the stated value of goodwill prior to the negotiations.
2. Eliminating goodwill completely from the balance sheet prior to negotiations.

c. From an ethical point of view, do you believe goodwill should be written down or left alone? Explain.

AICPA adapted

AD&J 13-70 Analyzing the Accounting for R&D, Software, and Oil Exploration Costs **LO6**

Communication Case Globe Inc. is an enterprise with interests in natural resources, high-tech enterprises, and publishing. Liz, the VP of Finance for Globe, needs your help (member of her accounting staff) in understanding why current GAAP requires different reporting treatment for seemingly similar costs.

> Liz: I just don't see why research and development, software development, and oil exploration costs are treated so differently in the accounting standards. After all, don't they all represent current expenditures in the hope of creating or finding future assets? Aren't they all subject to significant risk? They all seem like shooting in the dark hoping to make profits. I want to anticipate questions at the upcoming shareholders' meeting and would like to say something other than "because the FASB said so."

Required

Draft a brief email message to Liz giving your opinion on why GAAP treats these similar costs so differently.

AD&J 13-71 Defining Terms **LO1, 3, 4, 6**

Codification Skills How are the terms (1) intangible assets, (2) goodwill, (3) recoverable amount, (4) impairment, and (5) research and development defined in the Codification?

AD&J 13-72 Performing Accounting Research **LO1, 2, 4, 6**

Codification Skills Through research in the Codification, find the proper citation that provides guidance on each of the following topics.

a. Factors to consider in estimating the useful life of intangible assets. FASB ASC ___-___-___-___

b. Defining indefinite life intangible assets. FASB ASC ___-___-___-___

c. General standard to expense research and development costs. FASB ASC ___-___-___-___

d. Criteria for technological feasibility for software development. FASB ASC ___-___-___-___

e. Description of qualitative assessment of goodwill. FASB ASC ___-___-___-___

AD&J 13-73 Performing Accounting Research **LO1**

Codification Skills A company is preparing disclosures for its annual financial statements related to intangible assets recently purchased and held by the company. The company is registered with the Securities and Exchange Commission. The company is unsure as to whether a detailed breakdown of its various intangible assets is required. Identify the relevant authoritative guidance. FASB ASC ___-___-___-___

Answers to Review Exercises

Review 13-1

1. Finite life intangible asset
2. Expense
3. Finite life intangible asset
4. Expense
5. Indefinite life intangible asset other than goodwill
6. Expense
7. Finite life intangible asset
8. Goodwill
9. Indefinite life intangible asset other than goodwill

Review 13-2

Assets	= Liabilities +	Equity
−3,917		−3,917

Patent: Cr. 2,500; 1,417 — Amort Exp: Dr. 3,917

December 31, 2020—To record amortization expense

Amortization Expense	3,917	
Patent 1 ($50,000/15 × 9/12)		2,500
Patent 2 ($85,000/10 × 2/12)		1,417

(No amortization is required for the trademark, which has an indefinite life.)

Review 13-3

a. $35,000 ($365,000 − $330,000)

b. **January 1, 2020—To record purchase of Naperville Company**

Assets	= Liabilities +	Equity
+455,000	+90,000	
−365,000		

Cash: Dr. 15,000; Cr. 365,000 — Goodwill: Dr. 35,000 — Assets Other than Cash, Goodwill: Dr. 405,000 — Liabilities: Cr. 90,000

Cash	15,000	
Accounts Receivable	35,000	
Inventory	70,000	
Plant and Equipment	230,000	
Land	60,000	
License Agreement	10,000	
Goodwill	35,000	
Accounts Payable		25,000
Noncurrent Note Payable		65,000
Cash		365,000

c. $0

Review 13-4

a. Patent $190,667 ($220,000 − $29,333), Trademark $15,000, Goodwill $30,000

b. $7,500 loss ($2,500 impairment loss on trademark + $5,000 impairment loss on goodwill)

c. $18,500 gain on sale ($200,000 − $181,500)

Review 13-5

Assets	= Liabilities +	Equity
−4,469		−4,469

Patent: Bal. 46,552; Cr. 4,469; Bal. 42,083 — Amort Exp: Dr. 4,469

December 31, 2020—To record amortization expense on patent

Amortization Expense ($46,552*/125 months × 12 months)	4,469	
Patent		4,469

*(December 31, 2018 carrying value of $47,083 + $5,000) − [($47,083 + $5,000)/113 months × 12 months]

The carrying value of the patent on December 31, 2020, is $42,083 ($46,552 − $4,469).

Review 13-6

Part One

a. 2 *b.* 1 *c.* 2 *d.* 1 *e.* 2 *f.* 3 *g.* 1

Part Two

a. **2020—To capitalize costs for computer software product development**

Software Intangible Asset ($1,800,000 × 0.30)	540,000	
Cash		540,000

Assets	= Liabilities	+ Equity
+540,000		
−540,000		

Software Intang		Cash	
540,000			540,000

2020—To expense costs for computer software product development

Software Development Expense ($1,800,000 × 0.70)	1,260,000	
Cash		1,260,000

Assets	= Liabilities	+ Equity
−1,260,000		−1,260,000

Software Dev Exp		Cash	
1,260,000			1,260,000

b. **December 31, 2021—To amortize computer software product development costs**

Software Amortization Expense	108,000	
Software Intangible Asset		108,000

Assets	= Liabilities	+ Equity
−108,000		−108,000

Software Intang		Software Amort Exp	
540,000	108,000	108,000	

14 Investments in Debt and Equity Securities

Chipotle Mexican Grill, Inc.

Investments

Investments classified as trading securities are carried at fair value with any unrealized gain or loss being recorded in the consolidated statement of income. Investments classified as available-for-sale are carried at fair value with unrealized gains and losses, net of tax, included as a component of other comprehensive income (loss) on the statement of comprehensive income. Held-to-maturity securities are carried at amortized cost. Impairment charges on investments are recognized in interest and other income, net on the consolidated statement of income when management believes the decline in the fair value of the investment is other-than-temporary.

CHIPOTLE MEXICAN GRILL, INC.
CONSOLIDATED BALANCE SHEET
(in thousands, except per share data)

	December 31, 2017	December 31, 2016
Assets		
Current assets:		
Cash and cash equivalents	$ 184,569	$ 87,880
Accounts receivable, net of allowance for doubtful accounts of $0 and $259 as of December 31, 2017 and 2016, respectively	40,453	40,451
Inventory	19,860	15,019
Prepaid expenses and other current assets	50,918	44,080
Income tax receivable	9,353	5,108
Investments	324,382	329,836
Total current assets	629,535	522,374
Leasehold improvements, property and equipment, net	1,338,366	1,303,558
Long term investments	—	125,055
Other assets	55,852	53,177
Goodwill	21,939	21,939
Total assets	$2,045,692	$2,026,103

Chipotle Mexican Grill, Inc.

3. Investments

As of December 31, 2017 and 2016, our investments consisted of U.S. treasury notes with maturities up to approximately one year and were classified as available-for-sale. Fair value of U.S. treasury notes is measured on a recurring basis based on Level 1 inputs (quoted prices for identical assets in active markets).

The following is a summary of available-for-sale securities:

	December 31, 2017	December 31, 2016
Amortized cost	$324,875	$455,109
Unrealized gains (losses)	(493)	(218)
Fair value	$324,382	$454,891

xican Grill, Inc.

ng is a summary of unrealized gains (losses) on available-for-sale securities recorded in other comprehensive he consolidated statement of comprehensive income:

	Year ended December 31, 2017	2016	2015
Unrealized gains (losses) on available-for-sale securities	$ (274)	$ 2,251	$ (2,468)
Unrealized gains (losses) on available-for-sale securities, net of tax	$ (186)	$ 1,402	$ (1,522)

Realized gains and losses on available-for-sale securities are recorded in interest and other income on the consolidated statement of income. We had no realized gains or losses for the years ended December 31, 2017 and 2015, and $547 of realized gains on available-for-sale securities for the year ended December 31, 2016. During the year ended December 31, 2015, we recorded an other-than-temporary impairment charge of $244 in interest and other income in the consolidated statement of income in connection with a decline in the fair market value of certain available-for-sale securities.

Chapter Preview

In this chapter we describe the accounting for various classifications of debt and equity investments. The accounting treatment of a particular investment depends on that classification. We explain other topics related to investment accounting including the impact of impairment losses and the fair value option method. The appendices include a discussion on accounting for derivatives, which are financial instruments purchased to speculate on future prices or to hedge against risk.

Action Plan

LO	Topic/Subtopic	Page	Demos	Reviews	Assignments
LO 14–1	**Account for debt securities measured at amortized cost** HTM :: Amortized Cost :: Par :: Discount :: Premium :: Interest Revenue :: Effective Interest Method :: Straight-Line Interest Method	14-4	D14-1A D14-1B D14-1C D14-1D D14-1E	R14-1	16, 17, 36, 38, 39, 40, 41, 42, 43, 44, 68, 75, 76, 77, 78, 85, 90, 95, 100, 108, 110
LO 14–2	**Account for debt securities measured at FV-NI** TS :: Fair Value Option Election :: Interest Revenue :: Fair Value Adjustment :: Unrealized Gain or Loss—Income	14-12	D14-2A D14-2B	R14-2	18, 19, 20, 36, 38, 39, 40, 45, 46, 47, 48, 49, 68, 72, 73, 79, 80, 81, 85, 90, 93, 95, 100, 103, 104, 106, 108, 109
LO 14–3	**Account for debt securities measured at FV-OCI** AFS :: Interest Revenue :: Fair Value Adjustment :: Unrealized Gain or Loss—OCI :: Reclassification Adjustment	14-17	D14-3A D14-3B	R14-3	21, 22, 23, 24, 25, 36, 39, 40, 50, 51, 52, 53, 54, 68, 73, 76, 77, 82, 83, 84, 85, 90, 93, 95, 100, 103, 104, 108, 109
LO 14–4	**Account for equity securities measured at FV-NI** Equity Securities :: Insignificant Influence :: Dividend :: Fair Value Adjustment :: Unrealized Gain or Loss—Income	14-25	D14-4	R14-4	26, 27, 28, 29, 32, 39, 40, 55, 56, 57, 58, 59, 60, 61, 62, 68, 85, 86, 87, 88, 89, 90, 95, 105, 107, 108
LO14–5	**Account for equity securities following the equity method** Equity Securities :: Significant Influence :: Proportionate Share of Income :: Depreciation Adjustment :: Fair Value Option	14-29	D14-5	R14-5	30, 31, 32, 37, 39, 40, 62, 63, 64, 65, 66, 67, 68, 74, 89, 90, 91, 92, 94, 95, 97, 98, 99, 108
LO 14–6	**Adjust debt and equity securities for impairment** Impairment Loss :: HTM :: AFS :: Equity Method Investments	14-34	D14-6	R14-6	33, 34, 35, 69, 70, 71, 96, 108
LO 14–7	**APPENDIX 14A—Explain the accounting for transfers of investments** Transfer Investment Category :: No Retrospective Treatment :: Disclosure	14-37	D14-7	R14-7	101, 102, 103, 104, 106, 111, 112, 119, 120, 126
LO 14–8	**APPENDIX 14B—Describe accounting for special-purpose funds and investments in life insurance policies** Special-Purpose Funds :: Cash Surrender Value :: Whole-Life Policy	14-39	D14-8	R14-8	113, 114, 121, 127
LO 14–9	**APPENDIX 14C—Describe and account for derivatives** Speculative Instrument :: Call Option :: Hedging Instrument :: Put Option :: Interest Rate Swap :: Futures Contract	14-41	D14-9A D14-9B D14-9C D14-9D	R14-9	115, 116, 117, 118, 122, 123, 124, 125, 128, 129, 130

Expanded Chapter Preview

Companies invest in the securities of other companies and government agencies for a variety of reasons. Companies often have cash available that is not needed at present but will be needed in the near future. Rather than allow idle cash to remain in a nonearning account, companies find temporary investments where they can earn a return. These investments are usually low risk and can be quickly and easily converted to cash. They often include securities of federal, state, and local government agencies but can also include securities of other companies. A second reason companies invest in securities of other companies, especially in securities representing ownership interests, is to develop a beneficial intercompany relationship that will increase the profitability of the investing company, both directly and indirectly.

This chapter explains how to account for investments in debt and equity securities from the perspective of the *investor*. In general, a **security** is a share, participation, or interest that is (1) represented by an instrument or is registered, (2) commonly recognized or dealt with on exchanges or markets, and (3) either one of a class or is divisible. Debt and equity securities are **financial assets**.

ASC Glossary Financial Assets: Cash, evidence of an ownership interest in an entity, or a contract that conveys to one entity a right to do either of the following:

a. Receive cash or another financial instrument from a second entity.

b. Exchange other financial instruments on potentially favorable terms with the second entity.

The first step in accounting for investments in securities is to determine whether an investment is a **debt security** or an **equity security**, the differences of which are outlined below.

Investment	Definition	Examples
Debt security	**ASC Glossary** Any security representing a creditor relationship with an entity.	▪ U.S. Treasury securities ▪ Municipal securities ▪ Corporate bonds ▪ Securitized debt instruments ▪ Convertible debt ▪ Commercial paper
Equity security[1]	**ASC Glossary** Any security representing an ownership interest in an entity (for example, common, preferred, or other capital stock) or the right to acquire (for example, warrants, rights, forward purchase contracts, and call options) or dispose of (for example, put options and forward sale contracts) an ownership interest in an entity at fixed or determinable prices.	▪ Common, preferred, and other capital stock ▪ Stock options, warrants, and stock rights ▪ Options to purchase (call options) or to sell (put options) equity securities at fixed or determinable prices

[1] While ASC 321 describes the accounting for equity securities and other ownership interests in an entity such as investments in partnerships, the discussion in this chapter focuses on equity securities.

The next step is to determine the method to account for debt and equity securities, which *will have a direct impact on both recording of transactions and financial statement presentation.* Determining which method to use to account for debt investments requires an analysis of both the intent and the ability of the investor to trade or hold the securities until maturity. In the case of equity securities, extent of influence or control over the investee is important. We examine the accounting for investments in debt securities followed by equity securities. **For purposes of illustration in this chapter, we use bonds payable to illustrate debt securities and investments in common or preferred stock to illustrate equity securities.** Debt and equity securities are accounted for through the following methods.

Methods to Account for Debt Securities		
Amortized Cost **LO 14-1** Recognize at amortized cost. Ignore adjustment to fair value.	**FV-NI** **LO 14-2** Recognize at fair value with adjustment affecting NI.	**FV-OCI** **LO 14-3** Recognize at fair value with adjustment affecting OCI.

Methods to Account for Equity Securities		
FV-NI **Investor Lacks Significant Influence (< 20% Ownership Interest)** **LO 14-4** Recognize at fair value with adjustment affecting net income.	**Equity Method** **Investor Has Significant Influence (20% to 50% Ownership Interest)** **LO 14-5** Recognize at cost, adjusted for investor's share of net income and dividends.	**Consolidation** **Investor Has Controlling Influence (> 50% Ownership Interest)** **Advanced accounting courses** Financial statements of the investor and investee are consolidated for reporting purposes.

Account for debt securities measured at amortized cost

LO 14-1

HTM at Amortized Cost
- Recognize at amortized cost (par, discount, or premium)
- Ignore changes in fair value
- Recognize interest revenue in net income as earned (effective interest method or straight-line interest method)
- Recognize realized gain or loss from a sale in net income

LO 14-1 Overview

Of the three methods to account for debt investments, we begin with amortized cost. **Amortized cost** is relevant only if a security is actually held to maturity. For example, amortized cost is relevant for a bond investment with a 15-year term, where the investor holds the bond for the full 15 years. Debt investments accounted for at amortized cost are called **held-to-maturity securities (HTM)**. The HTM classification is determined at acquisition, where a company has both **the positive intent and ability to hold an investment to its maturity date.** This implies that the investor (1) intends to hold the security until maturity, and (2) does not anticipate a need to sell the security before its maturity date to access cash for reasons such as liquidity needs or interest rate changes. We will illustrate HTM securities in this section using a common type of debt investment—bonds issued by another company. **Exhibit 14-1** defines terms commonly used in accounting for bond investments.

EXHIBIT 14-1 Bond Investment Terminology

Amortized cost	Amount at which an investment is acquired, adjusted for amortization of a premium or a discount.
Discount	Amount equal to the excess of a bond investment's face value over its present value. A discount reduces the investment account to its amortized cost. A discount represents deferred interest revenue that will be recognized over the term of the bond investment.
Premium	Amount equal to the excess of the present value of a bond investment over its face value. A premium increases the investment account to its amortized cost. A premium represents a reduction of interest revenue that will be recognized over the term of the bond investment.
Fair value	ASC Glossary The price that would be received to sell an asset or paid to transfer a liability in an orderly transaction between market participants at the measurement date.
Face value (or par value or stated value)	Contractual cash flow receivable at a bond's maturity date.
Stated rate	Rate used to determine the cash interest receipts on a bond investment. Stated as an annual percentage of face value.
Market rate (or effective rate)	Rate on a similar bond investment in the market involving similar risk and where the issuer has a similar crediting rating. Stated as an annual percentage.

Held-to-Maturity Securities

HTM securities are recognized at amortized cost (not fair value). The HTM classification is further described in the accounting guidance.

Methods to Account for Debt Securities		
Amortized Cost LO 14-1	FV-NI LO 14-2	FV-OCI LO 14-3

320-10-25-3 Amortized cost is relevant only if a security is actually held to maturity. Use of the held-to-maturity category is restrictive because the use of amortized cost must be justified for each investment in a debt security. At acquisition, an entity shall determine if it has the positive intent and ability to hold a security to maturity, which is distinct from the mere absence of an intent to sell. If management's intention to hold a debt security to maturity is uncertain, it is not appropriate to carry that investment at amortized cost. In establishing intent, an entity shall consider pertinent historical experience, such as sales and transfers of debt securities classified as held-to-maturity. A pattern of sales or transfers of those securities is inconsistent with an expressed current intent to hold similar debt securities to maturity.

Because an investor must have the intent and ability to hold the HTM security for its entire life, a sale before maturity should be rare. However, due to unforeseen events an investor may decide to sell an HTM security before its maturity date. A sale of an HTM security due to *unforeseen circumstances* is not inconsistent with the original classification of HTM. For example, a company may sell an HTM debt security due to a downgrade of the investor's credit rating, or a tax law change. However, if a company sells an HTM security before maturity, without the justification of a major unforeseen event, the early sale may call into question the company's intention to hold to maturity. In such a case, the investor may be required to reclassify all of its debt securities as either trading or available for sale. The accounting guidance provides examples of unforeseen circumstances—three examples are provided below.

320-10-25-6 The following changes in circumstances may cause the entity to change its intent to hold a certain security to maturity without calling into question its intent to hold other debt securities to maturity in the future. The sale or transfer of a held-to-maturity security due to one of the following changes in circumstances shall not be considered inconsistent with its original classification:

a. Evidence of a significant deterioration in the issuer's creditworthiness (for example, a downgrading of an issuer's published credit rating).

b. A change in tax law that eliminates or reduces the tax-exempt status of interest on the debt security.

c. A major business combination or major disposition . . . that necessitates the sale or transfer of held-to-maturity securities to maintain the entity's existing interest rate risk position or credit risk policy.

EXPANDING YOUR KNOWLEDGE **Maturity of HTM Securities**

If a sale of the HTM debt security occurs near enough to its maturity date such that interest rate risk is substantially eliminated, or the sale occurs after substantial collection on the principal, the security is considered to be held the full-term for purposes of classification.

320-10-25-14 Sales of debt securities that meet either of the following conditions may be considered as maturities for purposes of the classification of securities and the disclosure requirements under this Subtopic:

a. The sale of a security occurs near enough to its maturity date . . . that interest rate risk is substantially eliminated as a pricing factor. That is, the date of sale is so near the maturity or call date (for example, within three months) that changes in market interest rates would not have a significant effect on the security's fair value.

b. The sale of a security occurs after the entity has already collected a substantial portion (at least 85 percent) of the principal outstanding at acquisition due either to prepayments on the debt security or to scheduled payments on a debt security payable in equal installments (both principal and interest) over its term.

Measurement of HTM Securities

HTM investments are initially measured at acquisition cost, which is equal to the price paid for the security. In the absence of an observable price, the acquisition cost may be measured as the present value of the cash principal and interest expected to be collected based upon the stated rate, discounted at the market rate in effect at the time of acquisition. The market rate fluctuates with investors' expectations and is based upon many factors including changes in risks, market conditions, and more. However, the stated rate, which determines the periodic cash interest receipts, is fixed based upon the bond agreement and therefore does not fluctuate based upon market conditions. Any incidental costs related to the acquisition such as brokerage fees and transfer costs are added to the acquisition cost.

In the case of a bond investment (a form of a debt security), if present value and face value do not differ materially, the bond investment is recognized at face value. If the face value of the bond investment is greater than its present value, a **discount** is recorded. If the face value of the bond investment is less than its present value, a **premium** is recorded. A discount (premium) is amortized over the life of the bond investment as an increase (decrease) to interest revenue. **In practice, companies generally record a net bond investment rather than record separate accounts for discounts or premiums.** Because the process of amortization of discounts and premiums is also used in accounting for debt instruments by the issuer, it is also addressed in Chapter 16. An HTM investment purchased at its face value is illustrated in **Demo 14-1A**, at a discount (< face value) is illustrated in **Demo 14-1B** and **Demo 14-1D**, and at a premium (> face value) is illustrated in **Demo 14-1C** and **Demo 14-1E.**

If a security is sold between interest payment dates, the company (investor) would pay both the purchase price of the security and the interest accrued from the most recent interest payment date to the purchase date. Then, on the next interest payment date, the company (investor) receives interest for the latest full interest period. We illustrate the accounting for a debt security sold between interest payment dates in LO 14-2, but the concept applies to all debt securities.

Subsequent measurement of HTM securities ignores changes in the fair value of the securities. **Therefore, no adjustment is made to the carrying value of the security over the life of the investment for changes in fair value.** Although there is no financial statement impact for changes in fair value, the aggregate fair value of an HTM investment and any unrecognized holding gain (loss) are disclosed in the notes accompanying the financial statements. However, if the investment is considered impaired, a loss may need to be recognized as discussed in LO 14-6.

Accounting for HTM Investment Purchased at Face Value

Demo 14-1A illustrates the case where the cost of a bond investment is equal to its face value.

HTM Investment Purchased at Par

LO14-1 **Demo 14-1A**

Demo MBC

On January 1, 2020, an investor purchased a 7% bond investment at an amount equal to its face value of $100,000. The bond matures in 5 years and pays interest annually on December 31. Record (a) the investor's purchase on January 1, 2020, assuming that the investor classified the investment as HTM and (b) the receipt of cash interest on December 31, 2020.

Solution

a. **Purchase of Bond Investment**

January 1, 2020—To record investment purchase

Investment in HTM Securities.	100,000	
Cash		100,000

Assets = Liabilities + Equity
+100,000
−100,000

Invest—HTM: 100,000 (debit)
Cash: 100,000 (credit)

b. **Interest Revenue**

The investor would receive periodic cash interest on the investment at the stated rate of 7%. Because the investment was purchased at its face value, the stated rate of 7% equals the market rate of 7%. Cash interest received equals interest revenue recognized over the term of the bond investment. On December 31, 2020, the investor would record the following entry to recognize interest of $7,000 or $100,000 × 7%.

December 31, 2020—To record receipt of interest

Cash ($100,000 × 0.07).	7,000	
Interest Revenue.		7,000

Assets = Liabilities + Equity
+7,000 +7,000

Cash: 7,000 (debit) | 100,000 (credit)
Interest Rev: 7,000 (credit)

Accounting for HTM Investment Purchased at a Discount—Effective Interest Method

The present value of payments (discounted at the market rate) does not equal the bond investment's face value when the stated rate is not equal to the market rate. More specifically, if the market rate is *greater* than the stated rate of the bond, the bond will sell at a discount as shown in **Exhibit 14-2**. This means the investor is expecting a *higher* rate of return than the stated rate, based upon expected returns on investments of similar risks. Thus, the investor who is not satisfied with the periodic cash interest receipts on the bond will counter by paying a lower price for the bond in order to *effectively* yield a higher rate of return. Regardless of the price paid up front for the bond, the investor will receive the face value of the bond upon maturity. The difference between the lower price paid for the bond and the face value of the bond is the **bond discount**.

EXHIBIT 14-2
Fluctuation in Bond Price

The amount of interest revenue to be recognized over the life of the bond is typically determined using the effective interest method. Under the **effective interest method**, the interest revenue each period is measured by multiplying the market rate at inception by the amortized cost of the bond investment of the bonds at the beginning of each interest period. Interest revenue increases each period because the interest revenue increases with the increasing amortized cost of the bond investment. In other words, the base for calculating interest revenue each period is increasing as the bond investment moves toward the face value.

The cash interest received each period is calculated by multiplying the face value of the bonds by the stated rate. The difference between the market interest expense and the cash interest received is used to increase the investment value each period until the investment reaches its face value.

Demo 14-1B LO14-1 HTM Investment Purchased at a Discount (Effective Interest)

Demo MBC

Montana Inc. acquires $100,000 of Timberlake Corporation 7% bonds on January 1, 2020. Montana has the ability and intends to hold the bonds until they mature on December 31, 2023. The bonds pay cash interest annually, each December 31. Montana has acquired the bonds at the market price, which yields a market rate of 7.59845%. Montana uses the effective interest method to amortize any discounts or premiums on HTM investments.

Required

a. Determine the classification, accounting method, and purchase price of the bond investment.
b. Record the entry to purchase the bond investment on January 1, 2020.
c. Prepare an effective interest schedule and record the December 31, 2020, entry for interest earned and discount amortized.
d. Record the entry at maturity of the bonds on December 31, 2023.
e. Assume that instead of holding Timberlake bonds until December 31, 2023, Montana sells Timberlake bonds on January 2, 2023, for $99,850 (due to a significant unforeseen event). Record the entry for the sale on January 2, 2023.

Solution

a. **Classification of a Bond Investment and Computation of Purchase Price**
The investment in bonds is classified as a held-to-maturity investment because Montana has both the intent and the ability to hold the bonds to maturity. HTM investments are accounted for at amortized cost. In exchange for the purchase price of the bonds, Montana will receive annual cash interest of $7,000 (7% × $100,000), and the face value of $100,000 at the end of the bond term. The purchase price of the bonds is calculated as the present value of the 7% cash interest payments and the face value of the bonds at maturity, discounted at the market rate of 7.59845%. The present value of $98,000, the purchase price of the bonds, is calculated using the PV function in Excel.

	RATE	NPER	PMT	PV	FV	Excel Formula
Given	7.59845%	4	7,000	?	100,000	*=PV(0.0759845,4,7000,100000)*
Solution				$(98,000)*		

* Rounded

b. **Purchase of Bond Investment**
The entry to record the debt investment classified as HTM securities purchased at a discount is recorded at a net value of $98,000. This means that the investment is recorded at an amount net of the discount of $2,000 ($100,000 − $98,000).

January 1, 2020—To record investment purchase

Investment in HTM Securities—Timberlake Bonds	98,000	
Cash		98,000

Assets	=	Liabilities	+	Equity
+98,000				
−98,000				

Invest—HTM		Cash	
98,000			98,000

c. **Effective Interest Schedule and Interest Revenue Recognition**
The following amortization schedule illustrates how the amortization of the bond discount impacts interest revenue recognition over the life of the bonds under the effective interest method. Interest revenue each period is measured by multiplying the market rate by the amortized cost of the bonds at the beginning of the period. For example, in the first year, interest revenue of $7,446 is equal to 7.59845% multiplied by $98,000. The difference between market interest of $7,446 and cash interest of $7,000 is the discount amortized in year one of $446. This amount increases the amortized cost of the bond to a balance of $98,446 on December 31, 2020. The components of the journal entries each period to record the receipt of cash interest and amortization of the discount can be found in this schedule.

Effective Interest Method—Discount

Date	Cash (Stated Interest)[a]	Interest Revenue (Market Interest)[b]	Discount Amortization[c]	Bond Investment, net (Amortized Cost)[d]
Jan. 1, 2020. . .				$ 98,000
Dec. 31, 2020. . .	$ 7,000	$ 7,446	$ 446	98,446
Dec. 31, 2021. . .	7,000	7,480	480	98,926
Dec. 31, 2022. . .	7,000	7,516	516	99,442
Dec. 31, 2023. . .	7,000	7,558*	558*	100,000
	$28,000	$30,000	$2,000	

*Rounded
[a] Bond face value × Stated rate
[b] Bond amortized cost, beginning of year × Market rate
[c] Market interest − Stated interest
[d] Bond amortized cost, beginning of year + Discount amortization

continued

continued from previous page

The entry to record interest revenue in 2020 follows. Because we have chosen not to use a separate account for the discount, the amortization of the discount results in a direct addition to the investment account of $446. The unamortized discount balance, not shown separately in the table, is simply the amortized cost minus the face value at the end of the period.

December 31, 2020—To record receipt of interest and amortization of discount

Cash	7,000	
Investment in HTM Securities—Timberlake Bonds	446	
Interest Revenue		7,446

Assets = Liabilities + Equity
+7,000 +7,446
+446

Cash: 7,000 | 98,000
Interest Rev: | 7,446
Invest—HTM: 98,000; 446 |

At December 31, 2020, the amortized cost of the bond investment is $98,446 ($98,000 + $446).

d. **Bond Retirement at Maturity**

The amortized cost of Timberlake Corporation bonds has increased $2,000 by the end of the four years; thus the amortized cost of the investment is equal to its face value of $100,000 at December 31, 2023. On this date, Montana receives the face value of the bonds and Timberlake retires the bonds.

December 31, 2023—To derecognize bond investment

Cash	100,000	
Investment in HTM Securities—Timberlake Bonds		100,000

Assets = Liabilities + Equity
+100,000
−100,000

Cash: 7,000; 7,000; 7,000; 7,000; 100,000 | 98,000
Invest—HTM: 98,000; 446; 480; 516; 558 | 100,000; bal. 0

e. **Sale of Bond Investment *Before* Maturity**

On January 2, 2023, Montana records a gain on the sale of the investment of $408 when the bonds are retired early at $99,850. The gain is the difference between the cash received of $99,850 and the amortized cost of the bonds of $99,442 (obtained from the amortization schedule). The realized gain on the sale of a security is included in other income in the income statement.

January 2, 2023—To record sale of bond investment before maturity

Cash	99,850	
Investment in HTM Securities—Timberlake Bonds		99,442
Gain on Sale of Investment ($99,850 − $99,442)		408

Assets = Liabilities + Equity
+99,850 +408
−99,442

Cash: 7,000; 7,000; 7,000; 99,850 | 98,000
Gain on Sale of Invest: | 408
Invest—HTM: Bal. 98,000; 446; 480; 516 | 99,442; bal. 0

Accounting for HTM Investment Purchased at a Premium—Effective Interest Method

If the market rate is *less* than the stated rate of the bonds, the bonds will sell at a premium. This means that the issuer of the bonds would be unwilling to sell the bonds for the face value when the market rate for debt securities of similar risk is less than the stated rate at which the bonds will pay interest to the investor. Pricing the bonds to yield a lower market rate results in a selling price that exceeds the face value.

Regardless of the price paid for the bonds, Montana will receive the face value of the bonds upon maturity. The excess of the price paid over the face value of the bonds is the **bond premium**. Over the term of the bonds, the premium is amortized, reducing interest revenue and the amortized cost of the bond by each period's amortization amount.

HTM Investment Purchased at a Premium (Effective Interest) LO14-1 Demo 14-1C

Demo MBC

Refer to the information in **Demo 14-1B** but now assume that Montana Inc. paid *more* than the face value of the 7%, $100,000 bonds because the market rate is 6.4172%

Required

a. Determine the purchase price of the bond investment.
b. Record the entry to purchase the bond investment on January 1, 2020.
c. Prepare an effective interest schedule and record the December 31, 2020, entry for interest earned and premium amortized.

continued

continued from previous page

d. Report the investment in bonds on the balance sheet on December 31, 2020, and the effects on the 2020 income statement.

e. Record the entry at the maturity of the bonds on December 31, 2023.

Solution

	RATE	NPER	PMT	PV	FV	Excel Formula
Given	6.4172%	4	7,000	?	100,000	=PV(0.064172,4,7000,100000)
Solution				$(102,000)		

* Rounded

a. **Computation of Bond Investment Purchase Price**
The present value of the cash interest payments of $7,000 per year and the bond face value of $100,000 is equal to $102,000, the purchase price of the bonds, and is calculated using the PV function in Excel.

b. **Purchase of Bond Investment**
The entry to record the bond investment purchase includes a debit to Investments in HTM Securities for the net proceeds of $102,000. This means that the investment is recorded at an amount reflecting the premium of $2,000 ($102,000 − $100,000).

Assets = Liabilities + Equity
+102,000
−102,000

Invest—HTM: 102,000 (debit)
Cash: 102,000 (credit)

January 1, 2020— To record investment purchase

Investment in HTM Securities—Timberlake Bonds	102,000	
Cash		102,000

c. **Effective Interest Schedule and Interest Revenue Recognition**
Utilizing the effective interest method, interest revenue each period is measured by multiplying the market rate by the amortized cost of the bonds at the beginning of the period. For example, in the first year, interest revenue of $6,545 is equal to 6.4172% multiplied by $102,000. Interest revenue decreases each period because the interest revenue is a function of the decreasing bond amortized cost.

Effective Interest Method—Premium

Date	Cash (Stated Interest)[a]	Interest Revenue (Market Interest)[b]	Premium Amortization[c]	Bond Investment, net (Amortized Cost)[d]
Jan. 1, 2020. . .				$102,000
Dec. 31, 2020. . .	$ 7,000	$ 6,545	$ 455	101,545
Dec. 31, 2021. . .	7,000	6,516	484	101,061
Dec. 31, 2022. . .	7,000	6,485	515	100,546
Dec. 31, 2023. . .	7,000	6,454*	546*	100,000
	$28,000	$26,000	$2,000	

*Rounded
[a] Bond face value × Stated rate
[b] Bond amortized cost, beginning of year × Market rate
[c] Stated interest − Market interest
[d] Bond amortized cost, beginning of year − Premium amortization

The entry to record interest revenue in 2020 follows. Because we have chosen not to use a separate account for the premium, amortization of the premium results in a direct reduction to the investment account of $455.

Assets = Liabilities + Equity
+7,000 +6,545
−455

Cash: 7,000 (debit) | 102,000 (credit)
Invest—HTM: 102,000 (debit) | 455 (credit)
Interest Rev: 6,545 (credit)

December 31, 2020—To record receipt of interest and amortization of premium

Cash	7,000	
Investment in HTM Securities—Timberlake Bonds		455
Interest Revenue.		6,545

At December 31, 2020, the amortized cost of the bond investment is $101,545 or $102,000 − $455.

d. **Financial Statement Presentation of Bond Investment**
The 2020 financial statements for Montana would include the following amounts.

Balance Sheet excerpt December 31, 2020	
Assets	
Investment in HTM securities	$101,545

Income Statement excerpt For Year Ended December 31, 2020	
Other revenues and gains	
Interest revenue	$6,545

continued

continued from previous page

e. **Bond Retirement at Maturity**

The amortized cost of Timberlake Corporation bonds has decreased $2,000 by the end of the four years; thus the amortized cost of the investment is its face value of $100,000 at December 31, 2023. On this date, Montana receives the face value of the bonds and Timberlake retires the bonds.

December 31, 2023—To derecognize bond investment

Cash	100,000	
Investment in HTM Securities—Timberlake Bonds		100,000

Assets	=	Liabilities	+	Equity
+100,000				
−100,000				

Cash (Dr.)	Cash (Cr.)	Invest—HTM (Dr.)	Invest—HTM (Cr.)
7,000	102,000	102,000	455
7,000			484
7,000			515
7,000			546
100,000			100,000
		0	

Accounting for HTM Investment—Straight-Line Interest Method

Although the effective interest method for amortizing discounts (and premiums) is the preferred method, there is an alternative method. The **straight-line interest method** can be used if the results are not materially different from the results using the effective interest method. Authoritative support follows.

835-30-55-2 Generally accepted accounting principles (GAAP) require use of the interest method. There is no basis for using an alternative to the interest method except if the results of alternative methods do not differ materially from those obtained by using the interest method. Therefore, methods other than the interest method, such as . . . straight-line interest methods shall not be used if their results materially differ from the interest method.

What would the amortization of the Timberlake bonds look like if instead the bonds were amortized using the straight-line interest method? Instead of computing the discount (premium) amortization as a function of the carrying value of the bonds, the discount (premium) is amortized evenly over the bond life. In other words, the total discount (premium) is divided and amortized equally over the term of the bonds. See **Demo 14-1D** for an illustration of straight-line amortization of a discount and **Demo 14-1E** for the illustration of straight-line amortization of a premium.

HTM Investment Purchased at a Discount (Straight-Line Interest) LO14-1 Demo 14-1D

Demo MBC

Referring to the Timberlake bonds in **Demo 14-1B**, prepare an amortization schedule using the straight-line interest method and record the December 31, 2020, entry for interest earned and discount amortized.

Solution

The following amortization schedule illustrates how the amortization of the bond discount impacts interest revenue recognition over the life of the bonds. For each period, cash interest ($100,000 x 7%) plus the discount amortization ($2,000 ÷ 4) equals interest revenue of $7,500.

Straight-Line Method—Discount

Date	Cash (Stated Interest)[a]	Interest Revenue (Market Interest)[b]	Discount Amortization[c]	Bond Investment, net (Amortized Cost)[d]
Jan. 1, 2020. . .				$ 98,000
Dec. 31, 2020. . .	$ 7,000	$ 7,500	$ 500	98,500
Dec. 31, 2021. . .	7,000	7,500	500	99,000
Dec. 31, 2022. . .	7,000	7,500	500	99,500
Dec. 31, 2023. . .	7,000	7,500	500	100,000
	$28,000	$30,000	$2,000	

[a] Bond face value × Stated rate
[b] Stated interest + Discount amortization
[c] Total discount/Number of periods
[d] Bond amortized cost, beginning of year + Discount amortization

The following entry records the receipt of interest and discount amortization on December 31, 2020. Montana would record this same entry each period for four years, at which time, the discount would be fully amortized.

continued

continued from previous page

Assets	=	Liabilities	+	Equity
+7,000				+7,500
+500				

Cash		Invest—HTM		Interest Rev	
7,000		98,000			7,500
7,000		500			7,500
7,000		500			7,500
7,000		500			7,500
		500			

December 31, 2020—To record receipt of interest and amortization of discount

Cash	7,000	
Investment in HTM Securities—Timberlake Bonds	500	
Interest Revenue.		7,500

Demo 14-1E LO14-1 HTM Investment Purchased at a Premium (Straight-Line Interest)

Demo MBC

Referring to the Timberlake bonds in **Demo 14-1C**, prepare an amortization schedule using the straight-line interest method and record the entry for interest earned and premium amortized on December 31, 2020.

Solution

The amortization schedule under the straight-line interest method is prepared as follows. For each period, cash interest ($100,000 × 7%) minus the premium amortization ($2,000 ÷ 4) equals interest revenue of $6,500.

Straight-Line Method—Premium

Date	Cash (Stated Interest)[a]	Interest Revenue (Market Interest)[b]	Premium Amortization[c]	Bond Investment, net (Amortized Cost)[d]
Jan. 1, 2020. . .				$102,000
Dec. 31, 2020. . .	$ 7,000	$ 6,500	$ 500	101,500
Dec. 31, 2021. . .	7,000	6,500	500	101,000
Dec. 31, 2022. . .	7,000	6,500	500	100,500
Dec. 31, 2023. . .	7,000	6,500	500	100,000
	$28,000	$26,000	$2,000	

[a] Bond face value × Stated rate
[b] Stated interest − Premium amortization
[c] Total premium/Number of periods
[d] Bond amortized cost, beginning of year − Premium amortization

The following entry records the receipt of interest and premium amortization on December 31, 2020. Montana would record the same entry each period for four years, at which time, the premium would be fully amortized.

Assets	=	Liabilities	+	Equity
+7,000				+6,500
−500				

Cash		Invest—HTM		Interest Rev	
7,000		Bal. 102,000	500		6,500
7,000			500		6,500
7,000			500		6,500
7,000			500		6,500

December 31, 2020—To record receipt of interest and amortization of premium

Cash	7,000	
Investment in HTM Securities—Timberlake Bonds		500
Interest Revenue.		6,500

Interest Revenue: Straight-line vs. Effective Interest Method

As shown in the demos of this section, how interest revenue is recognized over a bond term varies depending on (1) whether a company accounts for the investment using the effective interest method or the straight-line interest method and (2) whether the bond was acquired at a premium or a discount. The graphs to the right illustrate how interest revenue is recognized at a constant rate under the straight-line interest method. Under the effective interest method however, interest revenue increases each period for a bond acquired at a discount and decreases each period for a bond acquired at a premium due to the corresponding changes in the amortized cost of the bond investments (a factor in the calculation).

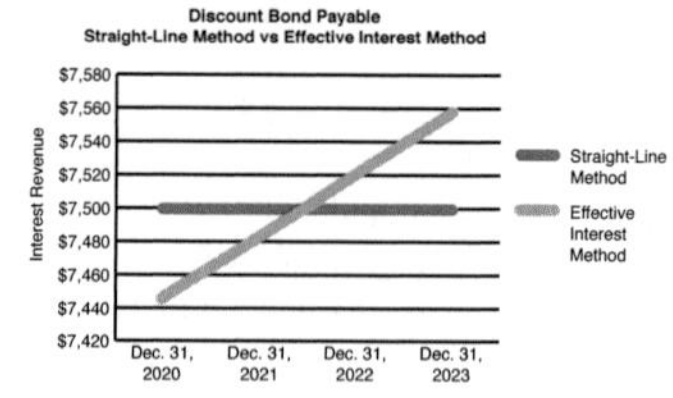

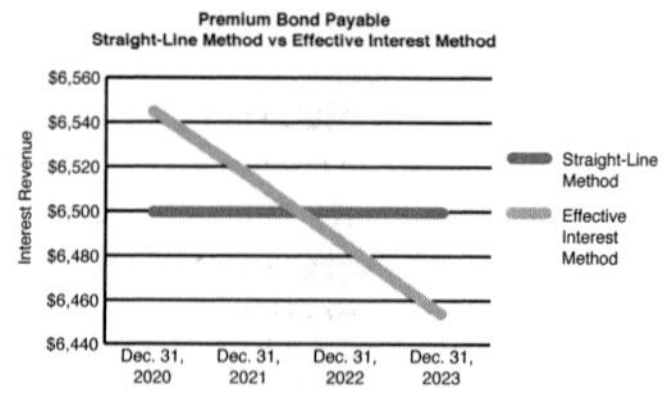

CHIPOTLE

Real World—HELD-TO-MATURITY SECURITIES

Chipotle Mexican Grill, Inc. described its investments in held-to-maturity securities in a recent report on Form 10-K.

Note 1 (excerpt): Investments classified as trading securities are carried at fair value with any unrealized gain or loss being recorded in the consolidated statement of income. Investments classified as available-for-sale are carried at fair value with unrealized gains and losses, net of tax, included as a component of other comprehensive income (loss) on the statement of comprehensive income. Held-to-maturity securities are carried at amortized cost. Impairment charges on investments are recognized in interest and other income, net on the consolidated statement of income when management believes the decline in the fair value of the investment is other-than-temporary.

CHIPOTLE MEXICAN GRILL, INC. [CMG]

Accounting for HTM Debt Investments at Amortized Cost LO14-1 REVIEW 14-1

On January 2, 2020, New Apple Inc. purchased for cash, six, $10,000 bonds of Mack Corporation. The bonds pay 6% cash interest, payable on an annual basis each December 31, and mature on December 31, 2027. The bonds are classified as held-to-maturity securities. The annual reporting period ends December 31. Complete the following table for the five separate scenarios.

Review MBC

	(1) Bonds Yield 6%	(2) Bonds Yield 8% (Account for using the effective interest method)	(3) Bonds Yield 8% (Account for using the straight-line interest method)	(4) Bonds Yield 5% (Account for using the effective interest method)	(5) Bonds Yield 5% (Account for using the straight-line interest method)
Indicate whether bonds will sell at par, discount, or premium					
Purchase price of HTM investment					
Interest revenue for 2020					
Interest revenue for 2021					

More Practice: 14-16, 14-17, 14-39, 14-41, 14-42, 14-43

Solution on p. 14-83.

Account for debt securities measured at FV-NI LO 14-2

Certain debt investments are measured at fair value with adjustments reflected in net income (**FV-NI**). This means that instead of recognizing investments at amortized cost, the amortized cost amount is adjusted to fair value. The resulting unrealized gain or loss is recognized in net income. The FV-NI method applies to (1) trading securities (**Demo 14-2A**) and (2) debt investments accounted for using the fair value option (**Demo 14-2B**).

TS Measured at FV-NI and Investments under Fair Value Option Election
- Recognize interest earned in net income
- Recognize adjustment to fair value (unrealized gain or loss) in net income

LO 14-2 Overview

Trading Securities

Debt securities that are bought and held primarily to be sold in the near term are classified as **trading securities (TS)**. Trading generally reflects active and frequent buying and selling with the objective of generating profits on short-term changes in price. Trading securities are generally classified as current assets on a classified balance sheet.

ASC Glossary Trading Securities: Securities that are bought and held principally for the purpose of selling them in the near term and therefore held for only a short period of time. Trading generally reflects active and frequent buying and selling, and trading securities are generally used with the objective of generating profits on short-term differences in price.

Methods to Account for Debt Securities		
Amortized Cost LO 14-1	FV-NI LO 14-2	FV-OCI LO 14-3

Trading securities are adjusted to fair value through the income statement. The total **unrealized holding gain (or loss)** is the difference between the amortized cost and fair value of an investment—*unrealized* because the asset has not been sold. The change in the unrealized gain or loss for the period is included in the determination of earnings in the income statement and is classified as other income. Amortized cost is equal to the cost of the bond if the bond is purchased at par. If the bond is purchased at a discount (premium), the discount (premium) is amortized as an adjustment to interest revenue as illustrated in LO 14-1. This means that the amortized cost of the bond changes over time.

320-10-35-1 Investments in debt securities that are classified as trading shall be measured subsequently at fair value in the statement of financial position. Unrealized holding gains and losses for trading securities shall be included in earnings.

320-10-35-4 Dividend and interest income, including amortization of the premium and discount arising at acquisition, for all three categories of investments in debt securities shall be included in earnings.

In computing changes in the fair value of trading securities, more than one security may be analyzed as part of an **investment portfolio**. By adjusting trading securities to fair value instead of waiting until the asset is sold, financial statement users have more timely information to assess the performance of the company's investment strategies. The fair value of an investment changes—sometimes multiple times in a given day. Companies may adjust the investment to fair value daily or simply at reporting dates. For example, a company that reports financial statements quarterly may only adjust investments to fair value at the end of each quarter. Regardless of the company's procedure to adjust its trading portfolio to fair value, all TS investments must be reflected at fair value at the reporting date and any resulting unrealized gains or losses are recognized in net income. For any TS sold during the period, the net effect on the income statement for the period reflects any change in fair value from the last report date to the date of sale.

320-10-40-1 With respect to trading securities, because all changes in a trading security's fair value are reported in earnings as they occur, the sale of a trading security does not necessarily give rise to a gain or loss. Generally, a debit to cash (or trade date receivable) is recorded for the sales proceeds, and a credit is recorded to remove the security at its fair value (or sales price). . . Some adjustment to this procedure will be necessary for entities that have not yet recorded the security's change in fair value up to the point of sale (perhaps because fair value changes are recorded at the end of each day).

Instead of directly adjusting the investment account to fair value, an investor may create a valuation account, the **Fair Value Adjustment (FVA)** account. *This balance sheet account is debited for holding gains and credited for holding losses.* The carrying value of TS is the net of its amortized cost and the Fair Value Adjustment account. A debit balance in the FVA account is added to the investment account whereas a credit in the FVA account is subtracted from the investment account. The Fair Value Adjustment account enables the accounting system to maintain a record of the amortized cost of the investment and the net amount of increase or decrease in carrying value recognized over time. **In this chapter, we assume the use of the Fair Value Adjustment account in all examples and end of chapter assignments.**

EXPANDING YOUR KNOWLEDGE — **Noncash Consideration**

When noncash consideration (property or services) is given for an investment, the cost assigned to the securities should be measured by the fair value of the consideration given or the fair value of the securities received, whichever can be more reliably determined.

Demo 14-2A **LO14-2** **Trading Security Investment**

Demo MBC

On November 1, 2020, Montana Inc. purchased for par, $30,000 of Upper Armour Co. 8% bonds that mature on June 30, 2025. Cash interest is paid semiannually on June 30 and December 31. Montana classifies the investment as trading securities (TS).

Required

a. Record the entry to purchase TS on November 1, 2020.
b. Record the receipt of cash interest on December 31, 2020.
c. Record the entry to adjust the TS to fair value assuming that the fair value of the Upper Armour bonds is $28,000 on December 31, 2020.
d. Report the investment in bonds on the balance sheet on December 31, 2020, and the effects on the 2020 income statement.

continued

continued from previous page

e. Assume that the investment in TS is sold on January 4, 2021, for $28,500. Ignoring interest revenue earned during the first four days of January for simplicity, record the sale under two treatments: ① Compute the gain or loss on sale as the difference between the cash received and the amortized cost of the investment; in this case, do not adjust the Fair Value Adjustment account. ② Adjust the investment to fair value at the date of sale using FV-NI; then, record the sale, eliminating the associated Fair Value Adjustment account balance.

f. Record the entry to adjust the Fair Value Adjustment account (if applicable) on December 31, 2021, assuming no additional investments in 2021.

Solution

a. **Purchase of Bond Investment Between Interest Payment Dates**

Because the bonds were purchased outside of an interest payment date, Montana would pay Upper Armour accrued interest from the last interest payment date to the purchase date. Montana would need to pay four months of interest up front because on December 31, 2020, Montana will automatically *receive the full six months of interest* totaling $1,200. Because Montana would have only *earned two months of interest* from November 1, 2020, to December 31, 2020, Montana must pay Upper Armour four months of interest at the date of purchase. The journal entry for Montana at the date of purchase is as follows.

November 1, 2020—To record investment purchase

Investment in TS—Upper Armour Bonds	30,000	
Interest Receivable ($30,000 × 0.08 × 4/12)	800	
Cash		30,800

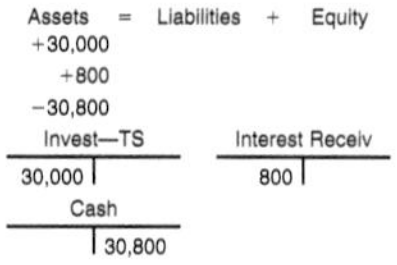

b. **Interest Revenue**

On December 31, 2020, Montana would record the full six months of interest received as cash, reverse the balance of interest receivable, and record two months of interest revenue. The journal entry is as follows.

December 31, 2020—To record receipt of interest

Cash ($30,000 × 0.08 × 6/12)	1,200	
Interest Receivable		800
Interest Revenue ($30,000 × 0.08 × 2/12)		400

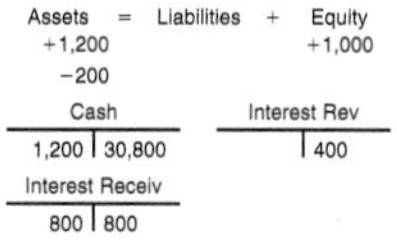

c. **Adjustment of Bond Investment to Fair Value**

At each balance sheet date, all securities classified as TS are to be reported at fair value. The unrealized holding loss on December 31, 2020, is measured and recorded as follows.

TS Investment	Amortized Cost	Fair Value Year-End	Unrealized Holding Gain (Loss)
Upper Armour bonds	$30,000	$28,000	$(2,000)
Existing balance in Fair Value Adjustment			0
Increase (decrease) to Fair Value Adjustment			$(2,000)

December 31, 2020—To adjust investment to fair value

Unrealized Gain or Loss—Income	2,000	
Fair Value Adjustment—TS		2,000

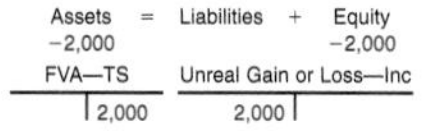

With this entry, the carrying value of TS has been adjusted to fair value and the net change, an unrealized loss of $2,000, has been recorded. For TS, the net unrealized holding gain (or loss) is treated as a component of other income on the income statement.

d. **Financial Statement Presentation of Bond Investment**

On the December 31, 2020, balance sheet and the 2020 income statement, Montana would report the following.

Balance Sheet excerpt December 31, 2020	
Current assets	
Investment in trading securities	$28,000

Income Statement excerpt For Year Ended December 31, 2020	
Other revenues and gains	
Interest revenue	$1,200
Other expenses and losses	
Unrealized holding loss on trading securities	(2,000)

continued

continued from previous page

Select Accounting Treatment

① Adjust FVA at Year-End

e. Sale of Bond Investment

The company recognizes a loss as the difference between cash received of $28,500 and the amortized cost of bonds of $30,000.

January 4, 2021—To record sale of bond investment

Cash	28,500	
Loss on Sale of Investment	1,500	
Investment in TS—Upper Armour Bonds		30,000

Cash		Invest—TS		Loss on Sale of Invest	
1,200	30,800	30,000	30,000	1,500	
28,500					

f. Adjustment of Fair Value Adjustment Account

At year-end, because Montana held no investments in TS, the balance in the Fair Value Adjustment account is derecognized.

Required FVA ending account balance	$ 0
Less existing FVA account balance	(2,000)
Increase to FVA account	$2,000

December 31, 2021—To eliminate fair value adjustment balance

Fair Value Adjustment—TS	2,000	
Unrealized Gain or Loss—Income		2,000

FVA—TS		Unreal Gain or Loss—Inc	
2,000	2,000	2,000	2,000

The loss on sale of $1,500 is recognized in the financial statements over the ownership period of the TS.

Loss in 2020 income statement	$(2,000)
Gain in 2021 income statement ($2,000 − $1,500)	500
Loss recognized over ownership period	$(1,500)

② Adjust FVA at Sale and Year-End

e. Sale of Bond Investment

At the sale date, the company first adjusts the investment to fair value (FV-NI).

Required FVA ending account balance*	$(1,500)
Less existing FVA account balance	(2,000)
Increase to FVA account	$ 500

*$28,500 fair value − $30,000 amortized cost.

January 4, 2021—To adjust investment to fair value

Fair Value Adjustment—TS	500	
Unrealized Gain or Loss—Income		500

FVA—TS		Unreal Gain or Loss—Inc	
500	2,000	2,000	500

Next, the company records the sale, eliminating the related Fair Value Adjustment credit balance of $1,500. No gain or loss is recorded upon the sale because the investment was adjusted to fair value in the prior entry. This means net income already reflects any difference between fair value and the amortized cost of bonds.

January 4, 2021—To record sale of bond investment

Cash	28,500	
Fair Value Adjustment—TS	1,500	
Investment in TS—Upper Armour Bonds		30,000

Cash		FVA—TS		Invest—TS	
1,200	30,800	500	2,000	30,000	30,000
28,500		1,500			

f. Adjustment of Fair Value Adjustment Account

No adjustment is required to the Fair Value Adjustment account (currently at a zero balance) because the company held no investments in TS at year-end.

The loss on sale of $1,500 is recognized in the financial statements over the ownership period of the TS.

Loss in 2020 income statement	$(2,000)
Gain in 2021 income statement	500
Loss recognized over ownership period	$(1,500)

GENERAL MOTORS

Real World—TRADING SECURITIES

General Motors Company included its trading securities in the category of marketable securities in the current asset section of its balance sheet as indicated by the following note in its annual report on Form 10-K.

Note 2 (excerpt) Marketable Securities—We classify marketable securities as available-for-sale or trading. Various factors, including turnover of holdings and investment guidelines, are considered in determining the classification of securities. Available-for-sale securities are recorded at fair value with unrealized gains and losses recorded net of related income taxes in Accumulated other comprehensive loss until realized. Trading securities are recorded at fair value with changes in fair value recorded in Interest income and other non-operating income, net. We determine realized gains and losses for all securities using the specific identification method.

GENERAL MOTORS [GM]

Fair Value Option—Debt Securities

Under the fair value option, an investment is adjusted to fair value through net income each reporting period (**FV-NI**). The fair value option is an election that may be applied to debt securities that would otherwise be recognized at amortized cost or where unrealized gains or losses are reflected in OCI (the category of debt investments reviewed in the next section). This election must be selected on the purchase date of the asset, applied to each investment individually, and the decision is generally irrevocable. The company must include a disclosure on the fair value option election (825-10-50-28).

Fair Value Option Accounting—Debt Security LO14-2 Demo 14-2B

Demo MBC

On July 1, 2020, Montana Inc. purchased at par, $30,000 of Upper Armour Co. 8% bonds that mature on June 30, 2025. Montana classifies the investment as HTM. However, on July 1, 2020, Montana chooses to account for the HTM investment using the fair value option. If the fair value of the Upper Armour bonds is $31,200 on December 31, 2020, record the year-end adjusting entry for Montana. (Assume that interest revenue has been recorded in 2020.)

Solution

December 31, 2020— To adjust investment to fair value

Fair Value Adjustment—Fair Value Option ($31,200 − $30,000)	1,200	
Unrealized Gain or Loss—Income		1,200

Assets	=	Liabilities	+	Equity
+1,200				+1,200
FVA—Fair Val Opt 1,200				Unreal Gain or Loss—Inc 1,200

Accounting for TS Debt Investment at FV-NI LO14-2 REVIEW 14-2

Review MBC

On September 30, 2020, New Apple Inc. purchased $20,000 of Mack Corp. bonds. These bonds pay 5% cash interest annually on September 30 and mature September 30, 2030. The investment is classified as a TS investment and the company uses the effective interest method to amortize any bond discount or premium. The market rate on the bonds is 6%.

a. Do Mack Corp. bonds sell at a discount or premium? Determine the selling price of the bonds.

b. Record the entry for the purchase of the bonds by New Apple Inc.

c. Record the entry on December 31, 2020, to record interest revenue.

d. Record the entry on December 31, 2020, to adjust the investment to fair value, determined to be $21,000 on December 31, 2020.

e. Record the entry to sell the bonds on January 1, 2021, for $21,000, plus accrued interest under two treatments: ① Compute the gain or loss on sale as the difference between the cash received and the amortized cost of the investment; in this case, do not adjust the Fair Value Adjustment account. Instead, adjust the Fair Value Adjustment account at December 31, 2021. ② Adjust the investment to fair value at the date of sale using FV-NI; then, record the sale, eliminating the associated Fair Value Adjustment account balance.

f. How would your answers to parts *a* to *e* change if instead, the bond investment were classified as an HTM security and the company elected to account for the bond using the fair value option on the acquisition date?

More Practice: 14-18, 14-19, 14-20, 14-45, 14-46, 14-47, 14-48, 14-49

Solution on p. 14-83.

LO 14-3 Account for debt securities measured at FV-OCI

LO 14-3 Overview

AFS Securities measured at FV-OCI
- Recognize interest earned in net income
- Recognize adjustment to fair value (unrealized gain or loss) in OCI
- Recognize realized gain or loss from a sale in net income

Certain debt investments are measured at fair value with adjustments reflected in other comprehensive income (**FV-OCI**). This means that instead of recognizing investments at amortized cost, the amortized cost amount is adjusted to fair value. The resulting unrealized gain or loss is recognized in other comprehensive income. The FV-OCI method applies to available-for-sale securities.

Available-for-Sale Securities

Debt investments that are *not* classified as trading securities or held-to-maturity securities are classified as **available–for-sale securities (AFS)**. The AFS category includes debt securities expected to be held for an unspecified period of time, such as those that might be sold to meet liquidity needs or to implement a company's risk management program. AFS investments are classified as short-term or long-term depending upon the intention and ability of the investor to sell the investment within the next year (or operating cycle, if longer).

Methods to Account for Debt Securities		
Amortized Cost LO 14-1	FV-NI LO 14-2	FV-OCI LO 14-3

ASC Glossary Available-for-Sale Securities: Investments not classified as either trading securities or as held-to-maturity securities.

Unlike trading securities, subsequent adjustments to fair value affect OCI (other comprehensive income) rather than net income as shown in **Demo 14-3A** and **14-3B**. Recall from Chapter 3 that comprehensive income includes all changes in equity during a period from transactions and other events and circumstances from nonowner sources, including unrealized holding gains and losses on available-for-sale securities. Comprehensive income consists of net income and OCI. At the end of each reporting period, other comprehensive income is closed to accumulated OCI and is reported in the stockholders' equity statement. Likewise, net income is closed to retained earnings and is reported in the stockholders' equity statement.

320-10-35-1 Available-for-sale securities. Investments in debt securities that are classified as available for sale shall be measured subsequently at fair value in the statement of financial position. Unrealized holding gains and losses for available-for-sale securities (including those classified as current assets) shall be excluded from earnings and reported in other comprehensive income until realized except [as indicated for securities designated as being hedged in a fair value hedge].

Justification for the different accounting treatment of unrealized holding gains or losses arising from trading securities and available-for-sale securities centers on the different purposes of the investments. Since the TS investments are actively managed and expected to be bought and sold continually, the inclusion of unrealized gains or losses in income reflects the economic consequences of TS investments in a timely manner. However, investments in AFS investments are often made for purposes other than profiting from increases in security prices, such as being part of a risk management strategy. The AFS investments and the liabilities of the investor interact to reduce the exposure of the investor to interest rate risk. Including in earnings only the unrealized gain or loss on the investment and not that on the related liabilities may result in misleading information in the financial statements about the impact of economic events on the overall financial condition of the company. Therefore, to avoid volatility to earnings, the gain or loss is instead included in AOCI, a separate component of stockholders' equity.

Only after the sale of an AFS investment is the change in fair value reflected in the income statement. At the time of sale of AFS securities, the company records a realized gain or loss included in other income in the income statement. The realized gain or loss is the difference between the cash received upon sale of the security and the amortized cost of the investment. Also, the corresponding fair value adjustment in Accumulated OCI is eliminated. In this situation, disclosure of the amount reclassified out of accumulated other comprehensive income and into net income is required for financial reporting. The amount of the reclassification adjustment from AOCI to net income must equal the realized gain or loss on the sale.

320-10-50-9d For each period for which the results of operations are presented, an entity shall disclose . . . The amount of the net unrealized holding gain or loss on available-for-sale securities for the period that has been included in accumulated other comprehensive income and the amount of gains and losses reclassified out of accumulated other comprehensive income into earnings for the period.

However, if the investment is considered impaired, a loss may need to be recorded as discussed in LO 14-6.

Available-for-Sale Securities—Bonds LO14-3 Demo 14-3A

Demo MBC

On July 1, 2020, Montana Inc. purchased for par, $30,000 of Upper Armour Co. 8% bonds that mature on June 30, 2025. Cash interest is paid semiannually on June 30 and December 31. Montana classifies the investment as AFS.

Required

a. Record the entry to purchase the investment on July 1, 2020.
b. Record the receipt of cash interest on December 31, 2020.
c. Record the entry to adjust AFS securities to fair value assuming that the fair value of the Upper Armour bonds is $28,000 on December 31, 2020.
d. Report the investment in AFS securities in the 2020 income statement, statement of comprehensive income, and the December 31, 2020, balance sheet for Montana.
e. Assume that Montana made no changes to the current holdings of AFS securities in 2021. Record the entry to adjust the AFS securities to fair value assuming that the fair value of the Upper Armour bonds is $31,000 on December 31, 2021.
f. Record the sale of AFS securities on January 2, 2022, for $31,800. Ignoring interest revenue earned during the first two days of January for simplicity, record the sale under two treatments: ① Compute the gain or loss on sale as the difference between the cash received and the amortized cost of the investment; in this case, do not adjust the Fair Value Adjustment account. ② Adjust the investment to fair value at the date of sale using FV-OCI; then, record the sale, including the reclassification of holding gains or losses in AOCI to net income and the elimination of the associated Fair Value Adjustment account balance.
g. Record the entry to adjust the Fair Value Adjustment account if applicable on December 31, 2022, assuming no additional investments in AFS securities in 2022.

Solutions

a. **Purchase of Bond Investment**

The entry to record the purchase of the AFS investment by Montana increases the Investment account by $30,000.

July 1, 2020—To record investment purchase

Investment in AFS Securities—Upper Armour Bonds	30,000	
Cash		30,000

Assets = Liabilities + Equity
+30,000
−30,000

Invest—AFS		Cash	
30,000			30,000

b. **Interest Revenue**

Upper Armour pays cash interest on December 31, 2020. As a result, Montana would record the following journal entry.

December 31, 2020—To record receipt of interest

Cash ($30,000 × 0.08 × 6/12)	1,200	
Interest Revenue.		1,200

Assets = Liabilities + Equity
+1,200 +1,200

Cash		Interest Rev	
1,200	30,000		1,200

continued

continued from previous page

c. **Adjustment of Bond Investment to Fair Value**
At each balance sheet date, all securities classified as AFS are to be reported at fair value. The difference between fair value ($28,000) and the amortized cost ($30,000) is recorded in a Fair Value Adjustment account and the unrealized holding loss is included in other comprehensive income (OCI) through the following journal entry.

Assets = Liabilities + Equity
−2,000 −2,000
FVA—AFS: | 2,000
Unreal Gain or Loss—OCI: 2,000 |

December 31, 2020—To adjust investment to fair value

Unrealized Gain or Loss—OCI	2,000	
Fair Value Adjustment—AFS ($30,000 − $28,000).		2,000

d. **Financial Statement Presentation of Bond Investment**
Montana would report the following on its December 31, 2020, balance sheet and 2020 statement of comprehensive income.

Balance Sheet excerpt December 31, 2020	
Assets	
Investment in available-for-sale securities	$28,000
Stockholders' equity	
Accumulated other comprehensive income (loss)	(2,000)

Income Statement excerpt For Year Ended December 31, 2020	
Other revenues and gains	
Interest revenue	$1,200

Statement of Comprehensive Income excerpt For Year Ended December 31, 2020	
Net income	$ ####
Other comprehensive income	
Unrealized holding loss on available-for-sale securities . . .	(2,000)
Comprehensive income	$ ####

e. **Adjustment of Bond Investment to Fair Value—2021**
The adjustment to fair value for AFS securities in 2021 is calculated as follows.

AFS Investment	Amortized Cost	Fair Value Year-End	Unrealized Holding Gain (Loss)
Upper Armour bonds	$30,000	$31,000	$ 1,000
Existing balance in Fair Value Adjustment			(2,000)
Increase (decrease) to Fair Value Adjustment			$ 3,000

Based on this summary, Montana would need to make the following entry to adjust its AFS investment to fair value.

Assets = Liabilities + Equity
+1,000 +1,000
FVA—AFS: 3,000 | 2,000
Unreal Gain or Loss—OCI: 2,000 | 3,000

December 31, 2021—To adjust investment to fair value

Fair Value Adjustment—AFS	3,000	
Unrealized Gain or Loss—OCI		3,000

continued

continued from previous page

Select Accounting Treatment

① Adjust FVA at Year-End

f. Sale of Bond Investment

The company recognizes a gain as the difference between cash received of $31,800 and the amortized cost of bonds of $30,000.

January 2, 2022—To record sale of bond investment

Cash	31,800	
Investment in AFS—Upper Armour Bonds		30,000
Loss on Sale of Investment		1,800

Account	Debit	Credit
Cash	31,800	30,800
Invest—AFS	30,000	30,000
Gain on Sale of Invest		1,800

g. Adjustment of Fair Value Adjustment Account

At year-end, because Montana held no investments in AFS securities, the balance in the Fair Value Adjustment account is derecognized.

Required FVA ending account balance	$ 0
Less existing FVA account balance	1,000
Decrease to FVA account	$(1,000)

December 31, 2022—To eliminate fair value adjustment balance

Unrealized Gain or Loss—OCI	1,000	
Fair Value Adjustment—AFS		1,000

Account	Debit	Credit
FVA—AFS	3,000	2,000 1,000
Unreal Gain or Loss—OCI	2,000 1,000	3,000

② Adjust FVA at Sale and Year-End

f. Sale of Bond Investment

At the sale date, the company first adjusts the investment to fair value (FV-NI).

Required FVA ending account balance*	$1,800
Less existing FVA account balance	1,000
Increase to FVA account	$ 800

*$31,800 fair value – $30,000 amortized cost.

January 2, 2022—To adjust investment to fair value

Fair Value Adjustment—AFS	800	
Unrealized Gain or Loss—OCI		800

Account	Debit	Credit
FVA—AFS	3,000 800	2,000
Unreal Gain or Loss—OCI	2,000	3,000 800

Next, the company records the loss on sale of $200 ($31,800 cash proceeds – $30,000 amortized cost) and reclassifies the loss of $1,800 from AOCI to net income, as required for an AFS investment.

January 2, 2022—To record sale of bond investment

Cash	31,800	
Unrealized Gain or Loss—OCI	1,800	
Investment in AFS—Upper Armour Bonds		30,000
Gain on Sale of Investment		1,800
Fair Value Adjustment—AFS		1,800

Account	Debit	Credit
Cash	31,800	30,000
Invest—AFS	30,000	30,000
Gain on Sale of Invest		1,800
FVA—AFS	3,000 800	2,000 1,800
Unreal Gain or Loss—OCI	2,000 1,800	3,000 800

g. Adjustment of Fair Value Adjustment Account

No adjustment is required to the Fair Value Adjustment account (currently at a zero balance) because the company held no investments in AFS securities at year-end.

continued

continued from previous page

While the gain on sale of $1,800 is fully recognized in net income in 2022, there is no cumulative effect on Accumulated OCI as shown in the following summary.

Loss recognized in 2020 OCI	$(2,000)
Gain recognized in 2021 OCI	3,000
Loss recognized in 2021 OCI	(1,000)*
Net effect in accumulated OCI	$ 0

*Equal to the adjustment of AFS securities to fair value in 2022 of $800 ($31,800 − $31,000) less reclassification adjustment to net income of $1,800 ($31,800 − $30,000). The reclassification adjustment equals the realized gain of $1,800.

While the gain on sale of $1,800 is fully recognized in net income in 2022, there is no cumulative effect on Accumulated OCI as shown in the following summary.

Loss recognized in 2020 OCI	$(2,000)
Gain recognized in 2021 OCI	3,000
Gain recognized in 2022 OCI	800
Reclassification adjustment to 2022 NI	(1,800)
Net effect in accumulated OCI	$ 0

PEPSI

Real World—AVAILABLE-FOR-SALE SECURITIES

PEPSICO [PEP]

An excerpt from a **PepsiCo, Inc.**'s recent annual report on Form 10-K described the treatment of unrealized gains and losses on available-for-sale securities.

> **Note 10 (excerpt): Financial Instruments** Investments in debt and marketable equity securities, other than investments accounted for under the equity method, are classified as available-for-sale. All highly liquid investments with original maturities of three months or less are classified as cash equivalents. Our investments in available-for-sale securities are reported at fair value. Unrealized gains and losses related to changes in the fair value of available-for-sale securities are recognized in accumulated other comprehensive loss within common shareholders' equity. Unrealized gains and losses on our investments in debt securities as of December 30, 2017 were not material.

Demo 14-3B LO14-3 Portfolio of Available-for-Sale Securities—Bonds

Demo MBC

Let's assume Montana Inc. had the following AFS portfolio consisting of investments in two bonds: Upper Armour bonds and Athletic Goods Inc. bonds.

The December 31, 2021, summary of the available-for-sale securities includes the following.

AFS Investment	Amortized Cost	Fair Value Year-End	Unrealized Holding Gain (Loss)
Upper Armour bonds	$ 30,000	$ 29,000	$ (1,000)
Athletic Goods bonds	100,500	120,000	19,500
	$130,500	$149,000	$18,500*

* Amount represents the December 31, 2021, balance in AOCI and FVA.

The Upper Armour bonds are sold on January 5, 2022, for $31,000. The remaining AFS investment in Athletic Goods bonds (originally purchased at par value) had a fair value of $116,500 on December 31, 2022. Besides the sale of the Upper Armour bonds on January 5, 2022, no other AFS transactions took place during the year.

a. Ignoring interest revenue earned during the first five days of January for simplicity, record the sale under two treatments: ① Compute the gain or loss on sale as the difference between the cash received and the amortized cost of the investment; in this case, do not adjust the Fair Value Adjustment account. ② Adjust the investment to fair value at the date of sale using FV-OCI; then, record the sale, including the reclassification of holding gains or losses in AOCI to net income and the elimination of the associated Fair Value Adjustment account balance.

b. Record the entry to adjust the Fair Value Adjustment account (if applicable) on December 31, 2022.

c. Prepare the disclosures required in the financial statements for the year ended December 31, 2022.

continued

continued from previous page

Solution

Select Accounting Treatment

① Adjust FVA at Year-End

a. Sale of Bond Investment

The company recognizes a gain as the difference between the cash received of $31,000 and the amortized cost of bonds of $30,000.

January 5, 2022—To record sale of bond investment

Cash	31,000	
Investment in AFS—Upper Armour Bonds		30,000
Gain on Sale of Investment		1,000

Cash	
31,000	

Invest—AFS	
Bal. 130,500	30,000

Gain on Sale of Invest	
	1,000

b. Adjustment of the Fair Value Adjustment Account

At year-end, Montana adjusts its holding in Athletic Good bonds to fair value.

Required FVA ending account balance*	$16,000
Less existing FVA account balance	18,500
Decrease to FVA account	$ (2,500)

*116,500 fair value – $100,500 amortized cost.

December 31, 2022—To adjust investment to fair value

Unrealized Gain or Loss—OCI	2,500	
Fair Value Adjustment—AFS		2,500

FVA—AFS	
Bal.18,500	2,500

Unreal Gain or Loss—OCI	
2,500	

② Adjust FVA at Sale and Year-End

a. Sale of Bond Investment

At the sale date, the company first adjusts the investment to fair value (FV-OCI).

Required FVA ending account balance*	$1,000
Less existing FVA account balance	(1,000)
Increase to FVA account	$2,000

*$31,000 fair value – $30,000 amortized cost.

January 5, 2022—To adjust investment to fair value

Fair Value Adjustment—AFS	2,000	
Unrealized Gain or Loss—OCI		2,000

FVA—AFS	
Bal. 18,500	
2,000	

Unreal Gain or Loss—OCI	
	2,000

Next, the company records the gain on sale of $1,000 ($31,000 cash proceeds – $30,000 amortized cost) and reclassifies the gain of $1,000 from AOCI to net income, as required for an AFS investment.

January 2, 2022—To record sale of bond investment

Cash	31,000	
Unrealized Gain or Loss—OCI	1,000	
Investment in AFS—Upper Armour Bonds		30,000
Gain on Sale of Investment		1,000
Fair Value Adjustment—AFS		1,000

Cash	
31,000	

Invest—AFS	
Bal. 130,500	30,000

Gain on Sale of Invest	
	1,800

FVA—AFS	
Bal.18,500	1,000
2,000	

Unreal Gain or Loss—OCI	
1,000	2,000

b. Adjustment of the Fair Value Adjustment Account

The company adjusts the Athletic Goods bonds held at year-end to fair value (FV-OCI).

Required FVA ending account balance*	$16,000
Less existing FVA account balance	19,500
Increase to FVA account	$ (3,500)

*$116,500 fair value – $100,500 amortized cost.

December 31, 2022—To adjust investment to fair value

Unrealized Gain or Loss—OCI	3,500	
Fair Value Adjustment—AFS		3,500

FVA—AFS	
Bal.18,500	1,000
2,000	3,500

Unreal Gain or Loss—OCI	
1,000	2,000
3,500	

c. Reclassification Adjustment Disclosure

The following reclassification adjustment disclosure is reported in the notes accompanying the 2022 financial statements. The 2022 loss in OCI of $2,500 is made up of two components: (1) the current year fair value adjustment for the Upper Armour and Athletic Goods bonds and (2) the reclassification adjustment related to the Upper Armour bonds sold during the year.

continued

continued from previous page

Reconciliation of Accumulated Other Comprehensive Income

Accumulated other comprehensive income, January 1, 2022		$18,500
Current period fair value loss for Athletic Goods bonds ($116,500 − $120,000)	$(3,500)	
Current period fair value gain for Upper Armour bonds ($31,000 − $29,000) . .	2,000	
Total change in fair value during the period		(1,500)
Reclassification adjustment for Upper Armour Bonds Sold		(1,000)
Accumulated other comprehensive income, December 31, 2022		$16,000

Real World—FAIR VALUE OF FINANCIAL INSTRUMENTS

APPLE INC. [AAPL]

Certain investment classifications require adjustments of investments to fair value on reporting dates. Financial statement disclosures provide information on how the fair value estimates are determined. This is communicated through disclosure on how the investments fall into the three levels of the fair value hierarchy introduced in Chapter 1. **Apple Inc.** in the following disclosure communicates how cash, cash equivalents, and marketable securities include both Level 1 and Level 2 investments. For example, a Level 1 investment may be publicly traded, while a Level 2 investment may be estimated based upon the quoted market price of a similar investment.

Note 2 – Financial Instruments

Cash, Cash Equivalents and Marketable Securities The following tables show the Company's cash and available-for-sale securities by significant investment category as of September 30, 2017 and September 24, 2016 (in millions):

At September 30, 2017	Adjusted Cost	Unrealized Gains	Unrealized Losses	Fair Value	Cash and Cash Equivalents	Short-Term Marketable Securities	Long-Term Marketable Securities
Cash	$ 7,982	$ —	$ —	$ 7,982	$ 7,982	$ —	$ —
Level 1:							
Money market funds	6,534	—	—	6,534	6,534	—	—
Mutual funds	799	—	(88)	711	—	711	—
Subtotal	7,333	—	(88)	7,245	6,534	711	—
Level 2:							
U.S. Treasury securities	55,254	58	(230)	55,082	865	17,228	36,989
U.S. agency securities	5,162	2	(9)	5,155	1,439	2,057	1,659
Non-U.S. government securities	7,827	210	(37)	8,000	9	123	7,868
Certificates of deposit and time deposits . . .	5,832	—	—	5,832	1,142	3,918	772
Commercial paper	3,640	—	—	3,640	2,146	1,494	—
Corporate securities	152,724	969	(242)	153,451	172	27,591	125,688
Municipal securities	961	4	(1)	964	—	114	850
Mortgage- and asset-backed securities	21,684	35	(175)	21,544	—	656	20,888
Subtotal	253,084	1,278	(694)	253,668	5,773	53,181	194,714
Total	$268,399	$1,278	$(782)	$268,895	$20,289	$53,892	$194,714

REVIEW 14-3 LO14-3 Accounting for AFS Debt Investment at FV-OCI

Review MBC

On January 1, 2020, Big Apple Inc. purchased for cash, eight $10,000 bonds of Mack Corporation to yield 5%. The bonds pay 6% interest, payable on an annual basis each January 1, and mature on January 1, 2025. The bonds are classified as AFS. The annual reporting period for Big Apple Inc. ends December 31. Big Apple uses the effective interest method to amortize discounts and premiums. Provide the entries and reporting for the following transactions for Big Apple.

a. Record the entry for the purchase of AFS securities on January 1, 2020.

b. Record adjusting entries on December 31, 2020. The bonds were quoted on the market on this date at 95.

c. Indicate the effects of this investment on the 2020 income statement, statement of comprehensive income, and its year-end balance sheet.

d. Record the receipt of interest on January 1, 2021.

continued

continued from previous page

e. After the interest payment on January 1, 2021, two of the bonds were sold for $19,000 cash. Record the sale under two treatments: ① Compute the gain or loss on sale as the difference between the cash received and the amortized cost of the investment; in this case, do not adjust the Fair Value Adjustment account. ② Record the sale, including the reclassification of holding gains or losses in AOCI to net income and the elimination of the associated Fair Value Adjustment account balance. (No adjustment to fair value is required before the sale because the fair value has not changed since December 31, 2020.)

f. Record adjusting entries on December 31, 2021. The bonds were quoted on the market on this date at 95.

Review MBC

More Practice: 14-21, 14-22, 14-50, 14-51, 14-52

Solution on p. 14-84.

Review of Accounting for Debt Securities

The following table compares journal entries in accounting for (1) held-to-maturity securities, (2) trading securities, and (3) available-for-sale securities.

Transaction	HTM LO 14-1	TS LO 14-2	AFS LO 14-3
Purchase of debt security	Dr. Investment in HTM Cr. Cash	Dr. Investment in TS Cr. Cash	Dr. Investment in AFS Cr. Cash
Receipt of interest for debt security purchased at par	Dr. Cash Cr. Interest Revenue	Dr. Cash Cr. Interest Revenue	Dr. Cash Cr. Interest Revenue
Receipt of interest for debt security purchased at a discount	Dr. Cash Dr. Investment in HTM Cr. Interest Revenue	Dr. Cash Dr. Investment in TS Cr. Interest Revenue	Dr. Cash Dr. Investment in AFS Cr. Interest Revenue
Receipt of interest for debt security purchased at a premium	Dr. Cash Cr. Investment in HTM Cr. Interest Revenue	Dr. Cash Cr. Investment in TS Cr. Interest Revenue	Dr. Cash Cr. Investment in AFS Cr. Interest Revenue
Adjust debt security to fair value with a gain	No entry	Dr. Fair Value Adjustment Cr. Unrealized Gain or Loss—Income	Dr. Fair Value Adjustment Cr. Unrealized Gain or Loss—OCI
Adjust debt security to fair value with a loss	No entry	Dr. Unrealized Gain or Loss—Income Cr. Fair Value Adjustment	Dr. Unrealized Gain or Loss—OCI Cr. Fair Value Adjustment

Financial Presentation and Disclosure Requirements for Debt Securities

An investment is recognized on the balance sheet as *current* or *noncurrent* depending upon when the investment matures or is expected to be sold. The investment amounts in the categories of HTM, TS, and AFS may be presented separately on the face of the balance sheet or in a note accompanying the financial statements.

320-10-45-1 An entity shall report its investments in available-for-sale securities and trading securities separately from similar assets that are subsequently measured using another measurement attribute on the face of the statement of financial position. To accomplish that, an entity shall do either of the following:

a. Present the aggregate of those fair value and non-fair-value amounts in the same line item and parenthetically disclose the amount of fair value included in the aggregate amount

b. Present two separate line items to display the fair value and non-fair-value carrying amounts.

Investing and Operating Activities

In the statement of cash flows, cash inflows from investing activities include receipts from the sale of debt securities of other entities (other than certain instruments the entity purchased with the intention to trade). Cash outflows from investing activities include payments to acquire debt securities of other entities (other than certain instruments the entity purchased with the intention to trade).

Cash inflows and outflows resulting from investments acquired specifically for resale and carried at fair value in a trading account are presented as operating activities in the cash flow statement. Investments held in trading accounts are acquired by companies as part of a trading operation (buying and selling securities). Authoritative support follows along with a description of trading account securities.

230-10-45-20 Cash receipts and cash payments resulting from purchases and sales of other securities and other assets shall be classified as operating cash flows if those assets are acquired specifically for resale and are carried at fair value in a trading account.

255-10-55-2 Trading account securities are securities of all types carried in a trading account that are held principally for resale. These securities generally are carried at fair value. Trading account investments include both fixed-income securities (for example, nonconvertible preferred stock, convertible bonds, and other bonds) and other securities (for example, common stock). Usually, trading account securities are held for extremely short periods of time—sometimes for only a few hours.

In the notes to the financial statements, the following items should be disclosed where applicable.

- Amortized cost and maturity dates
- Aggregate fair value
- Allowance for credit losses
- Gross realized and unrealized holding gains and losses
- Change in net unrealized holding gains and losses
- Information about contractual maturities of securities
- Impairment disclosures
- Inputs in determining fair value (Level 1, 2, or 3 in the fair value hierarchy) and other required fair value disclosures

LO 14-4 Account for equity securities measured at FV-NI

LO 18-4 Overview

Equity Securities Measured at FV-NI
- Adjust to fair value
- Recognize adjustment to fair value (unrealized gain or loss) in net income
- Recognize dividends declared in net income
- Record sale of investment
- Record no adjustment to FVA at time of sale *OR* adjust and eliminate FVA at time of sale

Methods to Account for Equity Securities		
FV-NI LO 14-4	Equity Method LO 14-5	Consolidation

In determining the appropriate accounting for equity investments, the extent of ownership interest is a critical factor. When the investor has *insignificant influence* over the investee and the fair value of the investment is *readily determinable*, the equity investment is measured at fair value with adjustments reflected in net income (**FV-NI**). It is generally presumed that investments in equity securities in which the investor holds generally less than 20% of the voting stock of the investee do not represent a **significant influence** over the investee. However, the key issue is influence, which can occur at lower ownership levels. In this case (as illustrated in **Demo 14-4**), the investment is initially recorded at its purchase price plus other incidental costs, such as brokerage fees, excise taxes, and other transfer costs incurred as part of the purchase. Subsequently, the investment is recognized at fair value and any unrealized holding gains and losses are included in net income (FV-NI).

321-10-35-1 Except [for investments without a readily determinable fair value] investments in equity securities shall be measured subsequently at fair value in the statement of financial position. Unrealized holding gains and losses for equity securities shall be included in earnings.

As is the case for debt securities, the fair value of equity securities changes. Companies may adjust the carrying value of equity securities daily or at reporting dates. Regardless of the procedure, all equity securities (with insignificant influence) must be reflected at fair value at the reporting date and any resulting unrealized gains or losses are recognized in net income. For any securities sold during the period, the net effect on the income statement for the reporting period reflects any change in fair value from the last report date to the date of sale.

321-10-40-1 With respect to equity securities, because all changes in an equity security's fair value are reported in earnings as they occur, the sale of an equity security does not necessarily give rise to a gain or loss. Generally, a debit to cash (or trade date receivable) is recorded for the sales proceeds, and a credit is recorded to remove the security at its fair value (or sales price). If the entity is not taxed on the changes in fair value, the deferred tax accounts would be adjusted. An entity that has not yet recorded the security's change in fair value to the point of sale (perhaps because fair value changes are recorded at the end of each day) will need to adjust this procedure.

Because the investor does not have significant influence over the investee, the investor is unable to direct whether net income will be retained in the company or distributed. In other words, the investee may choose to permanently retain capital and not pay dividends. Therefore, revenue is only recognized by the investor with a declaration of a dividend.

321-10-35-6 Dividend income from investments in equity securities shall be included in earnings.

Equity investments are classified as short-term or long-term depending upon the intention and ability of the investor to sell the investment within the next year (or operating cycle, if longer).

If the investor has significant influence (but not a controlling interest), the investment is accounted for under the equity method (**Demo 14-5**). If an investor has a controlling interest, the financial statements of the investor (parent) and investee (subsidiary) are consolidated and treated as one economic entity. (Generally, controlling interest occurs when a company controls more than 50% of the investee's voting common stock.) For example, the Coca-Cola consolidated financial statements are labeled "Coca-Cola Company and Subsidiaries." Accounting for consolidations is the subject of advanced accounting courses.

Equity Investments Measured at FV-NI — LO14-4 — Demo 14-4

On July 1, 2020, Montana Inc. purchases 5,000 of Northfast Inc.'s 50,000 outstanding shares of common stock for $20 per share. Commissions on the common stock purchase were $500. Montana's investment represents a 10% interest in Northfast (5,000 shares/50,000 shares). Montana does *not* have significant influence on Northfast. Provide the entries and reporting for the following transactions of Montana.

a. Record the entry to purchase the investment in equity securities on July 1, 2020.
b. Record the entry for the declaration and payment of dividends of $5,000 by Northfast Inc. on December 15, 2020.
c. Record the entry to adjust the investment of common stock to fair value assuming that the fair value of Northfast Inc.'s stock is $22 per share on December 31, 2020.
d. Report the investment in common stock on the December 31, 2020, balance sheet, and the 2020 income statement.
e. Record the sale of the investment in common stock on January 5, 2021, for $111,300 under two treatments: ① Compute the gain or loss on sale as the difference between the cash received and the original cost of the investment; in this case, do not adjust the Fair Value Adjustment account. ② Adjust the investment to fair value at the date of sale using FV-NI; then, record the sale, eliminating the associated Fair Value Adjustment account balance.
f. Record the entry to adjust the Fair Value Adjustment account on December 31, 2021, assuming no additional investments in common stock in 2021.

Solution

a. **Purchase of Equity Investment with Insignificant Influence**

The entry to record the purchase of common stock by Montana includes commissions as part of the purchase price.

July 1, 2020— To record investment purchase

Investment in Northfast Stock	100,500	
Cash ([5,000 × $20] + $500)		100,500

Assets = Liabilities + Equity
+100,500
−100,500

Invest—CS: 100,500 (debit)
Cash: 100,500 (credit)

continued

continued from previous page

b. **Dividend Revenue**

Because Montana doesn't have significant influence over Northfast, it is unable to direct whether net income will be retained in the company or distributed. Therefore, revenue is only recognized by Montana with a declaration of a dividend by Northfast. Montana would record the following journal entry for its share of declared and paid dividends of $500 ($5,000 × 10%).

Assets = Liabilities + Equity
+500 +500
Cash: 500 | 100,500
Dividend Rev: | 500

December 15, 2020—To record dividend revenue

Cash	500	
Dividend Revenue ($5,000 × 0.10)		500

c. **Adjustment of Investment to Fair Value**

At each balance sheet date, all securities held with insignificant influence are reported at fair value. The difference between fair value and the original cost is recorded in the Fair Value Adjustment account. The unrealized holding gain is measured as follows.

Investment	Cost	Fair Value Year-End	Unrealized Holding Gain (Loss)
Northfast common stock	$100,500	$110,000*	$9,500
Existing balance in Fair Value Adjustment			0
Increase (decrease) to Fair Value Adjustment			$9,500

* $22 × 5,000 shares

The unrealized gain of $9,500 is reflected in the following entry.

Assets = Liabilities + Equity
+9,500 +9,500
FVA—Eq Sec: 9,500 |
Unreal Gain or Loss—Inc: | 9,500

December 31, 2020—To adjust investment to fair value

Fair Value Adjustment—Equity Securities	9,500	
Unrealized Gain or Loss—Income		9,500

With this entry, the carrying value has been adjusted to its current fair value and the net change, an unrealized gain of $9,500, has been recorded. The net unrealized holding gain (or loss) is treated as a component of other income and is included in the determination of the earnings of the period in the income statement.

d. **Financial Statement Presentation of Investment in Common Stock**

On the December 31, 2020, balance sheet and 2020 income statement, Montana would report the following.

Balance Sheet excerpt December 31, 2020	
Assets	
Dividend receivable	$ 500
Investment in equity securities	110,000

Income Statement excerpt For Year Ended December 31, 2020	
Other revenues and gains	
Dividend revenue	$ 500
Unrealized holding gain on equity securities	9,500

continued

continued from previous page

Select Accounting Treatment

① Adjust FVA at Year-End

e. **Sale of Investment in Common Stock**

The company recognizes a gain as the difference between the cash received of $111,300 and the original cost of investment of $100,500.

January 5, 2021—To record sale of equity securities

Cash	111,300	
Investment in Northfast Stock		100,500
Gain on Sale of Investment		10,800

Cash		Invest—CS		Gain on Sale—of Invest	
500	100,500	100,500	100,500		10,800
111,300		0			

f. **Adjustment of the Fair Value Adjustment Account**

At year-end, because Montana held no investments in common stock, the balance in the Fair Value Adjustment account is no longer needed and is derecognized.

December 31, 2021—To eliminate fair value adjustment balance

Unrealized Gain or Loss—Income	9,500	
Fair Value Adjustment—Equity Securities		9,500

FVA—Eq Sec		Unreal Gain or Loss—Inc	
9,500	9,500	9,500	9,500
0			

The gain on sale of $10,800 is recognized in financial statements over the ownership period of the investment.

Unrealized gain in 2020 income statement	$ 9,500
Gain in 2021 income statement ($10,800 − $9,500)	1,300
Total gain recognized over ownership period	$10,800

② Adjust FVA at Sale and Year-End

e. **Sale of Investment in Common Stock**

At the sale date, the company first adjusts the investment to fair value (FV-NI).

Required FVA ending account balance*	$10,800
Less existing FVA account balance	9,500
Increase to FVA account	1,300

*$111,300 fair value − $100,500 original cost.

January 5, 2021—To adjust investment to fair value

Fair Value Adjustment—Equity Securities	1,300	
Unrealized Gain—Income		1,300

FVA—Eq Sec		Unreal Gain or Loss—Inc	
9,500			9,500
1,300			1,300

Next, the sale is recorded, including elimination of the associated Fair Value Adjustment balance. No gain is recorded at sale because the gain was recorded in the prior entry.

January 5, 2021—To record sale of equity securities

Cash	111,300	
Investment in Northfast Stock		100,500
Fair Value Adjustment—Equity Securities		10,800

Cash		Invest—CS		FVA—Eq Sec	
500	100,500	100,500	100,500	9,500	10,800
111,300		0		1,300	
				0	

f. **Adjustment of the Fair Value Adjustment Account**

No balance is required in the Fair Value Adjustment account (currently at a zero balance) because Montana holds no equity investments at year-end.

The gain on sale of $10,800 is recognized in financial statements over the ownership period of the investment.

Gain in 2020 income statement	$ 9,500
Gain in 2021 income statement	1,300
Total gain recognized over ownership period	$10,800

EXPANDING YOUR KNOWLEDGE **Fair Value is Not Readily Determinable**

What happens if the fair value of the equity investment is not readily determinable, such as with shares of stock of a private company? First, the Codification includes a practical expedient option that allows companies to measure the value of alternative investments using *net asset value per share*, typically used by investment companies.

820-10-15-4 [Practical expedient] shall apply only to an investment that meets both of the following criteria as of the reporting entity's measurement date:

a. The investment does not have a readily determinable fair value.

b. The investment is in an investment company within the scope of Topic 946 or is an investment in a real estate fund.

continued

continued from previous page

If, however, the equity investments do not have a readily determinable fair value and do not qualify for the practical expedient option, the investment may be accounted for at cost, less impairment, plus or minus subsequent adjustments for observable price changes.

321-10-35-2 An entity may elect to measure an equity security without a readily determinable fair value that does not qualify for the practical expedient to estimate fair value . . . at its cost minus impairment, if any, plus or minus changes resulting from observable price changes in orderly transactions for the identical or a similar investment of the same issuer.

For example, let's assume that a company had two classes of preferred stock, Series A and Series B. The two series have different dividend rates but all other features are the same. The Series A stock is actively traded and the Series B stock is not actively traded and does not have a readily determinable fair value. If the company determined that both series were similar, the company could choose to value the Series B shares at its cost plus or minus observable price changes in its Series A preferred shares. For example, if the Series A preferred stock increased in price by 5% for a given period, the company would record an unrealized gain for 5% for the Series B shares. For equity securities without readily determinable fair values, the company must disclose the carrying amount, the adjustments, and information describing the adjustment.

Estimating the value of an investment without a readily determinable value involves significant management judgment. This alternate approach, while it still involves judgment, is intended to provide relief to companies by basing the investment value on observable prices. However, management must still make judgments in order to determine whether an investment is similar and also must estimate impairment on the investment being measured.

REVIEW 14-4 LO14-4 Accounting for Investments Measured at FV-NI

Review MBC

On September 1, 2020, Big Apple Inc. purchased 2,500 shares of common stock of Mack Corp. for $250,000. Big Apple has insignificant influence over Mack Corp. On November 15, 2020, Big Apple sold 1,000 shares of Mack stock for $110 per share. At December 31, 2020, Mack Corp. declared and paid dividends of $3 per share. The fair value of the remaining investment in Mack Corp. was $162,000 on December 31, 2020. Prepare the following entries for Big Apple Inc.

a. Purchase on September 1, 2020.

b. Sale of shares on November 15, 2020, under the following two recording options: ① Compute the gain or loss on sale as the difference between the cash received and the original cost of the investment. Do not adjust the Fair Value Adjustment account at the sale date. ② Adjust the investment to fair value at the date of sale through FV-NI. Record the sale, eliminating the Fair Value Adjustment account.

c. Dividends declared and received on December 31, 2020.

d. Adjustment to fair value on December 31, 2020.

More Practice: 14-26, 14-27, 14-55, 14-56, 14-57

Solution on p. 14-86.

LO 14-5 Account for equity securities following the equity method

LO 14-5 Overview

Accounting for Investment Under the Equity Method
- Adjust investment and net income for proportionate share of investee's net income (loss)
- Record expense adjustment related to a basis difference when applicable
- Decrease investment for proportionate share of dividends declared
- Ignore changes in fair value of the security unless impaired

The **equity method** (**Demo 14-5**) differs from FV-NI in that the investors' proportionate share of the investee's income is recognized in the investor's net income and dividends are recorded as a return of the investor's investment rather than return on the investor's investment. The equity method is most appropriate if the investor's relationship with the investee enables the investor to influence the operating and financial decisions of the investee while having less than a controlling interest. Influence tends to be greater as the investor's ownership in the investee increases. If the investor holds between 20% and 50% of the voting stock of the investee, the investor is presumed to have **significant influence** over the investee. However, this is a rebuttable presumption. Based on facts and circumstances, an investor owning less than 20% of the voting shares may have significant influence, and an investor owning 20% or more of the voting shares may not have significant influence over the investee.

Methods to Account for Equity Securities		
FV-NI LO 14-4	Equity Method LO 14-5	Consolidation

The purposes for making equity method investments generally differ from those of fair value method securities, and the difference in accounting methods reflects this fact. Equity method investments tend to be long-term and to establish relationships between the investor and the investee. For example, the investor may use its influence to cause the investee to buy products or services from the investor. The equity method of accounting reflects this unique relationship.

EXPANDING YOUR KNOWLEDGE **Another Look at Significant Influence**

An investor may not be able to exercise significant influence over the investee's policies, even though the investor owns more than 20% interest when (1) opposition by the investee (such as litigation or complaints to governmental regulatory agencies) challenges the investor's ability to exercise influence; (2) the investor and investee sign an agreement under which the investor surrenders significant rights as a stockholder; (3) majority ownership of the investee is concentrated among a small group of stockholders who operate the company without regard to the views of the investor; or (4) the investor is unsuccessful in attempts to obtain representation on the investee's board of directors. This list, abstracted from FASB ASC 323-10-15-10, is intended to be illustrative and not all-inclusive. *This means that the 20% ownership cut-off percentage is a general guideline and other factors must be considered when determining whether an investor has significant influence over an investee.*

Conceptually, the equity method treats the accounts of the investee as if they were condensed into one balance sheet item and one income statement item and then merged into the investor at the proportion owned by the investor. The equity method is sometimes called the **one-line consolidation method** because it results in the same effect on earnings and retained earnings that would result from consolidating the financial statements of the investor and investee, but does so without combining both companies' financial statements, as in a complete consolidation.

For example, if an investor purchases an investment for $100, representing a 25% ownership interest under the equity method, the investor would debit the Investment account for $100. Periodically, the investor would record a debit to the Investment account for its proportionate share of net income of the investee. Let's say the investee's net income is $40, so the investor's share is $10. Also, the investor would periodically record a credit to the Investment account for the dividends it is entitled to receive from the investee. Let's say $2 in this example. The net balance in the Investment account at the end of the period would be $108. **Under the equity method, if an investment were purchased during the year, the entry to record the proportionate share of income would be prorated for the holding period of the investment. The entry to record dividends the investee is entitled to would only include dividends *declared* during the holding period.**

Investment			
Purchases	100		
		2	Dividends entitled to receive from investee
Proportionate share of earnings of investee	10		
Ending balance	108		

An adjusting entry is required when the fair value of *depreciable* assets of the investee exceeds the book value of depreciable assets of the investee. The excess of fair value over book value would result in additional depreciation expense that would result in a decrease to the investment account of the investor. In other words, simply recording a proportionate share of the investee's net income captures only depreciation on the book value of depreciable assets. In a similar way, an adjusting entry for additional amortization expense would be required for intangible assets for the excess of fair value over carrying value.

Unlike FV-NI that recognizes dividends as income, the equity method requires the investor to recognize in income a proportionate share of the investee's income, and to recognize dividends as a reduction of the carrying value of the investment. This is because an investor with significant influence can control the timing and amount of dividends. Because of this, dividends are not considered an objective measure of income related to the investee. Also unlike FV-NI, changes in the fair value of equity method investments are ignored. However, if the investment is considered impaired, an impairment loss may need to be recognized, as discussed in LO 14-6.

323-10-35-4 Under the equity method, an investor shall recognize its share of the earnings or losses of an investee in the periods for which they are reported by the investee in its financial statements rather than in the period in which an investee declares a dividend. An investor shall adjust the carrying amount of an investment for its share of the earnings or losses of the investee after the date of investment and shall report the recognized earnings or losses in income.

323-10-35-16 If an investee has outstanding cumulative preferred stock, an investor shall compute its share of earnings (losses) after deducting the investee's preferred dividends, whether or not such dividends are declared.

To record depreciation on the fair value of assets, an adjustment is required for the excess of fair value over book value. (If the investment purchase were made in the middle of the year, the depreciation expense would be prorated to correspond with the holding period.) No adjustments are necessary for items such as land and goodwill that are not depreciated.

350-20-35-58 The portion of the difference between the cost of an investment and the amount of underlying equity in net assets of an equity method investee that is recognized as goodwill… (equity method goodwill) shall not be amortized.

EXPANDING YOUR KNOWLEDGE — Share of Investee's Losses

What if an investee recognizes a net loss? The investor should *credit* the investment account for the proportionate share of the net loss of the investee. However, the investor would generally discontinue applying the equity method if the investment account is reduced to zero. (An exception would be if the investee is expected to be profitable in the future or the investor is committed to financially supporting the investee.) If the investee subsequently reports net income, the investor would resume applying the equity method only after its share of net income equals the share of net losses not recognized during the period the equity method was suspended.

323-10-35-20 The investor ordinarily shall discontinue applying the equity method if the investment (and net advances) is reduced to zero and shall not provide for additional losses unless the investor has guaranteed obligations of the investee or is otherwise committed to provide further financial support for the investee.

323-10-35-21 An investor shall, however, provide for additional losses if the imminent return to profitable operations by an investee appears to be assured. For example, a material, nonrecurring loss of an isolated nature may reduce an investment below zero even though the underlying profitable operating pattern of an investee is unimpaired.

Demo 14-5 LO14-5 Equity Method Accounting

Demo MBC

Montana Inc. makes an initial investment of $100,000 for 40% of the voting stock of Bear Claw Corp. on January 1, 2020. The investment amount is exactly equal to 40% of Bear Claw's stockholders' equity, and this amount also represents 40% of the fair value of net assets of Bear Claw. In 2020, Bear Claw has earnings of $30,000 and declares and pays dividends of $10,000 on December 31, 2020. The investment is accounted for under the equity method. Provide the entries and reporting for the following transactions of Montana.

a. Record the entry to purchase the investment in equity securities on January 1, 2020.
b. Record Montana's interest in Bear Claw's net income on December 31, 2020.
c. Record Montana's receipt of declared dividends on December 31, 2020.
d. Compute the ending balance of Montana's investment in Bear Claw on December 31, 2020.
e. Assume that Montana purchased Bear Claw on March 1, 2020, instead of January 1, 2020. Record Montana's interest in Bear Claw's net income and Montana's receipt of declared dividends on December 31, 2020.
f. Assume the original purchase date of January 1, 2020, but that the fair value exceeded the book value of Bear Claw's total assets by $5,000, attributable to a depreciable asset (equipment) with a 10-year useful life. Record the additional adjustment required for depreciation expense on December 31, 2020, assuming the straight-line depreciation method.

Solution

a. **Purchase of Common Stock under Equity Method**

January 1, 2020—To record investment purchase

Investment in Bear Claw Stock	100,000	
Cash		100,000

Assets = Liabilities + Equity
+100,000
−100,000

Invest—CS		Cash	
100,000			100,000

b. **Investment Income**

December 31, 2020—To record investment income

Investment in Bear Claw Stock	12,000	
Investment Income (0.40 × $30,000)		12,000

Assets = Liabilities + Equity
+12,000 +12,000

Invest—CS		Invest Inc	
100,000			12,000
12,000			

c. **Receipt of Declared Dividends**

December 31, 2020—To record receipt of dividends

Cash	4,000	
Investment in Bear Claw Stock (0.40 × $10,000).		4,000

Assets = Liabilities + Equity
+4,000
−4,000

Cash		Invest—CS	
4,000	100,000	100,000	4,000
		12,000	

continued

continued from previous page

d. **Computing the Ending Balance in the Investment Account**
At December 31, 2020, the value of the investment classified under the equity method is $108,000, calculated as follows:
$100,000 (original purchase) + $12,000 (share of net income) − $4,000 (share of dividends) = $108,000

Invest—CS	
Bal. 100,000	4,000
12,000	
108,000	

e. **Share of Net Income—Partial Period and the Receipt of Declared Dividends**
The proportionate share of net income is for 10 months or 10/12 of the year, representing the holding period of the investment.

December 31, 2020—To record investment income

Investment in Bear Claw Stock	10,000	
Investment Income (0.40 × $30,000 × 10/12)		10,000

Assets = Liabilities + Equity
+10,000 +10,000

Invest—CS		Invest Inc	
Bal. 100,000			10,000
10,000			

Dividends were declared and paid on December 31, 2020, when Montana owned a 40% interest in Bear Claw.

December 31, 2020—To record receipt of dividends

Cash	4,000	
Investment in Bear Claw Stock (0.40 × $10,000)		4,000

Assets = Liabilities + Equity
+4,000
−4,000

Invest—CS		Cash	
Bal. 100,000	4,000	4,000	
10,000			

f. **Additional Depreciation Expense**
Montana would need to record an adjustment for the excess depreciation that would not be reflected in Bear Claw's net income. The following adjusting entry would be required.

December 31, 2020—To record adjustment for additional depreciation expense

Investment Income [0.40 × ($5,000/10)]	200	
Investment in Bear Claw Stock		200

Assets = Liabilities + Equity
−200 −200

Invest—CS		Invest Inc	
Bal. 100,000	200	200	

Fair Value Option

Under the fair value option, an investment is adjusted to fair value through net income each reporting period (FV-NI). However, the fair value option must be selected on the purchase date of the asset, applied to each investment individually, and the decision is generally irrevocable. The fair value option may be applied to any security accounted for under the equity method. Recall when an asset is measured at FV-NI, the investment is adjusted to fair value at report dates and the unrealized gain or loss is recognized in net income. For recording purposes, a company may measure the investment directly as FV-NI or account for the investment under the equity method and record a fair value adjustment in net income at reporting dates.

Real World—REPORTING SHARE OF INCOME OF EQUITY INVESTMENT

In a recent annual report, **Telephone and Data Systems, Inc. (TDS)** reported $453 million in investments in unconsolidated entities, accounted for using the equity method. How is it possible for a company like TDS to report its share of income of an investee during the same time period its investees are also finalizing net income amounts for financial reporting? TDS, as an example, reports income on a one-quarter lag basis, which is supported by GAAP.

TELEPHONE AND DATA SYSTEMS, INC. [TDS]

323-10-35-6 If financial statements of an investee are not sufficiently timely for an investor to apply the equity method currently, the investor ordinarily shall record its share of the earnings or losses of an investee from the most recent available financial statements. A lag in reporting shall be consistent from period to period.

Note 1 (excerpt): Investments in Unconsolidated Entities For its equity method investments for which financial information is readily available, TDS records its equity in the earnings of the entity in the current period. For its equity method investments for which financial information is not readily available, TDS records its equity in the earnings of the entity on a one quarter lag basis.

REVIEW 14-5 LO14-5 Account for Investment in Common Stock under the Equity Method

Review MBC

On January 2, 2020, Big Apple Inc. purchased 4,000 of the 18,000 outstanding shares of common stock of Mack Corp. for $100,000 cash. Big Apple Inc. has the intention of holding the securities indefinitely and has a significant influence over Mack. On January 3, 2020, the balance sheet of Mack Corp. reflected the following: nondepreciable assets, $450,000 (same as fair value); depreciable assets (net), $80,000 (fair value, $90,000); total liabilities, $200,000; and stockholders' equity, $330,000. Assume a 10-year remaining life (straight-line depreciation) on the depreciable assets. Mack Corp. recognized net income of $90,000 in 2020. Record the following entries for Big Apple Inc.

a. Record the entry on January 2, 2020, to reflect the acquisition of Mack Corp. common stock.
b. Record the entry on December 31, 2020, to reflect the net income reported by Mack Corp.
c. Record the entry on December 31, 2020, to recognize additional depreciation expense.
d. Record the entry on December 31, 2020, to recognize the decrease in the fair value of Mack Corp. stock, given a quoted market price of $23 per share.
e. Record the entry on December 31, 2020, for a cash dividend of $1 per share declared and paid by Mack Corp.
f. Indicate the ending balance in the Investment in Mack Stock account as of December 31, 2020.

More Practice:
14-30, 14-63, 14-64, 14-65, 14-66, 14-67

Solution on p. 14-86.

EXPANDING YOUR KNOWLEDGE **Tax Effect**

While net income of the investor is increased when an investee earns income under the equity method, taxable income is increased when an investee pays dividends to the investor. The timing difference represents a deferred tax liability, when investment income exceeds declared dividends, which is explained in Chapter 18.

Review of Accounting for Equity Securities

The following table compares journal entries in accounting for equity securities under (1) FV-NI, and (2) the equity method.

Transaction	FV-NI LO 14-4	Equity Method LO 14-5
Purchase of equity security	Dr. Investment in Stock Cr. Cash	Dr. Investment in Stock Cr. Cash
Declaration of dividends	Dr. Cash Cr. Dividend Revenue	Dr. Cash Cr. Investment in Stock
Recognize proportionate share of net income	No entry	Dr. Investment in Stock Cr. Investment Income
Adjust equity security to fair value with a gain	Dr. Fair Value Adjustment Cr. Unrealized Gain or Loss—Income	No entry
Adjust equity security to fair value with a loss	Dr. Unrealized Gain or Loss—Income Cr. Fair Value Adjustment	No entry

Financial Presentation and Disclosure Requirements

An investment is recognized on the balance sheet as *current* or *noncurrent* depending upon when the investment is expected to be sold. Unrealized gains and losses on equity securities held at a reporting date must be disclosed.

321-10-50-4 For each period for which the results of operations are presented, an entity shall disclose the portion of unrealized gains and losses for the period that relates to equity securities still held at the reporting date.

Investing and Operating Activities

In the statement of cash flows, cash inflows from investing activities include receipts from the sale of equity securities of other entities (other than certain instruments carried in a trading account).

Cash outflows from investing activities include payments to acquire equity securities of other entities (other than certain instruments carried in a trading account). Cash inflows and outflows resulting from investments acquired specifically for resale and carried at fair value in a trading account are presented as operating activities. For investments accounted for under the equity method, the difference between investment income and dividends declared is an adjustment to net income in the operating section of the statement of cash flows under the indirect method. For example, if an investor's share of investment income and dividends are $1,000 and $400, respectively, the investor subtracts $600 ($1,000 less $400) in the operating section as an amount necessary to reconcile net income to cash provided by operating activities.

Inputs in determining fair value (Level 1, 2, or 3 in the fair value hierarchy) and other required fair value disclosures are also required.

Adjust debt and equity securities for impairment — LO 14-6

Investments in securities that are required to be recognized at fair value, with the *adjustment affecting net income,* need not be separately evaluated for impairment because any decline in value has already been recognized in net income. In contrast, investments that are not adjusted to fair value through net income including held-to-maturity debt investments, available-for-sale debt investments, and equity investments accounted for under the equity method must be evaluated to determine whether an impairment loss must be recognized as a charge against income.

LO 14-6 Overview

Accounting for Impairment of Investments
- Evaluate HTM, AFS, and equity method securities for impairment
- Recognize impairment losses in net income

Held-to-Maturity Debt Investment

Remember that held-to-maturity debt investments are accounted for at amortized cost with no adjustment to fair value. Similar to the accounting for the impairment of receivables, the **Current Expected Credit Loss Model** (CECL model) is used to estimate impairment losses of held-to-maturity debt investment accounts. The estimate of the impairment loss is forward-looking, which requires management to use forecasts about future economic conditions (along with historical information) to determine the expected credit loss over the remaining life of the investment. An allowance should be recorded for the excess of the amortized cost over the present value of amounts expected to be collected over the lifetime of the investment. No particular methodology is specified by GAAP in determining the estimated credit loss.

- A loss on impairment is reported as a charge against income.
- On the balance sheet, credit losses are recognized using the account, Allowance for Credit Losses—a contra asset account that is deducted from the amortized cost basis of the investment.
- Subsequent changes to the allowance (both favorable and unfavorable) are immediately recognized in net income. However, favorable reversals may not exceed the initial credit loss (the Allowance may not have a debit balance).

Available-for-Sale Debt Investment

A different model, the **AFS debt security model** outlined below is used to estimate impairment losses on AFS debt investments. Under the AFS debt security model, an AFS security is considered impaired if the fair value of the investment is less than its amortized cost, assessed every reporting period, on an individual security basis.

326-30-35-4 Impairment shall be assessed at the individual security level (referred to as an investment).

326-30-35-1 An investment is impaired if the fair value of the investment is less than its amortized cost basis.

If the company (investor) intends to sell the AFS debt security (or it is *more likely than not* that the company will be required to sell the security before recovery) a loss is recognized in net income and the fair value of the security becomes its new cost basis.

326-30-35-10 If an entity intends to sell the debt security (that is, it has decided to sell the security), or more likely than not will be required to sell the security before recovery of its amortized cost basis, any allowance for credit losses shall be written off and the amortized cost basis shall be written down to the debt security's fair value at the reporting date with any incremental impairment reported in earnings.

If, however, the company does not intend to sell (nor is it *more likely than not* that the company will be required to sell the security before recovery), then the company must determine whether the loss (difference between amortized cost and fair value) is due to **credit factors** or **noncredit factors**. The amount of loss due to credit factors is recognized in net income.

326-30-35-6 In assessing whether a credit loss exists, an entity shall compare the present value of cash flows expected to be collected from the security with the amortized cost basis of the security. If the present value of cash flows expected to be collected is less than the amortized cost basis of the security, a credit loss exists and an allowance for credit losses shall be recorded for the credit loss, limited by the amount that the fair value is less than amortized cost basis. Credit losses on an impaired security shall continue to be measured using the present value of expected future cash flows.

AFS Investment Information	Impairment or No Impairment	Accounting Treatment
Fair value > amortized cost	No impairment	Carrying value of investment adjusted through the FV-OCI adjustment.
Fair value < amortized cost and company intends to sell the investment or it is *more likely than not* that the investor will be required to sell before recovery of the unrealized loss	Asset is impaired	Debit Loss on Impairment and credit the Investment account for the difference between fair value and amortized cost. Eliminate a corresponding OCI loss (previously recorded through FV-OCI*) through a debit to the Fair Value Adjustment account and a credit to Unrealized Gain or Loss—OCI.
Fair value < amortized cost and doesn't meet criteria above	Asset is impaired	Debit Loss on Impairment and credit Allowance for Credit Losses for the portion of the unrealized loss due to credit risk, limited to the amount that the fair value is less than amortized cost. Eliminate a corresponding OCI loss (previously recorded through FV-OCI*) through a debit to the Fair Value Adjustment account and a credit to Unrealized Gain or Loss—OCI.

* In the illustrations in this chapter, we assume that the AFS investments have been adjusted to fair value through FV-OCI (as described in LO 14-3) before any impairment analysis.

Disclosure Requirements

Disclosure in the notes accompanying the financial statements includes the following:

- For HTM debt securities, disclose information about changes in the factors that influenced management's estimate of expected credit losses, including the reasons for those changes.
- For AFS debt securities, prepare a rollforward of the new allowance for credit losses.

Equity Method Investment

For equity method investments, a current fair value of an investment that is less than its carrying amount may indicate a loss in value of the investment. For example, the carrying amount of an investment may not be justified due to losses reported over several years by an investee. A loss in value of an investment that management estimates is other than a *temporary decline* is recognized as a loss in the income statement and a reduction of the investment's carrying value. Losses on impairment of equity method investments are not reversed in future periods.

323-10-35-32 A loss in value of an investment that is other than a temporary decline shall be recognized. Evidence of a loss in value might include, but would not necessarily be limited to, *absence of an ability to recover the carrying amount of the investment* or inability of the investee to sustain an earnings capacity that would justify the carrying amount of the investment. A current fair value of an investment that is less than its carrying amount may indicate a loss in value of the investment. However, a decline in the quoted market price below the carrying amount or the existence of operating losses is not necessarily indicative of a loss in value that is other than temporary. All are factors that shall be evaluated.

Loss on Impairment of Investments LO14-6 Demo 14-6

Part One—Impairment of HTM Investment
Montana Inc. holds a bond in Rainwear Co. with a carrying value of $30,000, classified as an HTM security. As of December 31, 2020, Montana determines that due to a potential bankruptcy of Rainwear Co. it is probable that Montana will not collect the full amount due on the bond. The present value of the probable collection amounts is $20,000, estimated using the CECL model. Record the loss on impairment on December 31, 2020.

Solution
The journal entry to record the impairment loss is

December 31, 2020—To record an impairment loss

Loss on Impairment	10,000	
Allowance for Credit Losses		10,000

Assets = Liabilities + Equity
−10,000 −10,000
Allow—Cred Loss: 10,000 (credit)
Loss—Impair: 10,000 (debit)

Part Two—Impairment of Available-for-Sale Debt Investment
Under the following three separate scenarios, Investor Inc. does not intend to sell and does not believe it is *more likely than not* that it will be required to sell the investment before recovery of any unrealized loss. Assume the company has already recorded the change in fair value in Other Comprehensive Income (FV-OCI).

Scenario	1	2	3
Fair value	$35,000	$25,000	$22,000
Amortized cost	30,000	30,000	30,000
Expected loss due to credit factors*	6,000	6,000	6,000

*Excess of amortized cost over the present value of expected cash flows.

Required
a. Determine the amount of impairment loss to recognize in net income under the three separate scenarios.
b. Record the journal entry (if any) for the impairment loss under the three separate scenarios.

Solution
a. **Measurement of Impairment Loss**
Scenario 1: **$0**(fair value exceeds amortized cost)
Scenario 2: **$5,000** (amortized cost exceeds fair value by $5,000, all of which relates to a credit loss)
Scenario 3: **$6,000** (amortized cost exceeds fair value by $8,000, of which $6,000 is due to a credit loss)
b. **Entry to Record Impairment Loss**
Scenario 1: No entry required
Scenario 2:

December 31, 2020—To record an impairment loss

Loss on Impairment	5,000	
Fair Value Adjustment—AFS	5,000	
Allowance for Credit Losses		5,000
Unrealized Gain or Loss—OCI		5,000

Assets = Liabilities + Equity
+5,000 +5,000
−5,000 −5,000
Allow—Cred Loss: 5,000 (credit)
Loss—Impair: 5,000 (debit)
FVA—AFS: 5,000 (debit)
Unreal Gain or Loss—OCI: 5,000 (credit)

Scenario 3:

December 31, 2020—To record an impairment loss

Loss on Impairment	6,000	
Fair Value Adjustment—AFS	6,000	
Allowance for Credit Losses		6,000
Unrealized Gain or Loss—OCI		6,000

Assets = Liabilities + Equity
+6,000 +6,000
−6,000 −6,000
Allow—Cred Loss: 6,000 (credit)
Loss—Impair: 6,000 (debit)
FVA—AFS: 6,000 (debit)
Unreal Gain or Loss—OCI: 6,000 (credit)

continued

continued from previous page

Part Three—Impairment of Equity Method Investment

Oasis Inc. has an equity investment in Caribbean Corp. accounted for under the equity method. The carrying value of the investment was $25,000 on December 31, 2020. At December 31, 2020, the fair value of Oasis's investment in Caribbean has declined to $22,000. Oasis management decides that the decline is other-than-temporary because Caribbean lost a significant market share to a major competitor. Record the journal entry on December 31, 2020, to recognize the impairment.

Solution

The loss considered other-than-temporary is recorded as follows.

Assets	=	Liabilities	+	Equity
−3,000				−3,000

Invest—CS: Cr. 3,000 | Loss—Impair: Dr. 3,000

December 31, 2020—To record an impairment loss

Loss on Impairment ($25,000 − $22,000)	3,000	
Investment in Caribbean Stock		3,000

REVIEW 14-6 LO14-6 Accounting for Impairment Loss on AFS Investments

Review MBC

Determine the amount of impairment loss to recognize in net income under the following three separate scenarios. In all three cases, the company does not intend to sell the AFS investment and does not believe it is *more likely than not* that it will be required to sell the investment before recovery of any unrealized loss. Assume that the company has already adjusted the AFS investments to fair through FV-OCI.

Scenario	1	2	3
Fair value	$250,000	$300,000	$225,000
Amortized cost	280,000	280,000	280,000
Expected credit loss	40,000	40,000	40,000

More Practice: 14-33, 14-34, 14-35, 14-69, 14-70, 14-71

Solution on p. 14-87.

Management Judgment

Classification of Debt Securities

Management judgment is required in the accounting for debt securities. First, the classification of debt securities is based on the intent and ability of management to hold a security (p. 14-3). While the classification categories have established criteria, management must apply the criteria to specific investments. As a result, the same 10-year bond purchased as an investment may be classified in three different ways (HTM, AFS, or TS) depending on management's determination of its intent and ability to hold the bond investment. The company documents the classification of the investment at acquisition.

320-10-25-2 At acquisition, an investor shall document the classification of debt securities.

A management decision to later sell an HTM security before maturity for reasons other than those outlined in the accounting guidance may require the company to reclassify its other HTM debt securities (p. 14-4). Accounting guidance indicates that the selling of an HTM security before maturity without justification calls into question or taints the investor's intent to hold other securities to maturity.

320-10-25-9 In addition to the changes in circumstances listed in paragraph 320-10-25-6(a) through (f), certain other events may cause the entity to sell or transfer a held-to-maturity security without necessarily calling into question (tainting) its intent to hold other debt securities to maturity.

Classification of Equity Securities

Determining whether a company (investor) has significant influence over an investee requires judgment. While a range of ownership percentages is provided of 20% to 50%, this is not a bright-line test. Investors must evaluate the facts and circumstances of the situation to determine whether or not they have significant influence over the investee. Some of the factors to consider in making this determination are included on page 14-30.

Estimating Fair Value

Estimating the value of equity securities requires judgment when the fair value is not readily determinable (p. 14-28). Disclosure is required of the levels of 1, 2, or 3 of the fair value hierarchy used in measuring all investments.

Impairment of Certain Securities

Because HTM securities are not recognized at fair value, management must estimate impairment losses using the CECL model (p. 14-34). The CECL model requires an estimate of all future losses over the life of the investment. For example, if the bond has a term of 20-years, management must estimate expected losses over the 20-year period using historical information and forecasts. Risk factors should be evaluated when a company is assessing how historical data may be different from current or future conditions. For example, an inventor analyzes risks specific to the investee, such as investor's credit rating, and risks at a macroeconomic level, such as unemployment rates.

AFS securities and equity method securities follow different models to estimate impairment losses (p. 14-34), but they also require management judgment in the evaluation process for impairment.

Explain the accounting for transfers of investments

APPENDIX 14A
LO 14-7

Transfer of Investments

- Update the investment account through the transfer date
- Transfer investment to the new category
- Account for investment according to the rules of the new investment category
- Apply no retrospective treatment

LO 14-7 Overview

A decision about the classification of an investment is made upon purchase. The accounting treatment is contingent upon such classification. At a later period, an investor may decide that a different classification is more appropriate, which may result in a transfer of the investment to a new category. **Transfers of securities between classifications are generally accounted for at fair value on the transfer date (Demo 14-7).** The following table summarizes the proper accounting treatment for transfers of investments, including effects on net income (NI) and other comprehensive income (OCI). Notes accompanying the financial statements should include a description of the circumstances leading to the transfer of a security to a different classification.

Type of Investment	Transfer Description	Impact on NI or OCI on Transfer Date	Future Impact on NI or OCI After Transfer Date
Debt	Transfer from AFS to HTM 320-10-35-10d	No effect on NI. Unrealized gain or loss in AOCI as of date of transfer amortized to interest income as a yield adjustment, similar to the treatment of premium or discount.	■ Amortize existing unrealized gain or loss in accumulated OCI to NI through interest income over the life of the investment. ■ Account for investment according to the rules for HTM investments.
Debt	Transfer from HTM to AFS 320-10-35-10c	No effect on NI. Carrying value is adjusted to fair value as of the date of transfer through OCI.	Account for investment according to the rules for AFS investments.
Debt	Transfer to TS 320-10-35-10b	Any unrecognized holding gain or loss existing as of the date of transfer is recognized in net income.	Account for investment according to the rules of TS investments.
Debt	Transfer from TS 320-10-35-10a	NI already adjusted for any unrealized gain or loss	Account for investment according to the rules of the new investment category.
Equity	Transfer to the Equity Method 323-10-35-33	Unrealized gain or loss existing as of the date of transfer is recognized in net income. Fair value becomes the new cost basis.	The new cost basis is adjusted according to the rules of the equity method.
Equity	Transfer from the Equity Method 323-10-35-36	Balance in Investment account is the new cost basis.	Balance in the investment account at the date of change becomes the cost basis under the new category and is adjusted according to the rules of the new investment category.

In general, transfers among the debt investment categories should be rare.

320-10-35-11 Transfers from the held-to-maturity category should be rare, except for transfers due to the changes in circumstances identified in [the Codification].

320-10-35-12 In addition, given the nature of a trading security, transfers into or from the trading category also should be rare.

320-10-35-13 Available-for-sale securities shall not be automatically transferred to the trading category because the passage of time has caused the maturity date to be within one year or because management intends to sell the security within one year.

A change to the equity method may result from an increase in the level of ownership through acquisition of additional shares by the investor, the acquisition or retirement of shares by the investee, or through other transactions. A change from the equity method may result from a decrease in the level of ownership through the sale of a portion of investments by the investor, the sale of additional stock by an investee, or other transactions leading to an investor's inability to influence policy.

Demo 14-7 LO14-7 Accounting for Transfer of Investment

Demo MBC

Montana Inc. makes the decision to change the classification of its current holding of Upper Armour bonds, with an amortized cost of $30,000, from AFS to TS on January 1, 2021. On January 1, 2021, the fair value of the Upper Armour investment is $25,000. Record the entry to transfer the security from AFS to TS on January 1, 2021. Assume the entry to recognize the unrealized loss in OCI has already been made at the date of transfer.

Solution

Montana would prepare the following journal entry to record the transfer at fair value.

January 1, 2021—To record transfer from AFS to TS

Investment in TS—Upper Armour Bonds	25,000	
Fair Value Adjustment—AFS	5,000	
Investment in AFS—Upper Armour Bonds		30,000
Unrealized Gain or Loss—Income	5,000	
Unrealized Gain or Loss—OCI		5,000

Assets	=	Liabilities	+	Equity
+25,000				−5,000
−30,000				+5,000
+5,000				

Invest—TS	
25,000	

Unreal Gain or Loss—Inc	
5,000	

Invest—AFS	
Bal. 30,000	30,000

Unreal Gain or Loss—OCI	
Bal. 5,000	5,000

FVA—AFS	
5,000	5,000 Bal.

Upon transfer, the company must derecognize the account balances relating to the AFS classification, which include the amortized cost of the bond ($30,000) and the fair value adjustment of $5,000. The fair value of $25,000 becomes the cost basis of the TS security, and the unrealized loss of $5,000 is reclassified from OCI and recognized in net income.

REVIEW 14-7 LO14-7 Accounting for Transfer of Investment

Review MBC

Big Apple Inc.'s holdings of 1,800 shares of the 10,000 shares outstanding of common stock of Mack Corp. was originally purchased for $15 per share and has been measured at FV-NI. However, on January 1, 2020, due to recent changes, Big Apple determined that it now has significant influence over Mack Corp. and should account for the investment as an equity investment. The fair value of Mack Corp. stock on December 31, 2019, was $30 per share. If Big Apple had accounted for the investment since the purchase date under the equity method, the investment account would have a balance of $45,000 on January 1, 2020.

Record the entry on January 1, 2020, to transfer the investment account from the accounting treatment of FV-NI to the equity method. Assume that the investment was adjusted to fair value on December 31, 2019.

More Practice: 14-111, 14-119, 14-120

Solution on p. 14-87.

Describe accounting for special-purpose funds and investments in life insurance policies

APPENDIX 14B
LO 14-8

This appendix and **Demo 14-8** cover accounting for investments that are less frequently encountered: special-purpose funds and the cash surrender value of life insurance.

Other Investments
- Special-purpose funds
  - Designated fund due to contract, law, or by choice
- Life insurance funds
  - Cash surrender value from whole-life insurance policies

LO 14-8 Overview

Special-Purpose Fund

Companies sometimes set aside cash or other assets in special-purpose funds for a particular future use. These assets are commonly noncurrent assets and are not directly related to current operations. They are recognized on the balance sheet under the noncurrent heading classification of investments. Note that a special fund does not meet the definition of a security, and for this reason is not included as part of the TS, AFS, or HTM securities portfolios. Funds may be set aside (1) by contract, as in the case of funds set aside to retire specific long-term liabilities such as a bond sinking fund, (2) by law, as in the case of rent deposits, or (3) voluntarily, as in the case of funds set aside to purchase major assets, such as land or a building or to reacquire shares of a company's outstanding stock.

Typically, special-purpose funds are deposited with an independent trustee, such as a financial institution, which agrees to pay a specified rate of interest each period on the balance in the fund. Special-purpose funds are generally disclosed in the notes to the financial statements.

Investment in Life Insurance Policies

Often a company insures the lives of its top executives, with the company as the beneficiary. A certain type of insurance policy, a whole-life policy, builds up value while the policy is in force. This policy has a stipulated loan value and cash surrender value. The **cash surrender value** of a policy is the amount that would be refunded should the policy be terminated at the request of the insured. This value increases over time as the company pays insurance premiums. Cash surrender value is a form of investment usually recognized on the balance sheet under investments as a long-term asset.

Each policy provides a schedule that indicates the cash surrender value and the loan value for each policy year. Because a portion of the premiums paid is refundable in the form of the cash surrender value, only a portion of the periodic premiums is expensed. The company's life insurance expense each period is the excess of the premium paid over the increase in the cash surrender value for the period.

Accounting for Other Investments LO14-8 **Demo 14-8**

Example One—Special-Purpose Fund

Demo MBC

Watt Corporation plans to build an addition to its office building in five years. The plans estimate the total construction cost to be $1,300,000 over a six-month construction period. The company decided to make five $231,000 cash deposits to a special construction fund each July 1, starting on July 1, 2020. An independent trustee will administer the fund. The trustee will increase the fund each June 30 at a 4% interest rate on the fund balance at that date. Watt Corporation's accounting period ends December 31.

a. Record the journal entry for the first fund payment on July 1, 2020.
b. Record the entry for the accrual of interest on December 31, 2020.
c. Record the entry for the receipt of interest on June 30, 2021.

Solution

a. **Funding Special-Purpose Fund**

July 1, 2020—To record first fund payment

Special-Purpose Fund—Building	231,000	
Cash		231,000

Assets = Liabilities + Equity
+231,000
−231,000

Spec-Purp Fund: 231,000 (debit)
Cash: 231,000 (credit)

continued

continued from previous page

b. **Interest Revenue on Special-Purpose Fund**

Assets = Liabilities + Equity
+4,620 +4,620
Receiv on Fund: 4,620 |
Interest Rev: | 4,620

December 31, 2020—To record accrual of interest revenue

Receivable on Building Fund	4,620	
Interest Revenue ($231,000 × 0.04 × 0.5)		4,620

c. **Interest Receipt on Special-Purpose Fund**

Assets = Liabilities + Equity
+9,240 +4,620
−4,620
Spec-Purp Fund: 231,000 | ; 9,240 |
Interest Rev: | 4,620 ; | 4,620
Receiv on Fund: 4,620 | 4,620

June 30, 2021—To record receipt of interest

Special-Purpose Fund—Building	9,240	
Receivable on Building Fund		4,620
Interest Revenue ($231,000 × 0.04 × 0.5)		4,620

Example Two—Cash Surrender Value

Assume that Zim Corporation purchased a $250,000 whole-life policy on its top executive several years ago. In 2020, which is the fourth year the policy has been in effect, the company pays an insurance premium in the amount of $20,200. The premium of $20,200 paid in 2020 results in an increase in cash surrender value of $1,000 to a total cash surrender value of $1,500 at the end of 2020. Assume that the executive dies at the end of 2020.

a. Record the entry for the life insurance payment in 2020.

b. Record the entry for the settlement of the whole-life policy due to the death of the executive.

Solution

a. **Whole-Life Insurance Payment**

Assets = Liabilities + Equity
+1,000 −19,200
−20,200
Cash Surr Value: Bal. 500 | ; 1,000 |
Life Ins Exp: 19,200 |
Cash: | 20,200

2020—To record whole-life insurance payment

Life Insurance Expense	19,200	
Cash Surrender Value of Life Insurance	1,000	
Cash		20,200

b. **Whole-Life Insurance Settlement**

Assets = Liabilities + Equity
+100,000 +98,500
−1,500
Cash: 100,000 | 20,200
Gain—Settlement: | 98,500
Cash Surr Value: 500 | 1,500 ; 1,000 |

2020—To record whole-life insurance settlement

Cash	100,000	
Cash Surrender Value of Life Insurance		1,500
Gain on Settlement of Life Insurance Indemnity		98,500

REVIEW 14-8 LO14-8 Accounting for Other Investments

Review MBC

On December 31, 2020, M4 Inc. decided to create a special-purpose fund to be identified as a special contingency fund. The resources in the fund will be used to settle an environmental obligation on December 31, 2024. The company desires to accumulate a $500,000 fund balance by the end of 2024 by making four equal annual deposits starting on January 1, 2021. The independent trustee handling the fund will increase the fund by 5% compound interest each December 31.

a. Compute the amount of the annual deposit.

b. Provide the entries relating to the fund that M4 Inc. should make on January 1, 2021, and December 31, 2021.

Example Two—Cash Surrender Value

M4 Inc. purchased a $200,000 whole-life policy on its top executive in 2014. In 2020, the company pays an insurance premium in the amount of $12,000. The premium of $12,000 paid in 2020 results in an increase in cash surrender value of $1,800 for a total cash surrender value of $3,300 at the end of 2020. Record the entry for the life insurance payment in 2020.

More Practice:
14-113, 14-114, 14-121

Solution on p. 14-87.

Describe and account for derivatives

APPENDIX 14C
LO 14-9

Accounting for Derivatives

- Recognize derivatives as assets or liabilities
- Value derivatives at fair value
- Generally reflect adjustment to fair value in net income (in one-line item)
- Reflect adjustment to fair value for cash flow hedges in other comprehensive income

LO 14-9 Overview

Over the years, companies have greatly expanded the number and forms of financial instruments and contracts used to conduct financial activities, many of which are called **derivative financial instruments** (often referred to simply as derivatives). Derivatives are so labeled because their value is derived from the value of some **underlying(s)** (the value of stocks, bonds, interest rates, or commodities).

The types of derivatives vary from straightforward, basic instruments, to complex multifaceted instruments. Derivatives may be purchased or sold for speculative purposes or to offset business risks such as those present in volatile domestic financial markets and global markets. To offset the risk of a particular financial holding, a future *positive* outcome of holding a derivative (an increase in fair value or cash flows) counters a future *negative* outcome of holding an instrument (a decrease in fair value or cash flows). Thus, the value of the derivative goes up when the value of the risky financial holding goes down (and vice versa).

This section explains the accounting entries as they apply to four derivative instruments: one held as a speculative instrument and three held as hedging instruments. A **speculative derivative instrument** is simply one that the company has not designated as a hedging derivative instrument. With a **hedging derivative instrument**, a company is taking an offsetting position through a derivative instrument in order to balance gains and losses to an underlying. Irrespective of classification, all derivatives are recognized at fair value.

ASC Glossary **Underlying:** A specified interest rate, security price, commodity price, foreign exchange rate, index of prices or rates, or other variable (including the occurrence or nonoccurrence of a specified event such as a scheduled payment under a contract). An underlying may be a price or rate of an asset or liability but is not the asset or liability itself. An underlying is a variable that, along with either a notional amount or a payment provision, determines the settlement of a derivative instrument.

815-10-05-4 This Topic requires that an entity recognize derivative instruments, including certain derivative instruments embedded in other contracts, as assets or liabilities in the statement of financial position and measure them at fair value.

Two types of derivatives are **option-based contracts** and **obligation-based contracts**. With an option-based contract, the holder of the derivative has an option, but not an obligation to exercise a contract. For example, a holder could have a call option to buy stock at a specified price or a put option to sell stock at a specified future price. An obligation-based contract requires a payment in the future of a specified price in exchange for an underlying asset. For example, two companies may agree to exchange payments based on a specified fixed rate and a variable interest rate. Or, a company may agree to purchase a specified number of euros 6 months from today at a specified price in U.S. dollars.

The four cornerstones underlying the accounting for derivatives and hedges follow.

815-10-10-1

a. Derivative instruments represent rights or obligations that meet the definitions of assets or liabilities and should be reported in financial statements.

b. Fair value is the most relevant measure for financial instruments and the only relevant measure for derivative instruments. Derivative instruments should be measured at fair value, and adjustments to the carrying amount of hedged items should reflect changes in their fair value (that is, gains or losses) that are attributable to the risk being hedged and that arise while the hedge is in effect.

c. Only items that are assets or liabilities should be reported as such in financial statements.

d. Special accounting for items designated as being hedged should be provided only for qualifying items. One aspect of qualification should be an assessment of the expectation of effective offsetting changes in fair values or cash flows during the term of the hedge for the risk being hedged

Speculative Derivative Instrument—Call Option on Stock

In this section we describe the accounting for a derivative not designated as a hedging instrument using a call option as an example. Important terms in the accounting for a call option are defined as follows.

Key Term	Definition
Call option	**ASC Glossary** A contract that allows the holder to buy a specified quantity of stock from the writer of the contract at a fixed price for a given period.
Strike price or exercise price	**ASC Glossary** The amount that must be paid for a share of common stock upon exercise of an option or warrant.
Notional amount	**ASC Glossary** A number of currency units, shares, bushels, pounds, or other units specified in a derivative instrument. Sometimes other names are used. For example, the notional amount is called a face amount in some contracts.

Demo 14-9A illustrates the accounting treatment of a call option held as a speculative derivative instrument. A call option provides the holder the right, but not the obligation, to purchase a specified quantity of securities (such as common stock) at a specified price (exercise price), within a specified period. The **call date** is the date that the holder of a call option chooses to exercise the call option. A call option is recognized at the price paid for the instrument and the carrying value is adjusted to fair value at each reporting date. The adjustments are recognized in net income in the period of the adjustment.

815-10-35-3 The gain or loss on a derivative instrument not designated as a hedging instrument shall be recognized currently in earnings.

Demo 14-9A LO14-9 Call Option as a Speculative Investment—Underlying is Fair Value of Stock

Montana purchases a call option contract for $250 on November 1, 2020, from Goldman Investors Inc. The contract allows Montana (the holder) to call (purchase) at any time in the next 12 months, 100 shares of Risky Inc. stock at a strike price of $50 per share. If the contract is exercised, it can be settled by payment (from Goldman Investors Inc. to Montana) for an amount equal to the difference between the market price of 100 shares of Risky Inc. stock on the call date and the strike price of $5,000 ($50 × 100 shares). The underlying instrument of this call option is the stock of Risky Inc. because the value of the call option depends on the value of the stock of Risky Inc. If the value of Risky Inc. remains below $50 a share, over the next 12 months the call option expires worthless. The notional amount is the 100 shares that can be called at $50 per share.

Required

a. Prepare the entry to record the purchase of the call option by Montana.

b. Record the adjusting entries on December 31, 2020, assuming the fair value of the option is now $1,350.

c. Montana chooses to settle the option on December 31, 2020. (In practice, the option contract does not typically require the actual transfer of shares upon the exercise of the contract. The issuer of the contract can settle with payment of cash in an amount equal to the net gain of the holder.) Record the entry for the settlement of the call option on December 31, 2020, assuming Risky Inc.'s stock value is $60 per share.

d. Present the impact on the 2020 income statement of the derivative transactions for Montana.

Solution

a. **Purchase of Call Option**

Montana records an asset, Call Option, for the amount paid under contract, or the option premium.

Assets = Liabilities + Equity
+250
−250
Call Option: 250 (debit) | Cash: 250 (credit)

November 1, 2020—To record option premium

Call Option	250	
Cash		250

b. **Adjustment of Call Option to Fair Value**

At December 31, 2020, Montana would record a gain equal to the change in the fair value of the call option of $1,100.

Assets = Liabilities + Equity
+1,100 +1,100
Call Option: 250, 1,100 (debit) | Unreal Gain or Loss—Inc: 1,100 (credit)

December 31, 2020—To record value of call option

Call Option	1,100	
Unrealized Gain or Loss—Income ($1,350 − $250)		1,100

continued

continued from previous page

c. **Settlement of Call Option**

After making the preceding adjustments to the fair value of the options, Montana would record the following entry on the call date. (A company will always record a loss if the option is exercised early.)

December 31, 2020—To record settlement of call option on call date

Cash [($60 − $50) × 100].	1,000	
Loss on Settlement of Call Option.	350	
Call Option.		1,350

Assets	=	Liabilities	+	Equity
+1,000				−350
−1,350				

Call Option

250	1,350
1,100	
0	

Loss on Settle

350	

Cash

1,000	250

d. **Financial Statement Presentation**

Montana would record the following in its 2020 income statement.

Income Statement excerpt **For Year Ended December 31, 2020**	
Other revenues and gains	
Net gain on call option ($1,100 − $350).	$750

Hedging Derivative Instrument—Put Option as a Fair Value Hedge

The terms fair value hedge and put option are defined as follows.

Key Term	Definition
Fair value hedge	ASC Glossary A hedge of the exposure to changes in the fair value of a recognized asset or liability, or of an unrecognized firm commitment, that are attributable to a particular risk.
Put option*	ASC Glossary A contract that allows the holder to sell a specified quantity of stock to the writer of the contract at a fixed price during a given period.

* Not all put options are fair value hedges.

Fair value hedges are purchased to offset the risk of holding certain assets or liabilities. **Demo 14-9B** illustrates the accounting treatment of a put option, held as a hedging derivative instrument. With a put option, the holder has the option to require the seller of the option to purchase an asset at a specified price and date. The holder can "put" the asset to the counterparty. For example, a company may purchase a put option allowing the company to sell a bond held at a designated price to a counterparty. The put option offsets the risk of a company holding a bond that unexpectedly decreases in fair value. A put option is recognized at the price paid for the instrument. Subsequently, the put option is adjusted to fair value with the adjustment recognized in net income. *At the same time when the put is designated as a hedging instrument, changes in the fair value of the hedged item are also recognized in net income* even though changes in fair value would not normally be recorded, for example a bond classified as HTM. In cases where the risk is completely offset, the impact on the income statement will be zero. In other words, if the market price of the stock goes down, the market price of the put option goes up. The offsetting changes are presented net in one line item on the income statement.

815-25-35-1 Gains and losses on a qualifying fair value hedge shall be accounted for as follows:

a. The gain or loss on the hedging instrument shall be recognized currently in earnings, except for amounts excluded from the assessment of effectiveness that are recognized in earnings through an amortization approach[1]. . . All amounts recognized in earnings shall be presented in the same income statement line item as the earnings effect of the hedged item.

b. The gain or loss (that is, the change in fair value) on the hedged item attributable to the hedged risk shall adjust the carrying amount of the hedged item and be recognized currently in earnings.

[1] If a company elects to exclude amounts from the assessment of effectiveness, the excluded amounts are reflected in earnings immediately or over the life of the option using a systematic and rational approach such as the straight-line interest method.

815-25-35-4 Any gain or loss on the hedging instrument that does not offset the gain or loss on the hedged item attributable to the hedged risk is recognized in earnings in the same income statement line item as the earnings effect of the hedged item.

In order for an instrument to qualify for hedge accounting, both at the inception of the hedge and on an ongoing basis, the hedge must be considered **highly effective** at offsetting the specified risk during the period the hedge is designated. Highly effective is interpreted in practice as a change in the fair value of the hedge being within 80% to 125% of the change in the fair value of the hedged item pertaining to the risk being hedged.

EXPANDING YOUR KNOWLEDGE — **Ongoing Assessment of Effectiveness**

Initially, an assessment of hedge effectiveness must be done through a *quantitative test*. However, subsequent assessment may be performed through a *qualitative test* if certain criteria are met.

815-20-35-2 If a fair value hedge or cash flow hedge initially qualifies for hedge accounting, the entity would continue to assess whether the hedge meets the effectiveness test on either a quantitative basis (using either a dollar-offset test or a statistical method such as regression analysis) or a qualitative basis... If the hedge fails the effectiveness test at any time (that is, if the entity does not expect the hedge to be highly effective at achieving offsetting changes in fair values or cash flows), the hedge ceases to qualify for hedge accounting. At least quarterly, the hedging entity shall determine whether the hedging relationship has been highly effective in having achieved offsetting changes in fair value or cash flows through the date of the periodic assessment.

815-20-35-2A An entity may qualitatively assess hedge effectiveness if both of the following criteria are met:

a. An entity performs an initial quantitative test of hedge effectiveness on a prospective basis . . . and the results of that quantitative test demonstrate highly effective offset.

b. At hedge inception, an entity can reasonably support an expectation of high effectiveness on a qualitative basis in subsequent periods.

Demo 14-9B LO14-9 Put Option as a Fair Value Hedge—Underlying is an Asset

Demo MBC

Montana Inc. would like to offset the risk of market declines of its holding of bonds issued by Rivendell Corp. Therefore, Montana enters into a put option agreement with Goldman Investors Inc., which allows Montana to sell the bonds at a fixed price to Goldman Investors Inc. Thus, Montana will benefit from potential increases in the fair value of Rivendell Corp. bonds while not being exposed to the risk of decreases in the fair value of Rivendell Corp. bonds. For simplicity, ignore interest on the bond.

Required

a. Record the entry by Montana, for the acquisition on January 2, 2020, of 100, $50, 5% bonds issued by Rivendell Corp. at par. Montana classifies the bonds as HTM and measures the bonds at amortized cost.

b. On June 30, 2020, to avoid exposure to possible declines in the fair value of the bond investment, Montana enters into a 2-year put option with Goldman Investors Inc. The agreement allows Montana to sell 100 bonds at a price of $50 each, the current fair value of each bond. The cost of the fair value hedge (put option) is zero. (Although there would typically be a cost for Montana to purchase this put option, the purchase price is assumed to be zero to simplify the illustration.) The put option is considered highly effective. Record the entry required for entering into the put option agreement.

c. On December 31, 2020, Rivendell Corp. bonds are trading at $40 per bond, which caused the fair value of the put option to increase from zero to $1,000. Record the entry to adjust the bond investment and put option to fair value.

d. Present the impact of the derivative transactions on the 2020 income statement and December 31, 2020, balance sheet.

Solution

a. **Purchase of the Underlying Asset—Debt Security**

January 2, 2020—To record purchase of debt investment

Assets	= Liabilities	+ Equity
+5,000		
−5,000		

Invest—HTM	
5,000	

Cash	
	5,000

Investment in HTM Securities—Rivendell Bonds	5,000	
Cash ($50 × 100)		5,000

b. **Put Option Purchase**

The cost of the fair value hedge (put option) is zero; thus no entry is required on June 30, 2020.

continued

continued from previous page

c. **Adjustment of Investment in Bonds and Put Option to Fair Value**

December 31, 2020—To adjust debt investment to fair value

Unrealized Gain or Loss—Income	1,000	
Fair Value Adjustment—HTM [($50 − $40) × 100]		1,000

Assets = Liabilities + Equity
−1,000 −1,000
FVA—HTM: 1,000 (credit) | Unreal Gain or Loss—Inc: 1,000 (debit)

December 31, 2020—To record fair value adjustment of put option

Put Option [($50 − $40) × 100 shares]	1,000	
Unrealized Gain or Loss—Income		1,000

Assets = Liabilities + Equity
+1,000 +1,000
Put Option: 1,000 (debit) | Unreal Gain or Loss—Inc: 1,000 (debit) 1,000 (credit)

The entries above match the change in the value of the put option (recorded in an asset account—Put Option) to the related change in the fair value of the underlying asset, the debt security. In this example, the net impact on the income statement is zero.

d. **Financial Statement Presentation**

In the December 31, 2020, balance sheet and 2020 income statement, Montana would recognize the following.

Balance Sheet excerpt December 31, 2020		Income Statement excerpt For Year Ended December 31, 2020	
Assets		Other revenues and gains	
Investment in debt securities	$4,000	Net unrealized holding gain or loss	
Put option	1,000	($1,000 − $1,000)	$0

Hedging Derivative Instrument—Interest Rate Swap as a Fair Value Hedge

The terms interest rate swap and LIBOR are defined as follows.

Key Term	Definition
Interest rate swap	A contractual agreement between two parties to exchange particular cash flows on particular dates in the future. Given a principal amount, one party makes payments based on fixed interest rates while the other party makes payments based on variable interest rates.
LIBOR	LIBOR (London Interbank Offer Rate) is a commonly used parameter upon which variable interest rates are linked. LIBOR is the rate a number of international banks use for interbank lending/borrowing. LIBOR represents an accepted measure of the current short-term interest rate.

An interest rate swap is a commonly used form of derivative to allow a company to offset the risk of paying fixed interest payments over a fixed period of time. A fixed rate liability has fair value risk. When rates go down, the value of the liability increases, and when rates go up, the value of the liability decreases. An interest rate swap helps to mitigate that risk by allowing the purchaser of the interest rate swap to make variable interest payments. As in the prior example, a hedge designed to offset fair value risk is treated as a fair value hedge. In this case the hedged item is a liability, rather than an asset, and the hedging instrument is a swap rather than a put option.

Demo 14-9C illustrates the accounting treatment of a hedge involving a benchmark interest rate treated as a fair value hedge. **Any unrealized gains or losses on holding an interest rate swap along with corresponding changes in the fair value of an underlying liability are reflected in the income statement.** When a swap meets the GAAP criteria of effectiveness in achieving offsetting changes in the fair value of the underlying (debt), the **shortcut method** is permitted. This method allows the holder of the swap to use the change in the fair value of the swap as an estimate for the offsetting change in the liability's fair value.

815-20-25-102 The conditions for the shortcut method do not determine which hedging relationships qualify for hedge accounting; rather, those conditions determine which hedging relationships qualify for a shortcut version of hedge accounting that assumes perfect hedge effectiveness. If all of the applicable conditions in the list in paragraph 815-20-25-104 are met, an entity may assume perfect effectiveness in a hedging relationship of interest rate risk.

Demo 14-9C LO14-9 Interest Rate Swap as a Fair Value Hedge—Underlying is a Liability

Montana Inc. issued a 5-year note payable to a bank for $10,000 on January 1, 2020, at a fixed interest rate of 7%. *Montana would like to offset the risk of paying fixed interest on the note over a 5-year period.* As a result, Montana enters into an interest rate swap contract on January 1, 2020, with Goldman Investors Inc., which allows Montana to effectively pay interest based on LIBOR over five years. The swap calls for Montana to receive fixed payments from the counterparty (Goldman Investors Inc.) equal to 7% on the notional amount of $10,000 and to make payments to the counterparty based upon the current market interest rate. Effectively, the note payable is converted from a fixed interest payment to a variable interest payment that fluctuates with the market. The hedge is considered to be highly effective. The cash settlement of the interest rate swap takes place annually on December 31, correlating with the interest payment date on the note payable to the bank and consists of the difference between the market interest and the fixed interest. At the date of the swap agreement, the swap has no value.

Required

a. Record the issuance of the note payable and the swap agreement on January 1, 2020.
b. Record the interest payment to the bank on December 31, 2020.
c. Record any payments related to the interest rate swap on December 31, 2020, assuming that the market rate is 6% on December 31, 2020.
d. The estimated fair value of the swap at December 31, 2020, is $400. Record any required adjusting entries on December 31, 2020, related to the fair value of the swap and underlying liability.
e. Present the impact of the derivative transactions on the December 31, 2020, balance sheet and the 2020 income statement.

Solution

a. **Issuance of Note Payable**

Montana records the following entry for the issuance of the note.

Assets = Liabilities + Equity
+10,000 +10,000
Cash: 10,000 (Dr) | Note Payable: 10,000 (Cr)

January 1, 2020—To record issuance of note

Cash	10,000	
Note Payable		10,000

At the date of the swap agreement, the swap has no value; thus no entry is required.

b. **Interest Expense on Note Payable**

At the end of 2020, Montana makes the payment to the bank for the interest on the note.

Assets = Liabilities + Equity
−700 −700
Cash: 10,000 (Dr) 700 (Cr) | Interest Exp: 700 (Dr)

December 31, 2020—To record interest on note payable

Interest Expense	700	
Cash (7% × $10,000)		700

c. **Payment Received on Interest Rate Swap**

The market rate declined to 6% causing an increase to the value of the interest rate swap. Interest based upon the market rate is $600 ($10,000 × 6%). Thus, the payment due to Montana at the settlement date of December 31, 2020, is the difference between the fixed and market interest of $100 ($700 − $600). Montana records the following entry for payment received based upon the swap agreement.

Assets = Liabilities + Equity
+100 +100
Cash: 10,000, 100 (Dr) 700 (Cr) | Interest Exp: 700 (Dr) 100 (Cr)

December 31, 2020—To record payment received on interest rate swap

Cash	100	
Interest Expense		100

d. **Adjustment of Swap and Underlying Liability to Fair Value**

Montana would record an entry for an unrealized gain on holding the swap along with a corresponding increase to the note payable to adjust it to fair value. In the case of an interest rate swap, GAAP requires a deviation in reporting the note payable from the amortized cost method to FV-NI.

continued

continued from previous page

December 31, 2020—To record fair value adjustment of interest rate swap

Interest Rate Swap Contract.	400	
Unrealized Gain or Loss—Income		400

Assets	=	Liabilities	+	Equity
+400				+400
Interest Rate Swap: 400 (debit)				Unreal Gain or Loss—Inc: 400 (credit)

December 31, 2020—To record fair value adjustment of note payable

Unrealized Gain or Loss—Income	400	
Note Payable		400

Assets	=	Liabilities	+	Equity
		+400		−400
Unreal Gain or Loss—Inc: 400 (debit) | 400 (credit)				Note Payable: 10,000 (credit); 400 (credit)

e. **Financial Statement Presentation**

In the December 31, 2020, balance sheet and the 2020 income statement, Montana would recognize the following.

Balance Sheet excerpt December 31, 2020	
Assets	
Interest rate swap contract	$400
Liabilities	
Note payable.	10,400

Income Statement excerpt For Year Ended December 31, 2020	
Other expenses and losses	
Interest expense ($700 − $100).	$600
Net unrealized hold gain or loss ($400 − $400).	$0

Hedging Derivative Instrument—Cash Flow Hedge

The terms cash flow hedge and futures contract are defined as follows.

Key Term	Definition
Cash flow hedge	**ASC Glossary** A hedge of the exposure to variability in the cash flows of a recognized asset or liability, or of a forecasted transaction, that is attributable to a particular risk.
Futures contract	**ASC Glossary** A standard and transferable form of contract that binds the seller to deliver to the bearer a standard amount and grade of a commodity to a specific location at a specified time. It usually includes a schedule of premiums and discounts for quality variation.

Demo 14-9D illustrates the accounting treatment of a cash flow hedge in the form of a futures contract. Cash flow hedges are purchased in order to offset a *future cash flow such as a future purchase of materials used for production that would otherwise be impacted by changes in the market price for those materials.* A cash flow hedge hedges exposure to cash flow risk resulting from the variability in expected future cash flows that is attributable to a particular, identifiable risk. **In the case of a cash flow hedge, unrealized gains or losses on a derivative instrument will be reflected in other comprehensive income and later reclassified into earnings in the period when the hedged transaction affects earnings (for example, when the inventory is sold).**

815-30-35-3 When the relationship between the hedged item and hedging instrument is highly effective at achieving offsetting changes in cash flows attributable to the hedged risk, an entity shall record in other comprehensive income the entire change in the fair value of the designated hedging instrument that is included in the assessment of hedge effectiveness. More specifically, a qualifying cash flow hedge shall be accounted for as follows:

a. An entity's defined risk management strategy for a particular hedging relationship may exclude a specific component of the gain or loss, or related cash flows, on the hedging derivative from the assessment of hedge effectiveness . . . That excluded component of the gain or loss shall be recognized in earnings either through an amortization approach . . . or through a mark-to-market approach.

b. Amounts in accumulated other comprehensive income related to the derivative designated as a hedging instrument included in the assessment of hedge effectiveness are reclassified to earnings in the same period or periods during which the hedged forecasted transaction affects earnings . . . and presented in the same income statement line item as the earnings effect of the hedged item.

815-30-35-39 If the hedged transaction results in the acquisition of an asset or the incurrence of a liability, the gains and losses in accumulated other comprehensive income that are included in the assessment of effectiveness shall be reclassified into earnings in the same period or periods during which the asset acquired or liability incurred affects earnings (such as in the periods that depreciation expense, interest expense, or cost of sales is recognized).

EXPANDING YOUR KNOWLEDGE **Contractually Specified Component**

The types of hedges that qualify for hedge accounting include contractually specified components of total price risk.

ASC Glossary Contractually Specified Component: An index or price explicitly referenced in an agreement to purchase or sell a nonfinancial asset other than an index or price calculated or measured solely by reference to an entity's own operations.

For example, a company may designate a commodity index as a component of price risk. In that way, only the changes in the hedged item relating to changes in future commodity prices are analyzed in the hedging relationship, not changes due to other factors affecting the hedged items such as quality or delivery locations.

Demo 14-9D LO14-9 Futures Contract as a Cash Flow Hedge—Underlying is the Market Price of a Purchase

Demo MBC

On October 30, 2020, Seattle's Best Coffee (SBC) projects a need to purchase 1,000 pounds of Brazilian coffee on July 1, 2021. The spot price or the current acquisition price of Brazilian coffee is $1.00 per pound. *SBC would like to offset the risk of potential price increases of coffee.* As a result, on October 30, 2020, SBC enters into a futures contract with Clearing House Inc. to take delivery of 1,000 pounds of coffee on July 1, 2021, at a price of $1.00 per pound. The underlying is the price of coffee. Under the contract, SBC purchases the coffee at the current market price when needed in July 2021. However, Clearing House Inc. must pay SBC for all market price increases over $1.00, while SBC must pay Clearing House Inc. for all market price decreases (under $1). Thus, the company shifts the risk of market price increases to Clearing House Inc. The cost of the fair value hedge (futures contract) is zero. The hedge is considered to be highly effective.

Required

a. Record the entry on October 30, 2020, for the initiation of the futures contract.
b. On December 31, 2020, the price of coffee rises to $1.20. Record the fair value adjustment of the futures contract.
c. On July 1, 2021, SBC executes the futures contract when the price of coffee is $1.25 per pound. Record the entries for the execution of the contract.
d. The entire inventory of coffee was sold to SBC's major customer on September 30, 2021, at $1.85 per pound. Prepare the entry to record the credit sale.
e. Present the impact of the sale on the 2021 income statement.

Solution

a. **Purchase of Futures Contract**
The cost of the fair value hedge (futures contract) is zero; thus no entry is required on October 30, 2020.

b. **Adjustment of Futures Contract to Fair Value**
The futures contract (recorded in an asset account) now has a value of $200 [($1.20 − $1.00) × 1,000 pounds]. The fair value adjustment will affect *other comprehensive income* rather than net income. The following entry is required on December 31, 2020.

Assets = Liabilities + Equity
+200 +200
Futures Contract 200 | Gain or Loss—OCI | 200

December 31, 2020—To record fair value adjustment of futures contract

Futures Contract	200	
Gain or Loss—OCI		200

c. **Execution of Futures Contract**
SBC acquires 1,000 pounds of coffee at a price of $1.25 per pound, for a total cost of $1,250. However, SBC is reimbursed by Clearing House Inc. for $250 or the difference between $1.25 and $1.00 per pound for the 1,000 pounds of coffee. If SBC had not entered into the hedge contract, it would have had to acquire the 1,000 pounds of coffee at $1.25 per pound, or a total of $1,250. SBC has a realized gain of $250 from the hedge.

Assets = Liabilities + Equity
+1,250
−1,250
Inventory 1,250 | Cash | 1,250

July 1, 2021—To record purchase of coffee at market

Coffee Inventory	1,250	
Cash ($1.25 × 1,000 pounds)		1,250

continued

continued from previous page

July 1, 2021—To record payment from Clearing House on settlement of futures contract

Cash [($1.25 − $1.00) × 1,000 pounds]	250	
Gain or Loss—OCI		50
Futures Contract		200

Assets = Liabilities + Equity
+250 +50
−200

Cash: 250 | 1,250
Gain or Loss—OCI: 200 | 50
Futures Contract: 200 | 200

d. **Sale of Merchandise**
SBC would record the following entry for the sale of coffee.

September 30, 2021—To record credit sale of coffee

Accounts Receivable	1,850	
Sales ($1.85 × 1,000 pounds)		1,850
Cost of Goods Sold	1,250	
Coffee Inventory		1,250
Gain or Loss—OCI	250	
Cost of Goods Sold		250

Assets = Liabilities + Equity
+1,850 +1,850
−1,250 −1,250
+250
−250

Accounts Rec: 1,850 |
Sales: | 1,850
Inventory: 1,250 | 1,250
COGS: 1,250 | 250
Gain or Loss—OCI: 200 | 200; 250 | 250

e. **Financial Statement Presentation**
With a cash flow hedge, gains or losses are deferred in OCI until earnings are affected by the hedged transaction. Earnings is affected in this scenario when the inventory was sold, at which time the company expenses inventory costs and reclassifies the gain in OCI to Cost of Goods Sold. In this case, the reclassification adjustment reduces Cost of Goods Sold by $250. SBC reports the following amounts in its 2021 income statement.

Income Statement excerpt **For Year Ended December 31, 2021**	
Sales	$1,850
Cost of goods sold on coffee ($1,250 – $250)	(1,000)
Gross profit	$ 850

Summary of Derivative Instruments

The following table summarizes the four derivative examples illustrated in this section consisting of one speculative derivative and three hedging derivatives.

Type of Financial Derivative	Illustrated Derivative Example	Income Statement Impact of the Derivative Transaction	Financial Presentation of Underlying
Speculative investment	Call Option **Demo 14-9A**	Net gain: $750	No underlying asset or liability
Fair value hedge	Put Option **Demo 14-9B**	Net gain/loss: $0 (Amounts are completely offsetting.)	Underlying—Bond investment, recognized at fair value at reporting dates for changes in fair value during the hedging period.
Fair value hedge	Interest Rate Swap **Demo 14-9C**	Net interest expense: $600 (Amount equals market interest.)	Underlying—Note payable, recognized at fair value at reporting dates for changes in fair value during the hedging period.
Cash flow hedge	Futures Contract **Demo 14-9D**	COGS (net): $1,000 (Amount equals the contract price.)	Underlying—Inventory, recognized at cost upon purchase

There are literally hundreds of different financial contracts that are being created today; thus there are many different kinds of derivatives. We provide illustrations of three fundamental types: options, swaps, and futures. Many derivative financial instruments are composed of a combination of these three fundamental types. In this text, it is not necessary or possible to show applications of the myriad of complex derivatives or of derivatives embedded in other contracts. More detailed review of derivatives will be covered in advanced accounting courses.

EXPANDING YOUR KNOWLEDGE — **Foreign Currency Hedges**

A company can hedge exposure to foreign currency risks. The hedged item can be a single unrecognized firm commitment (foreign currency fair value or cash flow hedge), an asset or liability such as an available-for-sale debt security (foreign currency fair value hedge), a forecasted transaction (foreign currency cash flow hedge), or a net investment in a foreign operation. The accounting guidance indicates that the following items may be designated as derivative instruments if certain conditions are met.

815-10-05-4c A hedge of the foreign currency exposure of any one of the following:

1. An unrecognized firm commitment (a foreign currency fair value hedge)
2. An available-for-sale debt security (a foreign currency fair value hedge)
3. A forecasted transaction (a foreign currency cash flow hedge)
4. A net investment in a foreign operation.

PEPSICO [PEP]

PEPSICO

Real World—DERIVATIVE INSTRUMENTS

In this section, examples were provided both of derivatives held as speculative investments and as hedges to offset risk. The following disclosure from a recent annual report of PepsiCo, Inc. indicates that derivatives were purchased for hedging purposes only.

> **Note 9 Financial Instruments** (excerpt) We do not use derivative instruments for trading or speculative purposes. We perform assessments of our counterparty credit risk regularly, including reviewing netting agreements, if any, and a review of credit ratings, credit default swap rates and potential nonperformance of the counterparty. Based on our most recent assessment of our counterparty credit risk, we consider this risk to be low. In addition, we enter into derivative contracts with a variety of financial institutions that we believe are creditworthy in order to reduce our concentration of credit risk.

REVIEW 14-9 LO14-9 Accounting for Derivatives

Review MBC

Example One—Speculative Derivative—Call Option

On January 1, 2020, Hyett Inc. purchased a call option for $40 which allows Hyett to purchase 75 shares of Seafood Inc. stock at a strike price of $40 per share through December 31, 2020. On January 1, 2020, the fair value of Seafood Inc. is $40 per share. On June 30, 2020, the fair value of each share of Seafood Inc. stock is $45 per share, and the fair value of the option is $380.

a. Record the entries to adjust the call option to fair value on June 30, 2020.
b. Assuming that Hyett settles the call option on June 30, 2020, record the journal entry.
c. What is the total impact on 2020 net income related to the call options?

Example Two—Accounting for Put Option

Hyett Inc. purchased at par, 200, $50, 5% bonds of Seafood Inc. classified as HTM securities on January 1, 2020. In order to avoid exposure to possible declines in the value of Seafood Inc. bonds, Hyett acquires a 12-month put option on January 1, 2020, to sell 200 bonds of Seafood Inc. at a price of $50 per bond. The hedge is considered to be highly effective. On December 31, 2020, the market price per share of Seafood bonds fell to $35 per bond while the value of the put option is estimated to be $2,800. For simplicity, ignore interest on the bonds and assume the purchase price of the put option is zero.

a. Prepare the entry to adjust the investment to fair value on December 31, 2020.
b. Prepare the entry to adjust the put option to fair value on December 31, 2020.
c. Calculate the net effect on the income statement of holding the put option and the debt securities in 2020.

continued

continued from previous page

Example Three—Accounting for Interest Rate Swap

Review MBC

On January 2, 2020, Hyett Inc. enters into a 5-year interest rate swap contract in order to effectively hedge against the fixed annual interest payments of a 3-year, 4%, $50,000 note. The swap calls for Hyett Inc. to receive payments annually on December 31 from the counterparty based upon a 4% interest rate for a notional amount of $50,000 and to make payments to the counterparty based upon LIBOR. LIBOR is 4.2% as of January 2, 2020, and the rate will be adjusted every 12 months to the current LIBOR rate. The swap has zero value on January 2, 2020, and on December 31, 2020. The hedge is considered to be highly effective.

a. Prepare the journal entry on January 2, 2020, to record the issuance of the note and the initiation of the interest rate swap agreement.

b. Prepare the entries related to the note payable and the interest rate swap on December 31, 2020, assuming LIBOR remains unchanged.

Example Four—Accounting for Futures Contract

Hyett Inc. is holding a futures contract classified as a cash flow hedge with an original cost of zero. The futures contract hedges the risk of future purchases of materials totaling 10,000 pounds. The futures contract provides that Hyett purchases the required materials at the future date needed at market price, but the counterparty must pay Hyett any differences above $5.00 per pound while Hyett pays to the counterparty any differences below $5.00 per pound. The hedge is considered to be highly effective. If the materials are selling for $5.10 per pound on December 31, 2020, the first reporting date, what adjusting entry is required?

More Practice: 14-122, 14-123, 14-124, 14-125

Solution on p. 14-88.

Questions

14-1. Define a security. Distinguish between debt and equity securities.

14-2. Briefly describe the methods to account for debt investments. How does an investor determine the appropriate accounting method to follow?

14-3. On July 1, 2020, Baker Company purchased $50,000 of LoCal Company 6% bonds at par value. The bonds pay interest semiannually on July 1 and January 1. At December 31, 2020, the bonds have a fair value of $51,000. Provide the journal entries (a) to record the purchase of the investment, assuming that the bonds are classified as trading securities, and (b) to record investment income and any other needed adjustments at December 31, 2020.

14-4. If an investor holds an equity security investment where the investor does not exert significant influence, explain the appropriate accounting for the investment.

14-5. What accounts are affected by a sale of a debt security classified as HTM?

14-6. What is the most significant difference in the accounting treatment of an available-for-sale debt security compared to a trading debt security?

14-7. Explain the basic features of the equity method of accounting for long-term investments. When is the equity method applicable?

14-8. Why is the equity method sometimes called the one-line consolidation method?

14-9. How would an investor typically report a dividend declared by a company in which it holds a 40% voting interest? A 10% voting interest?

14-10. Indicate reasons why a 30% ownership interest in another company may not be considered significant.

14-11. When are unrealized holding gains and losses on debt securities included in the determination of net income? When are unrealized holding gains and losses on equity securities included in the determination of net income?

14-12. Describe the balance sheet categorization and valuation within the asset section when an investment in securities is classified as

a. Trading debt securities.
b. Available-for-sale debt securities.
c. Held-to-maturity debt securities.
d. Equity securities measured at FV-NI.
e. Equity method securities.

14-13. What is the financial statement impact when an investment is reclassified from a trading debt security to an available-for-sale debt security? When an available-for-sale debt security is reclassified as a trading debt security?

14-14. Explain when the fair value option of accounting for equity investments is applicable. What is the financial statement impact of accounting for investments under the fair value option?

14-15. What approach(es) are used to analyze impairment on available-for-sale and held-to-maturity debt securities?

Brief Exercises

Brief Exercise 14-16
Recording Entries for Debt HTM Investments **LO1**
Hint: See Demo 14-1C

On January 1, 2020, Sharp Company purchased $50,000 of Sox Company 6% bonds, at a time when the market rate was 5%. The bonds mature on December 31, 2024, and pay interest annually on December 31. Sharp plans to and has the ability to hold the bonds until maturity. Assume that Sharp uses the effective interest method to amortize any premium or discount on investments in bonds. At December 31, 2020, the bonds are quoted at 98.

a. Prepare the entry for the purchase of the debt investment on January 1, 2020.
b. Prepare the entry for the receipt of interest on December 31, 2020.
c. Record the entry to adjust the investment to fair value on December 31, 2020, if applicable.

Brief Exercise 14-17
Recording Entries for Debt HTM Investments **LO1**
Hint: See Demo 14-1B

On January 1, 2020, Sharp Company purchased $50,000 of Sox Company 5% bonds, at a time when the market rate was 6%. The bonds mature on December 31, 2024, and pay interest semiannually on June 30 and December 31. Sharp plans to and has the ability to hold the bonds until maturity. Assume that Sharp uses the effective interest method to amortize any premium or discount on investments in bonds. At June 30, 2020, the bonds are quoted at 98.

a. Prepare the entry for the purchase of the debt investment on January 1, 2020.
b. Prepare the entry for the receipt of interest on June 30, 2020.
c. Record the entry to adjust the investment to fair value on June 30, 2020, if applicable.

Brief Exercise 14-18
Recording Entries for TS **LO2**
Hint: See Demo 14-2A

Henry Inc. purchased $5,000 of Container Corporation's 5% bonds at par. The purchase is made on January 1, 2020, and the investment is classified as a trading security. At June 30, 2020, Henry Inc. received semiannual interest of $125, and the fair value of the bonds was $4,800. Prepare Henry's journal entries for (*a*) the purchase of the investment, (*b*) the interest received, and (*c*) the fair value adjustment.

Brief Exercise 14-19
Recording Entry for Sale of TS Debt Trading Securities **LO2**

① Adjust FVA at Year-End Referring to information in Brief Exercise 14-18, assume that Henry Inc. sold its holdings of Container Corporation bonds on July 2, 2020, for $4,800.

a. Record the sale of the debt investment.
b. Adjust the Fair Value Adjustment account on December 31, 2020, the company's year-end.

Brief Exercise 14-20
Recording Entry for Sale of TS Debt Trading Securities **LO2**
Hint: See Demo 14-2A

② Adjust FVA at Sale and Year-End Referring to information in Brief Exercise 14-18, assume that Henry Inc. sold its holdings of Container Corporation bonds on July 2, 2020, for $4,800. Record the sale of the debt investment, eliminating the Fair Value Adjustment account upon sale.

Brief Exercise 14-21
Recording Entries for AFS Securities **LO3**
Hint: See Demo 14-3A

Assume the same facts as in Brief Exercise 14-16, except that Sharp Company does not intend to trade the bonds or to hold them until maturity.

a. Prepare the entry for the purchase of the debt investment on January 1, 2020.
b. Prepare the entry for the receipt of interest on December 31, 2020.
c. Record the entry to adjust the investment to fair value on December 31, 2020, if applicable.

Brief Exercise 14-22
Adjusting AFS Securities to Fair Value **LO3**
Hint: See Demo 14-3A

Tracking Co. holds an AFS bond investment in Fields Corp. The carrying value of the investment is $4,500 at December 31, 2020. Tracking Co. determines the fair value of the investment at the end of the year 2020 to be

$5,400. Prepare the journal entry, if any, to record the difference between the fair value and the carrying value. The Fair Value Adjustment account had a zero balance on January 1, 2020.

Brief Exercise 14-23 Adjusting AFS Securities to Fair Value **LO3**

The following information relates to an AFS security investment held by Gomez Inc.

	Dec. 31, 2019	Dec. 31, 2020
Fair value	$30,000	$33,000
Carrying value	28,000	30,000

Provide the journal entry to adjust the investment to fair value on December 31, 2020.

Brief Exercise 14-24 Determining Impact on Financial Reporting of Unrealized Losses **LO3**

Turbo Corporation had net income of $30,000 and other comprehensive income of $0 prior to the following two adjustments: Turbo Corporation discovered it has an unrealized holding loss of $1,000 related to available-for-sale debt securities and an unrealized holding loss of $500 related to trading debt securities. Ignoring income taxes, what are the adjusted totals for (*a*) net income, (*b*) other comprehensive income, and (*c*) comprehensive income?

Brief Exercise 14-25 Reporting Comprehensive Income with Reclassification Adjustments **LO3**

Phelps Company reported the following amounts this past year.

- Revenues, $50,000.
- Expenses, $30,000.
- Realized loss on sale of AFS debt investments, $5,000.
- Reclassification adjustment for AFS debt investments sold during the period, $5,000.
- Unrealized holding gain on currently held AFS debt investments, $1,000.

Ignoring income taxes, calculate (*a*) net income and (*b*) comprehensive income.

Brief Exercise 14-26 Recording Entries of Equity Securities: FV-NI **LO4** *Hint:* See Demo 14-4

① **Adjust FVA at Year-End** An investor purchased 100 shares of Mallard common stock at $20 per share on March 15, 2020. On December 31, 2020, the stock was quoted at $19 per share and declared and paid a dividend of $1.50 per share. On June 5, 2021, the investor sold the stock for $22 per share. On December 31, 2021, the Fair Value Adjustment account is adjusted. Assuming the investment is measured at FV-NI, provide the journal entries to be made at each of the following dates.

a. March 15, 2020.
b. December 31, 2020.
c. June 5, 2021.
d. December 31, 2021.

Brief Exercise 14-27 Recording Entries of Equity Securities: FV-NI **LO4**

② **Adjust FVA at Sale and Year-End** An investor purchased 100 shares of Mallard common stock at $20 per share on March 15, 2020. On December 31, 2020, the stock was quoted at $19 per share and declared and paid a dividend of $1.50 per share. On June 5, 2021, the investor sold the stock for $22 per share. Assuming the investment is measured at FV-NI, provide the journal entries to be made at each of the following dates. On the date of sale, update the Fair Value Adjustment account prior to the sale and eliminate its balance at the date of sale.

a. March 15, 2020.
b. December 31, 2020.
c. June 5, 2021.

Brief Exercise 14-28 Recording Entries for Equity Securities: FV-NI **LO4**

Lance Co. purchased 100 shares of Mallard common stock at $20 per share on March 15, 2020. Mallard declared and paid a dividend of $1.50 per share in 2020. The market price on December 31, 2020, is unavailable because the fair value of the stock is not readily determinable. Assume that the amount of $2,000 is a measure of cost less impairment, adjusted for observable price changes for an identical investment for this equity investment. Assuming the investment is measured at FV-NI, provide the journal entries to be made at each of the following dates.

a. March 15, 2020.
b. December 31, 2020.

Brief Exercise 14-29 Analyzing Fair Value Adjustment Account **LO4**

On December 31, 2020, Raven Company's portfolio of equity securities was valued at $1,800. The original cost of the investments in the portfolio was $1,600. Raven does not have significant influence on the investees in the portfolio. Prepare the journal entry to adjust the securities to fair value assuming that the Fair Value Adjustment account (unadjusted) has a

a. Credit balance of $90.
b. Debit balance of $90.

Brief Exercise 14-30
Recording Entries under the Equity Method **LO5**
Hint: See Demo 14-5

On January 1, 2020, Evergreen Inc. purchased 3,750 of the 15,000 outstanding shares of common stock of Nature Net Inc. obtaining significant influence of the company. The shares were purchased for $5,000 cash and Evergreen Inc. intends for it to be a long-term investment. During the year, Nature Net Inc. reported net income of $26,000 and declared and paid dividends of $12,000.

a. Prepare Evergreen Inc.'s entry on January 1, 2020, for the purchase of the equity investment.
b. Prepare Evergreen Inc.'s entries on December 31, 2020, to record investment income and declaration of dividends for 2020.
c. What is the ending balance of the Investment account on December 31, 2020?

Brief Exercise 14-31
Recording Entries under the Equity Method **LO5**
Hint: See Demo 14-5

On January 1, 2020, Hockey Unlimited Inc. purchased 2,500 of the 10,000 outstanding common shares of Goal Corporation for $14,000 cash obtaining significant influence of the company. Hockey Unlimited intends to hold the securities indefinitely. On January 1, 2020, the balance sheet of Goal Corporation reflected depreciable assets with a net book value of $30,000, and a 10-year remaining useful life. The fair value of the depreciable assets is $33,000 on January 1, 2020. Record the adjusting entry for depreciation expense on December 31, 2020, using the straight-line depreciation method.

Brief Exercise 14-32
Assessing Impact of Dividends under FV-NI vs. Equity Methods
LO4, 5

Clarkson Inc. purchased 10% of the 10,000 shares of common stock in Nashville Inc. for $40,000 in January 2020. Shelton Inc. purchased 35% of the 10,000 shares of common stock in Nashville Inc. for $140,000 in January 2020. In December 2020, Nashville Inc. declared and paid a dividend of $1 per share on its outstanding shares of common stock. For each investor, determine the dividend amount received, and the related impact on the Investment and Dividend Revenue accounts. Assume that Shelton Inc. (but not Clarkson Inc.) has significant influence over Nashville Inc.

Investor	Dividend Amount Declared and Received	Change in Investment Account	Increase in Dividend Revenue
Clarkson Inc.	$ ______	$ ______	$ ______
Shelton Inc.	______	______	______

Brief Exercise 14-33
Recording Entries for Impairment—HTM
LO6
Hint: See Demo 14-6

Tracking Co. holds an HTM bond investment in Fields Corp. The carrying value of the investment is $4,500 at December 31, 2020. Tracking Co. estimates the present value of the amounts expected to be collected on the bond investment to be $2,000. The company does not intend to sell the asset or would likely be required to sell the investment before recovery of any unrealized loss. Prepare the journal entry, if any, to record the impairment loss.

Brief Exercise 14-34
Recording Entries for Impairment—AFS **LO6**
Hint: See Demo 14-6

Determine the amount of impairment loss (if any) to record in income under the following three separate scenarios for an AFS debt investment. In all three cases, the company does not intend to sell and does not believe it is *more likely than not* that it will be required to sell the investment before recovery of any unrealized loss. Assume that the company has already adjusted the AFS investments to fair value through OCI.

Scenario	1	2	3
Fair value	$90,000	$70,000	$60,000
Amortized cost	80,000	80,000	80,000
Expected credit loss	15,000	15,000	15,000

Brief Exercise 14-35
Recording Entries for Impairment—AFS **LO6**

Refer to the information in Brief Exercise 14-34 except now assume that the company intends to sell the AFS securities. Determine the amount of impairment loss (if any) to record in income under the three separate scenarios.

Brief Exercise 14-36
Determining Adjustments to Debt Securities **LO1, 2, 3**

Tracking Co. holds a bond investment in Fields Corp. Tracking Company's carrying value of the bond investment is $4,500 at year-end. Tracking Co. determines the fair value of the bond investment at the end of the year 2020 to be $2,000. Prepare the journal entry (if any) to record the difference between the fair value and the carrying value for each of the following separate scenarios.

a. Tracking Co. has the intent and ability to hold the bond to maturity.
b. Tracking Co. has the intent and ability to hold the bond to maturity but elected to account for the investment using the fair value option on the purchase date.
c. Tracking Co. is uncertain as to how long it intends to hold the bond investment.

d. Tracking Co. is uncertain as to how long it intends to hold the bond investment but elected to account for the investment using the fair value option on the purchase date.

Brief Exercise 14-37
Recording Entries Using the Fair Value Option **LO5**

On January 1, 2020, Evergreen Inc. purchased 3,750 of the 15,000 outstanding shares of common stock of Nature Net Inc. resulting in significant influence over Nature Net Inc. The shares were purchased for $5,000 cash and Evergreen elected to account for the investment under the fair value option. During the year, Nature Net reported net income of $26,000 and declared and paid dividends of $12,000. The 3,750 shares of Nature Net Inc. stock had a fair value of $5,500 on December 31, 2020.

a. Prepare Evergreen's entry to record the purchase of the common stock of Nature Net Inc. on January 1, 2020.
b. Prepare Evergreen's entry to record the receipt of declared dividends on December 31, 2020.
c. Prepare Evergreen's entry to adjust the securities to fair value on December 31, 2020.
d. What is the carrying value of the investment on December 31, 2020?

Brief Exercise 14-38
Recognizing Income under the Fair Value Option **LO 1, 2**

On June 15, 2020, Diaz Inc. purchased $100,000 bonds at par value and elects to account for the bonds using the fair value option. On December 31, 2020, the bonds had a fair value of $104,000. Diaz Inc. sold the bonds on January 21, 2021, for $106,000.

a. What is the impact on the income statement in 2020 and 2021 for the transactions described above?
b. How would your answer to (*a*) change if the bonds were instead classified as HTM securities and not accounted for using the fair value option?

Brief Exercise 14-39
Classifying Financial Statement Amounts **LO1, 2, 3, 4, 5**

For the following six items, indicate which financial statement category would be affected: (1) net income or (2) other comprehensive income.

a. Realized gain on sale of AFS debt investment.
b. Realized loss on sale of HTM debt investment.
c. Unrealized gain on an AFS debt investment.
d. Unrealized loss on a TS debt investment.
e. Unrealized gain on an AFS debt investment accounted for using the fair value option.
f. Unrealized loss on an equity investment measured at FV-NI.

Exercises

Exercise 14-40
Classifying Investments in Securities **LO1, 2, 3, 4, 5**

Match each security listed below with its usual classification: (1) trading securities, (2) available-for-sale securities, (3) equity method securities, (4) held-to-maturity securities, or (5) equity security measured at FV-NI.

____ *a.* Abbot common stock, no-par; acquired to use temporarily idle cash with intent to sell next month.
____ *b.* 30% interest in Packaging Inc.; acquired to drive costs down through vertical integration.
____ *c.* Mack stock held in trading account.
____ *d.* Hasten Inc.'s 10-year bonds acquired. Hasten intends to hold to maturity, but may need to sell the bonds earlier for cash.
____ *e.* Staufer common stock, par $5; acquired to gain a significant influence, but not control.
____ *f.* Frazer bonds, 9%, mature at the end of 10 years; acquired with the intent and ability to hold for 10 years.
____ *g.* Foreign Corp. common stock; a 30% interest acquired, but difficulties encountered in an attempt to obtain representation on the Foreign Corporation's board of directors. Intent is to hold stock indefinitely.
____ *h.* Astroid common stock, par $1; acquired as an investment (with insignificant influence) that management plans to hold indefinitely.

Exercise 14-41
Recording Entries for HTM Debt Securities—Par **LO1**
Hint: See Demo 14-1A

On January 1, 2020, Lazer Inc. purchased for cash, ten $1,000, 4% bonds of Star Corp. at par. The bond interest is paid annually on January 1 of each year, and the bond maturity date is January 1, 2030. Lazer has the intent and ability to hold the bonds over the full term. The fair value of the bonds on December 31, 2020, is $9,800.

a. Record the entry for the purchase of the bonds on January 1, 2020.
b. Record the entry to accrue interest revenue on December 31, 2020.
c. Record the entry for the receipt of interest on January 1, 2021.

Exercise 14-42
Recording Entries for HTM Debt Securities—Effective Interest Method **LO1**
Hint: See Demo 14-1C

On January 1, 2020, Baker Corp. purchased $20,000 of Chocolate Inc. bonds. These bonds pay 5% interest annually on December 31 and mature December 31, 2029. The investment is classified as a held-to-maturity investment because Baker has the intent and the ability to hold the bonds for 10 years. The effective rate on the bonds is 4.5%.

Required

a. Were the bonds purchased at a discount or premium?
b. Prepare a bond amortization schedule for 2020 and 2021 using the effective interest method.
c. Prepare the journal entry for the purchase of the investment on January 1, 2020.
d. Prepare the journal entries to record interest received on December 31, 2020, and December 31, 2021.
e. Indicate the carrying value of the Chocolate bonds on Baker's December 31, 2021, balance sheet assuming that the fair value of the bonds on December 31, 2021, was $20,800.

Exercise 14-43
Recording Entries for HTM Debt Securities—Effective Interest Method **LO1**
Hint: See Demo 14-1B

On July 1, 2020, West Company purchased for cash, eight $10,000 bonds of North Corporation to yield 10%. The bonds pay 9% interest, payable on a semiannual basis each July 1 and January 1, and mature on July 1, 2023. The bonds are classified as held-to-maturity securities. The annual reporting period ends December 31. Assume the effective interest method of amortization of any discount or premium.

Required

a. Prepare a bond amortization schedule for 2020 and 2021 using the effective interest method.
b. Record the entry for the purchase of the bonds by West Company on July 1, 2020.
c. Record the adjusting entry by West Company on December 31, 2020. The fair value of the bonds at December 31, 2020, was $81,000.
d. Indicate the effects of this investment on the 2020 income statement and year-end balance sheet.
e. Record the receipt of interest on January 1, 2021.
f. After the interest payment on July 1, 2021, two of the bonds were sold for $19,300 cash. Provide the required entries on July 1, 2021.

Exercise 14-44
Recording Entries for HTM Debt Securities—Straight-Line Method **LO1**
Hint: See Demo 14-1D

Repeat Exercise 14-43, assuming discounts and premiums are amortized using the straight-line interest method.

Exercise 14-45
Recording Entries for TS—Effective Interest Method **LO2**

① Adjust FVA at Year-End On July 1, 2020, West Company purchased for cash, eight $10,000 bonds of North Corporation at a market rate of 6%. The bonds pay 5% interest, payable on a semiannual basis each July 1 and January 1, and mature on July 1, 2023. The bonds are classified as trading securities. The annual reporting period ends December 31. Assume the effective interest method of amortization of any discounts or premiums. Ignore income taxes.

Required

a. Prepare a bond amortization schedule for the life of the bonds using the effective interest method.
b. Record the entry for the purchase of the bonds by West Company on July 1, 2020.
c. Record the adjusting entries by West Company on December 31, 2020 to accrue interest revenue and record the unrealized gain or loss. The fair value of the bonds on December 31, 2020, was $83,000.
d. Record the receipt of interest on January 1, 2021.
e. Record the sale of all of the bonds on January 2, 2021, for $83,000.
f. Record the adjustment to the Fair Value Adjustment account on December 31, 2021, assuming no additional TS investments.

Exercise 14-46
Recording Entries for TS—Effective Interest Method **LO2**

② Adjust FVA at Sale and Year-End On July 1, 2020, West Company purchased for cash, eight $10,000 bonds of North Corporation at a market rate of 6%. The bonds pay 5% interest, payable on a semiannual basis each July 1 and January 1, and mature on July 1, 2023. The bonds are classified as trading securities. The annual reporting period ends December 31. Assume the effective interest method of amortization of any discounts or premiums. Ignore income taxes.

Required

a. Prepare a bond amortization schedule for the life of the bonds using the effective interest method.
b. Record the entry for the purchase of the bonds by West Company on July 1, 2020.

c. Record the adjusting entries by West Company on December 31, 2020, to accrue interest revenue and record the unrealized gain or loss. The fair value of the bonds on December 31, 2020, was $83,000.

d. Record the receipt of interest on January 1, 2021.

e. Record the sale of all of the bonds on January 2, 2021, for $83,050, eliminating the associated Fair Value Adjustment account balance. Prior to recording the sale, adjust the investment to fair value.

Exercise 14-47 Recording Entries for TS—Effective Interest Method **LO2**

② **Adjust FVA at Sale and Year-End** Repeat Exercise 14-45 except now assume that the market rate is 4% on July 1, 2020.

Exercise 14-48 Recording Entries for TS—Par Value **LO2**

① **Adjust FVA at Year-End** At December 31, 2020, the investments in the portfolio of the trading securities of Kennedy Company included the following.

Security	Purchase Date	Original Purchase Price
Atlanta Corp. bonds, 5%, $100,000	October 1, 2020	$100,000
Dallas Inc. bonds, 4%, $50,000	July 1, 2020	50,000

Required

a. Record the entry for the receipt of quarterly interest from the Atlanta Corp. bonds on December 31, 2020.

b. Record the entry for the receipt of semiannual interest from the Dallas Inc. bonds on December 31, 2020.

c. Record the entry to adjust the bonds to fair value on December 31, 2020. The fair value of the Atlanta Corp. bonds and the Dallas Inc. bonds on December 31, 2020, were $110,000 and $45,000, respectively.

d. Indicate the total amount to be included on the December 31, 2020, balance sheet of Kennedy Company as investments in trading securities.

e. Record the entry to sell the Atlanta Corp. bonds on January 2, 2021, for $112,500.

f. Record the entry to sell the Dallas Inc. bonds on January 3, 2021, for $44,500.

g. Adjust the Fair Value Adjustment account on December 31, 2021.

h. Determine the investment related impact on net income in 2020 and 2021.

Exercise 14-49 Recording Entries for TS—Par Value **LO2**

② **Adjust FVA at Sale and Year-End** At December 31, 2020, the investments in the portfolio of the trading securities of Kennedy Company included the following.

Security	Purchase Date	Original Purchase Price
Atlanta Corp. bonds, 5%, $100,000	October 1, 2020	$100,000
Dallas Inc. bonds, 4%, $50,000	July 1, 2020	50,000

Required

a. Record the entry for the receipt of quarterly interest from the Atlanta Corp. bonds on December 31, 2020.

b. Record the entry for the receipt of semiannual interest from the Dallas Inc. bonds on December 31, 2020.

c. Record the entry to adjust the bonds to fair value on December 31, 2020. The fair value of the Atlanta Corp. bonds and the Dallas Inc. bonds on December 31, 2020, were $110,000 and $45,000, respectively.

d. Indicate the total amount to be included on the December 31, 2020, balance sheet of Kennedy Company as investments in trading securities.

e. Record the entry to sell the Atlanta Corp. bonds on January 2, 2021, for $112,500. First adjust the bonds to fair value and then eliminate the associated Fair Value Adjustment account upon the sale of the securities.

f. Record the entry to sell the Dallas Inc. bonds on January 3, 2021, for $44,500. First adjust the bonds to fair value and then eliminate the associated Fair Value Adjustment account upon the sale of the securities.

g. Determine the investment related impact on net income in 2020 and 2021.

Exercise 14-50 Recording Entries for AFS Debt Securities—Effective Interest Method **LO3**

On January 1, 2020, Jules Company purchased for cash, $50,000 bonds (ten $5,000 bonds) of Android Corporation at a market rate of 6%. The bonds pay 6.5% interest, payable on a semiannual basis each June 30 and December 31, and mature on December 31, 2024. The bonds are classified as available-for-sale securities. The annual reporting period of Jules Company ends December 31. Assume the effective interest method of amortization of any discounts or premiums.

Required

a. Prepare a bond amortization schedule for the year 2020, using the effective interest method.
b. Record the entry for the purchase of the bonds by Jules Company on January 1, 2020.
c. Record the entry for the receipt of interest on June 30, 2020.
d. Record the entry for the receipt of interest on December 31, 2020.
e. Record the adjusting entry on December 31, 2020, to adjust the debt investment to fair value. The fair value of the bonds on December 31, 2020, was $49,000.
f. Determine the impact on the following financial statement categories, for 2020, assuming no transactions other than those of the AFS securities.
1. Other comprehensive income
2. Net income
3. Comprehensive income
4. Other revenues and gains
5. Other expenses and losses

g. Determine the balance in the Investment account on the balance sheet of December 31, 2020.

Exercise 14-51
Recording Entries for AFS Debt Securities—Effective Interest Method **LO3**

① **Adjust FVA at Year-End** On July 1, 2020, West Company purchased for cash, eight $10,000 bonds of North Corporation to yield 10%. The bonds pay 9% interest, payable on a semiannual basis each July 1 and January 1, and mature on July 1, 2023. The bonds are classified as held-to-maturity securities. The annual reporting period ends December 31. Assume the effective interest method of amortization of any discount or premium.

Required

a. Prepare a bond amortization schedule for 2020 and 2021 using the effective interest method.
b. Record the entry for the purchase of the bonds by West Company on July 1, 2020.
c. Record the adjusting entry by West Company on December 31, 2020. The fair value of the bonds at December 31, 2020, was $81,000.
d. Indicate the effects of this investment on the 2020 income statement and year-end balance sheet.
e. Record the receipt of interest on January 1, 2021.
f. After the interest receipt on July 1, 2021, two of the bonds were sold for $19,300 cash. Record the entry for (1) the receipt of interest and (2) the sale of the bond investment.
g. On December 31, 2021, the company's year-end, record the entry to eliminate the Fair Value Adjustment balance associated with the two bonds sold.

Exercise 14-52
Recording Entries for AFS Debt Securities—Effective Interest Method **LO3**

② **Adjust FVA at Sale and Year-End** On July 1, 2020, West Company purchased for cash, eight $10,000 bonds of North Corporation to yield 10%. The bonds pay 9% interest, payable on a semiannual basis each July 1 and January 1, and mature on July 1, 2023. The bonds are classified as held-to-maturity securities. The annual reporting period ends December 31. Assume the effective interest method of amortization of any discount or premium.

Required

a. Prepare a bond amortization schedule for 2020 and 2021 using the effective interest method.
b. Record the entry for the purchase of the bonds by West Company on July 1, 2020.
c. Record the adjusting entry by West Company on December 31, 2020. The fair value of the bonds at December 31, 2020, was $81,000.
d. Indicate the effects of this investment on the 2020 income statement and year-end balance sheet.
e. Record the receipt of interest on January 1, 2021.
f. After the interest receipt on July 1, 2021, two of the bonds were sold for $19,300 cash.
1. Record the receipt of interest on July 1, 2021.
2. Record the entry to adjust the two bonds to fair value (FV-OCI).
3. Record the sale, eliminating the associated Fair Value Adjustment account balance.

Exercise 14-53
Adjusting AFS Debt Securities to Fair Value
LO3

A portfolio of investments of available-for-sale securities held by Dow Inc. is as follows.

December 31, 2020	Cost	Fair Value
Eastern Corp. bonds.	$120,000	$128,000
Western Corp. bonds	200,000	205,000
Total	$320,000	$333,000

December 31, 2021	Cost	Fair Value
Eastern Corp. bonds.	$120,000	$140,000
Western Corp. bonds	200,000	190,000
Total	$320,000	$330,000

The Fair Value Adjustment account had a $0 balance on January 1, 2020. No sales or purchases took place in the available-for-sale investment portfolio in 2021.

Required

a. Record the adjusting entry on December 31, 2020, to adjust the debt investments to fair value.

b. Record the adjusting entry on December 31, 2021, to adjust the debt investments to fair value.

c. Indicate how the adjustment to fair value in (*b*) would be reflected in Dow's income statement for the year ended December 31, 2021.

Exercise 14-54
Recording and Reporting AFS Securities **LO3**

On December 31, 2020, Banff Company held an investment in Glacier Inc. bonds with an original cost of $23,000. The investment was classified as an available-for-sale security, had a fair value of $21,500 on December 31, 2020, and was the only investment in the available-for-sale security portfolio in 2020. In 2021, Banff sold the investment in Glacier Inc. bonds for $20,000. On December 31, 2021, assume that Banff Company has an $8,000 net unrealized holding gain on other available-for-sale securities purchased during 2021.

Required

a. Prepare the adjusting entry on December 31, 2020, to record the unrealized holding gain or loss on the Glacier Inc. bond investment.

b. Prepare the adjusting entry on December 31, 2021, to record the unrealized holding gain on Banff's available-for-sale portfolio.

c. Indicate the effect on net income and other comprehensive income in 2021 for these transactions.

d. Prepare the reclassification disclosure of accumulated other comprehensive income to include in the notes accompanying the financial statements of Banff Company for 2021.

Exercise 14-55
Recording and Reporting Equity Investment: FV-NI
LO4
Hint: See Demo 14-4

① **Adjust FVA at Year-End** On November 1, 2020, Drucker Co. acquired the following investments in equity securities measured at FV-NI.

Kelly Corporation—500 shares of common stock (no-par) at $60 per share.
Keefe Corporation—300 shares preferred stock ($10 par) at $20 per share.

On December 31, 2020, the company's year-end, the quoted market prices were as follows: Kelly Corporation common stock, $52, and Keefe Corporation preferred stock, $24. Following are the data for 2021.

Mar. 2, 2021	Dividends per share, declared and paid: Kelly Corp., $1, and Keefe Corp., $0.50.
Oct. 1, 2021	Sold 100 shares of Keefe Corporation preferred stock at $25 per share.
Dec. 31, 2021	Fair values: Kelly common, $46 per share, Keefe preferred, $26 per share.

Required

a. Prepare the entry for Drucker Company to record the purchase of the securities.

b. Prepare any adjusting entry needed at December 31, 2020.

c. Indicate the items and amounts that should be reported on the 2020 income statement of Drucker and its year-end balance sheet. Assume that the investments are classified as current.

d. Prepare the entries required in 2021 to record dividend revenue, the sale of stock, and the fair value adjustment. Assume that the Fair Value Adjustment account is adjusted for the investment portfolio on December 31, 2021.

e. Indicate items and amounts that should be reported on the 2021 income statement and year-end balance sheet.

Exercise 14-56
Recording and Reporting Equity Investment: FV-NI
LO4
Hint: See Demo 14-4

② **Adjust FVA at Sale and Year-End** On November 1, 2020, Drucker Co. acquired the following investments in equity securities measured at FV-NI.

Kelly Corporation—500 shares of common stock (no-par) at $60 per share.
Keefe Corporation—300 shares preferred stock ($10 par) at $20 per share.

On December 31, 2020, the company's year-end, the quoted market prices were as follows: Kelly Corporation common stock, $52, and Keefe Corporation preferred stock, $24. Following are the data for 2021.

Mar. 2, 2021	Dividends per share, declared and paid: Kelly Corp., $1, and Keefe Corp., $0.50.
Oct. 1, 2021	Sold 100 shares of Keefe Corporation preferred stock at $25 per share.
Dec. 31, 2021	Fair values: Kelly common, $46 per share, Keefe preferred, $26 per share.

Required

a. Prepare the entry for Drucker Company to record the purchase of the securities.
b. Prepare any adjusting entry needed at December 31, 2020.
c. Indicate the items and amounts that should be reported on the 2020 income statement of Drucker and its year-end balance sheet. Assume that the investments are classified as current.
d. Prepare the entries required in 2021 to record dividend revenue, the sale of stock, and the fair value adjustment. Update the Fair Value Adjustment account prior to recording any sale. Eliminate the associated Fair Value Adjustment account upon recording the sale of any investment.
e. Indicate items and amounts that should be reported on the 2021 income statement and year-end balance sheet.

Exercise 14-57
Recording Entries for Equity Investment: FV-NI **LO4**
Hint: See Demo 14-4

① **Adjust FVA at Year-End** On September 1, 2020, Tech Company purchased 2,000 shares of common stock of Eagle Inc. for $200,000, while not obtaining significant influence over Eagle Inc. On November 1, 2020, Tech Company sold 1,000 shares of the Eagle Inc. stock for $105 per share and incurred brokerage fees of $480 on the sale. At December 31, 2020, Eagle Inc. declared and paid dividends of $5 per share. The fair value of the remaining investment in Eagle Inc. was $110,000 on December 31, 2020.

Required

Prepare the following entries for Tech Company.

a. Purchase on September 1, 2020.
b. Sale of shares on November 1, 2020.
c. Dividends declared and received on December 31, 2020.
d. Adjustment to fair value on December 31, 2020.

Exercise 14-58
Recording Entries for Equity Investment: FV-NI **LO4**
Hint: See Demo 14-4

① **Adjust FVA at Year-End** At December 31, 2019, the portfolio of investments in equity securities measured at FV-NI held by Athletes Inc. is as follows.

Investment Security	Cost	Fair Value	Unrealized Holding Gain (Loss)
Badger Common Stock (1,000 shares)	$ 40,000	$ 39,500	$ (500)
Spartan Common Stock (1,600 shares)	50,000	51,000	1,000
Wildcat Common Stock (500 shares)	25,000	23,500	(1,500)
	$115,000	$114,000	$(1,000)

On June 1, 2020, Athletes Inc. sold 400 shares of Spartan stock for $33 per share and 100 shares of Wildcat stock for $55 per share. Athletes Inc. purchased 400 shares of Gopher common stock for $35 per share on August 1, 2020. The fair value of the remaining stock held on December 31, 2020, is Badger common stock, $42,000; Spartan common stock, $36,000; Wildcat common stock, $20,800; and Gopher common stock, $14,400.

Required

a. Prepare the entry for the sale of Spartan and Wildcat common stock on June 1, 2020.
b. Record the purchase of Gopher common stock on August 1, 2020.
c. Prepare any adjusting entry needed on December 31, 2020.

Exercise 14-59
Recording Entries for Equity Investment: FV-NI **LO4**
Hint: See Demo 14-4

② **Adjust FVA at Sale and Year-End** At December 31, 2019, the portfolio of investments in equity securities measured at FV-NI held by Athletes Inc. is as follows.

Investment Security	Cost	Fair Value	Unrealized Holding Gain (Loss)
Badger Common Stock (1,000 shares)	$ 40,000	$ 39,500	$ (500)
Spartan Common Stock (1,600 shares)	50,000	51,000	1,000
Wildcat Common Stock (500 shares)	25,000	23,500	(1,500)
	$115,000	$114,000	$(1,000)

On June 1, 2020, Athletes Inc. sold 400 shares of Spartan stock for $33 per share and 100 shares of Wildcat stock for $55 per share. Athletes Inc. purchased 400 shares of Gopher common stock for $35 per share on August 1, 2020. The fair value of the remaining stock held on December 31, 2020, is Badger common stock, $42,000; Spartan common stock, $36,000; Wildcat common stock, $20,800; and Gopher common stock, $14,400.

Required

a. Prepare the entry for the sale of Spartan and Wildcat common stock on June 1, 2020. Prior to recording the sale, update the investments to fair value. Eliminate the associated Fair Value Adjustment balances upon sale of the investments.

b. Record the purchase of Gopher common stock on August 1, 2020.

c. Prepare any adjusting entry needed on December 31, 2020.

Exercise 14-60
Adjusting Fair Value Adjustment Account—Equity Investments **LO4**

Five separate scenarios of equity investment holdings, measured at FV-NI are as follows.

Scenario	Original Cost of Investment	Fair Value at Dec. 31, 2019	Fair Value at Dec. 31, 2020
1	$10,000	$10,000	$10,500
2	10,000	10,500	11,000
3	10,000	8,500	9,200
4	10,000	12,000	9,500
5	10,000	8,200	7,900

Required

For each of the five separate scenarios, record the adjustment to fair value required on December 31, 2020. Assume that each investment was purchased in 2019 and that there were no purchases or sales related to the investment in 2020.

Exercise 14-61
Recording Entries for Equity Investment: FV-NI **LO4**

① **Adjust FVA at Year-End** 5M Corporation completed the following transactions, in the order given, relative to the portfolio of stocks held as equity investments measured at FV-NI.

Year 2020

1. Purchased 150 shares of Starbux Corporation common stock (par value $1) at $50 per share plus a brokerage commission of 4% and transfer costs of $50 on August 1, 2020.
2. Purchased 300 shares of Kolgate Corporation Class A common stock (par value $0.50) at $35 per share plus transfer costs of $75 on September 15, 2020.

Year 2021

1. Purchased 275 shares of Starbux Corporation common stock at $55 per share plus a brokerage commission of 4% and transfer costs of $60 on February 1, 2021.
2. Received declared cash dividends of $2.00 per share on the Kolgate Corporation Class A common stock on June 30, 2021.
3. Sold 75 shares of Starbux Corporation common stock at $58 per share on August 15, 2021.

Year-End Stock Prices	2020	2021
Starbux, common stock	$48	$60
Kolgate, Class A common stock	38	50

Required

a. Provide entries for 5M Corporation for the purchases of equity securities in 2020.
b. Provide entries for 5M Corporation to adjust securities to fair value on December 31, 2020.
c. Record the purchase of Starbux Corporation common stock in 2021.
d. Record the receipt of declared dividends on the Kolgate common stock in 2021.
e. Record the sale of Starbux common stock in 2021. Assume FIFO (first-in, first-out) order when shares are sold.
f. Provide the entry for 5M Corporation on December 31, 2021, to adjust the Fair Value Adjustment account.

Exercise 14-62
Recording Entries for Equity Investment: FV-NI and Equity Method **LO4, 5**

On January 1, 2020, Allen Corporation purchased 30% of the 30,000 outstanding common shares of Towne Corporation at $17 per share as a long-term investment. On the date of purchase, the book value and the fair value of the net assets of Towne Corporation were equal. During the year, Towne Corporation reported net income of $24,000 and declared and paid dividends of $8,000. As of December 31, 2020, common shares of Towne Corporation were trading at $20 per share.

Required

a. Assume that Allen Corporation had significant influence over Towne Corporation. Prepare the entries for 2020 to record the purchase of the investment, the receipt of declared dividends, and the proportionate share of net income.
b. Assume that Allen Corporation did not have significant influence over Towne Corporation. Record the entries in 2020 to record the purchase of the investment, the receipt of declared dividends, and the fair value adjustment.
c. Indicate the amount of income that would be reported on the 2020 income statement and the investment balance on the 2020 year-end balance sheet under requirement (*a*) and requirement (*b*).

Exercise 14-63
Analyzing Investment Account: Equity Method **LO5**
Hint: See Demo 14-5

Assume that Fleetwood Inc. purchased 40% of the voting stock of Mac Corporation on January 1, 2020, for $100,000, an amount equal to 40% of Mac's book value. Assume that the fair value and book value of all net assets of Mac were the same at that time. During the year, Fleetwood Inc. debited the Investment account for $12,000 and credited the Investment account for $4,000. The ending balance of Fleetwood's Investment account is $108,000 at December 31, 2020. Assume that Fleetwood Inc. has significant influence over Mac Corporation.

Required

a. What did Mac Corporation report as net income for the year 2020? What is Fleetwood's share of Mac Corporation's net income for the year?
b. What did Mac Corporation report as dividends for the year 2020? What is Fleetwood's share of Mac Corporation's dividends for the year?

Exercise 14-64
Recording Entries for Equity Investment: Equity Method **LO5**
Hint: See Demo 14-5

On January 1, 2020, Allen Corporation purchased 30% of the 30,000 outstanding common shares of Towne Corporation at $15 per share as a long-term investment. On the date of purchase, the book value and the fair value of the net assets of Towne Corporation were equal. During the year, Towne Corporation reported income of $24,000. Towne Corporation declared and paid cash dividends of $8,000 on December 30, 2020, to shareholders on record. As of December 31, 2020, common shares of Towne Corporation were trading at $20 per share.

Required

a. Record the entries in 2020 assuming that Allen Corporation had significant influence over Towne Corporation.
b. Indicate the effects of this investment on the 2020 income statement and year-end balance sheet.

Exercise 14-65
Recording Entries for Equity Investment: Equity Method **LO5**
Hint: See Demo 14-5

On January 1, 2020, Mercedez Company purchased 400 of the 1,000 outstanding shares of Auto Supplies Inc. for $40,000. At that date, the balance sheet of Auto Supplies Inc. showed the following values.

Assets not subject to depreciation	$40,000*
Assets subject to depreciation	26,000**
Liabilities	6,000*
Common stock (par $1)	50,000
Retained earnings	10,000

* Same as fair value. ** Fair value $30,000; the assets have a 10-year remaining useful life (straight-line depreciation).

Required

a. Provide the entry by Mercedez Company to record the acquisition at a cost of $40,000.

b. Assume that on December 31, 2020 (end of the accounting period), Auto Supplies Inc. reported net income of $12,000. Provide all year-end entries for Mercedez Company.

c. In February 2021, Auto Supplies Inc. declared and paid a $2 per share cash dividend. Provide the necessary entry for Mercedez Company.

Exercise 14-66
Recording Entries for Equity Investment: Equity Method **LO5**

On January 1, 2020, Case Corporation purchased 3,000 of the 10,000 outstanding shares of common stock of Dow Corporation for $28,000 cash. At that date, Dow's balance sheet reflected the following book values.

Assets not subject to depreciation	$25,000*
Assets subject to depreciation	30,000**
Liabilities	5,000*
Common stock (par $4)	40,000
Retained earnings, $10,000	10,000

* Same as fair value. ** Fair value $38,000; the assets have a 10-year remaining useful life (straight-line depreciation).

Dow Corporation reported net income of $18,000 in 2020 and declared and paid a $1 per share cash dividend.

Required

Assuming that the equity method is appropriate, determine the value of Case Corporation's Investment account on December 31, 2020, for its holding of common stock of Dow Corporation.

Exercise 14-67
Recording Entries for Equity Investment: Equity Method, Partial Year **LO5**
Hint: See Demo 14-5

On July 1, 2020, Allen Corporation purchased 30% of the 30,000 outstanding common shares of Towne Corporation at $17 per share as a long-term investment. On the date of purchase, the book value and the fair value of the net assets of Towne Corporation were equal. During the year, Towne Corporation reported net income of $24,000. Towne Corporation paid cash dividends of $8,000 on December 30, 2020, to shareholders on record. As of December 31, 2020, common shares of Towne Corporation were trading at $20 per share.

Required

a. Record Allen's entries in 2020 assuming that Allen Corporation had significant influence over Towne Corporation.

b. Indicate the effects of this investment on the 2020 income statement of Allen Corporation and its year-end balance sheet.

Exercise 14-68
Reporting Various Investment Securities **LO1, 2, 3, 4, 5**

Complete the following table for four types of investment securities.

Security Type	Carrying Value	Fair Value	Current Asset	Noncurrent Asset	Unrealized Gain/Loss-Income	Unrealized Gain/Loss-Equity
Example: AFS Debt Investment[1]	*$ 9,000*	*$ 8,000*	*n.a.*	*$8,000*	*n.a.*	*$(1,000)*
1. AFS Debt Investment[1]	3,000	3,300				
2. TS Debt Investment[2]	8,000	7,500				
3. HTM Debt Investment[3]	18,000	17,000				
4. Equity Investment—measured at FV-NI[2]	21,000	23,000				

[1] Investor intends to hold investment for at least one year but less than full term.
[2] Investor intends to hold for less than one year.
[3] Debt investment is purchased with a remaining term of 10 years.

Exercise 14-69
Recording Entries for Impairment of Investments—HTM **LO6**
Hint: See Demo 14-6

Atlanta Inc. holds an HTM bond investment in Falcons Corporation. The carrying value of the investment is $140,500 on December 31, 2020. Atlanta Inc. determines the present value of the amounts expected to be collected under the debt contract under the CECL model to be $120,000.

Required

a. Record the impairment loss on December 31, 2020.

b. Assume that Atlanta Inc. holds the HTM bond investment in Falcons Corporation on December 31, 2021. Record the adjusting entry if the present value of the amounts expected to be collected under the debt contract under the CECL model is now estimated to be $130,000.

Exercise 14-70
Recording Entries for Impairment of Investments—Equity Method **LO6**
Hint: See Demo 14-6

Eagle Software has an equity investment in Finch Enterprises accounted for under the equity method. The carrying value of the investment was $45,000 on December 31, 2020. At December 31, 2020, the fair value of Eagle's investment in Finch has declined to $32,000. Eagle management decides that the decline is other-than-temporary because Finch lost a patent protection suit during the year and can no longer profit from some of its products.

Required

a. Record the journal entry on December 31, 2020, to recognize the impairment.

b. What is the adjusted cost basis of the equity investment on December 31, 2020?

c. Assume that the fair value of the investment is $36,000 on December 31, 2021. Record the applicable journal entry.

Exercise 14-71
Recording Entries for Impairment of Investments—AFS **LO6**

Atlanta Inc. holds an AFS bond investment in Falcons Corporation. The amortized cost of the investment is $140,500 on December 31, 2020. Atlanta Inc. estimates the fair value of the bonds to be $130,000. The unrealized loss of $10,500 is partially due to a credit loss of $8,000, with the remaining portion due to other factors. The company adjusted the AFS bonds to fair value through OCI on December 31, 2020.

Required

a. Record the impairment loss on December 31, 2020, assuming that the company does not intend to sell the investment and does not believe it is *more likely than not* that it will be required to sell the investment before recovery of any unrealized loss.

b. Record the impairment loss on December 31, 2020, now assuming that the company intends to sell the investment.

Exercise 14-72
Recording Entries under the Fair Value Option—HTM **LO2**
Hint: See Demo 14-2B

On January 1, 2020, Josie Inc. purchased for cash ten, $1,000, 4% bonds of Star Corp. at par. The bond interest is paid annually on January 1 of each year, and the bonds mature on January 1, 2030. Josie has the intent and ability to hold the bonds over the full term and has elected to account for the bonds using the fair value option. The fair value of the bonds on December 31, 2020, is $9,500.

Required

Prepare the following entries for Josie Inc.

a. Record the entry for the purchase of the bonds on January 1, 2020.

b. Record any required adjusting entries on December 31, 2020.

c. Record the entry for the receipt of interest on January 1, 2021.

Exercise 14-73
Recording Entries under the Fair Value Option—AFS **LO2, 3**

On October 31, 2020, West Company purchased $10,000 of East Company bonds. West Company plans to hold the bonds for an indefinite period of time. West Company elects to account for the debt investment using the fair value option.

Required

a. If the fair value of the East Company bonds were $11,000 at year-end, what adjusting entry would West Company record at December 31, 2020?

b. If West Company had not elected the fair value option, what adjusting entry would West Company record at December 31, 2020?

Exercise 14-74
Recording Entries under the Fair Value Option—Equity Method **LO5**

Assume that Fireside Inc. purchased 30% of the common stock of Theater Supplies Corporation on January 1, 2020, for $100,000. Fireside Inc. elected to account for its investment using the fair value option. During the year, Fireside Inc. reported net income of $80,000 and declared and paid dividends of $15,000. The fair value of Fireside's investment in Theater Supplies common stock is $105,000. Assume that Fireside Inc. has significant influence over Theater Supplies Corporation.

Required

a. What amount would Fireside Inc. report on its balance sheet on December 31, 2020, for its investment in Theater Supplies Corporation?

b. What amount would Fireside Inc. report in its income statement for the year ended December 31, 2020, for its investment in Theater Supplies Corporation?

Problems

Problem 14-75
Recording and Reporting HTM Securities: Premium, Discount, Straight-Line, Accrued Interest **LO1**

On July 1, 2020, Scarlet Company acquired the following bonds, which Scarlet intends to hold to maturity.

Security	Price	Face Value Purchased
Gold 10% bonds, maturity date July 1, 2025	$101.5	$30,000
Green 8% bonds, maturity date December 31, 2022.............	97.0	40,000

Both bonds pay interest annually on December 31. Premiums and discounts are amortized on a straight-line basis.

Required

a. Provide the entries to record the purchase of the investments on July 1, 2020. Assume that cash payments for purchases include accrued interest.

b. Provide the entries on December 31, 2020, to record the receipt of interest.

c. Provide the items and amounts that would be reported in the 2020 income statement and end of year balance sheet related to the investments.

d. Provide the entries on December 31, 2021, to record the receipt of interest.

e. Provide the items and amounts that would be reported in the 2021 income statement and end of year balance sheet related to the investments.

Problem 14-76
Recording and Reporting HTM and AFS Securities: Discount, Semiannual, Effective Interest
LO1, 3

On January 1, 2020, Pitt Company acquired the following bonds, which Pitt intends to hold to maturity.

Security	Purchase Price	Face Value Purchased
Hollywood 5% bonds, maturity date January 1, 2030 ...	$277,684	$300,000

The bonds pay interest semiannually on June 30 and December 31. Premiums and discounts are amortized using the effective interest method and a market rate of 6%. The fair value of the bonds was $275,000 on December 31, 2020.

Required

a. Provide the entry to record the purchase of the investment on January 1, 2020.

b. Provide the entry on June 30, 2020, to record the receipt of interest.

c. Provide the entry on December 31, 2020, to record the receipt of interest and adjustment to fair value (if required).

d. Provide the items and amounts that would be reported in the 2020 income statement, 2020 comprehensive income statement, and year-end balance sheet related to this investment.

e. Provide the entry on June 30, 2021, to record the receipt of interest.

f. Provide the entry on December 31, 2021, to record the receipt of interest and adjustment to fair value (if required). The fair value of the bonds was $277,000 on December 31, 2021.

g. Provide the items and amounts that would be reported in the 2021 income statement, 2021 comprehensive income statement, and year-end balance sheet related to this investment.

h. Repeat *a* through *g* assuming that Pitt was uncertain as to how long to hold the security.

Problem 14-77
Recording and Reporting HTM and AFS Securities: Premium, Semiannual, Effective Interest
LO1, 3

On January 1, 2020, Pitt Company acquired the following bonds, which Pitt intends to hold to maturity.

Security	Purchase Price	Face Value Purchased
Hollywood 5% bonds, maturity date January 1, 2030 ...	$324,527	$300,000

The bonds pay interest semiannually on June 30 and December 31. Premiums are amortized using the effective interest method and a market rate of 4%. The fair value of the bonds was $325,000 on December 31, 2020.

Required

a. Provide the entry to record the purchase of the investment on January 1, 2020.

b. Provide the entry on June 30, 2020, to record the receipt of interest.

c. Provide the entry on December 31, 2020, to record the receipt of interest and adjustment to fair value (if required).

d. Provide the items and amounts that would be reported in the 2020 income statement, 2020 comprehensive income statement, and year-end balance sheet related to this investment.
e. Provide the entry on June 30, 2021, to record the receipt of interest.
f. Provide the entry on December 31, 2021, to record the receipt of interest and adjustment to fair value (if required). The fair value of the bonds was $323,000 on December 31, 2021.
g. Provide the items and amounts that would be reported in the 2021 income statement, 2021 comprehensive income statement, and year-end balance sheet related to this investment.
h. Repeat *a* through *g* assuming that Pitt was uncertain as to how long to hold the security.

Problem 14-78
Computing Selling Price and Bond Interest Revenue—Effective Interest and Straight-Line **LO1**

On January 1, 2020, Olympians Inc. purchased for cash, ten, $10,000 bonds of Ring Corporation. The bonds pay 4% interest, payable on an annual basis each December 31, and mature on December 31, 2029. The bonds are classified as held-to-maturity securities. The annual reporting period of Olympians Inc. ends December 31. The following table includes five separate scenarios pertaining to these bonds.

	(1) Bonds Yield 4%	(2) Bonds Yield 5% (Account for using the effective interest method.)	(3) Bonds Yield 5% (Account for using the straight-line interest method.)	(4) Bonds Yield 3% (Account for using the effective interest method.)	(5) Bonds Yield 3% (Account for using the straight-line interest method.)
Were the bonds sold at par, discount, or premium?					
Compute the purchase price of the bonds.					
Compute interest revenue for 2020.					
Compute interest revenue for 2021.					

Required
a. Prepare a bond amortization schedule for 2020 and 2021 for each of the five bond scenarios.
b. Complete each row and column of the table.

Problem 14-79
Recording and Reporting TS: Premium, Semiannual, Straight-Line **LO2**

On July 1, 2020, JB Enterprises purchased for cash eight, $1,000, 9% bonds of Star Corporation at 102 plus accrued interest. The bond interest is paid semiannually each May 1 and November 1, and the maturity date of the bonds is November 1, 2021. JB's annual reporting period ends on December 31. JB classifies this investment as a trading security and uses the straight-line interest method to amortize discounts and premiums on bonds. At December 31, 2020, the Star Corporation bonds were quoted at 97.

Required
a. Prepare the entry for JB Enterprises to record the purchase of the bonds on July 1, 2020.
b. Prepare the entry for interest collected during 2020.
c. Prepare any adjusting entry(ies) required on December 31, 2020.
d. Indicate what items and amounts should be reported on the 2020 income statement and December 31, 2020, balance sheet.

Problem 14-80
Recording and Reporting TS: Discount, Annual, Effective Interest **LO2**

① **Adjust FVA at Year-End** On January 1, 2020, New Edition Co. purchased for cash ten, $1,000, 4% bonds of Brown Corporation at a market rate of 5.5%. The bond interest is paid annually each January 1, and the bonds mature in 8 years. New Edition's annual reporting period ends on December 31. New Edition classifies this investment as a trading security and uses the effective interest method to amortize discounts and premiums on bonds. At December 31, 2020, the Brown bonds were quoted at 97.

Required
a. Prepare the entry for New Edition to record the purchase of the bonds on January 1, 2020.
b. Prepare any adjusting entries required on December 31, 2020.
c. Indicate what items and amounts should be reported on the 2020 income statement and the December 31, 2020, balance sheet.

d. New Edition sold the bonds on January 2, 2021, at 95. Record the sale of the investment.
e. On December 31, 2021, the company's year-end, record the entry to eliminate the Fair Value Adjustment account associated with the bonds.

Problem 14-81 Recording and Reporting TS: Discount, Annual, Effective Interest **LO2**

② **Adjust FVA at Sale and Year-End** On January 1, 2020, New Edition Co. purchased for cash ten, $1,000, 4% bonds of Brown Corporation at a market rate of 5.5%. The bond interest is paid annually each January 1, and the bonds mature in 8 years. New Edition's annual reporting period ends on December 31. New Edition classifies this investment as a trading security and uses the effective interest method to amortize discounts and premiums on bonds. At December 31, 2020, the Brown bonds were quoted at 97.

Required

a. Prepare the entry for New Edition to record the purchase of the bonds on January 1, 2020.
b. Prepare any adjusting entries required on December 31, 2020.
c. Indicate what items and amounts should be reported on the 2020 income statement and the December 31, 2020, balance sheet.
d. New Edition sold the bonds on January 2, 2021, at 95. First adjust the investment to fair value. Next, record the sale, eliminating the associated Fair Value Adjustment balance.

Problem 14-82 Recording and Reporting AFS Debt Securities, Reclassification **LO3**

① **Adjust FVA at Year-End** Universe Inc. had the following portfolio of available-for-sale securities on December 31, 2020, purchased at par.

AFS Investment	Amortized Cost	Fair Value at Dec. 31, 2020	Unrealized Holding Gain (Loss)
Saturn Inc. bonds . . .	$ 81,500	$ 85,000	$3,500
Venus bonds.	50,800	49,000	(1,800)
	$132,300	$134,000	1,700
Existing balance in Fair Value Adjustment			1,500
Increase (decrease) to Fair Value Adjustment for 2020			$ 200

The Saturn bonds are sold on January 5, 2021, for $85,500. At the end of 2021, the Venus bonds (originally purchased at par value) have a fair value of $50,000. Besides the sale of Saturn bonds on January 5, 2021, no other AFS transactions took place during the year.

Required

a. Record the fair value adjustment of the AFS bonds on December 31, 2020.
b. Record the sale of Saturn bonds on January 5, 2021.
c. Adjust the Fair Value Adjustment account on December 31, 2021.
d. Prepare a reconciliation of other comprehensive income from January 1, 2021, to December 31, 2021.

Problem 14-83 Recording and Reporting AFS Debt Securities, Reclassification **LO3**

② **Adjust FVA at Sale and Year-End** Refer to the information provided in Problem 14-82 and complete the following requirements.

Required

a. Record the fair value adjustment of the AFS bonds on December 31, 2020.
b. Record the fair value adjustment of the Saturn bonds on January 5, 2021, prior to the sale.
c. Record the sale of Saturn bonds on January 5, 2021, reversing the associated Fair Value Adjustment account balance.
d. Adjust the Fair Value Adjustment account on December 31, 2021.
e. Prepare a reconciliation of other comprehensive income from January 1, 2021, to December 31, 2021.

Problem 14-84 Recording Fair Value Adjustments of AFS Debt Investments **LO3**

Given the following amortization schedule for available-for-sale bonds, answer the questions that follow.

Date	Stated Interest	Market Interest	Amortization	Bond Amortized Cost
Jan. 1, 2020.				$2,922.69
Dec. 31, 2020.	$210.00	$233.81	$23.81	2,946.50
Dec. 31, 2021.	210.00	235.72	25.72	2,972.22
Dec. 31, 2022.	210.00	237.78	27.78	3,000.00

Required

a. Were the bonds purchased at a discount or premium?

b. Assume that the estimated fair value measures for the bonds were $3,100 and $2,800 on December 31, 2020, and December 31, 2021, respectively. Provide the adjusting entries to record the bonds at fair value on December 31, 2020, and December 31, 2021. Assume that the Fair Value Adjustment account had a balance of $0 at January 1, 2020.

Problem 14-85
Recording and Reporting Investments in Securities—Fair Value, HTM **LO1, 2, 3, 4**

During 2020, Shale Company purchased equity security shares of two corporations and debt securities of a third. Related transactions were as follows.

1. On February 1, 2020, Shale Company purchased 200 of the 10,000 shares outstanding of common stock of Tee Corporation at $31 per share plus a 4% brokerage fee and a transfer cost of $52. Shale Company intends to hold these shares for more than one year.
2. On March 3, 2020, Shale Company purchased 300 of 4,000 outstanding shares of preferred stock (nonvoting) of Stone Corporation at $78 per share plus a 3% brokerage fee and a transfer cost of $198. Shale Company intends to hold the stock for an indefinite period.
3. On August 15, 2020, Shale Company purchased an additional 20 shares of common stock of Tee Corporation at $35 per share plus a 4% brokerage fee and a transfer cost of $4. Shale Company intends to take advantage of short-term gains on these 20 shares.
4. Shale Company purchased $10,000 of Container Corporation 9% bonds at par plus accrued interest and a transfer fee of $200. The purchase is made on November 1; interest is paid semiannually on January 31 and July 31. The Shale Company intends to hold these bonds through maturity.
5. On December 31, 2020, Shale Company received $4 per share cash dividend on the Stone Corporation stock (declared December 15, 2020). Interest receivable on the Container bonds is accrued on December 31.
6. At December 31, 2020, the fair value of the shares held at the end of 2020 were Tee stock, $34, and Stone stock, $75. The Container Corporation bonds were quoted at 100.

Required

a. Provide the entries of Shale Company for each transaction listed above.

b. Indicate how the income statement and balance sheet for Shale Company would report relevant data concerning these investments for 2020. Assume a December 31 year-end.

Problem 14-86
Recording and Reporting Investments in Equity Securities—FV-NI **LO4**

① Adjust FVA at Year-End On January 1, 2020, Laker Company acquired the following equity securities and classified them as having insignificant influence.

Co.	Description	Quantity	Unit Cost
T	Common stock (no-par)	1,000 shares	$20
U	Common stock (par $10)	1,000 shares	15
V	Preferred stock (par $20, nonconvertible)	400 shares	30
W	Common stock (no-par)	1,000 shares	10

Per share data subsequent to the acquisition are as follows.

Dec. 31, 2020	Fair values: T stock, $16; U stock, $15; V stock, $35; and W stock, $9.90.
Feb. 10, 2021	Cash dividends declared and received: T stock, $1.50; U stock, $1; and V stock, $0.50.
Nov. 1, 2021	Sold the shares of V stock at $38.
Dec. 31, 2021	Fair values: T stock, $13; U stock, $17; and W stock, $10.15.

The company adjusts securities to fair value on annual reporting dates.

Required

a. Provide the following entries for Laker Company for 2020 and 2021, assuming that the Fair Value Adjustment account for the investment portfolio is updated annually on December 31.

1. Purchase of equity securities on January 1, 2020.
2. Adjustment to fair value on December 31, 2020.
3. Receipt of declared dividends on February 10, 2021.
4. Sale of V stock shares on November 1, 2021.
5. Adjustment to fair value on December 31, 2021.

b. Provide the income statement and balance sheet presentation for Laker Company that would reflect these investments for 2020 and 2021. Assume a December 31 year-end.

Problem 14-87 Recording and Reporting Investments in Equity Securities—FV-NI **LO4**

① **Adjust FVA at Year-End** On December 31, 2020, Raven Company's portfolio of securities measured at FV-NI (originally purchased on September 1, 2020) was as follows.

Security	Shares	Unit Cost	Unit Market Price
Bic Corp., common stock, no-par	50	$186	$187
Cross Corp., preferred stock, 6% par $40	200	40	35

Transactions relating to this portfolio during 2021 were as follows.

Jan. 25	Received a 6% declared dividend on the Cross shares.
Apr. 15	Sold 30 shares of Bic Corporation stock at $151 per share.
July 25	Received a $45 declared dividend on the Bic shares.
Oct. 1	Sold the remaining shares of Bic Corporation at $149.50 per share.
Dec. 1	Purchased 100 shares of Pilot Corporation common stock at $47 per share plus a $30 brokerage fee.
Dec. 5	Purchased 400 shares of Sanford Corporation common stock, par $1, at $15 per share.

On December 31, 2021, the following unit market prices were available: Bic stock, $140; Cross stock, $38; Pilot stock, $51; and Sanford stock, $14. Raven updates its Fair Value Adjustment account for its investment portfolio at year-end on December 31.

Required

a. Prepare entries that Raven Company should make on (1) September 1, 2020, and (2) December 31, 2020.

b. Provide the investment items and amounts that should be reported on the 2020 income statement and balance sheet.

c. Prepare the entries for the 2021 transactions described above, plus any required year-end adjusting entries.

d. Provide the investment items and amounts that should be reported on the 2021 income statement and balance sheet.

Problem 14-88 Recording and Reporting Investments in Equity Securities—FV-NI **LO4**

② **Adjust FVA at Sale and Year-End** Refer to the information provided in Problem 14-87 and complete the following requirements.

Required

a. Prepare entries that Raven Company should make on (1) September 1, 2020, and (2) December 31, 2020.

b. Provide the investment items and amounts that should be reported on the 2020 income statement and balance sheet.

c. Prepare the entries for the 2021 transactions described above, plus any required year-end adjusting entries. Record an entry to adjust to market any securities sold during the year. As part of the entry to record the sale, eliminate any associated balances in the Fair Value Adjustment account.

d. Provide the investment items and amounts that should be reported on the 2021 income statement and balance sheet.

Problem 14-89 Recording and Reporting Investments in Equity Securities—FV-NI, Equity Method **LO4, 5**

On January 3, 2020, American Company purchased 2,000 shares of the 10,000 outstanding shares of common stock of United Corporation for $14,600 cash with the intention of holding the securities indefinitely. At that date, the balance sheet of United Corporation reflected the following: nondepreciable assets, $50,000 (same as fair value); depreciable assets (net), $30,000 (fair value, $33,000); total liabilities, $20,000; and stockholders' equity, $60,000. Assume a 10-year remaining useful life (straight-line depreciation) on the depreciable assets. United Corporation recorded net income of $15,000 in 2020.

Required

a. Provide the entries, if any are required, on American's books for each item 1 through 5 below assuming that FV-NI is appropriate.

1. Entry at date of acquisition.
2. Entry on December 31, 2020, to record net income reported by United.
3. Entry on December 31, 2020, for additional depreciation expense.
4. Entry on December 31, 2020, to recognize the decrease in fair value of United stock, quoted market price, $7 per share

5. Entry on December 31, 2020, for a cash dividend of $1 per share declared and paid by United.

b. Repeat (*a*) above assuming that the equity method is appropriate.

c. Indicate the ending balance in the Investment account under each method as of December 31, 2020.

d. Indicate what items and amounts should be reported on the 2020 income statement and statement of cash flows (indirect method) under each method for 2020.

Problem 14-90
Recording Investments in Debt and Equity Securities—FV-NI, Equity Method **LO1, 2, 3, 4, 5**

① **Adjust FVA at Year-End** Spectrum Inc. is involved in a variety of investment transactions during the second quarter of 2020. To begin the quarter, Spectrum Inc. held shares of Atlanta Co. stock, the details of which are as follows.

Investment holdings on April 1, 2020
Atlanta Co.: 2,000 shares of common stock purchased at $20,000; accounted for under FV-NI

Second quarter transactions are as follows.

Apr.	**1**	Spectrum Inc. purchases $30,000 of face amount bonds issued by Madison Inc. at par plus accrued interest. The bonds have an interest rate of 5% and pay interest semiannually on April 30 and October 31. The investment is classified as AFS.
Apr.	**2**	Purchased 2,000 shares of a total of 8,000 shares outstanding of Detroit Inc. stock at $50 per share. Assume that Spectrum accounts for the investment using the equity method.
Apr.	**15**	Dividends of $1.00 per share are declared and received on the Atlanta Co. common shares.
Apr.	**30**	Received interest on the Madison bonds.
May	**5**	Sold 150 shares of Atlanta Co. stock for $15 a share.
June	**30**	Detroit Inc. reports net income of $20,000 for the second quarter of 2020.
June	**30**	Detroit Inc. pays dividends of $2.00 per share.
June	**30**	Market price per share of Atlanta Co. and Detroit Inc. is $18 and $54, respectively. The market price of the Madison Inc. bonds is 98.

Required

Record the entries for the second quarter of 2020, assuming a $10,000 debit balance in the Fair Value Adjustment account on March 30, 2020. Spectrum Inc. updates its Fair Value Adjustment account for its investment portfolio quarterly.

Problem 14-91
Recording Investments in Securities—Equity Method, Fair Value Option **LO5**

On January 1, 2020, Redmond Company purchased 3,000 of the 15,000 outstanding shares of common stock of Decca Computer (DC) Corporation for $80,000 cash as a long-term investment (the only long-term equity investment held). The assets and liabilities of DC Corporation at the date of purchase approximate fair value. During 2020, DC reported net income of $25,000 and declared and paid cash dividends of $10,000. The fair value of DC Corporation at December 31, 2020, was $25 per share.

Required

a. Prepare the journal entries to record the purchase of the investment, the receipt of dividends, and the year-end adjusting entry, assuming that the investment is recorded under the equity method.

b. Record the journal entries assuming instead that Redmond Company opted on the purchase date to account for the investments using the fair value option.

Problem 14-92
Recording Investments in Securities—Equity Method **LO5**

On January 1, 2020, Rae Company purchased 8,000 of the 40,000 shares outstanding of common stock (par $1) of Sundem Corporation for $80,000 cash. Assume that the fair value and book value of all net assets of Sundem were the same at that time. This is the only long-term equity investment held and the ownership of Sundem shares represents a significant interest. The accounting periods for both Rae and Sundem end on December 31.

Sundem Corporation	
Year 2020	
Income reported for 2020	$40,000
Cash dividend per share declared and paid on December 15, 2020	1.50
Market price per share of stock, December 31, 2020	12.00
Year 2021	
Income reported for 2021	$50,000
Cash dividend per share declared and paid on December 15, 2021	1.50
Market price per share of stock, December 31, 2021	11.00

Required

a. Provide all of the entries required for Rae Company for 2020 and 2021 including the investment purchase, receipt of declared dividends, and year-end adjusting entries.

b. Show how the long-term investments in equity securities and the related investment income would be reported on the balance sheet and income statement of Rae Company at the end of each year.

Problem 14-93 Recording and Reporting Investments in Debt Securities—AFS, Fair Value Option **LO2, 3**

② **Adjust FVA at Sale and Year-End** On January 1, 2020, Sage Company acquired $50,000 of 4% bonds of Thyme Company, purchased to yield 6% interest. Interest is received semiannually on June 30 and December 31. The bonds mature in 10 years on December 31, 2029. Sage Company intends to hold the bonds longer than one year but doesn't anticipate holding the bonds until maturity. The fair value of the bonds on December 31, 2020, is $41,000.

Required

a. Prepare an amortization schedule for 2020 and 2021 for the bonds purchased by Sage Company.
b. Provide the entry to record the purchase of the bonds on January 1, 2020.
c. Provide the entry to record interest received on June 30, 2020, and December 31, 2020.
d. Provide any necessary adjusting entries to reflect the fair value of the bonds at December 31, 2020.
e. On June 30, 2021, after interest was received, Sage Company sold the bonds for $44,000. Record the interest entry, the entry to adjust the bonds to fair value, the sale entry, and the entry to eliminate the Fair Value Adjustment account on June 30, 2021.
f. Repeat requirements *b* through *e*, assuming Sage Company elected to account for the bonds under the fair value option.
g. Summarize the income statement impact in 2020 and 2021 under each of the two methods utilized above.

Problem 14-94 Recording and Reporting Investments—Equity Method **LO5**

Refer to the information in Problem 14-82, but now assume that on January 1, 2020, Rae Company elects to account for the investment using the fair value option.

Required

a. Provide all of the entries required for Rae Company for 2020 and 2021 including the investment purchase, receipt of declared dividends, and year-end adjusting entries. Assume that Rae Company accounts for the investment similarly to an asset measured at FV-NI except that the investment account is adjusted directly for market adjustments.
b. Show how the long-term investments in equity securities and the related investment income would be reported on the financial statements of Rae Company at the end of each year.
c. Alternatively, Rae Company records entries for this investment under the equity method during the year and adjusts the Investment account to fair value at year-end. Provide all of the entries required for Rae Company for 2020 and 2021 under this approach.
d. Show how the long-term investments in equity securities and the related investment income would be reported on the financial statements of Rae Company at the end of each year according to the approach in requirement (*c*).
e. How do the net results on the balance sheet and income statement compare in requirement (*b*) as compared to requirement (*d*)?

Problem 14-95 Classifying Securities **LO1, 2, 3, 4, 5**

The following are descriptions of various debt and equity securities.

	Investment Description	Debt or Equity Security	Investment Classification	Current or Noncurrent Asset
1	**Starbucks Corporation**'s 50% ownership in **President Starbucks Coffee (Shanghai)**.			
2	**Starbucks Corporation**'s corporate debt securities, not held for short-term trading gains or expected to be retained for the full-term. The company does not intend to sell the security sooner than one year.			
3	**3M**'s long-term investment in a municipal bond with the City of Nevada, Missouri. The company does not intend to hold the bond to maturity.			
4	**General Electric** holds shares of corporate stock with intention of immediate resale.			
5	**3M**'s 3-month certificate of deposit, not held for short-term trading.			

continued

continued from previous page

	Investment Description	Debt or Equity Security	Investment Classification	Current or Noncurrent Asset
6	**U.S. Bancorp**'s mortgage-backed security investment that the company intends to hold for the full-term.			
7	**Kellogg's** 50% interest in **Multipro Singapore Pte. Ltd.**, a leading distributor of a variety of food products in Nigeria and Ghana.			
8	**Whole Foods** holds short-term investments in commercial paper (with an intent to hold longer than 3 months).			
9	**GM Corporation** holds a significant influence on its equity investment in a joint venture in China.			
10	**Lowe's** holds shares of a mutual fund held for short-term gains.			

Required

Complete the table by identifying the type of security (debt or equity), the investment classification, and whether the investment is a current or noncurrent asset. For the investment classifications, use the following categories: (1) investment in trading securities, (2) investment in available-for-sale securities, (3) investment in equity method securities, (4) investment in held-to-maturity securities, and (5) investment in FV-NI securities. Choose the most likely classification based upon the information provided.

Problem 14-96
Accounting for Impairment of Investments **LO6**

Olympians Inc. holds a bond investment in Los Angeles Corporation. The amortized cost of the investment is $280,000 at December 31, 2020. Olympians Inc. estimates the fair value of the bonds to be $250,000. The unrealized loss of $30,000 is partially due to a credit loss of $20,000 with the remaining portion due to other factors.

Required

Record any journal entries required for each of the following separate scenarios. Include the elimination of any fair value adjustment account with each entry if appropriate.

a. Record the impairment loss on December 31, 2020, assuming that (1) the company does not intend to sell the asset and does not believe it is *more likely than not* that it will be required to sell the investment before recovery of any unrealized loss, (2) the company classifies the investments as AFS, and (3) the AFS bonds were adjusted to fair value through OCI on December 31, 2020.

b. Record the impairment loss on December 31, 2020, assuming that (1) the company does not intend to sell the asset and does not believe it is *more likely than not* that it will be required to sell the investment before recovery of any unrealized loss, (2) the company classifies the investments as AFS, (3) the AFS bonds were adjusted to fair value through OCI on December 31, 2020, and (4) the estimated credit loss is $40,000.

c. Record the impairment loss on December 31, 2020, assuming that (1) the company intends to sell the asset, (2) the company classifies the investment as AFS, and (3) the AFS bonds were adjusted to fair value through OCI on December 31, 2020.

d. Record the impairment loss on December 31, 2020, assuming that (1) the company intends to sell the asset, (2) the company classifies the investment as HTM, and (3) an estimate of the allowance for credit losses is $20,000.

e. Record the impairment loss on December 31, 2020, assuming that (1) the company does not intend to sell the asset and does not believe it is *more likely than not* that it will be required to sell the investment before recovery of any unrealized loss, (2) the company classifies the investments as TS, and (3) the TS bonds were adjusted to fair value through net income on December 31, 2020.

Accounting Decisions and Judgments

AD&J 14-97
Analyzing Equity Method **LO5**

Real World Analysis In its Year 8 annual report, **Xerox Corporation**, a manufacturer of photocopying equipment, has several items in the financial statements that refer to investments measured using the equity method (which are labeled "affiliated companies" by Xerox).

$ millions	Year 8	Year 7
From the income statement:		
Equity in net income of unconsolidated affiliated companies and other income.......	$ 74	$ 127
From the balance sheet:		
Investment in affiliates, at equity	1,456	1,332
From the statement of cash flows:		
Adjustments to reconcile income to cash flows		
Undistributed equity in net income of affiliates:*	(27)	(84)

*These are amounts added back (subtracted from) net income to obtain cash flow from operations.

Assume that there are no adjustments required for differences between book value and fair value at the date of acquisition, associated with the affiliated companies.

Required

a. On the income statement, equity income is combined with "other income." From the information presented, what is the maximum amount that Xerox could have received in declared dividends from its affiliated companies in Year 8? In Year 7? Now suppose Xerox received no dividends from its affiliated companies in Year 8. In this case, how much of the $74 million is other income?

b. Did Xerox increase or decrease its investments in affiliated companies during Year 8 beyond the amount of Xerox's equity in earnings retained by the investee? If so, by how much?

c. What rate of return on average assets did Xerox earn on its investment in affiliated companies in Year 8? Assume that other income in Year 8 is zero.

d. Suppose there is only one affiliated company in Xerox's investment, and it is a 50% owned joint venture. What would you estimate the total stockholders' equity of that company to be at December 31, Year 8?

AD&J 14-98 Analyzing Equity Method **LO5**

Real World Analysis Kimberly-Clark is a global consumer products company with total assets in excess of $11 billion. In Year 8, total revenues were over $12 billion from sales in over 150 countries. To conduct its global operations, Kimberly-Clark has an equity interest in over 60 companies. Some of these are wholly (100%) owned, while others have various lesser percentages of ownership.

Data from the Year 8 annual report provide information referring to its investments measured using the equity method (which are labeled "equity companies" by Kimberly-Clark).

$ millions	Year 8	Year 7
From the Balance Sheet:		
Investments in equity companies	$ 813.1	$ 567.7
From the Income Statement:		
Share of net income of equity companies........	137.1	157.3
From the Statement of Cash Flows:		
Increases (decreases) to adjust net income to cash flows from operations		
Equity companies' earnings in excess of dividends paid........	(15.1)	(62.1)
Notes Disclosures:		
Net income of equity companies........	294.6	338.1
Total stockholders' equity of equity companies........	1,522.3	1,063.2

Required

a. In the notes, Kimberly-Clark provides information on the percentage ownership of its various affiliated companies. How would you expect Kimberly-Clark to account for each of the following companies, based on the percentage of ownership reported?

1. Kimberly-Clark Southern Africa Holdings Limited, Johannesburg, South Africa (50% plus one share)
2. Kimberly-Clark Canada, Inc. (100%)
3. Kimberly-Clark Pudumjee Limited, Pune, India (51%)
4. Hogla-Kimberly, Hadera, Israel (49.9%)
5. Tecnosura, Colombia (29%)

b. Based on the information given in the statement of cash flows, it is apparent that in Year 8 Kimberly-Clark received cash dividends from its equity companies of $122.0 million (equal to $137.1 minus the undistributed portion of $15.1). Provide the journal entries to record the recognition of Kimberly-Clark's share of net income of the equity companies and the receipt of dividends (assume declared and paid in current year) from these companies.

c. Kimberly-Clark increased its interest in equity companies during Year 8. Determine the amount of investment Kimberly-Clark made in the equity companies during Year 8.

d. For both Year 7 and Year 8, estimate the average percent ownership that Kimberly-Clark has in equity companies based on its share of net income. Is the direction of change in ownership consistent with increasing or decreasing investment in equity companies?

e. Suppose there was no change in percent ownership. What effect would consolidating the equity companies have on Kimberly-Clark's Year 8 net income? In general terms, what effect would consolidating have on the reported total assets of Kimberly-Clark?

AD&J 14-99
Analyzing Equity Method **LO5**

Real World Analysis Refer to Note 6 from the Year 4 Coca-Cola annual report provided below and answer the questions that follow.

NOTE 6: EQUITY METHOD INVESTMENTS

Our consolidated net income includes our Company's proportionate share of the net income or loss of our equity method investees. When we record our proportionate share of net income, it increases equity income (loss) — net in our consolidated statements of income and our carrying value in that investment. Conversely, when we record our proportionate share of a net loss, it decreases equity income (loss) — net in our consolidated statements of income and our carrying value in that investment. The Company's proportionate share of the net income or loss of our equity method investees includes significant operating and nonoperating items recorded by our equity method investees. These items can have a significant impact on the amount of equity income (loss) — net in our consolidated statements of income and our carrying value in those investments. Refer to Note 17 for additional information related to significant operating and nonoperating items recorded by our equity method investees. The carrying values of our equity method investments are also impacted by our proportionate share of items impacting the equity investee's AOCI.

We eliminate from our financial results all significant intercompany transactions, including the intercompany portion of transactions with equity method investees.

The Company's equity method investments include our ownership interests in Coca-Cola FEMSA, Coca-Cola Hellenic and Coca-Cola Amatil. As of December 31, Year 4, we owned 28 percent, 23 percent and 29 percent, respectively, of these companies' outstanding shares. As of December 31, Year 4, our investment in our equity method investees in the aggregate exceeded our proportionate share of the net assets of these equity method investees by $1,671 million. This difference is not amortized.

A summary of financial information for our equity method investees in the aggregate is as follows (in millions):

For Year Ended December 31	Year 4	Year 3	Year 2
Net operating revenues	**$52,627**	$53,038	$47,087
Cost of goods sold	**31,810**	32,377	28,821
Gross profit	**$20,817**	$20,661	$18,266
Operating income	**$ 4,489**	$ 4,380	$ 4,605
Consolidated net income	**$ 2,440**	$ 2,364	$ 2,993
Less: Net income attributable to noncontrolling interests	**74**	62	89
Net income attributable to common shareowners	**$ 2,366**	$ 2,302	$ 2,904
Equity income (loss) — net	**$ 769**	$ 602	$ 819

At December 31	Year 4	Year 3
Current assets	**$16,184**	$19,229
Noncurrent assets	**40,080**	40,427
Total assets	**$56,264**	$59,656
Current liabilities	**$12,477**	$14,386
Noncurrent liabilities	**16,657**	17,779
Total liabilities	**$29,134**	$32,165
Equity attributable to shareowners of investees	**$26,363**	$26,668
Equity attributable to noncontrolling interests	**767**	823
Total equity	**$27,130**	$27,491
Company equity investment	**$ 9,947**	$10,393

Net sales to equity method investees, the majority of which are located outside the United States, were $10,063 million, $9,178 million and $7,082 million in Year 4, Year 3 and Year 2, respectively. Total payments, primarily marketing, made to equity method investees were $1,605 million, $1,807 million and $1,587 million in Year 4, Year 3 and Year 2, respectively. In addition, purchases of finished products from equity method investees were $381 million, $415 million and $392 million in Year 4, Year 3 and Year 2, respectively.

If valued at the December 31, Year 4 quoted closing prices of shares actively traded on stock markets, the value of our equity method investments in publicly traded bottlers would have exceeded our carrying value by $5,443 million.

Total net receivables due from equity method investees were $1,448 million and $1,308 million as of December 31, Year 4 and Year 3, respectively. The total amount of dividends received from equity method investees was $398 million, $401 million and $393 million for the years ended December 31, Year 4, Year 3 and Year 2, respectively. Dividends received included a $35 million special dividend from Coca-Cola Hellenic during Year 2. We classified the receipt of the special dividend in cash flows from operating activities because our cumulative equity in earnings from Coca-Cola Hellenic exceeded the cumulative distributions received; therefore, the dividends were deemed to be a return on our investment and not a return of our investment.

Required

a. Does Coca-Cola have investments in affiliated companies for which it accounts using the equity method? What is the percentage ownership of each investee?

b. At December 31, Year 4, what is the total amount of assets over which Coca-Cola has "significant influence" as a result of its equity investments? What is the total amount of "investment" Coca-Cola reports in its financial statements for investees? What is the fair value for these investments?

c. What is the reported income from all of Coca-Cola's equity investments in Year 4? Considering only this income, does it appear that Coca-Cola is earning a large return on its equity investments?

d. In what additional ways does Coca-Cola benefit from its equity investments other than its equity in the earnings of these companies?

e. If all the equity method investments were consolidated into the Coca-Cola financial statements, what would be the effect on Coca-Cola's net income in Year 4? Assuming there are no intercompany receivables or payables to be eliminated, what would be the effect on Coca-Cola's total assets?

f. Comment on why Coca-Cola might use a strategy of acquiring a significant but less than a 50% ownership in its various bottlers.

AD&J 14-100
Classifying Investments in Debt Securities
LO1, 2, 3

Judgment Case GAAP requires investments in debt securities to be classified as held-to-maturity, as trading securities, or as available-for-sale securities.

Required

a. At what carrying value are investments in debt securities recorded for each of the three classifications? What treatment is given to differences between carrying value and original cost, if any, in terms of how they are reported in the financial statements?

b. Suppose a company makes an investment in a debt security at the beginning of its fiscal year. The debt security is acquired at face value (that is, there is no premium or discount), and the security matures in three years. At the purchase of the securities, management overlooks the issue of how to classify the investment security.

1. At year-end the market price of the security has declined significantly because of a substantial increase in interest rates for investment securities of similar risk. What are some reasons management might wish to classify this investment into each of the three categories to manage its reported earnings?
2. At year-end the market price of the security has increased significantly because of a substantial decline in interest rates for investment securities of similar risk. What are some reasons management might wish to classify this investment into each of the three categories to manage its reported earnings?

AD&J 14-101
Reclassifying Investments in Debt Securities **LO7**

Judgment Case Petersen Company purchased debt securities at a cost of $500,000 on March 1, 2020, and classified them as AFS, as it intended to hold them for more than one year. At December 31, 2020, the fair value of the securities was $470,000, and the investment was carried at this value on that balance sheet date. At the end of the third quarter of the next year (September 30, 2021), management is considering reclassifying the securities as trading securities. Alternatively, management is considering waiting until December 31, the end of the fiscal year, to record the reclassification.

Required

Suppose the securities have a fair value of $525,000 at September 30, 2021, $515,000 on December 31, 2021, and are sold on May 1, 2022, for $510,000.

a. What are the effects on 2021 income if the securities are (a) reclassified on September 30, (b) reclassified on December 31, or (c) not reclassified during 2021? What would be the effect of the May sale on 2022 income if the securities (a) were reclassified on September 30, (b) were reclassified on December 31, or (c) were not reclassified prior to their sale? Does the reclassification affect the total gain recorded over the two-year period?

b. The authoritative guidance indicates the following.

320-10-35-12 In addition, given the nature of a trading security, transfers into or from the trading category also should be rare.

How should the guidance inform management's decision in considering a reclassification?

AD&J 14-102
Reclassifying Investments from FV-NI to Equity Method **LO7**

Judgment Case Bell Company acquired a 20% ownership interest in the outstanding voting stock of Harris Inc. on January 1, 2017, at a cost of $800,000. At the time, Bell did not have significant influence over Harris, and so Bell measured the investment at FV-NI. As time passed, Bell gained more influence over Harris, culminating in the election of two members of Bell's management to the board of directors of Harris on December 31, 2020. The investment has a current carrying value of $840,000 on Bell's books. An analysis of Harris Inc. reveals that 20% of its net book value equals $750,000 and that 20% of its net assets measured at fair value equals $820,000.

Required

a. Should Bell continue to account for its investment in Harris using FV-NI, or should it use the equity method? What issues would influence the answer to this question?

b. Suppose Bell adopts the equity method effective December 31, 2020. What effect would the decision have on its 2020 income statement and balance sheet?

c. Suppose Bell adopts the equity method effective on January 1, 2021. What effect would the decision have on its 2021 income statement and balance sheet, relative to adoption on December 31, 2020?

d. By adopting the equity method, what are some of the changes that Bell will make in recording its investment income from its investment in Harris?

AD&J 14-103
Reclassifying Investments from TS to AFS: Management Incentives **LO2, 3, 7**

Ethics Case Ace Investors Company buys and sells various debt securities. These security investments represent approximately 90% of the company's total assets. Ace has a policy of classifying all its investments as trading securities, since it has traditionally sold any individual security when management felt it advantageous to do so. The company is reconsidering this classification policy because securities are often held for many accounting periods before they are sold. Many members of senior management feel that the entire investment portfolio should be classified as AFS debt securities. A number of managers, however, are opposed to the change in classification policy. They are concerned about the effects of the policy change on their retirement pay, which is based on a formula involving the three-year average earnings of the company in the year of retirement. We have been asked to advise Ace on its decision regarding changing its classification policy.

Required

a. What are the fundamental distinctions between the classifications as trading securities and as available-for-sale securities?

b. Give possible reasons why the Ace managers are concerned about their retirement pay.

c. Do you see any ethical issues involved in the assignment we have been asked to undertake?

AD&J 14-104
Recording and Reporting Investments in Debt Securities: Accrued Interest on Purchase and Sale, Transfer **LO2, 3, 7**

Challenge Problem ② **Adjust FVA at Sale and Year-End** On September 1, 2020, New Company purchased 20 bonds of Old Corporation ($1,000, 6%) as an investment in trading securities at par plus accrued interest. The bonds pay annual interest each July 1. New Company paid cash, including accrued interest. New Company's annual reporting period ends December 31. At December 31, 2020, Old Corporation's bonds were quoted at 99.

Required

a. Provide the journal entry for New Company to record the purchase of the bonds.

b. Provide any adjusting entries required at December 31, 2020.

c. Provide the items and amounts that should be reported on New Company's 2020 income statement and December 31, 2020, balance sheet.

d. Provide the required entry on July 1, 2021.

e. On August 1, 2021, New Company sold 8 of the bonds at 100.5 plus any accrued interest. The remaining 12 bonds were transferred to AFS securities portfolio. Provide the required entry(ies). First adjust investments to fair value and eliminate the associate Fair Value Adjustment balance upon sale or transfer.

f. At December 31, 2021, the Old Corporation bonds were quoted at 101.5. There were no additional transactions during 2021. Provide the entry(ies) to be made at December 31, 2021.

g. List the investment items and amounts that would be reported on the 2021 income statement and the December 31, 2021, balance sheet.

AD&J 14-105 Recording Investments in Equity Securities: Cash and Stock Dividends, Stock Split **LO4**

Challenge Problem Hewlett Company purchased common stock (par value $10, 50,000 shares outstanding) of Packard Corporation as a long-term investment. Transactions (which occurred in the order given) related to this investment were:

1. Purchased 600 shares of Packard common stock at $90 per share (designated lot 1).
2. Purchased 2,000 shares of Packard common stock at $96 per share (designated lot 2).
3. At the end of the first year, Packard Corporation reported net income of $52,000 and the stock was selling at $97 per share.
4. At the end of the year, Packard Corporation declared and paid a cash dividend of $2.00 per share.
5. After reporting net income of $5,000 for the second year, Packard Corporation issued a stock dividend whereby each stockholder received one additional share for every two shares owned. After the stock dividend at the end of the second year, the stock was selling at $85.
6. Packard Corporation revised its charter to provide for a stock split. The par value was reduced to $5. The old common stock was turned in, and the holders received in exchange two shares of the new stock for each old share turned in.

Required

Provide the entries for each transaction, as they should be made in the accounts of Hewlett Company. Hewlett has an insignificant influence over Packard.

AD&J 14-106 Recording and Reporting Investment in Trading Securities: Purchases, Sale, Accrued Interest, Reclassification **LO2, 7**

Challenge Problem At December 31, 2020, the portfolio of investments in trading securities held by Dow Company was as follows.

Security	Par Value	Interest Rate	Interest Payable	Cash Cost*	Date Purchased	Maturity Date
X Corp. Bonds	$30,000	6%	Nov. 1	$30,000	Sept. 1, 2020	Nov. 1, 2025
Y Corp. Bonds	20,000	9%	Dec. 31	20,000	Dec. 31, 2020	Dec. 31, 2022

*Excluding any accrued interest

Dow's annual reporting period ends on December 31. At December 31, 2020, the X Corporation bonds were selling at 100.5.

Transactions relating to the portfolio of short-term investments in debt securities during 2021 were as follows.

June 1 Sold the Y Corporation bonds at 103, plus any accrued interest.
Nov. 1 Collected interest on the X Corporation bonds.
Dec. 1 Purchased $30,000 of Z Corporation bonds at 99½ plus accrued interest. These bonds pay 8% interest, semiannually each March 1 and September 1, and mature on March 1, 2023. The investment is classified as trading securities.
Dec. 31 Transferred the X Corporation bonds, quoted at 101.5, to the AFS portfolio of securities.

Required

a. Provide the 2020 entries for Dow Company to record the purchase of the debt securities, collections of interest, and all related adjusting entries.

b. The Z Corporation bonds were quoted at 99 on December 31, 2021. Provide all of the 2021 entries, including interest collections and any adjusting entries assuming the use of the straight-line interest method for amortizing discounts or premiums. Adjust trading securities to fair value before sales and transfers. Reverse related fair value adjustment amount upon sale or transfer.

c. List the items and amounts that would be reported on the 2021 income statement and the current section of the balance sheet.

AD&J 14-107 Recording and Reporting Investment in Equity Securities: Cash and Stock Dividends, Lump Sum Purchase, Split **LO4**

Challenge Problem ① **Adjust FVA at Year-End** Allen Corporation completed the following transactions, in the order given, relative to the portfolio of stocks measured at FV-NI. The company adjusts the Fair Value Adjustment account annually at December 31.

Year 2018

1. Purchased 200 shares of Mountain Corporation common stock (par value $10) at $70 per share plus a brokerage commission of 4% and transfer costs of $20.
2. Purchased, for a lump sum of $96,000, the following stocks of Dew Corporation.

	Number of Shares	Market Price at Date of Purchase
Class A, common, par value $20	200	$ 50
Preferred, noncumulative, par value $50	300	100
Class B, no-par common stock (stated value $100).	400	150

Year 2019

1. Purchased 300 shares of Mountain Corporation common stock at $80 per share plus a brokerage commission of 4% and transfer costs of $60.
2. Received a stock dividend on the Mountain Corporation stock; for each share held, an additional share was received.
3. Sold 100 shares of Mountain Corporation stock at $45 per share (from first lot).

Year 2020

1. Received a two-for-one stock split on the Class A common stock of Dew Corporation.
2. Cash dividends declared and paid:
   a. Mountain Corporation common stock—$10 per share.
   b. Dew, Class A, common stock—$5 per share.
   c. Dew, preferred—6%.
   d. Dew, Class B, nopar common stock—$15 per share.

Year-End Stock Prices	2018	2019	2020
Mountain, common stock	$ 70	$ 40	$ 40
Dew, Class A, common.	51	47	24
Dew preferred stock	98	95	96
Dew, Class B, common	140	144	144

Required

a. Provide entries for Allen Corporation for the above transactions. Provide calculations and assume FIFO order when shares are sold.

b. What items, amounts would be shown on the 2018, 2019, and 2020 income statements and balance sheets by Allen Corporation with respect to these investments?

AD&J 14-108
Defining Terms **LO1, 2, 3, 4, 5, 6**

Codification Skills How are the terms (1) equity security, (2) fair value, (3) holding gain or loss, (4) readily determinable fair value, and (5) debt security defined in the Codification?

AD&J 14-109
Performing Accounting Research **LO2, 3**

Codification Skills Our audit client is trying to determine whether a debt security should be classified as a trading security or an available-for-sale security. Does the Codification provide guidance on a specific time period that an investor intends to hold a security? Is there a defined cut-off for an intended holding period?

Identify the relevant authoritative guidance.

FASB ASC ___-___-___-___

AD&J 14-110
Performing Accounting Research **LO1**

Codification Skills The Codification provides guidance on the criteria of holding a debt security as a held-to-maturity security. The holder must have a positive intent and ability to hold the security to maturity. If the security may be sold before its maturity date because of possible changes such as market rate changes or foreign currency risk changes, or due to liquidity needs, the holder should not classify the security as a held-to-maturity security.

Assume a company meets the requirements to classify a security as held-to-maturity in both intent and ability. What unanticipated circumstances may arise that could change the status of a particular held-to-maturity security, without calling into question other held-to-maturity classifications?

Identify the relevant authoritative guidance.

FASB ASC ___-___-___-___

Appendix—Brief Exercises

App—Brief Exercise 14-111
Recording the Transfer from FV-NI to Equity Method **LO7**

On January 1, 2020, Big Apple Inc.'s holding of 1,800 shares of the 10,000 shares outstanding of common stock of Mack Corporation was originally purchased for $15 per share and has been measured at FV-NI. However, due to recent changes, Big Apple Inc. determined that it now has significant influence over Mack Corporation and should account for the investment as an equity investment. The fair value of Mack Corporation stock on January 1, 2020, is $30 per share. If Big Apple had accounted for the investment since the purchase date under the equity method, the Investment account would have a balance of $45,000. Record the entry on January 1, 2020, to transfer the Investment account from the accounting treatment of FV-NI to the equity method. Assume that the investment was adjusted to fair value on December 31, 2019.

App—Brief Exercise 14-112
Recording the Transfer from AFS to TS **LO7**
Hint: See Demo 14-7

Franklin Inc. makes the decision to change the classification of its current holding of Washington bonds, with an amortized cost of $20,000, from AFS to TS on January 1, 2020. On January 1, 2020, the fair value of the Washington investment is $15,000. Record the entry to transfer the security from AFS to TS on January 1, 2020.

App—Brief Exercise 14-113
Recording Cash Surrender Value **LO8**

Rusch Inc. purchased a $500,000 whole-life policy on its top executive in 2014. On January 1, 2020, the company pays an insurance premium in the amount of $20,000. The premium of $20,000 paid in 2020 results in an increase in cash surrender value of $1,200 to a total cash surrender value of $5,500 at the end of 2020. Record the adjusting entry for the life insurance policy on December 31, 2020, assuming that the full payment made on January 1, 2020, increased prepaid insurance.

App—Brief Exercise 14-114
Recording Cash Surrender Value **LO8**
Hint: See Demo 14-8

Referring to the information in Brief Exercise 14-113, assume that the executive dies at the end of 2020. Record the entry for the settlement of the policy, assuming that year-end adjusting entries had been recorded.

App—Brief Exercise 14-115
Determining Gain or Loss on Call Option Settlement **LO9**
Hint: See Demo 14-9A

On January 1, 2020, a call option was purchased by Beats Co. for $40, which allows Beats Co. to purchase 50 shares of Bieber Inc. stock at a strike price of $25 per share through December 31, 2021. On January 1, 2020, the fair value of the stock is $25 per share. On June 30, 2020, the fair value of each share of Bieber Inc. stock is $28 per share, and the fair value of the option is $190. Assuming that Beats Co. settles the call option on June 30, 2020, what is the gain or loss (if any) recorded on June 30, 2020? Assume that the call option was adjusted to fair value before settlement.

App—Brief Exercise 14-116
Recording Entries for a Fair Value Hedge: Put Option **LO9**
Hint: See Demo 14-9B

Anchor Inc. is holding a put option classified as a fair value hedge, with an estimated value of $300 effective December 31, 2020. Assume that one month later, the fair value of the put option at $375. Record the entry (if any) required on January 31, 2021, to adjust the put option to fair value.

App—Brief Exercise 14-117
Recording Entries for a Fair Value Hedge: Interest Rate Swap **LO9**
Hint: See Demo 14-9C

Arial Inc. entered into a 3-year interest swap agreement, which requires Arial Inc. to make interest payments based on LIBOR and receive fixed interest payments based on 4.2% of a notional amount of $100,000. The interest rate swap hedges against Arial's $100,000 note payable, which calls for fixed interest payments over 3 years at 4.2%. The fair value of the interest rate swap at the initiation of the agreement is zero. Assuming that the interest rate swap meets the GAAP effectiveness criteria, record any required adjusting entries related to the fair value of the swap and underlying liability at the first reporting date of December 31, 2020, if at that time, the interest rate swap is valued at $1,200. Assume a LIBOR rate of 4% at the reporting date.

App—Brief Exercise 14-118
Recording the Entry to Adjust Futures Contract **LO9**
Hint: See Demo 14-9D

A-Plus Company is holding a futures contract classified as a cash flow hedge with a value of $500 effective December 31, 2020. Assume that one month later, the fair value of the futures contract is $300. Record the entry (if any) required on January 31, 2021, to adjust the futures contract to fair value.

Appendix—Exercises

App—Exercise 14-119
Accounting for Transfer from HTM to AFS **LO7**

Glacier Inc. held the following investments in an HTM security portfolio at December 31, 2020.

Security	Cost	Fair Value at Dec. 31, 2020	Unrealized Gain (Loss)
Rain Gear Company bonds	$ 57,000	$ 65,000	$ 8,000
Camping Unlimited Inc. bonds ...	76,000	86,000	10,000
Total	$133,000	$151,000	$18,000

Both bonds were purchased at par value. At January 1, 2021, Glacier Inc. changed its intent from holding the bonds to maturity to holding these securities for an indefinite period of time due to a decrease in the credit standings of both investees. As a result, Glacier Inc. will begin to account for the securities as AFS beginning January 1, 2021.

Required

Record the entry on January 1, 2021, the date of transfer.

App—Exercise 14-120
Accounting for Transfer from AFS to HTM **LO7**

Refer to the information in Exercise 14-111, but now assume that the bonds were originally recorded as AFS securities but are transferred to HTM bonds on January 1, 2021, due to a change in Glacier's ability and intent to now hold the securities to maturity. Both bonds have a remaining term of 10 years. Assume the company straight-line amortizes the unrealized gain to income.

Required

a. Record the entry on January 1, 2021, the date of transfer.

b. Record any required adjusting entries on December 31, 2021, related to the HTM bonds.

App—Exercise 14-121
Accounting for Special-Purpose Fund **LO8**

On January 1, 2020, Koke Company decided to create a special-purpose fund to be identified as the special contingency fund. The resources in the fund will be used to reimburse employees injured while on the job. The company desires to accumulate a $150,000 fund balance by the end of 2022 by making three equal annual deposits starting on January 1, 2020. The independent trustee handling the fund will increase the fund by 9% compound interest each December 31.

Required

a. Compute the amount of the annual deposit.

b. Provide entries relating to the fund that Koke Company should make each year through December 31, 2022.

c. Assume that on January 2, 2023, the trustee made the first payment from the fund in the amount of $1,000. Provide the entry, if any, that Koke Company should make.

App—Exercise 14-122
Accounting for Call Options **LO9**
Hint: See Demo 14-9A

On January 2, 2020, Starz Inc. established an agreement with Silver Co. allowing Starz Inc. to call 100 shares of Gold Inc. stock at a strike price of $45 per share through June 30, 2021. On January 2, 2020, the current market price of Gold Inc. is $45 and the option premium is $200. On June 30, 2020, the fair value of the option is $900.

Required

a. Prepare the journal entry on January 2, 2020, to record the purchase of the call option.

b. Prepare the entry to adjust the call option to fair value on June 30, 2020.

c. When will the call option become valuable to Starz Inc.?

App—Exercise 14-123
Accounting for Fair Value Hedge: Put Option **LO9**

PierTwo purchased at par, 100, $100, 5% bonds of Supplier Inc. on January 1, 2020. In order to avoid exposure to fluctuations in the fair value of Supplier Inc. bonds, PierTwo acquires a 12-month put option on January 1, 2020, to sell 100 bonds of Supplier Inc. at a price of $100 per bond. The hedge is considered to be highly effective. On December 31, 2020, the market price per share of Supplier Inc. bonds fell to $90 per bond while the value of the put option is estimated to be $980. For simplicity, ignore interest on the bonds and assume the purchase price of the put option is zero.

Required

a. Prepare the entry to adjust the investment to fair value on December 31, 2020.

b. Prepare the entry to adjust the put option to fair value on December 31, 2020.

c. Calculate the net effect on the income statement of holding the put option and the debt securities in 2020.

App—Exercise 14-124
Accounting for Fair Value Hedge: Interest Rate Swap **LO9**
Hint: See Demo 14-9C

On January 2, 2020, Badger Corp. enters into a 5-year interest rate swap contract in order to effectively hedge a 5-year, 5%, $10,000 note, issued on January 2, 2020. The swap calls for Badger Corp. to receive payments semi-annually on June 30 and December 31 from the counterparty at a 5% interest rate based on a notional amount of $10,000 and to make payments to the counterparty based upon LIBOR. LIBOR is 4.2% as of January 2, 2020, and the rate will be adjusted every 6 months to the current LIBOR rate. For simplicity, assume that the swap has zero value on January 2, 2020, and on June 30, 2020.

Required

a. Prepare the journal entry on January 2, 2020, to record the issuance of the note and initiation of the interest rate swap agreement.

b. Prepare the entries related to the note payable and the interest rate swap on June 30, 2020, assuming LIBOR is unchanged.

App—Exercise 14-125
Accounting for Cash Flow Hedge: Futures Contract **LO9**

In October 2020, Rye Company, a producer of a grain-based product, determined that it would need 10,000 bushels of grain near the end of February 2021. Rye Company expects the current price of $4 per bushel of grain to change and does not want to assume the risk of such market price changes. As a result, Rye Company enters into a futures contract with Chicago Clearing House Inc. (CCH) to hedge the risk of market price changes of grain. The cost of the fair value hedge (futures contract) is zero. The futures contract provides that Rye Company purchases the grain at the date needed at market price, but CCH must pay Rye Company any differences above $4/bushel while Rye Company pays to CCH any differences below $4/bushel. Assume that the market price of grain is $4.20/bushel on December 31, 2020, and that Rye Company settles the futures contract with CCH and purchases the 10,000 bushels on February 20, 2021, in the market for $4.30/bushel.

Required

a. Prepare the journal entry required on November 1, 2020 (if any) related to the purchase of the futures contract.

b. Prepare the journal entry required on December 31, 2020 (if any) for the futures contract.

c. Prepare the journal entry required on February 20, 2021, for the settlement of the futures contract and purchase of the grain.

d. Record the entry needed to reclassify any unrealized gain or loss when the inventory is sold.

Appendix—Problems

App—Problem 14-126
Accounting for Transfer from FV-NI to Equity Method **LO7**

Duluth Travel Adventures reported the following regarding its investment in Superior Company common stock on December 31, 2020.

Investments in Superior	$78,000
Less: Fair Value Adjustment	(6,000)
Investment in Superior, at fair value	$72,000

Duluth has only one security, Superior Company common stock, measured at FV-NI and purchased at the beginning of 2020. Duluth owns 1,000 of the 5,000 outstanding voting shares of Superior common but was not allowed to influence the company. On January 2, 2021, Duluth is able to elect two of its senior management to Superior's board of directors and determines that it can now exert significant influence over Superior.

Required

Provide the January 2, 2021, entry to record the reclassification of the investment in Superior from the FV-NI measurement to the equity method.

App—Problem 14-127
Accounting for Special-Purpose Fund **LO8**

On January 1, 2020, Case Corporation created a special building fund by depositing a single sum of $100,000 with an independent trustee. The purpose of the fund is to provide resources to build an addition to the older office building during the latter part of 2024. The company anticipates a total construction cost of $500,000 and completion by January 1, 2025. The company plans to make five equal annual deposits each December 31, 2020 through 2024, to accumulate the $500,000. The independent trustee will increase the fund each December 31 at an interest rate of 5%. The accounting periods of the company and the fund end on December 31.

Required

a. Compute the amount of the equal annual deposits that will be needed and prepare a fund accumulation schedule through December 31, 2024, for Case Corporation.

b. The total cash outlay by Case will be $____.
Total interest revenue will be $____.

c. Provide the entries for Case on (a) January 1, 2020, and (b) December 31, 2020.

d. Provide the entries for Case on January 3, 2025, when the addition is completed and the actual cost of $525,000 is paid in full. The trustee paid interest on the fund for two extra days at the fund rate.

e. Show what the 2021 Case income statement, balance sheet, and statement of cash flows should report in regard to the building addition program.

f. Assume that the accounting period of Case Corporation ends on October 31 (instead of December 31) and that the fund year-end is unchanged. Provide any adjusting entry(s) that Case should make at its 2022 year-end.

App—Problem 14-128
Accounting for Call Options **LO9**

Champion Inc. purchased a call option as a speculative investment on January 1, 2020, for $125, allowing Champion Inc. to purchase 200 of Rising Star Co. common shares at $100 per share through January 1, 2021. Champion Inc. prepared the following table to track the activity of this investment in 2020.

Date	Rising Star Co.: Market Price per Share	Call Option: Fair Value
Jan. 1, 2020	$100	$125
June 30, 2020	90	50
Dec. 31, 2020	102	400

Required

a. Prepare the following journal entries for Champion Inc.
1. Purchase of the call option on January 1, 2020.
2. Adjust the call option to fair value on June 30, 2020.
3. Adjust the call option to fair value on December 31, 2020.

b. What is the impact on the income statement of holding this speculative investment in 2020?

App—Problem 14-129
Accounting for Fair Value Hedge: Interest Rate Swap **LO9**

On January 1, 2019, Innovative Lab issued a 4-year, $50,000 note to a local bank with fixed interest payments based on 6%, payable annually on December 31. In order to hedge the risk of a fixed interest payment, Innovative Lab entered into a 4-year interest rate swap agreement on January 1, 2019, calling for interest payments tied to LIBOR to a counterparty, receipt of interest based on 6%, negotiated at a notional amount of $50,000. The settlement date for the net cash payment is on December 31 of each year. The following table provides additional information related to the interest rate swap as forecasted over the next 4 years.

	Dec. 31, 2019	Dec. 31, 2020	Dec. 31, 2021	Dec. 31, 2022
Fair value: Interest rate swap	$ 200	$ 400	$ 0	$ 0
Fair value: note payable	$50,200	$50,400	$50,000	$50,000
LIBOR	4.2%	4.0%	5.2%	5.8%

Required

a. Record the required journal entries for years 2019, 2020, 2021, and 2022 related to the note payable and interest rate swap agreement.

b. Compute the effect on net income for each year, 2019 through 2022, ignoring income tax.

c. What change(s) in the forecast would make the interest rate swap more valuable than it is projected to be currently?

App—Problem 14-130
Accounting for Cash Flow Hedge: Futures Contract **LO9**

Mellogs is a small company that produces corn-based breakfast foods. On November 1, 2020, the company obtains a contract to supply 2 million pounds of its corn-based breakfast product to a large customer based in Germany, with delivery to be made in May 2021. As a result, Mellogs will need to acquire 100,000 bushels of corn in March 2021, in order to fulfill this contract. The price of corn currently at $3.60 per bushel, could increase dramatically between November 1, 2020, and March 2021. As a result, Mellogs entered into a futures contract with Capitol Clearing House Inc. (CCH) to hedge the risk of market price changes of corn. The cost of the fair value hedge (futures contract) is zero. The futures contract provides that Mellogs Company purchases the corn needed at the date needed at market price, but CCH must pay Mellogs Company any differences above $3.60/bushel while Mellogs Company pays to CCH any differences below $3.60/bushel. Assume that the market price of corn is $3.80/bushel on December 31, 2020, and that Mellogs Company purchases the 100,000 bushels on March 3, 2021, for $3.50/bushel.

Required

a. Prepare the journal entry required on November 1, 2020, (if any) related to the purchase of the futures contract.

b. Prepare the journal entry required on December 31, 2020, (if any) for the futures contract.

c. Prepare the journal entry required on March 3, 2021, for the execution of the futures contract and purchase of the corn.

d. Assuming that the 100,000 bushels of corn were utilized to fulfill the order in May 2021, at what amount is the cost of the corn included in the reported COGS on the sale?

Answers to Review Exercise

Review 14-1

	Bonds Yield 6%	Bonds Yield 8% (effective interest method)	Bonds Yield 8% (straight-line method)	Bonds Yield 5% (effective interest method)	Bonds Yield 5% (straight-line method)
Par, discount, or premium. . .	Par	Discount	Discount	Premium	Premium
Purchase price of HTM.	$60,000	$53,104	$53,104	$63,878	$63,878
Interest revenue for 2020 . . .	3,600	4,248	4,462	3,194	3,115
Interest revenue for 2021 . . .	3,600	4,300	4,462	3,174	3,115

Review 14-2

a. Discount: $18,528 [PV(0.06,10,1000,20000)]

b. **September 30, 2020—To record purchase of investment**

Investment in TS—Mack Bonds	18,528	
Cash		18,528

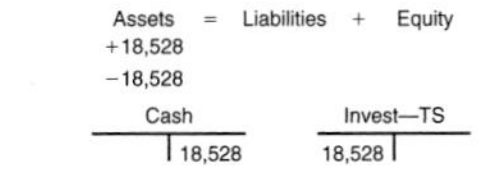

c. **December 31, 2020—To record interest revenue**

Interest Receivable ($1,000/4).	250	
Investment in TS—Mack Bonds ($112/4).	28	
Interest Revenue ($1,112/4).		278

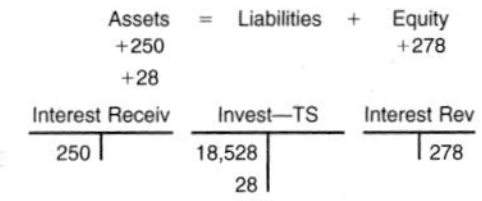

d. **December 31, 2020—To adjust investment to fair value**

Fair Value Adjustment—TS [$21,000 − ($18,528 + $28)]	2,444	
Unrealized Gain or Loss—Income		2,444

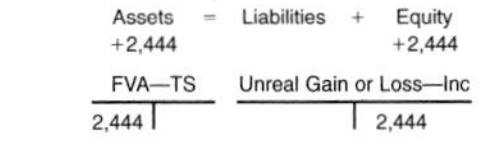

Select Accounting Treatment

① Adjust FVA at Year-End

e. **Sale of Bond Investment**

The company recognizes a gain as the difference between the cash received of $21,000 and the amortized cost of bonds of $18,556 ($18,528 + $28).

January 1, 2021—To record sale of bond investment

Cash ($21,500 + $250)	21,250	
Interest Receivable		250
Investment in TS—Mack Bonds		18,556
Gain on Sale of Investment		2,444

Cash: 21,250 | 18,528
Interest Receiv: 250 | 250
Invest—TS: 18,528, 28 | 18,556
Gain on Sale of Invest: | 2,444

December 31, 2021—To eliminate fair value adjustment balance

Unrealized Gain or Loss—Income	2,444	
Fair Value Adjustment—TS		2,444

FVA—TS: 2,444 | 2,444
Unreal Gain or Loss—Inc: 2,444 | 2,444

② Adjust FVA at Sale and Year-End

e. **Sale of Bond Investment**

The investment is recognized at fair value at the date of sale, so no adjustment to fair value is required on the sale date.

January 1, 2021—To record sale of bond investment

Cash ($21,000 + $250)	21,250	
Interest Receivable		250
Investment in TS—Mack Bonds		18,556
Fair Value Adjustment—TS		2,444

Cash: 21,250 | 18,528
Interest Receiv: 250 | 250
Invest—TS: 18,528, 28 | 18,556
FVA—TS: 2,444 | 2,444

No adjustment is required at year-end to the Fair Value Adjustment account (currently at a zero balance) because the company held no investments in TS at year-end.

f. The journal entries would generally be the same if an HTM security were accounted for under the fair value option. The account titles may be updated to reflect the fair value option election of an HTM security.

Review 14-3

a. **January 1, 2020—To record purchase of investment**

Assets = Liabilities + Equity: +83,464; −83,464
Cash: | 83,464
Invest—AFS: 83,464 |

Investment in AFS Securities—Mack Bonds (PV(0.05,5,−4800,−80000))	83,464	
Cash		83,464

b. **December 31, 2020—To record interest revenue**

Assets = Liabilities + Equity: +4,800; −627; Equity +4,173
Interest Receiv: 4,800 |
Invest—AFS: 83,464 | 627
Interest Rev: | 4,173

Interest Receivable ($80,000 × 0.06)	4,800	
Investment in AFS Securities—Mack Bonds		627
Interest Revenue ($83,464 × 0.05)		4,173

Partial Amortization Schedule

Date	Stated Interest	Market Interest	Discount Amortization	Bond Amortized Cost
Jan. 1, 2020				$83,464
Dec. 31, 2020	$4,800	$4,173	$627	82,837
Dec. 31, 2021	4,800	4,142	658	82,179

December 31, 2020—To adjust investment to fair value

Assets = Liabilities + Equity: −6,837; Equity −6,837
FVA—AFS: | 6,837
Unreal Gain or Loss—OCI: 6,837 |

Unrealized Gain or Loss—OCI [($83,464 − $627) − ($80,000 × 0.95)]	6,837	
Fair Value Adjustment—AFS		6,837

c.

Balance Sheet excerpt December 31, 2020	
Assets	
Interest receivable	$ 4,800
Investment in available-for-sale securities	76,000
Stockholders' equity	
Accumulated other comprehensive income (loss)	(6,837)

Income Statement excerpt For Year Ended December 31, 2020	
Other revenues and gains	
Interest revenue	$4,173

Statement of Comprehensive Income excerpt For Year Ended December 31, 2020	
Net income	$ ##
Other comprehensive income	
Unrealized holding loss on available-for-sale securities	(6,837)

d. **January 1, 2021—To record receipt of interest**

Cash	4,800	
Interest Receivable		4,800

Assets = Liabilities + Equity
+4,800
−4,800

Cash		Interest Receiv	
4,800	83,464	4,800	4,800

Select Accounting Treatment

① Adjust FVA at Year-End

e. Sale of Bond Investment

January 1, 2021—To record sale of bond investment

Cash	19,000	
Loss on Sale of Investment	1,709	
Investment in AFS Sec—Mack Bonds*		20,709

*2/8 × $82,837.

Cash		Invest—AFS		Loss on Sale of Invest	
4,800	83,464	83,464	627	1,709	
19,000			20,709		

f. Year-End Adjusting Entries

December 31, 2021—To adjust investment to fair value

Interest Receivable ($60,000 × 0.06)	3,600	
Investment in AFS—Mack Bonds ($658 × 0.75)		494
Interest Revenue ($4,142 × 0.75)		3,106

Interest Receiv		Invest—AFS		Interest Rev	
4,800	4,800	83,464	627		4,173
3,600			20,709		3,106
			494		
		61,634			

Required FVA ending account balance*	$(4,634)
Less existing FVA account balance	(6,837)
Increase to FVA account	$ 2,203

*$57,000 fair value (calculated as 0.95 × $60,000) − $61,634 amortized cost.

December 31, 2021—To adjust investment to fair value

Fair Value Adjustment—AFS	2,203	
Unrealized Gain or Loss—OCI		2,203

FVA—AFS		Unreal Gain or Loss—OCI	
2,203	6,837	6,837	2,203

② Adjust FVA at Sale and Year-End

e. Sale of Bond Investment

January 2, 2021—To record sale of bond investment

Cash	19,000	
Loss on Sale of Investment	1,709	
Fair Value Adjustment—AFS	1,709	
Investment in AFS—Mack Bonds		20,709
Unrealized Gain or Loss—OCI		1,709

Cash		Invest—AFS		Loss on Sale of Invest	
4,800	83,464	83,464	627	1,709	
19,000			20,709		

FVA—AFS		Unreal Gain or Loss—OCI	
1,709	6,837	6,837	1,709

f. Year-End Adjusting Entries

December 31, 2021—To adjust investment to fair value

Interest Receivable ($60,000 × 0.06)	3,600	
Investment in AFS—Mack Bonds ($658 × 0.75)		494
Interest Revenue ($4,142 × 0.75)		3,106

Interest Receiv		Invest—AFS		Interest Rev	
4,800	4,800	83,464	627		4,173
3,600			20,709		3,106
			494		
		61,634			

Required FVA ending account balance*	$(4,634)
Less existing FVA account balance	(5,128)
Increase to FVA account	$ 494

*$57,000 fair value (calculated as 0.95 × $60,000) − $61,634 amortized cost.

December 31, 2022—To adjust investment to fair value

Fair Value Adjustment—AFS	494	
Unrealized Gain or Loss—AFS		494

FVA—AFS		Unreal Gain or Loss—OCI	
1,709	6,837	6,837	1,709
494			494

Review 14-4

a. September 1, 2020—To record investment purchase

Assets	=	Liabilities	+	Equity
+250,000				
−250,000				

Cash		Invest—Mack Stock	
	250,000	250,000	

Investment in Mack Stock	250,000	
Cash		250,000

Select Accounting Treatment

① Adjust FVA at Year-End

b. Sale of Bond Investment

November 15, 2020—To record sale of bond investment

Cash	110,000	
Investment in Mack Stock		100,000
Gain on Sale of Investment		10,000

Cash		Invest—Mack Stock		Gain on Sale of Invest	
110,000	250,000	250,000	100,000		10,000

c. Receipt of Dividends

Cash ($3.00 × 1,500 shares)	4,500	
Dividend Revenue		4,500

Cash		Dividend Rev	
110,000	250,000		4,500
4,500			

d. Adjustment of Investment to Fair Value

Required FVA ending account balance*	$12,000
Less existing FVA account balance	0
Increase to FVA account	$12,000

*$162,000 fair value − $150,000 cost.

December 31, 2020—To adjust investment to fair value

Fair Value Adjustment—Equity Securities	12,000	
Unrealized Gain or Loss—Income		12,000

FVA—Eq Sec		Unreal Gain or Loss—Inc	
12,000			12,000

② Adjust FVA at Sale and Year-End

b. Sale of Bond Investment

Required FVA ending account balance*	$10,000
Less existing FVA account balance	0
Increase to FVA account	$10,000

*$110,000 fair value − $100,000 original cost.

November 15, 2020—To adjust investment to fair value

Fair Value Adjustment—Equity Securities	10,000	
Unrealized Gain or Loss—Income		10,000

FVA—Eq Sec		Unreal Gain or Loss—Inc	
10,000			10,000

November 15, 2020—To record sale of bond investment

Cash	110,000	
Investment in Mack Stock		100,000
Fair Value Adjustment—Equity Securities		10,000

Cash		Invest—Mack Stock		FVA—Eq Sec	
110,000	250,000	250,000	100,000	10,000	10,000

c. Receipt of Dividends

Cash ($3.00 × 1,500 shares)	4,500	
Dividend Revenue		4,500

Cash		Dividend Rev	
110,000	250,000		4,500
4,500			

d. Adjustment of Investment to Fair Value

Required FVA ending account balance*	$12,000
Less existing FVA account balance	0
Increase to FVA account	$12,000

*162,000 fair value − $150,000 cost.

December 31, 2020—To adjust investment to fair value

Fair Value Adjustment—Equity Securities	12,000	
Unrealized Gain or Loss—Income		12,000

FVA—Eq Sec		Unreal Gain or Loss—Inc	
12,000			12,000

Review 14-5

a. **January 2, 2020—To record investment purchase**

Investment in Mack Stock	100,000	
Cash		100,000

Assets	=	Liabilities	+	Equity
+100,000				
−100,000				

b. **December 31, 2020—To record investment income**

Investment in Mack Stock [(4,000/18,000) × $90,000]	20,000	
Investment Income		20,000

Assets	=	Liabilities	+	Equity
+20,000				+20,000

c. **December 31, 2020—To recognize depreciation expense**

Investment Income [($90,000 − $80,000) × (4,000/18,000)/10 years]	222	
Investment in Mack Stock		222

Assets	=	Liabilities	+	Equity
−222				−222

d. No entry required

e. **December 31, 2020—To record dividend receipt**

Cash ($1.00 × 4,000)	4,000	
Investment in Mack Stock		4,000

Assets	=	Liabilities	+	Equity
+4,000				
−4,000				

Cash: 4,000 | 100,000

Invest—CS: 100,000 | 222; 20,000 | 4,000; 115,778

Invest Inc: 222 | 20,000

f. December 31, 2020 balance . . . $115,778

Review 14-6

1. $30,000 loss
2. No loss is reported (FV > amortized cost)
3. $40,000 loss

Review 14-7

January 1, 2020—To record transfer from FV-NI to equity method

Investment in Mack—Equity Method (1,800 × $30)	54,000	
Investment in Mack—FV-NI		54,000

Assets	=	Liabilities	+	Equity
+54,000				
−54,000				

Review 14-8

Example One

a. $110,482 [PMT(0.05,4,0,−500000,1)]

b. **January 1, 2021—To record annual deposit in special-purpose fund**

Special-Purpose Fund	110,482	
Cash		110,482

Assets	=	Liabilities	+	Equity
+110,482				
−110,482				

December 31, 2021—To record interest revenue

Special-Purpose Fund ($110,482 × 0.05)	5,524	
Interest Revenue		5,524

Assets	=	Liabilities	+	Equity
+5,524				+5,524

Cash: | 110,482

Interest Rev: | 5,524

Spec-Purp Fund: 110,482; 5,524 |

Example Two

2020—To record payment on life insurance policy

Life Insurance Expense	10,200	
Cash Surrender Value of Life Insurance	1,800	
Cash		12,000

Assets	=	Liabilities	+	Equity
+1,800				−10,200
−12,000				

Cash Surr Value: 1,800 |

Life Ins Exp: 10,200 |

Cash: | 12,000

Review 14-9

Example One

a. **June 30, 2020—To adjust call option to fair value**

Assets = Liabilities + Equity
+380 +380

Call Option	380	
Unrealized Gain or Loss—Income		380

b. **June 30, 2020—To settle call option**

Assets = Liabilities + Equity
+375 −45
−420

Cash [($45 − $40) × 75 shares]	375	
Loss on Settlement of Call Option	45	
Call Option ($40 + $380)		420

Cash: 375 (debit)
Unreal Gain or Loss—Inc: 380 (credit)
Call Option: Bal. 40, 380 (debit); 420 (credit); 0
Loss on Settle: 45 (debit)

c. Net effect on net income .... $335 gain ($380 − $45)

Example Two

a. **December 31, 2020—To adjust debt investment to fair value**

Assets = Liabilities + Equity
−3,000 −3,000

Unrealized Gain or Loss—Income [($50 − $35) × 200]	3,000	
Fair Value Adjustment—HTM		3,000

b. **December 31, 2020—To adjust put option to fair value**

Assets = Liabilities + Equity
+2,800 +2,800

Put Option: 2,800 (debit)
FVA—HTM: 3,000 (credit)
Unreal Gain or Loss—Inc: 3,000 (debit); 2,800 (credit)

Put Option	2,800	
Unrealized Gain or Loss—Income		2,800

c. Net effect on net income .... $(200)

Example Three

a. **January 2, 2020—To record issuance of note payable**

Assets = Liabilities + Equity
+50,000 +50,000

Cash	50,000	
Note Payable		50,000

No entry required for the initiation of the swap agreement

b. **December 31, 2020—To record interest payment**

Assets = Liabilities + Equity
−2,000 −2,000

Interest Expense ($50,000 × 0.04)	2,000	
Cash		2,000

December 31, 2020—To record payment due to swap

Assets = Liabilities + Equity
−100 −100

Cash: 50,000 (debit); 2,000, 100 (credit)
Note Payable: 50,000 (credit)
Interest Exp: 2,000, 100 (debit)

Interest Expense	100	
Cash ($50,000 × 0.002)		100

Example Four

December 31, 2020—To adjust futures contract

Assets = Liabilities + Equity
+1,000 +1,000

Futures Contract: 1,000 (debit)
Gain or Loss—OCI: 1,000 (credit)

Futures Contract [($5.10 − $5.00) × 10,000]	1,000	
Gain or Loss—OCI		1,000

15 Current Liabilities and Contingencies

United Parcel Service, Inc.

	2017	2016
Current Liabilities:		
Current maturities of long-term debt and commercial paper	$ 4,011	$ 3,681
Accounts payable	3,872	3,042
Accrued wages and withholdings	2,521	2,317
Hedge margin liabilities	17	575
Self-insurance reserves	705	670
Accrued group welfare and retirement plan contributions	677	598
Other current liabilities	905	847
Total Current Liabilities	12,708	11,730

The Coca-Cola Company and Subsidiaries

	2017	2016
CURRENT LIABILITIES		
Accounts payable and accrued expenses	$ 8,748	$ 9,490
Loans and notes payable	13,205	12,498
Current maturities of long-term debt	3,298	3,527
Accrued income taxes	410	307
Liabilities held for sale	37	710
Liabilities held for sale — discontinued operations	1,496	—
TOTAL CURRENT LIABILITIES	27,194	26,532

3M Corporation

Warranties/Guarantees:

3M's accrued product warranty liabilities, recorded on the Consolidated Balance Sheet as part of current and long-term liabilities, are estimated at approximately $50 million at December 31, 2017, and $47 million at December 31, 2016. 3M does not consider this amount to be material. The fair value of 3M guarantees of loans with third parties and other guarantee arrangements are not material.

Target Corporation

Accrued and Other Current Liabilities (millions)	January 28, 2017	January 30, 2016
Wages and benefits	$ 812	$ 884
Gift card liability, net of estimated breakage	693	644
Real estate, sales, and other taxes payable	571	574
Dividends payable	334	337
Straight-line rent accrual (a)	271	262
Income tax payable	158	502
Workers' compensation and general liability (b)	141	146
Interest payable	71	76
Other	686	811
Total	$3,737	$4,236

Chapter Preview

In this chapter, we first review common current operating liabilities including accounts payable, sales taxes payable, customer deposits and advances, and employee payroll and compensated absences accruals. Next, we review current liabilities related to financing transactions including short-term notes payable, interest payable, and the reporting of current maturities of long-term debt. Issues related to the reporting of callable debt and short-term debt expected to be refinanced are discussed. We then explain contingencies, which involve a higher degree of estimation and judgment by management. We explore the accounting treatment of loss contingencies and how subsequent events affect financial reporting. We take a closer look at more common contingencies including litigation and warranties. We close with a review of reporting requirements and liquidity ratios.

Action Plan

LO	Topic/Subtopic	Page	Demos	Reviews	Assignments
LO 15–1	**Record accounts payable and sales taxes payable** Current Liability :: Unavoidable Obligation :: Accounts Payable :: Sales Taxes Payable	15-3	D15-1A D15-1B	R15-1	23, 24, 46, 47, 48, 69, 70, 73, 74, 75, 84, 85, 86, 87, 95
LO 15–2	**Record customer deposits and advances** Returnable Deposits :: Customer Advance Payments :: Deferred Revenue :: Gift Card Breakage :: Proportional Method	15-6	D15-2A D15-2B D15-2C	R15-2	25, 26, 49, 50, 51, 69, 70, 73, 74, 75, 84, 85, 86, 87, 95, 96
LO 15–3	**Measure and record employee payroll withholdings, employer payroll taxes, employee compensated absences, and bonus agreements** Payroll Withholdings :: Salaries Payable :: Payroll Taxes Payable :: FICA :: FUTA :: SUTA :: Compensated Absences Accrual :: Bonus Accrual	15-11	D15-3A D15-3B D15-3C D15-3D	R15-3	27, 28, 29, 52, 53, 54, 55, 69, 70, 73, 74, 75, 76, 84, 85, 86, 87, 92, 93, 95, 96
LO 15–4	**Account for short-term debt and classify debt on the balance sheet** Short-Term Note Payable :: Interest-Bearing :: Noninterest-Bearing :: Interest Payable :: Current Maturities :: Callable Debt :: Debt Refinance	15-15	D15-4A D15-4B D15-4C	R15-4	30, 31, 32, 33, 34, 56, 57, 58, 59, 60, 69, 70, 73, 74, 75, 77, 78, 84, 85, 86, 87, 88, 90, 95, 96
LO 15–5	**Describe accounting for subsequent events and contingencies including litigation, warranties, and other contingencies** Loss Contingency :: Probable :: Reasonably Estimable :: Reasonably Possible:: Remote :: Subsequent Event :: Recognized :: Nonrecognized :: Gain Contingency	15-23	D15-5A D15-5B D15-5C D15-5D	R15-5	35, 36, 37, 38, 39, 40, 41, 42, 43, 44, 60, 61, 62, 63, 64, 65, 66, 67, 68, 69, 70, 73, 74, 75, 79, 80, 81, 82, 83, 89, 91, 94, 95, 96, 97
LO 15–6	**Explain liability and contingency disclosures and analyses using liquidity ratios** Disclosures :: Liquidity Ratios :: Current Ratio :: Quick Ratio	15-34	D15-6	R15-6	45, 68, 69, 70, 71, 72, 74, 75

LO 15-1 Record accounts payable and sales taxes payable

LO 15-1 Overview

Current Liability
- Unavoidable obligations expected to be liquidated with current assets or creation of current liabilities
- Includes
  - Accounts payable
  - Sales taxes payable

A **liability** has three essential characteristics as indicated in Financial Accounting Concepts Statement No. 6.

SFAC No. 6 36 A liability has three essential characteristics:

a. it embodies a present duty or responsibility to one or more other entities that entails settlement by probable future transfer or use of assets at a specified or determinable date, on occurrence of a specified event, or on demand,

b. the duty or responsibility obligates a particular entity, leaving it little or no discretion to avoid the future sacrifice, and

c. the transaction or other event obligating the entity has already happened.

This means a liability is an *existing,* unavoidable obligation based upon a *past* transaction that must be fulfilled in the *future* when the company gives up resources.

The accounting guidance defines current liabilities as follows.

ASC Glossary **Current liabilities**—Current liabilities is used principally to designate obligations whose liquidation is reasonably expected to require the use of existing resources properly classifiable as current assets, or the creation of other current liabilities.

Liabilities that do not conform to this definition are called long-term, or noncurrent liabilities. Long-term liabilities are discussed in the next chapter. Current liabilities can influence operations in a different manner than long-term liabilities because current liabilities represent a claim on current resources. These claims differ from claims that mature years into the future, such as bonds. In the last section of this chapter, we review ratios that are critical in comparing current obligations to a company's currently available resources.

Current liabilities are typically recorded at maturity value or face amount rather than at fair value or present value. In general, the cost of an asset received and the maturity amount of a current liability coincide, supporting the case for recording a current liability at maturity value. Specifically, ASC 835-30-15-3 does not require separate accounting for interest in certain situations including (1) payables arising from transactions with suppliers in the normal course of business that are due within one year, (2) advance payments for the purchase of resources and raw materials, and (3) amounts intended to provide security for one party to an agreement (security deposits). However, significant financing components of contract liabilities with customers (deferred revenue) must be identified and related interest expense recorded. We will see instances in this chapter where we recognize interest expense on short-term notes.

At times, current liabilities must be estimated. Further, the identity of the payee may not be specifically identified as explained in the accounting guidance.

210-10-45-6 The concept of current liabilities includes estimated or accrued amounts that are expected to be required to cover expenditures within the year for known obligations the amount of which can be determined only approximately (as in the case of provisions for accruing bonus payments) or where the specific person or persons to whom payment will be made cannot as yet be designated (as in the case of estimated costs to be incurred in connection with guaranteed servicing or repair of products already sold).

During a normal operating cycle, companies often initiate transactions that create current liabilities. A company may acquire a product or a service from a supplier or vendor in advance of payment, which creates an accounts payable (**Demo 15-1A**). Or, a company may sell a product or service to a customer and collect the associated sales taxes, which creates sales taxes payable (**Demo 15-1B**).

Accounts Payable

Accounts payable or **trade accounts payable** are obligations arising from a company's ongoing operations related to the acquisition of inventories, supplies, and services used in the production and sale of goods or services. Of significant concern is achieving an accurate cut-off at the end of a reporting period, so that all liabilities are included in the proper accounting period. For example, items in transit may be included or excluded from inventory and accounts payable depending on when control of the goods has passed to the purchaser. (Recall the in-transit inventory discussion in Chapter 9.)

A transaction is documented through an invoice (on open account) with specific amounts and terms such as payment due within 30 days. Because of the short-term nature of accounts payable, typically no interest is due. However, terms can allow a discount for early payment. For example, terms of 2/10, n/30 allow for a 2% discount on purchases paid within 10 days, while the account balance is due in 30 days. For a review of journal entries for purchases in perpetual and periodic inventory systems, see Chapter 9.

EXPANDING YOUR KNOWLEDGE — Other Current Liabilities

While we highlight a number of current liabilities in this chapter, a few other current liabilities we sometimes see on a balance sheet follow.

Dividends payable Cash dividends declared but not yet paid are reported as a current liability if they are to be paid within the coming year or operating cycle. Declared dividends are reported as a liability between the date of declaration and the date of payment because declaration gives rise to an enforceable contract. Liabilities, however, are not recognized for undeclared dividends in arrears on cumulative preferred stock or any other dividends not formally declared by the board of directors.

Income tax payable Quarterly reports require a provision for both federal and state income tax liabilities. The estimated liability should be reported as a current liability based on the management's best estimates. Periodic payments, which will change through the year as the estimated tax changes, are required. Income taxes are covered in a later chapter.

Conditional expense payable A company may have an obligation based upon certain specified conditions in a contract. For example, rent payments may be partially fixed, and partially based upon sales revenue (such as 2% of sales over $100,000). Any unpaid rent payments for a given reporting period in which the conditions were met and the amounts were reasonably estimable, would be accrued.

Property tax payable Property taxes paid directly by a company are based on the assessed value of real and personal property and are levied to support school, city, county, and other designated activities. Unpaid taxes constitute a lien on the assessed property. Property taxes are typically assessed annually late in the year and paid in the following year. The accounting period during which these taxes should be recognized therefore precedes the period in which the taxes are paid. As a result, estimates are made (typically monthly) while revisions or changes in estimate are made prospectively.

Accounting for Accounts Payable — LO15-1 — Demo 15-1A

On January 1, 2020, Nakoma Co. purchases merchandise for resale. The merchandise has an invoice price of $5,000 and terms 3/10, n/60. Nakoma Co. accounts for inventory using the gross method in a perpetual inventory system and pays the balance in full on January 8, 2020. Record the entries on January 1, 2020, and January 8, 2020, for Nakoma Co.

Solution

January 1, 2020—To record purchase of inventory under perpetual method

Inventory	5,000	
Accounts Payable		5,000

Assets	=	Liabilities	+	Equity
+5,000		+5,000		

January 8, 2020—To record payment on account within discount period

Accounts Payable	5,000	
Inventory ($5,000 × 0.03)		150
Cash ($5,000 × 0.97)		4,850

Assets	=	Liabilities	+	Equity
−150		−5,000		
−4,850				

Inventory	
5,000	150

Accounts Payable	
5,000	5,000

Cash	
	4,850

Sales Taxes Payable

Acting as agents for taxing authorities, companies collect (or accrue) sales taxes at the time of sale on transfers of tangible personal property and on some services and subsequently remit the amounts to taxing authorities. Between the time of collection of sales taxes and remittance to governmental units, the company records an obligation of **sales taxes payable**. Sales taxes can be segregated and reported separately at the time of sale or recorded through a periodic adjusting entry.

Demo 15-1B **LO15-1** **Accounting for Sales Taxes Payable**

Demo MBC

Example One—Sales Taxes Payable Recorded at the Point of Sale

On January 8, 2020, Nakoma Co. sells merchandise with a sales price of $100 (cost of $80), and sales taxes of 5% to a customer on account (n/25). It is Nakoma's policy to record sales taxes payable with each sale. On January 31, the customer pays the balance on account. On April 30, 2020, Nakoma Co. remits the sales taxes to the appropriate governmental taxing units. Record the entries on January 8, January 31, and April 30 for Nakoma Co. Nakoma uses a perpetual inventory system.

Solution

Assets = Liabilities + Equity
+105 +5 +100

January 8, 2020—To record sales and sales taxes payable

Accounts Receivable ($100 + $5)	105	
Sales		100
Sales Taxes Payable ($100 × 0.05)		5

Assets = Liabilities + Equity
−80 −80

January 8, 2020—To record cost of sales

Cost of Goods Sold	80	
Inventory		80

Assets = Liabilities + Equity
+105
−105

January 31, 2020—To record payment from customer on account

Cash	105	
Accounts Receivable		105

Assets = Liabilities + Equity
−5 −5

Cash	
105	5

Accounts Receivable	
105	105

Inventory	
	80

Sales Tax Payable	
5	5

Sales	
	100

COGS	
80	

April 30, 2020—To record payment to taxing authorities

Sales Taxes Payable	5	
Cash		5

Example Two—Sales Taxes Payable Recorded as an Adjusting Entry

On January 8, 2020, Nakoma Co. sells merchandise with a sales price of $100 (cost of $80), and sales taxes of 5% to a customer on account (n/25). However, now assume that Nakoma Co. does *not* separate sales revenue and sales taxes payable at the time of sale. Record the entries for Nakoma Co. for (1) the sale on January 8 and (2) the adjusting entry on January 31 to identify amounts due to taxing authorities.

Solution

Assets = Liabilities + Equity
+105 +105

January 8, 2020—To record cash collected at time of sale

Cash	105	
Sales ($100 × 1.05)		105

Assets = Liabilities + Equity
−80 −80

January 8, 2020—To record cost of sales

Cost of Goods Sold	80	
Inventory		80

To identify the portion of the cash collected that pertains to sales revenue, simply divide the cash collected of $105 by 1 plus the sales tax rate ($105/1.05 = $100 in sales revenue). The difference of $5 ($105 − $100) is the amount of sales taxes payable.

continued

continued from previous page

January 31, 2020—To separately identify sales taxes payable amount

Sales.	5	
Sales Taxes Payable ($100 × 0.05).		5

Assets = Liabilities + Equity
+5 −5

Cash: 105 | ; Inventory: | 80
Sales Tax Payable: | 5 ; Sales: 5 | 105
COGS: 80 |

Recording Accounts Payable and Sales Taxes Payable

LO15-1 **Review 15-1**

Prepare journal entries for the following transactions for Retailer Inc. Retailer uses a perpetual inventory system.

a. On June 1, 2020, Retailer Inc. purchased merchandise for resale for $20,000 on credit terms 2/15, n/30 from a supplier. Retailer Inc. incurred a shipping charge of $300 on the purchase, which was immediately paid. Record the purchase using the gross method.

b. For the week ended June 7, 2020, Retailer Inc. sells $4,000 of inventory to customers for $8,000, with a sales tax rate of 6%. Of the total sales for the week, 25% are cash sales, and 75% are credit sales (n/30). Record the sales entries, with sales taxes payable recorded in a separate account.

c. On June 10, 2020, record Retailer Inc.'s payment of its account balance with its supplier.

d. Assume instead that Retailer Inc. sells $3,000 of inventory during the week ended June 7, 2020, to customers for $5,300, which includes a 6% sales tax. Of the total sales for the week, 25% are cash sales, and 75% are credit sales. Record the sales entries, with sales taxes payable recorded in a separate account.

More Practice: **15-23, 15-24, 15-46, 15-48**

Solution on p. 15-58.

3M

Real World—ACCOUNTS PAYABLE

3M Company included the following summary in its balance sheet found in its 2017 Form 10-K report. Accounts payable made up 25% and 29% of total current liabilities on December 31, 2017, and December 31, 2016, respectively.

3M [MMM]

3M Company and Subsidiaries—Consolidated Balance Sheet (Excerpt)

At December 31 ($ millions)	2017	2016
Current liabilities		
Short-term borrowings and current portion of long-term debt.	$1,853	$ 972
Accounts payable	1,945	1,798
Accrued payroll.	870	678
Accrued income taxes.	310	299
Other current liabilities	2,709	2,472
Total current liabilities	$7,687	$6,219

Record customer deposits and advances

LO 15-2

Companies can collect cash from customers resulting in an obligation from the company to the customer. In one case, cash collected is in the form of a deposit that will be returned to the customer as long as certain conditions are met (**Demo 15-2A**). In another case, cash collected is in the form of a prepayment for future services or products that the company will provide (**Demo 15-2B**) including the purchase of gift cards (**Demo 15-2C**). Revenue is not recognized until the company satisfies its performance obligation as discussed in the chapter on revenue recognition.

LO 15-2 Overview

Current Operating Liabilities
- Returnable deposits from customers
- Advance payments from customers
  - Prepayment for a good or service
  - Purchase of gift cards

Customer Returnable Deposits

A company can receive a **returnable deposit,** also called a **refundable deposit**, from a customer as a guarantee of a future payment or to guarantee performance on a contract or service. Deposits can also be received as a guarantee in case of noncollection or for possible damage to property. Such advances create liabilities for the company receiving the payment until the underlying transaction is completed and the deposit is returned to the customer. If the customer fails to perform as required, the deposit is forfeited and the company records the forfeited deposit as revenue. Deposits should be reported as current liabilities or long-term liabilities depending on the time involved between the date of deposit and the expected termination of the relationship.

Demo 15-2A **LO15-2** **Accounting for Returnable Deposits**

Demo MBC

Example One—Returnable Deposit

Unique Blinds Inc. supplies high-end, custom-fit blinds to approved customers, primarily residential builders. Unique Blinds Inc. collected a $2,000 deposit from a new customer on January 1, 2020, which will be held until full payment is received on the customer's initial three orders. The purpose of the deposit is to protect Unique Blinds Inc. from the cancellation of orders or for nonpayment. The customer fulfills the commitment through full payment of its first three orders on March 30, 2020, and the deposit is released to the customer. Prepare the entries on January 1, 2020, and March 30, 2020, for Unique Blinds Inc.

Solution

Assets = Liabilities + Equity
+2,000 +2,000

January 1, 2020—To record cash received for customer deposit

Cash	2,000	
Liability—Returnable Deposit		2,000

Assets = Liabilities + Equity
−2,000 −2,000

Cash		Deposit	
2,000	2,000	2,000	2,000

March 30, 2020—To record return of deposit to customer

Liability—Returnable Deposit	2,000	
Cash		2,000

Example Two—Returnable Deposit with Forfeiture

Ocean Properties Inc. in southern Florida rents out vacation units. The company offers its guests access to beach equipment including beach umbrellas and beach chairs for a returnable deposit. During March of 2020, the company collected $5,000 in customer deposits. Deposits forfeited (due to equipment not returned or damaged) amounted to $500. The inventory cost of the beach equipment is 75% of the deposit amount. It is the company's policy to include the beach equipment as inventory unless a deposit is forfeited. Provide summary entries for March 2020 for the following items.

a. Collection of the customer deposits.
b. Return of customer deposits.
c. Forfeiture of customer deposits.

Solution

Assets = Liabilities + Equity
+5,000 +5,000

March 2020—To record collection of customer deposits

Cash	5,000	
Liability—Returnable Deposit		5,000

Assets = Liabilities + Equity
−4,500 −4,500

March 2020—To record return of deposits to customer

Liability—Returnable Deposit	4,500	
Cash ($5,000 − $500)		4,500

continued

continued from previous page

March 2020—To recognize revenue on deposit forfeiture

Liability—Returnable Deposit	500	
Sales		500

Assets	=	Liabilities	+	Equity
		−500		+500

March 2020—To recognize COGS on deposit forfeiture

Cost of Goods Sold (0.75 × $500)	375	
Inventory		375

Assets	=	Liabilities	+	Equity
−375				−375

Cash	
5,000	4,500

Inventory	
	375

Deposit	
4,500	5,000
500	

COGS	
375	

Sales	
	500

Customer Advance Payments

In certain situations, customers prepay for a good or service. In the event of a customer advance payment, the seller will recognize deferred revenue (a form of a contract liability) in the amount of the prepayment for its performance obligation to transfer goods or services in the future. *This means a seller would record a liability if a customer's payment occurs before the transfer of control of the good or service to the customer.* Such transactions are recorded as a debit to Cash and a credit to Deferred Revenue. Subsequently, the seller recognizes revenue at the time the performance obligation is satisfied. Examples of revenues collected in advance include gift certificates, college tuition, rent, ticket sales, streaming movie subscriptions, and gift cards (also called a **prepaid stored-value product**). See Chapter 7 for examples of account titles of deferred liabilities. Deferred rent revenue relating to short-term leases is discussed in Chapter 17.

In the case of gift cards, revenue is recognized when gift cards are redeemed for a good or service. However, some gift cards will go unused—the value of unredeemed gift cards is called **gift card breakage**. Gift card breakage revenue is recorded under the **proportional method** if it is *probable* that a significant reversal of the recognized breakage amount will not subsequently occur. Under the proportional method, revenue on unused gift cards is recognized (in the account Gift Card Breakage Revenue) based upon the rate of actual gift card redemptions to total expected gift card redemptions. To use this method, companies need detailed information to reasonably estimate the total amount of gift card values that will not be redeemed. *If a company does not meet the requirements to use the proportional method, the company will not record revenue on gift card breakage until the chance of gift card redemption is remote.*

405-20-40-4 If an entity expects to be entitled to a breakage amount for a liability resulting from the sale of a prepaid stored-value product . . . the entity shall derecognize the amount related to the expected breakage in proportion to the pattern of rights expected to be exercised by the product holder only to the extent that it is probable that a significant reversal of the recognized breakage amount will not subsequently occur. If an entity does not expect to be entitled to a breakage amount for prepaid stored-value products . . . the entity shall derecognize the amount related to breakage when the likelihood of the product holder exercising its remaining rights becomes remote.

Accounting for Deferred Revenue — LO15-2 — Demo 15-2B

On November 1, 2020, Luxury Spas Inc. collects an advance payment of $900 from a customer for six months of spa services. The accounting period of Luxury Spas Inc. ends December 31. Record the entry on November 1, 2020, and the adjusting entry on December 31, 2020, for Luxury Spas Inc.

Solution

Luxury Spas Inc. would record the following entry upon receipt of payment.

November 1, 2020—To record advance payment

Cash	900	
Deferred Revenue		900

Assets	=	Liabilities	+	Equity
+900		+900		

On December 31, 2020, Luxury Spas Inc. would reduce its current liability (deferred revenue) for the two months of November and December 2020.

continued

continued from previous page

December 31, 2020—To recognize revenue

Assets = Liabilities + Equity
−300 +300

Deferred Revenue	300	
Service Revenue ($900 × 2/6)		300

Cash	
900	

Deferred Rev	
300	900

Service Rev	
	300

The remaining deferred revenue of $600 ($900 − $300) is reported as a current liability on Luxury Spa's December 31, 2020, balance sheet for its obligation to provide spa services for the following four months.

EXPANDING YOUR KNOWLEDGE Advances from Customers with Significant Financing

Chapter 7 explained that revenue contracts with significant financing components must take into account the time value of money. The following example illustrates an advance payment with a significant financing component.

Assume that on June 30, 2020, Water's Edge Hotel collected $1,335 in advance from a customer for a banquet room and catering services for a wedding scheduled in two years. The market rate is 6%, compounded annually. Record the entry for the advance payment on June 30, 2020, the adjusting entries on December 31, 2020, and December 31, 2021; and the recognition of revenue on June 30, 2022.

June 30, 2020—To record advance payment

Assets = Liabilities + Equity
+1,335 +1,335

Cash	1,335	
Deferred Revenue		1,335

December 31, 2020—To recognize interest expense

Assets = Liabilities + Equity
+40 −40

Interest Expense ($1,335 × 0.06/2)	40	
Interest Payable		40

December 31, 2021—To recognize interest expense

Assets = Liabilities + Equity
+82 −82

Interest Expense ($40 + [{$1,335 + $80} × 0.06/2])	82	
Interest Payable		82

June 30, 2022—To recognize revenue

Assets = Liabilities + Equity
−122 −43
−1,335 +1,500

Interest Expense ($1,415 × 0.06/2)	43	
Interest Payable ($40 + $82)	122	
Deferred Revenue	1,335	
Sales		1,500

Cash	
1,335	

Interest Payable	
122	40
	82

Deferred Rev	
1,335	1,335

Sales	
	1,500

Interest Exp	
40	
82	
43	

Demo 15-2C LO15-2 Accounting for Gift Cards

Pizza Toppers Inc. sold $500 of nonrefundable gift cards during the year 2020, its first year of operations. Customers redeemed $300 of the gift cards for restaurant purchases during 2020. On December 31, 2020, Pizza Toppers Inc. calculates the remaining balance of unredeemed gift cards is $200 ($500 less $300). Pizza Toppers Inc. estimates that 80% of the value of gift cards sold in 2020 will be redeemed, while 20% will remain unclaimed.

Required

a. Record the entry for the sale of gift cards during 2020.

b. Record the entry for the redemption of gift cards during 2020. Ignore the entry for cost of goods sold.

c. Record the adjusting entry on December 31, 2020, to recognize gift card breakage revenue under the proportional method.

d. Assume instead that the company does not meet the requirements to use the proportional method. However, there is only a *remote* chance that the remaining unredeemed gift cards of $200 will be redeemed. Record the adjusting entry on December 31, 2020.

continued

continued from previous page

Solution

a. Sale of Gift Cards

At the time of sale (2020)—To record sale of gift cards

Cash	500	
Deferred Gift Card Revenue		500

Assets	=	Liabilities	+	Equity
+500		+500		

Cash: 500 (debit) — Deferred Rev: 500 (credit)

b. Redemption of Gift Cards

At the time of redemption (2020)—To record redemption of gift cards

Deferred Gift Card Revenue	300	
Sales		300

Assets	=	Liabilities	+	Equity
		−300		+300

Deferred GC Rev: 300 (debit) | 500 (credit) — Sales: 300 (credit)

c. Gift Card Breakage Revenue—Proportional Method

The total gift card redemption is estimated to be $400 ($500 × 80%) and the total gift card breakage is estimated to be $100 ($500 × 20%). Under the proportional method, the rate of redemption for 2020 and the estimate of breakage revenue are calculated as follows.

To calculate rate of redemption in 2020

2020 redemptions	$300	= 75%
Total expected redemptions	$400	

To calculate proportional breakage revenue to recognize in 2020

Total estimated breakage revenue	$100
Gift card redemption rate	75%
Proportional breakage revenue to recognize	$ 75

The amount estimated as breakage revenue is recorded as an adjusting entry on December 31, 2020.

December 31, 2020—To recognize revenue due to gift card breakage

Deferred Gift Card Revenue	75	
Gift Card Breakage Revenue		75

Assets	=	Liabilities	+	Equity
		−75		+75

Deferred GC Rev: 300, 75 (debit) | 500 (credit) — GC Break Rev: 75 (credit)

d. Gift Card Breakage Revenue—Redemption is Remote

Because the chance of redemption is remote, the estimated gift card breakage of $200 is recognized as revenue immediately.

December 31, 2020—To recognize revenue due to gift card breakage

Deferred Gift Card Revenue	200	
Gift Card Breakage Revenue		200

Assets	=	Liabilities	+	Equity
		−200		+200

Deferred GCRev: 300, 200 (debit) | 500 (credit) — GC Break Rev: 200 (credit)

EXPANDING YOUR KNOWLEDGE — Gift Card Revenue Affected by Escheatment Laws

A number of states have enacted **escheatment laws** (abandoned property laws) for unredeemed gift card balances, typically after a waiting period of either three or five years. These states require companies to pay to the state either the full unredeemed value of gift cards, or a percentage of the unredeemed value, typically 60%. *Therefore, companies can recognize revenue for gift card breakage only to the extent that the state allows a company to retain the cash collected.* Let's say that Pizza Toppers Inc. in **Demo 15-2C (d)** must abide by a state law that requires 60% of unredeemed gift card revenue to be paid to the state. Taking into account escheatment law, the December 31, 2020, adjusting entry would be recorded as follows.

December 31, 2020—To recognize revenue due to gift card breakage

Deferred Gift Card Revenue	200	
Gift Card Breakage Revenue ($200 × 0.40)		80
Amount Due to State ($200 × 0.60)		120

Assets	=	Liabilities	+	Equity
		−200 +120		+80

Deferred GC Rev: 300, 200 (debit) | 500 (credit) — GC Break Rev: 80 (credit) — Due to State: 120 (credit)

REVIEW 15-2 LO15-2 Recording Customer Deposits and Advances

Review MBC

Party Planners Inc. sold $5,000 of gift cards during the month of January 2020. During January 2020, $2,000 of the gift cards sold were redeemed. Based on previous experience, Party Planners Inc. estimates gift card breakage to be 4% of total gift card sales. The company uses the proportional method to recognize revenue on gift card breakage.

The company also collected deposits totaling $1,000 from customers for equipment rentals in January. The company will return the deposits in full in February as long as there is no damage on the equipment during the rental period. Record the following entries in January 2020 for Party Planners Inc.

a. Record the entry for the sale of gift cards in January 2020.

b. Record the entry for the redemption of gift cards in January of 2020. Ignore the entry for cost of goods sold.

c. Record the adjusting entry for revenue recognized on January 31, 2020, due to gift card breakage using the proportional method.

d. Record the entry for the collection of deposits for equipment rentals in January.

More Practice: 15-50, 15-51

Solution on p. 15-59.

LO 15-3 Measure and record employee payroll withholdings, employer payroll taxes, employee compensated absences, and bonus agreements

LO 15-3 Overview

Current Operating Liabilities
- Payroll withholdings and salaries payable
- Payroll taxes payable: FICA, FUTA, SUTA
- Liability for compensated absences
- Salaries payable for future bonus payments

In addition to salaries, employers must pay various payroll taxes. Employers may also compensate for absences through vacation or sick pay or offer commission or bonus plans.

Four significant aspects of payroll accounting for companies are:

- Deductions from employees' pay for legally required deductions and voluntary deductions (**Demo 15-3A**).
- Employer's accrual of various payroll taxes (**Demo 15-3B**).
- Accrual for compensated absences (**Demo 15-3C**).
- Accrual for bonus agreements (**Demo 15-3D**).

Withholdings from Wages of Employees

Companies typically withhold a number of items from employees' pay. The amounts withheld are remitted to the appropriate third parties (such as federal or state governmental units) while the remaining pay is forwarded to the employees electronically or through printed checks. Some withholdings are *legally required* such as withholding taxes while others are *voluntary*, such as contributions to retirement plans, union dues, insurance premiums, health care savings plans, etc.

Legally required withholdings include federal and state income tax withholdings, as well as social security and Medicare tax withholdings authorized by **FICA** (Federal Insurance Contribution Act). Amounts withheld for federal taxes are based on tax tables provided by the Internal Revenue Service. The rate of withholdings varies depending upon earnings and the number of exemptions selected by the employee. Rates for the social security and Medicare tax withholdings change from time to time. The employer must deduct these taxes from the pay of each employee under specified conditions.

For example, in 2018, employers and employees each paid a tax of 1.45% on all wages for Medicare plus 6.20% on the first $128,400 of wages earned by each employee for social security. Thus, the combined rate on the first $128,400 earned by each employee was 7.65%. In addition, employees paid 0.9% in Medicare taxes on wages over $200,000. The primary purpose of these taxes is to provide retirement pay and health benefits for retirees and death benefits for retirees' survivors.

Recording Employee Payroll Withholdings — LO15-3 — Demo 15-3A

Top Consultants Inc. had a weekly payroll of $38,000 for the week ended January 31, 2020, with the following withholdings:

- Legal withholdings
  - Social security tax of 7.65% on the total weekly payroll.
  - Federal tax withholdings of $7,600.
  - State tax withholdings of $1,900.
- Voluntary withholdings
  - Voluntary retirement plan contributions of $1,000.
  - Health care premiums of $1,500.

Record the company's payroll entry on January 31, 2020.

Solution

January 31, 2020—To record weekly payroll

Salaries Expense	38,000	
Withholding Taxes Payable—Federal		7,600
Withholding Taxes Payable—State		1,900
FICA Taxes Payable (0.0765 × $38,000)		2,907
Retirement Contributions Payable		1,000
Health Care Premiums Payable		1,500
Salaries Payable (to balance)		23,093

Assets = Liabilities + Equity
+38,000 −38,000
Salaries Exp: 38,000 |
Payables: | 38,000

Accrual for Payroll Taxes

The employer's primary federal payroll taxes are **FICA** and **FUTA** (authorized by the Federal Unemployment Tax Act). In addition to the FICA taxes withheld from employees' pay, the employer remits their required 7.65% FICA tax to the U.S. Treasury. FUTA payroll tax is used to finance the cost of the federal-state unemployment compensation program. In most states, this payroll tax is paid only by the employer. The state portion of this tax is commonly referred to as **SUTA**. In 2018, the FUTA tax rate was 6.0% on the first $7,000 in wages paid to each employee, with 5.4% the maximum payable to the state and the remaining 0.6% payable to the U.S. Treasury. States grant discounts on the unemployment tax rate for low occurrences of employees seeking unemployment compensation.

Recording Employer Payroll Taxes — LO15-3 — Demo 15-3B

Assume the same information in **Demo 15-3A** for Top Consultants Inc. along with this additional data.

- FUTA tax rate: 0.6% on the full $38,000 of salaries expense.
- SUTA tax rate: 5.4% on the full $38,000 of salaries expense.

Record the company's payroll tax entry on January 31, 2020.

Solution

January 31, 2020—To record employer's weekly payroll tax expense

Payroll Tax Expense (to balance)	5,187	
FICA Taxes Payable (0.0765 × $38,000)		2,907
FUTA Taxes Payable (0.006 × $38,000)		228
SUTA Taxes Payable (0.054 × $38,000)		2,052

Assets = Liabilities + Equity
+5,187 −5,187
Payroll Tax Exp: 5,187 |
Payroll Tax Pay: | 5,187

Accrual for Compensated Absences

Companies often grant employees paid vacations and holidays, and paid absences for illness. When employees carry over unused time to future periods, any expense due to compensated absences is accrued in the year in which it is earned, provided four criteria are met as outlined in the accounting guidance.

710-10-25-1 An employer shall accrue a liability for employees' compensation for future absences if all of the following conditions are met:

a. The employer's obligation relating to employees' rights to receive compensation for future absences is attributable to employees' services already rendered.
b. The obligation relates to rights that vest or accumulate.
c. Payment of the compensation is probable.
d. The amount can be reasonably estimated.

If the first three criteria are met, but the amount cannot be reliably estimated, disclosure is required.

A benefit **vests** when it is no longer contingent on continuing employment. Thus, vested benefits are accrued because the benefit will be paid even if the employee is terminated. However, a benefit that **accumulates** does not necessarily vest. For example, an employee with six weeks of earned vacation pay accumulated over the last two years loses this benefit if it is unvested and the employee leaves the company before using the paid vacation time.

In the case of nonvested, accumulated benefits, the employer must assess the probability of paying the benefit. If the payment is probable, can be estimated, and relates to services already performed, the amount would be accrued. This becomes more complicated in the case of sickness leave. The employer must determine the probability of an employee becoming ill. If, however, companies allow employees to convert unused sick pay into personal days where it is highly probable that the employee will use the personal days, the sickness leave is accrued.

Implementing the accrual of compensated absences involves an adjusting entry at the end of each fiscal year to accrue all of the compensation costs that meet the above criteria. These entries recognize the cost of compensated absences as an expense in the period earned rather than when taken because the company has a probable obligation to transfer assets in the future as a result of events in the current period. Compensated absences are typically accrued at *current* employee wages rather than at uncertain, future wages expected in the period when the compensation for absences will occur. (GAAP does not specify whether to use current or future wages when estimating an accrual.) If the wage rates change, the pay difference would be debited (if an increase) or credited (if a decrease) to salaries expense during the time of the compensated absences. This wage rate change is considered a *change in estimate*.

Demo 15-3C **LO15-3** **Recording Compensated Absences**

Consider the carryover of vacation time for Conway Company, which has 500 employees. Each employee is granted three weeks paid vacation each year. Vacation time, up to a maximum accumulation of four weeks, may be carried over to subsequent years prior to termination of employment. At the end of 2020, the end of the annual accounting period, personnel records revealed the following information concerning carry-over vacation amounts: a total of 23 weeks of unused vacation for 13 employees, valued at $36,000 in salary costs.

a. Record the accrual for compensated absences on December 31, 2020.
b. During 2021, all vacation except for two weeks valued at $3,000 were used. Record the entry for used vacation in 2021.
c. Assume instead that the 2021 salaries for the employees of Conway Company who used their vacation carryovers during 2021 had increased by $1,000. Record the entry for used vacation in 2021.

continued

continued from previous page

Solution

a. **Accrual for Compensated Absences**

December 31, 2020—To accrue for compensated absences

Salaries Expense	36,000	
Accrued Compensation		36,000

Assets = Liabilities + Equity
+36,000 −36,000
Salaries Exp: 36,000 (debit)
Accrued Comp: 36,000 (credit)

b. **Recording of Vacation Time Used**

When the vacation time is taken, the liability account is debited at the time the employee is paid.

2021—To record vacation time used

Accrued Compensation	33,000	
Cash ($36,000 − $3,000)		33,000

Assets = Liabilities + Equity
−33,000 −33,000
Cash: 33,000 (credit)
Accrued Comp: 33,000 (debit) | 36,000 (credit)

c. **Change in Compensation Rates**

The increase in salaries of $1,000 is considered a change in estimate and is recorded as expense in the current period.

2021—To record vacation time used with adjusted salaries

Accrued Compensation	33,000	
Salaries Expense	1,000	
Cash ($36,000 − $3,000 + $1,000)		34,000

Assets = Liabilities + Equity
−34,000 −33,000 −1,000
Cash: 34,000 (credit)
Accrued Comp: 33,000 (debit) | 36,000 (credit)
Salaries Exp: 1,000 (debit)

Bonus Accrual

In addition to salaries, many companies pay cash bonuses, which are often contingent on meeting specified performance targets of the company, such as sales or earnings targets. Bonuses allow employers to compensate (and motivate) employees without a commitment to an ongoing increase in salaries. Bonuses earned but unpaid at year-end are recorded as an adjusting entry in the year earned.

Recording Bonus Accruals — LO15-3 — Demo 15-3D

Pleasant Ridge Co. has pretax income of $500,000 in 2020. The board of directors determined that the company will pay out $30,000 in annual bonuses on January 31, 2021, to compensate for services performed by employees in 2020. Record the adjusting entry on December 31, 2020.

Solution

December 31, 2020—To record bonus accrual

Salaries Expense	30,000	
Salaries Payable		30,000

Assets = Liabilities + Equity
+30,000 −30,000
Salaries Exp: 30,000 (debit)
Salaries Payable: 30,000 (credit)

EXPANDING YOUR KNOWLEDGE — **Bonus as a Percentage of Net Income**

Computing bonuses can be complex when bonuses are based on a percentage of net income. When earnings are involved, the adjusting entry to recognize the bonus cannot be established until all other adjusting entries affecting earnings have been made. The bonus is also an expense and must be deducted in determining the income on which the bonus is to be paid. The following example illustrates the bonus calculation. Pleasant Ridge Co. has pretax income of $500,000 in 2020 before establishing the year's bonus. The bonus agreement specifies that the employees are to be paid 10% of net income as this year's bonus. Ignoring income taxes, the bonus is 10% of income, with income first reduced by the bonus.

$$\begin{aligned} \text{Bonus} &= 0.10\,(\$500{,}000 - \text{Bonus}) \\ \text{Bonus} &= \$50{,}000 - 0.10(\text{Bonus}) \\ 1.1(\text{Bonus}) &= \$50{,}000 \\ \text{Bonus} &= \$45{,}455 \end{aligned}$$

REVIEW 15-3 LO15-3 Recording Payroll Withholding and Taxes, Compensated Absences, and Bonuses

Review MBC

Record entries for the following transactions for the month of June 2020 for Tokay Inc.

a. Payroll records for the month of June show the following:

	Employee			Employer		
Gross Wages	Withholdings	FICA	HSA*	FICA	SUTA	FUTA
$80,000.	$24,000	$6,120	$1,000	$6,120	$4,320	$480

*Health Savings Account

b. Employees' rights to paid vacation vest and are attributable to services already rendered. Payment is probable, and Tokay's obligation was reasonably estimated at $55,000 on June 30, 2020.

c. Employees' rights to sick pay benefits do not vest but accumulate for possible future use. The rights are attributable to services already rendered, the total accumulated sick pay was reasonably estimated at $10,000 on June 30, 2020, and payment is possible.

d. Executives of Tokay Inc. earn a bonus (payable in the following month) equal to 2% of the company's monthly sales over $500,000. Sales for the month of June were $580,000.

More Practice: 15-28, 15-29, 15-54, 15-76

Solution on p. 15-59.

UNITED PARCEL SERVICE

Real World—ACCRUED WAGES AND WITHHOLDINGS

UNITED PARCEL SERVICE [UPS]

United Parcel Service Inc. reported $2,521 million in accrued wages and withholdings as of December 31, 2017, on the face of its balance sheet in its 2017 Form 10-K.

Consolidated Balance Sheets—excerpt ($ Millions)

December 31	2017	2016
Current Liabilities:		
Current maturities of long-term debt and commercial paper.	$ 4,011	$ 3,681
Accounts payable	3,872	3,042
Accrued wages and withholdings	2,521	2,317
Hedge margin liabilities.	17	575
Self-insurance reserves	705	670
Accrued group welfare and retirement plan contributions.	677	598
Other current liabilities	905	847
Total Current Liabilities	$12,708	$11,730

LO 15-4 Account for short-term debt and classify debt on the balance sheet

LO 15-4 Overview

Financing Current Liabilities

- Short-term notes payable: interest-bearing and noninterest-bearing
- Interest payable
- Current maturities of long-term debt
- Callable long-term debt
- Debt expected to be refinanced

Notes payable are amounts due to a third party (such as a financial lending institution) based upon formal, written agreements with specific terms. Notes payable can be current or noncurrent depending on the length of the agreement.

Examples of **current notes payable** include lines of credit, interest-bearing notes, and noninterest-bearing notes. A **line of credit** is essentially a guarantee that a lender will make funds available as needed on a short-term basis. A *committed credit line* is an agreement between a financial institution and a company (borrower) requiring the financial institution to lend money (up to the credit line limit) in exchange for a fee.

An *uncommitted credit line* is an informal agreement between a financial institution and a company (borrower) where the financial institution makes available short-term funding for temporary needs (such as seasonal funding needs). The financial institution has no obligation to extend the loan. A current note payable is either **secured** (specific assets pledged as security), or **unsecured** (repayment is based only on the general creditworthiness of the debtor).

Commercial paper is an example of an unsecured note, issued by financial institutions or large corporations (such as manufacturers or retailers) to fund short-term working capital requirements. The notes are typically issued with maturity dates up to 270 days. Commercial paper does not have to be registered with the Securities and Exchange Commission for issuances that mature within 270 days. Because commercial paper is not typically backed by collateral, only companies with high-quality credit positions will issue commercial paper without significant interest costs.

TARGET

Real World—COMMERCIAL PAPER

TARGET CORPORATION [TGT]

Target Corporation included the following schedule in the Liquidity and Capital Resources section of a recent Form 10-K. The schedule includes the maximum daily amount of commercial paper outstanding that was used to generate cash during peak holiday sales periods.

In 2016, we funded our peak holiday sales period working capital needs through internally generated funds and the issuance of commercial paper. In 2015, we funded our peak holiday sales period working capital needs through internally generated funds.

Commercial Paper (dollars in millions)	2016	2015	2014
Maximum daily amount outstanding during the year	$89	$—	$590
Average amount outstanding during the year	1	—	129
Amount outstanding at year-end	—	—	—
Weighted average interest rate	0.43%	—%	0.11%

In this section, we record the issuance, interest accrual, and maturity of a short-term interest-bearing note in **Demo 15-4A** and of a short-term noninterest-bearing note in **Demo 15-4B**. Then, in **Demo 15-4C**, we review the balance sheet presentation of (1) maturing long-term debt, (2) callable debt, (3) short-term debt to be paid from long-term assets or stockholders' equity, and (4) debt expected to be refinanced. For an introduction to the terms used in accounting for notes payable, see **Exhibit 15-1**.

EXHIBIT 15-1 Note Payable Terminology

Note Terminology	Definition
Face value	Amount due at a note's maturity date.
Stated rate	Interest rate used to determine the cash interest payments which can be 0% if no cash interest payments are required. Stated as an annual rate.
Market rate (Effective rate)	Interest rate on a similar debt in the market involving similar risk and where the borrower has a similar crediting rating. Stated as an annual rate.
Interest-bearing note	Note requiring periodic cash interest payments based on terms of the note.
Noninterest-bearing note	Note requiring no periodic cash interest payments (the stated rate is equal to zero). Instead, all amounts are paid at maturity.
Discount on note payable	Contra account equal to the excess of the face value of a note over its present value. A discount decreases the carrying value of a note payable. Discount represents deferred interest expense that will be recognized over the term of the note.
Premium on note payable	Adjunct account equal to the excess of the present value of a note over its face value. A premium increases the carrying value of a note payable. Premiums represent a reduction of interest expense that will be recognized over the term of the note.

Short-Term Notes Payable—Interest-Bearing

An interest-bearing note payable explicitly states a rate of interest. This rate is called the **stated rate** and is presented as an annual rate. The debtor receives cash, other assets, or services and pays back the face amount of the note plus cash interest at the stated rate on one or more interest dates. When the stated rate appropriately reflects the note's risk, the stated and market rates are the same. This is the usual case.

The measurement basis for a note payable is the present value of the cash expected to be paid on the note, discounted at the market rate in effect at the inception of the note. The present value of payments equals the note's face value when the stated rate is equal to the market rate. In this case, the company records the note payable at its face value and accrues interest over the term of the note as illustrated in **Demo 15-4A**.

Demo 15-4A **LO15-4** **Short-Term Note Payable—Interest-Bearing**

On October 1, 2020, Blues Company borrows $10,000 cash on a one-year note with 6% cash interest payable at the maturity date. The accounting year of Blues Company ends December 31, and the maturity date of the note is September 30, 2021. Prepare the following entries and financial statement amounts for Blues Company.

a. Record the entry for the issuance of the note on October 1, 2020.
b. Record the entry for the accrual of interest on December 31, 2020.
c. Provide the financial statement presentation related to the note payable on December 31, 2020.
d. Prepare the entry for the full payment of the note on September 30, 2021.

Solution

a. **Issuance of a Short-Term Note Payable**

Assets = Liabilities + Equity
+10,000 +10,000
Cash: 10,000 (debit) | Note Payable: 10,000 (credit)

October 1, 2020—To record note payable issuance

Cash	10,000	
Note Payable		10,000

b. **Interest Accrual on Short-Term Note Payable**

The stated rate determines the amount of cash interest that will be paid on the principal amount of the debt at maturity. Interest is accrued on December 31 for the number of months that the note is outstanding. Because the stated rate is an *annual rate*, the annual interest of $1,200 ($10,000 × 0.06) is prorated for 3 months (October, November, and December) of the year.

Assets = Liabilities + Equity
+150 −150
Interest Exp: 150 (debit) | Interest Payable: 150 (credit)

December 31, 2020—To record accrual of interest

Interest Expense.	150	
Interest Payable ($10,000 × 0.06 × 3/12)		150

c. **Financial Statement Presentation**

Blues Company would report the following amounts related to its note payable transactions on its December 31, 2020, balance sheet and 2020 income statement.

Balance Sheet excerpt December 31, 2020	
Current liabilities	
Note payable.	$10,000
Interest payable	150

Income Statement excerpt For Year Ended December 31, 2020	
Other expenses	
Interest expense	$150

continued

continued from previous page

d. **Maturity of Short-Term Note Payable**
At the time the note is paid off, the note payable and interest payable amounts are reversed and the interest for the 9 months the note is outstanding during 2021 is expensed. The cash paid is equal to the $10,000 stated value of the note plus the stated interest for the term of the note of $600.

September 30, 2021—To record payment of note plus interest

Note Payable	10,000	
Interest Payable	150	
Interest Expense ($10,000 × 0.06 × 9/12)	450	
Cash ($10,000 + [$10,000 × 0.06])		10,600

Assets = Liabilities + Equity
−10,600 = −10,000 −150 + −450

Cash: 10,000 | 10,600
Note Payable: 10,000 | 10,000
Interest Payable: 150 | 150
Interest Exp: 150, 450 |

Short-Term Notes Payable—Issued at a Discount

The present value of payments (discounted at the market rate) does not equal a note's face value when the stated rate is not equal to the market rate. For example, the stated rate can be zero in the case of a noninterest-bearing note. In this case, the company credits the Note Payable at its face value and debits **Discount on Note Payable** (a contra account to note payable) for the difference between the face value and the present value of the note. This discount is amortized to interest expense over the term of the note payable.

Short-Term Note Payable—Issued at a Discount — LO15-4 — Demo 15-4B

On October 1, 2020, Blues Company signs a $10,600, one-year, noninterest-bearing note but receives only $10,000 cash. The **market rate** of the note is 6% due to the difference between the cash received and the amount to be paid back at the end of the term of the note. The present value of the note is $10,000, assuming a market rate of 6%, and is computed as shown.

	RATE	NPER	PMT	PV	FV	Excel Formula
Given	6%	1	0	?	(10,600)	=PV(0.06,1,0,−10600)
Solution				$10,000		

Prepare the following entries and financial statement amounts for Blues Company.

a. Record the entry for the issuance of the note on October 1, 2020.
b. Record the entry for the accrual of interest on December 31, 2020. Amortize the discount on the note using the straight-line method.
c. Provide the financial statement presentation related to the note payable on December 31, 2020.
d. Prepare the entry for the payment of the note on September 30, 2021.

Solution

a. **Issuance of a Short-Term Note Payable**

October 1, 2020—To record note payable issuance

Cash (present value of note)	10,000	
Discount on Note Payable ($10,600 − $10,000)	600	
Note Payable (face value of note)		10,600

Assets = Liabilities + Equity
+10,000 = +10,600 −600

Cash: 10,000 |
Note Payable: | 10,600
Discount on NP: 600 |

b. **Interest Accrual on Short-Term Note Payable**
The discount is expensed as interest over the life of the short-term note payable on a straight-line basis. Therefore, the discount of $600 is prorated for 3 months (October, November, and December) of the year.

December 31, 2020—To record accrual of interest

Interest Expense	150	
Discount on Note Payable ($600 × 3/12)		150

Assets = Liabilities + Equity
+150 + −150

Interest Exp: 150 |
Discount on NP: 600 | 150

continued

continued from previous page

c. **Financial Statement Presentation**

The net value of the note payable on December 31, 2020, is $10,150, which is the face value of the note of $10,600 less the unamortized discount of $450 ($600 – $150). Blues Company would record the following relating to its note payable transaction on its December 31, 2020, balance sheet and 2020 income statement.

Balance Sheet excerpt December 31, 2020	
Current liabilities	
Note payable, net	$10,150

Income Statement excerpt For Year Ended December 31, 2020	
Other expenses	
Interest expense	$150

d. **Maturity of Short-Term Note Payable**

At the time the note is paid off, Blues Company would record the following entry, which includes the recognition of the remaining 9 months of interest of $450.

Assets	=	Liabilities	+	Equity
−10,600		−10,600 +450		−450

Cash	
10,000	10,600

Note Payable	
10,600	10,600

Interest Exp	
150 450	

Discount on NP	
600	150 450

September 30, 2021—To record payment of note

Note Payable	10,600	
Interest Expense	450	
Cash		10,600
Discount on Note Payable ($600 × 9/12)		450

In summary, a note can be set up as interest-bearing or noninterest-bearing. As seen in **Demo 15-4A** and **Demo 15-4B**, with a market rate of 6%, a company may either borrow $10,000 and pay $600 interest on the note or borrow $10,000 and pay back a note of $10,600. In both cases, the cost of borrowing (interest) is $600.

Balance Sheet Classification of Debt

Typically, when debt payments are due within the next accounting period, the debt is classified as a current liability. However, sometimes long-term debt is classified as a current liability and current debt is classified as a noncurrent liability.

Type of Debt	Description	Balance Sheet Classification of Debt
Current maturities of long-term debt	Payment(s) on long-term debt due in the next accounting period.	Current liability, unless debt will be paid from long-term assets or stockholders' equity, or the debt meets the requirements for refinancing.
Callable long-term debt [1]	Long-term debt that is ▪ Due on demand by the creditor within the next accounting period. ▪ Callable by the creditor because of a violation of the terms of the debt at the date of the balance sheet. ▪ Callable by the creditor because a violation was not cured within a specified grace period.	Current liability
Short-term debt to be paid from long-term assets or stockholders' equity	Short-term debt to be extinguished through a long-term asset such as a bond sinking fund or through the issuance of stockholders' equity, such as common stock.	Noncurrent liability
Debt expected to be refinanced [2]	Long-term debt due in the next accounting period where the borrower has the intent and ability to refinance on a long-term basis.	Noncurrent liability

[1] Criteria to Evaluate Callable Long-Term Debt Obligations

Long-term debt that is callable by the creditor is classified on the balance sheet as short-term because the debtor cannot control the payment date. If the long-term obligation is callable because of a contract violation, the company can *avoid current liability classification* if either the creditor has waived or lost the right to demand repayment for more than one year or it is probable that the creditor will cure the violation within the grace period allotted.

470-10-45-11 Current liabilities shall include long-term obligations that are or will be callable by the creditor either because the debtor's violation of a provision of the debt agreement at the balance sheet date makes the obligation callable or because the violation, if not cured within a specified grace period, will make the obligation callable. Accordingly, such callable obligations shall be classified as current liabilities unless either of the following conditions is met:

a. The creditor has waived or subsequently lost (for example, the debtor has cured the violation after the balance sheet date and the obligation is not callable at the time the financial statements are issued or are available to be issued) . . . the right to demand repayment for more than one year (or operating cycle, if longer) from the balance sheet date . . .

b. For long-term obligations containing a grace period within which the debtor may cure the violation, it is probable that the violation will be cured within that period, thus preventing the obligation from becoming callable.

[2] Criteria to Evaluate Debt to be Refinanced

Current liabilities expected to be refinanced are reclassified as long-term liabilities on the balance sheet only if the debtor:

- Fully intends to refinance the specific short-term liability.
- Shows an ability to do so by
  - Actually refinancing debt on a long-term basis before the financial statements are issued.
  - Entering in good faith into a long-term, noncancelable refinancing agreement supported by a viable lender.
  - Issuing an equity instrument.

470-10-45-14 A short-term obligation shall be excluded from current liabilities if the entity intends to refinance the obligation on a long-term basis . . . and the intent to refinance the short-term obligation on a long-term basis is supported by an ability to consummate the refinancing demonstrated in either of the following ways:

a. Post-balance-sheet-date issuance of a long-term obligation or equity securities.

b. Financing agreement.

An ability to refinance is required to reduce the risk of a failure to refinance, which would result in the understatement of current liabilities on the balance sheet date. This ability can be demonstrated up to the point that the financial statements are issued, which may be several weeks after the balance sheet date.

Balance Sheet Classification of Debt **LO15-4** **Demo 15-4C**

Example One—Current Maturities of Long-Term Debt

Blues Company borrowed $500,000 through a 5% note payable dated December 31, 2020. Interest is due annually on December 31, and the principal is due annually in $100,000 installment payments, beginning on December 31, 2021. Show the balance sheet presentation for the note payable on December 31, 2020.

Solution

Because $100,000 of the total debt amount is due within the next year, this amount will be classified as current while the remaining amount of $400,000 ($500,000 − $100,000) will be classified as noncurrent.

Balance Sheet excerpt	Dec. 31, 2020
Liabilities	
Current liabilities	
Current payment on note payable (due in 2021)	$100,000
Noncurrent liabilities	
Note payable (less current portion of $100,000)	400,000

continued

continued from previous page

Example Two—Callable Debt

On December 31, 2020, Blues Company had a $100,000 note payable with First Choice Bank due January 15, 2025. The loan agreement with First Choice Bank requires Blues Company to maintain a minimum current ratio of 1.5 for each monthly reporting period, with a one-month grace period allowed to cure any violations. On December 31, 2020, Blues Company's current ratio slips to 1.25 (current assets of $250,000 divided by current liabilities of $200,000) assuming a classification of the note payable as long-term. Show the balance sheet presentation for the note payable on December 31, 2020, and compute an updated current asset ratio based upon the debt classification.

Solution

If First Choice Bank does not waive its right to call in the note and Blues Company did not cure the violation within the one-month grace period allotted per the loan agreement, Blues Company would report the debt as current.

Balance Sheet excerpt	Dec. 31, 2020
Current liabilities	
Note payable	$100,000

The updated current ratio would be 0.83 [current assets of $250,000 divided by current liabilities of $300,000 ($200,000 + $100,000)].

Example Three—Debt to be Repaid from Long-Term Assets

Blues Company borrowed $100,000 through a 7% note payable dated December 31, 2016. Interest is due annually on December 31, and the principal is due on December 31, 2021. The note will be paid on December 31, 2021, with amounts Blues Company accumulated in a long-term investment fund classified as a long-term asset. Show the balance sheet presentation of the note payable on December 31, 2020.

Solution

Blues Company would report the debt as noncurrent because the debt will be extinguished with a long-term asset.

Balance Sheet excerpt	Dec. 31, 2020
Noncurrent liabilities	
Note payable	$100,000

Example Four—Debt to be Refinanced

Blues Company uses cash to pay a $30,000 short-term note in February 2021. Blues Company subsequently issues a long-term note payable for $30,000 before the 2020 financial statements are issued. Show the balance sheet presentation for the note payable on December 31, 2020.

Solution

Short-term obligations refinanced after the balance sheet date but before the financial statement issue date are reported as short-term obligations if the funds used in the refinancing were short term, *even if long-term financing is ultimately obtained before the financial statement issue date.* Therefore, Blues Company would report the debt as current.

Balance Sheet excerpt	Dec. 31, 2020
Current liabilities	
Note payable	$30,000

REVIEW 15-4 LO15-4 Accounting for and Reporting Debt

Review MBC

Example One—Accounting for a Short-Term Note Payable

Emerald Inc. borrowed cash on March 1, 2020, and signed a $50,000 (face amount), six-month note payable, due on September 1, 2020. Assume an effective interest rate of 7%.

continued

continued from previous page

a. Prepare the following entries assuming that the note is interest-bearing at 7%, with interest due upon maturity of the note.
1. March 1, 2020, date of the loan.
2. June 30, 2020, end of Emerald Inc.'s accounting period.
3. September 1, 2020, payment of principal and interest on the note.

b. Repeat part *a* assuming that the note is noninterest-bearing and the present value of the note payable is $48,285. The company amortizes the discount using the straight-line method.

Example Two—Balance Sheet Reporting of Notes Payable

Complete the following table by indicating the amount of debt (ignoring any interest payable amounts) that would be classified as current and noncurrent on Blues Company's December 31, 2020, balance sheet. Assume financial statements were issued on March 1, 2021.

More Practice: 15-56, 15-57, 15-77, 15-78

	Debt Scenario	Current Liability	Noncurrent Liability
1.	Blues Company borrowed $500,000 through an 8% note payable dated December 31, 2016. Interest is due annually on December 31, and the principal is due on December 31, 2021. The company plans to pay for the amount due with cash.		
2.	On December 31, 2020, Blues Company had a $100,000 note payable with First Choice Bank due January 15, 2025. The loan agreement with First Choice Bank requires Blues Company to maintain a minimum current ratio of 1.5 for each monthly reporting period. On December 31, 2020, Blues Company's current ratio slips to 1.25 (current assets of $250,000 divided by current liabilities of $200,000) assuming that the note payable is classified as long-term. Blues Company obtains a letter from First Choice Bank, waiving its right to call the $100,000 loan in the next year.		
3.	Blues Company borrowed $500,000 through an 8% note payable dated January 31, 2016. Interest is due annually on January 31, and the principal is due on January 31, 2021. The company extinguished the debt through a common stock issuance in January 2021.		
4.	Blues Company has a $500,000 note payable due June 15, 2021. At the financial statement date of December 31, 2020, Blues Company signed an agreement to borrow up to $500,000 to refinance the note payable on a long-term basis. The financing agreement called for borrowings not to exceed 80% of the value of the collateral Blues Company was providing. Upon issuance of the December 31, 2020, financial statements, the value of the collateral was $600,000 and was not expected to fall below this amount during 2021.		

Solution on p. 15-59.

COCA-COLA

Real World—CURRENT MATURITIES OF LONG-TERM DEBT

In a recent Form 10-K, Coca-Cola Company reported on its 2017 balance sheet that current maturities of long-term debt totaled $3,298 million.

COCA-COLA CORPORATION [KO]

Consolidated Balance Sheets Excerpt December 31 ($ millions)	**2017**	**2016**
CURRENT LIABILITIES		
Accounts payable and accrued expenses	$ 8,748	$ 9,490
Loans and notes payable	13,205	12,498
Current maturities of long-term debt	3,298	3,527
Accrued income taxes	410	307
Liabilities held for sale	37	710
Liabilities held for sale — discontinued operations	1,496	—
TOTAL CURRENT LIABILITIES	$27,194	$26,532

LO 15-5 Describe accounting for subsequent events and contingencies including litigation, warranties, and other contingencies

LO 15-5 Overview

Loss Contingencies
- Accrue: Probable and reasonably estimable
- Disclose: Reasonably possible or probable but not reasonably estimable

Subsequent Events
- Recognize if material
- Disclose if required to avoid misleading statements

In the previous sections, we illustrated a number of current liabilities. Under certain circumstances, a loss contingency may also be accrued as a current liability. Additional criteria are considered however, due to the uncertainties surrounding a loss contingency. The accounting guidance defines a contingency as follows.

ASC Glossary **Contingency:** An existing condition, situation, or set of circumstances involving uncertainty as to possible gain (gain contingency) or loss (loss contingency) to an entity that will ultimately be resolved when one or more future events occur or fail to occur.

As an example, a company is involved in a legal dispute over an action that took place prior to a company's reporting period of December 31, 2020. Because this legal matter will not be settled until after the 2020 financial statements are issued in March of 2021, the litigation is a contingency for purposes of financial reporting for 2020. The definition of a contingency indicates that an uncertain outcome impacts the settlement of *an existing condition*. Therefore, in relating this to the litigation example, the event leading to the litigation needs to have taken place *on or before the balance sheet date*. Sometimes the future events happen after the balance sheet date but before financial statements are issued (subsequent events), and other times it may take years to resolve, making estimation difficult. In this section, we examine the accounting for (1) loss contingencies in general (**Demo 15-5A**), (2) subsequent events (**Demo 15-5B**), (3) specific loss contingencies (**Demo 15-5C**), and (4) gain contingencies (**Demo 15-5D**).

EXHIBIT 15-2
Common Types of Reported Loss Contingencies

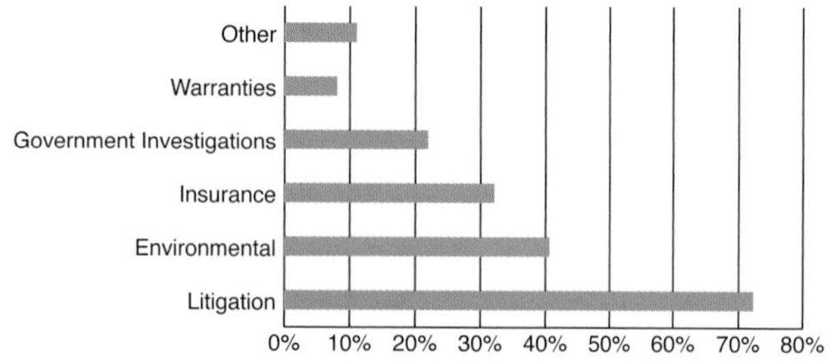

Percentage of companies reporting loss contingencies
Source: AICPA, U.S. GAAP Financial Statements: Best Practices in Presentation and Disclosure, 2012.

Loss Contingencies

Common types of loss contingencies reported in financial statements are shown in **Exhibit 15-2**.

Loss contingencies can have an impact on periodic financial reporting through accruals of losses or through disclosures. Whether and how a loss contingency is reported in the financial statements first depends on the likelihood of the future event or events that will resolve the contingency. The likelihood can be classified as remote, reasonably possible, or probable. These terms are defined as follows.

Likelihood of Contingency Resolution	Definition
Probable	**ASC Glossary** The future event or events are likely to occur.
Reasonably Possible	**ASC Glossary** The chance of the future event or events occurring is more than remote but less than likely.
Remote	**ASC Glossary** The chance of the future event or events occurring is slight.

The proper accounting treatment for the loss contingency depends on the likelihood of contingency resolution and whether the amount of the loss is reasonably estimable, as outlined in **Exhibit 15-3**.

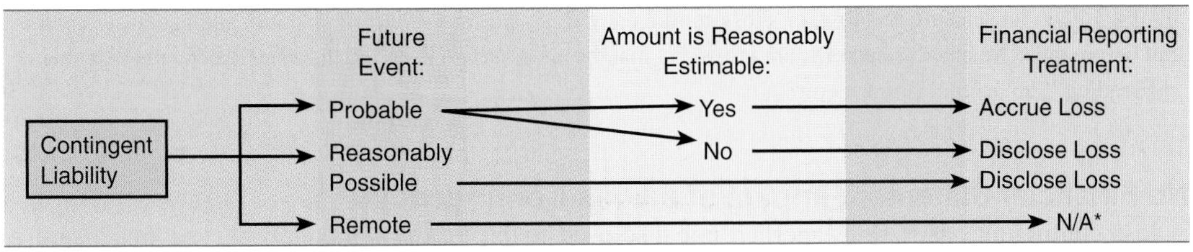

EXHIBIT 15-3 Accounting Treatment of a Contingent Liability

*Except in the case of certain guarantees where disclosure is required.

Accrual and Disclosure of a Loss Contingency

A loss contingency must be accrued (debit a loss or an expense and credit a liability or a contra-asset) if a loss is both probable and reasonably estimable.

450-20-25-2 An estimated loss from a loss contingency shall be accrued by a charge to income if both of the following conditions are met:

a. Information available before the financial statements are issued or are available to be issued . . . indicates that it is probable that an asset had been impaired or a liability had been incurred at the date of the financial statements. It is implicit in this condition that it must be probable that one or more future events will occur confirming the fact of the loss.

b. The amount of loss can be reasonably estimated.

Estimated liabilities may ultimately require expenditures that differ from the amount originally estimated to satisfy the actual liability. When the estimated liability varies from the actual settlement, the difference is accounted for as a change in estimate. If the loss can only be estimated within a range, with no better estimate within that range, the company accrues the *minimum* point in the range.

450-20-30-1 If some amount within a range of loss appears at the time to be a better estimate than any other amount within the range, that amount shall be accrued. When no amount within the range is a better estimate than any other amount, however, the minimum amount in the range shall be accrued. Even though the minimum amount in the range is not necessarily the amount of loss that will be ultimately determined, it is not likely that the ultimate loss will be less than the minimum amount.

Disclosure of a Loss Contingency

A loss contingency must be disclosed (and not accrued) if the loss is at least reasonably possible and *either* of the following conditions exists: (1) the loss is not both probable and estimable or (2) there is an exposure to a range of loss where only the minimum point in the range was accrued.

450-20-50-3 Disclosure of the contingency shall be made if there is at least a reasonable possibility that a loss or an additional loss may have been incurred and either of the following conditions exists:

a. An accrual is not made for a loss contingency because any of the conditions [loss is probable and estimable] are not met.

b. An exposure to loss exists in excess of the amount accrued [as a minimum amount in a range of loss].

The disclosure should include the nature of the contingency and an estimate of the loss (or range of loss) or a statement that an estimate is not possible at this time. Management is unlikely to disclose a belief that a contingent *legal loss* is probable and can be reliably estimated because generally the outcome of a lawsuit is hard to predict. In addition, doing so could imply that it may be advisable to settle out of court. To disclose a tacit expectation of loss in advance may prejudice the outcome of the trial. For this reason, lawyers vehemently object to such disclosures. The information would appear, if at all, in the notes to the financial statements. Even then, it is unusual for a company to mention specific amounts unless court judgments have already been rendered.

Even if the disclosure arises after the date of the company's financial statements, disclosure may be necessary. (Events arising after the balance sheet date are discussed further in the next section on subsequent events.)

450-20-50-9 Disclosure of a loss, or a loss contingency, arising after the date of an entity's financial statements but before those financial statements are issued . . . may be necessary to keep the financial statements from being misleading if an accrual is not required.

No Financial Statement Impact of a Loss Contingency

A loss contingency is neither accrued nor disclosed if the loss is remote. However, disclosure is required even if the contingent aspect of a guarantee is deemed to be remote as indicated in the accounting guidance.

460-10-50-2 An entity shall disclose certain loss contingencies even though the possibility of loss may be remote. The common characteristic of those contingencies is a guarantee that provides a right to proceed against an outside party in the event that the guarantor is called on to satisfy the guarantee. Examples include the following:

a. Guarantees of indebtedness of others, including indirect guarantees of indebtedness of others.
b. Obligations of commercial banks under standby letters of credit.
c. Guarantees to repurchase receivables (or, in some cases, to repurchase the related property) that have been sold or otherwise assigned
d. Other agreements that in substance have the same guarantee characteristic.

Demo 15-5A **LO15-5** **Accounting for Litigation Loss Contingencies**

Blues Brothers Inc. is subject to a lawsuit, initiated in the last quarter of the current year, 2020, because of an accident that occurred in 2020 involving a vehicle owned and operated by the company. Blues Brothers Inc.'s year-end is December 31, 2020, and the financial statements were issued on March 1, 2021. The plaintiff is seeking $100,000 in damages. Provide the information indicated for each of the following *separate* scenarios.

a. Blues Brothers Inc. determines that a reasonable estimate of a probable loss on the settlement of the lawsuit is $50,000, although a settlement had not been reached prior to the issuance of the financial statements. On March 15, 2021, the lawsuit was settled in a $40,000 cash settlement. Record the required journal entries on December 31, 2020, and on March 15, 2021.
b. Blues Brothers Inc. estimates that a loss on the lawsuit is probable but the company is not able to reasonably estimate the settlement prior to the issuance of the financial statements. On March 15, 2021, the suit was settled in a $40,000 cash settlement. Record the required journal entries on December 31, 2020, and on March 15, 2021.
c. Blues Brothers Inc. estimates that a loss on the lawsuit is reasonably possible and the company is not able to reasonably estimate the settlement prior to the issuance of the financial statements. On June 30, 2021, the suit was settled in a $25,000 cash settlement. Record the required journal entries on December 31, 2020, and on June 30, 2021.
d. Blues Brothers Inc. determines that a loss on the lawsuit is remote. Indicate the proper financial statement impact on December 31, 2020.

Solution

a. **Loss Contingency—Probable and Reasonably Estimable**
Because the loss is probable and reasonably estimable, Blues Brothers Inc. records an accrual on December 31, 2020, using the amount of loss reasonably estimated at year-end.

Assets = Liabilities + Equity
+50,000 −50,000
Litig Loss: 50,000 (Dr) | Litig Liab: 50,000 (Cr)

December 31, 2020—To accrue for a loss contingency

Loss on Litigation Settlement	50,000	
Estimated Litigation Liability		50,000

Assets = Liabilities + Equity
−40,000 −50,000 +10,000
Litig Liab: 50,000 (Dr) 50,000 (Cr) | Litig Gain: 10,000 (Cr)
Cash: 40,000 (Cr)

March 15, 2021—To record settlement of legal contingency

Estimated Litigation Liability	50,000	
Gain on Litigation Settlement		10,000
Cash		40,000

continued

continued from previous page

b. **Loss Contingency—Probable and Not Reasonably Estimable**

December 31, 2020

No entry is recorded because the loss is not reasonably estimable but the company would disclose information relating to the lawsuit in the notes accompanying the financial statements.

March 15, 2021—To record settlement of legal contingency

Loss on Litigation Settlement	40,000	
Cash		40,000

Assets	=	Liabilities	+	Equity
−40,000				−40,000

Litig Loss: 40,000 (debit) — Cash: 40,000 (credit)

c. **Loss Contingency—Reasonably Possible and Not Reasonably Estimable**

December 31, 2020

No entry is recorded because the loss is reasonably possible and not reasonably estimable, but the company would disclose information relating to the lawsuit in the notes accompanying the financial statements.

June 30, 2021—To record settlement of legal contingency

Loss on Litigation Settlement	25,000	
Cash		25,000

Assets	=	Liabilities	+	Equity
−25,000				−25,000

Litig Loss: 25,000 (debit) — Cash: 25,000 (credit)

d. **Loss Contingency—Remote**

Because the loss is considered remote, the company is not required to record an entry or disclose information relating to the lawsuit in the 2020 financial statements.

Financial Reporting of Subsequent Events

Subsequent events are material financial events that take place between the balance sheet date and the issuance date (or the date available to be issued) of the financial statements. The accounting guidance indicates two types of subsequent events: recognized and nonrecognized.

ASC Glossary **Subsequent events**—Events or transactions that occur after the balance sheet date but before financial statements are issued or are available to be issued. There are two types of subsequent events:

a. The first type consists of events or transactions that provide additional evidence about conditions that existed at the date of the balance sheet, including the estimates inherent in the process of preparing financial statements (that is, recognized subsequent events).

b. The second type consists of events that provide evidence about conditions that did not exist at the date of the balance sheet but arose subsequent to that date (that is, nonrecognized subsequent events).

Determining when financial statements are issued or are available to be issued is explained in the accounting guidance.

ASC Glossary **Financial statements are issued**—Financial statements are considered issued when they are widely distributed to shareholders and other financial statement users for general use and reliance in a form and format that complies with GAAP.

ASC Glossary **Financial statements are available to be issued**—Financial statements are considered available to be issued when they are complete in a form and format that complies with GAAP and all approvals necessary for issuance have been obtained, for example, from management, the board of directors, and/or significant shareholders.

The subsequent event period is outlined in **Exhibit 15-4**. Events taking place in the subsequent period may involve information that could influence a user's evaluation of the future prospects of a company. Some events can clarify or add additional information to conditions that existed at the balance sheet date. However, some events may be completely new, or unconnected to conditions existing at the balance sheet date. These events are important to a financial statement user who is forecasting balance sheet amounts into a future period.

EXHIBIT 15-4
Subsequent Event Period

Balance Sheet Date	Subsequent Event Period	Financial Statement Issuance*
Dec. 31, 2020	Jan. 1, 2021–Feb. 28, 2021 ▪ **Recognized subsequent event:** If the event reflects conditions existing during 2020, ***recognize*** the effects in the 2020 financial statements. ▪ **Nonrecognized subsequent event:** If the event does not reflect conditions existing during 2020 and is required to keep financial statements from being misleading, ***disclose*** the event in the 2020 financial statements.	Mar. 1, 2021

*Or available to be issued

Judgment is necessary to determine whether the likelihood of a loss based on the resolution of a contingency is remote, reasonably possible, or probable. In making this judgment, management will use all information that is available up to the date of the release of the financial statements. Because the release of the financial statements will take place weeks after year-end, events may take place during this period that will shed more light on the nature of a contingency that existed at the balance sheet date.

Recognized Subsequent Events The effects of subsequent events must be recognized in the financial statements if they provide additional evidence about conditions that existed at the balance sheet date or affect assumptions made in preparing the financial statements. For example, if the events that gave rise to litigation had taken place before December 31, 2020 (balance sheet date) and that litigation is settled after December 31, 2020, but before the financial statements are issued on March 1, 2021, then the settlement amount should be considered in estimating the amount of liability recognized on December 31, 2020. Subsequent events may also affect the realization of assets, such as inventories or receivables, or the settlement of estimated liabilities, and should be recognized in the financial statements when those events represent the culmination of conditions that existed over a relatively long period of time.

855-10-25-1 An entity shall recognize in the financial statements the effects of all subsequent events that provide additional evidence about conditions that existed at the date of the balance sheet, including the estimates inherent in the process of preparing financial statements.

855-10-55-1 The following are examples of recognized subsequent events addressed in paragraph 855-10-25-1:

a. If the events that gave rise to litigation had taken place before the balance sheet date and that litigation is settled after the balance sheet date but before the financial statements are issued or are available to be issued, for an amount different from the liability recorded in the accounts, then the settlement amount should be considered in estimating the amount of liability recognized in the financial statements at the balance sheet date.

b. Subsequent events affecting the realization of assets, such as inventories, or the settlement of estimated liabilities, should be recognized in the financial statements when those events represent the culmination of conditions that existed over a relatively long period of time.

Nonrecognized Subsequent Events Subsequent events are disclosed in the notes and not recognized within the financial statements if they (1) result from conditions that did not exist at the balance sheet date and (2) are required to keep the financial statements from being misleading. The following examples would typically require financial statement disclosure:

- The sale of a bond or issuance of capital stock after the date of the balance sheet.
- Litigation related to an event that transpired after the date of the balance sheet.
- Inventory losses due to a casualty occurring after the date of the balance sheet.
- Losses caused by a condition that arose after the balance sheet date, such as a fire or flood.

855-10-25-3 An entity shall not recognize subsequent events that provide evidence about conditions that did not exist at the date of the balance sheet but arose after the balance sheet date but before financial statements are issued or are available to be issued.

855-10-50-2 Some nonrecognized subsequent events may be of such a nature that they must be disclosed to keep the financial statements from being misleading. For such events, an entity shall disclose the following:
a. The nature of the event
b. An estimate of its financial effect, or a statement that such an estimate cannot be made.

Examples of subsequent events that are neither disclosed nor reported through financial statements (but may be communicated through other means) are changes in the market price of a company's stock, employee strike, new product development, management changes, recognition or decertification of a union, and new sales or marketing agreements.

Accounting for Subsequent Events — LO15-5 — Demo 15-5B

Example One—Recognized Subsequent Event
Blues Brothers Inc. is subject to a lawsuit initiated during the last quarter of the current year, 2020, because of an accident that occurred in 2020 involving a vehicle owned and operated by the company. Blues Brothers Inc.'s year-end is December 31, 2020, and the financial statements were issued on March 1, 2021. The plaintiff is seeking $100,000 in damages. A settlement in the amount of $50,000 was reached on February 1, 2021, prior to the issuance of the financial statements. Record the required journal entries on December 31, 2020, and on February 1, 2021.

Solution
Because the suit is settled before the financial statements are issued (considered a subsequent event) and the accident took place during 2020, Blues Brothers Inc. records an accrual on December 31, 2020, equal to the amount of the settlement.

December 31, 2020—To accrue for legal loss contingency

Loss on Litigation Settlement	50,000	
Estimated Litigation Liability		50,000

Assets = Liabilities + Equity: +50,000 (Liabilities); −50,000 (Equity)
Litig Loss: 50,000 (debit) | Litig Liab: 50,000 (credit)

The subsequent settlement of the lawsuit is recorded as follows.

February 1, 2021— To record settlement of legal contingency

Estimated Litigation Liability	50,000	
Cash		50,000

Assets = Liabilities + Equity: −50,000 (Assets); −50,000 (Liabilities)
Litig Liab: 50,000 (debit) 50,000 (credit) | Cash: 50,000 (credit)

Example Two—Nonrecognized Subsequent Event
Repeat the requirements of Example One except now assume that the accident took place on January 1, 2021, instead of in 2020.

Solution

December 31, 2020
No entry is recorded in 2020 because the actual event (accident) took place after the 2020 reporting period. However, the company would disclose information relating to this subsequent event in the notes accompanying the financial statements if required to keep the financial statements from being misleading.

The subsequent settlement of the lawsuit is recorded as follows.

February 1, 2021— To record settlement of legal contingency

Loss on Litigation Settlement	50,000	
Cash		50,000

Assets = Liabilities + Equity: −50,000 (Assets); −50,000 (Equity)
Litig Loss: 50,000 (debit) | Cash: 50,000 (credit)

COCA-COLA

Real World—SUBSEQUENT EVENT

COCA-COLA CORPORATION [KO]

Coca-Cola Company recorded the following note (excerpt below) related to a February 2016 event that occurred after the December 31, 2015, balance sheet date.

NOTE 21: SUBSEQUENT EVENT In February 2016, additional territories in North America met the criteria to be classified as held for sale. Therefore, we are required to record the related assets and liabilities at the lower of carrying value or fair value less any costs to sell based on the estimated sale price, which will result in a noncash loss of $296 million in 2016. This loss is primarily related to the write-down of intangible assets due to the accounting treatment for the contingent consideration that will be received in exchange for the grant of the exclusive territory rights. The Company expects these territories to be refranchised at various times throughout 2016. Refer to Note 2 for additional information about North America refranchising.

A Deeper Look at Certain Loss Contingencies

In our analysis of loss contingencies, further explanations are provided for the following items: (1) unasserted claims and assessments, (2) injury or damage caused by products sold, (3) risk of loss, (4) expropriation of assets, (5) coupons, and (6) warranties (**Demo 15-5C**).

Unasserted Claims and Assessments Disclosure or accrual is not required for a loss contingency involving an unasserted claim or assessment if there has been no indication of a claim unless it is considered probable that a claim will be asserted.

- If it is *probable* that an unasserted claim or assessment will be asserted, the company would then assess the contingency following the steps outlined in **Exhibit 15-3**.
- If it is *not probable* that an unasserted claim or assessment will be asserted, no accrual or disclosure is required.

450-20-50-6 Disclosure is not required of a loss contingency involving an unasserted claim or assessment if there has been no manifestation by a potential claimant of an awareness of a possible claim or assessment unless both of the following conditions are met: (a) It is considered probable that a claim will be asserted. (b) There is a reasonable possibility that the outcome will be unfavorable.

For example, Tyler Inc. owns a facility that sustained fire damage. There is a possibility that the company could be fined for noncompliance with certain laws. Assuming that a claim is only reasonably possible of materializing, no disclosure or accrual would be necessary at year-end related to the potential for a fine for noncompliance.

Injury or Damage Caused by Products Sold At times, companies become aware of potential litigation claims resulting from injury or damages caused by a product defect as in the case of a product recall for safety reasons. If claims are probable, accrual for losses may be necessary. For example, Pharmaceutical Inc. sells a drug product for which a safety hazard related to the product is discovered. If it is considered probable that a loss will occur and Pharmaceutical Inc.'s experience enables the company to make a reasonable estimate of the loss with respect to the drug product, the estimated loss would be accrued.

450-20-55-2 If it is probable that a claim resulting from injury or damage caused by a product defect will arise with respect to products or services that have been sold, accrual for losses may be appropriate.

Risk of Loss A company can choose not to purchase insurance against risk of loss that may result from injury to others, casualty losses (such as fire or natural disaster), interruption of its business operations, or other business risks. A contingency requires the existence of a condition as of a balance sheet date. Therefore, simply the risk of a future loss, not based upon an actual event, does not qualify as a contingency.

450-20-55-5 The absence of insurance does not mean that an asset has been impaired or a liability has been incurred at the date of an entity's financial statements.

For example, a company that operates manufacturing equipment should not accrue for injury to employees that might be caused by the use of the equipment in the future, even if the amount of those losses may be reasonably estimable.

In evaluating the accounting of a possible loss contingency, the company must consider the following conditions:

- An actual event must have taken place prior to the date of the financial statements, even though the company may not become aware of those matters until after that date.
- The experience of the entity or other information enables the company to make a reasonable estimate of the loss that was incurred prior to the release of its financial statements.

Expropriation of Assets The threat of expropriation of assets, where a government takes private property for the benefit of public interest, is a contingency because of the uncertainty about its outcome and effect. In evaluating the accounting for a loss contingency, the company must determine if the expropriation is imminent and compensation will be less than the carrying amount of the assets.

450-20-55-9 The threat of expropriation of assets is a contingency (as defined) because of the uncertainty about its outcome and effect. The condition [that the settlement of the loss is probable] is met if both of the following are true:

a. Expropriation is imminent.
b. Compensation will be less than the carrying amount of the assets.

Accrual would be required if the amount of loss can be reasonably estimated and both conditions above are met.

Coupons—Separate from a Revenue Contract Sometimes coupons are offered outside of a revenue contract (such as in newspapers). In this case, a company would record a liability for the estimated value of redeemed coupons at the time of coupon distribution if redemption is considered probable and the amount of redemption can be reasonably estimated. (Coupons offered as part of a revenue contract fall under the guidance of revenue recognition.)

EXPANDING YOUR KNOWLEDGE **Asset Retirement Obligations**

A company records an *asset retirement obligation* for an existing long-term legal obligation associated with costs that will take place upon retirement of a long-term asset, such as costs for remediation, dismantling, disposal, restoration, etc. Because of the difficulty in estimating these costs, an asset retirement obligation is a type of a loss contingency. See Chapter 11 for issues in evaluating this loss contingency.

Accounting for Warranties It is common for a company to offer a warranty in connection with the sale of a product or service. A **warranty** is a guarantee or a commitment by a company selling a product or providing a service, to provide repairs or substitutions in the event that the product or service does not function as planned or intended. Warranties can be included as part of a sales contract or warranties can be implied by legal requirements or as part of customary business practices. Warranties either (a) provide an assurance that the product or service will comply with agreed-upon specifications or (b) provide a service in addition to assurance that the product will comply with agreed-upon specifications.

Assurance-type Warranties provide assurance that the related product will function as intended because it complies with agreed-upon specifications. This type of warranty is connected to the sale of the product or service and the warranty is typically included as part of the selling price of the product. Assurance-type warranties are accounted for on an accrual basis and are considered loss contingencies.

606-10-55-32 If a customer does not have the option to purchase a warranty separately, an entity should account for the warranty in accordance with the guidance on product warranties in Subtopic 460-10 on guarantees, unless the promised warranty, or a part of the promised warranty, provides the customer with a service in addition to the assurance that the product complies with agreed-upon specifications.

In other words, the warranty expense should be estimated and recorded fully in the year of the sale of the related product or service (when probable and reasonably estimable) even though repairs or exchanges may take place in later periods. In cases where the warranty extends over two or more years and the probabilities of estimated future cash flows can be estimated, the expected cash flow approach may be used to estimate the warranty liability. See **Demo 6-3C** in Chapter 6 for an example of estimating a warranty liability using the expected cash flow method.

Service-type Warranties provide customers with a service in addition to the assurance that the product complies with agreed-upon specifications. Typically, a service-type warranty is sold separately from the product. Because the additional service is a separate performance obligation, the cash collected for service-type warranties is recorded initially as deferred revenue (a contract liability) and recognized subsequently as revenue on a straight-line basis over the service contract. Thus, **a service-type warranty is considered to be a separate performance obligation accounted for under revenue recognition and is not considered a loss contingency.**

606-10-55-31 If a customer has the option to purchase a warranty separately (for example, because the warranty is priced or negotiated separately), the warranty is a distinct service because the entity promises to provide the service to the customer in addition to the product that has the functionality described in the contract. In those circumstances, an entity should account for the promised warranty as a performance obligation.

How do you distinguish between an assurance-type warranty and a service-type warranty?

- If a customer has the option to purchase the warranty separately, the warranty is a service-type warranty.
- The longer the coverage period, the more likely it is that the warranty is a service-type warranty because it is more likely to be providing an *additional* service.
- If the entity is required by law to provide a warranty, the warranty is typically an assurance-type warranty because it is protecting customers from the risk of purchasing defective products.
- If the customer performs tasks to assure that a product complies with agreed-upon specifications such as a return shipping service for a defective product, the warranty is more likely to be an assurance-type warranty.

Recognition of revenue and expense related to assurance-type and service-type warranties is summarized in **Exhibit 15-5**.

EXHIBIT 15-5
Assurance-Type and Service-Type Warranty Recognition

Assurance-Type Warranty	Service-Type Warranty
At time of sale:	***At time of sale:***
▪ Recognize revenue on (combined) sales price of product and warranty	▪ Recognize revenue on product
▪ Recognize estimated warranty expense and warranty liability	▪ Recognize deferred revenue on warranty
Over warranty period:	***Over warranty period:***
▪ Recognize warranty costs incurred against liability	▪ Recognize warranty expense as costs are incurred
	▪ Recognize warranty revenue

Demo 15-5C **LO15-5** **Accounting for Warranty Loss Contingencies**

Example One—Assurance-Type Warranty
Rollex Company sells merchandise for $200,000 cash in 2020. The merchandise includes a two-year warranty against manufacturing defects as part of the selling price of the product. The company's experience has indicated that warranty costs will approximate 0.5% of sales.

a. Record the sale of merchandise in 2020, ignoring the cost entry.
b. Record the accrual of warranty costs on December 31, 2020. Assume no actual warranty costs were incurred in 2020.
c. Record the expenditures for actual warranty costs of $1,100 in 2021.

continued

continued from previous page

Solution

a. **Sale of Merchandise**

2020—To record sale of merchandise

Cash	200,000	
Sales		200,000

Assets = Liabilities + Equity
+200,000 +200,000
Cash: 200,000 | Sales: | 200,000

b. **Accrual of Warranty Costs**

December 31, 2020—To accrue warranty costs

Warranty Expense	1,000	
Warranty Liability ($200,000 × 0.005)		1,000

Assets = Liabilities + Equity
+1,000 −1,000
Warranty Exp: 1,000 | Warranty Liab: | 1,000

c. **Actual Warranty Costs**

2021—To record warranty services incurred

Warranty Liability	1,000	
Warranty Expense	100	
Cash (and other resources used)		1,100

Assets = Liabilities + Equity
−1,100 −1,000 −100
Warranty Liab: 1,000 | 1,000; Warranty Exp: 1,000, 100 |
Cash: 200,000 | 1,100

Example Two—Service-Type Warranty

Rollex sells merchandise for $10,000 cash on January 1, 2020, but also sells extended warranties for $50 per product for two years, beginning on January 1, 2020. The stand-alone selling price of the merchandise is $10,000 and the stand-alone selling price of the extended warranties is $50 per warranty. Rollex sold 10 extended warranties on January 1, 2020, and incurred costs of $200 related to servicing the warranties in 2020.

a. Record the sale of warranties and merchandise on January 1, 2020, ignoring the cost entry for the merchandise.
b. Record the expenditures for actual warranty costs of $200 in 2020.
c. Record the recognition of warranty revenue on a straight-line basis on December 31, 2020.

Solution

a. **Sale of Merchandise and Warranties**

Revenue on service-type warranties is initially deferred in Deferred Warranty Revenue, a current liability account.

January 1, 2020—To record sale of merchandise and extended warranties

Cash [$10,000 + ($50 × 10)]	10,500	
Deferred Warranty Revenue ($50 × 10)		500
Sales		10,000

Assets = Liabilities + Equity
+10,500 +500 +10,000
Cash: 10,500 | Def Warr Rev: | 500
Sales: | 10,000

b. **Actual Warranty Costs**

2020—To record warranty service costs incurred

Warranty Expense	200	
Cash (and other resources used)		200

Assets = Liabilities + Equity
−200 −200
Warranty Exp: 200 | Cash: 10,500 | 200

c. **Recognition of Warranty Revenue**

Deferred warranty revenue is recognized as revenue on a straight-line basis over the two-year service period.

December 31, 2020—To recognize warranty revenue

Deferred Warranty Revenue ($500/2)	250	
Warranty Revenue		250

Assets = Liabilities + Equity
−250 +250
Def Warr Rev: 250 | 500; Warranty Rev: | 250

3M [MMM]

Real World—WARRANTY CONTINGENCY

3M Corporation provided the following disclosure in its 2017 Form 10-K regarding warranty accruals.

Note 15 Commitments and Contingencies—Excerpt
Warranties/Guarantees: 3M's accrued product warranty liabilities, recorded on the Consolidated Balance Sheet as part of current and long-term liabilities, are estimated at approximately $50 million at December 31, 2017, and $47 million at December 31, 2016. 3M does not consider this amount to be material. The fair value of 3M guarantees of loans with third parties and other guarantee arrangements are not material.

EXPANDING YOUR KNOWLEDGE — Guarantees

A guarantee that a company makes may result in the recognition or disclosure of an obligation. For example, a guarantor may agree to make payments to a guaranteed party in the event that another entity fails to perform under an obligating agreement (such as a loan). The authoritative guidance considers two aspects to a guarantee:

460-10-25-2 The issuance of a guarantee obligates the guarantor (the issuer) in two respects:

a. The guarantor undertakes an obligation to stand ready to perform over the term of the guarantee in the event that the specified triggering events or conditions occur (the noncontingent aspect).

b. The guarantor undertakes a contingent obligation to make future payments if those triggering events or conditions occur (the contingent aspect).

The **stand ready aspect** of the guarantee, a noncontingent obligation, is recorded as a *liability at fair value.* The **potential credit loss aspect** of the agreement is treated as a *loss contingency* where the probability of default is assessed as outlined in **Exhibit 15-2**.

Gain Contingencies For a gain contingency to be *disclosed*, the characteristics of a contingency must be present: there must be a probable increase in assets or a decrease in liabilities, and the gain must depend upon the occurrence of future events. An example of a gain contingency is a probable favorable outcome in a pending legal dispute. **Contingent gains are not accrued but may be disclosed provided that the disclosure does not mislead as to the likelihood the gain will be realized.**

450-30-50-1 Adequate disclosure shall be made of a contingency that might result in a gain, but care shall be exercised to avoid misleading implications as to the likelihood of realization.

Demo 15-5D LO15-5 Accounting for a Gain Contingency

Bower Inc. sold its hockey apparel division in December 2020. The sale agreement provides for $100 million to be paid to the company at closing plus an amount contingent on sales of apparel over a 12-month period beginning Apri1 1, 2021. An estimate of the contingent amount based upon Bower's 20 years of experience is $500,000. Record the journal entry on December 31, 2020 related to the contingent amount.

Solution
The contingent gain (which is based on the level of sales of the hockey apparel business over a 12-month period beginning April 1, 2021) is not recorded in the financial statements as an asset or as income.

REVIEW 15-5 LO15-5 Reporting of Contingencies and Subsequent Events

Review MBC

Complete the following table by indicating whether each item *a* through *f* would result in the reporting of any revenue or expense in the income statement of 5M Inc. for the year ended December 31, 2020. Assume that 5M Inc. issued its financial statements on February 15, 2021.

continued

continued from previous page

Contingency Scenario	Revenue and/or Expense in 2020
a. 5M Inc. believes it is probable that it will incur $50,000 in additional charges in January 2021 related to its medical coverage for employees for medical conditions and related treatments occurring in 2020.	
b. 5M Inc. believes it is probable that it will incur $75,000 in additional charges in January 2021 related to its medical coverage for employees for medical conditions and related treatments occurring in early January 2021.	
c. 5M Inc. sells merchandise of $1 million in 2020 that includes a two-year limited warranty as part of the selling price. Warranty costs are estimated to be 1% of sales.	
d. 5M Inc. sells merchandise of $2 million in 2020, along with two-year warranties (for years 2020 and 2021) for $75 per product for 200 products. Warranty costs are estimated to be 1% of sales. The company incurred actual costs of $8,000 in 2020 related to the warranties. Warranty revenue is recognized on a straight-line basis.	
e. The company issued $250,000 of bonds payable at par on January 31, 2021.	
f. The attorneys for 5M Inc. believe that it is highly probable that the company will win a court settlement in the amount of $150,000, expected to be settled in the second quarter of 2021.	

More Practice: 15-64, 15-66, 15-82, 15-83

Solution on p. 15-60.

EXPANDING YOUR KNOWLEDGE **Revenue Contracts**

Revenue contracts can result in obligations to provide something in the future to a customer such as a rebate, discount on future product sales, or a free product. As we discussed in Chapter 7, these items are accounted for as part of the revenue contract; thus, they are not treated distinctly as a contingent liability.

- **Customer options** grant rights to customers to acquire additional goods and services as part of a revenue contract. Options include loyalty rewards programs, coupons affixed to a product, and premiums (such as a promotion where a toy is received in exchange for cereal box tops). In these cases, the customer option is considered to be a separate performance obligation (if material to the context of the contract), and revenue is deferred for the amount allocated to the customer option until control of the performance obligation is transferred to the customer.
- **Consideration payable** results from a payment to a customer as a result of a revenue contract. Examples include rebates, credits, and volume discounts. Consideration payable is treated as a reduction to the transaction price unless the payment is exchanged for a distinct good or service. Consideration paid for a distinct good or service is accounted for in the same way as a typical purchase from a supplier.
- **Refund liability** is recorded if a company receives consideration from a customer and expects to refund some or all of the consideration in the future (such as is the case with a sale with a right of return). The estimated amount of returns is recorded as a liability (refund liability) at the time of sale.

Explain liability and contingency disclosures and analyses using liquidity ratios

LO 15-6

In a classified balance sheet, current liabilities are included on the face of the balance sheet. The notes to the financial statements often include additional details on the composition of current liabilities. The balance sheet may include a line titled *Commitments and Contingencies*. Even though the balance may be zero on the balance sheet, this alerts the financial statement user to further information included in the notes. The notes will include additional information on contingencies accrued and on contingenices requiring disclosure but not accrual.

LO 15-6 Overview

Disclosures
- Current liabilities, contingencies

Liquidity ratios
- Current ratio

$$\frac{\text{Current assets}}{\text{Current liabilities}}$$

- Quick ratio

$$\frac{\text{Cash} + \text{Marketable securities} + \text{Receivables}}{\text{Current liabilities}}$$

Disclosure of Current Liabilities and Contingencies

The SEC requires that any item in excess of 5% of total current liabilities be stated separately on the balance sheet or in the notes.

210-10-S99-1 20 Other current liabilities. State separately, in the balance sheet or in a note thereto, any item in excess of 5 percent of total current liabilities. Such items may include, but are not limited to, accrued payrolls, accrued interest, taxes, indicating the current portion of deferred income taxes, and the current portion of long-term debt. Remaining items may be shown in one amount.

The following is an example of a disclosure of accrued and current liability amounts from a recent Form 10-K of **Target Corporation**.

Accrued and Other Current Liabilities (millions)	**January 28, 2017**	**January 30, 2016**
Wages and benefits	$ 812	$ 884
Gift card liability, net of estimated breakage	693	644
Real estate, sales, and other taxes payable	571	574
Dividends payable	334	337
Straight-line rent accrual[a]	271	262
Income tax payable	158	502
Workers' compensation and general liability[b]	141	146
Interest payable	71	76
Other	686	811
Total	$3,737	$4,236

[a] Straight-line rent accrual represents the amount of operating lease rent expense recorded that exceeds cash payments.

[b] We retain a substantial portion of the risk related to general liability and workers' compensation claims. Liabilities associated with these losses include estimates of both claims filed and losses incurred but not yet reported. We estimate our ultimate cost based on analysis of historical data and actuarial estimates. General liability and workers' compensation liabilities are recorded at our estimate of their net present value.

The methodology used to recognize breakage of gift cards and significant judgments made in applying the methodology must be disclosed.

405-20-50-2 An entity that recognizes a breakage amount [prepaid stored-value products or gift cards] shall disclose the methodology used to recognize breakage and significant judgments made in applying the breakage methodology.

Disclosures required for contingencies are also outlined in the accounting guidance.

450-20-50-4 The disclosure [for any contingencies meeting the requirements for disclosure] shall include both of the following:

a. The nature of the contingency

b. An estimate of the possible loss or range of loss or a statement that such an estimate cannot be made.

Certain remote contingencies (as named in an earlier section) require disclosure. In addition, a guarantor must disclose information for product warranties and other guarantee contracts including the nature of the guarantee and a schedule of changes in the guarantees

460-10-50-8 A guarantor shall disclose all of the following information for product warranties and other guarantee contracts.

a. The information required to be disclosed by paragraph 460-10-50-4 [see above].

b. The guarantor's accounting policy and methodology used in determining its liability for product warranties

c. A tabular reconciliation of the changes in the guarantor's aggregate product warranty liability for the reporting period.

An example of a litigation contingency disclosure for **Ford Motor Company** follows where the company disclosed an estimate of reasonably possible losses in a range of up to approximately $2.3 billion.

NOTE 27. Commitments and Contingencies

Various legal actions, proceedings, and claims (generally, "matters") are pending or may be instituted or asserted against us. These include but are not limited to matters arising out of alleged defects in our products; product warranties; governmental regulations relating to safety, emissions, and fuel economy or other matters; government incentives; tax matters; alleged illegal acts resulting in fines or penalties; financial services; employment-related matters; dealer, supplier, and other contractual relationships; intellectual property rights; environmental matters; shareholder or investor matters; and financial reporting matters. Certain of the pending legal actions are, or purport to be, class actions. Some of the matters involve or may involve claims for compensatory, punitive, or antitrust or other treble damages in very large amounts, or demands for field service actions, environmental remediation programs, sanctions, loss of government incentives, assessments, or other relief, which, if granted, would require very large expenditures.

The extent of our financial exposure to these matters is difficult to estimate. Many matters do not specify a dollar amount for damages, and many others specify only a jurisdictional minimum. To the extent an amount is asserted, our historical experience suggests that in most instances the amount asserted is not a reliable indicator of the ultimate outcome.

We accrue for matters when losses are deemed probable and reasonably estimable. In evaluating matters for accrual and disclosure purposes, we take into consideration factors such as our historical experience with matters of a similar nature, the specific facts and circumstances asserted, the likelihood that we will prevail, and the severity of any potential loss. We reevaluate and update our accruals as matters progress over time.

For the majority of matters, which generally arise out of alleged defects in our products, we establish an accrual based on our extensive historical experience with similar matters. We do not believe there is a reasonably possible outcome materially in excess of our accrual for these matters.

For the remaining matters, where our historical experience with similar matters is of more limited value (i.e., "nonpattern matters"), we evaluate the matters primarily based on the individual facts and circumstances. For nonpattern matters, we evaluate whether there is a reasonable possibility of a material loss in excess of any accrual that can be estimated. Our estimate of reasonably possible loss in excess of our accruals for all material matters currently reflects indirect tax and customs matters, for which we estimate the aggregate risk to be a range of up to about $2.3 billion. As noted, the litigation process is subject to many uncertainties, and the outcome of individual matters is not predictable with assurance. Our assessments are based on our knowledge and experience, but the ultimate outcome of any matter could require payment substantially in excess of the amount that we have accrued and/or disclosed.

In Note 15 of **General Motors'** 2015 Form 10-K the following table was reported, which summarizes information related to the liabilities recorded for commitments and contingencies.

	December 31, 2015
Litigation-related liability and tax administrative matters	$1,155
Product liability	712
Ignition Switch Recall compensation program	66
Credit card programs	
Redemption liability—recorded in Accrued liabilities	115
Deferred revenue—recorded in other liabilities	258
Environmental liability	124
Guarantees	72

Each item is explained in more detail in the disclosure and where applicable, ranges of possible losses are disclosed. For the ignition switch recall, the company disclosed a rollforward of activity for the program, explained as follows.

NOTE 15. Commitments and Contingencies

Ignition Switch Recall Compensation Program

In the three months ended June 30, 2014 we created a compensation program (the Program) for accident victims who died or suffered physical injury (or for their families) as a result of a faulty ignition switch related to the 2.6 million vehicles recalled in the three months ended March 31, 2014. The Program is being administered by an independent program administrator, who established a protocol that defined the eligibility requirements to participate in the Program. The Program accepted claims from August 1, 2014 through January 31, 2015 and received a total of 4,343 claims. The Program completed its claims review process in the three months ended September 30, 2015 and the independent program administrator determined that 399 claims were eligible for payment under the Program. Payments to eligible claimants began in the three months ended December 31, 2014 and will continue through the first quarter of 2016. At January 29, 2016 we had paid 345 eligible claimants $554 million out of the 362 claimants who accepted offers under the Program. The other 37 accident victims (or their families) chose not to participate in the Program and could pursue litigation against us. Accident victims (or their families) that accept a payment under the Program agree to settle all claims against GM related to the accident.

We recorded a charge of $400 million in the year ended December 31, 2014 and based on the Program's claims experience we recorded an additional $195 million in the year ended December 31, 2015. These charges were recorded in Automotive selling, general and administrative expense in Corporate and were treated as adjustments for EBIT-adjusted reporting purposes. Based on currently available information we believe our accrual at December 31, 2015 is adequate to cover the estimated costs under the Program. The following table summarizes the activity for the Program since its inception (dollars in millions):

	Activity
Balance at April 1, 2014	$ —
Provisions	400
Payments	(85)
Balance at December 31, 2014	315
Provisions	195
Payments	(444)
Balance at December 31, 2015	$ 66

Liquidity Ratios

$$\frac{\text{Current assets}}{\text{Current liabilities}}$$

The **current ratio** is a test of short-term liquidity. It indicates a company's ability to meet short-term obligations from current assets. Investors and creditors use this ratio to assess whether a company has the ability to pay debts coming due within the year. A higher ratio indicates a stronger level of liquidity. However, a large ratio, such as a ratio of 3, may indicate that the company has idle assets that should be invested or returned to the shareholders.

$$\frac{\text{Cash} + \text{Marketable securities} + \text{Receivables}}{\text{Current liabilities}}$$

The current ratio includes all current assets while the **quick ratio** includes *only* the most liquid assets of cash, cash equivalents, short-term investments, and accounts receivable. The intent of the quick ratio is to analyze the company's ability to pay its current debts with only its most liquid assets. Thus, this ratio is a more rigorous test of liquidity than the current ratio. The purpose of these two ratios is not to assess profitability or long-term debt paying ability, but instead to assess whether the company can remain solvent in the short-run. The current ratio and the quick ratio are illustrated in **Demo 15-6**.

Liquidity Ratios

LO15-6 **Demo 15-6**

The following financial information is provided for **Target Corporation**. Compute the current asset ratio and the quick ratio for the two years presented. Provide a brief analysis of your results.

($ millions)	2017	2016
Current assets		
Cash and cash equivalents, including short-term investments of $1,110 and $3,008	$ 2,512	$ 4,046
Inventory	8,309	8,601
Assets of discontinued operations	69	322
Other current assets	1,100	1,161
Total current assets	$11,990	$14,130
Current liabilities		
Accounts payable	$7,252	$7,418
Accrued and other current liabilities	3,737	4,236
Current portion of long-term debt and other borrowings	1,718	815
Liabilities of discontinued operations	1	153
Total current liabilities	$12,708	$12,622

Solution

Current Ratio

		2017	2016
Current Ratio =	$\frac{\text{Current assets}}{\text{Current liabilities}}$	$\frac{\$11,990}{\$12,708} = 0.94$	$\frac{\$14,130}{\$12,622} = 1.12$

Quick Ratio

		2017	2016
Quick Ratio =	$\frac{\text{Cash} + \text{Marketable securities} + \text{Receivables}}{\text{Current liabilities}}$	$\frac{\$2,512}{\$12,708} = 0.20$	$\frac{\$4,046}{\$12,622} = 0.32$

For the past two years, Target had a current ratio of approximately 1.0. This means that for every dollar of current liabilities, Target has approximately $1 of current assets. We see that the large decrease in the denominator for the quick ratio (relative to the current ratio) is due to the exclusion of inventory. Inventory takes longer to convert to cash because it first must be sold, and then the accounts receivable must be collected. The quick ratio decreased for Target from 2016 to 2017 mainly because of the excess cash from the sale of pharmacy and clinic businesses disclosed in its annual report. Because the sale was completed in late 2015, the company had not fully deployed the proceeds by the 2016 financial statement date. Without this one-time bump due to a non-recurring item, the quick ratio for Target was roughly 0.20 for 2016.

REVIEW 15-6 LO15-6 Calculating Liquidity Ratios

Review MBC

Compute the current asset ratio and the quick ratio for Starbucks Corporation for the two years presented.

$ millions	Oct. 1, 2017	Oct. 2, 2016
Current assets		
Cash and cash equivalents	$2,462.3	$2,128.8
Short-term investments	228.6	134.4
Accounts receivable, net	870.4	768.8
Inventories	1,364.0	1,378.5
Prepaid expenses and other current assets	358.1	347.4
Total current assets	$5,283.4	$4,757.9
Current liabilities		
Accounts payable	$ 782.5	$ 730.6
Accrued liabilities	1,934.5	1,999.1
Insurance reserves	215.2	246.0
Stored value card liability	1,288.5	1,171.2
Current portion of long-term debt	—	399.9
Total current liabilities	$4,220.7	$4,546.8

More Practice: 15-45, 15-71, 15-72
Solution on p. 15-60.

Management Judgment

Accounting for Contingencies

In applying the accounting guidance outlined in this chapter for contingencies, the judgment of management is important. Following are examples.

- Identifying contingencies is a subjective process—by their very nature, contingencies represent unrecorded circumstances with uncertain outcomes.
- Determination of whether the likelihood of the resolution of a future event resulting in a loss is probable, reasonably possible, or remote is complex. It requires in-depth analysis and consultation with legal experts and a final decision based on management discernment.
- Determining a reasonably estimable amount is not a straightforward process—such an amount is not on a vendor invoice as we see with accounts payable. Determining a warranty accrual or a legal accrual, for example, is a subjective process, resulting often-times in a range of losses (such as $250,000 to $500,000).

Ratio Analysis

Decisions made by management have a direct impact on ratio analysis. For example, management decisions result in the accrual, disclosure, or exclusion of contingencies in the financial statements. Financial statement users can assess whether contingencies not accrued (but disclosed) should be considered in ratio analysis.

Questions

15-1. Provide the definition of a liability.

15-2. Provide the definition of a current liability.

15-3. Explain how the measurement of a liability is related to its cause.

15-4. Why are most current liabilities recognized at maturity value at the beginning of their term?

15-5. Compute the present value of a $10,000, one-year note payable that specifies no interest, although 10% would be a realistic rate. Is the present value less than, greater than, or equal to the maturity value?

15-6. In evaluating a balance sheet, some creditors say the liability section is one of the most important sections. What are some reasons justifying this position?

15-7. Some liabilities are reported at their maturity amount. In general, when should liabilities, prior to the maturity date, be reported at less than their maturity amount?

15-8. Explain why the amount of cash salaries paid to employees does not equal salaries expense for the employer.

15-9. Differentiate between secured and unsecured liabilities. Explain the reporting procedures for each.

15-10. What are examples of secured and unsecured liabilities?

15-11. Distinguish between the stated rate and the market rate on a debt.

15-12. Briefly define the following terms related to a note payable: present value of the note and maturity value of the note.

15-13. Distinguish between an interest-bearing note and a noninterest-bearing note.

15-14. Assume that $4,000 cash is borrowed on a $4,000, 10%, one-year note payable that is interest-bearing and that another $4,000 cash is borrowed on a $4,400 one-year note that is noninterest-bearing. For each note, provide the following:

a. Present value of the note. *b.* Maturity amount. *c.* Total interest paid.

15-15. How is gift card breakage recognized as revenue using the proportional method?

15-16. Why is deferred revenue classified as a liability?

15-17. What is a compensated absence? When should the expense related to compensated absences be recognized?

15-18. What is the accounting definition of a contingency? What are the three characteristics of a contingency? Why is this concept important?

15-19. How is the likelihood of the outcome of a contingency measured? In general, how does this affect the accounting for and reporting of contingencies?

15-20. Briefly explain the accounting and reporting for loss contingencies.

15-21. What costs are recognized for environmental obligations?

15-22. Under what conditions may a debt due within the next year (as measured at year-end) be reported as a noncurrent liability? Under what conditions may a long-term debt (as measured at year-end) be reported as a current liability?

Brief Exercises

Brief Exercise 15-23
Recording Sales Tax Payable Entries **LO1**

Target Shoppers Inc. reported cash sales of $18,000 for the month of June 2020. Sales taxes payable are recorded at the point of sale.

a. Assume that sales of Target Shoppers Inc. are *subject to* a 6% sales tax. Record the sales entry.
b. Now assume that the cash collected on sales *includes* the 6% sales tax. Record the sales entry.

Brief Exercise 15-24
Recording Accounts Payable Entries **LO1**
Hint: See Demo 15-1A

On June 15, 2020, Red Buckle Inc. purchased merchandise for resale for $12,000 on credit terms 2/10, n/30. On June 20, Red Buckle paid for the merchandise. Record the entry on June 15 and the entry on June 20 using the perpetual inventory method.

Brief Exercise 15-25
Recording Customer Advances **LO2**
Hint: See Demo 15-2B

Jet Air Inc. collected $300 cash from a customer who purchased a one-way airline ticket on June 1, 2020, for a flight from Minneapolis to New York on August 15, 2020. Record the entry on June 1, and the entry on August 15 for Jet Air Inc.

Brief Exercise 15-26
Recording Gift Card Entries **LO2**
Hint: See Demo 15-2C

Chica's Inc. sold a $50 gift card on February 1, 2020. The gift card was redeemed on February 14, 2020. Record the entries on (1) February 1 and (2) February 14 for Chica's Inc.

Brief Exercise 15-27
Recording Payroll Entries **LO3**
Hint: See Demo 15-3A

BSW Inc. had a weekly payroll of $5,000 for three employees with mandatory withholdings of social security tax (7.65%), federal withholdings of $1,000, and state withholdings of $200. Voluntary withholdings included retirement plan contributions of $100, and health care savings account contributions of $150. Record BSW Inc.'s weekly payroll entry.

Brief Exercise 15-28
Recording Liability for Compensated Absences **LO3**
Hint: See Demo 15-3C

The following information relating to compensated absences was available from Graf Company's accounting records at December 31, 2020.

- Employees' rights to vacation pay vest and are attributable to services already rendered. Payment is probable, and Graf's obligation was reasonably estimated at $220,000.
- Employees' rights to sick pay benefits do not vest but accumulate for possible future use. The rights are attributable to services already rendered, the total accumulated sick pay was reasonably estimated at $100,000, and payment is possible.

a. What amount is Graf required to report as the liability for compensated absences on its December 31, 2020, balance sheet?
b. Record the appropriate journal entry on December 31, 2020.

Brief Exercise 15-29
Recording Bonus Payable **LO3**
Hint: See Demo 15-3D

On December 15, 2020, the board of directors of Limited Label Inc. approved a bonus payout of $70,000 to executives, based upon services performed in 2020. The bonus is payable on January 25, 2021. Record the entries required on (1) December 15, 2020, and (2) January 25, 2021.

Brief Exercise 15-30
Recording Interest-Bearing Note Payable Entries **LO4**
Hint: See Demo 15-4A

On August 31, 2020, Pine Company issued a 9-month, 12% note payable to National Bank in the amount of $900,000. Interest is due at maturity. Record the entries for Pine Company on the following dates.

a. Issuance of the note on August 31, 2020.
b. Adjusting entry on December 31, 2020, Pine Company's fiscal year-end.
c. Payment of the note payable on May 31, 2021.

Brief Exercise 15-31
Recording Noninterest-Bearing Note Payable Entries **LO4**

First Choice Company buys equipment on October 1, 2020, providing as payment a noninterest-bearing note for $20,000 to be paid one year from today. The equipment could be purchased for $18,182 in cash today. Record the entries for First Choice Company on the following dates.

a. Issuance of the note on October 1, 2020.
b. Adjusting entry on December 31, 2020, First Choice Company's fiscal year-end. Amortize the discount on the note using the straight-line method.
c. Payment of the note payable on October 1, 2021.

Brief Exercise 15-32
Recording Debt Issued at a Discount **LO4**
Hint: See Demo 15-4B

The face value of commercial paper borrowings at December 31, 2020, was $6 million. The six-month loan originated on September 1, 2020.

a. Prepare the journal entry for issuance of the loan on September 1, 2020, assuming that the loan is discounted at 5.7%. *Hint:* Discount on Note Payable is equal to 6 months of interest.
b. Prepare the adjusting entry at December 31, 2020. Amortize the discount on the note using the straight-line method.
c. Prepare the entry to repay the loan on February 28, 2021.
d. Calculate the market rate of the loan.

Brief Exercise 15-33
Classifying Refinanced Debt **LO4**
Hint: See Demo 15-4C

Maple Leaf Co. has a $50,000, 5%, 10-year note issued July 31, 2011.

a. How will the $50,000 be classified on the December 31, 2020, balance sheet?
b. If the $50,000 is refinanced into a five-year note on January 31, 2021 (before the 2020 financial statements are issued), how will the $50,000 note payable be classified on the December 31, 2020, balance sheet?

Brief Exercise 15-34
Classifying Callable Debt **LO4**
Hint: See Demo 15-4C

On December 31, 2020, Mainstreet Inc. has a $100,000 note payable due on demand or on June 30, 2025, whichever is earlier, to First Bank. The repayment of the note by First Bank is not expected at any point in 2021. How will the $100,000 note payable be classified on the December 31, 2020, balance sheet?

Brief Exercise 15-35
Recording Assurance-Type Warranty Liability **LO5**
Hint: See Demo 15-5C

Finisher Inc. sells merchandise of $250,000 in 2020 that includes a three-year limited warranty. Warranty costs are estimated to be 1% of sales. The company incurred actual costs of $800 in 2020 related to the warranties.

a. Record the warranty accrual at the time of sale in 2020.
b. Record the adjustment to the warranty accrual for actual warranty costs in 2020.

Brief Exercise 15-36
Recording Service-Type Warranty Liability **LO5**
Hint: See Demo 15-5C

Madison Co. sells merchandise of $250,000 in 2020, along with a two-year warranty (for years 2020 and 2021) for $25 per product. Warranty costs are estimated to be 0.5% of sales. The company sold $2,500 of warranties in 2020 and incurred actual costs of $800 in 2020 related to the warranties. The company uses straight-line recognition of warranty revenue.

a. Record the sale of the merchandise and warranties, ignoring the cost of goods sold entry.
b. Record the warranty service costs for 2020.
c. Record the warranty revenue recognized in 2020.

Brief Exercise 15-37 Reporting a Legal Contingency **LO5** *Hint:* See Demo 15-5A

On November 5, 2020, a Dunn Corporation truck was in an accident with an auto driven by R. Bell. Dunn received notice on January 12, 2021, of a lawsuit for $350,000 in damages for personal injuries suffered by Bell. Dunn Corporation's legal counsel believes it is probable that Bell will be awarded an estimated amount in the range between $100,000 and $225,000, and that $150,000 is a better estimate of potential liability than any other amount. Dunn's accounting year ends on December 31, and the 2020 financial statements were issued on March 2, 2021.

a. What liability should Dunn accrue on December 31, 2020?
b. How would your answer to *(a)* change if Dunn Corporation's legal counsel believes it is reasonably possible that Bell will be awarded a settlement?
c. How would your answer to *(a)* change if Dunn Corporation's legal counsel believes there is only a remote possibility that Bell will be awarded a settlement?

Brief Exercise 15-38 Recording and Reporting a Legal Contingency **LO5**

Pitt Company is the defendant in a lawsuit filed by Hoffman in 2020 disputing the validity of a copyright held by Pitt. At December 31, 2020, Pitt determined that Hoffman would probably be successful against Pitt for an estimated amount of $800,000. Appropriately, an $800,000 loss was accrued by a charge to income of Pitt for the year ended December 31, 2020. On December 15, 2021, Pitt and Hoffman agreed to a settlement providing for cash payment of $500,000 by Pitt to Hoffman and transfer of Pitt's copyright to Hoffman. The carrying amount of the copyright on Pitt's accounting records was $120,000 at December 15, 2021.

a. What would be the effect of the settlement of this liability on Pitt's income before income tax in 2021?
b. Record the entry on December 15, 2021 for Pitt Company.

Brief Exercise 15-39 Reporting a Loss Contingency **LO5**

The following information pertains to a fire insurance policy in effect during the calendar year 2020, covering Vail Company's inventory:

Face amount of policy	$400,000
Deductible	25,000
Amount of premium	2,000

Vail's inventory averages $500,000 uniformly throughout the year. How much of a contingent liability should Vail accrue at December 31, 2020, to cover possible future fire losses?

Brief Exercise 15-40 Recording Asset Retirement Obligation **LO5**

Marathon Inc. estimates that it will be required to spend approximately $40,000 to remove an underground storage tank in 10 years that was constructed in 2020 for $300,000. The present value of this obligation based on the company's discount rate of 8% is $18,528. Record the entry in 2020 (if any) related to the removal of the storage tank in 10 years.

Brief Exercise 15-41 Reporting a Loss Contingency **LO5**

A manufacturer of household appliances has potential losses due to the discovery of a possible defect in one of its products. The occurrence of the loss is reasonably possible, and the costs can be reasonably estimated at $50,000. How should this potential loss be treated for financial statement purposes?

Brief Exercise 15-42 Reporting a Loss Contingency **LO5**

The Occupational Safety and Health Administration (OSHA) is in the process of conducting a workplace inspection at Kenny's Corp. to determine whether the company is in compliance with standards on health and safety in the workplace. While the investigation is currently in process, Kenny's Corp. estimates that it is probable that an assessment will be made. The range of a reasonably possible assessment is between $25,000 and $100,000. How should this potential loss be treated for financial statement purposes?

Brief Exercise 15-43 Analyzing a Gain Contingency **LO5** *Hint:* See Demo 15-5D

During the year, a driver for Commuters Inc. was involved in an accident. Commuters Inc. brought a suit against the negligent party for $1 million. The suit is pending on December 31, 2020. Commuters Inc. believes it is virtually certain that it will receive a settlement of $1 million. How should this potential gain be treated for financial statement purposes on December 31, 2020?

Brief Exercise 15-44 Reporting Subsequent Events **LO5**

In January 2021, an explosion occurred at Nilo Company's plant, causing damage to area properties. In March 2021, Nilo received notification of lawsuits filed against the company. Nilo's management and legal counsel concluded that it was reasonably possible that Nilo would be held responsible for negligence and that $1,500,000 was a reasonable estimate of the damages. Nilo's $2,500,000 comprehensive public liability policy contains a

$150,000 deductible clause. In Nilo's December 31, 2020, financial statements, how should this casualty be reported if the financial statements were released on March 31, 2021?

Brief Exercise 15-45
Calculating Liquidity Ratios **LO6**
Hint: See Demo 15-6

Compute the (1) current ratio and the (2) quick ratio for **Nike, Inc.** using the following excerpt from the balance sheet reported in a recent 10-K of Nike, Inc.

At May 31 (in millions)	2015	At May 31 (in millions)	2015
Current assets		Current liabilities	
Cash and equivalents	$ 3,852	Current portion of long-term debt	$ 107
Short-term investments	2,072	Notes payable	74
Accounts receivable, net	3,358	Accounts payable	2,131
Inventories	4,337	Accrued liabilities	3,951
Deferred income taxes	389	Income taxes payable	71
Prepaid expenses and other current assets	1,968		
Total current assets	$15,976	Total current liabilities	$ 6,334

Exercises

Exercise 15-46
Recording Sales Taxes Payable **LO1**

Cash sales for Zeviae Inc. in 2020 were $9 million. The majority of sales were subject to a sales tax rate of 6%. Zeviae records sales taxes payable at the point of sale.

Required

a. Record the sales and sales tax entry for 2020 assuming that $180,000 of sales were not subject to tax.

b. Now assume that cash collections for 2020 were $9 million, which included a 6% sales tax along with the sales amount. Of the amount collected, $180,000 of sales were *not* subject to tax. Record the sales and sales tax entry for 2020.

Exercise 15-47
Recording Inventory Purchase **LO1**

On September 1, 2020, Global Tech Inc. purchased merchandise for resale for $8,000 on credit terms 2/15, n/60 using the gross method and a perpetual inventory system. Global Tech incurred a shipping charge of $300 on the purchase, which was immediately paid. On September 10, 2020, Global Tech paid for half of the merchandise. On October 25, 2020, Global Tech paid the remaining balance.

Required

Record the following entries for Global Tech related to the merchandise purchase.

a. Record the purchase of inventory on account and the freight payment on September 1, 2020.

b. Record the payment on September 10, 2020.

c. Record the payment on October 25, 2020.

d. Assume that instead of making payments on September 10 and October 25, Global Tech issued a 12-month note in payment of the $8,000 account balance on October 31, 2020. Interest on the note is 10%, due in full upon maturity of the note. Record the issuance of the note payable.

Exercise 15-48
Recording Inventory Purchases and Sales on Account **LO1**

Record the entries for the following transactions for Shoppers Inc. Shoppers uses a perpetual inventory system and records sales taxes payable at the point of sale.

a. On January 1, 2020, Shoppers Inc. purchased merchandise for resale for $35,000 on credit terms 1/15, n/30. Shoppers Inc. incurred a shipping charge of $180 on the purchase, which was immediately paid. Shoppers Inc. uses the gross method to purchases.

b. Shoppers Inc. sells $14,000 of inventory during the first week of January 2020, to customers for $25,000, with a sales tax rate of 5%. Of the total sales for the week, 30% are cash sales, and 70% are credit sales (n/30).

c. On January 14, 2020, Shoppers Inc. pays the balance for purchases on account.

d. Assume instead that Shoppers Inc. sells $15,000 of inventory during the first week of January 2020 to customers for $28,000, which includes a 5% sales tax. Of the total sales for the week, 30% are cash sales, and 70% are credit sales. Record the sales entry.

Exercise 15-49
Recording and Reporting Customer Advances **LO2**
Hint: See Demo 15-2B

Manchester Co. operates as a manufacturer of industrial equipment. On March 28, 2020, Manchester Co. required an advance payment of $100,000 from a customer on a special order of equipment. On May 1, 2020,

Manchester Co. prepared an invoice and delivered the industrial equipment to the customer. Total sales price is $400,000 and the remaining balance is due upon receipt of purchase.

Required

a. Record the entry on March 28, 2020, for Manchester Co.'s acceptance of the advance payment.

b. Indicate how the payment would be reported on Manchester's March 31, 2020, financial statements.

c. Record the entry on May 1, 2020, for the sale of the equipment assuming that the advance payment was applied to the balance due. Ignore the cost of goods sold entry.

Exercise 15-50 Recording Customer Deposits **LO2** *Hint:* See Demo 15-2A

In 2020, Neighbor Co-Op Inc. sells 500 beverages in glass bottles and receives a $1.00 deposit for each returnable bottle sold. As of December 31, 2020, a total of 400 glass bottles were returned, and deposits on 60 bottles were forfeited because it is the company's policy that a deposit must be claimed within 30 days. The remaining 40 bottles are still with customers within the 30-day claim period.

Required

a. Record the collection of deposits in 2020.

b. Record the return of glass bottles in 2020.

c. Record the forfeiture of deposits in 2020 assuming that the cost of each bottle is $0.80.

Exercise 15-51 Accounting for Gift Cards **LO2** *Hint:* See Demo 15-2C

Assume Ikeo Inc. sold $100,000 of gift cards during the last two weeks of December 2020. No gift cards were redeemed in 2020, while $90,000 of the gift cards were redeemed for store purchases during 2021. On December 31, 2021, Ikeo Inc. calculates the remaining balance of unredeemed gift cards of $10,000 ($100,000 less $90,000). Based on previous experiences, Ikeo estimates gift card breakage to be 5% of total gift card sales. Ikeo uses the proportional method to recognize income on gift card breakage.

Required

a. Record the sale of gift cards in 2020.

b. Record the redemption of gift cards in 2021.

c. Record revenue in 2021 due to gift card breakage using the proportional method.

Exercise 15-52 Recording and Reporting Compensated Absences **LO3**

Aloha Company has a personnel policy that allows each employee with at least one year's employment, 20 days vacation time and two holidays with regular pay. Unused days are carried over to the next year. If not taken during the next year, the vacation and holiday times are lost. Aloha's accounting period ends December 31. At the end of 2020, the personnel records showed the following:

Vacations Carried Over to 2021		Holidays Carried Over to 2021	
Total Days	**Total Salaries**	**Total Days**	**Total Salaries**
70	$16,800	10	$2,580

During 2021, all of the 2020 vacation time that was carried over and eight days of the holiday time that was carried over were taken. Salary increases in 2021 for these employees relating to the days carried over amounted to $1,600. Total cash wages paid were: 2020, $1,780,000; and 2021, $1,860,000. There was no carryover of vacation time earned in 2021.

Required

a. Provide all of the entries for Aloha Company related to salaries and compensated absences during 2020 and 2021. Disregard payroll taxes.

b. Show how the effects of the above transactions should be reported in the 2020 and 2021 financial statements of Aloha.

Exercise 15-53 Recording and Reporting Compensated Absences **LO3**

Ulta Inc. allows each employee to earn 15 paid vacation days each year with full pay. Unused vacation time can be carried over to the next year. If not taken during the next year, unused vacation time is lost. By the end of 2020, all but 3 of the 30 employees had taken their earned vacation time. The three employees carried over to 2021 a total of 20 vacation days, which represented 2020 salary of $6,000. During 2021, all of these three used their 2020 vacation carryover; none of them had received a pay rate change from 2020 until the time they used their carryover. Total cash wages paid: 2020, $700,000; 2021, $740,000. There was no carryover of vacation time earned in 2021.

Required

a. Provide the entry for Ulta Inc. to accrue compensated absences on December 31, 2020, and for the payment of vacation days in 2021. Disregard payroll taxes.

b. Compute the total amount of wage expense for 2020 and 2021. How would the vacation time carried over from 2020 affect the December 31, 2020 balance sheet?

Exercise 15-54
Recording Payroll and Related Deductions **LO3**

Urban Fit Corporation paid salaries and wages of $143,800 to its employees for the month. Of this amount, $3,800 was paid to employees who had already exceeded wages of $128,400. Also, $43,800 was paid to employees who had already been paid the SUTA maximum. FICA employee withholdings consist of a social security tax of 6.20% on the first $128,400 earned, plus a Medicare tax of 1.45% on all wages. Urban Fit pays employer taxes as follows: Its required FICA contribution, plus a FUTA tax of 6.0% on wages up to the SUTA maximum. Of this amount, 5.4% is payable to the state and 0.6% is payable to the U.S. Treasury. Employee income tax withholding was $35,000. Deductions included: union dues (in conformity with the union agreement), $3,000, and insurance premiums, $12,000.

Required

Provide the entries to:

a. Record liabilities for payroll deductions.

b. Record payroll expenses.

c. Record remittance of the payroll obligations.

Exercise 15-55
Determining Accrued Salaries **LO3**

Bloy Company pays all salaried employees on a biweekly basis. Overtime pay, however, is paid in the following biweekly period. Bloy accrues salaries expense only at its December 31 year-end. Data relating to salaries earned in December 2020 are:

- Last payroll was paid on December 26, 2020, for the two-week period ended on that day.
- Overtime pay earned in the two-week period ended December 26, 2020, was $8,400.
- Remaining work days in 2020 were December 29, 30, and 31, on which days there was no overtime.
- The recurring biweekly salaries total $150,000.

Required

Assuming a 5-day workweek, what should Bloy record as a liability at December 31, 2020, for accrued salaries?

Exercise 15-56
Recording Entries for Interest-Bearing and Noninterest-Bearing Notes **LO4**

Anne Taylor Company borrowed cash on August 1, 2020, and signed a $33,300 (face amount), one-year note payable, due on July 31, 2021. The accounting period of Anne Taylor ends December 31. Assume an effective interest rate of 11%.

Required

a. How much cash should Anne Taylor Company receive on the note, assuming the note is an interest-bearing note?

b. Provide the following entries and reporting amounts:
   1. August 1, 2020, date of the loan.
   2. December 31, 2020, adjusting entry.
   3. July 31, 2021, payment of the note.
   4. What liability amounts should be shown on the December 31, 2020, balance sheet?

c. Answer (*a*) and (*b*) above assuming that the note is noninterest-bearing. Use the straight-line method to amortize any discounts on note payable.

Exercise 15-57
Analyzing Interest-Bearing and Noninterest-Bearing Notes **LO4**

Consider the following three separate scenarios for a one-year, $100,000 note payable issued on September 1, 2020. Use the straight-line method to amortize any discount on note payable.

	$100,000 Note payable 12% Interest due at maturity 12% market rate Borrower's FYE*: Dec. 31	**$100,000 Note payable** 10% interest due at maturity 10% market rate Borrower's FYE: Nov. 30	**$100,000 Note payable** Noninterest-bearing 12% market rate Borrower's FYE: Dec. 31
Cash received upon note issuance			
Cash paid at maturity date			
Total interest paid (cash)			

continued

continued from previous page

	$100,000 Note payable 12% Interest due at maturity 12% market rate Borrower's FYE*: Dec. 31	**$100,000 Note payable** 10% interest due at maturity 10% market rate Borrower's FYE: Nov. 30	**$100,000 Note payable** Noninterest-bearing 12% market rate Borrower's FYE: Dec. 31
Interest expense in fiscal year 2020			
Interest expense in fiscal year 2021			
Amount of liabilities reported on fiscal year 2020 balance sheet:			
Note payable (net)			
Interest payable			

*FYE: Fiscal year-end

Required

Complete the table above based upon the information provided for the three *separate* scenarios.

Exercise 15-58 Recording Entries for Short-term Notes Payable **LO4**

Masy's Department Store supported its operations through short-term note financing in 2020 described as follows:

May 10 The Company entered into a new credit agreement with certain financial institutions providing for revolving credit borrowings and letters of credit in an aggregate amount not to exceed $1.5 million. Interest rates are adjustable.

Sep. 30 The Company borrowed $500,000 on the revolving credit line, payable in 6 months, at an interest rate of 7.25%, due upon maturity.

Nov. 30 Additional cash needed during peak holiday sale period was funded through the issuance of 60-day, $200,000 commercial paper, discounted at 4%.

Jan. 29 Paid off the commercial paper debt on due date.

Mar. 31 Paid off the balance of $500,000 on the revolving credit line plus interest.

Required

Record the following journal entries, assuming a 360-day year for interest computations:

a. May 10—Entering into credit line agreement.
b. September 30—Issuance of $500,000 note payable.
c. November 30—Issuance of $200,000 commercial paper. Compute the discount on note payable using 360 days as the base for prorating interest.
d. December 31—Adjusting entries.
e. January 29—Payment of $200,000 commercial paper.
f. March 31—Payment of $500,000 note payable.

Exercise 15-59 Calculating Accrued Interest Expense **LO4**

The following table includes five separate short-term note payable scenarios.

	Note Payable	Issuance Date	Term	Stated Rate	Fiscal Year-End	Accrued Interest at Fiscal Year-End
1	$5,000 note payable	September 1, 2020	6-month	6%	December 31	
2	$5,000 note payable	September 30, 2020	6-month	6%	December 31	
3	$2,000 note payable	November 1, 2020	3-month	8%	December 31	
4	$2,000 note payable	November 30, 2020	3-month	8%	December 31	
5	$10,000 note payable	May 31, 2020	12-month	10%	November 30	

Required

For each separate scenario, complete the last column in the table by calculating interest expense accrued at the relevant fiscal year-end.

Exercise 15-60 Classifying Debt **LO4, 5**

On December 31, 2020, Millers Grocery Inc. had a 10-year, 7% note payable balance of $100,000. The note payable was originally issued on June 30, 2011. The company will issue its financial statements on March 15, 2021.

Required

How will the note payable in each of the following separate scenarios be classified on the balance sheet of Millers Grocery on December 31, 2020?

a. The company intends to pay off the note payable when it comes due.
b. The company intends to refinance the note payable and will begin discussions with the lender in February 2021.
c. The company issues common stock in January 2021. $75,000 of the proceeds of the issuance plus $25,000 in cash are used to pay off the loan.
d. The company enters into a refinancing agreement dated January 31, 2021, which allows the issuance of debt up to 50% of the company's inventory balance, which is expected to be $175,000 during 2021. The interest rate in the refinancing agreement is 6.5% and the debt agreement expires on December 31, 2023.
e. The full $100,000 was extinguished on February 1, 2021, when it was paid off with a $100,000, 8%, interest-bearing note payable, due February 1, 2026.
f. Assume that the note payable was issued on June 30, 2020. The note payable includes a provision that allows for the lender to call the note at any time. However, the lender has indicated that it does not intend to call the note in 2021.
g. Assume that the note payable was issued June 30, 2019, instead of December 31, 2020. Millers Grocery Inc. is in violation of a debt covenant that requires a current ratio of 1.5. Millers obtained a waiver of the debt covenant through September 2021 because it expects to be back at 1.5 by mid-year.

Exercise 15-61
Recording and Reporting Warranties **LO5**

During 2020, Ward Company introduced a new product carrying a two-year warranty against defects, which is included in the selling price of the product. The estimated warranty costs are 2% of sales within the first 12 months following the sale and 4% in the second 12 months following the sale. Sales and actual warranty expenditures for the years ended December 31, 2020, and 2021 are:

	Sales	Actual Warranty Expenditures
2020	$ 600,000	$ 9,000
2021	1,000,000	30,000
	$1,600,000	$39,000

Required

a. At December 31, 2020, what would Ward report as estimated warranty liability on its balance sheet?
b. Record the journal entry required on December 31, 2020.
c. At December 31, 2021, what would Ward report as estimated warranty liability on its balance sheet?
d. Record the journal entry required on December 31, 2021.

Exercise 15-62
Recording and Reporting Warranties **LO5**
Hint: See Demo 15-5C

Assume the same information in Exercise 15-61, except that the warranty is for three years and has a separate purchase price. The company collected $20,000, and $35,000 for this extended warranty feature in the years 2020 and 2021, respectively. The company uses straight-line recognition of warranty revenue. For simplification, assume that sales occurred at the first of the year.

Required

a. Record the journal entries required for (1) the sale of the products and warranties, (2) incurred warranty costs, and (3) recognition of warranty revenue for 2020 and 2021.
b. What liability would be reported on the balance sheet at the end of 2020 and 2021?

Exercise 15-63
Recording and Reporting Warranties **LO5**

Macy Furniture sells a line of products that carry a three-year warranty against defects at no extra charge. Based on industry experience, the estimated warranty costs are as follows: first year following the year of sale, 1% of sales; second year following the year of sale, 3% of sales; and third year following the year of sale, 5% of sales. Sales and actual warranty expenditures for the first three-year period were:

	Cash Sales	Actual Warranty Expenditures
2020	$ 80,000	$1,000
2021	110,000	4,100
2022	120,000	9,800

Required

a. Provide entries for the three years for (1) sales, (2) estimated warranty expense, and (3) actual expenditures.
b. What amount should be reported as a liability on the balance sheet at the end of each year?

c. Assume instead that at the end of 2022, the company changed its estimate of the second year after sale to 2% of sales rather than 3%. Provide the entry to record the adjustment to the warranty liability (assuming all entries described above were recorded as planned).

Exercise 15-64
Reporting Litigation Contingencies **LO5**

Koll's Company is preparing its annual financial statements at December 31, 2020. During 2020, a customer fell while riding on the escalator and has filed a lawsuit for $150,000 because of a claimed back injury. The lawyer employed by the company has carefully assessed all of the implications. If the suit is lost, their attorney's reasonable estimate is that the $150,000 will be assessed by the court.

Required

How should the contingency be handled during 2020 in each of the following cases? Provide all necessary entries and any necessary disclosures.

a. Assume that the attorney and the management concluded that it is reasonably possible that the company will be liable.

b. Assume instead, that the attorney, the independent accountant, and management have reluctantly concluded that it is probable that the suit will be successful.

c. Assume that the conclusion of the legal counsel and management is that the chance of a contingency loss is remote. They believe the suit is without merit.

d. Assume that the company decided to accrue a loss of $150,000 in 2020 based upon their assessment. However, in 2021, the suit was settled for $175,000. How would this change be treated in the financial statements?

Exercise 15-65
Reporting Product Recall Contingency **LO5**

Stony Electronics, an electronics manufacturer, includes battery packs with its laptop computers that it sells. After a year of sales of the product, management learns that the battery packs have the potential to overheat, which may lead to burns or fire hazards. As a result of this issue, management has determined that the likelihood of recalling the battery packs is highly probable. The estimated cost of the recall (publishing the notice and replacing the batteries with other safer options) is $350,000.

Required

How should this potential product recall be treated in the Stony Electronics financial statements?

Exercise 15-66
Analyzing Various Contingencies **LO5**

Atlanta Corp. is preparing its 2020 financial statements (December 31 year-end) and is considering the following events:

a. Probable warranty costs on the company's products are estimated to be 1% of sales. The warranties are considered assurance-type warranties.

b. One of its manufacturing plants is located in a foreign country. There is a threat of expropriation of this plant. The threat of expropriation is deemed to be reasonably possible. Any compensation from the foreign government would be less than the carrying amount of the plant.

c. It is highly probable that the company will be awarded damages next year as a result of a lawsuit filed this year against a competitor.

d. Potential costs due to the discovery of a safety hazard related to one of its products are considered probable and can be reasonably estimated.

e. Potential costs are due to the discovery of a possible product defect related to one of its products. These costs are reasonably possible and can be reasonably estimated.

f. The closure and removal in 20 years of a storage tank used in the company's technology center is estimated to cost $2 million. The present value of this amount at the company's 7% discount rate is $516,838.

g. The company is under investigation by the Department of Labor related to its health care plan. Management believes it is probable that the company will receive an assessment and as a result, it is probable that the company will owe an amount totaling between $10,000 and $20,000.

h. The company is under investigation by the Department of Labor related to its health care plan. Management believes it is reasonably possible that the company will receive an assessment and as a result, it is probable that the company will owe an amount totaling between $10,000 and $20,000.

Required

For each item listed above, indicate whether the company should record a journal entry or make a disclosure in its 2020 financial statements.

Exercise 15-67
Analyzing Contingencies **LO5**

Boston Scientific Corporation is a worldwide developer, manufacturer and marketer of medical devices that are used in a broad range of interventional medical specialties. In a recent annual report on Form 10-K, the company reported the following regarding its legal expense accrual.

> **Note K: Commitments and Contingencies (excerpt)** Our accrual for legal matters that are probable and estimable was $1.936 billion as of December 31, 2015 and $1.577 billion as of December 31, 2014, and includes certain estimated costs of settlement, damages and defense.

Required

a. Record the entry for Boston Scientific Corporation for the accrual of legal expense during 2015. Assume that no settlement payments were made in 2015.

b. If legal matters unresolved at the end of 2015 were settled in 2016 for $1.736 billion, record the related entry. What impact would this settlement have on the 2015 financial statements?

Exercise 15-68
Reporting Subsequent Event **LO5, 6**

On January 17, 2021, an explosion occurred at a Cord Company plant, causing extensive property damage to area buildings. Although no claims had yet been asserted against Cord by March 10, 2021, the company believes it is probable that claims will be asserted. Cord's management and counsel concluded that it was reasonably possible that Cord would be responsible for damages and that $2,500,000 would be a reasonable estimate of its liability. Cord's $10,000,000 comprehensive public liability policy has a $500,000 deductible clause.

Required

In Cord's December 31, 2020, financial statements, which were issued on March 25, 2021, how should this item be reported?

Exercise 15-69
Reporting Liabilities and Contingencies
LO1, 2, 3, 4, 5, 6

The following transactions relate to topics in this chapter.

a. Purchased inventory on account, terms 2/n, n/30, accounted for using the perpetual method.
b. Collected sales taxes on a customer sale.
c. Received a deposit from a customer as a down payment on a large purchase.
d. Recorded a sale of gift cards to customers.
e. Recognized breakage revenue on gift cards.
f. Accrued weekly payroll including employee withholdings.
g. Accrued payroll tax expense.
h. Recorded vacation time paid that had been previously accrued.
i. Accrued year-end employee bonuses.
j. Accrued interest on a short-term, interest-bearing note payable.
k. Reclassified long-term debt due within the next year as current.
l. Accrued a loss contingency.
m. Settled a loss contingency for considerably less than previously accrued.
n. Recorded the sale of an extended warranty.
o. Discovered as a subsequent event that a large customer unexpectedly filed for bankruptcy. As a result, the accounts receivable balance is written off before the financial statements are issued.

Required

For each transaction above, indicate the impact on assets, liabilities, and stockholders' equity.

Exercise 15-70
Determining the Impact on Liabilities of the Balance Sheet
LO1, 2, 3, 4, 5, 6

The following transactions relate to topics in this chapter.

a. Coupons published in a newspaper that may be redeemed for merchandise or service.
b. Sales taxes payable.
c. Probable requirements to clean up toxic wastes.
d. Company contract promises to pay postretirement health benefits.
e. Probable awards (gain) based on product liability suits.
f. Cash dividends declared but not paid.
g. Customer payments for online newsletter subscriptions not yet delivered.
h. Notes payable (trade); due June 30, 2021.
i. Discount on short-term notes payable.
j. Bonds payable (25% installment due each April 1).
k. Accounts payable.
l. Accrued property taxes (estimated).

m. Note payable, due June 30, 2025.
n. Accrued interest on note payable.
o. Long-term debt that is callable by the lender at any time.
p. Customer deposit received in advance of purchase.
q. Gift certificates sold but not yet redeemed.
r. Employee FICA withholding.

Required

Which of these items should be considered liabilities and recognized on the balance sheet dated December 31, 2020? For items recognized as liabilities, would they be classified as current or long-term?

Exercise 15-71 Analyzing Liquidity Ratios **LO6**

Atlas Inc. issues short-term interest-bearing notes and uses the proceeds to purchase inventory. The company's profits for the year remain unchanged.

Required

Indicate how the use of the notes would affect the following ratios:

a. Current ratio
b. Quick ratio

Exercise 15-72 Calculating Liquidity Ratios **LO6** *Hint:* See Demo 15-6

The balance sheets for Red Oak Inc. and Birch Co. reflect the following:

	Red Oak	Birch
Current assets		
Cash	$ 5,000	$ 10,000
Short-term investments	3,000	0
Accounts receivable	25,000	18,000
Inventory	17,000	5,000
Other	5,000	6,000
Noncurrent assets	285,000	317,000
Total assets	$340,000	$356,000
Current liabilities	$ 30,000	$ 30,000
Long-term liabilities	30,000	230,000
Stockholders' equity	280,000	96,000
Total liabilities and stockholders' equity	$340,000	$356,000

Required

Calculate the following ratios and comment on the results.

a. Current ratio
b. Quick ratio

Problems

Problem 15-73 Identifying Current Liabilities **LO1, 2, 3, 4, 5**

Each of the following items describes a current obligation.

a. To pay an amount to employees as a benefit earned for prior services rendered.
b. To return cash back to a customer if specific conditions are met.
c. To pay for the use of borrowed funds.
d. For an acquisition on account.
e. To remit cash collected related to the sale of a product or service to taxing authorities.
f. To complete a performance obligation in the future.
g. To remit amounts for taxes to the federal or state government.
h. To pay an amount to employees for current services rendered.
i. To pay an amount to employees beyond salaries, usually contingent upon a company's profits.
j. To repay a loan due less than a year from now.
k. To repay a long-term loan that is callable by the lender.

Required

Identify the current liability that is best described by each item.

Problem 15-74
Recording and Reporting Liabilities **LO1, 2, 3, 4, 5, 6**

The following selected transactions of Johnson Motors Company were completed during the current accounting year ended December 31, 2020.

1. March 1, 2020, borrowed $25,000 on a two-year, 12% interest-bearing note. Interest is paid annually.
2. April 1, 2020, borrowed cash and signed a $20,000, two-year, noninterest-bearing note. The market rate for this level of risk was 12%.
3. June 1, 2020, purchased a special truck with a list price of $33,000. Paid $3,000 cash and signed a $30,000, one-year, noninterest-bearing note. The market rate for this level of risk was 12%.
4. During 2020, sold merchandise for $30,000 cash that carried a two-year warranty for parts and labor. A reasonable estimate of the cost of the warranty is 1.5% of sales revenue. By December 31, 2020, actual warranty costs amounted to $250.
5. June 1, 2020, Johnson cosigned and guaranteed payment of a $50,000, 14%, one-year note owed by a local supplier to City Bank. The bank required a cosignature; however, they believe that default by the debtor is only reasonably possible.
6. Property taxes for 2020 are recorded monthly.
   - Prior-year property taxes, $2,087; expected to increase by 15% during 2020.
   - December 10, 2020, final tax assessment received, $2,500; paid on February 1, 2021, the latest payment date without penalty.
7. December 2020, $20,000 cash dividends declared (not yet paid or issued).
8. December 2020, sales revenue (excluding sales taxes collected) for the month, $400,000. Sales tax, 5%, applicable to 98% of the sales. No unpaid sales tax carried over from November 2020.
9. December 31, 2020, accrual of interest payable.

Required

a. For each of the nine items above, provide the entries that Johnson should make in 2020.

b. List each current liability (account title and the amount) that should be reported on the December 31, 2020, balance sheet of Johnson Company (issued March 1, 2021).

Problem 15-75
Recording and Reporting Liabilities **LO1, 2, 3, 4, 5, 6**

The following selected transactions of AVC Corp. were completed during the accounting year ended December 31, 2020.

a. Merchandise was purchased on account; a $10,000, one-year, 8% interest-bearing note, dated April 1, 2020, was provided to the creditor. Assume a perpetual inventory system.

b. The company cosigned an $8,000 note payable for another party.

c. On July 1, the company borrowed cash; a one-year, noninterest-bearing note with a face amount of $28,750 was signed. Assume a discount rate of 8%.

d. Payroll records showed the following:

	Employee			Employer		
Gross Wages	**Withholdings**	**FICA**	**Union Dues**	**FICA**	**SUTA**	**FUTA**
$50,000	$15,000	$3,100	$500	$3,100	$1,350	$350

Remittances: Withholding taxes, $13,000; FICA, $6,000; SUTA, $1,200; FUTA, $340; and union dues, $280.

e. The company was sued for $150,000 in damages. A court judgment against the company that is reasonably estimated to be $125,000 is probable.

f. Cash dividends declared but not yet paid were $14,000.

g. Accrued interest on the notes at December 31.

Required

a. Provide the entry or entries for each of the above transactions and events.

b. Prepare a list (title and amount) of the disclosures related to the liabilities at December 31, 2020.

Problem 15-76
Recording Payroll and Related Deductions **LO3**

Ryan Company paid salaries for the month of June 2020, amounting to $120,000. Of this amount, $30,000 was received by employees who had already been paid the $128,400 maximum amount of annual earnings taxable in one year under FICA laws. Of the $120,000, $14,000 was paid to employees who had already reached the $7,000 maximum wages subject to unemployment taxes (rates: 5.4 % state and 0.6 % federal). Withholding taxes amounted to $36,000, and $1,450 was withheld for investment in company stock per an agreement with certain employees.

Required

Provide entries to record the following:

a. Salary payment and the liabilities for the payroll deductions.
b. Employer payroll expenses.
c. Remittance of the taxes.

Problem 15-77
Recording and Reporting Short-Term Notes Payable **LO4**

On October 1, 2020, Reed Travel Company borrowed $40,000 cash and signed a one-year note payable, due on September 30, 2021. The interest rate is 10%. The accounting period ends on December 31.

Required

a. Compute the face amount of the note assuming:
   1. An interest-bearing note.
   2. A noninterest-bearing note.
b. Complete the following table.

	Interest-Bearing Note	Noninterest-Bearing Note
Total cash received		
Face amount of note		
Total cash paid		
Total interest		
Interest expense, 2020		
Interest expense, 2021		
Note payable, Dec. 31, 2020		
Interest payable, Dec. 31, 2020		
Stated rate		
Market rate		

c. Provide entries for each case from October 1, 2020, through the maturity date.
d. Show how the liability and expense amounts should be reflected for each case on the December 31, 2020, balance sheet and the 2020 income statement.

Problem 15-78
Classifying Debt **LO4**

The following selected liabilities of Star Electronics Inc. were outstanding on December 31, 2020.

a. $50,000, ten-year, 10% note payable, originating September 30, 2011.
b. $100,000, five-year, 7% note payable with Gold Star Bank, originating December 15, 2019. Per the loan agreement, Gold Star has the right to demand immediate payment if Star Electronics falls short of the required current ratio of 1.8 for longer than three months. On the balance sheet date of December 31, 2020, Star Electronics has a current ratio of 1.75. By March 15, the issuance date of the financial statements, the current ratio is 1.85.
c. $100,000, 8% bonds payable outstanding, due on March 1, 2021. Star Electronics issues common stock in early January 2020 and used the proceeds to pay off the bonds. Cash in excess of the bonds payable of $100,000 amounted to $25,000.
d. $150,000, 15-year, 6%, noncallable note payable, originating September 15, 2018.

Required

Indicate whether each of the items above would be classified as a current liability or a noncurrent liability on the balance sheet dated December 31, 2020, of Star Electronics. Provide support for your classification.

Problem 15-79
Accounting for Warranties **LO5**

Habek Hardware Inc. provides a product warranty for defects on two major lines of items sold since the beginning of 2019. Line A carries a two-year warranty for all labor and service (but not parts). The company contracts the service for the warranty (both parts and labor). The fee is $60 per unit payable at the date of sale.

Line B carries a three-year warranty for parts and labor on service. Habek purchases the parts needed under the warranty and has service personnel who perform the work and are paid by the job. On the basis of experience, it is estimated that for Line B, the three-year warranty costs are 3% of sales for parts and 7% for labor and overhead.

Additional data follow.

	2019	2020
Sales in units, Line A	700	1,000
Sales price per unit, Line A	$ 610	$ 660
Sales in units, Line B	600	800
Sales price per unit, Line B	$ 700	$ 750
Actual warranty outlays, Line B:		
Parts	$3,000	$ 9,600
Labor and overhead	$7,000	$22,000

Required

a. Provide entries for annual sales and expenses for 2019 and 2020 separately by product line. Assume that all sales were for cash.

b. Determine the year-end estimated warranty liability and the year's warranty expense for 2019 and 2020.

Problem 15-80
Accounting for Warranties **LO5**

In 2020, Carpenter Inc. sells a product that carries a separate, three-year warranty for parts and labor on service for $50 per product. Sales of products totaled $50,000 where customers also purchased the $50 warranty, resulting in total warranty sales of $5,000. On the basis of experience, it is estimated that for the three-year warranty, costs are 2% of sales for parts and 3% for labor and overhead. Actual warranty service costs were $1,000 in 2020 and $800 in 2021. The company uses straight-line recognition of warranty revenue. For simplification, assume that sales occurred at the first of the year.

Required

a. Record the journal entries required for the following.
1. Sale of the products and warranties in 2020.
2. Incurred warranty costs in 2020 and 2021.
3. Recognition of warranty revenue for 2020 and 2021.

b. What liability would be reported on the balance sheet at the end of 2020 and 2021?

Problem 15-81
Estimating Contingencies—Product Recall **LO5**

Engines Unlimited discovered a defect on a certain type of engine manufactured and sold over the last 6 months resulting in a product recall. Engines Unlimited uses the expected cash flow method to value the fair value of its product recall. In using this method, Engines Unlimited assigns a probability to estimated cash flows over the recall period of two years.

Year	Estimate of Cash Outflow	Probability	Expected Cash Flow
2021	$500,000	30%	$150,000
	550,000	40%	220,000
	600,000	30%	180,000
Total		100%	$550,000
2022	$250,000	20%	$ 50,000
	300,000	60%	180,000
	325,000	20%	65,000
Total		100%	$295,000

Required

Assuming that the cash flows occurred at the end of each year, and the risk-free rate of interest is 5%, calculate the present value of the product recall costs.

Problem 15-82 Analyzing Subsequent Events **LO5**

The following items are separate subsequent events, occurring after the balance sheet date of December 31, 2020, but before the financial statements are issued on March 15, 2021.

1. Sale of 5,000 shares of 6% preferred stock ($1 par value) on February 1, 2021. Total proceeds were $50,000.
2. Assume that the sale in (1) took place, but $25,000 of the proceeds were used to liquidate a note payable for $25,000 due on February 15, 2021.
3. Smoke and fire damage due to an electrical storm caused fire in one area of the corporate facilities on January 15, 2021. Total damage is estimated to be $500,000.
4. The president of the company resigned unexpectedly on January 31, 2021.
5. It has come to the attention of the board of directors of the company on January 28, 2021, that a competitor will be filing a lawsuit within the next week regarding a patent infringement. The product in question yielded $1 million in sales revenue in 2020. Because the details are not known, management is not able to reasonably estimate the loss at this time but believes it is reasonably possible that a loss would be incurred.
6. Employees voted to strike at a meeting on January 15, 2021. The strike is expected to take place immediately. The financial impact on the company is unknown at this time.
7. A former employee of the company filed a lawsuit against the company for wrongful termination on January 5, 2021. Employment had been terminated September 2020. A settlement for the case is highly probable based upon the negotiations that have taken place through mid-March and the estimate of range of loss is $50,000 to $100,000.
8. A customer is threatening legal action against the company for an injury that took place on January 25, 2021, in the company's parking lot. The potential financial impact is not estimable at this time and the likelihood of a loss is remote.
9. On February 15, 2021, the company declared that it would be selling a division that will be classified as a discontinued operation.
10. The company was informed on March 1, 2021, that it would undergo an investigation by the state auditor because of some issues that had surfaced regarding sales tax collection and payments. The company has determined that it is probable that a claim will be asserted, but the company plans to aggressively defend its position and feels that the likelihood of an unfavorable outcome is remote.

Required

Evaluate each of the above separate transactions and events and recommend appropriate accounting and reporting actions for the 2020 financial statements.

Problem 15-83 Analyzing Multiple Contingencies **LO5**

Duke Corporation is preparing its first set of financial statements at December 31, 2020, along with the appropriate adjusting entries. Among the contingent losses under consideration are the following transactions and events.

1. Two of the major product lines sold during the year carry a one-year warranty for defects (both labor and parts cost). Sales of these items amounted to $20,000. On average, warranty expenditures approximate 4% of sales price. The warranty is classified as an assurance-type warranty.
2. Duke was sued by a shopper for $300,000 in damages due to an accident in the retail store. Legal counsel is of the opinion that it is probable that the plaintiff will prevail in court and that Duke will have to pay 10% of the claim; it is anticipated that the insurance company will pay the balance. The suit is expected to be resolved in mid-2021.
3. Duke Corporation endorsed and guaranteed a $15,000, 15%, one-year mortgage note given by a local supplier of merchandise to Duke. The bank required a guarantor. The bank indicated that the probability of default by the supplier was reasonably possible.
4. The comprehensive liability insurance policy carried by Duke Corporation covers all claims for damages to individuals or groups due to accident, negligence, and other injuries relating to the legitimate operations of the company. However, the insurance policy carries an escape clause that states, "When the insured is willfully negligent, as determined by an independent third party, 10% of the loss must be paid by the insured." A payment by Duke Corporation under the escape clause is considered remote.
5. A gain on the sale of equipment is virtually certain and its amount can be reasonably estimated at $5,000.

Required

a. Evaluate each of the above transactions and events and recommend appropriate accounting and reporting actions for the 2020 financial statements. Provide any entry or disclosure required for each item.

b. Identify each liability and the amount that should be reported on the December 31, 2020, balance sheet.

Accounting Decisions and Judgments

AD&J 15-84
Analyzing Current Liabilities **LO1, 2, 3, 4**

Real World Analysis Listed below are the current liability section and Note 7 of the Year 7 balance sheet of **Amoco Corporation**, a major oil company.

$ millions	**Year 7**	**Year 6**
Current Liabilities		
Current portion of long-term obligations	$ 146	$ 74
Short-term obligations	576	442
Accounts payable	2,497	2,663
Accrued liabilities	872	916
Taxes payable (including income taxes)	1,074	831
	$5,165	$4,926

Note 7 Short-Term Obligations

Amoco's "short-term obligations" consist of notes payable and commercial paper. Notes payable as of December 31, Year 7, totaled $85 million at an average annual interest rate of 5.7%, compared with $24 million at an average annual interest rate of 5.7% at year-end Year 6. Commercial paper borrowings at December 31, Year 7, were $699 million at an average annual interest rate of 5.7% compared with $217 million at an average annual interest rate of 5.9% as of December 31, Year 6.

Bank lines of credit available to support existing commercial paper borrowings of the corporation amounted to $490 million at both December 31, Year 7 and Year 6. All of these were supported by commitment fees.

The corporation also maintains compensating balances with a number of banks for various purposes. Such arrangements do not legally restrict withdrawal or usage of available cash funds. In the aggregate, they are not material in relation to total liquid assets.

Required

a. Explain the origin of the $146 million current portion of long-term obligations in current liabilities of Year 7.

b. What amount of Amoco's long-term debt reflected in its current liabilities did Amoco pay off in Year 7?

c. During Year 7, did Amoco reduce its average yearly interest incurred on its short-term obligations described in Note 7?

d. Do the lines of credit that Amoco holds at the end of Year 7 appear as liabilities on its balance sheet? Explain.

AD&J 15-85
Analyzing Current Liabilities **LO1, 2, 3, 4**

Real World Analysis The following is the liability section of **U.S. Bancorp's** 2017 comparative annual financial statements.

U.S. Bancorp, Consolidated Balance Sheet At December (Dollars in Millions)	**2017**	**2016**
Deposits		
Noninterest-bearing	$ 87,557	$ 86,097
Interest-bearing	259,658	248,493
Total deposits	347,215	334,590
Short-term borrowings	16,651	13,963
Long-term debt	32,259	33,323
Other liabilities	16,249	16,155
Total liabilities	$412,374	$398,031

Required

a. What is unusual about this balance sheet presentation?

b. How do "deposits" above differ from deposits classified as a current liability of a non-financial institution?

Real World Analysis A recent annual report of **General Motors Company** (GM) reports the following current liabilities.

AD&J 15-86
Analyzing Current Liabilities **LO1, 2, 3, 4**

Current liabilities

1. Accounts payable
2. Short-term debt and current portion of long-term debt
3. Accrued liabilities

In the notes to its financial statements, GM indicates the following obligations.

a. Payrolls (obligations)
b. Pension liability
c. Trade accounts payable
d. Deposits primarily from rental car companies
e. Environmental liabilities
f. Unsecured debt with terms of one year or less

Required
Which of the above six items *a* through *f* (or portions thereof) do you believe are included as part of one of the amounts in GM's current liabilities 1 through 3 provided above? For any item(s) not classified as a current liability, indicate the most likely classification.

Real World Analysis Beyond some of the general current liabilities reviewed in this chapter, certain industries will have certain specialized current liabilities accounts. In solving this problem, access the 2015 10-K of each company listed.

AD&J 15-87
Identifying Current Liabilities **LO1, 2, 3, 4**

_____ 1. Deferred and advance tuition	*a.* **The Boston Beer Company Inc.**
_____ 2. Casino outstanding chip liability	*b.* **United Parcel Service Inc.**
_____ 3. Customer advances and amounts in excess of costs incurred	*c.* **Electronic Arts Inc.**
	d. **Mattel Inc.**
_____ 4. Charter revenues received in advance	*e.* **Devry Education Group Inc.**
_____ 5. Self-insurance reserves	*f.* **United Airlines Inc.**
_____ 6. Product warranties	*g.* **Overseas Shipholding Group Inc.**
_____ 7. Accrued royalties	*h.* **MGM Resorts International**
_____ 8. Frequent flyer deferred revenue	*i.* **The Boeing Company**
_____ 9. Incentive compensation	*j.* **Lockheed Martin Corporation**
_____ 10. Accrued stale beer	

Required
Identify each liability 1 through 10 in the left-hand column with the reporting company *a* through *j* in the right-hand column. You will find information about the current liabilities on the face of the balance sheet or in the disclosure notes.

Judgment Case Evans Equipment Company sells new and used earth-moving equipment. Evans uses a perpetual inventory system, and its accounting period ends December 31. On December 28, 2020, Evans purchased used equipment for resale at a list price of $80,000. Terms of the purchase: cash down payment, $40,000, plus a note payable, face amount, $40,000, maturity date, December 28, 2022. On January 5, 2021, Evans received the equipment and the down payment was made in cash.

AD&J 15-88
Evaluating a Liability and Providing Recommendations **LO4**

The company recorded the above transactions as follows.

- The company reported no interest expense for 2020 because the note did not specify that any interest would be paid.
- The transaction was recorded on January 5, 2021, because it was on that date that Evans received the equipment and the down payment was paid.
- The company entered the equipment in the perpetual inventory account at $80,000.
- The company planned to record, on the maturity date of the note, a debit to Note Payable and a credit to Cash for $40,000.

Required

a. Evaluate the accounting treatment of the purchase of the equipment. Consider both theoretical and GAAP issues. State any assumptions that you make.
b. If the company's accounting seems in error, provide recommendations for what should be done. Also provide all the necessary journal entries through January 5, 2021. Assume a 12% risk-adjusted interest rate if necessary.

AD&J 15-89
Analyzing Contingencies—Four Scenarios **LO5**

Judgment Case Speedoo Company is preparing its annual financial statements at December 31, 2020, and is concerned about unrecorded contingencies. Three separate situations are under consideration:

1. During 2020, a shopper sued the Speedoo Company for $500,000 for a claimed injury that occurred on the premises owned by the company. No date for the trial has been set; however, the lawyer employed by the company has completed a thorough investigation. Because it can be proven that the customer did fall on the premises, the legal counsel believes it will not be difficult for the plaintiff to prove injury. There is some evidence that it was due, at least partially, to negligence by the plaintiff. The attorney believes that it is not probable, but is reasonably possible, that the suit will be successful for the plaintiff, but for a significantly smaller amount that cannot be reasonably estimated at this time.
2. An outside party has filed a suit against Speedoo for $25,000, claiming that certain actions by Speedoo caused the party to lose a contract on which the estimated profit was $25,000. In the opinion of the legal counsel engaged by Speedoo, the probability that the claim will be successful is remote. Counsel does not believe it will ever be brought to trial. If necessary, Speedoo will defend itself in court.
3. Speedoo owns a small plant in a foreign country that has a book value of $3 million and an estimated fair value of $4 million. The foreign government has indicated its unalterable intention to expropriate the plant during the coming year and to reimburse Speedoo for 50% of the estimated fair value.

Required

For each separate situation, indicate what should be done, considering the following two points.

a. What accounting recognition, if any, should be accorded each situation at the end of 2020? Explain why and provide journal entries.

b. Indicate how each situation should be reported on the December 31, 2020, balance sheet.

AD&J 15-90
Distinguishing Short-Term from Long-Term Liabilities **LO4**

Judgment Case A professional football player signed a contract at the end of 2019 to play quarterback for a professional team and would be compensated as follows:

- A $4.5 million signing bonus spread over six years.
- Base salaries of
    - $1,025 million for 2020–2021
    - $1,281 million for 2021–2022
    - $1,538 million for 2022–2023
    - $1,793 million for 2023–2024
    - $2,050 million for 2024–2025
    - $2,306 million for 2025–2026

Only the first three years are guaranteed. If the player achieved certain measurable performance standards, the contract could be reexamined and changed after three, four, and five years. (After three years the player could elect to become a free agent and sign with any team.)

Required

a. Did the football organization have a liability to the player when the contract was signed? Explain, indicating whether it met the conditions of a liability.

b. Assuming it was a liability:
   1. What parts, if any, constituted current liabilities?
   2. How should the team measure the amounts to be recorded over the life of the contract?

AD&J 15-91
Determining Contingencies **LO5**

Ethics Case Multiple legal cases have surfaced for workplace injuries related to the handling of toxic substances or chemicals such as asbestos. In other cases, future losses may exist for environmental cleanups if a company has not elected to clean up the area or if no federal or state order exists for it to do so.

Required

Do you think employers should recognize liabilities either for the potential cleanup process on prior disposals or for future claims by affected workers? Do you see any ethical issues? How might you resolve it?

AD&J 15-92
Computing Bonus with Tax Impact **LO3**

Challenge Problem Executives of JR Inc. earn a bonus equal to 2% of the company's 2020 net income over $1,000,000, payable in February of 2021. The company's 2020 pretax income is $3,500,000, and the company's tax rate is 40%.

Required

Calculate the current liability for bonuses taking into account the tax rate of 40%.

Challenge Problem Executives of Limited Label Inc. earn a bonus equal to 2% of the company's 2020 net income over $1,000,000, payable in February of 2021. The company's 2020 income is $3,500,000. Record the adjusting entry on December 31, 2020, ignoring taxes.

AD&J 15-93 Computing and Recording Bonus without Tax Impact **LO3**

Trueblood Case The Trueblood case series, prepared by Deloitte professionals, are based on recent accounting technical issues that require research and judgment. The cases may be accessed through the Deloitte foundation at the following website: https://www2.deloitte.com/us/en/pages/about-deloitte/articles/trueblood-case-studies-deloitte-foundation.html

The following case is relevant to the content provided in this chapter: Case: 14-7 eVade Pays Up. This case applies the concepts of derecognizing a liability and distinguishing the difference between a contractual or legal liability and a contingency.

AD&J 15-94 Analyzing Contingencies **LO5**

Codification Skills How are the terms (1) current liability, (2) breakage, (3) callable obligation, (4) gain contingency, (5) loss contingency, and (6) subsequent event defined in the Codification?

AD&J 15-95 Defining Terms **LO1, 2, 3, 4, 5**

Codification Skills Through research in the Codification, identify the specific citation for each of the following items included as guidance in this chapter:

a. Proportional method for recognizing breakage income. FASB ASC ___-___-___-___

b. Criteria for the accrual of compensated absences. FASB ASC ___-___-___-___

c. Criteria for evaluating short-term obligations expected to be refinanced. FASB ASC ___-___-___-___

d. Assurance and service-type warranty distinctions. FASB ASC ___-___-___-___

e. Criteria for accruing loss contingencies. FASB ASC ___-___-___-___

AD&J 15-96 Accounting Research **LO2, 3, 4, 5**

Codification Skills A company is preparing 2nd quarter financial statements on June 30, 2020. The company's year-end is December 31. The company has been informed of the potential of a suit to be filed against the company related to a price disagreement on a recently completed contract. The company's CFO is wondering what obligation the company has in reporting the contingency on the June 30th financial statements. What guidance is available in the Codification?

FASB ASC ___-___-___-___

AD&J 15-97 Accounting Research **LO5**

Answers to Review Exercises

Review 15-1

a. **June 1, 2020—To record inventory purchase**

Inventory	20,300	
Cash		300
Accounts Payable		20,000

Assets = Liabilities + Equity: +20,300, −300 = +20,000
Inventory: 20,300 (Dr) | Cash: 300 (Cr) | Accounts Payable: 20,000 (Cr)

b. **June 7, 2020—To record sales and sales taxes payable**

Cash ($8,480 × 0.25)	2,120	
Accounts Receivable ($8,480 × 0.75)	6,360	
Sales		8,000
Sales Taxes Payable ($8,000 × 0.06)		480

Assets = Liabilities + Equity: +2,120, +6,360 = +480 + +8,000
Cash: 2,120 (Dr) | 300 (Cr); Accounts Rec: 6,360 (Dr); Sales: 8,000 (Cr); Sales Tax Payable: 480 (Cr)

June 7, 2020—To record cost of goods sold

Cost of Goods Sold	4,000	
Inventory		4,000

Assets = Liabilities + Equity: −4,000 = −4,000
COGS: 4,000 (Dr); Inventory: 20,300 (Dr) | 4,000 (Cr)

c. **June 10, 2020—To record payment on account**

Accounts Payable	20,000	
Inventory ($20,000 × 0.02)		400
Cash ($20,000 × 0.98)		19,600

Assets = Liabilities + Equity: −400, −19,600 = −20,000
Accounts Payable: 20,000 (Dr) | 20,000 (Cr); Inventory: 20,300 (Dr) | 4,000, 400 (Cr); Cash: 2,120 (Dr) | 300, 19,600 (Cr)

Assets = Liabilities + Equity
+1,325 +300 +5,000
+3,975
Cash: 1,325 | 300; Accounts Rec: 3,975 |
Sales: | 5,000; Sales Tax Payable: | 300

d. **June 7, 2020—To record sales and sales taxes payable**

Cash ($5,300 × 0.25)	1,325	
Accounts Receivable ($5,300 × 0.75)	3,975	
Sales ($5,300/1.06)		5,000
Sales Taxes Payable ($5,300 − $5,000)		300

Assets = Liabilities + Equity
−3,000 −3,000
COGS: 3,000 |; Inventory: 20,300 | 3,000

June 7, 2020—To record cost of goods sold

Cost of Goods Sold	3,000	
Inventory		3,000

Review 15-2

Assets = Liabilities + Equity
+5,000 +5,000

a. **January 2020—To record gift card sales**

Cash	5,000	
Deferred Gift Card Revenue		5,000

Assets = Liabilities + Equity
−2,000 +2,000

b. **January 2020—To record gift card redemption**

Deferred Gift Card Revenue	2,000	
Sales		2,000

Assets = Liabilities + Equity
−83 +83
Cash: 5,000 |; Deferred GC Rev: 2,000 | 5,000; 83 |
Sales: | 2,000; GC Break Rev: | 83

c. **January 31, 2020—To record revenue on gift card breakage**

Deferred Gift Card Revenue	83	
Gift Card Breakage Revenue ($2,000/$4,800 × $200)		83

Assets = Liabilities + Equity
+1,000 +1,000
Cash: 1,000 |; Deposit: | 1,000

d. **January 2020—To record deposits collected**

Cash	1,000	
Liability—Returnable Deposit		1,000

Review 15-3

Assets = Liabilities + Equity
+80,000 −80,000
Salaries Exp: 80,000 |; Payables: | 80,000

a. **June 30, 2020—To record payroll withholdings**

Salaries Expense	80,000	
Withholding Taxes Payable		24,000
FICA Taxes Payable		6,120
HSA Payable		1,000
Salaries Payable (to balance)		48,880

Assets = Liabilities + Equity
+10,920 −10,920
Payroll Tax Exp: 10,920 |; Payroll Tax Pay: | 10,920

June 30, 2020—To record payroll tax expense

Payroll Tax Expense (to balance)	10,920	
FICA Taxes Payable		6,120
FUTA Taxes Payable		480
SUTA Taxes Payable		4,320

Assets = Liabilities + Equity
+55,000 −55,000
Salaries Exp: 55,000 |; Accrued Comp: | 55,000

b. **June 30, 2020—To record compensated absences accrual**

Salaries Expense	55,000	
Accrued Compensation		55,000

c. No accrual required because payment is not probable.

Assets = Liabilities + Equity
+1,600 −1,600
Salaries Exp: 1,600 |; Salaries Payable: | 1,600

d. **June 30, 2020—To record bonus accrual**

Salaries Expense [($580,000 − $500,000) × 0.02]	1,600	
Salaries Payable		1,600

Review 15-4

Example One

a. **March 1, 2020—To record issuance of note payable**

Cash	50,000	
Note Payable		50,000

Assets	=	Liabilities	+	Equity
+50,000		+50,000		

June 30, 2020—To record interest accrual

Interest Expense	1,167	
Interest Payable ($50,000 × 0.07 × 4/12)		1,167

Assets	=	Liabilities	+	Equity
		+1,167		−1,167

September 1, 2020—To record note maturity

Note Payable	50,000	
Interest Payable	1,167	
Interest Expense ($50,000 × 0.07 × 2/12)	583	
Cash [$50,000 + ($50,000 × 0.07/2)]		51,750

Assets	=	Liabilities	+	Equity
−51,750		−50,000 −1,167		−583

Cash		Interest Payable	
50,000	51,750	1,167	1,167

Note Payable		Interest Exp	
50,000	50,000	1,167 583	

b. **March 1, 2020—To record issuance of note payable**

Cash (present value of note)	48,285	
Discount on Note Payable ($50,000 − $48,285)	1,715	
Note Payable (face value of note)		50,000

Assets	=	Liabilities	+	Equity
+48,285		−1,715 +50,000		

June 30, 2020—To record interest accrual

Interest Expense	1,143	
Discount on Note Payable ($1,715 × 4/6)		1,143

Assets	=	Liabilities	+	Equity
		+1,143		−1,143

September 1, 2020—To record note maturity

Note Payable	50,000	
Interest Expense	572	
Discount on Note Payable ($1,715 × 2/6)		572
Cash		50,000

Assets	=	Liabilities	+	Equity
−50,000		+572 −50,000		−572

Cash		Note Payable	
48,285	50,000	50,000	50,000

Interest Exp		Discount on NP	
1,143 572		1,715	1,143 572

Example Two

1. $500,000 current
2. $100,000 noncurrent
3. $500,000 noncurrent
4. $20,000 current and $480,000 noncurrent*

*The note is due June 15, 2021, and normally the entire amount would be classified as current. However, Blues demonstrated its ability to refinance by entering into a financing agreement before the financial statements are issued. Blues expects to be able to refinance at least $480,000 (0.80 × $600,000) of the note. Therefore, that amount can be classified as long-term while the remaining $20,000 ($500,000 − $480,000) must be classified as short-term on December 31, 2020.

Review 15-5

a. Expense: $50,000

b. $0

c. Revenue: $1,000,000, Expense: $10,000

d. Revenue: $2,007,500, Expense: $8,000

e. $0

f. $0

Review 15-6

2017 Current Ratio: 1.25; Quick Ratio: 0.84
2016 Current Ratio: 1.05; Quick Ratio: 0.67

16 Long-Term Liabilities

Ford Motor Company

Note 13: Debt and Commitments

On January 22, 2014, we terminated the conversion rights of holders under the 4.25% Senior Convertible Notes due December 15, 2036 ("2036 Convertible Notes") in accordance with their terms and settled conversions occurring after notice of termination with cash. In 2014, $24 million of the 2036 Convertible Notes were converted by the holders, resulting in cash payments of $43 million and a $5 million loss recorded in Automotive interest income and other income/(loss), net.

Nike, Inc.

Note 8: Long-Term Debt

The bonds are redeemable at the Company's option prior to February 1, 2023 and November 1, 2042, respectively, at a price equal to the greater of (i) 100% of the aggregate principal amount of the notes to be redeemed or (ii) the sum of the present values of the remaining scheduled payments, plus in each case, accrued and unpaid interest. Subsequent to February 1, 2023 and November 1, 2042, respectively, the bonds also feature a par call provision, which allows for the bonds to be redeemed at a price equal to 100% of the aggregate principal amount of the notes being redeemed, plus accrued and unpaid interest.

PepsiCo, Inc.

Note 9: Debt Obligations and Commitments (excerpt)

The following table summarizes the Company's debt obligations:

	2016[a]	2015[b]
Short-term debt obligations[b]		
Current maturities of long-term debt	$ 4,401	$ 3,109
Commercial paper (0.6% and 0.3%)	2,257	770
Other borrowing (4.4% and 10.0%)	234	192
	$ 6,892	$ 4,071
Long-term debt obligations[b]		
Notes due 2016 (2.6%)	$ —	$ 3,087
Notes due 2017 (1.4% and 1.2%)	4,398	4,392
Notes due 2018 (2.3% and 3.6%)	2,561	4,122
Notes due 2019 (1.7% and 3.7%)	2,837	1,627
Notes due 2020 (2.6% and 2.4%)	3,816	3,830
Notes due 2021 (2.4% and 3.0%)	2,249	1,290
Notes due 2022–2046 (3.7% and 3.9%)	18,558	13,938
Notes due 2017–2026 (1.4% and 4.3%)	35	36
	34,454	32,322
Less: current maturities of long-term debt obligations	(4,401)	(3,109)
Total	$30,053	$29,213

[a] Amounts are shown net of unamortized net discounts of $142 million and $162 million for 2016 and 2015, respectively.

[b] The interest rates presented reflect weighted-average rates at year-end. Certain of our fixed rate indebtedness have been swapped to floating rates through the use of interest rate derivative instruments. See Note 9 for additional information regarding our interest rate derivative instruments.

Home Depot, Inc.

Note 4: Debt

In June 2014, the Company issued $1.0 billion of 2.00% senior notes due June 15, 2019 (the "2019 notes") at a discount of $4 million and $1.0 billion of 4.40% senior notes due March 15, 2045 (the "2045 notes") at a discount of $15 million (together, the "June 2014 issuance"). Interest on the 2019 notes is due semi-annually on June 15 and December 15 of each year, beginning December 15, 2014. Interest on the 2045 notes is due semi-annually on March 15 and September 15 of each year, beginning September 15, 2014. The net proceeds of the June 2014 issuance were used for general corporate purposes, including repurchases of shares of the Company's common stock. The $19 million discount associated with the June 2014 issuance is being amortized over the term of the notes using the effective rate method. Issuance costs associated with the June 2014 issuance were approximately $14 million and are being amortized over the term of the notes.

Chapter Preview

This chapter focuses on the accounting treatment for the initial recognition and subsequent measurement of long-term debt. We first explore the types and features of bonds. We examine the accounting for bonds at issuance and throughout the bond term from the *debtor's* perspective. (In Chapter 14, we accounted for debt investments from the *investor's* perspective.) We then explain the accounting for notes payable as an alternative form of debt financing. We examine the initial recording of a note payable and subsequent measurement through maturity, again from the debtor's perspective. Additional topics include the retirement of debt through cash, refunding, or conversion into equity securities. We also discuss debt issued with stock warrants, the fair value election, and leverage ratios.

Action Plan

LO	Topic/Subtopic	Page	Demos	Reviews	Assignments
LO 16–1	**Identify types and features of bonds** Corporate :: Secured :: Debenture :: Callable :: Redeemable :: Convertible :: Face Value :: Maturity Date :: Stated Rate :: Market Rate	16-3	D16-1A D16-1B	R16-1	25, 26, 48, 49, 50, 83, 100, 104, 118
LO 16–2	**Measure and record bonds at issuance** Face Value :: Discount :: Premium :: Accrued interest	16-6	D16-2	R16-2	27, 28, 29, 30, 48, 50, 51, 52, 53, 66, 83, 84, 85, 86, 87, 88, 89, 90, 91, 95, 100, 103, 104, 110, 118
LO 16–3	**Account for bonds issued at face value** Face Value :: Stated Interest :: Bonds Payable	16-10	D16-3	R16-3	31, 48, 52, 53, 100, 104, 118
LO 16–4	**Account for bonds issued at a discount** Effective interest method :: Straight-Line Interest Method :: Discount Amortization :: Debt Issuance Costs	16-11	D16-4A D16-4B D16-4C	R16-4	32, 34, 36, 37, 48, 54, 55, 56, 57, 58, 59, 62, 64, 66, 82, 84, 85, 86, 89, 90, 91, 95, 100, 101, 104, 106, 110, 111, 113, 118
LO 16–5	**Account for bonds issued at a premium** Effective interest method :: Straight-Line Interest Method :: Premium Amortization	16-17	D16-5A D16-5B	R16-5	33, 35, 48, 60, 61, 63, 65, 66, 87, 88, 100, 104, 112, 118
LO 16–6	**Measure and record notes at issuance and after issuance** Note Payable :: Interest-Bearing :: Zero-Interest-Bearing :: Non-Cash Consideration	16-21	D16-6A D16-6B	R16-6	38, 39, 40, 41, 42, 48, 67, 68, 69, 70, 96, 97, 98, 100, 114, 115
LO 16–7	**Account for extinguishment of debt** Debt Extinguishment :: Derecognition :: Early Redemption :: Bond Refunding	16-29	D16-7	R16-7	43, 48, 71, 72, 73, 84, 87, 88, 89, 91, 95, 100, 103, 119
LO 16–8	**Account for conversion of debt into equity** Convertible Bonds :: Straight-Debt Issuance :: Book Value Method :: Induced Conversion	16-32	D16-8	R16-8	44, 48, 74, 75, 92, 93, 95, 100, 102, 105, 108, 116
LO 16–9	**Account for bonds with stock warrants** Nondetachable Warrants :: Detachable Warrants :: Incremental Method :: Proportional Method	16-34	D16-9	R16-9	45, 48, 76, 77, 94, 100, 105, 119
LO 16–10	**Apply the fair value option for liabilities** Fair Value Option :: General Risk :: Net Income Adjustment :: Instrument Risk :: OCI Adjustment	16-37	D16-10	R16-10	46, 78, 79, 80, 99
LO 16–11	**Describe financing disclosures and analyses using leverage ratios** Disclosure :: Total Liabilities-to-Equity :: Total Liabilities-to-Total Assets :: Times Interest Earned	16-40	D16-11A D16-11B	R16-11	47, 81, 100, 107, 109, 119, 120
LO 16–12	**APPENDIX 16A—Account for debt settlement and debt restructuring** Debt Settlement :: Transfer of Assets :: Transfer of Equity :: Restructuring :: Debtor :: Creditor	16-43	D16-12A D16-12B	R16-12	117, 124, 125, 126, 127, 128, 129, 130, 131

LO 16-1 Identify types and features of bonds

LO 16-1 Overview

Types and Features of Bonds

- **Bond types include:**
  - Corporate, municipal
  - Secured, debenture
  - Callable
  - Convertible
- **Bond features include:**
  - Face value
  - Maturity date
  - Stated rate
  - Market rate

A **long-term liability** is an obligation that *does not meet the definition of a current liability*. The term **current liabilities** is used principally to designate obligations whose liquidation is reasonably expected to require the use of existing resources properly classifiable as current assets, or the creation of other current liabilities. Long-term liabilities extend beyond one year from the current balance sheet date or the operating cycle of the debtor (borrower), whichever is longer. In this chapter we focus on debt instruments. However, other types of long-term debt are addressed in later chapters: lease liability (Chapter 17), net deferred tax liability (Chapter 18), and net pension liability (Chapter 19).

Debt instruments provide legally enforceable interest payments, return of principal, and a prior claim to assets upon corporate liquidation. Debt capital is an attractive means of financing for the debtor. Creditors do not acquire voting privileges in the debtor company, and debt issuance causes no ownership dilution. Debt capital is obtained more easily than equity capital for many new and risky companies. Interest expense, unlike dividends, is tax-deductible. Furthermore, a company that earns a return on borrowed funds that exceeds the rate it must pay in interest is using debt to its advantage and is said to be successfully leveraged.

A **bond** is a debt security issued by companies and governmental units to secure large amounts of capital on a long-term basis. A bond represents a formal promise by the issuing company to pay principal and interest in return for the capital invested. Bonds are normally issued in small denominations, such as $1,000, $5,000, or $10,000. The small denominations increase the affordability of the bonds and increase the participation level of creditors. Unlike a note that is issued to one lender such as a financial institution, bonds are issued to multiple lenders (sometimes with the aid of an investment firm that acts as a selling agent or as an underwriter for the entire issue for a specified sum). The length of the bond term reflects the issuer's long-term cash needs, the purpose for which the funds will be used, and the issuer's expected ability to pay principal and interest.

Exhibit 16-1 illustrates the cash flows in a typical bond issue over the bond term. This chapter accounts for bonds from the perspective of the company issuing the bonds (debtor) to obtain capital.

EXHIBIT 16-1
Cash Flows of a Typical Bond

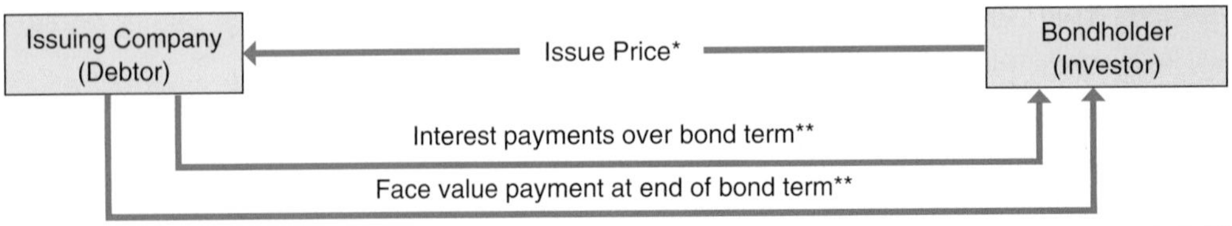

* Determined by general market and economic conditions, risk conditions, and supply and demand of the debt issuance.
** Determined by the bond indenture.

A formal bond agreement, or **bond indenture**, specifies the terms of the bonds and the rights and duties of the issuer and the bondholder. The indenture specifies **debt covenants** (restrictions on the issuing company to protect the interests of the bondholder), the dollar amount authorized for issuance, the interest rate and payment dates, the maturity date, and conversion and call privileges. Examples of debt covenants include compensating cash balances (or restricted deposits) and minimum ratio levels. Investors often receive **bond certificates**, which represent the contractual obligations of the issuer to the investors. Potential investors respond to the fixed terms of the bond indenture through the price they are willing to pay for the bonds. Depending on how favorably the market perceives the value of the bond features established in the bond indenture, *the issue price will adjust up or down from the face value at the time of issuance,* discussed more fully in LO 16-2.

Bond Types

Investors have a wide variety of investment goals, preferences, and policies. As a result, many different types of bonds are issued, some of which are described below and reviewed in **Demo 16-1A**.

Bond Type	Description
Corporate	Issued by private and public corporations.
Municipal	Issued by governmental entities.
Secured	Supported by a lien on specific assets where bondholders have first claim on the secured assets.
Debenture	Backed only by issuer's credit where bondholders are general creditors.
Term	Mature (pays principal) on a single, specified date.
Serial	Mature (pays principal) on several installment dates.
Callable (Redeemable)	Subject to early redemption at the option of the issuer.
Convertible	Convertible to equity securities at the option of the bondholders.

NIKE

Real World—BOND TYPE

NIKE [NKE]

Nike included a description of its redeemable corporate bonds in a recent annual report.

Long-Term Debt (excerpt) The bonds are redeemable at the Company's option prior to February 1, 2023 and November 1, 2042, respectively, at a price equal to the greater of (i) 100% of the aggregate principal amount of the notes to be redeemed or (ii) the sum of the present values of the remaining scheduled payments, plus in each case, accrued and unpaid interest. Subsequent to February 1, 2023 and November 1, 2042, respectively, the bonds also feature a par call provision, which allows for the bonds to be redeemed at a price equal to 100% of the aggregate principal amount of the notes being redeemed, plus accrued and unpaid interest.

Bond Types **LO16-1** **Demo 16-1A**

Demo MBC

For each separate bond example 1 through 4, identify the specific bond type(s) that apply.

		Bond Type
1.	Pier10 Inc. issued bonds to help finance store expansions.	**Corporate**
2.	Because of the exceptional creditworthiness of Gold Star Inc., the company did not allow bondholders to place liens on specific assets.	**Corporate debenture**
3.	Atwood Inc. issued bonds with an option for bondholders to convert the bonds to Atwood common stock any time after two years from the date of issuance at a conversion rate of 1 share for each $1,000 bond.	**Corporate convertible**
4.	The state of Ohio issued bonds with an option for the state to retire the bonds any time after two years from the date of issuance at a price of 103 (or 103% of the face value of the bonds).	**Municipal callable**

Bond Features

Several bond features affect the accounting for bonds. To illustrate, on January 1, 2020, Randolph Company issues $10,000 of 5% bonds dated January 1, 2020. Each of the 10 bonds has a $1,000 face value. The bonds mature December 31, 2024, and pay interest on June 30 and December 31. Five features of the Randolph Company bonds included in the bond indenture that *do not change over time* are outlined below.

Bond Feature	Description	Randolph Bonds
Face value (also called maturity value, principal amount, or par value)	Amount due at bond's maturity date.	**$10,000**
Maturity date	End of the bond term and the due date for the repayment of the face value.	**December 31, 2024**
Stated rate (also called coupon, nominal, or contractual rate)	Interest rate used to determine the cash interest payments which can be 0% if no cash payments are required. Stated as an annual rate.	**5% annual rate or 2.5% semiannual interest rate (5% ÷ 2)**
Interest payment dates	Dates the cash interest payments are due, typically on an annual or semiannual basis.	**June 30 and December 31**
Bond authorization rate	Earliest date the bonds can be issued and represents the planned date of the issuance.	**January 1, 2020**

The Randolph Company bonds are issued on January 1, 2020, for $9,573 when the market rate of interest is 6%. Features of this bond issue outlined below depend on market factors, and thus are *not* specified in the bond indenture and are *subject to change over time*. In **Demo 16-1B**, we identify the features of two bond issues.

Bond Feature	Definition	Randolph Bonds
Market rate (also called the effective rate, or yield)	Interest rate on a similar investment in the market involving similar risk and where the issuer has a similar credit rating. Stated as an annual rate.	**6% annual rate or 3% semiannual interest rate (6% ÷2)**
Bond selling price	Price of the bonds paid by the investor on the bond issue date which is not necessarily the same as the face value.	**$9,573**
Bond issue date	Date the bonds are sold to investors. Bonds can be issued after the bond authorization date to allow for additional time for processing or anticipated changes in market interest rates.	**January 1, 2020**

Demo 16-1B LO16-1 Bond Features

Demo MBC

Two separate bond scenarios are described below. Indicate the key features of the bonds in the table that follows.

1. **Annual interest-bearing bonds payable:** Goal Inc. authorizes and issues 5-year, $5,000 bonds on January 1, 2020, at 97 (or 97% of face value), bearing interest at 5%, payable annually on January 1.
2. **Semiannual interest-bearing bonds payable:** Goal Inc. authorizes and issues 5-year, $5,000 bonds on January 1, 2020, at 105 (or 105% of face value), bearing interest at 5%, payable semiannually on July 1 and January 1.

Solution

Bond Features	Annual Interest-Bearing Bonds	Semiannual Interest-Bearing Bonds
Face value	**$5,000**	**$5,000**
Maturity date	**January 1, 2025**	**January 1, 2025**
Stated rate per payment period	**5% (annual)**	**2.5% (semiannual)**
Interest payment date(s)	**January 1**	**July 1, January 1**
Bond authorization date	**January 1, 2020**	**January 1, 2020**
Bond selling price*	**$4,850 (0.97 × $5,000)**	**$5,250 (1.05 × $5,000)**
Bond issue date	**January 1, 2020**	**January 1, 2020**

* The market rate of interest implied for each bond sale is an annual rate of 5.71% [RATE(5,−250,4850,−5000)] for the annual interest-bearing bonds and a semiannual rate of 1.95% [RATE(10,−125,5250,−5000)] for the semiannual interest-bearing bonds.

Bond Types and Features **LO16-1** **REVIEW 16-1**

On January 1, 2020, the following bonds were authorized and issued by 5M Company, a manufacturer: $150,000, 10-year, 5% convertible bonds, interest payable semiannually on July 1 and January 1. The bonds sell for $138,842, yielding a market rate of 6%. For this bond issuance, indicate the following:

a. Bond type(s).
b. Face value.
c. Maturity date.
d. Stated rate per interest period.
e. Interest payment dates.
f. Authorization date.
g. Market rate per interest period.
h. Bond selling price.
i. Bond issue date.

Review MBC

More Practice: 16-25, 16-26, 16-49, 16-50

Solution on p. 16-72.

Measure and record bonds at issuance

LO 16-2

The issue price of bonds depends on the relation between the market and stated rates. *The two rates are frequently different at issuance.* The **stated rate** is determined at the time that the bond indenture is created and does not change over time. The **market rate** varies, depending on several interrelated factors, including the general rate of interest in the economy, the perceived risk of the bond issue, yields on bonds of similar risk, inflation expectations, the overall supply of and demand for bonds, and the bond term. Because these two rates can differ from each other, a bond can be sold above its face value (at a premium) or below its face value (at a discount).

Bond Issuance
- **Bonds issued at face value**
  Market rate = Stated rate
- **Bonds issued at a discount**
  Market rate > Stated rate
- **Bonds issued at a premium**
  Market rate < Stated rate
- **Bonds issued between interest dates**

LO 16-2 Overview

Bond Feature	Definition
Discount on bonds payable	Contra liability account equal to the excess of the face value of a bond over its present value. A discount decreases the carrying value of bonds payable. Discounts represent deferred interest expense that will be recognized over the term of the bond. On the balance sheet, discount on bonds payable is recognized as a deduction from the face value of bonds payable.
Premium on bonds payable	Adjunct liability account equal to the excess of the present value of a bond over its face value. A premium increases the carrying value of a bond. Premiums represent a reduction of interest expense that will be recognized over the term of the bond. On the balance sheet, premium on bonds payable is recognized as an addition to the face value of bonds payable.

Bond Selling Price at Issuance

The **selling price of a bond** is equal to the total of the following two components:

- Present value of the face value (principal) of the bond discounted at the market rate.
- Present value of the cash interest payments (determined by the stated rate) discounted at the market rate.

Because the market rate fluctuates, the following three scenarios for the issuance of bonds are possible.

1. **Present value = Face value** If the present value of the bond's face value and cash interest payments do not differ materially from the bond's face value, the bond is recognized at face value. In this case, the cash interest payments at the stated rate yield a return similar to the market rate for bonds of similar terms and risk. Thus, **when the market rate is equal to the stated rate of the bond, the bond will sell at face value.**

Bonds Sold at Par		
Stated rate	=	Market rate
Bond price	=	Face value

2. **Present value < Face value** If the present value of the bond's face value and cash interest payments is less than the bond's face value, a **Discount on Bonds Payable** is recognized for the difference. In this case, the issue price must be below face value to yield the investor a return equal to the market rate.

Bonds Sold at Discount		
Stated rate	<	Market rate
Bond price	<	Face value

In the previous section, the Randolph bonds sold at a discount because the market rate (6%) exceeded the stated rate (5%). Investors were unwilling to pay $10,000 for the bonds (a price that yields 5%) because competing debt securities of the same grade yield 6%. Instead, the investors paid $9,573 for the bonds. In sum, **when the market rate is greater than the stated rate of the bonds, the bonds will sell at a discount.**

Why would the market rate exceed the stated rate of 5%? The process for issuing bonds requires time for required registrations, negotiations with underwriters, accounting and legal services, and other activities. Although the company can make a solid estimate of the interest rate of 5% for the bond agreement, market conditions can change during the time required for the bond issuance process. If the market rate rises above the stated rate, investors would be unwilling to purchase the bonds for a 5% return and would demand a higher return. This demand for a higher return could be linked to general market factors or company-specific factors such as changes in income, financial position, and risk. When companies release a disappointing earnings announcement for example, the price of their bonds can decline due to a perception of increased risk.

Bonds Sold at Premium		
Stated rate	>	Market rate
Bond price	>	Face value

3. **Present value > Face value** If the present value of the bond's face value and cash interest payments is greater than the bond's face value, a **Premium on Bonds Payable** is recognized for the difference. Investors pay a price above face value because the stated rate exceeds the interest rate demanded by the market for similar grade bonds.

   For example, if the Randolph bonds in the previous section were sold at a market rate of 4%, an investor must pay more than $10,000 for the bonds. Randolph Company would be unwilling to sell the bonds for the face value of $10,000 when the market rate for debt securities of similar risk (4%) is less than the stated rate (5%) at which the bonds will pay interest to the investor. Pricing the bonds to yield the market rate of 4% results in a selling price that exceeds $10,000. In sum, **when the market or effective rate is less than the stated rate of the bonds, the bonds will sell at a premium.**

   Why would the market rate be below the stated rate of 5%? If the market rate drops below the stated rate, the investors are now willing to accept a return on this investment of less than 5% based upon interest rates of investments of similar risks. This acceptance of a lower market return could be linked to general market factors such as improving economic conditions or company-specific factors such as an upgrade on a bond rating based upon an independent bond-rating agency.

Accrued Interest at Bond Issuance

Bond prices exclude accrued interest, but the *proceeds* on bonds sold between interest payment dates include accrued interest at the stated rate since the last interest date. This means if a bond is not sold on an interest payment date, the **investor will pay the issuer the interest accrued from the most recent payment date to the bond issuance date.** At the next interest payment date, the investor will receive the *full cash interest payment*, even though they are only entitled to a portion of interest. The cash advanced by the investor at the bond issuance offsets the total amount of cash interest later received by the investor, resulting in a correct net amount of cash interest paid to the investor. This system facilitates the trading of bonds and ensures that each bondholder ultimately receives interest for the period the bond is held. In **Demo 16-2** we record entries for bonds issued at face value, at a discount, at a premium, and between interest payment dates.

Demo 16-2 **LO16-2** **Determining Selling Price of Bonds at Issuance**

Demo MBC

On January 1, 2020, Randolph Company authorizes and issues $10,000, 5% interest-bearing bonds. Each bond has a $1,000 face value. The bonds mature December 31, 2024, and pay interest semiannually on June 30 and December 31. Compute the selling price of the bonds and record the entry on January 1, 2020, for the following four *separate* scenarios.

a. Market rate for the Randolph Company bonds is 5%.
b. Market rate for the Randolph Company bonds is 6%.
c. Market rate for the Randolph Company bonds is 4%.
d. Market rate for the Randolph Company bonds is 5%, but the bonds are issued on February 1, 2020, instead of January 1, 2020.

continued

continued from previous page

Solution Because the bonds pay interest semiannually, the interest rates and number of periods must be adjusted to reflect semiannual compounding periods.

a. **Sale of Bonds at Face Value [Stated Rate = 5% and Market Rate = 5%]**
When bonds are issued, the issuer records the maturity value of the bonds in Bonds Payable, a long-term liability account. The selling price of the $10,000 of bonds is measured by taking the present value of the semiannual cash interest payments and the present value of the bond's maturity value, discounted at the semiannual market rate of 5%.

- Semiannual market rate: 5% ÷ 2 = 2.5%
- Semiannual periods: 5 years × 2 = 10 periods
- Semiannual cash interest payment: 5% × $10,000 ÷ 2 = $250

	RATE	NPER	PMT	PV	FV	Excel Formula
Given	2.5%	10	(250)	?	(10,000)	*=PV(0.025,10,−250,−10000)*
Solution				$10,000		

The present value of the principal and cash interest payments on January 1, 2020, is $10,000 (same as the maturity value) because the stated and market rates are equal. The entry to record the bond issuance at face value on January 1, 2020, follows.

January 1, 2020—To record bonds sold at face value

Cash	10,000	
Bonds Payable		10,000

Assets	=	Liabilities	+	Equity
+10,000		+10,000		

Cash		Bonds Payable	
10,000			10,000

b. **Sale of Bonds at a Discount [Stated Rate = 5% and Market Rate = 6%]**
The selling price of the bonds of $9,573 is measured by taking the present value of the semiannual cash interest payments and the present value of the bond's maturity value, discounted at the semiannual market rate of 6%.

- Semiannual market rate: 6% ÷ 2 = 3%
- Semiannual periods: 5 years × 2 = 10 periods
- Semiannual cash interest payment: 5% × $10,000 ÷ 2 = $250

The present value of the bonds of $9,573 is depicted graphically as the sum of the present value of the two components of cash interest payments and maturity value as follows.

	RATE	NPER	PMT	PV	FV	Excel Formula
Given	3%	10	(250)	?	(10,000)	=PV(0.03,10,−250,−10000)
Solution				$9,573		

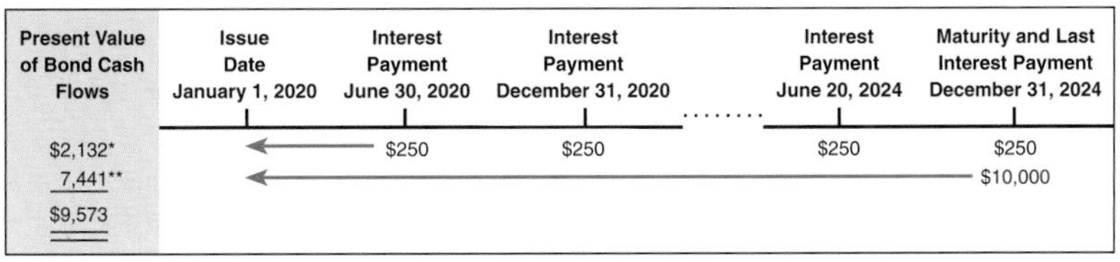

*

	RATE	NPER	PMT	PV	Excel Formula
Given	3%	10	(250)	?	=PV(0.03,10,−250)
Solution				$2,132 (rounded)	

**

	RATE	NPER	PV	FV	Excel Formula
Given	3%	10	?	(10,000)	=PV(0.03,10,0,−10000)
Solution			$7,441		

Upon the issuance of the bonds, Cash is recorded for the selling price of the bonds. Bonds Payable is recorded at the face value and represents the amount owed to the investors at the maturity of the bonds. The discount is recorded in the Discount on Bonds Payable account, which is the difference between the present value of the bonds and the face value of the bonds. The entry to record the bond issuance follows.

January 1, 2020—To record bonds sold at a discount

Cash	9,573	
Discount on Bonds Payable ($10,000 − $9,573)	427	
Bonds Payable		10,000

Assets	=	Liabilities	+	Equity
+9,573		−427 +10,000		

Cash		Bonds Payable	
9,573			10,000

Discount on BP	
427	

c. **Sale of Bonds at a Premium [Stated Rate = 5% and Market Rate = 4%]**
The selling price of the bonds of $10,449 is computed by discounting the semiannual cash interest payments and principal to the present value at the semiannual market rate of 2%.

- Semiannual market rate: 4% ÷ 2 = 2%
- Semiannual periods: 5 years × 2 = 10 periods
- Semiannual cash interest payment: 5% × $10,000 ÷ 2 = $250

	RATE	NPER	PMT	PV	FV	Excel Formula
Given	2%	10	(250)	?	(10,000)	=PV(0.02,10,−250,−10000)
Solution				$10,449		

Upon issuance of the bonds, Cash is recorded for the selling price of the bonds. Bonds Payable is recorded at the face value and represents the amount owed to the investors at the maturity of the bonds. The premium (difference between the present value of the bonds and the face value of the bonds) is recorded in the Premium on Bonds Payable account. The entry to record the bond issuance follows.

continued

continued from previous page

Assets = Liabilities + Equity
+10,449 +449
+10,000

Cash: 10,449 (Dr) | Bonds Payable: 10,000 (Cr) | Premium on BP: 449 (Cr)

January 1, 2020—To record bonds sold at a premium

Cash	10,449	
Premium on Bonds Payable ($10,449 − $10,000)		449
Bonds Payable		10,000

d. **Sale of Bonds at Face Value, Between Interest Payment Dates**

Investors who purchase the bonds on February 1 and hold the bonds five months to June 30 earn only five months of interest. Yet the investors will receive six months of interest on June 30. Therefore, Randolph Company will collect one month of interest from the investors on February 1, 2020 or $42 ($10,000 × 5% × 1/12), and subsequently pay the investors six months of interest on June 30, 2020.

The journal entry at the date of bond issuance follows.

Assets = Liabilities + Equity
+10,042 +10,000
+42

Cash: 10,042 (Dr) | Bonds Payable: 10,000 (Cr) | Interest Payable: 42 (Cr)

February 1, 2020—To record bonds sold at par between interest payment dates

Cash ($10,000 + $42)	10,042	
Bonds Payable		10,000
Interest Payable ($10,000 × 5% × 1/12)		42

Randolph Company will pay six months of interest on June 30, 2020, crediting Cash for $250 ($10,000 × 5% × 6/12). They will debit Interest Expense for five months of interest, or $208 ($10,000 × 2.5% × 5/12), and debit Interest Payable for the one month of interest collected when the bonds were sold on February 1.

STANDARD & POOR'S CORPORATION

Real World—STANDARD & POOR'S RATINGS

The market rate of a bond is influenced by risk perceived by the investors or potential investors of the bond holdings. Investors often rely on bond-rating agencies to assess the solvency of the companies issuing the bonds. An example of bond ratings provided by **Standard & Poor's Corporation** is included below.

Long-Term Issue Credit Ratings*

AAA	Highest rating. The obligor's capacity to meet its financial commitment on the obligation is extremely strong.
AA	The obligor's capacity to meet its financial commitment on the obligation is very strong.
A	More susceptible to the adverse effects of changes in circumstances and economic conditions than obligations in higher-rated categories, but obligor's capacity to meet its financial commitment on the obligation is still strong.
BBB	Exhibits adequate protection parameters. However, adverse economic conditions or changing circumstances are more likely to lead to a weakened capacity of the obligor to meet its financial commitment on the obligation.
BB	Less vulnerable to nonpayment than other speculative issues. However, it faces major ongoing uncertainties or exposure to adverse business, financial, or economic conditions, which could lead to the obligor's inadequate capacity to meet its financial commitment on the obligation.
B	More vulnerable to nonpayment than obligations rated 'BB,' but the obligor currently has the capacity to meet its financial commitment on the obligation. Adverse business, financial, or economic conditions will likely impair the obligor's capacity or willingness to meet its financial commitment on the obligation.
CCC	Currently vulnerable to nonpayment, and is dependent upon favorable business, financial, and economic conditions for the obligor to meet its financial commitment on the obligation. In the event of adverse business, financial, or economic conditions, the obligor is not likely to have the capacity to meet its financial commitment on the obligation.
CC	Highly vulnerable to nonpayment. Default has not yet occurred, but Standard & Poor's expects default to be a virtual certainty, regardless of the anticipated time to default.
C	Highly vulnerable to nonpayment, and the obligation is expected to have lower relative seniority or lower ultimate recovery compared to obligations that are rated higher.
D	In default or in breach of an imputed promise.

*Ratings from AA to CCC can be modified by the addition of a plus (+) or minus (−) sign to show relative standing within the major rating categories. Source: Adapted from Standard & Poor's Rating Definitions for Long-Term Issue Credit Ratings https://www.standardandpoors.com/en_US/web/guest/article/-/view/sourceId/504352

Pricing Bonds at Issuance — LO16-2 — REVIEW 16-2

Compute the selling price for each of the bond issuances outlined in the following separate scenarios. Round answers to two decimals.

a. 5M Corp. authorized and issued $150,000, 5%, 10-year bonds payable on January 1, 2020. Calculate the selling price of the bonds if the bonds pay cash interest semiannually on July 1 and January 1, and the market rate of interest on similar bonds is 7%.

b. 5M Corp. authorized and issued $50,000, 6%, 10-year bonds payable on January 1, 2020. Calculate the selling price of the bonds if the bonds pay cash interest semiannually on July 1 and January 1, and the market rate of interest on similar bonds is 5%.

c. 5M Corp. issued $50,000, 6%, 10-year bonds payable on April 30, 2020, at 97. The bonds were authorized on January 1, 2020. Calculate the selling price of the bonds (including interest) if the bonds pay cash interest semiannually on July 1 and January 1.

More Practice: 16-27, 16-28, 16-29, 16-30, 16-50, 16-51, 16-52

Solution on p. 16-72.

Account for bonds issued at face value — LO 16-3

If the present value and face value of issued bonds do not differ materially, the bonds are recognized at face value. This occurs when the interest rate and the market rate are equal. This means that investors consider the stated rate of the bonds as an acceptable measure of risk on the investment at the time of sale. Thus, interest expense for bonds issued at face value equals the stated interest amount as illustrated in **Demo 16-3**.

LO 16-3 Overview

Bonds Issued at Face value
- Stated rate = Market rate
- Proceeds = Face value
- Total interest expense = Total cash interest payments over bond term

Account for Bonds Issued at Face Value — LO16-3 — Demo 16-3

On January 1, 2020, Randolph Company authorizes and issues $10,000 of 5% interest-bearing bonds. The stated rate and market rate are equal (so the bonds were sold at face value). The bonds mature on December 31, 2024, and pay cash interest on June 30 and December 31.

a. Record the entry for the issuance of Randolph bonds on January 1, 2020.
b. Record the interest payment entry for Randolph Company on June 30, 2020.
c. Record the entry for Randolph Company upon maturity of the bonds on December 31, 2024. Ignore the final interest payment entry.

Solution

a. **Issuance of Bonds at Face Value**

The present value of the bonds on January 1, 2020, is $10,000 because the stated and market rates are equal. The carrying value of the bonds remains at $10,000 until the maturity of the bonds on December 31, 2024.

January 1, 2020—To record bonds sold at face value

Cash	10,000	
Bonds Payable		10,000

Assets = Liabilities + Equity
+10,000 = +10,000
Cash: 10,000 (debit) | Bonds Payable: 10,000 (credit)

b. **Interest Expense on Bonds**

On June 30, 2020, Randolph Company records the following journal entry for the first semiannual interest cash payment.

June 30, 2020—To record interest payment

Interest Expense	250	
Cash ($10,000× 2.5%)		250

Assets = Liabilities + Equity
−250 = −250
Cash: 250 (credit) | Interest Exp: 250 (debit)

Randolph Company records the *same entry* each semiannual period for five years, at which time the bonds would mature.

continued

continued from previous page

c. **Maturity of Bonds Payable**

Upon maturity, Randolph Company records the repayment of the face value of the bonds to the bondholders and derecognizes bonds payable.

Assets	=	Liabilities	+	Equity
−10,000		−10,000		

Cash: credit 10,000
Bonds Payable: debit 10,000 | credit 10,000

December 31, 2024—To derecognize bonds payable at maturity

Bonds Payable	10,000	
Cash		10,000

REVIEW 16-3 **LO16-3** **Account for Bonds Issued at Face Value**

Review MBC

5M Corp. authorized and issued $150,000, 5%, 10-year bonds on January 1, 2020, at face value. Cash interest is paid annually on December 31. Record the entries for (a) issuance of bonds on January 1, 2020, (b) the payment of interest on December 31, 2020, and (c) the payment of principal on December 31, 2029.

More Practice: 16-31, 16-52, 16-53

Solution on p. 16-72.

LO 16-4 Account for bonds issued at a discount

LO 16-4 Overview

Bonds Issued at a Discount
- Stated rate < Market rate
- Proceeds < Face value
- Total interest expense > Total cash interest payments over bond term
- Discount recognized as interest expense over the bond term
  - Effective interest method
  - Straight-line interest method

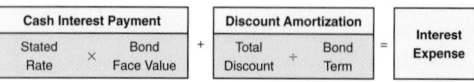

If the face value of bonds issued is greater than the proceeds of the issued bonds, a discount on bonds payable is recorded. When bonds are sold at a discount, the discount is initially recorded as a contra account to bonds payable. Over the term of the bonds, the discount is recognized as interest expense, resulting in total interest expense that is *greater* than total cash interest payments. The discount is amortized using the effective interest method.

Under the **effective interest method**, interest expense each period is determined by multiplying the market rate by the carrying value of the bonds at the *beginning* of the interest period. The difference between interest expense and the cash interest payment each period is the amount of discount amortized. As the discount is amortized over the term of the bonds, the carrying value of the bonds increases toward the face value. Interest expense *increases* each period because of the increasing carrying value of the bonds. See **Demo 16-4A**.

Effective interest method

Interest Expense (Market Rate × Bond Payable, Net (Beg. of Year)) − Cash Interest Payment (Stated Rate × Bond Face Value) = Discount Amortization

Although the effective interest method for amortizing discounts (and premiums) is the preferred method, there is an alternative method. The **straight-line interest method** can *only* be used, however, if the results are not materially different from the results using the preferred method.

835-30-55-2 Generally accepted accounting principles (GAAP) require use of the interest method. There is no basis for using an alternative to the interest method except if the results of alternative methods do not differ materially from those obtained by using the interest method. Therefore, methods other than the interest method, such as . . . straight-line interest methods shall not be used if their results materially differ from the interest method.

Straight-Line Interest Method

Cash Interest Payment (Stated Rate × Bond Face Value) + Discount Amortization (Total Discount ÷ Bond Term) = Interest Expense

Under the straight-line interest method, the discount is recognized as interest expense *evenly* over the bond term. Thus, this method produces a stable dollar amount of interest expense each period equal to the cash interest paid *plus* the straight-line discount amortized each interest period. The carrying value of the bonds is increased by the discount amortization each period until the carrying value of the bonds equals the face value, see **Demo 16-4B. Although interest expense per period varies depending upon the method followed, total interest expense over the life of the bonds is the same under both methods.**

Account for Bonds Issued at a Discount [Effective Interest Method] LO16-4 Demo 16-4A

Demo MBC

Randolph Company authorizes and issues $10,000 of 5% interest-bearing bonds on January 1, 2020. The bonds mature December 31, 2024, and pay cash interest on June 30 and December 31. The bonds were sold at a market rate of 6% and the company amortizes the bond discount using the effective interest method.

a. Prepare an amortization schedule over the term of the bonds.
b. Prepare the entry for the issuance of the bonds on January 1, 2020.
c. Prepare the journal entry for the semiannual interest payment and amortization of the bond discount on June 30, 2020, and December 31, 2020.
d. Show the December 31, 2020, balance sheet and the 2020 income statement impact from the bonds.
e. Assume that Randolph prepares financial statements for the month of January 2021. Record the entry for the accrual of bond interest and amortization of the discount on January 31, 2021.
f. Record the entry for Randolph Company upon maturity of the bonds, including the final interest payment, assuming no interest accrual since June 30, 2024.

Solution

a. **Amortization Schedule—Effective Interest Method [Stated Rate = 5% and Market Rate = 6%]**

Because the bonds pay interest semiannually, interest rates and periods must be adjusted to reflect semiannual compounding periods.

- Semiannual market rate: 6% ÷ 2 = 3%
- Semiannual periods: 5 years × 2 = 10 periods
- Semiannual cash interest payment: 5% × $10,000 ÷ 2 = $250

	RATE	NPER	PMT	PV	FV	Excel Formula
Given	3%	10	(250)	?	(10,000)	=PV(0.03,10,−250,−10000)
Solution				$9,573		

The following amortization schedule illustrates how interest expense is recognized over the term of the bonds using the effective interest method. The components of the journal entry for each period include Cash, Interest Expense, and Discount on Bonds Payable and are included in this schedule. The carrying value of the bond indicated for each period is always equal to the present value of the remaining cash flows discounted at the market rate in effect at the inception of the bond.

Let's review the calculations for June 30, 2020. As shown above, the semiannual cash interest payment is equal to $250. Interest expense of $287 is equal to the market rate of 3% multiplied by the bond carrying value at the beginning of the period of $9,573. The discount amortization of $37 is equal to interest expense of $287 less cash of $250. The carrying value of bonds payable increases to $9,610, or $9,573 plus $37. We see that over the bond term, stated interest is constant because it is contractual and is tied to the bond indenture. Interest expense each period increases because the basis of its measurement is an increasing bond carrying value. At the end of the bond term, the carrying value of the bonds equals the face value of $10,000 and the amortized discount in total equals the original discount of $427. We also see that total interest expense of $2,927 exceeds total cash interest of $2,500 over the term of the bonds when bonds are sold at a discount.

Effective Interest Method—Discount

Date	Cash (Stated Interest)[a]	Interest Expense (Market Interest)[b]	Discount on B.P. Amortization[c]	Bonds Payable, Net (Carrying Value)[d]
Jan. 1, 2020				$ 9,573
June 30, 2020	$ 250	$ 287	$ 37	9,610
Dec. 31, 2020	250	288	38	9,648
June 30, 2021	250	289	39	9,687
Dec. 31, 2021	250	291	41	9,728
June 30, 2022	250	292	42	9,770
Dec. 31, 2022	250	293	43	9,813
June 30, 2023	250	294	44	9,857
Dec. 31, 2023	250	296	46	9,903
June 30, 2024	250	297	47	9,950
Dec. 31, 2024	250	300*	50	10,000
Totals	$2,500	$2,927	$427	

*Rounded.
[a] Stated rate × Bond face value.
[b] Market rate × Bonds payable, net, beginning of period.
[c] Interest expense − Cash.
[d] Bonds payable, net, beginning of period + Discount amortization.

continued

continued from previous page

b. **Issuance of Bonds at a Discount**

January 1, 2020—To record bonds sold at a discount

Cash	9,573	
Discount on Bonds Payable ($10,000 − $9,573)	427	
Bonds Payable		10,000

Assets = Liabilities + Equity
+9,573 −427
+10,000

Cash: 9,573 (Dr)
Bonds Payable: 10,000 (Cr)
Discount on BP: 427 (Dr)

c. **Interest Expense and Discount Amortized on Bonds [Effective interest method]**
On June 30, 2020, Randolph Company records the following journal entry for the first semiannual cash interest payment, and amortization of the discount on bonds payable.

June 30, 2020—To record payment of interest and bond discount amortization

Interest Expense	287	
Discount on Bonds Payable		37
Cash		250

Assets = Liabilities + Equity
−250 +37 −287

Cash: 9,573 (Dr) | 250 (Cr)
Discount on BP: 427 (Dr) | 37 (Cr)
Interest Exp: 287 (Dr)

At June 30, 2020, Randolph Company carries the bonds at $9,610 ($9,573 + $37), which is the amortized cost of the bonds.

On December 31, 2020, Randolph Company records the following journal entry for the second semiannual cash interest payment, and amortization of the discount.

December 31, 2020—To record payment of interest and bond discount amortization

Interest Expense	288	
Discount on Bonds Payable		38
Cash		250

Assets = Liabilities + Equity
−250 +38 −288

Cash: 9,573 (Dr) | 250, 250 (Cr)
Discount on BP: 427 (Dr) | 37, 38 (Cr)
Interest Exp: 287, 288 (Dr)

Using the effective interest method, Randolph would continue to amortize the discount through the five years of the bond term by crediting the Discount on Bonds Payable account each period. Interest expense is computed each period based upon a constant percentage equal to the market rate. Upon maturity, Discount on Bonds Payable will be fully amortized.

d. **Financial Statement Presentation**
In the balance sheet on December 31, 2020, Randolph Corporation would record bonds payable of $10,000 net of the unamortized discount of $352 ($427 − $37 − $38). In the income statement for the 12 months ended December 31, 2020, Randolph Corporation would record 12 months of interest expense of $575 ($287 + $288).

Balance Sheet excerpt
December 31, 2020

Liabilities	
Bonds payable	$10,000
Less: Discount on bonds payable	352
Bonds payable, net	$ 9,648

Income Statement excerpt
For Year Ended December 31, 2020

Other expenses	
Interest expense	$575

e. **Accrual of Bond Interest**
In the previous example of Randolph Company, the interest payment dates were the same as the reporting dates of June 30 and December 31. On January 31, 2021, however, the financial reporting date does not match the cash interest payment date, so proration of interest is necessary. Randolph Company will record one month of interest, prorated from the six months of interest of $289 (see June 30, 2021, interest expense from the amortization schedule).

On January 31, 2021, Randolph Company records the following journal entry for accrual of interest and amortization of the discount.

January 31, 2021—To record accrual of bond interest expense

Interest Expense ($289 × 1/6)	48	
Discount on Bonds Payable ($39 × 1/6)		6
Interest Payable ($250 × 1/6)		42

Assets = Liabilities + Equity
+6 −48
+42

Interest Payable: 42 (Cr)
Discount on BP: 427 (Dr) | 37, 38, 6 (Cr)
Interest Exp: 287, 288, 48 (Dr)

continued

continued from previous page

f. **Derecognition of Bonds Payable**
Upon maturity, Randolph Company would record the final interest payment and the payment of the face value of the bonds to bondholders.

December 31, 2024—To record final interest payment

Interest Expense	300	
Discount on Bonds Payable		50
Cash		250

Assets = Liabilities + Equity
−250 +50 −300

December 31, 2024—To record retirement of bonds at maturity

Bonds Payable	10,000	
Cash		10,000

Assets = Liabilities + Equity
−10,000 −10,000

Cash: 250; 10,000 (credit)
Bonds Payable: 10,000 (debit) | 10,000 Bal. (credit)
Interest Exp: 300 (debit)
Discount on BP: Bal. 50 (debit) | 50 (credit)

EXPANDING YOUR KNOWLEDGE — **Correction of an Error**

Recall from earlier chapters that an accounting error occurs when a transaction or event is recorded incorrectly or is not recorded at all. A *material error* not discovered until after the release of the financial statements must be corrected through a **prior period adjustment and the results applied retrospectively in the presentation of the financial statements.** A prior period adjustment is an entry to correct an error through an adjustment of a balance sheet account and a retained earnings account. An example of an error relating to bonds payable would be an inaccurate (or missing) recording of an interest accrual at a reporting period or a failure to amortize a premium or discount on bonds payable. Also, the use of the straight-line interest method to amortize a discount or premium when the results are significantly different from using the effective interest method would be considered an accounting error.

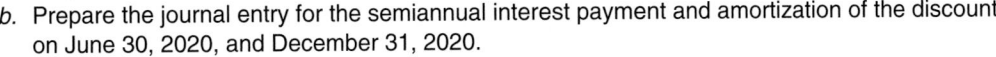

Account for Bonds Issued at a Discount [Straight-line Interest Method] LO16-4 **Demo 16-4B**

Demo MBC

Refer to the information in **Demo 16-4A** for Randolph Company. Now assume that the company amortizes the bond discount using the straight-line interest method.

a. Prepare an amortization schedule over the term of the bonds.
b. Prepare the journal entry for the semiannual interest payment and amortization of the discount on June 30, 2020, and December 31, 2020.
c. Record the entry for Randolph Company upon maturity of the bonds. Ignore the final interest payment.

Solution

a. **Amortization Schedule—Straight-Line Interest Method [Stated Rate = 5% and Market Rate = 6%]**
The following amortization schedule illustrates how interest expense is recognized over the term of the bonds under the straight-line interest method. The components of the journal entry for each period include Cash, Interest Expense, and Discount on Bonds Payable are included in this schedule.

Let's review the calculations for June 30, 2020. As shown above, the semiannual cash interest payment is equal to $250. The discount on bonds payable of $43 is equal to the total discount of $427 divided by 10 semiannual periods. Interest expense of $293 is equal to cash interest of $250 plus the amortized discount of $43. The carrying value of bonds payable increases to $9,616, or $9,573 plus $43. We see that over the bond term, stated interest is constant because it is contractual and is tied to the bond indenture. The amortized discount and interest expense are the same each period over the term of the bonds (except for a minor rounding difference). At the end of the bond term, the carrying value of the bonds equals the face value of $10,000 and the amortized discount in total equals the original discount of $427. We also see that total interest expense of $2,927 exceeds total cash interest of $2,500 over the term of the bonds when bonds are sold at a discount.

continued

continued from previous page

Straight-Line Interest Method—Discount

Date	Cash (Stated Interest)[a]	Interest Expense (Market Interest)[b]	Discount on B.P. Amortization[c]	Bonds Payable, Net (Carrying Value)[d]
Jan. 1, 2020. . .				$ 9,573
June 30, 2020. . .	$ 250	$ 293	$43	9,616
Dec. 31, 2020. . .	250	293	43	9,659
June 30, 2021. . .	250	293	43	9,702
Dec. 31, 2021. . .	250	293	43	9,745
June 30, 2022. . .	250	293	43	9,788
Dec. 31, 2022. . .	250	293	43	9,831
June 30, 2023. . .	250	293	43	9,874
Dec. 31, 2023. . .	250	293	43	9,917
June 30, 2024. . .	250	293	43	9,960
Dec. 31, 2024. . .	250	290	40*	10,000
	$2,500	$2,927	$427	

*Rounded.
[a] Stated rate × Bond face value.
[b] Stated interest + Discount amortization.
[c] Total bond discount / Number of periods.
[d] Bond amortized cost, beginning of year + Discount amortization.

b. **Interest Expense and Discount Amortized on Bonds [Straight-line interest method]**
On June 30, 2020, Randolph Company records the following journal entry for the first semiannual cash interest payment and amortization of the discount.

June 30, 2020—To record payment of interest and bond discount amortization

Interest Expense.	293	
Discount on Bonds Payable.		43
Cash		250

At June 30, 2020, Randolph Company carries the bonds at $9,616 ($9,573 + $43), which is the amortized cost of the bonds.

On December 31, 2020, Randolph Company records the following journal entry for the second semiannual cash interest payment and amortization of the discount.

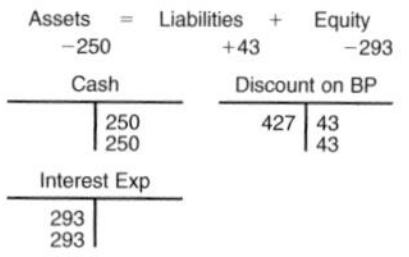

December 31, 2020—To record payment of interest and bond discount amortization

Interest Expense.	293	
Discount on Bonds Payable.		43
Cash		250

c. **Derecognition of Bonds Payable**
Under the straight-line interest method, Randolph would continue to amortize the discount through the five years of the bond term. Because interest expense is measured using the straight-line interest method, interest expense is constant over the term of the bond. Upon maturity, Discount on Bonds Payable will be fully amortized.

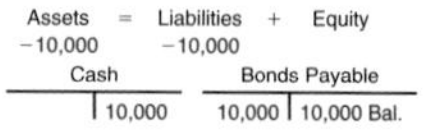

December 31, 2024—To record retirement of bonds at maturity

Bonds Payable	10,000	
Cash		10,000

Debt Issuance Costs

Debt issuance costs include legal, accounting, underwriting, commission, engraving, printing, registration, and promotion costs. These costs are paid by the issuer and reduce the net proceeds from the bond issue, thus raising the market rate for the issuer. By decreasing the cash received upon the sale of bonds, debt issuance costs increase the market rate on the transaction (meaning that borrowing costs go up).

Debt issuance costs are combined with the bond discount (subtracted from the premium) and recorded in a valuation account, Discount and Debt Issuance Costs (Premium and Debt Issuance Costs).

Amortization of debt issuance costs is recognized as interest expense over the term of the bonds. The new effective rate that equates the net bonds payable amount to the future cash flows must be calculated and applied to the amortization schedule in order to account for the bond.

835-30-45-1A Debt issuance costs related to a note shall be reported in the balance sheet as a direct deduction from the face amount of that note. The discount, premium, or debt issuance costs shall not be classified as a deferred charge or deferred credit.

835-30-45-3 Amortization of discount or premium shall be reported as interest expense in the case of liabilities or as interest income in the case of assets. Amortization of debt issuance costs also shall be reported as interest expense.

Account for Debt Issuance Costs — LO16-4 — Demo 16-4C

Refer to the information in **Demo 16-4A** for Randolph Company. Assume that the bonds were sold at a market rate of 6% and that the company amortizes the bond discount using the effective interest method. However, debt issuance costs are $500.

a. Record the entry upon issuance of the bonds, including the recording of debt issuance costs.
b. Prepare an amortization schedule over the term of the bonds.
c. Prepare the journal entry for the first semiannual interest payment and amortization of the discount and debt issuance costs on June 30, 2020.

Solution

a. **Issuance of Bonds at a Discount with Debt Issuance Costs**

Debt issuance costs are combined with the bond discount in the entry to record the issuance of the bonds. Cash is reduced by the debt issuance costs.

January 1, 2020—To record bonds sold at a discount

Cash ($9,573 − $500)	9,073	
Discount and Debt Issuance Costs ($10,000 − $9,073)	927	
Bonds Payable		10,000

Assets = Liabilities + Equity
+9,073 = −927 +10,000

Cash: 9,073 (debit)
Bonds Payable: 10,000 (credit)
Discount and Iss Cost: 927 (debit)

b. **Amortization Schedule—Effective Interest Method**

The carrying value of the bonds on January 1, 2020, is now $9,073. The market rate increases to 3.62%, as this is the rate that equates the present value of the bonds ($9,073) with the future value of the semiannual cash interest payments of $250 and the face value of $10,000.

	RATE	NPER	PMT	PV	FV	Excel Formula
Given	?	10	250	(9,073)	10,000	=RATE(10,250,−9073,10000)
Solution	3.62%					

Effective Interest Method—Discount and Debt Issuance Costs

Date	Cash (Stated Interest)[a]	Interest Expense (Market Interest)[b]	Discount on B.P. and Debt Issuance Costs Amortization[c]	Bonds Payable, Net (Carrying Value)[d]
Jan. 1, 2020				$ 9,073
June 30, 2020	$ 250	$ 328	$ 78	9,151
Dec. 31, 2020	250	331	81	9,232
June 30, 2021	250	334	84	9,316
Dec. 31, 2021	250	337	87	9,403
June 30, 2022	250	340	90	9,493
Dec. 31, 2022	250	344	94	9,587
June 30, 2023	250	347	97	9,684
Dec. 31, 2023	250	351	101	9,785
June 30, 2024	250	354	104	9,889
Dec. 31, 2024	250	361*	111	10,000
Totals	$2,500	$3,427	$927	

*Rounded.
[a] Stated rate × Bond face value.
[b] Market rate × Bond amortized cost, beginning of year.
[c] Stated interest − Market interest.
[d] Bond amortized cost, beginning of year + Discount amortization.

continued

continued from previous page

C. **Interest Expense and Discount Amortized on Bonds**

June 30, 2020—To record payment of interest and bond discount amortization

Interest Expense	328	
Discount and Debt Issuance Cost		78
Cash		250

Assets	=	Liabilities	+	Equity
−250		+78		−328

Cash: 9,073 | 250

Discount and Iss Cost: 927 | 78

Interest Exp: 328 |

HOME DEPOT [HD]

Real World—DISCOUNT ON NOTES PAYABLE

Home Depot, Inc. described the terms of its notes issued at a discount in a recent annual report. The disclosure includes the amount of the discount as well as the method used to amortize the discount. Discount on notes payable are accounted for in a similar way to discount on bonds payable.

> **Debt (excerpt)**—In June 2014, the Company issued $1.0 billion of 2.00% senior notes due June 15, 2019 (the "2019 notes") at a discount of $4 million and $1.0 billion of 4.40% senior notes due March 15, 2045 (the "2045 notes") at a discount of $15 million (together, the "June 2014 issuance"). Interest on the 2019 notes is due semi-annually on June 15 and December 15 of each year, beginning December 15, 2014. Interest on the 2045 notes is due semi-annually on March 15 and September 15 of each year, beginning September 15, 2014. The net proceeds of the June 2014 issuance were used for general corporate purposes, including repurchases of shares of the Company's common stock. The $19 million discount associated with the June 2014 issuance is being amortized over the term of the notes using the effective rate method. Issuance costs associated with the June 2014 issuance were approximately $14 million and are being amortized over the term of the notes.

REVIEW 16-4 LO16-4 Account for Bonds Issued at a Discount

Review MBC

More Practice: 16-32, 16-34, 16-36, 16-55, 16-56, 16-57, 16-58

Solution on p. 16-72.

5M Corp. authorized and issued $150,000, 5%, 10-year bonds on January 1, 2020. The bonds pay cash interest semiannually on July 1 and January 1, and are issued to yield 7%.

a. Record the entries for 5M Corp. on (1) January 1, 2020, for the issuance of the bonds, (2) July 1, 2020, for the payment of interest, and (3) December 31, 2020, for the accrual of interest, assuming that the company amortizes bond discount using the effective interest method.

b. Record the entries for 5M Corp. on (1) January 1, 2020, for the issuance of the bonds, (2) July 1, 2020, for the payment of interest, and (3) December 31, 2020, for the accrual of interest, assuming that the company amortizes bond discount using the straight-line interest method.

LO 16-5 Account for bonds issued at a premium

LO 16-5 Overview

Bonds Issued at a Premium
- Stated rate > Market rate
- Proceeds > Face value
- Total cash interest payments > Total interest expense over bond term
- Premium reduces interest expense over the bond term
  - Effective interest method
  - Straight-line interest method

If the proceeds of a bond issuance are greater than the face value of the issued bonds, a premium on bonds payable is recorded. When bonds are sold at a premium, the amount of premium is initially recorded as an adjunct account to bonds payable. Over the term of the bonds, the premium reduces interest expense, resulting in total interest expense that is *less than* total cash interest payments. The premium is amortized using the effective interest method.

Under the **effective interest method**, interest expense is equal to the market rate multiplied by the carrying value of the bonds at the *beginning* of the interest period. The difference between the cash interest payment and interest expense each period is the amount of premium amortized. As the premium is amortized over the term of the bonds, the carrying value of the bonds decreases toward the face value. Interest expense per period *declines* because the base for calculating interest expense each period (the carrying value of the bonds) declines as it is adjusted toward the face value of the bonds. See **Demo 16-5A**.

Effective interest method

Cash Interest Payment		Bond Interest Expense		
Stated Rate × Bond Face Value	−	Market Rate × Bond Payable, Net (Beg. of Year)	=	Premium Amortization

The **straight-line interest method** can be used if the results are not materially different from using the effective interest method. Under the straight-line interest method, the premium is amortized evenly over the bond term. Thus, this method produces a stable dollar amount of interest expense each period equal to the cash interest paid *less* the premium amortized each interest period. The carrying value of the bonds is decreased by the premium amortization each period until the carrying value of the bonds equals the face value, see **Demo 16-5B**.

Straight-Line Interest Method

Cash Interest Payment (Stated Rate × Bond Face Value) − Premium Amortization (Total Premium ÷ Bond Term) = Interest Expense

Account for Bonds Issued at a Premium [Effective interest method] LO16-5 Demo 16-5A

Demo MBC

Randolph Company authorizes and issues $10,000 of 5% interest-bearing bonds on January 1, 2020. The bonds mature December 31, 2024, and pay cash interest on June 30 and December 31. The bonds were sold at a market rate of 4% and the company amortizes the bond premium using the effective interest method.

a. Prepare an amortization schedule over the term of the bonds.
b. Prepare the entry for the issuance of the bonds on January 1, 2020.
c. Prepare the journal entry for the semiannual interest payment and amortization of the premium on June 30, 2020, and December 31, 2020.
d. Show the December 31, 2020, balance sheet and the 2020 income statement impact of the bonds.
e. Record the entry for Randolph Company upon maturity of the bonds, including the final interest payment.

Solution

a. **Amortization Schedule—Effective Interest Method [Stated Rate = 5% and Market Rate = 4%]**

Because the bonds pay interest semiannually, interest rates and periods must be adjusted to reflect semiannual compounding periods.

- Semiannual market rate: 4% ÷ 2 = 2%
- Semiannual periods: 5 years × 2 = 10 periods
- Semiannual cash interest payment: 5% × $10,000 ÷ 2 = $250

	RATE	NPER	PMT	PV	FV	Excel Formula
Given	2%	10	(250)	?	(10,000)	=PV(0.02,10,−250,−10000)
Solution				$10,449		

The following amortization schedule illustrates how interest expense is recognized over the term of the bonds using the effective interest method. The components of the journal entry for each period to record Cash, Interest Expense, and Premium on Bonds Payable are included in this schedule. We see that over the bond term, stated interest is constant because it is contractual and is tied to the bond indenture. Interest expense each period decreases because the basis of its measurement is a decreasing bond carrying value. The premium amortization is equal to the cash payment less interest expense. At the end of the bond term, the carrying value of the bonds equals the face value of $10,000 and the amortized premium in total equals the original premium of $449. We also see that total interest expense of $2,051 is less than total cash interest of $2,500 over the term of the bonds when bonds are sold at a premium.

Effective Interest Method—Premium

Date	Cash (Stated Interest)[a]	Interest Expense (Market Interest)[b]	Premium on B.P. Amortization[c]	Bonds Payable, Net (Carrying Value)[d]
Jan. 1, 2020.				$10,449
June 30, 2020.	$ 250	$ 209	$ 41	10,408
Dec. 31, 2020.	250	208	42	10,366
June 30, 2021.	250	207	43	10,323
Dec. 31, 2021.	250	206	44	10,279
June 30, 2022.	250	206	44	10,235
Dec. 31, 2022.	250	205	45	10,190
June 30, 2023.	250	204	46	10,144
Dec. 31, 2023.	250	203	47	10,097
June 30, 2024.	250	202	48	10,049
Dec. 31, 2024.	250	201	49	10,000
Totals	$2,500	$2,051	$449	

[a] Stated rate × Bond face value.
[b] Market rate × Bond amortized cost, beginning of year.
[c] Stated interest − Market interest.
[d] Bond amortized cost, beginning of year − Premium amortization.

continued

continued from previous page

b. Issuance of Bonds at a Premium

Assets = Liabilities + Equity
+10,449 = +449, +10,000

Cash: 10,449 (debit)
Bonds Payable: 10,000 (credit)
Premium on BP: 449 (credit)

January 1, 2020—To record bonds sold at a premium

Cash	10,449	
Premium on Bonds Payable ($10,449 – $10,000)		449
Bonds Payable		10,000

c. Interest Expense and Premium Amortized on Bonds [Effective interest method]

On June 30, 2020, Randolph Company records the following journal entry for the first semiannual cash interest payment and amortization of the premium.

Assets = Liabilities + Equity
−250 = −41 −209

Cash: 10,449 | 250
Premium on BP: 41 | 449
Interest Exp: 209 |

June 30, 2020—To record payment of interest and bond premium amortization

Interest Expense.	209	
Premium on Bonds Payable.	41	
Cash		250

At June 30, 2020, Randolph Company carries the bonds at $10,408 ($10,449 – $41), which is the carrying value of the bonds.

On December 31, 2020, Randolph Company records the following journal entry for the second semiannual cash interest payment and amortization of the premium.

Assets = Liabilities + Equity
−250 = −42 −208

Cash: 10,449 | 250, 250
Premium on BP: 41, 42 | 449
Interest Exp: 209, 208 |

December 31, 2020—To record payment of interest and bond premium amortization

Interest Expense.	208	
Premium on Bonds Payable.	42	
Cash		250

Under the effective interest method, Randolph would continue to amortize the premium through the five years of the bond term by debiting Premium on Bonds Payable each period. Upon maturity, Premium on Bonds Payable will be fully amortized, with a carrying value of zero.

d. Financial Statement Presentation

On the balance sheet on December 31, 2020, Randolph Corporation would record bonds payable of $10,000 plus the unamortized premium of $366 ($449 – $41 – $42). In the income statement for the 12 months ended December 31, 2020, Randolph Corporation would record 12 months of interest expense of $417 ($209 + 208).

Balance Sheet excerpt December 31, 2020	
Liabilities	
Bonds payable	$10,000
Plus: Premium on bonds payable.	366
Bonds payable, net.	$10,366

Income Statement excerpt For Year Ended December 31, 2020	
Other expenses	
Interest expense.	$417

e. Derecognition of Bonds Payable

Upon maturity, Randolph Company would record the final interest payment and the payment of the face value of the bonds to the investors.

Assets = Liabilities + Equity
−250 = −49 −201

December 31, 2024—To record final interest payment

Interest Expense.	201	
Premium on Bonds Payable.	49	
Cash		250

Assets = Liabilities + Equity
−10,000 = −10,000

Cash: | 250, 10,000
Bonds Payable: 10,000 | 10,000 Bal.
Interest Exp: 201 |
Premium on BP: 49 | 49 Bal.

December 31, 2024—To record retirement of bonds at maturity

Bonds Payable	10,000	
Cash		10,000

Account for Bonds Issued at a Premium [Straight-line Interest Method] LO16-5 Demo 16-5B

Refer to the information in **Demo 16-5A** for Randolph Company. Now assume that the company amortizes the bond premium using the straight-line interest method.

a. Prepare an amortization schedule over the term of the bonds.

b. Prepare the journal entry for the first semiannual cash interest payment and amortization of the premium on June 30, 2020.

Solution

a. **Amortization Schedule—Straight-Line Interest Method [Stated Rate = 5% and Market Rate = 4%]**

The following amortization schedule illustrates how interest expense is recognized over the term of the bonds under the straight-line interest method. The components of the journal entry for each period to record Cash, Interest Expense, and Premium on Bonds Payable are included in this schedule.

We see that over the bond term, stated interest is constant because it is contractual and is tied to the bond indenture. The amortized premium and interest expense are the same each period over the term of the bonds (except for a minor rounding difference). At the end of the bond term, the carrying value of the bonds equals the face value of $10,000 and the amortized premium in total equals the original premium of $449. We also see that total interest expense of $2,051 is less than total cash interest of $2,500 over the term of the bonds when bonds are sold at a premium.

Straight-Line Interest Method—Premium

Date	Cash (Stated Interest)[a]	Interest Expense (Market Interest)[b]	Premium on B.P. Amortization[c]	Bonds Payable, Net (Carrying Value)[d]
Jan. 1, 2020				$10,449
June 30, 2020. . .	$ 250	$ 205	$ 45	10,404
Dec. 31, 2020. . .	250	205	45	10,359
June 30, 2021. . .	250	205	45	10,314
Dec. 31, 2021. . .	250	205	45	10,269
June 30, 2022. . .	250	205	45	10,224
Dec. 31, 2022. . .	250	205	45	10,179
June 30, 2023. . .	250	205	45	10,134
Dec. 31, 2023. . .	250	205	45	10,089
June 30, 2024. . .	250	205	45	10,044
Dec. 31, 2024. . .	250	206	44*	10,000
	$2,500	$2,051	$449	

*Rounded

[a] Stated rate × Bond face value.

[b] Stated interest − Premium amortization.

[c] Total bond premium / Number of periods.

[d] Bond amortized cost, beginning of year − Premium amortization.

b. **Interest Expense and Premium Amortized on Bonds [Straight-line interest method]**

On June 30, 2020, Randolph Company records the following journal entry for the first semiannual cash interest payment and amortization of premium.

June 30, 2020—To record payment of interest and bond premium amortization

Interest Expense.	205	
Premium on Bonds Payable.	45	
Cash		250

Assets = Liabilities + Equity
−250 −45 −205
Cash: 250 (credit)
Premium on BP: 45 (debit) | 449 Bal.
Interest Exp: 205 (debit)

At June 30, 2020, Randolph Company carries the bonds at $10,404 ($10,449 − $45), which is the amortized cost of the bonds.

In both cases of a discount (**Demo 16-4**) and a premium (**Demo 16-5**), the carrying values of the Randolph Company bonds move toward the face value. Eventually at maturity, the bond carrying value equals the face value of the bonds both under the effective interest method and the straight-line interest method as illustrated below.

For both bonds issued at a discount and bonds issued at a premium, the carrying value moves toward the face value over the term of the bond using either the effective interest or straight-line amortization method. To illustrate, **Exhibit 16-2** shows the carrying value of the Randolph Company bonds issued at a discount (**Demo 16-4A**) and at a premium (**Demo 16-5A**) with the discount or premium amortized on a straight-line basis. Note that the carrying value of the bond issued at a discount is originally recorded at an amount less than the face value and gradually increases over the term of the bond. In contrast, the carrying value of the bond issued at a premium is originally recorded at an amount greater than the face value and gradually decreases over the term of the bond. At maturity, the carrying value equals the face value of the bonds regardless of whether the bonds were issued at par, a discount, or a premium.

EXHIBIT 16-2
Discount and Premium Amortization

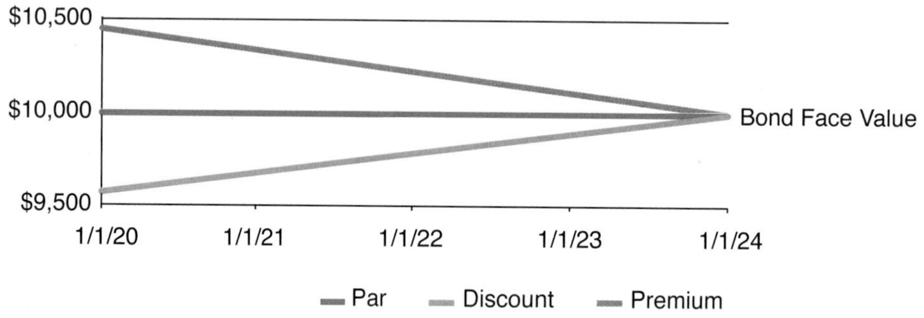

REVIEW 16-5 **LO16-5** **Account for Bonds Issued at a Premium**

Review MBC

5M Corp. authorized and issued $50,000, 6%, 10-year bonds on January 1, 2020. The bonds pay cash interest semiannually on July 1 and January 1, and were issued to yield 5%.

a. Record entries for 5M Corp. on (1) January 1, 2020, for issuance of the bonds, (2) July 1, 2020, for payment of interest, and (3) December 31, 2020, for accrual of interest, assuming that the company amortizes premiums using the *effective interest* method.

b. Record entries for 5M Corp. on (1) January 1, 2020, for issuance of the bonds, (2) July 1, 2020, for payment of interest, and (3) December 31, 2020, for accrual of interest, assuming that the company amortizes premiums using the *straight-line interest* method.

More Practice: 16-33, 16-35, 16-60, 16-61, 16-63, 16-65

Solution on p. 16-73.

LO 16-6 Measure and record notes at issuance and after issuance

LO 16-6 Overview

Notes Payable
- Note issued for cash
  - Measure note at present value of cash flows
- Note issued for non-cash consideration
  - Measure note at fair value of asset or debt, whichever is more reliable

A note is a formal document that specifies the terms of a debt. **Long-term notes** are often used for specific asset acquisitions while bonds are more likely to be used to raise large amounts of capital for general purposes. Notes typically have shorter maturities than bonds and are not traded on organized exchanges. A note typically is a contract with one creditor while bonds are contracts with multiple creditors.

The measurement basis for a note payable is the present value of the cash expected to be paid on the note, discounted at the market rate in effect at inception of the note. If present value and face value do not differ materially, the note is recognized at face value. If the face value of the note is greater than the present value of the note, a discount on note payable is recorded. If the face value of the note is less than the present value of the note, a premium on note payable is recorded. A discount (premium) is amortized over the life of the note as an increase (decrease) to interest expense.

Notes Payable Issued for Cash

The three examples in **Demo 16-6A** illustrate the accounting for a note payable exchanged for cash. The first example is a typical exchange where a company issues a note for cash (a form of a loan) at the note's face value. In this case, the market rate is equal to the stated rate. Although issuers usually attempt to set the stated rate close to the expected market rate at issuance (minimizing the discount or premium), a zero-interest-bearing note is an exception. A zero-interest-bearing note (illustrated in example two) provides no separate interest payments. Instead, upon issuance of the note, the face value of the note exceeds the present value of the note—the difference representing interest on the note. The note described in example three illustrates a case where the stated rate is less than the market rate causing the note to be issued at a discount. Although not illustrated below, if the present value of the cash flows exceeds the stated value of the note, the note is recorded at a premium. The difference between the present value and face value of the note decreases interest expense over the term of the note.

Note Payable Issued for Cash — LO16-6 — Demo 16-6A

Example One: Note Payable—Issued at Face Value [Stated Rate = 8% and Market Rate = 8%]
On January 1, 2020, Frazier Inc. borrowed $1,000 cash by issuing a three-year, $1,000 note payable to Seattle Corp. at face value, with cash interest payable annually on December 31 at 8%. Record the following entries for Frazier Inc. related to the note payable.

Demo MBC

a. Record the issuance of the note on January 1, 2020.
b. Record interest expense on the note payable on December 31, 2020, December 31, 2021, and December 31, 2022.
c. Record the entry upon maturity of the note payable on December 31, 2022.

Solution

a. **Issuance of Note Payable**
The issue price is equal to the present value of the note of $1,000, discounted at the market rate of 8%. The present value of the note on January 1, 2020, is equal to the face value of the note because the stated and market rates are equal.

	RATE	NPER	PMT	PV	FV	Excel Formula
Given	8%	3	(80)	?	(1,000)	=PV(0.08,3,-80,-1000)
Solution				$1,000		

Frazier Inc. records the following entry upon issuance of the note.

January 1, 2020—To record note payable issued at face value

Cash	1,000	
Note Payable		1,000

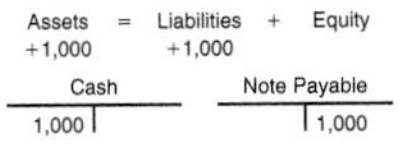

b. **Interest Expense on Note Payable**
Frazier Inc. recognizes interest expense each annual period as follows.

December 31, 2020, 2021 and 2022—To record payment of interest

Interest Expense ($1,000 × 8%)	80	
Cash		80

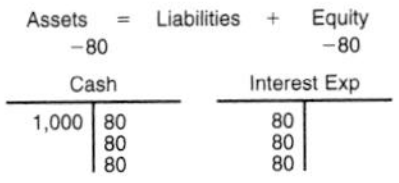

c. **Derecognition of Note Payable**
Upon maturity, Frazier Inc. would record the full payment of the face value of the note to Seattle Corp.

December 31, 2022—To record retirement of note

Note Payable	1,000	
Cash		1,000

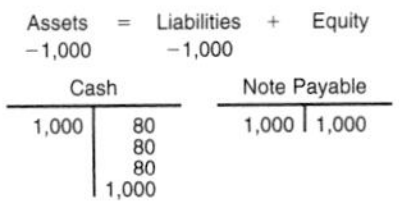

continued

continued from previous page

Example Two: Note Payable—Zero-Interest-Bearing [Stated Rate = 0% and Market Rate = 8%]
On January 1, 2020, Frazier Inc. issued a three-year, $1,000 zero-interest-bearing note payable to Seattle Corp for cash of $794. Record the following entries for Frazier Inc. related to the note payable, assuming that the market rate of interest on the note is 8%.

a. Record the issuance of the note on January 1, 2020.
b. Prepare an amortization schedule over the term of the note payable that uses the effective interest method to amortize the discount on note payable.
c. Record interest expense on the note payable on December 31, 2020, December 31, 2021, and December 31, 2022.
d. Record the entry upon maturity of the note payable.

Solution

a. **Issuance of Note Payable**

	RATE	NPER	PMT	PV	FV	Excel Formula
Given	8%	3	0	?	(1,000)	=PV(0.08,3,0,-1000)
Solution				$794		

Frazier Inc. borrows $794 in cash but will pay back the face value of the note of $1,000 at maturity. The difference of $206 is the discount which will be amortized to interest expense over the term of the note. Frazier Inc. recognizes the following entry upon issuance of the zero-interest-bearing note payable.

Assets = Liabilities + Equity
+794 −206
+1,000

Cash: 794 (debit)
Note Payable: 1,000 (credit)
Discount on NP: 206 (debit)

January 1, 2020—To record issuance of zero-interest-bearing note payable

Cash	794	
Discount on Note Payable ($1,000 − $794)	206	
Note Payable		1,000

b. **Amortization Schedule—Effective Interest Method [Stated Rate = 0% and Market Rate = 8%]**
The following amortization schedule illustrates how interest expense is recognized over the term of the note using the effective interest method. The components of the journal entry for each period to adjust Interest Expense and Discount on Note Payable are included in this schedule.

Effective Interest Method—Discount

Date	Cash (Stated Interest)	Interest Expense (Market Interest)	Discount on N.P. Amortization	Note Payable, Net (Carrying Value)
Jan. 1, 2020. . . .				$ 794
Dec. 31, 2020. . . .	$0	$ 64	$ 64	858
Dec. 31, 2021. . . .	0	69	69	927
Dec. 31, 2022. . . .	0	73*	73	1,000
Totals	$0	$206	$206	

* rounded

c. **Interest Expense on Note Payable**
Frazier Inc. recognizes interest expense at the end of the first year of the note as follows.

Assets = Liabilities + Equity
+64 −64

Interest Exp: 64, 69, 73 (debits)
Discount on NP: 206 (debit) | 64, 69, 73 (credits); balance 0

December 31, 2020—To record interest expense

Interest Expense.	64	
Discount on Note Payable		64

Assets = Liabilities + Equity
+69 −69

December 31, 2021—To record interest expense

Interest Expense.	69	
Discount on Note Payable		69

Assets = Liabilities + Equity
+73 −73

December 31, 2022—To record interest expense

Interest Expense.	73	
Discount on Note Payable		73

In this example, even though no interest is paid during the note term, the debtor still records interest expense as the discount is amortized.

continued

continued from previous page

d. **Derecognition of Note Payable**

Upon maturity, Frazier Inc. would record the payment of the face value of the note to Seattle Corp.

December 31, 2022—To record retirement of note at maturity

Note Payable	1,000	
Cash		1,000

Assets = Liabilities + Equity
−1,000 −1,000

Cash: 794 | 1,000
Note Payable: 1,000 | 1,000

Example Three: Note Payable—Interest-Bearing [Stated Rate = 8% and Market Rate = 9%]

On January 1, 2020, Frazier Inc. issued a three-year, $1,000 note payable to Seattle Corp. for $975 in cash, with cash interest payable annually on December 31 at 8%. The market rate of a note with similar risks is 9%. Record the following entries for Frazier Inc. related to the note payable.

a. Record the issuance of the note on January 1, 2020.
b. Prepare an amortization schedule over the term of the note payable that uses the effective interest method to amortize the discount on note payable.
c. Record interest expense on the note payable on December 31, 2020.
d. Record the entry upon maturity of the note payable (ignoring the interest entry) on December 31, 2022.

Solution

a. **Issuance of Note Payable**

The issue price of $975 is equal to the present value of the maturity amount ($1,000) plus the present value of the interest payments ($80 or $1,000 × 0.08). The difference between the cash received and the face value of the note is recorded as a discount on note payable.

	RATE	NPER	PMT	PV	FV	Excel Formula
Given	9%	3	(80)	?	(1,000)	=PV(0.09,3,-80,-1000)
Solution				$975		

January 1, 2020—To record issuance of interest-bearing note payable

Cash	975	
Discount on Note Payable ($1,000 − $975)	25	
Note Payable		1,000

Assets = Liabilities + Equity
+975 +1,000
−25

Cash: 975 |
Note Payable: | 1,000
Discount on NP: 25 |

b. **Amortization Schedule—Effective Interest Method [Stated Rate = 8% and Market Rate = 9%]**

The following amortization schedule illustrates how interest expense is recognized over the term of the note. The components of the journal entry for each period to record Cash, Interest Expense, and Discount on Note Payable are included in this schedule.

Effective Interest Method—Discount

Date	Cash (Stated Interest)	Interest Expense (Market Interest)	Discount on N.P. Amortization	Note Payable, Net (Carrying Value)
Jan. 1, 2020. . .				$ 975
Dec. 31, 2020. . .	$ 80	$ 88	$ 8	983
Dec. 31, 2021. . .	80	88	8	991
Dec. 31, 2022. . .	80	89	9	1,000
Totals	$240	$265	$25	

c. **Interest Expense on Note Payable**

Frazier Inc. recognizes interest expense at the end of the first year of the note as follows.

December 31, 2020—To record payment of interest and discount amortization

Interest Expense.	88	
Discount on Note Payable		8
Cash		80

Assets = Liabilities + Equity
−80 +8 −88

Cash: | 80
Discount on NP: 25 | 8
Interest Exp: 88 |

Frazier Inc. would record interest expense each period as indicated by the amortization schedule.

continued

continued from previous page

d. **Derecognition of Note Payable**
Upon maturity, Frazier Inc. would record the payment of the face value of the note to Seattle Corp.

December 31, 2022—To record retirement of note at maturity

Assets = Liabilities + Equity
−1,000 −1,000
Cash: | 1,000
Note Payable: 1,000 | 1,000

Note Payable	1,000	
Cash		1,000

Notes Payable Issued for Non-Cash Consideration [Property, Goods, or Services]

Although most notes represent loans, notes payable can also arise from normal purchases of goods or services or through extension of payment periods of accounts payable. Measuring the value of such transactions is more difficult because cash is not exchanged. In this case, the transaction should be recorded at the value of the asset or debt, whichever is more reliable.

If the value of the consideration given is known, the market rate can be measured by equating the present value of the cash flows called for in the note to the fair value of the consideration. **What happens when the fair value of the consideration received is not readily determinable?** The fair value of the debt can be used to measure the transaction. However, the interest rate stated in a note *may not equal* the market rate prevailing on obligations involving a similar credit rating or risk, although the stated rate is always used to determine the cash interest payments. *If the stated and market rates are different, the market rate (imputed interest rate) is used to measure the note and to measure interest expense.* The market rate is the rate accepted by two parties with opposing interests engaged in an arm's-length transaction.

835-30-05-2 Business transactions often involve the exchange of cash or property, goods, or service for a note or similar instrument. When a note is exchanged for property, goods, or service in a bargained transaction entered into at arm's length, there should be a general presumption that the rate of interest stipulated by the parties to the transaction represents fair and adequate compensation to the supplier for the use of the related funds. That presumption, however, must not permit the form of the transaction to prevail over its economic substance and thus would not apply if interest is not stated, the stated interest rate is unreasonable, or the stated face amount of the note is materially different from the current cash sales price for the same or similar items or from the fair value of the note at the date of the transaction.

The following three examples in **Demo 16-6B** illustrate the exchange of a note payable for non-cash consideration. In the first example, a note payable is exchanged for equipment with a determinable fair value. In the second example, the fair value of the equipment and the note are not determinable; therefore, the note is measured by discounting the note using the prevailing market rate of interest of notes with similar risks (also called the **imputed interest rate**). In the third example, rather than arranging to pay off the entire principal balance at the end of the loan as in the previous examples, the contract requires the debtor to make periodic, equal payments that include both principal and interest. This is similar to a typical house or vehicle loan where payments are made up of principal and interest. This type of note is an **installment note,** which allows for the obligation to be satisfied at the end of the note term through equal periodic payments.

Demo 16-6B **LO16-6** **Note Payable Issued for Non-Cash Consideration**

Demo MBC

Example One: Note Payable Exchanged for Equipment [Fair Value of Asset Determinable]
Frazier Inc. purchased equipment on January 1, 2020, and issued a two-year, $1,000 note with a 5% stated rate. Interest is payable each December 31, and the entire principal is payable December 31, 2022. The equipment has a fair value of $947. The market rate of 8% is implicit in this agreement. Record the following entries for Frazier Inc. related to the note payable.

a. Record the issuance of the note on January 1, 2020.
b. Prepare an amortization schedule over the term of the note payable that uses the effective interest method to amortize the discount on note payable.

continued

continued from previous page

c. Record interest expense on the note payable on December 31, 2020, and December 31, 2021.
d. Record the entry upon maturity of the note payable on December 31, 2021.

Solution

a. **Issuance of Note Payable**

The issuance of the note payable is recorded as follows based upon the fair value of the equipment received.

January 1, 2020—To record issuance of note payable

Equipment	947	
Discount on Note Payable ($1,000 − $947)	53	
Note Payable		1,000

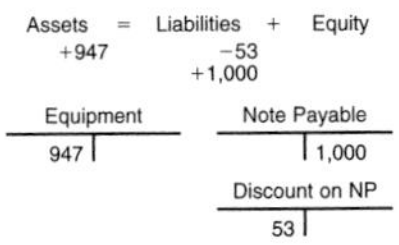

b. **Amortization Schedule—Effective Interest Method [Stated Rate = 5% and Market Rate = 8%]**

The following amortization schedule illustrates how interest expense is recognized over the term of the note, discounted at the market rate of 8% implicit in the agreement. The components of the journal entry for each period to record Cash, Interest Expense, and Discount on Note Payable are included in this schedule.

Effective Interest Method—Discount

Date	Cash (Stated Interest)	Interest Expense (Market Interest)	Discount on N.P. Amortization	Note Payable, Net (Carrying Value)
Jan. 1, 2020...				$ 947
Dec. 31, 2020...	$ 50	$ 76	$26	973
Dec. 31, 2021...	50	77*	27	1,000
Totals	$100	$153	$53	

* rounded

c. **Interest Expense on Note Payable**

Frazier Inc. recognizes interest expense at the end of each year as follows.

December 31, 2020—To record interest expense

Interest Expense (8% × $947)	76	
Discount on Note Payable ($76 − $50)		26
Cash (5% × $1,000)		50

December 31, 2021—To record interest expense

Interest Expense (8% × 973)	77	
Discount on Note Payable		27
Cash (5% × $1,000)		50

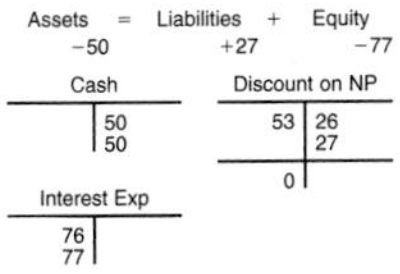

d. **Derecognition of Note Payable**

Along with interest, the principal of the note is paid on December 31, 2021.

December 31, 2021—To record retirement of note at maturity

Note Payable	1,000	
Cash		1,000

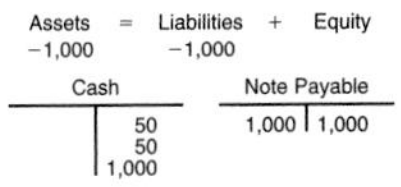

Example Two: Note Payable Exchanged for Equipment [Fair Value of Asset and Liability Not Determinable]

Frazier Inc. purchased used equipment on January 1, 2020, and issued a two-year, $1,000 note with a 3% stated rate. Interest is payable each December 31, and the entire principal is payable December 31, 2021. The equipment does not have a readily determinable fair value. The prevailing market rate of interest for similar notes is 8%. Record the following entries for Frazier Inc. related to the note payable.

continued

continued from previous page

a. Record the issuance of the note on January 1, 2020.
b. Prepare an amortization schedule over the term of the note payable that uses the effective interest method to amortize the discount on note payable.
c. Record interest expense on the note payable on December 31, 2020, and December 31, 2021.
d. Record the entry upon maturity of the note payable on December 31, 2021.

Solution

***a.* Issuance of Note Payable**

	RATE	NPER	PMT	PV	FV	Excel Formula
Given	8%	2	(30)	?	(1,000)	=PV(0.08,2,-30,-1000)
Solution				$911		

Because the fair value of the equipment (and the note) is not readily determinable, the present value of the note is measured by discounting the note using the prevailing market rate of interest of notes with similar risks. The present value of the note (principal of $1,000 and interest of $30 or 3% × $1,000) discounted at the market rate of 8% is computed as shown.

The entry for the issuance of the note payable is as follows.

Assets = Liabilities + Equity
+911 −89
+1,000

Equipment: 911 (debit)
Note Payable: 1,000 (credit)
Discount on NP: 89 (debit)

January 1, 2020—To record issuance of note payable

Equipment	911	
Discount on Note Payable ($1,000 − $911)	89	
Note Payable		1,000

***b.* Amortization Schedule—Effective Interest Method [Stated Rate = 5% and Market Rate = 8%]**

The following amortization schedule illustrates how interest expense is recognized over the term of the note. The components of the journal entry for each period to record Cash, Interest Expense, and Discount on Note Payable are included in this schedule.

Effective Interest Method—Discount

Date	Cash (Stated Interest)	Interest Expense (Market Interest)	Discount on N.P. Amortization	Note Payable, Net (Carrying Value)
Jan. 1, 2020 . . .				$ 911
Dec. 31, 2020 . . .	$30	$ 73	$43	954
Dec. 31, 2021 . . .	30	76	46	1,000
Totals	$60	$149	$89	

***c.* Interest Expense on Note Payable**

Assets = Liabilities + Equity
−30 +43 −73

Cash: 30 (credit)
Discount on NP: 89 (debit) | 43 (credit)
Interest Exp: 73 (debit)

December 31, 2020—To record interest expense

Interest Expense	73	
Discount on Note Payable		43
Cash		30

Assets = Liabilities + Equity
−30 +46 −76

Cash: 30, 30 (credit)
Discount on NP: 89 (debit) | 43, 46 (credit); balance 0
Interest Exp: 73, 76 (debit)

December 31, 2021—To record interest expense

Interest Expense	76	
Discount on Note Payable		46
Cash		30

***d.* Derecognition of Note Payable**

Assets = Liabilities + Equity
−1,000 −1,000

Cash: 1,000 (credit)
Note Payable: 1,000 (debit) | 1,000 (credit)

December 31, 2021—To record retirement of note at maturity

Note Payable	1,000	
Cash		1,000

continued

continued from previous page

Example Three: Installment Note Payable Exchanged for Equipment [Fair Value of Asset Determinable]

On January 1, 2020, Frazier Inc. purchases equipment with a cash price of $10,000 (representing fair value) in exchange for a note with the following payment schedule: $6,000 due December 31, 2020, and on December 31, 2021. The note does not explicitly require interest payments. However, the interest rate implied by this transaction is 13.07%, computed as shown.

	RATE	NPER	PMT	PV	FV	Excel Formula
Given	?	2	(6,000)	10,000	0	=RATE(2,-6000,10000,0)
Solution	13.07%					

To compute the payment if instead given the market rate of 13.07%, solve for PMT using the market rate (13.07%), number of periods (2), present value (10,000), and future value (0).

Record the following entries for Frazier Inc. related to the note payable.

a. Record the issuance of the note on January 1, 2020.

b. Prepare an amortization schedule over the term of the note payable using the effective interest method.

c. Record installment payments on the note payable on December 31, 2020, and December 31, 2021.

Solution

a. Issuance of Note Payable

This note is a form of an installment note with equal payments because each payment of $6,000 includes interest and principal. The reduction in principal is sufficient to pay off the note upon maturity. The entry for the issuance of the note payable is as follows.

January 1, 2020—To record issuance of installment note in exchange for equipment

Equipment	10,000	
Note Payable		10,000

Assets = Liabilities + Equity
+10,000 +10,000
Equipment: 10,000 (debit)
Note Payable: 10,000 (credit)

b. Amortization Schedule —Installment Note

For an installment note, the note carrying value is reduced to zero at the end of the note term. Each installment payment is allocated to market interest and the reduction of principal of the note as illustrated in the following amortization schedule. The components of the journal entry for each period to record Cash, Interest Expense, and Note Payable are included in this schedule.

Amortization Schedule—Installment Note

Date	Cash Payment[a]	Interest Expense (Market Interest)[b]	Note Payable (Reduction)[c]	Note Payable, Net (Carrying Value)[d]
Jan. 1, 2020				$10,000
Dec. 31, 2020	$ 6,000	$1,307	$ (4,693)	5,307
Dec. 31, 2021	6,000	693*	(5,307)	0
Totals	$12,000	$2,000	$(10,000)	

* rounded
[a] Installment payment (given).
[b] Note carrying value × Market rate ($10,000 × 13.07%).
[c] Installment payment − Market interest ($6,000 − $1,307).
[d] Note carrying value, beginning of year − Reduction in note payable ($10,000 − $4,693).

c. Installment Payments on Note Payable

December 31, 2020—To record interest expense

Interest Expense	1,307	
Note Payable	4,693	
Cash		6,000

Assets = Liabilities + Equity
−6,000 −4,693 −1,307
Cash: 6,000 (credit)
Note Payable: 4,693 (debit) | 10,000 (credit)
Interest Exp: 1,307 (debit)

December 31, 2021—To record interest expense

Interest Expense	693	
Note Payable	5,307	
Cash		6,000

Assets = Liabilities + Equity
−6,000 −5,307 −693
Cash: 6,000, 6,000 (credit)
Note Payable: 4,693, 5,307 (debit) | 10,000 (credit); balance 0
Interest Exp: 1,307, 693 (debit)

After the recording of this entry, the note payable is reduced to a zero balance ($10,000 − $4,693 − $5,307).

EXPANDING YOUR KNOWLEDGE — Mortgage Note Payable

A debtor can obtain financing for a real estate asset through a mortgage where the real estate asset serves as collateral for the mortgage loan. Mortgage notes secured by real property have longer terms than the previous notes discussed in this section (such as 15 or 30 years), but are otherwise similar. A mortgage note can have a fixed rate over its term, or a variable rate that readjusts to market rates at specified dates. Payments on mortgage notes would typically include both interest and principal as we illustrated with an installment note payable.

High and unstable interest rates gave rise to innovative mortgage notes, including point-system mortgages and adjustable-rate mortgages. The proceeds to the borrower are reduced in a point-system mortgage as a way of increasing the market rate. The monthly payment is based on the face amount of the note before the points are assessed. The interest rate on an adjustable-rate mortgage (ARM) fluctuates as market conditions change, periodically requiring a recalculation of the monthly payment based on the current loan balance, new interest rate, and remaining mortgage term.

REVIEW 16-6 LO16-6 Accounting for Notes Payable

Review MBC

5M Corp. purchased merchandise for resale on January 1, 2020, for $100,000 cash plus a note payable. The fair value of the inventory on January 1, 2020, is $149,108. The market rate of interest is 8%. 5M Corp. uses the effective interest method to amortize discounts and premiums. Record the entries over the term of the note payable for the following three *separate* scenarios for the structuring of the note payable.

a. The principal of $50,000 is due on December 31, 2021, and the note specified 7% interest payable each December 31 over a two-year period.

b. The face value of the note payable is instead $57,280 and is due on December 31, 2021. The note is structured as a zero-interest-bearing note payable over a two-year period.

c. The loan is extended to three years with equal payments of $19,055.55 due on each December 31 over the term of the note. The note will be fully paid upon maturity.

More Practice: 16-38, 16-39, 16-40,16-41, 16-42, 16-67, 16-68, 16-69,16-70

Solution on p. 16-73.

LO 16-7 Account for extinguishment of debt

LO 16-7 Overview

Account for Early Debt Extinguishment
- Update interest expense to retirement date
- Derecognize liability including unamortized discounts/premiums
- Record transfer of cash or other assets
- Record gain or loss
- Record bond refunding if applicable

Companies typically use the proceeds from long-term debt issuances for the duration of the debt term. At maturity, any discounts or premiums are fully amortized so that the carrying value of the debt is equal to the face value as illustrated earlier. The liability is then **derecognized** (removed) from the company's balance sheet at maturity.

Early Debt Extinguishment At times, however, a company may find it advantageous to extinguish debt early. This might be motivated by a desire to reduce interest costs, debt levels, or other reasons. For example, early retirement of debt decreases the debt-equity ratio and can facilitate future financing opportunities.

The incentives for retiring debt differ depending on whether interest rates have increased or decreased since the debt was issued. (When the call price is specified in the bond indenture, companies must decide whether it is more beneficial to extinguish the debt at the established price or issue new (additional) debt.) Let's look at an example for bonds payable.

- If market rates have *increased* since the issuance of bonds, the market price (the amount paid to retire the bonds early) has fallen, sometimes below net book value. The result is a gain recognized by the issuer on retirement.
- If market rates have *decreased* since the issuance of bonds, the market price of the bonds has increased. In this case, the issuing company retires higher-interest-rate bonds, thus reducing future interest costs. However, a loss is recognized because the market price of the bonds exceeds book value. Many companies take this opportunity to issue lower-rate debt in a refinancing of the higher-rate debt, just as homeowners do when they refinance their home mortgages when rates decline.

Accounting for Early Debt Extinguishment Accounting for debt extinguishment involves:

- Recording interest expense, discount, premium, and related issue costs (if applicable) to the retirement date.
- Removing the liability accounts including any unamortized discounts or premiums.
- Recording the transfer of cash, other resources, or debt securities.
- Recognizing a gain or loss in net income (see the following authoritative guidance).

470-50-40-2 A difference between the reacquisition price of debt and the net carrying amount of the extinguished debt shall be recognized currently in income of the period of extinguishment as losses or gains and identified as a separate item.

In **Demo 16-7** we review an extinguishment of bonds at maturity in Example One and a partial early extinguishment of bonds in Example Two. In Example Three, an early bond retirement is immediately followed by a new bond issue. When such a **bond refunding** takes place, one bond issue is replaced with another bond issue. One way of refunding is to issue new bonds in exchange for the old bonds. Cash is involved if the bond issues have different market values. A second more common way is where the proceeds from a new bond issue are used to retire the old issue because the holders of the old issue do not necessarily wish to become the new creditors. In both cases, the accounting for refunding is similar to all other forms of debt extinguishment where gains and losses are recognized in the period of refunding.

Extinguishment of Debt LO16-7 Demo 16-7

Demo MBC

Example One: Extinguishment of Debt at Maturity

On January 1, 2020, Frazier Inc. issued $10,000, 5%, 5-year bonds at a discount of $1,800. Assuming that Frazier holds the bonds to maturity, record the entry at maturity on December 31, 2024.

Solution

December 31, 2024—To record retirement of bonds at maturity

Bonds Payable	10,000	
Cash		10,000

Assets = Liabilities + Equity
−10,000 −10,000
Cash: | 10,000
Bond Payable: 10,000 | 10,000 Bal.

Example Two: Extinguishment of Debt Before Maturity

On January 1, 2020, Frazier Inc. issued a three-year, $10,000 bond payable for $9,485, with cash interest payable annually on December 31 at 6%. The market rate on the bond is 8% at the date of issue. Two years later, on December 31, 2021, after year-end adjusting entries were made, Frazier Inc. recalled 40% of the bonds at 101. At that time, the total unamortized discount was $184 as indicated in the following amortization schedule.

Effective Interest Method—Discount

Date	Cash (Stated Interest)	Interest Expense (Market Interest)	Discount on B.P. Amortization	Bonds Payable, Net (Carrying Value)
Jan. 1, 2020. . . .				$ 9,485
Dec. 31, 2020. . . .	$ 600	$ 759	$159	9,644
Dec. 31, 2021. . . .	600	772	172	9,816
Dec. 31, 2022. . . .	600	784*	184	10,000
Totals	$1,800	$2,315	$515	

* rounded

Required

a. Record Frazier Inc.'s entry upon recall of 40% of the bonds on December 31, 2021.

b. Record Frazier Inc.'s entry on December 31, 2022, to pay interest expense and to derecognize the remaining bonds.

continued

continued from previous page

Solution

a. **Early Redemption of Bonds Payable**

Frazier pays $4,040 upon redemption of the bonds or ($10,000 × 40% × 1.01). Frazier Inc. derecognizes 40% of the carrying value of the bonds on December 31, 2021. The unamortized bond discount in total is $184. However, only 40% of this amount (as well as the bonds payable amount) is derecognized. Frazier Inc. would record the following entry on redemption.

Assets = Liabilities + Equity
−4,040 = −4,000 +74 + −114

Cash: Cr. 4,040
Bonds Payable: Dr. 4,000 | Cr. 10,000 Bal.
Loss on Bond Red: Dr. 114
Discount on BP: Dr. Bal. 184 | Cr. 74

December 31, 2021—To record bond redemption

Bonds Payable ($10,000 × 40%)	4,000	
Loss on Redemption of Bonds ($4,040 − [$4,000 − $74])	114	
Discount on Bonds Payable ($184 × 40%)		74
Cash ($10,000 × 40% × 1.01)		4,040

b. **Interest Payment and Retirement of Remaining Bonds Payable**

Debt extinguishment does not affect the accounting for the remaining 60% of the bond issue; 60% of the values in the amortization schedule would be used to record entries over the remaining bond term.

Assets = Liabilities + Equity
−360 = +110 + −470

December 31, 2022—To record interest payment on bonds

Interest Expense ($784 × 60%)	470	
Discount on Bonds Payable ($184 × 60%)		110
Cash ($600 × 60%)		360

Assets = Liabilities + Equity
−6,000 = −6,000

Cash: Cr. 4,040, 360, 6,000
Bonds Payable: Dr. 4,000, 6,000 | Cr. 10,000; Bal. 0
Interest Exp: Dr. 470
Discount on BP: Dr. 184 | Cr. 74, 110; Bal. 0

December 31, 2022—To record retirement of remaining bonds at maturity

Bonds Payable	6,000	
Cash ($10,000 × 60%)		6,000

Example Three: Extinguishment of Debt Before Maturity with Refunding

On January 1, 2020, Frazier Inc. issues $10,000 of 10-year, 5% bonds at face value with cash interest payable each June 30 and December 31. On January 1, 2024, Frazier Inc. retires the 5% bond issue at 86, and immediately issues at face value, $8,600 of 20-year, 8% bonds with the same interest dates as the 5% bonds. Record Frazier's entry on January 1, 2024, to retire the 5% bonds and issue the new 8% bonds.

Solution

Assets = Liabilities + Equity
−8,600 = −10,000 + +1,400

January 1, 2024—To record retirement of the 5% bonds payable

Bonds Payable	10,000	
Cash ($10,000 × 0.86)		8,600
Gain on Bond Extinguishment ($10,000 − $8,600)		1,400

Assets = Liabilities + Equity
+8,600 = +8,600

Cash: Dr. 8,600 | Cr. 8,600
Bonds Payable: Dr. 10,000 | Cr. 10,000 Bal., 8,600
Gain on Bond Ext: Cr. 1,400

January 1, 2024—To record issuance of the 8% bonds payable

Cash	8,600	
Bonds Payable		8,600

REVIEW 16-7 LO16-7 Accounting for Extinguishment of Debt

On January 1, 2020, 5M Inc. issued $300,000 of bonds at 95. The bonds pay 5% cash interest semi-annually on June 30 and December 31. The bonds are scheduled to mature on December 31, 2024. The company retired $30,000 of the bonds on October 1, 2020, when the bonds were selling at 89 plus accrued interest. Assume the straight-line interest method is used to amortize the bond discount.

Required

a. Record the entry for the bond issuance on January 1, 2020.

b. Record the entry for the interest payment on June 30, 2020.

c. Provide the entry to recognize interest expense for the portion of the bond issue retired on October 1, 2020.

d. Provide the entry to record the bond retirement on October 1, 2020.

More Practice: 16-43, 16-71, 16-72, 16-73

Solution on p. 16-74.

Account for conversion of debt into equity

LO 16-8

A **convertible bond** is exchangeable for capital stock, usually common stock, of the issuer at the option of the investor. A convertible bond is a **hybrid security** because it is a security that has characteristics of both debt and equity. Convertible bonds often are marketable at lower interest rates than conventional bonds because investors assign a value to the conversion privilege.

The primary attraction of convertible bonds to investors is the potential for increased value if the stock appreciates. If it does not, the investor continues to receive both interest and principal (although usually at a lower rate than nonconvertible bonds would provide).

Convertible bonds are advantageous to the issuer for several reasons.

- Prospect for raising debt capital often is improved.
- Typically pay a lower interest rate than do nonconvertible bonds.
- If such bonds are converted, the face value is never paid.
- Fewer shares may be issued on conversion than in a direct sale of stock; thus, less control is given up.
- Call option protects issuer from having to issue stock with an aggregate value in excess of call price.

Convertible bonds are not without disadvantages. If the stock price rises, the issuing company forgoes the higher proceeds that would be possible from a direct sale of stock. If the stock price falls, the company must continue to service the debt.

LO 16-8 Overview

Account for a Debt Conversion
- Record issuance as a straight-debt issue
- Record conversion using book value method
- Record no gain or loss upon conversion
- Expense conversion inducement costs

FORD

Real World—CONVERTIBLE DEBT

FORD [F]

The following example found in a recent Ford Motor Company annual report illustrates a conversion of convertible debt to equity. In 2014, Ford Motor Company announced an election to terminate conversion rights on convertible notes. As a result, the majority of the outstanding notes were converted into Ford common stock.

> **Debt and Commitments (excerpt)**—On January 22, 2014, we terminated the conversion rights of holders under the 4.25% Senior Convertible Notes due December 15, 2036 ("2036 Convertible Notes") in accordance with their terms and settled conversions occurring after notice of termination with cash. In 2014, $24 million of the 2036 Convertible Notes were converted by the holders, resulting in cash payments of $43 million and a $5 million loss recorded in Automotive interest income and other income/(loss), net.

Accounting for Convertible Debt

Although convertible debt has an equity feature, it is typically recorded as a straight debt issuance. This means that there is no amount allocated to an equity account for the conversion feature of the debt. A separate market does not exist for either the bonds standing alone or the conversion privilege. There is no objective basis (such as a market or an exchange transaction) for allocating the bond price to the bonds and the conversion feature. The value of the conversion feature is contingent on a future stock price that cannot be predicted. The authoritative support follows, indicating an exception to the accounting treatment for beneficial conversion features, which is explored in the *Expanding Your Knowledge* box below.

470-20-25-12 No portion of the proceeds from the issuance of the types of convertible debt instruments described in the preceding two paragraphs [conversion features that are not beneficial] shall be accounted for as attributable to the conversion feature.

Book Value Method When the bonds are converted, the issuer updates interest expense and amortization of premium or discount to the date of conversion. Then, bonds payable and any unamortized discount or premium are derecognized. If the debt is converted into common stock, the **book value method** is used to record the conversion. Under the book value method, the stockholders' equity accounts replace the bond accounts for the issuer, and no gain or loss is recorded in net income.

Issuers of convertible debt sometimes change the conversion provisions after the bond issue date to induce prompt conversion. The inducement is an incentive over and above the original shares to be issued on conversion. Common inducements include an increase in the number of shares issued per bond, issuance of stock rights and cash or other consideration. Declining interest rates and a preference for lower debt levels can prompt an **induced conversion**. The issuer recognizes an expense equal to the fair value of consideration in excess of the fair value of the securities issuable under the original conversion terms as explained in the following guidance.

> **470-20-40-16** If a convertible debt instrument is converted to equity securities of the debtor pursuant to an inducement offer . . . the debtor shall recognize an expense equal to the fair value of all securities and other consideration transferred in the transaction in excess of the fair value of securities issuable pursuant to the original conversion terms. The fair value of the securities or other consideration shall be measured as of the date the inducement offer is accepted by the convertible debt holder

In **Demo 16-8** we account for conversion of bonds to stock (with an inducement) using the book value method. Although companies typically account for the conversion of debt through the book value method, an alternative method is to record stock at conversion at the fair value of stock or debt, whichever is more reliable. For example, let's assume that a company converted its bonds to common stock and the fair value of the common stock was available. The company would credit Common Stock at par and credit Paid-in Capital in Excess of Par for the excess of the fair value of the common stock over par. The bond (and any related discounts or premiums) is derecognized. Finally, a gain or loss is recognized equal to the difference between the fair value of the stock and the carrying value of the debt.

EXPANDING YOUR KNOWLEDGE — **Value of a Conversion Feature**

Accounting for the issuance of convertible bonds poses a conceptual problem. A popular view holds that the economic value of the conversion feature, reflected in the bond price, should be recorded as stockholders' equity. However, ASC 470 specifies that convertible bonds be recorded only as debt (unless it is a beneficial conversion feature described later in this section). The FASB reasoned that the debt and equity features of convertible bonds are inseparable and do not exist independently of each other.

Demo 16-8 LO16-8 Accounting for Convertible Debt

On January 1, 2020, Tollen Corporation sells $100,000 of 8% convertible bonds for $106,000. Each $1,000 bond is convertible to 10 shares of Tollen Corporation $10 par common stock on any interest date after the end of the second year from the date of issuance. (In practice, conversion is generally possible on any date within the conversion period. The restriction on conversion is used only to facilitate this example.) All of Tollen bonds are converted into common stock on December 31, 2021, when the unamortized premium is $3,000 and the common stock is trading at $110 per share.

Required

a. Record the issuance of convertible bonds on January 1, 2020.
b. Record the conversion of debt to common stock on December 31, 2021.
c. Record the conversion of debt to common stock on December 31, 2021, assuming Tollen makes a $5,000 payment to shareholders to induce conversion.

Solution

a. **Issuance of Convertible Debt**

January 1, 2020—To record issuance of bonds

Cash	106,000	
Premium on Bonds Payable ($106,000 − $100,000)		6,000
Bonds Payable		100,000

Assets	=	Liabilities	+	Equity
+106,000		+6,000		
		+100,000		

Cash	
106,000	

Bonds Payable	
	100,000

Premium on BP	
	6,000

continued

continued from previous page

b. Conversion of Convertible Debt to Equity

December 31, 2021—To record conversion of bonds

Bonds Payable	100,000	
Premium on Bonds Payable	3,000	
Common Stock ($100,000/$1,000 × 10 shares × $10 par)		10,000
Paid-in Capital in Excess of Par—Common Stock ($100,000 + $3,000 − $10,000)		93,000

Assets	=	Liabilities	+	Equity
		−100,000		+10,000
		−3,000		+93,000

Bonds Payable		Premium on BP	
100,000	100,000	3,000	3,000 Bal.

Common Stock		Paid-in Cap—CS	
	10,000		93,000

c. Induced Conversion of Convertible Debt

December 31, 2021—To record induced conversion of bonds

Bonds Payable	100,000	
Debt Conversion Expense	5,000	
Premium on Bonds Payable	3,000	
Common Stock ($100,000/$1,000 × 10 shares × $10 par)		10,000
Paid-in Capital in Excess of Par—Common Stock ($100,000 + $3,000 − $10,000)		93,000
Cash		5,000

Assets	=	Liabilities	+	Equity
−5,000		−100,000		−5,000
		−3,000		+10,000
				+93,000

Cash		Bonds Payable	
	5,000	100,000	100,000

Debt Convers Exp		Premium on BP	
5,000		3,000	3,000 Bal.

Common Stock		Paid-in Cap—CS	
	10,000		93,000

EXPANDING YOUR KNOWLEDGE — **Beneficial Conversion Feature**

The *beneficial conversion feature* allows an exception to the rule of recording convertible debt as a straight-debt issuance. If the market price of the stock at issuance of the convertible debt exceeds the exercise price to convert the debt, the conversion option has an intrinsic value that is recorded separately as equity.

470-20-25-5 An embedded beneficial conversion feature present in a convertible instrument shall be recognized separately at issuance by allocating a portion of the proceeds equal to the intrinsic value of that feature to additional paid-in capital.

For example, let's say a company issues at par, $4,500 of convertible bonds, which can be converted into 100 shares of common stock at the option of the holder. If the common stock is trading at $50 per share and the conversion price is $45 per share (or $4,500/100 shares), the intrinsic value of the conversion option is $5 per share. This means the debt proceeds allocated to equity would be $500 ($5 × 100 shares).

Accounting for Conversion of Debt — LO16-8 — REVIEW 16-8

5M Corp. issued $200,000 of 5%, 5-year convertible bonds. Each $1,000 bond is convertible into 5 shares of common stock ($1 par value per share) of 5M Corp. The bonds were sold at 98 on January 1, 2020.

Required

a. Provide the entry for 5M Corp. on January 1, 2020, for issuance of convertible bonds.

b. The conversion privilege for 50% of the bonds is exercised on December 31, 2021. Assume that any discount or premium has been amortized through the date of conversion using the straight-line interest method and that the common stock is selling at $125 per share at the conversion date. Provide the entry for conversion of the bonds to common stock, using the book value method.

Review MBC

More Practice: 16-44, 16-74, 16-75, 16-92

Solution on p. 16-75.

Account for bonds with warrants — LO 16-9

LO 16-9 Overview

Account for Bonds with Warrants

- Bonds with nondetachable warrants
  - Record as a straight-debt issue
- Bonds with detachable warrants
  - Record warrants as equity (separate from debt) following either the incremental or the proportional method

Companies can issue debt securities that include rights to acquire capital stock. In these cases the investor receives a right to become a shareholder (in the future) and then participate in stock price appreciation in addition to principal and cash interest payments.

One example of debt sold with rights is a bond sold with stock warrants attached. A **stock warrant** conveys the option to purchase from the issuer a specified number of shares of common stock at a designated price per share (the exercise price) within a stated time period (the exercise period). The warrant is valuable because it enables the holder to buy stock for less than fair value if the fair value rises above the exercise price. This means that warrants attached to a bond issue generally increase the bond price.

Accounting treatment for bonds with warrants depends on whether the warrants are detachable or nondetachable.

- **Nondetachable stock warrants** cannot be sold separately from the bond. Because no separate market for the warrants exists, the entire bond price is allocated to the bonds.
- **Detachable stock warrants** have a readily determinable fair value and are traded as separate securities. This means a portion of the bond price is allocated to equity through the incremental method or the proportional method.

470-20-25-2 Proceeds from the sale of a debt instrument with stock purchase warrants (detachable call options) shall be allocated to the two elements based on the relative fair values of the debt instrument without the warrants and of the warrants themselves at time of issuance. The portion of the proceeds so allocated to the warrants shall be accounted for as paid-in capital. The remainder of the proceeds shall be allocated to the debt instrument portion of the transaction. This usually results in a discount (or, occasionally, a reduced premium).

If bonds are sold with *detachable warrants*, and the fair value of only one security is known, the **incremental method** is used. Fair value is applied to the security with a known fair value. The remaining or incremental portion of the proceeds is allocated to the other security with an unknown fair value.

If bonds are sold with *detachable warrants*, and the fair value of both securities is known, the **proportional method** is used. Proceeds from the issuance are allocated based upon the relative fair value of the two securities.

In **Demo 16-9** we account for bond issuances with nondetachable and detachable stock purchase warrants.

Demo 16-9 LO16-9 Accounting for Bonds with Warrants

Demo MBC

Example One: Bonds with Nondetachable Warrants

Embassy Corporation issues $100,000 of 8%, 10-year nonconvertible bonds with *nondetachable* stock purchase warrants on January 1, 2020. Each $1,000 bond carries 10 warrants. Each warrant entitles the holder to purchase one share of $10 par common stock for $15. Assume the bond issue sells for 105. Record the entry for Embassy Corporation on January 1, 2020, to issue the bonds with nondetachable warrants.

Solution

Assets = Liabilities + Equity
+105,000 +5,000
+100,000

Cash: 105,000 (debit)
Bonds Payable: 100,000 (credit)
Premium on BP: 5,000 (credit)

January 1, 2020—To record issuance of bonds with nondetachable warrants

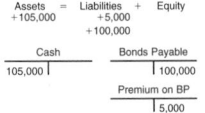

Cash ($100,000 × 1.05)	105,000	
Premium on Bonds Payable ($105,000 − $100,000)		5,000
Bonds Payable		100,000

Example Two: Bonds with Detachable Warrants–Incremental Method

Embassy Corporation issues $100,000 of 8%, 10-year nonconvertible bonds with *detachable* stock purchase warrants on January 1, 2020. Each $1,000 bond carries 10 warrants. Each warrant entitles the holder to purchase one share of $10 par common stock for $15. Assume the bonds with detachable stock warrants sell for 105. Shortly after issuance, the warrants trade for $4 each. Fair value is not determinable for the bonds selling without warrants. Record the entry for Embassy Corporation on January 1, 2020, to issue the bonds with detachable warrants using the incremental method.

Solution

Because the warrants are detachable, we determine a separate measurement for the warrants from the bonds. Also, because we only know the fair value of the warrants (and not the fair value of the bonds without the warrants), we use the incremental method to measure and record a separate value for the bonds and the warrants.

continued

continued from previous page

Incremental Method: Allocation of Selling Price to Bonds and Warrants	
Selling price of bonds with warrants ($100,000 × 1.05)	$105,000
Fair value of warrants ($100,000/$1,000 × 10 warrants × $4)	4,000
Allocation of proceeds to bonds	$101,000

At January 1, 2020, the entry for issuance of the bonds recorded by Embassy Corporation follows.

January 1, 2020—To record issuance of bonds with detachable warrants: Incremental method

Cash ($100,000 × 1.05)	105,000	
Paid-in Capital—Stock Warrants ($100,000/$1,000 × 10 × $4)		4,000
Premium on Bonds Payable ($101,000 − $100,000)		1,000
Bonds Payable		100,000

Assets = Liabilities + Equity
+105,000 = +100,000 +1,000 + +4,000

Cash: 105,000 (debit) | Bonds Payable: 100,000 (credit)
Premium on BP: 1,000 (credit) | Paid-in Cap—War: 4,000 (credit)

Example Three: Bonds with Detachable Warrants–Proportional Method

Embassy Corporation issues $100,000 of 8%, 10-year nonconvertible bonds with *detachable* stock purchase warrants on January 1, 2020. Each $1,000 bond carries 10 warrants. Each warrant entitles the holder to purchase one share of $10 par common stock for $15. Assume the bond issue sells for 105. Shortly after issuance, the warrants trade for $4 each and the bonds were quoted at 103 without warrants attached. Record the entry for Embassy Corporation on January 1, 2020, to issue the bonds with detachable warrants using the proportional method.

Solution

Because the warrants are detachable, we determine a separate measurement for the warrants from the bonds. Also, because we know the fair value of the warrants and the fair value of the bonds without the warrants, we use the proportional method to measure and record a separate value for the bonds and the warrants.

Proportional Method: Allocation of Selling Price to Bonds and Warrants

	Total	Proportion of Total
Fair value of bonds ($100,000 × 1.03)	$103,000	$103,000/$107,000
Fair value of warrants ($4 × 100 bonds × 10 warrants per bond)	4,000	$4,000/$107,000
	$107,000	
Allocation of proceeds to bonds ($105,000 × 103/107)	$101,075	
Allocation of proceeds to warrants ($105,000 × 4/107)	3,925	
	$105,000	

At January 1, 2020, the entry for issuance of the bonds recorded by Embassy Corporation follows.

January 1, 2020—To record issuance of bonds with detachable warrants: Proportional method

Cash	105,000	
Paid-in Capital—Stock Warrants		3,925
Premium on Bonds Payable ($101,075 − $100,000)		1,075
Bonds Payable		100,000

Assets = Liabilities + Equity
+105,000 = +800 +100,000 + +4,200

Cash: 105,000 (debit) | Bonds Payable: 100,000 (credit)
Premium on BP: 1,075 (credit) | Paid-in Cap—War: 3,925 (credit)

Example Four: Bonds with Detachable Warrants–Conversion and Expiration

Assume that Embassy Corporation accounted for its warrants using the incremental method (see Example 2) and that the warrants expire on January 31, 2021. On January 15, 2021, 900 warrants were exercised by warrant holders. Record the entry for Embassy Corporation on January 15, 2021, for the exercise of the 900 warrants, and the expiration of the remaining 100 warrants on January 31, 2021.

continued

continued from previous page

Solution

On January 15, 2021, a prorated amount of stock warrants is derecognized ($3,600 or 900 warrants/1,000 warrants × $4,000). One share of common stock is issued for each of the 900 warrants, totaling 900 shares. Par value of the common stock is recorded for $9,000 (900 shares × $10 par) and the entry is balanced through a credit to Paid-in Capital in Excess of Par—Common Stock. The entry for the exercise of 900 warrants for Embassy Corporation on January 15, 2021, is as follows.

Assets	=	Liabilities	+	Equity
+13,500				−3,600
				+9,000
				+8,100

Cash		Paid-in Cap—War	
13,500		3,600	4,000 Bal.

Common Stock		Paid-in Cap—CS	
	9,000		8,100

January 15, 2021—To record conversion of warrants to common stock

Cash (900 × $15)	13,500	
Paid-in Capital—Stock Warrants ($4,000 × 900/1,000)	3,600	
Common Stock (900 × 1 share × $10 par)		9,000
Paid-in Capital in Excess of Par—Common Stock (to balance)		8,100

An expiration entry is recorded at the end of the exercise period for any warrants that remain outstanding, whether through oversight or because of an unfavorable stock price. This entry simply reclassifies the equity amount in Paid-in Capital—Stock Warrants to Paid-in Capital in Excess of Par—Common Stock. The entry for the 100 expiring warrants follows.

Assets	=	Liabilities	+	Equity
				−400
				+400

Paid-in Cap—War		Paid-in Cap—CS	
3,600	4,000		8,100
400			400

January 31, 2021—To record expiration of 100 warrants

Paid-in Capital—Stock Warrants ($4,000 × 100/1,000)	400	
Paid-in Capital in Excess of Par—Common Stock		400

REVIEW 16-9 **LO16-9** **Accounting for Debt with Stock Warrants**

Review MBC

On January 1, 2020, CostKo Corporation issued $100,000 of 6%, 5-year nonconvertible bonds with *nondetachable* stock purchase warrants. Each $1,000 bond carried 10 warrants, each of which was for one share of CostKo common stock, par value $1, at a specified option price of $40 per share. The bonds (including the warrants) sold at 102. No bond price without warrants was available.

Required

a. Provide the entry for CostKo at the date of issuance of the bonds.

b. Provide the entry for CostKo at the date of issuance of the bonds assuming instead that the warrants are *detachable*. Immediately after the date of issuance, the detachable stock purchase warrants were selling at $5 each.

More Practice:
16-45, 16-76, 16-77, 16-94

Solution on p. 16-75.

LO 16-10 Apply the fair value option for liabilities

LO 16-10 Overview

Accounting for Fair Value Option
- Elect to value long-term liabilities at fair value
- Measure liability at fair value
  - General risk: Adjust NI
  - Instrument risk: Adjust OCI

The previous sections accounted for bonds and notes at amortized cost. Yet, debtors can opt to record most financial liabilities including bonds and notes payable under the **fair value option**. Under this method, a bond or note payable is adjusted to fair value each reporting date. The argument for reporting liabilities at fair value is that fair value enhances relevance and comparability and provides a better starting point for understanding and analyzing risks by reflecting changes in risks *in the period in which they occur*.

This decision to invoke the fair value option must be made on the issue date of the debt or established through a company policy. The decision is applied to each debt instrument individually, and the decision is generally irrevocable (decision to report at fair value cannot be changed). A company should apply the method consistently to each financial liability from period to period. A company may choose to account for some debt instruments at fair value and others at amortized cost. Authoritative support follows.

825-10-25-2 The decision about whether to elect the fair value option:

a. Shall be applied instrument by instrument.

b. Shall be irrevocable.

c. Shall be applied only to an entire instrument and not to only specified risks, specific cash flows, or portions of that instrument.

An entity may decide whether to elect the fair value option for each eligible item on its election date. Alternatively, an entity may elect the fair value option according to a preexisting policy for specified types of eligible items.

Fair value can be determined through market prices quoted on an exchange (readily observable). Otherwise, fair value can be measured by taking the present value of remaining cash flows, discounted at the market rate. Amortized cost of the debt is determined through the entries shown in previous sections. When adjusting liabilities to fair value from amortized cost, the adjustment is recorded in the **Fair Value Adjustment** account, which is a contra or adjunct account to the liability account. The offsetting debit or credit is an unrealized gain or loss recognized in either other comprehensive income or net income.

- **General Risk** Recognize the portion of the total change in the fair value of the liability that results from a change in general risk (such as a change in the risk-free rate or a benchmark interest rate) in *net income*.
- **Instrument-Specific Credit Risk** Recognize the portion of the total change in the fair value of the liability that results from a change in a company's own credit risk (called instrument-specific credit risk) in *other comprehensive income*. Instrument-specific credit risk is the risk that the bond issuer will not pay interest payments and the principal balance at the times and in the amounts specified in the bond indenture. The gain or loss recognized in accumulated other comprehensive income is reclassified to net income when the bond matures or is redeemed.

The accounting guidance follows.

825-10-45-5 If an entity has designated a financial liability under the fair value option in accordance with this Subtopic, the entity shall measure the financial liability at fair value with qualifying changes in fair value recognized in net income. The entity shall present separately in other comprehensive income the portion of the total change in the fair value of the liability that results from a change in the instrument-specific credit risk. The entity may consider the portion of the total change in fair value that excludes the amount resulting from a change in a base market risk, such as a risk-free rate or a benchmark interest rate, to be the result of a change in instrument-specific credit risk. Alternatively, an entity may use another method that it considers to faithfully represent the portion of the total change in fair value resulting from a change in instrument-specific credit risk. The entity shall apply the method consistently to each financial liability from period to period.

In general, a company reports a gain from an increase in risk or, alternatively, a loss from a decrease in risk related to the underlying instrument. For example, a general increase in interest rates (due to an increase in risk) will cause the fair value of a bond issued at its face value to decrease. (Discounting the bond to present value using a higher rate of interest causes a lower fair value.) A decrease in bonds payable or a debit to Fair Value Adjustment, causes a gain or a credit to Unrealized Gain—Income. The fair value option is illustrated in **Demo 16-10**.

EXPANDING YOUR KNOWLEDGE **Instrument-Specific Credit Risk**

Bonds associated with an increase in instrument-specific risk result in a recognized gain under the fair value option. (Discounting of bonds at a higher interest rate causes the value of the bonds to decrease, resulting in an unrealized gain.) Many financial statement users would consider recognizing a gain due to a decrease in credit standing to be *potentially misleading* because a company often lacks the ability to realize those gains by repurchasing the bonds at fair value. Thus, the inclusion of such gains in OCI (rather than net income) is supported by the FASB's observation that liabilities typically are not settled with a third party. This means that the fair value changes attributed to changes in a company's own credit risk usually are not realized. Plus, it is counterintuitive for a company to report an increase in its net income when its own credit risk increases and a decrease in net income if its own credit risk decreases.

Demo 16-10 LO16-10 Fair Value Option Accounting for Liabilities

Demo MBC

On January 1, 2020, Frazier Inc. issued three-year bonds to Seattle Corp. at face value for $10,000, with cash interest payable annually on December 31 at 4%. On January 1, 2020, Frazier Inc. chooses to account for the bonds using the *fair value option*. The fair value of the bonds on December 31, 2020, is $9,200 because the stated rate is now less than the market rate due to an increase in the risk-free rate. (A market rate increase will cause comparable debt instruments to now offer a higher interest rate.)

a. Record the adjusting entry on December 31, 2020, to adjust the bonds to fair value. Assume that interest expense has been recorded in 2020.

b. Now assume that the bonds were originally issued at a discount to yield a market rate of 5%. Record the adjusting entry on December 31, 2020, to adjust the bonds to fair value. Assume that interest expense has been recorded in 2020. *Hint:* First compute the amortized cost of the bonds using the effective interest method.

Solution

a. **Fair Value Adjustment—Bond Issued at Face Value**

At December 31, 2020, the year-end adjusting entry adjusts the bonds to the fair value of $9,200. Because the change in fair value is attributed to an increase in the risk-free rate, net income will be adjusted.

Assets = Liabilities + Equity
−800 +800
FVA—BP 800 | Unreal Gain—Inc | 800

December 31, 2020—To record fair value option adjustment and the net unrealized gain

Fair Value Adjustment—Bond Payable ($10,000 − $9,200)	800	
Unrealized Gain—Income		800

b. **Fair Value Adjustment—Bond Issued at a Discount**

The bonds originally sold at a price of $9,728 (PV(0.05,3,–400,–10000)). On December 31, 2020, the amortized cost of the bonds is $9,814 ($9,728 + ($486 – $400)). Frazier would record an entry to adjust the bonds to fair value from amortized cost.

Assets = Liabilities + Equity
−186 +186
FVA—BP 186 | Unreal Gain—Inc | 186

December 31, 2020—To record fair value option adjustment and the net unrealized gain

Fair Value Adjustment—Bond Payable ($10,000 − $9,814)	186	
Unrealized Gain—Income		186

AMERICAN INTERNATIONAL GROUP [AIG]

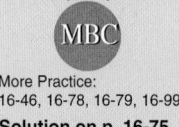

Real World—FAIR VALUE OPTION

American International Group, Inc. (AIG), an insurance organization, reported the following related to its election of the fair value method in a recent Form 10-K.

Fair Value Measurements (excerpt)—Under the fair value option, we may elect to measure at fair value financial assets and financial liabilities that are not otherwise required to be carried at fair value. Subsequent changes in fair value for designated items are reported in earnings . . . The following table presents the gains or losses recorded related to the eligible instruments for which we elected the fair value option:

Years Ended December 31 (in millions)	Gain (Loss) 2017	2016	2015
Liabilities:			
Long-term debt	$(49)	$(9)	$(38)
Other liabilities	(2)	—	(3)

REVIEW 16-10 LO16-10 Accounting for Debt Using the Fair Value Option

Review MBC

On January 1, 2020, Frazier Inc. issued three-year bonds to Seattle Corp. at face value for $10,000, with cash interest payable annually on December 31 at 4%. On January 1, 2020, Frazier Inc. chooses to account for the bonds using the *fair value option*. The fair value of the bonds on December 31, 2020, is $8,000 because Frazier Inc. was in violation of a debt covenant. Record the adjusting entry on December 31, 2020.

More Practice: 16-46, 16-78, 16-79, 16-99

Solution on p. 16-75.

Describe financing disclosures and analyses using leverage ratios

LO 16-11

Financing Disclosures and Ratios
- **Disclosures**
  - Interest rates, maturity dates
  - Debt provisions and restrictions
  - Pledged collateral
  - Fair value of debt
  - Five-year maturities
- **Leverage Ratios**
  - Total liabilities-to-equity ratio
  - Total liabilities-to-total assets ratio
  - Times interest earned ratio

LO 16-11 Overview

In general, notes accompanying financial statements provide information relevant to investors and creditors not conveniently disclosed within financial statements. Various aspects of debt agreements are disclosed in notes as they are relevant to investors and creditors.

Debt Disclosures with Financial Statements

The nature of debt, related interest rates, maturity dates, restrictions, call provisions, and conversion privileges are disclosed in notes to financial statements. Any assets pledged as collateral for debt, or other creditor restrictions also are disclosed in the notes.

If it is practical to estimate the fair value of long-term debt, fair value should be disclosed and the disclosure includes the following items as identified in the accounting guidance.

825-10-50-10 A reporting entity shall disclose all of the following:

a. Either in the body of the financial statements or in the accompanying notes, the fair value of financial instruments for which it is practicable to estimate that value.
b. The method(s) and significant assumptions used to estimate the fair value of financial instruments.
c. A description of the changes in the method(s) and significant assumptions used to estimate the fair value of financial instruments, if any, during the period.
d. The level of the fair value hierarchy within which the fair value measurements are categorized in their entirety (Level 1, 2, or 3).

EXPANDING YOUR KNOWLEDGE **Off-Balance-Sheet Financing**

Off-balance-sheet financing arises when commitments that expose the company to credit risk are not recorded on the balance sheet. For example, a company may be at risk for debt incurred by an unconsolidated subsidiary or a company may agree to pay the debt of another party (in return for a fee) if that party defaults. A *direct guarantee of indebtedness* is an agreement in which a guarantor states that if the debtor fails to make payment to the creditor when due, the guarantor will pay the creditor. If the debtor defaults, the creditor has a direct claim on the guarantor. *An indirect guarantee of indebtedness* is an agreement that obligates the guarantor to transfer funds to a debtor upon the occurrence of specified events under certain conditions. For example, a guarantor may be obligated to advance funds if a debtor's net income, coverage of fixed charges, or working capital falls below a specified minimum.

The SEC requires the disclosure of off-balance-sheet arrangements within the company's report on Form 10-K. Specifically, the SEC requires tabular disclosure of contractual obligations and either tabular or textual disclosure of contingent liabilities and commitments. The **Coca Cola Company** disclosed the following off-balance-sheet arrangement in a recent Form 10-K.

As of December 31, 2015, we were contingently liable for guarantees of indebtedness owed by third parties of $572 million, of which $263 million was related to VIEs (variable interest entities). These guarantees are primarily related to third-party customers, bottlers, vendors and container manufacturing operations and have arisen through the normal course of business. These guarantees have various terms, and none of these guarantees was individually significant. The amount represents the maximum potential future payments that we could be required to make under the guarantees; however, we do not consider it probable that we will be required to satisfy these guarantees. Management concluded that the likelihood of any significant amounts being paid by our Company under these guarantees is not probable. As of December 31, 2015, we were not directly liable for the debt of any unconsolidated entity, and we did not have any retained or contingent interest in assets as defined above.

Debt disclosures also include the aggregate amount of maturities and sinking-fund requirements for all long-term debt for each of the five years following the balance sheet date (illustrated in **Demo 16-11A**).

470-10-50-1 The combined aggregate amount of maturities and sinking fund requirements for all long-term borrowings shall be disclosed for each of the five years following the date of the latest balance sheet presented.

Debt Disclosures for Cash Flows Generally, proceeds from the issuance of long-term debt are reported as a cash inflow from *financing activities* while cash paid to retire long-term debt is reported as a cash outflow from financing activities. (If a debt is incurred to purchase inventory, repayment of that debt is classified as an operating outflow. This is true even for long-term debt.) Cash paid for interest is included in cash flows from *operating activities*. Interest expense is included in the computation of net income, the starting point of the operating activities section. Noncash adjustments to net income include (1) changes in interest payable, (2) amortization of discounts and premiums, and (3) gains and losses on the retirement of debt. Chapter 22 discusses the statement of cash flows in more detail.

Demo 16-11A LO16-11 Disclosure of Five-Year Debt Maturities

Demo MBC

Frazier Inc. had three debt obligations as of December 31, 2020, summarized as follows.

1. Unsecured note payable of $838,000, with full payment due on December 31, 2024.
2. Secured note payable of $555,000, with installment payments of $55,500 due over the next 10 years.
3. Redeemable bond issuance of $200,000, with full payment due on December 31, 2030.

Prepare a table to present debt maturities and prepare the related disclosure.

Solution

The following table summarizes the projected principal debt payments.

Debt	2021	2022	2023	2024	2025	Beyond 2025
1. Unsecured note payable				$838,000		
2. Secured note payable	$55,500	$55,500	$55,500	55,500	$55,500	$277,500
3. Redeemable bonds payable						200,000
Total	$55,500	$55,500	$55,500	$893,500	$55,500	$477,500

The following disclosure would be included in the financial statement disclosure notes of Frazier Inc. as of December 31, 2020.

December 31, 2020—Debt Disclosure

The annual requirements for principal payments on long-term debt are approximately $55,500, $55,500, $55,500, $893,500, and $55,500 for the years 2021 through 2025, respectively, and $477,500 thereafter.

PEPSICO [PEP]

Real World—LONG-TERM DEBT

PepsiCo Inc. Form 10-K illustrates disclosure of maturities of long-term debt obligations.

Debt Obligations and Commitments—The following table summarizes the Company's debt obligations:

	2014	2013
Short-term debt obligations		
Current maturities of long-term debt	$ 4,096	$ 2,224
Commercial paper (0.1% and 0.1%)	746	2,924
Other borrowings (17.7% and 12.4%)	234	158
	$ 5,076	$ 5,306

	2014	2013
Long-term debt obligations		
Notes due 2014 (5.3%)	$ —	$ 2,219
Notes due 2015 (1.4% and 1.2%)	4,093	4,116
Notes due 2016 (2.6% and 2.5%)	3,099	3,106
Notes due 2017 (1.6% and 2.0%)	2,004	1,258
Notes due 2018 (4.4% and 4.3%)	3,410	3,439
Notes due 2019 (3.7% and 3.7%)	1,631	1,635
Notes due 2020–2044 (3.9% and 4.0%)	13,640	10,738
Other, due 2015–2019 (4.4% and 4.4%)	40	46
	27,917	26,557
Less: current maturities of long-term debt obligations	(4,096)	(2,224)
Total	$23,821	$24,333

The interest rates in the above table reflect weighted-average rates at year-end.

Financial Leverage Ratios

The balance sheet provides information concerning liquidity and financial flexibility. For example, is a company in a position to finance new activities with relative ease without incurring excessive debt? Is a company in a position to pay interest on outstanding debt? Is a company able to respond to new competitive conditions? Is a company at risk of defaulting on its obligations? If a company carries a high debt load, it will be less flexible to incur unexpected expenses or take advantage of unexpected opportunities.

The balance sheet is the basis for calculating financial ratios measuring liquidity and financial flexibility. A number of ratios assist investors and creditors in analyzing the financial position of a company. The following three financial leverage ratios are illustrated in **Demo 16-11B**.

Total liabilities-to-equity ratio (total liabilities/total stockholders' equity) provides a direct comparison between debt and stockholders' equity. It measures the balance between resources provided by creditors and resources provided by owners (including retained earnings). The higher the ratio, the more **leverage** the company is using and the more risk that is borne by owners. Because interest payments are a required expense and creditors have a priority claim on the assets of the company, investors are concerned if this ratio is high relative to the inherent risk of the operations of the company. On the other hand, a company may also have too low a ratio if management is not using debt financing at an appropriate level. A more detailed analysis of a computed ratio would include a comparison to the following: prior year ratios, current year's forecasted or budgeted ratios, competitor ratios, and average industry ratios.

Total liabilities-to-total assets ratio (total liabilities/total assets) measures the proportion of assets provided by creditors (an indicator of leverage). This ratio measures the percentage of assets financed by creditors. Again, a higher ratio indicates higher risk of default on debt.

Times interest earned ratio (income before taxes and interest expense/interest expense) measures the number of times a company could pay for interest from its current earnings. This ratio helps creditors and investors determine whether a company can make its required interest payments. Generally, the lower the ratio, the more risk of a company's default on interest payments.

Calculating Leverage Ratios

LO16-11 **Demo 16-11B**

Demo MBC

The following financial information is provided for PepsiCo Inc. from a recent annual report. Compute the company's (a) total liabilities-to-equity ratio, (b) total liabilities-to-total assets ratio, and (c) times interest earned ratio for 2016.

Balances at December 31, 2016 ($ millions)	
Total assets	$74,129
Total liabilities	62,930
Total shareholders' equity	11,199

Results for Year Ended December 31, 2016 ($ millions)	
Operating profit before interest and taxes	$9,785
Interest expense	1,342

Solution

$$\textbf{Total liabilities-to-equity} = \frac{\text{Total liabilities}}{\text{Total stockholders' equity}} = \frac{\$62,930}{\$11,199} = 5.62$$

$$\textbf{Total liabilities-to-total assets} = \frac{\text{Total liabilities}}{\text{Total assets}} = \frac{\$62,930}{\$74,129} = 0.85$$

$$\textbf{Times interest earned} = \frac{\text{Income before taxes and interest expense}}{\text{Interest expense}} = \frac{\$9,785}{\$1,342} = 7.29$$

This analysis illustrates that PepsiCo relies heavily on debt from creditors for financing yet demonstrates an ability to pay interest on its debt out of current earnings.

REVIEW 16-11 **LO16-11** **Calculating Leverage Ratio**

Review MBC

Coca-Cola Company reported the following amounts (in millions) for 2016 in a recent Form 10-K.

Balance at December 31, 2016	
Total assets	$87,270
Total liabilities	64,050
Total stockholders' equity	23,220

Results for Year Ended December 31, 2016	
Total earnings	$6,550
Interest expense	733
Net earnings before taxes and interest	8,626

Compute the following ratios.

a. Total liabilities-to-equity
b. Total liabilities-to-total assets
c. Times interest earned

More Practice: 16-47, 16-81, 16-120
Solution on p. 16-75.

Management Judgment

There are many financing decisions that management must make related to debt issues. For example, management determines the type and features of new debt and the terms and timing of the issue. Management must also determine whether or not to extinguish debt early, refund debt with alternative debt, or entice debt holders to convert debt to equity in cases of convertible debt. Let's consider a sample of the judgments that management must make in accounting for long-term debt.

- Management determines the method to amortize discounts or premiums and whether a method other than the effective interest method produces results that are not materially different from the effective interest method (p. 16-11).
- In a case where a note is issued at a stated rate that does not equal the market rate, the market rate of a note with similar risks must be determined (p. 16-24).
- In a case where a note is issued for noncash consideration, management must determine whether the fair value of the debt or the fair value of the noncash consideration is more reliable. Further, in cases where the fair value of the debt is used to measure the transaction, a market rate must be determined (p. 16-25).
- When bonds with detachable warrants are issued, management must determine the fair value of warrants and the fair value of the bonds without the warrants (p. 16-35).
- Management must decide whether or not to elect the irrevocable fair value option on an individual, debt security basis (p. 16-37).
- If the fair value option is selected, management must determine whether a gain or loss is attributable to general or instrument-specific credit risk (p. 16-38).
- For disclosure purposes, management must estimate the fair value of long-term debt through the categories of the fair value hierarchy when it is practical to do so (p. 16-40).
- SEC registrants must identify off-balance sheet disclosures for the MD&A analysis (p. 16-40).

APPENDIX 16A LO 16-12 Account for debt settlement and debt restructuring

Rising interest rates, nonperforming loans, unsatisfactory return on investments, and lack of demand for a company's products and services contribute to troubled debt. Rather than write off nonperforming loans or pursue legal action, creditors frequently agree to a debt restructure, allowing the debtor to remain in operation in the hope that the debtor can resolve its financial difficulties. Creditors usually receive more on restructured debt than through bankruptcy by the debtor.

Typical debt restructuring includes a complete settlement of debt through cash payment or transfer of equity securities or a restructure of debt provisions. Modifications include changes such as a reduction in the interest rate, extension of the maturity date, reduction in the face amount of the debt, or reduction of accrued interest. In a ***troubled debt restructure***, *the creditor grants a concession to the debtor that it would not otherwise consider.* The concession is granted by the creditor in an attempt to protect its investment.

ASC Glossary Troubled debt restructuring: A restructuring of a debt constitutes a troubled debt restructuring if the creditor for economic or legal reasons related to the debtor's financial difficulties grants a concession to the debtor that it would not otherwise consider.

LO 16-12 Overview

Debt Settlement and Restructuring
- **Debtor perspective**
  - Settlement though transfer of assets or equity interest
  - Restructuring of debt terms
- **Creditor perspective**
  - Settlement though transfer of assets or equity interest
  - Restructuring of debt terms

Troubled Debt Restructure—Debtor

We review and illustrate in **Demo 16-12A** the following four scenarios as related to the debtor.

Settlement of Debt through Transfer of Assets In a full settlement of debt through the transfer of assets (such as land, receivables, building, or other assets), the debtor measures the assets given up at fair value, derecognizes the debt and the assets given up, and records a gain or loss on the income statement.

470-60-35-3 A difference between the fair value and the carrying amount of assets transferred to a creditor to settle a payable is a gain or loss on transfer of assets. The carrying amount of a receivable encompasses not only unamortized premium, discount, acquisition costs, and the like but also an allowance for uncollectible amounts and other valuation accounts, if any. The debtor shall include that gain or loss in measuring net income for the period of transfer.

Settlement of Debt through Transfer of Equity Interest In a full settlement of debt through the transfer of equity (such as common stock of the debtor), the debtor derecognizes the debt, records the equity issuance at fair value, and records a gain or loss on the income statement.

470-60-35-4 A debtor that issues or otherwise grants an equity interest to a creditor to settle fully a payable shall account for the equity interest at its fair value. The difference between the fair value of the equity interest granted and the carrying amount of the payable settled shall be recognized as a gain on restructuring of payables.

Restructuring of Debt When Payments Are Less than Debt Carrying Value In a debt restructuring where the future revised cash flows are less than the debt carrying value, the debtor reduces the carrying value of the debt to the future modified cash payments (undiscounted), and a gain is recognized.

470-60-35-6 If, however, the total future cash payments specified by the new terms of a payable, including both payments designated as interest and those designated as face amount, are less than the carrying amount of the payable, the debtor shall reduce the carrying amount to an amount equal to the total future cash payments specified by the new terms and shall recognize a gain on restructuring of payables equal to the amount of the reduction.

Restructuring of Debt When Payments Exceed Debt Carrying Value In a debt restructuring where the future revised cash flows exceed the debt carrying value, no gain is recognized by the debtor and the debtor does not adjust the carrying value of the debt. Instead, the debtor computes a new effective interest rate to equate the present value of the future cash flows with the debt carrying value. The new effective interest rate is used to prepare an amortization schedule, which becomes the basis for the recording of interest expense over the remaining term of the debt agreement.

470-60-35-5 A debtor in a troubled debt restructuring involving only modification of terms of a payable—that is, not involving a transfer of assets or grant of an equity interest—shall account for the effects of the restructuring prospectively from the time of restructuring, and shall not change the carrying amount of the payable at the time of the restructuring unless the carrying amount exceeds the total future cash payments specified by the new terms . . . Interest expense shall be computed in a way such that a constant effective interest rate is applied to the carrying amount of the payable at the beginning of each period between restructuring and maturity.

Demo 16-12A LO16-12 Debt Restructuring and Debt Settlement—DEBTOR Perspective

Demo MBC

On January 1, 2019, Debb Company issues a 10%, two-year, $500,000 note paying annual interest each December 31 to Credex Company in exchange for $500,000 of merchandise. Debb is unable to make the December 31, 2019, interest payment. Debb is a calendar-year company and accrued the 2019 interest.

We illustrate four possible debt restructuring arrangements at January 1, 2020, from the *debtor's perspective.*

- Example One: Settlement of debt through transfer of assets.
- Example Two: Settlement of debt through transfer of equity interest.
- Example Three: Restructuring of debt when payments exceed debt book value.
- Example Four: Restructuring of debt when payments are less than debt book value.

Example One: Settlement of Debt through Transfer of Assets

On January 1, 2020, Debb agrees to transfer land and a building to Credex in full settlement of the note. Information regarding the land and building follow.

	Land	Building
Fair value, January 1, 2020	$100,000	$250,000
Original cost to Debb	75,000	300,000
Accumulated depreciation through January 1, 2020		100,000
Book value, January 1, 2020	75,000	200,000

Required

Record the entries for Debb (debtor) related to the debt settlement on January 1, 2020.

Solution

Assets	=	Liabilities	+	Equity
+25,000				+75,000
+50,000				

January 1, 2020—To adjust assets to fair value for Debb (debtor)

Land ($100,000 − $75,000)	25,000	
Building ($250,000 − [$300,000 − $100,000])	50,000	
Gain on Disposal		75,000

Assets	=	Liabilities	+	Equity
+100,000		−500,000		+200,000
−100,000		−50,000		
−350,000				

Land	
Bal. 75,000	100,000
25,000	
0	

Building	
Bal. 300,000	350,000
50,000	
0	

Accum Deprec	
100,000	100,000 Bal.
	0

Interest Payable	
50,000	50,000 Bal.
	0

Note Payable	
500,000	500,000 Bal.
	0

Gain	
	75,000
	200,000

January 1, 2020—To record troubled debt restructure for Debb (debtor)

Note Payable	500,000	
Interest Payable ($500,000 × 10%)	50,000	
Accumulated Depreciation	100,000	
Land		100,000
Building		350,000
Gain on Restructuring of Debt (to balance)		200,000

Example Two: Settlement of Debt through Transfer of Equity Interest

Instead, let's assume that on January 1, 2020, Debb issues 2,500 shares of its $10 par common stock in full settlement of the note. The market price per share is $60 on January 1, 2020, and the increase in outstanding shares is not expected to affect the stock price appreciably.

Required

Record the entries for Debb (debtor) related to the debt settlement on January 1, 2020.

Solution

Assets	=	Liabilities	+	Equity
		−500,000		+25,000
		−50,000		+125,000
				+400,000

Interest Payable	
50,000	50,000 Bal.
	0

Note Payable	
500,000	500,000 Bal.
	0

Common Stock	
	25,000

Paid-in-Cap—CS	
	125,000

Gain—Debt Restr	
	400,000

January 1, 2020—To record troubled debt restructure for Debb (debtor)

Note Payable	500,000	
Interest Payable	50,000	
Common Stock (2,500 × $10)		25,000
Paid-in Capital in Excess of Par—Common Stock (2,500 × [$60 − $10])		125,000
Gain on Restructuring of Debt (to balance)		400,000

continued

continued from previous page

Example Three: Restructuring of Debt at Less than Debt Carrying Value

Now let's assume that on January 1, 2020, Debb and Credex agree to a debt restructure agreement with the following provisions:

- Face value of note is reduced to $400,000.
- Accrued interest for 2019 is forgiven.
- Maturity is extended to January 1, 2022 (a one-year extension).
- Interest rate is reduced to 5%; interest payments are due December 31, 2020, and 2021.

Required

Record the entries for Debb (debtor) related to the debt restructuring on January 1, 2020.

Solution

The excess of the debt book value over the restructured cash flows is calculated as follows.

Book value of debt, January 1, 2020 ($500,000 + $50,000)		$550,000
Sum of restructured cash flows:		
Face value payable, January 1, 2022	$400,000	
December 31, 2020, interest payment (5% × $400,000)	20,000	
December 31, 2021, interest payment (5% × $400,000)	20,000	440,000
Gain on structure for Debb (debtor)		$110,000

Debb (debtor) will reduce the value of the interest payable and note payable by $110,000.

January 1, 2020—To record troubled debt restructure for Debb (debtor)

Note Payable	500,000	
Interest Payable	50,000	
Note Payable		440,000
Gain on Restructuring of Debt (to balance)		110,000

Assets	=	Liabilities	+	Equity
		−500,000		+110,000
		−50,000		
		+440,000		

Interest Payable	
50,000	50,000 Bal.
	0

Note Payable	
500,000	500,000 Bal.
	440,000
	440,000

Gain—Debt Restr	
	110,000

Example Four: Restructuring of Debt when Restructured Payments Exceed Debt Carrying Value

Let's assume on January 1, 2020, Debb and Credex agree to a debt restructure agreement providing the following:

- Accrued interest for 2019 is forgiven.
- Maturity is extended to January 1, 2022 (a one-year extension), and regular interest payments are required December 31, 2020, and 2021.

Required

Record the entries for Debb (debtor) related to the (1) debt restructuring on January 1, 2020, (2) the interest payments on December 31, 2020, and 2021, and (3) the payment of the note on January 1, 2022.

Solution

The excess of the restructured cash flows over the debt book value is calculated as follows.

Sum of restructured cash flows		
Face value payable, January 1, 2022	$500,000	
December 31, 2020, interest payment (10% × $500,000)	50,000	
December 31, 2021, interest payment (10% × $500,000)	50,000	$600,000
Less book value of debt, January 1, 2020		550,000
Excess of restructured cash flows over debt book value		$ 50,000

Debb, the debtor, records no gain on the debt restructure. Instead, Debb computes a new effective interest rate using the revised debt payment schedule and this rate is computed as follows.

	RATE	NPER	PMT	PV	FV	Excel Formula
Given	?	2	50,000	(550,000)	500,000	=RATE(2,50000,550000,500000)
Solution	4.6487%					

continued

continued from previous page

Using the market rate of 4.6487%, Debb (the debtor) would prepare the following amortization schedule.

Debb (Debtor)

	Effective Interest Method			
Date	**Cash (Stated Interest)**	**Interest Expense (Market Interest)**	**Note Payable Reduction**	**Note Payable, Net (Carrying Value)**
Jan. 1, 2020. . .				$550,000
Dec. 31, 2021. . .	$ 50,000	$25,568	$24,432	525,568
Dec. 31, 2022. . .	50,000	24,432	25,568	500,000
Totals	$100,000	$50,000	$50,000	

On January 1, 2020, no gain is recorded. Any outstanding interest is combined with the outstanding principal into the new note payable account.

Assets	=	Liabilities	+	Equity
		−500,000 −50,000 +550,000		

January 1, 2020—To record troubled debt restructure for Debb (debtor)

Note Payable	500,000	
Interest Payable	50,000	
Note Payable		550,000

Assets	=	Liabilities	+	Equity
−50,000		−24,432		−25,568

December 31, 2020—To record interest payment for Debb (debtor)

Note Payable	24,432	
Interest Expense.	25,568	
Cash		50,000

Assets	=	Liabilities	+	Equity
−50,000		−25,568		−24,432

December 31, 2021—To record interest payment for Debb (debtor)

Note Payable	25,568	
Interest Expense.	24,432	
Cash		50,000

Assets	=	Liabilities	+	Equity
−500,000		−500,000		

Cash	
	50,000 50,000 500,000

Interest Payable	
50,000	50,000 Bal.
	0

Note Payable	
500,000 24,432 25,568 500,000	500,000 Bal. 550,000
	0

Interest Exp	
25,568 24,432	

January 1, 2022—To record principal payment for Debb (debtor)

Note Payable	500,000	
Cash		500,000

Troubled Debt Restructure—Creditor

Recall from the definition of a troubled debt restructuring that a creditor grants a *concession* based upon a debtor's *financial difficulties*. Factors for a creditor to consider in whether a debtor is experiencing financial difficulties include the following.

ASC 310-40-15-20 (a)The debtor is currently in payment default on any of its debt. In addition, a creditor shall evaluate whether it is probable that the debtor would be in payment default on any of its debt in the foreseeable future without the modification . . . (b) The debtor has declared or is in the process of declaring bankruptcy. (c) There is substantial doubt as to whether the debtor will continue to be a going concern. (d) The debtor has securities that have been delisted, are in the process of being delisted, or are under threat of being delisted from an exchange.

Factors to consider for a creditor in whether a concession was granted include the following.

ASC 310-40-15-13 A creditor has granted a concession when, as a result of the restructuring, it does not expect to collect all amounts due, including interest accrued at the original contract rate.

In **Demo 16-12B** we review the four scenarios from **Demo 16-12A** but now from the perspective of the *creditor.*

The accounting guidance for the creditor is different from the debtor and at times, delivers different results (such as carrying amounts and gains or losses).

Settlement of a Receivable If a receivable (such as a note receivable) is settled by the debtor making a payment of cash, or transferring asset(s) or equity, the creditor will record the amounts at fair value and record a loss on the settlement. The loss can be recorded as an offset to the allowance for doubtful accounts.

Modification of Terms of a Receivable A creditor measures the loss on a receivable by discounting the restructured future cash flows using the historical market rate of interest on the loan. (This is the same procedure that we used to account for an impairment of receivables in LO 8-9 except now we have officially modified cash flows while with an impairment we used expected future cash flows.)

310-40-35-12 The effective interest rate for a loan restructured in a troubled debt restructuring is based on the original contractual rate, not the rate specified in the restructuring agreement. It has been indicated that a troubled debt restructuring does not result in a new loan but rather represents part of a creditor's ongoing effort to recover its investment in the original loan. Therefore, the interest rate used to discount expected future cash flows on a restructured loan shall be the same interest rate used to discount expected future cash flows on an impaired loan.

Debt Restructuring and Debt Settlement—CREDITOR Perspective LO16-12 Demo 16-12B

Demo MBC

Refer to the information in **Demo 16-12A**, but now record the entries from the perspective of the creditor.

Example One: Settlement of Debt through Transfer of Assets

January 1, 2020—To record troubled debt restructure for Credex (creditor)

Land	100,000	
Building	250,000	
Loss on Restructuring of Debt* (to balance)	200,000	
Note Receivable		500,000
Interest Receivable ($500,000 × 10%)		50,000

*Can also debit Bad Debt Expense or offset the Allowance for Doubtful Accounts

Assets = Liabilities + Equity
+100,000 −200,000
+250,000
−500,000
−50,000

Interest Receiv: Bal. 50,000 | 50,000; 0
Note Receiv: Bal. 500,000 | 500,000; 0
Land: 100,000 |
Building: 250,000 |
Loss—Debt Restr: 200,000 |

Example Two: Settlement of Debt through Transfer of Equity Interest

January 1, 2020—To record troubled debt restructure for Credex (creditor)

Investment in Common Stock (2,500 × $60)	150,000	
Loss on Restructuring of Debt* (to balance)	400,000	
Note Receivable		500,000
Interest Receivable		50,000

*The company can also debit Bad Debt Expense or offset the Allowance for Doubtful Accounts.

Assets = Liabilities + Equity
+150,000 −400,000
−500,000
−50,000

Interest Receiv: Bal. 50,000 | 50,000; 0
Note Receiv: Bal. 500,000 | 500,000; 0
Inv—CS: 150,000 |
Loss—Debt Restr: 400,000 |

Example Three: Restructuring of Debt at Less than Debt Carrying Value

The creditor will treat the debt restructure as a loan impairment, which calls for a write-down of the note to the present value of expected future cash flows discounted at the original market rate (10%). The net carrying value of the note for Credex (creditor) after the restructure is calculated as follows:

	RATE	NPER	PMT	PV	FV	Excel Formula
Given	0.10	2	20,000	?	400,000	=PV(0.1,2,20000,400000)
Solution				$(365,289)		

Credex recognizes an immediate charge to bad debt expense of $184,711 ($550,000 − $365,289) and then recognizes interest at 10% over the remaining term of the restructure agreement using the effective interest method.

January 1, 2020—To record troubled debt restructure for Credex (creditor)

Note Receivable	550,000	
Bad Debt Expense	184,711	
Allowance for Doubtful Accounts		184,711
Interest Receivable		50,000
Note Receivable		500,000

Assets = Liabilities + Equity
+550,000 −184,711
−184,711
−50,000
−500,000

Interest Receiv: Bal. 50,000 | 50,000; 0
Note Receiv: Bal. 500,000 | 500,000; 550,000 |; 550,000
Bad Debt Exp: 184,711 |
AFDA: | 184,711

continued

continued from previous page

Example Four—Restructuring of Debt when Restructured Payments Exceed Debt Carrying Value

The creditor will treat the debt restructure as a loan impairment, which calls for a write-down of the note to the present value of expected future cash flows discounted at the original market rate (10%). The net carrying value of the note for Credex (creditor) after the restructure is calculated as follows.

	RATE	NPER	PMT	PV	FV	Excel Formula
Given	0.10	2	50,000	?	500,000	=PV(0.1,2,50000,500000)
Solution				$(500,000)		

Credex recognizes an immediate charge to bad debt expense of $50,000 ($550,000 – $500,000) and then recognizes interest at 10% over the remaining term of the restructure agreement (the effective interest method).

January 1, 2020—To record troubled debt restructure for Credex (creditor)

Assets	=	Liabilities	+	Equity
+550,000				−50,000
−50,000				
−50,000				
−500,000				

Interest Receiv

Bal. 50,000	50,000
0	

Note Receiv

Bal. 500,000	500,000
550,000	
550,000	

Bad Debt Exp

50,000	

AFDA

	50,000

	Debit	Credit
Note Receivable	550,000	
Bad Debt Expense	50,000	
Allowance for Doubtful Accounts		50,000
Interest Receivable		50,000
Note Receivable		500,000

REVIEW 16-12 LO16-12 Accounting for Debt Settlement and Debt Restructuring

Review MBC

Example One: Settling Debt through a Transfer of Assets

Atlanta Corporation is experiencing financial struggles and is negotiating a settlement of its $40,000, 8% note payable to Johnson Corporation. The note's carrying amount is $35,000, and its present value at the current market rate is $28,000. Atlanta agreed to give Johnson Company equipment in full settlement of a note payable on January 1, 2020. The equipment's original cost was $50,000. On January 1, 2020, the equipment's carrying amount is $28,000, and its fair value is $32,000. Record the entries by Atlanta Corporation to record the gain or loss on disposal of equipment and the settlement of the note. Interest has been paid through December 31, 2019.

Example Two: Settling Debt through a Transfer of Equity

Now assume that instead of settling the note with equipment, Atlanta Corporation settles the note with an equity interest. On January 1, 2020, Atlanta Corporation issues 3,000 shares of its $1 par common stock in full settlement of the note. The market price per share is $10 on January 1, 2020, and the increase in outstanding shares is not expected to affect the stock price appreciably. Record the entry by Atlanta Corporation to settle the note.

Example Three: Restructuring Debt at Less than Debt Carrying Value

Now assume that instead of settling the note, Johnson Company agrees to restructure the note. On January 1, 2020, Johnson Company agrees to reduce the note to $25,000, and decrease the interest rate to 5% (due annually). The note payable is due December 31, 2021. Record the entry by Atlanta Corporation to restructure the note.

Example Four: Restructuring Debt in Excess of Debt Carrying Value

Now assume that terms of the restructure are as follows. On January 1, 2020, Johnson Company agrees to reduce the note to $30,000, and decrease the interest rate to 9% (due annually). The note payable is due December 31, 2022. Record the entry by Atlanta Corporation to restructure the note.

More Practice: 16-124, 16-125, 16-126, 16-127

Solution on p. 16-75.

Questions

16-1. List and briefly explain the primary characteristics of long-term debt securities. What are the primary distinctions between a debt security and an equity security?

16-2. Explain the difference between the stated rate and the market rate on a long-term debt security.

16-3. How is the issue price of a zero-interest-bearing note payable determined?

16-4. Briefly explain the effects on interest recognized when the stated and market rates of interest are different.

16-5. What are the primary characteristics of a bond? What distinguishes it from capital stock?

16-6. Contrast the following classes of bonds: (a) corporate versus municipal, (b) secured versus unsecured, (c) term versus serial, and (d) callable versus convertible.

16-7. What are the principal advantages and disadvantages of issuing bonds versus common stock for (a) the issuer and (b) the investor?

16-8. Distinguish between the face value and the issue price of a bond. When are they the same? When are they different? Explain.

16-9. Explain the impact on interest of a bond discount and bond premium to (a) the issuer and (b) the investor.

16-10. Assume that a $1,000, 8% (payable semiannually), 10-year bond is sold at a market rate of 6%. Explain how to compute the price of this bond.

16-11. Explain why and how bond discount and bond premium affect (a) the balance sheet and (b) the income statement of the investor.

16-12. What is the primary conceptual difference between the straight-line and effective interest methods of amortizing bond discount and premium?

16-13. Under GAAP, when is it appropriate to use the (a) straight-line interest method and (b) effective interest method of amortization for bond discount or premium?

16-14. When the end of the accounting period of the issuer is not on a bond interest date, adjusting entries must be made for (a) accrued interest and (b) discount or premium amortization. Explain in general terms what each adjustment amount represents.

16-15. When bonds are sold (or purchased) between interest dates, accrued interest must be recognized. Explain why.

16-16. What are convertible bonds? What are the primary reasons for their use?

16-17. Define extinguishment of debt.

16-18. When may extinguishment of debt occur? List the various ways in which extinguishment of debt occurs.

16-19. Explain how an accounting gain or loss to the debtor may occur when a call privilege is exercised.

16-20. When the issuer purchases its own debt securities in the open market to extinguish the debt, two entries must usually be made. Explain.

16-21. What is meant by refunding?

16-22. Interest rates have increased since a company issued its bonds. Why would the company want to refund the bonds with another issue of bonds paying a higher rate?

16-23. A company retired a bond issue early, at a loss. Is the company in an economically worse position after the retirement?

16-24. Why is the accounting different for nonconvertible bonds with detachable stock purchase warrants and nonconvertible bonds with nondetachable stock purchase warrants?

Brief Exercises

Brief Exercise 16-25
Determining Bond Type **LO1**
Hint: See Demo 16-1A

For each of the following debt scenarios described below, identify the bond type that applies.

a.	Bonds issued by a public corporation	Corporate bonds or Municipal bonds
b.	Mortgage note issued for commercial property	Secured note or Debenture note
c.	Bonds issued at a discount, pays interest periodically and principal at bond maturity	Term bonds or Serial bonds
d.	Bonds which may be converted to equity securities at the option of the holder	Redeemable bonds or Convertible bonds

Brief Exercise 16-26
Determining Bond Features **LO1**
Hint: See Demo 16-1B

Rowe Corporation authorized $5,000 of 8% (cash interest payable semiannually) 10-year bonds. The bonds were dated January 1, 2020; interest dates are June 30 and December 31. Assume three different cases with respect to the sale of the bonds: Case A: Bonds sold on January 1, 2020, at par; Case B: Bonds sold on January 1, 2020, at 98; Case C: Bonds sold on February 1, 2020, at 102. Complete the following table.

	Case A	Case B	Case C
Face value of bonds			
Semiannual interest payment			
Bond selling price (excluding accrued interest)			
Bond issue date			

Brief Exercise 16-27 Computing Bond Selling Price **LO2**

An eight-year, 6%, $1,000 bond (cash interest payable annually) is sold to yield 6% interest. Compute the bond selling price.

Brief Exercise 16-28 Computing Bond Selling Price **LO2** *Hint:* See Demo 16-2

A 10-year, 7%, $1,000 bond (cash interest payable 3.5% semiannually) is sold to yield 6% interest. Compute the bond selling price.

Brief Exercise 16-29 Computing Bond Selling Price **LO2** *Hint:* See Demo 16-2

A 10-year, 6%, $1,000 bond (cash interest payable 3% semiannually) is sold to yield 8% interest. Compute the bond selling price.

Brief Exercise 16-30 Computing Bond Issue Price—Sold Between Interest Payment Dates **LO2** *Hint:* See Demo 16-2

Rowe Corporation authorized $600,000 of 8% (cash interest payable semiannually) 10-year bonds. The bonds were dated January 1, 2020. Interest dates are June 30 and December 31. Assuming that the bonds were sold on March 1, 2020, at face value, record the following journal entries.

a. March 1, 2020: Issuance of bonds.
b. June 30, 2020: Interest payment.

Brief Exercise 16-31 Recording Bonds Issued at Face Value **LO3** *Hint:* See Demo 16-3

Yale Corporation issued to Zap Corporation $60,000, 8% (cash interest payable semiannually on July 1 and January 1) 10-year bonds dated and sold on January 1, 2020. If the bonds were sold at face value, provide the journal entries to be made at each of the following dates. Yale's fiscal year ends on December 31.

a. January 1, 2020, for issuance of bonds.
b. July 1, 2020, for the interest payment.
c. December 31, 2020, for the adjusting entry.

Brief Exercise 16-32 Recording Bonds Issued at a Discount—Straight-Line **LO4** *Hint:* See Demo 16-4B

Yale Corporation issued to Zap Corporation $60,000, 8% (cash interest payable semiannually on June 30 and December 31) 10-year bonds dated and sold on January 1, 2020. Assume that the company uses the straight-line amortization method. If the bonds were sold at 97, provide journal entries to be made at each of the following dates.

a. January 1, 2020, for issuance of bonds.
b. June 30, 2020, for interest payment.

Brief Exercise 16-33 Recording Bonds Issued at a Premium—Straight-Line **LO5**

Yale Corporation issued to Zap Corporation $60,000, 8% (cash interest payable semiannually on June 30 and December 31) 10-year bonds dated and sold on January 1, 2020. Assume that the company uses the straight-line amortization method. If the bonds were sold at 103, provide journal entries to be made at each of the following dates.

a. January 1, 2020, for issuance of bonds.
b. March 31, 2020, for accrual of interest for quarterly reporting.
c. June 30, 2020, for interest payment.

Brief Exercise 16-34 Recording Bonds Issued at a Discount—Effective Interest **LO4** *Hint:* See Demo 16-4A

Yale Corporation issued to Zap Corporation $60,000, 8% (cash interest payable semiannually on June 30 and December 31) 10-year bonds dated and sold on January 1, 2020. Assume that the company uses the effective interest amortization method. If the bonds were sold to yield 9%, provide journal entries to be made at each of the following dates.

a. January 1, 2020, for issuance of bonds.
b. June 30, 2020, for the interest payment.

Brief Exercise 16-35 Recording Bonds Issued at a Premium—Effective Interest **LO5** *Hint:* See Demo 16-5A

Yale Corporation issued to Zap Corporation $60,000, 8% (cash interest payable semiannually on June 30 and December 31) 10-year bonds dated and sold on January 1, 2020. Assume that the company uses the effective interest amortization method. If the bonds were sold to yield 7%, provide journal entries to be made at each of the following dates.

a. January 1, 2020, for issuance of bonds.
b. June 30, 2020, for the interest payment.

Brief Exercise 16-36
Reporting Bonds on the Balance Sheet **LO4**
Hint: See Demo 16-4A

For the Yale Corporation bonds in Brief Exercise 16-34, show how the bonds and related accounts would be presented in the balance sheet as of June 30, 2020.

Brief Exercise 16-37
Recording Debt Issuance Costs **LO4**
Hint: See Demo 16-4C

Yale Corporation issued to Zap Corporation $60,000, 8% (cash interest payable semiannually on June 30 and December 31) 10-year bonds dated and sold on January 1, 2020. Assume that the company uses the effective interest amortization method and bond issuance costs are $1,500. If the bonds were sold to yield 9%, provide journal entries to be made at each of the following dates.

a. January 1, 2020, for issuance of bonds.
b. June 30, 2020, for the interest payment.

Brief Exercise 16-38
Recording Entries for Note Payable **LO6**
Hint: See Demo 16-6A

Lacey Corp. issued a three-year, $5,000 note with an 8% stated rate to Hayley Co. on January 1, 2020, and received cash of $5,000. The note requires semiannual interest payments on June 30 and December 31. Provide journal entries to be made at each of the following dates.

a. January 1, 2020, for issuance of the note.
b. June 30, 2020, for the interest payment.

Brief Exercise 16-39
Recording Entries for Zero-Interest-Bearing Note Payable **LO6**
Hint: See Demo 16-6A

On January 1, 2020, Landry Inc. issued a three-year, $5,000, zero-interest-bearing note to Dillon LLP, and received $4,198. The implied interest rate is 6% on this note transaction. Provide journal entries to be made at each of the following dates.

a. January 1, 2020, for issuance of the note.
b. December 31, 2020, for accrual of interest.

Brief Exercise 16-40
Recording Entries for Interest-Bearing Note Payable **LO6**
Hint: See Demo 16-6B

Fern Company purchased goods on January 1, 2020, and issued a two-year, $2,500 note with a 5% stated rate. The fair value of the goods is $2,366. The note requires annual interest payments on December 31. The market rate of interest appropriate for this note is 8%. Provide journal entries to be made at each of the following dates.

a. January 1, 2020, for issuance of the note.
b. December 31, 2020, for the interest payment.

Brief Exercise 16-41
Recording Entries for Note Payable Exchanged for Cash and Noncash Consideration **LO6**

On January 1, 2020, Allen Corp. issued a 3-year, zero-interest-bearing note payable for $10,000 to Town Corp. for a cash receipt of $10,000. In lieu of interest payments, Allen Corp. agreed to sell merchandise to Town Corp. at a discount and provide free shipping during the 3-year period. The appropriate market rate for this transaction is 8%. Record the journal entry for Allen Corp. upon issuance of the note payable.

Brief Exercise 16-42
Computing Installment Payment on Note Payable **LO6**

On January 1, 2020, a borrower signed a long-term note, face amount $50,000 with time to maturity of 6 years. The interest rate is 7% and equal annual installment payments will pay off the loan after six years.

a. How much is each annual installment payment?
b. Record the first installment payment on December 31, 2020.

Brief Exercise 16-43
Recording Bond Redemption **LO7**
Hint: See Demo 16-7

Darien Inc. redeemed $5,000 of its bonds at 102 on January 1, 2020. At this date, the unamortized discount was $690. Prepare the journal entry on January 1, 2020, for the bond redemption. Assume Darien has a December 31 year-end and all adjusting entries were made.

Brief Exercise 16-44
Recording the Issuance of Convertible Bonds **LO8**
Hint: See Demo 16-8

Stonewall Corporation issued $20,000 of 5%, 10-year convertible bonds. Each $1,000 bond is convertible to 10 shares of common stock (par $50) of Stonewall Corporation. The bonds were sold at 105 on January 1, 2020. Provide the entry for Stonewall Corporation on January 1, 2020, to record the issuance of the bonds.

Brief Exercise 16-45
Recording the Issuance of Bonds with Detachable Warrants **LO9**
Hint: See Demo 16-9

On December 1, 2020, Junction Company issued at 104, 4,000 of its 9%, 10-year, $1,000 par value, nonconvertible bonds with detachable stock purchase warrants. Each bond carried two detachable warrants; each warrant was for one share of common stock at a specified option price of $15 per share. Shortly after issuance, the warrants were quoted on the market for $3 each. No fair value can be determined for the bonds without the warrants. Interest is payable on December 1 and June 1. Provide the entry to record issuance of the bonds by Junction Company on December 1, 2020.

Brief Exercise 16-46
Adjusting Bonds Payable Under the Fair Value Option **LO10**

Josie Corporation issued 10-year, 8% interest-bearing bonds payable at face value for $10,000 on January 1, 2020. At that time, Josie Corporation elected to account for the bonds payable using the fair value option method. At December 31, 2020, the fair value of the bonds payable was $9,900 due to an increase in Josie Corporation's borrowing rate because of general market risk.

a. Prepare the journal entry to adjust the bonds payable under the fair value option method on December 31, 2020.

b. How would your answer to (a) change if the decrease in the fair value of bonds payable was instead due to an increase in Josie Corporation's borrowing rate due to a decline in corporate liquidity?

Brief Exercise 16-47
Calculating Leverage Ratios **LO11**
Hint: See Demo 16-11B

Target Corporation reported the following amounts (in millions) in a recent Form 10-K.

- Total assets: $44,553
- Total liabilities: $28,322
- Total noncurrent liabilities: $15,545
- Total stockholders' equity: $16,231
- Total earnings: $1,971
- Interest expense: $1,126
- Net earnings before taxes and interest: $4,229

Compute the following ratios.

a. Total liabilities-to-equity *b.* Total liabilities-to-total assets *c.* Times interest earned

Exercises

Exercise 16-48
Classifying Financial Statement Accounts
LO1, 2, 3, 4, 5, 6, 7, 8, 9

For each account *a* through *m* listed below, indicate the account type (asset, liability, or equity) and the financial statement (balance sheet or statement of comprehensive income) where the account would be reported.

a. Discount on Bonds Payable (10-year bonds)
b. Premium on Bonds payable (10-year bonds)
c. Bonds Payable (Due in 5 years)
d. Note Payable (Due in 2 years)
e. Interest Expense
f. Unrealized Gain or Loss—Income
g. Unrealized Gain or Loss—OCI
h. Gain on Redemption of Bonds
i. Debt Conversion Expense
j. Interest Payable
k. Gain on Extinguishment of Bonds
l. Mortgage Payable
m. Paid-in Capital—Stock Warrants

Exercise 16-49
Determining Bond Type
LO1
Hint: See Demo 16-1A

For each of the following bond scenarios *a* through *e* described below, identify a bond type that applies.

a. Harrison County Flood Control Improvement Bonds issued in the state of Texas.
b. Bonds backed by liens on equipment are issued.
c. Treasury bill where the registered owner receives the face value of the bill at maturity with no principal payments during the term.
d. Corporate bonds where the holder has the option to trade in the bonds for the company's common stock.
e. Corporate bond that may be retired early at the option of the issuer.

Exercise 16-50
Determining Bond Features and Selling Price **LO1, 2**

On January 1, 2020, the following debt was authorized and issued by Anderson Company.

1. $50,000, 5-year, 9% convertible bonds payable, cash interest payable semiannually to yield 10%.
2. $10,000, 8-year, 10% note payable, cash interest payable semiannually to yield 9.5%.
3. $30,000, 10-year, zero-interest-bearing bonds to yield 11% annually.

Required

For each debt, indicate the following:

a. Face value.
b. Stated rate per interest period.
c. Stated interest amount per interest period.
d. Market rate per interest period.
e. Number of interest periods over life of the bonds.
f. Selling price.
g. Maturity date.
h. Authorization date.

Exercise 16-51
Determining Bond Selling Price **LO2**

Calculate the bond selling price for the three separate scenarios that follow.

a. 33M Corp. authorized and issued $100,000, 6%, 20-year bonds payable on January 1, 2020. Calculate the selling price of the bonds if the bonds pay cash interest semiannually on July 1 and January 1, and the market rate of interest on similar bonds is 8%.

b. 33M Corp. authorized and issued $250,000, 7%, 10-year bonds payable on January 1, 2020. Calculate the selling price of the bonds if the bonds pay cash interest semiannually on July 1 and January 1, and the market rate of interest on similar bonds is 6%.

c. 33M Corp. issued $75,000, 5%, 10-year bonds payable on March 31, 2020. The bonds were authorized on January 1, 2020. Calculate the selling price of the bonds (including interest) if the bonds pay cash interest annually on January 1, beginning January 1, 2021, and the market rate of interest on similar bonds is 6%.

Exercise 16-52
Recording Entries for Bonds Sold Between Interest Dates **LO2, 3**

On May 1, 2020, Setup Inc. sold an issue of 5%, $1,000 bonds dated January 1, 2020, to yield 5%. The bonds pay interest every June 30 and December 31, and mature December 31, 2024.

Required

a. Provide journal entries to be made by Setup Inc. at each of the following dates.
   1. May 1, 2020, bond issuance.
   2. June 30, 2020, first interest payment.

b. Indicate the amount of interest expense to be recorded in the income statement of Setup Inc. for the six months ended June 30, 2020.

Exercise 16-53
Recording Journal Entries for At-Par-Bonds **LO2, 3**

On October 1, 2020, New Co. issued an eight-year, 6%, $1,000 bond at face value, with cash interest payable semiannually on April 1 and October 1.

Required

Provide journal entries to be made by New Co. at each of the following dates.

a. October 1, 2020—Issuance.
b. December 31, 2020—Interest expense adjusting entry.
c. April 1, 2021—Interest payment.

Exercise 16-54
Preparing an Amortization Schedule—Effective Interest Method **LO4**

On January 1, 2020, Williams Inc. issued 8-year, $50,000, 5% bonds, priced to yield 6%, with cash interest payable semiannually on June 30 and December 31. The company amortizes the bond discount using the effective interest method.

Required

Provide an amortization schedule of interest and discount amortization for the 8-year bond term. Round amounts to two decimals.

Exercise 16-55
Preparing an Amortization Schedule—Straight-Line Interest Method **LO4**
Hint: See Demo 16-4B

On January 1, 2020, Williams Inc. issued 8-year, $50,000, 5% bonds, priced to yield 6%, with cash interest payable semiannually on June 30 and December 31. The company amortizes the bond discount using the straight-line interest method.

Required

Provide an amortization schedule of interest and discount amortization for the 8-year bond term. Round amounts to two decimals.

Exercise 16-56
Recording Bond Entries and Preparing an Amortization Schedule—Effective interest method, Discount **LO4**

Mitchell Inc. issued 40, 6%, $1,000 bonds on January 1, 2020, for $38,950. The bonds pay cash interest annually each December 31 and were issued to yield 7%. The bonds mature December 31, 2022, and the company uses the effective interest method to amortize bond discounts or premiums.

Required

a. Prepare an amortization schedule for the full bond term. Round amounts to the nearest dollar.

b. Prepare journal entries on the following dates.
   1. January 1, 2020, bond issuance.
   2. December 31, 2020, interest payment.

c. Explain why, in economic terms, the interest expense recognized each year exceeds the cash interest paid.

Exercise 16-57
Recording Bond Entries and Preparing an Amortization Schedule—Effective interest method, Discount **LO4**
Hint: See Demo 16-4A

Mitchell Inc. issued 40, 6%, $1,000 bonds on January 1, 2020. The bonds pay cash interest semiannually each July 1, and December 31, and were issued to yield 7%. The bonds mature December 31, 2022, and the company uses the effective interest method to amortize bond discounts or premiums.

Required

a. Determine the selling price of the bonds.
b. Prepare an amortization schedule for the full bond term.
c. Prepare journal entries on the following dates.
   1. January 1, 2020, bond issuance.
   2. July 1, 2020, bond payment.
   3. December 31, 2020, interest payment.

Exercise 16-58
Recording Bond Entries and Preparing an Amortization Schedule—Effective interest method, Discount, Interest Accrual **LO4**
Hint: See Demo 16-4A

Refer to the information in Exercise 16-57. However, now assume that the interest payments are made on July 1, and January 1.

Required

a. Determine the selling price of the bonds.
b. Prepare an amortization schedule for the full bond term.
c. Prepare journal entries on the following dates.
1. January 1, 2020, bond issuance.
2. July 1, 2020, interest payment.
3. December 31, 2020, interest accrual.
4. January 1, 2021, interest payment.

Exercise 16-59
Recording Bond Entries and Preparing an Amortization Schedule—Debt Issuance Costs **LO4**
Hint: See Demo 16-4C

Mitchell Inc. issued 40, 6%, $1,000 bonds on January 1, 2020. The bonds pay cash interest semiannually each July 1, and December 31, and were issued to yield 7%. Debt issuance costs were $800. The bonds mature December 31, 2022, and the company uses the effective interest method to amortize bond discounts and debt issuance costs.

Required

a. Determine the selling price of the bonds, net of debt issuance costs.
b. Prepare an amortization schedule for the full bond term.
c. Prepare journal entries on the following dates.
1. January 1, 2020, bond issuance.
2. July 1, 2020, interest payment.
3. December 31, 2020, interest payment.

Exercise 16-60
Recording Bond Entries and Preparing an Amortization Schedule—Effective interest method, Premium **LO5**

Mitchell Inc. issued 60, 6%, $1,000 bonds on January 1, 2020. The bonds pay cash interest annually each December 31 and were issued to yield 5%. The bonds mature December 31, 2024, and the company uses the effective interest method to amortize bond discounts or premiums.

Required

a. Determine the selling price of the bonds.
b. Prepare an amortization schedule for the full bond term.
c. Prepare journal entries on the following dates.
1. January 1, 2020, bond issuance.
2. December 31, 2020, interest payment.
3. December 31, 2021, interest payment.

Exercise 16-61
Recording Bond Entries and Preparing an Amortization Schedule—Effective interest method, Premium **LO5**
Hint: See Demo 16-5A

Mitchell Inc. issued 60, 6%, $1,000 bonds on January 1, 2020. The bonds pay cash interest semiannually each June 30, and December 31, and were issued to yield 5%. The bonds mature December 31, 2024, and the company uses the effective interest method to amortize bond discounts or premiums.

Required

a. Determine the selling price of the bonds.
b. Prepare an amortization schedule for the full bond term.
c. Prepare journal entries on the following dates.
1. January 1, 2020, bond issuance.
2. June 30, 2020, interest payment.
3. December 31, 2020, interest payment.

Exercise 16-62
Recording Bond Entries and Preparing an Amortization Schedule—Straight-Line Interest Method, Discount **LO4**
Hint: See Demo 16-4B

Mitchell Inc., issued 40, 6%, $1,000 bonds on January 1, 2020. The bonds pay cash interest semiannually each June 30 and December 31, and were issued to yield 7%. The bonds mature December 31, 2022, and the company will use the straight-line interest method to amortize the bond discount or premium. Assume that the difference between the effective interest method and the straight-line interest method is not material.

Required

a. Determine the selling price of the bonds.
b. Prepare an amortization schedule for the full bond term.
c. Prepare journal entries on the following dates.
1. January 1, 2020, bond issuance.
2. June 30, 2020, interest payment.
3. December 31, 2020, interest payment.

Exercise 16-63 Recording Bond Entries and Preparing an Amortization Schedule—Straight-Line Interest Method, Premium **LO5**

Mitchell Inc., issued 70, 6%, $1,000 bonds on January 1, 2020. The bonds pay cash interest annually each January 1 (beginning January 1, 2021), and were issued to yield 4%. The bonds mature January 1, 2030, and the company will use the straight-line interest method to amortize the bond discount or premium. Assume that the difference between the effective interest method and the straight-line interest method is not material.

Required

a. Determine the selling price of the bonds.

b. Prepare an amortization schedule for the full bond term.

c. Prepare journal entries on the following dates.
1. January 1, 2020, bond issuance.
2. December 31, 2020, interest accrual.
3. January 1, 2021, interest payment.

Exercise 16-64 Recording Bond Entries and Reporting Bonds—Effective Interest, Straight-Line **LO4**

Master Corp. issued 5%, $300,000 bonds on January 1, 2020. The bonds pay cash interest semiannually each July 1 and January 1, and were issued to yield 6%. The bonds mature January 1, 2030, and the company uses the effective interest method to amortize bond discounts or premiums.

Required

a. Prepare journal entries on the following dates.
1. January 1, 2020—Issuance of bonds.
2. July 1, 2020—Interest payment.
3. December 31, 2020—Interest accrual.
4. January 1, 2021—Interest payment.

b. Answer part *a* assuming instead that the company uses the straight-line interest method to amortize discounts and premiums and the bonds were sold on March 1, 2020, for $277,482 (excluding accrued interest).

Exercise 16-65 Recording Bond Entries and Reporting Bonds—Effective interest method, Straight-Line **LO5**

Master Corp. issued 8%, $80,000 bonds on February 1, 2020. The bonds pay interest semiannually each July 31 and January 31 and were issued to yield 7%. The bonds mature January 31, 2030, and the company uses the effective interest method to amortize bond discounts or premiums.

Required

a. Prepare journal entries on the following dates.
1. February 1, 2020—Issuance of bonds.
2. July 31, 2020—Interest payment.
3. December 31, 2020—Interest accrual.
4. January 31, 2021—Interest payment.

b. Indicate how the balance sheet and income statement of Master Corp. for the year ended December 31, 2020 would reflect these transactions.

c. What is the total cost of financing assuming that the bonds remain outstanding for the full term?

d. What is the total cost of financing assuming that the bonds remain outstanding for the full term if the straight-line interest method was used to amortize the premium?

e. If the company were to have instead amortized the premium using the straight-line interest method, would interest expense recognized be lower or higher in 2020?

f. If the company were to have instead amortized the premium using the straight-line interest method, would interest expense recognized be lower or higher in 2030?

Exercise 16-66 Computing Amounts under Effective Interest and Straight-Line Interest Methods **LO2, 4, 5**

For the following *separate* bond issues, assume that the bonds are sold on January 1, 2020, interest is paid semiannually on July 1 and December 31, and the bond term is 5 years.

Case	Face Value of Bonds	Stated Rate	Market Rate	Amortization Method	Bond Selling Price	Interest Expense 2020	Interest Paid 2020
1	$ 10,000	5%	6%	Effective interest			
2	40,000	4%	5%	Effective interest			
3	130,000	5%	4%	Straight-line			
4	500,000	0%	7%	Straight-line			
5	80,000	7%	6%	Effective interest			
6	100,000	6%	8%	Straight-line			

Required

Complete the table by measuring the bond selling price on January 1, 2020, and interest expense and interest paid for 2020.

Exercise 16-67
Recording a Note Payable Issued for Non-Cash Consideration
LO6

Lathrop Inc. purchased equipment on January 1, 2020, for $75,000 cash plus a note payable. The fair value of the equipment on January 1, 2020, is $271,333. The market rate of interest is 6%. 5M Corp. uses the effective interest method to amortize discounts and premiums.

Required

Record the entries over the term of the note payable for the following three *separate* scenarios for the structuring of the note payable.

a. The principal of $200,000 is due on December 31, 2021, and the note specified 5% interest payable each December 31 over a two-year period.

b. The face value of the note payable is instead $220,600 and is due on December 31, 2021. The note is structured as a zero-interest-bearing note payable over a two-year period.

c. The loan is extended to three years with equal payments of $73,450.10 due on each December 31 over the term of the note. The note will be fully paid upon maturity.

Exercise 16-68
Recording a Note Payable Issued for Non-Cash Consideration
LO6
Hint: See Demo 16-6B

On January 1, 2020, Jet Air Inc. contracted with Systems Plus Inc. to manufacture heavy equipment. Jet Air Inc. issued a $75,000 note to Systems Plus Inc. in exchange for the equipment that required 5% interest payments annually over 3 years on December 31 of each year. Although the fair value of the customized heavy equipment was not reasonably determinable, it was determined that 10% was a reasonable rate of interest for such a transaction.

Required

Provide journal entries to be made by Jet Air Inc. at each of the following dates.

a. January 1, 2020—Date of note issuance.

b. December 31, 2020—Date of interest payment.

c. December 31, 2021—Date of interest payment.

d. December 31, 2022—Date of interest payment.

e. December 31, 2022—Date of note payment at maturity.

Exercise 16-69
Recording a Note Payable Issued for Non-Cash Consideration
LO6

On June 30, 2020, BMO Company purchased land for expansion with an assessed value of $108,661 by issuing a 5-year, zero-interest-bearing note. The face value of the note is $175,000.

Required

a. Compute the rate of interest implied by this transaction.

b. Prepare an amortization schedule for the full note term using the effective interest method.

c. Prepare the journal entries on the following dates.

1. June 30, 2020—Note issuance
2. December 31, 2020—Adjusting entry

Exercise 16-70
Recording Entries for an Installment Note Payable **LO6**

On January 1, 2020, a borrower signed a long-term note, face amount, $100,000; time to maturity, three years; stated rate of interest, 8%. The market rate of interest of 10% determined the cash received by the borrower. The note will be paid in three equal annual installments of $38,803 each December 31 (which is also the end of the accounting period for the borrower).

Required

a. Compute the cash received by the borrower and prepare a debt amortization schedule.

b. Provide the required entries for the borrower for the issuance of the note on January 1, 2020, and the interest payments in 2020, 2021, and 2022.

Exercise 16-71
Recording Bond Retirement **LO7**

On March 1, 2020, Sandollar Inc. issued $30,000 of bonds at 105, paying 8% cash interest semiannually on June 30 and December 31. The bonds are scheduled to mature December 31, 2023. On September 1, 2020, $10,000 of the bonds were retired when the bonds were selling at 89. Assume the straight-line interest method is used to amortize bond discounts and premiums.

Required

a. Provide the entry for the bond issuance on March 1, 2020.

b. Provide the entry for the interest payment on June 30, 2020.

c. Provide the entry to recognize interest expense for the portion of the bond issue retired on September 1, 2020.

d. Provide the entry to record the bond retirement on September 1, 2020.

Exercise 16-72 Recording the Refunding of Long-Term Debt **LO7**

On January 1, 2020, Rocket Corporation issued $250,000 of 6%, 20-year bonds at 98. The interest is payable each December 31. Rocket uses straight-line amortization. The company's accounting period ends December 31.

On January 1, 2029, Rocket issued $250,000, 5% 20-year, refunding bonds at par. On this date, the old 6% bonds could be purchased in the open market at 102. Rocket immediately purchased all of the 6% bonds.

Required

a. Provide the entry for issuance of the 6% bonds on January 1, 2020.
b. Provide the entry for issuance of the 5% bonds on January 1, 2029.
c. Provide the entry to record the extinguishment of the old bonds on January 1, 2029.

Exercise 16-73 Recording the Refunding of Long-Term Debt **LO7**

Dillon Corp. issued $100,000 of 6% (cash payable each December 31), 10-year bonds on January 1, 2020. The bonds are callable at any point after 2024 at 103. The bonds sold on January 1, 2020, at 98. Straight-line amortization of bond discounts and premiums is used. Due to a drop in interest rates, Dillon decided to call in half of the bonds and issue a new series of bonds in the amount of $50,000 (5% cash interest annually, five-year term) on January 1, 2025, at par.

Required

a. Provide the entry for issuance of the 6% bonds on January 1, 2020.
b. Provide the entry for issuance of the 5% bonds on January 1, 2025.
c. Provide the entry for redemption of the 6% bonds on January 1, 2025.

Exercise 16-74 Recording Entries for Convertible Bonds **LO8** *Hint:* See Demo 16-8

Stonewall Corporation issued $20,000 of 5%, 10-year convertible bonds. Each $1,000 bond is convertible to 10 shares of common stock (par $50) of Stonewall Corporation. The bonds were sold at 105 on January 1, 2020.

Required

a. Provide the entry for Stonewall Corporation on January 1, 2020, for the bond issuance.
b. Provide entries for Stonewall Corporation assuming that the conversion privilege is subsequently exercised immediately after the end of the third year. Assume that at the date of conversion, 30% of any premium or discount has been amortized and the common stock was selling at $125 per share. Use the book value method.

Exercise 16-75 Recording Entries for Convertible Bonds **LO8** *Hint:* See Demo 16-8

On January 1, 2020, Sierra Corp. issued 500, $1,000, 6% convertible bonds at face value. Each bond is convertible into 15 shares of $1 par value common stock. As an inducement to convert the bonds into common stock in 2022 prompted by a drop in interest rates, the company offered $35,000 to bondholders, payable upon conversion. All of the bondholders converted to common stock in June of 2022.

Required

a. Provide the entry for issuance of bonds on January 1, 2020.
b. Provide the entry for Sierra Corp. for conversion of the bonds in June of 2022, using the book value method.

Exercise 16-76 Recording Entries for Bonds with Warrants **LO9**

Harley Corporation issued $75,000 of 6%, 10-year, nonconvertible bonds with detachable stock purchase warrants. Each $1,000 bond carried 20 detachable warrants, each of which was for one share of Harley common stock, par $20, at a specified exercise price of $60. The bonds sold at 102 including the warrants (no bond price without warrants was available), and immediately after the date of issuance, the detachable stock purchase warrants were selling at $4 each. All indicated transactions occurred in the same fiscal year.

Required

a. Provide the entry for the issuer at the date of issuance of the bonds.
b. Provide the entry for Harley assuming subsequent tender of all of the warrants by the investors for exercise at the specified exercise price. At this date, the stock was selling at $75 per share.

Exercise 16-77 Recording Entries for Bonds with Warrants **LO9**

On July 1, 2020, Salem Corporation issued $2,000,000 of 7% bonds due in 10 years. The bonds pay cash interest semiannually. Each $1,000 bond includes a detachable stock purchase warrant. Each right gives the bondholder the right to purchase, for $30, one share of $1 par value common stock at any time during the next 10 years. The bonds were sold at 101. The value of the stock purchase warrants at the time of issuance was $100,000. The bonds would sell without warrants at $1,940,000.

Required

a. Record the entry for issuance of bonds using the proportional method.
b. Record the entry for issuance of bonds assuming instead that the warrants are not detachable.

Exercise 16-78
Reporting Bonds Using the Fair Value Option **LO10**

Mitchell Inc. issued 40, 6%, $1,000 bonds on January 1, 2020, for $38,934. The bonds pay cash interest semiannually each June 30, and December 31, and were issued to yield 7%. The bonds mature December 31, 2022, and the company uses the effective interest method to amortize bond discounts or premiums. On January 1, 2020, Mitchell Inc. elects to account for the bonds using the fair value option.

Required

a. Record the issuance of bonds on January 1, 2020.
b. Record the interest payment on June 30, 2020.
c. Record the interest payment on December 31, 2020.
d. At December 31, 2020, the market rate on the bonds drops to 7.5% due to a general increase in market risk. Record the adjustment of bonds payable to fair value.

Exercise 16-79
Reporting Bonds Using the Fair Value Option **LO10**

Royal Inc. issued 10-year, $100,000, 10% annual interest-bearing bonds with a carrying value of $88,800 as of December 31, 2020. Royal Inc. amortizes the discount using the effective interest method. At the time the bonds were issued on June 30, 2020, Royal Inc. elected to account for the bonds using the fair value option. In preparing financial statements for 2020, Royal Inc. will need to make an adjusting entry to reflect the change in the fair value of the bonds.

Required

a. Assume that the fair value of the $100,000 bonds is $80,000 on December 31, 2020. The decrease in fair value is due to general interest rate changes. Record the adjusting entry on December 31, 2020.
b. Assume instead that the fair value of the $100,000 bonds is $95,000 on December 31, 2020. The increase in the fair value of the bonds is due entirely to a change in the credit risk of the debt. Record the adjusting entry on December 31, 2020.

Exercise 16-80
Reporting a Note Payable Using the Fair Value Option **LO10**

On January 1, 2020, Nakoma Inc. issued an 8% note payable of $500,000 to a financial institution in order to finance an operational expansion through the acquisition of a competitor. Upon issuance of the note, Nakoma elected to account for the note using the fair value option. At the end of the first three years, 2020, 2021, and 2022, the note had a carrying value of $470,024, $472,326, and $474,835, respectively. At the end of the first three years, 2020, 2021, and 2022, the note had a fair value of $485,000, $476,000, and $474,000, respectively. Any differences between fair value and carrying value of the note are due to general interest rate changes.

Required

a. Prepare the adjusting journal entry on December 31 of 2020, 2021, and 2022.
b. Show the balance sheet presentation of the note payable on December 31 of 2020, 2021, and 2022.
c. What can generally be stated about the change in interest rate between the issuance of the note and the end of 2020?

Exercise 16-81
Preparing a Debt Disclosure **LO11**
Hint: See Demo 16-11A

As of December 31, 2020, Dole Company's long-term debt consisted of the following:

- $63,500—Unsecured note payable to bank due 2021.
- $225,000—Unsecured note payable to bank due 2023.
- $300,000—Unsecured note payable to bank due 2025.
- $45,000—Secured mortgage payable to bank due in equal installments 2021 through 2025.
- $80,000—Secured note payable to bank due in 2026.

Required

Prepare the required financial statement disclosure at December 31, 2020, indicating the amounts due in each of the next five years and thereafter.

Exercise 16-82
Correcting Error in Accounting for Bonds Payable **LO4**

On June 30, 2020, Williams Inc. issued 8-year, $500,000, 5% bonds, priced at $412,608 to yield 8%, with cash interest payable semiannually on June 30 and December 31. In 2021, after the financial statements had been issued, Williams discovered that the entry to record interest expense on December 31, 2020, was recorded incorrectly as follows: debit to Interest Expense for $12,500 and a credit to Cash for $12,500.

Required

Record the correcting entry in 2021, ignoring income taxes. Company policy is to amortize bond discounts or premiums using the effective interest method.

Problems

Problem 16-83
Valuing Bonds Payable **LO1, 2**

Majors Inc. has two bond issues outstanding today, each with (1) $1,000 face value, (2) a term of five years at issuance, (3) three years remaining to maturity, and (4) a 10% yield rate at issuance. Bond A is a zero-interest-bearing bond; bond B pays 10% cash annually and just paid interest yesterday. The yield rate today on both bonds is 12%.

Required

a. Determine the bond for which book value and fair value have changed the most since issuance.

b. Discuss the magnitude of the difference between changes in the values of these two bonds.

Problem 16-84
Analyzing Bond Issuance, Interest, and Early Retirement **LO2, 4, 7**

Answer the following requirements for these three separate scenarios.

a. On April 1, 2020, Felly Company issued 800 of its 10%, $1,000 bonds at 97 plus accrued interest. The bonds are dated January 1, 2020, and mature on January 1, 2030. Cash interest is payable semiannually on January 1 and July 1.

b. On July 1, 2020, Center Company issued 9% bonds in the face amount of $500,000, which mature on July 1, 2030. The bonds were issued for $469,277 to yield 10%, resulting in a bond discount of $30,723. Center uses the effective interest method of amortizing bond discount. Cash interest is payable annually on June 30.

c. On July 1, 2020, Fondue Company issued 1,000 of its 9%, $1,000 callable bonds for $960,000. The bonds are dated July 1, 2020, and mature on July 1, 2030. Cash interest is payable semiannually on January 1 and July 1. Fondue uses the straight-line interest method of amortizing bond discount. The bonds can be called by the issuer at 101 at any time after June 30, 2025. On July 1, 2026, Fondue called in all the bonds and retired them.

Required

a. Compute the total proceeds (including interest) on the Felly bond issue.

b. Compute the unamortized discount on the Center bond issue on July 1, 2022.

c. Provide the entry to record extinguishment of the Fondue bond issue.

AICPA adapted

Problem 16-85
Recording and Reporting Bond Issuance, Effective Interest, Bond Issuance Costs **LO2, 4**

Alpha Corporation sold and issued to Beta Corporation $400,000 of 8% (cash payable semiannually on June 30 and December 31), three-year bonds. The bonds were dated and sold on January 1, 2020, at a market rate of 10%. The accounting period for Alpha Corporation ends on December 31. Bond issuance costs incurred were $3,000.

Required

a. Compute the price of the bonds, without taking into account bond issuance costs.

b. Prepare an amortization schedule for the life of the bonds (use the effective interest method and round to the nearest dollar).

c. Prepare entries for Alpha Corporation on January 1, 2020, to record bond issuance, and on June 30, 2020, and December 31, 2020, to record interest payments.

d. Indicate how Alpha Corporation would report the bond transactions in the balance sheet and income statement for the year ended December 31, 2020.

Problem 16-86
Recording Entries for Bonds Sold Between Interest Payment Dates—Straight-Line Interest Method **LO2, 4**

Saturn Inc. sold an issue of 5%, $100,000 bonds dated January 1, 2020, on March 1, 2020, at 95. The bonds pay interest every June 30 and December 31, and mature December 31, 2024.

Required

a. Prepare an amortization schedule over the term of the bonds using the straight-line interest method.

b. Provide journal entries to be made by Saturn Inc. at each of the following dates.

1. March 1, 2020.
2. June 30, 2020.

c. Indicate the amount of interest expense reported in the income statement of Saturn Inc. for the six months ended June 30, 2020.

Problem 16-87
Recording Entries: Straight-Line Interest Method, Redemption **LO2, 5, 7**

On January 1, 2020, Skylar Company issued $400,000 of bonds payable with a stated rate of 5% payable annually each December 31. The bonds mature in 10 years and are callable after the fourth year at 101. The bonds originally sold on January 1, 2020, at 104. On June 30, 2025, the bonds were called at 101 plus accrued interest. The company uses straight-line amortization, and the company's accounting period ends December 31.

Required

a. Provide the bond issuance entry on January 1, 2020.

b. Provide journal entries to update the bond issue and pay the accrued interest, and to extinguish the bonds on June 30, 2025, the call date.

Problem 16-88
Recording Entries: Straight-Line and Effective interest methods, Redemption
LO2, 5, 7

On January 1, 2020, Quaid Company issued $100,000 of 10% debentures. The following information relates to these bonds:

Bond issuance date	January 1, 2020	Maturity date.	December 31, 2024
Market rate	8%	Interest payment date.	December 31

On March 1, 2021, Quaid retires $10,000 (face value) of the bonds when the market price is 110.

Required

Provide entries for Quaid on the following dates under both the effective interest and straight-line interest methods of amortization.

a. January 1, 2020, bond issuance.

b. December 31, 2020, first interest payment.

c. March 1, 2021, entries to update the portion of the bond issue retired and pay the accrued interest, and to extinguish the bonds.

d. Explain why the two methods result in differing interest amounts per period.

Problem 16-89
Recording Debt Extinguishment by Refunding **LO2, 4, 7**

Deenilli Corporation issued $100,000 of 4.5% (payable each December 31), 10-year bonds on January 1, 2020. The issuer may call them at any time after 2023 at 104. The bonds sold on January 1, 2020, at 98. Straight-line amortization is used. Due to a large increase in interest rates, similar bonds were being sold in the market at the end of 2024 at 86 (i.e., at a market rate of 8%). In view of this situation, Deenilli decided to issue a new series of bonds (a refunding issue) in the amount of $75,000 (8% cash payable annually, five-year term) on January 1, 2025. Deenilli had cash on hand sufficient to retire the old bonds.

Required

a. Provide the entry for Deenilli Corporation to record issuance of the bonds at 98 on January 1, 2020.

b. Assuming that the $75,000 refunding issue was sold at par, provide the required entry for Deenilli.

c. Assume that all of the old bonds were immediately purchased in the open market at 86 on January 2, 2025. Provide the required entry for Deenilli. How should the gain or loss be reported in the financial statements?

d. What was the economic gain or loss to the issuer and the investor?

Problem 16-90
Analyzing an Amortization Schedule
LO2, 4

The following amortization schedule relates to a bond issuance on January 1, 2020.

Date	Stated Interest	Market Interest	Amortization Amount	Bond Carrying Value
Jan. 1, 2020.				$ 9,298
Dec. 31, 2020.	$600	$651	$51	9,349
Dec. 31, 2021.	600	654	54	9,403
Dec. 31, 2022.	600	658	58	9,461
Dec. 31, 2023.	600	662	62	9,523
Dec. 31, 2024.	600	667	67	9,590
Dec. 31, 2025.	600	671	71	9,661
Dec. 31, 2026.	600	676	76	9,737
Dec. 31, 2027.	600	682	82	9,819
Dec. 31, 2028.	600	687	87	9,906
Dec. 31, 2029.	600	694	94	10,000

Required

a. What is the face amount of the bonds? What is the selling price of the bonds?

b. Were the bonds sold at a discount or premium? If so, what is the dollar amount?

c. Are the bonds amortized using the effective interest method or the straight-line interest method?

d. What is the stated rate of interest?

e. What is the market rate of interest?

f. What is the journal entry required on December 31, 2027, based on this amortization schedule?
g. Why do market interest amounts increase each year?

Problem 16-91 Recording Debt Extinguishment, Purchase in the Open Market **LO2, 4, 7**

On July 1, 2020, B. Shelton Corporation (BSC) issued \$300,000 of 5% (cash payable each June 30 and December 31) 10-year bonds payable. The bonds were issued at 97. Assume straight-line amortization of the bond discount. Due to an increase in interest rates, these bonds were selling in the market at the end of June 2023 at a market rate of 8%. Because the company had available cash, \$100,000 (face amount) of the bonds were purchased in the market and retired on July 1, 2023.

Required

a. Provide the entry by BSC to record issuance of the bonds on July 1, 2020.
b. Provide the entry by BSC to record the extinguishment of \$100,000 face value of the debt on July 1, 2023. How should the gain or loss be reported on the 2023 financial statements of BSC?
c. Was the extinguishment economically favorable to the issuer, investor, or neither?

Problem 16-92 Recording Entries for Convertible Debt **LO8**

On January 1, 2020, when its \$30 par value common stock was selling for \$80 per share, Ancil Corporation issued \$5,000,000 of 4% convertible debentures due in 10 years. The conversion option allowed the holder of each \$1,000 bond to convert the bond into five shares of the corporation's \$30 par value common stock. The debentures were issued for \$5,500,000. The present value of the bond payments at the time of issuance was \$4,250,000, and the corporation believes that the difference between the present value and the amount paid is attributable to the conversion feature.

On January 1, 2022, when the corporation's common stock was selling for \$90 per share, holders of 40% of the convertible debentures exercised their conversion options. For convenience, assume that the corporation uses the straight-line interest method for amortizing any bond discount or premium.

Required

a. Provide the entry to record the original issuance of convertible debentures.
b. Provide the entry to record the exercise of the conversion option, using the book value method.

Problem 16-93 Recording Entries for Convertible Debt with Induced Conversion **LO8**

Convee Company issued \$75,000 of 12% convertible bonds at face value on an interest payment date several years ago. The face value of each bond is \$1,000, and each bond is convertible into 15 shares of \$5 par common stock of Convee. Convee has embarked on a program of debt reduction; U.S. interest rates have declined during the term of the convertible bonds. Consequently, Convee offers the convertible bondholders \$50 cash per bond as an inducement to convert. The market price of Convee stock is currently \$70 per share. The bonds must be converted within a three-month period to receive the cash inducement. The bondholders accept the inducement and convert within the required period.

Required

a. Why did the bondholders convert bonds into common stock?
b. Record the conversion using the book value method.
c. Explain why induced conversion is not treated as debt extinguishment for purposes of classifying the inducement cost.

Problem 16-94 Recording Entries for Bonds with Detachable Warrants **LO9**

Friday's Corporation issued \$1,000,000 of 6%, nonconvertible bonds with detachable stock purchase warrants. Each \$1,000 bond carried 20 detachable stock purchase warrants, each of which called for the purchase of one share of Friday's common stock, par \$50, at the specified exercise price of \$60 per share. The bonds sold at 106 on January 1, 2020, the interest date of the bonds. The detachable stock purchase warrants were immediately quoted at \$1 each on the market and the bonds were quoted at 102 without the warrants.

Required

Provide the following entries for Friday's Corporation:

a. To record issuance of the bonds. Round allocation percentages to 3 decimals.
b. To record the subsequent exercise of the 20,000 stock purchase warrants.

Problem 16-95 Recording Entries for Convertible Debt, Redeemable Debt **LO2, 4, 7, 8**

On January 1, 2020, Grand Corporation issued \$100,000 of 9% (cash payable each June 30 and December 31) 10-year bonds payable (convertible and callable) at a 10% market rate of interest. Each \$1,000 bond is convertible, at the option of the holder, into Grand common stock (par \$10) as follows: first five years—25 shares for each bond tendered; second five years—20 shares for each bond. The bonds can be called, at the option of Grand, after the fifth year at 101.

On July 1, 2026, the market rate on comparable bonds is 8%, and the common stock is quoted on the market at $52 per share.

Required

a. Provide the entry to record issuance of bonds on January 1, 2020. Show computation of the bond issue price.

b. Provide the entry to record payment of bond interest and the amortization of bond premium or discount on June 30, 2020. Use the effective interest method.

c. Prepare the journal entries at July 1, 2026, to record each of the following separate assumptions (use straight-line amortization).

1. Assumption A: All of the bondholders converted their bonds to common stock. Use the book value method to record the conversion.
2. Assumption B: Grand called all of the bonds at the stipulated call price.
3. Assumption C: Grand refunded all of the outstanding 9% bonds by purchasing them in the open market at the current yield rate of interest. Cash for the refunding was obtained by issuing new 8% bonds (cash interest payable semiannually) at par; cash proceeds were $103,000 (face amount of bonds sold).

d. Which of the three alternative means of retiring the old 9% bonds is most likely to occur if each is available to investors? Why?

Problem 16-96
Recording and Reporting a Note Payable **LO6**

Sable Company purchased merchandise for resale on January 1, 2020, for $5,000 cash plus a $20,000, two-year note payable. The principal is due on December 31, 2021; the note specified 8% interest payable each December 31.

Assume that Sable's rate of interest for this type of debt was 15%. The accounting period ends December 31.

a. Provide the entry to record the purchase on January 1, 2020, for Sable Company.

b. Provide the entries at each year-end for Sable Company (the debtor).

c. Provide the entries at each year-end for the creditor.

d. Illustrate how Sable Company (the debtor) and the creditor should report or disclose the data related to the note on the income statement and balance sheet at each year-end.

e. Compute the following amounts to be reported by Sable Company (the debtor):

1. Amount of cash interest payable each December 31.
2. Total interest expense for the two-year period.
3. Amount of interest reported on the income statement for 2020.
4. Amount of liability reported on the balance sheet at December 31, 2020.

Problem 16-97
Recording Entries for a Zero-Interest-Bearing Note Payable **LO6**

Fox Co. purchases land on January 1, 2020, and issues a 3-year, $50,000 zero-interest-bearing note as payment. The market rate of interest is 10% and Fox Co. uses the effective interest method to amortize discounts and premiums.

Required

a. Prepare a debt amortization schedule for the note.

b. Prepare the entry for issuance of the note in exchange for land by Fox Co.

c. Prepare the entries subsequent to issuance of the note through maturity for Fox Co.

d. Does a zero-interest-bearing note bear no interest or cost of borrowing? Explain.

e. Repeat the requirements of parts *a* and *b* with the stated interest on the note as 5%. Does the total cost of borrowing change when the stated rate is 5% rather than 0%?

Problem 16-98
Recording Entries for an Installment Note Payable **LO6**

Cathy Company purchased a machine with a fair value of $250,000 on January 1, 2020, with a five-year, 8% note to the manufacturer. Cathy Company will make equal payments on June 30 and December 31 over the life of the note and the note will be fully paid upon maturity. Assume that the stated rate of the note approximates the market rate.

Required

a. Compute the semiannual cash payment required by Cathy Company on the installment note payable.

b. Prepare a debt amortization schedule for the installment note payable.

c. Prepare the entries in 2020 for Cathy Company for issuance of the note on January 1, 2020, and for the interest payments on June 30, 2020, and December 31, 2020.

Problem 16-99
Recording Entries Using the Fair Value Option **LO10**

On January 1, 2020, New Corporation issued to Old Corporation a $20,000 9% (cash interest payable semiannually on June 30 and December 31) 3-year bond, dated January 1, 2020. The bond was sold at an 8% effective rate. Upon issuance of the bond on January 1, 2020, New Corporation elected to account for the bond using the fair value option. On December 31, 2020, the fair value of the bond was $22,000 although general (risk free) interest rates had not changed since January 1, 2020.

Required

a. Prepare the journal entries required in 2020 related to the bond transaction including the issuance and interest payment entries. New Corporation used the effective interest method to account for discounts and premiums.

b. Record the fair value adjustment under the fair value option method on December 31, 2020.

Problem 16-100
Defining Debt Terms
LO1, 2, 3, 4, 5, 6, 7, 8, 9, 11

Terms relating to concepts discussed in this chapter along with descriptions of the terms are included in the following two lists.

Debt Terminology	Description of Terms
____ 1. Bond indenture	*a.* Subject to early retirement at the choice of the issuer.
____ 2. Municipal bond	*b.* Adjunct liability valuation account.
____ 3. Corporate bond	*c.* Bond contract.
____ 4. Debenture bond	*d.* Contra liability valuation account.
____ 5. Callable bond	*e.* Bond subject to a conversion to common stock at the choice of the holder.
____ 6. Redeemable bond	*f.* Typically issued for general capital purposes.
____ 7. Bond issue date	*g.* Bond issued by a governmental unit.
____ 8. Bond effective rate	*h.* Bond subject to early retirement at the choice of the holder.
____ 9. Bond selling price	*i.* To guarantee the debt of another company.
____10. Discount on bonds payable	*j.* Bond issued by a private or public company.
____11. Premium on bonds payable	*k.* Date of the actual sale of bonds.
____12. Long-term note payable	*l.* Typically issued for specific asset acquisition.
____13. Bonds payable	*m.* Market rate of interest on a bond payable.
____14. Installment note payable	*n.* Debt that requires equal payments of principal and interest over its term.
____15. Off-balance-sheet risk	*o.* Unsecured bond issuance.
____16. Convertible bonds payable	*p.* Present value of bond payments discounted using the market rate.

Required

Match each term, 1 through 16 with the most appropriate description *a* through *p*.

Accounting Decisions and Judgments

AD&J 16-101
Analyzing Zero Coupon Bonds **LO4**

Real World Analysis **Baxter International Inc.** is a manufacturer of surgical and medical instruments. Following is information adapted from the notes to Baxter's annual report.

Note 7 Long-Term Debt and Lease Obligations

December 31 ($ millions)	Year 2	Year 1
Zero coupon notes due in Year 7, market rate 10%.	$86	$78

The company had unamortized original issue discounts of $58 and $66 for the zero coupon notes due Year 7, at December 31, Year 2 and Year 1, respectively. Assume the notes were issued January 1 of a previous year and mature December 31.

Required

a. Reconstruct the Year 2 interest expense entry, rounding to the nearest million. Verify the December 31, Year 2, net note payable carrying value from the results of the entry.

b. Estimate the face value of the notes.

c. Using a present value approach, estimate the December 31, Year 2, net note payable balance using the result from part *b*.

AD&J 16-102
Analyzing Convertible Bonds **LO8**

Real World Analysis International Paper Company's long-term liability disclosure note to its Year 5 financial statements included the following.

$ millions	Year 5	Year 4
5¾% Convertible subordinated debentures	$0	$199

In July Year 5, the 5¾% debentures were converted into 5.8 million shares of common stock.

Additional information:

1. The average market price per share of the company's common stock was approximately $40 during Year 5.
2. The par value of its common stock is $1.

Required

a. Prepare the conversion entry assuming the book value method is used.
b. Why is no gain or loss recognized on conversion?

AD&J 16-103
Analyzing Bonds Payable and Debt Retirement **LO2, 7**

Real World Analysis The long-term liability disclosure note to the Year 2 annual report of Alaska Air Group Inc. included the following.

December 31 ($ millions)	Year 2	Year 1
6% Convertible senior debentures due Year 9 . . .	$132	$0

Additional assumptions:

1. The debentures were issued at par on January 1 in Year 2 and pay interest each December 31.
2. The debentures retired were scheduled to mature December 31, Year 9.
3. Assume instead that Alaska Air decides to retire the bonds at December 31, Year 2, paying the fair value of the bonds, which reflected a yield rate of 5%.

Required

a. Prepare the December 31, Year 2, interest payment entry.
b. Prepare the December 31, Year 2, bond retirement entry.
c. What factor may have contributed to recognition of a loss on early retirement?

AD&J 16-104
Analyzing Long-Term Liabilities **LO1, 2, 3, 4, 5**

Real World Analysis Refer to the 2014 financial statement excerpts of the Coca-Cola Company that follow and answer the following questions.

a. What was 2014 interest expense for Coca-Cola?
b. Using 2014 interest expense and relevant liability amounts, estimate the average 2014 interest rate for Coca-Cola. Assume that interest-bearing liabilities include (1) loans and notes payable, (2) current maturities of long-term debt, and (3) long-term debt.
c. Approximately reconcile debt issuances and debt payments on the statement of cash flows to the change in ending debt balances on the balance sheet.
d. What is the fair value of Coca Cola's long-term debt on December 31, 2014? What is the carrying value of Coca Cola's long-term debt on December 31, 2014? What does the difference between the fair value and carrying value of long-term debt indicate about the movement of interest rates between the time the debt was originally issued and December 31, 2014?

Excerpts from the Coca-Cola Company Consolidated 2014 Statements of Income

The Coca-Cola Company and Subsidiaries
Consolidated Statements of Income

Year Ended December 31 (In millions except per share data)	2014
Net operating revenues	$45,998
Cost of goods sold	17,889
Gross profit	28,109
Selling, general and administrative expenses	17,218
Other operating charges	1,183
Operating income	9,708
Interest income	594
Interest expense	483
Equity income (loss)—net	769
Other income (loss)—net	(1,263)
Income before income taxes	9,325
Income taxes	2,201
Consolidated net income	$ 7,124
Less: Net income attributable to noncontrolling interests	$ 26

Excerpt from the Coca-Cola Company 2014 Consolidated Balance Sheets

Liabilities	2014	2013
Current liabilities		
Accounts payable and accrued expenses	$ 9,234	$ 9,577
Loans and notes payable	19,130	16,901
Current maturities of long-term debt	3,552	1,024
Accrued income taxes	400	309
Liabilities held for sale	58	—
Total current liabilities	32,374	27,811
Long-term debt	19,063	19,154
Other liabilities	4,389	3,498
Deferred income taxes	5,636	6,152

Excerpt from the Coca-Cola Company 2014 Consolidated Statements of Cash Flows

Financing activities	2014	2013	2012
Issuances of debt	$41,674	$43,425	$42,791
Payments of debt	(36,962)	(38,714)	(38,573)
Issuances of stock	1,532	1,328	1,489
Purchases of stock for treasury	(4,162)	(4,832)	(4,559)
Dividends	(5,350)	(4,969)	(4,595)
Other financing activities	(363)	17	100
Net cash provided by (used in) financing activities	$ (3,631)	$(3,745)	$ (3,347)

Excerpt from the Coca-Cola Company 2014 Form 10K Disclosure Note

The fair value of our long-term debt is estimated using Level 2 inputs based on quoted prices for those instruments. Where quoted prices are not available, fair value is estimated using discounted cash flows and market-based expectations for interest rates, credit risk and the contractual terms of the debt instruments. As of December 31, 2014, the carrying amount and fair value of our long-term debt, including the current portion, were $22,615 million and $23,411 million, respectively. As of December 31, 2013, the carrying amount and fair value of our long-term debt, including the current portion, were $20,178 million and $20,352 million, respectively.

AD&J 16-105
Comparing Alternatives: Convertible Bonds versus Detachable Stock Warrants **LO8, 9**

Judgment Case & **Challenge Problem** Seton Corporation is considering the issuance of $100,000 of five-year bonds. Two alternatives are under consideration. Seton's management is considering which alternative to select. Management is concerned about several issues that may influence the decision. One such issue is the comparative impact of the two alternatives on financial statements. Our assistance in selecting an alternative has been requested. Assume in each case that the investor intends to hold the bonds to maturity.

Alternative A: At the beginning of 2020, issue 100 convertible bonds that would specify that each $1,000 bond can be tendered for conversion to 15 shares of Seton's common stock, par $10, at any time after the second year from the issue date of the convertible bonds. Seton's best estimate is that the convertible bonds can be sold to Investor X for $108,000 cash at the beginning of 2020 if the common stock is selling at that time for not less than $65 per share.

Alternative B: At the beginning of 2020, issue 100 nonconvertible $1,000 bonds with 15 detachable stock purchase warrants per bond. Each warrant can be tendered at any time after 2020 for one share of Seton's common stock, par $10, at an exercise price of $60 per share. Seton's best estimate is that the nonconvertible bonds can be sold to Investor X for $108,000 cash at the beginning of 2020 if the common stock is selling at that time for not less than $65 per share. The warrants are expected to have a fair value of $2 each immediately after issuance of the bonds; the bonds do not have a listed market price.

Required

a. Using Seton's best estimate, provide the journal entries for each alternative that each party (the issuer and the investor) would make at the beginning of 2020. Explain any differences in accounting values between the two alternatives.

b. Provide the entries for each alternative that each party would make at the beginning of 2023, assuming all of the bonds in alternative A are tendered for conversion and all of the warrants are turned in for shares in alternative B. Seton's common stock is selling for $75 per share. Seton uses the book value method for alternative A. Assume straight-line amortization of bond premium and assume that the fair value of the warrants has not changed.

c. Complete the following schedule, assuming that the transactions in parts *a* and *b* have taken place.

d. Respond to management's request for assistance in choosing between the two alternatives in a one-page memo. Consider the results from part *b*.

	A: Convertible Bonds		B: Detachable Warrants	
Items	**Issuer**	**Investor**	**Issuer**	**Investor**
Gain (loss) conversion				
Bond investment				
Common stock investment				
Bonds payable				
Premium on bonds payable				
Common stock				
Paid-in capital in excess of par				
Cash inflow				
Cash outflow				

AD&J 16-106
Comparing Straight-Line and Effective Interest Methods **LO4**

Judgment Case Shelby Company issues $10 million of bonds maturing 25 years after issuance. The bonds yield 10% but pay no interest.

Required

a. Why would Shelby issue bonds paying no interest?

b. Why would investors buy them?

c. Compute the issue price (assume annual compounding periods and assume that issue date and bond date are the same).

d. Compute interest expense for the 1st, 16th, and 25th years under the effective interest method.

e. Compute interest expense for the 1st, 16th, and 25th years under the straight-line interest method.

f. Comment on results from parts *d* and *e*. Why is the straight-line interest method inappropriate for Shelby bonds?

AD&J 16-107 Reporting Liabilities—an Ethical Perspective **LO11**

Ethics Case In December, Mr. Wilson, the controller of Fargo Company, a calendar-fiscal-year company, is faced with a tough situation. The bond indenture of a major issue of Fargo bonds requires maintaining a 3-to-1 current ratio as measured at each balance sheet date. Fargo has recently experienced cash shortages caused by a downturn in the general economy and in the demand for Fargo's products. However, leading economic indicators suggest that an upturn is expected.

A substantial account payable is due in January. Fargo does not have the cash to pay the debt before the end of the current year. Furthermore, the January cash budget based on a realistic estimate of sales and collections from accounts receivable indicates a cash shortage requiring short-term financing. The payable due in January is large enough to cause the current ratio at December 31 to fall below 3.0. The controller begins the search for a financial institution willing to refinance the payable on a long-term basis. If successful, the payable would be reclassified as long term, enabling Fargo to comply with the bond indenture. Several financial institutions are willing to refinance the payable, but none agree to do so on a noncancellable basis.

The controller is quite stressed by the situation. Noncompliance with the bond indenture may lead to technical default. If the bondholders exercise their right and call the bonds, Fargo may be forced into bankruptcy. The controller is confident that Fargo will rebound in the coming year and reasons that more harm will come to the company, its employees, and its shareholders if he does not take action that will result in compliance with the bond indenture. Mr. Wilson therefore decides to refinance the payable on a long-term basis and to report the payable as a long-term liability on the balance sheet.

Required

Prepare a one-page report regarding the following situation from an ethical and financial reporting viewpoint.

AD&J 16-108 Accounting for Convertible Bonds **LO8**

Communication Case Columbus Company's 10-year convertible bonds, issued and dated October 1, 2020, are convertible into 20 shares of Columbus's $25 par value common stock, at the holder's option. The bonds were issued at a premium when the common stock traded at $45 per share. After payment of interest on October 1, 2021, 30% of the bonds were tendered for conversion when the common stock was trading at $57 per share. Columbus uses the book value method to account for the conversion.

Required

In a one-page memo, discuss:

a. How the issue price of Columbus's convertible bonds would be determined.
b. How Columbus should account for issuance of the convertible bonds. Provide the rationale for this accounting practice.
c. How Columbus should account for conversion of the bonds into common stock.

AD&J 16-109 Assessing Off-Balance-Sheet Risk **LO11**

Communication Case The reported balances of certain liabilities carried on a corporation's books do not always indicate the maximum obligation potentially facing the company as a result of past transactions. In addition, a company may have potential obligations that are not recorded at all.

Required

For each of the following potential or actual liability items, explain whether the company is subject to off-balance-sheet risk of accounting loss and, if so, whether that risk arises from credit risk or market risk (or both). Explanation should be from the point of view of the company named.

a. Fixed-rate mortgage payable by Wellco Inc. and secured by real estate owned by Wellco.
b. Guarantee by Jolko Inc. of a $4 million loan obtained by one of Jolko's subsidiaries.
c. Bonds payable issued by Samson Inc. at a discount, due in five years.
d. Convertible bonds issued by Coastal Company, at a premium, due in two years.
e. Transfer of accounts receivable by Jenell Company, accounted for as a borrowing. The transfer is with recourse to Jenell.
f. Variable-rate mortgage payable by Angeles Inc. and secured by real estate owned by Angeles.
g. A loan commitment made by BCCJ Bank to a computer manufacturer, guaranteeing a fixed line of credit at a fixed rate of interest for one year from the commitment date.

AD&J 16-110 Recording Entries for Bonds Issued Between Interest Payment Dates; Partial Periods **LO2, 4**

Challenge Problem Radian Company issued to Silver Company $30,000 of four-year, 8% bonds dated November 30, 2019. Cash interest is payable semiannually on May 31 and November 30. The bonds were issued on March 1, 2020, for $28,163 plus accrued interest. The bonds would have sold at the market rate on the next interest date for $28,264. The accounting period ends December 31 for both companies. The effective interest rate was 10%. Round answers to the nearest dollar.

Required

a. Verify the bond price. Use straight-line interpolation between interest dates.
b. Prepare an amortization schedule using the effective interest method.
c. Provide entries for Radian for the following dates, March 1, 2021, and May 31, 2021. Use the effective interest method of amortization.

AD&J 16-111
Accounting for Bonds from a Debtor and Investor Perspective
LO4

Challenge Problem Jones Corporation issued bonds, face amount $100,000, three-year, 8% (cash payable semiannually on June 30 and December 31). The bonds were dated January 1, 2020, and were sold on November 1, 2020, for $100,739 (including interest of $2,667 and a bond price of $98,072) at an effective interest rate of 9%. The bonds would have sold at the market rate on December 31, 2020, for $98,210. The bonds mature on December 31, 2022. The bonds were purchased as a long-term investment by Smith Corporation, which intends to hold the bonds to maturity.

Required

a. Prepare an amortization schedule using the effective interest method.
b. Provide the entries at November 1, 2020, for the issuer and the investor.
c. Provide the entries for both the issuer and the investor for interest and amortization at the interest date, December 31, 2020. Use the effective interest method of amortization.
d. Assume that the accounting period for each entity ends on February 28. Provide the adjusting entries for each entity on February 28, 2021. Assume the effective interest method of amortization.
e. Compute the amount of amortization per month for each entity, assuming that straight-line amortization is used (the difference between amortization methods is immaterial).

AD&J 16-112
Accounting for Bonds from a Debtor and Investor Perspective
LO5

Challenge Problem Foyt Corporation sold and issued to Mears Corporation $100,000 of bonds on June 1, 2020, for $102,640 plus accrued interest. Mears intends to hold the bonds to maturity. The bond indenture provided the following information.

Maturity amount	$100,000	Stated rate	6.5%, cash payable semiannually
Date of bonds.........	April 1, 2020	Interest payments......	March 31 and September 30
Maturity date..........	March 31, 2022		

Required

a. Provide entries for the issuer and the investor from the date of sale to maturity. Use straight-line amortization of the bond premium. The accounting period for each company ends on December 31.
b. Indicate how the bonds would be reported on the balance sheet of each company at December 31, 2020.
c. What would be reported on the income statement for each company for the year ended December 31, 2020?

AD&J 16-113
Accounting for Bonds from a Debtor and Investor Perspective
LO4

Challenge Problem Randy Corporation issued $200,000 of 8%, four-year bonds (cash interest payable each February 28 and August 31). The bonds were dated March 1, 2020, and mature on February 28, 2024. The bonds were sold on August 1, 2020, to yield 8.5% interest. The bonds were purchased by Voss Corporation, which intends to hold the bonds to maturity. The accounting period for each company ends on December 31. The bonds were sold for $196,967 plus accrued interest of $6,667. The bonds would have sold on August 31, 2020, for $197,029.

Required

a. Prepare an amortization schedule using the effective interest method.
b. Provide entries for the issuer and the investor from the date of issuance through February 28, 2021. Use amortization results from part *a*.

AD&J 16-114
Accounting for Note Payable—Point-System Mortgage **LO6**

Challenge Problem On January 1, 2020, Derek Company borrowed cash from Patricia Finance Company on a $30,000, 12%, two-year note. The note will be paid off in two equal installments each December 31. Patricia assessed Derek two points, which means that the proceeds to Derek are reduced by 2% of the face value of the note. The annual payment, however, is computed on the face value. The accounting period for each company ends December 31.

Required

a. Compute the amount of each annual payment.
b. The market rate is 13.55%. Show how this rate was computed.
c. Prepare a debt amortization schedule for the two parties.
d. Provide all entries for each party from January 1, 2020, through maturity.

Challenge Problem On January 1, 2020, Baker Company borrowed cash from Alter Finance Company and signed a three-year, $30,000 note. Interest is payable each December 31 at a stated rate of "floating prime at January 1 of each year plus 2%." The principal is due on December 31, 2022. The following actual prime rates were used by Alter: January 1, 2020, 13%; January 1, 2021, 12%; and January 1, 2022, 15%. The accounting period for each company ends on December 31.

AD&J 16-115 Accounting for a Note Payable with an Adjustable Rate **LO6**

Required

a. Compute the total amount of interest paid, by year.
b. What was the difference between the stated and market rates? Explain.
c. Provide all entries for each company through the maturity date.
d. Provide the 2020 adjusting entry that would have been necessary had the accounting periods for each company ended on August 31 instead of December 31.

Challenge Problem Berlin Corporation issued 500, 6% convertible bonds at face value ($1,000). Each bond is convertible into 10 shares of $20 par common stock. Subsequent to the bond issuance, Berlin offers two additional shares of common stock for each bond as an inducement to convert. The offer is open for a two-month period. The bondholders accept the inducement within the required period. The market price of the common stock on the acceptance date (also an interest date) is $110.

AD&J 16-116 Accounting for Convertible Debt with Induced Conversion **LO8**

Required

Record entries to record the induced conversion under the book value method.

Trueblood Case The Trueblood case series, prepared by Deloitte professionals, are based on recent accounting technical issues that require research and judgment. The cases are accessed through the Deloitte foundation at the following website: https://www2.deloitte.com/us/en/pages/about-deloitte/articles/trueblood-case-studies-deloitte-foundation.html

The following case is relevant to the content provided in this chapter: Case 15-5, Trouble at the Resort. This case explores the valuation of a debt restructuring including troubled debt restructuring considerations, modification or extinguishment of debt, and treatment of fees related to the restructuring.

AD&J 16-117 Accounting for Debt Restructuring **LO12**

Codification Skills How is the term imputed interest defined in the Codification? What are the financial statement implications for the initial recognition of debt if using a stated rate to measure debt instead of an imputed rate when the rates are not the same?

AD&J 16-118 Defining Terms **LO1, 2, 3, 4, 5**

Codification Skills Locate the relevant section in the FASB Codification for each of the following topics related to accounting for long-term debt.

a. Specific disclosure requirements when a company guarantees the debt of another entity.
FASB ASC ___-___-___-___
b. Treatment of a gain or loss upon early extinguishment of a bond originally sold at a discount.
FASB ASC ___-___-___-___
c. Allocation to equity and debt of bonds with detachable warrants. FASB ASC ___-___-___-___

AD&J 16-119 Conducting Accounting Research **LO7, 9, 11**

Codification Skills Amazon.Com Inc. reported the following information in its December 31, 2014, Form 10-K report, Note 6.

AD&J 16-120 Conducting Accounting Research **LO11**

As of December 31, 2014, future principal payments for our total debt were as follows (in millions):

2015	$1,520
2016	36
2017	1,037
2018	38
2019	1,000
Thereafter	6,250
	$9,881

What guidance is Amazon.Com Inc. following from the Codification in reporting this information?
FASB ASC ___-___-___-___

Appendix—Questions

16-121. What is meant by troubled debt restructuring? What are some of the features of typical restructuring arrangements?

16-122. Explain the classification of gains and losses from troubled debt restructuring.

16-123. Differentiate between a debt restructure in which debt is settled and one in which it continues after the restructure.

Appendix—Brief Exercises

App—Brief Exercise 16-124
Settling Debt through Transfer of Assets
LO12

Nano Corporation agreed to give Rewind Company a machine in full settlement of a note payable to Rewind. The machine's original cost was $70,000. The note's face amount was $55,000. On the date of the agreement, the note's carrying amount was $52,500, and its present value at the current market rate was $48,000. In addition, the machine's carrying amount was $54,500, and its fair value was $48,000. What amounts of gain (loss) should Nano recognize, and how should these amounts be classified in its income statement?

App—Brief Exercise 16-125
Settling Debt through Transfer of Equity
LO12

Wild Company granted an equity interest to a creditor in full settlement of a $56,000 debt owed to the creditor. At the date of this transaction, the equity interest in common stock had a fair value of $50,000. What amount should Wild recognize as a gain on restructuring of debt?

App—Brief Exercise 16-126
Restructuring of Debt
LO12

During 2019, Camellia Company experienced financial difficulties and was likely to default on a $500,000, 15%, three-year note dated January 1, 2019, payable to Central National Bank. On January 15, 2020, the bank agreed to restructure the note and unpaid 2019 interest of $75,000 for $410,000 cash, payable on January 31, 2020. What is the amount of gain, before income taxes, from the debt restructuring recorded by Camellia on January 31, 2020?

App—Brief Exercise 16-127
Restructuring of Debt
LO12

In 2017, Marie Corporation acquired land by paying $37,500 down and signing a note with a maturity value of $500,000. On the note's due date, December 31, 2021, Marie owed $20,000 of accrued interest and $500,000 principal on the note. Marie was in financial difficulty and was unable to make any payments. Marie and the bank agreed to amend the note as follows.

- The $20,000 of interest due on December 31, 2021, was forgiven.
- The principal of the note was reduced from $500,000 to $475,000, and the maturity date was extended one year to December 31, 2022.

Marie would be required to make one interest payment totaling $15,000 on December 31, 2022. As a result of the troubled debt restructuring, Marie should report a gain, before taxes, in its 2021 income statement for what amount?

Appendix—Exercises

App—Exercise 16-128
Recording Entries for a Troubled Debt Settlement **LO12**
Hint: See Demo 16-12A, 16-12B

Down Company owed Super Bank a $50,000, 10%, three-year note dated January 1, 2017, with cash interest payable each December 31. During 2019, Down Company experienced unusual financial difficulties and was unable to pay the note or interest for 2019 that had been accrued. On January 1, 2020, the bank agreed to settle the debt and interest for $2,000 cash plus land that had a fair value of $30,000. At December 31, 2019, the records of Down Company showed the acquisition cost of the land to be $20,000. Super intends to sell the land and estimates $3,000 of direct selling costs.

Required

Provide all entries required on January 1, 2020, to record this debt restructure (a) for Down Company and (b) for Super Bank.

App—Exercise 16-129 Recording Entries for a Troubled Debt Restructure **LO12** *Hint:* See Demo 16-12A, 16-12B

Brown Company owed City Bank a $50,000, 10%, four-year note dated January 1, 2018, with cash interest payable each December 31. Early in 2019, it became clear that Brown Company was experiencing difficulty in making the annual interest payment, although the company did manage to make the 2018 and 2019 payments. Because of expected continuing difficulties, it appeared that there was a good chance the company would default on the note (as well as on other obligations). On January 2, 2020, the two parties agreed to restructure the debt by (a) reducing the remaining annual interest payments to $2,240 each and (b) reducing the principal amount (maturity amount) to $48,000.

Required

a. Compute the new market rate of interest for Brown.

b. Provide all entries required on date of restructure (January 2, 2020) for each company. If no entry is required, explain the reason.

c. Provide all entries required at December 31, 2020, and 2021, for each company. Assume that City Bank uses the effective interest method.

Appendix—Problems

App—Problem 16-130 Recording Entries for a Troubled Debt Settlement **LO12**

Slow Company owed Quick Finance Company a three-year, 10%, $100,000 note dated January 1, 2017, with cash interest payable annually each December 31. At December 31, 2019, Slow was experiencing serious financial problems and could not pay the principal and interest for 2019 that had been accrued. Quick agreed to settle the debt and interest in full for $12,000 cash plus a tract of land (Slow's acquisition cost was $7,000) plus 1,000 shares of Slow common stock, par $10, that had a fair value of $35 per share. The fair value of the land on January 1, 2020, was $20,000. The agreement was accepted by both entities, and settlement was effected on January 1, 2020.

Required

Provide all entries required to record the debt restructure for (a) Slow Company and (b) Quick Finance Company.

App—Problem 16-131 Recording Entries for a Troubled Debt Restructure **LO12**

Baker Company owed Cook Company a $20,000, 10% four-year note, dated January 1, 2018, with cash interest payable annually each December 31. Baker Company faced extreme financial difficulties. Both companies had accrued interest for the year 2019, but no interest was paid for 2019. On January 2, 2020, the entities agreed that the principal would be paid in full on maturity date and that the interest for 2019, 2020, and 2021 would be settled by payment of $3,340 cash on December 31, 2022 (maturity date).

Required

a. Compute the new market rate of interest for Baker.

b. Provide all entries required on the date of restructure (January 2, 2020) for each company.

c. Provide all entries required on December 31, 2020, and 2021, for each company. Cook uses the effective interest method.

Answers to Review Exercises

Review 16-1

a. Corporate, convertible
b. $150,000
c. January 1, 2030
d. 2.5%
e. July 1, January 1
f. January 1, 2020
g. 3%
h. $138,842
i. January 1, 2020

Review 16-2

a. $128,681.40
(PV(0.025,20,–50000*0.03,–50000))

b. $53,897.29
(PV(0.025,20,–50000*0.03,–50000))

c. $49,500.00
(($50,000 x 0.97) + ($50,000 x 4/12 x 0.06))

Review 16-3

January 1, 2020—To record bond issuance

Cash	150,000	
Bonds Payable		150,000

Assets = Liabilities + Equity
+150,000 +150,000

Assets = Liabilities + Equity
−7,500 −7,500

December 31, 2020—To record payment of interest

Interest Expense	7,500	
Cash ($150,000 × 5%)		7,500

Assets = Liabilities + Equity
−150,000 −150,000

Cash: 150,000 | 7,500, 150,000
Bonds Payable: 150,000 | 150,000
Interest Exp: 7,500 |

December 31, 2029—To record principal payment

Bonds Payable	150,000	
Cash		150,000

Review 16-4

Assets = Liabilities + Equity
+128,681 −21,319
+150,000

a. **January 1, 2020—To record bonds sold at a discount**

Cash	128,681	
Discount on Bonds Payable	21,319	
Bonds Payable		150,000

Assets = Liabilities + Equity
−3,750 +754 −4,504

July 1, 2020—To record payment of interest

Interest Expense	4,504	
Discount on Bonds Payable		754
Cash		3,750

Assets = Liabilities + Equity
+780 −4,530
+3,750

Cash: 128,681 | 3,750
Bonds Payable: | 150,000
Interest Payable: | 3,750
Discount on BP: 21,319 | 754, 780
Interest Exp: 4,504, 4,530 |

December 31, 2020—To record accrual of interest

Interest Expense	4,530	
Discount on Bonds Payable		780
Interest Payable		3,750

Assets = Liabilities + Equity
+128,681 −21,319
+150,000

b. **January 1, 2020—To record bonds sold at a discount**

Cash	128,681	
Discount on Bonds Payable	21,319	
Bonds Payable		150,000

Assets = Liabilities + Equity
−3,750 +1,066 −4,816

July 1, 2020—To record payment of interest

Interest Expense	4,816	
Discount on Bonds Payable		1,066
Cash		3,750

Assets = Liabilities + Equity
+1,066 −4,816
+3,750

Cash: 128,681 | 3,750
Bonds Payable: | 150,000
Interest Payable: | 3,750
Discount on BP: 21,319 | 1,066, 1,066
Interest Exp: 4,816, 4,816 |

December 31, 2020—To record accrual of interest

Interest Expense	4,816	
Discount on Bonds Payable		1,066
Interest Payable		3,750

Review 16-5

Assets = Liabilities + Equity
+53,987 +3,897
+50,000

a. **January 1, 2020—To record bonds sold at a premium**

Cash	53,897	
Premium on Bonds Payable		3,897
Bonds Payable		50,000

Assets = Liabilities + Equity
−1,500 −153 −1,347

July 1, 2020—To record payment of interest

Interest Expense	1,347	
Premium on Bonds Payable	153	
Cash		1,500

Assets = Liabilities + Equity
−1,500 −156 −1,344

Cash: 53,897 | 1,500
Bonds Payable: | 50,000
Interest Payable: | 1,500
Premium on BP: 153, 156 | 3,897
Interest Exp: 1,347, 1,344 |

December 31, 2020—To record payment of interest

Interest Expense	1,344	
Premium on Bonds Payable	156	
Interest Payable		1,500

Assets = Liabilities + Equity
+53,987 +3,897
+50,000

b. **January 1, 2020—To record bonds sold at a premium**

Cash	53,897	
Premium on Bonds Payable		3,897
Bonds Payable		50,000

July 1, 2020—To record payment of interest

Interest Expense	1,305	
Premium on Bonds Payable	195	
Cash		1,500

Assets = Liabilities + Equity
−1,500 −195 −1,305

December 31, 2020—To record payment of interest

Interest Expense	1,305	
Premium on Bonds Payable	195	
Interest Payable		1,500

Assets = Liabilities + Equity
−195 −1,305
+1,500

Cash: 53,897 | 1,500
Bonds Payable: | 50,000
Interest Payable: | 1,500
Premium on BP: 195, 195 | 3,897
Interest Exp: 1,305, 1,305 |

Review 16-6

a. **January 1, 2020—To record issuance of note**

Inventory ($100,000 + $49,108) (PV(0.08,2,−0.07*50000,−50000))	149,108	
Discount on Note Payable ($50,000 − $49,108)	892	
Cash		100,000
Note Payable		50,000

Assets = Liabilities + Equity
+149,108 −892
−100,000 +50,000

December 31, 2020—To record payment of interest

Interest Expense ($49,108 × 8%)	3,929	
Discount on Note Payable		429
Cash ($50,000 × 7%)		3,500

Assets = Liabilities + Equity
−3,500 +429 −3,929

December 31, 2021—To record payment of interest

Interest Expense ($49,537 × 8%)	3,963	
Discount on Note Payable		463
Cash ($50,000 × 7%)		3,500

Assets = Liabilities + Equity
−3,500 +463 −3,963

December 31, 2021—To record payment of note

Note Payable	50,000	
Cash		50,000

Assets = Liabilities + Equity
−50,000 −50,000

Cash: | 100,000, 3,500, 3,500, 50,000
Note Payable: 50,000 | 50,000
Discount on NP: 892 | 429, 463
Inventory: 149,108 |
Interest Exp: 3,929, 3,963 |

b. **January 1, 2020—To record issuance of note**

Inventory (fair value of inventory)	149,108	
Discount on Note Payable ($57,280 − $49,108)	8,172	
Cash		100,000
Note Payable		57,280

Assets = Liabilities + Equity
+149,108 −8,172
−100,000 +57,280

December 31, 2020—To record accrual of interest

Interest Expense ($49,108 × 8%)	3,929	
Discount on Note Payable		3,929

Assets = Liabilities + Equity
+3,929 −3,929

December 31, 2021—To record accrual of interest

Interest Expense ($53,037 × 8%)	4,243	
Discount on Note Payable		4,243

Assets = Liabilities + Equity
+4,243 −4,243

December 31, 2021—To record payment of note

Note Payable	57,280	
Cash		57,280

Assets = Liabilities + Equity
−57,280 −57,280

Cash: | 100,000, 57,280
Note Payable: 57,280 | 57,280; 0
Inventory: 149,108 |
Discount on NP: 8,172 | 3,929, 4,243; 0
Interest Exp: 3,929, 4,243 |

c. **January 1, 2020—To record issuance of note payable**

Inventory	149,108	
Cash		100,000
Note Payable (PV(0.08,3,−19055.55,0))		49,108

Assets = Liabilities + Equity
+149,108 +49,108
−100,000

December 31, 2020—To record payment of interest plus principal

Interest Expense ($49,108 × 8%)	3,929	
Note Payable	15,127	
Cash		19,056

Assets = Liabilities + Equity
−19,056 −15,127 −3,929

Assets = Liabilities + Equity
−19,056 = −16,337 + −2,719

December 31, 2021—To record payment of interest plus principal

Interest Expense ($33,981 × 8%) (amount rounded)	2,719	
Note Payable	16,337	
Cash		19,056

Assets = Liabilities + Equity
−19,056 = −17,644 + −1,412

Cash: (credit) 100,000; 19,056; 19,056; 19,056
Note Payable: (debit) 15,127; 16,337; 17,644 | (credit) 49,108 | balance 0
Inventory: (debit) 149,108
Interest Exp: (debit) 3,929; 2,719; 1,412

December 31, 2022—To record payment of interest plus principal

Interest Expense ($17,644 × 8%)	1,412	
Note Payable	17,644	
Cash		19,056

*Amount rounded

Review 16-7

Assets = Liabilities + Equity
+285,000 = −15,000, +300,000

a. **January 1, 2020—To record bond issuance**

Cash ($300,000 × 0.95)	285,000	
Discount on Bonds Payable ($300,000 − $285,000)	15,000	
Bonds Payable		300,000

Assets = Liabilities + Equity
−7,500 = +1,500 + −9,000

b. **June 30, 2020—To record payment of interest**

Interest Expense	9,000	
Discount on Bonds Payable ($15,000/10)		1,500
Cash ($300,000 × 5%/2)		7,500

Assets = Liabilities + Equity
−375 = +75 + −450

c. **October 1, 2020—To record payment of interest**

Interest Expense	450	
Discount on Bonds Payable ($15,000/60 × 3 × 0.10)		75
Cash ($30,000 × 5% × 3/12)		375

Assets = Liabilities + Equity
−26,700 = −30,000, +1,275 + +2,025

Cash: (debit) 285,000 | (credit) 7,500; 375; 26,700
Bonds Payable: (debit) 30,000 | (credit) 300,000
Interest Exp: (debit) 9,000; 450
Discount on BP: (debit) 15,000 | (credit) 1,500; 75; 1,275
Gain on Bond Ext: (credit) 2,025

d. **October 1, 2020—To record bond extinguishment**

Bonds Payable	30,000	
Discount on Bonds Payable ($15,000/60 × 51 × 0.10)		1,275
Cash ($30,000 × 0.89)		26,700
Gain on Bond Extinguishment ([$30,000 − $1,275] − $26,700)		2,025

Review 16-8

Assets = Liabilities + Equity
+196,000 = −4,000, +200,000

a. **January 1, 2020—To record bond issuance**

Cash ($200,000 × 0.98)	196,000	
Discount on Bonds Payable ($200,000 − $196,000)	4,000	
Bonds Payable		200,000

Assets = Liabilities + Equity
−100,000, +1,200 + +500, +98,300

Cash: (debit) 196,000
Bonds Payable: (debit) 100,000 | (credit) 200,000
Discount on BP: (debit) 4,000 | (credit) 1,200
Common Stock: (credit) 500
Paid in Cap—CS: (credit) 98,300

b. **December 31, 2021—To record conversion of bonds to common stock**

Bonds Payable ($200,000 × 0.50)	100,000	
Discount on Bonds Payable ($4,000 × 0.60 × 0.50)		1,200
Common Stock ($100,000/$1,000 × 5 shares × $1 par)		500
Paid-in Capital in Excess of Par—Common Stock (to balance)		98,300

Review 16-9

Assets = Liabilities + Equity
+102,000 = +100,000, +2,000

Cash: (debit) 102,000
Bonds Payable: (credit) 100,000
Premium on BP: (credit) 2,000

a. **To record issuance of bonds with nondetachable warrants**

Cash ($100,000 × 1.02)	102,000	
Premium on Bonds Payable ($102,000 − $100,000)		2,000
Bonds Payable		100,000

b. **To record issuance of bonds with detachable warrants**

Cash ($100,000 × 1.02)	102,000	
Discount on Bonds Payable ($100,000 + $5,000 − $102,000)	3,000	
Paid-in Capital—Stock Warrants ($100,000/$1,000 × 10 × $5)		5,000
Bonds Payable		100,000

Assets = Liabilities + Equity
+102,000 = −3,000 +100,000 + +5,000

Cash: 102,000 (Dr.) | Bonds Payable: 100,000 (Cr.)
Discount on BP: 3,000 (Dr.) | Paid in Cap—War: 5,000 (Cr.)

Review 16-10

December 31, 2020—To record fair value option adjustment

Fair Value Adjustment—Bond Payable	2,000	
Unrealized Gain—OCI		2,000

Assets = Liabilities + Equity
−2,000 + +2,000

FVA—BP: 2,000 (Dr.) | Unreal Gain—OCI: 2,000 (Cr.)

Review 16-11

a. 2.76 *b.* 0.73 *c.* 11.77

Review 16-12

Example One

January 1, 2020—Debtor: To record asset appreciation

Equipment	4,000	
Gain on Disposal ($32,000 − $28,000)		4,000

Assets = Liabilities + Equity
+4,000 + +4,000

January 1, 2020—Debtor: To record settlement of debt through asset transfer

Note Payable	35,000	
Accumulated Depreciation	22,000	
Equipment		54,000
Gain on Restructuring of Debt		3,000

Assets = Liabilities + Equity
−32,000 = −35,000 + +3,000

Equipment: Bal. 50,000, 4,000 (Dr.); 54,000 (Cr.); 0
Note Payable: 35,000 (Dr.); 35,000 Bal. (Cr.); 0
Accum Deprec: 22,000 (Dr.); 22,000 Bal. (Cr.)
Gain on Debt Restr: 3,000 (Cr.)
Gain on Disposal: 4,000 (Cr.)

Example Two

January 1, 2020—Debtor: To record settlement of debt through transfer of equity interest

Note Payable	35,000	
Common Stock ($1 × 3,000 shares)		3,000
Paid-in Capital in Excess of Par—Common Stock ($30,000 − $3,000)		27,000
Gain on Restructuring of Debt (to balance)		5,000

Assets = Liabilities + Equity
−35,000 + +3,000 +27,000 +5,000

Note Payable: 35,000 (Dr.); 35,000 Bal. (Cr.); 0
Gain on Debt Restr: 5,000 (Cr.)
Common Stock: 3,000 (Cr.)
Paid in Cap—CS: 27,000 (Cr.)

Example Three

Book value of debt		$35,000
Sum of restructured cash flows:		
Face value payable	$25,000	
Interest payments (2 x $25,000 x 5%)	2,500	27,500
Gain on restructure		$ 7,500

January 1, 2020—Debtor: To record restructuring of debt at less than debt book value

Note Payable	35,000	
Note Payable (restructured)		27,500
Gain on Restructuring of Debt		7,500

Assets = Liabilities + Equity
−35,000 +27,500 + +7,500

Note Payable: 35,000 (Dr.); 35,000 Bal., 27,500 (Cr.); 27,500
Gain on Debt Restr: 7,500 (Cr.)

Example Four

There is no entry by the debtor because the value of the restructured note ($35,400 or $30,000 plus interest of $5,400 (= $30,000 x 9% x 2)) exceeds the book value of the debt.

17 Accounting for Leases

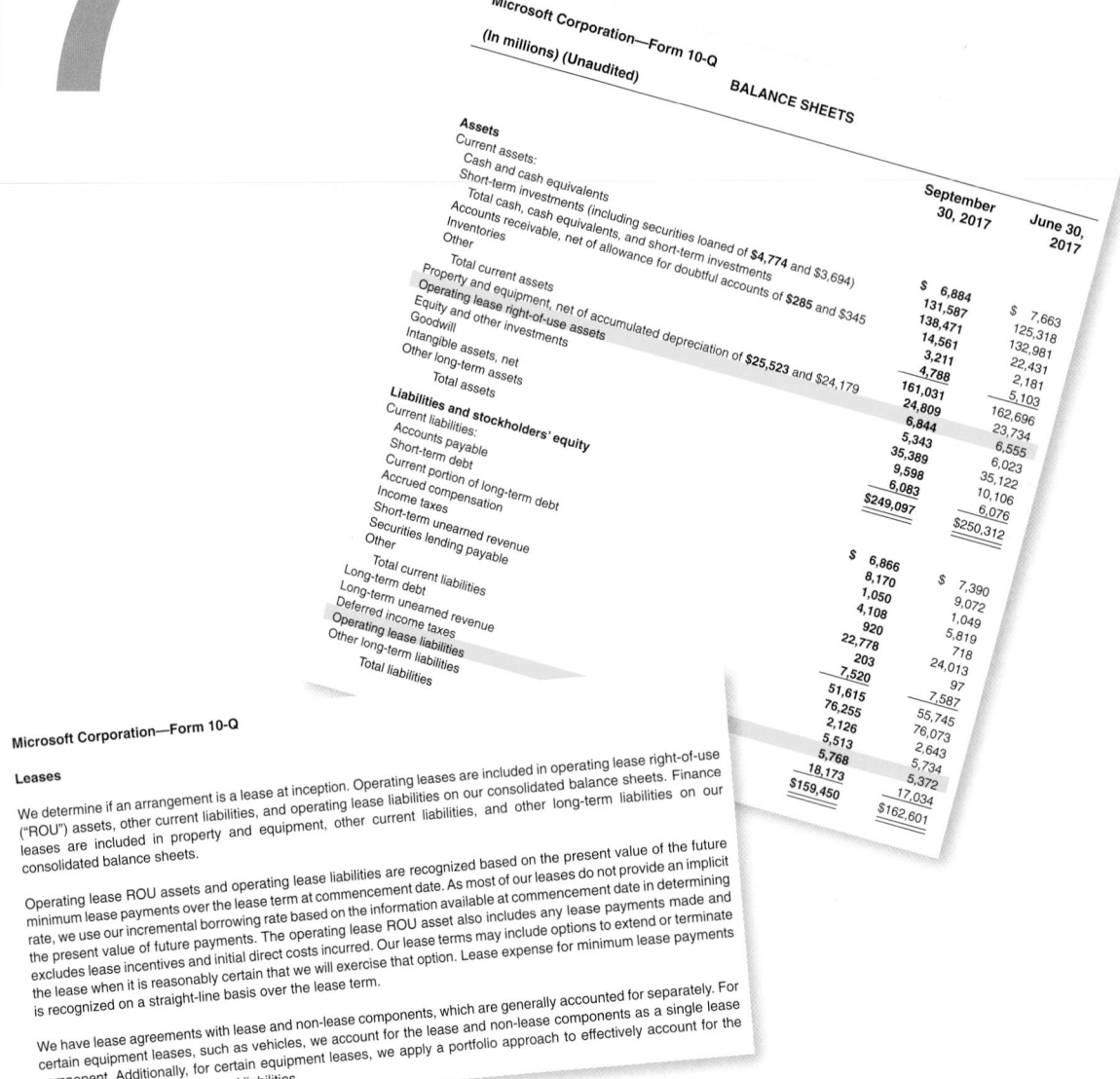

Microsoft Corporation—Form 10-Q

(In millions) (Unaudited)

BALANCE SHEETS

	September 30, 2017	June 30, 2017
Assets		
Current assets:		
Cash and cash equivalents	$ 6,884	$ 7,663
Short-term investments (including securities loaned of $4,774 and $3,694)	131,587	125,318
Total cash, cash equivalents, and short-term investments	138,471	132,981
Accounts receivable, net of allowance for doubtful accounts of $285 and $345	14,561	22,431
Inventories	3,211	2,181
Other	4,788	5,103
Total current assets	161,031	162,696
Property and equipment, net of accumulated depreciation of $25,523 and $24,179	24,809	23,734
Operating lease right-of-use assets	6,844	6,555
Equity and other investments	5,343	6,023
Goodwill	35,389	35,122
Intangible assets, net	9,598	10,106
Other long-term assets	6,083	6,076
Total assets	$249,097	$250,312
Liabilities and stockholders' equity		
Current liabilities:		
Accounts payable	$ 6,866	$ 7,390
Short-term debt	8,170	9,072
Current portion of long-term debt	1,050	1,049
Accrued compensation	4,108	5,819
Income taxes	920	718
Short-term unearned revenue	22,778	24,013
Securities lending payable	203	97
Other	7,520	7,587
Total current liabilities	51,615	55,745
Long-term debt	76,255	76,073
Long-term unearned revenue	2,126	2,643
Deferred income taxes	5,513	5,734
Operating lease liabilities	5,768	5,372
Other long-term liabilities	18,173	17,034
Total liabilities	$159,450	$162,601

Microsoft Corporation—Form 10-Q

Leases

We determine if an arrangement is a lease at inception. Operating leases are included in operating lease right-of-use ("ROU") assets, other current liabilities, and operating lease liabilities on our consolidated balance sheets. Finance leases are included in property and equipment, other current liabilities, and other long-term liabilities on our consolidated balance sheets.

Operating lease ROU assets and operating lease liabilities are recognized based on the present value of the future minimum lease payments over the lease term at commencement date. As most of our leases do not provide an implicit rate, we use our incremental borrowing rate based on the information available at commencement date in determining the present value of future payments. The operating lease ROU asset also includes any lease payments made and excludes lease incentives and initial direct costs incurred. Our lease terms may include options to extend or terminate the lease when it is reasonably certain that we will exercise that option. Lease expense for minimum lease payments is recognized on a straight-line basis over the lease term.

We have lease agreements with lease and non-lease components, which are generally accounted for separately. For certain equipment leases, such as vehicles, we account for the lease and non-lease components as a single lease component. Additionally, for certain equipment leases, we apply a portfolio approach to effectively account for the operating lease ROU assets and liabilities.

Chapter Preview

In this chapter, we explain lease accounting from the perspectives of both the lessor and the lessee. Accounting standards provide guidance on what is considered to be a lease in a recent accounting standard, ASC 842. The standard also provides criteria which guide companies in determining the proper classification of leases, which then determines the accounting and reporting of the related lease transactions. We discuss other related topics including lease modifications, short-term leases, and financial statement disclosures.

Action Plan

LO	Topic/Subtopic	Page	Demos	Reviews	Assignments
LO 17–1	**Determine lease types for lessees and lessors and classify leases using lease criteria** Finance Lease :: Operating Lease :: Sales-Type Lease :: Direct-Financing Lease :: Lease Classification Criteria	17-4	D17-1	R17-1	21, 22, 23, 24, 25, 52, 53, 88, 89, 90, 96, 97, 98, 99, 115, 116
LO 17–2	**Account for a finance lease for a lessee** Finance Lease :: Right-of-Use Asset :: Straight-Line Method :: Lease Liability :: Effective Interest Method	17-12	D17-2A D17-2B D17-2C	R17-2	26, 27, 28, 29, 30, 31, 32, 54, 55, 56, 57, 58, 59, 60, 61, 62, 69, 70, 72, 74, 88, 89, 90, 91, 92, 93, 96, 97, 98, 104, 107, 108, 109, 111, 112, 115, 116
LO 17–3	**Account for a sales-type lease for a lessor** Sales-Type Lease:: Lease Receivable :: Interest Revenue :: Effective Interest Method	17-25	D17-3A D17-3B	R17-3	33, 34, 35, 36, 37, 38, 39, 40, 41, 42, 43, 63, 64, 65, 66, 67, 68, 69, 70, 71, 72, 73, 75, 84, 88, 94, 95, 96, 97, 98, 111, 114, 115, 116
LO 17–4	**Account for an operating lease for a lessee** Operating Lease :: Right-of-Use Asset :: Lease Liability :: Lease Expense :: Straight-Line Basis	17-33	D17-4A D17-4B	R17-4	44, 45, 46, 47, 76, 77, 78, 79, 82, 88, 99, 100, 102, 103, 110, 112, 115, 116
LO 17–5	**Account for an operating lease for a lessor** Operating Lease :: Depreciation Expense :: Lease Revenue	17-42	D17-5	R17-5	48, 49, 80, 81, 83, 88, 101, 102, 114, 115, 116
LO 17–6	**Explain lease modifications and lease remeasurements** Lease Modification :: Standalone Price :: Remeasurement :: Reassessment of Lease Classification	17-44	D17-6	R17-6	50, 85, 86, 88, 105, 117
LO 17–7	**Explain the accounting policy election for short-term leases and other lease disclosures** Qualitative Disclosures :: Quantitative Disclosures :: Short-Term Lease Election :: Lease Expense :: Straight-Line Basis	17-47	D17-7	R17-7	51, 87, 88, 106, 113
LO 17–8	**APPENDIX 17A—Account for direct financing leases** Third Party Residual Guarantee:: Deferred Gross Profit :: Lease Receivable :: Interest Revenue :: Effective Interest Method	17-50	D17-8	R17-8	118, 119, 122
LO 17–9	**APPENDIX 17B—Describe the difference in accounting for a sale-leaseback versus a failed sale** Sale-Leaseback :: Sale and Lease :: Failed Sale :: Finance Liability	17-54	D17-9	R17-9	120, 121, 123, 124

Expanded Chapter Preview

Leasing is an important activity for many companies. A lease is a legal agreement where an owner of an asset (lessor) turns over the right to control the asset's use to a renter (lessee) for payment (consideration). Lessees are able to gain access to an asset, finance the use of that asset, and simplify the disposal of a used asset. This means that leasing reduces the risks of *full* ownership of an asset for the lessee. Lessors on the other hand, can earn profits on the leasing transactions.

It is essential that financial statement users understand a lessee's rights and obligations associated with leasing transactions. Financial statement information presented should also address a lessor's exposure to credit and asset risk as a result of these leasing transactions. This means that, these transactions must be faithfully represented in the financial statements. The FASB determined that faithful representation requires that **assets and liabilities be recognized for all leases with lease terms of more than 12 months** with the implementation of a new leasing standard, ASC 842 (effective for annual periods beginning after December 15, 2018).

This was not always the case—prior to the new standard, the SEC estimated $1.25 trillion of off-balance sheet lease obligations by SEC registrants (2005 Report and Recommendations Pursuant to Section 401(c) of the Sarbanes-Oxley Act of 2002 On Arrangements with Off-Balance Sheet Implications, Special Purpose Entities, and Transparency of Filings by Issuers). Under the new standard, the FASB determined that most leases create assets and liabilities. Thus, on the balance sheet, a lessee recognizes an *asset* for the right to use an underlying asset for the lease term and a *liability* for the obligation to make lease payments for the vast majority of leases.

ASU 2016-02 The core principle of Topic 842 is that a lessee should recognize the assets and liabilities that arise from leases. All leases create an asset and a liability for the lessee in accordance with FASB Concepts Statement No. 6, Elements of Financial Statements, and, therefore, recognition of those lease assets and lease liabilities represents an improvement over previous GAAP, which did not require lease assets and lease liabilities to be recognized for most leases.

Within this right-of-use model there are different lease classifications for the lessee and the lessor. The primary distinction in categories is that some leases are viewed essentially as a sale/purchase of an asset because the lease effectively transfers the remaining benefits of the asset to the lessee. For example, if we lease a new vehicle with a 6-year useful life for a period of 18 months, we obtain the right to use that vehicle for a period of time. However, if we lease that same vehicle for 6 years, we obtain substantially all of the remaining benefits of that vehicle—as if we purchased that vehicle. Lease criteria, described later in **Exhibit 17-3** are used to determine if a lease is economically similar to the purchase of a nonfinancial asset. **Exhibit 17-1** displays the classification alternatives.

Update 2016-02 Section C BC56 The lessee accounting model in Topic 842 classifies leases as finance or operating leases on the basis of whether the lease is economically similar to the purchase of a nonfinancial asset because the lessee, in effect, obtains control of the underlying asset (that is, the ability to direct the use of and obtain substantially all the remaining benefits from the underlying asset), in contrast to merely obtaining control over the use of the underlying asset for a period of time.

EXHIBIT 17-1
Lease Classifications

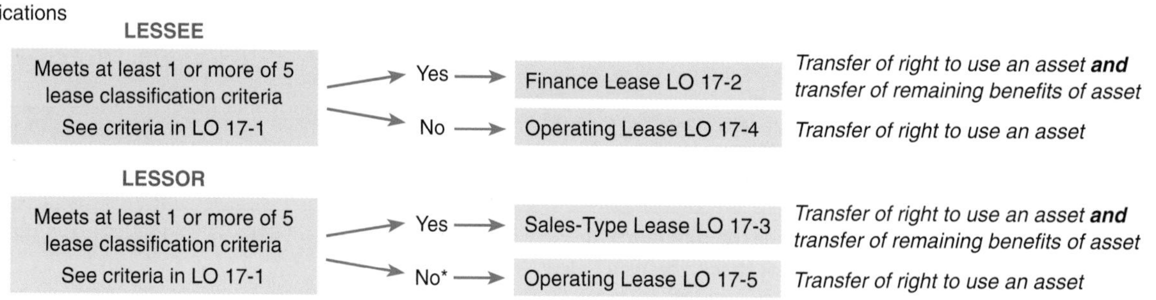

* Not classified as operating if it meets the criteria of direct financing lease—See Appendix 17A

In LO 17-1, we start with the definition of a lease, which is the right to control the use of an asset in exchange for consideration. Lease consideration is made up of five components: fixed payments, variable payments, purchase options, penalties, and guaranteed residual value. We then explain in depth the lease classification criteria referenced in **Exhibit 17-1** that determine lease classifications. In sections that follow, we describe the accounting of the four lease categories along with the short-term lease exception. An additional classification for lessors, direct financing, is discussed in an appendix.

Determine lease types for lessees and lessors and classify leases using lease criteria

LO 17-1

In this section, we start with a definition of a lease and explain the key components that comprise a lease. We then review the lease classification criteria that are used to determine how to classify a specific lease. Lease classifications include finance and operating for lessees and sales-type, operating, and direct-financing for lessors. We apply the lease classification criteria to a variety of leases in **Demo 17-1**. Although there is judgment involved in applying the lease classification criteria, the criteria help to provide consistency in lease classifications across leases and across companies. Key lease terms are defined as follows.

LO 17-1 Overview

Lease Types
- **Lessee**—Finance, operating
- **Lessor**—Sales-type, operating, direct-financing

Lease Classification Criteria
- Ownership transfer
- Purchase option
- Lease term length
- PV of lease payments
- Alternative use

Lease	**ASC Glossary** A contract, or part of a contract, that conveys the right to control the use of identified property, plant, or equipment (an identified asset) for a period of time in exchange for consideration.
Lessee	**ASC Glossary** An entity that enters into a contract to obtain the right to use an underlying asset for a period of time in exchange for consideration.
Lessor	**ASC Glossary** An entity that enters into a contract to provide the right to use an underlying asset for a period of time in exchange for consideration.
Underlying asset	**ASC Glossary** An asset that is the subject of a lease for which a right to use that asset has been conveyed to a lessee. The underlying asset could be a physically distinct portion of a single asset.
Commencement date of the lease	**ASC Glossary** The date on which a lessor makes an underlying asset available for use by a lessee.
Lease term	**ASC Glossary** The noncancellable period for which a lessee has the right to use an underlying asset, together with all of the following: *a.* Periods covered by an option to extend the lease if the lessee is reasonably certain to exercise that option *b.* Periods covered by an option to terminate the lease if the lessee is reasonably certain not to exercise that option *c.* Periods covered by an option to extend (or not to terminate) the lease in which exercise of the option is controlled by the lessor.
Residual value guarantee	**ASC Glossary** A guarantee made to a lessor that the value of an underlying asset returned to the lessor at the end of a lease will be at least a specified amount.
Unguaranteed residual asset	**ASC Glossary** The amount that a lessor expects to derive from the underlying asset following the end of the lease term that is not guaranteed by the lessee or any other third party unrelated to the lessor, measured on a discounted basis.

Definition of a Lease

A **lease** is identified at the **inception of a contract** or the date that the contract is signed or authorized. This means that at the time a contract is initiated, the company determines whether the contract is a lease or includes a lease. If so, the reporting requirements of ASC 842 apply.

842-10-15-2 At inception of a contract, an entity shall determine whether that contract is or contains a lease.

A **lease** is an agreement where the legal owner (**lessor**) of property, plant, or equipment, turns over the right to control the use of an identified asset to a renter (**lessee**) in exchange for consideration for a period of time. For example, Leasing Company leases equipment to Manufacturer Inc. for a five-year period in exchange for annual lease payments of $15,000 per year. During the five-year period, Manufacturer Inc. controls the right to

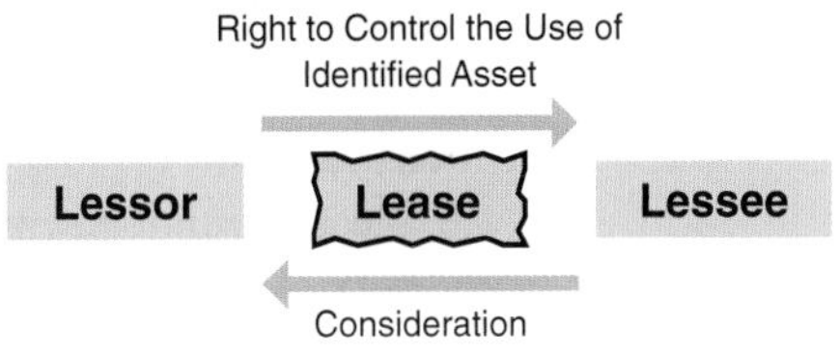

use the equipment in its manufacturing facility. At the end of the lease term, Manufacturer Inc. returns the equipment to Leasing Company.

Right to Control the Use of an Identified Asset

The accounting guidance provides two criteria in determining *whether a contract conveys the right to control the use of an asset.*

842-10-15-4 To determine whether a contract conveys the right to control the use of an identified asset . . . for a period of time, an entity shall assess whether, throughout the period of use, the customer has both of the following:

a. The right to obtain substantially all of the economic benefits from use of the identified asset.
b. The right to direct the use of the identified asset.

842-10-15-9 An asset typically is identified by being explicitly specified in a contract. However, an asset also can be identified by being implicitly specified at the time that the asset is made available for use by the lessee.

The two criteria apply to the period of use or the time that the underlying asset fulfills the contract. **Economic benefits** from the use of the identified asset include the asset's primary outputs (such as a produced product) and any by-products (such as tax credits that are generated through the use of the asset) including resulting cash payments. An identified asset can be either explicitly specified or implicitly identified or specified in a contract. An asset may be **explicitly identified** with a unique code such as a serial number. An asset may be **implicitly identified** if an asset must be used to fulfill a contract. For example, the parameters of a contract imply that a company uses its specialized equipment to fulfill the contract, even though the specialized equipment is not mentioned specifically in the contract.

A lessee has the right to **direct the use** of an identified asset when either (a) the lessee has the right to direct how and for what purpose the asset is used or (b) relevant decisions about how and for what purpose the asset is used are predetermined and the lessee either has the right to operate or direct the use of the asset or the lessee designed the asset to be used for a specific purpose. For example, a lessee has the right to change the output that is produced by a leased asset, such as what is sold in a leased retail space. Or, a lessee has the right to change when the output is produced, such as when a leased retail space is open for business.

Consideration

Consideration identified in a lease contract includes lease payments. **Lease payments** are defined in the lease standard as consisting of five amounts: fixed payments, variable payments, purchase option, lease termination penalty, and residual value guarantee—see **Exhibit 17-2**. **The concept of a lease payment is important because it is the basis for measuring the lease liability in later sections and is used in the determination of a lease classification later in this section.** Recall from the expanded introduction that a lease is classified differently for a lessee (and lessor) depending on whether certain lease criteria are met. As a result, accounting standards are specific about what is classified as a *lease payment.* A description of the five lease payment components follows.

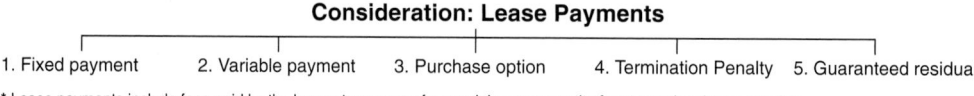

EXHIBIT 17-2
Lease Payment Components*

Consideration: Lease Payments

1. Fixed payment
2. Variable payment
3. Purchase option
4. Termination Penalty
5. Guaranteed residual

* Lease payments include fees paid by the lessee to owners of a special-purpose entity for structuring the transaction.

Lease Payments
1. **Fixed payment**
2. Variable payment
3. Purchase option
4. Penalty
5. Guaranteed residual

Fixed Payment **Fixed payments** are required payments in the lease contract. Fixed payments are known payments that are stable or change over time based upon a predetermined rate. For example, a fixed lease payment is $2,000 per month for the first 2 years and increases to $2,500 for the remaining 3 years of a 5-year lease.

842-10-30-5a Fixed payments, including in substance fixed payments [discussed below], less any lease incentives paid or payable to the lessee.

Lease incentives are incentives to encourage a lessee to sign a lease, such as an up-front cash payment to a lessee, reimbursement of lessee costs (such as moving expenses), or the payment by a lessor of a lessee's preexisting lease. Lease incentives are paid to the lessee before the commencement of the lease or during the lease term.

It is important for a lessee to identify the lease components and nonlease components of a contract because consideration is allocated separately to each **lease component** and **nonlease component**. Costs that contribute to obtaining control of a building (a leased asset) including insurance and real estate taxes should be included in lease payments. However, considerations allocated to a nonlease component such as maintenance costs are not classified as a lease payment.

842-10-15-30 The consideration in the contract shall be allocated to each separate lease component and nonlease component of the contract. . . . Components of a contract include only those items or activities that transfer a good or service to the lessee.

842-10-15-31 An entity shall account for each separate lease component separately from the nonlease components of the contract. . . . Nonlease components are not within the scope of this Topic and shall be accounted for in accordance with other Topics.

Payment Type	Example	Include as Lease Payment	Analysis
Fixed payment increases in later periods	Rent increases each year by 2% over five years	✔ (fixed)	**Because the rate increase is predetermined, the payments are considered fixed.**
Fixed payment includes charges for other services related to the transfer of the leased asset	Rent includes a charge for real estate taxes and insurance	✔ (fixed)	**Include charges as part of fixed payment unless it is a nonlease payment such as charges for cleaning or snow removal.**

For example, a lessor charges a lessee $10,000 to lease a building, $1,000 for real estate taxes, $500 for hazard insurance, and $800 for maintenance for the building. The charge to the lessee for maintenance of a leased building is a cost for a service, separate from obtaining control of the leased building, and thus would be considered a nonlease component. The fee for maintenance would *not* be included in the fixed lease payment but would be recorded for accounting purposes separately (for example, debit Maintenance Expense and credit Cash for the lessee). However, the charges for real estate taxes and insurance are fixed payments that relate to obtaining control of the leased building, and thus are included as part of the lease payment. The payments to the lessor are summarized as follows.

Fixed Lease Payment	
Rent	$10,000
Real estate taxes	1,000
Hazard insurance	500
Total fixed lease payment	$11,500

Nonlease Payment	
Maintenance fee	$800

EXPANDING YOUR KNOWLEDGE — **Nonlease Component Practical Expedient**

The accounting guidance allows an alternative accounting treatment (practical expedient) for the treatment of the nonlease component. A lessee *may elect* to combine the nonlease components with the lease components and classify the total as a lease payment. For example, a maintenance charge would be allocated to the fixed lease payment along with rent, insurance, and property tax charges.

842-10-15-37 As a practical expedient, a lessee may, as an accounting policy election by class of underlying asset, choose not to separate nonlease components from lease components and instead to account for each separate lease component and the nonlease components associated with that lease component as a single lease component.

Variable Payment **Variable payments** are payments for the right to use a leased asset that vary because of changes in factors or circumstances occurring *after* the lease commencement date. The fluctuation is due to items such as price changes, performance changes, or usage fluctuation. For example, variable payments include rent increases that fluctuate with changes in the Consumer Price Index (CPI) or with changes in the lessee's sales revenue. This allows rent to adjust based upon the outcome of future events.

Lease Payments
1. Fixed payment
2. Variable payment
3. Purchase option
4. Penalty
5. Guaranteed residual

842-10-30-5b Variable lease payments that depend on an index or a rate (such as the Consumer Price Index or a market interest rate), initially measured using the index or rate at the commencement date.

Variable payments are classified as *lease payments* only if the variability is based on an index or rate. In this case, the rate or index in effect at the time of the lease commencement is used to calculate the lease payment. Otherwise, the variable payment is excluded from what the authoritative standards define as a *lease payment*. Why only include variable payments based upon an index or a rate? Such payments are unavoidable and thus are similar to fixed lease payments—only the measurement of the payment varies, not the existence of a payment. Contingent payments not based on an index or rate are not classified as a *lease payment*; they are, however, expensed as incurred.

One exception to the exclusion of variable payments for the lease classification test is the occurrence of an **in-substance fixed payment**. For example, a lease payment may be variable or contingent on a future event (such as sales volumes) but the lease indicates a required minimum payment level. The minimum payment level is considered a fixed lease payment. The inclusion or exclusion of certain variable payments in the lease payment calculation is summarized below.

Payment Type	Example	Include as Lease Payment	Analysis
Variable payment, dependent on an index or rate	Rent increases based upon changes in the CPI.	✔ (variable)	**Include as a lease payment using the index or rate on the date of lease commencement.**
Variable payment, *not* dependent on an index or rate	Rent increases based upon the lessee's sales volume.		**Do not include as a lease payment because the variability is not based on a rate or index.**
In-substance, fixed payment	Rent increases based upon the lessee's sale volume, but the contract calls for a minimum annual payment.	✔ (fixed)	**Include the minimum annual rent as part of the lease payment because the payment is unavoidable.**

Lease Payments
1. Fixed payment
2. Variable payment
3. **Purchase option**
4. Penalty
5. Guaranteed residual

Purchase Option A **purchase option** (sometimes called a bargain purchase option in practice) is a provision of a lease contract giving the lessee an option to purchase the underlying asset for a specific price at a specific time or period of time. Only when it is *reasonably certain* that the lessee will exercise the option to purchase the underlying asset is the purchase option included as a lease payment. An option to purchase the asset for less than fair value is an indicator that the lessee would exercise the option. However the amount of discount that makes an exercise reasonably certain is subject to judgment. As an example, a lessee would be reasonably certain to exercise a purchase option for a vehicle (underlying asset) if the lease provision allowed the lessee to purchase the vehicle at the end of the lease for 70% of its fair value at lease end.

842-10-30-5c The exercise price of an option to purchase the underlying asset if the lessee is reasonably certain to exercise that option.

Lease Payments
1. Fixed payment
2. Variable payment
3. Purchase option
4. **Penalty**
5. Guaranteed residual

Lease Termination Penalty A payment for penalties for terminating a lease is included as a lease payment if the termination of the lease by the lessee is *reasonably certain*.

842-10-30-5d Payments for penalties for terminating the lease if the lease term . . . reflects the lessee exercising an option to terminate the lease.

In the case where a termination penalty is classified as a lease payment, the lessee must take into account the termination when identifying the lease term. This means that the lease term would end at the time of the expected termination.

ASC Glossary Penalty: Any requirement that is imposed or can be imposed on the lessee by the lease agreement or by factors outside the lease agreement to do any of the following:

a. Disburse cash
b. Incur or assume a liability
c. Perform services

d. Surrender or transfer an asset or rights to an asset or otherwise forego an economic benefit, or suffer an economic detriment . . .

Residual Value Guarantee A **guaranteed residual value** is a guarantee by a lessee to a lessor that a leased asset returned to the lessor at the end of a lease term will be valued at a minimum amount. The amount probable of being owed is equal to any excess of the *guaranteed* residual value over an estimate of the *expected* residual value. For example, a 3-year vehicle lease may require that a lessee return the vehicle at the end of 3 years with a fair value of $15,000 based upon its physical condition and mileage levels. If the lessee estimates that the fair value of the vehicle at lease-end will be $12,000, the lease payment is only $3,000 ($15,000 − $12,000). (This requirement differs from how a residual value guarantee is measured in the lease classification criteria in the next section.) If however, it is assumed that it is reasonably certain that the lessee will exercise a purchase option, a guaranteed residual value is not considered a payment because the leased asset would revert to the lessee at the end of the lease.

Lease Payments
1. Fixed payment
2. Variable payment
3. Purchase option
4. Penalty
5. **Guaranteed residual**

842-10-30-5f For a lessee only, amounts probable of being owed by the lessee under residual value guarantees.

An **unguaranteed residual value** is an amount estimated by the lessor of the value of an underlying asset returned to the lessor. Because there is no obligation on the part of the lessee to return an asset at this value, an unguaranteed residual is *not* considered to be a lease payment for the lessee. (For a discussion of lease contracts where the residual guarantee is guaranteed to the lessor by a third party, see Appendix 17A.)

EXHIBIT 17-3
Lease Classification Criteria

Lease Classification Criteria

1. Ownership transfer 2. Purchase option 3. Lease term length 4. PV of lease payments 5. Alternative use

Lease Classification Criteria

After it is determined that a contract includes a lease, the next step is to determine the proper classification of the lease. To determine the proper classification, it is necessary to determine the extent of control of the identified asset that is passed to the lessee. The economics of leases differ. A lease can be structured in ways similar to a purchase of an asset on credit where the lessee obtains control of the underlying asset, beyond obtaining merely the control of the use of the leased asset. This means that the lessee obtains substantially all of the *remaining* benefits from the asset and has obligations that are similar to those as if it purchased the asset through a loan. In both cases, an asset and liability are initially recognized, but subsequent reporting is different. If the lease meets at least one of the five criteria, it is classified as a finance lease (lessee) and a sales-type lease (lessor). **The five lease classification criteria outlined in Exhibit 17-3 are used to determine whether a particular lease is economically similar to an acquisition of the underlying asset.** A description of the five lease criteria follows.

Ownership Transfer

842-10-25-2a The lease transfers ownership of the underlying asset to the lessee by the end of the lease term.

Lease Classification Criteria
1. **Ownership transfer**
2. Purchase option
3. Lease term length
4. PV of lease payments
5. Alternative use

Transfer of ownership refers to a transfer of legal ownership from the lessor to the lessee at the end of the lease term. For example, a five-year lease arrangement for a vehicle could allow for the vehicle to transfer to the lessee automatically at the end of the lease term. Throughout the lease term however, the lessor legally owns the vehicle.

Purchase Option

842-10-25-2b The lease grants the lessee an option to purchase the underlying asset that the lessee is reasonably certain to exercise.

Lease Classification Criteria
1. Ownership transfer
2. **Purchase option**
3. Lease term length
4. PV of lease payments
5. Alternative use

A **purchase option** is an option to purchase the underlying asset at a specified time and price. A lessee may reasonably expect to exercise an option if a significant economic incentive exists. For example, if a lessee is able to purchase a vehicle at the end of a lease at a 20% discount off of the projected fair value of the vehicle at the end of the lease, it is reasonable to assume that the lessee will purchase the vehicle at lease-end. In another example, a lessee leases highly customized equipment for a 5-year period. The lessee may have a significant economic incentive to purchase the equipment at the end of the lease term at *fair value* because the equipment is vital to its business, and to replace the equipment may cause disruptions or halting of operations.

Lease Term Length

Lease Classification Criteria
1. Ownership transfer
2. Purchase option
3. **Lease term length**
4. PV of lease payments
5. Alternative use

842-10-25-2c The lease term is for the major part of the remaining economic life of the underlying asset. However, if the commencement date falls at or near the end of the economic life of the underlying asset, this criterion shall not be used for purposes of classifying the lease.

Although not a mandated approach, the lease standard offers one option, a 75% threshold, in defining a major part of the economic life of the asset. More specifically, companies would consider a lease term to be a major part of the economic life of the asset if the lease term is greater than or equal to 75% of the remaining economic life of the asset. If however, the lease commences near the end of the lease asset's economic life (such as the last 25% of its economic useful life), this criterion is not applicable. **For assignments in this chapter, use the 75% test unless information in the problem indicates that the 75% threshold is not a reasonable approach.**

842-10-55-2 When determining lease classification, one reasonable approach to assessing the [leasing criteria] would be to conclude: a. Seventy-five percent or more of the remaining economic life of the underlying asset is a major part of the remaining economic life of that underlying asset. b. A commencement date that falls at or near the end of the economic life of the underlying asset refers to a commencement date that falls within the last 25 percent of the total economic life of the underlying asset.

The **lease term** is the noncancelable period for which a lessee has the right to use an underlying asset. A lease term is impacted by (a) a lessee renewal option, (b) a lessee termination option, or (c) a lessor-controlled renewal or termination option. **Renewal or termination options should be included in the lease term if it is reasonably certain that the lessee will exercise the options.** For example, a lessee has an economic incentive to renew a lease if the price of the renewal is less than the expected price of rent for an alternative rental option. Or, a lessee may have an economic incentive to renew a lease if the lessee would face a substantial penalty for failure to renew the lease. Additionally, if the lessor controls the decision for renewal or termination, the lease term should reflect the renewal or termination in the lease term. If however, the lease contains a purchase option that the lessee will reasonably exercise, the renewal terms are not considered because they would not be relevant.

842-10-30-2 At the commencement date, an entity shall include the periods...in the lease term having considered all relevant factors that create an economic incentive for the lessee.

Present Value (PV) of Lease Payments

Lease Classification Criteria
1. Ownership transfer
2. Purchase option
3. Lease term length
4. **PV of lease payments**
5. Alternative use

842-10-25-2d The present value of the sum of the lease payments and any residual value guaranteed by the lessee that is not already reflected in the lease payments . . . equals or exceeds substantially all of the fair value of the underlying asset.

This means that control has effectively transferred to the lessee when the present value of the lessee's lease payments is substantially the same as the fair value of the underlying asset. Lease payments used for this classification criterion were identified in **Exhibit 17-2**. However, residual value guarantees are treated differently for the purposes of defining lease payments in order to classify the lease. **While "lease payments" include only the probable payment related to a guarantee, for the purposes of classifying the lease 100% of the guaranteed residual value is included when calculating the present value of the lease payments.**

When defining "substantially all of the fair value of the underlying asset" the lease standard offers an option to consider 90% of the lease asset's fair value as "substantially all" of the fair value. For example, let's assume that annual lease payments for a vehicle lease are $7,500 for 3 years (with the first payment due immediately), the fair value of the vehicle is $35,000, and the discount rate is 8%. The lease requires that the lessee return the vehicle at the end of 3 years with a fair value of $15,000 even though the lessee estimates that the residual value will be $12,000. We consider this full amount of $15,000 in calculating the present value of the lease payments, regardless of its estimated value at lease end of $12,000.

Present value of the lease payments:	$32,782
90% of the fair value of the lease asset:	$31,500 (0.90 × $35,000)

	RATE	NPER	PMT	PV	FV	TYPE	Excel Formula
Given	8%	3	(7,500)	?	(15,000)	1	=PV(0.08,3, −7500, −15000,1)
Solution				$32,872			

In this example, the present value of the lease payments of $32,782 exceeds $31,500, or 90% of the fair value of the lease asset. Therefore, the lessor has effectively transferred control of the asset to the lessee. If the present value of the payments were lower than $31,500, we may say that the control of the asset did not pass to the lessee over the lease term. **For assignments in this chapter, use the 90% test unless information in the problem indicates that the 90% threshold is not a reasonable approach.**

842-10-55-2 When determining lease classification, one reasonable approach to assessing the [leasing criteria] would be to conclude . . . Ninety percent or more of the fair value of the underlying asset amounts to substantially all the fair value of the underlying asset.

What discount rate is used to calculate the present value of the lease payments? The lease standard requires the lessee to use the **rate implicit in the lease** (the rate used by the lessor to establish the lease payments) if known. If a lessee has information regarding the fair value of the underlying asset, the residual value estimated by the lessor, and the initial direct costs incurred by the lessor, the lessee could calculate the implicit rate. *However, such information is rarely known by the lessee.* The lessor on the other hand, will always use the rate implicit in the lease for present value calculations.

If the implicit rate of the lease is not known, the lessee would use its **incremental borrowing rate**—the rate a lessee would have to pay to borrow on a collateralized basis with terms similar to the terms of the lease. For example, if an equipment lease has a 3-year term, the interest rate should relate to a hypothetical borrowing of an amount equal to the fair value of the equipment, with a loan term of 3 years, and using the equipment as collateral. The rate must be determined on a lease by lease basis unless the company identifies a **portfolio** of leases where the leases have similar terms (lease term) and where the lessee's credit rating and interest rate environment is stable. This means that there is not a material difference in results in choosing an interest rate at a portfolio level versus a contract level. In the case of a portfolio, the lessee applies one rate to the entire portfolio of leases.

842-20-30-3 A lessee should use the rate implicit in the lease whenever that rate is readily determinable. If the rate implicit in the lease is not readily determinable, a lessee uses its incremental borrowing rate.

Alternative Use

842-10-25-2e The underlying asset is of such a specialized nature that it is expected to have no alternative use to the lessor at the end of the lease term.

Lease Classification Criteria
1. Ownership transfer
2. Purchase option
3. Lease term length
4. PV of lease payments
5. Alternative use

The restrictions on the **alternative use** of an asset (use of the asset for other purposes at the end of the lease) may be due to contractual or practical restrictions. An enforceable contractual restriction may limit the lessor's ability to redirect the asset for other purposes. A practical limitation can be that it is not economically feasible to make modifications necessary to use the asset for other purposes at lease end. For example, equipment under a lease is highly specialized to meet a lessee's specific specifications and it is cost prohibitive to refit the equipment for other lessees. Thus, the lessee will receive substantially all of the remaining benefits of the underlying asset. This means that no other entities are expected to take control of the asset after the lease term ends.

Lease Classification

At the lease commencement, the classification of the lease, and thus the accounting for the lease is determined (see **Exhibit 17-4**). **The lease commencement date is used rather than the lease inception date because the lessor has not performed under the contract until the lease commencement date.** For example, let's assume that a lessee and lessor enter into a contract on January 1, 2020, but the lessor doesn't make the asset available for use until March 1, 2020. At the lease inception date (January 1) the lessee would determine that the contract contains a lease, but the lease classification (and measurement of the right-of-use asset and lease liability discussed in the next section) would not take place until the lease commencement (March 1).

842-10-25-1 An entity shall classify each separate lease component at the commencement date.

EXHIBIT 17-4
Lease Types for a Lessee and Lessor

Lessee	Lessor*
Finance Lease Meets *at least one* of the five lease classification criteria.	**Sales-Type Lease** Meets *at least one* of the five lease classification criteria.
Operating Lease Meets *none* of the five lease classification criteria.	**Operating Lease** Meets *none* of the five lease classification criteria.

*An additional option of lessor classification is the direct financing lease, which is addressed in Appendix 17A to this chapter.

Lessees and lessors perform lease classification analyses independently. The five lease classification criteria in **Exhibit 17-3** are assessed to determine whether a lease is a **finance lease** (lessee), a **sales-type lease** (lessor), or an **operating lease** (lessee or lessor). If at least one lease classification criterion at lease commencement is met indicating that the lease is economically similar to a purchase by the lessee, the lease is considered to be a finance or a sales-type lease. If no lease classification criteria are met at lease commencement, the lease is considered to be an operating lease (lessee and lessor), with the specific exception of a direct financing lease for a lessor discussed in Appendix 17A.

Demo 17-1 **LO17-1** **Analysis of Lease Classification Criteria**

For each of the five separate scenarios, determine whether the lease criterion indicated has been met and provide an explanation to support your answer.

Lease Scenario	Applicable Lease Criterion	Explanation	Lease Criterion Met
1. Lessee Inc. signs a lease to rent equipment for a 10-year period from Lessor Inc. At the end of the 10-year lease term, the legal title of the equipment automatically transfers from Lessor Inc. to Lessee Inc.	**Ownership transfer**	**The automatic transfer of ownership of the underlying asset from the lessor to the lessee indicates that the transfer of ownership criterion is met.**	✔
2. Lessee Inc. signs a lease contract to rent construction equipment for five years. The lease includes an option for the lessee to purchase the equipment at the end of the lease for 20% below fair value which the lessee would be reasonably certain to exercise.	**Purchase option**	**The discount on the option to purchase at year-end *makes it reasonably certain* that the lessee will exercise the purchase option at lease end.**	✔
3. Lessee Inc. signs a lease contract for an office building for 10 years. The contract includes an option for a 10-year renewal, with rents determined by market prices at the time of renewal. Due to the amount invested in leasehold improvements, the lessee expects to renew the lease. The estimated useful life of the office building is 20 years.	**Lease term length**	**There is an economic incentive to renew the lease, so the lease term is considered to be 20 years. Because the lease term is 100% of the building's estimated life, the lease term is a major part of the asset's economic life.**	✔
4. Lessee Inc. leases equipment for 5 years. For the first year, the annual payment is $3,000, with the first payment due immediately. After the first year, the lease payments increase by an amount equivalent to the percentage increase in the CPI. *Other information* ▪ Implicit interest rate: 5%. ▪ CPI in year 2 is expected to increase by 2%. ▪ Fair value of equipment: $15,000.	**Present value of lease payments**	**The present value of the lease payments ($13,638) is greater than 90% of the fair value ($13,500, or 0.90 × $15,000).** (see table below) **Effective control is considered transferred to the lessee based upon the significance of the present value of the lease payments. (Only the current index is used to compute the payment.)**	✔

	RATE	NPER	PMT	PV	TYPE	Excel Formula
Given	5%	5	(3,000)	?	1	=PV(0.05,5,−3000,0,1)
Solution				$13,638		

continued

continued from previous page

Lease Scenario	Applicable Lease Criterion	Explanation	Lease Criterion Met
5. Lessor Inc. entered into a lease agreement to rent specialized equipment to Lessee Inc. for five years. The equipment was tailored specifically to the Lessee's operations and would require significant adjustments to resell the equipment at lease end to another company, which the lessor would be reluctant to make.	**Alternative use**	**The specialized equipment meets this criterion because of the restrictions on the alternative use of the equipment at lease end.**	✔

Determine Lease Classification

LO17-1 **REVIEW 17-1**

Review MBC

Jefferson Inc. is in the process of negotiating a lease of equipment with a fair value of $200,000 and must determine the proper lease classification. The following table describes four scenarios under negotiation.

	Option One	Option Two	Option Three	Option Four
Ownership transfer	No	No	No	No
Purchase option	No	No	$40,000 purchase option, considered to be a discounted price.	No
Length of lease term.	8	10	8	8
Economic life of equipment	12	12	12	12
Alternative use of equipment at lease end	Yes	Yes	Yes	Yes
Annual lease payment	$25,000	$25,000	$25,000	$28,000
Guaranteed residual value	No	No	$50,000	No
Implicit rate of lease	Unknown to lessee	Unknown to lessee	5.4544%	Unknown to lessee
Incremental borrowing rate of lessee	6%	6%	6%	6%
Payment type	Beginning of period	Beginning of period	Beginning of period	End of period

Determine the proper classification for each of the four scenarios assuming that Jefferson Inc. is the lessee.

More Practice:
17-21, 17-22, 17-23, 17-52, 17-53
Solution on p. 17-81.

Account for a finance lease for a lessee

LO 17-2

With the exception of short-term leases discussed in a later section, all leases are initially recognized on the balance sheet in the form of a right-of-use asset and a lease liability. This concept is similar to a purchase of a fixed asset through debt where a noncurrent asset and a noncurrent liability are recognized. A lessee's financial obligation to make lease payments in the future for its right to use an underlying asset during a lease term meets the definition of a liability. Likewise, the right to use an underlying asset conveyed to a lessee by a lessor results in the recording of an asset. Subsequent to the initial recognition of a lease however, measurement will vary depending on the lease classification.

LO 17-2 Overview

Lessee Accounting—Finance Lease
- At least one of the lease classification criteria is met
- Establish a right-of-use asset and amortize the asset using the straight-line method
- Establish a lease liability and record interest expense using the effective interest method

842-20-25-1 At the commencement date, a lessee shall recognize a right-of-use asset and a lease liability.

We explain the lessee's accounting for a finance lease, applicable when at least one of the five lease classification criteria is met. We illustrate the accounting for (1) a finance lease with no residual value in **Demo 17-2A**, (2) a finance lease with a guaranteed residual value in **Demo 17-2B**, and (3) a finance lease with a purchase option expected to be exercised in **Demo 17-2C**. An overview of a lessee's accounting for a finance lease follows.

Balance Sheet	Income Statement
Recognize a right-of-use asset, net and test for impairment.	Recognize amortization expense on the right-of-use asset typically using the straight-line method. Amortize over the (a) lease term or (b) useful life if there is an ownership transfer or the exercise of a purchase option is reasonably certain.
Recognize a lease liability.	Recognize interest expense on the lease liability using the effective interest method.

Calculate Lease Liability

Present value of *remaining* lease payments
- Fixed payment
- Variable payment
- Purchase option
- Penalty
- Guaranteed residual: only probable amount owed

Lease Liability On the lease commencement date, the lessee records a **lease liability** equal to the present value of the *remaining* lease payments discounted using the rate implicit in the lease (or if that rate cannot be readily determined, the lessee's incremental borrowing rate). **Remaining lease payments are those lease payments that have yet to be paid at the time of the lease commencement.**

842-20-30-1 At the commencement date, a lessee shall measure both of the following:
a. The lease liability at the present value of the lease payments not yet paid, discounted using the discount rate for the lease at lease commencement.
b. The right-of-use asset as described in paragraph 842-20-30-5.

Lease payments used to measure the lease liability are the same lease payments used to determine the appropriate lease classification (see lease classification criterion #4) with the following two exceptions:

- To classify a lease, all lease payments are considered, including payments before the lease commencement date. On the other hand, in recording a lease liability, only *remaining* lease payments (net of any remaining lease incentives) are used to measure the lease liability.
- To classify a lease, 100% of the guaranteed residual value is included in lease payments. On the other hand, only *probable amounts* expected to be owed for a residual value guarantee are used to measure the lease liability.

Calculate Right-of-Use Asset

Initial measurement of lease liability
Add prepaid lease payment
Subtract lease incentive received
Add initial direct costs incurred
Right-of-use asset

Right-of-Use-Asset A **right-of-use asset** is recognized in the balance sheet as an asset at the measurement of the liability (calculated above) adjusted for the following items occurring *at or before the lease commencement date*: add lease prepayments, subtract lease incentives, and add initial direct costs. For example, if the lessee had prepaid lease payments to the lessor prior to the commencement of the lease (for example, debit Prepaid Rent and credit Cash), the prepaid rent would be reclassified to the right-of-use asset at the lease commencement date. Or, if the lessee had received a lease incentive prior to the commencement of the lease (for example, debit Cash and credit Lease Incentive Payable), the lease incentive payable would offset the right-of-use asset at the lease commencement date. (Lease incentives received by a lessee before the lease begins are recorded as a liability.) Or lastly, if the lessee had paid an initial direct cost (for example, debit Initial Direct Cost and credit Cash) the initial direct cost would be reclassified to the right-of-use asset at the lease commencement date.

Prepaid Rent	#	
Cash		#
Right-of-Use Asset	#	
Prepaid Rent		#
Cash	#	
Lease Incentiv Pay		#
Lease Incentiv Pay	#	
Right-of-Use Asset		#
Init Dir Cost	#	
Cash		#
Right-of-Use Asset	#	
Init Dir Cost		#

842-20-30-5 At the commencement date, the cost of the right-of-use asset shall consist of all of the following:
a. The amount of the initial measurement of the lease liability.
b. Any lease payments made to the lessor at or before the commencement date, minus any lease incentives received [at or before the commencement date].
c. Any initial direct costs incurred by the lessee.

Initial direct costs are incremental costs of a lease that would not have been incurred if the lease had not been obtained. This means that costs that would have been incurred regardless of whether the lease was obtained are not initial direct costs. Initial direct costs are *not* considered "lease payments" as defined in LO 17-1. Examples of what to include and exclude in initial direct costs are listed in the following table.

Items Included in Initial Direct Costs	Items Excluded from Initial Direct Costs
Commissions paid to secure a lease.	Fixed employee salaries.
Payments to an existing tenant as an incentive for the tenant to terminate its lease.	General overhead including depreciation, equipment costs, engineering costs, and unsuccessful origination efforts.
Legal fees incurred from the execution of the lease or after the execution of the lease.	Advertising, solicitation, and travel costs.
Consideration paid to an unrelated third party for a guarantee of a residual value.	Servicing of existing leases.
Lease document preparation fees.	Tax or legal fees for advice or assistance in negotiations before the lease is executed.

The right-of-use asset is amortized as expense over the period of economic benefit typically using the straight-line method. The period of economic benefit would typically be the lease term. **However, if ownership transfers at the end of the lease to the lessee or the exercise of a purchase option is reasonable, the lessee would amortize over the underlying asset's useful life.** A lessee assesses a right-of-use asset for impairment and recognizes any impairment losses following the procedures applicable to long-lived assets described in Chapter 12.

842-20-35-7 A lessee shall amortize the right-of-use asset on a straight-line basis, unless another systematic basis is more representative of the pattern in which the lessee expects to consume the right-of-use asset's future economic benefits.

842-20-35-8 A lessee shall amortize the right-of-use asset from the commencement date to the earlier of the end of the useful life of the right-of-use asset or the end of the lease term. However, if the lease transfers ownership of the underlying asset to the lessee or the lessee is reasonably certain to exercise an option to purchase the underlying asset, the lessee shall amortize the right-of-use asset to the end of the useful life of the underlying asset.

Along with a right-of-use asset, companies recognize leasehold improvements. **Leasehold improvements** are improvements made to leased property by a lessee that revert to the lessor at the end of the lease such as the construction of a new building, addition, or a modification to a leased space. As in the case with other fixed assets, the leasehold improvements are capitalized as long-term assets typically in property, plant, and equipment on the balance sheet and are depreciated over the shorter of their useful life or the lease term.

842-20-35-12 Leasehold improvements shall be amortized over the shorter of the useful life of those leasehold improvements and the remaining lease term, unless the lease transfers ownership of the underlying asset to the lessee or the lessee is reasonably certain to exercise an option to purchase the underlying asset, in which case the lessee shall amortize the leasehold improvements to the end of their useful life.

In summary, the accounting for a lease by a lessee is outlined in the following timeline. These steps are illustrated in the demonstrations that follow.

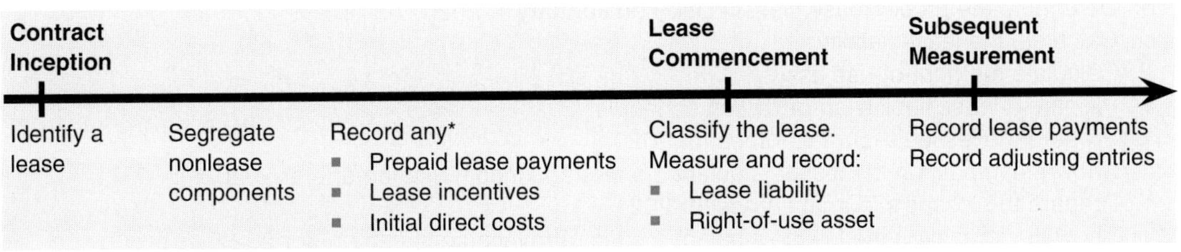

*Amounts recorded through the lease commencement enter into measurement of the right-of-use asset.

EXPANDING YOUR KNOWLEDGE **Benefits and Disadvantages of Leasing**

In considering options to finance the purchase of property, plant, and equipment, a lessee should consider the advantages and disadvantages of a leasing option.

Benefits of Leasing

- Financing option for up to 100% of the leased asset's value. (Bank loans are typically limited to 80% of the asset's value.)
- Fixed interest rate option. (Some bank loans feature only variable rates.)
- Ready-to-use leased equipment can be attractive over a lengthy build-to-order.
- Solution for temporary, seasonal, or sporadic needs.
- Protection from equipment obsolescence where upgrades to newer equipment is possible.
- Income tax advantages derived from accelerated depreciation and interest expense.
- Tailored lease payment schedules to coordinate with expected cash inflows from operations.

Disadvantages of Leasing

- 100% financing of leased assets also means a higher total dollar outlay for interest.
- Leasing ready-to-use (as opposed to custom-built) equipment may result in a lower-quality product and ultimately lost sales to the lessee.
- Equipment may be unavailable under lease when needed.
- Leasing interest rates may increase with market changes.
- Short-term leases may provide protection from product obsolescence, but short-term leasing rates are normally set at a premium over longer-term rates (to compensate the lessor for assuming the obsolescence risk).

Demo 17-2A **LO17-2** **Lessee—Finance Lease with No Residual Value**

Demo MBC

Let's review a lease example and record entries from the *lessee's perspective.* On December 31, 2019, Lessor Inc. and Lessee Inc. sign a three-year non-cancelable lease of equipment. Details of the lease agreement, with a commencement date of January 1, 2020, follow.

1. The equipment has an estimated economic life of three years.
2. Lessor Inc. routinely leases this type of equipment to other companies.
3. The three lease payments are $34,972.07, each payable January 1, 2020, 2021, and 2022.
4. The fair value of the asset at the lease commencement is $100,000.
5. The lease does not contain a renewal or purchase option, and the asset reverts to the lessor at the end of the three-year period.
6. The asset's residual value is estimated to be $0 and there is no guaranteed residual value.
7. The lessee's incremental borrowing rate is 5%.
8. Lessee Inc. depreciates assets using the straight-line method for book purposes.
9. The accounting year ends on December 31 for each entity.
10. The lessor's implicit interest rate, the rate that equates the present value of the payments to the asset's fair value, is 5% and is known by the lessee.
11. Initial direct costs of $800 (legal fees incurred related to the execution of the lease) were paid on December 31, 2019.
12. The lessor paid a lease incentive to the lessee of $1,200 on December 31, 2019, as an incentive to sign the lease by December 31, 2019.

Answer the following questions from the perspective of Lessee Inc.

a. Prepare journal entries to record the lease incentive received and the initial direct costs paid on December 31, 2019.
b. Determine the proper lease classification on January 1, 2020.
c. Calculate the lease liability.
d. Calculate the right-of-use asset.
e. Prepare a lease liability amortization schedule.
f. Prepare the lessee's journal entries for 2020.
g. Show the impact on the lessee's balance sheet and income statement for 2020.
h. Prepare the lessee's journal entries for 2021.
i. Show the impact on the lessee's balance sheet and income statement for 2021.
j. Prepare the lessee's journal entries for 2022.

continued

continued from previous page

Solution

Amounts in the following calculations and journal entries are rounded for simplicity.

a. **Lessee's Journal Entries—Prior to Lease Commencement**

The lessee records the following entries prior to the lease commencement.

December 31, 2019—To record lease incentive

Cash	1,200	
Lease Incentive Payable		1,200

Assets = Liabilities + Equity
+1,200 +1,200
Cash: 1,200 (debit) | Incent Pay: 1,200 (credit)

December 31, 2019—To record initial direct costs

Initial Direct Cost	800	
Cash		800

Assets = Liabilities + Equity
+800 +800
Init Dir Cost: 800 (debit) | Cash: 1,200 (debit) 800 (credit)

b. **Lease Classification**

At lease commencement, the lease is classified as a finance lease to the lessee because *at least one* of the lease classification criteria is met as shown in the following analysis.

	Classification Criteria	Analysis	Met
1	Ownership transfer	Asset reverts to the lessor at the end of the three-year period.	
2	Purchase option	Lease does not contain a purchase option.	
3	Lease term length	Three-year lease term is 100% of the equipment's three-year useful life.	✔
4	PV of lease payments	$98,800 (PV of lease payments of $100,000 − lease incentive of $1,200) > $90,000 (90% of fair value of $100,000).	✔
5	Alternative use	There are alternative uses for the equipment as the lessor often leases this equipment to other companies.	

	RATE	NPER	PMT	PV	TYPE	Excel Formula
Given	5%	3	(34,972.07)	?	1	=PV(0.05,3,−34972.07,0,1)
Solution				$100,000		

c. **Lease Liability**

The present value of the *remaining* lease payments (consisting only of fixed lease payments) is $100,000 using the rate implicit in the lease of 5% as calculated above in the lease classification test. (The lease incentive occurred prior to the lease commencement thus is not part of the *remaining* lease payments.)

d. **Right-of-Use-Asset**

There are two adjustments to the lease liability of $100,000 to arrive at the right-of-use asset of $99,600: A deduction for the lease incentive received by the lessee of $1,200; and an addition for initial direct costs incurred by the lessee of $800—both incurred at or before the lease commencement.

Calculate Right-of-Use Asset	
Initial measurement of lease liability	$100,000
Add prepaid lease payment	0
Subtract lease incentive received	(1,200)
Add initial direct costs incurred	800
Right-of-use asset	$ 99,600

e. **Lease Liability Amortization Schedule**

The lessee will prepare a lease liability amortization schedule using the effective interest method to record interest expense.

- The Lease Payment column includes the lease payment (determined by the lessor). The lease payment reduces cash and the lease liability.
- The Interest on Liability column includes interest which increases the lease liability and increases interest expense (however the first payment is all applied to the liability because the payment took place on day one of the lease). Interest is calculated by taking the interest rate multiplied by the beginning of period, net lease liability.
- The Lease Liability Reduction column is the net of the lease payment and the interest on the liability.
- The Net Lease Liability column shows the cumulative balance of the lease liability.

continued

continued from previous page

This schedule illustrates how each lease payment is allocated between interest and the reduction of the liability. Notice how after the first payment (applied completely to principal because it took place on day one of the lease) interest expense per period decreases due to the corresponding decrease in the net lease liability.

Lease Liability Amortization Schedule

Date	Lease Payment[a] Dr. Lease Liability Cr. Cash	Interest on Liability[b] Dr. Interest Expense Cr. Lease Liability	Lease Liability Reduction[c]	Net Lease Liability[d]
Jan. 1, 2020				$100,000
Jan. 1, 2020	$ 34,972	$ —	$ 34,972	65,028
Jan. 1, 2021	34,972	3,251	31,721	33,307
Jan. 1, 2022	34,972	1,665	33,307	0
	$104,916	$4,916	$100,000	

[a] Lease payment (given).
[b] Interest rate (5%) × Beginning of period net lease liability (with exception of first payment applied 100% to principal).
[c] Lease payment less interest on liability.
[d] Net lease liability (beginning of period) less net reduction of lease liability.

f. **Lessee's Journal Entries—Year One**
Lessee Inc. will record the following entries in year one.

Assets = Liabilities + Equity
−1,200 −1,200
R-of-U Asset: | 1,200
Incent Pay: 1,200 | 1,200

January 1, 2020—To reclassify lease incentive to the right-of-use asset

Lease Incentive Payable.	1,200	
Right-of-Use Asset.		1,200

Assets = Liabilities + Equity
+800
−800
R-of-U Asset: 800 | 1,200
Init Dir Cost: 800 | 800

January 1, 2020—To reclassify initial direct costs to the right-of-use asset

Right-of-Use Asset.	800	
Initial Direct Cost.		800

Assets = Liabilities + Equity
+100,000 +100,000
R-of-U Asset: 800, 100,000 | 1,200; 99,600
Lease Liab: | 100,000

January 1, 2020—To record right-of-use asset and lease liability

Right-of-Use Asset.	100,000	
Lease Liability		100,000

Assets = Liabilities + Equity
−34,972 −34,972
Cash: 1,200 | 800, 34,972
Lease Liab: 34,972 | 100,000

January 1, 2020—To record lease payment

Lease Liability	34,972	
Cash		34,972

Assets = Liabilities + Equity
+3,251 −3,251
Interest Exp: 3,251 |
Lease Liab: 34,972 | 100,000, 3,251; 68,279

December 31, 2020—To record interest expense

Interest Expense.	3,251	
Lease Liability		3,251

Assets = Liabilities + Equity
−33,200 −33,200
R-of-U Asset: 800, 100,000 | 1,200, 33,200; 66,400
Amort Exp: 33,200 |

December 31, 2020—To record amortization on the right-of-use asset

Amortization Expense	33,200	
Right-of-Use Asset ($99,600/3).		33,200

The company chooses to credit the right-of-use asset directly for the amortization expense instead of crediting an accumulated amortization account.

g. **Lessee's Financial Statements—Year One**
Lessee Inc. will recognize the following amounts in its financial statements in year one.

continued

continued from previous page

Balance Sheet	**Dec. 31, 2020**
Assets	
Noncurrent assets	
Right-of-use asset* ($99,600 − $33,200) . .	$66,400
Liabilities	
Current liabilities	
Lease liability ($3,251 + $31,721)	34,972
Noncurrent liabilities	
Lease liability ($68,279† − $34,972).	33,307

Income Statement	**2020**
Expenses	
Interest expense—lease liability	$ 3,251
Amortization expense—right-of-use asset . . .	33,200

* The right-of-use asset is shown net in the asset section.

†Total lease liability of $68,279 derived from the journal entries above equals $100,000 − $34,972 + $3,251. The noncurrent portion is equal to the total lease liability less the current lease liability.

h. **Lessee's Journal Entries—Year Two**

Lessee Inc. will record the following entries in year two.

January 1, 2021— To record lease payment

Lease Liability	34,972	
Cash		34,972

Cash is credited for the payment of $34,972. Lease Liability is debited for the same amount of $34,972, which is equal to lease liability reduction of $31,721 plus the reversal of the lease liability recorded on December 31, 2020, related to interest of $3,251.

December 31, 2021—To record interest expense

Interest Expense.	1,665	
Lease Liability		1,665

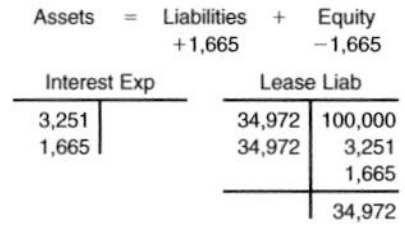

December 31, 2021—To record amortization on right-of-use asset

Amortization Expense	33,200	
Right-of-Use Asset ($99,600/3).		33,200

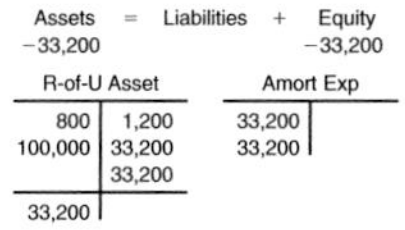

i. **Lessee's Financial Statements—Year Two**

Lessee Inc. will recognize the following amounts in its financial statements in year two.

Balance Sheet	**Dec. 31, 2021**
Assets	
Current assets	
Right-of-use asset ($66,400 − $33,200). . .	$33,200
Liabilities	
Current liabilities	
Lease liability ($1,665 + $33,307)	34,972
Noncurrent liabilities	
Lease liability.	—

Income Statement	**2021**
Expenses	
Interest expense—lease liability	$ 1,665
Amortization expense—right-of-use asset . . .	33,200

j. **Lessee's Journal Entries—Year Three**

Lessee Inc. will record the following entries in year three.

January 1, 2022—To record lease payment

Lease Liability	34,972	
Cash		34,972

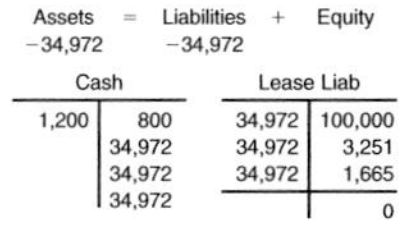

December 31, 2022—To record amortization on right-of-use asset

Amortization Expense	33,200	
Right-of-Use Asset ($99,600/3).		33,200

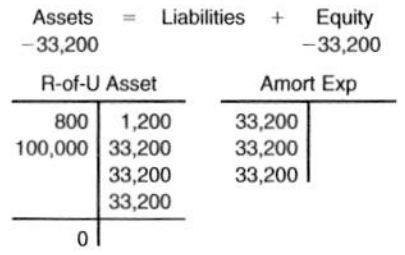

After the journal entries of year three and the expiration of the lease, the right-of-use asset has a value of $0 (December 31, 2021, balance of $33,200 less $33,200) and the lease liability has a value of $0 (December 31, 2021, balance of $34,972 less $34,972).

MICROSOFT

Real World—FINANCE LEASE DISCLOSURE

MICROSOFT CORPORATION [MSFT]

Microsoft Corporation disclosed amortization expense and interest expense related to its finance leases in a recent Form 10-Q.

> We have operating and finance leases for datacenters, corporate offices, research and development facilities, retail stores, and certain equipment. Our leases have remaining lease terms of 1 year to 20 years, some of which may include options to extend the leases for up to 5 years, and some of which may include options to terminate the leases within 1 year. As of September 30, 2017 and June 30, 2017, assets recorded under finance leases were $3.4 billion and $2.7 billion, respectively, and accumulated depreciation associated with finance leases was $209 million and $161 million, respectively. The components of lease expense were as follows:

Three Months Ended September 30 (in millions)	2017	2016
Operating lease cost	$388	$260
Finance lease cost		
Amortization of right-of-use assets	48	15
Interest on lease liabilities	30	12
Total finance lease cost	$ 78	$ 27

Demo 17-2B **LO17-2** **Lessee—Finance Lease with Guaranteed Residual Value**

Demo MBC

Let's review a lease example that includes a guaranteed residual value. On January 1, 2020, the lease commencement date, Lessor Inc. and Lessee Inc. sign a three-year non-cancelable lease for equipment. Details of the lease agreement follow.

1. The equipment has an estimated economic life of three years.
2. Lessor Inc. routinely leases this type of equipment to other companies.
3. The three lease payments are $33,461.73 each, payable January 1, 2020, 2021, and 2022.
4. The fair value of the asset at the commencement of the lease is $100,000.
5. The lease does not contain a renewal or purchase option, and the asset reverts to the lessor at the end of the three-year period.
6. The contract requires the lessee to guarantee the residual value of the equipment at the end of the lease for $5,000. Lessee Inc. estimates that the residual value of the equipment at the end of the lease will be $3,000.
7. The lessee's incremental borrowing rate is 4.5%.
8. Lessee Inc. depreciates assets using the straight-line method for book purposes.
9. The accounting year ends on December 31 for each entity.
10. The lessor's implicit interest rate, the rate that equates the present value of the payments to the asset's fair value, is 5% and is known by the lessee.
11. Initial direct costs of $800 were paid in cash (legal fees related to the execution of the lease) by the lessee on the lease commencement date.
12. The lessee received no lease incentive related to the lease.

Answer the following questions from the perspective of Lessee Inc.

a. Determine the proper lease classification on January 1, 2020.
b. Calculate the lease liability.
c. Calculate the right-of-use asset.
d. Prepare a lease liability amortization schedule.
e. Prepare the lessee's journal entries for 2020.
f. Show the impact on the lessee's balance sheet and income statement for 2020.
g. Prepare the lessee's journal entries for 2021.
h. Show the impact on the lessee's balance sheet and income statement for 2021.
i. Prepare the lessee's journal entries for 2022.

continued

continued from previous page

Solution

Amounts in the following calculations and journal entries are rounded for simplicity.

a. **Lease Classification**

First, the lease is classified as a finance lease to the lessee because at least one of the lease classification criteria is met as shown in the following analysis.

	Classification Criteria	Analysis	Met
1	Ownership transfer	The asset reverts to the lessor at the end of the three-year period.	
2	Purchase option	The lease does not contain a purchase option.	
3	Lease term length	Three-year lease term > 75% of the three-year useful life (2.25 years).	✔
4	PV of lease payments	$100,000 (PV of lease payments including full residual guarantee) > $90,000 (90% of fair value of $100,000).	✔
5	Alternative use	There are alternative uses for the equipment as the lessor often leases this equipment to other companies.	

	RATE	NPER	PMT	PV	FV	TYPE	Excel Formula
Given	5%	3	(33,461.73)	?	(5,000)	1	*=PV(0.05,3,−33461.73, −5000,1)*
Solution				$100,000			

b. **Lease Liability**

On the lease commencement date, the lessee records a lease liability. The present value of the lease payments from the lease classification test computed above is $100,000, which includes the full, guaranteed residual value. To calculate the lease liability however, only the *probable payment* on a residual guarantee is included or $2,000 ($5,000 − $3,000). Thus, the lease liability measurement is $97,408.

	RATE	NPER	PMT	PV	FV	Excel Formula
Given	5%	3	(33,461.73)	?	(2,000)	*=PV(0.05,3,−33461.73, −2000,1)*
Solution				$97,408		

c. **Right-of-Use-Asset**

The right-of-use asset measurement is equal to $98,208 after adding the initial direct costs of $800 to the liability balance of $97,408.

Calculate Right-of-Use Asset	
Initial measurement of lease liability. . .	$97,408
Add prepaid lease payment	0
Subtract lease incentive received.	0
Add initial direct costs incurred.	800
Right-of-use asset	$98,208

d. **Lease Liability Amortization Schedule**

The lessee will prepare a lease liability amortization schedule using the effective interest method to determine the allocation of the lease payment between interest expense and a reduction of the lease liability.

Lease Liability Amortization Schedule

Date	Lease Payment Dr. Lease Liability Cr. Cash	Interest on Liability Dr. Interest Expense Cr. Lease Liability	Lease Liability Reduction	Net Lease Liability
Jan. 1, 2020				$97,408
Jan. 1, 2020	$ 33,462	$ 0	$33,462	63,946
Jan. 1, 2021	33,462	3,197	30,265	33,681
Jan. 1, 2022	33,462	1,684	31,778	1,903
Jan. 1, 2023	2,000	97*	1,903	0
	$102,386	$4,978	$97,408	

*Amount adjusted due to rounding.

e. **Lessee's Journal Entries—Year One**

Lessee Inc. will record the following entries in year one.

continued

continued from previous page

Assets = Liabilities + Equity
+98,208 +97,408
−800

R-of-U Asset: 98,208 | ; Lease Liab: | 97,408 ; Cash: | 800

January 1, 2020—To record right-of-use asset and lease liability

Right-of-Use Asset.	98,208	
Lease Liability		97,408
Cash		800

Assets = Liabilities + Equity
−33,462 −33,462

Cash: 1,200 | 800, 33,462 ; Lease Liab: 33,462 | 97,408

January 1, 2020—To record first lease payment

Lease Liability	33,462	
Cash		33,462

Assets = Liabilities + Equity
+3,197 −3,197

Interest Exp: 3,197 | ; Lease Liab: 33,462 | 97,408, 3,197 ; | 67,143

December 31, 2020—To record interest expense

Interest Expense.	3,197	
Lease Liability		3,197

Assets = Liabilities + Equity
−32,736 −32,736

R-of-U Asset: 98,208 | 32,736 ; 65,472 | ; Amort Exp: 32,736 |

December 31, 2020—To record amortization on right-of-use asset

Amortization Expense	32,736	
Right-of-Use Asset ($98,208/3).		32,736

f. **Lessee's Financial Statements—Year One**
Lessee Inc. will recognize the following amounts in its financial statements in year one.

Balance Sheet	Dec. 31, 2020
Assets	
Noncurrent assets	
Right-of-use asset ($98,208 − $32,736). . .	$65,472
Liabilities	
Current liabilities	
Lease liability ($3,197 + $30,265)	33,462
Noncurrent liabilities	
Lease liability ($67,143* − $33,462).	33,681

*Total lease liability of $67,143 derived from the journal entries above equals $97,408 − $33,462 + $3,197. The noncurrent portion is equal to the total lease liability less the current lease liability.

Income Statement	2020
Expenses	
Interest expense—lease liability	$ 3,197
Amortization expense—right-of-use asset. . .	32,736

g. **Lessee's Journal Entries—Year Two**
Lessee Inc. will record the following entries in year two.

Assets = Liabilities + Equity
−33,462 −33,462

Cash: 1,200 | 800, 33,462, 33,462 ; Lease Liab: 33,462, 33,462 | 97,408, 3,197

January 1, 2021—To record lease payment

Lease Liability	33,462	
Cash		33,462

Assets = Liabilities + Equity
+1,684 −1,684

Interest Exp: 3,197, 1,684 | ; Lease Liab: 33,462, 33,462 | 97,408, 3,197, 1,684 ; | 35,365

December 31, 2021—To record interest expense

Interest Expense.	1,684	
Lease Liability		1,684

Assets = Liabilities + Equity
−32,736 −32,736

R-of-U Asset: 98,208 | 32,736, 32,736 ; 32,736 | ; Amort Exp: 32,736, 32,736 |

December 31, 2021—To record amortization on right-of-use asset

Amortization Expense	32,736	
Right-of-Use Asset ($98,208/3).		32,736

h. **Lessee's Financial Statements—Year Two**
Lessee Inc. will recognize the following amounts in its financial statements in year two.

continued

continued from previous page

Balance Sheet	Dec. 31, 2021
Assets	
Noncurrent assets	
Right-of-use asset ($65,472 − $32,736). . .	$32,736
Liabilities	
Current liabilities	
Lease liability.	33,462
Noncurrent liabilities	
Lease liability ($35,365* − $33,462).	1,903

*Total lease liability of $35,365 derived from the journal entries above equals $67,143 − $33,462 + $1,684. The noncurrent portion is equal to the total lease liability less the current lease liability.

Income Statement	2021
Expenses	
Interest expense—lease liability	$ 1,684
Amortization expense—right-of-use asset. . .	32,736

i. **Lessee's Journal Entries—Year Three**

Lessee Inc. will record the following entries in year three.

January 1, 2022— To record lease payment

Lease Liability	33,462	
Cash		33,462

Assets = Liabilities + Equity
−33,462 −33,462

Cash (Dr)	Cash (Cr)	Lease Liab (Dr)	Lease Liab (Cr)
	800	33,462	97,408
	33,462	33,462	3,197
	33,462	33,462	1,684
	33,462		

December 31, 2022—To record interest expense

Interest Expense.	97	
Lease Liability		97

Assets = Liabilities + Equity
+97 −97

Interest Exp (Dr)	Interest Exp (Cr)	Lease Liab (Dr)	Lease Liab (Cr)
3,197		33,462	97,408
1,684		33,462	3,197
97		33,462	1,684
			97
			2,000

December 31, 2022—To record amortization on right-of-use asset

Amortization Expense	32,736	
Right-of-Use Asset ($98,208/3).		32,736

Assets = Liabilities + Equity
−32,736 −32,736

R-of-U Asset (Dr)	R-of-U Asset (Cr)	Amort Exp (Dr)	Amort Exp (Cr)
98,208	32,736	32,736	
	32,736	32,736	
	32,736	32,736	
0			

After the journal entries of year three and the expiration of the lease, the right-of-use asset has a value of $0 (December 31, 2021, balance of $32,736 less $32,736) and the lease liability has a value of $2,000 (December 31, 2021, balance of $35,365 less $33,462 plus $97).

On January 1, 2023, upon the expiration of the lease, the lessee would record the following entry assuming that the value of the equipment was $3,000, which is $2,000 short of the guaranteed residual value of $5,000 as planned.

January 1, 2023—To record payment to satisfy guaranteed residual value

Lease Liability	2,000	
Cash		2,000

Assets = Liabilities + Equity
−2,000 −2,000

Cash (Dr)	Cash (Cr)	Lease Liab (Dr)	Lease Liab (Cr)
	800	33,462	97,408
	33,462	33,462	3,197
	33,462	33,462	1,684
	33,462	2,000	97
	33,462		0

Lessee—Finance Lease with Purchase Option Expected to Exercise LO17-2 Demo 17-2C

A lease incorporates a purchase option when the lessee can purchase the underlying asset at the end of the lease for a specified amount. The purchase option, if it is reasonably certain that the lessee will exercise the option, will be included as a lease payment in evaluating the lease for its proper classification and in valuing the lease liability at the start of the lease. The following two examples include a purchase option.

Example One—Finance Lease with Purchase Option

Let's assume the same facts from **Demo 17-2B** above, except that the lease contract now (a) includes a purchase option for $2,000 expected to be exercised and (b) excludes a guaranteed residual value. We also assume that Lessee Inc. intends to exercise the purchase option at lease end. Determine how the lessee's journal entries would change from the solution shown in **Demo 17-2B**.

Solution

In this case, the present value of the lease payments used to classify the lease is $97,408. The $2,000 purchase option is included as an additional payment on the lease (refer to **Exhibit 17-2**).

continued

continued from previous page

The present value of the lease payments would also be the appropriate amount to record as the lease liability because there are no adjustments to the lease liability. The lease liability of $97,408 matches the earlier example with a guaranteed residual value. There is no change to the initial recording of the right-of-use asset, which would still be depreciated over 3 years, which is the lease term and economic life of the asset. Therefore, the *journal entries and the financial statement presentation are identical to the solutions for* **Demo 17-2B**.

	RATE	NPER	PMT	PV	FV	TYPE	Excel Formula
Given	5%	3	(33,461.73)	?	(2,000)	1	=PV(0.05,3,−33461.73, −2000,1)
Solution				$97,408			

Example Two—Finance Lease with Purchase Option—Economic Life of Asset Differs from Lease Term

Let's assume the same information in Example One, except that the economic life of the equipment is estimated to be *4 years instead of 3 years.* Determine how the accounting for the lessee would change from the solution shown in **Demo 17-2B**.

Solution

If a lease indicates that the underlying asset automatically reverts to the lessee at the end of the lease, or if the lease includes a purchase option that the lessee is reasonably certain to exercise, *the right-of-use asset is expensed over the asset's economic life.* The initial direct costs would be amortized over the lease term.

Dec. 31, 2020	Amortization expense ($97,408/4 + $800/3)	$24,619
Dec. 31, 2021	Amortization expense ($97,408/4 + $800/3)	24,619
Dec. 31, 2022	Amortization expense ($97,408/4 + $800/3)	24,619
Dec. 31, 2023	Depreciation expense ($97,408/4)	24,351*

* Amount adjusted for rounding difference.

Upon the expiration of the lease, the remaining balance in the right-of-use asset of $24,352 would be transferred to an equipment account. The last year of expense would be depreciation expense rather than amortization expense.

The following table summarizes the treatment of guaranteed and unguaranteed residual value, purchase options, and termination penalties for the lessee.

Accounting for the Lessee	Guaranteed Residual Value	Unguaranteed Residual Value	Purchase Option or Penalty*
ASC 842 definition of a lease payment	Include only probable amount owed	Not included	Included
PV of lease payment criterion of the lease classification test	Included	Not included	Included
Lease liability and right-of-use asset	Include only probable amount owed	Not included	Included

* Assume that it is reasonably certain that the lessee will exercise the purchase option or it is reasonably certain that the lessee will terminate the lease. If a purchase option is included, residual value must be ignored in the lessee's calculations.

EXPANDING YOUR KNOWLEDGE **Multiple Lease Components**

After determining that a contract contains a lease, a company must identify separate lease components (or individual right-to-use assets) in a contract. The right-of-use of an asset is considered a *separate lease component* if both of the following criteria are met.

842-10-15-28

a. The lessee can benefit from the right of use either on its own or together with other resources that are readily available to the lessee. Readily available resources are goods or services that are sold or leased separately (by the lessor or other suppliers) or resources that the lessee already has obtained (from the lessor or from other transactions or events).

b. The right of use is neither highly dependent on nor highly interrelated with the other right(s) to use underlying assets in the contract. A lessee's right to use an underlying asset is highly dependent on or highly interrelated with another right to use an underlying asset if each right of use significantly affects the other.

After the separate lease components are identified, consideration in the contract is allocated to the separate lease components and nonlease components on a relative standalone selling price basis—see allocation methods in Chapter 7.

Management Judgment

Identifying a Lease

Leases are sometimes embedded in arrangements such as supply contracts, data center agreements, or outsourcing agreements. At the inception of a contract, judgment is involved in determining whether an arrangement includes an embedded lease. Recall that a lease turns over the right to control the use of an identified asset to a lessee in exchange for consideration for a period of time. Any *nonlease* components not meeting these criteria must be identified and separately accounted for (unless management elects the practical expedient explained on p. 17-6).

Classifying a Lease

In applying the lease classification test, management must determine whether the lease term is a *major part* of the remaining economic life of the underlying asset. Management must also determine whether the present value of the lease payments is *substantially all* of the fair value of the underlying asset. Although a bright-line threshold of 75% for the economic life test is described in the accounting guidance as a "reasonable approach" (along with the 90% threshold for the fair value test), the accounting standards do *not* require the bright-line test leaving room for management to define the *major part* of the remaining economic life. In addition, if the contract includes a renewal option or a purchase option, management must determine whether it is reasonably possible that the company will renew the lease or take advantage of a purchase option. These decisions are often not clear-cut in practice.

Accounting for a Lease

Management must value the following items, and each requires judgment.

- Estimated economic life of equipment and its estimated residual value
- Fair value of the leased asset at inception of the lease.
- Lessee's incremental borrowing rate.
- Lease term.

Amounts associated with these items require management to make assumptions and provide estimations. For example, the lease term includes any renewal or termination options that a lessee is *reasonably certain* to exercise. The estimated economic life of equipment depends on how a company plans to use and maintain the equipment. The fair value of a leased asset would be more difficult to determine if the asset were self-constructed or purchased years earlier. The residual value is subjective and influenced by the lease term and the expected usage of the asset. The lessee's incremental borrowing rate varies by leased asset and depends on a hypothetical borrowing under similar terms to the lease. The authoritative guidance requires disclosing qualitative and quantitative information about the judgments made in applying the lease standard.

Accounting for a Finance Lease by Lessee **LO17-2** **REVIEW 17-2**

Review MBC

Lessor Company and Lessee Company signed a four-year lease on January 1, 2020. The leased property cost Lessor Company $65,000, which was also its carrying value at commencement of the lease. The leased asset had an estimated life of six years, and the property reverts to Lessor Company at the end of the lease term. Lease payments of $15,999.49 are payable on January 1 of each year and were set to yield Lessor Company a return of 9%, which was known to Lessee Company. The estimated residual value at the end of the lease term is $12,000 and is guaranteed by Lessee Corporation. Lessee expects the residual value at the end of the lease term to be $12,000. The lease contains no purchase option. Round amounts to the nearest $1.

a. How would Lessee Company classify the lease? Support your answer.

b. Prepare an amortization schedule of the lease liability.

c. Prepare the entries for Lessee Company for 2020 to (1) record the right-of-use asset and liability, (2) record the first lease payment, and (3) record adjusting entries at year-end.

d. Repeat parts (*b*) and (*c*) but assume instead that Lessee Company expects the estimated residual value at the end of the lease term to be $3,500.

More Practice: 17-26, 17-27, 17-30, 17-31, 17-54, 17-55, 17-56, 17-59, 17-60, 17-61, 17-62, 17-74

Solution on p. 17-81.

LO 17-3 Account for a sales-type lease for a lessor

LO 17-3 Overview

Lessor Accounting—Sales-Type Lease
- At least one of the lease classification criteria is met
- Record selling profit (if applicable) at lease commencement
- Derecognize underlying asset
- Record a lease receivable and recognize interest revenue on the receivable using the effective interest method

We now consider lease accounting for the lessor. If a lease meets at least one of the five lease classification criteria in **Exhibit 17-3** and payments from the lessee are probable, the lessor accounts for the lease as a sales-type lease. If the lessor determines that payments are not **probable**, the lessor does not recognize a lease receivable or derecognize the asset. Instead, the lessor records lease payments as a deposit liability (for example, debit Cash and credit Deposit Liability) until payments are probable, the lease is terminated, or the underlying asset is repossessed.

842-30-25-3 If collectibility of the lease payments, plus any amount necessary to satisfy a residual value guarantee provided by the lessee, is not probable at the commencement date, the lessor shall not derecognize the underlying asset but shall recognize lease payments received—including variable lease payments—as a deposit liability.

If the lease does not meet any of the lease classification criteria outlined in **Exhibit 17-3**, the lease is classified as an operating lease (discussed in a later section) or as a direct financing lease (discussed in Appendix 17A to this chapter).

In a sales-type lease, the lessor effectively transfers ownership of the underlying asset to the lessee. We illustrate the accounting for a sales-type lease with no residual value in **Demo 17-3A** and a sales-type lease with a guaranteed residual value in **Demo 17-3B**. A summary of the accounting for the lessee for a sales-type lease follows.

Balance Sheet	Income Statement
Recognize a lease receivable and derecognize the underlying asset.	Recognize selling profit or loss at the commencement of the lease (if applicable).
Increase the lease receivable by interest revenue and decrease lease receivable for lease payments collected.	Recognize interest revenue on the lease receivable using the effective interest method.

Lease Receivable **The lease receivable is equal to the present value of the lease payments and any guaranteed or unguaranteed residual value, or the purchase and termination options when applicable.**

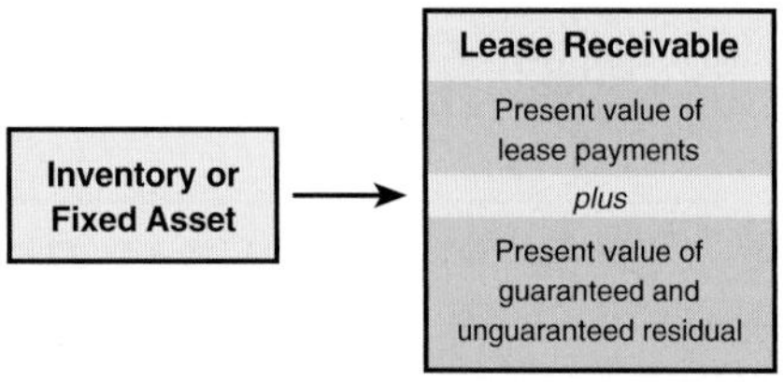

Sales revenue
− Cost of goods sold
= Gross profit

No gross profit:
Carrying value = Fair value

Upon initiation of the lease, the lessor derecognizes the asset to be leased (Cr. Inventory or Fixed Asset), records an investment in the lease (Dr. Lease Receivable), and recognizes gross profit by crediting Sales Revenue for the value of the lease receivable (present value of payments and residual value), and debiting Cost of Goods Sold for the carrying value of the asset. This means that any gross profit is recorded immediately in a sales-type lease, which is similar to a sale of the asset because the lessee obtains substantially all of the *remaining* benefits. If, however, the lessor's carrying value were to equal the fair value at the commencement of the lease, the lessor would simply derecognize the asset to be leased and record a lease receivable (Dr. Lease Receivable and Cr. Inventory or Fixed Asset). The lessor will prepare a lease receivable amortization schedule to recognize interest revenue as a function of the lease receivable balance using the effective interest method. (Sometimes, the lease receivable is defined as the present value of the lease payments plus the present value of the guaranteed residual value with the unguaranteed residual value being accounted for in separate entries. In this chapter, we define the lease receivable as including the present value of the lease payments plus guaranteed and unguaranteed residual values, without separate recording of the unguaranteed residual values.)

Calculation of Lease Payment A lessor determines the lease payment using the lessor's expected rate of return. The expected return varies across leases and lessees as the return depends upon factors specific to the contract and the lessee, such as the lessee's credit rating and the amount of expected residual value. In the determination of the lease payment, the number of lease payments includes reasonably certain renewals. The future value includes guaranteed residual, expected unguaranteed residual, and purchase and termination options expected to be exercised. In the case of a *guaranteed residual value*, the lease payments due over the lease term will originally be set lower by the lessor because contractually, the lessor can count on receiving the guaranteed residual value at lease end. If however, the residual value is unguaranteed, the amount entered as a future payment would be equal to the residual value that the lessor *expects to receive*. Additionally, if the lease includes a purchase or termination option that the lessor reasonably expects the lessee to exercise in the future, *the options are included as payments*. Any residual value is ignored when a purchase option is expected to be exercised.

Initial Direct Lease Costs In a sales-type lease, the lessor will expense initial direct costs as selling expense in cases where the lessor records a gross profit. However, in cases where there is no gross profit (the carrying value of the underlying asset on the lessor's records approximates the fair value of the asset), initial direct costs are deferred and expensed over the lease term.

Lessor—Sales-Type Lease with No Residual Value LO17-3 Demo 17-3A

Demo MBC

Let's review a lease example from a *lessor's perspective.* On January 1, 2020, the lease commencement date, Lessor Inc. and Lessee Inc. sign a three-year non-cancelable lease for equipment. Details of the lease agreement follow.

1. The equipment has an estimated economic life of three years and the lessor manufactured the equipment at a cost of $80,000.
2. Lessor Inc. routinely leases this type of equipment to other companies.
3. The three lease payments are $34,972.07 each, payable January 1, 2020, 2021, and 2022.
4. The fair value of the asset at the commencement of the lease is $100,000.
5. The lease does not contain a renewal or purchase option, and the asset reverts to the lessor at the end of the three-year period.
6. The asset's residual value is estimated to be $0 and there is no guaranteed residual value.
7. Lessor Inc. depreciates assets using the straight-line method for book purposes.
8. The accounting year ends on December 31 for each entity.
9. The lessor's implicit interest rate, which is the rate that equates the present value of the payments to the asset's fair value, is 5%.
10. Initial direct costs of the lessor were $800 (legal fees related to the execution of the lease paid in cash on January 1, 2020).

Answer the following questions from the perspective of Lessor Inc.

a. Determine the proper lease classification assuming that the receipt of lease payments is probable.
b. Confirm the lease payment of $34,972.
c. Calculate the lease receivable.
d. Record initial direct costs.
e. Prepare a lease receivable amortization schedule.
f. Prepare the lessor's journal entries for 2020.
g. Show the impact on the lessor's balance sheet and income statement for 2020.
h. Prepare the lessor's journal entries for 2021.
i. Show the impact on the lessor's balance sheet and income statement for 2021.
j. Prepare the lessor's journal entries for 2022.

Solution

Amounts in the following calculations and journal entries are rounded.

continued

continued from previous page

a. **Lease Classification**
The lease is classified as a sales-type lease because at least one of the lease classification criteria is met. The lease term is 100% of the useful life of the asset. Also, the present value of the lease payments of $100,000 is equal to the fair value of the underlying asset of $100,000.

Classification Criteria	Criteria Met
1. Transfer of ownership.	
2. Option to purchase	
3. Length of lease term.	✔
4. Present value of lease payments . . .	✔
5. Alternative use	

b. **Calculation of Lease Payment**
From the lessor's perspective, let's examine how the annual lease payment of $34,972 (rounded) was determined by the lessor. The lessor expected a return on investment of 5% (RATE) from leasing an asset with a fair value of $100,000 (PV) over three years (NPER), with no expected residual value (FV), and with beginning of period payments (TYPE, 1).

	RATE	NPER	PMT	PV	TYPE	Excel Formula
Given	5%	3	(34,972.07)	?	1	=PV(0.05,3,−34972.07,0,1)
Solution				$100,000		

	RATE	NPER	PMT	PV	FV	TYPE	Excel Formula
Given	5%	3	?	(100,000)	—	1	=PMT(0.05,3,−100000,0,1)
Solution			$34,972				

c. **Calculation of Lease Receivable**
The lease receivable is $100,000, or the present value of the annual lease payments of $34,972.07 for three years.

	RATE	NPER	PMT	PV	TYPE	Excel Formula
Given	5%	3	(34,972.07)	?	1	=PV(0.05,3,−34972.07,0,1)
Solution				$100,000		

d. **Initial Direct Costs**
Because this lease has a selling profit ($100,000, fair value less $80,000, carrying value), the initial direct costs are expensed directly.

Assets = Liabilities + Equity
−800 −800
Cash: Cr. 800 | Selling Exp: Dr. 800

January 1, 2020—To record initial direct costs

Selling Expense	800	
Cash		800

e. **Lease Receivable Amortization Schedule**
The lessor will prepare a lease receivable amortization schedule using the effective interest method in order to calculate interest revenue as a function of the net lease receivable balance. The schedule illustrates how the lease payment is allocated between interest revenue and a reduction to the lease receivable.

Date	Lease Payment[a] Dr. Cash Cr. Lease Receivable	Interest on Receivable[b] Dr. Lease Receivable Cr. Interest Revenue	Lease Receivable Net Reduction[c]	Net Lease Receivable[d]
Jan. 1, 2020. . .				$100,000
Jan. 1, 2020. . .	$ 34,972	$ 0	$ 34,972	65,028
Jan. 1, 2021. . .	34,972	3,251	31,721	33,307
Jan. 1, 2022. . .	34,972	1,665*	33,307	0
	$104,916	$4,916	$100,000	

* Amount adjusted due to rounding of amounts in table.
[a] Lease payment.
[b] Interest rate (5%) × Beginning of period net lease receivable (with exception of first payment applied 100% to principal).
[c] Lease payment less interest on receivable.
[d] Net lease receivable (beginning of period) less net reduction of lease receivable.

f. **Lessor's Journal Entries—Year One**
Lessor Inc. will record the following entries in year one.

Assets = Liabilities + Equity
+100,000 −80,000
−80,000 +100,000
Lease Receiv: Dr. 100,000 | COGS: Dr. 80,000
Inventory: Cr. 80,000 | Sales Rev: Cr. 100,000

Sales revenue	$100,000
− Cost of goods sold	(80,000)
= Gross profit	$ 20,000

January 1, 2020—To derecognize asset and record investment in lease

Lease Receivable	100,000	
Cost of Goods Sold	80,000	
Sales Revenue		100,000
Inventory		80,000

continued

continued from previous page

Lessor Inc. records gross profit of $20,000 ($100,000 less $80,000). The lessor also removes the asset to be leased (inventory) and records an investment in the lease (lease receivable).

January 1, 2020—To record lease payment

Cash	34,972	
Lease Receivable		34,972

Assets	=	Liabilities	+	Equity
+34,972				
−34,972				

Cash		Lease Receiv	
34,972	800	100,000	34,972

December 31, 2020—To recognize interest revenue

Lease Receivable	3,251	
Interest Revenue		3,251

Assets	=	Liabilities	+	Equity
+3,251				+3,251

Lease Receiv		Interest Rev	
100,000	34,972		3,251
3,251			
68,279			

g. **Lessor's Financial Statements—Year One**

Lessor Inc. will recognize the following amounts in its financial statements in year one.

Balance Sheet	**Dec. 31, 2020**
Assets	
Current assets	
Lease receivable ($3,251 + $31,721)	$34,972
Noncurrent assets	
Lease receivable ($68,279* − $34,972) . . .	33,307

*Total lease receivable of $68,279 derived from the journal entries above equals $100,000 − $34,972 + $3,251. The noncurrent portion is equal to the total lease liability less the current lease liability.

Income Statement	**2020**
Sales	
Sales revenue	$100,000
Less cost of goods sold . . .	80,000
Gross margin	$ 20,000
Other revenues and gains	
Interest revenue	3,251
Other expenses and losses	
Selling expense	800

h. **Lessor's Journal Entries—Year Two**

Lessor Inc. will record the following entries in year two.

January 1, 2021—To record lease payment

Cash	34,972	
Lease Receivable		34,972

Assets	=	Liabilities	+	Equity
+34,972				
−34,972				

Cash		Lease Receiv	
34,972	800	100,000	34,972
34,972		3,251	34,972

December 31, 2021—To recognize interest revenue

Lease Receivable	1,665	
Interest Revenue		1,665

Assets	=	Liabilities	+	Equity
+1,665				+1,665

Lease Receiv		Interest Rev	
100,000	34,972		3,251
3,251	34,972		1,665
1,665			
34,972			

i. **Lessor's Financial Statements—Year Two**

Lessor Inc. will recognize the following amounts in its financial statements in year two.

Balance Sheet	**Dec. 31, 2021**
Assets	
Current assets	
Lease receivable ($1,665 + $33,307)	$34,972
Noncurrent assets	
Lease receivable	0

Income Statement	**2021**
Other revenues and gains	
Interest revenue	$1,665

j. **Lessor's Journal Entries—Year Three**

Lessor Inc. will record the following entry in year three.

January 1, 2022— To record lease payment

Cash	34,972	
Lease Receivable		34,972

Assets	=	Liabilities	+	Equity
+34,972				
−34,972				

Cash		Lease Receiv	
34,972	800	100,000	34,972
34,972		3,251	34,972
34,972		1,665	34,972
		0	

After the journal entries of year three and the expiration of the lease, the lease receivable has a value of $0 (December 31, 2021, balance of $34,972 less $34,972).

Demo 17-3B LO17-3 Lessor—Sales-Type Lease with a Guaranteed Residual Value

Demo MBC

Let's review another lease example. In this case we modify the example to include a guaranteed residual value. On January 1, 2020, the lease commencement date, Lessor Inc. and Lessee Inc. sign a three-year non-cancelable lease for equipment. Details of the lease agreement follow.

1. The equipment has an estimated economic life of three years and the lessor manufactured the equipment at a cost of $80,000.
2. Lessor Inc. routinely leases this type of equipment to other companies.
3. The three lease payments are $33,461.73 each, payable January 1, 2020, 2021, and 2022.
4. The fair value of the asset at the commencement of the lease is $100,000.
5. The lease does not contain a renewal or purchase option, and the asset reverts to the lessor at the end of the three-year period.
6. The contract requires the lessee to guarantee the residual value of the equipment at the end of the lease for $5,000.
7. Lessor Inc. depreciates assets using the straight-line method for book purposes.
8. The accounting year ends December 31 for each entity.
9. The lessor's implicit interest rate, the rate that equates the present value of payments to the asset's fair value, is 5%.
10. Initial direct costs of the lessor were $800 (legal fees related to the execution of the lease, paid in cash on January 1, 2020).

Answer the following questions from the perspective of Lessor Inc.

a. Determine the proper lease classification assuming that lease payments are probable.
b. Confirm the lease payment of $33,462 (rounded).
c. Calculate the lease receivable.
d. Record initial direct costs.
e. Prepare a lease receivable amortization schedule.
f. Prepare the lessor's journal entries for 2020.
g. Show the impact on the lessor's balance sheet and income statement for 2020.
h. Prepare the lessor's journal entries for 2021.
i. Show the impact on the lessor's balance sheet and income statement for 2021.
j. Prepare the lessor's journal entries for 2022.
k. Show the impact on the lessor's balance sheet and income statement for 2022.
l. Prepare the lessor's journal entry on January 1, 2023. Assume that the inventory was returned with a value of $5,000.

Solution

Amounts in the following calculations and journal entries are rounded.

a. **Lease Classification**

First, the lease is classified as a *sales-type lease* because at least one of the lease classification criteria is met. The lease term is 100% of the useful life of the asset. Also, the present value of the lease payments of $100,000 is equal to the fair value of the underlying asset of $100,000 indicating that control of the underlying asset has transferred from the lessor to the lessee.

Classification Criteria	Criteria Met
1. Ownership transfer.	
2. Purchase option	
3. Lease term length.	✔
4. Present value of lease payments . . .	✔
5. Alternative use	

	RATE	NPER	PMT	PV	FV	TYPE	Excel Formula
Given	5%	3	(33,461.73)	?	(5,000)	1	=PV(0.05,3,−33461.73,−5000,1)
Solution				$100,000			

b. **Calculation of Lease Payment**

From the lessor's perspective, let's review how the lease payment of 33,462 (rounded) was determined by the lessor. The lessor expected a return on its investment of 5% (RATE) from leasing an asset with a fair value of $100,000 (PV) over three years (NPER), with a guaranteed residual value of $5,000 (FV). Because there is a guaranteed residual value, the lease payments to achieve a 5% return to the lessor ($33,462) are lower than in **Demo 17-3A** ($34,972). The first payment is due immediately (TYPE, 1).

	RATE	NPER	PMT	PV	FV	TYPE	Excel Formula
Given	5%	3	?	(100,000)	5,000	1	=PMT(0.05,3,−100000,5000,1)
Solution			$33,462				

continued

continued from previous page

c. **Calculation of Lease Receivable**
The lease receivable is equal to $100,000 calculated as the present value of the annual lease payments of $33,462 (PMT) and the guaranteed residual value of $5,000 (FV).

	RATE	NPER	PMT	PV	FV	TYPE	Excel Formula
Given	5%	3	(33,462)	?	(5,000)	1	=PV(0.05,3,−33462,−5000,1)
Solution				$100,000			

d. **Initial Direct Costs**
In a sales-type lease, the lessor will expense immediately initial direct costs as selling expense in cases where the lessor records a gross profit (in this case $20,000 or $100,000 minus $80,000).

January 1, 2020—To record initial direct costs

Selling Expense	800	
Cash		800

Assets = Liabilities + Equity
−800 −800
Cash: Cr. 800
Selling Exp: Dr. 800

e. **Lease Receivable Amortization Schedule**

Date	Lease Payment Dr. Cash Cr. Lease Receivable	Interest on Receivable Dr. Lease Receivable Cr. Interest Revenue	Lease Receivable Net Reduction	Net Lease Receivable
Jan. 1, 2020 . . .				$100,000
Jan. 1, 2020 . . .	$ 33,462	$ 0	$ 33,462	66,538
Jan. 1, 2021 . . .	33,462	3,327	30,135	36,403
Jan. 1, 2022 . . .	33,462	1,820	31,642	4,761
Jan. 1, 2023 . . .	5,000*	239**	4,761	0
	$105,386	$5,386	$100,000	

*Amount reclassified to inventory at lease end

** Amount adjusted due to rounding of amounts in table.

f. **Lessor's Journal Entries—Year One**

January 1, 2020—To record lease receivable and derecognize inventory

Lease Receivable	100,000	
Cost of Goods Sold	80,000	
Sales Revenue		100,000
Inventory		80,000

Assets = Liabilities + Equity
+100,000 −80,000
−80,000 +100,000
Lease Receiv: Dr. 100,000
COGS: Dr. 80,000
Inventory: Cr. 80,000
Sales Rev: Cr. 100,000

Gross profit of $20,000 is equal to sales revenue of $100,000 less cost of goods sold of $80,000.

January 1, 2020—To record lease payment

Cash	33,462	
Lease Receivable		33,462

Assets = Liabilities + Equity
+33,462
−33,462
Cash: Dr. 33,462 | Cr. 800
Lease Receiv: Dr. 100,000 | Cr. 33,462

December 31, 2020—To recognize interest revenue

Lease Receivable	3,327	
Interest Revenue.		3,327

Assets = Liabilities + Equity
+3,327 +3,327
Lease Receiv: Dr. 100,000, 3,327 | Cr. 33,462; balance 69,865
Interest Rev: Cr. 3,327

g. **Lessor's Financial Statements—Year One**
Lessor Inc. will recognize the following amounts in its financial statements in year one.

Balance Sheet	**Dec. 31, 2020**
Assets	
Current assets	
Lease receivable ($3,327 + $30,135)	$33,462
Noncurrent assets	
Lease receivable ($69,865* − $33,462). . .	36,403

*Total lease receivable of $69,865 derived from the journal entries above equals $100,000 − $33,462 + $3,327. The noncurrent portion is equal to the total lease liability less the current lease liability.

Income Statement	**2020**
Sales	
Sales revenue.	$100,000
Less cost of goods sold . . .	80,000
Gross margin	$ 20,000
Other revenues and gains	
Interest revenue	3,327
Other expenses and losses	
Selling expense.	800

continued

continued from previous page

h. Lessor's Journal Entries—Year Two

Lessor Inc. will record the following entries in year two.

January 1, 2021—To record lease payment

Account	Debit	Credit
Cash	33,462	
Lease Receivable		33,462

Assets = Liabilities + Equity
+33,462
−33,462

Cash (Dr)	Cash (Cr)	Lease Receiv (Dr)	Lease Receiv (Cr)
33,462	800	100,000	33,462
33,462		3,327	33,462

December 31, 2021—To recognize interest revenue

Account	Debit	Credit
Lease Receivable	1,820	
Interest Revenue		1,820

Assets = Liabilities + Equity
+1,820 +1,820

Lease Receiv (Dr)	Lease Receiv (Cr)	Interest Rev (Dr)	Interest Rev (Cr)
100,000	33,462		3,327
3,327	33,462		1,820
1,820			
38,223			

i. Lessor's Financial Statements—Year Two

Lessor Inc. will recognize the following amounts in its financial statements in year two.

Balance Sheet	**Dec. 31, 2021**
Assets	
Current assets	
Lease receivable ($1,820 + $31,642)	$33,462
Noncurrent assets	
Lease receivable ($38,223 − $33,462) . . .	4,761

Income Statement	**2021**
Other revenues and gains	
Interest revenue	$1,820

*Total lease receivable of $38,223 derived from the journal entries above equals $69,865 − $33,462 + $1,820. The noncurrent portion is equal to the total lease liability less the current lease liability.

j. Lessor's Journal Entries—Year Three

Lessor Inc. will record the following entries in year three.

January 1, 2022—To record lease payment

Account	Debit	Credit
Cash	33,462	
Lease Receivable		33,462

Assets = Liabilities + Equity
+33,462
−33,462

Cash (Dr)	Cash (Cr)	Lease Receiv (Dr)	Lease Receiv (Cr)
33,462	800	100,000	33,462
33,462		3,327	33,462
33,462		1,820	33,462

December 31, 2022—To recognize interest revenue

Account	Debit	Credit
Lease Receivable	239	
Interest Revenue		239

Assets = Liabilities + Equity
+239 +239

Lease Receiv (Dr)	Lease Receiv (Cr)	Interest Rev (Dr)	Interest Rev (Cr)
100,000	33,462		3,327
3,327	33,462		1,820
1,820	33,462		239
239			
5,000			

k. Lessor's Financial Statements—Year Three

Lessor Inc. will recognize the following amounts in its financial statements in year three.

Balance Sheet	**Dec. 31, 2022**
Assets	
Current assets	
Lease receivable.	$5,000

Income Statement	**2022**
Other revenues and gains	
Interest revenue	$239

l. Lessor's Journal Entry at Lease Termination

After the journal entries of year three and the expiration of the lease, the lease receivable has a value of $5,000. The lease receivable would be eliminated and the asset would return to inventory when the asset is returned to the lessor.

January 1, 2023—To record return of lease asset to lessor

Account	Debit	Credit
Inventory	5,000	
Lease Receivable		5,000

Assets = Liabilities + Equity
+5,000
−5,000

Inventory (Dr)	Inventory (Cr)	Lease Receiv (Dr)	Lease Receiv (Cr)
5,000		100,000	33,462
		3,327	33,462
		1,820	33,462
		239	5,000
		0	

EXPANDING YOUR KNOWLEDGE — **Unguaranteed Residual Value**

For a sales-type lease with an unguaranteed residual value, the lease standard requires that the lessor deduct the present value of the unguaranteed residual value from both sales revenue and cost of goods sold to avoid overstatement. *This treatment is necessary because of the lessor's uncertainty in receiving the unguaranteed residual value at the end of the lease term.* This does not affect the gross profit, the lease receivable, or annual interest revenue.

For example, if we assume the same information for Lessor Inc., except that the residual value of $5,000 were unguaranteed, the entry to record the lease receivable on January 1, 2020, follows.

January 1, 2020—To record lease receivable and derecognize inventory

Lease Receivable	100,000	
Cost of Goods Sold ($80,000 − $4,319*)	75,681	
Sales ($100,000 − $4,319)		95,681
Inventory		80,000

Sales revenue	$95,681
− Cost of goods sold	(75,681)
= Gross profit	$ 20,000

* Present value of unguaranteed residual value of $5,000 is $4,319 (**PV(0.05,3,0,5000)).**

In this example, the gross profit with a guaranteed residual value ($20,000 or $100,000 minus $80,000) is the same as with an unguaranteed residual value ($20,000 or $95,681 minus $75,681). At the end of the lease term, the company derecognizes the $5,000 lease receivable and recognizes $5,000 of inventory. If the inventory is returned for a value less than $5,000, this difference would be recorded as a loss.

The following table summarizes the treatment of guaranteed and unguaranteed residual value, purchase options, and termination penalties for the lessor.

Accounting for the Lessor	Guaranteed Residual Value	Unguaranteed Residual Value	Purchase Option or Penalty*
ASC 842 definition of a lease payment	Include only probable amount owed	Not included	Included
PV of lease payment criterion of the lease classification test	Included	Not included	Included
Lease receivable calculation	Included	Included	Included
Lease payment calculation (fixed payment)	Included	Include only expected value	Included

* Assume that it is reasonably certain that the lessee will exercise the purchase option or it is reasonably certain that the lessee will terminate the lease. If a purchase option is included, residual value must be ignored in the lessor's calculations.

Account for Sales-Type Lease by Lessor — LO17-3 — REVIEW 17-3

Lessor Company leased equipment (recorded as inventory) to Lessee Company for a three-year period. Lessor paid $300,000 for the equipment (its fair value) and immediately leased it on January 1, 2020 (estimated useful life is four years, and the estimated residual value at the end of the lease term is $60,000). Lessor used an expected rate of return of 8% (known by the Lessee). The lessee agreed to guarantee the estimated residual value of $60,000. The first lease payment is due on January 1, 2020, and the accounting periods for both entities end on December 31. At the lease termination date, an independent appraiser provided an estimated residual value of $25,000. The lessee immediately paid the difference of $35,000 ($60,000 guaranteed residual value minus $25,000, the actual residual value).

Required

a. Compute the lease payment for the lessor. Compute the lease receivable to be capitalized by the lessor.

b. Provide the entry for the lessor on January 1, 2020, to derecognize inventory and record the lease receivable.

c. Provide an amortization schedule of the lease receivable.

d. Provide the entries for the lessor through the lease term to record the lease payments, the year-end adjusting entries, and the lease termination.

More Practice: 17-33, 17-34, 17-35, 17-36, 17-37, 17-38, 17-39, 17-40, 17-41, 17-43

Solution on p. 17-83.

LO 17-4 Account for an operating lease for a lessee

LO 17-4 Overview

Operating Leases—Lessee
- Meets *none* of the lease classification criteria
- Establish a right-of-use asset and a lease liability
- Record lease expense on a straight-line basis to encompass both
  - Interest expense on the lease liability
  - Amortization of the right-of-use asset

From the perspective of the lessee, an operating lease is any lease other than a finance lease. In accounting for an operating lease, a lessee records a right-of-use asset and a lease liability on the balance sheet (calculated in the same way as presented earlier for a finance lease). Even though the control of the asset has not passed to the lessee, the lessee still has a right-of-use asset and an obligation to make lease payments.

However, unlike a finance lease, an equal amount of expense is recorded each period on the income statement, using the straight-line method for expense recognition. The lease expense reduces the lease asset and the lease liability until both values reach a zero balance, see **Demo 17-4A** and **Demo 17-4B**. A summary of the accounting for the lessee for an operating lease follows.

Balance Sheet	Income Statement
Recognize a right-of-use asset and test for impairment. Recognize a lease liability.	Recognize lease expense on a straight-line basis as a single line item combining both: ▪ Interest expense on the lease liability using the effective interest method. ▪ Amortization expense on the right-of-use asset as the difference between straight-line expense and interest expense.

Straight-Line Lease Expense As in previous examples, the lessee will prepare an amortization schedule of the lease liability to calculate interest expense each period, using the effective interest method. The right-of-use asset amortization schedule is created next to allocate straight-line lease expense to interest expense and amortization expense. **Straight-line lease expense** is measured by taking the total cost of the lease divided by the total number of lease periods.

Straight-Line Lease Expense Less **Interest Expense on Lease Liability** = **Amortization of Right-of-Use Asset**

Total cost of the lease at the commencement of the lease equals total lease payments (including those previously paid and not yet paid), plus total lessee initial direct costs, less lease incentives received as shown in **Demo 17-4B**. Next, the amortization of the right-of-use asset is determined by subtracting the interest expense on the lease liability from the straight-line lease expense to arrive at amortization expense of the right-of-use asset. The amortization of the right-of-use asset cannot be calculated independently—it is a plug figure when accounting for operating leases.

842-20-25-6 After the commencement date, a lessee shall recognize all of the following in profit or loss.

a. A single lease cost, calculated so that the remaining cost of the lease . . . is allocated over the remaining lease term on a straight-line basis unless another systematic and rational basis is more representative of the pattern in which benefit is expected to be derived from the right to use the underlying.

b. Variable lease payments not included in the lease liability in the period in which the obligation for those payments is incurred.

c. Any impairment of the right-of-use asset determined.

EXPAND YOUR KNOWLEDGE — **Variable Lease Payments**

If a lessee also pays variable lease payments (variable lease payments that do not depend on an index or rate), such payments are recognized in the period in which the achievement of the specified target that triggers the variable lease payments becomes probable. For example, if a portion of a lease payment in an operating lease is contingent upon a lessee's sales revenue, this portion of the lease payment is variable and is *not* included in the total lease payments recognized as expense on a straight-line basis. Instead, the variable lease payment is expensed when payment is probable (such as when it is probable that sales targets will be met).

842-20-55-1 A lessee should recognize costs from variable lease payments (in annual periods as well as in interim periods) before the achievement of the specified target that triggers the variable lease payments, provided the achievement of that target is considered probable.

Lessee—Operating Lease

LO17-4 **Demo 17-4A**

Demo MBC

Let's review an operating lease example and record entries from the *lessee's perspective*. On January 1, 2020, Lessor Inc. and Lessee Inc. sign a three-year non-cancelable lease for equipment. Details of the lease agreement with a commencement date of January 1, 2020, follow.

1. The equipment has an estimated economic life of six years.
2. Lessor Inc. routinely leases this type of equipment to other companies.
3. The three lease payments are $34,972.07 each, payable January 1, 2020, 2021, and 2022.
4. Fair value of the asset at the commencement of the lease is $150,000, which is also the carrying value (cost) on the lessor's books.
5. The lease does not contain a renewal or purchase option, and the asset reverts to the lessor at the end of the three-year period.
6. The asset's unguaranteed residual value is estimated to be $57,882.
7. The lessee's incremental borrowing rate is 5%.
8. The accounting year ends December 31 for each entity.
9. The lessor's implicit interest rate, the rate that equates the present value of the payments to the asset's fair value, is 5% and is known by the lessee.

Answer the following questions from the perspective of Lessee Inc.

a. Determine the proper lease classification.
b. Calculate the lease liability and the right-of-use asset.
c. Prepare a lease liability amortization schedule and a right-of-use asset amortization schedule.
d. Prepare the lessee's journal entries for 2020.
e. Show the impact on the lessee's balance sheet and income statement for 2020.
f. Prepare the lessee's journal entries for 2021.
g. Show the impact on the lessee's balance sheet and income statement for 2021.
h. Prepare the lessee's journal entries for 2022.

Solution

a. **Lease Classification**

The lease is classified as an operating lease to the lessee because none of the lease classification criteria is met as shown in the following analysis.

	Lease Classification Criteria	Analysis	Lease Criteria Met
1	Ownership transfer	Asset reverts to the lessor at the end of the three-year period.	
2	Purchase option	Lease does not contain a purchase option.	
3	Lease term length	Three-year lease term < 75% of the six-year useful life (4.5 years).	
4	PV of lease payments	PV of lease payments of $100,000 (rounded) < $135,000 (90% of fair value of $150,000).	
5	Alternative use	There are alternative uses for the equipment as the lessor often leases this equipment to other companies.	

RATE	NPER	PMT	TYPE	PV	Excel Formula
5%	3	(34,972.07)	1	?	=PV(0.05,3,−34972.07,0,1)
				$99,999.50	

b. **Calculation of the Lease Liability and the Right-of-Use Asset**

With an operating lease, a lease liability and a right-of-use asset are initially recognized on the balance sheet in the same way as a finance lease. The lease liability is equal to the present value of the *remaining* lease payments of $100,000 as calculated above in the lease classification test. The right-of-use asset is equal to the lease liability of $100,000 with no adjustments.

Calculate Right-of-Use Asset	
Initial measurement of lease liability. . .	$100,000
Add prepaid lease payment	0
Subtract lease incentive received.	0
Add initial indirect costs incurred	0
Right-of-use asset	$100,000

continued

continued from previous page

c. **Lease Liability Amortization Schedule**

The lease liability amortization schedule is prepared first. Interest expense determined in the lease liability amortization schedule is an input to the right-of-use asset amortization schedule below.

Date	Lease Payment	Interest on Liability	Lease Liability Reduction	Net Lease Liability
Jan. 1, 2020				$100,000
Jan. 1, 2020	$ 34,972	$ 0	$ 34,972	65,028
Jan. 1, 2021	34,972	3,251	31,721	33,307
Jan. 1, 2022	34,972	1,665	33,307	0
	$104,916	$4,916	$100,000	

Note: Certain amounts in table adjusted for rounding differences.

Right-of-Use Asset Amortization Schedule

Date	Lease Expense Straight-Line[a]	Interest on Liability[b]	Right-of-Use Asset Amortization[c]	Net Right-of-Use Asset[d]
Jan. 1, 2020				$100,000
Dec. 31, 2020	$ 34,972	$3,251	$ 31,721	68,279
Dec. 31, 2021	34,972	1,665	33,307	34,972
Dec. 31, 2022	34,972	—	34,972	0
	$104,916	$4,916	$100,000	

[a] Straight-line expense equals total lease payments divided by total number of periods ($34,972 + $34,972 + $34,972)/3 = $34,972).

[b] Interest on the liability is calculated in the lease liability amortization schedule. This interest expense amount is an identifiable portion of lease expense for the period.

[c] Amortization is the difference between 1 and 2 (Straight-line lease expense less interest on liability).

[d] Beginning right-of-use asset balance less amortization.

Lease expense recognized in the income statement each period is $34,972 (straight-line expense) and is made up of interest expense of the lease liability and the amortization expense of the right-of-use asset (calculated above).

	Interest Expense	Amortization Expense	Lease Expense
2020	$3,251	$ 31,721	$ 34,972
2021	1,665	33,307	34,972
2022	—	34,972	34,972
	$4,916	$100,000	$104,916

d. **Lessee's Journal Entries—Year One**

Lessee Inc. will record the following entries in year one.

January 1, 2020— To record right-of-use asset and lease liability

Right-of-Use Asset.	100,000	
Lease Liability		100,000

Assets = Liabilities + Equity
+100,000 +100,000

R-of-U Asset	
100,000	

Lease Liab	
	100,000

January 1, 2020— To record lease payment

Lease Liability	34,972	
Cash		34,972

Assets = Liabilities + Equity
−34,972 −34,972

Cash	
	34,972

Lease Liab	
34,972	100,000

December 31, 2020— To record lease expense

Lease Expense	34,972	
Lease Liability		3,251
Right-of-Use Asset.		31,721

Assets = Liabilities + Equity
−31,721 +3,251 −34,972

R-of-U Asset	
100,000	31,721
68,279	

Lease Liab	
34,972	100,000
	3,251
	68,279

Lease Exp	
34,972	

continued

continued from previous page

e. **Lessee's Financial Statements—Year One**

You may recall from the financial presentation earlier for a finance lease that the interest expense and the amortization expense were recognized as two separate line items in the income statement. For the operating lease however, the lessee will calculate the interest expense on the lease liability and the amortization expense on the right-of-use asset but will combine them into one expense line item on the income statement.

Lessee Inc. will recognize the following amounts in its financial statements in year one.

Balance Sheet	**Dec. 31, 2020**
Assets	
Noncurrent assets	
Right-of-use asset ($100,000 − $31,721). .	$68,279
Liabilities	
Current liabilities	
Lease liability.	34,972
Noncurrent liabilities	
Lease liability*	33,307

Income Statement	**2020**
Expenses	
Lease expense	$34,972

*Total lease liability of $68,279 derived from the journal entries above equals $100,000 − $34,972 + $3,251. The noncurrent portion is equal to the total lease liability less the current lease liability.

f. **Lessee's Journal Entries—Year Two**

Lessee Inc. will record the following entries in year two.

January 1, 2021—To record lease payment

Lease Liability	34,972	
Cash		34,972

Assets	=	Liabilities	+	Equity
−34,972		−34,972		

Cash	
	34,972
	34,972

Lease Liab	
34,972	100,000
34,972	3,251

December 31, 2021—To record lease expense

Lease Expense	34,972	
Lease Liability		1,665
Right-of-Use Asset.		33,307

Assets	=	Liabilities	+	Equity
−33,307		+1,665		−34,972

R-of-U Asset	
100,000	31,721
	33,307
34,972	

Lease Liab	
34,972	100,000
34,972	3,251
	1,665
	34,972

Lease Exp	
34,972	
34,972	

g. **Lessee's Financial Statements—Year Two**

Lessee Inc. will recognize the following amounts in its financial statements in year two.

Balance Sheet	**Dec. 31, 2021**
Assets	
Current assets	
Right-of-use asset ($68,279 − $33,307). . .	$34,972
Liabilities	
Current liabilities	
Lease liability.	34,972
Noncurrent liabilities	
Lease liability.	0

Income Statement	**2021**
Expenses	
Lease expense	$34,972

h. **Lessee's Journal Entries—Year Three**

Lessee Inc. will record the following entries in year three.

January 1, 2022—To record lease payment

Lease Liability	34,972	
Cash		34,972

Assets	=	Liabilities	+	Equity
−34,972		−34,972		

Cash	
	34,972
	34,972
	34,972

Lease Liab	
34,972	100,000
34,972	3,251
34,972	1,665
	0

December 31, 2022—To record amortization on right-of-use asset

Lease Expense	34,972	
Right-of-Use Asset.		34,972

Assets	=	Liabilities	+	Equity
−34,972				−34,972

R-of-U Asset	
100,000	31,721
	33,307
	34,972
0	

Lease Exp	
34,972	
34,972	
34,972	

After the journal entries of year three and the expiration of the lease, the right-of-use asset has a value of $0 (December 31, 2022) and the lease liability has a value of $0 (December 31, 2022).

Demo 17-4B LO17-4 Lessee—Operating Lease with Prepayment, Initial Cost, Incentive

Demo MBC

Let's review an operating lease example and record entries from the *lessee's perspective.* On December 20, 2019, Lessor Inc. and Lessee Inc. sign a three-year non-cancelable lease for equipment. Details of the lease agreement with a commencement date of January 1, 2020, follow.

1. The equipment has an estimated economic life of six years.
2. Lessor Inc. routinely leases this type of equipment to other companies.
3. The three lease payments are $34,972 each, payable January 1, 2020, 2021, and 2022. However, Lessee Inc. prepaid the first payment on December 28, 2019.
4. Fair value of the asset at the commencement of the lease is $150,000, which is also the carrying value (cost) on the lessor's books.
5. The lease does not contain a renewal or purchase option, and the asset reverts to the lessor at the end of the three-year period.
6. The asset's unguaranteed residual value is estimated to be $57,882.
7. The lessee's incremental borrowing rate is 5%.
8. The accounting year ends December 31 for each entity.
9. The lessor's implicit interest rate, the rate that equates the present value of the payments to the asset's fair value, is 5% and is known by the lessee.
10. The lessee incurred legal fees to execute the lease of $620 in cash on December 20, 2019.
11. On December 20, 2020, the lessee received $5,000 cash as a partial payment for the lessee's preexisting lease.

Answer the following questions from the perspective of Lessee Inc.

a. Record the entries in December 2019 for the lease prepayment, lease incentive received, and legal fees.
b. Determine the proper lease classification.
c. Calculate the lease liability and the right-of-use asset.
d. Prepare a lease liability amortization schedule and a right-of-use asset amortization schedule.
e. Prepare the lessee's journal entries for 2020.
f. Show the impact on the lessee's balance sheet and income statement for 2020.
g. Prepare the lessee's journal entries for 2021.
h. Show the impact on the lessee's balance sheet and income statement for 2021.
i. Prepare the lessee's journal entries for 2022.

Solution

a. **Lessee's Journal Entries—Prior to Lease Commencement**

December 20, 2019—To record lease incentive received

Assets = Liabilities + Equity
+5,000 +5,000
Cash: 5,000 (Dr) | Incent Pay: 5,000 (Cr)

Cash	5,000	
Lease Incentive Payable		5,000

December 20, 2019—To record initial direct costs

Assets = Liabilities + Equity
+620
−620
Cash: 5,000 (Dr) 620 (Cr) | Init Dir Cost: 620 (Dr)

Initial Direct Cost	620	
Cash		620

December 28, 2019—To record lease prepayment

Assets = Liabilities + Equity
+34,972
−34,972
Cash: 5,000 (Dr) 620, 34,972 (Cr) | Prepaid Lease: 34,972 (Dr)

Prepaid Lease Payment	34,972	
Cash		34,972

b. **Lease Classification**

First, the lease is classified as an operating lease to the lessee because none of the lease classification criteria is met as shown in the following analysis.

continued

continued from previous page

	Lease Classification Criteria	Analysis	Lease Criteria Met
1	Ownership transfer	Asset reverts to the lessor at the end of the three-year period.	
2	Purchase option	Lease does not contain a purchase option.	
3	Lease term length	Three-year lease term < 75% of the six-year useful life (4.5 years).	
4	PV of lease payments	$95,000 (PV of lease payments of $65,027.43 *plus* lease prepayment of $34,972.07 *less* lease incentive of $5,000) < $135,000 (90% of fair value of $150,000).	
5	Alternative use	There are alternative uses for the equipment as the lessor often leases this equipment to other companies.	

RATE	NPER	PMT	PV	Excel Formula
5%	2	(34,972.07)	?	=PV(0.05,2,−34972.07)
			$65,027.43	

c. **Calculation of the Lease Liability and the Right-of-Use Asset**

With an operating lease, a lease liability and a right-of-use asset are initially recognized on the balance sheet in the same way as a finance lease. The lease liability is equal to $65,027, the present value of the *remaining* lease payments as calculated above in the lease classification test. The right-of-use asset is equal to the lease liability of $65,027 adjusted for items incurred at or before the lease commencement: lease prepayment, lease incentive and initial direct costs.

Calculate Right-of-Use Asset	
Initial measurement of lease liability . . .	$65,027
Add prepaid lease payment	34,972
Subtract lease incentive received.	(5,000)
Add initial direct costs incurred.	620
Right-of-use asset	$95,619

d. **Lease Liability Amortization Schedule**

The lease liability amortization schedule is prepared first. Interest expense determined in the lease liability amortization schedule is an input to the right-of-use asset amortization schedule below.

Date	Lease Payment	Interest on Liability	Lease Liability Reduction	Net Lease Liability
Jan. 1, 2020				$65,027
Jan. 1, 2021	$34,972	$3,251	$31,721	33,306
Jan. 1, 2022	34,972	1,666	33,306	0
	$69,944	$4,917	$65,027	

Note: Certain amounts in table adjusted for rounding differences.

Right-of-Use Asset Amortization Schedule

Date	Lease Expense Straight-Line[a]	Interest on Liability[b]	Right-of-Use Asset Amortization[c]	Net Right-of-Use Asset[d]
Jan. 1, 2020				$95,619
Dec. 31, 2020	$ 33,512	$3,251	$30,261	65,358
Dec. 31, 2021	33,512	1,666	31,846	33,512
Dec. 31, 2022	33,512	—	33,512	0
	$100,536	$4,917	$95,619	

[a] Straight-line expense equals total lease payments divided by total number of periods ($34,972 + $34,972 + $34,972 + $620 − $5,000)/3 = $33,512).

[b] Interest on the liability is calculated in the lease liability amortization schedule. This interest expense amount is an identifiable portion of lease expense for the period (see table below) and also periodically reduces the lease liability.

[c] Amortization is the difference between 1 and 2 (Straight-line lease expense less interest on liability).

[d] Beginning right-of-use asset balance less amortization.

continued

continued from previous page

Lease expense recognized in the income statement each period is $33,512 (straight-line expense) and is made up of interest expense of the lease liability and the amortization expense of the right-of-use asset (calculated above).

	Interest Expense	Amortization Expense	Lease Expense
2020	$3,251	$30,261	$ 33,512
2021	1,666	31,846	33,512
2022	—	33,512	33,512
	$4,917	$95,619	$100,536

e. **Lessee's Journal Entries—Year One**

Lessee Inc. will record the following entries in year one. The following three accounts are reclassified to the right-of-use asset account through this entry: Lease Incentive Payable, Initial Direct Costs, and Prepaid Lease Payment.

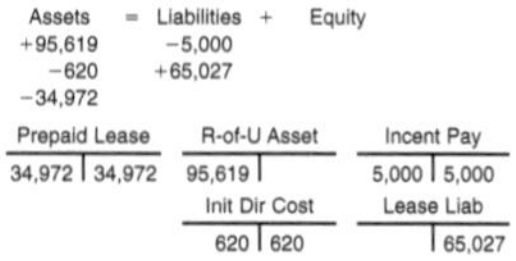

Assets = Liabilities + Equity
+95,619 −5,000
−620 +65,027
−34,972
Prepaid Lease
34,972 | 34,972
R-of-U Asset
95,619 |
Incent Pay
5,000 | 5,000
Init Dir Cost
620 | 620
Lease Liab
| 65,027

January 1, 2020—To record right-of-use asset and lease liability

Right-of-Use Asset.	95,619	
Lease Incentive Payable.	5,000	
Lease Liability		65,027
Initial Direct Cost.		620
Prepaid Lease Payment		34,972

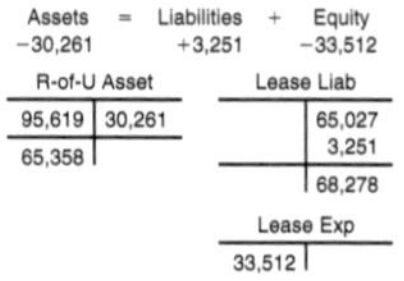

Assets = Liabilities + Equity
−30,261 +3,251 −33,512
R-of-U Asset
95,619 | 30,261
65,358 |
Lease Liab
| 65,027
| 3,251
| 68,278
Lease Exp
33,512 |

December 31, 2020—To record lease expense

Lease Expense	33,512	
Lease Liability		3,251
Right-of-Use Asset.		30,261

f. **Lessee's Financial Statements—Year One**

You may recall from the financial presentation earlier for a finance lease that the interest expense and the amortization expense were recognized as two separate line items in the income statement. For the operating lease however, the lessee will calculate the interest expense on the lease liability and the amortization expense on the right-of-use asset but will combine them into one expense line item on the income statement.

Lessee Inc. will recognize the following amounts in its financial statements in year one.

Balance Sheet	Dec. 31, 2020
Assets	
Noncurrent assets	
Right-of-use asset ($95,619 − $30,261). . .	$65,358
Liabilities	
Current liabilities	
Lease liability.	34,972
Noncurrent liabilities	
Lease liability*	33,306

*Total lease liability of $68,278 derived from the journal entries above equals $65,027 + $3,251. The noncurrent portion is equal to the total lease liability less the current lease liability.

Income Statement	2020
Expenses	
Lease expense	$33,512

g. **Lessee's Journal Entries—Year Two**

Lessee Inc. will record the following entries in year two.

January 1, 2021— To record lease payment

Lease Liability	34,972	
Cash		34,972

continued

continued from previous page

December 31, 2021— To record lease expense

Lease Expense	33,512	
Lease Liability		1,666
Right-of-Use Asset.		31,846

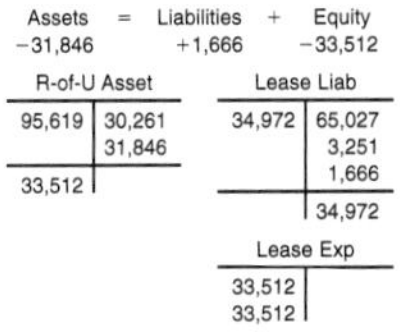

h. **Lessee's Financial Statements—Year Two**

Lessee Inc. will recognize the following amounts in its financial statements in year two.

Balance Sheet	Dec. 31, 2021
Assets	
Current assets	
Right-of-use asset ($65,358 − $31,846). . .	$33,512
Liabilities	
Current liabilities	
Lease liability.	34,972
Noncurrent liabilities	
Lease liability.	0

Income Statement	2021
Expenses	
Lease expense	$33,512

i. **Lessee's Journal Entries—Year Three**

Lessee Inc. will record the following entries in year three.

January 1, 2022— To record lease payment

Lease Liability	34,972	
Cash		34,972

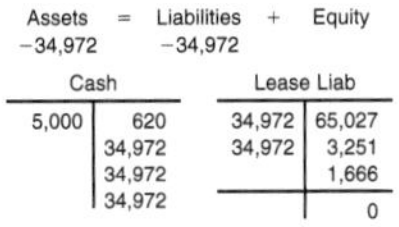

December 31, 2022—To record amortization on right-of-use asset

Lease Expense	33,512	
Right-of-Use Asset.		33,512

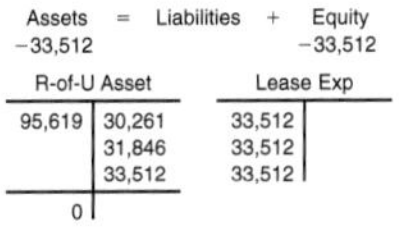

After the journal entries of year three and the expiration of the lease, the right-of-use asset has a value of $0 (December 31, 2022) and the lease liability has a value of $0 (December 31, 2022).

Income Statement Presentation—Operating Compared to Financing Lease Whether a lease is classified as an operating or a finance lease, an asset and liability are recorded on the balance sheet. However, the timing and presentation on the income statement differs between an operating and finance lease.

842-20-45-4 In the statement of comprehensive income, a lessee shall present both of the following:

a. For finance leases, the interest expense on the lease liability and amortization of the right-of-use asset are not required to be presented as separate line items and shall be presented in a manner consistent with how the entity presents other interest expense and depreciation or amortization of similar assets, respectively.

b. For operating leases, lease expense shall be included in the lessee's income from continuing operations.

Let's consider two scenarios: one where the lease is classified as operating and one where the same lease is classified as a finance lease (assuming a change in an estimate of useful life). Using the lease example in **Demo 17-4B**, lease expense is recorded on a straight-line basis, over the term of the lease, as one expense amount in income from operations. However, under the finance lease, interest expense is reported separately from the amortization of the right-of-use asset. Interest expense would be reported in other expense while the amortization would be reported as part of income from operations. In addition, expense is higher in earlier years (lower in later years) for a finance lease (under the effective interest method) versus for an operating lease (straight-line method). As a result, lessees would likely prefer the operating lease classification over the finance lease classification as it produces stronger operating results in the earlier years. We see, however, that while total expense recognized differs per year between the two methods, total lease expense recognized of $100,536 is the same under both methods.

	Operating Lease	Finance Lease		
	Lease Expense	Interest Expense	Amortization of Right-of-Use Asset	Total
2020 . . .	$ 33,512	$3,251	$31,873	$ 35,124
2021 . . .	33,512	1,666	31,873	33,538
2022 . . .	33,512	—	31,874	31,874
	$100,536	$4,917	$95,620	$100,536

Because the amortization of the right-of-use asset differs, the net balance in the right-of-use asset for the first two years also differs as follows.

	Operating Lease Right-of-Use Asset	Finance Lease Right-of-Use Asset
Dec. 31, 2020	$65,358	$63,746
Dec. 31, 2021	33,512	31,873
Dec. 31, 2022	0	0

EXPANDING YOUR KNOWLEDGE **Leases and Statement of Cash Flows**

On the statement of cash flows for an operating lease, the full lease payment is classified as an outflow from operating activities. Because the full lease payment is reported as expense each period, the cash outflows related to the full lease payment are incorporated into cash flows from operating activities. However, for a finance lease, only the interest portion of the lease payment is included in expense, and thus only the cash outflows related to interest are incorporated into cash flows from operating activities. The reduction in principal is reported as an outflow for financing activities. For a lessor, lease cash receipts are treated as a cash inflow from operating activities.

Guaranteed Residual Let's assume that the residual was guaranteed in our last example. As you may recall, a guaranteed residual value is considered an additional payment by the lessee. Therefore, the present value of lease payments criterion would be reevaluated.

	RATE	NPER	PMT	PV	FV	Excel Formula
Given	5%	2	(34,972.07)	?	(57,882)	=PV(0.05,2,−34972.07,−57882)
Solution				$117,528		

Present value of lease payments criterion:
$147,500 (PV of lease payments of $117,528 plus lease prepayment of $34,972 less lease incentive of $5,000) **>** **$135,000** (90% of the fair value of $150,000)

Because the present value of the lease payments is greater than 90% of the fair value of the asset, the lease would be considered a finance lease, *not an operating lease*, for the lessee.

REVIEW 17-4 **LO17-4** **Accounting for Operating Lease by Lessee**

On January 1, 2020, Lessee Inc. signed a ten-year lease for office space for $75,000 annually, with the first payment due immediately. Lessee Inc. has the option to renew the lease for an additional four-year period on or before January 1, 2030, at market lease rates at the time of renewal. Lessee Inc. intends to evaluate rental options at the time of the option to renew. The economic life of the rental space is 30 years and the fair value of the rental space is $1 million. Lessee Inc. is not aware of the implicit rate of the lease but has an incremental borrowing rate of 6%. Lessee Inc. paid $1,000 on January 1, 2020, in initial direct costs.

a. How would Lessee Inc. classify the lease?
b. Prepare an amortization schedule for the lease liability.
c. Prepare an amortization schedule for the right-of-use asset.
d. Prepare the entries for Lessee Inc. for years 2020 and 2021, to record the right-of-use asset and lease liability, to record the lease payments, and to record lease expense.

More Practice:
17-44, 17-45, 17-46, 17-47, 17-76, 17-77, 17-78, 17-79
Solution on p. 17-84.

Account for an operating lease for a lessor

LO 17-5

From the perspective of the lessor, an operating lease is any lease other than a sales-type lease or a direct financing lease. In accounting for an operating lease, a lessor continues to maintain the leased asset on its balance sheet as shown in **Demo 17-5**. The asset is depreciated over its economic useful life (unless the lessor classifies the asset as inventory) and lease revenue is recognized over the term of the lease. Revenue is generally recognized on a straight-line basis. This means that if lease payments were $1,000 for the first two years and $1,600 for the third year of a three-year lease, lease revenue would be recognized as $1,200 per year ($3,600 ÷ 3). With an operating lease, the lessor will defer and expense initial direct costs over the lease term.

LO 17-5 Overview

Operating Lease—Lessor
- Meets *none* of the lease classification criteria
- Continue to record asset on the balance sheet
- Record depreciation expense over asset's useful life
- Record lease revenue each period

842-30-25-11 After the commencement date, a lessor shall recognize all of the following:

a. The lease payments as income in profit or loss over the lease term on a straight-line basis unless another systematic and rational basis is more representative of the pattern in which benefit is expected to be derived from the use of the underlying asset, subject to paragraph 842-30-25-12

b. Variable lease payments as income in profit or loss in the period in which the changes in facts and circumstances on which the variable lease payments are based occur

c. Initial direct costs as an expense over the lease term on the same basis as lease income (as described in (a)).

A summary of the accounting for the lessor for an operating lease follows.

Balance Sheet	Income Statement
Underlying asset remains on the balance sheet.	Depreciate asset over its useful life. Recognize lease revenue and depreciation expense in the income statement.

Lessor—Operating Lease

LO17-5 **Demo 17-5**

Demo MBC

Let's review an operating lease example and record entries from the *lessor's perspective.* On January 1, 2020 (lease commencement date), Lessor Inc. and Lessee Inc. sign a three-year non-cancelable lease for equipment. Details of the lease agreement follow.

1. The equipment has an estimated economic life of six years.
2. Lessor Inc. routinely leases this type of equipment to other companies.
3. The three lease payments are $34,972.07 each, payable January 1, 2020, 2021, and 2022.
4. Fair value of the asset at the commencement of the lease is $150,000, which is also the carrying value (cost) on the lessor's books.
5. The lease does not contain a renewal or purchase option, and the asset reverts to the lessor at the end of the three-year period.
6. The asset's unguaranteed residual value is estimated to be $57,882 at the end of the lease term.
7. Lessor Inc. depreciates assets using the straight-line method for book purposes.
8. The accounting year ends on December 31 for each entity.
9. The lessor's implicit interest rate, the rate that equates the present value of the payments to the asset's fair value, is 5%.
10. Initial direct costs of the lessor were $900 (legal fees related to the execution of the lease, paid in cash on January 1, 2020).

Answer the following questions from the perspective of Lessor Inc.

a. Determine the proper lease classification.
b. Record initial direct costs.
c. Prepare the lessor's journal entries for 2020, 2021, and 2022.
d. Show the impact on the lessor's balance sheet and income statement for 2020.

continued

continued from previous page

Solution

a. **Lease Classification**

First, the lease is classified as an operating lease because none of the lease classification criteria is met.

	Lease Classification Criteria	Analysis	Lease Criteria Met
1	Ownership transfer	Asset reverts to the lessor at the end of the three-year period.	
2	Purchase option	Lease does not contain a purchase option.	
3	Lease term length	Three-year lease term < 75% of the six-year useful life (4.5 years).	
4	PV of lease payments	$100,000 (PV of lease payments) < $135,000 (90% of fair value of $150,000).	
5	Alternative use	There are alternative uses for the equipment as the lessor often leases this equipment to other companies.	

RATE	NPER	PMT	PV	Excel Formula
5%	3	(34,972.07)	?	*=PV(0.05,3,−34972.07,0,1)*
			$100,000	

b. **Initial Direct Costs**

The following entry is recorded when the initial direct costs of $900 are incurred.

Assets = Liabilities + Equity
+900
−900
Init Dir Cost: 900 |
Cash: | 900

January 1, 2020—To record initial direct cost

	Debit	Credit
Initial Direct Cost	900	
Cash		900

c. **Lessor's Journal Entries—Years One through Three**

Lessor Inc. will record the following entries in years one through three.

Assets = Liabilities + Equity
+34,972 +34,972
Cash: 34,972 | 900
Def Lease Rev: | 34,972

January 1, 2020, 2021, and 2022—To record receipt of lease payment

	Debit	Credit
Cash	34,972	
Deferred Lease Revenue		34,972

Assets = Liabilities + Equity
−34,972 +34,972
Def Lease Rev: 34,972 | 34,972
Lease Rev: | 34,972

December 31, 2020, 2021, and 2022—To record lease revenue

	Debit	Credit
Deferred Lease Revenue	34,972	
Lease Revenue		34,972

Assets = Liabilities + Equity
−25,000 −25,000
Accum Deprec: | 25,000
Deprec Exp: 25,000 |

December 31, 2020, 2021, and 2022—To record depreciation expense

	Debit	Credit
Depreciation Expense	25,000	
Accumulated Depreciation ($150,000/6)		25,000

The equipment is depreciated over its useful life of 6 years, rather than the lease term because the lessor has control of the asset over its useful life.

Assets = Liabilities + Equity
−300 −300
Selling Exp: 300 |
Init Dir Cost: 900 | 300

December 31, 2020, 2021, and 2022—To amortize deferred cost (initial direct cost)

	Debit	Credit
Selling Expense	300	
Initial Direct Cost ($900/3)		300

d. **Lessor's Financial Statements—Year One**

Lessor Inc. will recognize the following amounts in its financial statements in year one.

Balance Sheet		Dec. 31, 2020
Assets		
Current assets		
Initial direct cost		$ 300
Noncurrent assets		
Initial direct cost		300
Equipment	$150,000	
Accumulated depreciation	(25,000)	125,000

Income Statement	2020
Revenue	
Lease revenue	$34,972
Expenses	
Depreciation expense	25,000
Selling expense	300

Accounting for Operating Lease by Lessor **LO17-5** **REVIEW 17-5**

On January 1, 2020, Lessor Inc. purchased a building for $3 million to be leased. The building is expected to have a 50-year life with no salvage value. The building was leased immediately by Lessee Inc. for $180,000 a year payable January 1 of each year starting January 1, 2020. The lease term is seven years with no renewal or purchase option reasonably expected to be exercised. There are no uncertainties surrounding collection. The implicit rate of the lease is 6% known by Lessee Inc.

a. How would Lessor Inc. classify the lease?

b. Prepare the entries for Lessor Inc. for 2020 to record the lease payment received, lease revenue, and depreciation.

c. Prepare the entries for Lessor Inc. to record initial direct costs of $1,200 paid in cash on January 1, 2020, for the execution of the lease and the adjusting entry at year-end 2020.

Review MBC

More Practice:
17-48, 17-49, 17-80, 17-81, 17-83
Solution on p. 17-85.

Explain lease modifications and lease remeasurements — LO 17-6

Lease modifications are changes to the terms and conditions of a contract that take place after a lease is in effect. For example, a lease term may be extended or terminated, or the timing of lease payments may be adjusted. A lease modification is treated as (1) a separate lease or (2) a modification to an existing lease depending on whether the modification grants additional rights at a **standalone price** (price at which a lessee would purchase the right separately). The treatment of lease modifications, along with cases for lease classification reassessment and remeasurement, are described as follows and illustrated in **Demo 17-6.**

LO 17-6 Overview

Lease Modifications
- Does *not* grant the lessee additional rights at standalone price: Results in a reassessment of lease classification and remeasurement
- Does grant the lessee additional rights at standalone price: Results in a new lease

Lease Modifications

If a modification grants the lessee an additional right at a standalone price, a **separate lease** is recorded at the lease modification date. This means that a separate lease (apart from the original lease) is created with additional rights at standalone prices. If these conditions are not met, the lease is considered to be a **single, modified lease**. In the case of a single, modified lease, the lease classification is reassessed and the lease liability is remeasured accordingly.

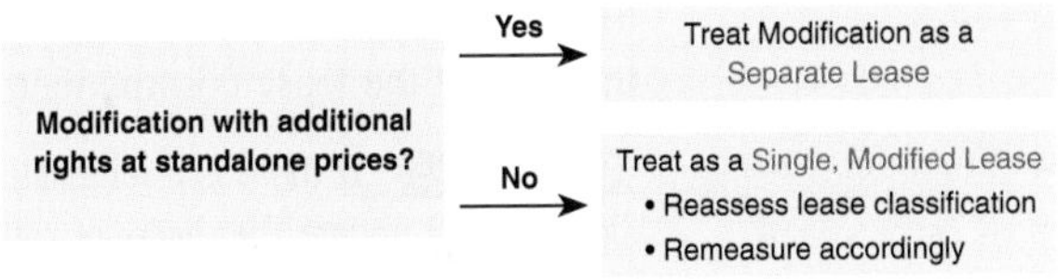

842-10-25-8 An entity shall account for a modification to a contract as a separate contract . . . when both of the following conditions are present:

a. The modification grants the lessee an additional right of use not included in the original lease.

b. The lease payments increase commensurate with the standalone price for the additional right of use, adjusted for the circumstances of the particular contract.

842-10-25-9 If a lease is modified and that modification is not accounted for as a separate contract in accordance with paragraph 842-10-25-8, the entity shall reassess the classification of the lease as of the effective date of the modification based on its modified terms and conditions and the facts and circumstances as of that date (for example, the fair value and remaining economic life of the underlying asset as of that date).

Additional Cases of Lease Classification Reassessment and Lease Remeasurement

For the lessee, a lease classification reassessment and/or a remeasurement of a lease liability may take place for reasons *other than a lease modification*. A lessor on the other hand, is not required to reassess a lease unless the lease contract is modified.

A lessee reassesses its lease classification and remeasures its lease payments in the following cases: change in lease term, and a change in whether the lessee is reasonably certain to exercise an option to purchase the underlying asset.

A lessee remeasures the lease payments (without a lease classification reassessment) in the following cases: resolution of a contingency affecting variable lease payments such that those payments become fixed, and a change in the probable amounts owed for a guaranteed residual value.

Remeasure a Lease Liability

- Modification not treated as a separate lease
- Change in assessment of lease term or exercise of purchase option
- Change in probable amount owed for guaranteed residual value
- Contingency resolution making variable payments fixed

842-10-25-1 In addition, a lessee also shall reassess the lease classification after the commencement date if there is a change in the lease term or the assessment of whether the lessee is reasonably certain to exercise an option to purchase the underlying asset.

842-10-35-4 A lessee shall remeasure the lease payments if any of the following occur:

a. The lease is modified, and that modification is not accounted for as a separate contract.

b. A contingency upon which some or all of the variable lease payments that will be paid over the remainder of the lease term are based is resolved such that those payments now meet the definition of lease payments. For example, an event occurs that results in variable lease payments that were linked to the performance or use of the underlying asset becoming fixed payments for the remainder of the lease term.

c. There is a change in any of the following:

1. The lease term . . . A lessee shall determine the revised lease payments on the basis of the revised lease term.
2. The assessment of whether the lessee is reasonably certain to exercise or not to exercise an option to purchase the underlying asset . . . A lessee shall determine the revised lease payments to reflect the change in the assessment of the purchase option.
3. Amounts probable of being owed by the lessee under residual value guarantees. A lessee shall determine the revised lease payments to reflect the change in amounts probable of being owed by the lessee under residual value guarantees.

In the case of remeasurement, the lease liability is remeasured and the adjustment to the lease liability is applied to the right-of-use asset. Generally, the lease liability is remeasured using the new information and any required changes are treated prospectively, similar to a change in estimate.

842-20-35-4 After the commencement date, a lessee shall remeasure the lease liability to reflect changes to the lease . . . A lessee shall recognize the amount of the remeasurement of the lease liability as an adjustment to the right-of-use asset.

The discount rate used for the remeasurement is updated at the time of remeasurement with the following exceptions. In the three cases outlined below in the authoritative guidance, the discount rate at the time of the lease commencement is used.

842-20-35-5 If there is a remeasurement of the lease liability in accordance with paragraph 842-20-35-4, the lessee shall update the discount rate for the lease at the date of remeasurement on the basis of the remaining lease term and the remaining lease payments unless the remeasurement of the lease liability is the result of one of the following:

a. A change in the lease term or the assessment of whether the lessee will exercise an option to purchase the underlying asset and the discount rate for the lease already reflects that the lessee has an option to extend or terminate the lease or to purchase the underlying asset.

b. A change in amounts probable of being owed by the lessee under a residual value guarantee (see paragraph 842-10-35-4(c)(3)).

c. A change in the lease payments resulting from the resolution of a contingency upon which some or all of the variable lease payments that will be paid over the remainder of the lease term are based (see paragraph 842-10-35-4(b)).

Demo 17-6 LO17-6 Lease Modifications and Lease Remeasurements

Demo MBC

Lease modifications resulting in a separate lease or modification to an existing lease for a lessee and a lessor are illustrated in the following three examples.

Example One—Lease Modification Resulting in a Separate (New) Lease

Lessee Corp. signs a 3-year lease contract to rent 500 square feet of office space from Lessor Corp. for $1,000 per month. At the end of the first year, Lessee Corp. and Lessor Corp. agree to amend the contract to include an additional 200 square feet of office space in the same building for the remaining two years of the lease. Lessee Corp pays an additional $400 per month for the additional space. The additional rent is the going rate for rental of office space ($2 per square foot).

continued

continued from previous page

Lessee Corp. will make one monthly payment of $1,400 per month after the modification. Determine whether the lease modification results in a separate lease or a lease remeasurement.

Solution

Lessee Corp. receives an additional right-of-use at a standalone price. Thus, the modification results in a new and separate lease. Lessee Corp. would account for the following items separately:

- Original lease for 3 years of 500 square feet.
- New lease for 2 years of 200 square feet.

The accounting for the original lease is not impacted. The new lease would be analyzed as any other new lease, starting with the lease classification analysis.

Example Two—Modification of an Existing Lease Leading to Lease Remeasurement

Lessee Corp. signs a 3-year lease contract to rent 500 square feet of office space with Lessor Corp. for $1,000 per month. At the end of the first year, Lessee Corp. and Lessor Corp. agree to amend the contract to include an additional 200 square feet of office space in the same building for the remaining two years of the lease. Lessee Corp. pays an additional $200 per month for the additional space. The additional rent at $1 per square foot is offered at a significant discount under the going rate of $2 per square foot. Lessee Corp. will make one monthly payment of $1,200 per month after the modification. Determine whether the lease modification results in a separate lease or a lease remeasurement.

Solution

In this case, the modification is considered an extension of the current lease because the additional rent is not at a standalone price. As a result, the current lease classification would be reassessed. After the lease classification is determined, the lease would be accounted for accordingly.

Example Three—Event Leading to Lease Remeasurement

On January 1, 2018, Lessee Corp. signs a lease contract with Lessor Corp. to lease equipment with an estimated useful life of six years. The lease has a 5-year term with no renewal option. Annual lease payments are $100,000 beginning on January 1, 2018. The lessee's discount rate is 5%. The lease contains a purchase option at the end of the lease for $30,000, but Lessee Corp. is not reasonably certain that it will exercise the purchase option. Lessee Corp. appropriately records the lease as a finance lease. The discount rate does not reflect the purchase option.

On January 1, 2020, Lessee Corp. now reasonably expects to purchase the equipment at the end of the lease term because of a significant increase in the sales forecasts of products produced by the equipment. After evaluating the classification criteria, Lessee Corp. determines that the lease remains a finance lease.

On the date of remeasurement of January 1, 2020 (before the lease payment is made), Lessee Corp's incremental borrowing rate is 4% and the carrying value of the right-of-use asset and lease liability are $272,757 and $185,941, respectively.

Record the entry required on January 1, 2020.

Solution

The lease liability would be remeasured using the updated discount rate because the lessee changed the assessment of whether to exercise a purchase option.

	RATE	NPER	PMT	PV	FV	TYPE	Excel Formula
Given	4%	3	(100,000)	?	(30,000)	1	=PV(0.04,3,–100000,–30000,1)
Solution				$315,279			

The revised lease liability is $315,279, which is an increase of $129,338 ($315,279 – $185,941). The increase to the liability is recorded as an adjustment to the right-of-use asset.

January 1, 2020—To remeasure lease liability

Right-of-Use Asset	129,338	
Lease Liability		129,338

Assets	=	Liabilities	+	Equity
+129,338		+129,338		

R-of-U Asset		Lease Liab	
Bal. 272,757			185,941 Bal.
129,338			129,338
402,095			315,279

REVIEW 17-6 **LO17-6** **Lease Modifications and Lease Remeasurements**

Review MBC

Determine whether the following changes would result in a (1) new lease, or a (2) reassessment of a lease classification and/or lease remeasurement.

Lease Scenario	New Lease, Remeasurement, Classification Reassessment and Remeasurement
a. Lessee Inc. guarantees the residual value of a vehicle (underlying) at the end of the lease term. The lessee now anticipates exceeding the allotted miles of the vehicle, causing the lessee's estimate of the residual value to drop by $5,000.	
b. A lessee of a manufacturing facility expands its current lease to include additional warehouse space at a standalone lease price.	
c. An existing lease was modified to extend the lease for an additional two years.	
d. Lessee Inc. unexpectedly disposed of a purchased vehicle in 2020. This event caused Lessee Inc. to now reasonably expect to exercise a purchase option on a leased vehicle at the end of its lease term in two years, while before, a purchase was not expected by the lessee.	

More Practice: 17-50, 17-85, 17-86, 17-105

Solution on p. 17-85.

LO 17-7 Explain the accounting policy election for short-term leases and other lease disclosures

LO 17-7 Overview

Short-term Lease Policy Election
- Lease with a duration of one year or less
- Lessee records lease expense on a straight-line basis over the lease term.
- Lessee does not record a right-of-use asset or a lease liability.

Disclosures
- Qualitative disclosures
- Quantitative disclosures

The accounting guidance provides information on requirements for recognition in the financial statements and for disclosure in the notes accompanying the financial statements for leases. We will highlight general reporting requirements in this section and also explain the policy election available for short-term leases (leases with a duration of one year or less).

Short-Term Leases

A **short-term lease** is defined by the lease standard as a lease with a duration of 12 months or less with no purchase option that the lessee is reasonably expected to exercise. You may recall that the lease criterion on the length of a lease requires lessees to consider renewal periods where the lessee is reasonably certain of renewal. Thus, a one-year lease where there is a reasonable certainty that the lessee will renew the lease is *not* considered a one-year lease under this short-term lease exception.

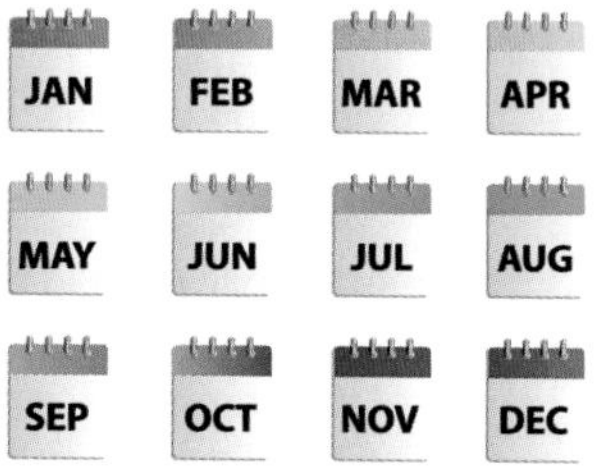

ASC Glossary Short-term lease: A lease that, at the commencement date, has a lease term of 12 months or less and does not include an option to purchase the underlying asset that the lessee is reasonably certain to exercise.

If a lessee identifies a short-term lease, the lessee may *elect* to expense the lease payments on a straight-line basis and not record a right-of-use asset and lease liability as illustrated in **Demo 17-7**. Once a lessee establishes a **short-term lease election** for a class of underlying assets, all future short-term leases for that class should consistently follow the lessee's policy. Otherwise, the company would need to account for a future change in policy as a change in accounting principle. A company would disclose a short-term lease disclosure along with a number of qualitative and quantitative disclosures in the notes accompanying the financial statements. (This exception applies only to the lessee, not the lessor.)

842-20-25-2 As an accounting policy, a lessee may elect not to apply the recognition requirements in this Subtopic to short-term leases. Instead, a lessee may recognize the lease payments in profit or loss on a straight-line basis over the lease term and variable lease payments in the period in which the obligation for those payments is incurred.

Short-Term Leases

LO17-7 **Demo 17-7**

Demo MBC

Lessee Inc. enters into a lease with Lessor Inc. for a 6-month rental of a storage unit for use during a construction project. The lease contract includes a 6-month renewal that the lessee is reasonably certain that it will exercise based upon the estimate of the construction project. Because the lease plus the renewal is one year or less (original lease term plus the renewal) the lessee has elected to account for the lease as a *short-term lease.* Record the entry for Lessee Inc. in year one if the monthly rent is $10,000. Assume each payment is made at the end of each month.

Solution

The lessee would record the following entry for each of the 12 months of the lease period.

To record monthly lease expense

Lease Expense	10,000	
Cash		10,000

Assets	= Liabilities +	Equity
−10,000		−10,000

Lease Exp		Cash	
10,000			10,000

Financial Statement Reporting of Leases

A lessee presents (or discloses) finance and operating right-of-use assets and liabilities on its balance sheet separately from each other and from other assets or liabilities.

842-20-45-1 A lessee shall either present in the statement of financial position or disclose in the notes all of the following:

a. Finance lease right-of-use assets and operating lease right-of-use assets separately from each other and from other assets

b. Finance lease liabilities and operating lease liabilities separately from each other and from other liabilities.

Right-of-use assets and lease liabilities shall be subject to the same considerations as other nonfinancial assets and financial liabilities in classifying them as current and noncurrent in classified statements of financial position.

Companies are prohibited from combining operating lease and finance lease right-to-use assets in a single line item or liabilities in a single line item.

842-20-45-3 In the statement of financial position, a lessee is prohibited from presenting both of the following:

a. Finance lease right-of-use assets in the same line item as operating lease right-of-use assets.

b. Finance lease liabilities in the same line item as operating lease liabilities.

In income, a lessee reports interest expense and amortization expense for a finance lease as it would report other such expenses. Lease expense for an operating lease would be reported in income from continuing operations.

The objective of lease disclosure is described in the authoritative guidance.

842-20-50-1 The objective of the disclosure requirements is to enable users of financial statements to assess the amount, timing, and uncertainty of cash flows arising from leases. To achieve that objective, a lessee shall disclose qualitative and quantitative information about all of the following:

a. Its leases.

b. The significant judgments made in applying the requirements in this Topic to those leases.

c. The amounts recognized in the financial statements relating to those leases.

A lessor of a sales-type (and direct financing) lease presents lease assets separately from other items on its balance sheet and identifies income arising from leases. Conversely, a lessor of an operating lease, continues to report assets according to other standards (such as continuing to report assets as property, plant, and equipment).

842-30-45-1 [For sales-type leases, a] lessor shall present lease assets (that is, the aggregate of the lessor's net investment in sales-type leases and direct financing leases) separately from other assets in the statement of financial position.

842-30-45-3 A lessor shall either present in the statement of comprehensive income or disclose in the notes income arising from leases. If a lessor does not separately present lease income in the statement of comprehensive income, the lessor shall disclose which line items include lease income in the statement of comprehensive income.

842-30-45-6 A lessor shall present the underlying asset subject to an operating lease in accordance with other Topics.

The following **qualitative items** should be disclosed in the notes accompanying the financial statements of both lessees and lessors:

1. Information about the nature of leases, including:
   - Lease description.
   - Basis on which variable lease payments are determined.
   - Terms and conditions of options to extend or terminate a lease.
   - Terms and conditions of residual value guarantees provided by a lessee.
   - The restrictions or covenants imposed by leases.
2. Information about leases creating significant rights and obligations that have not commenced.
3. Information about significant assumptions including determining whether a lease exists, allocation between lease and nonlease components, and the determination of a discount rate.

The following **quantitative items** should be disclosed in the notes accompanying the financial statements of lessees:

- Total lease costs including the following:
  - Finance lease cost.
  - Operating lease cost.
  - Short-term lease cost.
  - Variable lease cost.
- Cash paid for amounts included in the measurement of lease liabilities, segregated between operating and financing cash flows.
- Supplemental noncash information on lease liabilities due to obtaining right-of-use assets.
- Weighted-average remaining lease term and weighted-average discount rate.
- Maturity analysis showing the undiscounted cash flows on an annual basis for a minimum of each of the first five years and a total of the amounts for the remaining years (separately for finance and operating leases).

The following **quantitative items** should be disclosed in the notes accompanying the financial statements of lessors:

- Profit or loss recognized at the commencement date.
- Interest revenue either in aggregate or separated by components of the net investment in the lease.
- For operating leases, lease income relating to lease payments.
- Lease income relating to variable lease payments not included in the measurement of a lease receivable.
- Information about the management of risk associated with the residual value of leased assets.
- Significant changes in the balance of its unguaranteed residual assets and deferred selling profit on direct financing leases.
- Maturity analysis of its lease receivables, showing the undiscounted cash flows to be received on an annual basis for a minimum of each of the first five years and a total of the amounts for the remaining years.

MICROSOFT

Real World—DISCLOSURE OF FUTURE MINIMUM LEASE PAYMENTS

MICROSOFT CORPORATION [MSFT]

Microsoft Corporation disclosed the following future minimum lease payments in a recent Form 10-Q.

Future minimum lease payments under non-cancellable leases as of September 30, 2017 were as follows:

Year Ending June 30 (In millions)	Operating Leases	Finance Leases
2018 (excluding the three months ended September 30, 2017)	$1,110	$ 205
2019	1,385	281
2020	1,267	287
2021	1,022	293
2022	833	299
Thereafter	2,333	3,133
Total future minimum lease payments	7,950	4,498
Less imputed interest	(930)	(1,225)
Total	$7,020	$3,273

Accounting for a Short-Term Lease

LO17-7 REVIEW 17-7

Lessee Inc. entered into a contract on January 1, 2020, to lease a vehicle for one year, with monthly payments of $500, due at the end of each month. The vehicle has a fair value of $35,000. The lease agreement does not contain an option for purchase or renewal. The lessor's implicit rate of return is 6%. Gomez Inc. recognizes the lease under the short-term lease accounting election. Prepare the entries for Lessee Inc. for 2020 related to the lease.

Review MBC

More Practice: 17-51, 17-87, 17-107

Solution on p. 17-85.

Account for direct financing leases by the lessor

APPENDIX 17A
LO 17-8

Typically, a lease that does not meet any of the lease classification criteria would be classified as an operating lease by the lessor. However, there is an exception for lessors when a third-party guarantee of the residual value is involved. A lease is classified as a direct financing lease if the lessor determines that control of the underlying asset is transferred to the lessee when taking into account a guarantee of the residual value by a third party (typically an insurance company).

Lessor Accounting—Direct Financing Lease
- Control passes to the lessee with an involvement by a third party
- Defer selling profit at lease commencement
- Recognize selling loss at lease commencement
- Derecognize underlying asset and recognize lease receivable
- Recognize interest revenue over lease term using the effective interest method

LO 17-8 Overview

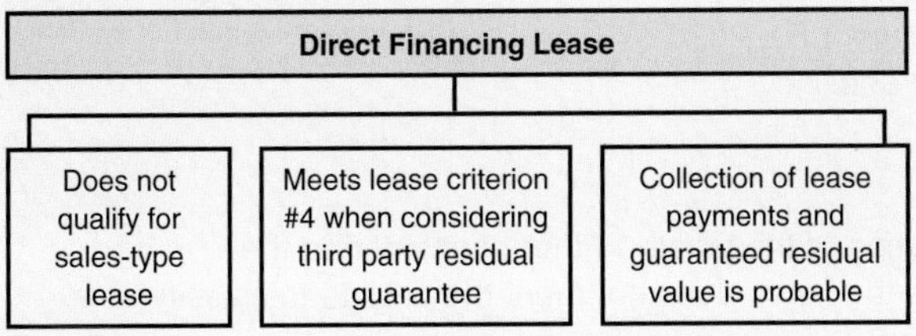
Direct Financing Lease
Does not qualify for sales-type lease
Meets lease criterion #4 when considering third party residual guarantee
Collection of lease payments and guaranteed residual value is probable

For a lease to be classified as a **direct financing lease**, it must first *not* qualify for a sales-type lease. Second, the lease must meet the present value of lease payments criterion **but** only by considering both the present value of the lease payments (as previously defined) *plus the present value of a residual guaranteed by a third party, arranged by the lessor*. In addition, the collection of the lease payments and any amounts necessary to satisfy a guaranteed residual value is considered probable.

Lease Classification Criteria
1. Ownership transfer
2. Purchase option
3. Lease term length
4. PV of lease payments
5. Alternative use

842-10-25-3b A lessor shall classify the lease as an operating lease unless both of the following criteria are met, in which case the lessor shall classify the lease as a direct financing lease:

1. The present value of the sum of the lease payments and any residual value guaranteed by the lessee that is not already reflected in the lease payments . . . and/or any other third party unrelated to the lessor equals or exceeds substantially all of the fair value of the underlying asset.
2. It is probable that the lessor will collect the lease payments plus any amount necessary to satisfy a residual value guarantee.

A summary of the accounting for the lessor for a direct financing lease follows.

Balance Sheet	Income Statement
Recognize a lease receivable (net of deferred gross profit) and derecognize the underlying asset.	Defer selling profit but recognize selling loss at the commencement of the lease.
Increase the lease receivable by interest revenue and decrease the lease receivable for lease payments collected.	Recognize interest revenue on the lease receivable using the effective interest method.

842-30-30-2 At the commencement date, for a direct financing lease, a lessor shall measure the net investment in the lease to include the [lease receivable] reduced by the amount of any selling profit.

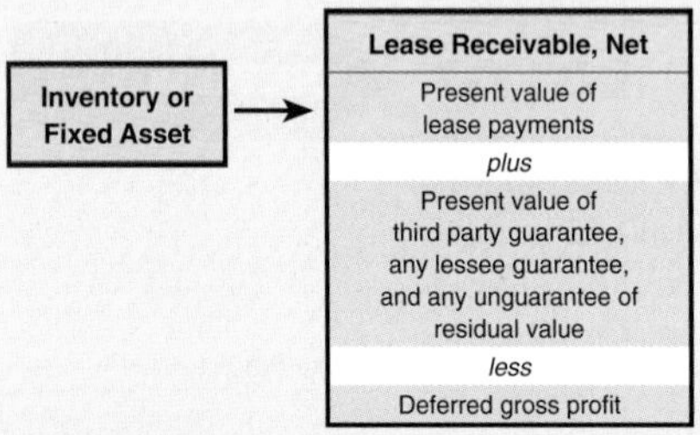

The lessor records a net lease receivable and derecognizes the leased asset. The lease receivable is equal to the lease receivable (including the present value of the third party guarantee) net of deferred gross profit. A selling loss would be recognized at the lease commencement. The decrease in the lease receivable causes the implicit rate of the lease to increase. The lessor computes the new discount rate that equates the balance in the net lease receivable to the lease payments and residual value. The new rate is used to produce an effective interest schedule in order to determine interest revenue recognized over the lease term.

Demo 17-8 **LO17-8** **Lessor—Direct Financing Lease**

Demo MBC

Consider the following lease contract from the *lessor's perspective.* Lessor Inc. enters into a 5-year lease of equipment with Lessee Inc. on January 1, 2020. The equipment is not specialized in nature, has a 10-year economic life, and ownership is not transferred to the lessee at lease end. In addition, the following information applies to this lease.

- Lease payments of $12,800 are due at the end of each year.
- The expected residual value of the equipment at lease end is $12,000. The lessor contracts with a third party (an insurance company) to insure the guaranteed residual value of $12,000.
- The rate implicit in the lease is 4.909%.
- The lessor concludes that the collection of lease payments (including the amount insured by a third party on the residual value) is probable.
- The fair value of the equipment is $65,000 and the carrying value of the equipment (recorded as inventory) to the lessor is $60,000.

Answer the following questions from the perspective of Lessor Inc.

a. Determine the proper lease classification.
b. Record the lease receivable (net) on January 1, 2020.
c. Prepare the lessor's journal entry on December 31, 2020.
d. Prepare the lessor's journal entry at lease end.

Solution

a. **Lease Classification**
The first step is to determine the classification of the lease. Without considering the guaranteed residual value by a third party, the lease does not meet the criteria to classify as a sales-type lease.

continued

continued from previous page

	Lease Classification Criteria	Analysis	Lease Criteria Met
1	Ownership transfer	Asset reverts to the lessor at the end of the five-year period.	
2	Purchase option	Lease does not contain a purchase option,	
3	Lease term length	Five-year length of the lease is < 75% of the equipment's useful life.	
4	PV of lease payments	$55,557 (PV of lease payments) < $58,500 (90% of fair value of $65,000).	
5	Alternative use	There are alternative uses for the equipment as the lessor often leases this equipment to other companies.	

	RATE	NPER	PMT	PV	Excel Formula
Given	4.909%	5	(12,800)	?	=PV(0.04909,5,−12800)
Solution				$55,557	

The lease does not meet any of the lease classification criteria, thus, it is not classified as a sales-type lease. However, in considering the guarantee by a third party for the residual value, the lease does meet the present value of lease payments test.

PV of lease payments	$65,000 (PV of lease payments) > $58,500 (90% of fair value of $65,000).	✔

Therefore, the lease meets the criteria of a direct financing lease, given that the payments are considered probable.

	RATE	NPER	PMT	PV	FV	Excel Formula
Given	4.909%	5	(12,800)	?	(12,000)	=PV(0.04909,5,−12800, −12000)
Solution				$65,000		

b. **Initial Recording of Lease Receivable, Net**

In the case of a direct financing lease, a net lease receivable is recorded of $60,000. The net lease receivable is equal to the lease receivable of $65,000, net of the deferred gross profit of $5,000 ($65,000 − $60,000).

January 1, 2020—To record lease receivable

Lease Receivable, Net	60,000	
Inventory		60,000

Assets = Liabilities + Equity
+60,000
−60,000

Lease Receiv, Net		Inventory	
60,000			60,000

Calculation of Lease Receivable, Net

Lease receivable	$65,000
Deferred gross profit	(5,000)
Lease receivable, net	$60,000

c. **Lessor's Journal Entry—Year One**

The net lease receivable is amortized over the lease term using the effective interest method, where the discount rate is a rate that will equate the balance in the net lease receivable to the lease payments and residual value.

Discount Rate	7.583%

We see that this rate is higher than the rate implicit in the lease of 4.909% because we are using the net lease receivable balance as the present value instead of the fair value of the equipment and recognizing the interest revenue of the deferred gross profit over the lease term. Using this discount rate of 7.583%, we can construct the amortization table of the net lease receivable using the effective interest method.

	RATE	NPER	PMT	PV	FV	Excel Formula
Given	?	5	12,800	(60,000)	12,000	=RATE(5, 12800, −60000, 12000)
Solution	7.583%					

continued

continued from previous page

Date	Lease Payment	Interest on Receivable		
	Dr. Cash Cr. Lease Receivable	Dr. Lease Receivable Cr. Interest Revenue[a]	Lease Receivable Net Reduction	Net Lease Receivable
Jan. 1, 2020 . . .				$60,000
Dec. 31, 2020 . . .	$ 12,800	$4,550	$ 8,250	51,750
Dec. 31, 2021 . . .	12,800	3,924	8,876	42,874
Dec. 31, 2022 . . .	12,800	3,251	9,549	33,325
Dec. 31, 2023 . . .	12,800	2,527	10,273	23,052
Dec. 31, 2024 . . .	24,800[b]	1,748	23,052	0

[a] Interest revenue is equal to 7.583% multiplied by the beginning of period lease receivable balance.

[b] Final payment includes the lease payment of $12,800 and the residual value of $12,000 to be reclassified to inventory.

The entry to record the first lease payment is recorded using amounts from the effective interest table above.

Assets = Liabilities + Equity
+12,800 +4,550

Cash: 12,800 |

Lease Receiv, Net: 60,000 | 8,250; 51,750 |

Interest Rev: | 4,550

December 31, 2020—To record lease payment

Cash	12,800	
Lease Receivable, Net ($12,800 − $4,550).		8,250
Interest Revenue.		4,550

The net lease receivable will be recorded in the balance sheet as $51,750* ($60,000 − $8,250) on December 31, 2020. The lessor will continue to derecognize the net lease receivable over the term of the lease.

*The net lease receivable of $51,750 is equal to the gross lease receivable of $55,391, less the deferred gross profit of $3,641. *Gross lease receivable* is equal to the original lease receivable of $65,000 less the amortization of $9,609 [($65,000 × 0.04909) − $12,800]. *Deferred gross profit* is equal to $5,000 (original gross profit) less the amortization of $1,359 [($65,000 × 0.04909) − ($60,000 × 0.07583)]. The components of net lease receivable will be disclosed in the notes accompanying the financial statements.

d. **Lessor's Journal Entry—Lease End**

At the end of the lease, assuming that the residual value was equal to $12,000, the lessor would record the following entry.

Assets = Liabilities + Equity
+12,000
−12,000

Inventory: 12,000 |

Lease Receiv, Net: Bal. 12,000 | 12,000; 0 |

December 31, 2024—To record inventory at lease-end

Inventory	12,000	
Lease Receivable, Net		12,000

REVIEW 17-8 LO17-8 Accounting for Direct Financing Leases

On January 1, 2020, Lessor Inc. entered into a 4-year lease agreement with Lessee Inc. to lease equipment with a useful life of 6 years. The equipment will be returned to the lessor at the end of the lease term and is expected to have alternative uses. The lessor obtained a guarantee from a third party (insurance company) for the expected residual of $5,000 at the end of the lease term. Lease payments are $10,000 due annually at the end of each year. The implicit rate of the lease is 6.65682%. The fair value of the equipment is $38,000 and the carrying value is $35,000.

a. Determine the proper classification of the lease for the lessor.

b. Record the lessor's entry on January 1, 2020.

c. Compute the discount rate used to amortize the net lease receivable.

d. Prepare the schedule to amortize the lease receivable.

e. Prepare the lessor's entry on December 31, 2020.

Review MBC

More Practice:
17-118, 17-119, 17-122

Solution on p. 17-86.

Describe the difference in accounting for a sale-leaseback versus a failed sale

APPENDIX 17B
LO 17-9

Sale-Leaseback or Failed Sale
- Sale-leaseback
  - Control of asset is transferred to the buyer
  - Lessee records a sale and accounts for an operating lease
- Failed sale
  - Control of asset is not transferred to the buyer
  - Lessee records a finance liability

LO 17-9 Overview

Sale-leaseback transactions are essentially financing transactions. In a sale-leaseback, one party (seller/lessee) sells an asset to another party (buyer/lessor) and then simultaneously leases the same asset back from the buyer.

Companies engage in sale-leaseback transactions for a variety of reasons. For a lessee, a sale-leaseback reduces exposure to the risk of owning assets and provides an immediate cash inflow. If a company owns fully depreciated assets that afford no tax savings beyond maintenance and insurance expenses, selling the equipment and leasing it back may increase tax benefits through deductible lease payments.

In the majority of sale-leaseback transactions, the sale of assets generates immediate cash. If liquidity is a problem, or if expansion capital is needed, the sale-leaseback of assets (without giving up operating possession) provides an immediate inflow of cash of up to 100% of the asset's current fair value. In contrast, asset-secured bank loans are typically limited to 75% or 80% of the asset's fair value. The lessor, on the other hand, is at an advantage in that the earnings on the leaseback arrangement may be higher than under conventional loans.

In accounting for a sale-leaseback, it is important to determine whether the buyer has obtained control of the asset in order to record a sale of the asset. In determining whether a sale has taken place, a review of the indicators in the revenue recognition standard may be helpful: buyer has a right to payment, legal title, physical possession, significant risks and rewards of ownership, and has accepted the asset. See Chapter 7 for further discussion on these indicators. Not all indicators must be met for a sale to have taken place. Another factor in determining whether control has transferred is through a review of the lease classification. If a seller classifies a leaseback as a finance lease, no sale has occurred and this would be considered a **failed sale**. Classifying a lease as a finance lease indicates an effective purchase of an asset and not a lease. On the other hand, if a seller classifies a leaseback as an operating lease, a sale has occurred and would be appropriately recorded as a lease. We illustrate the accounting for a sale-leaseback and a failed sale in **Demo 17-9**.

If a transfer of an asset is *considered a sale*, the seller/lessee accounts for the transaction as follows.

- Recognize the sales price when buyer/lessor takes control of asset.
- Derecognize the carrying amount of asset and record a gain or loss.
- Account for the operating lease as discussed previously in this chapter.

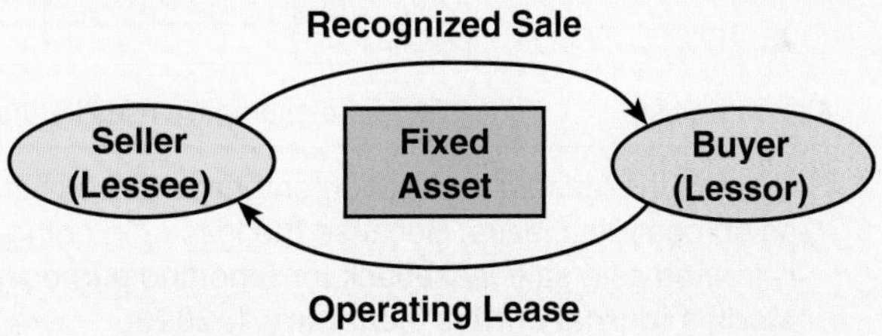

If a transfer of the asset is *not considered a sale* (such as a failed sale), the debtor/lessee accounts for the transaction as follows.

- Do not adjust the carrying value of asset at the transaction date but continue to depreciate the asset over its useful life.
- Recognize "sales" proceeds as a loan.
- Allocate payments to interest expense and to principal reduction of the loan over the lease term.

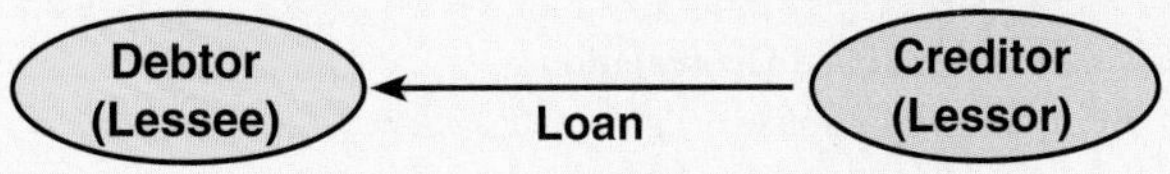

Demo 17-9 LO17-9 Sale-leaseback and Failed Sale

Example One—To Record Sale-Leaseback

To obtain an immediate cash flow, Merill Co. negotiated a sale-leaseback agreement with Leasing Solutions Inc. On January 1, 2020, Merill Co. sells a warehouse to Leasing Solutions Inc. for $95,000, the fair value of the warehouse. The warehouse is carried on Merill's books at $80,000 (cost of $200,000 less accumulated depreciation of $120,000) and has an estimated remaining useful economic life of 10 years (total life, 25 years).

In conjunction with the sale of the warehouse, Merill Co. and Leasing Solutions Inc. enter into a five-year lease. The lease contains no transfer of title, purchase option, and the warehouse could have alternative uses as the warehouse is used primarily for storage. The implicit rate of the lease is 8%, known by the lessee. Annual lease payments, starting January 1, 2020, are $16,890, due at the end of each year. The lessor estimates that the warehouse will have a $40,500 residual value that is *not* guaranteed by the lessee. Answer the following questions from the perspective of Merill Co.

a. Determine the appropriate lease classification.
b. Prepare Merill's journal entries at January 1, 2020.
c. Prepare Merill's journal entry at December 31, 2020.

Solution

a. **Lease Classification**

In order to determine whether control of the warehouse has transferred from Leasing Solutions Inc. (Lessor) to Merill Co. (Lessee) it is necessary to determine the classification of the lease.

	Lease Classification Criteria	Analysis	Lease Criteria Met
1	Ownership transfer	Asset reverts to the lessor at the end of the five-year period.	
2	Purchase option	Lease does not contain a purchase option.	
3	Lease term length	Length of the lease is only 50% of the economic life of warehouse.	
4	PV of lease payments	$67,437 (PV of lease payments) < $85,500 (90% of fair value of $95,000).	
5	Alternative use	There are alternative uses for the warehouse.	

	RATE	NPER	PMT	PV	Excel Formula
Given	8%	5	(16,890)	?	=PV(0.08,5,–16890)
Solution				$67,437	

None of the lease classification criteria is met which indicates that the lease will be classified as an operating lease. Because the lease did not transfer control to the lessee, the transaction is treated as a sale-leaseback for reporting purposes.

b. **Merill's journal entries—January 1, 2020**

Merill Inc. records a gain on the sale of the warehouse to Leasing Solutions Inc. as follows.

January 1, 2020—To record gain on sale of warehouse

Cash	95,000	
Accumulated Depreciation	120,000	
Warehouse		200,000
Gain on Sale-Leaseback		15,000

Assets = Liabilities + Equity
+95,000 / +120,000 / −200,000 = +15,000

Cash		Accum Deprec	
95,000		120,000	120,000 Bal.

Warehouse		Gain—Leaseback	
Bal. 200,000	200,000		15,000

Also, on the same day, Merill Inc. records a right-of-use asset and lease liability related to the operating lease.

January 1, 2020—To record right-of-use asset and lease liability

Right-of-Use Asset	67,437	
Lease Liability		67,437

Assets = Liabilities + Equity
+67,437 = +67,437

R-of-U Asset		Lease Liab	
67,437			67,437

continued

continued from previous page

c. **Merill's journal entry—December 31, 2020**
On December 31, 2020, Merill Inc. records the following entry related to the first lease payment obtained from the partial amortizations schedules included below.

December 31, 2020—To record lease expense

Lease Expense	16,890	
Lease Liability		5,395
Right-of-Use Asset		11,495

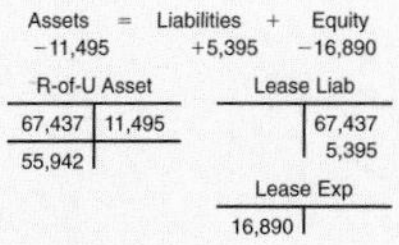

December 31, 2020—To record lease payment

Lease Liability	16,980	
Cash		16,980

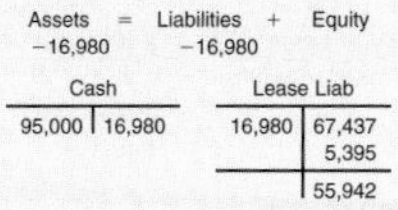

Assets = Liabilities + Equity
−16,980 −16,980
Cash
95,000 16,980
Lease Liab
16,980 67,437
5,395
55,942

Lease Liability Amortization Schedule (Partial)

Date	Lease Payment	Interest on Liability	Lease Liability Reduction	Net Lease Liability
Jan. 1, 2020 . . .				$67,437
Dec. 31, 2020 . . .	$16,890	$5,395	$11,495	55,942

Right-of-Use Asset Amortization Schedule (Partial)

Date	Lease Expense Straight-Line	Interest on Liability	Right-of-Use Asset Amortization	Net Right-of-Use Asset
Jan. 1, 2020 . . .				$67,437
Dec. 31, 2020 . . .	$16,890	$5,395	$11,495	55,942

Example Two—To Record a Failed Sale
Let's assume the same circumstances as Example 1, except that the lease term is 8 years and the payments are now $14,651. Answer the following questions from the perspective of Merill Co.

a. Determine the appropriate lease classification.
b. Prepare Merill's journal entry at January 1, 2020.
c. Prepare Merill's journal entry at December 31, 2020.

Solution
a. **Lease Classification**

	Lease Classification Criteria	Analysis	Lease Criteria Met
1	Ownership transfer	Asset reverts to the lessor at the end of the five-year period.	
2	Purchase option	Lease does not contain a purchase option.	
3	Lease term length	Length of the lease is 80% of the economic life of warehouse.	✔
4	PV of lease payments	$84,194 (PV of lease payments) < $85,500 (90% of fair value of $95,000).	
5	Alternative use	There are alternative uses for the warehouse.	

	RATE	NPER	PMT	PV	Excel Formula
Given	8%	8	(14,651)	?	*=PV(0.08,8,−14651)*
Solution				$84,194	

The lease qualifies as a finance lease because the lease term of 8 years is 80% of the economic life of 10 years. This qualification as a finance lease precludes the recording of a sale of the warehouse to Leasing Solutions Inc. Thus, this transaction will be recorded similarly to a loan.

b. **Merill's journal entry—January 1, 2020**
For a failed sale, the transaction results in the recording of a note payable by Merill.

continued

continued from previous page

Assets = Liabilities + Equity
+95,000 +95,000
Cash: 95,000 (Dr) | Note Payable: 95,000 (Cr)

January 1, 2020—To record note payable on failed sale

Cash	95,000	
Note Payable		95,000

c. **Merill's journal entry—December 31, 2020.**
On December 31, 2020, the lease payment and depreciation expense would be recorded as follows.

Assets = Liabilities + Equity
−14,651 −6,651 −8,000
Cash: 95,000 (Dr) | 14,651 (Cr); Note Payable: 6,651 (Dr) | 95,000 (Cr); Interest Exp: 8,000 (Dr)

December 31, 2020—To record lease payment

Interest Expense (0.08 × $100,000)	8,000	
Note Payable ($14,651 − $8,000)	6,651	
Cash		14,651

Assets = Liabilities + Equity
−8,000 −8,000
Accum Deprec: 8,000 (Cr); Deprec Exp: 8,000 (Dr)

December 31, 2020—To record depreciation expense

Depreciation Expense ($80,000/10)	8,000	
Accumulated Depreciation		8,000

REVIEW 17-9 LO17-9 Accounting for Sale-Leaseback

Review MBC

Wal-Market Inc. sells a building currently used to Diversified Investors for $9 million, its current fair value. Prior to the sale, the carrying value of the building was $7 million (original cost of $15 million). The estimated remaining useful life of the building is 20 years, with no estimated residual value; straight-line depreciation is used. On January 1, 2020, Wal-Market Inc. signed a 15-year noncancelable leaseback agreement that has an 8% implicit rate of interest for the lessor, known to the lessee. The lessee's incremental borrowing rate also is 7%. Annual payments of $1,051,466 start on December 31, 2020. The lease agreement does not contain a purchase option, the lessee does not guarantee a residual value, and the building does not revert to the lessee at lease end. The building would have alternative uses at lease end.

a. Determine the lease classification for Wal-Market Inc.

b. Record the journal entries for Wal-Market Inc. for 2020.

More Practice: 17-120, 17-121, 17-123, 17-124

Solution on p. 17-86.

Questions

17-1. What are the advantages of leasing from the lessee's perspective?

17-2. What is meant by capitalization of a lease from the viewpoint of the lessee?

17-3. What types of leases are capitalized by a lessee? Under what condition would a lessee not capitalize a lease?

17-4. From a lessee's standpoint, leases are classified as finance or operating leases. What criteria are used to identify a finance lease?

17-5. What lease payments are used in determining whether the present value of lease payments is greater than or equal to substantially all of the fair value of the underlying asset?

17-6. How is a lease liability calculated?

17-7. How is a right-of-use asset calculated?

17-8. How does a lessee determine what interest rate is appropriate to discount the lease liability?

17-9. How does an unguaranteed residual value in a sales-type lease affect the lessor's accounting in recording the entries at the date of inception of the lease?

17-10. How is a guaranteed residual value treated differently by the lessee when determining the classification of leases as compared to the recording of a lease liability?

17-11. Define initial direct costs.

17-12. How does a lessee derecognize a right-of-use asset and lease liability over the term of an operating lease?

17-13. How does a lessee derecognize a right-of-use asset and lease liability over the term of a finance lease?

17-14. If a lessee records a right-of-use asset related to a finance lease, over what period would the lessee recognize amortization expense? What conditions impact your answer?

17-15. How does a lessor account for an operating lease?

17-16. How does a lessor account for a sales-type lease?

17-17. If a lessor determines that payments from a lessee pertaining to a sales-type lease are not probable, how would the lessor account for the lease?

17-18. What qualifies as a short-term lease and how would a lessee account for a short-term lease?

17-19. What determines whether a lease modification results in a separate lease or in a modification of an existing lease?

17-20. What types of qualitative information should be disclosed about a company's leases?

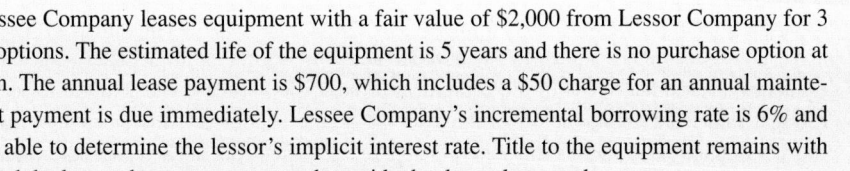

Brief Exercises

Brief Exercise 17-21 Classifying Leases **LO1**

On January 1, 2020, Lessee Company leases equipment with a fair value of $2,000 from Lessor Company for 3 years, with no renewal options. The estimated life of the equipment is 5 years and there is no purchase option at the end of the lease term. The annual lease payment is $700, which includes a $50 charge for an annual maintenance contract. The first payment is due immediately. Lessee Company's incremental borrowing rate is 6% and the lessee is not readily able to determine the lessor's implicit interest rate. Title to the equipment remains with the lessor at lease end and the lessee does not guarantee the residual value at lease end.

a. Determine the classification of the lease for Lessee Company.

b. Determine the classification of the lease for Lessor Company.

Brief Exercise 17-22 Classifying Leases **LO1**

On January 1, 2020, Lessee Company leases a vehicle with a fair value of $30,000 from Lessor Company for 3 years, with no renewal options. The estimated life of the vehicle is 6 years and Lessee Company has an option to purchase the vehicle at lease end at the vehicle's fair value which the lessee is not expected to exercise. The monthly lease payment is $520, with the first payment due immediately. Lessee Company's incremental borrowing rate is 6% and the lessee is not readily able to determine the lessor's implicit interest rate. Title to the equipment remains with the lessor at lease end and the lessee does not guarantee the residual value at lease end. Lessee Company will pay for the maintenance of the vehicle separately from the lease.

a. Determine the classification of the lease for Lessee Company.

b. Determine the classification of the lease for Lessor Company.

Brief Exercise 17-23 Classifying Leases **LO1**

A lessee is evaluating whether a lease term is a major part of the remaining life of an asset in order to determine the proper lease classification. The lessee leases office space through a lease with a 10-year term. The lease has a renewal option for an additional 5 years at a rental price that is adjusted to market at time of renewal. The office building has a remaining useful life of 20 years from the commencement of the lease. The lessee plans to make a significant investment in leasehold improvements (useful life of 15 years) at the commencement of the lease. Based on this information only, how would the lessee classify this lease?

Brief Exercise 17-24 Identifying Lease Payments **LO1**

For each of the following four *separate* finance lease scenarios, determine the lease payment that the lessee should use to determine the appropriate lease classification.

a. Lease payments are $3,000 per month plus 5% of lessee net sales. Lessee sales for year one are estimated to be $100,000.

b. Lease payments are computed as the *greater of* (a) 5% of lessee net sales or (b) $3,000. Lessee sales for year one are estimated to be $100,000.

c. Annual lease payments are 10% of lessee annual sales, with no fixed portion. Lessee sales for year one are estimated to be $100,000.

d. Lease payments total $5,000 in year one and increase each year based on the annual increase in the CPI at the end of the preceding year. The CPI at the end of the current year is expected to be 2%.

Brief Exercise 17-25 Identifying Lease Payments **LO1**

For each of the following four *separate* finance lease scenarios, determine the lease payment that the lessee should use to determine the appropriate lease classification.

a. An annual lease payment for equipment was $50,000 and included a fee of $5,000 for maintenance of the equipment.

b. An annual lease payment for equipment was $55,000 and included both a fee of $4,000 for maintenance and $5,000 for insurance on the equipment.

c. An annual lease for a building was $120,000 and included $10,000 for property taxes and $6,000 for parking lot maintenance.

Brief Exercise 17-26 Recording Finance Lease Journal Entries—No Residual Value **LO2** *Hint:* See Demo 17-2A

Pier10 Inc. entered into a 5-year lease and recorded a right-of-use asset and lease liability of $88,000 on January 1, 2020. Pier10 Inc. was aware of the lessor's implicit rate of interest of 5%. The equipment under lease had an estimated 5-year useful life with no residual value. The first lease payment of $19,358 was due upon commencement of the lease. Record Pier10 Inc.'s journal entries during the year of 2020 assuming that the lease is properly classified as a finance lease.

a. January 1, 2020 Record the right-of-use asset and lease liability.

b. January 1, 2020 Record the lease payment.

c. December 31, 2020 Record the adjusting entries.

Brief Exercise 17-27 Reporting a Finance Lease **LO2** *Hint:* See Demo 17-2A

Referring to the information in Brief Exercise 17-26, show the balance sheet presentation on December 31, 2020, and the income statement presentation for the year ended December 31, 2020.

Brief Exercise 17-28 Computing Lease Liability **LO2**

Lessee Company enters into a 6-year finance lease of non-specialized equipment with Lessor Company on January 1, 2020. Lessee has agreed to pay $28,000 annually beginning immediately on January 1, 2020. The lessor estimates the residual value of the equipment to be $5,000 at lease end, but the lessee has not guaranteed the residual value. The economic life of the asset is 7 years. The lessee's incremental borrowing rate is 7% and the lessor's implicit rate is not readily determinable by the lessee company. What is the value of the lease liability on January 1, 2020, assuming that the lease is properly classified as a finance lease?

Brief Exercise 17-29 Computing Lease Liability **LO2**

Referring to the information in Brief Exercise 17-28, assume the same information except that the lessee guaranteed the residual value for $5,000 at the end of the lease term. Compute the value of the lease liability for the lessee on January 1, 2020, under the following separate scenarios.

a. The lessee estimates that the underlying asset will have a fair value of $5,000 at the end of the lease.

b. The lessee estimates that the underlying asset will have a fair value of $2,000 at the end of the lease.

Brief Exercise 17-30 Recording Finance Lease Journal Entries—Purchase Option **LO2** *Hint:* See Demo 17-2C

Lessee Company enters into a 6-year finance lease of non-specialized equipment with Lessor Company on January 1, 2020. Lessee has agreed to pay $28,000 annually beginning immediately on January 1, 2020. The lease includes an option for the lessee to purchase the equipment at $3,000, which is $2,000 below the estimated fair value at lease end. Lessee Company is reasonably certain that it will exercise the purchase option. The economic life of the asset is 7 years. The lessee's incremental borrowing rate is 7% and the lessor's implicit rate is not readily determinable by the lessee. Record Lessee Company's journal entries on (a) January 1, 2020, and (b) December 31, 2020, assuming that the lease is properly classified as a finance lease.

Brief Exercise 17-31 Recording Finance Lease Journal Entries—Guaranteed Residual Value **LO2** *Hint:* See Demo 17-2B

Smith, the lessee, signs an 8-year lease agreement of a floor of a building on December 31, 2020 that requires annual payments of $70,000, beginning immediately. The residual value is guaranteed to the lessor of $50,000 at the end of the lease term. Smith estimates that the residual will have a value of $30,000 at the end of the lease term. Smith is aware of the lessor's implicit rate of interest of 7%. Record Smith's journal entries on December 31, 2020, assuming that the lease is properly classified as a finance lease.

Brief Exercise 17-32 Recording Finance Lease Journal Entries—Nonlease and Initial Direct Costs **LO2**

Frontier Inc. enters into an 8-year lease contract to lease equipment with a useful life of 8 years. Annual lease payments are due with the first payment made immediately on January 1, 2020, the commencement of the lease. No residual value is expected or guaranteed of the underlying equipment. Lease payments consist of (a) fixed lease payment of $33,000, (b) insurance on the equipment of $1,000, and (c) maintenance on the equipment of $1,200. Frontier Inc. also paid legal fees of $850 related to the execution of the lease on January 1, 2020. Record Frontier's journal entries at the commencement of the finance lease assuming an implicit interest rate of 6%, known by Frontier.

Brief Exercise 17-33 Recording Sales-Type Lease Journal Entries—No Residual Value **LO3** *Hint:* See Demo 17-3A

Franklin Co. leased its manufactured equipment to Parker Inc. for a 4-year term. Franklin Co. reported a book value of $55,000 for the equipment in its inventory account. The lease commenced on January 1, 2020, with the first annual payment of $18,500 due immediately. The equipment has a useful life of 4 years, an estimated fair value of $68,880, and no residual or salvage value. The implicit rate of the lease is 5% and collectibility of the lease payments from Parker is probable. Record Franklin's journal entries at the commencement of the sales-type lease.

Brief Exercise 17-34 Recording Sales-Type Lease Journal Entries—No Residual Value **LO3** *Hint:* See Demo 17-3A

Referring to the information in Brief Exercise 17-33, record Franklin's required journal entry to record interest revenue on December 31, 2020.

Brief Exercise 17-35 Recording Sales-Type Lease Journal Entries—No Residual Value **LO3**

Referring to the information in Brief Exercise 17-33, record Franklin's required journal entry at the commencement of the lease, assuming that the collectibility of payments is not probable.

Brief Exercise 17-36 Recording Sales-Type Lease Journal Entries—Residual Value **LO3** *Hint:* See Demo 17-3B

Kelly Inc. leased equipment, originally reported in inventory, to General Engines Inc. for a 4-year lease term and recorded the lease as a sales-type lease. At the expiration of the lease, the equipment had a fair value equal to the guaranteed residual value of $13,000, and was returned to Kelly Inc. Record Kelly Inc.'s journal entry for the return of the equipment.

Brief Exercise 17-37 Recording Sales-Type Lease Journal Entries—Residual Value **LO3** *Hint:* See Demo 17-3B

Referring to the information in Brief Exercise 17-31, record the lessor's journal entries on December 31, 2020, assuming that the lease is properly classified as a sales-type lease. The carrying value of the equipment is $450,000 at the commencement of the lease.

Brief Exercise 17-38 Reporting a Sales-Type Lease **LO3**

A lessor, Ace Corp. enters into an equipment lease with a lessee, Spades Inc. The terms of the lease require annual lease payments of $48,000 over a 10-year period, with the first payment due immediately upon the commencement of the lease on January 1, 2020. There is no estimated residual value. The implicit rate of the lease is 5%. What amount would the lessor report in its income statement (ignoring taxes) for the year ended December 31, 2020?

Brief Exercise 17-39 Reporting a Sales-Type Lease **LO3**

Hearts Inc. (Lessor) enters into a 10-year lease of equipment with Spades Inc. (Lessee) on January 1, 2020. Hearts Inc. sells and leases the equipment, which is not specialized in nature and is expected to have alternative use to Hearts Inc. at the end of the 10-year lease term. Under the lease, Hearts Inc. receives annual lease payments of $15,000, payable at the beginning of each year. Lessor expects no residual value of the equipment at the end of the 10-year lease term. The equipment has an estimated remaining economic life of 11 years, a carrying amount of $100,000, and a fair value of $115,000. Hearts Inc. incurred and paid costs of $2,000 for a broker's commission as a result of obtaining the lease. The rate implicit in the lease is 6.4632%. What amounts would the lessor report in its income statement (ignoring taxes) for the year ended December 31, 2020?

Brief Exercise 17-40 Calculating Lessor Payment—No Residual Value **LO3** *Hint:* See Demo 17-3A

Konverse Inc. is negotiating an agreement to lease equipment to a lessee for 6 years. The fair value of the equipment is $50,000 and the lessor expects a rate of return of 7% on the lease contract and no residual value. If the first annual payment is required at the commencement of the lease, what fixed lease payment should Konverse Inc. charge in order to earn its expected rate of return on the contract?

Brief Exercise 17-41 Calculating Lessor Payment—Purchase Option **LO3**

Armstrong Inc. is negotiating an agreement to lease equipment to a lessee for 5 years. The fair value of the equipment is $150,000 and the lessor expects a rate of return of 6% on the lease contract. The lessee has an option to purchase the equipment at the end of the 5-year term at $25,000, which is 20% under the estimated fair value at that time. If the first annual payment is required at the commencement of the lease, what fixed lease payment should Armstrong Inc. charge in order to earn its expected rate of return on the contract?

Brief Exercise 17-42 Calculating Lessor Payment—Unguaranteed Residual Value **LO3**

Marshall Inc. is negotiating an agreement to lease equipment to a lessee for 5 years. The equipment has a useful life of 8 years. The fair value of the equipment is $80,000 and the lessor expects a rate of return of 5% on the lease contract. Marshall Inc. expects the equipment to have a fair value of $30,000 at the end of 5 years; however, the lessee does not guarantee the residual amount. If the first annual payment is required at the commencement of the lease, what fixed lease payment should Marshall Inc. charge in order to earn its expected rate of return on the contract?

Brief Exercise 17-43 Calculating Lessor Payment—Guaranteed Residual Value **LO3** *Hint:* See Demo 17-3B

Quest Inc. is negotiating an agreement to lease equipment to a lessee for 8 years. The equipment has a useful life of 10 years. The fair value of the equipment is $40,000 and the lessor expects a rate of return of 8% on the lease contract. The lessee guarantees a residual value of $10,000 at the end of the 8-year lease term. If the first annual payment is required at the end of the first year following the commencement of the lease, what fixed lease payment should Quest Inc. charge in order to earn its expected rate of return on the contract?

Brief Exercise 17-44
Reporting Operating Lease **LO4**
Hint: See Demo 17-4A

Solutions Inc. signs a 10-year lease for a building owned by Property Inc. that is appropriately classified as an operating lease by both the lessee and lessor. Lease payments are $150,000 per year. The building has an estimated useful life of 30 years with no salvage value. What amount would Solutions Inc. report in its income statement (ignoring taxes) for the year ended December 31, 2020?

Brief Exercise 17-45
Recording Operating Lease Journal Entries—Lessee **LO4**
Hint: See Demo 17-4A

Gomez Inc. leases a vehicle from CareMax Inc. on January 1, 2020, for a three-year period, appropriately classified by Gomez Inc. as an operating lease. Gomez agrees to make $6,000 annual payments beginning on January 1, 2020. Prepare the journal entries for Gomez in 2020 assuming that Gomez is aware of the rate implicit in the lease of 6%.

a. January 1, 2020—Record the right-of-use asset.
b. January 1, 2020—Record the lease payment.
c. December 31, 2020—Record the adjusting entry.

Brief Exercise 17-46
Recording Operating Lease Journal Entries—Lessee **LO4**
Hint: See Demo 17-4A

Lessor Co. enters into an operating lease of property with Lessee Co. on January 1, 2020, for a five-year term at an annual fixed lease payment of $10,000 (beginning of period payments). Prepare the journal entries in 2020 for the lessee assuming that the lessee is aware of the rate implicit in the lease of 5%.

a. January 1, 2020—Record the right-of-use asset.
b. January 1, 2020—Record the lease payment.
c. December 31, 2020—Record the adjusting entry.

Brief Exercise 17-47
Determining Amounts in Operating Lease **LO4**
Hint: See Demo 17-4B

Kulver's Inc. leases equipment from Equip Inc. on January 1, 2020, under a 3-year *operating lease*. Kulver's agrees to pay Equip Inc. $15,000 annually with the first payment due on January 1, 2020. As an incentive for Kulver's to sign the lease by January 1, Equip Inc. paid Kulver's Inc. $700. Kulver's also incurred legal fees for the review of the lease agreement ($200) and salaries for employees involved in negotiating the lease ($1,300). Assuming an incremental borrowing rate of 7% for Kulver's Inc., determine the value of the lease liability and the right-of-use asset on January 1, 2020, for Kulver's.

Brief Exercise 17-48
Reporting Operating Lease—Lessor **LO5**
Hint: See Demo 17-5

Referring to the information in Brief Exercise 17-44, and assuming that the building has a fair value of $2,000,000 at the commencement of the lease, what amount would Property Inc. recognize in its income statement (ignoring taxes) for the year ended December 31, 2020? Assume that Property Inc. is using the straight-line method to depreciate buildings.

Brief Exercise 17-49
Recording Operating Lease—Lessor **LO5**
Hint: See Demo 17-5

Referring to the information in Brief Exercise 17-45, prepare the journal entries in 2020 for CareMax Inc. assuming that the fair value of the vehicle is $28,000 and it has a useful life of 6 years with no salvage value (depreciated using the straight-line method).

Brief Exercise 17-50
Remeasuring a Lease Liability **LO6**
Hint: See Demo 17-6

Universal Inc. signed a contract to lease equipment for a 4-year term on January 1, 2020, for $20,000 annually beginning immediately. The lease included a purchase option at the end of the lease for $8,000, that at the commencement of the lease, Universal did not believe would exercise. However, on December 31, 2021, two years later, circumstances had changed causing Universal to now reasonably expect to exercise the option. Universal's incremental borrowing rate changes from 5% at the lease commencement date to 7% currently. The incremental borrowing rate at lease commencement did not reflect the purchase option. On December 31, 2021, the lease liability and right-of-use asset had balances of $37,188 and $37,233, respectively. What is the adjusted lease liability on December 31, 2021?

Brief Exercise 17-51
Recording Entries for Short-Term Leases **LO7**
Hint: See Demo 17-7

On January 1, 2020, Baker Inc. enters into an operating lease of equipment for one year for $1,000 per month on January 1, 2020. The equipment cost $200,000 and has a useful life of 10 years. Assuming that Baker Inc. elects to account for the lease under the short-term lease option, prepare Baker's monthly entry for 2020 assuming payments are made at the end of each month.

Exercises

Exercise 17-52
Classifying Leases **LO1**

Tropical Products Inc. is in the process of negotiating a lease of equipment with a fair value of $50,000, and it must determine the proper lease classification. The following table describes four scenarios under negotiation.

	Option One	Option Two	Option Three	Option Four
Ownership transfer	No	No	No	No
Purchase option	No	No	No	Yes, for $10,000 which is a discounted price
Lease term length, in years	4	3	4	3
Economic life of equipment, in years	5	5	5	5
Alternative use of equipment at lease end	Yes	Yes	Yes	Yes
Annual lease payment	$11,000	$11,000	$11,000	$11,000
Guaranteed residual value	No	No	$15,000	No
Implicit rate of lease	Unknown to lessee	Unknown to lessee	8.4%	Unknown to lessee
Incremental borrowing rate of lessee	8%	8%	8%	8%
Payment type	Beginning of year	Beginning of year	Beginning of year	End of year

Required

Determine the proper classification for each of the four separate scenarios assuming that Tropical Products Inc. is the lessee.

Exercise 17-53
Classifying Leases
LO1

The following *separate* scenarios relate to a 5-year lease, pertaining to equipment with a fair value of $25,000. Assume in all scenarios that payments are made at the beginning of the period.

1. Lease payments include a fixed payment of $5,000 per year.
2. Lease payments include a fixed payment of $5,000 per year, plus $250 for insurance and $300 for a maintenance contract.
3. Lease payments will be $5,000 in the first year and will increase by 3% (calculated on the previous year's payment) for each of the following 4 years.
4. Lease payments will be $5,000 in the first year and will increase each of the following years by the increase in the CPI from the preceding year. The current CPI is 120 and is expected to increase to 122 at the end of the next year.
5. Lease payments will be $5,000 in the first year and will increase each of the following years by (a) the increase in the CPI from the preceding year, or (b) 3%, whichever is greater. The current CPI is 120 and is expected to increase to 122 at the end of the next year.
6. Lease payments include a fixed payment of $5,000 per year. In addition, the lessee has guaranteed the residual value of the equipment for $1,000 at the end of the lease.

Required

For each of the six separate scenarios outlined above, and considering only the fair value lease criterion, determine how the lessee would classify the lease, assuming a discount rate of 7%.

Exercise 17-54
Recording Entries for Finance Lease—No Residual **LO2**
Hint: See Demo 17-2A

On January 1, 2020, Ashe Company entered into a 5-year equipment lease (with no renewal options) requiring payments of $10,000, with the first payment due immediately. The lessor's implicit interest rate, known to Ashe, is 6%. Ownership of the equipment remains with the lessor at expiration of the lease. There is no option to purchase the property at the end of the lease term and the equipment is expected to have no residual value. The equipment has an estimated economic life of 5 years.

Required

a. How would Ashe Company classify the lease?
b. Prepare an amortization schedule of the lease liability.
c. Prepare the entries for Ashe Company for 2020.

Exercise 17-55
Recording Entries for Finance Lease—No Residual, Renewal Terms **LO2**

On January 1, 2020, Lessee Inc. enters into a 5-year equipment lease agreement for $15,000 annually (first payment due immediately). The lease grants the lessee an option to renew the lease for an additional 3 years. Lease payments adjust to current market rates for equivalent rentals at the time of renewal. Lessee Inc. is reasonably certain that it will exercise the renewal option due to the customization of the equipment. The estimated useful life of the equipment is 10 years. The lessee is not aware of the implicit rate of the lease, but the lessee's incremental borrowing rate is 6%.

Required

a. How would Lessee Inc. classify the equipment lease?
b. Prepare an amortization schedule of the lease liability.
c. Prepare the entries for Lessee Inc. for years 2020 and 2021.

Exercise 17-56
Recording Entries for Finance Lease—No Residual, Payments Increase at a Defined Rate **LO2**

On December 30, 2019, Drew Company leased equipment under a lease for a period of 5 years. Drew contracted to pay $90,000 on December 31, 2019, with an annual increase of 3% (calculated on the previous year's lease payment) for each of the next four years due on December 31. The leased equipment has a useful life of 7 years, a fair value of $450,000, and the interest rate implicit in the lease is 8% and is known to Drew Company.

Required

a. How would Drew Company classify the lease?
b. Prepare an amortization schedule of the lease liability.
c. Prepare the entries for Drew Company for years 2020 and 2021.

Exercise 17-57
Reporting Finance Lease, Unguaranteed Residual—Lessee **LO2**

On January 1, 2020, Alex Company signed a 5-year lease contract for equipment with Abel Company. The equipment had a normal selling price of $55,000 and an estimated useful life of 6 years. Five annual payments of $11,815 are payable by Abel on January 1, beginning in 2020. The asset reverts to Alex at the end of the lease term, December 31, 2022, and is estimated to have an unguaranteed residual value on that date of $3,000. Alex's implicit interest rate is 6%, which is known to Abel.

Required

a. How would Abel Company classify the lease?
b. Prepare an amortization schedule of the lease liability.
c. Prepare the entries for Abel Company for 2020.

Exercise 17-58
Recording Finance Lease, Unguaranteed Residual, Initial Direct Costs—Lessee **LO2**

Assume the same information in Exercise 17-57 except that the lessee also paid legal fees in the execution of the lease of $1,800 on January 1, 2020.

Required

a. How would Abel Company classify the lease?
b. Prepare an amortization schedule of the lease liability.
c. Prepare the entries for Abel Company for 2020.

Exercise 17-59
Reporting Finance Lease, Guaranteed Residual—Lessee **LO2**
Hint: See Demo 17-2B

Mac Leasing Company (lessor) and Ash Corporation (lessee) signed a four-year lease on January 1, 2020. The underlying asset has an estimated life of six years, and the property reverts to Mac at the end of the lease term. Lease payments of $11,923 are payable on January 1 of each year and were set to yield Mac a return of 8%, which was known to Ash. The estimated residual value at the end of the lease term is $10,000 and is guaranteed by Ash Corporation. Ash expects the estimated residual value at the end of the lease term to be $10,000. The lease contains no purchase option.

Required

a. How would Ash Corporation classify the lease?
b. Prepare an amortization schedule of the lease liability.
c. Prepare the entries for Ash Corporation for 2020.
d. Let's now assume that Ash Corporation expects the estimated residual value at the end of the lease term to be $3,500 instead. Prepare the entries for Ash Corporation for 2020.

Exercise 17-60
Reporting Finance Lease, Guaranteed Residual—Lessee **LO2**
Hint: See Demo 17-2B

On the first day of its accounting year, January 1, 2020, Lessee Inc. leased a building at an annual payment of $138,847.84 to be paid at the beginning of each year for 10 years. The first payment was paid immediately. The building, which is new, cost $1,100,000 and has an estimated useful life of 12 years. The lessor's implicit rate is 6% and is known to Lessee Inc. The residual value of the building of $30,000 was guaranteed by Lessee Inc. who expects the residual value to approximate $20,000. Lessee Inc. incurred the following additional costs and received the following incentives pertaining to this lease on January 1, 2020:

- Paid legal fees of $1,000 related to the execution of the lease.
- Paid a fixed lease payment of $138,847.84 plus a $3,500 recurring payment to the lessor for hazard insurance on the building.
- Received a lease incentive of $1,500 to sign the lease.

Required

a. How would Lessee Inc. classify the lease?
b. Prepare an amortization schedule of the lease liability.
c. Compute the value of the right-of-use asset.
d. Prepare the entries for Lessee Inc. for years 2020 and 2021. Assume legal fees were paid and the lease incentive was received in 2019.

e. What would be the value of the lease liability if the lessor charged a market price for hazard insurance, which changed from year to year?

Exercise 17-61
Reporting Finance Lease, Purchase Option—Lessee **LO2**

On January 1, 2020, lessor Marcy and lessee Lenox contract for the lease of a machine for five payments of $7,000 each. The $7,000 payments are to be paid at the end of each year. They also agree that at the time of the fifth payment, for an added $6,000 purchase option payment, Lenox can buy the property. Lenox reasonably expects to exercise the purchase option as the amount is well under the expected fair value at that time. Lenox's incremental borrowing rate is 6% per year and Lenox is unaware of the implicit rate of the lease. The economic life of the asset is six years.

Required

a. How would Lenox classify the lease?
b. Compute the value of the lease liability.
c. Prepare an amortization schedule of the lease liability.
d. Prepare the entries for Lenox for years 2020 and 2021.

Exercise 17-62
Reporting Finance Lease—Lessee **LO2**
Hint: See Demo 17-2A

On the first day of its accounting year, Lessee Inc. leased certain property at a semiannual payment of $60,000 receivable at the beginning of each period for 8 years. The first payment was paid immediately. The leased property, which is new, cost $1,100,000 and has an estimated useful life of 10 years and no guaranteed residual value. The lessee's incremental borrowing rate is 7% and the lessee is not aware of the lessor's implicit rate.

Required

a. How would Lessee Inc. classify the lease?
b. What balances (account titles, amounts) appear on Lessee Inc.'s balance sheet at the end of the first year, related to the lease?
c. What balances (account titles, amounts) appear on Lessee Inc.'s income statement for the first year, related to the lease?

Exercise 17-63
Recording Sales-Type Lease, Unguaranteed Residual Value—Lessor **LO3**

Flint Company leased equipment to Land Company for a five-year period. Flint paid $46,965 for the equipment, its current carrying value (estimated useful life five years). The lease started on January 1, 2020. Flint uses a target rate of return of 8% in all lease contracts. The first payment was on January 1, 2020, and the accounting periods end on December 31. The equipment reverts to the lessor at the end of the lease term at which time the lessor estimates that the equipment will have an unguaranteed residual value of $2,000.

Required

a. Compute the annual payment for the lessor.
b. Prepare an amortization schedule of the lease receivable for the lessor.
c. Provide journal entries for 2020 and 2021 for the lessor assuming that the equipment is held in the lessor's Inventory account.
d. Record the entry on January 1, 2025, for the return of the equipment assuming the equipment had a fair value of $2,000.

Exercise 17-64
Recording Sales-Type Lease, Purchase Option—Lessor **LO3**

Use the same information from Exercise 17-63 but assume instead that the lease contract contains a purchase option stating that Land Company can purchase the equipment for $4,000 on January 1, 2025, at which time its estimated residual value is $6,500. It is reasonably certain that Land Company will exercise the purchase option at the end of the lease term.

Required

a. Compute the annual payment for the lessor.
b. Prepare an amortization schedule of the lease receivable for the lessor.
c. Prepare journal entries for 2020 and 2021 for the lessor.

Exercise 17-65
Recording Sales-Type Lease, Residual Value—Lessor **LO3**

Dunlap Company leased a large copier to Rust Company for a three-year period. Dunlap paid $30,000 for the copier and immediately leased it on January 1, 2020 (estimated useful life is four years, and Dunlap expects the residual value at the end of the lease term to be $6,000). Dunlap used an expected rate of return of 6% (known by Rust). The lessee agreed to guarantee two-thirds ($4,000) of the residual value. The first lease payment is due on January 1, 2020, and the accounting periods for both entities end on December 31. At the lease termination date, an independent appraiser provided an estimated residual value of $3,000. The lessee immediately paid the difference of $1,000 ($4,000 guaranteed residual value minus $3,000, the actual residual value).

Required

a. Compute the lease payment for the lessor and the lease receivable to be capitalized by the lessor.
b. Provide the entries for the lessor on January 1, 2020.
c. Provide the entries for the lessor through the lease term.
d. Instead assume that the collectibility of the lease payments by Rust Company was not probable. How would your answer to part (*b*) change?

Exercise 17-66
Reporting Sales-Type Lease, Initial Direct Costs—Lessor **LO3**

Rex Corporation (lessor) and Lee Company (lessee) agreed to a lease with the following information:

- Rex's carrying value of the underlying asset (inventory item) was $400,000.
- Lease term is four years, beginning January 1, 2020. Lease payments are made each January 1, beginning January 1, 2020.
- Estimated useful life of the underlying asset is four years. Estimated residual value at the end of the lease is zero.
- Sales price of the underlying asset on January 1, 2020, was $460,000.
- Rex's implicit interest rate is 8% on retail price (known to Lee).
- Rex paid commission and legal fees in securing the lease of $5,000 on January 1, 2020.
- Rex expects to collect all payments from Lee.

Required

a. Compute the lease payment for the lessor and the lease receivable to be capitalized by the lessor.
b. Provide the entries for the lessor during 2020.

Exercise 17-67
Reporting a Sales-Type Lease—Lessor **LO3**
Hint: See Demo 17-3A

On January 1, 2020, the first day of its accounting year, Lessor Inc., leased certain equipment at an annual payment of $10,254.19, receivable at the beginning of each year for 10 years. The first payment was received immediately. The equipment has an estimated useful life of 12 years and no residual value. Lessor's implicit rate is 6%. Lessor had no other costs associated with this lease and properly classified the lease as a sales-type lease. The leased equipment was carried on Lessor Inc.'s books at $65,000.

Required

a. Calculate the value of the lease receivable at the commencement of the lease.
b. What amounts would be presented in the balance sheet as of December 31, 2020, related to this lease?
c. What amounts would be presented in the income statement for the year ended December 31, 2020, related to this lease?

Exercise 17-68
Reporting a Sales-Type Lease—Lessor **LO3**

On January 1, 2020, the first day of its accounting year, Lessor Inc., leased certain property at an annual payment of $20,000 receivable at the beginning of each year for 5 years. The first payment was received immediately. The leased property, which is new, has an estimated useful life of 8 years and an estimated residual value of $15,000 (expected to be received by lessor but not guaranteed by the lessee). Lessor's implicit rate is 6%. Lessor had no other costs associated with this lease and properly classified the lease as a sales-type lease.

Required

a. Calculate the value of the lease receivable at the commencement of the lease
b. What amounts would be presented in the balance sheet as of December 31, 2020, related to this lease?
c. What amounts would be presented in the income statement for the year ended December 31, 2020, related to this lease?

Exercise 17-69
Computing Lease Payment—Lessor; Computing Right-of-Use Asset and Lease Liability—Lessee
LO2, 3

Information for four *separate* finance/sales-type lease scenarios is provided as follows:

	A	B	C	D
Lessor's desired rate of return	6%	7%	8%	7.5%
Implicit rate known by the lessee	yes	no	yes	no
Lessee's incremental borrowing rate	7%	6%	7%	8%
Lease term	5	8	5	8
Fair value of underlying asset	$100,000	$45,000	$275,000	$18,000
Beginning or end of year payments	Beginning	Beginning	Beginning	End

Required

Answer the following questions for each separate scenario, assuming that the lessee is aware of the lessor's implicit lease rate.

a. Compute the lessor's lease payment.
b. Compute the lessee's balance of the lease liability at the commencement of the lease.
c. Compute the lessee's balance of the right-of-use asset at the commencement of the lease.

Exercise 17-70 Computing Lease Payment—Lessor; Computing Right-of-Use Asset and Lease Liability—Lessee **LO2, 3**

Information for four *separate* finance/sales-type lease scenarios is provided as follows:

	A	B	C	D
Lessor's desired rate of return	6%	7%	6%	8%
Lease term	5	10	8	4
Fair value of underlying asset	$35,000	$140,000	$18,000	$230,000
Beginning or end of year payments	Beginning	Beginning	Beginning	End
Guaranteed residual value	—	12,000	—	80,000
Residual value *expected* by lessee		—		30,000
Unguaranteed residual value expected by lessor	—	—	3,500	—
Initial direct costs paid by lessee	250	1,000	—	1,200
Prepaid lease payment	—	1,500	—	—

Required

Answer the following questions for each separate scenario assuming that the lessee is aware of the lessor's implicit lease rate.

a. Compute the lessor's lease payment.
b. Compute the balance of the lessee's lease liability at the commencement of the lease, prior to the first payment.
c. Compute the balance of the lessee's right-of-use asset at the commencement of the lease.

Exercise 17-71 Recording Entries for Sales-Type Lease: Lease Payment Calculation **LO3**

A lessor entered into a 5-year lease appropriately classified as a sales-type lease. The cost of the underlying asset was $40,000 and the fair value of the asset was $50,000. The lease included a purchase option that allowed the lessee to purchase the underlying asset for $5,000 at the end of the lease. Because of the discount offered in the purchase option from the expected residual value of $7,000, the lessor is reasonably certain that the lessee will exercise the purchase option. The first lease payment will be made immediately, with annual payments due throughout the lease term.

Required

a. Assuming that the lessor had a desired rate of return of 6%, compute the annual lease payment.
b. Assume the same facts (original scenario) except that the exercise of the option is not reasonably certain. Compute the annual lease payment.
c. Assume the same facts (original scenario) except that lessor's desired rate of return is 8%. Compute the annual lease payment.
d. Assume the same facts (original scenario) except that the lease allows the ownership of the leased asset to revert to the lessee at lease end. Compute the annual lease payment.

Exercise 17-72 Recording Entries for Finance Lease: Lessee **LO2, 3**

Try-Star Leasing Company enters into a contract with LLX Corporation for equipment under lease for a three-year period. The equipment will have no residual value when the lease term ends and has an economic life of 3 years. Try-Star expects to collect all payments from LLX Corporation. The carrying value of the equipment was $120,000 at the inception of the lease, but the fair value was $140,000. The three equal annual payments (amount to be determined) are to be paid each January 1, starting January 1, 2020, (at which time the equipment was delivered). In addition to the fixed lease payment, LLX Corporation has agreed to pay Try-Star $1,000 annually for taxes and insurance throughout the lease term, at the time fixed lease payments are due. Try-Star expects an 8% return (known to LLX Corporation). LLX incurred $1,000 in legal fees for the execution of the lease on January 1, 2020, to be paid in 30 days. The accounting year of both companies ends December 31.

Required

a. Determine the annual lease payment.
b. Determine the classification of the lease to LLX Corporation.
c. Provide all journal entries relating to the lease for LLX Corporation for 2020–2022.

d. How would the following items change if the LLX Corporation was not aware of the implicit rate of the lease? Assume that LLX Corporation's borrowing rate for debt with similar terms would be 9%.
   1. Lease payment
   2. Lease classification
   3. Initial value of the right-of-use-asset
   4. Initial value of the lease liability

e. How would your answers change to (*a*) and (*b*) if the lease agreement included a 3-year service contract to provide maintenance on the machine as needed? The annual cost of $6,000 will be paid by LLX Corporation at the time fixed lease payments are due.

Exercise 17-73
Recording Entries for Sales-type Lease—Lessor **LO3**

Using the information from Exercise 17-72, complete the following requirements from the lessor's perspective.

Required

a. Determine the classification of the lease to Try-Star Leasing Company.

b. Provide all journal entries relating to the lease for Try-Star Leasing Company for 2020–2022. Assume that Try-Star classifies the equipment as inventory.

c. What would be the entry at the commencement of the lease if Try-Star Leasing Company determined that the collection of lease payments was not probable?

d. How would your answers to parts (*a*) and (*b*) change if future increases in lease payments (starting in 2021) would be based on the changes in CPI from the prior period? Assume that if the CPI remains stable or decreases, the lease payment remains at the level in effect during the previous year. The CPI in 2020 was 120 and is expected to increase by 2% every year.

Exercise 17-74
Recording Entries for Finance Lease—Lessee **LO2**
Hint: See Demo 17-2A

Lessory Corporation, a manufacturer of equipment, enters into a lease of specialized equipment with LesseeX Corp. Title to the asset remains with Lessory Corp upon lease expiration. LesseeX Corp does not guarantee the residual value of the specialized equipment at the end of the lease term, and the lease contains no renewal or purchase options. The following information pertains to the lease.

Lease term	5 years
Economic life of the leased equipment	6 years
Annual lease payments	$1,098
Payment date	Annually on January 1
Fair value of the leased equipment	$5,200
Lessory Corp's carrying value of the leased equipment	$4,500
Rate implicit in the lease (known by lessee)	6.02%
Estimated fair value of the equipment at the end of the lease term	$400

Required

a. Determine the classification of the lease to LesseeX Corporation.

b. Prepare an amortization schedule of the lease liability.

c. Provide all journal entries relating to the lease for LesseeX Corporation for 2020 and 2021.

Exercise 17-75
Recording Entries for Sales-Type Lease—Lessor **LO3**

Using the information from Exercise 17-74, complete the following requirements from the lessor's perspective. Assume that lessor classifies the equipment as inventory prior to the lease arrangement.

Required

a. Determine the classification of the lease to Lessory Corporation.

b. Determine the lease receivable balance at the lease commencement.

c. Prepare an amortization schedule of the lease receivable.

d. Provide all journal entries relating to the lease for Lessory Corporation for 2020 and 2021.

e. What is the gross profit recorded for this lease in 2020? If the lessor determined that the unguaranteed residual value were $0 (instead of $400), what gross profit would be recorded in 2020?

Exercise 17-76
Recording Entries for Operating Lease—Lessee **LO4**
Hint: See Demo 17-4A

On January 1, 2020, Frozen Yogart Inc. signed a 10-year lease for its retail outlet. The lease payments, paid semiannually, are based upon semiannual sales and will equal 5% of sales with a semiannual sale minimum of $500,000. Based upon the previous three years, average sales per semiannual period are $600,000. Frozen Yogart's incremental borrowing rate is 6% and is unaware of the rate implicit in the lease. The lease is considered an operating lease for Frozen Yogart. A $25,000 payment (5% of $500,000) is due immediately on January 1, 2020. Frozen Yogart's accounting year ends June 30.

Required

a. Calculate the lease liability recorded by Frozen Yogart Inc. on January 1, 2020.

b. Calculate the right-of-use asset recorded by Frozen Yogart Inc. on January 1, 2020.
c. Prepare an amortization schedule of the lease liability.
d. Prepare an amortization schedule of the right-of-use asset.
e. Prepare the entries for Frozen Yogart Inc. on January 1, 2020, June 30, 2020, and July 1, 2020.
f. On July 21, 2020, Frozen Yogart reported to the lessor its sales of $575,000 for the semiannual period ended June 30, 2020. Any rent adjustments are due to the lessor at the end of the following month after the sales. Record the adjusting entry required on July 31, 2020.

Exercise 17-77
Recording Entries for Operating Lease—Lessee **LO4**

On January 2, 2020, Wayne Inc. signed an eight-year lease for office space for $24,000 annually, with the first payment due immediately. Wayne has the option to renew the lease for an additional four-year period on or before January 2, 2028, at market lease rates at the time of renewal. Wayne intends to evaluate rental options at the time of the option to renew. The remaining economic life of the office is 30 years. Wayne Inc. is not aware of the implicit rate of the lease but has an incremental borrowing rate of 7%. Wayne Inc. paid $1,000 on January 2, 2020, for initial direct costs.

Required

a. How would Lessee Inc. classify the lease?
b. Prepare an amortization schedule of the lease liability.
c. Prepare an amortization schedule of the right-of-use asset.
d. Prepare the entries for Wayne Inc. for years 2020 and 2021, assuming Wayne Inc.'s accounting year ends December 31.

Exercise 17-78
Reporting Operating Lease—Lessee **LO4**
Hint: See Demo 17-4A

On January 1, 2020, Lessee Inc. leased equipment at an annual payment of $85,099 payable at the beginning of each year for 4 years. The equipment had a fair value of $400,000, a book value of $375,000, and was commonly purchased or leased by customers. The lessor estimates that the equipment has an estimated useful life of 8 years and an estimated residual value of $125,000, not guaranteed by the lessee. Lessor's implicit rate is 7.5%, which is unknown to the lessee. The lessee's incremental borrowing rate is 8%. The lease does not contain a purchase option or a renewal option. The lessee had no other costs associated with this lease.

Required

a. How would Lessee Inc. classify the lease? Support your answer.
b. Prepare an amortization schedule of the lease liability.
c. Prepare an amortization schedule of the right-of-use asset.
d. Prepare the entries for Lessee Inc. for the years 2020 and 2021, assuming Lessee Inc.'s accounting year ends December 31.

Exercise 17-79
Reporting Operating Lease—Lessee **LO4**
Hint: See Demo 17-4A

Renewable Co. uses leasing as a secondary means of selling its products. The company contracted with Green Corporation to lease a machine with an economic life of 12 years to be used by Green Corporation in its operations. The fair value of the asset at the inception of the lease was $400,000; it cost Renewable Co. $360,000 and is carried as equipment at that value. Payments of $44,925 are to be made by Green Corporation at the beginning of each of the eight years of the lease. Renewable Co.'s implicit interest rate is 6% per year, which is not known by Green Corporation. Green Corporation's incremental borrowing rate is 7%. Renewable Co. estimates the residual value of the leased asset to be $166,217 at the end of the lease term. The residual value is not guaranteed by Green Corporation. Renewable Co. will depreciate the equipment on a straight-line basis (assume no salvage value).

Required

a. How would Green Corporation classify the lease?
b. What balances (account titles, amounts) appear on Green's balance sheet at the end of the first year, related to the lease?
c. What balances (account titles, amounts) appear on Green's income statement for the first year, related to the lease?

Exercise 17-80
Reporting Operating Lease—Lessor **LO5**
Hint: See Demo 17-5

Using the information from Exercise 17-79, answer the following question from the perspective of the lessor.

Required

a. How would Renewable Co. classify the lease?
b. What balances (account titles, amounts) appear on Renewable's balance sheet at the end of the first year, related to the lease?
c. What balances (account titles, amounts) appear on Renewable's income statement for the first year, related to the lease?

Exercise 17-81
Recording Operating Lease Entries—Lessor
LO5
Hint: See Demo 17-5

Using the information from Exercise 17-78, answer the following question from the perspective of the lessor.

Required

a. Recalculate the lessor's lease payment.

b. Prepare the entries for the lessor for 2020, assuming that the lessor uses the straight-line method to depreciate fixed assets.

c. If the lessor incurred a commission to secure the acceptance of the lease agreement for $1,000, what entry would be required by the lessor on January 1, 2020, and December 31, 2020?

d. How would the lease payment and accounting for the lease be affected for the lessor if the lessee guaranteed the residual value of $80,000?

Exercise 17-82
Recording Operating Lease Entries—Lessee
LO4

On January 1, 2020, Merick Inc. purchased a building for $2 million to be leased. The building is expected to have a 45-year life with no salvage value. The building was leased immediately by Kregor Construction for $130,000 a year payable January 1 of each year starting January 1, 2020. The lease term is five years with no renewal or purchase option reasonably expected to be exercised. There are no uncertainties surrounding collection. The implicit rate of the lease is 7% known by Kregor Construction.

Required

a. How would Kregor Construction classify the lease?

b. Prepare an amortization schedule of the lease liability.

c. Prepare an amortization schedule of the right-of-use asset.

d. Prepare the entries for Kregor Construction for years 2020 and 2021, assuming Kregor Construction's accounting year ends December 31.

Exercise 17-83
Recording Operating Lease Entries—Lessor
LO5
Hint: See Demo 17-5

Using the information from Exercise 17-82, answer the following question from the perspective of the lessor.

Required

a. How would Merick Inc. classify the lease?

b. Prepare the entries for Merick Inc. for 2020.

c. Prepare the entries for Merick Inc. to record legal fees of $1,000 incurred on January 1, 2020, for the execution of the lease and the related adjusting entry on December 31, 2020.

Exercise 17-84
Computing Lease Payment, Lease Receivable—Sales-Type Lease **LO3**

Information for four separate sales-type lease scenarios is provided as follows.

	A	B	C	D
Lessor's desired rate of return	6%	7%	8%	7.5%
Lease term (years)	5	8	5	8
Fair value of underlying asset	$100,000	$45,000	$275,000	$18,000
Beginning or end of year payments	Beginning	Beginning	Beginning	End
Guaranteed residual value	$ 10,000	$ —	$ 25,000	$ —
Expected fair value of the residual	10,000	2,500	10,000	—

Required

Answer the following questions for each separate scenario from the perspective of the lessor.

a. Compute the lessor's annual fixed lease payment.

b. Compute the balance of the lease receivable at the commencement of the lease.

Exercise 17-85
Remeasuring Leases
LO6

On January 1, 2020, Lessee Corp. commences a finance lease contract for equipment with the following terms.

- Lease term: 5 years
- Economic life: 6 years
- Annual lease payments: $100,000 (due at the beginning of each period)
- Guaranteed residual value: $15,000
- Lessee's incremental borrowing rate: 6% (lessor's implicit rate unknown to the lessee)

At the commencement of the lease, Lessee Corp. did not anticipate having to make a payment for the guaranteed residual value requirement. However, on January 1, 2022, the company determined that a payment would be due to the lessor as a result of a change in technology, which lowered the estimated fair value of the residual, causing an expected $10,000 payment.

Required

a. Will the change in expected payment on the guaranteed residual value result in a lease reclassification assessment or a lease remeasurment?

b. What is the value of the right-of-use asset and lease liability of the existing lease on January 1, 2022, prior to the change in the estimated residual value?

c. If applicable, calculate the remeasured value of the lease liability on January 1, 2022. Use the discount rate of 6% at the time of the lease commencement to compute remeasurement differences, if applicable.

d. Record the entry required on January 1, 2022.

e. What are the adjusted balances for the lease liability and right-of-use asset after the entry recorded in (*d*) above?

f. What is the income statement *impact* for 2022 related to the lease?

Exercise 17-86 Identifying Remeasurement **LO6** *Hint:* See Demo 17-6

Determine whether the following changes would result in a new lease, or a lease classification reassessment and/or a lease remeasurement.

a. Lessee and Lessor enter into a 10-year lease for 10,000 square feet of office space in a building with a remaining economic life of 50 years. Annual payments are $100,000, paid in arrears. Lessee's incremental borrowing rate at the commencement date is 6%. The lease is classified as an operating lease. At the beginning of Year 6, Lessee and Lessor agree to modify the lease such that the total lease term increases from 10 years to 15 years. The annual lease payments increase to $110,000 per year for the remaining 10 years after the modification. Lessee's incremental borrowing rate is 7% at the date the modification is agreed to by the parties.

b. Lessee enters into a 10-year lease for 10,000 square feet of office space. At the beginning of Year 6, Lessee and Lessor agree to modify the lease for the remaining 5 years to include an additional 10,000 square feet of office space in the same building. The increase in the lease payments is commensurate with the market rate of office space at the date the modification became effective.

Exercise 17-87 Preparing Lessee Journal Entries: Short-term Lease Election **LO7** *Hint:* See Demo 17-7

Gomez Inc. entered into a contract on January 1, 2020, to lease a vehicle for one year, with monthly payments of $650, due at the beginning of each month. The vehicle has a fair value of $30,000. The lease agreement does not contain an option for purchase or renewal. The lessor's implicit rate of return is 5%. Gomez Inc. elects the short-term leasing option.

Required

Prepare the entries for Gomez Inc. for 2020 related to the lease.

Exercise 17-88 Defining Lease Concepts **LO1, 2, 3, 4, 5, 6, 7**

Terms relating to concepts discussed in this chapter along with descriptions of the terms are included in the following two lists.

Terms	Description of Terms
____ 1. Identified asset	*a.* Unavoidable costs of executing a lease agreement.
____ 2. Right to use	*b.* Date on which an underlying asset is made available to lessee.
____ 3. Lessee	*c.* Interest rate on debt applicable to a lessee for terms similar to a lease.
____ 4. Lessor	*d.* Explicit or implicit specification of a leased asset.
____ 5. Lease commencement	*e.* Charge by a lessor for a distinct good or service.
____ 6. Finance lease	*f.* Lessee lease classification where at least one lease criterion is met.
____ 7. Operating lease	*g.* Entity obtaining right to use an asset.
____ 8. Sales-type lease	*h.* Lessor lease classification where at least one lease criterion is met.
____ 9. Implicit lease rate	*i.* Value at the end of a lease that a lessee is obligated to transfer to lessor.
____ 10. Incremental borrowing rate	*j.* Entity providing right to use an asset.
____ 11. Nonlease component	*k.* To direct the use of or obtain benefits of an identified asset.
____ 12. In-substance fixed payment	*l.* Lease payment that fluctuates based upon a rate or index.
____ 13. Variable payment	*m.* Lease classification where no lease criteria are met.
____ 14. Guaranteed residual value	*n.* Lease payment that varies but includes a minimum payment level.
____ 15. Initial direct costs	*o.* Lessor desired rate of return on lease.

Required

Match each term, 1 through 15 with the most appropriate description *a* through *o*.

Problems

Problem 17-89
Reporting Entries for a Finance Lease—Lessee **LO1, 2**

On January 1, 2020, Tiffany Company leased new equipment to Masy's Corporation. The equipment cost Tiffany $180,000. The lease agreement specified that Masy's is to make five annual lease payments (on January 1, beginning January 1, 2020) to yield Tiffany a 5% return. The equipment has a five-year useful life with an unguaranteed residual value of $9,000. In December 2019, Tiffany paid Masy's $1,000 as an incentive to sign the lease and Masy's paid legal fees of $500 related to the execution of the lease. Ownership of the lease asset remains with Tiffany at the end of the lease term. Masy's is aware of the implicit interest rate used by Tiffany. The accounting period for Masy's ends December 31.

Required

a. Compute the annual fixed lease payment.
b. What type of lease is this to the lessee? Explain.
c. Provide all journal entries associated with this lease for the lessee for the years ended December 31, 2020, and 2021.

Problem 17-90
Reporting Entries for a Finance Lease—Lessee **LO1, 2**

On January 1, 2020, Shell Leasing Company leased to Last Service Company a new machine that cost $45,500 and has an economic life of 5 years. Shell computed the annual payments (first payment due immediately) at an amount that will yield an annual return of 6%, and the lessee, being aware of this rate, also uses it to record the lease and calculate interest expense. Last Service Company guaranteed a residual value of $10,000 at the end of the four-year lease term. Last Service Company estimates that the residual value at the end of the lease will be $7,000. The lessee has an accounting year ending December 31.

Required

a. Compute the annual fixed lease payment.
b. What type of lease is this to the lessee?
c. Provide all journal entries associated with this lease for the lessee for the years ended December 31, 2020, and 2021.
d. Assume instead, that Last Service Company made a payment of $2,500 (a portion of the first fixed lease payment) on December 20, 2019. Record the required entries for Last Service Company on December 20, 2019, and January 1, 2020.

Problem 17-91
Reporting and Recording Entries for a Finance Lease—Lessee **LO2**

On January 1, 2020, lessor Berkley leased a machine to lessee Columbia on a three-year lease. The machine cost Berkley $300,000 immediately prior to the lease. The machine has a five-year estimated useful life and an estimated residual value of $100,000. The lessor used a 6% target rate of return. The three annual lease payments start on January 1, 2020. The lessee has an option to purchase the machine at the end of the lease term for $75,000 and the lessee is reasonably certain to exercise this option. The accounting period for the lessee ends on December 31.

Required

a. Compute the annual fixed lease payments.
b. What type of lease is this to the lessee? Explain.
c. Provide all journal entries associated with this lease for the lessee for the years ended December 31, 2020, and 2021.
d. What balances (account titles, amounts) appear on Columbia's balance sheet on December 31, 2020, related to the lease?
e. What balances (account titles, amounts) appear on Columbia's income statement for 2020 related to the lease?
f. How would your answer to (*c*) change if Columbia also signed a three-year service contract with Berkley for $1,200 a year for maintenance services on the machine for the lease term?

Problem 17-92
Preparing Lessee Amortization Schedule—Quarterly Payments **LO2**

Apollo leases equipment from Baxter Inc. over a 3-year period, agreeing to make quarterly payments beginning on the commencement of the lease on January 1, 2020. The equipment has a fair value of $87,500 and has a guaranteed residual value of $15,000. The equipment has a 4-year useful life and ownership remains with the lessor at the end of the lease term.

Required

Compute the lease payment and prepare Apollo's lease liability amortization schedule for the following 3 separate scenarios for Apollo.

a. Baxter Inc. has an implicit rate of interest of 6%, known to Apollo. Apollo estimates the fair value of the residual to be $15,000.

b. Baxter Inc. has an implicit rate of interest of 8%, known to Apollo. Apollo estimates the fair value of the residual to be $5,000.

c. Baxter Inc. has an implicit rate of interest of 6%, known to Apollo. Apollo estimates the fair value of the residual to be $15,000. The first lease payment is due at the end of the first quarter.

Problem 17-93
Reporting Finance Lease—Lessee **LO2**

The following data are available regarding a noncancelable lease.

1. Lease term is five years, beginning June 1, 2020.
2. The leased property cost the lessor $400,000, its fair value, on June 1, 2020.
3. Estimated useful life of the asset is six years; residual value at the end of the five-year useful life is $20,000, unguaranteed.
4. No purchase option is available to the lessee. Ownership is retained by lessor at the end of the lease term.
5. Five annual lease payments are payable on June 1 of each year (starting January 1, 2020) to yield the lessor a 6% return (implicit interest rate). Lessee does not know and cannot reliably estimate the lessor's yield rate. Lessee's incremental borrowing rate is 7%.
6. Lessee's credit rating is excellent. The accounting year-end for the lessee is December 31.

Required

a. Compute the annual payment.

b. What type of lease is this to the lessee?

c. Provide all journal entries associated with this lease for the lessee for the year ended December 31, 2020.

d. What balances (account titles, amounts) appear on the lessee's balance sheet on December 31, 2020, related to the lease?

e. What balances (account titles, amounts) appear on the lessee's income statement for 2020, related to the lease?

Problem 17-94
Reporting a Sales-Type Lease—Lessor **LO3**

On December 31, 2020, a lessor acquired a machine at a cost of $35,000 to be held for lease, and classified as inventory. The machine was leased on January 1, 2021, for five years in a sales-type lease that requires annual payments of $14,099 at the end of each year. At inception of the lease, the sales value of the leased asset was $55,000. The machine will revert to the lessor at the end of the lease term, at which time the estimated residual value will be $2,500 (none of which is guaranteed by the lessee). The lessor's implicit rate of interest was 10% on the investment. The estimated fair value of the residual at lease end is $2,500.

Required

a. Show how the lessor computed the annual payment of $14,099.

b. What type of lease is this to the lessor?

c. Prepare a lease receivable amortization schedule for the lessor.

d. Provide all journal entries associated with this lease for the lessor for the years ended December 31, 2021, and 2022.

e. Provide the journal entry at termination of the lease on December 31, 2025, the last payment, interest revenue, and return of the asset, assuming the estimate of residual value is confirmed.

Problem 17-95
Reporting a Sales-Type Lease—Lessor **LO3**

On January 1, 2020, Lansing Leasing Company leased equipment to a lessee for an eight-year term during which $59,139 is payable each January 1, starting on January 1, 2020. The guaranteed residual value of the equipment at the end of the lease term is $41,000. The interest rate implicit in the lease is 6%. The accounting period for the lessor ends on December 31. Lansing Leasing Company manufactured the equipment at a cost of $380,000 and the fair value at the commencement of the lease was $415,000.

Required

a. Show how the lessor computed the annual payment of $59,139.

b. What type of lease is this to the lessor? Explain.

c. Prepare a lease receivable amortization schedule for the lessor.

d. Provide all journal entries associated with this lease for the lessor for the years ended December 31, 2020, and 2021.

e. What balances (account titles, amounts) appear on the lessor's balance sheet on December 31, 2020, related to the lease?

f. What balances (account titles, amounts) appear on the lessor's income statement for 2020, related to the lease?

Problem 17-96
Determining Lease Type and Recording Journal Entries—Lessee and Lessor
LO1, 2, 3

Rentals Inc. leases a vehicle to United Inc. for four years on January 1, 2020, requiring equal annual payments on each January 1. The leased asset, recently purchased new, cost the lessor $45,000. The estimated unguaranteed value of the asset at the end of the lease term is $5,000. The annual lease payments were computed to yield Rentals Inc. 6%, a rate known to United Inc. The leased asset has a six-year life with zero residual value at the end of year 6. There is no purchase option, and the asset is retained by Rentals Inc. at the end of the lease term. The accounting period for both lessor and lessee ends December 31.

Required

a. Compute the annual lease payment.
b. What type of lease is this to the lessor and lessee? Explain.
c. Prepare amortization schedules for the lessee and for the lessor.
d. Provide all journal entries associated with this lease for the lessee for the years ended December 31, 2020, and 2021.
e. Provide all journal entries associated with this lease for the lessor for the years ended December 31, 2020, and 2021.
f. What balances (account titles, amounts) appear on the lessee's balance sheet on December 31, 2020, related to the lease?
g. What balances (account titles, amounts) appear on the lessee's income statement for 2020, related to the lease?
h. What balances (account titles, amounts) appear on the lessor's balance sheet on December 31, 2020, related to the lease?
i. What balances (account titles, amounts) appear on the lessor's income statement for 2020, related to the lease?

Problem 17-97
Determining Lease Type and Recording Journal Entries—Lessee and Lessor
LO1, 2, 3

Key Company uses leasing as a secondary means of selling its products. On January 1, 2020, it contracted with Lock Corporation to lease machinery for six years that had a sales price of $90,000 and that cost Key $60,000 (its carrying value in inventory). Equal annual lease payments of $18,786 are to be made each January 1, starting on January 1, 2020. Key's implicit interest rate, based on the sales price, is 10% (known to Lock). There is no residual value expected at the end of the lease term. The accounting period for both companies ends on December 31. The economic life of the machinery is six years. Both parties paid $500 in legal fees to execute the lease on the lease commencement date.

Required

a. What type of lease is this for the lessee and the lessor?
b. Provide all journal entries associated with this lease for the lessee for the years ended December 31, 2020, and 2021.
c. Provide all journal entries associated with this lease for the lessor for the years ended December 31, 2020, and 2021.

Problem 17-98
Determining Lease Type and Recording Journal Entries—Lessee and Lessor
LO1, 2, 3

On January 1, 2020, lessor Alpha and lessee Beta signed a four-year lease. The equipment, recorded as inventory, cost Alpha $900,000 and the sales price is $1,400,000. The equipment has a six-year estimated useful life. Estimated residual values were the following: end of 2023, $200,000, and end of 2025, $80,000. The lease provides Beta an option to buy the equipment at the end of 2023 for $150,000 cash and Beta is reasonably expected to exercise the option. The lease requires four equal annual payments starting on January 1, 2020. Alpha's expected rate of return on the lease is 6%, and the incremental borrowing rate for Beta is 5%. Beta is aware of Alpha's rate.

On December 31, 2023, the lessee exercises the purchase option, at which time a new estimate of residual value was $175,000.

Required

a. Compute the annual lease payment.
b. What type of lease is this? Explain.
c. Prepare amortization schedules for the lessee and for the lessor.
d. Provide all journal entries associated with this lease for the lessee for the years ended December 31, 2020, and 2021.
e. Provide all journal entries associated with this lease for the lessor for the years ended December 31, 2020, and 2021.
f. Record the entries for the lessee and lessor on December 31, 2023, for the exercise of the purchase option.

Problem 17-99
Recording Entries for Operating Lease—Lessee **LO1, 4**

The following data are available about a noncancelable lease that involves a leased asset that was new at the inception date of the lease term, January 1, 2020.

Lease term	2 years
Interest rate implicit in the lease	6%
Lessee's incremental borrowing rate	6%
Amount of each lease payment	$ 7,718.45
Lessor's cost of asset (fair value)	$15,000

Lessee has no way of knowing the interest rate implicit in the lease. Each lease payment occurs at the beginning of each period.

Estimated useful life of asset	6 years
Estimated residual value at end of lease term (unguaranteed)	$4,000

The accounting period for both entities ends on December 31.

Required

a. Show how the lessor computed the annual lease payment of $7,718.45.
b. What type of lease is this to the lessee? Explain.
c. Prepare an amortization schedule of the lease liability and an amortization schedule of the right-of-use asset.
d. Provide all journal entries associated with this lease for the lessee for the years ended December 31, 2020, and 2021.

Problem 17-100
Recording Entries for Operating Lease—Lessee **LO4**

Lessor and lessee agreed to a noncancelable lease for which the following information is available.

1. The leased asset with a fair value of $25,000 was new at the inception of the lease term.
2. Lease term is four years starting January 1, 2020.
3. Estimated useful life of the leased asset is eight years.
4. On January 1, 2020, lessor and lessee estimated that the residual value of the leased asset will be $9,000 on the purchase option date and zero at the end of its useful life. The residual value is not guaranteed.
5. Lessee's incremental borrowing rate is 7%.
6. Lessor's interest rate implicit in the lease is 7%.
7. Purchase option price of leased asset exercisable on January 1, 2024, is $9,000. It is not reasonably certain that the lessee will purchase the asset at the end of the lease at the purchase option, which equals the estimated residual value.
8. Title to the leased asset is retained by the lessor unless the purchase option is exercised.
9. Sales value of leased asset on January 1, 2020, is $30,000.
10. Four annual lease payments will be made each January 1 during the lease term, and the first payment is due at inception of the lease term.

Required

a. Calculate the annual lease payment.
b. Is this an operating lease or a finance lease to the lessee?
c. Prepare a lease liability amortization schedule and right-of-use asset amortization schedule for the lessee.
d. Provide all journal entries associated with this lease for the lessee for the years ended December 31, 2020, and 2021.

Problem 17-101
Recording Entries for Operating Lease—Lessor **LO5**

On July 1, 2020, Stanley Company leased a small building and its site to East Company on a five-year contract. The lease provides for an annual fixed lease payment of $40,000 payable each July 1 starting in 2020. There is no renewal agreement. Stanley's accounts showed the following data on January 1, 2020: initial cost of the building, $250,000 (accumulated depreciation, $60,000); estimated remaining life, 15 years; and estimated residual value, $10,000. The accounting period for each company ends December 31. Stanley Company appropriately classifies the lease as operating.

Required

a. Provide all journal entries associated with this lease for the lessor for the years ended December 31, 2020, and 2021. Assume adjusting entries are recorded annually at December 31.
b. Instead, assume that the initial payment is still $40,000, but the payment increases by $1,000 each year of the lease. Provide all journal entries associated with this lease for the lessor for the years ended December 31, 2020, and 2021.

Problem 17-102
Analyzing and Recording Entries for Operating Lease—Lessee and Lessor
LO4, 5

Lessor Sales Company and Lessee Manufacturing Company agreed to a noncancelable lease. The following information is available to both entities regarding the lease terms and the leased asset.

1. Lessor's cost of the leased asset was $30,000. The asset was new at the inception of the lease term.
2. Lease term is three years starting January 1, 2020.
3. Estimated useful life of the leased asset is six years. Estimated residual value at end of six years is zero.
4. On January 1, 2023, the estimated unguaranteed residual value of the leased asset one day after the end of the lease term is $10,000.
5. Lessor's implicit rate is 7%.
6. Lessee's incremental borrowing rate on January 1, 2020, is 8% and the lessee is unaware of the lessor's implicit rate.
7. Title to the leased asset is retained by the lessor.
8. The fair value of the leased asset on January 1, 2020, is $45,000.
9. Three annual lease payments are due on January 1 of each year during the lease term, and the first payment is due at the inception of the lease term.
10. The accounting period for the lessor and the lessee ends on December 31.

Required

a. Compute the annual lease payment.
b. What type of lease is this for the lessee and lessor?
c. Provide all journal entries associated with this lease for the lessee for the years ended December 31, 2020, and 2021.
d. Provide all journal entries associated with this lease for the lessor for the years ended December 31, 2020, and 2021.

Problem 17-103
Recording Operating Lease Entries—Lessee
LO4

Box Retailer Inc. leases a building from Lessor Corp. The following is a summary of information about the lease and the leased building.

Lease term: 5 years with no options for renewal
Annual lease payments: $1,100,000
Payment date: Annually in advance on January 1
Fair value of the underlying asset: $40,000,000
Box Retailer Inc.'s incremental borrowing rate: 4.5%
Remaining economic life of the building: 35 years
Purchase option: None

Additional information:

- The rate implicit in the lease that Lessor Corp charges Box Retailer Inc. is not readily determinable by Box Retailer Inc.
- Title to the building remains with Lessor Corp throughout the period of the lease and upon lease expiration.
- Box Retailer Inc. does not guarantee the residual value of the building.
- Box Retailer Inc. pays for all property taxes, insurance, and maintenance of the building separate from lease payments.
- Lessor Corp pays Box Retailer Inc. $125,000 prior to the lease commencement date for packing and moving expenses as a lease incentive, recorded as a liability by Box Retailer.

Required

a. Is this an operating lease or a finance lease to the lessee?
b. Prepare a lease liability amortization schedule and right-of-use asset amortization schedule for the lessee.
c. Provide all journal entries associated with this lease for the lessee for the years ended December 31, 2020, and 2021.

Problem 17-104
Reporting Interest Expense **LO2**

Spectrum Inc. reported the following information.

Liability account balances at December 31, 2019, included:	
Note payable to bank	$800,000
Liability under finance lease	354,595

Additional information:

1. The note payable, dated October 1, 2019, bears interest at an annual rate of 10% payable semiannually on April 1 and October 1. Principal payments are due annually on October 1 (beginning October 1, 2020) in four equal installments.

2. The finance lease is for a 10-year period beginning December 31, 2014, with payment due in advance. Equal annual payments of $100,000 are due on December 31 of each year. The 5% interest rate implicit in the lease is known by Spectrum.
3. On July 1, 2020, Spectrum issued $1,000,000 face amount of 10-year, 4% bonds for $922,000, to yield 5%. Interest is payable annually on July 1. Bond discount is amortized by the effective interest method.
4. All required principal and interest payments were made on schedule in 2021.

Required

a. What is the theoretical basis for requiring lessees to capitalize certain long-term leases? Do not discuss the specific criteria for classifying a lease as a finance lease.

b. Prepare the long-term liabilities section of Spectrum's balance sheet at December 31, 2020.

c. Prepare a schedule showing interest expense that should appear in Spectrum's income statement for the year ended December 31, 2020.

Problem 17-105
Remeasuring a Lease Liability **LO6**

Old Co. (lessor) enters into a lease agreement with New Co. (lessee) to lease retail space in an outlet mall. The 5-year lease commenced on January 1, 2020, with no renewal options. The lease payments of $105,000 are due at the beginning of each period and the lessee incurred initial direct costs of $10,000. The lessee's incremental borrowing rate is 5% and the lease is properly classified as an operating lease.

On January 1, 2021, the lease is amended to decrease the lease term to 3 years and increase the annual rent to $110,000. The lease continues to qualify as an operating lease.

Required

a. Determine the balance of the lease liability and right-of-use asset on January 1, 2021.

b. Determine the proper treatment of the modification of the lease for the lessee.

c. Record the entry to adjust the lease liability and right-of-use asset, if applicable, using the lessee's current discount rate of 6%.

d. Determine the adjusted balances of the lease liability and right-of-use asset on January 1, 2021.

Problem 17-106
Recording Entries for a Short-Term Lease **LO7**

On January 1, 2020, lessor First Star Leasing Inc. leased equipment to lessee Convers Inc. The equipment cost the lessor $400,000, and the lessor's expected rate of return was 8%. Lease payments of $12,500 are due at the end of each quarter over the lease term of one year.

Required

a. What options does Convers Inc. have in accounting for the lease?

b. Prepare the entry for the lease assuming that the company elects the short-term lease election.

c. If the lease had an option for annual renewals at market prices, and the lessee was reasonably certain to exercise such option, how would your answer to part (*a*) change?

Accounting Decisions and Judgments

AD&J 17-107
Estimating Lease Liability **LO2**

Real World Analysis Norfolk & Southern is a major transportation company. This is an excerpt (adapted by the authors) from Note 6 to Norfolk & Southern's Year 8 annual report.

> **Long-Term Debt** The Company's noncancelable long-term leases generally include options to purchase at fair value and to extend the terms. Finance leases have been discounted at rates ranging from 3.09% to 14.26% and are collateralized by assets with a net book value of $332 million at December 31, Year 8. Minimum commitments, exclusive of nonlease costs borne by the Company are:

$ millions	Finance Leases
Year 9	$ 92
Year 10	76
Year 11	60
Year 12	57
Year 13	52
Year 14 through Year 28	194
Total	$531
Imputed interest on finance lease at an average rate of 8.4%	(140)
Lease liability included in debt	$391

Required

Provided that lease payments occur evenly throughout the year, estimate the decline in the finance lease liability in Year 8.

AD&J 17-108
Performing Lease Calculations **LO2**

Real World Analysis **Turner Broadcasting Company** sponsors CNN. Note 6 to Turner's Year 5 annual statements, dealing with long-term debt, includes the following information:

December 31 ($ thousand)	Year 5	Year 4
Bank credit facilities	$1,435,044	$1,490,000
8 3/8% Senior Notes due July 1, Year 23, net of unamortized discount of $2,558 and $2,619	297,442	297,381
7.4% Senior Notes due Year 14, net of unamortized discount of $334 and $363	249,666	249,637
8.4% Senior Debentures due Year 34, net of unamortized discount of $154 and $155	199,846	199,845
Zero coupon subordinated convertible notes, 7.25% yield, due February 13, Year 17, net of unamortized discount of $318,362 and $336,487	263,694	245,569
Convertible subordinated debentures of a wholly owned subsidiary	29,075	29,075
Obligations under finance leases due in varying amounts through Year 9, net of imputed interest of $684 and $931	5,254	6,200
Other debt, net of imputed interest of $1,175 and $29, due in varying amounts through Year 9, interest at fixed rates ranging from 6.00% to 9.49%	1,336	1,386
	$2,481,313	$2,519,093
Less current portion	1,543	1,345
	$2,479,770	$2,517,748

Other information obtained from Note 6 to Turner Broadcasting Company's financial statements:

> Included in the maturities of long-term debt amounts are obligations under finance lease of $1,492,000; $1,798,000; $1,534,000; $1,097,000; and $17,000 for each of the five years following December 31, Year 5.

Required

Estimate the company's average implicit interest rate on its lease liability. Assume there are no further long-term lease obligations after December 31, Year 13. All payments are made at the end of the year.

AD&J 17-109
Analyzing Lease Reporting Entries **LO2**

Real World Analysis **United Airlines** leases aircraft, airport passenger terminal space, aircraft hangars and related maintenance facilities, cargo terminals, other airport facilities, real estate, office and computer equipment and vehicles. Portions of the United Airlines (UAL) liability section of its Year 8 annual report and portions of Note 10 (adapted by the authors) are provided below.

Balance Sheet Liabilities at Dec. 31, $ millions	Year 8	Year 7
Current obligations under finance leases	$ 176	$ 171
Long-term obligations under finance leases	2,113	1,679

Note 10: Lease Obligations Payable during	Finance Leases
Year 9	$ 317
Year 10	308
Year 11	399
Year 12	341
Year 13	242
After Year 13	1,759
Total lease payments	3,366
Imputed interest (at rates of 5.3% to 12.2%)	(1,077)
Lease liability	2,289
Current portion	(176)
Long-term obligations under finance leases	$2,113

The statement of cash flows statement reports principal payments under finance lease obligations of $322 million.

Required

a. What was the value of the equipment acquired under finance lease obligations in Year 8?
b. What principal was paid on these new leases in Year 8?

AD&J 17-110 Assessing the Capitalization of Operating Leases **LO4**

Communication Case Prior to the recent lease standard (ASC 824), operating leases were not required to be shown on the balance sheet. For example, prior to the updated lease standard, if United Airlines' operating leases on December 31, Year 8, were added to its liabilities, its current ratio would decline from 0.69 to 0.57, while its total debt would increase from $239 million to $1,105 million. There would also be significant changes in the measured return on assets because assets would be increased and the related increase in amortization and interest expense exceeds the lease expense included in its Year 8 income statement.

Comment on this situation with regard to economic reality and the provision of useful information to decision makers. Do you support the capitalization of operating leases? Why or why not? Put your answer in the form of a memo to the FASB.

AD&J 17-111 Analyzing Interest Rates Implicit in Leases **LO2, 3**

Judgment Case If the rate implicit in the lease is not readily determinable, the lessee will use its incremental borrowing rate when determining the present value of lease payments. A lessor assesses a lease's classification using the rate implicit in the lease.

> **ASC Glossary** **Rate Implicit in the Lease**—The rate of interest that, at a provided date, causes the aggregate present value of (a) the lease payments and (b) the amount that a lessor expects to derive from the underlying asset following the end of the lease term to equal the sum of (1) the fair value of the underlying asset minus any related investment tax credit retained and expected to be realized by the lessor and (2) any deferred initial direct costs of the lessor.

> **ASC Glossary** **Incremental Borrowing Rate**—The rate of interest that a lessee would have to pay to borrow on a collateralized basis over a similar term an amount equal to the lease payments in a similar economic environment.

Required

Evaluate the foregoing criteria in light of each of the following assertions.

a. Asking a lessor what interest rate is inherent in a lease transaction would be similar to asking a farmer what rate is implicit in the price the farmer can expect now for next fall's corn crop. There are varying degrees of risk in any operation having a distant future; the higher the farmer's future risks are thought to be, the higher the farmer will set his or her rate, and the lessor will do likewise.
b. The assumption that a lease has an implicit interest rate, in many cases, represents circular reasoning in that the fair value of the leased asset itself (that is, the benchmark value used in determining the implicit rate) is determined by market forces. The value of the property stems from the payments it will command rather than the payments stemming from the value of the property.
c. One determinant of the implicit interest rate in a lease is the residual value of the property to be leased. This is a subjective judgment that, depending on the property, can be substantially in error. Lessors will not disclose what their guess is.

AD&J 17-112 Analyzing Debt Ratios **LO2, 4**

Judgment Case Speedware Corporation has entered into a debt agreement that restricts its debt-to-equity ratio to less than 2 to 1. The corporation is planning to expand its facilities, creating a need for additional financing. The board of directors is considering leasing the additional facilities but is concerned that leasing may violate its existing debt agreement; a violation would place the corporation in default. Speedware's board has asked you to analyze the following alternatives:

Alternative A—Speedware would enter into a lease that qualifies as a finance lease (to Speedware). If this alternative is selected, Speedware's reported debt-to-equity ratio would be 1.9, and its ability to issue debt in the future would be seriously constrained.

Alternative B—Speedware would enter into a lease that would be structured in such a way as to qualify as an operating lease to Speedware and as a finance lease to the lessor.

Required

Analyze and explain the consequences of each scenario.

AD&J 17-113 Analyzing Lease Disclosures **LO7**

Judgment Case The following excerpts are from disclosure of a telecommunications company for the year ended December 31, 2020.

Long-Term Debt Note The following table sets forth interest rates and other information on long-term debt outstanding at December 31 (in thousands).

Interest Rates	Maturities	2020	2019
4.5%–6.5%.	2022-2029	$1,800	$ 650
6.6%–8.0%.	2023-2039	2,500	2,400
8.1%–9.0%.	2022-2027	45	180
9.1%–9.5%.	2027-2038	90	90
		4,435	3,320
Finance lease obligations. . . .		400	450
Other.		2	1
Unamortized discount, net . . .		(36)	(40)
Total		$4,801	$3,731

Commitments—Finance Lease	
Years	
2021	$150
2022	100
2023	150
2024	50
2025	50
Thereafter.	50
Total rental commitments	550
Less interest costs	40
Present value of lease payments. . .	$510

Required

a. Is the company a lessee or lessor?

b. Where would the lease liabilities appear on the 2020 balance sheet, and in what amounts?

c. What entries would the company make to account for its finance leases during 2021 based on those leases currently on the company's balance sheet?

AD&J 17-114
Accounting for Leases by Lessor **LO3, 5**

Trueblood Case The Trueblood case series, prepared by Deloitte professionals, are based on recent accounting technical issues that require research and judgment. The cases may be accessed through the Deloitte foundation at the following website: https://www2.deloitte.com/us/en/pages/about-deloitte/articles/trueblood-case-studies-deloitte-foundation.html

The following case is relevant to the content provided in this chapter: Case: 15-11 Deal for a Dozer. In this case, classification and accounting for leases is explored from a lessor perspective.

AD&J 17-115
Defining Terms **LO1, 2, 3, 4, 5**

Codification Skills How are the terms (1) lease, (2) lessee, (3) lessor, (4) underlying asset, and (5) unguaranteed residual asset, defined in the Codification?

AD&J 17-116
Performing Accounting Research **LO1, 2, 3, 4, 5**

Codification Skills Through research in the Codification, identify the specific citation for each of the following items included as guidance in this chapter.

a. Specific topics not covered by ASC 842 (lease standard) FASB ASC ☐-☐-☐-☐

b. Explicit or implicit specification of an underlying asset in a contract FASB ASC ☐-☐-☐-☐

c. Variable rates depending on an index or rate FASB ASC ☐-☐-☐-☐

d. Lease classification criteria FASB ASC ☐-☐-☐-☐

AD&J 17-117
Performing Accounting Research **LO6**

Codification Skills A company is preparing annual financial statements, which includes the valuation of a finance lease. The lease was modified during the current year from the original term of 5 years to a modified term of 10 years. The extension was not part of a renewal option. The company believes that it needs to remeasure the lease liability but is uncertain as to what interest rate to use to discount the lease liability. What guidance is available in the Codification?

FASB ASC ☐-☐-☐-☐

Appendix—Brief Exercises

App—Brief Exercise 17-118
Classifying a Lease **LO8**
Hint: See Demo 17-8

Lessor Inc. entered into a 5-year lease agreement with Lessee Inc. to lease equipment with a useful life of 7 years. The equipment will be returned to the lessor at the end of the lease term and is expected to have alternative uses. The lessor obtained a guarantee from a third party (insurance company) for the expected residual of $5,000 at the end of the lease term. Lease payments are $3,500 due annually at the end of each annual period. The implicit rate of the lease is 5.117%. The fair value of the equipment is $19,000 and the carrying value is $17,000. Determine the proper classification of the lease for the lessor.

App—Brief Exercise 17-119
Recording a Direct Financing Lease **LO8**
Hint: See Demo 17-8

Using the information from Brief Exercise 17-118, record the lessor's entry at the commencement of the lease.

App—Brief Exercise 17-120
Recording a Sale-Leaseback **LO9**
Hint: See Demo 17-9

Olympia Co. owns a building with a current carrying value on January 1, 2020, of $450,000, an original cost of $700,000, a 10-year remaining useful life, and no residual value. On this date, it was sold to Beta Investor Inc. for $500,000 cash. Simultaneously, the two parties executed a 5-year lease with a 7% implicit rate of interest, known by both parties. Each annual payment of $78,000 is due on December 31. Assuming that the lease is classified as an operating lease, record Olympia's journal entry(s) on January 1, 2020.

App—Brief Exercise 17-121
Recording a Failed Sale-Leaseback **LO9**
Hint: See Demo 17-9

Olympia Co. owns a building with a current carrying value on January 1, 2020, of $450,000, an original cost of $700,000, a 10-year remaining useful life, and no residual value. On this date, it was sold to Beta Investor Inc. for $500,000 cash. Simultaneously, the two parties executed a 10-year lease with a 7% implicit rate of interest, known by both parties. Each annual payment of $75,000 is due on December 31. Assuming that the lease is classified as a finance lease, record Olympia's journal entry(s) on January 1, 2020.

Appendix—Exercises

App—Exercise 17-122
Recording a Direct Financing Lease **LO8**
Hint: See Demo 17-8

On January 1, 2020, Lessor Inc. entered into a 5-year lease agreement with Lessee Inc. to lease equipment with a useful life of 7 years. The equipment will be returned to the lessor at the end of the lease term and is expected to have alternative uses. The lessor obtained a guarantee from a third party (insurance company) for the expected residual of $100,000 at the end of the lease term. Lease payments are $95,000 due annually at the end of each annual period. The implicit rate of the lease is 4.3265%. The fair value of the equipment is $500,000 and the carrying value is $475,000.

Required

a. Determine the proper classification of the lease for the lessor.
b. Record the lessor's entry on January 1, 2020.
c. Compute the discount rate used to amortize the lease receivable.
d. Prepare the schedule to amortize the lease receivable.
e. Prepare the lessor's entry on December 31, 2020.

App—Exercise 17-123
Recording a Sale-Leaseback **LO9**
Hint: See Demo 17-9

On January 1, 2020, Metalwork Manufacturing Inc. enters into a sales agreement with 4M Inc. to sell a building for $950,000 with a simultaneous agreement to lease the building back for five years. Other information about the transactions is as follows.

- The net carrying amount of the building at the date of sale is $800,000 (original cost, $1.2 million).
- The lease payment is $100,000 (end of year payments).
- Annual depreciation on the building is $75,000.
- Metalwork does not guarantee the residual value at the end of the lease term, but the agreement allows for Metalwork to repurchase the building at market price for equivalent property.
- Metalwork's incremental borrowing rate is 8% and the implicit rate on the lease is unknown to Metalwork.
- There are no alternative assets readily available.

Required

a. Determine the lease classification for Metalwork Manufacturing.
b. Record the journal entries for Metalwork Manufacturing for 2020.
c. Record the journal entry on January 1, 2025, at the conclusion of the lease.

App—Exercise 17-124
Recording a Sale-Leaseback **LO9**
Hint: See Demo 17-9

On January 1, 2020, Wal-Market Inc. sells a building to Diversified Investors for $9,000,000, its current fair value. Prior to the sale, the carrying value of the building was $7,000,000 (original cost of $15 million). The estimated remaining useful life of the building is 20 years, with no residual value; straight-line depreciation is used. On January 1, 2020, Wal-Market Inc. signed a 10-year noncancelable leaseback agreement that has an 8% implicit rate of return for the lessor, unknown to the lessee. The lessee's incremental borrowing rate is 7%. The annual payments of $992,000 start on December 31, 2020. The lease agreement does not contain a purchase option, the lessee does not guarantee a residual value, and the building does not revert to the lessee at lease end. The building would have alternative uses at lease end.

Required

a. Determine the lease classification for Wal-Market Inc.
b. Record the journal entries for Wal-Market Inc. for 2020.

Answers to Review Exercises

Review 17-1

Option One	
1. Ownership transfer	Title does not transfer
2. Purchase option	No purchase option
3. Lease term length	8 < 9 (75% of life of 12)
4. Present value of lease payments	PV of lease payments of $164,559[1] < 90% of fair value of $200,000
5. Alternative use	No indication of limited use
Lease Classification	
Lessee: Operating Lease	No criteria met

[1] PV(0.06,8,–25000,0,1)

Option Two	
1. Ownership transfer	Title does not transfer
2. Purchase option	No purchase option
3. Lease term length	10 > 9 (75% of life of 12)
4. Present value of lease payments	PV of lease payments of $195,042[2] > 90% of fair value of $200,000
5. Alternative use	No indication of limited use
Lease Classification	
Lessee: Finance Lease	Two criteria met (#3, #4)

[2] PV(0.06,10,–25000,0,1)

Option Three	
1. Ownership transfer	Title does not transfer
2. Purchase option	Yes, discounted purchase option
3. Lease term length	8 < 9 (75% of life of 12)
4. Present value of lease payments	PV of lease payments of $200,000[3] > 90% of fair value of $200,000
5. Alternative use	No indication of limited use
Lease Classification	
Lessee: Finance Lease	Two criteria met (#2, #4)

[3] PV(0.054544,8,–25000,–50000,1)

Option Four	
1. Ownership transfer	Title does not transfer
2. Purchase option	No purchase option
3. Lease term length	8 < 9 (75% of life of 12)
4. Present value of lease payments	PV of lease payments of $173,874[4] < 90% of fair value of $200,000
5. Alternative use	No indication of limited use
Lease Classification	
Lessee: Operating Lease	No criteria met

[4] PV(0.06,8,–28000,0,0)

Review 17-2

a.

1. Ownership transfer	Title does not transfer
2. Purchase option	No purchase option
3. Lease term length	4 < 4.5 (75% of life of 6)
4. Present value of lease payments	PV of lease payments of $65,000* = 100% of fair value of $65,000
5. Alternative use	No information indicating customization
Lease Classification	
Lessee: Finance Lease	One criterion met (#4)

*PV(0.09,4,–15999.49,–12000,1)

b.

Date	Lease Payment	Interest on Liability	Lease Liability Reduction	Net Lease Liability
Jan. 1, 2020				$56,499[1]
Jan. 1, 2020	$15,999	$ 0	$15,999	40,500
Jan. 1, 2021	15,999	3,645	12,354	28,146
Jan. 1, 2022	15,999	2,533	13,466	14,680
Jan. 1, 2023	15,999	1,319[2]	14,680	0
	$63,996	$7,497	$56,499	

[1] Rounded [2] PV(0.09,4,–15999.49,0,1)

c. **January 1, 2020—To record right-of-use asset and lease liability**

Right-of-Use Asset	56,499	
Lease Liability		56,499

Assets = Liabilities + Equity
+56,499 +56,499
R-of-U Asset: 56,499 | ; Lease Liab: | 56,499

January 1, 2020—To record lease payment

Lease Liability	15,999	
Cash		15,999

Assets = Liabilities + Equity
−15,999 −15,999
Cash: | 15,999 ; Lease Liab: 15,999 | 56,499

December 31, 2020—To record interest expense

Interest Expense	3,645	
Lease Liability		3,645

Assets = Liabilities + Equity
+3,645 −3,645
Interest Exp: 3,645 | ; Lease Liab: 15,999 | 56,499, 3,645; balance 44,145

December 31, 2020—To record amortization of right-of-use asset

Amortization Expense	14,125	
Right-of-Use Asset ($56,499/4)		14,125

Assets = Liabilities + Equity
−14,125 −14,125
Amort Exp: 14,125 | ; R-of-U Asset: 56,499 | 14,125; balance 42,374

d. The result of the lease classification test does not change because the total guaranteed residual value is used in the present value of lease payment test. Therefore, the lease is still classified as a finance lease.

Date	Lease Payment	Interest on Liability	Lease Liability Reduction	Net Lease Liability
Jan. 1, 2020				$62,521[2]
Jan. 1, 2020	$15,999	$ 0	$15,999	46,522
Jan. 1, 2021	15,999	4,187	11,812	34,710
Jan. 1, 2022	15,999	3,124	12,875	21,835
Jan. 1, 2023	15,999	1,965	14,034	7,801
Jan. 1, 2024	8,500	701[1]	7,801	0
	$72,496	$9,977	$62,521	

[1] rounded. [2] =PV(0.09,4,–15999.49,–8500,1)

January 1, 2020— To record right-of-use asset and lease liability

Right-of-Use Asset	62,521	
Lease Liability		62,521

Assets = Liabilities + Equity
+62,521 +62,521
R-of-U Asset: 62,521 | ; Lease Liab: | 62,521

January 1, 2020—To record lease payment

Lease Liability	15,999	
Cash		15,999

Assets = Liabilities + Equity
−15,999 −15,999
Cash: | 15,999 ; Lease Liab: 15,999 | 62,521

December 31, 2020—To record interest expense

Interest Expense	4,187	
Lease Liability		4,187

Assets = Liabilities + Equity
+4,187 −4,187
Interest Exp: 4,187 | ; Lease Liab: 15,999 | 62,521, 4,187; balance 50,709

Assets	=	Liabilities	+	Equity
−15,630				−15,630

R-of-U Asset		Amort Exp	
62,521	15,630	15,630	
46,891			

December 31, 2020—To record amortization of right-of-use asset

Amortization Expense	15,630	
Right-of-Use Asset ($62,521/4)		15,630

Review 17-3

a. Lease payment: $90,674.11 (PMT(0.08,3,-300000,60000,1))
Lease receivable: $300,000 (PV(0.08,3,-90674.11,-60000,1))

Assets	=	Liabilities	+	Equity
+300,000				
−300,000				

Lease Receiv		Inventory	
300,000			300,000

b. **January 1, 2020—To derecognize asset and record investment in lease**

Lease Receivable	300,000	
Inventory		300,000

c.

Date	Lease Payment	Interest on Receivable	Lease Receivable Net Reduction	Net Lease Receivable
Jan. 1, 2020				$300,000
Jan. 1, 2020	$ 90,674	$ 0	$ 90,674	209,326
Jan. 1, 2021	90,674	16,746	73,928	135,398
Jan. 1, 2022	90,674	10,832	79,842	55,556
Jan. 1, 2023	60,000	4,444	55,556	0
	$332,022	$32,022	$300,000	

d.

Assets	=	Liabilities	+	Equity
+90,674				
−90,674				

Cash		Lease Receiv	
90,674		300,000	90,674

January 1, 2020—To record lease payment

Cash	90,674	
Lease Receivable		90,674

Assets	=	Liabilities	+	Equity
+16,746				+16,746

Lease Receiv		Interest Rev	
300,000	90,674		16,746
16,746			

December 31, 2020—To recognize interest revenue

Lease Receivable	16,746	
Interest Revenue		16,746

Assets	=	Liabilities	+	Equity
+90,674				
−90,674				

Cash		Lease Receiv	
90,674		300,000	90,674
90,674		16,746	90,674

January 1, 2021—To record lease payment

Cash	90,674	
Lease Receivable		90,674

Assets	=	Liabilities	+	Equity
+10,832				+10,832

Lease Receiv		Interest Rev	
300,000	90,674		16,746
16,746	90,674		10,832
10,832	90,674		

December 31, 2021—To recognize interest revenue

Lease Receivable	10,832	
Interest Revenue		10,832

Assets	=	Liabilities	+	Equity
+90,674				
−90,674				

Cash		Lease Receiv	
90,674		300,000	90,674
90,674		16,746	90,674
90,674		10,832	90,674

January 1, 2022—To record lease payment

Cash	90,674	
Lease Receivable		90,674

Assets	=	Liabilities	+	Equity
+4,444				+4,444

Lease Receiv		Interest Rev	
300,000	90,674		16,746
16,746	90,674		10,832
10,832			4,444
4,444			

December 31, 2022—To recognize interest revenue

Lease Receivable	4,444	
Interest Revenue		4,444

Assets	=	Liabilities	+	Equity
+25,000				
+35,000				
−60,000				

Cash		Lease Receivable	
90,674		300,000	90,674
90,674		16,746	90,674
90,674		10,832	90,674
35,000		4,444	60,000
		0	

Inventory	
25,000	

December 31, 2022—To record lease termination

Inventory	25,000	
Cash	35,000	
Lease Receivable		60,000

Review 17-4

a. Operating Lease—no lease classification criteria met.

b. **Lease Liability Amortization Schedule**

Date	Lease Payment	Interest on Liability	Lease Liability Reduction	Net Lease Liability
Jan. 1, 2020				$585,127*
Jan. 1, 2020	$ 75,000	$ —	$ 75,000	510,127
Jan. 1, 2021	75,000	30,608	44,392	465,735
Jan. 1, 2022	75,000	27,944	47,056	418,679
Jan. 1, 2023	75,000	25,121	49,879	368,800
Jan. 1, 2024	75,000	22,128	52,872	315,928
Jan. 1, 2025	75,000	18,956	56,044	259,884
Jan. 1, 2026	75,000	15,593	59,407	200,477
Jan. 1, 2027	75,000	12,029	62,971	137,506
Jan. 1, 2028	75,000	8,250	66,750	70,756
Jan. 1, 2029	75,000	4,244	70,756	0
	$750,000	$164,873	$585,127	

* =PV(0.06,10,–75000,0,1)

c. **Right-of-Use Asset Amortization Schedule**

Date	Lease Expense*	Interest on Liability	Right-of-Use Asset Amortization	Net Right-of-Use Asset
Jan. 1, 2020		0		$586,127**
Dec. 31, 2020	$ 75,100	$ 30,608	$ 44,492	541,635
Dec. 31, 2021	75,100	27,944	47,156	494,479
Dec. 31, 2022	75,100	25,121	49,979	444,500
Dec. 31, 2023	75,100	22,128	52,972	391,528
Dec. 31, 2024	75,100	18,956	56,144	335,384
Dec. 31, 2025	75,100	15,593	59,507	275,877
Dec. 31, 2026	75,100	12,029	63,071	212,806
Dec. 31, 2027	75,100	8,250	66,850	145,956
Dec. 31, 2028	75,100	4,244	70,856	75,100
Dec. 31, 2029	75,100	—	75,100	0
	$751,000	$164,873	$586,127	

* (($75,000 × 10) + $1,000)/10

** $585,127 + $1,000

d. **January 1, 2020—To record right-of-use asset and lease liability**

Right-of-Use Asset.	586,127	
Lease Liability		585,127
Cash		1,000

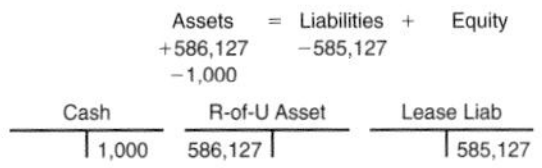

January 1, 2020—To record lease payment

Lease Liability	75,000	
Cash		75,000

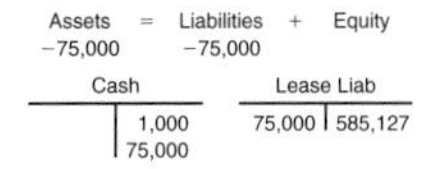

December 31, 2020—To record lease expense

Lease Expense	75,100	
Lease Liability		30,608
Right-of-Use Asset.		44,492

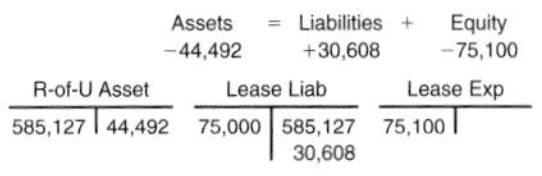

January 1, 2021—To record lease payment

Lease Liability	75,000	
Cash		75,000

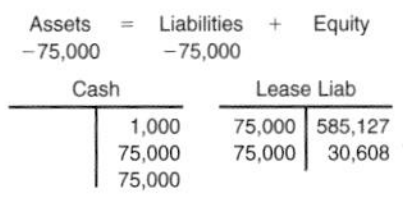

Assets = Liabilities + Equity
−47,156 +27,944 −75,100
R-of-U Asset: 586,127 | 44,492; 47,156
Lease Liab: 75,000; 75,000 | 585,127; 30,608; 27,944
Lease Exp: 75,100; 75,100 |

December 31, 2021—To record lease expense

Lease Expense	75,100	
Lease Liability		27,944
Right-of-Use Asset		47,156

Review 17-5

a.

1. Ownership transfer	Title does not transfer
2. Purchase option	No purchase option
3. Lease term length	7 < 37.5 (75% of life of 50)
4. PV of lease payments	PV of lease payments of $1,065,118 < 90% of fair value of $3 million
5. Alternative use	No indication of limited use
Lease Classification	
Lessor: Operating Lease	No criteria met

Assets = Liabilities + Equity
+180,000 +180,000
Cash: 180,000 |
Def Lease Rev: | 180,000

b. **January 1, 2020—To record receipt of lease payment**

Cash	180,000	
Deferred Lease Revenue		180,000

Assets = Liabilities + Equity
−180,000 +180,000
Def Lease Rev: 180,000 | 180,000
Lease Rev: | 180,000

December 31, 2020—To record lease revenue

Deferred Lease Revenue	180,000	
Lease Revenue		180,000

Assets = Liabilities + Equity
−60,000 −60,000
Accum Deprec: | 60,000
Deprec Exp: 60,000 |

December 31, 2020—To record depreciation

Depreciation Expense ($3,000,000/50)	60,000	
Accumulated Depreciation		60,000

Assets = Liabilities + Equity
+1,200
−1,200
Cash: 180,000 | 1,200
Init Dir Cost: 1,200 |

c. **January 1, 2020—To record initial direct cost**

Initial Direct Cost	1,200	
Cash		1,200

Assets = Liabilities + Equity
−171 −171
Init Dir Cost: 1,200 | 171
Selling Exp: 171 |

December 31, 2020—To amortize deferred cost

Selling Expense	171	
Initial Direct Cost ($1,200/7)		171

Review 17-6

a. Remeasurement.

b. New lease (lessee continues to record the original lease as planned, but records a new lease related to the rent of the warehouse space).

c. Reassessment of lease classification with remeasurement.

d. Reassessment of lease classification with remeasurement.

Review 17-7

Assets = Liabilities + Equity
−500 −500
Cash: | 500
Lease Exp: 500 |

To record rent expense each month in 2020

Lease Expense	500	
Cash		500

Review 17-8

a.

			Criteria Met?
1. Ownership transfer	Title does not transfer		No
2. Purchase option	No purchase option		No
3. Lease term length	Lease term is 67% of the economic life		No
4. PV of lease payments	PV of lease payments.	$34,136 *	No
	90% of fair value.	$34,200	
5. Alternative use	No		No

*=PV(0.0665682,4,−10000)

Considering the third-party residual guarantee			
4. PV of lease payments	PV of lease payments.	$38,000**	Yes
	90% of fair value.	$34,200	
Lease Classification			
Direct financing lease			

**PV(0.0665682,4,−10000,−5000)

b. **January 1, 2020—To record lease receivable**

Lease Receivable, Net ($38,000 − $3,000).	35,000	
Inventory		35,000

Assets = Liabilities + Equity
+35,000
−35,000
Lease Receiv, Net: 35,000 |
Inventory: | 35,000

c. Discount rate: RATE(4,10000,−35000,5000) 10.14070%

d.

Date	Lease Payment	Interest on Receivable	Lease Receivable Net Reduction	Net Lease Receivable
Jan. 1, 2020.				$35,000
Dec. 31, 2020.	$10,000	$3,549	$ 6,451	28,549
Dec. 31, 2021.	10,000	2,895	7,105	21,444
Dec. 31, 2022.	10,000	2,175	7,825	13,619
Dec. 31, 2023.	15,000	1,381	13,619	0

e. **December 31, 2020—To record lease payment**

Cash	10,000	
Lease Receivable, Net		6,451
Interest Revenue.		3,549

Assets = Liabilities + Equity
+10,000 +3,549
−6,451
Cash: 10,000 |
Interest Rev: | 3,549
Lease Receiv, Net: 35,000 | 6,451

Review 17-9

a. The lease is a finance lease (Criteria 3: 15/20 = 75%; Criteria 4: PV = $8,784,291 > 90% of $9,000,000), thus the transaction is accounted for as a loan by the lessor to the lessee.

b. **January 1, 2020—To record note payable on failed sale**

Cash	9,000,000	
Note Payable		9,000,000

Assets = Liabilities + Equity
+9,000,000 +9,000,000
Cash: 9,000,000 |
Note Payable: | 9,000,000

December 31, 2020—To record lease payment

Interest Expense ($9,000,000 × 0.08).	720,000	
Note Payable	331,466	
Cash		1,051,466

Assets = Liabilities + Equity
−1,051,466 −331,466 −720,000
Cash: 9,000,000 | 1,051,466
Note Payable: 331,466 | 9,000,000
Interest Exp: 720,000 |

December 31, 2020—To record depreciation expense

Depreciation Expense ($7,000,000/20)	350,000	
Accumulated Depreciation.		350,000

Assets = Liabilities + Equity
−350,000 −350,000
Accum Deprec: | 350,000
Deprec Exp: 350,000 |

18 Income Taxes

THE COCA-COLA COMPANY AND SUBSIDIARIES

Income taxes from continuing operations consisted of the following for the years ended December 31, 2017, 2016 and 2015 (in millions):

2017	United States	State and Local	International	Total
Current	$5,438	$121	$1,257	$6,816
Deferred	(1,783)	14	513	(1,256)

THE COCA-COLA COMPANY AND SUBSIDIARIES

The tax effects of temporary differences and carryforwards that give rise to deferred tax assets and liabilities consist of the following (in millions):

December 31,	2017	2016
Deferred tax assets:		
Property, plant and equipment	$ 99	$ 144
Trademarks and other intangible assets	98	114
Equity method investments (including foreign currency translation adjustment)	300	684
Derivative financial instruments	387	193
Other liabilities	861	1,141
Benefit plans	977	1,599
Net operating/capital loss carryforwards	520	461
Other	163	135
Gross deferred tax assets	3,405	4,471
Valuation allowances	(501)	(530)
Total deferred tax assets[1,2]	$2,904	$3,941
Deferred tax liabilities:		
Property, plant and equipment	$(819)	$(1,176)
Trademarks and other intangible assets	(978)	(2,694)
Equity method investments (including foreign currency translation adjustment)	(1,835)	(1,718)
Derivative financial instruments	(436)	(1,121)
Other liabilities	(50)	(149)
Benefit plans	(289)	(487)
Other	(688)	(635)
Total deferred tax liabilities[3]	(5,095)	(7,980)
Net deferred tax liabilities[4]	$(2,191)	$(4,039)

[1] Current deferred tax assets of $80 million were included in the line item prepaid expenses and other assets in our consolidated balance sheet as of December 31, 2016.

[2] Noncurrent deferred tax assets of $331 million and $326 million were includ… other assets in our consolidated balance sheets as of December 31, 2017 and 2016, respectively.

[3] Current deferred tax liabilities of $692 million were included in the line item …lidated balance sheet as of December 31, 2016.

[4] The decrease in the net deferred tax liabilities was primarily the result of t… refranchising certain bottling territories in North America. Refer to Note 2.

A reconciliation of the statutory U.S. federal tax rate and our effective tax rate is as follows:

Year Ended December 31,	2017	2016	2015
Statutory U.S. federal tax rate	35.0%	35.0%	35.0%
State and local income taxes—net of federal benefit	1.2	1.2	1.2
Earnings in jurisdictions taxed at rates different from the statutory U.S. federal rate	(9.7)	(17.5)	(12.7)
Equity income or loss	(3.4)	(3.0)	(1.7)
Tax Reform Act	53.5	—	—
Other—net	5.9	3.8	1.5
Effective tax rate	82.5%	19.5%	23.3%

Chapter Preview

The focus of this chapter is how to record and report income taxes on financial statements. While we are not preparing a tax return, we will explore how some events are recognized differently for financial reporting and tax purposes. We begin with a discussion on temporary differences that result in deferred tax liabilities, deferred tax assets, and valuation allowances. Next, we explain what are known as *permanent differences* and other items that reduce or increase a corporation's reported effective tax rate. We then explore how a change in tax rates enacted into law impacts the accounting for deferred taxes and reported financial accounting income. We also examine the accounting for loss carryforwards and the accounting for uncertain tax positions. Throughout the chapter, we discuss the financial reporting and disclosure requirements for these topics. Our focus is on U.S. corporations with only U.S. earnings. However, in an *Expanding Your Knowledge* section, we describe accounting for income taxes on foreign earnings of a U.S. multinational corporation. The U.S. has enacted a major tax reform, Tax Cuts and Jobs Act (TCJA), and we explain relevant issues arising from TCJA.

Action Plan

LO	Topic/Subtopic	Page	Demos	Reviews	Assignments
LO 18–1	**Describe taxable temporary differences that lead to deferred tax liabilities and related income tax expense** Taxable Temporary Differences :: Deferred Tax Liabilities :: Income Tax Payable :: Income Tax Expense	18-4	D18-1	R18-1	18, 19, 20, 21, 22, 23, 29, 35, 36, 37, 38, 44, 45, 46, 47, 48, 50, 51, 52, 53, 54, 55, 56, 57, 59, 60, 63, 64, 65, 67, 68, 69, 79, 80, 82, 83, 84, 85, 90, 92, 94, 95, 97, 98, 100, 101
LO 18–2	**Describe deductible temporary differences that lead to deferred tax assets and related income tax expense** Deductible Temporary Differences :: Deferred Tax Assets :: Income Tax Payable :: Income Tax Expense	18-9	D18-2	R18-2	19, 20, 24, 25, 26, 27, 28, 29, 36, 48, 49, 50, 51, 52, 53, 54, 56, 57, 58, 59, 60, 65, 66, 68, 69, 81, 83, 84, 86, 87, 90, 92, 94, 95, 98, 99, 100
LO 18–3	**Explain how to record and report a valuation allowance for deferred tax assets** Valuation Allowance:: Contra Asset :: More Likely than Not :: Negative and Positive Evidence	18-13	D18-3	R18-3	30, 31, 32, 48, 61, 62, 92, 96, 98, 99, 100, 101
LO 18–4	**Describe *permanent differences* and other items that impact the reported effective tax rate** Permanent Difference:: No Deferred Tax Effect :: Reconciliation of Statutory Tax Rate to Effective Tax Rate	18-16	D18-4A D18-4B	R18-4	33, 34, 35, 36, 48, 58, 59, 60, 77, 83, 84, 95, 98, 100
LO 18–5	**Explain how a change in tax rates impacts deferred taxes** Enacted Future Tax Rates :: Period of Change :: Deferred Tax Accounts	18-21	D18-5	R18-5	37, 38, 48, 60, 63, 64, 65, 66, 67, 68, 69, 80, 85, 86, 87, 93, 98, 100
LO 18–6	**Describe accounting for net operating loss carryforwards** Net Operating Loss Carryforward:: Deferred Tax Asset :: Valuation Allowance	18-24	D18-6	R18-6	39, 40, 48, 70, 71, 72, 73, 74, 75, 88, 91, 94, 98, 100, 101
LO 18–7	**Explain and demonstrate accounting for uncertainty in income tax decisions** Uncertain Tax Position :: Two-Step Process :: Recognition Threshold :: Measurement of Tax Benefit	18-27	D18-7	R18-7	41, 48, 76, 89, 98, 100, 101, 102
LO 18–8	**Describe financial statement disclosure for deferred taxes and income tax expense** Net Deferred Tax Amount :: Noncurrent Presentation :: Disclosure Requirements	18-31	D18-8	R18-8	42, 43, 48, 52, 53, 55, 58, 78, 81, 82, 83, 84, 90, 94, 97, 98
LO 18–9	**APPENDIX 18A—Apply intraperiod tax allocation** Allocation of Tax Expense (Benefit) :: Continuing Operations :: Discontinued Operations :: Comprehensive Income	18-33	D18-9	R18-9	48, 101, 103, 104, 108, 112
LO 18–10	**APPENDIX 18B—Apply tax effects to changes in accounting principle and error corrections** Change in Accounting Principle :: Error Correction :: Retrospective Treatment :: Tax Effects	18-35	D18-10A D18-10B	R18-10	105, 106, 107, 109, 110, 111, 113, 114

Expanded Chapter Preview

For a U.S. company with earnings only in the U.S., **taxable income** is income determined by applying the measurement rules found in the U.S. tax code (Internal Revenue Code). Taxable income is multiplied by the U.S. corporate income tax rate to determine the amount of income taxes a company must pay for the year. In this chapter, we use a 25% tax rate. The U.S. Federal tax rate is currently 21%. We assume a tax rate of 25% for ease in math.

Pretax GAAP income (financial accounting income or income recognized for financial reporting purposes) on the other hand is the amount of income before income taxes determined under GAAP.

Let's assume that the tax bases and the GAAP carrying values of the assets and liabilities of Vail Inc. on December 31, 2020 are the same and that no other differences between accounting and taxable incomes exist. Pretax GAAP income of $40,000 equals taxable income of $40,000, and the tax rate is 25%. In this case, income tax expense of $10,000 on the financial statements *would equal* the total tax for the year computed on the income tax return illustrated as follows.

Financial Accounting	
Pretax GAAP income	$40,000
Tax rate.	× 25%
Income tax expense (financial statements)	**$10,000**

Tax Return	
Taxable income.	$40,000
Tax rate.	× 25%
Income tax (tax return). . .	**$10,000**

However, the reality is that pretax GAAP income and taxable income almost always differ. There are several reasons for this. For example, the rules for determining what is a taxable revenue and what is a tax-deductible expense can and often do differ from what are defined as revenues and expenses by GAAP. The goals and motivation for the development of tax laws differ from the development of GAAP. As discussed earlier in this text, financial accounting is intended to provide information to external users about the financial performance of the company. The information presented to external users should faithfully represent the performance of the company. In contrast, the tax code is written to raise revenue to fund public finance and also to encourage and discourage certain behaviors. For example, the U.S. government encourages corporations to invest more in plant and equipment, with the aim of increasing employment in the economy by putting people to work building plants and equipment. The government encourages such behavior by allowing companies investing in plant and equipment to deduct the cost for tax purposes at a rapid rate and over a shorter period than the expected useful life of the assets. *In many cases accelerated or even immediate expensing is allowed.* This allows a company to recover its investment rapidly by reducing the amount of income taxes paid early in the asset's life. For financial reporting purposes, however, GAAP requires companies to depreciate assets over their estimated useful life. This is an example of how the measurement rules for determining taxable income differ from GAAP rules. In addition, companies choose among GAAP alternatives so as to present fairly financial conditions and results of operations. Companies generally choose among alternatives allowed by tax laws to minimize the company's tax obligation.

Because the objectives of these two sets of rules (Internal Revenue Code and U.S. GAAP) are different and because reporting incentives are different, *it is no surprise that taxable income is usually different from pre-tax accounting income and that the GAAP basis of assets and liabilities often differs from the tax basis of assets and liabilities.* For example, the tax basis (original cost less depreciation deductions allowed) of an asset at the end of the first full year in service that, upon acquisition, was allowed a 100% cost deduction for tax purposes (full expensing) is zero. For financial accounting, however, the carrying value is greater than zero because the asset is depreciated over the useful life and, thus, the carrying value at the end of the first year is the original cost less only the first year GAAP depreciation.

In this chapter we discuss the accounting for *temporary differences*—differences between taxable income and accounting income that reverse over time, such as the asset depreciation example. A **temporary difference** exists when the tax basis of an asset or liability differs from the basis (or the carrying value) for financial accounting purposes.

740-10-25-20 An assumption inherent in an entity's statement of financial position prepared in accordance with generally accepted accounting principles (GAAP) is that the reported amounts of assets and liabilities will be recovered and settled, respectively. Based on that assumption, a difference between the tax basis of an asset or a liability and its reported amount in the statement of financial position will result in taxable or deductible amounts in some future year(s) when the reported amounts of assets are recovered and the reported amounts of liabilities are settled.

Temporary differences are accounted for using a **balance sheet approach** which focuses on the differences between the **tax basis** of a company's assets and liabilities and the **GAAP basis**, the reported amounts under GAAP on the balance sheet. The differences are temporary because they originate in one or more periods and then reverse and have the opposite effect in one or more future periods. Temporary differences must be accounted for in income tax expense to report net income on an accrual basis. To only record income taxes paid would overlook the tax impact of the reported net income under GAAP. Recall, financial accounting records tax expense related to reported accounting earnings whether the tax is due in a tax payment for the current period or in a future period. Accruals for some parts of tax expense are required.

740-10-05-7 A temporary difference refers to a difference between the tax basis of an asset or liability, determined based on recognition and measurement requirements for tax positions, and its reported amount in the financial statements that will result in taxable or deductible amounts in future years when the reported amount of the asset or liability is recovered or settled, respectively.

We also discuss items that are not temporary in nature but that either are differences between taxable income and accounting income that do not reverse (items known as *permanent differences*) and other items that affect income tax expense but do not affect either taxable income or pretax accounting income (such as tax credits and state income taxes that are required to be paid).

Describe taxable temporary differences that lead to deferred tax liabilities and related income tax expense reporting — LO 18-1

Taxable temporary differences are temporary differences that, when the differences reverse in a future period, *increase future taxable income* relative to pretax GAAP income. In other words, to continue on with our depreciation example from above, in the year an asset is purchased, taxable income is lower (relative to financial accounting income in that period) because tax depreciation is more accelerated (either full expensing or accelerated depreciation) than depreciation for financial accounting income. However, in future periods, when financial accounting depreciation is still being expensed but tax depreciation is much smaller or even zero, the company will have higher taxable income relative to financial accounting income (all else constant).

LO 18-1 Overview

Deferred Tax Liability
- Created from taxable temporary differences that *increase* future taxable income
- Asset GAAP basis > Asset tax basis
- Liability GAAP basis < Liability tax basis

Creation of Future Taxable Amounts

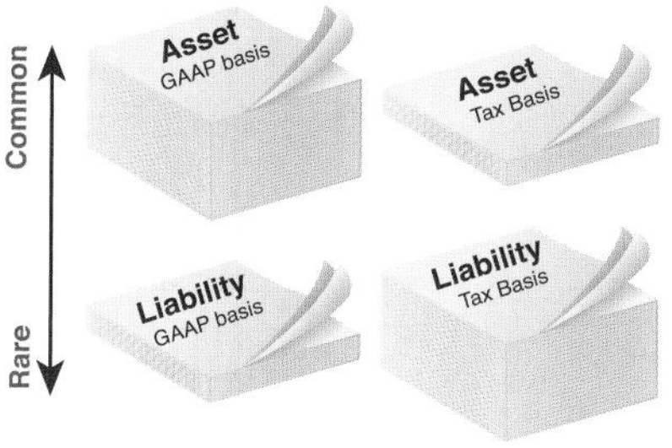

A future taxable amount results when either (a) the reported value of an asset (GAAP basis) is greater than the tax basis of an asset or (2) when the reported value of a liability (GAAP basis) is less than the tax basis of a liability. (However, cases where the GAAP basis of a liability is less than its tax basis are rare and involve complex transactions outside the scope of this text.)

740-10-25-23 Temporary differences that will result in taxable amounts in future years when the related asset or liability is recovered or settled are often referred to as taxable temporary differences.

A taxable temporary difference creates a deferred tax liability. **Deferred tax liabilities** are expected future tax obligations arising from temporary taxable differences existing at the end of the accounting period. A deferred tax liability is calculated by multiplying the enacted tax rate that will be in effect when the taxable temporary difference reverses by the taxable temporary difference in asset bases. We discuss changes in tax rates in a later section.

ASC Glossary Deferred tax liability—The deferred tax consequences attributable to taxable temporary differences. A deferred tax liability is measured using the applicable enacted tax rate and provisions of the enacted tax law.

Taxable temporary differences resulting in deferred tax liabilities result when either revenues are recognized in taxable income *after* GAAP income or when expenses are recognized in taxable income *before* GAAP income. The **Tax Cuts and Jobs Act** requires taxpayers to recognize income no later than the taxable year in which such income is taken into account as income on the taxpayer's applicable financial statement (but this requirement does not apply for most special methods of accounting such as installment sales). Thus, such cases where revenue is recognized for tax purposes later in time relative to financial accounting income are less common in 2018 and after. If they exist, they create deferred tax liabilities as discussed here.

COCA COLA

Real World—DEFERRED TAX LIABILITIES

COCA COLA [KO]

Coca Cola Company provided the following summary of deferred tax liabilities in a recent Form 10-K.

Note 14 (excerpt): Income Taxes The tax effects of temporary differences and carryforwards that give rise to deferred tax assets and liabilities consist of the following:

December 31 (In millions)	2017	2016
Deferred tax liabilities:		
Property, plant and equipment	**$ (819)**	$(1,176)
Trademarks and other intangible assets	**(978)**	(2,694)
Equity method investments (including foreign currency translation adjustment)	**(1,835)**	(1,718)
Derivative financial instruments	**(436)**	(1,121)
Other liabilities	**(50)**	(149)
Benefit plans	**(289)**	(487)
Other	**(688)**	(635)
Total deferred tax liabilities	**$(5,095)**	$(7,980)

Taxable Temporary Differences: Revenues in Taxable Income *After* GAAP Income

740-10-25-20a Revenues or gains that are taxable after they are recognized in financial income. An asset (for example, a receivable from an installment sale) may be recognized for revenues or gains that will result in future taxable amounts when the asset is recovered.

GAAP basis asset > Tax basis asset

Basis of installment sale receivable on installment sale Installment sales where payments are made over time are recorded on an accrual basis under GAAP. For tax purposes, installment sales are recorded on a cash basis (later) when installment payments are collected.

Basis of installment sale receivable (asset) is higher for GAAP than for tax.

GAAP basis asset > Tax basis asset

Investment—FV-NI Unrealized holding gains for investments accounted for under FV-NI are accrued under GAAP. For tax purposes, gains are recorded on a cash basis (later) when an actual sale occurs; the tax basis remains at cost.

Basis of investment account (asset) is higher for GAAP than for tax.

GAAP basis asset > Tax basis asset

Investment—Equity method Investments are reported under the equity method for GAAP purposes where revenue is recognized based upon a proportionate share of an investee's net income. For tax purposes, revenue is recognized when dividends are received. A taxable temporary difference results when the proportionate share of income included for financial reporting under the equity method is greater than the dividends received. (From a balance sheet perspective, the investment account for financial reporting increases by the proportionate share of earnings from the investee and decreases by the dividend received from the investee; for tax purposes, the investment remains at cost.)

Basis of investment account (asset) is higher for GAAP than for tax.

Taxable Temporary Differences: Expenses in Taxable Income *Before* GAAP Income

740-10-25-20d Expenses or losses that are deductible before they are recognized in financial income. The cost of an asset (for example, depreciable personal property) may have been deducted for tax purposes faster than it was depreciated for financial reporting. Amounts received upon future recovery of the amount of the asset for financial reporting will exceed the remaining tax basis of the asset, and the excess will be taxable when the asset is recovered.

Prepaid expenses Under GAAP, prepaid expenses such as prepaid insurance are reported as assets and expensed over the period of usage. For tax purposes, prepaid expenses are generally deductible immediately when paid.

Basis of prepaid expense (asset) is higher for GAAP than for tax.

GAAP basis asset > Tax basis asset

Fixed assets Under GAAP, fixed assets are depreciated over their useful life using the straight-line method (or other methods such as sum-of-the-years'-digits or double-declining balance). For tax purposes, fixed assets may be depreciated using accelerated tax methods such as MACRS—modified accelerated cost recovery system—or even 100% immediate expensing (also called bonus depreciation). Tax depreciation amounts typically exceed GAAP depreciation amounts in the earlier years of an asset's useful life.

Basis of fixed assets (asset) is higher for GAAP than for tax.

GAAP basis asset > Tax basis asset

Purchased intangible assets If the company engages in a certain type of acquisition (taxable asset purchase), the intangibles acquired are amortizable for tax purposes over 15 years (again, this is only for this certain type of acquisition). However, for financial accounting purposes some of these assets may have a different amortization period.

Basis of purchased intangible (asset) is higher for GAAP than for tax.

GAAP basis asset > Tax basis asset

In **Demo 18-1**, we illustrate the accounting for an expense that is deductible for tax purposes before it is recognized as an expense for financial reporting, which results in the recognition of a deferred tax liability. An increase (decrease) in a deferred tax liability over the accounting period results in an increase (decrease) in **deferred income tax expense** (for that period). The amount computed as total tax on the tax return, increases income tax payable (we assume it is paid in cash later) and **current tax expense**.

Taxable Temporary Difference Leading to Deferred Tax Liability LO18-1 Demo 18-1

Demo MBC

Vail Inc. pays an insurance premium of $15,000 on December 31, 2020, for casualty insurance coverage for the following year, 2021. For GAAP purposes, Vail Inc. would record prepaid insurance (debit Prepaid Insurance and credit Cash). Tax laws, however, allow a tax-deductible expense in 2020. Thus, Vail Inc. has a tax deduction in 2020, but for financial reporting, would report an expense in 2021.

GAAP basis asset > Tax basis asset

The records of Vail Inc. include the following.

Pretax GAAP Income	2020	2021	Total
Revenues	$100,000	$100,000	
Insurance premium	0	(15,000)	
Other expenses	(60,000)	(60,000)	
Pretax GAAP income	$ 40,000	$ 25,000	$65,000

Taxable Income	2020	2021	Total
Revenues	$100,000	$100,000	
Insurance premium	(15,000)	0	
Other expenses	(60,000)	(60,000)	
Taxable income	$ 25,000	$ 40,000	$65,000

Required

a. Compute the increase in Income Tax Payable in 2020 and 2021. Assume a tax rate of 25%. The income tax payable increase is the income tax as computed on the tax return—for brevity, we use "income tax payable increase" to indicate this throughout the chapter.

b. Prepare a schedule to compute the Deferred Tax Liability balance on December 31, 2020, and 2021. Assume a zero-beginning balance in the Deferred Tax Liability account on January 1, 2020.

c. Record the income tax journal entry required on December 31, 2020.

d. Indicate amounts that are reported on the balance sheet on December 31, 2020, and on the 2020 income statement. Indicate the disclosure of current and deferred tax expense. Classify all deferred accounts as *noncurrent* on the balance sheet.

e. Record the income tax journal entry required on December 31, 2021.

continued

continued from previous page

Solution

a. **Computation of the Increase in Income Tax Payable**

The increase in income tax payable is calculated by multiplying taxable income by the tax rate of 25%.

Calculation of Income Tax Payable Increase (Dec. 31)	2020	2021
Taxable income	$25,000	$40,000
Tax rate	× 25%	× 25%
Income tax payable increase	$ 6,250	$10,000

b. **Tax Basis and GAAP Basis of Prepaid Insurance**

For financial reporting purposes, the company would record an asset of $15,000 for prepaid insurance on December 31, 2020. However, for tax purposes, the amount paid for insurance is deducted in 2020; therefore, the tax basis of prepaid insurance on December 31, 2020, is zero. In 2021, prepaid insurance for financial reporting is reduced to $0 when insurance is expensed. In 2020, there is a $15,000 temporary difference that will result in future taxable amounts that originate from the difference between the GAAP basis of prepaid insurance of $15,000 and the tax basis of prepaid insurance of $0.

Measurement of Deferred Tax Liability (Dec. 31)	2020	2021
GAAP basis of prepaid insurance	$15,000	$ 0
Tax basis of prepaid insurance	0	0
Difference between GAAP and tax bases	15,000	0
Tax rate	× 25%	× 25%
Deferred tax liability, ending balance	$ 3,750	$ 0

This table illustrates that the deferred tax liability is created in 2020 and reverses in 2021 such that at the end of 2021, the deferred tax liability is zero.

c. **Income Tax Journal Entry—2020**

The following entry would establish the deferred tax liability of $3,750 and the income tax payable of $6,250. Income tax expense of $10,000 is the sum of current income tax expense of $6,250 and deferred tax expense of $3,750 (change in deferred tax liability). In this simple case there are no permanent differences, and income tax expense† may be confirmed by multiplying the tax rate of 25% by pretax GAAP income of $40,000. This illustrates how income tax expense recorded for financial reporting purposes aligns with pretax GAAP income rather than taxable income.

Pretax GAAP income	$40,000
Tax rate	× 25%
Income tax expense	$10,000

†We compute income tax expense directly in this case. This is not easy for more complex cases such as when tax rates change or when multiple tax rates apply. For this reason, it is common to plug for income tax expense when preparing journal entries.

Taxable income	$25,000
Tax rate	× 25%
Income tax (tax return)	$ 6,250

While it is the convention to show the income tax entry as a combined entry as illustrated in this chapter, it is likely recorded in two parts.

Current Income Tax Expense	6,250	
Income Tax Payable		6,250

Deferred Income Tax Expense	3,750	
Deferred Tax Liability		3,750

December 31, 2020—To record income tax expense

Income Tax Expense ($6,250 + $3,750)	10,000	
Deferred Tax Liability		3,750
Income Tax Payable		6,250

Assets = Liabilities + Equity
+3,750 −10,000
+6,250

Def Tax Liab: | 3,750
Income Tax Exp: 10,000 |
Inc Tax Payable: | 6,250

d. **Financial Statement Presentation**

The following amounts would be recognized on the December 31, 2020, balance sheet and 2020 income statement. (Deferred tax assets and liabilities are classified as noncurrent, see later discussion.)

Balance Sheet (excerpt)	Dec. 31, 2020
Liabilities	
Current liabilities	
Income tax payable	$6,250
Noncurrent liabilities	
Deferred tax liability	3,750

Income Statement (excerpt)	2020
Income tax expense	$10,000

Financial Statement Disclosure	2020
Income tax expense	
Current	$ 6,250
Deferred	3,750
	$10,000

continued

continued from previous page

e. **Income Tax Journal Entry—2021**

As insurance is expensed for financial reporting, the deferred tax liability is reversed leaving a zero balance by year-end. For the year 2021 the entry to reflect this includes a debit to the Deferred Tax Liability account and a credit to Deferred Tax Expense account for $3,750. The complete entry including the recording of the current tax expense and income tax payable for the year follows.

Pretax GAAP income	$25,000
Tax rate	× 25%
Income tax expense	$ 6,250

Taxable income	$40,000
Tax rate	× 25%
Income tax (tax return)	$10,000

December 31, 2021—To record income tax expense

Income Tax Expense ($10,000 − $3,750)	6,250	
Deferred Tax Liability	3,750	
Income Tax Payable		10,000

Assets	=	Liabilities	+	Equity
		−3,750		−6,250
		+10,000		

Def Tax Liab	
3,750	3,750

Inc Tax Payable	
	10,000

Income Tax Exp	
10,000	
6,250	

EXPANDING YOUR KNOWLEDGE **Computing Ratios Considering Deferred Tax Liabilities**

Recall that the **total liabilities-to-equity** ratio measures the proportion of liabilities to equity in a company's capital structure. It indicates how much a company relies on debt financing compared to equity financing. *As the liabilities-to-equity ratio increases, risk increases, and solvency decreases.* A ratio greater than 1.0 indicates that total liabilities exceed total stockholders' equity. Deferred tax liabilities are classified as liabilities and would seemingly be included as part of total liabilities in computing the debt-to-equity ratio. However, some analysts exclude deferred tax liabilities from total liabilities for ratio analyses. More specifically, if it is uncertain that the deferred tax liability will reverse over time, some financial analysts exclude the deferred tax liability from the numerator of the ratio. For example, continually replenishing fixed assets can cause tax depreciation to be indefinitely lower than GAAP depreciation, delaying the realization of the tax liability.

Taxable Temporary Difference Leading to Deferred Tax Liability LO18-1 REVIEW 18-1

Review MBC

Staples Corporation purchased a depreciable asset that cost $60,000 in 2020. For accounting purposes, the straight-line method over a useful life of four years is used (that is, $15,000 per year). Assume this is the only temporary difference. The accounting and tax periods both end December 31. There were no deferred taxes at the beginning of 2020. The tax rate for each year was 25%. Pretax GAAP income amounts for each of the four years are as follows.

2020	$145,000	2021	$160,000	2022	$160,000	2023	$155,000

Example One—Accelerated Depreciation for Tax Purposes

The asset of Staples Corp was depreciated for income tax purposes using the following amounts: 2020, $20,000; 2021, $27,000; 2022, $9,000; and 2023, $4,000.

a. Compute the increase in income tax payable on December 31, 2020, 2021, 2022, and 2023.
b. Prepare a schedule to compute the deferred tax liability balance on December 31, 2020, 2021, 2022, and 2023.
c. Record the journal entry to record income tax expense for the years 2020 through 2023.

Example Two—100% Expensing for Tax Purposes

100% of the asset of Staples Corp was depreciated for income tax purposes in 2020.

a. Compute the increase in income tax payable on December 31, 2020, 2021, 2022, and 2023.
b. Prepare a schedule to compute the deferred tax liability balance on December 31, 2020, 2021, 2022, and 2023.
c. Record the journal entry to record income tax expense for the years 2020 through 2023.

More Practice: 18-21, 18-22, 18-23, 18-44, 18-45, 18-46, 18-47

Solution on p. 18-60.

LO 18-2 Describe deductible temporary differences that lead to deferred tax assets and related income tax expense

LO 18-2 Overview

Deferred Tax Asset
- Created from deductible temporary differences that *decrease* future taxable income
  - Asset GAAP basis < Asset tax basis
  - Liability GAAP basis > Liability tax basis

Deductible temporary differences are temporary differences that *decrease taxable income* relative to pretax GAAP income in future periods. In other words, a company experiences higher taxes today, but will pay less tax later (relative to an amount calculated using reported financial accounting income). **A future deductible amount results when either (1) the reported value of an asset (GAAP basis) is less than the tax basis of an asset or (2) when the reported value of a liability (GAAP basis) is greater than the tax basis.**

Creation of Future Deductible Amounts

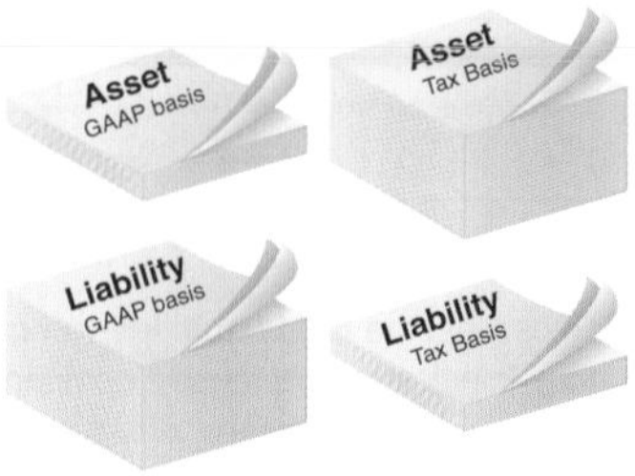

740-10-25-23 Temporary differences that will result in deductible amounts in future years are often referred to as deductible temporary differences.

A deductible temporary difference creates a deferred tax asset. **Deferred tax assets** are expected (estimated) future tax benefits arising from temporary deductible differences existing at the end of the accounting period. A deferred tax asset is calculated by multiplying the taxable temporary difference in asset bases by the enacted tax rate that will be in effect when the taxable temporary difference reverses.

ASC Glossary Deferred Tax Asset—The deferred tax consequences attributable to deductible temporary differences and carryforwards. A deferred tax asset is measured using the applicable enacted tax rate and provisions of the enacted tax law.

Deductible temporary differences result when either revenues are recognized in taxable income *before* GAAP income or when expenses are recognized in taxable income *after* GAAP income. For example, customer advances (cash received from a customer before the satisfaction of a performance obligation) result in the recording of deferred revenue (a liability) for GAAP purposes. For tax purposes, however, generally such payments are taxable when received, so there is no liability on a tax basis. The balance in deferred revenue under GAAP represents the cumulative deductible temporary difference because this revenue will not appear on any future income tax returns. If it is probable that the company will satisfy its performance obligation and record GAAP revenue in the future, then a deductible temporary difference exists and a deferred tax asset is required to be recorded for financial accounting purposes.

A deferred tax asset also results from carryforwards. This occurs when a company carries forward operating tax losses to offset future taxable income, reducing taxes in future years. Carryforwards are covered in LO 18-6.

Deductible Temporary Differences: Revenues in Taxable Income *Before* GAAP Income

740-10-25-20c Revenues or gains that are taxable before they are recognized in financial income. A liability (for example, subscriptions received in advance) may be recognized for an advance payment for goods or services to be provided in future years. For tax purposes, the advance payment is included in taxable income upon the receipt of cash. Future sacrifices to provide goods or services (or future refunds to those who cancel their orders) will result in future tax deductible amounts when the liability is settled.

GAAP basis liability > Tax basis liability

Customer advances Advances from customers are deferred for GAAP, but are taxable when cash is collected (up-front).
Basis of deferred revenue (liability) is higher for GAAP than for tax.

GAAP basis liability > Tax basis liability

Deferred rent revenue Rental receipts received in advance are deferred for GAAP, but are taxable when cash is collected (up-front).
Basis of deferred rent revenue (liability) is higher for GAAP than for tax.

GAAP basis liability > Tax basis liability

Deferred subscription revenue Subscriptions received in advance are deferred for GAAP, but are taxable when cash is collected (up-front).
Basis of deferred subscription revenue (liability) is higher for GAAP than for tax.

GAAP basis liability > Tax basis liability

Deferred contract revenue Prepaid contracts received are deferred for GAAP, but are taxable when cash is collected (up-front).
Basis of deferred contract revenue (liability) is higher for GAAP than for tax.

Deductible Temporary Differences: Expenses in Taxable Income *After* GAAP Income

740-10-25-20b Expenses or losses that are deductible after they are recognized in financial income. A liability (for example, a product warranty liability) may be recognized for expenses or losses that will result in future tax deductible amounts when the liability is settled.

Warranty expense For GAAP, warranty expense is recognized when sales are recorded. However, warranty costs are deductible for tax when actually paid (later).
Basis of warranty liability (liability) is higher for GAAP than for tax.

GAAP basis liability > Tax basis liability

Investment—FV-NI Unrealized holding loss on an investment accounted for under FV-NI is recorded for GAAP. However, for tax purposes, a loss is deducted only if realized on the sale of the investment (later).
Basis of investment (asset) is lower for GAAP than for tax.

GAAP basis asset < Tax basis asset

Inventory Inventory is adjusted to the lower-of-cost-or-net realizable value for GAAP purposes, but losses are not realized for tax purposes until the inventory is sold at an amount below cost.
Basis of inventory, net (asset) is lower for GAAP than for tax.

GAAP basis asset < Tax basis asset

Accounts receivable Bad debt expense estimated at the time of sale for GAAP purposes is deducted when the account is written off for tax purposes.
Basis of accounts receivable, net (asset) is lower for GAAP than for tax.

GAAP basis asset < Tax basis asset

In **Demo 18-2**, we illustrate the accounting of an expense that is recognized for financial reporting before it is tax deductible, which results in the recognition of a deferred tax asset. An increase (decrease) in a deferred tax asset over the accounting period results in a decrease (increase) in **deferred income tax expense**. The amount computed as total tax on the tax return increases income tax payable (we assume it is paid in cash later) and current tax expense.

EXPANDING YOUR KNOWLEDGE — **Identifying Temporary Differences**

Temporary differences originate from differences between the GAAP and tax basis of an asset or liability. Thus, a good way to identify temporary differences is to compare a GAAP balance sheet to a tax basis balance sheet.

Comparison of GAAP to Tax Basis	Example	Temporary Difference
GAAP and tax bases are the same	Accounts payable where the GAAP basis is identical to the tax basis.	
GAAP and tax bases are different	Equipment where GAAP and tax depreciation methods differ.	✔
GAAP and tax bases are different	Accrued litigation expense that is not tax deductible until paid.	✔
GAAP and tax bases are different	Organization costs—expensed immediately for GAAP but deferred for tax.	✔

Deductible Temporary Differences Leading to a Deferred Tax Asset — LO18-2 — Demo 18-2

Aspen Inc. estimates assurance-type warranty costs of $30,000 related to 2020 sales. During the year, $10,000 warranty costs are incurred. On December 31, 2020, Aspen Inc. recorded a warranty accrual (debit Warranty Expense and credit Warranty Liability) for future estimated claims of $20,000 ($30,000 − $10,000). For tax purposes, however, only the $10,000 of actual warranty costs is deductible. Assume that the $20,000 of claims results in actual costs in 2021. Aspen Inc. had no beginning balances (January 1, 2020) in deferred tax accounts.

GAAP basis liability > Tax basis liability

The records of Aspen Inc. include the following.

Pretax GAAP Income	2020	2021	Total
Revenues	$100,000	$100,000	
Expenses	(60,000)	(60,000)	
Warranty expense	(30,000)	0	
Pretax GAAP income	$ 10,000	$ 40,000	$50,000

Taxable Income	2020	2021	Total
Revenues	$100,000	$100,000	
Expenses	(60,000)	(60,000)	
Warranty expense	(10,000)	(20,000)	
Taxable income	$ 30,000	$ 20,000	$50,000

Required

a. Compute the increase in income tax payable for 2020 and 2021. Assume a tax rate of 25%.
b. Prepare a schedule to compute the Deferred Tax Asset balance on December 31, 2020, and 2021. Assume a zero-beginning balance in the Deferred Tax Asset account on January 1, 2020.

continued

continued from previous page

c. Record the income tax journal entry required on December 31, 2020.

d. Indicate the amounts that would be included on the balance sheet on December 31, 2020, and on the 2020 income statement. Indicate the disclosure of current and deferred tax expense. Classify all deferred accounts as *noncurrent* on the balance sheet.

e. Record the income tax journal entry required on December 31, 2021.

Solution

a. **Computation of the Increase in Income Tax Payable**

To calculate the increase in income tax payable, multiply taxable income by the tax rate of 25% for each year.

Calculation of Income Tax Payable Increase (Dec. 31)	2020	2021
Taxable income	$30,000	$20,000
Tax rate	× 25%	× 25%
Income tax payable increase	$ 7,500	$ 5,000

b. **Tax Basis and GAAP Basis of Warranty Expense**

For financial reporting purposes, the company would record $20,000 for accrued warranty expense on December 31, 2020. However, on a tax basis, the amount paid for servicing warranties is deducted only when paid; therefore, the tax basis of the warranty liability on December 31, 2020, is zero. In 2021, the warranty liability for GAAP purposes is reduced to $0 when warranty costs are paid (the liability is reduced). The $20,000 temporary difference that results in future deductible amounts originates from the difference between the GAAP amount of warranty liability of $20,000 and the tax amount of warranty liability of $0.

Measurement of Deferred Tax Asset (Dec. 31)	2020	2021
GAAP basis of warranty liability	$20,000	$ 0
Tax basis of warranty liability	0	0
Difference between GAAP and tax bases	20,000	0
Tax rate	× 25%	× 25%
Deferred tax asset, ending balance	$ 5,000	$ 0

c. **Income Tax Journal Entry—2020**

The following entry would establish the deferred tax asset of $5,000 and the income tax payable of $7,500. Income tax expense is the net of current income tax payable of $7,500 and deferred tax benefit of $5,000 (change in deferred tax asset). Again, in this simple case, the amount of income tax expense can be checked as the tax rate of 25% multiplied by pretax GAAP income of $10,000.

Pretax GAAP income	$10,000
Tax rate	× 25%
Income tax expense	$ 2,500

Taxable income	$30,000
Tax rate	× 25%
Income tax (tax return)	$ 7,500

While it is the convention to show the income tax entry as a combined entry as illustrated in this chapter, it is likely recorded in two parts.

Current Income Tax Expense	7,500	
Income Tax Payable		7,500

Deferred Tax Asset	5,000	
Deferred Income Tax Expense		5,000

December 31, 2020—To record income tax expense

Income Tax Expense ($7,500 − $5,000)	2,500	
Deferred Tax Asset	5,000	
Income Tax Payable		7,500

Assets = Liabilities + Equity
+5,000 = +7,500 + −2,500

Def Tax Asset	
5,000	

Inc Tax Payable	
	7,500

Income Tax Exp	
2,500	

d. **Financial Statement Presentation**

The following amounts would be recognized on the December 31, 2020, balance sheet and 2020 income statement.

Balance Sheet (excerpt)	Dec. 31, 2020
Assets	
Noncurrent assets	
Deferred tax asset	$5,000
Liabilities	
Current liabilities	
Income tax payable	7,500

Income Statement (excerpt)	2020
Income tax expense	$2,500

Financial Statement Disclosure	2020
Income tax expense	
Current	$ 7,500
Deferred	(5,000)
	$ 2,500

continued

continued from previous page

e. **Income Tax Journal Entry—2021**

As the warranty costs are actually paid, the deferred tax asset reverses. The entry that is made to reflect this includes a credit to the Deferred Tax Asset Account and a Debit to Deferred Tax Expense of $5,000. Along with the entry to reflect the current income tax expense and income tax payable of $5,000 for 2021, the combined entry follows.

Pretax GAAP income.....	$40,000
Tax rate................	× 25%
Income tax expense.....	$10,000

December 31, 2021—To record income tax expense

Income Tax Expense ($5,000 + $5,000)...	10,000	
Deferred Tax Asset ($5,000 – $0)....		5,000
Income Tax Payable...............		5,000

Taxable income..........	$20,000
Tax rate................	× 25%
Income tax (tax return)...	$ 5,000

Assets = Liabilities + Equity
−5,000 +5,000 −10,000

Def Tax Asset	
5,000	5,000

Inc Tax Payable	
	5,000

Income Tax Exp	
2,500	
10,000	

COCA COLA

Real World—DEFERRED TAX ASSETS

COCA COLA [KO]

Coca Cola Company provided the following summary of deferred tax assets in a recent Form 10-K. The most significant difference between GAAP and tax reporting in 2017 is due to benefit plans. The funding deductions on a cash basis were less than amounts recorded as pension expense. In later periods, this will reverse where the funding tax deductions will be greater than pension expense.

Note 14: Income Taxes (excerpt) The tax effects of temporary differences and carryforwards that give rise to deferred tax assets and liabilities consist of the following:

December 31 (In millions)	2017	2016
Deferred tax liabilities:		
Property, plant and equipment	$ 99	$ 144
Trademarks and other intangible assets.........	98	114
Equity method investments (including foreign currency translation adjustment)	300	684
Derivative financial instruments	387	193
Other liabilities	861	1,141
Benefit plans.........	977	1,599
Net operating/capital loss carryforwards.........	520	461
Other.........	163	135
Gross deferred tax assets	3,405	4,471
Valuation allowances	(501)	(530)
Total deferred tax assets	$2,904	$3,941

Deductible Temporary Difference Leading to Deferred Tax Asset LO18-2 REVIEW 18-2

Review MBC

On January 1, 2020, Staples Corporation collected $200,000 cash in advance of the satisfaction of performance obligations of a revenue contract and recognized $200,000 in deferred revenue. Staples Corporation recognized GAAP revenue of $50,000, $50,000, $50,000, and $50,000 in December 2020, 2021, 2022, and 2023, respectively. For tax purposes, the full $200,000 was recognized as taxable income in 2020. The accounting and tax periods both end December 31. There were no deferred tax account balances at the beginning of 2020. The tax rate for each year was 25%.

Pretax GAAP income amounts for each of the four years were as follows.

2020..... $145,000	2021..... $155,000	2022..... $150,000	2023..... $148,000

a. Compute the increase in income tax payable on December 31, 2020, 2021, 2022, and 2023.

b. Prepare a schedule to compute the deferred tax asset balance on December 31, 2020, 2021, 2022, and 2023.

c. Record the income tax journal entry required for the years 2020 through 2023.

More Practice:
18-24, 18-25, 18-26, 18-27, 18-28, 18-49
Solution on p. 18-62.

LO 18-3 Explain how to record and report a valuation allowance for deferred tax assets

LO 18-3 Overview

Valuation Allowance for Deferred Tax Assets
- Record as a contra asset to deferred tax asset
- Record when it is *more likely than not* that the deferred tax won't be realized
- Consider the impact of negative and positive evidence

To realize the benefit of a deferred tax asset, there must be future taxable income against which the future deductible amounts (the deferred tax assets) can be applied. Possible sources of future taxable income are reversals of taxable temporary differences, forecasted future taxable income, and the application of tax-planning strategies. If sufficient future taxable income is not likely, a company must reduce the carrying value of the deferred tax asset through a **valuation allowance**.

ASC Glossary Valuation Allowance—The portion of a deferred tax asset for which it is more likely than not that a tax benefit will not be realized.

740-10-30-18 The following four possible sources of taxable income may be available under the tax law to realize a tax benefit for deductible temporary differences and carryforwards:

a. Future reversals of existing taxable temporary differences
b. Future taxable income exclusive of reversing temporary differences and carryforwards
c. Taxable income in prior carryback year(s) if carryback is permitted under the tax law
d. Tax-planning strategies

If, based on the weight of available evidence, it is ***more likely than not*** (>50%) that some portion of the deferred tax asset will not be realized, the deferred tax asset is reduced by a valuation allowance. The **Valuation Allowance for Deferred Tax Assets** is a contra asset account sufficient to reduce the deferred tax asset to the amount *more likely than not* to be realized. **Demo 18-3** illustrates the establishment and adjustment of the valuation allowance.

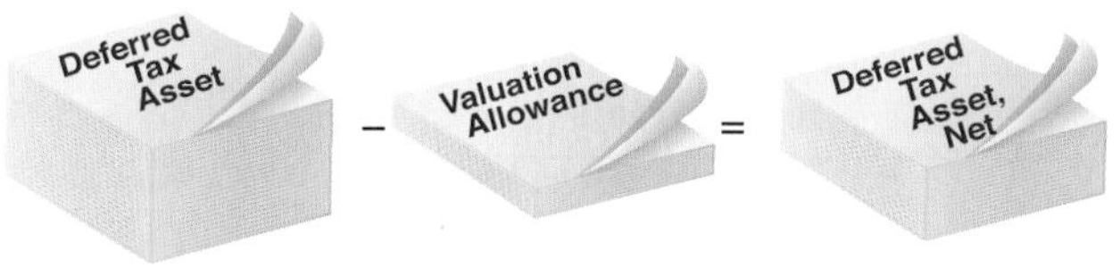

740-10-30-5e Reduce deferred tax assets by a valuation allowance if, based on the weight of available evidence, it is more likely than not (a likelihood of more than 50 percent) that some portion or all of the deferred tax assets will not be realized. The valuation allowance shall be sufficient to reduce the deferred tax asset to the amount that is more likely than not to be realized.

To realize a deferred tax asset means that the company has positive taxable income in the future that offsets its deferred deductions. That is, a deferred tax asset related to future tax deductions of $10,000 can only be realized if the company has at least $10,000 of future taxable income before considering the deferred deductions. A company must consider all available evidence, both positive and negative, to make a determination of whether a deferred tax asset will be realized. For example, a strong history of profitability is **positive evidence** that a company would realize the deferred tax asset. A loss expected in the following year would be **negative evidence** indicating that the company may not realize the deferred tax asset. The valuation allowance is evaluated and adjusted at the end of each reporting period.

An entity shall use judgment in considering the relative impact of negative and positive evidence. The weight given to the potential effect of negative and positive evidence shall be commensurate with the extent to which it can be objectively verified. The more negative evidence that exists, the more positive evidence is necessary and the more difficult it is to support a conclusion that a valuation allowance is not needed for some portion or all of the deferred tax asset. A cumulative loss in recent years is a significant piece of negative evidence that is difficult to overcome.

Assessing the realizability of deferred tax assets is arguably more difficult following the Tax Cuts and Jobs Act. Tax net operating losses (losses for tax purposes that are carried forward) can now be carried forward indefinitely but cannot be carried back. See LO 18-6 for further discussion. In addition, limitations were placed on interest expense deductibility. If such limitations apply to a company they can carry forward any unused deductions to future years. Both of these create deferred tax assets and the indefinite carryforward period rules make the assessment of a need for a valuation allowance more difficult.

EXPANDING YOUR KNOWLEDGE **Negative and Positive Evidence—Valuation Allowance**

The authoritative guidance includes a list of items that could be considered negative and positive evidence when considering whether or how much to reserve as a deferred tax valuation allowance.

Negative Evidence

740-10-30-21 Forming a conclusion that a valuation allowance is not needed is difficult when there is negative evidence such as cumulative losses in recent years. Other examples of negative evidence include, but are not limited to, the following:

a. A history of operating loss or . . . tax credit carryforwards expiring unused.

b. Losses expected in early future years (by a presently profitable entity).

c. Unsettled circumstances that, if unfavorably resolved, would adversely affect future operations and profit levels on a continuing basis in future years.

d. A carryback, carryforward period that is so brief it would limit realization of tax benefits if a significant deductible temporary difference is expected to reverse in a single year or the entity operates in a traditionally cyclical business.

Positive Evidence

740-10-30-22 Examples (not prerequisites) of positive evidence that might support a conclusion that a valuation allowance is not needed when there is negative evidence include, but are not limited to, the following:

a. Existing contracts or firm sales backlog that will produce more than enough taxable income to realize the deferred tax asset based on existing sales prices and cost structures.

b. An excess of appreciated asset value over the tax basis of the entity's net assets in an amount sufficient to realize the deferred tax asset.

c. A strong earnings history exclusive of the loss that created the future deductible amount (tax loss carryforward or deductible temporary difference) coupled with evidence indicating that the loss (for example, an unusual or infrequent item) is an aberration rather than a continuing condition.

Account for Deferred Tax Asset Valuation Allowance LO18-3 Demo 18-3

Denver Inc. recorded a deferred tax asset on December 31, 2020, for $50,000. The company has a beginning balance of zero in its Valuation Allowance for Deferred Tax Asset account.

Required

a. On December 31, 2020, Denver Inc. determined that it was *more likely than not* that $10,000 of the deferred tax asset would not be realized. Record the entry required to establish a valuation allowance.

b. In the following year, Denver Inc. evaluates its Deferred Tax Asset account ($48,000 balance) to determine whether it is *more likely than not* that the deferred tax asset will not be realized. On December 31, 2021, the company determines that it is *more likely than not* that half of the balance will not be realized. The company used all available evidence to make this determination, which is based on judgment. Record the entry required to adjust the valuation allowance.

Solution

a. **Valuation Allowance for Deferred Tax Asset**

December 31, 2020—To establish deferred tax asset valuation allowance

Income Tax Expense	10,000	
Valuation Allowance for Deferred Tax Asset		10,000

Assets = Liabilities + Equity
−10,000 −10,000
Def Tax Asset Allow: 10,000 (credit)
Income Tax Exp: 10,000 (debit)

The valuation allowance is a contra asset account that is subtracted from the deferred tax asset amount on the balance sheet. Thus, the net deferred tax asset on the balance sheet on December 31, 2020, is $40,000 ($50,000 − $10,000).

b. **Valuation Allowance for Deferred Tax Asset Adjustment**

Because Denver Inc. has a beginning balance in the valuation allowance account of $10,000, a credit of $14,000 to the valuation account is required to arrive at an ending balance of $24,000 ($48,000 × 50%).

continued

continued from previous page

Valuation Allowance for Deferred Tax Asset		
	10,000	Jan. 1, 2021
	14,000	**Adjustment**
	24,000	Dec. 31, 2021 Desired ending balance: $48,000 × 50%

Denver Inc. would record the following entry to adjust the valuation allowance.

Assets = Liabilities + Equity
−14,000 −14,000

Def Tax Asset Allow	Income Tax Exp
10,000 14,000	10,000 14,000

December 31, 2021—To adjust deferred tax asset valuation allowance

Income Tax Expense	14,000	
Valuation Allowance for Deferred Tax Asset		14,000

To obtain the value of the net deferred tax asset, the valuation allowance is subtracted from the deferred tax asset on the balance sheet. Thus, the net deferred tax asset on the balance sheet on December 31, 2021, is $24,000 ($48,000 − $24,000).

COCA COLA

Real World—DEFERRED TAX ASSET VALUATION ALLOWANCE

COCA COLA [KO]

Coca Cola Company provided the following reconciliation of its deferred tax asset valuation allowance in a recent Form 10-K. The allowance balances as a percentage of total gross deferred tax assets were 14.7%, 11.9%, and 11.1% for the years ended 2017, 2016, and 2015, respectively. This deferred tax allowance is due to the company's inability to use tax loss carryforwards to offset taxable income in future years.

Note 14: Income Taxes (excerpt) An analysis of our deferred tax asset valuation allowances is as follows:

Year Ended December 31 ($ millions)	2017	2016	2015
Balance at beginning of year	**$530**	$477	$649
Additions.	**184**	68	42
Decrease due to reclassification to assets held for sale.	**—**	(9)	(163)
Deductions	**(213)**	(6)	(51)
Balance at end of year	**$501**	$530	$477

The Company's deferred tax asset valuation allowances are primarily the result of uncertainties regarding the future realization of recorded tax benefits on tax loss carryforwards from operations in various jurisdictions. Current evidence does not suggest we will realize sufficient taxable income of the appropriate character within the carryforward period to allow us to realize these deferred tax benefits. If we were to identify and implement tax planning strategies to recover these deferred tax assets or generate sufficient income of the appropriate character in these jurisdictions in the future, it could lead to the reversal of these valuation allowances and a reduction of income tax expense. The Company believes that it will generate sufficient future taxable income to realize the tax benefits related to the remaining net deferred tax assets in our consolidated balance sheet.

REVIEW 18-3 LO18-3 Tax Asset Valuation Allowance

Review MBC

Dallas Corp. has a deferred tax asset balance of $300,000 on December 31, 2020, due to a temporary difference related to a warranty expense accrual that is not deductible for tax purposes. The deferred tax asset balance has increased $20,000 over the 2019 ending balance of $280,000. Taxable income for 2020 is $880,000 and the tax rate is 25%.

a. Record the income tax journal entry on December 31, 2020, assuming that it is *more likely than not* that the deferred tax asset will be realized.

b. Record the income tax journal entries on December 31, 2020, assuming that it is *more likely than not* that 30% of the deferred tax asset will not be realized.

More Practice:
18-30, 18-31, 18-62

Solution on p. 18-62.

Describe *permanent differences* and other items that impact the reported effective tax rate

LO 18-4

> **Permanent Differences**
> - Affects taxable income but never affects pretax GAAP income *or* affects pretax GAAP income but never affects taxable income
> - Impacts the effective tax rate
> - Does not impact deferred taxes
>
> LO 18-4 Overview

There are also differences between taxable income and pre-tax GAAP income that are not temporary. These are commonly known as *permanent differences*. FASB no longer uses the term but we will use it here for simplicity. A **permanent difference** between pretax GAAP income and taxable income is created when an income element—a revenue, gain, expense, or loss—enters the computation of either taxable income or pretax GAAP income but *never* enters into the computation of the other.

740-10-10-1 There are two primary objectives related to accounting for income taxes:

a. To recognize the amount of taxes payable or refundable for the current year.

b. To recognize deferred tax liabilities and assets for the future tax consequences of events that have been recognized in an entity's financial statements or tax returns. As it relates to the second objective, some events do not have tax consequences. Certain revenues are exempt from taxation and certain expenses are not deductible. In some tax jurisdictions, for example, interest earned on certain municipal obligations is not taxable and fines are not deductible.

Let's assume that a company invests in tax-exempt municipal bonds and receives $10,000 of interest. Interest is recognized as revenue for financial reporting. However, interest received on investments from these tax-exempt municipal bonds is not taxable by the federal government. The interest appears as revenue for pretax GAAP income (where we debit Cash, credit Interest Revenue), but because it is tax-exempt income, it is *never* considered as revenue for federal tax purposes.

The following are examples of permanent differences.

- Most state and local government bonds (referred to as municipal bonds) pay interest that is *not* taxable at the federal level but is recognized as interest revenue in GAAP income. ☑ GAAP Revenue ☐ Taxable Revenue
- Investment expenses related to obtaining tax-exempt income are *not* deductible for tax purposes but are recognized as expenses in GAAP income. ☑ GAAP Expense ☐ Taxable Expense
- Fines and expenses related to violation of laws/regulations are *not* tax deductible but are recognized as expense in GAAP income. ☑ GAAP Expense ☐ Taxable Expense
- Proceeds from life insurance due to the death of an insured member of the company are *not* recognized as revenue for tax purposes but are recognized as a gain in GAAP income. ☑ GAAP Revenue ☐ Taxable Revenue
- The premiums paid on life insurance policies for members of a company are *not* tax deductible but are recognized as expense for GAAP purposes. ☑ GAAP Expense ☐ Taxable Expense
- Some portion of dividends received from U.S. corporations is *not* taxable (such as 65% for a less than 20% ownership interest), but dividends received from entities less than 20% owned are fully recognized as revenue for GAAP purposes. ☑ GAAP Revenue ☐ Taxable Revenue
- Total tax deductions allowed for depletion of natural resources through the percentage depletion method exceed total GAAP expense determined through cost depletion. ☐ GAAP Expense ☑ Taxable Expense

Permanent differences never reverse so there is no deferred tax accounting required for permanent differences (meaning, no deferred tax asset and no deferred tax liability). As a result, when the company only has permanent differences, then *income tax expense for financial reporting is equal to the amount computed as total income taxes on the tax return for the period.*

Companies are required to disclose their effective tax rate in their financial statements. This rate will often be different from the statutory tax rate, and one reason for the difference is the existence of permanent differences. The **statutory tax rate** is the legally imposed tax rate of a jurisdiction. The **effective tax rate** for GAAP is income tax expense as a percentage of pretax GAAP income. When a company has permanent differences such as nontaxable revenue or deductions for tax purposes not reportable in the financial statements, the effective tax rate is reduced. On the other hand, permanent differences such as nondeductible expenses increase the effective tax rate. Companies must disclose a **rate reconciliation**, which is a reconciliation (in dollars or in percentages) between the U.S. statutory tax rate and the effective tax rate as illustrated in **Demo 18-4A**. While permanent differences impact the effective tax rate, temporary differences do not. Temporary differences only affect the timing of when taxes are paid.

Other Items that Impact Effective Tax Rate

There are several items that impact the rate reconciliation beyond permanent differences between taxable income and accounting income. For example, in addition to the federal income taxes, most companies have to pay state income taxes. This increases the company's effective tax rate beyond the U.S. federal income tax rate. Thus, a reconciling item for the effect of state income taxes is often necessary in the rate reconciliation. Tax credits are sometimes allowed and these also can impact a company's effective tax rate. The credit reduces the tax the company owes to the tax authority, now and forever, but is not technically a difference between income measures. It's essentially a reduction in the tax rate but via a tax credit. Thus, a reconciling item is required for certain tax credits as well. A change in management's estimate for the valuation allowance in a reporting period after the deferred tax asset is recorded also impacts the effective tax rate. Management is just changing the accounting accrual in this case, so there is no change in the actual taxes paid during the period. Thus, a change in the valuation allowance is often required as an item in the rate reconciliation as well.

Demo 18-4A **LO18-4** **Permanent Difference**

Demo MBC

Springs Inc. has taxable revenues of $105,000 and tax-deductible expenses of $60,000 for the year ended December 31, 2020. In addition, Springs Inc. receives interest from municipal bonds in the amount of $10,000, not subject to income taxation. All of these revenues and expenses are included in pretax GAAP income for the period. Assume that the tax rate is 25%.

a. Record the income tax journal entry on December 31, 2020.
b. Prepare a reconciliation disclosure of the statutory tax rate to the effective tax rate.

Solution

a. **Income Tax Journal Entry**

Taxable income of $45,000 is equal to taxable revenues of $105,000 less tax-deductible expenses of $60,000. The increase to income tax payable is equal to $45,000 multiplied by the tax rate of 25%. Income tax expense is calculated by taking pretax GAAP income of $55,000 (or $105,000 − $60,000 + $10,000) less the permanent difference of $10,000 multiplied by the tax rate of 25%. We subtract the permanent difference because there will never be tax on this income of $10,000, so we do not accrue tax expense for it. On December 31, 2020, Springs Inc. would record the following journal entry.

Pretax GAAP income	$55,000
Less: Permanent difference	(10,000)
GAAP income adjusted for permanent differences	$45,000
Tax rate	× 25%
Income tax expense	$11,250

Taxable income	$45,000
Tax rate	× 25%
Income tax (tax return)	$11,250

December 31, 2020—To record income tax expense

Income Tax Expense	11,250	
Income Tax Payable		11,250

Assets = Liabilities + Equity
+11,250 −11,250
Inc Tax Payable 11,250 | Income Tax Exp 11,250

b. **Reconciliation of Statutory Tax Rate to the Effective Tax Rate**

The following reconciliation begins with the statutory rate of 25%. The permanent difference of interest on the municipal bonds is never taxed, which decreases the effective tax rate. The decrease of 4.5% is equal to the tax on the permanent difference (25% of $10,000) divided by pretax GAAP income of $55,000. The effective tax rate of 20.5% is calculated by dividing tax expense ($11,250) by pretax GAAP income ($55,000).

Dec. 31, 2020 Reconciliation of statutory U.S. federal tax rate and effective tax rate

	Percentage	
Statutory tax rate	25.0%	Statutory rate
Tax-exempt income	(4.5)%	($10,000 × 25%)/$55,000
Effective tax rate	20.5%	$11,250 ÷ $55,000

Illustration of Permanent and Temporary Differences

In previous sections, we accounted for temporary differences leading to deferred tax assets and deferred tax liabilities as well as permanent differences. It is important to be able to distinguish among these types of differences because companies will have both types and the accounting varies by type of difference. **Demo 18-4B** combines both types of differences, permanent and temporary.

Multiple Temporary and Permanent Differences — LO18-4 — Demo 18-4B

For its first year of operations, Altitude Inc. reports pretax GAAP income of $100,000 in 2020. Assume pretax GAAP income in 2021 and 2022 of $125,000 and $90,000, respectively. The enacted income tax rate for all years is 25%. The following additional information is available for the first three years of operations.

- Prepaid rent in the amount of $20,000 was recorded on December 31, 2020, for 2021 rent. Rent is deductible for tax purposes in the year paid. *(GAAP basis asset > Tax basis asset)*
- A warranty accrual of $30,000 recorded on December 31, 2020, is not deductible for tax purposes until the warranty costs are paid. The amount is paid evenly over the years 2021–2023. *(GAAP basis liability > Tax basis liability)*
- The company recorded interest revenue of $500 each year (2020–2022) on municipal bonds. Interest revenue on municipal bonds is not taxable. *(Permanent)*

Required

a. Prepare a schedule to compute the increase in income tax payable on December 31, 2020, 2021, and 2022.

b. Prepare a schedule to compute the deferred tax liability balance and a schedule to compute the deferred tax asset balance on December 31, 2020, 2021, and 2022.

c. Record the income tax journal entries required in years 2020 through 2022.

Solution

a. **Computation of the Increase in Income Tax Payable**

The differences in the GAAP bases and tax bases of prepaid rent and the warranty accrual are both temporary differences because the differences reverse in later years. Interest revenue on municipal bonds is never taxable; therefore, it is a permanent difference.

Calculation of Income Tax Payable Increase (Dec. 31)	2020	2021	2022
Pretax GAAP income	$100,000	$125,000	$90,000
Rent expense adjustment	(20,000)	20,000	
Warranty expense adjustment	30,000	(10,000)	(10,000)
Interest revenue—municipal bond	(500)	(500)	(500)
Taxable income	109,500	134,500	79,500
Tax rate	× 25%	× 25%	× 25%
Income tax payable increase	$ 27,375	$ 33,625	$19,875

b. **Schedule of Deferred Tax Balances**

Measurement of Deferred Tax Liability (Dec. 31)	2020	2021	2022
GAAP basis of prepaid rent	$20,000	$ 0	$ 0
Tax basis of prepaid rent	0	0	0
Difference between GAAP and tax bases	20,000	0	0
Tax rate	× 25%	× 25%	× 25%
Deferred tax liability, ending balance	$ 5,000	$ 0	$ 0

continued

continued from previous page

Measurement of Deferred Tax Asset (Dec. 31)	2020	2021	2022
GAAP basis of accrued warranty liability	$30,000	$20,000	$10,000
Tax basis of accrued warranty liability	0	0	0
Difference between GAAP and tax bases	30,000	20,000	10,000
Tax rate	× 25%	× 25%	× 25%
Deferred tax asset, ending balance	$ 7,500	$ 5,000	$ 2,500

c. **Income Tax Journal Entries**

Altitude Inc. would record the following entries in the years 2020–2022.

Assets = Liabilities + Equity: Assets +7,500; Liabilities +5,000, +27,375; Equity −24,875

Def Tax Asset: 7,500 | ; Inc Tax Payable: | 27,375; Income Tax Exp: 24,875 | ; Def Tax Liab: | 5,000

December 31, 2020

Income Tax Expense ($27,375 − $2,500)	24,875	
Deferred Tax Asset	7,500	
Deferred Tax Liability		5,000
Income Tax Payable		27,375

Assets = Liabilities + Equity: Assets −2,500; Liabilities −5,000, +33,625; Equity −31,125

Def Tax Asset: 7,500 | 2,500; Inc Tax Payable: | 33,625; Income Tax Exp: 24,875, 31,125 | ; Def Tax Liab: 5,000 | 5,000

December 31, 2021

Income Tax Expense ($33,625 − $2,500)	31,125	
Deferred Tax Liability ($5,000 − $0)	5,000	
Deferred Tax Asset ($7,500 − $5,000)		2,500
Income Tax Payable		33,625

Assets = Liabilities + Equity: Assets −2,500; Liabilities +19,875; Equity −22,375

Def Tax Asset: 7,500 | 2,500, 2,500; Inc Tax Payable: | 19,875

December 31, 2022

Income Tax Expense ($19,875 + $2,500)	22,375	
Deferred Tax Asset ($5,000 − $2,500)		2,500
Income Tax Payable		19,875

Income Tax Exp: 24,875, 31,125, 22,375 |

At the end of year 2022, the deferred tax liability has a zero balance because the entire liability reverses in 2021. The deferred tax asset has a balance of $2,500 ($7,500 − $2,500 − $2,500), which represents one-third of the warranty liability balance expected to reverse in the year 2023. The permanent difference produces neither a deferred tax asset nor a deferred tax liability because the difference never reverses.

$$\frac{\text{GAAP income before taxes}}{\text{Taxable income}}$$

Financial Statement Analysis While companies try to maximize profits, they also try to minimize or at least defer tax payments. One way to potentially assess a) the extent to which managers have used discretion in reporting financial accounting earnings and/or b) the extent to which managers have employed aggressive tax strategies is by computing the *conservatism ratio* (GAAP income before taxes divided by taxable income). The higher the ratio, the less conservative the accounting earnings and/or the more aggressive the tax strategies employed that defer (or eliminate in the case of permanent differences) tax payments to future periods. In our previous example for Altitude Inc., the conservatism ratio for 2020 is 0.91, which is pretax GAAP income in 2020 of $100,000 divided by taxable income of $109,500.

Let's apply the conservatism ratio to **Coca-Cola Company** using amounts reported in recent financial statements.

Coca-Cola ($ millions)	2017	2016	2015
GAAP income before taxes	$ 6,742	$8,136	$9,605
Taxable income*	$19,474	$6,977	$6,189
Conservatism ratio	0.35	1.17	1.55

* A rough way to estimate taxable income (which can vary greatly from actual), is to divide current tax expense by the statutory tax rate).

For Coca-Cola, the most aggressive tax policy year was 2015, where GAAP income before taxes was 155% of taxable income. In 2017, however, the company had *higher* taxable income than GAAP income. The years 2016 and 2015 seem to show less conservative financial accounting or more aggressive tax reporting relative to 2017. Remember that taxable income is the basis for the tax payment computations for the current year. This ratio could also inform us about the quality of financial accounting in some cases.

HARTFORD

Real World—PERMANENT TAX DIFFERENCES

HARTFORD [HIG]

The **Hartford Financial Services Group, Inc.** provided the following income tax rate reconciliation for the years 2015-2017 in a recent Form 10-K. The pre-tax GAAP income on its income statement for 2017 is $723 million. Thus, the rate reconciliation below for 2017 starts with this amount of income multiplied by the U.S. statutory tax rate in effect for 2017, 35%, for a provision at the U.S. statutory rate of $253 million ($723 × 35%). Then, you can see some of the items discussed above over the three years—the tax effect of tax-exempt (municipal) interest, changes in the valuation allowance, the effects of solar credits, and some others. The effective tax rate for Hartford for 2017 is 136% (= $985/$723). It is over 100% in this year because of U.S. tax reform. We discuss the effects of changing tax rates, such as in the recent U.S. tax reform, and foreign earnings of U.S. multinationals later in the chapter.

Income Tax Rate Reconciliation

For the years ended December 31	2017	2016	2015
Tax provision at U.S. federal statutory rate	$253	$157	$517
Tax-exempt interest	(123)	(124)	(132)
Decrease in deferred tax valuation allowance	—	(79)	(102)
Stock-based compensation	(15)	—	—
Solar credits	—	(79)	—
Sale of HFPI and foreign rate differential	5	(37)	—
Tax Reform	877	—	—
Other	(12)	(4)	6
Provision (benefit) for income taxes	**$985**	**$(166)**	**$289**

In addition to the effect of tax-exempt interest, the Company's effective tax rate for the year ended December 31, 2017 reflects a federal income tax benefit of $15 related to a deduction for stock-based compensation that vested at a fair value per share greater than the fair value on the date of grant.

The Company recognized an $877 increase in income tax expense in 2017 due to the effects of Tax Reform (see LO 18-5), primarily due to the reduction in net deferred tax assets as a result of the reduction in the Federal corporate income tax rate from 35% to 21%.

Additionally, reflected above is a benefit of $79 in 2016 due to the investment in solar energy partnerships. The total tax benefit from the transaction was $113 which includes the tax effects of the related financial statement realized loss from writing down the investments in the partnerships. Also included in 2016 is a tax benefit primarily due to the sale of the Company's U.K. property and casualty run-off subsidiaries.

EXPANDING YOUR KNOWLEDGE — Foreign Earnings of a U.S. Multinational

A complicated topic in accounting for income taxes is how to account for taxes on foreign earnings of U.S. multinationals. Prior to the TCJA, the U.S. was on a worldwide tax system, with deferral. This meant that worldwide earnings of the company were taxable in the U.S. (as well as subject to the tax rules in the foreign country). However, the operating earnings of a foreign subsidiary were not taxed currently; the U.S. taxation was deferred, until the company repatriated those earnings to the U.S. parent company (meaning it paid the earnings back to the U.S. parent as a dividend). Thus, many U.S. multinationals chose to not repatriate the earnings and to leave them in the foreign subsidiary. This resulted in temporary differences unless the company did not expect to repatriate the funds in the foreseeable future, in which case, the amounts were treated as permanent differences under GAAP.

The TCJA of 2017 fundamentally changed the tax treatment of foreign earnings of U.S. multinationals. The changes moved the U.S. to a modified territorial system. The territorial system means that earnings of a U.S. multinational that are earned in a foreign jurisdiction are not taxable in the U.S. In this case, foreign earnings are a *permanent difference* between financial accounting and tax.

However, the U.S. revised and added new rules, known as base erosion provisions, *that require some of the foreign earnings to be taxable currently in the U.S. under certain conditions.* Details are beyond the scope of this text, but in general these rules operate so that companies do not shift too much passive or high return income to low tax jurisdictions.

Upon transition to the new system, companies must pay a mandatory tax on unrepatriated earnings earned prior to 2018 (and after 1986). This tax is assessed at two rates (15.5% if the foreign earnings are held in cash and 8% if the foreign earnings held in non-cash assets). The tax is payable over eight years. FASB provided guidance that this tax is required to be recorded in the companies' accounting records as a tax expense and liability in the accounting period in which the tax law was enacted (December 2017), without discounting for the time value of money (even though the amount is not payable for up to eight years). For 2017, many companies' tax expense and effective tax rates were high but much of the cash taxes will not be paid until later in time.

REVIEW 18-4 **LO18-4** **Multiple Temporary and Permanent Differences**

Review MBC

For 2020, Raleigh Corporation had pretax GAAP income of $250,000 and an income tax rate of 25%. Raleigh had a $5,000 credit balance in its Deferred Tax Liability account on January 1, 2020, and a zero balance in its Deferred Tax Asset account on January 1, 2020. The company summarized the following items for 2020.

- Depreciation for accounting purposes, $80,000, and for income tax purposes, $110,000. The related fixed asset was acquired for $400,000 at the beginning of 2020, and had an estimated 5-year life at that time.
- Installment sales revenue for accounting purposes, $80,000, and for income tax purposes, $40,000. The collection period for the $40,000 receivable is the following four years with equal amounts expected each year.
- Payment of life insurance premiums on executive officers totaled $4,000 in 2020.

More Practice:
18-33, 18-35, 18-51, 18-52, 18-53, 18-58

Solution on p. 18-63.

Required

a. Compute the increase in income tax payable on December 31, 2020.
b. Record the income tax journal entry required on December 31, 2020.

LO 18-5 Explain how a change in tax rates impacts deferred taxes

LO 18-5 Overview

Tax Rate Changes
- Use new tax rate only if enacted into law
- Recognize income statement effect of a change in tax rate in period the new tax rate was enacted
- Apply new tax rate(s) to temporary taxable amounts in the year(s) of reversal

In our previous examples, one tax rate applied for all years. However, tax rates can change through the legislature, which impacts the tax calculations and the accounting for income taxes. In 2017 as part of the TCJA, a new federal tax rate was enacted into law that significantly reduced the federal corporate statutory tax rate from 35% to 21%. As mentioned, deferred tax assets and liabilities are valued at the enacted tax rate that will be in effect when temporary differences reverse. Thus, any 2017 existing deferred tax assets or liabilities needed to be reduced to reflect the change in the enacted tax rate. Rate adjustments are reflected in net income *in the period of change in the enacted tax rate*, which in this example was 2017. In **Demo 18-5**, we examine how to measure a deferred tax amount when multiple rate changes are enacted. We also examine how a change in an enacted tax rate affects existing deferred tax accounts.

740-10-25-47 The effect of a change in tax laws or rates shall be recognized at the date of enactment.

740-10-35-4 Deferred tax liabilities and assets shall be adjusted for the effect of a change in tax laws or rates. A change in tax laws or rates may also require a reevaluation of a valuation allowance for deferred tax assets.

Demo 18-5 **LO18-5** **Change in Enacted Tax Rate**

Demo MBC

GAAP basis liability > Tax basis liability

Example One—Enacted Tax Rate Change—Impact on Existing Deferred Tax Asset Account

Boulder Inc. has one deductible temporary difference of $50,000 due to a GAAP accrual for a pending lawsuit with a tax basis of zero. The deferred tax asset has a balance of $20,000 ($50,000 × 40% current tax rate) on December 1, 2020. On December 15, 2020, a new tax rate of 25% was enacted into law, effective in 2021.

a. Prepare a schedule to compute the deferred tax asset balance on December 31, 2020.
b. Record the income tax journal entry required on December 31, 2020, assuming taxable income of $100,000.

Solution

a. **Schedule of Deferred Tax Asset Balance**

The enacted tax rate is used to determine the deferred tax asset value in the following calculation.

continued

continued from previous page

Measurement of Deferred Tax Asset (Dec. 31)	**2020**
GAAP basis of estimated litigation liability	$50,000
Tax basis of estimated litigation liability	0
Difference between GAAP and tax bases	$50,000
Tax rate	× 25%
Deferred tax asset, ending balance	$12,500

The Deferred Tax Asset account will require an adjustment of $7,500 (credit).

Deferred Tax Asset			
Dec. 1, 2020	20,000		
		7,500	**Adjustment**
Dec. 31, 2020	12,500		

b. **Income Tax Journal Entry**
Boulder Inc., would record the following entry to recognize income tax expense for 2020. The *decrease* in the tax rate caused an *increase* in income tax expense due to the adjustment required to the existing deferred tax asset. Specifically, an asset is now valued at a lower amount and this devaluation of an asset reduces income.

December 31, 2020—To record income tax expense

Income Tax Expense ($40,000 + $7,500)	47,500	
Deferred Tax Asset		7,500
Income Tax Payable ($100,000 × 40%)		40,000

Assets	=	Liabilities	+	Equity
−7,500		+40,000		−47,500

Def Tax Asset: Bal. 20,000 | 7,500

Inc Tax Payable: | 40,000

Income Tax Exp: 47,500 |

Example Two—Enacted Tax Rate Change—Impact on Existing Deferred Tax Liability Account

GAAP basis asset > Tax basis asset

Boulder Inc. has one taxable temporary difference of $40,000 related to fixed assets with a GAAP basis of $40,000 and with a tax basis of zero. The Deferred Tax Liability account has a balance of $16,000 ($40,000 × 40% current tax rate) on December 1, 2020. On December 15, 2020, a new tax rate of 25% was enacted into law, effective in 2021.

a. Prepare a schedule to compute the deferred tax liability balance on December 31, 2020.
b. Record the income tax journal entry required on December 31, 2020, assuming taxable income of $100,000.

Solution

a. **Schedule of Deferred Tax Liability Balance**
The enacted tax rate is used to determine the deferred tax liability value.

Measurement of Deferred Tax Liability (Dec. 31)	**2020**
GAAP basis of fixed assets	$40,000
Tax basis of fixed assets	0
Difference between GAAP and tax bases	$40,000
Tax rate	× 25%
Deferred tax liability, ending balance	$10,000

The Deferred Tax Liability account will require an adjustment of $6,000 (debit).

Deferred Tax Liability			
		16,000	Dec. 1, 2020
Adjustment	**6,000**		
		10,000	Dec. 31, 2020

b. **Income Tax Journal Entry**
Boulder Inc., would record the following entry to recognize income tax expense for 2020. The *decrease* in the tax rate caused a *decrease* in income tax expense due to the adjustment required to the existing deferred tax liability.

continued

continued from previous page

Assets = Liabilities + Equity
+40,000 −34,000
−6,000

Def Tax Liab: 6,000 | 16,000 Bal.
Income Tax Exp: 34,000 |
Inc Tax Payable: | 40,000

December 31, 2020—To record income tax expense

Income Tax Expense ($40,000 − $6,000).	34,000	
Deferred Tax Liability	6,000	
Income Tax Payable ($100,000 × 40%)		40,000

Example Three—Enacted Tax Rate Change, Multiple Tax Rates

Springs Inc. has taxable income of $40,000 for the year ended December 31, 2020. In addition, Springs Inc. calculates a temporary taxable difference of $5,000 due to the excess of the carrying value of depreciable assets over the tax basis. The $5,000 temporary difference will result in future taxable amounts of $2,000 in 2021, $2,000 in 2022, and $1,000 in 2023. The current year tax rate is 25%. Newly enacted future tax rates are as follows: 2021: 25%, 2022: 30%, and 2023: 35%.

GAAP basis asset > Tax basis asset

a. Prepare a schedule to compute the deferred tax liability balance on December 31, 2020. Assume a beginning balance of zero for the tax liability.

b. Record the income tax journal entry on December 31, 2020.

Solution

a. **Schedule to Compute Deferred Tax Liability**

The future enacted tax rates are matched to the temporary taxable amounts in the relevant *years of reversal* as follows.

Measurement of Deferred Tax Liability (Dec. 31)	2021	2022	2023	Total
Reversal of differences between GAAP and tax bases	$2,000	$2,000	$1,000	$5,000
Tax rate.	× 25%	× 30%	× 35%	
Deferred tax liability, ending balance	$ 500	$ 600	$ 350	$1,450

b. **Income Tax Journal Entry**

The current tax rate is used to calculate the increase in income tax payable (the current tax expense) of $10,000 ($40,000 × 25%). The journal entry to record income tax expense is as follows.

Recall that while it is the convention to show the income tax entry as a combined entry as illustrated in this chapter, it is likely recorded in two parts.

Current Income Tax Expense	10,000	
Income Tax Payable		10,000
Deferred Income Tax Expense . . .	1,450	
Deferred Tax Liability.		1,450

Assets = Liabilities + Equity
+1,450 −11,450
+10,000

Def Tax Liab: | 1,450
Income Tax Exp: 11,450 |
Inc Tax Payable: | 10,000

December 31, 2020—To record income tax expense

Income Tax Expense ($1,450 + $10,000).	11,450	
Deferred Tax Liability		1,450
Income Tax Payable ($40,000 × 25%)		10,000

HARTFORD

Real World—CHANGES IN TAX RATES FOR A COMPANY WITH DEFERRED TAX ASSETS

HARTFORD [HIG]

Recall the rate reconciliation for **Hartford** on page 18-20. Hartford reports an item in the rate reconciliation for "Tax Reform" of $877 million. This amount is an *increase* to its income tax expense. This might seem puzzling because the U.S. tax rate *decreased*! However, Hartford had large deferred tax assets recorded on its balance sheet. When the U.S. tax rate is reduced, the value of those deferred tax assets is also reduced. Thus, the company must record a journal entry to reduce deferred tax assets (a credit) and increase deferred tax expense (a debit). There were no changes to the underlying non-tax assets and non-tax liabilities. The only change was the tax rate, affecting the valuation of the deferred tax assets and liabilities. Hartford reports the following in its Form 10-K tax note.

The Company recognized an $877 increase in income tax expense in 2017 due to the effects of Tax Reform, primarily due to the reduction in net deferred tax assets as a result of the reduction in the Federal corporate income tax rate from 35% to 21%.

BOEING

Real World—CHANGES IN TAX RATES FOR A COMPANY WITH DEFERRED TAX LIABILITIES

BOEING [BA]

Boeing had net deferred tax liabilities recorded when the TCJA was passed, and Boeing was required to revalue these liabilities at the new lower rate. As a result, the company showed a reduction in their effective tax rate.

> In the fourth quarter of 2017, we recorded provisional tax benefits of $1,210 related to the remeasurement of our net U.S. deferred tax liabilities to reflect the reduction in the corporate tax rate. We also recorded a provisional tax expense of $159 related to tax on non-U.S. activities resulting from the TCJA.

COCA COLA

Real World—ESTIMATING IMPACT OF THE TAX CUTS AND JOB ACTS

COCA COLA [KO]

Staff Accounting Bulletin No. 118 was issued by the SEC in December 2017 to assist registrants in accounting for the Tax Cuts and Job Acts (Act) enacted on December 22, 2017. The guidance requires registrants to

- Reflect the income tax effects of the Act in which the accounting is complete.
- Recognize a provisional amount for specific income tax effects of the Act that are incomplete but where a reasonable estimate can be determined.
- Continue to apply ASC Topic 740 based on the tax law prior to the Act when a reasonable estimate cannot be determined.

Coca Cola Company disclosed the following in its 2017 Form 10-K related to its provisional estimates recognized due to the Act.

> The Company has determined that the net tax charge of $3.6 billion recorded in connection with the tax effect of the Tax Reform Act is a provisional amount and a reasonable estimate as of December 31, 2017. Additional work is necessary to finalize the calculation for certain income tax effects of the Tax Reform Act. Additionally, certain of our equity method investees are impacted by the Tax Reform Act and have recorded provisional tax amounts. To the extent their provisional amounts are refined in 2018, we will record our proportionate share in the line item equity income (loss)—net in our consolidated statement of income.

Change in Enacted Tax Rate — LO18-5 — REVIEW 18-5

Billboard Company has a deferred tax liability in the amount of $6,900 at December 31, 2020, relating to a $23,000 installment sale receivable, $10,000 of which is collected in 2021. The tax rate in 2021 is 30%. However, the rate for 2022 and thereafter is changed during 2021 to 25%. Warranty expense in 2021 included in the determination of pretax GAAP income is $22,000, with these amounts expected to be incurred and deductible for tax purposes in 2022. Pretax GAAP income is $112,000 in 2021. Prepare the journal entry to record income taxes in 2021.

Review MBC

More Practice: 18-37, 18-38, 18-63, 18-64, 18-65

Solution on p. 18-63.

Describe accounting for net operating loss carryforwards — LO 18-6

When a company has negative taxable income in a period, it has a **net operating loss** (NOL). As a result, the company has no income tax obligation in the current period. The company can carry such tax losses forward to offset future taxable income and thus, reduce taxes in future years.

ASC Glossary **Carryforwards**: Deductions or credits that cannot be utilized on the tax return during a year that may be carried forward to reduce taxable income or taxes payable in a future year.

LO 18-6 Overview

Net Operating Loss Carryforward
- Losses offset taxable income (maximum of 80%) in future years
- No limit on the number of years losses may be carried forward
- Record a deferred tax asset for loss carryforward
- Determine whether an allowance is required

Under current federal tax laws, a company may carry federal income tax losses forward indefinitely. In future years, the company can use the losses to offset taxable income (earned in those future

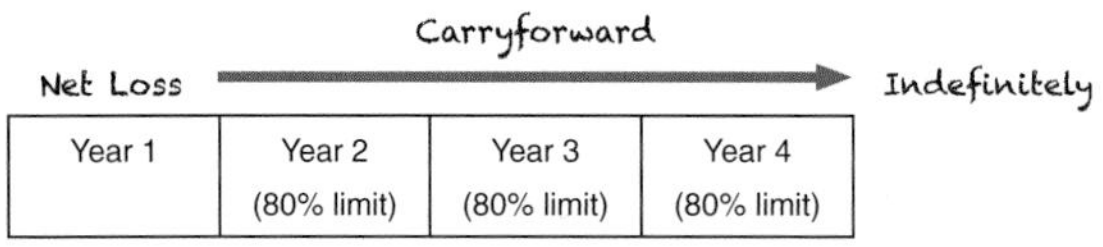

years); however, net operating loss carryforwards can only offset a maximum of 80% of taxable income in each of the future years. The loss carryforward requires the recording of a deferred tax asset as illustrated in **Demo 18-6**. (Recall that the ASC Glossary definition of a deferred tax asset included earlier directly references "carryforwards.") The realization of a future tax savings from loss carryforwards depends on a company's ability to earn profits in the future. As a result, the company must assess whether a valuation allowance is necessary as described earlier in LO 18-3.

Demo 18-6 **LO18-6** **Net Operating Loss Carryforward**

Whitewater Inc. experiences an operating loss for tax purposes of $65,000 in 2020. Management estimates future taxable income of $10,000, $5,000, $50,000, and $60,000, in years 2021, 2022, 2023, and 2024, respectively. An enacted tax law in 2020 decreases the current statutory tax rate of 35% to 25% in 2022 and thereafter.

a. Calculate Whitewater's deferred tax asset balance on December 31, 2020, related to its NOL carryforward.

b. Record the effect of the NOL carryforward. Assume that evidence indicates that it is *more likely than not* that the deferred tax asset will be realized.

c. Show the income statement presentation of the NOL carryforward in 2020.

d. Whitewater becomes profitable in 2021 (actual taxable income of $15,000). Record the income tax expense entry for 2021. Assume that evidence indicates that it is *more likely than not* that only 70% of the deferred tax asset will be realized.

Solution

a. **Measurement of Deferred Tax Asset**

The full $65,000 loss is carried forward to future years to create a deferred tax asset. The $65,000 NOL is estimated to be allocated as follows, along with the associated tax savings per year.

	Future Earnings	80% Limit	Enacted Tax Rate	Estimated Tax Savings
2021	$ 10,000	$ 8,000	35%	$ 2,800
2022	5,000	4,000	25%	1,000
2023	50,000	40,000	25%	10,000
2024	60,000	13,000*	25%	3,250
	$125,000	$65,000		$17,050

*$65,000 – $8,000 – $4,000 – $40,000.

b. **Recording Effect of Net Operating Loss Carryforward**

Whitewater records a deferred tax asset of $17,050, the estimated future tax savings from the carryforward. No valuation allowance is recorded because evidence indicates that it is *more likely than not* that the deferred tax asset will be realized. Income tax expense is credited for the net benefit due to the recognition of the deferred tax asset related to the net operating loss carryforward. For presentation purposes, when income tax expense has a credit balance, it is called Income Tax Benefit on the income statement.

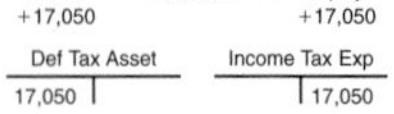

December 31, 2020—To record income tax benefit

Deferred Tax Asset	17,050	
Income Tax Expense		17,050

c. **Income Statement Presentation**

Partial Income Statement	2020
Operating loss before income taxes	$(65,000)
Income tax benefit	17,050
Net loss	$(47,950)

continued

continued from previous page

d. **Recording Effect of Net Operating Loss Carryforward—Year Two**

In 2021, the company would apply (use up) a carryforward loss of $12,000 or 80% of taxable income of $15,000. The $65,000 loss carryforward is reduced to $53,000. Thus, the deferred tax asset would be reduced to $13,250 ($53,000 × 25%). The company would pay income tax on 20% of taxable income for the year.

Deferred Tax Asset			
Jan. 1, 2021	17,050		
		3,800	**Adjustment**
Dec. 31, 2021	13,250		

December 31, 2021—To record income tax expense

Income Tax Expense ($3,800 + $1,050)	4,850	
Deferred Tax Asset (see adjustment above)		3,800
Income Tax Payable ($15,000 × 20% × 35%)		1,050

Assets	=	Liabilities	+	Equity
−3,800		+1,050		−4,850

Def Tax Asset	
17,050	3,800

Inc Tax Payable	
	1,050

Income Tax Exp	
4,850	17,050

December 31, 2021—To adjust deferred tax asset valuation allowance

Income Tax Expense ($13,250 × 30%)	3,975	
Valuation Allowance for Deferred Tax Asset		3,975

Assets	=	Liabilities	+	Equity
−3,975				−3,975

Def Tax Asset Allow	
	3,975

Income Tax Exp	
4,800 3,975	17,050

EXPANDING YOUR KNOWLEDGE — Pre-2018 Losses

Based upon previous tax legislation, *pre-2018 losses* are either carried back two years and forward up to 20 years *or* are carried forward only up to 20 years. In a loss carryback, losses are carried back two years (in order of years, starting with the earliest year) to secure a refund of prior years' taxes. For example, a 2017 loss would first offset 2015 income, and then 2016 income if applicable. If the NOL is so large that the carryback to the prior two years does not fully absorb it, the remaining loss can be carried forward a maximum of 20 years to reduce taxable income in future years until it is fully absorbed. Under these rules, there is a total of 22 years available to absorb the NOL. Under the prior rules, there were no limitations on the amount of losses that could offset income in a profitable year (i.e., no 80% limitation).

While new legislation is in effect post-2017, many companies will have existing tax assets related to loss carryforwards that will be treated under the prior tax law. Therefore, companies will need to account for deferred tax assets originating before 2018 separately from those originating in 2018 and later.

UNITED CONTINENTAL

Real World—NET OPERATING LOSSES

UNITED CONTINENTAL [UAL]

United Continental Holdings Inc., a holding company of United Airlines Inc., included the following summary in its disclosure of income taxes in a recent Form 10-K. A significant item in the company's deferred tax asset balance is the inclusion of federal and state operating loss carryforwards. The company has evidence to support the use of the remaining balance of carryforwards as evidenced by the low balance in the valuation allowance in 2017. Because these net operating losses contributing to the carryforwards took place prior to 2018 (when the new tax law went into effect), these carryforwards expire 20 years after their origination.

Deferred income tax asset (liability), in millions	**2017**	**2016**
Federal and state net operating loss ("NOL") carryforwards	$ 601	$1,613
Deferred revenue	1,069	2,096
Employee benefits, including pension, postretirement and medical	1,051	1,662
Alternative minimum tax credit carryforwards	—	116
Other	351	523
Less: Valuation allowance	(63)	(68)
Total deferred tax assets	$3,009	$5,942

REVIEW 18-6 **LO18-6** **Net Operating Loss Carryforward**

Review MBC

More Practice:
18-39, 18-40, 18-70,
18-71, 18-72

Solution on p. 18-63.

Tyson Corporation has no differences between financial accounting and taxable incomes. In 2021, the corporation experienced an $18,000 pretax loss from operations. Assume an income tax rate of 25%.

Provide the 2021 income tax entry for Tyson. Assume that on December 31, 2021, there is evidence that it is *more likely than not* that 60% of the deferred tax asset would not be realized.

LO 18-7 Explain and demonstrate accounting for uncertainty in income tax decisions

LO 18-7 Overview

Uncertain Tax Benefits
- **Recognition threshold**: Recognize uncertain tax position if it is *more likely than not* the company will sustain it
- **Measurement of tax benefit**: Measure tax benefit as the largest amount greater than 50% likely of being realized

At times, companies can take a tax position on how tax revenues or tax expenses are shown on the tax return that may later be subject to a different interpretation by taxing authorities. For example, a company and a tax authority can arrive at different conclusions about how the taxpayer should treat a particular transaction, a valuation computation that affects taxable income, or the timing of when an expense is taken (among other positions). The dispute can be solved through negotiation between the taxing authority and the taxpayer or through litigation if a settlement cannot be reached. The accounting for income taxes must consider the types of tax positions where the outcome is not certain, known as uncertain tax positions.

740-10-55-4 Relatively few disputes are resolved through litigation, and very few are taken to the court of last resort. Generally, the taxpayer and the taxing authority negotiate a settlement to avoid the costs and hazards of litigation. As a result, the measurement of the tax position is based on management's best judgment of the amount the taxpayer would ultimately accept in a settlement with taxing authorities.

The intuition behind an uncertain tax benefit is that if a company takes a tax position that provides tax savings but those tax savings might not be retained upon a tax dispute with a tax authority, then the financial accounting rules require the taxpayer to accrue an expense for the estimated amount that might not be retained. An uncertain tax benefit is essentially a contingent liability of the company; they may be liable for additional taxes in the future for positions taken in the current or prior periods. Determining the amount to record for the unrecognized tax benefit requires management judgment in assessing how likely it is that a position is maintained and also in measuring the amount that is likely to be sustained. The decision process for the accounting treatment of uncertain tax positions is a two-step process that separates recognition from measurement (**Demo 18-7** illustrates this).

Step One: Recognition The first step is to determine whether a tax position has met the recognition threshold. It is met if it is *more likely than not* (> 50%) that the taxpayer will maintain the tax position in a dispute with taxing authorities, based on the technical merits of the company's position. When making this determination the company is to assume that the taxing authority will audit the position and has full knowledge of all relevant information. In other words, the company cannot take the probability of audit into account. If more likely than not the condition is met, the company measures the tax benefit as described in step two. If this condition is not met, the company cannot recognize the tax benefit based upon the uncertain tax position.

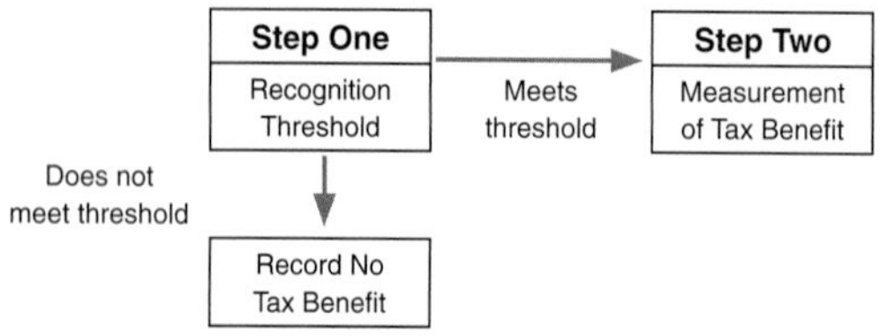

Step Two: Measurement The second step is to determine the measurement of the tax benefit that meets the *more likely than not* recognition threshold. The benefit is measured as the largest amount of tax benefit that is greater than 50% likely of being realized.

740-10-55-3 The application of the requirements of this Subtopic related to tax positions requires a two-step process that separates recognition from measurement. The first step is determining whether a tax position has met the recognition threshold; the second step is measuring a tax position that meets the recognition threshold. The recognition threshold is met when the taxpayer (the reporting entity) concludes that . . . it is more likely than not that the taxpayer will sustain the benefit taken or expected to be taken in the tax return in a dispute with taxing authorities if the taxpayer takes the dispute to the court of last resort.

740-10-25-6 An entity shall initially recognize the financial statement effects of a tax position when it is more likely than not, based on the technical merits, that the position will be sustained upon examination. The term more likely than not means a likelihood of more than 50 percent; the terms examined and upon examination also include resolution of the related appeals or litigation processes, if any. For example, if an entity determines that it is certain that the entire cost of an acquired asset is fully deductible, the more-likely-than-not recognition threshold has been met. The more-likely-than-not recognition threshold is a positive assertion that an entity believes it is entitled to the economic benefits associated with a tax position. The determination of whether or not a tax position has met the more-likely-than-not recognition threshold shall consider the facts, circumstances, and information available at the reporting date. The level of evidence that is necessary and appropriate to support an entity's assessment of the technical merits of a tax position is a matter of judgment that depends on all available information.

740-10-55-5 The recognition and measurement requirements of this Subtopic related to tax positions require that the entity recognize the largest amount of benefit that is greater than 50 percent likely of being realized upon settlement.

Uncertain Tax Positions

LO18-7 **Demo 18-7**

Example One—Uncertain Tax Position—Does Not Meet Recognition Threshold

In applying the first step, Boulder Inc. determined that a tax position resulting in a tax benefit due to a tax-deductible amount of $100 does *not* meet the threshold of recognition. In other words, Boulder Inc. is less than 50% certain that the tax position supporting the deductibility of the $100 will be sustained if challenged by taxing authorities. Boulder Inc. paid taxes based upon the tax position that it had taken: Boulder's income tax payable is $5,000 on December 31, 2020, after considering the $100 deductible amount. Record the income tax expense entry on December 31, 2020, assuming a tax rate of 25%.

Solution

Although Boulder Inc. paid taxes based upon the tax position that it had taken, the income tax expense reported in the financial statements will account for the position as if it will not be sustained.

December 31, 2020—To record income tax expense

Income Tax Expense	5,025	
Income Tax Payable.		5,000
Liability for Unrecognized Tax Benefits ($100 × 25%).		25

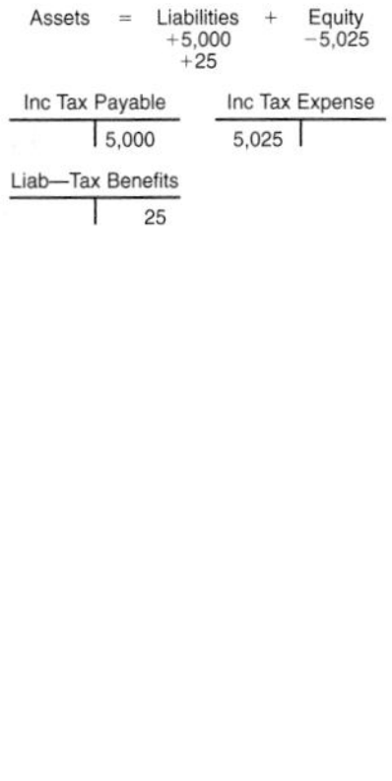

Example Two—Uncertain Tax Position—Meets Recognition Threshold

Not let's assume that Boulder Inc. does meet the recognition threshold (>50% probability that the tax position will be sustained). There is limited information about how a taxing authority will view the position. However, based upon judgment, management of Boulder Inc. believes it is likely Boulder would settle for less than the full amount of the entire position when examined by the taxing authority. Management has considered the amounts and the probabilities of the possible estimated outcomes and concluded the following.

Possible Estimated Outcome (Allowable Tax Deduction)	Individual Probability of Occurring	Cumulative Probability of Occurring
$100	25%	25%
70	40%	65%
50	30%	95%
0	5%	100%

Boulder Inc. paid taxes based upon the tax position that it had taken: Boulder's income tax payable is $5,000 on December 31, 2020, after considering the $100 benefit. Record the income tax expense entry that Boulder would record on December 31, 2020, assuming a tax rate of 25%.

continued

continued from previous page

Solution

To make the determination, the company is to compute the cumulative probability for the possible estimated outcomes. The outcome with the largest benefit that has a cumulative probability greater than 50% is what is allowed to continue to be recorded as a benefit. The remainder is the amount required to be recorded as an unrecognized tax benefit (a contingent liability). Because $70 is the largest amount of benefit that has a greater than 50% cumulative probability of being realized upon settlement, the entity would recognize a tax benefit of $70 in the financial statements. In other words, at a $100 outcome, the probability is 25%. At a $70 outcome, the probability is 40%, and on a cumulative basis of 65% (25% + 40%), the probability of being allowed at least a $70 deduction is greater than the 50% threshold defined in the measurement principle. Boulder Inc. would record a liability for the unrecognized tax benefit of $30 ($100 − $70) multiplied by the tax rate of 25%.

Assets = Liabilities + Equity: Liabilities +5,000, +8; Equity −5,008
Inc Tax Payable: 5,000 (credit); Inc Tax Exp: 5,008 (debit); Liab—Tax Benefit: 8 (credit)

December 31, 2020—To record income tax expense

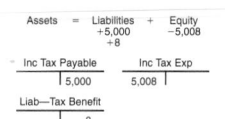

Income Tax Expense ($5,000 + $8 [rounded])	5,008	
Income Tax Payable (given)		5,000
Liability for Unrecognized Tax Benefits ($30 × 25%)		8

Determining the possible estimated outcomes and the associated probabilities requires *management judgment.* For example, in the probability table above, management estimated that there is a 25% probability of an outcome where the full $100 would be allowed as a tax deduction. Let's instead assume that management estimated that there is a 55% probability of an outcome where the full $100 is allowed as a tax deduction. In that case, no liability would be recorded for unrecognized tax benefits and thus the amount of income tax expense would be $5,000. Estimates prepared by management have a direct impact on net income reported in the financial statements.

Example Three—Uncertain Tax Position—Resolution

Resolution of the uncertain tax position could take on a number of forms: (a) full benefit is lost, (b) full benefit is realized, or (c) some portion of the benefit is realized. In all three cases, assume that the company previously accrued $8 ($30 × 25%) as the liability for the unrecognized tax benefit.

a. **Full Tax Benefit Is Lost**

Assume that in December 2021, after negotiations with taxing authorities, Boulder Inc. does not sustain its tax position regarding the $100 tax deduction. Record Boulder's entry resolving the uncertain tax position on December 31, 2021.

Solution

Assets = Liabilities + Equity: Liabilities −8, +25; Equity −17
Inc Tax Payable: 25 (credit); Inc Tax Exp: 17 (debit); Liab—Tax Benefit: 8 (debit) | 8 Bal.

December 31, 2021—To record failure to sustain tax position

Liability for Unrecognized Tax Benefits	8	
Income Tax Expense ($25 − $8)	17	
Income Tax Payable ($100 × 25%)		25

In this case the effect on tax expense in this period is only $17 because the company expensed $8 in a prior period when it accrued a liability for the uncertain tax position.

b. **Full Tax Benefit Is Realized**

Assume that in December 2021, after negotiations with taxing authorities, Boulder Inc. sustains its full tax position regarding the $100 tax deduction. Record Boulder's entry resolving the uncertain tax position on December 31, 2021.

Solution

Assets = Liabilities + Equity: Liabilities −8; Equity +8
Liab—Tax Benefit: 8 (debit) | 8 Bal.; Inc Tax Exp: 8 (credit)

December 31, 2021—To record favorable resolution of tax position

Liability for Unrecognized Tax Benefits	8	
Income Tax Expense		8

In this case, we decrease income tax expense to offset the increase to income tax expense of $8 in the initial entry on December 31, 2020.

c. **Portion of Tax Benefit Is Realized**

Assume that in December 2021, after negotiations with taxing authorities, Boulder Inc. realizes $70 of the tax deduction. Record Boulder's entry resolving the uncertain tax position on December 31, 2021.

continued

continued from previous page

Solution

December 31, 2021—To record negotiated resolution of tax position

Liability for Unrecognized Tax Benefits	8	
Income Tax Payable ($30 × 25%)		8

Assets	=	Liabilities	+	Equity
		−8 +8		

Liab—Tax Benefit		Inc Tax Payable	
8	8 Bal.		8

In this case there is no effect on the income statement. The company is essentially moving the liability from a contingent liability to a payable that is certain.

TARGET

Real World—UNCERTAIN TAX POSITION

TARGET [TGT]

In a recent Form 10-K, **Target Corporation** recorded $325 million of unrecognized tax benefits on December 31, 2017, based upon the uncertainty of some tax positions. The following required disclosure reconciles the beginning of year balance to the end of year balance of the Liability for Unrecognized Tax Benefits. The company also reserved for potential interest and penalties that could result if the company does not sustain their position with taxing authorities. Target shows a substantial increase in the liability during 2017.

Reconciliation of Liability for Unrecognized Tax Benefits (millions)	2017	2016	2015
Balance at beginning of period	**$153**	$153	$155
Additions based on tax positions related to the current year	**112**	12	10
Additions for tax positions of prior years	**142**	6	14
Reductions for tax positions of prior years	**(71)**	(16)	(26)
Settlements	**(11)**	(2)	—
Balance at end of period	**$325**	$153	$153

If we were to prevail on all unrecognized tax benefits recorded, $261 million of the $325 million reserve would benefit the effective tax rate. In addition, the reversal of accrued penalties and interest would also benefit the effective tax rate. Interest and penalties associated with unrecognized tax benefits are recorded within income tax expense. During the years ended February 3, 2018, January 28, 2017, and January 30, 2016, we recorded a (benefit)/expense from accrued penalties and interest of $(12) million, $1 million, and $5 million, respectively. As of February 3, 2018, January 28, 2017, and January 30, 2016 total accrued interest and penalties were $29 million, $45 million, and $44 million, respectively. It is reasonably possible that the amount of the unrecognized tax benefits with respect to our other unrecognized tax positions will increase or decrease during the next twelve months; however, an estimate of the amount or range of the change cannot be made at this time.

Uncertain Tax Benefit **LO18-7** **REVIEW 18-7**

Review MBC

Leah Inc. considered the probability of a recent tax position taken related to the deduction of $30,000 from taxable revenue. Leah determined that this position is *more likely than not* to be sustained in future discussions with taxing authorities. Using available information, Leah Inc. created the following summary of the probabilities of sustaining its tax position.

Individual probability of occurring	15%	20%	25%	20%	20%
Estimated allowable tax deduction	$30,000	$22,000	$20,000	$10,000	$5,000

Assuming taxable income of $450,000 (reflecting the inclusion of the uncertain tax expense in deductible expenses) and a tax rate of 25%, record the income tax journal entry for 2020.

More Practice: 18-41, 18-76

Solution on p. 18-64.

LO 18-8 Describe financial statement disclosure for deferred taxes and income tax expense

LO 18-8 Overview

Income Tax Presentation and Disclosure
- Present on balance sheet the net deferred tax amount as noncurrent
- Provide disclosure in notes including
  - Current and deferred amount and totals
  - Changes in valuation allowance
  - Major sources of deferred accounts

Though we have presented some disclosures throughout the chapter, this section provides an overall discussion of the reporting of income tax expense and related balance sheet accounts. We explain how multiple deferred tax asset and liability accounts are classified on the balance sheet. We also outline a variety of income tax disclosures required to provide information to investors and creditors who are making decisions based on information in financial statements. A number of disclosures, including reconciliations of balances, are required to support the deferred tax and income tax payable amounts on the balance sheet as well as income tax expense/benefit on the income statement.

Financial Statement Presentation

Income tax payable (income tax receivable) is recognized as a current liability (current asset) on a classified balance sheet. Deferred tax assets, valuation allowances, and deferred tax liabilities are merged into either a net noncurrent tax asset or a net noncurrent tax liability on a classified balance sheet as illustrated in **Demo 18-8**. Deferred amounts are offset; however, if components of a company are distinguishable as separate companies for tax purposes, or the company pays taxes in different jurisdictions, there is an exception as noted in the following accounting guidance.

740-10-45-4 In a classified statement of financial position, an entity shall classify deferred tax liabilities and assets as noncurrent amounts.

740-10-45-6 For a particular tax-paying component of an entity and within a particular tax jurisdiction, all deferred tax liabilities and assets, as well as any related valuation allowance, shall be offset and presented as a single noncurrent amount. However, an entity shall not offset deferred tax liabilities and assets attributable to different tax-paying components of the entity or to different tax jurisdictions.

As an example, Fastenal Company recognized a net deferred tax liability on its balance sheet as a noncurrent liability in the amount of $50.6 million (labeled deferred tax liabilities). A note accompanying the financial statements (shown below) included the balance of deferred income tax assets and deferred income tax liabilities of $24.6 and $75.2 million, respectively, making up the net balance of $50.6 million. Based on this disclosure, financial statement users are informed that there will be higher taxable amounts in the future due to lower taxable depreciation on property and equipment. We see that the company has several types of deferred tax assets (leading to taxable income lower than accounting income in the future). These consist of loss carryforwards in foreign jurisdictions, insurance, reserves, bad debt reserves, and inventory losses. We also see that the company has recorded a valuation allowance on its foreign deferred tax assets.

Fastenal Company (Note 7 excerpt) Deferred income tax assets (liabilities), in millions	2017
Inventory costing and valuation methods	$ 3.6
Allowance for doubtful accounts	3.0
Insurance reserves	8.4
Promotions payable	1.3
Stock-based compensation	5.2
Federal and state benefit of uncertain tax positions	0.9
Foreign net operating loss and credit carryforwards	4.2
Foreign valuation allowances	(2.8)
Other, net	0.8
Total deferred income tax assets	24.6
Property and equipment	(75.2)
Total deferred income tax liabilities	(75.2)
Deferred income tax liabilities	$(50.6)

On the income statement, the tax effect is presented as an expense or as a benefit (current and deferred portions). Income effects are allocated to sections of the income statement through intraperiod tax allocation—see Appendix 18A.

EXPANDING YOUR KNOWLEDGE **Simplifying Deferred Tax Presentation**

Classifying deferred tax assets and liabilities all as noncurrent is relatively new. While the FASB acknowledged that simplifying the presentation of deferred taxes presentation was not as accurate as breaking out current and noncurrent amounts, the benefits do not outweigh the cost and complexity. Previous guidance required presentation of current and noncurrent deferred tax amounts based upon the period of reversals.

SC Update No. 2015-17 BC7 The Board acknowledged that the noncurrent classification for all deferred tax liabilities and assets is not pure conceptually. However, this simplification will reduce cost and complexity without decreasing the usefulness of information provided to users of financial statements. In addition, the Board noted that the income taxes disclosures are being evaluated as part of the disclosure framework project and that project would be a better place to consider whether there is enhanced information about accounting for income taxes that could be provided to users that cannot be adequately communicated through classification.

Disclosure Requirements for Income Tax

Notes to the financial statements should provide the following supplemental disclosures regarding income taxes (ASC 740-10-50).

- Total of all deferred tax liabilities and assets.
- Total adjustments to and net change in the valuation allowance.
- Approximate tax effect of each major source of temporary difference and carryforward that gives rise to significant portions of deferred tax assets and liabilities.
- Reconciliation between the effective tax rate and the U.S. statutory rate.
- Current portion of income tax expense or benefit.
- Deferred portion of income tax expense or benefit.
- Tax credits.
- Government grants to the extent they are used as reductions of income tax expense.
- Benefits of and expiration dates of operating loss carryforwards.
- Adjustments of deferred tax assets or liabilities as a result of enacted tax law or rate changes or changes in the tax status of the company.

Balance Sheet Classification of Deferred Tax Assets and Liabilities **LO18-8** **Demo 18-8**

Aspen Co. reports temporary differences resulting in a deferred tax asset of $100,000, a valuation allowance of $50,000 and a total deferred tax liability of $120,000. How would the company report deferred taxes on its balance sheet?

Solution

The company reports a net noncurrent deferred tax liability of $70,000 ($120,000 – [$100,000 – $50,000]).

FASTENAL

Real World—DISCLOSURE

FASTENAL [FAST]

Fastenal Company included the following summary of current and deferred taxes in its disclosure of income taxes in a recent Form 10-K.

Components of income tax expense (benefit) were as follows:

2017 ($ millions)	Current	Deferred	Total
Federal	$270.6	$(33.1)	$237.5
State	33.2	3.3	36.5
Foreign	20.5	—	20.5
Income tax expense	$324.3	$(29.8)	$294.5

continued

continued from previous page

Total income tax expense is also shown on the face of the income statement:

Components of income tax expense (benefit) were as follows ($ millions):

Consolidated Statement of Earnings (excerpt)	**2017**
Earnings before income taxes	$873.1
Income tax expense	294.5
Net earnings	$578.6

While numerous detailed journal entries go into producing the disclosures a financial statement user sees, we can infer that the net of all these entries would be the following entry at an aggregated level ($ millions).

Assets	= Liabilities	+ Equity
+29.9	+324.3	−294.5

Income Tax Expense	294.5	
Net Deferred Tax Asset	29.8	
Income Tax Payable		324.3

REVIEW 18-8 **LO18-8** **Financial Statement Presentation of Deferred Taxes**

Review MBC

The following items create deferred tax assets and deferred tax liabilities at December 31, 2020.

1. Prepaid operating expenses of $40,000 are tax deductible when paid.
2. Excess tax depreciation (MACRS) over GAAP depreciation (straight-line) is $30,000.
3. Bad debt expense amount of $10,000 is tax deductible when actual losses are incurred.
4. Installment sales of $35,000 are recorded on an accrual basis for reporting purposes and taxed when collected.
5. Valuation allowance for deferred tax asset is estimated to be 50% of the deferred tax asset balance.
6. Taxable income for 2020 is $333,000.

Required

Show how all tax-related items would be recognized on the company's December 31, 2020, balance sheet. The tax rate is 25%.

More Practice: 18-42, 18-78

Solution on p. 18-64.

Management Judgment

Deferred Tax Asset Valuation Allowance

Determining whether it is *more likely than not* that some or all of the balance of deferred tax assets will not be realized requires management judgment. Recall that deferred tax assets are realized only if the company has positive taxable income in the future to offset the deferred deductions (p. 18-13). Management must evaluate both positive and negative evidence to determine the portion (if not all of) the deferred tax asset for which an allowance is required.

740-10-30-24 Future realization of a tax benefit sometimes will be expected for a portion but not all of a deferred tax asset, and the dividing line between the two portions may be unclear. In those circumstances, application of judgment based on a careful assessment of all available evidence is required to determine the portion of a deferred tax asset for which it is more likely than not a tax benefit will not be realized.

The decisions made by management regarding the amount of the allowance impacts financial reporting. An adjustment to the allowance in a period results in lower or higher tax expense and thus higher or lower reported financial accounting income.

Uncertain Tax Position

The measurement of an uncertain tax position is based on management's judgment of the amount that the company will settle with the taxing authority. Management must determine whether the company meets the recognition threshold, and if so, management must measure the tax benefit (p. 18-27). Both steps require management judgment depending on what factors management determines are relevant and the weight assigned to the factors based on all information available at the time. The uncertain tax position is revaluated as new information becomes available.

740-10-25-14 Subsequent recognition shall be based on management's best judgment given the facts, circumstances, and information available at the reporting date. A tax position need not be legally extinguished and its resolution need not be certain to subsequently recognize the position. Subsequent changes in judgment that lead to changes in recognition shall result from the evaluation of new information and not from a new evaluation or new interpretation by management of information that was available in a previous financial reporting period.

Apply intraperiod tax allocation

APPENDIX 18A
LO 18-9

Intraperiod tax allocation is the allocation of tax expense (benefit) to different income statement segments. Intraperiod tax allocation is required for income (loss) from continuing operations and discontinued operations. In addition, income tax expense (benefit) related to items charged or credited directly to other comprehensive income are shown in other comprehensive income. This is done by showing the item net of the tax effect as illustrated in **Demo 18-9**.

Allocate Tax Expense (Benefit)
- To income (loss) from continuing operations
- To income (loss) from discontinued operations
- To other comprehensive income

LO 18-9 Overview

Intraperiod Tax Allocation — LO18-9 — Demo 18-9

In 2020, Hikers Corp. reports pretax GAAP income of $6,000, resulting from income of $8,000 from continuing operations and a loss from discontinued operations of $2,000. Unrealized loss on available-for-sale debt securities totaled $500 before tax. The tax rate is 25%. Present the income statement and the statement of comprehensive income for 2020.

Solution
The income statement for Hikers Corp. would include the following.

Income Statement	2020
Income before income taxes	$ 8,000
Income tax expense ($8,000 × 25%)	2,000
Income from continuing operations	6,000
Discontinued operations	
Loss from discontinued operations, net of tax ($2,000 × 75%)	(1,500)
Net income	$ 4,500

The statement of comprehensive income for Hikers Corp. would include the following.

Statement of Comprehensive Income	2020
Net income	$ 4,500
Other comprehensive income	
Unrealized loss on securities ($500 × 75%)	(375)
Comprehensive income	$ 4,125

TARGET [TGT]

Real World—INTRAPERIOD TAX ALLOCATION

Target Corporation recognized (a) income from operations of discontinued segments net of tax and (b) other comprehensive income items net of tax in a recent Form 10-K, applying intraperiod tax allocation.

Consolidated Statements of Operations (millions)	2017	2016	2015
Earnings from continuing operations before income taxes	$3,646	$3,965	$4,923
Provision for income taxes	718	1,296	1,602
Net earnings from continuing operations	2,928	2,669	3,321
Discontinued operations, net of tax	6	68	42
Net earnings	$2,934	$2,737	$3,363

Consolidated Statements of Comprehensive Income (millions)	2017	2016	2015
Net earnings	$2,934	$2,737	$3,363
Other comprehensive income/(loss), net of tax			
Pension and other benefit liabilities, net of tax provision/(benefit) of $12, $(9), and $(18)	2	(13)	(27)
Currency translation adjustment and cash flow hedges, net of provision for taxes of $4, $2, and $2	6	4	(3)
Other comprehensive income/(loss)	8	(9)	(30)
Comprehensive income	$2,942	$2,728	$3,333

REVIEW 18-9 **LO18-9** **Intraperiod Tax Allocation**

Review MBC

Athletics Inc. had the following pretax balances in its accounts on December 31, 2020.

Revenues	$180,000
Cost of goods sold	99,000
Operating expenses	15,000
Loss from discontinued operations	(14,000)
Unrealized gain on available-for-sale debt securities	3,000

More Practice:
18-103, 18-104, 18-108
Solution on p. 18-64.

Assuming an income tax rate of 25% and a simple company structure (with no differences between accounting and taxable income, no state taxes, no foreign earnings or taxes, and no tax credits), prepare a combined statement of comprehensive income using intraperiod tax allocation.

APPENDIX 18B
LO 18-10

Apply tax effects to changes in accounting principle and error corrections

LO 18-10 Overview

Retrospective Accounting Treatment
- Tax effects
  - Change in accounting principle
  - Error corrections

In earlier chapters, we reviewed the accounting for changes in accounting principle and errors as they relate to topics such as property, plant, and equipment, and inventory. We will expand on those discussions in this section by taking into account the *tax effect* of retrospective adjustments for changes in accounting principle (**Demo 18-10A**) and error corrections (**Demo 18-10B**).

Change in Accounting Principle

Accounting principles include methods, techniques, and procedures applied to transactions or information for purposes of measurement, recognition, and disclosure. When a company changes an accounting principle, it substitutes one generally accepted accounting principle for another. Examples include changing from LIFO to FIFO or changing from FIFO to the weighted-average inventory method. Maintaining the relevance of financial accounting information in light of new information and changing circumstances is one objective of reporting for accounting changes. In some instances, an accounting change can improve the relevance of reported information. *Most changes in accounting principle are reported retrospectively*, where all prior period reporting reflects the new accounting principle. In applying a

retrospective adjustment, a company will present the cumulative effect of the change in prior periods (net of tax) as an adjustment to beginning retained earnings of the earliest reporting year presented.

Change in Accounting Principle **LO18-10** **Demo 18-10A**

Lawrence Inc. decided to change from FIFO to the average-cost method in 2020 for financial reporting purposes. If the average-cost method had been used in all previous periods, the inventory balance would have been $50,000 less than was recorded using FIFO. Assuming a tax rate of 25% and that the company continues to use FIFO for tax purposes, record the entry in the accounting records for the effect of the change in accounting principle.

Solution

The Inventory account is reduced for the change from FIFO to average-cost. The cumulative effect is an increase in cost of goods sold, reducing net income reflected in retained earnings by $37,500 ($50,000 – $12,500). The carrying value of inventory for reporting purposes is lower than the tax carrying value, creating a deferred tax asset. (If, instead, the company changed from the average-cost method to the FIFO inventory method resulting in a $50,000 increase in the carrying value of inventory, a deferred tax liability would result.)

January 1, 2020—To record the effect of change in accounting principle

Retained Earnings ($50,000 – $12,500)	37,500	
Deferred Tax Asset ($50,000 × 25%)	12,500	
Inventory		50,000

Assets = Liabilities + Equity
+12,500 −37,500
−50,000

Inventory: 50,000 (credit)
Ret Earnings: 37,500 (debit)
Def Tax Asset: 12,500 (debit)

EXPANDING YOUR KNOWLEDGE **Accounting for Change from the LIFO Inventory Method**

Recall that the primary reason to use LIFO is to save taxes and that the LIFO conformity rule requires that if LIFO is used for tax purposes it must be used for financial accounting. Thus, if a company is using LIFO for financial accounting, it is safe to assume it uses LIFO for tax purposes. As a result, if a company changes methods from LIFO to something else for financial reporting, it would also have to change for tax purposes. The Internal Revenue Code requires that taxes saved in previous years under LIFO must be repaid over a certain period of time when changing to another inventory method. This means the entry to adjust inventory to the new basis of accounting will include a credit to Income Tax Payable.

Error Correction

An accounting error occurs when a transaction or event is recorded incorrectly or is not recorded at all. For example, an accounting error results from an incorrect application of an accounting principle, from a clerical error, or from fraud. *Error corrections are applied retrospectively*. To compute the tax implications of an error correction, it is necessary to understand whether the error was also reflected on the tax return and whether the method applied on the tax return aligns with the method applied for financial reporting purposes.

Error Correction **LO18-10** **Demo 18-10B**

On January 1, 2020, Coe pays $5,000 for ordinary repairs and erroneously debits the Equipment account. The straight-line depreciation rate on equipment is 10% per year. Coe discovers the error in 2021. Assume a tax rate of 25%, the GAAP depreciation rate of 10% is the same as the tax depreciation rate, and the error carried over to the tax return. Record the journal entry to correct the error on January 1, 2021.

Solution

The company determines that expenses were understated in 2020 by $4,500, measured as follows.

Correct repair expense for 2020	$5,000
Depreciation expense recorded in 2020 ($5,000 × 10%)	500
Understated expense in 2020	$4,500

continued

continued from previous page

For 2020, repair expense is understated by \$5,000 and depreciation expense is overstated by \$500. The net impact is an understatement of expenses of \$4,500. The tax impact of \$1,125 is recorded as income tax receivable because taxable income would have also been overstated causing a tax overpayment. As a result, income is overstated by \$3,375 after tax (\$4,500 × 75%). To correct the error, the company would record the following entry.

Assets	=	Liabilities	+	Equity
+500				−3,375
+1,125				
−5,000				

Equipment		Inc Tax Receiv	
	5,000	1,125	

Accum Deprec		Ret Earnings—PPA	
500		3,375	

January 1, 2021—To correct for repair expense improperly capitalized

Accumulated Depreciation (10% × \$5,000)	500	
Retained Earnings—Prior Period Adjustment (\$4,500 − \$1,125)	3,375	
Income Tax Receivable (\$4,500 × 25%)	1,125	
Equipment		5,000

REVIEW 18-10 LO18-10 Change in Accounting Principle and Error Correction

Review MBC

Example One—Change in Accounting Principle

Lawrence Inc. decided to change from average-cost to the FIFO inventory method in 2020 for reporting purposes. If the FIFO cost method had been used in all previous periods, the inventory balance would have been \$50,000 more than was reported using the average-cost method. Assume a tax rate of 25% and that the company continues to use average-cost for tax purposes. Prepare the entry to record the effect of the change in accounting principle.

Example Two—Error Correction

During June 2021, Ace Company discovers that depreciation expenses for 2019 and 2020 were understated each year by \$5,000 for both accounting and income tax purposes; total pretax understatement, \$10,000. Record the entry on January 1, 2021, in the accounting records to correct for the error assuming a tax rate of 25%.

More Practice: 18-105, 18-106, 18-107, 18-109, 18-110, 18-111, 18-114, 18-115

Solution on p. 18-65.

Questions

18-1. Briefly explain intraperiod tax allocation.

18-2. Briefly describe the balance sheet approach in accounting for income taxes.

18-3. Explain why deferred income tax can be either an asset or a liability.

18-4. Explain the main overriding reasons why pretax GAAP income and taxable income are often quite different.

18-5. Differentiate between a temporary difference and a permanent difference.

18-6. Landend Corporation (a) uses straight-line depreciation for its financial accounting and uses accelerated depreciation on its income tax return and (b) holds a \$50,000 investment in tax-free municipal bonds. What kind of tax difference is caused by each of these items? Explain.

18-7. How are deferred tax accounts presented on the balance sheet?

18-8. ATW Corporation has completed an analysis of its pretax GAAP income, its taxable income, and temporary differences. Taxable income is \$100,000, and there are several temporary differences that result in (a) a deferred tax asset of \$15,000 and (b) a deferred tax liability of \$20,000. The income tax rate for the current period and all future periods is 25%. There were no deferred tax assets or deferred tax liabilities as of the beginning of the current year. Provide the entry to record income taxes and indicate how the amounts were determined.

18-9. Explain the difference between a taxable temporary difference and a deductible temporary difference.

18-10. Suppose Wilson Company has one item that gives rise to a temporary difference and that item is expected to continue indefinitely. Specifically, Wilson prepays the following year's annual rent of \$100,000 each December 31. In years subsequent to the first year, what will the effects be of this temporary difference on the income statement and the balance sheet? Assume a constant tax rate of 25%.

18-11. Explain the difference between a deferred tax liability and a deferred tax asset.

18-12. Define net operating loss (NOL) carryforwards. Briefly explain the process of a tax loss carryforward.

18-13. With respect to NOL carryforwards, how does uncertainty affect the accounting treatment?
18-14. Is deferred tax arising from an NOL carryforward classified as current or noncurrent?
18-15. Explain the limitation on the carrying value of deferred income tax assets.
18-16. How does a company account for a change in tax rates?
18-17. Describe the two-step process required when uncertain tax positions are taken.

Brief Exercises

Brief Exercise 18-18 Computing Net Income **LO1**

4M Inc. showed income tax on its tax return of $4,800 on December 31, 2020, and had a tax rate of 25%. If taxable income were equal to pretax GAAP income for 2020, determine the amount of net income that 4M Inc. recognized in 2020 on its financial statements.

Brief Exercise 18-19 Recording Income Tax Expense **LO1, 2**

Aquafena Inc. recognized taxable income of $100,000 for the year ended December 31, 2020. Aquafena calculated a deferred tax asset and a deferred tax liability of $12,000 and $8,000, respectively, on December 31, 2020. The tax rate is 25%. Assume zero beginning balances in deferred tax accounts.

a. Determine the income tax payable on December 31, 2020.
b. Prepare the income tax expense journal entry on December 31, 2020.

Brief Exercise 18-20 Recording Income Tax Expense **LO1, 2**

Alexa Inc. recorded the following deferred tax amounts.

	December 31, 2019	December 31, 2020
Deferred tax liability	$ 5,000	$8,500
Deferred tax asset	13,000	6,000

If the company had current tax expense of $26,000 in 2020, determine total income tax expense for 2020.

Brief Exercise 18-21 Reporting a Deferred Tax Liability **LO1**

On December 31, 2020, Lexxus Inc. recorded an unrealized gain in income of $5,000 related to its trading debt securities originally purchased on December 15, 2020, for $20,000. Lexxus recognized pretax GAAP income of $80,000 in 2020 and had a tax rate of 25%.

a. Determine the reported amount of trading securities in the financial statements of Lexxus on December 30, 2020.
b. Determine the tax basis of the trading securities on December 30, 2020.
c. Calculate the deferred tax balance and show how it would be reported in the December 31, 2020, balance sheet of Lexxus.

Brief Exercise 18-22 Recording Income Tax Expense **LO1**

Assuming the same information from Brief Exercise 18-21, record the income tax journal entry on December 31, 2020. Assume zero beginning balances in deferred tax accounts.

Brief Exercise 18-23 Recording Income Tax Expense **LO1**

Alexa Inc. purchased equipment in 2018 for $50,000 with no residual value. On December 31, 2020, accumulated depreciation using the straight-line method for financial reporting was $15,000. For tax purposes, Alexa uses MACRS depreciation resulting in $35,600 in accumulated depreciation for tax purposes on December 31, 2020. Taxable income was $100,000 for 2020 and the company's tax rate is 25%.

a. Determine the GAAP basis of equipment (net) on December 30, 2020.
b. Determine the tax basis of equipment on December 30, 2020.
c. Assuming a deferred tax liability balance of $4,900 on December 31, 2019, record income tax expense for 2020.

Brief Exercise 18-24 Calculating Income Tax Expense **LO2**

Underwood Co. had current tax expense of $20,000 for the year ended December 31, 2020. The ending deferred tax asset balance was $6,000, which was a $4,000 increase from January 1, 2020. The tax rate is 25%. Calculate income tax expense for 2020.

Brief Exercise 18-25 Calculating Deferred Tax Asset Balance **LO2**

On December 31, 2020, Delta Inc. recorded $28,000 of deferred revenue (a liability) on customer deposits received in advance of the satisfaction of performance obligations. However, this amount is taxable in 2020 when cash was received. Assume a tax rate of 25% and pretax GAAP income of $160,000 for 2020.

a. Determine the GAAP basis of deferred revenue on December 30, 2020.
b. Determine the tax basis of deferred revenue on December 30, 2020.
c. Determine Delta Inc.'s deferred tax asset balance on December 31, 2020.

Brief Exercise 18-26 Recording Income Tax Expense **LO2**

Assuming the same information in Brief Exercise 18-25, record the income tax journal entry on December 31, 2020. Assume zero beginning balances in deferred tax accounts and there are no other differences between accounting and tax incomes.

Brief Exercise 18-27 Recording Income Tax Expense **LO2**

Rangee Rover Inc. recorded pretax GAAP income of $89,000 in 2020. The GAAP basis of accounts receivable (net) is $6,000 less than the tax basis of accounts receivable. Assuming a tax rate of 25%, record the income tax journal entry on December 31, 2020. Assume zero beginning balances in deferred tax accounts.

Brief Exercise 18-28 Recording Income Tax Expense **LO2**

Assume the same information as in Brief Exercise 18-27 except that the Deferred Tax Asset account had a December 31, 2019, balance of $1,800. Record the income tax journal entry on December 31, 2020.

Brief Exercise 18-29 Preparing Income Tax Section of Income Statement **LO1, 2**

Bell Corp. recognized $38,000 in current income tax expense in 2020. Pretax GAAP income was $89,000 and deferred income tax expense is $6,000 for 2020. Prepare (a) the income tax section of the income statement for Bell Corp. for 2020 and (b) the disclosure of current and deferred income tax expense.

Brief Exercise 18-30 Recording Tax Valuation Allowance **LO3** *Hint:* See Demo 18-3

Maui Resort Inc. determined that the balance in its deferred tax asset account on December 31, 2020, was $50,000. Management reviewed all available positive and negative evidence to estimate that 30% of the deferred tax asset was *more likely than not* to be realized. The valuation allowance for deferred tax assets has a December 31, 2020, unadjusted balance of $4,000 (credit). Record the entry to adjust the allowance on December 31, 2020.

Brief Exercise 18-31 Analyzing Deferred Taxes **LO3**

Assume Company A and Company B each had a balance in deferred tax assets of $250,000. However, Company A has a valuation allowance related to the deferred tax asset of $200,000 while Company B has a valuation allowance of $5,000. What can you infer about Company A and B based upon this information?

Brief Exercise 18-32 Analyzing Deferred Valuation Allowance **LO3**

Starbucks Corporation recognized the following amounts in a recent annual report on Form 10-K.

$ millions	October 2, 2016	September 27, 2015
Deferred tax asset	$1,651.1	$1,660.0
Valuation allowance	70.3	143.7
Net income attributable to Starbucks	2,817.7	2,757.4

a. Calculate the deferred tax asset valuation allowance as a percentage of deferred tax assets for fiscal years 2016 and 2015.

b. Based on your results in part *a*, does it appear that the company considers deferred tax benefits to be realized at a higher or lower rate than 2015?

Brief Exercise 18-33 Analyzing Permanent Differences **LO4**

Baltimore Inc. reported pretax GAAP income of $45,000 in 2020. In analyzing differences between GAAP income and taxable income, the company determined that it had deducted $5,000 in nondeductible fines and added $2,800 in tax-exempt municipal interest revenue to GAAP income. Given a statutory tax rate of 25%, determine the following.

a. Taxable income
b. Income tax payable
c. Income tax expense
d. Net income
e. Effective tax rate

Brief Exercise 18-34 Reconciling between Effective and Statutory Tax Rates **LO4**

Refer to information in Brief Exercise 18-33. Prepare a reconciliation between Baltimore Inc.'s effective and statutory tax rates.

Brief Exercise 18-35 Recording Income Tax Expense **LO1, 4**

Lake Company has pretax GAAP income of $100,000 in 2020, its first year of operations. Lake Company has depreciation expense in 2020 for GAAP purposes that is $60,000 less than the amount of depreciation expense for tax purposes. In addition, $5,000 of regulatory fines included in the determination of pretax GAAP income are not tax deductible. Lake Company's tax rate is 25%. Prepare Lake Company's income tax entry on December 31, 2020.

Brief Exercise 18-36 Calculating Deferred Tax Balance **LO1, 2, 4**

Evergreen Company's 2020 reconciliation between pretax GAAP income and taxable income is as follows.

Pretax GAAP income	$ 200,000
Depreciation adjustment	(40,000)
Permanent difference	1,250
Taxable income	$161,250

The company had one temporary difference due to the GAAP basis of equipment exceeding the tax basis of the equipment. Record the income tax journal entry for 2020, assuming an enacted tax rate of 25%. Assume that the December 31, 2019, deferred tax liability balance was $5,000.

Brief Exercise 18-37 Calculating a Deferred Tax Liability Balance **LO1, 5**

In 2020, Explorers Inc. completed installment sales of $80,000, recorded in full as accounts receivable and as revenue. For tax purposes, it recognizes income when cash is received. Cash related to the installment sales is expected to be received in the following years: 2021 of $10,000; 2022 of $40,000; 2023 of $30,000. The enacted tax rate for 2020 and 2021 is 25%. The newly enacted tax rate for 2023 is 40%. Compute the value of the deferred tax liability on December 31, 2020.

Brief Exercise 18-38 Recording Income Tax with Changing Tax Rates **LO1, 5** *Hint:* See Demo 18-5

The Jets Company recorded a deferred tax liability in the amount of $18,750 in December 2020, due to the book value of equipment exceeding the tax basis of equipment by $75,000. The difference will reverse equally over the next three years. In late 2020, the enacted tax rate increased to 42.5% beginning 2022.

a. Determine the income tax rate that is the enacted rate for 2020.

b. What journal entry should the Jets record to adjust the deferred tax liability, if any?

Brief Exercise 18-39 Recording Net Operating Loss Carryforward **LO6**

In 2020, Lambeau Inc. suffered a loss of $100,000. The enacted tax rate is 25%. Prepare Lambeau's entry for the loss carryforward on December 31, 2020, assuming that management determined that it was *more likely than not* that the deferred tax asset would be realized.

Brief Exercise 18-40 Recording Net Operating Loss Carryforward **LO6**

In 2020, Cardinals Company operated at a tax loss, totaling $88,000 during its first year of business. Assuming a tax rate of 25%, and that income is expected in 2021, record the entry to reflect the tax benefit of the net operating loss on December 31, 2020. Cardinals Company determined that it was *more likely than not* that 75% of the deferred tax asset would not be realized.

Brief Exercise 18-41 Recording Income Tax Expense with Tax Uncertainty **LO7**

Springs Inc. has taken a tax position in 2020 that it believes is based on fairly clear tax law for the payment of $80,000 in salaries and benefits to employees. There are no limits on deductibility and all amounts were fully paid within the statutory time limit, although there is some question on the company's policies for capitalization of a portion of the salaries. Management has a fairly high confidence level in the technical merits of this position. It is clear that it is greater than 50% likely that the full amount of the tax position will be ultimately realized, but it is less than 100%. Springs estimates the probability of sustaining the entire tax position with taxing authorities at 60%. Springs Inc. taxable income is $100,000, which includes the salary deduction of $80,000 referenced above. If the Springs Inc. tax rate is 25% (with no other deferred items), record the income tax journal entry required on December 31, 2020.

Brief Exercise 18-42 Reporting Deferred Taxes in Balance Sheet **LO8** *Hint:* See Demo 18-8

Kate Club Inc. has determined that there are four temporary differences between the tax basis and the GAAP book value of assets and liabilities that resulted in the following deferred taxes: (a) deferred tax liability related to accelerated tax depreciation over straight-line depreciation: $20,000; (b) deferred tax asset related to deferred contract (one-year contracts) revenue collected in advance, $24,000; (c) deferred tax asset related to bad debt expense recognized on an allowance basis, $10,000; and (d) deferred tax liability related to prepaid automobile insurance, $8,000. Prepare the balance sheet presentation of deferred taxes.

Brief Exercise 18-43 Computing Ratios **LO8**

The following information was obtained from recent annual reports on 10-K for **American Eagle Outfitters, Inc.** Compute the debt-to-equity ratio (a) including deferred tax liabilities as part of total liabilities, and (b) excluding deferred tax liabilities as part of total liabilities.

$ thousands	Jan. 28, 2017	Jan. 30, 2016	Jan. 31, 2015
Deferred tax liabilities	$ 71,468	$ 67,332	$ 36,289
Total liabilities	578,091	560,870	557,162
Total stockholders' equity	1,204,569	1,051,376	1,139,746

Exercises

Exercise 18-44 Recording and Reporting Temporary Difference **LO1** *Hint:* See Demo 18-1

Staples Corporation would have had identical income before taxes on both its income tax returns and its income statements for the years 2020 through 2023 except for a depreciable asset that cost $120,000. The asset was depreciated for income tax purposes using the following amounts: 2020, $48,000; 2021, $36,000; 2022, $24,000;

and 2023, $12,000. However, for accounting purposes the straight-line method was used (that is, $30,000 per year). The accounting and tax periods both end December 31. There were no deferred taxes at the beginning of 2020. The depreciable asset has a four-year estimated life and no residual value. The tax rate for each year was 25%. Pretax GAAP income amounts for each of the four years were as follows.

2020 . . . . . $230,000	2021 . . . . . $250,000	2022 . . . . . $240,000	2023 . . . . . $240,000

Required

a. Prepare a schedule to compute the increase to income tax payable on December 31, 2020, 2021, 2022, and 2023.

b. Prepare a schedule to determine the deferred tax balances on December 31, 2020, 2021, 2022, and 2023. Assume a zero-beginning balance in the deferred tax liability account on January 1, 2020.

c. Record the income tax journal entry on December 31, 2020, 2021, 2022, and 2023.

d. For each year show how the deferred income tax amount would be reported on the balance sheet.

e. Prepare the income tax section of the income statement for 2020 and provide the disclosure of current and deferred tax expense.

Exercise 18-45
Recording and Reporting Temporary Difference **LO1**

Repeat the requirements of Exercise 18-44, but now assume that the asset was 100% expensed for tax purposes in 2020.

Exercise 18-46
Reporting a Temporary Difference **LO1**

For 2020, Trendy Inc. calculated taxable income of $30,000 after taking into account one temporary difference: prepaid insurance expense on a GAAP basis exceeds prepaid insurance on a tax basis by $5,000. The tax rate is 25% and there were no balances in deferred tax accounts at the beginning of 2020.

Required

a. Indicate the deferred income tax amount that would be recognized on the balance sheet on December 31, 2020.

b. Prepare the income tax section of the income statement for 2020 and provide the disclosure of current and deferred tax expense.

Exercise 18-47
Recording and Reporting Temporary Difference **LO1**

On December 31, 2020, for GAAP purposes, Clubs Inc. reported a balance of $70,000 in Prepaid Maintenance Expense for services to be received over the following year. For tax purposes, however, prepaid costs are deducted immediately when paid. Pretax GAAP income is $300,000 and the tax rate is 25%. Assume no other temporary differences or any beginning balances in deferred tax accounts.

Required

a. Record the income tax journal entry on December 31, 2020.

b. Prepare the income tax section of the income statement for 2020 and provide the disclosure of current and deferred tax expense.

Exercise 18-48
Defining Tax Terminology **LO1, 2, 3, 4, 5, 6, 7, 8, 9**

Terms frequently used in accounting for income tax along with descriptions of the terms are included in the following two lists.

Terms

__ 1. Deferred tax asset
__ 2. Taxable temporary difference
__ 3. Permanent difference
__ 4. Valuation allowance
__ 5. Temporary difference
__ 6. Taxable income
__ 7. Noncurrent deferred tax asset, net
__ 8. Income tax expense
__ 9. NOL carryforward
__ 10. Intraperiod income tax allocation

Descriptions

a. Current tax expense plus net changes in the deferred tax liability, deferred tax asset, valuation allowance, and the unrecognized tax benefit balance sheet accounts.

b. An amount used to compute the cash taxes owed to the taxing authority.

c. The net of deferred tax assets, liabilities, and valuation allowance (relating to the same tax jurisdiction) presented on the balance sheet as a noncurrent asset.
d. May result in a reduction of income tax paid to taxing authorities in future periods.
e. Accounted for using a balance-sheet approach.
f. A deferred tax balance sheet amount that has a debit balance.
g. A difference between accounting and taxable incomes that does not reverse.
h. An allocation of tax among the components in the income statement and the statement of comprehensive income.
i. A contra asset account used to reduce deferred tax assets to the portion *more likely than not* to be realized.
j. An amount that represents a difference between GAAP and tax basis of an asset (liability) that will increase taxable income in future periods relative to financial accounting income.

Required
Match each of the terms 1 through 10 with the most closely aligned description *a* through *j*.

Exercise 18-49
Recording a Temporary Difference **LO2**
Hint: See Demo 18-2

On December 31, 2020, for GAAP purposes, Clubs Inc. reported a balance of $40,000 in a warranty liability for anticipated costs to satisfy future warranty claims. No claims were paid in 2020. Pretax GAAP income is $300,000 and the tax rate is 25%. Assume no other differences between the tax bases and GAAP bases of assets and liabilities, or any beginning balances in deferred tax accounts.

Required
a. Record the income tax journal entry on December 31, 2020.
b. Assume that there was a December 31, 2019, balance of $4,000 in the deferred tax asset account. How would your answer to part *a* change?

Exercise 18-50
Recording Multiple Temporary Differences
LO1, 2

The records of Anderson Inc. provide the following information for the tax year 2020.

- There was no beginning balance in deferred tax account(s).
- Taxable income for 2020 was $60,000.
- Tax rate is 25%.
- Three temporary differences were identified:
  1. Estimated litigation accrual of $20,000, not deductible for tax purposes. Settlement not expected to take place until 2022.
  2. Excess of accelerated depreciation over GAAP depreciation of $12,000 caused a difference in the $50,000 GAAP basis and the $38,000 tax basis of equipment. One-third of the difference will reverse in 2021.
  3. Unrealized holding gain on equity securities of $3,500 not recognized for tax purposes. Anderson Inc. intends to sell the security in early 2021. The investment (accounted for under FV-NI) is reported at its fair value of $10,000 at year-end in its financial statements.

Required
a. Record the income tax journal entry on December 31, 2020.
b. Record the income tax journal entry on December 31, 2021, assuming taxable income of $125,000.

Exercise 18-51
Recording and Reporting Multiple Temporary Differences
LO1, 2

Lake Company has the following results of operations on December 31, 2020.

1. Pretax GAAP income in 2020, its first year of operations, totals $100,000. Taxable income is $90,000.
2. Lake Company recorded an installment sale receivable totaling $60,000, with a tax basis of $0. This amount will be included in taxable income in future years.
3. The company accrued in its 2020 financial statements $50,000 as a provision for future warranty costs. This amount was not deductible for tax purposes in 2020 but will be deductible in future years.
4. The enacted tax rate for 2020 and all future years is 25%.

Required
a. Provide the journal entry to record income tax expense for 2020.
b. Prepare the income tax section of the income statement for 2020 and provide the disclosure of current and deferred tax expense.
c. Compute the effective tax rate for 2020.

Exercise 18-52
Recording and Reporting Multiple Temporary Differences
LO1, 2, 8

The records of Cross Corporation provided the following reconciliation between taxable income and pretax GAAP income.

	2020	2021	2022	2023
Taxable income.	$60,000	$80,000	$85,000	$75,000
Depreciation expense.	15,000	(5,000)	(5,000)	(5,000)
Bad debt expense.	(20,000)	(10,000)	(18,000)	25,000
Pretax GAAP income	$55,000	$65,000	$62,000	$95,000

- The depreciation adjustment results from a difference between the GAAP basis and tax basis of depreciable equipment.
- The bad debt expense adjustment results from a difference between the GAAP basis and tax basis of net accounts receivable.
- The deferred tax accounts have a zero balance at the start of 2020. Tax rate is 25%.

Required

a. Record the income tax journal entry on December 31, 2020.
b. Record the income tax journal entry on December 31, 2021.
c. Record the income tax journal entry on December 31, 2022.
d. Record the income tax journal entry on December 31, 2023.
e. Prepare the income tax section of the income statement for 2020 and provide the disclosure of current and deferred tax expense.
f. Indicate the deferred income tax amount that would be recognized on the balance sheet at December 31, 2020.

Exercise 18-53
Recording and Reporting Multiple Temporary Differences
LO1, 2, 8

The records of TNA Corporation at the end of 2020 provided the following data related to income taxes.

- Unrealized gain on the company's investment portfolio, $50,000; recognized in net income for accounting purposes at the end of 2020. Amount will be considered for tax purposes when sold, estimated to be in 2022. Fair value of the investment portfolio on December 31, 2020, is $400,000.
- Estimated litigation expense, $30,000; accrued for accounting purposes at the end of 2020. Amount will be considered for income tax purposes when paid, estimated to be at the end of 2021.
- Taxable income (from the tax return) at the end of 2020, $100,000; the enacted income tax rate is 25%. There were no deferred tax amounts at the beginning of 2020.

Required

a. Prepare a schedule to determine difference between the tax basis and the GAAP basis for the investment account and the accrued litigation liability account, and the related deferred tax balance(s) on December 31, 2020.
b. Determine pretax GAAP income for 2020.
c. Prepare the journal entry to record income tax expense in 2020.
d. Prepare the income tax section of the income statement for 2020 and provide the disclosure of current and deferred tax expense.
e. Indicate the deferred income tax amount that would be recognized on the balance sheet on December 31, 2020.

Exercise 18-54
Recording Multiple Temporary Differences
LO1, 2

The following information is available for Rapper Inc.

- Taxable income in 2020: $115,000
- Accounts receivable on installment sales
  - GAAP basis: $150,000
  - Tax basis: $0
- Tax rate: 25%
- Deferred revenue on services
  - GAAP basis: $35,000
  - Tax basis: $0
- No deferred tax balances at the beginning of 2020

Required

a. Prepare a schedule to determine deferred tax balances on December 31, 2020.
b. Compute pretax GAAP income.
c. Record the income tax journal entry on December 31, 2020.

Exercise 18-55 Reporting Multiple Temporary Differences **LO1, 8**

For 2020, Raleigh Corporation had taxable income of $100,000 and an income tax rate of 25%. Raleigh had a $75,000 credit balance in its Deferred Tax Liability account. This credit balance was due to the following two temporary differences.

- Carrying value of equipment for accounting purposes, $300,000, tax basis of equipment, $200,000. The equipment has a five-year remaining life.
- Installment sale receivable for accounting purposes, $200,000, and for income tax purposes, $0. The collection period for the $200,000 receivable is the following four years with equal amounts each year.

Required

Indicate how the deferred tax amounts would be reported on Raleigh's 2020 balance sheet.

Exercise 18-56 Recording Multiple Temporary Differences **LO1, 2**

Cruse Corporation started operations on January 1, 2020. Taxable income from the tax return is $2,850,000. Income tax rate is 25%. There were no beginning balances in deferred tax accounts.

Additional information

- On December 31, 2020, GAAP basis of installment sale receivables, $330,000; tax basis, $0. Receivables will be collected equally over the years 2021, 2022, and 2023.
- On December 31, 2020, GAAP basis of litigation accrual, $270,000; tax basis, $0. Management expects the litigation loss to be recorded in the tax return in 2023.

Required

a. Prepare a schedule to determine deferred tax balances on December 31, 2020.

b. Record the income tax journal entry on December 31, 2020.

c. Record the income tax journal entry on December 31, 2020, assuming the following *separate* situations.

1. Taxable income is $1,650,000 for 2020.
2. Deferred tax liability had a January 1, 2020, balance of $50,000.
3. Deferred tax asset had a January 1, 2020, balance of $28,000.
4. Litigation loss was estimated at $170,000 instead of $270,000.
5. Profit on installment sale was $440,000 instead of $330,000.

Exercise 18-57 Computing Taxable Income **LO1, 2**

A-1 Company had pretax GAAP income of $50,000 for the tax year ended December 31, 2020.

Required

a. Determine taxable income given the following *separate* situations.

1. Excess accelerated depreciation for tax purposes, $5,000
2. Unrealized holding gain on securities accounted for under FV-NI, $2,000
3. Unrealized holding loss on securities accounted for under FV-NI, $2,000
4. Rental receipts received in advance, $30,000
5. Litigation contingency accrual, $10,000
6. Six-month prepaid rent deposit, $12,000

b. Label each of the items in part *a* as one of the following:

1. GAAP revenue before taxable revenue
2. Taxable revenue before GAAP revenue
3. GAAP expense before taxable expense
4. Taxable expense before GAAP expense

Exercise 18-58 Recording and Reporting Multiple Differences **LO2, 4, 8**

The income statements for Prince Inc. for two years (summarized) follow.

	GAAP		Tax	
	2020	2021	2020	2021
Service revenue	$ 0	$ 10,000	$ 10,000	$ 0
Sales revenue	180,000	190,000	180,000	190,000
Environmental fines	(10,000)	(10,000)	0	0
Warranty expense	(8,000)	0	0	(8,000)
Other expenses	(134,000)	(171,000)	(134,000)	(171,000)
Pretax GAAP income	$ 28,000	$ 19,000		
Taxable income			$ 56,000	$ 11,000

Additional information

- Environmental fines are not deductible for income tax purposes.
- The amount collected in 2020 related to deferred service revenue ($10,000) was taxable in 2020.
- Accrued warranty costs of $8,000 are not deductible for income tax purposes until 2021 when the expenditures are made.
- Income tax rate is 25% for both years.
- At the beginning of 2020, deferred tax asset and liability balances were zero.

Required

a. Prepare a schedule to determine deferred tax balances on December 31, 2020.
b. Prepare a schedule to determine income tax payable on December 31, 2020, and 2021.
c. Record the income tax journal entry on December 31, 2020.
d. Record the income tax journal entry on December 31, 2021.
e. Show how the tax accounts would be reported on the income statement and balance sheet for 2020 and 2021. Include the disclosure of current and deferred tax expense.
f. Compute the effective tax rate for 2020.

Exercise 18-59
Identifying Tax Differences **LO1, 2, 4**

Listed below are ten separate situations. For each item indicates whether the difference is (1) temporary creating a deferred tax asset or a deferred tax liability or (2) permanent.

Item	Deferred Income Tax Account Would Be: Asset	Liability	Permanent
1. Pension fund contributions are less than pension expense for the current year, resulting in a pension liability on the company's balance sheet.	____	____	____
2. Dividend revenue recognized for accounting while a portion is deductible for taxes (dividends received deduction).	____	____	____
3. Estimated warranty costs: accrual basis for accounting and cash basis for income tax.	____	____	____
4. Fines expensed for accounting but not deductible for tax purposes.	____	____	____
5. Straight-line depreciation for accounting and accelerated depreciation for income tax.	____	____	____
6. Unrealized gain on investments: FV-NI recognized for accounting, but gain recognized only on disposal of the asset for income tax.	____	____	____
7. Rent revenue collected in advance: accrual basis for accounting, cash basis for income tax.	____	____	____
8. Unrealized loss on investments: FV-NI recognized for accounting, but loss recognized only on disposal of the asset for income tax.	____	____	____
9. Probable and estimable litigation contingency: accrual basis for accounting and cash basis for income tax.	____	____	____
10. Interest received on investments in municipal bonds is not taxable.	____	____	____

Exercise 18-60
Recording Income Tax Journal Entry: Temporary and Permanent Differences **LO1, 2, 4, 5**

Fox Corporation purchased a machine on January 1, 2020, that cost $40,000. The machine had an estimated service life of five years and no residual value. Fox uses straight-line depreciation for accounting purposes and accelerated depreciation for the income tax return as follows: 2020, 30%; 2021, 25%; 2022, 20%; 2023, 15%; and 2024, 10%. Taxable income on the tax return for 2020 was $150,000. The 2020 income statement also showed a $15,000 expense for premiums paid for life insurance policies on company executive officers. The income tax rate is 25% in 2020 and 35% in all subsequent years.

Required

a. Prepare a schedule to determine deferred tax balances on December 31, for the years 2020 through 2024.
b. Record the income tax journal entry on December 31, 2020.
c. Repeat requirements *a* and *b* assuming instead that the machine is 100% expensed in 2020 for tax purposes.

Exercise 18-61
Recording a Deferred Tax Allowance **LO3**

Allied Corp. has a deferred tax asset balance of $50,000 on December 31, 2020, due to a temporary difference related to a warranty expense accrual that is not deductible for tax purposes. The deferred tax asset balance has increased $10,000 over the prior year ending balance of $40,000. Taxable income for 2020 is $210,000 and the tax rate is 25%. There was no valuation allowance recorded on December 31, 2019.

Required

a. Record the income tax journal entry on December 31, 2020, assuming that it is *more likely than not* that the deferred tax asset will be realized.

b. Record the income tax journal entries on December 31, 2020, assuming that it is *more likely than not* that only 60% of the deferred tax asset will be realized.

Exercise 18-62
Recording a Deferred Tax Allowance **LO3**

Assume the same information in Exercise 18-61, except that there is a $12,000 beginning balance in the valuation allowance.

Required

a. Record the income tax journal entries on December 31, 2020, assuming that it is *more likely than not* that the deferred tax asset will be realized.

b. Record the income tax journal entries on December 31, 2020, assuming that it is *more likely than not* that only 60% of the deferred tax asset will be realized.

Exercise 18-63
Recording Multiple Temporary Differences, Change in Enacted Tax Rate **LO1, 5**

Wittco Company reports pretax GAAP income in 2020, its first year of operations, of $100,000. Temporary differences in the GAAP basis and tax basis of assets arose in 2020 from the following two sources.

- Prepayment of 2021 rent in the amount of $24,000 in 2020.
- An installment sale totaling $36,000, with cash collections expected in two equal amounts in 2022 and 2023.

The enacted tax rates are 25% in 2020, 30% in 2021, and 40% in 2022 and thereafter.

Required

a. Record the income tax journal entry on December 31, 2020.

b. Record the income tax journal entry on December 31, 2020, assuming that a new tax law is passed in 2020 decreasing the tax rate to 20% for 2020 and all years thereafter.

Exercise 18-64
Recording Multiple Temporary Differences, Change in Enacted Tax Rate **LO1, 5**

On January 1 of each of the first four years of its existence, Allway Company purchases a new unit of equipment. Each unit has a four-year life and zero salvage value, costs $100,000, and is depreciated for GAAP and tax purposes as shown below. The income tax rate is 25%. Allway has a deferred tax liability of $12,500 at the end of year 3. The current year is year 4, and pretax GAAP income is $30,000. Amounts are in thousands.

	Past Years			Current Year	Future Years		
	1	2	3	4	5	6	7
Equipment							
Beginning balance	$ 0	$100	$200	$300			
Purchases at January 1	100	100	100	100			
Retirements at December 31	0	0	0	(100)			
Ending balance	$100	$200	$300	$300			
GAAP depreciation							
Equipment 1	$ 25	$ 25	$ 25	$ 25			
Equipment 2		25	25	25	$25		
Equipment 3			25	25	25	$25	
Equipment 4				25	25	25	$25
Annual total	$ 25	$ 50	$ 75	$100	$75	$50	$25
Tax depreciation							
Equipment 1	$ 40	$ 30	$ 20	$ 10			
Equipment 2		40	30	20	$10		
Equipment 3			40	30	20	$10	
Equipment 4				40	30	20	$10
Annual total	$ 40	$ 70	$ 90	$100	$60	$30	$10

Required

a. Record the income tax entry at the end of year 4.

b. Assume that during year 4 the tax rate is increased to 30% effective as of the beginning of year 4. Repeat (*a*) under this assumption.

c. Assume that during year 4 the tax rate is increased to 30% effective in year 5 and to 35% thereafter. Repeat (*a*) under this assumption.

Exercise 18-65
Recording Multiple Temporary Differences, Change in Enacted Tax Rate **LO1, 2, 5**

The Billboard Company has a deferred tax liability in the amount of $14,000 at December 31, 2020, relating to a $40,000 installment sale receivable, $20,000 of which is collected in 2021. The tax rate in 2021 is 35%. However, the rate for 2022 and thereafter is changed during 2021 to 25%. Warranty expense in 2021 included in the determination of pretax GAAP income is $100,000, with these amounts expected to be incurred and deductible for tax purposes in 2022. Pretax GAAP income is $280,000 in 2021.

Required

Prepare the journal entry to record income taxes in 2021.

Exercise 18-66
Recording Temporary Difference, Multiple Tax Rates **LO2, 5**

In 2020, Adele Company accrued a legal liability of $500,000 for payments expected to be paid (and will be deducted when paid) as follows: 2021: $250,000; 2022: $150,000; and 2023: $100,000. The company's pretax GAAP income is $5 million. Enacted tax rates are as follows: 2020: 25%; 2021: 25%; 2022: 30%; 2023 and beyond: 30%. The company had no other differences between GAAP and tax, and its deferred tax accounts had zero balances at the beginning of 2020.

Required

Prepare the journal entry to record income taxes in 2020.

Exercise 18-67
Recording Temporary Difference, Multiple Tax Rates **LO1, 5**

A plant asset purchased by Krest Inc. for $100,000 late in 2018 is to be depreciated as follows.

Year	Tax Depreciation	GAAP Depreciation
2019	$ 40,000	$ 20,000
2020	30,000	20,000
2021	20,000	20,000
2022	10,000	20,000
2023	0	20,000
	$100,000	$100,000

In 2020, taxable income was $450,000 and the tax rate is 25%. Future enacted tax rates are as follows: 2021: 25%; 2022: 30%; and 2023: 30%. The deferred tax liability balance on January 1, 2020, was $5,000.

Required

a. Prepare a schedule to compute the deferred tax liability as of December 31, 2020.

b. Calculate the tax basis of the plant asset on December 31, 2020 and its reported amount in the financial statements.

c. Prepare the journal entry to record income tax expense in 2020.

Exercise 18-68
Recording Multiple Temporary Differences, Multiple Tax Rates **LO1, 2, 5**

On December 31, 2020, Colgait Inc. had an installment sale receivable balance of $90,000 recognized on its financial statements, while the amount was not recognized for tax purposes. Colgait Inc. also had a warranty accrual of $20,000 on December 31, 2020, that is not deductible for tax purposes. The accounts receivable will be settled equally over the next three years. The warranty will be settled equally over the next two years. Taxable income in 2020 was $500,000. Enacted tax rates are 25% for years 2020–2021, and 30% for years thereafter.

Required

a. Prepare a schedule to compute deferred tax balances as of December 31, 2020.

b. Prepare the journal entry to record income tax expense in 2020, assuming zero beginning balances in deferred tax accounts.

Exercise 18-69
Recording Multiple Temporary Differences, Multiple Tax Rates **LO1, 2, 5**

Aim Inc. had the following activity for the years 2020–2022.

- Prepaid maintenance contract: $30,000 on January 1, 2020, for a three-year period beginning January 1, 2020.
- Deferred revenue: $45,000 on January 1, 2020, for a three-year period beginning January 1, 2020.
- Pretax GAAP income is $500,000, $388,000, and 425,000 for the years 2020, 2021, and 2022, respectively.
- Enacted tax rates are 25% for years 2020 and 2021, and 30% for the year 2022.
- There were no balances in the deferred tax accounts on January 1, 2020.

Required

a. Compute the increase to income tax payable on December 31, 2020, 2021, and 2022.
b. Prepare a schedule to compute deferred tax accounts on December 31, 2020.
c. Prepare the journal entry to record income taxes in the following years: 2020, 2021, and 2022.

Exercise 18-70 Recording NOL Carryforward **LO6**

Tyson Corporation reported pretax income from operations in 2020 of $80,000 (the first year of operations). In 2021, the corporation experienced a $40,000 NOL (pretax loss from operations). Management is confident the company will have taxable income in excess of $50,000 in 2022. Assume an income tax rate of 25% in 2020 and thereafter. Tyson has no other temporary differences.

Required

a. Provide the 2020 and 2021 income tax entries that Tyson should make.
b. Show how all tax-related items would be reported on the 2020 and 2021 income statements and balance sheets.

Exercise 18-71 Recording and Reporting NOL Carryforward **LO6**

Decker Corporation experienced a loss in 2020. Additional information for Decker Corporation follows.

	2020
Taxable income (loss).	$(65,000)
Income tax rate.	25%

There were no temporary differences from 2018 to 2020 other than any related to a net operating loss carryforward.

Required

a. Record income taxes for 2020 and 2021 assuming the following.
- For 2021, the company computed taxable income of $45,000 and recognized a deferred tax liability balance of $2,250 related to acquisition of depreciable assets in its year-end financial statements. These amounts were consistent with management's expectations.
- The income tax rate enacted in 2020 and effective for 2021 and thereafter is 30%.
- Management estimates the valuation allowance on the deferred tax asset related to its 2020 NOL to be zero.

b. List the amounts that should be reported on the income statements and balance sheets for 2020 and 2021.

Exercise 18-72 Recording NOL Carryforward **LO6**

Toner Corporation computed the following taxable income and loss: 2020 taxable income, $10,000 and 2021 taxable loss, $40,000. At the end of 2021, Toner made the following estimates: 2022 taxable income, $4,000, 2023 taxable income, $11,000, and 2024 taxable income, $50,000. On the basis of these estimates, Toner believes the full amount of tax loss carryforward benefit is *more likely than not* to be realized. There are no other temporary differences. The tax rates are 25% for years 2020, 2021, and 2022; and 30% for years 2023 and 2024.

Required

a. Provide the income tax entry for 2021.
b. Provide the income tax entry for 2022, assuming that the actual taxable income was $6,000 (tax rate, 25%).
c. Provide the income tax entry for 2023, assuming that 2022 results were as described in (*c*), and that the actual 2023 taxable income was $13,000.
d. Provide the entry for 2024, assuming results for 2022 and 2023 as described above and assuming that the actual 2024 taxable income was $45,000.

Exercise 18-73 Recording NOL Carryforward, Valuation Allowance **LO6**

DNSE Inc. began operations in 2019. In its first year the company had a net operating loss of $10,000, which was carried forward and used to reduce income tax payable in 2020. In 2020, DNSE had taxable income of $40,000 before the use of the NOL carryforward. At December 31, 2020, DNSE Inc. determines that it should have a deferred tax asset ending balance of 25,000 related to 2020 deferred revenue. The income tax rate is 25%. No valuation allowance has been established.

Required

a. Provide the journal entry to record income taxes in 2020, assuming that no valuation allowance is required.
b. Now assume DNSE has encountered stiff competition and is uncertain whether it will have any taxable income in the foreseeable future. DNSE determined that it was *more likely than not* that none of the deferred tax asset would be realized. Assume that the temporary differences that give rise to the deferred tax asset are expected to reverse in 2021 and 2022. Determine what amount, if any, should be recorded as a valuation

allowance at December 31, 2020, and make the appropriate entry. Assume DNSE has already recorded the entry in part *a*.

c. Show how the December 31, 2020, balance sheet and income statement would present the information above, assuming that a valuation allowance is recorded.

Exercise 18-74
Recording and Reporting NOL Carryforward, Valuation Allowance **LO6**

The financial statements of Gibson Corporation for the first two years of operations reflected the following amounts.

	2020	2021
Revenues	$295,000	$330,000
Expenses	320,000	315,000
Pretax income (loss)	$ (25,000)	$ 15,000

Assume a tax rate of 25% for 2020 and 2021.

Estimates of future earnings at the end of each year, 2020 and 2021 are zero. There are no temporary differences.

Required

a. Provide entries to record the NOL income tax effects for 2020 and 2021.

b. Present Gibson's 2020 and 2021 financial statements, incorporating the income tax effects.

Exercise 18-75
Recording NOL Carryforward **LO6**

ABC Inc. reported taxable income for the years 2019–2023 as follows.

2019	$ 65,000
2020	(100,000)
2021	$(50,000)
2022	80,000
2023	$100,000

The enacted tax rate is 25%. There are no differences between taxable income/loss and GAAP income/loss. Management believes that the full amount of tax loss carryforward benefit is *more likely than not* to be realized.

Required

Prepare the journal entries to record income tax expense for the years 2019–2023.

Exercise 18-76
Recording Income Tax Expense with an Uncertain Tax Position **LO7**
Hint: See Demo 18-7

Randolph Inc. considered the probability of a recent tax position taken related to the exclusion of certain revenues of $10,000 from taxable revenue. Randolph determined that this position is *more likely than not* to be sustained in future discussions with taxing authorities. Using available information, Randolph Inc. created the following summary of the probabilities of sustaining its tax position:

Possible Estimated Outcome (Allowable Revenue Exclusion)	Individual Probability of Occurring
$10,000	10%
8,000	20
6,000	25
5,000	30
1,000	15

Required

Assuming taxable income of $50,000 (reflecting the exclusion of the $10,000 uncertain tax revenue) and a tax rate of 25%, record the income tax journal entry for 2020.

Exercise 18-77
Reconciling Effective and Statutory Tax Rate **LO4**

In 2020, Rafting Inc. had pretax GAAP income of $100,000 and the federal statutory tax rate is 25%. Rafting Inc. has no temporary differences, and so there is no deferred tax component to income tax expense. However, Rafting Inc. has the following permanent difference items.

- Interest revenue of $20,000 resulting from an investment in tax-exempt municipal bonds.
- Fines paid of $30,000 relating to several environmental laws that were violated. The fines are not tax-deductible.

Required

a. Compute the increase to income tax payable and record the income tax expense journal entry.

b. Prepare a reconciliation of the statutory tax rate to the effective tax rate.

Exercise 18-78
Reporting Tax Amounts on the Balance Sheet
LO8
Hint: See Demo 18-8

The following items create deferred tax assets and deferred tax liabilities at December 31, 2020.

1. Prepaid operating expenses of $25,000 are tax deductible when paid.
2. Excess tax depreciation (MACRS) over GAAP depreciation (straight-line) is $22,000.
3. Warranty liability of $8,000 is tax deductible when incurred.
4. Installment sales of $80,000 are recorded on an accrual basis for book purposes and taxed when collected.
5. Taxable income is $320,000 for 2020 and the tax rate is 25%.

Required

Show how all tax-related items would be reported on the December 31, 2020, balance sheet.

Problems

Problem 18-79
Recording Temporary Differences **LO1**

On January 1, 2020, Keefe Corporation purchased equipment at a cost of $100,000. The equipment has a five-year life and no salvage value. The depreciation schedule for tax and accounting purposes follows.

Year	GAAP Depreciation	Tax Depreciation
2020	$20,000	$25,000
2021	20,000	38,000
2022	20,000	37,000
2023	20,000	0
2024	20,000	0

Pretax GAAP income for each year 2020 through 2023 is $120,000 and the tax rate is 25%. There are no other differences between tax and financial accounting income.

a. Prepare a schedule calculating the deferred tax balance at the end of years 2020–2023.
b. Record the income tax journal entry on December 31, 2020.
c. Record the income tax journal entry on December 31, 2021.
d. Record the income tax journal entry on December 31, 2022.
e. Record the income tax journal entry on December 31, 2023.
f. Repeat (*a*) through (*d*) instead assuming that the company expensed 100% of the equipment in 2020 for tax purposes.

Problem 18-80
Reporting Changes in Enacted Tax Rates
LO1, 5

Refer to the data and information given in Problem 18-79 for Keefe Corporation. Assume that the tax rate for 2020 through 2022 is known to be 25%, but that a new law is passed in 2020 that will raise the tax rate in 2023 and thereafter to 30%. Assume pretax GAAP income equals $120,000 in 2020 and 2021.

Required

a. Record the income tax journal entry on December 31, 2020 (assuming the original tax depreciation schedule provided).
b. Record the income tax journal entry on December 31, 2021 (assuming the original tax depreciation schedule provided).

Problem 18-81
Recording and Reporting Temporary Differences **LO2, 8**

Whirlpools Corporation provided the following information: taxable income based on its 2020 tax return, $47,600; income tax rate, 25%. There were two temporary differences.

- December 31, 2020, collected rent in advance for 2021, resulting in deferred rent revenue of $5,000. The $5,000 is included on the 2020 tax return.
- On December 31, 2020, the company recorded a $10,000 estimated expense, accrued as a liability to be paid in 2021. The $10,000 is not deductible for tax purposes.

Required

a. Prepare a schedule to determine the deferred tax balance on December 31, 2020.
b. Record the income tax journal entry on December 31, 2020. Assume a zero-beginning balance in the deferred tax asset account on January 1, 2020.
c. Show how the income tax accounts should be reported on the balance sheet and income statement for 2020. Include the disclosure of current and deferred tax expense.

Problem 18-82
Recording and Reporting Temporary Differences **LO1, 8**

The financial statements of Drake Corporation for a four-year period reflected the following pretax amounts.

	2020	2021	2022	2023
Income statement (summarized)				
Revenues	$120,000	$134,000	$154,000	$174,000
Expenses other than depreciation	(80,000)	(92,000)	(95,000)	(128,000)
Depreciation expense (straight-line)	(20,000)	(20,000)	(20,000)	(20,000)
Pretax GAAP income	$ 20,000	$ 22,000	$ 39,000	$ 26,000
Balance sheet (partial)				
Equipment (four-year life, no residual value), at cost	$ 80,000	$ 80,000	$ 80,000	$ 80,000
Less accumulated depreciation	(20,000)	(40,000)	(60,000)	(80,000)
Net book value	$ 60,000	$ 40,000	$ 20,000	$ 0

Drake has a tax rate of 25% each year and deducts accelerated depreciation for income tax purposes as follows: 2020, $32,000; 2021, $24,000; 2022, $16,000; and 2023, $8,000. There are no deferred tax assets or liabilities at January 1, 2020.

Required

a. Prepare a schedule to compute deferred tax balances on December 31, 2020, 2021, 2022, and 2023.
b. Prepare the journal entries to record income tax expense for the years 2020, 2021, 2022, and 2023.
c. For each year show the deferred income tax amount that should be reported on the balance sheet.

Problem 18-83
Recording and Reporting Temporary and Permanent Differences **LO1, 2, 4, 8**

The records of Lane Corporation provided the following income tax-related information.

	2020	2021	2022	2023
Pretax GAAP income	$90,000	$92,000	$95,000	$98,000

The income tax rate is 25%. The company identified the following differences between the GAAP basis and tax basis of installment accounts receivable and warranty accrued expense.

- For reporting purposes, installment sales in accounts receivable is $30,000 on December 31, 2020. On the tax return, $10,000 will be recognized each year, 2021 through 2023, as cash is collected.
- For reporting purposes, warranty expenses of $4,000 are accrued in 2020. On the tax return, $1,000 will be deducted each year, 2020 through 2023, as expenditures are made related to warranties.

In addition, the company recorded interest revenue of $1,250 each year on municipal bonds, which are not taxable.

Required

a. Prepare a schedule to compute deferred tax balances on December 31, 2020, 2021, 2022, and 2023.
b. Prepare a schedule to compute the increase to income tax payable on December 31, 2020, 2021, 2022, and 2023.
c. Record the journal entries to record income tax expense for the years 2020, 2021, 2022, and 2023.
d. For each year show the income tax amounts that should be reported on the income statement and balance sheet each year. Include the disclosure of current and deferred tax expense.

Problem 18-84
Recording and Reporting Temporary and Permanent Differences **LO1, 2, 4, 8**

The first year of operations for Blair Corporation is 2020. The accounting and income tax periods end on December 31. The records of the company provided the following income tax-related data at the end of 2020.

- Tax rate is 25% for 2020–2022 and becomes 30% in 2023. All of these rates are enacted as of 2020.
- 2020 taxable income: $150,000.
- Temporary differences:
  - A $300,000 estimated expense was accrued at the end of 2020 for accounting purposes and recorded as a liability; the expected settlement date is 2024 for income tax purposes.
  - A $200,000 gain on a special installment sale was recognized for accounting purposes at the end of 2020; the amount will be included in the income tax return as collected in equal amounts for years 2021 through 2024.
  - A depreciable asset that cost $200,000 (estimated useful life five years and no residual value) is depreciated as follows:

	2020	2021	2022	2023	2024
Accounting purposes	$ 40,000	$ 40,000	$40,000	$40,000	$40,000
Income tax purposes	66,000	54,000	40,000	26,000	14,000
Difference	$(26,000)	$(14,000)	$ 0	$14,000	$26,000

- Rent revenue collected in advance at the end of 2020 is $40,000; rent revenue is recognized for accounting purposes evenly in 2021 and 2022. The full amount must be included in the 2020 income tax return.

■ Permanent differences:

- Fines paid in 2020 and 2023 were $5,000 and $4,000, respectively.

Required

a. Prepare a schedule to compute deferred tax balances on December 31, 2020.
b. Record the journal entries to record income tax expense for 2020.
c. Show the amounts that should be reported on the December 31, 2020, balance sheet and 2020 income statement. Include the disclosure of current and deferred tax expense.

Problem 18-85
Recording Temporary Differences: Change in Enacted Rate **LO1, 5**

The records of Morgan Corporation provided the following data at the end of years 2020 through 2023 relating to income tax allocation.

	2020	2021	2022	2023
Pretax GAAP income	$58,000	$70,000	$80,000	$88,000
Taxable income	28,000	80,000	90,000	98,000

The above amounts include only one temporary difference; no other changes occurred. At the end of 2020, the company prepaid an expense of $30,000, which will be amortized for accounting purposes over the next three years (straight line). The full amount is included in 2020 for income tax purposes. At the end of 2020, the enacted tax rate was 35%. During 2021, the enacted tax rate was changed to 25%, retroactive to the beginning of 2021, and was to remain in effect through 2023.

Required

Provide the entry to record income taxes for the years 2020 through 2023.

Problem 18-86
Recording Temporary Differences: Change in Enacted Tax Rates **LO2, 5**

The records of Castle Corporation provided the following income tax allocation data.

	2020	2021	2022	2023
Pretax GAAP income	$40,000	$70,000	$90,000	$100,000

The deferred tax account has a zero balance at the start of 2020. There was only one source of temporary differences, estimated warranty expenses, which were recorded (i.e., accrued) for accounting purposes in 2020 for $20,000. The income tax rate is 25%. The balance in the warranty liability for financial reporting purposes is estimated as follows.

	2020	2021	2022	2023
Warranty liability	$20,000	$30,000	$25,000	$0

Required

a. Provide the entry to record income taxes at the end of 2020.
b. During 2021, tax legislation was passed that changed the enacted tax rate to 40% for years 2022 and 2023. Provide the journal entry on 2021.
c. Assume instead that during 2021, tax legislation was passed that changed the enacted tax rate to 20% for years 2022 and 2023. Provide the journal entry on 2021.

Problem 18-87
Recording Temporary Differences: Change in Enacted Tax Rates **LO2, 5**

Beetle Corporation reported pretax GAAP income as follows: 2020, $150,000 and 2021, $176,000. Taxable income for each year would have been the same as pretax GAAP income except for the tax effects, arising for the first time in 2020 of $600 per month for rent revenue collected in advance on October 1, 2020, to be applied to the six months ended March 31, 2021. Rent revenue is taxable in the year collected. The tax rate for 2020 and 2021 is 25% and the year-end for both accounting and tax purposes is December 31. The rent revenue collected in advance is the only difference, and it is not repeated in October 2021.

Required

a. Prepare the income tax journal entry for 2020.

b. Now assume that during 2020, the tax rate changes to 35% for years 2021 and future years. Prepare the journal entry for income taxes in 2020.

Problem 18-88
Recording NOL Carryforward **LO6**

The financial statements of Bixler Corporation for the first four years of operations reflected the following pretax amounts.

Income statement (summarized)	2020	2021	2022	2023
Revenue	$125,000	$155,000	$180,000	$250,000
Expenses	120,000	195,000	160,000	200,000
Pretax income (loss)	$ 5,000	$ (40,000)	$ 20,000	$ 50,000

There are no temporary differences other than those created by tax loss carryforwards. The income tax rate is 25%. Assume that future income is very uncertain at the end of each year, so a valuation allowance is needed for any recognized deferred tax asset.

Required

a. Provide entries to record the NOL income tax effects for each year.

b. Prepare income statements for the years 2020–2023 (including income tax expense).

Problem 18-89
Recording Income Tax Expense: Uncertain Tax Position **LO7**

Randolph Inc. considered the probability of a recent tax position taken related to a tax deduction of $250,000 on a research and development project. The company had uncertainty about the classification of some costs associated with the project. However, Randolph determined that this position is *more likely than not* to be sustained in a future investigation by taxing authorities. Using available information, Randolph Inc. created the following summary of the probabilities of sustaining the tax position.

Possible Estimated Outcome (Allowable Deductible Expense)	Individual Probability of Occurring
$250,000	15%
200,000	25
180,000	40
100,000	10
80,000	10

Required

a. Assuming taxable income of $1,000,000 (with the research and development tax deduction taken) and a tax rate of 25%, record the income tax journal entry for 2020. Assume Randolph has no temporary differences between GAAP and taxable income.

b. In 2021, if the full benefit is realized, record the journal entry required.

c. In 2021, if the full benefit is lost, record the journal entry required.

Accounting Decisions and Judgments

AD&J 18-90
Analyzing Texaco—Income Tax Disclosure
LO1, 2, 8

Real World Analysis In the notes to its Year 8 financial statements, Texaco Inc., a major U.S. oil producer, provides the following disclosure regarding the deferred tax asset and liability accounts at December 31, Year 8.

$ millions	Asset (Liability)
Depreciation	$(1,079)
Depletion	(429)
Intangible drilling costs	(726)
Other deferred tax liabilities	(686)
Total	(2,920)
Employee benefit plans	532
Tax loss carryforwards	641
Tax credit carryforwards	368
Environmental liabilities	116
Other deferred tax assets	639
Total	2,296
Total before valuation allowance	(624)
Valuation allowance	(815)
Total—net	$(1,439)

Required

a. What is the total amount of deferred tax liability at December 31, Year 8? The total amount of deferred tax asset? The net amount of deferred tax asset or liability reported on Texaco's December 31, Year 8 balance sheet?

b. Assuming a federal tax rate of 35%, estimate the amount of temporary difference arising from GAAP/tax differences for depreciable assets that exists for Texaco at December 31, Year 8.

AD&J 18-91 Analyzing Applied Technology Laboratories—Income Tax Disclosure LO6

Real World Analysis Applied Technology Laboratories (ATL) a medical equipment manufacturer, reported a loss before income taxes of $20.9 million in Year 4, yet the income tax effect was a tax benefit of $0.7 million. The effective income tax rate was only 3.3% ($0.7 million/$20.9 million). ATL reported a loss before income taxes of $1.7 million in Year 3 yet had income tax expense of $1.6 million. Assume a statutory income tax rate of 35%.

This schedule from the notes to the Year 4 ATL annual report explains its deferred tax assets and deferred tax liabilities.

$ thousands	Year 4	Year 3
Deferred tax assets		
Receivables	$ 3,230	$ 2,936
Inventories	11,564	8,800
Net operating loss carryforwards	3,969	3,157
State taxes	3,106	2,087
Compensation	2,623	2,171
Provision for litigation claim	1,700	—
Research and experimentation credit carryforwards	6,602	6,425
Other	3,032	3,107
Gross deferred tax assets	$35,826	$28,683
Less valuation allowance	(27,249)	(19,709)
Net deferred tax assets	$ 8,577	$ 8,974
Deferred tax liabilities, primarily depreciation and intangible assets	(4,472)	(4,628)
Net deferred income taxes	$ 4,105	$ 4,346

Required

a. What are some reasons why ATL's effective tax rate might be so low in Year 4?

b. Why might ATL show an income tax expense in a year when it has a loss before income taxes for financial reporting?

c. In general terms, explain why ATL has such a large amount reported as a valuation allowance.

d. What effect did the increase in the valuation allowance from Year 3 to Year 4 have on ATL's income tax expense computation in fiscal Year 4?

e. Using a tax rate of 35%, estimate the amount of net operating loss carryforwards that ATL has as of December 31, Year 4.

f. Using a tax rate of 35%, estimate the amount of "research and experimentation credit carryforwards" that ATL has as of December 31, Year 4.

g. Using a tax rate of 35%, estimate the amount of accrued liability for litigation claim that ATL has as of December 31, Year 4.

AD&J 18-92
Analyzing Coca Cola—Income Tax Disclosure
LO1, 2, 3

Real World Analysis Refer to the following three 2015 **Coca-Cola Company** financial statement excerpts below to answer the following questions.

a. If Coca-Cola had no permanent or temporary differences and all earnings were subject to the federal statutory income tax rate, for what amount would Coca-Cola record income tax expense in 2015?

b. Identify three sources and their percentage effects on income taxes that caused Coca-Cola's effective tax rate in 2015 to differ from the federal statutory rate of 35%.

c. By how much did Coca-Cola increase or decrease its valuation allowance in 2015? How did the valuation allowance as a percentage of deferred tax assets (gross) change from 2014 to 2015? Analyze the results.

Note 14: Income Taxes Income before income taxes consisted of the following (in millions).

Year Ended December 31	2015	2014	2013
United States	$1,801	$1,567	$ 2,451
International	7,804	7,758	9,026
Total	$9,605	$9,325	$11,477

A reconciliation of the statutory U.S. federal tax rate and our effective tax rate is as follows:

Year Ended December 31	2015	2014	2013
Statutory U.S. federal tax rate	35.0%	35.0%	35.0%
State and local income taxes—net of federal benefit	1.2	1.0	1.0
Earnings in jurisdictions taxed at rates different from the statutory U.S. federal rate	(12.7)	(11.5)	(10.3)
Equity income or loss	(1.7)	(2.2)	(1.4)
Other operating charges	1.2	2.9	1.2
Other—net	0.3	(1.6)	(0.7)
Effective tax rate	23.3%	23.6%	24.8%

December 31	2015	2014
Deferred tax assets:		
Property, plant and equipment	$ 192	$ 96
Trademarks and other intangible assets	68	68
Equity method investments (including foreign currency translation adjustment)	694	462
Derivative financial instruments	161	134
Other liabilities	1,056	1,082
Benefit plans	1,541	1,673
Net operating/capital loss carryforwards	413	729
Other	175	196
Gross deferred tax assets	$4,300	$4,440
Valuation allowances	(477)	(649)
Total deferred tax assets	$3,823	$3,791

AD&J 18-93
Analyzing a Change in Enacted Tax Rate **LO5**

Communication Case The statutory federal tax rate had been 35% for a number of years. Assume that late in the third quarter of 2020, a new rate, 40%, was approved as the new enacted rate, effective as of January 1, 2020. You are an assistant controller with Zenics Inc., a manufacturer of laser printers. The CEO of the company is concerned about what effect, if any, the new tax rate will have on 2020 earnings.

At the beginning of the year, Zenics had a deferred tax asset of $10 million and a deferred tax liability of $6 million. There was no need for a valuation allowance, nor is it expected that any will be needed this year. You estimate that pretax GAAP income will be approximately $5 million in 2020 and that taxable income will be about $7 million. The company is publicly traded, with 500,000 shares outstanding all year.

Required

Write a memo to the CEO, Rihanna Star, explaining what effect the tax rate increase will have on the balance sheet and income statement for the company for 2020. Be as specific as you can, especially with regard to the effect the change will have on the balance sheet accounts, income statement accounts, net income, and earnings per share. If there is likely to be a negative impact on earnings, Rhianna would like your advice on what actions the company might consider taking in the last few days of 2020 to minimize the impact. You should also comment on what effect, if any, you think the tax rate change will have on the company's stock price.

Ethics Case A company had a tax refund of $2,000 but it reported income tax expense of $5,000 on its income statement.

AD&J 18-94 Explaining Tax Accounting and Financial Reporting **LO1, 2, 6, 8**

Required

a. Is it appropriate and legal for a company to keep two sets of books: one for tax purposes and one for financial reporting purposes?

b. Explain how a company might have an income tax refund at the time it is reporting income tax expense.

Judgment Case Rimes Inc. has each of the following items on its balance sheet at December 31, 2020. The prepaid expenses have already been deducted for tax purposes; none of the other items have yet been deducted. The current and future income tax rate is 35%.

AD&J 18-95 Analyzing Deferred Income Taxes **LO1, 2, 4**

Current assets: Prepaid expenses	$ 50,000
Current liabilities: Warranty liability	100,000
Current liabilities: Insurance liability*	10,000
Noncurrent liabilities: Postretirement liability other than pensions	1,000,000

*Not tax deductible.

Required

a. Explain which of the above items requires a deferred tax amount to be recorded, in what amount, and whether it is a deferred tax asset or deferred tax liability.

b. Determine how the amounts of deferred tax asset and deferred tax liability would be reported on the balance sheet.

Judgment Case Soderstrom Company has a deferred tax asset of $1,000,000 at December 31, 2020, arising from its recording of its liability for postretirement benefits other than pensions. Soderstrom's CPA asks management whether a valuation allowance to reduce the deferred tax asset to zero should be recorded.

AD&J 18-96 Analyzing Valuation Allowance for Deferred Tax Assets **LO3**

Required

a. Why would Soderstrom not want to report a valuation allowance? Outline what evidence, assuming it existed, that Soderstrom might use to argue against recording a valuation allowance.

b. Suppose in the final analysis it is determined that a valuation allowance of $400,000 is needed. How would the company have arrived at this determination, and what effect will it have on net income in fiscal 2020?

Challenge Problem The following are descriptions of long-term debt for SuperK.

AD&J 18-97 Reporting Comprehensive Long-Term Debt **LO1, 8**

Income Tax—SuperK Corporation had identical income before taxes on both its income tax return and its income statement for 2020 except for a temporary difference related to the difference between tax and GAAP depreciation. A depreciable asset that cost $250,000 was depreciated for income tax purposes using the following amounts: 2020, $128,000; 2021, $64,000; 2022, $34,000; 2023, $16,000; and 2024, $8,000. However, for accounting purposes the straight-line method was used (5 years, no salvage value). The accounting and tax periods both end December 31. There were no deferred taxes at the beginning of 2020. Taxable income was $298,000 and the income tax rate is 40% for 2020.

Lease—On December 31, 2020, SuperK Corporation completed the first year of a 3-year lease. The lease is considered a finance lease. Annual payments of $36,556 are due on January 1, with the first payment due on January 1, 2020. The incremental borrowing rate of SuperK is 10% and the fair value of the equipment at the origination of the lease was $100,000.

Long-term Debt—On January 1, 2020, SuperK issued $250,000 of bonds with a stated rate of 6%, accounted for using the effective interest method. The 10-year bonds pay interest annually on December 31 to yield 8%.

Pension—SuperK sponsors a defined benefit plan. December 31, 2020, ending balances for the projected benefit obligation, and fair value of plan assets totaled $800,000 and $725,000, respectively. The accumulated benefit obligation on December 31, 2020 was $700,000.

Required

a. Provide the entry to record income taxes at the end of 2020.

b. Compute the amounts to be included in long-term debt on the balance sheet on December 31, 2020.

Challenge Problem The Duesing Company began operations in 2015, engaging in a number of business activities ranging from manufacturing and marketing durable goods to editing technical business publications on which the company collects royalty income. The accounting for these many activities resulted in a number of differences between reporting for book and tax purposes. For financial reporting purposes, the company accrued estimated warranty costs when it sold products under warranty, deferred advance royalty payments it received, and prepaid many operating expenses. For tax purposes, it recognized warranty costs when paid, royalty income when cash was received,

AD&J 18-98 Reporting Income Tax Expense: Comprehensive Example **LO1, 2, 3, 4, 5, 6, 7, 8**

and operating expenses when cash was paid. The opening and closing balances in these accounts for 2020 were as follows. Assume that each of these has a tax basis of zero and each is expected to reverse in 2021.

Debit (Credit)	January 1	December 31	Change During Year
Accrued warranty costs	$(50,000)	$(40,000)	$10,000
Deferred royalty income	(10,000)	(40,000)	(30,000)
Prepaid expenses	33,000	25,000	(8,000)

The company depreciates its manufacturing equipment using an accelerated method for tax purposes and a straight-line method for financial reporting. The schedule of GAAP and tax depreciation for 2020 and all remaining years for the company's existing equipment is as follows.

Year	GAAP Depreciation	Tax Depreciation
2020	$ 9,000	$14,000
2021	9,000	9,000
2022	9,000	6,000
2023	9,000	3,000
Total	$36,000	$32,000

The company's 2020 pretax GAAP income was $8,000. This includes $2,000 of interest revenue on municipal bonds that is not taxable.

- The tax rate the company expected to be effective in 2020 and 2021 (and for all prior years) is 34%. However, during 2020 a tax law was enacted that will change the tax rate to 40% for 2022 and subsequent years.
- There are no prior taxes currently payable or any prior tax refunds currently receivable.
- At January 1, 2020, there are opening balances in the deferred tax asset account of $29,240, in the valuation allowance of $5,100, and in the deferred tax liability account of $15,980.
- The company determines that it is *more likely than not* that any deferred tax asset on December 31, 2020, will not be realized.

Required

a. Prepare the journal entry to record the company's income tax expense for 2020.

b. Determine the deferred tax amount to be reported on the company's balance sheet.

AD&J 18-99
Accounting for Income Taxes **LO2, 3**

Trueblood Case The Trueblood case series, prepared by Deloitte professionals, are based on recent accounting technical issues that require research and judgment. The cases may be accessed through the Deloitte foundation at the following website: https://www2.deloitte.com/us/en/pages/about-deloitte/articles/trueblood-case-studies-deloitte-foundation.html

The following case is relevant to the content provided in this chapter: Case 13-10 Income Taxes. This case examines the sources of taxable income to support a deferred tax asset and management's assertions on future taxable income and valuation of deferred tax assets.

AD&J 18-100
Defining Terms **LO1, 2, 3, 4, 5, 6, 7**

Codification Skills How are the terms (1) deferred tax asset, (2) deferred tax liability, (3) tax position, (4) valuation allowance, (5) income tax expense (or benefit), (6) carryforwards defined in the Codification?

AD&J 18-101
Performing Accounting Research **LO1, 3, 6, 7, 9**

Codification Skills Through research in the Codification, identify the specific citation for each of the following items included as guidance in this chapter for income tax accounting.

a. *More likely than not* threshold in recording a valuation allowance FASB ASC ___-___-___-___

b. Recording deferred tax liabilities using enacted tax rates FASB ASC ___-___-___-___

c. *More likely than not* threshold in evaluating tax positions FASB ASC ___-___-___-___

d. Loss carryforwards resulting in deferred tax assets FASB ASC ___-___-___-___

e. Intraperiod tax allocation FASB ASC ___-___-___-___

AD&J 18-102
Performing Accounting Research **LO7**

Codification Skills When a company is uncertain as to the disposition of a tax position, it becomes a question as to the amount of tax benefit to recognize in the financial statements. Resolution of tax positions may take years. A company is trying to determine how to estimate the benefit to recognize related to an anticipated tax settlement with a taxing authority.

What guidance is available in the Codification in reporting this information?

FASB ASC ___-___-___-___

Appendix—Brief Exercises

In 2020, Roberts Inc. reports pretax GAAP income of $60,000, resulting from income from continuing operations of $65,000 and $5,000 from a loss from discontinued operations. If the company's tax rate is 25%, what amount will the company report for the loss from discontinued operations and net income in its income statement?

App—Brief Exercise 18-103
Reporting Intraperiod Tax Allocation **LO9**
Hint: See Demo 18-9

Bye Corporation is preparing its 2020 financial statements. Its pretax amounts are income before discontinued operations, $300,000 and gain from discontinued operations, $20,000. How much income tax should be allocated to each of the intraperiod amounts assuming a tax rate of 25%?

App—Brief Exercise 18-104
Reporting Intraperiod Tax Allocation **LO9**
Hint: See Demo 18-9

In 2020, Equafax Company decided to change the inventory costing method used from FIFO to the average-cost method for financial reporting. The annual reporting period ends December 31. The tax rate is 25%. The decrease in December 31, 2019, inventory, had the inventory been recorded using the average-cost method, was $400,000. Record the journal entry in 2020 to account for the change in accounting principle.

App—Brief Exercise 18-105
Recording Change in Accounting Principle **LO10**
Hint: See Demo 18-10A

In 2020, Fleetwood Company decided to change its inventory costing method used from LIFO to the average-cost method for book and tax. The annual reporting period ends December 31. The tax rate is 25%. The increase in December 31, 2019, inventory, had the inventory been recorded using the average-cost method, was $375,000. Record the journal entry in 2020 to account for the change in accounting principle.

App—Brief Exercise 18-106
Recording Change in Accounting Principle **LO10**
Hint: See Demo 18-10A

Whitney Company purchased equipment on January 1, 2020, for $90,000. This equipment has a useful life of ten years and a residual value of $5,000. The company uses the straight-line depreciation method. In 2021, the company discovered that it had incorrectly recorded depreciation for 2020 as $5,800. Assume a tax rate of 25%, that the company uses the same method for tax purposes, and that the error carried over to the tax return. Record the correcting entry on January 1, 2021.

App—Brief Exercise 18-107
Recording Error Correction **LO10**
Hint: See Demo 18-10B

Appendix—Exercises

Apple Inc. had the following balances in its accounts on December 31, 2020.

Revenues	$500,000
Cost of goods sold	210,000
Operating expenses	75,000
Loss from discontinued operations	(40,000)
Unrealized gain on available-for-sale debt securities	4,000

Required

Assuming an income tax rate of 25%, prepare a combined statement of comprehensive income using intraperiod tax allocation.

App—Exercise 18-108
Reporting Intraperiod Tax Allocation **LO9**
Hint: See Demo 18-9

Key Company changed its method of accounting for inventory from LIFO to FIFO in 2020 for both tax and financial accounting purposes. The 2019 ending inventory was $40,000 under LIFO and $55,000 under FIFO. The 2019 ending retained earnings was $300,000, before accounting for the change in accounting principle. Key Company discloses 2019 and 2020 results comparatively. The tax rate is 25%.

App—Exercise 18-109
Recording and Reporting Change from LIFO to FIFO **LO10**
Hint: See Demo 18-10A

Required

a. Record the entry for the change in accounting principle.

b. In the comparative income statement presentation in 2020, which method will be used in 2019? Which method will be used in 2020?

c. How will the presentation of retained earnings be affected in 2020 based on the change in accounting principle?

On January 1, 2020, Baker Company decided to change the inventory costing method used from LIFO to FIFO, for book and tax purposes. The annual reporting period ends on December 31. The income tax rate is 30%. The following related data were developed.

App—Exercise 18-110
Recording and Reporting Change from LIFO to FIFO: Entries, Reporting **LO10**
Hint: See Demo 18-10A

	LIFO Basis	FIFO Basis
Beginning inventory, 2019	$ 20,000	$30,000
Ending inventory		
2019	40,000	70,000
2020	44,000	76,000
Net income		
2019: LIFO basis	80,000	
2020: FIFO basis		90,000
Retained earnings		
2019 beginning balance	120,000	
Dividends declared and paid		
2019	64,000	
2020		70,000
Common shares outstanding, 10,000		

Required

a. Provide the journal entry on January 1, 2020, to record the effect of the change in accounting principle.

b. Prepare a schedule to indicate the relevant effects on the 2019 and 2020 comparative balance sheet, income statement, and retained earnings section of the statement of shareholders' equity assuming 2019 restated net income under FIFO is $94,000.

App—Exercise 18-111
Recording and Reporting Change from FIFO to Average Cost: Entries, Reporting **LO10**
Hint: See Demo 18-10A

Marshall Company began operations in 2018. In 2020, Marshall Company decided to change from FIFO to average cost in reporting inventory for financial reporting purposes. The company's tax rate is 25%. The following information is available.

	Pretax Income—FIFO	Pretax Income—Average Cost
2018	$30,000	$20,000
2019	45,000	33,000
2020	70,000	58,000

Required

a. Provide the journal entry on January 1, 2020, to record the effect of the change in accounting principle, assuming Marshall continues to use FIFO for tax purposes.

b. Indicate the net income amounts to be reported in 2020 assuming that comparative statements (2019, 2020) are reported.

c. How would the change in accounting principle affect retained earnings in the statement of stockholders' equity, assuming two years of activity are included in the statement of stockholders' equity?

Appendix—Problems

App—Problem 18-112
Reporting Intraperiod Tax Allocation **LO9**

Information for Lake Inc. for the year ended December 31, 2020, is as follows.

- Revenues, costs of goods sold, and operating expenses are $800,000, $350,000, and $100,000, respectively.
- One timing difference originating in 2020 results in future taxable amounts of $40,000.
- Fines paid of $2,500 included in operating expenses are not deductible.
- Loss from discontinued operations that is tax deductible in the current year of $10,000 is not included in the amounts above.
- Tax rate is 25% for all years.

Required

a. Prepare the journal entry to record income tax expense.

b. Prepare an income statement using intraperiod tax allocation.

App—Problem 18-113
Recording and Reporting Change in Inventory Costing Method **LO10**

Atlanta Company changed its method of accounting for inventory from LIFO to FIFO in 2020 for both tax and financial accounting purposes. The 2019 ending inventory was $40,000 under LIFO and $55,000 under FIFO. Atlanta discloses 2019 and 2020 results comparatively. Retained earnings at the end of 2018 and 2019 are $380,500 and $387,000, respectively, as previously reported. However, if the FIFO method had been used, the balances in retained earnings at the end of 2018 and 2019 would have been $355,500 and $364,500. Net income as previously reported under LIFO in 2019 was $46,500. However, if FIFO were used, net income in 2019 would have been $49,000. Net income following FIFO in 2020 was $55,000. Dividends of $40,000 were declared and paid in each year. The tax rate is 30%. 10,000 shares are outstanding in years 2019 and 2020.

Required

a. Prepare the entry to record the change in accounting principle on January 1, 2020.

b. Indicate the net income and earnings per share to be recorded in comparative income statements (2020 and 2019).

c. Prepare a retained earnings statement that would be incorporated in a statement of stockholders' equity for the years 2019 and 2020.

App—Problem 18-114
Recording and Reporting Error Correction **LO10**
Hint: See Demo 18-10B

In 2020, Arrow Company, which has a calendar fiscal year, discovered that depreciation expense was erroneously overstated by $2,000 in both 2018 and 2019 for financial reporting purposes but not for tax purposes. The tax rate is 30%. Additional information follows.

	2019	2020
Beginning retained earnings, as previously reported	$36,000	$ 0
Net income (as previously reported for 2019)	32,000	36,000
Dividends declared	12,000	16,000

Required

a. Record the entry in 2020 to correct the error.

b. Provide the comparative retained earnings statements, included in the 2019 and 2020 statements of stockholders' equity, including any required note disclosure.

Answers to Review Exercises

Review 18-1

Example One

a.

Calculation of Income Tax Payable Increase (Dec. 31)	2020	2021	2022	2023
Pretax GAAP income	$145,000	$160,000	$160,000	$155,000
Accelerated depreciation adjustment	(5,000)	(12,000)	6,000	11,000
Taxable income	140,000	148,000	166,000	166,000
Tax rate	× 25%	× 25%	× 25%	× 25%
Income tax payable increase	$ 35,000	$ 37,000	$ 41,500	$ 41,500

b.

Measurement of Deferred Tax Liability, at Dec. 31	2020	2021	2022	2023
GAAP basis of depreciable asset	$45,000	$30,000	$15,000	$ 0
Tax basis of depreciable asset	40,000	13,000	4,000	0
Difference between GAAP and tax bases	5,000	17,000	11,000	0
Tax rate	× 25%	× 25%	× 25%	× 25%
Deferred tax liability, ending balance	$ 1,250	$ 4,250	$ 2,750	$ 0

c. **December 31, 2020—To record income tax expense**

Income Tax Expense ($35,000 + $1,250)	36,250	
Deferred Tax Liability		1,250
Income Tax Payable		35,000

Assets = Liabilities + Equity
+1,250 −36,250
+35,000

Def Tax Liab		Inc Tax Payable		Income Tax Exp	
	1,250		35,000	36,250	

Assets = Liabilities + Equity: Liabilities +3,000, +37,000; Equity −40,000

Def Tax Liab: 1,250; 3,000 | Inc Tax Payable: 37,000 | Income Tax Exp: 36,250; 40,000

December 31, 2021—To record income tax

Income Tax Expense ($37,000 + $3,000).	40,000	
Deferred Tax Liability ($4,250 − $1,250)		3,000
Income Tax Payable.		37,000

Assets = Liabilities + Equity: Liabilities −1,500, +41,500; Equity −40,000

Def Tax Liab: 1,500 | 1,250; 3,000 | Inc Tax Payable: 41,500 | Income Tax Exp: 36,250; 40,000; 40,000

December 31, 2022—To record income tax expense

Income Tax Expense ($41,500 − $1,500).	40,000	
Deferred Tax Liability ($4,250 − $2,750)	1,500	
Income Tax Payable.		41,500

Assets = Liabilities + Equity: Liabilities −2,750, +41,500; Equity −38,750

Def Tax Liab: 1,500; 2,750 | 1,250; 3,000; 0 | Inc Tax Payable: 41,500 | Income Tax Exp: 36,250; 40,000; 40,000; 38,750

December 31, 2023—To record income tax expense

Income Tax Expense ($41,500 − $2,750).	38,750	
Deferred Tax Liability ($0 − $2,750)	2,750	
Income Tax Payable.		41,500

Example Two

a.

Calculation of Income Tax Payable Increase (Dec. 31)	2020	2021	2022	2023
Pretax GAAP income	$145,000	$160,000	$160,000	$155,000
Expense adjustment.	(45,000)	15,000	15,000	15,000
Taxable income.	100,000	175,000	175,000	170,000
Tax rate.	× 25%	× 25%	× 25%	× 25%
Income tax payable increase	$ 25,000	$ 43,750	$ 43,750	$ 42,500

b.

Measurement of Deferred Tax Liability, at Dec. 31	2020	2021	2022	2023
GAAP basis of depreciable asset.	$45,000	$30,000	$15,000	$ 0
Tax basis of depreciable asset	0	0	0	0
Difference between GAAP and tax bases	45,000	30,000	15,000	0
Tax rate.	× 25%	× 25%	× 25%	× 25%
Deferred tax liability, ending balance	$11,250	$ 7,500	$ 3,750	$ 0

c.

Assets = Liabilities + Equity: Liabilities +11,250, +25,000; Equity −36,250

Def Tax Liab: 11,250 | Inc Tax Payable: 25,000 | Income Tax Exp: 36,250

December 31, 2020—To record income tax expense

Income Tax Expense ($25,000 + $11,250).	36,250	
Deferred Tax Liability		11,250
Income Tax Payable.		25,000

Assets = Liabilities + Equity: Liabilities −3,750, +43,750; Equity −40,000

Def Tax Liab: 3,750 | 11,250 | Inc Tax Payable: 43,750 | Income Tax Exp: 36,250; 40,000

December 31, 2021—To record income tax expense

Income Tax Expense ($43,750 − $3,750).	40,000	
Deferred Tax Liability ($11,250 − $7,500)	3,750	
Income Tax Payable.		43,750

Assets = Liabilities + Equity: Liabilities −3,750, +43,750; Equity −40,000

Def Tax Liab: 3,750; 3,750 | 11,250 | Inc Tax Payable: 43,750 | Income Tax Exp: 36,250; 40,000; 40,000

December 31, 2022—To record income tax expense

Income Tax Expense ($43,750 − $3,750).	40,000	
Deferred Tax Liability ($7,500 − $3,750)	3,750	
Income Tax Payable.		43,750

Assets = Liabilities + Equity: Liabilities −3,750, +42,500; Equity −38,750

Def Tax Liab: 3,750; 3,750; 3,750 | 11,250; 0 | Inc Tax Payable: 42,500 | Income Tax Exp: 36,250; 40,000; 40,000; 38,750

December 31, 2023—To record income tax expense

Income Tax Expense ($42,500 − $3,750).	38,750	
Deferred Tax Liability ($3,750 − $0)	3,750	
Income Tax Payable.		42,500

Review 18-2

a.

Calculation of Income Tax Payable Increase (Dec. 31)	2020	2021	2022	2023
Pretax GAAP income	$145,000	$155,000	$150,000	$148,000
Revenue adjustment	150,000	(50,000)	(50,000)	(50,000)
Taxable income	295,000	105,000	100,000	98,000
Tax rate	× 25%	× 25%	× 25%	× 25%
Income tax payable increase	$ 73,750	$ 26,250	$ 25,000	$ 24,500

b.

Measurement of Deferred Tax Asset, at Dec. 31	2020	2021	2022	2023
GAAP basis of deferred revenue	$150,000	$100,000	$50,000	$ 0
Tax basis of deferred revenue	0	0	0	0
Difference between GAAP and tax bases	150,000	100,000	50,000	0
Tax rate	× 25%	× 25%	× 25%	× 25%
Deferred tax asset, ending balance	$ 37,500	$ 25,000	$12,500	$ 0

c. **December 31, 2020—To record income tax expense**

Income Tax Expense ($73,750 − $37,500)	36,250	
Deferred Tax Asset	37,500	
Income Tax Payable		73,750

Assets = Liabilities + Equity
+37,500 = +73,750 − 36,250
Def Tax Asset: 37,500 | ; Inc Tax Payable: | 73,750; Income Tax Exp: 36,250 |

December 31, 2021—To record income tax expense

Income Tax Expense ($26,250 + $12,500)	38,750	
Deferred Tax Asset ($37,500 − $25,000)		12,500
Income Tax Payable		26,250

Assets = Liabilities + Equity
−12,500 = +26,250 − 38,750
Def Tax Asset: 37,500 | 12,500; Inc Tax Payable: | 73,750, 26,250; Income Tax Exp: 36,250, 38,750 |

December 31, 2022—To record income tax expense

Income Tax Expense ($25,000 + $12,500)	37,500	
Deferred Tax Asset ($25,000 − $12,500)		12,500
Income Tax Payable		25,000

Assets = Liabilities + Equity
−12,500 = +25,000 − 37,500
Def Tax Asset: 37,500 | 12,500, 12,500; Inc Tax Payable: | 73,750, 26,250, 25,000; Income Tax Exp: 36,250, 38,750, 37,500 |

December 31, 2023—To record income tax expense

Income Tax Expense ($24,500 + $12,500)	37,000	
Deferred Tax Asset ($12,500 − $0)		12,500
Income Tax Payable		24,500

Assets = Liabilities + Equity
−12,500 = +24,500 − 37,000
Def Tax Asset: 37,500 | 12,500, 12,500, 12,500; Inc Tax Payable: | 73,750, 26,250, 25,000, 24,500; Income Tax Exp: 36,250, 38,750, 37,500, 37,000 |

Review 18-3

a. **December 31, 2020—To record income tax expense**

Income Tax Expense ($220,000 − $20,000)	200,000	
Deferred Tax Asset	20,000	
Income Tax Payable ($880,000 × 0.25)		220,000

Assets = Liabilities + Equity
+20,000 = +220,000 − 200,000
Def Tax Asset: Bal. 280,000, 20,000 | ; Inc Tax Payable: | 220,000; Income Tax Exp: 200,000 |

b. **December 31, 2020—To record income tax expense**

Income Tax Expense ($220,000 − $20,000)	200,000	
Deferred Tax Asset	20,000	
Income Tax Payable ($880,000 × 0.25)		220,000

Assets = Liabilities + Equity
+20,000 = +220,000 − 200,000
Def Tax Asset: Bal. 280,000, 20,000 | ; Inc Tax Payable: | 220,000; Income Tax Exp: 200,000 |

December 31, 2020—To record valuation allowance

Income Tax Expense	90,000	
Valuation Allowance for Deferred Tax Asset*		90,000

Assets = Liabilities + Equity
−90,000 = − 90,000
Def Tax Asset Allow: | 90,000; Income Tax Exp: 90,000 |

*(30% × $300,000).

Review 18-4

a.

Calculation of Income Tax Payable Increase (Dec. 31)	2020
Pretax GAAP income	$250,000
Depreciation adjustment	(30,000)
Installment sales adjustment	(40,000)
Insurance premiums	4,000
Taxable income	184,000
Tax rate	× 25%
Income tax payable increase	$ 46,000

b. **December 31, 2020**

Assets = Liabilities + Equity
+17,500 (Liabilities); +46,000 (Liabilities); −63,500 (Equity)

Def Tax Liab: Cr 17,500
Inc Tax Payable: Cr 46,000
Income Tax Exp: Dr 63,500

Income Tax Expense ($46,000 + $12,500)	58,500	
Deferred Tax Liability ($17,500* − $5,000)		12,500
Income Tax Payable		46,000

*	Fixed Asset	Installment Receivable	Total
GAAP	$320,000	$40,000	
Tax	290,000	0	
	30,000	40,000	
	× 25%	× 25%	
Deferred tax liability bal.	$ 7,500	$10,000	$17,500

Review 18-5

Calculation of Income Tax Payable Increase (Dec. 31)	2021
Pretax GAAP income	$112,000
Installment sales adjustment	10,000
Warranty expense adjustment	22,000
Taxable income	144,000
Tax rate	× 30%
Income tax payable increase	$ 43,200

Deferred Tax Liability Adjustment, at Dec. 31	2021
Installment receivable ($13,000 × 0.25)	$ 3,250
Beginning balance	6,900
Deferred tax liability adjustment	$(3,650)

December 31, 2021—To record income tax expense

Assets = Liabilities + Equity
+5,500 (Assets); −3,650, +43,000 (Liabilities); −34,050 (Equity)

Def Tax Asset: Dr 5,500
Income Tax Exp: Dr 34,050
Inc Tax Payable: Cr 43,200
Def Tax Liab: Dr 3,650 | Cr 6,900 Bal.

Income Tax Expense ($43,200 − $9,150)	34,050	
Deferred Tax Asset ($22,000 × 25%)	5,500	
Deferred Tax Liability	3,650	
Income Tax Payable		43,200

Review 18-6

December 31, 2021—To record income tax benefit

Assets = Liabilities + Equity
+4,500 (Assets); +4,500 (Equity)

Def Tax Asset: Dr 4,500
Income Tax Exp: Dr 2,500 | Cr 4,500

Deferred Tax Asset ($18,000 × 25%)	4,500	
Income Tax Expense		4,500

December 31, 2021—To record valuation allowance

Assets = Liabilities + Equity
−2,700 (Assets); −2,700 (Equity)

Def Tax Asset Allow: Cr 2,700
Inc Tax Exp: Dr 2,500, 2,700 | Cr 4,500

Income Tax Expense ($4,500 × 60%)	2,700	
Valuation Allowance for Deferred Tax Asset		2,700

Review 18-7

December 31, 2020—To record income tax expense

Income Tax Expense	115,000	
Liability for Unrecognized Tax Benefits*		2,500
Income Tax Payable ($450,000 × 25%)		112,500

Assets = Liabilities + Equity
+2,500 −115,000
+112,500

Liab—Tax Benefit: 2,500
Inc Tax Payable: 112,500
Income Tax Exp: 115,000

* The outcome at a cumulative probability of 50% is $20,000 where the probability is 60% (15% + 20% + 25%). Liability for unrecognized tax benefits is $2,500, computed as 25% × $10,000 (= $30,000 − $20,000).

Review 18-8

	Deferred Tax Asset (Liability)
Prepaid operating expense	$10,000
Excess accelerated depreciation	(7,500)
Bad debt expense	2,500
Installment sales	(8,750)
Valuation allowance (50% × $12,500)	(6,250)
Net deferred tax liability	$(10,000)

Balance Sheet (excerpt)	
Liabilities	
Current	
Income tax payable	$83,250
Noncurrent	
Deferred tax liability, net	10,000

Review 18-9

Athletics Inc.
Statement of Comprehensive Income
For Year Ended December 31, 2020

Revenues	$180,000
Cost of goods sold	99,000
Gross margin	81,000
Operating expenses	15,000
Income from continuing operations before income tax	66,000
Income tax expense ($66,000 × 25%)	16,500
Income from continuing operations	49,500
Discontinued operations	
Loss from discontinued operations, net of tax ($14,000 × 75%)	10,500
Net income	39,000
Other comprehensive income	
Unrealized gain on debt securities ($3,000 × 75%)	2,250
Comprehensive income	$ 41,250

Review 18-10

Example One

Assets	=	Liabilities	+	Equity
+50,000		+12,500		+37,500

Inventory		Def Tax Liab		Ret Earnings—PPA	
50,000			12,500		37,500

January 1, 2021—Change in accounting principle

Inventory	50,000	
Deferred Tax Liability ($50,000 × 25%)		12,500
Retained Earnings—Prior Period Adjustment		37,500

Example Two

Assets	=	Liabilities	+	Equity
+2,500		+1,250		−7,500
−10,000		+35,000		

Accum Deprec		Inc Tax Receiv		Ret Earnings—PPA	
	10,000	2,500		7,500	

January 1, 2021—To correct for depreciation error

Retained Earnings—Prior Period Adjustment	7,500	
Income Tax Receivable ($10,000 × 25%)	2,500	
Accumulated Depreciation		10,000

19 Pensions and Postretirement Benefits

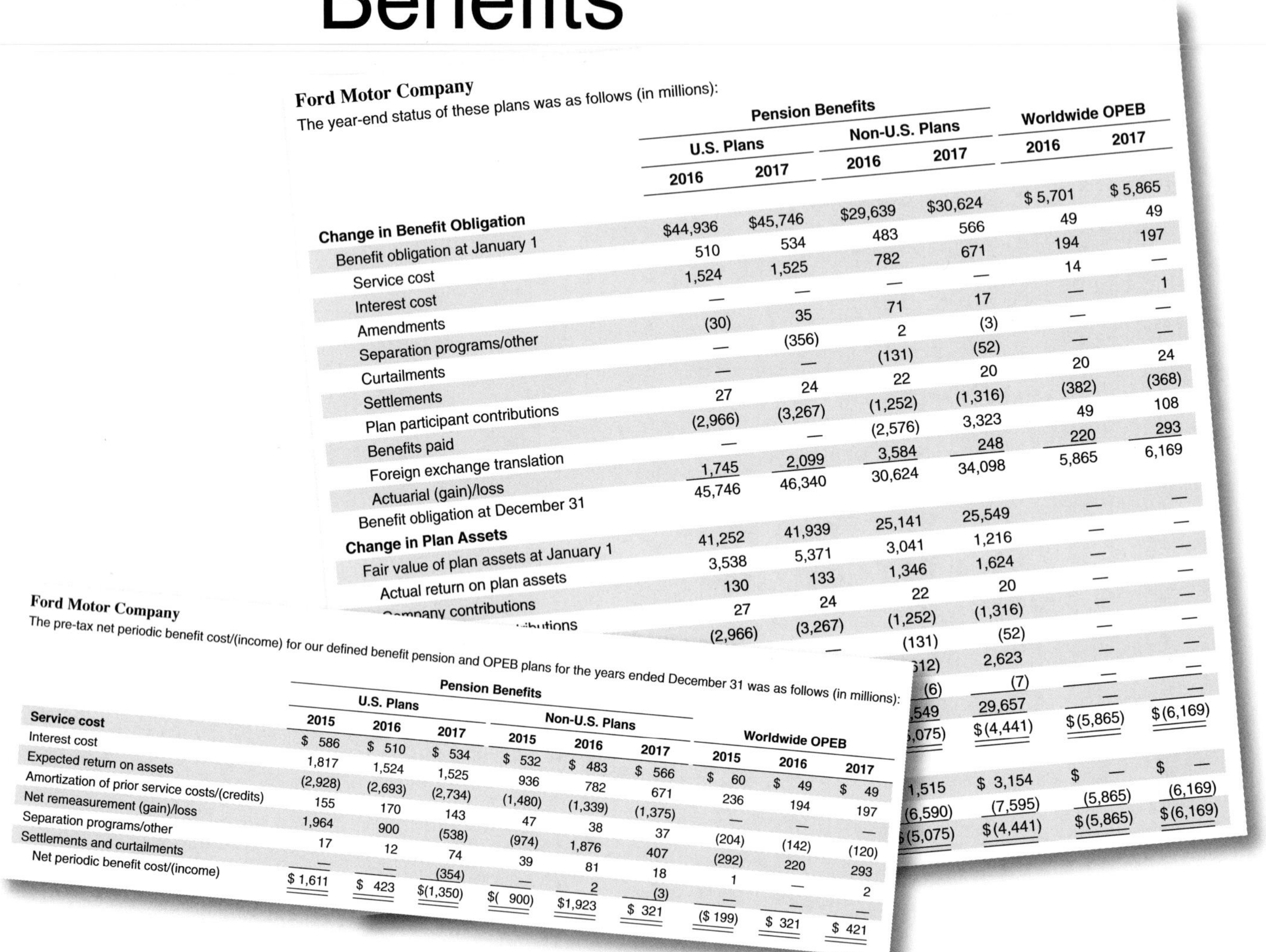

Ford Motor Company

The year-end status of these plans was as follows (in millions):

	Pension Benefits				Worldwide OPEB	
	U.S. Plans		Non-U.S. Plans			
	2016	2017	2016	2017	2016	2017
Change in Benefit Obligation						
Benefit obligation at January 1	$44,936	$45,746	$29,639	$30,624	$ 5,701	$ 5,865
Service cost	510	534	483	566	49	49
Interest cost	1,524	1,525	782	671	194	197
Amendments	—	—	—	—	14	—
Separation programs/other	(30)	35	71	17	—	1
Curtailments	—	(356)	2	(3)	—	—
Settlements	—	—	(131)	(52)	—	—
Plan participant contributions	27	24	22	20	20	24
Benefits paid	(2,966)	(3,267)	(1,252)	(1,316)	(382)	(368)
Foreign exchange translation	—	—	(2,576)	3,323	49	108
Actuarial (gain)/loss	1,745	2,099	3,584	248	220	293
Benefit obligation at December 31	45,746	46,340	30,624	34,098	5,865	6,169
Change in Plan Assets						
Fair value of plan assets at January 1	41,252	41,939	25,141	25,549	—	—
Actual return on plan assets	3,538	5,371	3,041	1,216	—	—
Company contributions	130	133	1,346	1,624	—	—

Ford Motor Company

The pre-tax net periodic benefit cost/(income) for our defined benefit pension and OPEB plans for the years ended December 31 was as follows (in millions):

	Pension Benefits						Worldwide OPEB		
	U.S. Plans			Non-U.S. Plans					
	2015	2016	2017	2015	2016	2017	2015	2016	2017
Service cost	$ 586	$ 510	$ 534	$ 532	$ 483	$ 566	$ 60	$ 49	$ 49
Interest cost	1,817	1,524	1,525	936	782	671	236	194	197
Expected return on assets	(2,928)	(2,693)	(2,734)	(1,480)	(1,339)	(1,375)	—	—	—
Amortization of prior service costs/(credits)	155	170	143	47	38	37	(204)	(142)	(120)
Net remeasurement (gain)/loss	1,964	900	(538)	(974)	1,876	407	(292)	220	293
Separation programs/other	17	12	74	39	81	18	1	—	2
Settlements and curtailments	—	—	(354)	—	2	(3)	—	—	—
Net periodic benefit cost/(income)	$ 1,611	$ 423	$(1,350)	$(900)	$1,923	$ 321	($ 199)	$ 321	$ 421

Chapter Preview

Financial presentation of pension plans and postretirement benefits is a critical part of financial statements of many companies. Most employers offer some type of benefit plan, and depending on the plan, the accounting and related disclosures can be extensive. We begin by describing the differences between defined contribution pension plans and defined benefit pension plans. After this, the chapter is devoted to the more complex topic of accounting for defined benefit pension plans. We explore the five components of the projected benefit obligation, prepare a reconciliation of plan assets, and learn how these two amounts help us determine the funded status of a pension plan. We then analyze the five components of pension expense. After exploring the assets, liabilities, and expenses related to pension plans, we record the related journal entries and demonstrate the various components in a pension worksheet. The financial statement presentation of pension amounts is explained as well as disclosure requirements. Appendices 19A and 19B are devoted to accounting for postretirement benefit plans.

Action Plan

LO	Topic/Subtopic	Page	Demos	Reviews	Assignments
LO 19–1	**Describe defined contribution plans and defined benefit plans and the measurement of related pension obligations** Defined Contribution :: Defined Benefit :: Pension Benefit Formula :: Projected Benefit Obligation :: Accumulated Benefit Obligation :: Vested Benefit Obligation	19-4	D19-1A D19-1B	R19-1	21, 22, 38, 39, 59, 60, 61, 62, 80, 83, 87,88, 90
LO 19–2	**Determine the five components of change in projected benefit obligation** Service Cost :: Interest Cost :: Prior Service Cost Adjustment :: Actuarial Gain/Loss on PBO :: Benefit Payments	19-9	D19-2	R19-2	23, 24, 25, 40, 41, 43, 59, 60, 64, 81, 82, 87
LO 19–3	**Reconcile pension plan assets and determine funded status** Plan Asset Reconciliation :: Plan Funded Status :: Underfunded :: Overfunded	19-11	D19-3A D19-3B	R19-3	26, 27, 28, 41, 42, 43, 45, 47, 59, 60, 64, 66, 69, 73, 74, 75, 76, 77, 81
LO 19–4	**Determine the five components of pension expense** Service Cost :: Interest Cost :: Expected Return on Plan Assets :: Prior Service Cost Amortization :: Pension Gain or Loss Amortization	19-15	D19-4	R19-4	29, 30, 31, 41, 44, 46, 47, 48, 49, 50, 59, 60, 63, 64, 65, 66, 69, 74, 75, 76, 78, 81, 89
LO 19–5	**Record prior service cost amendment, pension expense, gains and losses, funding, and benefits paid** Prior Service Cost Amendment :: Pension Expense :: Gain/Loss Deferral :: Funding Payment :: Benefit Payment	19-19	D19-5	R19-5	32, 33, 47, 49, 51, 52, 53, 54, 55, 56, 57, 58, 59, 60, 63, 66, 67, 71, 72, 73, 79, 81, 84, 86, 89
LO 19–6	**Describe the reporting of pensions in financial statements** Financial Statement Presentation :: Disclosure Requirements	19-23	D19-6	R19-6	34, 35, 36, 45, 52, 54, 58, 59, 60, 76, 77, 78, 84, 85, 89
LO 19–7	**Use a pension worksheet to record pension journal entries** Pension Worksheet :: Organizational Tool :: Presentation of Funded Status :: Journal Entries	19-26	D19-7	R19-7	37, 47, 51, 52, 53, 54, 55, 56, 57, 67, 68, 70, 71, 72, 84
LO 19–8	**APPENDIX 19A—Explain postretirement benefit plans and differences from pensions plans** Expected Postretirement Benefit Obligation :: Accumulated Postretirement Benefit Obligation :: Attribution Period	19-28	D19-8	R19-8	77, 89, 91, 92, 97, 102, 106, 107
LO 19–9	**APPENDIX 19B—Record postretirement benefit expense, gains and losses, funding, and benefits paid** Prior Service Cost Amendment :: Postretirement Benefit Expense :: Gain/Loss Deferral :: Funding Payment :: Benefit Payment	19-31	D19-9	R19-9	77, 93, 94, 95, 96, 99, 100, 101, 104
LO 19–10	**APPENDIX 19C—Allocate prior service cost using the service method** Prior Service Cost Amortization :: Service Method :: Service Years :: Straight-Line Method :: Average Service Period	19-34	D19-10	R19-10	98, 103, 105

Expanded Chapter Preview

Employers commonly offer pension benefits to employees as part of compensation packages. As we will see in LO 19-1, there has been a shift from defined benefit plans (where the *ultimate benefit* to the employee is established by a pension benefit formula) to defined contribution plans (where the employer's *contribution* to the plan is defined by formula). It is challenging for an employer to estimate a current obligation for how much will ultimately be paid to employees eligible to receive benefits at retirement (which could be 40 or more years into the future for an individual employee). The accounting requirements for *defined benefit plans* make up the bulk of this chapter starting with LO 19-2.

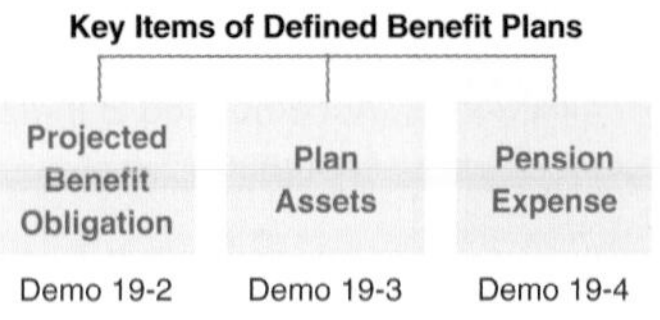

Key items in a defined benefit plan include:

- Employer's obligation to pay benefits to retirees called the **projected benefit obligation.**
- **Plan assets** or funds set aside and maintained with a trustee to pay the amounts due to retirees.
- Periodic **pension expense** which reduces net income for the current cost of having the plan.

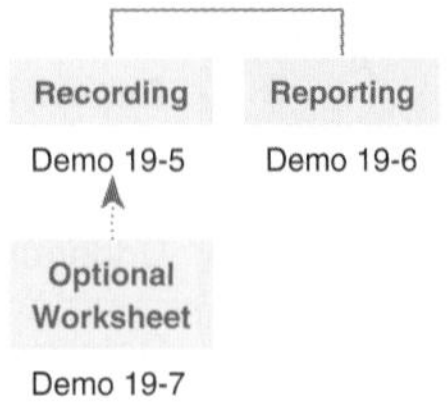

Once we explain these key items, we demonstrate the recording of journal entries, the reporting requirements, and preparing a pension worksheet. *To illustrate the accounting for defined benefit plans, we use the same company Taser Inc. in **Demo 19-2** through **Demo 19-7**.* To see how the pieces fit together for Taser Inc. let's preview these sections.

Taser Inc. PBO $118,550

Demo 19-2

We calculate the balance of the **projected benefit obligation** (PBO) for Taser Inc. to be $118,550 as of December 31, 2020. This is Taser Inc.'s best estimate of the present value of benefits that must be paid to employees when they retire.

Taser Inc. Plan Assets $120,000

Demo 19-3

We then calculate Taser's balance in **plan assets** to be $120,000 as of December 31, 2020. These are the funds set aside today to fulfill the pension obligation to be settled in the future. For Taser, its plan assets of $120,000 exceeds its estimated obligation of $118,550. This difference of $1,450 is recognized on the balance sheet as a *single net amount* (a net asset). (This is unusual for typical accounting practices where both assets and liabilities are reported at gross amounts on the balance sheet.)

Taser Inc. Pension Expense $16,300

Demo 19-4

We calculate total **pension expense** for 2020 to be $16,300 for Taser Inc. This represents the amount of pension cost allocated to the 2020 reporting period, and Taser's net income is reduced by this amount. It is the amount incurred as employees render services that earn the pension benefits. We explain certain changes in plan assets and the PBO that affect pension expense.

Recording

Demo 19-5

We then show recording of journal entries for Taser Inc. The ending account balances in the PBO ($118,550), plan assets ($120,000), and pension expense ($16,300) tie to the ending balances in the related T-accounts in Demo 19-5. While many pension related items affect pension expense, there are certain items that are deferred in OCI when incurred. This means that the impact of some items is not immediately reflected in the income statement but instead is shown as part of OCI. The process of moving deferred amounts from OCI to net income in a reporting period is completed through an amortization process. *This means we will see circumstances where a portion of the amounts deferred in Accumulated OCI is amortized (transferred) to pension expense.*

Reporting

Demo 19-6

We next illustrate the impact of the defined benefit plan on the company's financial statements: income statement, statement of comprehensive income, and balance sheet. We previewed some of these above such as the net asset amount of $1,450 on the balance sheet and pension expense of $16,300 on the income statement. We describe the detailed disclosure requirements for defined benefit plans.

Optional Worksheet

Demo 19-7

We conclude by illustrating the use of a pension worksheet. Use of a worksheet is optional and is used to summarize the steps described above in determining amounts to recognize in financial statements. Our final step is to report the impact of the pension plan on financial statements. This information is required for financial statement users to assess the status of the employer's pension arrangement and the effects on the company's financial position and results of operations. These disclosures enable financial statement users to better understand why reported items changed from period to period. This is especially important for defined benefit plans because only a single net amount is reported on the balance sheet as a net asset or a net liability. Disclosure requirements include a reconciliation of the PBO, a reconciliation of plan assets, and a presentation of pension expense components as described in LO 19-2, 19-3, and 19-4. This again highlights the importance of these three key components of a defined benefit plan.

Describe defined contribution plans and defined benefit plans and the measurement of related pension obligations

LO 19-1

Pension Plans
- **Defined Contribution Plan**
  - Employer's obligation established by contract
  - Retiree bears risk of fund performance
- **Defined Benefit Plan**
  - Retiree's benefit established by a pension benefit formula
  - Employer's obligation measured as the projected benefit obligation

LO 19-1 Overview

Company-sponsored retirement plans provide cash payments to employees during retirement. This is a benefit provided to employees in return for service to the company. The company contributes to investment accounts (through a trustee) as the employee is earning the retirement benefits.

Plans are **contributory** or **noncontributory**. A plan is contributory if the employees must provide the funding or if the employees voluntarily make payments to increase retirement benefits. In a noncontributory plan, the employer bears the full cost of the pension plan. A **qualified pension plan** offers certain tax benefits such as the deductibility of employer pension contributions and tax-free pension fund earnings. For a plan to be qualified, it must meet a number of requirements, including coverage of a minimum of 70% of employees.

A bank or trust company serving as the **trustee** invests the employer's contributions in a pension fund, makes retirement payments from the fund, and provides the employer with periodic updates. The **pension fund** is a *separate legal and reporting entity*, outside of the employer. A pension fund prepares its own separate set of financial statements. **Exhibit 19-1** summarizes relations among the parties in a pension plan when a trustee is used. **The focus of this chapter is on the accounting procedures of the employer only.**

Companies establish pension plans to increase employee motivation and productivity, reduce turnover, and compete for skilled workers. Pension costs can be a substantial part of total compensation costs for companies, and pension benefits are a significant portion of total income for many retirees.

EXHIBIT 19-1
Parties of a Pension Plan

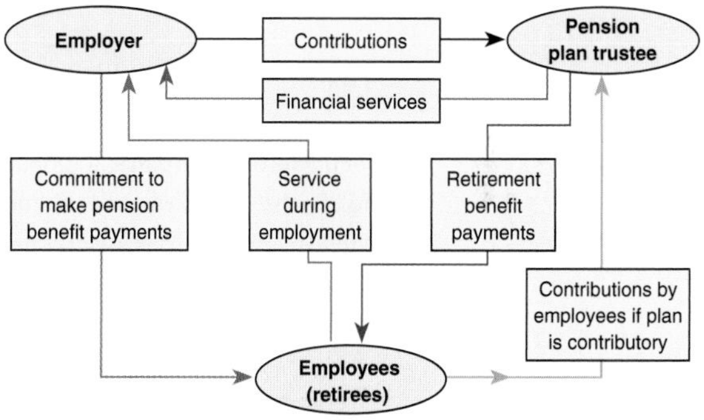

Defined Contribution Plan

In a **defined contribution plan**, contributions by an employer are established by formula. For example, a defined contribution plan might require an employer to contribute 3% of each eligible employee's monthly salary into a 401(k) plan. A 401(k) plan is a qualified defined contribution plan established under Section 401 of the Internal Revnue Code. In another example, an employer *matches* its contribution to the amount that the employee contributes. With a defined contribution plan, the employer makes no promise about the amount of future retirement benefits. Instead, the employee chooses how to invest the retirement funds and bears the risks and rewards of the fund's performance.

DEFINED CONTRIBUTION PLAN

Defined contribution plans are popular for employers because these plans shift the risk of investment performance to the employee. This means that the employer has no further responsibility regarding the benefit after the employer makes its required contribution to the plan. A portability feature is popular for employees because it allows an employee to maintain full pension benefits when changing employers. This is particularly important given the increasing frequency with which employees change jobs.

Pension expense is equal to the specified contribution paid or payable for the period as illustrated in **Demo 19-1A**. The company would record a pension asset (liability) if the company paid more (less) than the required contribution at a financial reporting date.

715-70-05-2 An employer's present obligation under the terms of a [defined contribution] plan is fully satisfied when the contribution for the period is made, provided that costs (defined contributions) are not being deferred and recognized in periods after the related service period of the individual to whose account the contributions are to be made.

A company must disclose the cost recognized for a defined contribution plan separately along with a description of significant changes as described in the accounting guidance.

715-70-50-1 An employer shall disclose the amount of cost recognized for defined contribution pension plans and for other defined contribution postretirement benefit plans for all periods presented separately from the amount of cost recognized for defined benefit plans. The disclosures shall include a description of the nature and effect of any significant changes during the period affecting comparability, such as a change in the rate of employer contributions, a business combination, or a divestiture.

Demo 19-1A **LO19-1** **Accounting for Defined Contribution Plan**

Demo MBC

IBN established a defined contribution plan in which the company contributes 5% of five full-time employees' salaries to a traditional 401(k) plan for each completed year of service. The amount of salaries eligible for the contribution totaled $500,000 in 2020. If IBN contributed the designated amount on December 15, 2020, record the related journal entry. Assume that financial statements are prepared annually.

Solution

Assets = Liabilities + Equity
−25,000 −25,000

Pension Expense 25,000 | Cash | 25,000

December 15, 2020—To record contribution to defined contribution plan

Pension Expense ($500,000 × 5%)	25,000	
Cash		25,000

FORD

Real World—DEFINED CONTRIBUTION PLAN

FORD MOTOR [F]

Ford Motor Company, a global automotive and mobility company based in Dearborn, Michigan, outlines the expense incurred on its defined contribution plans in a recent Form 10-K. While the defined benefit note extends across approximately *nine pages* in the Form 10-K, the following paragraph is the *only* disclosure related to the defined contribution plan. The obligation of the company is straightforward with a defined contribution plan.

Note 17 (excerpt): Retirement Benefits—*Defined Contribution and Savings Plans.* We also have defined contribution and savings plans for hourly and salaried employees in the United States and other locations. Company contributions to these plans, if any, are made from general Company cash and are expensed as incurred. The expense for our worldwide defined contribution and savings plans was $291 million, $340 million, and $377 million for the years ended December 31, 2015, 2016, and 2017, respectively. This includes the expense for Company-matching contributions to our primary employee savings plan in the United States of $124 million, $132 million, and $142 million for the years ended December 31, 2015, 2016, and 2017, respectively.

Defined Benefit Plan

A **defined benefit plan** commits the employer to specified retirement benefits. The benefits are established by a **pension benefit formula**. The employer's contributions must be sufficient, together with earnings from plan assets, to fund the benefits established by the pension benefit formula. *The employer bears the risk of pension fund performance.* The employer's responsibilities in a defined benefit plan differ significantly from its responsibilities in a defined contribution plan as shown in **Exhibit 19-2**. In a defined contribution plan, the employer must make contractually specified payment amounts into the pension fund. The employee directs the investments. If investment performance is poor and the fund loses value, the employee will have less money available at retirement. In a defined benefit plan, the employee is guaranteed to receive payments of a certain amount as defined by the pension benefit formula. The employer must manage the pension fund contributions and investments to assure sufficient money is available to pay the retirees the amounts to which they are entitled. If the pension plan investments perform poorly, the employer must increase the amount of its contributions to the plan. The contributions necessary to fund the benefits required under the plan must be estimated.

EXHIBIT 19-2
Defined Benefit vs. Defined Contribution: Employer Perspective

	CASH FLOW To Fund Pension Plan	CASH FLOW To Retirees for Benefits
Defined Contribution Plan	Specified *Employer funding is a contractual amount*	*Employer not involved*
Defined Benefit Plan	Estimated *Amount of funding changes each period*	Specified *Employer makes payment per benefit formula*

DEFINED BENEFIT PLAN

Consider the problem of forecasting the pension benefit payments for employees who will retire 20 years from now. Many plans base benefit payments on an employee's total service period and on salary levels near retirement. These future salary amounts must be estimated. The employer must also estimate when employees will actually retire and how many years of service the employees will have completed upon retirement. Inflation and interest rate changes also must be factored into the calculation. How long will employees receive benefit payments in retirement? A large number of estimates and assumptions must be made to measure a company's defined benefit pension liability.

Actuaries (professionals trained in a specific branch of mathematics and statistics) develop estimates of future retirement benefit payments needed to compute the employer's pension obligation for defined benefit plans. These estimates involve statistical models incorporating multiple variables, including turnover, inflation, future compensation levels, final retirement age, life expectancy, the interest rate used for discounting benefit payments, and administrative costs. Actuaries are an important part of pension accounting.

Pension Vesting

Exhibit 19-3 summarizes three different measures of the liability for pension benefits. Each of these alternatives was considered by standard setters when they required pension liabilities to be recognized. Current accounting standards require companies to estimate and recognize as a liability the pension benefit obligation (PBO). The PBO reflects the company's best estimate of the present value of benefits that must be paid to employees when they retire. As such, it includes estimates of future salary increases the employee will earn over his or her tenure with the company, as well as the probability that the employee will vest in those benefits by working for the required number of service years. However, there exist other measures of the pension obligation. The accumulated benefit obligation (ABO) is an estimate of the present value of benefits that would need to be paid to employees if their salary amounts remained constant until retirement. The estimated ABO is necessarily smaller than the PBO. Some feel the ABO is a more valid measure because it reflects only salary events that have happened as of the measurement date, while the PBO reflects salary events that have not yet happened. The vested benefit obligation (VBO) is that portion of the ABO in which the employees are vested as of the measurement date. The VBO is necessarily smaller than the ABO. The VBO is an estimate of the benefits the employees would be entitled to should they cease working for the firm at the measurement date. Some view the VBO as the most appropriate measure of the benefit liability as of the measurement date, while others view the assumption that employees cease working as incompatible with the going concern principle.

EXHIBIT 19-3
Measurement of Pension Obligations

Pension Obligation	Definition	Relevance
Vested benefit obligation (VBO)	Actuarial present value of the benefits attributed to employee service rendered to date, as measured by the benefit formula using *current salary levels, limited to vested benefits.*	Considered a measure of the minimum pension obligation at the measurement date.
Accumulated benefit obligation (ABO)	Actuarial present value of the benefits attributed to employee service rendered to date, as measured by the benefit formula using *current salary levels.*	A measure of pension obligation based on salary events that have occurred as of the measurement date. Required to be disclosed.
Projected benefit obligation (PBO)	Actuarial present value of the benefits attributed to employee service rendered to date, as measured by the benefit formula using *estimated future salary levels.* (If a pension benefit formula does not incorporate future salary levels, ABO and PBO are equal.)	Basis for measuring the pension obligation at the measurement date.

715-30-55-60 The projected benefit obligation reflects the actuarial present value of all benefits attributed to employee service rendered before the date of the employer's fiscal year-end statement of financial position . . . The measurement of that obligation shall be based on actuarial assumptions appropriate for the date of the employer's fiscal year-end statement of financial position (for example, turnover, mortality, discount rates, and so forth) and census data as of that date.

715-30-35-2 The accumulated benefit obligation differs from the projected benefit obligation in that it includes no assumption about future compensation levels. For plans with flat-benefit or non-pay-related pension benefit formulas, the accumulated benefit obligation and the projected benefit obligation are the same. The accumulated benefit obligation and the vested benefit obligation provide information about the obligation the employer would have if the plan were discontinued.

We quantify the three pension liability measures in **Demo 19-1B**. The calculation of the PBO has three steps:

1. Calculate the annual retirement annuity to be received based on the pension benefit formula, the years of service, and the expected ending salary.
2. Calculate the present value of the retirement annuity at the date of retirement.
3. Discount the amount determined in step 2 to calculate its present value as of the measurement date.

Calculation of ABO is identical to that of PBO except the current salary rather than the expected ending salary is used in step 1. Calculation of VBO is identical to that of ABO except the result obtained in step 3 is multiplied by the appropriate vesting percentage.

Demo 19-1B LO19-1 Estimating Pension Obligations

Nicole (age 40) started working at 5M on January 1, 2020, at a starting annual salary of $45,000. Nicole's expected retirement date is December 31, 2044, when her annual salary is estimated to be $150,000. Benefits vest as follows: 10% after the first year, 15% after the second year, and 20% each year after until 100%. Nicole's expected retirement period is 10 years. The relevant discount rate is 10%. 5M offers to its retired employees an annual pension equal to 2% of their final annual salary for each year worked.

Annual benefit payment during retirement = 2% × Number of service years × Final salary

a. Compute the annual benefit payment under (1) VBO, (2) ABO, and (3) PBO pension liability measurements. Assume pension benefits are paid at the end of each retirement year.

b. Compute the present value at retirement date of the retirement cash flow stream under (1) VBO, (2) ABO, and (3) PBO pension liability measurements.

c. Compute present value on December 31, 2020, of the retirement cash flow stream under (1) VBO, (2) ABO, and (3) PBO pension liability measurements.

Solution

a. **Annual Benefit Payment**

First, using the pension benefit formula, the annual benefit payment would be computed differently under the three obligation measurements.

1. VBO: $90 2% × 1 year × $45,000 (current salary) × 10% (vesting percentage)
2. ABO: $900 2% × 1 year × $45,000 (current salary)
3. PBO: $3,000 2% × 1 year × $150,000 (estimated future salary)

b. **Present Value of Retirement Cash Flow Stream at Retirement Date**

We compute the present value (at retirement date) of a 10-year, retirement cash flow stream (annuity) at a discount rate of 10%.

1. Present Value of the VBO Retirement Cash Flow Stream at Retirement Date

	RATE	NPER	PMT	PV	Excel Formula
Given	10%	10	(90)	?	=PV(0.1,10,−90)
Solution				$553	

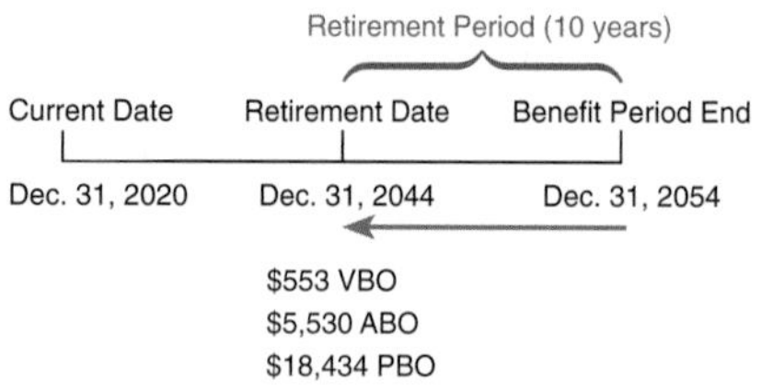

2. Present Value of the ABO Retirement Cash Flow Stream at Retirement Date

	RATE	NPER	PMT	PV	Excel Formula
Given	10%	10	(900)	?	=PV(0.1,10,−900)
Solution				$5,530	

3. Present Value of the PBO Retirement Cash Flow Stream at Retirement Date

	RATE	NPER	PMT	PV	Excel Formula
Given	10%	10	(3,000)	?	=PV(0.1,10,−3000)
Solution				$18,434	

continued

continued from previous page

c. **Present Value of Retirement Cash Flow Stream on December 31, 2020**

We discount the 10-year cash flow stream back to December 31, 2020, 24 years earlier.

1. Present Value of the VBO Retirement Cash Flow Stream on December 31, 2020

	RATE	NPER	PV	FV	Excel Formula
Given	10%	24	?	(553)	=PV(0.1,24,0,−553)
Solution			$56		

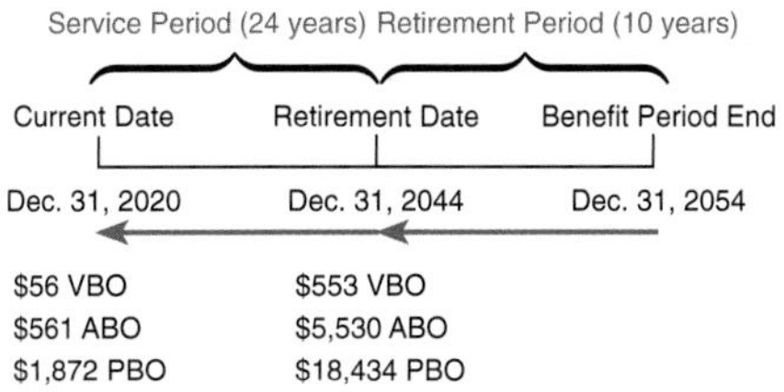

2. Present Value of the ABO Retirement Cash Flow Stream on December 31, 2020

	RATE	NPER	PV	FV	Excel Formula
Given	10%	24	?	(5,530)	=PV(0.1,24,0,−5530)
Solution			$561		

3. Present Value of the PBO Retirement Cash Flow Stream on December 31, 2020

	RATE	NPER	PV	FV	Excel Formula
Given	10%	24	?	(18,434)	=PV(0.1,24,0,−18434)
Solution			$1,872		

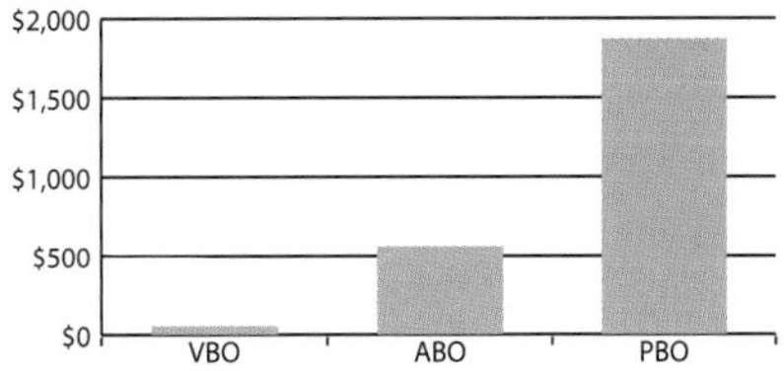

The PBO measure of $1,872 is the largest measure of the liability when compared to VBO and ABO as illustrated in the chart. This simplified example provides the foundation for the complex calculations performed by actuaries.

EXPANDING YOUR KNOWLEDGE **Shift to Defined Contribution Plan**

Defined contribution plans have grown in popularity at the expense of defined benefit plans. Regulatory and reporting burdens have increased for defined benefit pension plans. Defined benefit plans are costly and involve much risk to the employer. On the other hand, defined contribution plans are more flexible for the employee because the benefits are portable. Also, the ease of administering defined contribution plans makes them a popular choice for small businesses. The overall trend is for companies to establish new defined contribution plans and to settle or terminate existing defined benefit plans. Upon termination of a defined benefit plan, any effects on net income are recorded immediately.

ASC Glossary Settlement of a Pension or Postretirement Benefit Obligation: A transaction that is an irrevocable action, relieves the employer (or the plan) of primary responsibility for a pension or postretirement benefit obligation, and eliminates significant risks related to the obligation and the assets used to effect the settlement.

715-30-35-82 Recognition in earnings of gains or losses from settlements is required if the cost of all settlements during a year is greater than the sum of the service cost and interest cost components of net periodic pension cost for the pension plan for the year.

Defined Contribution and Defined Benefit Pension Plans LO19-1 REVIEW 19-1

Review MBC

Example One—Defined Contribution Plan

Jude Company established a defined contribution plan in which the company contributes 5% of full-time employees' salaries to a traditional 401(k) plan. The company made a specified cash payment of $300,000 to the plan on June 15, 2020. The amount of salaries eligible for the contribution totaled $600,000 in 2020. The company's final cash payment to the plan is due in January of the following year.

a. Record the entry on June 15, 2020, for the company's cash contribution to the plan.

b. Record any adjusting entries required on December 31, 2020.

Example Two—Defined Benefit Plan

Jude Company sponsors a pension plan with the following pension benefit.

continued

continued from previous page

$$\text{Benefit paid at each year-end during retirement} = \frac{(\text{Number of years worked} \times \text{Annual salary at retiremer}}{25}$$

Jude would like to estimate the pension obligation related to a new employee, Smith. Credit for service began January 1, 2010, Smith's first day with the company. Smith is expected to work a total of 25 years with an annual salary at retirement of $200,000. Smith is expected to draw 15 years of retirement benefits. The discount rate is 6%.

More Practice: 19-21, 19-22, 19-38, 19-39

a. Calculate the PBO on December 31, 2019, after which Smith has completed 10 years of service. Smith's current salary is $80,000.

Solution on p. 19-61.

b. Calculate the ABO on December 31, 2019.

LO 19-2 Determine the five components of change in projected benefit obligation

LO 19-2 Overview

PBO Reconciliation

	PBO, beginning balance
+	Service cost
+	Interest cost
+	Prior service cost adjustment
−/+	Actuarial gain/loss on PBO
−	Benefit payments
=	PBO, ending balance

The prior section estimated the PBO for one employee considering the pension benefit formula (using future salaries) and the time value of money. In practice the PBO is estimated by actuaries who must estimate the PBO for many employees simultaneously using much more complex assumptions. While the PBO at a point in time reflects the liability for pension obligations at that date, changes in the PBO over the period reflect changes, or flows occurring during the period. Some changes in the PBO are recognized as pension expense immediately, while other changes are recognized as a component of other comprehensive income.

715-30-35-1A The projected benefit obligation as of a date is the actuarial present value of all benefits attributed by the plan's benefit formula to employee service rendered before that date. The projected benefit obligation is measured using an assumption as to future compensation levels if the pension benefit formula is based on those future compensation levels . . . The projected benefit obligation is a measure of benefits attributed to service to date assuming that the plan continues in effect and that estimated future events (including compensation increases, turnover, and mortality) occur.

Component Changes in the Projected Benefit Obligation

The change in the projected benefit obligation (liability) over a period consists of five components: service cost, interest cost, prior service cost adjustment, actuarial gain or loss on the PBO, and benefit payments.

Service Cost

ASC Glossary Service cost— A component of net periodic pension cost recognized in a period determined as the actuarial present value of benefits attributed by the pension benefit formula to services rendered by employees during that period. The service cost component is a portion of the projected benefit obligation and is unaffected by the funded status of the plan.

Increase PBO
Increase Pension Exp

Service cost is the actuarial present value of additional pension benefits earned by employees based upon employee service in the current year actuarial present value of additional pension benefits earned by employees based upon employee service in the current year. It is based on the pension benefit formula and is influenced by factors such as changes in plan participants through promotions or early retirements, and salary increases. The amount of service cost is estimated by actuaries.

Interest Cost

ASC Glossary Interest cost—The amount recognized in a period determined as the increase in the projected benefit obligation due to the passage of time.

Increase PBO
Increase Pension Exp

Interest cost increases the PBO during a reporting period. Because the PBO is discounted to present value, the carrying value of the PBO will increase due to the passage of time. The recognition of interest cost on the PBO is similar to the accrual of interest on bonds issued at a discount and results in an increase to the liability and an increase in pension expense. (Interest cost is equal to the adjusted PBO balance at the beginning of the year multiplied by the discount rate—explained in more detail in a later section.)

Prior Service Cost Adjustment

ASC Glossary Prior service cost—The cost of retroactive benefits granted in a plan amendment. Retroactive benefits are benefits granted in a plan amendment (or initiation) that are attributed by the benefit formula to employee services rendered in periods before the amendment.

Increase PBO
Decrease OCI

Prior service costs (PSC) result from the granting of pension benefits for service provided *before* the pension plan began or from plan amendments granting increased pension benefits for service provided *before* a plan amendment. For example, if a company increases a payout percentage in its pension benefit formula retroactively to the past five years of service for all current employees, the company incurs prior service costs. A prior service cost adjustment results in an increase to the company's PBO. Prior service cost amendments will also impact other comprehensive income (instead of directly impacting net income), illustrated later in **Demo 19-5**. If on the other hand, a change in the pension benefit formula applies only to future years of service, the company records no prior service cost adjustment.

Actuarial Gain/Loss on PBO

ASC Glossary Gain or loss—A change in the value of either the benefit obligation . . . resulting from experience different from that assumed or from a change in an actuarial assumption, or the consequence of a decision to temporarily deviate from the other postretirement benefit substantive plan.

Increase PBO
Decrease OCI
or
Decrease PBO
Increase OCI

The PBO at any balance sheet date is the result of estimates and assumptions about employee turnover, life expectancy, interest rates, and other factors. Increases in the PBO due to changes in assumptions are called losses while decreases due to assumption changes are called gains. For example, an increase in beneficiaries' life expectancy will increase the PBO because benefits will be paid over a longer period of time. The opposite would happen if life expectancies decreased. To avoid fluctuations in pension expense, actuarial gains or losses on the PBO are recognized in other comprehensive income rather than directly in pension expense, as discussed in LO 19-5.

Benefit Payments

Decrease PBO
Decrease Plan assets

As employees reach retirement age and the company satisfies its obligation through cash payments made by the trust fund to employees, the PBO decreases. Thus, payments of benefits to retirees reduce the PBO.

In summary, PBO at the end of a reporting period is calculated as follows and is illustrated in **Demo 19-2**.

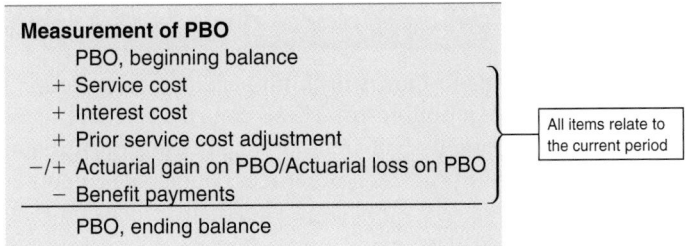

Measurement of PBO

	PBO, beginning balance
+	Service cost
+	Interest cost
+	Prior service cost adjustment
−/+	Actuarial gain on PBO/Actuarial loss on PBO
−	Benefit payments
	PBO, ending balance

All items relate to the current period

Recognizing Changes in the Projected Benefit Obligation **LO19-2** **Demo 19-2**

Demo MBC

Taser Inc. sponsored a defined benefit plan for full-time employees. Taser made contributions to plan assets that are maintained by a trustee. The purpose of the plan asset fund is to pay benefits to retired employees. The defined benefit plan has a PBO balance on January 1, 2020, of $95,000. Actuaries provided the following information for 2020: service cost, $12,000; interest cost, $8,550; actuarial loss on the PBO, $4,000; and benefits paid to retirees, $1,000. No changes were made to the plan in 2020 that created new prior service cost adjustments. Determine the projected benefit obligation balance on December 31, 2020.

continued

continued from previous page

Solution

PBO on December 31, 2020, is computed as follows.

Measurement of PBO

PBO, Jan. 1, 2020	$ 95,000
Service cost	12,000
Interest cost	8,550
Prior service cost adjustment	0
Actuarial loss on PBO	4,000
Benefit payments	(1,000)
PBO, Dec. 31, 2020	$118,550

EXPANDING YOUR KNOWLEDGE

Pension Protection Act of 2006 *and* Employment Retirement Income Security Act of 1974 (ERISA)

Among other things, the Pension Protection Act and ERISA protect pension holders in the following ways.

- Set minimum pension funding requirements for employers.
- Establish minimum vesting requirements (such as full vesting within 5 years or 20% within 3 years with 20% each subsequent year until 100%).
- Establish the Pension Benefit Guaranty Corporation to administer and make retirement payments for terminated pension plans. If a covered pension plan terminates with liabilities exceeding assets, the PBGC guarantees certain minimum benefits.
- Mandate extensive reporting to regulatory authorities that evaluate the plan's funded status and require pension fund audits.

REVIEW 19-2 **LO19-2** **Determine Changes in the Components of PBO**

Review MBC

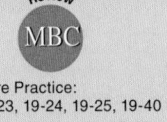

More Practice: 19-23, 19-24, 19-25, 19-40

Solution on p. 19-62.

University Inc. sponsors a defined benefit plan covering all employees. Benefits are based on years of service and compensation levels at the time of retirement. University's January 1, 2020, trial balance included a projected benefit obligation balance of $375,000. Assuming service cost of $85,000, interest cost of $22,000, an actuarial loss on the PBO of $2,800, and benefit payments of $46,000, what was the December 31, 2020, balance in the projected benefit obligation account?

LO 19-3 Reconcile pension plan assets and determine funded status

LO 19-3 Overview

Plan Assets Reconciliation

Plan assets, beginning balance
+/− Actual return on plan assets
\+ Employer contributions
− Benefit payments
= Plan assets, ending balance

Plan Funded Status

Underfunded
- PBO > Plan assets
- Recognize as a net liability

Overfunded
- Plan assets > PBO
- Recognize as a net asset

Setting aside resources to fulfill pension obligations is important both for planning and legal purposes. These contributions are recorded in the **Plan Assets** account. Certain regulations are in place that quantify minimum funding requirements for the protection of retirees. Companies report how investments measure up to the current estimate of a company's Pension Benefit Obligation when reporting funded status.

Reconciliation of Plan Assets

Plan assets are restricted to the payment of pension benefits and payment of costs for administering the pension plan. Plan assets are maintained by the trustee, not the employer. The trustee (such as a bank or trust company) is responsible for accepting employer contributions, investing the funds, accumulating the returns on the investments, and paying the retirees. The trustee prepares an annual report showing the beginning balance in plan assets, all changes during the year, and the ending balance.

ASC Glossary Plan Assets: Assets—usually stocks, bonds, and other investments—that have been segregated and restricted, usually in a trust, to provide for pension benefits. The amount of plan assets includes amounts contributed by the employer, and by employees for a contributory plan, and amounts earned from investing the contributions, less benefits paid.

Actual Return on Plan Assets

Plan assets measured at the end of a reporting period are adjusted for the actual return on investments. The actual return includes interest and dividend revenue and realized and unrealized gains and losses on plan assets. In a year when the markets are down, a company may have a negative return on investments. The reconciliation of changes in plan assets over a reporting period is illustrated below in **Demo 19-3A**.

Positive return:
Increase Plan assets
Increase OCI
or
Negative return:
Decrease Plan assets
Decrease OCI

Employer Contributions

The employer funds the pension plan by making cash contributions to the fund that is administered by the trustee. Contributions increase the plan assets (maintained by the trustee) and decrease the cash balance of the employer. The employer pays cash to the fund and not directly to the retirees.

Increase Plan assets
Decrease Cash

Benefit Payments

Benefit payments made to eligible retirees through the actions of the plan's administrator decrease plan assets. Retirees are paid directly from the fund resulting in no direct impact on the company's cash balance.

Decrease Plan assets
Decrease PBO

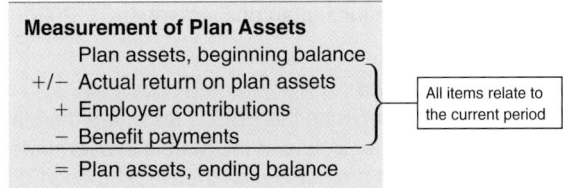

Measurement of Plan Assets

Plan assets, beginning balance
+/− Actual return on plan assets
\+ Employer contributions
− Benefit payments
= Plan assets, ending balance

All items relate to the current period

Reconcile Pension Plan Assets **LO19-3** **Demo 19-3A**

Continuing our example with Taser Inc. from **Demo 19-2**, the company's plan assets had a January 1, 2020, balance of $100,000. The 2020 actual return on plan assets is 6%. The company contributed $15,000 to the plan through the trustee. The trustee paid $1,000 of benefits to retirees of Taser. Calculate the balance of plan assets on December 31, 2020.

Solution

The December 31, 2020, balance in plan assets is calculated as follows.

Measurement of Plan Assets

Plan assets, Jan. 1, 2020	$100,000
Actual return on plan assets (6% × $100,000)	6,000
Employer contributions	15,000
Benefits paid	(1,000)
Plan assets, Dec. 31, 2020	$120,000

Financial Statement Reporting of Funded Status

On the balance sheet, companies will report the assets and liabilities related to the pension plan on a *net basis* as illustrated in **Demo 19-3B**. The net balance indicates the funded status of the pension plan. If the PBO is greater than plan assets, the plan is *underfunded* and the company reports a *net liability* balance on the balance sheet. If the PBO is less than plan assets, the plan is *overfunded* and the company reports a *net asset* on the balance sheet. If the PBO equals plan assets, the plan is *fully-funded*, and the net recognized amount on the balance sheet is zero. Most plans are underfunded. For example, the estimated aggregate funding level of pension plans sponsored by S&P 1,500 companies was 89% in May 2018. This means that, on average, pension funds were underfunded.

715-30-25-1 If the projected benefit obligation exceeds the fair value of plan assets, the employer shall recognize in its statement of financial position a liability that equals the unfunded projected benefit obligation. If the fair value of plan assets exceeds the projected benefit obligation, the employer shall recognize in its statement of financial position an asset that equals the overfunded projected benefit obligation.

Defined Benefit Pension Fund Information

$ millions	PBO Balance	Funded Status
Ford Motor	$80,438	$ (6,621)
Boeing	80,393	(16,382)
United Parcel Service. . . .	47,498	(4,233)

As a result of net presentation on the face of the balance sheet, financial statement users must review the notes accompanying the financial statements to obtain the gross PBO and Plan Asset balances. **These balances are required for a more complete understanding of a company's asset and liability position and may be required to update ratio analyses performed by financial statement users.**

Demo 19-3B LO19-3 Determination of Funded Status

Demo MBC

Taser Inc. calculated a December 31, 2020, projected benefit obligation balance of $118,550, and a plan asset balance of $120,000.

a. Determine the funded status and the balance sheet presentation of the defined benefit plan on December 31, 2020.

b. If instead, Taser calculated the fair value of plan assets of $115,000, and the projected benefit obligation balance of $118,550, determine the funded status and the balance sheet presentation of the defined benefit plan on December 31, 2020.

c. If instead, Taser calculated the fair value of plan assets of $118,550, and the projected benefit obligation balance of $118,550, determine the funded status and the balance sheet presentation of the defined benefit plan on December 31, 2020.

Solution

a. **Funded Status—Overfunded**

Taser's plan is overfunded because the PBO is less than the plan asset's fair value, as indicated in the following table. Because the plan is in overfunded status, the net balance of $1,450 would be reported as a *net asset* on the December 31, 2020, balance sheet of Taser.

Overfunded plan: PBO < Plan assets

Determination of Funded Status

Projected benefit obligation	$118,550
Plan assets at fair value	120,000
Funded status, Dec. 31, 2020	$ 1,450

b. **Funded Status—Underfunded**

If instead, Taser calculated ending plan assets at fair value of $115,000, Taser would report a *net liability* of $3,550 ($118,550 − $115,000) on its balance sheet.

Underfunded plan: PBO > Plan assets

Determination of Funded Status

Projected benefit obligation	$118,550
Plan assets at fair value	115,000
Funded status, Dec. 31, 2020	$ (3,550)

c. **Funded Status—Fully-Funded**

If Taser calculated the ending balance of plan assets at fair value of $118,550, no balance would be reported on the balance sheet on December 31, 2020, because the difference between the plan assets ($118,550) and the PBO ($118,550) is zero. Similar to unrecognized contingencies, a line item for funded status would appear in the liability section with a reference to the notes to financial statements for more information.

PBO ≈ Plan assets

Determination of Funded Status

Projected benefit obligation	$118,550
Plan assets at fair value	118,550
Funded status, Dec. 31, 2020	$ 0

FORD

Real World—FUNDED STATUS

FORD MOTOR [F]

Ford Motor Company reported the following information in a recent Form 10-K summarizing its funded status for its defined benefit plans. The U.S. Plans, the Non-U.S. Plans, and the Worldwide OPEB (other postretirement benefit) plans are all in underfunded status for the past two years.

Note 17 (excerpt): Retirement Benefits The year-end status of these plans was as follows (in millions):

	Pension Benefits					
	U.S. Plans		Non-U.S. Plans		Worldwide OPEB	
Change in Benefit Obligation	**2016**	**2017**	**2016**	**2017**	**2016**	**2017**
Benefit obligation at January 1	$44,936	$45,746	$29,639	$30,624	$ 5,701	$ 5,865
Service cost	510	534	483	566	49	49
Interest cost	1,524	1,525	782	671	194	197
Amendments	—	—	—	—	14	—
Separation programs/other	(30)	35	71	17	—	1
Curtailments	—	(356)	2	(3)	—	—
Settlements	—	—	(131)	(52)	—	—
Plan participant contributions	27	24	22	20	20	24
Benefits paid	(2,966)	(3,267)	(1,252)	(1,316)	(382)	(368)
Foreign exchange translation	—	—	(2,576)	3,323	49	108
Actuarial (gain)/loss	1,745	2,099	3,584	248	220	293
Benefit obligation at December 31	45,746	46,340	30,624	34,098	5,865	6,169
Change in Plan Assets						
Fair value of plan assets at January 1	41,252	41,939	25,141	25,549	—	—
Actual return on plan assets	3,538	5,371	3,041	1,216	—	—
Company contributions	130	133	1,346	1,624	—	—
Plan participant contributions	27	24	22	20	—	—
Benefits paid	(2,966)	(3,267)	(1,252)	(1,316)	—	—
Settlements	—	—	(131)	(52)	—	—
Foreign exchange translation	—	—	(2,612)	2,623	—	—
Other	(42)	(40)	(6)	(7)	—	—
Fair value of plan assets at December 31	41,939	44,160	25,549	29,657	—	—
Funded status at December 31	$ (3,807)	$ (2,180)	$ (5,075)	$ (4,441)	$(5,865)	$(6,169)

Reconciliation of Plan Assets and Determination of Plan's Funded Status LO19-3

REVIEW 19-3

Review MBC

Example One—Plan Asset Reconciliation

Raspberry Inc. implemented a defined benefit pension plan for its employees. The following data are provided for 2020.

Balance	Jan. 1, 2020	Activity	2020
Projected Benefit Obligation	$280,000 Cr.	Actual return on plan assets	$12,000
Plan Assets	300,000 Dr.	Benefits paid to employees	30,000
		Employer contributions	22,000

Calculate the fair value of plan assets on December 31, 2020.

Example Two—Funded Status

As of December 31, 2020, the projected benefit obligation and plan assets of a noncontributory defined benefit plan sponsored by Randall Inc. were

Projected Benefit Obligation	$480,000 Cr.
Plan Assets	466,000 Dr.

Determine the funded status of Randall Inc.'s pension plan.

More Practice:
19-26, 19-27, 19-28, 19-42

Solution on p. 19-62.

LO 19-4 Determine the five components of pension expense

LO 19-4 Overview

Components of Pension Expense
+ Service cost
+ Interest cost
− Expected return on plan assets
+ Amortization of prior service cost
−/+ Amortization of pension gain/loss

Pension expense (also referred to as **net periodic pension cost** for reporting purposes) is the amount of total pension cost allocated to each reporting period. Periodic pension expense is the sum of the five elements shown in the figure below.

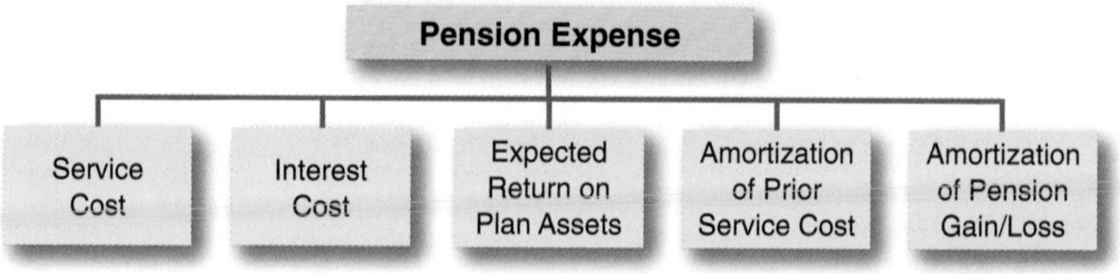

Defined Benefit Pension Fund Information

$ millions	Pension Exp. (Inc)	Pension Exp. (Inc) Divided by Revenue
Ford Motor	$(1,029)	−0.7%
Boeing	639	0.7%
United Parcel Service	1,449	2.2%

Service Cost

Service cost is the actuarial present value of additional pension benefits earned by employees as a result of completing additional service in the current year. Service cost increases pension expense and the PBO balance.

Interest Cost

Interest cost is the interest on the PBO for a given period. Interest cost is equal to the PBO balance at the beginning of the year (adjusted for any prior service cost amendment and pension gain or loss dated as of the beginning of the year), multiplied by the discount rate. Interest cost increases pension expense and the PBO balance. The interest rate or discount rate used to determine interest cost should reflect the rate at which the pension benefits could be effectively settled (this is why the discount rate is often referred to as the *settlement rate*). In estimating the discount rate, companies should look to available information about rates implicit in current prices of annuity contracts that could be used to settle the pension obligation.

715-30-35-8 The interest cost component of net periodic pension cost is interest on the projected benefit obligation, which is a discounted amount. Measuring the projected benefit obligation as a present value requires accrual of an interest cost at rates equal to the assumed discount rates.

715-30-35-43 Assumed discount rates shall reflect the rates at which the pension benefits could be effectively settled.

Expected Return on Plan Assets

Expected return on plan assets is calculated by multiplying the **expected rate of return** on plan assets by the **market-related value of plan assets** at the beginning of the reporting period, defined as follows.

ASC Glossary Market-Related Value of Plan Assets—A balance used to calculate the expected return on plan assets. The market-related value of plan assets is either fair value or a calculated value that recognizes changes in fair value in a systematic and rational manner over not more than five years.

The market-related value of plan assets reflects a smoothed average of fair values over a number of years; however, **for simplicity, we use fair value as the market-related value for pension calculations in this chapter.**

The expected rate of return on plan assets should reflect long-term expected yields of asset classes in which plan assets are invested. A company investing in less risky assets should expect a lower rate of return than a company investing in more risky assets. A positive *expected* return on plan assets reduces the computation of pension expense. When expected and actual returns on plan assets differ, a **gain/loss on plan assets** results. Pension expense is adjusted for expected return on plan assets and the gain/loss on plan assets is deferred as an adjustment to accumulated other comprehensive income as discussed in LO 19-5. However, in certain cases, amortization of pension gains/losses accumulated in OCI can affect pension expense as described below.

Amortization of Prior Service Cost

Recall that prior service cost increases the PBO (and decreases OCI) and results from the granting of additional pension benefits for services provided by employees in *prior years*. Although the entire adjustment is added to projected benefit obligation immediately (assuming increased benefits), the adjustment is amortized to pension expense over time. (This does impact interest cost for the year because interest is based on the PBO balance.)

Employers who increase pension benefits attributable to prior service are assumed to benefit in future periods from improved employee productivity and morale, reduced turnover, and reduced demand for pay raises. Therefore, the cost of retroactive benefits is subject to delayed recognition and is expensed or matched against the periods of benefit to the company (the average remaining service life of the employees affected by the prior service adjustment). While the accounting guidance suggests companies use the service method to allocate pension expense (illustrated in Appendix 19C) the guidance also indicates the **straight-line method** is acceptable, as long as more rapid amortization results.

715-30-35-11 A plan amendment that retroactively increases benefits (including benefits that are granted to retirees) increases the projected benefit obligation. The cost of the benefit improvement shall be recognized as a charge to other comprehensive income at the date of the amendment. . . That prior service cost shall be amortized as a component of net periodic pension cost by assigning an equal amount to each future period of service of each employee active at the date of the amendment who is expected to receive benefits under the plan.

715-30-35-13 To reduce the complexity and detail of the computations required, consistent use of an alternative approach that more rapidly amortizes the cost of retroactive amendments is acceptable. For example, a straight-line amortization of the cost over the average remaining service period of employees expected to receive benefits under the plan is acceptable.

Amortization of Pension Gain/Loss

We introduced two sources of pension gain/loss: actuarial gain/loss on the PBO (see LO 19-2) and gain/loss on plan assets (earlier in this section). Unlike typical gains and losses that are recognized in income when they occur, pension gains and losses are recognized in other comprehensive income. The rationale is that recognizing pension gains and losses as part of periodic pension expense in the period in which they occur would add too much volatility to pension expense. Deferring income statement recognition of gains and losses achieves **income smoothing**. Over time, incurred gains may offset incurred losses resulting in a relatively small net unrecognized gain or loss in accumulated other comprehensive income. However, if the balance grows too large, the company must begin amortizing it.

How does the FASB define whether an accumulated pension gain/loss is too large? If the unrecognized amount exceeds either 10% of the greater of the PBO at the beginning of the year (adjusted for any prior service cost amendment and pension gain or loss dated as of the beginning of the year) or the market-related value of plan assets at the beginning of the year, then the gain or loss is considered to be too large. Because balances that are less than 10% of the greater of plan assets or the PBO are not considered large, the 10% limit is called the acceptable **corridor**. Larger balances that fall outside the corridor limit are subject to amortization. Amortization of a net loss increases pension expense and increases other comprehensive income. Amortization of a net gain decreases pension expense and decreases other comprehensive income.

The minimum required amortization to be recognized (illustrated in **Exhibit 19-4**) is computed as follows.

$$\frac{\textbf{Accumulated OCI—Pension Gain/Loss, beginning of year in excess of Corridor lin}}{\textbf{Average remaining service period of employees expected to receive benefits}}$$

EXHIBIT 19-4
Corridor Approach

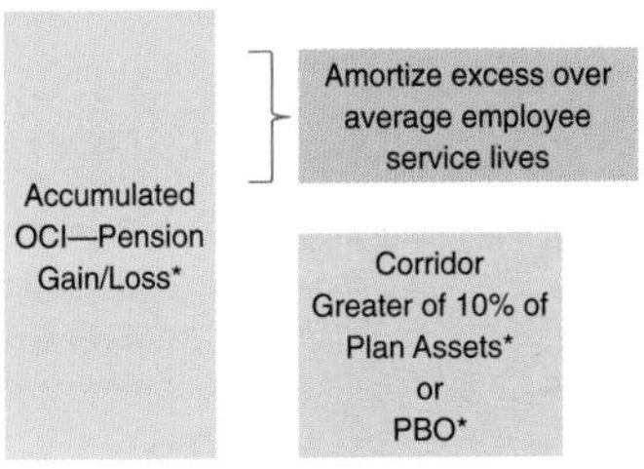

* Beginning of year balance

715-30-35-24 As a minimum, amortization of a net gain or loss included in accumulated other comprehensive income (excluding asset gains and losses not yet reflected in market-related value) shall be included as a component of net pension cost for a year if, as of the beginning of the year, that net gain or loss exceeds 10 percent of the greater of the projected benefit obligation or the market-related value of plan assets. If amortization is required, the minimum amortization shall be that excess divided by the average remaining service period of active employees expected to receive benefits under the plan. The amortization must always reduce the beginning-of-the-year balance. Amortization of a net gain results in a decrease in net periodic pension cost; amortization of a net loss results in an increase in net periodic pension cost.

The FASB allows a company to adopt any systematic method under certain conditions that results in faster recognition than the corridor approach as indicated in the accounting guidance. Based upon this guidance, companies can even elect to recognize the entire gain or loss directly on the income statement—see the excerpt from Ford Motor Company in the Real World segment below.

715-30-35-25 Any systematic method of amortizing gains or losses may be used in lieu of the minimum specified in the preceding paragraph provided that all of the following conditions are met:

a. The minimum is used in any period in which the minimum amortization is greater (reduces the net balance included in accumulated other comprehensive income by more).

b. The method is applied consistently.

c. The method is applied similarly to both gains and losses.

In summary, pension expense is calculated as follows as illustrated below in **Demo 19-4**.

Measurement of Pension Expense

+ Service cost
+ Interest cost
− Expected return on plan assets
+ Amortization of prior service cost
−/+ Amortization of pension gain/loss

Total pension expense*

*Net amount of net periodic pension cost recognized could be income rather than expense. Ford Motor Company reported net periodic pension income in 2017 of $1.4 billion. This was a result of expected return on plan assets and pension gains exceeding other components of pension expense.

FORD

Real World—IMMEDIATE RECOGNITION OF REMEASUREMENT GAINS/LOSSES

FORD MOTOR [F]

The following excerpt from Ford Motor Company describes the company's move from the corridor approach to immediate income statement recognition for remeasurement gains and losses on plan assets.

Note 1 (excerpt)—Presentation On December 31, 2015, we adopted a change in accounting method for certain components of expense related to our defined benefit pension and OPEB plans. Under the new method, we recognize remeasurement gains and losses immediately in net income and use fair value to calculate the expected return on plan assets. Historically, we recognized remeasurement gains and losses as a component of accumulated other comprehensive income/(loss) and amortized them as a component of net periodic benefit cost, subject to a corridor, over the remaining service period of our active employees.

Demo 19-4 **LO19-4** **Components of Pension Expense**

Demo MBC

Taser Inc. reports the following related to its defined benefit pension plan.

Account Balances	Jan. 1, 2020
Projected Benefit Obligation	$ 95,000 Cr.
Plan Assets (at fair value)	100,000 Dr.
Accumulated OCI—Prior Service Cost	12,500 Dr.
Accumulated OCI—Pension Gain/Loss	25,000 Dr.

Activity	2020
Service cost	$12,000
Actual return on plan assets	6,000
Actuarial loss on PBO (determined Dec. 31, 2020)	4,000
Contribution amount	15,000
Benefits paid	1,000
Prior service cost amortization	1,250

Other	
Expected rate of return on plan assets	7%
Discount (Settlement) rate	9%
Average remaining service period	10 years

continued

continued from previous page

Determine the following components of pension expense for Taser Inc. for 2020.

a. Service cost
b. Interest cost
c. Expected return on plan assets
d. Amortization of prior service cost—straight-line method
e. Amortization of pension gain/loss—corridor method
f. Calculation of total pension expense

Solution

a. **Service Cost**

Component of Pension Expense	
Service cost	$12,000

b. **Interest Cost**

Interest cost is calculated by multiplying the discount rate by the PBO balance at the beginning of the reporting period.

Component of Pension Expense	
Interest cost ($95,000 × 0.09)	$8,550

c. **Expected Return on Plan Assets**

Expected return on plan assets is calculated by multiplying the expected rate of return on plan assets by the fair value of plan assets at the beginning of the reporting period.

Component of Pension Expense	
Expected return on plan assets ($100,000 × 0.07)	$(7,000)

Taser incurred an unexpected loss of $1,000 (expected return on plan assets of $7,000 less actual return on plan assets of $6,000). This is not recognized as part of current period pension expense. See **Demo 19-5** to see how this is recorded.

d. **Amortization of Prior Service Cost**

The prior service cost is amortized over the average remaining service period.

Component of Pension Expense	
Prior service cost amortization ($12,500/10 service years)	$1,250

e. **Amortization of Pension Gain/Loss—Corridor Method**

The corridor is calculated as follows.

10% × $100,000* = $10,000

*Greater of the beginning of year PBO ($95,000) or plan assets ($100,000).

The excess of the beginning balance of Accumulated OCI—Pension Gain/Loss over the corridor of $10,000 is amortized over the average remaining service years of 10.

$$\frac{\text{Accumulated OCI—Pension Gain/Loss, January 1, 2020} - \text{Corridor}}{\text{Average remaining service period}} = \frac{\$25{,}000 - \$10{,}000}{10 \text{ years}} = \frac{\$15{,}000}{10} = \$1,$$

Component of Pension Expense	
Amortization of Accumulated OCI—Pension Gain/Loss	$1,500*

* Amount represents a loss.

f. **Calculation of Total Pension Expense**

The five components of pension expense for Taser Inc. are totaled below.

Components of Pension Expense (2020)	
Service cost	$12,000
Interest cost	8,550
Expected return on plan assets	(7,000)
Amortization of prior service cost	1,250
Amortization of net pension loss	1,500
Total pension expense	$16,300

UPS

Real World—PENSION EXPENSE

UNITED PARCEL SERVICE [UPS]

United Parcel Service (UPS) reported the following information regarding its benefit plans in a recent Form 10-K. Included in its pension expense total of $1,394 million for 2017 are the five components of pension expense described in LO 19-4.

Note 4 Company-Sponsored Employee Benefit Plans Information about net periodic benefit cost for the company-sponsored pension and postretirement benefit plans is as follows (in millions).

U.S. Pension Benefits	2017	2016	2015
Net Periodic Benefit Cost:			
Service cost	$1,543	$1,412	$1,527
Interest cost	1,813	1,828	1,694
Expected return on assets	(2,883)	(2,516)	(2,489)
Amortization of prior service cost	192	166	168
Actuarial (gain) loss	729	2,520	70
Curtailment and settlement loss	—	—	—
Net periodic benefit cost	$1,394	$3,410	$ 970

REVIEW 19-4 **LO19-4** **Components of Pension Expense**

Review MBC

Alexa Company started a noncontributory, defined benefit pension plan on January 1, 2019. The records of Alexa Company indicate the following for the year of 2020.

Account Balances	Jan. 1, 2020
Projected Benefit Obligation	$75,000 Cr.
Plan Assets	81,000 Dr.
Accumulated OCI—Pension Gain/Loss	12,900 Dr.
Accumulated OCI—Prior Service Cost	8,000 Dr.

Activity	2020
Service cost	$18,000
Amortization of prior service cost	1,000
Pension benefits paid	(500)
Actual earnings on plan assets (same as expected return)	4,000
Employer contribution	15,000

More Practice: 19-29, 19-30, 19-31, 19-44

Solution on p. 19-62.

Compute net pension expense for 2020 using the corridor approach to amortize any applicable pension gain/loss over a 10-year average remaining service period. Assume a discount rate of 6%.

LO 19-5 Record prior service cost amendment, pension expense, gains and losses, funding, and benefits paid

LO 19-5 Overview

Pension Plan Recording (as applicable)
- Record prior service cost amendment
- Record pension expense
- Record deferral of pension gain/loss
- Record employer contributions
- Record benefits paid

In the last section we examined the types of adjustments that affect accumulated OCI: prior service cost and pension gain/loss. In this section, we explain the journal entries to record these items for the pension plan of Taser Inc. in **Demo 19-5**. We also present journal entries related to funding the plan and paying benefits.

Recording Prior Service Cost Amendment

OCI—Prior Service Cost . . . . . . #
PBO . . . . #

When a company retroactively grants credit for prior service, the company debits OCI—Prior Service Cost and credits Projected Benefit Obligation to recognize the cost (assuming an increase in benefits). The adjusted beginning of year PBO balance (after the effect of the prior service cost amendment) is then used for any calculations requiring the beginning of year PBO, such as the interest cost calculation. The adjustment for a prior service cost amendment is illustrated in **Review 19-5**.

Recording Pension Expense

We summarize the effect on pension expense in a single entry in **Demo 19-5**. We explain each component of that entry as follows.

- Service cost: Debit Pension Expense and credit PBO.
- Interest cost: Debit Pension Expense and credit PBO.
- Expected return on plan assets: For an expected positive return, debit Plan Assets and credit Pension Expense. (In the next section, Plan Assets is adjusted to reflect *actual* return instead of *expected* return on plan assets.)
- Amortization of prior service cost: debit Pension Expense and credit OCI—Prior Service Cost.
- Amortization of pension gain/loss: credit (debit) Pension Expense and debit(credit) OCI—Pension Gain/Loss.

Pension Expense	#
Plan Assets	#
PBO	#
OCI—PSC	#
OCI—Gain/Loss	# or #

Recording Deferral of Pension Gains and Losses

We discussed how gain/loss on the PBO and gain/loss on plan assets do *not* affect net income unless they fall outside the acceptable corridor and must be amortized. Instead these gains or losses are deferred in other comprehensive income when incurred. To record an unexpected gain(loss) on plan assets, other comprehensive income and plan assets are both increased(decreased). As a result, the account Plan Assets, is now adjusted to reflect actual return on plan assets. To defer an actuarial gain(loss) on the PBO determined by the actuaries, other comprehensive income is increased(decreased), and the projected benefit obligation is decreased(increased).

To defer gain:
Plan Assets .... #
OCI—Pension Gain/Loss .... #

To defer loss:
OCI—Pension Gain/Loss .... #
Plan Assets .... #

To defer gain:
PBO .... #
OCI—Pension Gain/Loss .... #

To defer loss:
OCI—Pension Gain/Loss .... #
Plan Assets .... #

Recording Employer Contributions

When a company funds its pension plan, an amount is paid to the trustee who manages the fund investments. The company records a debit to Plan Assets and a credit to Cash. The amount of funding is based upon factors including legal minimum funding requirements, tax consequences, and cash flow capabilities.

Plan Assets .... #
Cash .... #

Recording Benefits Paid

A trustee will make payments from the plan assets to eligible retirees based upon the pension benefit formula. The payment of benefits reduces the company's pension obligation and plan assets resulting in a debit to Projected Benefit Obligation and a credit to Plan Assets.

PBO .... #
Plan Assets .... #

Recording the Impact of Defined Benefit Plan — LO19-5 — Demo 19-5

Using the information from **Demo 19-4** for Taser Inc., provide the following journal entries for 2020 to record the activity related to its defined benefit plan. Taser Inc. did not incur a *new* amendment for prior service cost in 2020.

a. Record pension expense.
b. Record the deferral of current year pension losses.
c. Record the funding of plan assets.
d. Record the payment of retiree benefits.

Solution

a. **Recording Pension Expense**

Recall our analysis from Demo 19-4 where we determined the components of pension expense.

Components of Pension Expense (2020)	
Service cost	$12,000
Interest cost	8,550
Expected return on plan assets	(7,000)
Amortization of prior service cost	1,250
Amortization of net pension loss	1,500
Total pension expense	$16,300

continued

continued from previous page

Assets = Liabilities + Equity
+7,000 +20,550 −16,300 +1,250 +1,500

The journal entry to record pension expense follows.

December 31, 2020—To record pension expense

Pension Expense	16,300	
Plan Assets	7,000	
Projected Benefit Obligation ($12,000 + $8,550)		20,550
OCI—Prior Service Cost		1,250
OCI—Pension Gain/Loss		1,500

b. **Recording Deferral of Pension Gains and Losses**
The following entries are required to defer (1) the unexpected loss on plan assets of $1,000 and (2) the actuarial loss on the PBO of $4,000. First, to defer the unexpected loss on plan assets of $1,000, other comprehensive income (rather than net income) and plan assets are both reduced. As a result, the account Plan Assets, is now adjusted for actual return on plan assets. The $7,000 expected return on plan assets from the pension expense entry (above) less the $1,000 unexpected gain (below), results in a net increase to plan assets of $6,000 which is equal to the actual return on plan assets.

Assets = Liabilities + Equity
−1,000 −1,000

December 31, 2020—To defer unexpected loss on plan assets to OCI

OCI—Pension Gain/Loss	1,000	
Plan Assets ($7,000 − $6,000)		1,000

Secondly, to defer the actuarial loss on the PBO (determined by the actuaries as of December 31, 2020) other comprehensive income is decreased (rather than net income) and the projected benefit obligation is increased.

Assets = Liabilities + Equity
+4,000 −4,000

December 31, 2020—To defer actuarial loss on PBO to OCI

OCI—Pension Gain/Loss	4,000	
Projected Benefit Obligation		4,000

(While these current year losses are recorded in OCI, remember that a portion of the *beginning* balance of Accumulated OCI—Pension Gain/Loss was amortized in the pension expense entry above because it exceeded the corridor. Amortization is always based on the beginning balance of Accumulated OCI—Pension Gain/Loss, therefore adjustments made during the year will not affect amortization.)

c. **Recording Employer Contributions**
Taser Inc. records the following entry for the funding of its pension plan.

Assets = Liabilities + Equity
+15,000
−15,000

December 31, 2020—To record funding of pension plan

Plan Assets	15,000	
Cash		15,000

d. **Recording Benefits Paid**
Taser Inc. records the following entry for the payment of benefits to retirees.

Assets = Liabilities + Equity
−1,000 −1,000

December 31, 2020—To record benefits paid to retirees

Projected Benefit Obligation	1,000	
Plan Assets		1,000

The following T-accounts for Taser Inc. illustrate how pension expense is affected by changes in the PBO, plan assets, and accumulated OCI accounts.

- Service cost and interest cost directly affect pension expense.
- While *expected* return on plan assets of $7,000 impacts pension expense, plan assets is adjusted for *actual* return on plan assets of $6,000 (equal to $7,000 minus $1,000) and the unexpected loss of $1,000 is deferred in OCI.
- Adjustments to prior service cost are deferred in OCI and only amortization of PSC affects pension expense.
- While current year losses (on the PBO and on plan assets) are deferred in OCI, the only impact on pension expense is for amortization of the beginning balance of accumulated OCI using the corridor approach.

continued

continued from previous page

Plan Assets

Beg. bal.	**100,000**		
(a) Expected returns	7,000	1,000	(b) Loss on plan assets
(c) Plan contrib.	15,000	1,000	(d) Benefits pd.
End. bal.	**120,000**		

Demo 19-3A

Cash

		15,000	(c) Plan contrib.
		15,000	**End. bal.**

PBO

(b) Benefits paid	1,000	**95,000**	**Beg. bal.**
		12,000	(a) Serv. cost
		8,550	(a) Int. cost
		4,000	(b) Act. loss on PBO
		118,550	**End. bal.**

Demo 19-2

Pension Expense

(a) Service cost	12,000	7,000	(a) Expected return
(a) Interest cost	8,550		
(a) PSC amort.	1,250		
(a) Pens. gain/loss adjust	1,500		
End. bal.	**16,300**		

Demo 19-4

OCI—Prior Service Cost

Close to AOCI	1,250	1,250	(a) Amort.
		0	**End. bal.**

OCI—Pension Gain/Loss

(b) Act. loss on PBO	4,000	1,500	(a) Amort.
(b) Loss on plan assets	1,000	3,500	Close to AOCI
End. bal.	**0**		

Just as net revenue and expense accounts are closed out to retained earnings at the end of a reporting period, OCI accounts are closed out to Accum. OCI accounts:

Accum. OCI—PSC

Beg. Bal.	**12,500**	1,250	Close OCI—Pens G/L
End. Bal.	**11,250**		

Accum. OCI—Pension Gain/Loss

Beg. Bal.	**25,000**		
Close OCI—Pens G/L	3,500		
End. Bal.	**28,500**		

EXPANDING YOUR KNOWLEDGE — Recording as Pension Asset (Liability)

Instead of separately recording in journal entries the pension asset and projected benefit obligation as we have demonstrated, some companies record amounts in a net account: Pension Asset (Liability). In either case, the *net amount* of pension asset and projected benefit obligation (PBO) is always recognized on the balance sheet.

Recording the Impact of a Defined Benefit Plan

LO19-5 **REVIEW 19-5**

Review MBC

The following data relate to a pension plan for BMXX Inc.

Account Balances	Jan. 1, 2020
Projected Benefit Obligation	$300,000 Cr.
Plan Assets	350,000 Dr.
Accumulated OCI—Pension Gain/Loss	5,000 Dr.

Activity	2020
Service cost	$33,000
Contributions to pension fund	40,000
Benefits paid to retirees	22,000
Expected return on plan assets	15,000
Actual return on plan assets	16,000

Other	
Prior service cost amendment on January 1, 2020 (relates to an employee group with an average remaining service period of 10 years; use straight-line method)	$30,000

Provide the entries to record pension activity for 2020 assuming a discount rate of 5%. Instead of using the corridor approach to amortize Accumulated OCI—Pension Gain/Loss, we amortize the account using the straight-line method over 10 years (an alternative, systematic approach resulting in a higher amortization amount).

More Practice: 19-32, 19-33, 19-50

Solution on p. 19-62.

LO 19-6 Describe the reporting of pensions in financial statements

LO 19-6 Overview

Pension Reporting
- Income statement
- Statement of comprehensive income
- Stockholders' equity statement
- Balance sheet
- Disclosure requirements

The entries in the prior section result in account balances that are reported in a company's financial reports and note disclosures. We summarize how pensions are reported in the income statement, statement of comprehensive income, stockholders' equity statement, and the balance sheet. We then continue with the Taser Inc. example to illustrate how accounts are shown on its financial statements in **Demo 19-6**.

Income Statement

Components of pension expense are recognized in the income statement as follows: service cost is included with other employee compensation costs within operations (if the subtotal is presented) while the remaining components of pension expense are included outside of operating income.

Sales
Operating expenses (includes service costs)
Operating income
Other revenue (expenses), net
Other components of net periodic pension cost
Net income

715-20-45-3A An employer shall report in the income statement:

a. The service cost component of net periodic pension cost and net periodic postretirement benefit cost in the same line item or items as other compensation costs arising from services rendered by the pertinent employees during the period (except for the amount being capitalized, if appropriate, in connection with the production or construction of an asset such as inventory or property, plant, and equipment).

b. The other components. . . separately from the service cost component and outside a subtotal of income from operations, if one is presented. If a separate line item or items are used to present the other components, that line item or items shall be described appropriately.

Statement of Comprehensive Income and Statement of Stockholders' Equity

Other comprehensive income is affected by the following pension related items (net of tax) within a statement of comprehensive income.

Net income
Other comprehensive income
(Deferral of pension loss)
Amortization of pension loss
Deferral of pension gain
(Amortization of pension gain)
(Prior service cost adjustment for additional benefits)
Amortization of prior service cost
Comprehensive income

The other comprehensive income (OCI) accounts are accumulated in accumulated OCI accounts. Both the activity during the period and the balances in the accumulated OCI accounts are shown on the statement of stockholders' equity. The ending balances of the accumulated OCI accounts are carried over to the balance sheet.

Balance Sheet

The net pension asset or net pension liability is recognized on the balance sheet. A net pension asset is presented as a noncurrent asset labeled **Prepaid pension cost, net**. A net pension liability is presented as current or noncurrent depending on whether the benefit obligation is due within the next 12 months. A net pension liability is labeled **Accrued pension cost, net.** If a company has more than one pension plan, plans with a net asset balance may be combined together while plans with a net liability balance may be combined together. Companies may *not* combine a plan with a net asset balance with a plan with a net liability balance on the balance sheet.

Net pension asset: Plan assets > PBO

Net pension liability: PBO > Plan assets

Note disclosure: PBO ≈ Plan assets

715-30-25-2 The employer shall aggregate the statuses of all overfunded plans and recognize that amount as an asset in its statement of financial position. It also shall aggregate the statuses of all underfunded plans and recognize that amount as a liability in its statement of financial position.

A net pension asset is presented as a noncurrent asset, while a net pension liability may be recorded as a current liability, noncurrent liability, or as a combination of both as indicated in the accounting guidance.

715-20-45-3 An employer that presents a classified statement of financial position shall classify the liability for an underfunded plan as a current liability, a noncurrent liability, or a combination of both. The current portion (determined on a plan-by-plan basis) is the amount by which the actuarial present value of benefits included in the benefit obligation payable in the next 12 months, or operating cycle if longer, exceeds the fair value of plan assets. The asset for an overfunded plan shall be classified as a noncurrent asset in a classified statement of financial position. The amount classified as a current liability is limited to the amount of the plan's unfunded status recognized in the employer's statement of financial position.

The ending balance in accumulated OCI accounts would be included on the balance sheet. (Although not emphasized in this chapter, the contributions to the pension plan would be included in the operating section of the statement of cash flows. In addition, an increase (decrease) to the net pension cost asset/liability is added (subtracted) to (from) net income in the operating section of the statement of cash flows.)

Pension Plan Reporting

LO19-6 **Demo 19-6**

Demo MBC

Considering the entries for Taser Inc. from **Demo 19-5**, present the effect on the following financial statements.

a. Income statement *b.* Statement of comprehensive income *c.* Balance sheet

Solution

a. **Income Statement** The following income statement excerpt illustrates the inclusion of pension expense ($16,300 shown in two parts as $12,000 and $4,300) related to Taser's defined benefit plan.

Income Statement	2020
Revenue	$ #
Operating expenses (includes $12,000 of service costs)	#
Operating income	#
Other components of net periodic pension cost	4,300
Net income	$ #

b. **Statement of Comprehensive Income** The following abbreviated statement of comprehensive income illustrates the presentation of other comprehensive income accounts related to Taser's defined benefit plan. This example ignores income taxes but other comprehensive income should be shown net of tax.

Statement of Comprehensive Income	2020
Net income	$ #
Other comprehensive income (loss)	
Loss due to actuarial change in PBO	(4,000)
Unexpected loss on plan assets	(1,000)
Amortization of prior service cost	1,250
Amortization of pension loss	1,500
Comprehensive income	$ #

continued

continued from previous page

c. **Balance Sheet** The following balance sheet excerpt illustrates the inclusion of pension related accounts in the noncurrent asset section and the stockholders' equity section.

Balance Sheet	Dec. 31, 2020
Assets	
Noncurrent assets	
Prepaid pension cost, net ($118,550 − $120,000) . . .	$ 1,450
Liabilities	
Stockholders' equity	
Accumulated other comprehensive income	
Net pension loss	(28,500)
Prior service cost.	(11,250)

Disclosure Requirements

Disclosure requirements for defined benefit pension plans are extensive so as to provide useful information to investors and creditors who are trying to assess the company's obligation to fulfill pension requirements. Due to the volatility of the liability and the nature of the assumptions needed to estimate the liability, a number of items are reported by companies in their annual reports. Disclosure requirements (outlined in ASC 715-20-50-1) include the following.

- Reconciliation of beginning and ending balances of the PBO.
- Reconciliation of beginning and ending balances of the fair value of plan assets.
- Funded status of the plans and the amounts recognized on the balance sheet.
- Information on how investment allocation decisions are made.
- Fair value of each class of plan assets.
- Description of rate assumptions used.
- Accumulated benefit obligation.
- Benefits expected to be paid in each of the next five years, and in the aggregate for the next five years.
- Estimate of contributions expected to be paid to the plan during the next year.
- Amount (and components) of net benefit cost recognized.
- Pension gain/loss and net prior service cost or credit recognized in OCI.
- Amounts in accumulated OCI.
- On a weighted-average basis, assumptions used in accounting for the plans.
- Explanation of significant changes made in assumptions.

Nonpublic companies are not required to provide a reconciliation of the beginning and ending balance of the PBO and fair value of plan assets.

Management Judgment

Nearly every aspect of accounting for defined benefit plans requires judgment. The assumptions used directly impact the derived pension amounts. In the Taser Inc. example, let's consider how just three changes in assumptions would change the accounting results.

1. A change in the service cost estimate from $12,000 to $18,000 would increase pension expense and the PBO. Service cost is not an objective value as it is based on many assumptions such as the assumption of the final salary of an employee (before retirement).
2. The discount rate could change from 9% to 10%. This may increase or decrease pension expense and the PBO. For example, a higher rate is applied to the PBO which will be lower because the present value of the pension obligations will be discounted at a lower rate.

3. The expected rate of return could change from 7% to 6.5%. This would increase pension expense without affecting the PBO.

Changes in assumptions not only impact the amounts recognized on financial statements (pension expense and net pension asset/liability), but changes in assumptions impact the amount of funding contributions to the pension fund required by the company.

FORD

Real World—EXPECTED FUTURE BENEFIT PAYMENTS

FORD MOTOR [F]

Ford Motor Company reported the following expected future benefit payments for five years in a recent Form 10-K.

Note 17 (excerpt): Retirement Benefits—The expected future benefit payments at December 31, 2017 were as follows (in millions):

	Pension		
Benefit Payments	**U.S. Plans**	**Non-U.S. Plans**	**Worldwide OPEB**
2018	$ 2,960	$1,360	$ 350
2019	2,860	1,240	350
2020	2,850	1,260	340
2021	2,840	1,280	340
2022	2,820	1,290	340
2023–2027	14,200	6,850	1,690

Reporting a Defined Benefit Pension Plan

LO19-6 REVIEW 19-6

Review MBC

The following data relate to a pension plan for Vilas Inc.

Account Balances	Dec. 31, 2020
Projected Benefit Obligation	$310,000 Cr.
Plan Assets	350,000 Dr.
Accumulated OCI—Prior Service Cost	40,000 Dr.
Accumulated OCI—Pension Gain/Loss	12,000 Dr.

Activity	2020
Pension expense, including service cost of $50,000	$75,000
Unexpected gain on plan assets	8,500
Amortization of prior service costs	2,500

Use the information for Vilas Inc. to present the effect on the following financial statements.

a. Income statement *b.* Statement of comprehensive income c. Balance sheet

More Practice: 19-35, 19-36

Solution on p. 19-63.

Use a pension worksheet to record pension journal entries

LO 19-7

Pension Worksheet
- Organizational tool
- Presentation of funded status
- Source for recording end of period pension journal entries

LO 19-7 Overview

A pension worksheet is a tool used to organize the effects on pension accounts and for calculating ending balances in pension accounts—see **Demo 19-7**. The worksheet illustrates the changes in plan assets, projected benefit obligation, pension expense, and accumulated other comprehensive income accounts examined in this chapter. The worksheet also provides the funded status both at the beginning and end of the period. The information provided in the worksheet can be used to record end of period pension entries.

In completing the worksheet, first enter beginning balances. Next, enter both sides of the journal entries for the prior service cost amendment, service cost, interest cost, expected return on plan assets, unexpected gain or loss on plan assets, gain or loss on the PBO (provided by actuaries), prior service cost amortization, net pension gain or loss amortization, fund contributions, and benefit payments. Fill in the *Net Pension Asset/Liability* column by subtracting the projected benefit obligation from plan assets. Total all columns (except for the cash column) to arrive at ending balances.

Demo 19-7 LO19-7 Preparation of a Pension Worksheet

Demo MBC

Assume the following information for Taser Inc. used in previous demonstrations.

Account Balance Jan. 1, 2020	
Projected Benefit Obligation	$ 95,000 Cr.
Plan Assets	100,000 Dr.
Accumulated OCI—Prior Service Cost	12,500 Dr.
Accumulated OCI—Pension Gain/Loss	25,000 Dr.

Activity	2020
Service cost	$12,000
Actual return on plan assets	6,000
Actuarial loss on PBO (determined December 31, 2020)	4,000
Contribution to pension fund	15,000
Benefit payments	1,000
Prior service cost amortization	1,250

Other	
Expected rate of return on plan assets	7%
Discount rate	9%
Average remaining service period	10 years

Required

Record the pension activity directly into a pension worksheet for Taser Inc.

Solution

	Reported Net in Financial Statements		Reported in Balance Sheet				Reported in Comprehensive Income		
	A	B	(A-B)	Accumulated OCI				OCI	
	Plan Assets	PBO	Net Pension Asset/ Liability	Prior Service Cost	Pension Gain/Loss	Cash Outflow	Pension Expense	Prior Service Cost	Pension Gain/Loss
1. Balance, Jan. 1, 2020	$100,000	$ (95,000)	$ 5,000	$12,500	$25,000				
2. Service cost		(12,000)	(12,000)				$12,000		
Interest cost		(8,550)	(8,550)				8,550		
3. Expected return on plan assets	7,000		7,000				(7,000)		
4. Unexpected loss on plan assets	(1,000)		(1,000)		1,000				1,000
5. Actuarial loss on PBO		(4,000)	(4,000)		4,000				4,000
6. Prior service cost amortization				(1,250)			1,250	(1,250)	
7. Net pension loss amortization					(1,500)		1,500		(1,500)
8. Contributions to fund	15,000		15,000			$(15,000)			
9. Retiree benefits paid	(1,000)	1,000							
10. Balance, Dec. 31, 2020	$120,000	$(118,550)	$1,450	$11,250	$28,500		$16,300	$(1,250)	$3,500

Steps to Complete Pension Worksheet

1. Enter beginning balances for Plan Assets, PBO, Net Pension Asset/Liability, AOCI—Prior Service Cost, and AOCI—Pension Gain/Loss.
2. Enter service cost, $12,000 (given) and interest cost, $8,550 (0.09 × $95,000) as a credit to Projected Benefit Obligation and a debit to Pension Expense.
3. Enter expected return on plan assets, $7,000 (0.07 × $100,000) as debit to Plan Assets and a credit to Pension Expense.
4. Enter unexpected loss on return, $1,000 ($6,000 − $7,000) as a debit to Pension Gain/Loss in both the OCI column and the Accumulated OCI column and a credit to Plan Assets. This loss would be shown in OCI for 2020 in the statement of comprehensive income. The OCI for the year would be closed out to AOCI and the ending balance of AOCI would be shown on the balance sheet. While not illustrated in this worksheet, the amount of pension expense would be included in the end of year retained earnings balance on the balance sheet through the process of closing net income to retained earnings at year-end.
5. Enter actuarial loss on the PBO, $4,000 as a debit to Pension Gain/Loss in both the OCI column and the Accumulated OCI column and a credit to Projected Benefit Obligation.
6. Enter prior service cost amortization, $1,250 as a debit to Pension Expense and a credit to Prior Service Cost in both the OCI column and the Accumulated OCI column.
7. Enter amortization of pension loss, $1,500, as a debit to Pension Expense and a credit to Pension Gain/Loss in both the OCI column and the Accumulated OCI column. (Amortization equals beginning of year AOCI—Pension Gain/Loss of $25,000 less the corridor of $10,000, divided by service years of 10. Corridor is 10% of the greater of beginning of year PBO or Plan Assets [$100,000 × 10%].)

continued

continued from previous page

8. Enter contributions of $15,000 as a debit to Plan Assets and a credit to Cash.
9. Enter benefits of $1,000 as a debit to Projected Benefit Obligation and a credit to Plan Assets.
10. Total all columns (except the cash column) to arrive at ending balances. Funded status (net pension asset) is $1,450, which is pension assets of $120,000 less the PBO of $118,550.

Record Pension Entries Using a Pension Worksheet — LO19-7 — REVIEW 19-7

Review MBC

Fox Company has a noncontributory, defined benefit pension plan. The following information pertains to the pension plan.

Account Balances	Jan. 1, 2020
Projected Benefit Obligation,(before amendment)	$223,000 Cr.
Plan Assets	200,000 Dr.
Accumulated OCI—Prior Service Cost (before amendment)	0 Dr.
Accumulated OCI—Pension Gain/Loss	30,000 Dr.

Activity	2020
Service cost	$80,000
Pension benefits paid	30,000
Contributions to pension fund	70,000
Actual return on plan assets	10,000
Loss on PBO due to changes in actuarial assumptions*	8,000

*Determined December 31, 2020

Other	
Prior service benefits granted through plan amendment on Jan. 1, 2020 (present value)	$15,000
Average remaining service period	10 years
Discount rate	8%
Expected rate of return on plan assets	7%

Required

a. Record amounts above directly into a pension worksheet for Fox Company. Assume Fox uses corridor amortization.

b. Record journal entries using the pension worksheet.

More Practice: 19-37, 19-53, 19-55, 19-57

Solution on p. 19-63.

Explain postretirement benefit plans and differences from pensions plans

APPENDIX 19A LO 19-8

Employer Accounting for Postretirement Benefit Plans

- Determine expected postretirement benefit obligation
  - Assign equally over attribution period
- Recognize accumulated postretirement benefit obligation

LO 19-8 Overview

Postretirement benefit plans other than pensions provide benefits to retirees in exchange for service at a company. These benefits may include health-care coverage (medical and dental), life insurance, tuition assistance, legal services, and housing subsidies. Benefits are often extended to the employee and the employee's spouse and dependents. For employers, health-care benefits are generally the most significant benefit.

An employee is fully eligible for postretirement benefits when the employee renders the service necessary to receive expected benefits. Full eligibility is attained by fulfilling age and service requirements, depending on the plan. For example, an employee may earn certain postretirement healthcare coverage if he or she provides at least 15 years of service with the company and reaches the age of 60 years old.

The company determines the EPBO (**expected postretirement benefit obligation**) or the present value of the expected postretirement benefits to be paid to retirees. An APBO (**accumulated postretirement benefit obligation**) is recognized for the expected benefits attributed to the employee's services rendered to date and expense is recognized through an attribution process. **Attribution** is the process of assigning the postretirement benefit costs to employee service periods. The attribution period typically extends from the employee's hire date to the full eligibility date (when the employee has met the requirements to receive the postretirement benefit). The employee may continue to provide service after the point of full eligibility, which does not impact (increase) postretirement benefits.

The obligation is generally assigned equally to each year of service during the attribution period as illustrated in **Demo 19-8**.

ASC Glossary Expected Postretirement Benefit Obligation—The actuarial present value as of a particular date of the postretirement benefits expected to be paid by the employer's plan to or for each employee, the employee's beneficiaries, and any covered dependents pursuant to the terms of the plan.

ASC Glossary Accumulated Postretirement Benefit Obligation—The actuarial present value as of a particular date of all future benefits attributed to an employee's service rendered to that date assuming the plan continues in effect and that all assumptions about future events are fulfilled. The accumulated postretirement benefit obligation generally reflects a ratable allocation of expected future benefits to employee service already rendered in the attribution period.

ASC Glossary Attribution period—The period of an employee's service to which the expected postretirement benefit obligation for that employee is assigned. The beginning of the attribution period is the employee's date of hire unless the plan's benefit formula grants credit only for service from a later date, in which case the beginning of the attribution period is generally the beginning of that credited service period. The end of the attribution period is the full eligibility date. Within the attribution period, an equal amount of the expected postretirement benefit obligation is attributed to each year of service unless the plan's benefit formula attributes a disproportionate share of the expected postretirement benefit obligation to employees' early years of service. In that case, benefits are attributed in accordance with the plan's benefit formula.

Key differences between pension plans and postretirement benefit plans that affect financial statement reporting are described as follows.

Comparison of Pension Plans and Postretirement Benefit Plans

	Pension Plans (LO 19-1 through LO 19-7)	Postretirement Benefit Plans (LO 19-8 and LO 19-9)
Determination of retiree benefit amount and employer's obligation	Benefit is calculated based upon a pension benefit formula.	The benefit is undefined, hard to estimate, based upon many factors, and varies by individual. As a result, prediction of expense is more difficult than under pension plans.
Typical vesting period	Total pension obligation typically changes (increases) for each year of service driven by the pension benefit formula.	Benefits are typically 100% earned when the employee meets the criteria. Therefore, the EPBO is generally assigned through attribution where the employee earns an equal amount of benefit for each year of service from the date of hire to the full eligibility date.
	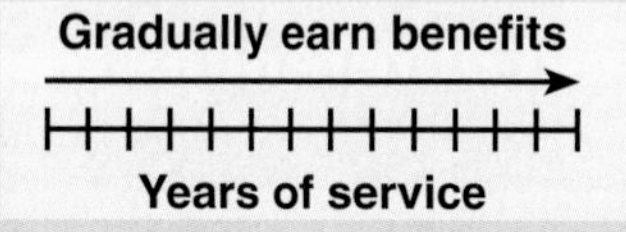	
Measurement of Service Cost	Actuarial present value of additional pension benefits earned by employees based upon employee service in the current year.	EPBO equally assigned (through the attribution process) to each year of service from date of hire until date of 100% eligibility.

Disclosure

In addition to the disclosures required for pension plans, disclosures for postretirement benefit plans include the assumed cost trend rate(s) and assumed pattern of changes used to measure the expected cost of benefits covered by the plan (gross eligible charges), along with the effect of a one-percentage-point increase (and decrease) in the assumed cost trend rates on the cost analysis. For health plans, accounting guidance requires the following:

715-20-50-1l The assumed health care cost trend rate(s) for the next year used to measure the expected cost of benefits covered by the plan (gross eligible charges), and a general description of the direction and pattern of change in the assumed trend rates thereafter, together with the ultimate trend rate(s) and when that rate is expected to be achieved.

715-20-50-1m The effect of a one-percentage-point increase and the effect of a one-percentage-point decrease in the assumed health care cost trend rates on the aggregate of the service and interest cost components of net periodic postretirement health care benefit costs and the accumulated postretirement benefit obligation for health care benefits.

EXPAND YOUR KNOWLEDGE **Drivers of Postretirement Health-Care Plan Payments**

Net incurred claims cost by age are the employer's share of the cost of providing postretirement health care for one year at each age plan participants are expected to receive benefits. The cost equals future gross eligible charges reduced by expected Medicare reimbursement, expected employee contributions (cost sharing), and deductibles. The net incurred claims cost amounts by age are the cash flow inputs into the actuarial present-value models. These cash estimates are affected by the following:

- Past and present claims data for the plan, or the experience of other employers.
- Health care trend rates or assumptions about annual rate of change of health-care costs for the benefits provided. These assumptions include health-care inflation, changes in utilization, technological advances, and health-care status of participants.
- Plan demographics or characteristics of a plan population, including geographical distribution, age, gender, and marital status.

Determining Obligations for Postretirement Benefit Plan LO19-8 Demo 19-8

Demo MBC

Rayovak Corp. sponsors a postretirement plan that provides postretirement health care coverage to employees who serve 15 years and reach the age of 60. On January 1, 2020, a 45-year-old employee, Michael has worked for the company for 5 years and is expected to retire at age 67. The postretirement plan provides benefits for 5 years and the benefit is estimated to be $5,000 per year.

Required

a. Determine the attribution period.
b. Calculate the expected postretirement benefit obligation (EPBO) on January 1, 2020 assuming the discount rate is 10%.
c. Calculate the accumulated postretirement benefit obligation (APBO) on January 1, 2020.
d. Compute service cost for one year.

Solution

a. **Attribution Period**
The attribution period of 20 years begins at date of hire (January 1, 2015) and ends at the full eligibility date of January 1, 2035 (the date Michael reaches the age of 60). On January 1, 2035, Michael has met both requirements of service years and age.

b. **Expected Postretirement Benefit Obligation (EPBO)**
To calculate the EPBO, we will first compute the present value (at retirement date) of a 5-year, postretirement benefit cash flow stream (annuity), assuming a discount rate of 10%.

Present Value of Postretirement Benefit Cash Flow Stream at Retirement Date

	RATE	NPER	PMT	PV	Excel Formula
Given	10%	5	5,000	?	=PV(0.1,5,5000)
Solution				**$18,954**	

We then discount the cash flow stream to January 1, 2020 (the current date).

Present Value of Postretirement Benefit Cash Flow Stream on January 1, 2020

	RATE	NPER	PV	FV	Excel Formula
Given	10%	20	?	18,954	=PV(0.1,22,0,18954)
Solution			**$2,328**		

The expected postretirement benefit obligation for Michael is $2,328 on January 1, 2020.

c. **Accumulated Postretirement Benefit Obligation (APBO)**
The APBO on January 1, 2020, is calculated as follows.

EPBO × (Years of service/Years in full attribution period)
$2,328 × 5/20 = $582

The APBO is the portion of the EPBO attributed to service rendered. On the full eligibility date of January 1, 2035, the APBO and the EPBO will be equal.

continued

continued from previous page

d. **Service Cost**
EPBO ÷ Years in Attribution Period
$2,328 ÷ 20 = $116
The service cost for one year is equal to the attribution of the EPBO to one year of service during the attribution period of 20 years.

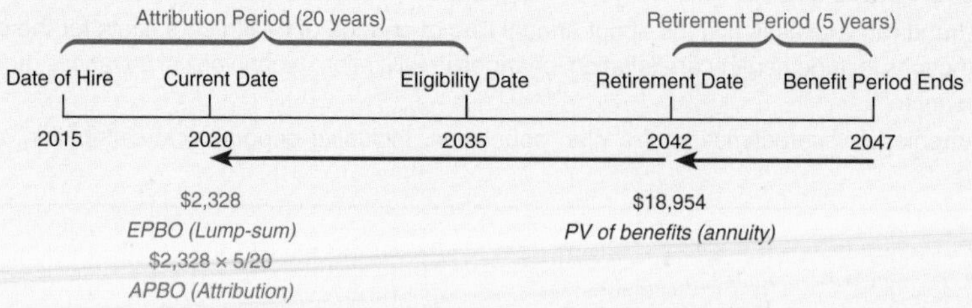

REVIEW 19-8 **LO19-8** **Determining Obligations for Postretirement Benefit Plan**

Review MBC

A postretirement plan promises 100% health care coverage for all employees who retire after age 62. Leah, employed on January 1, 2016, is expected to render a total of 14 years of service before reaching age 62. Expected benefits are $7,500 per year for an estimated 10 years commencing at an estimated retirement age of 67 years.

a. Calculate the attribution period.

b. Calculate the expected postretirement benefit obligation (EPBO) on January 1, 2020, using an interest rate of 6%.

c. Calculate the accumulated postretirement benefit obligation (APBO) on January 1, 2020, using an interest rate of 6%.

More Practice: 19-91, 19-92, 19-97, 19-102

Solution on p. 19-65.

APPENDIX 19B LO 19-9 Record postretirement benefit expense, gains and losses, funding, and benefits paid

LO 19-9 Overview

Postretirement Benefit Plan Recording (as applicable)
- Record prior service cost amendment
- Record postretirement benefit expense
- Record deferral of benefit gain/loss
- Record employer contributions
- Record benefit payments

The accounting for postretirement benefit plans is similar to the accounting for pension plans. The APBO is treated in a similar way for accounting purposes as the PBO. **Postretirement benefit expense**, or **net periodic postretirement benefit cost**, includes the same components as pension expense. For example, service cost is still recognized as expense for the period as under a pension plan even though the underlying calculations to derive service cost differ as illustrated in Appendix 19A. The amortization period, however, differs under a postretirement plan. Instead of amortizing over the remaining service years, amounts will be amortized over the remaining service years up to the point of full eligibility. (Recall from Appendix 19A that an employee may continue employment after the date of full eligibility.) **Demo 19-9** illustrates the similarities in the accounting treatment of postretirement benefits and pension plans.

Demo 19-9 **LO19-9** **Recording Entries for Postretirement Benefit Plan**

Assume that MTV Inc. has a health-care benefit plan for retirees and the following information is available regarding the plan.

- Plan Assets, January 1, 2020: $200,000 Dr.
- Accumulated OCI—Prior Service Cost, January 1, 2020: $60,000 Dr.
- Accumulated OCI—Benefit Gain/Loss, January 1, 2020: $0

continued

continued from previous page

- APBO, January 1, 2020: $288,000 Cr.
- Expected 5% return on plan assets: $10,000
- Actual return on plan assets in 2020: $9,500
- Service cost for 2020: $40,000
- Contribution to fund in 2020: $75,000
- Benefit payments in 2020: $45,000
- Increase in estimated health care cost trends results in a $50,000 increase in the APBO on December 31, 2020
- Average remaining service years to full eligibility for active plan participants: 10 years
- Discount rate: 9%

Required

a. Compute postretirement benefit expense for 2020.
b. Compute accumulated postretirement benefit obligation as of December 31, 2020.
c. Record postretirement benefit expense for 2020.
d. Record deferral of gain or loss on plan assets and on the APBO.
e. Record the funding of plan assets.
f. Record the benefits paid.
g. Prepare a postretirement benefit worksheet for 2020.

Solution

a. **Measuring Postretirement Benefit Expense**
Postretirement benefit expense for MTV Inc. is measured as follows, using the same guidance as determined under pension plans.

Measurement of Postretirement Benefit Expense (2020)	
Service cost	$40,000
Interest cost ($288,000 × 9%)	25,920
Expected return on plan assets	(10,000)
Amortization of prior service cost	6,000
Total postretirement benefit expense	$61,920

No amortization is recorded on the Accumulated OCI—Benefit Gain/Loss because there is a zero balance on January 1, 2020.

b. **Reconciliation of Accumulated Postretirement Benefit Obligation**
Accumulated postretirement benefit obligation for MTV Inc. is computed as follows, using the same guidance in determining the PBO under pension plans.

Measurement of APBO	
APBO, Jan. 1, 2020	$288,000
Service cost	40,000
Interest cost	25,920
Prior service cost adjustment	0
Loss on APBO	50,000
Payment of benefits	(45,000)
APBO, Dec. 31, 2020	$358,920

c. **Recording Postretirement Benefit Expense**
The journal entry to record postretirement benefit expense will include the following.

- A debit to Postretirement Benefit Expense for total postretirement benefit expense.
- A debit to Plan Assets for the expected return on plan assets.
- A credit to APBO for service cost plus interest cost.
- A credit to OCI—Prior Service Cost for amortization of prior service cost.
- A credit to OCI—Benefit Gain/Loss for amortization of gain/loss (not applicable in this example).

continued

continued from previous page

Assets = Liabilities + Equity
+10,000 +65,920 −61,920
+6,000

December 31, 2020—To record postretirement benefit expense

Postretirement Benefit Expense	61,920	
Plan Assets	10,000	
Accumulated Postretirement Benefit Obligation		65,920
OCI—Prior Service Cost		6,000

d. **Recording Deferral of Benefit Gain/Loss**
The following entries are required to defer (1) the unexpected loss on plan assets of $500 and (2) the actuarial loss on the APBO of $50,000.

Assets = Liabilities + Equity
−500 −500

December 31, 2020—To defer unexpected loss on plan assets

OCI—Benefit Gain/Loss	500	
Plan Assets ($10,000 − $9,500)		500

Assets = Liabilities + Equity
+50,000 −50,000

December 31, 2020—To defer actuarial loss on APBO

OCI—Benefit Gain/Loss	50,000	
Accumulated Postretirement Benefit Obligation		50,000

e. **Recording Funding of Plan Assets**
At the time that MTV Inc. funds its postretirement benefit plan by making a payment to increase plan assets, MTV Inc. would record the following entry.

Assets = Liabilities + Equity
+75,000
−75,000

December 31, 2020—To record funding of postretirement benefit plan

Plan Assets	75,000	
Cash		75,000

The amount of funding is based upon factors including legal minimum funding requirements, tax consequences, and cash flow capabilities. Amounts are paid to the trustee who manages the fund investments.

f. **Recording Benefits Paid**
The trustee, on behalf of MTV Inc., will make payments to eligible retirees based upon the benefit payout ratio. As payments are made, both plan assets and the APBO decrease.

Assets = Liabilities + Equity
−45,000 −45,000

Cash	
	75,000

OCI—PSC	
	6,000

APBO	
45,000	288,000 Bal.
	65,920
	50,000
	358,920

Plan Assets	
Bal. 200,000	500
10,000	45,000
75,000	
239,500	

OCI—Benefit G/L	
500	
50,000	

Postret Benefit Exp	
61,920	

December 31, 2020—To record benefits paid to retirees

Accumulated Postretirement Benefit Obligation	45,000	
Plan Assets		45,000

g. **Postretirement Benefit Worksheet**

	Reported Net in Financial Statements		Reported on the Balance Sheet				Reported in Comprehensive Income		
	A	B	(A-B)	Accumulated OCI				OCI	
	Plan Assets	APBO	Net Postretirement Asset/Liability	Prior Service Cost	Benefit Gain/Loss	Cash Outflow	Postretirement Benefit Expense	Prior Service Cost	Benefit Gain/Loss
Balance, Jan. 1, 2020	$200,000	$(288,000)	$ (88,000)	$60,000					
Service cost		(40,000)	(40,000)				$40,000		
Interest cost		(25,920)	(25,920)				25,920		
Expected return on plan assets	10,000		10,000				(10,000)		
Unexpected loss on assets	(500)		(500)		$ 500				$ 500
Loss on APBO		(50,000)	(50,000)		50,000				50,000
Prior service cost amortization				(6,000)			6,000	$(6,000)	
Contributions to fund	75,000		75,000			$(75,000)			
Retiree benefits paid	(45,000)	45,000							
Balance, Dec. 31, 2020	$239,500	$(358,920)	$(119,420)	$54,000	$50,500		$61,920	$(6,000)	$50,500

BOEING

Real World—POSTRETIREMENT BENEFIT EXPENSE

BOEING [BA]

The **Boeing Company**, one of the world's major aerospace firms, sponsors defined benefit pension plans. However, nonunion and the majority of union employees that had participated in defined benefit pension plans transitioned to a company-funded defined contribution retirement savings plan in 2016. Components of net periodic benefit cost for defined benefit and other postretirement benefits from 2015 to 2017 are summarized below. We see the decrease in annual net periodic benefit cost from 2015 to 2017. Other postretirement benefits consist primarily of health care coverage for eligible retirees and qualifying dependents, and to a lesser extent, life insurance to certain groups of retirees.

Note 14 excerpt-Postretirement Plans—The components of net periodic benefit cost were as follows:

	Pension			Other Postretirement Benefits		
Years ended December 31	**2017**	**2016**	**2015**	**2017**	**2016**	**2015**
Service cost	$ 402	$ 604	$1,764	$106	$128	$140
Interest cost	2,991	3,050	2,990	229	262	248
Expected return on plan assets	(3,847)	(3,999)	(4,031)	(7)	(8)	(8)
Amortization of prior service (credits)/costs	(39)	38	196	(137)	(126)	(136)
Recognized net actuarial loss	804	790	1,577	10	22	31
Settlement/curtailment/other losses	1	40	290			10
Net periodic benefit cost	$ 312	$ 523	$2,786	$201	$278	$285

Recording Entries for Postretirement Benefit Plan — LO19-9 — REVIEW 19-9

Levii Corp. sponsors a postretirement benefit plan for health care. The following information relates to this plan.

Activity	2020
Service cost	$320,000
Contributions to the plan	150,000
Benefits paid to retirees	50,000
Amortization of prior service cost	10,000
Interest cost	15,000

Account Balances	Dec. 31, 2019
Plan Assets	$125,000 Dr.
APBO	250,000 Cr.
Accumulated OCI—Prior Service Cost	60,000 Dr.

Other	
Expected (and actual) rate of return on plan assets	6%

Review MBC

More Practice: 19-94, 19-95, 19-96, 19-99, 19-100

Record entries for postretirement benefit expense, benefit payments, and funding in 2020.

Solution on p. 19-65.

Allocate prior service cost using the service method

APPENDIX 19C
LO 19-10

Prior service cost is deferred and recognized over time through either the service method, or through an alternative approach such as the straight-line method.

- **Service method**—allocates an equal amount of prior service cost to each service year and results in declining amortization as employees retire.
- **Straight-line method**—allocates an equal amount of prior service cost over the employees' average service period.

Allocation of Prior Service Cost
- Service method
  - Allocation over employee service years
- Straight-line method
  - Allocation over average service period

LO 19-10 Overview

The service method is preferable because it logically relates prior service cost to years of service as rendered, with more expense allocated to the early years. The benefits the employer realizes are also greatest during those years. More employees are working, and the effect of the grant on performance is at its peak soon after the award. Both methods are illustrated in **Demo 19-10**.

Demo 19-10 **LO19-10** **Allocation of Prior Service Cost**

A plan amendment for BWW Company results in a $48,000 prior service cost adjustment on January 1, 2020. The amendment affects 5 employees with service years estimated as follows: 5, 4, 2, and 1, for the years 2020, 2021, 2022, and 2023, respectively. This means that 5 employees are expected to work in 2020, 4 employees in 2021, 2 employees in 2022, and 1 employee in 2023. Total service years are equal to 12 years (5 + 4 + 2 + 1). Average service years are equal to 2.4 year (12 service years / 5 employees).

Required

a. Compute prior service cost amortization in years 2020 through 2023 using the service method.

b. Compute prior service cost amortization in years 2020 through 2023 using the straight-line method.

Solution

a. **Service Method**

Under the service method, $20,000 of prior service cost (5/12 × $48,000) is amortized in 2020, when 5 of the total 12 service years are rendered. Pension expense is increased by $20,000 in 2020. Similarly, in each of the remaining years, the amount of prior service cost is allocated based upon the number of employee service years.

Year	Service Years	Annual Amortization	
2020	5	$48,000 × 5/12 =	$20,000
2021	4	$48,000 × 4/12 =	16,000
2022	2	$48,000 × 2/12 =	8,000
2023	1	$48,000 × 1/12 =	4,000
	12		$48,000

b. **Straight-Line Method**

Under the straight-line method, prior service cost is amortized over the average service years of 2.4.

Year	Annual Amortization	
2020	$48,000/2.4 years	$20,000
2021	$48,000/2.4 years	20,000
2022	$8,000 (remaining)	8,000
2023		0
		$48,000

REVIEW 19-10 **LO19-10** **Allocation of Prior Service Costs**

Review MBC

On January 1, 2020, Oracle Company amended its defined benefit pension plan by granting retroactive pension benefits for work performed before that date. The present value of those benefits was determined to be $80,000 at that date. The following employees expect to receive benefits under the plan, and they have the indicated expected number of years remaining in their careers at January 1, 2020: Jake: two years, Julia: five years.

Determine the amortization of prior service cost to be recognized in 2022 under the following two methods.

More Practice: 19-98, 19-103

a. Service method that associates an equivalent amount of prior service cost to each service year.

b. Straight-line method based on the average remaining service period of employees.

Solution on p. 19-65.

Questions

19-1. Distinguish between a defined contribution pension plan and a defined benefit pension plan.

19-2. Describe the role and responsibilities of the employer, the trustee, and the employees in their involvement in a defined benefit pension plan.

19-3. What are actuarial assumptions used to develop estimates of future retirement benefit payments of a pension plan?

19-4. Distinguish between a contributory pension plan and a noncontributory pension plan.

19-5. Employer Mac sponsors a defined benefit pension plan. The estimated pension expense for 2020 is $100,000, the first year of the plan. Provide the balance sheet presentation for each of the following separate scenarios.

a. Mac contributes 100% of the pension expense

b. Mac contributes 80% of the expense

c. Mac contributes 120% of the expense

19-6. Employee Justin will receive an annual pension benefit of $12,000 for five years, starting on December 31, 2021. Assuming an interest rate of 8%, how much must be in the pension fund on January 1, 2021? Explain why the answer is not $60,000.

19-7. Employer Beeber must build a pension fund of $50,000 by December 31, 2024. Five equal annual payments are made into the fund starting on December 31, 2020. The fund will earn 8%. What is the amount of each payment? Explain why it is not $10,000.

19-8. Explain why accounting for defined benefit plans must be based on assumptions and estimates.

19-9. What is the pension benefit formula?

19-10. Explain why pension expense is not simply recognized when benefits are paid to employees.

19-11. What does attribution mean in pension accounting?

19-12. Two special features of pension accounting are (a) income smoothing in the income statement, and (b) offsetting in the balance sheet. Explain each feature.

19-13. What is the vested benefit obligation?

19-14. List and define the five components of pension expense.

19-15. Define and explain the projected benefit obligation (PBO).

19-16. What information is typically found in the report from the trustee on plan assets?

19-17. Explain what is meant by underfunded pension plan.

19-18. Explain the difference between the projected benefit obligation and the accumulated benefit obligation.

19-19. Explain the primary approaches for amortizing unrecognized pension costs.

19-20. In the case of unrecognized prior service cost, first incurred during 2020, amortization may or may not be appropriate at the end of 2020. Explain why.

Brief Exercises

Brief Exercise 19-21 Recording Entry for Defined Contribution Plan **LO1** *Hint:* See Demo 19-1A

Aguilera Co. established a defined contribution plan in which the company contributes 3% of full-time employees' salaries to a traditional 401(k) plan for each completed year of service. The amount of salaries eligible for the contribution totaled $150,000 in 2020. Record the entry for Aguilera Co. for the contribution to the plan, assuming 100% funding.

Brief Exercise 19-22 Computing Annual Benefit Payment **LO1** *Hint:* See Demo 19-1B

Michael (age 35) commenced employment at Larkin Supplies Inc. on January 1, 2020. Larkin sponsors a defined benefit plan where employees vest 5% after year one, an additional 10% after year two, and an additional 15% each year after until 100%. Michael's current salary is $90,000 per year, and he is expected to retire in 20 years, at which time his salary is estimated to be $175,000 per year. The annual benefit formula is equal to 2.5% × number of years of service × final salary. Determine the gross annual benefit payment earned as of December 31, 2021, under a (1) VBO, (2) ABO, and (3) PBO pension liability measurement.

Brief Exercise 19-23 Analyzing Change in PBO Balance **LO2** *Hint:* See Demo 19-2

Sharks Company implemented a defined benefit pension plan for its employees. The following data are provided for 2021 and 2020. Determine the benefit payments to retirees in 2021, assuming no PSC adjustment or gain or loss on the PBO in 2021 and a discount rate of 7%.

	2021	2020
Projected Benefit Obligation, December 31	$187,500	$175,000
Plan Assets, December 31	168,750	150,000
Service cost	22,500	

Brief Exercise 19-24
Analyzing Change in PBO Balance **LO2**
Hint: See Demo 19-2

Gaap Company sponsors a defined benefit plan covering all employees. Benefits are based on years of service and compensation levels at the time of retirement. Gaap determined that as of December 31, 2020, its accumulated benefit obligation was $270,000 and its plan assets had a $290,000 fair value. Gaap's December 31, 2020, trial balance included a projected benefit obligation balance of $297,075. Assuming service cost of $50,000, interest cost of $1,875, and benefit payments of $4,800, what was the January 1, 2020, balance of the PBO?

Brief Exercise 19-25
Analyzing Change in PBO Balance **LO2**

Alpha Company sponsors a defined benefit plan covering all employees. Benefits are based on years of service and compensation levels at the time of retirement. Alpha's December 31, 2020, trial balance included a projected benefit obligation balance of $983,000, adjusted for an actuarially determined pension loss due to projected changes in interest rates. Assuming service cost of $155,000, discount rate of 5% applicable during the year (prior to the change in rates), benefit payments of $118,000, and a January 1, 2020, balance of $840,000 for the PBO, what was the loss recorded on the PBO in 2020?

Brief Exercise 19-26
Analyzing Change in Plan Asset Balance **LO3**
Hint: See Demo 19-3A

Blues Company implemented a defined benefit pension plan for its employees. The following data are provided for 2021 and 2020. Determine the employer's contribution in 2021.

	2021	2020
Projected Benefit Obligation, December 31 . . .	$187,500	$175,000
Plan Assets, December 31	168,750	150,000
Actual return on plan assets	9,000	
Benefits paid to employees	3,000	

Brief Exercise 19-27
Analyzing Change in Plan Asset Balance **LO3**
Hint: See Demo 19-3A

The Blackhawk Company implemented a defined benefit pension plan for its employees. The following data are provided for 2021.

Account Balances, Dec. 31	2021
Projected Benefit Obligation . . .	$280,000
Plan Assets	280,020

Activity	2021
Actual return on plan assets . . .	$ 8,120
Benefits paid to employees . . .	12,000
Employer contributions	15,000

a. Determine the balance in Plan Assets on January 1, 2021.
b. Determine the actual rate of return on plan assets for 2021.

Brief Exercise 19-28
Determining Funded Status **LO3**
Hint: See Demo 19-3B

As of December 31, 2020, the projected benefit obligation and plan assets of a noncontributory defined benefit plan sponsored by Durasell Inc. were as follows. Determine the funded status of Durasell Inc.'s pension plan.

Projected benefit obligation	$312,000
Plan assets at fair value	300,000

Brief Exercise 19-29
Determining Pension Expense **LO4**
Hint: See Demo 19-4

The following information pertains to Qdobe Corporation's defined benefit pension plan for 2020. Assume no beginning balance in Accumulated OCI—Pension Gain/Loss. What amount should Qdobe report as pension expense in its 2020 income statement?

Service cost	$160,000
Actual and expected gain on plan assets	35,000
Actuarial loss on PBO incurred during 2020	40,000
Amortization of unrecognized prior service cost	5,000
Annual interest on pension obligation	50,000

Brief Exercise 19-30 Analyzing Prior Service Cost **LO4** *Hint:* See Demo 19-4

Clark Kent Co. approved a prior service obligation of $120,000 on January 1, 2020, which granted retroactive benefit to employees. Assuming an average remaining service period of 10 years for all active plan participants, what is the effect on pension expense of the prior service cost?

Brief Exercise 19-31 Amortizing Pension Gain/Loss **LO4** *Hint:* See Demo 19-4

On June 1, 2018, West Corporation established a defined benefit pension plan for its employees. The following information was available in 2020:

Balance	Jan. 1, 2020
Projected Benefit Obligation	$3,625,000 Cr.
Plan Assets	3,750,000 Dr.
Accumulated OCI—Pension Gain/Loss	637,500 Cr.

For 2021, compute the amortization of the account, Accumulated OCI—Pension Gain/Loss, assuming that the company uses the corridor approach in determining the minimum amortization to recognize. Assume that the average remaining service life of employees is 10 years.

Brief Exercise 19-32 Recording Pension Expense and Plan Funding **LO5** *Hint:* See Demo 19-5

Kidman Inc. sponsors a defined benefit plan and determined that for the current year of 2020, service cost was $10,000, interest cost was $2,100, and the expected (and actual) return on plan assets was $2,000. Kidman will contribute $1,800 to the plan on December 31, 2020. Record the journal entries for pension expense and to fund the plan for 2020, assuming no benefits are paid during the year.

Brief Exercise 19-33 Recording Pension Expense, Plan Funding, Benefit Payments **LO5** *Hint:* See Demo 19-5

LetsGo Inc. sponsors a defined benefit plan and determined that for the current year of 2020, service cost was $250,000, amortization of prior service cost was $1,800, interest cost was $21,100, and the expected (and actual) return on plan assets was $18,000. LetsGo will contribute $45,000 to the plan for 2020 and payments to retirees totaled $15,000 in 2020. Record the journal entries for pension expense, to fund the plan, and to pay benefits for 2020.

Brief Exercise 19-34 Computing Net Pension Asset (Liability) **LO6**

The following pension-related values are determined on December 31, 2020, for BNW Inc. Compute the net pension asset (liability) to be recorded on the balance sheet on December 31, 2020.

Projected benefit obligation	$100,000
Accumulated benefit obligation	80,000
Plan assets at fair value	90,000
Accumulated OCI—Prior Service Cost (Dr.)	12,000

Brief Exercise 19-35 Reporting the Impact of Pension Fund **LO6**

At the end of 2020, after recording pension expense, Talent Co. has the following balances: Accumulated OCI—Pension Gain/Loss $6,000 (debit) and Projected Benefit Obligation $100,000 (credit). During the year 2021, Talent Co. experienced a $500 actuarial gain on its PBO and an unexpected loss on plan assets of $80. Net income for the year totaled $3,800. Talent Co. did not record amortization expense on the pension gain/loss because the beginning balance in Accumulated OCI—Pension Gain/Loss did not exceed the corridor. The company has no other items affecting OCI besides pension related items.

a. What is Talent's other comprehensive income for 2020, reported in the financial statements?
b. What is Talent's comprehensive income for 2020, reported in the financial statements?
c. What is the balance of accumulated other comprehensive income as of December 31, 2021, reported in the financial statements?

Brief Exercise 19-36 Reporting the Impact of Pension Fund **LO6** *Hint:* See Demo 19-6

Pharrell Inc. sponsored a defined pension plan for its employees. For the year ended December 31, 2020, Pharrell recorded pension expense of $2,500 (including service cost of $1,500) and a $200 unexpected loss on plan assets. Pharrell calculated the December 31, 2020, balance in Accumulated OCI—Gain/Loss account to be $400 (debit) and calculated a net pension asset/liability of $250 (credit). Assuming no amortization of pension gain/loss, what is the impact of this plan on the (a) balance sheet, (b) income statement, and (c) statement of comprehensive income?

Brief Exercise 19-37 Preparing a Pension Worksheet **LO7** *Hint:* See Demo 19-7

Levine Co. sponsored a defined benefit plan, which included January 1, 2020, balances of $5,000 and $4,800 in Plan Assets and Projected Benefit Obligation, respectively. During 2020, the company incurred $1,000 in service cost, made plan contributions of $210, and paid benefits to retirees for $150. The discount rate is 9% and the expected and actual rate of return on plan assets is 10%. Prepare a pension worksheet for 2020.

Exercises

Exercise 19-38
Recording Entries for Defined Contribution Plan **LO1**

Hewlatt Inc. sponsors a defined contribution plan for its employees. In 2020, salaries eligible for a 3% payment toward defined contribution plans of employees are $880,000. Hewlatt funded 100% of its obligation to fund 3% toward contribution plans as of the end of the year. Hewlatt Inc. will also match contributions made by employees by the end of the year, up to 5% of salaries. Hewlatt estimates the obligation to match up to 5% of salaries to be $15,000 on December 31, 2020. The amount will be paid to defined contribution plan in January of 2021. Record Hewlatt Inc.'s journal entries related to its defined contribution plan in 2020.

Exercise 19-39
Computing ABO, PBO **LO1**
Hint: See Demo 19-1B

Mallard Company sponsors a pension plan with the following pension benefit:

$$\text{Benefit paid at each year-end during retirement} = \frac{\text{Number of years worked} \times \text{Annual salary at retirement}}{25}$$

Credit for service began January 1, 2010, Josie's first day with the company. Josie is expected to work a total of 30 years with an annual salary at retirement of $100,000. She is expected to draw 10 years of retirement benefits. The discount rate is 10%.

Required

a. Compute the PBO on December 31, 2019, if Josie's current salary is $30,000.
b. Compute the ABO on December 31, 2019, if Josie's current salary is $30,000.

Exercise 19-40
Analyzing Changes in PBO **LO2**
Hint: See Demo 19-2

Garcia Co. has a PBO balance on January 1, 2020, of $146,000. The actuaries provided the following information: PBO December 31, 2020, balance, $140,000; interest cost, $13,000; actuarial gain on the PBO, $24,000; prior service cost amendment (causing additional obligations) $8,000; benefits paid to retirees, $19,000.

Required

Compute service cost for 2020.

Exercise 19-41
Determining Amounts Affecting Pension Expense, PBO, and Plan Assets **LO2, 3, 4**

The following items are related to a defined pension plan:

Items relate to 2020 unless otherwise indicated

____ *a.* December 31, 2020, projected benefit obligation balance
____ *b.* December 31, 2020, plan asset balance
____ *c.* Loss (gain) related to changes in actuarial assumptions
____ *d.* Cash funding by the employer
____ *e.* Prior service cost amendment
____ *f.* Net periodic pension expense
____ *g.* Actual return on plan assets
____ *h.* Interest cost on PBO
____ *i.* Amortization of prior service cost
____ *j.* January 1, 2020, pension plan asset balance
____ *k.* Pension benefits paid to retirees
____ *l.* January 1, 2020, projected benefit obligation balance
____ *m.* Expected return on plan assets
____ *n.* Amortization of pension gain/loss
____ *o.* Service cost

Required

Indicate whether each item *a* through *o* would be included in (1) a plan asset reconciliation, (2) a PBO reconciliation, and/or (3) a schedule of pension expense. An item may appear in more than one place.

Exercise 19-42
Analyzing Changes in Plan Assets **LO3**
Hint: See Demo 19-3A

Kulver's Inc. sponsored a defined benefit plan in 2020. Plan assets had a January 1, 2020, balance at fair value of $130,000 and a December 31, 2020, balance at fair value of $134,800. The actual return on plan assets is 6%. The trustee paid $18,000 of benefits to retirees.

Required

Compute Kulver's 2020 contribution to the defined benefit plan.

Exercise 19-43
Analyzing Changes in Plan Assets and PBO **LO2, 3**

The following information pertains to a company's defined benefit plan.

Balance	
Fair value of plan assets, Jan. 1, 2020	$5,000 Dr.
Fair value of plan assets, Dec. 31, 2020	5,625 Dr.
Projected benefit obligation, Jan. 1, 2020	5,000 Cr.
Net pension asset (liability), Dec. 31, 2020	200 Cr.

Activity	2020
Actual return on plan assets	$300
Contributions to plan assets	450
Service cost	500

Other	
Discount rate	8%
Expected rate of return on plan assets	7%

Required

a. Calculate benefits paid to retirees in 2020.

b. Calculate any actuarial gain or loss on the PBO in 2020.

Exercise 19-44
Calculating Pension Expense **LO4**
Hint: See Demo 19-4

Stars Inc. has a noncontributory defined pension plan for its employees. During 2020, the company had service cost of $60,000, an expected return on plan assets of $9,280, amortization of prior service cost of $2,000, amortization of net pension loss of $2,222, and benefits paid to employees of $40,000. The January 1, 2020, balance in its projected benefit obligation was $194,000. The discount rate is 10%.

Required

Calculate pension expense for 2020.

Exercise 19-45
Determining and Reporting Funded Status **LO3, 6**

Determine how the following three defined benefit plans would be reported on Brittany Inc.'s balance sheet given the following information on December 31, 2020 (assuming all amounts are noncurrent).

Plan #1		Plan #2		Plan #3	
PBO	$100,000	PBO	$540,000	PBO	$85,000
ABO	60,000	ABO	450,000	ABO	50,000
Plan assets at fair value	80,000	Plan assets at fair value	600,000	Plan assets at fair value	95,000

Exercise 19-46
Analyzing Pension Gain/Loss **LO4**

Spears Company presents the following information related to its pension plan for 2020, before recording pension expense.

Account Balances	
Projected Benefit Obligation, Jan. 1, 2020	$300,000 Cr.
Projected Benefit Obligation, Dec. 31, 2020	325,000 Cr.
Accumulated OCI—Pension Gain/Loss, Jan. 1, 2020	12,000 Cr.
Plan Assets, Jan. 1, 2020	280,000 Dr.
Plan Assets, Dec. 31, 2020	295,000 Dr.

Activity	
Actuarial loss on PBO, determined at Dec. 31, 2020	$ 4,200
Contributions to pension fund in 2020	10,000
Benefits paid in 2020	15,000

Other	
Average remaining service period of employees, 2020 and 2021	20 years
Expected rate of return	10%

Required

a. Determine the amortization of Accumulated OCI—Pension Gain/Loss for 2020, using (1) corridor (minimum amortization) and (2) straight-line amortization based on average remaining service period.

b. Determine the Accumulated OCI—Pension Gain/Loss balance at January 1, 2021, assuming straight-line amortization.

c. Determine the impact on pension expense in 2020 based upon the information provided, assuming straight-line amortization of accumulated pension gain/loss. What information is missing in order to calculate total pension expense?

d. Determine the amortization of Accumulated OCI—Pension Gain/Loss for 2021, assuming straight-line amortization.

Exercise 19-47
Determining Funded Status, Recording Pension Expense, Preparing Worksheet **LO3, 4, 5, 7**

Rico Corporation initiated a defined benefit pension plan on January 1, 2020. The plan does not provide any retroactive benefits for existing employees. The pension funding payment is made to the trustee on December 31 of each year. The following information is available for 2020 and 2021.

	2020	2021
Service cost	$75,000	$82,500
Funding payment (contribution)	85,000	92,500
Interest on projected benefit obligation.		7,500
Actual and expected return on plan assets		9,000

Required

a. In its December 31, 2020, balance sheet, Rico should report what amount of net pension asset/liability?
b. In its December 31, 2021, balance sheet, Rico should report what amount of net pension asset/liability?
c. Prepare the journal entries to record pension expense and plan funding for 2021.
d. Create a worksheet to summarize the pension data at the end of 2021.

AICPA adapted

Exercise 19-48
Computing Amortization of Pension Gain/Loss **LO4**

On January 1, 2020, K. Crew Inc. reported a $6,000 credit balance in its Accumulated OCI—Pension Gain/Loss account related to its pension plan. During 2020, the following events occurred.

- Actual return on plan assets was $8,000, and expected return on plan assets was $10,000.
- A gain on the PBO of $4,000 was determined by the actuary at December 31, 2020, based on changes in actuarial assumptions.

K. Crew amortizes unrecognized gains and losses using the corridor approach over the average remaining service life of active employees (20 years for 2020 and 2021). Further information on this plan follows.

	Jan. 1, 2020	Dec. 31, 2020
PBO	$50,000	$56,000
Fair value of plan assets.	30,000	34,000

Required

a. Compute amortization of Accumulated OCI—Pension Gain/Loss for 2020 using the corridor approach.
b. Compute the balance in Accumulated OCI—Pension Gain/Loss on December 31, 2020.
c. Compute amortization of Accumulated OCI—Pension Gain/Loss for 2021 using the corridor approach.
d. Instead, now assume that K. Crew elects to amortize Accumulated OCI—Pension Gain/Loss using the straight-line method. Compute amortization of Accumulated OCI—Pension Gain/Loss for 2020 and 2021.

Exercise 19-49
Computing Pension Expense, Gain/Loss Amortization, PBO, and Plan Asset Balances **LO4, 5**

The following data relate to a defined benefit pension plan for Hollistir Co.

Fair value of plan assets, Jan. 1, 2020.	$16,000
PBO Jan. 1, 2020, not including any items below	20,000
PSC from amendment dated Jan. 1, 2020, (10 years is the amortization period)	10,000
Gain from change in actuarial assumptions, computed as of Jan. 1, 2020	3,000
Actual return on plan assets, 2020.	2,000
Contributions to plan assets in 2020	4,000
Benefits paid to retirees in 2020.	5,000
Service cost for 2020	9,000
Discount rate	8%
Expected rate of return on plan assets.	10%

Required

a. Compute pension expense for 2020. Hollistir amortizes the full pension gain/loss over average service life of 15 years, using the straight-line method.
b. Compute the PBO at December 31, 2020.
c. Compute fair value of plan assets at December 31, 2020.

Exercise 19-50
Computing Amortization of Pension Gain/Loss
LO4

Everglade Co. reported the following balances related to its noncontributory defined pension plan.

Account Balance	PBO	Plan Assets
Jan. 1, 2020	$120,000	$ 95,000
Jan. 1, 2021	194,000	116,000
Jan. 1, 2022	221,400	219,200
Jan. 1, 2023	248,000	233,000

Additional information related to the plan.

Account Balance	Current Year OCI—Pension Gain/Loss	Average Service Life
Dec. 31, 2020	$50,000 Dr.	10
Dec. 31, 2021	20,000 Dr.	10
Dec. 31, 2022	12,000 Cr.	9
Dec. 31, 2023	8,000 Dr.	9

The January 1, 2020, balance in OCI—Pension Gain/Loss is zero.

Required

Using the corridor approach, compute the following.

a. Amortization of OCI—Pension Gain/Loss for each of the years 2020–2023.
b. Balance of Accumulated OCI—Pension Gain/Loss on December 31 for each of the years 2020–2023.

Exercise 19-51
Recording Pension Expense, Gains/Losses, Funding, Benefit Payments and Preparing Worksheet
LO5, 7

Amex Company started a noncontributory defined benefit pension plan on January 1, 2019. The records of Amex Company indicate the following for the year 2020.

Account Balances	Jan. 1, 2020
Projected Benefit Obligation	$30,000 Cr.
Plan Assets	27,500 Dr.
Accumulated OCI—Pension Gain/Loss	1,500 Cr.

Activity	2020
Service cost	$10,000
Interest cost (interest rate, 10%)	3,000
Gain in PBO due to change in actuarial assumption	2,000
Pension benefits paid	500
Actual earnings on plan assets (same as expected return)	2,500
Plan funding payment (contributions)	15,000

Required

a. Compute net pension expense for 2020 assuming that the January 1, 2020, Accumulated OCI—Pension Gain/Loss is amortized in 2020 over a 15-year average remaining service period.
b. Prepare the 2020 pension expense, deferral of gain, funding, and benefits paid entries for Amex Company.
c. Compute the underfunded (overfunded) pension balance as of December 31, 2020.
d. Create a worksheet to summarize the pension data at the end of 2020.

Exercise 19-52
Recording and Reporting Pension Accounts; Preparing Worksheet **LO5, 6, 7**

2020 records of Lexxus Company provided the following data related to its noncontributory defined benefit pension plan.

Account Balances	Jan. 1, 2020
Projected Benefit Obligation	$3,000
Plan Assets	2,400
Accumulated OCI—Prior Service Cost	0
Accumulated OCI—Pension Gain/Loss	0

Activity	2020
Service cost	$1,200
Interest cost	240
Pension benefits paid	400
Actual return on plan assets	168
Contributions	1,024

Other	
Expected rate of return of plan assets	7%
Discount rate	8%

Required

a. Compute 2020 net periodic pension expense reported by Lexxus.
b. Prepare a 2020 reconciliation for (1) plan assets and (2) projected benefit obligation.
c. Provide the 2020 entries for Lexxus Company to record pension expense, funding, and payment of benefits.
d. Determine the plan's funded status at the beginning and end of 2020.
e. Indicate the amounts that would appear on the income statement and balance sheet in 2020 for Lexxus Company.
f. Create a worksheet to summarize the pension data at the end of 2020.

Exercise 19-53
Preparing Pension Journal Entries and Pension Worksheet
LO5, 7
Hint: See Demo 19-7

Mac Company has a noncontributory defined benefit pension plan, with the following data available.

Account Balances	Jan. 1, 2020
PBO balance, before PSC adjustment . . .	$45,000 Cr.
Prior service cost (due to plan amendment on Jan. 1, 2020)	5,000 Dr.
Plan Asset balance	52,500 Dr.

Activity	2020
Service cost	$32,500
Pension benefits paid	0
Actual and expected return on plan assets	2,500
Cash funding (contributions).	25,000
Pension benefits paid to retirees	0

Required

a. Provide the computation for interest cost assuming a discount rate of 8%.
b. Compute net pension expense. Assume that prior service cost will be amortized over a 10-year average remaining service period.
c. Provide the 2020 entries for Mac Company related to the defined benefit pension plan.
d. Provide the same entries in (*c*) assuming cash funding from the employer of $35,500 and no other changes.
e. Determine the plans' fund balance for (*c*) and (*d*), at December 31, 2020.
f. Create a worksheet to summarize the pension data at the end of 2020 based upon part (*c*).

Exercise 19-54
Preparing and Recording Pension Entries and Preparing Pension Worksheet
LO5, 6, 7

The following data relate to a pension plan for ISPN Inc.

Account Balances	Jan. 1, 2020
Projected Benefit Obligation.	$30,000 Cr.
Plan Assets.	30,000 Dr.
Accumulated OCI—Pension Gain/Loss . . .	5,000 Cr.
Accumulated OCI—Prior Service Cost. . . .	8,000 Dr.

Activity	2020
Service cost	$7,000
Contributions	9,000
Prior service cost amortization . . .	1,000
Expected return on plan assets . .	2,000
Actual return on plan assets.	3,000

Required

a. Provide the entries related to the defined pension plan for 2020 assuming a discount rate of 8%. Amortize Accumulated OCI—Pension Gain/Loss using the straight-line method over 15 years.
b. Assuming pension expenses are not capitalized as part of inventory or other assets, indicate the effect on the income statement for the year ended December 31, 2020.
c. Indicate the changes in balance sheet accounts between January 1 and December 31, 2020.
d. Create a worksheet to summarize the pension data at the end of 2020.

Exercise 19-55
Preparing Pension Entries and Pension Worksheet **LO5, 7**
Hint: See Demo 19-7

Rollo Company has a defined benefit pension plan. At the end of the current reporting period, December 31, 2020, the following information was available:

Projected benefit obligation	
Balance, Jan. 1, 2020	$150,000
Service cost	40,000
Interest cost ($150,000 × 10% discount rate)	15,000
Change in actuarial assumptions on Dec. 31, 2020	(400)
Pension benefits paid	(42,000)
Balance, Dec. 31, 2020	$162,600
Accumulated benefit obligation	$120,000
Vested benefit obligation	$ 40,000

Plan assets	
Balance, Jan. 1, 2020	$160,000
Actual return on plan assets (same as expected)	16,000
Funding of plan by Rollo	30,000
Pension benefits paid to retirees	(42,000)
Balance, Dec. 31, 2020	$164,000
Accumulated other comprehensive income Jan. 1, 2020	
Accumulated OCI—Prior Service Cost	$20,000 Dr.
Accumulated OCI—Pension Gain/Loss	2,000 Cr.

Required

a. Create a worksheet to summarize the pension data at the end of 2020. Assume that Rollo uses the corridor approach in amortizing the pension gain/loss. Assume an average remaining service period of 10 years.

b. Provide Rollo's pension entries at December 31, 2020.

Exercise 19-56
Preparing Pension Entries and Pension Worksheet **LO5, 7**

Information for the Jenkins Company defined benefit pension plan follows. Jenkins uses the straight-line method to amortize prior service cost and corridor amortization for gains and losses.

Account Balances	Jan. 1, 2020
Projected Benefit Obligation	$700,000 Cr.
Plan Assets	500,000 Dr.
Accumulated OCI—Pension Gain/Loss	160,000 Cr.
Accumulated OCI—PSC	120,000 Dr.

Activity	
Service cost, 2020	$ 60,000
Actuarial loss determined Dec. 31, 2020	40,000
Actual return on plan assets, 2020	55,000
Funding, 2020	88,000
Benefits paid, 2020	0

Other	
Discount rate	8%
Expected rate of return on plan assets	10%
Average remaining service period of active plan participants	10 years

Required

a. Prepare the December 31, 2019, presentation of funded status.

b. Prepare the entries to record 2020 pension expense, gain and loss deferral (if any), contributions, and benefits.

c. Prepare the December 31, 2020, presentation of funded status.

d. Determine whether amortization of net unrecognized gain or loss is required for 2021.

e. Prepare a pension worksheet for 2020.

Exercise 19-57
Preparing Pension Entries and Pension Worksheet **LO5, 7**
Hint: See Demo 19-7

Laker Company has a noncontributory defined benefit pension plan. The company must record its pension expense for the year ended December 31, 2020. The following data are available ($ thousands).

Activity	2020
Service cost	$ 60
Interest cost (at 8%)	48
Loss on PBO due to actuarial changes determined Dec. 31, 2020	20
Pension benefit paid to retirees	200
Actual return on plan assets	36
Employer contributions	120
Pension benefits paid	200

Account Balances	Jan 1, 2020
Accumulated OCI—Prior Service Cost	$ 72 Dr.
Accumulated OCI—Pension Gain/Loss	8 Dr.
Projected Benefit Obligation	600 Cr.
Plan Assets	400 Dr.

Other	
Average remaining service period	10 years
Expected return on plan assets	10%

Required

a. Create a worksheet to summarize the pension data at the end of 2020. Assume that Laker uses the corridor approach in amortizing any pension gain/loss.

b. Provide Laker's pension entries at December 31, 2020.

Exercise 19-58
Determining Reporting Amounts and Preparing Disclosures **LO5, 6**

The following information relates to the contributory, defined pension plan of Klarbrun Inc.

Account Balances	Jan. 1, 2020
Projected Benefit Obligation	$75,000 Cr.
Plan Assets	78,750 Dr.
Accumulated OCI—Prior Service Cost	49,500 Dr.

Activity	2020
Service cost	$ 49,000
Interest cost	6,000
Prior service cost amortization	500
Actual return on plan assets (same as expected return)	4,725
Cash funding by company	37,500
Cash funding by plan participants	10,000
Pension benefits paid to retirees	5,000
Net income	500,000

Required

a. Prepare the portion of the pension disclosure showing the components of pension expense.

b. Prepare the portion of the pension disclosure showing the reconciliation of the projected benefit obligation, plan assets, and funded balance.

c. Prepare the statement of comprehensive income, assuming there are no other OCI items except those related to pensions.

d. Determine the ending balance in accumulated other comprehensive loss.

Exercise 19-59
Defining Pension Terminology **LO1, 2, 3, 4, 5, 6**

Terms relating to concepts discussed in this chapter along with descriptions of the terms are included in the following two lists.

____ 1. Projected benefit obligation
____ 2. Expected return on plan assets
____ 3. Amortization of gains and losses
____ 4. Pension plan assets
____ 5. Pension expense
____ 6. Fair value (of plan assets)
____ 7. Amortization of prior service costs
____ 8. Net pension asset
____ 9. Accumulated benefit obligation
____10. Interest cost
____11. Discount rate
____12. Service cost
____13. Vested benefit obligation
____14. Actual return on plan assets

a. Amount reported as pension expense for the period; has five components
b. Allocation of the cost of retroactive pension benefits to periodic expense
c. Actuarial present value of future pension benefits earned as of the measurement date excluding the effects of expected future compensation levels
d. Cost of future pension benefits earned during the current accounting period
e. The interest rate used to compute the present value of future pension benefits earned by employees.
f. Present value of the employee's benefits at the measurement date not contingent on future employee service
g. Allocation of the difference between expected return and actual return on plan assets and changes in actuarial assumptions to periodic expense
h. Cumulative fund assets in excess of the PBO
i. Difference between plan assets at fair value at the beginning and end of the period minus contributions and plus distributions during the accounting period
j. The value of plan assets between a willing buyer and a willing seller (not a forced sale)
k. Actuarial present value of future pension benefits earned as of the measurement date, including the effects of current and future compensation levels
l. Projected benefit obligation at the beginning of the current accounting period multiplied by the discount rate
m. Resources set aside to provide future pension benefits to retirees
n. Beginning market-related value of pension plan assets multiplied by the beginning of year plan assets

Required

Match each term, 1 through 14, with the most appropriate description *a* through *n*.

Exercise 19-60
Determining How Pension Items Affect Accounts **LO1, 2, 3, 4, 5, 6**

Pension items discussed in this chapter along with account effects are included in the following two lists.

Account Effects	Pension Items
____ 1. Increase pension expense	*a.* Service cost
____ 2. Decrease pension expense	*b.* Expected return on plan assets
____ 3. Increase projected benefit obligation	*c.* Excess of expected return over actual return on plan assets
____ 4. Decrease projected benefit obligation	*d.* Excess of actual return over expected return on plan assets
____ 5. Increase plan assets	*e.* Amortization of prior service cost
____ 6. Decrease plan assets	*f.* Actuarial loss on the PBO (deferral)
____ 7. Increase other comprehensive income	*g.* Amendment to prior service cost (increase benefits)
____ 8. Decrease other comprehensive income	*h.* Payment of retirement benefits
____ 9. Decrease cash	*i.* Actuarial gain on the PBO (deferral)
	j. Employer contributions
	k. Interest cost on the PBO
	l. Amortization of actuarial pension loss

Required

Match each pension item, *a* through *l* with the account effect *1* through *9*. More than one account effect may apply to a pension item.

Problems

Problem 19-61
Calculating ABO and PBO Balances **LO1**
Hint: See Demo 19-1B

L. Bryan is a participant in a pension plan. Information on the plan and Bryan's involvement follows.

Plan inception: Jan. 1, 2020
Bryan's first day with the company: Jan. 1, 2020
Bryan's expected service period: 20 years
Bryan's expected final salary: $100,000
Retirement period: 10 years
Brian's salary for 2020 and 2021: $30,000
Discount rate: 10%
Pension benefit formula: Yearly benefit during retirement = (number of years worked)(final salary)/25

Required

a. Compute projected benefit obligation at December 31, 2020.
b. Compute accumulated benefit obligation at December 31, 2020.
c. Compute projected benefit obligation at December 31, 2021.
d. Compute accumulated benefit obligation at December 31, 2021.

Problem 19-62
Calculating ABO and PBO Balances **LO1**
Hint: See Demo 19-1B

The Jets Company sponsors a pension plan with the following pension benefit formula:

Benefit paid at each year-end during retirement = 2% × (Number of service years) × (Annual salary at retirement)

Credit for service began January 1, 2019, Shuler's first day with the company with a starting salary of $45,000. Shuler is expected to work a total of 25 years with an annual salary at retirement of $150,000. He is expected to draw 10 years of retirement benefits. The discount rate is 10%. Starting January 1, 2021, Shuler's new salary is $47,250 after a 5% raise.

Required

a. Considering the information above, compute the following amounts:
1. PBO on January 1, 2020.
2. ABO on January 1, 2020.
3. PBO on January 1, 2021.
4. ABO on January 1, 2021.

b. Consider the following three additional, separate scenarios and compute the following amounts:
1. PBO on January 1, 2020, assuming that the discount rate is 8%.
2. PBO on January 1, 2020, assuming that the starting salary is $100,000 and final salary is $325,000.
3. PBO on January 1, 2020, assuming that the retirement period is 20 years instead of 10.

Problem 19-63
Computing Pension Expense, Two Years
LO4, 5

The following information pertains to a pension plan for Gucci Company that recognizes only the minimum amortization of unrecognized gains and losses through the corridor method.

Account Balances	Jan. 1, 2020
Accumulated OCI—Pension Gain/Loss . . .	$ 0
Projected Benefit Obligation, not considering 2020 actuarial loss.	60,000
Plan assets.	24,000
Accumulated OCI—Prior Service Cost (average remaining service life of employees covered under prior service cost grant: 2 years).	8,000

Activity	
Actuarial loss, 2020 (determined Jan. 1, 2020).	$12,000
Service cost, 2020	12,000
Service cost, 2021	14,000
Funding amount, 2020	16,000
Funding amount, 2021	20,000
Actual return on fund in 2020	1,800
Actual return on fund in 2021	2,400

Other	
Discount rate:	10%
Expected rate of return on fund assets:	12%
No benefits were paid in either year.	
Average remaining service period in years for amortization of any pension gain/loss . . .	12

Required

a. Compute Gucci's pension expense for 2020.

b. For 2021, compute the following amounts:
1. Plan asset balance, January 1, 2021.
2. PBO balance, January 1, 2021.
3. Accumulated Pension Gain/Loss balance, January 1, 2021.
4. Pension expense, 2021.

Problem 19-64
Calculating PBO, Plan Assets, and Underfunding or Overfunding **LO2, 3, 4**

Netflicks Inc. has a noncontributory defined benefit pension plan.

Projected Benefit Obligation	
Balance, Jan. 1, 2020.	$164,000
Balance, Dec. 31, 2020	214,000

Plan Assets (at Fair Value)	
Balance, Jan. 1, 2020.	$ 80,000
Balance, Dec. 31, 2020	140,000

Required

a. How much did the PBO increase during 2020? Name five items that could have caused the PBO to change.

b. How much did pension plan assets change during 2020? Name three items that could have caused the change in plan assets.

c. Compute the plan's funded balance at (1) January 1, 2020, and (2) December 31, 2020. Explain what these amounts mean.

Problem 19-65
Computing Pension Gain/Loss **LO4**

Information for a pension plan for J. Q. Morgan Inc. follows.

Account Balances	
Accumulated OCI—Pension Gain/Loss, Jan. 1, 2020	$ 7,000 Cr.
Plan assets, Jan. 1, 2020.	200,000 Dr.
Plan assets, Dec. 31, 2020.	220,000 Dr.

Activity	2020
Contributions	$40,000
Benefits paid.	32,000
Actuarial loss on PBO (computed on Dec. 31, 2020)	8,000

J. Q. Morgan Inc. elects to amortize pension gain/loss into income for the period using the straight-line method (10-year average remaining service period) without applying the corridor approach. The expected rate of return on plan assets is 7%.

Required

Compute Accumulated OCI—Pension Gain/Loss at January 1, 2021.

Problem 19-66 Preparing Entries and Reconciliations for Pension Plan **LO3, 4, 5**

Mason Company has a noncontributory defined benefit pension plan. On December 31, 2020, information about the pension plan included the following.

Projected Benefit Obligation, Jan. 1, 2020	$ 40,000
Service cost	60,000
Interest cost	3,600
Pension benefits paid	0
Projected Benefit Obligation, Dec. 31, 2020	103,600
Plan Assets, Jan. 1, 2020	50,000
Funding of plan	37,000
Actual return and expected return on plan assets	10,000
Discount rate	9%

Required

a. Prepare a reconciliation of plan assets for 2020.
b. Compute the plan's funded balance on the beginning and ending dates.
c. Provide the 2020 entries for Mason Company to record the defined benefit pension plan.
d. Provide the same entries in (c), assuming cash funding of $55,000 (instead of $37,000).
e. Provide the computation for the $3,600 of interest.

Problem 19-67 Preparing Entries and Worksheet for Pension Plan **LO5, 7**

Luloo Inc. has a defined benefit pension plan. At the end of the current reporting period, December 31, 2020, the following information was available.

Account Balances	Jan. 1, 2020
PBO	$2,400 Cr.
Plan Assets	2,000 Dr.
Accumulated OCI—Prior Service Cost	180 Dr.
Accumulated OCI—Pension Gain/Loss	144 Dr.

Activity	2020
Service cost	$ 312
Interest cost ($2,400 × 7% discount rate)	168
Loss on PBO due to a change in actuarial assumptions determined Dec. 31, 2020	72
Pension benefits paid	(160)
Actual return on plan assets (same as expected)	120
Pension funding payment	280

Required

a. Create a worksheet to summarize the pension data at the end of 2020. Assume that the company amortizes accumulated prior service costs over a nine-year service period. The company amortizes its accumulated pension gain/loss using the corridor approach and amortizes over a nine-year average remaining service period.
b. Provide Luloo Inc's pension entries at December 31, 2020.

Problem 19-68 Preparing Worksheet for Pension Plan and Analyze Changes **LO7**

Cruise Company has a noncontributory defined benefit pension plan. The annual accounting period ends on December 31. The following plan information relates to the year 2020.

Projected Benefit Obligation	
Balance, Jan. 1, 2020	$16,000
Service cost	1,920
Interest cost ($16,000 × 8% discount rate)	1,280
Loss (gain) change in actuarial assumptions determined Dec. 31, 2020	660
Pension benefit paid to retirees	(1,600)
Balance, Dec. 31, 2020	$18,260

Plan Assets	
Balance, Jan. 1, 2020	$12,600
Actual return on plan assets	1,000
Funding to plan by Cruise	3,000
Pension benefits paid to retirees	(1,600)
Balance, Dec. 31, 2020	$15,000

Other Information	
Accumulated OCI—Prior Service Cost, Jan. 1, 2020	$1,980 Dr.
Accumulated OCI—Pension Gain/Loss, Jan. 1, 2020	440 Cr.
Expected return on plan assets	1,000
Average remaining service period	11 years

Required

a. Create a worksheet to summarize the pension data at the end of 2020. Assume that Cruise uses the corridor approach in amortizing any pension gain/loss.

b. The company president asked the following question: We paid $3,000 cash to the pension fund, but the projected benefit obligation increased over $2,000. Why? Prepare a written response with data and explanation.

Problem 19-69
Analyzing Pension Information for Two Years **LO3, 4**

The following schedule provides two years of information for Rhino Inc. related to its defined benefit plan.

	Dec. 31, 2020	Dec. 31, 2021
Projected Benefit Obligation	$120,000 Cr.	$194,000 Cr.
Plan Assets	95,000 Dr.	116,000 Dr.
Accumulated OCI—Prior Service Cost	0 Dr.	18,000 Dr.
Accumulated OCI—Pension Gain/Loss	1,000 Cr.	3,450 Cr.

In 2021, Rhino Inc. made a contribution to pension plan assets. Payout to retirees in 2021 totaled $40,000. The discount rate is 8%. Expected return on plan assets is 9%. Assume no amortization of prior service cost or pension gain/loss in 2021 and no new actuarial changes to the PBO in 2021.

Required

Based on the information provided for Rhino Inc., measure the following amounts:

a. Funded balance as of December 31, 2020.

b. Funded balance as of December 31, 2021.

c. Actual return on plan assets.

d. Employer contributions.

e. Service cost.

f. Total pension expense.

Problem 19-70
Preparing Pension Worksheets for Two Years **LO7**

Voss Company has a noncontributory defined benefit pension plan for its employees. The data available at year-end are as follows.

Balance, Jan. 1,	2020	2021
Projected Benefit Obligation	$1,520 Cr.	$1,752 Cr.
Plan Assets	940 Dr.	1,084 Dr.
Accumulated OCI—Prior Service Cost	100 Dr.	108 Dr.
Accumulated OCI—Pension Gain/Loss	182 Dr.	199 Dr.

Activity	2020	2021
Service cost	$200	$238
Interest cost	152	140
Prior service cost amendment, Jan. 1 (increase to PBO)	20	13
Loss on PBO due to actuarial changes, Dec. 31	10	6
Pension benefits paid	150	170
Actual return on plan assets	84	92
Plan funding	210	320

Other	2020	2021
Expected return on plan assets	10%	10%
Average remaining service period	10 years	9 years

Required

Prepare worksheets to summarize the pension data at the end of 2020 and 2021. Assume that Voss Company uses the corridor approach in amortizing any pension gain/loss.

Problem 19-71
Preparing Pension Worksheets for Two Years **LO5, 7**

Andros Company has a noncontributory defined benefit pension plan. The data for the two years are as follows.

Balance, Jan. 1	2020	2021
Projected Benefit Obligation	$1,700 Cr.	$2,215 Cr.
Plan Assets	1,000 Dr.	1,210 Dr.
Accumulated OCI—Prior Service Cost	0 Dr.	216 Dr.
Accumulated OCI—Pension Gain/Loss	150 Dr.	180 Dr.

Activity	2020	2021
Service cost	$180	$210
Prior service cost (plan amended, Jan. 1, 2020)	240	
Increase in PBO due to actuarial change (Dec. 31)	20	5
Pension benefits paid	80	125
Actual return on plan assets	90	110
Contributions (funding)	200	440

Other	2020	2021
Expected return on plan assets	10%	10%
Discount rate	8%	9%
Average remaining service period	10 years	9 years

Required

a. Prepare worksheets to summarize the pension data at the end of 2020 and 2021. Assume that Andros Company uses the corridor approach in amortizing any pension gain/loss.

b. Provide journal entries for each year based upon the worksheet amounts.

Problem 19-72
Preparing Pension Worksheet **LO5, 7**

Jack Company has a noncontributory defined benefit pension plan. The company will record its pension expense for the year ended December 31, 2020.

Balance	Jan. 1, 2020
Projected Benefit Obligation	$300 Cr.
Plan Assets	170 Dr.
Accumulated OCI—Prior Service Cost	40 Dr.
Accumulated OCI—Pension Gain/Loss	80 Dr.

Activity	2020
Service cost	$ 50
Gain on PBO due to change in actuarial assumption (determined Dec. 31, 2020)	10
Pension benefit paid to retirees	124
Actual return on plan assets	8
Contributions	110
Pension benefits paid	124

Other	
Expected return on plan assets	6%
Discount rate	8%
Average remaining service period	10 years

Required

a. Prepare a worksheet to summarize the pension data at the end of 2020. Assume that Jack uses the corridor approach in amortizing any pension gain/loss.

b. Provide journal entries based upon the worksheet amounts.

Problem 19-73
Preparing Pension Entries for Three Years
LO3, 5

This problem involves three years of accounting for the defined benefit pension plan of Americo's Inc. The pension plan for the company has been in existence for several years before January 1, 2020. The following data relates to the plan.

Discount rate and expected rate of return	10%
PBO, Jan. 1, 2020, (before amendment)	$1,965
Plan assets at fair value, Jan. 1, 2020	$2,094
Average remaining service period − Prior service cost	4 years
Average remaining service period − Pension gain/loss	10 years

	2020	2021	2022
Service cost	$ 800	$1,400	$1,700
Contributions	1,100	1,600	1,700
Actual return on plan assets	209	300	600
Benefits paid	0	0	0

On January 1, 2020, the company retroactively granted three employees an increase in benefits based on work performed before that date. The immediate present value of those benefits is $3,000.

On January 1, 2020, the actuaries inform the company that on the basis of new estimates, the actuarial gain on the PBO is $1,200. The company elects minimum amortization of the net unrecognized gain or loss using the corridor approach.

On January 1, 2022, the actuaries inform the company that on the basis of new estimates, average life expectancy of retirees and current employees is expected to be higher than previously anticipated. The immediate effect on the actuarial present value of benefits based on the budget formula is a $1,400 loss on the PBO.

Required

For each of the three years 2020 through 2022:

a. Record the pension related journal entries.

b. Prepare the end of year presentation of funded status.

c. Determine the year-end balance in the accumulated other comprehensive income accounts.

Accounting Decisions and Judgments

AD&J 19-74
Analyzing Retirement Benefits **LO3, 4**

Real World Analysis **Ford Motor Company** (Ford) is a global automotive and mobility company based in Dearborn, Michigan. Below is an excerpt from its 2015 Form 10-K.

NOTE 12. RETIREMENT BENEFITS The year-end status of these plans was as follows (in millions):

Pension Benefits U.S. Plans	2015	2014
Change in Benefit Obligation		
Benefit obligation at January 1	$47,103	$43,182
Service cost	586	507
Interest cost	1,817	1,992
Amendments	99	—
Separation programs and other	(27)	(50)
Plan participant contributions	26	26
Benefits paid	(2,949)	(3,028)
Actuarial (gain)/loss	(1,719)	4,474
Benefit obligation at December 31	44,936	47,103
Change in Plan Assets		
Fair value of plan assets at January 1	44,844	41,217
Actual return on plan assets	(755)	6,542
Company contributions	130	130
Plan participant contributions	26	26
Benefits paid	(2,949)	(3,028)
Other	(44)	(43)
Fair value of plan assets at December 31	41,252	44,844
Funded status at December 31	$ (3,684)	$ (2,259)
Amounts Recognized on the Balance Sheet		
Prepaid assets	$ —	$ 76
Other liabilities	(3,684)	(2,335)
Total	$ (3,684)	$ (2,259)
Amounts Recognized in Accumulated Other Comprehensive Loss (pre-tax)		
Unamortized prior service costs/(credits)	$ 553	$ 609

Required

a. What is the funded status of the plan in the most current year?

b. Estimate the discount rate.

c. Determine as many components of 2015 pension expense as possible from the information provided.

AD&J 19-75 Analyzing Defined Pension Plan **LO3, 4**

Real World Analysis United Parcel Service Inc. (UPS), a package delivery company, reported the following in its annual report regarding its pension plans (company-sponsored employee benefit plans).

> The UPS Retirement Plan is noncontributory and includes substantially all eligible employees of participating domestic subsidiaries who are not members of a collective bargaining unit, as well as certain employees covered by a collective bargaining agreement. This plan generally provides for retirement benefits based on average compensation levels earned by employees prior to retirement. Benefits payable under this plan are subject to maximum compensation limits and the annual benefit limits for a tax-qualified defined benefit plan as prescribed by the Internal Revenue Service ("IRS").

	2015
Discount rate	4.40%
Rate of compensation increase	4.29%
Expected return on assets	8.75%

U.S. Pension Benefits	2015	2014
Funded status:		
Fair value of plan assets	$28,887	$28,828
Benefit obligation	(36,846)	(37,521)
Funded status recognized at December 31	$ (7,959)	$ (8,693)
Funded Status Recognized in our Balance Sheet:		
Other non-current assets	$ 0	$ 0
Other current liabilities	(16)	(17)
Pension and postretirement benefit obligations	(7,943)	(8,676)
Net liability at December 31	$ (7,959)	$ (8,693)
Amounts Recognized in AOCI:		
Unrecognized net prior service cost	$ (954)	$ (1,122)
Unrecognized net actuarial gain (loss)	(3,263)	(3,752)
Gross unrecognized cost at December 31	(4,217)	(4,874)
Deferred tax assets (liabilities) at December 31	1,585	1,833
Net unrecognized cost at December 31	$ (2,632)	$ (3,041)

The company also reported accumulated benefit obligation for U.S. pension plans as of the measurement dates in 2015 and 2014 of $34.210 and $34.725 billion, respectively.

Required

a. Estimate 2015 interest cost based upon the information provided.

b. Estimate the 2015 expected return on plan assets based upon the information provided.

c. What is the funded status of the plan in the most current year?

d. What is the funded status in the most current year comparing ABO to plan assets? Why is this different from your answer to part *c*?

AD&J 19-76 Analyzing Pension Plans **LO3, 4, 6**

Real World Analysis 3M Company is a diversified technology company with a global presence in the following businesses: Industrial; Safety and Graphics; Electronics and Energy; Health Care; and Consumer. In its 2013–2015 annual reports, 3M Company shows the following regarding its defined benefit plans.

> 3M has company-sponsored retirement plans covering substantially all U.S. employees and many employees outside the United States. In total, 3M has over 80 defined benefit plans in 28 countries. Pension benefits associated with these plans generally are based on each participant's years of service, compensation, and age at retirement or termination. The primary U.S. defined benefit pension plan was closed to new participants effective January 1, 2009.

U.S. Defined Pension Plans ($ millions)	2015	2014	2013	2012
Projected benefit obligation	$15,856	$16,435	$13,967	$14,830
Accumulated benefit obligation	14,834	15,319	13,357	14,127
Fair value of plan assets	13,966	14,623	13,889	13,781
Pension Costs				
Service cost	$ 293	$ 241	$ 258	$ 254
Interest cost	655	676	598	587
Expected return on plan assets	(1,069)	(1,043)	(1,046)	(992)
Amortization of prior service cost (benefit)	(24)	4	5	5
Amortization of net actuarial (gain) loss	409	243	399	470
Other	2	—	—	26
Pension Expense	$ 266	$ 121	$ 214	$ 350
Changes to Other Comprehensive Income				
Prior service cost (benefit)	$ —	$ (266)	$ —	$ —
Amortization of prior service cost (benefit)	24	(4)	(5)	(5)
Net actuarial (gain) loss	312	2,167	(743)	(470)
Amortization of net actuarial (gain) loss	(409)	(243)	(399)	(470)
	$ (73)	$ 1,654	$(1,147)	$ (945)
Assumptions[1]	**2015**	**2014**	**2013**	**2012**
Discount rate	4.10%	4.98%	4.14%	4.15%
Return on plan assets	7.75%	7.75%	8.00%	8.25%
Cash Flow Information				
Pension and postretirement contributions	$(267)	$(215)	$(482)	$(1,146)
Financial Statement Information				
Total assets	$32,718	$31,209	$33,550	$33,876
Total liabilities	20,971	18,067	15,602	15,836
Total equity	11,747	13,142	17,948	18,040
Net income	4,841	4,998	4,721	4,511
Total other comprehensive income	(72)	(2,395)	755	231
Net cash provided by operating activities	6,420	6,626	5,817	5,300

[1] Weighted-average assumption used to determine net cost

Required

a. What is the funded status of the plan using the PBO over the four years presented? Comment on your results.

b. What is recorded in 3M's liabilities on the balance sheet related to the pension plans over the four years presented? Calculate the percentage of these amounts over the company's total liabilities. Calculate the percentage of the PBO over the company's total liabilities. Comment on your results.

c. Compute the funded status of the plan using the ABO for 2012–2015. How does this differ from your results in part *a*? Why?

d. Calculate the interest cost and expected return on plan assets for 2013, 2014, and 2015.

e. When did 3M record prior period cost amendment(s) in the four years presented and for what amount? What was the impact on prior service cost amortization (if any)? Estimate the average service life related to the plan amendment.

f. Calculate the cash impact of pension plan contributions as a percentage of net cash provided by operating activities over the past four years. Comment on your results.

g. Calculate comprehensive income for the four years presented and compare to net income for the four years presented. Comment on the deferral of any significant amounts in other comprehensive income based upon your analysis. How do you think the company treats the allocation of pension gains/losses?

h. 3M reported the following in its 2015 Form 10-K note on pension plans. How does 3M's shift from offering new employees defined pension plans to now offering 401(k) plans affect its pension plan accounting?

The Company also sponsors employee savings plans under Section 401(k) of the Internal Revenue Code. These plans are offered to substantially all regular U.S. employees. For eligible employees hired prior to January 1, 2009, employee 401(k) contributions of up to 6% of eligible compensation were matched in cash at rates of 60% or 75%, depending on the plan in which the employee participates. Employees hired on or after January 1, 2009, received a cash match of 100% for employee 401(k) contributions of up to 6% of eligible compensation and also received an employer retirement income account cash contribution of 3% of the participant's total eligible compensation.

AD&J 19-77 Analyzing Postretirement Benefit Plans **LO3, 6, 8, 9**

Real World Analysis In its 2013, 2014, and 2015 annual reports, **3M Company** shows the following regarding its postretirement benefit plans.

The Company also provides certain postretirement health care and life insurance benefits for substantially all of its U.S. employees who reach retirement age while employed by the Company. Most international employees and retirees are covered by government health care programs.

Postretirement Benefits ($ millions)	2015	2014	2013	2012
Change in benefit obligation				
Postretirement Benefits				
Benefit obligation at beginning of year	$2,462	$2,017	$2,205	$2,108
Service cost	75	65	80	78
Interest cost	98	97	88	86
Participant contributions	14	18	30	52
Foreign exchange rate changes	(22)	(11)	(13)	(2)
Plan amendments	(211)	—	(20)	—
Actuarial (gain)loss	(80)	415	(225)	31
Medicare Part D Reimbursement	1	1	2	8
Benefit payments	(122)	(140)	(130)	(156)
Other	1	—	—	—
Benefit obligation at end of year	$2,216	$2,462	$2,017	$2,205
Change in plan assets				
Fair value of plan assets at beginning of year	$1,436	$1,405	$1,321	$1,209
Actual return on plan assets	36	148	178	149
Company contributions	3	5	6	67
Participant contributions	14	18	30	52
Benefit payments	(122)	(140)	(130)	(156)
Fair value of plan assets at end of year	$1,367	$1,436	$1,405	$1,321

Required

a. What is the funded status of the plan using the APBO over the four years presented? Comment on your results.

b. What is recorded in 3M's assets and/or liabilities on the balance sheet related to the postretirement plans over the four years presented?

c. In Note 11 of the 3M Company's 2015 Form 10-K, the company reported the following. Comment on this change as it relates to the estimation of postretirement pension obligations.

The Company is in the process of transitioning all current and future retirees in the U.S. postretirement health care benefit plans to a savings account benefits-based plan. The contributions provided by the Company to the health savings accounts increase 3% per year for employees who retired prior to January 1, 2016 and increase 1.5% for employees who retire on or after January 1, 2016. Therefore, the Company no longer has material exposure to health care cost inflation.

AD&J 19-78 Analyzing Components of Pension Loss **LO4, 6**

Communication Case At December 31, 2020, as a result of its defined benefit pension plan, Creste Company had a balance in Accumulated OCI—Pension Loss and an underfunded pension balance. Creste's pension plan and its actuarial assumptions have not changed since it began operations in 2010. Creste has made annual contributions to the plan.

Required

Write a one-page report addressing the following questions.

a. Identify the components of net pension expense that should be recognized in Creste's 2020 financial statements.

b. What circumstances caused Creste's (1) net pension loss and (2) underfunded pension balance?

AD&J 19-79
Assessing the Delayed Recognition in Pension Accounting **LO5**

Ethics Case GAAP accounting for pension plans has been criticized by those who maintain that it provides a wealth of opportunity for sponsors to manipulate and smooth earnings. Would you propose changes to these standards?

Required

Briefly discuss the provisions of the accounting standards that contribute to opportunities for income smoothing or manipulation. For each point, give your opinion as to whether the provision is appropriate in terms of optimal measurement and reporting (as opposed to the economic consequences of such reporting).

AD&J 19-80
Recording Pension Expense Based on Funding **LO1**

Judgment Case An alternative conceptualization of pension expense that had been proposed at various times before the current standards, would have based annual pension expense on the required annual contribution needed to fully fund the estimated total pension benefit at retirement. It is called the cost approach because pension expense for a period is considered to be the contribution (annuity amount) required in that year to fund the plan. This approach is not allowed under GAAP.

Required

a. Using the following example developed in the text, determine 2020 pension expense using the cost approach, where funding is assumed to take place equally over Nicole's service period.

Nicole (age 40) started working at 5M on January 1, 2020, at a starting annual salary of $45,000. Nicole's expected retirement date is December 31, 2044, with an annual salary of $150,000. Benefits vest as follows: 10% after the first year, 15% after the second year, and 20% each year after until 100%. Nicole's expected retirement period is 10 years. The relevant discount rate is 10%. The applicable pension benefit formula for the defined benefit plan is

Annual benefit payment during retirement = 2% × Number of service years × Final salary

b. Assume the company funds its obligation to Nicole at the date she retires. How much funding is required?

c. Based on your findings above and your knowledge of GAAP, provide your opinion as to whether the cost approach would be a better approach to measuring pension expense than the current standards.

AD&J 19-81
Considering Opportunities for Managing Pension Expense and Liabilities **LO2, 3, 4, 5**

Ethics Case We are the auditors for Frito Inc., which is in considerable financial difficulty. In particular, debt covenants may be violated if liabilities are increased. In addition, the client's balance in retained earnings is minimal as a result of excessively high dividends and diminished earnings in the past several years.

Frito Inc. is dominated by its CEO, a person who has served the company for 30 years. The CEO makes most of the major decisions in the company. This person is the company's primary representative working with the audit staff. There has been considerable turnover of audit committee members in the last two years. The CEO is very aggressive with respect to earnings.

From the minutes, we have discovered that extreme emphasis has been placed on meeting earnings projections. Department officers have been fired for not meeting earnings goals for two successive years. We know that, through PCAOB Audit Standard No. 8, part of our responsibility as an auditor is to develop an audit plan that is sensitive to audit risk. Audit risk is the probability that we may unknowingly fail to modify our audit report on financial statements that are materially misstated. Our audit plan should be designed to provide reasonable assurance that material errors and fraud are detected.

Required

We understand that the pressures faced by Frito Inc. may create incentives for unethical and fraudulent financial reporting. In a report of not more than two pages, discuss the aspects of pension accounting that should be considered with special care. What pension-related variables might be changed, and in what direction, to achieve reduced pension expense and liabilities? Include in your discussion reasons why you chose these variables.

AD&J 19-82
Analyzing Pension Expense; Assumed Rate of Salary Increase **LO2**

Communication Case Rogers Inc., has a defined benefit pension plan for its 2,000 employees. It provides covered employees with a pension equal to 1.5% of their average salary during the two calendar years of highest pay times the number of years of service, with a maximum of 30 years. Benefits are based on an assumed retirement age of 65 and are reduced or increased to their actuarial equivalents for those employees who retire before or after age 65. The projected benefit obligation of Rogers' plan on December 31, 2020, was $180 million, and the fair value of assets in the fund was $207 million.

Early in 2021 Joel Stave, CFO of Rogers Inc., received a report from the actuaries of Rogers' pension plan that recommended an increase in the assumed rate of increase in future salaries among other things. An annual rate of 3% per year had been used for several years; according to the actuaries' experience during the last five years, a period of relatively low inflation, average salaries increased considerably more than that. Actuaries recommended a 6% rate that would increase Rogers' year-end projected benefit obligation by 40%. The actuaries also sent a copy of the report to Aaron Rogers, CEO of Rogers Inc.

Several days after receiving the report, Joel and Aaron were having lunch when the subject of the report came up. Rogers began by saying that initially he feared that a 40% increase in the pension obligation would wipe out 2020 profits, but after discussing the astronomical rise in the stock market in 2020 with his broker, he began to think that since Rogers Inc.'s pension fund is heavily invested in equities, the effect of the increase in the salary increase rate might be offset to some extent by the large increase in return on plan assets in 2020. His broker had mentioned to him that the bull market of 2020 caused his company's plan to go from underfunded to overfunded. Rogers then asked Joel what he thought a revision of the salary increase rate would do to 2020 profits, but before he had a chance to respond, they were interrupted and did not have a chance to get back to the subject.

Later that day Joel received an email from Rogers asking him to write a memo explaining what the proposed revision in the salary increase rate would do to profits. Joel will be out of town for several days so he has asked you, his assistant, to draft an email to Rogers.

Required

Prepare a draft of the requested email.

AD&J 19-83 Calculating Funding Payment, Multiple Employees **LO1**

Challenge Problem Plans are being made to fund the prospective pension benefits of a group of employees of Forever 31 Inc. due to retire in nine years and to be paid in these amounts from one to five years after retirement.

End of year 1	$ 90,000
End of year 2	50,000
End of year 3	30,000
End of year 4	15,000
End of year 5	5,000
Thereafter	0
Total of pension payments	$190,000

Funds deposited with the pension fund trustee will earn 6% per year. The pension plan contract calls for the deposit of an amount sufficient to fund all of the expected payments from the fund by the date the employees retire.

Required

a. Compute the amount required by the trustee on the employees' retirement date, assuming that the first pension payment is one year after retirement and prepare an amortization schedule showing principal and interest payments on the pension liability over the 5 years.

b. Assuming that eight equal payments are made to the trustee, with the last payment coinciding with the retirement date, compute the amount of the equal payment.

AD&J 19-84 Preparing Pension Worksheet for Two Years with Corridor (Minimum) Amortization **LO5, 6, 7**

Challenge Problem Voss Company has a noncontributory defined benefit pension plan for its employees. The data available at year-end, December 31, 2020, and 2021, are as follows.

$ thousands	2020	2021
Projected benefit obligation, beginning	$1,520	?
Service cost	200	$238
Interest cost	152	140
Loss (gain), actuarial changes, Dec. 31	10	6
Average remaining service period*	10 years	9 years
Plan assets, balance at beginning	1,450	?
Actual return on plan assets	135	155
Funding of plan	210	320
Pension benefits paid to retirees	(150)	(170)
Expected return on plan assets	10%	10%
Accumulated OCI—Prior Service Cost, Jan. 1	100 Dr.	?
Accumulated OCI—Pension Gain/Loss, Jan. 1	182 Dr.	?

*Assume this for all unrecognized pension costs.

Required

a. Prepare a worksheet to summarize the pension data at the end of 2020 and 2021. Assume that Voss uses the corridor approach in amortizing any pension gain/loss.

b. Provide the following disclosures for both years: (1) the amount of pension expense for each period with separate disclosure of service cost, interest cost, actual return on plan assets, and net total of other components and (2) the presentation of funded status.

AD&J 19-85
Determining Change in Principle, Estimation, or Error Correction
LO6

Challenge Problem Pension plan disclosures provide useful information for investors and creditors that is not available in the financial statements.

Required

For each of the following separate scenarios, briefly explain how the event would be treated (as a change in principle, correction of an error, or a change in estimate).

a. Recognition of pension gains/losses in net income rather than including in accumulated other comprehensive income and amortizing according to the corridor approach.

b. The expected rate of return of plan assets drops from 6.75% to 6.70%.

c. Employee contributions to a contributory plan were not included in the PBO reconciliation in the prior year.

d. The discount rate used by the actuary changed by a full percentage point from one year to the next.

e. The company disclosed estimated gross benefit payments for the next five years and the aggregate amount for the next five years after that. The amount disclosed for the next year does not match exactly to the actual payment.

AD&J 19-86
Assessing the Tax Effect of Pension Entries **LO5**

Challenge Problem Mac Company has a noncontributory defined benefit pension plan. On December 31, 2020, the following data (all presented before tax) are available.

PBO balance, Jan. 1, 2020	$45,000
Plan Asset balance, Jan. 1, 2020	52,500
Actuarial loss on PBO determined Dec. 31, 2020	5,000
Prior service cost (10-year average service life)	5,000
Service cost	32,500
Interest cost	4,000
Pension benefits paid	3,500
Actual return on plan assets (same as expected return)	2,500
Cash funding	35,500
Tax rate	25%

Required

Prepare the year-end pension journal entries including the income tax effect. Assume that the pension is considered overfunded for tax purposes. Tax assets and/or liabilities will need to be established for the timing differences between book and tax. *Hint*: Record items in other comprehensive income net of tax.

AD&J 19-87
Analyzing the Effects of a Pension Freeze
LO1, 2

Trueblood Case The Trueblood case series, prepared by Deloitte professionals, are based on recent accounting technical issues that require research and judgment.The cases may be accessed through the Deloitte foundation at the following website: https://www2.deloitte.com/us/en/pages/about-deloitte/articles/trueblood-case-studies-deloitte-foundation.html. The following case is relevant to the content provided in this chapter: Case 16-8 Frozen. This case requires an analysis of options faced by a struggling company to either amend a pension plan by eliminating the future earnings of pension benefits or reduce head count.

AD&J 19-88
Defining Terms **LO1**

Codification Skills How are the terms (1) attribution, (2) projected benefit obligation, (3) accumulated benefit obligation, (4) net periodic pension cost, (5) defined contribution plan, and (6) defined benefit plan defined in the Codification?

AD&J 19-89
Performing Accounting Research **LO4, 5, 6, 8**

Codification Skills Through research in the Codification, identify the specific citation for each of the following items included as guidance in this chapter for pension accounting.

a. Amortizing of gains/losses using the corridor approach FASB ASC ___-___-___-___

b. Disclosure of defined contribution plans FASB ASC ___-___-___-___

c. Components of net periodic pension cost FASB ASC ___-___-___-___

d. Disclosure of the accumulated benefit obligation for public companies FASB ASC ☐-☐-☐-☐

e. Attribution in postretirement benefit plan accounting FASB ASC ☐-☐-☐-☐

AD&J 19-90 Performing Accounting Research LO1

Codification Skills A settlement is a transaction that is an irrevocable action, relieves the employer (or the plan) of primary responsibility for a pension or postretirement benefit obligation, and eliminates significant risks related to the obligation and the assets used to effect the settlement. How is a settlement recognized in the financial statements? Through research in the Codification, identify the specific citation where guidance is included.

FASB ASC ☐-☐-☐-☐

Appendix—Brief Exercises

App—Brief Exercise 19-91 Explaining Terms LO8 *Hint:* See Demo 19-8

Explain the difference between expected postretirement benefit obligation (EPBO) and accumulated postretirement benefit obligation (APBO) in accounting for postretirement benefits other than pensions.

App—Brief Exercise 19-92 Determining Attribution Period LO8 *Hint:* See Demo 19-8

A postretirement plan promises 100% health care coverage for all employees who retire after age 62. It is expected that participants will have rendered an average of 15 years of service at age 62.

a. What is the full eligibility date for a participant?

b. What is the attribution period (the period to which the expected postretirement benefit obligation is assigned)?

App—Brief Exercise 19-93 Reporting of Postretirement Benefit Plans LO9

The following information is for a postretirement benefit plan where the average remaining service period for active plan participants is 15 years. What is the impact on the balance sheet?

Accumulated Postretirement Benefit Obligation	Plan Assets at Fair Value	Net Postretirement Asset/Liability
$100,000	$200,000	$100,000

App—Brief Exercise 19-94 Computing Postretirement Benefit Expense LO9 *Hint:* See Demo 19-9

Targets Corp. sponsored a postretirement benefit plan for health care. The following information related to this plan. Compute postretirement benefit expense for 2020 assuming an expected (and actual) return on plan assets of 10%.

Activity	2020
Service cost	$30,000
Contributions to the plan	75,000
Benefits paid to retirees	45,000
Amortization of prior service cost	6,000
Interest cost	25,920

Account Balances	Dec. 31, 2019
Plan assets	$ 15,000
APBO	228,000

App—Brief Exercise 19-95 Recording Entries for Postretirement Benefit Plans LO9 *Hint:* See Demo 19-9

Refer to information in Brief Exercise 19-94. Record the entry for postretirement benefit expense, funding, and benefit payments in 2020.

App—Brief Exercise 19-96 Determining APBO Balance LO9 *Hint:* See Demo 19-9

Refer to information in Brief Exercise 19-94. Calculate the APBO balance as of December 31, 2020.

App—Brief Exercise 19-97 Calculating APBO LO8 *Hint:* See Demo 19-8

At December 31, 2019, Atlanta Inc. estimated the present value of postretirement health benefits of $75,000 for an employee. The employee is 50 years old and has been working for Atlanta Inc. for 8 years and is expected to retire at age 65. In order to be fully eligible, the employee must work for Atlanta Inc. for 15 years and remain at the company until age 55. Calculate the accumulated postretirement benefit obligation at December 31, 2019, for this employee.

App—Brief Exercise 19-98
Amortizing Prior Service Costs **LO10**
Hint: See Demo 19-10

On January 1, 2020, Allied Co. amended its postretirement benefit plan to grant retroactive benefits for services already performed in prior years. The present value of the benefits on January 1, 2020, is $50,000 and it relates to two employees with the following expected years of service: Jeff, 2 years and Eric, 4 years. Determine the amortization to be recognized in 2020 by allocating an equivalent amount of prior service cost to each service year.

Appendix—Exercises

App—Exercise 19-99
Recording Postretirement Benefit Expense and Determining Funded Status **LO9**
Hint: See Demo 19-9

The following information pertains to YNCA Inc.

APBO: Jan. 1, 2020	$100,000
Plan assets: Jan. 1, 2020	$75,000
Actual (and expected) return on plan assets	$7,500
Discount rate	12%
Service cost, 2020	$25,000
Contribution to asset fund, Dec. 31, 2020	$35,000
Benefit payments, Dec. 31, 2020	$10,000

Required

a. Provide the entry to record 2020 postretirement benefit expense.

b. Prepare a presentation of funded status on December 21, 2020.

App—Exercise 19-100
Recording Postretirement Benefit Expense and Determining Funded Status **LO9**
Hint: See Demo 19-9

The December 31, 2020, presentation of funded status and accrued postretirement benefit cost for Aude Inc. with a postretirement benefit plan is as follows.

Balance	Dec. 31, 2020
APBO	$(224,000)
Plan assets at fair value	203,000
Underfunded APBO (funded status)	$ (21,000)

Activity	2021
Service cost	$50,000
Actual return on plan assets	20,000
Contributions (end of year)	75,000
Benefit payments (end of year)	85,000

At the beginning of 2021, the plan was amended to increase future health-care benefits for retirees. The increase is attributable to service performed before 2021. As a result, the APBO increased $56,000. The discount rate is 12%, and the expected rate of return on plan assets is 10%. The average remaining years of service to full eligibility for active plan participants is 15 years.

Required

a. Provide the entry for Aude Inc. to record 2021 postretirement benefit expense.

b. Provide a presentation of funded status at December 31, 2021.

App—Exercise 19-101
Calculating Postretirement Benefit—Gain/Loss and Postretirement Benefit Expense **LO9**

Information for the Krysler Company postretirement health care plan is available as follows.

APBO, Jan. 1, 2020	$300,000
Plan assets at fair value, Jan, 1, 2020	100,000
Accumulated OCI—Postretirement Benefit Gain/Loss, Jan. 1, 2020	80,000*
Actual return on plan assets, 2020	6,000
Service cost, 2020	60,000

Discount rate	8%
Expected rate of return on plan assets	7%
Average service period	10 years

* Amount represents an accumulated loss.

Required

a. Calculate the amount of amortization related to Accumulated OCI—Postretirement Benefit Gain/Loss (if any) for 2020. Krysler uses the corridor approach for the amortization of postretirement gains and losses.

b. Compute postretirement benefit expense for 2020.

App—Exercise 19-102
Calculating EPBO and APBO **LO8**
Hint: See Demo 19-8

A plan provides life insurance benefits to employees who serve 20 years, at which time the employees become fully eligible. The benefit equals $50,000. On December 31, 2020, a 45-year-old employee has worked 15 years for the company. He is expected to retire at age 65. The discount rate is 7%.

Required

a. What is the expected postretirement benefit obligation on December 31, 2020?

b. What is the accumulated postretirement benefit obligation on December 31, 2020?

App—Exercise 19-103
Allocating Prior Service Cost **LO10**
Hint: See Demo 19-10

On January 1, 2020, Oracle Company amended its postretirement benefit plan by granting retroactive pension benefits for work performed before that date. The present value of those benefits was determined to be $100,000 at that date. The following employees expect to receive benefits under the plan, and they have the indicated expected number of years remaining in their careers at January 1, 2020: Jake: three years and Julia: five years.

Required

Determine the amortization of prior service cost to be recognized in 2024 under:

a. The method that associates an equivalent amount of prior service cost to each service year.

b. Straight-line method based on the average remaining service period of employees.

Appendix—Problems

App—Problem 19-104
Recording Postretirement Benefit Expense, Funded Status, Preparing Worksheet **LO9**

The December 31, 2020, balances for CTS Inc. with a postretirement benefit plan are as follows.

Account Balances	Dec. 31, 2020
APBO	$450,000 Cr.
Plan assets at fair value	425,000 Dr.
Accumulated OCI—Prior Service Cost	48,000 Dr.
Accumulated OCI—Benefit Gain/Loss	62,000 Dr.

Additional information

- Expected return on plan assets: 10%
- Discount rate: 8%
- Remaining years to amortize prior service cost: 8
- Average remaining service period: 10
- CTS Inc. recognizes the minimum amortization of gains and losses through the corridor approach.
- Service cost, 2021: $80,000
- Actual return on plan assets, 2021: $40,000
- APBO increased $100,000 on Dec. 31, 2021, due to an increase in health-care cost trend rates.
- Contributions to fund, Dec. 31, 2021: $100,000
- Benefit payments, Dec. 31, 2021: $80,000

Required

a. Prepare a worksheet to summarize the postretirement benefit data at the end of 2021. Assume that CTS Inc. uses the corridor approach in amortizing any benefit gain/loss.

b. Provide CTS Inc's postretirement benefit entries at December 31, 2021.

App—Problem 19-105
Allocating Prior Service Cost **LO10**

Pepsee Inc. amended its postretirement plan on January 1, 2020, by increasing health-care benefits attributable to services rendered by employees before the amendment date. The accumulated postretirement benefit obligation increased $90,000 (prior service cost). The three employees affected and their remaining years to full eligibility follow.

Remaining Years to Full Eligibility at Date of Amendment (January 1, 2020)

Employee	2020	2021	2022	2023	2024
Miley	1	1	1	1	1
Justin	1	1	—	—	—
Will	1	1	—	—	—
Total	3	3	1	1	1

The average remaining service period for all active plan participants is 10 years.

Required

a. Determine amortization of prior service cost for each remaining year to full eligibility, using the service method.

b. Determine the amortization of prior service cost for each remaining year to full eligibility, using the straight-line method.

App—Problem 19-106
Calculating EPBO and APBO **LO8**

At December 31, 2020, Gyro Inc. estimated the following net incurred claims costs for one of its employees for each year of the employee's postretirement period to which the plan applies.

At Age	Estimated Net Incurred Claims Cost by Age
64	$4,194
65	4,640
66	1,284
67	1,421
68	1,577

The postretirement plan of Gyro Inc. provides no benefits after age 68. For full eligibility, an employee must serve 20 years. The employee in question is 51 years old at December 31, 2020, and has served 15 years at that date. The employee is expected to retire at age 63. Gyro's discount rate for postretirement benefit accounting purposes is 8%.

Required

a. Determine the expected postretirement benefit obligation and accumulated postretirement benefit obligation at December 31, 2020, for this employee.

b. Assuming that the employee works another five years after December 31, 2020, and that there are no changes in expected net incurred claims costs, determine the expected postretirement benefit obligation and accumulated postretirement benefit obligation at December 31, 2025, for this employee.

App—Problem 19-107
Assessing Differences between Accounting for Pensions and Nonpension Postretirement Benefits **LO8**

Accounting for pensions is similar to accounting for nonpension postretirement benefits in many ways. However, there are some significant differences.

Required

Prepare a list of the differences and discuss some of these differences and their financial statement effects.

Answers to Review Exercises

Review 19-1

Example One

Assets = Liabilities + Equity
−10,000 −10,000

June 15, 2020—To record contribution to pension plan

Pension Expense	10,000	
Cash		10,000

Assets = Liabilities + Equity
+20,000 −20,000

Pension Exp: 10,000 | 20,000 (debits)
Acc. Pension Liab: | 20,000 (credit)
Cash: | 20,000 (credit)

December 31, 2020—To record pension expense

Pension Expense	20,000	
Accrued Pension Liability (0.05 × $600,000 − $10,000)		20,000

Example Two

Annual pension benefit: (10 years worked × $200,000 final salary)/25.	$ 80,000
PV of Ordinary Annuity: PV(0.06,15,−80000,0).	776,980
PBO: PV(0.06,15,0,−776980)	$324,207

Annual pension benefit: (10 years worked × $80,000 current salary)/25	$ 32,000
PV of Ordinary Annuity: PV(0.06,15,−32000,0)	310,792
ABO: PV(0.06,15,0,−310792)	$129,683

Review 19-2

Measurement of PBO	
PBO, Jan. 1, 2020	$375,000
Service cost	85,000
Interest cost	22,000
Actuarial loss on PBO	2,800
Benefit payments	(46,000)
PBO, Dec. 31, 2020	$438,800

Review 19-3

Example One

Measurement of Plan Assets	
Plan assets, Jan. 1, 2020	$300,000
Actual return on plan assets	12,000
Employer contributions	22,000
Benefit payments	(30,000)
Plan assets, Dec. 31, 2020	$304,000

Example Two

Determination of Funded Status	
Projected benefit obligation	$480,000
Plan assets at fair value	466,000
Funded status, Dec. 31, 2020	$ (14,000)

Review 19-4

Measurement of Net Pension Expense (2020)	
Service cost	$18,000
Interest cost ($75,000 × 0.06)	4,500
Expected return on plan assets	(4,000)
Amortization of prior service costs	1,000
Amortization of net loss (($12,900 − $8,100)/10)	480
Net pension expense	$19,980

Review 19-5

January 1, 2020—To record deferral of prior service cost

OCI—Prior Service Cost	30,000	
Projected Benefit Obligation		30,000

Assets = Liabilities + Equity
+30,000 −30,000

December 31, 2020—To record pension expense

Pension Expense	38,000	
Plan Assets (expected gain)	15,000	
OCI—Pension Gain/Loss ($5,000/10)		500
Projected Benefit Obligation ($33,000 + (0.05 × $330,000))		49,500
OCI—Prior Service Cost ($30,000/10)		3,000

Assets = Liabilities + Equity
+15,000 +49,500 −38,000
+500
+3,000

Assets	=	Liabilities	+	Equity
+1,000				+1,000

December 31, 2020—To record deferral of unexpected gain on plan assets

Plan Assets ($16,000 − $15,000)	1,000	
OCI—Pension Gain/Loss		1,000

Assets	=	Liabilities	+	Equity
+40,000 −40,000				

December 31, 2020—To record funding of plan assets

Plan Assets	40,000	
Cash		40,000

Assets	=	Liabilities	+	Equity
−22,000		−22,000		

Cash		Plan Assets		PBO		OCI—Pension G/L	
	40,000	Bal. 350,000	22,000	22,000	300,000 Bal.		500
		15,000			30,000		1,000
		1,000			49,500		
		40,000			357,500		
		384,000					

OCI—PSC		Pension Exp	
30,000	3,000	38,000	

December 31, 2020—To record benefits paid to retirees

Projected Benefit Obligation	22,000	
Plan Assets		22,000

Review 19-6

Income Statement	
Operating expenses	
Periodic pension cost, net	$50,000
Nonoperating expenses	
Other components of periodic pension cost, net	25,000

Statement of Comprehensive Income	
Other comprehensive income (loss)	
Unexpected gain on plan assets	$ 8,500
Amortization of prior service cost	2,500

Balance Sheet	
Noncurrent assets	
Net pension asset ($350,000 − $310,000)	$ 40,000
Liabilities	
Stockholders' equity	
Accumulated other comprehensive income	
Net pension loss	(12,000)
Prior service cost	(40,000)

Review 19-7

	Reported Net in Financial Statements		Reported in Balance Sheet				Reported in Comprehensive Income		
				Accumulated OCI				OCI	
	Plan Assets	PBO	Net Pension Asset/ Liability	Prior Service Cost	Pension Gain/Loss	Cash Outflow	Pension Expense	Prior Service Cost	Pension Gain/Loss
Balance, Jan. 1, 2020	$200,000	$(223,000)	$(23,000)	$ 0	$30,000				
Prior service cost amendment		(15,000)	(15,000)	15,000				$15,000	
Service cost		(80,000)	(80,000)				$80,000		
Interest cost [0.08 × ($223,000 + $15,000)]		(19,040)	(19,040)				19,040		
Expected return on plan assets (0.07 × $200,000)	14,000		14,000				(14,000)		
Unexpected loss on assets ($10,000 − $14,000)	(4,000)		(4,000)		4,000				$ 4,000
Actuarial loss on PBO		(8,000)	(8,000)		8,000				8,000
Prior service cost amortization				(1,500)			1,500	(1,500)	
Pension gain/loss amortization					(620)		620		(620)
Contributions to fund	70,000		70,000			$(70,000)			
Retiree benefits paid	(30,000)	30,000							
Balance, Dec. 31, 2020	$250,000	$(315,040)	$(65,040)	$13,500	$41,380		$87,160	$13,500	$11,380

1. Beginning balances for Plan Assets, PBO, Net Pension Asset/Liability and AOCI—Pension Gain/Loss.
2. Prior service cost amendment, $15,000 debit to Prior Service Cost in both the AOCI and OCI columns and credit to Projected Benefit Obligation.
3. Service cost, $80,000 (given) and interest cost, $19,040 (0.08 × $238,000 ($223,000 + $15,000)) credit to Projected Benefit Obligation and a debit to Pension Expense. *Interest cost is calculated based upon the adjusted PBO balance as of January 1, 2020.*
4. Expected return on plan assets, $14,000 (0.07 × $200,000) debit to Plan Assets and credit to Pension Expense.
5. Unexpected loss, $4,000 ($10,000 − $14,000) debit to Pension Gain/Loss in both the AOCI and OCI columns and credit to Plan Assets.
6. Actuarial loss on the PBO, $8,000 debit to Pension Gain/Loss in both the AOCI and OCI columns and credit to Projected Benefit Obligation.
7. Prior service cost amortization, $1,500 ($15,000/10 years) debit to Pension Expense and credit to Prior Service Cost in both the AOCI and OCI columns.
8. Amortization of pension loss, $620, debit to Pension Expense and credit to Pension Gain/Loss in both the AOCI and OCI columns. (Amortization equals beginning of year AOCI—Pension Gain/Loss of $30,000 less the corridor of $23,800, divided by service years of 10. Corridor is 10% of the greater of *the adjusted beginning of year PBO* or Plan Assets ($238,000 × 10%).)
9. Contributions, $70,000 debit to Plan Assets and credit to Cash.
10. Benefits, $30,000 debit to Projected Benefit Obligation and credit to Plan Assets.

January 1, 2020—To record prior service cost amendment

OCI—Prior Service Cost	15,000	
Projected Benefit Obligation		15,000

Assets	=	Liabilities	+	Equity
		+15,000		−15,000

December 31, 2020—To record pension expense

Pension Expense	87,160	
Plan Assets	14,000	
Projected Benefit Obligation		99,040
OCI—Pension Gain/Loss		620
OCI—Prior Service Cost		1,500

Assets	=	Liabilities	+	Equity
+14,000		+99,040		−87,160 +620 +1,500

December 31, 2020—To record deferral of unexpected loss on plan assets

OCI—Pension Gain/Loss	4,000	
Plan Assets		4,000

Assets	=	Liabilities	+	Equity
−4,000				−4,000

December 31, 2020—To record deferral of actuarial loss on PBO

OCI—Pension Gain/Loss	8,000	
Projected Benefit Obligation		8,000

Assets	=	Liabilities	+	Equity
		+8,000		−8,000

December 31, 2020—To record funding of plan assets

Plan Assets	70,000	
Cash		70,000

Assets	=	Liabilities	+	Equity
+70,000 −70,000				

December 31, 2020—To record benefits paid

Projected Benefit Obligation	30,000	
Plan Assets		30,000

Assets	=	Liabilities	+	Equity
−30,000		−30,000		

Cash (Dr)	Cash (Cr)
	70,000

Plan Assets (Dr)	Plan Assets (Cr)
Bal. 200,000	4,000
14,000	30,000
70,000	
250,000	

OCI—Pension G/L (Dr)	OCI—Pension G/L (Cr)
4,000	620
8,000	

PBO (Dr)	PBO (Cr)
30,000	223,000 Bal.
	15,000
	99,040
	8,000
	315,040

OCI—PSC (Dr)	OCI—PSC (Cr)
15,000	1,500

Pension Exp (Dr)	Pension Exp (Cr)
87,160	

Illustration of Closing Entries

Pension Exp (Dr)	Pension Exp (Cr)
87,160	87,160

Acc Earning (Dr)	Acc Earning (Cr)
87,160	

OCI—Pension G/L (Dr)	OCI—Pension G/L (Cr)
4,000	620
8,000	11,380
0	

AOCI—Pension G/L (Dr)	AOCI—Pension G/L (Cr)
Bal. 30,000	
11,380	
41,380	

OCI—PSC (Dr)	OCI—PSC (Cr)
15,000	1,500
	13,500
0	

AOCI—PSC (Dr)	AOCI—PSC (Cr)
Bal. 0	
13,500	
13,500	

Review 19-8

a. 15 years

b.

Present value benefit stream	$55,201	(PV of annuity of $7,500/year for 10 years, 6%)
Present value on January 1, 2020	23,033	(PV of $23,033 received at end of 15 years, 6%)

c.

APBO ($23,033 × 5/14).	$ 8,226

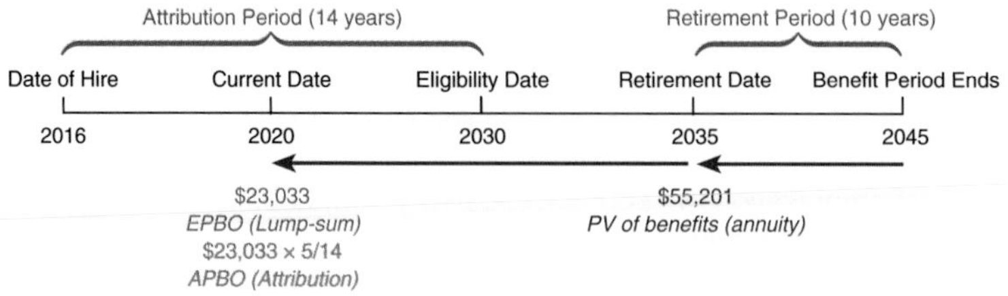

Review 19-9

Measurement of Postretirement Benefit Expense (2020)	
Service cost	$320,000
Interest cost	15,000
Expected return on plan assets (0.06 × $125,000)	(7,500)
Amortization of prior service cost	10,000
Total postretirement benefit expense	$337,500

Assets = Liabilities + Equity
+7,500 +335,000 −337,500
+10,000

December 31, 2020—To record postretirement benefit plan expense

Postretirement Benefit Expense.	337,500	
Plan Assets.	7,500	
Accumulated Postretirement Benefit Obligation.		335,000
OCI—Prior Service Cost.		10,000

Assets = Liabilities + Equity
+150,000
−150,000

December 31, 2020—To record funding of plan assets

Plan Assets.	150,000	
Cash		150,000

Assets = Liabilities + Equity
−50,000 −50,000

December 31, 2020—To record benefits paid

Accumulated Postretirement Benefit Obligation.	50,000	
Plan Assets.		50,000

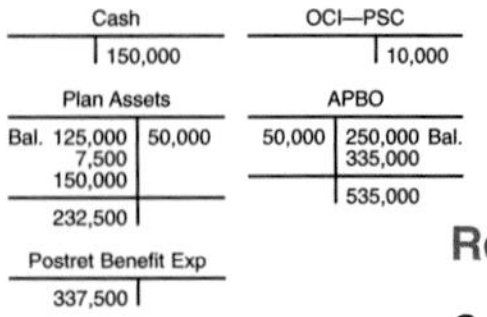

Cash
150,000
OCI—PSC
10,000
Plan Assets
Bal. 125,000
7,500
150,000
50,000
232,500
APBO
50,000
250,000 Bal.
335,000
535,000
Postret Benefit Exp
337,500

Review 19-10

a.

Year	Service Years	Annual Amortization	
2020	2	$80,000 × 2/7 =	$22,857
2021	2	$80,000 × 2/7 =	22,857
2022	1	$80,000 × 1/7 =	11,429
2023	1	$80,000 × 1/7 =	11,429
2024	1	$80,000 × 1/7 =	11,428
			$80,000

b. **Average service years**
(2 + 5)/2 employees = 3.5 years

2020 ($80,000 / 3.5)	$22,857
2021 ($80,000 / 3.5)	22,857
2022 ($80,000 / 3.5)	22,857
2023 ($80,000 – [3 × $22,857])	11,429
	$80,000

20 Stockholders' Equity

PepsiCo, Inc. and Subsidiaries
Consolidated Balance sheet (excerpt)
Fiscal years ended December 30, 2017, December 31, 2016 and December 26, 2015 (in millions)

	2017		2016		2015	
	Shares	Amount	Shares	Amount	Shares	Amount
Preferred Stock	0.8	$ 41	0.8	$ 41	0.8	$ 41
Repurchased Preferred Stock						
Balance, beginning of year	(0.7)	(192)	(0.7)	(186)	(0.7)	(181)
Redemptions	—	(5)	—	(6)	—	(5)
Balance, end of year	(0.7)	(197)	(0.7)	(192)	(0.7)	(186)
Common Stock						
Balance, beginning of year	1,428	24	1,448	24	1,488	25
Change in repurchased common stock	(8)	—	(20)	—	(40)	(1)
Balance, end of year	1,420	24	1,428	24	1,448	24
Capital in Excess of Par Value						
Balance, beginning of year		4,091		4,076		4,115
Share-based compensation expense		290		289		299
Stock option exercises, RSUs, PSUs and PEPunits converted [a]		(236)		(138)		(182)
Withholding tax on RSUs, PSUs and PEPunits converted		(145)		(130)		(151)
Other		(4)		(6)		(5)
Balance, end of year		3,996		4,091		4,076
Retained Earnings						
Balance, beginning of year		52,518		50,472		49,092
Net income attributable to PepsiCo		4,857		6,329		5,452
Cash dividends declared - common		(4,536)		(4,282)		(4,071)
Cash dividends declared - preferred		—		(1)		(1)
Balance, end of year		52,839		52,518		50,472
Accumulated Other Comprehensive Loss						
…beginning of year		(13,919)		(13,319)		(10,669)
…/(loss) attributable		862		(600)		(2,650)
		(13,057)		(13,919)		(13,319)
…k						
	(438)	(31,468)	(418)	(29,185)	(378)	(24,985)
	(18)	(2,000)	(29)	(3,000)	(52)	(4,999)
…SUs, PSUs and	10	708	9	712	12	794
	—	3	—	5	—	5
	(446)	(32,757)	(438)	(31,468)	(418)	(29,185)
…Shareholders' Equity		11,045		11,246		12,068
…year		104		107		110
…e to noncontrolling interests		51		50		49
…ntrolling interests		(62)		(55)		(48)
…adjustment		—		4		(2)
Other, net		(1)		(2)		(2)
Balance, end of year		92		104		107
Total Equity		$10,981		$11,199		$12,030

[a] Includes total tax benefits of $110 million in 2016 and $107 million in 2015.
See accompanying notes to the consolidated financial statements.

PepsiCo, Inc. and Subsidiaries
Consolidated Balance sheet (excerpt)

December 31	2017	2016
Preferred Stock, no par value	41	41
Repurchased Preferred Stock	(197)	(192)
PepsiCo Common Shareholders' Equity		
Common stock, par value 1 2/3¢ per share (authorized 3,600 shares, issued, net of repurchased common stock at par value: 1,420 and 1,428 shares, respectively)	24	24
Capital in excess of par value	3,996	4,091
Retained earnings	52,839	52,518
Accumulated other comprehensive loss	(13,057)	(13,919)
Repurchased common stock, in excess of par value (446 and 438 shares, respectively)	(32,757)	(31,468)
Total PepsiCo Common Shareholders' Equity	11,045	11,246
Noncontrolling interests	92	104
Total Equity	10,981	11,199
Total Liabilities and Equity	$79,804	$73,490

Chapter Preview

In this chapter, we identify five main components of stockholders' equity and illustrate how these components are reported in the stockholders' equity statement. We then examine in more detail common stock, preferred stock, and the related additional paid-in capital accounts, as well as treasury stock, which is a contra equity account. We examine the effect on retained earnings from different kinds of dividends: cash, property, liquidating, and stock. We also examine stock splits. Accumulated comprehensive income, a segment of stockholders' equity, is discussed, as well as the required reporting of the statement of comprehensive income. We wrap up the topic of equity with a discussion of required financial statement disclosures and the use of equity-based ratio analyses.

Action Plan

LO	Topic/Subtopic	Page	Demos	Reviews	Assignments
LO 20–1	**Describe and report stockholders' equity key components** Paid-in Capital :: Retained Earnings :: Accumulated OCI :: Treasury Stock :: Noncontrolling Interest	20-3	D20-1	R20-1	31, 32, 33, 55, 56, 79, 81, 86, 87, 88, 90, 91, 92, 94, 95, 96, 98, 102, 103
LO 20–2	**Account for common stock issuance including par and no-par, cash and noncash, and issue costs** Par Value :: No-Par :: Stated Value :: Noncash Consideration :: Multiple Securities Issuance :: Stock Issue Costs	20-8	D20-2A D20-2B D20-2C D20-2D D20-2E	R20-2	34, 35, 36, 37, 38, 57, 58, 59, 60, 61, 69, 71, 79, 86, 89, 90, 92, 96, 101, 102, 103, 107, 115, 119
LO 20–3	**Account for reacquisition of common stock** Treasury Stock :: Cost Method :: Direct Retirement	20-12	D20-3A D20-3B	R20-3	39, 40, 41, 42, 62, 63, 64, 65, 66, 67, 68, 69, 79, 86, 89, 90, 91, 92, 96, 101, 102, 106, 109, 110, 119
LO 20–4	**Describe and account for preferred stock** Callable :: Redeemable :: Convertible :: Cumulative Dividend Preference	20-16	D20-4	R20-4	43, 70, 71, 72, 75, 79, 86, 87, 89, 99, 100, 104, 105, 108, 113, 114, 119
LO 20–5	**Record dividend distributions, including cash, property, and liquidating** Cash Dividends :: Property Dividends :: Liquidating Dividends :: Declaration Date	20-19	D20-5A D20-5B D20-5C	R20-5	44, 45, 46, 47, 70, 73, 74, 75, 76, 79, 86, 87, 89, 90, 93, 97, 99, 105, 111, 112, 113, 114, 116
LO 20–6	**Account for stock dividends and stock splits** Small Stock Dividend :: Fractional Shares :: Stock Split Effected in the Form of Stock Dividend :: Stock Split :: Reverse Stock Split	20-24	D20-6A D20-6B D20-6C	R20-6	48, 49, 50, 77, 78, 79, 80, 81, 86, 87, 94, 101, 112, 117, 118, 120
LO 20–7	**Describe comprehensive income, its components, and how it is reported** Net Income :: Retained Earnings :: Other Comprehensive Income :: Accumulated Other Comprehensive Income	20-29	D20-7	R20-7	51, 52, 79, 81, 82, 83, 88, 96, 118, 119
LO 20–8	**Explain stockholders' equity disclosures and key analyses** Disclosures :: Book Value per Share :: Payout Ratio :: Return on Equity :: Price-to-Earnings Ratio	20-32	D20-8	R20-8	53, 54, 84, 85, 88, 92, 95, 97, 98, 102, 103, 104

LO 20-1 Describe and report stockholders' equity key components

LO 20-1 Overview

Key Components of Stockholders' Equity
- Paid-in capital
  - Capital stock and additional paid-in capital
- Retained earnings
- Accumulated other comprehensive income
- Treasury stock
- Noncontrolling interest

The corporate form of business has both advantages and disadvantages. An advantage of a public corporation is its ability to obtain funds from investors in the market. The corporation is a separate entity from the owners, which means that the owners have limited personal liability for the debt of a corporation. The corporation's creditors cannot settle debt by collecting investors' personal assets. The disadvantages of a corporation include increased taxation and regulation, and extensive reporting requirements. Owners or shareholders of the corporation are able to easily transfer ownership interests but are not able to exercise active control over management actions.

The advantages of the corporate form of business often outweigh the disadvantages, making it a popular choice for businesses. The corporate form of business is the dominant form of U.S. business organization in terms of total capital invested. Generally accepted accounting principles apply to all forms of business organizations, whether a sole proprietorship, partnership, or corporation. Corporations, however, have legal and contractual implications that result in different accounting and reporting requirements for stockholders' equity. This chapter focuses on the corporate form of business and the accounting for its equity.

Stockholders' equity (also called **net assets** or **shareholders' equity**) is the difference between recorded assets and recorded liabilities for a corporation. Stockholders' equity is a residual interest and has no existence without the presence of assets. Stockholders' equity is not a claim on specific assets but rather a claim on total assets after liabilities are recognized.

Key Components of Stockholders' Equity

Stockholders' equity consists of *five* components.

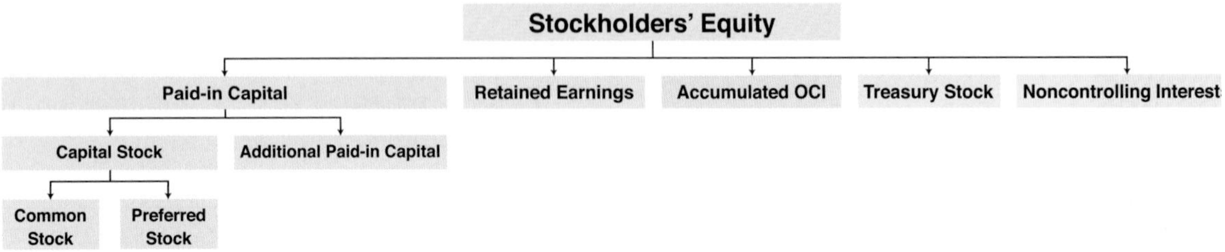

The end of period balances of components of stockholders' equity are recognized in the stockholders' equity section of the balance sheet. Changes in separate equity accounts for the periods reported are typically presented in a separate **statement of stockholders' equity**, although disclosure is an option as indicated in authoritative guidance. A statement of stockholders' equity shows the beginning balance, additions, deductions, and ending balance for each major stockholders' equity component. See the statement of stockholders' equity for the Coca-Cola Company later in this section as one example.

505-10-50-2 If both financial position and results of operations are presented, disclosure of changes in the separate accounts comprising shareholders' equity (in addition to retained earnings) and of the changes in the number of shares of equity securities during at least the most recent annual fiscal period and any subsequent interim period presented is required to make the financial statements sufficiently informative. Disclosure of such changes may take the form of separate statements or may be made in the basic financial statements or notes thereto.

Paid-in Capital

Paid-in capital or **contributed capital** consists of capital stock (common stock and preferred stock) and additional paid-in capital.

Capital Stock The following table defines the terms used to describe capital stock.

Term	Explanation
Par value	Value per share of stock designated in the articles of incorporation.
Authorized shares	Number of shares of stock that can be issued legally, as specified in the charter of the corporation.
Issued shares	Number of shares of authorized capital stock that has been issued to stockholders.
Unissued shares	Number of shares of authorized capital stock that has not been issued, that is, the difference between authorized shares and issued shares.
Outstanding shares	Number of shares issued, less the number of shares repurchased and currently held by the company as treasury stock. Outstanding shares are used for earnings per share calculations.
Treasury shares	Shares previously issued and later repurchased by the corporation that are still held (also, the difference between issued shares and outstanding shares).

Common stock is the primary issue of shares. When there is only one class of stock, all the shares are common stock (whether so designated or not). Although common stock is usually voting stock, some corporations issue two (or more) classes of common stock: one class has voting rights (often identified as Class A), and any other stock (Class B and other classes) is nonvoting. When two or more classes of common stock are issued, the Class B stock usually is traded publicly, while the Class A stock is often held by a smaller ownership group and traded privately. This arrangement permits greater control by that smaller group (perhaps as protection against takeovers) and still allows access to capital markets.

Common stockholders are the residual owners of the corporation. Their position is less secure than that of creditors and preferred stockholders because they are not guaranteed dividends or assets if the business fails. However, common stockholders often benefit most from a company's success.

Ownership of common stock normally entitles the holder the right to:

- Vote in stockholder meetings and influence management.
- Receive dividends declared by the board of directors.
- Share in the distribution of assets upon liquidation.
- Purchase new shares of common stock on a pro rata basis when new issues are offered for sale. This **preemptive right** gives each stockholder the opportunity to maintain a proportional ownership in the corporation.

The first three rights generally hold in all states. The fourth right is less consistently required across states, and in many instances may not exist. These rights are shared proportionately by all stockholders unless the charter or bylaws say otherwise. When there are two or more classes of stock, ownership rights vary depending on the class of stock.

The number of authorized shares is reported either on the face of the balance sheet or in the notes, while the number of shares issued or outstanding (as appropriate) is reported on the face of the balance sheet as indicated in the accounting guidance.

210-10-S99-1 29 Common stocks. For each class of common shares state, on the face of the balance sheet, the number of shares issued or outstanding, as appropriate . . . and the dollar amount thereof. If convertible, this fact should be indicated on the face of the balance sheet. For each class of common shares state, on the face of the balance sheet or in a note, the title of the issue, the number of shares authorized, and, if convertible, the basis of conversion... Show in a note or statement the changes in each class of common shares for each period for which an income statement is required to be filed.

Preferred stock has preferences, or specific rights, that distinguish it from common stock. In return, the preferred stock may restrict certain rights held by common shareholders. The most common preference is a priority claim on dividends, usually at a stated rate or amount. This means that if the board declares a dividend, preferred shareholders will receive the stated dividend before common stockholders receive dividends. The number of authorized shares, issued or outstanding (as appropriate), is recognized on the face of the balance sheet or in a note as indicated in the accounting guidance.

210-10-S99-1 28 Non-Redeemable Preferred Stocks. Preferred stocks which are not redeemable or are redeemable solely at the option of the issuer. State on the face of the balance sheet, or if more than one issue is outstanding state in a note, the title of each issue and the dollar amount thereof . . . State on the face of the balance sheet or in a note, for each issue, the number of shares authorized and the number of shares issued or outstanding, as appropriate . . . Show in a note or separate statement the changes in each class of preferred shares reported under this caption for each period for which an income statement is required to be filed.

Additional Paid-in Capital **Additional paid-in capital**, or **paid-in capital in excess of par**, reports the value of assets received by the corporation above par or stated value. For financial reporting, the various types of additional paid-in capital accounts are aggregated and reported as one item in the equity section of the balance sheet. Examples of additional paid-in capital accounts include, Paid-in Capital in Excess of Par—Common Stock, Paid-In Capital in Excess of Par—Preferred Stock, Paid-in Capital—Treasury Stock, and Paid-in Capital—Retired Stock. Other paid-in capital accounts are introduced throughout the text as needed.

Retained Earnings

	Retained earnings, beginning balance
+/−	Prior period adjustment (net of tax)
+/−	Net income (loss)
−	Dividends (Cash, property, stock)
	Retained earnings, ending balance

Retained earnings, or **reinvested earnings**, is the company's accumulated net income or net loss from its inception (including prior period adjustments net of tax) less accumulated dividends and other amounts transferred to contributed capital (paid-in capital) accounts. If the accumulated losses and distributions of retained earnings exceed accumulated earnings, a deficit exists (represented by a debit balance) in retained earnings.

Accumulated Other Comprehensive Income

	Accumulated OCI, beginning balance
+/−	Other comprehensive income (loss)
	Accumulated OCI, ending balance

Accumulated Other Comprehensive Income (Accumulated OCI or AOCI) represents changes in equity defined as other comprehensive income (OCI) that have accumulated over the years. Items affecting other comprehensive income are changes in equity during a period resulting from non-owner sources that are *not* included as part of net income. This accumulated amount, net of tax, is reported as a separate section of stockholders' equity after retained earnings. Accumulated OCI is either added or subtracted in the stockholders' equity section of the balance sheet depending on whether it represents accumulated income or losses.

Treasury Stock

Treasury stock is preferred or common stock that has been issued and reacquired by the issuing corporation but has not been resold or retired. The purchase of treasury stock does not reduce the number of issued shares but does reduce the number of outstanding shares. Treasury shares subsequently may be resold or, in some cases, retired. Treasury stock, a contra equity account, is deducted to arrive at total stockholders' equity.

Noncontrolling Interest

Noncontrolling interest represents the amount of the company's net assets (assets less liabilities) owned by outside investors in one of a company's subsidiaries that are not part of the controlling stockholders' interest. A controlling interest is typically achieved when a company owns more than 50% of the outstanding shares of another company. In this case, a parent company has a controlling interest in separate companies (subsidiaries). Generally, the full financial results of the subsidiaries are consolidated into the results of the parent company. The noncontrolling interest is the amount of net assets of any subsidiaries *owned by investors other than the parent company*. The equity attributable to noncontrolling interests is shown separately from the equity attributable to the controlling interest.

In the stockholders' equity section of the balance sheet, the relevant components of stockholders' equity would typically be presented in the same order as presented here. Equity attributable to stockholders is totaled before adding equity attributable to noncontrolling interests, to arrive at total stockholders' equity as illustrated in **Demo 20-1**.

Stockholders' Equity Key Components

LO20-1 Demo 20-1

Demo MBC

On December 31, 2020, Polar Inc. had the following account balances.

Preferred stock, $15 par, 20,000 shares authorized	$ 30,000 Cr.
Paid-in capital in excess of par—preferred stock	25,000 Cr.
Common stock, $1 par, 100,000 shares authorized	8,000 Cr.
Paid-in capital in excess of par—common stock	192,000 Cr.
Retained earnings	140,000 Cr.
Accumulated other comprehensive income (loss)	25,000 Dr.
Treasury stock, 500 shares	15,000 Dr.
Noncontrolling interests	10,000 Cr.

Prepare the stockholders' equity section of the balance sheet for Polar Inc. on December 31, 2020. State the par value per share, and the number of shares authorized, issued, and outstanding of common stock and preferred stock on the *face* of the balance sheet.

Solution

In describing common shares, while 8,000 shares were issued ($8,000 par value/$1 par value per share), only 7,500 is considered outstanding due to 500 shares being held as treasury shares. In describing preferred stock, 2,000 shares were issued ($30,000 par value/$15 par value per share). Additional paid-in capital accounts for common stock and preferred stock are combined into one single amount of $217,000. The accumulated other comprehensive loss and treasury stock both have debit balances, and are deducted within the stockholders' equity section. Total equity attributable to Polar Inc. stockholders is totaled before adding noncontrolling interests.

Balance Sheet (excerpt)
December 31, 2020

Common stock, $1 par value, 100,000 shares authorized, 8,000 shares issued, 7,500 shares outstanding	$ 8,000
Preferred stock, $15 par value, 20,000 shares authorized, 2,000 shares issued and outstanding	30,000
Paid-in capital in excess of par	217,000
Retained earnings	140,000
Accumulated other comprehensive loss	(25,000)
Less: Treasury stock, 500 shares	(15,000)
Total equity attributable to Polar Inc. stockholders	**355,000**
Equity attributable to noncontrolling interests	10,000
Total stockholders' equity	**$365,000**

Components of Stockholders' Equity

LO20-1 REVIEW 20-1

Review MBC

Match each of the financial statement items *a* through *k* with its proper stockholders' equity classification 1 through 5.

Stockholders' Equity Components

1. Paid-in capital
2. Retained earnings
3. Accumulated other comprehensive income
4. Treasury stock
5. Noncontrolling interest

Financial Statement Items

____ *a.* Net income
____ *b.* Foreign currency translation loss adjustment
____ *c.* Paid-in capital in excess of par—preferred stock
____ *d.* Cash dividends declared and paid
____ *e.* Reacquired common shares
____ *f.* Unrealized holding loss on securities classified as available-for-sale
____ *g.* Prior period adjustment—error correction
____ *h.* Common stock at par value
____ *i.* Preferred stock at par value
____ *j.* Paid-in capital in excess of par—common stock
____ *k.* Net assets owned by non-parent investors

More Practice: 20-31, 20-32, 20-33, 20-55, 20-56

Solution on p. 20-61.

COCA-COLA

Real World—COCA-COLA COMPANY– STOCKHOLDERS' EQUITY

COCA-COLA [KO]

The following financial statement excerpt of Coca-Cola Company illustrates the various components of stockholders' equity described in LO 20-1. We see differences in terminology: *shareowners' equity* is used for stockholders' equity, *capital surplus* is used for paid-in capital in excess of par, and *reinvested earnings* is used for retained earnings.

Coca-Cola Company—Balance Sheets (excerpt) December 31 (in millions except par value)	**2017**	**2016**
Common stock, $0.25 par value; authorized—11,200 shares; issued—7,040 and 7,040 shares, respectively	$ 1,760	$ 1,760
Capital surplus	15,864	14,993
Reinvested earnings	60,430	65,502
Accumulated other comprehensive income (loss)	(10,305)	(11,205)
Treasury stock, at cost—2,781 and 2,752 shares, respectively	(50,677)	(47,988)
Equity attributable to shareowners of the Coca-Cola company	17,072	23,062
Equity attributable to noncontrolling interests	1,905	158
Total equity	$18,977	$23,220

We see how each of the ending balances provided above, along with the activity for the year, is presented on the consolidated statement of shareowners' equity shown below.

THE COCA-COLA COMPANY AND SUBSIDIARIES
CONSOLIDATED STATEMENTS OF SHAREOWNERS' EQUITY

Year Ended December 31 (in millions except per share data)	**2017**	**2016**	**2015**
Equity attributable to shareowners of the Coca-Cola company			
Number of common shares outstanding			
Balance at beginning of year	**$ 4,288**	$ 4,324	$ 4,366
Treasury stock issued to employees related to stock compensation plans	**53**	50	44
Purchases of stock for treasury	**(82)**	(86)	(86)
Balance at end of year	**4,259**	4,288	4,324
Common stock	**$ 1,760**	$1,760	$ 1,760
Capital surplus			
Balance at beginning of year	**$14,993**	$14,016	$13,154
Stock issued to employees related to stock compensation plans	**655**	589	532
Tax benefit (charge) from stock compensation plans	**—**	130	94
Stock-based compensation expense	**219**	258	236
Other activities	**(3)**	—	—
Balance at end of year	**15,864**	14,993	14,016
Reinvested earnings			
Balance at beginning of year	**65,502**	65,018	63,408
Net income attributable to shareowners of the Coca-Cola company	**1,248**	6,527	7,351
Dividends (per share—$1.48, $1.40 and $1.32 in 2017, 2016 and 2015, respectively)	**(6,320)**	(6,043)	(5,741)
Balance at end of year	**60,430**	65,502	65,018
Accumulated other comprehensive income (loss)			
Balance at beginning of year	**(11,205)**	(10,174)	(5,777)
Net other comprehensive income (loss)	**900**	(1,031)	(4,397)
Balance at end of year	**(10,305)**	(11,205)	(10,174)
Treasury stock			
Balance at beginning of year	**(47,988)**	(45,066)	(42,225)
Treasury stock issued to employees related to stock compensation plans	**909**	811	696
Purchases of stock for treasury	**(3,598)**	(3,733)	(3,537)
Balance at end of year	**(50,677)**	(47,988)	(45,066)
Total equity attributable to shareowners of the Coca-Cola company	**$17,072**	$23,062	$25,554

continued

continued from previous page

THE COCA-COLA COMPANY AND SUBSIDIARIES
CONSOLIDATED STATEMENTS OF SHAREOWNERS' EQUITY

Year Ended December 31 (in millions except per share data)	2017	2016	2015
Equity attributable to noncontrolling interests			
Balance at beginning of year	**$ 158**	$ 210	$ 241
Net income attributable to noncontrolling interests	**35**	23	15
Net foreign currency translation adjustment	**38**	(13)	(18)
Dividends paid to noncontrolling interests	**(15)**	(25)	(31)
Contributions by noncontrolling interests	**—**	1	—
Business combinations	**1,805**	—	(3)
Deconsolidation of certain entities	**(157)**	(34)	—
Other activities	**41**	(4)	6
Total equity attributable to noncontrolling interests	**$ 1,905**	$ 158	$ 210

Account for common stock issuance including par and no-par, cash and noncash, and issue costs

LO 20-2

Accounting for Stock Issuance
- Par value common stock issuance
- No-par common stock issuance
- Stated value common stock issuance
- Noncash consideration
- Multiple securities issuance
- Stock issue costs

LO 20-2 Overview

Articles of incorporation are prepared by a corporation's organizers to meet the legal requirements of the state that issues a **corporate charter.** The articles of incorporation describe the nature and purpose of the corporation and specify the number of shares of capital stock authorized. An initial **board of directors** is selected to approve corporate bylaws, to supplement the provisions of the charter, and to select corporate officers. While state laws vary regarding corporate procedures, many states have adopted the **Model Business Corporation Act,** which is a model corporate law established by the American Bar Association. Having a model act for guidance allows for some consistency and clarity across state statutes in the U.S.

Par Value Common Stock

No journal entry is made when stock is authorized with a company's state of incorporation. From the authorized shares, a company can issue shares to shareholders for cash or noncash consideration. In the articles of incorporation, authorized shares may have a **par value** designated per share of stock. Par value has *no particular relation to the fair value* of the company's stock. For example, **Facebook Inc.** has a par value per common share of $0.000006, which does not (and was not intended to) correlate with its stock price per share.

In the case of par value common stock, legal capital is specified in most states as the par value of the issued or outstanding shares. **Legal capital** is the minimum amount (defined by state law) which must be maintained in the company for the protection of its creditors. Generally, corporate laws prohibit a distribution of assets to shareholders if the distribution would reduce the remaining total capital below legal capital. For example, a corporation must refrain from paying dividends when the effect would be to impair legal capital. Further, any shareholders who purchased stock at an amount below par value would be liable for any shortages under par in the case of a company's liquidation. However, over time, par value has become less relevant (and in many cases irrelevant) because the assigned par value is typically very low, affording little, if any, protection for creditors.

When par value stock is issued, Common Stock is credited for the par value of stock issued. Any excess amount of cash over the par value is credited to Paid-in Capital in Excess of Par—Common Stock as illustrated in **Demo 20-2A**.

Demo 20-2A **LO20-2** **Par Value Stock Issuance**

Demo MBC

Assets = Liabilities + Equity
+102,000 +10,000
+92,000

Cash: 102,000 (debit)
Common Stock: 10,000 (credit)
Paid-in Cap—CS: 92,000 (credit)

Lopez Inc. issued 10,000 shares of common stock, $1 par value per share, for cash at $10.20 per share on January 2, 2020. Record the issuance of stock on January 2, 2020.

Solution

January 2, 2020—To record par value common stock issuance

Cash (10,000 × $10.20)	102,000	
Common Stock (10,000 × $1)		10,000
Paid-in Capital in Excess of Par—Common Stock (10,000 × [$10.20 − $1])		92,000

PEPSICO FACEBOOK

Real World—PAR VALUE OF COMMON STOCK

PEPSICO [PEP]
FACEBOOK [FB]

PepsiCo and Facebook reported the following par values of common stock in recent annual reports.

PepsiCo, Inc.	Facebook, Inc.
Common stock, 1 2/3 ¢	Common stock, $0.000006 par value
Preferred stock, no-par value	

For PepsiCo Inc., total par value of common stock was $24 million, reported in its December 26, 2017, balance sheet. This represents 0.03% of its total assets of $79.8 billion. For Facebook Inc., the par value of common stock was below the rounding materiality threshold for reporting in the balance sheet. Assets reported on December 31, 2017, were $84.5 billion. Both cases illustrate how par value is typically assigned a nominal amount, that does not have any connection to the market price, nor does it provide much protection for creditors in the form of legal capital.

No-Par and Stated Value Common Stock

Many state statutes permit two types of no-par stock: true no-par stock and stated value no-par stock. When true no-par stock is sold, the capital stock account is credited for the full amount received, with no impact on additional paid-in capital accounts. In some states, the full proceeds from the sale of no-par stock is considered legal capital, thus restricting a company's ability to distribute earnings in the future. Some states instead require no-par stock to be associated with a minimum amount or stated value. If shares of no-par stock are assigned a minimum **stated value**, the stated amount is credited to the capital stock account, with any remainder credited to the additional paid-in capital account. No-par stock with a stated value is accounted for in the same manner as par value stock as illustrated in **Demo 20-2B**.

Demo 20-2B **LO20-2** **No-Par Common Stock Issuance**

Demo MBC

Assets = Liabilities + Equity
+102,000 +102,000

Cash: 102,000 (debit)
Common Stock: 102,000 (credit)

Example One—No-Par Stock

Lopez Inc. issued 10,000 shares of common stock, no-par, for cash at $10.20 per share on January 2, 2020. Record the issuance of stock on January 2, 2020.

Solution

January 2, 2020—To record no-par common stock issuance

Cash (10,000 × $10.20)	102,000	
Common Stock		102,000

Example Two—Stock with a Stated Value

Let's instead assume that Lopez Inc. issued 10,000 shares of common stock, no-par, stated value of $1 per share, for cash at $10.20 per share on January 2, 2020. Record the issuance of stock on January 2, 2020.

continued

continued from previous page

Solution

January 2, 2020—To record no-par, stated-value common stock issuance

Cash (10,000 × $10.20)	102,000	
Common Stock (10,000 × $1)		10,000
Paid-in Capital in Excess of Stated Value—Common Stock (10,000 × [$10.20 − $1])		92,000

Assets = Liabilities + Equity
+102,000 +10,000
+92,000

Cash: 102,000 |
Common Stock: | 10,000
Paid-in Cap—CS: | 92,000

Common Stock Issued for Noncash Consideration

Corporations sometimes issue capital stock for noncash assets as illustrated in **Demo 20-2C**. The fair value of the stock issued or the noncash consideration received, whichever is the most reliably determinable, is used to record the transaction. If the current market value of neither the capital stock issued nor the noncash consideration received can be reliably determined, appraised values are used. If neither market values nor appraisals are reliable, values are established by the corporation's board of directors using available data such as comparable asset sales or discounted expected future cash flows.

Common Stock Issuance for Noncash Consideration — LO20-2 — Demo 20-2C

On January 1, 2020, Fields Corp. privately issued 100,000, $1 par, common shares in exchange for land. The value of the common shares is not reliably determinable. However, a recent appraisal indicates that the land is valued at $240,000. Record the issuance of stock on January 1, 2020.

Solution

January 1, 2020—To record common stock issuance for noncash consideration

Land	240,000	
Common Stock (100,000 × $1)		100,000
Paid-in Capital in Excess of Par—Common Stock ($240,000 − $100,000)		140,000

Assets = Liabilities + Equity
+240,000 +100,000
+140,000

Land: 240,000 |
Common Stock: | 100,000
Paid-in Cap—CS: | 140,000

Multiple Securities Issuance

Although most corporations sell one class of stock when obtaining financing, they may sell two or more classes of capital stock for one lump-sum amount as illustrated in **Demo 20-2D**. In the case of a sale of multiple securities, the total proceeds must be allocated logically among the securities. Two approaches are used. (1) When the fair value of each individual security is known, the lump sum received is allocated proportionately among the classes of stock on the basis of the *relative fair value* of each security. (2) When the fair value of one security is known, the known value is used as a basis for that security, with the remainder of the lump sum allocated to the other class. A decision on which approach to use should be the one that produces the most reliable results for the data available.

Multiple Securities Issuance — LO20-2 — Demo 20-2D

Example One—Proportional Allocation

On January 2, 2020, Vale Inc. issued 1,000 shares of common stock, $10 par, and 500 shares of preferred stock, $8 par. The common stock is selling at $40 per share, and the preferred stock at $20 per share. Total cash received is $48,000. Record the issuance of stock on January 2, 2020.

Solution

Because fair value is known, proportional allocation is preferable as a basis for allocating the lump-sum amount.

continued

continued from previous page

Fair value of stock		
Fair value of common stock (1,000 shares × $40)	$40,000	($40,000/$50,000) or 80%
Fair value of preferred stock (500 shares × $20)	10,000	($10,000/$50,000) or 20%
	$50,000	

Proportional allocation of lump-sum sale price of $48,000	
Common stock allocation ($48,000 × 80%)	$38,400
Preferred stock allocation ($48,000 × 20%)	9,600
	$48,000

The following entry records the issuance of securities.

Assets = Liabilities + Equity
+48,000 +48,000

Cash: 48,000 (Dr)
Common Stock: 10,000 (Cr)
Preferred Stock: 4,000 (Cr)
Paid-in Cap—CS: 28,400 (Cr)
Paid-in Cap—PS: 5,600 (Cr)

January 2, 2020—To record multiple securities stock issuance—proportional allocation

Cash	48,000	
Common Stock (1,000 × $10)		10,000
Paid-in Capital in Excess of Par—Common Stock ($38,400 − $10,000)		28,400
Preferred Stock (500 × $8)		4,000
Paid-in Capital in Excess of Par—Preferred Stock ($9,600 − $4,000)		5,600

Example Two—Incremental Allocation

On January 2, 2020, Vale Inc. issued 1,000 shares of common stock, $10 par, and 500 shares of preferred stock, $8 par. The common stock of Vale Inc. is selling at $40 per share but the market for the preferred stock has not been established. Record the issuance of stock on January 2, 2020.

Solution

Because the fair value of only the common stock is known, incremental allocation is appropriate for allocating the lump-sum amount.

Incremental allocation of lump-sum sale price of $48,000	
Common stock allocation ($40 × 1,000 shares)	$40,000
Preferred stock allocation ($48,000 − $40,000)	8,000
	$48,000

The following entry records the issuance of securities.

Assets = Liabilities + Equity
+48,000 +48,000

Cash: 48,000 (Dr)
Common Stock: 10,000 (Cr)
Preferred Stock: 4,000 (Cr)
Paid-in Cap—CS: 30,000 (Cr)
Paid-in Cap—PS: 4,000 (Cr)

January 2, 2020—To record multiple securities stock issuance—incremental allocation

Cash	48,000	
Common Stock (1,000 × $10)		10,000
Paid-in Capital in Excess of Par—Common Stock ($40,000 − $10,000)		30,000
Preferred Stock (500 × $8)		4,000
Paid-in Capital in Excess of Par—Preferred Stock ($8,000 − $4,000)		4,000

Stock Issue Costs

Issues of capital stock can entail substantial expenditures including registration fees, underwriter commissions, attorney and accountant fees, printing costs, administrative costs, and promotional costs. These expenditures are called **stock issue costs.**

Stock issue costs are treated as a reduction to paid-in capital in excess of par as shown in **Demo 20-2E**. The cash received from the stock issuance is the net cash received (selling price less stock issue costs). Because the stock issue costs relate to the issuance of stock, not the operations of the company, they should not affect net income. The authoritative guidance follows.

505-10-25-2 The following shall be excluded from the determination of net income or the results of operations under all circumstances: Adjustments or charges or credits resulting from transactions in the entity's own capital stock.

Common Stock Issue Costs **LO20-2** **Demo 20-2E**

Vale Inc. issued 10,000 shares of common stock, $1 par, for cash of $10.20 per share on January 2, 2020. Vale also incurred $5,000 in stock issue costs. Record the issuance of stock on January 2, 2020.

Solution

January 2, 2020—To record par value common stock issuance and stock issue costs

Cash ((10,000 × $10.20) − $5,000)	97,000	
Common Stock (10,000 × $1)		10,000
Paid-in Capital in Excess of Par—Common Stock ([10,000 × {$10.20 − $1}] − $5,000)		87,000

Assets = Liabilities + Equity
+97,000 +97,000

Cash: 97,000 |
Common Stock: | 10,000
Paid-in Cap—CS: | 87,000

EXPANDING YOUR KNOWLEDGE **Types of Business Organizations**

There are many different types of corporations, each organized by different parties for different purposes. The focus in this chapter is on privately and publicly held corporations, organized to earn a profit. (In a private corporation, stock is held by a small number of investors and shares are not available for public sale.) Although the accounting is similar in many ways, this text does not address, for example, differences in accounting for equity in not-for-profit organizations, sole proprietorships, partnerships, and hybrid corporations. Hybrid corporations (such as S corporations, limited liability companies, and limited liability partnerships) combine certain aspects of corporations and partnerships. These business forms differ in tax treatment and the exposure to liability of its owners or shareholders as compared to either a straight corporation or partnership.

Accounting for Common Stock Issuance **LO20-2** **REVIEW 20-2**

Seven unrelated stock issue scenarios follow.

a. Issue 20,000 shares of common stock at $20 per share ($1 par).
b. Issue 20,000 shares of common stock at $20 per share (no-par value).
c. Issue 20,000 shares of common stock at $20 per share (no-par value), with a stated value of $1 per share.
d. Issue 10,000 shares of common stock ($1 par) in exchange for equipment with a fair value of $180,000.
e. Issue 5,000 shares of common stock ($1 par) and 2,000 shares of preferred stock ($5 par) at a price of $160,000. At the time of issuance, the market price of the common stock is $20 per share, and the market price of the preferred stock is $35 per share.
f. Issue 5,000 shares of common stock ($1 par) and 2,000 shares of preferred stock ($5 par) at a price of $175,000. At the time of issuance, the market price of the common stock is $18 per share, and the market price of the preferred stock is unknown.
g. Issue 20,000 shares of common stock at $20 per share ($1 par). Related to this transaction, the company incurred legal and administrative costs totaling $4,000.

Record journal entries for each of the seven *separate* scenarios described and dated as of January 1, 2020. Round to the nearest percentage when prorating the issuance price.

More Practice: 20-57, 20-58, 20-59, 20-60, 20-61

Solution on p. 20-62.

Account for reacquisition of common stock **LO 20-3**

It is common practice for a company to buy back its own shares of outstanding stock for a variety of reasons that include the following.

- Shares may be repurchased and later reissued to satisfy stock compensation awards to employees or for business acquisitions, avoiding the dilution caused by issuing new shares for these purposes.
- Management may choose to buy back stock as a way to increase the market price of the stock. When stock is acquired, the number of

LO 20-3 Overview

Reacquisition of Common Stock
- Treasury stock—Cost Method
  - Deduct treasury stock from equity
  - Shares remain issued
- Direct retirement of stock
  - Derecognize capital accounts
  - Shares reclassified to unissued

outstanding shares decreases. This reduction in supply of stock results in an increase in fair value per share (and earnings per share) of the remaining shares outstanding.

- Repurchasing shares distributes excess cash to shareholders through the purchase of shares at a favorable price to the investors.
- An acquisition of stock is used to thwart takeover attempts by allowing existing owners (remaining shareholders) to increase ownership interest. This allows existing owners a larger impact on the future plans of the company.

A company accounts for the purchase of its own outstanding stock by either holding the shares as **treasury stock**—see **Demo 20-3A** or through **direct retirement**—see **Demo 20-3B**. Shares held as treasury stock are deducted from stockholders' equity and the shares remain as *issued* shares. However, treasury stock generally does not carry voting, dividend, preemptive, or liquidation rights and is not an asset of the company. On the other hand, in a direct retirement, the capital accounts are derecognized and the shares are reclassified as *unissued*. These shares revert to the pool of authorized but unissued shares.

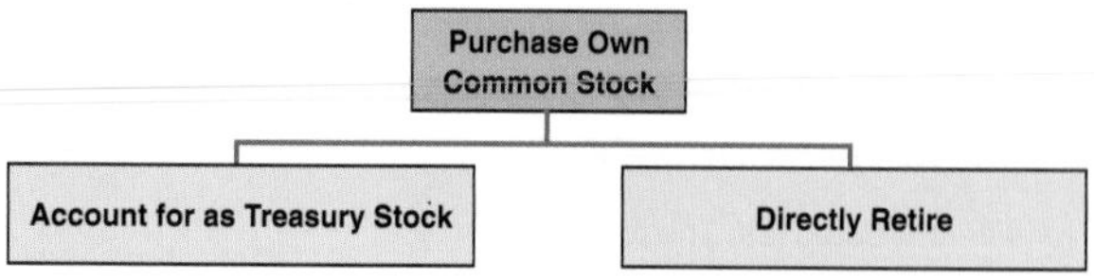

Treasury Stock

Under the **cost method**, treasury stock is reported as a deduction from total paid-in capital and retained earnings in the stockholders' equity section of the balance sheet, at its acquisition cost. The entry to record the repurchase of shares for treasury stock is a debit to Treasury Stock, a contra stockholders' equity account, and a credit to Cash. The purchase of treasury stock decreases both assets and stockholders' equity.

505-30-45-1 If a corporation's stock is acquired for purposes other than retirement (formal or constructive), or if ultimate disposition has not yet been decided, the cost of acquired stock may be shown separately as a deduction from the total of capital stock, additional paid-in capital, and retained earnings, or may be accorded the accounting treatment appropriate for retired stock.

A company may later sell the treasury stock. If a company decides to sell the treasury stock, Cash is debited for the selling price and Treasury Stock is credited for the original cost of acquiring the treasury stock. If a company has multiple purchases of treasury stock, purchased at different times and at different prices, the acquisition cost of the shares must be determined. A company may use any of the cost flow assumptions used in inventory: FIFO, LIFO, or the weighted average method to measure the cost of treasury shares. If the selling price is not equal to the treasury stock amount, the company will balance the journal entry as follows:

- When treasury stock is sold for ***more*** than its acquisition cost, the difference is credited to Paid-in Capital—Treasury Stock.
- When treasury stock is sold for an amount ***less*** than its acquisition cost, the difference is debited to Paid-in Capital—Treasury Stock if the prior credit balance in that account is sufficient to absorb the debit. Any excess is debited to Retained Earnings.

505-30-30-10 Gains on sales of treasury stock not previously accounted for as constructively retired shall be credited to additional paid-in capital; losses may be charged to additional paid-in capital to the extent that previous net gains from sales or retirements of the same class of stock are included therein, otherwise to retained earnings.

Subsequent Retirement of Treasury Stock Treasury stock is sometimes subsequently retired. In this case the company debits Common Stock and Paid-in Capital in Excess of Par—Common Stock at the amount of the original issuance of the shares, and credits Treasury Stock for its account balance. Any amounts needed to balance the entry are determined through the same procedures described above.

(Alternatively, a company may account for treasury stock using the **par value method** in which treasury stock is recognized as a deduction in the capital section of the stockholders' equity statement. Because this method is used rarely in practice, only the cost method is demonstrated.)

Reacquisition of Common Stock—Treasury Stock

LO20-3 **Demo 20-3A**

Demo

On January 1, 2020, Star Corp. sold 10,000 of its 50,000 authorized shares of common stock, par $1, at $26 per share. On June 30, 2020, Star Corp. reacquires 2,000 common shares for the treasury at $28 per share.

a. Record reacquisition of 2,000 shares of common stock on June 30, 2020.
b. Record sale of 500 shares of treasury stock on September 30, 2020, at $30 per share.
c. Record sale of 500 shares of treasury stock on December 31, 2020, at $19 per share.
d. Present the stockholders' section of the balance sheet on December 31, 2020. Assume a balance in retained earnings of $40,000 before any adjustments due to treasury stock.
e. The remaining 1,000 treasury shares (2,000 − 500 − 500) are retired and returned to unissued status on March 1, 2021. Record the necessary entry.

Solution

a. **Treasury Stock Acquisition**
The following entry records the acquisition of 2,000 shares of treasury stock at $28 per share.

June 30, 2020—To record acquisition of treasury stock

Treasury Stock (2,000 × $28)	56,000	
Cash		56,000

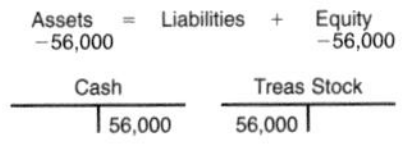

b. **Sale of Treasury Stock**
The sale of treasury stock at $30 per share is recorded as follows.

September 30, 2020—To record sale of treasury stock (above acquisition cost)

Cash (500 × $30)	15,000	
Treasury Stock (500 × $28)		14,000
Paid-in Capital—Treasury Stock (to balance)		1,000

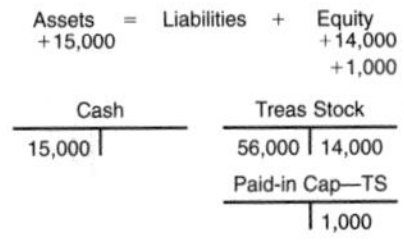

c. **Sale of Treasury Stock**
The sale of treasury stock at $19 per share is recorded as follows.

December 31, 2020—To record sale of treasury stock (below acquisition cost)

Cash (500 × $19)	9,500	
Paid-in Capital—Treasury Stock†	1,000	
Retained Earnings (to balance)	3,500	
Treasury Stock (500 × $28)		14,000

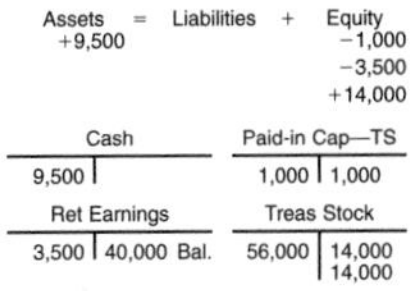

†The credit balance of $1,000 in Paid-in Capital—Treasury Stock is eliminated. The debit to Paid-in Capital—Treasury Stock is limited to its previous $1,000 credit balance. The remaining difference of $3,500 to balance the journal entry is debited to Retained Earnings.

d. **Financial Statement Presentation of Treasury Stock**
The stockholders' equity section of the balance sheet on December 31, 2020, follows.

Stockholders' Equity	
Common stock, $1 par value, 50,000 shares authorized, 10,000 shares issued, 9,000 shares outstanding	$ 10,000
Paid-in capital in excess of par	250,000
Retained earnings	36,500*
Less: Treasury stock, 1,000 shares	(28,000)†
Total stockholders' equity	**$268,500**

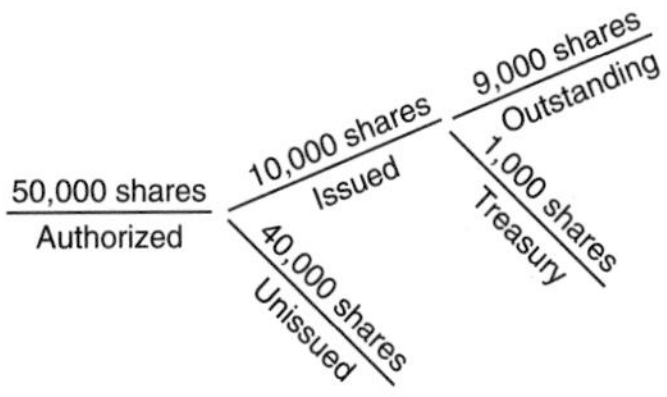

*$40,000 − $3,500. † $56,000 − $14,000 − $14,000.

e. **Subsequent Retirement of Treasury Stock**
Treasury stock is credited for $28,000 (its ending balance) and common stock and paid-in capital are derecognized for the original issue amounts. Because there is no remaining balance in Paid-in Capital—Treasury Stock, the debit amount required to balance the entry is

continued

continued from previous page

debited to Retained Earnings. The retirement of the stock does not affect the net balance in stockholders' equity. However, it does reduce the number of shares issued by the number of shares retired.

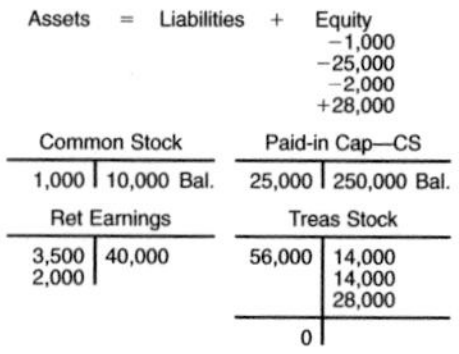

Assets = Liabilities + Equity
−1,000
−25,000
−2,000
+28,000
Common Stock
1,000 | 10,000 Bal.
Paid-in Cap—CS
25,000 | 250,000 Bal.
Ret Earnings
3,500 | 40,000
2,000
Treas Stock
56,000 | 14,000
14,000
28,000
0

March 1, 2021—To record subsequent retirement of treasury stock

Common Stock (1,000 × $1)	1,000	
Paid-in Capital in Excess of Par—Common Stock (1,000 × [$26 − $1])	25,000	
Retained Earnings (to balance)	2,000	
Treasury Stock (1,000 × $28)		28,000

Direct Retirement of Stock

Instead of holding repurchased shares in the treasury, a company can choose to directly retire the shares. In this case, the company debits Common Stock and Paid-in Capital in Excess of Par—Common Stock at the amount of its original issuance and credits Cash. If the acquisition cost of the stock is not equal to the original issuance amount, the company will balance the journal entry as follows:

- When stock is retired for ***less*** than its original issuance price, the difference is credited to Paid-in Capital—Retired Stock.
- When stock is retired for an amount ***more*** than its original issuance price, the difference is debited to Paid-in Capital—Retired Stock as long as the credit balance in that account is sufficient to absorb the debit. Any excess is debited to Retained Earnings.

Demo 20-3B **LO20-3** **Reacquisition of Common Stock—Direct Retirement**

On January 1, 2020, Star Corp. sold 10,000 shares of common stock, par $1, at $26 per share. On June 30, 2020, Star Corp. acquires 1,000 shares of its common stock at $28 per share and immediately retires the shares.

a. Record the entry for immediate retirement on June 30, 2020.

b. Instead, assume that Star Corp. acquires 1,000 shares at $24 per share for retirement. Record the entry for immediate retirement on June 30, 2020.

Solution

a. **Immediate Retirement—Above Acquisition Cost**

Star Corp. records the following journal entry on the repurchase and immediate retirement of common shares. Because there is no credit balance in Paid-in Capital—Retired Stock, the difference between the cash paid and the amount of the original issuance of the stock is debited to Retained Earnings.

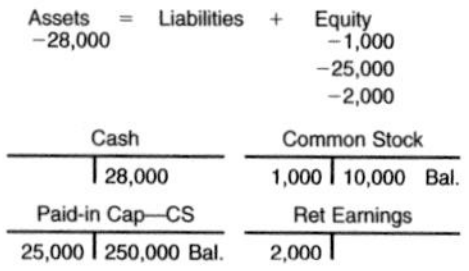

Assets = Liabilities + Equity
−28,000
−1,000
−25,000
−2,000
Cash
| 28,000
Common Stock
1,000 | 10,000 Bal.
Paid-in Cap—CS
25,000 | 250,000 Bal.
Ret Earnings
2,000 |

June 30, 2020—To record direct retirement of treasury stock

Common Stock (1,000 × $1)	1,000	
Paid-in Capital in Excess of Par—Common Stock (1,000 × [$26 − $1])	25,000	
Retained Earnings (to balance)	2,000	
Cash (1,000 × $28)		28,000

b. **Immediate Retirement— Below Acquisition Cost**

Star Corp. records the following journal entry on the repurchase and immediate retirement of common shares.

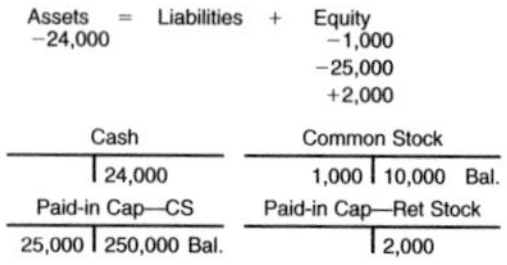

June 30, 2020—To record direct retirement of treasury stock

Common Stock (1,000 × $1)	1,000	
Paid-in Capital in Excess of Par—Common Stock (1,000 × [$26 − $1])	25,000	
Paid-in Capital—Retired Stock (to balance)		2,000
Cash (1,000 × $24)		24,000

Reacquisition of Common Stock

LO20-3 REVIEW 20-3

Review MBC

On January 1, 2020, Baker Corporation issued 5,000 shares of $1 par value common stock at $25 per share. On June 15, 2020, Baker reacquired 1,000 shares of its common stock at $30 per share for the treasury. On November 15, 2020, the company sold 250 treasury shares for $33 per share.

a. Record the entry on January 1, 2020, for the issuance of common stock.
b. Record the entry on June 15, 2020, for the purchase of common shares for the treasury.
c. Record the entry on November 15, 2020, for the sale of treasury shares at $33 per share.
d. Assume that on December 31, 2020, all remaining treasury stock shares are retired. Provide the entry for *subsequent retirement* of treasury shares.
e. Alternatively, assume that Baker Corporation purchased 1,000 shares on June 15, 2020, for $30 and immediately retired the shares rather than holding the shares as treasury shares. Provide the entry for *immediate retirement* of common shares.

More Practice: 20-62, 20-63, 20-64, 20-67

Solution on p. 20-62.

Describe and account for preferred stock

LO 20-4

Preferred stock has preferences, or specific rights, that distinguish it from common stock. Preferred stock typically is par value stock with a dividend preference expressed as a percentage of par. For example, 6% preferred stock would pay a dividend of 6% of the par value of each share per year if the board of directors declares dividends. In exchange for this preference, the preferred stockholders often sacrifice voting rights and the right to dividends beyond the stated rate or amount. Preferred stockholders also typically have preference over common stockholders in the case of a company liquidation.

The following terms are used to describe preferred stock.

Features of Preferred Stock
- Callable
- Redeemable
- Mandatorily redeemable
- Convertible
- Cumulative dividend preference

LO 20-4 Overview

Preferred Stock Feature	Description
Callable	Allows the issuer an option to recall (buy back) shares at a specified price.
Redeemable	Allows the stockholder an option to redeem stock (return stock to issuer for payment) at a specified price.
Mandatorily redeemable	**ASC Glossary** Mandatorily Redeemable Financial Instrument—Any of various financial instruments issued in the form of shares that embody an unconditional obligation requiring the issuer to redeem the instrument by transferring its assets at a specified or determinable date (or dates) or upon an event that is certain to occur.
Convertible	**ASC Glossary** Convertible security—A security that is convertible into another security based on a conversion rate. For example, convertible preferred stock that is convertible into common stock on a two-for-one basis (two shares of common for each share of preferred).
Cumulative dividend preference	Requires dividends not declared in a given year to accumulate at the preference rate for the stock. The issuer must pay cumulative dividends in full before dividends can be paid on the common stock. If preferred dividends are not declared in a given year, they are said to have been passed and are called **dividends in arrears** on the cumulative preferred stock, see LO 20-5.

Initial Recognition of Preferred Stock

Other than mandatorily redeemable preferred stock, preferred stock is recognized initially as *equity* as illustrated in **Demo 20-4**. As with common stock, Cash is debited and Preferred Stock is credited for the par value of the shares issued and the excess cash received over the par value is credited to Paid-in Capital in Excess of Par—Preferred Stock.

Mandatorily redeemable preferred shares have financial characteristics of both debt and equity. They resemble equity securities in that dividend payments are not mandatory and redeemable preferred shareholders are paid after debt holders in the event of liquidation. However, **they are more**

similar to a debt instrument in that they must be either retired or refunded by the issuer at a specified or determinable date or upon an event that is certain to occur. Therefore, the accounting standards require that mandatorily redeemable preferred stock be classified as a *liability* (measured at present value of payments) on the balance sheet as indicated in the accounting guidance.

480-10-25-4 A mandatorily redeemable financial instrument shall be classified as a liability unless the redemption is required to occur only upon the liquidation or termination of the reporting entity.

480-10-35-3 [M]andatorily redeemable financial instruments shall be measured subsequently in either of the following ways:

a. If both the amount to be paid and the settlement date are fixed, those instruments shall be measured subsequently at the present value of the amount to be paid at settlement, accruing interest cost using the rate implicit at inception.

b. If either the amount to be paid or the settlement date varies based on specified conditions, those instruments shall be measured subsequently at the amount of cash that would be paid under the conditions specified in the contract if settlement occurred at the reporting date. . .

Subsequent Recognition of Preferred Stock

Subsequent recognition for specific types of preferred stock follows.

- **Callable and Redeemable**—In the event that preferred stock is called in or redeemed, the preferred stockholder exchanges shares of preferred stock for cash. The issuer derecognizes preferred stock and its related paid-in capital account and reduces the cash balance (with any debit differences recorded in retained earnings and any credit differences in additional paid-in capital). *The net impact is a decrease to equity and to assets.*
- **Convertible**—In the event that preferred stock is converted into common stock, the preferred shareholder exchanges shares of preferred stock for common stock. The issuer derecognizes preferred stock and its related paid-in capital account and increases common stock and its related paid-in capital account (with any debit differences recorded in retained earnings and any credit differences in additional paid-in capital). This means that if the carrying value of preferred stock exceeds the par value of common stock, credit Paid-in Capital in Excess of Par—Common Stock for the remainder. If the carrying value of preferred stock is less than the par value of the common stock, debit Retained Earnings for the remainder. *There is no net change to equity.*

EXPANDING YOUR KNOWLEDGE — Temporary Equity

SEC registrants have additional guidance to consider in determining whether to classify preferred stock as equity or as a liability. If preferred stock is not mandatorily redeemable (when it is required to be classified as a *liability*) but redemption is outside of the issuer's control (or triggered by the occurrence of an event that is not solely within the control of the issuer), the preferred stock is classified as **temporary equity** on the balance sheet. In this case, the preferred stock is shown between the liability and equity sections of the balance sheet. The balance sheet presentation of temporary equity is illustrated as follows.

Balance Sheet

Total assets	$200	
Total liabilities	75	
Redeemable preferred stock	25	[Temporary equity]
Total stockholders' equity	100	
Total liabilities, redeemable preferred stock, and stockholders' equity	$200	

480-10-S99-3A 4 ASR 268 requires equity instruments with redemption features that are not solely within the control of the issuer to be classified outside of permanent equity (often referred to as classification in "temporary equity."

Accounting for Preferred Stock LO20-4 Demo 20-4

Demo MBC

Example One—Callable Preferred Stock

On January 1, 2020, Ace Corp. issued 2,500 shares of callable preferred stock ($10 par value) at $104 per share. Ace Corp. has the option to repurchase the preferred stock from the shareholders at any point in the next five years at $104 per share. Record the entry for issuance of the preferred stock on January 1, 2020, and for the recall of preferred stock on March 15, 2021.

Solution

January 1, 2020—To record issuance of preferred stock

Cash (2,500 × $104)	260,000	
Preferred Stock (2,500 × $10)		25,000
Paid-in Capital in Excess of Par—Preferred Stock (2,500 × [$104 − $10])		235,000

Assets = Liabilities + Equity
+260,000 +25,000 +235,000

Cash: 260,000 (debit)
Preferred Stock: 25,000 (credit)
Paid-in Cap—PS: 235,000 (credit)

March 15, 2021—To record recall of preferred stock

Preferred Stock	25,000	
Paid-in Capital in Excess of Par—Preferred Stock	235,000	
Cash ($104 × 2,500)		260,000

Assets = Liabilities + Equity
−260,000 −25,000 −235,000

Cash: 260,000 | 260,000
Preferred Stock: 25,000 | 25,000
Paid-in Cap—PS: 235,000 | 235,000

Example Two—Mandatorily Redeemable and Redeemable Preferred Stock

Eagle Inc. issued for cash 5,000 shares of 5%, $20 par value, preferred stock that is mandatorily redeemable on January 1, 2025, at a fixed price.

a. Indicate in which section of the balance sheet the preferred stock would be presented on a reporting date.

b. How would the answer to part *a* change if preferred stock can instead be redeemed at a fixed price at the option of the stockholder?

Solution

a. The preferred stock would be reported in the noncurrent liability section of the company's balance sheet.

b. The preferred stock would be reported in the stockholders' equity section of the company's balance sheet.

Example Three—Convertible Preferred Stock

On January 1, 2020, Ace Corp. issued 2,500 shares of preferred stock ($10 par value) at $104 per share. Each share of preferred stock is convertible into 5 shares of common stock ($1 par value) at the option of the holder. Record the entry for issuance of preferred stock on January 1, 2020, and for the conversion of all preferred stock into common stock on March 15, 2021.

Solution

January 1, 2020—To record issuance of convertible preferred stock

Cash (2,500 × $104)	260,000	
Preferred Stock (2,500 × $10)		25,000
Paid-in Capital in Excess of Par—Preferred Stock (2,500 × [$104 − $10])		235,000

Assets = Liabilities + Equity
+260,000 +25,000 +235,000

Cash: 260,000 (debit)
Preferred Stock: 25,000 (credit)
Paid-in Cap—PS: 235,000 (credit)

In the following entry, Preferred Stock and Paid-in Capital in Excess of Par—Preferred Stock are derecognized. Common Stock is credited for the par value of 12,500 shares (or 2,500 shares × conversion ratio of 5) and the remainder is credited to Paid-in Capital in Excess of Par—Common Stock.

March 15, 2021—To record conversion of preferred stock to common stock

Preferred Stock	25,000	
Paid-in Capital in Excess of Par—Preferred Stock	235,000	
Common Stock (2,500 × 5 × $1)		12,500
Paid-in Capital in Excess of Par—Common Stock (to balance)		247,500

Assets = Liabilities + Equity
−25,000 −235,000 +12,500 +247,500

Preferred Stock: 25,000 | 25,000
Paid-in Cap—PS: 235,000 | 235,000
Common Stock: 12,500 (credit)
Paid-in Cap—CS: 247,500 (credit)

EXPANDING YOUR KNOWLEDGE — **Why Issue Preferred Stock Over Debt?**

If redeemable preferred stock is really debt, why don't corporations just issue debt in the first place? After all, preferred dividends are not tax-deductible, and interest payments normally are. One answer lies in the requirements affecting debt capacity in debt agreements and covenants. The issuance of redeemable preferred stock instead of debt may avoid a debt covenant violation. A second answer is the issuer might obtain capital at rates below the market rate of interest. Corporate buyers are willing to accept a dividend rate on redeemable preferred stock that is less than the market rate of interest because corporations can exclude a significant portion of their dividend income from taxable income. No such exclusion is available for interest income.

REVIEW 20-4 **LO20-4** **Accounting for Preferred Stock**

Review MBC

Two unrelated scenarios follow for the issuance of preferred stock.

a. Bell Inc. issues 1,000 shares of 6% convertible preferred stock ($10 par value) on December 31, 2020, for $100,000.

b. Bell Inc. issues 1,000 shares of 6% redeemable preferred stock ($10 par value) on December 31, 2020, for $100,000.

Required

For each separate scenario, (1) record the issuance of preferred stock, and (2) indicate the financial statement presentation of preferred stock at December 31, 2020.

More Practice: 20-43, 20-70, 20-72
Solution on p. 20-63.

LO 20-5 Record dividend distributions, including cash, property, and liquidating

LO 20-5 Overview

Accounting for Dividend Distributions
- Cash (reduce retained earnings)
  - Common stock dividends
  - Preferred stock dividends
- Property (reduce retained earnings)
- Liquidating (reduce additional paid-in capital)

A corporation has two alternative uses for the company's earnings:

1. Reinvest in the operations of the company.
2. Distribute to shareholders in the form of a dividend.

A **dividend** is a distribution of retained earnings to shareholders in the form of assets or shares of the issuing company's stock. A consistent dividend payment over time can create demand in a company's stock, especially for investors seeking a steady flow of income. Corporations are not *required* to pay dividends. It is rare that 100% of a company's current period earnings are distributed as dividends. Some state laws and contracts restrict the amount of retained earnings that can be distributed as dividends.

If a company has investment opportunities in which it expects to earn excess profits, management may advise that the earnings be retained and used as capital for financing the investment. Retaining earnings is a common way for a company to provide capital for growth. Many start-up companies pay little or no dividends. Generally, investors are not disappointed when a company retains earnings and reinvests them, so long as the investment earns a high return or the company is building a buffer against possible cash shortages. In this section, we review the accounting for cash dividends (**Demo 20-5A**), property dividends (**Demo 20-5B**), and liquidating dividends (**Demo 20-5C**).

Cash Dividends

When the decision is to pay out retained earnings through a cash dividend, cash is distributed to shareholders. Cash dividends are the most common form of distributions to stockholders. Cash dividends depend on the corporation having sufficient cash available for distribution. Before a cash dividend can be paid to common shareholders, any preference in dividends (including those in arrears) must be paid to preferred stockholders.

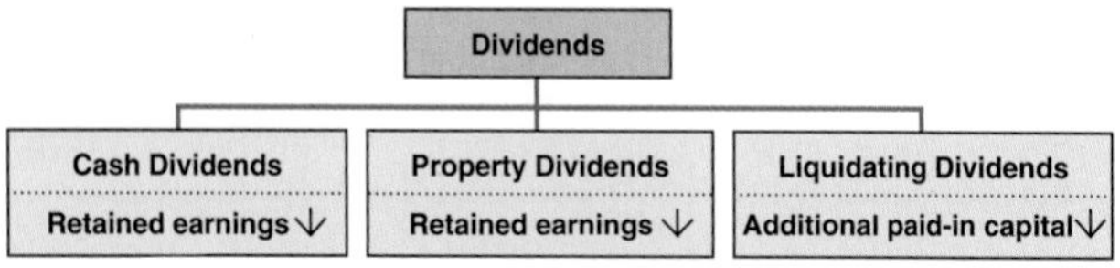

A corporation's board of directors approves and announces a dividend payment on the **date of declaration**, for shareholders of record at a specified date, to be paid on a specified date. This timeline is illustrated in **Exhibit 20-1**.

- Declaration is recorded as a debit to Retained Earnings and a credit to Dividends Payable. A liability is recorded because declaration of a cash dividend constitutes an enforceable contract between the corporation and the stockholders.
- The **ex-dividend date** is the first day shares are traded without the right to receive declared dividends. Thus, holders of the stock on the day prior to the stipulated ex-dividend date receive the dividend. This allows time for the determination of the owners as of the date of record. Investors who buy shares on and after the ex-dividend date do not receive the dividend. *No entry is made on the ex-dividend date.*
- Those holding stock on the **date of record** receive the dividend regardless of sales or purchases of stock after the record date. No entry is made on the date of record. The record date selected by the board of directors is stated in the declaration. Usually the record date follows the declaration date by two to three weeks.
- **Date of payment** is determined by the board of directors and typically follows the declaration date by four to six weeks.

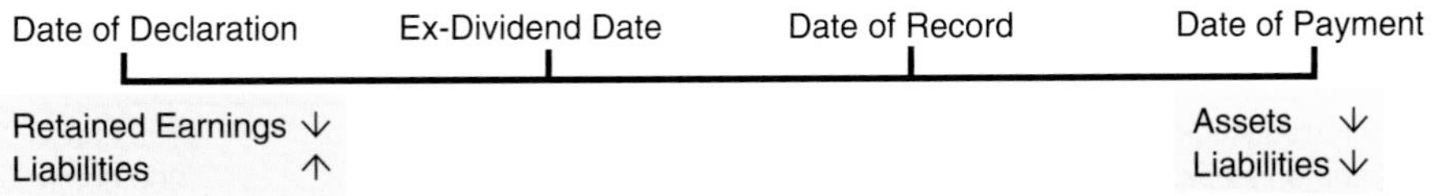

EXHIBIT 20-1
Cash Dividend Timeline

If a company declares a dividend, the dividend is allocated in a predetermined way to preferred and common shareholders. In the previous section, we identified a certain feature of preferred stock that would influence this allocation: cumulative dividend preference. The current year dividend on preferred stock and any cumulative dividends in arrears must be paid out to preferred shareholders before common shareholders are paid. After these obligations are satisfied, and unless the preferred shares are participating, the common shareholders receive the remainder of declared dividends. **Participating preference**, however, allows the preferred stockholder to share in additional dividends on a pro rata basis with common shareholders in the way defined by the company's charter.

EXPANDING YOUR KNOWLEDGE **Ex-Dividend Date and Market Reaction**

Between the declaration date and the ex-dividend date, the market price of the stock reflects the dividend. On the stipulated ex-dividend date, the price of the stock usually drops because the purchaser of the stock will not receive the dividend. For example, **AT&T** declares dividends on a quarterly basis. The ex-dividend dates shown in the chart below relate to four quarterly dividend payments: a dividend was paid to owners of stock identified before the ex-dividend dates of April 6, 2016, January 6, 2016, October 7, 2015, and July 8, 2015. In all four cases, the market price of the stock was lower on the close of the ex-dividend date as compared to the close of the day before.

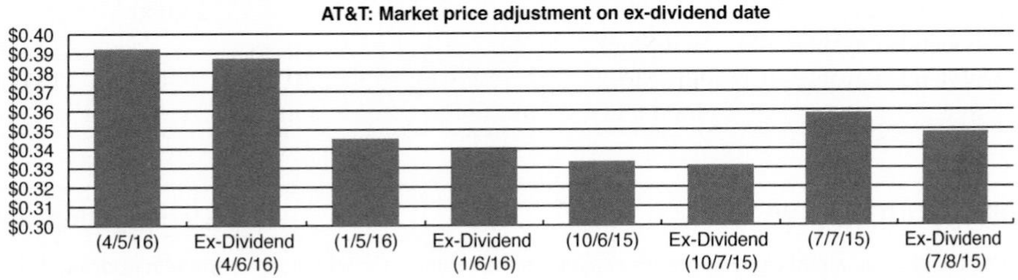

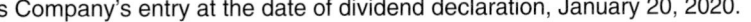

Cash Dividend Distributions **LO20-5** **Demo 20-5A**

Demo MBC

Example One—Common Stock Dividends
The board of directors of Bass Company, at its meeting on January 20, 2020, declares a cash dividend of 50 cents per share, payable March 20, 2020, to stockholders of record on March 1, 2020. There are 10,000 shares of no-par common stock outstanding. The cash dividends are paid on March 20, 2020.

a. Record Bass Company's entry at the date of dividend declaration, January 20, 2020.
b. Record Bass Company's entry at the date of record, March 1, 2020.
c. Record Bass Company's entry at the date of payment, March 20, 2020.

continued

continued from previous page

Solution

a. **Date of Dividend Declaration**

Assets = Liabilities +5,000 + Equity −5,000
Ret Earnings 5,000 | Div Payable | 5,000

January 20, 2020—To record cash dividends declared

Retained Earnings (10,000 × $0.50)	5,000	
Dividends Payable		5,000

b. **Date of Record**

No entry is made on the date of record.

c. **Date of Dividend Payment**

At the date of payment of cash on March 20, 2020, the transaction is recorded as follows.

Assets −5,000 = Liabilities −5,000 + Equity
Cash | 5,000 ; Div Payable 5,000 | 5,000

March 20, 2020—To record cash dividend payment

Dividends Payable	5,000	
Cash		5,000

Example Two—Cumulative Preferred Stock Dividends

Sprite Inc. has the following capital structure.

Preferred stock, 5%, $10 par, 10,000 shares issued and outstanding	$100,000
Common stock, $5 par, 40,000 shares issued and outstanding	200,000
Total	$300,000

The preferred stock is cumulative and dividends are in arrears for two preceding years. Cash dividends of $28,000 are declared on December 31, 2020. Determine the allocation of dividends between common and preferred shareholders, and record the declaration entry.

Solution

The annual preferred stock dividend is $5,000 ($100,000 × 5%). The declared dividend of $28,000 is allocated as follows.

	Preferred Dividends	Common Dividends
Preferred dividends in arrears (2 × $5,000)	$10,000	
Preferred current dividend	5,000	
Balance to common		$13,000
Total	$15,000	$13,000

Assets = Liabilities +15,000 +13,000 + Equity −28,000
Ret Earnings 28,000 | ; Div Payable | 15,000 13,000

December 31, 2020—To record cash dividends declared

Retained Earnings ($15,000 + $13,000)	28,000	
Dividends Payable—Preferred Stock		15,000
Dividends Payable—Common Stock		13,000

EXPANDING YOUR KNOWLEDGE — **Participating Dividends**

Depending on the charter, a participating preference allows the preferred stockholder to share in additional dividends on a pro rata basis with common shareholders after receiving the stated amount. Let's assume the same capital structure for Sprite Inc. in Example Two of **Demo 20-5A** *except* that the preferred stock is fully participating and noncumulative. Cash dividends of $28,000 are declared. Allocation between the common and preferred shareholders is determined as follows.

	Preferred Dividends	Common Dividends
Preferred current dividend	$5,000	
Common to match (5% × $200,000)		$10,000
Allocation of remaining dividend of $13,000 ($28,000 − $15,000) based upon par:		
Preferred ($100,000/$300,000 × $13,000)	4,333	
Common ($200,000/$300,000 × $13,000)		8,667
Total	$9,333	$18,667

Property Dividends

Corporations occasionally pay **property dividends** with noncash assets. The property can be securities of *other* companies held by the corporation, real estate, or any other noncash asset designated by the board of directors. Most property dividends are the securities of other companies held as an investment because this kind of property dividend reduces the problem of indivisibility of units that would occur with most other noncash assets. For example, a mining company issues common shares of its fully owned subsidiary to shareholders as a property dividend equivalent to one share of its investment in subsidiary to every 200 shares held of the mining company.

A property dividend is recorded at the fair value of the assets transferred. When the corporation's carrying value of the property to be distributed as a dividend is different from its fair value on the declaration date, the corporation first recognizes a gain or loss on disposal of the asset before recording the dividend declaration. Any changes in asset value after the dividend declaration date are unrecorded.

Property Dividend Distributions — LO20-5 — Demo 20-5B

Demo MBC

On June 2, 2020, the board of directors of Sun Co. declares a property dividend of 1,000 shares of its investment in Nic Inc., originally purchased on January 1, 2020 for $10,000 (which is also the current carrying value). The property dividends are payable on June 30, 2020, to stockholders of record on June 15, 2020. The fair value of Sun Co.'s investment in Nic Inc. is $12,000 on June 2, 2020.

a. Record the declaration of property dividend on January 2, 2020.
b. Record the transfer of property on January 31, 2020.

Solution

a. **Declaration of Property Dividend**

Sun Co. must first recognize the gain in fair value over carrying value ($12,000 less $10,000, or $2,000) before recording the property dividend.

June 2, 2020—To record gain on disposal of investment

Investment in Common Stock—Nic	2,000	
Gain on Disposal of Investment ($12,000 − $10,000)		2,000

Assets = Liabilities + Equity
+2,000 +2,000

Invest—CS		Gain on Disposal	
Bal. 10,000			2,000
2,000			

June 2, 2020—To record property dividend on date of declaration

Retained Earnings	12,000	
Property Dividends Payable (at fair value)		12,000

Assets = Liabilities + Equity
+12,000 −12,000

Ret Earnings		Prop Div Payable	
12,000			12,000

b. **Transfer of Property**

Upon transfer of the investment property to its shareholders, Sun Co. records the following entry.

June 30, 2020—To record property dividend payment

Property Dividends Payable	12,000	
Investment in Common Stock—Nic		12,000

Assets = Liabilities + Equity
−12,000 −12,000

Invest—CS		Prop Div Payable	
10,000	12,000	12,000	12,000
2,000			

Liquidating Dividends

Liquidating dividends are a return of stockholders' investment rather than a distribution of a company's profits. Stockholders must be informed of the portion of any dividend that represents a return of capital. For example, a liquidating dividend might be issued when a company is dissolving and is using the dividend as a way to distribute assets.

Demo 20-5C LO20-5 Liquidating Dividend Distributions

Demo MBC

On May 31, 2020, Miners Inc. declared a cash dividend of $40,000 and informs the stockholders that 75% of it is a liquidating dividend. The dividends are payable June 25, 2020, to stockholders of record on June 10, 2020.

a. Record the declaration of liquidating dividend on May 31, 2020.
b. Record the dividend payment on June 25, 2020.

Solution

a. **Declaration of Liquidating Dividend**

The dividend declaration includes a debit to Retained Earnings for $10,000 (25% × $40,000) and a debit to Paid-in Capital in Excess of Par—Common Stock for $30,000 (75% × $40,000).

Assets	=	Liabilities	+	Equity
		+40,000		−10,000
				−30,000

Ret Earnings		Paid-in Cap—CS	
10,000		30,000	

Div Payable	
	40,000

May 31, 2020—To record liquidating dividend on date of declaration

Retained Earnings ($40,000 × 25%)	10,000	
Paid-in Capital in Excess of Par—Common Stock ($40,000 × 75%)	30,000	
Dividends Payable		40,000

b. **Dividend Payment**

Assets	=	Liabilities	+	Equity
−40,000		−40,000		

Cash		Div Payable	
	40,000	40,000	40,000

June 25, 2020—To record liquidating dividend payment

Dividends Payable	40,000	
Cash		40,000

TOOTSIE ROLL

Real World—DIVIDENDS

TOOTSIE ROLL [TR]

In its *Highlights of 2017* section of a recent report on Form 10-K, Tootsie Roll Industries Inc. reported:

- Cash dividends were paid for the seventy-fifth consecutive year.
- Our fifty-third consecutive annual 3% stock dividend was distributed.

In the Selected Financial Data section of its annual report, Tootsie Roll Industries reported that cash dividends declared were $0.36, $0.36, $0.35, $0.32, and $0.32 in the years 2017, 2016, 2015, 2014, and 2013, respectively. Although not legally required to pay a dividend to shareholders each year, the long history of dividend payments by Tootsie Roll Industries sets up an expectation for investors for stable dividend payments projecting into future years.

REVIEW 20-5 LO20-5 Recording Dividend Distributions

Review MBC

Following are four separate dividend scenarios.

a. On June 1, 2020, Sox Inc. declared a cash dividend of $2.50 per share on its 50,000 outstanding shares of common stock ($0.10 par). The dividend is payable on June 15, 2020, to stockholders of record on June 1, 2020.

b. FX Inc. holds 1,000 shares of Den Co. common stock, purchased in May of 2020 for $19 a share. On June 1, 2020, FX Inc. declared a property dividend of 1,000 shares of Den Co. common stock when the shares were selling at $22 per share.

c. Lox Inc. declared a common stock dividend of $80,000 on August 15, 2020. Lox Inc. announced to shareholders that $20,000 of the dividend amount was a return of capital.

d. Vox Inc. has issued and outstanding 2,000 shares of $10 par, cumulative, 5% preferred stock and 10,000 shares of $1 par common stock. Dividends are in arrears for the past year (not including the current year). On June 1, 2020, the board of directors of Vox Inc. declared dividends of $25,000 to be paid to shareholders at the end of the fiscal year.

Record the entry for declaration of dividends for each of the four separate scenarios.

More Practice:
20-45, 20-46, 20-47, 20-73, 20-74, 20-76

Solution on p. 20-63.

Account for stock dividends and stock splits

LO 20-6

Another form of dividend called a **stock dividend** may be declared. A stock dividend is a proportional distribution of additional shares of a company's stock to shareholders. The accounting treatment of stock dividends differs depending on the size of the stock dividend. A small stock dividend is illustrated in **Demo 20-6A** and a large stock dividend called a *stock split effected in the form of a dividend* is illustrated in **Demo 20-6B**. A **stock split** is a change in the number of shares outstanding accompanied by an offsetting change in the par or stated value per share. A stock split is illustrated in **Demo 20-6C**.

LO 20-6 Overview

Stock Dividends and Stock Splits
- Small stock dividend
  - Record at fair value
- Stock split effected in the form of a dividend (large stock dividend)
  - Record at par value
- Stock split/reverse stock split
  - No journal entry

Stock Dividends

A stock dividend proportionally grants new shares of stock to current shareholders without requiring consideration from the shareholders. For example, if a company has 400 shares of stock outstanding, after a 10% stock dividend, it would have an additional 40 shares (or 400 shares × 10%) resulting in a total of 440 shares of stock outstanding.

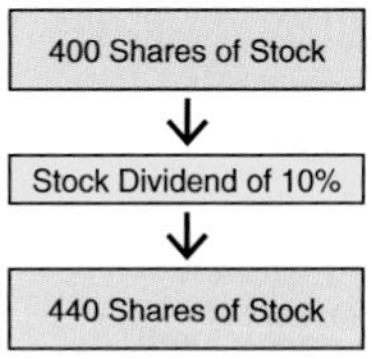

With the exception of cash payouts for fractional shares described below, a stock dividend does not result in a net change in total assets, liabilities, or stockholders' equity. The components of stockholders' equity change, but the net value does not change. The ownership percentage of *each investor* remains *exactly the same* before and after a stock dividend as illustrated below.

Investor	Shares Before 10% Stock Dividend	Ownership %	Shares After 10% Stock Dividend	Ownership %
Investor A	120	30%	132	30%
Investor B	40	10%	44	10%
Investor C	100	25%	110	25%
Investor D	140	35%	154	35%
Totals	400	100%	440	100%

Companies issue stock dividends for several reasons, including the following.

- To continue dividend distributions without disbursing cash needed for operations. Shareholders may be willing to accept a stock dividend representing accumulated earnings because they can sell these additional shares.
- To increase the number of shares outstanding, reducing the market price per share and possibly leading to increased trading of shares in the market.
- To convey that the company plans to retain a portion of earnings permanently in the business because a stock dividend results in a shift from retained earnings to paid-in capital. (State law often restricts the extent of retained earnings that may be distributed in dividends.)

There is debate about the amounts that should be used in recognizing stock dividends. The issue is whether the stock issued for the dividend should be recorded at fair value, at par or stated value, or at some other value. In support of the par value method, it is generally recognized that if a company doubles the number of shares outstanding by issuing a stock dividend, the competitive market price will roughly fall to one-half its previous level, absent any other market factors. At the time of the issuance of the accounting guidance on stock dividends, it was believed that the market price did *not* automatically adjust for the issuance of small stock dividends thus supporting the recording at fair value—as indicated in the following accounting guidance.

505-20-05-2 Many recipients of stock dividends look upon them as distributions of corporate earnings, and usually in an amount equivalent to the fair value of the additional shares received. If the issuances of stock dividends are so small in comparison with the shares previously outstanding, such issuances generally do not have any apparent effect on the share market price and, consequently, the fair value of the shares previously held remains substantially unchanged.

This authoritative standard does not come without controversy because of evidence of market adjustments for small stock dividends coupled with the fact that the company does not receive any new assets upon distribution of a stock dividend. Nonetheless, this is the basis of the accounting treatment of stock dividends which treats a small stock dividend differently from a large stock dividend: **the accounting standards require *small* stock dividends to be recorded at fair value and *large* stock dividends to be recorded at par value.**

Small Stock Dividends

If the proportion of the additional shares issued is small in relation to the shares previously outstanding (**small stock dividend**), the *fair value* of the additional shares is capitalized. Small in the accounting standards is generally defined as less than 20% to 25% of the outstanding shares.

> **505-20-25-3** The point at which the relative size of the additional shares issued becomes large enough to materially influence the unit market price of the stock will vary with individual entities and under differing market conditions and, therefore, no single percentage can be established as a standard for determining when capitalization of retained earnings in excess of legal requirements is called for and when it is not. Except for a few instances, the issuance of additional shares of less than 20 or 25 percent of the number of previously outstanding shares would call for treatment as a [small] stock dividend.

A small common stock dividend is recorded by a debit to Retained Earnings (at fair value) and a credit to Common Stock Dividends Distributable (at par value) and Paid-in Capital in Excess of Par—Common Stock (for the remainder). When the shares are officially issued, the company debits Common Stock Dividends Distributable and credits Common Stock. **With offsetting increases and decreases to stockholders' equity accounts, the net balance in stockholders' equity remains unchanged.**

> **05-20-30-3** In accounting for a stock dividend, the corporation shall transfer from retained earnings to the category of capital stock and additional paid-in capital an amount equal to the fair value of the additional shares issued. Unless this is done, the amount of earnings that the shareholder may believe to have been distributed to him or her will be left, except to the extent otherwise dictated by legal requirements, in retained earnings subject to possible further similar stock issuances or cash distributions.

When a stock dividend is issued, not all shareholders may own exactly the number of shares needed to receive whole shares. For example, if a company issues a 10% stock dividend and a shareholder owns 15 shares, the stockholder is entitled to 1.5 shares (15 shares × 10%). The shareholder has a right to 1 full share plus a **fractional share** of ½ share. A company often pays cash to shareholders for the fair value of the fractional shares to which they are entitled.

Demo 20-6A **LO20-6** **Accounting for Small Stock Dividends**

Demo MBC

Example One— Small Stock Dividend

WayMart Inc. issued a 10% common stock dividend on 100,000 shares of $1 par common stock issued and outstanding on May 1, 2020. The market price of the common stock is $5 per share. The small stock dividend will be distributed on May 25, 2020, to stockholders of record on May 10, 2020. Record the entry on (1) the date of declaration and (2) the date of distribution.

Solution

The small stock dividend is recorded at fair value, with the excess of the fair value of $50,000 over the par value of $10,000 recorded as an increase to additional paid-in capital for $40,000.

May 1, 2020—To record small stock dividend on date of declaration

Retained Earnings (100,000 × 10% × $5)	50,000	
Common Stock Dividends Distributable (100,000 × 10% × $1)		10,000
Paid-in Capital in Excess of Par—Common Stock (to balance)		40,000

Assets = Liabilities + Equity −50,000 +10,000 +40,000

Ret Earnings: 50,000 (Dr) | CS Div Distrib: 10,000 (Cr) | Paid-in Cap—CS: 40,000 (Cr)

May 25, 2020—To record distribution of small stock dividend

Common Stock Dividends Distributable	10,000	
Common Stock		10,000

Assets = Liabilities + Equity +10,000 −10,000

CS Div Distrib: 10,000 (Dr) 10,000 (Cr) | Common Stock: 10,000 (Cr)

continued

continued from previous page

Example Two— Small Stock Dividend with Fractional Shares

Let's assume from Example One that of the 10,000 stock dividend shares, 9,200 were whole shares and 800 were fractional shares. The market price of common stock is $5 per share. The company's policy is to pay cash to shareholders for fractional shares. Record the entry on (1) the date of declaration and (2) the date of distribution.

Solution

The company will pay cash of $4,000 for the fractional shares (or 800 fractional shares × $5) and distribute a stock dividend of 9,200 shares recorded as follows.

May 1, 2020—To record small stock dividend on date of declaration

Retained Earnings (100,000 × 10% × $5)	50,000	
Dividends Payable (800 × $5)		4,000
Common Stock Dividends Distributable (9,200 × $1)		9,200
Paid-in Capital in Excess of Par—Common Stock (9,200 × [$5 − $1])		36,800

Assets	=	Liabilities	+	Equity
		+4,000		−50,000
				+9,200
				+36,800

May 25, 2020—To record distribution of small stock dividend

Common Stock Dividends Distributable	9,200	
Common Stock		9,200

Assets	=	Liabilities	+	Equity
				−9,200
				+9,200

May 25, 2020—To record cash distribution

Dividends Payable	4,000	
Cash		4,000

Assets	=	Liabilities	+	Equity
−4,000		−4,000		

Account	Debit	Credit
Cash		4,000
Div Payable	4,000	4,000
CS Div Distrib	9,200	9,200
Paid-in Cap—CS		36,800
Common Stock		9,200
Ret Earnings	50,000	

Stock Split Effected in the Form of a Dividend (Large Stock Dividend)

When the proportion of the additional shares issued is large in relation to the total shares previously outstanding (more than 20% to 25%), no less than the legal minimum (usually par, or stated value, or average paid-in for no-par stock) is capitalized. Because this is more in line with a stock split, a large stock dividend must *not* be referred to as a dividend. Instead, a large stock dividend is often referred to as a **stock split effected in the form of a dividend** in the financial statements. (As discussed in the next section, a stock split results in a distribution of new shares with an offsetting decrease in par value per share.)

505-20-25-2 The number of additional shares issued as a stock dividend may be so great that it has, or may reasonably be expected to have, the effect of materially reducing the share market value. In such a situation… the substance of the transaction is clearly that of a stock split.

505-20-50-1 Paragraph 505-20-25-2 identifies a situation in which a stock dividend in form is a stock split in substance. In such instances every effort shall be made to avoid the use of the word dividend in related corporate resolutions, notices, and announcements and that, in those cases in which because of legal requirements this cannot be done, the transaction be described, for example, as a stock split effected in the form of a dividend.

A *stock split effected in the form of a dividend* is recorded through a debit to Retained Earnings (at par value) and a credit to Common Stock Dividends Distributable (at par value). A large stock dividend does not change the par value per share. Instead, more shares are issued, resulting in an increase to the stock account. When the shares are officially issued, the company debits Common Stock Dividends Distributable and credits Common Stock. **With offsetting increases and decreases to stockholders' equity accounts, the net balance in stockholders' equity remains unchanged.** The fair value of the stock is not relevant to the recording of the entry. A company might choose to debit Paid-in Capital in Excess of Par—Common Stock instead of Retained Earnings *if legally acceptable*.

505-20-30-6 In the case of a stock split, there is no need to capitalize retained earnings, other than to the extent occasioned by legal requirements.

Management Judgment

Management judgment is sometimes needed to classify a stock dividend as a small stock dividend or a stock split effected in the form of a dividend. The accounting guidance provides a minimum range of

20% to 25% where a stock issuance becomes large enough to materially influence the unit market price of the stock. However, this is a range (not a bright line) and the guidance allows for some exceptions outside of this range.

Assume that WayMart Inc. issued a 24% common stock dividend on 100,000 shares of $1 par common stock issued and outstanding on May 1, 2020. The market price of the common stock is $5 per share. The impact on financial statements of these two options follows.

	Capital Stock	Paid-in Capital in Excess of Par	Retained Earnings	Total Stockholders' Equity
Small stock dividend.	$24,000	$96,000	$(120,000)	No change
Stock split effected through dividend . . .	24,000	—	(24,000)	No change

Retained earnings would be $96,000 lower ($120,000 less $24,000) had the dividend been classified as a small stock dividend rather than a stock split effected in the form of a dividend. If the balance in Retained Earnings before the stock dividend were $500,000, adjusted retained earnings would be $380,000 with a small stock dividend versus $476,000 with a stock split effected in the form of a dividend. Reporting a 20% lower retained earnings balance with a small stock dividend can have broad implications such as lowering the availability of future cash dividend distributions or affecting debt covenant compliance requiring a minimum retained earnings balance.

Demo 20-6B **LO20-6** **Accounting for a Stock Split Effected in the Form of a Dividend**

Demo MBC

WayMart Inc. declares a 50% common stock dividend on 100,000 common shares ($1 par value) on May 1, 2020. The market price of the common stock is $5 per share. The stock split effected in the form of a stock dividend will be distributed to shareholders on May 25, 2020, to stockholders of record on May 10, 2020. Record the entry on (1) the date of declaration and (2) the date of distribution.

Solution

The stock split effected in the form of a stock dividend is recorded at par value.

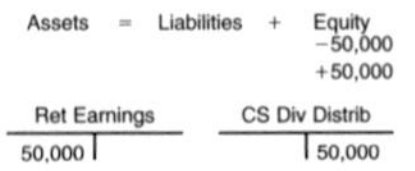

May 1, 2020—To record stock split effected in the form of a dividend on date of declaration

Retained Earnings (100,000 × 50% × $1)	50,000	
Common Stock Dividends Distributable		50,000

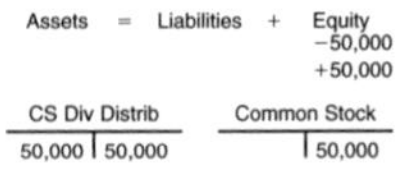

Assets = Liabilities + Equity
−50,000
+50,000
CS Div Distrib
50,000 | 50,000
Common Stock
50,000

May 25, 2020—To record stock split effected in the form of a dividend on date of distribution

Common Stock Dividends Distributable	50,000	
Common Stock.		50,000

Stock Splits

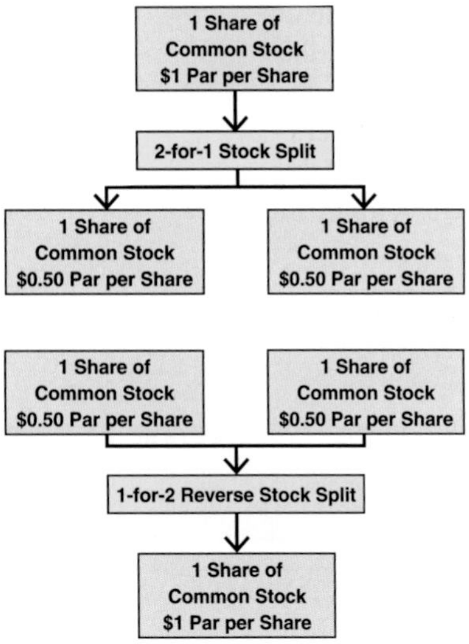

A large distribution of stock might also be achieved through a **stock split**. A stock split is a change in the number of shares outstanding accompanied by an offsetting change in the par or stated value per share. For example, in a 2-for-1 stock split, the number of outstanding and unissued shares doubles (1 share becomes 2 shares) and the par value per share is reduced by one-half (such as $1.00 par becomes $0.50 par). The effect of a stock split is to increase the number of shares outstanding and *decrease* the market price per share. The lower market price after a stock split might increase potential investor participation. Increasing the number of shares outstanding reduces earnings per share.

A company might also initiate a **reverse stock split** that will result in an *increase* in market price per share. For example, in a reverse 2-for-1 split, a company drops the number of shares by one-half (2 shares become 1 share) and doubles the par value per share (such as $0.50 par becomes $1.00 par). A company might initiate a reverse stock split to increase market price to a minimum price level to remain on a major stock exchange.

In a stock split or a reverse stock split, no accounting entry is needed because there is no change in the dollar amounts in capital stock, additional paid-in capital, or retained earnings. The increase (decrease) in the number of shares is exactly counterbalanced by a proportional reduction (increase) in the par or stated value per share. The only items changed are par (or stated) value per share, and shares issued, outstanding, and in the treasury. The ownership percentage of *each investor* remains *exactly the same* as illustrated below.

Investor	Shares Before 2-for-1 Stock Split	Ownership %	Shares After 2-for-1 Stock Split	Ownership %
Investor A	120	30%	240	30%
Investor B	40	10%	80	10%
Investor C	100	25%	200	25%
Investor D	140	35%	280	35%
Totals	400	100%	800	100%

Impact of Dividends and Stock Splits

We have reviewed the accounting for different types of dividends and stock splits. Dividends can be distributed through cash, property, or a company's own stock. A split either increases outstanding shares or in the case of a reverse split, decreases the number of outstanding shares. The impact on a corporation's capital structure is summarized in **Exhibit 20-2**. These changes are reflected on the financial statements (including disclosures) of a company. These events will also have an impact on the market price of shares, which is not reflected in financial statements.

EXHIBIT 20-2
Impact of a Dividend or Split

	Number of Shares Outstanding	Par Value per Share	Capital Stock	Paid-in Capital in Excess of Par	Retained Earnings	Total Stockholders' Equity
Declaration of cash dividend . . .	No change	No change	No change	No change	Decrease	Decrease
Payment of cash dividend	No change	No change	No change	No change	No change	No change
Declaration and distribution:						
Property dividend[1]	No change	No change	No change	No change	Decrease	Decrease
Liquidating dividend	No change	No change	No change	Decrease	No change	Decrease
Small stock dividend	Increase	No change	Increase[2]	Increase[3]	Decrease[4]	No change
Large stock dividend	Increase	No change	Increase[2]	No change	Decrease[2]	No change
Stock split	Increase	Decrease	No change	No change	No change	No change
Reverse stock split	Decrease	Increase	No change	No change	No change	No change

[1] Assets distributed are first adjusted to fair value.
[2] Par value (or stated value).
[3] Excess of fair value over par value (or stated value).
[4] Fair value.

Accounting for Stock Splits

LO20-6 **Demo 20-6C**

Cruz Co is authorized to issue 200,000 shares of common stock, $1 par, of which 40,000 shares were issued initially at $11 per share. Retained earnings has a balance of $450,000. Show the effect of a 2-for-1 stock split on the stockholders' equity section of the balance sheet.

Solution

In the following stockholders' equity presentation, the effects of a 2-for-1 stock split are demonstrated.

Stockholders' Equity	Before 2-for-1 Stock Split	After 2-for-1 Stock Split
Common stock, $1 par value; 200,000 shares authorized; 40,000 shares issued and outstanding	$ 40,000	
Common stock, $0.50 par value; 400,000 shares authorized; 80,000 shares issued and outstanding		$ 40,000
Paid-in capital in excess of par	400,000	400,000
Retained earnings	450,000	450,000
Total stockholders' equity	$890,000	$890,000

KROGER [KR]

KROGER

Real World—STOCK SPLIT

The Kroger Co. reported the following regarding a stock split effected in the form of a stock dividend in a recent annual report.

> **Note 1 (excerpt): Accounting Policies**—On June 25, 2015, the Company's Board of Directors approved a two-for-one stock split of The Kroger Co.'s common shares in the form of a 100% stock dividend, which was effective July 13, 2015. All share and per share amounts in the Company's Consolidated Financial Statements and related notes have been retroactively adjusted to reflect the stock split for all periods presented.

REVIEW 20-6 LO20-6 Account for Stock Dividends and Stock Splits

Review MBC

The records of Round Corporation showed the following account balances on March 1, 2020.

Common stock, $1 par, 50,000 shares outstanding	$ 50,000
Paid-in capital in excess of par	200,000
Retained earnings	175,000

The fair value of its common stock is $24 per share. Prepare journal entries for the following four separate scenarios.

a. The company declares (March 1, 2020) and issues (March 15, 2020) a 5% stock dividend.

b. The company declares (March 1, 2020) and issues (March 15, 2020) a 5% stock dividend. Of the stock dividend shares distributed, 200 shares are fractional shares. It is Round Corporation's policy to pay out fractional shares in cash.

c. The company declares (March 1, 2020) and issues (March 15, 2020) a stock split in the form of a 100% stock dividend.

d. The company declares (March 1, 2020) and issues (March 15, 2020) a 3-for-1 stock split.

More Practice: 20-48, 20-49, 20-50, 20-77, 20-78

Solution on p. 20-64.

LO 20-7 Describe comprehensive income, its components, and how it is reported

LO 20-7 Overview

Comprehensive Income Components
- Net income (loss)
  - Accumulate in retained earnings
- Other comprehensive income (loss)
  - Accumulate in accumulated other comprehensive income (loss)

Total **comprehensive income (or loss)** represents the change in equity (net assets) of a business entity *during a period* from transactions and other events and circumstances from nonowner sources. A statement of comprehensive income (illustrated in **Demo 20-7**) is required as part of a full set of financial statements.

Total comprehensive income is divided into two categories:

- Net income
- Other comprehensive income

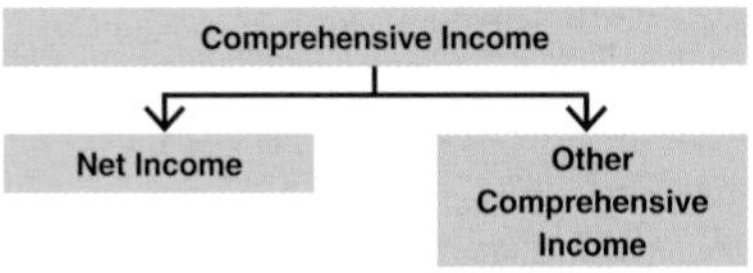

Other comprehensive income includes gains and losses that are excluded from net income, but which are recognized separately in the category of **other comprehensive income (or loss)**—often abbreviated OCI. The components of other comprehensive income are displayed as reconciling items between net income and comprehensive income. Gains and losses (net of tax) commonly reported in other comprehensive income include:

1. Unrealized holding gains or losses on available-for-sale debt securities (Chapter 14).
2. Gains or losses related to postretirement benefit plans (Chapter 19).
3. Gains or losses from foreign currency translation adjustments (Chapter 3).
4. Gains or losses from adjustments to a cash flow hedge (Chapter 14).

GAAP requires the reporting of comprehensive income in the financial statements either as a **single continuous statement of comprehensive income** *or* as **two separate statements of income and comprehensive income**. The expectation is that financial statement users are able to understand the relation between net income and comprehensive income and that this understanding leads to increased comparability of financial statements across companies.

At the end of an accounting period, the process of closing out other comprehensive income differs from the process of closing out net income. While net income is closed to a permanent account, retained earnings, at the end of an accounting period, other comprehensive income is closed to a permanent account called **accumulated other comprehensive income (or loss)**—often abbreviated AOCI—at the end of an accounting period. Accumulated other comprehensive income is a separate component of stockholders' equity.

Reporting of Comprehensive Income and Accumulated OCI — LO20-7 — Demo 20-7

Whitefish Inc. recognizes net income of $50,000 for the year ended December 31, 2020. The company's tax rate is 25%. Whitefish Inc. also reports a pretax net unrealized gain on available-for-sale debt securities of $4,000 ($3,000 after-tax) and a pretax loss on derivatives (cash flow hedges) of $6,400 ($4,800 after-tax) in 2020. Its December 31, 2019, balances (all credit balances) in common stock, paid-in capital in excess of par, retained earnings, and accumulated other comprehensive income are $1,000, $300,000, $200,000 and $3,000, respectively. The company paid no dividends and had no transactions affecting common stock during 2020.

a. Prepare a separate statement of comprehensive income for 2020.
b. Prepare a statement of stockholders' equity for 2020. Use a columnar format with the account types as the column titles.
c. Prepare the stockholders' equity section of the balance sheet at December 31, 2020.

Solution

a. **Separate Statement of Comprehensive Income**
A separate statement of comprehensive income begins with net income, and adds/subtracts other comprehensive income to arrive at total comprehensive income. Other comprehensive income items are shown net of tax.

Whitefish Inc.
Statement of Comprehensive Income
For Year Ended December 31, 2020

Net income		$50,000
Other comprehensive income, net of tax		
Net unrealized holding gain on available-for-sale securities	$3,000	
Loss on cash flow hedges	(4,800)	
Other comprehensive loss		(1,800)
Comprehensive income		$48,200

b. **Statement of Stockholders' Equity**

Whitefish Inc.
Statement of Stockholders' Equity

	Common Stock	Paid-in Capital in Excess of Par	Retained Earnings	Accumulated Other Comprehensive Income	Total
Balance, Dec. 31, 2019	$1,000	$300,000	$200,000	$3,000	$504,000
Net income			50,000		50,000
Other comprehensive loss				(1,800)	(1,800)
Balance, Dec. 31, 2020	$1,000	$300,000	$250,000	$1,200	$552,200

continued

continued from previous page

c. **Stockholders' Equity Presentation**

Whitefish Inc.
Balance Sheet (excerpt)
December 31, 2020

Stockholders' Equity	
Common stock	$ 1,000
Paid-in capital in excess of par	300,000
Retained earnings	250,000
Accumulated other comprehensive income	1,200
Total stockholders' equity	$552,200

PEPSICO

Real World—STATEMENT OF COMPREHENSIVE INCOME

PEPSICO [PEP]

PepsiCo Inc. reported the following statement of comprehensive income in a recent annual report. PepsiCo Inc. chose to report comprehensive income in a statement separate from the income statement. The following statement includes all four types of other comprehensive income adjustments discussed in this section.

Consolidated Statement of Comprehensive Income
PepsiCo, Inc. and Subsidiaries

Fiscal Years Ended Dec. 30, 2017, Dec. 31, 2016, and Dec. 26, 2015 (in millions)	**2017**	**2016**	**2015**
Net income	**$4,908**	$6,379	$5,501
Other comprehensive income/(loss), net of taxes:			
Net currency translation adjustment	**1,109**	(302)	(2,827)
Net change on cash flow hedges	**(36)**	46	3
Net pension and retireee medical adjustments	**(159)**	(316)	171
Net change on securities	**(68)**	(24)	1
Other	**16**	—	—
	862	(596)	(2,652)
Comprehensive income	**5,770**	5,783	2,849
Comprehensive income attributable to noncontrolling interests	**(51)**	(54)	(47)
Comprehensive income attributable to PepsiCo	**$5,719**	$5,729	$2,802

REVIEW 20-7 **LO20-7** **Comprehensive Income and Accumulated OCI**

Review MBC

Fox Corporation recognizes net income of $250,000 along with an other comprehensive gain of $55,000 (net of tax) for the year ended December 31, 2020. The December 31, 2019, balance in accumulated other comprehensive income is $114,000 (credit balance) and the balance in retained earnings is $80,000 (credit balance).

a. Prepare a statement of comprehensive income for 2020.

b. Determine the ending balance in accumulated other comprehensive income on December 31, 2020.

More Practice:
20-51, 20-52, 20-82, 20-83
Solution on p. 20-64.

Explain stockholders' equity disclosures and key analyses

LO 20-8

Stockholders' equity is an important component of financial statement presentation, disclosures, and analyses. Financial statement users find useful information in financial statements and in notes to financial statements that explain elements of equity. Using this information, ratios are computed to assess financial strength and long-run solvency.

Equity Analysis
- Disclosure
  - Number of shares
  - Changes in equity categories
  - Rights and privileges of outstanding securities
- Ratios
  - Book value per share
  - Payout ratio
  - Return on equity
  - Price-to-earnings ratio

LO 20-8 Overview

Equity Disclosures

For each issuance of equity, companies report the number of shares authorized, the number of shares issued or outstanding, and any par value. A company must also disclose changes in the stockholders' equity categories and changes in the number of shares of equity securities.

Disclosure also includes the rights and privileges associated with a company's outstanding securities. Dividend and liquidation preferences, participation rights, call prices and dates, sinking fund requirements, and conversion rates are examples of information disclosed. For example, in notes to financial statements in a recent Form 10-K of Bank of America, the company described a liquidation preference for a preferred stock issuance of $1,000 per share. This means that preferred shareholders have a right to $1,000 per share in the event of a liquidation before common shareholders would be paid, but after creditors would be paid.

Accounting standards also require companies to provide the following additional specific disclosures for equity, several of which pertain to preferred stock.

1. Relevant rights and privileges of the various securities.*
2. Number of shares issued from the conversion, exercise of securities, or satisfaction of required conditions during the period.
3. Liquidation preference of preferred or of other senior stock *must be disclosed in the equity section of the balance sheet* when that preference is significantly greater than par or stated value.
4. Aggregate or per-share amounts at which preferred stock may be called or is subject to redemption.
5. Aggregate and per-share amounts of cumulative preferred stock dividends in arrears.
6. Significant terms (quantitative and qualitative) of the conversion features of contingently convertible securities.
7. Redemption requirement for all capital stock redeemable at fixed or determinable prices on fixed or determinable dates in each of the five years following the date of the balance sheet.

* **505-10-50-3** An entity shall explain, in summary form within its financial statements, the pertinent rights and privileges of the various securities outstanding. Examples of information that shall be disclosed are dividend and liquidation preferences, participation rights, call prices and dates, conversion or exercise prices or rates and pertinent dates, sinking-fund requirements, unusual voting rights, and significant terms of contracts to issue additional shares or terms that may change conversion or exercise prices (excluding standard antidilution provisions).

A portion of retained earnings may be **restricted** for a certain purpose. Retained earnings are restricted primarily to protect the cash position of the corporation by reducing the amount of cash dividends that otherwise might be paid. The restriction may be the result of a legal contract or a state law. For example, a company may have signed a debt agreement that protects the creditors by restricting the amount of retained earnings that can be paid out in dividends while the debt is outstanding. Restrictions of retained earnings are typically indicated in notes to financial statements.

Management of a company may restrict retained earnings more formally through an appropriation of retained earnings. In this case, the restricted amount of retained earnings is transferred to an account, **appropriated retained earnings**, which is clearly identified separately in financial statements. This means that the company would report retained earnings in two components: appropriated retained earnings and unappropriated retained earnings. Disclosure in the notes accompanying the financial statements should include the nature of the appropriation and the amount restricted.

505-10-45-3 Appropriation of retained earnings is permitted, provided that it is shown within the shareholders' equity section of the balance sheet and is clearly identified as an appropriation of retained earnings.

Equity Ratios

We examine the following ratios in **Demo 20-8**: book value per share, payout ratio, return on equity, and price-to-earnings ratio.

Book Value per Share

$$\frac{\text{Common stock equity}}{\text{Number of common shares outstanding}}$$

This ratio measures the common shareholder investment per share. Common stockholders' equity is total stockholders' equity less preferred stockholder claims such as liquidation value and dividends in arrears on cumulative preferred stock. The amount per common share represents the liquidation value per share of common stock based on historical cost and other accounting principles affecting measurement and recognition in the financial statements. The ratio is less relevant as an estimation of liquidation value, however, if the amounts on the balance sheet do not reflect fair value.

Payout Ratio

$$\frac{\text{Cash common dividends}}{\text{Net income available to common stockholders}}$$

The payout ratio computes the proportion of income paid as dividends to common shareholders. A higher ratio indicates that a larger percentage of income was paid out in dividends. If preferred shareholders receive a portion of profits through dividends (or preferred dividends are cumulative), this amount is subtracted from net income to arrive at the net income that is available to common shareholders.

Return on Equity

$$\frac{\text{Net income available to common stockholders}}{\text{Average common stockholders' equity}}$$

This ratio computes the return on investment by the company's owners or the dollars of income earned for each investment dollar of the owners. Average common stockholders' equity is a simple average of beginning and ending total common stockholders' equity. A higher ratio indicates a higher return on investment of the shareholders. If preferred shareholders receive a portion of profits through dividends (or preferred dividends are cumulative), this amount is subtracted from net income to arrive at the net income that is available to common shareholders.

Price-to-Earnings Ratio

$$\frac{\text{Market price per share}}{\text{Earnings per share}}$$

The price-to-earnings ratio measures the amount an investor is willing to pay (market price of stock) per each dollar of earnings per share. As this ratio increases, an investor would assume to have a higher expectation for the profitability of the company in the future.

Demo 20-8 **LO20-8** **Equity Ratios**

The following financial information is provided for **Target Corporation**.

$ millions†	Fiscal Year 2017	Fiscal Year 2016	Fiscal Year 2015
Total assets	$38,999	$37,431	$40,262
Total liabilities	27,290	26,478	27,305
Shareholders' investment (common)	11,709	10,953	12,957

†Target fiscal year-ends: Feb. 3, 2018, Jan. 28, 2017, Jan. 30, 2016

Additional information ($ millions)	2017	2016
Common dividends paid	$1,338	$1,348
Net income	2,934	2,737
Earnings per share	5.33	4.70

Compute the book value per share, the payout ratio, the return on equity, and the price earnings ratio for fiscal years 2017 and 2016. Market price per share of its stock was $72.95 on Feb. 3, 2018, and $63.70 on Jan. 28, 2017. Common shares outstanding were 541,682,000 in fiscal year 2017 and 556,156,000 in fiscal year 2016.

continued

continued from previous page

Solution

		2017	2016
Book value per share =	$\frac{\text{Common stock equity}}{\text{Number of common shares outstanding}}$	$\frac{\$11,709}{\$41.682} = \$21.62$	$\frac{\$10,953}{556.156} = \$19.69$
Payout ratio =	$\frac{\text{Cash common dividends}}{\text{Net income available to common}}$	$\frac{\$1,338}{\$2,934} = 0.46$	$\frac{\$1,348}{\$2,737} = 0.49$
Return on equity =	$\frac{\text{Net income available to common}}{\text{Average common stockholders' equity}^{\dagger}}$	$\frac{\$2,934}{\$11,331} = 0.26$	$\frac{\$2,737}{\$11,955} = 0.23$
Price to earnings =	$\frac{\text{Market price per share}}{\text{Earnings per share}}$	$\frac{\$72.95}{\$5.33} = 13.69$	$\frac{\$63.70}{\$4.70} = 13.55$

† Average common stockholders' equity: For 2017 = ($11,709 + $10,953) / 2. For 2016 = ($10,953 + $12,957) / 2.

Target increased book value per share by approximately 10% over the prior year. Target returned approximately 48% of profits in dividends on average over the two years, indicating stability and maturity in the company's operations to maintain this sizeable dividend payment. Target investors had a higher rate of return on their investment, receiving 26 cents on each dollar invested compared to 23 cents per dollar in the prior year. Price to earnings also increased slightly over the prior year (approximately 1%).

GOLDMAN SACHS

Real World—FINANCIAL STATEMENT RATIOS

GOLDMAN SACHS [GS]

The Goldman Sachs Group Inc. provided the following ratios in its Management's Discussion and Analysis section in a recent annual report on Form 10-K. Two ratios discussed above (return on equity and the payout ratio) are included in the three-year, comparative ratio analysis.

Year Ended December	2017	2016	2015
Return on average common shareholders' equity	**4.9%**	9.4%	7.4%
Net earnings to average total assets	**0.5%**	0.8%	0.7%
Return on average total shareholders' equity	**5.0%**	8.5%	7.0%
Total average shareholders' equity to average total assets	**9.5%**	9.8%	9.9%
Dividend payout ratio	**32.2%**	16.0%	21.0%

Computing Equity Ratios

LO20-8 **REVIEW 20-8**

The following information is provided for **Starbucks Corporation**.

$ millions	Oct. 1, 2017	Oct. 2, 2016	Sept. 27, 2015
Common stock	$ 1.4	$ 1.5	$ 1.5
Additional paid-in capital	41.1	41.1	41.1
Retained earnings	5,563.2	5,949.8	5,974.8
Accumulated other comprehensive loss	(155.6)	(108.4)	(199.4)
Total shareholders' equity	$5,450.1	$5,884.0	$5,818.0
Common shares outstanding	1,431.6	1,460.5	1,485.1
Cash common dividends	$1,450.4	$1,178.0	$ 928.6
Net income	$2,884.7	$2,817.7	$2,757.4

Compute the following ratios for its fiscal years 2017 and 2016.

a. Book value per share *b.* Payout ratio *c.* Return on equity

More Practice: 20-53, 20-54, 20-84, 20-85
Solution on p. 20-64.

Questions

20-1. Identify four basic rights of stockholders. How may one or more of these rights be withheld from the stockholders?

20-2. Explain the meaning of authorized capital stock, issued capital stock, unissued capital stock, outstanding capital stock, and treasury stock.

20-3. Describe the main categories of stockholders' equity in accounting for corporate capital.

20-4. What is a noncontrolling interest and how is it presented in a company's statement of stockholders' equity?

20-5. Define legal capital.

20-6. Distinguish between par and no-par stock. Distinguish between common and preferred stock.

20-7. Identify and explain a transaction that causes paid-in capital to increase but does not result in any increase in the assets or decrease in the liabilities of the corporation.

20-8. Explain the difference between cumulative and noncumulative preferred stock.

20-9. Under what conditions is preferred stock reported as a liability?

20-10. Distinguish between callable and redeemable preferred stock.

20-11. How are assets valued when shares of stock are given in payment to acquire these assets?

20-12. Briefly describe the accounting for stock issue costs.

20-13. Define treasury stock.

20-14. What is the effect on the amounts of assets, liabilities, and stockholders' equity of (a) the purchase of treasury stock and (b) the sale of treasury stock?

20-15. Total stockholders' equity is not affected by the use of the cost method of accounting for treasury stock, yet some components of stockholders' equity are affected. Is this statement correct? Explain.

20-16. Why may states limit purchases of treasury stock to the amount reported as retained earnings?

20-17. In recording treasury stock transactions, explain why "gains" are recorded in additional paid-in capital account, whereas "losses" may involve a debit to retained earnings.

20-18. How is treasury stock reported on the balance sheet under the cost method?

20-19. When treasury stock is formally retired, retained earnings may be affected. Explain how this situation may occur.

20-20. What are the principal sources and uses of retained earnings?

20-21. Explain the significance of the declaration date, record date, and payment date related to dividends.

20-22. Distinguish between cash dividends and property dividends.

20-23. What is a liquidating dividend? What is the proper accounting treatment for such dividends?

20-24. What is the difference between a cash or property dividend and a stock dividend?

20-25. Explain this statement: When property dividends are declared and paid, a loss or gain often must be reported.

20-26. Contrast the effects of a stock dividend (declared and issued) versus a cash dividend (declared and paid) on assets, liabilities, and total stockholders' equity.

20-27. Contrast the effects of a typical small stock dividend (declared and issued and ignoring fractional shares) versus a typical cash dividend (declared and paid) on the components of stockholders' equity.

20-28. Explain why the amount of retained earnings reported on the balance sheet is often not the net amount of all accumulated earnings (and losses) less all accumulated cash and property dividends.

20-29. Distinguish between a stock split effected in the form of a dividend and a stock split.

20-30. What are the primary reasons for appropriating and for restricting retained earnings?

Brief Exercises

Brief Exercise 20-31
Preparing a Stockholders' Equity Section **LO1**
Hint: See Demo 20-1

On December 31, 2020, Polar Inc. had the following account balances.

Preferred stock, $10 par value	$150,000
Paid in capital in excess of par—Preferred stock	12,000
Common stock, $1 par value	8,000
Paid in capital in excess of par—Common stock	40,000
Retained earnings	220,000
Accumulated other comprehensive loss	(6,000)

Prepare the stockholders' equity section of the balance sheet for Polar Inc. at December 31, 2020. Ignore disclosure of number of shares.

Brief Exercise 20-32 Determining issued and outstanding shares **LO1**

From the following information, determine (1) the number of common shares issued, (2) the number of common shares outstanding, and (3) the number of common shares unissued.

Common stock, $2 par value, 10,000 shares authorized.	$8,000
Treasury stock, 250 shares	2,500

Brief Exercise 20-33 Classifying Stockholders' Equity Accounts **LO1**

Match each of the items *a* through *n* with its proper classification 1 through 7.

Stockholders' Equity Component	Financial Statement Item
1. Capital stock	____ *a.* Net loss
2. Additional paid-in capital	____ *b.* Restriction on retained earnings
3. Retained earnings	____ *c.* Goodwill
4. Accumulated other comprehensive income	____ *d.* Gain from foreign currency translation adjustment
	____ *e.* Cash dividends declared, not paid
5. Treasury stock	____ *f.* Bond sinking fund
6. Noncontrolling interests	____ *g.* Treasury stock, cost method
7. None of the above	____ *h.* Unrealized gain on available-for-sale debt securities
	____ *i.* Net income
	____ *j.* Correction of accounting error affecting prior years' net income
	____ *k.* Legal capital
	____ *l.* Net assets owned by investors other than the parent
	____ *m.* Preferred stock
	____ *n.* Paid-in capital in excess of par

Brief Exercise 20-34 Preparing Entry to Issue Common Stock **LO2** *Hint:* See Demo 20-2A

On June 30, 2020, Ebae Inc. issued 120 shares of $1 par value common stock for $12 per share. Prepare Ebae's journal entry.

Brief Exercise 20-35 Preparing Entry to Issue Common Stock **LO2** *Hint:* See Demo 20-2B

On June 30, 2020, Ebae Inc. issued 120 shares of no-par common stock for $15 per share.

a. Prepare Ebae's journal entry.

b. Prepare Ebae's journal entry assuming instead that the company designated a stated value of $2 per share for common stock.

Brief Exercise 20-36 Preparing Entry for Multiple Securities Issuance **LO2** *Hint:* See Demo 20-2D

Amazing Inc. issued 1,000 shares of common stock ($1 par) and 1,000 shares of preferred stock ($10 par) at a price of $150,000 on April 1, 2020. At the time of issuance, the market price of the common stock is $60 per share, and the market price of the preferred stock is $120 per share. Prepare the journal entry required on April 1, 2020. Round allocation rates to 3 decimal points.

Brief Exercise 20-37 Preparing Entry to Issue Stock for Noncash Consideration **LO2**

Ranier Corp. authorized the issuance of 400,000 shares of no-par common stock. The state of incorporation requires a minimum stated value of $4 per share of common stock issued. On February 1, 2020, Ranier issued 50 shares of common stock to a local law firm for legal services related to the start-up of the company with an estimated value of $1,500. Prepare the journal entry required on February 1, 2020. *Hint:* Start-up costs are expensed.

Brief Exercise 20-38 Preparing Entry to Issue Common Stock with Stock Issue Costs **LO2** *Hint:* See Demo 20-2E

On January 1, 2020, Vera Clothing Inc. issued 5,000 shares of common stock, $5 par for $100,000. Related to this issuance, the company incurred legal and accounting fees of $2,500 and administrative fees of $2,500. Prepare the journal entry required on January 1, 2020.

Brief Exercise 20-39 Preparing Entry for Direct Retirement of Reacquired Shares **LO3** *Hint:* See Demo 20-3B

Refer to the information in Brief Exercise 20-38. On June 30, 2020, Vera Clothing Inc. reacquired 500 shares of common stock at $21 per share and immediately retired the shares. Prepare the journal entry required on June 30, 2020.

Brief Exercise 20-40 Preparing Entry for Direct Retirement of Reacquired Shares **LO3**
Hint: See Demo 20-3B

On June 30, 2020, Pier5 Inc. issued 500 shares of $1 common stock for $15 per share. On June 30, 2020, Pier5 Inc. reacquired 50 shares of common stock at $12 per share and immediately retired the shares. On December 15, 2020, Pier5 Inc. reacquired 100 shares of common stock at $17 per share and immediately retired the shares. By what amount did retained earnings decrease as a result of the reacquisition of common stock on December 15, 2020?

Brief Exercise 20-41 Preparing Entries for Treasury Stock Transactions **LO3**
Hint: See Demo 20-3A

Harlee Inc. has 60,000 shares of $5 par common stock outstanding at the beginning of the year 2020. Prepare entries for the following transactions affecting stockholders' equity. Assume Paid-in Capital—Treasury Stock has a zero beginning balace.

a. January 15, 2020: Purchased common stock as treasury shares, 2,000 shares at $20.
b. June 15, 2020: Sold common treasury stock, 800 shares at $14.

Brief Exercise 20-42 Preparing Entries for Treasury Stock Transactions **LO3**
Hint: See Demo 20-3A

Charter Inc. has 600,000 shares of $1 par common stock outstanding at the beginning of the year 2020. Prepare entries for the following transactions affecting stockholders' equity. Assume Paid-in Capital—Treasury Stock has a zero beginning balace.

a. January 31, 2020: Purchased common stock as treasury shares, 1,200 shares at $15.
b. September 15, 2020: Sold common treasury stock, 200 shares at $17.
c. December 20, 2020: Sold common treasury stock, 250 shares at $13.

Brief Exercise 20-43 Preparing Entry to Issue Preferred Stock **LO4**
Hint: See Demo 20-4

Regency Inc. issued 800 shares of $20 par value, 8%, cumulative preferred stock for $48,000 on June 30, 2020. Prepare Regency's journal entry on June 30, 2020.

Brief Exercise 20-44 Determining Dividend Distributions **LO5**

Urban Inc. had the following capital outstanding. In 2020, Urban Inc. distributes $80,000 in cash dividends to shareholders.

Common, $1 par, 30,000 shares issued and outstanding . . . .
8% Preferred, $10 par, 20,000 shares issued and outstanding . . .

a. If the preferred stock is cumulative and dividends are in arrears for the past three years, what is the cash distribution to common shareholders and preferred shareholders?
b. What is the cash distribution to common shareholders and preferred shareholders if the preferred stock is noncumulative?

Brief Exercise 20-45 Preparing Dividend Entries **LO5**
Hint: See Demo 20-5A

On September 1, 2020, Fox Corporation declared a cash dividend of $1 per share on its 800,000 outstanding shares of common stock ($1 par). The dividend is payable on October 15, 2020, to stockholders of record on October 1, 2020. Provide all journal entries directly related to this dividend.

Brief Exercise 20-46 Preparing Entry for Property Dividends **LO5**
Hint: See Demo 20-5B

Zerizon Inc. holds 6,000 shares of Cable Co. common stock, which it acquired for $25 per share in May of 2020. On June 1, 2020, Zerizon Inc. declares a property dividend of 500 shares of Cable Co. common stock when the shares are selling at $28 per share. Provide the journal entry on June 1, 2020, for the declaration of the property dividend.

Brief Exercise 20-47 Preparing Entry for Liquidating Dividend Declaration **LO5**
Hint: See Demo 20-5C

Wellington Corp. declared a dividend on common stock of $250,000 on May 18, 2020. Wellington announced to shareholders that $175,000 of the dividend amount was a return of capital. Provide the journal entry on May 18, 2020, for the dividend declaration.

Brief Exercise 20-48 Preparing Entries for Small Stock Dividends **LO6**
Hint: See Demo 20-6A

Landry Inc. has 10,000 shares of common stock, $1 par outstanding. On September 30, 2020, Landry declares a 10% stock dividend when the fair value of its common stock is $30 per share. Distribution of the dividend will be on October 15, 2020.

a. Prepare the journal entry for the declaration of the stock dividend on September 30, 2020.
b. Prepare the journal entry for the distribution of the stock dividend on October 15, 2020.

Brief Exercise 20-49 Preparing Entries for Stock Split Effected in the Form of a Dividend **LO6**
Hint: See Demo 20-6B

Landry Inc. has 10,000 shares of common stock, $1 par outstanding. On September 30, 2020, Landry declares a stock split effected in the form of a 100% stock dividend when the fair value of its common stock is $30 per share. Distribution of the dividend will be on October 15, 2020.

a. Prepare the journal entry for the declaration of the stock dividend on September 30, 2020.
b. Prepare the journal entry for the distribution of the stock dividend on October 15, 2020.

Brief Exercise 20-50 Analyzing a Stock Split **LO6**

Refer to the information in Brief Exercise 20-49. Instead Landry announces a 2-for-1 stock split *not* effected through a stock dividend.

a. Prepare the journal entry for the declaration of the stock split on September 30, 2020.
b. Prepare the journal entry for the distribution of the stock split on October 15, 2020.
c. What is the total par value of common stock before and after the stock split?
d. What is the par value per share before and after the stock split?
e. What are the total number of shares before and after the stock split?

Brief Exercise 20-51 Determining the Balance in Accumulated OCI **LO7** *Hint:* See Demo 20-7

Fastco Corp. reports net income of $20,000, and other comprehensive income of $5,000 (net of tax) for the year ended December 31, 2020. The December 31, 2019, balance in accumulated other comprehensive income is $18,000 (credit balance) and the balance in retained earnings is $100,000 (credit balance). What is the ending balance in accumulated other comprehensive income on December 31, 2020?

Brief Exercise 20-52 Identifying Net Income and Other Comprehensive Income Amounts **LO7**

Identify whether the following items *a* through *j* are part of (1) net income or (2) other comprehensive income.

____ *a.* Sales revenue
____ *b.* Bad debt expense
____ *c.* Loss from foreign current translation adjustment
____ *d.* Gain on sale of an available-for-sale debt investment
____ *e.* Unrealized gain on an available-for-sale debt investment
____ *f.* Unrealized gain on an equity investment where investor lacks significant influence
____ *g.* Prior service cost amortization expense for a defined benefit plan
____ *h.* Unrealized loss on cash flow hedge
____ *i.* Loss on impairment of investment
____ *j.* Loss on sale of land

Brief Exercise 20-53 Analyzing Payout Ratio **LO8**

Bucky's Apparel Inc. is considering paying a dividend on December 31, 2020. A loan covenant stipulates that the payout ratio must be less than or equal to 10%. If the company has no preferred stock outstanding, and net income is expected to be $80,000, what is the maximum value that Bucky may pay out in dividends to the common shareholders?

Brief Exercise 20-54 Computing Equity Ratios **LO8** *Hint:* See Demo 20-8

The following information is provided for the Coca-Cola Company ($ millions).

Total common stockholders' equity on Dec. 31, 2017	$17,072
Total common stockholders' equity on Dec. 31, 2016	23,062
Net income, 2017	1,248

Compute the following ratios for 2017, assuming total number of 2017 common shares outstanding of 4.259 billion.

a. Book value per share
b. Return on equity

Exercises

Exercise 20-55 Reporting Stockholders' Equity **LO1**

The following data are from the accounts of Mitar Corporation at December 31, 2020 ($ thousands).

Retained earnings, beginning balance	$ 900
Common stock, $__ par, 100,000 shares authorized, 50,000 shares issued	1,000
Treasury stock, 1,000 shares	20
Paid-in capital in excess of par	400
Bonds payable	200
Net income for 2020 (not included in retained earnings above)	190
Dividends declared and paid during 2020 (not included in retained earnings above)	80

Required

a. Determine the value of the following items.
1. Total retained earnings at end of 2020
2. Par value per share
3. Number of shares outstanding

4. Total stockholders' equity
5. Average original selling price per share
6. Cost per share of treasury stock

b. Prepare the stockholders' equity section of the balance sheet at December 31, 2020.

Exercise 20-56
Reporting Stockholders' Equity **LO1**
Hint: See Demo 20-1

On December 31, 2020, Nakoma Inc. had the following account balances.

Preferred stock, $100 par, 5,000 shares authorized.	$ 20,000 Cr.
Paid in capital in excess of par—Preferred stock.	80,000 Cr.
Common stock, $1 par, 250,000 shares authorized.	35,000 Cr.
Paid in capital in excess of par—Common stock.	480,000 Cr.
Retained earnings	360,000 Cr.
Accumulated other comprehensive income	48,000 Cr.
Treasury stock, 1,200 shares.	55,000 Dr.
Noncontrolling interests	5,000 Cr.

Prepare the stockholders' equity section of the balance sheet for Nakoma Inc. on December 31, 2020. State the par value per share, and the number of shares authorized, issued, and outstanding for common stock and preferred stock on the face of the statement.

Exercise 20-57
Recording Entries for Common Stock Issuance **LO2**

Record journal entries for the following separate transactions.

a. Max Inc. issued 5,000 shares of $1 par value common stock for $20 per share on January 1, 2020.
b. Max Inc. issued 1,000 shares of no-par common stock for $25 on January 1, 2020. The state of incorporation requires a minimum value per share of $2.
c. Max Inc. issued 500 shares of no-par common stock for $18 per share on January 1, 2020.
d. Max Inc. issued 5,000 shares of $1 par value common stock for $18 per share on January 1, 2020, and incurred $1,000 in legal fees related to the stock issuance.
e. Max Inc. issued 10,000 shares of common stock ($1 par) in exchange for equipment with a fair value of $178,000.
f. Max Inc. issued 3,000 shares of Class A common stock ($1 par) and 4,000 shares of Class B common stock ($2 par) at a price of $80,000. At the time of issuance, the market price of the Class A common stock is $15 per share, and the market price of the Class B common stock is $10 per share.
g. Max Inc. issued 3,000 shares of Class A common stock ($1 par) and 4,000 shares of Class B common stock ($2 par) at a price of $85,000. At the time of issuance, the market price of the Class A common stock is $16 per share, and the market price of the Class B common stock is unknown.

Exercise 20-58
Recording Entries for Common Stock Issuance **LO2**

Trident Corporation is authorized to issue 100,000 shares of $5 par value common stock. The shares of stock are not publicly traded. During 2020, the company completed the following transactions.

Jan. 8, 2020	Issued 40,000 shares of common stock at $12 per share.
Jan. 30, 2020	Issued 10,500 shares of common stock in exchange for equipment with an appraised value of $136,500.

Required

a. Prepare the journal entry on January 8, 2020.
b. Prepare the journal entry on January 30, 2020.
c. Would the answer to part *b* change if the stock were traded on a registered stock exchange at $14 per share on January 30, 2020? If yes, prepare the journal entry on January 30, 2020.

Exercise 20-59
Recording Entry for Stock Issuance **LO2**

In May of 2012, **Facebook** raised over $16 billion in its initial public offering. Approximately 421.2 million shares of Class A common stock, $0.000006 par value were sold for $38 a share.

Required

Ignoring stock issue costs, record the journal entry for this stock issuance.

Exercise 20-60
Recording Entries for Multiple Securities Issuance **LO2**

Gilmore Company has 20,000 authorized shares of common stock, $2 par, and 20,000 authorized shares of preferred stock, $10 par. On April 10, 2020, Gilmore sold 600 shares of common stock and 400 shares of preferred stock in one transaction for a total cash price of $20,000. The common stock recently had been selling at $26 per share while the preferred stock recently had been selling at $16 per share.

Required

a. Prepare the entry on April 10, 2020, for the issuance of common and preferred stock.

b. Assume instead that only the market price of the common stock is known ($26 per share). Prepare the entry on April 10, 2020, for the issuance of common and preferred stock.

Exercise 20-61 Recording Stock Issue Costs **LO2**

Stellar Inc. issues 20,000 shares of common stock, $0.01 par value, for $28 per share on March 28, 2020. Related to this transaction, Stellar incurred legal and administrative costs totaling $4,000, paid in cash.

Required

Prepare the journal entry on March 28, 2020, for the issuance of common shares.

Exercise 20-62 Recording Common Stock Direct Retirement **LO3**
Hint: See Demo 20-3B

Laser Inc. has the following account balances on December 31, 2019.

Common stock, $1 par, 10,000 shares issued	$ 10,000
Paid-in capital in excess of par.	140,000

Required

Prepare journal entries for the following three separate scenarios.

a. On January 15, 2020, Laser Inc. acquires and immediately retires 1,000 shares of stock at $15 per share.

b. On January 15, 2020, Laser Inc. acquires and immediately retires 1,000 shares of stock at $17 per share.

c. On January 15, 2020, Laser Inc. acquires and immediately retires 1,000 shares of stock at $14 per share.

Exercise 20-63 Recording Common Stock Direct Retirement **LO3**

M4 Inc. issued 50,000 shares of $0.01 par value common stock for $15 per share on January 1, 2020, the day of its initial stock offering.

Required

a. Record entries for the following subsequent transactions assuming that the company's policy is to directly retire any reacquired shares.
   1. On March 30, 2020, M4 Inc. reacquires and retires 1,000 shares of common stock at $13.50 per share.
   2. On August 20, 2020, M4 Inc. reacquires and retires 1,000 shares of common stock at $17.25 per share.
   3. On December 1, 2020, M4 Inc. issues 5,000 shares of common stock at $17.00 per share.

b. Determine the number of shares issued and the number of shares outstanding on the following dates (after transactions have been recorded).
   1. March 30, 2020.
   2. August 20, 2020.
   3. December 1, 2020.

Exercise 20-64 Recording Treasury Stock Transactions **LO3**

On January 2, 2020, Liberty Corporation was authorized to issue 100,000 shares of $5 par value common stock. Liberty issued 20,000 shares of common stock on January 15, 2020, at $15 per share.

Required

a. Record the entry on June 30, 2020, for purchase of 2,200 common shares for the treasury at $18 per share.

b. Record the entry on September 20, 2020, for sale of 800 treasury shares at $21 per share.

c. Record the entry on November 3, 2020, for sale of 500 treasury shares at $17 per share.

d. Record the entry on December 15, 2020, for sale of 400 treasury shares at $13 per share.

e. Determine the number of shares issued and the number of shares outstanding on the following dates (after transactions have been recorded): June 30, 2020; September 20, 2020; November 3, 2020; and December 15, 2020.

Exercise 20-65 Recording Treasury Stock Transactions **LO3**
Hint: See Demo 20-3A

On January 2, 2020, Zeviae Corporation was authorized to issue 200,000 shares of $1 par value common stock. Zeviae issued 50,000 shares of common stock on January 8, 2020, at $10 per share. In addition, the company completed the following transactions in 2020.

Mar. 30	Purchased 5,000 shares of common stock for the treasury at $12 per share.
Apr. 20	Purchased 5,000 shares of common stock for the treasury at $9 per share.
Oct. 31	Sold 8,000 shares of treasury stock at $11 per share.

Required

a. Record the entry on March 30, 2020, for the purchase of common shares for the treasury.

b. Record the entry on April 20, 2020, for the purchase of common shares for the treasury.

c. Record the entry on October 31, 2020, for the sale of treasury shares at $11 per share. Assume a FIFO cost flow in accounting for the sale of treasury shares.

d. Repeat part *c* but instead assume a weighted average cost flow in accounting for the sale of treasury shares.

Exercise 20-66
Recording and Reporting Treasury Stock Transactions **LO3**

On January 1, 2020, M. Jordan Corporation issued 20,000 shares of $1 par value common stock at $50 per share. On January 15, 2020, M. Jordan purchased 50 shares of its own common stock at $55 per share. On March 1, 2020, 20 of the treasury shares were resold at $58. The balance in retained earnings was $25,000 prior to these transactions.

Required

a. Record the entry on January 1, 2020, for issuance of common stock. What is the impact on stockholders' equity of this transaction?

b. Record the entry on January 15, 2020, for purchase of common shares for the treasury. What is the impact on stockholders' equity of this transaction?

c. Record the entry on March 1, 2020, for sale of treasury shares at $58 per share. What is the impact on stockholders' equity of this transaction?

d. Provide the ending balances for each of the stockholders' equity accounts affected by these entries.

e. Assume that on March 30, 2020, all remaining treasury stock shares are retired. Provide the entry for retirement of treasury shares.

Exercise 20-67
Recording: Treasury Stock vs. Direct Stock Retirement **LO3**

On December 31, 2020, the records for Lakers Inc. provided the following data on stockholders' equity.

Common stock, $10 par, 30,000 shares issued	$300,000
Additional paid-in capital on common stock, $0.30 per share	9,000
Treasury stock, 3,000 shares (cost $9.80 per share)	29,400

The stockholders vote to retire all of the treasury stock immediately and to purchase for direct retirement another 4,000 shares of common stock currently trading at $12.50 per share.

Required

a. Provide the journal entry for the purchase and immediate retirement of the 4,000 shares of outstanding common stock.

b. Provide the journal entry for the retirement of all of the remaining treasury shares.

c. Assume instead for part (*a*) that the company holds the 4,000 shares in the treasury rather than retiring immediately. Record the journal entry and indicate how stockholders' equity is impacted. Is the impact on stockholders' equity different if the shares were immediately retired?

Exercise 20-68
Analyzing Common Stock Reacquisition Methods **LO3**

Lakers Inc. reacquired a number of its own shares in one transaction in December of 2020. (Assume no previous reacquisitions of stock.) Lakers Inc. could account for the reacquisition transaction using two different methods, illustrated as Option One and Option Two.

Stockholders' Equity Section at December 31, 2020	Option One	Option Two
Common stock, $1 par, 100,000 shares authorized	$ 8,000	$ 10,000
Paid-in capital in excess of par	120,000	150,000
Retained earnings	31,000	35,000
Treasury stock, 2,000 shares	0	(36,000)
Total stockholders' equity	$159,000	$159,000

Required

a. Identify which method the company used in Option One to account for the reacquisition of common stock. Recreate the accounting entry to record the reacquisition of common stock.

b. Identify which method the company used in Option Two to account for the reacquisition of common stock. Recreate the accounting entry to record the reacquisition of common stock.

c. Determine the shares issued and shares outstanding on December 31, 2020 under Option One.

d. Determine the shares issued and shares outstanding on December 31, 2020 under Option Two.

Exercise 20-69 Correcting Stockholders' Equity Account **LO2, 3**

In our review of the accounting records of Crew Corp., we discover that during 2020, stockholders' equity transactions were all recorded in the common stock account. Our first step is to recreate the journal entries for the year that affected equity.

Common Stock			
		0	Beginning balance
		7,500	June 1: Sold 500 shares of common stock ($1 par) at $15 per share
		5,400	July 31: Sold 300 shares of common stock ($1 par) at $18 per share
Oct. 15: Purchased 200 shares for treasury at $20 per share	4,000		
		2,100	Dec. 1: Sold 100 shares treasury stock at $21
		11,000	Ending balance

Required

a. Provide the correct journal entries for the stockholders' equity transactions for 2020.

b. What is the correct ending balance of common stock?

Exercise 20-70 Recording and Reporting Preferred Stock **LO4, 5**

Cedar Corporation is authorized to issue 10,000 shares of 6%, $10 par, cumulative preferred stock. During 2020, it sold 2,000 shares of preferred stock for $25 per share.

Required

a. Record the entry for the issuance of preferred stock during 2020.

b. Assume the company is preparing financial statements for the year ended 2023. If the company had not declared or paid dividends in any year to preferred shareholders, what would the company report as dividends in arrears on December 31, 2023?

Exercise 20-71 Recording Common and Preferred Stock Transactions **LO2, 4**

Gilmore Company has 20,000 authorized shares of common stock, $2 par, and also 20,000 authorized shares of preferred stock, $10 par.

Required

Record journal entries for the following *separate* transactions. Analyze and record each transaction separately.

a. On January 1, 2020, Gilmore sold 400 shares of common stock and 200 shares of preferred stock for a lump sum of $12,300. The common stock had been selling during the current week at $25 per share, and the preferred at $12 per share. Round amounts to the nearest dollar.

b. On January 1, 2020, Gilmore issued 180 shares of preferred stock for used equipment. The equipment had been appraised at $2,400, and the book value recorded by the seller was $1,200. A reliable determinable fair value on the preferred stock has not been established.

c. Assume that the 20,000 shares of preferred stock are callable for $12 per share at the option of the issuer, Gilmore. After issuing 500 shares of callable preferred stock on January 1, 2020, for $12, Gilmore recalled 100 shares of preferred stock on June 30, 2020, for $12. Record the entries for Gilmore on January 1, 2020, and on June 30, 2020.

d. Assume that each of the 20,000 shares of preferred stock is convertible into 2 shares of common stock at the option of the stockholder. After issuing 500 shares of convertible preferred stock on January 1, 2020 for $12, 100 shares of preferred stock were converted into common stock on June 30, 2020. Record the entries for Gilmore on January 1, 2020, and on June 30, 2020, assuming that the fair value of the preferred stock was $16 per share on June 30, 2020.

Exercise 20-72 Determining Preferred Stock Financial Statement Presentation **LO4**

On December 31, 2020, Costko Corporation had 50,000 shares of 6%, $10 par, cumulative preferred stock.

Required

Indicate where the preferred stock is reported in the balance sheet for each separate scenario.

a. Preferred shares of Costko are nonredeemable.

b. Preferred shares of Costko will be called in by Costko on December 31, 2024, for a fixed price. Although not obligated to pay dividends each year, Costko intends to pay the 6% dividend to the preferred shareholders over the next 5 years.

c. Preferred shares of Costko may be redeemed by shareholders at a predetermined price at any point in time.

d. Preferred shares of Costko may be called in by Costko at any point in time.

Exercise 20-73
Recording Dividend Declarations **LO5**

Following are four separate dividend scenarios.

a. On April 1, 2020, Meriter Corporation declared a cash dividend of $5.00 per share on its 32,000 outstanding shares of common stock ($1 par). The dividend is payable on April 21, 2020, to stockholders of record on April 14, 2020.

b. Axe Co. has issued and outstanding 1,000 shares of $100 par, cumulative, 5% preferred stock and 20,000 shares of $5 par common stock. Dividends are in arrears for the past year (not including the current year). On December 15, 2020, the board of directors of Axe Co. declared dividends of $25,000 to be paid to shareholders at the end of its fiscal year.

c. Siri Corp. holds 1,000 shares of Mobile Co. common stock, purchased at the beginning of the year for $30 a share (carrying value on February 1, 2020). On February 1, 2020, Siri Corp. declared a property dividend of 450 shares of Mobile Co. common stock when the shares were selling at $28 per share.

d. Treck Corporation declared a common stock dividend of $45,000 on April 1, 2020. Treck Corporation announced to shareholders that 70% of the dividend amount was a return of capital.

Required

Record the entry for the declaration of dividends for each of the four separate scenarios.

Exercise 20-74
Determining Preferred Dividend Distributions **LO5**

Olivia Inc. had 30,000 outstanding shares of common stock, $0.01 par, and 8,000 outstanding shares of 7%, cumulative preferred stock, $50 par throughout its initial four years of operations. The company declared dividends of $0, $40,000, $40,000, $40,000, in years 1, 2, 3, and 4, respectively.

Required

a. Determine how the dividends were shared between the preferred and common shareholders in year 2 in total and on a per share basis.

b. Determine how the dividends were shared between the preferred and common shareholders in year 3 in total and on a per share basis.

c. Determine how the dividends were shared between the preferred and common shareholders in year 4 in total and on a per share basis.

Exercise 20-75
Analyzing Preferred Dividend Disclosure **LO4, 5**

Following is an excerpt from a recent Form 10-K of **Pandora Media Inc.** on its redeemable preferred stock.

> In June 2017, we entered into an agreement with Sirius XM Radio, Inc. ("Sirius XM") to sell 480,000 shares of Series A for $1,000 per share, with gross proceeds of $480.0 million. The Series A shares were issued in two rounds: an initial closing of 172,500 shares for $172.5 million that occurred on June 9, 2017 upon signing the agreement with Sirius XM, and an additional closing of 307,500 shares for $307.5 million that occurred on September 22, 2017. In the year ended December 31, 2017, total proceeds from the initial and additional closing, net of preferred stock issuance costs of $29.3 million, was $450.7 million.
>
> Conversion Feature. Holders of the Series A shares have the option to convert their shares plus any accrued dividends into common stock. We have the right to settle the conversion in cash, common stock or a combination thereof. The conversion rate for the Series A is initially 95.2381 shares of common stock per each share of Series A, which is equivalent to an initial conversion price of approximately $10.50 per share of our common stock, and is subject to adjustment in certain circumstances. Dividends on the Series A will accrue on a daily basis, whether or not declared, and will be payable on a quarterly basis at a rate of 6% per year. We have the option to pay dividends in cash when authorized by the Board and declared by the Company or accumulate dividends in lieu of paying cash. Dividends accumulated in lieu of paying cash will continue to accrue and accumulate at rate of 6% per year.
>
> Redemption Feature As of December 31, 2017, there is no ability to redeem or require redemption of the Series A. Under certain circumstances, we will have the right to redeem the Series A on or after September 22, 2020. The Series A holders will have the right to require us to redeem the Series A on or after September 22, 2022. Any optional redemption of the Series A will be at a redemption price equal to 100% of the liquidation preference, or $1,000 per share, plus accrued and unpaid dividends to, but excluding, the redemption date. In the event of a future redemption, whether initiated by us or by the holders, we will have the option to redeem the Series A in cash, common stock or a combination thereof.

Required

Referring to the excerpt provided, answer the following questions.

a. Would we expect the redeemable preferred stock to be presented on the balance sheet as a liability or as equity?

b. Provide the summary entry for the issuance of the Series A redeemable stock in 2017, assuming that the preferred stock has a par value of $0.0001 per share. Indicate how the stock issue costs affect the journal entry.

c. Provide the entry if 100,000 shares of Series A preferred stock were converted to common stock, assuming that the common stock has a par value of $0.001 per share.

d. Determine the amount of dividends that would be in arrears for a full year, assuming no dividend declaration, no change in the number of preferred shares outstanding, and that the dividend rate applies to the net preferred stock proceeds (not the par value).

Exercise 20-76
Recording Liquidating Dividends **LO5**

On November 1, 2020, Toni Corp. declared a cash dividend of $3.00 per share on its 20,000 outstanding shares of common stock ($1 par, originally sold at $10 per share). The dividend is payable on January 5, 2021, to its stockholders of record on December 30, 2020. On its declaration date, the balance in the retained earnings account was $46,000; this balance had not been corrected for a $6,000 overstatement of the 2019 net income (caused by an understatement of 2019 depreciation expense). The annual accounting period ends December 31.

Required

a. Provide the entry for declaration of the dividend on November 1, 2020.
b. Provide the entry for distribution of the dividend on January 5, 2021.
c. Are there any issues in recording the cash dividend? Explain.

Exercise 20-77
Recording Stock Dividends and Stock Splits **LO6**

The records of Dixie Corporation showed the following balances on November 1, 2020. The fair value of its stock is $18 per share.

Common stock, $10 par, 30,000 shares outstanding	$300,000
Paid-in capital in excess of par	102,000
Retained earnings	200,000

Required

Prepare journal entries for the following six separate scenarios.

a. The company declares (November 1, 2020) and issues (November 20, 2020) a 10% stock dividend.
b. The company declares (November 1, 2020) and issues (November 20, 2020) a 10% stock dividend. Of the 3,000 stock dividend shares, 2,800 shares are whole shares and 200 shares are fractional shares. It is the company's policy to pay out fractional shares in cash.
c. The company declares (November 1, 2020) and issues (November 20, 2020) a stock split effected in the form of a 100% stock dividend.
d. The company declares (November 1, 2020) and issues (November 20, 2020) a 2-for-1 stock split. Determine the total number of shares and the par value per share after the stock split.
e. The company declares (November 1, 2020) and issues (November 20, 2020) a 5-for-1 stock split. Determine the total number of shares and the par value per share after the stock split.
f. The company declares (November 1, 2020) and issues (November 20, 2020) a 3-for-1 reverse stock split. Determine the total number of shares and the par value per share after the stock split.

Exercise 20-78
Recording Stock Dividends, Fractional Shares **LO6**

Tech Inc. issues a 5% common stock dividend on 50,000 shares of $1 par common stock issued and outstanding on August 1, 2020. The market price of its common stock is $20 per share. The small stock dividend will be distributed on August 15, 2020, to stockholders of record on August 7, 2020.

Required

a. Record the entry on (1) the date of declaration and (2) the date of distribution.
b. Assume that of the 2,500 stock dividend shares, 2,200 were whole shares and the remaining were fractional shares making up 300 equivalent whole shares. The company's policy is to pay cash to shareholders for fractional shares. Record the entry on (1) the date of declaration and (2) the date of distribution.

Exercise 20-79
Reporting Impact of Equity Transactions **LO1, 2, 3, 4, 5, 6, 7**

Fourteen equity transactions are included in the following table.

	Transaction	Paid-in Capital	Retained Earnings	Accumulated OCI	Treasury Stock	Total Stockholders' Equity	Total Assets	Total Liabilities
1	Issue common stock for cash							
2	Issue common stock for land							
3	Retire common stock from the treasury							
4	Issue preferred stock for cash							

continued

continued from previous page

	Transaction	Paid-in Capital	Retained Earnings	Accumulated OCI	Treasury Stock	Total Stockholders' Equity	Total Assets	Total Liabilities
5	Incur stock issue costs							
6	Purchase shares for the treasury.							
7	Resale of treasury stock above cost.							
8	Declare a cash dividend							
9	Pay a previously declared cash dividend							
10	Declare a liquidating dividend. .							
11	Declare a 5% stock dividend . .							
12	Declare stock split effected in the form of a dividend.							
13	Declare a 2-for-1 stock split . . .							
14	Record an unrealized gain on available-for-sale debt securities							

Required

Indicate how each transaction affects each financial statement category: increase, decrease, or remain unchanged.

Exercise 20-80
Reporting a Stock Split **LO6**

Starbucks Corporation disclosed the following on a recent stock split in its annual Form 10-K report for the year ended September 27, 2015.

> **Stock Split (excerpt from Note 1)**—On April 9, 2015, we effected a 2-for-1 stock split of our $0.001 par value common stock for shareholders of record as of March 30, 2015. All share and per-share data in our consolidated financial statements and notes has been retroactively adjusted to reflect this stock split. We adjusted shareholders' equity to reflect the stock split by reclassifying an amount equal to the par value of the additional shares arising from the split from retained earnings to common stock during the second quarter of fiscal 2015, resulting in no net impact to shareholders' equity on our consolidated balance sheets.
>
> In addition, the statement of equity for Starbucks on September 27, 2015, reported the following: the company increased common shares by 749.4 million shares, increased the common stock account by $0.8 million, and decreased retained earnings by $0.8 million related to this effected stock split.

Required

a. What journal entry did the company record for this effected stock split?

b. What was the impact of the effected stock split on (1) the number of common shares, (2) par value per common share, (3) retained earnings, (4) paid-in capital, (5) net income, (6) stockholders' equity, and (7) market price?

c. How would the transaction have been different if the company distributed a 2-for-1 stock split?

Exercise 20-81
Calculating the Balance in Retained Earnings **LO1, 6, 7**

The following information is provided for Fey Corp. for the year ended December 31, 2020.

Sales.	$110,000
Cost of goods sold	45,000
General and administrative expenses	25,000
Unrealized gain on available for sale securities	2,000
Dividends declared and paid	12,000
Prior period adjustment, net of tax (expense understatement). . . .	2,200
Stock dividends distributed.	6,000
Treasury stock at cost	4,000
Retained earnings, beginning balance	130,000

Required

Assuming a 25% statutory tax rate, calculate the ending balance in retained earnings for the year ended December 31, 2020.

Exercise 20-82
Reporting Comprehensive Income, Retained Earnings, Accumulated OCI **LO7**

The following excerpts are from the annual financial statements of KPNG, Inc.

KPNG, Inc.
Statement of Comprehensive Income
For Year Ended December 31, 2020

Net Income		$100,000
Other comprehensive income, net of tax		
Net unrealized holding loss on available-for-sale securities		(12,000)
Gain on pension benefit plan		1,200
Other comprehensive loss		(10,800)
Comprehensive income		$ 89,200

KPNG, Inc.
Stockholders' Equity Section

As of December 31	2020	2019
Common stock	$ 1,000	$ 1,000
Paid-in capital in excess of par	300,000	300,000
Retained earnings	250,000	150,000
Accumulated other comprehensive income (loss)	(7,800)	3,000
Total stockholders' equity	$543,200	$454,000

Required

a. What is comprehensive income (loss) for the year ended December 31, 2020? What is the accumulated other comprehensive income (loss) as of December 31, 2020?

b. Prepare a reconciliation of retained earnings from 2019 to 2020 assuming that no dividends were declared in 2020.

c. Prepare a reconciliation of accumulated other comprehensive income (loss) from December 31, 2019, to December 31, 2020.

Exercise 20-83
Analyzing Amounts Affecting Net Income and Other Comprehensive Income **LO7**

The following items are included in the statement of comprehensive income of Raft Inc.

____ *a.* Dividend revenue
____ *b.* Unrealized loss on available-for-sale securities
____ *c.* Realized loss on available-for-sale securities
____ *d.* Gain on sale of short-term investments
____ *e.* Gain from foreign currency translation adjustment
____ *f.* Loss on disposal of equipment
____ *g.* Gain on sale of discontinued operations
____ *h.* Interest revenue
____ *i.* Loss on postretirement benefit plan
____ *j.* Gain on cash flow hedge derivative instrument
____ *k.* Insurance gain on casualty (fire)

Required

For each item *a* through *k*, indicate whether the amount is included in comprehensive income as (1) net income or (2) other comprehensive income. Also indicate whether the item is accumulated in (3) retained earnings or in (4) accumulated other comprehensive income.

Exercise 20-84
Computing and Analyzing Stockholders' Equity Ratios **LO8**

The balance sheets for Crosby Inc. and Gretzky Company reflect the following.

	Crosby Inc.	Gretzky Inc.
Current liabilities	$ 30,000	$ 30,000
Long-term liabilities	30,000	230,000
Stockholders' equity		
Common stock, $5 par	170,000	46,000
6% Preferred stock, $10 par, cumulative	50,000	20,000
Retained earnings	60,000	30,000
Total liabilities and stockholders' equity	$340,000	$356,000
Net income, included in above retained earnings amount	$ 40,000	$ 20,000
Common stockholders' equity, prior year	225,000	90,000

Required

a. Compute the debt to equity ratio.
b. Compute the return on equity ratio.
c. Compute book value per share of common stock.
d. Interpret the results from parts *a*, *b*, and *c*.

Exercise 20-85
Computing Stockholders' Equity Ratios **LO8**

The following information is provided for ABC Retail Inc.

Shareholders' Equity ($ thousands)	Dec. 31, 2020
Preferred stock, $50 par, 4,000,000 shares authorized, 61,000 shares outstanding...	$ 3,050
Common stock, $1 par, 1,000,000 shares authorized, 800,000 shares outstanding...	800
Paid-in capital in excess of par...	200
Retained earnings ...	35,730
Total shareholders' equity...	$39,780

Additional information	
Preferred dividends paid in 2020 ...	$ 240,000
Common dividends paid in 2020 ...	1,840,000
Net income for year ended December 31, 2020...	2,250,000
Average common shareholders' equity ...	35,000,000

Required

a. Compute book value per share of common stock.
b. Compute the payout ratio.
c. Compute the return on equity ratio.

Problems

Problem 20-86
Recording Equity Journal Entries and Reporting Stockholders' Equity **LO1, 2, 3, 4, 5, 6**

Haywood Co. is a publicly owned company whose shares are traded on a national stock exchange. At December 31, 2019, Haywood had 50 million shares of $10 par value common stock authorized, of which 30 million shares were issued and 28 million shares were outstanding.

The stockholders' equity accounts at December 31, 2019, had the following balances ($ millions).

Common stock...	$300
Paid-in capital in excess of par...	160
Retained earnings ...	100
Treasury stock ...	(36)

During 2020, Haywood had the following transactions.

1. On February 1, 2020, a secondary distribution of 4 million shares of $10 par value common stock was completed. The stock was sold to the public at $18 per share, net of issue costs.
2. On February 15, 2020, Haywood issued, at $110 per share, 200,000 shares of $100 par value, 8% cumulative preferred stock.
3. On March 1, 2020, Haywood reacquired 40,000 shares of its common stock for $18.50 per share for the treasury.
4. On March 31, 2020, Haywood declared a semi-annual cash dividend on common stock of 10 cents per share, payable on April 30, 2020, to stockholders of record on April 10, 2020.
5. On May 31, 2020, when the market price of the common stock was $20 per share, Haywood declared a 5% stock dividend distributable on July 1, 2020, to stockholders of record on June 1, 2020.
6. On June 30, 2020, Haywood sold the 40,000 treasury shares reacquired on March 1, 2020, and an additional 560,000 treasury shares costing $11.2 million that were on hand at the beginning of the year. The selling price was $25 per share.

7. On September 30, 2020, Haywood declared a semi-annual cash dividend on common stock of 10 cents per share and the yearly dividend on preferred stock, both payable on October 30, 2020, to stockholders of record on October 10, 2020.
8. Net income for 2020 was $50.0 million.

Required

a. Provide entries for each of the transactions.

b. Provide a summary of the ending balances of Haywood's stockholders' equity accounts for 2020.

Problem 20-87
Recording Equity Journal Entries and Reporting Stockholders' Equity **LO1, 4, 5, 6**

The Gilmore Company had the following stockholders' equity section as of December 31, 2019.

Stockholders' Equity	
Preferred stock, $100 par, 8% cumulative, 10,000 shares issued and outstanding. . . .	$1,000,000
Common stock, $20 par, 70,000 shares issued and outstanding.	1,400,000
Paid-in capital in excess of par.	800,000
Retained earnings	3,000,000
Total stockholders' equity	$6,200,000

There are no dividends in arrears on preferred shares. During 2020 the following events or transactions occurred:

- Earnings during 2020 total $600,000. The board of directors declares a cash dividend totaling $280,000 to be paid as appropriate to preferred and common shareholders. Later, a stock dividend of 10% is declared on common stock. The fair value of common stock is $68 per share on the date the stock dividend is declared.
- To familiarize stockholders with one of the company's new products, the board declares a property dividend of one ounce of a new perfume the company produces for every share of outstanding common stock (before the above stock dividend). The cost of the perfume is 60 cents per ounce, and the product has a wholesale market value of $1 per ounce. Any gain or loss on this transaction is already included in the earnings reported above.
- At the end of 2020, the board declares a 3-for-2 stock split of its common stock, effected in the form of a dividend. At the date of the stock split, the fair value of common stock is $75 per share.

Required

a. Prepare entries to record the transactions.

b. Prepare the stockholders' equity section as of December 31, 2020.

Problem 20-88
Reporting Stockholders' Equity **LO1, 7, 8**

The following information is available for Croton Corporation at December 31, 2020.

Retained earnings appropriated for bond sinking fund.	$ 40,000
Preferred stock, 6%, $100 par, 1,000 shares authorized, cumulative	90,000
Bonds payable, 7%.	200,000
Common stock, no-par, 5,000 shares authorized and outstanding	250,000
Paid-in capital in excess of par—Preferred stock.	15,000
Discount on bonds payable	1,000
Retained earnings	250,000
Accumulated other comprehensive income	5,000

Required

Prepare the stockholders' equity section of the balance sheet for Croton Corporation at December 31, 2020.

Problem 20-89
Recording Stock Issuances, Dividends, and Retirement **LO2, 3, 4, 5**

On June 2, 2020, Aerial Corporation issued 100,000 shares of $0.01 par value common stock for $1,000,000. One share of Aerial 5% preferred stock ($5 par) was issued with every 10 shares of common stock. The market price per share for the common stock was $6, and the market price per share for the preferred stock was $50 per share.

Required

a. Record the journal entry for issuance of common and preferred stock. When determining the proportionate shares, round allocations to the nearest dollar.

b. Assume that the market price for the common stock was $8 but the market price for the preferred stock was not easily determinable because the shares are not traded publicly. Also, Aerial incurred stock issue costs of

$7,000. Record the journal entry for the issuance of common and preferred stock. Allocate stock issue costs proportionately to the common and preferred stock accounts.

c. On June 30, 2020, Aerial declares a cash dividend of $15,000. What is the allocation between common and preferred shareholders? Record the journal entry for the dividend declaration.

d. On December 31, 2020, Aerial purchases and immediately retires 5,000 shares of common stock at $8 per share. Record the journal entry for the purchase and retirement of the 5,000 shares. Assume the stock issuance was recorded as in part *a.*

Problem 20-90
Correcting Entries on Stock issuance **LO1, 2, 3, 5**

T. Woods Corporation was organized on January 1, 2018, and began operations immediately.

- For years 2018 through 2020, the company incorrectly presented an annual balance sheet that reported only one amount for stockholders' equity: 2018, $137,700; 2019, $156,600; and 2020, $185,000.
- Its condensed income statement reported: 2018, net loss, $17,500; 2019, net profit, $12,000; and 2020, net profit, $40,930 (cumulative earnings of $35,430).
- Given cumulative earnings of $35,430, the president recommended to the board of directors that a cash dividend of $35,000 be declared and paid in January 2021.
- An outside director on the board has objected on the basis that the company's financial statements contain significant errors (and there has never been an audit).

We have been engaged to clarify the situation. The single stockholders' equity account, provided by the company, follows.

Stockholders' Equity

2018 Stock issue cost	1,300	160,000	2018 Common stock, $5 par, 20,000 shares issued
2018 Net loss	17,500		
2019 Bought 100 shares of company stock from stockholder Doe	700	22,000	2019 Net profit (including $10,000 land write-up to appraisal)
Depreciation expense* 2018, $1,500; 2019, $1,700; 2020, $2,300	5,500	1,800	2019 Common stock, 200 shares issued
Cash Over and Short* 2018, $2,000; 2019; $2,500; 2020, $500	5,000	270	2020 Sold 30 of the Doe shares
2020 Cash loan to the company president	10,000	40,930	2020 Net profit
	40,000	225,000	

* Recorded as expense but not shown on income statement.

Required

Based on concerns of the outside director, we must address three major questions.

a. What amount of retained earnings is available to support a cash dividend? Assume that the above amounts are found to be arithmetically accurate and that there is no change in income tax.

b. Based on calculations in part *a*, what journal entries should be made for declaration and later payment of the amount available as a cash dividend?

c. What entry, prior to the dividend entries in part *b*, is necessary (1) to close the above single stockholders' equity account and (2) to record the various components of stockholders' equity in separate accounts?

Problem 20-91
Recording Treasury Stock Transactions **LO1, 3**

Han Tire Corporation has outstanding 10,000 shares of preferred stock, $10 par, and also 10,000 shares of no-par common stock sold initially for $20 per share. Paid-in capital in excess of par on the preferred stock is $40,000; the retained earnings balance is $81,600. The company then entered into the following transactions in 2020.

Jan. 15, 2020 Purchased 500 shares of its common stock at $30 per share for the treasury.
Mar. 1, 2020 Sold 100 shares of the common treasury stock for $26 per share.
Oct. 15, 2020 Sold 50 shares of the common treasury stock for $32 per share.
Dec. 31, 2020 Sold 50 shares of the common treasury stock for $29 per share.

Required

a. Provide entries to record these treasury stock transactions.

b. Prepare the resulting stockholders' equity section of the balance sheet after these transactions.

Problem 20-92
Recording, Reporting Treasury Stock Transactions **LO1, 2, 3, 8**

At January 1, 2020, the records of Frazer Corporation provided the following.

Common stock, $10 par, 60,000 shares outstanding	$600,000
Paid-in capital in excess of par	240,000
Retained earnings	160,000

During the year, the following transactions affecting shareholders' equity were recorded.

- On January 15, 2020, purchased 1,000 shares of common stock for the treasury at $20 per share.
- On March 1, 2020, purchased 1,000 shares of common stock for the treasury at $22 per share.
- On June 30, 2020, sold 1,200 shares of treasury stock at $25.
- Net income for 2020 was $45,000.

State law places a restriction on retained earnings equal to the cost of treasury stock held.

Required

a. Provide entries for each of the transactions. Assume a FIFO flow for treasury stock.
b. Determine the ending balance for each capital account.
c. Draft any required disclosure related to the treasury stock.
d. Provide the journal entry on January 15, 2020, assuming instead that the company purchased and immediately retired the 1,000 shares of common stock at $20 per share.
e. Repeat part *a* but instead assume a weighted average flow for treasury stock.

Problem 20-93
Determining Dividend Preferences **LO5**

The records of Palmer Corporation showed the following at the end of 2020.

Preferred stock, 6% cumulative, nonparticipating, $20 par	$200,000
Common stock, no-par value, 50,000 shares issued and outstanding. . . .	240,000
Paid-in capital in excess of par—Preferred stock.	30,000
Retained earnings	125,000
Investment in stock of Ace Corporation (500 shares).	30,000
Preferred stock has dividends in arrears for 2018 and 2019	

On January 15, 2020, the board of directors approved the following resolution: "The 2020 dividend, to stockholders of record on February 1, 2020, shall be 6% on the preferred stock and $1.00 per share on the common stock; the dividends in arrears are to be paid on March 1, 2020, by issuing a property dividend using the requisite amount of Ace Corporation stock. All current dividends for 2020 are to be paid in cash on March 1, 2020."

On January 15, 2020, the stock of Ace Corporation was selling at $60 per share; on February 1, 2020, $61 per share; and on March 1, 2020, $62 per share.

Required

a. Compute the dividends to be paid to each class of stockholders, including the number of shares of Ace Corporation stock and the cash required by the declaration. Assume that divisibility of the shares of Ace Corporation poses no problem.
b. Provide journal entries to record all aspects of the dividend declaration and its subsequent payment.

Problem 20-94
Recording and Reporting Stock Dividends and Stock Splits **LO1, 6**

Bailey Corporation has the following stockholders' equity account balances.

Common stock, $12 par, 20,000 shares outstanding.	$240,000
Paid-in capital in excess of par.	70,000
Retained earnings	500,000
Total stockholders' equity	$810,000

The corporation will triple the number of shares currently outstanding (to 60,000 shares) by taking one of the following separate actions.

1. Issue a 200% stock dividend (40,000 additional shares) and capitalize retained earnings on the basis of par value.
2. Issue a stock split (3-for-1 stock split; that is, three new shares are issued for each old share replaced) by changing par value per share proportionately.

Required

a. Provide the journal entry that should be made for each alternative action.
b. Complete the following schedule that compares the effects of the two alternative actions.

Item	Before Change	Option One	Option Two
Number of shares outstanding			
Par value per share			
Common stock			
Paid-in capital in excess of par			
Total paid-in capital			
Retained earnings			
Total stockholders' equity			

Problem 20-95
Preparing Income Statement, Retained Earnings LO1, 8

The following annual data were taken from the records of Baker Corporation at December 31, 2020.

Sales revenue	$450,000
Cost of goods sold	230,000
General and administrative expenses	85,000
Gain on sale of equipment	30,000
Stock dividend issued	80,000
Cash dividend declared and paid	25,000
Correction of accounting error involving understatement of depreciation expense from prior period (net of tax)	8,000
Current restriction for bond sinking fund	10,000
Current appropriation for plant expansion	40,000

Assume an average income tax rate of 25% on all items except the prior period adjustment.

	Jan. 1, 2020
Retained earnings, unappropriated	$120,000 Cr.
Retained earnings, restricted for bond sinking fund	20,000 Cr.
Retained earnings, appropriated for plant expansion	60,000 Cr.

Required

a. Prepare a single-step income statement for the year ended December 31, 2020. Disregard EPS.

b. Prepare the retained earnings section of the statement of stockholders' equity for the year ended December 31, 2020, that separately discloses each restriction on total retained earnings.

Problem 20-96
Analyzing an Equity Financial Statement LO1, 2, 3, 7

Included below is an excerpt from the **Fastenal Company**'s Form 10-K statement from its consolidated statement of stockholders' equity.

Consolidated Statements of Stockholders' Equity (in thousands)	Common Stock Shares	Common Stock Amount	Additional Paid-In Capital	Retained Earnings	Accumulated Other Comprehensive Income (Loss)	Total Stockholders' Equity
Balance as of December 31, 2014	295,868	$2,959	$33,744	$1,886,350	$ (7,836)	$1,915,217
Dividends paid in cash	—	—	—	(327,101)	—	(327,101)
Purchases of common stock	(7,100)	(71)	(60,042)	(232,838)	—	(292,951)
Stock options exercised	814	8	19,091	—	—	19,099
Stock-based compensation	—	—	5,841	—	—	5,841
Excess tax benefits from stock-based compensation	—	—	3,390	—	—	3,390
Net earnings	—	—	—	516,361	—	516,361
Other comprehensive income (loss)	—	—	—	—	(38,567)	(38,567)
Balance as of December 31, 2015	**289,582**	**$2,896**	**$ 2,024**	**$1,842,772**	**$(46,403)**	**$1,801,289**

Required

a. What types of capital stock have been issued by Fastenal? What is the par value per share? Provide support for the answer.

b. What is Fastenal's (1) net income, (2) other comprehensive income, and (3) comprehensive income, for the year ended December 31, 2015?

c. What activities in 2015 are indicated by the change in the retained earnings account?

d. Obtain more details about the source of other comprehensive income for Fastenal by accessing the Fastenal Form 10-K for the year ended December 31, 2015. List the source of the amount of other comprehensive income included in this statement.

Problem 20-97
Reporting Stockholders' Equity Including Disclosures **LO5, 8**

On November 1, 2020, the board of directors of Jax Mining Company declared the maximum cash dividend permitted by state law. The company had never declared a dividend before this time. There were 100 stockholders, each holding 400 shares of stock with a par value of $5 per share. The laws of the state provide that "dividends may be paid equal to all accumulated profits prior to the recorded depletion expense." Retained earnings showed a correct balance of $120,000; depletion for the year amounted to $24,000 (accumulated depletion was $40,000). The dividend was payable 60 days after declaration date.

Required

a. Provide all entries related to this dividend through the payment date.

b. What special notification, if any, should be reported to stockholders?

c. What items related to the dividend declaration are reported on the balance sheet dated December 31, 2020, assuming net income for 2020 of $15,000 (included in the $60,000 balance of retained earnings given above)? Draft any note that may be needed to fully disclose the dividend.

Accounting Decisions and Judgments

AD&J 20-98
Analyzing a Statement of Stockholders' Equity **LO1, 8**

Real World Analysis In its 2015 annual report, **General Dynamics Corporation** showed the following regarding stockholders' equity.

Consolidated Statements of Shareholders' Equity

$ millions	Common Stock Par	Common Stock Surplus	Retained Earnings	Treasury Stock	Accumulated Other Comprehensive Loss	Total Shareholders' Equity
December 31, 2014	$482	$2,548	$21,127	$ (9,396)	$(2,932)	$11,829
Net earnings	—	—	2,965	—	—	2,965
Cash dividends declared	—	—	(888)	—	—	(888)
Equity-based awards	—	182	—	237	—	419
Shares purchased	—	—	—	(3,233)	—	(3,233)
Other comprehensive loss	—	—	—	—	(354)	(354)
December 31, 2015	$482	$2,730	$23,204	$(12,392)	$(3,286)	$10,738

On December 31, 2015, we had 481,880,634 shares of common stock issued and 312,987,277 shares of common stock outstanding, including unvested restricted stock of 1,391,275 shares. On December 31, 2014, we had 481,880,634 shares of common stock issued and 332,164,097 shares of common stock outstanding. We repurchased 22.8 million of our outstanding shares for $3.2 billion in 2015.

Required

a. What appears to be the par value, if any, of General Dynamics Corporation common stock? What amount was paid for purchases of stock for the treasury? What was the average price paid per share for these treasury shares?

b. What is the book value per common share of General Dynamics at December 31, 2014? At December 31, 2015?

c. At December 31, 2015, General Dynamics common stock had a market price of $136.36 per share. Briefly discuss why investors might pay so much, relative to the company's book value per share, for General Dynamics Corporation common stock.

d. How does the amount paid for treasury shares calculated in part *a* differ from the market price at December 31, 2015, included in part *c*?

AD&J 20-99
Analyzing Preferred Stock Dividends **LO4, 5**

Real World Analysis **Unocal** is the parent company of Union Oil, a fully integrated energy resources company. In its Year 5 annual report, Unocal showed the following regarding stockholders' equity.

December 31 ($ millions)	Year 5	Year 4
Stockholders' equity		
Preferred stock, $0.10 par value; stated at liquidation value of $50 per share		
Shares authorized: 100,000,000		
Shares outstanding: 10,250,000 in Year 5 and Year 4	$513	$513
Common stock, $1 par value		
Shares authorized: 750,000,000		
Shares outstanding: 247,310,376 in Year 5; 244,198,701 in Year 4	247	244
Capital in excess of par value	319	237

In notes to financial statements, the following is provided regarding preferred stock.

Preferred Stock—The company has authorized 100,000,000 shares of preferred stock with a par value of $0.10 per share. In July Year 2, the company issued 10,250,000 shares of $3.50 convertible preferred stock. The convertible preferred stock is redeemable on and after July 15, Year 6, in whole or in part, at the option of the company, at a redemption price of $52.10 per share declining to $50 per share on and after July 15, Year 12, together with accumulated but unpaid dividends. The convertible preferred stock has a liquidation value of $50 per share and is convertible at the option of the holder into common stock of the company at a conversion price of $30.75 per share, subject to adjustment in certain events. Dividends on the preferred stock at an annual rate of $3.50 per share are cumulative and are payable quarterly in arrears, when and as declared by Unocal's Board of Directors (the Board). Holders of the preferred stock have no voting rights. However, there are certain exceptions, including the right to elect two additional directors if the equivalent of six quarterly dividends payable on the preferred stock are in default.

Required

a. Suppose Unocal decides to redeem the outstanding preferred stock on July 15, Year 6. Show the entry to record the transaction. Assume that dividends for the quarter ending June 30, Year 6, have not been paid and that the shares were originally issued at their liquidation value.

b. Assume all preferred stock is converted to common stock on January 1, Year 6. Show the entry to record this transaction. Assume that the shares were originally issued at their liquidation value.

c. Suppose that Unocal does *not* declare and pay the preferred dividends for Year 11 and the first half of Year 12. On July 15, Year 12, Unocal calls and redeems the preferred stock. Show the entry to record this redemption.

AD&J 20-100
Analyzing Preferred Stock **LO4**

Real World Analysis Con Ed is a large public utility company that provides New York City with electric service. Similar to many other public utilities, Con Ed uses preferred stock for a portion of its financing. In its Year 5 annual report, Con Ed provided the following schedule regarding its capitalization.

Consolidated Statement of Capitalization
Consolidated Edison Company of New York, Inc.

	Shares Outstanding			
At December 31 ($ in thousands)	**Year 5**	**Year 4**	**Year 5**	**Year 4**
Common shareholders' equity (Note B)				
Common stock, $2.50 par value, authorized 340,000,000 shares	234,956,299	234,905,235	$1,464,305	$1,463,913
Retained earnings			4,097,305	3,888,010
Capital stock expense			(38,606)	(38,926)
Total common shareholders' equity			$5,522,734	$5,312,997
Preferred stock (Note B)				
Subject to mandatory redemption				
Cumulative Preferred, $100 par value,				
7.20% Series I	500,000	500,000	$ 50,000	$ 50,000
6 1/8 % Series J	500,000	500,000	50,000	50,000
Total subject to mandatory redemption			100,000	100,000
Other preferred stock				
$5 Cumulative Preferred, without par value, authorized 1,915,319 shares	1,915,319	1,915,319	175,000	175,000

continued

continued from previous page

Consolidated Statement of Capitalization
Consolidated Edison Company of New York, Inc.

	Shares Outstanding			
At December 31 ($ in thousands)	**Year 5**	**Year 4**	**Year 5**	**Year 4**
Cumulative Preferred, $100 par value authorized 6,000,000 shares*				
5 3/4% Series A	600,000	600,000	$ 60,000	$ 60,000
5 1/4 % Series B	750,000	750,000	75,000	75,000
4.65% Series C	600,000	600,000	60,000	60,000
4.65% Series D	750,000	750,000	75,000	75,000
5 3/4% Series E	500,000	500,000	50,000	50,000
6.20% Series F	400,000	400,000	40,000	40,000
Cumulative Preference, $100 par value, authorized 2,250,000 shares 6% Convertible Series B	49,174	53,102	4,917	5,310
Total other preferred stock			539,917	540,310
Total preferred stock			$639,917	$640,310

* Represents total authorized shares of cumulative preferred stock, $100 par value, including preferred stock subject to mandatory redemption.

In the notes to the financial statements, Con Ed provides the following information regarding its preferred stock.

> **Note B Capitalization**—Common Stock and Preferred Stock Not Subject to Mandatory Redemption Each share of Series B preference stock is convertible into 13 shares of common stock at a conversion price of $7.69 per share. During Year 5, Year 4 and Year 3, 1,993, 3,928 shares, 4,176 shares and 5,208 shares of Series B preference stock were converted into 51,064 shares, 54,288 shares and 67,704 shares of common stock, respectively.
>
> At December 31, Year 5, 639,262 shares of unissued common stock were reserved for conversion of preference stock. The preference stock is subordinate to the $5 Cumulative Preferred Stock and Cumulative Preferred Stock with respect to dividends and liquidation rights.
>
> Redemption prices of preferred stock other than Series I and Series J (in each case, plus accrued dividends) are as follows:

$5 Cumulative Preferred Stock	$105.00
Cumulative Preferred Stock	
Series A	$102.00
Series B	102.00
Series C	101.00
Series D	101.00
Series E	101.00
Series F	102.50
Cumulative Preference Stock	
6% Convertible Series B	$100.00

> Preferred Stock Subject to Mandatory Redemption The Company is required to redeem 25,000 of the Series I shares on May 1 of each year in the five-year period commencing with Year 12 and to redeem the remaining Series I shares on May 1, Year 17. The Company is required to redeem the Series J shares on August 1, 2, Year 12. In each case, the redemption price is $100 per share plus accrued and unpaid dividends to the redemption date. In addition, the Company may redeem Series I shares at a redemption price of $105.04 per share, plus accrued dividends, if redeemed prior to May 1, Year 6 (and thereafter at prices declining annually to $100 per share, plus accrued dividends, after April 30, Year 12); provided, however, that prior to May 1, Year 7, the Company may not redeem any Series I shares with borrowed funds or proceeds from certain securities issuances having a cost to the Company of less than 7.20% per annum.

Required

a. Outline the preference differences between the various types of preferred stock issued by Con Ed. Which of these issues is most like a debt issue? Which is most like a common equity issue? Explain.

b. What were the proceeds per share for the preferred stock identified as $5 Cumulative Preferred, without par value? What were the proceeds per share for each of the Cumulative Preferred, $100 par value series (A through F)?

c. Show the entry Con Ed would make if it elects to redeem the entire Series I preferred stock on April 30, Year 6. Assume all preferred dividends are paid as of April 30.

d. If Con Ed had not redeemed the preferred stock as stated in part *c*, show the entry Con Ed would make on May 1, Year 12, for mandatory redemption of its Series I Cumulative Preferred Stock.

e. Suppose that during Year 6, a total of 5,000 shares of the 6% Convertible Series B preference stock is tendered to the company for conversion into common stock. Provide the entry to record this transaction.

AD&J 20-101
Analyzing Common Stock and Repurchased Stock **LO2, 3, 6**

Real World Analysis T. Rowe Price's (TRP) primary business is providing investment information services to Price Funds and individual private accounts. The Year 5 annual report for the company included the following Consolidated Statement of Stockholders' Equity.

$ thousands	Common Stock Shares	Common Stock Par Value	Capital in Excess of Par Value	Retained Earnings	Accumulated Other Comprehensive Income	Total Stockholders' Equity
Balance at December 31, Year 2	14,429,315	$2,886	$1,171	$150,141		$154,198
Common stock issued under stock-based compensation plans	254,629	51	2,963			3,014
2-for-1 stock split	14,491,095	2,898	(1,997)	(901)		
Purchases of common stock	(80,000)	(16)	(940)	(1,295)		(2,251)
Net income				48,539		48,539
Dividends declared				(12,892)		(12,892)
Unrealized security holding gains					$5,345	5,345
Balance at December 31, Year 3	**29,095,039**	**5,819**	**1,197**	**183,592**	**5,345**	**195,953**
Common stock issued under stock-based compensation plans	366,880	74	4,277			4,351
Purchases of common stock	(892,500)	(179)	(3,539)	(22,831)		(26,549)
Net income				61,151		61,151
Dividends declared				(15,876)		(15,876)
Decrease in unrealized security holding gains					(2,791)	(2,791)
Balance at December 31, Year 4	**28,569,419**	**5,714**	**1,935**	**206,036**	**2,554**	**216,239**
Common stock issued under stock-based compensation plans	465,553	93	5,555	(2)		5,646
Purchases of common stock	(369,500)	(74)	(4,578)	(8,789)		(13,441)
Net income				75,409		75,409
Dividends declared				(19,720)		(19,720)
Increase in unrealized security holding gains					10,099	10,099
Balance at December 31, Year 5	**28,665,472**	**$5,733**	**$2,912**	**$252,934**	**$12,653**	**$274,232**

Required

a. From the information provided at December 31, Year 2, estimate the par value of a share of common stock on that date. From the information provided at December 31, Year 3, estimate the par value of a share of common stock on that date. Did TRP really split the par value of its shares two for one?

b. When TRP purchases common stock, is it held as treasury stock or as retired stock? If as treasury stock, is TRP using the cost method or the par value method or some variation of one of these methods for accounting for treasury stock? *Hint:* The par value method treats treasury stock as if it had been retired.

c. Determine the average price per share TRP paid for common stock repurchased during Year 5. Determine the average price per share TRP received for common stock issued under the stock-based compensation plans.

d. On December 31, Year 5, TRP common stock had a market price of $48 per share. What is the company's total fair value on this date? What is the company's net book value on this date? Why do these two amounts differ?

AD&J 20-102
Analyzing Stockholders' Equity **LO1, 2, 3, 8**

Real World Analysis Gtech Holdings Corporation is a technology and communications services company. Its consolidated statement of shareholders' equity provides the following information.

$ thousands	Common Stock Shares	Common Stock Par Value	Additional Paid-in Capital	Other	Retained Earnings	Treasury Stock	Total
Balance at February 29, Year 2	36,293,642	$363	$31,570	$(6,783)	$ 5,595	$(30)	$ 30,715
Purchase of 73,463 shares of common stock				(113)		(113)	(113)
Common stock issued	5,900,000	59	90,294				90,353
Common stock issued under stock award plans	765,867	8	8,747				8,755
Tax benefit from stock compensation			17,467				17,467
Net income					21,694		21,694
Foreign currency translation				(816)			(816)
Balance at February 27, Year 3	42,959,509	$430	$148,078	$(7,599)	$27,289	$(143)	$168,055

Required

a. What is the par value of Gtech common stock?

b. Record the entry for the issuance of 5,900,000 shares of stock in Year 3.

c. What is the book value per share of Gtech at February 29, Year 2, assuming shares in the treasury total 40,090 shares? At February 27, Year 3? Explain why book value per share changed so much from February 29, Year 2, to February 27, Year 3.

d. What was the average price per share paid for common shares acquired during the year ending February 27, Year 3? What were the average proceeds per share for shares issued, other than those issued under stock award plans, during the year ending February 27, Year 3? List any possible reasons why these amounts might significantly differ.

AD&J 20-103 Analyzing Stockholders' Equity **LO1, 2, 8**

Real World Analysis The following information is included in the consolidated statement of equity for **Starbucks Corporation** in a recent Form 10-K.

STARBUCKS CORPORATION
CONSOLIDATED STATEMENTS OF EQUITY

	Common Stock		Additional Paid-in Capital	Retained Earnings	Accumulated Other Comprehensive Income/(Loss)	Shareholders' Equity
in millions, except per share data	**Shares**	**Amount**				
Balance, September 28, 2014	749.5	$0.7	$ 39.4	$5,206.6	$ 25.3	$5,272.0
Net earnings	—	—	—	2,757.4	—	2,757.4
Other comprehensive income/(loss)					(193.6)	(193.6)
Stock-based compensation expense	—	—	211.7	—	—	211.7
Exercise of stock options/vesting of RSUs, including tax benefit of $131.3	14.6	—	224.4	—	—	224.4
Sale of common stock, including tax benefit of $0.2	0.6	—	23.5	—	—	23.5
Repurchase of common stock	(29.0)	—	(459.6)	(972.2)	—	(1,431.8)
Cash dividends declared, $0.680 per share	—	—	—	(1,016.2)	—	(1,016.2)
Two-for-one stock split	749.4	0.8	—	(0.8)	—	—
Noncontrolling interest resulting from acquisition	—	—	—	—	—	—
Purchase of noncontrolling interest	—	—	1.7	—	(31.1)	(29.4)
Balance, September 27, 2015	1,485.1	$1.5	$ 41.1	$5,974.8	$(199.4)	$5,818.0

Required

a. Does Starbucks have a par value for its common stock that can be determined from the information provided? If so, what is it?

b. Ignoring the tax benefit, record the entry for the sale of common stock during fiscal 2015. Assume that the par value per common share is $0.001. What was the average price per share for which this stock was sold?

c. Compute Starbucks's book value per share at September 27, 2015, assuming that the number of outstanding shares is 1,499.1 million. What is the relation between the stock trading price at September 27, 2015, of $57.99 per share and its book value? What factors might explain this difference?

AD&J 20-104 Analyzing Stockholders' Equity Disclosure **LO4, 8**

Real World Analysis Consider the following excerpt from a 2015 Form 10-K of **Bank of America Corporation**.

Note 13—Shareholders' Equity (excerpt)

Series: Series L
Description: 7.25% Non-Cumulative Perpetual Convertible
Initial Issuance date: January 2008

Total Shares Outstanding: 3,080,182
Liquidation preference per share: $1,000
Carrying value: $3,080,000,000

The 7.25% Non-Cumulative Perpetual Convertible Preferred Stock, Series L (Series L Preferred Stock) listed in the Preferred Stock Summary table does not have early redemption/call rights. Each share of the Series L Preferred Stock may be converted at any time, at the option of the holder, into 20 shares of the Corporation's common stock plus cash in lieu of fractional shares. The Corporation may cause some or all of the Series L Preferred Stock, at its option, at any time or from time to time, to be converted into shares of common stock at the then-applicable conversion rate if, for 20 trading days during any period of 30 consecutive trading days, the closing price of common stock exceeds 130 percent of the then-applicable conversion price of the Series L Preferred Stock. If a conversion of Series L Preferred Stock occurs at the option of the holder, subsequent to a dividend record date but prior to the dividend payment date, the Corporation will still pay any accrued dividends payable. All series of preferred stock in the Preferred Stock Summary table have a par value of $0.01 per share, are not subject to the operation of a sinking fund, have no participation rights... All outstanding series of preferred stock of the Corporation have preference over the Corporation's common stock with respect to the payment of dividends and distribution of the Corporation's assets in the event of a liquidation or dissolution.

Required

Complete the following table by identifying the relevant disclosure from the financial statement excerpt of Bank of America, related to the disclosure requirement listed.

Disclosure Requirements	Relevant Disclosure for the Bank of America
a. Par value	
b. Number of shares outstanding	
c. Liquidation preference	
d. Dividend preferences	
e. Dividends in arrears	
f. Call prices and dates	
g. Sinking fund requirements	
h. Conversion rates	
i. Contingent conversion terms	

AD&J 20-105
Determining Participating Preferred Dividend Distributions **LO4, 5**

Challenge Problem Alexa Inc. has the following capital structure.

Common stock, $10 par, 6,000 shares issued and outstanding......	$60,000
6% Preferred stock, $100 par, 200 shares issued and outstanding...	20,000

Required

Alexa declared a cash dividend distribution of $20,000. Calculate the allocation of dividends between preferred and common shareholders under the following separate scenarios.

a. Preferred stock is cumulative and nonparticipating. Dividends are in arrears for the preceding year.
b. Preferred stock is noncumulative and fully participating.
c. Preferred stock is cumulative and fully participating. Dividends for the preferred stock are in arrears for the preceding two years.

AD&J 20-106
Classifying Treasury Stock **LO3**

Communication Case Arguments are made that treasury stock is an asset because it is purchased, owned, and paid for in cash like any other asset. Also, as with other assets, it can be sold for cash at any time in an established market. One possible conclusion is that because treasury stock has the overriding attributes of an asset, it should be reported and classified on the balance sheet as an asset.

Required

a. Assuming that we have no GAAP constraints to consider, explain in a memo how we believe treasury stock should be classified and why.
b. Assume that the issuing company has a bond sinking fund being accumulated to retire outstanding bonds payable at maturity date. It is administered by an independent outside trustee in accordance with the bond agreement. Assume that the sinking fund investments include stock of the issuing company. How should that particular stock be classified? Explain the basis for that conclusion.

AD&J 20-107
Issuing Capital Stock **LO2**

Communication Case C. Banfield, an engineer, developed a special safety device to be installed in backyard swimming pools; when turned on, it would set off an alarm if anything fell into the water. Over a two-year period, Banfield's spare time was spent developing and testing the device. After receiving a patent, three of Banfield's friends, including an attorney, considered plans to produce and market the device. Accordingly, a charter was obtained, which authorized 200,000 shares of $10 par value stock. Each of the four organizers contributed $20,000, and each received in return 2,000 shares of stock. They also agree that for other consideration, each would receive 5,000 additional shares. The remaining shares were to be held as unissued stock. Each organizer made a proposal concerning how the additional 5,000 shares would be paid for. These individual proposals were made independently; then the group considered them as a package. The four proposals were:

Banfield: Patent would be turned over to the corporation as payment for the 5,000 shares. An independent appraisal of the patent could not be obtained.

Attorney: 1,000 shares would be received for legal services already rendered during organization, 1,000 shares would be received as advance payment for legal retainer fees for the next three years, and the balance would be paid for in cash at par.

Friend #2: A small building, suitable for operations, would be given to the corporation for the 5,000 shares of stock. It was estimated that $20,000 would be needed for renovation prior to use. The owner estimates that the fair value of the building is $750,000, and there is a $580,000 loan on it to be assumed by the corporation.

Friend #3: To pay $10,000 cash on the stock and to give a 12% (the going rate) interest-bearing note for the total price of $40,000 (subscriptions receivable) to be paid out of dividends over the next five years.

Required

a. How would each of the above proposals be recorded? Assess the valuation basis for each, including alternatives.

b. What are your recommendations for an agreement that would be equitable to each organizer? Explain the basis for such recommendations.

AD&J 20-108 Analyzing Preferred Stock: Equity versus Debt **LO4**

Communication Case Onray Corporation reported the following items on its balance sheet dated December 31, 2020.

Liabilities	
Long-term note payable, 12% interest payable each June 30 and December 31 (maturity date December 31, 2025)	$ 500,000
Stockholders' equity	
Common stock, no-par	6,000,000
Preferred stock, $100 par, nonvoting, 9% cumulative, nonparticipating, and mandatory redemption at par no later than December 31, 2025; 4,000 shares authorized and outstanding	400,000
Retained earnings	800,000

Required

Evaluate the reporting classifications applied by Onray. Did Onray violate current GAAP? Explain.

AD&J 20-109 Analyzing Treasury Stock Transactions **LO3**

Communication Case Ellis Corporation purchased equipment (cash price of $144,000) for $107,000 cash and a promise to deliver an indeterminate number of shares of its $5 par common stock, with a fair value of $15,000, on January 1 of each year for the next four years. Hence, $60,000 in fair value of shares will be required to discharge the $37,000 balance due on the equipment.

The corporation then acquired 5,000 shares of its own stock (which became treasury shares) in the expectation that the fair value of the stock would increase substantially before the delivery date.

Required

a. Discuss the propriety of recording the equipment at the following values.
1. $107,000 (the cash payment).
2. $144,000 (the cash price of the equipment).
3. $167,000 (the $107,000 cash payment plus the $60,000 fair value of treasury stock that must be transferred to the vendor to settle the obligation per the agreement). Assume an ordinary annuity.

b. Discuss the arguments for treating the balance due as:
1. A liability.
2. Treasury stock subscribed. *Hint:* To subscribe treasury stock, we debit Subscriptions Receivable (contra equity account) and credit paid-in capital accounts.

c. Assuming that legal requirements do not affect the decisions, discuss the arguments for treating the corporation's treasury shares as follows:
1. An asset awaiting ultimate disposition.
2. A capital element awaiting ultimate disposition.

AICPA Adapted

AD&J 20-110 Analyzing Use of Debt and Equity Securities to Purchase an Asset **LO3**

Judgment Case On January 1, 2020, Crefax Corporation purchased a tract of land, for long-term use as a possible future plant site, in exchange for $50,000 cash plus a five-year note with no interest, even though the current interest for similar debt is 15%. The note is to be paid in $20,000 annual amounts; the first $20,000 is due one year from the date of the land purchase, and the last $20,000 is due at the end of five years. The note also specifies (quite unusually) that instead of being payable in cash, each $20,000 annual amount is to be settled by issuance of 20,000 shares of Crefax common stock, $1 par, to the holder of the note. On the date land was purchased, the fair value of the stock set aside to be issued on the five dates by Crefax Corporation was $180,000.

Required

a. Prepare and explain the basis for the journal entry that Crefax should make on January 1, 2020.

b. Prepare and explain the basis for the entry(ies) that Crefax should make on December 31, 2020.

c. Explain how the following items should be reported on the 2020 financial statements of Crefax Corporation: (1) interest expense, (2) land, (3) debt, and (4) paid-in capital.

AD&J 20-111
Determining Whether to Declare a Dividend **LO5**

Judgment Case Drake Company was started in 2005 to manufacture a wide range of plastic products from three basic components. The company was originally owned by 23 stockholders; however, in late 2015 the capital structure was expanded considerably, at which time preferred stock was issued. The preferred is nonvoting, cumulative, nonparticipating, 6% stock. The company has experienced a substantial growth in business over the years. This growth was due to two principal factors: (a) the dynamic management and (b) the geographical location. The company served a rapidly expanding area with relatively few regionally situated competitors.

The December 31, 2020, audited balance sheet showed the following (summarized):

Cash	$ 11,000	Current liabilities	$ 38,000
Other current assets	76,000	Long-term notes payable	60,000
Investment in Kile Co. stock	30,000	Preferred stock, $100 par, 500 shares*	50,000
Plant and equipment (net)	310,000	Common stock, $15 par, 10,000 shares*	150,000
Intangible assets	15,000	Premium on preferred stock	2,000
Other assets	8,000	Retained earnings	25,000
		Profits invested in plant	125,000
Total assets	$450,000	Total liabilities and equity	$450,000

*Authorized shares—preferred, 2,000; common, 20,000.

The board of directors has not declared any dividends since organization. Instead, profits were used to expand the company. This decision was based on the fact that the original capital was small and the number of stockholders was limited. At present, the common stock is held by slightly fewer than 50 individuals. Each of these individuals also owns preferred shares; their total holdings approximate 46% of the outstanding preferred. The preferred was issued at the time of the capital expansion.

The board of directors had been planning to declare a dividend during the early part of 2021, payable June 30. However, the cash position as shown by the balance sheet has raised serious doubts about the advisability of a dividend in 2021. The president has explained that most of the cash will be needed shortly to pay for inventory already purchased. The company has a chief accountant but no controller. The board relies on an outside CPA for advice concerning financial management. The CPA was asked to advise about the contemplated dividend declaration. Four of the seven members of the board felt very strongly that some kind of dividend must be declared and paid and that all stockholders "should get something."

Required

We have been asked to analyze the situation and make whatever dividend proposals appear worthy of consideration by the board. Show amounts to support our recommendations in a written form suitable for consideration by the board in reaching a decision. Provide the basis for all proposals and indicate any preferences that we may have in a memo to the board.

AD&J 20-112
Recording Stock and Property Dividends **LO5, 6**

Challenge Problem To date, 3,000 shares of preferred stock (6%, $100 par value, cumulative, nonparticipating) and 100,000 shares of common stock (no-par) of Gomez Inc. have been issued. Authorized shares were as follows: common, 200,000; preferred, 3,000. No dividends were in arrears as of December 31, 2019. During 2020, the following transactions affected stockholders' equity:

- **February 1:** Declared and immediately issued one share of the company's investment in AC Corporation stock for each share of preferred stock as a property dividend. The fair value of the AC stock was $3.50 per share. Original cost of the AC stock was $3.50 per share. In addition, a cash dividend was paid to complete payment of the dividends.
- **December 1:** Declared and issued a stock dividend, payable in common stock to holders of both preferred and common stock. The preferred holders are to receive value equivalent to 6%, and the common holders are to receive one share for each five shares held. The value and the amount to be capitalized per share as a debit to Retained Earnings is the fair value. The price per share of the common stock immediately after the stock dividend was $1.50.

Required

a. Provide the entry for declaration and distribution of the property and cash dividend on February 1.
b. Provide the entry for declaration and distribution of the stock dividend on December 1.

Challenge Problem Able Corporation has the following stock outstanding:

AD&J 20-113
Computing Participating Preferred Dividend Distributions **LO4, 5**

Common, $50 par, 6,000 shares
Preferred, 6%, $100 par, 1,000 shares

Required

Compute dividends payable in total and per share on the common stock and the preferred stock for each separate case:

a. Preferred is cumulative and nonparticipating; two years in arrears; dividends declared, $34,000.
b. Preferred is noncumulative and fully participating; dividends declared, $40,000.
c. Preferred is cumulative and partially participating up to an additional 3%; three years in arrears; dividends declared, $60,000.
d. Preferred is cumulative and fully participating; three years in arrears; dividends declared, $50,000.

Challenge Problem The charter of Crew Corporation authorized: (1) 5,000 shares of 6% preferred stock, $20 par, and (2) 8,000 shares of common stock, $50 par. All of the authorized shares have been issued. In a five-year period, annual dividends paid in chronological order were (from oldest to most current) $4,000, $40,000, $32,000, $5,000, and $36,000, respectively.

AD&J 20-114
Computing Participating Preferred Dividend Distributions **LO4, 5**

Required

Compute the amount of dividends that would be paid to each class of stock for each year under the following separate cases.

a. Preferred stock is noncumulative and nonparticipating.
b. Preferred stock is cumulative and nonparticipating.
c. Preferred stock is noncumulative and fully participating.
d. Preferred stock is cumulative and fully participating.
e. Preferred stock is cumulative and partially participating up to an additional 2%; *also* assume that the dividend for year 5 was $42,000 instead of $36,000.

Challenge Problem Rather Corporation had authorized an outstanding 100,000 shares of common stock, $2 par value. The stockholders approved the exchange of two new shares for each share of the old stock. *Hint:* Do not decrease paid-in capital accounts below zero; instead, debit retained earnings.

AD&J 20-115
Recording Exchanges of Stock **LO2**

Required

Provide the journal entries to record the change under each of the following separate cases (assume a sufficient balance in retained earnings).

a. Old stock was sold at par, and the new stock was no-par stock with no stated or assigned value.
b. Old stock was sold at a premium of $3 per share, and the new stock was no-par stock with a stated value of $2 per share.
c. Old stock was sold at a premium of $1.50 per share, and the new stock was no-par stock with a stated value of $2 per share.
d. Old stock was sold at par, and the new stock was no-par stock with a stated value of $1.50 per share.
e. Old stock originally was sold at a premium of $1.50 per share, and the new stock was $1 par value.
f. Old stock was sold at a premium of $3 per share, and the new stock was no-par stock with no stated or assigned value.
g. Old stock was sold at a premium of $1 per share, and the new stock was no-par stock with no stated or assigned value.

Challenge Problem On June 1, 2020, Ward Corporation had outstanding 10,000 shares of capital stock, $10 par. The shares were held by 10 stockholders, each having an equal number of shares. The retained earnings account showed a credit balance of $60,000, although the company was short of cash.

AD&J 20-116
Recording and Reporting Scrip Dividends **LO5**

The company owned 20,000 shares (2%) of the common stock of Carson Corporation that had been purchased as an investment. The fair value of this stock is $1.25 per share, an increase of $0.25 per share over its value at the beginning of the year.

On June 1, 2020, the board of directors of Ward Corporation declared a dividend of $4 per share "to be paid with the Carson stock 30 days after declaration date and scrip to be issued for the difference. The scrip will be payable at the end of 12 months from payment date of the property dividend and will earn 12% interest per annum." The accounting period ends December 31.

Required

a. Provide all entries related to the dividends through date of payment of the scrip, including accounts relating to the investment in Carson. *Hint:* Use the account, Script Dividends Payable.

b. Illustrate how all items related to the dividend declaration should be reported by Ward on (1) the balance sheet and (2) the income statement at the end of 2020, including any notes needed for full disclosure.

AD&J 20-117
Recording Adjustments to Investments **LO6**

Challenge Problem On January 1, 2020, Lambo Inc. purchased 200 shares of Farve Industries' common stock at $100 per share. The investment is measured as FV-NI. On June 30, 2020, Lambo received a 15% stock dividend on the Farve investment.

Required

Record the entry to adjust the investment to fair value on December 31, 2020, assuming that the Lambo stock is trading at $101 per share on December 31, 2020.

AD&J 20-118
Defining Terms **LO6, 7**

Codification Skills How are the terms (1) comprehensive income, (2) other comprehensive income, (3) dividend, (4) stock dividend, and (5) stock split defined in the Codification?

AD&J 20-119
Performing Accounting Research **LO2, 3, 4, 7**

Codification Skills Through research in the Codification, identify the specific citation for each of the following items included as guidance in this chapter for the accounting for equity.

a. Specific amounts included in other comprehensive income. FASB ASC ___-___-___-___

b. Determination of value recorded for noncash consideration in a stock issuance. FASB ASC ___-___-___-___

c. Treatment of common stock issue costs. FASB ASC ___-___-___-___

d. Financial reporting of treasury stock. FASB ASC ___-___-___-___

e. Preferred stock reported as a liability. FASB ASC ___-___-___-___

AD&J 20-120
Performing Accounting Research **LO6**

Codification Skills Ellis Company has experienced a sustained growth in its market price of common stock such that the company is considering either offering a stock dividend or stock split. The company understands that adding new shares to the market place will result in a decrease in price per share of common stock, which would make the stock more attractive to an average investor. Every indication points to a continued growth in stock price over the next three years. The company has no experience with stock dividends but had heard that options include stock splits, small stock dividends, and large stock dividends. What research supports these options in the Codification? FASB ASC ___-___-___-___

Answers to Review Exercises

Review 20-1

a. 2
b. 3
c. 1
d. 2
e. 4
f. 3
g. 2
h. 1
i. 1
j. 1
k. 5

Review 20-2

a. **January 1, 2020—To record issuance of par value stock**

Cash (20,000 × $20)	400,000	
Common Stock (20,000 × $1)		20,000
Paid-in Capital in Excess of Par—Common Stock ($400,000 − $20,000)		380,000

Assets = Liabilities + Equity
+400,000 +20,000 +380,000
Cash: 400,000 | Common Stock: | 20,000
Paid-in Cap—CS: | 380,000

b. **January 1, 2020—To record issuance of no-par stock**

Cash (20,000 × $20)	400,000	
Common Stock		400,000

Assets = Liabilities + Equity
+400,000 +400,000
Cash: 400,000 | Common Stock: | 400,000

c. **January 1, 2020—To record issuance of no-par stock with a stated value**

Cash (20,000 × $20)	400,000	
Common Stock (20,000 × $1)		20,000
Paid-in Capital in Excess of Stated Value—Common Stock ($400,000 − $20,000)		380,000

Assets = Liabilities + Equity
+400,000 +20,000 +380,000
Cash: 400,000 | Common Stock: | 20,000
Paid-in Cap—CS: | 380,000

d. **January 1, 2020—To record issuance of stock for noncash consideration**

Equipment	180,000	
Common Stock (100,000 × $1)		10,000
Paid-in Capital in Excess of Par—Common Stock ($180,000 − $10,000)		170,000

Assets = Liabilities + Equity
+180,000 +10,000 +170,000
Equipment: 180,000 | Common Stock: | 10,000
Paid-in Cap—CS: | 170,000

e. **January 1, 2020—To record issuance of multiple securities—proportional allocation**

Cash	160,000	
Common Stock (5,000 × $1)		5,000
Paid-in Capital in Excess of Par—Common Stock ($94,400 − $5,000)		89,400
Preferred Stock (2,000 × $5)		10,000
Paid-in Capital in Excess of Par—Preferred Stock ($65,600 − $10,000)		55,600

Assets = Liabilities + Equity
+160,000 +160,000
Cash: 160,000 | Common Stock: | 5,000
Preferred Stock: | 10,000 Paid-in Cap—PS: | 89,400 55,600

f. **January 1, 2020—To record issuance of multiple securities—incremental allocation**

Cash	175,000	
Common Stock (5,000 × $1)		5,000
Paid-in Capital in Excess of Par—Common Stock ([$18 × 5,000] − $5,000)		85,000
Preferred Stock (2,000 × $5)		10,000
Paid-in Capital in Excess of Par—Preferred Stock (to balance)		75,000

Assets = Liabilities + Equity
+175,000 +175,000
Cash: 175,000 | Common Stock: | 5,000
Preferred Stock: | 10,000 Paid-in Cap—CS: | 85,000
Paid-in Cap—PS: | 75,000

g. **January 1, 2020—To record stock issue costs**

Cash ([20,000 × $20] − $4,000)	396,000	
Common Stock (20,000 × $1)		20,000
Paid-in Capital in Excess of Par—Common Stock ($396,000 − $20,000)		376,000

Assets = Liabilities + Equity
+396,000 +20,000 +376,000
Cash: 396,000 | Common Stock: | 20,000
Paid-in Cap—CS: | 376,000

Review 20-3

a. **January 1, 2020—To record issuance of common stock**

Cash (5,000 shares × $25)	125,000	
Common Stock (5,000 shares × $1)		5,000
Paid-in Capital in Excess of Par—Common Stock ($125,000 − $5,000)		120,000

Assets = Liabilities + Equity
+125,000 +5,000 +120,000

b. **June 15, 2020—To record acquisition of treasury stock**

Treasury Stock (1,000 shares × $30)	30,000	
Cash		30,000

Assets = Liabilities + Equity
−30,000 −30,000

c. **November 15, 2020—To record sale of treasury stock**

Cash (250 shares × $33)	8,250	
Paid-in Capital—Treasury Stock (to balance)		750
Treasury Stock (250 shares × $30)		7,500

Assets = Liabilities + Equity
+8,250 +750 +7,500

Assets = Liabilities + Equity −750 −18,000 −750 −3,000 +22,500
Cash: 125,000, 8,250 | 30,000
Common Stock: 750 | 5,000
Paid-in Cap—CS: 18,000 | 120,000
Ret Earnings: 3,000 |
Paid-in Cap—TS: 750 | 750; | 0
Treasury Stock: 30,000 | 7,500, 22,500; 0 |

d. **December 31, 2020—To record retirement of treasury stock**

Common Stock (750 shares × \$1)	750	
Paid-in Capital in Excess of Par (750 shares × \$24)	18,000	
Paid-in Capital—Treasury Stock	750	
Retained Earnings	3,000	
Treasury Stock (750 shares × \$30)		22,500

Assets −30,000 = Liabilities + Equity −30,000
Cash: | 30,000
Common Stock: 750 | 5,000 Bal.
Paid-in Cap—CS: 24,000 | 120,000 Bal.
Ret Earnings: 5,250 |

e. **June 15, 2020—To record direct retirement of stock**

Common Stock (1,000 shares × \$1)	750	
Paid-in Capital in Excess of Par (1,000 shares × \$24)	24,000	
Retained Earnings	5,250	
Cash (1,000 shares × \$30)		30,000

Review 20-4

Assets +100,000 = Liabilities + Equity +10,000 +90,000
Cash: 100,000 |
Preferred Stock: | 10,000
Paid-in Cap—PS: | 90,000

a. **December 31, 2020—To record issuance of convertible preferred stock**

Cash	100,000	
Preferred Stock (1,000 × \$10)		10,000
Paid-in Capital in Excess of Par—Preferred Stock (to balance)		90,000

Financial statement presentation: \$100,000 reported in paid-in capital in the stockholders' equity section.

Assets +100,000 = Liabilities + Equity +10,000 +90,000
Cash: 100,000 |
Preferred Stock: | 10,000
Paid-in Cap—PS: | 90,000

b. **December 31, 2020—To record issuance of redeemable preferred stock**

Cash	100,000	
Preferred Stock (1,000 × \$10)		10,000
Paid-in Capital in Excess of Par—Preferred Stock (to balance)		90,000

Financial statement presentation: \$100,000 reported in paid-in capital in the stockholders' equity section.

Review 20-5

Assets = Liabilities +125,000 + Equity −125,000
Ret Earnings: 125,000 |
Div Payable: | 125,000

a. **June 1, 2020—To record declaration of cash dividends**

Retained Earnings (50,000 shares × \$2.50)	125,000	
Dividends Payable		125,000

Assets +3,000 = Liabilities + Equity +3,000
Inv—CS: 3,000 |
Gain on Disposal: | 3,000

b. **June 1, 2020—To adjust investment to fair value**

Investment in Den Co. Stock	3,000	
Gain on Disposal of Investment (1,000 × [\$22 − \$19])		3,000

Assets = Liabilities +22,000 + Equity −22,000
Ret Earnings: 22,000 |
Prop Div Payable: | 22,000

June 1, 2020—To record declaration of property dividends

Retained Earnings	22,000	
Property Dividends Payable		22,000

Assets = Liabilities +80,000 + Equity −60,000 −20,000
Ret Earnings: 60,000 |
Paid-in Cap—CS: 20,000 |
Div Payable: | 80,000

c. **August 15, 2020—To record a partial liquidating dividend**

Retained Earnings (\$80,000 − \$20,000)	60,000	
Paid-in Capital in Excess of Par—Common Stock	20,000	
Dividends Payable		80,000

Assets = Liabilities +2,000 +23,000 + Equity −25,000
Ret Earnings: 25,000 |
Div Payable: | 25,000

d. **June 1, 2020—To record preferred and common stock dividend declaration**

Retained Earnings	25,000	
Dividends Payable—Preferred Stock (20,000 × 0.05 × 2 years)		2,000
Dividends Payable—Common Stock (\$25,000 − \$2,000)		23,000

Review 20-6

a. **March 1, 2020—To record declaration of stock dividend**

Retained Earnings (50,000 × 5% × $24)	60,000	
Common Stock Dividends Distributable (50,000 × 5% × $1)		2,500
Paid-in Capital in Excess of Par—Common Stock (to balance)		57,500

Assets = Liabilities + Equity
−60,000
+2,500
+57,500

March 15, 2020—To record issuance of stock dividend

Common Stock Dividends Distributable	2,500	
Common Stock		2,500

Assets = Liabilities + Equity
+2,500
−2,500

Ret Earnings: 60,000 |
CS Div Distrib: 2,500 | 2,500
Common Stock: | 2,500
Paid-in Cap—CS: | 57,500

b. **March 1, 2020—To record declaration of stock dividend**

Retained Earnings (50,000 × 5% × $24)	60,000	
Dividends Payable (200 shares × $24)		4,800
Common Stock Dividends Distributable (2,300 × $1)		2,300
Paid-in Capital in Excess of Par—Common Stock (2,300 × $23)		52,900

Assets = Liabilities + Equity
+4,800 −60,000
+2,300
+52,900

March 15, 2020—To record issuance of stock dividend

Common Stock Dividends Distributable	2,300	
Common Stock		2,300

Assets = Liabilities + Equity
−2,300
+2,300

March 15, 2020—To record issuance of cash dividend

Dividends Payable	4,800	
Cash		4,800

Assets = Liabilities + Equity
−4,800 −4,800

Cash: | 4,800
Div Payable: 4,800 | 4,800
Common Stock: | 2,300
CS Div Distrib: 2,300 | 2,300
Paid-in Cap—CS: | 52,900
Ret Earnings: 60,000 |

c. **March 1, 2020—To record declaration of stock dividend**

Retained Earnings (50,000 × 100% × $1)	50,000	
Common Stock Dividends Distributable		50,000

Assets = Liabilities + Equity
−50,000
+50,000

March 15, 2020—To record issuance of stock dividend

Common Stock Dividends Distributable	50,000	
Common Stock		50,000

Assets = Liabilities + Equity
−50,000
+50,000

Ret Earnings: 50,000 |
CS Div Distrib: 50,000 | 50,000
Common Stock: | 50,000

d. There are no journal entries required on the declaration date or the date of the distribution. Total par value is the same before and after the stock split. Round Company would disclose that they have 50,000 × 3 = 150,000 common shares outstanding with a par value per share of $1/3 = $0.3333.

Review 20-7

a.

Net Income	$250,000
Other comprehensive gain, net of tax	55,000
Comprehensive income	$305,000

b.

Accumulated OCI, beginning balance	$114,000
Other comprehensive gain, net of tax	55,000
Accumulated OCI, ending balance	$169,000

Review 20-8

	2017		2016	
Book value per share	$3.81	($5,450.1 ÷ 1,431.6)	$4.03	($5,884.0 ÷ 1,460.5)
Payout ratio	0.50	(1,431.6 ÷ $2,884.7)	0.42	($1,178.0 ÷ $2,817.7)
Return on equity	0.51	$2,884.7 ÷ (($5,450.1 + $5,884.0)/2)	0.48	$2,817.7 ÷ (($5,884.0 + $5,818.0)/2)

21 Share-Based Compensation and Earnings per Share

THE HOME DEPOT, INC.
CONSOLIDATED STATEMENTS OF EARNINGS

in millions, except per share data	Fiscal 2017	Fiscal 2016	Fiscal 2015
Net sales	$100,904	$94,595	$88,519
Cost of sales	66,548	62,282	58,254
Gross profit	34,356	32,313	30,265
Operating expenses:			
Selling, general and administrative	17,864	17,132	16,801
Depreciation and amortization	1,811	1,754	1,690
Total operating expenses	19,675	18,886	18,491
Operating income	14,681	13,427	11,774
Interest and other (income) expense:			
Interest and investment income	(74)	(36)	(166)
Interest expense	1,057	972	919
Interest and other, net	983	936	753
Earnings before provision for income taxes	13,698	12,491	11,021
Provision for income taxes	5,068	4,534	4,012
Net earnings	$ 8,630	$ 7,957	$ 7,009
Basic weighted-average common shares	1,178	1,229	1,277
Basic earnings per share	$ 7.33	$ 6.47	$ 5.49
Diluted weighted-average common shares	1,184	1,234	1,283
Diluted earnings per share	$ 7.29	$ 6.45	$ 5.46

THE HOME DEPOT, INC.
8. EMPLOYEE STOCK PLANS

Stock Options. Under the terms of the Plans, incentive stock options and nonqualified stock options must have an exercise price at or above the fair market value of our stock on the date of the grant. Typically, incentive stock options and nonqualified stock options vest at the rate of 25% per year commencing on the first or second anniversary date of the grant, and expire on the tenth anniversary date of the grant. Additionally, certain stock options may become non-forfeitable upon the associate reaching age 60, provided the associate has had five years of continuous service.

Restricted Stock and Performance Shares. Restrictions on the restricted stock issued under the Plans generally lapse according to one of the following schedules:

- the restrictions on the restricted stock lapse over various periods up to five years;
- the restrictions on 25% of the restricted stock lapse upon the third and sixth anniversaries of the date of issuance with the remaining 50% of the restricted stock lapsing upon the associate's attainment of age 62; or
- the restrictions on 25% of the restricted stock lapse upon the third and sixth anniversaries of the date of issuance with the remaining 50% of the restricted stock lapsing upon the earlier of the associate's attainment of age 60 or the tenth anniversary of the grant date.

We have also granted performance shares under the Plans, the payout of which is dependent on our performance against target average ROIC and operating profit over a three-year performance cycle. Additionally, certain awards may become non-forfeitable upon the associate's attainment of age 60, provided the associate has had five years of continuous service. The fair value of the restricted stock and performance shares is expensed over the period during which the restrictions lapse.

THE HOME DEPOT, INC.
10. WEIGHTED-AVERAGE COMMON SHARES

The reconciliation of our basic to diluted weighted-average common shares follows.

in millions	Fiscal 2017	Fiscal 2016	Fiscal 2015
Basic weighted-average common shares	1,178	1,229	1,277
Effect of potentially dilutive securities	6	5	6
Diluted weighted-average common shares	1,184	1,234	1,283
Anti-dilutive securities excluded from diluted weighted-average common shares	1	1	1

Chapter Preview

In this chapter we explain the accounting for share-based compensation plans where compensation is paid in a form other than a straight cash payment. We examine the accounting for restricted stock awards, restricted stock unit plans, stock option plans, and employee share purchase plans. We then describe the calculation of basic earnings per share, including the effects of dividends, share issuances, share buybacks, stock dividends, and stock splits. We also describe the diluted earnings per share calculation, which considers any financial instrument with a potential to increase common shares outstanding.

Action Plan

LO	Topic/Subtopic	Page	Demos	Reviews	Assignments
LO21–1	**Account for restricted stock plans** Restricted Stock Shares :: Restricted Stock Units :: Compensation Expense :: Requisite Service Period :: Forfeitures	21-3	D21-1A D21-1B	R21-1	23, 24, 46, 47, 48, 49, 73, 83
LO21–2	**Account for stock options** Stock Options :: Fair Value :: Option-Pricing Model :: Compensation Expense :: Forfeitures	21-8	D21-2	R21-2	25, 26, 27, 28, 29, 30, 31, 50, 51, 52, 74, 75, 48, 49, 91, 95
LO21–3	**Account for employee share purchase plans** Employee Share Purchase Plan :: Noncompensatory :: Compensatory	21-13	D21-3	R21-3	32, 33, 53, 75
LO21–4	**Compute earnings per share (EPS) with a simple capital structure** Net Income Available to Common Shareholders :: Weighted-Average Common Shares	21-15	D21-4	R21-4	34, 54, 76, 85, 86, 87, 88, 89, 90, 97, 98, 99
LO21-5	**Compute EPS given share issuances, buybacks, dividends, and splits** Weighted-Average Number of Common Shares :: Stock Issuance :: Treasury Stock :: Stock Dividends :: Stock Split	21-16	D21-5	R21-5	34, 35, 36, 37, 38, 55, 56, 57, 58, 59, 65, 66, 67, 70, 76, 77, 78, 79, 80, 81, 85, 86, 87, 88, 89, 90, 93, 94, 97, 98, 99
LO21–6	**Compute EPS using *if-converted* method for convertible securities** Diluted EPS :: Convertible Preferred Stock :: Convertible Debt :: *If-Converted* Method	21-20	D21-6A D21-6B	R21-6	39, 40, 55, 61, 62, 66, 67, 70, 76, 77, 79, 80, 81, 85, 86, 87, 88, 89, 90, 92, 93, 94, 97, 98, 99
LO21–7	**Compute EPS using treasury stock method for options, warrants, and restricted stock** Diluted EPS :: Stock Options :: Stock Warrants :: Restricted Stock :: Treasury Stock Method	21-25	D21-7A D21-7B	R21-7	41, 42, 63, 66, 68, 70, 77, 78, 79, 81, 83, 85, 86, 87, 88, 89, 90, 94, 96, 97, 98, 99
LO21–8	**Compute EPS using *contingent* methods** Diluted EPS :: Contingently Issuable Shares :: Satisfaction of Conditions	21-30	D21-8	R21-8	43, 69, 70, 82, 85, 86, 87, 88, 89, 90, 97, 98, 99
LO21–9	**Compute EPS given multiple securities and describe EPS financial statement presentation** Multiple Securities :: Rank Securities :: Dilutive Effect :: EPS Presentation	21-31	D21-9	R21-9	44, 45, 60, 64, 66, 71, 72, 76, 77, 79, 80, 84, 85, 86, 87, 88, 89, 90, 94, 97, 98, 99
LO21–10	**APPENDIX 21A—Describe accounting for stock appreciation rights** Stock Appreciation Rights (SARs) :: Equity :: Liability	21-35	D21-10	R21-10	100, 101, 102, 103, 104, 105

LO 21-1 Account for restricted stock plans

LO 21-1 Overview

Restricted Stock Plans
- Grant restricted stock share or units
- Determine total compensation at fair value at the date of grant
- Recognize compensation expense in net income over the requisite service period of the employees
- Account for forfeitures

An increasing number of companies have established plans under which employees receive compensation in a form other than cash such as shares of restricted stock or options to acquire shares of stock. We refer to the entire set of such plans as *share-based compensation plans*. **Share-based compensation plans**, also called stock-based compensation plans, are often awarded to select employees to encourage superior performance, and to help recruit and retain outstanding employees. Two types of share-based compensation plans are restricted stock share awards and restricted stock unit awards. These are *restricted awards* because stock (or rights to stock) is awarded only after certain conditions are met. We illustrate the accounting for (1) **restricted stock share awards** (awards of restricted stock) in **Demo 21-1A** and (2) **restricted stock unit awards** (awards for the right to receive a specified number of shares of stock) in **Demo 21-1B**.

Key terms related to restricted stock plans are defined as follows.

Grant date	ASC Glossary The date at which an employer and an employee reach a mutual understanding of the key terms and conditions of a share-based payment award.
Vest	ASC Glossary To earn the rights to. A share-based payment award becomes vested at the date that the employee's right to receive or retain shares, other instruments, or cash under the award is no longer contingent on satisfaction of either a service condition or a performance condition. Market conditions are not vesting conditions.
Requisite service period	ASC Glossary The period or periods during which an employee is required to provide service in exchange for an award under a share-based payment arrangement. The service that an employee is required to render during that period is referred to as the requisite service. The requisite service period for an award that has only a service condition is presumed to be the vesting period, unless there is clear evidence to the contrary.
Vesting date	Date that a share-based compensation plan is exercisable by an employee.
Vesting period	Period from the grant date to the vesting date. Typically, the vesting period would align with the requisite service period.

Compensation Award Mix

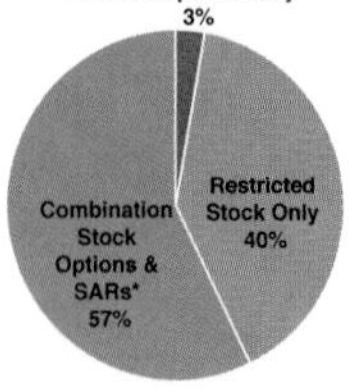

*SARs plans grant the right to compensation equal to the appreciation in market price of stock above a specified price level. See Appendix 21A.

Source: "Stock Compensation: 2017 Assumption and Disclosure Study," PricewaterhouseCoopers (August 2017).

A restricted stock plan gives an employee shares (or rights to own shares) that cannot be awarded to the employee until the employee has satisfied vesting requirements. Such restrictions provide an incentive to the employee to stay with the company through the vesting date and to act in the best interest of shareholders. Thus, if an employee were to leave the company before the vesting period, the restricted shares (units) would be forfeited. Typically, the employee would be restricted from selling these shares during the vesting period.

Restricted Stock SHARE Awards

When a company compensates an employee through restricted stock shares, the company issues stock to the employee at the grant date but holds the stock through the vesting period. **Unearned Compensation—Equity** (also called Deferred Compensation), a contra-equity account, is debited for the *fair value* of the shares at the **grant date**. Changes in the fair value of the shares after the grant date are irrelevant for purposes of valuation of the share award. Unearned Compensation—Equity is reversed to Compensation Expense over the employee's **requisite service period** (typically the vesting period), using the straight-line amortization method.

718-10-30-6 The measurement objective for equity instruments awarded to employees is to estimate the fair value at the grant date of the equity instruments that the entity is obligated to issue when employees have rendered the requisite service and satisfied any other conditions necessary to earn the right to benefit from the instruments (for example, to exercise share options).

718-10-35-2 The compensation cost for an award of share-based employee compensation classified as equity shall be recognized over the requisite service period, with a corresponding credit to equity (generally, paid-in capital). The requisite service period is the period during which an employee is required to provide service in exchange for an award, which often is the vesting period. The requisite service period is estimated based on an analysis of the terms of the share-based payment award.

Restricted Stock UNIT Awards

When a company chooses to compensate employees through restricted stock units, the employee is granted the *right* to receive stock at a future date under certain conditions. After the employee meets the conditions, the company distributes the common shares. Unlike restricted stock awards, the issuance of shares is delayed until after the vesting period. However, the fair value of the compensation is still determined at the date of grant, as is the case with restricted stock award plans. Compensation expense (along with an increase in **Paid-in Capital—Restricted Stock**) is recognized over the employee's requisite service period using the straight-line amortization method. Paid-in Capital—Restricted Stock is credited instead of Common Stock and Paid-in Capital—Common Stock because the employee receives a right to receive stock in the future. This means the stock is not yet issued. After the employee meets the vesting requirements, Paid-in Capital—Restricted Stock is replaced with the accounts Common Stock and Paid-in Capital—Common Stock.

Forfeitures

What if an employee does not meet the specified conditions and the restricted stock shares or units are forfeited? The accounting standards allow two different options in accounting for forfeitures.

- **Recording an estimate of forfeitures** Under this option, the fair value of the restricted stock award is reduced by the percentage of shares estimated to be forfeited. Thus, compensation expense recorded each period is based on the net expected stock award. If the estimate changes in a later period, the *cumulative effect* of the change in estimate is recorded in the current period.
- **Recording forfeitures as they are incurred** The accounting standards allow for a practical expedient, where a company may record forfeitures (due to employee turnover) in the period incurred.

718-10-35-3 To determine the amount of compensation cost to be recognized in each period, an entity shall make an entity-wide accounting policy election for all share-based payment awards to do either of the following:

a. Estimate the number of awards for which the requisite service will not be rendered (that is, estimate the number of forfeitures expected to occur). The entity shall base initial accruals of compensation cost on the estimated number of instruments for which the requisite service is expected to be rendered. The entity shall revise that estimate if subsequent information indicates that the actual number of instruments is likely to differ from previous estimates. The cumulative effect on current and prior periods of a change in the estimated number of instruments for which the requisite service is expected to be or has been rendered shall be recognized in compensation cost in the period of the change.

b. Recognize the effect of awards for which the requisite service is not rendered when the award is forfeited (that is, recognize the effect of forfeitures in compensation cost when they occur). Previously recognized compensation cost for an award shall be reversed in the period that the award is forfeited.

Accounting for Restricted Stock Shares **LO21-1** **Demo 21-1A**

On January 1, 2020, Jax Inc. grants 1,000, $1 par, restricted shares of its common stock to one senior corporate officer. The shares vest if the officer stays with the company for three years, which is the requisite service period. The fair value of the shares on January 1, 2020, is $15 per share.

a. Record the journal entry on January 1, 2020, the date of grant, for this compensatory plan.
b. Record the journal entry on December 31, 2020, to recognize compensation expense.
c. Show the December 31, 2020, financial statement presentation resulting from the restricted stock award.

continued

continued from previous page

d. Assume that the senior corporate officer resigned on January 1, 2021. Record the entry on January 1, 2021, to reflect the financial statement impact of the resignation. Assume that the company elects to record forfeitures as incurred.

Solution

a. **Issuance of Restricted Stock**

The journal entry at the date of grant follows.

Assets = Liabilities + Equity
−15,000
+1,000
+14,000

Unearned Comp—Eq: 15,000 (debit)
Common Stock: 1,000 (credit)
Paid-in Cap—CS: 14,000 (credit)

January 1, 2020—To record issuance of restricted stock

Unearned Compensation—Equity (1,000 × $15)	15,000	
Common Stock (1,000 × $1)		1,000
Paid-in Capital in Excess of Par—Common Stock ($15,000 − $1,000)		14,000

b. **Recognition of Compensation Expense**

Compensation expense is recognized over the next three years or the requisite service period. Jax Inc. recognizes compensation expense at the end of the first year as follows.

Assets = Liabilities + Equity
−5,000
+5,000

Comp Exp: 5,000 (debit)
Unearned Comp—Eq: 15,000 (debit) | 5,000 (credit)

December 31, 2020—To record compensation expense

Compensation Expense	5,000	
Unearned Compensation—Equity ($15,000/3 years)		5,000

Jax Inc. also records compensation expense of $5,000 in both 2021 and 2022.

c. **Financial Statement Presentation**

In the financial statements for December 31, 2020, Jax Inc. would record the following for its restricted stock transactions for 2020.

Balance Sheet	
Stockholders' equity	
Common stock	$ 1,000
Paid-in capital in excess of par	14,000
Unearned compensation—equity ($15,000 − $5,000)	(10,000)

Income Statement	
Expense	
Compensation expense	$5,000

d. **Restricted Stock Forfeiture**

The related equity accounts are derecognized and compensation expense previously recorded is now credited.

Assets = Liabilities + Equity
−1,000
−14,000
+10,000
+5,000

Unearned Comp—Eq: 15,000 (debit) | 5,000, 10,000 (credit)
Common Stock: 1,000 (debit) | 1,000 (credit)
Paid-in Cap—CS: 14,000 (debit) | 14,000 (credit)
Comp Exp: 5,000 (debit) | 5,000 (credit)

January 1, 2021—To record restricted stock forfeiture

Common Stock	1,000	
Paid-in Capital in Excess of Par—Common Stock	14,000	
Unearned Compensation—Equity ($15,000 − $5,000)		10,000
Compensation Expense		5,000

Demo 21-1B LO21-1 Accounting for Restricted Stock Units

Demo MBC

On January 1, 2020, Jax Inc. grants a total of 5,000 restricted stock units to five senior corporate officers. Each stock unit may be exchanged for 1 share of $1 par common stock. Each corporate officer will receive 1,000 shares if the officer stays with the company for three years, which is the requisite service period. The fair value of the shares on January 1, 2020, is $15 per share.

a. Record compensation expense in 2020, 2021, and 2022, related to the award of the restricted stock units on January 1, 2020.

b. Record the issuance of the shares of restricted stock on January 1, 2023, assuming all five officers received the designated stock awards.

c. Assume the same information in the original scenario except that Jax Inc. now expects forfeitures due to employee turnover and Jax's policy is to recognize estimated forfeitures. On January 1, 2020, Jax Inc. estimates 1,000 shares will be forfeited due to employee turnover during the three-year requisite service period.

continued

continued from previous page

1. Record the entry on December 31, 2020, to recognize compensation expense.
2. Record the entry on December 31, 2021, to recognize compensation expense, assuming that one officer left the company on that date and no further forfeitures are expected.

d. Assume the same information in the original scenario except that Jax Inc. now expects forfeitures due to employee turnover and Jax elected to record forfeitures as incurred.

1. Record the required entry on December 31, 2020, to recognize compensation expense.
2. Record the entry on December 31, 2021, to recognize compensation expense, assuming that one officer left the company on that date.

e. Assume the same information as in c. Record the entry on December 31, 2021, assuming that the estimate of forfeitures increases to 2,000 restricted stock units and no forfeitures have occurred.

Solution

a. **Recognition of Compensation Expense**

No journal entry is required on January 1, 2020 (the date of grant). However, the total compensation expense is calculated at that time as 5,000 units multiplied by $15 per share or $75,000. Compensation expense will be recognized at the end of each of the next three years or the requisite service period as follows.

December 31, 2020, 2021, and 2022—To record compensation expense

Compensation Expense	25,000	
Paid-in Capital—Restricted Stock ($75,000/3 years)		25,000

Assets = Liabilities + Equity −25,000 +25,000
Comp Exp: 25,000 / 25,000 / 25,000 | Paid-in Cap—RS: 25,000 / 25,000 / 25,000

b. **Issuance of Vested Restricted Stock Units**

On January 1, 2023, the restricted stock units would be fully vested and the shares would be awarded to the corporate officer.

January 1, 2023—To record issuance of restricted stock

Paid-in Capital—Restricted Stock ($25,000 × 3 years)	75,000	
Common Stock (5,000 × $1)		5,000
Paid in Capital in Excess of Par—Common Stock ($75,000 − $5,000)		70,000

Assets = Liabilities + Equity −75,000 +5,000 +70,000
Paid-in Cap—RS: 75,000 | 25,000 / 25,000 / 25,000; Paid-in Cap—CS: | 70,000; Common Stock: | 5,000

c. **Restricted Stock Unit Forfeitures—Estimated**

1. The fair value of the compensation related to the restricted stock units would be reduced by the estimate of forfeiture of 1,000 units or 20%. Thus, compensation would be estimated to be $60,000 ($75,000 × 80%). Jax Inc. recognizes compensation expense at the end of the first year of the requisite service period as follows.

December 31, 2020—To record compensation expense

Compensation Expense	20,000	
Paid-in Capital—Restricted Stock ($60,000/3 years)		20,000

Assets = Liabilities + Equity −20,000 +20,000
Comp Exp: 20,000 | Paid-in Cap—RS: | 20,000

2. Considering the forfeiture in 2021, total compensation is $60,000 or $75,000 less $15,000 for the forfeiture. Paid-in Capital—Restricted Stock should be $40,000 (or $60,000 × 2/3). Because $20,000 was expensed in 2020, an additional $20,000 is expensed in 2021.

December 31, 2021—To record compensation expense

Compensation Expense	20,000	
Paid-in Capital—Restricted Stock ($40,000 − $20,000)		20,000

Assets = Liabilities + Equity −20,000 +20,000
Comp Exp: 20,000 / 20,000 | Paid-in Cap—RS: | 20,000 / 20,000

d. **Restricted Stock Unit Forfeitures—Recognized as Incurred**

1. Total compensation expense is calculated at that time as 5,000 shares multiplied by $15 shares or $75,000. One-third of the total amount is expensed in 2020 as follows.

December 31, 2020—To record compensation expense

Compensation Expense	25,000	
Paid-in Capital—Restricted Stock ($75,000/3 years)		25,000

Assets = Liabilities + Equity −25,000 +25,000
Comp Exp: 25,000 | Paid-in Cap—RS: | 25,000

continued

continued from previous page

2. The company would record the forfeiture as incurred in 2021. Considering the forfeiture, total compensation is $60,000 or $75,000 less $15,000 for the forfeiture. Paid-in Capital—Restricted Stock should be $40,000 (or $60,000 × 2/3). Because $25,000 was expensed in 2020, an additional $15,000 is expensed in 2021.

Assets	= Liabilities	+ Equity
		−15,000
		+15,000

Comp Exp	Paid-in Cap—RS
25,000	25,000
15,000	15,000
	40,000

December 31, 2021—To record compensation expense

Compensation Expense	15,000	
Paid-in Capital—Restricted Stock ($40,000 − $25,000)		15,000

We see from parts *c* and *d* that total compensation expense is $40,000 over the two-year period of 2020 to 2021. Only the timing of revenue recognition differs.

e. **Change in Estimate in Accounting for Forfeitures**
On December 31, 2021, the estimate of forfeitures increases to 2,000 units or 40% of the total compensation (2,000 shares/5,000 shares). The total compensation with a 40% reduction is $45,000 ($75,000 × 60%). Thus, on December 31, 2021, after two years, total Paid-in Capital—Restricted Stock should be $30,000 ($45,000 × 2/3). Because $20,000 was expensed in the prior year, an additional $10,000 is expensed in 2021.

Assets	= Liabilities	+ Equity
		−10,000
		+10,000

Comp Exp	Paid-in Cap—RS
20,000	20,000
10,000	10,000
	30,000

December 31, 2021—To record compensation expense

Compensation Expense	10,000	
Paid-in Capital—Restricted Stock		10,000

FORD

Real World—RESTRICTED STOCK UNITS

FORD MOTOR [F]

Ford Motor Company described the issuance of restricted stock units as compensation for key employees in a recent Form 10-K. Some units are time-based and some are performance-based.

> We issue to our employees restricted stock units ("RSUs"), which consist of time-based and performance-based awards. RSUs provide the recipients with the right to shares of Common Stock following a specified performance period and/or vesting period. Time-based awards generally have a vesting feature whereby one-third of each grant of RSUs vests after the first anniversary of the grant date, one-third after the second anniversary, and one-third after the third anniversary. Performance-based RSUs vest at the end of the specified performance period, generally three years, assuming required metrics are met. Performance-based RSUs have two components: one based on Ford's internal financial performance metrics, and the other based on Ford's total shareholder return relative to total shareholder returns of an industrial and automotive peer group. We issue new shares of Common Stock upon vesting of RSUs. At the time of vest, RSU awards are net settled (shares are withheld to cover the employee tax obligation).

REVIEW 21-1 LO21-1 Accounting for Restricted Stock Plans

Review MBC

On January 1, 2020, the board of directors of Instagraham Inc. granted restricted stock shares to 5 key employees to acquire 5,000 shares each under the following terms.

- Restricted stock share awards vest on December 31, 2021. Grantees must remain employed with the company to receive the common shares of stock without restriction. The requisite service period is considered to be 2 years.
- Each stock share award represents one share of $1 par, common stock of Instagraham Inc.
- No forfeitures are anticipated.

On the date of grant, the common shares were trading at $75 per share. During 2020 and 2021, the average price of common stock was $70 and $80 per share, respectively.

a. Prepare the journal entry on the date of grant, January 1, 2020.
b. Prepare the adjusting journal entry on December 31, 2020.
c. Assume instead that the board of directors granted 5,000 restricted stock units instead of restricted stock shares. Each restricted stock unit may be exchanged for one share of common stock of Instagraham Inc. Prepare the related journal entries on January 1, 2020, and on December 31, 2020.

More Practice:
21-46, 21-47, 21-48, 21-49, 21-73

Solution on p. 21-58.

Account for stock options

LO 21-2

A stock option plan is another form of share-based compensation. **Stock options** give an employee the right to buy a specified number of shares of stock of the employer at an established price (**exercise price**) over a specified time period. The accounting for stock option plans is illustrated in **Demo 21-2**.

Stock Option
- Determine total compensation at the date of grant using option-pricing model
- Recognize compensation expense in net income over the requisite service period of the employees
- Account for forfeitures

LO 21-2 Overview

Stock option plans are designed to provide incentives to employees to increase productivity and the share price of the company's stock. For example, an option awarded to an employee to purchase stock at the current market price that is exercisable in five years provides an incentive to increase the market price of the stock over the next five years. The employee reaps a reward equal to the increase in the share price times the number of shares under option. In this way, stock options are designed to align the interests of shareholders with the interests of employees. However, stock options are short-term focused as the holders benefit from an increase in stock price in a certain time period. Decisions made by management that lead to an increase in stock price in the short-term may be detrimental to the company in the long-term.

Key terms related to stock option plans are defined as follows.

Option	ASC Glossary Unless otherwise stated, a call option that gives the holder the right to purchase shares of common stock from the reporting entity in accordance with an agreement upon payment of a specified amount. Options include, but are not limited to, options granted to employees and stock purchase agreements entered into with employees. Options are considered securities.
Exercise price (Strike price)	ASC Glossary The amount that must be paid for a share of common stock upon exercise of an option or warrant.
Expiration date	Date that marks the point where the employee may no longer exercise the award under a share-based payment arrangement.
Performance condition	ASC Glossary A condition affecting the vesting, exercisability, exercise price, or other pertinent factors used in determining the fair value of an award that relates to both of the following: *a.* An employee's rendering service for a specified (either explicitly or implicitly) period of time *b.* Achieving a specified performance target that is defined solely by reference to the employer's own operations (or activities).

The measurement of the cost of compensation is determined at the grant date, based on the fair value of the options as determined by applying an option-pricing model such as the **Black-Scholes option-pricing model**. Changes in assumptions or in a selected valuation technique are applied *prospectively* as explained in the authoritative guidance.

> **718-10-55-27** Assumptions used to estimate the fair value of equity and liability instruments granted to employees shall be determined in a consistent manner from period to period . . . The valuation technique an entity selects to estimate fair value for a particular type of instrument also shall be used consistently and shall not be changed unless a different valuation technique is expected to produce a better estimate of fair value. A change in either the valuation technique or the method of determining appropriate assumptions used in a valuation technique is a change in accounting estimate . . . and shall be applied prospectively to new awards.

Option-pricing models consider several variables in valuing compensation expense including the expected price of the option, current market price of the stock, risk-free rate of interest, expected term of the options, expected volatility of the stock price, and expected dividend yield of the stock. Thus, an option-pricing model considers prospective information in deriving a fair value. For example, let's assume that a stock option with an exercise price of $20 per share was granted at a time when the related stock was trading at $20 per share. The intrinsic value (or the amount by which the fair value of the underlying stock exceeds the exercise price of the option) is $0. However, the option-pricing model estimates the fair value of each option to be $5, based upon the variables considered in the option-pricing model. While the fair value of the stock options is determined on the grant date, no journal entry is recorded at this time.

The amount determined to be the fair value of the stock options is expensed over the requisite service period, ending when the employee has no further service obligations or constraints imposed by the stock option plan. The entry includes a debit to **Compensation Expense** and a credit to **Paid-in Capital—Stock Options**. The compensation plan may specify the requisite service period; otherwise, the grantor must use a best estimate. A company may estimate forfeitures or elect to record forfeitures as incurred as described in LO 21-1.

Stock option plans may be structured to award shares based upon certain performance conditions or market conditions.

Performance conditions In cases where a stock option award is based upon performance conditions, the company recognizes compensation expense when the company determines that it is *probable* that the performance condition will be met. Revisions of estimates of probability that affect the amounts previously recorded are reflected *fully* in the year of the estimate revision.

Market conditions In cases where a stock option award is based upon a market condition such as a target stock price, the share price models such as Black Scholes, have already taken market factors into account so no adjustments to fair values determined by the models are required. This means that the company recognizes compensation expense as if there is no target.

718-10-25-20 Accruals of compensation cost for an award with a performance condition shall be based on the probable outcome of that performance condition—compensation cost shall be accrued if it is probable that the performance condition will be achieved and shall not be accrued if it is not probable that the performance condition will be achieved.

718-10-30-14 Some awards contain a market condition. The effect of a market condition is reflected in the grant-date fair value of an award.

Upon exercise of the stock options (after the requisite service period), the employer debits Cash for the contractual amount paid by the employee, debits Paid-in Capital—Stock Options and credits the Capital Stock accounts. If instead, the stock options expire, the company transfers the balance of Paid-in Capital—Stock Options to Paid-in Capital—Expired Stock Options.

A stock option agreement may be structured to allow a performance obligation to be met *after* the employee retires. In this case, compensation is recognized when the company determines that it is probable that the condition is met, even if the condition is met after the employee retires.

718-10-30-28 In some cases, the terms of an award may provide that a performance target that affects vesting could be achieved after an employee completes the requisite service period. That is, the employee would be eligible to vest in the award regardless of whether the employee is rendering service on the date the performance target is achieved. A performance target that affects vesting and that could be achieved after an employee's requisite service period shall be accounted for as a performance condition. As such, the performance target shall not be reflected in estimating the fair value of the award at the grant date.

EXPANDING YOUR KNOWLEDGE **Shift from Stock Option Plans to Restricted Stock Plans**

As illustrated in the graph below, the mix is shifting from stock options to restricted stock in recent years. For example, in 2016, 54% of the units granted were stock options compared to 59% in 2012 (in relation to restricted stock). Why has the popularity of restricted stock increased over time while the popularity of stock options has decreased?

First, less shares are typically granted with restricted stock awards than with stock option plans, resulting in less dilution on current shareholder ownership. For example, a company may grant to an executive officer, stock options to purchase 500 shares of stock at a predetermined price. On the other hand, an executive officer may be just as satisfied with 200 shares of restricted stock.

Second, restricted shares will generally retain some value despite market volatility, whereas stock options may become worthless in a market downturn. Executives are assured of receiving value when restricted shares are awarded (as long as the stock has some value on the market). However, under a stock option plan, there is less certainty in a share price exceeding an exercise price, which may result in short-term decisions to inflate stock prices.

continued

continued from previous page

Mix of Awards–Units of Awards Granted of Stock Options vs. Restricted Stock*

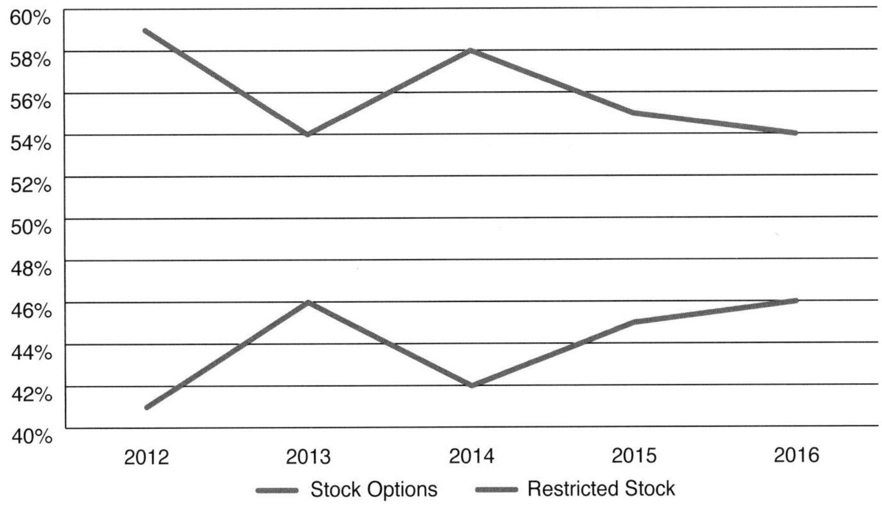

*Percent of Median # of Units Awarded.
Source: "Stock Compensation: 2017 Assumption and Disclosure Study," PWC (August 2017).

Accounting for Stock Options

LO21-2 **Demo 21-2**

Demo MBC

On January 1, 2020, Ram Co. awards a total of 100,000 stock options to acquire 100,000 shares of common stock ($1 par value) to 1,000 employees at an exercise price of $5 per share. The market price of Ram Co. common stock on the grant date is $5 per share. The options are exercisable after January 1, 2023, and expire when an employee leaves the company or on December 31, 2029, whichever is first. The requisite service period is three years. Management estimates through a fair value option-pricing model that total compensation expense is $540,000 related to the stock options.

a. Record an entry (if applicable) on the date of grant.
b. Recognize compensation expense in 2020 related to the stock options.
c. Employees exercised 90,000 options (90% of the options) that vested on January 1, 2023. On that date, the market price of Ram Co. stock was $7 per share. The amount collected from the employees totaled $450,000 or $5 × 90,000 options. Record the required journal entry on January 1, 2023.
d. The remaining 10,000 options (10% of the options) were *not* exercised before the expiration date of December 31, 2029. Record the required journal entry on December 31, 2029.
e. Assume the original scenario except that 20,000 options were associated with employees who left the company in 2021. Record the required journal entry on December 31, 2021, assuming that the company recognizes forfeitures as incurred.
f. Assume the original scenario except that the company estimates forfeitures to be 10%. Record the compensation expense related to the stock options in 2020 assuming that it is the company's policy to recognize estimated forfeitures.
g. Assume the original scenario except that the awards will only be granted to employees if sales of the company increase by 5% in each of the following three years: 2020, 2021, and 2022. Management believes that it is probable that the company will achieve this performance target. Recognize compensation expense in 2020.
h. Assume the original scenario except that the awards will only be granted to employees if sales of the company increase by 5% in each of the following three years: 2020, 2021, and 2022. Management believes that it is *not* probable that the company will achieve this performance target. Recognize compensation expense in 2020.

continued

continued from previous page

Solution

a. **Issuance of Stock Options**

While the total cost of compensation of $540,000 is determined at the grant date, no journal entry is recorded at this time.

b. **Recognition of Compensation Expense**

The compensation expense of $540,000 determined at the grant date is recognized over the three-year requisite service period. This is the period that the employees earn the compensation.

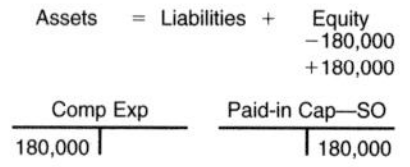

December 31, 2020—To record compensation expense

Compensation Expense	180,000	
Paid-in Capital—Stock Options ($540,000/3 years)		180,000

Ram Co. records compensation expense of $180,000 in both 2021 and 2022 as well.

c. **Exercise of Stock Options**

Ram Co. records the following entry upon the exercise of stock options by employees.

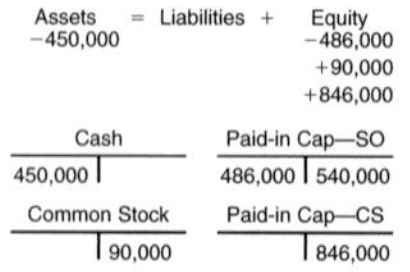

January 1, 2023—To record exercise of stock options

Cash (90,000 × $5)	450,000	
Paid-in Capital—Stock Options ($540,000 × 90%)	486,000	
Common Stock (90,000 × $1)		90,000
Paid-in Capital in Excess of Par—Common Stock (to balance)		846,000

d. **Expiration of Stock Options—Time Lapse**

On December 31, 2029, the company transfers the balance of Paid-in Capital—Stock Options to Paid-in Capital—Expired Stock Options.

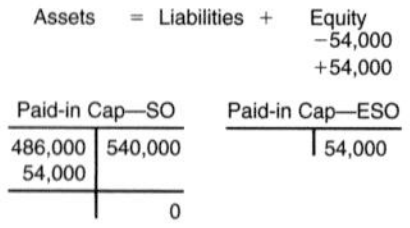

December 31, 2029—To record expiration of stock options

Paid-in Capital—Stock Options ($540,000 × 10%)	54,000	
Paid-in Capital—Expired Stock Options		54,000

e. **Stock Option Forfeitures—Recognized as Incurred**

The company will recognize the forfeiture in 2021 when incurred. The forfeiture of 20,000 options is a 20% (20,000 options/100,000 options) reduction of compensation costs. Total compensation reflecting the forfeiture is $432,000 or $540,000 × 80%. Total Paid-in Capital—Stock Options should be $288,000 or $432,000 × 2/3. Because $180,000 was expensed in 2020, an additional $108,000 is expensed in 2021.

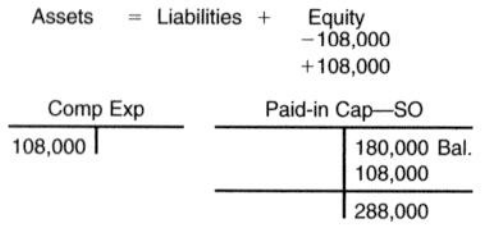

December 31, 2021—To record compensation expense adjusted for expiration of stock options

Compensation Expense	108,000	
Paid-in Capital—Stock Options ($288,000 − $180,000)		108,000

f. **Stock Option Forfeitures—Estimated**

Forfeitures are estimated to be 10%, which reduces total compensation costs to $486,000 ($540,000 × 90%). Thus, compensation expense is now $162,000 per year (or $486,000/3 years), recorded in 2020 as follows.

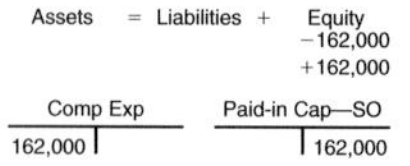

December 31, 2020—To record compensation expense

Compensation Expense	162,000	
Paid-in Capital—Stock Options ($486,000/3 years)		162,000

g. **Performance Based Measure**

Because the company believes that it is probable that it will achieve the performance target, compensation expense is recorded for the year 2020 based on the allocation of the estimated fair value.

continued

continued from previous page

December 31, 2020—To record compensation expense

Compensation Expense	180,000	
Paid-in Capital—Stock Options ($540,000/3 years)		180,000

Assets	=	Liabilities	+	Equity
				−180,000
				+180,000

Comp Exp		Paid-in Cap—SO	
180,000			180,000

h. **Performance Based Measure**
Because the company believes that it is *not* probable that it will achieve the performance target, compensation expense is not recorded for the year 2020.

EXPANDING YOUR KNOWLEDGE — Graded Vesting of Stock Option Plans

Stock option plans may vest over several dates instead of on one particular date, which is called **graded vesting**. (**Cliff vesting**, as illustrated in **Demo 21-2**, is when *all* awards vest at the end of the vesting period.) In the case of graded vesting, a company may value each vesting group (or tranche) *separately* or in the *aggregate* using an average expected term. Compensation may be recognized using an accelerated approach or straight-line method, as long as the cumulative amount recognized each year is at least equal to the value of the awards vested to that date. For example, AAA Co. awards stock options that vest over a three-year period. The fair value of each group of options that vest is estimated to be $5,000, $12,000, and $21,000, for years 1, 2, and 3, respectively. The amounts are separately recognized as expense on a straight-line basis as follows.

Compensation Costs to be Recognized	Year 1	Year 2	Year 3	Total
Shares vesting in Year 1	$ 5,000	$ —	$ —	$5,000
Shares vesting in Year 2	6,000	6,000	—	12,000
Shares vesting in Year 3	7,000	7,000	7,000	21,000
	$18,000	$13,000	$7,000	$38,000

Under this approach, each year of expense exceeds the actual value of the awards vested to date:

In year 1, compensation expense of $18,000 exceeds vested expense of $5,000.

In year 2, compensation expense of $31,000 ($18,000 + $13,000) exceeds vested expense of $17,000 ($5,000 + $12,000).

Alternatively, the company may calculate amortization expense in the aggregate as $12,667 each year or $38,000/3.

PEPSICO

Real World—EMPLOYEE STOCK OPTIONS

PEPSICO [PEP]

PepsiCo Inc. described the assumptions that were used to calculate the fair value of stock options at the date of grant in a recent annual report.

Note 6 (excerpt)—A stock option permits the holder to purchase shares of PepsiCo common stock at a specified price. We account for our employee stock options under the fair value method of accounting using a Black-Scholes valuation model to measure stock option expense at the date of grant. All stock option grants have an exercise price equal to the fair market value of our common stock on the date of grant and generally have a 10-year term. Our weighted-average Black-Scholes fair value assumptions are as follows:

	2017	2016	2015
Expected life	**5 years**	6 years	7 years
Risk-free interest rate	**2.0%**	1.4%	1.8%
Expected volatility	**11.0%**	12.0%	15.0%
Expected dividend yield	**2.7%**	2.7%	2.7%

The expected life is the period over which our employee groups are expected to hold their options. It is based on our historical experience with similar grants. The risk-free interest rate is based on the expected U.S. Treasury rate over the expected life. Volatility reflects movements in our stock price over the most recent historical period equivalent to the expected life. Dividend yield is estimated over the expected life based on our stated dividend policy and forecasts of net income, share repurchases and stock price.

REVIEW 21-2 **LO21-2** **Accounting for Stock Options**

Review MBC

On April 1, 2020, Badger Corp. announced a stock option incentive plan for its top executives. The plan provides certain executives stock options for the company's common stock. Each option allows for the purchase of one share of common stock, par $1, at a standard option price of $25 per share. The rights are nontransferable and are exercisable three years after the grant date and prior to five years from the grant date. Continuing employment is required through the exercise date, and the requisite service period ends on the first possible exercise date.

On April 1, 2020, 2,000 options were granted to employees when the market price was $30 per share. Using an option-pricing model, the fair value of the options granted was $18,000. Employees exercised 1,200 options on June 30, 2023, when the market price of the stock was $45 per share.

a. Compute the total amount of compensation cost for the grant made on April 1, 2020.

b. Record the entry for compensation expense on December 31, 2020, Badger's year-end.

c. Record the entry for the exercise of options on June 30, 2023.

More Practice: 21-25, 21-50, 21-51

Solution on p. 21-58.

LO 21-3 Account for employee share purchase plans

LO 21-3 Overview

Employee Share Purchase Plan
- Noncompensatory plan
  - Meets criteria
  - Recognize no compensation expense
- Compensatory plan
  - Does not meet criteria
  - Recognize compensation expense for employee discount on stock purchase

Employee share purchase plans allow employees the opportunity to purchase shares of stock of their employer at a discounted price. The company records no compensation expense in this situation if all of the following conditions are met as outlined in the authoritative guidance.

718-50-25-1 An employee share purchase plan that satisfies all of the following criteria does not give rise to recognizable compensation cost (that is, the plan is noncompensatory):

a. The plan satisfies either of the following conditions:
1. The terms of the plan are no more favorable than those available to all holders of the same class of shares.
2. Any purchase discount from the market price does not exceed the per-share amount of share issuance costs that would have been incurred to raise a significant amount of capital by a public offering. A purchase discount of 5 percent or less from the market price shall be considered to comply with this condition without further justification.

b. Substantially all employees that meet limited employment qualifications may participate on an equitable basis.

c. The plan incorporates no option features, other than the following:
1. Employees are permitted a short period of time—not exceeding 31 days—after the purchase price has been fixed to enroll in the plan.
2. The purchase price is based solely on the market price of the shares at the date of purchase, and employees are permitted to cancel participation before the purchase date and obtain a refund of amounts previously paid (such as those paid by payroll withholdings).

If all of the conditions outlined above are met, no compensation is recorded related to the plan as illustrated in **Demo 21-3** (Example One). However, if any of the conditions are *not* met, the company must recognize compensation expense for the amount of the stock discount extended to employees—see **Demo 21-3** (Example Two).

EXPANDING YOUR KNOWLEDGE **Disclosure of Compensation Plans**

Companies with a share-based payment arrangement(s) must disclose the following information described in the authoritative guidance.

718-10-50-1

a. The nature and terms of such arrangements that existed during the period and the potential effects of those arrangements on shareholders.

b. The effect of compensation cost arising from share-based payment arrangements on the income statement.

c. The method of estimating the fair value of the goods or services received, or the fair value of the equity instruments granted (or offered to grant), during the period.

d. The cash flow effects resulting from share-based payment arrangements.

HOME DEPOT

Real World—EMPLOYEE STOCK PURCHASE PLANS

HOME DEPOT [HD]

Home Depot Inc. described employee stock purchase plans (ESPPs) in a recent annual report. The discount provided to employees is 15% and the related compensation expense is noted.

Note 8 (excerpt) Employee Stock Purchase Plans—We maintain two ESPPs (U.S. and non-U.S. plans). The plan for U.S. associates is a tax-qualified plan under Section 423 of the Internal Revenue Code. The non-U.S. plan is not a Section 423 plan. At January 28, 2018, there were 20 million shares available under the U.S. plan and 19 million shares available under the non-U.S. plan. The purchase price of shares under the ESPPs is equal to 85% of the stock's fair market value on the last day of the purchase period, which is a six-month period ending on December 31 and June 30 of each year. During fiscal 2017, there were 1 million shares purchased under the ESPPs at an average price of $143.71. Under the outstanding ESPPs at January 28, 2018, employees have contributed $17 million to purchase shares at 85% of the stock's fair market value on the last day of the current purchase period (June 30, 2018). Recognized stock-based compensation expense related to ESPPs follows.

in millions, for Fiscal Years	2017	2016	2015
Stock-based compensation expense related to ESPPs.	$28	$26	$23

Accounting for Employee Share Purchase Plans

LO21-3 **Demo 21-3**

Demo MBC

Example One—Shares Issuance Under a Noncompensatory Employee Share Purchase Plan
Evergreen Inc. has an employee stock purchase plan for all eligible employees. Under the plan, shares of the company's $1 par value common stock may be purchased at 95% of the fair value on the last day of each six-month period. On January 31, 2020, employees purchased 5,000 shares at a price of $18 per share, less the 5% discount. The plan is determined to be noncompensatory because it meets the criteria of a noncompensatory plan. Record the journal entry for the issuance of stock on January 31, 2020.

Solution
On January 31, 2020, Evergreen Inc. records the following journal entry for issuance of stock through the employee share purchase plan.

January 31, 2020—To record issuance of stock for employee share purchase plan

Cash (5,000 × $18 × 95%).	85,500	
Common Stock (5,000 × $1).		5,000
Paid-in Capital in Excess of Par—Common Stock (to balance)		80,500

Assets	=	Liabilities	+	Equity
+85,500				+5,000 +80,500

Cash: 85,500 (debit)
Paid-in Cap—CS: 80,500 (credit)
Common Stock: 5,000 (credit)

Example Two—Shares Issuance Under a Compensatory Employee Share Purchase Plan
Let's assume the same facts described in Example One, except now the plan allows for the shares to be purchased at 90% of the fair value on the last day of each six-month period. In this case, the discount exceeds 5% of the stock price and the plan is considered compensatory. Record the journal entry for the issuance of stock on January 31, 2020.

Solution
On January 31, 2020, Evergreen Inc. records the following journal entry for the issuance of stock through the employee share purchase plan.

January 31, 2020—To record issuance of stock for employee share purchase plan

Cash (5,000 × $18 × 90%).	81,000	
Compensation Expense (5,000 × $18 × 10%).	9,000	
Common Stock (5,000 × $1).		5,000
Paid-in Capital in Excess of Par—Common Stock (to balance)		85,000

Assets	=	Liabilities	+	Equity
+81,000				−9,000 +5,000 +85,000

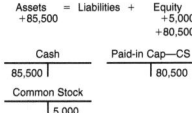

Cash: 81,000 (debit)
Comp Exp: 9,000 (debit)
Common Stock: 5,000 (credit)
Paid-in Cap—CS: 85,000 (credit)

REVIEW 21-3 **LO21-3** **Accounting for Employee Share Purchase Plans**

Review MBC

Safe Inc. employees are all eligible to participate in a stock purchase plan. The plan allows employees to purchase $1 par value common stock at a 5% discount. On January 1, 2020, employees purchased 500 shares of common stock when the market price of the stock was $10 per share.

a. Record the journal entry for Safe Inc. on January 1, 2020, assuming the plan is determined to be noncompensatory.

b. Assume instead that only certain employees are eligible for the plan and that the discount is 15% on the market price of the stock. Record the entry on January 1, 2020, when employees purchased 500 shares of common stock when the market price of the stock was $10 per share.

More Practice: 21-32, 21-33, 21-53

Solution on p. 21-59.

LO 21-4 Compute earnings per share (EPS) with a simple capital structure

LO 21-4 Overview

EPS—Simple Capital Structure
- Earnings attributable to each share of common stock
- Divide net income available to common stockholders by weighted-average common shares outstanding

Earnings per share (EPS) is the amount of earnings attributable to each share of common stock. This measure is important to investors because it is a factor in determining the market price of stock. Given the emphasis of this measure, the FASB, the SEC, and other investment regulatory agencies are concerned with how this financial statistic is measured. We begin with a discussion of basic earnings per share.

ASC Glossary Basic earnings per share: The amount of earnings for the period available to each share of common stock outstanding during the reporting period.

In its most elementary form, **basic earnings per share** (EPS) for a period of time is calculated as follows and illustrated in **Demo 21-4**.

$$\textbf{Basic earnings per share} = \frac{\textbf{Net income available to common stockholders}}{\textbf{Weighted-average common shares outstanding}}$$

One implication of this expression is that preferred dividends declared in the period must be deducted from net income because these dividends are a part of net income that does not belong to common stockholders. The impact of preferred dividends on this calculation is explained in the next section. If a company records a net loss (instead of net income), the net loss is divided by weighted-average common shares to arrive at a net loss per share. Net income excludes the income attributable to the noncontrolling interest in subsidiaries.

A company has a **simple capital structure** if stockholders' equity consists only of common stock or if no common stock exists that upon a potential conversion or exercise could dilute (decrease) earnings per common share. We will explore in a later section how to reflect the impact on EPS of owning financial instruments or employee share-based awards that could result in an increase in common stock. If a company has several classes of common stock, the total of the weighted-average shares of the classes of common stock are used to compute basic EPS. **For a simple capital structure, a single EPS presentation showing basic earnings per share is appropriate on the face of the income statement.**

Demo 21-4 **LO21-4** **Earning per Share Calculation—Simple Capital Structure**

Demo MBC

Atlanta Co. has 300,000 common shares outstanding for the entire year of 2020, and after-tax net income of $2 million.

a. Compute basic earnings per share for 2020.

b. Show how basic earnings per share is presented in the financial statements.

continued

continued from previous page

Solution

a. **Computation of Basic EPS**

	Net Income Available to Common Stockholders		Weighted-Average Common Shares Outstanding		Per Share
Basic EPS . . .	$2,000,000	÷	300,000	=	$6.67

b. **Financial Statement Presentation of Basic EPS**

In the income statement for December 31, 2020, the company would report the following.

Income Statement	
Net income	$2,000,000
Basic earnings per share	$ 6.67

Calculation of Basic EPS **LO21-4** **REVIEW 21-4**

Compute basic earnings per share considering the following information.

Common stock, par $1, outstanding throughout 2020	100,000 shares
Net income	$245,000

Review MBC

More Practice: 21-34, 21-54

Solution on p. 21-59.

Compute EPS given share issuances, buybacks, dividends, and splits **LO 21-5**

Factors Affecting EPS Calculation

- Denominator
  - Weight shares by the fraction of the period outstanding for issuances and buybacks
  - Weight shares from the beginning of the periods presented for stock dividends and stock splits
- Numerator
  - Reduce net income for preferred dividends

LO 21-5 Overview

A number of factors cause adjustments to the numerator and the denominator in the computation of basic EPS. In the denominator, weighted-average common shares are adjusted for share issuances and share buybacks, stock splits and stock dividends. In the numerator, net income is adjusted for the impact of preferred dividends. The impact on EPS for these factors is illustrated in **Demo 21-5**.

Share Issuances and Buybacks

To properly reflect weighted-average number of shares in the denominator, shares issued and reacquired must be weighted for the portion of the period that they were outstanding. The resources made available by the issuance (or buyback) of shares during the period were available only for the part of the year for which the shares were outstanding.

260-10-45-10 Basic EPS shall be computed by dividing income available to common stockholders (the numerator) by the weighted-average number of common shares outstanding (the denominator) during the period. Shares issued during the period and shares reacquired during the period shall be weighted for the portion of the period that they were outstanding.

Stock Dividends and Stock Splits

Stock dividends and stock splits are *not* treated the same as the issuance of new stock because stock dividends and splits do not generate additional capital for the company. Current shareholders received additional shares of common stock without making any new contributions to the company. Shares issued as dividends or split shares are treated as subdivisions of the shares already outstanding. *As such, stock dividends and splits are taken into consideration by adjusting the number of shares outstanding retroactively to the beginning of the period of the earliest financial statements presented.* This means they are treated as if the new shares had always been outstanding.

To report EPS figures in comparative financial statements, all years shown are adjusted for all stock dividends and splits since the company started operations. Thus, all stock dividends and splits are automatically considered when EPS is computed for prior years. Sometimes stock dividends and splits occur after the balance sheet date but before the issuance of financial statements. In this situation, all EPS amounts shown for the period just ended and for any previous periods shown comparatively must reflect the stock dividend or split. Restatement provides the most current and relevant information for the user. A description of the effects of such dividends and splits is disclosed in notes to financial statements.

260-10-55-12 If the number of common shares outstanding increases as a result of a stock dividend or stock split . . . or decreases as a result of a reverse stock split, the computations of basic . . . EPS shall be adjusted retroactively for all periods presented to reflect that change in capital structure. If changes in common stock resulting from stock dividends, stock splits, or reverse stock splits occur after the close of the period but before the financial statements are issued or are available to be issued . . . the per-share computations for those and any prior-period financial statements presented shall be based on the new number of shares. If per-share computations reflect such changes in the number of shares, that fact shall be disclosed.

Preferred Stock Dividends

The adjustment to the numerator for preferred dividends depends on whether the preferred stock is cumulative and whether a dividend was declared. If the preferred stock is *noncumulative*, only the dividends declared for the current period are subtracted. If the preferred stock is *cumulative*, one year's dividend claim is subtracted from earnings whether or not declared. Undeclared cumulative preferred dividends must be paid before current common dividends, which is why they are subtracted even if not declared. However, only the current-year claim is subtracted. Prior years' cumulative preferred stock dividends were subtracted in computing EPS in prior years and should not be subtracted again.

260-10-45-11 Income available to common stockholders shall be computed by deducting both the dividends declared in the period on preferred stock (whether or not paid) and the dividends accumulated for the period on cumulative preferred stock (whether or not earned) from income from continuing operations (if that amount appears in the income statement) and also from net income. If there is a loss from continuing operations or a net loss, the amount of the loss shall be increased by those preferred dividends.

If the company declared *common* stock dividends, there will be no impact on the calculation above. EPS calculates the income per common share available to common shareholders. The company may choose to distribute a portion of earnings as dividends, or to retain the earnings for internal growth. In either case, there is no adjustment to the EPS calculation.

Demo 21-5 **LO21-5** **EPS Calculations—Simple Capital Structure**

Demo MBC

Example One—Basic EPS Calculation with Share Issuance

Atlanta Co. has 100,000 common shares outstanding as of January 1, 2020, and after-tax net income of $300,000 for 2020. On October 1, 2020, the company issues an additional 50,000 shares of common stock. Calculate Atlanta Co.'s basic EPS for 2020.

Solution

First, the company calculates weighted-average common shares for 2020.

Inclusive Dates	A Actual Shares Outstanding	Months Outstanding	B Percentage of Full Year*	(A × B) Weighted-Average Shares Outstanding
Jan.–Sept.	100,000	9	75%	75,000
Oct.–Dec.	150,000	3	25%	37,500
		12	100%	112,500

* Divide months outstanding by total months of 12.

continued

continued from previous page

The weighted-average number of shares outstanding is 112,500 shares and reflects the number of months shares were outstanding. This means more weight (75%) is given to 100,000 shares (than 150,000 shares) because it represents outstanding shares for a full nine months of the twelve-month period. The weighted-average common shares of 112,500 is used to calculate basic EPS.

	Net Income Available to Common Stockholders	Weighted-Average Common Shares Outstanding	Per Share
Basic EPS	$300,000	112,500	$2.67

Example Two—Basic EPS Calculation with Share Buyback

To extend Example One, let's now assume the same facts except that Atlanta Co. also purchased 5,000 common shares for the treasury on March 31, 2020. The company started the year with 100,000 shares; reduced the number of shares to 95,000 on March 31, 2020 (100,000 − 5,000) and increased the number of shares to 145,000 (95,000 + 50,000) on October 1, 2020. Calculate Atlanta Co.'s basic EPS for 2020.

Solution

First, we calculate weighted-average common shares for 2020. Again, any changes in the number of common shares outstanding must be reflected in the calculation of EPS and weighted according to the period outstanding.

Inclusive Dates	A Actual Shares Outstanding	Months Outstanding	B Percentage of Full Year*	(A × B) Weighted-Average Shares Outstanding
Jan.–Mar.	100,000	3	25%	25,000
Apr.–Sept.	95,000	6	50%	47,500
Oct.–Dec.	145,000	3	25%	36,250
		12	100%	108,750

* Divide months outstanding by total months of 12.

The weighted-average common shares of 108,750 is used to calculate basic EPS.

	Net Income Available to Common Stockholders	Weighted-Average Common Shares Outstanding	Per Share
Basic EPS	$300,000	108,750	$2.76

Example Three—Basic EPS Calculation with Stock Dividends and Stock Splits

a. To extend Example Two, let's now assume that Atlanta Co. also distributed a stock dividend of 40% on October 31, 2020. On October 31, 2020, the shares outstanding increase by 40% to 203,000 shares (145,000 × 1.4). Calculate Atlanta Co.'s basic EPS for 2020.

b. Instead of a stock dividend on October 31, 2020, now assume that Atlanta Co. declared a 2-for-1 stock split. Calculate Atlanta Co.'s basic EPS for 2020.

Solution

a. **Stock Dividend**

The company would calculate weighted-average common shares for 2020 as follows, applying the retroactive restatement adjustment of 140% (1.4) to all periods prior to the stock dividend.

Inclusive Dates	Actual Shares Outstanding	Retroactive Restatement for Stock Dividend	A Equivalent Shares Outstanding*	Months Outstanding	B Fraction of Year	(A × B) Weighted-Average Shares Outstanding
Jan.–Mar.	100,000	1.4	140,000	3	3/12	35,000
Apr.–Sept.	95,000	1.4	133,000	6	6/12	66,500
Oct.	145,000	1.4	203,000	1	1/12	16,917
Nov.–Dec.	203,000		203,000	2	2/12	33,833
				12	100.0%	152,250

* Shares outstanding × Retroactive restatement.

continued

continued from previous page

The weighted-average common shares of 152,250 is used to calculate basic EPS.

	Net Income Available to Common Stockholders	Weighted-Average Common Shares Outstanding	Per Share
Basic EPS	$300,000	152,250	$1.97

b. **Stock Split**

If the stock dividend were instead a 2-for-1 stock split on October 31, 2020, the retroactive restatement factor would be 2.0. (Had the stock dividend been instead a reverse, 1-for-2 stock split on October 31, 2020, the retroactive restatement factor would be 0.5.)

Inclusive Dates	Actual Shares Outstanding	Retroactive Restatement for Stock Dividend	A Equivalent Shares Outstanding*	Months Outstanding	B Fraction of Year	(A × B) Weighted-Average Shares Outstanding
Jan.–Mar.	100,000	2.0	200,000	3	3/12	50,000
Apr.–Sept..	95,000	2.0	190,000	6	6/12	95,000
Oct..	145,000	2.0	290,000	1	1/12	24,167
Nov.–Dec..	290,000		290,000	2	2/12	48,333
				12	100.0%	217,500

* Shares outstanding × Retroactive restatement.

The weighted-average common shares of 217,500 is used to calculate basic EPS.

	Net Income Available to Common Stockholders	Weighted-Average Common Shares Outstanding	Per Share
Basic EPS	$300,000	217,500	$1.38

Example Four—Basic EPS Calculation with Cash Dividends (Noncumulative Preferred)

Madison Co. has 100,000 common shares outstanding during 2020, and an after-tax net income of $300,000 for 2020. During the year, the company also has 20,000 shares of 4%, $10 par value preferred stock outstanding. The preferred stock is *noncumulative* and preferred dividends of $6,000 were declared and paid in 2020. Calculate Madison Co.'s basic EPS for 2020.

Solution

The preferred dividends of $6,000 are subtracted from net income in calculating basic earnings per share. With noncumulative preferred stock, dividends are subtracted in the current year when dividends are declared in the current year. (Had the company declared no dividends on noncumulative preferred stock, no adjustment for dividends would have been required.)

December 31, 2020—To calculate basic EPS with noncumulative preferred stock

	Net Income Available to Common Stockholders	Weighted-Average Common Shares Outstanding	Per Share
Basic EPS	$294,000[1]	100,000	$2.94

[1] $300,000 (net income) – $6,000 (preferred dividends).

Example Five—Basic EPS Calculation with Cash Dividends (Cumulative Preferred)

Let's now assume Madison Co. has 100,000 common shares outstanding during 2020, and an after-tax net income of $300,000 for 2020. During the year, the company also had 20,000 shares of 4%, $10 par value preferred stock outstanding. The preferred stock is *cumulative* and no preferred stock dividends were declared in 2020. Calculate Madison Co.'s basic EPS for 2020.

continued

continued from previous page

Solution

Even though no dividends were declared, because the preferred stock is cumulative, one year of dividends is subtracted in the numerator of the EPS calculation. The annual preferred stock dividend is $8,000 (4% × 20,000 × $10).

	Net Income Available to Common Stockholders	Weighted-Average Common Shares Outstanding	Per Share
Basic EPS	$292,000[1]	100,000	$2.92

[1] $300,000 (net income) − $8,000 (preferred dividends).

Calculation of Basic EPS **LO21-5** **REVIEW 21-5**

Seco Corporation was incorporated on January 2, 2020. The following information pertains to Seco's common stock transactions for 2020.

Jan.	2	Number of shares issued	150,000
Mar.	31	Number of shares issued	60,000
Jul.	1	Number of shares reacquired but not canceled	5,000
Nov.	1	150% common stock dividend	

Net income for 2020 for Seco Corporation was $825,000. The company also had 5,000 shares of noncumulative, preferred stock outstanding and paid $3,500 in preferred dividends to shareholders in 2020. Compute basic EPS for 2020.

Review MBC

More Practice: 21-35, 21-36, 21-58

Solution on p. 21-59.

Compute EPS using *if-converted* method for convertible securities

LO 21-6

To this point, we assumed that the company had a simple capital structure. *What if the company owns financial instruments that upon exercise or conversion could result in an increase to common shares?* A **complex capital structure** exists when a company owns financial instruments that have the *potential* to increase common shares. The exercise or conversion of such instruments could result in a decrease to EPS in the future. We consider the potential dilution of stockholders' interest in the company's earnings when we calculate **diluted EPS**.

LO 21-6 Overview

Convertible Bonds: Effect on Diluted EPS
- Numerator: Add back interest expense, net of tax
- Denominator: Add new common shares

Convertible Preferred Stock: Effect on Diluted EPS
- Numerator: Add back preferred dividends
- Denominator: Add new common shares

ASC Glossary Diluted earnings per share: The amount of earnings for the period available to each share of common stock outstanding during the reporting period and to each share that would have been outstanding assuming the issuance of common shares for all dilutive potential common shares outstanding during the reporting period.

260-10-10-2 The objective of diluted EPS is consistent with that of basic EPS—to measure the performance of an entity over the reporting period—while giving effect to all dilutive potential common shares that were outstanding during the period.

260-10-45-16 The computation of diluted EPS is similar to the computation of basic EPS except that the denominator is increased to include the number of additional common shares that would have been outstanding if the dilutive potential common shares had been issued. In addition, in computing the dilutive effect of convertible securities, the numerator is adjusted to add back any convertible preferred dividends and the after-tax amount of interest recognized in the period associated with any convertible debt.

A security is **dilutive** if EPS is reduced as a result of incorporating the effects of an *assumed* conversion or exercise of common stock into the EPS calculation. A security is **antidilutive** if EPS is *not* reduced as a result of incorporating the effects of an *assumed* conversion or exercise of common stock into the EPS calculation. **If a security is determined to be antidilutive, the effects of the security are *not* considered in the diluted EPS calculation.** This means we only want to consider securities that have the potential to *decrease* earnings per share without offsetting this impact by a security with a potential to increase earnings per share. At this point, we will consider only one potentially dilutive security at a time. In a later section, we will explore the impact of multiple potentially dilutive securities in a company's diluted earnings per share calculation.

Convertible Bonds and Convertible Preferred Stock

Convertible bonds (or other forms of convertible debt) and convertible preferred stock are instruments that have the potential to convert into common stock. Therefore, the effect of conversion must be considered in computing diluted earnings per share. This is accomplished by using the ***if-converted* method** to determine whether the convertible securities are dilutive and, if so, the amount needed to adjust diluted EPS.

The *if-converted* method assumes that conversion occurs as of the beginning of the period or at the date of issue, if later. This is a hypothetical calculation—no conversion to common stock has taken place during the year, but a conversion could have taken place during the year. The impact of such hypothetical conversions on EPS is shown in the **diluted EPS** calculation.

ASC Glossary If-Converted Method: A method of computing EPS data that assumes conversion of convertible securities at the beginning of the reporting period (or at time of issuance, if later).

Convertible Bonds

Convertible bonds are assumed to have been converted into common stock as of the beginning of the period (or the issue date if later) under the *if-converted* method. If we assume that the bonds are converted, the company would not incur interest expense. As a result, interest expense, adjusted for tax savings, is added back to the numerator of the basic EPS calculation and the new common shares are added to the denominator of the basic EPS calculation as we show in **Demo 21-6A**.

Effect on Diluted EPS Calculation of Convertible Bonds
Numerator: Add back interest expense, net of tax
Denominator: Add new common shares

260-10-45-40b If an entity has convertible debt outstanding:

1. Interest charges applicable to the convertible debt shall be added back to the numerator.
2. To the extent nondiscretionary adjustments based on income made during the period would have been computed differently had the interest on convertible debt never been recognized, the numerator shall be appropriately adjusted.
3. The numerator shall be adjusted for the income tax effect of (b)(1) and (b)(2).

260-10-45-40c The convertible preferred stock or convertible debt shall be assumed to have been converted at the beginning of the period (or at time of issuance, if later), and the resulting common shares shall be included in the denominator.

Impact of Net Losses on Calculation of Diluted EPS

If a company reports a *net loss* from continuing operations, the basic earnings per share amount will be negative. The dilutive earnings per share calculations will always result in a lower net loss, thus will have an antidilutive effect. Therefore, in the case of a loss from continuing operations, no potentially dilutive securities are considered; thus, **basic EPS and diluted EPS will be reported as the same amount.**

260-10-45-19 Including potential common shares in the denominator of a diluted per-share computation for continuing operations always will result in an antidilutive per-share amount when an entity has a loss from continuing operations or a loss from continuing operations available to common stockholders (that is, after any preferred dividend deductions). Although including those potential common shares in the other diluted per-share computations may be dilutive to their comparable basic per-share amounts, no potential common shares shall be included in the computation of any diluted per-share amount when a loss from continuing operations exists, even if the entity reports net income.

260-10-50-1 For each period for which an income statement is presented, an entity shall disclose . . . Securities (including those issuable pursuant to contingent stock agreements) that could potentially dilute basic EPS in the future that were not included in the computation of diluted EPS because to do so would have been antidilutive for the period(s) presented. Full disclosure of the terms and conditions of these securities is required even if a security is not included in diluted EPS in the current period.

EXPANDING YOUR KNOWLEDGE **Convertible Bonds Sold at a Discount or Premium**

If a convertible bond is sold at a discount or premium, interest expense on the income statement factors into the amortization of the discount or premium for the reporting period. This means the adjustment to the numerator described above should reflect *effective interest*. For example, let's assume that a $50,000, 10-year, 5% bond, is sold at $48,000 on January 1, 2020, and that the company's tax rate is 25%. What is the adjustment to the numerator in the diluted EPS calculation assuming that the discount is amortized using the straight-line method? *Answer*: The after-tax interest expense adjustment including the amortization of the discount of $200 [($50,000 − $48,000)/10 years] is: $2,025, computed as ([$50,000 × 5%] + $200) × 0.75.

EPS Calculations—Convertible Bonds

LO21-6 **Demo 21-6A**

Demo MBC

Net income for 2020 for Gridley Inc. is $600,000. During the entire year, 1,000, 6%, $1,000 bonds, issued at par, were outstanding, each convertible into 20 common shares. The weighted-average shares outstanding before considering potentially dilutive securities is 200,000, and the tax rate is 25%.

a. Compute basic EPS for Gridley Inc. for 2020.
b. Compute diluted EPS for 2020 using the *if-converted* method. Indicate the EPS amount(s) that the company would report in its 2020 income statement.
c. Compute diluted EPS for 2020 using the *if-converted* method, assuming instead that the convertible bonds were issued on October 1, 2020. Indicate the EPS amount(s) that the company would report in its 2020 income statement.
d. Repeat the requirements of parts *a* and *b*, but now assume that the company reported a net loss of $600,000.

Solution

a. **Basic EPS Calculation**

	Net Income Available to Common Stockholders	Weighted-Average Common Shares Outstanding	Per Share
Basic EPS	$600,000	200,000	$3.00

b. **Diluted EPS Calculation with Convertible Bond**

The impact on EPS *assuming* that all of the bonds were converted into common stock as of January 1, 2020, follows.

- **Adjustment to numerator:** After-tax interest of $45,000 is added, computed as (1,000 bonds × $1,000 par × 6%) × (1 − 25%). Had the bonds been converted at the beginning of the year, no interest would have been paid, causing earnings after tax to increase $45,000.
- **Adjustment to denominator:** 20,000 new common shares are added based on the assumed conversion (1,000 bonds × 20 shares per bond).

The impact on diluted EPS follows.

	Net Income Available to Common Stockholders	Weighted-Average Common Shares Outstanding	Per Share
Basic EPS	$600,000	200,000	$3.00
Effect of convertible bonds:			
Add back interest, net of tax	45,000		
Add new common shares		20,000	
Diluted EPS	$645,000	220,000	$2.93

continued

continued from previous page

The convertible bonds are considered dilutive because EPS drops from $3.00 (basic EPS) to $2.93 (diluted EPS). The company would report both basic EPS of $3.00 and diluted EPS of $2.93 in its 2020 income statement.

c. **Diluted EPS Calculation with Convertible Bonds (Partial Year)**
Because the bonds were issued on October 1, 2020, the number of shares assumed converted is weighted by the period over which the new shares are assumed outstanding.

- **Adjustment to numerator:** After-tax interest of $45,000 is prorated: $45,000 × 3/12, or $11,250.
- **Adjustment to denominator:** 20,000 new common shares are prorated: 20,000 shares × 3/12, or 5,000.

	Net Income Available to Common Stockholders	Weighted-Average Common Shares Outstanding	Per Share
Basic EPS	$600,000	200,000	$3.00
Effect of convertible bonds:			
Add back prorated interest, net of tax. . . .	11,250		
Add new prorated common shares.		5,000	
Diluted EPS.	$611,250	205,000	$2.98

The convertible bonds issued on October 1, 2020, are considered dilutive because EPS drops from $3.00 (basic EPS) to $2.98 (diluted EPS). The company would report both basic EPS of $3.00 and diluted EPS of $2.98 in its 2020 income statement.

d. **Basic and Diluted EPS Calculations with a Net Loss**

	Net Income Available to Common Stockholders	Weighted-Average Common Shares Outstanding	Per Share	
Basic EPS	$(600,000)	200,000	$(3.00)	
Effect of convertible bonds:				
Add back interest, net of tax . . .	45,000			
Add new common shares		20,000		
Diluted EPS.	$(555,000)	220,000	$(2.52)	antidilutive

Given a net loss, the convertible bonds are considered antidilutive because EPS increases from $(3.00) for basic EPS to $(2.93) for diluted EPS. The company would report basic and diluted EPS as $3.00 and disclose the information related to the convertible bonds with an *antidilutive* effect.

EXPANDING YOUR KNOWLEDGE **Conversion of a Convertible Bond before Year-End**

How is the diluted EPS calculation impacted if a convertible bond converts to common shares before year-end? Because a conversion is assumed to have happened on January 1, the diluted EPS amount will reflect a full 12-months of dilution. For example, let's assume Gridley Inc. has 1,000, 6%, $1,000 bonds, each convertible into 20 common shares. Assume that all of these bonds were converted to common stock on May 1, 2020. The diluted EPS calculation would include the following adjustments for the period from January 1 to May 1, 2020, assuming a tax rate of 25%.

Adjustment to numerator: $1,000,000 × 6% × 0.75 × 4/12 = $15,000.

Adjustment to denominator: 1,000 bonds × 20 common shares × 4/12 = 6,667 shares.

With these adjustments, diluted EPS will now reflect *a full-year of dilution.* This means diluted EPS will be the same in 2020, regardless if an actual conversion took place on a different day of the year or not at all.

Convertible Preferred Stock

Convertible preferred stock is assumed to have been converted into common stock as of the beginning of the period (or the issue date if later) under the *if-converted* method. If we assume that preferred stock is converted, the company would no longer pay preferred dividends. As a result, preferred dividends are added back to the numerator of the basic EPS calculation, if they were deducted when computing basic EPS, and the new common shares are added to the denominator of the basic EPS calculation as we show in **Demo 21-6B**.

260-10-45-40a The dilutive effect of convertible securities shall be reflected in diluted EPS by application of the if-converted method. Under that method: If an entity has convertible preferred stock outstanding, the preferred dividends applicable to convertible preferred stock shall be added back to the numerator. The amount of preferred dividends added back will be the amount of preferred dividends for convertible preferred stock deducted from income from continuing operations (and from net income) in computing income available to common stockholders.

Effect on Diluted EPS Calculation of Convertible Preferred Stock
Numerator: Add back preferred dividends
Denominator: Add new common shares

EPS Calculations—Convertible Preferred Stock

LO21-6 **Demo 21-6B**

Demo MBC

Let's now assume that instead of convertible debt, Gridley Inc. owns convertible preferred stock. Because convertible preferred stock has the potential to increase common shares upon conversion, the company has a complex capital structure. Current-year net income for the company is \$600,000. During the entirety of this year, 10,000 shares of 4%, \$100 par, cumulative convertible preferred stock were outstanding, each convertible into five common shares. Dividends are paid at the end of each quarter. The weighted-average shares outstanding before considering potentially dilutive securities is 200,000, and the tax rate is 25%.

a. Compute basic EPS for Gridley Inc. for 2020.

b. Compute diluted EPS for 2020 using the *if-converted* method, assuming that the preferred stock is converted into common stock as of January 1, 2020. Indicate the EPS amount(s) that the company would report in its 2020 income statement.

Solution

a. **Basic EPS Calculation**

Preferred dividends of \$40,000 (or 10,000 shares × \$100 par × 4%) are subtracted from the numerator.

	Net Income Available to Common Stockholders	Weighted-Average Common Shares Outstanding	Per Share
Basic EPS	\$560,000[1]	200,000	\$2.80

[1] \$600,000 (net income) − \$40,000 (preferred dividends).

b. **Diluted EPS Calculation with Convertible Preferred Stock**

The impact on basic EPS assuming that the preferred stock is converted into common stock as of January 1, 2020, follows.

Adjustment to numerator: Dividends saved equal \$40,000 (10,000 preferred shares × \$100 par × 4%).

Adjustment to denominator: 50,000 common shares are added (10,000 preferred shares × 5 common shares).

	Net Income Available to Common Stockholders	Weighted-Average Common Shares Outstanding	Per Share
Basic EPS	\$560,000	200,000	\$2.80
Effect of convertible preferred stock:			
Add back preferred dividends	40,000		
Add new common shares		50,000	
Diluted EPS	\$600,000	250,000	\$2.40

The convertible preferred stock is considered dilutive because EPS drops from \$2.80 (basic EPS) to \$2.40 (diluted EPS). The company would report both basic EPS of \$2.80 and diluted EPS of \$2.40 in its 2020 income statement.

FORD MOTOR

Real World—DILUTED EARNINGS PER SHARE

FORD MOTOR [F]

Ford Motor Company's basic and diluted earnings per share amounts included on the face of its income statement for the most recent year were $1.91 and $1.90, respectively. A note accompanying the financial statements included the detail necessary to recalculate the EPS calculations.

Basic EPS: $7,602/3,975 shares = $1.91

Diluted EPS: $7,602/3,998 shares = $1.90

Note 8 (Excerpt): Earnings Per Share Attributable to Ford Motor Company Common and Class B Stock
Basic and diluted income per share were calculated using the following (in millions):

Basic and Diluted Income Attributable to Ford Motor Company	2017
Basic income	$7,602
Diluted income	7,602
Basic and Diluted Shares	
Basic shares (average shares outstanding)	3,975
Net dilutive options and unvested restricted stock units	23
Diluted shares	$3,998

REVIEW 21-6

LO21-6 Calculation of EPS—Convertible Bonds and Convertible Preferred Stock

Review MBC

Example One—Calculation of EPS with Convertible Bonds

A company has outstanding $100,000 of 5% convertible bonds due in five years. Each $1,000 convertible bond is convertible into 60 shares of common stock. Net income for the year was $365,000. Common shares outstanding for the year were 205,000. The relevant tax rate is 25%.

a. Compute basic earnings per share.

b. Compute diluted earnings per share. Indicate the EPS amount(s) that the company would report in its 2020 income statement.

Example Two—Calculation of EPS with Convertible Preferred Stock

Charter Company earned net income of $248,000 in 2020. The company had 85,000 shares of common stock outstanding during the year and 1,000 shares of noncumulative preferred stock, each preferred share convertible into 4 shares of common stock, $5 par value per share. The relevant tax rate is 25%. During the year, Charter Company paid $15,000 in preferred dividends and no common stock dividends.

a. Compute basic earnings per share.

b. Compute diluted earnings per share. Indicate the EPS amount(s) that the company would report in its 2020 income statement.

More Practice: 21-39, 21-40, 21-61, 21-62

Solution on p. 21-59.

LO 21-7 Compute EPS using treasury stock method for options, warrants, and restricted stock

LO 21-7 Overview

Stock Options, Warrants, Restricted Stock: Effect on Diluted EPS
- Numerator: No effect
- Denominator: Add incremental common shares

Equity contracts, including stock options and warrants (security giving the holder the right to purchase shares of common stock), are typically exercisable at the option of the holder. Restricted stock shares are granted to employees but are restricted until the employee completes a vesting period. These potentially dilutive securities enter into the calculation of diluted earnings per share if they result in a dilution of EPS.

Stock Options and Warrants

Stock options and warrants are assumed to have been exercised as of the beginning of the period (or at time of issuance, if later). In most situations, there are no adjustments to the

Effect on Diluted EPS Calculation of Stock Options and Warrants
Numerator: No effect
Denominator: Add incremental common shares

numerator of basic EPS on the assumed exercise of options and warrants. Assumed exercise of options and warrants increases the number of common shares outstanding following the treasury stock method as we show in **Demo 21-7A**.

Recall that if an employee chooses to exercise stock options, the employee pays a designated amount of cash for those shares (presumably less than the fair value if the employee is electing to exercise the options). The accounting standards (through the treasury stock method) designate that this assumed cash receipt is treated similarly across all companies measuring diluted earnings per share. This cash is presumed to be used to help purchase shares for the treasury to then be distributed to the employees exercising the options.

Under the required **treasury stock method**, *incremental* common shares are added to the denominator of the diluted EPS calculation. Incremental common shares are calculated as new assumed common shares less shares assumed purchased for the treasury. Companies are *assumed* to use cash received upon exercise of stock options or warrants to repurchase their own common shares at an average market price for the treasury. In this chapter, assume that stock options are fully vested unless otherwise stated. Fully vested means that an employee's right to receive shares is not contingent on a service or performance condition.

ASC Glossary Treasury stock method: A method of recognizing the use of proceeds that could be obtained upon exercise of options and warrants in computing diluted EPS. It assumes that any proceeds would be used to purchase common stock at the average market price during the period.

260-10-45-23 Under the treasury stock method:

a. Exercise of options and warrants shall be assumed at the beginning of the period (or at time of issuance, if later) and common shares shall be assumed to be issued.
b. The proceeds from exercise shall be assumed to be used to purchase common stock at the average market price during the period.
c. The incremental shares (the difference between the number of shares assumed issued and the number of shares assumed purchased) shall be included in the denominator of the diluted EPS computation.

Increases in the average market price enhance the dilutive effect of options because the number of treasury shares declines. This result is consistent with the higher probability of exercise as the market price increases. On the other hand, a decrease in market price, where the market price is equal to or less than the option price, causes EPS to increase. Such options would *not* be exercised under such conditions by the investor because it would be less expensive to purchase shares directly on the market. **Therefore, equity contracts are not assumed to be exercised when the average market price is less than or equal to the exercise price.**

EPS Calculations—Stock Options   LO21-7   Demo 21-7A

Demo MBC

Options to purchase 1,000 shares of common stock are outstanding at the beginning of the year at Lax Inc. The exercise price of the options is $30 per share. The average market price of Lax Inc.'s common stock is $50 for the year. Net income for the year is $4,000 and 2,000 common shares were outstanding the entire year.

a. Compute basic EPS for 2020.
b. Compute diluted EPS for 2020 using the treasury stock method. Indicate the EPS amount(s) that the company would report in its 2020 income statement.
c. Compute diluted EPS for 2020 using the treasury stock method but now assume that the average market price of Lax Inc.'s common stock is $10 for the year. Indicate the EPS amount(s) that the company would report in its 2020 income statement.

Solution

a. **Basic EPS Calculation**

	Net Income Available to Common Stockholders	Weighted-Average Common Shares Outstanding	Per Share
Basic EPS	$4,000	2,000	$2.00

continued

continued from previous page

b. **Diluted EPS Calculation with Stock Options**
Rather than use the entire 1,000 option shares as the new shares, the assumed proceeds are used to purchase treasury shares, which reduces the 1,000 option shares to 400 incremental shares. Cash of $30,000 is calculated by taking the 1,000 options multiplied by the exercise price of $30. Then, the $30,000 is divided by $50 (average market price) to arrive at 600 shares assumed purchased for the treasury. Incremental shares are 400 or the option shares of 1,000 less the treasury shares of 600.

New shares upon exercise of stock options	1,000
Less treasury shares (1,000 shares × $30)/$50	(600)
Incremental shares	400

The impact on diluted EPS is as follows.
- **Adjustment to numerator:** No effect.
- **Adjustment to denominator:** 400 incremental common shares are added based on the treasury stock method.

	Net Income Available to Common Stockholders	Weighted-Average Common Shares Outstanding	Per Share
Basic EPS	$4,000	2,000	$2.00
Effect of stock options:			
Add incremental common shares		400	
Diluted EPS	$4,000	2,400	$1.67

The stock options are considered dilutive because EPS drops from $2.00 (basic EPS) to $1.67 (diluted EPS). The company would report both basic EPS of $2.00 and diluted EPS of $1.67 in its 2020 income statement.

c. **Stock Options—Market Price is Less than the Exercise Price**
If the market price were $10, the number of treasury shares purchased would be 3,000 [(1,000 × $30)/10], resulting in a negative 2,000 incremental shares (or 1,000 − 3,000) thereby causing EPS to increase. Therefore, in this case, the options do *not* have a dilutive effect on EPS and no diluted EPS would be reported. The company would report only basic EPS of $2.00 in its 2020 income statement.

EXPANDING YOUR KNOWLEDGE **Stock Options Exercised Before Year-End**

How is the diluted EPS calculation impacted if stock options are exercised before year-end? Because a conversion is assumed to have happened on January 1, the diluted EPS amount must reflect a full 12-months of dilution. This means diluted EPS will require an adjustment for the portion of the year *before* the conversion. (Basic EPS will reflect the new shares issued after the conversion date.)

Let's assume that 5,000 stock options are granted to executives prior to 2020, allowing the acquisition of common stock at an exercise price of $15 per share. On March 31, 2020, executives exercised all of the options. The average market price for the period of January 1 to March 31 was $22 per share. *When calculating diluted EPS, what adjustment is required to basic EPS to account for the stock options?* Answer: To reflect dilution for the full-year, an adjustment to diluted EPS is required for the months *before* conversion consisting of an addition of 398 incremental shares to the denominator, calculated as follows:

New shares upon exercise of stock options	5,000 shares
Less treasury shares (5,000 shares × $15)/$22	(3,409)
Net shares	1,591
Prorated shares for partial year (3/12 × 1,591 shares)	398 shares

Unvested Restricted Stock

While vested restricted stock is issued to employees (via outstanding shares) and included in basic EPS, unvested restricted stock is considered only in the diluted EPS calculation. Unvested restricted

Effect on Diluted EPS Calculation of Unvested Restricted Stock
Numerator: No effect
Denominator: Add incremental common shares

stock is assumed to have been exercised as of the beginning of the period (or at time of issuance, if later). In most situations, there are no adjustments to the numerator of basic EPS on the assumed issuance of unvested restricted stock. Assumed exercise of restricted stock increases the number of common shares outstanding following the treasury stock method as we show in **Demo 21-7B**. (Refer to LO 21-1 to review the reporting for restricted stock and unit awards that affect the diluted EPS calculation.)

Under the **treasury stock method**, *incremental* common shares are added to the denominator of the diluted EPS calculation. Incremental common shares are calculated as new assumed shares of restricted stock less shares assumed purchased for the treasury. **The amount of unearned compensation at a reporting date is used to calculate an assumed purchase of shares for the treasury at an average market price.** The unearned compensation is equal to the amount of compensation expense yet to be recognized on the unvested restricted stock.

260-10-45-32 Fixed employee stock options (fixed awards) and nonvested stock (including restricted stock) shall be included in the computation of diluted EPS based on the provisions for options and warrants in paragraphs 260-10-45-22 through 45-27. Even though their issuance may be contingent upon vesting, they shall not be considered to be contingently issuable shares.

EPS Calculations—Restricted Stock **LO21-7** **Demo 21-7B**

Demo MBC

100 restricted common stock shares are outstanding at the beginning of 2020 and will vest after 4 years of service. Net income for the year is $4,000, and 2,000 common shares were outstanding the entire year. The fair value of the shares on January 1, 2020, is $10 per share. For simplicity, assume that the average market price of common shares in 2020 is also $10 per share.

a. Compute basic EPS for 2020.
b. Compute diluted EPS for 2020. Indicate the EPS amount(s) that the company would report in its 2020 income statement.

Solution
a. **Basic EPS Calculation**

	Net Income Available to Common Stockholders	Weighted-Average Common Shares Outstanding	Per Share
Basic EPS	$4,000	2,000	$2.00

b. **Diluted EPS Calculation with Restricted Stock**
Rather than use the entire 100 shares as new shares in the diluted EPS calculation, the 100 unvested restricted shares are reduced by an assumed purchase of treasury shares. The treasury shares are purchased with the amount of *compensation that has not yet been expensed.* Total compensation of $1,000 is calculated by multiplying 100 shares by the market price at grant date of $10. One year of compensation has been expensed in 2020 for $250 ($1,000/4 years) leaving $750 of remaining compensation expense. Next, the $750 is divided by $10 (average market price) to arrive at 75 shares assumed purchased for the treasury. Incremental shares are 25 or the restricted shares of 100 less the treasury shares of 75.

New shares upon vesting of the restricted shares	100
Less treasury shares ($1,000 − $250)/$10	(75)
Incremental shares.	25

The impact on diluted EPS follows.
- **Numerator:** No effect.
- **Denominator:** 25 common shares are added based on the treasury stock method.

continued

continued from previous page

	Net Income Available to Common Stockholders	Weighted-Average Common Shares Outstanding	Per Share
Basic EPS	$4,000	2,000	$2.00
Effect of restricted stock:			
Add incremental common shares		25	
Diluted EPS	$4,000	2,025	$1.98

The restricted stock is considered dilutive because EPS drops from $2.00 (basic EPS) to $1.98 (diluted EPS). The company would report both basic EPS of $2.00 and diluted EPS of $1.98 in its 2020 income statement.

EXPANDING YOUR KNOWLEDGE — Stock Options Not Fully Vested

How is the diluted EPS calculation impacted if stock options are not fully vested? The treasury shares are considered purchased with the amount of compensation that has not yet been expensed along with the cash expected to be collected by the employees holding the stock options. (Refer to LO 21-2 for the computation of compensation expense and its recognition over time.) Let's assume options to purchase 1,000 shares of common stock are outstanding at the beginning of the year at Lax Inc. The exercise price of the options is $30 per share. The average market price of Lax Inc.'s common stock is $50 for the year. In addition, compensation not yet expensed related to the stock options totals $5,000. *When calculating diluted EPS, what adjustment is required to basic EPS to account for the stock options?* Answer: Incremental shares of 300 to adjust the numerator of the diluted EPS using the treasury stock method are calculated as follows.

New shares upon exercise of stock options	1,000
Less treasury shares [(1,000 shares × $30) + $5,000]/$50	(700)
Incremental shares	300

HOME DEPOT [HD]

HOME DEPOT

Real World—BASIC AND DILUTED EPS

Home Depot Inc. included both basic and diluted earnings per share on the face of its consolidated statements of earnings in a recent Form 10-K.

	2017	2016	2015
Basic weighted-average common shares	1,178	1,229	1,227
Basic earnings per share	$7.33	$6.47	$5.49
Diluted weighted-average common shares	1,184	1,234	1,283
Diluted earnings per share	$7.29	$6.45	$5.46

REVIEW 21-7 LO21-7 EPS Calculations—Options and Restricted Stock

Review MBC

Example One—EPS Calculation with Options

Lazer Inc. reported net income of $450,000 for 2020. During the year, 300,000 shares were outstanding on average and Lazer's common stock sold at an average market price of $40 per share in 2020. In addition, Lazer had 2,000 stock options outstanding as part of executive compensation. The options allow certain executives the right to purchase a total of 8,000 common shares at $25 for each share of stock under option.

a. Compute basic EPS for 2020.

b. Compute diluted EPS for 2020. Indicate the EPS amount(s) that the company would report in its 2020 income statement.

continued

continued from previous page

Example Two—EPS Calculation with Restricted Stock

Lazer Inc. granted 2,000 shares of restricted stock (common shares, $1 par) to its president on January 1, 2020, when the stock was trading at $25 per share. Net income for 2020 was $480,000 and 220,000 shares were outstanding throughout 2020. On average, the fair value of common shares in 2020 was $25 per share. The restricted shares vest after 3 years if the president remains with the company.

a. Compute basic EPS for 2020.

b. Compute diluted EPS for 2020. Indicate the EPS amount(s) that the company would report in its 2020 income statement.

More Practice: 21-41, 21-42, 21-63, 21-68

Solution on p. 21-60.

Compute EPS using *contingent* methods

LO 21-8

Contingently issuable shares are common shares of stock that will be issued only if certain conditions are satisfied such as a target income level or a target stock price. If all necessary conditions have been satisfied by the end of the period, the contingently issuable shares are considered outstanding for purposes of computing diluted EPS.

If all necessary conditions have *not* been satisfied by the end of the period, the number of contingently issuable shares included in diluted EPS shall be based on the number of shares, if any, that would be issuable if the end of the reporting period were the end of the contingency period. See **Demo 21-8.**

LO 21-8 Overview

Contingently Issuable Shares: Effect on Diluted EPS

- Denominator
  - Add shares if conditions were satisfied by period end
  - Add shares assuming the reporting period-end is the contingency period-end and conditions were satisfied at that point

260-10-45-48 Shares whose issuance is contingent upon the satisfaction of certain conditions shall be considered outstanding and included in the computation of diluted EPS as follows:

a. If all necessary conditions have been satisfied by the end of the period (the events have occurred), those shares shall be included as of the beginning of the period in which the conditions were satisfied (or as of the date of the contingent stock agreement, if later).

b. If all necessary conditions have not been satisfied by the end of the period, the number of contingently issuable shares included in diluted EPS shall be based on the number of shares, if any, that would be issuable if the end of the reporting period were the end of the contingency period (for example, the number of shares that would be issuable based on current period earnings or period-end market price) and if the result would be dilutive. Those contingently issuable shares shall be included in the denominator of diluted EPS as of the beginning of the period (or as of the date of the contingent stock agreement, if later).

Effect on Diluted EPS Calculation of Contingently Issuable Shares
Numerator: No effect
Denominator: Add new common shares meeting criteria

In these cases, the contingently issuable shares shall be included as of the beginning of the period or as of the date of the contingent stock agreement, if later.

Compute EPS Given Contingently Issuable Shares

LO21-8 **Demo 21-8**

Demo MBC

Assume Gridley Inc. reported net income for 2020 of $100,000, and 10,000 common shares were outstanding the entire year. The company had a contingent stock agreement that granted 1,000 common shares to the company's chief executive officer if net income in 2021 reached $95,000. Compute diluted EPS in 2020 and indicate the EPS amount(s) that the company would report in its 2020 income statement.

Solution

Because the company surpassed the $95,000 net income target in 2020, it is presumed that the company will reach this target level in 2021. In other words, we assume that the end of 2020 is the end of the contingency period and determine that the contingency is met at that point. Therefore, the denominator will be increased by 1,000 shares in calculating diluted EPS.

continued

continued from previous page

	Net Income Available to Common Stockholders	Weighted-Average Common Shares Outstanding	Per Share
Basic EPS	$100,000	10,000	$10.00
Effect of contingently issuable stock:			
Add new common shares		1,000	
Diluted EPS	$100,000	11,000	$ 9.09

The company would report both basic EPS of $10.00 and diluted EPS of $9.09 in its 2020 income statement.

REVIEW 21-8 **LO21-8** **Calculation of EPS Given Contingently Issuable Shares**

Review MBC

In 2020, Case Inc. initiated an agreement with its shareholders that if 2021 net income exceeded $600,000, an additional 42,000 shares of Case Inc. stock would be issued to shareholders in 2022 as a stock dividend. Compute Case Inc's basic and diluted EPS in 2020 assuming net income of $500,000 and weighted-average common shares of 385,000 in 2020. Indicate the EPS amount(s) that the company would report in its 2020 income statement.

More Practice: 21-43, 21-69
Solution on p. 21-61.

LO 21-9 Compute EPS given multiple securities and describe EPS financial statement presentation

LO 21-9 Overview

Diluted EPS with Multiple Securities
- Rank securities from most dilutive to least dilutive
- Determine the cumulative dilutive effect on EPS for each additional security

Financial Statement Presentation of EPS
- Face of the income statement
  - Income (loss) from continuing operations
  - Net income (loss)
- Face of the income statement or note
  - Income (loss) from discontinued operations

To this point, we have considered only one potentially dilutive security at a time. Diluted EPS was reported only if it resulted in a decline relative to basic EPS. If not, the security is **antidilutive** and no further disclosure is required.

In practice, companies can have several potentially dilutive securities outstanding at any one time. The order by which multiple securities are included in the diluted EPS calculation can affect the final amount reported. In response to this issue, the FASB requires that potentially dilutive securities be considered for inclusion in diluted EPS in sequence *from the most dilutive to the least dilutive*. It can be shown that this approach achieves maximum dilution (the lowest diluted EPS) as we show in **Demo 21-9**.

260-10-45-18 Convertible securities may be dilutive on their own but antidilutive when included with other potential common shares in computing diluted EPS. To reflect maximum potential dilution, each issue or series of issues of potential common shares shall be considered in sequence from the most dilutive to the least dilutive. That is, dilutive potential common shares with the lowest earnings per incremental share shall be included in diluted EPS before those with a higher earnings per incremental share... Options and warrants generally will be included first because use of the treasury stock method does not affect the numerator of the computation.

Demo 21-9 **LO21-9** **Compute EPS Given Multiple Securities**

Demo MBC

For the Palmento Company, net income for 2020 was $124,000, and 94,000 common shares were outstanding the entire year. Palmento Company holds four potentially dilutive securities. The numerator and denominator effects on the basic EPS calculation for the potentially dilutive securities are summarized and ranked as follows. The potentially dilutive securities are ranked from the most dilutive (lowest ratio of the numerator to the denominator) to the least dilutive.

continued

continued from previous page

Ranking of Potentially Dilutive Securities

Potentially Dilutive Security	Increase in Income	Increase in Number of Common Shares	Earnings per Incremental Share
Stock options	$ 0	400	$0.00
Convertible preferred stock	7,000	8,000	0.88
Series B convertible bonds.	30,000	25,000	1.20
Series A convertible bonds	9,600	6,000	1.60

Required

a. Compute basic EPS for 2020.
b. Compute diluted EPS for 2020.
c. Show the financial statement presentation of earnings per share.

Solution

a. **Basic EPS Calculation—Multiple Securities**

	Net Income Available to Common Stockholders	Weighted-Average Common Shares Outstanding	Per Share
Basic EPS	$124,000	94,000	$1.32

b. **Diluted EPS—Multiple Securities**

Now consider the effect of potentially dilutive securities on the diluted EPS calculation, in the order previously established in the ranking from most dilutive to least dilutive.

	Net Income Available to Common Stockholders	Weighted Average Common Shares Outstanding	Per Share	
Basic EPS	$124,000	94,000	$1.32	
Effect of stock options:				
Additional common shares		400		
Tentative diluted EPS.	$124,000	94,400	$1.31	dilutive
Effect of convertible preferred stock:				
Add back preferred dividends	7,000			
Additional common shares		8,000		
Tentative diluted EPS.	$131,000	102,400	$1.28	dilutive
Effect of convertible bonds—series B:				
Add back prorated interest	30,000			
Additional prorated common shares . .		25,000		
Tentative diluted EPS.	$161,000	127,400	$1.26	dilutive
Effect of convertible bonds—series A:				
Add back prorated interest	9,600			
Additional prorated common shares . .		6,000		
Tentative diluted EPS.	$170,600	133,400	$1.28	antidilutive
Diluted EPS.	$161,000	127,400	$1.26	

After considering stock options, the tentative diluted EPS is $1.31 (which is less than basic EPS of $1.32) before considering the remaining securities. Next, we consider convertible preferred stock, which results in a tentative EPS of $1.28, which is less than $1.31. This means the convertible preferred stock is dilutive and is included in the diluted EPS calculation. Next, we consider series B convertible bonds, which results in an EPS of $1.26, which is less than $1.28. This means the convertible securities are dilutive and are included in the diluted EPS calculation. This is the final value for diluted EPS because adding the remaining Series A convertible bonds (ranked fourth) would create a larger EPS amount of $1.28 which exceeds $1.26. Including the Series A bonds would be antidilutive.

continued

continued from previous page

c. **Financial Statement Presentation**

Income Statement	
Basic earnings per share	$1.32
Diluted earnings per share	1.26

Presentation and Disclosure of EPS

Companies with simple and complex capital structures must disclose basic EPS on the face of the income statement for the following, net of tax.

1. **Income (loss) from continuing operations**
2. **Net income (loss)**

EPS data must be presented for all periods for which an income statement or summary of earnings is presented. The EPS amounts for an annual period must equal the weighted-average of the EPS amounts reported on interim (quarterly) financial statements. In comparative disclosures, if any period reports diluted EPS, then all periods must report diluted EPS even if it is the same as basic EPS. If basic and diluted EPS are the same for all years presented, dual presentation can be accomplished in one line on the income statement.

260-10-45-2 Entities with simple capital structures, that is, those with only common stock outstanding, shall present basic per-share amounts for income from continuing operations and for net income on the face of the income statement. All other entities shall present basic and diluted per-share amounts for income from continuing operations and for net income on the face of the income statement with equal prominence.

Earnings per share in prior periods should be restated as a result of a declaration of stock dividends and stock splits, or a prior period adjustment due to an error or change in accounting principle. Income from continuing operations and net income exclude the income attributable to the noncontrolling interest in subsidiaries.

Income (loss) from discontinued operations must also be disclosed on a per-share basis (net of tax), either on the face of the income statement or in the notes accompanying the financial statements for simple and complex capital structures.

260-10-45-3 An entity that reports a discontinued operation in a period shall present basic and diluted per-share amounts for that line item either on the face of the income statement or in the notes to the financial statements.

For example, Target Corporation reported the following earnings per share information related to continuing and discontinued operations on the face of its Consolidated Statement of Operations in its recent report on Form 10-K.

Basic earnings per share	**2017**	**2016**	**2015**
Continuing operations	$5.35	$4.62	$5.29
Discontinued operations	0.01	0.12	0.07
Net earnings per share	$5.36	$4.74	$5.35

Diluted earnings per share			
Continuing operations	$5.32	$4.58	$5.25
Discontinued operations	0.01	0.12	0.07
Net earnings per share	$5.33	$4.70	$5.31

In a case where a company has discontinued operations, the company makes the determination of whether to report diluted EPS by considering the impact of potentially dilutive securities on income from continuing operations as indicated in the accounting guidance.

260-10-45-20 The control number for determining whether including potential common shares in the diluted EPS computation would be antidilutive should be income from continuing operations (or a similar line item above net income if it appears on the income statement). As a result, if there is a loss from continuing operations, diluted EPS would be computed in the same manner as basic EPS is computed, even if an entity has net income after adjusting for a discontinued operation.

Other disclosures required include the following:

260-10-50-1a A reconciliation of the numerators and the denominators of the basic and diluted per-share computations for income from continuing operations.

260-10-50-1b The effect that has been given to preferred dividends in arriving at income available to common stockholders in computing basic EPS.

260-10-50-1c Securities (including those issuable pursuant to contingent stock agreements) that could potentially dilute basic EPS in the future that were not included in the computation of diluted EPS because to do so would have been antidilutive for the period(s) presented.

260-10-50-2 For the latest period for which an income statement is presented, an entity shall provide a description of any transaction that occurs after the end of the most recent period but before the financial statements are issued or are available to be issued . . . that would have changed materially the number of common shares or potential common shares outstanding at the end of the period if the transaction had occurred before the end of the period.

HOME DEPOT

Real World—ANTIDILUTIVE SECURITIES

HOME DEPOT [HD]

Home Depot Inc. illustrates the calculation of diluted earnings per share in a recent annual report. Included in the notes was a description of options that were not included in the calculation of diluted earnings per share because the impact was not dilutive.

WEIGHTED AVERAGE COMMON SHARES. The reconciliation of our basic to diluted weighted-average common shares follows:

	2017	2016	2015
Basic weighted-average common shares	1,178	1,229	1,227
Effect of potentially dilutive securities	6	5	6
Diluted weighted-average common shares	1,184	1,234	1,283
Anti-dilutive securities excluded from diluted weighted-average common shares	1	1	1

Calculation of EPS—Multiple Securities

LO21-9 **REVIEW 21-9**

Review MBC

The following information relates to Jones Corporation on December 31, 2020.

Common stock, outstanding shares	140,000 shares
Convertible preferred stock, outstanding shares	25,000 shares
5% Convertible bonds	$300,000

During 2020, Jones paid dividends of $2.50 per share on its preferred stock. The preferred shares are convertible into 75,000 shares of common stock. The 5% bonds are convertible into 25,000 shares of common stock. Net income for 2020 is $820,000. Assume that the income tax rate is 25% and that the common stock, preferred stock, and the bonds were outstanding all year.

a. Compute basic EPS for 2020.

b. Compute diluted EPS for 2020.

c. Show the financial statement presentation of earnings per share for 2020.

More Practice: 21-44, 21-45, 21-60, 21-64, 21-71

Solution on p. 21-61.

Management Judgment

Share-Based Compensation

Management must make decisions on how to compensate employees (for example, through salaries, bonuses, restricted stock share awards, restricted stock unit awards, or stock options). In accounting for employee compensation, management judgment is required as shown in the following examples.

- For restricted stock awards, management must determine the fair value of the shares at the date of grant. If shares are publicly traded, estimating the fair value is not complicated. However, in cases when a company is not public or has been delisted from the market, estimating fair value requires judgment.
- Management must determine how to account for forfeitures of share-based awards: Record an estimate of forfeitures or record forfeitures as incurred. If management decides to record an estimate of forfeitures, management will need to apply judgment to determine the estimate (p. 21-4).
- For stock options, compensation expense is based on the fair value of the awards determined through an option-pricing model. The model is chosen by management and should be used consistently from period to period. The variables that are entered into the model are subjective, often including prospective information (p. 21-8). The significant assumptions are disclosed in the notes to the financial statements.
- If a stock option plan is based upon employees meeting certain performance conditions, management must determine when it is probable that the conditions will be met requiring an accrual of compensation expense (p. 21-9).

EPS Calculations

Management judgment is crucial in EPS calculations.

- The EPS calculation starts with net income. Therefore, all estimates that we have discussed in this text that impact net income through the recognition of revenues and expenses impact the calculation of EPS.
- In the use of the treasury stock method in computing EPS, companies must determine the fair value of common shares by determining the average market price (p. 21-26). As explained, when shares are not traded publicly, determining fair value is more difficult.

APPENDIX 21A LO 21-10 Describe accounting for stock appreciation rights

LO 21-10 Overview

Stock Appreciation Rights (SARs)
- Record as equity (Employer may settle with stock)
  - Estimate fair value at grant date
  - Accrue as compensation expense over requisite service period
- Record as liability (Settled with cash or employee chooses stock or cash)
  - Continually adjust liability (and corresponding expense) to align with expected cash payment

Stock appreciation rights (SARs) were developed primarily to provide cash incentives to employees and to take advantage of favorable income tax provisions. SARs plans allow executives the right to compensation equal to the appreciation in market price of stock above a specified price level.

From the point of view of the employee, stock appreciation rights have two potential advantages over stock options.

- First, the employee does not have to purchase shares of stock as is required with stock options. If a large number of shares are involved, amassing the cash necessary to exercise a stock option may be difficult for the employee.
- Second, the difference between the market price and the exercise price for the acquired shares is usually taxable income for the employee when the shares are acquired. The employee must have the resources to pay this income tax, which presents another cash-flow problem, especially if the employee plans to hold the newly acquired shares. SARs minimize these cash flow problems. While this receipt of cash is taxable, the employee has the cash with which to pay the tax.

Recording SARs as Equity

When the *employer* (not the employee) has the right to settle the SARs agreement in stock (rather than cash), the SARs is recorded as an equity instrument—see **Demo 21-10 Example One**. Similar to the accounting for restricted stock unit plans discussed in a previous section, total fair value is estimated at grant date, and compensation expense is recognized over the requisite service period on a straight-line basis. Because a transfer of assets is *not required,* no liability is recorded. In addition, no adjustment is made for changes in fair value of stock over the requisite service period.

Recording SARs as a Liability

When the *employee* has the right to settle the SARs agreement in *cash*, the SARs is recorded as a liability over the requisite service period as compensation is expensed—see **Demo 21-10 Example Two**. Because of the ultimate cash payment and the classification as a liability, the company must continually adjust the liability account to align with the expected cash payment.

718-10-25-11 Options or similar instruments on shares shall be classified as liabilities if either of the following conditions is met:

a. The underlying shares are classified as liabilities.

b. The entity can be required under any circumstances to settle the option or similar instrument by transferring cash or other assets.

EXPANDING YOUR KNOWLEDGE **Other Examples of Liability Recognition**

Besides the SARs agreements, there are other compensation awards that result in the recording of a liability because the employee has the right to settle the agreement with cash.

- **Restricted stock units with option to settle in cash** Restricted stock awards structured with a cash settlement election by employees are recorded as a *liability* (restricted stock—liability), adjusted at reporting periods for the change in the value of the common stock.
- **Stock option reward with stock sell-back option** Other times, a reward may allow the employee to sell back newly acquired shares for cash. For example, a stock option reward may be structured to allow the employee to sell back shares to the company, up to 6 months after the exercise date. The authoritative literature provides guidance on recording shares with repurchase agreements as liabilities.

718-10-25-9 A puttable (or callable) share awarded to a grantee as compensation shall be classified as a liability if either of the following conditions is met:

a. The repurchase feature permits the grantee to avoid bearing the risks and rewards normally associated with equity share ownership for a reasonable period of time from the date the good is delivered or the service is rendered and the share is issued.

b. It is probable that the grantor would prevent the grantee from bearing those risks and rewards for a reasonable period of time from the date the share is issued. For this purpose, a period of six months or more is a reasonable period of time.

Stock Appreciation Rights **LO21-10** **Demo 21-10**

Example One—Stock Appreciation Rights: Recorded as Equity

On January 1, 2020, Serenity Corporation began a stock appreciation rights plan. For each stock appreciation right, the grantee receives cash for the difference between the fair value per share of the company's common stock on the date the SARs are exercised and the market price per share on the grant date. The rights require continuing employment and may be exercised at any time between the end of the fourth year after the grant date and the expiration date. The rights expire at the end of the sixth year after the grant date or when employment is terminated, whichever is earlier. The requisite service period is from the grant date to the earliest exercise date (the vesting date), or in this case, four years.

On January 1, 2020, the company's common stock has a market price of $10 per share, and Ann Killian, CEO of Serenity, is granted 5,000 SARs under the incentive plan. The fair value of the SARs is estimated to be $25,000 as of January 1, 2020.

The fair value of the SARs is estimated to be $1.00, $3.50, $2,00 and $4.00 per unit for the years ended 2020, 2021, 2022, and 2023 respectively.

The SARs may be settled by the employer, Serenity, through the issuance of stock. Record the journal entry required for the SARs on December 31, 2020, 2021, 2022, and 2023. Assume that Killian exercises the SARs on December 3,1 2023, when the market price of the stock is $14 per share and Serenity settles the SARs in cash for $20,000 (the difference between the fair value of common stock on the exercise date and date of grant).

continued

continued from previous page

Solution

Total compensation cost is expensed over a requisite service period that is from the date of grant to the vesting date.

December 31, 2020—To record compensation expense

Compensation Expense	6,250	
Paid-in Capital—SARs Plan ($25,000/4 years)		6,250

Assets = Liabilities + Equity −6,250 +6,250
Comp Exp: 6,250 | Paid-in Cap—SARs: | 6,250

Serenity records compensation expense of $6,250 for the years 2021, 2022, and 2023.

December 31, 2023—To record the exercise of SARs

Paid-in Capital—SARs Plan	25,000	
Cash ([$14 − $10] × 5,000)		20,000
Compensation Expense		5,000

Assets −15,000 = Liabilities + Equity −20,000 +5,000
Cash: | 20,000 | Comp Exp: 6,250, 6,250, 6,250, 6,250 | 5,000
Paid-in Cap—SARs: 25,000 | 6,250, 6,250, 6,250, 6,250; balance 0

Example Two—Stock Appreciation Rights: Recorded as Liability

Refer to the information in Example One *except* now assume that the *employee* has the right to settle the SARs agreement in cash. Record the journal entry required for the SARs on December 31, 2020, 2021, 2022, and 2023. Assume that the employee settled the SARs contract in cash on December 31, 2023 for $20,000, the difference between the fair value of common stock on the exercise date and date of grant..

Solution

This method for determining annual compensation expense for SARs is illustrated in this table.

Date	A Year-End Fair Value	B (A × 5,000 SARs) Aggregate Compensation	C % of Service Period Accrued	D (B × C) Total SARs Liability Accrued	E (D − Previous Liability) Annual Expense
Dec. 31, 2020	$1.00	$ 5,000	25%	$ 1,250	$ 1,250
Dec. 31, 2021	3.50	17,500	50%	8,750	7,500
Dec. 31, 2022	2.00	10,000	75%	7,500	(1,250)
Dec. 31, 2023	4.00	20,000	100%	20,000	12,500

December 31, 2020—To record compensation expense

Compensation Expense	1,250	
SARs Liability		1,250

Assets = Liabilities +1,250 + Equity −1,250
Comp Exp: 1,250 | SARs Liab: | 1,250

December 31, 2021—To record compensation expense

Compensation Expense	7,500	
SARs Liability		7,500

Assets = Liabilities +7,500 + Equity −7,500
Comp Exp: 1,250, 7,500 | SARs Liab: | 1,250, 7,500

December 31, 2022—To record compensation expense

SARs Liability	1,250	
Compensation Expense		1,250

Assets = Liabilities −1,250 + Equity +1,250
Comp Exp: 1,250, 7,500 | 1,250 SARs Liab: 1,250 | 1,250, 7,500

December 31, 2023—To record compensation expense

Compensation Expense	12,500	
SARs Liability		12,500

Assets = Liabilities +12,500 + Equity −12,500
Comp Exp: 1,250, 7,500, 12,500 | 1,250 SARs Liab: 1,250 | 1,250, 7,500, 12,500

December 31, 2023—To record exercise of SARs plan

SARs Liability	20,000	
Cash		20,000

Assets −20,000 = Liabilities −20,000 + Equity
Cash: | 20,000 SARs Liab: 1,250, 20,000 | 1,250, 7,500, 12,500; balance 0

Accounting for Stock Appreciation Rights **LO21-10** **REVIEW 21-10**

Brum Inc. established a SARs plan on January 1, 2020, that extends rights to certain company executives that can be redeemed for cash by the employee, equal to the difference between the market price of the company's common stock ($1 par) at a pre-determined price of $15 and market price at the first exercise date. The 400 SARs can be exercised two years from the grant date and expire one year from the first eligible exercise date or when employment is terminated, if earlier. The requisite service period is considered to be two years because exercise is expected (highly probable) to occur on December 31, 2021. The fair value of the SARs is estimated to be $5.50, $3.00, and $5.00 per unit on January 1, 2020, December 31, 2020, and December 31, 2021, respectively.

a. Record Brum Inc.'s entries for 2020 and 2021, assuming that the SARs are settled for $2,000 in cash on December 31, 2021.

b. Assume the same information *except* now Brum may settle the SARs contract with common stock. Record Brum's entries for 2020 and 2021, assuming that the SARs are settled for common stock on December 31, 2021. The market price of common stock per share on December 31, 2021, is $20 per share.

Review MBC

More Practice: 21-101, 21-102, 21-103, 21-104

Solution on p. 21-62.

Questions

21-1. What is the difference between a restricted stock award plan and a restricted stock unit plan?

21-2. Explain how a company classifies share-based compensation plans for employees as either noncompensatory or compensatory.

21-3. What are the required disclosures for share-based compensation plans?

21-4. What are some factors used in the estimation of fair value in the accounting for stock option plans using a pricing model?

21-5. What is the fundamental difference in EPS computations and reporting between a simple capital structure and a complex capital structure?

21-6. Is the undeclared annual dividend on cumulative convertible preferred stock outstanding all year subtracted from net income in computing basic EPS? Why or why not?

21-7. Explain the treasury stock method as it is applied to stock options.

21-8. Is the treasury stock method's use of average market price consistent with the overall objective of EPS reporting? Explain.

21-9. Briefly, how are stock dividends and splits reflected in the calculation of basic EPS if the dividend or split occurs (a) before the balance sheet date or (b) after the balance sheet date but before the issuance of the statements?

21-10. Why are dividends from dilutive convertible preferred stock added back to the numerator of basic EPS without tax effect, while interest recognized on dilutive convertible bonds is added back to the numerator on an after-tax basis?

21-11. What is the difference between a dilutive security and an antidilutive security? Why is the distinction important in EPS computations?

21-12. A company split its common stock two-for-one on June 30 of its accounting year ended December 31. Before the split, there were 4,000 shares of common stock outstanding. How many shares of common stock should be used in computing EPS for the year? How many shares of common stock should be used in computing a comparative EPS amount for the preceding year?

21-13. Explain why nonconvertible securities do not cause a complex capital structure, whereas convertible securities do cause a complex capital structure.

21-14. Explain why and when dividends on nonconvertible preferred stock must be subtracted from income to compute EPS in both simple and complex capital structures.

21-15. Suppose a company has a convertible bond outstanding among other dilutive securities. What calculations must be made to establish an impact on EPS?

21-16. Why are potentially dilutive securities ranked (in cases of multiple security holdings), and why is it useful?

21-17. What are contingent shares, and do they need to be considered in computing EPS?

21-18. A dilutive convertible bond was issued at a premium. Explain how to compute the numerator effect for such a bond when computing dilutive EPS.

21-19. Explain in general how to handle actual conversions of convertible dilutive securities for basic and diluted EPS purposes (denominator effect only).

21-20. Shares of a parent corporation will be issued in the future based on the number of retail outlets opened by a recently acquired subsidiary. The subsidiary predicts that 10 new outlets will be opened in the next three years. However, to date, no outlets have been opened. Describe how the contingent shares would be calculated for the parent company's diluted EPS in this situation.

21-21. Would antidilutive securities be included in the calculation of diluted earnings per share?

21-22. Are the following items required to be disclosed on the face of the financial statements, or either on the face or in the notes to the financial statements?

1. Income (loss) from continuing operations
2. Net income (loss)
3. Income (loss) from discontinued operations

Brief Exercises

Brief Exercise 21-23
Recording Entries for Restricted Shares **LO1**
Hint: See Demo 21-1A

On January 1, 2020, Alaska Inc. issued a total of 1,000 shares of $10 par, restricted common stock to five executives. The fair value of the shares of stock on January 1, 2020, is $60,000. The restricted shares require a vesting period of 3 years, which is the requisite service period, and no forfeitures are anticipated.

a. Prepare the journal entry (if any) required on January 1, 2020.
b. Prepare the adjusting journal entry required on December 31, 2020.

Brief Exercise 21-24
Recording Entries for Restricted Stock Units **LO1**
Hint: See Demo 21-1B

On January 1, 2020, Alaska Inc. granted restricted stock units to five executives for a total of 1,000 shares of $10 par common stock. The fair value of the shares of stock on January 1, 2020, is $60,000. The restricted shares require a vesting period of 3 years, which is the requisite service period, and no forfeitures are anticipated.

a. Prepare the journal entry (if any) required on January 1, 2020.
b. Prepare the adjusting journal entry required on December 31, 2020.

Brief Exercise 21-25
Recording Stock Options: Compensation Expense, Exercise **LO2**
Hint: See Demo 21-2

On January 1, 2020, Holiday Inc. offered a stock option incentive plan to a top executive. The plan provided the executive 300 stock options for Holiday Inc. $1 par value, common stock at an option price of $15 per share through the expiration date of January 1, 2026. The fair value of the options based upon an option-pricing model on January 1, 2020, is $9,000. The market price at year-end of Holiday Inc. stock is $15 per share on January 1, 2020, and $18 on December 31, 2020. The requisite service period is 3 years. The options were exercised on March 1, 2023, when the market price of the stock was $20 per share.

a. Prepare the journal entry (if any) required on January 1, 2020.
b. Prepare the adjusting journal entry required on December 31, 2020, the company's year-end.
c. Prepare the journal entry required on March 1, 2023.

Brief Exercise 21-26
Recording Forfeiture of Stock Options **LO2**

Refer to the information in Brief Exercise 21-25. The options were granted as described, but instead the executive left the company on January 1, 2022. Prepare the journal entry required on January 1, 2022, assuming that the company's policy is to record forfeitures as incurred.

Brief Exercise 21-27
Determining Compensation Expense Considering Forfeitures of Options **LO2**

On January 1, 2020, Spring Co. awards 10,000 stock options to acquire 10,000 shares of common stock ($1 par value) to executives at an exercise price of $30 per share. The market price of Spring Co. common stock on the grant date is $30 per share. The options are exercisable after January 1, 2024, and expire when the employee leaves the company or on December 31, 2026, whichever is first. Management estimates through a fair value option-pricing model that total compensation expense is $130,000. The requisite service period is considered to be 4 years. Spring Co.'s policy is to record forfeitures as they are incurred. Determine compensation expense in 2021 considering 1,500 shares were forfeited in that year.

Brief Exercise 21-28
Recording Expiration of Stock Options **LO2**
Hint: See Demo 21-2

Assume the same information in Brief Exercise 21-25, except that the employees did *not* exercise the stock options due to the stock price remaining below $15 after the vesting period. Record the entry on January 1, 2026, for the expiration of the stock options.

Brief Exercise 21-29 Recording Performance Based Stock Options **LO2** *Hint:* See Demo 21-2

Through a performance share option plan, Anderson Inc. granted executives and other key employees share option awards where vesting is contingent upon meeting company-wide performance goals, including decreasing time for a new product launch and specified sales targets. The options vest over a three-year period (considered the requisite service period) and expire in 6 years. The company granted 10,000 options on January 1, 2020, for the purchase of 10,000 shares at $30 per share. The company estimates the fair value of the options to be $3 per share based upon an option-pricing model. Management believes it is probable that the company will achieve the specified performance targets defined in the performance share option plan. Record compensation expense (if any) for 2020.

Brief Exercise 21-30 Recording Performance Based Stock Options **LO2**

Assume the same information in Brief Exercise 21-29 except that in 2021, management's view changed in that it now does *not* believe that it was probable that the company will achieve the specified performance targets defined in the performance share option plan. Record any entry required in 2021 based upon the estimate change.

Brief Exercise 21-31 Recording Market Based Stock Options **LO2**

Anderson Co. approved a 10,000 share option plan for executives on January 1, 2020, for the purchase of 10,000 shares of $1 par value common stock at $30 per share *if the stock price of Anderson Co. is at least $45 a share in two years*. The options vest over a two-year period (considered the requisite service period) and expire in 3 years. The company estimates the fair value of the options to be $3 per share based upon an option-pricing model. Management does *not* believe that it is probable that the stock price will appreciate to $45 in two years. Record compensation expense (if any) for 2020.

Brief Exercise 21-32 Recording Employee Stock Purchase Plans **LO3** *Hint:* See Demo 21-3

Safe Inc. employees are all eligible to participate in a stock purchase plan. The plan allows employees to purchase $1 par value stock at a 5% discount. On January 1, 2020, employees purchased 100 shares of common stock when the market price of the stock was $30 per share. Record the journal entry for Safe Inc. on January 1, 2020.

Brief Exercise 21-33 Recording Employee Stock Purchase Plans **LO3** *Hint:* See Demo 21-3

Safe Inc. employees are all eligible to participate in a stock purchase plan. The plan allows employees to purchase $1 par value stock at a 15% discount. On January 1, 2020, employees purchased 100 shares of common stock when the market price of the stock was $30 per share. Record the journal entry for Safe Inc. on January 1, 2020.

Brief Exercise 21-34 Computing Basic EPS **LO4, 5**

At December 31, 2019, and 2020, Jet Corp. had 100,000 shares of common stock and 10,000 shares of 5%, $100 par value noncumulative preferred stock outstanding. No dividends were declared on either the preferred or the common stock in 2020 or 2019. Net income for 2020 was $1,000,000. Compute basic earnings per common share for 2020.

Brief Exercise 21-35 Computing Basic EPS **LO5** *Hint:* See Demo 21-5

Refer to the information in Brief Exercise 21-34. Assume now that the preferred stock is cumulative, no dividends were declared in 2020, and there were $50,000 dividends in arrears related to 2019. Compute basic earnings per common share for 2020.

Brief Exercise 21-36 Computing Weighted-Average Common Shares **LO5** *Hint:* See Demo 21-5

On January 1, 2020, Case Inc., had 300,000 shares of common stock issued and outstanding. Case issued a 10% stock dividend on July 1, 2020. On October 1, 2020, Case purchased 24,000 shares of its common stock for the treasury. What is the number of shares that should be used in computing basic earnings per share for the year ended December 31, 2020?

Brief Exercise 21-37 Computing Weighted-Average Common Shares **LO5** *Hint:* See Demo 21-5

Knight Company, a calendar-year firm with 100,000 shares of common stock outstanding at the start of the year, declares a three-for-one stock split halfway through the year. The next day, Knight issues 200,000 new shares in conjunction with the acquisition of a new plant. What is the number of shares that should be used in computing basic earnings per share for the year?

Brief Exercise 21-38 Determining Weighted-Average Common Shares and Computing Basic EPS **LO5** *Hint:* See Demo 21-5

Seco Corporation was incorporated on January 2, 2020. The following information pertains to Seco's common stock transactions for 2020.

Jan. 2	Number of shares authorized	80,000
Jan. 2	Number of shares issued	60,000
July 1	Number of shares reacquired but not canceled	5,000
Dec. 1	Two-for-one stock split	
Dec. 31	Net income for 2020 for Seco is $488,000	

At December 31, 2020, what is Seco's earnings per share?

Brief Exercise 21-39 Computing EPS: Convertible Bonds **LO6** *Hint:* See Demo 21-6A

A company has outstanding $100,000 of 8% convertible bonds due in five years. Each $1,000 convertible bond is convertible into 40 shares of common stock. Net income for the year was $640,000. Common shares outstanding for the year were 250,000. The relevant tax rate is 25%.

a. Compute basic earnings per share.
b. Compute diluted earnings per share.

Brief Exercise 21-40
Computing EPS: Convertible Preferred Stock **LO6**
Hint: See Demo 21-6B

Charter Company earned net income of $48,000 in 2020. The company had 10,000 shares of common stock outstanding during the year and 1,000 shares of noncumulative preferred stock, each convertible into 5 shares of common stock with $10 par value per share. The relevant tax rate is 25%. During the year, Charter Company paid $5,000 in preferred dividends and no common stock dividends.

a. Compute basic earnings per share.
b. Compute diluted earnings per share.

Brief Exercise 21-41
Computing Shares Used in EPS Calculation: Stock Options **LO7**
Hint: See Demo 21-7A

Mann Inc., had 300,000 shares of common stock issued and outstanding at December 31, 2019. On July 1, 2020, an additional 50,000 shares of common stock were issued for cash. Mann also had unexercised stock options to purchase 40,000 shares of common stock at $15 per share outstanding at the beginning and end of 2020. The average market price of Mann's common stock was $20 during 2020. What is the number of shares that should be used in computing diluted earnings per share for the year ended December 31, 2020?

Brief Exercise 21-42
Computing EPS: Restricted Stock Awards **LO7**
Hint: See Demo 21-7B

West Inc. granted 5,000 shares of restricted common stock shares at the beginning of 2020 to company managers that will vest after 4 years of service. Net income for the year is $360,000, and 250,000 common shares were outstanding the entire year. The fair value of the shares on January 1, 2020, is $25 per share. The average market price of common shares in 2020 is $25 per share.

a. Compute basic earnings per share.
b. Compute diluted earnings per share.

Brief Exercise 21-43
Computing EPS: Contingently Issuable Shares **LO8**
Hint: See Demo 21-8

On January 1, 2020, to motivate top management, Resume Inc. granted 1,000 options to purchase common stock at $10 per share to key officers if net income increased by 5% in 2020 over the prior year. The fair value of the options on January 1, 2020, is estimated to be $5,000. Resume Inc. reported net income of $50,000 in 2020, which represented a 7% increase over the prior year. How will the options affect the calculation of the company's 2020 diluted earnings per share?

Brief Exercise 21-44
Computing EPS: Multiple Securities **LO9**
Hint: See Demo 21-9

Rio Inc. had 192,500 shares of common stock outstanding throughout 2020. Net income for 2020 was $580,000. Rio Inc. had 3 potentially dilutive securities.

Potentially Dilutive Security	Numerator Effect	Denominator Effect
1	$28,000	8,250 shares
2	7,000	14,000 shares
3	0	3,000 shares

a. Compute basic earnings per share.
b. Compute diluted earnings per share.

Brief Exercise 21-45
Presenting EPS in Financial Statements **LO9**
Hint: See Demo 21-9

Lee Corp. had 200,000 weighted-average common shares outstanding in 2020 and 5,000 weighted-average preferred shares outstanding in 2020. Lee Corp. reported net income of $450,000 in 2020 and declared and paid $50,000 and $10,000 of common stock and preferred stock dividends, respectively. Lee Corp. also reported a loss from discontinued operations of $20,000, after tax. Prepare the company's presentation of earnings per share on the income statement.

Exercises

Exercise 21-46
Recording Entries for Restricted Stock Share Award Plan **LO1**
Hint: See Demo 21-1A

Restricted stock awards for 5,000 shares of common stock (par $5) are granted to the CEO of Siri Inc. The restricted shares will be awarded to the CEO after 4 years from the date of grant. The shares vest if the CEO remains with the company for the full 4 years. The market price of the stock at the date of grant, January 2, 2020, is $20 per share and increases to $25 per share on December 31, 2020. Siri records forfeitures as they occur.

Required

a. Prepare the journal entry on the date of grant, January 2, 2020.
b. Prepare the journal entry on December 31, 2020.

c. On July 1, 2023, the CEO leaves Siri Inc. Prepare the entry on July 1, 2023, to account for the forfeiture of the restricted shares of stock by the CEO. Assume that the last adjusting entry recorded for the restricted stock was on December 31, 2022.

Exercise 21-47
Recording Entries for Restricted Stock Unit Plan **LO1**
Hint: See Demo 21-1B

In late 2020, the board of directors of Arches Corp. approved a restricted stock unit plan to be awarded to select employees, including the following general terms.

- Each restricted stock unit is equivalent to one share of $5 par value, common stock of Arches Corp.
- The restricted stock units vest two years after the date of grant.
- Shares are distributed after the vesting period if the employee is still employed by the company.

On December 31, 2020, 6,000 restricted stock units were granted to key employees under this plan when the market price of the common stock was $18 per share.

Required

a. Compute the total amount of compensation cost for the restricted stock unit plan.
b. Prepare the journal entry on the date of grant, December 31, 2020.
c. Prepare the journal entry on December 31, 2021.
d. Prepare the journal entry on December 31, 2022, including the issuance of the shares of stock.

Exercise 21-48
Recording Entries for Restricted Stock Unit Plan with Estimated Forfeitures **LO1**
Hint: Demo 21-1B

On December 31, 2020, 5M Inc. approved a restricted stock unit plan to be awarded to executives, including the following general terms:

- Each restricted stock unit is equivalent to one share of $1 par value, common stock of 5M Inc.
- Restricted stock units vest three years after the date of grant, subject to forfeiture if employment is terminated prior to the end of the vesting period.
- Shares are distributed after the vesting period if the employee is still employed by the company.

On December 31, 2020, 30,000 restricted stock units were granted to key employees under this plan when the market price of the common stock was $25 per share. The company estimates that 15% of the restricted stock units will be forfeited and it is the company's policy to estimate forfeitures.

Required

a. Compute the total amount of compensation cost for the restricted stock unit plan.
b. Prepare the journal entry on the date of grant, December 31, 2020.
c. Prepare the journal entry on December 31, 2021.
d. Prepare the journal entry on December 31, 2022. At that time, the company adjusts its estimate of forfeitures to 10%.
e. Prepare the journal entries on December 31, 2023 to record compensation expense and distribution of shares, assuming actual forfeitures of 2,400 shares in 2023.

Exercise 21-49
Recording Entries for Restricted Stock Unit Plan and Forfeitures as Incurred **LO1**
Hint: See Demo 21-1B

On December 31, 2020, 85M Inc. approved a restricted stock unit plan that included the following general terms.

- Each restricted stock unit is equivalent to one share of $1 par value, common stock of 85M Inc.
- Restricted stock units vest three years after the date of grant, subject to forfeiture if employment is terminated prior to the end of the vesting period.
- Shares are distributed after the vesting period if the employee is still employed by the company.

On December 31, 2020, 30,000 restricted stock units were granted to key employees under this plan when the market price of the common stock was $25 per share. The company estimates that 15% of the restricted stock units will be forfeited and the company's policy is to record forfeitures as incurred.

Required

a. Compute the total amount of compensation cost for the restricted stock unit plan.
b. Prepare the journal entry on the date of grant, December 31, 2020.
c. Prepare the journal entry on December 31, 2021.
d. Prepare the journal entry on December 31, 2022. In 2022, 2,000 shares are forfeited.
e. Prepare the journal entries on December 31, 2023 to record compensation expense and distribution of shares, assuming an additional 400 shares are forfeited in 2023.

Exercise 21-50
Recording Stock Options: Issuance and Exercise **LO2**
Hint: See Demo 21-2

Rex Corporation is authorized to issue 300,000 shares of common stock, $1 par, of which 140,000 shares had been issued. The corporation initiated a stock bonus plan during 2020 for designated managers. Under the plan, options vest with the grantee if still employed by the company two years from the date of grant. The rights are nontransferable and expire immediately after December 31, 2024. The exercise price is $20 per share. Assume that manager Ruth Roe receives stock options on January 1, 2020, to purchase 1,000 shares of Rex common stock. The market price of Rex common stock on the date of grant was $24 per share. Using an option-pricing model, the fair value of the options granted to Roe is computed to be $12 per option.

Required

a. Compute the total amount of compensation cost for the grant made to Roe.
b. What entry should be made on the date of the grant?
c. What entry should be made at December 31, 2020?
d. Provide the entry to record the exercise of the options held by Roe on December 31, 2024, when the stock of Rex Corporation was trading at $35 per share.

Exercise 21-51
Recording Stock Options: Issuance and Exercise **LO2**
Hint: See Demo 21-2

In October 2019, Meno Corp. announced a stock option incentive plan for its top executives. The plan provides each executive 3,000 stock options for Meno's common stock, $1 par, at an exercise price of $36 per share reduced by the percentage increase in EPS from December 31, 2019, to December 31, 2021. The rights are nontransferable and are exercisable three years after the grant date and prior to five years from the grant date. Continuing employment is required through exercise date, and the requisite service period ends on the first possible exercise date.

On January 1, 2020, Martha Smith was granted 3,000 options when the market price was $30 per share. Using an option-pricing model, the fair value of the options granted to Smith was valued at $9 per option. On December 31, 2020, Meno's management believed that Smith would exercise her options at the first exercise date. By December 31, 2021, Meno's EPS had increased by 20%.

Smith exercised her options at December 31, 2022, when the market price of the stock was $60 per share.

Required

a. Compute the total amount of compensation cost for the grant made to Smith.
b. What entry should be made on the date of the grant?
c. What entry should be made at December 31, 2020?
d. Provide the entry to record the exercise of the options held by Smith on December 31, 2022.

Exercise 21-52
Recording Stock Options: Issuance and Forfeiture **LO2**

Stacy Corporation offered a stock option incentive plan to six of its top executives. During the second year from the date of the grant, but prior to the permissible exercise date, one of the six executives resigned and accepted employment with a competitor. In accordance with the provisions of the incentive plan, the stock option award for the resigned executive lapsed. At the date of lapse, the relevant account balance for all six executives combined was Paid-in Capital—Stock Options, $675,000. The requisite service period extends for three more years. The company's policy is to record forfeitures as incurred.

Required

Provide the journal entry directly related to the forfeited options.

Exercise 21-53
Recording Shares Issued through an Employee Share Purchase Plan **LO3**

Rice Corporation has a stock purchase plan with the following provision. Each full-time employee with a minimum of one year's service may acquire from Rice Corporation, its common stock, $10 par, through payroll deductions at 5% below the market price on the date selected by the employee for a stock purchase (the exercise date). The exercise decision must be made within one year from the payroll deduction date.

Employee Adams signed a payroll deduction agreement form on January 1, 2020, for $60 per month. At that date, the market price of the stock was $27 per share. At the end of 2020, Adams requested that stock be purchased equal to the amount Adams accumulated as a deposit. At that date, the market price of the stock was $25 per share.

Required

Prepare the journal entry on December 31, 2020, for the issuance of shares to Adams. *Hint:* The company credited Liability—Employee Stock Purchase Plan at the time of each payroll deduction.

Exercise 21-54
Computing Basic Earnings per Share **LO4**
Hint: See Demo 21-4

Compute basic earnings per share considering the following information.

Common stock, $10 par, outstanding throughout 2020	9,000 shares
Common stock dividends paid, 2020	$27,000
Net income	$34,000

Required

Compute the required EPS amounts.

Exercise 21-55 Computing EPS: Simple Capital Structure **LO5, 6**

At the end of 2020, the records of Block Corporation reflected the following.

Common stock, $5 par, authorized 500,000 shares	
Outstanding January 1, 2020, 400,000 shares	$2,000,000
Sold and issued April 1, 2020, 2,000 shares	10,000
Issued 5% stock dividend, September 30, 2020; 20,100 shares	100,500
Preferred stock, 6%, $10 par, nonconvertible, noncumulative, authorized 50,000 shares, outstanding during year, 20,000 shares	200,000
Paid-in capital in excess of par, common stock	180,000
Paid-in capital in excess of par, preferred stock	100,000
Retained earnings (after the effects of current preferred dividends declared during 2020)	640,000
Bonds payable, 6.5%, nonconvertible, issued at par January 1, 2020	1,000,000
Net income	164,000
Income tax rate, 25%	

Required

a. What EPS presentation is required—basic, diluted, or both?

b. Compute the required EPS amounts.

c. Compute the required EPS amounts, assuming that the preferred stock is cumulative.

Exercise 21-56 Calculating EPS: Simple Capital Structure and 3 years **LO5**
Hint: See Demo 21-5

C-Bay Inc.'s accounting year ends on December 31. During the following three years, its common shares outstanding changed as follows.

	2022	2021	2020
Shares outstanding, January 1	150,000	120,000	100,000
Sales of shares, April 1, 2020			20,000
25% stock dividend, July 1, 2021		30,000	
2-for-1 stock split, July 1, 2022	150,000		
Shares sold, October 1, 2022	50,000		
Shares outstanding, December 31	350,000	150,000	120,000

Required

a. For purposes of calculating EPS at the end of each year, determine the number of shares outstanding. *Hint:* Consider each reporting year separately.

b. For purposes of calculating EPS at the end of 2022, when comparative statements are being prepared on a three-year basis, determine the number of shares outstanding for each year.

c. Compute EPS for each year based on computations in part *b*. Assume net income is $375,000, $330,000, and $299,000, for years 2022, 2021, and 2020, respectively.

Exercise 21-57 Calculating EPS: Simple Capital Structure **LO5**
Hint: See Demo 21-5

Select Corporation was incorporated on January 2, 2020. The following information pertains to Select Corporation's 2020 common stock transactions.

Jan. 2	Number of shares authorized	250,000
Jan. 2	Number of shares issued	85,000
Jul. 1	Number of shares reacquired but not canceled	5,000
Sept. 1	Two-for-one stock split	
Dec. 1	Reissued shares of treasury stock	5,000

Required

a. Determine the weighted-average number of shares of Select Corporation's common stock outstanding.

b. Compute earnings per share for 2020 considering the following additional information:

1. Net income: $330,000
2. Preferred stock, 5%, cumulative, 5,000 shares, $10 par value per share
3. Preferred dividends declared in 2020: $0

Exercise 21-58
Calculating EPS: Simple Capital Structure **LO5**

On December 31, 2020, Americana Inc. had 175,000 shares of common stock issued and outstanding. Americana Inc. issued a 40% stock dividend on July 1, 2020. On October 1, 2020, the company purchased 20,000 shares of its common stock for the treasury, and declared a 2-for-1 stock split on December 31, 2020. American also had 10,000 shares of 5%, $20 par value cumulative preferred stock outstanding. No dividends were declared on either the preferred or the common stock in 2019 or 2020. Net income for 2020 was $1,000,000.

Required

a. Compute the required EPS amount.
b. Compute the required EPS amount assuming instead that Americana Inc. declared and paid the current year preferred dividend and one year of dividends in arrears in December 2020.
c. Compute the required EPS amount assuming instead that the preferred stock is noncumulative.

Exercise 21-59
Computing EPS: Simple Capital Structure and Net Loss **LO5**

Grace Corp. suffered a net loss in 2020 of $100,000. The company has 100,000 common shares outstanding as of January 1, 2020, and declared a 1-for-2 reverse stock split on March 31. In addition, the company bought 5,000 shares for the treasury on August 31, 2020, and 2,000 shares of stock were issued on November 1, 2020, in exchange for legal services. The company had 1,000 shares of 5%, $10 par, cumulative, nonconvertible preferred stock for the year 2020. No common or preferred stock dividends were declared in 2020. Weighted average shares outstanding in 2020 were 110,000 shares for common stock and 10,000 shares for preferred stock.

Required

Compute the required EPS amount.

Exercise 21-60
Computing Diluted EPS: Convertible Bonds and Convertible Preferred Stock **LO9**

Jones Corporation's capital structure follows.

December 31	2020
Outstanding shares of stock	
Common stock, outstanding shares	110,000
Convertible preferred stock, outstanding shares	10,000
8% Convertible bonds	$1,000,000

During 2020, Jones paid dividends of $3.00 per share on its preferred stock. The preferred shares are convertible into 20,000 shares of common stock. The 8% bonds are convertible into 30,000 shares of common stock. Net income for 2020 is $850,000. Assume that the income tax rate is 25%.

Required

a. Compute basic EPS for 2020.
b. Compute diluted EPS for 2020.

Exercise 21-61
Computing EPS: Convertible Debt **LO6**
Hint: See Demo 21-6A

Shaffer Corporation issued 100, $1,000, 10% convertible bonds in 2019 at face value. Each bond is convertible into 100 shares of common stock. Shaffer's net income for 2020 is $1,824,000 ($2,432,000 before tax). Considering all factors except convertible bonds, average common shares outstanding for 2020 are 1,010,000.

Required

a. Compute basic EPS.
b. Compute diluted EPS.
c. How do the answers to parts *a* and *b* change if the bonds were issued on July 1, 2020?
d. Ignoring part *c*, how do the answers to parts *a* and *b* change if *one-half* of the bonds were converted on July 1, 2020?

Exercise 21-62
Computing EPS: Convertible Preferred with Partial Conversion **LO6**

Bridgeman Company, headquartered in San Francisco, reported the following data for the current year.

- Net income, $2,220,000.
- Common shares outstanding at the beginning of the year, 800,000.
- Nonconvertible cumulative preferred stock, $100 par, $8 dividend per share per year, 100,000 shares outstanding all year.
- Issued 200,000 shares of common stock on October 1.
- Convertible cumulative preferred stock, $100 par, $7 dividend per share per year, 50,000 shares outstanding at the beginning of the year. On March 31, 20,000 shares of preferred stock converted to 40,000 common shares.
- For both preferred stock issues, assume dividends are paid for time held.

Required

a. Compute basic EPS.

b. Compute diluted EPS.

Exercise 21-63 Computing Diluted EPS: Stock Options **LO7** *Hint:* See Demo 21-7A

Rand Inc. had a net income of $800,000. During the year, 200,000 shares were outstanding on average and Rand's common stock sold at an average market price of $50. In addition, Rand had 20,000 stock options outstanding to purchase a total of 20,000 common shares at $25 for each option exercised.

Required

a. Compute basic EPS.

b. Compute diluted EPS.

Exercise 21-64 Computing EPS with Multiple Potentially Dilutive Securities **LO9** *Hint:* See Demo 21-9

Spencer Inc.'s 2020 earnings of $500,000 reflect a tax rate of 25%. During the entire year, Spencer had the following securities outstanding:

120,000 shares of common stock.
5,000 shares of 6%, $100 par, nonconvertible, cumulative preferred stock.
5,000 shares of 6%, $100 par, cumulative preferred stock, each convertible into 1.75 shares of common stock.
500 bonds, $1,000 face value, 8% interest, each convertible into 30 shares of common stock (issued at face value).
200 bonds, $1,000 face value, 6% interest, each convertible into 20 shares of common stock (issued at face value).

Required

a. Compute basic EPS.

b. Compute diluted EPS.

Exercise 21-65 Correcting EPS Calculation **LO5**

Zolar Corporation reported basic earnings per share of $2.18 ($22,875,000/10,500,000) based on the following data.

Net income	$22,875,000
Common shares	
January 1, 2020	12,000,000
December 31, 2020	9,000,000
Average number of shares outstanding	10,500,000

After examining Zolar's records, we note that Zolar acquired and retired 4 million shares on April 1, 2020, and issued 1,000,000 shares on September 30, 2020. No equity securities besides common stock are outstanding, and Zolar has no convertible securities or stock options outstanding.

Required

a. Is Zolar's basic EPS calculation of $2.18 per share accurate?

b. Revise the EPS calculation if we believe it is incorrect.

c. Now assume that in addition to the information provided above, Zolar has outstanding 100,000 shares of $100 par, 5% cumulative preferred, issued on September 9, 2014. The annual dividend was paid in 2020. Revise the EPS calculation.

Exercise 21-66 Calculating EPS with Multiple Securities **LO5, 6, 7, 9**

At the end of 2020, the records of Wolverine Corporation reflected the following.

Common stock, $10 par; authorized 100,000 shares: issued and outstanding throughout the year, 50,000 shares	$500,000
Preferred stock, $50 par, 7%, cumulative, convertible into common stock, share for share; authorized, 10,000 shares; issued and outstanding throughout year, 2,000 shares	100,000
Contributed capital in excess of par, common stock	80,000
Retained earnings (no dividends declared during the year)	470,000
Bonds payable, 10% nonconvertible, issued at par in 2016	150,000
Net income	120,000
Stock options outstanding (all year for 10,000 shares of common stock at $15 per share).	
Income tax rate, 25%.	
Average market price of the common stock during 2020, $25 per share.	

Required

a. Is this a simple or a complex capital structure?

b. Compute the required EPS amounts.

Exercise 21-67
Calculating EPS with Convertible Debt **LO5, 6**

At the end of 2020, the records of Ruso Corporation reflected the following.

Common stock, no-par, authorized 250,000 shares: issued and outstanding throughout the period to December 1, 2020, 60,000 shares. A 2-for-1 stock split was issued on December 1, 2020.	$840,000
Preferred stock, 5%, $10 par, nonconvertible, cumulative, nonparticipating, shares authorized, issued, and outstanding during year, 10,000 shares	100,000
Contributed capital in excess of par, preferred stock	30,000
Retained earnings (no cash or property dividends during year)	570,000
Bonds payable, 8%, issued January 1, 2020; each $1,000 bond is convertible into 60 shares of common stock after the stock split on December 1, 2020 (bonds initially sold at par)	200,000
Net income	72,000
Income tax rate, 25%.	

Required

a. Is this a simple or a complex capital structure?
b. Compute the required EPS amounts.

Exercise 21-68
Calculating EPS with Restricted Stock **LO7**
Hint: See Demo 21-7B

StarStruck Inc. granted 500 shares of restricted stock (common shares, $1 par) to its president on January 1, 2020, when the stock was trading at $40 per share. Net income for 2020 was $250,000 and 40,000 shares were outstanding throughout 2020. On average, the fair value of common shares in 2020 was $40 per share. The restricted shares vest after 3 years if the president remains with the company.

Required

a. Compute basic EPS.
b. Compute diluted EPS

Exercise 21-69
Calculating Diluted EPS: Contingent Shares **LO8**
Hint: See Demo 21-8

In 2020, Xonacs acquired Realtest Service. The acquisition agreement included a commitment by Xonacs to the shareholders of Realtest that if 2021 net income exceeded $250,000, an additional 50,000 shares of Xonacs stock would be issued to the shareholders in 2022. Realtest's net income in 2020 was $255,000.

Required

a. How many contingent shares would Xonacs recognize in its calculation of 2020 diluted EPS?
b. Suppose Realtest's earnings in 2020 were $200,000. How many contingent shares would Xonacs recognize in its calculation of 2020 diluted EPS?

Exercise 21-70
Analyzing EPS **LO5, 6, 7, 8**

Match each separate scenario to the list of possible impacts on the EPS calculation below. Assume a simple capital structure unless the scenario indicates otherwise. Ignore the possibility of antidilutive securities and the initial impact on net income of a particular transaction.

Scenario	Impact on EPS Calculation
____ 1. Noncumulative, 7% preferred stock dividend with no dividend declaration.	*a.* Effects numerator in basic EPS calculation.
____ 2. Cumulative, 7% preferred stock dividend with no dividend declaration.	*b.* Effects denominator in basic EPS calculation.
____ 3. Issuance of stock options.	
____ 4. Retirement of common shares.	*c.* Effects numerator in diluted EPS calculation.
____ 5. Stock dividend declared during the year.	
____ 6. Stock dividend declared after the calendar year but before financial statements are issued.	*d.* Effects denominator in diluted EPS calculation.
____ 7. Stock split.	*e.* No impact on EPS calculation.
____ 8. Issuance of convertible noncumulative preferred stock with no dividend declaration.	
____ 9. Issuance of convertible bonds.	
____ 10. Conditions for issuance are met for unissued contingent shares.	
____ 11. Purchase of shares for the treasury.	
____ 12. Granting of restricted common stock (not vested).	

Required

Match each term, 1 through 12 with its impact on the EPS calculation, *a* through *e*. A scenario may have more than one impact on the EPS calculation.

Exercise 21-71 Financial Statement Presentation of EPS **LO9**

To illustrate EPS reporting for various combinations of gains and losses, assume that 1,000 weighted-average shares of common stock for basic EPS are outstanding for each of the four cases below. Also assume preferred stock dividends of $2,500 were paid during the year.

	Case A	Case B	Case C	Case D
Income (loss) continuing operations.	$10,000	$(10,000)	$10,000	$(10,000)
Income (loss) from discontinued operations.	3,000	(3,000)	(3,000)	6,000

Required

Show the EPS financial statement presentation for basic EPS for each Case *A* through *D*.

Exercise 21-72 Reporting EPS: Discontinued Operations **LO9**

Taft Corporation had after-tax income from continuing operations of $6.7 million for 2020. Taft also reported a $1.23 million after-tax loss on the disposal of its textile subsidiary. Taft uses a calendar-year reporting period. Taft's capital structure consists of the following.

- Preferred: 100,000 shares of $100 par, 8% cumulative nonconvertible preferred issued in 2020. No dividends were paid in the current year.
- Common: Outstanding January 1, 2020, 4,271,865 shares, $1 par. Dividends of $1.00 per share were paid in 2020. On July 1, 2020, a three-for-one stock split was declared and the shares were issued.

Required

a. What type of capital structure does Taft have (simple or complex)?
b. Compute relevant EPS amounts.
c. Show the EPS presentation for financial reporting.

Problems

Problem 21-73 Recording Entries for Restricted Stock Share Awards and Restricted Stock Unit Awards **LO1**

On January 1, 2020, the board of directors of Bunting Inc. granted restricted stock awards to 10 key employees to acquire 2,000 shares each under the following terms.

- Restricted stock awards vest on December 31, 2021. Grantees must remain employed with Bunting Inc. to receive the common shares of stock without restrictions. The requisite service period is considered to be 2 years.
- Each stock award represents one share of $10 par, common stock of Bunting Inc.

On the date of grant, the common shares were trading at $40 per share. During 2020 and 2021, the average price of common stock was $45 and $50 per share, respectively.

Required

a. Prepare the journal entry on the date of grant, January 1, 2020.
b. Prepare the journal entry on December 31, 2020.
c. Assume instead that the board of directors granted each of the 10 employees 2,000 restricted stock units instead of restricted stock awards. Each restricted stock unit represents one share of common stock of Bunting Inc. Prepare the journal entries on January 1, 2020, and on December 31, 2020.
d. What is the net impact on stockholders' equity on December 31, 2020, for restricted stock awards in part *a*? What is the net impact on stockholders' equity on December 31, 2020, for restricted stock units in part *c*?

Problem 21-74 Recording Entries for Stock Options **LO2**

Baxter Furniture Corporation is authorized to issue 30,000 shares of common stock, $1 par, of which 16,000 are outstanding; issue price $8 per share. On January 1, 2020, the company initiated a stock incentive plan for many employees. The plan provides for each qualified executive to receive options for 200 shares of the common stock. Subject to continued employment, the option is exercisable at any time after four years and prior to expiration, which is five years from the date of grant. The options are nontransferable, and the specified exercise price for the options is to be set equal to the grant date market price of the stock. The option is compensation, and any compensation cost is to be prorated equally for the period from the date of grant to the first exercise (vesting) date, which is four years or the requisite service period. The company's policy is to record forfeitures as incurred.

On January 1, 2020, 10 employees were each granted options to acquire 200 shares (per employee) under the plan when the market price of the stock was $30. The Black-Scholes option-pricing model is used, with estimates provided by management, to compute the fair value of an option. The fair value at the grant date of the options is $30,000.

All vested options are exercised just prior to their expiration on December 28, 2024, when the market price of the stock was $50 per share.

Required

a. Record the entry to record compensation cost for 2020.

b. At December 31, 2022, 2 grantees are no longer employed by the company. Record the entries to record the forfeiture by 2 grantees and to record compensation costs on December 31, 2022.

c. Record the entries for the exercise of all remaining vested options on December 28, 2024.

Problem 21-75
Recording and Analyzing Stockholders' Equity Transactions **LO2, 3**

Haywood Publishing Corporation is a publicly owned company whose shares are traded on a national stock exchange. At December 31, 2019, Haywood had 50 million shares of $10 par value common stock authorized, of which 30 million shares were issued and 28 million shares were outstanding. The stockholders' equity accounts at December 31, 2019, had the following balances ($ millions).

Common stock	$300
Paid-in capital in excess of par	160
Retained earnings	100
Treasury stock (at cost)	(36)

During 2020, Haywood had the following transactions.

Feb. 1	Another distribution of 4,000,000 shares of $10 par value common stock was completed. The stock was sold to the public at $18 per share.
Mar. 1	Haywood reacquired 40,000 shares of its common stock for $18.50 per share.
Mar. 31	Haywood declared a semiannual cash dividend on common stock of $.10 per share, payable on April 30, 2020, to stockholders of record on April 10, 2020.
Apr. 15	When the option price of outstanding stock options was $20 each and the market price of the common stock was $22 per share, 60,000 stock options were exercised. The fair value of the options at the date of grant was determined to be $1 per option. Haywood issued new shares to settle the transaction.
Apr. 30	Employees purchased 200,000 shares under a noncompensatory stock purchase plan at a 5% discount. The shares were trading at $20 per share at the date of purchase. Haywood issued new shares to settle the transaction.
May 31	When the market price of the common stock was $23 per share, Haywood declared a 5% stock dividend distributable on July 1, 2020, to stockholders of record on June 1, 2020. Immediately after issuance of the dividend shares, the market price of the common stock was $20.

Required

a. Prepare the journal entries for the stockholders' equity transactions.

b. Determine whether Haywood's net stockholders' equity increases, decreases, or remains unchanged for each transaction above.

Problem 21-76
Presenting Earnings per Share: Convertible Bonds **LO4, 5, 6, 9**

At the end of 2020, the records of Richardson Corp. included the following.

Common stock, no-par, authorized 400,000 shares:	
Outstanding January 1, 2020, 250,000 shares	$1,650,000
Treasury shares acquired June 1, 2020, 1,000 shares (at cost)	(15,000)
Stock dividend issued, November 1, 2020, 24,900 shares (10%, one additional share for each 10 shares outstanding)	398,000
Preferred stock, 4%, $20 par, noncumulative, nonconvertible, authorized, issued, and outstanding throughout the year, 10,000 shares	200,000
Paid-in capital in excess of par, preferred stock	75,000
Retained earnings (no cash or property dividends declared during 2020)	942,000
Bonds payable, Series A, 7%, each $1,000 bond is convertible to 20 shares of common stock after stock dividend (bonds issued at par in 2017)	50,000
Bonds payable, Series B, 6%, each $1,000 bond is convertible to 57 shares of common stock after stock dividend (bonds issued at par in 2018)	400,000
Net income	395,000
Income tax rate for 2020, 25%.	

Required

a. Is this a simple or a complex capital structure?

b. Prepare the EPS presentation.

Problem 21-77
Presenting Earnings per Share: Stock Options, Convertible Preferred Stock, and Convertible Bonds **LO5, 6, 7, 9**

Sharp Inc. is preparing its EPS presentation at December 31, 2020. The records of the company provide the following information.

Liabilities	
Convertible bonds payable, 7% (each $1,000 bond is convertible to 100 shares of common stock)	$150,000
Stockholders' Equity	
Common stock, no-par, authorized 100,000 shares:	
Outstanding January 1, 2020, 59,000 shares	214,000
Sold and issued 10,000 shares on April 1, 2020	40,000
Preferred stock, $10 par, 6%, cumulative, convertible (each share is convertible into 0.50 share of common stock), authorized 10,000 shares, outstanding during 2020, 5,000 shares	50,000
Contributed capital in excess of par, preferred stock	15,000
Retained earnings	452,000

Additional data

- Stock options: 4,000 options with an option price of $4 per share; average market price of the common stock during 2020, $6.
- Convertible bonds: issue price, par.
- Net income: $130,000.
- Income tax rate, 25%.

Required

a. Is this a simple or a complex capital structure?
b. What kind of EPS presentation is required?
c. Prepare the required EPS presentation for 2020.

Problem 21-78
Computing Earnings per Share: Stock Options **LO5, 7**

Falcon Company has a compensatory stock option plan under which options to buy 255,000 common shares were issued in 2019. These options are exercisable during 2020 and 2021 at $16 per share. In 2020, Falcon reported net income of $500,000; the company's capital structure remained unchanged that year.

Outstanding stock consists of 1 million common shares, which traded at an average price of $20 per share throughout 2020. The company's long-term debt consists of a $2,500,000 bond issue sold at par, which pays 12% annual interest and was outstanding throughout 2020. Falcon had no other debt. Falcon's income tax rate is 25%.

Required

a. Compute basic and diluted EPS for 2020.
b. Assume instead that Falcon issued the stock options on July 1, 2020 and that the market price of Falcon's stock averaged $22 per share throughout the last half of 2020. Compute diluted EPS for 2020.

Problem 21-79
Presenting Earnings per Share: Convertible Bonds and Stock Options **LO5, 6, 7, 9**

The records of Jefferson Corporation reflected the following data at the end of 2020.

Liabilities	
Bonds payable, 5%, convertible (each $1,000 bond is convertible to 40 shares of common stock)	$150,000
Stockholders' Equity	
Common stock, $2 par, authorized 400,000 shares	
Outstanding January 1, 2020, 150,000 shares	300,000
Sold and issued on October 1, 2020, 20,000 shares	40,000
Preferred stock, 6%, $5 par, nonconvertible, cumulative; authorized 100,000 shares;	
Outstanding during 2020, 20,000 shares	100,000
Paid-in capital in excess of par, common stock	375,000
Paid-in capital in excess of par, preferred stock	45,000
Retained earnings	280,000
Additional Information	
Net income	150,000
Common stock options outstanding (all year for 6,000 shares).	
Stock options: option price, $3 per share; average market price of common stock during 2020, $3.60 per share.	
Convertible bonds: issue price, par.	
Income tax rate, 25%	

Required

1. Is this a simple or a complex capital structure?
2. What kind of EPS presentation is required?
3. Prepare the required EPS presentation for 2020.

Problem 21-80 Presenting Earnings per Share: Convertible Bonds **LO5, 6, 9**

At the end of 2020, the records of Luholtz Corporation showed the following.

Common stock, no-par, authorized 500,000 shares; issued and outstanding throughout period, 100,000 shares	$680,000
Stock dividend issued, December 31, 2020, 50,000 shares (not included in the 100,000 shares above).	340,000
Retained earnings (after effect of dividends on all shares)	500,000
Bonds payable, 4.5%; each $1,000 bond is convertible to 80 shares of common stock after the stock dividend (bonds issued at par in 2018)	100,000
Bonds payable, 6.5%; each $1,000 bond is convertible to 90 shares of common stock after the stock dividend (bonds issued at par in 2018)	300,000
Net income	222,000
Income tax rate, 25%.	

Required

Prepare the required EPS presentation for 2020.

Problem 21-81 Computing Earnings per Share with a Net Loss **LO5, 6, 7**

Wilson Corporation's financial statements at December 31, 2020, reported the following.

Accrued interest payable	$ 1,000
Long-term notes payable, 10%, due 2023	50,000
Bonds payable, 7%; each $1,000 of face value is convertible into 90 shares of common stock; bonds mature in 2014, issued at par in 2018	800,000
Preferred stock, 5%, nonconvertible, cumulative, $100 par, issued in 2011	300,000
Common stock, $5 par, outstanding all year	700,000
Common stock options outstanding all year entitling holders to acquire 40,000 shares of common stock at $9 per share	200,000
Net loss for 2020	(125,000)

Additional data

- 1,000 shares of preferred stock were issued at par on July 1, 2020. Dividends are paid semiannually, on May 31 and November 30. On newly issued shares, dividends are prorated from issue date.
- Average market price of common stock during 2020 was $10.
- Wilson's income tax rate is 25%.

Required

a. Compute the basic EPS amount that Wilson must report on the income statement for 2020.
b. Compute the diluted EPS amount that Wilson must report on the income statement for 2020.

Problem 21-82 Computing EPS: Contingently Issuable Shares **LO8**

PellCo is subject to an agreement whereby it must issue shares to shareholders of a company it acquired in 2020, if certain conditions are met. These shares are issuable the year following the year in which the relevant conditions are met. The agreement specifies:

1. PellCo will issue 20 shares for each $1,000 in net income of the combined enterprise in excess of $100,000.
2. PellCo will issue 1,000 shares for each new patent awarded to the recently acquired subsidiary (a research enterprise) during the year.
3. PellCo will issue 50 shares for each $5 increase in the market price of PellCo's stock above the price at the beginning of the year.

Data for 2020 follows.

Year	Patents Awarded	Beginning Stock Price	Ending Stock Price	Earnings
2020	3	$30	$41	$190,000

Required

a. Determine the contingent shares to be included in basic EPS for 2020.
b. Determine the contingent shares to be included in diluted EPS for 2020.

Problem 21-83
Calculating EPS and Recording Entries for Restricted Stock Awards **LO1, 7**

As an incentive to retain key employees, on January 1, 2020, the board of directors of Master Corp. awarded restricted stock awards to 5 executives to acquire 500 shares each under the following terms.

- Restricted stock awards vest on December 31, 2022. Grantees must remain employed with Master Corp. to receive the common shares of stock for 3 years (the requisite service period) for the shares to be fully vested.
- Each stock award represents one share of $10 par, common stock of Master Corp.

Master Corp. has 10,000 common shares outstanding during 2020. Net income for 2020 was $50,000. On the date of grant, the common shares were trading at $20 per share. During 2020, the average price of common stock was $20.

Required

a. Prepare the journal entry on the date of grant, January 1, 2020.
b. Prepare the journal entry on December 31, 2020.
c. Calculate 2020 basic EPS.
d. Calculate 2020 diluted EPS.

Problem 21-84
Reporting EPS: Discontinued Operations **LO9**

Moore Inc., an international tea merchant, has a complex capital structure with several potentially dilutive securities. The following information pertains to the current year.

- Common stock, 10,000 shares
- Options to purchase 2,000 shares at $8. The average market price of common stock for the year was $12.
- 500, 6%, $1,000 bonds, each convertible into 10 shares of common stock (issued at face value)
- 200, 8%, $1,000 bonds, each convertible into 30 shares of common stock (issued at face value)
- 1,000 shares of 9%, $100 par cumulative preferred stock, each convertible into 6 shares of common stock
- No options or warrants were exercised or converted during the period.
- Tax rate is 25%.
- Income from continuing operations, $60,000
- Gain from discontinued operations, net of tax, $10,000

Required

Prepare the required EPS presentation for the current year. Assume all per-share amounts are shown in the income statement.

Accounting Decisions and Judgments

AD&J 21-85
Analyzing EPS through Financial Statement Reporting **LO4, 5, 6, 7, 8, 9**

Real World Analysis This assignment should be worked using the most recent available annual financial statements of PepsiCo and Coca Cola. Consider the data on each company's EPS. If we were constrained to consider only the EPS data, how would we respond to the question as to which company appears to be more successful? If, as would be the case in practice, we could consider the additional material in the financial statements, what would we conclude? Can we identify other sources of relevant data? Do EPS amounts necessarily indicate how effectively a company is managing its resources?

AD&J 21-86
Analyzing EPS through Financial Statement Presentation **LO4, 5, 6, 7, 8, 9**

Real World Analysis Home Depot Inc. reported the following information in its fiscal year ended January 31, 2016, consolidated statement of earnings.

Net earnings	$ 7,009 million
Basic earnings per share	5.49
Diluted earnings per share	5.46

Required

a. Estimate the average number of common shares outstanding for its fiscal year ended January 31, 2016.
b. Does Home Depot have a simple or a complex capital structure?
c. If diluted weighted-average common shares were 1,283 million, recompute diluted EPS.
d. Based on part *c*, what type(s) of dilutive securities would we assume Home Depot reported in its financial statements?

AD&J 21-87
Recalculating and Analyzing EPS from Financial Report **LO4, 5, 6, 7, 8, 9**

Real World Analysis Locate the December 31, 2015, Form 10-K for the **Coca-Cola Company** and answer the following questions.

a. What EPS values for net income did the Coca-Cola Company report for 2015?

b. Recalculate Coca-Cola Company's basic earnings per share and diluted earnings per share for 2015.

c. Does Coca-Cola have any convertible securities? Does it have any stock options outstanding on December 31, 2015?

d. Does Coca-Cola have a simple or a complex capital structure?

e. What is the fair value of options granted during 2015? *Hint:* See Note 12 accompanying the financial statements.

AD&J 21-88
Analyzing EPS Presentation and Dilutive Securities **LO4, 5, 6, 7, 8, 9**

Real World Analysis In its 2014 annual statement, **Pfizer** reports the following information on its income statement.

Net income before allocation to noncontrolling interests ($ millions)	$9,168
Earnings per common share—basic	
Income from continuing operations	$ 1.43
Discontinued operations, net of tax	0.01
Net income	$ 1.44
Earnings per common share—diluted	
Income from continuing operations	$ 1.41
Discontinued operations, net of tax	0.01
Net income	$ 1.42
Weighted-average shares—basic	6,346
Weighted-average shares—diluted	6,424

The 2013–2014 section of Pfizer's Consolidated Statement of Stockholders' Equity is shown below.

	Pfizer Inc. Shareholders											
	Preferred Stock		Common Stock			Treasury Stock						
(Millions, Except Preferred Shares)	Shares	Stated Value	Shares	Par Value	Add'l Paid-In Capital	Shares	Cost	Retained Earnings	Accum. Other Comp. Loss	Share-holders' Equity	Non-controlling Interests	Total Equity
Balance, December 31, 2013	829	$33	9,051	$453	$77,283	(2,652)	$(67,923)	$69,732	$(3,271)	$76,307	$313	$76,620
Net income								9,135		9,135	32	9,168
Other comprehensive income/(loss), net of tax									(4,045)	(4,045)	3	(4,042)
Cash dividends declared:												
Common stock								(6,690)		(6,690)		(6,690)
Preferred stock								(2)		(2)		(2)
Noncontrolling interests											(6)	(6)
Share-based payment transactions			59	3	1,693	(2)	(100)			1,597		1,597
Purchases of common stock						(165)	(5,000)			(5,000)		(5,000)
Preferred stock conversions and redemptions	(112)	(4)			(4)	—	1			(8)		(8)
Other	—	—	—	(1)	5	—	—	—	—	5	(22)	(17)
Balance, December 31, 2014	717	$29	9,110	$455	$78,977	(2,819)	$(73,021)	$72,176	$(7,316)	$71,301	$321	$71,622

Required

a. Pfizer reports EPS for discontinued operations net of tax of $48 million.
1. Is Pfizer required to report both basic and diluted EPS for discontinued operations?
2. Is Pfizer required to report EPS for discontinued operations in its financial statement?

b. Pfizer's balance sheet shows that 9,110 million common shares were issued through December 31, 2014. Why is this amount of 9,110 materially different from the weighted-average shares of 6,346? Explain.

c. Suppose that among Pfizer's outstanding long-term debt there is a $400 million, 10-year, 6% convertible bond that was issued April 1, 2014, at 106. One $1,000 bond is convertible into 20 shares of Pfizer common stock. Determine the additional impact of this bond issue alone, if any, on the items below (use a tax rate of 25%). Assume the bond premium is amortized using the straight-line method.
1. Basic EPS for 2014?
2. Diluted EPS for 2014?

d. Suppose that Pfizer has contingently issuable shares. What effect, if any, would this have on basic EPS? Explain.

e. We see that Pfizer does not report EPS amounts for comprehensive income. Why?

AD&J 21-89 Estimating EPS from Statement of Equity **LO4, 5, 6, 7, 8, 9**

Real World Analysis Below is an excerpt from the Consolidated Statement of Equity for PepsiCo Inc. for the fiscal year ended 2014.

Consolidated Statement of Equity†
PepsiCo, Inc. and Subsidiaries

Fiscal Year Ended December 27, 2014	Shares	Amount
Preferred Stock	0.8	$ 41
Repurchased Preferred Stock		
Balance, beginning of year	(0.6)	(171)
Redemptions	(0.1)	(10)
Balance, end of year	(0.7)	$ (181)
Common Stock		
Balance, beginning of year	1,529	$ 25
Repurchased common stock	(41)	—
Balance, end of year	1,488	$ 25
Capital in Excess of Par Value		
Balance, beginning of year		$ 4,095
Stock-based compensation expense		297
Stock option exercises, RSUs, PSUs and PEPunits converted		(200)
Withholding tax on RSUs and PSUs converted		(91)
Other		14
Balance, end of year		$ 4,115
Retained Earnings		
Balance, beginning of year		$46,420
Net income attributable to PepsiCo		6,513
Cash dividends declared—common		(3,814)
Cash dividends declared—preferred		(1)
Cash dividends declared—RSUs and PSUs		(26)
Balance, end of year		$49,092

† Definitions: RSU: restricted stock units; PSU: performance stock units; PEPunits: PepsiCo equity performance units.

Required

a. Using this information, estimate basic earnings per share. What additional information would be required to compute the reported basic earnings per share?

b. Would we expect the company to report diluted earnings per share? Why or why not?

AD&J 21-90 Explaining the Impact of Dilutive Securities on EPS **LO4, 5, 6, 7, 8, 9**

Judgment Case Many believe that earnings per share is crucial to most financial statement users. Together with earnings, it is also the most commonly reported statistic about a company's yearly activities. Discuss the following issues.

a. If a convertible debenture exists, when is it considered in calculating EPS? Why?

b. When a convertible debenture exists, if it is dilutive, what calculations must be made?

c. In applying the treasury stock method, why must the company first use the funds to repurchase common shares for the treasury?

d. If a 10% stock dividend is issued halfway through the year, how many additional shares are added to the denominator of the EPS calculation? Does the answer change if the same number of shares is issued for cash? Why?

AD&J 21-91 Analyzing a Stock Option Compensation Plan **LO2**

Judgment Case

a. When is a stock option plan compensatory?

b. Is it possible for a stock option plan to qualify as a compensatory plan according to the criteria yet require no compensation expense to be recorded? Explain.

c. Is total compensation expense recorded for a compensatory plan for a grantee typically equal to the actual compensation received by the grantee?

AD&J 21-92
Presenting EPS: Issuance of Convertible Bonds Sold at a Premium; Partial Year **LO6**

Challenge Problem Records of Watson Corporation reflected the following information for 2020.

Common stock, no-par, authorized 500,000 shares	
Outstanding January 1, 2020, 150,000 shares	$256,000
Sold and issued on August 1, 2020, 15,000 shares	30,000
Bonds payable, 6% convertible	150,000
Premium on bonds payable	13,800
Retained earnings	900,000
Net income	360,000

The convertible bonds were issued on July 1, 2020, to yield 4.03%. Interest is paid semiannually on January 1 and July 1. Each $1,000 bond is convertible to 20 shares of common stock. Premium amortization related to the bonds during 2020 was $1,200. Watson's income tax rate during 2020 was 25%.

Required

a. Is this a simple or a complex capital structure?
b. Prepare the required EPS presentation for 2020.

AD&J 21-93
Computing EPS: Cumulative Preferred Stock, Stock Dividends, Partial Year **LO5, 6**

Challenge Problem Zorbas Inc. must compute EPS for its 2020 reports. The following information is available to the controller.

- Net income is $30 million (before tax it is $50 million).
- Common stock (20 million shares authorized; 15 million shares outstanding January 1, 2020).
- Cumulative convertible preferred stock (2 million shares issued August 1, 2017, and outstanding January 1, 2020). The stock was issued at $50 a share with a yearly $4 dividend paid semiannually on June 30 and December 31. The stock is convertible on a share-for-share basis adjusted automatically for any stock dividends or splits. Dividends are paid for time stock is held.
- March 1, 2020: Half of the preferred stock was converted to common stock.
- April 1, 2020: Zorbas declared a 10% stock dividend.
- July 1, 2020: One million shares of stock were issued in the acquisition of Tande Corporation. The stock's fair value at this time was $15 a share.
- October 1, 2020: Zorbas purchased and retired 600,000 shares of its common stock for $700,000.
- All preferred dividends were declared and paid.

Required

a. Compute the number of shares to be used in computing basic EPS for 2020.
b. Compute the number of shares to be used in computing diluted EPS for 2020.
c. Compute basic EPS.
d. Compute diluted EPS.

AD&J 21-94
Calculating EPS: Convertible Debentures, Convertible Preferred Stock, Warrants; and Partial Year **LO5, 6, 7, 9**

Challenge Problem The following facts pertain to Conway Company's year ended on December 31, 2020.

From the income statement:	
Net income	$10,500,000
From the balance sheet:	
Long-term debt	
10% convertible debentures, due October 2029	10,000,000
Stockholders' equity (Note 1):	
Convertible voting preferred stock of $1 par value, $0.20 cumulative dividend. Authorized, 600,000 shares; issued and outstanding, 600,000. Liquidation value $22 per share, aggregating $13,200,000	600,000
Common stock of $1 par value per share; authorized, 5,000,000 shares; issued and outstanding, 3,400,000 for the entire year	3,400,000

Note 1—The $0.20 convertible preferred stock is callable by the company after March 31, 2022, at $53 per share. Each share is convertible into one share of common stock. Warrants to acquire 500,000 shares of the company's stock at $60 per share were outstanding at the end of 2020.

Additional information

- Average fair value of the common stock during 2020 was:

  First quarter . . . . $50 Second quarter . . . . $60 Third quarter . . . . $70 Fourth quarter $70
- Cash dividends of $0.125 per common share were declared and paid for each quarter of 2020.
- 10% convertible debentures with a principal amount of $10,000,000 due October 1, 2029, were sold for cash at a price of $98 on October 1, 2019. Each $100 debenture is convertible into two shares of common stock. Discount is amortized on a straight-line basis.
- 600,000 shares of convertible preferred stock were issued for assets in a purchase transaction on April 1, 2020. The annual dividend on each share of this convertible preferred stock is $0.20. Each share is convertible into one share of common stock. The fair value of the convertible preferred stock was $53 at the time of issuance. Dividends are paid for time stock is held.
- Warrants to buy 500,000 shares of common stock at $60 per share for a period of five years were issued along with the convertible preferred stock mentioned previously.
- 3.4 million shares of common stock were outstanding at the end of 2019. There have been no conversions or warrants exercised in 2020.
- Income tax rate is 25%.

Required

a. Calculate basic EPS.

b. Calculate diluted EPS.

AD&J 21-95 Recognizing Graded Vesting of Stock Options **LO2**

Challenge Problem On January 1, 2020, Wayfare Inc. granted 40,000 stock options to executives under a stock option incentive plan (option price of $28), when the market price of common stock was $30 per share ($1 par per share). Continuing employment is required through exercise date. Shares vest each year as follows: 25% in year 1, 30% in year 2, and 45% in year 3. The fair value of the share awards vesting in year 1, year 2, and year 3, are $8, $9, and $10, per share, respectively.

Required

a. Determine compensation expense per year assuming straight-line allocation of compensation costs to each separate vesting award by year.

b. Determine compensation expense per year assuming straight-line allocation of compensation costs in the aggregate.

AD&J 21-96 Computing Diluted EPS with Restricted Stock Units **LO7**

Trueblood Case The Trueblood case series, prepared by Deloitte professionals, are based on recent accounting technical issues that require research and judgment. The cases may be accessed through the Deloitte foundation at the following website: https://www2.deloitte.com/us/en/pages/about-deloitte/articles/trueblood-case-studies-deloitte-foundation.html. The following case is relevant to the content provided in this chapter: **Case 16-4, To Dilute or Not to Dilute**. This case requires an analysis of diluted earnings per share for a company issuing restricted stock units.

AD&J 21-97 Defining Terms **LO4, 5, 6, 7, 8, 9**

Codification Skills How are the terms (1) weighted-average number of common shares outstanding and (2) diluted earnings per share defined in the Codification? What is meant by the term "dilutive potential common shares"?

AD&J 21-98 Performing Accounting Research **LO4, 5, 6, 7, 8, 9**

Codification Skills For the following items, indicate whether the Codification requires reporting on the (1) face of the income statement (2) notes to the income statement or (3) either the face *or* the notes to the income statement. In addition, for each item, record the Codification reference.

	Face of income statement	Notes to income statement	Either on face or in notes to financial statements	Codification reference
Basic EPS for income from continuing operations				FASB ASC ___-___-___-___
Basic EPS for net income				FASB ASC ___-___-___-___

continued

continued from previous page

	Face of income statement	Notes to income statement	Either on face or in notes to financial statements	Codification reference
Basic EPS for income from discontinued operations				FASB ASC ___-___-___-___
Diluted EPS for income from discontinued operations				FASB ASC ___-___-___-___
Reconciliation of the numerators and denominators of basic EPS for income from continuing operations				FASB ASC ___-___-___-___
Extent of antidilutive securities not included in the diluted EPS calculation				FASB ASC ___-___-___-___
Adjustments to basic and diluted EPS because of stock splits				FASB ASC ___-___-___-___
Effect of preferred dividends on the EPS calculation				FASB ASC ___-___-___-___
Diluted EPS for income from continuing operations				FASB ASC ___-___-___-___
Diluted EPS for net income				FASB ASC ___-___-___-___

AD&J 21-99
Performing Accounting Research **LO4, 5, 6, 7, 8, 9**

Codification Skills Are the following statements true or false? Indicate the Codification reference that supports your answer.

a. Cumulative preferred dividends for the current year are subtracted from net income even though a company did not declare a preferred dividend payment. FASB ASC ___-___-___-___

b. Basic EPS should be restated in prior years for the effects of contingently issuable shares when conditions change that result in these shares becoming issuable. FASB ASC ___-___-___-___

c. A company that reports a discontinued operation in a period shall use income from continuing operations as the control number in determining whether those potential common shares are dilutive or antidilutive. FASB ASC ___-___-___-___

d. Stock options will have a dilutive effect under the treasury stock method only when the average market price of the common stock during the period is less than the exercise price of the stock options. FASB ASC ___-___-___-___

e. In calculating diluted EPS, convertible preferred stock is considered to have been converted to common stock as of the beginning of the year, regardless of the issuance date of the preferred stock. FASB ASC ___-___-___-___

f. When there is a year-to-date loss, potential common shares should never be included in the computation of diluted EPS, because to do so would be antidilutive. FASB ASC ___-___-___-___

Appendix—Brief Exercises

App—Brief Exercise 21-100
LO10

What are stock appreciation rights?

App—Brief Exercise 21-101
Computing Compensation Expense for SARs Plan **LO10**
Hint: See Demo 21-10

Kelly Corporation established a stock appreciation rights plan on January 1, 2020, that extends rights to certain company officers that can be redeemed for cash equal to the difference between the market price of the company's common stock at the grant date, which is $10, and the market price at the first exercise date. The 100 SARs can be exercised two years from the grant date and expire three years from the grant date or when employment is terminated, if earlier. The requisite service period is considered to be two years because exercise is expected (highly probable) to occur on December 31, 2021. The fair value of the SARs is estimated to be $14, $12, and $15 on January 1, 2020, December 31, 2020, and 2021, respectively. Compute Kelly Corporation's compensation expense for 2020 and 2021.

App—Brief Exercise 21-102 Computing Compensation Expense for SARs Plan **LO10** *Hint:* See Demo 21-10

Refer to the information in Brief Exercise 21-101, except now assume that the awards may be settled with common stock or cash at the option of the employer. Compute Kelly Corporation's compensation expense for 2020 and 2021.

Appendix—Exercises

App—Exercise 21-103 Recording Entries for SARs Plan **LO10** *Hint:* See Demo 21-10

On January 1, 2020, Kelly Corporation established a stock appreciation rights plan that offers to selected executives rights (SARs) that can be redeemed for cash equal to the difference between the market price of the company's common stock at the grant date and market price at the first exercise date. The rights can be exercised three years from the grant date and expire four years from the grant date or when employment is terminated, if earlier. The requisite service period is considered to be three years because exercise is expected (highly probable) to occur on December 31, 2022.

Executive Brown was granted 2,000 SARs on January 1, 2020 (when the common stock price was $20) and exercised the rights on December 31, 2022. Fair value at year-end of the SARs were 2020, $3; 2021, $7; 2022, $10; and 2023, $6.

Required

a. Determine the following.
   1. Requisite service period.
   2. Total compensation expense.
   3. Total cash paid by grantor to grantee.

b. Prepare necessary journal entries for the years 2020 through 2022 related to the SARs plan.

App—Exercise 21-104 Recording Cash Settlement of Restricted Stock Units **LO10** *Hint:* See Demo 21-10

In late 2019, the board of directors of Arches Corp. approved a restricted stock unit plan to be awarded to select employees, including the following general terms:

- Each restricted stock unit is equivalent to one share of $1 par value, common stock of Arches Corp or the cash equivalent at the option of the employee.
- Restricted stock units vest three years after the date of grant.
- Shares are distributed after the vesting period if the employee is still employed by the company.

On January 1, 2020, 6,000 restricted stock units were granted to key employees under this plan. The market price of the common stock was $18, $15, $20 per share on December 31, 2020, December 31, 2021, and December 31, 2022, respectively.

Required

a. Prepare the journal entries on December 31, 2020, December 31, 2021, and December 31, 2022.

b. Prepare the journal entry for the settlement of the restricted stock units on January 1, 2023, assuming that the executives elect a cash settlement.

Appendix—Problems

App—Problem 21-105 Recording Entries for SARs Plan **LO10**

On January 1, 2020, McClain Control Corporation employed a new president, Serina Miller, with the following compensation package: (1) salary, $200,000 per year (minimum employment period, three years), (2) an annual bonus of 10% of the dollar increase in accrual basis income, and (3) 10,000 stock appreciation rights (SARs) tied to the market price of McClain's common stock. This problem focuses on the SARs granted to Miller on January 1, 2020, when the market price per share was $30. Four other executives also participate in this SAR plan.

The SAR plan specifies that each SAR will earn for the grantee cash equal to the difference between the market prices of McClain's common stock on the grant date and on the exercise date. The SARs may be exercised at any time after the end of the fourth year from the grant date, and they expire at the end of the fifth year from the grant date, or at the date of termination of employment, if before the end of the fifth year. The requisite service period is from the grant date to the expected (a high probability) exercise (vesting) date, December 31, 2023.

Miller exercised the SARs on January 4, 2024, when the market price per share was $40. Relevant year-end SARs fair value were as follows: 2020, $3; 2021, $8; 2022, $8; 2023, $10; and January 4, 2024, $10. The accounting period ends December 31.

a. Respond to the following questions:
1. Is this plan compensatory? Why?
2. What is total compensation expense?
3. What is the requisite service period?
4. How is total compensation expense allocated to annual periodic expense?

b. Provide all entries related to the SARs granted to Miller from the grant date through the exercise date.

Answers to Review Exercise

Review 21-1

Assets = Liabilities + Equity: −1,875,000; +25,000; +1,850,000

a. **January 1, 2020—To record restricted stock award**

Unearned Compensation—Equity (5 × 5,000 × $75)	1,875,000	
Common Stock (5 × 5,000 × $1)		25,000
Paid-in Capital in Excess of Par—Common Stock (to balance)		1,850,000

Assets = Liabilities + Equity: −937,500; +937,500
Unearn Comp—Eq: 1,875,000 | 937,500; Common Stock: | 25,000
Paid-in Cap—CS: | 1,850,000; Comp Exp: 937,500 |

b. **December 31, 2020—To record compensation expense**

Compensation Expense ($1,875,000/2)	937,500	
Unearned Compensation—Equity		937,500

c. No entry is recorded at the date of grant; however, the total cost of compensation is measured at the grant date: $1,875,000 (5 × 5,000 × $75)

December 31, 2020—To record compensation expense

Assets = Liabilities + Equity: −937,500; +937,500
Comp Exp: 937,500 |; Paid-in Cap—RS: | 937,500

Compensation Expense ($1,875,000/2)	937,500	
Paid-in Capital—Restricted Stock		937,500

Review 21-2

a. Total Compensation Cost $18,000

b. **December 31, 2020—To record compensation expense**

Assets = Liabilities + Equity: −4,500; +4,500
Comp Exp: 4,500 |; Paid-in Cap—SO: | 4,500

Compensation Expense ([$18,000/3] × 9/12)	4,500	
Paid-in Capital—Stock Options		4,500

c. **June 30, 2023—To record exercise of stock options**

Assets +30,000 = Liabilities + Equity: −10,800; +1,200; +39,600
Cash: 30,000 |; Paid-in Cap—SO: 10,800 | 18,000 Bal.
Common Stock: | 1,200; Paid-in Cap—CS: | 39,600

Cash (1,200 × $25)	30,000	
Paid-in Capital—Stock Options ($18,000 × 1,200/2,000)	10,800	
Common Stock (1,200 × $1)		1,200
Paid-in Capital in Excess of Par—Common Stock (to balance)		39,600

Review 21-3

a. **January 1, 2020—To record issuance of stock for employee share purchase plan**

Assets +4,750 = Liabilities + Equity: +500; +4,250

Cash (500 × $10 × 0.95)	4,750	
Common Stock (500 × $1)		500
Paid-in Capital in Excess of Par—Common Stock (to balance)		4,250

b. **January 1, 2020—To record issuance of stock for employee share purchase plan**

Assets +4,250 = Liabilities + Equity: −750; +500; +4,500
Cash: 4,250 |; Comp Exp: 750 |
Common Stock: | 500; Paid-in Cap—CS: | 4,500

Cash (500 × $10 × 0.85)	4,250	
Compensation Expense (500 × $10 × 0.15)	750	
Common Stock (500 × $1)		500
Paid-in Capital in Excess of Par—Common Stock (to balance)		4,500

Review 21-4

	Net Income Available to Common Stockholders	Weighted-Average Common Shares Outstanding	Per Share
Basic EPS	$245,000	100,000	$2.45

Review 21-5

Inclusive Dates	Actual Shares Outstanding	Retroactive Restatement for Stock Dividend	Equivalent Shares Outstanding	Months Outstanding	Percentage of Full Year	Weighted-Average Shares Outstanding
Jan.–Mar. . .	150,000	2.5	375,000	3	25.0%	93,750
Apr.–Jun. . .	210,000	2.5	525,000	3	25.0%	131,250
Jul.–Oct. . . .	205,000	2.5	512,500	4	33.3%	170,663
Nov.–Dec. . .	512,500		512,500	2	16.7%	85,588
				12	100.0%	481,251

	Net Income Available to Common Stockholders	Weighted-Average Common Shares Outstanding	Per Share
Basic EPS	$821,500†	481,251	$1.71

† $825,000 − $3,500.

Review 21-6

Example One

a. **Basic EPS**

	Net Income Available to Common Stockholders	Weighted-Average Common Shares Outstanding	Per Share
Basic EPS	$365,000	205,000	$1.78

b. **Diluted EPS**

	Net Income Available to Common Stockholders	Weighted-Average Common Shares Outstanding	Per Share
Basic EPS	$365,000	205,000	$1.78
Effect of convertible bonds:			
Add back prorated interest, net of tax. . . .	3,750		
Add new prorated common shares.		6,000	
Diluted EPS	$368,750	211,000	$1.75

The convertible bonds are dilutive. Thus, diluted EPS is $1.75. The company would report both basic EPS of $1.78 and diluted EPS of $1.75 in its 2020 income statement.

Example Two

a. **Basic EPS**

	Net Income Available to Common Stockholders	Weighted-Average Common Shares Outstanding	Per Share
Basic EPS	$233,000	85,000	$2.74

b. **Diluted EPS**

	Net Income Available to Common Stockholders	Weighted-Average Common Shares Outstanding	Per Share
Basic EPS	$233,000	85,000	$2.74
Effect of convertible preferred stock:			
Add back preferred dividends	15,000		
Add new common shares		4,000	
Diluted EPS	$248,000	89,000	$2.79 antidilutive

The convertible preferred shares are not dilutive. The company would report basic and diluted EPS of $2.74 in its 2020 income statement.

Review 21-7

Example One

a.

	Net Income Available to Common Stockholders	Weighted-Average Common Shares Outstanding	Per Share
Basic EPS	$450,000	300,000	$1.50

b.

	Net Income Available to Common Stockholders	Weighted-Average Common Shares Outstanding	Per Share
Basic EPS	$450,000	300,000	$1.50
Effect of stock options:			
Add incremental common shares		3,000†	
Diluted EPS	$450,000	303,000	$1.49

† 8,000 shares under option less 5,000 treasury shares computed as ((8,000 shares × $25)/$40)).

The stock options are dilutive. This means diluted EPS is $1.49. The company would report both basic EPS of $1.50 and diluted EPS of $1.49 in its 2020 income statement.

Example Two

a.

	Net Income Available to Common Stockholders	Weighted-Average Common Shares Outstanding	Per Share
Basic EPS	$480,000	220,000	$2.18

b.

	Net Income Available to Common Stockholders	Weighted-Average Common Shares Outstanding	Per Share
Basic EPS	$480,000	220,000	$2.18
Effect of restricted stock:			
Add incremental common shares		667‡	
Diluted EPS	$480,000	220,667	$2.18

‡ 2,000 restricted shares less 1,333 treasury shares computed as (($50,000 − $16,667)/$25)).

The company would report basic and diluted EPS of $2.18 in its 2020 income statement. (The dilutive EPS did not differ from basic EPS considering rounding to 2 decimals.)

Review 21-8

	Net Income Available to Common Stockholders	Weighted-Average Common Shares Outstanding	Per Share
Basic EPS	$500,000	385,000	$1.30

Basic EPS is $1.30. There are no additional potentially dilutive securities to consider in calculating diluted EPS because the conditions for the contingently issuable shares were not met at the end of 2020 (assumed end of contingency period).

The company would report only basic EPS of $1.30 in its 2020 income statement.

Review 21-9

a. **Basic EPS**

	Net Income Available to Common Stockholders	Weighted-Average Common Shares Outstanding	Per Share
Basic EPS	$757,500*	140,000	$5.41

* $820,000 − ($2.50 × 25,000).

b. **Diluted EPS**

Ranking of Potentially Dilutive Securities

Potentially Dilutive Security	Increase in Income	Increase in Number of Common Shares	Earnings per Incremental Share
Convertible bonds.	$11,250[1]	25,000	$0.45
Convertible preferred stock	62,500[2]	75,000	0.83

[1] $300,000 × 0.05 × 0.75. [2] $2.50 × 25,000.

	Net Income Available to Common Stockholders	Weighted-Average Common Shares Outstanding	Per Share	
Basic EPS	$757,500	140,000	$5.41	
Effect of convertible bonds:				
Add back prorated interest	11,250			
Additional prorated common shares . .		25,000		
Tentative diluted EPS.	$768,750	165,000	$4.66	Dilutive
Effect of convertible preferred stock:				
Add back preferred dividends	62,500			
Additional common shares		75,000		
Tentative diluted EPS.	$831,250	240,000	$3.46	Dilutive
Diluted EPS.	$831,250	240,000	$3.46 ←	

c. **Income Statement**

Basic earnings per share	$5.41
Diluted earnings per share	3.46

Review 21-10

a.

Year-End	Year-End Fair Value	Aggregate Compensation	% of Service Period Accrued	Total SARs Liability Accrued	Annual Expense
2020	$3.00	$1,200	50%	$ 600	$ 600
2021	5.00	2,000	100%	2,000	1,400

Assets = Liabilities + Equity
+600 −600

December 31, 2020—To record compensation expense

Compensation Expense	600	
SARs Liability		600

Assets = Liabilities + Equity
+1,400 −1,400

December 31, 2021—To record compensation expense

Compensation Expense	1,400	
SARs Liability		1,400

Assets = Liabilities + Equity
−2,000 −2,000

Comp Exp: 600 | ; 1,400 |

SARs Liab: 2,000 | 600; | 1,400; | 0

Cash: | 2,000

December 31, 2021—To record exercise of SARs plan

SARs Liability	2,000	
Cash		2,000

Assets = Liabilities + Equity
−1,100
+1,100

b. **December 31, 2020—To record compensation expense**

Compensation Expense	1,100	
Paid-in Capital—SARs Plan ($5.50 × 400/2)		1,100

Assets = Liabilities + Equity
−1,100
+1,100

December 31, 2021—To record compensation expense

Compensation Expense	1,100	
Paid-in Capital—SARs Plan ($2,200/2)		1,100

Assets = Liabilities + Equity
−2,200
+100
+2,100

Comp Exp: 1,100 | ; 1,100 |

Common Stock: | 100

Paid-in Cap—CS: | 2,100

Paid-in Cap—SARs: 2,200 | 1,100; | 1,100; | 0

December 31, 2021—To settle SARs plan

Paid-in Capital—SARs Plan	2,200	
Common Stock $1 par × [($20 − $15) × 400]/$20		100
Paid-in Capital in Excess of Par—Common Stock		2,100

22 Statement of Cash Flows Revisited

Consolidated Statement of Cash Flows
PepsiCo, Inc. and Subsidiaries
Fiscal years ended December 30, 2017, December 31, 2016 and December 26, 2015
(in millions)

	2017	2016	2015
Operating Activities			
Net income	$ 4,908	$ 6,379	$ 5,501
Depreciation and amortization	2,369	2,368	2,416
Share-based compensation expense	292	284	295
Restructuring and impairment charges	295	160	230
Cash payments for restructuring charges	(113)	(125)	(208)
Charges related to the transaction with Tingyi	—	373	73
Venezuela impairment charges	—	—	1,359
Pension and retiree medical plan expenses	221	501	467
Pension and retiree medical plan contributions	(220)	(695)	(205)
Deferred income taxes and other tax charges and credits	619	452	78
Provisional net tax expense related to the TCJ Act	2,451	—	—
Change in assets and liabilities:			
Accounts and notes receivable	(202)	(349)	(461)
Inventories	(168)	(75)	(244)
Prepaid expenses and other current assets	20	10	(50)
Accounts payable and other current liabilities	201	997	1,692
Income taxes payable	(338)	329	55
Other, net	(341)	64	(134)
Net Cash Provided by Operating Activities	9,994	10,673	10,864
Investing Activities			
Capital spending	(2,969)	(3,040)	(2,758)
Sales of property, plant and equipment	180	99	86
Acquisitions and investments in noncontrolled affiliates	(61)	(212)	(86)
Reduction of cash due to Venezuela deconsolidation	—	—	(568)
Divestitures	267	85	76
Short-term investments, by original maturity:			
More than three months—purchases	(18,385)	(12,504)	(4,428)
More than three months—maturities	15,744	8,399	4,111
More than three months—sales	790	—	—
Three months or less, net	2	16	3
Other investing, net	29	9	(5)
Net Cash Used for Investing Activities	(4,403)	(7,148)	(3,569)
Financing Activities			
Proceeds from issuances of long-term debt	7,509	7,818	8,702
Payments of long-term debt	(4,406)	(3,105)	(4,095)
Debt redemptions	—	(2,504)	—
Short-term borrowings, by original maturity:			
More than three months—proceeds	91	59	15
More than three months—payments	(128)	(27)	(43)
Three months or less, net	(1,016)	1,505	53
Cash dividends paid	(4,472)	(4,227)	(4,040)
Share repurchases—common	(2,000)	(3,000)	(5,000)
Share repurchases—preferred	(5)	(7)	(5)
Proceeds from exercises of stock options	462	465	504
Withholding tax payments on RSUs, PSUs and PEPunits converted	(145)	(130)	(151)
Other financing	(76)	(58)	(52)
Net Cash Used for Financing Activities	(4,186)	(3,211)	(4,112)
Effect of exchange rate changes on cash and cash equivalents	47	(252)	(221)
Net Increase in Cash and Cash Equivalents	1,452	62	2,962
Cash and Cash Equivalents, Beginning of Year	9,158	9,096	6,134
Cash and Cash Equivalents, End of Year	$10,610	$ 9,158	$ 9,096

See accompanying notes to the consolidated financial statements.

Chapter Preview

This chapter builds on the introduction of the statement of cash flows presented in Chapter 5. We begin with a brief review of the format and content of the statement of cash flows using the indirect method. We then prepare each of the three cash flow sections: operating, investing, and financing. We describe disclosures required with the statement of cash flows including the disclosure of noncash investing and financing activities. Next, we introduce a tool that can be useful in preparing the statement of cash flows: a cash flow worksheet. We conclude by explaining the direct method, which is another generally accepted method to present the operating activities section in the statement of cash flows.

Action Plan

LO	Topic/Subtopic	Page	Demos	Reviews	Assignments
LO 22–1	**Identify operating, investing, and financing activities, and the statement of cash flows format** Cash Flows from Operating Activities :: Cash Flows from Investing Activities :: Cash Flows from Financing Activities	22-3	D22-1	R22-1	21, 22, 40, 41, 75, 97, 98, 99, 101, 105
LO 22–2	**Prepare the operating activities section of the statement of cash flows using the indirect method** Net Income :: Noncash Revenue and Expense Adjustments :: Changes in Operating Assets and Liabilities	22-7	D22-2	R22-2	21, 23, 24, 25, 27, 29, 31, 40, 42, 43, 44, 45, 46, 47, 49, 53, 54, 55, 56, 57, 58, 59, 60, 70, 74, 75, 76, 77, 78, 79, 80, 81, 82, 83, 85, 91, 92, 94, 95, 96, 97, 98, 99, 100, 101, 102
LO 22–3	**Prepare the investing activities section of the statement of cash flows** Property, Plant and Equipment :: Investments :: Intangible Assets	22-15	D22-3	R22-3	26, 27, 32, 46, 50, 51, 52, 53, 54, 55, 56, 57, 58, 59, 60, 73, 74, 76, 77, 78, 79, 80, 81, 82, 91, 95, 96, 99, 101, 103, 106
LO 22–4	**Prepare the financing activities section of the statement of cash flows** Equity :: Nontrade Debt :: Dividend Payments	22-17	D22-4	R22-4	28, 29, 30, 47, 48, 49, 50, 51, 52, 53, 54, 55, 56, 57, 58, 59, 60, 73, 74, 76, 77, 78, 79, 80, 81, 82, 83, 84, 91, 96, 101, 106
LO 22–5	**Describe required disclosures including that for noncash transactions** Disclosure Requirements :: Interest and Income Tax Paid :: Noncash Investing and Financing Transactions	22-22	D22-5	R22-5	32, 40, 49, 52, 56, 57, 58, 60, 75, 76, 77, 78, 79, 80, 81, 82, 96, 101, 102, 103, 104, 106
LO 22–6	**Utilize a worksheet to prepare the statement of cash flows** Cash Flow Worksheet :: Optional Tool for Cash Flow Preparation	22-26	D22-6	R22-6	33, 61, 62, 63, 80, 81, 101, 103, 106, 107
LO 22–7	**Prepare the operating cash flow section of the statement of cash flows using the direct method** Cash Receipts from Customers :: Cash Payments to Suppliers :: Cash Payments for Operating Expenses	22-29	D22-7	R22-7	34, 35, 36, 37, 38, 39, 64, 65, 66, 67, 68, 69, 70, 71, 72, 73, 74, 83, 85, 86, 87, 88, 89, 90, 91, 93, 95, 96, 97, 100
LO 22–8	**APPENDIX 22A—Prepare a statement of cash flows using the cash T-account approach** Cash T-Account Approach :: Optional Tool for Cash Flow Preparation	22-36	D22-8	R22-8	108, 109

LO 22-1 Identify operating, investing, and financing activities, and the statement of cash flows format

LO 22-1 Overview

Indirect Statement of Cash Flows
- Classify cash flows into operating, investing, and financing sections
- Total cash flow sections to determine change in cash for the period
- Reconcile the change in cash from beginning to end of period
- Include in the "cash" balance: cash, cash equivalents, and restricted cash

Accrual accounting is important in measuring a company's performance and financial condition. Cash-flow information is also an important part of assessing financial performance and condition. Cash flows indicate whether a borrower will produce sufficient cash to pay its debts. Both creditors and investors are interested in the historical record of cash inflows and outflows for the same reasons that a mortgage lender insists on knowing a borrower's credit history and cash income. Further, the trend of cash flows over several periods allows an assessment of **financial flexibility**—the ability to use cash flows to meet unexpected needs and opportunities.

All cash inflows and outflows on the statement of cash flows are classified into one of three categories: **operating, investing, or financing.** *Classification of cash flows is important for evaluating past cash flows and predicting future flows.* The ability of a company to generate positive cash flow from operations is critical to its survival. A company cannot indefinitely sell its assets or incur additional debt if it is not operating successfully.

Classification enables the financial statement user to distinguish between repetitive ongoing activities and long-term strategic changes. For example, did *cash inflows* result from daily operations or from a specific event such as a sale of stock? Were *cash outflows* used for daily operations of the company or for reduction of debt? The three sections of the statement of cash flows provide a meaningful framework for investors and creditors in their analysis of companies. The three sections of operating, investing, and financing are defined in the accounting guidance as follows.

Cash Flow Section	Definition
Operating activities	**ASC Glossary** Operating activities include all transactions and other events that are not defined as investing or financing activities . . . Operating activities generally involve producing and delivering goods and providing services. Cash flows from operating activities are generally the cash effects of transactions and other events that enter into the determination of net income.
Investing activities	**ASC Glossary** Investing activities include making and collecting loans and acquiring and disposing of debt or equity instruments and property, plant, and equipment and other productive assets, that is, assets held for or used in the production of goods or services by the entity (other than materials that are part of the entity's inventory). Investing activities exclude acquiring and disposing of certain loans or other debt or equity instruments that are acquired specifically for resale.
Financing activities	**ASC Glossary** Financing activities include obtaining resources from owners and providing them with a return on, and a return of, their investment; receiving restricted resources that by donor stipulation must be used for long-term purposes; borrowing money and repaying amounts borrowed, or otherwise settling the obligation; and obtaining and paying for other resources obtained from creditors on long-term credit.

Cash Flows from Operating Activities

Cash flows from operating activities include all cash flows not defined as investing or financing activities. Activities classified as operating are mainly those where the cash effects of transactions and other events enter into the determination of net income, however there are exceptions. Some operating cash flows, including cash proceeds or cash used to purchase trading securities do not enter into determination of net income. Common operating cash flows are listed in **Exhibit 22-1**. Items with an * do not enter into the determination of net income.

The difference between operating cash inflows and outflows is called the **net cash provided (used) by operating activities**. Typically, the net amount is an inflow because, over the long term, cash collections from operations must exceed cash outflows for a going concern. Many analysts consider this the most important subtotal in the statement of cash flows because it provides a measure similar to net income on a cash basis.

EXHIBIT 22-1
Typical Cash Flows from Operating Activities

Cash Inflows—Cash Received from:	Cash Outflows—Cash Paid for:
Sale of goods or services.	Purchase of goods for resale.
Refunds from suppliers.	Salaries and other operating expenses.
Dividends from investments.	Income taxes, duties, and fines.
Interest on receivables.	Interest on liabilities.
Refund on pension plan payments.*	Funding of pension plan.*
Settlement of lawsuit.	Settlement of lawsuit.
Proceeds from sale of investments held for resale in a trading account.*	Settlement of asset retirement obligation.
	Purchases of investments held for resale in a trading account.*

* Items not included in determination of net income.

EXPAND YOUR KNOWLEDGE **Other Items Affecting Cash Flows from Operating Activities**

The accounting guidance references cash flows included in the operating activities section that are not included in determination of net income.

Investments held for resale Selling and purchasing investments acquired specifically for resale by banks, brokers, and dealers is more similar to the inventory transactions of a typical merchandiser or manufacturer. Thus, the accounting guidance requires such investments to be reported in the operating activities section.

230-10-45-18 Banks, brokers and dealers in securities, and other entities may carry securities and other assets in a trading account.

230-10-45-20 Cash receipts and cash payments resulting from purchases and sales of other securities and other assets shall be classified as operating cash flows if those assets are acquired specifically for resale and are carried at fair value in a trading account.

230-10-45-21 Some loans are similar to debt securities in a trading account in that they are originated or purchased specifically for resale and are held for short periods of time. Cash receipts and cash payments resulting from acquisitions and sales of loans also shall be classified as operating cash flows if those loans are acquired specifically for resale and are carried at fair value or at the lower of amortized cost basis or fair value.

Note issued for an operating activity Cash amounts collected (or paid) on a note extended for an operating transaction such as to fund the sale or purchase of merchandise inventory are reported in the operating activities section. If notes are issued for reasons other than operating activities such as for a fixed asset, the cash flows are *not* classified as operating. The following are cash inflows (outflows) for operating activities as described in the accounting guidance.

230-10-45-16a Cash receipts from sales of goods or services, including receipts from collection or sale of accounts and both short- and long-term notes receivable from customers arising from those sales.

230-10-45-17a Cash payments to acquire materials for manufacture or goods for resale, including principal payments on accounts and both short- and long-term notes payable to suppliers for those materials or goods.

Cash Flows from Investing Activities

Cash flows from investing activities include cash inflows and outflows related to disposing of or acquiring property, plant, and, equipment; the sale or purchase of investments and other long-term assets; and the extension and collection of loans (nontrade). Typical investing cash flows are listed in **Exhibit 22-2**. The difference between investing cash inflows and outflows is called **net cash provided (used) by investing activities.**

EXHIBIT 22-2
Cash Flows from Investing Activities

Cash Inflows—Cash Received from:	Cash Outflows—Cash Paid for:
Sale of property, plant, and equipment.	Purchase of property, plant, and equipment.
Sale of debt and equity investments in other companies.*	Investments in debt and equity investments in other companies.*
Collection of a loan (excluding interest, which is an operating activity).	Loans to other entities.
Sale of patents or other intangible assets.	Purchase of patents or other intangible assets.

*Cash flows from investments held specifically for resale are classified as operating activities as discussed in the previous section.

Cash Flows from Financing Activities

Cash flows from financing activities include both cash inflows and outflows related to issuances of debt and equity. Cash inflows occur by borrowing from creditors or by issuing stock to owners to obtain cash for financing the business. Cash outflows occur when principal is repaid to creditors and when distributions are made to owners. Typical financing cash flows are listed in **Exhibit 22-3**. The difference between these cash inflows and outflows is called **net cash provided (used) by financing activities**.

EXHIBIT 22-3
Cash Flows from Financing Activities

Cash Inflows—Cash Received from:	Cash Outflows—Cash Paid for:
Issuance of a company's own stock.	Dividends and other cash distributions to owners.
Issuance of bonds or other debt (short-term and long-term).	Reacquiring previously issued capital stock.
Sale of treasury stock.	Principal payments on loans, payments to retire bonds or other debt, debt issue costs, and principal payments on finance leases.

In sum, the change from one balance sheet date to another is a result of operating, investing, and financing activities.

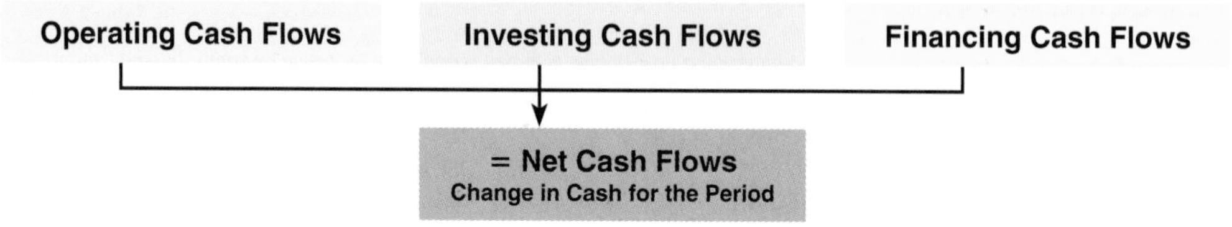

Format of Statement of Cash Flows

In the statement of cash flows, the operating section is listed first followed by the investing and financing sections where positive amounts represent cash inflows and negative amounts represent cash outflows. Except when the indirect method is used for the operating section, cash inflows and cash outflows *are reported separately*. For example, increases to equipment (purchases) are reported separately from decreases in equipment (sales).

230-10-45-26 Except for items described in paragraphs 230-10-45-8 through 45-9, both investing cash inflows and outflows and financing cash inflows and outflows shall be reported separately in a statement of cash flows—for example, outlays for acquisitions of property, plant, and equipment shall be reported separately from proceeds from sales of property, plant, and equipment; proceeds of borrowings shall be reported separately from repayments of debt; and proceeds from issuing stock shall be reported separately from outlays to reacquire the entity's stock.

The totals from the operating, investing, and financing sections are added together to account for the total change in cash from the beginning of the period to the end of the period. This means cash at the beginning of the period is reconciled to cash at the end of the period through operating, investing, and financing activities as shown in the following table. "Cash" includes cash, cash equivalents, and restricted cash. Cash equivalents (highly liquid investment with little credit risk) and restricted cash (cash not available for general use) were explained in Chapter 4.

+/−	Net cash flows from operating activities for the period
+/−	Net cash flows from investing activities for the period
+/−	Net cash flows from financing activities for the period
+/−	Net change in cash during the period
+	Cash at the beginning of the period
=	Cash at the end of the period

230-10-45-24 A statement of cash flows for a period shall report net cash provided or used by operating, investing, and financing activities and the net effect of those flows on the total of cash, cash equivalents, and amounts generally described as restricted cash or restricted cash equivalents during the period. The statement of cash flows shall report that information in a manner that reconciles beginning and ending totals of cash, cash equivalents, and amounts generally described as restricted cash or restricted cash equivalents.

In **Demo 22-1** we classify items into the sections of operating, investing, and financing, and we reconcile the sections of the statement of cash flows to the change in cash.

Identify Operating, Investing, and Financing Activities — LO22-1 — Demo 22-1

Demo MBC

Part One

Wilson Inc. has the following cash flows, 1 through 12, in 2020. For each item, indicate the type of cash flow (inflow or outflow), as well as the classification of the cash flow (operating, investing, or financing).

	Cash Inflow or Cash Outflow	Operating, Investing, or Financing Activity
1. Proceeds from issuance of preferred stock	Inflow	Financing
2. Payment for the early extinguishment of long-term debt issued for capital projects	Outflow	Financing
3. Cash sale of merchandise inventory	Inflow	Operating
4. Nontrade loan made to another entity	Outflow	Investing
5. Sale of patent for cash	Inflow	Investing
6. Purchase of equity securities	Outflow	Investing
7. Proceeds from issuance of bonds	Inflow	Financing
8. Payments to purchase capital stock for treasury	Outflow	Financing
9. Sale of land for cash	Inflow	Investing
10. Issuance of short-term note payable for operations	Inflow	Operating
11. Declaration and payment of dividends	Outflow	Financing
12. Payment of operating expenses with cash	Outflow	Operating

Part Two

Wilson Inc. determined the following amounts for the year ended December 31, 2020.

Cash and cash equivalents balance, Dec. 31, 2020	$ 58,000
Net cash provided by operating activities	245,000
Net cash provided by financing activities	45,000
Net cash used by investing activities	(250,000)

Using this information, determine Wilson's *beginning* cash balance on January 1, 2020.

Solution

The cash balance on January 1, 2020, is $18,000 computed as follows.

Net cash provided by operating activities	$ 245,000
Net cash used by investing activities	(250,000)
Net cash provided by financing activities	45,000
Net change in cash	40,000
Cash at the end of the period	58,000
Cash at the beginning of the period ($58,000 − $40,000)	**$ 18,000**

Identify Operating, Investing, and Financing Activities — LO22-1 — REVIEW 22-1

Review MBC

Sonic Company has the following items, 1 through 10, in the current year. For each item, indicate the appropriate classification on the statement of cash flows, selecting from *a* through *f*.

continued

continued from previous page

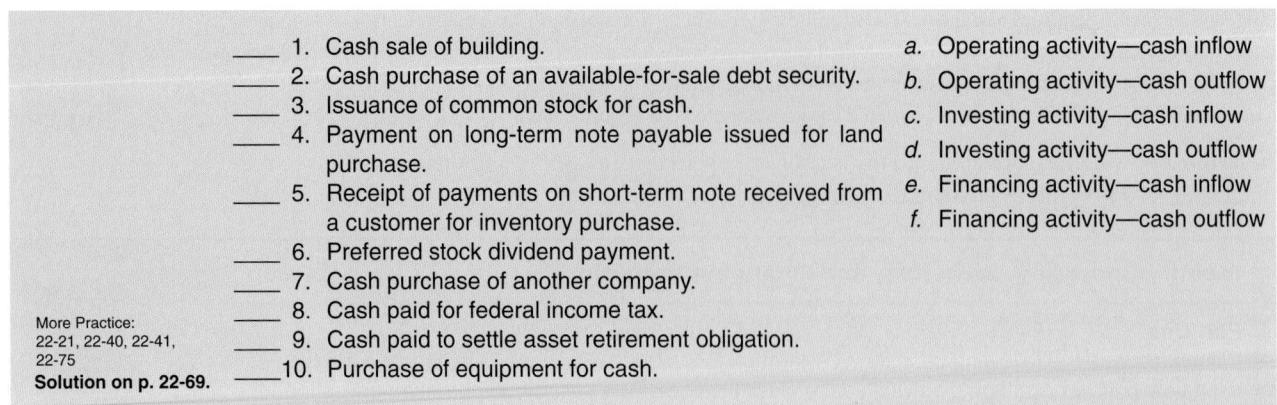

____ 1. Cash sale of building.
____ 2. Cash purchase of an available-for-sale debt security.
____ 3. Issuance of common stock for cash.
____ 4. Payment on long-term note payable issued for land purchase.
____ 5. Receipt of payments on short-term note received from a customer for inventory purchase.
____ 6. Preferred stock dividend payment.
____ 7. Cash purchase of another company.
____ 8. Cash paid for federal income tax.
____ 9. Cash paid to settle asset retirement obligation.
____10. Purchase of equipment for cash.

a. Operating activity—cash inflow
b. Operating activity—cash outflow
c. Investing activity—cash inflow
d. Investing activity—cash outflow
e. Financing activity—cash inflow
f. Financing activity—cash outflow

More Practice: 22-21, 22-40, 22-41, 22-75
Solution on p. 22-69.

LO 22-2 Prepare the operating activities cash flow section of the statement of cash flows using the indirect method

LO 22-2 Overview

Operating Activities Section—Indirect Method
- Section begins with net income
- Adjust net income for:
  - Noncash revenue and expense
  - Changes in noncash operating assets and noncash operating liabilities
- Adjust for operating cash flows not included in determination of net income

We now explain the preparation of the statement of cash flows beginning with the operating activities section. In general, preparing a statement of cash flows requires more information than is available simply from a review of an adjusted trial balance. To determine the cash consequences of transactions recorded in the accounting system on an accrual basis, we must review and analyze the income statement, comparative balance sheets, and other data from the accounting records.

Operating Activities Cash Flow Section—Indirect Method

One of the more important uses of the statement of cash flows is to help financial statement users understand the difference between net income, an *accrual measure*, and net cash provided by operations, a *cash-basis measure*. In many cases, these two amounts are markedly different. The operating activities section under the **indirect method** helps to explain the difference between net income and operating cash flows.

Under the indirect method, the operating activities section starts with net income. Adjustments are made to net income to arrive at net cash flows from operating activities, a cash-based amount. If a company were to report a *net loss*, the amount of the net loss would be the starting point for the operating activities section.

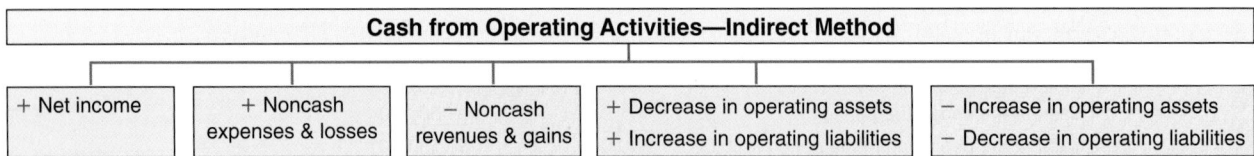

Cash from Operating Activities—Indirect Method

- + Net income
- + Noncash expenses & losses
- − Noncash revenues & gains
- + Decrease in operating assets
+ Increase in operating liabilities
- − Increase in operating assets
− Decrease in operating liabilities

The majority of items typically shown in the operating activities section are adjustments to net income including (1) noncash revenue and expense adjustments, and (2) changes in operating assets and operating liabilities. We can add a third category consisting of operating cash flows that do not enter into determination of net income.

Net income	
+ Noncash expenses and losses − Noncash revenues and gains	1) Noncash revenue/gain and expense/loss adjustments
− Increase in operating assets (other than cash) + Decrease in operating assets (other than cash) − Decrease in operating liabilities + Increase in operating liabilities	2) Changes in operating assets and operating liabilities
+/− Cash flows classified as operating, but not included in net income	3) Cash flows not included in income
= Net cash flows from operating activities	

Noncash Revenue and Expense Adjustments

Through accrual accounting, certain revenues and gains, and expenses and losses, affect net income, but not operating cash flows. These items require an adjustment in the operating activities section. *This adjustment is necessary because the related cash flows are accounted for in another section in the statement of cash flows, or because the related cash flows occur in a different time period, or because no cash flow is associated with the accrual at all.* The following are examples of **noncash items requiring adjustments to net income in the operating activities** section of the statement of cash flows.

Examples of Noncash Revenues and Gains

- Gain on disposition of fixed asset
- Gain on settlement of nonoperating liability
- Unrealized gain—income*

Examples of Noncash Expenses and Losses

- Loss on disposition of fixed asset
- Depreciation expense or Amortization expense
- Stock compensation expense
- Unrealized loss—income*
- Loss on settlement of nonoperating liability

*Unrealized holding gains and losses on investments affecting net income.

To reconcile net income to cash provided by operating activities, noncash revenues and gains are subtracted from net income. Gains on the sale of investments, including investments in property, plant, and equipment, or the settlement of nonoperating liabilities are reversed from net income because the full cash effects of these transactions are classified as investing or financing activities. This means the gain must be eliminated from the operating section.

Expenses and losses not involving cash payments are added back to net income to arrive at cash from operating activities. The more common adjustments include depreciation and amortization expense. If, for example, a fixed asset is depreciated, the original purchase of the asset (not the periodic depreciation) is shown as an investing activities cash outflow. Losses on the sale of investments, including investments in property, plant, and equipment, or the settlement of nonoperating liabilities are added back to net income because the cash effects of these transactions are classified as investing or financing activities.

Changes in Operating Assets (Other than Cash) and Noncash Operating Liabilities

Changes in operating assets and liabilities impact net income. For example, an increase in accounts receivable (an operating asset) increases revenue, which increases net income. Similarly, an increase in accounts payable (an operating liability) increases expense and decreases net income. Operating assets and liabilities are typically *current assets* and *current liabilities*, examples of which follow.

Examples of Operating Assets

- Accounts receivable
- Supplies
- Income tax receivable
- Misc. prepaid expenses
- Inventory
- Prepaid insurance

Examples of Operating Liabilities

- Accounts payable
- Income tax payable
- Deferred revenue
- Salaries payable
- Interest payable
- Accrued liabilities

To reconcile net income to cash provided by operating activities, changes in operating assets (other than cash) are subtracted from net income. **Subtracting a negative change means that decreases in noncash operating assets are added to net income. Subtracting a positive change means that increases in noncash operating assets are subtracted from net income.** For example, an increase in accounts receivable is subtracted from net income because

> Add **decrease in operating asset**
> Deduct **increase in operating asset**

the corresponding sales increased net income, but did not result in the collection of cash. A decrease in accounts receivable is added to net income because it reflects cash received from customers that was not included in income this period.

To reconcile net income to cash provided by operating activities, changes in operating liabilities are added to net income. This means **increases in operating liabilities are added back to net income and decreases in operating liabilities are subtracted from net income.** For example, an increase in accounts payable is added to net income because the corresponding expense decreased net income without affecting cash. A decrease in accounts payable is subtracted from net income because it reflects a cash payment on account but not an expense of the current period.

Add **increase in operating liability**
Deduct **decrease in operating liability**

In **Demo 22-2** we prepare the operating activities section of the cash flows statement.

Demo 22-2 **LO22-2** **Net Cash Flows from Operating Activities**

Demo MBC

The balance sheet, income statement, and selected additional information are provided for Gilmore Inc. The information provided here will be used to complete the operating, investing, and financing sections of the statement of cash flows for Gilmore Inc. in **Demo 22-2**, **Demo 22-3,** and **Demo 22-4.**

Balance Sheets (December 31)	2019	2020	Difference
Cash	$200,000	$62,000	$(138,000)
Accounts receivable	65,000	86,000	21,000
Allowance for doubtful accounts	(5,000)	(6,000)	(1,000)
Inventory	12,000	20,000	8,000
Prepaid expenses	6,000	5,000	(1,000)
Equipment	400,000	640,000	240,000
Accumulated depreciation	(100,000)	(140,000)	(40,000)
Patent, net	90,000	70,000	(20,000)
Total assets	**$668,000**	**$737,000**	**$ 69,000**
Accounts payable	$ 40,000	$ 60,000	$ 20,000
Salaries payable	60,000	50,000	(10,000)
Interest payable	6,000	9,000	3,000
Income tax payable	12,000	20,000	8,000
Mortgage payable	120,000	110,000	(10,000)
Bonds payable	200,000	100,000	(100,000)
Premium on bonds payable	8,000	3,000	(5,000)
Common stock, no-par	150,000	170,000	20,000
Retained earnings	72,000	215,000	143,000
Total liabilities and stockholders' equity	**$668,000**	**$737,000**	**$ 69,000**

Income Statement	2020
Sales	$820,000
Cost of goods sold	(380,000)
Depreciation expense	(100,000)
Amortization of patent	(20,000)
Other expenses	(51,000)
Gain on insurance settlement	10,000
Loss on bond retirement	(3,000)
Interest expense	(22,000)
Income tax expense	(71,000)
Net income	$183,000

Additional information

1. The company declared $40,000 of cash dividends in 2020.
2. Equipment (cost of $100,000 and accumulated depreciation of $60,000) was destroyed by fire; cash proceeds from insurance totaled $50,000.
3. Bonds with a stated value of $100,000 were retired on January 1, 2020, at 107.
4. All sales are on account.

Prepare the cash flows from operating activities section of the 2020 statement of cash flows for Gilmore Inc. following the indirect method of presentation.

continued

continued from previous page

Solution

Cash Flows from Operating Activities
For Year Ended December 31, 2020

Net income	$183,000	
Depreciation expense (1)	100,000	Noncash revenue/gain and expense/loss adjustments
Amortization of patent (2)	20,000	
Amortization of bond premium (3)	(1,000)	
Gain on insurance settlement (4)	(10,000)	
Loss on bond retirement (5)	3,000	
Increase in accounts receivable (6)	(20,000)	Changes in operating assets and operating liabilities
Increase in inventory (6)	(8,000)	
Decrease in prepaid expenses (6)	1,000	
Increase in accounts payable (6)	20,000	
Decrease in salaries payable (6)	(10,000)	
Increase in interest payable (6)	3,000	
Increase in income tax payable (6)	8,000	
Net cash provided by operating activities	$289,000	

Adjustments to the $183,000 of net income in the operating activities section are explained below.

1. **Noncash Expense Adjustment—Depreciation Expense (Equipment)**

Accumulated Depreciation

		100,000	Beg. bal.
Accumulated dep. on damaged equipment	60,000	**100,000**	Depreciation expense
		140,000	End. bal.

Cash Flows from Operating Activities

Net income	$ #
Add depreciation expense	**100,000**

Depreciation expense is a noncash expense that reduced net income. Although depreciation expense is sometimes separately listed in the income statement, the reconciliation of the accumulated depreciation account from the beginning to the end of the year illustrates that depreciation expense increases Accumulated Depreciation while removing accumulated depreciation associated with equipment sold or disposed of decreases it.

2. **Noncash Expense Adjustment—Amortization Expense (Patent)**

Patents, Net

Beg. bal.	90,000		
		20,000	Amortization expense
End. bal.	70, 000		

Cash Flows from Operating Activities

Net income	$ #
Add amortization expense of intangible asset	**20,000**

Amortization expense on a patent (a limited-life intangible asset) is a noncash expense that reduced net income. Because there were no references to a sale of patents in the data of the problem, we can assume that the full change in net patents is attributed to amortization. Amortization expense is also listed separately in the income statement in this example.

3. **Noncash Expense Adjustment—Amortization Expense (Bond Premium)**

Premium on Bonds Payable

		8,000	Beg. bal.
Premium on bonds redeemed*	4,000		
Amortization of bond premium	**1,000**		
		3,000	End. bal.

*Half of the bonds were retired on January 1, 2020 ($100,000/$200,000), therefore half of the premium is eliminated ($8,000/2 = $4,000). Alternatively, given the loss reported in the income statement, calculate as $107,000 − ($100,000 + $3,000) = $4,000.

Cash Flows from Operating Activities

Net income	$ #
Subtract premium amortized on bonds payable	**(1,000)**

Amortization of the premium of a bond *reduces* interest expense and *increases* net income. However, amortization of a premium does not affect cash flow so the required adjustment is negative. Premium amortization is subtracted because interest expense is less than the cash paid for interest during the period.

If Gilmore Inc. had instead recorded amortization of a discount on bonds payable, the amortization of the discount would be positive or *added back* to net income in cash flows from operating activities. The amount is added because interest expense is greater than the cash paid for interest during the period.

continued

continued from previous page

4. **Noncash Gain Adjustment—Gain on Insurance Settlement**

Cash Flows from Operating Activities		
Net income	$	#
Subtract gain on insurance settlement		(10,000)

Proceeds from the insurance settlement	$50,000
Less book value of equipment: ($100,000 − $60,000)	40,000
Gain on insurance settlement	$10,000

The gain on insurance settlement increased net income. Therefore, the gain is subtracted from net income in cash flows from operating activities. The gain is subtracted in arriving at cash provided by operating activities because the proceeds from the insurance settlement are considered investing cash flows. (The cash inflow from the insurance proceeds on damaged equipment will be addressed later in the investing section.)

5. **Noncash Loss Adjustment—Loss on Bond Retirement**

Cash Flows from Operating Activities		
Net income	$	#
Add loss on bond retirement		3,000

Bond redemption (1.07 × $100,000)	$(107,000)
Less book value of bond: [$100,000 + $4,000 ($8,000/2)]	(104,000)
Loss on bond retirement	$ (3,000)

The loss on bond retirement decreased net income. Therefore, the loss is added to net income in cash flows from operating activities. The loss is added back in arriving at cash provided by operating activities because the repayment of bonds is considered a financing transaction. (The cash outflow from the bond redemption will be addressed later in the financing section.)

6. **Adjustment for Changes in Operating Assets and Operating Liabilities**

Change in Account	Operating Asset or Liability	Adjustment to Operating Activities †	Reason for Adjustment
Increase in accounts receivable, net	**Increase** in operating asset	**Subtract** from cash from operating activities $(20,000)*	Increase in accounts receivable indicates sales on an accrual basis are *greater* than cash collected. Thus, the increase in accounts receivable is *subtracted* from net income.
Increase in inventory	**Increase** in operating asset	**Subtract** from cash from operating activities $(8,000)	Increase in inventory indicates that purchases are *greater* than cost of goods sold (accrual). Thus, the increase in inventory is *subtracted* from net income.
Decrease in prepaid expense	**Decrease** in operating asset	**Add** to cash from operating activities $1,000	Decrease in prepaid expense indicates that expenses on an accrual basis are *greater* than cash paid. Thus, the decrease in prepaid expenses is *added* to net income.
Increase in accounts payable	**Increase** in operating liability	**Add** to cash from operating activities $20,000	Increase in accounts payable indicates that expenses on an accrual basis are *greater* than cash paid for expenses. Thus, the increase in accounts payable is *added* to net income.
Increase in interest payable	**Increase** in operating liability	**Add** to cash from operating activities $3,000	Increase in interest payable indicates that interest expense on an accrual basis is *greater* than cash paid for interest. Thus, the increase in interest payable is *added* to net income.
Increase in income tax payable	**Increase** in operating liability	**Add** to cash from operating activities $8,000	Increase in income tax payable indicates that income tax expense on an accrual basis is *greater* than cash paid for income tax expense. Thus, the increase in income tax payable is *added* to net income.
Decrease in salaries payable	**Decrease** in operating liability	**Subtract** from cash from operating activities $(10,000)	Decrease in salaries payable indicates that cash paid for salaries is *greater* than salaries expense on an accrual basis. Thus, the decrease in salaries payable is *subtracted* from net income.

*Net change in accounts receivable can be calculated as follows:

Accounts receivable, net January 1, 2020	$60,000 ($65,000 − $5,000)
Accounts receivable, net December 31, 2020	80,000 ($86,000 − $6,000)
Increase in accounts receivable, net	$20,000

†

Cash Flows from Operating Activities		
Net income	$	#
Subtract increase in operating assets		
Increase in accounts receivable, net		(20,000)
Increase in inventory		(8,000)
Add decrease in operating asset		
Decrease in prepaid expense		1,000
Add increase in operating liabilities		
Increase in accounts payable		20,000
Increase in interest payable		3,000
Increase in income tax payable		8,000
Subtract decrease in operating liability		
Decrease in salaries payable		(10,000)
Net cash flows from operating activities	$	#

Reconciling the Net Change in Accounts Receivable

In **Demo 22-2** we calculated the change in *net* accounts receivable or accounts receivable (gross) less the allowance for doubtful accounts. Does the change in *net* accounts receivable account for noncash changes due to bad debt expense considering any write-offs of customer accounts? Let's reconstruct an accounts receivable analysis to answer this question. Assume the following additional information pertaining to Gilmore Inc.

Bad debt expense	$ 4,000
Recoveries of accounts previously written off	2,000
Accounts written off	5,000
Collections on account	796,000

T-accounts can be used to reconstruct the activity for the year.

Accounts Receivable

	Debit	Credit	
Beg. bal.	65,000		
Credit sales	820,000		
		796,000	Cash collection
Recoveries	2,000	5,000	Write-offs
End. bal.	86,000		

Allowance for Doubtful Accounts

	Debit	Credit	
		5,000	Beg. bal.
Write-offs	5,000	2,000	Recoveries
		4,000	Bad debt expense
		6,000	End. bal.

The net change in accounts receivable of $20,000 consists of the following two *noncash* components.

Increase in gross accounts receivable before write-offs	$24,000	($820,000 − $796,000)
Increase in bad debt expense	4,000	(given)
Reconciling item to net income in the operating activities section	$20,000	

Thus, using the *change in net accounts receivable* to reconcile net income in the operating section of the statement of cash flows will adjust for changes in gross accounts receivable, bad debt expense, and write-offs of accounts.

Other Items Affecting Cash Flows from Operating Activities

The following adjustments found in the operating activities section are *not* included as part of the Gilmore Inc. example but do warrant further explanation.

Noncash Expense Adjustment—Compensation expense for Share-Based Compensation Plans

Assume: A company recognizes compensation expense of $30,000 related to stock options granted to its employees. The company would increase compensation expense and increase Paid-in Capital—Stock Options *without* an impact on cash. This means a noncash adjustment of **$30,000** must be added back to net income to arrive at cash flows from operating activities.

Cash Flows from Operating Activities	
Net income	$ #
Add compensation expense (noncash)	30,000

Noncash Adjustment—Net Unrealized Gain or Loss—Income

Companies often report unrealized holding gains and losses on investments in debt and equity securities in net income. Unrealized gains or losses reported in net income are noncash items that require adjustments to the operating activities section of the statement of cash flows.

Assume: A company had an *unrealized* loss on equity securities (accounted for at fair value) of **$5,000** that resulted in a decrease in net income. This noncash unrealized loss would be added back to net income in the operating section.

Cash Flows from Operating Activities	
Net income	$ #
Add unrealized loss—income	5,000
Subtract unrealized gain—income	n.a.

Net Unrealized Gain or Loss—OCI

Unrealized holding gains or losses on available-for-sale debt securities are recognized in other comprehensive income. No adjustment to the statement of cash flows is required for these unrealized holding gains or losses because there is no impact on net income.

Noncash Expense Adjustment—Pension Expense on Postretirement Benefit Plans

Pension expense consists of a number of items including service costs and interest on the projected benefit obligation. However, this is a noncash expense because cash outflows relate only to the funding of the pension plan. This means when pension expense exceeds the plan funding, the excess is added back to net income in the statement of cash flows. On the other hand, if plan funding exceeds pension expense, the excess would be subtracted from net income in the statement of cash flows.

Assume: A company had a defined benefit pension plan where recorded pension expense was \$10,000 but cash contributions were only \$8,000. The amount of noncash pension expense of **\$2,000** (\$10,000 − \$8,000) would be added back to net income in the operating activities section of the statement of cash flows. The net effect is that the \$8,000 funding of the benefit pension plan (cash amount) is deducted in the operating section of the statement of cash flows.

Cash Flows from Operating Activities	
Net income	\$ #
Add excess of pension expense over cash contributions	2,000
Subtract excess of cash contributions over pension expense	n.a.

Noncash Revenue Adjustment under the Equity Method

When a company has an investment in another company reported using the equity method, adjustments are required to the operating section of the statement of cash flows.

Assume: Lanta Company had an investment (35% interest) in another entity, Ashton Company. The investment was appropriately accounted for under the *equity method*. If Ashton Company reported net income of \$50,000 and paid dividends of \$12,000, the Lanta Company would have recorded the following.

- Investment income for this investment of \$17,500 (0.35 × \$50,000), along with a corresponding increase to the investment account. This represents noncash revenue for Lanta Company.
- Cash dividends received on the investment in Ashton Company of \$4,200 (0.35 × \$12,000) would increase cash and decrease the investment. Although cash increased, there is no impact on net income.

The excess of investment income over the cash dividend of **\$13,300** (\$17,500 − \$4,200) would be *deducted from* net income in the operating activities section of the statement of cash flows. If cash dividends received exceeded investment income, the excess must be *added* to net income. The accounting literature specifies that a "return of investment" should be classified as an investing activity. This occurs when an investor's *cumulative* dividends received exceed *cumulative* recognized investment income.

Cash Flows from Operating Activities	
Net income	\$ #
Subtract excess of share of revenue over dividends from equity investments	(13,300)
Add excess of share of dividends over revenue from equity investments	n.a.

230-10-45-21D When a reporting entity applies the equity method, it shall make an accounting policy election to classify distributions received from equity method investees using either of the following approaches:

a. Cumulative earnings approach: Distributions received are considered returns on investment and shall be classified as cash inflows from operating activities unless the investor's cumulative distributions received less distributions received in prior periods that were determined to be returns of investment exceed cumulative equity in earnings recognized by the investor (as adjusted for amortization of basis differences). When such an excess occurs, the current-period distribution up to this excess is considered a return of investment and shall be classified as cash inflows from investing activities.

b. Nature of the distribution approach: Distributions received shall be classified on the basis of the nature of the activity or activities of the investee that generated the distribution as either a return on investment (classified as a cash inflow from operating activities) or a return of investment (classified as a cash inflow from investing activities) when such information is available.

Noncash Income Tax Expense Adjustment Related to Changes in Deferred Tax Assets and Liabilities

Changes in tax expense may be the result of changes in deferred tax assets or deferred tax liabilities. Noncash adjustments to tax expense due to changes in deferred taxes are eliminated in the operating section of the statement of cash flows.

Change in Deferred Tax Account	Adjustment to Operating Section	Explanation
Increase in deferred tax liability	Add to net income	An increase in a deferred tax liability indicates that tax expense on an accrual basis is greater than taxes paid. Because the cash is not paid now, the amount is added to net income.
Decrease in deferred tax liability	Subtract from net income	A decrease in a deferred tax liability indicates that taxes previously accrued are now paid. Thus, the amount is deducted from net income because the cash outflow is not currently reflected in tax expense.
Increase in a deferred tax asset	Subtract from net income	An increase in a deferred tax asset indicates that taxes paid are greater than tax expense on an accrual basis. Because cash is paid now, the amount is subtracted from net income.
Decrease in a deferred tax asset	Add to net income	A decrease in a deferred tax asset indicates that taxes paid in previous periods are not expensed. Because the amounts were paid in a previous period, the decrease in deferred tax asset is added to net income.

Cash Flows from Operating Activities	
Net income	$ #
Add increase in deferred tax liability	+#
Subtract decrease in deferred tax liability	−#
Subtract increase in deferred tax asset	−#
Add decrease in deferred tax asset	+#
Net cash flows from operating activities	$ #

APPLE

Real World—CASH FLOWS FROM OPERATING ACTIVITIES

APPLE [AAPL]

Apple Inc. reported the following cash flows from operating activities in its recent report on Form 10-K.

Consolidated Statements of Cash Flows (In millions)	**September 30, 2017**
Operating activities:	
Net income	$48,351
Adjustments to reconcile net income to cash generated by operating activities:	
Depreciation and amortization	10,157
Share-based compensation expense	4,840
Deferred income tax expense	5,966
Other	(166)
Changes in operating assets and liabilities:	
Accounts receivable, net	(2,093)
Inventories	(2,723)
Vendor non-trade receivables	(4,254)
Other current and non-current assets	(5,318)
Accounts payable	9,618
Deferred revenue	(626)
Other current and non-current liabilities	(154)
Cash generated by operating activities	$63,598

REVIEW 22-2 **LO22-2** **Prepare the Operating Activities Section**

Review MBC

The following is Vegas Corporation's comparative balance sheets for 2019 and 2020 ($ thousands).

Assets	**2019**	**2020**	**Difference**
Cash and cash equivalents	$ 3,500	$ 4,845	$1,345
Accounts receivable, net	5,840	5,640	(200)
Inventory	8,575	9,250	675
Property, plant, and equipment	14,835	16,535	1,700
Accumulated depreciation	(5,200)	(5,825)	(625)
Investment in Belle Co.	1,375	1,555	180
Loan receivable (nontrade)	0	1,350	1,350
Total assets	$28,925	$33,350	$4,425
Liabilities and Stockholders' Equity			
Accounts payable	$ 4,775	$ 5,075	$ 300
Salaries payable	250	150	(100)
Dividends payable	450	400	(50)
Long-term debt	0	2,000	2,000
Common stock, $1 par	2,500	2,500	0
Paid-in capital in excess of par	7,500	7,512	12
Retained earnings	13,450	15,713	2,263
Total liabilities and stockholders' equity	$28,925	$33,350	$4,425

Additional information

1. On December 31, 2019, Vegas Corp. acquired 30% of Belle Company's common stock for $1,375. On that date, the carrying value of Belle's net assets and liabilities, which approximated fair value, was $5,500. Belle reported income of $600 for the year ended December 31, 2020. No dividend was paid on Belle's common stock during the year.
2. During 2020, Vegas Corp. loaned $1,500 to Chase Company, an unrelated company. Chase made the first semiannual principal repayment of $150, plus interest at 10% on October 1, 2020.
3. On January 2, 2020, Vegas Corp. sold equipment with an original cost of $300 and with a carrying value of $175 for $245 cash.
4. Vegas Corp.'s net income for 2020 was $2,713.
5. Compensation expense recorded on restricted stock awards for 2020 totaled $12.

Required

Prepare the operating activities section of the company's 2020 statement of cash flows following the indirect method.

More Practice:
22-23, 22-24, 22-25, 22-42, 22-43, 22-44
Solution on p. 22-69.

LO 22-3 Prepare the investing activities section of the statement of cash flows

LO 22-3 Overview

Investing Activities
- Reports cash flows due to changes in assets including fixed assets, intangible assets, and investments in other companies
- Gross cash inflows and outflows are reported separately

Investing activities include the acquisition and disposal of assets such as property, plant, and equipment, investments (other than those in trading accounts), intangible assets, and nontrade receivables (transaction outside of normal operations with a customer). Unlike the operating activities section under the indirect method where net income is adjusted to cash, items in the investing section are simply listed as either *a cash inflow* or *a cash outflow*. This means that gross cash inflows and outflows for investing activities are generally represented separately in the statement of cash flows.

The accounting guidance provides examples of cash inflows and cash outflows from investing activities including the following items.

230-10-45-12a Receipts from collections or sales of loans made by the entity and of other entities' debt instruments . . .

230-10-45-12b Receipts from sales of equity instruments of other entities . . .

230-10-45-12c Receipts from sales of property, plant, and equipment and other productive assets

230-10-45-13a Disbursements for loans made by the entity and payments to acquire debt instruments of other entities (other than cash equivalents and certain debt instruments that are acquired specifically for resale . . .)

230-10-45-13b Payments to acquire equity instruments of other entities (other than certain equity instruments carried in a trading account . . .)

230-10-45-13c Payments at the time of purchase or soon before or after purchase to acquire property, plant, and equipment and other productive assets, including interest capitalized as part of the cost of those assets. Generally, only advance payments, the down payment, or other amounts paid at the time of purchase or soon before or after purchase of property, plant, and equipment and other productive assets are investing cash outflows.

Included in the investing section as part of the payment to acquire fixed assets is capitalized cash interest paid. These items are reflected in the following graphic.

Cash from Investing Activities

- − Cash paid for fixed assets
- − Cash paid for investments
- − Cash paid for intangible assets
- + Cash paid for sale of fixed assets
- + Cash received for sale of investments
- + Cash received for sale of intangible assets

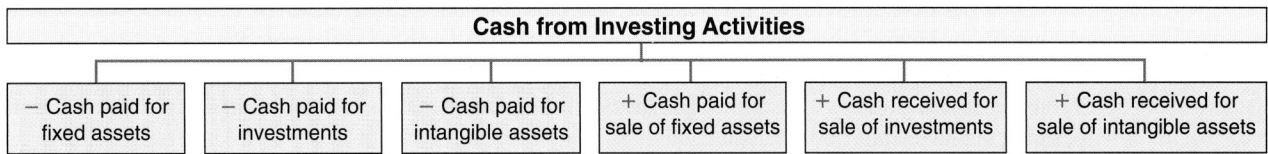

In **Demo 22-3** we continue with Gilmore Inc. by preparing the investing activities section of the statement of cash flows. After this Demo, we examine other items that may be found in the investing activities section.

Net Cash Flows from Investing Activities — LO22-3 — Demo 22-3

Prepare the cash flows from investing activities section of the 2020 statement of cash flows for Gilmore Inc. using the information provided in **Demo 22-2**.

Solution

Cash Flows from Investing Activities	
Proceeds from insurance settlement (1).	$ 50,000
Purchase of equipment (2).	(340,000)
Net cash used by investing activities	$ 290,000

Amounts included in cash flows from investing activities are described below.

1. **Proceeds from Insurance Settlement**

Proceeds from the insurance settlement.	$50,000
Less book value of destroyed equipment ($100,000 − $60,000). . .	40,000
Gain on insurance settlement.	$10,000

Cash Flows from Investing Activities	
Add proceeds from insurance settlement.	$50,000

The proceeds from the insurance settlement received in cash are recognized as a cash inflow in the investing section because the settlement is intended to compensate Gilmore for loss of the building. Recall that the gain was eliminated from net income in the operating section, this means the full $50,000 cash proceeds is recorded as an investing activity.

2. **Purchase of Equipment**

Property, Plant, and Equipment			
Beg. bal.	400,000		
		100,000	Original cost of destroyed equipment
Purchase(s) of equipment	**340,000**		
End. bal.	640,000		

Cash Flows from Investing Activities	
Subtract purchase of equipment.	$(340,000)

The property, plant and equipment account increases by $240,000 during the year. The account is reduced by the $100,000 original cost of the destroyed equipment, so equipment purchases must be $340,000. The purchase(s) of equipment is recorded as a cash outflow in the investing section.

Other Item Affecting Cash Flows from Investing Activities

The following adjustment in the investing activities section is not included as part of the Gilmore Inc. example but does warrant further explanation.

Purchase or Sale of Investments in Other Companies The cash inflows from the sale of an investment in another company or the cash outflows from the purchase of an investment in another company *are generally treated as investing activities.* Unless investments are held specifically for resale as explained in the previous section, related cash flows are classified as investing activities.

Assume: A company purchases equity investments (accounted for under the fair value method) in another company for $10,000 and that these assets are *not* acquired specifically for resale. In the same annual period, the company sold half of the investments for $5,000. The purchase price and sale proceeds of these investments would be included as cash flows in the investing section of the statement of cash flows. (Any gains or losses on sales would be reported as reconciling items in the operating activities section.)

Cash Flows from Investing Activities	
Subtract purchase price of investments	$(10,000)
Add proceeds from sale of investments	5,000

In the case of a business combination, a company (the acquirer) purchases a controlling interest in another business. Cash flows from investing activities include a single line item, cash paid to purchase a business (net of cash acquired) or cash received from the sale of a business (net of cash sold). In addition, the non-cash effects of the business combination would be disclosed. (Subsequent to the acquisition of a business, cash flows of the acquirer and the newly acquired business are combined and presented within operating, investing, and financing activities as appropriate.)

APPLE [AAPL]

APPLE

Real World—CASH FLOWS FROM INVESTING ACTIVITIES

Apple Inc. reported the following cash flows from investing activities in a recent report on Form 10-K.

Consolidated Statements of Cash Flows (In millions)	**September 30, 2017**
Investing activities:	
Purchases of marketable securities	$(159,486)
Proceeds from maturities of marketable securities.	31,775
Proceeds from sales of marketable securities	94,564
Payments made in connection with business acquisitions, net	(329)
Payments for acquisition of property, plant and equipment	(12,451)
Payments for acquisition of intangible assets.	(344)
Payments for strategic investments, net.	(395)
Other.	220
Cash used in investing activities	$(46,446)

REVIEW 22-3 **LO22-3** **Prepare the Investing Activities Section**

Using the information for Vegas Corporation in **Review 22-2**, prepare the investing activities section of the company's 2020 statement of cash flows.

Review MBC

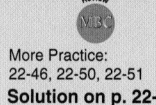

More Practice:
22-46, 22-50, 22-51

Solution on p. 22-70.

LO 22-4 Prepare the financing activities section of the statement of cash flows

LO 22-4 Overview

Financing Activities

- Reports cash flows due to changes in equity, nontrade debt, and payment of dividends
- Gross cash inflows and outflows are reported separately

Financing activities include cash receipts and payments for equity financing through common and preferred stock issuances, and principal payments and proceeds on both short-term and long-term debt (excluding trade debt), as well as dividend payments. Similar to the investing activities section, items in the financing activities section are simply listed as either *a cash inflow* or *a cash outflow*.

The accounting guidance provides examples of cash inflows and cash outflows from financing activities including the following items.

230-10-45-14a Proceeds from issuing equity instruments.

230-10-45-14b Proceeds from issuing bonds, mortgages, notes, and from other short- or long-term borrowing.

230-10-45-15a Payments of dividends or other distributions to owners, including outlays to reacquire the entity's equity instruments.

230-10-45-15b Repayments of amounts borrowed.

230-10-45-15c Other principal payments to creditors who have extended long-term credit. See paragraph 230-10-45-13(c), which indicates that most principal payments on seller-financed debt directly related to a purchase of property, plant, and equipment or other productive assets are financing cash outflows.

230-10-45-15e Payments for debt issue costs.

These items are reflected in the following graphic.

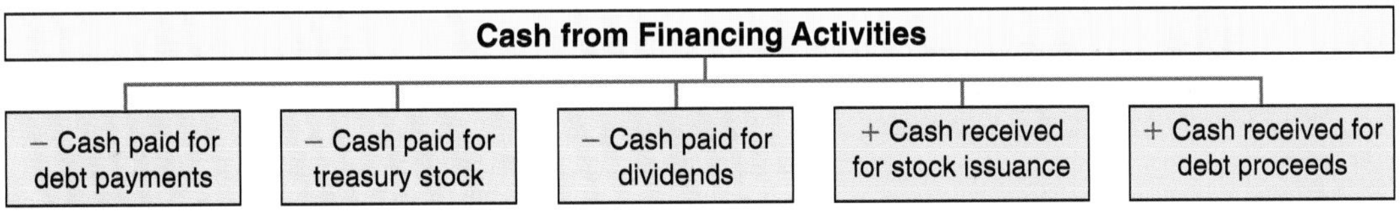

In **Demo 22-4** we continue with Gilmore Inc. by preparing the financing activities section of the statement of cash flows. After this Demo, we examine other items that might be found in the financing activities section.

EXPANDING YOUR KNOWLEDGE **Exception: Presenting Cash Flows on a Net Basis**

While financing and investing activities are generally presented as gross cash inflows and outflows on the statement of cash flows, the accounting guidance provides an exception. In cases where maturities of debt, investments, or loan receivables have a maturity of three months or less, preparers report cash flows on a *net basis*. For example, the borrowings and payments on a revolving line of credit where the payable is due on demand or within a 3 month time period would qualify for net reporting.

230-10-45-9 Providing that the original maturity of the asset or liability is three months or less, cash receipts and payments pertaining to any of the following qualify for net reporting for the reasons stated in the preceding paragraph:

a. Investments (other than cash equivalents)
b. Loans receivable
c. Debt.

For purposes of this paragraph, amounts due on demand are considered to have maturities of three months or less.

Net Cash Flows from Financing Activities **LO22-4** **Demo 22-4**

Demo MBC

Answer the following requirement using the information from **Demo 22-2** for Gilmore Inc.

a. Prepare the cash flows from financing activities section of the 2020 statement of cash flows.
b. Prepare the full statement of cash flows for 2020.

Solution

a. **Cash Flows from Financing Activities**

Payment to retire bonds (1)	$(107,000)
Dividend payment (2)	(40,000)
Principal payments on mortgage (3)	(10,000)
Issuance of common stock (4)	20,000
Net cash used by financing activities	$(137,000)

Each of the financing activities is explained below.

continued

continued from previous page

1. **Payment to Retire Bonds**

Cash Flows from Financing Activities	
Subtract payment to retire bonds	$(107,000)

Bond redemption (1.07 × $100,000)	**$107,000**
Less book value of bond ($100,000 + $4,000 [$8,000/2])	104,000
Loss on bond retirement	$ 3,000

The cash paid to retire the bond is included as an outflow in the financing section. If the indirect method is used for the operating section, the $3,000 loss is added back to net income to arrive at cash provided by operating activities.

2. **Dividend Payment**

Cash Flows from Financing Activities	
Subtract payment of dividends	$(40,000)

Retained Earnings			
		72,000	Beg. bal.
Dividends	**40,000**	183,000	Net income
		215,000	End. bal.

Dividends paid to stockholders are included as an outflow in the financing section. The amount of dividends of $40,000 is required to balance the beginning and ending retained earnings given a net income amount of $183,000.

3. **Principal Payments on Mortgage**

Cash Flows from Financing Activities	
Subtract principal payments on mortgage	$(10,000)

Mortgage Payable			
		120,000	Beg. bal.
Payment on mortgages	**10,000**		
		110,000	End. bal.

Mortgage payable decreased by $10,000 suggesting that the mortgage principal payments were $10,000 (assuming no additions to mortgage debt). This amount is included as a cash outflow in the financing section. See that if there were additions to mortgage debt, the additions and payments would be shown on separate lines in the statement of cash flows.

4. **Common Stock Issuance**

Cash Flows from Financing Activities	
Add proceeds from the issuance of common stock	$20,000

Common Stock			
		150,000	Beg. bal.
		20,000	Issuance of common stock
		170,000	End. bal.

Common stock increased by $20,000, suggesting that common stock was issued (assuming no stock buybacks). This stock issuance is included as a cash inflow in the financing section of the statement of cash flows.

b. **Complete Statement of Cash Flows**

The complete statement of cash flows where the total of the three sections (operating, investing, financing) are reconciled to the change in cash follows. The total of three sections of $(138,000) reconciles the beginning and ending cash balances on the balance sheet of $200,000 and $62,000, respectively.

Cash Flows from Operating Activities	
Net income	$ 183,000
Depreciation expense	100,000
Amortization of patent	20,000
Amortization of bond premium	(1,000)
Gain on insurance settlement	(10,000)
Loss on bond retirement	3,000
Increase in accounts receivable	(20,000)
Increase in inventory	(8,000)
Decrease in prepaid expenses	1,000
Increase in accounts payable	20,000
Decrease in salaries payable	(10,000)
Increase in interest payable	3,000
Increase in income tax payable	8,000
Net cash provided by operating activities	289,000

continued

continued from previous page

Cash Flows from Investing Activities	
Proceeds from insurance settlement	50,000
Purchase of equipment	(340,000)
Net cash used by investing activities	(290,000)
Cash Flows from Financing Activities	
Payment to retire bonds	(107,000)
Dividends payment	(40,000)
Principal payments on mortgage	(10,000)
Issuance of common stock	20,000
Net cash used by financing activities	(137,000)
Net decrease in cash	(138,000)
Cash, January 1, 2020	200,000
Cash, December 31, 2020	$ 62,000

Other Financing Activities

The following adjustments in the financing activities section are not included as part of the Gilmore Inc. example but do warrant further explanation.

Leases

When a lessee initiates a finance lease, the lessee reports the right-of-use asset and lease liability as a noncash transaction. A lessor would also report a noncash transaction for the shift from a long-term asset (or inventory) to a leased asset. The classification of lease payments is illustrated in **Exhibit 22-4**.

EXHIBIT 22-4
Classification of Lease Payments

Lease Type	Lessee	Lessor
Operating Lease	Operating activity	Operating activity
Finance Lease (lessee) Sales-Type Lease (lessor)	Operating activity: Interest Financing activity: Principal	Operating activity

Assume: A lessee makes an annual lease payment on a finance lease for $15,000, where $3,800 of the payment represents interest expense. The annual lease payment would be recorded in two sections: $3,800 would be recorded as part of net income in the operating activities section while **$11,200** ($15,000 − $3,800) would be recorded as a cash outflow in the financing activities section.

Cash Flows from Financing Activities	
Subtract lease principal payment	$(11,200)

Dividends Payable

A change in dividends payable is *not* an adjustment necessary to reconcile net income to cash provided by operating activities because accrued dividends payable have no effect on net income. Cash dividends paid are a financing outflow. To compute the amount of cash dividends paid during the period, the change in dividends payable is subtracted from dividends declared as shown in the following example.

Assume: A company declares dividends of $40,000. In addition, assume that dividends payable on January 1, 2020, was $4,000 and dividends payable at the end of the year was $10,000. Cash dividends paid would be $40,000 less the increase in dividends payable of $6,000 or $34,000 as shown in the following T-account. An increase in dividends payable is subtracted from dividends declared because an increase in dividends payable implies dividends declared were greater than dividends paid. Conversely, a decrease in dividends payable implies dividends paid were greater than dividends declared. A decrease in dividends payable would be added to dividends declared to arrive at dividends paid.

Cash Flows from Financing Activities	
Subtract payment of dividends	$(34,000)

Dividends Payable			
		4,000	Beg. bal.
Dividends paid	34,000	40,000	Dividends declared
		10,000	End. bal.

Installment Note Payable

A company may sign an installment note, which is repaid through equal payments over the term of the note, where the payments include both principal and interest. The portion of the payment that is interest will reduce net income as an expense, and thus is included in net cash flows from operating activities. However, the portion of the payment that is a reduction of the note balance is recorded as an outflow from financing activities.

Assume: A company signs a 5-year installment note that requires annual payments of $20,000. In the current year, the payment of $20,000 is made up of $7,000 interest, and $13,000 as a reduction in principal. The amount of interest expense of $7,000 would be reported as interest expense that would reduce net income. The reduction in principal of **$13,000** would be reported in the financing activities section of the statement of cash flows as a cash outflow.

Cash Flows from Financing Activities	
Subtract principal payments on installment note	$(13,000)

EXPANDING YOUR KNOWLEDGE — Effect of Foreign Exchange Rate Fluctuations

The Gap Inc. included the *effect of foreign exchange rate fluctuation* in determining the net increase (decrease) in cash and cash equivalents. ASC 830 requires that companies report the effect of exchange rate changes on cash, cash equivalents, and restricted cash held in foreign currencies as a separate part of the reconciliation in the statement of cash flows. The following table was constructed from information included in Gap's Consolidated Statements of Cash Flows in its recent report on Form 10-K.

$ millions	**Fiscal Year 2017**
Net cash provided by operating activities.............................	$1,380
Net cash used for investing activities................................	(668)
Net cash used for financing activities................................	(731)
Effect of foreign exchange rate fluctuations on cash and cash equivalents...	19
Net increase (decrease) in cash and cash equivalents	—
Cash and cash equivalents at beginning of period......................	1,783
Cash and cash equivalents at end of period	$1,783

APPLE

Real World—CASH FLOWS FROM FINANCING ACTIVITIES

APPLE [AAPL]

Apple Inc. reported the following cash flows from financing activities in a recent report on Form 10-K.

Consolidated Statements of Cash Flows (In millions)	**September 30, 2017**
Financing activities:	
Proceeds from issuance of common stock...........................	$ 555
Excess tax benefits from equity awards	627
Payments for taxes related to net share settlement of equity awards	(1,874)
Payments for dividends and dividend equivalents	(12,769)
Repurchases of common stock.....................................	(32,900)
Proceeds from issuance of term debt, net	28,662
Repayments of term debt	(3,500)
Change in commercial paper, net..................................	3,852
Cash used in financing activities	$(17,347)

Prepare the Financing Activities Section

LO22-4 REVIEW 22-4

Part One—Financing Activities Section

Using the information for Vegas Corporation from **Review 22-2**, (a) prepare the financing activities section of the company's 2020 statement of cash flows and (b) reconcile the totals of the operating, investing, and financing activities sections to the change in cash for the year.

Review MBC

Part Two—Complete Statement of Cash Flows

Comparative balance sheets along with some additional information is provided for Eagle Company.

Balance Sheets, December 31	2019	2020	Difference
Cash and cash equivalents	$ 100	$ 65	$ (35)
Restricted cash	20	30	10
Accounts receivable, net	280	170	(110)
Inventory	100	300	200
Equipment	2,000	2,700	700
Accumulated depreciation	(200)	(500)	(300)
Total assets	$2,300	$2,765	$465
Accounts payable	$ 275	$ 240	$ (35)
Salaries payable	50	25	(25)
Bonds payable	600	700	100
Common stock, no-par	1,100	1,200	100
Retained earnings	275	600	325
Total liabilities and stockholders' equity	$2,300	$2,765	$465

Additional information

- Net income for the year ended December 31, 2020, was $515.
- Depreciation expense for the year ended December 31, 2020, was $400.
- Equipment with an original cost of $400 and accumulated depreciation of $100 was sold for $100.
- Equipment purchases in 2020 were made with cash.
- All dividends declared were cash dividends.

Present the statement of cash flows following the indirect method for Eagle Company for 2020.

More Practice: 22-28, 22-50, 22-51, 22-53, 22-54, 22-55
Solution on p. 22-70.

Describe required disclosures including that for noncash transactions

LO 22-5

A company has a number of reporting requirements when presenting the statement of cash flows. Among the disclosures required is information regarding a company's noncash transactions where investing and/or financing activities do not involve the receipt or payment of cash.

Reporting Requirements

- Reconciliation of net income to operating cash flow
- Report investing and financing inflows and outflows
- Disclose interest and income taxes paid
- Disclose noncash investing and financing transactions
- Disclose nature and amounts of restricted cash and cash equivalents

LO 22-5 Overview

Cash Flow Reporting

Under the indirect method, the reconciliation of net income to cash flows from operating activities is provided either on the face of the statement of cash flows or in a disclosure note. Reconciliation of net income to operating cash should include all major classes of deferrals and accruals including changes during the period in receivables, inventory, and accounts payable pertaining to operating activities.

230-10-45-31 If the indirect method is used, the reconciliation may be either reported within the statement of cash flows or provided in a separate schedule, with the statement of cash flows reporting only the net cash flow from operating activities.

Under the indirect method, the amount of interest paid (net of amounts capitalized) and income taxes paid during the period shall be disclosed.

230-10-50-2 If the indirect method is used, amounts of interest paid (net of amounts capitalized) . . . and income taxes paid during the period shall be disclosed.

The following items are required disclosures relating to cash flows, regardless of the method used.

- Both investing and financing cash inflows and outflows should be reported separately.

- Information about all noncash investing and financing activities of an entity shall be disclosed as discussed below.
- Information about the nature of restrictions on its cash, cash equivalents, and amounts generally described as restricted cash or restricted cash equivalents shall be disclosed.

230-10-50-7 An entity shall disclose information about the nature of restrictions on its cash, cash equivalents, and amounts generally described as restricted cash or restricted cash equivalents.

Noncash Transactions

Noncash investing and financing transactions are transactions that involve no exchange of cash. For example, the purchase of equipment can be made through issuance of a note payable.

Examples of noncash investing and financing transactions follow.

- Conversion of debt securities to equity securities.
- Acquisition of assets by assuming directly related liabilities.
- Securing a right-of-use asset in exchange for a lease liability.
- Obtaining a beneficial interest as consideration for transferring financial assets.
- Refinancing a long-term note payable.
- Obtaining a building or investment asset by receiving a gift.
- Exchanging noncash assets or liabilities for other noncash assets or liabilities.

230-10-50-4 Examples of noncash investing and financing transactions are converting debt to equity; acquiring assets by assuming directly related liabilities, such as purchasing a building by incurring a mortgage to the seller; obtaining a right-of-use asset in exchange for a lease liability; obtaining a beneficial interest as consideration for transferring financial assets (excluding cash), including the transferor's trade receivables, in a securitization transaction; obtaining a building or investment asset by receiving a gift; and exchanging noncash assets or liabilities for other noncash assets or liabilities.

Noncash investing and financing transactions are omitted from the statement of cash flows because they do not reflect cash flows. This leads to different reporting outcomes for similar transactions. For example if a firm first buys an asset with cash and then later needs to borrow on its line of credit to replenish the cash on hand, the statement of cash flows will show an investing cash outflow for purchase of the asset, and a financing cash inflow when the proceeds from borrowing are received. However, if the firm acquires an asset by signing a directly related loan, no investing outflow or financing inflow will be shown on the statement of cash flows because the exchange of a promise to pay cash in the future in return for a noncash asset is considered a noncash transaction at the time of the exchange. For this reason, noncash transactions should be disclosed when material. The disclosure may be included on the same page as the statement of cash flows. Otherwise, the transactions may be disclosed in the notes accompanying financial statements.

230-10-50-3 Information about all investing and financing activities of an entity during a period that affect recognized assets or liabilities but that do not result in cash receipts or cash payments in the period shall be disclosed. Those disclosures may be either narrative or summarized in a schedule, and they shall clearly relate the cash and noncash aspects of transactions involving similar items.

230-10-50-6 If there are only a few such noncash transactions, it may be convenient to include them on the same page as the statement of cash flows. Otherwise, the transactions may be reported elsewhere in the financial statements, clearly referenced to the statement of cash flows.

Management Judgment

Classification of Cash Flows

Certain cash inflows and outflows may have aspects of more than one class of cash flows. For example, insurance proceeds received may provide lump sum fixed compensation for business losses as a result of a hurricane. The types of losses incurred may include damage to buildings, damage to inventory, lost profits, and the inability to make loan payments. In the absence of specific guidance in accounting standards, a company classifies each separately identifiable cash flow as an operating, investing, or financing activity on the basis of the nature of the underlying cash flows. If a cash flow has attributes of more than one class of cash flows that cannot be separately identified, classification is based on the primary source or use. Both identifying the nature of the items and identifying the cash amount requires management judgment.

230-10-45-22 Certain cash receipts and payments may have aspects of more than one class of cash flows. The classification of those cash receipts and payments shall be determined first by applying specific guidance in this Topic and other applicable Topics. In the absence of specific guidance, a reporting entity shall determine each separately identifiable source or each separately identifiable use within the cash receipts and cash payments on the basis of the nature of the underlying cash flows, including when judgment is necessary to estimate the amount of each separately identifiable source or use. A reporting entity shall then classify each separately identifiable source or use within the cash receipts and payments on the basis of their nature in financing, investing, or operating activities.

230-10-45-22A In situations in which cash receipts and payments have aspects of more than one class of cash flows and cannot be separated by source or use (for example, when a piece of equipment is acquired or produced by an entity to be rented to others for a period of time and then sold), the appropriate classification shall depend on the activity that is likely to be the predominant source or use of cash flows for the item.

Transactions Affecting Cash Flow Presentation

Transactions initiated by management can have a direct impact on the net cash flows reported in the statement of cash flows. For example, a company may accelerate collections from customers on account by offering discounts or by selling the receivables to a factor. A company may delay payments to suppliers on account to report a more favorable cash position. A company may also choose to delay or decrease discretionary spending items to report a more favorable cash position. In most of these cases, the positive impact reported in cash flows affects only the current period (and potentially a shift from some other period).

While the transactions described above increase cash for the current period, in some other cases, transactions are initiated by management, that change cash flow classification but not overall cash flows. For example, if an item is purchased and recorded as expense, the cash outflow is recognized within net cash flows from operating activities. However, if the item is capitalized and depreciated, the initial outflow is recognized as a net cash flow from investing activities. Likewise, if R&D is developed internally, the costs are expensed as research and development and are included within net cash flows from operating activities. However, if the patent is purchased, it is classified as an intangible asset and the cash outflow is recorded as an investing activity.

This means certain actions by management can impact how a cash flow is classified. Such transactions can be subject to the latitude in standards because management may have an incentive to bolster cash reported from operating activities (an important measure tracked by analysts).

Disclosure of Noncash Transactions LO22-5 Demo 22-5

Demo MBC

The investing and financing activities section of the statement of cash flows for Gilmore Inc. follow.

Cash Flows from Investing Activities	
Proceeds from insurance settlement . . .	$ 50,000
Purchase of equipment.	(340,000)
Net cash used by investing activities . . .	$(290,000)

Cash Flows from Financing Activities	
Payment to retire bonds	$(107,000)
Dividends payment.	(40,000)
Principal payments on mortgage	(10,000)
Issuance of common stock.	20,000
Net cash used by financing activities . . .	$(137,000)

Assume that we discover that the stock issuance of $20,000 (1,000 shares) was used to purchase equipment of $20,000. In other words, common stock was not issued for cash and only $320,000 of the equipment purchases were made with cash.

a. Prepare the investing and financing cash flows sections of the cash flows statement updated for the noncash items.
b. Prepare the disclosure of noncash items.

continued

continued from previous page

Solution

a. **Investing and Financing Cash Flow Sections**

The statement of cash flows would be adjusted to eliminate these noncash items as follows.

Cash Flows from Investing Activities	
Proceeds from insurance settlement . . .	$ 50,000
Purchase of equipment.	(320,000)
Net cash used by investing activities . . .	$(270,000)

Cash Flows from Financing Activities	
Payment to retire bonds	$(107,000)
Dividends payment.	(40,000)
Principal payments on mortgage	(10,000)
Net cash used by financing activities . . .	$(157,000)

After the adjustment to the investing and financing sections, the sum of the totals of the two sections are equivalent. This means there is no net impact on the reconciliation of cash on the statement of cash flows.

	Prior to Noncash Adjustment	After Noncash Adjustment
Net cash used by investing activities	$(290,000)	$(270,000)
Net cash used by financing activities	(137,000)	(157,000)
Total	$(427,000)	$(427,000)

b. **Noncash Disclosure**

Noncash investing and financing activities

Purchased equipment for $340,000 through the payment of cash and the issuance of 1,000 shares of common stock.

Cost of equipment.	$340,000
Cash payment for equipment	320,000
Issuance of common stock for equipment	$ 20,000

AMERICAN EAGLE OUTFITTERS

Real World—CASH FLOW DISCLOSURES

AMERICAN EAGLE OUTFITTERS [AEO]

American Eagle Outfitters Inc. reported the following disclosure of cash flow information in a recent report on Form 10-K.

Supplemental Disclosures of Cash Flow Information The table below shows supplemental cash flow information for cash amounts paid during the respective periods:

For the Years Ended (In thousands)	February 3, 2018	January 28, 2017	January 30, 2016
Cash paid during the periods for:			
Income taxes	$47,094	$126,592	$116,765
Interest	$ 1,098	$ 1,155	$ 1,173

REVIEW 22-5 **LO22-5** **Disclosure of Noncash Transactions**

Review MBC

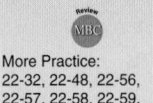

More Practice: 22-32, 22-48, 22-56, 22-57, 22-58, 22-59, 22-60

Solution on p. 22-71.

Using the information for Vegas Corporation from **Review 22-2**, now assume that of the total equipment purchases for the year, $1,000 was purchased through issuance of a $1,000 note payable (included in the ending balance of note payable on the balance sheet).

Prepare the adjusted investing and financing activities sections of the statement of cash flows for Vegas Corporation. Prepare the required noncash disclosure.

Utilize a worksheet to prepare the statement of cash flows

LO 22-6

Statement of Cash Flows Worksheet

- Optional tool to prepare statement of cash flows
- Tracks changes in balance sheet accounts by reconstructing transaction entries
- Identify balance sheet changes that impact the statement of cash flows and classify as operating, investing or financing

LO 22-6 Overview

A **cash flow worksheet** is an optional tool for preparing a statement of cash flows. The worksheet provides an organized format for documenting the preparation process and for subsequent cash flow analysis. A worksheet tracks changes in balance sheet accounts and ensures that all account changes are explained. For complex problems, this formal tracking can be beneficial.

A complete cash flow worksheet for the Gilmore Inc. example is included in **Demo 22-6**. In applying the cash flow worksheet tool, a transaction entry is reconstructed and entered into a worksheet to explain changes in balance sheet account balances. As cash flows are identified, they are entered into one of the cash-flow activity sections in the lower half of the worksheet.

Inflows are debits (a cash inflow is a debit to cash), and outflows are credits (a cash outflow is a credit to cash). The corresponding debit or credit is entered into the appropriate balance sheet account as an adjustment in the upper half of the worksheet. **Debits and credits of each adjustment must balance so the totals at the bottom of the worksheet are always in balance.** The entries are recreated for the purpose of preparing the worksheet only and are *not* entered into the accounting system as entries.

The process is completed when all balance sheet account changes are explained. In other words, all of the changes identified as debits and credits added to the beginning balance sheet amounts must equal the ending balance sheet amounts. The information from the three activity sections in the lower half of the worksheet is transferred to the statement of cash flows.

Cash Flow Worksheet LO22-6 **Demo 22-6**

Prepare a cash flow worksheet for Gilmore Inc. using the financial statement information from **Demo 22-2**. Input each entry into the worksheet along with a brief explanation.

Solution

Cash Flow Worksheet—Gilmore Inc.

Comparative Balance Sheets, December 31	2019		Dr.	Cr.		2020
Cash	$200,000			$ 138,000	(a)	$ 62,000
Accounts receivable	65,000	(b)	$ 21,000			86,000
Allowance for doubtful accounts	(5,000)			1,000	(b)	(6,000)
Inventory	12,000	(c)	8,000			20,000
Prepaid expenses	6,000			1,000	(d)	5,000
Equipment	400,000	(f)	340,000	100,000	(e)	640,000
Accumulated depreciation	(100,000)	(e)	60,000	100,000	(g)	(140,000)
Patent, net	90,000			20,000	(h)	70,000
Total assets	**$668,000**					**$737,000**
Accounts payable	40,000			20,000	(i)	60,000
Salaries payable	60,000	(j)	10,000			50,000
Interest payable	6,000			3,000	(k)	9,000
Income tax payable	12,000			8,000	(l)	20,000
Mortgage payable	120,000	(m)	10,000			110,000
Bonds payable	200,000	(n)	100,000			100,000
Premium on bond payable	8,000	(n)	4,000			
		(o)	1,000			3,000
Common stock, no-par	150,000			20,000	(p)	170,000
Retained earnings	72,000	(r)	40,000	183,000	(q)	215,000
Total liabilities and stockholders' equity	**$668,000**					**$737,000**

continued

continued from previous page

Cash Flows from Operating Activities					
Net income	(q)	183,000			Net cash provided by operating activities . . . $289,000
Depreciation expense	(g)	100,000			
Amortization expense	(h)	20,000			
Amortization of bond premium			1,000	(o)	
Gain on insurance settlement			10,000	(e)	
Loss on bond retirement	(n)	3,000			
Increase in accounts receivable			20,000	(b)	
Increase in inventory			8,000	(c)	
Decrease in prepaid expenses	(d)	1,000			
Increase in accounts payable	(i)	20,000			
Decrease in salaries payable			10,000	(j)	
Increase in interest payable	(k)	3,000			
Increase in income tax payable	(l)	8,000			
Cash Flows from Investing Activities					
Insurance proceeds for equipment fire	(e)	50,000			Net cash used by investing activities . . . $(290,000)
Purchase of equipment			340,000	(f)	
Cash Flows from Financing Activities					
Payment for bond retirement			107,000	(n)	Net cash used by financing activities . . . $(137,000)
Dividends paid			40,000	(r)	
Principal payment, mortgage			10,000	(m)	
Issuance of stock	(p)	20,000			
Net cash decrease	(a)	138,000			
Total		**$1,140,000**	**$1,140,000**		

Adjustments to the cash flow worksheet are explained as follows.

a. **Change in cash** The $138,000 credit explains the decrease in cash in the balance sheet. This amount will be used to reconcile the beginning and ending cash balances to the change in cash for the period on the statement of cash flows.

Decrease in Cash—Reconciliation in Statement of Cash Flows	138,000	
Cash		138,000

b. **Change in accounts receivable, net** The increase in net accounts receivable of $20,000 (debit) computed as $21,000 − $1,000 is also included as a credit in the income statement or a deduction from net income in the operating section.

Accounts Receivable	21,000	
Allowance for Doubtful Account		1,000
Increase in Accounts Receivable—Operating Section		20,000

c. **Change in inventory** The $8,000 debit explains the increase in inventory on the balance sheet. This amount is included as a reduction from net income in the operating section.

Inventory	8,000	
Increase in Inventory—Operating Section		8,000

d. **Change in prepaid expenses** The $1,000 credit explains the decrease in prepaid expenses on the balance sheet. This amount is included as an increase to net income in the operating section.

Decrease in Prepaid Expenses—Operating Section	1,000	
Prepaid Expenses		1,000

e. **Insurance proceeds from equipment fire** The insurance proceeds from the equipment fire of $50,000 are included in the investing section while the gain on insurance proceeds is a noncash adjustment, which reduces net income in the operating section. The entry to record the loss of the equipment is recreated and entered into the worksheet as follows.

Insurance Proceeds from Equipment Fire—Investing Section	50,000	
Accumulated Depreciation	60,000	
Equipment		100,000
Gain on Insurance Settlement—Operating Section		10,000

continued

continued from previous page

f. **Purchases of equipment** The debit to equipment of $340,000 represents an increase to equipment resulting from purchases. This amount is also included in the investing section of the statement of cash flows as an outflow. The $340,000 difference is needed to balance the equipment account after considering the $100,000 credit to the equipment account due to the write-off of the cost of equipment destroyed in the fire.

Equipment	340,000	
Purchase of Equipment—Investing Section		340,000

g. **Depreciation expense** Depreciation expense of $100,000 is shown as a credit to accumulated depreciation and also as an increase to net income in the operating section of the statement of cash flows. The $100,000 difference is needed to balance the equipment account after considering the $60,000 write-off of accumulated depreciation due to the loss of equipment due to a fire.

Depreciation Expense—Operating Section	100,000	
Accumulated Depreciation		100,000

h. **Amortization of patent** The $20,000 credit explains the decrease in patent on the balance sheet. This amount represents the amortization on the patent, which is included as an addition to net income in the operating section of the statement of cash flows.

Amortization Expense—Operating Section	20,000	
Patent		20,000

i. **Change in accounts payable** The $20,000 credit to accounts payable reconciles the beginning and ending accounts payable balance. This increase in accounts payable is also shown as an addition to net income in the operating section of the statement of cash flows.

Increase in Accounts Payable—Operating Section	20,000	
Accounts Payable		20,000

j. **Change in salaries payable** The $10,000 debit explains the decrease in salaries payable from $60,000 to $50,000. This $10,000 change is also included as a deduction from net income in the operating section of the income statement.

Salaries Payable	10,000	
Decrease in Salaries Payable—Operating Section		10,000

k. **Change in interest payable** The $3,000 credit to interest payable explains the increase in interest payable on the balance sheet. The increase in interest payable is also included as an addition to net income in the operating section of the income statement.

Increase in Interest Payable—Operating Section	3,000	
Interest Payable		3,000

l. **Change in income tax payable** The $8,000 credit to interest payable explains the increase in income tax payable on the balance sheet. The increase in income tax payable is also included as an addition to net income in the operating section of the income statement.

Increase in Income Tax Payable—Operating Section	8,000	
Income Tax Payable		8,000

m. **Payment on mortgage** The deduction in mortgage payable of $10,000 due to principal payments is shown as a debit to mortgage payable on the balance sheet and as an outflow of cash in the financing section of the statement of cash flows.

Mortgage Payable	10,000	
Principal Payment, Mortgage—Financing Section		10,000

n. **Loss on bond retirement** The loss on bond retirement of $3,000 is included as a noncash adjustment to net income in the operating section while the payment for the bond retirement is included as an outflow in the financing section of the statement of cash flows. The entry to record the bond retirement is recreated and entered into the worksheet as follows.

Bonds Payable	100,000	
Premium on Bonds Payable	4,000	
Loss on Bond Retirement—Operating Section	3,000	
Payment for Bond Retirement—Financing Section		107,000

continued

continued from previous page

o. **Amortization of bond premium** The $1,000 debit required to balance the premium on bonds payable account reflects the amortization of the premium. The amortization is a noncash adjustment to net income in the operating section of the statement of cash flows.

Premium on Bond Payable	1,000	
Amortization of Bond Premium—Operating Section		1,000

p. **Issuance of stock** The $20,000 credit to balance the common stock account in the balance sheet is shown as a cash inflow in the financing section of the statement of cash flows.

Issuance of Stock—Financing Section	20,000	
Common Stock		20,000

q. **Net income** Net income of $183,000 is included as a credit to the retained earnings account on the balance sheet and as an addition and starting point to the operating section of the statement of cash flows.

Net Income—Operating Section	183,000	
Retained Earnings		183,000

r. **Payment of dividends** The debit of $40,000 representing dividends paid is required to reconcile the retained earnings account from the beginning to the end of the period. The offsetting credit or outflow is presented in the financing section of the statement of cash flows.

Retained Earnings	40,000	
Dividends Paid—Financing Section		40,000

The amounts in the lower half of the worksheet would be entered into a formal statement of cash flows creating a statement of cash flows under the indirect method that is identical to the Gilmore Inc. statement of cash flows presented earlier in LO 22-4.

REVIEW 22-6 LO22-6 Preparing Cash Flow Worksheet Entries

Review MBC

Indicate the entries that would be included on an accounting worksheet for each of the following items assuming the indirect method of cash flow presentation.

a. Decrease in accounts receivable of $8,500 and an increase in the allowance for doubtful accounts of $500.

b. Increase in supplies of $1,000.

c. Sale of equipment (original cost of $80,000 and accumulated depreciation of $50,000) for $22,000.

d. Depreciation expense of $12,000.

e. Issuance of $50,000 bonds payable at 90.

More Practice: 22-33, 22-61, 22-62, 22-63

Solution on p. 22-71.

LO 22-7 Prepare the operating cash flow section of the statement of cash flows using the direct method

LO 22-7 Overview

Cash Flows from Operating Activities—Direct Method

- Reports major classes of cash receipts and cash payments
- Reports same *total* of net cash flows from operating activities as under the indirect method
- Requires disclosure of a reconciliation of net income to cash flows from operating activities

The previous sections outlined the preparation of the operating section of the statement of cash flows using the indirect method. The **direct method** is mandatory for the investing and financing sections, but may be elected for the operating section. If elected for the operating section, the direct method requires the reporting of *major classes* of gross operating cash receipts and cash payments that sum to net cash flows from operating activities. **This means that accrual items on the income statement are converted to a cash basis and reported separately.** For example, sales revenue reported on an accrual basis is converted to cash received from customers and then reported on the statement of cash flows. Cost of goods sold also reported on an accrual basis is converted to cash paid to suppliers and then reported on the statement of cash flows.

Major required classes of cash receipts and cash payments under the direct method include cash receipts from customers, interest and dividend receipts, other operating cash receipts, cash paid to suppliers, cash paid for interest, cash paid for taxes, and other operating cash payments. Recall that the purpose of the statement of cash flows is to show cash flows rather than accruals. Therefore, noncash items will not appear. If material, they will be disclosed.

230-10-45-25 In reporting cash flows from operating activities, entities are encouraged to report major classes of gross cash receipts and gross cash payments and their arithmetic sum—the net cash flow from operating activities (the direct method) . . . Entities that do so shall, at a minimum, separately report the following classes of operating cash receipts and payments:

a. Cash collected from customers, including lessees, licensees, and the like.
b. Interest and dividends received.
c. Other operating cash receipts, if any.
d. Cash paid to employees and other suppliers of goods or services, including suppliers of insurance, advertising, and the like.
e. Interest paid.
f. Income taxes paid.
g. Other operating cash payments, if any.

Entities are encouraged to provide further breakdowns of operating cash receipts and payments that they consider meaningful and feasible. For example, a retailer or manufacturer might decide to further divide cash paid to employees and suppliers (category (d) in the preceding paragraph) into payments for costs of inventory and payments for selling, general, and administrative expenses.

These items are reflected in the following graphic.

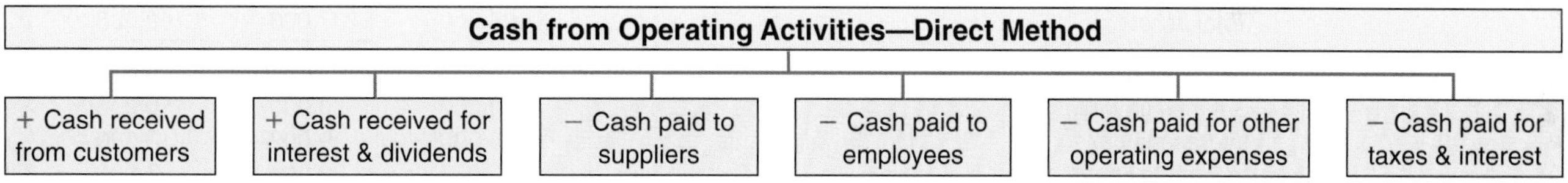

The option to use the indirect method applies only to operating activities. *Thus, our discussion on the direct method simply outlines the change in the operating activities cash flow section.* In **Demo 22-7** we prepare the operating activities section of the statement of cash flows following the direct method using the information for Gilmore Inc. from **Demo 22-2**.

While the direct method is encouraged by FASB (as indicated in the accounting guidance presented above) most companies opt to report cash flows under the indirect method. Arguably, the direct method presentation is more useful for predicting future net operating cash flows. Unlike the indirect method, the direct method reports collections from sales and other operating cash flows that analysts need to assess cash-generating ability. However, the added information required under the direct method comes with a cost to the preparers because accounting systems may not readily provide gross operating receipts and payments. In addition, companies are reluctant to divulge more information than required. On the other hand, ledger account balances provide most of the reconciling items under the indirect method.

Cash Flows from Operating Activities under Direct Method LO22-7 Demo 22-7

The following income statement is from Gilmore Inc. with five items identified for inclusion on the direct method statement of cash flows presentation after a conversion from accrual to cash. Noncash reconciling items appearing on the indirect method statement will not appear in the direct method statement because they represent adjustments necessary to reconcile net income to cash provided by operating activities. Noncash reconciling items appear on the indirect method statement because they are included in income but are not cash flows. For example, depreciation expense is added back to net income in the indirect method because it reduces income but is not a cash outflow. *In contrast, the direct method statement shows only the flows that are cash.* Because depreciation is not a cash ouflow, it will not appear on the direct method statement. The same is true of other reconciling items, including gains and losses and bond amortization. For the direct method we begin with the income statement and comparative balance sheets as follows.

continued

continued from previous page

Income Statement, for Year Ended December 31	2020
Sales (1)	$820,000
Cost of goods sold (2)	(380,000)
Depreciation expense (*noncash*)	(100,000)
Amortization of patent (*noncash*)	(20,000)
Operating expenses including $4,000 bad debt expense (3)	(51,000)
Gain on insurance settlement (*noncash*)	10,000
Loss on bond retirement (*noncash*)	(3,000)
Interest expense (4)	(22,000)
Income tax expense (5)	(71,000)
Net income	$183,000

The comparative balance sheets along with differences for Gilmore Inc. follows.

Comparative Balance Sheets, December 31	2019	2020	Difference
Cash	$200,000	$ 62,000	$(138,000)
Accounts receivable	65,000	86,000	21,000
Allowance for doubtful accounts	(5,000)	(6,000)	(1,000)
Inventory	12,000	20,000	8,000
Prepaid expenses	6,000	5,000	(1,000)
Equipment	400,000	640,000	240,000
Accumulated depreciation	(100,000)	(140,000)	(40,000)
Patent, net	90,000	70,000	(20,000)
Total assets	$668,000	$737,000	$ 69,000
Accounts payable	$ 40,000	$ 60,000	$ 20,000
Salaries payable	60,000	50,000	(10,000)
Interest payable	6,000	9,000	3,000
Income tax payable	12,000	20,000	8,000
Mortgage payable	120,000	110,000	(10,000)
Bonds payable	200,000	100,000	(100,000)
Premium on bonds payable	8,000	3,000	(5,000)
Common stock, no-par	150,000	170,000	20,000
Retained earnings	72,000	215,000	143,000
Total liabilities and stockholders' equity	$668,000	$737,000	$ 69,000

Required

Prepare the operating activities section of the statement of cash flows following the direct method. Assume that operating expenses of $51,000 on the income statement consists of $4,000 of bad debt expense, $30,000 of salaries expense and $17,000 of other expenses.

Solution

The cash flows from operating activities section for Gilmore Inc. presented under the direct method follows.

Cash Flows from Operating Activities—Direct Method	
Collections from customers (1)	$796,000
Payments to suppliers (2)	(368,000)
Other payments (3)	(56,000)
Interest payments (4)	(20,000)
Tax payments (5)	(63,000)
Net cash provided by operating activities	$289,000

The five components of cash flows from operating activities are explained as follows.

continued

continued from previous page

1. **Cash Collections from Customers**

The amount of cash receipts from customers is determined by analyzing the change in accounts receivable as shown in the following T-account.

Accounts Receivable			
Beg. balance	65,000		
Recoveries previously written off	2,000	**796,000**	Cash collections
Sales	820,000	5,000	Write offs
End. balance	86,000		

Cash collected from customers	
Sales	$820,000
Subtract increase in accounts receivable	(21,000)
Add decrease in accounts receivable	—
Subtract write-offs	(5,000)
Add collection of AR previously written off	2,000
Cash collections	**$796,000**

Only the cash collected from customers is included in the operating section of the direct method statement of cash flows. The write-offs of $5,000 and the recoveries of $2,000 were noncash changes in accounts receivable. Therefore they are not included in cash collected from customers in the direct method statement. Additionally, an increase in the allowance for doubtful accounts through an increase in bad debt expense is a noncash expense. Thus, the $4,000 of bad debt expense is excluded from cash from operating activities under the direct method as shown below.

2. **Cash Payments to Suppliers**

To calculate cash paid to suppliers, first total purchases must be computed. Cost of goods sold of $380,000 is adjusted for the increase in inventory of $8,000 ($20,000 less $12,000). The result is total purchases of $388,000 as illustrated in the following T-account.

Inventory			
Beg. balance	12,000		
		380,000	Cost of goods sold
Purchases	388,000		
End. balance	20,000		

Next, cash payments for purchases is calculated by adjusting total purchases of $388,000 for the increase in accounts payable of $20,000 ($60,000 less $40,000). The result is cash payments of $368,000 as illustrated in the following T-account.

Accounts Payable			
		40,000	Beg. balance
		388,000	Purchases
Cash payments for purchases	**368,000**		
		60,000	End. balance

Cash payments to suppliers	
Cost of goods sold	$380,000
Add increase in inventory balance	8,000
Subtract decrease in inventory balance	—
Add decrease in accounts payable	—
Subtract increase in accounts payable	(20,000)
Cash payments to suppliers	**$368,000**

3. **Cash Payments, Other**

Starting with $51,000 of other expenses, we subtract bad debt expense (a noncash expense and a credit to the allowance for doubtful accounts) of $4,000. The change in prepaid expenses is subtracted because the decline in the prepaid expense account implies the expense recognized exceeded cash payments by $1,000.

Prepaid Expenses			
Beg. balance	6,000		
		17,000	Other expenses
Cash payments	**16,000**		
End. balance	5,000		

Salaries expense of $30,000 is adjusted from an accrual to a cash basis by adjusting for the change in salaries payable.

Salaries Payable			
		60,000	Beg. balance
		30,000	Salaries expense
Cash payments for salaries	**40,000**		
		50,000	End. balance

Total cash payments equal $56,000 ($16,000 + $40,000).

Cash payments for other operating expenses	
Other operating expenses	$51,000
Subtract bad debt expense (noncash)	(4,000)
Subtract decrease in prepaid expenses	(1,000)
Add increase in prepaid expenses	—
Add decrease in salaries payable	10,000
Subtract increase in accrued liabilities	—
Cash payments to suppliers	**$56,000**

continued

continued from previous page

4. Cash Payments for Interest

Cash payments for interest	
Interest expense	$22,000
Add premium amortization	1,000
Subtract discount amortization	—
Add decrease in interest payable	—
Subtract increase in interest payable	(3,000)
Cash paid for interest	**$20,000**

Interest paid of $20,000 is calculated by subtracting the increase in interest payable of $3,000 ($9,000 less $6,000) from $23,000 ($22,000 interest expense plus $1,000 premium amortization). The calculation is illustrated in the following T-account.

Interest Payable			
		6,000	Beg. balance
Payment for interest	**20,000**	23,000	Interest expense + premium amortization
		9,000	End. balance

5. Cash Payments for Taxes

Cash payments for taxes	
Income tax expense	$71,000
Add decrease in income tax payable	—
Subtract increase in income tax payable	(8,000)
Add decrease in deferred tax liabilities	—
Subtract increase in deferred tax liabilities	—
Subtract decrease in deferred tax assets	—
Add increase in deferred tax assets	—
Cash paid for taxes	**$63,000**

Taxes paid of $63,000 is calculated by adding the increase in income tax payable of $8,000 ($20,000 less $12,000) to income tax expense of $71,000. The calculation is illustrated in the following T-account.

Income Tax Payable			
		12,000	Beg. balance
Payment for taxes	**63,000**	71,000	Income tax expense
		20,000	End. balance

EXPANDING YOUR KNOWLEDGE — **Reconciliation of Accounts Receivable**

In reconciling accounts receivable, why do we include total sales rather than sales on account? *Answer:* This is an analytic short-cut that provides the number we want to derive. In this problem, cash received from customers is the sum of two amounts: 1) Cash Sales, and 2) Cash collected on account. When we subtract the increase in accounts receivable net of write-offs and recoveries, we obtain the sum of these two numbers. For example, assume we know that credit sales during the period are $720,000 and cash sales are $100,000. The increase in accounts receivable is actually equal to credit sales of $720,000 minus write-offs of $5,000 plus recoveries of $2,000 minus cash collections. We solve for cash collections on account of $696,000. Total cash collected from customers is this number plus cash sales of $100,000 or $796,000. This is the amount of cash collections we calculate if we include total sales of $820,000 in the T-account. Thus, using total sales in the reconciliation saves a step. This reconciliation short-cut works even if the amounts of cash sales and credit sales are unknown.

Accounts Receivable			
Beg. balance	65,000		
Sales on account	720,000	696,000	Cash collected on account
Recoveries	2,000	5,000	Write-offs
End. balance	86,000		

Reconciliation of Net Income and Operating Cash Flows

For companies using the direct method, a supporting schedule equivalent to the operating activities section under the *indirect method* is a required disclosure. This schedule is called **the reconciliation of net income and operating cash flows.**

230-10-45-30 If an entity other than an NFP [not-for-profit entities] uses the direct method of reporting net cash flow from operating activities, the reconciliation of net income to net cash flow from operating activities shall be provided in a separate schedule.

For Gilmore Inc. the reconciliation schedule is the cash from operating activities section that we calculated previously under the indirect method. **The total of the cash inflow from operating activities under the indirect method of $289,000 equals the total under the direct method.**

Reconciliation of Net Income and Operating Cash Flows	
Net income	$183,000
Depreciation expense	100,000
Amortization expense	20,000
Amortization of bond premium	(1,000)
Gain on insurance settlement	(10,000)
Loss on bond retirement	3,000
Increase in accounts receivable	(20,000)
Increase in inventory	(8,000)
Decrease in prepaid expenses	1,000
Increase in accounts payable	20,000
Decrease in salaries payable	(10,000)
Increase in interest payable	3,000
Increase in income tax payable	8,000
Net cash provided by operating activities	$289,000

Bond Interest—Direct and Indirect Method Presentation

When a company issues a bond at a discount (premium), the proceeds are less than (greater than) the bond's face value. The net proceeds are included as a cash inflow in the *financing section* of the statement of cash flows. Over the term of the bond, the interest expense is greater than (less than) the interest paid due to the amortization of the discount (premium). The actual interest paid, based on the stated rate of the bond, is included as a deduction in the *operating section* either directly as interest paid through the direct method, or as part of net income through the indirect method. In the indirect method of cash flow presentation, the amortization of the discount (premium) is added (subtracted) to (from) net income.

Assume that a company issues $100,000, 10-year bonds with a market rate of 8% and a stated rate of 6% on January 1. Cash interest payments are made semiannually on June 30 and December 31. Because the market rate is greater than the stated rate, the bond will sell at a discount. The selling price of the bond of $86,410 is computed as **=PV(0.04,20,0.03*100000,100000)**.

Under both the direct and indirect methods, an inflow of cash would be recorded in the financing activities section of the statement of cash flows.

Cash Flows from Financing Activities	
Add cash proceeds from the issuance of bonds	$86,410
Net cash flows from financing activities	$ #

During the term of the bonds, the cash interest payments would be reported in the operating section of the statement of cash flows. A partial amortization scheduled follows.

Effective Interest Amortization—Discount

Date	Cash (Stated Interest)	Interest Expense (Market Interest)	Discount on B.P. Amortization	Bonds Payable, Net (Carrying Value)
Jan. 1				$86,410
June 30	$3,000	$3,456	$456	86,866
Dec. 31	3,000	3,475	475	87,341

Direct Method Under the direct method in the operating activities section, the company records an outflow for cash interest paid of $6,000 ($3,000 + $3,000) at the end of the first year.

Cash Flows from Operating Activities—Direct Method	
Cash payment for interest	$(6,000)
Net cash flows from operating activities	$ #

Indirect Method Under the indirect method in the operating activities section, the company includes interest expense of $6,931 ($3,456 + $3,475), as a deduction to arrive at net income. Because the discount amortization is noncash, the amount of $931 ($456 + $475) is included as an addition to net income as a reconciling item. This means the net effect would be a cash outflow of $6,000 for cash interest or $(6,931) + $931.

Cash Flows from Operating Activities—Indirect Method	
Net income	$ #
Amortization of bond discount ($456 + $475)	931
Net cash flows from operating activities	$ #

Upon redemption of the bond at the end of the bond term, the company will present a cash outflow of $100,000 as a financing activity.

Debt Settlement of a Zero-Coupon Bond

A company would classify the accreted interest portion of the cash payment made to settle a *zero-coupon bond* or a *bond with a coupon rate insignificant in relation to the effective rate* as a cash outflow for operating activities. The portion of the cash payment attributable to the principal would be classified as a financing activity. The following is defined as a cash outflow for *operating activities* in the accounting guidance.

230-10-45-17d Cash payments to lenders and other creditors for interest, including the portion of the payments made to settle zero-coupon debt instruments that is attributable to accreted interest related to the debt discount or the portion of the payments made to settle other debt instruments with coupon interest rates that are insignificant in relation to the effective interest rate of the borrowing that is attributable to accreted interest related to the debt discount. For all other debt instruments, an issuer shall not bifurcate cash payments to lenders and other creditors at settlement for amounts attributable to accreted interest related to the debt discount, nor classify such amounts as cash outflows for operating activities.

REVIEW 22-7 **LO22-7** **Cash Flows from Operating Activities Using the Direct Method**

Review MBC

The following information for Washington Inc. includes an income statement and a partial balance sheet for 2020.

Income Statement For Year Ended December 31	2020
Sales revenue	$98,000
Cost of goods sold	39,000
Depreciation expense	8,800
Salaries expense	16,000
Rent expense	5,500
Insurance expense	3,600
Interest expense	3,600
Utilities expense	3,200
Net income	$18,300

Selected Balance Sheet Accounts December 31	2019	2020
Accounts receivable	$2,800	$2,600
Inventory	3,000	3,200
Accounts payable	4,600	4,400
Accrued salaries	450	500
Utilities payable	160	220
Prepaid insurance	320	300
Prepaid rent	450	480
Interest payable	0	300

More Practice: 22-64, 22-67, 22-68, 22-69

Solution on p. 22-71.

Prepare the cash flows from operating activities section of the company's 2020 statement of cash flows using the direct method.

Prepare a statement of cash flows using the cash T-Account approach

APPENDIX 22A
LO 22-8

T-Account Approach
- Optional tool to prepare statement of cash flows
- Recreates entries in T-accounts
- Tracks cash effects in a cash T-account
- Provides statement of cash flows information through cash T-account

LO 22-8 Overview

The double-entry accounting system ensures that the change in cash is algebraically equal to the net change in all other accounts as explained in Chapter 5 and repeated here.

$$\Delta\text{Cash} = -\Delta\text{Noncash Assets} + \Delta\text{Liabilities} + \Delta\text{Equity}$$

The change in cash and cash equivalents for the period from the comparative balance sheets equals the change disclosed in the statement of cash flows. Except for the operating section of the indirect method, each line item in the statement of cash flows describes a cash flow.

Under the **Cash Flow T-Account method** for preparing the statement of cash flows, a cash T-account is reconstructed to reflect the cash effects of operating, investing, and financing activities. T-accounts for the balance sheet and income statement accounts are used to reflect the offsetting side of the entries as we show in **Demo 22-8**.

Cash T-Account Approach

LO22-8 **Demo 22-8**

Comparative balance sheets, an income statement, along with additional information follows for Eagle Heights Company.

Comparative Balance Sheets December 31	**2019**	**2020**	**Difference**
Cash and cash equivalents	$ 100	$ 65	$ (35)
Restricted cash	20	30	10
Accounts receivable, net	280	170	(110)
Inventory	100	300	200
Equipment	2,000	2,700	700
Accumulated depreciation	(200)	(500)	(300)
Total assets	$2,300	$2,765	$465
Accounts payable	$ 275	$ 240	$ (35)
Salaries payable	50	25	(25)
Bonds payable	600	700	100
Common stock, no-par	1,100	1,200	100
Retained earnings	275	600	325
Total liabilities and stockholders' equity	$2,300	$2,765	$465

Income Statement For Year Ended December 31, 2020	
Sales revenue	$3,000
Cost of goods sold	(1,700)
Salary expense	(125)
Interest expense	(60)
Depreciation expense	(400)
Loss on equipment sale	(200)
Net income	$ 515

Additional information for 2020
- Equipment with an original cost of $400 and accumulated depreciation of $100 was sold for $100.
- Equipment purchases were made with cash.
- All dividends declared were paid in cash.

Required

Prepare and complete the cash T-account and then report the statement of cash flows for 2020 following the direct method for the operating activities section.

Solution

The following *reconstructed* journal entries are recreated from the financial information above.

		Debit	Credit
a.	Cash	3,110	
	Accounts Receivable		110
	Sales Revenue		3,000
b.	Cost of Goods Sold	1,700	
	Inventory	200	
	Accounts Payable	35	
	Cash		1,935
c.	Salary Expense	125	
	Salaries Payable	25	
	Cash		150

continued

continued from previous page

		Debit	Credit
d.	Interest Expense	60	
	Cash		60
e.	Cash	100	
	Accumulated Depreciation	100	
	Loss on Sale of Equipment	200	
	Equipment		400
f.	Equipment	1,100	
	Cash		1,100
g.	Cash	100	
	Bonds Payable		100
h.	Cash	100	
	Common Stock		100
i.	Retained Earnings	190	
	Cash		190
j.	Depreciation Expense	400	
	Accumulated Depreciation		400

The recreated entries from above are entered into T-accounts as follows.

Cash and cash equivalents and restricted cash

		25	(Net change in cash)
Operating Activities			
(a) From customers	3,110	1,935	(b) To suppliers
		150	(c) To employees
		60	(d) For interest
Investing Activities			
(e) Sale of equipment	100		
		1,100	(f) Purchase of equipment
Financing Activities			
(g) Issuance of bonds	100	190	(h) Payment of dividends
(i) Issuance of common stock	100		

Accounts Receivable, Net

		110	
		110	(a)

Inventory

	200		
(b)	200		

Equipment

	700		
(f)	1,100	400	(e)

Accumulated Depreciation

		300	
(e)	100	400	(j)

Accounts Payable

	35		
(b)	35		

Salaries Payable

	25		
(c)	25		

Bonds Payable

		100	
		100	(g)

Common Stock

		100	
		100	(i)

Retained Earnings

		325	
(h)	190	515	(NI)

Sales Revenue

		3,000	
		3,000	(a)

Loss on Sale of Equipment

	200		
(e)	200		

Depreciation Expense

	400		
(j)	400		

Cost of Goods Sold

	1,700		
(b)	1,700		

Salaries Expense

	125		
(c)	125		

Interest Expense

	60		
(d)	60		

continued

continued from previous page

The following statement of cash flows is constructed from the cash flow T-account following the direct method.

Cash Flows from Operating Activities	
Collections from customers	$3,110
Payments to suppliers	(1,935)
Payments to employees	(150)
Interest payments	(60)
Net cash provided by operating activities	965
Cash Flows from Investing Activities	
Proceeds from sale of equipment	100
Purchase of equipment	(1,100)
Net cash used by investing activities	(1,000)
Cash Flows from Financing Activities	
Issuance of bonds	100
Dividends paid	(190)
Issuance of stock	100
Net cash provided by financing activities	10
Net decrease in cash and cash equivalents and restricted cash	(25)
Cash and cash equivalents and restricted cash, Jan. 1, 2020	120
Cash and cash equivalents and restricted cash, Dec. 31, 2020	$ 95

Cash T-Account Approach

LO22-8 **REVIEW 22-8**

Review MBC

The following income statement and comparative balance sheets are from Redd Inc.

Balance Sheets, December 31	2019	2020
Cash	$ 3,500	$ 4,600
Accounts receivable	2,800	2,750
Inventory	3,000	3,300
Investments	1,000	1,600
Total assets	$10,300	$12,250
Accounts payable	$ 1,750	$ 1,400
Accrued expense	1,450	1,900
Retained earnings	2,575	4,325
Common stock	4,525	4,625
Total liabilities and stockholders' equity	$10,300	$12,250

Income Statement For Year Ended December 31	2020
Sales revenue	$9,800
Cost of goods sold	3,900
Operating expense	4,150
Net income	$1,750

Construct the cash T-account only and prepare the statement of cash flows for 2020 using the direct method for the operating activities section.

More Practice: 22-108, 22-109
Solution on p. 22-72.

Questions

22-1. Explain the purpose of the statement of cash flows.

22-2. Explain the basic difference between the three activities reported in the statement of cash flows: operating, investing, and financing.

22-3. List three major cash inflows and three major cash outflows under (a) operating activities, (b) investing activities, and (c) financing activities.

22-4. Define a noncash investing activity. Give examples of two possible cases.

22-5. Define a noncash financing activity. Give examples of two possible cases.

22-6. Define a cash equivalent.

22-7. Explain the basic difference between the direct and indirect methods of reporting on the statement of cash flows. Use net income, $5,000, sales revenue, $100,000, and an increase in net accounts receivable, $10,000, to illustrate the basic difference. Which method provides the most relevant information to investors and creditors?

22-8. Explain why cash paid during the period for purchases and for salaries is not specifically reported on the statement of cash flows, indirect method, as cash outflows.

22-9. Explain why a $50,000 increase in inventory during the year must be considered when developing disclosures for operating activities under both the direct method and the indirect method.

22-10. What three reconciling amounts must be reported at the bottom of the statement of cash flows? Which one(s) must agree with a key amount in another financial statement? Use assumed amounts for illustrative purposes.

22-11. One of the criticisms of the statement of cash flows indirect method is that it does not report each of the three activities consistently. Explain the basis for this argument.

22-12. Explain why an adjustment must be made to compute cash flow from operating activities for depreciation expense, bad debt expense, amortization of intangibles (such as patents, copyrights, franchises), and bond discount.

22-13. Explain why gains and losses reported on the income statement usually must be omitted (or removed) from operating activities to compute cash flow from operating activities.

22-14. A corporation's records showed the following: sales, $80,000, and gross accounts receivable decrease, $10,000, after the write-off of a $3,000 bad debt. Assuming the direct method, compute the cash inflow from customers.

22-15. Why are cash, cash equivalents, and restricted cash grouped together for purposes of the statement of cash flows?

22-16. Why is a two-year Treasury note purchased three months before maturity a cash equivalent for cash flow purposes, although the same security purchased one year before maturity is not?

22-17. If the intent is to hold an investment in common stock less than three months, why is the investment not a cash equivalent?

22-18. What general disclosure requirements are required related to the statement of cash flows?

22-19. How is a lease payment (after inception) on a finance lease classified in the statement of cash flows of a lessee?

22-20. Certain equity securities and trading debt securities are treated differently in the statement of cash flows. What are the major differences in treatment?

Brief Exercises

Brief Exercise 22-21
Identifying Cash Flows **LO1, 2**

For each of the items listed below, indicate whether it would be included as an adjustment in the (1) operating, (2) investing, or (3) financing section of the statement of cash flows. Assume the indirect method is used.

_____ *a.* Decrease in accounts receivable
_____ *b.* Proceeds from the sale of equipment
_____ *c.* Cash dividend payment
_____ *d.* Depreciation expense
_____ *e.* Principal payments on a note payable
_____ *f.* Increase in accounts payable

Brief Exercise 22-22
Solving for Statement of Cash Flows Amounts **LO1**
Hint: See Demo 22-1

Complete the following table for each of the four *separate* scenarios *a* through *d*.

	Net cash flows from operating activities	Net cash flows from investing activities	Net cash flows from financing activities	Cash at the beginning of the period	Cash at the end of the period
a.	$ 50,000	$ (40,000)	$ (4,500)	$5,000	$?
b.	250,000	(200,000)	(55,000)	?	45,000
c.	45,000	(50,000)	?	8,000	11,000
d.	?	5,000	(1,000)	6,000	6,500

Brief Exercise 22-23
Preparing Operating Activities Section **LO2**
Hint: See Demo 22-2

Quest Company reported net income of $45,000, which included depreciation expense of $2,000 and a loss on sale of equipment of $600. On the balance sheet, the company reported the following: increases in accounts receivable of $2,200 and accounts payable of $4,400, and decreases in inventory of $1,200 and in salaries payable of $800. Prepare the operating activities section of the statement of cash flows using the indirect method.

Brief Exercises 22-24
Preparing Operating Activities Section **LO2**
Hint: See Demo 22-2

Konverse Company reported net income of $200,000 in 2020. Depreciation expense was $15,000 and amortization expense on patents was $2,500 in 2020. In addition, the balance sheet reported the following balance changes during 2020.

Decrease in accounts receivable	$5,000
Increase in debt investments classified as available-for-sale securities	4,500
Decrease in prepaid expenses	2,000
Decrease in accounts payable	8,000
Increase in accrued expenses	4,500
Decrease in short-term nontrade notes payable	8,000

Prepare the operating activities section of the statement of cash flows using the indirect method.

Brief Exercise 22-25
Preparing Operating Activities Section **LO2**

Quest Company reported a net loss of $15,000, which included depreciation expense of $2,000 and a gain on sale of equipment of $800. On the balance sheet, the company reported the following: increases in accounts receivable of $650 and accounts payable of $2,300, and a decrease in inventory of $1,200. Prepare the operating activities section of the statement of cash flows using the indirect method.

Brief Exercise 22-26
Identifying Investing Cash Flows **LO3**

Indicate items from the following list that would be included in the investing activities section of the statement of cash flows. Indicate whether items would be added or subtracted in the investing section.

____ *a.* Patent amortization recognized amounted to $30,000.
____ *b.* Plant assets costing $4,000 were purchased with cash.
____ *c.* Sold a long-term investment in another company's common stock for $5,000.
____ *d.* Borrowed $40,000 cash for capital projects on a note payable.
____ *e.* Paid a cash dividend of $5,000.
____ *f.* Depreciation recognized amounted to $80,000.
____ *g.* Purchased land for $85,000 cash.
____ *h.* Issued common stock, $1 par, for $200,000.
____ *i.* Purchased a 3-month U.S. Treasury bill, $5,000. The company's accounting policy treats such securities as cash equivalents.
____ *j.* Purchased a patent for $5,000.
____ *k.* Purchased treasury stock, $3,500.

Brief Exercise 22-27
Analyzing Cash Flow Effects of Equipment Sale **LO2, 3**
Hint: See Demo 22-3

Frontier Company sold equipment on June 30, 2020, for $30,000. The equipment had been depreciated $1,500 for the first six months of 2020, contributing to an accumulated depreciation balance of $10,000 on June 30, 2020. The original cost of the equipment was $50,000. Indicate how the statement of cash flows would be impacted for the equipment for 2020 under the indirect method.

Brief Exercise 22-28
Identifying Financing Cash Flows **LO4**

Considering the information provided in Brief Exercise 22-26, indicate items that would be included in the financing section of a statement of cash flows. Indicate whether items would be added or subtracted in the financing section.

Brief Exercise 22-29
Classifying Bond Transactions on Statement of Cash Flows **LO2, 4**

Cambell Inc. issued $100,000, 6%, 10-year bonds on January 1, 2020, for $86,580, with interest payments due annually at the end of each year. The amount of the discount amortization in year one is $926 using the effective interest rate method. Indicate the impact on the (a) operating activities section and the (b) financing activities section of the 2020 statement of cash flows, assuming the indirect method is used.

Brief Exercise 22-30
Presenting Installment Payment on Statement of Cash Flows **LO4**

Tiffany Inc. issued a 9% note payable to First Choice Bank for $100,000 with 10 equal payments of $15,582 (principal plus interest) due at the end of each year. Indicate the impact on the financing activity section of the statement of cash flows of the first installment payment.

Brief Exercise 22-31
Adjusting Cash Flows for Changes in Accounts Receivable **LO2**

Marshall Inc. had beginning balances (January 1) of $200,000 and $5,000 for accounts receivable and the allowance for doubtful accounts, respectively. During the year, the company had the following transactions.

Sales.	$900,000
Write-off of accounts.	1,000
Cash collections on account receivable	850,000
Bad debt expense recorded	2,800

a. Determine the ending balance (December 31) in accounts receivable and the allowance for doubtful accounts.

b. Determine the adjustment in the operating activities section in the statement of cash flows assuming the indirect method.

Brief Exercise 22-32
Analyzing Noncash Transactions **LO3, 5**

Pier2 Company purchased equipment with a useful life of 10 years for $36,000. Pier2 paid one-third down and signed a two-year, interest-bearing note for the balance. Indicate how the transaction would be reported in the statement of cash flows and/or related disclosure.

Brief Exercise 22-33
Preparing Entries for an Accounting Worksheet **LO6**
Hint: See Demo 22-6

Indicate the entries that would be included on an accounting worksheet for each of the following items.

a. Depreciation expense of $10,000.
b. Increase in prepaid expenses of $2,500.
c. Purchase of equipment of $100,000.
d. Dividend payment, $12,000.

Brief Exercise 22-34
Determining Cash Receipts—Direct Method **LO7**
Hint: See Demo 22-7

Universal Company reported revenue in its income statement for the year of $350,000. The beginning and ending balances of accounts receivable, gross were $35,000 and $42,000, respectively. What amount would be reported as cash receipts from customers in the operating activities section of the statement of cash flows using the direct method?

Brief Exercise 22-35
Determining Cash Receipts—Direct Method **LO7**
Hint: See Demo 22-7

Using the information from Brief Exercise 22-31, determine the cash receipts from customers reported in the operating activities section in the statement of cash flows assuming the direct method.

Reconcile sales to cash receipts from customers.

Brief Exercise 22-36
Computing Cash Paid to Supplier—Direct Method **LO7**
Hint: See Demo 22-7

Park Place Company reported cost of goods sold of $280,000 for the year 2020. Park Place also reported the following amounts on its balance sheets.

	Jan. 1, 2020	**Dec. 31, 2020**
Inventory.	$50,000	$55,000
Accounts payable	30,000	29,000

What amount would be reported as cash paid to suppliers in the operating activities section of the statement of cash flows using the direct method?

Brief Exercise 22-37
Computing Cash Paid to Employees—Direct Method **LO7**
Hint: See Demo 22-7

Park Place Company reported salaries expense of $100,000 for the year 2020. Park Place also reported salaries payable of $18,000 and $12,000 on January 1, 2020, and December 31, 2020, respectively. What amount would be reported as cash paid to employees in the operating activities section of the statement of cash flows using the direct method?

Brief Exercise 22-38
Classifying Bond Transactions—Direct Method **LO7**

Using the information in Brief Exercise 22-29, indicate the impact on the (a) operating activity section and the (b) financing activity section of the statement of cash flows, assuming the direct method.

Brief Exercise 22-39
Classifying a Sale of Equipment—Direct Method **LO7**

Frontier Company sold equipment on June 30, 2020, for $30,000. The equipment had been depreciated $1,500 for the first six months of 2020, contributing to an accumulated depreciation balance of $10,000 on June 30, 2020. The original cost of the equipment was $50,000. Indicate how the statement of cash flows would be impacted for the equipment for 2020 under the direct method.

Exercises

Exercise 22-40
Classifying Cash Flow Activities **LO1, 2, 5**

Sonic Company had the following activities during the current year ended December 31, 2020.

____ 1. Purchased treasury stock.
____ 2. Issuance of finance lease liability for equipment.
____ 3. Depreciation expense on equipment.
____ 4. Loss on sale of land.
____ 5. Increase in accounts receivable.
____ 6. Increase in accounts payable.
____ 7. Pension expense in excess of cash funded to plan.
____ 8. Exchange of common stock for a building.
____ 9. Unrealized gain—income on equity securities.
____10. Increase in a current deferred tax asset.
____11. Decrease in deferred tax liability.
____12. Issued a short-term nontrade note payable for cash.
____13. Amortization expense on discount for a bond payable.
____14. Excess of the company's share of its investee's net income over the company's share of dividend payments (accounted for under the equity method).
____15. Decrease in interest payable.
____16. Decrease in prepaid expenses.
____17. Decrease in income taxes payable.
____18. Exchange of currently held equipment with replacement equipment.
____19. Proceeds from sale of a business segment.
____20. Purchase of land for cash.

Required

Assuming that the company uses the indirect method for the statement of cash flows, classify each activity as follows:

a. Operating activity—add to net income
b. Operating activity—subtract from net income
c. Investing activity—cash inflow
d. Investing activity—cash outflow
e. Financing activity—cash inflow
f. Financing activity—cash outflow
g. Noncash transaction

Exercise 22-41
Classifying Cash Flow Activities **LO1**
Hint: See Demo 22-1

Savers Company had the following cash receipts and cash payments during the current year ended December 31, 2020.

____ 1. Cash receipt for issuance of preferred stock.
____ 2. Cash payment for dividends to shareholders.
____ 3. Cash outflow for a nontrade loan advanced to another entity.
____ 4. Cash payment for the redemption of bonds.
____ 5. Cash receipt from customers for services performed.
____ 6. Cash paid to the federal government for federal income taxes.
____ 7. Cash receipt for sale of a patent.
____ 8. Cash receipt for issuance of bonds at a premium.
____ 9. Cash receipt from dividends from investments.
____10. Cash payment on nontrade note payable (principal balance).
____11. Cash payment for interest on debt.
____12. Cash receipt from sale of equity securities (not held in trading account).
____13. Cash receipt for sale of equipment.
____14. Cash payment for employee salaries

Required

Indicate in which of the following three sections, each of the items listed above would be included on a statement of cash flows.

a. Operating activity
b. Investing activity
c. Financing activity

Exercise 22-42
Preparing the Operating Activities Section **LO2**
Hint: See Demo 22-2

The data below were provided by the accounting records of Franklin Company.

Net income (accrual basis)	$40,000	Increase in long-term liabilities	$10,000
Depreciation expense	8,000	Sale of capital stock for cash	25,000
Decrease in salaries payable	1,200	Amortization of premium on bonds payable	200
Decrease in trade accounts receivable	1,800	Accounts payable increase	4,000
Increase in merchandise inventory	2,500	Stock dividend issued	10,000
Amortization of patent	100		

Required

Prepare the reconciliation of net income with cash flow from operations for inclusion in the statement of cash flows (indirect method).

Exercise 22-43
Preparing the Operating Activities Section **LO2**
Hint: See Demo 22-2

The data below were provided by the accounting records of Marshall Company.

Net income (accrual basis)	$25,000	Amortization of patent	$ 100
Depreciation expense	3,000	Decrease in long-term liabilities	5,000
Increase in salaries payable	500	Sale of capital stock for cash	12,500
Increase in trade accounts receivable	900	Amortization of discount on bonds payable	150
Decrease in merchandise inventory	1,150		

Required

Prepare the reconciliation of net income with cash flow from operations for inclusion in the statement of cash flows (indirect method).

Exercise 22-44
Preparing the Operating Activities Section **LO2**
Hint: See Demo 22-2

The following items are relevant to the preparation of a statement of cash flows for Maxwell Inc.

1. Net loss for the year was $20,000. Depreciation expense was $50,000.
2. Wrote off a $4,000 account. During the year, gross accounts receivable increased $100,000, and the allowance for doubtful accounts increased $10,000. All sales of $600,000 are on account.
3. Pension expense is $100,000 while funding for the pension plan was $80,000.
4. Deferred tax liability increased $80,000, income taxes payable decreased $20,000, and income tax expense was $220,000.
5. $20,000 of interest was capitalized. Interest expense is $100,000. There is no change in interest payable.
6. Sold short-term investments (not held in a trading account) at a $4,000 gain, proceeds $16,000.
7. Merchandise inventory decreased by $10,000, accounts payable decreased by $5,000, and salaries payable increased by $14,000.

Required

Prepare the reconciliation of net income with cash flow from operations for inclusion in the statement of cash flows (indirect method).

Exercise 22-45
Presenting Pension Funding on Statement of Cash Flows **LO2**

Appleton Corporation initiated a defined benefit pension plan on January 1, 2020. The plan does not provide any retroactive benefits for existing employees. The pension funding payment is made to the trustee on December 31 of each year. The following information is available for 2020 and 2021.

	2020	2021
Service cost	$75,000	$82,500
Funding payment (contribution)	85,000	92,500
Interest on projected benefit obligation		7,500
Actual (and expected) return on plan assets		9,000

Required

a. Prepare the journal entries to record pension expense and the funding of plan assets for 2021.

b. Assuming that the company uses the indirect method in accounting for cash flows, what adjustment (if any) to net income would the company make in the operating activities section of the statement of cash flows?

Exercise 22-46
Presenting Investment Revenue on Statement of Cash Flows **LO2, 3**

On January 1, 2020, Allen Corporation purchased 30% of the 30,000 outstanding common shares of Towne Corporation at $17 per share as a long-term investment. On the date of purchase, the book value and the fair value of the net assets of Towne Corporation were equal. During the year, Towne Corporation reported income of $24,000 and paid dividends of $8,000. As of December 31, 2020, common shares of Towne Corporation were trading at $20 per share.

Required

a. Assume that Allen Corporation had significant influence over Towne Corporation. Record the entries for 2020 for Allen Corporation.

b. Indicate how the investment transactions would affect the statement of cash flows for 2020, assuming that the company uses the indirect method.

Exercise 22-47 Presenting Installment Note on Statement of Cash Flows **LO2, 4**

United Company signed an 8% installment note with Bank One on January 1, 2020, for $100,000. The installment note calls for 5 equal payments at the end of 5 years beginning on December 31, 2020.

Required

a. Calculate the amount of each installment payment.

b. Indicate how the installment note transactions would affect the statement of cash flows for 2020, assuming that the company uses the indirect method.

Exercise 22-48 Presenting Bond Payable on Statement of Cash Flows **LO4**

Yale Corporation issued a $60,000 5-year bond dated January 1, 2020, at 8% with 6% interest payable annually on December 31. Assume that the company uses the effective interest amortization method.

Required

a. Provide journal entries to be made on January 1, 2020, and December 31, 2020.

b. Indicate how the bond transactions would affect the statement of cash flows for 2020, assuming that the company uses the indirect method.

Exercise 22-49 Classifying Lessee Transactions in Statement of Cash Flows **LO2, 4, 5**

On January 1, 2020, Less Inc. signs a three-year non-cancelable agreement to lease equipment (no residual value) from Lessor Inc. Lessee Inc. accounts for the lease as a finance lease, which requires three lease payments of $34,972 each, payable January 1, 2020, December 31, 2020, and December 31, 2021. The lessor's implicit rate is 5%, which is known to the lessee, resulting in the recording of right-to-use asset and lease liability of $100,000 (or =PV(0.05,3,34972.07,0,1) at the inception of the lease. As a result, the lessee recorded the following entries in 2020 (amounts rounded).

January 1, 2020—To record right-of-use asset and lease liability

Right-of-Use Asset	100,000	
Lease Liability		100,000

January 1, 2020—To record lease payment

Lease Liability	34,972	
Cash		34,972

December 31, 2020—To record lease payment

Interest Expense	3,251	
Lease Liability	31,721	
Cash		34,972

December 31, 2020—To record amortization on right-of-use asset

Amortization Expense	33,333	
Right-of-Use Asset ($100,000/3)		33,333

Required

Determine the effects on the statement of cash flows of Lessee Inc. for 2020 assuming that the company follows the indirect method of cash flows.

Exercise 22-50 Determining Investing and Financing Activities **LO3, 4**

The following items are relevant to the preparation of a statement of cash flows for Pier Imports Inc.

1. Comparative balance sheets show a decrease of $6,000 in accrued utilities payable for the current year.
2. Nontrade short-term notes payable to banks increased $80,000 during the current year due to new borrowings.

3. The following end-of-year adjusting entry was recorded. No other interest-related transactions or entries occurred during the year.

Interest Expense.	12,000	
Premium on Bonds Payable.	800	
Interest Payable		12,800

4. $500 payment was made to reduce the principal balance of a nontrade loan from a bank.
5. Gross equipment account increased $20,000 during the year, accumulated depreciation increased $8,000, and depreciation expense for the period is $10,000. One item of equipment (cost $10,000, accumulated depreciation $2,000) was sold during the year; a gain of $1,000 on the sale was recognized.
6. Purchase of treasury stock, $30,000.
7. Distribution of cash dividends, $5,000.
8. Sale of available-for-sale debt securities for $16,000, at a loss of $3,000.

Required

a. Determine the amount of net cash flows that would be reported in the investing section of the statement of cash flows.

b. Determine the amount of net cash flows that would be reported in the financing section of the statement of cash flows.

Exercise 22-51
Determining Investing and Financing Activities LO3, 4

The following items are relevant to the preparation of a statement of cash flows for Tropical Products Inc.

1. Sale of common stock, $500,000.
2. Retirement of bonds payable, $355,000.
3. Purchase of land, $10,000.
4. Sale of equipment for $24,000, at a loss of $5,000.
5. Purchase of equity securities (not held in a trading account), $10,000.
6. Declaration of cash dividends, $40,000.
7. Loan of $30,000 resulting in a note receivable, nontrade.
8. Purchase of a patent, $20,000.
9. Proceeds from the issuance of a short-term nontrade note, $10,000.

Required

a. Determine the amount of net cash flows that would be reported in the investing section of a statement of cash flows.

b. Determine the amount of net cash flows that would be reported in the financing section of a statement of cash flows.

Exercise 22-52
Determining Cash Flow Impact of Retained Earnings Changes LO3, 4, 5

The following items affected the retained earnings account for 2020 for Walker Inc.

1. Net loss, $15,000.
2. Cash dividend distributed, $3,000.
3. Stock dividend, $5,000 (1,000 shares, $1 par value common stock).
4. Property dividend, $4,000 (100 shares of common stock held as an investment).
5. Sale of treasury shares for $5,000, previously purchased for $6,000.

Required

Indicate how each of the retained earnings transactions would affect the statement of cash flows for 2020 assuming that Walker uses the indirect method.

Exercise 22-53
Preparing Statement of Cash Flows—Indirect Method **LO2, 3, 4**

The accounting records of Zale Inc. provided the following data for the current year.

Balance Sheet, December 31	2019	2020	Difference
Cash	$ 100	$ 265	$165
Accounts receivable	300	200	(100)
Merchandise inventory	100	300	200
Equipment, net	1,800	2,100	300
Total assets	$2,300	$2,865	$565
Accounts payable	$ 275	$ 240	$(35)
Salaries payable	50	25	(25)
Bonds payable	600	800	200
Common stock (no-par)	1,100	1,200	100
Retained earnings	275	600	325
Total liabilities and stockholders' equity	$2,300	$2,865	$565

Income Statement, For Year Ended December 31	2020
Revenues	$3,000
Costs of goods sold	(1,700)
Depreciation	(400)
Other expenses	(385)
Net income	$ 515

Additional information for 2020

1. Equipment was sold for its book value of $500.
2. Equipment was purchased during the year for $1,200.
3. Dividends declared and paid were $190.

Required

Prepare the statement of cash flows following the indirect method for Zale Inc. for the year ended December 31, 2020.

Exercise 22-54
Preparing Statement of Cash Flows—Indirect Method **LO2, 3, 4**

Pier2 Inc. reported the following comparative balance sheets for the current year.

Balance Sheets	January 1	December 31
Cash	$ 4,000	$ 9,750
Restricted cash	1,000	1,000
Accounts receivable	3,000	2,000
Equipment	9,000	15,000
Accumulated depreciation	(1,000)	(2,000)
Total assets	$16,000	$25,750
Salaries payable	$ 1,000	$ 2,000
Long-term notes payable	5,000	5,000
Capital stock	8,000	8,000
Retained earnings	2,000	10,750
Total liabilities and stockholders' equity	$16,000	$25,750

Additional information

1. Net income for the current year was $10,000.
2. No disposals of equipment took place during the year.

Required

Prepare the statement of cash flows following the indirect method for Pier2 Inc.

Exercise 22-55
Preparing a Statement of Cash Flows—Indirect Method **LO2, 3, 4**

Denton Corporation's balance sheet accounts as of December 31, 2019, and 2020, and information relating to 2020 activities are presented below.

Balance Sheets, December 31	2020	2019
Assets		
Cash	$ 230,000	$ 100,000
Short-term investments	300,000	—
Accounts receivable (net)	510,000	510,000
Inventory	680,000	600,000
Long-term investments	200,000	300,000
Plant assets	1,700,000	1,000,000
Accumulated depreciation	(450,000)	(450,000)
Patent	90,000	100,000
Total assets	$3,260,000	$2,160,000
Liabilities and Stockholders' Equity		
Accounts payable and accrued liabilities	$ 825,000	$ 720,000
Short-term debt to financial institutions	325,000	—
Common stock, $10 par	800,000	700,000
Additional paid-in capital	370,000	250,000
Retained earnings	940,000	490,000
Total liabilities and stockholders' equity	$3,260,000	$2,160,000

Information relating to 2020 activities

1. Net income for 2020 was $690,000.
2. Cash dividends of $240,000 were declared and paid in 2020.
3. Equipment costing $400,000 and having a carrying amount of $150,000 was sold in 2020 for $150,000.
4. A long-term investment was sold in 2020 for $135,000. There were no other transactions affecting long-term investments in 2020.
5. 10,000 shares of common stock were issued in 2020 for $22 per share.
6. Short-term investments consist of Treasury bills maturing on June 30, 2021, and are reported at fair value. Assume no change in fair value from the date of purchase.

Required

Prepare the statement of cash flows following the indirect method for Denton Corporation for the year ended December 31, 2020.

Exercise 22-56
Preparing a Statement of Cash Flows—Indirect Method **LO2, 3, 4, 5**

Exon Corporation's recent comparative balance sheet and income statement follow.

Balance Sheets, December 31	2020	2019
Assets		
Cash	$ 49,000	$ 53,000
Cash equivalents	10,000	7,000
Accounts receivable (net)	34,000	24,000
Plant assets	277,000	247,000
Accumulated depreciation	(178,000)	(167,000)
Total assets	$192,000	$164,000
Liabilities and Stockholders' Equity		
Bonds payable	$ 49,000	$ 46,000
Dividends payable	8,000	5,000
Common stock, $1 par	22,000	19,000
Additional paid-in capital	9,000	3,000
Retained earnings	104,000	91,000
Total liabilities and stockholders' equity	$192,000	$164,000

Income Statement, For Year Ended December 31	2020
Sales revenue	$155,000
Cost of goods sold	(107,000)
Gross margin	48,000
Depreciation expense	(33,000)
Gain on sale of equipment	13,000
Net income	$ 28,000

Additional information

1. During 2020, equipment costing $40,000 was sold for cash.
2. During 2020, $20,000 of bonds payable was issued in exchange for property, plant, and equipment. There was no amortization of bond discount or premium.

Required

Prepare the statement of cash flows following the indirect method for Exon Corporation for the year ended December 31, 2020.

Sketchers Corporation's recent comparative balance sheet and income statement follow.

Exercise 22-57
Preparing a Statement of Cash Flows—Indirect Method **LO2, 3, 4, 5**

Balance Sheets, December 31	2019	2020
Assets		
Cash and cash equivalents	$ 16,000	$ 68,000
Accounts receivable (net)	20,000	36,000
Inventory	40,000	48,000
Investment, long-term	8,000	—
Plant assets	120,000	188,000
Accumulated depreciation	(20,000)	(28,000)
Total assets	$184,000	$312,000
Liabilities and Stockholders' Equity		
Accounts payable	$ 12,000	$ 20,000
Notes payable, short-term (nontrade)	16,000	12,000
Notes payable, long-term	40,000	72,000
Common stock, no-par	100,000	160,000
Retained earnings	16,000	48,000
Total liabilities and stockholders' equity	$184,000	$312,000

Income Statement, For Year Ended December 31	2020
Sales revenue	$600,000
Cost of goods sold	(360,000)
Gross margin	240,000
Depreciation expense	(8,000)
Other operating expenses	(128,000)
Net income	$104,000

Additional Information

1. Sold the long-term investment at cost, for cash.
2. Declared and paid a cash dividend of $28,000.
3. Purchased plant assets that cost $68,000; gave a $48,000 long-term note payable and paid $20,000 cash.
4. Paid a $16,000 long-term note payable by issuing common stock; fair value, $16,000.
5. Issued a stock dividend, $44,000.

Required

Prepare the statement of cash flows following the indirect method for Sketchers Corporation for the year ended December 31, 2020.

Sterling Corporation's recent comparative balance sheet and income statement follow.

Exercise 22-58
Preparing a Statement of Cash Flows—Indirect Method **LO2, 3, 4, 5**

Balance Sheets, December 31	2019	2020	Difference
Assets			
Cash and cash equivalents	$ 34,000	$ 33,500	$ (500)
Accounts receivable (net)	12,000	17,000	5,000
Inventory	16,000	14,000	(2,000)
Investment, long-term	6,000	—	(6,000)
Fixed assets	80,000	98,000	18,000
Accumulated depreciation	(48,000)	(39,000)	9,000
Total assets	$100,000	$123,500	$23,500
Liabilities and Stockholders' Equity			
Accounts payable	19,000	12,000	(7,000)
Bonds payable	10,000	30,000	20,000
Common stock, no-par	50,000	65,000	15,000
Retained earnings	21,000	28,000	7,000
Treasury stock	—	(11,500)	(11,500)
Total liabilities and stockholders' equity	$100,000	$123,500	$23,500

Income Statement, For Year Ended December 31	2020
Sales revenue	$70,000
Cost of goods sold	(42,000)
Gross margin	28,000
Depreciation expense	(5,000)
Other operating expenses	(18,000)
Gain on sale of investments	3,000
Loss on sale of fixed assets	(1,000)
Net income	$ 7,000

Analysis of selected accounts and transactions

1. Sold fixed assets for cash; cost, $21,000, and two-thirds depreciated.
2. Purchased fixed assets for cash, $9,000.
3. Purchased fixed assets; exchanged unissued bonds of $30,000 (face value and fair value) in payment.
4. Sold the long-term investments for cash. Assume carrying value of the investment is equal to its original purchase price.
5. Purchased treasury stock for cash, $11,500.
6. Retired bonds payable at maturity date by issuing common stock, $10,000.
7. Sold unissued common stock for cash, $5,000.

Required

Prepare the statement of cash flows following the indirect method for Sterling Corporation for the year ended December 31, 2020.

Exercise 22-59
Preparing a Statement of Cash Flows—Indirect Method **LO2, 3, 4**

5M Corporation's recent comparative balance sheets and income statement follow.

Balance Sheets, December 31	2019	2020
Assets		
Cash and cash equivalents	$ 42,000	$ 76,000
Accounts receivable (net)	31,000	39,000
Plant assets	82,000	81,000
Accumulated depreciation	(20,000)	(14,000)
Total assets	$135,000	$182,000
Liabilities and Stockholders' Equity		
Salaries payable	$ 3,000	$ 5,000
Notes payable, long-term	46,000	40,000
Common stock, par $10	61,000	101,000
Additional paid-in capital	9,000	17,000
Retained earnings	16,000	27,000
Treasury stock	—	(8,000)
Total liabilities and stockholders' equity	$135,000	$182,000

Income Statement, For Year Ended December 31	2020
Sales revenue	$66,000
Salaries expense	(28,000)
Depreciation expense	(4,000)
Administrative and selling expenses	(12,000)
Net income	$22,000

Additional information

1. Plant assets were sold for $21,000 with an original cost of $31,000 and accumulated depreciation of $10,000.
2. Borrowed cash for $40,000 and made principal payments of $46,000 on long-term notes for the year.

Required

Prepare the statement of cash flows following the indirect method for 5M Corporation for the year ended December 31, 2020.

Exercise 22-60
Analyzing the Statement of Cash Flows **LO2, 3, 4, 5**

K. Crew Company recorded the following amounts in the selected accounts below.

Equipment			
Jan. 1, 2020	100,000		
Purchase of equipment	80,000	25,000	Cost of equipment sold
Dec. 31, 2020	155,000		

Retained earnings			
		88,000	Jan. 1, 2020
Dividends	2,000	14,000	Net income
		100,000	Dec. 31, 2020

Accumulated depreciation			
		35,000	Jan. 1, 2020
		12,000	Depreciation expense
Accumulated depreciation on equipment sold	15,000		
		32,000	Dec. 31, 2020

Common stock			
		100,000	Jan. 1, 2020
		40,000	Stock issuance
		140,000	Dec. 31, 2020

Additional Information

1. Equipment was sold for $12,500 during the year.
2. Dividends payable increased by $500 from the beginning of the year.
3. $10,000 of the equipment purchases were made by issuing common stock.

Required

a. Indicate items that would be included in the operating, investing, and financing sections of the statement of cash flows based upon the information provided (indirect method).

b. Indicate any noncash disclosures that would be required based upon the information above.

Exercise 22-61
Preparing a Cash Flow Worksheet **LO6**
Hint: See Demo 22-6

Taser Corporation's recent comparative balance sheet and income statement follow.

Balance Sheets, December 31	2019	2020
Assets		
Cash and cash equivalents	$ 39,000	$ 63,800
Accounts receivable (net)	68,000	68,000
Merchandise inventory	156,000	170,000
Investments, long-term	—	20,000
Plant assets	337,000	361,000
Accumulated depreciation	(88,000)	(68,000)
Total assets	$512,000	$614,800
Liabilities and Stockholders' Equity		
Accounts payable	$ 42,000	$ 38,000
Salaries payable	3,000	1,000
Income taxes payable	4,000	7,000
Bonds payable	200,000	200,000
Premium on bonds payable	8,000	7,400
Common stock, no-par	240,000	311,000
Retained earnings	15,000	50,400
Total liabilities and stockholders' equity	$512,000	$614,800

Income Statement, For Year Ended December 31	2020
Sales revenue	$240,000
Cost of goods sold	(96,000)
Depreciation expense	(12,000)
Salaries expense	(44,000)
Income tax expense	(20,000)
Interest expense	(14,000)
Other expenses	(4,600)
Gain on sale of plant assets	6,000
Net income	$ 55,400

Additional information

1. Purchased a plant asset, $60,000; issued capital stock in full payment.
2. Purchased a long-term investment in equity securities for cash, $20,000.
3. Declared and paid cash dividend, $20,000.
4. Sold a plant asset for $10,000 cash (cost, $36,000; accumulated depreciation, $32,000).
5. Sold capital stock, 1,000 shares at $11 per share cash.

Required

a. Prepare a cash flow worksheet.

b. Prepare a reconciliation of the total of the three sections of net cash flows from operating, investing, and financing activities to the change in cash and the noncash disclosure note.

Exercise 22-62
Preparing a Cash Flow Worksheet **LO6**
Hint: See Demo 22-6

Guccii Corporation's recent comparative balance sheet and income statement follow:

Balance Sheets, December 31	2019	2020
Assets		
Cash and cash equivalents	$ 30,000	$ 43,000
Investments, short-term	—	6,000
Accounts receivable (net)	34,000	42,000
Merchandise inventory	20,000	30,000
Investments, long-term	—	20,000
Plant assets, net	120,000	118,000
Patents	6,000	5,400
Other assets	14,000	14,000
Total assets	$224,000	$278,400
Liabilities and Stockholders' Equity		
Accounts payable	$ 24,000	$ 44,000
Accrued expenses payable	—	17,400
Bonds payable	80,000	40,000
Common stock, par $10	70,000	80,000
Additional paid-in capital	—	9,000
Retained earnings	50,000	88,000
Total liabilities and stockholders' equity	$224,000	$278,400

Income Statement, For Year Ended December 31	2020
Sales revenue	$208,000
Cost of goods sold	(110,000)
Depreciation expense	(16,000)
Patent amortization	(600)
Other operating expenses	(35,400)
Net income	$ 46,000

Additional information for 2020

1. Retired bonds paying $40,000 cash.
2. Bought long-term debt investment in securities, $20,000 cash.
3. Purchased a plant asset, $14,000 cash.
4. Purchased short-term investment in securities (not held in a trading account), $6,000 cash.
5. Declared and paid cash dividends, $8,000.
6. Issued capital stock, 1,000 shares at $19 cash per share.

Required

a. Prepare a cash flow worksheet.

b. Prepare a reconciliation of the total of the three sections of net cash flows from operating, investing, and financing activities to the change in cash.

Exercise 22-63
Preparing a Cash Flow Worksheet **LO6**

ISPN Corporation's recent comparative balance sheet and income statement follow.

Balance Sheets, December 31	2019	2020
Assets		
Cash	$ 16,000	$ 32,000
Accounts receivable	56,000	52,000
Allowance for doubtful accounts	(6,000)	(5,000)
Other receivables (nontrade)	3,000	2,000
Inventory	30,000	32,000
Equipment	80,000	77,000
Accumulated depreciation	(6,000)	(5,000)
Intangibles, net	55,000	53,000
Total assets	$228,000	$238,000
Liabilities and Stockholders' Equity		
Accounts payable	$ 50,000	$ 60,000
Income taxes payable	70,000	50,000
Interest payable	2,000	1,000
Bonds payable	32,000	
Discount on bonds payable	(2,000)	
Common stock, no-par	70,000	80,000
Retained earnings	6,000	47,000
Total liabilities and stockholders' equity	$228,000	$238,000

Income Statement, For Year Ended Dec. 31	2020
Sales revenue	$300,000
Cost of goods sold	(80,000)
Depreciation expense	(45,000)
Patent amortization	(2,000)
Other expenses	(44,000)
Interest expense	(3,000)
Income tax expense	(65,000)
Net income	$ 61,000

Additional information

1. $20,000 of dividends was declared and paid in 2020.
2. Equipment costing $66,000, with a book value of $20,000, was sold at book value. New equipment also was purchased; common stock was issued in partial payment, $10,000.
3. Bonds were retired at book value; $500 of bond discount was amortized in 2020.

Required

a. Prepare a cash flow worksheet.

b. Prepare a reconciliation of the total of the three sections of net cash flows from operating, investing, and financing activities to the change in cash and the noncash disclosure note.

Exercise 22-64
Determining Operating Cash Flows—Direct Method **LO7**
Hint: See Demo 22-7

Adjusted trial balances for Garboz Company, an industrial recycler, at December 31, 2020, and 2019, follow.

Debits, December 31	2020	2019
Cash	$ 35,000	$ 32,000
Accounts receivable	33,000	30,000
Inventory	31,000	47,000
Property, plant, and equipment	100,000	95,000
Discount on bonds payable	4,500	5,000
Cost of goods sold	250,000	380,000
Selling expenses	141,500	172,000
General and administrative expenses	137,000	151,300
Interest expense	4,300	2,600
Income tax expense	20,400	61,200
Total debits	$756,700	$976,100

Credits, December 31	2020	2019
Allowance for doubtful accounts	$ 1,300	$ 1,100
Accumulated depreciation	16,500	15,000
Trade accounts payable	25,000	17,500
Income taxes payable	21,000	27,100
Deferred income tax liability	5,300	4,600
Callable bonds payable, 8%	45,000	20,000
Common stock	50,000	40,000
Additional paid-in capital	9,100	7,500
Retained earnings	44,700	64,600
Sales	538,800	778,700
Total credits	$756,700	$976,100

Additional information

1. Purchased $5,000 of equipment in 2020.
2. Allocated one-third of its depreciation expense to selling expenses and the remainder to general and administrative expenses.
3. Assume no accounts receivable were written off or recovered during the year.

Required

What amounts should Garboz report in its statement of cash flows for the year ended December 31, 2020, for the following?

a. Cash collected from customers
b. Cash paid to suppliers
c. Cash paid for interest
d. Cash paid for income taxes
e. Cash paid for selling expenses

Exercise 22-65 Analyzing Cash Flows: Sales **LO7**

The records of J.Q. Morgan Company reported sales revenue of $100,000 (on the income statement) and a change in the balance of accounts receivable. To demonstrate the effect of changes in accounts receivable on cash inflows from customers, five separate cases are used.

Case	Sales Revenue (From Income Statement)	Accounts Receivable Increase (Decrease)	Cash Flows
A.	$100,000	$ 0	$____
B.	100,000	10,000	____
C.	100,000	(10,000)	____
D.	100,000	9,000*	____
E.	100,000	(9,000)*	____

*Includes the effect of a $1,000 write-off of an uncollectible account.

Required

Complete the table above for each separate case.

Exercise 22-66 Analyzing Cash Flows: Cost of Goods Sold **LO7**

The records of Atlas Company showed cost of goods sold (on the income statement) of $60,000 and a change in the inventory and accounts payable balances. To demonstrate the effect of these changes on cash outflow for cost of goods sold (i.e., payments to suppliers), eight separate cases are used.

Case	Cost of Goods Sold (From Income Statement)	Inventory Increase (Decrease)	Accounts Payable Increase (Decrease)	Cash Flows
A.	$60,000	$ 0	$ 0	$____
B.	60,000	6,000	0	____
C.	60,000	(6,000)	0	____
D.	60,000	0	4,000	____
E.	60,000	0	(4,000)	____
F.	60,000	6,000	4,000	____
G.	60,000	(6,000)	(4,000)	____
H.	60,000	(6,000)	(6,000)	____

Required

Complete the table above for each separate case.

Exercise 22-67 Determining Operating Cash Flows—Direct Method **LO7** *Hint:* See Demo 22-7

Using the information provided in Exercise 22-61, prepare the operating activities section of the statement of cash flows, using the direct method.

Exercise 22-68 Determining Operating Cash Flows—Direct Method **LO7** *Hint:* See Demo 22-7

Using the information provided in Exercise 22-58, prepare the operating activities section of the statement of cash flows, using the direct method. Assume there is no bad debt expense.

Exercise 22-69 Determining Operating Cash Flows—Direct Method **LO7** *Hint:* See Demo 22-7

Using the information provided in Exercise 22-62, prepare the operating activities section of the statement of cash flows, using the direct method. Assume there is no bad debt expense

Exercise 22-70
Analyzing Changes in Accounts Receivable LO2, 7

The following information pertains to Medicoil Inc., producers of medical hardware, for the current year just ended.

Balance Sheet Excerpts	January 1	December 31
Accounts receivable	$20,000	$35,000
Allowance for doubtful accounts	(1,000)	(2,000)
Net accounts receivable	$19,000	$33,000

Income Statement Excerpts	
Net sales	$80,000
Bad debt expense	5,500

Additional information

1. $6,000 of accounts receivable were written off during the year.
2. $1,500 was collected on accounts receivable written off in previous years.

Required

a. Determine the adjustment(s) to net income appearing in the operating section of the statement of cash flows for the current year under the *indirect* method.

b. Determine the cash collections appearing in the operating section of the statement of cash flows for the current year under the *direct* method.

Exercise 22-71
Analyzing Cash Flows: Bond Interest LO7

The records of Atlas Company showed bond interest expense (on the income statement) of $20,000 and a change in the bond interest payable, premium, and discount balances. To demonstrate the effect of these changes on cash outflow for bond interest (i.e., payments to creditors) reported under the direct cash flow method, six separate cases are used.

Case	Interest Expense	Change in Interest Payable	Change in Unamortized Discount	Change in Unamortized Premium	Cash Flows
A.	$20,000	$ 0	$ 0	n/a	$_____
B.	20,000	500	(1,000)	n/a	_____
C.	20,000	(500)	(1,800)	n/a	_____
D.	20,000	0	n/a	$(2,000)	_____
E.	20,000	800	(1,000)	n/a	_____
F.	20,000	(500)	n/a	(2,000)	_____

Required

Complete the table above for each separate case. Assume the only change affecting the unamortized premium and discount accounts is amortization for the period.

Exercise 22-72
Analyzing Cash Flows: Income Taxes LO7

The records of Atlas Company showed income tax expense (on the income statement) of $20,000 and a change in the income taxes payable and deferred tax accounts. To demonstrate the effect of these changes on cash outflow for income taxes, six separate cases are used.

Case	Income Tax Expense	Change in Income Taxes Payable	Change in Deferred Tax Asset	Change in Deferred Tax Liability	Cash Flows
A.	$20,000	$ 0	$ 0	$ 0	$_____
B.	20,000	1,000	0	0	_____
C.	20,000	1,000	800	0	_____
D.	20,000	1,000	0	800	_____
E.	20,000	(1,000)	500	(800)	_____
F.	20,000	1,000	(600)	700	_____

Required

Complete the table above for each separate case.

Exercise 22-73
Preparing a Statement of Cash Flows—Direct Method LO3, 4, 7

Using the information from Exercises 22-62 and 22-69, prepare a statement of cash flows using the direct method. Assume there is no bad debt expense.

The following three statements relate to Aude Company.

Exercise 22-74 Analyzing Interrelations of Financial Statements **LO2, 3, 4, 7**

Net Cash Flows from Operating Activities—Direct Method For Year Ended December 31, 2020	
Collections from customers	$240,000
Payments to suppliers	(114,000)
Payments for salaries	(46,000)
Payments for income taxes	(17,000)
Payments for interest	(14,600)
Other operating expenses	(4,600)
Net cash provided by operating activities	$ 43,800

Income Statement For Year Ended December 31, 2020	
Sales revenue	$x
Cost of goods sold	x
Depreciation expense	x
Salaries expense	x
Income tax expense	x
Interest expense	x
Other expenses	x
Gain on sale of fixed assets	x
Net income	$x

Net Cash Flows from Operating Activities—Indirect Method For Year Ended December 31, 2020	
Net income	$ x
Depreciation expense	12,000
Amortization of bond premium	(600)
Gain on sale of fixed assets	(6,000)
Increase in inventory	(14,000)
Decrease in accounts payable	(4,000)
Decrease in salaries payable	(2,000)
Increase in income taxes payable	3,000
Net cash provided by operating activities	$43,800

Required

Determine the missing amounts indicated by an "x" in the statements above.

Problems

Harlee Company had the following activities during the current year ended December 31, 2020.

Problem 22-75 Identifying Operating, Investing, and Financing Activities **LO1, 2, 5** *Hint:* See Demo 22-1

____ 1. Payment of a dividend.
____ 2. Amortization expense on patent.
____ 3. Compensation expense recognized for stock options.
____ 4. Decrease in accounts payable.
____ 5. Cash funded to pension plan in excess of pension expense.
____ 6. Purchase of land through the issuance of common stock.
____ 7. Unrealized loss—income on equity securities.
____ 8. Increase in deferred tax liability.
____ 9. Increase in deferred tax asset.
____ 10. Conversion of bonds payable to common stock.
____ 11. Decrease in supplies.

____ 12. Issued a short-term, nontrade note.
____ 13. Increase in salaries payable.
____ 14. Acquisition of equipment through an increase in bonds payable.
____ 15. Proceeds from sale of a patent.
____ 16. Purchase of equipment for cash.
____ 17. Excess of the company's share of its investee's net income over the company's share of dividend payments (accounted for under the equity method).
____ 18. Proceeds from an insurance settlement on a property loss.
____ 19. Increase in inventory.
____ 20. Principal payment on a mortgage payable.
____ 21. Collection of a nontrade note receivable.
____ 22. Proceeds from long-term nontrade note payable.
____ 23. Amortization expense on premium for a bond payable.
____ 24. Sale of available-for-sale debt securities.
____ 25. Retirement of preferred stock for cash.
____ 26. Collection on a trade note receivable (note received for inventory purchase).

Required

Assuming that the company uses the indirect method for the statement of cash flows, classify each activity as follows:

a. Operating activity—addition
b. Operating activity—subtraction
c. Investing activity—cash inflow
d. Investing activity—cash outflow
e. Financing activity—cash inflow
f. Financing activity—cash outflow
g. Noncash transaction

Problem 22-76 Preparing a Statement of Cash Flows—Indirect Method **LO2, 3, 4, 5**

Limit Label Corporation's recent comparative balance sheet and income statement, along with additional information follow.

Balance Sheets, December 31	**2019**	**2020**
Assets		
Cash and cash equivalents	$ 15,000	$ 31,000
Accounts receivable	30,000	28,500
Allowance for doubtful accounts	(1,500)	(2,000)
Inventory	10,000	15,000
Prepaid insurance	2,400	1,400
Fixed assets	80,000	81,000
Accumulated depreciation	(20,000)	(16,000)
Land	40,100	81,100
Total assets	$156,000	$220,000
Liabilities and Stockholders' Equity		
Accounts payable	$ 10,000	$ 11,000
Salaries payable	2,000	1,000
Interest payable	—	1,000
Notes payable, long-term	20,000	46,000
Common stock, no-par	100,000	136,000
Retained earnings	24,000	25,000
Total liabilities and stockholders' equity	$156,000	$220,000

Income Statement, For Year ended December 31	**2020**
Sales revenue	$80,000
Cost of goods sold	(35,000)
Depreciation expense	(5,000)
Bad debt expense	(1,000)
Insurance expense	(1,000)
Interest expense	(2,000)
Salaries expense	(12,000)
Income tax expense	(3,000)
Other expenses, including loss on sale of fixed assets	(15,000)
Net income	$ 6,000

Additional information

1. Wrote off $500 accounts receivable as uncollectible.
2. Sold an operating asset for $4,000 cash (cost, $15,000; accumulated depreciation, $9,000).
3. Issued common stock for $5,000 cash.
4. Declared and paid a cash dividend, $5,000.
5. Purchased land, $20,000 cash.

6. Acquired land for $21,000 and issued common stock as payment in full.
7. Acquired fixed assets, cost $16,000; issued a $16,000, three-year, interest-bearing note payable.
8. Paid a $10,000 long-term note installment by issuing common stock to the creditor.
9. Borrowed cash on long-term note, $20,000.

Required

Prepare a statement of cash flows using the indirect method.

Problem 22-77 Preparing a Statement of Cash Flows—Indirect Method **LO2, 3, 4, 5**

The income statement and balance sheets of Kenwood Company and related analysis are provided below.

Balance Sheets, December 31	2020	2019
Assets		
Cash and cash equivalents	$ 100,000	$ 90,000
Accounts receivable (net of allowance for doubtful accounts of $10,000 and $8,000, respectively)	210,000	140,000
Inventory	260,000	220,000
Land	325,000	200,000
Plant and equipment	580,000	633,000
Accumulated depreciation	(90,000)	(100,000)
Patents	30,000	33,000
Total assets	$1,415,000	$1,216,000
Liabilities and Stockholders' Equity		
Accounts payable	$ 260,000	$ 200,000
Salaries payable	200,000	210,000
Income tax payable	140,000	100,000
Bonds payable (due December 15, 2029)	130,000	180,000
Common stock, par value $5, authorized 100,000 shares, issued and outstanding 50,000 and 42,000 shares, respectively	250,000	210,000
Additional paid-in capital	233,000	170,000
Retained earnings	202,000	146,000
Total liabilities and stockholders' equity	$1,415,000	$1,216,000

Income Statement, For Year Ended December 31	2020
Sales revenue	$1,000,000
Expenses and losses	
Cost of goods sold	(560,000)
Salaries	(190,000)
Depreciation	(20,000)
Patent amortization	(3,000)
Loss on sale of equipment	(4,000)
Interest expense	(16,000)
Miscellaneous expenses	(8,000)
Gain on early extinguishment of debt	12,000
Income tax expense	(90,000)
Net income	$ 121,000

Analysis of selected accounts and transactions

1. On February 2, 2020, issued a 10% stock dividend to stockholders of record on January 15, 2020. The market price per share of the common stock on February 2, 2020, was $15.
2. On March 1, 2020, issued 3,800 shares of common stock for land. The common stock had a fair value of approximately $40,000 on March 1, 2020.
3. On April 15, 2020, repurchased its long-term bonds payable with a face value of $50,000 for cash.
4. On June 30, 2020, sold equipment that cost $53,000, with a book value of $23,000, for $19,000 cash.
5. On September 30, 2020, declared and paid a 4 cents per share cash dividend to stockholders of record on August 1, 2020.
6. On October 10, 2020, purchased land for $85,000 cash.

Required

Prepare a statement of cash flows using the indirect method.

Problem 22-78
Preparing a Statement of Cash Flows—Indirect Method **LO2, 3, 4, 5**

The following is Orem Corporation's comparative balance sheets for 2020 and 2019.

Balance Sheets, December 31	2020	2019
Assets		
Cash and cash equivalents	$ 400,000	$ 350,000
Accounts receivable (net)	564,000	584,000
Inventory	925,000	857,500
Right-of-use asset	200,000	—
Property, plant, & equipment	1,453,500	1,483,500
Accumulated depreciation	(582,500)	(520,000)
Investment in Belle Co.	152,500	137,500
Loan receivable	135,000	—
Total assets	$3,247,500	$2,892,500
Liabilities and Stockholders' Equity		
Accounts payable	$ 507,500	$ 477,500
Income taxes payable	15,000	25,000
Dividends payable	40,000	45,000
Lease liability	200,000	—
Capital stock, common, $1 par	250,000	250,000
Additional paid-in capital	750,000	750,000
Retained earnings	1,485,000	1,345,000
Total liabilities and stockholders' equity	$3,247,500	$2,892,500

Additional information

1. On December 31, 2019, acquired 25% of Belle Company's common stock for $137,500. On that date, the carrying value of Belle's net assets and liabilities, which approximated fair value, was $550,000. Belle reported income of $60,000 for the year ended December 31, 2020. No dividend was paid on Belle's common stock during the year.
2. During 2020, loaned $150,000 to Chase Company, an unrelated company. Chase made the first semi-annual principal repayment of $15,000, plus interest at 10% on October 1, 2020.
3. On January 2, 2020, sold equipment costing $30,000, with a carrying value of $17,500, for $20,000 cash.
4. On December 31, 2020, entered into a finance lease for an office building. Orem recorded a right-of-use asset and a lease liability for $200,000 at the lease commencement. Orem made the first rental payment of $30,000 when due on January 2, 2021.
5. Net income for 2020 was $180,000. Taxes paid in 2020 were $70,000.

Required

Prepare a statement of cash flows using the indirect method.

Problem 22-79
Preparing a Statement of Cash Flows—Indirect Method **LO2, 3, 4, 5**

The differences between the Boole Inc. balance sheet accounts of December 31, 2019, and 2020, follow.

Balance Sheet Changes	Difference	Balance Sheet Changes	Difference
Assets		**Liabilities and Stockholders' Equity**	
Cash and cash equivalents	$ 60,000	Accounts payable and accrued liabilities	$ (2,500)
Short-term investments	150,000	Dividends payable	80,000
Accounts receivable, net	—	Short-term debt (nontrade)	162,500
Inventory	40,000	Long-term debt	55,000
Investment, long-term	(50,000)	Common stock, $5 par	50,000
Plant assets	350,000	Additional paid-in capital	60,000
Accumulated depreciation	—	Retained earnings	145,000
Total assets	$550,000	Total liabilities and stockholders' equity	$550,000

Additional information for 2020

1. Both short- and long-term investments are reported at fair value. The fair value of the short-term investments and long-term investments did not change during 2020. Investments were not held in a trading account.
2. A building costing $300,000 and having a carrying amount of $175,000 was sold for $175,000.
3. Equipment costing $55,000 was acquired through the issuance of long-term debt.
4. A long-term investment was sold for $67,500. There were no other transactions affecting long-term investments.
5. 10,000 shares of common stock were issued for $11 a share.

6. Net income was $395,000.
7. Interest and taxes paid in 2020 were $30,000 and $160,000, respectively.

Required

Prepare Boole's statement of cash flows under the indirect method assuming that cash on January 1, 2020, was $30,000.

Problem 22-80
Preparing a Statement of Cash Flows—Indirect Method **LO2, 3, 4, 5, 6**

At December 31, 2020, the following data for Lincoln Company were available.

Balance Sheets, December 31	2019	2020	Difference
Assets			
Cash	$ 7,000	$ 19,000	$ 12,000
Cash equivalents	1,000	3,000	2,000
Accounts receivable (net)	18,000	24,000	6,000
Inventory	16,000	10,000	(6,000)
Investment, long-term	4,000	—	(4,000)
Plant	60,000	60,000	—
Equipment	40,000	44,000	4,000
Land	20,000	80,000	60,000
Patents	16,000	14,000	(2,000)
Accumulated depreciation—plant	(14,000)	(20,000)	(6,000)
Accumulated depreciation—equipment	(20,000)	(16,000)	4,000
Total assets	$148,000	$218,000	$ 70,000
Liabilities and Stockholders' Equity			
Accounts payable	$ 16,000	$ 4,000	$(12,000)
Salaries payable	2,000	—	(2,000)
Notes payable, long-term	20,000	38,000	18,000
Common stock, no-par	100,000	150,000	50,000
Retained earnings	10,000	26,000	16,000
Total liabilities and stockholders' equity	$148,000	$218,000	$ 70,000

Income Statement, For Year Ended December 31	2020
Sales revenue	$180,000
Cost of goods sold	(110,000)
Depreciation expense, plant	(6,000)
Depreciation expense, equipment	(4,000)
Patent amortization	(2,000)
Other operating expenses	(40,000)
Loss on sale of equipment	(2,000)
Gain on sale of long-term investment	16,000
Income tax expense	(8,000)
Net income	$ 24,000

Analysis of selected accounts and entries

1. At the end of the year, sold equipment that cost $16,000 (50% depreciated) for $6,000 cash.
2. Purchased land that cost $20,000; paid $4,000 cash, issued a long-term note for the balance.
3. Paid $8,000 to retire a long-term note payable at maturity.
4. Sold $20,000 of common stock.
5. Purchased equipment costing $20,000; paid half in cash, balance due in three years (interest-bearing note).
6. Issued 3,000 shares of common stock, fair value $30,000, for land that cost $40,000; the balance was paid in cash.
7. Sold the long-term investment for $20,000 cash. The investments were debt securities classified as available-for-sale. The securities were purchased December 31, 2019; therefore, no valuation allowance was established.
8. Declared and paid dividends, $8,000.
9. Income taxes paid and interest paid in 2020 were $8,000 and $2,000, respectively.

Required

a. Prepare a cash flow worksheet for Lincoln for 2020.

b. Prepare Lincoln's statement of cash flows under the indirect method.

Problem 22-81
Preparing a Statement of Cash Flows—Indirect Method **LO2, 3, 4, 5, 6**

The records of Lopez Co. provided the following data for the accounting year ended December 31, 2020.

Balance Sheets, December 31	2019	2020
Assets		
Cash and cash equivalents	$ 30,000	$ 69,000
Investments, short term	10,000	8,000
Accounts receivable	56,000	86,000
Allowance for doubtful accounts	(6,000)	(7,000)
Inventory	20,000	30,000
Prepaid rent	—	2,000
Land	60,000	25,000
Equipment	80,000	90,000
Accumulated depreciation	(20,000)	(26,900)
Other assets	29,000	39,000
Total assets	$259,000	$315,100
Liabilities and Stockholders' Equity		
Accounts payable	$ 33,000	$ 45,000
Salaries payable	5,000	2,000
Income taxes payable	2,000	8,000
Bonds payable	70,000	55,000
Discount on bonds payable	(1,000)	(900)
Common stock, no-par	100,000	131,000
Preferred stock, no-par	20,000	30,000
Retained earnings	30,000	45,000
Total liabilities and stockholders' equity	$259,000	$315,100

Income Statement, For Year Ended December 31	2020
Sales revenue	$180,000
Cost of goods sold	(90,000)
Depreciation expense	(6,900)
Bad debt expense	(1,000)
Salaries	(32,900)
Other operating expenses	(4,000)
Interest expense	(6,100)
Gain on sale of land	18,000
Loss on bond retirement	(1,000)
Income tax expense	(12,100)
Net income	$ 44,000

Analysis of selected accounts and transactions

1. Issued bonds payable for cash, $5,000. The bonds payable account represents more than one bond issue.
2. Sold land for $53,000 cash; book value, $35,000.
3. Purchased equipment for cash, $10,000.
4. Purchased short-term investments (not held in a trading account) for cash, $2,000.
5. Declared a property dividend on the preferred stock and paid it with a short-term investment; fair value and carrying value are the same, $4,000.
6. Prior to maturity date, retired $20,000 (face) of bonds payable by issuing common stock; the common stock had a fair value of $21,000. The bonds retired had been issued at face value.
7. Acquired other assets by issuing preferred stock with a fair value of $10,000.
8. Cash dividends declared and paid were $15,000. A stock dividend with a fair value of $10,000 was issued on the common stock.

Required

a. Prepare a cash flow worksheet for Lopez Co. for 2020.

b. Prepare the statement of cash flows under the indirect method for Lopez Co.

Problem 22-82
Preparing a Statement of Cash Flows—Indirect Method **LO2, 3, 4, 5**

The income statement, balance sheet and analysis of selected accounts of Cruz Co. are provided below.

Balance Sheets, December 31	2019	2020	Difference
Assets			
Cash and cash equivalents	$ 80,000	$ 89,800	$ 9,800
Accounts receivable (net)	120,000	105,000	(15,000)
Inventory	360,000	283,200	(76,800)
Prepaid insurance	4,800	2,400	(2,400)
Investment, long-term	60,000	—	(60,000)
Land	20,000	76,800	56,800
Plant assets	500,000	518,000	18,000
Accumulated depreciation	(130,000)	(158,000)	(28,000)
Patent (net)	3,200	2,800	(400)
Total assets	$1,018,000	$920,000	$ (98,000)
Liabilities and Stockholders' Equity			
Accounts payable	$ 100,000	$106,000	$ 6,000
Salaries payable	4,000	3,000	(1,000)
Income taxes payable	18,000	26,800	8,800
Bonds payable	200,000	100,000	(100,000)
Premium on bonds payable	10,000	3,400	(6,600)
Common stock, par $10	600,000	612,000	12,000
Additional paid-in capital	30,000	36,000	6,000
Retained earnings	56,000	32,800	(23,200)
Total liabilities and stockholders' equity	$1,018,000	$920,000	$ (98,000)

Income Statement, For Year Ended December 31	2020
Sales revenue	$800,000
Cost of goods sold	(448,800)
Depreciation expense	(28,000)
Patent amortization	(400)
Gain on sale of long-term investment	20,000
Other expenses, including interest of $3,400 and taxes of $23,800	(306,000)
Net income	$ 36,800

Analysis of selected accounts and entries

1. Purchased plant assets; cost, $18,000; payment by issuing 1,200 shares of stock.
2. Payment at maturity date to retire bonds payable, $100,000.
3. Sold the long-term investments for $80,000. The fair value of these securities reported at fair value had not changed until 2020.
4. Purchased land, $56,800; paid cash.
5. Analysis of the retained earnings account follows.

Retained earnings, beginning balance	$56,000
Net income, 2020	36,800
Cash dividend paid	(60,000)
Retained earnings, ending balance	$32,800

Required

Prepare the statement of cash flows under the indirect method.

Problem 22-83
Recording the Effects of Bonds and Leases **LO2, 4, 7**

Central Corporation issued a $100,000, 6% 10-year bonds (interest payable semiannually on June 30 and December 31) dated on January 1, 2020, at 7%. Assume that the company uses the effective interest amortization method.

Central Corporation also leased equipment on January 1, 2020 recording a right-of-use asset and lease liability for $50,000. The lease calls for beginning of the year payments beginning on January 1, 2020, for five years. The implicit rate of interest (known by Central Corporation) is 10%. The estimated useful life of the equipment is five years and no salvage value is estimated.

Required

Part One

a. Indicate how the bond transactions would affect the statement of cash flows for 2020, assuming that the company uses the indirect method.

b. Indicate how the lease transactions would affect the statement of cash flows for 2020, assuming that the company uses the indirect method.

Part Two

a. Indicate how the bond transactions would affect the statement of cash flows for 2020, assuming that the company uses the direct method.

b. Indicate how the lease transactions would affect the statement of cash flows for 2020, assuming that the company uses the direct method.

Problem 22-84
Analyzing Financing Activities **LO4**

The following items affected the retained earnings account for 2020.

1. Net income, $35,000.
2. Cash dividend distributed, $10,000.
3. Stock dividend, $5,000 (1,000 shares, $1 par value common stock).
4. Retirement of common shares for $45,000, resulting in a settlement of $4,500 in excess of the stock carrying value.

Required

Indicate how the retained earnings transactions would affect the statement of cash flows for 2020, assuming that the company uses the indirect method.

Problem 22-85
Determining Operating Activities—Direct and Indirect Approaches **LO2, 7**

The following information is provided for Vale Inc. for the year ended December 31, 2020.

Balance Sheets, December 31	2019	2020	Difference
Assets			
Cash and cash equivalents	$ 45,000	$105,000	$ 60,000
Accounts receivable, net	75,000	65,000	(10,000)
Inventory	100,000	78,000	(22,000)
Equipment	200,000	180,000	(20,000)
Accumulated depreciation	(40,000)	(20,000)	20,000
Land	30,000	35,000	5,000
Total assets	$410,000	$443,000	$ 33,000
Liabilities and Stockholders' Equity			
Accounts payable	$ 70,000	$ 87,000	$ 17,000
Other current liabilities	10,000	8,000	(2,000)
Bonds payable	100,000	100,000	0
Premium on bonds payable	10,000	8,000	(2,000)
Common stock, no-par	120,000	90,000	(30,000)
Retained earnings	100,000	150,000	50,000
Total liabilities and stockholders' equity	$410,000	$443,000	$ 33,000

Income Statement, For Year Ended December 31	2020
Sales revenue	$255,000
Cost of goods sold	(125,000)
Depreciation expense	(20,000)
Other operating expenses	(40,000)
Interest expense	(10,000)
Gain on sale of equipment	25,000
Net income	$ 85,000

Other information

Equipment with an original cost of $60,000 and accumulated depreciation of $40,000 was sold for $45,000. Assume there is no bad debt expense.

Required

a. Prepare the operating activities section of the statement of cash flows using the direct method.

b. Prepare the operating activities section of the statement of cash flows using the indirect method.

Problem 22-86
Preparing a Statement of Cash Flows—Direct Method **LO7**

Using the information provided in Problem 22-76, prepare the operating activities section of the statement of cash flows using the direct method. Do not include a disclosure reconciling net income to cash flows from operating activities.

Problem 22-87
Preparing a Statement of Cash Flows—Direct Method **LO7**

Using the information provided in Problem 22-77, prepare the statement of cash flows using the direct method for the operating activities section. Assume no accounts receivable were written off or recovered during the year. Do not include a disclosure reconciling net income to cash flows from operating activities.

Problem 22-88
Preparing a Statement of Cash Flows—Direct Method **LO7**

Using the information provided in Problem 22-80, prepare the statement of cash flows using the direct method for the operating activities section. Do not include a disclosure reconciling net income to cash flows from operating activities.

Problem 22-89
Preparing a Statement of Cash Flows—Direct Method **LO7**

Using the information provided in Problem 22-81, prepare the statement of cash flows using the direct method for the operating activities section. Assume no accounts receivable were written off or recovered during the year. Do not include a disclosure reconciling net income to cash flows from operating activities.

Problem 22-90
Preparing a Statement of Cash Flows—Direct Method **LO7**

The following information is provided for DHS Inc. for the year ended December 31, 2020.

Balance Sheets, December 31	2019	2020
Assets		
Cash	$ 35,000	$ 49,582
Cash equivalents	20,000	10,000
Investment, short-term	8,000	5,000
Accounts receivable	50,000	75,000
Allowance for doubtful accounts	(2,000)	(3,000)
Inventory	120,000	40,000
Prepaid insurance	20,000	30,000
Long-term investment	40,000	45,000
Land	250,000	350,000
Equipment	100,000	130,000
Right-of-use asset	—	60,653
Accumulated depreciation, equipment	(50,000)	(64,837)
Intangible assets, net	45,000	35,000
Total assets	$636,000	$762,398
Liabilities and Stockholders' Equity		
Accounts payable	$ 40,000	$ 70,000
Income taxes payable	5,000	8,000
Dividends payable	6,000	12,000
Lease liability, long-term	—	63,398
Deferred tax liability	20,000	25,000
Mortgage payable	—	80,000
Note payable	—	100,000
Bonds payable	180,000	—
Unamortized bond discount	(12,000)	—
Common stock	300,000	300,000
Retained earnings	97,000	104,000
Total liabilities and stockholders' equity	$636,000	$762,398

Income Statement, For Year Ended December 31	2020
Sales revenue	$620,000
Cost of goods sold	(400,000)
Depreciation expense	(26,837)
Bad debt expense	(18,000)
Interest expense	(23,000)
Amortization of right-of-use asset	(15,163)
Amortization of intangibles	(10,000)
Other operating expenses	(85,000)
Gain on sale of short-term investments	3,000
Gain on equipment sale	7,000
Gain on bond retirement	20,000
Investment income	30,000
Income tax expense	(25,000)
Net income	$ 77,000

Additional information about events in 2020

1. On January 1, 2020, the fair value of the portfolio of short-term investments in debt securities, classified as available-for-sale, equaled cost. During 2020, investments carried at $3,000 were sold for $6,000. No securities were purchased during 2020. At December 31, 2020, the fair value of the portfolio is $5,000.
2. Cash equivalents were continually purchased and sold at cost. No gains or losses were incurred.
3. $20,000 of accounts receivable was written off in 2020, and $3,000 was collected on an account written off in 2019. All sales are on account.

4. The long-term investment represents a 25% equity interest in Wickens Company and is accounted for under the equity method, purchased at book value. During 2020, Wickens paid $100,000 of dividends and earned $120,000.
5. At the end of 2020, DHS Inc. acquired land for $100,000 by assuming an $80,000 mortgage and paying the balance in cash.
6. Equipment (cost, $20,000; book value, $8,000) was sold for $15,000.
7. Started and completed construction of equipment for its own use in 2020. The cost of the finished equipment, $50,000, includes $5,000 of capitalized interest.
8. Entered into a finance lease on January 1, 2020 recording a right-of-use asset and a lease liability for $75,816. The interest rate used to capitalize the lease is 10%. Equal annual payments of $20,000 are due each December 31 for five years. Interest expense in the 2020 income statement includes interest on the lease liability of $7,582.
9. The bonds were retired before maturity at a $20,000 gain, before taxes. Discount amortized in 2020, $4,000.
10. Declared $70,000 of dividends in 2020.

Required

Prepare the statement of cash flows using the direct method for the operating section. Include a disclosure reconciling net income to cash flows from operating activities.

Problem 22-91
Analyzing Interrelations of Financial Statements—Direct and Indirect Method **LO2, 3, 4, 7**

The following three statements relate to Sterling Co.

Income Statement
For Year Ended December 31, 2020

Sales revenue	$x
Cost of goods sold	x
Depreciation expense	x
Salaries	x
Other operating expenses	x
Interest expense	x
Gain on sale of equipment	x
Loss on bond retirement	x
Income tax expense	x
Net income	$x

Net Cash Flows from Operating Activities, Direct Method
For Year Ended December 31, 2020

Collections from customers	$165,000
Payments to suppliers	(88,000)
Payments for salaries	(35,900)
Payments for other operating expenses	(4,900)
Payments for interest	(6,000)
Payments for income tax	(6,100)
Net cash provided by operating activities	$ 24,100

Net Cash Flows from Operating Activities, Indirect Method
For Year Ended December 31, 2020

Net income	$ x
Adjustments:	
Depreciation expense	8,000
Gain on sale of equipment	(18,000)
Loss on bond retirement	1,000
Amortization of bond discount	100
Increase in accounts receivable, net	(29,000)
Increase in inventory	(10,000)
Increase in prepaid rent	(2,000)
Increase in accounts payable	12,000
Decrease in salaries payable	(3,000)
Increase in income taxes payable	6,000
Net cash provided by operating activities	$ x

Required

Determine the missing amounts indicated by an "x" in the statements above.

Accounting Decisions and Judgments

AD&J 22-92 Interpreting the Statement of Cash Flows **LO2**

Real World Analysis A portion of the operating activities section of a telecommunication firm's Year 8 statement of cash flows is reproduced below ($ millions).

Cash flows from operating activities	
Net income	$3,606
Adjustments to net income	
Depreciation and amortization	2,717
Deferred income taxes, net (#1)	305
Investment tax credits, net (#2)	(25)
Change in accounts receivable, net	26
Change in material and supplies	(95)
Change in other current assets	(213)
Change in accounts payable	(50)
Change in certain other current liabilities (#3)	1,322
Change in certain noncurrent assets and liabilities (#4)	(959)
Gain on sale of TCNZ shares (#5)	(1,543)
(Combined other items—deleted by authors)	(281)
Net cash provided by operating activities	$4,810

The firm uses the deferral method to account for investment tax credits: the company amortizes part of the deferred investment tax credit account as a reduction in income tax expense over the lives of related plant assets.

Required

Using only the information provided, explain why each of the five numbered reconciling items appears in the operating section and why it is added or subtracted.

AD&J 22-93 Interpreting the Statement of Cash Flows **LO7**

Real World Analysis The **Dole Food Company** is one of the largest international food processing and distribution companies. Partial information from the Year 8 annual report appears below ($ thousands).

Consolidated Statement of Income For Year Ended December 31, Year 8 ($ thousands)	
Revenue	$4,424,160
Cost of products sold	3,785,745
Gross margin	638,415
Selling, marketing and administrative expenses	433,509
Hurricane loss	100,000
Citrus charge	20,000
Operating income	84,906
Interest income	9,312
Other income (expense)—net	(7,996)
Earnings before interest and taxes	86,222
Interest expense	68,943
Income from operations before income taxes	17,279
Income taxes	5,200
Net income	$ 12,079

From the December 31 balance sheets ($ thousands)	Year 8	Year 7
Current assets		
Cash and short-term investments	$ 35,352	$ 31,202
Receivables—net	616,579	534,844
Inventories	475,524	468,692
Prepaid expenses	43,200	48,438
Total current assets	$1,170,655	$1,083,176

continued

continued from previous page

	Year 8	Year 7
Current liabilities		
Notes payable	$ 29,637	$ 11,290
Current portion of long-term debt	6,451	2,326
Accounts payable	264,732	230,143
Accrued liabilities	504,058	432,680
Total current liabilities	$ 804,878	$ 676,439

Additional information

1. Payments for selling, marketing, and administrative expenses and other income expense—net can be determined by analyzing the change in prepaid expenses and accrued expenses.
2. Notes payable are due to financial institutions.
3. Net deferred tax liability increased $2,000 during Year 8.

Required

Use the information in this case to prepare the operating activities section of the Year 8 statement of cash flows, using the direct method. List any assumptions necessary to prepare this report.

AD&J 22-94
Interpreting the Statement of Cash Flows **LO2**

Real World Analysis **Johnson & Johnson** is a leading personal care products manufacturer. The company's Year 2 statement of cash flow, prepared under the indirect method, disclosed the following two reconciling adjustments in the operating activity section ($ thousands).

Imputed interest on note	$134
Increase in cash surrender value of life insurance	(251)

Required

Explain why the reconciliation includes these two adjustments and why they are added to or subtracted from net income.

AD&J 22-95
Reconstructing an Income Statement from a Statement of Cash Flows **LO2, 3, 7**

Real World Analysis **Collins Industries Inc.**, based in Missouri, is a manufacturer of specialty vehicles, such as ambulances and school and shuttle buses. The company uses the direct method to prepare its statement of cash flows. Reproduced below from the Year 5 statement of cash flows are (1) the operating activities section and (2) the reconciliation schedule.

Operating Activities	
Cash received from customers	$141,425,892
Cash paid to suppliers and employees	(132,956,101)
Interest paid, net	(3,209,818)
Cash provided by operations	$ 5,259,973

Reconciliation of Net Loss to Net Cash Provided by Operations	
Net loss	$ (340,759)
Depreciation and amortization	2,513,541
Common stock issued for benefit of employees	106,365
Decrease in receivables, net	700,827
Decrease in inventories	1,614,442
Decrease in prepaid expenses	329,517
Increase (decrease) in accounts payable	276,782
Increase (decrease) in accrued expenses	(261,519)
Gain on sale of vacant land	(99,667)
Loss on early extinguishment of debt	420,444
Cash provided by operations	$5,259,973

Required

Reconstruct the Year 5 income statement for Collins Industries. Assume that accrued and prepaid expenses do not relate to interest or to income taxes, and that Collins had no interest income in Year 5. *Hint:* Aggregate cost of goods sold and operating expenses in one category.

Real World Analysis Obtain an electronic copy of the Form 10-K for the **Coca-Cola Company** for the year ended December 31, 2015, which can be found on the SEC Edgar website (https://www.sec.gov/edgar/searchedgar/companysearch.html). Answer the following questions.

AD&J 22-96 Analyzing a Statement of Cash Flows **LO2, 3, 4, 5, 7**

a. Is Coca Cola's statement of cash flows prepared under the direct method or the indirect method?
b. Were all the 2015 declared dividends paid in 2015?
c. Provide an estimate of cash receipts from sales for 2015, assuming that all net operating revenues are credit sales and that there were no write-offs of receivables in 2015.
d. What is the company's policy with respect to classification of investments fulfilling the definition of cash equivalents?
e. Did the company fulfill the requirement to disclose certain operating cash flows for 2015?
f. Can we estimate the amount of dividends received from investments accounted for under the equity method in 2015? Why is this amount not shown in the statement of cash flows?

Communication Case The principal advantage of the direct method is that it shows operating cash receipts and payments relating to the major classes of revenues and expenses in the income statement. The principal advantage of the indirect method is that it focuses on reconciling items between net income and net cash flow from operating activities. There has been discussion over the years of requiring companies to use the direct method to be more consistent with the objective of a statement of cash flows—to provide information about cash receipts and cash payments—than the indirect method, which does not directly report operating cash receipts and payments. Assume the following are items separately reported in a company's financial statements.

AD&J 22-97 Comparing Direct and Indirect Methods **LO1, 2, 7**

Cash Inflows and Outflows (and related changes)	Direct Method	Indirect Method	Comparative Balance Sheet
1. Cash inflow from sales			
2. Cash inflow from services			
3. Cash inflow from interest			
4. Cash inflow from dividend received			
5. Accounts receivable increase or decrease			
6. Interest receivable increase or decrease			
7. Payments to suppliers (cash purchases)			
8. Inventory increase or decrease			
9. Accounts payable increase or decrease			
10. Payments for salaries			
11. Salaries payable increase or decrease			
12. Payments for income taxes			
13. Income taxes payable increase or decrease			
14. Net income			
15. Net cash flow from operating activities			
16. Cash flows from investing activities			
17. Cash flows from financing activities			
18. Net increase or decrease in cash during the period			
19. Cash, beginning balance			
20. Cash, ending balance			

Required

a. Complete the table indicating whether each item 1 through 20 is included in a statement of cash flows prepared using the direct method, indirect method, and/or on a comparative balance sheet.
b. Prepare a memorandum on the advantages of each method (direct and indirect).

Ethics Case Honore Company has competed for many years in product lines that have recently experienced a great increase in global competition. Their products have long been dominated by U.S. firms. Honore has no foreign operations and few personnel with experience in international trade. Honore has made few product changes in recent years and is not actively engaged in product innovation or research and development. The following information is taken from the company's financial statements and notes for the period 2018 to 2020 ($ thousands).

AD&J 22-98 Interpreting the Statement of Cash Flows **LO1, 2**

	2018	2019	2020
Net income	$50,000	$30,000	$10,000
Net accounts receivable (ending)	40,000	12,000	6,000
Inventory (ending)	19,000	14,000	7,000
Net cash provided by operating activities	15,000	7,000	4,500
Capital expenditures	9,000	7,000	6,000
Proceeds from sale of plant assets	15,000	10,000	18,000
Net gain on sales of plant assets	16,000	12,000	15,000

The company has:

1. Recently negotiated with banks to extend payment terms on short-term loans.
2. Maintained very low levels of accounts payable during this period.
3. Significant investments in corporate bonds (interest revenue on bonds in 2021 was $3,000).
4. Paid no dividends during this period.
5. Issued no stock or bonds during this period.

Statement of Cash Flows
For Year Ended December 31, 2021 (in thousands)

Cash flows from operating activities:		
Net income	$ 7,000	
Items reconciling net income and net cash inflow from operating activities		
Accounts receivable decrease	1,000	
Inventory decrease	1,500	
Loss from building fire	8,000	
Dividends received (equity investment)	6,000	
Investment revenue (equity investment)	(10,000)	
Gains on sales of plant assets	(14,000)	
Depreciation, amortization	4,000	
Net cash provided by operating activities		$ 3,500
Cash flows from investing activities:		
Purchase of plant assets	(4,000)	
Insurance proceeds on building fire	20,000	
Sale of plant assets	25,000	
Purchase of corporate bonds	(5,000)	
Purchase of corporate stocks	(10,000)	
Net cash provided by investing activities		26,000
Cash flows from financing activities:		
Principal payments on short-term notes to financial institutions	(15,000)	
Purchase of treasury stock	(6,000)	
Net cash used by financing activities		(21,000)
Net cash increase		8,500
Beginning cash balance		12,000
Ending cash balance		$20,500

Required

Provide an interpretation of the statement of cash flows in light of Honore's situation. Weigh ethical considerations in terms of company strategy and financial disclosure.

AD&J 22-99
Reporting Cash Flow for Investments in Securities **LO1, 2, 3**

Judgment Case The following transactions and end-of-year fair values refer to investments of BankOne Inc.

a. BankOne purchased securities of Smith Company for $10,000 in late December 2020. The investment is held in a trading account.

b. The December 31, 2020, fair value of the investment in Smith Company is $12,000.

c. During January 2021, BankOne sold the trading investment for $12,000.

Required

For each of the above transactions and end-of-year adjusting entries, describe how the transaction will be reported under the indirect method in the statement of cash flows.

AD&J 22-100 Reconciling Net Income and Net Operating Cash Flow **LO2, 7**

Judgment Case The reconciliation of a company's earnings and its net cash flow from operating activities is a required disclosure regardless of the method chosen to prepare the statement of cash flows. If the direct method is used, the reconciliation appears as a supporting schedule. If the indirect method is used, the reconciliation appears either as the operating activity section of the statement of cash flow or as a supporting schedule. This case asks us to look more closely at the reconciliation.

Required

Answer the following questions about the reconciliation.

a. What is the purpose of the reconciliation?
b. Why does the reconciliation result in the same amount for net operating cash flow as does the list of operating cash flows found in the operating activities section under the direct method?
c. One of the most common adjustments found in the reconciliation is the change in operating working capital accounts, such as accounts receivable and prepaid expenses. Why are changes in dividends payable and short-term non-trade notes to financial institutions not found in the reconciliation?
d. Are the reconciliation adjustments referred to in part *c* limited to changes in current assets and liabilities? Explain.
e. Why is a cash flow not a common adjustment to be found in the reconciliation? Can we think of any cash flows that would appear in the reconciliation?

AD&J 22-101 Improving the Statement of Cash Flows **LO1, 2, 3, 4, 5, 6**

Judgment Case Do you feel that the principles governing the statement of cash flows have produced the most useful statement possible? If you were a member of the FASB, would you suggest any changes to the statement of cash flows? Provide your thoughts to the Board on how the statement of cash flows might be improved.

AD&J 22-102 Interpreting Interest Disclosures in the Statement of Cash Flows **LO2, 5**

Rubbermaid Inc., a manufacturer of home products, begins its Year 8 statement of consolidated cash flows with the line:

Net earnings	$142,536,000

In a supplement to its statement of cash flows, Rubbermaid reports:

Interest paid during the year.	$33,407,000

Required

a. Interest expense of $37,944,000 was reported in the income statement and no interest was capitalized during the period. Where is the $4,537,000 difference between interest expense and interest paid reported on the statement of cash flows?
b. Now assume that interest expense of $28,870,000 is reported in the income statement, interest was capitalized during the period, and there was no change in interest payable from the beginning to the end of the year. Where is the $4,537,000 difference between interest expense and interest paid reported on the statement of cash flows?

AD&J 22-103 Presenting Payments to Employees in Statement of Cash Flows **LO3, 5, 6**

Trueblood Case The Trueblood case series, prepared by Deloitte professionals, are based on recent accounting technical issues that require research and judgment. The cases are accessed through the Deloitte foundation at the following website: https://www2.deloitte.com/us/en/pages/about-deloitte/articles/trueblood-case-studies-deloitte-foundation.html. The following case is relevant to the content provided in this chapter: **Case 17-8 Justified Wages**. This case requires an analysis of the cash flow presentation of amounts related to the sale and purchase of common stock related to share-based compensation awards.

AD&J 22-104 Presenting Debt Advances and Payments in Statement of Cash Flows **LO5**

Trueblood Case The Trueblood case series, prepared by Deloitte professionals, are based on recent accounting technical issues that require research and judgment. The cases are accessed through the Deloitte foundation at the following website: https://www2.deloitte.com/us/en/pages/about-deloitte/articles/trueblood-case-studies-deloitte-foundation.html. The following case is relevant to the content provided in this chapter: **Case 13-2: Buck's Dilemma: Gross or Net?** This case requires an analysis of the presentation for advances and payments under a revolving credit line in the statement of cash flows.

AD&J 22-105 Defining Terms **LO1**

Codification Skills How are the terms (1) operating activities, (2) investing activities, (3) financing activities, and (4) cash equivalents defined in the Codification?

AD&J 22-106
Performing Accounting Research **LO3, 4, 5, 6**

Codification Skills Through research in the Codification, identify the specific citation for each of the following items.

a. Cash flow classification of available-for-sale debt securities. FASB ASC ___-___-___-___
b. Examples of items classified as outflows from financing activities. FASB ASC ___-___-___-___
c. Describing the change in cash to include cash, cash equivalents, and restricted cash. FASB ASC ___-___-___-___
d. Requirement to disclose interest and taxes paid if specifically using the indirect method. FASB ASC ___-___-___-___

AD&J 22-107
Performing Accounting Research **LO6**

Codification Skills A company is preparing annual financial statements including the statement of cash flows. The controller would like to report trends of cash flow on a per share basis over the last five years. What guidance is available in the Codification regarding such a presentation?

FASB ASC ___-___-___-___

Appendix—Exercise

App—Exercise 22-108
Preparing a Statement of Cash Flows—T-Account Method **LO8**
Hint: See Demo 22-8

Using the data referenced in Exercise 22-73, determine net cash flows from operating, investing, and financing activities using the T-Account method.

Appendix—Problem

App—Problem 22-109
Preparing a Statement of Cash Flows—T-Account Method **LO8**
Hint: See Demo 22-8

Using the data referenced in Problem 22-88, determine net cash flows from operating, investing, and financing activities using the T-Account method.

Answers to Review Exercises

Review 22-1

1. c	3. e	5. a	7. d	9. b
2. d	4. f	6. f	8. b	10. d

Review 22-2

Cash Flows from Operating Activities ($ thousands)	
Net income	$2,713
Adjustments:	
Depreciation expense (see T-account below)	750[1]
Gain on sale of equipment ($245 − $175)	(70)
Investment revenue (0.30 × $600)	(180)
Compensation expense	12
Decrease in accounts receivable, net	200
Increase in inventory	(675)
Increase in accounts payable	300
Decrease in salaries payable	(100)
Net cash provided by operating activities	$2,950

Accumulated Depreciation ($ thousands)

Accum. dep. on equipment sold	125	5,200	Beg. balance
		750[1]	Depreciation expense
		5,825	End. balance

Review 22-3

Cash Flows from Investing Activities ($ thousands)	
Loan to Chase Company	$(1,500)
Collection of principal payment on loan	150
Purchase of property, plant, and equipment (see T-account below)	(2,000)[2]
Proceeds from sale of equipment	245
Net cash used by investing activities	$(3,105)

Property, Plant, and Equipment ($ thousands)			
Beg. balance	14,835		
		300	Orig. cost of equipment sold
Purchase(s) of equipment	2,000[2]		
End. balance	16,535		

Review 22-4

Part One

a.

Cash Flows from Financing Activities ($ thousands)	
Dividends paid*	$ (500)
Issuance of long-term debt	2,000
Net cash provided by financing activities	$1,500

*Dividends declared = $15,713 – $13,450 – $2,713 = $450.
Dividends paid = $400 – $450 – $450 = $(500)

b.

Net cash provided by operating activities	$2,950
Net cash used by investing activities	(3,105)
Net cash provided by financing activities	1,500
Net increase in cash and cash equivalents during 2020	1,345
Cash and cash equivalents, January 1, 2020	3,500
Cash and cash equivalents, December 31, 2020	$4,845

Part Two

Statement of Cash Flows For Year Ended December 31, 2020	
Cash Flows from Operating Activities	
Net income	$ 515
Depreciation expense	400
Loss on sale of equipment	200[1]
Decrease in accounts receivable	110
Increase in inventory	(200)
Decrease in accounts payable	(35)
Decrease in salaries payable	(25)
Net cash provided by operating activities	965
Cash Flows from Investing Activities	
Proceeds from sale of equipment	100
Purchase of equipment	(1,100)[2]
Net cash used by investing activities	(1,000)
Cash Flows from Financing Activities	
Issuance of bonds	100
Issuance of stock	100
Dividends paid	(190)[3]
Net cash provided by financing activities	10
Net decrease in cash, cash equivalents, and restricted cash	(25)
Cash, cash equivalents, and restricted cash, January 1, 2020	120
Cash, cash equivalents, and restricted cash, December 31, 2020	$ 95

[1] $100 (proceeds on sale) − $300 (book value computed as $400 − $100) = $(200) (loss on sale of equipment).
[2] $2,700 (equipment end. bal.) − $2,000 (equipment beg. bal.) + $400 (cost of equipment sold) = $1,100 (purchases).
[3] $600 (retained earnings end. bal.) − $275 (retained earnings beg. bal) − $515 (net income) = $(190) (dividends).

Review 22-5

Cash Flows from Investing Activities ($ thousands)	
Loan to Chase Company	$(1,500)
Collection of principal payment on loan	150
Purchase of property, plant, and equipment [$(2,000) + $1,000]	(1,000)
Proceeds from sale of equipment	245
Net cash used by investing activities	$(2,105)

Cash Flows from Financing Activities ($ thousands)	
Dividends paid	$ (500)
Issuance of long-term debt ($2,000 − $1,000)	1,000
Net cash provided by financing activities	$ 500

Noncash disclosure:

Purchased equipment for $2,000 through payment of cash and issuance of a note payable.

Cost of equipment	$2,000
Cash payment for equipment	(1,000)
Issuance of note payable	$1,000

Review 22-6

a.	Decrease in Accounts Receivable—Operating Section	9,000	
	Accounts Receivable		8,500
	Allowance for Doubtful Accounts		500

b.	Supplies	1,000	
	Increase in Supplies—Operating Section		1,000

c.	Proceeds from Sale of Equipment—Investing Section	22,000	
	Accumulated Depreciation	50,000	
	Loss on Sale of Equipment—Operating Section	8,000	
	Equipment		80,000

d.	Depreciation Expense—Operating Section	12,000	
	Accumulated Depreciation		12,000

e.	Issuance of Bonds Payable—Financing Section	45,000	
	Bonds Payable		45,000

Review 22-7

Cash Flows from Operating Activities—Direct Method	
Collections from customers ($98,000 + $200)	$98,200
Payments to suppliers ($39,000 + $200 + $200)	(39,400)
Payment for salaries ($16,000 – $50)	(15,950)
Payment for rent ($5,500 + $30)	(5,530)
Payment for insurance ($3,600 – $20)	(3,580)
Payment for utilities ($3,200 – $60)	(3,140)
Payment for interest ($3,600 – $300)	(3,300)
Net cash provided by operating activities	$27,300

Review 22-8

Cash			
		1,100	Net change in cash
Operating Activities			
From customers	9,850	4,550	To suppliers
		3,700	To pay other operating expenses
Investing Activities			
		600	Purchase of investment
Financing Activities			
Issuance of common stock	100		

Cash Flows from Operating Activities	
Collections from customers	$9,850
Payments to suppliers	(4,550)
Payments for other operating expenses	(3,700)
Net cash provided by operating activities	1,600
Cash Flows from Investing Activities	
Purchase of investments	(600)
Net cash used by investing activities	(600)
Cash Flows from Financing Activities	
Issuance of stock	100
Net cash provided by financing activities	100
Net increase in cash	1,100
Cash, Dec. 31, 2019	3,500
Cash, Dec. 31, 2020	$4,600

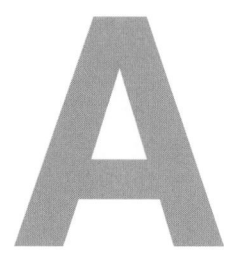

A Accounting Changes and Error Analysis Revisited

Change in Accounting Principle—Lowe's Companies, Inc.

In May 2014, the FASB issued ASU 2014–19, *Revenue from Contracts with Customers*. The ASU is a comprehensive new revenue recognition model that requires a company to recognize revenue to depict the transfer of goods or services to customers in an amount that reflects the consideration to which the entity expects to be entitled in exchange for those goods or services. In addition, the ASU has expanded disclosure requirements regarding revenue. In August 2015, the FASB issued ASU 2015–14, which deferred the effective date in the ASU to fiscal years beginning after December 15, 2017, and interim periods within those fiscal years. Early adoption is permitted for fiscal years beginning after December 15, 2016. Companies may use either a full retrospective or a modified retrospective approach to adopt this ASU.

The Company will adopt this ASU in the first quarter of fiscal 2018, using modified retrospective approach to adoption. Based on the Company's assessment of the standard and its subsequent related amendments and interpretations, the standard will not materially affect our consolidated financial statements. The Company has determined the adoption of the guidance will impact the timing of recognition of its stored value card breakage. Currently, breakage is recognized using the remote method and will be recognized using the proportional method upon adoption of the guidance. The Company will also change the presentation of the sales return reserve on the consolidated balance sheet, as it is currently reported on a net basis, as well as change the timing of how installation services are recognized. In addition, the Company has evaluated its principal versus agent conclusions relating to certain arrangements with third parties and concluded there are no significant changes impacting the presentation of revenue on a gross or net basis. The Company is currently still evaluating any impacts the s[...]ating to the classification of profit sharing income earned in connection with our private label credit card programs which is currently include[...]ot identified any significant modifications to existing systems or material changes in the Company's internal controls over fina[...]ult in increased footnote disclosure requirements.

Change in Estimate—The Gap, Inc.

We record an allowance for estimated returns based on our historical return patterns and various other assumptions that management believes to be reasonable. We do not believe there is a reasonable likelihood that there will be a material change in the future estimates or assumptions we use to calculate our sales return allowance. However, if the actual rate of sales returns increases significantly, our operating results could be adversely affected. We have not made any material changes in the accounting methodology used to estimate future sales returns in the past three fiscal years.

Error Correction—KBR, Inc.

Prior Period Adjustments

During the second quarter of 2017, we corrected cumulative errors resulting in an increase to "Equity in earnings of unconsolidated affiliates" and "Net income attributable to KBR" within our consolidated statements of operations of $9 million and $11 million, respectively. The errors in equity in earnings of unconsolidated affiliates primarily related to our accounting for derivatives in one of our unconsolidated VIEs in our GS segment from the first quarter of 2016 through the first quarter of 2017.

During the fourth quarter of 2016, we corrected a cumulative error related to contract cost estimates on an LNG project in Australia within our E&C business segment. The cumulative error occurred throughout the period beginning in 2009 and through the third quarter of 2016 and resulted in a $13 million reduction to revenues and gross profit on our consolidated statements of operations and a decrease to "CIE" on our consolidated balance sheets during the fourth quarter of 2016.

During the second quarter of 2015, we corrected cumulative error related to transactions between unconsolidated affiliates associated with our Mexican offshore maintenance joint venture within our E&C business segment. The cumulative error occurred throughout the period beginning in 2007 and through the first quarter of 2015 and resulted in a $15 million increase to "equity in earnings of unconsolidated affiliates" on our consolidated statements of operations and an increase to "equity in and advances to unconsolidated affiliates" on our consolidated balance sheets during the second quarter of 2015.

We evaluated these cumulative errors on both a quantitative and qualitative basis under the guidance of ASC 250—Accounting Changes and Error Corrections. We determined that the cumulative impact of the errors described above did not affect the trend of net income, cash flows or liquidity and therefore did not have a material impact to previously issued financial statements. Additionally, we determined that the cumulative impact of the errors did not have a material impact to our consolidated financial statements for the fiscal year ended December 31, 2017.

Appendix Preview

Chapter 3 provided a framework for accounting changes and the correction of material accounting errors. In subsequent chapters we applied that framework to a variety of topics such as inventory and depreciation. This appendix summarizes the accounting treatment and reporting requirements for accounting changes and error corrections, and provides references to previous examples in the text.

Action Plan

LO	Topic/Subtopic	Page	Demos	Reviews	Assignments
LO A–1	Demonstrate the accounting for a change in accounting estimate and a change in accounting estimate effected by a change in principle	A-4	D3-7A, D8-4B, D12-4, D12-5, D13-5		3-28, 3-48, 3-49, 3-59, 7-105, 7-106, 7-107, 7-109, 7-110, 7-111, 7-112, 7-113, 7-114, 8-46, 8-62, 8-63, 8-66, 12-32, 12-33, 12-34, 12-35, 12-61, 12-62, 12-63, 12-64, 12-65, 12-66, 12-67, 12-68, 12-69, 12-73, 12-92, 12-93, 12-94, 12-95, 12-96, 12-97, 12-98, 13-35, 13-36, 13-53, 13-54, 13-61, 15-61, 15-63, 15-64, 19-85, A-13, A-14, A-15, A-16, A-19, A-20, A-21, A-22, A-25, A-26, A-29
LO A–2	Demonstrate the accounting for a change in accounting principle	A-5	D3-7B, D10-6A, D10-6B, D18-10A		3-29, 3-49, 3-59, 10-32, 10-33, 10-34, 10-58, 10-59, 10-60, 10-61, 10-78, 10-79, 10-80, 10-81, 18-105, 18-106, 18-109, 18-110, 18-111, 18-113, 19-85, A-13, A-14, A-15, A-16, A-19, A-20, A-21, A-23, A-24, A-25, A-26, A-28, A-29
LO A–3	Demonstrate the accounting for an error correction	A-9	D3-7C, D10-7, D12-6, D18-10B		3-30, 3-47, 3-49, 3-58, 3-59, 8-64, 10-35, 10-36, 10-62, 10-63, 10-64, 10-82, 10-83, 12-36, 12-37, 12-38, 12-70, 12-71, 12-72, 12-73, 12-96, 12-97, 12-98, 13-59, 16-82, 18-107, 18-114, 19-85, A-13, A-14, A-15, A-16, A-17, A-18, A-20, A-21, A-22, A-25, A-26, A-27
LO A–4	Describe the accounting for a change in reporting entity	A-12	DA-4		A-13, A-14, A-15, A-16, A-19, A-25, A-29

Expanded Appendix Overview

In this Appendix we summarize the accounting treatment underlying accounting changes and errors, and the associated reporting requirements. Examples of accounting changes and error corrections are listed in **Exhibit A-1**.

EXHIBIT A-1 Examples of Accounting Changes and Error Corrections

Change in Accounting Estimate	Change in Accounting Principle	Error Correction	Change in Reporting Entity
▪ Change in useful life of asset for depreciation purposes ▪ Change in depreciation method ▪ Change in estimate of sales returns ▪ Change in warranty accrual estimate	▪ Change from LIFO to FIFO inventory costing method ▪ Adoption of new leasing standard ▪ Change from the equity method to fair value method ▪ Change in accounting for pension gains and losses	▪ Mathematical errors ▪ Misapplication of GAAP principle ▪ Adopting an unrealistic assumption in depreciation calculation ▪ Failure to accrue for end of period expenses	▪ Consolidation of entities previously accounted for individually ▪ Change in composition of consolidated subsidiaries ▪ Change in entities included in combined financial statements

A mapping of the coverage of these topics to this text is in **Exhibit A-2**.

EXHIBIT A-2 Coverage of Accounting Changes and Error Correction

Type	Description	Accounting Treatment	Coverage
Change in estimate	Change an accounting estimate due to changes in circumstance or new facts.	Prospective treatment	**LO 3-7.** Introduction **LO 8-4.** Change in allowance for doubtful account estimates **LO 12-4.** Change in depreciation estimates **LO 13-5.** Change in intangible estimates **Appendix A.** Recap
Change in accounting estimate effected by a change in principle	Effects of a change in accounting principle are inseparable from the effects of a change in accounting estimate.	Prospective treatment	**LO 3-7.** Introduction **LO 12-5.** Change in depreciation method **Appendix A.** Recap
Change in accounting principle	Substitution of one generally accepted accounting principle for another.	▪ Retrospective treatment typically applied. ▪ Prospective treatment applied only if it is impractical to use retrospective treatment. ▪ Retrospective, prospective, or modified retrospective treatment applied in implementing a new standard or update as required.	**LO 3-7.** Introduction **LO 10-6.** Change in inventory method **LO 18-10.** Tax effects of change in accounting principle **Appendix A.** Recap
Error correction	Correction of a transaction that is recorded incorrectly or not at all.	▪ Retrospective treatment. ▪ Restatement of previously issued financial statements if error is discovered in a subsequent accounting period.	**LO 3-7.** Introduction **LO 10-7.** Inventory errors **LO 12-6.** Property, plant and equipment errors **LO 18-10.** Tax effects of error corrections **Appendix A.** Recap
Change in reporting entity	Presentation of financial statements that are effectively those of a *different* reporting entity.	Retrospective treatment	**LO 3-7.** Introduction **Appendix A.** Recap

Demonstrate the accounting for a change in accounting estimate and a change in accounting estimate effected by a change in principle

LO A-1

LO A-1 Overview

Change in Accounting Estimate *and* Change in Accounting Estimate Effected by a Change in Accounting Principle

- Prospective treatment
  - Use the new method in the current year and going forward
  - No change to prior reporting

Most accounting entries involve estimations that require management judgment as a necessary part of the steps in the accounting process. These estimates are subject to change and require periodic revision(s) over time as new information becomes available.

Changes in accounting estimate are recorded prospectively. The *prospective approach* is supported by the notion that good-faith estimates are valid until conditions change. New estimates are not applied to the results of previous periods because the information supporting the estimate change was not available or applicable until the current period.

By their nature, estimates require judgment and those estimates almost always change over time as more information becomes available. The **prospective approach** applies revised accounting estimates *to current and future periods affected by the change*. Prior financial statements remain unchanged, and no cumulative effect on prior years' income is computed. Although the results of previous periods reflect different estimates, disclosing the effect of the change on current income (described below) partially offsets the reduced consistency in reporting from year to year.

ASC Glossary **Change in Accounting Estimate:** A change that has the effect of adjusting the carrying amount of an existing asset or liability or altering the subsequent accounting for existing or future assets or liabilities. A change in accounting estimate is a necessary consequence of the assessment, in conjunction with the periodic presentation of financial statements, of the present status and expected future benefits and obligations associated with assets and liabilities. Changes in accounting estimates result from new information. Examples of items for which estimates are necessary are uncollectible receivables, inventory obsolescence, service lives and salvage values of depreciable assets, and warranty obligations.

Examples of accounts that require estimations that are subject to changes include the allowance for doubtful accounts (**Demo 8-4B**), measuring inventory at the lower of cost or net realizable value (**Demo 10-1**), intangible asset estimates (**Demo 13-5**), depreciation expense (**Demo 3-7A** and **Demo 12-4**), recognizing revenue over time (**Demo 7-10A**), certain liabilities and contingencies, such as a warranty liability (**Demo 15-5C**), and tax asset valuation allowance (**Demo 18-3**). Estimations are present in nearly all accounting entries—many other examples of estimations are included throughout this text.

KELLOGG

Real World—ESTIMATION IN FINANCIAL STATEMENTS

KELLOGG [K]

Kellogg Company included the following note in a recent annual report regarding estimations included in its financial statements.

Note 1—Accounting Policies (excerpt) Use of estimates: The preparation of financial statements in conformity with accounting principles generally accepted in the United States of America requires management to make estimates and assumptions that affect the reported amounts of assets and liabilities, the disclosure of contingent liabilities at the date of the financial statements and the reported amounts of revenues and expenses during the periods reported. Actual results could differ from those estimates.

Under certain circumstances, a company can change from one depreciation method to another depreciation method such as from sum-of-the-years'-digits depreciation method to straight-line depreciation method. Generally, when this happens, a company treats this as a change in accounting estimate, accounted for prospectively. The accounting standards refer to a change in depreciation method more specifically as a **change in accounting estimate effected by a change in accounting principle**.

ASC Glossary **Change in Accounting Estimate Effected by a Change in Accounting Principle:** A change in accounting estimate that is inseparable from the effect of a related change in accounting principle. An example of a change in estimate effected by a change in principle is a change in the method of depreciation, amortization, or depletion for long-lived, nonfinancial assets.

While other changes in accounting methods are accounted for retrospectively, the standards distinguish a change in depreciation method from other changes. In this case, management would not be able to separately determine the effects of changing the accounting principle from the effects of changing its estimate. In other words, the change in estimate is accomplished by changing the method. A change in depreciation relates to the continuing process of obtaining additional information and revising estimates and, therefore, is treated as other changes in estimates with prospective treatment—**see Demo 12-5**. Just as with fixed assets, a change in amortization method for intangible assets and bond premium or discount, for example, is considered a change in accounting estimate effected by a change in accounting principle that requires *prospective* treatment.

While the general rule is to apply prospective treatment to changes in estimates, estimates that are made in error (such as the use of an unrealistic estimate or not using reasonably available information due to management inexperience, or a mathematical mistake) will be treated as accounting errors (see later section).

Disclosure

The accounting standards require disclosure of the impact on income and per-share amounts for a change in estimate when the change affects several periods and is material. This disclosure is required because the change in estimate could impact the comparability of financial information from year to year.

250-10-50-4 The effect on income from continuing operations, net income (or other appropriate captions of changes in the applicable net assets or performance indicator), and any related per-share amounts of the current period shall be disclosed for a change in estimate that affects several future periods, such as a change in service lives of depreciable assets. Disclosure of those effects is not necessary for estimates made each period in the ordinary course of accounting for items such as uncollectible accounts or inventory obsolescence; however, disclosure is required if the effect of a change in the estimate is material.

LO A-2 Demonstrate the accounting for a change in accounting principle

LO A-2 Overview

Change in Accounting Principle
- **Retrospective adjustment**—Most often used
- **Prospective adjustment**—Exception basis only
  - Use if impractical to use retrospective method or if retrospective treatment is not required for a new or updated standard
- **Modified retrospective adjustment**—Exception basis only
  - Use if retrospective treatment is not required for a new or updated standard

Financial reporting requirements for accounting changes are in effect to enhance consistency, comparability, and confidence in financial reporting and full disclosure. Accounting principles include methods, techniques, and procedures applied to transactions or information for purposes of measurement, recognition, or disclosure.

When a company makes a **change in an accounting principle,** it substitutes one generally accepted accounting principle for another.

ASC Glossary **Change in Accounting Principle:** A change from one generally accepted accounting principle to another generally accepted accounting principle when there are two or more generally accepted accounting principles that apply or when the accounting principle formerly used is no longer generally accepted. A change in the method of applying an accounting principle also is considered a change in accounting principle.

A change in accounting principle is supported by one of two reasons: (1) the company can justify the use of an alternative accounting principle on the basis that it is **preferable** or (2) the change is required by a Codification update. Common justifications for a change to a *preferable* method include more faithfully representational results, enhanced asset valuation, providing of new information, and as a response to changing economic or market conditions. In the case of a change initiated by a Codification update, the accounting change is required (if applicable) and follows the effective date and transition requirements specified in the update.

250-10-45-12 An entity may change an accounting principle only if it justifies the use of an allowable alternative accounting principle on the basis that it is preferable.

Neither of the following is considered a change in accounting principle.

1. Initial adoption of an accounting principle based upon new transactions or based upon transactions that were immaterial in the past.
2. Adoption of a new accounting principle because transactions changed from those previously occurring.

In addition, if a company changes from a principle that is *not* generally accepted to a GAAP principle, this would be considered an error and is discussed in the next section.

Voluntary Change in Accounting Principle—Retrospective Approach

For most voluntary accounting principle changes, changes are reported retrospectively. The **retrospective approach** adjusts all prior period financial statement information presented on a comparative basis to conform to the new principle as illustrated in **Demo 3-7B** and **Demo 10-6A**. The cumulative, after-tax income difference for any earlier affected periods adjusts the beginning retained earnings balance (or another component of stockholders' equity if appropriate), and the balance of any affected asset and liability accounts as of the earliest year presented. *When the prior financial statement information is updated, all information presented in the comparative financial statements follows the new accounting principle.*

Restating previously issued financial statements to reflect a new accounting method results in comparative financial statements based on the same principles. Consistency, the conformity of accounting principles and procedures across periods, makes accounting information more useful by facilitating an understanding of information and relationships across time periods and companies. A disadvantage of the retrospective approach is that updating prior financial statements conflicts with the public's expectations that previous financial statements should not change. In other words, financial statement users expect that except for error corrections, financial statements are final. Another disadvantage is the cost for companies to restate the prior period amounts based on the new standard.

In the accounting records, an entry is recorded for the cumulative income difference for prior periods (net of tax), adjusting retained earnings (or another component of stockholders' equity if appropriate) and an asset or liability account. Recall that all prior years are closed, which prevents a company from recording direct adjustments to prior period income accounts; thus for record-keeping purposes, retained earnings is adjusted. Tax effects are illustrated in **Demo 18-10A**.

KELLOGG **Real World—VOLUNTARY CHANGE IN ACCOUNTING POLICY**

KELLOGG [K]

Kellogg Company included the following note accompanying a recent annual report on Form 10-K (referenced in the preferability letter in the Expand Your Knowledge section below).

Note 1—Accounting Policies (excerpt) Pension and nonpension postretirement benefits. In the fourth quarter of 2012, the Company elected to change its policy for recognizing expense for pension and nonpension postretirement benefits. Previously, the Company recognized actuarial gains and losses associated with benefit obligations in accumulated other comprehensive income in the consolidated balance sheet upon each plan remeasurement, amortizing them into operating results over the average future service period of active employees in these plans. Under the new policy, the Company has elected to immediately recognize actuarial gains and losses in operating results in the year in which they occur, eliminating the amortization. Experience gains and losses will be recognized annually as of the measurement date, which is the Company's fiscal year-end, or when remeasurement is otherwise required under generally accepted accounting principles. The Company believes the new policy provides greater transparency to on-going operating results and better reflects the Company's obligations to its employees and the impact of the current market conditions on those obligations.

Voluntary Change in Accounting Principle—Prospective Approach

The prospective treatment, however, is applied if it is impracticable to use retrospective treatment. Sometimes it is impossible to determine the cumulative income difference for prior years' income between the old and new methods. The accounting guidance indicates when applying retrospective treatment is impracticable.

250-20-45-9 It shall be deemed impracticable to apply the effects of a change in accounting principle retrospectively only if any of the following conditions exist:

a. After making every reasonable effort to do so, the entity is unable to apply the requirement.
b. Retrospective application requires assumptions about management's intent in a prior period that cannot be independently substantiated.
c. Retrospective application requires significant estimates of amounts, and it is impossible to distinguish objectively information about those estimates that both:
  1. Provides evidence of circumstances that existed on the date(s) at which those amounts would be recognized, measured, or disclosed under retrospective application
  2. Would have been available when the financial statements for that prior period were issued.

Generally, companies that change to the LIFO method report the change **prospectively,** as shown in **Demo 10-6B**. Past costs and purchase prices necessary for reconstructing inventory layers are typically unavailable for any prior period. Instead, the beginning inventory balance in the current year serves as the base layer or beginning balance for LIFO. Prospective treatment for the impracticality exception is described in the accounting guidance.

250-10-45-6 If the cumulative effect of applying a change in accounting principle to all prior periods can be determined, but it is impracticable to determine the period-specific effects of that change on all prior periods presented, the cumulative effect of the change to the new accounting principle shall be applied to the carrying amounts of assets and liabilities as of the beginning of the earliest period to which the new accounting principle can be applied. An offsetting adjustment, if any, shall be made to the opening balance of retained earnings (or other appropriate components of equity or net assets in the statement of financial position) for that period.

250-10-45-7 If it is impracticable to determine the cumulative effect of applying a change in accounting principle to any prior period, the new accounting principle shall be applied as if the change was made prospectively as of the earliest date practicable.

Required Change in Accounting Principle Based on a Codification Update

An update to the Codification can result in a change in the accounting for a particular transaction or event. When this happens, we look to the standards to see whether we make a retrospective adjustment, or follow a prospective approach or a modified retrospective approach. The **modified retrospective approach** is where the new standard is applied to the current period only (prior financial statements are not restated) and a cumulative effect adjustment is added to or subtracted from beginning retained earnings of the current period. The required approach depends on the circumstances of the standard update—at times, standard updates even allow the preparer to choose among alternative approaches. The FASB will often push out the effective date of a more extensive standard change in order to allow companies a chance to not only implement the standard on the effective date, but to apply the standard update to past results for comparative reporting purposes.

KELLOGG

Real World—CHANGE IN ACCOUNTING POLICY DUE TO CODIFICATION UPDATE

KELLOGG [K]

Kellogg Company included the following note in a recent annual report regarding a change mandated through a standard update. The update allowed companies to either report the change prospectively or retrospectively.

Note 1—Accounting Policies (excerpt) Balance sheet classification of deferred taxes. In November 2015, the FASB issued an ASU to simplify the presentation of deferred income taxes. The ASU requires that deferred tax liabilities and assets be classified as noncurrent in a classified statement of financial position. Entities should apply the new guidance either prospectively to all deferred tax liabilities and assets or retrospectively to all periods presented. The Company early adopted the updated standard in the first quarter of 2016, on a prospective basis. The year-end 2015 balance for current deferred tax assets and liabilities was $227 million and $(9) million, respectively. Please see Note 13 for more information on the Company's deferred tax assets and liabilities. Prior period balances have not been adjusted.

Direct and Indirect Effects

Many companies that change accounting principles report both **direct** and **indirect effects** as illustrated in **Demo 10-6A**.

The *direct effects* of the change are those adjustments made to account balances and earnings amounts (plus any related income tax effects) to reflect the new principle. For example, in **Demo 10-6A**, inventory and retained earnings were retrospectively adjusted.

ASC Glossary **Direct Effects of a Change in Accounting Principle:** Those recognized changes in assets or liabilities necessary to effect a change in accounting principle. An example of a direct effect is an adjustment to an inventory balance to effect a change in inventory valuation method. Related changes, such as an effect on deferred income tax assets or liabilities or an impairment adjustment resulting from applying the subsequent measurement guidance in Subtopic 330-10 to the adjusted inventory balance, also are examples of direct effects of a change in accounting principle.

Had the new accounting principle been in effect in prior years, certain nondiscretionary items based on earnings, including bonus arrangements and royalties, may have been different. These are indirect effects of the accounting principle change. Indirect costs are not retrospectively applied to financial statements. Instead, any indirect costs are recorded in the *current period as incurred.* For example, in **Demo 10-6A**, a bonus that was retroactively adjusted based on the inventory change, was reported in the current year and not retrospectively applied to the financial statements.

ASC Glossary **Indirect Effects of a Change in Accounting Principle:** Any changes to current or future cash flows of an entity that result from making a change in accounting principle that is applied retrospectively. An example of an indirect effect is a change in a nondiscretionary profit sharing or royalty payment that is based on a reported amount such as revenue or net income.

Disclosure Requirements

Accounting standards provide guidance for disclosure.

250-10-50-1 An entity shall disclose all of the following in the fiscal period in which a change in accounting principle is made:

a. The nature of and reason for the change in accounting principle, including an explanation of why the newly adopted accounting principle is preferable.

b. The method of applying the change, including all of the following:
   1. A description of the prior-period information that has been retrospectively adjusted, if any.
   2. The effect of the change on income from continuing operations, net income (or other appropriate captions of changes in the applicable net assets or performance indicator), any other affected financial statement line item, and any affected per-share amounts for the current period and any prior periods retrospectively adjusted. Presentation of the effect on financial statement subtotals and totals other than income from continuing operations and net income (or other appropriate captions of changes in the applicable net assets or performance indicator) is not required.
   3. The cumulative effect of the change on retained earnings or other components of equity or net assets in the statement of financial position as of the beginning of the earliest period presented.
   4. If retrospective application to all prior periods is impracticable, disclosure of the reasons therefore, and a description of the alternative method used to report the change (see paragraphs 250-10-45-5 through 45-7).

c. If indirect effects of a change in accounting principle are recognized both of the following shall be disclosed:
   1. A description of the indirect effects of a change in accounting principle, including the amounts that have been recognized in the current period, and the related per-share amounts, if applicable.
   2. Unless impracticable, the amount of the total recognized indirect effects of the accounting change and the related per-share amounts, if applicable, that are attributable to each prior period presented. Compliance with this disclosure requirement is practicable unless an entity cannot comply with it after making every reasonable effort to do so.

EXPAND YOUR KNOWLEDGE **SEC Preferability Letter**

To emphasize the need for transparency of material voluntary changes in accounting principles, the Securities and Exchange Commission requires that registered companies file a ***preferability letter*** from their independent auditors. The letter includes a description of the change, indicates that the new method is in accordance with GAAP, and indicates whether the auditors concur with management's assessment of preferability. The letter is required to be filed with the first quarterly (10-Q) or annual report (10-K) after the change. The following is an example of a preferability letter filed with the Securities and Exchange Commission.

February 26, 2013

Board of Directors of Kellogg Company
One Kellogg Square, P.O. Box 3599
Battle Creek, MI 49016

Dear Directors:

We are providing this letter to you for inclusion as an exhibit to your Form 10-K filing pursuant to Item 601 of Regulation S-K.

We have audited the consolidated financial statements included in the Company's Annual Report on Form 10-K for the year ended December 29, 2012 and issued our report thereon dated February 26, 2013. Note 1 to the financial statements describes a change in accounting principle for pension and nonpension postretirement benefits. It should be understood that the preferability of one acceptable method of accounting over another for pension and nonpension post-retirement benefits has not been addressed in any authoritative accounting literature, and in expressing our concurrence below we have relied on management's determination that this change in accounting principle is preferable. Based on our reading of management's stated reasons and justification for this change in accounting principle in the Form 10-K, and our discussions with management as to their judgment about the relevant business planning factors relating to the change, we concur with management that such change represents, in the Company's circumstances, the adoption of a preferable accounting principle in conformity with Accounting Standards Codification 250, *Accounting Changes and Error Corrections.*

Very truly yours,

/s/ PricewaterhouseCoopers LLP
PricewaterhouseCoopers LLP
Detroit, Michigan

Management Judgment

Management judgment is relied on for the selection of accounting methods and in the estimation process. Often, GAAP allows companies to choose from a number of options or provides criteria that a company must analyze when choosing a method. Both the initial selection of an accounting method and subsequent changes to an accounting method warrant review by financial statement users for a number of reasons:

- If comparing one company to another company, are the companies using the same methods?
- Is the company using the method most common to its industry?
- If a company has changed methods, was there a motivation to make financial results look more favorable or to smooth income over time?

It is nearly impossible to think of an entry that does not involve some type of estimation. An original estimate and subsequent adjustments to the estimate require management judgment. Disclosures required under GAAP related to estimations help financial statement users better understand the judgments supporting the numbers that on the surface, are a simple sum of assets equating to liabilities plus equity.

LO A-3 Demonstrate the accounting for an error correction

LO A-3 Overview

Accounting for Error Correction
- Retrospective adjustment for material errors
- Restatement of prior period financial statements

An accounting error occurs when a transaction or event is recorded incorrectly or is not recorded at all. (Disclosures related to fraud and illegal acts are discussed in Chapter 4.) Material errors are not a common occurrence. Larger companies discover most material errors before completing the financial statements. All of the following are examples of accounting errors.

- Use of an inappropriate or unacceptable accounting principle and mistakes in applying GAAP. For example, the use of the fair value method to account for an investment when the equity method is appropriate is an error.
- Use of an unrealistic accounting estimate or gross negligence in making estimates. For example, adopting an unrealistic depreciation rate requires an error correction.
- Misstating or misclassifying an account balance.
- Delay in or failure to recognize accruals, deferrals, and other transactions.
- Mathematical mistakes.

EXPANDING YOUR KNOWLEDGE **Common Types of Errors**

The most common types of restatements due to errors are classified into the following types.

- Recording debt and equity securities (conversion options, valuation, and derivative requirements).
- Recognition of revenue (improperly interpreting sales contracts and treating sales returns and allowances).
- Tax related errors in calculating obligations and benefits (foreign tax, specialty tax, tax planning issues, failure to identify book and tax differences).
- Errors in the statement of cash flows (misclassification errors).
- Failure to record liabilities (pension, leases, deferred revenue, other accruals).
- Expense recording issues (failure to record expenses, payables, or reconcile accounts).

Source: 2017 Financial Restatements: A Seventeen Year Comparison, Audit Analytics (May 2018).

ASC Glossary **Error in Previously Issued Financial Statements:** An error in recognition, measurement, presentation, or disclosure in financial statements resulting from mathematical mistakes, mistakes in the application of generally accepted accounting principles (GAAP), or oversight or misuse of facts that existed at the time the financial statements were prepared. A change from an accounting principle that is not generally accepted to one that is generally accepted is a correction of an error.

250-10-45-27 In determining materiality for the purpose of reporting the correction of an error, amounts shall be related to the estimated income for the full fiscal year and also to the effect on the trend of earnings.

Correction of an error in previously issued financial statements is required if the error is **material.** Management and auditors use judgment in determining whether an adjustment reaches the level of materiality requiring correcting entries and restatement of previously issued financial statements. See **LO 3-7** for a discussion on materiality. A **prior period adjustment** is an entry to correct an error through an adjustment of a balance sheet account and, in many cases, retained earnings account and is recorded in the period that the error is discovered. Tax effects should also be recorded.

A change in principle and an error correction are similar in that that they both require retrospective treatment. This means that in presenting comparative financial statements, any effects on the financial statement amounts in all periods presented are corrected. The cumulative income difference (net of tax) for prior periods not presented, adjusts the beginning retained earnings balance, and the balance of any affected asset and liability accounts as of the earliest year presented. However, a change in principle and an error correction are dissimilar in that only an error correction requires a **restatement** or an *amendment of prior periodic reports* to report the changes necessary to correct the error.

ASC Glossary **Restatement:** The process of revising previously issued financial statements to reflect the correction of an error in those financial statements.

If the error is material, the accounting for the error will depend on timing of when the error was made and discovered, what accounts are affected, and whether the error counterbalances (automatically self-corrects) within two accounting periods as applied to inventory in **Exhibit A-3** (originally included in Chapter 10). **Demo 3-7C** and **Demo 12-6** illustrated the correction of depreciation errors, **Demo 10-7** illustrates the correction of inventory errors, and the tax effects of error corrections are illustrated in **Demo 18-10B**.

Disclosure

When financial statements are *restated* to correct an error, the entity shall disclose a description of the nature of the error causing the restatement. In addition, disclosure includes the effect of the correction on each financial statement line item (and affected per-share amounts) along with the cumulative effect of the change on retained earnings as of the beginning of the earliest period presented. Such disclosures do not need to be repeated in subsequent periods.

250-10-50-7 When financial statements are restated to correct an error, the entity shall disclose that its previously issued financial statements have been restated, along with a description of the nature of the error. The entity also shall disclose both of the following:

a. The effect of the correction on each financial statement line item and any per-share amounts affected for each prior period presented.

b. The cumulative effect of the change on retained earnings or other appropriate components of equity or net assets in the statement of financial position, as of the beginning of the earliest period presented.

250-10-50-8 When prior period adjustments are recorded, the resulting effects (both gross and net of applicable income tax) on the net income of prior periods shall be disclosed in the annual report for the year in which the adjustments are made and in interim reports issued during that year after the date of recording the adjustments.

EXHIBIT A-3
Accounting for an Error

Type of Error	Financial Statement Presentation	Entries	Example
Error discovered in same accounting period.	No impact on prior periods.	Reverse incorrect entry and record correct entry.	Inadvertently include consigned inventory in the merchandise inventory account. (Discovered in the current accounting period.)
Error discovered in subsequent accounting period: affects balance sheet only or income statement only.	Restatement of all financial statements presented.	Record reclassification entry (if amount currently on the balance sheet).	Misclassify work-in-process as finished goods inventory. (Discovered in a subsequent accounting period.)
Error discovered in subsequent accounting period: affects balance sheet and income statement and is **counterbalancing** (or an error that self-corrects within two consecutive accounting periods).	Restatement of all financial statements presented.	Record correcting entry only if discovered before self-correction of the error.	Overstate ending inventory due to a mathematical error. (Discovered in a subsequent accounting period.)
Error discovered in subsequent accounting period: affects balance sheet and income statement and is **noncounterbalancing** (or an error that does not self-correct within two consecutive accounting periods).	Restatement of all financial statements presented.	Record an entry to correct the error.	Inadvertently record an inventory purchase as equipment to be depreciated over 10 years. (Discovered in a subsequent accounting period.)

KBR

Real World—PRIOR PERIOD ADJUSTMENT

KBR INC. [KBR]

KBR Inc. is a global engineering, construction and services company supporting various market segments. KBR Inc. filed Amendment No. 1 (Form 10-K/A) to the annual Form 10-K for the fiscal year ended December 31, 2013 (originally filed on February 27, 2014) to restate its consolidated financial statements as of and for the year ended December 31, 2013, and to amend related disclosures, including controls and procedures. The correction for the error is noted throughout the report including references to affected accounts in the MD&A section and throughout the financial reports and notes accompanying the financial statements. An excerpt from the revised annual report follows.

> **Note 1. Description of Company and Significant Accounting Policies (excerpt)** Prior Period Adjustment: We corrected an error in our Gas Monetization business segment, originating in periods prior to 2013, which resulted in a net unfavorable impact to gross profit of $25 million and an after tax unfavorable impact to net income of $17 million for the year ended December 31, 2013. The error related to the accounting over the

continued

continued from previous page

last several years for foreign currency in the determination of revenue on one of our long term construction projects with multiple currencies. We evaluated the cumulative error on both a quantitative and qualitative basis under the guidance of ASC 250—Accounting Changes and Error Corrections. We determined that the cumulative impact of the error did not affect the trend of net income, cash flows or liquidity and therefore did not have a material impact to previously issued financial statements for the years ended December 31, 2012 and 2011. Additionally, we determined our consolidated financial statements for the fiscal year ended December 31, 2013 were not materially impacted by the error correction.

Describe the accounting for a change in reporting entity

LO A-4

A change in the reporting entity results in financial statements that, in effect, are those of a different reporting entity.

Change in Reporting Entity

- Retrospective adjustment
- Applies when there is a change to consolidation or in the composition of consolidated companies

LO A-4 Overview

ASC Glossary **Change in the Reporting Entity:** A change that results in financial statements that, in effect, are those of a different reporting entity. A change in the reporting entity is limited mainly to the following:

a. Presenting consolidated or combined financial statements in place of financial statements of individual entities

b. Changing specific subsidiaries that make up the group of entities for which consolidated financial statements are presented

c. Changing the entities included in combined financial statements.

Neither a business combination accounted for by the acquisition method nor the consolidation of a variable interest entity (VIE) pursuant to Topic 810 is a change in reporting entity

To allow meaningful comparisons across reporting periods, the **retrospective approach** is applied to these changes. The results of all prior periods presented are restated as if the consolidated group represented the current combination of entities during those periods. Consolidation is explained in advanced accounting courses.

250-10-45-21 When an accounting change results in financial statements that are, in effect, the statements of a different reporting entity, the change shall be retrospectively applied to the financial statements of all prior periods presented to show financial information for the new reporting entity for those periods. Previously issued interim financial information shall be presented on a retrospective basis.

The acquisition of another company is *not* considered a change in reporting entity. In other words, if a company purchases another company, financial results are combined for the current year but prior periods are not adjusted. Because this makes it difficult for financial statement users to compare results from year to year, certain disclosures are required to show results as if the companies had been consolidated in prior periods.

Disclosure

The nature and justification for the change are reported, as well as the effect on income from operations, net income, other comprehensive income, and related per-share amounts for all periods presented. Subsequent financial statements need not repeat the disclosures.

250-10-50-6 When there has been a change in the reporting entity, the financial statements of the period of the change shall describe the nature of the change and the reason for it. In addition, the effect of the change on income from continuing operations, net income (or other appropriate captions of changes in the applicable net assets or performance indicator), other comprehensive income, and any related per-share amounts shall be disclosed for all periods presented. Financial statements of subsequent periods need not repeat the disclosures required by this paragraph. If a change in reporting entity does not have a material effect in the period of change but is reasonably certain to have a material effect in later periods, the nature of and reason for the change shall be disclosed whenever the financial statements of the period of change are presented.

Demo A-4 **Identification of a Change in Reporting Entity**

Determine whether each of the following items qualifies as a change in reporting entity. If the change qualifies as a change in reporting entity, indicate the appropriate accounting treatment.

	Item	Change in Reporting Entity	Accounting Treatment
1.	A subsidiary that previously was not consolidated, now meets the criteria for consolidation. With the change, the subsidiary financial statements are now consolidated with the parent company's financial statements.	✔	**Retrospectively applied**
2.	A subsidiary that was previously consolidated, now does not meet the criteria for consolidation. With the change, the subsidiary is reported as a separate entity.	✔	**Retrospectively applied**
3.	A newly purchased company is consolidated with the purchaser's other existing subsidiaries to report as a single entity.		**Does not qualify as a change in reporting entity**

MEDALLION

Real World—REPORTING A CHANGE IN ENTITY

MEDALLION FINANCIAL CORP. [MFIN]

Medallion Financial Corp. (the Company) is a specialty finance company that has a leading position in originating, acquiring, and servicing loans that finance taxicab medallions (city-issued license to operate a taxicab) and various types of commercial businesses. Medallion Bank (MB), a wholly-owned portfolio company, also originates consumer loans for the purchase of recreational vehicles, boats, motorcycles, trailers, and to finance small scale home improvements. Medallion Financial Corp. reported the following change in reporting entity that required retrospective treatment in an annual report on Form 10-K.

> **Note 3: Change in the Reporting Entity** Since MB commenced operations in December 2003, the Company had historically consolidated MB's financial statements with those of its own. Although MB is not an investment company, and SEC rules generally do not permit investment companies such as the Company to consolidate the financial statements of non-investment companies, such as MB, the Company had sought and obtained a letter from the SEC in March 2004 permitting such consolidation. We believed that consolidating MB provided a more complete and accurate representation of the Company's full scope of operations, and its complete financial position and results of operations.
>
> During August 2006, the Company filed a registration statement on Form N-2 which the SEC staff reviewed and on which they provided comments, including those relating to the consolidation of the accounts of MB. Based on discussion with the SEC staff, the Company determined during the 2006 fourth quarter to voluntarily not consolidate MB and present MB as a portfolio company. We determined that this change represents a change in the reporting entity as described in SFAS No. 154, "Accounting Changes and Error Corrections." Accordingly the Company has retrospectively applied this change to the financial statements of all prior periods presented, including previously issued interim periods presented. The effect of this retrospective application is to present the Company's financial position and results of operations as if MB had not been consolidated for all periods presented and to present MB as an unconsolidated portfolio investment. Although this creates changes in the reported levels of assets, liabilities, revenues, and expenses, our net increase in net assets resulting from operations, shareholders' equity, and the related amounts per common share are unchanged.

Questions

A-1. Distinguish among the following: (a) change in principle, (b) change in estimate, (c) change in reporting entity, and (d) accounting error.

A-2. What are the two basic ways to account for the effects of accounting changes and error corrections?

A-3. Complete the following schedule:

	Method of Reflecting the Effect	
	Prospectively	Retrospectively
Change in estimate		
Change in principle		
Correction of error		

A-4. Explain the basic difference between an accounting change and an error correction.

A-5. The three types of accounting changes involve (*a*) principles, (*b*) estimates, and (*c*) reporting entities. Using these letters and (*d*) for error corrections, identify each of the following changes.

1. A lessor discovers during the term of a finance lease that an estimated material unguaranteed residual value of the leased property has probably become zero.
2. A corporation with foreign subsidiaries has used the cost method of accounting for its investments in the subsidiary companies because economic conditions in the countries in which the subsidiary companies operate have been unstable and exchange of foreign currency into dollars has been restricted. Under changed, improved conditions, it has become feasible for the controlling entity to prepare consolidated statements instead, thereby eliminating the foreign investment account from the balance sheet of the corporation.
3. After five years of use, an asset originally estimated to have a 15-year life is now to be depreciated on the basis of a 20-year life.
4. Office equipment purchased last year is discovered to have been debited to office expense when acquired. Appropriate accounting is to be applied at the discovery date.
5. A company that has been using the FIFO inventory method is changing to LIFO.
6. A company that used 5% of accounts receivable to estimate its expected credit losses discovers that losses are running higher than expected and changes to 6%.

A-6. How is the book value of a plant asset at the beginning of the year of a change in estimated life used in the accounting for the change?

A-7. What is the difference between a counterbalancing error and a noncounterbalancing error? Why is the distinction significant in the analysis of errors?

A-8. Complete the schedule below by entering a plus sign to indicate overstatement, a minus sign to indicate understatement, or a zero for no effect.

	Effect of Error On			
	Income	Assets	Liabilities	Equity
a. Ending inventory for 2020 understated:				
2020 financial statements.				
2021 financial statements.				
b. Ending inventory for 2021 overstated:				
2021 financial statements.				
2022 financial statements.				
c. Failed to record depreciation in 2020:				
2020 financial statements.				
2021 financial statements.				
d. Failed to record a liability for cash advances received in 2020 related to 2021 revenue; instead, credited revenue in full erroneously in 2020:				
2020 financial statements.				
2021 financial statements.				

A-9. Provide two examples of each of the following types of errors:

a. Affects the income statement only.
b. Affects the balance sheet only.
c. Affects both income statement and balance sheet.

A-10. A company failed to accrue $12,000 of salaries at the end of 2020. Explain (*a*) why the discovery of the error in 2021, after the issuance of the 2020 statements, requires a correcting entry and (*b*) why discovery of the error in 2022, after the issuance of the 2021 statements, does not require a correcting entry.

A-11. What is the difference between retrospective treatment with a change in accounting principle and a retrospective restatement with an error correction?

A-12. What are the similarities and differences between a cumulative effect on prior years of applying a new accounting principle and a prior period adjustment due to the discovery of an error?

Brief Exercises

Brief Exercise A-13
LO1, 2, 3, 4

Indicate whether the following items are a (*a*) change in accounting principle, (*b*) change in accounting estimate, (*c*) change in reporting entity, or (*d*) correction of an error.

1. The controller of H&P Company discovered that inventory held on consignment was counted as part of ending inventory.
2. An investment in another company is now considered a subsidiary (due to an increase in ownership interest) and will be consolidated in the financial statement of the H&P Company.
3. H&P Company decided to change its inventory cost method from FIFO to the average-cost method.

Brief Exercise A-14
LO1, 2, 3, 4

Indicate whether the following items are a (*a*) change in accounting principle, (*b*) change in accounting estimate, (*c*) change in reporting entity, or (*d*) correction of an error.

1. The salvage value of a building being depreciated over 30 years is adjusted from $15,000 to $5,000 due to the unexpected deterioration of the building.
2. A company discovered that depreciation expense was overstated by $50,000 in the prior year's financial statements due to incorrect asset valuation amounts entered into the fixed asset depreciation software.
3. A company changes its depreciation method from the straight-line method to the double-declining balance method for the long-term asset category of equipment.

Exercises

Exercise A-15
Identification of Accounting Changes and Errors **LO1, 2, 3, 4**

The following items are accounting changes and errors.

1. Recorded expense, $87,000; should be $78,000.
2. Changed useful life of a machine.
3. Changed from single-company to consolidated financial statements.
4. Changed from straight-line to accelerated depreciation.
5. Change in residual value of an intangible asset.
6. Changed from cash-basis to accrual-basis in accounting for bad debts.
7. Changed from FIFO to average-cost method in accounting for inventory.
8. Due to a change in ownership percentage, a company previously consolidated will no longer be consolidated for financial statement purposes.
9. Changed to a new accounting principle required by the FASB.
10. Change in the rate of expected uncollectible accounts applied to accounts receivable in determining the allowance for doubtful account adjustment.

Required

For each item above, indicate whether the item is a (*a*) change in accounting principle, (*b*) change in accounting estimate, (*c*) change in accounting entity, or (*d*) error.

Exercise A-16
Identification of Accounting Changes and Errors **LO1, 2, 3, 4**

The following items are accounting changes and errors.

1. Changed the residual value of an asset.
2. Changed from LIFO to FIFO for inventory.

3. Changed from straight-line depreciation to accelerated.
4. Changed percentages of uncollectibility of accounts receivable aging categories for allowance for doubtful account estimation.
5. Changed to LIFO (layers cannot be determined).
6. Changed to a new accounting method mandated by a Codification update.
7. A new subsidiary is included in the consolidated financial statements that were appropriately not previously consolidated.
8. An accrual for taxes was not included in the year-end financial statements causing an overstatement of net income.
9. An occurrence of an unexpected write-off of accounts receivable that was not reflected in the allowance for doubtful accounts at year-end.
10. An in-transit sale (for a significant amount) at year-end with terms F.O.B. destination, was inadvertently recorded as a sale at year-end.

Required

a. For each item above, indicate whether the item is a (1) change in accounting principle, (2) change in accounting estimate, (3) change in accounting entity, or (4) correction of an error.

b. Indicate whether each item would require (1) retrospective treatment, (2) retrospective treatment with restatement, or (3) prospective treatment. Assume all items are considered material.

Exercise A-17
Analysis of Errors: Correcting Entries and Correct Pretax Income **LO3**

Travis Inc. has just completed its financial statements for the reporting year ended December 31, 2020. The pretax income amount is $160,000. The accounts have not been closed for December 31, 2020. Further consideration and review of the records revealed the following items related to the 2020 statements.

1. On January 1, 2016, a machine was acquired that cost $10,000. The estimated useful life was 10 years, and the residual value was $2,000. At the time of acquisition, the full cost of the machine was incorrectly debited to the land account. Use straight-line depreciation.
2. On January 1, 2018, a long-term investment of $18,000 was made by purchasing a $20,000, 8% bond of Tiffany Corporation. The investment account was debited for $18,000. Each year, starting on December 31, 2018, the company has recognized and reported investment revenue on these bonds of $1,600. The bonds mature in 10 years from the date of purchase. Assume that any amortization would be straight-line, and that Travis intends to hold the bonds to maturity.
3. The 2019 ending inventory was overstated by $7,000 (periodic inventory system).
4. An $11,000 credit purchase of merchandise occurred on December 18, 2019. Because the merchandise was on hand on December 31, 2019, it was included in the 2019 ending inventory. The purchase was recorded on January 18, 2020, when the invoice was paid (periodic inventory system).

Required

a. Prepare any correcting and adjusting entries that should be made on December 31, 2020. Ignore income tax.

b. Compute the correct pretax income for 2020.

Exercise A-18
Impact of Errors on Income Statement **LO3**

Trinity Company discovered the following errors in 2020.

1. Interest expense of $3,000 was not accrued at the end of 2019. Amount was paid and expensed in 2020 instead.
2. Supplies account at the end of 2019 was not adjusted for supplies used. The supplies account was reduced in 2020.
3. An error in the input of salvage values and useful lives into the depreciation system resulted in an overstatement of depreciation expense by $5,000 in 2019. Depreciation expense was calculated correctly in 2020.
4. An accrual for vacation ($5,000) earned in 2019 (taken in 2020) was not included in the financial statements in 2019.
5. The January 2020 insurance premium of $800 paid in December of 2019 was expensed in 2019.

Required

a. Indicate how each item would impact net income in 2019 (overstatement, understatement, or no effect).

b. Indicate how each item would impact net income in 2020 (overstatement, understatement, or no effect).

Problems

Problem A-19
Analysis of Accounting Changes **LO1, 2, 4**

A business entity may change its method of accounting for certain items. The change may be classified as a change in accounting principle, accounting estimate, or reporting entity. Listed below are three separate, unrelated situations.

Case 1: Able Company determined that the depreciable lives currently used for its fixed assets were too long to best match the cost of using the assets with the revenue produced. At the beginning of the current year, the company decided to reduce the depreciable lives of all its existing fixed assets by five years.

Case 2: On December 31, 2019, Baker Company owned 51% of the voting stock of Allen Company. At that time Baker reported its investment using the cost method due to political uncertainties in the country in which Allen was located. On January 2, 2020, the management of Baker Company was satisfied that the political uncertainties had been resolved and that the assets of the company were in no danger of nationalization. Accordingly, Baker will prepare consolidated financial statements for Baker and Allen for the year ended December 31, 2020.

Case 3: Charlie Company decides in January 2020 to adopt the FIFO method in accounting for inventory. The cost of inventory had been computed based upon the average-cost method.

Required

For each case described above, indicate the following:

a. Type of accounting change.
b. Manner of reporting the change under current GAAP, including a discussion, for cases 1 and 3 only, of how amounts are computed.
c. Effect of the change on the balance sheet and income statement (cases 1 and 3 only).
d. Note disclosures which would be necessary (cases 1 and 3 only).

AICPA adapted

Problem A-20
Accounting Changes and Errors: Analysis and Correction, Entries **LO1, 2, 3**

General Sales Company recently was acquired by a new owner, who has decided to correct the prior accounting records during the current reporting period, which ends December 31, 2020. The accounts have been partially adjusted but not closed for 2020. The following additional items have been discovered.

1. The merchandise inventory at December 31, 2019, was overstated by $10,000 (periodic inventory system).
2. During January 2018, improvements on equipment were debited to repair expense; the $15,000 should have been debited to equipment, which is being depreciated 15% per year on cost (no residual value).
3. A patent that cost $9,350 has been amortized (straight line) for the past 10 years (excluding 2020) over its legal life of 20 years. It is now clear that its economic life will not be more than 12 years from the initial acquisition date.
4. At the end of 2019, sales revenue collected in advance of $3,000 was included in 2019 sales revenue. The performance obligation was fulfilled in 2020.
5. Paid $8,000 during January 2018 for ordinary repairs on a machine that was acquired during January 2018. The repairs were erroneously capitalized. The machine has an estimated life of five years and no residual value. Assume straight-line depreciation.
6. The rate used for bad debts has been ½% of credit sales, which has proved to be too low; therefore, for 2020 and thereafter, the rate used will be 1% of credit sales. The amount of the expense recorded per year under the old rate was $800 in 2018 and $1,000 in 2019. (The amount for 2020 has not been entered in the accounts because the adjusting entries have not been made.) Credit sales for 2020 exceeded 2019 credit sales by 20%.
7. During January 2018, a five-year insurance premium of $750 was paid, which was debited in full to insurance expense at that time.
8. At the end of 2019, accrued salaries payable of $1,800 were not recorded; they were first recorded when paid early in 2020. Unpaid salaries at the end of 2020 were $2,100.

Required

a. For each of the eight items, identify whether it is an error correction or an accounting change and briefly explain how each should be accounted for.
b. Provide the appropriate pretax entry to record any change or correction and provide any adjusting entry needed in each instance at the end of 2020. Show computations. If no entry is needed, explain why.

Problem A-21
Multiple Accounting Changes—Entries and Reporting **LO1, 2, 3**

The year 2020 was not a good one for Zealand Company accountants. The company made several financial accounting changes that year. Assume a 30% tax rate where appropriate.

First, the company changed the total useful life from 20 years to 13 years on an asset purchased January 1, 2017, for $350,000. The asset was originally expected to be sold for $50,000 at the end of its useful life, but that amount also was changed in 2020 to $200,000. Zealand applies the straight-line method of depreciation to this asset.

Second, the company changed from FIFO to LIFO but is unable to recreate LIFO inventory layers. The FIFO 2020 beginning and ending inventories are $30,000 and $45,000, respectively. The company expects LIFO to render income numbers more useful for prediction.

Third, the company changed to the straight-line method from the sum-of-years'-digits method on equipment purchased for $650,000 on January 1, 2016. The equipment has a $100,000 residual value and 10-year useful life. These values were not changed. The change in depreciation method was made to provide a better measure of expired equipment cost because the annual benefits derived from the asset have been relatively constant.

Fourth, an error in amortizing patents was discovered in 2020. Patents costing $510,000 on January 1, 2018, were amortized over their legal life (20 years). The accountant neglected to obtain an estimate of the patent's economic life, which totals only 5 years. The entire cost of the patents was deducted for tax purposes when acquired.

Required

Record the entries in 2020 necessary to make the accounting changes. Assume a tax rate of 30%.

Problem A-22
Multiple Accounting Changes—Entries and Reporting **LO1, 3**

Answer the following three *separate* questions.

1. Gear Company records $2,000 of depreciation under the sum-of-years'-digits method in 2019, the company's first year of operations. In 2020, the company decides to change to the straight-line method for accounting purposes. If the straight-line method were used in 2019, depreciation would have been $1,500. Depreciation in 2020 under the straight-line method is $1,800 (depreciated based on the book value on January 1, 2020). The tax rate is 25%. Income from continuing operations before tax and before deducting depreciation in 2020 is $12,000.

Required

Provide the 2020 entry to record this change and calculate 2020 net income.

2. Helms Company purchases a delivery truck for $12,000 on January 1, 2019. Helms expects to use the truck only two years and to sell it for $4,000. The company's policy is to use straight-line depreciation but depreciation in 2019 is not recorded. Rather, the accountant charges the entire cost to delivery expense in 2019. The controller discovers the error late in 2020.

Required

Provide the 2020 entries to record depreciation and the error correction and indicate the amounts of the prior period adjustments appearing in the 2019 and 2020 retained earnings sections of the statement of stockholders' equity. The tax rate is 25%.

3. On July 1, 2018 a full year's insurance premium of $2,400, covering the period July 1, 2018, to June 30, 2019 was paid and debited to insurance expense. Assume the following:
   - The company has a calendar fiscal year.
   - January 1, 2018, retained earnings balance is $20,000.
   - 2018 reported net income (assuming the error is not discovered) is $22,800.
   - 2019 net income (assuming the error is not discovered) is $30,000.
   - 2020 net income is $40,000. Ignore taxes.

Required

a. List the effects of the error on affected accounts and on net income in 2018 and 2019, assuming no adjusting entry is made on December 31, 2018.

b. Prepare the entry to record the error if discovered in 2018.

c. Prepare the entry to record the error if discovered in 2019, and the 2018 and 2019 retained earnings sections of the statement of stockholders' equity.

d. Prepare the entry (if needed) to record the error if discovered in 2020, and the 2019 and 2020 retained earnings sections of the statement of stockholders' equity.

Analyzing Financial Statements

AD&J A-23
Change in Accounting Principle **LO2**

Real World Analysis Obtain an electronic copy of the 10-K for the **Coca-Cola Company** for the year ended December 31, 2015, which can be found on the SEC Edgar website (https://www.sec.gov/edgar/searchedgar/companysearch.html). Answer the following questions.

Required

a. How many updates to accounting standards are discussed in the notes to the financial statements?

b. Briefly indicate the company's perspective on impact of each of the anticipated standard changes on the company's financial reporting.

AD&J A-24
Change in Accounting Principle **LO2**

Real World Analysis Obtain an electronic copy of the preferability letter filed with the 10-Q for the quarterly period ended November 30, 2013, by **Schnitzer Steel Industries Inc.** on the SEC Edgar website (https://www.sec.gov/edgar/searchedgar/companysearch.html).

Required

Include the body of the letter in your solution, and answer the following questions.

a. What is the purpose of the preferability letter?

b. What change in accounting principle is highlighted in the preferability letter?

c. How is preferability supported by management? By the auditors? *Hint*: Obtain an electronic copy of the 10-Q to answer this question.

d. Since the posting of this preferability letter, the SEC has indicated that a preferability letter is not required for a change in the test date of goodwill if a registrant determines that a change in goodwill impairment testing date does not represent a *material change* to its method of applying an accounting principle. However, the change must be prominently disclosed in the registrant's financial statements. What may have caused this change by the SEC?

AD&J A-25
Defining Terms **LO1, 2, 3, 4**

Codification Skills How are the terms (1) accounting change, (2) change in accounting estimate, (3) change in accounting principle, (4) change in the reporting entity, (5) change in accounting estimate effected by a change in accounting principle, (6) restatement, (7) retrospective application defined in the Codification?

AD&J A-26
Performing Accounting Research **LO1, 2, 3**

Codification Skills Through research in the Codification, identify the specific citation for each of the following items included as guidance in this chapter.

a. Retrospective treatment of changes in accounting principles FASB ASC ___-___-___-___

b. Restatement required for corrections of errors FASB ASC ___-___-___-___

c. Impractical changes in accounting principles—proper treatment FASB ASC ___-___-___-___

d. Prospective treatment of changes in accounting estimates FASB ASC ___-___-___-___

AD&J A-27
Performing Accounting Research **LO3**

Codification Skills A company is preparing interim financial statements where an error was discovered. The company is unsure as to what items need to be disclosed on an interim basis. What guidance is available in the Codification?

FASB ASC ___-___-___-___

AD&J A-28
Ethical Considerations: Accounting Changes **LO2**

Ethics Case A manufacturer of electric power transmission and distribution equipment more than doubled its EPS by changing depreciation methods. In justifying the change, management supported the change as follows: In comparison to direct competitors, the previous depreciation method was more conservative and thus had a negative impact on earnings.

Although difficult to prove, there is considerable evidence that accounting changes are made for reasons other than improved financial reporting. GAAP are flexible in the initial selection of accounting methods and in making subsequent changes. However, the accounting standards specifically require that only changes to preferable accounting methods be made.

Required

Comment on the appropriateness of making accounting changes to fulfill financial reporting objectives. Consider relevant ethical issues in your response.

AD&J A-29 Conflicting Issues in Accounting Changes **LO1, 2, 4**

Judgment Case Consistency, comparability, and the need to maintain public confidence in the financial reporting process (defined in terms of the expectation that prior financial statements will not be changed except for error) are arguably conflicting objectives.

Required

Write a memo to a new accounting employee discussing the extent to which the two approaches to accounting changes (retrospective and prospective) fulfill these objectives.

B IFRS

This appendix can be downloaded from this book's website.

C Data Analytics

This appendix can be downloaded from this book's website.

Index

Exhibits included in the index with a corresponding “e” following the page numbers.

D

Exhibits included in the index with a corresponding "e" following the page numbers.

E

F

Exhibits included in the index with a corresponding "e" following the page numbers.

Exhibits included in the index with a corresponding "e" following the page numbers.

K

L

M

N

O

P

Exhibits included in the index with a corresponding "e" following the page numbers.

Q

R

Exhibits included in the index with a corresponding "e" following the page numbers.

Exhibits included in the index with a corresponding "e" following the page numbers.

Exhibits included in the index with a corresponding “e” following the page numbers.